CENTURY READINGS
FOR A COURSE IN
ENGLISH LITERATURE

𝔘𝔫𝔦𝔣𝔬𝔯𝔪 𝔚𝔦𝔱𝔥 𝔗𝔥𝔦𝔰

———

STUDENTS' HANDBOOK
OF THE FACTS OF
ENGLISH LITERATURE

BY

J. F. A. PYRE, Ph.D.
THOMAS H. DICKINSON, Ph.D.
KARL YOUNG, Ph.D.

CENTURY READINGS
FOR A COURSE IN
ENGLISH LITERATURE

EDITED AND ANNOTATED BY

J. W. CUNLIFFE, D.Lit.
PROFESSOR OF ENGLISH AND DIRECTOR OF THE
SCHOOL OF JOURNALISM, COLUMBIA UNIVERSITY

J. F. A. PYRE, Ph.D.
PROFESSOR OF ENGLISH, UNIVERSITY OF WISCONSIN

KARL YOUNG, Ph.D.
PROFESSOR OF ENGLISH, YALE UNIVERSITY

NEW YORK
THE CENTURY CO.
1926

PRINTED IN U. S. A.

PREFACE

The method of CENTURY READINGS FOR A COURSE IN ENGLISH LITERATURE has been so widely adopted since the publication of the first edition in 1910 that it needs no longer to be explained or justified. The editors have received the compliment of imitation by numerous competitors, but the book has more than held its own, partly on account of the sound principles on which the original issue was based, partly, no doubt, owing to the improvements introduced into successive later editions. The collection aims at selecting the most important authors and their most significant works, in wholes rather than in samples, and it makes no attempt to include plays or novels. The scheme of combined lectures and reading assignments (including drama and fiction), as originally outlined in *A Chronological Study Course*, has been supplemented by a *Course by Types*, which some teachers prefer, though the editors cling to their personal preference for the historical method, which seems to them to have manifest advantages. Of this they are so convinced that in this edition the older texts, originally presented in translation in an Appendix, have been moved to their chronological position at the beginning of the book, with the addition of 'Pearl' and 'Noah's Flood,' which will, it is hoped, make this section of increased value and usefulness.

For the translation of 'Pearl' the editors are indebted to The Century Company. They wish also to acknowledge their obligations to the Houghton Mifflin Company and to Professor R. E. N. Dodge for permission to use the latter's Cambridge edition of Spenser. In the modern field they offer sincere thanks for the generosity of numerous authors and publishers, who have permitted the reproduction of a large amount of copyright material. They wish, in particular, to make the following acknowledgments:

D. Appleton & Co., for 'Emancipation: Black and White' by T. H. Huxley.

Brentano's, for 'The Case for the Critic-Dramatist' by George Bernard Shaw.

Lord Burghclere, for 'Aftermath.'

Cambridge University Press, for 'All the Hills and Vales Along' by Charles Hamilton Sorley.

Century Magazine, for 'William and Mary' by Max Beerbohm.

Country Life, for 'The Defenders' by John Drinkwater; 'The Wykhamist' by Nora Griffiths; 'Canadians' by W. H. Ogilvie.

Doran & Co., for 'Salary Earning Girls' by Arnold Bennett.

Doubleday, Page & Co., for 'The Ballad of Iskander' by James Elroy Flecker.

Duffield & Co., for 'The Death of Ailill' by Francis Ledwidge.

E. P. Dutton & Co., for 'My First Visit to Buenos Ayres' by W. H. Hudson; 'The Spires of Oxford' by Winifred M. Letts; 'The Old Huntsman' by Siegfried Sassoon.

The Fortnightly Review, for 'The First Battle of Ypres' by Margaret L. Woods.

Four Seas Company, for 'The Mountainy Singer' by Joseph Campbell.

Harcourt, Brace and Howe, for 'English Hills,' 'Happy is England Now' and 'The Return' by John Freeman; 'Europe Before the War' by John Maynard Keynes.

Harper & Bros., for 'With the Marseilles Pilots' by Joseph Conrad; 'What England Thinks of America' by Sir Philip Gibbs; 'The Contemporary Novel' by H. G. Wells.

The Harrovian, for 'A Harrow Grave in Flanders' by Lord Crewe.

Henry Holt & Co., for 'The Plougher' and 'What the Shuiler Said as She Lay by the Fire in the Farmer's House' by Padraic Colum; 'All That's Past' and 'Miss Loo' by Walter de la Mare; 'Sowing,' 'Bright Clouds' and 'The Gallows' by Edward Thomas; 'Romance and Realism' by Hugh Walpole.

Houghton Mifflin Co., for 'For the Fallen' by Laurence Binyon.

B. W. Huebsch, for 'The Bride' and 'Study' by D. H. Lawrence.

Mitchell Kennerley, for selections from 'The Note Books' by Samuel Butler, and 'The South Country' by Hilaire Belloc.

Alfred Knopf, for 'Leisure,' 'Money,' 'Sheep' and 'The Muse' by William H. Davies; 'Goliath and David' and 'Not Dead' by Robert Graves.

John Lane Co., for 'The Old Vicarage, Grantchester' and 'The Soldier' by Rupert Brooke; 'The Return of the Barbarian' and 'The Wife of Flanders' by G. K. Chesterton; 'Thirty Bob a Week' by John Davidson; 'An Idol of the Market Place' and 'Ars Immortalis' by Helen Parry Eden; 'A Shropshire Lad' by A. E. Housman; 'Clifton Chapel,' 'Drake's Drum' and 'Vitai Lampada' by Sir Henry Newbolt; 'Revenge for Rheims' by Stephen Phillips; 'Wordsworth's Grave' by Sir William Watson.

The Macmillan Co., for 'The Earth Breath' by 'A.E.'; 'His Father,' 'The Question,' and 'Raining' by Wilfred Wilson Gibson; 'Afterwards,' 'For Life I had Never Cared Greatly' and 'The Coming of the End' by Thomas Hardy; 'Eve' and 'The Bull' by Ralph Hodgson; 'The Island of Skyros' and 'Sea-Fever' by John Masefield; 'What Tomas An Buile Said in a Pub' by James Stephens; 'Into the Twilight,' 'The Lake Isle of Innisfree,' 'Red Hanrahan's Song about Ireland,' and 'Song from the Land of Heart's Desire' by William Butler Yeats.

The Poetry Book Shop, for 'Over the Brazier' by Robert Graves; 'Milk for the Cat,' 'Suburb,' 'The Rebellious Vine,' and 'Change of Mind' by Harold Monro.

The Poetry Review, for 'The Airman' by Gregg Goddard.

G. P. Putnam's Sons, for 'Soldier, Soldier' by Maurice Hewlett.

Grant Richards, for 'Socks' by Jessie Pope.

Chas. Scribner's Sons, for 'The Lost Dog' by John Galsworthy; 'Parted,' 'The Lady Poverty,' and 'The Shepherdess,' by Alice Meynell.

Martin Secker, for 'The English Novel' by Gilbert Cannan.

Selwyn and Blount, for 'English Hills,' 'Happy Is England Now' and 'The Return' by John Freeman.

Sidgwick & Jackson, for 'A Legend of Ypres' by Elinor Jenkins; 'Form Fours' by Frank Sidgwick, and 'A Girl's Song' by Katharine Tynan.

The Spectator, for 'Master and Pupil' by O. M., and 'England's Dead' by Frank Taylor.

Fred A. Stokes, for 'Kilmeny,' 'The Search-Lights' and 'Wireless' by Alfred Noyes.

The Talbot Press, Ltd., for 'Ambition in Cuffe Street' and 'How Would It Be?' by Susan L. Mitchell.

The Westminster Gazette, for 'Many Sisters to Many Brothers' by Rose Macaulay, and 'Non-Combatant' by Cicely Hamilton.

The London *Times,* for 'How Sleep the Brave' by Walter de la Mare; 'Into Battle' by Julian Grenfell; 'The Old Way' by Ronald A. Hopwood; 'Sailor, What of the Debt We Owe You?' by Viscount Stuart.

CONTENTS

CONTENTS

CONTENTS

CONTENTS

CONTENTS

CONTENTS

CONTENTS

P*

CONTENTS

CONTENTS

CONTENTS

CONTENTS

CONTENTS

CONTENTS

CONTENTS

CONTENTS

CONTENTS

CONTENTS

PLANS OF STUDY

I. A CHRONOLOGICAL STUDY COURSE

As the editors have explained in the Prefatory Note, Century Readings was compiled to meet primarily the needs of students in the general, or "Survey," course in English literature offered in most American colleges. For the convenience of teachers using this book the editors offer the following plan for a chronological course covering the academic year.

PRELIMINARY EXPLANATIONS

The course consists of two parts: (1) lectures on the history of English literature, and (2) study, in small tutorial groups, of the works of representative authors.

Every student must possess the following books:

Students' Handbook of the Facts of English Literature.
> Compiled by J. F. A. Pyre, Thomas H. Dickinson, and Karl Young (Century Company).

Century Readings for a Course in English Literature.
> Edited and annotated by J. W. Cunliffe, J. F. A. Pyre, and Karl Young (Century Company).

Shakspere's *Hamlet.*
Sheridan's *The Rivals.*
Scott's *Old Mortality.*
Dickens' *David Copperfield.*
Thackeray's *Vanity Fair.*
Eliot's *Middlemarch.*
Shaw's *Saint Joan.*

In the following list of assignments the reading prescribed for each meeting of the class is printed in italics. Lectures are marked with a star. The "Outlines" mentioned are found in the *Students' Handbook. Readings* refers to *Century Readings.*

PROGRAMME OF ASSIGNMENTS

(It is understood that the teacher may reduce the number of assignments in accordance with the number of recitations available.)

FIRST SEMESTER

I. From the Beginning to the Renaissance

*1. Anglo-Saxon Literature. See Outlines I, II, III, and IV.
 2. Beowulf.
> *Readings, pp. i-xxxiii.*
 3. Geoffrey Chaucer: Prologue, lines 1-308.
> *Readings, pp. 4-7.*
*4. The Norman Period. See Outline V.
 5. Chaucer's Prologue, lines 309 to the end.
> *Readings, pp. 7-12.*
 6. Chaucer's Nun's Priest's Tale, lines 1-301.
> *Readings, pp. 12-15.*
*7. Chaucer: Life and Works. See Outlines IX and X.
 8. Chaucer's Nun's Priest's Tale, lines 302 to the end.
> *Readings, pp. 15-18.*
 9. Sir Gawain and the Green Knight.
> *Readings, pp. xxxiv-lvi.*
*10. Sir Thomas Malory and Mediæval Romance.
> See Outlines VI, VII, and XII.
> *Readings, pp. 19-33.*
 11. Ballads. See Outline XIII.
> *Readings, pp. 34-53.*

II. The Renaissance

12. William Shakspere: Sonnets.
     Readings, pp. 150-155.
*13. The Renaissance. See Outlines XV and XVI.
     Readings, pp. 71-90.
14. Elizabethan Lyrics.
     Readings, pp. 133-159.
15. Edmund Spenser: The Faery Queen, Book I, Canto I.
     Readings, pp. 109-117.
*16. The Elizabethan Age. See Outlines, XVII, XVIII, XIX, and XX.
     Readings, pp. 91-103.
17. Spenser: The Faery Queen, Book I, Canto II, and Other Poems.
     Readings, pp. 117-132.
18. Shakspere's Hamlet.
*19. The Drama before Shakspere, See Outlines XXI, XXII, and XXIII.
     Noah's Flood, Readings, pp. lxiv-lxix.
20. Hamlet.
21. Hamlet.
*22. Shakspere: Life and Works, See Outlines XXIV, XXV, XXVI, and XXVII.
23. Hamlet.
24. Hamlet.
*25. Shakspere's Later Contemporaries. See Outlines XXVIII and XXIX.
     Beaumont and Fletcher's *Philaster.*

III. The Seventeenth Century

26. Francis Bacon: The Essays.
     Readings, pp. 187-199.
27. Seventeenth Century Prose. See Outline XXXI.
     Readings, pp. 200-224.
*28. The English Bible. See Outline XXX.
     Genesis i, ii; *Book of Ruth; I Samuel* xvii; *Psalm* xxiii; *Ecclesiastes* xii; *Isaiah* xl;
       Job i-iii; *Matthew* v-vii; *Luke* ii, 1-20.
29. Seventeenth Century Lyrics. See Outline XXXII.
     Readings, pp. 160-186.
30. John Milton: Early Poems.
     Readings, pp. 236-242.
*31. Milton: Life and Works. See Outlines XXXIII and XXXIV.
     Readings, pp. 242-244, 260-265.
32. Milton: Paradise Lost, Book I.
     Readings, pp. 244-254.
33. Milton: Paradise Lost, Book II, lines 1-505.
     Readings, pp. 254-260.
*34. John Dryden and the Restoration Drama. See Outlines XXXV and XXXVI.
     Congreve's *The Way of the World.*
35. Dryden.
     Readings, pp. 266-285.
36. John Bunyan. See Outline XXXVII.
     Readings, pp. 225-235.

IV. The Eighteenth Century

*37. Daniel Defoe and the Beginnings of Journalism. See Outline XXXVIII.
     Readings, pp. 286-298.
38. Jonathan Swift.
     Readings, pp. 299-323.
39. Joseph Addison and Richard Steele.
     Readings, pp. 324-349.
*40. Swift and the Essayists. See Outlines XXXIX and XL.
41. Alexander Pope: An Essay on Criticism. See Outline XLI.
     Readings, pp. 350-357.
42. Pope: The Rape of the Lock.
     Readings, pp. 358-368.
*43. The Eighteenth Century Novel. See Outline XLII.
     Henry Fielding's *Tom Jones.*

44. Thomas Gray.
    Readings, pp. 396-404.
45. James Boswell.
    Readings, pp. 423-442.
*46. Dr. Johnson and His Circle. See Outlines XLIII and XLIV.
    Readings, pp. 405-422, 463-469.
47. Richard Brinsley Sheridan.
    The Rivals.
48. Robert Burns. See Outline XLVIII.
    Readings, pp. 490-496.
*49. The Beginnings of Romanticism. See Outlines XLV, XLVI, and XLVII.
    Readings, pp. 369-395, 470-489.
50. Burns.
    Readings, pp. 496-502.

SECOND SEMESTER

I. The Early Nineteenth Century

*1. William Wordsworth. See Outline XLIX.
    Readings, pp. 503-515.
 2. Wordsworth.
    Readings, pp. 516-521.
 3. Wordsworth.
    Readings, pp. 521-529.
*4. Wordsworth and Coleridge. See Outline L.
    Readings, pp. 542-553.
 5. Wordsworth.
    Readings, pp. 530-541.
 6. Samuel Taylor Coleridge.
    Readings, pp. 553-566.
*7. Sir Walter Scott. See Outline LI.
    Readings, pp. 579-585.
 8. Scott.
    Old Mortality.
 9. Early Nineteenth Century Essayists. See Outline LVI.
    Readings, pp. 567-578, 683-690.
*10. Lord Byron. See Outline LII.
    Readings, pp. 600-605.
11. Byron.
    Readings, pp. 586-600.
12. Byron.
    Readings, pp. 605-613.
*13. Percy Bysshe Shelley, See Outline LIII.
    Readings, pp. 614-625.
14. Shelley.
    Readings, pp. 625-628.
15. Shelley.
    Readings, pp. 629-638.
*16. John Keats. See Outline LIV.
    Readings, pp. 639-645.
17. Keats.
    Readings, pp. 645-649.
18. Keats.
    Readings, pp. 649-655.

II. The Victorian Age

*19. Thomas Carlyle. See Outline LVII.
    Readings, pp. 714-724.
20. Carlyle.
    Readings, pp. 724-732.
21. John Henry Newman. See Outline LIX.
    Readings, pp. 702-713.
*22. John Ruskin. See Outline LXIV.
    Readings, pp. 733-744.

23. Charles Dickens.
    David Copperfield.
24. William Makepeace Thackeray.
    Vanity Fair.
*25. The Victorian Novel. See Outlines LXII and LXIII.
26. George Eliot.
    Middlemarch.
27. Alfred Tennyson.
    Readings, pp. 747-757.
*28. Tennyson. See Outline LX.
    Readings, pp. 745-747; 769-784.
29. Tennyson.
    Readings, pp. 757-769.
30. Robert Browning.
    Readings, pp. 785-791; 802-811.
*31. Browning. See Outline LXI.
    Readings, pp. 791-802.
32. Browning.
    Readings, pp. 811-822.
33. Matthew Arnold.
    Readings, pp. 823-837.
*34. Arnold. See Outline LXV.
    Readings, pp. 840-852.
35. Arnold.
    Readings, pp. 837-840; 852-858.
36. Dante Gabriel Rossetti. See Outline LXVI.
    Readings, pp. 859-876.
*37. William Morris. See Outline LXVI.
    Readings, pp. 877-894.
38. Algernon Charles Swinburne. See Outline LXVII.
    Readings, pp. 895-915.
39. George Meredith.
    Readings, pp. 949-966.
*40. The Later Nineteenth Century Novel.
    Thomas Hardy's *The Return of the Native.*
41. Walter Horatio Pater.
    Readings, pp. 916-927.
42. Robert Louis Stevenson.
    Readings, pp. 928-948.
*43. Later Victorian Essayists.
    Readings, pp. 967-974.
44. Later Victorian Poetry.
    Readings, pp. 994-1006.

III. The Twentieth Century

45. Contemporary Essayists.
    Readings, pp. 974-993.
*46. The Contemporary Novel.
    Arnold Bennett's *The Old Wives' Tale.*
47. The Contemporary Drama.
    George Bernard Shaw's *Saint Joan.*
48. Poems of the Great War.
    Readings, pp. 1012-1025.
*49. Contemporary Poetry.
    Readings, pp. 1006-1011; 1047-1063.
50. Contemporary Prose.
    Readings, pp. 1026-1046.

II. A STUDY COURSE BY TYPES

Teachers who prefer a course in which English literature is studied by types, without particular reference to chronology, will be aided in their use of the book by the following classified list of its contents. The scheme of classification as a whole may be conveniently seen in the following table:

POETRY	**Lyric**		**Occasions**	**Tale**
	Love		Conviviality	Satire
	Nature		Satire	
	Childhood		Vers de Société	**Dramatic**
	Patriotism			Story
	The Great War		**Narrative**	Character
	Devotion		Epic	Ideas
	Reflection		Romance	**Didactic**
	Elegy		Ballad	Description
	Persons		History	Instruction

PROSE	**Narrative**		**Exposition**
	History		Criticism
	Biography		Literature and Art
	Travel		Society
	Romance		Education
	Allegory		Controversy
	Satire		Familiar Essay
			Oratory
	Letters		Meditation

The distribution of literary pieces in this scheme appears in the following list:

POETRY

LYRIC—Love

LYRIC—Nature

LYRIC—Childhood

LYRIC—The Great War

LYRIC—Reflection

LYRIC—Elegy

PLANS OF STUDY

LYRIC—Vers de Société

NARRATIVE—BALLAD

NARRATIVE—HISTORY

NARRATIVE—TALE

NARRATIVE—Satire

DRAMATIC—Story

DRAMATIC—Character

DRAMATIC—Ideas

DIDACTIC—Description

DIDACTIC—Instruction

PROSE
NARRATIVE—History

NARRATIVE—Biography

NARRATIVE—Travel

NARRATIVE—Romance

NARRATIVE—Allegory

NARRATIVE—Satire

EXPOSITION—Criticism: *Literature and Art*

EXPOSITION—Criticism: *Society*

EXPOSITION—Criticism: *Education*

EXPOSITION—Controversy

EXPOSITION—Familiar Essay

EXPOSITION—Oratory

EXPOSITION—Meditation

LETTERS

EARLY ENGLISH POEMS IN MODERN VERSIONS

BEOWULF

It is supposed that Beowulf, the hero of this poem, was a real person. Although Beowulf himself does not appear in sober history, his uncle, Hygelac of the poem, is identified with a historical Scandinavian hero who invaded the land of enemies on the Lower Rhine about 512 A. D. (See Section XL of the text below.) Even though the uncle was disastrously defeated in this foray, the nephew Beowulf seems to have distinguished himself for bravery and for astounding feats of endurance. We infer that, as a result of his prowess, Beowulf was cele-brated in song and story, and that one generation of narrators after another enhanced his achievements, the enhancement consisting largely, no doubt, in the attachment to our hero of exploits originally associated with other personages,—heroes or gods. Such a natural process of story growth seems to account for the presence in our poem of some four sepa-rate stories: (1) a fight with Grendel, (2) a fight with Grendel's mother, (3) the vic-torious return of the hero to his home, and (4) a fight with a dragon. These four stories, originally, no doubt, told or sung separately, were probably combined into a form ap-proaching that of the present poem, in the course of the seventh century. The events of the poem take place in Denmark and southern Sweden, and since England is nowhere men-tioned, it seems likely that the main elements of the story had been gathered together before the last migration of the Angles to the island. The present form of the poem, however, with its unfortunate admixture of Christian elements, is due to a final recension in England.

The chief merit of *Beowulf* will hardly escape him who reads the poem as a vigorous nar-rative of stirring adventure, heroic endeavor, and elevated sentiments. Imagination and de-scriptive power are not lacking, and the charm of picturesque phrasing pervades the poem.

BEOWULF

THE FIRST PART

PROLOGUE. THE CHIVALRY OF THE DANISH EMPIRE. THE COMING OF SCYLD AND HIS GLORIOUS CAREER. THE BIRTH OF HIS YOUTH. THE PASSING OF SCYLD.

What ho! we have heard tell of the grandeur of the imperial kings of the spear-bearing Danes in former days, how those ethelings promoted bravery. Often did Scyld of the Sheaf wrest from harry-ing bands, from many tribes, their con-vivial seats; the dread of him fell upon warriors, whereas he had at the first been a lonely foundling; — of all that (humilia-tion) he lived to experience solace; he waxed great under the welkin, he flour-ished with trophies, till that every one of the neighboring peoples over the sea were constrained to obey him, and pay trewage: — that was a good king!

To him was born a son to come after him, a young (prince) in the palace, whom God sent for the people's com-fort. He (God) knew the hard calamity, what they had erst endured when they were without a king for a long while; and in consideration thereof the Lord of Life, the Ruler of Glory accorded to them a time of prosperity.

Beowulf was renowned, his fame sprang wide; heir of Scyld in the Scede-lands. So ought a young chief to work with his wealth, with gracious largesses, while in his father's nurture; that in his riper age willing comrades may in re-turn stand by him at the coming of war, and that men may do his bidding. Em-inence must, in every nation, be attained by deeds (worthy) of praise.

As for Scyld, he departed, at the des-tined hour, full of exploit, to go into the Master's keeping. They then car-ried him forth to the shore of the sea,

i

his faithful comrades, as he himself had requested, while he with his words held sway as lord of the Scyldings; dear chief of the land, he had long tenure of power.

There at lithe stood the ship with ringed prow, glistening fresh, and outward bound; convoy for a prince. Down laid they there the loved chief, dispenser of jewels, on the lap of the ship, the illustrious (dead) by the mast. There was store of precious things, ornaments from remote parts, brought together; never heard I of craft comelier fitted with slaughter weapons and campaigning harness, with bills and breast-mail: — in his keeping lay a multitude of treasures, which were to pass with him far away into the watery realm. Not at all with less gifts, less stately opulence, did they outfit him, than those had done, who at the first had sent him forth, lone over the wave, when he was an infant. Furthermore they set up by him a gold-wrought banner, high over his head; they let the holm bear him, gave him over to ocean; sad was their soul, mourning their mood. Men do not know to say of a sooth, not heads of halls, men of mark under heaven, who received that burden!

I

KING HROTHGAR. HIS POPULARITY. THE BUILDING OF HEOROT AND THE HAPPY LIFE OF THE COURT. GRENDEL.

Then was in the towers Beowulf of the Scyldings, the dear king of his people, for a long time famous among the nations — his father was gone otherwhere, patriarch from family seat — till in succession to him was born the lofty Healfdene; he governed while he lived, old and warlike, contented Scyldings. To him four children, one after another, awoke in the world: Heorogar, commander of armies, and Hrothgar, and Halga the good: I heard that Elan queen was consort of the warlike Scylding.

To Hrothgar was given martial spirit, warlike ambition; insomuch that his cousins gladly took him for leader, until the young generation grew up, a mighty regiment of clansmen. Into his mind it came, that he would give orders for men to construct a hall-building, a great mead-house, (greater) than the children·

of men had ever heard tell of; and that therewithin he would freely deal out to young and old what God should give him, save people's land and lives of men.

Then I heard of work widely proclaimed to many a tribe throughout this world, to make a fair gathering-place of people. His plan was in good time accomplished, with a quickness surprising to men; so that it was all ready, the greatest of hall-buildings. He gave it the name of Heorot, he who with his word had wide dominion. He belied not his announcement; — rings he distributed, treasure at the banquet. The hall towered aloft, high and with pinnacles spanning the air; awaited the scathing blasts of destructive flame. No appearance was there as yet of knife-hatred starting up between son-in-law and father-in-law in revenge of blood.

Then the outcast creature, he who dwelt in darkness, with torture for a time endured that he heard joyance day by day, loud sounding in hall; there was the swough of the harp, the ringing song of the minstrel.

Said one who was skilled to narrate from remote time the primeval condition of men; quoth he — 'The Almighty made the earth, the country radiant with beauty, all that water surroundeth, delighting in magnificence. He ordained sun and moon, luminaries for light to the dwellers on earth, and adorned the rustic regions with branches and leaves; life also he created for all the kinds that live and move.'

Thus they, the warrior-band, in joyance lived and full delight; — until that one began to work atrocity, a fiend in the hall. The grim visitant was called Grendel, the dread mark-ranger, he who haunted moors, fen and fastness: — the unblessed man had long time. kept the abode of monsters, ever since the Creator had proscribed them. On Cain's posterity did the eternal Lord wreak that slaughter, for that he slew Abel. He profited not by that violence; but He banished him far away, the Maker for that crime banished him from mankind. From that origin all strange broods awoke, eotens and elves and ogres, as well as giants who warred against God long time; — He repaid them due retribution.

II

GRENDEL. HIS SUCCESSFUL RAID. THE DE-
JECTION OF HROTHGAR AND HIS COURT.

He set out then as soon as night was
come, to explore the lofty house; how the
mailed Danes had after carousal bestowed themselves in it. So he found
therein a princely troop sleeping after
feast; they knew not sorrow, desolation 10
of men. The baleful wight, grim and
greedy, was ready straight, fierce and furious, and in their sleep he seized thirty
of the thanes; thence hied him back,
yelling over his prey, to go to his home 15
with the war-spoils, and reach his habitation. Then was in the dawning and with
early day the war-craft of Grendel plain
to the grooms; then was upraised after
festivity the voice of weeping, a great 20
cry in the morning. The illustrious
ruler, the honored prince, sat woebegone;
majestic rage he tholed, he endured sorrow for his thanes: — since they had
surveyed the track of the monster, of the 25
accursed goblin; — that contest was too
severe, horrible, and prolonged. It was
not a longer space, but the interval of
one night, that he again perpetrated a
huger carnage; and he recked not of it 30
— outrage and atrocity; he was too fixed
in those things. Then was it not hard
to find some who sought a resting-place
elsewhere more at large, a bed among
the castle-bowers, when to them was 35
manifested and plainly declared by conspicuous proof the malice of the hell-
thane; — whoever had once escaped the
fiend did from thenceforward hold himself farther aloof and closer. So dom- 40
ineered and nefariously warred he single
against them all, until that the best of
houses stood empty. The time was long;
twelve winters' space did the friend of
the Scyldings suffer indignity, woes of 45
every kind, unbounded sorrows; and so
in process of time it became openly
known to the sons of men through ballads in lamentable wise, that Grendel
warred continually against Hrothgar; he 50
waged malignant hostilities, violence and
feud, many seasons, unremitting strife;
he would not have peace with any man
of the Danish power, or remove the life-
bale, or compound for tribute; nor could 55
any of the senators expect worthy compensation at the hands of the destroyer;

the foul ruffian, a dark shadow of death,
was pursuing the venerable and the
youthful alike. He prowled about and
lay in wait; at nights he continually held
the misty moors; — men do not know in
what direction hell's agents move in their
rounds.

Many were the atrocities which the foe
of mankind, the grisly prowler, oft accomplished, hard indignities,— Heorot he
occupied, the richly decorated hall, in
dark nights — yet was he by no means
able to come nigh the throne, sacred to
God, nor did he share the sentiment
thereof.

That was a huge affliction for the
friend of the Scyldings, heart breaking.
Many a time and oft did the realm sit
in conclave; they meditated on a remedy,
what course it were best for them, soul-
burdened men, to take against these
awful horrors. Sometimes they vowed
at idol fanes, honors of sacrifice; with
words they prayed that the goblin-queller
would afford them relief against huge
oppressions. Such was their custom,
heathens' religion; they thought of hell
in their imagination; they were not
aware of the Maker, the Judge of actions,
they knew not God the Governor, nor did
they at all understand how to glorify the
Crowned Head of the heavens, the Ruler
of glory.

It is woe for him who is impelled by
headlong perversity to plunge his soul
into the gulf of fire; not to believe in
consolation nor in any way turn: — well
is it for him who is permitted, after
death-day, to visit the Lord, and claim
sanctuary in the Father's arms.

III

THE VOYAGE OF THE HERO. A PARLEY.

Thus was the son of Healfdene perpetually tossed with the trouble of that
time; the sapient man was unable to
avert the woe. Too heavy, horrible, and
protracted was the struggle which had
overtaken that people; tribulation cruel,
hugest of nocturnal pests.

That in his distant home learnt a thane
of Hygelac's, a brave man among the
Goths; he learnt the deeds of Grendel;
he was of mankind strongest in might
in the day of this life; he was of noble
birth and of robust growth. He ordered

a wave-traveler, a good one, to be prepared for him; said he would pass over the swan-road and visit the gallant king, the illustrious ruler, inasmuch as he was in need of men. That adventure was little grudged him by sagacious men, though he was dear to them; they egged on the dareful spirit, they observed auguries. The brave man had selected champions of the leeds of the Goths, the keenest whom he could find; with fourteen in company he took to ship;—a swain for pilot, a water-skilled man, pointed out the landmarks.

Time went on; the floater was on the waves, the boat under the cliff. Warriors ready dight mounted on the prow; currents eddied, surf against the beach; lads bore into the ship's lap bright apparel, gallant harness of war; the men, the brave men on adventure, shoved off the tight-timbered craft. So the foamy-necked floater went forth over the swelling ocean urged by the wind, most like to a bird; till that in due time, on the next day, the coily-stemmed cruiser had made such way that the voyagers saw land, sea-cliffs gleaming, hills towering, headlands stretching out to sea; then was the voyage accomplished, the water-passage ended. Then lightly up the Weder Leeds and sprang ashore, they made fast the sea-wood, they shook out their sarks, their war-weeds, they thanked God for that their seafaring had been easy.

Then from his rampart did the Scyldings' warden, he who had to guard the sea-cliffs, espy men bearing over bulwark bright shields, accoutrements ready for action;—curiosity urged him with impassioned thought (to learn) who those men were. Off he set then to the shore, riding on horseback, thane of Hrothgar; powerfully he brandished a huge lance in his hands, and he demanded with authoritative words—'Who are ye arm-bearing men, fenced with mail-coats, who have come thus with proud ship over the watery highway, hither over the billows? Long time have I been in fort, stationed on the extremity of the country; I have kept the coast-guard, that on the land of the Danes no enemy might be able to do hurt: never have shield-bearing men more openly attempted to land here; nor do

ye know beforehand the pass-word of our warriors, the confidential token of kinsmen. I never saw, of eorls upon ground, a finer figure in harness than is one of yourselves; he is no mere goodman bedizened with armor, unless his look belies him, his unique aspect. Now I am bound to know your nationality, before ye on your way hence as explorers at large proceed any further into the land of the Danes. Now ye foreigners, mariners of the sea, ye hear my plain meaning; haste is best to let me know whence your comings are.'

IV

BEOWULF EXPLAINS THEIR VISIT TO THE WARDEN'S SATISFACTION. THEREUPON HE GUIDES THEIR MARCH TO HEOROT. THE WARDEN RETURNS.

To him the chiefest gave answer; the captain of the band unlocked the treasure of words: 'We are people of Gothic race, and hearth-fellows of Hygelac. My father was celebrated among the nations, a noble commander by the name of Ecgtheow; he lived to see many years, ere he departed an aged man out of his mansion; he is quickly remembered by every worshipful man all over the world. We with friendly intent have come to visit thy lord, the son of Healfdene, the guardian of his people; be thou good to us with instructions! We have for the illustrious prince of the Danes a great message; there is no need to be dark about the matter, as I suppose. Thou knowest if it is so as we have heard say for a truth, that among the Scyldings some strange depredator, a mysterious author of deeds, in the darkness of night inflicts in horrible wise monstrous atrocity, indignity, and havoc. Of this I can, in all sincerity of heart, teach Hrothgar a remedy; how he, so wise and good, shall overpower the enemy; if for him the fight of afflictions was ever destined to take a turn, better times to come again, and the seethings of anguish grow calmer; or else for ever hereafter tholeth he a time of tribulation, sore distress, so long as the best of houses resteth there upon her eminence.'

The warden addressed them, where he sat on his horse, an officer undaunted: 'Of every particular must a sharp esquire know the certainty as to words and works — any one who hath a sense of duty. I gather from what I hear that this is a friendly band to the lord of the Scyldings. March ye forward, bearing weapons and weeds; I will guide you: likewise I will command my kinsmen thanes honorably to keep against every foe your vessel, the newly dight, the boat on the beach: until the neck-laced craft shall bear back again over the water-streams her dear lord to Wedermark. To such a benign adventurer is it given, that he passeth unscathed through the encounter of battle.'

They proceeded then on their march; the vessel remained still, rode on her cable, the wide-bosomed ship, at anchor fast; — the boar-figures shone over the cheek-guards, pranked with gold, ornate and hard-welded; — the farrow kept guard. In fighting mood they raged along, the men pushed forward; down-hill they ran together, until they could see the hall structure, gallant and gold-adorned; that was to dwellers on earth the most celebrated of all mansions under the sky, that in which the ruler dwelt; the gleam of it shot over many lands. Then did the warrior point out to them the court of the valiant, which was now conspicuous; — that they could go straight to it. Like a man of war, he wheeled about his horse, and spake a parting word: 'It is time for me to go; may the allwielding Father graciously keep you safe in adventures! I will to the sea, to keep guard against hostile force.'

V

ARRIVAL AND ACCOST. BEOWULF SENDS IN
HIS NAME.

The street was stone-paven; the path guided the banded men. The war-corslet shone, hard, hand-locked; the polished ring-iron sang in its meshes, when they in grim harness now came marching to the hall. The sea-weary men set down their broad shields, bucklers mortal hard, against the terrace of that mansion. Then they seated themselves on the bench; — their mail-coats rang, harness of warriors; — the spears stood, sea-men's artillery, stacked together, ash-timber with tip of gray; the iron troop was accoutred worthily.

Then a proud officer there questioned the martial crew as to their kindred: — 'Whence bring ye damasked shields, gray sarks, and visored helms; — a pile of war shafts? I am Hrothgar's herald and esquire. Never saw I foreigners, so many men, loftier looking. I think that ye for daring, not at all of desperate fortune, but for courageous emprise, have come to visit Hrothgar.'

To him then with gallant bearing answered the proud leed of the Wederas; words spake he back, firm under helmet: —'We are Hygelac's table-fellows; my name is Beowulf. I will expound mine errand to the son of Healfdene, to the illustrious prince, to thy lord, if he will deign us that we may approach him so good.'

Wulfgar addressed them — that was a leed of the Wendlas; his courage had been witnessed by many, his valor and wisdom: —'Thereanent will I ask the friend of the Danes, the Scyldings' lord, the ring-dispenser, according as thou dost petition, the illustrious chief (will I ask) concerning thy visit; and to thee promptly declare the answer, which the brave prince is pleased to give me.'

Thereupon he returned briskly to where Hrothgar sat, old and hoary, with his guard of warriors: he went with gallant bearing till he took his stand before the shoulders of the Danish prince; he knew the custom of nobility. Wulfgar addressed himself to his liege lord: 'Here are arrived, come from far, over the circuit of ocean, men of the Goths; the companions name their chief Beowulf. They make petition, that they, my prince, may be permitted to exchange discourse with thee: do not thou award them a refusal of thy conversation, benignant Hrothgar! They by their war-harness appear worthy of the reverence of eorls; certainly the chief is a valiant man, he who has conducted those martial comrades hither.'

VI

THE OLD KING KNOWS ALL ABOUT HIM.
AND ORDERS HIM TO BE ADMITTED. BE-
OWULF EXPLAINETH HIS VISIT AND EN-
TERPRISETH THE BATTLE TO FIGHT THE
FOE. HE WILL REMOVE THE SCOURGE, OR
DIE IN THE ATTEMPT.

Hrothgar, crown of Scyldings, uttered speech: 'I knew him when he was a page. His good old father was Ecgtheow by name; to whose home Hrethel of the Goths gave over his only daughter: it is his offspring surely, his grown-up son, that is hither come, come to visit a loyal friend. Sure enough they did say that — the sailors who carried thither for compliment the presents to the Goths — that he hath thirty men's strength in his handgrip, a valiant campaigner. Him hath holy God of high grace sent to us, sent to the western Danes, as I hope, against Grendel's terror; I must proffer the brave man treasures for his great-heartedness. Be thou full of alacrity, request the banded friends to enter, one and all, into my presence. Say to them moreover expressly with words, that they are welcome visitors to the Danish leeds.' [Then to the door of the hall Wulfgar went] he announced his message: — 'To you I am commanded to say by my chieftain the lord of the eastern Danes, that he knoweth your noble ancestry, and ye to him are, over the sea-waves, men of hardihood, welcome hither. Now ye can go, in your warlike equipage, with helm on head, to the presence of Hrothgar; leave the war-boards, here to abide, and the wooden battle-shafts till the parley is over.' Up then arose the prince: about him many a trooper, a splendid band of thanes; some remained there, they kept the armor, as their brave captain bade. They formed all together, as the officer (Wulfgar) showed the way, under the roof of Heorot; [he went with courage high] with a firm look under his helmet, till he took his stand in the royal chamber. Beowulf uttered a speech — on him his byrnie shone, a curious net-work linked by cunning device of the artificer — 'To Hrothgar hail! I am Hygelac's kinsman and cousin-thane; I have undertaken many exploits in young-sterhood. To me on my native soil the affair of Grendel became openly known; seafaring men say that this hall do stand, fabric superb, of every trooper empty and useless, as soon as the light of evening under the cope of heaven is hidden from view. Then did my people, the best of them, sagacious fellows, O royal Hrothgar, insense me that I should visit thee; because they knew the strength of my might; they had themselves been spectators when I came off my campaign battered by foes, where I bound five monsters, humbled the eoten brood; and in the waves I slew nickers in the night-time, I ran narrow risks, avenged the grievance of the Wederas — they had been acquainted with grief — a grinding I gave the spoilers; — and now against Grendel I am bound, against that formidable one, single-handed, to champion the quarrel against the giant. Wherefore I will now petition thee, prince of the glorious Danes, thou roof-tree of the Scyldings, one petition; that thou refuse me not, oh thou shelter of warriors, thou imperial lord of nations, now I have come from such a distance, that I may have the task alone — I and my band of eorls, this knot of hardy men — to purge Heorot. I have learnt too that the terrible one out of bravado despises weapons; I therefore will forgo the same — as I hope that Hygelac my prince may be to me of mood benignant,— that I bear not sword or broad shield, or yellow buckler, to the contest; but with handgrip I undertake to encounter the enemy, and contend for life, foe to foe; there shall he whom death taketh resign himself to the doom of the Lord. 'I suppose that he will, if he can have his way, in the hall of battle devour fearlessly the men of the Goths, just as he often did the power of the Hrethmen. Thou wilt not need to cover my head (with a mound), but he will have me all blood-besprent, if death taketh me; he will bear away the gory corpse with intent to feast upon it, the solitary ranger will eat it remorselessly, will stain the moor-swamps; no need wilt thou have to care any longer for the disposal of my body. Send to Hygelac, if Hild take me, the matchless armor that protects my breast, bravest of jackets; — that is a relic of Hrethla's, a work of Weland's. Wyrd goeth ever as she is bound.'

VII

HROTHGAR EMBRACES HIS VISITOR'S OFFER AND POURS OUT THE TALE OF HIS MISERY. THE NEWCOMERS ARE FEASTED IN THE HALL.

Hrothgar, crown of Scyldings, uttered speech: 'For pledged rescue thou, Beowulf my friend, and at honor's call, hast come to visit us. Thy father did fight out a mighty feud; he was the banesman of Heatholaf among the Wylfings; then the nation could not keep him for dread of invasion. Therefrom he went over the yeasty waves to visit the Southron folk of the Danes, of the honorable Scyldings, at the time when I had just then become king over the Danish folk, and in my prime swayed the jewel-stored treasure-city of heroes: when Heorogar my elder brother was dead, no longer living, Healfdene's son. He was better than I! Afterwards I composed the feud for money; I sent to the Wylfings over the water's ridge ancient treasures; he swore oaths (of homage) to me.

'It is a sorrow for me in my soul to tell to any mortal men what humiliation, what horrors Grendel hath brought upon me in Heorot with his malignant stratagems. My hall-troop, my warrior band, is reduced to nothing; Wyrd hath swept them away in the hideous visitation of Grendel. God unquestionably can arrest the fell destroyer in his doings. Full oft they boasted when refreshed with beer, troop-fellows over the ale-can, that they in the beer-hall would receive Grendel's onset with clash of swords. Then was this mead-hall at morning-tide, this royal saloon bespattered with gore, at blush of dawn, all the bench-timber was reeking with blood, the hall with deadly gore; so much the less owned I of trusty lieges, of dear nobility, when death had taken those away.

'Sit now to banquet, and merrily share the feast, brave captain, with (thy) fellows, as thy mind moves thee.'

Then was there for the Goth-men all together, in the beer-hall, a table cleared; there the resolute men went to sit in the pride of their strength. A thane attended to the service; one who bore in his hand a decorated ale-can; he poured forth the sheer nectar. At times a minstrel sang, clear-voiced in Heorot; there was social merriment, a brave company of Danes and Wederas.

VIII

UNFERTH THE KING'S ORATOR IS JEALOUS. HE BAITS THE YOUNG ADVENTURER AND IN A SCOFFING SPEECH DARES HIM TO A NIGHTWATCH FOR GRENDEL. BEOWULF IS ANGERED AND THUS HE IS DRAWN OUT TO BOAST OF HIS YOUTHFUL FEATS.

Unferth made a speech, Ecglaf's son; he who sat at the feet of the Scyldings' 5 lord, broached a quarrelsome theme—the adventure of Beowulf the high-souled voyager was great despite to him, because he grudged that any other man should ever in the world achieve more exploits 10 under heaven than he himself:—'Art thou that Beowulf, he who strove with Breca on open sea in swimming-match, where ye twain out of bravado explored the floods, and foolhardily in deep water 15 jeoparded your lives? nor could any man, friend or foe, turn the pair of you from the dismal adventure! What time ye twain plied in swimming, where ye twain covered with your arms the awful stream, 20 meted the sea-streets, buffeted with hands, shot over ocean; the deep boiled with waves, a wintry surge. Ye twain in the realm of waters toiled a sennight; he at swimming outvied thee, had greater force. 25 Then in morning hour the swell cast him ashore on the Heathoram people, whence he made for his own patrimony, dear to his leeds he made for the land of the Brondings, a fair stronghold, where he 30 was lord of folk, of city, and of rings. All his boast to thee-ward, Beanstan's son soothly fulfilled. Wherefore I anticipate for thee worse luck—though thou wert everywhere doughty in battle- 35 shocks, in grim war-tug—if thou darest bide in Grendel's way a night-long space.'

Beowulf, son of Ecgtheow, uttered speech:—'Lo, big things hast thou, my friend Unferth, beer-exalted, spoken 40 about Breca; hast talked of his adventure! Rightly I claim, that I have proved more sea-power, more buffetings in waves, than any other man. He and I used to talk when we were pages, and we used to 45 brag of this—we were both of us at that time in youngsterhood—how that we two would out on the main and put our lives in jeopardy; and that we matched so. Drawn sword we had, as we at 50 swimming plied, firm in hand: we meant to guard us against the whale-fishes. Not a whit from me could he further fleet on sea-waves, swifter on holm; not from him would I. So we twain kept 55 together in the sea for the space of five nights, till the flood parted us, the seething billows, coldest weather, darkening night, and a fierce wind from the north came dead against us; rough were the waves. The sea-fishes' temper was stirred; and then it was that my body-sark, firm, hand-locked, gave me help against the spiteful ones; the plaited war-jacket lay about my breast, gold-pranked. Me to bottom dragged a spotty monster, tight the grim thing had me in grip; nathless 't was given me that I got at the vermin with point, with hand-bill; combat despatched the mighty sea-brute by my hand.

IX

BEOWULF CONTINUES HIS STORY AND TELLS HOW HE MADE HAVOC OF THE SEA-MONSTERS. HE WAXES WARM AND FLOUTS THE ORATOR. HE VOWS TO FACE GRENDEL. RESTORATION OF SOCIAL HARMONY WHEREOF THE QUEEN IS THE CENTER. HROTHGAR SOLEMNLY COMMITS TO BEOWULF THE NIGHTWARD OF HEOROT.

'As repeatedly as the spiteful assailants shrewdly pressed me, I served them (liberally) with precious sword as was meet. They did not have their slaughterous revel, the foul brigands, that they should eat me up sitting around their supper, by the floor of the sea; but (on the contrary) next morning, wounded with weapons along the wrack of the wave, they lay high and dry; by swords they had their quietus, so that never afterwards about the swelling highway should they let seafaring men of their destined course.

'Light came from the east, the bright signal of God; the waves grew calm, so that I was able to see the forelands, the windy walls. Fortune often rescues the warrior, if he is not fated to die; provided that his courage is sound! Anyhow 't was my good luck, that I slew with the sword nine nickers. Never did I hear of a harder fight under heaven's roof in the night-time, nor of a man more distressed in ocean streams; howbeit I escaped the clutch of foes with my life, though worn and spent. Me the sea upcast, the swirling flood, upon the land of the Finns, the heaving billow. I never heard say aught by thee of such deadly fightings, sword-clashings: Breca never yet, at war play, not he nor you, deed achieved so valorously with flashing swords — of that I brag not much —

though thou wast banesmen to thy brother, thy next of kin; for which thou shalt in hell damnation dree, though doughty be thy wit. I say to thee of a sooth, thou son of Ecglaf, that never had Grendel the foul ruffian made such a tale of horrors for thy prince, such disgrace in Heorot, if thy courage were, if thy spirit were, so formidable as thou thyself claimest. But he hath found out that he need not greatly fear reprisals, grisly edge-clash, from your people, the mighty Scyldings; he taketh blackmail, respecteth no one of the people of the Danes, but maketh a sport of war, slaughtereth and feasteth : — no thought hath he of a fight with the spear-Danes. But now shall the Goth show him erelong puissance and emprise in the way of war After that, he who can shall go proud into the mead-hall, when over the sons of men the morning light of another day, the sun, with radiance clothed, shall shine from the south.'

Then was in bliss the dispenser of wealth, gray-haired and militant; he believed in help; the prince of the glorious Danes, the shepherd of the people, perceived in Beowulf a resolute purpose. There was laughter of mighty men; music sounded; the words (of song) were jovial.

Wealhtheow moved forward, Hrothgar's queen, mindful of ceremonies; she greeted in her gold array the men in Hall; and then the noble lady presented the beaker first to the sovereign of the East-Danes, wished him blithe at the banquet, and dear to his leeds; — he merrily enjoyed the feast and the hall-cup, valiant king. Then the Helming princess went the round, to elder and to younger, every part; handed the jeweled cup; till the moment came, that she, the diademed queen, with dignity befitting brought the mead-cup nigh to Beowulf; she greeted the leed of the Goths, she thanked God with wise choice of words, for that her desire was come to pass, that she in any warrior believed for remedy of woes. He, the death-doing warrior, accepted the beaker at Wealhtheow's hand, and then he descanted, elate for battle; — Beowulf, son of Ecgtheow, uttered speech: 'I undertook that, when I went on board, and sat on the sea-boat, with the company of my fel-

lows, that I once for all would work out
the will of your leeds, or fall in the
death-struggle, in the grip of the fiend.
I am bound as an eorl to fulfill the emprise, or in this mead-hall to meet my 5
death-day.' To the lady the words were
well-liking, the vaunt-speech of the Goth;
she walked gold-arrayed, high-born queen
of the nation, to sit by her lord.

Then was again as erst within the hall 10
the lofty word outspoken, the company
was happy, the sound was that of a
mighty people; until that sudden the son
of Healfdene was minded to retire to his
nightly rest; he knew that against the 15
high hall war was determined by the
monster, from the time when they could
[not] see the sun's light or shrouding
night came over all, and the creatures
of darkness came stalking abroad; he 20
warred in obscurity. All the company
arose. Then did man greet man, Hrothgar greeted Beowulf, bespake him luck,
mastery in the house of hospitality; and
delivered this speech: ' Never before, 25
since I could heave hand and shield, did
I confide the guard-house of the Danes
to any man, but only to thee now on this
occasion. Have now and hold the best
of houses; resolve on success: show valor 30
amain; be vigilant against the foe!
Thou shalt not have any desire unfulfilled, if thou that mighty work with life
achievest.'

X

BEOWULF DOFFS HIS ARMOR AND WATCHES
    UNARMED. A POINT OF HONOR. HIS
    COMPANIONS SLEEP.

So Hrothgar, chief of Scyldings, took
his departure with retinue of men, out of
hall; he was minded to join Wealhtheow,
his queen and consort. The glory of
kings had — so men told one another — 45
set up a hall-warden against Grendel;
he had undertaken the single service
about the patriarch of the Danes, offered
watch against the monster; — assuredly
the Gothic leed with joyous mien trusted 50
in valorous might and the smile of
Providence.

Then put he off from him his iron
byrnie, helmet from head; delivered to
his esquire the richly-dight sword, choic- 55
est steel; and charged him with the care
of his war-harness. Then did the valiant

man Beowulf the Goth utter some vaunting words ere he mounted on bed: ' I
reckon myself to be in the fury of battle,
in warlike feats, no wise below the pretensions of Grendel; for that reason I
will not with sword give him his quietus,
deprive him of life, although I very well
may. Naught knoweth he of those
gentle practices, to give and take sword-
cuts, to hew the shield, dread though
he be in feats of horror: — but we twain
shall in the night-time supersede the
blade, if he dare to court war without
weapon; and thereafter may the allwise
God, the holy Lord, adjudge success on
which side soever may to him appear
meet!'

Then the daring warrior laid him
down; the pillow received the countenance of the eorl; and round about him
many a smart sea-warrior couched to his
hall-rest. Not one of them thought that
from that place he should ever again visit
his own estate, his folk and castle, where
he was brought up; but they had been informed that before now a bloody death
had all too much reduced them, the Danish
people, in that festive hall. But to them,
the leeds of Wedermark, did the Lord
grant webs of war-speed, strength and
support, that they by the force of one,
by his single prowess, should all be victorious over their foe. For a truth it
is shown, that the mighty God has governed mankind in every age! 35

He came in dim night, marching along,
ranger of the dark. The defenders slept,
they whose duty it was to guard that
gabled mansion — all slept but one! 40

It was very well known to all men,
that the ruthless destroyer might not
against the will of God whirl them under
darkness; but (all the same) he, vigilant
in defiance of the foe, awaited in full-
fraught mood the arbitrament of battle.

XI

GRENDEL'S LAST MEAL. THE BATTLE BE-
    GINS.

Then came Grendel marching from the
moor under the misty brows; he bore
the wrath of God. The assassin meant
to catch some one of human-kind in that
lofty hall; he tore along under heaven
in the direction where he knew the hospitable building, the gold-hall of men,

metal-spangled, ever ready for his en-tainment; — that was not the first time he had visited Hrothgar's homestead. Never had he in his life-days, earlier or later, met so tough a warrior, such hall-guards!

Came then journeying to the hall the felon mirth-bereft; suddenly the door, fastened with bars of wrought iron, sprang open as soon as he touched it with his hands; thus bale-minded and big with rage he wrecked the vestibule of the hall. Quickly after that the fiend was treading on the paven floor; he went ravening; out of his eyes there stood likest to flame an eerie light. He perceived in the hall many warriors, a troop of kinsmen, grouped together, a band of cousins, asleep. Then was his mood exalted to laughter; he counted, the fell ruffian, that he should sever, ere day came, the life of each one of them from his body, seeing that luck had favored him to gratify his slaughterous appetite. That was not, however, so destined, that he should be permitted to eat any more of mankind after that night.

Mighty rage the kinsman of Hygelac curbed, considering how the assassin meant to proceed in the course of his ravenings. Nor was the marauder minded to delay it; but he seized promptly at his first move a sleeping warrior, tore him in a moment, crunched the bony frame, drank blood of veins, swallowed huge morsels; in a trice he had devoured the lifeless body, feet, hands, and all. He stepped up nearer forward; he was then taking with his hand the great-hearted warrior on his bed. The fiend reached towards him with his fang: — he promptly seized with shrewd design and grappled his arm. Quickly did the boss of horrors discover that, that never in all the world, all the quarters of the earth, had he met man more strange with bigger hand-grip; he in mood became alarmed in spirit; but never the quicker could he get away. His mind was to be going; he wanted to flee into darkness; rejoin the devils' pack; his entertainment there was not such as he before had met with in bygone days. Then did the brave kinsman of Hygelac remember his dis-course of the evening; up he stood full length, and grappled with him amain; his fingers cracked as they would burst.

The monster was making off; the eorl followed him up. The oaf was minded, if so be he might, to fling himself loose, and away therefrom to flee into fen-hol-lows; he knew that the control of his fingers was in the grip of a terrible foe; that was a rash expedition which the devastator had made to Heorot!

The guard-hall roared; — upon all the Danes, upon the inhabiters of the castle, upon every brave man, upon the eorls, came mortal panic. Furious were both the maddened champions; the building re-sounded; it was a great wonder that the genial saloon endured the combatants, that it did not fall to ground, that fair ornament of the country; only that it was inwardly and outwardly so firmly be-smithied with iron staunchions of mas-terly skill! There, from the sill started — as my story tells — many a mead-bench adorned with gold, where the ter-rible ones contended. Thereanent had the Scylding senators weened at the first, that never would any man by mortal force be able to wreck it, the beautiful and ivoried house, or by craft to disjoint it; — leastwise fire's embrace should swal-low it up in vapory reek.

The noise rose high, with renewed violence; the North-Danes were stricken with eldritch horror every one, whoso-ever heard even out on the wall the dole-ful cry, the adversary of God yelling a dismal lay, a song unvictorious: — the thrall of hell howling for his wound. He held him too fast, he who was in main the strongest of men in the day of this life.

XII

GRENDEL'S FLIGHT. HIS ARM REMAINS WITH BEOWULF AND IS SET UP AS A TROPHY. HEOROT IS PURGED.

The shelter of eorls was not by any means minded to let the murderous visit-ant escape alive; he did not reckon his life-days useful to any one of the leeds. There did many an eorl of Beowulf's unsheath his old heirloom; — would res-cue the life of their master, their great captain; if so be they might. They knew it not, — when they plunged into the fight, the stouthearted companions, and thought to hack him on every side, reach his life, — that no choicest blade upon earth, no war-bill would touch that destroyer, but he had by enchantment secured himself against victorious weapons, edges of all kinds. His life-parting [in the day of this life] was destined to be woeful, and the outcast spirit must travel far off into the realm of fiends. Then discovered he that, he who erst in wanton mood had wrought huge atrocity upon mankind — he was out of God's peace — that his body was not at his command, but the valiant kinsman of Hygelac had got hold of him by the hand; to either was the other's life loathsome. A deadly wound the foul warlock got; on his shoulder the fatal crack appeared; the sinews sprang wide, the bone-coverings burst. To Beowulf was victory given; Grendel must flee life-sick therefrom to the coverts of the fen, must make for a cheerless habitation; — full well he knew that the end of his life was reached, the number of his days. All the Danes had in the issue of that dire struggle the fulfilment of their desire.

He had then purged, he who but now came from far, sagacious and resolute, Hrothgar's hall; he had rescued it from danger; had succeeded in his night-task with brilliant achievement. The leed of the Gothic companions had made good his vaunt to the East-Danes; likewise he had entirely remedied the horror, the harrowing sorrow, which they were enduring before, and of dire necessity were forced to suffer; — huge indignity. That was a token conspicuous, when the hero of battle had affixed the hand, arm, and shoulder — that was the whole affair of Grendel's fang — under the gabled roof.

XIII

HORSEMEN UPON GRENDEL'S TRACK. RIDING, RACING AND TALE-TELLING. BEOWULF'S ADVENTURE A MINSTREL'S THEME; HIS FAME COUPLED WITH SIGEMUND'S; CONTRASTED WITH HEREMOD'S.

Then was in the morning — so goes my story — about the gift-hall many a warrior; the chiefs of the folk came from far and near, through divers ways, to survey the prodigy, the traces of the loathed one. His life-ending was no grief whatever to any of those who surveyed the track of the vanquished, how he in doleful mood away from that place.

in buffets worsted, had, death-doomed and fugitive, fled in mortal terror to the nickers' mere. There was the face of the lake surging with blood, the gruesome 5 plash of waves all turbid with reeking gore, with sword-spilth; — the death-doomed (Grendel) had discolored it; — presently he, void of joyance, in fenny covert yielded up his life, his heathen 10 soul; there did Hela receive him.

Thence back home went the old companions along with many a bachelor from the pleasure-trip; from the mere in high spirits riding on horses, barons on jen-15 nets. There was Beowulf's achievement rehearsed; many a one often said that south nor north between the seas all the wide world over, other none of shield-bearing warriors under the compass of 20 the firmament preferable were or worthier of sovereignty. They did not, however, at all disparage their natural lord, gracious Hrothgar; but he was a good king!

25 Now and then the gallant warriors loosened their russet nags for a gallop, to run a match, where the turfways looked fair, or were favorably known. Otherwhiles a thane of the king's, bom-30 bastic groom, his mind full of ballads, the man who remembered good store of old-world tales — word followed word by the bond of truth — began anon to rehearse, cunningly to compose, the adven-35 ture of Beowulf, and fluently to pursue the story in its order, with interlacing words. At large he detailed, what he had heard say of Sigemund's exploits, much that was strange, the battle-toil 40 of the Wælsing, distant expeditions, things the sons of men quite knew not of, feud and atrocity; — none but Fitela by his side, when he would say aught of such matter, uncle to nephew, as they 45 had ever stood by one another in every struggle: they had with swords laid low many of the monster brood. To Sigemund there sprang up after his death-day no little fame; forasmuch as he, 50 hardy in fight, had quelled the dragon, the keeper of treasure; he, the son of a prince, in under the hoary rock, single-handed enterprised the perilous deed; — Fitela was not with him. Nathless he 55 succeeded so well that the sword sped through the stupendous worm, till it stuck in the bank, noble iron! the dragon

died the death. The champion had by valor attained that he might enjoy the jewel-hoard at his own discretion; he laded the sea-boat, the son of Wæls bore to the bosom of the ship the bright ornaments; the worm dissolved with heat. He was by daring exploits the most famous of adventurers far and wide over the world, shelter of warriors; such eminence he won.

When Heremod's warfare had slackened, his puissance and emprise, he among the Eotens was decoyed forth into the power of enemies, promptly sent out of the way. Him did billows of sorrow disable too long; he to his leeds, to all his princes, became a loyal anxiety. Moreover, in his earlier times, many a wise countryman had often deplored the adventurous life of the ardent soul, such a one as had trusted to him for remedy of grievances, that the royal child might grow powerful, succeed to the state of his fathers, protect the people, the treasure and the castle, realm of heroes, patrimony of the Scyldings. There was he, Hygelac's kinsman, to all mankind, and to his friends, more acceptable; the other was seized with fury.

At intervals racing they with their horses measured the fallow streets. Then was the light of morning launched and advanced; there was many a varlet going eager-minded to the lofty hall to see the strange prodigy; — likewise the king himself from his domestic lodge, keeper of jeweled hoards, trod with glorious mien, gorgeously distinguished in the midst of a great retinue; — and his queen with him, measured the path to the mead-hall with a bevy of ladies.

XIV

A PATRIARCHAL THANKSGIVING. BEO-WULF'S ACCOUNT OF THE FRAY. EFFECT UPON UNFERTH.

Hrothgar uttered speech — he was going to Hall; he stood on the staple; he beheld the steep roof gold-glittering and the hand of Grendel.

'For this spectacle a thanksgiving to the Almighty be done without delay! Much despite I endured, capturings by Grendel; always can God work wonder after wonder, the Lord of Glory! It was but now that I thought I should never see a remedy for any of my woes, while the best of houses stood blood-stained, soaked in slaughter; the woe had scattered all my senators, as men who weened 5 not that they ever should rescue the national edifice of my leeds from the hateful ones, the demons and bogles.

'Now hath a lad, through might of God, achieved the deed which we all ere- 10 while were unable with our wisdom to compass. Lo! that may she say, what lady soever mothered that child by human generation, if yet she liveth, that to her was the Ancient Master favorable in her 15 child-bearing!

'Now I will heartily love thee, Beowulf, youth most excellent, as if thou wert my son; from this time forth keep thou up the new relation. There shall 20 be no lack to thee of any desires in the world, so far as I have power. Full oft have I for less service decreed recompense, honor from the treasury, to a less distinguished hero, less prompt to fight. 'Thou thyself hast by deeds achieved 25 that thy fame will live ever and always. May the Almighty reward thee with good, as he hath just now done!'

Beowulf uttered speech, Ecgtheow's 30 son: 'We discharged that high task, fighting with right good heart; shrewdly we enterprised the terror of the unknown. I had liked it vastly better, that thou hadst seen his very self, the fiend in full 35 gear, ready to drop. I thought quickly to fix him on a bloody bed with hard grapplings, that he for my hand-grip should lie death-struggling, unless his body vanished; I could not, as the An- 40 cient would not, balk his passage; I did not stick close enough to him, the manqueller; the fiend was too over-mighty in his making off. However he left his fist — to save his life and mark his track 45 — his arm and shoulder: not thereby however has the wretched being bought reprieve; none the longer will he live, the loathsome pest burdened with crimes; but the wound hath him, in deadly grip 50 close pinioned, in baleful bands; in that condition must he, crime-stained wretch, abide the great doom, according as the Ancient One may will to assign his portion.'

A silenter man was then the son of 55 Ecglaf in the brag of martial exploits; since it was by the hero's valor the ethelings beheld the hand, the fiendish fingers, over the high roof, every one straight before him. Each one of the nail-places was likest to steel, hand-spur of the heathenish marauder, horrible spikes; every one declared there was nothing so hard would graze them, no sword of old celebrity that would take off the monster's bloody war-fist.

XV

HEOROT RESTORED. REJOICINGS AND GIV-ING OF GIFTS.

Then was order promptly given that the interior of Heorot should be decorated; many they were, of men and of women, who garnished that genial palace, hospitable hall. Gold-glistering shone the brocaded tapestries along the walls, pictures many for the wonder of all people who have an eye for such. That bright building was terribly wrecked in its whole interior, though it had been strengthened with iron fastenings; the hinges were wrenched away; the roof alone had escaped altogether unhurt, when the destroyer, stained with atrocities, took to flight in desperation of life. It is not easy to elude [death], try it who will; but every living soul of the sons of men, of dwellers upon ground, must of necessity approach the destined spot, where his body, bedded in fast repose, shall sleep after supper.

Then was the time and the moment, that Healfdene's son should go to hall; the king was minded himself to share the feast. Never that I heard of did that nation in stronger force about their bounty-giver more bravely muster. They went to bench in merry guise — while their kinsmen enjoyed the copious feast, and with fair courtesy quaffed many a mead-bowl — mighty men in the lofty hall, Hrothgar and Hrothulf. The interior of Heorot was wholly filled with friends; no treachery had imperial Scyldings at that early date attempted.

Then did the son of Healfdene present to Beowulf a golden ensign in reward of victory, decorated staff-banner, helmet and mail-coat; many beheld when they brought the grand treasure-sword before the hero. Beowulf tasted the beaker on the hall-floor; no need had he to be ashamed of that bounty-giving before the

archers. I heard not many instances of men giving to other at ale-bench four treasures gold-bedight in friendlier wise. About the helmet's roof the crest was fastened with wire-bound fencing for the head, in order that file-wrought war-scoured blades might not cruelly scathe it, when the shielded fighter had to go against angry foes.

Then did the shelter of eorls command to bring eight horses gold-cheeked into the court within the palings; on one of them stood the saddle gaily caparisoned and decorated with silver, which was the war-seat of the high king, when the son of Healfdene was minded to exercise the play of swords; — never failed in the front the charger of the famous (king) when the slain were falling. And then did the chief of the Ingwines deliver unto Beowulf possession of both at once, both horses and arms; — bade him enjoy them well. So manfully did the illustrious chieftain, the hoard-warden of heroes, reward battle-risks with horses and treasures, so as never will any mispraise them who is minded to speak sooth according to right.

XVI

GIFTS TO BEOWULF'S COMRADES. MUSIC AND SONG.

Moreover, to each one of those who had made the voyage with Beowulf, did the captain of warriors give a precious gift at the mead-bench, an old heirloom; and gave orders to compensate with gold for that (missing) one, that one whom Grendel had atrociously killed, as he would have killed more of them, had not the providence of God, had not Wyrd, stood in his way; — and, the courage of that man. The Ancient One ruled then, as he now and always doth, over all persons of human race; therefore is prudence eachwhere best, forecast of soul. Much experience of pleasant and of painful must he make, who long here in these struggling days brooks the world.

Then was song and instrumental music together blended, concerning Healfdene's war-chief, — the harp was struck, a ballad often recited, what time the hall-joy along the mead-bench was invoked by Hrothgar's minstrel.

* * *

XVII

A PICTURE OF SOCIAL PLEASURE. SPEECH
OF THE QUEEN TO THE KING.

* * *

Enjoyment rose high as before, bright
was the sound of revelry, the drawers
served wine out of curious flagons.
Then came Wealhtheow forward, moving under her golden diadem, to where
the two brave men sat, uncle and nephew;
up to that time was their natural affection undisturbed, either to other true.
Likewise there Unferth the speaker sat
at the feet of the Scyldings' lord; every
man of them trusted his spirit that he
had great courage, though he had not
been loyal to his kindred at sword-play.
Spake then the lady of the Scyldings:
—'Receive this beaker, sovereign mine,
wealth-dispenser! be thou merry, a mu-
nificent friend of men, and speak to the
Goths with comfortable words. So it
behooves one to do! Near and far, thou
now hast peace! To me it hath been
said, that thou wouldest have the hero for
thy son. Heorot is purged, the bright
ring-hall; dispense whilst thou mayest
many bounties;—and to thy children
leave folk and realm, when thou must
away to see Eternity. I know my gracious Hrothulf that he will honorably
govern the younger ones, if thou earlier
than he, O friend of the Scyldings,
quittest the world. I think that he will
repay our children with good, if he that
fully remembers, what gracious atten-
tions thou and I bestowed for his comfort
and advantage in the time past when he
was an infant.' She turned then towards
the bench where her boys were, Hrethric
and Hrothmund, and the sons of mighty
men, the youth all together; there the
brave man sat, Beowulf of the Goths, by
the two brothers.

XVIII

GIFTS OF THE QUEEN TO THE HERO AND
HER SPEECH TO HIM. THE HALL IS AR-
RANGED AS A DORMITORY.

To him the cup was borne; and friendly
invitation (to drink) was offered with
words; and twisted gold was graciously
presented, armlets two, a mantle and
rings; the grandest of carcanets that I
have heard of on earth. None superior

among the treasures of men heard I ever
of under heaven, since Hama bore away
to the bright fortress the necklace of the
Brisings — jewel and casket; he fled the
toils of Eormanric; chose eternal counsel.
That collar had Hygelac of the Goths,
grandson (or nephew) of Swerting, on
his latest expedition, when under his flag
he defended his prize, guarded the spoil;
him Fate took off, when he for wantonness challenged woe, feud with the Frisians; he carried that decoration, the
costly stones over the wave-bowl, the
mighty chieftain; he fell shield in hand;
so then came into the power of the
Franks the corpse of the king, the breast
apparel, and the collar along with the
rest: inferior combatants stripped the
slain by the fortune of war; the people
of the Goths tenanted the bed of death.
— The hall echoed with sound (of
music).
Wealhtheow uttered speech; she spake
before that company: 'Brook this collar,
Beowulf, beloved youth, with luck, and
make use of this mantle; stately possessions; and prosper well; make thyself
famous by valor, and to these boys be
thou a kind adviser! I will reward thee
for it. Thou hast attained, that far and
near, for all future time, men will celebrate thee, even as widely as the sea
encircleth windy walls. Be thou, whilst
thou live, a happy prince! With good
will I accord thee precious possessions.
Be thou to my son loyal with deeds, sustaining joyance. Here is each warrior to
other true, kindly disposed, loyal to their
chief; the thanes are obedient, the people
all ready! Retainers, be merry, do as I
bid you.'
She went then to her chair. There was
high festivity; men drank wine, Wyrd
they knew not, the cruel destiny, as it
had gone forth, for many a noble. By
and by the evening came, and Hrothgar
betook him to his lodge, the prince to his
repose.
Countless nobles guarded the hall, as
they had often done in earlier time: they
cleared away the bench-boards; it was
strewn throughout with beds and bolsters.
One of the revelers, whose end was near,
lay down to rest in hall a doomed man.
At their heads they set the shields, the
bright bucklers; there on the bench was
over each etheling, plain to be seen, the

towering war-helmet, the ringed mail-coat, the shaft of awful power. Their custom was that they were constantly ready for war, whether at home or in the field, in both cases alike, whatever the occasion on which their liege lord had need of their services;— it was a good people.

THE SECOND PART

XIX

IN THE NIGHT THE OLD WATER-HAG COMES, SEIZES ONE OF THE SLEEPERS, AND FETCHES AWAY GRENDEL'S ARM. BEO-WULF IS HASTILY SUMMONED TO THE KING AT EARLY DAWN.

So they sank down to sleep. One there was who sorely paid for that night's rest, in the manner that had very often happened to them, since Grendel had occupied the gold-hall, had perpetrated violence, until his end arrived, death after crimes. That became manifest, widely known to men, that an avenger still lived after the (slain) foe; long to remember the disaster; Grendel's mother, beldam troll-wife, thought of her desolation, creature that had to dwell in the dreariness of water, cold streams, ever since Cain was the knife-bane of his only brother, his father's son; he then went forth an outlaw, marked with murder, shunning human society; he kept the wilderness. Thence grew a number of branded creatures;— one of those was Grendel, horrible ban-wolf; he at Heorot found a vigilant man waiting for battle. There did the monster grapple with him; he, however, remembered the strength of his might, the marvelous gift which God had given to him, and he trusted to the Supreme for grace, courage, and support; therefore he overcame the fiend, subdued the hellish demon; so he departed crestfallen, void of joyance, to see his death-place, foe of man. And yet his mother, nevertheless, bloodthirsty and gallows-minded, was going to enter upon a sorrow-fraught way to wreak the death of her son.

So the hag came to Heorot where the jeweled Danes slept throughout the hall. Then was it for the eorls a sudden upset, when Grendel's mother burst into their midst. The terror was less just in the same proportion as female strength, woman's war-terror, is (of less account) with an armed man; when the well-hafted steel, hammer-toughened, the bloodstained sword, with edge effective, sheareth resisting boar on helmet. Then was the hard-edged sword drawn throughout the benches, many a wide buckler raised firm in hand; many one thought not of helmet, nor of spacious byrnie, when the alarm surprised him.

The hag was in a hurry; it wanted to get out from there with life, because it was discovered; promptly it had seized one of the ethelings tight, and then it went to fen. That man was to Hrothgar, in quality of comrade, dearest of warriors between the seas, mighty shield-combatant;— him the hag crushed in his sleep, illustrious baron. Beowulf was not there; but another lodging had been assigned, after the gift-giving, to the distinguished Goth. A cry was heard in Heorot; the blood-sprent hag took away the well-known hand; anxiety was renewed, was set up in the castle. That barter was not good, which they on both sides were compelled to pay for with lives of friends.

Then was the venerable king, the hoary man of war, in embittered mood, when he knew that his chiefest thane no longer lived, that the man most dear to him was dead. Hastily to (the king's) bower was Beowulf fetched, the victorious stripling. At early dawn, he went with his warriors, the noble champion, he and his comrades, where the sapient king was waiting to be resolved, whether the Almighty will ever, after the spell of woe, bring about a change. He then marched along the flooring, the expedite man, with his little band,— hall-timbers echoed — until he accosted with words the wise lord of the Ingwines, and inquired if, according to his sincere wish, he had had a restful night.

XX

HROTHGAR'S ANSWER TO BEOWULF'S MORNING SALUTATION. HE DEPLORES THE FATE OF ÆSCHERE AND DESCRIBES THE HAUNT OF THE WATER-DEMONS.

Hrothgar, crown of Scyldings, uttered speech: 'Ask not thou after welfare! Grief is renewed for the Danish leeds.

Æschere is dead, Yrmenlaf's elder brother, my secretary and my counselor; my body-squire, when we in battle defended our heads, what time foot-fighters closed, boar-crests clashed; — such should a warrior be, a long-tried etheling, such as Æschere was. In Heorot hath he met his death at the hands of the raging destroyer; I know not in what direction the gruesome corpse-exulting thing took its return-way leaving tracks of its forage. She hath wreaked the feud, for that thou yesternight didst quell Grendel in masterful wise with stern grapplings; for that he too long had wasted and destroyed my people. He in fight succumbed with forfeiture of life; and now hath come the other, a mighty ravager, would avenge her kin; — yea, hath further aggravated the feud, as may well appear to many a thane, who along with his sovereign groans in spirit, in cruel heart-grief; now the hand of him who was the promoter of all your desires lies still in death.

'That I did hear say by land-owners, leeds of mine, heads of halls, that they saw a pair of such, huge mark-stalkers, keeping the moors, creatures of strange fashion; one of them was, according to the clearest they could make out, a beldam's likeness, the other miscreated thing trod lonely tracks in man's figure; only he was huger than any other man; him in old times the country folk used to call Grendel: they know not about any father, whether they had any in pedigree before them of mysterious goblins. They inhabit unvisited land, wolf-crags, windy bluffs, the dread fen-track, where the mountain waterfall amid precipitous gloom vanished beneath, flood under earth; not far hence it is, reckoning by miles, that the mere standeth, and over it hang rimy groves; a wood with clenched roots overshrouds the water. There may every night a fearful portent be seen, fire on the flood; none so wise liveth of the children of men as to know the depth. Though the heath-roamer, when exhausted by hounds, the hart strong in his horns, make for the wood-coverts, driven from afar; sooner will he resign his breath, his life on the bank, sooner than he will there in plunge his head. That is no comfortable place; therefrom mount up the raging waves,

murky to the clouds, when wind stirreth foul weather, till the air thickens, the skies crack. Now is it again to thee alone that we look for counsel! The haunt as yet thou knowest not, the dreadful place, where thou mayest find the guilty felon; go for it if thou dare! I will recompense thee for that warfare with treasure, with old stored wealth, as I did before, with coiled gold, if thou comest away.'

XXI

BEOWULF SOOTHES THE KING AND GAILY UNDERTAKES THE NEW ADVENTURE. THE CAVALCADE TO THE MERE. THE LOOK OF IT. BEOWULF ARMS; HIS SWORD IS DESCRIBED.

Beowulf, son of Ecgtheow, uttered speech: 'Sorrow not, experienced sire! better is it for every man that he should avenge his friend, than that he should greatly mourn. Every one of us must look for the end of worldly life; he who has the chance should achieve renown before death; that is for a mighty man, when life is past, the best memorial. Rouse thee, guardian of the kingdom! let us promptly set forth to explore the route of Grendel's kin. I vow it to thee; he shall by no means escape to covert; neither in the bowels of the earth, nor in the haunted wood, nor in ocean's depth — go where he will! This day have thou patience of all thy woes, as I have high confidence in thy behalf.'

Up sprang then the aged (king); he thanked God, the mighty Lord, for what that man had spoken. Then Hrothgar's horse was bridled, the crull-maned charger. The wise monarch rode forth stately; the foot-force marched, of shield-bearing men. Traces there were broadly visible along the slopes of the weald, the track (of the foe) over the grounds; right forward (the warlock) had gone, over the murky moor, it had carried off, lifeless, the most beloved of kindred thanes, of those who kept home with Hrothgar.

Then did the scion of ethelings pass lightly over steep stone-banks, narrow gullies, strait lonesome paths, an untraveled route, sheer bluffs, many habitations of nickers. He with few companions, practised men, went forward to explore the ground, until that he of a sudden perceived the gloomy trees overhanging the grisly rock, a joyless wood; beneath it was a standing water, dreary and troubled. All the Danes, all the friends of the Scyldings, had a shock of feeling, many a thane had to suffer; horror seized each warrior, when on that lake-cliff they came across the head of Æschere. The pool seethed with blood — the folk beheld it — with hot gore.

The horn sounded from time to time a spirited bugle-blast. The troop all sat them down; there saw they along the water many things of serpent kind, monstrous sea-snakes at their swimming gambols; and likewise on the jutting slopes nickers lying, those that in the early hours of the morning often procure disastrous going on the sailroad; dragons and strange beasts: — they tumbled away, spitish and rage-blown; they had caught sound of the racket, the clarion's clang. The leed of the Goths with an arrow out of his bow detached one of them from life, and from all future swimming matches; insomuch that in his vitals stood fixed the inexorable war-shaft; he in the element was the slacker at swimming, from the circumstance that death had caught him. Promptly was he on the waves with boar-poles harpoon-armed, tightly nipped — barred of his tricks — and landed on the point, the prodigious wave-tosser; — the men beheld the grisly goblin.

Beowulf geared himself in knightly armor; in no wise was he anxious for his life; now must the war-byrnie, hand-woven, spacious and decorated, make trial of swimming; the byrnie which knew to protect the body, that his breast, his life, might not be scathed by the grip of battle, the spiteful clutch of the furious one. Moreover the white helmet guarded his head, the helmet that was to plunge into the depths of the pool, to face buffeting waters, with all its decoration of silver, encircled with princely wreathings, as a weapon-smith in ancient days wrought it, wonderfully executed it, set it round with boar figures, so that never might brand nor war-blades make any impression upon it.

That moreover was not the least important of helps to his valor, which Hrothgar's orator lent to him at his need; — the name of that hafted blade was Hrunting, it was preëminently one of old heirlooms; — the edge was iron, mottled with poison-twigs, hardened with battle-gore; never had it in conflict proved false to any man who brandished it with hands, such man as durst adventure on paths of terror, where nations meet as foes; that was not the first occasion on which it had been required to discharge heroic work. Manifestly Ecglaf's son, of doughty puissance, remembered not what he had recently uttered when flushed with wine, seeing now he made loan of that weapon to a rarer sword-gallant; — for himself he durst not adventure his life among the turmoil of waves, to fulfil mastery; — there he fell short of glory, of high achievement. It was not so with the other, when he had harnessed him for combat.

XXII

BEOWULF'S NUNCUPATORY WILL. HE PLUNGES INTO THE ABYSS AND MEETS THE TROLL-WIFE. THE BATTLE BEGINS.

Beowulf, son of Ecgtheow, uttered speech: 'Bethink thee now, great son of Healfdene, sapient monarch, now I am ready to start, oh, thou gold-friend of men, what we two lately talked of; — If I in thy service had to quit life, that thou to me wouldest ever be, after my departure, in the place of a father; — be thou protector to my kindred thanes, my familiar comrades, if Hild should take me; in such a case do thou, beloved Hrothgar, forward the presents which thou hast given me, to Hygelac. So will the master of the Goths be able to understand by that gold, Hrethel's son will be able to see for himself when he gazeth upon that treasure, that I had found a bountifully good distributor of jewels, and was in luck while my fortune lasted. And do thou let Unferth have the ancient heir-loom, the curious damasked sword; let the far-famed man have Hardedge; I will with Hrunting achieve for myself renown, or death shall take me.'

After these words the leed of the Weder-Goths dashed bravely off, would await no answer; — the eddying flood engulfed the warrior. It was then a main while of the day ere he could reach the country at the bottom.

Soon was that perceived by the blood-thirsty creature, grim and greedy, which for a hundred seasons had kept the watery region, that one of the children of men was exploring from above the hab- 5 itation of goblins. It made a grab then towards him; it caught the brave man with grisly talons; nevertheless it pierced not to wound the wholeness of his body; ring-mail outside fenced him about, in- 10 somuch that the hag could not get through that jacket of service, well-knit limb-sark, with its loathsome fingers. Then did the she-wolf of the lake, when she came to the bottom, bear the jeweled 15 prince to her mansion, so that he had no power at all — courage enough he had — to wield his weapons; but so many monsters harassed him in swimming, many a water-beast with hostile tusks 20 battered his war-sark, the brigands were in pursuit.

Then did the eorl perceive that he was in some strange abysmal hall, where no water at all molested him, nor could 25 the violence of the flood touch him, being kept off by the roofed hall; firelight he saw, an eerie luster, shining bright. Then the hero knew it was the she-wolf of the abyss, the mighty carline of the 30 mere; — onset he delivered with slaughter-bill, his hand delayed not the stroke, so that about her head the costly blade resounded a greedy war-song. Then did the visitor discover that the battle- 35 gleamer would not bite, not scathe life, but the edge failed the master at need; it had in times past supported many encounters, had often cleft helmet, war-harness of the doomed; — that was the 40 first time for the honored treasure, that its fame broke down. Again he was for action, in courage never faltering, mindful of exploits, Hygelac's kinsman. Away did the wrathful combatant then 45 fling the damascened blade cunningly bedizened, insomuch that it lay along on the earth, stark and steel-edged; he trusted to his strength, the hand-grip of his might.

So it behooves a man to act, when he in battle thinks to attain enduring praise; — he will not be caring about his life.

Then did the leed of the warlike Goths — naught recked he of deadly peril — 55 seize Grendel's dam by the shoulder; then did the man valiant in fight, as he

was full of rage, sway his deadly adversary so that she sank on the pavement. The hag swiftly paid him back reprisal with fell grapplings, and closed in upon him: — then staggered he with spirits exhausted, he the strongest of warriors, the champion-soldier, insomuch that he fell prostrate. Then did the hag sit upon the visitant of her hall, and drew her knife, broad and brown-edged; would revenge her bairn, her only offspring. About his shoulder lay the breast-net interlaced; that fenced his life; against point and against edge it barred the entrance.

Then had the son of Ecgtheow, the champion of the Goths, miscarried under the vast profound, had not his campaigning byrnie, his hard war-net, afforded help; — and holy God controlled the victory, the Lord of providence, the heavenly Ruler, he determined it aright, and that with ease; — presently he again stood erect on his feet.

XXIII

BEOWULF FINISHES THE BUSINESS. THE KING'S PARTY GIVE HIM UP AND GO HOME. BEOWULF'S COMRADES REMAIN ON THE CLIFF. FIDELITY REWARDED. AN AFTER-DINNER SURPRISE.

Then saw he among the armor a monumental cutlass, an old eotenish sword, of edge effective, a trophy of warriors; — that was the very pride of weapons, only then it was huger than any other man could bear to the battle-game; it was good and gallant, handiwork of giants. Then did he, the champion of the Scyldings, grasp Fetelhilt; exasperate and greedy of fight he drew the jeweled arm; despairing of his life, he smote in his fury; insomuch that the hard steel caught her by the neck, broke through the bone-rings, the bill sped all through the doomed flesh-jacket; — she dropped on the pavement; the sword was gory; the lad was fain of his work.

The glimmer flashed up, light filled the place, even as when from heaven serenely shineth the candle of the firmament. He scanned the apartment with his eye, then took his way along by the wall; stubborn the thane of Hygelac swung his weapon aloft by the hilt, fierce and aggressive. That blade was not flung away by the hero, but he was forthwith minded to repay Grendel the many fatal assaults he had wrought on the West Danes oftener far than a single once, when he slew Hrothgar's hearth-comrades in their slumber; sleeping men of the Danish folk he devoured fifteen, and an equal number he conveyed away, hideous spoil. He had paid him his recompense for that, the furious cham- 10 pion had; insomuch that he now beheld him at rest, weary of war, even Grendel he saw lying, bereft of life, so deadly for him had erst the conflict at Heorot been. The carcass gaped wide, when it 15 after death received the blow, the hard sword-slash; then did he cut the head from off him.

Forthwith was that perceived by the observant men who with Hrothgar were 20 watching over the water, that the wave-plash was all turbid, the surf was tinged with blood: the men of grizzled locks, the old men, spake together about the brave man, how that they expected not 25 the etheling back again, did not expect that he would come radiant with victory to seek the illustrious prince; inasmuch as the more part were of opinion, that the she-wolf of the mere had torn him 30 in pieces.

Then came the ninth hour of the day. The impetuous Scyldings quitted the bluff; the gold-friend of men took his departure homeward thence. The for- 35 eigners sat fast, sick at heart, and upon the pool they gazed; they wished and did not expect, that they might ever get sight of their lord and captain in the body. 40

Then did that sword begin — under spilth of blood in fearful clots — the war-bill began to waste away; — that was a marvelous thing that it melted all away, likest to ice when the Father dis- 45 solveth the rigor of frost and unwind-eth the ropes of the torrent, he who hath control of times and seasons; that is the true Governor.

The leed of the Weder-Goths took 50 not of rare possessions in those halls — though he saw many there — aught more than the head, and with it the hilt that was metal-spangled; the sword had al-ready melted away, the decorated 55 weapon had burnt up; — so fiercely hot was that blood, and so venomous the strange goblin which had perished there in that habitation.

Soon was he swimming, he who erst had strugglingly encountered the onset 5 of furious beasts; up through the water he dived; the wave-depths were all puri-fied, spacious haunts; now that the goblin had quitted life, and this transitory scene.

Then came he to land, the crown of the men from over the sea, bravely swim-ming; — he exulted in his lake-spoil, in the mighty burden which he had with him. Then went they to meet him, they 15 thanked God, the valiant band of thanes, they rejoiced over their captain, for that they had been so happy as to get sight of him whole and sound. Then was from the ardent hero his helmet and 20 byrnie promptly slackened: — sullenly the mere subsided, water under welkin, dusk with battle-gore.

Forth thence they fared upon the tracks of their (former) march, fain in 25 their souls, they passed over the country, and along the public highways; men of kingly courage bore the head-piece away from the mere-cliff, toilsomely for every one of them: of the lusty and stalwart 30 fellows four were required to convey with much ado on the gory pole the head of Grendel to the gold-hall; (and so they went) till that unexpectedly to hall the brave adventurers arrived, fourteen of 35 Goths marching; their captain withal, glorious in their midst, trod the grounds of the mead-hall. Then did the com-mander of the thanes proceed to enter, deed-keen man, adorned with glory, war- 40 like hero, to accost Hrothgar: then was Grendel's head borne by the hair into the hall where men drank; — startling for the nobles and the lady withal; a visage indescribable did men behold.

XXIV

BEOWULF REPORTS HIS EXPERIENCE TO HROTHGAR AND GIVES HIM THE WON-DROUS HILT WHICH IS EXAMINED AND DESCRIBED. HROTHGAR'S PATERNAL DIS-COURSE.

Beowulf, son of Ecgtheow, uttered speech: 'Lo and behold! we unto thee, oh, son of Healfdene, leed of the Scyld-ings, have joyfully brought these mere-spoils which thou here lookest on, in token of achievement! Not easily did I fight it through with life: in battle under water I had hardly faced out the task, well-nigh had the struggle failed, only that God shielded me. I could not in conflict accomplish aught with Hrunting, though that be a good weapon; but the Ruler of men vouchsafed to me that I on the wall saw smilingly hanging an old sword of huge size — oftenest hath He guided men when they have no other friend — insomuch that I grasped at that weapon. Then smote I in that campaign — occasion favoring me — the keepers of the house. Then did that battle-bill consume away, that twisted piece, by reason of that blood which gushed forth, hottest of battle-gore; I brought away from the enemy that hilt as a trophy; I avenged the atrocities, the death-agony of Danes, as it was meet. Accordingly I promise it to thee that thou in Heorot mayest sleep free from care with the regiment of thy troopers; and so may every thane of thy leeds, of the seniority and of the juniority, for that thou needest not on their account apprehend danger, O chief of Scyldings, in that quarter, life-bale to warriors; as erewhile thou didst.'

Then was the gilded hilt given to the veteran soldier, the hoary leader in battle, given into his hand, ancient workmanship of giants; it passed, after the demons were quelled, into the possession of the prince of the Danes, a work of mystic smiths; and so when the atrocious creature, God's enemy, murder-criminous, left this world, and his mother too, it went into the possession of the best of worldly kings between the seas, of all that even in Scania distributed wealth.

Hrothgar uttered speech; — he surveyed the hilt, the old relic; upon it was written the origin of the primeval quarrel, what time the flood, the rushing ocean, destroyed the giant's brood; they got for themselves a bitter fate; that was a tribe estranged from the Eternal Captain, to them did the Ruler assign final retribution with whelming water. Likewise on the mounting of sheer gold there was with rune-staves rightly inscribed, set down, and said, for whom that sword had erst been wrought, best of steely fabrics, with wreathen hilt, and dragon ornament.

Then did the wise son of Healfdene utter speech — all held their peace —: 'That, lo! may a man say, a man who promoteth truth and right among folk, — he remembereth all long ago, the old housemaster — that this eorl was born superior! The fame is spread through distant parts, my friend Beowulf, the fame of thee over every nation. Withal thou dost carry it modestly thy prowess with discretion of mind. I shall make good to thee my plighted love, according as was before said betwixt us two; thou art destined to prove a comfort sure and lasting to thy leeds, a help to mankind.

'Heremod did not prove so to the descendants of Ecgwela, to the honorable Scyldings; he waxed great not for their pleasure, but for mortal fray and for death-blows to the Danish leeds; he in his ungoverned mood crushed his boon companions, the squires of his body; until that at last he wandered forth alone, the illustrious monarch, away from human society; notwithstanding that the mighty God had with the attractions of strength, with puissance, exalted him, promoted him, above all men. Nevertheless in his soul there grew a blood-thirsty passion; — far was he from giving rings to the Danes according to merit; he continued estranged from social joy, so that he suffered the penalty of that outrage in the settled disaffection of his people.

'Do thou take warning by that; understand the ornament of man! It is about thee that I being old in years and experience have told this tale.

'Wonderful it is to tell, how the mighty God with large intelligence dispenses understanding to mankind, dispenses position and prowess — he holds the disposition of all things. Sometimes he lets the purpose of a man of noble race turn towards possession, he giveth to him earthly joy on his estate, to hold the citadel of men, he assigns to him regions of the world so extensive, a realm so wide, that he in his unwisdom is not able to carry his thought to the end of it; he dwelleth in prosperity, not anything annoys him, not sickness nor age nor carking care darkens his spirits, no quarrel on any side, no feud appears; but all the world moves to his mind, he knows not reverse.

XXV

THE CONCLUSION OF HROTHGAR'S DIS-
COURSE. MORE FEASTING AND THEN
CAME BED-TIME FOR WHICH THE HERO
HAD HUGE DESIRE. BEOWULF SLEPT TILL
THE VOICE OF THE BIRD PROCLAIMED
SUNRISE. PREPARING TO RETURN HOME
HE RESTORES HRUNTING TO UNFERTH
COURTEOUSLY.

'Until at length within the man himself
something of arrogancy grows and develops; then sleepeth the guardian, the
soul's keeper; it is too fast that sleep,
awfully profound, the assassin is very
nigh, he who from his arrow-bow malig-
nantly shooteth. Then is he, helmeted
man, smitten in the breast with a bitter
shaft: he cannot defend himself from the
crooked exorbitant counsels of the
damned sprite; he fancies that it is too
little, all that he has so long enjoyed;
he is covetous, and malignant; glorieth
not in the pomp of bestowing gilded
decorations; and he forgetteth the ulte-
rior consequences; he too lightly considers how that God the Dispenser of
glory had erewhile given him the post
of dignity. Then at the end of the chapter it returns to this, that the body
shrunken falls away, the outgoing life
drops; — another fills his room, one who
ungrudgingly distributes treasure, the
eorl's old accumulations; — timid prudence he despises.

'Guard thee against the fatal grudge,
beloved Beowulf, youth most excellent,
and choose for thee the better course,
enduring counsels! incline not to arrogancy, thou mighty champion! Now is
thy strength in full bloom for one while;
eftsoons it will happen that sickness or
sword will bereave thee of puissance; —
either clutch of fire or whelm of flood,
either assault of knife or flight of javelin, either wretched eld or glance of eyes,
will mar and darken all; without more
ado it will come to pass that death will
subdue thee, thou captain of men!

'For example, I myself during fifty
years ruled beneath the welkin over the
jeweled Danes, and I by valor made them
secure against many a nation throughout
this world with spears and swords, insomuch that I had no apprehension of
any rival under the circuit of the sky.

When lo! in my ancestral seat there
came a change over all that; — distress
where mirth was before, as soon as
Grendel, the old adversary, became an
inmate of mine; because of that visitation
I continually carried great anxiety at
heart. Thanks therefore be to the Governor, the Eternal Captain, for that which
I have lived to see, that I, the old tribulation past, upon that severed, that bloody
headpiece, with mine eyes do gaze!

'Go now to settle, share the festive
joy, crowned with honors of war! Thou
and I must have dealings together in
many many treasures, when to-morrow
comes.'

The Goth was glad of mood; he moved
promptly off, drawing to settle, as the
sapient king ordained him. Then was
again as before, to the gallant warriors,
to the company in hall, fair banquet
served afresh.

Night's covering grew dim, dark over
the banded men. Uprose all the seniors:
— it was that the gray-haired king, the
venerable Scylding, was minded to draw
to his bed. Vastly well did the Goth, the
illustrious warrior, like the thought of
repose; promptly was he, now weary of
adventure, the man of far country, marshaled forth by the chamberlain, one who
with meet ceremony supplied all the
wants of a gentleman, such things as in
that day the lords of the main required
to have.

So the great-hearted hero rested him;
— high in air loomed the edifice, wide-
spanning and gold-gleaming: — the
stranger slept within, until the black
raven announced heaven's glory with a
blithe heart. Then came bright light
striding over shadow; fiends scampered
off. The ethelings were ready dight to
fare back to their leeds; — the magnanimous visitor was minded to take ship,
for a voyage far away.

Then did the hero bid the son of Ecglaf bear away Hrunting, bade him take
his sword, beloved weapon; said his
thanks for the loan; quoth that he
counted that war-mate a good one, war-
serviceable; with his words did not blame
the faulchion's edge; that was a high-
souled lad!

And when the departing warriors were
equipped in harness, the etheling honored

by the Danes went up to the dais, where the other warlike hero was;—he greeted Hrothgar.

XXVI

BEOWULF'S PARTING INTERVIEW WITH HROTHGAR WHO IS MOVED TO TEARS.

Beowulf, son of Ecgtheow, uttered speech:—'Now we sea-voyagers wish to say, we who have come from far, that we are purposing to go to Hygelac. Here we have been well entertained to our satisfaction; thou hast been to us very generous. If I therefore may by any means upon earth undertake for thy further gratification, O captain of men, labors of war beyond what I have yet done, I shall be ready promptly. If they bring me word over the circuit of the floods that neighbors press thee with alarm as whilom thy haters did, I will bring thee a thousand thanes, warriors to help thee. I can undertake for Hygelac, captain of the Goths, young though he be, shepherd of people, that he will forward me by words and by works, so that I may do high service to thee, and for thy support bring a forest of spears, a mighty subsidy, when thou shalt have need of men:—if moreover Hrethric, princely child, is in treaty for admission at the courts of the Goths, he may there find many friends; foreign countries are best visited by him who is of high worth in himself.'

Hrothgar bespake him in answer: 'These considerate words hath the All-wise Lord put into thy mind; never heard I a man so young in life speak more to purpose; thou art strong in might and ripe in understanding; wise in discourse of speech. I count it likely, if it cometh to pass that the spear, the grim despatch of battle, taketh away Hrethel's offspring, if ailing or iron taketh thy chieftain, the shepherd of the people, and thou hast thy life, that the sea-faring Goths have not any thy better to choose for king, for treasurer of warriors, if thou art willing to hold the realm of thy kinsfolk. To me thy disposition is well-liking more and more, beloved Beowulf; thou hast achieved, that the nations — Gothic leeds and spear-bearing Danes — shall have mutual friendship, and strife shall cease, the hostile surprises whence they suffered erewhile;—they shall be, while I rule the wide realm, a community of treasure: many friends shall greet one another with gifts across the bath of the gannet; the ringed ship shall bring over ocean presents and tokens of love. I know the people to be equally as towards foe so towards friend constant in mind, either way irreproachable, in olden wise.'

Then did the shelter of warriors, the son of Healfdene, further give into his possession twelve hoarded jewels; he bade him go with the presents, visit his own people in comfort, and soon come back again. Then did the king of noble ancestry, the chief of the Scyldings, kiss the incomparable thane and clasp him by the neck; tears from him fell, the gray-haired man; forecast was both ways to the man of old experience, but one way stronger than the other, namely, that they might never meet again, proud men in the assembly. To him the man was so dear, that he could not restrain the passion of his breast, but deep in the affections of his soul a secret longing after the beloved man stemmed the current of his blood.

Beowulf, departing thence, a warrior gold-bedight, trod the grassy earth conscious of wealth:—the seagoer, which was riding at anchor, awaited his owner and lord. Then upon the march was the liberality of Hrothgar often praised; that was a king, every way without reproach; until old age had bereft him of the vantage of his prowess,—him who had often been a terror to many.

XXVII

THE WARDEN OF THE PORT, HIS RESPECTFUL DEMEANOR. HOW BEOWULF RECOMPENSED THE CARE OF THE BOAT-WARDEN. THE HOME-BOUND VOYAGE.

So the troop of gallant bachelors came to the water; they wore ring-armor, netted limb-sarks. The land warden observed the return-march of the eorls, just as he had done before;—not with suspicion from the peak of the cliff did he greet the visitors, but he rode towards them; he said to the leeds of the Wederas that the bright-mailed explorers came welcome to their ships. Then was on the beach the roomy sea-boat laden with war-harness, the ring-prowed ship with horses and treasures; the mast rose high over wealth from Hrothgar's hoard. 5

He to the boat-warden presented a gold-bound sword insomuch that ever after he was on the mead-bench the more worshipful by reason of that decoration, that sword of pedigree. 10

[The Gothic captain with his band of warriors] betook him to ship, ploughing deep water; the Danes' land he quitted. Then was by the mast a manner of sea-garment, a sail with sheet made fast; the 15 sea-timber hummed. There did the wind over the billows not baffle the wavefloater of her course; the sea-goer marched, scudded with foamy throat forward over the swell, with gorgeous prow 20 over the briny currents, till they were able to espy the Gothic cliffs, familiar headlands. The keel grated up ashore, with way on her from the wind; she stood on land. Quickly was the hithe-25 warden ready at the strand, he who already for a long time expectant at the water's edge had eyed the craft of the beloved men; he bound to the shore the wide-bosomed ship with anchor-cables 30 fast, lest the violence of the waves might snatch the winsome craft away from them.

* * *

XXXI

BÉOWULF COMES TO THE THRONE.

* * *

Consequently the broad realm came to the hand of Beowulf; he governed well fifty-winters — that was a venerable king, an ethel-warden — until one began in dark nights, even a dragon, to have mastery; one that on a high heath kept a hoard, a steep stone-castle; a path lay beneath, unfrequented by people. Therewithin had gone some man or other, [deftly] he took of the heathen hoard, [took a thing] glistening with precious metal; — that he afterwards [rued], that he had tricked the horrid keeper while 55 sleeping, with thievish dexterity , ○ . that he was infuriate.

THE THIRD PART

XXXII

HOW IT HAPPENED THAT THE MAN ROBBED THE DRAGON'S HOARD. THAT TREASURE WAS ACCUMULATED STORE OF ANCIENT AND FORGOTTEN WARRIORS. THE DRAGON PREPARES REVENGE. THE BEGINNING OF THE FATAL WAR.

Not of set purpose nor by his own free choice had he visited the dragon's hoard, he who brought sore trouble on himself; but for dire necessity had he, the slave of some one or other of the 15 sons of men, fled from outrageous stripes a houseless wretch, and into that place had blundered like a man in guilty terror. [Here four (or five) mutilated lines seem to say that the fugitive, though 20 quickly horror-struck at his new danger, still by the impetus of despair borne forward had espied a cup of precious metal.] There was a quantity of such things in that earth-cavern, ancient acquisitions; 25 just as some unknown man in days of yore had in pensive thought hidden them there, the prodigious legacy of a noble race, treasures of worth. Death had carried them all off previously, and that 30 solitary one then of the proud company who had there longest kept afoot, a possessor mourning lost friends, would fain survive, if only that he might for a little space enjoy the long-accumulated 35 wealth.

A barrow already existed on the down, nigh by the waves, sheer over the cliff, cunningly secured; therein did the owner of rings carry a ponderous quantity of 40 beaten gold: a few words he spake: 'Hold thou now, O earth, now that the heroes could not, the possessions of mighty men. Lo! in thee at first the brave men found it; a violent death car-45 ried them away, a fearful slaughter carried off every one of the men, my peers, who surrendered this life; they attained the joy of the (supernal) hall. Not one have I to wear a sword, or furbish the 50 bossy tankard, the precious drink-stoup; the valiant are departed otherwhere. Now must the hard helmet, damascened with gold, shed its intayled foliations; the furbishers sleep, they whose task it was to 55 keep the masks of war; likewise the war-coat which in battle and through the crash of shields was proof against the bite of swords, shall molder like the warrior. No longer can the ringed mail along with the war-chief widely travel by the hero's side; — no delight of harp, no joy of gleewood, no good hawk swinging through the hall, no swift horse tramping in the castle-court. Destructive death hath sent many generations far away.' Thus did he with sorrowful heart lament his unhappiness, sole survivor of all he sadly wept, by day and by night, until that death's ripple touched at his heart.

The dazzling hoard was found open 15 standing by the old pest of twilight, the flaming one that haunteth barrows, the scaly spiteful dragon, that flieth by night, surrounded with fire, whom country-folk hold in awful dread. His portion is to 20 resort to the hoard under ground, where he with winters aged shall guard heathen gold; he will be no whit the better for it. So had that wide-ravager for three hundred winters held in the earth an 25 enormous treasure-house, until that one angered him, a man angered his mood; — to his chieftain the man bore a tankard bossed with gold, and prayed his lord for a covenant of peace. Then was the 30 hoard rifled, quantity of jewels carried off; the friendless man had his petition granted. The lord contemplated men's ancient work for the first time.

When the worm woke, the quarrel was 35 begun; forthwith he sniffed the scent along the rock; the marble-hearted one found the enemy's track; — he had stepped forth abroad with undetected craft, hard by the dragon's head. So may 40 that man who retains the fealty of the Supreme, elude death and freely escape both harm and pursuit. The hoard-keeper sought diligently over the ground, he wanted to find the man, the man who had 45 wrought him mischief in his sleep; fiery and in raging mood he often swung around the mound, all out round about; there was not any man there in that desert waste. Nevertheless he exulted in 50 purpose of battle, of bloody work; at intervals he would dash back into the barrow, would seek the costly vessel; presently he had satisfied himself of that, that some one of manfolk had invaded 55 the gold, the mighty treasures. The hoard-keeper waited with difficulty until

evening came; so enraged was the master of the barrow, the malignant one designed with fire to revenge the loss of the precious tankard. Presently the day was gone, the worm had his will; no longer would he bide in fenced wall, but he issued forth with burning, equipped with fire. The commencement of it was frightful to the people in the country; likewise it speedily had a sore ending upon their benefactor.

XXXIII

THE DRAGON'S DEVASTATION. THE KING'S MANSION BURNT. BEOWULF'S PROUD RESOLVE TO FIGHT THE DRAGON SINGLE-HANDED.

Then the monster began to spirt fire-gleeds, to burn the cheerful farmsteads; the flame-light glared aloft, in defiance of man; the hostile air-flyer would leave nothing there alive. The war-craft of the worm was manifest in all parts; the rage of the deadly foe was seen far and near: how the ravaging invader hated and ruined the Gothic people; to his hoard he shot back again, to his dark mansion, before the hour of day. He had encompassed the landfolk with flame, with fire and conflagration; he trusted in his mountain, his war-craft and his rampart; that confidence deceived him.

Then was the crushing news reported to Beowulf with swiftness and certainty, that his own mansion, best of buildings, was melting away in fiery eddies, even the gift-seat of the Goths. That was to the goodman a rude experience in his breast, hugest of heart-griefs; the wise man felt as if he should, in despite of venerable law, break out against Providence, against the Eternal Lord, with bitter outrage; his breast within him surged with murky thoughts, in a manner unwonted with him. The fire-drake had desolated the stronghold of the nobles, the sea-board front, that enclosed pale, with fiery missiles. For him therefore the war-king, the lord of the Storm-folk, studied revenge. He gave orders, that they should make for him, the shelter of warriors, the captain of knights, wholly of iron, a war-shield, a master-piece; he knew assuredly, that forest-timber would not serve him, linden-wood against flame! Destined he was, the prince of proved valor, to meet the end of his allotted days, of his worldly life; — and the worm (was to die) at the same time, long though he had held the hoarded wealth.

Then did he, of rings the patron, think it scorn that he should go seek the wide-flyer with a band, with a large host; he had no fear of the encounter for him-self, nor did the worm's war-craft at all subdue his puissance and enterprise; for-asmuch as he whilere, in shrewd jeopardy, had carried him safe through many a con-test, many a battle-clash, since the time that he, a victorious boy, had purged Hrothgar's hall, and with battle-grip had done for Grendel's kinsfolk, a loathsome brood.

* * *

XXXV

FURTHER DISCOURSES OF BEOWULF. HE GIVES A GREAT SHOUT AND THE DRAGON COMES FORTH. THE FIGHT BEGINS; BEO-WULF IN DISTRESS.

* * *

Beowulf uttered speech, with boastful words he spake, for the last time: 'I hazarded many wars in youth; yet again will I, the aged keeper of the folk, seek strife, and do famously; if the fell rav-ager out of his earthen dome will come forth to meet me.' Then did he address a word of greeting to each of his men, the keen helm-wearers, for the last time, his own familiar comrades. 'I would not bear sword or weapon to meet the worm, if I knew how I might otherwise main-tain my vaunt against the monster, as I formerly did against Grendel. But there I expect fire, deadly scorching, blast and venom; for that reason I have upon me shield and byrnie. I will not flee away from the keeper of the mountain, no, not a foot space; but it shall be decided be-tween us two on this rampart, as Wyrd allots us, (and) the Governor of every man. I am in spirit so eager for action, that I cut short bragging against the wingy warrior. Await ye on the moun-tain, with your byrnies about you, men-at-arms, to see which of us twain may after deadly tussle best be able to survive his hurt. That is not your mission, nor any man's task save mine alone, that he try strength against the monster, achieve heroism. I must with daring conquer

gold, or else war carrieth, pitiless life-bale carrieth away your lord!'

Up rose then by the brink the resolute warrior, stern under his helmet, he wore battle-sark among rugged cliffs, he trusted the strength of his single manhood; such is not the way of a craven. Then he be-held near the rampart — he who, excellent in accomplishments, had survived a great number of wars, of battle-clashes, when armed men close — beheld where stood a rocky arch, and out of it a stream break-ing from the barrow, the surface of that burn was steaming hot with cruel fire; nigh to the hoard could not the hero un-scorched any while survive for the flame of the dragon.

Then did the prince of the Storm-Goths, being elate with rage, let forth word out of his breast, the strong-hearted stormed; the shout penetrated within (the cavern), vibrating clear as a battle-cry, under the hoary rock. Fury was stirred; the hoard-warder recognized speech of man; opportunity was there no more, to stickle for terms of peace. In advance first of all there came the reeking breath of the monster, out from the rock, a hot jet of defiance; the ground trembled. The warrior under the barrow side, the Gothic captain, swung his mighty shield against the hideous customer; therewithal was the heart of the ringy worm incited to seek battle. Already the brave war-king had drawn sword, ancient heirloom of speedy edge; each of the belligerents had a dread of the other. Resolute in mind the prince of friends took stand well up to his hoised shield, while the worm buckled suddenly in a bow; — he stood to his weapons.

Then did the flaming foe, curved like an arch, advance upon him with headlong shuffle. The shield effectually protected life and limb a less while for the glorious chieftain than his sanguine hope ex-pected, supposing he, that time, early in the morning, was to achieve glory in the strife; — so had Wyrd not ordained it. Up swung he his hand, the Gothic captain, he smote the spotted horror with the mighty heirloom, that its brown edge turned upon the bony crust; less effec-tually bit than was required by the king's need, who was sorely pressed. Then was the keeper of the barrow after that shrewd assault furious with rage, cast forth devouring fire, the deadly sparks sprang every way: the gold-friend of the Goths plumed him not on strokes of vantage; the war-bill had failed him with its bared edge on the foe, as it had not been expected to do, metal of old renown. That was no light experience, inducing the mighty son of Ecgtheow to relinquish that emprise; he must consent to inhabit a dwelling otherwhere; — so must every man resign allotted days.

Then was it not long until the combatants closed again. The hoard-warder rallied his courage, out of his breast shot steam, as beginning again; — direly suffering, encompassed with fire, was he who erewhile had ruled men. Not (alas!) in a band did his life-guardsmen, sons of ethelings, stand about him with war-custom of comrades; no, to the wood they slunk, to shelter life. In one only of them did his soul surge in a tumult of grief; — kindred may never be diverted from duty, for the man who is rightly minded.

XXXVI

BEOWULF HAD ONE FAITHFUL FOLLOWER IN THE DESPERATE STRUGGLE. HIS FATAL WOUND.

Wiglaf was his name, Weohstan's son, a beloved warrior, a leed of the Scylfings, a kinsman of Ælfhere: he beheld his liege-lord under helmet, distressed by the heat. Then did he remember the (territorial) honor which he (Beowulf) had formerly given him, the well-stocked homestead of the Wægmundings, every political prerogative which his father had enjoyed; then could he not refrain; hand grasped shield, yellow linden, drew the old sword, known among men as the relic of Eanmund, son of Ohthere, whom, when a lordless exile, Weohstan had slain, in fair fight, with weapon's edge; and from his kindred had carried off the brown-mottled helmet, ringed byrnie, old mysterious sword; which Onela yielded to him, his nephew's war-harness, accoutrement complete; not a word spake he (Onela) about the feud, although he (Weohstan) had killed his brother's son. He (Weohstan) retained the spoils many years, bill and byrnie, until when his boy was able to claim warrior's rank, like his father before him: then gave he to him before the

Goths armor untold of every sort; after which he departed out of life, ripe for the parting journey.

Now this was the first adventure for 5 the young champion wherein he had with his liege lord to enterprise the risk of war; his courage did not melt in him, nor did his kinsman's heirloom prove weak in the conflict; a fact which the 10 worm experienced, as soon as they had come to close quarters.

Wiglaf discoursed much that was fitting; he said to his comrades that his soul was sad: — 'I recall the time, when 15 we enjoyed the mead, then did we promise our lord in the festive hall, to him who gave us rings, that we would repay him the war-harness, if any need of this kind should befall him, would repay him for 20 helmets and tempered swords. That is why he chose us of his host for this adventure by his own preference, reminded us of glory and promised rewards, because he counted us brave warriors, keen 25 helm-wearers; although our lord had designed single-handed to accomplish this mighty work, the shepherd of his people, forasmuch as he of all men had achieved most of famous exploits, of desperate 30 deeds. Now is the day come, that our liege lord behooves the strength of brave warriors; let us go to him, help our war-chief, while the scorching heat is on him, the grim fiery terror! God knows of me, 35 that I had much liever the flame should swallow my body with my gold-giver. Me thinketh it indecent, that we bear our shields back to our home, unless we can first quell the foe, and rescue the life of 40 the Storm-folk's ruler. I know well those were not the old habits of service, that he alone of the Gothic nobles should bear the brunt, should sink in fight; our sovereign must be requited for sword and 45 helm, byrnie and stately uniform, and so he shall by me, though a common death take us both.'

Then he sped through the deadly reek, he came with helm on head to his lord's 50 assistance; few words spake he: 'My liege Beowulf, now make good all that which thou once saidst in time of youth, that thou never by thy lifetime wouldest let thy glory decline; now must thou, 55 glorious in deeds, etheling impetuous, with all thy might defend life; I shall support thee to the utmost.'

After these words were spoken, the
worm came on in fury, the fell malignant
monster came on for the second time,
with fire-jets flashing, to engage his
enemies, hated men; with the waves of
flame the shield was consumed all up to
the boss; the mail-coat could not render
assistance to the young warrior; but the
young stripling valorously went forward
under his kinsman's shield when his own 10
was reduced to ashes by the gleeds.
Then once more the warlike king remembered glory, remembered his forceful
strength, so smote with battle-bill that it
stood in the monster's head, desperately 15
impelled. Nægling flew in splinters, Beowulf's sword betrayed him in battle,
though old and monumental gray. To
him was it not granted that edges of iron
should help him in fight; too strong was 20
the hand of the man who with his stroke
overtaxed (as I have heard say) all
swords whatsoever; so that when he carried to conflict a weapon preternaturally
hard, he was none the better for it.   25

Then for the third time was the monstrous ravager, the infuriated fire-drake,
roused to vengeance; he rushed on the
heroic man, as he had yielded ground,
fiery and destructive, his entire neck he 30
enclosed with lacerating teeth; he was
bloodied over with the vital stream; gore
surged forth in waves.

XXXVII

THE DRAGON SLAIN. BEOWULF IN MORTAL AGONY.

Then I heard tell how, in the glorious
king's extremity, the young noble put 40
forth exemplary prowess of force and
daring, as was his nature to; he regarded
not that (formidable) head, but the
valiant man's hand was scorched, while
he helped his kinsman, insomuch that he 45
smote the fell creature a little lower down,
the man-at-arms did, with such effect that
the sword penetrated, the chased and
gilded sword, yea, with such effect that
the fire began to subside from that mo- 50
ment.

Then once more the beloved king recovered his senses, drew the war-knife,
biting and battle-sharp, which he wore
on his mail-coat; the crowned head of the 55
Storm-folk gashed the worm in the

middle. They had quelled the foe, death-
daring prowess had executed revenge,
and they two together, cousin ethelings,
had destroyed him; — such should a fellow be, a thane at need. To the chieftain
that was the supreme triumphal hour of
his career — by his own deeds — of his
life's completed work.

Then began the wound which the earth-
dragon had just now inflicted on him, to
inflame and swell. That he soon discovered, that in his breast fatal mischief was
working, venom in the inward parts.
Then the etheling went until he sat him
on a stone by the mound, thoughtfully
pondering; he looked upon the cunning
work of dwarfs, how there the world-old
earth-dome do contain within it stone
arches firmly set upon piers. Upon him
then, gory from conflict, illustrious monarch, the thane immeasurably good, ladled
water with hand upon his natural chieftain, battle-worn; — and unloosened his
helmet. Beowulf discoursed — in spite of
his hurt he spake, his deadly exhausting
wound; he knew well that he had spent
his hours, his enjoyment of earth; surely
all was gone of the tale of his days,
death immediately nigh —' Now I would
have given my war-weeds to my son, had
it so been that any heir had been given
to come after me, born of my body. I
have ruled this people fifty winters; —
there was not the king, not any king of
those neighboring peoples, who dared to
greet me with war-mates, to menace with
terror. I in my habitation observed social obligations, I held my own with justice, I have not sought insidious quarrels,
nor have I sworn many false oaths. Considering all this, I am able, though sick
with deadly wounds, to have comfort;
forasmuch as the Ruler of men cannot
charge me with murder-bale of kinsmen,
when my life quitteth the body.

' Now quickly go thou, to examine the
treasure, under the hoary rock, beloved
Wiglaf, now the worm lieth dead, sleepeth sore wounded, of riches bereaved.
Be now on the alert, that I may ascertain
the ancient wealth, the golden property,
may fully survey the brilliant, the curious gems; that I may be able the more
contentedly, after (seeing) the treasured
store, to resign my life, and the lordship
which I long have held.'

XXXVIII

BEOWULF IS GRATIFIED WITH SEEING THE
TREASURES. HE DEMISES THE CROWN
AND DIES.

Then I heard tell how the son of
Weohstan after the injunction promptly
obeyed his wounded death-sick lord; bore
his ring-mail, linked war-sark, under the
roof of the barrow. Then the victorious 10
youth, as he went along by the stony
bench, the true and courageous thane, beheld many jewels of value, gold glistening, indenting the ground, wondrous
things in the barrow;— and the lair of 15
the worm, the old dawn-flyer — vases
standing, choice vessels of men of old,
with none to burnish them,— their in-
crustations fallen away. There was
many a helmet, old and rusty, many a 20
bracelet, with appendage of trinkets.
Treasure may easily, gold in the earth,
may easily make a fool of any man;
heed it who will! Likewise he saw
looming above the hoard a banner all 25
golden, greatest marvel of handiwork,
woven with arts of incantation; out of
it there stood forth a gleam of light, insomuch that he was able to discern the
surface of the floor, and survey the 30
strange curiosities. Of the worm there
was not any appearance, but the knife
had put him out of the way.

Then heard I how in the chambered
mound the old work of dwarfs was spoiled 35
by a single man, how he gathered into
his lap cups and platters at his own discretion; the banner also he took, the most
brilliant of ensigns; the sword with its
iron edge had even now despatched the 40
old proprietor, the one who had been the
possessor of these treasures for a long
while; a hot and flaming terror he had
waged for the hoard, gushing with destruction at midnights; until he died the 45
death.

The messenger was in haste, eager to
return, fraught with spoils; painfully he
wondered in his brave soul whether he
should find alive the prince of the Storm- 50
folk, on the open ground where he left
him erst, chivalrously dying. He then
bearing the treasures, found the illustrious king, his captain, bleeding from his
wounds, at the extremity of life; he be- 55
gan again to sprinkle him with water,
until the point of speech forced open the
treasures of his breast. Beowulf discoursed, the old man in pain, he contemplated the gold: 'I do utter a
thanksgiving to the Lord of all, to the
king of glory, to the eternal captain, for 5
those spoils upon which I here do gaze;
to think that I have been permitted to
acquire such for my leeds before the day
of my death. Now I have sold my expiring life-term for a hoard of treasure; 10
ye now shall provide for the requirements
of the leeds; I cannot be any longer
here. Order my brave warriors to erect
a lofty cairn after the bale-fire, at the
headland over the sea; it shall tower 15
aloft on Hronesness for a memorial to
my leeds, that sea-faring men in time to
come may call it Beowulf's Barrow, those
who on distant voyages drive their foamy
barks over the scowling floods.' 20

The brave-hearted monarch took off
from his neck the golden collar and gave
it to the thane, to the young spear-fighter,
his gold-hued helmet, coronet, and byrnie;
bade him brook them well: 'Thou art 25
the last remnant of our stock, of the
Wægmundings; Fate has swept all my
kinsmen away into eternity, princes in
chivalry; I must after them.'

That was the aged man's latest word, 30
from the meditations of his breast, before he chose the bale-fire, the hot consuming flames;— out of his bosom the
soul departed, to enter into the lot of 35
the just.

XXXIX

A BRIEF REVIEW OF THE SITUATION. WIG-
LAF UPBRAIDS THE RECREANT COMPAN-
IONS. HE PRONOUNCES UPON THEM AND
THEIR KIN A SENTENCE OF DEGRADATION.

Thus had a hard experience overtaken
the inexperienced youth, that he saw
upon the ground the man who was dear- 45
est to him at his life's end in a helpless
condition. His destroyer likewise lay
dead, the horrible earth-dragon, bereft of
life, crushed in ruin; no longer was the
coiled worm to be lord of the jewel- 50
treasures, but they had been wrested
from him with weapons of iron, hard
battle-sharp relics of hammers, insomuch
that the wide-flyer tamed by wounds had
fallen on earth nigh to the hoard-cham- 55
ber; no more through the regions of air
did he sportively whirl at midnights, and

elate over his treasured property, display his presence; but on earth he collapsed, through mighty hand of warrior-prince.

Howbeit, that has rarely in the world 5 prospered with men, even men of fame, — by my information,— daring though a man might be in all deeds whatsoever; that he should rush against the breath of the poisonous destroyer, or with hands 10 molest the ring-hall, if he found the keeper waking, at home in the barrow. Beowulf had purchased the gain of princely treasures with his death; he had howsoever reached the end of transitory 15 life.

Then was it not long until the war-laggards quitted the wood, the faint-hearted traitors, ten all together, those who whilere durst not sport their lances 20 in the great need of their liege lord; but they in shame bore their shields, their war-weeds, to the place where the aged warrior lay dead;— they looked upon Wiglaf!   25

He sat wearied out, the active champion, nigh his lord's shoulder; was refreshing him with water; his care availed nothing; he could not retain upon earth, well as he would have wished it, 30 that chieftain's life; nor turn the Almighty's will; the dispensation of God would take effect upon men of all conditions, just as it does at present. Then had the young man a grim answer 35 promptly ready for such as erst had failed in courage. Wiglaf discoursed, Weohstan's son; the youth with sorrowful heart looked upon men whom he no longer loved: 40

'That, look you, may a man say, a man who is minded to speak the truth, that the chieftain who gave you those decorations, military apparel, which ye 45 there stand upright in,— when he at ale-bench often presented to inmates of his hall helmet and byrnie, as a prince to thanes, of such make as he far or near could procure most trusty — that he 50 utterly threw away those war-weeds miserably. When stress of battle overtook him, the folk-king had by no means cause to boast of his companions-in-arms; nevertheless it was accorded to him by 55 God, the ordainer of victories, that he avenged himself single-handed with his weapon, when his valor was put to the

proof. Little protection could I afford him in the conflict, and I attempted nevertheless what was beyond my ability, to help my kinsman;— ever was he (the 5 dragon) the feebler, when I with sword smote the destroyer, the fire less violently gushed from his inwards. Defenders too few pressed round their prince, when the dire moment overtook him. Now 10 must (all) sharing of treasure, and presentation of swords, all patrimonial wealth and estate, escheat from your kin; every man of that family may roam destitute of land-right, as soon as ethel-15 ings at a distance are informed of your desertion, your ignominious conduct. Death is preferable, for every warrior, rather than a life of infamy.'

XL

ANNOUNCEMENT OF THE EVENT TO THE ARMED HOST. THE ENVOY ADDS A DISCOURSE REVIEWING THE SITUATION.

Orders gave he then to announce the issue of the conflict to the camp up over the seacliff, where the host of eorls, from morning all day long, had with anxious hearts sat by their shields, in divided 30 antic̲i̲p̲a̲t̲i̲o̲n̲ ... a fatal return of the ... icent was he of the latest tidings, he who rode up the bluff; he truthfully spake out in the hearing of all: 'Now is 35 the bounteous chief of the leeds of the Stormfolk, the captain of the Goths, motionless on bed of death, he dwells in war-like repose by the deeds of the worm! with him in even case lieth his 40 mortal antagonist, smitten with dirk-wounds: — with sword he could not upon the monster by any means effect a wound. Over Beowulf sitteth Wiglaf, Weohstan's boy, a living eorl over a dead; over his 45 unconscious head he holdeth guard against friend and foe.

'Now the leeds may expect a time of war, as soon as the king's fall is published abroad among Franks and Fris-50 ians. The obstinate quarrel with the Hugas was set up when Hygelac came with embarked army upon the Frisian land, where the Hetware in battle vanquished him; resolutely they struck with 55 overwhelming force, insomuch that the mailed warrior was compelled to bow his head: he fell among the fighting men:

far was he from giving spoils as chieftain to his veterans; — to us ever since that time has the favor of the Merwing been unaccorded.

'Nor do I anywise count upon peace or good understanding on the side of Sweden; — indeed, it was a far-famed story, how that Ongentheow slew Hætheyn the son of Hrethel, by Ravenswood, whenas the warlike Scylfings had been the first to invade for sheer insolence the people of the Goths. Promptly did the veteran, the father of Ohthere, old and awful, deliver his onslaught, demolished the sea-king (Hæthcyn), rescued his consort, the aged man rescued the wife of his youth, though plundered of her jewels, the mother of Onela and of Ohthere, and then pursued his deadly foes, until they got away, with great difficulty, into Ravensholt, bereaved of their lord. Then did he, with host drawn out, surround those whom the sword had left, men exhausted with wounds, he repeatedly threatened woe to the poor band all the livelong night: he said that in the morning he would reach them with the edge of the sword, and (hang) some on gal~~low~~ ~~...~~ to please the birds.

~~. . . . . day,~~ when they heard Hygelac's horn, and the sound of his trumpet; presently the brave (prince) came marching upon their track with the best of his leeds.

XLI

CONCLUSION OF THE ENVOY'S DISCOURSE. THE BATTALION VISITS THE SCENE OF THE SUPREME CONFLICT.

'Then was the gory track of Swedes and Goths, the deadly strife of men, widely conspicuous, how the folk on either side revived the feud. Then did the valiant man proceed with his comrades, the solemn veteran, to seek a place of strength; the warrior Ongentheow turned towards the hill; he had heard tell of the warfare of Hygelac, the war-craft of the valiant; he trusted not in resistance, that he could defy the seamen, the travelers of the deep, could protect his treasure, his children, and his wife; so he retired back therefrom, the old king retired behind the earth-wall. Then was chase given to the Swedish leeds; the banners of Hygelac moved forward over that peaceful plain, and presently the Hrethlings massed themselves upon the garrison. Then was Ongentheow, the gray-haired, driven to bay with sword-edges, insomuch that the mighty king was constrained to put up with the one-handed decision of Eofor. Him (Ongentheow) had Wulf, son of Wonred, fiercely attacked with weapon, so effectually, that with the stroke his blood flew from his veins out from under his hair. He was not daunted, however, the aged Scylfing; but he quickly repaid that deadly assault with worse barter, as soon as the mighty king had collected himself. The brisk son of Wonred failed to give counter-blow to the old veteran, but he (Ongentheow) had first shorn the helmet on his head, so that blood-sprinkled he was forced to bow, he fell on the ground; — he was not at that time death-doomed as yet, but he recovered from it, though the wound had touched him close. Then did Hygelac's valiant thane let his broad blade, gigantesque old sword, his dwarf-wrought helmet, break over the shield-wall; then crouched the king, the people's shepherd, he was fatally smitten. Then were there many who bound up his brother's wounds (of Wulf the brother of Eofor), who quickly raised him up, when they had got the ground cleared, so that they had command of the place of battle. Meanwhile warrior stripped warrior; he (Eofor) captured on Ongentheow the iron breast-mail, his hard sword with hilt, and his helmet likewise, the gray-beard's accoutrements; — to Hygelac he bare them. He accepted the spoils, and made him a fair promise of rewards before his leeds, and he kept his word; he, the lord of the Goths, the son of Hrethel, when he arrived at his mansion, repaid Eofor and Wulf for that war-brunt, with treasure extraordinary; he gave to each of them a hundred thousand of land and collars of filigree; none could jeer at them for those rewards, not a man in the world, since they had achieved those exploits; — and moreover he bestowed upon Eofor, his only daughter, to make his home honorable, and for a pledge of loyalty.

'Such is the feud and the enmity and the deadly grudge of the men, even the

Swedish leeds, who, as I apprehend, will attack us, as soon as they shall learn that our prince is dead, he who whilere hath upheld against hostilities, our treasure and our realm, was master of public counsel, or won ever-increasing glory in war. Now is quickness best, that we should there look upon the mighty king, and bring him who gave us bracelets, on to the funeral-pile. It is not meet that some trifling matter be consumed with the high-souled man; but yonder is a hoard of precious things, gold uncounted, frightfully bargained for, and now at last jewels purchased with the hero's own life; those must fire devour, the flame must enfold them; never a warrior wear ornament for memorial, nor maiden sheen have on her neck the decorated collar, but on the contrary must in dejected mood and stripped of gold ornaments tread often and often the land of the stranger, now the army leader hath laid aside laughter, game, and glee. Therefore shall many a spear in the cold of the morning be clutched in men's grasp, hoisted in the hand; no swough of harp shall waken the warriors: but the bleak raven fluttering over carnage shall chatter abundantly, recount to the eagle of his luck at the spread, while alongside of the wolf he stripped the slain.'

Thus was the ardent youth discoursing of painful themes; he erred not widely of events or words. All the troop arose, they went unjoyous, under the Eagle's Crag, with gushing tears, to behold the tremendous sight. They found there, on the sand, bereft of life, and keeping his helpless bed, the man who had given them rings in times bygone; there had the final day come to the valiant, in that the warlike king, the prince of the Wederas, had perished with a death heroic.

. . . never saw they frightfuller object — the dragon on the ground there right before their face, the loathsome beast lying dead; all scorched with flames was the fire-drake, the grisly gruesome pest; it was fifty foot-measurements long where it lay; in the pride of the air he had been supreme during the hours of night, and then down would he return back again to reconnoitre his lair: — now he was there stock dead, had made his last use of earthly caverns. By the side of it stood pots and bowls; there dishes lay about, and swords of price, rusty and corroded, as if they in earth's lap a thousand winters there had sojourned; forasmuch as that patrimony, huge and vast, that gold of ancient men, had been closed about with enchantment; and therefore that treasure-chamber might not be touched by any one of mankind, save in so far as God himself, the true king of achievements, should grant to the man of his choice to open the hoard, the sorcerers' hold: — even to such one of mankind whomso he deemed to be meet.

XLII

REFLECTIONS UPON THE GREAT EVENT. WIGLAF PUBLISHES BEOWULF'S DYING ORDERS. PREPARATIONS FOR THE BALEFIRE. THE CAVERN IS RIFLED AND THE TREASURES ARE PILED ON A WAGON TO FOLLOW THE BIER. THE LAST OF THE DRAGON.

Then was it manifest, that good luck attended not upon the course of them who by unlawful means had closely safeguarded valuables under the mound. At first the keeper slew one here and there; at length the feud had grown to be expiated furiously. By a heroic death therefore in some manner should a brave warrior accomplish the end of life's record, seeing that he cannot much longer as a man in the midst of his kinsfolk inhabit the mead-hall. Such was Beowulf's lot, when he went forth to seek the keeper of the barrow, went to seek deadly strife, he himself knew not by what means his severance from the world was destined to happen, according as the mighty captains, when they that deposited there, had uttered a deep spell to hold till doomsday, that the man who invaded that ground should be criminally guilty, cabined in heathen fanes, fast bound with hell-bands, penally doomed; yet never did he at any previous time more effectually experience the gold-bestowing favor of God.

Wiglaf, son of Weohstan, lifted up his voice: 'Often must many a brave man, by the will of one, endure tribulation, as it hath happened to us. We were not able to convince our beloved master, the shepherd of the kingdom, by any reasoning, that he should not challenge you gold-warden, but should leave him to lie where he had long been, and to dwell in his haunts till the end of the world, fulfil high destiny. The hoard is laid open to our view, fearfully purchased; too overpowering was that boon which attracted our prince thither. I was in the interior of the place, and I explored the whole of it, the stores of the chamber, inasmuch as the way had been opened for me and that by no gentle means, passage was permitted in under the earthern dome. Hurriedly I grappled with my hands a huge mighty burden of hoarded treasures; out hither I bore them to the feet of my king. He was still alive then, wise and sensible; freely did he talk, the aged one in death-pang; and he commanded me to give you his greeting, he bade that you should construct, in memory of your chieftain's deeds, upon the scene of the bale-fire, a barrow of the highest, mighty and magnifical, according as he was of all men the warrior most famous, through the wide earth, so long as he might enjoy the wealth of his castle.

'Go to, let us now hasten, a second time, to see and to visit the ruck of jewels, the spectacle beneath the earthwork. I will be your guide, so that ye shall have your fill of seeing close at hand, collars and bullion gold.

'Let the bier be ready, promptly equipped, attending us as we go forth of this place, and so let us convey our master, the beloved man, to the place where he shall tarry long in the safe keeping of the Almighty.'

Then did the son of Weohstan order his brave warriors that they should issue commands to many homestead-owners, for them to haul pyre-timber from far to meet the occasion of the ruler of men: — ' Now must fire devour, the scowling flame must wash, the pillar of warriors, him who often stood the shock of the iron shower, what time the storm of missiles, urged by bow-strings, hurtled over the shield-wall, the shaft did its duty, with feather-fittings eager it backed up the arrow's point.'

Thereupon the prudent son of Weohstan called out of the squadron some thanes of the king, seven of them together, the choicest; he made the eighth, and went with them under the dangerous roof; a

warrior bore in hand a flaming torch, and he walked in front. It was not staked upon lot who should have the looting of that hoard, when the warriors had partly taken a view of it in its keeperless state occupying the chamber, lying helpless. Little did any man scruple that they should with all despatch convey abroad the valuable treasures; the dragon moreover they haled, they shoved the worm over the precipitous cliff, they let the wave take him, the flood engulf him, that warder of precious spoils.

There was coiled gold laden upon wagon, countless in quantity of every kind; — the etheling was borne on a bier, the hoary warrior, to Hronesness.

XLIII

THE FUNERAL AND THE EPITAPH.

For him then did the leeds of the Goths construct a pyre upon the earth, one of no mean dimensions, hung about with helmets, with battle-boards, with bright byrnies, as he had requested; then did they, heaving deep sighs, lay in the midst of it the illustrious chieftain, the hero, the beloved lord. Then began the warriors to kindle upon the hill the hugest of bale-fires; the wood-smoke mounted up black over the combustive mass, the roaring blaze shot aloft, mingled with the howling of the windcurrents; until the sweltering element had demolished the bone-house. With hearts distressed and care-laden minds they mourned their liege lord's death; likewise a dirge of sorrow [was sung in honor of Beowulf by the aged dame, her hair bound up, her soul sorrowing; she said repeatedly, that she sorely dreaded for herself evil days, much bloodshed, the warrior's horror, shame and captivity]. Heaven swallowed the smoke.

Then did the people of the Wederas construct a mound on the hill; it was high and broad, to sea-voyagers widely conspicuous; and during ten days they labored about the building of the warhero's beacon: they surrounded the ashes of the conflagration with an embankment in such wise as men of eminent skill could contrive it with noblest effect. They deposited in the barrow collars and brilliants, the whole of such trappings as war-breathing men had recently captured in the hoard; they abandoned the accumulated wealth of eorls for the earth to retain it, gold in marl, where it now still continues to be as useless to mankind as it was erst.

Then there rode round the mound war-chiefs, sons of ethelings, twelve in all; they would bewail their loss, bemoan the king, recite an elegy, and celebrate his name. They admired his manhood, and they loftily appraised his daring work; as it is fitting that a man should with words extol his liege lord, should cherish him in his affections, when he must take his departure from the ten-5 emental body.

Thus did the leeds of the Goths, the companions of his hearth, lament the fall of their lord; — they said that he was of all kings in the world, the mildest 10 and most affable to his men; most genial to his leeds; and most desirous of praise.

SIR GAWAIN AND THE GREEN KNIGHT (c. 1375)

The romantic stories cherished by the Norman conquerors of England found equal favor, in course of time, among the English. By the time of Chaucer's birth, English romances in verse were in full bloom, and during the course of that poet's life appeared the finest of all English romances, the anonymous *Sir Gawain and the Green Knight*. This romance as we have it combines two stories that were originally separate: the test of Sir Gawain's bravery through the compact with the Green Knight, and the test of Sir Gawain's honor and chastity through the wife of his host of the castle. Although the English author probably drew materials for his story directly from French sources, many of the structural and rhetorical excellencies of the present poem are certainly his own. A tale of daring, loyalty, courtesy, and religious devotion is presented in a spirit of refinement not to be exceeded. The poet's power of language is best shown in the scenery through which Sir Gawain is set a-wandering,— the winter scenery, not of conventional romance, but of Arthur's own Britain.

SIR GAWAIN AND THE GREEN KNIGHT

I

After the siege and the assault of Troy, when that burg was destroyed and burnt to ashes, and the traitor tried for his treason, the noble Æneas and his kin sailed forth to become princes and patrons of well-nigh all the Western Isles. Thus Romulus built Rome (and gave to the city his own name, which it bears even to this day); and Ticius turned him to Tuscany; and Langobard raised him up dwellings in Lombardy; and Felix Brutus sailed far over the French flood, and founded the kingdom of Britain, wherein have been war and waste and wonder, and bliss and bale, ofttimes since.

And in that kingdom of Britain have been wrought more gallant deeds than in any other; but of all British kings Arthur was the most valiant, as I have heard tell; therefore will I set forth a wondrous adventure that fell out in his time. And if ye will listen to me, but for a little while, I will tell it even as it stands in story stiff and strong, fixed in the letter, as it hath long been known in the land.

King Arthur lay at Camelot upon a Christmas-tide, with many a gallant lord and lovely lady, and all the noble brotherhood of the Round Table. There they held rich revels with gay talk and jest; 35 one while they would ride forth to joust and tourney, and again back to the court to make carols; for there was the feast holden fifteen days with all the mirth that men could devise, song and glee, glorious to hear, in the daytime, and dancing at night. Halls and chambers were crowded with noble guests, the bravest of knights and the loveliest of ladies, and Arthur himself was the comeliest king that ever held a court. For all this fair folk were in their youth, the fairest and most fortunate under heaven, and the king himself of such fame that it were hard now to name so valiant a hero.

Now the New Year had but newly come in, and on that day a double portion was served on the high table to all the noble guests, and thither came the king with all his knights, when the service in the chapel had been sung to an end. And they greeted each other for the New Year, and gave rich gifts, the one to the other (and they that received them were not wroth, that may ye well believe!), and the maidens laughed and made mirth till it was time to get them to meat. Then they washed and sat them down to the feasting in fitting rank and order, and Guinevere the queen, gaily clad, sat on the high daïs. Silken was her seat, with a fair canopy over her head, of rich tapestries of Tars, embroidered, and studded with costly gems; fair she was to look upon, with her shining gray eyes, a fairer woman might no man boast himself of having seen.

But Arthur would not eat till all were served, so full of joy and gladness was he, even as a child; he liked not either to lie long, or to sit long at meat, so worked upon him his young blood and his wild brain. And another custom he had also, that came of his nobility, that he would never eat upon an high day till he had been advised of some knightly deed, or some strange and marvelous tale, of his ancestors, or of arms, or of other ventures. Or till some stranger knight should seek of him leave to joust with one of the Round Table, that they might set their lives in jeopardy, one against another, as fortune might favor them. Such was the king's custom when he sat in hall at each high feast with his noble knights; therefore on that New Year tide, he abode, fair of face, on the throne, and made much mirth withal.

Thus the king sat before the high tables, and spake of many things; and there good Sir Gawain was seated by Guinevere the queen, and on her other side sat Agravain, *à la dure main;* both were the king's sister's sons and full gallant knights. And at the end of the table was Bishop Bawdewyn, and Ywain, King Urien's son, sat at the other side alone. These were worthily served on the daïs, and at the lower tables sat many valiant knights. Then they bare the first course with the blast of trumpets and waving of banners, with the sound of drums and pipes, of song and lute, that many a heart was uplifted at the melody. Many were the dainties, and rare the meats; so great was the plenty they might scarce find room on the board to set on the dishes. Each helped himself as he liked best, and to each two were twelve dishes, with great plenty of beer and wine.

Now I will say no more of the service, but that ye may know there was no lack, for there drew near a venture that the folk might well have left their labor to gaze upon. As the sound of the music ceased, and the first course had been fitly served, there came in at the hall door one terrible to behold, of stature greater than any on earth; from neck to loin so strong and thickly made, and with limbs so long and so great that he seemed even as a giant. And yet he was but a man, only the mightiest that might mount a steed; broad of chest and shoulders and slender of waist, and all his features of like fashion; but men marveled much at his color, for he rode even as a knight, yet was green all over.

For he was clad all in green, with a straight coat, and a mantle above; all decked and lined with fur was the cloth and the hood that was thrown back from his locks and lay on his shoulders. Hose had he of the same green, and spurs of bright gold with silken fastenings richly worked; and all his vesture was verily green. Around his waist and his saddle were bands with fair stones set upon silken work, 't were too long to tell of all the trifles that were embroidered thereon — birds and insects in gay gauds of green and gold. All the trappings of his steed were of metal of like enamel, even the stirrups that he stood in stained of the same, and stirrups and saddle-bow alike gleamed and shone with green stones. Even the steed on which he rode was of the same hue, a green horse, great and strong, and hard to hold, with broidered bridle, meet for the rider.

The knight was thus gaily dressed in green, his hair falling around his shoulders; on his breast hung a beard, as thick and green as a bush, and the beard and the hair of his head were clipped all round above his elbows. The lower part of his sleeves was fastened with clasps in the same wise as a king's mantle. The horse's mane was crisp and plaited with many a knot folded in with gold thread about the fair green, here a twist of the hair, here another of gold. The tail was twined in like manner, and both were bound about with a band of bright green set with many a precious stone; then they were tied aloft in a cunning knot, whereon rang many bells of burnished gold. Such a steed might no other ride, nor had such ever been looked upon in that hall ere that time; and all who saw that knight spake and said that a man might scarce abide his stroke.

The knight bore no helm nor hauberk, neither gorget nor breast-plate, neither shaft nor buckler to smite nor to shield, but in one hand he had a holly-bough, that is greenest when the groves are bare, and in his other an axe, huge and uncomely, a cruel weapon in fashion, if one would picture it. The head was an ell-yard long, the metal all of green steel and gold, the blade burnished bright, with a broad edge, as well shapen to shear as a sharp razor. The steel was set into a strong staff, all bound round with iron, even to the end, and engraved with green in cunning work. A lace was twined about it, that looped at the head, and all adown the handle it was clasped with tassels on buttons of bright green richly broidered.

The knight rideth through the entrance of the hall, driving straight to the high daïs, and greeted no man, but looked ever upwards; and the first words he spake were, 'Where is the ruler of this folk? I would gladly look upon that hero, and have speech with him.' He cast his eyes on the knights, and mustered them up and down, striving ever to see who of them was of most renown.

Then was there great gazing to behold that chief, for each man marveled what it might mean that a knight and his steed should have even such a hue as the green grass; and that seemed even greener than green enamel on bright gold. All looked on him as he stood, and drew near unto him, wondering greatly what he might be; for many marvels had they seen, but none such as this, and phantasm and faërie did the folk deem it. Therefore were the gallant knights slow to answer, and gazed astounded, and sat stone still in a deep silence through that goodly hall, as if a slumber were fallen upon them. I deem it was not all for doubt, but some for courtesy that they might give ear unto his errand.

Then Arthur beheld this adventurer before his high daïs, and knightly he greeted him, for fearful was he never. 'Sir,' he said, 'thou art welcome to this place — lord of this hall am I, and men call me Arthur. Light thee down, and tarry awhile, and what thy will is, that shall we learn after.'

'Nay,' quoth the stranger, 'so help me he that sitteth on high, 'twas not mine errand to tarry any while in this dwelling; but the praise of this thy folk and thy city is lifted up on high, and thy warriors are holden for the best and the most valiant of those who ride mail-clad to the fight. The wisest and the worthiest of this world are they, and well

proven in all knightly sports. And here, as I have heard tell, is fairest courtesy; therefore have I come hither as at this time. Ye may be sure by the branch that 5 I bear here that I come in peace, seeking no strife. For had I willed to journey in warlike guise I have at home both hauberk and helm, shield and shining spear, and other weapons to mine hand, but 10 since I seek no war, my raiment is that of peace. But if thou be as bold as all men tell, thou wilt freely grant me the boon I ask.'

And Arthur answered, 'Sir Knight, if 15 thou cravest battle here thou shalt not fail for lack of a foe.'

And the knight answered, 'Nay, I ask no fight; in faith here on the benches are but beardless children; were I clad in 20 armor on my steed there is no man here might match me. Therefore I ask in this court but a Christmas jest, for that it is Yule-tide, and New Year, and there are here many fain for sport. If any 25 one in this hall holds himself so hardy, so bold both of blood and brain, as to dare strike me one stroke for another, I will give him as a gift this axe, which is heavy enough, in sooth, to handle as he 30 may list, and I will abide the first blow, unarmed as I sit. If any knight be so bold as to prove my words, let him come swiftly to me here, and take this weapon; I quit claim to it, he may keep it as his 35 own, and I will abide his stroke, firm on the floor. Then shalt thou give me the right to deal him another, the respite of a year and a day shall he have. Now haste, and let see whether any here dare 40 say aught.'

Now if the knights had been astounded at the first, yet stiller were they all, high and low, when they had heard his words. The knight on his steed straightened him-45 self in the saddle, and rolled his eyes fiercely round the hall; red they gleamed under his green and bushy brows. He frowned and twisted his beard, waiting to see who should rise, and when none 50 answered he cried aloud in mockery, 'What, is this Arthur's hall, and these the knights whose renown hath run through many realms? Where are now your pride and your conquests, your 55 wrath, and anger, and mighty words? Now are the praise and the renown of the Round Table overthrown by one man's speech, since all keep silence for dread ere ever they have seen a blow!'

With that he laughed so loudly that the blood rushed to the king's fair face for very shame; he waxed wroth, as did all his knights, and sprang to his feet, and drew near to the stranger and said, 'Now by heaven, foolish is thy asking, and thy folly shall find its fitting answer. I know no man aghast at thy great words. Give me here thine axe and I shall grant thee the boon thou hast asked.' Lightly he sprang to him and caught at his hand, and the knight, fierce of aspect, lighted down from his charger.

Then Arthur took the axe and gripped the haft, and swung it round, ready to strike. And the knight stood before him, taller by the head than any in the hall; he stood, and stroked his beard, and drew down his coat, no more dismayed for the king's threats than if one had brought him a drink of wine.

Then Gawain, who sat by the queen, leaned forward to the king and spake, 'I beseech ye, my lord, let this venture be mine. Would ye but bid me rise from this seat, and stand by your side, so that my liege lady thought it not ill, then would I come to your counsel before this goodly court. For I think it not seemly when such challenges be made in your hall that ye yourself should undertake it, while there are many bold knights who sit beside ye, none are there, methinks, of readier will under heaven, or more valiant in open field. I am the weakest, I wot, and the feeblest of wit, and it will be the less loss of my life if ye seek sooth. For save that ye are mine uncle, naught is there in me to praise, no virtue is there in my body save your blood, and since this challenge is such folly that it beseems ye not to take it, and I have asked it from ye first, let it fall to me, and if I bear myself ungallantly, then let all this court blame me.'

Then they all spake with one voice that the king should leave this venture and grant it to Gawain.

Then Arthur commanded the knight to rise, and he rose up quickly and knelt down before the king, and caught hold of the weapon; and the king loosed his hold of it, and lifted up his hand, and gave him his blessing, and bade him be strong both of heart and hand. 'Keep thee

well, nephew,' quoth Arthur, 'that thou give him but the one blow, and if thou redest him rightly I trow thou shalt well abide the stroke he may give thee after.'

Gawain stepped to the stranger, axe in hand, and he, never fearing, awaited his coming. Then the Green Knight spake to Sir Gawain, 'Make we our covenant ere we go further. First, I ask thee, knight, what is thy name? Tell me truly, that I may know thee.'

'In faith,' quoth the good knight, 'Gawain am I, who give thee this buffet, let what may come of it; and at this time twelvemonth will I take another at thine hand with whatsoever weapon thou wilt, and none other.'

Then the other answered again, 'Sir Gawain, so may I thrive as I am fain to take this buffet at thine hand,' and he quoth further, 'Sir Gawain, it liketh me well that I shall take at thy fist that which I have asked here, and thou hast readily and truly rehearsed all the covenant that I asked of the king, save that thou shalt swear me, by thy troth, to seek me thyself wherever thou hopest that I may be found, and win thee such reward as thou dealest me to-day, before this folk.'

'Where shall I seek thee?' quoth Gawain. 'Where is thy place? By him that made me, I wot never where thou dwellest, nor know I thee, knight, thy court, nor thy name. But teach me truly all that pertaineth thereto, and tell me thy name, and I shall use all my wit to win my way thither, and that I swear thee for sooth, and by my sure troth.'

'That is enough in the New Year, it needs no more,' quoth the Green Knight to the gallant Gawain, 'if I tell thee truly when I have taken the blow, and thou hast smitten me; then will I teach thee of my house and home, and mine own name, then mayest thou ask thy road and keep covenant. And if I waste no words then farest thou the better, for thou canst dwell in thy land, and seek no further. But take now thy toll, and let see how thou strikest.'

'Gladly will I,' quoth Gawain, handling his axe.

Then the Green Knight swiftly made him ready, he bowed down his head, and laid his long locks on the crown that his bare neck might be seen. Gawain gripped his axe and raised it on high, the left foot he set forward on the floor, and let the blow fall lightly on the bare neck. The sharp edge of the blade sundered the bones, smote through the neck, and clave it in two, so that the edge of the steel bit on the ground, and the fair head fell to the earth that many struck it with their feet as it rolled forth. The blood spurted forth, and glistened on the green raiment, but the knight neither faltered nor fell; he started forward with out-stretched hand, and caught the head, and lifted it up; then he turned to his steed, and took hold of the bridle, set his foot in the stirrup, and mounted. His head he held by the hair, in his hand. Then he seated himself in his saddle as if naught ailed him, and he were not headless. He turned his steed about, the grim corpse bleeding freely the while, and they who looked upon him doubted them much for the covenant.

For he held up the head in his hand, and turned the face towards them that sat on the high daïs, and it lifted up the eyelids and looked upon them and spake as ye shall hear. 'Look, Gawain, that thou art ready to go as thou hast promised, and seek loyally till thou find me, even as thou hast sworn in this hall in the hearing of these knights. Come thou, I charge thee, to the Green Chapel; such a stroke as thou hast dealt thou hast deserved, and it shall be promptly paid thee on New Year's morn. Many men know me as the knight of the Green Chapel, and if thou askest, thou shalt not fail to find me. Therefore it behooves thee to come, or to yield thee as recreant.'

With that he turned his bridle, and galloped out at the hall door, his head in his hands, so that the sparks flew from beneath his horse's hoofs. Whither he went none knew, no more than they wist whence he had come; and the king and Gawain they gazed and laughed, for in sooth this had proved a greater marvel than any they had known aforetime.

Though Arthur the king was astonished at his heart, yet he let no sign of it be seen, but spake in courteous wise to the fair queen: 'Dear lady, be not dismayed, such craft is well suited to Christmas-tide when we seek jesting, laughter, and song, and fair carols of knights and ladies. But now I may well get me to meat, for I have seen a marvel I may not forget.' Then he looked on Sir Gawain, and said gaily, 'Now, fair nephew, hang up thine axe, since it has hewn enough,' and they hung it on the dossal above the daïs, where all men might look on it for a marvel, and by its true token tell of the wonder. Then the twain sat them down together, the king and the good knight, and men served them with a double portion, as was the share of the noblest, with all manner of meat and of minstrelsy. And they spent that day in gladness, but Sir Gawain must well bethink him of the heavy venture to which he had set his hand.

II

This beginning of adventures had Arthur at the New Year; for he yearned to hear gallant tales, though his words were few when he sat at the feast. But now had they stern work on hand. Gawain was glad to begin the jest in the hall, but ye need have no marvel if the end be heavy. For though a man be merry in mind when he has well drunk, yet a year runs full swiftly, and the beginning but rarely matches the end.

For Yule was now over-past, and the year after, each season in its turn following the other. For after Christmas comes crabbed Lent, that will have fish for flesh and simpler cheer. But then the weather of the world chides with winter; the cold withdraws itself, the clouds uplift, and the rain falls in warm showers on the fair plains. Then the flowers come forth, meadows and grove are clad in green, the birds make ready to build, and sing sweetly for solace of the soft summer that follows thereafter. The blossoms bud and blow in the hedgerows rich and rank, and noble notes enough are heard in the fair woods.

After the season of summer, with the soft winds, when zephyr breathes lightly on seeds and herbs, joyous indeed is the growth that waxes thereout when the dew drips from the leaves beneath the blissful glance of the bright sun. But then comes harvest and hardens the grain, warning it to wax ripe ere the winter. The drought drives the dust on high, flying over the face of the land; the angry wind of the welkin wrestles with the sun; the leaves fall from the trees and light upon the ground, and all brown are the groves that but now were green, and ripe is the fruit that once was flower. So the year passes into many yesterdays, and winter comes again, as it needs no sage to tell us.

When the Michaelmas moon was come in with warnings of winter, Sir Gawain bethought him full oft of his perilous journey. Yet till All Hallows Day he lingered with Arthur, and on that day they made a great feast for the hero's sake, with much revel and richness of the Round Table. Courteous knights and comely ladies, all were in sorrow for the love of that knight, and though they spake no word of it, many were joyless for his sake.

And after meat, sadly Sir Gawain turned to his uncle, and spake of his journey, and said, 'Liege lord of my life, leave from you I crave. Ye know well how the matter stands without more words; to-morrow am I bound to set forth in search of the Green Knight.'

Then came together all the noblest knights, Ywain and Erec, and many another. Sir Dodinel le Sauvage, the Duke of Clarence, Launcelot and Lionel, and Lucan the Good, Sir Bors and Bedivere, valiant knights both, and many another hero, with Sir Mador de la Porte, and they all drew near, heavy at heart, to take counsel with Sir Gawain. Much sorrow and weeping was there in the hall to think that so worthy a knight as Gawain should wend his way to seek a deadly blow, and should no more wield his sword in fight. But the knight made ever good cheer, and said, 'Nay, wherefore should I shrink? What may a man do but prove his fate?'

He dwelt there all that day, and on the morn he arose and asked betimes for his armor; and they brought it unto him on this wise: first, a rich carpet was stretched on the floor (and brightly did the gold gear glitter upon it), then the knight stepped upon it, and handled the steel; clad he was in a doublet of silk, with a close hood, lined fairly throughout. Then they set the steel shoes upon his feet, and wrapped his legs with greaves, with polished knee-caps, fastened with knots of gold. Then they cased his thighs in cuisses closed with thongs, and brought him the byrnie of bright steel rings sewn upon a fair stuff. Well burnished braces they set on each arm with good elbow-pieces, and gloves of mail, and all the goodly gear that should shield him in his need. And they cast over all a rich surcoat, and set the golden spurs on his heels, and girt him with a trusty sword fastened with a silken bawdrick. When he was thus clad his harness was costly, for the least loop or latchet gleamed with gold. So armed as he was he hearkened Mass and made his offering at the high altar. Then he came to the king, and the knights of his court, and courteously took leave of lords and ladies, and they kissed him, and commended him to Christ.

With that was Gringalet ready, girt with a saddle that gleamed gaily with many golden fringes, enriched and decked anew for the venture. The bridle was all barred about with bright gold buttons, and all the covertures and trappings of the steed, the crupper and the rich skirts, accorded with the saddle; spread fair with the rich red gold that glittered and gleamed in the rays of the sun.

Then the knight called for his helmet, which was well lined throughout, and set it high on his head, and hasped it behind. He wore a light kerchief over the ventail, that was broidered and studded with fair gems on a broad silken ribbon, with birds of gay color, and many a turtle and true-lover's knot interlaced thickly, even as many a maiden had wrought diligently for seven winters long. But the circlet which crowned his helmet was yet more precious, being adorned with a device in diamonds. Then they brought him his shield, which was of bright red, with the pentangle painted thereon in gleaming gold. And why that noble prince bare the pentangle I am minded to tell you, though my tale tarry thereby. It is a sign that Solomon set ere-while, as betokening truth; for it is a figure with five points and each line overlaps the other, and nowhere hath it beginning or end, so that in English it is called 'the endless knot.' And therefore was it well suiting to this knight and to his arms, since Gawain was faithful in five and five-fold, for pure was he as gold, void of all villainy and endowed with all virtues. Therefore he bare the pentangle on shield and surcoat as truest of heroes and gentlest of knights.

For first he was faultless in his five senses; and his five fingers never failed him; and all his trust upon earth was in the five wounds that Christ bare on the cross, as the Creed tells. And wherever this knight found himself in stress of battle he deemed well that he drew his strength from the five joys which the Queen of Heaven had of her Child. And for this cause did he bear an image of Our Lady on the one half of his shield, that whenever he looked upon it he might not lack for aid. And the fifth five that the hero used were frankness and fellowship above all, purity and courtesy that never failed him, and compassion that surpasses all; and in these five virtues was that hero wrapped and clothed. And all these, five-fold, were linked one in the other, so that they had no end, and were fixed on five points that never failed, neither at any side were they joined or sundered, nor could ye find beginning or end. And therefore on his shield was the knot shapen, red-gold upon red, which is the pure pentangle. Now was Sir Gawain ready, and he took his lance in hand, and bade them all farewell, he deemed it had been for ever.

Then he smote the steed with his spurs, and sprang on his way, so that sparks flew from the stones after him. All that saw him were grieved at heart, and said one to the other, 'By Christ, 't is great pity that one of such noble life should be lost! I' faith, 't were not easy to find his equal upon earth. The king had done better to have wrought more warily. Yonder knight should have been made a duke; a gallant leader of men is he, and such a fate had beseemed him better than to be hewn in pieces at the will of an elfish man, for mere pride. Who ever knew a king to take such counsel as to risk his knights on a Christmas jest?' Many were the tears that flowed from their eyes when that goodly knight rode from the hall. He made no delaying, but went his way swiftly, and rode many a wild road, as I heard say in the book.

So rode Sir Gawain through the realm of Logres, on an errand that he held for no jest. Often he lay companionless at night, and must lack the fare that he liked. No comrade had he save his steed, and none save God with whom to take counsel. At length he drew nigh to North Wales, and left the isles of Anglesey on his left hand, crossing over the fords by the foreland over at Holyhead, till he came into the wilderness of Wirral, where but few dwell who love God and man of true heart. And ever he asked, as he fared, of all whom he met, if they had heard any tidings of a Green Knight in the country thereabout, or of a Green Chapel? And all answered him, Nay, never in their lives had they seen any man of such a hue. And the knight wended his way by many a strange road and many a rugged path, and the fashion of his countenance changed full often ere he saw the Green Chapel.

Many a cliff did he climb in that unknown land, where afar from his friends he rode as a stranger. Never did he come to a stream or a ford but he found a foe before him, and that one so marvelous, so foul and fell, that it behooved him to fight. So many wonders did that knight behold, that it were too long to tell the tenth part of them. Sometimes he fought with dragons and wolves; sometimes with wild men that dwelt in the rocks; another while with bulls, and bears, and wild boars, or with giants of the high moorland that drew near to him. Had he not been a doughty knight, enduring, and of well-proved valor, and a servant of God, doubtless he had been slain, for he was oft in danger of death. Yet he cared not so much for the strife; what he deemed worse was when the cold clear water was shed from the clouds, and froze ere it fell on the fallow ground. More nights than enough he slept in his harness on the bare rocks, near slain with the sleet, while the stream leapt bubbling from the crest of the hills, and hung in hard icicles over his head.

Thus in peril and pain, and many a hardship, the knight rode alone till Christmas Eve, and in that tide he made his prayer to the Blessed Virgin that she would guide his steps and lead him to some dwelling. On that morning he rode by a hill, and came into a thick forest, wild and drear; on each side were high hills, and thick woods below them of great hoar oaks, a hundred together, of hazel and hawthorn with their trailing boughs interwined, and rough ragged moss spreading everywhere. On the bare twigs the birds chirped piteously, for pain of the cold. The knight upon Gringalet rode lonely beneath them, through marsh and mire, much troubled at heart lest he should fail to see the service of the Lord, who on that self-same night was born of a maiden for the cure of our grief; and therefore he said, sighing, 'I beseech thee, Lord, and Mary thy gentle Mother, for some shelter where I may hear Mass, and thy matins at morn. This I ask meekly, and thereto I pray my Paternoster, Ave, and Credo.' Thus he rode praying, and lamenting his misdeeds, and he crossed himself, and said, 'May the Cross of Christ speed me.'

Now that knight had crossed himself but thrice ere he was aware in the wood of a dwelling within a moat, above a lawn, on a mound surrounded by many mighty trees that stood round the moat. 'T was the fairest castle that ever a knight owned; built in a meadow with a park all about it, and a spiked palisade, closely driven, that enclosed the trees for more than two miles. The knight was ware of the hold from the side, as it shone through the oaks. Then he lifted off his helmet, and thanked Christ and Saint Julian that they had courteously granted his prayer, and hearkened to his cry. 'Now,' quoth the knight, 'I beseech ye, grant me fair hostel.' Then he pricked Gringalet with his golden spurs, and rode gaily towards the great gate, and came swiftly to the bridge end.

The bridge was drawn up and the gates close shut; the walls were strong and thick, so that they might fear no tempest. The knight on his charger abode on the bank of the deep double ditch that surrounded the castle. The walls were set deep in the water, and rose aloft to a wondrous height; they were of hard hewn stone up to the corbels, which were adorned beneath the battlements with fair carvings, and turrets set in between with many a loophole; a better barbican Sir Gawain had never looked upon. And within he beheld the high hall, with its tower and many windows with carven cornices, and chalk-white chimneys on the turreted roofs that shone fair in the sun. And everywhere, thickly scattered on the castle battlements, were pinnacles, so many that it seemed as if it were all wrought out of paper, so white was it.

The knight on his steed deemed it fair enough, if he might come to be sheltered within it to lodge there while that the holy-day lasted. He called aloud, and soon there came a porter of kindly countenance, who stood on the wall and greeted this knight and asked his errand.

'Good sir,' quoth Gawain, 'wilt thou go mine errand to the high lord of the castle, and crave for me lodging?'

'Yea, by Saint Peter,' quoth the porter. 'In sooth I trow that ye be welcome to dwell here so long as it may like ye.'

Then he went, and came again swiftly, and many folk with him to receive the knight. They let down the great drawbridge, and came forth and knelt on their knees on the cold earth to give him worthy welcome. They held wide open the great gates, and courteously he bade them rise, and rode over the bridge. Then men came to him and held his stirrup while he dismounted, and took and stabled his steed. There came down knights and squires to bring the guest with joy to the hall. When he raised his helmet there were many to take it from his hand, fain to serve him, and they took from him sword and shield.

Sir Gawain gave good greeting to the noble and the mighty men who came to do him honor. Clad in his shining armor they led him to the hall, where a great fire burnt brightly on the floor; and the lord of the household came forth from his chamber to meet the hero fitly. He spake to the knight, and said: 'Ye are welcome to do here as it likes ye. All that is here is your own to have at your will and disposal.'

'Gramercy!' quoth Gawain, 'may Christ requite ye.'

As friends that were fain each embraced the other; and Gawain looked on the knight who greeted him so kindly, and thought 't was a bold warrior that owned that burg.

Of mighty stature he was, and of high age; broad and flowing was his beard, and of a bright hue. He was stalwart or limb, and strong in his stride, his face fiery red, and his speech free: in sooth he seemed one well fitted to be a leader of valiant men.

Then the lord led Sir Gawain to a chamber, and commanded folk to wait upon him, and at his bidding there came men enough who brought the guest to a fair bower. The bedding was noble, with curtains of pure silk wrought with gold, and wondrous coverings of fair cloth all embroidered. The curtains ran on ropes with rings of red gold, and the walls were hung with carpets of Orient, and the same spread on the floor. There with mirthful speeches they took from the guest his byrnie and all his shining armor, and brought him rich robes of the choicest in its stead. They were long and flowing, and became him well, and when he was clad in them all who looked on the hero thought that surely God had never made a fairer knight: he seemed as if he might be a prince without peer in the field where men strive in battle.

Then before the hearth-place, whereon the fire burned, they made ready a chair for Gawain, hung about with cloth and fair cushions; and there they cast around him a mantle of brown samite, richly embroidered and furred within with costly skins of ermine, with a hood of the same, and he seated himself in that rich seat, and warmed himself at the fire, and was cheered at heart. And while he sat thus, the serving men set up a table on trestles, and covered it with a fair white cloth, and set thereon salt-cellar, and napkin, and silver spoons; and the knight washed at his will, and set him down to meat.

The folk served him courteously with many dishes seasoned of the best, a double portion. All kinds of fish were there, some baked in bread, some broiled on the embers, some sodden, some stewed and savored with spices, with all sorts of cunning devices to his taste. And often he called it a feast, when they spake gaily to him all together, and said, 'Now take ye this penance, and it shall be for your amendment.' Much mirth thereof did Sir Gawain make.

Then they questioned that prince courteously of whence he came; and he told them that he was of the court of Arthur, who is the rich royal king of the Round Table, and that it was Gawain himself who was within their walls, and would keep Christmas with them, as the chance had fallen out. And when the lord of the castle heard those tidings he laughed aloud for gladness, and all men in that keep were joyful that they should be in the company of him to whom belonged all fame, and valor, and courtesy, and whose honor was praised above that of all men on earth. Each said softly to his fellow, 'Now shall we see courteous bearing, and the manner of speech befitting courts. What charm lieth in gentle speech shall we learn without asking, since here we have welcomed the fine father of courtesy. God has surely shown us his grace since he sends us such a guest as Gawain! When men shall sit and sing, blithe for Christ's birth, this knight shall bring us to the knowledge of fair manners, and it may be that hearing him we may learn the cunning speech of love.'

By the time the knight had risen from dinner it was near nightfall. Then chaplains took their way to the chapel, and rang loudly, even as they should, for the solemn evensong of the high feast. Thither went the lord, and the lady also, and entered with her maidens into a comely closet, and thither also went Gawain. Then the lord took him by the sleeve and led him to a seat, and called him by his name, and told him he was of all men in the world the most welcome. And Sir Gawain thanked him truly, and each kissed the other, and they sat gravely together throughout the service. Then was the lady fain to look upon that knight; and she came forth from her closet with many fair maidens. The fairest of ladies was she in face, and figure, and coloring, fairer even than Guinevere, so the knight thought. She came through the chancel to greet the hero; another lady held her by the left hand, older than she, and seemingly of high estate, with many nobles about her. But unlike to look upon were those ladies, for if the younger were fair, the elder was yellow. Rich red were the cheeks of the one, rough and wrinkled those of the other; the kerchiefs of the one were broidered with many glistening pearls, her throat and neck bare, and whiter than the snow that lies on the hills; the neck of the other was swathed in a gorget, with a white wimple over her black chin. Her forehead was wrapped in silk with many folds, worked with knots, so that naught of her was seen save her black brows, her eyes, her nose, and her lips, and those were bleared, and ill to look upon. A worshipful lady in sooth one might call her! In figure was she short and broad, and thickly made — far fairer to behold was she whom she led by the hand.

When Gawain beheld that fair lady, who looked at him graciously, with leave of the lord he went towards them, and, bowing low, he greeted the elder, but the younger and fairer he took lightly in his arms, and kissed her courteously, and greeted her in knightly wise. Then she hailed him as friend, and he quickly prayed to be counted as her servant, if she so willed. Then they took him between them, and talking, led him to the chamber, to the hearth, and bade them bring spices, and they brought them in plenty with the good wine that was wont to be drunk at such seasons. Then the lord sprang to his feet and bade them make merry, and took off his hood, and hung it on a spear, and bade him win the worship thereof who should make most mirth that Christmas-tide. 'And I shall try, by my faith, to fool it with the best, by the help of my friends, ere I lose my raiment.' Thus with gay words the lord made trial to gladden Gawain with jests that night, till it was time to bid them light the tapers, and Sir Gawain took leave of them and gat him to rest.

In the morn when all men call to mind how Christ our Lord was born on earth to die for us, there is joy, for his sake, in all dwellings of the world; and so was there here on that day. For high feast was held, with many dainties and cunningly cooked messes. On the daïs sat gallant men, clad in their best. The ancient dame sat on the high seat, with the lord of the castle beside her. Gawain and the fair lady sat together, even in the midst of the board when the feast was served; and so throughout all the hall each sat in his degree, and was served in order. There was meat, there was mirth, there was much joy, so that to tell thereof would take me too long, though peradventure I might strive to declare it. But Gawain and that fair lady had much joy of each other's company through her sweet words and courteous converse. And there was music made before each prince, trumpets and drums, and merry pipings; each man hearkened his minstrel, and they too hearkened theirs

So they held high feast that day and the next, and the third day thereafter, and the joy on Saint John's Day was fair to hearken, for 't was the last of the feast and the guests would depart in the gray of the morning. Therefore they awoke early, and drank wine, and danced fair carols, and at last, when it was late, each man took his leave to wend early on his way. Gawain would bid his host farewell, but the lord took him by the hand, and led him to his own chamber beside the hearth, and there he thanked him for the favor he had shown him in honoring his dwelling at that high season, and gladdening his castle with his fair countenance. 'I wis, sir, that while I live I shall be held the worthier that Gawain has been my guest at God's own feast.' 'Gramercy, sir,' quoth Gawain, 'in good faith, all the honor is yours, may the High King give it you, and I am but at your will to work your behest, inasmuch as I am beholden to you in great and small by rights.'

Then the lord did his best to persuade the knight to tarry with him, but Gawain answered that he might in no wise do so. Then the host asked him courteously what stern behest had driven him at the holy season from the king's court, to fare all alone, ere yet the feast was ended?

'Forsooth,' quoth the knight, 'ye say but the truth: 't is a high quest and a pressing that hath brought me afield, for I am summoned myself to a certain place, and I know not whither in the world I may wend to find it; so help me Christ, I would give all the kingdom of Logres an I might find it by New Year's morn. Therefore, sir, I make request of you that ye tell me truly if ye ever heard word of the Green Chapel, where it may be found, and the Green Knight that keeps it. For I am pledged by solemn compact sworn between us to meet that knight at the New Year if so I were on life; and of that same New Year it wants but little — I' faith, I would look on that hero more joyfully than on any other fair sight! Therefore, by your will, it behooves me to leave you, for I have but barely three days, and I would as fain fall dead as fail of mine errand.'

Then the lord quoth, laughing, 'Now must ye needs stay, for I will show you your goal, the Green Chapel, ere your term be at an end, have ye no fear! But ye can take your ease, friend, in your bed, till the fourth day, and go forth on the first of the year and come to that place at mid-morn to do as ye will. Dwell here till New Year's Day, and then rise and set forth, and ye shall be set in the way; 't is not two miles hence.'

Then was Gawain glad, and he laughed gaily. 'Now I thank you for this above all else. Now my quest is achieved I will dwell here at your will, and otherwise do as ye shall ask.'

Then the lord took him, and set him beside him, and bade the ladies be fetched for their greater pleasure, tho' between themselves they had solace. The lord, for gladness, made merry jest, even as one who wist not what to do for joy; and he cried aloud to the knight, 'Ye have promised to do the thing I bid ye: will ye hold to this behest, here, at once?'

'Yea, forsooth,' said that true knight, 'while I abide in your burg I am bound by your behest.'

'Ye have traveled from far,' said the host, 'and since then ye have waked with me, ye are not well refreshed by rest and sleep, as I know. Ye shall therefore abide in your chamber, and lie at your ease to-morrow at Mass-tide, and go to meat when ye will with my wife, who shall sit with you, and comfort you with her company till I return; and I shall rise early and go forth to the chase.' And Gawain agreed to all this courteously.

'Sir knight,' quoth the host, 'we will make a covenant. Whatsoever I win in the wood shall be yours, and whatever may fall to your share, that shall ye exchange for it. Let us swear, friend, to make this exchange, however our hap may be, for worse or for better.'

'I grant ye your will,' quoth Gawain the good; 'if ye list so to do, it liketh me well.'

'Bring hither the wine-cup, the bargain is made,' so said the lord of that castle. They laughed each one, and drank of the wine, and made merry, these lords and ladies, as it pleased them. Then with gay talk and merry jest they rose, and stood, and spoke softly, and kissed courteously, and took leave of each other. With burning torches, and many a serving-man, was each led to his couch; yet ere they gat them to bed the old lord oft repeated their covenant, for he knew well how to make sport.

III

Full early, ere daylight, the folk rose up; the guests who would depart called their grooms, and they made them ready, and saddled the steeds, tightened up the girths, and trussed up their mails. The knights, all arrayed for riding, leapt up lightly, and took their bridles, and each rode his way as pleased him best.

The lord of the land was not the last. Ready for the chase, with many of his men, he ate a sop hastily when he had heard Mass, and then with blast of the bugle fared forth to the field. He and his nobles were to horse ere daylight glimmered upon the earth.

Then the huntsmen coupled their hounds, unclosed the kennel door, and called them out. They blew three blasts gaily on the bugles, the hounds bayed fiercely, and they that would go a-hunting checked and chastised them. A hundred hunters there were of the best, so I have heard tell. Then the trackers gat them to the trysting-place and uncoupled the hounds, and the forest rang again with their gay blasts.

At the first sound of the hunt the game quaked for fear, and fled, trembling, along the vale. They betook them to the heights, but the liers in wait turned them back with loud cries; the harts they let pass them, and the stags with their spreading antlers, for the lord had forbidden that they should be slain, but the hinds and the does they turned back, and drave down into the valleys. Then might ye see much shooting of arrows. As the deer fled under the boughs a broad whistling shaft smote and wounded each sorely, so that, wounded and bleeding, they fell dying on the banks. The hounds followed swiftly on their tracks, and hunters, blowing the horn, sped after them with ringing shouts as if the cliffs burst asunder. What game escaped those that shot was run down at the outer ring. Thus were they driven on the hills, and harassed at the waters, so well did the men know their work, and the greyhounds were so great and swift that they ran them down as fast as the hunters could slay them. Thus the lord passed the day in mirth and joyfulness, even to nightfall.

So the lord roamed the woods, and Gawain, that good knight, lay ever a-bed, curtained about, under the costly coverlet, while the daylight gleamed on the walls. And as he lay half slumbering, he heard a little sound at the door, and he raised his head, and caught back a corner of the curtain, and waited to see what it might be. It was the lovely lady, the lord's wife; she shut the door softly behind her, and turned towards the bed; and Gawain was shamed, laid him down softly and made as if he slept. And she came lightly to the bedside, within the curtain, and sat herself down beside him, to wait till he wakened. The knight lay there awhile, and marveled within himself what her coming might betoken; and he said to himself, ''T were more seemly if I asked her what hath brought her hither.' Then he made feint to waken, and turned towards her, and opened his eyes as one astonished, and crossed himself; and she looked on him laughing, with her cheeks red and white, lovely to behold, and small smiling lips.

'Good morrow, Sir Gawain,' said that fair lady; 'ye are but a careless sleeper, since one can enter thus. Now are ye taken unawares, and lest ye escape me I shall bind you in your bed; of that be ye assured!' Laughing, she spake these words.

'Good morrow, fair lady,' quoth Gawain blithely. 'I will do your will, as it likes me well. For I yield me readily, and pray your grace, and that is best, by my faith, since I needs must do so.' Thus he jested again, laughing. 'But an ye would, fair lady, grant me this grace that ye pray your prisoner to rise. I would get me from bed, and array me better, then could I talk with ye in more comfort.'

'Nay, forsooth, fair sir,' quoth the lady, 'ye shall not rise, I will rede ye better. I shall keep ye here, since ye can do no other, and talk with my knight whom I have captured. For I know well that ye are Sir Gawain, whom all the world worships, wheresoever ye may ride. Your honor and your courtesy are praised by lords and ladies, by all who live. Now ye are here and we are alone, my lord and his men are afield; the serving men in their beds, and my maidens also, and the door shut upon us. And since in this hour I have him that all men love, I shall use my time well with speech, while it lasts. Ye are welcome to my company, for it behooves me in sooth to be your servant.'

'In good faith,' quoth Gawain, 'I think me that I am not him of whom ye speak, for unworthy am I of such service as ye here proffer. In sooth, I were glad if I might set myself by word or service to your pleasure; a pure joy would it be to me!'

'In good faith, Sir Gawain,' quoth the gay lady, 'the praise and the prowess that pleases all ladies I lack them not, nor hold them light; yet are there ladies enough who would liever now have the knight in their hold, as I have ye here, to dally with your courteous words, to bring them comfort and to ease their cares, than much of the treasure and the gold that are theirs. And now, through the grace of Him who upholds the heavens, I have wholly in my power that which they all desire!'

Thus the lady, fair to look upon, made him great cheer, and Sir Gawain, with modest words, answered her again: 'Madam,' he quoth, 'may Mary requite ye, for in good faith I have found in ye a noble frankness. Much courtesy have other folk shown me, but the honor they have done me is naught to the worship of yourself, who knoweth but good.'

'By Mary,' quoth the lady, 'I think otherwise; for were I worth all the women alive, and had I the wealth of the world in my hand, and might choose me a lord to my liking, then, for all that I have seen in ye, Sir Knight, of beauty and courtesy and blithe semblance, and for all that I have hearkened and hold for true, there should be no knight on earth to be chosen before ye.'

'Well I wot,' quoth Sir Gawain, 'that ye have chosen a better; but I am proud that ye should so prize me, and as your servant do I hold ye my sovereign, and your knight am I, and may Christ reward ye.'

So they talked of many matters till mid-morn was past, and ever the lady made as though she loved him, and the knight turned her speech aside. For though she were the brightest of maidens, yet had he forborne to show her love for the danger that awaited him and the blow that must be given without delay.

Then the lady prayed her leave from him, and he granted it readily. And she gave him good-day, with laughing glance, but he must needs marvel at her words:

'Now He that speeds fair speech reward ye this disport; but that ye be Gawain my mind misdoubts me greatly.'

'Wherefore?' quoth the knight quickly, fearing lest he had lacked in some courtesy.

And the lady spake: 'So true a knight as Gawain is holden, and one so perfect in courtesy, would never have tarried so long with a lady but he would of his courtesy have craved a kiss at parting.'

Then quoth Gawain, 'I wot I will do even as it may please ye, and kiss at your commandment, as a true knight should who forbears to ask for fear of displeasure.'

At that she came near and bent down and kissed the knight, and each commended the other to Christ, and she went forth from the chamber softly.

Then Sir Gawain rose and called his chamberlain and chose his garments, and when he was ready he gat him forth to Mass, and then went to meat, and made merry all day till the rising of the moon, and never had a knight fairer lodging than had he with those two noble ladies, the elder and the younger.

And ever the lord of the land chased the hinds through holt and heath till eventide, and then with much blowing of bugles and baying of hounds they bore the game homeward; and by the time daylight was done all the folk had returned to that fair castle. And when the lord and Sir Gawain met together, then were they both well pleased. The lord commanded them all to assemble in the great hall, and the ladies to descend with their maidens, and there, before them all, he bade the men fetch in the spoil of the day's hunting, and he called unto Gawain, and counted the tale of the beasts, and showed them unto him, and said, 'What think ye of this game, Sir Knight? Have I deserved of ye thanks for my woodcraft?'

'Yea, I wis,' quoth the other, 'here is the fairest spoil I have seen this seven year in the winter season.'

'And all this do I give ye, Gawain,' quoth the host, 'for by accord of covenant ye may claim it as your own.'

'That in sooth,' quoth the other, 'I grant you that same; and I have fairly won this within walls, and with as good will do I yield it to ye.' With that he clasped his hands round the lord's neck and kissed him as courteously as he might. 'Take ye here my spoils, no more have I won; ye should have it freely, though it were greater than this.'

''T is good,' said the host, 'gramercy thereof. Yet were I fain to know where ye won this same favor, and if it were by your own wit?'

'Nay,' answered Gawain, 'that was not in the bond. Ask me no more: ye have taken what was yours by right, be content with that.'

They laughed and jested together, and sat them down to supper, where they were served with many dainties; and after supper they sat by the hearth, and wine was served out to them; and oft in their jesting they promised to observe on the morrow the same covenant that they had made before, and whatever chance might betide, to exchange their spoil, be it much or little, when they met at night. Thus they renewed their bargain before the whole court, and then the night-drink was served, and each courteously took leave of the other and gat him to bed.

By the time the cock had crowed thrice the lord of the castle had left his bed; Mass was sung and meat fitly served. The folk were forth to the wood ere the day broke, with hound and horn they rode over the plain, and uncoupled their dogs among the thorns. Soon they struck on the scent, and the hunt cheered on the hounds who were first to seize it, urging them with shouts. The others hastened to the cry, forty at once, and there rose such a clamor from the pack that the rocks rang again. The huntsmen spurred them on with shouting and blasts of the horn; and the hounds drew together to a thicket betwixt the water and a high crag in the cliff beneath the hillside. There where the rough rock fell ruggedly they, the huntsmen, fared to the finding, and cast about round the hill and the thicket behind them. The knights wist well what beast was within, and would drive him forth with the bloodhounds. And as they beat the bushes, suddenly over the beaters there rushed forth a wondrous great and fierce boar, long since had he left the herd to roam by himself. Grunting, he cast many to the ground, and fled forth at his best speed, without more mischief. The men hallooed loudly and cried, 'Hay! Hay!' and blew the horns to urge on the hounds, and rode swiftly after the boar. Many a time did he turn to bay and tare the hounds, and they yelped, and howled shrilly. Then the men made ready their arrows and shot at him, but the points were turned on his thick hide, and the barbs would not bite upon him, for the shafts shivered in pieces, and the head but leapt again wherever it hit.

But when the boar felt the stroke of the arrows he waxed mad with rage, and turned on the hunters and tare many, so that, affrightened, they fled before him. But the lord on a swift steed pursued him, blowing his bugle; as a gallant knight he rode through the woodland chasing the boar till the sun grew low.

So did the hunters this day, while Sir Gawain lay in his bed lapped in rich gear; and the lady forgat not to salute him, for early was she at his side, to cheer his mood.

She came to the bedside and looked on the knight, and Gawain gave her fit greeting, and she greeted him again with ready words, and sat her by his side and laughed, and with a sweet look she spoke to him:

'Sir, if ye be Gawain, I think it a wonder that ye be so stern and cold, and care not for the courtesies of friendship, but if one teach ye to know them ye cast the lesson out of your mind. Ye have soon forgotten what I taught ye yesterday, by all the truest tokens that I knew!'

'What is that?' quoth the knight. 'I trow I know not. If it be sooth that ye say, then is the blame mine own.'

'But I taught ye of kissing,' quoth the fair lady. 'Wherever a fair countenance is shown him, it behooves a courteous knight quickly to claim a kiss.'

'Nay, my dear,' said Sir Gawain, 'cease that speech; that durst I not do lest I were denied, for if I were forbidden I wot I were wrong did I further entreat.'

'I' faith,' quoth the lady merrily, 'ye may not be forbid, ye are strong enough to constrain by strength an ye will, were any so discourteous as to give ye denial.'

'Yea, by heaven,' said Gawain, 'ye speak well; but threats profit little in the land where I dwell, and so with a gift that is given not of good will! I am at your commandment to kiss when ye like, to take or to leave as ye list.'

Then the lady bent her down and kissed him courteously.

And as they spake together she said, 'I would learn somewhat from ye, an ye would not be wroth, for young ye are and fair, and so courteous and knightly as ye are known to be, the head of all chivalry, and versed in all wisdom of love and war—'t is ever told of true knights how they adventured their lives for their true love, and endured hardships for her favors, and avenged her with valor, and eased her sorrows, and brought joy to her bower; and ye are the fairest knight of your time, and your fame and your honor are everywhere, yet I have sat by ye here twice, and never a word have I heard of love! Ye who are so courteous and skilled in such love ought surely to teach one so young and unskilled some little craft of true love! Why are ye so unlearned who art otherwise so famous? Or is it that ye deemed me unworthy to hearken to your teaching? For shame, Sir Knight! I come hither alone and sit at your side to learn of ye some skill; teach me of your wit, while my lord is from home.'

'In good faith,' quoth Gawain, 'great is my joy and my profit that so fair a lady as ye are should deign to come hither, and trouble ye with so poor a man, and make sport with your knight with kindly countenance, it pleaseth me much. But that I, in my turn, should take it upon me to tell of love and such like matters to ye who know more by half, or a hundred fold, of such craft than I do, or ever shall in all my lifetime, by my troth 't were folly indeed! I will work your will to the best of my might as I am bounden, and evermore will I be your servant, so help me Christ!'

Then often with guile she questioned that knight that she might win him to woo her, but he defended himself so fairly that none might in any wise blame him, and naught but bliss and harmless jesting me this grace: give me some gift, if it were but thy glove, that I may bethink me of my knight, and lessen my mourning.'

'Now, I wis,' quoth the knight, 'I would that I had here the most precious thing that I possess on earth that I might leave ye as love-token, great or small, for ye have deserved forsooth more reward than I might give ye. But it is not to your honor to have at this time a glove for reward as gift from Gawain, and I am here on a strange errand, and have no man with me, nor mails with goodly things — that mislikes me much, lady, at this time; but each man must fare as he is taken, if for sorrow and ill.'

'Nay, knight highly honored,' quoth that lovesome lady, 'though I have naught of yours, yet shall ye have somewhat of mine.' With that she reached him a ring of red gold with a sparkling stone therein, that shone even as the sun (wit ye well, it was worth many marks); but the knight refused it, and spake readily,

'I will take no gift, lady, at this time. I have none to give, and none will I take.'

She prayed him to take it, but he refused her prayer, and sware in sooth that he would not have it.

The lady was sorely vexed, and said, 'If ye refuse my ring as too costly, that ye will not be so highly beholden to me, I will give you my girdle as a lesser gift.' With that she loosened a lace that was fastened at her side, knit upon her kirtle under her mantle. It was wrought of green silk, and gold, only braided by the fingers, and that she offered to the knight, and besought him though it were of little worth that he would take it, and he said nay, he would touch neither gold nor gear ere God give him grace to achieve the adventure for which he had come hither. 'And therefore, I pray ye, displease ye not, and ask me no longer, for I may not grant it. I am dearly beholden to ye for the favor ye have shown me, and ever, in heat and cold, will I be your true servant.'

'Now,' said the lady, 'ye refuse this silk, for it is simple in itself, and so it seems, indeed; lo, it is small to look upon and less in cost, but whoso knew the vir-

tue that is knit therein he would, peradventure, value it more highly. For whatever knight is girded with this green lace, while he bears it knotted about him there is no man under heaven can overcome him, for he may not be slain for any magic on earth.'

Then Gawain bethought him, and it came into his heart that this were a jewel for the jeopardy that awaited him when he came to the Green Chapel to seek the return blow — could he so order it that he should escape unslain, 't were a craft worth trying. Then he bare with her chiding, and let her say her say, and she pressed the girdle on him and prayed him to take it, and he granted her prayer, and she gave it him with good will, and besought him for her sake never to reveal it but to hide it loyally from her lord; and the knight agreed that never should any man know it, save they two alone. He thanked her often and heartily, and she kissed him for the third time.

Then she took her leave of him, and when she was gone Sir Gawain rose, and clad him in rich attire, and took the girdle, and knotted it round him, and hid it beneath his robes. Then he took his way to the chapel, and sought out a priest privily and prayed him to teach him better how his soul might be saved when he should go hence; and there he shrived him, and showed his misdeeds, both great and small, and besought mercy and craved absolution; and the priest assoiled him, and set him as clean as if doomsday had been on the morrow. And afterwards Sir Gawain made him merry with the ladies, with carols, and all kinds of joy, as never he did but that one day, even to nightfall; and all the men marveled at him, and said that never since he came thither had he been so merry.

Meanwhile the lord of the castle was abroad chasing the fox; awhile he lost him, and as he rode through a spinney he heard the hounds near at hand, and Reynard came creeping through a thick grove, with all the pack at his heels. Then the lord drew out his shining brand, and cast it at the beast, and the fox swerved aside for the sharp edge, and would have doubled back, but a hound was on him ere he might turn, and right before the horse's feet they all fell on him, and worried him fiercely, snarling the while.

Then the lord leapt from his saddle, and caught the fox from the jaws, and held it aloft over his head, and hallooed loudly, and many brave hounds bayed as they beheld it; and the hunters hied them thither, blowing their horns; all that bare bugles blew them at once, and all the others shouted. 'T was the merriest meeting that ever men heard, the clamor that was raised at the death of the fox. They rewarded the hounds, stroking them and rubbing their heads, and took Reynard and stripped him of his coat; then blowing their horns, they turned them homewards, for it was nigh nightfall.

The lord was gladsome at his return, and found a bright fire on the hearth, and the knight beside it, the good Sir Gawain, who was in joyous mood for the pleasure he had had with the ladies. He wore a robe of blue, that reached even to the ground, and a surcoat richly furred, that became him well. A hood like to the surcoat fell on his shoulders, and all alike were done about with fur. He met the host in the midst of the floor, and jesting, he greeted him, and said, ' Now shall I be first to fulfil our covenant which we made together when there was no lack of wine.' Then he embraced the knight, and kissed him thrice, as solemnly as he might.

' Of a sooth,' quoth the other, ' ye have good luck in the matter of this covenant, if ye made a good exchange!'

' Yet, it matters naught of the exchange,' quoth Gawain, ' since what I owe is swiftly paid.'

' Marry,' said the other, ' mine is behind, for I have hunted all this day, and naught have I got but this foul foxskin, and that is but poor payment for three such kisses as ye have here given me.'

' Enough,' quoth Sir Gawain, ' I thank ye, by the Rood.'

Then the lord told them of his hunting, and how the fox had been slain.

With mirth and minstrelsy, and dainties at their will, they made them as merry as a folk well might till 't was time for them to sever, for at last they must needs betake them to their beds. Then the knight took his leave of the lord, and thanked him fairly.

' For the fair sojourn that I have had here at this high feast may the High King give ye honor. I give ye myself, as one of your servants, if ye so like; for I must needs, as you know, go hence with the morn, and ye will give me, as ye promised, a guide to show me the way to the Green Chapel, an God will suffer me on New Year's Day to deal the doom of my weird.'

' By my faith,' quoth the host, ' all that ever I promised, that shall I keep with good will.' Then he gave him a servant to set him in the way, and lead him by the downs, that he should have no need to ford the stream, and should fare by the shortest road through the groves; and Gawain thanked the lord for the honor done him. Then he would take leave of the ladies, and courteously he kissed them, and spake, praying them to receive his thanks, and they made like reply; then with many sighs they commended him to Christ, and he departed courteously from that fold. Each man that he met he thanked him for his service and his solace, and the pains he had been at to do his will; and each found it as hard to part from the knight as if he had ever dwelt with him.

Then they led him with torches to his chamber, and brought him to his bed to rest. That he slept soundly I may not say, for the morrow gave him much to think on. Let him rest awhile, for he was near that which he sought, and if ye will but listen to me I will tell ye how it fared with him thereafter.

IV

Now the New Year drew nigh, and the night passed, and the day chased the darkness, as is God's will; but wild weather wakened therewith. The clouds cast the cold to the earth, with enough of the north to slay them that lacked clothing. The snow drave smartly, and the whistling wind blew from the heights, and made great drifts in the valleys. The knight, lying in his bed, listened, for though his eyes were shut, he might sleep but little, and hearkened every cock that crew.

He arose ere the day broke, by the light

of a lamp that burned in his chamber, and called to his chamberlain, bidding him bring his armor and saddle his steed. The other gat him up, and fetched his garments, and robed Sir Gawain.

First he clad him in his clothes to keep off the cold, and then in his harness, which was well and fairly kept. Both hauberk and plates were well burnished, the rings of the rich byrnie freed from rust, and all as fresh as at first, so that the knight was fain to thank them. Then he did on each piece, and bade them bring his steed, while he put the fairest raiment on himself; his coat with its fair cogni- zance, adorned with precious stones upon velvet, with broidered seams, and all fur- red within with costly skins. And he left not the lace, the lady's gift, that Gawain forgot not, for his own good. When he had girded on his sword he wrapped the gift twice about him, swathed around his waist. The girdle of green silk set gaily and well upon the royal red cloth, rich to behold, but the knight ware it not for pride of the pendants, polished though they were with fair gold that gleamed brightly on the ends, but to save himself from sword and knife, when it behooved him to abide his hurt without question. With that the hero went forth, and thanked that kindly folk full often.

Then was Gringalet ready, that was great and strong, and had been well cared for and tended in every wise; in fair con- dition was that proud steed, and fit for a journey. Then Gawain went to him, and looked on his coat, and said by his sooth, 'There is a folk in this place that think- eth on honor; much joy may they have, and the lord who maintains them, and may all good betide that lovely lady all her life long. Since they for charity cherish a guest, and hold honor in their hands, may he who holds the heaven on high requite them, and also ye all. And if I might live anywhile on earth, I would give ye full reward, readily, if so I might.' Then he set foot in the stirrup and bestrode his steed, and his squire gave him his shield, which he laid on his shoulder. Then he smote Gringalet with his golden spurs, and the steed pranced on the stones and would stand no longer.

By that his man was mounted, who bare his spear and lance, and Gawain quoth, 'I commend this castle to Christ, may he give it ever good fortune.' Then the drawbridge was let down, and the broad gates unbarred and opened on both sides; the knight crossed himself, and passed through the gateway, and praised the porter, who knelt before the prince, and gave him good-day, and commended him to God. Thus the knight went on his way with the one man who should guide him to that dread place where he should receive rueful payment.

The two went by hedges where the boughs were bare, and climbed the cliffs where the cold clings. Naught fell from the heavens, but 't was ill beneath them; mist brooded over the moor and hung on the mountains; each hill had a cap, a great cloak, of mist. The streams foamed and bubbled between their banks, dashing sparkling on the shores where they shelved downwards. Rugged and dan- gerous was the way through the woods, till it was time for the sun-rising. Then were they on a high hill; the snow lay white beside them, and the man who rode with Gawain drew rein by his master.

'Sir,' he said, 'I have brought ye hither, and now ye are not far from the place that ye have sought so specially. But I will tell ye for sooth, since I know ye well, and ye are such a knight as I well love, would ye follow my counsel ye would fare the better. The place whither ye go is accounted full perilous, for he who liveth in that waste is the worst on earth, for he is strong and fierce; and loveth to deal mighty blows; taller he is than any man on earth, and greater of frame than any four in Arthur's court, or in any other. And this is his custom at the Green Chapel; there may no man pass by that place, however proud his arms, but he does him to death by force of his hand, for he is a discourteous knight, and shows no mercy. Be he churl or chaplain who rides by that chapel, monk or mass-priest, or any man else, he thinks it as pleasant to slay them as to pass alive himself. Therefore, I tell ye, as sooth as ye sit in saddle, if ye come there and that knight know it, ye shall be slain, though ye had twenty lives; trow me that truly! He has dwelt here full long and seen many a combat; ye may not defend ye against his blows. Therefore, good Sir Gawain, let the man be, and get ye away some other road; for God's sake seek ye another land, and there may Christ speed ye! And I will hie me home again, and I promise ye further that I will swear by God and the saints, or any other oath ye please, that I will keep counsel faithfully, and never let any wit the tale that ye fled for fear of any man.'

'Gramercy,' quoth Gawain, but ill-pleased. 'Good fortune be his who wishes me good, and that thou wouldst keep faith with me I will believe; but didst thou keep it never so truly, an I passed here and fled for fear as thou sayest, then were I a coward knight, and might not be held guiltless. So I will to the chapel let chance what may, and talk with that man, even as I may list, whether for weal or for woe as fate may have it. Fierce though he may be in fight, yet God knoweth well how to save his servants.'

'Well,' quoth the other, 'now that ye have said so much that ye will take your own harm on yourself, and ye be pleased to lose your life, I will neither let nor keep ye. Have here your helm and the spear in your hand, and ride down this same road beside the rock till ye come to the bottom of the valley, and there look a little to the left hand, and ye shall see in that vale the chapel, and the grim man who keeps it. Now fare ye well, noble Gawain; for all the gold on earth I would not go with ye nor bear ye fellowship one step further.' With that the man turned his bridle into the wood, smote the horse with his spurs as hard as he could, and galloped off, leaving the knight alone.

Quoth Gawain, 'I will neither greet nor moan, but commend myself to God, and yield me to his will.'

Then the knight spurred Gringalet, and rode adown the path close in by a bank beside a grove. So he rode through the rough thicket, right into the dale, and there he halted, for it seemed him wild enough. No sign of a chapel could he see, but high and burnt banks on either side and rough rugged crags with great stones above. An ill-looking place he thought it.

Then he drew in his horse and looked round to seek the chapel, but he saw none and thought it strange. Then he saw as it were a mound on a level space

of land by a bank beside the stream where it ran swiftly; the water bubbled within as if boiling. The knight turned his steed to the mound, and lighted down and tied the rein to the branch of a linden; and he turned to the mound and walked round it, questioning with himself what it might be. It had a hole at the end and at either side, and was overgrown with clumps of grass, and it was hollow within as an old cave or the crevice of a crag; he knew not what it might be.

'Ah,' quoth Gawain, 'can this be the Green Chapel? Here might the devil say his matins at midnight! Now I wis there is wizardry here. 'T is an ugly oratory, all overgrown with grass, and 't would well beseem that fellow in green to say his devotions on devil's wise. Now feel I in five wits, 't is the foul fiend himself who hath set me this tryst, to destroy me here! This is a chapel of mischance: ill-luck betide it, 't is the cursedest kirk that ever I came in!'

Helmet on head and lance in hand, he came up to the rough dwelling, when he heard over the high hill beyond the brook, as it were in a bank, a wondrous fierce noise, that rang in the cliff as if it would cleave asunder. 'T was as if one ground a scythe on a grindstone, it whirred and whetted like water on a mill-wheel and rushed and rang, terrible to hear. 'By God,' quoth Gawain, 'I trow that gear is preparing for the knight who will meet me here. Alas! naught may help me, yet should my life be forfeit, I fear not a jot!' With that he called aloud. 'Who waiteth in this place to give me tryst. Now is Gawain come hither: if any man will aught of him let him hasten hither now or never.'

'Stay,' quoth one on the bank above his head, 'and ye shall speedily have that which I promised ye.' Yet for a while the noise of whetting went on ere he appeared, and then he came forth from a cave in the crag with a fell weapon, a Danish axe newly dight, wherewith to deal the blow. An evil head it had, four feet large, no less, sharply ground, and bound to the handle by the lace that gleamed brightly. And the knight himself was all green as before, face and foot, locks and beard, but now he was afoot. When he came to the water he would not wade it, but sprang over with the pole of his axe, and strode boldly over the bent that was white with snow.

Sir Gawain went to meet him, but he made no low bow. The other said, ' Now, fair sir, one may trust thee to keep tryst. Thou art welcome, Gawain, to my place. Thou hast timed thy coming as befits a true man. Thou knowest the covenant set between us: at this time twelve months agone thou didst take that which fell to thee, and I at this New Year will readily requite thee. We are in this valley, verily alone, here are no knights to sever us, do what we will. Have off thy helm from thine head, and have here thy pay; make me no more talking than I did then when thou didst strike off my head with one blow.'

' Nay,' quoth Gawain, ' by God that gave me life, I shall make no moan whatever befall me, but make thou ready for the blow and I shall stand still and say never a word to thee, do as thou wilt.'

With that he bent his head and showed his neck all bare, and made as if he had no fear, for he would not be thought a-dread.

Then the Green Knight made him ready, and grasped his grim weapon to smite Gawain. With all his force he bore it aloft with a mighty feint of slaying him: had it fallen as straight as he aimed he who was ever doughty of deed had been slain by the blow. But Gawain swerved aside as the axe came gliding down to slay him as he stood, and shrank a little with the shoulders, for the sharp iron. The other heaved up the blade and rebuked the prince with many proud words:

' Thou art not Gawain,' he said, ' who is held so valiant, that never feared he man by hill or vale, but thou shrinkest for fear ere thou feelest hurt. Such cowardice did I never hear of Gawain! Neither did *I* flinch from thy blow, or make strife in King Arthur's hall. My head fell to my feet, and yet I fled not; but thou didst wax faint of heart ere any harm befell. Wherefore must I be deemed the braver knight.'

Quoth Gawain, ' I shrank once, but so will I no more; though an my head fall on the stones I cannot replace it. But haste, Sir Knight, by thy faith, and bring me to the point, deal me my destiny, and do it out of hand, for I will stand thee a stroke and move no more till thine axe have hit me — my troth on it.'

' Have at thee, then,' quoth the other, and heaved aloft the axe with fierce mien, as if he were mad. He struck at him fiercely but wounded him not, withholding his hand ere it might strike him.

Gawain abode the stroke, and flinched in no limb, but stood still as a stone or the stump of a tree that is fast rooted in the rocky ground with a hundred roots.

Then spake gaily the man in green, ' So now thou hast thine heart whole it behooves me to smite. Hold aside thy hood that Arthur gave thee, and keep thy neck thus bent lest it cover it again.'

Then Gawain said angrily, ' Why talk on thus? Thou dost threaten too long. I hope thy heart misgives thee.'

' For sooth,' quoth the other, ' so fiercely thou speakest I will no longer let thine errand wait its reward.' Then he braced himself to strike, frowning with lips and brow, 't was no marvel that it pleased but ill him who hoped for no rescue. He lifted the axe lightly and let it fall with the edge of the blade on the bare neck. Though he struck swiftly, it hurt him no more than on the one side where it severed the skin. The sharp blade cut into the flesh so that the blood ran over his shoulder to the ground. And when the knight saw the blood staining the snow, he sprang forth, swift-foot, more than a spear's length, seized his helmet and set it on his head, cast his shield over his shoulder, drew out his bright sword, and spake boldly (never since he was born was he half so blithe), ' Stop, Sir Knight, bid me no more blows. I have stood a stroke here without flinching, and if thou give me another, I shall requite thee, and give thee as good again. By the covenant made betwixt us in Arthur's hall but one blow falls to me here. Halt, therefore.'

Then the Green Knight drew off from him and leaned on his axe, setting the shaft on the ground, and looked on Gawain as he stood all armed and faced him fearlessly — at heart it pleased him well. Then he spake merrily in a loud voice, and said to the knight, ' Bold sir, be not so fierce; no man here hath done thee wrong, nor will do, save by covenant, as we made at Arthur's court. I promised thee a blow and thou hast it — hold thyself well paid! I release thee of all other claims. If I had been so minded I might perchance have given thee a rougher buffet. First I menaced thee with a feigned one, and hurt thee not for the covenant that we made in the first night, and which thou didst hold truly. All the gain didst thou give me as a true man should. The other feint I proffered thee for the morrow: my fair wife kissed thee, and thou didst give me her kisses — for both those days I gave thee two blows without scathe — true man, true return. But the third time thou didst fail, and therefore hadst thou that blow. For 't is *my* weed thou wearest, that same woven girdle, my own wife wrought it, that do I wot for sooth. Now know I well thy kisses, and thy conversation, and the wooing of my wife, for 't was mine own doing. I sent her to try thee, and in sooth I think thou art the most faultless knight that ever trod earth. As a pearl among white peas is of more worth than they, so is Gawain, i' faith, by other knights. But thou didst lack a little, Sir Knight, and wast wanting in loyalty, yet that was for no evil work, nor for wooing neither, but because thou lovedst thy life — therefore I blame thee the less.'

Then the other stood a great while, still sorely angered and vexed within himself; all the blood flew to his face, and he shrank for shame as the Green Knight spake; and the first words he said were, 'Cursed be ye, cowardice and covetousness, for in ye is the destruction of virtue.' Then he loosed the girdle, and gave it to the knight. 'Lo, take there the falsity, may foul befall it! For fear of thy blow cowardice bade me make friends with covetousness and forsake the customs of largess and loyalty, which befit all knights. Now am I faulty and false and have been afeared: from treachery and untruth come sorrow and care. I avow to thee, Sir Knight, that I have ill done; do then thy will. I shall be more wary hereafter.'

Then the other laughed and said gaily, 'I wot I am whole of the hurt I had, and thou hast made such free confession of thy misdeeds, and hast so borne the penance of mine axe edge, that I hold thee absolved from that sin, and purged as clean as if thou hadst never sinned since

thou wast born. And this girdle that is wrought with gold and green, like my raiment, do I give thee, Sir Gawain, that thou mayest think upon this chance when thou goest forth among princes of renown, and keep this for a token of the adventure of the Green Chapel, as it chanced between chivalrous knights. And thou shalt come again with me to my dwelling and pass the rest of this feast in gladness.' Then the lord laid hold of him, and said, 'I wot we shall soon make peace with my wife, who was thy bitter enemy.'

'Nay, forsooth,' said Sir Gawain, and seized his helmet and took it off swiftly, and thanked the knight: 'I have fared ill, may bliss betide thee, and may he who rules all things reward thee swiftly. Commend me to that courteous lady, thy fair wife, and to the other my honored ladies, who have beguiled their knight with skilful craft. But 't is no marvel if one be made a fool and brought to sorrow by women's wiles, for so was Adam beguiled by one, and Solomon by many, and Samson all too soon, for Delilah dealt him his doom; and David thereafter was wedded with Bathsheba, which brought him much sorrow — if one might love a woman and believe her not, 't were great gain! And since all they were beguiled by women, methinks 't is the less blame to me that I was misled! But as for thy girdle, that will I take with good will, not for gain of the gold, nor for samite, nor silk, nor the costly pendants, neither for weal nor for worship, but in sign of my frailty. I shall look upon it when I ride in renown and remind myself of the fault and faintness of the flesh; and so when pride uplifts me for prowess of arms, the sight of this lace shall humble my heart. But one thing would I pray, if it displease thee not: since thou art lord of yonder land wherein I have dwelt, tell me what thy rightful name may be, and I will ask no more."

'That will I truly,' quoth the other 'Bernlak de Hautdesert am I called in this land. Morgain le Fay dwelleth in mine house, and through knowledge of clerkly craft hath she taken many. For long time was she the mistress of Merlin, who knew well all you knights of the court. Morgain the goddess is she called therefore, and there is none so haughty but she can bring him low. She sent me in this guise to yon fair hall to test the truth of the renown that is spread abroad of the valor of the Round Table. She taught me this marvel to betray your wits, to vex Guinevere and fright her to death by the man who spake with his head in his hand at the high table. That is she who is at home, that ancient lady, she is even thine aunt, Arthur's half-sister, the daughter of the Duchess of Tintagel, who after- 10 ward married King Uther. Therefore I bid thee, knight, come to thine aunt, and make merry in thine house; my folk love thee, and I wish thee as well as any man on earth, by my faith, for thy true deal- 15 ing.'

But Sir Gawain said nay, he would in no wise do so; so they embraced and kissed, and commended each other to the Prince of Paradise, and parted right there, 20 on the cold ground. Gawain on his steed rode swiftly to the king's hall, and the Green Knight got him whithersoever he would.

Sir Gawain, who had thus won grace 25 of his life, rode through wild ways on Gringalet; oft he lodged in a house, and oft without, and many adventures did he have and came off victor full often, as at this time I cannot relate in tale. The 30 hurt that he had in his neck was healed, he bare the shining girdle as a baldric bound by his side, and made fast with a knot 'neath his left arm, in token that he was taken in a fault — and thus he came 35 in safety again to the court.

Then joy awakened in that dwelling when the king knew that the good Sir Gawain was come, for he deemed it gain. King Arthur kissed the knight, and the 40 queen also, and many valiant knights

sought to embrace him. They asked him how he had fared, and he told them all that had chanced to him — the adventure of the chapel, the fashion of the knight, the love of the lady — at last of the lace. He showed them the wound in the neck which he won for his disloyalty at the hand of the knight; the blood flew to his face for shame as he told the tale.

'Lo, lady,' he quoth, and handled the lace, 'this is the bond of the blame that I bear in my neck, this is the harm and the loss I have suffered, the cowardice and covetousness in which I was caught, the token of my covenant in which I was taken. And I must needs wear it so long as I live, for none may hide his harm, but undone it may not be, for if it hath clung to thee once, it may never be severed.'

Then the king comforted the knight, and the court laughed loudly at the tale, and all made accord that the lords and the ladies who belonged to the Round Table, each hero among them, should wear bound about him a baldric of bright green for the sake of Sir Gawain. And to this was agreed all the honor of the Round Table, and he who ware it was honored the more thereafter, as it is testified in the book of romance. That in Arthur's days this adventure befell, the book of Brutus bears witness. For since that bold knight came hither first, and the siege and the assault were ceased at Troy, I wis

Many a venture herebefore
Hath fallen such as this:
May He that bare the crown of thorn
Bring us unto His bliss.
                              Amen.

PEARL (c. 1375)

Pearl is found in the same manuscript with *Sir Gawain and the Green Knight*, and is commonly ascribed to the same author; but it differs entirely from this romance in its nature. *Pearl* is essentially not a narrative, but an elegy. The lament is uttered by a mature person, possibly a father, and the object of his sorrow is a beloved young girl, perhaps a daughter, who had died before reaching the age of two years. Though the poem is elegiac in its intention, it takes the form of a vision of the other world. This vision falls into three parts. In the first, the mourner recounts his falling asleep upon the grave of the child, and the departure of his spirit to a marvelous landscape in the midst of which appears the beloved maiden arrayed in supernatural brilliance (Stanzas I to XIX below). The second part consists in a long dialogue in which the transfigured maiden conveys to the dreamer a substantial amount of theological instruction (Stanzas XX to XL). Finally in the third part the poet recounts his vision of the New Jerusalem, and his awaking from his dream (Stanzas XLI to XLVI). Aside from its remarkable theological learning, most of which is omitted from Dr. Mitchell's translation, the poem is notable, if not unique, among medieval works in England for descriptive beauty and sincerity of personal feeling.

PEARL

I

Pearl, for a prince's pleasance fair enow,
Right cleanly housed in gold so clear,
No orient pearl I dare avow
Was ever yet her precious peer.
So rounded, in such rare array,   5
So small, of smoothen comeliness,
I judged her of all jewels gay
As singly set in singleness.
Lost in mine arbour,—woe is me!
'Neath earth she lies with grass o'ergrown, 10
I mourn love's sweet anxiety
That spotless pearl had made my own.

II

There have I tarried ofttimes where below
It left my sight, to seek again the joy
That once was wont to scatter all my woe, 15
And lift my life above the world's annoy.
About my heart do ceaseless sorrows throng,
That constant grief must ever constant be—
Yet, thought I, never was so sweet a song
As the still hours thither brought to me. 20
Ah me! what thoughts are mine! I sit and dream
Of those fair colours clad, alas! in clay.
O earth! why hast thou marred this tender theme—
My spotless pearl, that was mine own alway?

III

What lavish fragrance here is spread   25
By herb and flower, newly won!
Of blossoms white and blue and red,
No gayer rise to greet the sun.
Here nor fruit nor flower may fade,
Where passed my pearl to night of ground;
From dead grain cometh fruitful blade, 31
Else never wheat had harvest found.
Ever 't is good that good doth bring,
Such seemly seed it faileth not;
Here ever-fragrant flowers shall spring 35
O'er thee, my pearl without a spot.

IV

That place I sweeten with gentle rhyme,
I came to, where was my arbour green,
In the high season of August time,
When corn is cut with the sickle keen. 40
Where pearl lay under the grassy mead,
Shadowed it was with leafage green,
Gillyflower, ginger, and gromwell seed,
And peonies powdered all between.
Fair and seemly the sight was seen, 45
Fairer fragrance earth knoweth not;
Worthily won it was, I ween,
Of pearl, the precious, without a spot.

V

I gazed, my hands together pressed,
For, chilled with care and sorrow caught, 50

My heart beat wildly in my breast,
Though reason sager counsel taught.
I wept my pearl in earthy cell,
And timid reason fought with doubt;
Though Christ did comfort me full well, 55
Weak will with woe me cast about.
Such soothing scents the air did fill
That, lulled on this rose-peopled plot,
By sleep o'ercome, I rested still
Above my pearl without a spot. 60

VI

Thence sped my spirit far through space,
My body tranced upon the ground,
My soul's quick ghost by God's sure grace
Adventuring where be marvels found.
I wist not where on earth that place 65
With cloven cliffs, so high and sheer,
But toward a wood I set my face,
Borne whither radiant rocks appear.
Their light more golden than the sun,
A gleaming glory glinted thence: 70
Was never web of mortals spun
So wondrous fair to mortal sense.

VII

The hill-sides there were brightly crowned
With crystal cliffs so clear of kind,
And wood-sides, set with boles around, 75
Shone blue as is the blue of Inde.
On every branch, with light between,
The leaves of quivering silver hung;
Through gleaming glades with shimmering
sheen
The light fell glistering them among. 80
The gravel rolled upon the shore
Was precious pearls of Orient.
The sun's bright beams were pale before
That sight so fair of wonderment.

VIII

My spirit there forgot its woe, 85
So wondrous were those charmèd hills.
Rare flavoured fruits thereon did grow,
Fit food to cure all human ills.
In fair accord the birds flew by,
Like wingèd flames, both great and small, 90
Nor cittern string nor minstrelsy
Might hope to match their joyous call:
For when the air their red wings beat,
Full choir sang they rapturously.
No greater joy a man could greet 95
Than this to hear, and that to see.

IX

Past all that eye of man has seen,
Past any wealth of words he hath,
The beauty of those wood-ways green,
The witchery of that wooing path. 100
Still on I pressed, as one who goes
Companioned by a joyous mood,
Through deepening dells where richly rose
Fair flowers by winsome breezes wooed.
Hedge-rows and marsh where wild fowl
breed 105
I saw, and lo! a golden band—
A wonder that did all exceed—
A sunlit river cleft the strand.

X

O marvellous river, broad and deep,
With banks that beam with beryl bright! 110
As music sweet the waters sweep,
Or gently murmur low and light.
From darkened depths shone jewels fine,
As gleams through glowing glass the light,
As quivering stars in the welkin shine, 115
When tired men sleep of a winter night.
Each little stone that stream below
Was emerald green, or sapphire gent;
From them the light did leap and glow,
To daze a man with wonderment. 120

XI

Wondrous glamour of down and vale,
Wood and water and noble plain,
Did build me bliss and made me hale,
Routed sorrow and cured my pain.
Low bowed beside the stream I strayed, 125
With breed of joys my mind was glad;
The more I walked by mere and glade,
More strength of joy my spirit had.
Fortune fares where likes she still,
Sends she solace or evil sore, 130
The wight on whom she works her will
Hath ever of either more and more.

XII

More and more, and yet far more,
I longed to see beyond the strand;
For if 't was fair on the nearer shore, 135
More lovelike was that farther land.
I stayed my steps,—I stood at gaze,
To find a ford I sought,—alas!
Beside the strand, as in a maze,
I won not any way to pass. 140
Though peril in my path might stand,
I recked not, where such treasures were;

But fresh delights were nigh at hand,
That did my wondering spirit stir.

XIII

What wonder more did daunt my sight? 145
I saw beyond that mystic mere
A shining cliff of crystal bright,
With royal rays, as morning clear.
At foot there sat a little maid—
A maid of grace, and debonair; 150
In glistening white was she arrayed,
Well known long ere I saw her there.
More radiant than refinèd gold,
She stood in sunshine on the shore.
Long did my sight that vision hold, 155
And more I knew her, more and more.

XIV

Long feasted I on her dear face,
The lissome curves her figure wore,
Until the gladness of her grace
My heart's guest was as ne'er before. 160
Her gentle name I fain had called,
But stayed was I with wonderment,
So strange the place I stood appalled,
My eager gaze upon her bent.
Then turned on me her visage fair,— 165
As ivory white the face she wore.
Heart-struck was I to see her there,
And still I loved her more and more.

XV

Yearning had I by dread opposed.
I stood full still, I durst not call, 170
With eyes wide open and mouth full closed,
Like to a well-trained hawk in hall.
Hope had I for my soul's behoof;
Fear had I it might thus befall,
That she I longed for might stay aloof, 175
Or pass forever beyond recall.
Lo! uprose that child of grace,
Slender, small, and seemly slight,—
Rose right royal with lifted face,
A precious maid, with pearls bedight. 180

XVI

When, fresh as dewy fleur-de-lys,
Adown the bank she moved toward me,
High fortuned he on earth that sees
Such peerless pearls of empery.
As white as snow her amice gleams, 185
Her waist a lustrous broidery
Of pearls a man might see in dreams,
But never else on earth could see.

Full ample hung her sleeves, I ween;
Twain braided they with pearlës bright. 190
Her kirtle green alike was seen,
With pearls of price around bedight.

XVII

A crown did wear that maiden girl
Of margerys, and none other stone.
High pinnacled, of clear white pearl, 195
It glowed with flowers wrought thereon.
Her head no other gem did grace;
Her hair half hid her neck from view.
In statelihood of mighty place
She stood more white than whale tooth's hue.
Her loosened locks, that gold exceed, 201
Flowed wandering, o'er her shoulders curled;
Though dark their gold, they scarce did need
For contrast fair her robe impearled.

XVIII

Bravely broidered was every hem, 205
On sleeve and vest fair broidery lay
Of white pearls and no other gem,
And glossy shone her white array.
A wonder pearl without a taint
Lay moon-white where her bodice met; 210
Soul of man might falter and faint
Ere mind of man its price could set.
Tongue of man might ne'er be sure
With fitting words to tell aright
How spotless white and virgin pure 215
Was that rare pearl, my soul's delight.

XIX

Decked with pearls, that precious piece
Of Heaven's make came down the strand;
My grief won wings of glad release
When that I saw her nearer stand. 220
None else of kin were dear as she,
And joyful then was my surprise
When seemed it she would speak to me,
And courteous bowed in woman wise.
She doffed her crown of jewels bright, 225
With low obeisance bending blithe.
Leave to answer that pearl of light
Made worth it well to be alive.

XX

'O Pearl, so gay with pearls,' quoth I,—
'O Pearl that in my loneliness 230
Art yearned for when at night I lie
Sole comrade of my own distress,—
Since over thee the grasses twine,
No love to mine with love replies.

May liking, love, and joy be thine,—   235
The strifeless bourne of Paradise.
Such weird as brought thee hither here,
With plight of sorrow hath me undone;
Now are we twayned that were so dear,
And in love's life were but as one.'   240

XXI

High crowned with pearls of Orient,
Looked up at me with fair blue eyes
That gracious maid with grave intent,
And sober spake in courtly wise.
'Sir, the tale is by half mistold   245
To say thy pearl is all perdue,
That a comely coffer in guard doth hold,
In flowered gardens, gay to view,
Where she may ever dwell and play,
Where sin nor sorrow come never near.   250
Safe should such treasury seem alway
If thou didst love thy jewel dear.

XXII

'Gentle Sir,' said the maiden gem,
'Why do men jest? Distraught ye be.
Three words hast said, and all of them   255
Forsooth are folly,—yea, all the three.
Thou knowest not what thy words may
      mean;
Quick words thy tardy wits outfly.
Dost surely think that I here am seen
Because thou seest with mortal eye.   260
Thou sayest, too, that thou, alas!
May bide with me in this domain.
The way this stream to freely pass
No living wight may know to gain.

XXIII

'Small praise that man would have of me   265
That trusts the wisdom of the eye.
Much to be blamed and graceless he
That thinks the Lord could speak a lie,—
Our Lord who promised thy life to raise,
Though fortune bid thy body die!   270
Ye read his words in crooked ways
To trust alone what sees the eye:
And that is a fault of haughtiness
Doth ill a righteous man beseem,
To trow no tale has worthiness   275
Unless his reason so may deem.

XXIV

'Think now thyself if it be well
Of God such words as thine to say.
Dost think in this fair land to dwell?

Methinks 't were better his leave to pray:
And yet might fail thine eager quest.   281
Ere thou shalt pass that watery way
Thou first must find another rest,
And cold must lie thy corse in clay;
For it was marred in Paradise,   285
Where our yore-father wrought it loss,—
Through dreary death thy journey lies
Ere God will give thee leave to cross.

XXV

'Thou thinkest sorrow is naught but dole.
Why dost thou make this vain pretence?   290
For lesser loss the wailing soul
May lose far more than he laments.
Shouldst rather hold thee blessed by it,
And love thy God in weal and woe,
For anger helpeth thee no whit,   295
And man must bear what all must know.
Though thou shouldst prance as any doe,
And fret and chafe in mad unrest,
Thou canst not any further go,—
Abide thou must what He thinks best.'   300

XXVI

Then spake I to that demoiselle—
'Let not my Lord be wroth with me.
As from a spring quick waters well,
Leaps forth my speech so wild and free.
My lonely heart is sorrow-scarred,   305
In misericorde of Christ I rest,
Rebuke me not with words so hard,
Forlorn am I, adored and best.
Thy kindly comfort me afford
With piteous thinking upon this—   310
Of care and me ye made accord
Who once were ground of all my bliss.

XXVII

'Thou hast been both my bale and bliss,
But greater is the bale I moan.
On every field my pearl I miss,   315
I wist not where my pearl has flown.
With clearer sight is sorrow eased.
Ere parting came we were at one.
Forbid it, God, we be displeased,
Though meet we not beneath the sun.   320
Though tender sweet thy courtesy,
I am but earth, my joy is gone;
Gone every hope of help for me
Save mercy of Christ, Marie, and John.

XXVIII

'I see thee with thy comrade, joy.   325
Ah, think of me when thou art glad;

Sad hours my ageing life annoy,
A lonely man bereft and sad.
But now, within thy presence here
I fain would bide, and patient wait   330
That ye may tell—ah, pearl most dear—
What life ye have both early and late.
Full glad am I that thy estate
Is changed to worship and to weal;
Where thou hast passed to lofty state—   335
There lies the only joy I feel.'

XXIX

'To know if here the life is led
Be glad, will that thy grief.assuage.
Thou knowest when thy pearl lay dead
Full young was I, of tender age.   340
Lo! I am bride of Christ the Lamb!
Through sacred Godhead wedded sure;
A crownèd queen of bliss I am,
Through days that shall for aye endure.
Who have his love do hold in fee   345
This heritage. I am his alone;
His priceless glory is to me
The source of every joy I own.'

XXX

'Ah, Pearl of bliss, can this be true?
Let not●my error bid me rue.   350
Art thou the Queen of heaven's blue
That all the world does honour to?
Art her we worship, the spring of grace,
Who bare a Child of virgin flower?
Ah, none can take her crown and place,   355
That pass her not in worth and power.
For singleness of gentillesse
We call her phenix of Araby,—
The bird none match in stateliness,
Like to that Queen of Courtesy.'   360

XXXI

'Ay, Queen of Courtesy!' she said;
And lowly knelt and hid her face.
'Matchless mother and merriest maid!
Blest beginner of all our grace.'
Then rose she up and 'gan to speak,   365
And looked at me across the space.
'Though many find what here they seek,
None here may take another's place.
The heavens do her empire make,
Of earth and hell the Queen is she;   370
Her heritage may no one take,
For she is Queen of Courtesy.'

XXXII

'Yea, courtesy, I well believe,
And charity do here belong.
Let not my words thy goodness grieve— 375
To me thy speech still seemeth wrong.
Thyself to set so high in heaven
As queen to make of one so young—
What honour more might him be given
That in the world by grief was wrung, 380
And bought his bliss by years of bale—
Yea, lived in penance wearily?
No lesser honour him could fail
Than King be crowned by courtesy.

XXXIII

'Such courtesy too free appears,   385
If that be sooth which thou dost say.
On earth were thine but two brief years,
Never couldst thou God please or pray,
Knew never neither pater nor creed,—
But queen outright on thy death day,— 390
I may not trow it, so God me speed,
That God should rule so wrong a way.
Countess or demoiselle, par ma fay,
Were fair to be in heaven's estate,
Or else a lady of less array,—   395
But queen! it were too high a fate.'

XXXIV

'His goodness hath nor mete nor bound,'
Said then to me this worthsome wight;
'For all is truth where he is found,
Nought can he do but that is right.   400
This Matthew doth for thee express,
Writ clear in gospel sooth aright,
Ensampled plain for easy guess,
A parable of heavenly light.'
'My realm,' saith Christ, 'is like, on high,
A lord's that had a vineyard fair,   406
When lo! the vintage time was nigh,
And men must to his vines repair.

XXXV

'Right well his men the season know,
So up full early that lord arose   410
To send them where his vines did grow,
And unto some did there propose
A penny a day to be their gain.
With this accord forthwith they go,
And toil and labour with honest pain, 415
And prune and carry, go to and fro.
At noon this lord the market seeks,
And finds men standing idle here.

"Why stand ye idle?" thus he speaks
"Now know ye not the time of year?"   420

XXXVI

' "We hither came ere day begun,"
This was their answer, one and all.
"Here have we stood since rose the sun,
And no man yet on us doth call."
"Go to my vineyard, work aright,   425
And rest ye sure," that lord did say,
"What wages fair ye earn by night,
In very sooth I will surely pay."
Into his vines they went and wrought,
The while he came, and came again,   430
And new men into his vineyard brought,
Until the day was on the wane.

XXXVII

'At close of day, at evensong,
An hour before the sun had fled,
He saw their idle men and strong,   435
And unto them he gently said:
"Why stand ye idle all day long?"
"No man," they said, "has come to hire."
"Go to my vines, ye yeomen strong,
And work your best, as I desire."   440
Soon the world grew dusk and gray,
The sun went down, it waxèd late;
He summoned them to take their pay—
The hour had come for which they wait.

XXXVIII

'That lord well knew the time of day,   445
And bade his steward pay them all.
"Give every man his proper pay;
And that no blame on me may fall,
Set ye all of them in a row,
And give alike a penny to each.   450
Begin with him that stands most low,
Until the first his wage shall reach."
Thereon the first did quick complain:
"My lord, we toiled full long and sore;
These last have had but little pain,   455
Our wage should justly be far more."

XXXIX

'Then said this lord, "In sooth, I try
To use mine own as seemeth meet.
Why turn on me an evil eye,
Who justice seek and no man cheat?"   460
Quoth Christ, "I now do thus decree,
The first shall be the last, and those
Who latest came the first shall be,—
Of many called but few be chose."

Thus do poor men win their way,   465
Though late they come and low their state;
If brief has been their labour day,
The more of grace doth them await.

XL

'More bliss have I, and joy herein
Of ladyship, and life's delight,   470
Than all the men on earth might win
If all they sought were theirs by right.
Although the night was nigh at hand
When came I to the vines at even,
Among the first God bade me stand,   475
And fullest wage to me was given.
Yet others waited there in vain,
Who toiled and sweated long of yore,
And still no wage repaid their pain,
And may not for a year or more.'   480

XLI

The Lamb's delight none doubted there.
Though seemed he hurt and wounded sore,
Yet glorious glad his glances were,
And nought of pain his semblance bore.
I looked among his radiant host,   485
Quick with eternal life,—and lo!
I saw my pearlës gentle ghost,
I loved and lost so long ago.
Lord! much of mirth that maiden made
Among her peers, so pure and white.   490
I yearned to cross—all unafraid,
So longed my love—so dear the sight.

XLII

Delight held captive eye and ear;
My mortal mind toward madness drave,
I would be there where stayed my dear,   495
Beyond that river's mystic wave.
Methought that none would do so ill
As me to halt, if now I tried;
And if at start none checked my will,
Fain would I venture though I died.   500
Anon, from bold resolve I fell
When I would take that peril's chance;
In that rash mood I dare not dwell—
Not so my Prince's fair pleasance.

XLIII

It pleased not God that I come near,   505
Or think to cross that guarding mere,
Aghast I stood, alone with fear—
Alone, and she no longer here.
For, as I stood beside the stream,
I wakened in that arbour's shade.   510

Gone was the gladness of my dream!
My head was on that hillock laid
Where over her the roses grow.
Heartsore I lay upon the sod,
And to myself I murmured low: 515
'Blest be my maid in care of God.'

XLIV

So hard it was to drift away
From that fair region all too soon,
From sights so gallant, blithe and gay,
That weak with hurt I seemed to swoon,   520
And ruefully my head I bowed.
'O Pearl,' said I, 'of rare renown!
O, news of joy!" I cried aloud,
'In this glad vision sent me down.
And if thy tale in sooth be so,   525
And thou art clad in joy's delight,
Well am I in this home of woe,
Since thou hast pleased the Prince's sight.'

XLV

If to God's pleasure I had but bent,
And craved no more than man is given,   530

And held me humble, with this content,
As prayed that pearl in goodness thriven,—
Then by God's grace I were less amiss,
More mysteries my soul had won;
But man doth have more greed of bliss   535
Than life may give ere life be done.
Therefore too soon my joy was riven,
And I exiled from realms eterne.
Lord! mad are they with thee have striven,
For what doth not thy pleasure earn!   540

XLVI

To win the Prince's love aright
For Christen men is an easy end.
Yea, I have found him, by day and night,
A God, a Lord, full firm a friend.
Befell me this on that mound's green
    sod,—   545
For sorrow of Pearl there lay I prone,
And this my jewel gave o'er to God,
In Christ's dear blessing and eke mine own.
Christ, that in form of bread and wine,
The priest doth show, wherein God grants 550
To us his servants here a sign
That we be pearls of his pleasance.

THE CHESTER PLAYS

NOAH'S FLOOD

The drama of the middle ages in Western Europe was prevailingly religious, and in the hands of the Church it normally appeared in the form of relatively brief scenes written in Latin and presented by the clergy in close association with the liturgy. Although our records are scanty, we may be sure that liturgical plays of this sort were performed in England from the tenth century to the fourteenth, and even later. By the fourteenth century, however, the religious drama had largely passed from within the church into secular surroundings outside. Under the new circumstances the language employed was English, the actors were chiefly laymen, and the dramatic incidents were sometimes taken from other than religious sources. Under the auspices of associations of guilds this English religious drama usually took the form of large cycles of short plays, the typical cycle including the whole of sacred history, beginning with the Fall of the Angels and the Creation, proceeding through parts of the Old and New Testaments, and ending with the Last Judgment. This kind of drama is well exemplified by the Chester Plays, which were presented by the guilds of Chester from time to time during the fourteenth, fifteenth, and sixteenth centuries. The twenty-five separate plays of this cycle were commonly performed on the first three week-days of Whitsuntide: nine on Monday, nine on Tuesday, and seven on Wednesday. Each play was assigned to a separate guild, or group of guilds, and the remarkable aptness of some of these assignments is shown by the fact that *Noah's Flood*, printed below, was played by the carriers of water from the River Dee, on the banks of which the city of Chester stands. Each play was performed upon a wagon, or 'pageant,' described in the records as 'a high place made like a house, with two rooms, being open on the top. [In] the lower room they apparelled and dressed themselves, and in the higher room they played.' Each pageant-wagon was drawn about the city and halted at each of the several stations where its play was to be presented. The way in which the succession of wagons was managed is well described in one of the Chester manuscripts: 'The places where they played them was in every street. They began first at the Abbey gates, and when the pageant was played, it was wheeled to the High Cross, before the Mayor; and so to every street, and so every street had a pageant playing before them till all the pageants for the day appointed were played. And when one pageant was near ended, word was brought from street to street, that so the [next] might come in place thereof, exceeding orderly. And all the streets had their pageant before them, all at one time playing together.' In *Noah's Flood* the farcical rôle of Noah's wife illustrates the freedom and levity with which the unknown playwrights of the cycles occasionally enlivened the Biblical narrative.

THE WATERLEADERS AND DRAWERS OF
DEE

*First, in some high place, or in the clouds,
if it may be done,* GOD *speaks to* NOAH
standing with all his family outside the ark.

GOD

I, God, that all the world have wrought,
Heaven and earth, and all of nought,
I see my people in deed and thought
  Are foully set in sin.
My ghost shall not remain in man   5
That through fleshly liking is my fone,
But till six score years be gone,
  To look if they will blyn.

Man that I made I will destroy,
Beast, worm, and fowl that fly,   10
For on earth they do me annoy,
  The folk that are thereon;
It harms me so hurtfully,
The malice now that does multiply,
That sore it grieveth me inwardly   15
  That ever I made man.

Therefore, Noah, my servant free,
That righteous man art, as I see
A ship right soon thou shalt make thee
  Of trees both dry and light;   20
Little chambers therein do make,
And binding pitch also do take:
Within and out do thou not slake
  To anoint it through thy might,

Three hundred cubits it shall be long,   25
And fifty of breadth, to make it strong,
Of height fifty, the range do thou fonge;
 Thus measure it about.
One window fashion through thy wit,
One cubit of length and breadth make it;   30
Upon the side a door shall sit,
 For to come in and out.

Eating places make thou also,
Three roofed chambers, one or two,
For with water I think to flow   35
 Man that I did make;
Destroyed all the world shall be,
Save thou, thy wife, and thy sons three,
And all their wives also with thee,
 Shall saved be for thy sake.   40

NOAH

Ah, Lord, I thank thee loud and still,
That to me art in such good will,
And sparest me and my house to spill,
 As now I soothly find;
Thy bidding, Lord, I shall fulfill,   45
And never more thee grieve nor grill,
That such a grace hast sent me till,
 Among all mankind.

[NOAH *speaks to his family.*]

Have done, you men and women all!
Help, for aught that may befall,   50
To make this ship, chamber and hall,
 As God hath bidden us do.

SHEM

Father, I am already bowne:
An axe I have here, by my crown,
As sharp as any in all this town,   55
 For to go thereto.

HAM

I have a hatchet wonder keen
To bite right well, as may be seen;
A better ground one, as I ween,
 Is not in all this town.   60

JAPHET

And I can well now make a pin,
And with this hammer knock it in;
Go and work without more din,
 And I am ready bowne.

NOAH'S WIFE

And we shall bring the timber too,   65
For we may nothing other do:
Women be weak to undergo
 Any great travail.

SHEM'S WIFE

Here is a right good chopping-block,
On this you may well hew and knock;   70
Shall none be idle in this flock,
 Nor now may no man fail.

HAM'S WIFE

And I will go to gather slich
The ship here for to clean and pitch:
Anointed it must be each stitch,   75
 Board, tree, and pin.

JAPHET'S WIFE

And I will gather chips up here
To make a fire for you in fere,
And for to dight you your dinner
 Against that you come in.   80

*Then they make motions as if they were
working with various tools.*

NOAH

Now in the name of God I will begin
To make the ship that we shall go in,
That we be ready for to swim
 At the coming of the flood:
These boards I join up here together   85
To keep us safe from all the weather,
That we may row both hither and thither,
 And safe be from this flood.

Of this tree will I make the mast,
Tied with cables that will last,   90
With a sailyard for each blast,
 And each thing in their kind;
With topcastle and bowsprit,
With cords and ropes I have all meet
To sail forth at the next weete: 95
 This ship is at an end.

*Then NOAH and all his family again make
motions of working with various tools.*

Wife, in this castle we shall be kept;
My children and thou I would in leapt.

NOAH'S WIFE

In faith, Noah, I had as lief thou slept.
 For all thy frankish fare,   100
I will not do after thy rede.

NOAH

Good wife, do now as I thee bid.

NOAH'S WIFE

By Christ! not ere I see more need,
  Though thou stand all the day and stare.

NOAH

Lord, that women be crabbed aye,   105
And never are meek, that dare I say;
This is well seen by me today
  In witness of you each one.
Good wife, let be all this bere
That thou makest in this place here,   110
For all they ween thou art master—
  And so thou art, by St. John!

GOD

Noah, take thou thy company,
And in the ship hie that you be,
For none so righteous man to me   115
  Is now on earth living.
Of clean beasts do thou with thee take
Seven and seven, ere thou slake,
He and she, and make to make,
  Quickly in do thou bring.   120

Of beasts unclean, two and two,
Male and female, without mo,
Of clean fowls seven also,
  The he and she together;
Of fowls unclean, two and no more,   125
As I of beasts did say before,
That shall be saved through my lore,
  Against I send the weather.

Of all the meats that must be eaten
Into the ship look there be getten,   130
For that no way may be forgetten,
  And do all this bydene,
To sustain man and beast therein,
Aye till this water cease and blyn.
This world is filled full of sin,   135
  And that is now well seen.

Seven days be yet coming,
You shall have space them in to bring;
After that is my liking
  Mankind for to annoy: 140
Forty days and forty nights
Rain shall fall for their unrights,
And what I have made through my mights,
  Now think I to destroy.

NOAH

Lord, at your bidding I am bayne;   145
Since nothing else your grace will gain,
It will I fulfill fain,
  For gracious I thee find.
A hundred winters and twenty
This ship making tarried have I,   150
If through amendment thy mercy
  Would fall unto mankind.

[NOAH *summons his family.*]

Have done, you men and women all!
Hie you, lest this water fall.
That each beast were in his stall,   155
  And into the ship brought!
Of clean beasts seven there shall be,
Of unclean two, this God bade me.
This flood is nigh, well may we see;
  Therefore tarry you not.   160

Then NOAH *shall enter the ark, and his
family shall exhibit and name all the
animals painted on sheets of parchment, and
after each one has spoken his part, he shall
go into the ark, except* NOAH'S WIFE.
*The animals painted must conform to the
words spoken. And thus let the first son
begin.*

SHEM

Sir, here are lions, leopards in,
Horses, mares, oxen, and swine,
Goats, calves, sheep, and kine,
  Here sitting thou mayst see.

HAM

Camels, asses, men may find,   165
Buck, doe, hart, and hind,
And beasts of all manner of kind
  Here be, it seems to me.

JAPHET

Take here cats, and dogs too,
Otter, fox, fulmart also,   170
Hares hopping gaily can go,
  Have cowle here for to eat.

NOAH'S WIFE

And here are bears, and wolves set,
Apes, and owls, and marmoset,
Weasels, squirrels, and ferret;   175
  Here they eat their meat.

SHEM'S WIFE

Yet more beasts are in this house:
Here the cats make it full crowse,
Here a rat and here a mouse,
    They all stand nigh together.   180

HAM'S WIFE

And here fowls, both less and more:
Herons, cranes, and bittour,
Swans, peacocks; and them before
    Meat for this weather.

JAPHET'S WIFE

Here are cocks and kites and crows,   185
Rooks and ravens, many rows;
Ducks, curlews: whoever knows
    Each one in his kind?
And here are doves and ducks and drakes,
Redshanks, running through the lakes;   190
And each fowl that language makes
    In this ship men find.

NOAH

Wife, come in! why standest thou here?
Thou art ever froward, dare I swear.
Come in, on God's half! time it were,   195
    For fear lest that we drown.

NOAH'S WIFE

Yea, sir, set up your sail,
And row forth with evil hail!
For without any fail
    I will not from this town.   200

Unless I have my gossips every one
One foot further I will not gone;
They shall not drown here, by St. John!
    If I may save their life!
They loved me full well, by Christ!   205
Unless thou'lt let them in thy chest,
Row forth, Noah, whither thou list,
    And get thee a new wife.

NOAH

Shem, son, lo! thy mother is wraw:
Forsooth, such another I do not know!   210

SHEM

Father, I'll fetch her in, I trow,
    Without any fail.

    [Goes to where his mother is sitting.]

Mother, my father after thee sent,
And bids thee into yon ship wend.
Look up and see the wind,   215
    For we be ready to sail.

NOAH'S WIFE

Son, go back to him and say
I will not come therein today.

NOAH

Come in, wife, in twenty devils' way!
    Or else stand there without.   220

HAM

Shall we all fetch her in?

NOAH

Yea, sons, in Christ's blessing and mine!
I would you hied you betime,
    For of this flood I am in doubt.

THE GOOD GOSSIPS [*Singing*]
The flood comes in full fleeting fast,   225
On every side it spreadeth full far;
For fear of drowning I am aghast,
Good gossip, let us draw near.
And let us drink ere we depart,
For oftentimes we have done so;   230
For at a draught thou drink'st a quart,
    And so will I do ere I go.

JAPHET

Mother, we pray you altogether,
For we are here, your own childer,
Come into the ship for fear of the weather,
    For his love that you bought.   236

NOAH'S WIFE

That will I not for all your call,
Unless I have my gossips all.

SHEM

In faith, mother, yet you shall,
    Whether you will or not!   240

                    Then she will go.

NOAH

Welcome, wife, into this boat!

NOAH'S WIFE
And have thou that for thy mote!

                    She deals NOAH *a blow.*

NOAH

Aha, marry, this is hot!
  It is good to be still.
Ah, children, methinks my boat removes! 245
Our tarrying here hugely me grieves;
Over the land the water spreads,—
  God do as he will!

Ah, great God, that art so good;
Who works not thy will is wood.   250
Now all this world is in a flood,
  As I see well in sight;
This window I will shut anon,
And into my chamber will I gone,
Till this water, so great one,   255
  Be slakèd through thy might.

Then let NOAH *close the window of the ark,
and after remaining within for a short time,
let them sing the psalm, 'Save me, O
God.' Then let* NOAH *open the window
and look out.*

Now forty days are fully gone.
Send a raven I will anon,
To see if earth or tree or stone,
  Be dry in any place;   260
And if this fowl come not again,
It is a sign, the sooth to sayne,
That dry it is on hill or plain,
  And God hath done some grace.

*Then let him send forth a raven, and tak-
ing a dove in his hands, let him speak.*

Ah, Lord, where'er this raven be,   265
Somewhere is dry, right well I see.
But yet a dove, by my loyalty,
  After I will send.
Thou wilt turn again to me,
     *   *   *
For of all fowls that may fly,   270
  Thou art most meek and hend.

*Then let him send forth the dove. And there
shall be on the ship another dove bearing
an olive branch in its mouth, which some
one shall let down from the mast by a
cord into* NOAH'S *hand. And afterwards
let* NOAH *speak.*

Ah, Lord, blessed be thou aye,
That me hast comforted thus today!
By this sight I may well say
  This flood begins to cease: 275
My sweet dove to me brought has
A branch of olive from some place;

This betokeneth God has done us some grace,
  And is a sign of peace.

Ah, Lord, honored may thou be!   280
All earth dries now, I see,
But yet till thou commandest me,
  Hence will I not hie.
All this water is away;
Therefore as soon as I may,   285
Sacrifice I shall do in fay
  To thee devoutly.

GOD

Noah, take thy wife anon,
And thy children every one;
Out of the ship thou shalt gone   290
  And they all with thee;
Beasts and all that can fly
Out anon they shall hie,
On earth to grow and multiply;
  I will that it so be.   295

NOAH

Lord, I thank thee, through thy might,
Thy bidding shall be done in hight,
And as fast as I may dight
  I will do thee honor,
And to thee offer sacrifice.   300
Therefore comes in all wise,
For of these beasts here that be his
  Offer I will this store.

*Then coming forth from the ark with all his
family,* NOAH *shall take his animals and
fowls and make an offering, and slay
them.*

Lord God in majesty,
That such grace hast granted me   305
Where all was lost, safe to be,
  Therefore now I am bowne,
My wife, my children, my company,
With sacrifice to honor thee,
With beasts and fowls, as thou mayst see.
  I offer here right soon.   311

GOD

Noah, to me thou art full able,
And thy sacrifice acceptable,
For I have found thee true and stable;
  On thee now must I myn.   315
Curse the earth will I no more
For man's sin that grieves me sore,
For of youth man full yore
  Has been inclined to sin.

You shall now grow and multiply,   320
And earth again you edify;
Each beast and fowl that may fly
   Shall be afraid of you;
And fish in sea that may flytte
Shall sustain you, I you behite;   325
To eat of them do you not let,
   That clean be you may know.

Whereas you have eaten before
Grass and roots since you were bore,
Of clean beasts, less and more,   330
   I give you leave to eat;
Save blood and flesh both in fere
Of wrong dead carrion that is here:
Eat not of that in no manner,
   For that aye shall you let.   335

Manslaughter also you shall flee,
For that is not pleasant to me.
Who sheds blood, he or she,
   Any where amongst mankind,
That blood foully shed shall be,   340
And vengeance have that men shall see.
Therefore beware now all ye,
   You fall not in that sin.

A foreword now with thee I make,
And all thy seed too for thy sake,   345

From such vengeance for to slake,   .
   For now I have my will;
Here I promise thee a hest:
That man nor woman, fowl nor beast
With water, while the world shall last,   350
   I will no more spill.

My bow between you and me
In the firmament shall be,
By very token that you may see
   That such vengeance shall cease;   355
That man nor woman shall never more
Be wasted by water as is before;
But for sin, that grieveth me sore,
   Therefore this vengeance was.

Where clouds in the welkin been   360
That same bow shall now be seen,
In token that my wrath and teen
   Shall never thus wreaked be;
The string is turned toward you,
And toward me is bent the bow,   365
That such weather shall never show,
   And this I promise thee.

My blessing now I give thee here,
To thee, Noah, my servant dear,
For vengeance shall no more appear.   370
And now, farewell, my darling dear.

CENTURY READINGS FOR A COURSE IN
ENGLISH LITERATURE

CENTURY READINGS FOR A COURSE IN ENGLISH LITERATURE

GEOFFREY CHAUCER (c. 1340–1400)

Since Chaucer's father, John Chaucer, was not only a successful London vintner, but also, probably, an occasional servant of the king, it is not surprising that at an early age our poet himself entered the service of royalty. Our earliest records concerning him show that in April, 1357, he was occupied, perhaps as page, in the household of Elizabeth, wife of Prince Lionel, son of Edward III, where he continued to serve throughout that year and probably into the next. During this service, Chaucer accompanied the princess to Hatfield, in Yorkshire, to London, and probably to other parts of England. We surmise that he witnessed more than one brilliant chivalric entertainment, and that at Hatfield, during Christmastide of 1357, he met his future friend and patron, John of Gaunt. During the year 1359, Chaucer served as a soldier in the army of Edward III, in France. Having been taken prisoner, not far from Reims, he was released through a ransom to which the king himself contributed the substantial sum of sixteen pounds. After the conclusion of this expedition, with the Peace of Brétigny, May 8, 1360, Chaucer returned to England, where he seems to have increased in favor at court, for in 1367 he was granted a life pension of twenty marks as a valet of the king. During the next ten or fifteen years, Chaucer took part in a considerable number of diplomatic missions to the Continent, of which the most important, from a literary point of view, are a secret embassy to Genoa and Florence (Dec., 1372, to April, 1373), and a mission to Milan (May to September, 1378). Although Petrarch and Boccaccio were both living at the time of Chaucer's first visit to Italy, we have no evidence that the English poet met either of them. To these Italian journeys, however, may be due Chaucer's subsequent devotion to Italian literature. Aside from his diplomatic employment, the poet had official duties at home in connection with the customs of the port of London. In 1374 he was appointed comptroller of the customs and subsidy of wools, skins, and tanned hides, and in 1382 he received the additional appointment of comptroller of the petty customs. In the autumn of 1386, Chaucer sat for a short time in parliament as a knight of the shire for Kent. In the political eclipse of Richard, from the latter part of 1386 to 1389, Chaucer lost his offices, a loss that left him, presumably, much leisure for writing. During this period he may have written a considerable part of *The Canterbury Tales*. In 1389, Chaucer was again in the service of the government as clerk of the king's works, and although the loss of this appointment, in 1391, left him in straitened circumstances, a royal pension of twenty pounds, in 1394, and a yearly gift of a tun of wine, in 1398, contributed somewhat toward his comfort. When Henry IV, son of Chaucer's old patron, John of Gaunt, came to the throne in 1399, the poet promptly addressed to him a balade entitled *The Compleynt of Chaucer to his Empty Purse*. To this pleasant bit of begging the king responded readily with a pension of forty marks, in addition to the annuity of twenty pounds that had been granted in 1394. Chaucer spent his last days, then, in comparative comfort, and on his death, October 25, 1400, he was buried in the south transept of West-minster Abbey, which has since become the 'Poets' Corner.'

Although the exact chronology of Chaucer's works is far from certain, the literary influences under which he wrote are clearly defined. As a courtier, diplomat, and man of the world, he was familiar with literary fashions at home and abroad,— literary fashions definitely embodied in his works. His first poems are imitations or translations of French poems popular at court both in France and in England. To an early stage of his career is assigned his translation of at least part of the *Roman de la Rose*, a French poem composed during the thirteenth century and popular in the fourteenth. French in style is *The Book of the Duchess*, written in 1369 as a lament for the death of Blanche, wife of John of Gaunt. Upon French models Chaucer composed his early poem, *A. B. C.*, and numerous shorter poems 'that highten balades, roundels, virelayes.' The *Parliament of Fowls*, written, probably, in 1382, in honor of the

3

marriage of Richard II and Anne of Bohemia, is conspicuously influenced by French poetical taste. During his journeys to Italy, or before, Chaucer acquired a new source of literary inspiration in the works of Dante, Petrarch, and Boccaccio. Although from Dante and Petrarch his literal borrowings are few, his extensive verbal obligations to Boccaccio are shown in *Troilus and Criseyde*, written about 1383, and in the *Knight's Tale*. *The House of Fame*, written, perhaps, about 1379, clearly shows the influence of Dante, as well as of French allegorical poetry. To the last fifteen years or so of Chaucer's life, without specification, may be assigned the *Legend of Good Women* and the *Canterbury Tales*. Although in these works Chaucer used a multiplicity of sources, the poems themselves show vigorous increase in English spirit and in literary originality.

THE CANTERBURY TALES

THE PROLOGUE

Whan that Aprille with his shoures soote
The droghte of Marche hath percèd to the roote,
And bathèd every veyne in swich licour,
Of which vertu engendrèd is the flour;
Whan Zephirus eek with his swete breeth   5
Inspirèd hath in every holt and heeth
The tendre croppes, and the yonge sonne
Hath in the Ram his halfe cours y-ronne,
And smale fowles maken melodye,
That slepen al the night with open yë,   10
(So priketh hem nature in hir corages):
Than longen folk to goon on pilgrimages,
And palmers for to seken straunge strondes,
To ferne halwes, couthe in sondry londes;
And specially, from every shires ende   15
Of Engelond, to Caunterbury they wende,
The holy blisful martir for to seke,
That hem hath holpen, whan that they were seke.
  Bifel that, in that sesoun on a day,
In Southwerk at the Tabard as I lay   20
Redy to wenden on my pilgrimage
To Caunterbury with ful devout corage,
At night was come in-to that hostelrye
Wel nyne and twenty in a compaignye,
Of sondry folk, by aventure y-falle   25
In felawshipe, and pilgrims were they alle,
That toward Caunterbury wolden ryde;
The chambres and the stables weren wyde,
And wel we weren esèd atte beste.
And shortly, whan the sonne was to reste, 30
So hadde I spoken with hem everichon,
That I was of hir felawshipe anon,
And made forward erly for to ryse,
To take our wey, ther as I yow devyse.
  But natheles, whyl I have tyme and space,
Er that I ferther in this tale pace,   36
Me thinketh it acordaunt to resoun,
To telle yow al the condicioun
Of ech of hem, so as it semèd me,   39
And whiche they weren, and of what degree;
And eek in what array that they were inne:

And at a knight than wol I first biginne.
  A KNIGHT ther was, and that a worthy man,
That fro the tyme that he first bigan
To ryden out, he lovèd chivalrye,   45
Trouthe and honour, fredom and curteisye.
Ful worthy was he in his lordes werre,
And thereto hadde he riden (no man ferre)
As wel in cristendom as hethenesse,
And evere honourèd for his worthinesse. 5ª
At Alisaundre he was, whan it was wonne;
Ful ofte tyme he hadde the bord bigonne
Aboven alle naciouns in Pruce.
In Lettow hadde he reysèd and in Ruce,
No cristen man so ofte of his degree.   55
In Gernade at the sege eek hadde he be
Of Algezir, and riden in Belmarye.
At Lyeys was he, and at Satalye,
Whan they were wonne; and in the Grete See
At many a noble aryve hadde he be.   6ª
At mortal batailles hadde he been fiftene,
And foughten for our feith at Tramissene
In listes thryes, and ay slayn his foo.
This ilke worthy knight hadde been also
Somtyme with the lord of Palatye,   65
Ageyn another hethen in Turkye:
And everemore he hadde a sovereyn prys.
And though that he were worthy, he was wys,
And of his port as meek as is a mayde.
He nevere yet no vileinye ne sayde   70
In al his lyf, un-to no maner wight.
He was a verray parfit gentil knight.
But for to tellen yow of his array,
His hors were goode, but he was nat gay.
Of fustian he werèd a gipoun   75
Al bismotered with his habergeoun.
For he was late y-come from his viage,
And wente for to doon his pilgrimage.
  With him ther was his sone, a yong SQUYER,
A lovyer, and a lusty bacheler,   80
With lokkes crulle, as they were leyd in presse.

Of twenty yeer of age he was, I gesse.
Of his stature he was of evene lengthe,
And wonderly delivere, and greet of
  strengthe.
And he hadde been somtyme in chivachye, 85
In Flaundres, in Artoys, and Picardye,
And born him wel, as of so litel space,
In hope to stonden in his lady grace.
Embrouded was he, as it were a mede
Al ful of fresshe floures, whyte and rede. 90
Singinge he was, or floytinge, al the day;
He was as fresh as is the month of May.
Short was his goune, with sleves longe and
  wyde.
Wel coude he sitte on hors, and faire ryde.
He coude songes make and wel endyte, 95
Iuste and eek daunce, and wel purtreye and
  wryte.
So hote he lovede, that by nightertale
He sleep namore than doth a nightingale.
Curteys he was, lowly, and servisable,
And carf biforn his fader at the table. 100
  A YEMAN hadde he, and servaunts namo
At that tyme, for him liste ryde so;
And he was clad in cote and hood of grene;
A sheef of pecok arwes brighte and kene
Under his belt he bar ful thriftily, 105
(Wel coude he dresse his takel yemanly:
His arwes droupèd noght with fetheres
  lowe),
And in his hand he bar a mighty bowe.
A not-heed hadde he, with a broun visage.
Of wode-craft wel coude he al the usage. 110
Upon his arm he bar a gay bracer,
And by his syde a swerd and a bokeler,
And on that other syde a gay daggere,
Harneisèd wel, and sharp as point of spere;
A Cristofre on his brest of silver shene. 115
An horn he bar, the bawdrik was of grene;
A forster was he, soothly, as I gesse.
  Ther was also a Nonne, a PRIORESSE,
That of hir smyling was ful simple and coy;
Hir gretteste ooth was but by sëynt Loy; 120
And she was clepèd madame Eglentyne.
Ful wel she song the service divyne,
Entunèd in hir nose ful semely;
And Frensh she spak ful faire and fetisly,
After the scole of Stratford atte Bowe, 125
For Frensh of Paris was to hir unknowe.
At mete wel y-taught was she with-alle;
She leet no morsel from hir lippes falle,
Ne wette hir fingres in hir sauce depe.
Wel coude she carie a morsel, and wel kepe,
That no drope ne fille up-on hir brest. 131
In curteisye was set ful moche hir lest.
Hir over lippe wypèd she so clene,
That in hir coppe was no ferthing sene

Of grece, whan she dronken hadde hir
  draughte. 135
Ful semely after hir mete she raughte,
And sikerly she was of greet disport,
And ful plesaunt, and amiable of port,
And peynèd hir to countrefete chere
Of court, and been estatlich of manere, 140
And to ben holden digne of reverence.
But, for to speken of hir conscience,
She was so charitable and so pitous,
She wolde wepe, if that she sawe a mous
Caught in a trappe, if it were deed or bledde.
Of smale houndes had she, that she fedde 146
With rostèd flesh, or milk and wastel breed.
But sore weep she if oon of hem were deed,
Or if men smoot it with a yerde smerte:
And al was conscience and tendre herte. 150
Ful semely hir wimpel pinchèd was;
Hir nose tretys; hir eyen greye as glas;
Hir mouth ful smal, and ther-to softe and
  reed;
But sikerly she hadde a fair forheed.
It was almost a spanne brood, I trowe; 153
For, hardily, she was nat undergrowe.
Ful fetis was hir cloke, as I was war.
Of smal coral aboute hir arm she bar
A peire of bedes, gauded al with grene;
And ther-on heng a broche of gold ful shene,
On which ther was first write a crownèd A,
And after, *Amor vincit omnia*. 162
  Another NONNE with hir hadde she,
That was hir chapeleyne, and PREESTES thre.
  A MONK ther was, a fair for the maistrye,
An out-rydere, that lovede venerye; 166
A manly man, to been an abbot able.
Ful many a deyntee hors hadde he in stable:
And, whan he rood, men mighte his brydel
  here
Ginglen in a whistling wynd as clere, 170
And eek as loude as doth the chapel-belle,
Ther as this lord was keper of the celle.
The reule of seint Maure or of seint Beneit,
By-cause that it was old and som-del streit,
This ilke monk leet olde thinges pace, 175
And held after the newe world the space.
He yaf nat of that text a pullèd hen,
That seith, that hunters been nat holy men;
Ne that a monk, whan he is cloisterlees,
Is liknèd til a fish that is waterlees; 180
This is to seyn, a monk out of his cloistre.
But thilke text held he nat worth an oistre.
And I seyde his opinioun was good.
What sholde he studie, and make him-selven
  wood,
Upon a book in cloistre alwey to poure, 185
Or swinken with his handes, and laboure,
As Austin bit? How shal the world be
  servèd?

Lat Austin have his swink to him reservèd.
Therfor he was a pricasour aright;
Grehoundes he hadde, as swifte as fowel in
    flight;
Of priking and of hunting for the hare   191
Was al his lust, for no cost wolde he spare.
I seigh his sleves purfiled at the hond
With grys, and that the fyneste of a lond;
And, for to festne his hood under his chin,
He hadde of gold y-wroght a curious pin:
A love-knot in the gretter ende ther was.   197
His heed was balled, that shoon as any glas,
And eek his face, as he hadde been anoint.
He was a lord ful fat and in good point;   200
His eyen stepe, and rollinge in his heed,
That stemèd as a forneys of a leed;
His botes souple, his hors in greet estat.
Now certeinly he was a fair prelat;
He was nat pale as a for-pynèd goost.   205
A fat swan loved he best of any roost.
His palfrey was as broun as is a berye.
  A FRERE ther was, a wantown and a merye,
A limitour, a ful solempne man.
In alle the ordres foure is noon that can   210
So moche of daliaunce and fair langage.
He hadde maad ful many a mariage
Of yonge wommen, at his owne cost.
Un-to his ordre he was a noble post.
Ful wel biloved and famulier was he   215
With frankeleyns over-al in his contree,
And eek with worthy wommen of the toun:
For he had power of confessioun,
As seyde him-self, more than a curat,
For of his ordre he was licentiat.   220
Ful swetely herde he confessioun,
And plesaunt was his absolucioun;
He was an esy man to yeve penaunce
Ther as he wiste to han a good pitaunce;
For unto a povre ordre for to yive   225
Is signe that a man is wel y-shrive.
For if he yaf, he dorste make avaunt,
He wiste that a man was repentaunt.
For many a man so hard is of his herte,
He may nat wepe al-thogh him sore smerte.
Therfore, in stede of weping and preyeres,
Men moot yeve silver to the povre freres.   232
His tipet was ay farsèd ful of knyves
And pinnes, for to yeven faire wyves.
And certeinly he hadde a mery note;   235
Wel coude he singe and pleyen on a rote.
Of yeddinges he bar utterly the prys.
His nekke whyt was as the flour-de-lys.
There-to he strong was as a champioun.
He knew the tavernes wel in every toun,   240
And everich hostiler and tappestere
Bet than a lazar or a beggestere;
For un-to swich a worthy man as he
Acorded nat, as by his facultee,

To have with seke lazars aqueyntaunce.   245
It is nat honest, it may nat avaunce
For to delen with no swich poraille,
But al with riche and sellers of vitaille.
And over-al, ther as profit sholde aryse,
Curteys he was, and lowly of servyse.   250
Ther nas no man nowher so vertuous.
He was the beste beggere in his hous;
For thogh a widwe hadde noght a sho,
So plesaunt was his *In principio*,
Yet wolde he have a ferthing, er he wente.
His purchas was wel bettre than his rente.   256
And rage he coude as it were right a whelpe.
In love-dayes ther coude he mochel helpe.
For ther he was nat lyk a cloisterer,
With a thredbare cope, as is a povre scole ,
But he was lyk a maister or a pope.   261
Of double worsted was his semi-cope,
That rounded as a belle out of the presse.
Somwhat he lipsèd, for his wantownesse,
To make his English swete up-on his tonge;
And in his harping, whan that he had songe,
His eyen twinklèd in his heed aright,   267
As doon the sterres in the frosty night.
This worthy limitour was cleped Huberd.
  A MARCHANT was ther with a forkèd berd,
In mottelee, and hye on horse he sat,   271
Up-on his heed a Flaundrish bever hat;
His botes claspèd faire and fetisly.
His resons he spak ful solempnely,
Sowninge alway thencrees of his winning.   275
He wolde the see were kept for any thing
Bitwixe Middelburgh and Orewelle.
Wel coude he in eschaunge sheeldes selle.
This worthy man ful wel his wit bisette;
Ther wiste no wight that he was in dette,   280
So estatly was he of his governaunce,
With his bargaynes, and with his chevisaunce.
For sothe he was a worthy man with-alle,
But sooth to seyn, I noot how men him calle.
  A CLERK ther was of Oxenford also,   285
That un-to logik hadde longe y-go.
As lene was his hors as is a rake,
And he nas nat right fat, I undertake;
But lokèd holwe, and ther-to soberly.
Ful thredbar was his overest courtepy;   290
For he had geten him yet no benefice,
Ne was so worldly for to have office.
For him was levere have at his beddes heed
Twenty bokes, clad in blak or reed
Of Aristotle and his philosophye,   295
Than robes riche, or fithele, or gay sautrye.
But al be that he was a philosophre,
Yet hadde he but litel gold in cofre;
But al that he mighte of his frendes hente,
On bokes and on lerninge he it spente,   300
And bisily gan for the soules preye
Of hem that yaf him wher-with to scoleye

Of studie took he most cure and most hede.
Noght o word spak he more than was nede,
And that was seyd in forme and reverence,
And short and quik, and ful of hy sentence.
Sowninge in moral vertu was his speche, 307
And gladly wolde he lerne, and gladly teche.

A SERGEANT OF THE LAWE, war and wys,
That often hadde been at the parvys, 310
Ther was also, ful riche of excellence.
Discreet he was, and of greet reverence:
He semèd swich, his wordes weren so wyse,
Iustice he was ful often in assyse,
By patente, and by pleyn commissioun; 315
For his science, and for his heigh renoun
Of fees and robes hadde he many oon.
So greet a purchasour was nowher noon.
Al was fee simple to him in effect,
His purchasing mighte nat been infect. 320
Nowher so bisy a man as he ther nas,
And yet he semèd bisier than he was.
In termes hadde he caas and domes alle,
That from the tyme of king William were
falle. 324
Thereto he coude endyte, and make a thing,
Ther coude no wight pinche at his wryting;
And every statut coude he pleyn by rote.
He rood but hoomly in a medlee cote
Girt with a ceint of silk, with barres smale;
Of his array telle I no lenger tale. 330

A FRANKELEYN was in his compaignye;
Whyt was his berd, as is the dayesye.
Of his complexioun he was sangwyn.
Wel loved he by the morwe a sop in wyn.
To liven in delyt was evere his wone, 335
For he was Epicurus owne sone,
That heeld opinioun that pleyn delyt
Was verraily felicitee parfyt.
An housholdere, and that a greet, was he;
Seynt Iulian he was in his contree. 340
His breed, his ale, was alwey after oon;
A bettre envyned man was nevere noon.
With-oute bake mete was nevere his hous,
Of fish and flesh, and that so plentevous,
It snewèd in his hous of mete and drinke,
Of alle deyntees that men coude thinke. 346
After the sondry sesons of the yeer,
So chaungèd he his mete and his soper.
Ful many a fat partrich hadde he in mewe,
And many a breem and many a luce in stewe.
Wo was his cook, but-if his sauce were 351
Poynaunt and sharp, and redy al his gere.
His table dormant in his halle alway
Stood redy covered al the longe day.
At sessiouns ther was he lord and sire. 355
Ful ofte tyme he was knight of the shire.
An anlas and a gipser al of silk
Heng at his girdel, whyt as morne milk.
A shirreve hadde he been, and a countour;

Was nowher such a worthy vavasour. 360
An HABERDASSHER and a CARPENTER,
A WEBBE, a DYERE, and a TAPICER,
And they were clothèd alle in o liveree,
Of a solempne and greet fraternitee.
Ful fresh and newe hir gere apykèd was; 365
Hir knyves were y-chapèd noght with bras,
But al with silver wroght ful clene and weel,
Hir girdles and hir pouches everydeel.
Wel semèd ech of hem a fair burgeys,
To sitten in a yeldhalle on a deys. 370
Everich, for the wisdom that he can,
Was shaply for to been an alderman.
For catel hadde they ynogh and rente,
And eek hir wyves wolde it wel assente;
And elles certein were they to blame. 375
It is ful fair to been y-clept ma dame,
And goon to vigilyès al bifore,
And have a mantel roialliche y-bore.

A COOK they hadde with hem for the nones,
To boille chiknes with the mary-bones, 380
And poudre-marchant tart, and galingale.
Wel coude he knowe a draughte of London
ale.
He coude roste, and sethe, and broille, and
frye,
Maken mortreux, and wel bake a pye.
But greet harm was it, as it thoughte me, 385
That on his shine a mormal hadde he;
For blankmanger, that made he with the
beste.

A SHIPMAN was ther, woning fer by
weste:
For aught I woot, he was of Dertemouthe.
He rood up-on a rouncy, as he couthe, 390
In a gowne of falding to the knee.
A daggere hanging on a laas hadde he
Aboute his nekke under his arm adoun.
The hote somer had maad his hewe al
broun;
And, certeinly, he was a good felawe. 395
Ful many a draughte of wyn had he y-drawe
From Burdeux-ward, whyl that the chapman
sleep.
Of nyce conscience took he no keep.
If that he faught, and hadde the hyer hond,
By water he sente hem hoom to every lond.
But of his craft to rekene wel his tydes, 401
His stremes and his daungers him bisydes,
His herberwe and his mone, his lodemenage,
Ther nas noon swich from Hulle to Cartage.
Hardy he was, and wys to undertake; 405
With many a tempest hadde his berd been
shake.
He knew wel alle the havenes, as they were,
From Gootlond to the cape of Finistere,
And every cryke in Britayne and in Spayne;
His barge y-clepèd was the Maudelayne. 410

With us ther was a DOCTOUR OF PHISYK,
In al this world ne was ther noon him lyk
To speke of phisik and of surgerye;
For he was grounded in astronomye.
He kepte his pacient a ful greet del   415
In houres, by his magik naturel.
Wel coude he fortunen the ascendent
Of his images for his pacient.
He knew the cause of everich maladye,
Were it of hoot or cold, or moiste, or drye,
And where engendrèd, and of what humour;
He was a verrey parfit practisour.   422
The cause y-knowe, and of his harm the rote,
Anon he yaf the seke man his bote.
Ful redy hadde he his apothecaries,   425
To sende him drogges, and his letuaries,
For ech of hem made other for to winne;
Hir frendschipe nas nat newe to biginne.
Wel knew he the olde Esculapius,
And Deiscorides, and eek Rufus;   430
Old Ypocras, Haly, and Galien;
Serapion, Razis, and Avicen;
Averrois, Damascien, and Constantyn;
Bernard, and Gatesden, and Gilbertyn.
Of his diete mesurable was he,   435
For it was of no superfluitee,
But of greet norissing and digestible.
His studie was but litel on the Bible.
In sangwin and in pers he clad was al,
Lynèd with taffata and with sendal;   440
And yet he was but esy of dispence;
He kepte that he wan in pestilence.
For gold in phisik is a cordial,
Therfor he lovede gold in special.   444
  A good WYF was ther of bisyde BATHE,
But she was som-del deef, and that was
    scathe.
Of cloth-making she hadde swiche an haunt,
She passèd hem of Ypres and of Gaunt.
In al the parisshe wyf ne was ther noon
That to the offring bifore hir sholde goon;
And if ther dide, certeyn, so wrooth was she,
That she was out of alle charitee.   452
Hir coverchiefs ful fyne were of ground;
I dorste swere they weyeden ten pound
That on a Sonday were upon hir heed.   455
Hir hosen weren of fyn scarlet reed,
Ful streite y-teyd, and shoos ful moiste and
    newe.
Bold was hir face, and fair, and reed of
    hewe.
She was a worthy womman al hir lyve,
Housbondes at chirche-dore she hadde fyve,
Withouten other compaignye in youthe;   461
But therof nedeth nat to speke as nouthe.
And thryes hadde she been at Ierusalem;
She hadde passèd many a straunge streem;
At Rome she hadde been, and at Boloigne,

In Galice at seint Iame, and at Coloigne.   466
She coude moche of wandring by the weye,
Gat-tothèd was she, soothly for to seye.
Up-on an amblere esily she sat,
Y-wimplèd wel, and on hir heed an hat   470
As brood as is a bokeler or a targe;
A foot-mantel aboute hir hipes large,
And on hir feet a paire of spores sharpe.
In felaweschip wel coude she laughe and
    carpe.   474
Of remedies of love she knew per-chaunce,
For she coude of that art the olde daunce.
  A good man was ther of religioun,
And was a povre PERSOUN of a toun;
But riche he was of holy thoght and werk.
He was also a lernèd man, a clerk,   480
That Cristes gospel trewely wolde preche;
His parisshens devoutly wolde he teche.
Benigne he was, and wonder diligent,
And in adversitee ful pacient;
And swich he was y-prevèd ofte sythes.   484
Ful looth were him to cursen for his tythes,
But rather wolde he yeven, out of doute,
Un-to his povre parisshens aboute
Of his offring, and eek of his substaunce.
He coude in litel thing han suffisaunce.   490
Wyd was his parisshe, and houses fer a-son-
    der,
But he ne lafte nat, for reyn ne thonder,
In siknes nor in meschief to visyte
The ferreste in his parisshe, moche and lyte,
Up-on his feet, and in his hand a staf.   495
This noble ensample to his sheep he yaf,
That first he wroghte, and afterward he
    taughte;
Out of the gospel he tho wordes caughte;
And this figure he added eek ther-to,
That if gold ruste, what shal yren do?   500
For if a preest be foul, on whom we truste,
No wonder is a lewèd man to ruste;
And shame it is, if a preest take keep,
A [dirty] shepherde and a clene sheep.
Wel oghte a preest ensample for to yive,   505
By his clennesse, how that his sheep shold
    live.
He sette nat his benefice to hyre,
And leet his sheep encombrèd in the myre,
And ran to London, un-to sëynt Poules,
To seken him a chaunterie for soules,   510
Or with a bretherhed to been withholde;
But dwelte at hoom, and kepte wel his folde,
So that the wolf ne made it nat miscarie;
He was a shepherde and no mercenarie.
And though he holy were, and vertuous,   515
He was to sinful man nat despitous,
Ne of his speche daungerous ne digne,
But in his teching discreet and benigne,
To drawen folk to heven by fairnesse

By good ensample, this was his bisynesse:
But it were any persone obstinat, 521
What so he were, of heigh or lowe estat,
Him wolde he snibben sharply for the nones.
A bettre preest, I trowe that nowher non is.
He wayted after no pompe and reverence,
Ne makèd him a spycèd conscience, 526
But Cristes lore, and his apostles twelve,
He taughte, but first he folwèd it him-selve.

  With him ther was a PLOWMAN, was his
    brother,
That hadde y-lad of dong ful many a fother,
A trewe swinkere and a good was he, 531
Livinge in pees and parfit charitee.
God loved he best with al his hole herte
At alle tymes, thogh him gamed or smerte,
And thanne his neighebour right as him-
    selve. 535
He wolde thresshe, and ther-to dyke and
    delve,
For Cristes sake, for every povre wight,
Withouten hyre, if it lay in his might.
His tythes payèd he ful faire and wel,
Bothe of his propre swink and his catel. 540
In a tabard he rood upon a mere.

Ther was also a Reve and a Millere,
A Somnour and a Pardoner also,
A Maunciple, and my-self; ther were namo.

  The MILLER was a stout carl, for the nones,
Ful big he was of braun, and eek of bones;
That provèd wel, for over-al ther he cam, 547
At wrastling he wolde have alwey the ram.
He was short-sholdrèd, brood, a thikke
    knarre
Ther nas no dore that he nolde heve of
    harre, 550
Or breke it, at a renning, with his heed.
His berd as any sowe or fox was reed,
And ther-to brood, as though it were a spade.
Up-on the cop right of his nose he hade
A werte, and ther-on stood a tuft of heres,
Reed as the bristles of a sowes eres; 556
His nose-thirles blake were and wyde.
A swerd and bokeler bar he by his syde;
His mouth as greet was as a greet forneys.
He was a Ianglere and a goliardeys, 560
And that was most of sinne and harlotryes.
Wel coude he stelen corn, and tollen thryes;
And yet he hadde a thombe of gold, pardee.
A whyt cote and a blew hood werèd he.
A baggepype wel coude he blowe and sowne,
And therwithal he broghte us out of towne.

  A gentil MAUNCIPLE was ther of a temple,
Of which achatours mighte take exemple 568
For to be wyse in bying of vitaille.
For whether that he payde, or took by taille,
Algate he wayted so in his achat, 571
That he was ay biforn and in good stat.

Now is nat that of God a ful fair grace,
That swich a lewèd mannes wit shal pace
The wisdom of an heep of lernèd men? 575
Of maistres hadde he mo than thryes ten,
That were of lawe expert and curious;
Of which ther were a doseyn in that hous,
Worthy to been stiwardes of rente and lond
Of any lord that is in Engelond, 580
To make him live by his propre good,
In honour dettelees, but he were wood,
Or live as scarsly as him list desire;
And able for to helpen al a shire
In any cas that mighte falle or happe; 585
And yit this maunciple sette hir aller cappe.

  The REVE was a sclendre colerik man,
His berd was shave as ny as ever he can.
His heer was by his eres round y-shorn.
His top was dokkèd lyk a preest biforn. 590
Ful longe were his legges, and ful lene,
Y-lyk a staf, ther was no calf y-sene.
Wel coude he kepe a gerner and a binne;
Ther was noon auditour coude on him winne.
Wel wiste he, by the droghte, and by the
    reyn, 595
The yeldyng of his seed, and of his greyn,
His lordes sheep, his neet, his dayerye,
His swyn, his hors, his stoor, and his pultrye,
Was hoolly in this reves governing,
And by his covenaunt yaf the rekening, 600
Sin that his lord was twenty yeer of age;
Ther coude no man bringe him in arrerage.
Ther nas baillif, ne herde, ne other hyne,
That he ne knew his sleighte and his covyne;
They were adrad of him, as of the deeth. 605
His woning was ful fair up-on an heeth,
With grene treës shadwèd was his place.
He coude bettre than his lord purchace.
Ful riche he was astorèd prively,
His lord wel coude he plesen subtilly, 610
To yeve and lene him of his owne good,
And have a thank, and yet a cote, and hood.
In youthe he lernèd hadde a good mister;
He was a wel good wrighte, a carpenter.
This reve sat up-on a ful good stot, 615
That was al pomely grey, and highte Scot.
A long surcote of pers up-on he hade,
And by his syde he bar a rusty blade.
Of Northfolk was this reve, of which I telle,
Bisyde a toun men clepen Baldeswelle. 620
Tukkèd he was, as is a frere, aboute,
And evere he rood the hindreste of our
    route.

  A SOMNOUR was ther with us in that place,
That hadde a fyr-reed cherubinnes face,
For sauceflem he was, with eyen narwe. 625
As hoot he was, and lecherous as a sparwe,
With scallèd browes blake, and pilèd berd;
Of his visage children were aferd.

Ther nas quik-silver, litarge, ne brimstoon,
Boras, ceruce, ne oille of tartre noon,   630
Ne oynement that wolde clense and byte,
That him mighte helpen of his whelkes
    whyte,
Ne of the knobbes sitting on his chekes.
Wel loved he garleek, oynons, and eek lekes,
And for to drinken strong wyn, reed as
    blood.   635
Thanne wolde he speke, and crye as he were
    wood. *
And whan that he wel dronken hadde the
    wyn,
Than wolde he speke no word but Latyn.
A fewe termes hadde he, two or thre,
That he had lernèd out of som decree;   640
No wonder is, he herde it al the day;
And eek ye knowen wel, how that a Iay
Can clepen 'Watte,' as well as can the pope.
But who-so coude in other thing him grope,
Thanne hadde he spent al his philosophye;
Ay 'Questio quid iuris' wolde he crye.   646
He was a gentil harlot and a kynde;
A bettre felawe sholde men noght fynde.
He wolde suffre for a quart of wyn
A good felawe to have his concubyn   650
A twelf-month, and excuse him atte fulle:
And prively a finch eek coude he pulle.
And if he fond owher a good felawe,
He wolde techen him to have non awe,
In swich cas, of the erchedeknes curs,   655
But-if a mannes soule were in his purs;
For in his purs he sholde y-punisshed be.
'Purs is the erchedeknes helle,' seyde he.
But wel I woot he lyèd right in dede;
Of cursing oghte ech gulty man him drede—
For curs wol slee right as assoilling sav-
    eth—   661
And also war him of a significavit.
In daunger hadde he at his owne gyse
The yonge girles of the diocyse,
And knew hir counseil, and was al hir reed.
A gerland hadde he set up-on his heed,   666
As greet as it were for an ale-stake;
A bokeler hadde he maad him of a cake.
    With him ther rood a gentil Pardoner
Of Rouncivale, his frend and his compeer,
That streight was comen fro the court of
    Rome.   671
Ful loude he song, 'Come hider, love, to
    me.'
This somnour bar to him a stif burdoun,
Was nevere trompe of half so greet a soun.
This pardoner hadde heer as yelow as wex,
But smothe it heng, as doth a strike of flex;
By ounces henge his lokkes that he hadde,
And there-with he his shuldres overspradde;
But thinne it lay, by colpons oon and oon;

But hood, for Iolitee, ne wered he noon,   680
For it was trussèd up in his walet.
Him thoughte he rood al of the newe Iet;
Dischevele, save his cappe, he rood al bare.
Swiche glaringe eyen hadde he as an hare.
A vernicle hadde he sowèd on his cappe.   685
His walet lay biforn him in his lappe,
Bret-ful of pardoun come from Rome al
    hoot.
A voys he hadde as smal as hath a goot.
No berd hadde he, ne nevere sholde have,
As smothe it was as it were late y-shave;   690

*   *   *

But of his craft, fro Berwik into Ware,
Ne was ther swich another pardoner.
For in his male he hadde a pilwe-beer,
Which that, he seyde, was our lady veyl: 695
He seyde he hadde a gobet of the seyl
That sëynt Peter hadde, whan that he wente
Up-on the see, til Iesu Crist him hente.
He hadde a croys of latoun, ful of stones,
And in a glas he hadde pigges bones.   700
But with thise relikes, whan that he fond
A povre person dwelling up-on lond,
Up-on a day he gat him more moneye
Than that the person gat in monthes tweye.
And thus with feynèd flaterye and Iapes,   705
He made the person and the peple his apes.
But trewely to tellen, atte laste,
He was in chirche a noble ecclesiaste.
Wel coude he rede a lessoun or a storie,
But alderbest he song an offertorie;   710
For wel he wiste, whan that song was songe,
He moste preche, and wel affyle his tonge,
To winne silver, as he ful wel coude;
Therefore he song so meriely and loude.
    Now have I told you shortly, in a clause,
Thestat, tharray, the nombre, and eek the
    cause   716
Why that assemblèd was this compaignye
In Southwerk, at this gentil hostelrye,
That highte the Tabard, faste by the Belle.
But now is tyme to yow for to telle   720
How that we baren us that ilke night,
Whan we were in that hostelrye alight.
And after wol I telle of our viage,
And al the remenaunt of our pilgrimage.
But first I pray yow of your curteisye,   725
That ye narette it nat my vileinye,
Thogh that I pleynly speke in this matere,
To telle yow hir wordes and hir chere;
Ne thogh I speke hir wordes proprely.
For this ye knowen al-so wel as I,   730
Who-so shal telle a tale after a man,
He moot reherce, as ny as evere he can,
Everich a word, if it be in his charge,
Al speke he never so rudeliche and large;
Or elles he moot telle his tale untrewe,   735

Or feyne thing, or fynde words newe.
He may nat spare, al-thogh he were his
   brother;
He moot as wel seye o word as another.
Crist spak him-self ful brode in holy writ,
And wel ye woot, no vileinye is it.   740
Eek Plato seith, who-so that can him rede,
The wordes mote be cosin to the dede.
Also I prey yow to foryeve it me,
Al have I nat set folk in hir degree
Here in this tale, as that they sholde stonde;
My wit is short, ye may wel understonde. 746
   Greet chere made our hoste us everichon,
And to the soper sette he us anon;
And servèd us with vitaille at the beste.
Strong was the wyn, and wel to drinke us
   leste.   750
A semely man our hoste was with-alle
For to han been a marshal in an halle;
A large man he was with eyen stepe,
A fairer burgeys was ther noon in Chepe:
Bold of his speche, and wys, and wel
   y-taught,   755
And of manhood him lakkede right naught.
Eek thereto he was right a mery man,
And after soper pleyen he bigan,
And spak of mirthe amonges othere thinges,
Whan that we hadde maad our rekeninges;
And seyde thus: ' Now, lordinges, trewely
Ye ben to me right welcome hertely: 762
For by my trouthe, if that I shal nat lye,
I ne saugh this yeer so mery a compaignye
At ones in this herberwe as is now.   765
Fayn wolde I doon yow mirthe, wiste I how.
And of a mirthe I am right now bithoght,
To doon yow ese, and it shal coste noght.
   Ye goon to Caunterbury; God yow spede,
The blisful martir quyte yow your mede. 770
And wel I woot, as ye goon by the weye,
Ye shapen yow to talen and to pleye;
For trewely, confort ne mirthe is noon
To ryde by the weye doumb as a stoon;
And therfore wol I maken yow disport, 775
As I seyde erst, and doon yow som confort.
And if yow lyketh alle, by oon assent,
Now for to stonden at my Iugement,
And for to werken as I shal yow seye,
To-morwe, whan ye ryden by the weye, 780
Now, by my fader soule, that is deed,
But ye be merye, I wol yeve yow myn heed.
Hold up your hond, withoute more speche.'
Our counseil was nat longe for to seche;
Us thoughte it was noght worth to make it
   wys,   785
And grauntèd him with-outen more avys,
And bad him seye his verdit, as him leste.
   'Lordinges,' quod he, ' now herkneth for
   the beste;

But tak it not, I prey yow, in desdeyn;
This is the poynt, to speken short and pleyn,
That ech of yow, to shorte with our weye, 791
In this viage, shal telle tales tweye,
To Caunterbury-ward, I mene it so,
And hom-ward he shal tellen othere two,
Of aventures that whylom han bifalle. 795
And which of yow that bereth him best of
   alle,
That is to seyn, that telleth in this cas
Tales of best sentence and most solas,
Shal han a soper at our aller cost
Here in this place, sitting by this post, 800
Whan that we come agayn fro Caunterbury.
And for to make yow the more mery,
I wol my-selven gladly with yow ryde,
Right at myn owne cost, and be your gyde.
And who-so wol my Iugement withseye 805
Shal paye al that we spenden by the weye.
And if ye vouche-sauf that it be so,
Tel me anon, with-outen wordes mo,
And I wol erly shape me therfore.'
   This thing was graunted, and our othes
   swore   810
With ful glad herte, and preyden him also
That he wold vouche-sauf for to do so,
And that he wolde been our governour,
And of our tales Iuge and reportour,
And sette a soper at a certeyn prys;   815
And we wold reulèd been at his devys,
In heigh and lowe; and thus, by oon assent,
We been acorded to his Iugement.
And ther-up-on the wyn was fet anoon;
We dronken, and to reste wente echoon, 820
With-outen any lenger taryinge.
A-morwe, whan that day bigan to springe,
Up roos our host, and was our aller cok,
And gadrede us togidre, alle in a flok,
And forth we riden, a litel more than pas,
Un-to the watering of seint Thomas.   826
And there our host bigan his hors areste,
And seyde; ' Lordinges, herkneth if yow
   leste.
Ye woot your forward, and I it yow recorde.
If even-song and morwe-song acorde,   830
Lat se now who shal telle the firste tale.
As evere mote I drinke wyn or ale,
Who-so be rebel to my Iugement
Shal paye for al that by the weye is spent.
Now draweth cut, er that we ferrer twinne;
He which that hath the shortest shal be-
   ginne.'
' Sire knight,' quod he, ' my maister and my
   lord,   837
Now draweth cut, for that is myn acord.
Cometh neer,' quod he, ' my lady prioresse;
And ye, sir clerk, lat be your shamfastnesse,
Ne studieth noght; ley hond to, every man.'

Anon to drawen every wight bigan, 842
And shortly for to tellen, as it was,
Were it by aventure, or sort, or cas,
The sothe is this, the cut fil to the knight, 845
Of which ful blythe and glad was every
    wight;
And telle he moste his tale, as was resoun,
By forward and by composicioun,
As ye han herd; what nedeth wordes mo?
And whan this goode man saugh it was so,
As he that wys was and obedient 851
To kepe his forward by his free assent,
He seyde: 'Sin I shal beginne the game,
What, welcome be the cut, a Goddes name!
Now lat us ryde, and herkneth what I seye.'
    And with that word we riden forth our
    weye; 856
And he bigan with right a mery chere
His tale anon, and seyde in this mannere.

* * *

THE NUN'S PRIEST'S TALE

A povre widwe somdel stope in age,
Was whylom dwelling in a narwe cotage,
Bisyde a grove, stondyng in a dale.
This widwe, of which I telle yow my tale,
Sin thilke day that she was last a wyf, 5
In pacience ladde a ful simple lyf,
For litel was hir catel and hir rente;
By housbondrye, of such as God hir sente,
She fond hir-self, and eek hir doghtren two.
Three large sowes hadde she, and namo, 10
Three kyn, and eek a sheep that highte Malle.
Ful sooty was hir bour, and eek hir halle,
In which she eet ful many a sclendre meel.
Of poynaunt sauce hir neded never a deel,
No deyntee morsel passèd thrugh hir throte;
Hir dyete was accordant to hir cote. 16
Repleccioun ne made hir nevere syk;
Attempree dyete was al hir phisyk,
And exercyse, and hertes suffisaunce.
The goute lette hir no-thing for to daunce, 20
Ne poplexye shente nat hir heed;
No wyn ne drank she, neither whyt ne reed;
Hir bord was servèd most with whyt and
    blak,
Milk and broun breed, in which she fond no
    lak,
Seynd bacoun, and somtyme an ey or tweye,
For she was as it were a maner deye. 26
A yerd she hadde, enclosèd al aboute
With stikkes, and a drye dich with-oute,
In which she hadde a cok, hight Chaunte-
    cleer,
In al the land of crowing nas his peer. 30
His vois was merier than the merye orgon
On messe-dayes that in the chirche gon;

Wel sikerer was his crowing in his logge,
Than is a clokke, or an abbey orlogge.
By nature knew he ech ascencioun 33
Of equinoxial in thilke toun;
For whan degrees fiftene were ascended,
Thanne crew he, that it mighte nat ben
    amended.
His comb was redder than the fyn coral,
And batailed, as it were a castel-wal. 40
His bile was blak, and as the Ieet it shoon;
Lyk asur were his legges, and his toon;
His nayles whytter than the lilie flour,
And lyk the burnèd gold was his colour.
This gentil cok hadde in his governaunce 45
Sevene hennes, for to doon al his pleasaunce,
Whiche were his sustres and his paramours,
And wonder lyk to him, as of colours.
Of whiche the faireste hewèd on hir throte
Was clepèd faire damoysele Pertelote. 50
Curteys she was, discreet, and debonaire,
And compaignable, and bar hir-self so faire
Sin thilke day that she was seven night old,
That trewely she hath the herte in hold
Of Chauntecleer loken in every lith; 55
He loved hir so, that wel him was therwith.
But such a Ioye was it to here hem singe,
Whan that the brighte sonne gan to springe,
In swete accord, 'my lief is faren in londe.'
For thilke tyme, as I have understonde, 60
Bestes and briddes coude speke and singe.
    And so bifel, that in a dawenynge,
As Chauntecleer among his wyves alle
Sat on his perche, that was in the halle,
And next him sat this faire Pertelote, 65
This Chauntecleer gan gronen in his throte,
As man that in his dreem is drecchèd sore.
And whan that Pertelote thus herde him
    rore,
She was agast, and seyde, 'O herte deere,
What eyleth yow, to grone in this manere?
Ye ben a verray sleper, fy for shame!' 71
And he answerde and seyde thus, 'Madame,
I pray yow, that ye take it nat agrief:
By God, me mette I was in swich meschief
Right now, that yet myn herte is sore afright.
Now God,' quod he, 'my swevene rede
    aright, 76
And keep my body out of foul prisoun!
Me mette, how that I romèd up and doun
Withinne our yerde, wher as I saugh a beste,
Was lyk an hound, and wolde han maad
    areste 80
Upon my body, and wolde han had me deed.
His colour was bitwixe yelwe and reed;
And tippèd was his tail, and bothe his eres
With blak, unlyk the remenant of his heres;
His snowte smal, with glowinge eyen tweye.
Yet of his look for fere almost I deye; 86

This causèd me my groning, douteles.'
'Avoy!' quod she, 'fy on yow, herteles!
Allas!' quod she, 'for, by that God above,
Now han ye lost myn herte and al my love;
I can nat love a coward, by my feith.   91
For certes, what so any womman seith,
We alle desyren, if it mighte be,
To han housbondes hardy, wyse, and free,
And secree, and no nigard, ne no fool,   95
Ne him that is agast of every tool,
Ne noon avauntour, by that God above!
How dorste ye sayn for shame unto youre
love,
That any thing mighte make yow aferd?
Have ye no mannes herte, and han a berd?
Alias! and conne ye been agast of swevenis?
No-thing, God wot, but vanitee, in sweven is.
Swevenes engendren of replecciouns,   103
And ofte of fume, and of complecciouns,
Whan humours been to habundant in a
wight.   105
Certes this dreem, which ye han met to-
night,
Cometh of the grete superfluitee
Of youre rede *colera*, pardee,
Which causeth folk to dremen in here
dremes
Of arwes, and of fyr with rede lemes,   110
Of grete bestes, that they wol hem byte,
Of contek, and of whelpes grete and lyte;
Right as the humour of malencolye
Causeth ful many a man, in sleep, to crye,
For fere of blake beres, or boles blake, 115
Or elles, blake develes wole him take.
Of othere humours coude I telle also,
That werken many a man in sleep ful wo;
But I wol passe as lightly as I can.   119
     Lo Catoun, which that was so wys a man,
Seyde he nat thus, ne do no fors of dremes?
Now, sire,' quod she, 'whan we flee fro the
bemes,
For Goddes love, as tak som laxatyf;
Up peril of my soule, and of my lyf,
I counseille yow the beste, I wol nat lye, 125
That both of colere, and of malencolye
Ye purge yow; and for ye shul nat tarie,
Though in this toun is noon apotecarie,
I shal my-self to herbes techen yow,
That shul ben for your hele, and for your
prow;   130
And in our yerd tho herbes shal I fynde,
The whiche han of here propretee, by kynde,
To purgen yow binethe, and eek above.
Forget not this, for Goddes owene love!
Ye been ful colerik of compleccioun.   135
Ware the sonne in his ascencioun
Ne fynde yow nat repleet of humours hote;
And if it do. I dar wel leye a grote,

That ye shul have a fevere terciane,
Or an agu, that may be youre bane.   140
A day or two ye shul have digestyves
Of wormes, er ye take your laxatyves,
Of lauriol, centaure, and fumetere,
Or elles of ellebor, that groweth there,
Of catapuce, or of gaytres beryis,   145
Of erbe yve, growing in our yerd, that mery
is;
Pekke hem up right as they growe, and
ete hem in.
Be mery, housbond, for your fader kyn!
Dredeth no dreem; I can say yow namore.'
     'Madame,' quod he, '*graunt mercy* of your'
lore.   150
But natheles, as touching daun Catoun,
That hath of wisdom such a gret renoun,
Though that he bad no dremes for to drede,
By God, men may in olde bokes rede
Of many a man, more of auctoritee   155
Than evere Catoun was, so moot I thee,
That al the revers seyn of this sentence,
And han wel founden by experience,
That dremes ben significaciouns,
As wel of Ioye as tribulaciouns   160
That folk enduren in this lyf present.
Ther nedeth make of this noon argument;
The verray preve sheweth it in dede.
Oon of the gretteste auctours that men rede
Seith thus, that whylom two felawes wente
On pilgrimage, in a ful good entente;   166
And happèd so, they come into a toun,
Wher as ther was swich congregacioun
Of peple, and eek so streit of herbergage,
That they ne founde as muche as o cotage,
In which they bothe mighte y-loggèd be. 171
Wherfor thay mosten, of necessitee,
As for that night, departen compaignye;
And ech of hem goth to his hostelrye,
And took his logging as it wolde falle.   175
That oon of hem was loggèd in a stalle,
Fer in a yerd, with oxen of the plough;
That other man was loggèd wel y-nough,
As was his aventure, or his fortune,
That us governeth alle as in commune.   180
And so bifel, that, long er it were day,
This man mette in his bed, ther as he lay,
How that his felawe gan up-on him calle,
And seyde, "Allas! for in an oxes stalle
This night I shal be mordrèd ther I lye. 185
Now help me, dere brother, or I dye;
In alle haste com to me," he sayde.
This man out of his sleep for fere abrayde;
But whan that he was waknèd of his sleep,
He turnèd him, and took of this no keep,
Him thoughte his dreem nas but a vanitee.
Thus twyes in his sleping dremèd he.   192
And atte thridde tyme yet his felawe

Com, as him thoughte, and seide, "I am now
  slawe;
Bihold my bloody woundes, depe and wyde!
Arys up erly in the morwe-tyde,   196
And at the west gate of the toun," quod he,
"A carte ful of donge ther shaltow see,
In which my body is hid ful prively;
Do thilke carte arresten boldely.   200
My gold causèd my mordre, sooth to sayn;"
And tolde him every poynt how he was slayn,
With a ful pitous face, pale of hewe.
And truste wel, his dreem he fond ful trewe;
For on the morwe, as sone as it was day, 205
To his felawes in he took the way;
And whan that he cam to this oxes stalle,
After his felawe he bigan to calle.
The hostiler answerde him anon,
And seyde, "Sire, your felawe is agon, 210
As sone as day he wente out of the toun."
This man gan fallen in suspecioun,
Remembring on his dremes that he mette,
And forth he goth, no lenger wolde he lette,
Unto the west gate of the toun, and fond
A dong-carte, as it were to donge lond, 216
That was arrayèd in that same wyse
As ye han herd the dede man devyse;
And with an hardy herte he gan to crye
Vengeaunce and Iustice of this felonye:—
"My felawe mordrèd is this same night, 221
And in this carte he lyth gapinge upright.
I crye out on the ministres," quod he,
"That sholden kepe and reulen this citee;
Harrow! allas! her lyth my felawe slayn!"
What sholde I more un-to this tale sayn? 226
The peple out-sterte, and caste the cart to
  grounde,
And in the middel of the dong they founde
The dede man, that mordrèd was al newe.
'O blisful God, that art so Iust and trewe!
Lo, how that thou biwreyest mordre alway!
Mordre wol out, that se we day by day. 232
Mordre is so wlatsom and abhominable
To God, that is so Iust and resonable,
That he ne wol nat suffre it helèd be; 235
Though it abyde a yeer, or two, or three,
Mordre wol out, this my conclusioun.
And right anoon, ministres of that toun
Han hent the carter, and so sore him pynèd,
And eek the hostiler so sore engynèd, 240
That thay biknewe hir wikkednesse anoon,
And were an-hangèd by the nekke-boon.
'Here may men seen that dremes been
  to drede.
And certes, in the same book I rede,
Right in the nexte chapitre after this, 245
(I gabbe nat, so have I Ioye or blis,)
Two men that wolde han passèd over see,
For certeyn cause, in-to a fer contree,

If that the wind ne hadde been contrarie,
That made hem in a citee for to tarie, 250
That stood ful mery upon an haven-syde.
But on a day, agayn the even-tyde,
The wind gan chaunge, and blew right as
  hem leste.
Iolif and glad they wente un-to hir reste,
And casten hem ful erly for to saille; 255
But to that oo man fel a greet mervaille.
That oon of hem, in sleping as he lay,
Him mette a wonder dreem, agayn the day;
Him thoughte a man stood by his beddes
  syde,
And him comaunded, that he sholde abyde,
And seyde him thus, "If thou to-morwe
  wende,   261
Thou shalt be dreynt; my tale is at an
  ende."
He wook, and tolde his felawe what he
  mette,
And preyde him his viage for to lette;
As for that day, he preyde him to abyde. 265
His felawe, that lay by his beddes syde,
Gan for to laughe, and scornèd him ful faste.
"No dreem," quod he, "may so myn herte
  agaste,
That I wol lette for to do my thinges.
I sette not a straw by thy dreminges, 270
For swevenes been but vanitees and Iapes.
Men dreme al-day of owles or of apes,
And eek of many a mase therwithal;
Men dreme of thing that nevere was ne shal.
But sith I see that thou wolt heer abyde, 275
And thus for-sleuthen wilfully thy tyde,
God wot it reweth me; and have good day."
And thus he took his leve, and wente his way.
But er that he hadde halfe his cours y-seylèd,
Noot I nat why, ne what mischaunce it
  eylèd,   280
But casuelly the shippes botme rente,
And ship and man under the water wente
In sighte of othere shippes it byside,
That with hem seylèd at the same tyde.
And therfor, faire Pertelote so dere, 285
By swiche ensamples olde maistow lere,
That no man sholde been to recchelees
Of dremes, for I sey thee, doutelees,
That many a dreem ful sore is for to drede.
'Lo, in the lyf of seint Kenelm, I rede, 290
That was Kenulphus sone, the noble king
Of Mercenrike, how Kenelm mette a thing;
A lyte er he was mordrèd, on a day,
His mordre in his avisioun he say.
His norice him expounèd every del 295
His swevene, and bad him for to kepe him
  wel
For traisoun; but he nas but seven yeer old,
And therfore litel tale hath he told

Of any dreem, so holy was his herte.
By God, I hadde levere than my sherte 300
That ye had rad his legende, as have I.
Dame Pertelote, I sey yow trewely,
Macrobeus, that writ the avisioun
In Affrike of the worthy Cipioun,
Affermeth dremes, and seith that they been
Warning of thinges that men after seen. 306
And forther-more, I pray yow loketh wel
In the olde testament, of Daniel,
If he held dremes any vanitee.
Reed eek of Ioseph, and ther shul ye see 310
Wher dremes ben somtyme (I sey nat alle)
Warning of thinges that shul after falle.
Loke of Egipt the king, daun Pharao,
His bakere and his boteler also,
Wher they ne felte noon effect in dremes.
Who so wol seken actes of sondry remes, 316
May rede of dremes many a wonder thing.
'Lo Cresus, which that was of Lyde king,
Mette he nat that he sat upon a tree,
Which signified he sholde anhangèd be? 320
Lo heer Andromacha, Ectores wyf,
That day that Ector sholde lese his lyf,
She dremèd on the same night biforn,
How that the lyf of Ector sholde be lorn,
If thilke day he wente in-to bataille; 325
She warnèd him, but it mighte nat availle;
He wente for to fighte natheles,
But he was slayn anoon of Achilles.
But thilke tale is al to long to telle,
And eek it is ny day, I may nat dwelle. 330
Shortly I seye, as for conclusioun,
That I shal han of this avisioun
Adversitee; and I seye forther-more,
That I ne telle of laxatyves no store,
For they ben venimous, I woot it wel; 335
I hem defye, I love hem nevere a del.
'Now let us speke of mirthe, and stinte al
this;
Madame Pertelote, so have I blis,
Of o thing God hath sent me large grace;
For whan I see the beautee of your face, 340
Ye ben so scarlet-reed about youre yën,
It maketh al my drede for to dyen;
For, also siker as *In principio,*
Mulier est hominis confusio;
Madame, the sentence of this Latin is — 345
Womman is mannes Ioye and al his blis.
* * *
I am so ful of Ioye and of solas 350
That I defye bothe sweven and dreem.'
And with that word he fley doun fro the
beem,
For it was day, and eek his hennes alle;
And with a chuk he gan hem for to calle,
For he had founde a corn, lay in the yerd.
Roial he was, he was namore aferd; 356
* * *

He loketh as it were a grim leoun;
And on his toos he rometh up and doun, 360
Him deynèd not to sette his foot to grounde.
He chukketh, whan he hath a corn y-founde,
And to him rennen thanne his wyves alle.
Thus roial, as a prince is in his halle,
Leve I this Chauntecleer in his pasture; 365
And after wol I telle his aventure.
Whan that the month in which the world
bigan,
That highte March, whan God first makèd
man,
Was complet, and y-passèd were also,
Sin March bigan, thritty dayes and two, 370
Bifel that Chauntecleer, in al his pryde,
His seven wyves walking by his syde,
Caste up his eyen to the brighte sonne,
That in the signe of Taurus hadde y-ronne
Twenty degrees and oon, and somwhat
more; 375
And knew by kynde, and by noon other lore,
That it was pryme, and crew with blisful
stevene.
'The sonne,' he sayde, 'is clomben up on
hevene
Fourty degrees and oon, and more, y-wis.
Madame Pertelote, my worldes blis, 380
Herkneth thise blisful briddes how they
singe,
And see the fresshe floures how they
springe;
Ful is myn hert of revel and solas.'
But sodeinly him fil a sorweful cas;
For evere the latter ende of Ioye is wo. 385
Got woot that worldly Ioye is sone ago;
And if a rethor coude faire endyte,
He in a chronique saufly mighte it write,
As for a sovereyn notabilitee.
Now every wys man, lat him herkne me; 390
This storie is al-so trewe, I undertake,
As is the book of Launcelot de Lake,
That wommen holde in ful gret reverence.
Now wol I torne agayn to my sentence.
A col-fox, ful of sly iniquitee, 395
That in the grove hadde wonèd yeres three,
By heigh imaginacioun forn-cast,
The same night thurgh-out the hegges brast
Into the yerd, ther Chauntecleer the faire
Was wont, and eek his wyves, to repaire; 400
And in a bed of wortes stille he lay,
Til it was passèd undern of the day,
Wayting his tyme on Chauntecleer to falle
As gladly doon thise homicydes alle,
That in awayt liggen to mordre men. 405
O false mordrer, lurking in thy den!
O newe Scariot, newe Genilon!
False dissimilour, O Greek Sinon,
That broghtest Troye al outrely to sorwe!
O Chauntecleer, acursèd be that morwe. 410

That thou into that yerd flough fro the
   bemes!
Thou were ful wel y-warnèd by thy dremes,
That thilke day was perilous to thee.
But what that God forwot mot nedes be,
After the opinioun of certeyn clerkis.   415
Witnesse on him, that any perfit clerk is,
That in scole is gret altercacioun
In this matere, and greet disputisoun,
And hath ben of an hundred thousand men.
But I ne can not bulte it to the bren,   420
As can the holy doctour Augustyn,
Or Boece, or the bishop Bradwardyn,
Whether that Goddes worthy forwiting
Streyneth me nedely for to doon a thing,
(Nedely clepe I simple necessitee) ;   425
Or elles, if free choys be graunted me
To do that same thing, or do it noght,
Though God forwot it, er that it was
   wroght ;
Or if his witing streyneth nevere a del
But by necessitee condicionel.   430
I wol not han to do of swich matere ;
My tale is of a cok, as ye may here,
That took his counseil of his wyf, with
   sorwe,
To walken in the yerd upon that morwe 434
That he had met the dreem, that I of tolde.
Wommennes counseils been ful ofte colde ;
Wommannes counseil broghte us first to wo,
And made Adam fro paradys to go,
Ther as he was ful mery, and wel at ese.
But for I noot, to whom it mighte displese,
If I counseil of wommen wolde blame,   441
Passe over, for I seyde it in my game.
Rede auctours, wher they trete of swich
   matere,
And what thay seyn of wommen ye may
   here.
Thise been the cokkes wordes, and nat myne ;
I can noon harme of no womman divyne.
  Faire in the sond, to bathe hire merily, 447
Lyth Pertelote, and alle hir sustres by,
Agayn the sonne ; and Chauntecleer so free
Song merier than the mermayde in the see ;
For Phisiologus seith sikerly,   451
How that they singen wel and merily.
And so bifel, that as he caste his yë,
Among the wortes, on a boterflye,
He was war of this fox that lay ful lowe. 455
No-thing ne liste him thanne for to crowe,
But cryde anon, 'cok, cok,' and up he sterte,
As man that was affrayèd in his herte.
For naturelly a beest desyreth flee
Fro his contrarie, if he may it see,   460
Though he never erst had seyn it with his
   yë.

  This Chauntecleer, whan he gan him espye,
He wolde han fled, but that the fox anon
Seyde. 'Gentil sire, allas! wher wol ye gon?
Be ye affrayed of me that am your freend ?
Now certes, I were worse than a feend,   466
If I to yow wolde harm or vileinye.
I am nat come your counseil for tespye ;
But trewely, the cause of my cominge
Was only for to herkne how that ye singe.
For trewely ye have as mery a stevene,   471
As eny aungel hath, that is in hevene ;
Therwith ye han in musik more felinge
Than hadde Boece, or any that can singe.
My lord your fader (God his soule blesse !)
And eek your moder, of hir gentilesse,   476
Han in myn hous y-been, to my gret ese ;
And certes, sire, ful fayn wolde I yow plese.
But for men speke of singing, I wol saye,
So mote I brouke wel myn eyen tweye,   480
Save yow, I herde nevere man so singe,
As dide your fader in the morweninge ;
Certes, it was of herte, al that he song.
And for to make his voys the more strong,
He wolde so peyne him, that with both his
   yën   485
He moste winke, so loude he wolde cryen,
And stonden on his tiptoon therwithal,
And strecche forth his nekke long and smal.
And eek he was of swich discrecioun,
That ther nas no man in no regioun   490
That him in song or wisdom mighte passe.
I have weel rad in daun Burnel the Asse,
Among his vers, how that ther was a cok,
For that a prestes sone yaf him a knok
Upon his leg, whyl he was yong and nyce,
He made him for to lese his benefyce.   496
But certeyn, ther nis no comparisoun
Bitwix the wisdom and discrecioun
Of your fader, and of his subtiltee.
Now singeth, sire, for seinte charitee,   500
Let se, conne ye your fader countrefete ?'
This Chauntecleer his winges gan to bete,
As man that coude his tresoun nat espye,
So was he ravisshed with his flaterye.
  Allas ! ye lordes, many a fals flatour   505
Is in your courtes, and many a losengeour,
That plesen yow wel more, by my feith,
Than he that soothfastnesse unto yow seith.
Redeth Ecclesiaste of flaterye ;
Beth war, ye lordes, of hir trecherye.   510
  This Chauntecleer stood hye up-on his
   toos,
Strecching his nekke, and held his eyen cloos,
And gan to crowe loude for the nones ;
And daun Russel the fox sterte up at ones,
And by the gargat hente Chauntecleer,   515
And on his bak toward the wode him beer,

For yet ne was ther no man that him sewèd.
O destinee, that mayst nat ben eschewèd!
Allas, that Chauntecleer fleigh fro the bemes!
Allas, his wyf ne roghte nat of dremes! 520
And on a Friday fil al this meschaunce.
O Venus, that art goddesse of plesaunce,
Sin that thy servant was this Chauntecleer,
And in thy service dide al his poweer,
More for delyt, than world to multiplye, 525
Why woldestow suffre him on thy day to dye?
O Gaufred, dere mayster soverayn,
That, whan thy worthy king Richard was slayn
With shot, compleynedest his deth so sore,
Why ne hadde I now thy sentence and thy lore, 530
The Friday for to chide, as diden ye?
(For on a Friday soothly slayn was he.)
Than wolde I shewe yow how that I coude pleyne
For Chauntecleres drede, and for his peyne.
Certes, swich cry ne lamentacioun 535
Was nevere of ladies maad, whan Ilioun
Was wonne, and Pirrus with his streite swerd,
Whan he hadde hent king Priam by the berd,
And slayn him (as saith us *Eneydos*),
As maden alle the hennes in the clos, 540
Whan they had seyn of Chauntecleer the sighte.
But sovereynly dame Pertelote shrighte,
Ful louder than dide Hasdrubales wyf,
Whan that hir housbond hadde lost his lyf,
And that the Romayns hadde brend Cartage,
She was so ful of torment and of rage, 546
That wilfully into the fyr she sterte,
And brende hir-selven with a stedfast herte.
O woful hennes, right so cryden ye,
As, whan that Nero brende the citee 550
Of Rome, cryden senatoures wyves,
For that hir housbondes losten alle hir lyves;
Withouten gilt this Nero hath hem slayn.
Now wol I torne to my tale agayn:
  This sely widwe, and eek hir doghtres two,
Herden thise hennes crye and maken wo, 556
And out at dores sterten thay anoon,
And syen the fox toward the grove goon,
And bar upon his bak the cok away;
And cryden, 'Out! harrow! and weylaway!
Ha, ha, the fox!' and after him they ran,
And eek with staves many another man; 562
Ran Colle our dogge, and Talbot, and Gerland,
And Malkin, with a distaf in hir hand; 564
Ran cow and calf, and eek the verray hogges

So were they fered for berking of the dogges
And shouting of the men and wimmen eke,
They ronne so, hem thoughte hir herte breke.
They yelleden as feendes doon in helle;
The dokes cryden as men wolde hem quelle;
The gees for fere flowen over the trees; 571
Out of the hyve cam the swarm of bees;
So hidous was the noyse, a! *benedicite!*
Certes, he Iakke Straw, and his meynee,
Ne maden nevere shoutes half so shrille, 575
Whan that they wolden any Fleming kille,
As thilke day was maad upon the fox.
Of bras thay broghten bemes, and of box,
Of horn, of boon, in whiche they blewe and poupèd,
And therwithal thay shrykèd and they houpèd; 580
It semèd as that hevene sholde falle.
Now, gode men, I pray yow herkneth alle!
Lo, how fortune turneth sodeinly
The hope and pryde eek of hir enemy!
This cok, that lay upon the foxes bak, 585
In al his drede, un-to the fox he spak,
And seyde, 'Sire, if that I were as ye,
Yet sholde I seyn (as wis God helpe me),
"Turneth agayn, ye proude cherles alle!
A verray pestilence up-on yow falle! 590
Now am I come un-to this wodes syde,
Maugree your heed, the cok shal heer abyde;
I wol him ete in feith, and that anon."'
The fox answerde, 'In feith, it shal be don,'
And as he spak that word, al sodeinly 595
This cok brak from his mouth deliverly,
And heighe up-on a tree he fleigh anon.
And whan the fox saugh that he was y-gon,
'Allas!' quod he, 'O Chauntecleer, allas!
I have to yow,' quod he, 'y-doon trespas,
In-as-muche as I makèd yow aferd, 601
Whan I yow hente, and broghte out of the yerd;
But, sire, I dide it in no wikke entente;
Com doun, and I shal telle yow what I mente.
I shal seye sooth to yow, God help me so.'
'Nay than,' quod he, 'I shrewe us bothe two,
And first I shrewe my-self, bothe blood and bones, 607
If thou bigyle me ofter than ones.
Thou shalt namore, thurgh thy flaterye
Do me to singe and winke with myn yë. 610
For he that winketh, whan he sholde see,
Al wilfully, God lat him never thee!'
'Nay,' quod the fox, 'but God yive him meschaunce,
That is so undiscreet of governaunce,
That iangleth whan he sholde holde his pees.'

Lo, swich it is for to be recchelees, 616
And necligent, and truste on flaterye.
But ye that holden this tale a folye,
As of a fox, or of a cok and hen,
Taketh the moralitee, good men. 620
For seint Paul seith, that al that writen is,
To our doctryne it is y-write, y-wis.
Taketh the fruyt, and lat the chaf be stille.
Now, gode God, if that it be thy wille, 624
As seith my lord, so make us alle good men;
And bringe us to his heighe blisse. Amen.

CHAUCERS WORDES UNTO ADAM HIS OWNE SCRIVEYN

Adam scriveyn, if ever it thee bifalle
Boece or Troilus to wryten newe,
Under thy lokkes thou most have the scalle,
But after my making thou wryte trewe.
So ofte a daye I mot thy werk renewe, 5
Hit to correcte and eek to rubbe and scrape;
And al is through thy negligence and rape.

LAK OF STEDFASTNESSE

BALADE

Som tyme this world was so stedfast and
stable
That mannes word was obligacioun,
And now hit is so fals and deceivable,
That word and deed, as in conclusioun,
Ben no-thing lyk, for turnèd up so doun 5
Is al this world for mede and wilfulnesse,
That al is lost, for lak of stedfastnesse.

What maketh this world to be so variable
But lust that folk have in dissensioun?
Among us now a man is holde unable, 10
But-if he can, by som collusioun,
Don his neighbour wrong or oppressioun.
What causeth this, but wilful wrecchednesse,
That al is lost, for lak of stedfastnesse?

Trouthe is put doun, resoun is holden
fable; 15
Vertu hath now no dominacioun,
Pitee exyled, no man is merciable.
Through covetyse is blent discrecioun;

The world hath mad a permutacioun
Fro right to wrong, fro trouthe to fikelnesse,
That al is lost, for lak of stedfastnesse. 21

Lenvoy to King Richard

O prince, desyre to be honourable,
Cherish thy folk and hate extorcioun!
Suffre no thing, that may be reprevable 25
To thyn estat, don in thy regioun.
Shew forth thy swerd of castigacioun,
Dred God, do law, love trouthe and worthi-
nesse,
And wed thy folk agein to stedfastnesse.

THE COMPLEINT OF CHAUCER TO HIS EMPTY PURSE

To you, my purse, and to non other wight
Compleyne I, for ye be my lady dere!
I am so sory, now that ye be light;
For certes, but ye make me hevy chere,
Me were as leef be leyd up-on my bere; 5
For whiche un-to your mercy thus I crye:
Beth hevy ageyn, or elles mot I dye!

Now voucheth sauf this day, or hit be night,
That I of you the blisful soun may here,
Or see your colour lyk the sonne bright, 10
That of yelownesse hadde never pere.
Ye be my lyf, ye be myn hertes stere,
Quene of comfort and of good companye:
Beth hevy ageyn, or elles mot I dye!

Now purs, that be to me my lyves light, 15
And saveour, as doun in this world here,
Out of this toune help me through your
might,
Sin that ye wole nat been my tresorere;
For I am shave as nye as any frere.
But yit I pray un-to your curtesye: 20
Beth hevy ageyn, or elles mot I dye!

Lenvoy de Chaucer

O conquerour of Brutes Albioun!
Which that by lyne and free eleccioun
Ben verray king, this song to you I sende;
And ye, that mowen al our harm amende, 26
Have minde up-on my supplicacioun!

SIR THOMAS MALORY (c. 1400–1471)

Concerning the life of the author of the *Morte d'Arthur* little is known. He was born about the year 1400, lived at Newbold Revell, was knighted, and represented Warwickshire in parliament in 1445. He was 'a gentleman of an ancient house and a soldier,' belonging to the most highly cultivated society of his day. Malory was prominent on the Lancastrian side in the Wars of the Roses, and his military service extended to France, where he was associated with Richard Beauchamp, Earl of Warwick, a knight distinguished throughout Europe as the embodiment of the chivalric ideal and as 'the father of courtesy.' Certain of the Earl of Warwick's exploits provide a rapid and highly colored narrative not unlike that of the *Morte d'Arthur* itself. It would seem, then, that Sir Thomas Malory was in every way endowed for composing the chivalric compilation by which he is now chiefly known.

William Caxton (c. 1422–1491) deserves a place by the side of Malory in the literary history of the fifteenth century not only because he edited and published the *Morte d'Arthur*, but also because he brought into print numerous other works of romance. After a considerable period of activity as a merchant, Caxton began his career as printer, translator, and editor by issuing at Bruges, about 1475, the first book printed in English, *The Recuyell of the Histories of Troy*. Caxton translated this work himself, from the French of Raoul le Fevre. In 1476 he returned to England, and set up his press in Westminster, where he finished printing, on November 18, 1477, *The Dictes and Sayings of the Philosophers*, the first dated book issued in England. From his press in Westminster, Caxton issued some seventy-one separate works, of which Malory's *Morte d'Arthur* was the fifty-second.

LE MORTE D'ARTHUR

PREFACE OF WILLIAM CAXTON

After that I had accomplished and finished divers histories, as well of contemplation as of other historical and worldly acts of great conquerors and princes, and also certain books of ensamples and doctrine, many noble and divers gentlemen of this realm of England came and demanded me, many and ofttimes, wherefore that I have not do made and enprint the noble history of the Sangreal, and of the most renowned christian king, first and chief of the three best christian and worthy, King Arthur, which ought most to be remembered among us Englishmen to-fore all other christian kings. For it is notoriously known through the universal world that there be nine worthy and the best that ever were. That is to wit three paynims, three Jews, and three christian men. As for the paynims they were to-fore the Incarnation of Christ, which were named, the first, Hector of Troy, of whom the history is come both in ballad and in prose; the second, Alexander the Great; and the third, Julius Cæsar, Emperor of Rome, of whom the histories be well known and had. And as for the three Jews which also were to-fore the Incarnation of our Lord, of whom the first was Duke Joshua which brought the children of Israel into the land of behest; the second, David, King of Jerusalem; and the third, Judas Maccabæus: of these three the Bible rehearseth all their noble histories and acts. And since the said Incarnation have been three noble christian men stalled and admitted through the universal world into the number of the nine best and worthy, of whom was first the noble Arthur, whose noble acts I purpose to write in this present book here following. The second was Charlemagne, or Charles the Great, of whom the history is had in many places, both in French and English; and the third and last was Godfrey of Boloine, of whose acts and life I made a book unto the excellent prince and king of noble memory, King Edward the Fourth. The said noble gentlemen instantly required me to enprint the history of the said noble king and conqueror, King Arthur, and of his knights, with the history of the Sangreal, and of the death and ending of the said Arthur; affirming that I ought rather to enprint his acts and noble 5 feats, than of Godfrey of Boloine, or any of the other eight, considering that he was a man born within this realm, and king and emperor of the same; and that there be in French divers and many noble vol- 10 umes of his acts, and also of his knights. To whom I answered, that divers men hold opinion that there was no such Arthur, and that all such books as been made of him be feigned and fables, because that 15 some chronicles make of him no mention, nor remember him no thing, nor of his knights. Whereto they answered, and one in special said, that in him that should say or think that there was never such a 20 king called Arthur, might well be aretted great folly and blindness; for he said that there were many evidences of the contrary: first ye may see his sepulture in the monastery of Glastonbury. And also in 25 *Polichronicon,* in the fifth book the sixth chapter, and in the seventh book the twenty-third chapter, where his body was buried, and after found, and translated into the said monastery. Ye shall see 30 also in the history of Bochas, in his book *De Casu Principum,* part of his noble acts, and also of his fall. Also Galfridus in his British book recounteth his life; and in divers places of England many remem- 35 brances be yet of him and shall remain perpetually, and also of his knights. First in the Abbey of Westminster, at Saint Edward's shrine, remaineth the print of his seal in red wax closed in beryl, in 40 which is written *Patricius Arthurus, Britannie, Gallie, Germanie, Dacie, Imperator.* Item in the castle of Dover ye may see Gawaine's skull and Craddock's mantle: at Winchester the Round Table: in other 45 places Launcelot's sword and many other things. Then all these things considered, there can no man reasonably gainsay but there was a king of this land named Arthur. For in all places, christian and 50 heathen, he is reputed and taken for one of the nine worthy, and the first of the three christian men. And also he is more spoken of beyond the sea, more books made of his noble acts, than there be in 55 England, as well in Dutch, Italian, Spanish, and Greek, as in French. And yet of record remain in witness of him in Wales,

in the town of Camelot, the great stones and marvelous works of iron, lying under the ground, and royal vaults, which divers now living have seen. Wherefore it is a marvel why he is no more renowned in his own country, save only it accordeth to the Word of God, which saith that no man is accept for a prophet in his own country.

Then all these things foresaid alleged, I could not well deny but that there was such a noble king named Arthur, and reputed one of the nine worthy, and first and chief of the christian men; and many noble volumes be made of him and of his noble knights in French, which I have seen and read beyond the sea, which be not had in our maternal tongue, but in Welsh be many and also in French, and some in English, but nowhere nigh all. Wherefore, such as have late been drawn out briefly into English I have after the simple conning that God hath sent to me, under the favor and correction of all noble lords and gentlemen, emprised to enprint a book of the noble histories of the said King Arthur, and of certain of his knights, after a copy unto me delivered, which copy Sir Thomas Malory did take out of certain books of French, and reduced it into English. And I, according to my copy, have done set it in enprint, to the intent that noble men may see and learn the noble acts of chivalry, the gentle and virtuous deeds that some knights used in those days, by which they came to honor; and how they that were vicious were punished and oft put to shame and rebuke; humbly beseeching all noble lords and ladies, with all other estates, of what estate or degree they been of, that shall see and read in this said book and work, that they take the good and honest acts in their remembrance, and to follow the same. Wherein they shall find many joyous and pleasant histories, and noble and renowned acts of humanity, gentleness, and chivalries. For herein may be seen noble chivalry, courtesy, humanity, friendliness, hardiness, love, friendship, cowardice, murder, hate, virtue, and sin. Do after the good and leave the evil, and it shall bring you to good fame and renown. And for to pass the time this book shall be pleasant to read in; but for to give faith and belief that all is true that is contained herein, ye be at your liberty: but all is written for our doctrine, and for to beware that we fall not to vice nor sin; but to exercise and follow virtue; by which we may come and attain to good fame and renown in this life, and after this short and transitory life, to come unto 5 everlasting bliss in heaven, the which he grant us that reigneth in heaven, the blessed Trinity. Amen.

Then to proceed forth in this said book, which I direct unto all noble princes, lords, 10 and ladies, gentlemen or gentlewomen, that desire to read or hear read of the noble and joyous history of the great conqueror and excellent king, King Arthur, sometime king of this noble realm, then 15 called Britain. I, William Caxton, simple person, present this book following, which I have emprised to enprint; and treateth of the noble acts, feats of arms of chivalry, prowess, hardiness, humanity, 20 love, courtesy and very gentleness, with many wonderful histories and adventures. And for to understand briefly the content of this volume, I have divided it into twenty-one books, and every book chap- 25 tered as hereafter shall by God's grace follow. The first book shall treat how Uther Pendragon gat the noble conqueror King Arthur, and containeth twenty-eight chapters. The second book treateth of 30 Balin the noble knight, and containeth nineteen chapters. The third book treateth of the marriage of King Arthur to Queen Guenever, with other matters, and containeth fifteen chapters. The fourth 35 book, how Merlin was assotted, and of war made to King Arthur, and containeth twenty-nine chapters. The fifth book treateth of the conquest of Lucius the emperor, and containeth twelve chapters. 40 The sixth book treateth of Sir Launcelot and Sir Lionel, and marvelous adventures, and containeth eighteen chapters. The seventh book treateth of a noble knight called Sir Gareth, and named by 45 Sir Kay, Beaumains, and containeth thirty-six chapters. The eighth book treateth of the birth of Sir Tristram the noble knight, and of his acts, and containeth forty-one chapters. The ninth book treat- 50 eth of a knight named by Sir Kay, Le Cote Male Taille, and also of Sir Tristram, and containeth forty-four chapters. The tenth book treateth of Sir Tristram and other marvelous adventures, and 55 containeth eighty-eight chapters. The eleventh book treateth of Sir Launcelot and Sir Galahad, and containeth four-

teen chapters. The twelfth book treateth of Sir Launcelot and his madness, and containeth fourteen chapters. The thirteenth book treateth how Galahad came first to King Arthur's court, and the quest how the Sangreal was begun, and containeth twenty chapters. The fourteenth book treateth of the quest of the Sangreal, and containeth ten chapters. The fifteenth book treateth of Sir Launcelot, and containeth six chapters. The sixteenth book treateth of Sir Bors and Sir Lionel his brother, and containeth seventeen chapters. The seventeenth book treateth of the Sangreal, and containeth twenty-three chapters. The eighteenth book treateth of Sir Launcelot and the queen, and containeth twenty-five chapters. The nineteenth book treateth of Queen Guenever and Launcelot, and containeth thirteen chapters. The twentieth book treateth of the piteous death of Arthur, and containeth twenty-two chapters. The twenty-first book treateth of his last departing, and how Sir Launcelot came to revenge his death, and containeth thirteen chapters. The sum is twenty-one books, which contain the sum of five hundred and seven chapters, as more plainly shall follow hereafter.

* * *

BOOK XXI

CHAPTER I

HOW SIR MORDRED PRESUMED AND TOOK ON HIM TO BE KING OF ENGLAND, AND WOULD HAVE MARRIED THE QUEEN, HIS UNCLE'S WIFE

As Sir Mordred was ruler of all England, he did do make letters as though that they came from beyond the sea, and the letters specified that King Arthur was slain in battle with Sir Launcelot. Wherefore Sir Mordred made a parliament, and called the lords together, and there he made them to choose him king; and so was he crowned at Canterbury, and held a feast there fifteen days; and afterward he drew him unto Winchester, and there he took the Queen Guenever, and said plainly that he would wed her which was his uncle's wife and his father's wife. And so he made ready for the feast, and a day prefixed that they should be wedded; wherefore Queen Guenever was passing heavy. But she durst not discover her heart, but spake fair, and agreed to Sir Mordred's will. Then she desired of Sir Mordred for to go to London, to buy all manner of things that longed unto the wedding. And because of her fair speech, Sir Mordred trusted her well enough, and gave her leave to go. And so when she came to London, she took the Tower of London, and suddenly in all haste possible she stuffed it with all manner of victual, and well garnished it with men, and so kept it. Then when Sir Mordred wist and understood how he was beguiled, he was passing wroth out of measure. And a short tale for to make, he went and laid a mighty siege about the Tower of London, and made many great assaults thereat, and threw many great engines unto them, and shot great guns. But all might not prevail Sir Mordred, for Queen Guenever would never for fair speech nor for foul, would never trust to come in his hands again. Then came the Bishop of Canterbury, the which was a noble clerk and an holy man, and thus he said to Sir Mordred: 'Sir, what will ye do? will ye first displease God and sithen shame yourself, and all knighthood? Is not King Arthur your uncle, no farther but your mother's brother, and on her himself King Arthur begat you upon his own sister, therefore how may you wed your father's wife? Sir,' said the noble clerk, 'leave this opinion or I shall curse you with book and bell and candle.' 'Do thou thy worst,' said Sir Mordred, 'wit thou well I shall defy thee.' 'Sir,' said the bishop, 'and wit you well I shall not fear me to do that me ought to do. Also where ye noise where my lord Arthur is slain, and that is not so, and therefore ye will make a foul work in this land.' 'Peace, thou false priest,' said Sir Mordred, 'for an thou chafe me any more, I shall make strike off thy head.' So the bishop departed and did the cursing in the most orgulist wise that might be done. And then Sir Mordred sought the Bishop of Canterbury, for to have slain him. Then the bishop fled, and took part of his goods with him, and went nigh unto Glastonbury; and there he was as priest hermit in a chapel, and lived in poverty and in holy prayers, for well he understood that mischievous war was at hand. Then Sir Mordred sought on Queen Guenever by letters and sonds, and by fair means and foul means, for to have her to come out of the Tower of London; but all this availed not, for she answered him shortly, openly and privily, that she had liefer slay herself than to be married with him. Then came word to Sir Mordred that King Arthur had araised the siege for Sir Launcelot, and he was coming homeward with a great host, to be avenged upon Sir Mordred; wherefore Sir Mordred made write writs to all the barony of this land, and much people drew to him. For then was the common voice among them that with Arthur was none other life but war and strife, and with Sir Mordred was great joy and bliss. Thus was Sir Arthur depraved and evil said of. And many there were that King Arthur had made up of naught, and given them lands, might not then say him a good word. Lo ye all Englishmen, see ye not what a mischief here was! for he that was the most king and knight of the world, and most loved the fellowship of noble knights, and by him they were all upholden, now might not these Englishmen hold them content with him. Lo thus was the old custom and usage of this land; and also men say that we of this land have not yet lost nor forgotten that custom and usage. Alas, this is a great default of us Englishmen, for there may no thing please us no term. And so fared the people at that time, they were better pleased with Sir Mordred than they were with King Arthur; and much people drew unto Sir Mordred, and said they would abide with him for better and for worse. And so Sir Mordred drew with a great host to Dover, for there he heard say that Sir Arthur would arrive, and so he thought to beat his own father from his lands; and the most part of all England held with Sir Mordred, the people were so new-fangle.

CHAPTER II

HOW AFTER THAT KING ARTHUR HAD TIDINGS, HE RETURNED AND CAME TO DOVER, WHERE SIR MORDRED MET HIM TO LET HIS LANDING; AND OF THE DEATH OF SIR GAWAINE

And so as Sir Mordred was at Dover with his host, there came King Arthur with a great navy of ships, and galleys, and carracks. And there was Sir Mordred ready awaiting upon his landing, to let his own father to land upon the land that he was king over. Then there was launching of great boats and small, and full of noble men of arms; and there was much slaughter of gentle knights, and many a full bold baron was laid full low, on both parties. But King Arthur was so courageous that there might no manner of knights let him to land, and his knights fiercely followed him; and so they landed maugre Sir Mordred and all his power, and put Sir Mordred aback, that he fled and all his people.

So when this battle was done, King Arthur let bury his people that were dead. And then was noble Sir Gawaine found in a great boat, lying more than half dead. When Sir Arthur wist that Sir Gawaine was laid so low, he went unto him; and there the king made sorrow out of measure, and took Sir Gawaine in his arms, and thrice he there swooned. And then when he awaked, he said: 'Alas, Sir Gawaine, my sister's son, here now thou liest, the man in the world that I loved most; and now is my joy gone, for now, my nephew Sir Gawaine, I will discover me unto your person: in Sir Launcelot and you I most had my joy, and mine affiance, and now have I lost my joy of you both; wherefore all mine earthly joy is gone from me.' 'Mine uncle King Arthur,' said Sir Gawaine, 'wit you well my death-day is come, and all is through mine own hastiness and wilfulness; for I am smitten upon the old wound the which Sir Launcelot gave me, on the which I feel well I must die; and had Sir Launcelot been with you as he was, this unhappy war had never begun; and of all this am I causer, for Sir Launcelot and his blood, through their prowess, held all your cankered enemies in subjection and danger. And now,' said Sir Gawaine, 'ye shall miss Sir Launcelot. But, alas, I would not accord with him, and therefore,' said Sir Gawaine, 'I pray you, fair uncle, that I may have paper, pen, and ink, that I may write to Sir Launcelot a cedle with mine own hands.' And then when paper and ink was brought, then Gawaine was set up weakly by King Arthur, for he was shriven a little to-fore; and then he wrote thus, as the French book maketh mention: 'Unto Sir Launcelot, flower of all noble knights that ever I heard of or saw by my days,

I, Sir Gawaine, King Lot's son of Orkney, sister's son unto the noble King Arthur, send thee greeting, and let thee have knowledge that the tenth day of May I was smitten upon the old wound that thou gavest me afore the city of Benwick, and through the same wound that thou gavest me I am come to my death-day. And I will that all the world wit, that I, Sir Gawaine, knight of the Table Round, sought my death, and not through thy deserving, but it was mine own seeking; wherefore I beseech thee, Sir Launcelot, to return again unto this realm, and see my tomb, and pray some prayer, more or less, for my soul. And this same day that I wrote this cedle, I was hurt to the death in the same wound, the which I had of thy hand, Sir Launcelot; for of a more nobler man might I not be slain. Also, Sir Launcelot, for all the love that ever was betwixt us, make no tarrying, but come over the sea in all haste, that thou mayest with thy noble knights rescue that noble king that made thee knight, that is my lord Arthur; for he is full straitly bestead with a false traitor, that is my half-brother, Sir Mordred; and he hath let crown him king, and would have wedded my lady Queen Guenever, and so had he done had she not put herself in the Tower of London. And so the tenth day of May last past, my lord Arthur and we all landed upon them at Dover; and there we put that false traitor, Sir Mordred, to flight, and there it misfortuned me to be stricken upon thy stroke. And at the date of this letter was written, but two hours and a half afore my death, written with mine own hand, and so subscribed with part of my heart's blood. And I require thee, most famous knight of the world, that thou wilt see my tomb.' And then Sir Gawaine wept, and King Arthur wept; and then they swooned both. And when they awaked both, the king made Sir Gawaine to receive his Saviour. And then Sir Gawaine prayed the king for to send for Sir Launcelot, and to cherish him above all other knights. And so at the hour of noon Sir Gawaine yielded up the spirit; and then the king let inter him in a chapel within Dover Castle; and there yet all men may see the skull of him, and the same wound is seen that Sir Launcelot gave him in battle. Then was it told the king that Sir Mordred had pight a new field upon Barham Down. And upon the morn the king rode thither to him, and there was a great battle betwixt them, and much people was slain on both parties; but at the last, Sir Arthur's party stood best, and Sir Mordred and his party fled unto Canterbury.

CHAPTER III

HOW AFTER, SIR GAWAINE'S GHOST APPEARED TO KING ARTHUR, AND WARNED HIM THAT HE SHOULD NOT FIGHT THAT DAY

And then the king let search all the towns for his knights that were slain, and interred them; and salved them with soft salves that so sore were wounded. Then much people drew unto King Arthur. And then they said that Sir Mordred warred upon King Arthur with wrong. And then King Arthur drew him with his host down by the seaside westward toward Salisbury; and there was a day assigned betwixt King Arthur and Sir Mordred, that they should meet upon a down beside Salisbury, and not far from the seaside; and this day was assigned on a Monday after Trinity Sunday, whereof King Arthur was passing glad, that he might be avenged upon Sir Mordred. Then Sir Mordred araised much people about London, for they of Kent, Southsex, and Surrey, Estsex, and of Southfolk, and of Northfolk, held the most part with Sir Mordred; and many a full noble knight drew unto Sir Mordred and to the king: but they that loved Sir Launcelot drew unto Sir Mordred.

So upon Trinity Sunday at night, King Arthur dreamed a wonderful dream, and that was this: that him seemed he sat upon a chaflet in a chair, and the chair was fast to a wheel, and thereupon sat King Arthur in the richest cloth of gold that might be made; and the king thought there was under him, far from him, an hideous deep black water, and therein were all manner of serpents, and worms, and wild beasts, foul and horrible; and suddenly the king thought the wheel turned up-so-down, and he fell among the serpents and every beast took him by a limb; and then the king cried as he lay on his bed and slept: 'Help!' And then knights, squires, and yeomen,

awaked the king; and then he was so amazed that he wist not where he was; and then he fell a-slumbering again, not sleeping nor thoroughly waking. So the king seemed verily that there came Sir Gawaine unto him with a number of fair ladies with him. And when King Arthur saw him, then he said: 'Welcome, my sister's son; I weened thou hadst been dead, and now I see thee alive, much am I beholding unto almighty Jesu. O fair nephew and my sister's son, what be these ladies that hither be come with you?' 'Sir,' said Sir Gawaine, 'all these be ladies for whom I have foughten when I was man living, and all these are those that I did battle for in righteous quarrel; and God hath given them that grace at their great prayer, because I did battle for them, that they should bring me hither unto you: thus much hath God given me leave, for to warn you of your death; for an ye fight as to-morn with Sir Mordred, as ye both have assigned, doubt ye not ye must be slain, and the most part of your people on both parties. And for the great grace and goodness that Almighty Jesu hath unto you, and for pity of you, and many more other good men there shall be slain, God hath sent me to you of his special grace, to give you warning that in no wise ye do battle as to-morn, but that ye take a treaty for a month day; and proffer you largely, so as to-morn to be put in a delay. For within a month shall come Sir Launcelot with all his noble knights, and rescue you worshipfully, and slay Sir Mordred, and all that ever will hold with him.' Then Sir Gawaine and all the ladies vanished.

And anon the king called upon his knights, squires, and yeomen, and charged them wightly to fetch his noble lords and wise bishops unto him. And when they were come, the king told them his avision, what Sir Gawaine had told him, and warned him that if he fought on the morn he should be slain. Then the king commanded Sir Lucan the Butler, and his brother Sir Bedivere, with two bishops with them, and charged them in any wise, an they might, 'Take a treaty for a month day with Sir Mordred, and spare not, proffer him lands and goods as much as ye think best.' So then they departed, and came to Sir Mordred, where he had a grim host of an hundred thousand men. And there they entreated Sir Mordred long time; and at the last Sir Mordred was agreed for to have Cornwall and Kent, by Arthur's days: after, all England, after the days of King Arthur.

CHAPTER IV

HOW BY MISADVENTURE OF AN ADDER THE BATTLE BEGAN, WHERE MORDRED WAS SLAIN, AND ARTHUR HURT TO THE DEATH

Then were they condescended that King Arthur and Sir Mordred should meet betwixt both their hosts, and everych of them should bring fourteen persons; and they came with this word unto Arthur. Then said he: 'I am glad that this is done:' and so he went into the field. And when Arthur should depart, he warned all his host that an they see any sword drawn: 'Look ye come on fiercely, and slay that traitor, Sir Mordred, for I in no wise trust him.' In like wise Sir Mordred warned his host that: 'An ye see any sword drawn, look that ye come on fiercely, and so slay all that ever before you standeth; for in no wise I will not trust for this treaty, for I know well my father will be avenged on me.' And so they met as their appointment was, and so they were agreed and accorded thoroughly; and wine was fetched, and they drank. Right soon came an adder out of a little heath bush, and it stung a knight on the foot. And when the knight felt him stung, he looked down and saw the adder, and then he drew his sword to slay the adder, and thought of none other harm. And when the host on both parties saw that sword drawn, then they blew beams, trumpets, and horns, and shouted grimly. And so both hosts dressed them together. And King Arthur took his horse, and said: 'Alas, this unhappy day!' and so rode to his party. And Sir Mordred in like wise. And never was there seen a more dolefuller battle in no christian land; for there was but rushing and riding, foining and striking, and many a grim word was there spoken either to other, and many a deadly stroke. But ever King Arthur rode throughout the battle of Sir Mordred many times, and did full nobly as a noble king should, and at all times he fainted never; and Sir Mordred that day put him

in devoir, and in great peril. And thus they fought all the long day, and never stinted till the noble knights were laid to the cold earth; and ever they fought still till it was near night, and by that time was there an hundred thousand laid dead upon the down. Then was Arthur wood wroth out of measure, when he saw his people so slain from him.

Then the king looked about him, and then was he ware, of all his host and of all his good knights, were left no more alive but two knights; that one was Sir Lucan the Butler, and his brother Sir Bedivere, and they were full sore wounded. 'Jesu mercy,' said the king, 'where are all my noble knights become? Alas that ever I should see this doleful day, for now,' said Arthur, 'I am come to mine end. But would to God that I wist where were that traitor Sir Mordred, that hath caused all this mischief.' Then was King Arthur ware where Sir Mordred leaned upon his sword among a great heap of dead men. 'Now give me my spear,' said Arthur unto Sir Lucan, 'for yonder I have espied the traitor that all this woe hath wrought.' 'Sir, let him be,' said Sir Lucan, 'for he is unhappy; and if ye pass this unhappy day, ye shall be right well revenged upon him. Good lord, remember ye of your night's dream, and what the spirit of Sir Gawaine told you this night, yet God of his great goodness hath preserved you hitherto. Therefore, for God's sake, my lord, leave off by this, for, blessed be God, ye have won the field, for here we be three alive, and with Sir Mordred is none alive; and if ye leave off now, this wicked day of destiny is past.' 'Tide me death, betide me life,' saith the king, 'now I see him yonder alone he shall never escape mine hands, for at a better avail shall I never have him.' 'God speed you well,' said Sir Bedivere.

Then the king gat his spear in both his hands, and ran toward Sir Mordred, crying: 'Traitor, now is thy death-day come.' And when Sir Mordred heard Sir Arthur, he ran until him with his sword drawn in his hand. And there King Arthur smote Sir Mordred under the shield, with a foin of his spear, throughout the body, more than a fathom. And when Sir Mordred felt that he had his death wound, he thrust himself with the might that he had up to the bur of King Arthur's spear. And right so he smote his father Arthur, with his sword holden in both his hands, on the side of the head, that the sword pierced the helmet and the brain-pan, and therewithal Sir Mordred 5 fell stark dead to the earth; and the noble Arthur fell in a swoon to the earth, and there he swooned ofttimes. And Sir Lucan the Butler, and Sir Bedivere, ofttimes heaved him up. And so weakly they 10 led him betwixt them both, to a little chapel not far from the seaside. And when the king was there, he thought him well eased.

Then heard they people cry in the field. 15 'Now go, thou, Sir Lucan,' said the king, 'and do me to wit what betokens that noise in the field.' So Sir Lucan departed, for he was grievously wounded in many places. And so as he yede, he saw 20 and hearkened by the moonlight, how that pillers and robbers were come into the field, to pill and to rob many a full noble knight of brooches, and beads, of many a good ring, and of many a rich jewel; 25 and who that were not dead all out, there they slew them for their harness and their riches. When Sir Lucan understood this work, he came to the king as soon as he might, and told him all what he had 30 heard and seen. 'Therefore by my rede,' said Sir Lucan, 'it is best that we bring you to some town.' 'I would it were so,' said the king.

CHAPTER V

HOW KING ARTHUR COMMANDED TO CAST HIS SWORD EXCALIBUR INTO THE WATER, AND HOW HE WAS DELIVERED TO LADIES IN A BARGE

'But I may not stand, mine head works so. Ah, Sir Launcelot,' said King Arthur, 'this day have I sore missed thee: alas, that ever I was against thee, for now 45 have I my death, whereof Sir Gawaine me warned in my dream.' Then Sir Lucan took up the king the one part, and Sir Bedivere the other part, and in the lifting the king swooned; and Sir Lucan 50 fell in a swoon with the lift, that the part of his guts fell out of his body, and therewith the noble knight's heart brast. And when the king awoke, he beheld Sir Lucan, how he lay foaming at the mouth, 55 and part of his guts lay at his feet. 'Alas,' said the king, 'this is to me a full heavy sight, to see this noble duke so die for my sake, for he would have holpen

me, that had more need of help than I. Alas, he would not complain him, his heart was so set to help me: now Jesu have mercy upon his soul!' Then Sir 5 Bedivere wept for the death of his brother. 'Leave this mourning and weeping,' said the king, 'for all this will not avail me, for wit thou well, an I might live myself, the death of Sir Lucan would grieve me 10 evermore; but my time hieth fast,' said the king. 'Therefore,' said Arthur unto Sir Bedivere, 'take thou Excalibur, my good sword, and go with it to yonder waterside, and when thou comest there, I 15 charge thee throw my sword in that water, and come again and tell me what thou there seest.' 'My lord,' said Bedivere, 'your commandment shall be done, and lightly bring you word again.'

So Sir Bedivere departed, and by the 20 way he beheld that noble sword, that the pommel and the haft was all of precious stones; and then he said to himself: 'If I throw this rich sword in the water, 25 thereof shall never come good, but harm and loss.' And then Sir Bedivere hid Excalibur under a tree. And so, as soon as he might, he came again unto the king, and said he had been at the water, and 30 had thrown the sword in the water. 'What saw thou there?' said the king. 'Sir,' he said, 'I saw nothing but waves and winds.' 'That is untruly said of thee,' said the king, 'therefore go thou 35 lightly again, and do my commandment; as thou art to me lief and dear, spare not, but throw it in.' Then Sir Bedivere returned again, and took the sword in his hand; and then him thought sin and shame 40 to throw away that noble sword, and so eft he hid the sword, and returned again, and told to the king that he had been at the water, and done his commandment. 'What saw thou there?' said the king. 45 'Sir,' he said, 'I saw nothing but the waters wap and waves wan.' 'Ah, traitor untrue,' said King Arthur, 'now hast thou betrayed me twice. Who would have weened that, thou that hast been to me so 50 lief and dear? and thou art named a noble knight, and would betray me for the richness of the sword. But now go again lightly, for thy long tarrying putteth me in great jeopardy of my life, for I have 55 taken cold. And but if thou do now as I bid thee, if ever I may see thee, I shall slay thee with mine own hands; for thou wouldst for my rich sword see me dead.' Then Sir Bedivere departed, and went to the sword, and lightly took it up, and went to the waterside; and there he bound the girdle about the hilts, and then he threw the sword as far into the water as he might; and there came an arm and 5 an hand above the water and met it, and caught it, and so shook it thrice and brandished, and then vanished away the hand with the sword in the water. So Sir Bedivere came again to the king, and told 10 him what he saw. 'Alas,' said the king, 'help me hence, for I dread me I have tarried over long.' Then Sir Bedivere took the king upon his back, and so went with him to that water side. And when 15 they were at the water side, even fast by the bank hoved a little barge with many fair ladies in it, and among them all was a queen, and all they had black hoods, and all they wept and shrieked when they saw 20 King Arthur. 'Now put me into the barge,' said the king. And so he did softly; and there received him three queens with great mourning; and so they set them down, and in one of their laps 25 King Arthur laid his head. And then that queen said: 'Ah, dear brother, why have ye tarried so long from me? alas, this wound on your head hath caught over-much cold.' And so then they rowed 30 from the land, and Sir Bedivere beheld all those ladies go from him. Then Sir Bedivere cried: 'Ah, my lord Arthur, what shall become of me, now ye go from me and leave me here alone among mine 35 enemies?' 'Comfort thyself,' said the king, 'and do as well as thou mayest, for in me is no trust for to trust in; for I will into the vale of Avilion to heal me of my grievous wound: and if thou hear 40 never more of me, pray for my soul.' But ever the queens and ladies wept and shrieked, that it was pity to hear. And as soon as Sir Bedivere had lost the sight of the barge, he wept and wailed, and so 45 took the forest; and so he went all that night, and in the morning he was ware betwixt two holts hoar, of a chapel and an hermitage.

CHAPTER VI

HOW SIR BEDIVERE FOUND HIM ON THE MORROW DEAD IN AN HERMITAGE, AND HOW HE ABODE THERE WITH THE HERMIT

Then was Sir Bedivere glad, and thither he went; and when he came into the chapel, he saw where lay an hermit groveling on all four, there fast by a tomb was new graven. When the hermit saw Sir Bedivere he knew him well, for he was but little to-fore Bishop of Canterbury, that Sir Mordred flemed. 'Sir,' said Bedivere, 'what man is there interred that ye pray so fast for?' 'Fair son,' said the hermit, 'I wot not verily, but by deeming. But this night, at midnight, here came a number of ladies, and brought hither a dead corpse, and prayed me to bury him; and here they offered an hundred tapers, and they gave me an hundred besants.' 'Alas,' said Sir Bedivere, 'that was my lord King Arthur, that here lieth buried in this chapel.' Then Sir Bedivere swooned; and when he awoke he prayed the hermit he might abide with him still there, to live with fasting and prayers. 'For from hence will I never go,' said Sir Bedivere, 'by my will, but all the days of my life here to pray for my lord Arthur.' 'Ye are welcome to me,' said the hermit, 'for I know ye better than ye ween that I do. Ye are the bold Bedivere, and the full noble duke, Sir Lucan the Butler, was your brother.' Then Sir Bedivere told the hermit all as ye have heard to-fore. So there bode Sir Bedivere with the hermit that was to-fore Bishop of Canterbury, and there Sir Bedivere put upon him poor clothes, and served the hermit full lowly in fasting and in prayers.

Thus of Arthur I find never more written in books that be authorized, nor more of the very certainty of his death heard I never read, but thus was he led away in a ship wherein were three queens; that one was King Arthur's sister, Queen Morgan le Fay; the other was the Queen of Northgalis; the third was the Queen of the Waste Lands. Also there was Nimue, the chief lady of the lake, that had wedded Pelleas the good knight; and this lady had done much for King Arthur, for she would never suffer Sir Pelleas to be in no place where he should be in danger of his life; and so he lived to the uttermost of his days with her in great rest. More of the death of King Arthur could I never find, but that ladies brought him to his burials; and such one was buried there, that the hermit bare witness that sometime was Bishop of Canterbury, but yet the hermit knew not in certain that he was verily the body of King Arthur: for this tale Sir Bedivere, knight of the Table Round, made it to be written.

CHAPTER VII

OF THE OPINION OF SOME MEN OF THE DEATH OF KING ARTHUR; AND HOW QUEEN GUENEVER MADE HER A NUN IN ALMESBURY

Yet some men say in many parts of England that King Arthur is not dead, but had by the will of our Lord Jesu into another place; and men say that he shall come again, and he shall win the holy cross. I will not say it shall be so, but rather I will say: here in this world he changed his life. But many men say that there is written upon his tomb this verse: *Hic jacet Arthurus, Rex quondam, Rexque futurus* [Here lies Arthur, king once, and king to be]. Thus leave I here Sir Bedivere with the hermit, that dwelled that time in a chapel beside Glastonbury, and there was his hermitage. And so they lived in their prayers, and fastings, and great abstinence.

And when Queen Guenever understood that King Arthur was slain, and all the noble knights, Sir Mordred and all the remnant, then the queen stole away, and five ladies with her, and so she went to Almesbury; and there she let make herself a nun, and ware white clothes and black, and great penance she took, as ever did sinful lady in this land, and never creature could make her merry; but lived in fasting, prayers, and alms-deeds, that all manner of people marveled how virtuously she was changed. Now leave we Queen Guenever in Almesbury, a nun in white clothes and black, and there she was abbess and ruler, as reason would; and turn we from her, and speak we of Sir Launcelot du Lake.

CHAPTER VIII

HOW WHEN SIR LAUNCELOT HEARD OF THE DEATH OF KING ARTHUR, AND OF SIR GAWAINE, AND OTHER MATTERS, HE CAME INTO ENGLAND

And when he heard in his country that Sir Mordred was crowned king in England, and made war against King Arthur, his own father, and would let him to land in his own land; also it was told Sir Launcelot how that Sir Mordred had laid siege about the Tower of London, because the queen would not wed him; then was Sir Launcelot wroth out of measure, and said to his kinsmen: 'Alas, that double traitor Sir Mordred, now me repenteth that ever he escaped my hands, for much shame hath he done unto my lord Arthur; for all I feel by the doleful letter that my lord Sir Gawaine sent me, on whose soul Jesu have mercy, that my lord Arthur is full hard bestead. Alas,' said Sir Launcelot, 'that ever I should live to hear that most noble king that made me knight thus to be overset with his subject in his own realm. And this doleful letter that my lord, Sir Gawaine, hath sent me afore his death, praying me to see his tomb, wit you well his doleful words shall never go from mine heart, for he was a full noble knight as ever was born; and in an unhappy hour was I born that ever I should have that unhap to slay first Sir Gawaine, Sir Gaheris the good knight, and mine own friend Sir Gareth, that full noble knight. Alas, I may say I am unhappy,' said Sir Launcelot, 'that ever I should do thus unhappily, and, 'alas, yet might I never have hap to slay that traitor, Sir Mordred.' 'Leave your complaints,' said Sir Bors, 'and first revenge you of the death of Sir Gawaine; and it will be well done that ye see Sir Gawaine's tomb, and secondly that ye revenge my lord Arthur, and my lady, Queen Guenever.' 'I thank you,' said Sir Launcelot, 'for ever ye will my worship.' Then they made them ready in all the haste that might be, with ships and galleys, with Sir Launcelot and his host to pass into England. And so he passed over the sea till he came to Dover, and there he landed with seven kings, and the number was hideous to behold. Then Sir Launcelot spered of men of Dover where was King Arthur become. Then the people told him how that he was slain, and Sir Mordred and an hundred thousand died on a day; and how Sir Mordred gave King Arthur there the first battle at his landing, and there was good Sir Gawaine slain; and on the morn Sir Mordred fought with the king upon Barham Down, and there the king put Sir Mordred to the worse. 'Alas,' said Sir Launcelot, 'this is the heaviest tidings that ever came to me. Now, fair sirs,' said Sir Launcelot, 'shew me the tomb of Sir Gawaine.' And then certain people of the town brought him into the Castle of Dover, and shewed him the tomb. Then Sir Launcelot kneeled down and wept, and prayed heartily for his soul. And that night he made a dole, and all they that would come had as much flesh, fish, wine and ale, and every man and woman had twelve pence, come who would. Thus with his own hand dealt he this money, in a mourning gown; and ever he wept, and prayed them to pray for the soul of Sir Gawaine. And on the morn all the priests and clerks that might be gotten in the country were there, and sang mass of *Requiem;* and there offered first Sir Launcelot, and he offered an hundred pound; and then the seven kings offered forty pound apiece; and also there was a thousand knights, and each of them offered a pound; and the offering dured from morn till night, and Sir Launcelot lay two nights on his tomb in prayers and weeping. Then on the third day Sir Launcelot called the kings, dukes, earls, barons, and knights, and said thus: 'My fair lords, I thank you all of your coming into this country with me, but we came too late, and that shall repent me while I live, but against death may no man rebel. But sithen it is so,' said Sir Launcelot, 'I will myself ride and seek my lady, Queen Guenever, for as I hear say she hath had great pain and much disease; and I heard say that she is fled into the West. Therefore ye all shall abide me here, and but if I come again within fifteen days, then take your ships and your fellowship, and depart into your country, for I will do as I say to you.'

CHAPTER IX

HOW SIR LAUNCELOT DEPARTED TO SEEK THE QUEEN GUENEVER, AND HOW HE FOUND HER AT ALMESBURY

Then came Sir Bors de Ganis, and said: 'My lord, Sir Launcelot, what think ye for to do, now to ride in this realm? wit ye well ye shall find few friends,' 'Be as be may,' said Sir Launcelot, 'keep you still here, for I will forth on my journey, and no man nor child shall go with me.' So it was no boot to strive, but he departed and rode westerly, and there he sought a seven or eight days; and at the last he came to a nunnery, and then was Queen Guenever ware of Sir Launcelot as he walked in the cloister. And when she saw him there

she swooned thrice, that all the ladies and gentlewomen had work enough to hold the queen up. So when she might speak, she called ladies and gentlewomen to her, and said: 'Ye marvel, fair ladies, why I make this fare. Truly,' she said, 'it is for the sight of yonder knight that yonder standeth; wherefore I pray you all call him to me.' When Sir Launcelot was brought to her, then she said to all the ladies: 'Through this man and me hath all this war been wrought, and the death of the most noblest knights of the world; for through our love that we have loved together is my most noble lord slain. Therefore, Sir Launcelot, wit thou well I am set in such a plight to get my soul-heal; and yet I trust through God's grace that after my death to have a sight of the blessed face of Christ, and at doomsday to sit on his right side, for as sinful as ever I was are saints in heaven. Therefore, Sir Launcelot, I require thee and beseech thee heartily, for all the love that ever was betwixt us, that thou never see me more in the visage; and I command thee, on God's behalf, that thou forsake my company, and to thy kingdom thou turn again, and keep well thy realm from war and wrack; for as well as I have loved thee, mine heart will not serve me to see thee, for through thee and me is the flower of kings and knights destroyed; therefore, Sir Launcelot, go to thy realm, and there take thee a wife, and live with her with joy and bliss; and I pray thee heartily, pray for me to our Lord that I may amend my misliving.' 'Now, sweet madam,' said Sir Launcelot, 'would ye that I should now return again unto my country, and there to wed a lady? Nay, madam, wit you well that shall I never do, for I shall never be so false to you of that I have promised; but the same destiny that ye have taken you to, I will take me unto, for to please Jesu, and ever for you I cast me specially to pray.' 'If thou wilt do so,' said the queen, 'hold thy promise, but I may never believe but that thou wilt turn to the world again.' 'Well, madam,' said he, 'ye say as pleaseth you, yet wist you me never false of my promise, and God defend but I should forsake the world as ye have done. For in the quest of the Sangreal I had forsaken the vanities of the world had not your lord been. And if I had done so at that time, with my heart, will, and thought, I had

passed all the knights that were in the
Sangreal except Sir Galahad, my son.
And therefore, lady, sithen ye have taken
you to perfection, I must needs take me to
perfection, of right. For I take record of
God, in you I have had mine earthly joy;
and if I had found you now so disposed,
I had cast to have had you into mine
own realm.

CHAPTER X

HOW SIR LAUNCELOT CAME TO THE HER-
MITAGE WHERE THE ARCHBISHOP OF
CANTERBURY WAS, AND HOW HE TOOK
THE HABIT ON HIM

'But sithen I find you thus disposed, I
ensure you faithfully, I will ever take me
to penance, and pray while my life last-
eth, if I may find any hermit, either gray
or white, that will receive me. Wherefore, madam, I pray you kiss me and
never no more.' 'Nay,' said the queen,
'that shall I never do, but abstain you
from such works;' and they departed.
But there was never so hard an hearted
man but he would have wept to see the
dolor that they made; for there was lamentation as they had been stung with
spears; and many times they swooned,
and the ladies bare the queen to her chamber.

And Sir Launcelot awoke, and went
and took his horse, and rode all that day
and all night in a forest, weeping. And
at the last he was ware of an hermitage
and a chapel stood betwixt two cliffs; and
then he heard a little bell ring to mass,
and thither he rode and alighted, and tied
his horse to the gate, and heard mass.
And he that sang mass was the Bishop
of Canterbury. Both the bishop and Sir
Bedivere knew Sir Launcelot, and they
spake together after mass. But when Sir
Bedivere had told his tale all whole, Sir
Launcelot's heart almost brast for sorrow,
and Sir Launcelot threw his arms abroad,
and said: 'Alas, who may trust this
world.' And then he kneeled down on
his knee, and prayed the bishop to shrive
him and assoil him. And then he besought the bishop that he might be his
brother. Then the bishop said: 'I will
gladly'; and there he put an habit upon
Sir Launcelot, and there he served God
day and night with prayers and fastings.

Thus the great host abode at Dover.
And then Sir Lionel took fifteen lords
with him, and rode to London to seek Sir
Launcelot; and there Sir Lionel was slain
and many of his lords. Then Sir Bors
de Ganis made the great host for to go
home again; and Sir Bors, Sir Ector de
Maris, Sir Blamore, Sir Bleoberis, with
more other of Sir Launcelot's kin, took on
them to ride all England overthwart and
endlong, to seek Sir Launcelot. So Sir
Bors by fortune rode so long till he came
to the same chapel where Sir Launcelot
was; and so Sir Bors heard a little bell
knell, that rang to mass; and there he
alighted and heard mass. And when
mass was done, the bishop, Sir Launcelot, and Sir Bedivere, came to Sir Bors.
And when Sir Bors saw Sir Launcelot in
that manner clothing, then he prayed the
Bishop that he might be in the same suit.
And so there was an habit put upon him,
and there he lived in prayers and fasting.
And within half a year, there was come Sir
Galihud, Sir Galihodin, Sir Blamore, Sir
Bleoberis, Sir Villiars, Sir Clarras, and
Sir Gahalantine. So all these seven noble knights there abode still. And when
they saw Sir Launcelot had taken him to
such perfection, they had no lust to depart, but took such an habit as he had.
Thus they endured in great penance six
years; and then Sir Launcelot took the
habit of priesthood of the bishop, and a
twelvemonth he sang mass. And there
was none of these other knights but they
read in books, and holp for to sing mass,
and rang bells, and did bodily all manner
of service. And so their horses went
where they would, for they took no regard
of no worldly riches. For when they saw
Sir Launcelot endure such penance, in
prayers, and fastings, they took no force
what pain they endured, for to see the noblest knight of the world take such abstinence that he waxed full lean. And
thus upon a night, there came a vision to
Sir Launcelot, and charged him, in remission of his sins, to haste him unto
Almesbury: 'And by then thou come
there, thou shalt find Queen Guenever
dead. And therefore take thy fellows
with thee, and purvey them of an horse
bier, and fetch thou the corpse of her,
and bury her by her husband, the noble
King Arthur.' So this avision came to
Sir Launcelot thrice in one night.

CHAPTER XI

HOW SIR LAUNCELOT WENT WITH HIS
SEVEN FELLOWS TO ALMESBURY, AND
FOUND THERE QUEEN GUENEVER DEAD,
WHOM THEY BROUGHT TO GLASTONBURY

Then Sir Launcelot rose up or day,
and told the hermit. 'It were well done,'
said the hermit, 'that ye made you ready,
and that you disobey not the avision.'
Then Sir Launcelot took his seven fellows
with him, and on foot they yede from
Glastonbury to Almesbury, the which is
little more than thirty mile. And thither
they came within two days, for they were
weak and feeble to go. And when Sir
Launcelot was come to Almesbury within
the nunnery, Queen Guenever died but
half an hour afore. And the ladies told
Sir Launcelot that Queen Guenever told
them all or she passed, that Sir Launcelot had been priest near a twelvemonth,
'And hither he cometh as fast as he may
to fetch my corpse; and beside my lord,
King Arthur, he shall bury me.' Wherefore the queen said in hearing of them all:
'I beseech Almighty God that I may
never have power to see Sir Launcelot
with my worldly eyes.' 'And thus,' said
all the ladies, 'was ever her prayer these
two days, till she was dead.' Then Sir
Launcelot saw her visage, but he wept
not greatly, but sighed. And so he did all
the observance of the service himself, both
the *Dirige,* and on the morn he sang mass.
And there was ordained an horse bier;
and so with an hundred torches ever brenning about the corpse of the queen, and
ever Sir Launcelot with his seven fellows
went about the horse bier, singing and
reading many an holy orison, and frankincense upon the corpse incensed. Thus
Sir Launcelot and his seven fellows went
on foot from Almesbury unto Glastonbury.
And when they were come to the chapel
and the hermitage, there she had a *Dirige,*
with great devotion. And on the morn,
the hermit that sometime was Bishop of
Canterbury sang the mass of *Requiem*
with great devotion. And Sir Launcelot
was the first that offered, and then also
his seven fellows. And then she was
wrapped in cered cloth of Raines, from
the top to the toe, in thirtyfold; and after
she was put in a web of lead, and then in
a coffin of marble. And when she was
put in the earth, Sir Launcelot swooned,
and lay long still, while the hermit came

and awaked him, and said: 'Ye be to
blame, for ye displease God with such
manner of sorrow-making.' 'Truly,' said
Sir Launcelot, 'I trust I do not displease
God, for he knoweth mine intent. For
my sorrow was not, nor is not, for any
rejoicing of sin, but my sorrow may never
have end. For when I remember of her
beauty, and of her noblesse, that was both
with her king and with her, so when I
saw his corpse and her corpse so lie together, truly mine heart would not serve
to sustain my careful body. Also when I
remember me how by my default, mine
orgulity, and my pride, that they were
both laid full low, that were peerless that
ever was living of christian people, wit
you well,' said Sir Launcelot, 'this remembered, of their kindness and mine unkindness, sank so to mine heart, that I
might not sustain myself.' So the French
book maketh mention.

CHAPTER XII

HOW SIR LAUNCELOT BEGAN TO SICKEN, AND
AFTER DIED, WHOSE BODY WAS BORNE TO
JOYOUS GARD FOR TO BE BURIED

Then Sir Launcelot never after ate but
little meat, ne drank, till he was dead.
For then he sickened more and more, and
dried, and dwined away. For the bishop
nor none of his fellows might not make
him to eat, and little he drank, that he was
waxen by a cubit shorter than he was, that
the people could not know him. For evermore, day and night, he prayed, but sometime he slumbered a broken sleep; ever he
was lying groveling on the tomb of King
Arthur and Queen Guenever. And there
was no comfort that the bishop, nor Sir
Bors, nor none of his fellows, could make
him, it availed not. So within six weeks
after, Sir Launcelot fell sick, and lay in
his bed; and then he sent for the Bishop
that there was hermit, and all his true
fellows. Then Sir Launcelot said with
dreary steven: 'Sir Bishop, I pray you
give to me all my rites that longeth to a
christian man.' 'It shall not need you,'
said the hermit and all his fellows, 'it
is but heaviness of your blood; ye shall
be well mended by the grace of God to-
morn.' 'My fair lords,' said Sir Launcelot, 'wit you well my careful body will
into the earth, I have warning more than
now I will say; therefore give me my
rites.' So when he was houseled and

anealed, and had all that a christian man ought to have, he prayed the bishop that his fellows might bear his body to Joyous Gard. Some men say it was Alnwick, and some men say it was Bamborough. 'Howbeit,' said Sir Launcelot, 'me repenteth sore, but I made mine avow sometime, that in Joyous Gard I would be buried. And because of breaking of mine avow, I pray you all, lead me thither.' Then there was weeping and wringing of hands among his fellows.

So at a season of the night they all went to their beds, for they all lay in one chamber. And so after midnight, against day, the bishop [that] then was hermit, as he lay in his bed asleep, he fell upon a great laughter. And therewith all the fellowship awoke, and came to the bishop, and asked him what he ailed. 'Ah, Jesu mercy,' said the bishop, 'why did ye awake me? I was never in all my life so merry and so well at ease.' 'Wherefore?' said Sir Bors. 'Truly,' said the bishop, 'here was Sir Launcelot with me with more angels than ever I saw men in one day. And I saw the angels heave up Sir Launcelot unto heaven, and the gates of heaven opened against him.' 'It is but dretching of swevens,' said Sir Bors, 'for I doubt not Sir Launcelot aileth nothing but good.' 'It may well be,' said the Bishop; 'go ye to his bed, and then shall ye prove the sooth.' So when Sir Bors and his fellows came to his bed, they found him stark dead, and he lay as he had smiled, and the sweetest savor about him that ever they felt.

Then was there weeping and wringing of hands, and the greatest dole they made that ever made men. And on the morn the bishop did his mass of *Requiem;* and after, the bishop and all the nine knights put Sir Launcelot in the same horse bier that Queen Guenever was laid in to-fore that she was buried. And so the bishop and they all together went with the body of Sir Launcelot daily, till they came to Joyous Gard; and ever they had an hundred torches brenning about him. And so within fifteen days they came to Joyous Gard. And there they laid his corpse in the body of the quire, and sang and read many psalters and prayers over him and about him. And ever his visage was laid open and naked, that all folks might behold him. For such was the custom in those days, that all men of worship should so lie with open visage till that they were buried. And right thus as they were at their service, there came Sir Ector de Maris, that had seven years sought all England, Scotland, and Wales, seeking his brother, Sir Launcelot.

CHAPTER XIII

HOW SIR ECTOR FOUND SIR LAUNCELOT HIS BROTHER DEAD, AND HOW CONSTANTINE REIGNED NEXT AFTER ARTHUR; AND OF THE END OF THIS BOOK

And when Sir Ector heard such noise and light in the quire of Joyous Gard, he alighted and put his horse from him, and came into the quire, and there he saw men sing and weep. And all they knew Sir Ector, but he knew not them. Then went Sir Bors unto Sir Ector, and told him how there lay his brother, Sir Launcelot, dead; and then Sir Ector threw his shield, sword, and helm from him. And when he beheld Sir Launcelot's visage, he fell down in a swoon. And when he waked, it were hard any tongue to tell the doleful complaints that he made for his brother. 'Ah Launcelot,' he said, 'thou were head of all christian knights, and now I dare say,' said Sir Ector, 'thou Sir Launcelot, there thou liest, that thou were never matched of earthly knight's hand. And thou were the courteoust knight that ever bare shield. And thou were the truest friend to thy lover that ever bestrad horse. And thou were the truest lover of a sinful man that ever loved woman. And thou were the kindest man that ever struck with sword. And thou were the goodliest person that ever came among press of knights. And thou was the meekest man and the gentlest that ever ate in hall among ladies. And thou were the sternest knight to thy mortal foe that ever put spear in the rest.' Then there was weeping and dolor out of measure.

Thus they kept Sir Launcelot's corpse aloft fifteen days, and then they buried it with great devotion. And then at leisure they went all with the Bishop of Canterbury to his hermitage, and there they were together more than a month. Then Sir Constantine, that was Sir Cador's son of Cornwall, was chosen king of England. And he was a full noble knight, and worshipfully he ruled this realm. And then this King Constantine sent for the Bishop of Canterbury, for he heard say where he was. And so he was restored unto his bishopric, and left that hermitage. And Sir Bedivere was there ever still hermit to his life's end. Then Sir Bors de Ganis, Sir Ector de Maris, Sir Gahalantine, Sir Galihud, Sir Galihodin, Sir Blamore, Sir Bleoberis, Sir Villiars le Valiant, Sir Clarrus of Clermont, all these knights drew them to their countries. Howbeit King Constantine would have had them with him, but they would not abide in this realm. And there they all lived in their countries as holy men. And some English books make mention that they went never out of England after the death of Sir Launcelot, but that was but favor of makers. For the French book maketh mention, and is authorized, that Sir Bors, Sir Ector, Sir Blamore, and Sir Bleoberis, went into the Holy Land thereas Jesu Christ was quick and dead, and anon as they had stablished their lands. For the book saith, so Sir Launcelot commanded them for to do, or ever he passed out of this world. And these four knights did many battles upon the miscreants or Turks. And there they died upon a Good Friday for God's sake.

Here is the end of the book of King Arthur, and of his noble knights of the Round Table, that when they were whole together there was ever an hundred and forty. And here is the end of the death of Arthur. I pray you all, gentlemen and gentlewomen that readeth this book of Arthur and his knights, from the beginning to the ending, pray for me while I am alive, that God send me good deliverance, and when I am dead, I pray you all pray for my soul. For this book was ended the ninth year of the reign of King Edward the Fourth, by Sir Thomas Maleore, knight, as Jesu help him for his great might, as he is the servant of Jesu both day and night.

Thus endeth this noble and joyous book entitled Le Morte Darthur. Notwithstanding it treateth of the birth, life, and acts of the said King Arthur, of his noble knights of the Round Table, their marvelous enquests and adventures, the achieving of the Sangreal, and in the end the dolorous death and departing out of this world of them all. Which book was reduced into English by Sir Thomas Malory, knight, as afore is said, and by me divided into twenty-one books, chaptered and enprinted, and finished in the abbey, Westminster, the last day of July, the year of our Lord MCCCCLXXXV.
Caxton me fieri fecit.

THE NUT-BROWN MAID (c. 1500)

This charming anonymous lyric, worthy in itself of a conspicuous place in any survey of English poetry, serves significantly as a link between an earlier and a later period. In its suggestion of the 'débat' form, it recalls the middle ages; in versification and sentiment, it is definitely modern.

THE NUTBROWNE MAIDE

'Be it right or wrong, these men among on
   women do complaine,
Affermyng this, how that it is a labour
   spent in vaine
To love them wele, for never a dele they
   love a man agayne;
For lete a man do what he can ther favour
   to attayne,
Yet yf a newe do them pursue, ther furst
   trew lover than   5
Laboureth for nought, and from her thought
   he is a bannished man.'

'I say not nay but that all day it is bothe
   writ and sayde
That woman's fayth is, as who sayth, all
   utterly decayed;
But nevertheless, right good witnes in this
   case might be layde,
That they love trewe and contynew,— recorde
   the Nutbrowne Maide,   10
Whiche from her love, whan, her to prove,
   he cam to make his mone,
Wolde not departe, for in her herte she lovyd
   but hym allone.'

'Than betwene us lete us discusse what was
   all the maner
Betwene them too, we wyl also telle all the
   peyne and fere
That she was in. Now I begynne, see that
   ye me answere.   15
Wherefore [all] ye that present be, I pray
   you geve an eare.
I am a knyght, I cum be nyght, as secret as
   I can,
Sayng, "Alas! thus stondyth the case: I am
   a bannisshed man."'

'And I your wylle for to fulfylle, in this
   wyl not refuse,
Trusting to shewe, in wordis fewe, that men
   have an ille use,   20
To ther owne shame wymen to blame, and
   causeles them accuse.
Therfore to you I answere now, alle wymen
   to excuse:
"Myn own hert dere, with you what chiere?
   I prey you telle anoon;
For in my mynde of all mankynde I love
   but you allon."'

'It stondith so, a deed is do wherof moche
   harme shal growe.   25
My desteny is for to dey a shamful dethe,
   I trowe,
Or ellis to flee; the ton must bee, none other
   wey I knowe
But to withdrawe as an outlaw and take me
   to my bowe.
Wherfore, adew, my owne hert trewe, none
   other red I can;
For I muste to the grene wode goo, alone,
   a bannysshed man.'   30

'O Lorde, what is this worldis blisse, that
   chaungeth as the mone?
My somers day in lusty May is derked before the none.
I here you saye "farwel;" nay, nay, we departe not soo sone.
Why say ye so? wheder wyl ye goo? alas!
   what have ye done?
Alle my welfare to sorow and care shulde
   chaunge if ye were gon;   35
For in my mynde of all mankynde I love
   but you alone.'

'I can beleve it shal you greve, and somwhat you distrayne;
But aftyrwarde your paynes harde within a
   day or tweyne
Shal sone aslake, and ye shal take confort
   to you agayne.

34

Why shuld ye nought? for to take thought,
  your labur were in vayne.   40
And thus I do, and pray you, too, as hertely
  as I can;
For I muste too the grene wode goo, alone,
  a bannysshed man.'

' Now syth that ye have shewed to me the
  secret of your mynde,
I shalbe playne to you agayne, lyke as ye
  shal me fynde;
Syth it is so that ye wyll goo, I wol not leve
  behynde;   45
Shal never be sayd the Nutbrowne Mayd
  was to her love unkind.
Make you redy, for soo am I, all though it
  were anoon;
For in my mynde of all mankynde I love but
  you alone.'

' Yet I you rede to take good hede, what
  men wyl thinke and sey;
Of yonge and olde it shal be told that ye be
  gone away,   50
Your wanton wylle for to fulfylle, in grene
  wood you to play,
And that ye myght from your delyte noo
  lenger make delay.
Rather than ye shuld thus for me be called
  an ylle woman,
Yet wolde I to the grenewodde goo, alone,
  a banysshed man.'

' Though it be songe of olde and yonge
  that I shuld be to blame,   55
Theirs be the charge that speke so large in
  hurting of my name;
For I wyl prove that feythful love it is de-
  voyd of shame,
In your distresse and hevynesse to parte
  wyth you the same;
And sure all thoo that doo not so, trewe
  lovers ar they noon;
But in my mynde of all mankynde I love
  but you alone.'   60

' I counsel yow, remember how it is noo
  maydens lawe
Nothing to dought, but to renne out to wod
  with an outlawe;
For ye must there in your hande bere a
  bowe to bere and drawe,
And as a theef thus must ye lyeve ever in
  drede and awe,
By whiche to yow gret harme myght grow;
  yet had I lever than   65
That I had too the grenewod goo, alone, a
  banysshyd man.'

' I thinke not nay, but as ye saye, it is noo
  maydens lore;
But love may make me for your sake, as ye
  have said before,
To com on fote, to hunte and shote to gete
  us mete and store;
For soo that I your company may have, I
  aske noo more;   70
From whiche to parte, it makith myn herte
  as colde as ony ston;
For in my mynde of all mankynde I love but
  you alone.'

' For an outlawe this is the lawe, that men
  hym take and binde,
Wythout pytee hangèd to bee, and waver
  wyth the wynde.
Yf I had neede, as God forbede, what rescous coude ye finde?   75
For sothe I trowe, you and your bowe shuld
  drawe for fere behynde;
And noo merveyle, for lytel avayle were in
  your councel than;
Wherfore I too the woode wyl goo, alone,
  a banysshed man.'

' Ful wel knowe ye that wymen bee ful febyl
  for to fyght;
Noo womanhed is it indeede to bee bolde
  as a knight;   80
Yet in suche fere yf that ye were, amonge
  enemys day and nyght,
I wolde wythstonde, with bowe in hande, to
  greeve them as I myght,
And you to save, as wymen have, from deth
  many one;
For in my mynde of all mankynde I love but
  you alone.'

' Yet take good hede, for ever I drede that
  ye coude not sustein   85
The thorney wayes, the depe valeis, the
  snowe, the frost, the reyn,
The colde, the hete; for, drye or wete, we
  must lodge on the playn,
And, us aboove, noon other rove but a brake,
  bussh, or twayne;
Whiche sone shulde greve you, I beleve, and
  ye wolde gladly than
That I had too the grenewode goo, alone,
  a banysshyd man.'   90

' Syth I have here been partynere with you
  of joy and blysse,
I muste also parte of your woo endure, as
  reason is:
Yet am I sure of oo plesure, and shortly it
  is this,

That where ye bee, me semeth, perdé, I
    coude not fare amysse.
Wythout more speche, I you beseche that we
    were soon agone;   95
For in my mynde of all mankynde I love but
    you alone.'

'Yf ye goo thedyr, ye must consider, whan
    ye have lust to dyne,
Ther shel no mete be fore to gete, nor
    drinke, bere, ale, ne wine,
Ne shetis clene to lye betwene, made of thred
    and twyne,
Noon other house but levys and bowes, to
    kever your hed and myn.   100
Loo! myn herte swete, this ylle dyet shuld
    make you pale and wan;
Wherfore I to the wood wyl goo, alone, a
    banysshid man.'

'Amonge the wylde dere suche an archier
    as men say that ye bee
Ne may not fayle of good vitayle, where is
    so grete plenté;
And watir cleere of the ryvere shal be ful
    swete to me,   105
Wyth whiche in hele I shal right wele en-
    dure, as ye shal see;
And, er we goo, a bed or too I can provide
    anoon;
For in my mynde of all mankynde I love but
    you alone.'

'Loo! yet before ye must doo more, yf ye
    wyl goo with me,—
As cutte your here up by your ere, your
    kirtel by the knee,   110
Wyth bowe in hande, for to withstonde your
    enmys, yf nede be,
And this same nyght before daylight to
    woodward wyl I flee;
And if ye wyl all this fulfylle, doo it shortely
    as ye can;
Ellis wil I to the grenewode goo, alone, a
    banysshyd man.'

'I shal, as now, do more for you than long-
    eth to womanhede,   115
To short my here, a bowe to bere to shote
    in tyme of nede.
O my swete moder, before all other, for you
    have I most drede;
But now adiew! I must ensue, wher for-
    tune duth me leede:
All this make ye; now lete us flee, the day
    cums fast upon;
For in my mynde of all mankynde I love but
    you alone.'   120

'Nay, nay, not soo, ye shal not goo! and
    I shal telle you why:
Your appetyte is to be lyght of love, I wele
    aspie;
For right as ye have sayd to me, in lyke-
    wise hardely
Ye wolde answere, whosoever it were, in
    way of company.
It is sayd of olde, "sone hote, sone colde,"
    and so is a woman;   125
Wherfore I too the woode wyl goo, alone,
    a banysshid man.'

'Yef ye take hede, yet is noo nede, suche
    wordis to say bee me,
For oft ye preyd, and longe assayed, or I
    you lovid, perdé!
And though that I of auncestry a barons
    doughter bee,
Yet have you proved how I you loved, a
    squyer of lowe degree,   130
And ever shal, what so befalle, to dey ther-
    fore anoon;
For in my mynde of all mankynde I love but
    you alone.'

'A barons childe to be begyled, it were a
    curssèd dede,
To be felaw with an outlawe, almyghty
    God forbede!
Yet bettyr were the power squyer alone to
    forest yede,   135
Than ye shal saye, another day, that be my
    wyked dede
Ye were betrayed; wherfore, good maide,
    the best red that I can,
Is that I too the greenewode goo, alone, a
    banysshed man.'

'Whatsoever befalle, I never shal of this
    thing you upbraid;
But yf ye goo and leve me so, than have
    ye me betraied.   140
Remembre you wele how that ye dele, for
    yf ye, as ye sayde,
Be so unkynde to leve behynd your love,
    the Notbrowne Maide,
Trust me truly that I shal dey sone after ye
    be gone;
For in my mynde of all mankynde I love but
    you alone.'

'Yef that ye went, ye shulde repent, for in
    the forest now   145
I have purveid me of a maide, whom I love
    more than you,—
Another fayrer than ever ye were, I dare
    it wel avowe:

And of you bothe, eche shulde be wrothe with
    other, as I trowe.
It were myn ease to lyve in pease; so wyl
    I, yf I can;
Wherfore I to the wode wyl goo, alone, a
    banysshid man.'   150

'Though in the wood I undirstode ye had a
    paramour,
All this may nought remeve my thought, but
    that I wil be your;
And she shal fynde me soft and kynde, and
    curteis every our,
Glad to fulfylle all that she wylle com-
    maunde me, to my power;
For had ye, loo! an hundred moo, yet wolde
    I be that one;   155
For in my mynde of all mankynde I love but
    you alone.'

'Myn oune dere love, I see the prove that ye
    be kynde and trewe;
Of mayde and wyf, in all my lyf, the best
    that ever I knewe!
Be mery and glad, be no more sad, the case
    is chaungèd newe;
For it were ruthe that for your trouth you
    shuld have cause to rewe.   160
Be not dismayed, whatsoever I sayd, to you
    whan I began,
I wyl not too the grenewod goo, I am noo
    banysshyd man.'

'Theis tidingis be more glad to me than to
    be made a quene,

Yf I were sure they shuld endure; but it is
    often seen,
When men wyl breke promyse, they speke
    the wordis on the splene.   165
Ye shape some wyle, me to begyle, and stele
    fro me, I wene.
Then were the case wurs than it was, and I
    more woo-begone;
For in my mynde of all mankynde I love but
    you alone.'

'Ye shall not nede further to drede, I wyl
    not disparage
You, God defende, sith you descende of so
    grete a lynage.   170
Nou understonde, to Westmerlande, whiche
    is my herytage,
I wyle you bringe, and wyth a rynge, be wey
    of maryage,
I wyl you take, and lady make, as shortly
    as I can;
Thus have ye wone an erles son, and not
    a banysshyd man.'

Here may ye see that wymen be in love
    meke, kinde, and stable,   175
Late never man repreve them than, or calle
    them variable,
But rather prey God that we may to them
    be confortable,
Whiche somtyme provyth suche as he loveth,
    yf they be charitable.
For sith men wolde that wymen sholde be
    meke to them echeon,
Moche more ought they to God obey, and
    serve but hym alone.   180

ENGLISH AND SCOTTISH POPULAR BALLADS

The popular ballad is a short, anonymous poem, in simple meter, recounting a simple narrative, and adapted, originally, for singing to a recurrent melody. The true ballad shows no traces of individual authorship: the story is told impersonally, without a suggestion of sentiment or reflection from the story-teller. Ballads originate in a naïve, homogeneous community, and it may fairly be said that they are composed not by any individual, but by the community as a whole. Ballads are to be thought of as beginning, ultimately and normally, in a choral throng, in which, to the accompaniment of dancing and singing, one person after another contributes an improvised verse, couplet, or short stanza to a simple but ever increasing story. The story grows by 'incremental repetition'; that is, in his improvisation, each singer in succession both repeats a part of the preceding improvisation and adds to the story a new element of his own. After contributing their bits to the narrative, the several singers disappear as individuals, leaving as a result a simple narrative poem, which is henceforth regarded as the composition not of one person or of particular persons, but of the gathering as a whole. Although such a process of composition can be securely inferred, no extant ballad shows so simple a form as would result immediately from such communal authorship. Since all true ballads are transmitted orally, variations in style and alterations of the narrative are inevitable; and the hand of a dominating individual may often be inferred. A large proportion of the ballads actually preserved do, however, bear unmistakable marks of their ultimate choral and community origin, and all ballads worthy of the name are the actual possession of the folk as a whole.

From the fact that ballads are transmitted orally, and are committed to writing only by happy accident, the body of preserved and published ballads of any people will represent, inevitably, only a small proportion of the whole sum of ballads produced during the history of that people. The English language, including Scottish, is fortunate in the preservation of at least three hundred and six ballads. Although the greater part of these ballads are recorded only in comparatively modern documents, many of the stories themselves are of very ancient origin. The oldest English ballad completely recorded dates from the thirteenth century. The most important of ballad manuscripts,— the so-called Percy Folio,— was written about the year 1650. Only some eleven of our ballads are preserved in documents older than the seventeenth century.

On the theory of 'communal authorship' one can readily explain the chief formal characteristics of popular ballads: refrain, repetition, and dialogue.

ROBIN HOOD AND GUY OF GISBORNE

1. When shawes beene sheene, and shradds
      full fayre,
   And leeves both large and longe,
   It is merry, walking in the fayre fforrest,
   To heare the small birds songe.

2. The woodweele sang, and wold not
      cease,   5
   Amongst the leaves a lyne;
   And it is by two wight yeomen.
   By deare God, that I meane.

      .   .   .

3. 'Me thought they did mee beate and
      binde,
   And tooke my bowe mee froe;   10

If I bee Robin alive in this lande,
   I'le be wrocken on both them towe.'

4. 'Sweavens are swift, master,' quoth
      John,
   'As the wind that blowes ore a hill;
   Ffor if itt be never soe lowde this night,
   To-morrow it may be still.'   16

5. 'Buske yee, bowne yee, my merry men
      all,
   Ffor John shall goe with mee;
   For I'le goe seeke yond wight yeomen
   In greenwood where they bee.'   20

6. They cast on their gowne of greene,
   A shooting gone are they.

Untill they came to the merry green-
    wood,
Where they had gladdest bee;
There were they ware of a wight yeo-
    man, 25
His body leaned to a tree.

7. A sword and a dagger he wore by his
    side,
Had beene many a mans bane,
And he was cladd in his capull-hyde,
Topp, and tayle, and mayne. 30

8. 'Stand you still, master,' quoth Litle
    John,
'Under this trusty tree,
And I will goe to yond wight yeoman,
To know his meaning trulye.'

9. 'A, John, by me thou setts noe store, 35
And that's a ffarley thinge;
How offt send I my men beffore,
And tarry my-selfe behinde?

10. 'It is noe cunning a knave to ken;
And a man but heare him speake 40
And itt were not for bursting of my
    bowe,
John, I wold thy head breake.'

11. But often words they breeden bale;
That parted Robin and John.
John is gone to Barnesdale, 45
The gates he knowes eche one.

12. And when hee came to Barnesdale,
Great heavinesse there hee hadd;
He ffound two of his fellowes
Were slaine both in a slade, 50

13. And Scarlett a-ffoote flyinge was,
Over stockes and stone,
For the sheriffe with seven score men
Fast after him is gone.

14. 'Yett one shoote I'le shoote,' sayes Litle
    John, 55
'With Crist his might and mayne;
I'le make yond fellow that flyes soe fast
To be both glad and ffaine.'

15. John bent up a good veiwe bow,
And ffetteled him to shoote; 60
The bow was made of a tender boughe,
And fell downe to his foote.

16. 'Woe worth thee, wicked wood,' sayd
    Litle John,

'That ere thou grew on a tree!
Ffor this day thou art my bale, 65
My boote when thou shold bee!'

17. This shoote it was but looselye shott,
The arrowe flew in vaine,
And it mett one of the sheriffes men;
Good William a Trent was slaine. 70

18. It had beene better for William a Trent
To hange upon a gallowe
Then for to lye in the greenwoode,
There slaine with an arrowe.

19. And it is sayd, when men be mett, 75
Six can doe more then three:
And they have tane Litle John,
And bound him ffast to a tree.

20. 'Thou shalt be drawen by dale and
    downe,' quoth the sheriffe,
'And hanged hye on a hill:' 80
'But thou may ffayle,' quoth Litle John,
'If itt be Christs owne will.'

21. Let us leave talking of Litle John,
For hee is bound fast to a tree,
And talke of Guy and Robin Hood 85
In the green woode where they bee.

22. How these two yeomen together they
    mett,
Under the leaves of lyne,
To see what marchandise they made
Even at that same time. 90

23. 'Good morrow, good fellow,' quoth Sir
    Guy;
'Good morrow, good ffellow,' quoth
    hee;
'Methinkes by this bow thou beares in
    thy hand,
A good archer thou seems to bee.'

24. 'I am wilfull of my way,' quoth Sir
    Guye, 95
'And of my morning tyde:'
'I'le lead thee through the wood,' quoth
    Robin,
'Good ffellow, I'le be thy guide.'

25. 'I seeke an outlaw,' quoth Sir Guye,
'Men call him Robin Hood; 100
I had rather meet with him upon a day
Than forty pound of golde.'

26. 'If you tow mett, itt wold be seene
    whether were better

Afore yee did part awaye;
Let us some other pastime find,   105
Good ffellow, I thee pray.

27. 'Let us some other masteryes make,
And wee will walke in the woods even;
Wee may chance meet with Robin Hoode
Att some unsett steven.'   110

28. They cutt them downe the summer
shroggs
Which grew both under a bryar,
And sett them three score rood in twinn,
To shoote the prickes full neare.

29. 'Leade on, good ffellow,' sayd Sir Guye,
'Lead on, I doe bidd thee:'   116
'Nay, by my faith,' quoth Robin Hood,
'The leader thou shalt bee.'

30. The first good shoot that Robin ledd,
Did not shoote an inch the pricke
ffroe;
Guy was an archer good enoughe,   121
But he cold neere shoote soe.

31. The second shoote Sir Guy shott,
He shott within the garlande;
But Robin Hoode shott it better then
hee,   125
For he clove the good pricke-wande.

32. 'Gods blessing on thy heart!' sayes
Guye,
'Goode ffellow, thy shooting is goode;
For an thy hart be as good as thy hands,
Thou were better then Robin Hood.

33. 'Tell me thy name, good ffellow,' quoth
Guy,   131
'Under the leaves of lyne:'
'Nay, by my faith,' quoth good Robin,
'Till thou have told me thine.'

34. 'I dwell by dale and downe,' quoth
Guye,   135
'And I have done many a curst turne;
And he that calles me by my right
name,
Calles me Guye of good Gysborne.'

35. 'My dwelling is in the wood,' sayes
Robin;
'By thee I set right nought;   140
My name is Robin Hood of Barnesdale,
A ffellow thou has long sought.'

36. He that had neither beene a kithe nor
kin
Might have seene a full fayre sight,
To see how together these yeomen
went,   145
With blades both browne and bright;

37. To have seene how these yeomen to-
gether fought
Two howers of a summers day;
Itt was neither Guy nor Robin Hood
That ffettled them to flye away.   150

38. Robin was reacheles on a roote,
And stumbled at that tyde,
And Guy was quicke and nimble withall,
And hitt him ore the left side.

39. 'Ah, deere Lady!' sayd Robin Hoode,
'Thou art both mother and may!   156
I thinke it was never mans destinye
To dye before his day.'

40. Robin thought on Our Lady deere,
And soone leapt up againe,   160
And thus he came with an awkwarde
stroke;
Good Sir Guy hee has slayne.

41. He tooke Sir Guys head by the hayre,
And sticked itt on his bowes end:
'Thou hast beene traytor all thy liffe,
Which thing must have an ende.'   166

42. Robin pulled forth an Irish kniffe,
And nicked Sir Guy in the fface,
That hee was never on a woman borne
Cold tell who Sir Guye was.   170

43. Saies, 'Lye there, lye there, good Sir
Guye,
And with me be not wrothe;
If thou have had the worse stroakes at
my hand,
Thou shalt have the better cloathe.'

44. Robin did off his gowne of greene,   175
Sir Guye hee did it throwe;
And hee put on that capull-hyde
That cladd him topp to toe.

45. 'The bowe, the arrowes, and litle horne,
And with me now I'le beare;   18c
Ffor now I will goe to Barnesdale
To see how my men doe ffare.'

46. Robin sett Guyes horne to his mouth,
A lowd blast in it he did blow;

That beheard the sheriffe of Nottingham,   185
As he leaned under a lowe.

47. 'Hearken! hearken!' sayd the sheriffe,
  'I heard noe tydings but good;
For yonder I heare Sir Guyes horne
  blowe,
For he hath slaine Robin Hoode. 190

48. 'For yonder I heare Sir Guyes horne
  blow,
Itt blowes soe well in tyde,
For yonder comes that wighty yeoman,
  Cladd in his capull-hyde.

49. 'Come hither, thou good Sir Guy,
  Aske of mee what thou wilt have:'
'I'le none of thy gold,' sayes Robin
  Hood,   197
'Nor I'le none of itt have.

50. 'But now I have slaine the master,' he
  sayd,
  'Let me goe strike the knave;   200
This is all the reward I aske,
  Nor noe other will I have.'

51. 'Thou art a madman,' said the shiriffe,
  'Thou sholdest have had a knights
    ffee;
Seeing thy asking hath beene soe badd,
  Well granted it shall be.'   206

52. But Litle John heard his master speake,
  Well he knew that was his steven;
'Now shall I be loset,' quoth Litle John,
  'With Christs might in heaven.'   210

53. But Robin hee hyed him towards Litle
  John,
  Hee thought hee wold loose him
    belive;
The sheriffe and all his companye
  Fast after him did drive.

54. 'Stand abacke! stand abacke!' sayd
  Robin;   215
  'Why draw you mee soe neere?
Itt was never the use in our countrye
  Ones shrift another shold heere.'

55 But Robin pulled forth an Irysh kniffe,
  And losed John hand and ffoote,   220
And gave him Sir Guyes bow in his
  hand,
  And bade it be his boote.

56. But John tooke Guyes bow in his hand—
  His arrowes were rawstye by the
    roote;
The sherriffe saw Little John draw a
  bow   225
And ffettle him to shoote.

57. Towards his house in Nottingam
  He ffled full fast away,
And soe did all his companye,
  Not one behind did stay.   230

58. But he cold neither soe fast goe,
  Nor away soe fast runn,
But Litle John, with an arrow broade,
  Did cleave his heart in twinn.

ROBIN HOOD'S DEATH AND BURIAL

1. When Robin Hood and Little John
  Down a down a down a down
Went oer yon bank of broom,
  Said Robin Hood bold to Little John,
'We have shot for many a pound.'   5
Hey down, a down, a down.

2. 'But I am not able to shoot one shot
    more,
  My broad arrows will not flee;
But I have a cousin lives down below,
  Please God, she will bleed me.'   10

3. Now Robin he is to fair Kirkly gone,
  As fast as he can win;
But before he came there, as we do hear,
  He was taken very ill.

4. And when he came to fair Kirkly-hall,
  He knockd all at the ring,   16
But none was so ready as his cousin
    herself
For to let bold Robin in.

5. 'Will you please to sit down, cousin
    Robin,' she said,
  'And drink some beer with me?'   20
'No, I will neither eat nor drink,
  Till I am blooded by thee.'

6. 'Well, I have a room, cousin Robin,'
    she said,
  'Which you did never see,
And if you please to walk therein,   25
  You blooded by me shall be.'

7. She took him by the lily-white hand,
   And led him to a private room,
   And there she blooded bold Robin Hood,
   While one drop of blood would run
   down.   30

8. She blooded him in a vein of the arm,
   And locked him up in the room;
   Then did he bleed all the live-long day,
   Until the next day at noon.

9. He then bethought him of a casement
   there,   35
   Thinking for to get down;
   But was so weak he could not leap,
   He could not get him down.

10. He then bethought him of his bugle-
    horn,
    Which hung low down to his knee;   40
    He set his horn unto his mouth,
    And blew out weak blasts three.

11. Then Little John, when hearing him,
    As he sat under a tree,
    'I fear my master is now near dead, 45
    He blows so wearily.'

12. Then Little John to fair Kirkly is gone,
    As fast as he can dree;
    But when he came to Kirkly-hall,
    He broke locks two or three: 50

13. Until he came bold Robin to see,
    Then he fell on his knee;
    'A boon, a boon,' cries Little John,
    'Master, I beg of thee.'

14. 'What is that boon,' said Robin Hood,
    'Little John, thou begs of me?'   56
    'It is to burn fair Kirkly-hall,
    And all their nunnery.'

15. 'Now nay, now nay,' quoth Robin Hood,
    'That boon I 'll not grant thee;   60
    I never hurt woman in all my life,
    Nor men in woman's company.

16. 'I never hurt fair maid in all my time,
    Nor at mine end shall it be;
    But give me my bent bow in my hand, 65
    And a broad arrow I 'll let flee
    And where this arrow is taken up,
    There shall my grave digged be.

17. 'Lay me a green sod under my head,
    And another at my feet;   70

And lay my bent bow by my side,
Which was my music sweet;
And make my grave of gravel and green,
Which is most right and meet.

18. 'Let me have length and breadth
    enough,   75
    With a green sod under my head;
    That they may say, when I am dead,
    Here lies bold Robin Hood.'

19. These words they readily granted him,
    Which did bold Robin please: 80
    And there they buried bold Robin Hood,
    Within the fair Kirkleys.

THE BATTLE OF OTTERBURN

1. Yt felle abowght the Lamasse tyde,
   Whan husbondes wynnes ther haye,
   The dowghtye Dowglasse bowynd hym
   to ryde,
   In Ynglond to take a praye.

2. The yerlle of Fyffe, wythowghten stryffe,
   He bowynd hym over Sulway;   6
   The grete wolde ever to-gether ryde;
   That raysse they may rewe for aye.

3. Over Hoppertope hyll they cam in,
   And so down by Rodclyffe crage;   10
   Upon Grene Lynton they lighted dowyn,
   Styrande many a stage.

4. And boldely brente Northomberlond,
   And haryed many a towyn;
   They dyd owr Ynglyssh men grete
   wrange,   15
   To battell that were not bowyn.

5. Then spake a berne upon the bent,
   Of comforte that was not colde,
   And sayd, 'We have brente Northom-
   berlond,
   We have all welth in holde.   20

6. 'Now we have haryed all Bamborowe
   schyre,
   All the welth in the worlde have wee;
   I rede we ryde to Newe Castell,
   So styll and stalworthlye.'

7. Upon the morowe, when it was day, 25
   The standerds schone fulle bryght;
   To the Newe Castell they toke the waye,
   And thether they cam full ryght.

8. Syr Henry Perssy laye at the New
    Castell,
  I tell yow wythowtten drede;   30
  He had byn a march-man all hys dayes,
  And kepte Barwyke upon Twede.

9. To the Newe Castell when they cam,
  The Skottes they cryde on hyght,
  'Syr Hary Perssy, and thow byste
    within,   35
  Com to the fylde, and fyght.

10. 'For we have brente Northomberlonde,
  Thy erytage good and ryght,
  And syne my logeyng I have take,
  Wyth my brande dubbyd many a
    knyght.'   40

11. Syr Harry Perssy cam to the walles,
  The Skottyssch oste for to se,
  And sayd, 'And thow hast brente North-
    omberlond,
  Full sore it rewyth me.

12. 'Yf thou hast haryed all Bamborowe
    schyre,   45
  Thow hast done me grete envye;
  For the trespasse thow hast me done,
  The tone of us schall dye.'

13. 'Where schall I byde the?' sayd the
    Dowglas,
  'Or where wylte thow com to me?' 50
  'At Otterborne, in the hygh way,
  Ther mast thow well logeed be.

14. 'The roo full rekeles ther sche rinnes,
  To make the game and glee;
  The fawken and the fesaunt both, 55
  Amonge the holtes on hye.

15. 'Ther mast thow have thy welth at wyll,
  Well loogèd ther mast be;
  Yt schall not be long or I com the tyll,'
  Sayd Syr Harry Perssye. 60

16. 'Ther schall I byde the,' sayd the Dow-
    glas,
  'By the fayth of my bodye.'
  'Thether schall I com,' sayd Syr Harry
    Perssy
  'My trowth I plyght to the.'

17. A pype of wyne he gave them over the
    walles, 65
  For soth as I yow saye;
  Ther he mayd the Dowglasse drynke,
  And all hys ost that daye.

18. The Dowglas turnyd hym homewarde
    agayne,
  For soth withowghten naye; 70
  He toke his logeyng at Oterborne,
  Upon a Wedynsday.

19. And ther he pyght hys standerd dowyn,
  Hys gettyng more and lesse,
  And syne he warned hys men to goo 75
  To chose ther geldynges gresse.

20. A Skottysshe knyght hoved upon the
    bent,
  A wache I dare well saye;
  So was he ware on the noble Perssy,
  In the dawnyng of the daye. 80

21. He prycked to hys pavyleon-dore,
  As faste as he myght ronne;
  'Awaken, Dowglas,' cryed the knyght,
  'For hys love that syttes in trone.

22. 'Awaken, Dowglas,' cryed the knyght, 85
  'For thow maste waken wyth wynne;
  Yender have I spyed the prowde Perssye,
  And seven stondardes wyth hym.'

23. 'Nay by my trowth,' the Dowglas sayed,
  'It ys but a faynèd taylle; 90
  He durst not loke on my brede banner
  For all Ynglonde so haylle.

24. 'Was I not yesterdaye at the Newe
    Castell,
  That stondes so fayre on Tyne?
  For all the men the Perssy had, 95
  He coude not garre me ones to dyne.'

25. He stepped owt at his pavelyon-dore,
  To loke and it were lesse:
  'Araye yow, lordynges, one and all,
  For here bygynnes no peysse. 100

26. 'The yerle of Mentaye, thow arte my
    eme,
  The forwarde I gyve to the:
  The yerlle of Huntlay, cawte and kene,
  He schall be wyth the.

27. 'The lorde of Bowghan, in armure
    bryght, 105
  On the other hand he schall be;
  Lord Jhonstoune and Lorde Maxwell,
  They to schall be wyth me.

28. 'Swynton, fayre fylde upon your pryde!
  To batell make yow bowen 110
  Syr Davy Skotte, Syr Water Stewarde,
  Syr Jhon of Agurstone!'

29. The Perssy cam byfore hys oste,
    Wych was ever a gentyll knyght;
    Upon the Dowglas lowde can he crye, 115
    'I wyll holde that I have hyght.

30. 'For thou haste brente Northomber-
    londe,
    And done me grete envye;
    For thys trespasse thou hast me done,
    The tone of us schall dye.'   120

31. The Dowglas answerde hym agayne,
    Wyth grett wurdes upon hye,
    And sayd, 'I have twenty agaynst thy
    one,
    Byholde, and thou maste see.'

32. Wyth that the Perssy was grevyd sore,
    For soth as I yow saye;   126
    He lyghted dowyn upon his foote,
    And schoote hys horsse clene awaye.

33. Every man sawe that he dyd soo,
    That ryall was ever in rowght;   130
    Every man schoote hys horsse hym froo,
    And lyght hym rowynde abowght.

34. Thus Syr Hary Perssye toke the fylde,
    For soth as I yow saye;
    Jhesu Cryste in hevyn on hyght   135
    Dyd helpe hym well that daye.

35. But nyne thowzand, ther was no moo,
    The cronykle wyll not layne;
    Forty thowsande of Skottes and fowre
    That day fowght them agayne,   140

36. But when the batell byganne to joyne,
    In hast ther cam a knyght;
    The letters fayre furth hath he tayne,
    And thus he sayd full ryght:

37. 'My lorde your father he gretes yow
    well,   145
    Wyth many a noble knyght;
    He desyres yow to byde
    That he may see thys fyght.

38. 'The Baron of Grastoke ys com out of
    the west,
    With hym a noble companye;   150
    All they loge at your fathers thys nyght,
    And the batell fayne wolde they see.'

39. 'For Jhesus love,' sayd Syr Harye
    Perssy,
    'That dyed for yow and me,
    Wende to my lorde my father agayne, 155
    And saye thow sawe me not with yee.

40. 'My trowth ys plyght to yonne Skottysh
    knyght,
    It nedes me not to layne,
    That I schulde byde hym upon thys bent,
    And I have hys trowth agayne.   160

41. 'And if that I weynde of thys growende,
    For soth, onfowghten awaye,
    He wolde me call but a kowarde knyght
    In hys londe another daye.

42. 'Yet had I lever to be rynde and rente,
    By Mary, that mykkel maye,   166
    Then ever my manhood schulde be re-
    provyd
    Wyth a Skotte another daye.

43. 'Wherefore schote, archars, for my sake,
    And let scharpe arowes flee;   170
    Mynstrells, playe up for your waryson,
    And well quyt it schall bee.

44. 'Every man thynke on hys trewe-love,
    And marke hym to the Trenité;
    For to God I make myne avowe   173
    Thys day wyll I not flee.'

45. The blodye harte in the Dowglas armes,
    Hys standerde stood on hye,
    That every man myght full well knowe;
    By syde stode starrës thre.   180

46. The whyte lyon on the Ynglyssh perte,
    For soth as I yow sayne,
    The lucettes and the cressawntes both;
    The Skottes faught them agayne.

47. Upon Sent Androwe lowde can they crye
    And thrysse they schowte on hyght, 186
    And syne merked them one owr Yng-
    lysshe men,
    As I have tolde yow ryght.

48. Sent George the bryght, owr Ladyes
    knyght,
    To name they were full fayne;   190
    Owr Ynglyssh men they cryde on hyght,
    And thrysse the schowtte agayne.

49. Wyth that scharpe arowes bygan to flee,
    I tell yow in sertayne;
    Men of armes byganne to joyne,   195
    Many a dowghty man was ther slayne,

50. The Perssy and the Dowglas mette,
    That ether of other was fayne;
    They swapped together whyll that the
    swette,
    Wyth swordes of fyne collayne: 200

51. Tyll the bloode from ther bassonnettes
      ranne,
    As the roke doth in the rayne;
    'Yelde the to me,' sayd the Dowglas,
      'Or elles thow schalt be slayne.

52. 'For I see by thy bryght bassonet,   205
    Thow arte sum man of myght;
    And so I do by thy burnysshed brande;
    Thow arte an yerle, or elles a knyght.'

53. 'By my good faythe,' sayd the noble
      Perssye,
    'Now haste thow rede full ryght;   210
    Yet wyll I never yelde me to the,
    Whyll I may stonde and fyght.'

54. They swapped together whyll that they
      swette,
    Wyth swordës scharpe and long;
    Ych on other so faste thee beette,   215
    Tyll ther helmes cam in peyses dowyn.

55. The Perssy was a man of strenghth,
    I tell yow in thys stounde;
    He smote the Dowglas at the swordës
      length
    That he felle to the growynde.   220

56. The sworde was scharpe, and sore can
      byte,
    I tell yow in sertayne;
    To the harte he cowde hym smyte,
    Thus was the Dowglas slayne.

57. The stonderdes stode styll on eke a syde,
    Wyth many a grevous grone;   226
    Ther they fowght the day, and all the
      nyght,
    And many a dowghty man was slayne.

58. Ther was no freke that ther wolde flye,
    But styffely in stowre can stond,   230
    Ychone hewyng on other whyll they
      myght drye,
    Wyth many a baylleful bronde.

59. Ther was slayne upon the Skottës syde,
    For soth and sertenly,
    Syr James a Dowglas ther was slayne,
    That day that he cowde dye.   236

60. The yerlle of Mentaye he was slayne,
    Grysely groned upon the growynd;
    Syr Davy Skotte, Syr Water Stewarde,
    Syr Jhon of Agurstoune.   240

61. Syr Charllës Morrey in that place,
    That never a fote wold flee;

62. Ther was slayne upon the Skottës syde,
    For soth as I yow saye,   246
    Of fowre and forty thowsande Scottes
    Went but eyghtene awaye.

63. Ther was slayne upon the Ynglysshe
      syde,
    For soth and sertenlye,   250
    A gentell knyght, Syr Jhon Fechewe,
    Yt was the more pety.

64. Syr James Hardbotell ther was slayne,
    For hym ther hartes were sore;
    The gentyll Lovell ther was slayne,   255
    That the Perssys standerd bore.

65. Ther was slayne upon the Ynglyssh pert
    For soth as I yow saye,
    Of nyne thowsand Ynglyssh men
    Fvye hondert cam awaye.   260

66. The other were slayne in the fylde;
    Cryste kepe ther sowlles from wo!
    Seyng ther was so fewe fryndes
    Agaynst so many a foo.

67. Then on the morne they mayde them
      beerys   265
    Of byrch and haysell graye;
    Many a wydowe, wyth wepyng teyres,
    Ther makes they fette awaye.

68. Thys fraye bygan at Otterborne,
    Bytwene the nyght and the day;   270
    Ther the Dowglas lost hys lyffe,
    And the Perssy was lede awaye.

69. Then was ther a Scottysh prisoner tayne.
    Syr Hewe Mongomery was hys name;
    For soth as I yow saye,   275
    He borowed the Perssy home agayne.

70. Now let us all for the Perssy praye
    To Jhesu most of myght,
    To bryng hys sowlle to the blysse of
      heven,
    For he was a gentyll knyght.   280

CAPTAIN CAR OR EDOM O GORDON

1. It befell at Martynmas,
   When wether waxèd colde,
   Captaine Care said to his men,
   'We must go take a holde.'

Syr Hewe Maxwell, a lord he was,
    Wyth the Dowglas dyd he dye.

Syck, sike, and to-towe sike, 5
  And sike and like to die;
The sikest nighte that ever I abode,
  God Lord have mercy on me!

2. 'Haille, master, and wether you will,
  And wether ye like it best;' 10
'To the castle of Crecrynbroghe,
  And there we will take our reste.'

3. 'I knowe wher is a gay castle,
  Is builded of lyme and stone;
Within their is a gay ladie, 15
  Her lord is riden and gone.'

4. The ladie she lend on her castle-walle,
  She lokèd upp and downe;
There was she ware of an host of men,
  Come riding to the towne. 20

5. 'Se yow, my meri men all,
  And se yow what I see?
Yonder I see an host of men,
  I muse who they shold bee.'

6. She thought he had ben her wed lord, 25
  As he comd riding home;
Then was it traitur Captaine Care
  The lord of Ester-towne.

7. They wer no soner at supper sett,
  Then after said the grace, 30
Or Captaine Care and all his men
  Were lighte aboute the place.

8. 'Gyve over thi howsse, thou lady gay,
  And I will make the a bande; 34
To-nighte thou shall ly within my armes,
  To-morrowe thou shall ere my lande.'

9. Then bespacke the eldest sonne,
  That was both whitt and redde:
'O mother dere, geve over your howsse,
  Or elles we shalbe deade.' 40

10. 'I will not geve over my hous,' she
  saithe,
'Not for feare of my lyffe;
It shalbe talked throughout the land,
  The slaughter of a wyffe.

11. 'Fetch me my pestilett, 45
  And charge me my gonne,
That I may shott at this bloddy butcher,
  The lord of Easter-towne.'

12. Styfly upon her wall she stòde,
  And lett the pellettes flee; 50

But then she myst the blody bucher,
  And she slew other three.

13. 'I will not geve over my hous,' she
  saithe,
'Netheir for lord nor lowne;
Nor yet for traitour Captaine Care, 55
  The lord of Easter-towne.

14. 'I desire of Captaine Care,
  And all his bloodye band,
That he would save my eldest sonne,
  The eare of all my lande.' 60

15. 'Lap him in a shete,' he sayth,
  'And let him downe to me,
And I shall take him in my armes,
  His waran shall I be.'

16. The captayne sayd unto him selfe; 65
  Wyth sped, before the rest,
He cut his tonge out of his head,
  His hart out of his brest.

17. He lapt them in a handkerchef,
  And knet it of knotes three, 70
And cast them over the castell-wall,
  At that gay ladye.

18. 'Fye upon the, Captayne Care,
  And all thy bloddy band!
For thou hast slayne my eldest sonne, 75
  The ayre of all my land.'

19. Then bespake the yongest sonne,
  That sat on the nurses knee,
Sayth, 'Mother gay, geve over your
  house;
  It smoldereth me.' 80

20. 'I wold geve my gold,' she saith,
  'And so I wolde my ffee,
For a blaste of the westryn wind,
  To dryve the smoke from thee.

21. 'Fy upon the, John Hamleton, 85
  That ever I paid the hyre!
For thou hast broken my castle-wall,
  And kyndled in the ffyre.'

22. The lady gate to her close parler,
  The fire fell aboute her head; 90
She toke up her children thre,
  Seth, 'Babes, we are all dead.'

23. Then bespake the hye steward,
  That is of hye degree;
Saith, 'Ladie gay, you are in close, 95
  Wether ye fighte or flee.'

24. Lord Hamleton dremd in his dream,
    In Carvall where he laye,
    His halle were all of fyre,
    His ladie slayne or daye.   100

25. 'Busk and bowne, my mery men all,
    Even and go ye with me;
    For I dremd that my haal was on fyre,
    My lady slayne or day.'

26. He buskt him and bownd hym,   105
    And like a worthi knighte;
    And when he saw his hall burning,
    His harte was no dele lighte.

27. He sett a trumpett till his mouth,
    He blew as it plesd his grace;   110
    Twenty score of Hamlentons
    Was light aboute the place.

28. 'Had I knowne as much yesternighte
    As I do to-daye,
    Captaine Care and all his men   115
    Should not have gone so quite.

29. 'Fye upon the, Captaine Care,
    And all thy blody bande!
    Thou haste slayne my lady gay,
    More wurth then all thy lande.   120

30. 'If thou had ought eny ill will,' he saith,
    'Thou shoulde have taken my lyffe,
    And have saved my children thre,
    All and my lovesome wyffe.'

THE WIFE OF USHER'S WELL

1. There lived a wife at Usher's Well,
   And a wealthy wife was she;
   She had three stout and stalwart sons,
   And sent them oer the sea.

2. They hadna been a week from her,   5
   A week but barely ane,
   Whan word came to the carline wife
   That her three sons were gane.

3. They hadna been a week from her,
   A week but barely three,   10
   Whan word came to the carlin wife
   That her sons she 'd never see.

4. 'I wish the wind may never cease,
   Nor fashes in the flood,
   Till my three sons come hame to me, 15
   In earthly flesh and blood.'

5. It fell about the Martinmass,
   When nights are lang and mirk,
   The carlin wife's three sons came hame,
   And their hats were o the birk.   20

6. It neither grew in syke nor ditch,
   Nor yet in ony sheugh;
   But at the gates o Paradise,
   That birk grew fair eneugh.

7. 'Blow up the fire, my maidens,   25
   Bring water from the well;
   For a' my house shall feast this night,
   Since my three sons are well.'

8. And she has made to them a bed,
   She 's made it large and wide,   30
   And she 's taen her mantle her about,
   Sat down at the bed-side.

9. Up then crew the red, red cock,
   And up and crew the gray;
   The eldest to the youngest said,   35
   ''T is time she were away.'

10. The cock he hadna crawd but once,
    And clappd his wings at al,
    When the youngest to the eldest said,
    'Brother, we must awa.   40

11. 'The cock doth craw, the day doth daw,
    The channerin worm doth chide;
    Gin we be mist out o our place,
    A sair pain we maun bide.

12. 'Faer ye weel, my mother dear!   45
    Fareweel to barn and byre!
    And fare ye weel, the bonny lass
    That kindles my mother's fire!'

KEMP OWYNE

1. Her mother died when she was young,
   Which gave her cause to make great
     moan;
   Her father married the warst woman
   That ever lived in Christendom.

2. She servèd her with foot and hand, 5
   In every thing that she could dee,
   Till once, in an unlucky time,
   She threw her in ower Craigy's sea.

3. Says, 'Lie you there, dove Isabel,
   And all my sorrows lie with thee;

Till Kemp Owyne come ower the sea,
  And borrow you with kisses three
Let all the warld do what they will,
  Oh borrowed shall you never be!'

4. Her breath grew strang, her hair grew
    lang,   15
  And twisted thrice about the tree,
And all the people, far and near,
  Thought that a savage beast was she.

5. These news did come to Kemp Owyne,
  Where he lived, far beyond the sea; 20
He hasted him to Craigy's sea,
  And on the savage beast lookd he.

6. Her breath was strang, her hair was lang,
  And twisted was about the tree,
And with a swing she came about: 25
  'Come to Craigy's sea, and kiss with
    me.'

7. 'Here is a royal belt,' she cried,
  'That I have found in the green sea;
And while your body it is on,
  Drawn shall your blood never be;   30
But if you touch me, tail or fin,
  I vow my belt your death shall be.'

8. He stepped in, gave her a kiss,
  The royal belt he brought him wi;
Her breath was strang, her hair was
    lang,   35
  And twisted twice about the tree,
And with a swing she came about:
  'Come to Craigy's sea, and kiss with
    me.

9. 'Here is a royal ring,' she said,
  'That I have found in the green
    sea;   40
And while your finger it is on,
  Drawn shall your blood never be;
But if you touch me, tail or fin,
  I swear my ring your death shall be.'

10. He stepped in, gave her a kiss,   45
  The royal ring he brought him wi;
Her breath was strang, her hair was lang,
  And twisted ance about the tree,
And with a swing she came about:
  'Come to Craigy's sea, and kiss with
    me.   50

11. 'Here is a royal brand,' she said,
  'That I have found in the green sea;
And while your body it is on,
  Drawn shall your blood never be;

But if you touch me, tail or fin,   55
  I swear my brand your death shall be.'

12. He stepped in, gave her a kiss,
  The royal brand he brought him wi;
Her breath was sweet, her hair grew
    short,
  And twisted nane about the tree,   60
And smilingly she came about,
  As fair a woman as fair could be.

THE DÆMON LOVER

1. 'O where have you been, my long, long
    love,
  This long seven years and mair?'
'O I'm come to seek my former vows
  Ye granted me before.'

2. 'O hold your tongue of your former
    vows,   5
  For they will breed sad strife;
O hold your tongue of your former vows,
  For I am become a wife.'

3. He turned him right and round about,
  And the tear blinded his ee: 10
'I wad never hae trodden on Irish
    ground,
  If it had not been for thee.

4. 'I might hae had a king's daughter,
  Far, far beyond the sea;
I might have had a king's daughter,   15
  Had it not been for love o thee.'

5. 'If ye might have had a king's daughter,
  Yersel ye had to blame;
Ye might have had taken the king's
    daughter,
  For ye kend that I was nane.   20

6. 'If I was to leave my husband dear,
  And my two babes also,
O what have you to take me to,
  If with you I should go?'

7. 'I hae seven ships upon the sea —   25
  The eighth brought me to land —
With four-and-twenty bold mariners,
  And music on every hand.'

8. She has taken up her two little babes,
  Kissd them baith cheek and chin: 30
'O fair ye weel, my ain two babes,
  For I'll never see you again.'

9. She set her foot upon the ship,
   No mariners could she behold;
   But the sails were o the taffetie,   35
   And the masts o the beaten gold.

10. She had not sailed a league, a league,
    A league but barely three,
    When dismal grew his countenance,   40
    And drumlie grew his ee.

11. They had not saild a league, a league,
    A league but barely three,
    Until she espied his cloven foot,
    And she wept right bitterlie.   45

12. 'O hold your tongue of your weeping,'
       says he,
    'Of your weeping now let me be;
    I will shew you how the lilies grow
    On the banks of Italy.'

13. 'O what hills are yon, yon pleasant hills,
    That the sun shines sweetly on?'   51
    'O yon are the hills of heaven,' he said,
    'Where you will never win.'

14. 'O whaten a mountain is yon,' she said,
    'All so dreary wi frost and snow?'   55
    'O yon is the mountain of hell,' he cried,
    'Where you and I will go.'

15. He strack the tap-mast wi his hand,
    The fore-mast wi his knee,
    And he brake that gallant ship in twain,
    And sank her in the sea.   61

LORD RANDAL

1. 'O where hae ye been, Lord Randal, my
       son?
   O where hae ye been, my handsome
       young man?'
   'I hae been to the wild wood; mother,
       make my bed soon,
   Fir I 'm weary wi hunting, and fain wald
   lie down.'

2. 'Where gat ye your dinner, Lord Randal,
       my son?   5
   Where gat ye your dinner, my hand-
       some young man?'
   'I dined wi my true-love; mother, make
       my bed soon,
   For I 'm weary wi hunting, and fain wald
   lie down.'

3. 'What gat ye to your dinner, Lord Ran-
       dal, my son?
   What gat ye to your dinner, my hand-
       some young man?'   10
   'I gat eels boiled in broo; mother make
       my bed soon,
   For I 'm weary wi hunting, and fain wald
   lie down.'

4. 'What became of your bloodhounds,
       Lord Randal, my son?
   What became of your bloodhounds, my
       handsome young man?'
   'O they swelld and they died; mother,
       make my bed soon,   15
   For I 'm weary wi hunting, and fain wald
   lie down.'

5. 'O I fear ye are poisond, Lord Randal,
       my son!
   O I fear ye are poisond, my handsome
       young man!'
   'O yes! I am poisond; mother, make
       my bed soon,
   For I 'm sick at the heart and I fain
   wald lie down.'   20

SIR PATRICK SPENS

1. The king sits in Dumferling toune,
   Drinking the blude-reid wine:
   'O whar will I get guid sailor,
   To sail this schip of mine?'

2. Up and spak an eldern knicht,   5
   Sat at the kings richt kne:
   'Sir Patrick Spence is the best sailor,
   That sails upon the se.'

3. The king has written a braid letter,
   And signd it wi his hand,   10
   And sent it to Sir Patrick Spence,
   Was walking on the sand.

4. The first line that Sir Patrick red,
   A loud lauch lauchèd he;
   The next line that Sir Patrick red,   15
   The teir blinded his ee.

5. 'O wha is this has don this deid,
   This ill deid don to me,
   To send me out this time o' the yeir,
   To sail upon the se!   20

6. 'Mak hast, mak haste, my mirry men all,
   Our guid schip sails the morne:'

'O say na sae, my master deir,
  For I feir a deadlie storme.

7. 'Late, late yestreen I saw the new
    moone,   25
  Wi the auld moone in hir arme,
  And l feir, I feir, my deir master,
  That we will cum to harme.'

8. O our Scots nobles wer richt laith
  To weet their cork-heild schoone; 30
  Bot lang owre a' the play wer playd,
  Thair hats they swam aboone.

9. O lang, lang may their ladies sit,
  Wi thair fans into their hand,
  Or eir they se Sir Patrick Spence 35
  Cum sailing to the land.

10. O lang, lang may the ladies stand,
  Wi thair gold kems in their hair,
  Waiting for thar ain deir lords,
  For they 'll se thame na mair. 40

11. Haf owre, haf owre to Aberdour,
  It 's fiftie fadom deip,
  And thair lies guid Sir Patrick Spence,
  Wi the Scots lords at his feit.

THOMAS RYMER

1. True Thomas lay oer yond grassy bank,
  And he beheld a ladie gay,
  A ladie that was brisk and bold,
  Come riding oer the fernie brae.

2. Her skirt was of the grass-green silk, 5
  Her mantel of the velvet fine,
  At ilka tett of her horse's mane
  Hung fifty silver bells and nine.

3. True Thomas he took off his hat
  And bowed him low down till his
    knee: 10
  'All hail, thou mighty Queen of Heaven!
  For your peer on earth I never did see.'

4. 'O no, O no, True Thomas,' she says,
  'That name does not belong to me;
  I am but the queen of fair Elfland, 15
  And I 'm come here for to visit thee.

5. 'But ye maun go wi me now, Thomas,
  True Thomas, ye maun go wi me,
  For ye maun serve me seven years, 19
  Thro weel or wae as may chance to be.'

6. She turned about her milk-white steed,
  And took True Thomas up behind,
  And aye wheneer her bridle rang,
  The steed flew swifter than the wind.

7. For forty days and forty nights 25
  He wade thro red blude to the knee,
  And he saw neither sun nor moon,
  But heard the roaring of the sea.

8. O they rade on and further on,
  Until they came to a garden green: 30
  'Light down, light down, ye ladie free,
  Some of that fruit let me pull to thee.'

9. 'O no, O no, True Thomas,' she says,
  'That fruit maun not be touched by
    thee,
  For a' the plagues that are in hell 35
  Light on the fruit of this countrie.

10. 'But I have a loaf here in my lap,
  Likewise a bottle of claret wine,
  And here ere we go farther on,
  We 'll rest a while, and ye may dine.' 40

11. When he had eaten and drunk his fill,
  'Lay down your head upon my knee,'
  The lady sayd, 'ere we climb yon hill,
  And I will show you fairlies three.

12. 'O see ye not yon narrow road, 45
  So thick beset wi thorns and briers?
  That is the path of righteousness,
  Tho after it but few enquires.

13. 'And see not ye that braid braid road,
  That lies across yon lillie leven? 50
  That is the path of wickedness,
  Tho some call it the road to heaven.

14. 'And see ye not that bonny road,
  Which winds about the fernie brae?
  That is the road to fair Elfland, 55
  Where you and I this night maun gae.

15. 'But Thomas, ye maun hold your tongue,
  Whatever ye may hear or see,
  For gin ae word you should chance to
    speak,
  You will neer get back to your air
    countrie.' 60

16. He has gotten a coat of the even cloth,
  And a pair of shoes of velvet green,
  And till seven years were past and gone
  True Thomas on earth was never seen.

BONNY BARBARA ALLAN

1. It was in and about the Martinmas time,
   When the green leaves were a falling,
That Sir John Græme, in the West
      Country,
   Fell in love with Barbara Allan.

2. He sent his man down through the town,
   To the place where she was dwelling: 6
'O haste and come to my master dear,
   Gin ye be Barbara Allan.'

3. O hooly, hooly rose she up,
   To the place where he was lying,   10
And when she drew the curtain by,
   'Young man, I think you 're dying.'

4. 'O it 's I 'm sick, and very, very sick,
   And 't is a' for Barbara Allan:'
'O the better for me ye 's never be,   15
   Tho your heart's blood were a spilling.

5. 'O dinna ye mind, young man,' said she,
   'When ye was in the tavern a drink-
      ing,
That ye made the healths gae round and
      round,
   And slighted Barbara Allan?'   20

6. He turnd his face unto the wall,
   And death was with him dealing:
'Adieu, adieu, my dear friends all,
   And be kind to Barbara Allan.'

7. And slowly, slowly raise she up,   25
   And slowly, slowly left him,
And sighing said, she could not stay,
   Since death of life had reft him.

8. She had not gane a mile but twa,   29
   When she heard the dead-bell ringing,
And every jow that the dead-bell geid,
   It cryd, Woe to Barbara Allan!

9. 'O mother, mother, make my bed!
   O make it saft and narrow!
Since my love died for me to-day,   35
   I 'll die for him to-morrow.'

THE TWA SISTERS

1. There was twa sisters in a bowr,
   Edinburgh, Edinburgh
There was twa sisters in a bowr,
   Stirling for ay
There was twa sisters in a bowr,   5

There came a knight to be their wooer,
Bonny Saint Johnston stands upon Tay.

2. He courted the eldest wi glove an ring,
   But he lovd the youngest above a' thing.

3. He courted the eldest wi brotch an knife,
   But lovd the youngest as his life.   11

4. The eldest she was vexèd sair,
   And much envied her sister fair.

5. Into her bowr she could not rest,
   Wi grief an spite she almos brast.   15

6. Upon a morning fair an clear,
   She cried upon her sister dear:

7. 'O sister, come to yon sea stran,
   An see our father's ships come to lan.'

8. She 's taen her by the milk-white han,   20
   An led her down to yon sea stran.

9. The youngest stood upon a stane,
   The eldest came an threw her in.

10. She tooke her by the middle sma,
    And dashd her bonny back to the jaw.   25

11. 'O sister, sister, tak my han,
    An Ise mack you heir to a' my lan.

12. 'O sister, sister, tak my middle,
    An yes get my goud and my gouder
       girdle.

13. 'O sister, sister, save my life,   30
    An I swear Ise never be nae man's wife.

14. 'Foul fa the han that I should tacke,
    It twind me an my wardles make.

15. 'Your cherry cheeks an yallow hair
    Gars me gae maiden for evermair.'   35

16. Sometimes she sank, an sometimes she
       swam,
    Till she came down yon bonny mill-dam

17. O out it came the miller's son,
    An saw the fair maid swimmin in.

18. 'O father, father, draw your dam,   40
    Here's either a mermaid or a swan.'

19. The miller quickly drew the dam,
    An there he found a drownd woman.

20. You coudna see her yallow hair
For gold and pearle that were so rare. 45

21. You coudna see her middle sma
For gouden girdle that was sae braw.

22. You coudna see her fingers white,
For gouden rings that was sae gryte.

23. An by there came a harper fine,   50
That harpèd to the king at dine.

24. When he did look that lady upon,
He sighd and made a heavy moan.

25. He's taen three locks o her yallow hair,
And wi them strung his harp sae fair. 55

26. The first tune he did play and sing,
Was, 'Farewell to my father the king.'

27. The nextin tune that he playd syne,
Was, 'Farewell to my mother the queen.'

28. The lasten tune that he playd then,   60
Was, 'Wae to my sister, fair Ellen.'

THE CRUEL BROTHER

1. There was three ladies playd at the ba,
With a hey ho and a lillie gay
There came a knight and played oer
them a'.
As the primrose spreads so sweetly.

2. The eldest was baith tall and fair,   5
But the youngest was beyond compare.

3. The midmost had a graceful mien,
But the youngest lookd like beautie's
queen.

4. The knight bowd low to a' the three,
But to the youngest he bent his knee. 10

5. The ladie turned her head aside,
The knight he wooed her to be his bride.

6. The ladie blushd a rosy red,
And sayd, 'Sir knight, I 'm too young
to wed.'

7. 'O ladie fair, give me your hand,   15
And I 'll make you ladie of a' my land.'

8. 'Sir knight, ere ye my favor win,
You maun get consent frae a' my kin.'

9. He 's got consent frae her parents dear,
And likewise frae her sisters fair.   20

10. He 's got consent frae her kin each one,
But forgot to spiek to her brother John.

11. Now, when the wedding day was come,
The knight would take his bonny bride
home.

12. And many a lord and many a knight   25
Came to behold that ladie bright.

13. And there was nae man that did her see
But wishd himself bridegroom to be.

14. Her father dear led her down the stair,
And her sisters twain they kissd her
there.   30

15. Her mother dear led her thro the closs,
And her brother John set her on her
horse.

16. She leand her oer the saddle-bow,
To give him a kiss ere she did go.

17. He has taen a knife, baith lang and
sharp,   35
And stabbed that bonny bride to the
heart.

18. She hadno ridden half thro the town,
Until her heart's blude staind her gown.

19. 'Ride softly on,' says the best young
man,
'For I think our bonny bride looks pale
and wan.'   40

20. 'O lead me gently up yon hill,
And I 'll there sit down, and make my
will.'

21. 'O what will you leave to your father
dear?'
'The silver-shode steed that brought me
here.'

22. 'What will you leave to your mother
dear?'   45
'My velvet pall and my silken gear.'

23. 'What will you leave to your sister
Anne?'
'My silken scarf and my gowden fan.'

24. 'What will you leave to your sister
        Grace?'
    'My bloody cloaths to wash and dress.' 50

25. 'What will you leave to your brother
        John?'
    'The gallows-tree to hang him on.'

26. 'What will you leave to your brother
        John's wife?'
    'The wilderness to end her life.'

27. This ladie fair in her grave was laid,   55
    And many a mass was oer her said.

28. But it would have made your heart right
        sair,
    To see the bridegroom rive his haire.

EDWARD

1. 'Why dois your brand sae drap wi bluid,
        Edward, Edward,
   Why dois your brand sae drap wi bluid,
        And why sae sad gang yee O?'
   'O I hae killed my hauke sae guid,   5
        Mither, mither,
   O I hae killed my hauke sae guid,
        And I had nae mair bot hee O.'

2. 'Your haukis bluid was nevir sae reid,
        Edward, Edward, 10
   Your haukis bluid was nevir sae reid,
        My deir son I tell thee O.'
   'O I hae killed my reid-roan steid,
        Mither, mither,
   O I hae killed my reid-roan steid,   15
        That erst was sae fair and frie O.'

3. 'Your steid was auld, and ye hae got
        mair,
        Edward, Edward,
   Your steid was auld, and ye hae got mair,
        Sum other dule ye drie O.'   20
   'O I hae killed my fadir deir,
        Mither, mither,

O I hae killed my fadir deir,
    Alas, and wae is mee O!'

4. 'And whatten penance wul ye drie for
        that,   25
        Edward, Edward,
   And whatten penance will ye drie for
        that?
        My deir son, now tell me O.'
   'Ile set my feit in yonder boat,
        Mither, mither,   30
   Ile set my feit in yonder boat,
        And Ile fare ovir the sea O.'

5. 'And what wul ye doe wi your towirs
        and your ha,
        Edward, Edward?
   And what wul you doe wi your towirs
        and your ha,   35
        That were sae fair to see O?'
   'Ile let thame stand tul they doun fa,
        Mither, mither,
   Ile let thame stand tul they down fa,
        For here nevir mair maun I bee O.'   40

6. 'And what wul ye leive to your bairns
        and your wife,
        Edward, Edward?
   And what wul ye leive to your bairns
        and your wife,
        Whan ye gang ovir the sea O?'
   'The warldis room, late them beg thrae
        life,   45
        Mither, mither,
   The warldis room, late them beg thrae
        life,
        For thame nevir mair wul I see O.'

7. 'And what wul ye leive to your ain
        mither deir,
        Edward, Edward?   50
   And what wul ye leive to your ain
        mither deir?
        My deir son. now tell me O.'
   'The curse of hell frae me sall ye beir,
        Mither, mither,
   The curse of hell frae me sall ye beir,   55
        Sic counseils ye gave to me O.'

SIR THOMAS WYATT (1503?–1542)

Wyatt was preëminently a courtier. Well educated at Cambridge, and, possibly, also at Oxford, he began his career at court in several offices connected with the person of the king, from which he advanced speedily to diplomatic services, during the period 1525–1540, in France, Italy, Spain, and Flanders. In 1536, Wyatt was knighted, and in 1542, he represented Kent in parliament. A vigorous tradition persists that Wyatt was attached to the English court not only through his official appointments, but also, indirectly, as the youthful lover of Anne Boleyn.

Well-read in Italian, French, and classical literature, Wyatt deliberately formed his style by imitating Italian and French models. He is conspicuous in the history of English literature chiefly from the fact that he introduced into English the sonnet form, with its refining influence upon English meter and diction. Several of Wyatt's sonnets are direct translations from Petrarch, upon whom, throughout, he drew largely for his rime-scheme, his vocabulary, and his conventional ideas. Besides sonnets, Wyatt wrote other lyrics, epigrams, satires, and devotional verse. In his lyrics other than sonnets, is found his finest work. A collection of Wyatt's poems was printed in *Songs and Sonnets written by the right honorable Lord Henry Howard, late Earl of Surrey, and others,* published by Richard Tottel in 1557, and commonly known as *Tottel's Miscellany.*

THE LOVER FOR SHAME-FASTNESS HIDETH HIS DESIRE WITHIN HIS FAITHFUL HEART

The long love that in my thought I harbor,
And in my heart doth keep his residence,
Into my face presseth with bold pretence,
And there campeth displaying his banner.
She that me learns to love and to suffer, 5
And wills that my trust, and lust's negligence
Be reined by reason, shame, and reverence,
With his hardiness takes displeasure.
Wherewith love to the heart's forest he fleeth,
Leaving his enterprise with pain and cry, 10
And there him hideth, and not appeareth.
What may I do, when my master feareth?
But in the field with him to live and die?
For good is the life, ending faithfully.

THE LOVER COMPARETH HIS STATE TO A SHIP IN PERILOUS STORM TOSSED ON THE SEA

My galley chargèd with forgetfulness
Thorough sharp seas, in winter nights doth pass,
'Tween rock and rock; and eke my foe, alas,
That is my lord, steereth with cruelness,
And every hour, a thought in readiness, 5
As though that death were light in such a case.
An endless wind doth tear the sail apace
Of forcèd sighs, and trusty fearfulness.
A rain of tears, a cloud of dark disdain
Hath done the wearied cords great hinderance, 10
Wreathèd with error, and with ignorance.
The stars be hid that led me to this pain;
Drowned is reason that should be my comfort,
And I remain, despairing of the port.

THE LOVER HAVING DREAMED OF ENJOYING OF HIS LOVE, COMPLAINETH THAT THE DREAM IS NOT EITHER LONGER OR TRUER

Unstable dream, according to the place,
Be steadfast once, or else at least be true.
By tasted sweetness make me not to rue
The sudden loss of thy false feignèd grace.
By good respect in such a dangerous case 5
Thou broughtst not her into these tossing seas,
But madest my spirit to live, my care t'encrease,
My body in tempest her delight t'embrace.
The body dead, the spirit had his desire;

Painless was th' one, the other in delight. 10
Why then, alas! did it not keep it right,
But thus return to leap into the fire,
And where it was at wish, could not remain?
Such mocks of dreams do turn to deadly
   pain!

A RENOUNCING OF LOVE

Farewell, Love, and all thy laws for ever!
Thy baited hooks shall tangle me no more:
Senec and Plato call me from thy lore
To perfect wealth my wit for to endeavor.
In blind error when I did persèver, 5
Thy sharp repulse, that pricketh aye so sore,
Taught me in trifles that I set no store;
But 'scape forth thence, since liberty is
   lever.
Therefore, farewell! go trouble younger
   hearts,
And in me claim no more authority. 10
With idle youth go use thy property,
And thereon spend thy many brittle darts;
For hitherto though I have lost my time,
Me list no longer rotten boughs to climb.

THE LOVER BESEECHETH HIS MIS-TRESS NOT TO FORGET HIS STEADFAST FAITH AND TRUE IN-TENT

Forget not yet the tried intent
Of such a truth as I have meant;
My great travail so gladly spent,
Forget not yet!

Forget not yet when first began 5
The weary life ye know, since whan
The suit, the service none tell can;
Forget not yet!

Forget not yet the great assays,
The cruel wrong, the scornful ways, 10
The painful patience in delays,
Forget not yet!

Forget not! O, forget not this,
How long ago hath been, and is,
The mind that never meant amiss — 15
Forget not yet!

Forget not then thine own approved,
The which so long hath thee so loved,
Whose steadfast faith yet never moved:
Forget not this! 20

AN EARNEST SUIT TO HIS UNKIND MISTRESS NOT TO FORSAKE HIM

And wilt thou leave me thus?
Say nay, say nay, for shame!
To save thee from the blame
Of all my grief and grame.
And wilt thou leave me thus? 5
Say nay! say nay!

And wilt thou leave me thus,
That hath loved thee so long
In wealth and woe among:
And is thy heart so strong 10
As for to leave me thus?
Say nay! say nay!

And wilt thou leave me thus,
That hath given thee my heart
Never for to depart 15
Neither for pain nor smart:
And wilt thou leave me thus?
Say nay! say nay!

And wilt thou leave me thus,
And have no more pity 20
Of him that loveth thee?
Alas, thy cruelty!
And wilt thou leave me thus?
Say nay! say nay!

THE LOVER COMPLAINETH THE UN-KINDNESS OF HIS LOVE

My lute, awake, perform the last
Labor that thou and I shall waste,
And end that I have now begun.
And when this song is sung and past,
My lute, be still, for I have done. 5

As to be heard where ear is none,
As lead to grave in marble stone,
My song may pierce her heart as soon.
Should we then sigh, or sing, or moan?
No, no, my lute, for I have done. 10

The rocks do not so cruelly
Repulse the waves continually,
As she my suit and affection;
So that I am past remedy,
Whereby my lute and I have done. 15

Proud of the spoil that thou hast got
Of simple hearts through Lovës shot,
By whom unkind thou hast them won,
Think not he hath his bow forgot,
Although my lute and I have done. 20

Vengeance shall fall on thy disdain
That makest but game on earnest pain.
Think not alone under the sun
Unquit to cause thy lovers playn,
Although my lute and I have done.   25

May chance thee lie withered and old
In winter nights that are so cold,
Playning in vain unto the moon;
Thy wishes then dare not be told.
Care then who list, for I have done.   30

And then may chance thee to repent
The time that thou hast lost and spent
To cause thy lovers sigh and swoon;
Then shalt thou know beauty but lent,
And wish and want, as I have done.   35

Now cease, my lute, this is the last
Labor that thou and I shall waste,
And ended is that we begun.
Now is the song both sung and past,
My lute, be still, for I have done.   40

OF THE MEAN AND SURE ESTATE

WRITTEN TO JOHN POINS

My mother's maids, when they did sew and
     spin,
They sung sometime a song of the field
     mouse
That, for because her livelihood was but
     thin,
Would needs go seek her townish sister's
     house.
She thought herself endurèd too much
     pain;   5
The stormy blasts her cave so sore did
     souse
That when the furrows swimmèd with the
     rain,
She must lie cold and wet in sorry plight;
And worse than that, bare meat there did
     remain
To comfort her when she her house had
     dight;   10
Sometime a barley corn; sometime a bean,
For which she labored hard both day and
     night
In harvest time whilst she might go and
     glean;
And when her store was stroyèd with the
     flood,
Then welaway! for she undone was clean.   15
Then was she fain to take, instead of food,
Sleep, if she might, her hunger to beguile.
'My sister,' quoth she, 'hath a living good,

And hence from me she dwelleth not a mile.
In cold and storm she lieth warm and dry   20
In bed of down, the dirt doth not defile
Her tender foot, she laboreth not as I.
Richly she feedeth, and at the rich man's
     cost,
And for her meat she needs not crave nor
     cry.
By sea, by land, of the delicates, the most   25
Her cater seeks and spareth for no peril,
She feedeth on boiled bacon, meat, and
     roast,
And hath thereof neither charge nor travail;
And, when she list, the liquor of the grape
Doth glad her heart till that her belly
     swell.'   30
And at this journey she maketh but a jape;
So forth she goeth, trusting of all this wealth
With her sister her part so for to shape,
That if she might keep herself in health,
To live a lady while her life doth last.   35
And to the door now is she come by stealth,
And with her foot anon she scrapeth full fast.
Th' other, for fear, durst not well scarce
     appear,
Of every noise so was the wretch aghast.
At last she askèd softly who was there,   40
And in her language as well as she could.
'Peep!' quoth the other sister, 'I am here.'
'Peace,' quoth the town mouse, 'why speak-
     est thou so loud?'
And by the hand she took her fair and well.
'Welcome,' quoth she, 'my sister, by the
     Rood!'   45
She feasted her, that joy it was to tell
The fare they had; they drank the wine so
     clear,
And, as to purpose now and then it fell,
She cheerèd her with 'How, sister, what
     cheer!'
Amid this joy befell a sorry chance,   50
That, welaway! the stranger bought full
     dear
The fare she had, for, as she looked askance,
Under a stool she spied two steaming eyes
In a round head with sharp ears. In France
Was never mouse so feared, for, though un-
     wise   55
Had not y-seen such a beast before,
Yet had nature taught her after her guise
To know her foe and dread him evermore.
The towny mouse fled, she knew whither to
     go;
Th' other had no shift, but wonders sore   60
Feared of her life. At home she wished her
     tho,
And to the door, alas! as she did skip,

The heaven it would, lo! and eke her chance
    was so,
At the threshold her silly foot did trip;
And ere she might recover it again,   65
The traitor cat had caught her by the hip,
And made her there against her will remain,
That had forgot her poor surety and rest
For seeming wealth wherein she thought to
    reign.
Alas, my Poins, how men do seek the best 70
And find the worst by error as they stray!
And no marvel; when sight is so opprest,
And blinds the guide, anon out of the way
Goeth guide and all in seeking quiet life.
O wretched minds, there is no gold that may
Grant that you seek; no war, no peace, no
    strife.   76
No, no, although thy head were hooped with
    gold,
Sergeant with mace, halberd, sword, nor
    knife,
Cannot repulse the care that follow should.
Each kind of life hath with him his dis-
    ease.   80
Live in delight even as thy lust would,
And thou shalt find, when lust doth most
    thee please,
It irketh straight, and by itself doth fade.
A small thing is it that may thy mind ap-
    pease.
None of ye all there is that is so mad   85
To seek for grapes on brambles or on briars;
Nor none, I trow, that hath his wit so bad
To set his hay for conies over rivers,

Nor ye set not a drag-net for an hare;
And yet the thing that most is your de-
    sire   90
Ye do mis-seek with more travail and care.
Make plain thine heart, that it be not knotted
With hope or dread, and see thy will be
    bare
From all effects whom vice hath ever spotted.
Thyself content with that is thee assigned, 95
And use it well that is to thee allotted.
Then seek no more out of thyself to find
The thing that thou hast sought so long be-
    fore,
For thou shalt feel it sticking in thy mind.
Mad, if ye list to continue your sore,   100
Let present pass and gape on time to come,
And deep yourself in travail more and
    more.
    Henceforth, my Poins, this shall be all and
    some,
These wretched fools shall have naught else
    of me;
But to the great God and to his high dome,
None other pain pray I for them to be,   106
But, when the rage doth lead them from the
    right,
That, looking backward, virtue they may
    see,
Even as she is so goodly fair and bright,
And whilst they clasp their lusts in arms'
    across,   110
Grant them, good Lord, as thou mayst of
    thy might,
To fret inward for losing such a loss.

HENRY HOWARD, EARL OF SURREY (1517?–1547)

Henry Howard, or, as he is commonly called, Surrey, was, like Wyatt, actively connected with the English court. His courtly occupations, however, were not so much administrative and diplomatic as military and chivalric. From his early years up to manhood, Surrey was the companion of princes, and more than once his elders bargained for his marriage with a princess. As a boy of some fifteen years, Surrey accompanied the king to France, and remained eleven months at the French court. At the age of twenty, by striking a courtier who had accused him of seditious intentions, he landed himself in confinement for a few months at Windsor. These months Surrey spent in versifying, a diversion for which he had been well prepared by previous practice and by considerable reading in classical and contemporary literature. After having distinguished himself from time to time in jousts, he was made knight of the garter in 1541. Surrey's impulsive and adventurous spirit, which established him as 'the most foolish proud boy that is in England,' led him to eminent military service in France, during which he called forth the king's reprimand by exposing himself needlessly to danger. By numerous angry and trenchant utterances, he eventually brought upon himself the charge of treason, which he vigorously denied, but which led, ultimately, to his beheading on Tower Hill, January 21, 1547.

Although Surrey composed verse during most of his life-time, his poems first appeared in print in 1557, when Richard Tottel published *Songs and Sonnets written by the right honorable Lord Henry Howard, late Earl of Surrey, and others.* During the same year appeared Surrey's translation of the second and fourth books of Virgil's *Æneid,* a translation in which blank verse is used for the first time, in any notable way, in English. Although Surrey was the poetical disciple of his friend Wyatt, he excelled his master in all points. In particular, this superiority is apparent in range of subject, in refinement and variety of versification, and in delicacy of feeling.

DESCRIPTION OF SPRING, WHEREIN EACH THING RENEWS, SAVE ONLY THE LOVER

The soote season that bud and bloom forth
  brings,
With green hath clad the hill and eke the
  vale;
The nightingale with feathers new she sings;
The turtle to her mate hath told her tale:
Summer is come, for every spray now
  springs;   5
The hart hath hung his old head on the pale;
The buck in brake his winter coat he flings;
The fishes flete with new repairèd scale;
The adder all her slough away she slings;
The swift swallow pursueth the flies smale;
The busy bee her honey now she mings.   11
Winter is worn, that was the flowers' bale:
And thus I see among these pleasant things
Each care decays, and yet my sorrow springs!

COMPLAINT OF A LOVER REBUKED

Love, that liveth and reigneth in my thought,
That built his seat within my captive breast,
Clad in the arms wherein with me he fought,
Oft in my face he doth his banner rest.
She that me taught to love, and suffer pain,
My doubtful hope and eke my hot desire   6
With shamefast cloak to shadow and refrain,
Her smiling grace converteth straight to ire.
The coward Love then to the heart apace
Taketh his flight, whereas he lurks and
  plains,   10
His purpose lost, and dare not show his face.
For my lord's guilt thus faultless bide I
  pains.
Yet from my lord shall not my foot remove;
Sweet is his death that takes his end by
  love.

DESCRIPTION AND PRAISE OF HIS LOVE GERALDINE

From Tuscan came my lady's worthy race;
Fair Florence was sometime her ancient
  seat;
The Western isle whose pleasant shore doth
  face
Wild Camber's cliffs did give her lively
  heat;

Fostered she was with milk of Irish breast;
Her sire, an earl; her dame, of princes'
    blood; 6
From tender years, in Britain she doth rest,
With a king's child, where she tasteth costly
    food;
Hunsdon did first present her to mine eyen;
Bright is her hue, and Geraldine she hight;
Hampton me taught to wish her first for
    mine; 11
And Windsor, alas, doth chase me from her
    sight:
Her beauty of kind, her virtues from above.
Happy is he that can obtain her love!

COMPLAINT OF THE LOVER DIS-
DAINED

In Cyprus springs, whereas dame Venus
    dwelt,
A well so hot, that whoso tastes the same,
Were he of stone, as thawèd ice should melt,
And kindled find his breast with firèd flame;
Whose moist poison dissolvèd hath my heart.
With creeping fire my cold limbs are sup-
    prest, 6
Feeleth the heart that harbored freedom,
    smart:
Endless despair long thraldom hath imprest.
Another well of frozen ice is found,
Whose chilling venom of repugnant kind, 10
The fervent heat doth quench of Cupid's
    wound,
And with the spot of change infects the
    mind;
Whereof my dear hath tasted, to my pain:
Whereby my service grows into disdain.

A COMPLAINT BY NIGHT OF THE
LOVER NOT BELOVED

Alas, so all things now do hold their peace!
Heaven and earth disturbèd in nothing;
The beasts, the air, the birds their song do
    cease,
The nightès chair the stars about doth bring.
Calm is the sea; the waves work less and
    less; 5
So am not I, whom love, alas, doth wring,
Bringing before my face the great increase
Of my desires, whereat I weep and sing,
In joy and woe, as in a doubtful ease.
For my sweet thoughts sometime do pleasure
    bring; 10
But by and by, the cause of my disease
Gives me a pang, that inwardly doth sting,

When that I think what grief it is again,
To live and lack the thing should rid my
    pain.

VOW TO LOVE FAITHFULLY HOW-
SOEVER HE BE REWARDED

Set me whereas the sun doth parch the
    green,
Or where his beams do not dissolve the ice;
In temperate heat, where he is felt and seen;
In presence prest of people, mad or wise;
Set me in high, or yet in low degree; 5
In longest night, or in the longest day;
In clearest sky, or where clouds thickest be;
In lusty youth, or when my hairs are gray;
Set me in heaven, in earth, or else in hell;
In hill, or dale, or in the foaming flood; 10
Thrall, or at large, alive whereso I dwell;
Sick or in health, in evil fame or good;
Hers will I be, and only with this thought
Content myself, although my chance be
    naught.

COMPLAINT OF THE ABSENCE OF
HER LOVER BEING UPON THE SEA

O happy dames! that may embrace
The fruit of your delight;
Help to bewail the woeful case,
And eke the heavy plight,
Of me, that wonted to rejoice 5
The fortune of my pleasant choice:
Good ladies, help to fill my mourning voice.

In ship freight with rememberance
Of thoughts and pleasures past,
He sails that hath in governance 10
My life, while it will last;
With scalding sighs, for lack of gale,
Furthering his hope, that is his sail,
Toward me, the sweet port of his avail.

Alas, how oft in dreams I see 15
Those eyes that were my food;
Which sometime so delighted me,
That yet they do me good;
Wherewith I wake with his return,
Whose absent flame did make me burn: 20
But when I find the lack, Lord, how I
    mourn!

When other lovers in arms across,
Rejoice their chief delight,
Drownèd in tears to mourn my loss,
I stand the bitter night 25

In my window, where I may see
Before the winds how the clouds flee:
Lo, what a mariner love hath made me!

And in green waves when the salt flood
Doth rise by rage of wind,   30
A thousand fancies in that mood,
Assail my restless mind.
Alas, now drencheth my sweet foe,
That with the spoil of my heart did go,
And left me; but, alas, why did he so?   35

And when the seas wax calm again,
To chase from me annoy,
My doubtful hope doth cause me pain;
So dread cuts off my joy.
Thus is my wealth mingled with woe,   40
And of each thought a doubt doth grow;
Now he comes! Will he come? Alas, no,
no!

A PRAISE OF HIS LOVE WHEREIN HE REPROVETH THEM THAT COMPARE THEIR LADIES WITH HIS

Give place, ye lovers, here before
That spent your boasts and brags in vain;
My lady's beauty passeth more
The best of yours, I dare well sayn,
Than doth the sun the candle light,   5
Or brightest day the darkest night.

And thereto hath a troth as just
As had Penelope the fair;
For what she saith, ye may it trust
As it by writing sealèd were: 10
And virtues hath she many mo
Than I with pen have skill to show.

I could rehearse, if that I would,
The whole effect of Nature's plaint,
When she had lost the perfect mold,   15
The like to whom she could not paint:
With wringing hands, how she did cry,
And what she said, I know it, I.

I know she swore with raging mind,
Her kingdom only set apart,   20
There was no loss by law of kind
That could have gone so near her heart.
And this was chiefly all her pain:
She could not make the like again.

Sith Nature thus gave her the praise,   25
To be the chiefest work she wrought;
In faith, methink, some better ways

On your behalf might well be sought,
Than to compare, as ye have done,
To match the candle with the sun.   30

DESCRIPTION OF THE RESTLESS STATE OF A LOVER

The sun hath twice brought forth his tender
green
And clad the earth in lively lustiness,
Once have the winds the trees despoilèd
clean,
And new again begins their cruelness,
Since I have hid under my breast the harm
That never shall recover healthfulness.   6
The winter's hurt recovers with the warm,
The parchèd green restored is with the
shade.
What warmth, alas, may serve for to disarm
The frozen heart that mine in flame hath
made?   10
What cold again is able to restore
My fresh green years, that wither thus and
fade?
Alas, I see, nothing hath hurt so sore,
But time in time reduceth a return;
In time my harm increaseth more and
more,   15
And seems to have my cure always in scorn.
Strange kinds of death, in life that I do try,
At hand to melt, far off in flame to burn;
And like as time list to my cure apply,
So doth each place my comfort clean re-
fuse.   20
All thing alive that seeth the heavens with
eye
With cloak of night may cover and excuse
Itself from travail of the day's unrest,
Save I, alas, against all others' use,
That then stir up the torments of my
breast,   25
And curse each star as causer of my fate.
And when the sun hath eke the dark op-
prest,
And brought the day, it doth nothing abate
The travails of mine endless smart and pain;
For then, as one that hath the light in
hate,   30
I wish for night, more covertly to plain,
And me withdraw from every haunted place,
Lest by my cheer my chance appear too plain.
And in my mind I measure, pace by pace,
To seek the place where I myself had lost,
That day that I was tangled in the lace,   36
In seeming slack, that knitteth ever most.
But never yet the travail of my thought
Of better state could catch a cause to boast;

For if I found, sometime that I have sought,
Those stars by whom I trusted of the port, 41
My sails do fall, and I advance right naught,
As anchored fast, my spirits do all resort
To stand agazed, and sink in more and more
The deadly harm which she doth take in
    sport. 45
Lo, if I seek, how do I find my sore!
And if I flee I carry with me still
The venomed shaft, which doth ·his force
    restore
By haste of flight, and I may plain my fill ·
Unto myself, unless this careful song 50
Print in your heart some parcel of my teen;
For I, alas, in silence all too long
Of mine old hurt yet feel the wound but
    green.
Rue on my life, or else your cruel wrong 54
Shall well appear, and by my death be seen!

THE MEANS TO ATTAIN HAPPY LIFE

Martial, the things that do attain
The happy life be these, I find:
The riches left, not got with pain;
The fruitful ground; the quiet mind;
The egall friend; no grudge, no strife; 5
No charge of rule, no governance;
Without disease, the healthful life;
The household of continuance;
The mean diet, no delicate fare;
True wisdom joined with simpleness; 10
The night dischargèd of all care,
Where wine the wit may not oppress;
The faithful wife, without debate;
Such sleeps as may beguile the night: ·
Contentèd with thine own estate, 15
Ne wish for death, ne fear his might.

OF THE DEATH OF SIR T[HOMAS] W[YATT]

W. resteth here, that quick could never rest;
Whose heavenly gifts, encreasèd by disdain,
And virtue sank the deeper in his breast;
Such profit he by envy could obtain. 4
A head where wisdom mysteries did frame;
Whose hammers beat still in that lively brain
As on a stithe where that some work of
    fame
Was daily wrought to turn to Britain's gain.
A visage stern and mild, where both did
    grow,
Vice to condemn, in virtue to rejoice; 10
Amid great storms, whom grace assurèd so

To live upright and smile at fortune's choice.
A hand that taught what might be said in
    rime;
That reft Chaucer the glory of his wit: 14
A mark, the which (unperfected, for time)
Some may approach, but never none shall
    hit.
A tongue that served in foreign realms his
    king;
Whose courteous talk to virtue did enflame
Each noble heart; a worthy guide to bring
Our English youth by travail unto fame. 20
An eye whose judgment none affect could
    blind,
Friends to allure, and foes to reconcile;
Whose piercing look did represent a mind
With virtue fraught, reposèd, void of guile,
A heart where dread was never so imprest,
To hide the thought that might the truth ad-
    vance;
In neither fortune lost, nor yet represt, 27
To swell in wealth, or yield unto mischance.
A valiant corse, where force and beauty met;
Happy, alas, too happy, but for foes! 30
Lived, and ran the race that Nature set:
Of manhood's shape, where she the mold did
    lose.
But to the heavens that simple soul is fled,
Which left with such as covet Christ to
    know
Witness of faith that never shall be dead, 35
Sent for our health, but not receivèd so.
Thus for our guilt, this jewel have we lost;
The earth his bones, the heavens possess his
    ghost!

VIRGIL'S ÆNEID

BOOK II

They whistèd all, with fixèd face attent,
When Prince Æneas from the royal seat
Thus gan to speak: 'O Queen, it is thy will
I should renew a woe cannot be told;
How that the Greeks did spoil and over-
    throw 5
The Phrygian wealth and wailful realm of
    Troy.
Those ruthful things that I myself beheld,
And whereof no small part fell to my share;
Which to express, who could refrain from
    tears?
What Myrmidon? or yet what Dolopës? 10
What stern Ulysses' wagèd soldier?
And lo! moist night now from the welkin
    falls,
And stars declining counsel us to rest.

But since so great is thy delight to hear
Of our mishaps and Troyës last decay,   15
Though to record the same my mind abhors
And plaint eschews, yet thus will I begin:—
The Greekës chieftains, all irked with the
      war,   •
Wherein they wasted had so many years,
And oft repulsed by fatal destiny,   20
A huge horse made, high raisèd like a hill,
By the divine science of Minerva,—
Of cloven fir compacted were his ribs,
For their return a feignèd sacrifice,—   24
The fame whereof so wandered it at point.
In the dark bulk they closed bodies of men
Chosén by lot, and did enstuff by stealth
The hollow womb with armèd soldiers.
    There stands in sight an isle hight Tene-
      don,
Rich, and of fame while Priam's kingdom
      stood,   30
Now but a bay and road unsure for ship.
Hither them secretly the Greeks withdrew,
Shrouding themselves under the desert
      shore;
And, weening we they had been fled and
      gone,
And with that wind had fet the land of
      Greece,   35
Troy discharged her long continued dole.
The gates cast up, we issued out to play,
The Greekish camp desirous to behold,
The places void and the forsaken coasts.
Here Pyrrhus' band, there fierce Achilles
      pight;   40

Here rode their ships, there did their battles
      join.
Astonied some the scathful gift beheld,
Behight by vow unto the chaste Minerve,
All wondering at the hugeness of the horse.
    And first of all, Timœtes gan advise   45
Within the walls to lead and draw the
      same,
And place it eke amid the palace court,
Whether of guile, or Troyës fate it would.
Capys, with some of judgment more discreet,
Willed it to drown, or underset with flame,
The suspect present of the Greeks' deceit,
Or bore and gauge the hollow caves un-
      couth;
So diverse ran the giddy people's mind.   53
    Lo! foremost of a rout that followed him,
Kindled Laöcoön hasted from the tower,
Crying far off: "O wretched citizens,   56
What so great kind of frenzy fretteth you?
Deem ye the Greeks, our enemies, to be
      gone?
Or any Greekish gifts can you suppose
Devoid of guile? Is so Ulysses known?   60
Either the Greeks are in this timber hid,
Or this an engine is to annoy our walls,
To view our towers, and overwhelm our
      town.
Here lurks some craft. Good Troyans give
      no trust
Unto this horse, for, whatsoever it be,   65
I dread the Greeks, yea, when they offer
      gifts."'

* * *

THOMAS SACKVILLE, LORD BUCKHURST (1536–1608)

About the year 1553, certain English printers projected a continuation of John Lydgate's *Fall of Princes*, a version of Boccaccio's *De Casibus Virorum Illustrium*, the design of these printers being to add stories of famous unfortunates from the period with which Boccaccio ended ' unto this presente time.'   The project, under the general title *A Mirror for Magistrates*, was printed in gradually enlarged editions between the years 1555 and 1610.   Although probably not a partner to the original plan, Sackville early became an associate and a contributor. *The Induction*, written as an introduction to such stories as he should contribute, and *The Complaint of Henry, Duke of Buckingham*, the only ' tragedy ' actually contributed by Sackville, appeared in the edition of 1563.

The Induction is commonly accounted the best achievement in English poetry between Chaucer and Spenser.   Although in writing his description of the lower world Sackville evidently had in mind both the sixth book of Virgil's *Æneid* and medieval allegory, the superb vivifying of such abstractions as Remorse of Conscience, Dread, Revenge, and the like, is to be credited to the genius of the English poet.   Sackville owes his inspiration, perhaps, to Virgil, and his verse form, certainly, to Chaucer; his masterly control of his material and his power of phrasing are surely his own.

THE INDUCTION

The wrathful Winter, 'proaching on apace,
With blustering blasts had all ybared the
   treen,
And old Saturnus, with his frosty face,
With chilling cold had pierced the tender
   green;   4
The mantles rent, wherein enwrappèd been
The gladsome groves that now lay over-
   thrown,
The tapets torn, and every bloom down
   blown.

The soil, that erst so seemly was to seen,
Was all despoilèd of her beauty's hue;
And soote fresh flowers, wherewith the sum-
   mer's queen   10
Had clad the earth, now Boreas' blasts down
   blew;
And small fowls flocking, in their song did
   rue
The winter's wrath, wherewith each thing
   defaced
In woeful wise bewailed the summer past.

Hawthorn had lost his motley livery,   15
The naked twigs were shivering all for cold,
And dropping down the tears abundantly;
Each thing, methought, with weeping eye me
   told
The cruel season, bidding me withhold
Myself within; for I was gotten out   20
Into the fields, whereas I walked about.

When lo, the night with misty mantles
   spread,
Gan dark the day, and dim the azure skies;
And Venus in her message Hermes sped
To bloody Mars, to will him not to rise,   25
While she herself approached in speedy
   wise;
And Virgo hiding her disdainful breast,
With Thetis now had laid her down to rest.

Whiles Scorpio dreading Sagittarius' dart,
Whose bow prest bent in fight, the string
   had slipped,   30
Down slid into the ocean flood apart,
The Bear, that in the Irish seas had dipped
His grisly feet, with speed from thence he
   whipped:
For Thetis, hasting from the Virgin's bed,
Pursued the Bear, that ere she came was
   fled.   35

And Phaeton now, near reaching to his race
With glist'ring beams, gold streaming where
   they bent,
Was prest to enter in his resting place:
Erythius, that in the cart first went,
Had even now attained his journey's stent:
And, fast declining, hid away his head,   41
While Titan couched him in his purple bed.

And pale Cynthea, with her borrowed light,
Beginning to supply her brother's place   44
Was past the noonstead six degrees in sight,
When sparkling stars amid the heaven's face,

With twinkling light shone on the earth
    apace,
That, while they brought about the nightës
    chare,
The dark had dimmed the day ere I was
    ware.

And sorrowing I to see the summer flowers,
The lively green, the lusty leas forlorn,   51
The sturdy trees so shattered with the
    showers,
The fields so fade, that flourished so beforn,
It taught me well, all earthly things be born
To die the death, for naught long time may
    last;   55
The summer's beauty yields to winter's blast.

Then looking upward to the heaven's leams,
With nightës stars thick powdered every-
    where,
Which erst so glistened with the golden
    streams
That cheerful Phœbus spread down from his
    sphere,   60
Beholding dark oppressing day so near:
The sudden sight reducèd to my mind,
The sundry changes that in earth we find.

That musing on this worldly wealth in
    thought,
Which comes, and goes, more faster than we
    see   65
The flickering flame that with the fire is
    wrought,
My busy mind presented unto me
Such fall of peers as in this realm had be;
That oft I wished some would their woes
    descrive,
To warn the rest whom fortune left alive.

And straight forth stalking with redoubled
    pace,   71
For that I saw the night drew on so fast,
In black all clad, there fell before my face
A piteous wight, whom woe had all fore-
    waste;
Forth from her eyen the crystal tears out
    brast;   75
And sighing sore, her hands she wrung and
    fold,
Tare all her hair, that ruth was to behold.

Her body small, forewithered, and forespent,
As is the stalk that summer's drought op-
    pressed;
Her welkèd face with woeful tears besprent;
Her color pale; and, as it seemed her best,
In woe and plaint reposèd was her rest;   82

And, as the stone that drops of water wears,
So dented were her cheeks with fall of tears.

Her eyes swollen with flowing streams
    afloat,   85
Wherewith, her looks thrown up full pite-
    ously,
Her forceless hands together oft she smote,
With doleful shrieks, that echoed in the sky;
Whose plaint such sighs did straight ac-
    company,
That, in my doom, was never man did see
A wight but half so woe-begone as she.   91

I stood aghast, beholding all her plight,
'Tween dread and dolor, so distrained in
    heart,
That, while my hairs upstarted with the
    sight,
The tears outstreamed for sorrow of her
    smart: 95
But, when I saw no end that could apart
The deadly dewle which she so sore did
    make,
With doleful voice then thus to her I spake:

'Unwrap thy woes, whatever wight thou be,
And stint in time to spill thyself with
    plaint: 100
Tell what thou art, and whence, for well I
    see
Thou canst not dure, with sorrow thus at-
    taint:'
And, with that word of sorrow, all fore-
    faint
She lookèd up, and, prostrate as she lay,
With piteous sound, lo, thus she gan to say:

'Alas, I wretch, whom thus thou seest dis-
    trained   106
With wasting woes, that never shall aslake,
Sorrow I am, in endless torments pained
Among the Furies in the infernal lake,
Where Pluto, god of hell, so grisly black,
Doth hold his throne, and Lethe's deadly
    taste   111
Doth reave remembrance of each thing fore-
    past:

'Whence come I am, the dreary destiny
And luckless lot for to bemoan of those
Whom fortune, in this maze of misery,   115
Of wretched chance, most woeful mirrors
    chose;
That, when thou seest how lightly they did
    lose
Their pomp, their power, and that they
    thought most sure.

Thou mayst soon deem no earthly joy may
    dure.'

Whose rueful voice no sooner had out
    brayed   120
Those woeful words wherewith she sor-
    rowed so,
But out, alas, she shright, and never stayed,
Fell down, alas, and all to-dashed herself for
    woe:
The cold pale dread my limbs gan overgo,
And I so sorrowed at her sorrows eft, 125
That, what with grief and fear, my wits
    were reft.

I stretched myself, and straight my heart
    revives,
That dread and dolor erst did so appale;
Like him that with the fervent fever strives,
When sickness seeks his castle health to
    scale;   130
With gathered spirits so forced I fear to
    avale:
And, rearing her, with anguish all fore-
    done,
My spirits returned, and then I thus begun:

'O Sorrow, alas, sith Sorrow is thy name,
And that to thee this drear doth well per-
    tain,   135
In vain it were to seek to cease the same:
But, as a man himself with sorrow slain,
So I, alas, do comfort thee in pain,
That here in sorrow art foresunk so deep,
That at thy sight I can but sigh and weep.'

I had no sooner spoken of a stike,   141
But that the storm so rumbled in her
    breast,
As Æölus could never roar the like;
And showers down rainèd from her eyen so
    fast,
That all bedrent the place, till at the last,
Well easèd they the dolor of her mind, 146
As rage of rain doth swage the stormy
    wind:

For forth she pacèd in her fearful tale:
'Come, come,' quoth she, 'and see what I
    shall show,
Come, hear the plaining and the bitter bale
Of worthy men by Fortune overthrow: 151
Come thou, and see them ruing all in row,
They were but shades that erst in mind thou
    rolled:
Come, come with me, thine eyes shall them
    behold.'

What could these words but make me more
    aghast,   155
To hear her tell whereon I mused whilere?
So was I mazed therewith, till, at the last,
Musing upon her words, and what they
    were,
All suddenly well lessoned was my fear;
For to my mind returnèd, how she telled
Both what she was, and where her won she
    held.   161

Whereby I knew that she a goddess was,
And, therewithal, resorted to my mind
My thought, that late presented me the glass
Of brittle state, of cares that here we find,
Of thousand woes to silly men assigned: 166
And how she now bid me come and behold,
To see with eye that erst in thought I rolled.

Flat down I fell, and with all reverence
Adorèd her, perceiving now that she, 170
A goddess, sent by godly providence,
In earthly shape thus showed herself to me,
To wail and rue this world's uncertainty:
And, while I honored thus her godhead's
    might
With plaining voice these words to me she
    shright: 175

'I shall thee guide first to the grisly lake,
And thence unto the blissful place of rest,
Where thou shall see, and hear, the plaint
    they make
That whilom here bare swing among the
    best:
This shalt thou see: but great is the unrest
That thou must bide, before thou canst at-
    tain   181
Unto the dreadful place where these remain.'

And, with these words, as I upraisèd stood,
And gan to follow her that straight forth
    paced,
Ere I was ware, into a desert wood 185
We now were come, where, hand in hand
    embraced,
She led the way, and through the thick so
    traced,
As, but I had been guided by her might,
It was no way for any mortal wight.

But lo, while thus amid the desert dark 190
We passèd on with steps and pace unmeet,
A rumbling roar, confused with howl and
    bark
Of dogs, shook all the ground under our
    feet.

And struck the din within our ears so deep,
As, half distraught, unto the ground I fell,
Besought return, and not to visit hell.   196

But she, forthwith, uplifting me apace,
Removed my dread, and, with a steadfast
   mind,
Bade me come on; for here was now the
   place,
The place where we our travail end should
   find: 200
Wherewith I rose, and to the place assigned
Astoined I stalk, when straight we ap-
   proached near
The dreadful place, that you will dread to
   hear.

An hideous hole all vast, withouten shape,
Of endless depth, o'erwhelmed with ragged
   stone,   205
With ugly mouth, and grisly jaws doth gape,
And to our sight confounds itself in one:
Here entered we, and yeding forth, anon
An horrible loathly lake we might discern,
As black as pitch, that clepèd is Avern: 210

A deadly gulf, where naught but rubbish
   grows,
With foul black swelth in thickened lumps
   that lies,
Which up in th' air such stinking vapors
   throws,
That over there may fly no fowl but dies
Choked with the pestilent savors that arise:
Hither we come; whence forth we still did
   pace,   216
In dreadful fear amid the dreadful place:

And, first, within the porch and jaws of
   hell,
Sat deep Remorse of Conscience, all be-
   sprent
With tears; and to herself oft would she
   tell   220
Her wretchedness, and cursing never stent
To sob and sigh; but ever thus lament,
With thoughtful care, as she that, all in
   vain,
Would wear, and waste continually in pain.

Her eyes unsteadfast, rolling here and there,
Whirled on each place, as place that ven-
   geance brought,   226
So was her mind continually in fear,
Tossed and tormented with the tedious
   thought
Of those detested crimes which she had
   wrought;

With dreadful cheer, and looks thrown to
   the sky,   230
Wishing for death, and yet she could not
   die.

Next saw we Dread, all trembling how he
   shook,
With foot uncertain, proffered here and
   there:
Benumbed of speech, and, with a ghastly
   look
Searched every place, all pale and dead for
   fear,   235
His cap borne up with staring of his hair,
'Stoined and amazed at his own shade for
   dread,
And fearing greater dangers than was need.

And next, within the entry of this lake,
Sat fell Revenge, gnashing her teeth for
   ire,   240
Devising means how she may vengeance
   take,
Never in rest, till she have her desire:
But frets within so far forth with the fire
Of wreaking flames, that now determines
   she   245
To die by death, or venged by death to be.

When fell Revenge, with bloody foul pre-
   tence
Had showed herself, as next in order set,
With trembling limbs we softly parted
   thence,
Till in our eyes another sight we met:
When from my heart a sigh forthwith I
   fet,   250
Ruing, alas! upon the woeful plight
Of Misery, that next appeared in sight.

His face was lean, and somedeal pined
   away,
And eke his hands consumèd to the bone,
But what his body was, I cannot say,   255
For on his carcass raiment had he none,
Save clouts and patches, piecèd one by one;
With staff in hand, and scrip on shoulders
   cast,
His chief defence against the winter's blast.

His food, for most, was wild fruits of the
   tree,   260
Unless sometimes some crumbs fell to his
   share,
Which in his wallet long, God wot, kept he,
As on the which full daint'ly would he fare:
His drink, the running stream: his cup, the
   bare

Of his palm closed; his bed, the hard cold
    ground: 265
To this poor life was Misery ybound.

Whose wretched state when we had well be-
    held,
With tender ruth on him, and on his fears,
In thoughtful cares forth then our pace we
    held;
And, by and by, another shape appears, 270
Of greedy Care, still brushing up the breres,
His knuckles knobbed, his flesh deep dented
    in,
With tawèd hands, and hard ytannèd skin.

The morrow gray no sooner hath begun
To spread his light, even peeping in our
    eyes,   275
When he is up, and to his work yrun:
But let the night's black misty mantles
    rise,
And with foul dark never so much dis-
    guise
The fair bright day, yet ceaseth he no while,
But hath his candles to prolong his toil. 280

By him lay heavy Sleep, the cousin of
    Death,
Flat on the ground, and still as any stone,
A very corpse, save yielding forth a breath:
Small keep took he, whom Fortune frownèd
    on,
Or whom she lifted up into the throne 285
Of high renown; but, as a living death,
So, dead alive, of life he drew the breath.

The body's rest, the quiet of the heart,
The travail's ease, the still night's fear was
    he,
And of our life in earth the better part; 290
Reaver of sight, and yet in whom we see
Things oft that tide, and oft that never be;
Without respect, esteeming equally
King Crœsus' pomp, and Irus' poverty.

And next, in order sad, Old Age we found:
His beard all hoar, his eyes hollow and
    blind,   296
With drooping cheer still poring on the
    ground,
As on the place where Nature him assigned
To rest, when that the Sisters had untwined
His vital thread, and ended with their
    knife   300
The fleeting course of fast declining life.

There heard we him with broke and hollow
    plaint

Rue with himself his end approaching fast,
And all for naught his wretched mind tor-
    ment
With sweet remembrance of his pleasures
    past,   305
And fresh delights of lusty youth fore-
    waste;
Recounting which, how would he sob and
    shriek,
And to be young again of Jove beseek!

But and the cruel fates so fixèd be,
That time forepast cannot return again, 310
This one request of Jove yet prayèd he:
That, in such withered plight, and wretched
    pain,
As eld, accompanied with his loathsome
    train,
Had brought on him, all were it woe and
    grief,
He might a while yet linger forth his life,

And not so soon descend into the pit, 316
Where Death, when he the mortal corpse
    hath slain,
With reckless hand in grave doth cover it,
Thereafter never to enjoy again
The gladsome light, but in the ground
    ylain,   320
In the depth of darkness waste and wear to
    naught,
As he had never into the world been
    brought.

But who had seen him sobbing, how he
    stood
Unto himself, and how he would bemoan
His youth forepast, as though it wrought
    him good   325
To talk of youth, all were his youth fore-
    gone,
He would have mused, and marveled much,
    whereon
This wretched Age should life desire so
    fain,
And knows full well life doth but length his
    pain.

Crookbacked he was, tooth-shaken, and
    blear-eyed,   330
Went on three feet, and sometime crept on
    four,
With old lame bones that rattled by his
    side,
His scalp all pilled, and he with eld for-
    lore:
His withered fist still knocking at Death's
    door.

Fumbling, and driveling, as he draws his
   breath: 335
For brief, the shape and messenger of
   Death.

And fast by him pale Malady was placed,
Sore sick in bed, her color all foregone,
Bereft of stomach, savor, and of taste,
Ne could she brook no meat, but broths
   alone: 340
Her breath corrupt, her keepers every one
Abhorring her, her sickness past recure,
Detesting physic, and all physic's cure.

But, oh, the doleful sight that then we see!
We turned our look, and, on the other side,
A grisly shape of Famine might we see, 346
With greedy looks, and gaping mouth that
   cried
And roared for meat, as she should there
   have died;
Her body thin and bare as any bone, 349
Whereto was left naught but the case alone.

And that, alas, was gnawn on every where,
All full of holes, that I ne might refrain
From tears, to see how she her arms could
   tear,
And with her teeth gnash on the bones in
   vain,
When, all for naught, she fain would so
   sustain   355
Her starven corpse, that rather seemed a
   shade,
Than any substance of a creature made.

Great was her force, whom stone wall could
   not stay,
Her tearing nails snatching at all she saw;
With gaping jaws, that by no means ymay
Be satisfied from hunger of her maw, 361
But eats herself as she that hath no law:
Gnawing, alas, her carcass all in vain,
Where you may count each sinew, bone, and
   vein.

On her while we thus firmly fixed our
   eyes,   365
That bled for ruth of such a dreary sight,
Lo, suddenly she shrieked in so huge wise,
As made hell-gates to shiver with the might:
Wherewith, a dart we saw, how it did light
Right on her breast, and, therewithal, pale
   Death   370
Enthrilling it, to reave her of her breath.

And by and by, a dumb dead corpse we saw,
Heavy, and cold, the shape of Death aright,

That daunts all earthly creatures to his
   law;   374
Against whose force in vain it is to fight:
Ne peers, ne princes, nor no mortal wight,
No towns, ne realms, cities, ne strongest
   tower,
But all, perforce, must yield unto his power.

His dart, anon, out of the corpse he took,
And in his hand (a dreadful sight to see)
With great triumph eftsoons the same he
   shook,   381
That most of all my fears affrayèd me:
His body dight with naught but bones,
   pardé.
The naked shape of man there saw I plain,
All save the flesh, the sinew, and the vein.

Lastly, stood War, in glittering arms yclad,
With visage grim, stern looks, and blackly
   hued;   387
In his right hand a naked sword he had,
That to the hilts was all with blood im-
   brued;
And in his left (that kings and kingdoms
   rued)   390
Famine and fire he held, and therewithal
He razèd towns, and threw down towers and
   all.

Cities he sacked, and realms that whilom
   flowered
In honor, glory, and rule, above the best,
He overwhelmed, and all their fame devoured,   395
Consumed, destroyed, wasted and never
   ceased,
Till he their wealth, their name, and all oppressed:
His face forehewed with wounds, and by his
   side
There hung his targe, with gashes deep and
   wide.

In mids of which, depainted there, we found
Deadly Debate, all full of snaky hair, 401
That with a bloody fillet was ybound,
Out breathing naught but discord every-
   where:
And round about were portrayed, here and
   there,
The hugy hosts, Darius and his power, 405
His kings, princes, his peers, and all his
   flower,

Whom great Macedo vanquished there in
   sight,
With deep slaughter, despoiling all his pride

Pierced through his realms, and daunted all
   his might:
Duke Hannibal beheld I there beside, 410
In Canna's field, victor how he did ride,
And woeful Romans that in vain withstood,
And consul Paulus covered all in blood.

Yet saw I more the fight at Thrasimene,
And Treby field, and eke when Hannibal 415
And worthy Scipio last in arms were seen
Before Carthago gate, to cry for all
The world's empire, to whom it should be-
   fall:
There saw I Pompey and Cæsar clad in
   arms,   419
Their hosts allied and all their civil harms:

With conquerors' hands, forebathed in their
   own blood,
And Cæsar weeping over Pompey's head;
Yet saw I Sulla and Marius where they
   stood,
Their great cruelty, and the deep bloodshed
Of friends: Cyrus I saw and his host dead,
And how the queen with great despite hath
   flung   426
His head in blood of them she overcome.

Xerxes, the Persian king, yet saw I there,
With his huge host, that drank the rivers
   dry,
Dismounted hills, and made the vales up-
   rear,   430
His host and all yet saw I slain, pardé:
Thebës I saw, all razed how it did lie
In heaps of stones, and Tyrus put to spoil,
With walls and towers flat evened with the
   soil.

But Troy, alas, methought, above them
   all,   435
It made mine eyes in very tears consume:
When I beheld the woeful word befall,
That by the wrathful will of gods was come;
And Jove's unmovèd sentence and fore-
   doom
On Priam king, and on his town so bent,
I could not lin, but I must there lament. 441

And that the more, sith destiny was so
   stern
As, force perforce, there might no force
   avail,
But she must fall: and, by her fall, we
   learn,
That cities, towers, wealth, world, and all
   shall quail;

No manhood, might, nor nothing might prevail;
All were there pressed full many a prince,
   and peer,
And many a knight that sold his death full
   dear.

Not worthy Hector, worthiest of them all,
Her hope, her joy, his force is now for
   naught: 450
O Troy, Troy, Troy, there is no boot but
   bale,
The hugy horse within thy walls is brought;
Thy turrets fall, thy knights, that whilom
   fought
In arms amid the field, are slain in bed,
Thy gods defiled, and all thy honor dead. 455

The flames up spring, and cruelly they creep
From wall to roof, till all to cinders waste:
Some fire the houses where the wretches
   sleep,
Some rush in here, some run in there as
   fast;
In every where or sword or fire they taste:
The walls are torn, the towers whirled to
   the ground;   461
There is no mischief but may there be
   found.

Cassandra yet there saw I how they haled
From Pallas' house, with spercled tress un-
   done,
Her wrists fast bound, and with Greeks'
   rout empaled: 465
And Priam eke, in vain how he did run
To arms, whom Pyrrhus with despite hath
   done
To cruel death, and bathed him in the baign
Of his son's blood, before the altar slain.

But how can I describe the doleful sight, 470
That in the shield so livelike fair did shine?
Sith in this world, I think was never wight
Could have set forth the half, not half so
   fine:
I can no more, but tell how there is seen
Fair Ilium fall in burning red gledes down,
And, from the soil, great Troy, Neptunus'
   town.   476

Herefrom when scarce I could mine eyes
   withdraw,
That filled with tears as doth the springing
   well,
We passèd on so far forth till we saw
Rude Acheron, a loathsome lake to tell, 480

That boils and bubs up swelth as black as
hell;
Where grisly Charon, at their fixèd tide,
Still ferries ghosts unto the farther side.

The agèd God no sooner Sorrow spied,
But, hasting straight unto the bank apace,
With hollow call unto the rout he cried,   486
To swerve apart, and give the goddess place:
Straight it was done, when to the shore we
pace,
Where, hand in hand as we then linkèd
fast,
Within the boat we are together placed.   490

And forth we launch full fraughted to the
brink:
When, with the unwonted weight, the rusty
keel
Began to crack as if the same should sink:
We hoise up mast and sail, that in a while
We fetched the shore, where scarcely we
had while   495
For to arrive, but that we heard anon
A three-sound bark confounded all in one.

We had not long forth passed, but that we
saw
Black Cerberus, the hideous hound of hell,
With bristles reared, and with a three-
mouthed jaw   500
Foredinning the air with his horrible yell,
Out of the deep dark cave where he did
dwell.
The goddess straight he knew, and by and
by,
He peased and couched, while that we passèd
by.

Thence come we to the horror and the
hell,   505
The large great kingdoms, and the dreadful
reign
Of Pluto in his throne where he did dwell,
The wide waste places, and the hugy plain,

The wailings, shrieks, and sundry sorts of
pain,
The sighs, the sobs, the deep and deadly
groan;   510
Earth, air, and all, resounding plaint and
moan.

Here puled the babes, and here the maids
unwed
With folded hands their sorry chance bewailed;
Here wept the guiltless slain, and lovers
dead,
That slew themselves when nothing else
availed;   515
A thousand sorts of sorrows here, that
wailed
With sighs, and tears, sobs, shrieks, and all
yfear,
That, of, alas, it was a hell to hear.

We staid us straight, and with a rueful
fear,
Beheld this heavy sight; while from mine
eyes   520
The vapored tears down stillèd here and
there,
And Sorrow eke, in far more woeful wise,
Took on with plaint, upheaving to the skies
Her wretched hands, that, with her cry, the
rout   524
Gan all in heaps to swarm us round about.

'Lo here' quoth Sorrow, 'princes of re-
nown,
That whilom sat on top of Fortune's wheel,
Now laid full low; like wretches whirlèd
down,
Even with one frown, that stayed but with a
smile:
And now behold the thing that thou, ere-
while,   530
Saw only in thought; and, what thou now
shalt hear,
Recount the same to kesar, king, and peer.'

* * *

ROGER ASCHAM (1515–1568)

Ascham was prepared for his career by gentle birth and by a thorough humanistic education at St. John's College, Cambridge. His studying of Greek resulted in his being one of the most enthusiastic advocates of the new classical learning. In 1531, he became a fellow of St. John's College, and subsequently held the appointments of reader in Greek and of public orator. Ascham's *Toxophilus* (1545), full of patriotism, learning, and human feeling, won for him the favor of Henry VIII, who granted him a pension, later renewed by Edward VI. In 1548, he became tutor of the Princess Elizabeth, and, soon after, secretary to an embassy to the court of Charles V. He became secretary to Queen Mary, and later received preferment from Queen Elizabeth. Ascham's vigorous humanism is emphatically expressed in his *Schoolmaster*, written late in life, and published posthumously in 1570.

THE SCHOOLMASTER

From BOOK I

But I am afraid that over-many of our travelers into Italy do not eschew the way to Circe's Court, but go and ride, and run, and fly thither; they make great haste to come to her; they make great suit to serve her; yea, I could point out some with my finger that never had gone out of England but only to serve Circe in Italy. Vanity and vice and any licence to ill living in England was counted stale and rude unto them. And so, being mules and horses before they went, returned very swine and asses home again; yet everywhere very foxes with subtle and busy heads; and where they may, very wolves with cruel malicious hearts. A marvelous monster, which, for filthiness of living, for dulness to learning himself, for wiliness in dealing with others, for malice in hurting without cause, should carry at once, in one body, the belly of a swine, the head of an ass, the brain of a fox, the womb of a wolf. If you think we judge amiss and write too sore against you, hear what the Italian saith of the Englishman, what the master reporteth of the scholar; who uttereth plainly what is taught by him, and what is learned by you, saying, '*Inglese Italianato è un diabolo incarnato,*' that is to say, you remain men in shape and fashion, but become devils in life and condition. This is not the opinion of one for some private spite, but the judgment of all in a common proverb, which riseth of that learning and those manners which you gather in Italy: a good schoolhouse of wholesome doctrine, and worthy masters of commendable scholars, where the master had rather defame himself for his teaching, than not shame his scholar for his learning. A good nature of the master, and fair conditions of the scholars. And now choose you, you Italian Englishmen, whether you will be angry with us for calling you monsters, or with the Italians for calling you devils, or else with your own selves that take so much pains and go so far to make yourselves both. If some yet do not well understand what is an Englishman Italianated, I will plainly tell him. He that by living and traveling in Italy bringeth home into England out of Italy the religion, the learning, the policy, the experience, the manners of Italy. That is to say, for religion, papistry or worse; for learning, less, commonly, than they carried out with them; for policy, a factious heart, a discoursing head, a mind to meddle in all men's matters; for experience, plenty of new mischiefs never known in England before; for manners, variety of vanities and change of filthy living. These be the enchantments of Circe, brought out of Italy to mar men's manners in England; much by example of ill life, but more by precepts of fond books of late translated out of Italian into English, sold in every shop in London, commended by honest titles, the sooner to corrupt honest manners; dedicated overboldly to virtuous and honorable personages, the easier to beguile simple and innocent wits. It is pity that those which have authority and charge to allow and disallow books to be printed, be no more circumspect herein than they are. Ten sermons at Paul's Cross do not so much good for moving men to true doctrine, as one of those books do harm with enticing men to ill living. Yea, I say farther, those books tend not so much to corrupt honest living, as they do to subvert true religion. More papists be made by your merry books of Italy than by your earnest books of Louvain. And because our great physicians do wink at the matter, and make no count of this sore, I, though not admitted one of their fellowship, yet having been many years a prentice to God's true religion, and trust to continue a poor journeyman therein all days of my life, for the duty I owe and love I bear both to true doctrine and honest living, though I have no authority to amend the sore myself, yet I will declare my good-will to discover the sore to others.

St. Paul saith that sects and ill opinions be the works of the flesh and fruits of sin. This is spoken no more truly for the doctrine than sensible for the reason. And why? For ill doings breed ill thinkings. And of corrupted manners spring perverted judgments. And how? There be in man two special things: man's will, man's mind. Where will inclineth to goodness, the mind is bent to truth. Where will is carried from goodness to vanity, the mind is soon drawn from truth to false opinion. And so the readiest way to entangle the mind with false doctrine is first to entice the will to wanton living. Therefore, when the busy and open papists abroad could not by their contentious books turn men in England fast enough from truth and right judgment in doctrine, then the subtle and secret papists at home procured bawdy books to be translated out of the Italian tongue, whereby over-many young wills and wits, allured to wantonness, do now boldly contemn all severe books that sound to honesty and godliness. In our forefathers' time, when papistry, as a standing pool, covered and overflowed all England, few books were read in our tongue, saving certain books [of] chivalry, as they said, for pastime and pleasure, which, as some say, were made in monasteries by idle monks or wanton canons: as one, for example, *Morte Arthur,* the whole pleasure of which book standeth in two special points — in open manslaughter and bold bawdry. In which book those be counted the noblest knights that do kill most men without any quarrel, and commit foulest adulteries by subtlest shifts: as Sir Launcelot with the wife of King Arthur, his master; Sir Tristram with the wife of King Mark, his uncle; Sir Lamerock with the wife of King Lot, that was his own aunt. This is good stuff for wise men to laugh at, or honest men to take pleasure at! Yet I know when God's Bible was banished the court, and *Morte Arthur* received into the prince's chamber. What toys the daily reading of such a book may work in the will of a young gentleman or a young maid that liveth wealthily and idly, wise men can judge and honest men do pity. And yet ten *Morte Arthurs* do not the tenth part so much harm as one of these books made in Italy and translated in England. They open not fond and common ways to vice, but such subtle, cunning, new, and diverse shifts to carry young wills to vanity and young wits to mischief, to teach old bawds new schoolpoints, as the simple head of an Englishman is not able to invent, nor never was heard of in England before; yea, when papistry overflowed all. Suffer these books to be read, and they shall soon displace all books of godly learning. For they, carrying the will to vanity and marring good manners, shall easily corrupt the mind with ill opinions and false judgment in doctrine: first, to think nothing of God himself — one special point that is to be learned in Italy and Italian books. And that which is most to be lamented, and therefore more needful to be looked to, there be more of these ungracious books set out in print within these few months than have been seen in England many score years before. And because our Englishmen made Italians cannot hurt but certain persons and in certain places, therefore these Italian books are made English to bring mischief enough openly and boldly to all states, great and mean, young and old, everywhere.

And thus you see how will enticed to wantonness doth easily allure the mind to false opinions; and how corrupt manners in living, breed false judgment in doctrine; how sin and fleshliness bring forth sects and heresies. And, therefore, suffer not vain books to breed vanity in men's wills, if you would have God's truth take root in men's minds.

That Italian that first invented the Italian proverb against our Englishmen Italianated, meant no more their vanity in living than their lewd opinion in religion. For in calling them devils, he carrieth them clean from God; and yet he carrieth them no farther than they willingly go themselves — that is, where they may freely say their minds — to the open contempt of God and all godliness, both in living and doctrine.

And how? I will express how, not by a fable of Homer, nor by the philosophy of Plato, but by a plain truth of God's Word, sensibly uttered by David thus: ' These men, *abominabiles facti in studiis suis,* think verily and sing gladly the verse before, *Dixit insipiens in corde suo, non est Deus '*— that is to say, they giving themselves up to vanity, shaking off the motions of grace, driving from them the fear of God, and running headlong into all sin, first lustily contemn God, then scornfully mock his Word, and also spitefully hate and hurt all well-willers thereof. Then they have in more reverence the *Triumphs* of Petrarch than the *Genesis* of Moses. They make more account of Tully's *Offices* than St. Paul's *Epistles;* of a tale in Boccaccio than a story of the Bible. Then they count as fables the holy mysteries of christian religion. They make Christ and his Gospel only serve civil policy. Then neither religion cometh amiss to them. In time they be promoters of both openly : in place, again, mockers of both privily, as I wrote once in a rude rime : —

Now new, now old, now both, now neither,
To serve the world's course, they care not with whether.

For where they dare, in company where they like, they boldly laugh to scorn both protestant and papist. They care for no Scripture ; they make no count of general councils ; they contemn the consent of the church ; they pass for no doctors ; they mock the Pope ; they rail on Luther ; they allow neither side ; they like none, but only themselves. The mark they shoot at, the end they look for, the heaven they desire, is only their own present pleasure and private profit : whereby they plainly declare of whose school, of what religion they be — that is, epicures in living and ἄθεοι [godless] in doctrine. This last word is no more unknown now to plain Englishmen than the person was unknown some time in England, until some Englishman took pains to fetch that devilish opinion out of Italy. These men, thus Italianated abroad, cannot abide our godly Italian church at home ; they be not of that parish ; they be not of that fellowship ; they like not that preacher ; they hear not his sermons, except sometimes for company they come thither to hear the Italian tongue naturally spoken, not to hear God's doctrine truly preached.

And yet these men in matters of divinity openly pretend a great knowledge, and have privately to themselves a very compendious understanding of all, which, nevertheless, they will utter when and where they list. And that is this : all the mysteries of Moses, the whole law and ceremonies, the Psalms and prophets, Christ and his Gospel, God and the devil, heaven and hell, faith, conscience, sin, death, and all they shortly wrap up, they quickly expound with this one half verse of Horace :

Credat Judaeus Apella.
[Let the Jew Apella believe it]

Yet though in Italy they may freely be of no religion, as they are in England in very deed to, nevertheless, returning home into England, they must countenance the profession of the one or the other, however inwardly they laugh to scorn both. And though for their private matters they can follow, fawn, and flatter noble personages contrary to them in all respects, yet commonly they ally themselves with the worst papists, to whom they be wedded, and do well agree together in three proper opinions : in open contempt of God's Word ; in a secret security of sin ; and in a bloody desire to have all taken away by sword and burning that be not of their faction. They that do read with indifferent judgment Pygius and Machiavelli, two indifferent patriarchs of these two religions, do know full well what I say true.

Ye see what manners and doctrine our Englishmen fetch out of Italy. For, finding no other there, they can bring no other hither. And, therefore, many godly and excellent learned Englishmen, not many years ago, did make a better choice, when open cruelty drove them out of this country, to place themselves there where Christ's doctrine, the fear of God, punishment of sin, and discipline of honesty were had in special regard.

I was once in Italy myself; but I thank God my abode there was but nine days. And yet I saw in that little time, in one city, more liberty to sin than ever I heard tell of in our noble city of London in nine years. I saw it was there as free to sin not only without all punishment, but also without any man's marking, as it is free in the city of London to choose without all blame whether a man lust to wear shoe or pantocle. And good cause why; for, being unlike in truth of religion, they must needs be unlike in honesty of living. For blessed be Christ, in our city of London commonly the commandments of God be more diligently taught, and the service of God more reverently used, and that daily in many private men's houses, than they be in Italy once a week in their common churches; where making ceremonies to delight the eye, and vain sounds to please the ear, do quite thrust out of the churches all service of God in spirit and truth. Yea, the Lord Mayor of London, being but a civil officer, is commonly, for his time, more diligent in punishing sin, the bent enemy against God and good order, than all the bloody inquisitors in Italy be in seven years. For their care and charge is not to punish sin, not to amend manners, not to purge doctrine, but only to watch and oversee that Christ's true religion set no sure footing where the Pope hath any jurisdiction. I learned, when I was at Venice, that there it is counted good policy, when there be four or five brethren of one family, one only to marry, and all the rest to welter with as little shame in open lechery as swine do here in the common mire. Yea, there be as fair houses of religion, as great provision, as diligent officers to keep up this misorder, as Bridewell is and all the masters there to keep down misorder. And, therefore, if the Pope himself do not only grant pardons to further these wicked purposes abroad in Italy, but also (although this present Pope in the beginning made some show of misliking thereof) assign both meed and merit to the maintenance of stews and brothel-houses at

home in Rome, then let wise men think Italy a safe place for wholesome doctrine and godly manners, and a fit school for young gentlemen of England to be brought up in!

Our Italians bring home with them other faults from Italy, though not so great as this of religion, yet a great deal greater than many good men can well bear. For commonly they come home common contemners of marriage and ready persuaders of all others to the same; not because they love virginity, nor yet because they hate pretty young virgins, but, being free in Italy to go whithersoever lust will carry them, they do not like that law and honesty should be such a bar to their like liberty at home in England. And yet they be the greatest makers of love, the daily dalliers, with such pleasant words, with such smiling and secret countenances, with such signs, tokens, wagers, purposed to be lost before they were purposed to be made, with bargains of wearing colors, flowers, and herbs, to breed occasion of ofter meeting of him and her, and bolder talking of this and that, etc. And although I have seen some, innocent of all ill and staid in all honesty, that have used these things without all harm, without all suspicion of harm, yet these knacks were brought first into England by them that learned them before in Italy in Circe's court; and how courtly courtesies soever they be counted now, yet, if the meaning and manners of some that do use them were somewhat amended, it were no great hurt neither to themselves nor to others.

Another property of this our English Italians is to be marvelous singular in all their matters: singular in knowledge, ignorant of nothing; so singular in wisdom (in their own opinion) as scarce they count the best counselor the prince hath comparable with them; common discoursers of all matters; busy searchers of most secret affairs; open flatterers of great men; privy mislikers of good men; fair speakers, with smiling countenances and much courtesy openly to all men; ready backbiters, sore nippers, and spiteful reporters privily of good men. And being brought up in Italy in some free city, as all cities be there, where a man may freely discourse against what he will, against whom he lust, against any prince, against any government, yea, against God himself and his whole religion; where he must be either Guelph or Ghibelin, either French or Spanish, and always compelled to be of some party, of some faction, he shall never be compelled to be of any religion; and if he meddle not over-much with Christ's true religion, he shall have free liberty to embrace all religions, and become, if he lust, at once, without any let or punishment, Jewish, Turkish, papish, and devilish.

A young gentleman thus bred up in this goodly school, to learn the next and ready way to sin, to have a busy head, a factious heart, a talkative tongue, fed with discoursing of factions, led to contemn God and his religion, shall come home into England but very ill taught, either to be an honest man himself, a quiet subject to his prince, or willing to serve God under the obedience of true doctrine, or within the order of honest living.

I know none will be offended with this my general writing, but only such as find themselves guilty privately therein: who shall have good leave to be offended with me, until they begin to amend themselves. I touch not them that be good; and I say too little of them that be not; and so, though not enough for their deserving, yet sufficiently for this time, and more else when if occasion so require.

And thus far have I wandered from my first purpose of teaching a child, yet not altogether out of the way, because this whole talk hath tended to the only advancement of truth in religion and honesty of living; and hath been wholly within the compass of learning and good manners, the special points belonging in the right bringing up of youth.

But to my matter, as I began plainly and simply with my young scholar, so will I not leave him, God willing, until I have brought him a perfect scholar out of the school, and placed him in the university, to become a fit student for logic and rhetoric: and so after to physic, law, or divinity, as aptness of nature, advice of friends, and God's disposition shall lead him.

JOHN LYLY (1554?-1606)

Of the events of Lyly's life little is known. After taking his degree from Oxford, thus securing for himself the somewhat invidious title of 'university wit,' he supported himself in London by his pen. Although his nine plays had an important influence in the development of pre-Shaksperean drama, and although they represent his most valuable contribution to English literature, Lyly is best known, probably, through the extravagant style of his *Euphues, the Anatomy of Wit* (1578) and *Euphues and his England* (1580). These two works, usually referred to in combination as *Euphues*, constitute, ostensibly, a romance. The story, however, meager at best, is almost infinitely attenuated by letters, 'model' conversations, and moral preachments. The interest of Euphues,— an interest more curious and historical than human,— lies in its unremitting artificiality of style, characterized especially by balance, alliteration, citations of classical examples, and references to natural history.

From EUPHUES AND HIS ENGLAND

This queen being deceased, Elizabeth, being of the age of twenty-two years, of more beauty than honor, and yet of more honor than any earthly creature, was called from a prisoner to be a prince, from the castle to the crown, from the fear of losing her head, to be supreme head. And here, ladies, it may be you will move a question, why this noble lady was either in danger of death, or cause of distress, which, had you thought to have passed in silence, I would, notwithstanding, have revealed.

This lady all the time of her sister's reign was kept close, as one that tendered not those proceedings which were contrary to her conscience, who, having divers enemies, endured many crosses, but so patiently as in her deepest sorrow she would rather sigh for the liberty of the Gospel than her own freedom. Suffering her inferiors to triumph over her, her foes to threaten her, her dissembling friends to undermine her, learning in all this misery only the patience that Zeno taught Eretricus to bear and forbear, never seeking revenge, but, with good Lycurgus, to lose her own eye rather than to hurt another's eye.

But being now placed in the seat royal, she first of all established religion, banished popery, advanced the Word, that before was so much defaced, who having in her hand the sword to revenge, used rather bountifully to reward, being as far from rigor when she might have killed, as her enemies were from honesty when they could not, giving a general pardon when she had cause to use particular punishments, preferring the name of pity before the remembrance of perils, thinking no revenge more princely than to spare when she might spill, to stay when she might strike, to proffer to save with mercy when she might have destroyed with justice. Here is the clemency worthy commendation and admiration, nothing inferior to the gentle disposition of Aristides, who, after his exile, did not so much as note them that banished him, saying with Alexander that there can be nothing more noble than to do well to those that deserve ill.

This mighty and merciful queen, having many bills of private persons that sought beforetime to betray her, burnt them all, resembling Julius Cæsar, who, being presented with the like complaints of his commons, threw them into the fire, saying that he had rather not know the names of rebels than have occasion to revenge, thinking it better to be ignorant of those that hated him than to be angry with them.

This clemency did her Majesty not only show at her coming to the throne, but also throughout her whole government, when she hath spared to shed their bloods that sought to spill hers, not racking the laws to extremity, but mitigating the rigor with mercy, insomuch as it may be said of that royal monarch as it was of Antoninus, surnamed the godly Emperor, who reigned many years without the effusion of blood. What greater virtue can there be in a prince than mercy; what greater praise than to abate the edge which she should whet, to pardon where she should punish, to reward where she should revenge?

I myself being in England when her Majesty was for her recreation in her barge upon the Thames, heard of a gun that was shot off, though of the party unwittingly, yet to her noble person dangerously, which fact she most graciously pardoned, accepting a just excuse before a great amends, taking more grief for her poor bargeman, that was a little hurt, than care for herself that stood in greatest hazard. O rare example of pity, O singular spectacle of piety.

Divers besides have there been which by private conspiracies, open rebellions, close wiles, cruel witchcrafts, have sought to end her life, which saveth all their lives, whose practices by the divine providence of the Almighty, have ever been disclosed, insomuch that he hath kept her safe in the whale's belly when her subjects went about to throw her into the sea, preserved her in the hot oven, when her enemies increased the fire, not suffering a hair to fall from her, much less any harm to fasten upon her. These injuries and treasons of her subjects, these policies and undermining of foreign nations so little moved her, that she would often say, 'Let them know that, though it be not lawful for them to speak what they list, yet it is lawful for us to do with them what we list,' being always of that merciful mind, which was in Theodosius, who wished rather that he might call the dead to life than put the living to death, saying with Augustus when she should set her hand to any condemnation, 'I would to God we could not write.' Infinite were the examples that might be alleged, and almost incredible, whereby she hath shown herself a lamb in meekness, when she had cause to be a lion in might, proved a dove in favor, when she was provoked to be an eagle in fierceness, requiting injuries with benefits, revenging grudges with gifts, in highest majesty bearing the lowest mind, forgiving all that sued for mercy, and forgetting all that deserved justice.

O divine nature, O heavenly nobility, what thing can there more be required in a prince, than in greatest power to show greatest patience, in chiefest glory to bring forth chiefest grace, in abundance of all earthly pomp to manifest abundance of all heavenly piety? O fortunate England that hath such a Queen, ungrateful if thou pray not for her, wicked if thou do not love her, miserable if thou lose her.

* * *

Touching the beauty of this prince, her countenance, her personage, her majesty, I cannot think that it may be sufficiently commended, when it cannot be too much marveled at; so that I am constrained to say as Praxitiles did, when he began to paint Venus and her son, who doubted whether the world could afford colors good enough for two such fair faces, and I, whether our tongue can yield words to blaze that beauty, the perfection whereof none can imagine; which seeing it is so, I must do like those that want a clear sight, who, being not able to discern the sun in the sky, are enforced to behold it in the water. Zeuxis, having before him fifty fair virgins of Sparta whereby to draw one amiable Venus, said that fifty more fairer than those could not minister sufficient beauty to show the goddess of beauty; therefore, being in despair either by art to shadow her, or by imagination to comprehend her, he drew in a table a fair temple, the gates open, and Venus going in so as nothing could be perceived but her back, wherein he used such cunning that Apelles himself, seeing this work, wished that Venus would turn her face, saying that if it were in all parts agreeable to the back, he would become apprentice to Zeuxis, and slave to Venus. In the like manner fareth it with me, for having all the ladies in Italy, more than fifty hundred, whereby to color Elizabeth, I must say with Zeuxis that as many more will not suffice, and therefore in as great an agony paint her court with her back towards you, for that I cannot by art portray her beauty, wherein, though I want the skill to do it as Zeuxis did, yet viewing it narrowly, and comparing it wisely, you all will say that if her face be answerable to her back, you will like my handicraft and become her handmaids. In the mean season, I leave you gazing until she turn her face, imagining her to be such a one as nature framed to that end, that no art should imitate, wherein she hath proved herself to be exquisite, and painters to be apes.

This beautiful mold when I beheld to be indued with chastity, temperance, mildness, and all other good gifts of nature (as hereafter shall appear), when I saw her to surpass all in beauty, and yet a virgin, to excel all in piety, and yet a prince, to be inferior to none in all the lineaments of the body, and yet superior to every one in all gifts of the mind, I began thus to pray, that as she hath lived forty years a virgin in great majesty, so she may live four score years a mother with great joy, that as with her we have long time had peace and plenty, so by her we may ever have quietness and abundance, wishing this even from the bottom of a heart that wisheth well to England, though feareth ill, that either the world may end before she die, or she live to see her children's children in the world; otherwise how fickle their state is that now triumph, upon what a twist they hang that now are in honor, they that live shall see, which I to think on, sigh! But God for his mercy's sake, Christ for his merits' sake, the Holy Ghost for his name's sake, grant to that realm comfort without any ill chance, and the prince they have without any other change, that the longer she liveth, the sweeter she may smell, like the bird Ibis, that she may be triumphant in victories, like the palm tree, fruitful in her age like the vine, in all ages prosperous, to all men gracious, in all places glorious, so that there be no end of her praise until the end of all flesh.

Thus did I often talk with myself, and wish with mine whole soul.

Why should I talk of her sharp wit, excellent wisdom, exquisite learning, and all other qualities of the mind, wherein she seemeth as far to excel those that have been accounted singular, as the learned have surpassed those that have been thought simple.

In questioning, not inferior to Nicaulia, the queen of Saba, that did put so many hard doubts to Solomon; equal to Nicostrata in the Greek tongue, who was thought to give precepts for the better perfection; more learned in the Latin than Amalasuuta; passing Aspasia in philosophy, who taught Pericles; exceeding in judgment Themistoclea, who instructed Pythagoras. Add to these qualities, those that none of these had; the French tongue, the Spanish, the Italian, not mean in every one, but excellent in all; readier to correct escapes in those languages than to be controlled; fitter to teach others than learn of any; more able to add new rules than to err in the old; insomuch as there is no ambassador that cometh into her court but she is willing and able both to understand his message and utter her mind; not like unto the kings of Assyria, who answered ambassadors by messengers, while they themselves either daily in sin or snort in sleep. Her godly zeal to learning, with her great skill, hath been so manifestly approved that I cannot tell whether she deserve more honor for her knowledge, or admiration for her courtesy, who in great pomp hath twice directed her progress unto the universities, with no less joy to the students than glory to her state. Here, after long and solemn disputations in law, physic, and divinity, not as one wearied with scholars's arguments, but wedded to their orations, when every one feared to offend in length, she in her own person, with no less praise to her Majesty than delight to her subjects, with a wise and learned conclusion, both gave them thanks, and put herself to pains. O noble pattern of a princely mind, not like to the kings of Persia, who in their progresses did nothing else but cut sticks to drive away the time, nor like the delicate lives of the Sybarites who would not admit any art to be exercised within their city that might make the least noise. Her wit so sharp, that if I should repeat the apt answers, the subtle questions, the fine speeches, the pithy sentences, which on the sudden she hath uttered, they would rather breed admiration than credit. But such are the gifts that the living God hath indued her withal, that look in what art or language, wit or learning, virtue or beauty any one hath particularly excelled most, she only hath generally exceeded every one in all, insomuch that there is nothing to be added that either man would wish in a woman, or God doth give to a creature.

I let pass her skill in music, her knowledge in all the other sciences, whenas I fear lest by my simplicity I should make them less than they are, in seeking to show how great they are, unless I were praising her in the gallery of Olympia, where giving forth one word, I might hear seven.

But all these graces, although they be to be wondered at, yet her politic government, her prudent counsel, her zeal to religion, her clemency to those that submit, her stoutness to those that threaten, so far exceed all other virtues that they are more easy to be marveled at than imitated.

Two and twenty years hath she borne the sword with such justice, that neither offenders could complain of rigor, nor the innocent of wrong; yet so tempered with mercy as malefactors have been sometimes pardoned upon hope of grace, and the injured requited to ease their grief, insomuch that in the whole course of her glorious reign, it could never be said that either the poor were oppressed without remedy, or the guilty repressed without cause, bearing this engraven in her noble heart, that justice without mercy were extreme injury, and pity without equity, plain partiality, and that it is as great tyranny not to mitigate laws, as iniquity to break them.

Her care for the flourishing of the Gospel hath well appeared whenas neither the curses of the Pope (which are blessings to good people) nor the threatenings of kings (which are perilous to a prince) nor the persuasions of papists (which are honey to the mouth) could either fear her or allure her to violate the holy league contracted with Christ, or to maculate the blood of the ancient Lamb, which is Christ. But always constant in the true faith, she hath to the exceeding joy of her subjects, to the unspeakable comfort of her soul, to the great glory of God, established that religion the maintenance whereof she rather seeketh to confirm by fortitude, than leave off for fear, knowing that there is nothing smelleth sweeter to the Lord than a sound spirit, which neither the hosts of the ungodly nor the horror of death can either remove or move.

This Gospel with invincible courage, with rare constancy, with hot zeal, she hath maintained in her own countries without change, and defended against all kingdoms that sought change insomuch that all nations round about her, threatening alteration, shaking swords, throwing fire, menacing famine, murder, destruction, desolation, she only hath stood like a lamp on the top of a hill, not fearing the blasts of the sharp winds, but trusting in his providence that rideth upon the wings of the four winds. Next followeth the love she beareth to her subjects, who no less tendereth them than the apple of her own eye, showing herself a mother to the afflicted, a physician to the sick, a sovereign and mild governess to all.

Touching her magnanimity, her majesty, her estate royal, there was neither Alexander, nor Galba the Emperor, nor any, that might be compared with her.

This is she that, resembling the noble queen of Navarre, useth the marigold for her flower, which at the rising of the sun openeth her leaves, and at the setting shutteth them, referring all her actions and endeavors to him that ruleth the sun. This is that Cæsar, that first bound the crocodile to the palm tree, bridling those that sought to rein her. This is that good pelican, that to feed her people spareth not to rend her own person. This is that mighty eagle, that hath thrown dust into the eyes of the hart that went about to work destruction to her subjects, into whose wings although the blind beetle would have crept, and so being carried into her nest, destroyed her young ones, yet hath she with the virtue of her feathers, consumed that fly in his own fraud. She hath exiled the swallow that sought to spoil the grasshopper, and given bitter almonds to the ravenous wolves that endeavored to devour the silly lambs, burning even with the breath of her mouth like the princely stag, the serpents that were engendered by the breath of the huge elephant, so that now all her enemies are as whist as the bird Attagen, who never singeth any tune after she is taken, nor they being so overtaken.

But whither do I wade, ladies, as one forgetting himself, thinking to sound the depth of her virtues with a few fathoms, when there is no bottom; for I know not how it cometh to pass that, being in this labyrinth, I may sooner lose myself than find the end.

Behold, ladies, in this glass a queen, a woman, a virgin in all gifts of the body, in all graces of the mind, in all perfection of either, so far to excel all men, that I know not whether I may think the place too bad for her to dwell among men.

To talk of other things in that court were to bring eggs after apples, or after the setting out of the sun, to tell a tale of a shadow. But this I say, that all offices are looked to with great care, that virtue is embraced of all, vice hated, religion daily increased, manners reformed, that whoso seeth the place there, will think it rather a church for divine service than a court for princes' delight.

This is the glass, ladies, wherein I would have you gaze, wherein I took my whole delight; imitate the ladies in England, amend your manners, rub out the wrinkles of the mind, and be not curious about the weams in the face. As for their Elizabeth, since you can neither sufficiently marvel at her, nor I praise her, let us all pray for her, which is the only duty we can perform, and the greatest that we can proffer.

Yours to command,
EUPHUES.

* * *

APELLES' SONG

(From ALEXANDER AND CAMPASPE)

Cupid and my Campaspe played
At cards for kisses; Cupid paid.
He stakes his quiver, bows and arrows,
His mother's doves and team of sparrows;
Loses them too; then down he throws   5
The coral of his lip, the rose
Growing on's cheek (but none knows how);
With these, the crystal of his brow,
And then the dimple of his chin;
All these did my Campaspe win.   10
At last he set her both his eyes;
She won, and Cupid blind did rise.
O Love, has she done this to thee?
What shall, alas! become of me?

SPRING'S WELCOME

(From ALEXANDER AND CAMPASPE)

What bird so sings, yet so does wail?
O 'tis the ravished nightingale.
'Jug, jug, jug, jug, tereu,' she cries,
And still her woes at midnight rise.
Brave prick-song! who is 't now we hear?   5
None but the lark so shrill and clear:
Now at heaven's gates she claps her wings,
The morn not waking till she sings

Hark, hark, with what a pretty throat
Poor robin redbreast tunes his note!   10
Hark how the jolly cuckoos sing,
'Cuckoo,' to welcome in the spring!
'Cuckoo,' to welcome in the spring!

SAPPHO'S SONG

(From SAPPHO AND PHAO)

O cruel Love! on thee I lay
My curse, which shall strike blind the day;
Never may sleep with velvet hand
Charm thine eyes with sacred wand:
Thy jailors still be hopes and fears;   5
Thy prison-mates groans, sighs, and tears;
Thy play to wear out weary times,
Fantastic passions, vows, and rimes;
Thy bread be frowns; thy drink be gall;
Such as when you Phao call;   10
The bed thou liest on be despair;
Thy sleep, fond dreams; thy dreams, long care;
Hope (like thy fool) at thy bed's head,
Mock thee, till madness strikes thee dead,
As, Phao, thou dost me, with thy proud eyes.   15
In thee poor Sappho lives, in thee she dies.

SONG

(From GALLATHEA)

TELUSA: O yes, O yes! if any maid
Whom leering Cupid has betrayed
To frowns of spite, to eyes of scorn,
And would in madness now see torn
The boy in pieces,—

ALL THREE: Let her come
Hither, and lay on him her doom.

EUROTA: O yes, O yes! has any lost
A heart which many a sigh hath cost;
Is any cozened of a tear   10
Which, as a pearl, disdain does wear?

ALL THREE: Here stands the thief; let her but come
Hither, and lay on him her doom.

LARISSA: Is any one undone by fire,
And turned to ashes through desire?   15
Did ever any lady weep,
Being cheated of her golden sleep
Stol'n by sick thoughts?

ALL THREE: The pirate's found
And in her tears he shall be drowned.
Read this indictment, let him hear   21
What he's to trust to. Boy, give ear!

SIR PHILIP SIDNEY (1554–1586)

Sidney's parents were Sir Henry Sidney, subsequently lord deputy in Ireland, and Lady Mary Dudley, daughter of the Duke of Northumberland. After an agreeable schooling at Shrewsbury, Sidney took up residence at Christ Church, Oxford, a residence which he cut short in order to travel abroad, after the fashion of young men of rank. At the time of the Massacre of St. Bartholomew, August 23–4, 1572, he was in Paris, and subsequently his travels, during about four years, extended to Germany, Italy, and other parts of the Continent. Of these travels, one interesting legacy is his Latin correspondence with the distinguished Huguenot, Hubert Languet. In 1576–77, Sidney was abroad on a diplomatic mission to the Emperor Rudolf II. As a courtier he was esteemed and honored on the continent, both for his personal charm and for his genuine talent. Although he was a favorite of Queen Elizabeth, his opposition to her proposed marriage with the Duke of Anjou may have been the cause of his retirement, for a time, to Wilton, where he wrote *Arcadia*, a pastoral romance (published 1590), in honor of his sister, the countess of Pembroke, and *An Apology for Poetry* (published 1595). During this period of retirement, also, he may have begun writing the sonnets and songs addressed to Penelope Devereux, and published, in 1591, as *Astrophel and Stella*. In 1582, Sidney was knighted by the queen, who is said to have interfered later against his being offered the Polish crown. In 1585, the queen appointed him governor of Flushing, on the coast of the Netherlands. During the siege of Zutphen, in an expedition to intercept a Spanish convoy, he was mortally wounded, and died, October 17, 1586.

Short-lived as he was, Sidney acquired a substantial place in English literature, as a masterly poet of the courtly order, as a charming romancer, and as a gentle but firm critic. The charm of his poetry and romance extended to his criticism, and gave to his somewhat too orthodox canons, a permanent allurement of frankness, gentleness, and humor.

FROM AN APOLOGY FOR POETRY

But since I have run so long a career in this matter, methinks, before I give my pen a full stop, it shall be but a little 5 more lost time to inquire, why England, the mother of excellent minds, should be grown so hard a step-mother to poets, who certainly in wit ought to pass all others, since all only proceeds from their 10 wit, being, indeed, makers of themselves, not takers of others. How can I but exclaim,

Musa, mihi causas memora, quo numine 15
laeso?
[Muse, bring to my mind the reasons:
for the injury of what divinity?]

Sweet poesy! that hath anciently had 20 kings, emperors, senators, great captains, such as besides a thousand others, David, Adrian, Sophocles, Germanicus, not only to favor poets, but to be poets; and of our nearer times can present for her 25 patrons, a Robert, King of Sicily; the great King Francis of France: King James of Scotland; such cardinals as Bembus and Bibiena; such famous preachers and teachers as Beza and Melancthon; so learned philosophers as 5 Fracastorius and Scaliger; so great orators as Pontanus and Muretus; so piercing wits as George Buchanan; so grave councilors as, besides many, but before all, that Hospital of France, than whom, 10 I think, that realm never brought forth a more accomplished judgment, more firmly builded upon virtue; I say these, with numbers of others, not only to read others' poesies, but to poetize for others' reading: 15 that poesy, thus embraced in all other places, should only find in our time a hard welcome in England, I think the very earth laments it, and therefore decks our soil with fewer laurels than it was accustomed. For heretofore poets have in England also flourished; and, which is to be noted, even in those times when the trumpet of Mars did sound loudest. And now that an over-faint quietness should 25 seem to strew the house for poets, they are almost in as good reputation as the mountebanks at Venice. Truly, even

81

that, as of the one side it giveth great praise to poesy, which, like Venus (but to better purpose), had rather be troubled in the net with Mars, than enjoy the homely quiet of Vulcan; so serves it for a piece of a reason why they are less grateful to idle England, which now can scarce endure the pain of a pen. Upon this necessarily followeth that base men with servile wits undertake it, who think it enough if they can be rewarded of the printer; and so as Epaminondas is said, with the honor of his virtue, to have made an office by his exercising it, which before was contemptible, to become highly respected; so these men, no more but setting their names to it, by their own disgracefulness, disgrace the most graceful poesy. For now, as if all the Muses were got with child, to bring forth bastard poets, without any commission, they do post over the banks of Helicon, until they make their readers more weary than post-horses; while, in the meantime, they,

> Queis meliore luto finxit praecordia Titan,
> [Whose heart-strings the Titan fastened
>   with a better clay]

are better content to suppress the out-flowings of their wit than by publishing them to be accounted knights of the same order.

But I that, before ever I durst aspire unto the dignity, am admitted into the company of the paper-blurrers, do find the very true cause of our wanting estimation is want of desert, taking upon us to be poets in despite of Pallas. Now, wherein we want desert, were a thank-worthy labor to express. But if I knew, I should have mended myself; but as I never desired the title, so have I neglected the means to come by it; only, overmastered by some thoughts, I yielded an inky tribute unto them. Marry, they that delight in poesy itself, should seek to know what they do, and how they do, and, especially, look themselves in an unflattering glass of reason, if they be inclinable unto it.

For poesy must not be drawn by the ears, it must be gently led, or rather it must lead; which was partly the cause that made the ancient learned affirm it was a divine gift, and no human skill, since all other knowledges lie ready for any that have strength of wit; a poet no industry can make, if his own genius be not carried into it. And therefore is it an old proverb, *Orator fit, poeta nasci-tur* [The orator is made, the poet born]. Yet confess I always, that, as the fertilest ground must be manured, so must the highest flying wit have a Dædalus to guide him. That Dædalus, they say, both in this and in other, hath three wings to bear itself up into the air of due commendation; that is, art, imita-tion, and exercise. But these, neither artificial rules, nor imitative patterns, we much cumber ourselves withal. Exer-cise, indeed, we do, but that very fore-backwardly; for where we should exer-cise to know, we exercise as having known; and so is our brain delivered of much matter which never was begotten by knowledge. For there being two principal parts, matter to be expressed by words, and words to express the mat-ter, in neither we use art or imitation rightly. Our matter is *quodlibet* [what you will], indeed, although wrongly, per-forming Ovid's verse,

> Quicquid conabor dicere, versus erit;
> [Whatever I shall try to say will be verse]

never marshaling it into any assured rank, that almost the readers cannot tell where to find themselves.

Chaucer, undoubtedly, did excellently in his *Troilus and Criseyde;* of whom, truly, I know not whether to marvel more, either that he in that misty time could see so clearly, or that we in this clear age go so stumblingly after him. Yet had he great wants, fit to be forgiven in so reverend antiquity. I account the *Mirror for Magistrates* meetly furnished of beautiful parts. And in the Earl of Surrey's lyrics, many things tasting of a noble birth, and worthy of a noble mind. The *Shepherd's Calendar* hath much poetry in its eclogues, indeed, wor-thy the reading, if I be not deceived. That same framing of its style to an old rustic language, I dare not allow; since neither Theocritus in Greek, Virgil in Latin, nor Sannazaro in Italian, did af-fect it. Besides these, I do not remember to have seen but few (to speak boldly) printed that have poetical sinews in them. For proof whereof, let but most of the verses be put in prose, and then ask the meaning, and it will be found that one verse did but beget another, without ordering at the first what should be at the last; which becomes a confused mass of words, with a tinkling sound of rime, barely accompanied with reason.

Our tragedies and comedies (not without cause, cried out against) observing rules neither of honest civility nor of skilful poetry, excepting *Gorboduc* (again I say of those that I have seen), which notwithstanding, as it is full of stately speeches and well-sounding phrases, climbing to the height of Seneca's style, and as full of notable morality, which it does most delightfully teach, and so obtain the very end of poesy; yet, in truth, it is very defectious in the circumstances, which grieves me, because it might not remain as an exact model of all tragedies. For it is faulty both in place and time, the two necessary companions of all corporal actions. For where the stage should always represent but one place, and the uttermost time presupposed in it should be, both by Aristotle's precept, and common reason, but one day, there is both many days and many places inartificially imagined.

But if it be so in *Gorboduc,* how much more in all the rest? where you shall have Asia of the one side, and Afric of the other, and so many other under kingdoms, that the player, when he comes in, must ever begin with telling where he is, or else the tale will not be conceived. Now you shall have three ladies walk to gather flowers, and then we must believe the stage to be a garden. By and by, we hear news of shipwreck in the same place, and then we are to blame if we accept it not for a rock. Upon the back of that comes out a hideous monster, with fire and smoke, and then the miserable beholders are bound to take it for a cave; while, in the meantime, two armies fly in, represented with four swords and bucklers, and then, what hard heart will not receive it for a pitched field?

Now, of time they are much more liberal; for ordinary it is, that two young princes fall in love; after many traverses she is got with child; delivered of a fair boy; he is lost, groweth a man, falls in love, and is ready to get another child; and all this in two hours' space; which, how absurd it is in sense, even sense may

imagine; and art hath taught and all ancient examples justified, and at this day the ordinary players in Italy will not err in. Yet will some bring in an example of the *Eunuch* in Terence, that containeth matter of two days, yet far short of twenty years. True it is, and so was it to be played in two days, and so fitted to the time it set forth. And though Plautus have in one place done amiss, let us hit it with him, and not miss with him.

But they will say, How then shall we set forth a story which contains both many places and many times? And do they not know that a tragedy is tied to the laws of poesy, and not of history; not bound to follow the story, but having liberty either to feign a quite new matter, or to frame the history to the most tragical conveniency? Again, many things may be told, which cannot be showed: if they know the difference betwixt reporting and representing. As, for example, I may speak, though I am here, of Peru, and in speech digress from that to the description of Calicut; but in action I cannot represent it without Pacolet's horse. And so was the manner the ancients took, by some *Nuntius* [Messenger] to recount things done in former time, or other place.

Lastly, if they will represent an history, they must not, as Horace saith, begin *ab ovo,* [from the egg] but they must come to the principal point of that one action which they will represent. By example this will be best expressed. I have a story of young Polydorus, delivered, for safety's sake, with great riches, by his father Priamus to Polymnestor, King of Thrace, in the Trojan war time. He, after some years, hearing the overthrow of Priamus, for to make the treasure his own, murdereth the child; the body of the child is taken up by Hecuba; she, the same day, findeth a sleight to be revenged most cruelly of the tyrant. Where, now, would one of our tragedy-writers begin, but with the delivery of the child? Then should he sail over into Thrace, and so spend I know not how many years, and travel numbers of places. But where doth Euripides? Even with the finding of the body; leaving the rest to be told by the spirit of Polydorus. This needs no further to be enlarged; the dullest wit may conceive it.

But, besides these gross absurdities,

how all their plays be neither right
tragedies nor right comedies, mingling
kings and clowns, not because the matter
so carrieth it, but thrust in clowns by
head and shoulders to play a part in 5
majestical matters, with neither decency
nor discretion; so as neither the admiration and commiseration, nor the right
sportfulness, is by their mongrel tragi-
comedy obtained. I know Apuleius did 10
somewhat so, but that is a thing recounted with space of time, not represented in one moment: and I know the
ancients have one or two examples of
tragi-comedies, as Plautus hath *Amphi-* 15
truo. But, if we mark them well, we shall
find that they never, or very daintily,
match hornpipes and funerals. So falleth it out, that, having, indeed, no·right
comedy in that comical part of our 20
tragedy, we have nothing but scurrility,
unworthy of any chaste ears; or some extreme show of doltishness, indeed fit to
lift up a loud laughter, and nothing else;
where the whole tract of a comedy should 25
be full of delight as the tragedy should be
still maintained in a well-raised admiration.

But our comedians think there is no
delight without laughter, which is very 30
wrong; for though laughter may come
with delight, yet cometh it not of delight,
as though delight should be the cause of
laughter; but well may one thing breed
both together. Nay, in themselves, they 35
have, as it were, a kind of contrariety.
For delight we scarcely do, but in things
that have a conveniency to ourselves, or
to the general nature. Laughter almost
ever cometh of things most dispropor- 40
tioned to ourselves and nature: delight
hath a joy in it, either permanent or
present; laughter hath only a scornful
tickling. For example: we are ravished
with delight to see a fair woman, and yet 45
are far from being moved to laughter; we
laugh at deformed creatures, wherein certainly we cannot delight; we delight in
good chances; we laugh at mischances;
we delight to hear the happiness of our 50
friends or country, at which he were
worthy to be laughed at that would
laugh: we shall, contrarily, laugh sometimes to find a matter quite mistaken, and
go down the hill against the bias, in the 55
mouth of some such men, as for the respect of them, one shall be heartily sorry,
yet he cannot choose but laugh, and so is

rather pained than delighted with laughter. Yet deny I not, but that they may
go well together; for, as in Alexander's
picture well set out, we delight without
laughter, and in twenty mad antics we
laugh without delight: so in Hercules,
painted with his great beard and furious
countenance, in a woman's attire, spinning at Omphale's commandment, it
breedeth both delight and laughter; for
the representing of so strange a power in
love procures delight, and the scornful-
ness of the action stirreth laughter.

But I speak to this purpose, that all the
end of the comical part be not upon such
scornful matters as stir laughter only, but
mix with it that delightful teaching which
is the end of poesy. And the great fault,
even in that point of laughter, and forbidden plainly by Aristotle, is, that they
stir laughter in sinful things, which are
rather execrable than ridiculous; or in
miserable, which are rather to be pitied
than scorned. For what is it to make
folks gape at a wretched beggar, and a
beggarly clown; or against the law of
hospitality, to jest at strangers, because
they speak not English so well as we do?
what do we learn? since it is certain,

Nil habet infelix paupertas durius in se,
Quam quod ridiculos, homines facit.
[Of all the griefs that harass the distrest,
Sure the most bitter is a scornful jest]

But rather a busy loving courtier, a heartless threatening Thraso; a self-wise-seem-
ing schoolmaster; a wry-transformed
traveler: these, if we saw walk in stage
names, which we play naturally, therein
were delightful laughter, and teaching delightfulness: as in the other, the tragedies
of Buchanan do justly bring forth a
divine admiration.

But I have lavished out too many words
of this play matter; I do it, because, as
they are excelling parts of poesy, so is
there none so much used in England, and
none can be more pitifully abused; which,
like an unmannerly daughter, showing a
bad education, causeth her mother Poesy's
honesty to be called in question.

Other sorts of poetry, almost have we
none, but that lyrical kind of songs and
sonnets, which, if the Lord gave us so
good minds, how well it might be employed, and with how heavenly fruits,
both private and public in singing the

praises of the immortal beauty, the immortal goodness of that God, who giveth us hands to write, and wits to conceive; of which we might well want words, but never matter; of which we could turn our eyes to nothing, but we should ever have new budding occasions. But, truly, many of such writings as come under the banner of irresistible love, if I were a mistress, would never persuade me they were in love; so coldly they apply fiery speeches, as men that had rather read lovers' writings, and so caught up certain swelling phrases, which hang together — like a man which once told me, ' the wind was at northwest and by south,' because he would be sure to name winds enough — than that, in truth, they feel those passions, which easily, as I think, may be bewrayed by the same forcibleness, or *energia* (as the Greeks call it), of the writer. But let this be a sufficient, though short note, that we miss the right use of the material point of poesy.

Now for the outside of it, which is words, or, as I may term it, diction, it is even well worse; so is that honey-flowing matron Eloquence, appareled, or rather disguised, in a courtesan-like painted affectation. One time with so far-fetched words, that may seem monsters, but must seem strangers to any poor Englishman: another time with coursing of a letter, as if they were bound to follow the method of a dictionary: another time with figures and flowers, extremely winter-starved.

But I would this fault were only peculiar to versifiers, and had not as large possession among prose printers: and, which is to be marveled, among many scholars, and, which is to be pitied, among some preachers. Truly, I could wish (if at least I might be so bold to wish, in a thing beyond the reach of my capacity) the diligent imitators of Tully and Demosthenes, most worthy to be imitated, did not so much keep Nizolian paperbooks of their figures and phrases, as by attentive translation, as it were, devour them whole, and make them wholly theirs. For now they cast sugar and spice upon every dish that is served to the table: like those Indians, not content to wear earrings at the fit and natural place of the ears, but they will thrust jewels through their nose and lips, because they will be sure to be fine. Tully, when he was to drive out Catiline, as it were with a thun-

derbolt of eloquence, often used the figure of repetition.

Vivit. Vivit? imo in Senatum venit, etc. [He lives. Lives? nay comes to the Senate]

Indeed, inflamed with a well-grounded rage, he would have his words, as it were, double out of his mouth; and so do that artificially which we see men do in choler naturally. And we, having noted the grace of those words, hale them in sometimes to a familiar epistle, when it were too much choler to be choleric.

How well, store of ' similiter cadences ' doth sound with the gravity of the pulpit, I would but invoke Demosthenes' soul to tell, who with a rare daintiness useth them. Truly, they have made me think of the sophister, that with too much subtlety would prove two eggs three, and, though he might be counted a sophister, had none for his labor. So these men bringing in such a kind of eloquence, well may they obtain an opinion of a seeming fineness, but persuade few, which should be the end of their fineness.

Now for similitudes in certain printed discourses, I think all herbalists, all stories of beasts, fowls, and fishes are rifled up, that they come in multitudes to wait upon any of our conceits, which certainly is as absurd a surfeit to the ears as is possible. For the force of a similitude not being to prove anything to a contrary disputer, but only to explain to a willing hearer: when that is done, the rest is a most tedious prattling, rather overswaying the memory from the purpose whereto they were applied, than any whit informing the judgment, already either satisfied, or by similitudes not to be satisfied.

For my part, I do not doubt, when Antonius and Crassus, the great forefathers of Cicero in eloquence, the one (as Cicero testifieth of them) pretended not to know art, the other not to set by it, because with a plain sensibleness they might win credit of popular ears, which credit is the nearest step to persuasion (which persuasion is the chief mark of oratory); I do not doubt, I say, but that they used these knacks very sparingly; which who doth generally use, any man may see, doth dance to his own music; and so to be noted by the audience, more careful to speak curiously than to speak truly. Undoubtedly (at least to my opinion, undoubtedly) I have found in divers small-learned courtiers a more sound style than in some professors of learning; of which I can guess no other cause, but that the courtier following that which by practice he findeth fittest to nature, therein (though he know it not) doth according to art, though not by art: where the other, using art to show art, and not to hide art (as in these cases he should do), flieth from nature, and indeed abuseth art.

But what! methinks I deserve to be pounded for straying from poetry to oratory: but both have such an affinity in the wordish considerations, that I think this digression will make my meaning receive the fuller understanding: which is not to take upon me, to teach poets how they should do, but only finding myself sick among the rest, to show some one or two spots of the common infection grown among the most part of writers; that, acknowledging ourselves somewhat awry, we may bend to the right use both of matter and manner: whereto our language giveth us great occasion, being, indeed, capable of any excellent exercising of it. I know some will say, it is a mingled language: and why not so much the better, taking the best of both the other? Another will say, it wanteth grammar. Nay, truly, it hath that praise, that it wanteth not grammar; for grammar it might have, but it needs it not; being so easy in itself, and so void of those cumbersome differences of cases, genders, moods, and tenses; which, I think, was a piece of the Tower of Babylon's curse, that a man should be put to school to learn his mother tongue. But for the uttering sweetly and properly the conceits of the mind, which is the end of speech, that hath it equally with any other tongue in the world, and is particularly happy in compositions of two or three words together, near the Greek, far beyond the Latin; which is one of the greatest beauties can be in a language.

Now, of versifying there are two sorts, the one ancient, the other modern; the ancient marked the quantity of each syllable, and according to that, framed its verse; the modern, observing only number, with some regard of the accent, the chief life of it standeth in that like sounding of the words, which we call rime. Whether of these be the more excellent, would bear many speeches; the ancient, no doubt more fit for music, both words and tune observing quantity; and more fit lively to express divers passions, by the low and lofty sound of the well-weighed syllable. The latter, likewise, with his rime striketh a certain music to the ear; and, in fine, since it doth delight, though by another way. it obtains the same purpose; there being in either, sweetness, and wanting in neither, majesty. Truly the English, before any other vulgar language I know, is fit for both sorts; for, for the ancient, the Italian is so full of vowels, that it must ever be cumbered with elisions. The Dutch so of the other side with consonants, that they cannot yield the sweet sliding fit for a verse. The French, in his whole language, hath not one word that hath its accent in the last syllable, saving two, called antepenultima; and little more hath the Spanish; and, therefore, very gracelessly may they use dactyls. The English is subject to none of these defects.

Now for rime, though we do not observe quantity, yet we observe the accent very precisely, which other languages either cannot do, or will not do so absolutely. That cæsura, or breathing-place, in the midst of the verse, neither Italian nor Spanish have, the French and we never almost fail of. Lastly, even the very rime itself the Italian cannot put in the last syllable, by the French named the masculine rime, but still in the next to the last, which the French call the female; or the next before that, which the Italians term *sdrucciola:* the example of the former is, *buono, suono;* of the *sdrucciola* is, *femina, semina.* The French, of the other side, hath both the male, as *bon, son,* and the female, as *plaise, taise;* but the *sdrucciola* he hath not; where the English hath all three, as 'due,' 'true,' 'father,' 'rather,' 'motion,' 'potion'; with much more which might be said, but that I find already the triflingness of this discourse is much too much enlarged.

So that since the ever praiseworthy poesy is full of virtue-breeding delightfulness, and void of no gift that ought to be in the noble name of learning; since the blames laid against it are either false or feeble; since the cause why it is not esteemed in England is the fault of poet-apes, not poets; since, lastly, our tongue is most fit to honor poesy, and to be honored by poesy; I conjure you all that have had the evil luck to read this ink-wasting toy of mine, even in the name of the Nine Muses, no more to scorn the sacred mysteries of poesy; no more to laugh at the name of poets, as though they were next inheritors to fools; no more to jest at the reverend title of a rimer; but to believe, with Aristotle, that they were the ancient treasurers of the Grecians' divinity; to believe, with Bembus, that they were the first bringers in of all civility; to believe, with Scaliger, that no philosopher's precepts can sooner make you an honest man, than the reading of Virgil; to believe, with Clauserus, the translator of Cornutus, that it pleased the heavenly deity by Hesiod and Homer, under the veil of fables, to give us all knowledge, logic, rhetoric, philosophy natural and moral, and *Quid non?* [Why not] to believe, with me, that there are many mysteries contained in poetry, which of purpose were written darkly, lest by profane wits it should be abused; to believe, with Landin, that they are so beloved of the gods that whatsoever they write proceeds of a divine fury. Lastly, to believe themselves, when they tell you they will make you immortal by their verses.

Thus doing, your names shall flourish in the printers' shops: thus doing, you shall be of kin to many a poetical preface: thus doing, you shall be most fair, most rich, most wise, most all: thus doing, though you be *Libertino patre natus* [Born of a freedman father], you shall suddenly grow *Herculea proles* [Descendant of Hercules],

Si quid mea Carmina possunt: 40
[If my poems are good for anything]

Thus doing, your soul shall be placed with Dante's Beatrice, or Virgil's Anchises.

But if (fie of such a but!) you be born so near the dull-making cataract of Nilus, that you cannot hear the planet-like music of poetry; if you have so earth-creeping a mind, that it cannot lift itself up to look to the sky of poetry, or rather, by a certain rustical disdain, will become such a Mome, as to be a Momus of poetry; then, though I will not wish unto you the ass's ears of Midas, nor to be driven by a poet's verses, as Bubonax was, to hang himself; nor to be rimed to death, as is said to be done in Ireland; yet thus much curse I must send you in the behalf of all poets; that while you live, you live in love, and never get favor, for lacking skill of a sonnet; and when you die, your memory die from the earth for want of an epitaph.

ASTROPHEL AND STELLA

I

Loving in truth, and fain in verse my love to show,
That she, dear she, might take some pleasure of my pain,—
Pleasure might cause her read, reading might make her know,
Knowledge might pity win, and pity grace obtain,—
I sought fit words to paint the blackest face of woe, 5
Studying inventions fine, her wits to entertain,
Oft turning others' leaves, to see if thence would flow
Some fresh and fruitful showers upon my sunburnt brain.
But words came halting forth, wanting Invention's stay;
Invention, Nature's child, fled step-dame Study's blows; 10
And others' feet still seemed but strangers' in my way.
Thus, great with child to speak, and helpless in my throes,
Biting my truant pen, beating myself for spite;
'Fool,' said my Muse to me, 'look in thy heart, and write.'

VII

When Nature made her chief work, Stella's eyes,
In color black why wrapt she beams so bright?
Would she, in beamy black, like painter wise,
Frame daintiest luster, mixed of shades and light?
Or did she else that sober hue devise, 5
In object best to knit and strength our sight;
Lest, if no veil these brave gleams did disguise,
They, sunlike, should more dazzle than delight?
Or would she her miraculous power show,
That, whereas black seems Beauty's contrary 10

She even in black doth make all beauties
   flow?
Both so, and thus,— she, minding Love
   should be
Placed ever there, gave him this mourning
   weed
To honor all their deaths which for her
   bleed.

xv

You that do search for every purling spring
Which from the ribs of old Parnassus
   flows,
And every flower, not sweet perhaps, which
   grows
Near thereabouts, into your poesy wring;
You that do dictionary's method bring   5
Into your rimes, running in rattling rows;
You that poor Petrarch's long-deceasèd
   woes
With new-born sighs and denizened wit do
   sing;
You take wrong ways; those far-fet helps
   be such
As do bewray a want of inward touch,   10
And sure, at length stolen goods do come to
   light:
But if, both for your love and skill, your
   name
You seek to nurse at fullest breasts of
   Fame,
Stella behold, and then begin to endite.

xxi

Your words, my friend, right healthful
   caustics, blame
My young mind marred, whom Love doth
   windlass so;
That mine own writings, like bad servants,
   show
My wits quick in vain thoughts, in virtue,
   lame;
That Plato I read for naught but-if he
   tame   5
Such coltish years; that to my birth I owe
Nobler desires, lest else that friendly foe,
Great Expectation, wear a train of shame:
For since mad March great promise made
   of me,
If now the May of my years much decline, 10
What can be hoped my harvest-time will
   be?
Sure, you say well, 'Your wisdom's golden
   mine
Dig deep with Learning's spade.' Now tell
   me this —
Hath this world aught so fair as Stella is?

xxxi

With how sad steps, O Moon, thou climb'st
   the skies!
How silently, and with how wan a face!
What, may it be that even in heavenly place
That busy archer his sharp arrows tries!
Sure, if that long-with-love-acquainted eyes 5
Can judge of love, thou feel'st a lover's
   case,
I read it in thy looks; thy languished grace,
To me, that feel the like, thy state descries.
Then, even of fellowship, O Moon, tell me,
Is constant love deemed there but want of
   wit?   10
Are beauties there as proud as here they
   be?
Do they above love to be loved, and yet
Those lovers scorn whom that love doth
   possess?
Do they call virtue there ungratefulness?

xxxii

Morpheus, the lively son of deadly Sleep,
Witness of life to them that living die,
A prophet oft, and oft an history,
A poet eke, as humors fly or creep;
Since thou in me so sure a power dost
   keep,   5
That never I with closed-up sense do lie,
But by thy work my Stella I descry,
Teaching blind eyes both how to smile and
   weep;
Vouchsafe, of all acquaintance, this to tell,
Whence hast thou ivory, rubies, pearl, and
   gold,   10
To show her skin, lips, teeth, and head so
   well?
'Fool!' answers he; 'no Indes such treas-
   ures hold;
But from thy heart, while my sire charmeth
   thee,
Sweet Stella's image I do steal to me.'

xxxix

Come, Sleep! O Sleep, the certain knot of
   peace,
The baiting-place of wit, the balm of woe,
The poor man's wealth, the prisoner's re-
   lease,
Th' indifferent judge between the high and
   low;
With shield of proof shield me from out
   the press   5
Of those fierce darts Despair at me doth
   throw;
O make in me those civil wars to cease;
I will good tribute pay, if thou do so.

Take thou of me smooth pillows, sweetest
    bed,
A chamber deaf of noise and blind of light,
A rosy garland and a weary head: 11
And if these things, as being thine by right,
Move not thy heavy grace, thou shalt in
    me,
Livelier than elsewhere, Stella's image see.

XLI

Having this day my horse, my hand, my
    lance
Guided so well that I obtained the prize,
Both by the judgment of the English eyes
And of some sent from that sweet enemy,
    France;   4
Horsemen my skill in horsemanship advance,
Town folks my strength; a daintier judge
    applies
His praise to sleight which from good use
    doth rise;
Some lucky wits impute it but to chance;
Others, because of both sides I do take   9
My blood from them who did excel in this,
Think Nature me a man-at-arms did make.
How far they shot awry! the true cause
    is,
Stella looked on, and from her heavenly face
Sent forth the beams which made so fair
    my race.

LXIV

No more! My Dear, no more these counsels
    try!
O give my passions leave to run their race!
Let Fortune lay on me her worst disgrace!
Let folk o'ercharged with brain, against me
    cry!
Let clouds bedim my face, break in mine
    eye!   5
Let me no steps but of lost labor trace!
Let all the earth in scorn recount my case;
But do not will me from my love to fly!
I do not envy Aristotle's wit;
Nor do aspire to Cæsar's bleeding fame;   10
Nor ought do care, though some above me
    sit;
Nor hope, nor wish another course to
    frame:
But that which once may win thy cruel
    heart.
Thou art my wit, and thou my virtue art.

CVII

Stella, since thou so right a princess art
Of all the powers which life bestows on me;
That ere by them ought undertaken be,

The first resort unto that sovereign part.
Sweet, for a while give respite to my heart, 5
Which pants as though it still should leap
    to thee;
And on my thoughts give thy lieutenancy
To this great cause, which needs both use
    and art.
And as a queen, who from her presence
    sends
Whom she employs, dismiss from thee my
    wit!   10
Till it have wrought what thy own will at-
    tends.
On servants' shame oft master's blame doth
    sit.
O let not fools in me thy works reprove;
And scorning, say, 'See, what it is to love!'

ELEVENTH SONG

'Who is it that this dark night
Underneath my window plaineth?'
It is one who from thy sight
Being, ah! exiled, disdaineth
Every other vulgar light.   5

'Why, alas! and are you he?
Be not yet those fancies changed?'
Dear, when you find change in me,
Though from me you be estranged,
Let my change to ruin be.   10

'Well, in absence this will die;
Leave to see, and leave to wonder.'
Absence sure will help, if I
Can learn how myself to sunder
From what in my heart doth lie.   15

'But time will these thoughts remove;
Time doth work what no man knoweth.'
Time doth as the subject prove;
With time still the affection groweth
In the faithful turtle-dove.   20

'What if we new beauties see?
Will not they stir new affection?'
I will think they pictures be,
(Image-like, of saint's perfection)
Poorly counterfeiting thee.   25

'But your reason's purest light
Bids you leave such minds to nourish,'
Dear, do reason no such spite;
Never doth thy beauty flourish
More than in my reason's sight.   30

'But the wrongs Love bears will make
Love at length leave undertaking,'

No, the more fools it do shake,
In the ground of so firm making,
Deeper still they drive the stake.   35

'Peace, I think that some give ear!
Come no more, lest I get anger!'
Bliss, I will my bliss forbear;
Fearing, sweet, you to endanger;
But my soul shall harbor there.   40

'Well, be gone! be gone, I say,
Lest that Argus' eyes perceive you!'
O unjust is Fortune's sway,
Which can make me thus to leave you;
And from louts to run away.   45

SONG: THE NIGHTINGALE

The nightingale, as soon as April bringeth
Unto her rested sense a perfect waking,
While late bare earth, proud of new cloth-
     ing, springeth,
Sings out her woes, a thorn her song-book
     making,
And mournfully bewailing,   5
Her throat in tunes expresseth
What grief her breast oppresseth
For Tereus' force on her chaste will pre-
     vailing.
O Philomela fair, O take some gladness,
That here is juster cause of painful sad-
     ness: 10
Thine earth now springs, mine fadeth;
Thy thorn without, my thorn my heart in-
     vadeth.

LOVE IS DEAD

Ring out your bells, let mourning shows be
     spread;
     For Love is dead:
All Love is dead, infected
With plague of deep disdain:
     Worth, as naught worth, rejected,   5
And Faith fair scorn doth gain.
     From so ungrateful fancy,
     From such a female franzie,
     From them that use men thus,
     Good Lord, deliver us!   10

Weep, neighbors, weep; do you not hear it
     said
     That Love is dead?
His death-bed, peacock's folly;
His winding-sheet is shame;
     His will, false-seeming holy;   15
His sole exec'tor, blame.

From so ungrateful fancy,
From such a female franzie,
From them that use men thus,
Good Lord, deliver us!   20

Let dirge be sung, and trentals rightly read.
     For Love is dead;
     Sir Wrong his tomb ordaineth
My mistress' marble heart;
     Which epitaph containeth,   25
'Her eyes were once his dart.'
     From so ungrateful fancy,
     From such a female franzie,
     From them that use men thus,
     Good Lord, deliver us!   30

Alas, I lie: rage hath this error bred;
     Love is not dead;
     Love is not dead, but sleepeth
In her unmatchèd mind,
     Where she his counsel keepeth,   35
Till due deserts she find.
     Therefore from so vile fancy,
     To call such wit a franzie,
     Who Love can temper thus,
     Good Lord, deliver us!   40

DORUS TO PAMELA

(From ARCADIA)

My sheep are thoughts, which I both guide
     and serve;
Their pasture is fair hills of fruitless love,
On barren sweets they feed, and feeding
     sterve.
I wail their lot, but will not other prove;
My sheep-hook is wan hope, which all up-
     holds;   5
My weeds, desire, cut out in endless folds;
What wool my sheep shall bear, whilst thus
     they live,
In you it is, you must the judgment give.

A DITTY

My true-love hath my heart and I have his,
By just exchange one for the other given:
I hold his dear, and mine he cannot miss,
There never was a better bargain driven:
     My true-love hath my heart, and I have
          his.   5

His heart in me keeps him and me in one,
My heart in him his thoughts and senses
     guides:
He loves my heart, for once it was his
     own,
I cherish his because in me it bides:
     My true-love hath my heart, and I have
          his.   10

HAKLUYT'S VOYAGES

Richard Hakluyt (1553–1616) has been well termed by Professor Raleigh 'the Homer of our heroic age'; yet his aim was not so much to record great deeds as to inspire them, to urge his countrymen to explore and colonize unknown countries, to encourage trade with the distant parts of the earth, and to furnish maps and other helps to navigation. A clergyman and a student, he had no experience of the adventures he described and prompted; but he was much more than a mere compiler. He brought to his self-appointed task the devotion and enthusiasm of a lofty purpose, and must be given a high rank among those who founded the British Empire and established the Anglo-Saxon race beyond the seas. It was fortunate for posterity that the Elizabethan age of commercial enterprise and romantic adventure found a chronicler with leisure and ability to save its achievements from oblivion, for the voyagers themselves were, as a rule, too busy making history to write it. Most of them were much readier with the sword than with the pen; Grenville's desperate resolution, Gilbert's religious valor, and Drake's restless daring would have been lost to literature, and perhaps even to history, if we had had to depend on their own records. Raleigh must be mentioned as a conspicuous exception; he combined with the spirit of adventure a literary power which makes his narratives a strange contrast to the matter-of-fact or garrulous reports of his less gifted fellows.

DEDICATORY EPISTLE TO SIR FRANCIS WALSINGHAM

(From the first edition of the Voyages, 1589)

Right honorable, I do remember that being a youth, and one of her Majesty's scholars at Westminster, that fruitful nursery, it was my hap to visit the chamber of Mr. Richard Hakluyt, my cousin, a 10 gentleman of the Middle Temple, well known unto you, at a time when I found lying open upon his board certain books of cosmography, with a universal map. He, seeing me somewhat curious in the 15 view thereof, began to instruct my ignorance by showing me the division of the earth into three parts after the old account, and then according to the latter, and better distribution, into more. He 20 pointed with his wand to all the known seas, gulfs, bays, straits, capes, rivers, empires, kingdoms, dukedoms, and territories of each part, with declaration also of their special commodities, and particu- 25 lar wants, which, by the benefit of traffic and intercourse of merchants, are plentifully supplied. From the map he brought me to the Bible, and turning to the 107th Psalm, directed me to the 23rd and 24th 30 verses, where I read, that they which go down to the sea in ships and occupy by the great waters, they see the works of the Lord, and his wonders in the deep, &c. Which words of the prophet, together with my cousin's discourse (things of high and rare delight to my young nature), took in 5 me so deep an impression that I constantly resolved, if ever I were preferred to the university, where better time and more convenient place might be ministered for these studies, I would by God's assistance prosecute that knowledge and kind of literature, the doors whereof, after a sort, were so happily opened before me.

According to which my resolution, when, not long after, I was removed to 15 Christ Church in Oxford, my exercises of duty first performed, I fell to my intended course, and by degrees read over whatsoever printed or written discoveries and voyages I found extant either in the 20 Greek, Latin, Italian, Spanish, Portugal, French, or English languages, and in my public lectures was the first that produced and showed both the old imperfectly composed, and the new lately reformed maps, 25 globes, spheres, and other instruments of this art for demonstration in the common schools, to the singular pleasure and general contentment of my auditory. In continuance of time, and by reason principally 30 of my insight in this study, I grew familiarly acquainted with the chiefest captains at sea, the greatest merchants, and the best mariners of our nation; by which means having gotten somewhat more than common knowledge, I passed at length the narrow seas into France with Sir Edward Stafford, her Majesty's careful and discreet Ligier, where during my five years' abode with him in his dangerous and chargeable residence in her Highness' service, I both heard in speech, and read· in books other nations miraculously extolled for their discoveries and notable enterprises by sea, but the English of all others for their sluggish security, and continual neglect of the like attempts, especially in so long and happy a time of peace, either ignominiously reported, or exceedingly condemned; which singular opportunity, if some other people, our neighbors, had been blessed with, their protestations are often and vehement, they would far otherwise have used. * * * Thus both hearing and reading the obloquy of our nation, and finding few or none of our own men able to reply herein; and further, not seeing any man to have care to recommend to the world the industrious labors and painful travels of our countrymen: for stopping the mouths of the reproachers, myself being the last winter returned from France with the honorable the Lady Sheffield, for her passing good behavior highly esteemed in all the French court, determined notwithstanding all difficulties to undertake the burden of that work wherein all others pretended either ignorance or lack of leisure, or want of sufficient argument, whereas (to speak truly) the huge toil and the small profit to ensue were the chief causes of the refusal. I call the work a burden in consideration that these voyages lay so dispersed, scattered, and hidden in several hucksters' hands, that I now wonder at myself to see how I was able to endure the delays, curiosity, and backwardness of many from whom I was to receive my originals, so that I have just cause to make that complaint of the maliciousness of divers in our time which Pliny made of the men of his age: At nos elaborata iis abscondere atque supprimere cupimus, et fraudare vitam etiam alienis bonis, &c. [But we desire to hide away and suppress their achievements, and to rob life even of the glories of others.]

To harp no longer upon this string, and to speak a word of that just commendation which our nation do indeed deserve: it cannot be denied. but as in all former ages they have been men full of activity, stirrers abroad, and searchers of the remote parts of the world, so in this most famous and peerless government of her most excellent Majesty, her subjects, through the special assistance and blessing of God, in searching the most opposite corners and quarters of the world, and to speak plainly, in compassing the vast globe of the earth more than once, have excelled all the nations and people of the earth. For which of the kings of this land before her Majesty had their banners ever seen in the Caspian sea? which of them hath ever dealt with the emperor of Persia as her Majesty hath done, and obtained for her merchants large and loving privileges? who ever saw, before this regiment, an English Ligier in the stately porch of the Grand Signor at Constantinople? who ever found English consuls and agents at Tripolis in Syria, at Aleppo, at Babylon, at Balsara, and which is more, who ever heard of Englishman at Goa before now? what English ships did heretofore ever anchor in the mighty river of Plate? pass and repass the unpassable (in former opinion) Strait of Magellan, range along the coast of Chili, Peru, and all the backside of Nova Hispania, further than any christian ever passed, traverse the mighty breadth of the South Sea, land upon the Luzones in despite of the enemy, enter into alliance, amity, and traffic with the princes of the Moluccas and the isle of Java, double the famous cape of Bona Speranza, arrive at the isle of St. Helena, and last of all return home most richly laden with the commodities of China, as the subjects of this now flourishing monarchy have done?

* * *

THE LAST FIGHT OF THE REVENGE

(From 'a report of the truth of the fight about the isles of Azores, the last of August, 1591, betwixt the *Revenge,* one of her Majesty's ships and an armada of the king of Spain. Penned by the honorable Sir Walter Raleigh, knight.')

The Lord Thomas Howard with six of her Majesty's ships, six victualers of London, the bark *Raleigh,* and two or three other pinnaces riding at anchor near unto Flores, one of the westerly islands of th⸱

Azores, the last of August in the afternoon, had intelligence by one Captain Middleton of the approach of the Spanish armada. Which Middleton, being in a very good sailer, had kept them company three days before, of good purpose both to discover their forces the more, as also to give advice to my Lord Thomas of their approach. He had no sooner delivered the news but the fleet was in sight; many of our ships' companies were on shore in the island, some providing ballast for their ships, others filling of water and refreshing themselves from the land with such things as they could, either for money, or by force, recover. By reason whereof, our ships being all pestered and rummaging, every thing out of order, very light for want of ballast, and that which was most to our disadvantage, the one half part of the men of every ship sick and utterly unserviceable; for in the *Revenge* there were ninety diseased, in the *Bonaventure* not so many in health as could handle her mainsail. For had not twenty men been taken out of a bark of Sir George Carey's, his being commanded to be sunk, and those appointed to her, she had hardly ever recovered England. The rest, for the most part, were in little better state. The names of her Majesty's ships were these, as followeth: the *Defiance,* which was admiral; the *Revenge,* viceadmiral; the *Bonaventure,* commanded by Captain Cross; the *Lion* by George Fenner; the *Foresight* by Mr. Thomas Vavasour; and the *Crane* by Duffield. The *Foresight* and the *Crane* being but small ships, only the others were of the middle size; the rest, besides the bark *Raleigh,* commanded by Captain Thin, were victualers, and of small force or none. The Spanish fleet, having shrouded their approach by reason of the island, were now so soon at hand as our ships had scarce time to weigh their anchors, but some of them were driven to let slip their cables and set sail. Sir Richard Grenville was the last that weighed, to recover the men that were upon the island, which otherwise had been lost. The Lord Thomas with the rest very hardly recovered the wind, which Sir Richard Grenville not being able to do, was persuaded by the master and others to cut his mainsail and cast about, and to trust to the sailing of the ship, for the squadron of Seville were on his weather bow. But Sir Richard utterly refused to turn from the enemy, alleging that he would rather choose to die than to dishonor himself, his country, and her Majesty's ship, persuading his company that he would pass through the two squadrons in despite of them and enforce those of Seville to give him way. Which he performed upon divers of the foremost, who, as the mariners term it, sprang their luff, and fell under the lee of the *Revenge.* But the other course had been the better, and might right well have been answered in so great an impossibility of prevailing. Notwithstanding, out of the greatness of his mind, he could not be persuaded. In the meanwhile, as he attended those which were nearest him, the great *San Philip,* being in the wind of him and coming towards him, becalmed his sails in such sort, as the ship could neither make way nor feel the helm; so huge and high carged was the Spanish ship, being of a thousand and five hundred tons. Who after laid the *Revenge* aboard. When he was thus bereft of his sails, the ships that were under his lee, luffing up, also laid him aboard, of which the next was the admiral of the Biscayans, a very mighty and puissant ship commanded by Brittandona. The said *Philip* carried three tiers of ordnance on a side, and eleven pieces in every tier. She shot eight forth right out of her chase, besides those of her stern ports.

After the *Revenge* was entangled with this *Philip,* four others boarded her, two on her larboard, and two on her starboard. The fight, thus beginning at three of the clock in the afternoon, continued very terrible all that evening. But the great *San Philip,* having received the lower tier of the *Revenge,* discharged with crossbar shot, shifted herself with all diligence from her sides, utterly misliking her first entertainment. Some say that the ship foundered, but we cannot report it for truth, unless we were assured. The Spanish ships were filled with companies of soldiers,— in some two hundred besides the mariners, in some five, in others eight hundred. In ours there were none at all beside the mariners but the servants of the commanders and some few voluntary gentlemen only. After many interchanged volleys of great ordnance and small shot, the Spaniards deliberated to enter the *Revenge,* and made divers attempts, hoping to force her by the multitudes of their armed soldiers and musketeers, but were still repulsed again and again, and at all times beaten back into their own ships, or into the seas. In the beginning of the fight, the *George Noble* of London, having received some shot through her by the armadas, fell under the lee of the *Revenge,* and asked Sir Richard what he would command him, being but one of the victualers and of small force. Sir Richard bade him save himself, and leave him to his fortune. After the fight had thus, without intermission, continued while the day lasted and some hours of the night, many of our men were slain and hurt, and one of the great galleons of the armada, and the admiral of the hulks both sunk, and in many other of the Spanish ships great slaughter was made. Some write that Sir Richard was very dangerously hurt almost in the beginning of the fight, and lay speechless for a time ere he recovered. But two of the *Revenge's* own company brought home in a ship of Lima from the islands, examined by some of the lords and others, affirmed that he was never so wounded as that he forsook the upper deck, till an hour before midnight, and then, being shot into the body with a musket, as he was dressing was again shot into the head, and withal his surgeon wounded to death. This agreeth also with an examination, taken by Sir Francis Godolphin, of four other mariners of the same ship, being returned, which examination the said Sir Francis sent unto Master William Killigrew, of her Majesty's privy chamber.

But to return to the fight: the Spanish ships which attempted to board the *Revenge,* as they were wounded and beaten off, so always others came in their places, she having never less than two mighty galleons by her sides and aboard her. So that ere the morning, from three of the clock the day before, there had fifteen several armadas assailed her; and all so ill approved their entertainment as they were by the break of day far more willing to hearken to a composition than hastily to make any more assaults or entries. But as the day increased, so our men decreased; and as the light grew more and more, by so much more grew our discomforts. For none appeared in sight but enemies, saving one small ship called the *Pilgrim,* commanded by Jacob Whiddon, who hovered all night to see the success,

but in the morning, bearing with the *Revenge,* was hunted like a hare amongst many ravenous hounds, but escaped.

All the powder of the *Revenge* to the last barrel was now spent, all her pikes broken, forty of her best men slain, and the most part of the rest hurt. In the beginning of the fight she had but one hundred free from sickness, and fourscore and ten sick, laid in hold upon the ballast: a small troop to man such a ship, and a weak garrison to resist so mighty an army. By those hundred all was sustained, the volleys, boardings, and enterings of fifteen ships of war, besides those which beat her at large. On the contrary, the Spanish were always supplied with soldiers brought from every squadron, all manner of arms and powder at will. Unto ours there remained no comfort at all, no hope, no supply either of ships, men, or weapons; the masts all beaten overboard, all her tackle cut asunder, her upper work altogether razed, and in effect evened she was with the water, but the very foundation or bottom of a ship, nothing being left overhead, either for flight or defence. Sir Richard, finding himself in this distress, and unable any longer to make resistance, having endured, in this fifteen hours' fight, the assault of fifteen several armadas, all by turns aboard him, and by estimation eight hundred shot of great artillery, besides many assaults and entries; and that himself and the ship must needs be possessed by the enemy, who were now all cast in a ring round about him, (the *Revenge* not able to move one way nor other, but as she was moved with the waves and billows of the sea), commanded the master gunner, whom he knew to be a most resolute man, to split and sink the ship, that thereby nothing might remain of glory or victory to the Spaniards, seeing in so many hours' fight, and with so great a navy, they were not able to take her, having had fifteen hours' time, above ten thousand men, and fifty and three sail of men-of-war to perform it withal; and persuaded the company, or as many as he could induce, to yield themselves unto God, and to the mercy of none else; but as they had, like valiant resolute men, repulsed so many enemies, they should not now shorten the honor of their nation by prolonging their own lives for a few hours or a few days. The master gunner readily condescended and divers others; but the captain and the master were of another opinion, and besought Sir Richard to have care of them, alleging that the Spaniard would be as ready to entertain a composition as they were willing to offer the same, and that there being divers sufficient and valiant men yet living, and whose wounds were not mortal, they might do their country and prince acceptable service hereafter. And whereas Sir Richard had alleged that the Spaniards should never glory to have taken one ship of her Majesty, seeing they had so long and so notably defended themselves, they answered, that the ship had six foot water in hold, three shot under water, which were so weakly stopped as with the first working of the sea, she must needs sink, and was besides so crushed and bruised as she could never be removed out of the place.

And as the matter was thus in dispute, and Sir Richard refusing to hearken to any of those reasons, the master of the *Revenge* (while the captain won unto him the greater party) was convoyed aboard the General Don Alfonso Bazan. Who (finding none over hasty to enter the *Revenge* again, doubting lest Sir Richard would have blown them up and himself, and perceiving by the report of the master of the *Revenge* his dangerous disposition) yielded that all their lives should be saved, the company sent for England, and the better sort to pay such reasonable ransom as their estate would bear, and in the mean season to be free from galley or imprisonment. To this he so much the rather condescended as well, as I have said, for fear of further loss and mischief to themselves, as also for the desire he had to recover Sir Richard Grenville, whom for his notable valor he seemed greatly to honor and admire.

* *

From LINSCHOTEN'S TESTIMONY

The 13th of September 'the said armada arrived at the island of Corvo, where the Englishmen with about 16 ships as then lay, staying for the Spanish fleet, whereof some or the most part were come, and there the English were in good hope to have taken them. But when they perceived the king's army to be strong, the admiral, being the Lord Thomas Howard, commanded his fleet not to fall upon them,

nor any of them once to separate their ships from him, unless he gave commission so to do. Notwithstanding the vice-admiral, Sir Richard Grenville, being in the ship called the *Revenge,* went into the Spanish fleet and shot among them, doing them great hurt, and thinking the rest of the company would have followed; which they did not, but left him there, and sailed away. The cause why could not be known. Which the Spaniards perceiving, with 7 or 8 ships they boarded her, but she withstood them all, fighting with them, at the least 12 hours together, and sunk two of them, one being a new double flyboat of 600 tons, and admiral of the flyboats, the other a Biscayan. But in the end, by reason of the number that came upon her, she was taken, but to their great loss, for they had lost in fighting and by drowning above 400 men, and of the English were slain about 100, Sir Richard Grenville himself being wounded in his brain, whereof afterwards he died. He was carried into the ship called *San Paul,* wherein was the admiral of the fleet, Don Alonzo de Bazan. There his wounds were dressed by the Spanish surgeons, but Don Alonzo himself would neither see him nor speak with him. All the rest of the captains and gentlemen went to visit him, and to comfort him in his hard fortune, wondering at his courage and stout heart, for that he showed not any sign of faintness nor changing of color. But feeling the hour of death to approach, he spake these words in Spanish, and said: Here die I, Richard Grenville, with a joyful and quiet mind, for that I have ended my life as a true soldier ought to do, that hath fought for his country, queen, religion, and honor, whereby my soul most joyful departeth out of this body, and shall always leave behind it an everlasting fame of a valiant and true soldier, that hath done his duty, as he was bound to do. When he had finished these or such other like words, he gave up the ghost, with great and stout courage, and no man could perceive any true sign of heaviness in him.

* * *

THE LOSS OF SIR HUMPHREY GILBERT

(From a report of the voyage and success thereof, attempted in the year of our

Lord, 1583, by Sir Humphrey Gilbert, knight, with other gentlemen assisting him in that action, intended to discover and to plant christian inhabitants in place convenient, upon those large and ample countries extended northward from the cape of Florida, lying under very temperate climes, esteemed fertile and rich in minerals, yet not in the actual possession of any christian prince, written by Mr. Edward Haie, gentleman, and principal actor in the same voyage, who alone continued to the end, and by God's special assistance returned home with his retinue safe and entire.')

So upon Saturday in the afternoon, the 31st of August, we changed our course and returned back for England, at which very instant, even in winding about, there passed along between us and towards the land which we now forsook, a very lion to our seeming, in shape, hair, and color, not swimming after the manner of a beast, by moving of his feet, but rather sliding upon the water with his whole body (excepting the legs) in sight; neither yet diving under, and again rising above the water, as the manner is of whales, dolphins, tunnies, porpoises, and all other fish, but confidently showing himself above water without hiding. Notwithstanding, we presented ourselves in open view and gesture to amaze him, as all creatures will be commonly at a sudden gaze and sight of men. Thus he passed along turning his head to and fro, yawning and gaping wide, with ugly demonstration of long teeth and glaring eyes, and to bid us a farewell (coming right against the *Hind*) he sent forth a horrible voice, roaring or bellowing as doth a lion, which spectacle we all beheld so far as we were able to discern the same, as men prone to wonder at every strange thing, as this doubtless was, to see a lion in the ocean sea, or fish in shape of a lion. What opinion others had thereof, and chiefly the general himself, I forbear to deliver. But he took it for *bonum omen* [a good omen], rejoicing that he was to war against such an enemy, if it were the devil.

The wind was large for England at our return, but very high, and the sea rough, insomuch as the frigate wherein the general went was almost swallowed up. Monday in the afternoon (Sept. 2), we passed in the sight of Cape Race, having made as much way in little more than two

days and nights back again, as before we had done in eight days from Cape Race unto the place where our ship perished, which hindrance thitherward and speed back again, is to be imputed unto the swift current, as well as to the winds, which we had more large in our return.

This Monday the general came aboard the *Hind* to have the surgeon of the *Hind* to dress his foot, which he hurt by treading upon a nail. At what time we comforted each other with hope of hard success to be all past, and of the good to come. So agreeing to carry out lights always by night, that we might keep together, he departed into his frigate, being by no means to be entreated to tarry in the *Hind,* which had been more for his security. Immediately after followed a sharp storm which we overpassed for that time. Praised be God.

The weather fair, the general came aboard the *Hind* again to make merry together with the captain, master, and company, which was the last meeting. and continued there from morning until night. During which time there passed sundry discourses, touching affairs past and to come, lamenting greatly the loss of his great ship, more of the men, but most of all of his books and notes, and what else I know not; for which he was out of measure grieved, the same doubtless being some matter of more importance than his books, which I could not draw from him, yet by circumstance I gathered the same to be the ore which Daniel the Saxon had brought unto him in the New-found-land. Whatsoever it was, the remembrance touched him so deep as not able to contain himself, he beat his boy in great rage, even at the same time, so long after the miscarrying of the great ship, because upon a fair day, when we were becalmed upon the coast of the New-found-land, near unto Cape Race, he sent his boy aboard the admiral to fetch certain things, amongst which, this being chief, was yet forgotten, and left behind. After which time, he could never conveniently send again aboard the great ship; much less he doubted her ruin so near at hand.

Herein my opinion was better confirmed diversely, and by sundry conjectures, which maketh me have the greater hope of this rich mine. For whereas the general had never before good conceit of these north parts of the world, now his mind was wholly fixed upon the New-found-land. And as before he refused not to grant assignments liberally to them that required the same into these north parts, now he became contrarily affected. refusing to make any so large grants, especially of St. John's, which certain English merchants made suit for, offering to employ their money and travel upon the same. Yet neither by their own suit, nor of others of his own company, whom he seemed willing to pleasure, it could be obtained.

Also laying down his determination in the spring following, for disposing of his voyage then to be re-attempted, he assigned the captain and master of the *Golden Hind* unto the south discovery, and reserved unto himself the north, affirming that this voyage had won his heart from the south, and that he was now become a northern man altogether.

Last, being demanded what means he had at his arrival in England to compass the charges of so great preparation as he intended to make the next spring, having determined upon two fleets, one for the south, another for the north: Leave that to me (he replied), I will ask a penny of no man. I will bring good tidings unto her Majesty, who will be so gracious to lend me 10,000 pounds, willing us therefore to be of good cheer, for he did thank God (he said) with all his heart for that he had seen, the same being enough for us all, and that we needed not to seek any further. And these last words he would often repeat, with demonstration of great fervency of mind, being himself very confident and settled in belief of inestimable good by this voyage, which the greater number of his followers nevertheless mistrusted altogether, not being made partakers of those secrets, which the general kept unto himself. Yet all of them that are living may be witnesses of his words and protestations, which sparingly I have delivered.

Leaving the issue of this good hope unto God, who knoweth the truth only, and can at his good pleasure bring the same to light, I will hasten to the end of this tragedy, which must be knit up in the person of our general. And as it was God's ordinance upon him, even so the vehement persuasion and entreaty of his friends could nothing avail to divert him from a wilful resolution of going through in his frigate, which was overcharged upon their decks, with fights, nettings, and small artillery, too cumbersome for so small a boat that was to pass through the ocean sea at that season of the year, when by course we might expect much storm of foul weather, whereof indeed we had enough.

But when he was entreated by the captain, master, and other his well-willers of the *Hind,* not to venture in the frigate, this was his answer: I will not forsake my little company going homeward, with whom I have passed so many storms and perils. And in very truth, he was urged to be so over hard, by hard reports given of him, that he was afraid of the sea, albeit this was rather rashness than advised resolution, to prefer the wind of a vain report to the weight of his own life.

Seeing he would not bend to reason, he had provision out of the *Hind,* such as was wanting aboard his frigate. And so we committed him to God's protection, and set him aboard his pinnace, we being more than 300 leagues onward of our way home.

By that time we had brought the islands of Azores south of us; yet we then keeping much to the north, until we had got into the height and elevation of England, we met with very foul weather and terrible seas, breaking short and high, pyramid wise. The reason whereof seemed to proceed either of hilly grounds, high and low, within the sea, (as we see hills and dales upon the land), upon which the seas do mount and fall; or else the cause proceedeth of diversity of winds, shifting often in sundry points, all which having power to move the great ocean, which again is not presently settled, so many seas do encounter together as there had been diversity of winds. Howsoever it cometh to pass, men which all their life time had occupied the sea, never saw more outrageous seas. We had also upon our mainyard, an apparition of a little fire by night, which seamen do call Castor and Pollux. But we had only one, which they take an evil sign of more tempest; the same is usual in storms.

Monday the ninth of September, in the afternoon, the frigate was near cast away, oppressed by waves; yet at that time recovered; and giving forth signs of joy the general sitting abaft with a book in his hand, cried out unto us in the *Hind* (so oft as we did approach within hearing):

We are as near to heaven by sea as by land. Reiterating the same speech, well beseeming a soldier, resolute in Jesus Christ, as I can testify he was.

The same Monday night, about twelve of the clock, or not long after, the frigate being ahead of us in the *Golden Hind,* suddenly her lights were out, whereof, as it were in a moment, we lost the sight, and withal our watch cried, the general was cast away, which was too true. For in that moment, the frigate was devoured and swallowed up of the sea. Yet still we looked out all that night and ever after, until we arrived upon the coast of England, omitting no small sail at sea, unto which we gave not the tokens between us agreed upon, to have perfect knowledge of each other, if we should at any time be separated.

In great torment of weather and peril of drowning, it pleased God to send safe home the *Golden Hind,* which arrived in Falmouth, the 22nd day of September, being Sunday, not without as great danger escaped in a flaw, coming from the southeast, with such thick mist that we could not discern land, to put in right with the haven.

A REPORT OF VIRGINIA

(From 'a brief and true report of the new-found land of Virginia, of the commodities there found and to be raised, as well merchantable as others. Written by Thomas Heriot, servant to Sir Walter Raleigh, a member of the colony and there employed in discovering a full twelve-month.')

There is an herb which is sowed apart by itself, and is called by the inhabitants *uppowoc.* In the West Indies it hath divers names, according to the several places and countries where it groweth and is used; the Spaniards generally call it *tobacco.* The leaves thereof being dried and brought into powder, they use to take the fume or smoke thereof by sucking it, through pipes made of clay, into their stomach and head, from whence it purgeth superfluous phlegm and other gross humors, and opens all the pores and passages of the body; by which means the use thereof not only preserveth the body from obstructions, but also (if any be, so that they have not been of too long continuance) in short time breaketh them, whereby their bodies are notably preserved in health, and know not many grievous diseases, wherewithal we in England are often times afflicted.

This *uppowoc* is of so precious estimation amongst them, that they think their gods are marvelously delighted therewith. Whereupon sometimes they make hallowed fires, and cast some of the powder therein for a sacrifice. Being in a storm upon the waters, to pacify their gods, they cast some up into the air and into the water. So a weir for fish being newly set up, they cast some therein and into the air. Also, after an escape of danger, they cast some into the air likewise; but all done with strange gestures, stamping, sometime dancing, clapping of hands, holding up of hands, and staring up into the heavens, uttering therewithal, and chattering strange words and noises.

We ourselves, during the time we were there, used to suck it after their manner, as also since our return, and have found many rare and wonderful experiments of the virtues thereof, of which the relation would require a volume by itself. The use of it by so many of late, men and women of great calling, as else, and some learned physicians also, is sufficient witness.

* * *

From RALEIGH'S DISCOVERY OF GUIANA

Upon this river one Captain George, that I took with Berreo, told me there was a great silver mine, and that it was near the banks of the said river. But by this time as well Orinoco, Caroli, as all the rest of the rivers were risen four or five feet in height so as it was not possible by the strength of any men, or with any boat whatsoever to row into the river against the stream. I therefore sent Captain Thyn, Captain Grenville, my nephew John Gilbert, my cousin Butshead Gorges, Captain Clark, and some thirty shot more to coast the river by land, and to go to a town some twenty miles over the valley called Amnatapoi. And they found guides there to go farther towards the mountain foot to another great town called Capurepana, belonging to a casique called Haharacoa (that was a nephew to old To piawari, king of Arromaia, our chiefest friend) because this town and province of Capurepana adjoined to Macureguarai, which was a frontier town of the empire. And the meanwhile myself with Captain Gifford, Captain Calfield, Edward Hancock, and some half a dozen shot marched overland to view the strange overfalls of the river of Caroli which roared so far off, and also to see the plains adjoining, and the rest of the province of Canuri. I sent also Captain Whiddon, William Connocke, and some eight shot with them, to see if they could find any mineral stone alongst the riverside. When we were come to the tops of the first hills of the plains adjoining to the river, we beheld that wonderful breach of waters which ran down Caroli, and might from that mountain see the river how it ran in three parts, above twenty miles off. And there appeared some ten or twelve overfalls in sight, every one as high over the other as a church-tower, which fell with that fury, that the rebound of water made it seem as if it had been all covered over with a great shower of rain; and in some places we took it at the first for a smoke that had risen over some great town. For mine own part, I was well persuaded from thence to have returned, being a very ill footman, but the rest were all so desirous to go near the said strange thunder of waters, as they drew me on by little and little, till we came into the next valley, where we might better discern the same. I never saw a more beautiful country, nor more lively prospects, hills so raised here and there over the valleys, the river winding into divers branches, the plains adjoining without bush or stubble, all fair green grass, the ground of hard sand, easy to march on, either for horse or foot, the deer crossing in every path, the birds towards the evening singing on every tree with a thousand several tunes, cranes, and herons of white, crimson, and carnation perching in the riverside, the air fresh with a gentle easterly wind, and every stone that we stooped to take up, promised either gold or silver by its complexion. Your lordship shall see of many sorts, and I hope some of them cannot be bettered under the sun; and yet we had no means but with our daggers and fingers to tear them out here and there, the rocks being most hard, of that mineral spar aforesaid, which is like

a flint, and is altogether as hard or harder; and besides the veins lie a fathom or two deep in the rocks. But we wanted all things requisite, save only our desires and good will, to have performed more if it had pleased God. To be short, when both our companies returned, each of them brought also several sorts of stones that appeared very fair, but were such as they found loose on the ground, and were for the most part but colored, and had not any gold fixed in them; yet such as had no judgment or experience kept all that glistered, and would not be persuaded but it was rich because of the luster, and brought of those and of marquesite withal, from Trinidad, and have delivered of those stones to be tried in many places, and have thereby bred an opinion that all the rest is of the same. Yet some of these stones I showed afterward to a Spaniard of the Caracas, who told me that it was *el madre del oro*, that is, the mother of gold, and that the mine was farther in the ground.

* * *

I will enter no further into discourse of their manners, laws, and customs, and because I have not myself seen the cities of Inca, I cannot avow on my credit what I have heard, although it be very likely that the Emperor Inca hath built and erected as magnificent palaces in Guiana as his ancestors did in Peru, which were for their riches and rareness most marvelous and exceeding all in Europe, and I think of the world, China excepted; which also the Spaniards (which I had) assured me to be true, as also the nations of the borderers, who, being but savages to those of the inland, do cause much treasure to be buried with them. For I was informed of one of the casiques of the valley of Amariocapana, which had buried with him, a little before our arrival, a chair of gold most curiously wrought, which was made either in Macureguaray adjoining, or in Manoa. But if we should have grieved them in their religion at the first, before they had been taught better, and have digged up their graves, we had lost them all. And therefore I held my first resolution that her Majesty should either accept or refuse the enterprise ere anything should be done that might in any sort hinder the same. And if Peru had so many heaps of gold, whereof those Incas were princes, and that they delighted so much therein: no doubt but this which

of the country, having their houses close by the water's side, showed themselves unto us, and sent a present to our general.

When they came unto us, they greatly wondered at the things that we brought, but our general (according to his natural and accustomed humanity) courteously entreated them, and liberally bestowed on them necessary things to cover their nakedness, whereupon they supposed us to be gods, and would not be persuaded to the contrary. The presents which they sent to our general were feathers and cauls of network.

Their houses are digged round about with earth, and have from the uttermost brims of the circle clifts of wood set upon them, joining close together at the top like a spire steeple, which by reason of that closeness are very warm.

Their beds is the ground with rushes strewed on it, and lying about the house, have the fire in the midst. The men go naked, the women take bulrushes and comb them after the manner of hemp, and thereof make their loose garments, which being knit about their middles, hang down about their hips, having also about their shoulders a skin of deer with the hair upon it. These women are very obedient and serviceable to their husbands.

After they were departed from us, they came and visited us the second time and brought with them feathers and bags of tobacco for presents. And when they came to the top of the hill (at the bottom whereof we had pitched our tents) they stayed themselves, where one appointed for speaker wearied himself with making a long oration, which done, they left their bows upon the hill, and came down with their presents.

In the meantime the women, remaining on the hill, tormented themselves lamentably, tearing their flesh from their cheeks, whereby we perceived that they were about a sacrifice. In the meantime our general with his company went to prayer and to reading of the Scriptures, at which exercise they were attentive, and seemed greatly to be affected with it. But when they were come unto us, they restored again unto us those things which before we bestowed upon them.

The news of our being there being spread through the country, the people that inhabited round about came down,

and amongst them the king himself, a man of goodly stature and comely personage, with many other tall and warlike men; before whose coming were sent two ambassadors to our general to signify that their king was coming, in doing of which message their speech was continued about half an hour. This ended, they by signs requested our general to send some thing by their hand to their king as a token that his coming might be in peace, wherein our general having satisfied them, they returned with glad tidings to their king, who marched to us with a princely majesty, the people crying continually after their manner; and as they drew near unto us, so did they strive to behave themselves in their actions with comeliness.

In the fore-front was a man of goodly personage, who bore the scepter or mace before the king, whereupon hung two crowns, a less and a bigger, with three chains of a marvelous length. The crowns were made of knit work wrought artificially with feathers of divers colors; the chains were made of a bony substance, and few be the persons among them that are admitted to wear them; and of that number also the persons are stinted, as some ten, some twelve, and so forth. Next unto him which bare the scepter was the king himself with his guard about his person, clad with coney skins, and other skins. After them followed the naked common sort of people, everyone having his face painted, some with white, some with black, and other colors, and having in their hands one thing or another for a present, not so much as their children, but they also brought their presents.

In the meantime our general gathered his men together and marched within his fenced place, making against their approaching a very warlike show. They being trooped together in their order and a general salutation being made, there was presently a general silence. Then he that bare the scepter before the king, being informed by another, whom they assigned to that office, with a manly and lofty voice proclaimed that which the other spoke to him in secret, continuing half an hour; which ended, and a general amen, as it were, given, the king with the whole number of men and women (the children excepted) came down without any weapon; who descending to the foot of the hill, set themselves in order.

In coming towards our bulwarks and tents, the scepter-bearer began a song, observing his measures in a dance, and that with a stately countenance; whom the king with his guard, and every degree of persons, following, did in like manner sing and dance, saving only the women, which danced and kept silence. The general permitted them to enter within our bulwark, where they continued their song and dance a reasonable time. When they had satisfied themselves, they made signs to our general to sit down, to whom the king and divers others made several orations, or rather supplications, that he would take their province and kingdom into his hand, and become their king, making signs that they would resign unto him their right and title of the whole land, and become his subjects. In which, to persuade us the better, the king and the rest with one consent and with great reverence, joyfully singing a song, did set the crown upon his head, enriched his neck with all their chains, and offered unto him many other things, honoring him by the name of *Hioh,* adding thereunto, as it seemed a sign of triumph, which thing our general thought not meet to reject, because he knew not what honor and profit it might be to our country. Wherefore in the name and to the use of her Majesty he took the scepter, crown, and dignity of the said country into his hands, wishing that the riches and treasure thereof might so conveniently be transported to the enriching of her kingdom at home, as it aboundeth in the same.

The common sort of people leaving the king and his guard with our general, scattered themselves together with their sacrifices among our people, taking a diligent view of every person; and such as pleased their fancy, (which were the youngest) they, inclosing them about, offered their sacrifices unto them with lamentable weeping, scratching, and tearing the flesh from their faces with their nails, whereof issued abundance of blood. But we used signs to them of disliking this, and stayed their hands from force, and directed them upwards to the living God, whom only they ought to worship. They showed unto us their wounds, and craved help of them at our hands, whereupon we gave them lotions, plasters, and ointments, agreeing to the state of their griefs, beseeching God to cure their diseases. Every third day they brought their sacrifices to us, until they understood our meaning that we had no pleasure in them. Yet they could not be long absent from us, but daily frequented our company to the hour of our departure, which departure seemed so grievous unto them that their joy was turned into sorrow. They entreated us that being absent we would remember them, and by stealth provided a sacrifice, which we misliked.

Our necessary business being ended, our general with his company traveled up into the country to their villages, where we found herds of deer by 1000 in a company, being most large and fat of body.

We found the whole country to be a warren of a strange kind of conies, their bodies in bigness as be the Barbary conies, their heads as the heads of ours, the feet of a want, and the tail of a rat, being of great length. Under her chin is on either side a bag, into the which she gathereth her meat, when she hath filled her belly abroad. The people eat their bodies and make great account of their skins, for their king's coat was made of them.

Our general called this country Nova Albion, and that for two causes: the one in respect of the white banks and cliffs which lie towards the sea; and the other because it might have some affinity with our country in name, which sometime was so called.

There is no part of earth here to be taken up, wherein there is not some probable show of gold or silver.

At our departure hence our general set up a monument of our being there, as also of her Majesty's right and title to the same, namely a plate, nailed upon a fair great post, whereupon was engraven her Majesty's name, the day and year of our arrival there, with the free giving up of the province and people into her Majesty's hands, together with her highness' picture and arms in a piece of six pence of current English money under the plate, whereunder was also written the name of our general.

* * *

EDMUND SPENSER (1552–1599)

Although Spenser's father was 'a gentleman by birth,' he seems to have lacked adequate resources for bringing up his son. In spite of insufficient means, however, Spenser received a thoroughly good education, first as a 'poor scholar' in the Merchant Tailors' School in London, under Richard Mulcaster, and later, during seven years, as a sizar, or needy student, at Pembroke Hall, Cambridge. At the university he gained not only a high standing in classical studies, but also the permanent friendship of Gabriel Harvey, Fellow of Pembroke, the Hobbinol of Spenser's pastoral verse. After leaving the university, in 1576, Spenser seems to have retired for a year or so into the country, where, according to a persistent tradition, he met the Rosalind of the *Shepherd's Calendar*. He began his active career as a private secretary, first, perhaps, to Sir Henry Sidney, in Ireland, certainly to Bishop Young of Rochester, in 1578, and finally to the Earl of Leicester, in 1579. In this last position he met Leicester's nephew, Sir Philip Sidney, and Sir Edward Dyer, with both of whom he formed an intimate literary and personal friendship. His friendship with Sidney, Spenser recorded in *Astrophel: A Pastoral Elegy* (1595). Under Leicester's roof was completed the *Shepherd's Calendar*, published in 1579. The enthusiastic reception of the poem among men of letters promptly established Spenser as the chief of English poets then living. In 1580, Spenser went to Ireland as secretary to the lord deputy, Arthur Grey, and, except for two visits to England, he remained in Ireland until a month before his death. In 1581, he became clerk of the faculties in the Court of Chancery, and in the succeeding years prospered sufficiently to acquire land and to buy the office of clerk of the council of Munster, in 1588, when, probably, he began to reside upon his new estate at Kilcolman Castle. In 1589, Sir Walter Raleigh visited Spenser, who showed him the first three books of the *Faery Queen*, and who departed with his eminent visitor during that same year for London, there to present his work to the queen and to publish it. If the poet expected reward in the form of a government office in London, he was disappointed, for in 1591, after obtaining a pension of fifty pounds, he returned home. Raleigh's visit and the sojourn in London are reflected in *Colin Clout's Come Home Again* (1595). After his return to Ireland, Spenser seems to have worked assiduously upon the *Faery Queen*, for the second three books were completed before June 11, 1594, when he married Elizabeth Boyle, the inspiration of the *Amoretti* and of *Epithalamion*. In 1596, Spenser again visited London, to publish Books IV–VI of the *Faery Queen*, and, no doubt, to seek office,— once more unsuccessfully. To this London visit is assigned the writing of the *Four Hymns*, the *Prothalamion*, and the prose tract, *View of the Present State of Ireland*. In this last work the poet vigorously records his contempt for the Irish, a contempt that must have grown into bitter hatred when, in 1598, Irish rebels burned Kilcolman Castle and drove Spenser and his family to Cork. After having prepared for the queen an account of the situation in Ireland, Spenser set out with dispatches for London, where he died, January 16, 1599.

From THE SHEPHEARDES CALENDAR

FEBRUARIE

ÆGLOGA SECUNDA

CUDDIE. THENOT.

Cud. Ah for pittie! wil rancke winters
    rage
These bitter blasts never ginne tasswage?
The kene cold blowes through my beaten
    hyde,
All as I were through the body gryde.
My ragged rontes all shiver and shake.   5

As doen high towers in an earthquake:
They wont in the wind wagge their wrigle
    tailes,
Perke as peacock: but nowe it avales.
   The. Lewdly complainest thou, laesie
    ladde,
Of winters wracke, for making thee sadde.
Must not the world wend in his commun
    course,   11
From good to badd, and from badde to
    worse,
From worse unto that is worst of all,
And then returne to his former fall?
Who will not suffer the stormy time,   15

Where will he live tyll the lusty prime?
Selfe have I worne out thrise threttie
  yeares,
Some in much joy, many in many teares;
Yet never complained of cold nor heate,
Of sommers flame, nor of winters threat; 20
Ne ever was to fortune foeman,
But gently tooke that ungently came:
And ever my flocke was my chiefe care;
Winter or sommer they mought well fare.
  Cud. No marveile, Thenot, if thou can
  beare   25
Cherefully the winters wrathfull cheare:
For age and winter accord full nie,
This chill, that cold, this crooked, that wrye;
And as the lowring wether lookes downe,
So semest thou like Good Fryday to frowne.
But my flowring youth is foe to frost, 31
My shippe unwont in stormes to be tost.
  The. The soveraigne of seas he blames
  in vaine,
That, once seabeate, will to sea againe.
So loytring live you little heardgroomes, 35
Keeping your beastes in the budded broomes:
And when the shining sunne laugheth once,
You deemen the spring is come attonce.
Tho gynne you, fond flyes, the cold to
  scorne,
And crowing in pypes made of greene
  corne,   40
You thinken to be lords of the yeare.
But eft, when ye count you freed from
  feare,
Comes the breme winter with chamfred
  browes,
Full of wrinckles and frostie furrowes,
Drerily shooting his stormy darte, 45
Which cruddles the blood, and pricks the
  harte.
Then is your carelesse corage accoied,
Your carefull heards with cold bene an-
  noied:
Then paye you the price of your surquedrie,
With weeping, and wayling, and misery. 50
  Cud. Ah, foolish old man! I scorne thy
  skill,
That wouldest me my springing youngth to
  spil.
I deeme thy braine emperished bee
Through rusty elde, that hath rotted thee:
Or sicker thy head veray tottie is, 55
So on thy corbe shoulder it leanes amisse.
Now thy selfe hast lost both lopp and topp,
Als my budding braunch thou wouldest
  cropp:
But were thy yeares greene, as now bene
  myne,
To other delights they would encline. 60

Tho wouldest thou learne to caroll ot love,
And hery with hymnes thy lasses glove:
Tho wouldest thou pype of Phyllis prayse:
But Phyllis is myne for many dayes:
I wonne her with a grydle of gelt, 65
Embost with buegle about the belt:
Such an one shepeheards woulde make full
  faine,
Such an one would make thee younge
  againe.
  The. Thou art a fon, of thy love to boste;
All that is lent to love wyll be lost. 70
  Cud. Seest howe brag yond bullocke
  beares,
So smirke, so smoothe, his prickèd eares?
His hornes bene as broade as rainebowe
  bent,
His dewelap as lythe as lasse of Kent.
See howe he venteth into the wynd. 75
Weenest of love is not his mynd?
Seemeth thy flocke thy counsell can,
So lustlesse bene they, so weake, so wan,
Clothed with cold, and hoary wyth frost.
Thy flocks father his corage hath lost: 80
Thy ewes, that wont to have blowen bags,
Like wailefull widdowes hangen their crags:
The rather lambes bene starved with cold,
All for their maister is lustlesse and old.
  The. Cuddie, I wote thou kenst little good,
So vainely tadvaunce thy headlessehood. 86
For youngth is a bubble blown up with
  breath,
Whose witt is weakenesse, whose wage is
  death,
Whose way is wildernesse, whose ynne
  penaunce,
And stoopegallaunt age, the hoste of gree-
  vaunce.   90
But shall I tel thee a tale of truth,
Which I cond of Tityrus in my youth,
Keeping his sheepe on the hils of Kent?
  Cud. To nought more, Thenot, my mind
  is bent,
Then to heare novells of his devise: 95
They bene so well thewed, and so wise,
What ever that good old man bespake.
  The. Many meete tales of youth did he
  make,
And some of love, and some of chevalrie:
But none fitter then this to applie. 100
Now listen a while, and hearken the end.
  There grewe an agèd tree on the greene,
A goodly Oake sometime had it bene,
With armes full strong and largely dis-
  playd,
But of their leaves they were disarayde: 105
The bodie bigge, and mightely pight,
Throughly rooted, and of wonderous hight:

Whilome had bene the king of the field,
And mochell mast to the husband did yielde,
And with his nuts larded many swine. 110
But now the gray mosse marred his rine,
His bared boughs were beaten with
 stormes,
His toppe was bald, and wasted with
 wormes,
His honor decayed, his braunches sere. 114
 Hard by his side grewe a bragging Brere,
Which proudly thrust into thelement,
And seemed to threat the firmament.
Yt was embellisht with blossomes fayre,
And thereto aye wonned to repayre 119
The shepheards daughters, to gather flowres,
To peinct their girlonds with his colowres:
And in his small bushes used to shrowde
The sweete nightingale singing so lowde:
Which made this foolish Brere wexe so
 bold,
That on a time he cast him to scold 125
And snebbe the good Oake, for he was old.
 'Why standst there,' quoth he, 'thou
 brutish blocke?
Nor for fruict nor for shadowe serves thy
 stocke.
Seest how fresh my flowers bene spredde,
Dyed in lilly white and cremsin redde, 130
With leaves engrained in lusty greene
Colours meete to clothe a mayden queene?
Thy wast bignes but combers the grownd,
And dirks the beauty of my blossomes
 round.
The mouldie mosse, which thee accloieth,
My sinamon smell too much annoieth. 136
Wherefore soone, I rede thee, hence remove,
Least thou the price of my displeasure
 prove.'
So spake this bold Brere with great dis-
 daine:
Little him answered the Oake againe, 140
But yielded, with shame and greefe adawed,
That of a weede he was overawed.
 Yt chaunced after upon a day,
The husbandman selfe to come that way,
Of custome for to survewe his grownd, 145
And his trees of state in compasse rownd.
Him when the spitefull Brere had espyed,
Causlesse complained, and lowdly cryed
Unto his lord, stirring up sterne strife:
'O my liege Lord, the god of my life, 150
Pleaseth you ponder your suppliants plaint,
Caused of wrong, and cruell constraint,
Which I your poore vassall dayly endure:
And but your goodnes the same recure,
Am like for desperate doole to dye, 155
Through felonous force of mine enemie.'
 Greatly aghast with this piteous plea,

Him rested the goodman on the lea,
And badde the Brere in his plaint proceede.
With painted words tho gan this proude
 weede 160
(As most usen ambitious folke)
His colowred crime with craft to cloke.
 'Ah my soveraigne, lord of creatures all,
Thou placer of plants both humble and tall,
Was not I planted of thine owne hand, 165
To be the primrose of all thy land,
With flowring blossomes to furnish the
 prime,
And scarlot berries in sommer time?
How falls it then, that this faded Oake,
Whose bodie is sere, whose braunches
 broke, 170
Whose naked armes stretch unto the fyre,
Unto such tyrannie doth aspire;
Hindering with his shade my lovely light,
And robbing me of the swete sonnes sight?
So beate his old boughes my tender side, 175
That oft the bloud springeth from wounds
 wyde:
Untimely my flowres forced to fall,
That bene the honor of your coronall.
And oft he lets his cancker wormes light
Upon my braunches, to worke me more
 spight: 180
And oft his hoarie locks downe doth cast,
Where with my fresh flowretts bene defast.
For this, and many more such outrage,
Craving your goodlihead to aswage
The ranckorous rigour of his might, 185
Nought aske I, but onely to hold my right;
Submitting me to your good sufferance,
And praying to be garded from greevance.'
 To this the Oake cast him to replie
Well as he couth: but his enemie 190
Had kindled such coles of displeasure,
That the good man noulde stay his leasure,
But home him hasted with furious heate,
Encreasing his wrath with many a threate.
His harmefull hatchet he hent in hand, 195
(Alas, that it so ready should stand!)
And to the field alone he speedeth,
(Ay little helpe to harme there needeth.)
Anger nould let him speake to the tree,
Enaunter his rage mought cooled bee; 200
But to the roote bent his sturdy stroke,
And made many wounds in the wast Oake.
The axes edge did oft turne againe,
As halfe unwilling to cutte the graine:
Semed, the sencelesse yron dyd feare, 205
Or to wrong holy eld did forbeare.
For it had bene an auncient tree,
Sacred with many a mysteree,
And often crost with the priestes crewe,
And often halowed with holy water dewe.

But sike fancies weren foolerie,   211
And broughten this Oake to this miserye.
For nought mought they quitten him from
 decay:
For fiercely the goodman at him did laye.
The blocke oft groned under the blow,   215
And sighed to see his neare overthrow.
In fine, the steele had pierced his pitth:
Tho downe to the earth he fell forthwith:
His wonderous weight made the grounde to
 quake,
Thearth shronke under him, and seemed to
 shake.   220
There lyeth the Oake, pitied of none.
 Now stands the Brere like a lord alone,
Puffed up with pryde and vaine pleasaunce:
But all this glee had no continuaunce.
For eftsones winter gan to approche,   225
The blustring Boreas did encroche,
And beate upon the solitarie Brere:
For nowe no succoure was seene him nere.
Now gan he repent his pryde to late:
For naked left and disconsolate,   230
The byting frost nipt his stalke dead,
The watrie wette weighed downe his head,
And heaped snowe burdned him so sore,
That nowe upright he can stand no more:
And being downe, is trodde in the durt 235
Of cattell, and brouzed, and sorely hurt.
Such was thend of this ambitious Brere,
For scorning eld —
 Cud. Now I pray thee, shepheard, tel it
 not forth:
Here is a long tale, and little worth.   240
So longe have I listened to thy speche,
That graffèd to the ground is my breche:
My hartblood is welnigh frorne, I feele,
And my galage growne fast to my heele:
But little ease of thy lewd tale I tasted. 245
Hye thee home, shepheard, the day is nigh
 wasted.

THENOTS EMBLEME.

Iddio, perchè è vecchio,
Fa suoi al suo essempio.

CUDDIES EMBLEME.

Niuno vecchio
Spaventa Iddio.

OCTOBER

ÆGLOGA DECIMA

PIERCE. CUDDIE.

 Piers. Cuddie, for shame! hold up thy
 heavye head,
And let us cast with what delight to chace
And weary thys long lingring Phœbus race.

Whilome thou wont the shepheards laddes
 to leade
In rymes, in ridles, and in bydding base: 5
Now they in thee, and thou in sleepe art
 dead.

 Cud. Piers, I have pypèd erst so long with
 payne,
That all mine oten reedes bene rent and
 wore:
And my poore Muse hath spent her sparèd
 store,
Yet little good hath got, and much lesse
 gayne.   10
Such pleasaunce makes the grashopper so
 poore,
And ligge so layd, when winter doth her
 straine.

The dapper ditties that I wont devise,
To feede youthes fancie and the flocking
 fry,
Delighten much: what I the bett forthy? 15
They han the pleasure, I a sclender prise:
I beate the bush, the byrds to them doe flye:
What good thereof to Cuddie can arise?
 Piers. Cuddie, the prayse is better then
 the price,
The glory eke much greater then the gayne:
O what an honor is it, to restraine   21
The lust of lawlesse youth with good ad-
 vice,
Or pricke them forth with pleasaunce of
 thy vaine,
Whereto thou list their traynèd willes en-
 tice!

Soone as thou gynst to sette thy notes in
 frame,   25
O how the rurall routes to thee doe cleave!
Seemeth thou doest their soule of sense
 bereave,
All as the shepheard, that did fetch his dame
From Plutoes balefull bowre withouten
 leave:
His musicks might the hellish hound did
 tame.   30

 Cud. So praysen babes the peacoks spotted
 traine,
And wondren at bright Argus blazing eye;
But who rewards him ere the more forthy?
Or feedes him once the fuller by a graine?
Sike prayse is smoke, that sheddeth in the
 skye,   35
Sike words bene wynd, and wasten soone in
 vayne.

Piers. Abandon then the base and viler
    clowne:
Lyft up thy selfe out of the lowly dust,
And sing of bloody Mars, of wars, of giusts:
Turne thee to those that weld the awful
    crowne,   40
To doubted knights, whose woundlesse ar-
    mour rusts,
And helmes unbruzèd wexen dayly browne.

There may thy Muse display her fluttryng
    wing,
And stretch her selfe at large from east to
    west:
Whither thou list in fayre Elisa rest,   45
Or if thee please in bigger notes to sing,
Advaunce the worthy whome shee loveth
    best,
That first the white beare to the stake did
    bring.

And when the stubborne stroke of stronger
    stounds
Has somewhat slackt the tenor of thy
    string,   50
Of love and lustihead tho mayst thou sing,
And carrol lowde, and leade the myllers
    rownde,
All were Elisa one of thilke same ring.
So mought our Cuddies name to heaven
    sownde.

Cud. Indeede the Romish Tityrus, I
    heare,   55
Through his Mecœnas left his oaten reede,
Whereon he earst had taught his flocks to
    feede,
And laboured lands to yield the timely eare,
And eft did sing of warres and deadly
    drede,
So as the heavens did quake his verse to
    here.   60

But ah! Mecœnas is yclad in claye,
And great Augustus long ygoe is dead,
And all the worthies liggen wrapt in leade,
That matter made for poets on to play:
For, ever, who in derring doe were dreade,
The loftie verse of hem was lovèd aye.   66

But after vertue gan for age to stoupe,
And mighty manhode brought a bedde of
    ease,
The vaunting poets found nought worth a
    pease
To put in preace emong the learnèd troupe.
Tho gan the streames of flowing wittes to
    cease,   71
And sonnebright honour pend in shamefull
    coupe.

And if that any buddes of poesie
Yet of the old stocke gan to shoote agayne,
Or it mens follies mote be forst to fayne,   75
And rolle with rest in rymes of rybaudrye,
Or, as it sprong, it wither must agayne:
Tom Piper makes us better melodie.

Piers. O pierlesse Poesye, where is then
    thy place?
If nor in princes pallace thou doe sitt,   80
(And yet is princes pallace the most fitt)
Ne brest of baser birth doth thee embrace.
Then make thee winges of thine aspyring
    wit,
And, whence thou camst, flye backe to
    heaven apace.

Cud. Ah, Percy! it is all to weake and
    wanne,   85
So high to sore, and make so large a flight;
Her peecèd pyneons bene not so in plight:
For Colin fittes such famous flight to
    scanne:
He, were he not with love so ill bedight,
Would mount as high and sing as soote as
    swanne.   90

Piers. Ah, fon! for love does teach him
    climbe so hie,
And lyftes him up out of the loathsome
    myre:
Such immortall mirrhor as he doth admire
Would rayse ones mynd above the starry
    skie,
And cause a caytive corage to aspire;   95
For lofty love doth loath a lowly eye.

Cud. All otherwise the state of poet
    stands:
For lordly Love is such a tyranne fell,
That, where he rules, all power he doth ex-
    pell.
The vaunted verse a vacant head demaundes.
Ne wont with crabbèd Care the Muses
    dwell: 101
Unwisely weaves, that takes two webbes in
    hand.

Who ever casts to compasse weightye prise,
And thinks to throwe out thondring words
    of threate,
Let powre in lavish cups and thriftie bitts
    of meate;   105
For Bacchus fruite is frend to Phœbus wise,
And when with wine the braine begins to
    sweate,
The nombers flowe as fast as spring doth
    ryse.

Thou kenst not, Percie, howe the ryme
    should rage.
O if my temples were distain'd with wine,
And girt in girlonds of wild yvie twine, 111
How I could reare the Muse on stately
    stage,
And teache her tread aloft in buskin fine,
With queint Bellona in her equipage!

But ah! my corage cooles ere it be warme;
Forthy content us in thys humble shade, 115
Where no such troublous tydes han us
    assayde.
Here we our slender *pipes may safely
    charme.
    Piers. And when my gates shall han their
    bellies layd,
Cuddie shall have a kidde to store his

T   UEENE,
                      NIGHT

L   did
A   hards
A
F   oaten
A   gentle
              5
V   e long,
N   reeds
]   earnèd
]   l mor-
             9
]   f nyne,
          will;
]   cryne
         hidden
(quill,
        ince so
         15
Sought through the world, and suffered so
    much ill.

That I must rue his undeservèd wrong:
O helpe thou my weake wit, and sharpen
    my dull tong.

III

And thou, most dreaded impe of highest
    Jove,
Faire Venus sonne, that with thy cruell
    dart   20
At that good knight so cunningly didst
    rove,
That glorious fire it kindled in his hart,
Lay now thy deadly heben bowe apart,
And with thy mother mylde come to mine
    ayde:
Come both, and with you bring triumphant
    Mart,   25
In loves and gentle jollities arraid,
After his murdrous spoyles and bloudie rage
    allayd.

IV

And with them eke, O Goddesse heavenly
    bright,
Mirrour of grace and majestie divine,
Great Ladie of the greatest Isle, whose
    light   30
Like Phœbus lampe throughout the world
    doth shine,
Shed thy faire beames into my feeble eyne,
And raise my thoughtes, too humble and
    too vile,
To thinke of that true glorious type of
    thine,
The argument of mine afflicted stile: 35
The which to heare vouchsafe, O dearest
    dread, a while.

CANTO I

The patrone of true Holinesse
Foule Errour doth defeate:
Hypocrisie, him to entrappe,
Doth to his home entreate.

I

A gentle knight was pricking on the
    plaine,
Ycladd in mightie armes and silver shielde,
Wherein old dints of deepe woundes did
    remaine,
The cruell markes of many a bloody fielde;
Yet armes till that time did he never wield:
His angry steede did chide his foming
    bitt,   6
As much disdayning to the curbe to yield:
Full jolly knight he seemd, and faire did
    sitt,

As one for knightly giusts and fierce encounters fitt.

II

But on his brest a bloodie crosse he bore, 10
The deare remembrance of his dying Lord,
For whose sweete sake that glorious badge
he wore,
And dead as living ever him ador'd:
Upon his shield the like was also scor'd,
For soveraine hope, which in his helpe he
had: 15
Right faithfull true he was in deede and
word,
But of his cheere did seeme too solemne
sad;
Yet nothing did he dread, but ever was
ydrad.

III

Upon a great adventure he was bond,
That greatest Gloriana to him gave,   20
That greatest glorious queene of Faery
Lond,
To winne him worshippe, and her grace to
have,
Which of all earthly thinges he most did
crave;
And ever as he rode his hart did earne
To prove his puissance in battell brave   25
Upon his foe, and his new force to learne;
Upon his foe, a dragon horrible and stearne.

IV

A lovely ladie rode him faire beside,
Upon a lowly asse more white then snow,
Yet she much whiter, but the same did
hide   30
Under a vele, that wimpled was full low,
And over all a blacke stole shee did throw:
As one that inly mournd, so was she sad,
And heavie sate upon her palfrey slow:
Seemèd in heart some hidden care she had;
And by her in a line a milkewhite lambe
she lad.   36

V

So pure and innocent, as that same lambe,
She was in life and every vertuous lore,
And by descent from royall lynage came
Of ancient kinges and queenes, that had of
yore   40
Their scepters stretcht from east to west-
erne shore,
And all the world in their subjection held,
Till that infernall feend with foule uprore

Forwasted all their land, and them expeld:
Whom to avenge, she had this knight from
far compeld.   45

VI

Behind her farre away a dwarfe did lag,
That lasie seemd, in being ever last,
Or wearièd with bearing of her bag
Of needments at his backe. Thus as they
past,
The day with cloudes was suddeine over-
cast,   50
And angry Jove an hideous storme of raine
Did poure into his lemans lap so fast,
That everie wight to shrowd it did con-
strain,
And this faire couple eke to shroud them-
selves were fain.

VII

Enforst to seeke some covert nigh at hand,
A shadie grove not farr away they spide, 56
That promist ayde the tempest to withstand:
Whose loftie trees, yclad with sommers
pride,
Did spred so broad, that heavens light did
hide,
Not perceable with power of any starr;   60
And all within were pathes and alleies wide,
With footing worne, and leading inward
farr:
Faire harbour that them seemes, so in they
entred ar.

VIII

And foorth they passe, with pleasure for-
ward led,
Joying to heare the birdes sweete har-
mony,   65
Which, therein shrouded from the tempest
dred,
Seemd in their song to scorne the cruell
sky.
Much can they praise the trees so straight
and hy,
The sayling pine, the cedar proud and tall,
The vine-propp elme, the poplar never dry,
The builder oake, sole king of forrests all,
The aspine good for staves, the cypresse
funerall,   72

IX

The laurell, meed of mightie conquerours
And poets sage, the firre that weepeth still,
The willow worne of forlorne paramours,
The eugh obedient to the benders will,   76

The birch for shaftes, the sallow for the
  mill,
The mirrhe sweete bleeding in the bitter
  wound,
The warlike beech, the ash for nothing ill,
The fruitfull olive, and the platane round, 80
The carver holme, the maple seeldom in-
  ward sound.

X

Led with delight, they thus beguile the way,
Untill the blustring storme is overblowne;
When, weening to returne whence they did
  stray,
They cannot finde that path, which first was
  showne, 85
But wander too and fro in waies unknowne,
Furthest from end then, when they neerest
  weene,
That makes them doubt, their wits be not
  their owne:
So many pathes, so many turnings seene,
That which of them to take, in diverse
  doubt they been. 90

XI

At last resolving forward still to fare,
Till that some end they finde, or in or out,
That path they take, that beaten seemd most
  bare,
And like to lead the labyrinth about;
Which when by tract they hunted had
  throughout, 95
At length it brought them to a hollowe
  cave,
Amid the thickest woods. The champion
  stout
Eftsoones dismounted from his courser
  brave,
And to the dwarfe a while his needlesse
  spere he gave.

XII

'Be well aware,' quoth then that ladie milde,
'Least suddaine mischiefe ye too rash pro-
  voke: 101
The danger hid, the place unknowne and
  wilde,
Breedes dreadfull doubts: oft fire is with-
  out smoke,
And perill without show: therefore your
  stroke,
Sir knight, with-hold, till further tryall
  made.' 105
'Ah, ladie,' sayd he, 'shame were to revoke
The forward footing for an hidden shade:
Vertue gives her selfe light, through darke-
  nesse for to wade'

XIII

'Yea, but,' quoth she, 'the perill of this
  place
I better wot then you; though nowe too
  late 110
To wish you backe returne with foule disgrace,
Yet wisedome warnes, whilest foot is in the
  gate,
To stay the steppe, ere forcèd to retrate.
This is the wandring wood, this Errours
  den,
A monster vile, whom God and man does
  hate: 115
Therefore I read beware.' 'Fly, fly!' quoth
  then
The fearefull dwarfe: 'this is no place for
  living men.'

XIV

But full of fire and greedy hardiment,
The youthfull knight could not for ought
  be staide,
But forth unto the darksom hole he went, 120
And lookèd in: his glistring armor made
A litle glooming light, much like a shade,
By which he saw the ugly monster plaine,
Halfe like a serpent horribly displaide,
But th' other halfe did womans shape re-
  taine, 125
Most lothsom, filthie, foule, and full of vile
  disdaine.

XV

And as she lay upon the durtie ground,
Her huge long taile her den all overspred,
Yet was in knots and many boughtes up-
  wound,
Pointed with mortall sting. Of her there
  bred 130
A thousand yong ones, which she dayly fed,
Sucking upon her poisnous dugs, eachone
Of sundrie shapes, yet all ill favorèd:
Soone as that uncouth light upon them
  shone,
Into her mouth they crept, and suddain all
  were gone. 135

XVI

Their dam upstart, out of her den effraide,
And rushèd forth, hurling her hideous taile
About her cursèd head, whose folds dis-
  plaid
Were stretcht now forth at length without
  entraile.
She lookt about, and seeing one in mayle

Armèd to point, sought backe to turne
    againe;   141
For light she hatèd as the deadly bale,
Ay wont in desert darknes to remaine,
Where plain none might her see, nor she
    see any plaine.

XVII

Which when the valiant elfe perceiv'd, he
    lept   145
As lyon fierce upon the flying pray,
And with his trenchand blade her boldly
    kept
From turning backe, and forcèd her to stay:
Therewith enrag'd she loudly gan to bray,
And turning fierce, her speckled taile ad-
    vaunst,   150
Threatning her angrie sting, him to dis-
    may:
Who, nought aghast, his mightie hand en-
    haunst:
The stroke down from her head unto her
    shoulder glaunst.

XVIII

Much daunted with that dint, her sence was
    dazed,
Yet kindling rage her selfe she gathered
    round,   155
And all attonce her beastly bodie raizd
With doubled forces high above the ground:
Tho, wrapping up her wrethèd sterne
    arownd,
Lept fierce upon his shield, and her huge
    traine
All suddenly about his body wound,   160
That hand or foot to stirr he strove in
    vaine:
God helpe the man so wrapt in Errours
    endlesse traine.

XIX

His lady, sad to see his sore constraint,
Cride out, ' Now, now, sir knight, shew
    what ye bee;
Add faith unto your force, and be not
    faint: 165
Strangle her, els she sure will strangle
    thee.'
That when he heard, in great perplexitie,
His gall did grate for griefe and high dis-
    daine;
And knitting all his force, got one hand
    free,
Wherewith he grypt her gorge with so great
    paine,   170
That soone to loose her wicked bands did
    her constraine.

XX

Therewith she spewd out of her filthie maw
A floud of poyson horrible and blacke,
Full of great lumps of flesh and goblets
    raw,
Which stunck so vildly, that it forst him
    slacke   175
His grasping hold, and from her turne him
    backe:
Her vomit full of bookes and papers was,
With loathy frogs and toades, which eyes
    did lacke,
And creeping sought way in the weedy gras:
Her filthie parbreake all the place defilèd
    has.   180

XXI

As when old father Nilus gins to swell
With timely pride above the Aegyptian vale,
His fattie waves doe fertile slime outwell,
And overflow each plaine and lowly dale:
But when his later spring gins to avale, 185
Huge heapes of mudd he leaves, wherin
    there breed
Ten thousand kindes of creatures, partly
    male
And partly femall, of his fruitful seed;
Such ugly monstrous shapes elswher may
    no man reed.

XXII

The same so sore annoyèd has the knight, 190
That, welnigh chokèd with the deadly stinke,
His forces faile, ne can no lenger fight.
Whose corage when the feend perceivd to
    shrinke,
She pourèd forth out of her hellish sinke
Her fruitfull cursèd spawne of serpents
    small,   195
Deformèd monsters, fowle, and blacke as
    inke,
Which swarming all about his legs did crall,
And him encombred sore, but could not
    hurt at all.

XXIII

As gentle shepheard in sweete eventide,
When ruddy Phebus gins to welke in west,
High on an hill, his flocke to vewen wide, 201
Markes which doe byte their hasty supper
    best;
A cloud of cumbrous gnattes doe him mo-
    lest,
All striving to infixe their feeble stinges
That from their noyance he no where can
    rest.   205

But with his clownish hands their tender
    wings
He brusheth oft, and oft doth mar their
    murmurings.

XXIV

Thus ill bestedd, and fearefull more of
    shame
Then of the certeine perill he stood in,
Halfe furious unto his foe he came,   210
Resolvd in minde all suddenly to win,
Or soone to lose, before he once would lin;
And stroke at her with more then manly
    force,
That from her body, full of filthie sin,
He raft her hatefull heade without re-
    morse: 215
A streame of cole black blood forth gushèd
    from her corse.

XXV

Her scattred brood, soone as their parent
    deare
They saw so rudely falling to the ground,
Groning full deadly, all with troublous
    feare,
Gathred themselves about her body round,
Weening their wonted entrance to have
    found   221
At her wide mouth: but being there with-
    stood,
They flockèd all about her bleeding wound,
And suckèd up their dying mothers bloud,
Making her death their life, and eke her
    hurt their good.   225

XXVI

That detestable sight him much amazde,
To see th' unkindly impes, of heaven ac-
    curst,
Devoure their dam; on whom while so he
    gazd,
Having all satisfide their bloudy thurst,
Their bellies swolne he saw with fulnesse
    burst,   230
And bowels gushing forth; well worthy end
Of such as drunke her life, the which them
    nurst!
Now needeth him no lenger labour spend;
His foes have slaine themselves, with whom
    he should contend.

XXVII

His lady, seeing all that chaunst, from
    farre,   235
Approcht in hast to greet his victorie,

And saide, 'Faire knight, borne under hap-
    pie starre,
Who see your vanquisht foes before you
    lye,
Well worthie be you of that armory,
Wherein ye have great glory wonne this
    day,   240
And proov'd your strength on a strong eni-
    mie,
Your first adventure: many such I pray,
And henceforth ever wish that like succeed
    it may.'

XXVIII

Then mounted he upon his steede againe,
And with the lady backward sought to
    wend;   245
That path he kept which beaten was most
    plaine,
Ne ever would to any by way bend,
But still did follow one unto the end,
The which at last out of the wood them
    brought.   249
So forward on his way (with God to frend)
He passèd forth, and new adventure sought:
Long way he travelèd, before he heard of
    ought.

XXIX

At length they chaunst to meet upon the
    way
An agèd sire, in long blacke weedes yclad,
His feete all bare, his beard all hoarie
    gray,   255
And by his belte his booke he hanging had;
Sober he seemde, and very sagely sad,
And to the ground his eyes were lowly bent,
Simple in shew, and voide of malice bad,
And all the way he prayèd as he went,   260
And often knockt his brest, as one that did
    repent.

XXX

He faire the knight saluted, louting low,
Who faire him quited, as that courteous
    was;
And after askèd him, if he did know
Of straunge adventures, which abroad did
    pas.   265
'Ah! my dear sonne,' quoth he, 'how should,
    alas!
Silly old man, that lives in hidden cell,
Bidding his beades all day for his trespas,
Tydings of warre and worldly trouble tell?
With holy father sits not with such thinges
    to mell.   270

XXXI

'But if of daunger, which hereby doth dwell,
And homebredd evil ye desire to heare,
Of a straunge man I can you tidings tell,
That wasteth all his countrie farre and
    neare.'
'Of such,' saide he, 'I chiefly doe inquere,
And shall you well rewarde to shew the
    place,   276
In which that wicked wight his dayes doth
    weare:
For to all knighthood it is foule disgrace,
That such a cursèd creature lives so long a
    space.'

XXXII

'Far hence,' quoth he, 'in wastfull wilder-
    nesse,   280
His dwelling is, by which no living wight
May ever passe, but thorough great dis-
    tresse.'
'Now,' saide the ladie, 'draweth toward
    night,
And well I wote, that of your later fight
Ye all forwearied be: for what so strong, 285
But, wanting rest, will also want of might?
The Sunne, that measures heaven all day
    long,
At night doth baite his steedes the ocean
    waves emong.

XXXIII

'Then with the Sunne take, sir, your timely
    rest,
And with new day new worke at once be-
    gin: 290
Untroubled night, they say, gives counsell
    best.'
'Right well, sir knight, ye have advisèd
    bin,'
Quoth then that agèd man; 'the way to
    win
Is wisely to advise: now day is spent;
Therefore with me ye may take up your
    in   295
For this same night.' The knight was well
    content:
So with that godly father to his home they
    went.

XXXIV

A litle lowly hermitage it was,
Downe in a dale, hard by a forests side,
Far from resort of people, that did pas   300
In traveill to and froe: a litle wyde
There was an holy chappell edifyde.

Wherein the hermite dewly wont to say
His holy thinges each morne and even-tyde:
Thereby a christall streame did gently play,
Which from a sacred fountaine wellèd
    forth alway.   306

XXXV

Arrivèd there, the little house they fill,
Ne looke for entertainement, where none
    was:
Rest is their feast, and all thinges at their
    will;
The noblest mind the best contentment
    has.   310
With faire discourse the evening so they
    pas:
For that olde man of pleasing wordes had
    store,
And well could file his tongue as smooth
    as glas:
He told of saintes and popes, and ever-
    more   314
He strowd an Ave-Mary after and before.

XXXVI

The drouping night thus creepeth on them
    fast,
And the sad humor loading their eye liddes,
As messenger of Morpheus, on them cast
Sweet slombring deaw, the which to sleep
    them biddes:
Unto their lodgings then his guestes he
    riddes: ·   320
Where when all drownd in deadly sleepe
    he findes,
He to his studie goes, and there amiddes
His magick bookes and artes of sundrie
    kindes,
He seekes out mighty charmes, to trouble
    sleepy minds.

XXXVII

Then choosing out few words most horri-
    ble,   325
(Let none them read) thereof did verses
    frame;
With which and other spelles like terrible,
He bad awake blacke Plutoes griesly dame,
And cursèd heven, and spake reproachful
    shame   329
Of highest God, the Lord of life and light;
A bold bad man, that dar'd to call by name
Great Gorgon, prince of darknes and dead
    night,
At which Cocytus quakes, and Styx is put
    to flight.

XXXVIII

And forth he cald out of deepe darknes
  dredd
Legions of sprights, the which, like litle
  flyes 335
Fluttring about his ever damnèd hedd,
Awaite whereto their service he applyes,
To aide his friendes, or fray his enimies:
Of those he chose out two, the falsest twoo,
And fittest for to forge true-seeming lyes;
The one of them he gave a message too, 341
The other by him selfe staide, other worke
  to doo.

XXXIX

He, making speedy way through spersèd
  ayre,
And through the world of waters wide and
  deepe,
To Morpheus house doth hastily repaire. 345
Amid the bowels of the earth full steepe,
And low, where dawning day doth never
  peepe,
His dwelling is; there Tethys his wet bed
Doth ever wash, and Cynthia still doth
  steepe
In silver deaw his ever-drouping hed, 350
Whiles sad Night over him her mantle black
  doth spred.

XL

Whose double gates he findeth lockèd fast,
The one faire fram'd of burnisht yvory,
The other all with silver overcast;
And wakeful dogges before them farre doe
  lye, 355
Watching to banish Care their enimy,
Who oft is wont to trouble gentle Sleepe.
By them the sprite doth passe in quietly,
And unto Morpheus comes, whom drownèd
  deepe
In drowsie fit he findes: of nothing he
  takes keepe. 360

XLI

And more, to lulle him in his slumber soft,
A trickling streame from high rock tum-
  bling downe,
And ever drizling raine upon the loft,
Mixt with a murmuring winde, much like
  the sowne
Of swarming bees, did cast him in a
  swowne:
No other noyse, nor peoples troublous cryes,
As still are wont t'annoy the wallèd towne,
Might there be heard: but carelesse Quiet
  lyes.

Wrapt in eternall silence farre from eni-
  myes.

XLII

The messenger approching to him spake, 370
But his waste wordes retourned to him in
  vaine:
So sound he slept, that nought mought him
  awake.
Then rudely he him thrust, and pusht with
  paine,
Whereat he gan to stretch: but he againe
Shooke him so hard, that forcèd him to
  speake. 375
As one then in a dreame, whose dryer braine
Is tost with troubled sights and fancies
  weake,
He mumbled soft, but would not all his
  silence breake.

XLIII

The sprite then gan more boldly him to
  wake,
And threatened unto him the dreaded name
Of Hecate: whereat he gan to quake, 381
And, lifting up his lompish head, with blame
Halfe angrie askèd him, for what he came.
'Hether,' quoth he, 'me Archimago sent,
He that the stubborne sprites can wisely
  tame; 385
He bids thee to him send for his intent
A fit false dreame, that can delude the
  sleepers sent.'

XLIV

The god obayde, and calling forth straight
  way
A diverse dreame out of his prison darke,
Delivered it to him, and downe did lay 390
His heavie head, devoide of careful carke;
Whose sences all were straight benumbd
  and starke.
He, backe returning by the yvorie dore,
Remounted up as light as chearful larke,
And on his litle winges the dreame he bore
In hast unto his lord, where he him left
  afore. 396

XLV

Who all this while, with charmes and hid-
  den artes,
Had made a lady of that other spright,
And fram'd of liquid ayre her tender partes,
So lively and so like in all mens sight, 400
That weaker sence it could have ravisht
  quight:
The maker selfe, for all his wondrous witt,

Was nigh beguilèd with so goodly sight:
Her all in white he clad, and over it
Cast a black stole, most like to seeme for
    Una fit.   405

XLVI

Now when that ydle dreame was to him
    brought,
Unto that Elfin knight he bad him fly,
Where he slept soundly, void of evil thought,
And with false shewes abuse his fantasy,
In sort as he him schoolèd privily: 410
And that new creature, borne without her
    dew,
Full of the makers guyle, with usage sly
He taught to imitate that lady trew,
Whose semblance she did carrie under
    feignèd hew.

XLVII

Thus well instructed, to their worke they
    haste,   415
And comming where the knight in slom-
    ber lay,
The one upon his hardie head him plaste,
And made him dreame of loves and lust-
    full play,
That nigh his manly hart did melt away,
Bathèd in wanton blis and wicked joy.   420
Then seemèd him his lady by him lay,
And to him playnd, how that false wingèd
    boy
Her chaste hart had subdewd to learne
    Dame Pleasures toy.

XLVIII

And she her selfe, of beautie soveraigne
    queene,   424
Fayre Venus, seemde unto his bed to bring
Her, whom he, waking, evermore did weene
To bee the chastest flowre that aye did
    spring
On earthly braunch, the daughter of a king,
Now a loose leman to vile service bound:
And eke the Graces seemèd all to sing   430
Hymen iö Hymen, dauncing all around,
Whylst freshest Flora her with yvie girlond
    crownd.

XLIX

In this great passion of unwonted lust,
Or wonted feare of doing ought amis,
He started up, as seeming to mistrust   435
Some secret ill, or hidden foe of his:
Lo! there before his face his ladie is,
Under blacke stole hyding her bayted hooke,
And as halfe blushing offred him to kis,
With gentle blandishment and lovely looke,

Most like that virgin true, which for her
    knight him took.   441

L

All cleane dismayd to see so uncouth sight,
And halfe enragèd at her shamelesse guise,
He thought have slaine her in his fierce de-
    spight;
But hastie heat tempring with sufferance
    wise,   445
He stayde his hand, and gan himselfe ad-
    vise
To prove his sense, and, tempt her faignèd
    truth.
Wringing her hands in wemens pitteous
    wise,
Tho can she weepe, to stirre up gentle ruth,
Both for her noble blood, and for her
    tender youth.   450

LI

And sayd, 'Ah sir, my liege lord and my
    love,
Shall I accuse the hidden cruell fate,
And mightie causes wrought in heaven
    above,
Or the blind god, that doth me thus amate,
For hopèd love to winne me certaine hate?
Yet thus perforce he bids me do, or die   456
Die is my dew: yet rew my wretched state
You, whom my hard avenging destinie
Hath made judge of my life or death in-
    differently.

LII

'Your owne deare sake forst me at first to
    leave   460
My fathers kingdom'—There she stopt
    with teares;
Her swollen hart her speech seemed to be-
    reave;
And then againe begonne: 'My weaker
    yeares,
Captiv'd to fortune and frayle worldly
    feares,   464
Fly to your fayth for succour and sure ayde:
Let me not die in languor and long teares.'
'Why, dame,' quoth he, 'what hath ye thus
    dismayd?
What frayes ye, that were wont to comfort
    me affrayd?'

LIII

'Love of your selfe,' she saide, 'and deare
    constraint,
Lets me not sleepe, but waste the wearie
    night   470

In secret anguish and unpittied plaint,
Whiles you in careless sleepe are drownèd
quight.'
Her doubtfull words made that redoubted
knight
Suspect her truth: yet since no' untruth he
knew,
Her fawning love with foule disdainefull
spight   475
He would not shend, but said, 'Deare dame,
I rew,
That for my sake unknowne such griefe
unto you grew.

LIV

'Assure your selfe, it fell not all to ground;
For all so deare as life is to my hart,
I deeme your love, and hold me to you
bound;   480
Ne let vaine feares procure your needlesse
smart,
Where cause is none, but to your rest de-
part.'
Not all content, yet seemd she to appease
Her mournfull plaintes, beguilèd of her
art,
And fed with words, that could not chose
but please;   485
So slyding softly forth, she turnd as to her
ease.

LV

Long after lay he musing at her mood,
Much griev'd to thinke that gentle dame so
light,
For whose defence he was to shed his blood.
At last dull wearines of former fight   490
Having yrockt a sleepe his irkesome spright,
That troublous dreame gan freshly tosse
his braine
With bowres, and beds, and ladies deare
delight:
But when he saw his labour all was vaine,
With that misformèd spright he backe re-
turnd againe,

CANTO II

The guilefull great enchaunter parts
The Redcrosse Knight from Truth:
Into whose stead faire Falshood steps,
And workes him woefull ruth.

I

By this the northerne wagoner had set
His sevenfold teme behind the stedfast
starre,

That was in ocean waves yet never wet,
But firme is fixt, and sendeth light from
farre
To al that in the wide deepe wandring arre:
And chearefull Chauntclere with his note
shrill   6
Had warnèd once, that Phoebus fiery carre
In hast was climbing up the easterne hill,
Full envious that night so long his roome
did fill:

II

When those accursèd messengers of hell, 10
That feigning dreame, and that faire-forgèd
spright,
Came to their wicked maister, and gan tel
Their bootelesse paines, and ill succeeding
night:
Who, all in rage to see his skilfull might
Deluded so, gan threaten hellish paine   15
And sad Proserpines wrath, them to af-
fright.
But when he saw his threatning was but
vaine,
He cast about, and searcht his baleful bokes
againe.

III

Eftsoones he tooke that miscreated faire,
And that false other spright, on whom he
spred   20
A seeming body of the subtile aire,
Like a young squire, in loves and lustyhed
His wanton daies that ever loosely led,
Without regard of armes and dreaded fight:
Those twoo he tooke, and in a secrete bed, 25
Covered with darkenes and misdeeming
night,
Them both together laid, to joy in vaine
delight.

IV

Forthwith he runnes with feignèd faithfull
hast
Unto his guest, who, after troublous sights
And dreames, gan now to take more sound
repast;   30
Whom suddenly he wakes with fearful
frights,
As one aghast with feends or damnèd
sprights,
And to him cals: 'Rise, rise, unhappy
swaine,
That here wex old in sleepe, whiles wicked
wights
Have knit themselves in Venus shameful
chaine: 35

Come see, where your false lady doth her
honor staine.'

V

All in amaze he suddenly up start
With sword in hand, and with the old man
went;
Who soone him brought into a secret part,
Where that false couple were full closely
ment   40
In wanton lust and leud enbracement:
Which when he saw, he burnt with gealous
fire,
The eie of reason was with rage yblent,
And would have slaine them in his furious
ire,
But hardly was restreinèd of that agèd
sire.   45

VI

Retourning to his bed in torment great,
And bitter anguish of his guilty sight,
He could not rest, but did his stout heart
eat,
And wast his inward gall with deepe de-
spight,
Yrkesome of life, and too long lingring
night.   50
At last faire Hesperus in highest skie
Had spent his lampe, and brought forth
dawning light;
Then up he rose, and clad him hastily;
The dwarfe him brought his steed: so both
away do fly.

VII

Now when the rosy fingred Morning faire,
Weary of agèd Tithones saffron bed,   56
Had spred her purple robe through deawy
aire,
And the high hils Titan discoverèd,
The royall virgin shooke of drousyhed,
And rising forth out of her baser bowre, 60
Lookt for her knight, who far away was
fled,
And for her dwarfe, that wont to wait each
howre:
Then gan she wail and weepe, to see that
woeful stowre.

VIII

And after him she rode with so much
speede,
As her slowe beast could make; but all in
vaine: 65
For him so far had borne his light-foot
steede,

Prickèd with wrath and fiery fierce dis-
daine,
That him to follow was but fruitlesse paine;
Yet she her weary limbes would never rest,
But every hil and dale, each wood and
plaine,   70
Did search, sore grievèd in her gentle brest,
He so ungently left her, whome she lovèd
best.

IX

But subtill Archimago, when his guests
He saw divided into double parts,
And Una wandring in woods and forrests,
Th' end of his drift, he praisd his divel-
ish arts,   76
That had such might over true meaning
harts:
Yet rests not so, but other meanes doth
make,
How he may worke unto her further smarts:
For her he hated as the hissing snake, 80
And in her many troubles did most pleasure
take.

X

He then devisde himselfe how to disguise;
For by his mighty science he could take
As many formes and shapes in seeming
wise,
As ever Proteus to himselfe could make: 85
Sometime a fowle, sometime a fish in lake,
Now like a foxe, now like a dragon fell,
That of himselfe he ofte for feare would
quake,
And oft would flie away. O who can tell
The hidden powre of herbes, and might of
magick spel?   90

XI

But now seemde best, the person to put on
Of that good knight, his late beguilèd guest:
In mighty armes he was yclad anon,
And silver shield; upon his coward brest
A bloody crosse, and on his craven crest 95
A bounch of heares discolourd diversly:
Full jolly knight he seemde, and wel ad-
drest,
And when he sate uppon his courser free,
Saint George himselfe ye would have
deemèd him to be.

XII

But he, the knight whose semblaunt he did
beare,   100
The true Saint George, was wandred far
away,

Still flying from his thoughts and gealous
 feare;
Will was his guide, and griefe led him
 astray.
At last him chaunst to meete upon the way
A faithlesse Sarazin, all armde to point, 105
In whose great shield was writ with letters
 gay
Sans foy: full large of limbe and every
 joint
He was, and carèd not for God or man a
 point.

XIII

Hee had a faire companion of his way,
A goodly lady clad in scarlot red, 110
Purfled with gold and pearle of rich assay;
And like a Persian mitre on her hed
Shee wore, with crowns and owches gar-
 nishèd,
The which her lavish lovers to her gave:
Her wanton palfrey all was overspred 115
With tinsell trappings, woven like a wave,
Whose bridle rung with golden bels and
 bosses brave.

XIV

With faire disport and courting dalliaunce
She intertainde her lover all the way:
But when she saw the knight his speare
 advaunce, 120
Shee soone left of her mirth and wanton
 play,
And bad her knight addresse him to the
 fray:
His foe was nigh at hand. He, prickte with
 pride
And hope to winne his ladies hearte that
 day,
Forth spurrèd fast: adowne his coursers
 side 125
The red bloud trickling staind the way, as
 he did ride.

XV

The Knight of the Redcrosse, when him he
 spide
Spurring so hote with rage dispiteous,
Gan fairely couch his speare, and towards
 ride:
Soone meete they both, both fell and furi-
 ous, 130
That, daunted with theyr forces hideous,
Their steeds doe stagger, and amazèd stand,
And eke themselves, too rudely rigorous,
Astonied with the stroke of their owne
 hand,

Doe backe rebutte, and ech to other yealdeth
 land. 135

XVI

As when two rams, stird with ambitious
 pride,
Fight for the rule of the rich fleecèd flocke,
Their hornèd fronts so fierce on either
 side
Doe meete, that, with the terror of the
 shocke
Astonied, both stand sencelesse as a blocke,
Forgetfull of the hanging victory: 141
So stood these twaine, unmovèd as a rocke,
Both staring fierce, and holding idely
The broken reliques of their former cruelty.

XVII

The Sarazin, sore daunted with the buffe,
Snatcheth his sword, and fiercely to him
 flies; 146
Who well it wards, and quyteth cuff with
 cuff:
Each others equall puissaunce envies,
And through their iron sides with cruell
 spies
Does seeke to perce: repining courage
 yields 150
No foote to foe. The flashing fier flies,
As from a forge, out of their burning
 shields,
And streams of purple bloud new dies the
 verdant fields.

XVIII

'Curse on that Crosse,' quoth then the Sara-
 zin,
'That keepes thy body from the bitter fitt!
Dead long ygoe, I wote, thou haddest bin,
Had not that charme from thee forwarnèd
 itt: 157
But yet I warne thee now assurèd sitt,
And hide thy head.' Therewith upon his
 crest
With rigor so outrageous he smitt, 160
That a large share it hewd out of the rest,
And glauncing downe his shield, from blame
 him fairely blest.

XIX

Who thereat wondrous wroth, the sleeping
 spark
Of native vertue gan eftsoones revive,
And at his haughty helmet making mark,
So hugely stroke, that it the steele did rive,
And cleft his head. He, tumbling downe
 alive, 167

With bloudy mouth his mother earth did
    kis,
Greeting his grave: his grudging ghost did
    strive
With the fraile flesh; at last it flitted is,
Whether the soules doe fly of men that live
    amis.   171

XX

The lady, when she saw her champion fall,
Like the old ruines of a broken towre,
Staid not to waile his woefull funerall,
But from him fled away with all her powre;
Who after her as hastily gan scowre,   176
Bidding the dwarfe with him to bring away
The Sarazins shield, signe of the conquer-
    oure.
Her soone he overtooke, and bad to stay,
For present cause was none of dread her
    to dismay.   180

XXI

Shee, turning backe with ruefull counte-
    naunce,
Cride, 'Mercy, mercy, sir, vouchsafe to
    showe
On silly dame, subject to hard mischaunce,
And to your mighty will!' Her humblesse
    low,
In so ritch weedes and seeming glorious
    show,   185
Did much emmove his stout heroïcke heart,
And said, 'Deare dame, your suddein over-
    throw
Much rueth me; but now put feare apart,
And tel, both who ye be, and who that tooke
    your part.'

XXII

Melting in teares, then gan shee thus la-
    ment: 190
'The wreched woman, whom unhappy howre
Hath now made thrall to your commande-
    ment,
Before that angry heavens list to lowre,
And Fortune false betraide me to your
    powre,   194
Was, (O what now availeth that I was?)
Borne the sole daughter of an emperour,
He that the wide west under his rule has,
And high hath set his throne where Tiberis
    doth pas.

XXIII

'He, in the first flowre of my freshest age,
Betrothèd me unto the onely haire   200
Of a most mighty king, most rich and sage;

Was never prince so faithfull and so faire,
Was never prince so meeke and debonaire;
But ere my hopèd day of spousall shone,
My dearest lord fell from high honors
    staire,   205
Into the hands of hys accursèd fone,
And cruelly was slaine, that shall I ever
    mone.

XXIV

'His blessèd body, spoild of lively breath,
Was afterward, I know not how, convaid
And fro me hid: of whose most innocent
    death   210
When tidings came to mee, unhappy maid,
O how great sorrow my sad soule assaid!
Then forth I went his woefull corse to find,
And many yeares throughout the world I
    straid,
A virgin widow, whose deepe wounded mind
With love, long time did languish as the
    striken hind.   216

XXV

'At last it chauncèd this proud Sarazin
To meete me wandring; who perforce me
    led
With him away, but yet could never win
The fort, that ladies hold in soveraigne
    dread.   220
There lies he now with foule dishonor
    dead,
Who, whilse he livde, was callèd proud
    Sansfoy:
The eldest of three brethren, all three bred
Of one bad sire, whose youngest is Sansjoy,
And twixt them both was born the bloudy
    bold Sansloy.   225

XXVI

'In this sad plight, friendlesse, unfortunate,
Now miserable I Fidessa dwell,
Craving of you, in pitty of my state,
To doe none ill, if please ye not doe well.'
He in great passion al this while did dwell,
More busying his quicke eies, her face to
    view,   231
Then his dull eares, to heare what shee did
    tell;
And said, 'Faire lady, hart of flint would
    rew
The undeservèd woes and sorrows which
    ye shew.

XXVII

'Henceforth in safe assuraunce may ye
    rest,   235

Having both found a new friend you to
aid,
And lost an old foe, that did you molest:
Better new friend then an old foe is said.'
With chaunge of chear the seeming simple
maid
Let fal her eien, as shamefast, to the earth,
And yeelding soft, in that she nought gain-
said,   241
So forth they rode, he feining seemely
merth,
And shee coy lookes: so dainty, they say,
maketh derth.

XXVIII

Long time they thus together traveilèd,
Til, weary of their way, they came at last
Where grew two goodly trees, that faire
did spred   246
Their armes abroad, with gray mosse over-
cast,
And their greene leaves, trembling with
every blast,
Made a calme shadowe far in compasse
round: 249
The fearefull shepheard, often there aghast,
Under them never sat, ne wont there sound
His merry oaten pipe, but shund th' unlucky
ground.

XXIX

But this good knight, soone as he them can
spie,
For the coole shade him thither hastly got:
For golden Phoebus, now ymounted hie, 255
From fiery wheeles of his faire chariot
Hurlèd his beame so scorching cruell hot,
That living creature mote it not abide;
And his new lady it endurèd not.
There they alight, in hope themselves to
hide   260
From the fierce heat, and rest their weary
limbs a tide.

XXX

Faire seemely pleasaunce each to other
makes,
With goodly purposes, there as they sit:
And in his falsèd fancy he her takes
To be the fairest wight that livèd yit;   265
Which to expresse, he bends his gentle wit,
And thinking of those braunches greene to
frame
A girlond for her dainty forehead fit,
He pluckt a bough; out of whose rifte there
came
Smal drops of gory bloud, that trickled
down the same.   270

XXXI

Therewith a piteous yelling voice was heard,
Crying, 'O spare with guilty hands to teare
My tender sides in this rough rynd em-
bard;
But fly, ah! fly far hence away, for feare
Least to you hap that happened to me
heare,   275
And to this wretched lady, my deare love;
O too deare love, love bought with death
too deare!'
Astond he stood, and up his heare did hove,
And with that suddein horror could no
member move.

XXXII

At last, whenas the dreadfull passion
Was overpast, and manhood well awake,
Yet musing at this straunge occasion,   281
And doubting much his sence, he thus be-
spake:
'What voice of damnèd ghost from Limbo·
lake,
Or guilefull spright wandring in empty aire,
Both which fraile men doe oftentimes mis-
take,   286
Sends to my doubtfull eares these speaches
rare,
And ruefull plaints, me bidding guiltlesse
blood to spare?'

XXXIII

Then groning deep: 'Nor damnèd ghost,'
quoth he,
'Nor guileful spirite to thee these words
doth speake,   290
But once a man, Fradubio, now a tree;
Wretched man, wretched tree! whose na-
ture weake
A cruell witch, her cursèd will to wreake,
Hath thus transformd, and plast in open
plaines,
Where Boreas doth blow full bitter bleake,
And scorching sunne does dry my secret
vaines: 296
For though a tree I seme, yet cold and heat
me paines.'

XXXIV

'Say on, Fradubio, then, or man or tree,'
Quoth then the knight; 'by whose mis-
chievous arts
Art thou misshapèd thus, as now I see?
He oft finds med'cine who his griefe im-
parts;   301
But double griefs afflict concealing harts,
As raging flames who striveth to suppresse.'

'The author then,' said he, 'of all my
  smarts,
Is one Duessa, a false sorceresse,   305
That many errant knights hath broght to
  wretchednesse.

XXXV

'In prime of youthly yeares, when corage
  hott
The fire of love and joy of chevalree
First kindled in my brest, it was my lott
To love this gentle lady, whome ye see 310
Now not a lady, but a seeming tree;
With whome as once I rode accompanyde,
Me chauncèd of a knight encountred bee,
That had a like faire lady by his syde;
Lyke a faire lady, but did fowle Duessa
  hyde.   315

XXXVI

'Whose forgèd beauty he did take in hand
All other dames to have exceded farre;
I in defence of mine did likewise stand,
Mine, that did then shine as the morning
  starre:
So both to batteill fierce arraungèd arre;
In which his harder fortune was to fall 321
Under my speare; such is the dye of warre:
His lady, left as a prise martiall,
Did yield her comely person, to be at my
  call.

XXXVII

'So doubly lov'd of ladies unlike faire, 325
Th' one seeming such, the other such in-
  deede,
One day in doubt I cast for to compare,
Whether in beauties glorie did exceede;
A rosy girlond was the victors meede.
Both seemde to win, and both seemde won
  to bee,   330
So hard the discord was to be agreede:
Frælissa was as faire as faire mote bee,
And ever false Duessa seemde as faire as
  shee.

XXXVIII

'The wicked witch, now seeing all this
  while   334
The doubtfull ballaunce equally to sway,
What not by right, she cast to win by
  guile;
And by her hellish science raisd streight
  way
A foggy mist, that overcast the day,
And a dull blast, that, breathing on her
  fac..

Dimmèd her former beauties shining ray,
And with foule ugly forme did her disgrace: 341
Then was she fayre alone, when none was
  faire in place.

XXXIX

'Then cride she out, "Fye, fye! deformèd
  wight,
Whose borrowèd beautie now appeareth
  plaine
To have before bewitchèd all mens sight;
O leave her soone, or let her soone be
  slaine."   346
Her loathly visage viewing with disdaine,
Eftsoones I thought her such as she me
  told,
And would have kild her; but with faignèd
  paine
The false witch did my wrathfull hand
  with-hold: 350
So left her, where she now is turnd to
  treen mould.

XL

'Thensforth I tooke Duessa for my dame,
And in the witch unweeting joyd long time,
Ne ever wist but that she was the same:
Till on a day (that day is everie prime, 355
When witches wont do penance for their
  crime)
I chaunst to see her in her proper hew,
Bathing her selfe in origane and thyme:
A filthy foule old woman I did vew,
That ever to have toucht her I did deadly
  rew.   360

XLI

'Her neather partes misshapen, monstruous,
Were hidd in water, that I could not see,
But they did seeme more foule and hideous,
Then womans shape man would beleeve to
  bee.
Thensforth from her most beastly com-
  panie   365
I gan refraine, in minde to slipp away,
Soone as appeard safe opportunitie:
For danger great, if not assurd decay,
I saw before mine eyes, if I were knowne
  to stray.

XLII

'The divelish hag, by chaunges of my
  cheare,   370
Perceiv'd my thought; and drownd in
  sleepie night,

With wicked herbes and oyntments did be-
smeare
My body all, through charmes and magicke
might,
That all my senses were bereavèd quight:
Then brought she me into this desert waste,
And by my wretched lovers side me pight,
Where now enclosd in wooden wals full
faste,   377
Banisht from living wights, our wearie
daies we waste.'

XLIII

'But how long time,' said then the Elfin
knight,
'Are you in this misformèd hous to
dwell?'   380
'We may not chaunge,' quoth he, 'this evill
plight
Till we be bathèd in a living well;
That is the terme prescribèd by the spell.'
'O how,' sayd he, 'mote I that well out
find,   384
That may restore you to your wonted well?'
'Time and suffisèd fates to former kynd
Shall us restore; none else from hence may
us unbynd.'

XLIV

The false Duessa, now Fidessa hight,
Heard how in vaine Fradubio did lament,
And knew well all was true. But the good
knight   390
Full of sad feare and ghastly dreriment,
When all this speech the living tree had
spent,
The bleeding bough did thrust into the
ground,
That from the blood he might be innocent,
And with fresh clay did close the wooden
wound: 395
Then turning to his lady, dead with feare
her fownd.

XLV

Her seeming dead he fownd with feignèd
feare,
As all unweeting of that well she knew,
And paynd himselfe with busie care to
reare
Her out of carelesse swowne. Her eyelids
blew,   400
And dimmèd sight, with pale and deadly
hew,
At last she up gan lift: with trembling
cheare
Her up he tooke, too simple and too trew,

And oft her kist. At length, all passèd
feare,
He set her on her steede, and forward
forth did beare.   405

* * *

AMORETTI

I

Happy ye leaves! when as those lilly hands,
Which hold my life in their dead doing
might,
Shall handle you, and hold in loves soft
bands,
Lyke captives trembling at the victors sight.
And happy lines! on which, with starry
light,   5
Those lamping eyes will deigne sometimes
to look,
And reade the sorrowes of my dying
spright,
Written with teares in harts close bleeding
book.
And happy rymes! bath'd in the sacred
brooke
Of Helicon, whence she derivèd is,   10
When ye behold that angels blessèd looke,
My soules long lackèd foode, my heavens
blis.
Leaves, lines, and rymes, seeke her to
please alone,
Whom if ye please, I care for other none.

VIII

More then most faire, full of the living
fire
Kindled above unto the Maker neere:
No eies, but joyes, in which al powers con-
spire,
That to the world naught else be counted
deare:
Thrugh your bright beams doth not the
blinded guest   5
Shoot out his darts to base affections
wound;
But angels come, to lead fraile mindes to
rest
In chast desires, on heavenly beauty bound.
You frame my thoughts, and fashion me
within,
You stop my toung, and teach my hart to
speake,   10
You calme the storme that passion did be-
gin,
Strong thrugh your cause, but by your vertue weak.

Dark is the world where your light shinèd
    never;
Well is he borne that may behold you ever.

XXIV

When I behold that beauties wonderment,
And rare perfection of each goodly part,
Of Natures skill the onely complement,
I honor and admire the Makers art.
But when I feele the bitter balefulle smart 5
Which her fayre eyes unwares doe worke
    in mee,
That death out of theyr shiny beames doe
    dart,
I thinke that I a new Pandora see;
Whom all the gods in councell did agree,
Into this sinfull world from heaven to
    send,   10
That she to wicked men a scourge should
    bee,
For all their faults with which they did
    offend.
But since ye are my scourge, I will intreat
That for my faults ye will me gently beat.

XXXIV

Lyke as a ship, that through the ocean
    wyde
By conduct of some star doth make her
    way,
Whenas a storme hath dimd her trusty
    guyde,
Out of her course doth wander far astray;
So I, whose star, that wont with her bright
    ray   5
Me to direct, with cloudes is overcast,
Doe wander now in darknesse and dismay,
Through hidden perils round about me plast.
Yet hope I well, that when this storme is
    past,
My Helice, the lodestar of my lyfe,   10
Will shine again, and looke on me at last,
With lovely light to cleare my cloudy grief.
Till then I wander carefull comfortlesse,
In secret sorrow and sad pensivenesse.

LXIII

After long stormes and tempests sad assay,
Which hardly I endurèd heretofore,
In dread of death, and daungerous dis-
    may,
With which my silly barke was tossèd sore,
I doe at length descry the happy shore, 5
In which I hope ere long for to arryve:
Fayre soyle it seemes from far, and fraught
    with store
Of all that deare and daynty is alyve.

Most happy he that can at last atchyve
The joyous safety of so sweet a rest;   10
Whose least delight sufficeth to deprive
Remembrance of all paines which him op-
    prest.
All paines are nothing in respect of this,
All sorrowes short that gaine eternall blisse.

LXX

Fresh Spring, the herald of loves mighty
    king,
In whose cote-armour richly are displayd
All sorts of flowers the which on earth do
    spring,
In goodly colours gloriously arrayd,
Goe to my love, where she is carelesse
    layd,   5
Yet in her winters bowre, not well awake;
Tell her the joyous time wil not be staid,
Unlesse she doe him by the forelocke take:
Bid her therefore her selfe soone ready
    make,
To wayt on Love amongst his lovely crew, 10
Where every one that misseth then her
    make
Shall be by him amearst with penance dew.
Make hast therefore, sweet love, whilest it
    is prime;
For none can call againe the passèd time.

LXXII

Oft when my spirit doth spred her bolder
    winges,
In mind to mount up to the purest sky,
It down is weighd with thoght of earthly
    things,
And clogd with burden of mortality:
Where, when that soverayne beauty it doth
    spy,   5
Resembling heavens glory in her light,
Drawne with sweet pleasures bayt, it back
    doth fly,
And unto heaven forgets her former flight.
There my fraile fancy, fed with full delight,
Doth bath in blisse, and mantleth most at
    ease;   10
Ne thinks of other heaven, but how it might
Her harts desire with most contentment
    please.
Hart need not wish none other happinesse,
But here on earth to have such hevens
    blisse.

LXXIX

Men call you fayre, and you doe credit it,
For that your selfe ye dayly such doe
    see:

But the trew fayre, that is the gentle wit
And vertuous mind, is much more praysd
    of me.
For all the rest, how ever fayre it be,   5
Shall turne to nought and loose that glori-
    ous hew:
But onely that is permanent, and free
From frayle corruption, that doth flesh en-
    sew.
That is true beautie: that doth argue you
To be divine, and borne of heavenly seed, 10
Deriv'd from that fayre Spirit from whom
    al true
And perfect beauty did at first proceed.
He onely fayre, and what he fayre hath
    made;
All other fayre, lyke flowres, untymely fade.

EPITHALAMION

Ye learnèd sisters, which have oftentimes
Beene to me ayding, others to adorne,
Whom ye thought worthy of your gracefull
    rymes,
That even the greatest did not greatly
    scorne
To heare theyr names sung in your simple
    layes,   5
But joyèd in theyr praise;
And when ye list your owne mishaps to
    mourne,
Which death, or love, or fortunes wreck
    did rayse,
Your string could soone to sadder tenor
    turne,
And teach the woods and waters to la-
    ment   10
Your dolefull dreriment:
Now lay those sorrowfull complaints aside,
And having all your heads with girland
    crownd,
Helpe me mine owne loves prayses to re-
    sound;
Ne let the same of any be envide: 15
So Orpheus did for his owne bride:
So I unto my selfe alone will sing;
The woods shall to me answer, and my
    eccho ring.

Early, before the worlds light giving lampe
His golden beame upon the hils doth spred,
Having disperst the nights unchearefull
    dampe,   21
Doe ye awake, and, with fresh lustyhed,
Go to the bowre of my belovèd love,
My truest turtle dove:

Bid her awake; for Hymen is awake,   25
And long since ready forth his maske to
    move,
With his bright tead that flames with many
    a flake,
And many a bachelor to waite on him,
In theyr fresh garments trim.
Bid her awake therefore, and soone her
    dight,   30
For lo! the wishèd day is come at last,
That shall, for al the paynes and sorrowes
    past,
Pay to her usury of long delight:
And whylest she doth her dight,
Doe ye to her of joy and solace sing,   35
That all the woods may answer, and your
    eccho ring.

Bring with you all the nymphes that you
    can heare,
Both of the rivers and the forrests greene,
And of the sea that neighbours to her
    neare,
Al with gay girlands goodly wel beseene.   40
And let them also with them bring in hand
Another gay girland,
For my fayre love, of lillyes and of roses,
Bound truelove wize with a blew silke
    riband.
And let them make great store of bridale
    poses,   45
And let them eeke bring store of other
    flowers,
To deck the bridale bowers.
And let the ground whereas her foot shall
    tread,
For feare the stones her tender foot should
    wrong,
Be strewed with fragrant flowers all along,
And diapred lyke the discolored mead.   51
Which done, doe at her chamber dore awayt
For she will waken strayt;
The whiles doe ye this song unto her sing
The woods shall to you answer, and your
    eccho ring.   55

Ye nymphes of Mulla, which with carefull
    heed
The silver scaly trouts doe tend full well,
And greedy pikes which use therein to feed,
(Those trouts and pikes all others doo ex-
    cell)
And ye likewise which keepe the rushy lake,
Where none doo fishes take,   61
Bynd up the locks the which hang scatterd
    light,
And in his waters, which your mirror make,

Behold your faces as the christall bright,
That when you come whereas my love doth
  lie,   65
No blemish she may spie.
And eke ye lightfoot mayds which keepe
  the dere
That on the hoary mountayne use to towre,
And the wylde wolves, which seeke them
  to devoure,
With your steele darts doo chace from com-
  ming neer,   70
Be also present heere,
To helpe to decke her, and to help to sing,
That all the woods may answer, and your
  eccho ring.

Wake now, my love, awake! for it is time:
The rosy Morne long since left Tithones
  bed,   75
All ready to her silver coche to clyme,
And Phœbus gins to shew his glorious hed.
Hark how the cheerefull birds do chaunt
  theyr laies,
And carroll of loves praise!
The merry larke hir mattins sings aloft,   80
The thrush replyes, the mavis descant
  playes,
The ouzell shrills, the ruddock warbles soft,
So goodly all agree, with sweet consent,
To this dayes merriment.
Ah! my deere love, why doe ye sleepe thus
  long,   85
When meeter were that ye should now
  awake,
T 'awayt the comming of your joyous mate,
And hearken to the birds love-learnèd song,
The deawy leaves among?
For they of joy and pleasance to you sing,
That all the woods them answer, and theyr
  eccho ring.   91

My love is now awake out of her dreame,
And her fayre eyes, like stars that dimmèd
  were
With darksome cloud, now shew theyr good-
  ly beams
More bright then Hesperus his head doth
  rere.   95
Come now, ye damzels, daughters of de-
  light,
Helpe quickly her to dight.
But first come ye, fayre Houres, which
  were begot,
In Joves sweet paradice, of Day and Night,
Which doe the seasons of the year allot, 100
And al that ever in this world is fayre
Do make and still repayre.
And ye three handmayds of the Cyprian
  Queene.

The which doe still adorne her beauties
  pride,   104
Helpe to addorne my beautifullest bride:
And as ye her array, still throw betweene
Some graces to be seene:
And as ye use to Venus, to her sing,
The whiles the woods shal answer, and your
  eccho ring.

Now is my love all ready forth to come: 110
Let all the virgins therefore well awayt,
And ye fresh boyes, that tend upon her
  groome,
Prepare your selves, for he is comming
  strayt.
Set all your things in seemely good aray,
Fit for so joyfull day,   115
The joyfulst day that ever sunne did see.
Faire Sun, shew forth thy favourable ray,
And let thy lifull heat not fervent be,
For feare of burning her sunshyny face,
Her beauty to disgrace.   120
O fayrest Phœbus, father of the Muse,
If ever I did honour thee aright,
Or sing the thing that mote thy mind de-
  light,
Doe not thy servants simple boone refuse,
But let this day, let this one day be myne,
Let all the rest be thine.   126
Then I thy soverayne prayses loud wil sing,
That all the woods shal answer, and theyr
  eccho ring.

Harke how the minstrels gin to shrill aloud
Their merry musick that resounds from
  far,   130
The pipe, the tabor, and the trembling croud,
That well agree withouten breach or jar,
But most of all the damzeis doe delite,
When they their tymbrels smyte,
And thereunto doe daunce and carrol sweet,
That all the sences they doe ravish quite, 136
The whyles the boyes run up and downe
  the street,
Crying aloud with strong confusèd noyce,
As if it were one voyce.
'Hymen, Iö Hymen, Hymen,' they do shout,
That even to the heavens theyr shouting
  shrill   141
Doth reach, and all the firmament doth fill;
To which the people, standing all about,
As in approvance doe thereto applaud,
And loud advaunce her laud,   145
And evermore they 'Hymen. Hymen' sing,
That al the woods them answer, and theyr
  eccho ring.

Loe! where she comes along with portly
  pace.

Lyke Phœbe, from her chamber of the east,
Arysing forth to run her mighty race, 150
Clad all in white, that seemes a virgin best.
So well it her beseemes, that ye would
    weene
Some angell she had beene. .
Her long loose yellow locks lyke golden
    wyre,
Sprinckled with perle, and perling flowres
    atweene,   155
Doe lyke a golden mantle her attyre,
And being crownèd with a girland greene,
Seeme lyke some mayden queene.
Her modest eyes, abashèd to behold
So many gazers as on her do stare,   160
Upon the lowly ground affixèd are;
Ne dare lift up her countenance too bold,
But blush to heare her prayses sung so
    loud,
So farre from being proud.
Nathlesse doe ye still loud her prayses
    sing,   165
That all the woods may answer, and your
    eccho ring.

Tell me, ye merchants daughters, did ye
    see
So fayre a creature in your towne before,
So sweet, so lovely, and so mild as she,
Adornd with beautyes grace and vertues
    store?   170
Her goodly eyes lyke saphyres shining
    bright,
Her forehead yvory white,
Her cheekes lyke apples which the sun hath
    rudded,
Her lips lyke cherryes charming men to
    byte,
Her brest like to a bowle of creame uncrud-
    dèd,   175
Her paps lyke lyllies budded,
Her snowie necke lyke to a marble towre,
And all her body like a pallace fayre,
Ascending uppe, with many a stately stayre,
To honors seat and chastities sweet bowre.
Why stand ye still, ye virgins, in amaze, 181
Upon her so to gaze,
Whiles ye forget your former lay to sing,
To which the woods did answer, and your
    eccho ring.

But if ye saw that which no eyes can see,
The inward beauty of her lively spright, 186
Garnisht with heavenly guifts of high de-
    gree,
Much more then would ye wonder at that
    sight,
And stand astonisht lyke to those which
    red

Medusaes mazeful hed.   190
There dwels sweet Love and constant Chas-
    tity,
Unspotted Fayth, and comely Womanhood,
Regard of Honour, and mild Modesty;
There Vertue raynes as queene in royal
    throne,
And giveth lawes alone,   195
The which the base affections doe obay,
And yeeld theyr services unto her will;
Ne thought of thing uncomely ever may
Thereto approch to tempt her mind to ill.
Had ye once seene these her celestial threa-
    sures,   200
And unrevealèd pleasures,
Then would ye wonder, and her prayses
    sing,
That al the woods should answer, and your
    echo ring.

Open the temple gates unto my love,
Open them wide that she may enter in, 205
And all the postes adorne as doth behove,
And all the pillours deck with girlands trim,
For to receyve this saynt with honour dew,
That commeth in to you.
With trembling steps and humble rever-
    ence,   210
She commeth in before th' Almighties vew:
Of her, ye virgins, learne obedience,
When so ye come into those holy places,
To humble your proud faces.
Bring her up to th' high altar, that she
    may   215
The sacred ceremonies there partake,
The which do endlesse matrimony make;
And let the roring organs loudly play
The praises of the Lord in lively notes,
The whiles with hollow throates   220
The choristers the joyous antheme sing,
That al the woods may answere, and their
    eccho ring.

Behold, whiles she before the altar stands,
Hearing the holy priest that to her speakes,
And blesseth her with his two happy
    hands,   225
How the red roses flush up in her cheekes,
And the pure snow with goodly vermill
    stayne,
Like crimsin dyde in grayne:
That even th' angels, which continually
About the sacred altare doe remaine,   230
Forget their service and about her fly,
Ofte peeping in her face, that seemes more
    fayre,
The more they on it stare.
But her sad eyes, still fastened on the
    ground.

Are governèd with goodly modesty,   235
That suffers not one looke to glaunce awry,
Which may let in a little thought unsownd.
Why blush ye, love, to give to me your
hand,
The pledge of all our band?
Sing, ye sweet angels, Alleluya sing,   240
That all the woods may answere, and your
eccho ring.

Now al is done; bring home the bride
againe,
Bring home the triumph of our victory,
Bring home with you the glory of her
gaine,
With joyance bring her and with jollity. 245
Never had man more joyfull day then this,
Whom heaven would heape with blis.
Make feast therefore now all this live long
day;
This day for ever to me holy is;
Poure out the wine without restraint or
stay,   250
Poure not by cups, but by the belly full,
Poure out to all that wull,
And sprinkle all the postes and wals with
wine,
That they may sweat, and drunken be with-
all.
Crowne ye God Bacchus with a coronall.
And Hymen also crowne with wreathes of
vine;   256
And let the Graces daunce unto the rest,
For they can doo it best:
The whiles the maydens doe theyr carroll
sing,
The which the woods shal answer, and theyr
eccho ring.   260

Ring ye the bels, ye yong men of the
towne,
And leave your wonted labors for this day:
This day is holy; doe ye write it downe,
That ye for ever it remember may.
This day the sunne is in his chiefest hight,
With Barnaby the bright,   266
From whence declining daily by degrees,
He somewhat loseth of his heat and light,
When once the Crab behind his back he
sees.
But for this time it ill ordainèd was,   270
To chose the longest day in all the yeare,
And shortest night, when longest fitter
weare:
Yet never day so long, but late would passe.
Ring ye the bels, to make it weare away,
And bonefires make all day,   275
And daunce about them, and about them
sing:

That all the woods may answer, and your
eccho ring.

Ah! when will this long weary day have
end,
And lende me leave to come unto my
love?
How slowly do the houres theyr number
spend!   280
How slowly does sad Time his feather
move!
Hast thee, O fayrest planet, to thy home
Within the westerne fome:
Thy tyrèd steedes long since have need of
rest.
Long though it be, at last I see it gloome,
And the bright evening star with golden
creast   286
Appeare out of the east.
Fayre childe of beauty, glorious lampe of
love,
That all the host of heaven in rankes doost
lead,
And guydest lovers through the nightes
dread,   290
How chearefully thou lookest from
above,
And seemst to laugh atweene thy twinkling
light,
As joying in the sight
Of these glad many, which for joy doe
sing,
That all the woods them answer, and their
echo ring!   .   295

Now ceasse, ye damsels, your delights fore-
past;
Enough is it that all the day was youres:
Now day is doen, and night is nighing
fast:
Now bring the bryde into the brydall
boures.
The night is come, now soone her disaray,
And in her bed her lay;   301
Lay her in lillies and in violets,
And silken courteins over her display,
And odourd sheetes, and Arras coverlets.
Behold how goodly my faire love does ly,
In proud humility!   306
Like unto Maia, when as Jove her tooke
In Tempe, lying on the flowry gras,
Twixt sleepe and wake, after she weary
was
With bathing in the Acidalian brooke. 310
Now it is night, ye damsels may be gon,
And leave my love alone.
And leave likewise your former lay to sing:
The woods no more shal answere, nor your
echo ring.

Now welcome, night! thou night so long
   expected,
That long daies labour doest at last de-
   fray,
And all my cares, which cruell Love col-
   lected,
Hast sumd in one, and cancellèd for aye:
Spread thy broad wing over my love and
   me,
That no man may us see,   320
And in thy sable mantle us enwrap,
From feare of perrill and foule horror free.
Let no false treason seeke us to entrap,
Nor any dread disquiet once annoy
The safety of our joy: 325
But let the night be calme and quietsome,
Without tempestuous storms or sad afray:
Lyke as when Jove with fayre Alcmena
   lay,
When he begot the great Tirynthian
   groome:
Or lyke as when he with thy selfe did
   lie,   330
And begot Majesty.
And let the mayds and yongmen cease to
   sing:
Ne let the woods them answer, nor theyr
   eccho ring.

Let no lamenting cryes, nor dolefull teares,
Be heard all night within, nor yet without:
Ne let false whispers, breeding hidden
   feares,   336
Breake gentle sleepe with misconceivèd
   dout.
Let no deluding dreames, nor dreadful
   sights,
Make sudden sad affrights;
Ne let house-fyres, nor lightnings helplesse
   harmes,   340
Ne let the Pouke, nor other evill sprights,
Ne let mischivous witches with theyr
   charmes,
Ne let hob goblins, names whose sense we
   see not,
Fray us with things that be not.
Let not the shriech oule, nor the storke be
   heard,   345
Nor the night raven that still deadly yels,
Nor damnèd ghosts cald up with mighty
   spels,
Nor griesly vultures make us once affeard:
Ne let th' unpleasant quyre of frogs still
   croking
Make us to wish theyr choking.   350
Let none of these theyr drery accents
   sing;
Ne let the woods them answer, nor theyr
   eccho ring.

But let stil Silence trew night watches
   keepe,
That sacred Peace may in assurance rayne,
And tymely Sleep, when it is tyme to
   sleepe,   355
May poure his limbs forth on your pleasant
   playne,
The whiles an hundred little wingèd loves,
Like divers fethered doves,
Shall fly and flutter round about our bed,
And in the secret darke, that none reproves,
Their prety stealthes shall worke, and
   snares shal spread   361
To filch away sweet snatches of delight,
Conceald through covert night.
Ye sonnes of Venus, play your sports at
   will:
For greedy Pleasure, careless of your toyes,
Thinks more upon her paradise of joyes,
Then what ye do, albe it good or ill.   367
All night therefore attend your merry play,
For it will soone be day:
Now none doth hinder you, that say or sing,
Ne will the woods now answer, nor your
   eccho ring.   371

Who is the same which at my window
   peepes?
Or whose is that faire face that shines so
   bright?
Is it not Cinthia, she that never sleepes,
But walkes about high heaven al the night?
O fayrest goddesse, do thou not envy   376
My love with me to spy:
For thou likewise didst love, though now
   unthought,
And for a fleece of woll, which privily
The Latmian shephard once unto thee
   brought,   380
His pleasures with thee wrought.
Therefore to us be favorable now;
And sith of wemens labours thou hast
   charge,
And generation goodly dost enlarge,
Encline thy will t' effect our wishfull vow,
And the chast wombe informe with timely
   seed,   386
That may our comfort breed:
Till which we cease our hopefull hap to sing,
Ne let the woods us answere, nor our eccho
   ring.

And thou, great Juno, which with awful
   might   390
The lawes of wedlock still dost patronize,
And the religion of the faith first plight
With sacred rites hast taught to solemnize,
And eeke for comfort often callèd art
Of women in their smart.   395

Eternally bind thou this lovely band,
And all thy blessings unto us impart.
And thou, glad Genius, in whose gentle hand
The bridale bowre and geniall bed remaine,
Without blemish or staine,   400
And the sweet pleasures of theyr loves
    delight
With secret ayde doest succour and supply,
Till they bring forth the fruitfull progeny,
Send us the timely fruit of this same night.
And thou, fayre Hebe, and thou, Hymen
    free,   405
Grant that it may so be.
Til which we cease your further prayse to
    sing,
Ne any woods shal answer, nor your eccho
    ring.

And ye high heavens, the temple of the
    gods,   409
In which a thousand torches flaming bright
Doe burne, that to us wretched earthly clods
in dreadful darknesse lend desirèd light,
And all ye powers which in the same re-
    mayne,
More then we men can fayne,
Poure out your blessing on us plentiously,
And happy influence upon us raine,   416
That we may raise a large posterity,
Which from the earth, which they may
    long possesse
With lasting happinesse,
Up to your haughty pallaces may mount, 420
And for the guerdon of theyr glorious merit,
May heavenly tabernacles there inherit,
Of blessèd saints for to increase the count.
So let us rest, sweet love, in hope of this,
And cease till then our tymely joyes to sing:
The woods no more us answer, nor our
    eccho ring.   426

Song, made in lieu of many ornaments
With which my love should duly have bene
    dect,
Which cutting off through hasty accidents,
Ye would not stay your dew time to expect,
But promist both to recompens,   431
Be unto her a goodly ornament,
And for short time an endlesse moniment.

PROTHALAMION

Calme was the day, and through the trem-
    bling ayre
Sweete breathing Zephyrus did softly play,
A gentle spirit, that lightly did delay
Hot Titans beames, which then did glyster
    fayre ·

When I, whom sullein care,   5
Through discontent of my long fruitlesse
    stay
In princes court, and expectation vayne
Of idle hopes, which still doe fly away,
Like empty shaddowes, did aflict my brayne,
Walkt forth to ease my payne   10
Along the shoare of silver streaming
    Themmes;
Whose rutty bancke, the which his river
    hemmes,
Was paynted all with variable flowers,
And all the meades adornd with daintie
    gemmes,
Fit to decke maydens bowres,   15
And crowne their paramours,
Against the brydale day, which is not long:
    Sweete Themmes, runne softly, till I end
    my song.

There, in a meadow, by the rivers side,
A flocke of nymphes I chauncèd to espy,   20
All lovely daughters of the flood thereby,
With goodly greenish locks all loose untyde,
As each had bene a bryde:
And each one had a little wicker basket,
Made of fine twigs entraylèd curiously,   25
In which they gathered flowers to fill their
    flasket;
And with fine fingers cropt full feateously
The tender stalkes on hye.
Of every sort, which in that meadow grew,
They gathered some; the violet pallid blew,
The little dazie, that at evening closes, 31
The virgin lillie, and the primrose trew,
With store of vermeil roses,
To decke their bridegromes posies
Against the brydale day, which was not
    long: 3~
    Sweete Themmes, runne softly, till I end
    my song.

With that I saw two swannes of goodly
    hewe
Come softly swimming downe along the
    lee;
Two fairer birds I yet did never see:
The snow which doth the top of Pindus
    strew   40
Did never whiter shew,
Nor Jove himselfe, when he a swan would
    be
For love of Leda, whiter did appear:
Yet Leda was, they say, as white as he,
Yet not so white as these, nor nothing
    neare: 45
So purely white they were,
That even the gentle streame, the which
    them bare.

Seem'd foule to them, and bad his billowes
    spare
To wet their silken feathers, least they
    might
Soyle their fayre plumes with water not so
    fayre,   50
And marre their beauties bright,
That shone as heavens light,
Against their brydale day, which was not
    long:
    Sweete Themmes, runne softly, till I end
        my song.

Eftsoones the nymphes, which now had
    flowers their fill,   55
Ran all in haste to see that silver brood,
As they came floating on the christal flood;
Whom when they sawe, they stood amazèd
    still,
Their wondring eyes to fill.
Them seem'd they never saw a sight so
    fayre,   60
Of fowles so lovely, that they sure did
    deeme
Them heavenly borne, or to be that same
    payre
Which through the skie draw Venus silver
    teeme;
For sure they did not seeme
To be begot of any earthly seede,   65
But rather angels or of angels breede:
Yet were they bred of Somers-heat, they
    say,
In sweetest season, when each flower and
    weede
The earth did fresh aray;
So fresh they seem'd as day,   70
Even as their brydale day, which was not
    long:
    Sweete Themmes, runne softly, till I end
        my song.

Then forth they all out of their baskets
    drew
Great store of flowers, the honour of the
    field,
That to the sense did fragrant odours yield,
All which upon those goodly birds they
    threw,   76
And all the waves did strew,
That like old Peneus waters they did
    seeme,
When downe along by pleasant Tempes
    shore,
Scattred with flowres, through Thessaly
    they streeme,   80
That they appeare, through lillies plenteous
    store,
Like a brydes chamber flore.

Two of those nymphes, meane while, two
    garlands bound
Of freshest flowres which in that mead
    they found,
The which presenting all in trim array,   85
Their snowie foreheads therewithall they
    crowned,
Whil'st one did sing this lay,
Prepar'd against that day,
Against their brydale day, which was not
    long:
    Sweete Themmes, runne softly, till I end
        my song.   90

'Ye gentle birdes, the worlds faire orna-
    ment,
And heavens glorie, whom this happie
    hower
Doth leade unto your lovers blissfull bower,
Joy may you have and gentle hearts con-
    tent
Of your loves couplement: 95
And let faire Venus, that is Queene of
    Love,
With her heart-quelling sonne upon you
    smile,
Whose smile, they say, hath vertue to
    remove
All loves dislike, and friendships faultie
    guile
For ever to assoile.   100
Let endlesse peace your steadfast hearts
    accord,
And blessèd plentie wait upon your lord;
And let your bed with pleasures chast
    abound,
That fruitfull issue may to you afford,
Which may your foes confound,   105
And make your joyes redound,
Upon your brydale day, which is not long:
    Sweete Themmes, run softlie, till I end
        my song.'

So ended she; and all the rest around
To her redoubled that her undersong,   110
Which said, their bridale daye should not
    be long.
And gentle Eccho from the neighbour
    ground
Their accents did resound.
So forth those joyous birdes did passe along,
Adowne the lee, that to them murmurde
    low,   115
As he would speake, but that he lackt a
    tong,
Yeat did by signes his glad affection show,
Making his streame run slow.
And all the foule which in his flood did
    dwell

Gan flock about these twaine, that did ex-
　cell　　　　　　　　　　　　　　　120
The rest so far as Cynthia doth shend
The lesser starres. So they, enrangèd well,
Did on those two attend,
And their best service lend,
Against their wedding day, which was not
　long:　　　　　　　　　　　　　125
　　Sweete Themmes, run softly, till I end
　　my song.

At length they all to mery London came,
To mery London, my most kyndly nurse,
That to me gave this lifes first native
　sourse:
Though from another place I take my name,
An house of auncient fame.　　　131
There when they came, whereas those
　bricky towres,
The which on Themmes brode agèd backe
　doe ryde,
Where now the studious lawyers have their
　bowers,
There whylome wont the Templer Knights
　to byde,　　　　　　　　　135
Till they decayd through pride:
Next whereunto there standes a stately
　place,
Where oft I gaynèd giftes and goodly grace
Of that great lord which therein wont to
　dwell,
Whose want too well now feeles my
　freendles case:　　　　　　140
But ah! here fits not well
Olde woes, but joyes to tell,
Against the bridale daye, which is not long:
　　Sweete Themmes, runne softly, till I end
　　my song.

Yet therein, now doth lodge a noble peer,
Great Englands glory and the worlds wide
　wonder,　　　　　　　　　146
Whose dreadfull name late through all
　Spaine did thunder,
And Hercules two pillors standing neere
Did make to quake and feare.

Faire branch of honor, flower of chevalrie,
That fillest England with thy triumphes
　fame,　　　　　　　　　　　151
Joy have thou of thy noble victorie,
And endlesse happinesse of thine owne
　name
That promiseth the same:
That through thy prowesse and victorious
　armes　　　　　　　　　　155
Thy country may be freed from forraine
　harmes;
And great Elisaes glorious name may ring
Through al the world, fil'd with thy wide
　alarmes,
Which some brave Muse may sing
To ages following,　　　　　　160
Upon the brydale day, which is not long:
　　Sweete Themmes, runne softly, till I end
　　my song.

From those high towers this noble lord
　issuing,
Like radiant Hesper when his golden hayre
In th' ocean billows he hath bathèd fayre,
Descended to the rivers open vewing,　166
With a great traine ensuing.
Above the rest were goodly to bee seene
Two gentle knights of lovely face and
　feature,　　　　　　　　　169
Beseeming well the bower of anie queene,
With gifts of wit and ornaments of nature,
Fit for so goodly stature:
That like the twins of Jove they seem'd in
　sight,
Which decke the bauldricke of the heavens
　bright.
They two, forth pacing to the rivers side,
Received those two faire brides, their loves
　delight,　　　　　　　　　176
Which, at th' appointed tyde,
Each one did make his bryde,
Against their brydale day, which is not
　long:
　　Sweete Themmes, runne softly, till I end
　　my song.　　　　　　　　180

ELIZABETHAN LYRICS

As a whole, the brilliant lyrical effluence of the Elizabethan period may fairly be regarded as the product of English courtly life, and particularly, in its beginning, the product of the Renaissance court of Henry VIII. Wyatt and Surrey were conspicuous courtiers, and scarcely one of the contributors to *Tottel's Miscellany* (1557) was free from court influence. An inevitable result of courtliness in literature is convention, a too conscious refinement, and, often, a baffling veil of literary pretence. These qualities are salient and inherent in the Elizabethan sonnet. After its introduction into English literature by Sir Thomas Wyatt, and after its chastening in the hands of Surrey and others, this poetical form was first used in masterly fashion by Sir Philip Sidney in his *Astrophel and Stella*, the earliest sonnet sequence in English, composed a good while before its publication in 1591. During the decade 1590–1600, the sonnet was, apparently, the prevailing literary fashion, a fashion to which Shakspere submitted without restraint. Of the total number of these sonnets,— which ' far exceeds two thousand,'— the larger proportion are found in sonnet collections, or sonnet sequences, of which the most important, after those of Shakspere and Sidney, are the following: *Delia* (1592), by Samuel Daniel; *Idea* (1594), by Michael Drayton; and *Amoretti* (1595), by Edmund Spenser. With few exceptions, these sonnets, like those of Wyatt and Surrey, are imitations of Continental models.

But since lyric is essentially the expression of personal emotion, the lyrist inevitably breaks out, at times, into a frank, intimate, and spontaneous utterance which is of all sorts of expression the most immediately pleasurable. Free, fresh, and various are the lyrics found in the series of miscellanies which began with *Tottel's Miscellany*, and continued with *The Paradise of Dainty Devices* (1576), *A Gorgeous Gallery of Gallant Inventions* (1578), *A Handful of Pleasant Delights* (1584), *The Phoenix' Nest* (1593), *The Passionate Pilgrim* (1599), *England's Helicon* (1600), and Francis Davison's *Poetical Rhapsody* (1602). In one or other of these collections are represented the chief lyrical writers of the Elizabethan period.

In a group apart from the lyrical miscellanies, though not conspicuously different from some of them in content, may be reckoned the Elizabethan song books. William Byrd's *Psalms, Sonnets, and Songs of Sadness and Piety* (1587) and *Songs of Sundry Natures* (1589) were followed, during the next decade or two, by some scores of similar collections, such as John Dowland's *The First Book of Songs or Airs* (1597), and Thomas Campion's *A Book of Airs* (1601). Along with the songs in song books should be mentioned those that delightfully enliven many of the plays of the period, eminently those of Lyly and of Shakspere.

GEORGE GASCOIGNE
(1525?–1577)

A STRANGE PASSION OF A LOVER

Amid my bale I bathe in bliss,
I swim in heaven, I sink in hell:
I find amends for every miss,
And yet my moan no tongue can tell.
I live and love, what would you more?　　5
As never lover lived before.

I laugh sometimes with little lust,
So jest I oft and feel no joy;
Mine eye is builded all on trust,
And yet mistrust breeds mine annoy.　　10

I live and lack, I lack and have;
I have and miss the thing I crave.

These things seem strange, yet are they true.
Believe me, sweet, my state is such,
One pleasure which I would eschew,　　15
Both slakes my grief and breeds my grutch.
So doth one pain which I would shun,
Renew my joys where grief begun.

Then like the lark that passed the night
In heavy sleep with cares opprest;　　20
Yet when she spies the pleasant light,
She sends sweet notes from out her breast.
So sing I now because I think
How joys approach, when sorrows shrink.

133

And as fair Philomene again   25
Can watch and sing when others sleep;
And taketh pleasure in her pain,
To wray the woe that makes her weep.
So sing I now for to bewray
The loathsome life I lead alway.   30

The which to thee, dear wench, I write,
That know'st my mirth, but not my moan:
I pray God grant thee deep delight,
To live in joys when I am gone.
I cannot live; it will not be: 35
I die to think to part from thee.

SIR EDWARD DYER (1550?–1607)

MY MIND TO ME A KINGDOM IS

My mind to me a kingdom is,
  Such present joys therein I find
That it excels all other bliss
  That earth affords or grows by kind:
Though much I want which most would
    have,   5
Yet still my mind forbids to crave.

No princely pomp, no wealthy store,
  No force to win the victory,
No wily wit to salve a sore,
  No shape to feed a loving eye;   10
To none of these I yield as thrall:
For why? My mind doth serve for all.

I see how plenty [surfeits] oft,
  And hasty climbers soon do fall;
I see that those which are aloft   15
  Mishap doth threaten most of all;
They get with toil, they keep·with fear:
Such cares my mind could never bear.

Content to live, this is my stay;
  I seek no more than may suffice;   20
I press to bear no haughty sway;
  Look, what I lack my mind supplies:
Lo, thus I triumph like a king,
Content with that my mind doth bring.

Some have too much, yet still do crave;   25
  I little have, and seek no more.
They are but poor, though much they have,
  And I am rich with little store:
They poor, I rich; they beg, I give;
They lack, I leave; they pine, I live.   30

I laugh not at another's loss;
  I grudge not at another's pain;
No worldly waves my mind can toss;
  My state at one doth still remain:
I fear no foe, I fawn no friend;   35
I loathe not life, nor dread my end.

Some weigh their pleasure by their lust,
  Their wisdom by their rage of will;
Their treasure is their only trust;
  A cloakèd craft their store of skill: 40
But all the pleasure that I find
Is to maintain a quiet mind.

My wealth is health and perfect ease;
  My conscience clear my chief defence;
I neither seek by bribes to please,   45
  Nor by deceit to breed offence:
Thus do I live; thus will I die;
Would all did so as well as I!

SIR WALTER RALEIGH
(1552?–1618)

THE SILENT LOVER

I

Passions are likened best to floods and
    streams:
  The shallow murmur, but the deep are
    dumb.
So, when affection yields discourse, it seems
  The bottom is but shallow whence they
    come.
They that are rich in words, in words dis-
    cover   5
That they are poor in that which makes a
    lover.

II

Wrong not, sweet empress of my heart,
  The merit of true passion,
With thinking that he feels no smart,
  That sues for no compassion.

Silence in love bewrays more woe   5
  Than words, though ne'er so witty:
A beggar that is dumb, you know,
  May challenge double pity.

Then wrong not, dearest to my heart,
  My true, though secret passion;   10
He smarteth most that hides his smart,
  And sues for no compassion.

HIS PILGRIMAGE

Give me my scallop-shell of quiet,
  My staff of faith to walk upon,
My scrip of joy, immortal diet,
  My bottle of salvation,
My gown of glory, hope's true gauge;   5
And thus I'll take my pilgrimage.

Blood must be my body's balmer;
No other balm will there be given;
Whilst my soul, like a quiet palmer,
   Traveleth towards the land of heaven,   10
Over the silver mountains,
Where spring the nectar fountains.
     There will I kiss
     The bowl of bliss;
And drink mine everlasting fill   15
Upon every milken hill.
My soul will be a-dry before;
But, after, it will thirst no more.

Then by that happy blissful day
   More peaceful pilgrims I shall see,
That have cast off their rags of clay,
   And walk appareled fresh like me.
     I 'll take them first,
     To quench their thirst   24
   And taste of nectar suckets,
     At those clear wells
     Where sweetness dwells,
Drawn up by saints in crystal buckets.

And when our bottles and all we
   Are filled with immortality,   30
Then the blessèd paths we 'll travel,
Strowed with rubies thick as gravel;
Ceilings of diamonds, sapphire floors,
High walls of coral, and pearly bowers.

From thence to heaven's bribeless hall,
Where no corruptèd voices brawl;
No conscience molten into gold;
No forged accuser bought or sold;
No cause deferred, no vain-spent journey,
For there Christ is the King's attorney,
Who pleads for all, without degrees,   41
And he hath angels but no fees.
   And when the grand twelve million jury
Of our sins, with direful fury,
Against our souls black verdicts give,
Christ pleads his death; and then we live.

Be Thou my speaker, taintless pleader!
Unblotted lawyer! true proceeder!
Thou giv'st salvation, even for alms,
Not with a bribèd lawyer's palms.   50

And this is mine eternal plea
To him that made heaven and earth and sea:
That, since my flesh must die so soon,
And want a head to dine next noon,
Just at the stroke, when my veins start and
    spread,
Set on my soul an everlasting head!   56

Then am I ready, like a palmer fit,
To tread those blest paths; which before I
   writ

A VISION UPON THIS CONCEIT OF THE FAERY QUEEN

Methought I saw the grave where Laura
   lay,
Within that temple where the vestal flame
Was wont to burn: and, passing by that
   way,
To see that buried dust of living fame,
Whose tomb fair Love and fairer Virtue
   kept,   5
All suddenly I saw the Faery Queen;
At whose approach the soul of Petrarch
   wept,
And from thenceforth those graces were not
   seen,
For they this queen attendèd; in whose
   stead
Oblivion laid him down on Laura's hearse.
Hereat the hardest stones were seen to
   bleed,   11
And groans of buried ghosts the heavens
   did pierce:
Where Homer's sprite did tremble all for
   grief,
And cursed the access of that celestial thief.

THE CONCLUSION

Even such is time, that takes in trust
   Our youth, our joys, our all we have,
And pays us but with earth and dust;
   Who, in the dark and silent grave,
When we have wandered all our ways,   5
Shuts up the story of our days:
But from this earth, this grave, this dust,
My God shall raise me up, I trust.

GEORGE PEELE (1558?–1597?)

SONG from THE ARRAIGNMENT OF PARIS

ŒNONE. Fair and fair, and twice so fair,
     As fair as any may be;
     The fairest shepherd on our green,
     A love for any lady.

PARIS. Fair and fair, and twice so fair,   5
     As fair as any may be;
     Thy love is fair for thee alone,
     And for no other lady.

ŒN. My love is fair, my love is gay,
     As fresh as bin the flowers in
     May,   10
     And of my love my roundelay,
     My merry, merry roundelay,
     Concludes with Cupid's curse,—

'They that do change old love for
        new,
    Pray gods they change for worse!'
AMBO SIMUL.   They that do change, etc.
ŒN.   Fair and fair, etc.
PAR.   Fair and fair, etc.
         Thy love is fair, etc.
ŒN.   My love can pipe, my love can sing,
         My love can many a pretty thing,
         And of his lovely praises ring
         My merry, merry roundelays,
         Amen to Cupid's curse,—
         'They that do change,' etc.   25
PAR.   They that do change, etc.
AMBO.   Fair and fair, etc.

HARVESTMEN A-SINGING

FROM THE OLD WIVES' TALE

All ye that lovely lovers be,
Pray you for me:
Lo, here we come a-sowing, a-sowing,
And sow sweet fruits of love;
In your sweet hearts well may it prove!   5

Lo, here we come a-reaping, a-reaping,
To reap our harvest-fruit!
And thus we pass the year so long,
And never be we mute.

ROBERT GREENE (1560?–1592)

SONG FROM THE FAREWELL TO FOLLY

Sweet are the thoughts that savor of con-
        tent;
The quiet mind is richer than a crown;
Sweet are the nights in careless slumber
        spent;
The poor estate scorns fortune's angry
        frown:
Such sweet content, such minds, such sleep,
        such bliss,   5
Beggars enjoy, when princes oft do miss.

The homely house that harbors quiet rest;
The cottage that affords no pride nor care;
The mean that 'grees with country music
        best;
The sweet consort of mirth and music's
        fare;   10
Obscurèd life sets down a type of bliss:
A mind content both crown and kingdom
        is.

PHILOMELA'S ODE

FROM PHILOMELA

Sitting by a river's side,
Where a silent stream did glide,
Muse I did of many things
That the mind in quiet brings.
I gan think how some men deem
Gold their god; and some esteem
Honor is the chief content
That to man in life is lent.
And some others do contend,
Quiet none like to a friend.   10
Others hold there is no wealth
Compared to a perfect health.
Some man's mind in quiet stands,
When he is lord of many lands.
But I did sigh, and said all this
Was but a shade of perfect bliss;
And in my thoughts I did approve,
Naught so sweet as is true love.
Love 'twixt lovers passeth these,
When mouth kisseth and heart 'grees,   20
With folded arms and lips meeting,
Each soul another sweetly greeting;
For by the breath the soul fleeteth,
And soul with soul in kissing meeteth.
If love be so sweet a thing,
That such happy bliss doth bring,
Happy is love's sugared thrall,
But unhappy maidens all,
Who esteem your virgin blisses
Sweeter than a wife's sweet kisses.   30
No such quiet to the mind
As true love with kisses kind;
But if a kiss prove unchaste,
Then is true love quite disgraced.
Though love be sweet, learn this of me
No sweet love but honesty.

SONG FROM MENAPHON

Weep not, my wanton, smile upon my knee,
When thou art old there's grief enough for
        thee.
    Mother's wag, pretty boy,
    Father's sorrow, father's joy;
    When thy father first did see   5
    Such a boy by him and me,
    He was glad, I was woe,
    Fortune changèd made him so,
    When he left his pretty boy
    Last his sorrow, first his joy.   10

Weep not, my wanton, smile upon my knee,
When thou art old there's grief enough for
        thee.

Streaming tears that never stint,
Like pearl-drops from a flint,
Fell by course from his eyes,   15
That one another's place supplies;
Thus he grieved in every part,
Tears of blood fell from his heart,
When he left his pretty boy,
Father's sorrow, father's joy.   20

Weep not, my wanton, smile upon my
    knee,
When thou art old there's grief enough for
    thee.
The wanton smiled, father wept,
Mother cried, baby leapt;
More he crowed, more he cried,   25
Nature could not sorrow hide:
He must go, he must kiss
Child and mother, baby bless,
For he left his pretty boy,
Father's sorrow, father's joy.   30
Weep not, my wanton, smile upon my
    knee,
When thou art old there's grief enough for
    thee.

SONG FROM MENAPHON

Some say Love,
Foolish Love,
    Doth rule and govern all the gods:
I say Love,
Inconstant Love,   5
    Sets men's senses far at odds.
Some swear Love,
Smooth-faced Love,
    Is sweetest sweet that men can have:
I say Love,   10
Sour Love,
    Makes virtue yield as beauty's slave.
A bitter sweet, a folly worst of all,
That forceth wisdom to be folly's thrall.

Love is sweet,   15
Wherein sweet?
    In fading pleasures that do pain.
Beauty sweet:
Is that sweet
    That yieldeth sorrow for a gain?   20
If Love's sweet,
Herein sweet,
    That minutes' joys are monthly woes:
'Tis not sweet,
That is sweet   25
    Nowhere but where repentance grows.
Then love who list, if beauty be so sour;
Labor for me, Love rest in prince's bower.

THE SHEPHERD'S WIFE'S SONG

FROM THE MOURNING GARMENT

Ah, what is love? It is a pretty thing,
As sweet unto a shepherd as a king;
    And sweeter too:
For kings have cares that wait upon a
    crown,
And cares can make the sweetest love to
    frown.
        Ah then, ah then,
If country loves such sweet desires do gain,
What lady would not love a shepherd swain?

His flocks are folded, he comes home at
    night,
As merry as a king in his delight;   10
    And merrier too:
For kings bethink them what the state re-
    quire,
Where shepherds careless carol by the fire.
        Ah then, ah then,
If country loves such sweet desires do
    gain,   15
What lady would not love a shepherd swain?

He kisseth first, then sits as blithe to eat
His cream and curds as doth the king his
    meat;
    And blither too:
For kings have often fears when they do
    sup,   20
Where shepherds dread no poison in their
    cup.
        Ah then, ah then,
If country loves such sweet desires do gain,
What lady would not love a shepherd swain?

To bed he goes, as wanton then, I ween,   25
As is a king in dalliance with a queen;
    More wanton too:
For kings have many griefs affects to move,
Where shepherds have no greater grief than
    love.
        Ah then, ah then,   30
If country loves such sweet desires do gain,
What lady would not love a shepherd swain?

Upon his couch of straw he sleeps as sound,
As doth the king upon his bed of down;
    More sounder too: 35
For cares cause kings full oft their sleep to
    spill,
Where weary shepherds lie and snort their
    fill.
        Ah then, ah then,

If country loves such sweet desires do
 gain,   39
What lady would not love a shepherd
 swain?

Thus with his wife he spends the year, as
 blithe
As doth the king at every tide or sithe;
  And blither too:
For kings have wars and broils to take in
 hand
When shepherds laugh and love upon the
 land.
  Ah then, ah then,   46
If country loves such sweet desires do
 gain,
What lady would not love a shepherd
 swain?

ROBERT SOUTHWELL
(1561?–1595)

THE BURNING BABE

As I in hoary winter's night stood shivering in the snow,
Surprised I was with sudden heat which
 made my heart to glow;
And lifting up a fearful eye to view what
 fire was near,
A pretty babe, all burning bright, did in
 the air appear,
Who scorchèd with exceeding heat such
 floods of tears did shed,   5
As though his floods should quench his
 flames with what his tears were fed;
'Alas!' quoth he, 'but newly born in fiery
 heats I fry,
Yet none approach to warm their hearts or
 feel my fire but I!
My faultless breast the furnace is, the fuel
 wounding thorns;
Love is the fire and sighs the smoke, the
 ashes shame and scorns;   10
The fuel Justice layeth on, and Mercy
 blows the coals;
The metal in this furnace wrought are
 men's defilèd souls;
For which, as now on fire I am, to work
 them to their good,
So will I melt into a bath, to wash them in
 my blood:'
With this he vanished out of sight, and
 swiftly shrunk away,   15
And straight I callèd unto mind that it
 was Christmas-day.

SAMUEL DANIEL (1562–1619)
SONNETS FROM DELIA

XIX

Restore thy treasure to the golden ore;
Yield Cytherea's son those arcs of love:
Bequeath the heavens the stars that I adore;
And to the orient do thy pearls remove.
Yield thy hands' pride unto the ivory
 white;   5
To Arabian odors give thy breathing sweet;
Restore thy blush unto Aurora bright;
To Thetis give the honor of thy feet.
Let Venus have the graces she resigned;
And thy sweet voice yield to Hermonius'
 spheres: 10
But yet restore thy fierce and cruel mind
To Hyrcan tigers and to ruthless bears.
Yield to the marble thy hard heart again;
So shalt thou cease to plague and I to
 pain.

XXIII

False Hope prolongs my ever certain grief,
Traitor to me, and faithful to my Love.
A thousand times it promised me relief,
Yet never any true effect I prove.
Oft, when I find in her no truth at all, 5
I banish her, and blame her treachery:
Yet, soon again, I must her back recall,
As one that dies without her company.
Thus often, as I chase my Hope from me,
Straightway, she hastes her unto Delia's
 eyes: 10
Fed with some pleasing look, there shall she
 be;
And so sent back. And thus my fortune
 lies.
Looks feed my Hope, Hope fosters me in
 vain;
Hopes are unsure, when certain is my pain.

XXVIII

Oft do I marvel, whether Delia's eyes
Are eyes, or else two radiant stars that
 shine?
For how could Nature ever thus devise
Of earth, on earth, a substance so divine?
Stars, sure, they are, whose motions rule
 desires;   5
And calm and tempest follow their aspects:
Their sweet appearing still such power in-
 spires,
That makes the world admire so strange
 effects.
Yet whether fixed or wandering stars are
 they.

Whose influence rules the orb of my poor
  heart?   10
Fixed, sure, they are, but wandering, make
  me stray
In endless errors, whence I cannot part.
Stars, then, not eyes, move you, with
  milder view,
Your sweet aspect on him that honors
  you!

XXXVIII

Thou canst not die, whilst any zeal abound
In feeling hearts, that can conceive these
  lines:
Though thou, a Laura, hast no Petrarch
  found:
In base attire, yet, clearly, Beauty shines,
And I, though born within a colder clime,
Do feel mine inward heat as great, I know
  it.   6
He never had more faith, although more
  rime:
I love as well, though he could better show
  it.
But I may add one feather to thy fame,
To help her flight throughout the fairest
  Isle;   10
And if my pen could more enlarge thy
  name,
Then should'st thou live in an immortal
  style.
For though that Laura better limnèd be,
Suffice, thou shalt be loved as well as she!

XLIX

Care-charmer Sleep, son of the sable Night,
Brother to Death, in silent darkness born:
Relieve my anguish, and restore the light;
With dark forgetting of my care, return!
And let the day be time enough to mourn 5
The shipwreck of my ill-adventured youth:
Let waking eyes suffice to wail their scorn,
Without the torment of the night's untruth.
Cease, dreams, the images of day-desires,
To model forth the passions of the mor-
  row;   10
Never let rising sun approve you liars,
To add more grief to aggravate my sor-
  row.
Still let me sleep, embracing clouds in vain;
And never wake to feel the day's disdain.

L

Let others sing of Knights and Paladins
In agèd accents and untimely words;
Paint shadows in imaginary lines
Which well the reach of their high wits
  records·

But I must sing of thee, and those fair
  eyes   5
Authentic shall my verse in time to come;
When yet th' unborn shall say, 'Lo, where
  she lies
Whose beauty made him speak that else
  was dumb.'
These are the arcs, the trophies I erect,
That fortify thy name against old age;   10
And these thy sacred virtues must pro-
  tect
Against the dark, and Time's consuming
  rage.
Though the error of my youth in them ap-
  pear,
Suffice they show I lived and loved thee
  dear.

MICHAEL DRAYTON (1563–1631)

SONNETS FROM IDEA

TO THE READER OF THESE SONNETS

Into these loves, who but for passion looks,
At this first sight, here let him lay them
  by,
And seek elsewhere in turning other books,
Which better may his labor satisfy.
No far-fetched sigh shall ever wound my
  breast;   5
Love from mine eye a tear shall never
  wring;
Nor in 'Ah me's!' my whining sonnets
  drest!
A libertine! fantasticly I sing!
My verse is the true image of my mind,
Ever in motion, still desiring change;   10
And as thus, to variety inclined,
So in all humors sportively I range!
My Muse is rightly of the English strain,
That cannot long one fashion entertain.

IV

Bright Star of Beauty, on whose eyelids sit
A thousand nymph-like and enamored
  Graces,
The Goddesses of Memory and Wit,
Which there in order take their several
  places;
In whose dear bosom, sweet delicious Love
Lays down his quiver, which he once did
  bear,   6
Since he that blessèd paradise did prove;
And leaves his mother's lap, to sport him
  there.
Let others strive to entertain with words!
My soul is of a braver mettle made·   10

I hold that vile, which vulgar wit affords;
In me's that faith which time cannot in-
      vade!
Let what I praise be still made good by
      you!
Be you most worthy, whilst I am most
      true!

IX

As other men, so I myself, do muse
Why in this sort I wrest invention so?
And why these giddy metaphors I use,
Leaving the path the greater part do go?
I will resolve you. I am lunatic!   5
And ever this in madmen you shall find,
What they last thought of, when the brain
      grew sick,
In most distraction, they keep that in
      mind.
Thus talking idly, in this Bedlam fit,
Reason and I, you must conceive, are twain;
'Tis nine years now, since first I lost my
      wit.   11
Bear with me, then, though troubled be my
      brain!
What diet and correction, men distraught,
Not too far past, may to their wits be
      brought.

XX

An evil Spirit (your Beauty) haunts me
      still,
Wherewith, alas, I have been long possest;
Which ceaseth not to attempt me to each
      ill,
Nor give me once, but one poor minute's
      rest.
In me it speaks, whether I sleep or wake; 5
And when by means to drive it out I try,
With greater torments then it me doth take,
And tortures me in most extremity.
Before my face, it lays down my despairs,
And hastes me on unto a sudden death;   10
Now tempting me to drown myself in tears,
And then in sighing to give up my breath.
Thus am I still provoked to every evil,
By this good-wicked Spirit, sweet Angel-
      Devil.

XLIV

Whilst thus my pen strives to eternize thee,
Age rules my lines with wrinkles in my
      face,
Where, in the map of all my misery,
Is modeled out the world of my disgrace;
Whilst in despite of tyrannizing times,   5
Medea-like, I make thee young again.

Proudly thou scorn'st my world-outwearing
      rimes,
And murder'st Virtue with thy coy dis-
      dain!
And though in youth my youth untimely
      perish
To keep thee from oblivion and the grave,
Ensuing ages yet my rimes shall cherish,
Where I entombed, my better part shall
      save;   12
And though this earthly body fade and die,
My name shall mount upon Eternity!

LXI

Since there's no help, come, let us kiss and
      part!
Nay, I have done; you get no more of
      me!
And I am glad, yea, glad, with all my heart,
That thus so cleanly I myself can free.
Shake hands for ever! Cancel all our
      vows!
And when we meet at any time again,   5
Be it not seen in either of our brows,
That we one jot of former love retain!
Now at the last gasp of Love's latest
      breath,
When, his pulse failing, Passion speechless
      lies;   10
When Faith is kneeling by his bed of
      death,
And Innocence is closing up his eyes,—
Now, if thou wouldst, when all have given
      him over,
From death to life thou might'st him yet
      recover!

ODE XI

TO THE VIRGINIAN VOYAGE

You brave heroic minds,
Worthy your country's name,
    That honor still pursue;
    Go and subdue!
Whilst loitering hinds
Lurk here at home with shame.

Britons, you stay too long;
Quickly aboard bestow you!
    And with a merry gale
    Swell your stretched sail,   10
With vows as strong
As the winds that blow you!

Your course securely steer,
West-and-by-south forth keep!

Rocks, lee-shores, nor shoals,   15
When Eolus scowls,
You need not fear,
So absolute the deep.

And, cheerfully at sea,
Success you still entice,   20
  To get the pearl and gold;
  And ours to hold,
Virginia,
Earth's only Paradise.

Where Nature hath in store   25
Fowl, venison, and fish;
  And the fruitful'st soil,—
  Without your toil,
Three harvests more,
All greater than your wish.   30

And the ambitious vine
Crowns with his purple mass
  The cedar reaching high
  To kiss the sky,
The cypress, pine,   35
And useful sassafras.

To whom, the Golden Age
Still Nature's laws doth give:
  Nor other cares attend,
  But them to defend   40
From winter's rage,
That long there doth not live.

When as the luscious smell
Of that delicious land,
  Above the seas that flows,   45
  The clear wind throws,
Your hearts to swell,
Approaching the dear strand.

In kenning of the shore
(Thanks to God first given!)   50
  O you, the happiest men,
  Be frolic then!
Let cannons roar,
Frightening the wide heaven!

And in regions far,   55
Such heroes bring ye forth
  As those from whom we came!
  And plant our name
Under that star
Not known unto our North!   60

And as there plenty grows
The laurel everywhere,
  Apollo's sacred tree
  You may it see

A poet's brows   65
To crown, that may sing there.

Thy Voyages attend,
Industrious Hakluyt!
  Whose reading shall inflame
  Men to seek fame;   70
And much commend
To after times thy wit.

ODE XII

TO THE CAMBRO-BRITONS AND THEIR HARP HIS BALLAD OF AGINCOURT

Fair stood the wind for France,
When we our sails advance;
Nor now to prove our chance
  Longer will tarry;
But putting to the main,   5
At Caux, the mouth of Seine,
With all his martial train
  Landed King Harry.

And taking many a fort,
Furnished in warlike sort,   10
Marcheth towards Agincourt
  In happy hour;
Skirmishing, day by day,
With those that stopped his way,
Where the French general lay   15
  With all his power.

Which, in his height of pride,
King Henry to deride,
His ransom to provide,
  To the King sending;   20
Which he neglects the while,
As from a nation vile,
Yet, with an angry smile,
  Their fall portending.

And turning to his men,   25
Quoth our brave Henry then:
'Though they to one be ten
  Be not amazed!
Yet have we well begun:
Battles so bravely won   30
Have ever to the sun
  By Fame been raised!

'And for myself,' quoth he,
'This my full rest shall be:
England ne'er mourn for me,   35
  Nor more esteem me!
Victor I will remain.

Or on this earth lie slain;
Never shall she sustain
    Loss to redeem me!   40

'Poitiers and Cressy tell,
When most their pride did swell,
Under our swords they fell.
    No less our skill is,
Than when our Grandsire great,   45
Claiming the regal seat,
By many a warlike feat
    Lopped the French lilies.'

The Duke of York so dread
The eager vanward led;   50
With the main, Henry sped
    Amongst his henchmen;
Exeter had the rear,
A braver man not there!
O Lord, how hot they were   55
    On the false Frenchmen!

They now to fight are gone;
Armor on armor shone;
Drum now to drum did groan:
    To hear, was wonder;   60
That, with the cries they make,
The very earth did shake;
Trumpet to trumpet spake;
    Thunder to thunder.

Well it thine age became,   65
O noble Erpingham,
Which didst the signal aim
    To our hid forces!
When, from a meadow by,
Like a storm suddenly,   70
The English archery
    Stuck the French horses.

With Spanish yew so strong;
Arrows a cloth-yard long,
That like to serpents stung,   75
    Piercing the weather.
None from his fellow starts;
But, playing manly parts,
And like true English hearts,
    Stuck close together.   80

When down their bows they threw,
And forth their bilboes drew,
And on the French they flew:
    Not one was tardy.
Arms were from shoulders sent,   85
Scalps to the teeth were rent,
Down the French peasants went:
    Our men were hardy.

This while our noble King,
His broad sword brandishing,   90
Down the French host did ding,
    As to o'erwhelm it.
And many a deep wound lent;
His arms with blood besprent,
And many a cruel dent   95
    Bruisèd his helmet.

Gloucester, that duke so good,
Next of the royal blood,
For famous England stood
    With his brave brother.   100
Clarence, in steel so bright,
Though but a maiden knight,
Yet in that furious fight
    Scarce such another!

Warwick in blood did wade;   105
Oxford, the foe invade,
And cruel slaughter made,
    Still as they ran up.
Suffolk his axe did ply;
Beaumont and Willoughby   110
Bare them right doughtily;
    Ferrers, and Fanhope.

Upon Saint Crispin's Day
Fought was this noble fray;
Which Fame did not delay   115
    To England to carry.
O, when shall English men
With such acts fill a pen?
Or England breed again
    Such a King Harry?   120

CHRISTOPHER MARLOWE
(1564–1593)

HERO AND LEANDER

From THE FIRST SESTIAD

On Hellespont, guilty of true love's blood,
In view and opposite two cities stood,
Sea-borderers, disjoined by Neptune's
    might;
The one Abydos, the other Sestos hight.
At Sestos Hero dwelt; Hero the fair,   5
Whom young Apollo courted for her hair,
And offered as a dower his burning throne,
Where she should sit, for men to gaze upon.
The outside of her garments were of lawn,
The lining purple silk, with gilt stars
    drawn;   10

Her wide sleeves green, and bordered with
   a grove,
Where Venus in her naked glory strove
To please the careless and disdainful eyes
Of proud Adonis, that before her lies;
Her kirtle blue, whereon was many a stain,
Made with the blood of wretched lovers
   slain.   16
Upon her head she ware a myrtle wreath,
From whence her veil reached to the
   ground beneath;
Her veil was artificial flowers and leaves,
Whose workmanship both man and beast
   deceives.   20
Many would praise the sweet smell as she
   past,
When 'twas the odor which her breath forth
   cast;
And there, for honey, bees have sought in
   vain,
And, beat from thence, have lighted there
   again.
About her neck hung chains of pebble-
   stone,   25
Which, lightened by her neck, like dia-
   monds shone.
She ware no gloves; for neither sun nor
   wind
Would burn or parch her hands, but, to
   her mind,
Or warm or cool them, for they took de-
   light
To play upon those hands, they were so
   white.   30
Buskins of shells, all silvered, usèd she,
And branched with blushing coral to the
   knee;
Where sparrows perched of hollow pearl
   and gold,
Such as the world would wonder to behold:
Those with sweet water oft her handmaid
   fills,   35
Which as she went, would chirrup through
   the bills.
Some say, for her the fairest Cupid pined,
And, looking in her face, was strooken
   blind.
But this is true; so like was one the other,
As he imagined Hero was his mother;   40
And oftentimes into her bosom flew,
About her naked neck his bare arms threw,
And laid his childish head upon her breast,
And, with still panting rock, there took his
   rest.
So lovely-fair was Hero, Venus' nun,   45
As Nature wept, thinking she was undone,
Because she took more from her than she
   left,
And of such wondrous beauty her bereft:

Therefore, in sign her treasure suffered
   wrack,
Since Hero's time hath half the world been
   black.   50
   Amorous Leander, beautiful and young
(Whose tragedy divine Musæus sung),
Dwelt at Abydos; since him dwelt there
   none
For whom succeeding times make greater
   moan.
His dangling tresses, that were never shorn,
Had they been cut, and unto Colchos borne,
Would have allured the venturous youth of
   Greece   57
To hazard more than for the golden fleece.
Fair Cynthia wished his arms might be her
   sphere;
Grief makes her pale, because she moves
   not there.   60
His body was as straight as Circe's wand;
Jove might have sipt out nectar from his
   hand.
Even as delicious meat is to the taste,
So was his neck in touching, and surpast
The white of Pelops' shoulder: I could tell
   ye,   65
How smooth his breast was, and how white
   his belly;
And whose immortal fingers did imprint
That heavenly path with many a curious
   dint
That runs along his back; but my rude pen
Can hardly blazon forth the loves of men,
Much less of powerful gods: let it suffice
That my slack Muse sings of Leander's
   eyes;   72
Those orient cheeks and lips, exceeding his
That leapt into the water for a kiss
Of his own shadow, and, despising many,
Died ere he could enjoy the love of any.   76
Had wild Hippolytus Leander seen,
Enamored of his beauty had he been.
His presence made the rudest peasant melt,
That in the vast uplandish country dwelt;
The barbarous Thracian soldier, moved
   with naught,   81
Was moved with him, and for his favor
   sought.
Some swore he was a maid in man's attire,
For in his looks were all that men desire,—
A pleasant-smiling cheek, a speaking eye,   85
A brow for love to banquet royally;
And such as knew he was a man, would
   say,
'Leander, thou art made for amorous play;
Why art thou not in love, and loved of all?
Though thou be fair, yet be not thine own
   thrall.'   90
   The men of wealthy Sestos every year.

For his sake whom their goddess held so
dear,
Rose-cheeked Adonis, kept a solemn feast.
Thither resorted many a wandering guest
To meet their loves; such as had none at
all,   95
Came lovers home from this great festival;
For every street, like to a firmament,
Glistered with breathing stars, who, where
they went,
Frighted the melancholy earth, which
deemed
Eternal heaven to burn, for so it seemed 100
As if another Phaëton had got
The guidance of the sun's rich chariot.
But, far above the loveliest, Hero shined,
And stole away th' enchanted gazer's mind;
For like sea-nymphs' inveigling harmony,
So was her beauty to the standers by;   106
Nor that night-wandering, pale, and watery
star
(When yawning dragons draw her thirling
car
From Latmus' mount up to the gloomy sky,
Where, crowned with blazing light and
majesty,   110
She proudly sits) more over-rules the flood
Than she the hearts of those that near her
stood.
Even as, when gaudy nymphs pursue the
chase,
Wretched Ixion's shaggy-footed race,
Incensed with savage heat, gallop amain 115
From steep pine-bearing mountains to the
plain,
So ran the people forth to gaze upon her,
And all that viewed her were enamored on
her.
And as, in fury of a dreadful fight,
Their fellows being slain or put to flight,
Poor soldiers stand with fear of death
dead-strooken,   121
So at her presence all surprised and tooken,
Await the sentence of her scornful eyes;
He whom she favors lives; the other dies.
There might you see one sigh; another
rage;   125
And some, their violent passions to assuage,
Compile sharp satires; but, alas, too late!
For faithful love will never turn to hate.
And many, seeing great princes were
denied,
Pined as they went, and thinking on her
died.   130
In this feast-day — O cursèd day and
hour! —

Went Hero thorough Sestos, from her
tower
To Venus' temple, where unhappily,
As after chanced, they did each other
spy.
So fair a church as this had Venus none:
The walls were of discolored jasper-stone,
Wherein was Proteus carved; and over-
head   137
A lively vine of green sea-agate spread,
Where by one hand light-headed Bacchus
hung,
And with the other wine from grapes out-
wrung.   140
Of crystal shining fair the pavement was;
The town of Sestos called it Venus' glass:
There might you see the gods in sundry
shapes,
Committing heady riots, incest, rapes:
                    * * *
Blood-quaffing Mars, heaving the iron
net,   145
Which limping Vulcan and his Cyclops set;
Love kindling fire, to burn such towns as
Troy:
Silvanus weeping for the lovely boy
That now is turned into a cypress-tree,
Under whose shade the wood-gods love
to be.   150
And in the midst a silver altar stood:
There Hero, sacrificing turtles' blood,
Vailed to the ground, veiling her eyelids
close;
And modestly they opened as she rose.
Thence flew Love's arrow with the golden
head;   155
And thus Leander was enamorèd.
Stone-still he stood, and evermore he gazed,
Till with the fire that from his counte-
nance blazed
Relenting Hero's gentle heart was strook:
Such force and virtue hath an amorous
look.   160
   It lies not in our power to love or hate,
For will in us is over-ruled by fate.
When two are stript long ere the course
begin,
We wish that one should lose, the other
win;
And one especially do we affect   165
Of two gold ingots, like in each respect:
The reason no man knows, let it suffice,
What we behold is censured by our eyes.
Where both deliberate, the love is slight:
Who ever loved, that loved not at first
sight?   171

WILLIAM SHAKSPERE
(1564–1616)

From VENUS AND ADONIS

Lo, here the gentle lark, weary of rest,
From his moist cabinet mounts up on high,
And wakes the morning, from whose silver
breast
The sun ariseth in his majesty;
  Who doth the world so glorious behold 5
  That cedar-tops and hills seem burnished
  gold.

Venus salutes him with this fair good-morrow:
'O thou clear god, and patron of all light,
From whom each lamp and shining star
doth borrow
The beauteous influence that makes him
bright,   10
  There lives a son that sucked an earthly
  mother,
  May lend thee light, as thou dost lend to
  other.

This said, she hasteth to a myrtle grove,
Musing the morning is so much o'erworn,
And yet she hears no tidings of her love: 15
She hearkens for his hounds and for his
horn:
  Anon she hears them chant it lustily,
  And all in haste she coasteth to the cry.

And as she runs, the bushes in the way
Some catch her by the neck, some kiss her
face,   20
Some twine about her thigh to make her
stay:
She wildly breaketh from their strict embrace,
  Like a milch doe, whose swelling dugs
  do ache,
  Hasting to feed her fawn hid in some
  brake.

By this, she hears the hounds are at a bay;
Whereat she starts, like one that spies an
adder   26
Wreathed up in fatal folds just in his way,
The fear whereof doth make him shake and
shudder;
  Even so the timorous yelping of the
  hounds
  Appals her senses and her spirit con-
  founds.   30

For now she knows it is no gentle chase,
But the blunt boar, rough bear, or lion
proud,

Because the cry remaineth in one place,
Where fearfully the dogs exclaim aloud:
  Finding their enemy to be so curst, 35
  They all strain courtesy who shall cope
  him first.

This dismal cry rings sadly in her ear,
Through which it enters to surprise her
heart;
Who, overcome by doubt and bloodless fear,
With cold-pale weakness numbs each feel-
ing part: 40
  Like soldiers, when their captain once
  doth yield,
  They basely fly and dare not stay the
  field.

Thus stands she in a trembling ecstasy;
Till, cheering up her senses all dismayed,
She tells them 'tis a causeless fantasy, 45
And childish error, that they are afraid;
  Bids them leave quaking, bids them fear
  no more:—
  And with that word she spied the hunted
  boar,

Whose frothy mouth, bepainted all with
red,
Like milk and blood being mingled both together,   50
A second fear through all her sinews
spread,
Which madly hurries her she knows not
whither:
  This way she runs, and now she will no
  further,
  But back retires to rate the boar for
  murther.

A thousand spleens bear her a thousand
ways: 55
She treads the path that she untreads again;
Her more than haste is mated with delays,
Like the proceedings of a drunken brain,
  Full of respects, yet naught at all re-
  specting;
  In hand with all things, naught at all
  effecting.   60

Here kenneled in a brake she finds a
hound,
And asks the weary catitiff for his master,
And there another licking of his wound,
'Gainst venomed sores the only sovereign
plaster;
  And here she meets another sadly scowl-
  ing   65
  To whom she speaks, and he replies with
  howling.

When he hath ceased his ill-resounding
  noise,
Another flap-mouthed mourner, black and
  grim,
Against the welkin volleys out his voice,
Another and another answer him,   70
    Clapping their proud tails to the ground
      below,
    Shaking their scratched ears, bleeding as
      they go.

Look, how the world's poor people are
  amazed
At apparitions, signs, and prodigies,
Whereon with fearful eyes they long have
  gazed,   75
Infusing them with dreadful prophecies;
    So she at these sad signs draws up her
      breath
    And sighing it again, exclaims on Death.

'Hard-favored tyrant, ugly, meager, lean,
Hateful divorce of love,'—thus chides she
  Death,—   . 80
'Grim-grinning ghost, earth's worm, what
  dost thou mean
To stifle beauty and to steal his breath,
    Who when he lived, his breath and
      beauty set
    Gloss on the rose, smell to the violet?

'If he be dead,— O no, it cannot be,   85
Seeing his beauty, thou shouldst strike at
  it:—
O yes, it may; thou hast no eyes to see,
But hatefully at random dost thou hit.
    Thy mark is feeble age, but thy false dart
    Mistakes that aim and cleaves an in-
      fant's heart.   90

Hadst thou but bid beware, then he had
  spoke,
And, hearing him, thy power had lost his
  power.
The Destinies will curse thee for this
  stroke;
They bid thee crop a weed, thou pluck'st a
  flower:
    Love's golden arrow at him should have
      fled,   95
    And not Death's ebon dart, to strike him
      dead.

'Dost thou drink tears, that thou provok'st
  such weeping?
What may a heavy groan advantage thee?
Why hast thou cast into eternal sleeping
Those eyes that taught all other eyes to
  see?   100

Now Nature cares not for thy mortal
  vigor,
Since her best work is ruined with thy
  rigor.'

Here overcome, as one full of despair,
She vailed her eyelids, who, like sluices,
  stopt
The crystal tide that from her two cheeks
  fair   105
In the sweet channel of her bosom dropt;
    But through the flood-gates breaks the
      silver rain,
    And with his strong course opens them
      again.

O, how her eyes and tears did lend and
  borrow!
Her eyes seen in the tears, tears in her eye;
Both crystals, where they viewed each
  other's sorrow,
Sorrow that friendly sighs sought still to
  dry;   112
    But like a stormy day, now wind, now
      rain,
    Sighs dry her cheeks, tears make them
      wet again.

Variable passions throng her constant woe,
As striving who should best become her
  grief;   116
All entertained, each passion labors so,
That every present sorrow seemeth chief,
    But none is best: then join they all to-
      gether,
    Like many clouds consulting for foul
      weather.   120

By this, far off she hears some huntsman
  hallo;
A nurse's song ne'er pleased her babe so
  well:
The dire imagination she did follow
This sound of hope doth labor to expel;
    For now reviving joy bids her rejoice, 125
    And flatters her it is Adonis' voice.

Whereat her tears began to turn their tide,
Being prisoned in her eye like pearls in
  glass;
Yet sometimes falls an orient drop beside,
Which her cheek melts, as scorning it
  should pass,   130
    To wash the foul face of the sluttish
      ground,
    Who is but drunken when she seemeth
      drowned.

O hard-believing love, how strange it seems
Not to believe, and yet too credulous!
Thy weal and woe are both of them ex-
    tremes;   135
Despair and hope makes thee ridiculous:
  The one doth flatter thee in thoughts un-
    likely,
  In likely thoughts the other kills thee
    quickly.

Now she unweaves the web that she hath
    wrought;
Adonis lives, and Death is not to blame;
It was not she that called him all to naught:
Now she adds honors to his hateful name;
  She clepes him king of graves and grave
    for kings,   143
  Imperious supreme of all mortal things.

'No, no,' quoth she, 'sweet Death, I did
    but jest;   145
Yet pardon me I felt a kind of fear
When-as I met the boar, that bloody beast,
Which knows no pity, but is still severe;
  Then, gentle shadow,— truth I must con-
    fess,—
  I railed on thee, fearing my love's de-
    cease.   150

''Tis not my fault: the boar provoked my
    tongue;
Be wreaked on him, invisible commander;
'Tis he, foul creature, that hath done thee
    wrong;
I did but act, he's author of thy slander;
  Grief hath two tongues, and never
    woman yet   155
  Could rule them both without ten women's
    wit.'

Thus hoping that Adonis is alive,
Her rash suspect she doth extenuate;
And that his beauty may the better thrive,
With Death she humbly doth insinuate; 160
  Tells him of trophies, statues, tombs, and
    stories;
  His victories, his triumphs, and his
    glories.

'O Jove,' quoth she, 'how much a fool was
    I
To be of such a weak and silly mind
To wail his death who lives and must not
    die   165
Till mutual overthrow of mortal kind!
  For he being dead, with him is beauty
    slain,
  And, beauty dead, black chaos comes
    again.

'Fie, fie, fond love, thou art as full of fear
As one with treasure laden, hemmed with
    thieves;   170
Trifles, unwitnessèd with eye or ear,
Thy coward heart with false bethinking
    grieves.'
  Even at this word she hears a merry
    horn,
  Whereat she leaps that was but late for-
    lorn.

As falcon to the lure, away she flies; 175
The grass stoops not, she treads on it so
    light;
And in her haste unfortunately spies
The foul boar's conquest on her fair de
    light;
  Which seen, her eyes, as murdered with
    the view,
  Like stars ashamed of day, themselves
    withdrew;   180

Or, as the snail, whose tender horns being
    hit,
Shrinks backward in his shelly cave with
    pain,
And there, all smothered up, in shade doth
    sit,
Long after fearing to creep forth again;
  So, at his bloody view, her eyes are fled
  Into the deep dark cabins of her head: 186

Where they resign their office and their
    light
To the disposing of her troubled brain;
Who bids them still consort with ugly night,
And never wound the heart with looks
    again;   190
  Who, like a king perplexèd in his throne.
  By their suggestion gives a deadly groan,

Whereat each tributary subject quakes;
As when the wind, imprisoned in the
    ground,
Struggling for passage, earth's foundation
    shakes,   195
Which with cold terror doth men's minds
    confound.
  This mutiny each part doth so surprise
  That from their dark beds once more
    leap her eyes;

And, being opened, threw unwilling light
Upon the wide wound that the boar had
    trenched   200
In his soft flank; whose wonted lily white
With purple tears, that his wound wept,
    was drenched

No flower was nigh, no grass, herb, leaf,
  or weed,
But stole his blood and seemed with him
  to bleed.   204

This solemn sympathy poor Venus noteth;
Over one shoulder doth she hang her head;
Dumbly she passions, franticly she doteth;
She thinks he could not die, he is not dead:
  Her voice is stopt, her joints forget to
    bow;
  Her eyes are mad that they have wept
    till now.   210

Upon his hurt she looks so steadfastly,
That her sight dazzling makes the wound
  seem three;
And then she reprehends her mangling eye,
That makes more gashes where no breach
  should be:
  His face seems twain, each several limb
    is doubled;   215
  For oft the eye mistakes, the brain be-
    ing troubled.

'My tongue cannot express my grief for
  one,
And yet,' quoth she, 'behold two Adons
  dead!
My sighs are blown away, my salt tears
  gone,
Mine eyes are turned to fire, my heart to
  lead: 220
  Heavy heart's lead, melt at mine eyes'
    red fire!
  So shall I die by drops of hot desire.

'Alas, poor world, what treasure hast thou
  lost!
What face remains alive that's worth the
  viewing?
Whose tongue is music now? what canst
  thou boast   225
Of things long since, or anything ensuing?
  The flowers are sweet, their colors fresh
    and trim;
  But true-sweet beauty lived and died with
    him.

'Bonnet nor veil henceforth no creature
  wear!
Nor sun nor wind will ever strive to kiss
  you: 230
Having no fair to lose, you need not fear;
The sun doth scorn you and the wind doth
  hiss you:
  But when Adonis lived, sun and sharp
    air

Lurked like two thieves, to rob him of
  his fair.

'And therefore would he put his bonnet on,
Under whose brim the gaudy sun would
  peep;   236
The wind would blow it off and, being
  gone,
Play with his locks: then would Adonis
  weep;
  And straight, in pity of his tender years,
  They both would strive who first should
    dry his tears.   240

'To see his face the lion walked along
Behind some hedge, because he would not
  fear him;
To recreate himself when he hath sung,
The tiger would be tame and gently hear
  him;
  If he had spoke, the wolf would leave his
    prey   245
  And never fright the silly lamb that day.

'When he beheld his shadow in the brook,
The fishes spread on it their golden gills;
When he was by, the birds such pleasure
  took,
That some would sing, some other in their
  bills   250
  Would bring him mulberries and ripe-red
    cherries;
  He fed them with his sight, they him
    with berries.

'But this foul, grim, and urchin-snouted
  boar,
Whose downward eye still looketh for a
  grave,
Ne'er saw the beauteous livery that he wore;
Witness the entertainment that he gave: 256
  If he did see his face, why then I know
  He thought to kiss him, and hath killed
    him so.

''Tis true, 'tis true; thus was Adonis slain:
He ran upon the boar with his sharp spear,
Who did not whet his teeth at him again,
But by a kiss thought to persuade him
  there;   262
  And nuzzling in his flank, the loving
    swine
  Sheathed unaware the tusk in his soft
    groin.

'Had I been toothed like him, I must confess,   265
With kissing him I should have killed him
  first;

But he is dead, and never did he bless
My youth with his; the more am I accurst.'
  With this, she falleth in the place she
    stood,
  And stains her face with his congealèd
    blood.   270

She looks upon his lips, and they are pale;
She takes him by the hand, and that is cold;
She whispers in his ears a heavy tale,
As if they heard the woeful words she told;
  She lifts the coffer-lids that close his
    eyes,   275
  Where, lo, two lamps, burnt out, in dark-
    ness lies;

Two glasses, where herself herself beheld
A thousand times, and now no more re-
  flect;
Their virtue lost, wherein they late excelled,
And every beauty robbed of his effect: 280
  'Wonder of time,' quoth she, 'this is my
    spite,
  That, thou being dead, the day should yet
    be light.

'Since thou art dead, lo, here I prophesy:
Sorrow on love hereafter shall attend:
It shall be waited on with jealousy,   285
Find sweet beginning, but unsavory end,
  Ne'er settled equally, but high or low,
  That all love's pleasure shall not match
    his woe.

'It shall be fickle, false, and full of fraud,
Bud and be blasted in a breathing-while; 290
The bottom poison, and the top o'erstrawed
With sweets that shall the truest sight be-
  guile:
  The strongest body shall it make most
    weak,
  Strike the wise dumb and teach the fool
    to speak.

'It shall be sparing and too full of riot 295
Teaching decrepit age to tread the measures;
The staring ruffian shall it keep in quiet,
Pluck down the rich, enrich the poor with
  treasures;
  It shall be raging-mad and silly-mild,
  Make the young old, the old become a
    child.   300

'It shall suspect where is no cause of fear;
It shall not fear where it should most mis-
  trust;
It shall be merciful and too severe,
And most deceiving when it seems most
  just;

Perverse it shall be where it shows most
  toward;   305
Put fear to valor, courage to the coward,

'It shall be cause of war and dire events,
And set dissension 'twixt the son and sire;
Subject and servile to all discontents,
As dry combustious matter is to fire: 310
  Sith in his prime Death doth my love
    destroy,
  They that love best their loves shall not
    enjoy.'

By this, the boy that by her side lay killed
Was melted like a vapor from her sight,
And in his blood that on the ground lay
  spilled,   315
A purple flower sprung up, chequered with
  white,
  Resembling well his pale cheeks and the
    blood
  Which in round drops upon their white-
    ness stood.

She bows her head, the new-sprung flower
  to smell,
Comparing it to her Adonis' breath, 320
And says, within her bosom it shall dwell,
Since he himself is reft from her by death:
  She crops the stalk, and in the breach ap-
    pears
  Green dropping sap, which she compares
    to tears.

'Poor flower,' quoth she, 'this was thy
  father's guise —   325
Sweet issue of a more sweet-smelling sire —
For every little grief to wet his eyes:
To grow unto himself was his desire,
  And so 'tis thine; but know, it is as good
  To wither in my breast as in his blood.

'Here was thy father's bed, here in my
  breast;   331
Thou art the next of blood, and 'tis thy
  right:
Lo, in this hollow cradle take thy rest,
My throbbing heart shall rock thee day and
  night;
  There shall not be one minute in an
    hour   335
  Wherein I will not kiss my sweet love's
    flower.'

Thus weary of the world, away she hies,
And yokes her silver doves; by whose swift
  aid
Their mistress mounted through the empty
  skies

In her light chariot quickly is conveyed; 340
  Holding their course to Paphos, where
    their queen
  Means to immure herself and not be seen.

SONNETS

XII

When I do count the clock that tells the
    time,
And see the brave day sunk in hideous
    night;
When I behold the violet past prime,
And sable curls all silvered o'er with white;
When lofty trees I see barren of leaves, 5
Which erst from heat did canopy the herd,
And summer's green all girded up in
    sheaves
Borne on the bier with white and bristly
    beard,
Then of thy beauty do I question make,
That thou among the wastes of time must
    go,   10
Since sweets and beauties do themselves
    forsake
And die as fast as they see others grow;
And nothing 'gainst Time's scythe can make
    defence
Save breed, to brave him when he takes
    thee hence.

XV

When I consider every thing that grows
Holds in perfection but a little moment,
That this huge stage presenteth naught but
    shows
Whereon the stars in secret influence com-
    ment;
When I perceive that men as plants in-
    crease,   5
Cheerèd and checked even by the self-same
    sky,
Vaunt in their youthful sap, at height de-
    crease,
And wear their brave state out of memory;
Then the conceit of this inconstant stay
Sets you most rich in youth before my
    sight,   10
Where wasteful Time debateth with Decay,
To change your day of youth to sullied
    night;
And all in war with Time for love of you,
As he takes from you, I engraft you new.

XVIII

Shall I compare thee to a summer's day?
Thou art more lovely and more temperate:
Rough winds do shake the darling buds of
    May,
And summer's lease hath all too short a
    date:
Sometime too hot the eye of heaven shines,
And often is his gold complexion dimmed;
And every fair from fair sometime de-
    clines,   7
By chance or nature's changing course un-
    trimmed;
But thy eternal summer shall not fade
Nor lose possession of that fair thou
    owest;   10
Nor shall Death brag thou wander'st in his
    shade,
When in eternal lines to time thou growest:
So long as men can breathe or eyes can
    see,
So long lives this and this gives life to
    thee.

XXV

Let those who are in favor with their stars
Of public honor and proud titles boast,
Whilst I, whom fortune of such triumph
    bars,
Unlooked for joy in that I honor most.
Great princes' favorites their fair leaves
    spread   5
But as the marigold at the sun's eye,
And in themselves their pride lies buried,
For at a frown they in their glory die.
The painful warrior famoused for fight,
After a thousand victories once foiled,   10
Is from the book of honor razèd quite,
And all the rest forgot for which he toiled:
Then happy I, that love and am beloved
Where I may not remove nor be removed.

XXIX

When in disgrace with fortune and men's
    eyes,
I all alone beweep my outcast state
And trouble deaf heaven with my bootless
    cries
And look upon myself and curse my fate,
Wishing me like to one more rich in hope,
Featured like him, like him with friends
    possessed,   6
Desiring this man's art and that man's
    scope,
With what I most enjoy contented least;

Yet in these thoughts myself almost despising,
Haply I think on thee, and then my state,
Like to the lark at break of day arising   11
From sullen earth, sings hymns at heaven's gate;
For thy sweet love remembered such wealth brings
That then I scorn to change my state with kings.

XXX

When to the sessions of sweet silent thought
I summon up remembrance of things past,
I sigh the lack of many a thing I sought,
And with old woes new wail my dear time's waste:
Then can I drown an eye, unused to flow, 5
For precious friends hid in death's dateless night,
And weep afresh love's long since canceled woe,
And moan the expense of many a vanished sight:
Then can I grieve at grievances foregone,
And heavily from woe to woe tell o'er   10
The sad account of fore-bemoanèd moan,
Which I new pay as if not paid before.
But if the while I think on thee, dear friend,
All losses are restored and sorrows end.

XXXIII

Full many a glorious morning have I seen
Flatter the mountain-tops with sovereign eye,
Kissing with golden face the meadows green,
Gilding pale streams with heavenly alchemy;
Anon permit the basest clouds to ride   5
With ugly rack on his celestial face,
And from the forlorn world his visage hide,
Stealing unseen to west with this disgrace:
Even so my sun one early morn did shine
With all-triumphant splendor on my brow;
But out, alack! he was but one hour mine;
The region cloud hath masked him from me now.   12
Yet him for this my love no whit disdaineth;
Suns of the world may stain when heaven's sun staineth.

LIV

O, how much more doth beauty beauteous seem
By that sweet ornament which truth doth give!
The rose looks fair, but fairer we it deem
For that sweet odor which doth in it live.
The canker blooms have full as deep a dye
As the perfumèd tincture of the roses,   6
Hang on such thorns, and play as wantonly
When summer's breath their maskèd buds discloses;
But, for their virtue only is their show,
They live unwooed and unrespected fade, 10
Die to themselves. Sweet roses do not so;
Of their sweet deaths are sweetest odors made:
And so of you, beauteous and lovely youth,
When that shall fade, my verse distills your truth.

LV

Not marble, nor the gilded monuments
Of princes, shall outlive this powerful rime;
But you shall shine more bright in these contents
Than unswept stone besmeared with sluttish time.
When wasteful war shall statues overturn, 5
And broils root out the work of masonry,
Nor Mars his sword nor war's quick fire shall burn
The living record of your memory.
'Gainst death and all-oblivious enmity
Shall you pace forth; your praise shall still find room   10
Even in the eyes of all posterity
That wear this world out to the ending doom.
So, till the judgment that yourself arise,
You live in this, and dwell in lovers' eyes.

LX

Like as the waves make towards the pebbled shore,
So do our minutes hasten to their end;
Each changing place with that which goes before,
In sequent toil all forwards do contend.
Nativity, once in the main of light,   5
Crawls to maturity, wherewith being crowned,
Crookèd eclipses 'gainst his glory fight,
And Time that gave doth now his gift confound.
Time doth transfix the flourish set on youth
And delves the parallels in beauty's brow,
Feeds on the rarities of nature's truth,   11
And nothing stands but for his scythe to mow:
And yet to times in hope my verse shall stand,
Praising thy worth, despite his cruel hand.

LXIV

When I have seen by Time's fell hand de-
faced
The rich proud cost of outworn buried
age;
When sometime lofty towers I see down-
razed
And brass eternal slave to mortal rage;
When I have seen the hungry ocean gain 5
Advantage on the kingdom of the shore,
And the firm soil win of the watery main,
Increasing store with loss and loss with
store;
When I have seen such interchange of state,
Or state itself confounded to decay; 10
Ruin hath taught me thus to ruminate,
That Time will come and take my love
away.
This thought is as a death, which cannot
choose
But weep to have that which it fears to
lose.

LXV

Since brass, nor stone, nor earth, nor bound-
less sea,
But sad mortality o'er-sways their power,
How with this rage shall beauty hold a
plea,
Whose action is no stronger than a flower?
O, how shall summer's honey breath hold
out 5
Against the wreckful siege of battering
days,
When rocks impregnable are not so stout,
Nor gates of steel so strong, but Time de-
cays?
O fearful meditation! where, alack,
Shall Time's best jewel from Time's chest
lie hid? 10
Or what strong hand can hold his swift
foot back?
Or who his spoil of beauty can forbid?
O, none, unless this miracle have might,
That in black ink my love may still shine
bright.

LXVI

Tired with all these, for restful death I
cry,—
As, to behold desert a beggar born,
And needy nothing trimmed in jollity,
And purest faith unhappily forsworn,
And gilded honor shamefully misplaced, 5
And maiden virtue rudely strumpeted,
And right perfection wrongfully disgraced,
And strength by limping sway disablèd,
And art made tongue-tied by authority,

And folly doctor-like controlling skill, 10
And simple truth miscalled simplicity,
And captive good attending captain ill:
Tired with all these, from these would I
be gone,
Save that, to die, I leave my love alone.

LXXI

No longer mourn for me when I am dead
Than you shall hear the surley sullen bell
Give warning to the world that I am fled
From this vile world, with vilest worms to
dwell:
Nay, if you read this line, remember not 5
The hand that writ it; for I love you so
That I in your sweet thoughts would be
forgot
If thinking on me then should make you
woe.
O, if, I say, you look upon this verse
When I perhaps compounded am with clay,
Do not so much as my poor name re-
hearse, 11
But let your love even with my life decay.
Lest the wise world should look into your
moan
And mock you with me after I am gone.

LXXIII

That time of year thou mayst in me behold
When yellow leaves, or none, or few, do
hang
Upon those boughs which shake against the
cold,
Bare ruined choirs, where late the sweet
birds sang.
In me thou see'st the twilight of such day
As after sunset fadeth in the west, 6
Which by and by black night doth take
away,
Death's second self, that seals up all in
rest.
In me thou see'st the glowing of such fire
That on the ashes of his youth doth lie, 10
As the death-bed whereon it must expire,
Consumed with that which it was nourished
by.
This thou perceiv'st, which makes thy love
more strong,
To love that well which thou must leave
ere long.

LXXVI

Why is my verse so barren of new pride,
So far from variation or quick change?
Why with the time do I not glance aside
To new-found methods and to compounds
strange?

Why write I still all one, ever the same, 5
And keep invention in a noted weed,
That every word doth almost tell my name,
Showing their birth and where they did
proceed?
O, know, sweet love, I always write of
you,
And you and love are still my argument; 10
So all my best is dressing old words new,
Spending again what is already spent:
For as the sun is daily new and old,
So is my love still telling what is told.

XCVII

How like a winter hath my absence been
From thee, the pleasure of the fleeting year!
What freezings have I felt, what dark days
seen!
What old December's bareness everywhere!
And yet this time removed was summer's
time, 5
The teeming autumn, big with rich increase,
Bearing the wanton burden of the prime,
Like widowed wombs after their lord's de-
cease:
Yet this abundant issue seemed to me
But hope of orphans and unfathered fruit;
For summer and his pleasures wait on thee,
And, thou away, the very birds are mute; 12
Or, if they sing, 'tis with so dull a cheer
That leaves look pale, dreading the winter's
near.

XCVIII

From you have I been absent in the spring,
When proud-pied April dressed in all his
trim
Hath put a spirit of youth in every thing,
That heavy Saturn laughed and leaped with
him.
Yet nor the lays of birds nor the sweet
smell 5
Of different flowers in odor and in hue
Could make me any summer's story tell,
Or from their proud lap pluck them where
they grew;
Nor did I wonder at the lily's white,
Nor praise the deep vermilion in the rose;
They were but sweet, but figures of de-
light, 11
Drawn after you, you pattern of all those.
Yet seemed it winter still, and, you away,
As with your shadow, I with these did play.

XCIX

The forward violet thus did I chide:
Sweet thief. whence didst thou steal thy
sweet that smells

If not from my love's breath? The purple
pride
Which on thy soft cheek for complexion
dwells
In my love's veins thou hast too grossly
dyed. 5
The lily I condemnèd for thy hand,
And buds of marjoram had stol'n thy hair.
The roses fearfully on thorns did stand,
One blushing shame, another white despair;
A third, nor red nor white, had stol'n of
both 10
And to his robbery had annexed thy breath;
But, for his theft, in pride of all his growth
A vengeful canker eat him up to death.
More flowers I noted, yet I none could see
But sweet or color it had stol'n from thee.

CIV

To me, fair friend, you never can be old,
For as you were when first your eye I eyed,
Such seems your beauty still. Three win-
ters cold
Have from the forests shook three sum-
mers' pride,
Three beauteous springs to yellow autumn
turned 5
In process of the seasons have I seen,
Three April perfumes in three hot Junes
burned
Since first I saw you fresh, which yet are
green.
Ah! yet doth beauty, like a dial-hand,
Steal from his figure and no pace perceived;
So your sweet hue, which methinks still
doth stand, 11
Hath motion and mine eye may be deceived:
For fear of which, hear this, thou age un-
bred:
Ere you were born was beauty's summer
dead.

CVI

When in the chronicle of wasted time
I see descriptions of the fairest wights,
And beauty making beautiful old rime
In praise of ladies dead and lovely knights,
Then, in the blazon of sweet beauty's
best, 5
Of hand, of foot, of lip, of eye, of brow,
I see their antique pen would have ex-
pressed
Even such a beauty as you master now.
So all their praises are but prophecies
Of this our time, all you prefiguring; 10
And, for they looked but with divining
eyes,
They had not skill enough your worth to
sing:

For we, which now behold these present
days,
Have eyes to wonder, but lack tongues to
praise.

CVII

Not mine own fears, nor the prophetic soul
Of the wide world dreaming on things to
come,
Can yet the lease of my true love control,
Supposed as forfeit to a confined doom.
The mortal moon hath her eclipse endured
And the sad augurs mock their own pre-
sage;   6
Incertainties now crown themselves assured
And peace proclaims olives of endless age.
Now with the drops of this most balmy
time
My love looks fresh, and Death to me sub-
scribes,   10
Since, spite of him, I'll live in this poor
rime,
While he insults o'er dull and speechless
tribes:
And thou in this shalt find thy monument,
When tyrants' crests and tombs of brass
are spent.

CIX

O, never say that I was false of heart,
Though absence seemed my flame to qual-
ify.
As easy might I from myself depart
As from my soul, which in thy breast doth
lie:
That is my home of love: if I have ranged,
Like him that travels I return again,   6
Just to the time, not with the time ex-
changed,
So that myself bring water for my stain.
Never believe, though in my nature reigned
All frailties that besiege all kinds of blood,
That it could so preposterously be stained,
To leave for nothing all thy sum of good;
For nothing this wide universe I call,   13
Save thou, my rose; in it thou art my all.

CX

Alas, 'tis true I have gone here and there
And made myself a motley to the view,
Gored mine own thoughts, sold cheap what
is most dear,
Made old offences of affections new;
Most true it is that I have looked on truth
Askance and strangely; but, by all above,   6
These blenches gave my heart another
youth,
And worse essays proved thee my best of
love.

Now all is done, have what shall have no
end:
Mine appetite I never more will grind   10
On newer proof, to try an older friend,
A god in love, to whom I am confined.
Then give me welcome, next my heaven the
best,
Even to thy pure and most most loving
breast.

CXI

O, for my sake do you with Fortune chide,
The guilty goddess of my harmful deeds,
That did not better for my life provide
Than public means which public manners
breeds
Thence comes it that my name receives a
brand,   5
And almost thence my nature is subdued
To what it works in, like the dyer's hand.
Pity me then and wish I were renewed;
Whilst, like a willing patient, I will drink
Potions of eisel 'gainst my strong infec-
tion;   10
No bitterness that I will bitter think,
Nor double penance, to correct correction
Pity me then, dear friend, and I assure ye
Even that your pity is enough to cure me.

CXVI

Let me not to the marriage of true minds
Admit impediments. Love is not love
Which alters when it alteration finds,
Or bends with the remover to remove:
O, no! it is an ever-fixèd mark   5
That looks on tempests and is never shaken;
It is the star to every wandering bark,
Whose worth's unknown, although his
height be taken.
Love's not Time's fool, though rosy lips
and cheeks
Within his bending sickle's compass come;
Love alters not with his brief hours and
weeks,   11
But bears it out even to the edge of doom.
If this be error and upon me proved,
I never writ, nor no man ever loved.

CXIX

What potions have I drunk of Siren tears,
Distilled from limbecks foul as hell within,
Applying fears to hopes and hopes to fears,
Still losing when I saw myself to win!
What wretched errors hath my heart com-
mitted,
Whilst it hath thought itself so blessèd
never!
How have mine eyes out of their spheres
been fitted

In the distraction of this madding fever!
O benefit of ill! now I find true
That better is by evil still made better;   10
And ruined love, when it is built anew,
Grows fairer than at first, more strong, far
     greater.
So I return rebuked to my content,
And gain by ills thrice more than I have
     spent.

CXXVIII

How oft, when thou, my music, music
     play'st,
Upon that blessèd wood whose motion
     sounds
With thy sweet fingers, when thou gently
     sway'st
The wiry concord that mine ear confounds,
Do I envy those jacks that nimble leap   5
To kiss the tender inward of thy hand,
Whilst my poor lips, which should that har-
     vest reap,
At the wood's boldness by thee blushing
     stand!
To be so tickled, they would change their
     state
And situation with those dancing chips,   10
O'er whom thy fingers walk with gentle
     gait,
Making dead wood more blest than living
     lips.
Since saucy jacks so happy are in this,
Give them thy fingers, me thy lips to kiss.

CXXX

My mistress' eyes are nothing like the sun;
Coral is far more red than her lips' red;
If snow be white, why then her breasts are
     dun;
If hairs be wires, black wires grow on her
     head.
I have seen roses damasked, red and white,
But no such roses see I in her cheeks;   6
And in some perfumes is there more de-
     light
Than in the breath that from my mistress
     reeks.
I love to hear her speak, yet well I know
That music hath a far more pleasing sound;
I grant I never saw a goddess go;   10
My mistress, when she walks, treads on the
     ground:
And yet, by heaven, I think my love as rare
As any she belied with false compare.

CXLVI

Poor soul, the center of my sinful earth,
Thrall to these rebel powers that thee
     array

Why dost thou pine within and suffer
     dearth,
Painting thy outward walls so costly gay?
Why so large cost, having so short a lease,
Dost thou upon thy fading mansion spend?
Shall worms, inheritors of this excess,   5
Eat up thy charge? is this thy body's end?
Then, soul, live thou upon thy servant's loss,
And let that pine to aggravate thy store;   10
Buy terms divine in selling hours of dross;
Within be fed, without be rich no more:
So shalt thou feed on Death, that feeds on
     men,
And Death once dead, there's no more
     dying then.

SONGS FROM THE PLAYS

From LOVE'S LABOR'S LOST

When icicles hang by the wall,
     And Dick the shepherd blows his nail,
And Tom bears logs into the hall,
     And milk comes frozen home in pail,
When blood is nipped and ways be foul,   5
Then nightly sings the staring owl,
'Tu-whit, tu-who!' a merry note,
While greasy Joan doth keel the pot.

When all aloud the wind doth blow,
     And coughing drowns the parson's saw,   10
And birds sit brooding in the snow,
     And Marian's nose looks red and raw,
When roasted crabs hiss in the bowl,
Then nightly sings the staring owl,
'Tu-whit, tu-who!' a merry note,   15
While greasy Joan doth keel the pot

From TWO GENTLEMEN OF VERONA

Who is Silvia? what is she,
     That all our swains commend her?
Holy, fair, and wise is she;
     The heaven such grace did lend her,
That she might admirèd be.   5

Is she kind as she is fair?
     For beauty lives with kindness.
Love doth to her eyes repair
     To help him of his blindness,
And, being helped, inhabits there.   10

Then to Silvia let us sing,
     That Silvia is excelling;
She excels each mortal thing
     Upon the dull earth dwelling:
To her let us garlands bring.   15

From THE MERCHANT OF VENICE

Tell me, where is fancy bred,
Or in the heart, or in the head?
How begot, how nourishèd?
    Reply, reply.
It is engendered in the eyes,   5
With gazing fed; and fancy dies
In the cradle where it lies:
Let us all ring fancy's knell;
I 'll begin it,— Ding-dong, bell.
        Ding, dong, bell.   10

From AS YOU LIKE IT

Under the greenwood tree
Who loves to lie with me,
And turn his merry note
Unto the sweet bird's throat,
Come hither! come hither! come hither!   5
    Here shall he see
    No enemy
But winter and rough weather.

Who doth ambition shun
And loves to live i' the sun,   10
Seeking the food he eats
And pleased with what he gets,
Come hither! come hither! come hither!
    Here shall he see
    No enemy   15
But winter and rough weather.

From AS YOU LIKE IT

Blow, blow, thou winter wind!
Thou art not so unkind
As man's ingratitude;
Thy tooth is not so keen,
Because thou art not seen,   5
Although thy breath be rude.

Heigh ho! sing, heigh ho! unto the green
    holly:
Most friendship is feigning, most loving
    mere folly:
    Then, heigh ho, the holly!
    This life is most jolly.   10

Freeze, freeze, thou bitter sky!
That dost not bite so nigh
    As benefits forgot;
Though thou the waters warp,
Thy sting is not so sharp   15
    As friend remembered not.

Heigh ho! sing, heigh ho! etc.

From MUCH ADO ABOUT NOTHING

Sigh no more, ladies, sigh no more!
Men were deceivers ever.

One foot in sea and one on shore,
    To one thing constant never:
Then sigh not so, but let them go,   5
    And be you blithe and bonny,
Converting all your sounds of woe
    Into Hey nonny, nonny!

Sing no more ditties, sing no moe
    Of dumps so dull and heavy!   10
The fraud of men was ever so,
    Since summer first was leafy:
Then sigh not so, but let them go,
    And be you blithe and bonny,
Converting all your sounds of woe   15
    Into Hey nonny, nonny!

From TWELFTH NIGHT

O Mistress mine, where are you roaming?
O, stay and hear; your true love 's coming,
    That can sing both high and low:
Trip no further, pretty sweeting,
Journeys end in lovers meeting,   5
    Every wise man's son doth know.

What is love? 't is not hereafter;
Present mirth hath present laughter;
    What 's to come is still unsure:
In delay there lies no plenty;   10
Then come kiss me, sweet and twenty,
    Youth 's a stuff will not endure.

From MEASURE FOR MEASURE

Take, O, take those lips away,
    That so sweetly were forsworn;
And those eyes, the break of day,
    Lights that do mislead the morn:
But my kisses bring again,   5
        Bring again;
Seals of love, but sealed in vain,
        Sealed in vain!

From CYMBELINE

Hark, hark! the lark at heaven's gate sings,
    And Phœbus 'gins arise,
His steeds to water at those springs
    On chaliced flowers that lies;
And winking Mary-buds begin
    To ope their golden eyes:
With every thing that pretty is,
    My lady sweet, arise!
        Arise, arise!

From CYMBELINE

Fear no more the heat o' th' sun,
    Nor the furious winter's rages;
Thou thy worldly task hast done,
    Home art gone, and ta'en thy wages:

Golden lads and girls all must,   5
As chimney-sweepers, come to dust.

Fear no more the frown o' th' great;
  Thou art past the tyrant's stroke;
Care no more to clothe and eat;
  To thee the reed is as the oak: 10
The Scepter, Learning, Physic, must
All follow this, and come to dust.

Fear no more the lightning-flash,
  Nor th' all-dreaded thunder-stone;
Fear not slander, censure rash;   15
  Thou hast finished joy and moan:
All lovers young, all lovers must
Consign to thee, and come to dust.

No exorciser harm thee!
  Nor no witchcraft charm thee!   20
Ghost unlaid forbear thee!
  Nothing ill come near thee!
Quiet consummation have;
And renownèd be thy grave!

FROM THE TEMPEST
ARIEL'S SONG

Full fathom five thy father lies:
  Of his bones are coral made;
Those are pearls that were his eyes;
  Nothing of him that doth fade
But doth suffer a sea-change   5
Into something rich and strange.
Sea-nymphs hourly ring his knell:
                          Ding-dong!
Hark! now I hear them,—Ding-dong, bell!

ENGLAND'S HELICON (1600)
PHYLLIDA AND CORYDON

In the merry month of May,
In a morn by break of day,
Forth I walked by the wood-side,
When as May was in her pride:
There I spièd all alone,   5
Phyllida and Corydon.
Much ado there was, God wot!
He would love and she would not.
She said, never man was true;
He said, none was false to you.   10
He said, he had loved her long;
She said, love should have no wrong.
Corydon would kiss her then;
She said, maids must kiss no men,
Till they did for good and all;   15
Then she made the shepherd call
All the heavens to witness truth:
Never loved a truer youth.

Thus with many a pretty oath,
Yea and nay, and faith and troth,   20
Such as silly shepherds use
When they will not love abuse,
Love which had been long deluded,
Was with kisses sweet concluded;
And Phyllida, with garlands gay,   25
Was made the Lady of the May.
                          N. BRETON

AS IT FELL UPON A DAY

As it fell upon a day,
In the merry month of May,
Sitting in a pleasant shade,
Which a group of myrtles made,
Beasts did leap and birds did sing,   5
Trees did grow and plants did spring,
Everything did banish moan,
Save the nightingale alone,
She, poor bird, as all forlorn,
Leaned her breast against a thorn,   10
And there sung the dolefull'st ditty,
That to hear it was great pity.
'Fie, fie, fie!' now would she cry;
'Teru, teru!' by-and-by.
That to hear her so complain   15
Scarce I could from tears refrain;
For her griefs so lively shown
Made me think upon mine own.
Ah, thought I, thou mourn'st in vain,
None takes pity on thy pain.   20
Senseless trees, they cannot hear thee;
Ruthless beasts, they will not cheer thee;
King Pandion he is dead,
All thy friends are lapped in lead;
All thy fellow birds do sing,   25
Careless of thy sorrowing;
Even so, poor bird, like thee,
None alive will pity me.
                          IGNOTO

TO COLIN CLOUT

Beauty sat bathing in a spring,
  Where fairest shades did hide her;
The winds blew calm, the birds did sing,
  The cool streams ran beside her.
My wanton thoughts enticed mine eye,   5
  To see what was forbidden,
But better memory said, fie:
  So, vain desire was chidden.
  Hey nonny, nonny, etc.

Into a slumber then I fell,   10
  When fond Imagination
Seemed to see, but could not tell,
  Her feature or her fashion.
But even as babes in dreams do smile,
  And sometimes fall a-weeping,   15

So I awaked, as wise this while
As when I fell a-sleeping.
Hey nonny, nonny, etc.

SHEPHERD TONY

HAPPY SHEPHERDS, SIT AND SEE

Happy shepherds, sit and see,
　　With joy,
　The peerless wight
For whose sake Pan keeps from ye
　　　　Annoy,　　　　　　　5
　And gives delight,
Blessing this pleasant spring.
Her praises must I sing;
List, you swains, list to me,
The whiles your flocks feeding be.　10

First, her brow a beauteous globe
　　I deem,
　And golden hair;
And her cheek Aurora's robe
　　　Doth seem,　　　　　15
　But far more fair.
Her eyes like stars are bright,
And dazzle with their light;
Rubies her lips to see,
But to taste nectar they be.　　20

Orient pearls her teeth, her smile
　　Doth link
　The Graces three;
Her white neck doth eyes beguile
　　　To think　　　　　25
　It ivory.
Alas! her lily hand
How it doth me command!
Softer silk none can be,
And whiter milk none can see.　30

Circe's wand is not so straight
　　As is
　Her body small;
But two pillars bear the weight
　　　Of this　　　　　35
　Majestic hall.
Those be, I you assure,
Of alabaster pure,
Polished fine in each part;
Ne'er Nature yet showed like art.　40

How shall I her pretty tread
　　Express,
　When she doth walk?
Scarce she does the primrose head
　　　Depress,　　　　45
　Or tender stalk
Of blue-veined violets.

Whereon her foot she sets.
Virtuous she is, for we find
In body fair beauteous mind.　　50

Live fair Amargana still
　　　Extolled
　In all my rime;
Hand want art, when I want will
　　　T' unfold　　　　55
　Her worth divine.
But now my muse doth rest,
Despair closed in my breast.
Of the valor I sing;
Weak faith that no hope doth
　　bring.　　　　　　60

W. H.

THE SHEPHERD'S COMMENDATION
OF HIS NYMPH

What shepherd can express
The favor of her face,
To whom in this distress
I do appeal for grace?
　A thousand Cupids fly　　　5
　About her gentle eye.

From which each throws a dart
That kindleth soft sweet fire
Within my sighing heart,
Possessèd by desire;　　　　10
　No sweeter life I try
　Than in her love to die.

The lily in the field,
That glories in his white,
For pureness now must yield,　15
And render up his right;
　Heaven pictured in her face
　Doth promise joy and grace.

Fair Cynthia's silver light,
That beats on running streams,　20
Compares not with her white,
Whose hairs are all sunbeams.
　So bright my nymph doth shine
　As day unto my eyne.

With this there is a red,　　25
Exceeds the damask-rose,
Which in her cheeks is spread,
Where every favor grows;
　In sky there is no star,
　But she surmounts it far.　30

When Phœbus from the bed
Of Thetis doth arise,
The morning blushing red,
In fair carnation-wise,
　He shows in my nymph's face　35
　As queen of every grace

This pleasant lily white,
This taint of roseate red,
This Cynthia's silver light,
This sweet fair Dea spread,   40
  These sunbeams in mine eye,
  These beauties make me die.
                    EARL OF OXFORD

THE HERDMAN'S HAPPY LIFE

What pleasure have great princes
  More dainty to their choice
Than herdmen wild, who careless
  In quiet life rejoice?
And fortune's fate not fearing,   5
Sing sweet in summer morning.

Their dealings plain and rightful,
  Are void of all deceit;
They never know how spiteful
  It is to kneel and wait   10
On favorite presumptuous,
Whose pride is vain and sumptuous.

All day their flocks each tendeth,
  At night they take their rest,
More quiet than who sendeth   15
  His ship into the east,
Where gold and pearl are plenty,
But getting very dainty.

For lawyers and their pleading,
  They 'steem it not a straw;   20
They think that honest meaning,
  Is of itself a law;
Where conscience judgeth plainly,
They spend no money vainly.

Oh, happy who thus liveth!   25
  Not caring much for gold;
With clothing which sufficeth,
  To keep him from the cold.
Though poor and plain his diet,
Yet merry it is and quiet.   30
        OUT OF MR. BIRD'S SET SONGS

A NYMPH'S DISDAIN OF LOVE

'Hey, down, a down!' did Dian sing,
  Amongst her virgins sitting;
'Than love there is no vainer thing,
  For maidens most unfitting.'
And so think I, with a down, down, derry.

When women knew no woe,   6
  But lived themselves to please,
Men's feigning guiles they did not know,
  The ground of their disease.
Unborn was false suspect,   10
  No thought of jealousy;
From wanton toys and fond affect.

The virgin's life was free.
'Hey, down, a down!' did Dian sing, etc.

At length men usèd charms,   15
  To which what maids gave ear,
Embracing gladly endless harms,
  Anon enthrallèd were.
Thus women welcomed woe,
  Disguised in name of love,   20
A jealous hell, painted show:
  So shall they find that prove.
'Hey, down, a down!' did Dian sing,
  Amongst her virgins sitting;
'Than love there is no vainer thing,   25
  For maidens most unfitting.'
And so think I, with a down, down, derry.
                            IGNOTO

ROSALIND'S MADRIGAL

Love in my bosom like a bee,
  Doth suck his sweet;
Now with his wings he plays with me,
  Now with his feet.
Within mine eyes he makes his nest,   5
  His bed amidst my tender breast;
My kisses are his daily feast,
And yet he robs me of my rest.
  Ah, wanton, will ye?

And if I sleep, then percheth he,   10
  With pretty slight,
And makes his pillow of my knee,
  The livelong night.
Strike I my lute, he tunes the string;
He music plays if I but sing;   15
He lends me every lovely thing;
Yet cruel he my heart doth sting.
  Whist, wanton, still ye!

Else I with roses every day
  Will whip ye hence,   20
And bind ye, when ye long to play,
  For your offence.
I 'll shut my eyes to keep ye in,
I 'll make you fast it for your sin,
I 'll count your power not worth a pin, 25
Alas! what hereby shall I win
  If he gainsay me?

What if I beat the wanton boy
  With many a rod?
He will repay me with annoy,   30
  Because a god.
Then sit thou safely on my knee,
And let thy bower my bosom be;
Lurk in mine eyes, I like of thee.
O Cupid! so thou pity me,   35
  Spare not, but play thee.
                        THOMAS LODGE

SEVENTEENTH CENTURY LYRICS

Among the lyrics of the earlier part of the seventeenth century, one discerns, somewhat clearly, at least three poetical manners, which emanated, respectively, from Edmund Spenser, Ben Jonson, and John Donne. The sensuous beauty, playful imagery, and fluent melody of Spenser are clearly present in the poems of William Browne and George Wither. The fine finish, poise, and chastened sweetness of Jonson are a refining influence in the shorter lyrics of Robert Herrick, Thomas Carew, John Suckling, and Richard Lovelace. In John Donne, incisive and subtle thinking finds fantastic, and sometimes harsh, expression in far-fetched analogies, mystifying metaphors, and dimly suggestive images. The poetical apparatus of Donne, often, and his fancy, still more often, are essential in the passionate, soaring, and mystical outbursts of George Herbert, Richard Crashaw, and Henry Vaughan. One notices, however, that Spenser, Jonson, and Donne did not exclusively dominate the poetical output of their conscious or unconscious disciples.

Toward the middle of the century appears a new influence in poetical form, the 'heroic,' or 'closed,' couplet, practiced by Edmund Waller, John Denham, Abraham Cowley, and Andrew Marvell. This verse-form, best adapted to epic and satire, had no important influence upon lyric, except, indirectly, through repression.

THOMAS CAMPION (d. 1619)

CHANCE AND CHANGE

What if a day, or a month, or a year,
Crown thy delights, with a thousand sweet
  contentings!
Cannot a chance of a night, or an hour,
Cross thy desires, with as many sad torment-
  ings?
Fortune, honor, beauty, youth,   5
  Are but blossoms dying!
Wanton pleasure, doting love,
  Are but shadows flying!
All our joys are but toys;
  Idle thoughts deceiving!   10
None have power, of an hour,
  In their life's bereaving.

Earth's but a point to the world; and a
  man
Is but a point to the world's comparèd
  center!
Shall then, a point of a point be so vain
As to triumph in a silly point's adventure!
All is hazard that we have!   17
  There is nothing biding!
Days of pleasure are like streams,
  Through fair meadows gliding!   20
Weal and woe, Time doth go!
  Time is never turning!
Secret fates guide our states;
  Both in mirth and mourning!

BASIA

Turn back, you wanton flyer,
And answer my desire
  With mutual greeting.
Yet bend a little nearer,—
True beauty still shines clearer   5
  In closer meeting!
Hearts with hearts delighted
Should strive to be united,
Each other's arms with arms enchaining,—
  Hearts with a thought,   10
Rosy lips with a kiss still entertaining.

What harvest half so sweet is
As still to reap the kisses
  Grown ripe in sowing?
And straight to be receiver   15
Of that which thou art giver,
  Rich in bestowing?
There's no strict observing
Of times' or seasons' swerving,
There is ever one fresh spring abiding;— 20
Then what we sow with our lips
Let us reap, love's gains dividing.

A RENUNCIATION

Thou art not fair, for all thy red and white,
  For all those rosy ornaments in thee,—
Thou art not sweet, though made of mere
  delight,

Nor fair, nor sweet — unless thou pity
    me!
I will not soothe thy fancies; thou shalt
    prove   5
That beauty is no beauty without love.

Yet love not me, nor seek not to allure
    My thoughts with beauty, were it more
        divine:
Thy smiles and kisses I cannot endure,
    I 'll not be wrapped up in those arms of
        thine: 10
Now show it, if thou be a woman
    right —
Embrace and kiss and love me, in de-
    spite!

SIC TRANSIT

Come, cheerful day, part of my life to me;
    For while thou view'st me with thy fading
        light
Part of my life doth still depart with thee,
    And I still onward haste to my last
        night:
Time's fatal wings do ever forward fly — 5
So every day we live a day we die.

But O ye nights, ordained for barren rest,
    How are my days deprived of life in
        you
When heavy sleep my soul hath dispossest,
    By feignèd death life sweetly to renew!
Part of my life in that, you life deny: 11
So every day we live, a day we die.

BEN JONSON (1573?–1637)

SONG TO CELIA

Drink to me only with thine eyes,
    And I will pledge with mine;
Or leave a kiss but in the cup,
    And I 'll not look for wine.
The thirst that from the soul doth rise   5
    Doth ask a drink divine;
But might I of Jove's nectar sup,
    I would not change for thine.

I sent thee late a rosy wreath,
    Not so much honoring thee   10
As giving it a hope, that there
    It could not withered be.
But thou thereon didst only breathe,
    And sent'st it back to me;
Since when it grows, and smells, I swear,
    Not of itself, but thee.

SONG: TO CELIA

Come, my Celia, let us prove,
While we can, the sports of love.
Time will not be ours for ever;
He, at length, our good will sever;
Spend not then his gifts in vain.   5
Suns that set may rise again;
But if once we lose this light,
'T is with us perpetual night.
Why should we defer our joys?
Fame and rumor are but toys.   10
Cannot we delude the eyes
Of a few poor household spies?
Or his easier ears beguile,
Thus removèd by our wile?
'T is no sin love's fruits to steal;   15
But the sweet theft to reveal,
To be taken, to be seen,
These have crimes accounted been.

TO HEAVEN

Good and great God! can I not think of
    thee,
But it must straight my melancholy be?
Is it interpreted in me disease,
That, laden with my sins, I seek for ease?
O be thou witness, that the reins dost
    know   5
And hearts of all, if I be sad for show;
And judge me after, if I dare pretend
To aught but grace, or aim at other end.
As thou art all, so be thou all to me,
First, midst, and last, converted One and
    Three!   10
My faith, my hope, my love; and, in this
    state,
My judge, my witness, and my advocate!
Where have I been this while exiled from
    thee,
And whither rapt, now thou but stoop'st
    to me?
Dwell, dwell here still! O, being every-
    where,   15
How can I doubt to find thee ever here?
I know my state, both full of shame and
    scorn,
Conceived in sin, and unto labor born,
Standing with fear, and must with horror fall,
And destined unto judgment, after all.   20
I feel my griefs too, and there scarce is
    ground
Upon my flesh t' inflict another wound;
Yet dare I not complain or wish for death
With holy Paul, lest it be thought the
    breath
Of discontent; or that these prayers be   25
For weariness of life, not love of thee.

THE TRIUMPH OF CHARIS

See the chariot at hand here of Love,
　　Wherein my Lady rideth!
Each that draws is a swan or a dove,
　　And well the car Love guideth.
As she goes, all hearts do duty　　5
　　Unto her beauty;
And enamored, do wish, so they might
　　But enjoy such a sight,
That they still were to run by her side,
Through swords, through seas, whither she
　　would ride.　　10

Do but look on her eyes, they do light
　　All that Love's world compriseth!
Do but look on her hair, it is bright
　　As Love's star when it riseth!
Do but mark, her forehead's smoother　　15
　　Than words that soothe her;
And from her arched brows, such a grace
　　Sheds itself through the face
As alone there triumphs to the life
All the gain, all the good, of the elements'
　　strife.　　20

Have you seen but a bright lily grow
　　Before rude hands have touched it?
Have you marked but the fall of the snow
　　Before the soil hath smutched it?
Have you felt the wool of the beaver?　　25
　　Or swan's down ever?
Or have smelt o' the bud of the briar?
　　Or the nard in the fire?
Or have tasted the bag of the bee?
Oh so white! Oh so soft! Oh so sweet is
　　she!　　30

AN EPITAPH ON SALATHIEL PAVY

　Weep with me, all you that read
　　This little story:
　And know, for whom a tear you shed
　　Death's self is sorry.
　'T was a child that so did thrive　　5
　　In grace and feature,
　As heaven and nature seemed to strive
　　Which owned the creature.
　Years he numbered scarce thirteen
　　When fates turned cruel,　　10
　Yet three filled zodiacs had he been
　　The stage's jewel;
　And did act, what now we moan,
　　Old men so duly,
　As, soth, the Parcæ thought him one,　　15
　　He played so truly.
　So, by error, to his fate
　　They all consented;

But viewing him since, alas, too late!
　　They have repented;　　20
And have sought, to give new birth,
　　In baths to steep him;
But being so much too good for earth,
　　Heaven vows to keep him.

EPITAPH ON ELIZABETH, L. H.

Would'st thou hear what man can say
In a little? Reader, stay.

　Underneath this stone doth lie
As much beauty as could die:
Which in life did harbor give　　5
To more virtue than doth live.

　If at all she had a fault,
Leave it buried in this vault.
One name was Elizabeth,
The other, let it sleep with death!　　10
Fitter, where it died, to tell,
Than that it lived at all. Farewell!

TO THE MEMORY OF MY BELOVED, MASTER WILLIAM SHAKSPERE

To draw no envy, Shakspere, on thy name,
Am I thus ample to thy book and fame;
While I confess thy writings to be such
As neither man, nor muse, can praise too
　　much.
'T is true, and all men's suffrage. But
　　these ways　　5
Were not the paths I meant unto thy
　　praise;
For silliest ignorance on these may light,
Which, when it sounds at best, but echoes
　　right;
Or blind affection, which doth ne'er ad-
　　vance
The truth, but gropes, and urgeth all by
　　chance;　　10
Or crafty malice might pretend this praise,
And think to ruin, where it seemed to
　　raise.
These are, as some infamous bawd or whore
Should praise a matron. What could hurt
　　her more?　　14
But thou art proof against them, and, indeed,
Above the ill fortune of them, or the need.
I therefore will begin. Soul of the age!
The applause, delight, the wonder of our
　　stage!
My Shakspere, rise! I will not lodge thee
　　by
Chaucer, or Spenser, or bid Beaumont lie

A little further, to make thee a room: 21
Thou art a monument without a tomb,
And art alive still while thy book doth live
And we have wits to read and praise to
give.
That I not mix thee so, my brain ex-
cuses, 25
I mean with great, but disproportioned
Muses;
For if I thought my judgment were of
years,
I should commit thee surely with thy peers,
And tell how far thou didst our Lyly out-
shine,
Or sporting Kyd, or Marlowe's mighty
line. 30
And though thou hadst small Latin and less
Greek,
From thence to honor thee, I would not
seek
For names; but call forth thundering
Æschylus,
Euripides, and Sophocles to us;
Pacuvius, Accius, him of Cordova dead, 35
To life again, to hear thy buskin tread,
And shake a stage; or, when thy socks were
on,
Leave thee alone for the comparison
Of all that insolent Greece or haughty
Rome
Sent forth, or since did from their ashes
come. 40
Triumph, my Britain, thou hast one to
show
To whom all scenes of Europe homage
owe.
He was not of an age, but for all time!
And all the Muses still were in their prime,
When, like Apollo. he came forth to warm
Our ears, or like a Mercury to charm! 46
Nature herself was proud of his designs
And joyed to wear the dressing of his
lines!
Which were so richly spun, and woven so
fit,
As, since, she will vouchsafe no other wit.
The merry Greek, tart Aristophanes, 51
Neat Terence, witty Plautus, now not
please;
But antiquated and deserted lie,
As they were not of Nature's family.
Yet must I not give Nature all; thy art, 55
My gentle Shakspere, must enjoy a part.
For though the poet's matter nature be,
His art doth give the fashion; and, that he
Who casts to write a living line, must
sweat,
(Such as thine are) and strike the second
heat 60

Upon the Muses' anvil; turn the same
(And himself with it) that he thinks to
frame,
Or, for the laurel, he may gain a scorn;
For a good poet's made, as well as born.
And such wert thou! Look how the fa-
ther's face 65
Lives in his issue, even so the race
Of Shakspere's mind and manners brightly
shines
In his well turnèd, and true filèd lines;
In each of which he seems to shake a lance,
As brandished at the eyes of ignorance. 70
Sweet Swan of Avon! what a sight it were
To see thee in our waters yet appear,
And make those flights upon the banks of
Thames,
That so did take Eliza, and our James!
But stay, I see thee in the hemisphere 75
Advanced, and made a constellation there!
Shine forth, thou Star of poets, and with
rage
Or influence, chide or cheer the drooping
stage,
Which, since thy flight from hence, hath
mourned like night,
And despairs day, but for thy volume's
light. 80

A PINDARIC ODE

*To the immortal memory and friendship of
that noble pair, Sir Lucius Cary and Sir
H. Morison.*

I

The Strophe, or Turn

Brave infant of Saguntum, clear
Thy coming forth in that great year,
When the prodigious Hannibal did crown
His rage with razing your immortal town.
    Thou looking then about, 5
    Ere thou wert half got out,
    Wise child, didst hastily return,
    And mad'st thy mother's womb thine urn,
How summed a circle didst thou leave man-
kind
Of deepest lore, could we the center find! 10

The Antistrophe, or Counter-Turn

Did wiser nature draw thee back,
From out the horror of that sack;
Where shame, faith, honor, and regard of
right,
Lay trampled on? the deeds of death and
night
    Urged, hurried forth, and hurled 15
    Upon the affrighted world;

Fire, famine, and fell fury met,
And all on utmost ruin set:
As, could they but life's miseries foresee,
No doubt all infants would return like
    thee.   20

The Epode, or Stand

For what is life, if measured by the space,
        Not by the act?
Or maskèd man, if valued by his face,
        Above his fact?
    Here's one outlived his peers   25
    And told forth fourscore years:
He vexèd time, and busied the whole
        state;
    Troubled both foes and friends;
    But ever to no ends:
What did this stirrer but die late?   30
How well at twenty had he fallen or stood!
For three of his four score he did no good.

II

The Strophe, or Turn

He entered well by virtuous parts,
Got up, and thrived with honest arts,
He purchased friends, and fame, and hon-
        ors then,   35
And had his noble name advanced with
        men;
    But weary of that flight,
    He stooped in all men's sight
To sordid flatteries, acts of strife,
And sunk in that dead sea of life,   40
So deep, as he did then death's waters sup,
But that the cork of title buoyed him up.

The Antistrophe, or Counter-Turn

Alas! but Morison fell young!
He never fell,—thou fall'st, my tongue.
He stood a soldier to the last right end, 45
A perfect patriot and a noble friend;
    But most, a virtuous son.
    All offices were done
By him, so ample, full, and round,
In weight, in measure, number, sound, 50
As, though his age imperfect might appear,
His life was of humanity the sphere.

The Epode, or Stand

Go now, and tell our days summed up with
        fears,
        And make them years;
Produce thy mass of miseries on the stage,
        To swell thine age;   56
    Repeat of things a throng,
    To show thou hast been long,
Not lived; for life doth her great actions
        spell

By what was done and wrought   6
    In season, and so brought
To light: her measures are, how well
Each syllabe answered, and was formed,
        how fair;
These make the lines of life, and that's
        her air!

III

The Strophe, or Turn

    It is not growing like a tree   65
    In bulk, doth make men better be;
Or standing long an oak, three hundred
        year,
To fall a log at last, dry, bald, and sear:
        A lily of a day,
        Is fairer far, in May,   7c
Although it fall and die that night;
It was the plant and flower of light.
In small proportions we just beauties see;
And in short measures life may perfect be.

The Antistrophe, or Counter-Turn

Call, noble Lucius, then, for wine,   75
And let thy looks with gladness shine;
Accept this garland, plant it on thy head,
And think, nay know, thy Morison's not
        dead.
        He leaped the present age,
        Possest with holy rage,   8
To see that bright eternal day;
Of which we priests and poets say
Such truths as we expect for happy men;
And there he lives with memory and
        Ben——

The Epode, or Stand

Jonson, who sung this of him, ere he went,
        Himself, to rest,   86
Or taste a part of that full joy he meant
        To have exprest,
        In this bright asterism;—
        Where it were friendship's schism, 90
Were not his Lucius long with us to
        tarry,
        To separate these twi-
        Lights, the Dioscuri;
And keep the one half from his Harry.
But fate doth so alternate the design,   95
Whilst that in heaven, this light on earth
        must shine,—

IV

The Strophe, or Turn

And shine as you exalted are;
Two names of friendship, but one star:
Of hearts the union, and those not by

Made, or indenture, or leased out t' advance
    The profits for a time.   101
    No pleasures vain did chime,
Of rimes, or riots, at your feasts,
Orgies of drink, or feigned protests;
But simple love of greatness and of good,
That knits brave minds and manners more
      than blood.   106

The Antistrophe, or Counter-Turn

This made you first to know the why
You liked, then after, to apply
That liking; and approach so one the t'
    other,
Till either grew a portion of the other;   110
    Each stylèd by his end,
    The copy of his friend.
You lived to be the great sir-names
And titles by which all made claims
Unto the Virtue: nothing perfect done,   115
But as a Cary or a Morison.

The Epode, or Stand

And such a force the fair example had,
    As they that saw
The good and durst not practise it, were
    glad
    That such a law   120
    Was left yet to mankind;
Where they might read and find
Friendship, indeed, was written not in
    words;
    And with the heart, not pen,
    Of two so early men,   125
Whose lines her rolls were, and records,
Who, ere the first down bloomèd on the
    chin,
Had sowed these fruits, and got the har-
    vest in.

JOHN DONNE (1573–1631)

SONG

Go and catch a falling star,
    Get with child a mandrake root,
Tell me where all past years are,
    Or who cleft the devil's foot;
Teach me to hear mermaids singing,   5
    to keep off envy's stinging,
      And find
      What wind
Serves to advance an honest mind.

If thou be'st born to strange sights,   10
    Things invisible go see,
Ride ten thousand days and nights
    Till Age snow white hairs on thee;

Thou, when thou return'st, wilt tell me
All strange wonders that befell thee,   15
      And swear
      No where
Lives a woman true and fair.

If thou find'st one, let me know;
    Such a pilgrimage were sweet.   20
Yet do not; I would not go,
    Though at next door we might meet.
Though she were true when you met her,
And last till you write your letter,
      Yet she   25
      Will be
False, ere I come, to two or three.

THE INDIFFERENT

I can love both fair and brown;
Her whom abundance melts, and her whom
    want betrays;
Her who loves loneness best, and her who
    masks and plays;
Her whom the country formed, and whom
    the town;
Her who believes, and her who tries;   5
Her who still weeps with spongy eyes,
And her who is dry cork and never cries.
I can love her, and her, and you, and you;
I can love any, so she be not true.

Will no other vice content you?   10
Will it not serve your turn to do as did
    your mothers?
Or have you all old vices spent and now
    would find out others?
Or doth a fear that men are true torment
    you?
O we are not, be not you so;
Let me — and do you — twenty know;   15
Rob me, but bind me not, and let me go.
Must I, who came to travel thorough you,
Grow your fixed subject, because you are
    true?

Venus heard me sigh this song;
And by love's sweetest part, variety, she
    swore,   20
She heard not this till now; it should be
    so no more.
She went, examined, and returned ere long,
And said, 'Alas! some two or three
Poor heretics in love there be,
Which think to stablish dangerous con-
    stancy.   25
But I have told them, "Since you will be
    true,
You shall be true to them who're false to
    you."'

THE CANONIZATION

For God's sake hold your tongue, and let
    me love;
Or chide my palsy, or my gout;
My five gray hairs, or ruined fortune
    flout;
With wealth your state, your mind with
    arts improve;
    Take you a course, get you a place, 5
    Observe his Honor, or his Grace;
Or the king's real, or his stamped face
Contemplate; what you will, approve,
So you will let me love.

Alas! alas! who's injured by my love? 10
    What merchant's ships have my sighs
    drowned?
    Who says my tears have overflowed his
    ground?
When did my colds a forward spring re-
    move?
    When did the heats which my veins fill
    Add one more to the plaguy bill? 15
Soldiers find wars, and lawyers find out
    still
    Litigious men, which quarrels move,
    Though she and I do love.

Call's what you will, we are made such by
    love;
    Call her one, me another fly, 20
    We're tapers too, and at our own cost
    die,
And we in us find th' eagle and the dove.
    The phoenix riddle hath more wit
    By us; we two being one, are it;
So, to one neutral thing both sexes fit. 25
    We die and rise the same, and prove
    Mysterious by this love.

We can die by it, if not live by love,
    And if unfit for tomb or hearse
Our legend be, it will be fit for verse; 30
And if no piece of chronicle we prove,
    We'll build in sonnets pretty rooms;
    As well a well-wrought urn becomes
The greatest ashes, as half-acre tombs,
    And by these hymns all shall approve 35
    Us canonized for love;

And thus invoke us, 'You, whom reverend
    love
    Made one another's hermitage;
    You, to whom love was peace, that now
    is rage;
Who did the whole world's soul contract,
    and drove 40
    Into the glasses of your eyes;
    So made such mirrors, and such spies,

That they did all to you epitomize —
    Countries, towns, courts beg from above
    A pattern of your love.' 45

THE DREAM

Dear love, for nothing less than thee
Would I have broke this happy dream;
    It was a theme
For reason, much too strong for fantasy.
Therefore thou waked'st me wisely; yet 5
My dream thou brok'st not, but continued'st
    it.
Thou art so true that thoughts of thee suf-
    fice
To make dreams truths and fables his-
    tories;
Enter these arms, for since thou thought'st
    it best
Not to dream all my dream, let's act the
    rest. 10

As lightning, or a taper's light,
Thine eyes, and not thine noise, waked me;
    Yet I thought thee —
For thou lov'st truth — an angel, at first
    sight;
But when I saw thou saw'st my heart, 15
And knew'st my thoughts beyond an angel's
    art,
When thou knew'st what I dreamt, when
    thou knew'st when
Excess of joy would wake me, and cam'st
    then,
I must confess it could not choose but be
Profane to think thee anything but thee. 20

Coming and staying showed thee thee,
But rising makes me doubt that now
    Thou art not thou.
That love is weak where fear's as strong
    as he;
'T is not all spirit pure and brave 25
If mixture it of fear, shame, honor have.
Perchance as torches, which must ready be,
Men light and put out, so thou deal'st with
    me.
Thou cam'st to kindle, go'st to come: then I
Will dream that hope again, but else would
    die. 30

LOVE'S DEITY

I long to talk with some old lover's ghost
    Who died before the god of love was
    born.
I cannot think that he who then loved most

Sunk so low as to love one which did
    scorn.
But since this god produced a destiny,   5
And that vice-nature, custom, lets it be,
I must love her that loves not me.

Sure they which made him god, meant not
    so much,
Nor he in his young godhead practised it.
But when an even flame two hearts did
    touch,   10
His office was indulgently to fit
Actives to passives. Correspondency
Only his subject was; it cannot be
Love till I love her who loves me.

But every modern god will now extend   15
    His vast prerogative as far as Jove.
To rage, to lust, to write to, to commend,
All is the purlieu of the god of love.
O! were we wakened by this tyranny
To ungod this child again, it could not be
I should love her who loves not me.   21

Rebel and atheist too, why murmur I,
    As though I felt the worst that love
    could do?
Love may make me leave loving, or might
    try
    A deeper plague, to make her love me
    too;   25
Which, since she loves before, I'm loth to
    see.
Falsehood is worse than hate; and that
    must be,
If she whom I love, should love me.

THE FUNERAL

Whoever comes to shroud me, do not harm
    Nor question much
That subtle wreath of hair about mine arm;
The mystery, the sign you must not touch,
    For 't is my outward soul,   5
Viceroy to that which, unto heav'n being
    gone,
    Will leave this to control
And keep these limbs, her provinces, from
    dissolution.

For if the sinewy thread my brain lets fall
    Through every part   10
Can tie those parts, and make me one of
    all;
Those hairs, which upward grew, and
    strength and art
    Have from a better brain,
Can better do 't: except she meant that I
    By this should know my pain,   15

As prisoners then are manacled, when
    they 're condemned to die.
Whate'er she meant by 't, bury it with me,
    For since I am
Love's martyr, it might breed idolatry
If into other hands these reliques came.   20
    As 't was humility
T' afford to it all that a soul can do,
    So 't is some bravery
That, since you would have none of me, I
    bury some of you.

THE COMPUTATION

For my first twenty years, since yesterday,
I scarce believed thou couldst be gone away;
For forty more I fed on favors past,
And forty on hopes, that thou wouldst they
    might last;
Tears drowned one hundred, and sighs blew
    out two;   5
A thousand I did neither think nor do.
Or not divide, all being one thought of you;
Or in a thousand more, forgot that too.
Yet call not this long life; but think that I
Am, by being dead, immortal; can ghosts
    die?   10

FORGET

If poisonous minerals, and if that tree
Whose fruit threw death on else immortal us,
If lecherous goats, if serpents envious
Cannot be damned, alas! why should I be?
Why should intent or reason, born in me,   5
Make sins, else equal, in me more heinous?
And, mercy being easy and glorious
To God, in his stern wrath why threatens
    he?
But who am I, that dare dispute with thee?
O God, O! of thine only worthy blood   10
And my tears make a heavenly Lethean
    flood,
And drown in it my sin's black memory.
That thou remember them, some claim as
    debt;
I think it mercy if thou wilt forget.

DEATH

Death, be not proud, though some have
    callèd thee
Mighty and dreadful, for thou art not so;
For those whom thou think'st thou dost
    overthrow
Die not, poor Death; nor yet canst thou
    kill me.

From rest and sleep, which but thy picture
    be,   5
Much pleasure; then from thee much more
    must flow;
And soonest our best men with thee do
    go —
Rest of their bones and souls' delivery!
Thou 'rt slave to fate, chance, kings, and
    desperate men,
And dost with poison, war, and sickness
    dwell;   10
And poppy or charms can make us sleep
    as well
And better than thy stroke. Why swell'st
    thou then?
One short sleep past, we wake eternally,
And Death shall be no more: Death, thou
    shalt die!

A HYMN TO GOD THE FATHER

Wilt thou forgive that sin where I begun,
    Which was my sin, though it were done
        before?
Wilt thou forgive that sin through which
    I run,
    And do run still, though still I do de-
        plore?
When thou hast done, thou hast not done;
    For I have more.   6

Wilt thou forgive that sin which I have
    won
Others to sin, and made my sins their
    door?
Wilt thou forgive that sin which I did
  . shun
    A year or two, but wallowed in a score?
When thou hast done, thou hast not done;
    For I have more.   12

I have a sin of fear, that when I 've spun
    My last thread, I shall perish on the
        shore;
But swear by thyself that at my death thy
    Son   15
    Shall shine as he shines now and hereto-
        fore;
And having done that, thou hast done;
    I fear no more.

JOHN FLETCHER (1579–1625)

LOVE'S EMBLEMS

Now the lusty spring is seen;
    Golden yellow, gaudy blue,
    Daintily invite the view,

Everywhere on every green,
Roses blushing as they blow,   3
    And enticing men to pull
Lilies whiter than the snow,
    Woodbines of sweet honey full:
All love's emblems, and all cry,
    'Ladies, if not plucked, we die.'   10

Yet the lusty spring hath stayed;
    Blushing red and purest white
    Daintily to love invite
Every woman, every maid.
Cherries kissing as they grow,   15
    And inviting men to taste,
Apples even ripe below,
    Winding gently to the waist:
All love's emblems, and all cry,
    'Ladies, if not plucked, we die.'   20

MELANCHOLY

Hence, all you vain delights,
As short as are the nights
    Wherein you spend your folly!
There 's naught in this life sweet,
If man were wise to see 't,   5
    But only melancholy;
    O sweetest melancholy!

Welcome, folded arms and fixèd eyes,
A sigh that piercing mortifies,
A look that 's fastened to the ground, 10
A tongue chained up without a sound!
Fountain heads and pathless groves,
Places which pale passion loves!
Moonlight walks, when all the fowls
Are warmly housed save bats and owls!   15
A midnight bell, a parting groan,
These are the sounds we feed upon.
Then stretch our bones in a still gloomy
    valley;
Nothing 's so dainty sweet as lovely melan-
    choly.

SONG TO BACCHUS

God Lyæus, ever young,
Ever honored, ever sung;
Stained with blood of lusty grapes.
In a thousand lusty shapes,
Dance upon the mazer's brim,   5
In the crimson liquor swim;
From thy plenteous hand divine
Let a river run with wine;
God of youth, let this day here
Enter neither care nor fear!   10

BEAUTY CLEAR AND FAIR

Beauty clear and fair,
  Where the air
Rather like a perfume dwells;
  Where the violet and the rose
  Their blue veins and blush disclose,   5
And come to honor nothing else.

Where to live near,
  And planted there,
Is to live, and still live new;
  Where to gain a favor is   10
  More than light, perpetual bliss,—
Make me live by serving you.

Dear, again back recall
  To this light
A stranger to himself and all;   15
  Both the wonder and the story
  Shall be yours, and eke the glory:
I am your servant, and your thrall.

WEEP NO MORE

Weep no more, nor sigh, nor groan,
Sorrow calls no time that's gone;
Violets plucked the sweetest rain
Makes not fresh nor grow again;
Trim thy locks, look cheerfully;   5
Fate's hid ends eyes cannot see;
Joys as wingèd dreams fly fast,
Why should sadness longer last?
Grief is but a wound to woe;
Gentlest fair, mourn, mourn no mo.   10

ASPATIA'S SONG

  Lay a garland on my hearse
    Of the dismal yew;
  Maidens, willow branches bear;
    Say, I dièd true.

  My love was false, but I was firm   5
    From my hour of birth.
  Upon my buried body lie
    Lightly, gentle earth!

FRANCIS BEAUMONT
(1584–1616)

ON THE LIFE OF MAN

Like to the falling of a star,
Or as the flights of eagles are,
Or like the fresh spring's gaudy hue,
Or silver drops of morning dew,

Or like a wind that chafes the flood,   5
Or bubbles which on water stood:
Even such is man, whose borrowed light
Is straight called in and paid to night:
The wind blows out, the bubble dies,
The spring intombed in autumn lies;   10
The dew's dried up, the star is shot,
The flight is past, and man forgot.

LINES ON THE TOMBS IN WESTMINSTER

Mortality, behold and fear!
What a change of flesh is here!
Think how many royal bones
Sleep within this heap of stones;
Here they lie had realms and lands,   5
Who now want strength to stir their
  hands;
Where from their pulpits sealed with
  dust
They preach, 'In greatness is no trust.'
Here's an acre sown indeed
With the richest royal'st seed   10
That the earth did e'er suck in,
Since the first man died for sin;
Here the bones of birth have cried,
'Though gods they were, as men they
  died.'
Here are sands, ignoble things,   15
Dropt from the ruined sides of kings.
Here's a world of pomp and state,
Buried in dust, once dead by fate.

GEORGE WITHER (1588–1667)

THE LOVER'S RESOLUTION

Shall I, wasting in despair,
Die, because a woman's fair?
Or make pale my cheeks with care,
'Cause another's rosy are?
Be she fairer than the day,   5
Or the flowery meads in May!
  If she be not so to me,
  What care I how fair she be?

Should my heart be grieved or pined,
'Cause I see a woman kind?   10
Or a well disposèd nature
Joinèd with a lovely feature?
Be she meeker, kinder than
Turtle dove, or pelican!
  If she be not so to me,   15
  What care I how kind she be?

Shall a woman's virtues move
Me to perish for her love?
Or her well deserving known,
Make me quite forget mine own?   20
Be she with that goodness blest
Which may gain her, name of best!
   If she be not such to me,
   What care I how good she be?

'Cause her fortune seems too high,   25
Shall I play the fool, and die?
Those that bear a noble mind,
Where they want of riches find,
Think 'What, with them, they would do
That, without them, dare to woo!'   30
   And unless that mind I see,
   What care I though great she be?

Great, or good, or kind, or fair,
I will ne'er the more despair!
If she love me (this believe!)   35
I will die, ere she shall grieve!
If she slight me, when I woo,
I can scorn, and let her go!
   For if she be not for me,
   What care I for whom she be?   40

WHEN WE ARE UPON THE SEAS

From HALLELUJAH

On those great waters now I am,
Of which I have been told,
That whosoever thither came
Should wonders there behold.
In this unsteady place of fear,   5
Be present, Lord, with me;
For in these depths of water here,
I depths of danger see.

A stirring courser now I sit,
A headstrong steed I ride,   10
That champs and foams upon the bit
Which curbs his lofty pride.
The softest whistling of the winds
Doth make him gallop fast;
And as their breath increased he finds   15
The more he maketh haste.

Take thou, Oh Lord! the reins in hand,
Assume our Master's room;
Vouchsafe thou at our helm to stand,
And pilot to become.   20
Trim thou the sails, and let good speed
Accompany our haste;
Sound thou the channels at our need
And anchor for us cast.

A fit and favorable wind   25
To further us, provide;
And let it wait on us behind,
Or lackey by our side.
From sudden gusts, from storms, from sands,
And from the raging wave;   30
From shallows, rocks, and pirates' hands,
Men, goods, and vessel save.

Preserve us from the wants, the fear,
And sickness of the seas;
But chiefly from our sins, which are   35
A danger worse than these.
Lord! let us, also, safe arrive
Where we desire to be;
And for thy mercies let us give
Due thanks and praise to thee.   40

THE PRAYER OF OLD AGE

From HALLELUJAH

As this my carnal robe grows old,
Soiled, rent, and worn by length of years,
Let me on that by faith lay hold
Which man in life immortal wears:
   So sanctify my days behind,   5
   Do let my manners be refined,
That when my soul and flesh must part,
There lurk no terrors in my heart.

So shall my rest be safe and sweet
When I am lodgèd in my grave;   10
And when my soul and body meet,
A joyful meeting they shall have;
   Their essence, then, shall be divine,
   This muddy flesh shall starlike shine,
And God shall that fresh youth restore   15
Which will abide for evermore.

WILLIAM BROWNE (1591–1643)

BRITANNIA'S PASTORALS

From BOOK II, SONG I

Glide soft, ye silver floods,
And every spring:
Within the shady woods
Let no bird sing!
Nor from the grove a turtle-dove   5
Be seen to couple with her love.
But silence on each dale and mountain dwell,
Whilst Willy bids his friend and joy farewell.

But, of great Thetis' train,
Ye mermaids fair   10
That on the shores do plain
Your sea-green hair,
As ye in trammels knit your locks,
Weep ye; and so enforce the rocks
In heavy murmurs through the broad shores
    tell,   15
How Willy bade his friend and joy fare-
    well.

Cease, cease ye murd'ring winds,
To move a wave;
But if with troubled minds
You seek his grave,   20
Know 't is as various as yourselves
Now in the deep, then on the shelves,
His coffin tossed by fish and surges fell,
Whilst Willy weeps, and bids all joy fare-
    well.

Had he, Arion-like   25
Been judged to drown,
He on his lute could strike
So rare a sown,
A thousand dolphins would have come
And jointly strive to bring him home.   30
But he on shipboard died, by sickness fell,
Since when his Willy paid all joy farewell.

Great Neptune, hear a swain!
His coffin take,
And with a golden chain   35
For pity make
It fast unto a rock near land!
Where ev'ry calmy morn I 'll stand,
And ere one sheep out of my fold I tell,
Sad Willy's pipe shall bid his friend fare-
    well.   40

* * *

From BOOK II, SONG V

Now was the Lord and Lady of the May
Meeting the May-pole at the break of day,
And Cælia, as the fairest on the green,
Not without some maids' envy chosen
    queen.
Now was the time com'n, when our gentle
    swain   5
Must in his harvest, or lose all again.
Now must he pluck the rose lest other
    hands,
Or tempests blemish what so fairly stands:
And therefore, as they had before decreed,
Our shepherd gets a boat, and with all
    speed,   10

In night, that doth on lovers' actions smile,
Arrivèd safe on Mona's fruitful isle.
    Between two rocks (immortal, without
        mother),
That stands as if out-facing one another,
There ran a creek up, intricate and blind, 15
As if the waters hid them from the wind;
Which never washed but at a higher tide
The frizzled coats which do the mountains
    hide;
Where never gale was longer known to stay
Than from the smooth wave it had swept
    away   20
The new divorcèd leaves, that from each
    side
Left the thick boughs to dance out with the
    tide.
At further end the creek a stately wood
Gave a kind shadow to the brackish flood
Made up of trees, not less kenned by each
    skiff   25
Than that sky-scaling peak of Teneriffe,
Upon whose tops the hernshaw bred her
    young,
And hoary moss upon their branches hung;
Whose rugged rinds sufficient were to show,
Without their height, what time they 'gan
    to grow;   30
And if dry eld by wrinkled skin appears,
None could allot them less than Nestor's
    years.
As under their command the throngèd
    creek
Ran lessened up. Here did the shepherd
    seek
Where he his little boat might safely hide,
Till it was fraught with what the world be-
    side   36
Could not outvalue; nor give equal weight
Though in the time when Greece was at her
    height.
    The ruddy horses of the rosy Morn
Out of the eastern gates had newly borne 40
Their blushing mistress in her golden chair,
Spreading new light throughout our hemi-
    sphere,
When fairest Cælia with a lovelier crew
Of damsels than brave Latmus ever knew
Came forth to meet the youngsters, who
    had here   45
Cut down an oak that long withouten peer
Bore his round head imperiously above
His other mates there, consecrate to Jove.
The wishèd time drew on: and Cælia now,
That had the fame for her white archèd
    brow,   50
While all her lovely fellows busied were
In picking off the gems from Tellus' hair,

Made tow'rds the creek, where Philocel, un-
    sped
Of maid or shepherd that their May-games
    plied
Received his wished-for Cælia, and begun
To steer his boat contrary to the sun,   56
Who could have wished another in his
    place
To guide the car of light, or that his race
Were to have end (so he might bless his
    hap)
In Cælia's bosom, not in Thetis' lap.   60
The boat oft danced for joy of what it
    held:
The hoist-up sail not quick but gently
    swelled,
And often shook, as fearing what might
    fall,
Ere she delivered what she went withal.
Wingèd Argestes, fair Aurora's son,   65
Licensed that day to leave his dungeon,
Meekly attended and did never err,
Till Cælia graced our land, and our land
    her.
As through the waves their love-fraught
    wherry ran,
A many Cupids, each set on his swan,   70
Guided with reins of gold and silver twist
The spotless birds about them as they
    list:
Which would have sung a song 'ere they
    were gone
Had unkind Nature given them more than
    one;
Or in bestowing that had not done wrong,
And made their sweet lives forfeit one sad
    song.   76

* * *

ON THE COUNTESS DOWAGER OF PEMBROKE

Underneath this sable hearse
Lies the subject of all verse:
Sidney's sister, Pembroke's mother:
Death, ere thou hast slain another
Fair and learned and good as she,   5
Time shall throw a dart at thee.

Marble piles let no man raise
To her name: for after days
Some kind woman, born as she,
Reading this, like Niobe   10
Shall turn marble, and become
Both her mourner and her tomb.

ROBERT HERRICK (1591–1674)

CORINNA'S GOING A-MAYING

Get up, get up for shame, the blooming
    morn
Upon her wings presents the god unshorn.
    See how Aurora throws her fair
    Fresh-quilted colors through the air:
    Get up, sweet slug-a-bed, and see   5
    The dew bespangling herb and tree.
Each flower has wept and bowèd toward the
    east
Above an hour since: yet you not dressed;
    Nay! not so much as out of bed?
    When all the birds have matins said   10
    And sung their thankful hymns, 't is
    sin,
    Nay, profanation, to keep in,
Whenas a thousand virgins on this day
Spring, sooner than the lark, to fetch in
    May.

Rise, and put on your foliage, and be seen
To come forth, like the spring-time, fresh
    and green,   16
    And sweet as Flora. Take no care
    For jewels for your gown or hair:
    Fear not; the leaves will strew
    Gems in abundance upon you: 20
Besides, the childhood of the day has kept,
Against you come, some orient pearls un-
    wept;
    Come and receive them while the light
    Hangs on the dew-locks of the night:
    And Titan on the eastern hill   25
    Retires himself, or else stands still
Till you come forth. Wash, dress, be brief
    in praying:
Few beads are best when once we go a-May-
    ing.

Come, my Corinna, come; and, coming
    mark
How each field turns a street, each street a
    park   30
    Made green and trimmed with trees;
    see how
    Devotion gives each house a bough
    Or branch: each porch, each door ere
    this
    An ark, a tabernacle is,
Made up of white-thorn, neatly interwove;
As if here were those cooler shades of love.
    Can such delights be in the street   37
    And open fields and we not see 't?
    Come, we 'll abroad; and let 's obey
    The proclamation made for May: 40

And sin no more, as we have done, by staying;
But, my Corinna, come, let's go a-Maying.

There's not a budding boy or girl this day
But is got up, and gone to bring in May.
    A deal of youth, ere this, is come   45
Back, and with white-thorn laden home.
Some have despatched their cakes and
    cream
Before that we have left to dream:
And some have wept, and wooed, and
    plighted troth,
And chose their priest, ere we can cast off
    sloth: 50
    Many a green-gown has been given;
    Many a kiss, both odd and even:
    Many a glance too has been sent
    From out the eye, love's firmament;
Many a jest told of the keys betraying 55
This night, and locks picked, yet we're not
    a-Maying.

Come, let us go while we are in our prime;
And take the harmless folly of the time.
    We shall grow old apace, and die
    Before we know our liberty.   60
    Our life is short, and our days run
    As fast away as does the sun;
And, as a vapor or a drop of rain,
Once lost, can ne'er be found again,
    So when or you or I are made   65
    A fable, song, or fleeting shade,
    All love, all liking, all delight
Lies drowned with us in endless night.
Then while time serves, and we are but de-
    caying,   69
Come, my Corinna, come let's go a-Maying.

UPON JULIA'S CLOTHES

Whenas in silks my Julia goes,
Then, then, methinks, how sweetly flows
The liquefaction of her clothes.

Next, when I cast mine eyes, and see
That brave vibration, each way free,   5
O, how that glittering taketh me!

TO THE VIRGINS TO MAKE MUCH OF TIME

Gather ye rosebuds while ye may,
    Old Time is still a-flying;
And this same flower that smiles to-day,
    To-morrow will be dying.

The glorious lamp of heaven, the sun,   5
    The higher he's a-getting,
The sooner will his race be run,
    And nearer he's to setting.

That age is best which is the first,
    When youth and blood are warmer;   10
But being spent, the worse and worst
    Times still succeed the former.

Then be not coy, but use your time,
    And while ye may, go marry;
For, having lost but once your prime   15
    You may forever tarry.

TO DAFFODILS

Fair Daffodils, we weep to see
    You haste away so soon;
As yet the early rising sun
    Has not attained his noon.
        Stay, stay,   5
        Until the hasting day
        Has run
    But to the even-song;
And, having prayed together, we
    Will go with you along.   10

We have short time to stay, as you,
    We have as short a spring;
As quick a growth to meet decay,
    As you, or anything.
        We die   15
        As your hours do, and dry
        Away,
    Like to the summer's rain;
Or as the pearls of morning's dew,
    Ne'er to be found again.

TO MUSIC

Charm me asleep, and melt me so
With thy delicious numbers,
That being ravished, hence I go
Away in easy slumbers.
Ease my sick head,
And make my bed,
Thou power that canst sever
From me this ill;
And quickly still,
Though thou not kill
My fever.

Thou sweetly canst convert the same
From a consuming fire,
Into a gentle-licking flame,
And make it thus expire.
Then make me weep

My pains asleep,
And give me such reposes,
That I, poor I,
May think, thereby,   20
I live and die
'Mongst roses.

Fall on me like a silent dew,
Or like those maiden showers,
Which, by the peep of day, do strew   25
A baptism o'er the flowers.
Melt, melt my pains
With thy soft strains;
That having ease me given,
With full delight,   30
I leave this light,
And take my flight
For heaven.

AN ODE FOR BEN JONSON

Ah, Ben!
Say how or when
Shall we, thy guests,
Meet at those lyric feasts,
Made at the Sun,   5
The Dog, the Triple Tun;
Where we such clusters had,
As made us nobly wild, not mad?
And yet each verse of thine
Out-did the meat, out-did the frolic wine. 10

My Ben!
Or come again,
Or send to us
Thy wit's great overplus;
But teach us yet   15
Wisely to husband it,
Lest we that talent spend;
And having once brought to an end
That precious stock, the store
Of such a wit the world should have no
     more.   20

A THANKSGIVING TO GOD FOR HIS HOUSE

Lord, thou hast given me a cell
     Wherein to dwell,
A little house, whose humble roof
     Is weather-proof,
Under the spars of which I lie   5
     Both soft and dry;
Where thou, my chamber for to ward,
     Hast set a guard
Of harmless thoughts to watch and keep
     Me, while I sleep.   10

Low is my porch, as is my fate,
     Both void of state;
And yet the threshold of my door
     Is worn by th' poor,
Who thither come and freely get   15
     Good words, or meat.
Like as my parlor, so my hall
     And kitchen's small;
A little buttery, and therein
     A little bin,   20
Which keeps my little loaf of bread
     Unchipped, unflead;
Some brittle sticks of thorn or briar
     Make me a fire,
Close by whose living coal I sit,   25
     And glow like it.
Lord, I confess, too, when I dine,
     The pulse is thine,
And all those other bits that be
     There placed by thee;   30
The worts, the purslain, and the mess
     Of water-cress,
Which of thy kindness thou hast sent;
     And my content ·
Makes those, and my belovèd beet,   35
     To be more sweet.
'T is thou that crown'st my glittering hearth
     With guiltless mirth,
And giv'st me wassail bowls to drink,
     Spiced to the brink.   40
Lord, 't is thy plenty-dropping hand
     That soils my land,
And giv'st me, for my bushel sown,
     Twice ten for one;
Thou mak'st my teeming hen to lay   45
     Her egg each day;
Besides my healthful ewes to bear
     Me twins each year;
The while the conduits of my kine
     Run cream, for wine.   50
All these, and better thou dost send
     Me, to this end,
That I should render, for my part,
     A thankful heart,
Which, fired with incense, I resign,   55
     As wholly thine;
But the acceptance, that must be,
     My Christ, by thee.

GRACE FOR A CHILD

Here, a little child, I stand,
Heaving up my either hand:
Cold as paddocks though they be,
Here I lift them up to thee,
For a benison to fall
On our meat, and on us all. Amen.

HIS PRAYER FOR ABSOLUTION

For those my unbaptizèd rimes,
Writ in my wild unhallowed times,
For every sentence, clause, and word,
That's not inlaid with thee, my Lord
Forgive me, God, and blot each line   5
Out of my book that is not thine.
But if, 'mongst all, thou find'st here one
Worthy thy benediction,
That one of all the rest shall be
The glory of my work and me.   10

GEORGE HERBERT (1593-1633)

VIRTUE

Sweet day, so cool, so calm, so bright,
    The bridal of the earth and sky!
The dew shall weep thy fall to-night;
    For thou must die.

Sweet rose, whose hue, angry and brave,   5
    Bids the rash gazer wipe his eye,
Thy root is ever in its grave,
    And thou must die.

Sweet spring, full of sweet days and roses,
    A box where sweets compacted lie,
My music shows ye have your closes,
    And all must die.

Only a sweet and virtuous soul,
    Like seasoned timber, never gives;
But though the whole world· turn to coal,
    Then chiefly lives.   16

LOVE

Love bade me welcome; yet my soul drew
        back,
    Guilty of dust and sin.
But quick-eyed Love, observing me grow
        slack
    From my first entrance in,
Drew nearer to me, sweetly questioning,   5
    If I lacked anything.

'A guest,' I answered, 'worthy to be here:'
    Love said, 'You shall be he.'
'I, the unkind, ungrateful? Ah, my dear,
    I cannot look on thee!'   10
Love took my hand and smiling did reply,
    'Who made the eyes but I?'

'Truth, Lord; but I have marred them: let
        my shame
    Go where it doth deserve.'

'And know you not,' says Love, 'who bore
        the blame?'   15
    'My dear, then I will serve.'
'You must sit down,' says Love, 'and taste
        my meat.'
    So I did sit and eat.

THE COLLAR

I struck the board, and cried, 'No more;
    I will abroad!
What! shall I ever sigh and pine?
My lines and life are free; free as the road,
    Loose as the wind, as large as store. 5
        Shall I be still in suit?
Have I no harvest but a thorn
To let me blood, and not restore
What I have lost with cordial fruit?
        Sure there was wine   10
Before my sighs did dry it; there was
        corn
    Before my tears did drown it;
Is the year only lost to me?
Have I no bays to crown it,
No flowers, no garlands gay? all blasted, 15
        All wasted?
Not so, my heart, but there is fruit,
        And thou hast hands.
Recover all thy sigh-blown age
On double pleasures; leave thy cold dispute
Of what is fit and not; forsake thy cage, 21
        Thy rope of sands
Which petty thoughts have made; and made
        to thee
Good cable, to enforce and draw,
        And be thy law,   25
While thou didst wink and wouldst not
        see.
        Away! take heed;
        I will abroad.
Call in thy death's head there, tie up thy
        fears:
        He that forbears   30
    To suit and serve his need
        Deserves his load.'
But as I raved, and grew more fierce and
        wild
        At every word,
Methought I heard one calling, 'Child';
    And I replied, 'My Lord.'   36

THE QUIP

The merry World did on a day
    With his train-bands and mates agree
To meet together where I lay,
    And all in sport to jeer at me.

First Beauty crept into a rose,   5
   Which when I pluckt not, 'Sir,' said she,
'Tell me, I pray, whose hands are those?'
   But Thou shalt answer, Lord, for me.

Then Money came, and chinking still,
   'What tune is this, poor man?' said he:
'I heard in Music you had skill;'   11
   But Thou shalt answer, Lord, for me.

Then came brave Glory puffing by
   In silks that whistled, who but he!
He scarce allowed me half an eye;   15
   But Thou shalt answer, Lord, for me.

Then came quick Wit and Conversation,
   And he would needs a comfort be,
And, to be short, make an oration:
   But Thou shalt answer, Lord, for me.   20

Yet when the hour of Thy design
   To answer these fine things shall come,
Speak not at large; say, 'I am Thine,'
   And then they have their answer home.

THE WORLD

Love built a stately house, where Fortune
    came;
   And spinning fancies, she was heard to say
That her fine cobwebs did support the
    frame,
Whereas they were supported by the same;
   But Wisdom quickly swept them all away.

Then Pleasure came, who, liking not the
    fashion,   6
   Began to make balconies, terraces,
Till she had weakened all by alteration;
   But reverend laws, and many a proclama-
    tion,
Reformèd all at length with menaces.   10

Then entered Sin, and with that sycamore
   Whose leaves first sheltered man from
    drought and dew,
Working and winding slily evermore,
The inward walls and summers cleft and
    tore;
   But Grace shored these, and cut that as it
    grew.   15

Then Sin combined with Death in a firm
    band
   To raze the building to the very floor:
Which they effected, none could them with-
    stand;
   But Love and Grace took Glory by the
    hand,
    And built a braver palace than before.   20

THE PULLEY

When God at first made man,
   Having a glass of blessing standing by;
'Let us,' said he, 'pour on him all we
    can:
Let the world's riches, which dispersèd lie,
   Contract into a span.'   5

So Strength first made a way;
   Then Beauty flowed; then Wisdom, Honor,
    Pleasure.
   When almost all was out, God made a
    stay,
Perceiving that alone, of all his treasure,
   Rest in the bottom lay.   10

'For if I should,' said he,
'Bestow this jewel also on my creature,
   He would adore my gifts instead of me,
And rest in Nature, not the God of Na-
    ture;
   So both should losers be.   15

'Yet let him keep the rest,
   But keep them with repining restlessness;
   Let him be rich and weary, that at least,
If goodness lead him not, yet weariness
   May toss him to my breast.'   20

THOMAS CAREW (1598?–1639?)

SONG

Ask me no more where Jove bestows,
When June is past, the fading rose,
For in your beauty's orient deep
These flowers, as in their causes, sleep.

Ask me no more whither do stray   5
The golden atoms of the day,
For, in pure love, heaven did prepare
Those powders to enrich your hair.

Ask me no more whither doth haste
The nightingale when May is past,   10
For in your sweet dividing throat
She winters and keeps warm her note.

Ask me no more where those stars light
That downwards fall in dead of night,
For in your eyes they sit, and there   15
Fixèd become as in their sphere.

Ask me no more if east or west
The Phœnix builds her spicy nest,
For unto you at last she flies,
And in your fragrant bosom dies.   20

SONG

Would you know what's soft? I dare
Not bring you to the down, or air,
Nor to stars to show what's bright,
Nor to snow to teach you white;

Nor, if you would music hear,   5
Call the orbs to take your ear;
Nor, to please your sense, bring forth
Bruisèd nard, or what's more worth;

Or on food were your thoughts placed,
Bring you nectar for a taste;   10
Would you have all these in one,
Name my mistress, and 't is done.

THE PROTESTATION

No more shall meads be decked with flow-
    ers,
Nor sweetness dwell in rosy bowers,
Nor greenest buds on branches spring,
Nor warbling birds delight to sing,
Nor April violets paint the grove,   5
If I forsake my Celia's love.

The fish shall in the ocean burn,
And fountains sweet shall bitter turn,
The humble oak no flood shall know
When floods shall highest hills o'erflow,   10
Black Lethe shall oblivion leave,
If e'er my Celia I deceive.

Love shall his bow and shaft lay by,
And Venus' doves want wings to fly,
The Sun refuse to show his light,   15
And day shall then be turned to night,
And in that night no star appear,
If once I leave my Celia dear.

Love shall no more inhabit earth,
Nor lovers more shall love for worth,   20
Nor joy above in heaven dwell,
Nor pain torment poor souls in hell,
Grim death no more shall horrid prove,
If e'er I leave bright Celia's love.

PERSUASIONS TO JOY: A SONG

If the quick spirits in your eye
Now languish and anon must die;
If every sweet and every grace
Must fly from that forsaken face;

Then, Celia, let us reap our joys   5
Ere Time such goodly fruit destroys.

Or if that golden fleece must grow
For ever free from agèd snow;
If those bright suns must know no shade
Nor your fresh beauties ever fade;   10
Then fear not, Celia, to bestow
    What, still being gathered, still must
    grow.

Thus either Time his sickle brings
In vain, or else in vain his wings.

INGRATEFUL BEAUTY THREAT-ENED

Know, Celia, since thou art so proud,
    'T was I that gave thee thy renown.
Thou hadst in the forgotten crowd
    Of common beauties lived unknown,
Had not my verse extolled thy name,   5
And with it imped the wings of Fame.

That killing power is none of thine:
    I gave it to thy voice and eyes;
Thy sweets, thy graces, all are mine;
    Thou art my star, shin'st in my skies; 10
Then dart not from thy borrowed sphere
Lightning on him that fixed thee there.

Tempt me with such affrights no more,
    Lest what I made I uncreate;
Let fools thy mystic form adore,   15
    I know thee in thy mortal state.
Wise poets, that wrapt Truth in tales,
Knew her themselves through all her veils.

AN EPITAPH

This little vault, this narrow room,
Of love and beauty is the tomb;
The dawning beam, that 'gan to clear
Our cloudèd sky, lies darkened here,
For ever set to us: by death   5
Sent to enflame the world beneath.
    'T was but a bud, yet did contain
More sweetness than shall spring again;
A budding star, that might have grown
Into a sun when it had blown.   10
This hopeful beauty did create
New life in love's declining state;
But now his empire ends, and we
From fire and wounding darts are free;
    His brand, his bow, let no man fear: 15
    The flames, the arrows, all lie here.

SIR WILLIAM DAVENANT
(1606–1668)

SONG

The lark now leaves his wat'ry nest,
  And climbing, shakes his dewy wings.
He takes this window for the East,
  And to implore your light he sings—
Awake, awake! the morn will never rise 5
Till she can dress her beauty at your eyes.

The merchant bows unto the seaman's star,
  The ploughman from the sun his season
    takes;
But still the lover wonders what they are
  Who look for day before his mistress
    wakes. 10
Awake, awake! break thro' your veils of
    lawn!
And draw your curtains, and begin the
    dawn!

PRAISE AND PRAYER

Praise is devotion fit for mighty minds,
  The diff'ring world's agreeing sacrifice;
Where Heaven divided faiths united finds:
  But prayer in various discord upward
    flies.

For Prayer the ocean is where diversely 5
  Men steer their course, each to a sev'ral
    coast;
Where all our interests so discordant be
  That half beg winds by which the rest
    are lost.

By penitence when we ourselves forsake,
  'T is but in wise design on piteous
    Heaven; 10
In praise we nobly give what God may
    take,
  And are, without a beggar's blush, for-
    given.

EDMUND WALLER (1606–1687)

THE STORY OF PHŒBUS AND
DAPHNE APPLIED

Thyrsis, a youth of the inspirèd train,
Fair Sacharissa loved, but loved in vain.
Like Phœbus sung the no less amorous boy;
Like Daphne she, as lovely, and as coy!
With numbers he the flying nymph pur-
  sues. 5

With numbers such as Phœbus' self might
  use!
Such is the chase when Love and Fancy
  leads,
O'er craggy mountains, and through flow-
  ery meads;
Invoked to testify the lover's care,
Or form some image of his cruel fair. 10
Urged with his fury, like a wounded deer,
O'er these he fled; and now approaching
  near,
Had reached the nymph with his harmoni-
  ous lay,
Whom all his charms could not incline to
  stay.
Yet, what he sung in his immortal strain,
Though unsuccessful, was not sung in vain;
All, but the nymph that should redress his
  wrong, 17
Attend his passion, and approve his song.
Like Phœbus thus, acquiring unsought
  praise,
He catched at love, and filled his arms with
  bays. 20

TO PHYLLIS

Phyllis! why should we delay
Pleasures shorter than the day?
Could we (which we never can)
Stretch our lives beyond their span,
Beauty like a shadow flies, 5
And our youth before us dies.
Or would youth and beauty stay,
Love hath wings, and will away.
Love hath swifter wings than Time;
Change in love to heaven does climb. 10
Gods that never change their state,
Vary oft their love and hate.
  Phyllis! to this truth we owe
All the love betwixt us two.
Let not you and I inquire 15
What has been our past desire;
On what shepherds you have smiled,
Or what nymphs I have beguiled;
Leave it to the planets too,
What we shall hereafter do; 20
For the joys we now may prove,
Take advice of present love.

ON A GIRDLE

That which her slender waist confined,
Shall now my joyful temples bind;
No monarch but would give his crown,
His arms might do what this has done.

It was my heaven's extremest sphere, 5
The pale which held that lovely deer.
My joy, my grief, my hope, my love,
Did all within this circle move!

A narrow compass! and yet there
Dwelt all that's good, and all that's fair;
Give me but what this ribband bound, 11
Take all the rest the sun goes round.

GO LOVELY ROSE!

Go, lovely Rose!
Tell her that wastes her time and me,
That now she knows,
When I resemble her to thee,
How sweet and fair she seems to be. 5

Tell her that's young,
And shuns to have her graces spied,
That hadst thou sprung
In deserts, where no men abide,
Thou must have uncommended died. 10

Small is the worth
Of beauty from the light retired;
Bid her come forth,
Suffer herself to be desired,
And not blush so to be admired. 15

Then die! that she
The common fate of all things rare
May read in thee;
How small a part of time they share
That are so wondrous sweet and fair! 20

SIR JOHN SUCKLING (1609–1642)

A DOUBT OF MARTYRDOM

O for some honest lover's ghost,
  Some kind unbodied post
    Sent from the shades below!
    I strangely long to know
Whether the noble chaplets wear, 5
Those that their mistress' scorn did bear
  Or those that were used kindly.

For whatsoe'er they tell us here
  To make those sufferings dear,
    'T will there, I fear, be found 10
    That to the being crowned
T' have loved alone will not suffice,
Unless we also have been wise
  And have our loves enjoved.

What posture can we think him in 15
  That, here unloved, again
    Departs, and 's thither gone
    Where each sits by his own?
Or how can that Elysium be
Where I my mistress still must see 20
  Circled in other's arms?

For there the judges all are just,
  And Sophonisba must
    Be his whom she held dear,
    Not his who loved her here. 25
The sweet Philoclea, since she died,
Lies by her Pirocles his side,
    Not by Amphialus.

Some bays, perchance, or myrtle bough
  For difference crowns the brow 30
    Of those kind souls that were
    The noble martyrs here:
And if that be the only odds
(As who can tell?), ye kinder gods,
    Give me the woman here! 35

THE CONSTANT LOVER

Out upon it, I have loved
  Three whole days together!
And am like to love three more,
  If it prove fair weather.

Time shall moult away his wings 5
  Ere he shall discover
In the whole wide world again
  Such a constant lover.

But the spite on't is, no praise
  Is due at all to me: 10
Love with me had made no stays,
  Had it any been but she.

Had it any been but she,
  And that very face,
There had been at least ere this 15
  A dozen dozen in her place.

WHY SO PALE AND WAN?

Why so pale and wan, fond lover?
  Prithee, why so pale?
Will, when looking well can't move her,
  Looking ill prevail?
  Prithee, why so pale? 5

Why so dull and mute, young sinner?
  Prithee, why so mute?

Will, when speaking well can't win her,
  Saying nothing do 't?
  Prithee, why so mute?   10

Quit, quit for shame! This will not move;
  This cannot take her.
If of herself she will not love,
  Nothing can make her:
  The devil take her!   15

RICHARD CRASHAW (1613?–1649)

IN THE HOLY NATIVITY OF OUR LORD GOD

A HYMN SUNG AS BY THE SHEPHERDS

CHORUS

Come, we shepherds, whose blest sight
Hath met Love's noon in Nature's night;
Come, lift we up our loftier song
And wake the sun that lies too long.

To all our world of well-stol'n joy   5
He slept, and dreamt of no such thing;
While we found out heaven's fairer eye
And kissed the cradle of our King.
Tell him he rises now, too late
To show us aught worth looking at.   10

Tell him we now can show him more
Than he e'er showed to mortal sight;
Than he himself e'er saw before;
Which to be seen needs not his light.
Tell him, Tityrus, where th' hast been   15
Tell him, Thyrsis, what th' hast seen.

TITYRUS. Gloomy night embraced the place
  Where the noble infant lay,
    The babe looked up and showed
      his face;
  In spite of darkness, it was day.   20
    It was thy day, sweet! and did rise
  Not from the east, but from thine
    eyes.

CHORUS. It was thy day, sweet, etc.

THYRSIS. Winter chid aloud; and sent
  The angry North to wage his wars.
  The North forgot his fierce in-
    tent;   26
  And left perfumes instead of scars.
    By those sweet eyes' persuasive
      powers,
  Where he meant frost he scattered
  flowers.

CHO. By those sweet eyes', etc.   30

BOTH. We saw thee in thy balmy nest,
  Young dawn of our Eternal Day!
  We saw thine eyes break from
    their east
  And chase the trembling shades away.
  We saw thee, and we blest the
    sight,   35
  We saw thee by thine own sweet
    light.

TIT. Poor World, said I, what wilt thou do
  To entertain this starry stranger?
    Is this the best thou canst bestow?
  A cold, and not too cleanly, manger?
  Contend, the powers of heaven and
    earth, –   41
  To fit a bed for this huge birth!

CHO. Contend the powers, etc.

THYR. Proud World, said I; cease your
    contest
  And let the mighty babe alone;   45
    The phœnix builds the phœnix'
      nest,
  Love's architecture is his own;
    The babe whose birth embraves
      this morn,
  Made his own bed e'er he was born.

CHO. The babe whose, etc.   50

TIT. I saw the curled drops, soft and slow,
  Come hovering o'er the place's head;
    Off'ring their whitest sheets of
      snow
  To furnish the fair infant's bed.
  Forbear, said I; be not too bold;
  Your fleece is white, but 't is too
    cold.   56

CHO. Forbear, said I, etc.

THYR. I saw the obsequious seraphim
  Their rosy fleece of fire bestow,
    For well they now can spare their
      wing,   60
  Since heaven itself lies here below.
    Well done, said I; but are you
      sure
  Your down so warm, will pass for
    pure?

CHO. Well done, said I, etc.

TIT. No, no, your king's not yet to seek 65
  Where to repose his royal head;
    See, see how soon his new-bloomed
    cheek

'Twixt 's mother's breasts is gone to
    bed!
    Sweet choice, said we! no way but
    so
Not to lie cold, yet sleep in snow. 70

CHO.   Sweet choice, said we, etc.

BOTH.   We saw thee in thy balmy nest,
    Bright dawn of our Eternal Day!
      We saw thine eyes break from their
      east
    And   chase   the   trembling   shades
      away.   75
      We saw thee, and we blest the
      sight,
    We saw thee by thine own sweet
      light.

CHO.   We saw thee, etc.

FULL CHORUS

Welcome all wonders in one night!
Eternity shut in a span,   80
    Summer in winter, day in night,
Heaven in earth, and God in man.
    Great Little One, whose all-embracing
      birth
Lifts earth to heaven, stoops heaven to
    earth!

Welcome, though nor to gold nor silk, 85
To more than Cæsar's birthright is;
    Two sister-seas of virgin-milk
With many a rarely-tempered kiss
    That breathes at once both maid and
      mother,
Warms in the one, cools in the other.   90

Welcome, though not to those gay flies
Gilded i' th' beams of earthly kings,
    Slippery souls in smiling eyes,
But to poor shepherds, homespun things,
    Whose wealth 's their flock, whose wit 's
      to be   95
Well read in their simplicity.

Yet when young April's husband showers
Shall bless the fruitful Maia's bed,
We 'll bring the first-born of her flowers
To kiss thy feet and crown thy head.   100
    To thee, dread Lamb! Whose love must
      keep
The shepherds, more than they the sheep.

To Thee, meek Majesty! soft King
Of simple graces and sweet loves!

Each of us his lamb will bring,   105
Each his pair of silver doves!
    Till burnt at last in fire of thy fair eyes,
Ourselves become our own best sacrifice!

SIR JOHN DENHAM (1615–1669)

FROM COOPER'S HILL

My eye, descending from the hill, surveys
Where Thames amongst the wanton val-
    leys strays;
Thames, the most loved of all the Ocean's
    sons,
By his old sire, to his embraces runs,
Hasting to pay his tribute to the sea,   5
Like mortal life to meet eternity;
Though with those streams he no resem-
    blance hold,
Whose foam is amber, and their gravel
    gold,
His genuine and less guilty wealth t' ex-
    plore,
Search not his bottom, but survey his shore,
O'er which he kindly spreads his spacious
    wing,   11
And hatches plenty for th' ensuing spring;
Nor then destroys it with too fond a stay,
Like mothers which their infants overlay,
Nor, with a sudden and impetuous wave, 15
Like profuse kings, resumes the wealth he
    gave;
No unexpected inundations spoil
The mower's hopes, nor mock the plough-
    man's toil,
But godlike his unwearied bounty flows,
First loves to do, then loves the good he
    does;   20
Nor are his blessings to his banks con-
    fined,
But free and common as the sea or wind;
When he to boast or to disperse his stores,
Full of the tributes of his grateful shores,
Visits the world, and in his flying towers,
Brings home to us, and makes both Indies
    ours,   26
Finds wealth where 't is, bestows it where
    it wants,
Cities in deserts, woods in cities plants;
So that to us no thing, no place is strange,
While his fair bosom is the world's ex-
    change.   30
O could I flow like thee, and make thy
    stream
My great example, as it is my theme!

Though deep, yet clear, though gentle, yet
  not dull,
Strong without rage, without o'erflowing
  full.

* * *

ON MR. ABRAHAM COWLEY'S DEATH AND BURIAL AMONGST THE ANCIENT POETS

Old Chaucer, like the morning star,
To us discovers day from far.
His light those mists and clouds dissolved,
Which our dark nation long involved;
But he descending to the shades,   5
Darkness again the age invades.
Next, like Aurora, Spenser rose,
Whose purple blush the day foreshows;
The other three, with his own fires
Phœbus, the poets' god inspires;   10
By Shakspere's, Jonson's, Fletcher's lines,
Our stage's luster Rome's outshines:
These poets near our princes sleep,
And in one grave their mansion keep;
They lived to see so many days,   15
Till time had blasted all their bays;
But cursèd be the fatal hour
That plucked the fairest, sweetest flower
That in the muses' garden grew,
And amongst withered laurels threw.   20
Time, which made them their fame out-
  live,
To Cowley scarce did ripeness give.
Old mother wit, and Nature, gave
Shakspere and Fletcher all they have;
In Spenser, and in Jonson, Art   25
Of slower Nature got the start;
But both in him so equal are,
None knows which bears the happiest
  share;
To him no author was unknown,
Yet what he wrote was all his own;   30
He melted not the ancient gold,
Nor, with Ben Jonson, did make bold
To plunder all the Roman stores
Of poets, and of orators:
Horace's wit, and Virgil's state,   35
He did not steal, but emulate:
And when he would like them appear,
Their garb, but not their clothes, did wear:
He not from Rome alone, but Greece,
Like Jason brought the golden fleece;   40
To him that language, though to none
Of th' others, as his own was known.
On a stiff gale, as Flaccus sings,
The Theban swan extends his wings,
When through th' ethereal clouds he flies,

To the same pitch our swan doth rise.   46
Old Pindar's flights by him are reached,
When on that gale his wings are stretched.
His fancy and his judgment such,
Each to the other seemed too much,   50
His severe judgment, giving law,
His modest fancy, kept in awe,
As rigid husbands jealous are
When they believe their wives too fair.

* * *

RICHARD LOVELACE (1618–1658)

TO LUCASTA GOING TO THE WARS

Tell me not, Sweet, I am unkind,
  That from the nunnery
Of thy chaste breast and quiet mind
  To war and arms I fly.

True, a new mistress now I chase,   5
  The first foe in the field;
And with a stronger faith embrace
  A sword, a horse, a shield.

Yet this inconstancy is such
  As thou too shalt adore;   10
I could not love thee, Dear, so much,
  Loved I not Honor more.

TO ALTHEA, FROM PRISON

When Love with unconfinèd wings
  Hovers within my gates,
And my divine Althea brings
  To whisper at the grates;
When I lie tangled in her hair   5
  And fettered to her eye,
The birds that wanton in the air
  Know no such liberty.

When flowing cups run swiftly round
  With no allaying Thames,   10
Our careless heads with roses bound,
  Our hearts with loyal flames;
When thirsty grief in wine we steep,
  When healths and draughts go free,
Fishes that tipple in the deep   15
  Know no such liberty.

When, like committed linnets, I
  With shriller throat will sing
The sweetness, mercy, majesty,
  And glories of my king;   20

When I shall voice aloud how good
  He is, how great should be,
Enlargèd winds, that curl the flood,
  Know no such liberty.

Stone walls do not a prison make,   25
  Nor iron bars a cage;
Minds innocent and quiet take
  That for an hermitage;
If I have freedom in my love
  And in my soul am free,   30
Angels alone, that soar above,
  Enjoy such liberty.

THE ROSE

Sweet, serene, sky-like flower,
Haste to adorn her bower,
  From thy long cloudy bed
  Shoot forth thy damask head.

New-startled blush of Flora,   5
The grief of pale Aurora
  (Who will contest no more),
  Haste, haste to strew her floor!

Vermilion ball that's given
From lip to lip in heaven,   10
  Love's couch's coverled,
  Haste, haste to make her bed.

Dear offspring of pleased Venus
And jolly plump Silenus,
  Haste, haste to deck the hair   15
  Of th' only sweetly fair!

See! rosy is her bower,
Her floor is all this flower,
  Her bed a rosy nest
  By a bed of roses pressed!   20

But early as she dresses,
Why fly you her bright tresses?
Ah! I have found, I fear,—
  Because her cheeks are near.

TO LUCASTA

Lucasta, frown, and let me die!
  But smile, and, see, I live!
The sad indifference of your eye
  Both kills and doth reprieve;
You hide our fate within its screen;   5
  We feel our judgment, e'er we hear;
So in one picture I have seen
  An angel here, the devil there!

ABRAHAM COWLEY (1618–1667)

THE SWALLOW

Foolish Prater, what do'st thou
So early at my window do
With thy tuneless serenade?
Well 't had been had Tereus made
Thee as dumb as Philomel: 5
There his knife had done but well.
In thy undiscovered nest
Thou dost all the winter rest,
And dreamest o'er thy summer joys,
Free from the stormy season's noise: 10
Free from th' ill thou 'st done to me;
Who disturbs, or seeks out thee?
Had'st thou all the charming notes
Of the wood's poetic throats,
All thy art could never pay   15
What thou 'st ta'en from me away;
Cruel bird, thou 'st ta'en away
A dream out of my arms to-day,
A dream that ne'er must equaled be
By all that waking eyes may see.   20
Thou this damage to repair,
Nothing half so sweet or fair,
Nothing half so good can'st bring,
Though men say, 'Thou bring'st the
  spring?'

THE WISH

Well then! I now do plainly see
This busy world and I shall ne'er agree.
The very honey of all earthly joy
Does of all meats the soonest cloy;
  And they, methinks, deserve my pity 5
Who for it can endure the stings,
The crowd and buzz and murmurings,
  Of this great hive, the city.

Ah, yet, ere I descend to the grave
May I a small house and large garden
  have;
And a few friends, and many books, both
  true,   11
Both wise, and both delightful too!
  And since love ne'er will from me flee,
A mistress moderately fair,
And good as guardian angels are,   15
  Only beloved and loving me.

O fountains! when in you shall I
Myself eased of unpeaceful thoughts espy?
O fields! O woods! when, when shall I be
  made

The happy tenant of your shade?   20
  Here's the spring-head of pleasure's
    flood:
Here's wealthy Nature's treasury,
Where all the riches lie that she
  Has coined and stamped for good.

Pride and ambition here   25
Only in far-fetched metaphors appear;
Here naught but winds can hurtful mur-
    murs scatter,
And naught but Echo flatter.
  The gods, when they descended, hither
From heaven did always choose their way:
And therefore we may boldly say   31
  That 't is the way too thither.

How happy here should I
And one dear She live, and embracing die!
She who is all the world, and can exclude
In deserts solitude.   36
  I should have then this only fear:
Lest men, when they my pleasures see,
Should hither throng to live like me,
  And so make a city here.   40

ANDREW MARVEL (1621–1678)

THE GARDEN

How vainly men themselves amaze,
To win the palm, the oak, or bays,
And their incessant labors see
Crowned from some single herb or tree
Whose short and narrow-vergèd shade   5
Does prudently their toils upbraid,
While all the flowers and trees do close
To weave the garlands of repose!

Fair Quiet, have I found thee here,
And Innocence, thy sister dear?   10
Mistaken long, I sought you then
In busy companies of men.
Your sacred plants, if here below,
Only among the plants will grow;
Society is all but rude   15
To this delicious solitude.

No white nor red was ever seen
So amorous as this lovely green.
Fond lovers, cruel as their flame,
Cut in these trees their mistress' name.   20
Little, alas! they know or heed,
How far these beauties hers exceed!

Fair trees! wheres'e'r your barks I wound
No name shall but your own be found.

When we have run our passion's heat,   25
Love hither makes his best retreat.
The gods, that mortal beauty chase,
Still in a tree did end their race;
Apollo hunted Daphne so,
Only that she might laurel grow;   30
And Pan did after Syrinx speed,
Not as a nymph, but for a reed.

What wondrous life is this I lead!
Ripe apples drop about my head;
The luscious clusters of the vine   35
Upon my mouth do crush their wine;
The nectarine, and curious peach,
Into my hands themselves do reach;
Stumbling on melons, as I pass,
Insnared with flowers, I fall on grass.   40

Meanwhile the mind, from pleasure less,
Withdraws into its happiness:—
The mind, that ocean where each kind
Does straight its own resemblance find;
Yet it creates, transcending these,   45
Far other worlds, and other seas,
Annihilating all that 's made
To a green thought in a green shade.

Here at the fountain's sliding foot,
Or at some fruit-tree's mossy root,   50
Casting the body's vest aside,
My soul into the boughs does glide:
There, like a bird, it sits and sings,
Then whets and combs its silver wings,
And, till prepared for longer flight,   55
Waves in its plumes the various light.

Such was that happy garden-state,
While man there walked without a mate
After a place so pure and sweet.
What other help could yet be meet!   60
But 't was beyond a mortal's share
To wander solitary there:
Two paradises 't were in one,
To live in paradise alone.

How well the skilful gardener drew   65
Of flowers, and herbs, this dial new;
Where, from above, the milder sun
Does through a fragrant zodiac run,
And, as it works, the industrious bee
Computes its time as well as we!   70
How could such sweet and wholesome
    hours
Be reckoned but with herbs and flowers?

TO HIS COY MISTRESS

Had we but world enough, and time,
This coyness, Lady, were no crime,
We would sit down and think which way
To walk and pass our long love's day.
Thou by the Indian Ganges' side   5
Shouldst rubies find; I by the tide
Of Humber would complain. I would
Love you ten years before the Flood,
And you should, if you please, refuse
Till the conversion of the Jews.   10
My vegetable love should grow
Vaster than empires, and more slow;
An hundred years should go to praise
Thine eyes and on thy forehead gaze;
Two hundred to adore each breast,   15
But thirty thousand to the rest;
An age at least to every part,
And the last age should show your heart.
For, Lady, you deserve this state,
Nor would I love at lower rate.   20
   But at my back I always hear
Time's wingèd chariot hurrying near;
And yonder all before us lie
Deserts of vast eternity.
Thy beauty shall no more be found,   25
Nor, in thy marble vault, shall sound
My echoing song; then worms shall try
That long preserved virginity,
And your quaint honor turn to dust,
And into ashes all my lust: 30
The grave's a fine and private place,
But none, I think, do there embrace.
   Now therefore, while the youthful hue
Sits on thy skin like morning dew,
And while thy willing soul transpires   35
At every pore with instant fires,
Now let us sport us while we may,
And now, like amorous birds of prey,
Rather at once our time devour
Than languish in his slow-chapt power.   40
Let us roll all our strength and all
Our sweetness up into one ball,
And tear our pleasures with rough strife
Thorough the iron gates of life:
Thus, though we cannot make our sun   45
Stand still, yet we will make him run.

HENRY VAUGHAN (1622–1695)

THE RETREAT

Happy those early days, when I
Shined in my angel-infancy!
Before I understood this place

Appointed for my second race,
Or taught my soul to fancy aught   5
But a white, celestial thought;
When yet I had not walked above
A mile or two from my first love,
And looking back, at that short space,
Could see a glimpse of his bright face;   10
When on some gilded cloud or flower
My gazing soul would dwell an hour,
And in those weaker glories spy
Some shadows of eternity;
Before I taught my tongue to wound   15
My conscience with a sinful sound,
Or had the black art to dispense,
A several sin to every sense,
But felt through all this fleshly dress
Bright shoots of everlastingness.   20
   O, how I long to travel back,
And tread again that ancient track,
That I might once more reach that plain,
Where first I left my glorious train;
From whence the enlightened spirit sees   25
That shady city of palm trees.
But ah! my soul with too much stay
Is drunk, and staggers in the way!
Some men a forward motion love,
But I by backward steps would move;   30
And when this dust falls to the urn,
In that state I came, return.

THE WORLD

I saw Eternity the other night,
Like a great ring of pure and endless light,
      All calm, as it was bright;
And round beneath it, Time, in hours, days,
      years,
      Driv'n by the spheres   5
Like a vast shadow moved; in which the
      world
      And all her train were hurled.
The doting lover in his quaintest strain
      Did there complain;
Near him, his lute, his fancy, and his
      flights,   10
      Wit's four delights,
With gloves, and knots, the silly snares of
      pleasure,
      Yet his dear treasure,
All scattered lay, while he his eyes did pour
      Upon a flower.   15

The darksome statesman, hung with weights
      and woe,
Like a thick midnight-fog, moved there so
      slow,
      He did not stay, nor go;

Condemning thoughts, like sad eclipses, scowl
    Upon his soul,   20
And clouds of crying witnesses without
    Pursued him with one shout.
Yet digged the mole, and lest his ways be found,
    Worked under ground,
Where he did clutch his prey; but one did see   25
    That policy;
Churches and altars fed him; perjuries
    Were gnats and flies;
It rained about him blood and tears, but he
    Drank them as free.   30

The fearful miser on a heap of rust
Sat pining all his life there, did scarce trust
    His own hands with the dust,
Yet would not place one piece above, but lives
    In fear of thieves.   35
Thousands there were as frantic as himself,
    And hugged each one his pelf;
The downright epicure placed heaven in sense,
    And scorned pretence;
While others, slipt into a wide excess,   40
    Said little less;
The weaker sort, slight, trivial wares enslave,
    Who think them brave;
And poor, despisèd Truth sat counting by
    Their victory.   45

Yet some, who all this while did weep and sing,
And sing and weep, soared up into the ring;
    But most would use no wing.
O fools, said I, thus to prefer dark night
    Before true light!   50
To live in grots and caves, and hate the day
    Because it shows the way,
The way, which from this dead and dark abode
    Leads up to God;
A way there you might tread the sun, and be   55
    More bright than he!
But, as I did their madness so discuss,
    One whispered thus
'This ring the Bridegroom did for none provide,
    But for his bride.'   60

DEPARTED FRIENDS

They are all gone into the world of light!
    And I alone sit lingering here;
Their very memory is fair and bright,
    And my sad thoughts doth clear.

It glows and glitters in my cloudy breast,   5
    Like stars upon some gloomy grove,
Or those faint beams in which this hill is drest,
    After the sun's remove.

I see them walking in an air of glory,
    Whose light doth trample on my days: 10
My days, which are at best but dull and hoary,
    Mere glimmering and decays.

O holy Hope! and high Humility,
    High as the heavens above!
These are your walks, and you have showed them me,   15
    To kindle my cold love.

Dear, beauteous Death! the jewel of the just,
    Shining nowhere, but in the dark,
What mysteries do lie beyond thy dust,
    Could man outlook that mark!   20

He that hath found some fledged bird's nest, may know
    At first sight if the bird be flown;
But what fair well or grove he sings in now,
    That is to him unknown.

And yet, as angels in some brighter dreams
    Call to the soul, when man doth sleep, 26
So some strange thoughts transcend our wonted themes,
    And into glory peep.

If a star were confined into a tomb,
    The captive flames must needs burn there;   30
But when the hand that locked her up, gives room,
    She 'll shine through all the sphere.

O Father of eternal life, and all
    Created glories under Thee,
Resume Thy spirit from this world of thrall
    Into true liberty.   36

Either disperse these mists, which blot and fill
    My perspective still as they pass;
Or else remove me hence unto that hill,
    Where I shall need no glass.   40

FRANCIS BACON (1561–1626)

Bacon was connected through both his parents with the governing classes. His father was lord keeper of the great seal, and the queen used to call the boy her 'young lord keeper.' At twelve he went to Trinity College, Cambridge, and as a youth he studied law at Gray's Inn. He was in the diplomatic service at Paris when his father died, leaving him but ill provided for. In 1584 he was elected to the House of Commons, but in spite of conspicuous ability and powerful connections, his political preferment was slow. He became solicitor-general in 1607, attorney-general 1613, privy councillor 1616, lord keeper 1617, lord chancellor and baron Verulam 1618, viscount St. Albans 1621. But hostile political influences in this last year brought about his fall. He was accused of bribery, and admitted receiving gifts, but denied that they had influenced him in the administration of justice. He was deprived of all his offices, fined £200,000, imprisoned, and excluded from court and parliament. All the penalties except the last were immediately remitted by the king, but he was not allowed to return to public life. He retired to the estate he had inherited from his elder brother, and gave himself to literature and philosophy, which had always occupied his leisure. While still a young man, he said, 'I have as vast contemplative ends as I have moderate civil ends: for I have taken all knowledge to be my province.' *The Advancement of Learning*, published in English in 1605, is mainly an attempt to review what was then known; the *Novum Organum* (in Latin, 1620) is an exposition of the means by which the bounds of knowledge may be extended. His philosophical work was of great influence on account of the stress he laid on observation of facts and the testing of hypothesis by experiment. He met his death through a chill contracted by leaving his coach on a winter's day to gather snow to stuff a fowl in order to try the effect of cold on the preservation of meat. His *History of Henry VII* (1622) is an important work, but his most notable contribution to literature was the *Essays* — a title probably suggested by the French *Essais* of Montaigne (1580). Bacon's first edition of 10 essays appeared in 1597, an enlarged edition, containing 38, in 1612, and the final issue (58 essays) in 1625. Though they reveal only at times the philosophical bent of Bacon's genius, they illustrate fully the extraordinary keenness of his mind, his practical worldly wisdom, and the terse incisiveness of his style.

ESSAYS

I.— OF TRUTH

'What is truth?' said jesting Pilate; and would not stay for an answer. Certainly there be that delight in giddiness, and count it a bondage to fix a belief, affecting free-will in thinking, as well as in acting. And though the sects of philosophers of that kind be gone, yet there remain certain discoursing wits which are of the same veins, though there be not so much blood in them as was in those of the ancients. But it is not only the difficulty and labor which men take in finding out of truth; nor again, that when it is found, it imposeth upon men's thoughts, that doth bring lies in favor: but a natural though corrupt love of the lie itself. One of the later school of the Grecians examineth the matter, and is at a stand to think what should be in it, that men should love lies: where neither they make for pleasure, as with poets; nor for advantage, as with the merchant; but for the lie's sake. But I cannot tell: this same truth is a naked and open daylight, that doth not show the masques, and mummeries, and triumphs of the world half so stately and daintily as candle-lights. Truth may perhaps come to the price of a pearl, that showeth best by day; but it will not rise to the price of a diamond or carbuncle, that showeth best in varied lights. A mixture of a lie doth ever add pleasure. Doth any man doubt that if there were taken out of men's minds vain opinions, flattering hopes, false valuations, imaginations as one would, and the like, but it would leave the minds of a number

187

of men poor shrunken things, full of melancholy and indisposition, and unpleasing to themselves? One of the fathers, in great severity, called poesy *vinum daemonum* [devils' wine], because it filleth the imagination, and yet it is but with the shadow of a lie. But it is not the lie that passeth through the mind, but the lie that sinketh in and settleth in it that doth the hurt, such as we spake of before. But howsoever these things are thus in men's depraved judgments and affections, yet truth, which only doth judge itself, teacheth that the inquiry of truth, which is the love-making, or wooing of it; the knowledge of truth, which is the presence of it; and the belief of truth, which is the enjoying of it, is the sovereign good of human nature. The first creature of God, in the works of the days, was the light of the sense; the last was the light of reason; and his Sabbath work, ever since, is the illumination of his spirit. First he breathed light upon the face of the matter, or chaos; then he breathed light into the face of man; and still he breatheth and inspireth light into the face of his chosen. The poet, that beautified the sect, that was otherwise inferior to the rest, saith yet excellently well, 'It is a pleasure to stand upon the shore, and to see ships tost upon the sea; a pleasure to stand in the window of a castle, and to see a battle, and the adventures thereof below; but no pleasure is comparable to the standing upon the vantage ground of truth (a hill not to be commanded, and where the air is always clear and serene), and to see the errors, and wanderings, and mists, and tempests, in the vale below'; so always that this prospect be with pity, and not with swelling or pride. Certainly it is heaven upon earth to have a man's mind move in charity, rest in providence, and turn upon the poles of truth.

To pass from theological and philosophical truth to the truth of civil business, it will be acknowledged, even by those that practice it not, that clear and round dealing is the honor of man's nature, and that mixture of falsehood is like alloy in coin of gold and silver, which may make the metal work the better, but it embaseth it; for these winding and crooked courses are the goings of the serpent, which goeth basely upon

the belly, and not upon the feet. There is no vice that doth so cover a man with shame as to be found false and perfidious; and therefore Montaigne saith prettily, when he inquired the reason why the word of the lie should be such a disgrace, and such an odious charge, 'If it be well weighed, to say that a man lieth, is as much as to say that he is brave towards God, and a coward towards man.' For a lie faces God, and shrinks from man. Surely the wickedness of falsehood and breach of faith cannot possibly be so highly expressed as in that it shall be the last peal to call the judgments of God upon the generations of men: it being foretold, that when Christ cometh, 'he shall not find faith upon the earth.'

V.— OF ADVERSITY

It was a high speech of Seneca, after the manner of the Stoics, that 'the good things which belong to prosperity are to be wished, but the good things that belong to adversity are to be admired.' *Bona rerum secundarum optabilia, adversarum mirabilia.* Certainly if miracles be the command over Nature, they appear most in adversity. It is yet a higher speech of his than the other, much too high for a heathen, 'It is true greatness to have in one the frailty of a man and the security of a God' *(Vere magnum, habere fragilitatem hominis, securitatem Dei).* This would have done better in poesy, where transcendencies are more allowed. And the poets, indeed, have been busy with it; for it is in effect the thing which is figured in that strange fiction of the ancient poets which seemeth not to be without mystery; nay, and to have some approach to the state of a christian: that Hercules, when he went to unbind Prometheus, by whom human nature is represented, sailed the length of the great ocean in an earthen pot or pitcher; lively describing christian resolution that saileth in the frail bark of the flesh through the waves of the world. But to speak in a mean, the virtue of prosperity is temperance, the virtue of adversity is fortitude, which in morals is the more heroical virtue. Prosperity is the blessing of the Old Testament, adversity is the blessing of the New, which carrieth the greater benediction and the clearer revelation of God's favor. Yet, even in the Old Testament, if you listen to David's harp you shall hear as many hearse-like airs as carols. And the pencil of the Holy Ghost hath labored more in describing the afflictions of Job than the felicities of Solomon. Prosperity is not without many fears and distastes, and adversity is not without comforts and hopes. We see in needleworks and embroideries it is more pleasing to have a lively work upon a sad and solemn ground than to have a dark and melancholy work upon a lightsome ground. Judge, therefore, of the pleasure of the heart by the pleasure of the eye. Certainly virtue is like precious odors, most fragrant when they are incensed or crushed; for prosperity doth best discover vice, but adversity doth best discover virtue.

VII.— OF PARENTS AND CHILDREN

The joys of parents are secret, and so are their griefs and fears; they cannot utter the one, nor they will not utter the other. Children sweeten labors, but they make misfortunes more bitter; they increase the cares of life, but they mitigate the remembrance of death. The perpetuity by generation is common to beasts; but memory, and merit, and noble works are proper to men; and surely a man shall see the noblest works and foundations have proceeded from childless men, which have sought to express the images of their minds where those of their bodies have failed; so the care of posterity is most in them that have no posterity. They that are the first raisers of their houses are most indulgent towards their children, beholding them as the continuance, not only of their kind, but of their work, and so both children and creatures.

The difference in affection of parents towards their several children is many times unequal, and sometimes unworthy, especially in the mother; as Solomon saith, 'A wise son rejoiceth the father, but an ungracious son shames the mother.' A man shall see, where there is a house full of children, one or two of the eldest respected, and the youngest made wantons; but in the midst, some that are as it were forgotten, who, many times, nevertheless, prove the best. The illiberality of parents, in allowance towards their children, is a harmful error, and makes them base, acquaints them with shifts, makes them sort with mean company, and makes them surfeit more when they come to plenty; and therefore the proof is best when men keep their authority towards their children, but not their purse. Men have a foolish manner (both parents, and schoolmasters, and servants), in creating and breeding an emulation between brothers during childhood, which many times sorteth to discord when they are men, and disturbeth families. The Italians make little difference between children and nephews, or near kinsfolk; but so they be of the lump they care not, though they pass not through their own body. And, to say truth, in nature it is much a like matter; insomuch that we see a nephew sometimes resembleth an uncle, or a kinsman, more than his own parent, as the blood happens. Let parents choose betimes the vocations and courses they mean their children should take, for then they are most flexible; and let them not too much apply themselves to the disposition of their children, as thinking they will take best to that which they have most mind to. It is true, that if the affection, or aptness, of the children be extraordinary, then it is good not to cross it; but generally the precept is good. *Optimum elige, suave et facile illud faciet consuetudo* [Choose the best; custom will make it pleasant and easy]. Younger brothers are commonly fortunate, but seldom or never where the elder are disinherited.

VIII.— OF MARRIAGE AND SINGLE LIFE

He that hath wife and children hath given hostages to fortune; for they are impediments to great enterprises, either of virtue or mischief. Certainly the best works, and of greatest merit for the public, have proceeded from the unmarried or childless men, which, both in affection and means, have married and endowed the public. Yet it were great reason that those that have children should have greatest care of future times, unto which they know they must transmit their dearest pledges.

Some there are, who, though they lead a single life, yet their thoughts do end with themselves, and account future times impertinences; nay, there are some other that account wife and children but as bills of charges. Nay, more, there are some foolish rich covetous men that take a pride in having no children, because they may be thought so much the richer; for, perhaps, they have heard some talk. 'Such a one is a great rich man,' and another except to it, 'Yea, but he hath a great charge of children,' as if it were an abatement to his riches. But the most ordinary cause of a single life is liberty, especially in certain self-pleasing and humorous minds, which are so sensible of every restraint, as they will go near to think their girdles and garters to be bonds and shackles. Unmarried men are best friends, best masters, best servants, but not always best subjects; for they are light to run away, and almost all fugitives are of that condition. A single life doth well with churchmen, for charity will hardly water the ground where it must first fill a pool. It is indifferent for judges and magistrates, for if they be facile and corrupt you shall have a servant five times worse than a wife. For soldiers, I find the generals commonly, in their hortatives, put men in mind of their wives and children. And I think the despising of marriage amongst the Turks maketh the vulgar soldier more base. Certainly, wife and children are a kind of discipline of humanity; and single men, though they be many times more charitable, because their means are less exhaust, yet, on the other side, they are more cruel and hard-hearted, good to make severe inquisitors, because their tenderness is not so oft called upon. Grave natures, led by custom, and therefore constant, are commonly loving husbands; as was said of Ulysses, '*Vetulam suam praetulit immortalitati*' [He preferred his old wife to immortality]. Chaste women are often proud and froward, as presuming upon the merit of their chastity. It is one of the best bonds, both of chastity and obedience, in the wife if she think her husband wise, which she will never do if she find him

jealous. Wives are young men's mistresses, companions for middle age, and old men's nurses; so as a man may have a quarrel to marry when he will. But yet he was reputed one of the wise men that made answer to the question when a man should marry, 'A young man not yet, an elder man not at all.' It is often seen that bad husbands have very good wives; whether it be that it raiseth the price of their husband's kindness when it comes, or that the wives take a pride in their patience; but this never fails, if the bad husbands were of their own choosing, against their friends' consent; for then they will be sure to make good their own folly.

X.—OF LOVE

The stage is more beholden to love than the life of man. For as to the stage love is ever a matter of comedies and now and then of tragedies, but in life it doth much mischief, sometimes like a siren, sometimes like a fury. You may observe that amongst all the great and worthy persons whereof the memory remaineth, either ancient or recent, there is not one that hath been transported to the mad degree of love, which shows that great spirits and great business do keep out this weak passion. You must except, nevertheless, Marcus Antonius, the half-partner of the empire of Rome, and Appius Claudius, the decemvir and lawgiver; whereof the former was indeed a voluptuous man and inordinate, but the latter was an austere and wise man; and therefore it seems, though rarely, that love can find entrance, not only into an open heart, but also into a heart well fortified, if watch be not well kept. It is a poor saying of Epicurus: *Satis magnum alter alteri theatrum sumus* [We are to each other a theater large enough], as if man, made for the contemplation of heaven and all noble objects, should do nothing but kneel before a little idol and make himself subject, though not of the mouth, as beasts are, yet of the eye, which was given him for higher purposes. It is a strange thing to note the excess of this passion, and how it braves the nature and value of things by this, that the speaking in a perpetual hyperbole is comely in nothing but in love. Neither is it merely in the phrase; for whereas it hath been well said that the arch-flatterer, with whom all the petty flatterers have intelligence, is a man's self, certainly the lover is more. For there was never proud man thought so absurdly well of himself as the lover doth of the person loved, and, therefore, it was well said that it is impossible to love and to be wise. Neither doth this weakness appear to others only, and not to the party loved, but to the loved most of all, except the love be reciprocal. For it is a true rule that love is ever rewarded either with the reciproque or with an inward and secret contempt; by how much the more men ought to beware of this passion, which loseth not only other things but itself. As for the other losses, the poet's relation doth well figure them, that he that preferred Helena quitted the gifts of Juno and Pallas; for whosoever esteemeth too much of amorous affection quitteth both riches and wisdom. This passion hath its floods in the very times of weakness, which are great prosperity and great adversity (though this latter hath been less observed), both which times kindle love and make it more fervent, and, therefore, show it to be the child of folly. They do best who, if they cannot but admit love, yet make it keep quarter, and sever it wholly from their serious affairs and actions of life; for if it check once with business, it troubleth men's fortunes and maketh men that they can nowise be true to their own ends. I know not how, but martial men are given to love; I think it is but as they are given to wine, for perils commonly ask to be paid in pleasures. There is in man's nature a secret inclination and motion towards love of others, which, if it be not spent upon some one or a few, doth naturally spread itself towards many, and maketh men become humane and charitable, as it is seen sometimes in friars. Nuptial love maketh mankind, friendly love perfecteth it, but wanton love corrupteth and embaseth it.

XII.—OF BOLDNESS

It is a trivial grammar-school text, but yet worthy a wise man's considera-

tion: question was asked of Demosthenes, what was the chief part of an orator? He answered, Action: what next? Action: what next again? Action. He said it that knew it best, and had by nature himself no advantage in that he commended. A strange thing, that that part of an orator which is but superficial, and rather the virtue of a player, should be placed so high above those other noble parts, of invention, elocution, and the rest — nay, almost alone, as if it were all in all. But the reason is plain. There is in human nature generally more of the fool than of the wise; and, therefore, those faculties by which the foolish part of men's minds is taken are most potent. Wonderful like is the case of boldness in civil business. What first? — Boldness. What second and third? — Boldness. And yet boldness is a child of ignorance and baseness, far inferior to other parts. But, nevertheless, it doth fascinate and bind hand and foot those that are either shallow in judgment or weak in courage, which are the greatest part — yea, and prevaileth with wise men at weak times. Therefore, we see it hath done wonders in popular states, but with senates and princes less; and more ever upon the first entrance of bold persons into action than soon after; for boldness is an ill keeper of promise. Surely, as there are mountebanks for the natural body, so there are mountebanks for the politic body; men that undertake great cures, and perhaps have been lucky in two or three experiments, but want the grounds of science, and therefore cannot hold out — nay, you shall see a bold fellow many times do Mahomet's miracle. Mahomet made the people believe that he would call a hill to him, and from the top of it offer up his prayers for the observers of his law. The people assembled; Mahomet called the hill to come to him again and again; and when the hill stood still he was never a whit abashed, but said, 'If the hill will not come to Mahomet, Mahomet will go to the hill.' So these men, when they have promised great matters, and failed most shamefully, yet, if they have the perfection of boldness, they will but slight it over, and make a turn, and no more ado. Certainly to men of great judgment bold persons are a sport to behold — nay, and to the vulgar also boldness hath somewhat of the ridiculous; for if absurdity be the subject of laughter, doubt you not but great boldness is seldom without some absurdity. Especially it is a sport to see when a bold fellow is out of countenance, for that puts his face into a most shrunken and wooden posture, as needs it must, for in bashfulness the spirits do a little go and come; but with bold men, upon like occasion, they stand at a stay, like a stale at chess, where it is no mate, but yet the game cannot stir; but this last were fitter for a satire than for a serious observation. This is well to be weighed, that boldness is ever blind: for it seeth not dangers and inconveniences. Therefore it is ill in counsel, good in execution; so that the right use of bold persons is that they never command in chief, but be seconds, and under the direction of others. For in counsel it is good to see dangers; and in execution not to see them, except they be very great.

XVII.— OF SUPERSTITION

It were better to have no opinion of God at all, than such an opinion as is unworthy of him; for the one is unbelief, the other is contumely: and certainly superstition is the reproach of the Deity. Plutarch saith well to that purpose: 'Surely,' saith he, 'I had rather a great deal, men should say there was no such a man at all as Plutarch, than that they should say that there was one Plutarch, that would eat his children as soon as they were born'; as the poets speak of Saturn. And as the contumely is greater towards God, so the danger is greater towards men. Atheism leaves a man to sense, to philosophy, to natural piety, to laws, to reputation — all which may be guides to an outward moral virtue, though religion were not; but superstition dismounts all these, and erecteth an absolute monarchy in the minds of men. Therefore atheism did never perturb states; for it makes men wary of themselves, as looking no further; and we see the times inclined to atheism, as the time of Augustus Cæsar, were civil times; but superstition hath been the confusion of many states, and bringeth in a new *primum mobile,* that ravisheth all the spheres of government. The master of supersti-

tion is the people; and in all superstition wise men follow fools; and arguments are fitted to practice in a reversed order. It was gravely said, by some of the prelates in the Council of Trent, where the doctrine of the schoolmen bare great sway, that the schoolmen were like astronomers, which did feign eccentrics and epicycles, and such engines of orbs, to save the phenomena, though they knew there were no such things; and, in like manner, that the schoolmen had framed a number of subtle and intricate axioms and theorems to save the practice of the church. The causes of superstition are pleasing and sensual rites and ceremonies, excess of outward and pharisaical holiness, over-great reverence of traditions, which cannot but load the church; the stratagems of prelates for their own ambition and lucre; the favoring too much of good intentions, which openeth the gate to conceits and novelties; the taking an aim at divine matters by human, which cannot but breed mixture of imaginations; and, lastly, barbarous times, especially joined with calamities and disasters. Superstition without a veil is a deformed thing, for as it addeth deformity to an ape to be so like a man, so the similitude of superstition to religion makes it the more deformed. And as wholesome meat corrupteth to little worms, so good forms and orders corrupt into a number of petty observances. There is a superstition in avoiding superstition, when men think to do best if they go farthest from the superstition formerly received. Therefore care would be had that, as it fareth in ill purgings, the good be not taken away with the bad, which commonly is done when the people is the reformer.

XXIII.— OF WISDOM FOR A MAN'S SELF

An ant is a wise creature for itself, but it is a shrewd thing in an orchard or garden; and certainly men that are great lovers of themselves waste the public. Divide with reason between selflove and society; and be so true to thyself as thou be not false to others, especially to thy king and country. It is a poor center of a man's actions, himself. It is right earth: for that only stands fast upon its own center; whereas all things that have affinity with the heavens move upon the center of another, which they benefit. The referring of all to a man's self is more tolerable in a sovereign prince, because themselves are not only themselves, but their good and evil is at the peril of the public fortune: but it is a desperate evil in a servant to a prince, or a citizen in a republic; for whatsoever affairs pass such a man's hands, he crooketh them to his own ends, which must needs be often eccentric to the ends of his master or state. Therefore, let princes or states choose such servants as have not this mark, except they mean their service should be made but the accessory. That which maketh the effect more pernicious is that all proportion is lost. It were disproportion enough for the servant's good to be preferred before the master's; but yet it is a greater extreme, when a little good of the servant shall carry things against a great good of the master's. And yet that is the case of bad officers, treasurers, ambassadors, generals, and other false and corrupt servants, which set a bias upon their bowl, of their own petty ends and envies, to the overthrow of their master's great and important affairs. And for the most part, the good such servants receive is after the model of their own fortune, but the hurt they sell for that good is after the model of their master's fortune. And certainly it is the nature of extreme self-lovers, as they will set a house on fire and it were but to roast their eggs; and yet these men many times hold credit with their masters, because their study is but to please them, and profit themselves; and for either respect they will abandon the good of their affairs.

Wisdom for a man's self is, in many branches thereof, a depraved thing; it is the wisdom of rats, that will be sure to leave a house somewhat before it fall; it is the wisdom of the fox, that thrusts out the badger, who digged and made room for him; it is the wisdom of crocodiles, that shed tears when they would devour. But that which is specially to be noted is that those which (as Cicero says of Pompey) are *sui amantes sine rivali* [lovers of themselves without a rival] are many times unfortunate; and whereas they have all

their time sacrificed to themselves, they become in the end themselves sacrifices to the inconstancy of fortune, whose wings they thought by their self-wisdom to have pinioned.

XXV.— OF DISPATCH

Affected dispatch is one of the most dangerous things to business that can be. It is like that which the physicians call *predigestion,* or hasty digestion, which is sure to fill the body full of crudities and secret seeds of diseases. Therefore measure not dispatch by the times of sitting, but by the advancement of the business. And as in races, it is not the large stride, or high lift, that makes the speed, so in business, the keeping close to the matter, and not taking of it too much at once, procureth dispatch. It is the care of some, only to come off speedily for the time, or to contrive some false periods of business, because they may seem men of dispatch; but it is one thing to abbreviate by contracting, another by cutting off; and business so handled at several sittings or meetings goeth commonly backward and forward in an unsteady manner. I knew a wise man that had it for a byword, when he saw men hasten to a conclusion, ' Stay a little, that we may make an end the sooner.'

On the other side, true dispatch is a rich thing; for time is the measure of business, as money is of wares; and business is bought at a dear hand where there is small dispatch. The Spartans and Spaniards have been noted to be of small dispatch: *Mi venga la muerte de Spagna,* ' Let my death come from Spain,' for then it will be sure to be long in coming.

Give good hearing to those that give the first information in business; and rather direct them in the beginning than interrupt them in the continuance of their speeches; for he that is put out of his own order will go forward and backward, and be more tedious while he waits upon his memory, than he could have been if he had gone on in his own course. But sometimes it is seen that the moderator is more troublesome than the actor.

Iterations are commonly loss of time; but there is no such gain of time as to iterate often the state of the question; for it chaseth away many a frivolous speech as it is coming forth. Long and curious speeches are as fit for dispatch as a robe or mantle with a long train is for a race. Prefaces, and passages, and excusations, and other speeches of reference to the person are great wastes of time; and though they seem to proceed of modesty, they are bravery. Yet beware of being too material when there is any impediment or obstruction in men's wills; for pre-occupation of mind ever requireth preface of speech, like a fomentation to make the unguent enter.

Above all things, order and distribution, and singling out of parts is the life of dispatch, so as the distribution be not too subtle; for he that doth not divide will never enter well into business, and he that divideth too much will never come out of it clearly. To choose time is to save time; and an unseasonable motion is but beating the air. There be three parts of business — the preparation, the debate, or examination, and the perfection; whereof, if you look for dispatch, let the middle only be the work of many, and the first and last the work of few. The proceeding upon somewhat conceived in writing doth for the most part facilitate dispatch; for though it should be wholly rejected, yet that negative is more pregnant of direction than an indefinite, as ashes are more generative than dust.

XXVI.— OF SEEMING WISE

It hath been an opinion that the French are wiser than they seem, and the Spaniards seem wiser than they are. But howsoever it be between nations, certainly it is so between man and man. For as the Apostle saith of godliness, 'having a show of godliness, but denying the power thereof,' so certainly there are in points of wisdom and sufficiency that do nothing or little very solemnly — *magno conatu nugas* [trifles with great effort]. It is a ridiculous thing, and fit for a satire to persons of judgment, to see what shifts these formalists have, and what prospectives to make superficies to seem body that hath depth and bulk. Some are so close and reserved as they will not show their wares but by a dark

light, and seem always to keep back somewhat; and when they know within themselves they speak of that they do not well know would, nevertheless, seem to others to know of that which they may not well speak. Some help themselves with countenance and gesture, and are wise by signs, as Cicero saith of Piso, that when he answered him he fetched one of his brows up to his forehead and bent the other down to his chin — *respondes, altero ad frontem sublato altero ad mentum depresso supercilio, crudelitatem tibi non placere.* Some think to bear it by speaking a great word and being peremptory, and go on and take by admittance that which they cannot make good. Some, whatsoever is beyond their reach, will seem to despise or make light of it as impertinent or curious, and so would have their ignorance seem judgment. Some are never without a difference, and commonly, by amusing men with a subtlety, blanch the matter, or whom A. Gellius saith, *Hominem delirum, qui verborum minutiis rerum frangit pondera* [a foolish man who breaks up important business with small points about words]. Of which kind also Plato, in his *Protagoras,* bringeth in Prodicus in scorn, and maketh him make a speech that consisteth of distinctions from the beginning to the end. Generally, such men, in all deliberations, find ease to be of the negative side, and affect a credit to object and foretell difficulties; for when propositions are denied, there is an end of them; but if they be allowed, it requireth a new work; which false point of wisdom is the bane of business. To conclude, there is no decaying merchant, or inward beggar, hath so many tricks to uphold the credit of their wealth, as these empty persons have to maintain the credit of their sufficiency. Seeming wise men may make shift to get opinion; but let no man choose them for employment; for, certainly, you were better take for business a man somewhat absurd than over-formal.

XXVIII.— OF EXPENSE

Riches are for spending, and spending for honor and good actions. Therefore extraordinary expense must be limited by the worth of the occasion; for voluntary undoing may be as well for a man's country as for the kingdom of heaven. But ordinary expense ought to be limited by a man's estate, and governed with such regard as it be within his compass, and not subject to deceit and abuse of servants, and ordered to the best show, that the bills may be less than the estimation abroad. Certainly, if a man will keep but of even hand, his ordinary expenses ought to be but to the half of his receipts, and if he think to wax rich, but to the third part. It is no baseness for the greatest to descend and look into their own estate. Some forbear it, not upon negligence alone, but doubting to bring themselves into melancholy, in respect they shall find it broken. But wounds cannot be cured without searching. He that cannot look into his own estate at all had need both choose well them whom he employeth, and change them often, for new are more timorous and less subtle. He that can look into his estate but seldom, it behoveth him to turn all to certainties. A man had need, if he be plentiful in some kind of expense, to be as saving again in some other: as if he be plentiful in diet, to be saving in apparel; if he be plentiful in the hall, to be saving in the stable; and the like. For he that is plentiful in expenses of all kinds will hardly be preserved from decay. In clearing of a man's estate, he may as well hurt himself in being too sudden, as in letting it run on too long, for hasty selling is commonly as disadvantageable as interest. Besides, he that clears at once will relapse, for, finding himself out of straits, he will revert to his customs; but he that cleareth by degrees induceth a habit of frugality, and gaineth as well upon his mind as upon his estate. Certainly, who hath a state to repair may not despise small things: and, commonly, it is less dishonorable to abridge petty charges than to stoop to petty gettings. A man ought warily to begin charges which, once begun, will continue; but in matters that return not, he may be more magnificent.

XXXII.— OF DISCOURSE

Some in their discourse desire rather commendation of wit, in being able to hold all arguments, than of judgment, in discerning what is true; as if it were a praise to know what might be said, and not what should be thought. Some have certain commonplaces and themes, wherein they are good, and want variety; which kind of poverty is for the most part tedious, and, when it is once perceived, ridiculous. The honorablest part of talk is to give the occasion; and again to moderate, and pass to somewhat else, for then a man leads the dance. It is good in discourse and speech of conversation to vary and intermingle speech of the present occasion with arguments, tales with reasons, asking of questions with telling of opinions, and jest with earnest, for it is a dull thing to tire, and as we say now, to jade anything too far. As for jest, there be certain things which ought to be privileged from it, namely, religion, matters of state, great persons, any man's present business of importance, and any case that deserveth pity. Yet there be some that think their wits have been asleep, except they dart out somewhat that is piquant and to the quick: that is a vein which would be bridled.

Parce, puer, stimulis, et fortius utere loris.
[Spare, boy, the whip, and tighter hold the reins.]

And generally men ought to find the difference between saltness and bitterness. Certainly he that hath a satirical vein, as he maketh others afraid of his wit, so he had need be afraid of others' memory. He that questioneth much shall learn much and content much; but especially if he apply his questions to the skill of the persons whom he asketh, for he shall give them occasion to please themselves in speaking, and himself shall continually gather knowledge. But let his questions not be troublesome, for that is fit for a poser. And let him be sure to leave other men their turns to speak. Nay, if there be any that would reign, and take up all the time, let him find means to take them off and to bring others on; as musicians used to do with those that danced too long galliards. If you dissemble sometimes your knowledge of that you are thought to know, you shall be thought another time to know that you know not. Speech of a man's self ought to be seldom and well chosen. I knew one was wont to say in scorn, ' He must needs be a wise man, he speaks so much of himself.' And there is but one case wherein a man may commend himself with good grace, and that is in commending virtue in another, especially if it be such a virtue whereunto himself pretendeth. Speech of touch towards others should be sparingly used, for discourse ought to be as a field, without coming home to any man. I knew two noblemen of the west part of England, whereof the one was given to scoff, but kept ever royal cheer in his house. The other would ask of those that had been at the other's table, ' Tell truly, was there never a flout or dry blow given?' To which the guest would answer, such and such a thing passed. The lord would say, ' I thought he would mar a good dinner.' Discretion of speech is more than eloquence, and to speak agreeably to him with whom we deal is more than to speak in good words or in good order. A good continued speech, without a good speech of interlocution, shows slowness; and a good reply, or second speech, without a good settled speech, showeth shallowness and weakness. As we see in beasts, that those that are weakest in the course are yet nimblest in the turn, as it is betwixt the greyhound and the hare. To use too many circumstances ere one come to the matter is wearisome; to use none at all is blunt.

XXXIV.— OF RICHES

I cannot call riches better than the baggage of virtue. The Roman word is better, *impedimenta*, for as the baggage is to an army so is riches to virtue. It cannot be spared, nor left behind, but it hindereth the march, yea, and the care of it sometimes loseth or disturbeth the victory. Of great riches there is no real use, except it be in the distribution; the rest is but conceit. So saith Solomon, ' Where much is, there are many to consume it; and what hath the owner but the sight of it with his eyes?' The personal fruition in any man cannot reach to feel great riches; there is a custody of them, or a power of dole and donative of them, or a fame of them, but no solid use to the owner. Do you not see what feigned prices are set upon little stones and rarities? And what works of ostentation are undertaken, because there might seem to be some use of great riches? But then you will say, they may be of use, to buy men out of dangers or troubles. As Solomon saith, ' Riches are as a stronghold in the imagination of the rich man.' But this is excellently expressed, that it is in imagination, and not always in fact. For certainly great riches have sold more men than they have bought out. Seek not proud riches, but such as thou mayest get justly, use soberly, distribute cheerfully, and leave contentedly. Yet have no abstract or friarly contempt of them, but distinguish, as Cicero saith well of Rabirius Posthumus, *In studio rei amplificandae, apparebat, non avaritiae praedam, sed instrumentum bonitati quaeri* [In his efforts to increase his wealth, it was clear that he did not seek a prey for avarice but an instrument for doing good]. Hearken also to Solomon, and beware of hasty gathering of riches: *Qui festinat ad divitias, non erit insons* [He that maketh haste to be rich shall not be innocent]. The poets feign that when Plutus (which is riches) is sent from Jupiter, he limps, and goes slowly, but when he is sent from Pluto, he runs, and is swift of foot; meaning that riches gotten by good means and just labor pace slowly, but when they come by the death of others (as by the course of inheritance, testaments, and the like), they come tumbling upon a man: but it might be applied likewise to Pluto taking him for the devil; for when riches come from the devil (as by fraud, and oppression, and unjust means) they come upon speed. The ways to enrich are many, and most of them foul; parsimony is one of the best, and yet is not innocent, for it withholdeth men from works of liberality and charity. The improvement of the ground is the most natural obtaining of riches, for it is our great mother's blessing, the earth's; but it is slow: and yet, where men of great wealth do stoop to husbandry, it multiplieth riches exceedingly. I knew a nobleman in England that had the greatest audits of any man in my time,— a great grazier, a great sheep master, a great timber man, a great collier, a great corn master, a great lead man. and so of iron and a number of the like points of husbandry; so as the earth seemed a sea to him in respect of the perpetual importation. It was truly observed by one, 'That himself came very hardly to a little riches, and very easily to great riches'; for when a man's stock is come to that, that he can expect the prime of markets, and overcome those bargains, which for their greatness are few men's money, and be partner in the industries of younger men, he cannot but increase mainly. The gains of ordinary trades and vocations are honest, and furthered by two things chiefly: by diligence, and by a good name for good and fair dealing; but the gains of bargains are of a more doubtful nature, when men shall wait upon others' necessity; broke by servants, and instruments to draw them on; put off others cunningly that would be better chapmen, and the like practices, which are crafty and naught. As for the chopping of bargains, when a man buys not to hold, but to sell over again, that commonly grindeth double, both upon the seller and upon the buyer. Sharings do greatly enrich, if the hands be well chosen that are trusted. Usury is the certainest means of gain, though one of the worst, as that whereby a man doth eat his bread *in sudori vultus alieni* [in the sweat of another man's brow]; and besides, doth plough upon Sundays. But yet certain though it be, it hath flaws, for that the scriveners and brokers do value unsound men, to serve their own turn. The fortune in being the first in an invention, or in a privilege, doth cause sometimes a wonderful overgrowth in riches, as it was with the first sugarman in the Canaries. Therefore, if a man can play the true logician, to have as well judgment as invention, he may do great matters, especially if the times be fit. He that resteth upon gains certain shall hardly grow to great riches. And he that puts all upon adventures, doth oftentimes break, and come to poverty: it is good therefore to guard adventures with certainties that may uphold losses. Monopolies, and co-emption of wares for resale, where they are not restrained, are great means to enrich, especially if the party have intelligence what things are like to come into request, and so store himself beforehand. Riches gotten by service, though it be of

the best rise, yet when they are gotten by flattery, feeding humors, and other servile conditions, they may be placed amongst the worst. As for fishing for testaments and executorships, as Tacitus saith of Seneca, *Testamenta et orbos tanquam indagine capi* [he took in bequests and wardships as with a net]; it is yet worse, by how much men submit themselves to meaner persons than in service. Believe not much them that seem to despise riches, for they despise them that despair of them, and none worse when they come to them. Be not penny-wise; riches have wings, and sometimes they fly away of themselves, sometimes they must be set flying to bring in more. Men leave their riches either to their kindred, or to the public; and moderate portions prosper best in both. A great estate left to an heir is as a lure to all the birds of prey round about to seize on him, if he be not the better stablished in years and judgments. Likewise glorious gifts and foundations are like sacrifices without salt, and but the painted sepulchers of alms, which soon will putrefy and corrupt inwardly. Therefore measure not thine advancements by quantity, but frame them by measure: and defer not charities till death; for, certainly, if a man weigh it rightly, he that doth so is rather liberal of another man's than of his own.

XLII.— OF YOUTH AND AGE

A man that is young in years may be old in hours if he have lost no time. But that happeneth rarely. Generally youth is like the first cogitations, not so wise as the second. For there is a youth in thoughts as well as in ages. And yet the invention of young men is more lively than that of old; and imaginations stream into their minds, better and, as it were, more divinely. Natures that have much heat, and great and violent desires and perturbations, are not ripe for action till they have passed the meridian of their years, as it was with Julius Cæsar and Septimius Severus, of the latter of whom it is said, *Juventutem egit erroribus, imo furoribus plenam* [he spent a youth full of errors, and even of acts of madness]. And yet he was the ablest emperor almost of all the list. But reposed natures may do well in youth, as it is seen in Augustus Cæsar, Cosmos, Duke of Florence, Gaston de Fois, and others. On the other side, heat and vivacity in age is an excellent composition for business. Young men are fitter to invent than to judge, fitter for execution than for counsel, and fitter for new projects than for settled business. For the experience of age, in things that fall within the compass of it, directeth them; but in new things abuseth them. The errors of young men are the ruin of business; but the errors of aged men amount but to this, that more might have been done, or sooner. Young men, in the conduct and manage of actions, embrace more than they can hold; stir more than they can quiet; fly to the end, without consideration of the means and degrees; pursue some few principles, which they have chanced upon, absurdly; care not to innovate, which draws unknown inconveniences; use extreme remedies at first; and, that which doubleth all errors, will not acknowledge or retract them, like an unready horse, that will neither stop nor turn. Men of age object too much, consult too long, adventure too little, repent too soon, and seldom drive business home to the full period, but content themselves with a mediocrity of success. Certainly it is good to compound employments of both, for that will be good for the present, because the virtues of either age may correct the defects of both; and good for succession, that young men may be learners, while men in age are actors; and, lastly, good for extern accidents, because authority followeth old men, and favor and popularity youth. But for the moral part perhaps youth will have the preëminence, as age hath for the politic. A certain rabbin upon the text, 'Your young men shall see visions, and your old men shall dream dreams,' inferreth that young men are admitted nearer to God than old, because vision is a clearer revelation than a dream. And certainly the more a man drinketh of the world the more it intoxicateth; and age doth profit rather in the powers of understanding than in the virtues of the will and affections. There be some have an over-early ripeness in their years, which fadeth betimes; these are, first, such as have brittle wits,

the edge whereof is soon turned — such as was Hermogenes, the rhetorician, whose books are exceeding subtle, who afterwards waxed stupid. A second sort is of those that have some natural dispositions, which have better grace in youth than in age, such as is a fluent and luxuriant speech, which becomes youth well, but not age; so Tully saith of Hortensius, *Idem manebat, neque idem decebat.* [He continued the same, when it was no longer becoming]. The third is of such as take too high a strain at the first, and are magnanimous more than tract of years can uphold; as was Scipio Africanus, of whom Livy saith in effect, *Ultima primis cedebant* [His end fell below his beginning].

XLVII.— OF NEGOTIATING

It is generally better to deal by speech than by letter, and by the mediation of a third than by a man's self. Letters are good, when a man would draw an answer by letter back again; or when it may serve for a man's justification afterwards to produce his own letter; or where it may be danger to be interrupted, or heard by pieces. To deal in person is good, when a man's face breedeth regard, as commonly with inferiors; or in tender cases, where a man's eye upon the countenance of him with whom he speaketh may give him a direction how far to go; and generally, where a man will reserve to himself liberty, either to disavow or to expound. In choice of instruments, it is better to choose men of a plainer sort, that are like to do that that is committed to them, and to report back again faithfully the success, than those that are cunning to contrive out of other men's business somewhat to grace themselves, and will help the matter in report, for satisfaction sake. Use also such persons as affect the business wherein they are employed, for that quickeneth much; and such as are fit for the matter, as bold men for expostulation, fair-spoken men for persuasion, crafty men for inquiry and observation, froward and absurd men for business that doth not well bear out itself. Use also such as have been lucky, and prevailed before in things wherein you have employed them; for that breeds confidence, and they will strive to maintain their prescription.

It is better to sound a person with whom one deals, afar off, than to fall upon the point at first, except you mean 5 to surprise him by some short question. It is better dealing with men in appetite, than with those that are where they would be. If a man deal with another upon conditions, the start or first per- 10 formance is all; which a man cannot reasonably demand, except either the nature of the thing be such which must go before; or else a man can persuade the other party, that he shall still need 15 him in some other thing; or else that he be counted the honester man. All practice is to discover, or to work. Men discover themselves in trust, in passion, at unawares; and of necessity, 20 when they would have somewhat done, and cannot find an apt pretext. If you would work any man, you must either know his nature and fashions, and so lead him, or his ends, and so persuade 25 him, or his weakness and disadvantages, and so awe him, or those that have interest in him, and so govern him. In dealing with cunning persons, we must ever consider their ends to interpret 30 their speeches, and it is good to say little to them, and that which they least look for. In all negotiations of difficulty a man may not look to sow and reap at once, but must prepare business, and so 35 ripen it by degrees.

L.— OF STUDIES

Studies serve for delight, for ornament, and for ability. Their chief use for delight is in privateness and retiring; for ornament is in discourse; and for ability is in the judgment and disposition 45 of business. For expert men can execute, and perhaps judge of particulars, one by one; but the general counsels and the plots and marshalling of affairs come best from those that are learned. 50 To spend too much time in studies is sloth; to use them too much for ornament is affectation; to make judgment wholly by their rules is the humor of a scholar. They perfect nature, and are 55 perfected by experience. For natural abilities are like natural plants, that need pruning by study; and studies themselves do give forth directions too much at large, except they be bounded in by experience. Crafty men contemn studies, simple men admire them, and wise men use them. For they teach not their own use; but that is a wisdom without them, and above them, won by observation. Read not to contradict and confute; nor to believe and take for granted; nor to find talk and discourse; but to weigh and consider. Some books are to be tasted, others to be swallowed, and some few to be chewed and digested — that is, some books are to be read only in parts, others to be read, but not curiously, and some few to be read wholly, and with diligence and attention. Some books also may be read by deputy, and extracts made of them by others; but that would be only in the less important arguments and the meaner sort of books; else distilled books are like common distilled waters, flashy things. Reading maketh a full man, conference a ready man, and writing an exact man. And therefore if a man write little he had need have a great memory; if he confer little he had need have a present wit; and if he read little he had need have much cunning to seem to know that he doth not. Histories make men wise, poets witty, the mathematics subtle, natural philosophy deep, moral grave, logic and rhetoric able to contend, *Abeunt studia in mores* [Studies develop into habits]. Nay, there is no stond or impediment in the wit but may be wrought out by fit studies, like 40 as diseases of the body may have appropriate exercises. Bowling is good for the stone and reins, shooting for the lungs and breast, gentle walking for the stomach, riding for the head, and the like. So if a man's wit be wandering, let him study the mathematics, for in demonstrations, if his wit be called away never so little, he must begin again; if his wit be not apt to distinguish or find differences, let him study the schoolmen, for they are *cymini sectores* [hairsplitters]; if he be not apt to beat over matters and to call up one thing to prove and illustrate another, let him study the lawyer's cases. So every defect of the mind may have a special receipt.

SIR THOMAS BROWNE (1605–1682)

Browne is described by Mr. Saintsbury as 'the greatest prose-writer perhaps, when all things are taken together, in the whole range of English,' and all critics are agreed that he is one of the greatest. He was educated at Winchester and Oxford, studied medicine abroad, and took his doctor's degree at Leyden. He was only thirty when he wrote the work by which he is best known, *Religio Medici*, or A Physician's Religion. Circulated at first in manuscript, it was twice printed surreptitiously in 1642, and an authorized edition was published in 1643. It at once attracted attention and was translated into Latin, Dutch, French, and German. In 1637 Browne settled at Norwich, and there he spent the rest of his life in the enjoyment of a wide fame, both as a scholar and as a physician. He was knighted when Charles II visited the city in 1671. He wrote a great deal, and left many tracts, which were published after his death. His most considerable work is an exposure of popular superstitions entitled *Pseudodoxia Epidemica* or Vulgar and Common Errors (1648). Ten years later appeared *Hydriotaphia Urn Burial, or a Discourse of the Sepulchral Urns lately found in Norfolk* and *The Garden of Cyrus, or the Quincuncial Lozenge, net-work plantations of the Ancients, artificially, naturally, mystically considered.* Of the latter Coleridge says that Browne finds 'quincunxes in heaven above, quincunxes in earth below, quincunxes in the mind of man, quincunxes in tones, in optic nerves, in roots of trees, in leaves, in everything.' Browne has, however, much rarer virtues than curious learning and quaintness of phrase: he expresses the deep thoughts of an unusually well-balanced mind in a style not merely clear and dignified, but rich with a sustained and subtle harmony as of solemn music.

RELIGIO MEDICI

For my religion though there be several circumstances that might persuade the world I have none at all, as the general scandal of my profession, the natural course of my studies, the indifferency of my behavior and discourse in matters of religion, neither violently defending one, nor with that common ardor and contention opposing another; yet in despite hereof, I dare, without usurpation, assume the honorable style of a christian. Not that I merely owe this title to the font, my education, or clime wherein I was born, as being bred up either to confirm those principles my parents instilled into my understanding, or by a general consent proceed in the religion of my country: but having in my riper years and confirmed judgment, seen and examined all, I find myself obliged by the principles of grace, and the law of mine own reason, to embrace no other name but this: neither doth herein my zeal so far make me forget the general charity I owe unto humanity, as rather to hate than pity Turks, Infidels, and (what is worse) Jews; rather contenting myself to enjoy that happy style, than maligning those who refuse so glorious a title.

But because the name of a christian is become too general to express our faith, there being a geography of religion as well as lands, and every clime distinguished not only by their laws and limits, but circumscribed by their doctrines and rules of faith; to be particular, I am of that reformed new-cast religion, wherein I dislike nothing but the name; of the same belief our Savior taught, the apostles disseminated, the fathers authorized, and the martyrs confirmed, but by the sinister ends of princes, the ambition and avarice of prelates, and the fatal corruption of times, so decayed, impaired, and fallen from its native beauty, that it required the careful and charitable hands of these times to restore it to its primitive integrity. Now the accidental occasion whereupon, the slender means whereby, the low and abject condition of the person by whom so good a work was set on foot, which in our adversaries beget contempt and scorn, fills me with wonder, and is the very same objection the insolent pagans first cast at Christ and his disciples.

Yet have I not so shaken hands with those desperate resolutions, who had rather venture at large their decayed bottom, than bring her in to be new trimmed in the dock; who had rather promiscuously retain all, than abridge any, and obstinately be what they ·are, than what they have been, as to stand in diameter and swords point with them. We have reformed from them, not against them; for omitting those improperations, and terms of scurrility betwixt us, which only difference our affections, and not our cause, there is between us one common name and appellation, one faith and necessary body of principles common to us both. And therefore I am not scrupulous to converse and live with them, to enter their churches in defect of ours, and either pray with them, or for them. I could never perceive any rational consequence from those many texts which prohibit the Children of Israel to pollute themselves with the temples of the heathens; we being all christians, and not divided by such detested impieties as might profane our prayers, or the place wherein we make them; or that a resolved conscience may not adore her Creator anywhere, especially in places devoted to his service; where if their devotions offend him, mine may please him; if theirs profane it, mine may hallow it; holywater and crucifix (dangerous to the common people) deceive not my judgment, nor abuse my devotion at all. I am, I confess, naturally inclined to that which misguided zeal terms superstition: my common conversation I do acknowledge austere, my behavior full of rigor, sometimes not without morosity; yet at my devotion I love to use the civility of my knee, my hat, and hand, with all those outward and sensible motions which may express or promote my invisible devotion. I should violate my own arm rather than a church, nor willingly deface the name of saint or martyr. At the sight of a cross or crucifix I can dispense with my hat, but scarce with the thought or memory of my Savior: I cannot laugh at, but rather pity the fruitless journeys of pilgrims, or contemn the miserable condition of friars; for though though misplaced in circumstances, there is something in it of devotion. I could never hear the Ave-Mary bell [1] without an elevation, or think it a sufficient warrant, because they erred in one circumstance, for me to err in all, that is, in silence and dumb contempt. Whilst therefore they direct their devotions to her, I offer mine to God, and rectify the errors of their prayers, by rightly ordering mine own. At a solemn procession I have wept abundantly, while my consorts, blind with opposition and prejudice, have fallen into an excess of scorn and laughter. There are questionless, both in Greek, Roman, and African churches, solemnities and ceremonies, whereof the wiser zeals do make a christian use, and stand condemned by us, not as evil in themselves, but as allurements and baits of superstition to those vulgar heads that look asquint on the face of truth, and those unstable judgments that cannot resist in the narrow point and center of virtue without a reel or stagger to the circumference.

As there were many reformers, so likewise many reformations; every country proceeding in a particular way and method, according as their national interest, together with their constitution and clime inclined them; some angrily, and with extremity; others calmly, and with mediocrity, not rending but easily dividing the community, and leaving an honest possibility of a reconciliation; which though peaceable spirits do desire, and may conceive that revolution of time and the mercies of God may effect, yet that judgment that shall consider the present antipathies between the two extremes, their contrarieties in condition, affection and opinion, may with the same hopes expect a union in the poles of heaven.

But to difference myself nearer, and draw into a lesser circle: there is no church, whose every part so squares unto my conscience; whose articles, constitutions, and customs, seem so consonant unto reason, and as it were framed to my particular devotion, as this whereof I hold my belief, the Church of England,

[1] A church bell that tolls every day at six and twelve of the clock; at the hearing whereof, every one in what place soever, either of house or street, betakes himself to his prayer, which is commonly directed to the Virgin.

to whose faith I am a sworn subject; and therefore in a double obligation subscribe unto her articles, and endeavor to observe her constitutions. Whatsoever is beyond, as points indifferent, I observe according to the rules of my private reason, or the humor and fashion of my devotion; neither believing this, because Luther affirmed it, or disproving that, because Calvin hath disavouched it. I condemn not all things in the Council of Trent, nor approve all in the Synod of Dort. In brief, where the Scripture is silent, the church is my text; where that speaks, 't is but my comment: where there is a joint silence of both, I borrow not the rules of my religion from Rome or Geneva, but the dictates of my own reason. It is an unjust scandal of our adversaries, and a gross error in ourselves, to compute the nativity of our religion from Henry the Eighth, who though he rejected the Pope, refused not the faith of Rome, and effected no more than what his own predecessors desired and assayed in ages past, and was conceived the state of Venice would have attempted in our days. It is as uncharitable a point in us to fall upon those popular scurrilities and opprobrious scoffs of the Bishop of Rome, to whom as temporal prince, we owe the duty of good language. I confess there is a cause of passion between us; by his sentence I stand excommunicated, heretic is the best language he affords me; yet can no ear witness, I ever returned him the name of Antichrist, Man of sin, or Whore of Babylon. It is the method of charity to suffer without reaction: those usual satires and invectives of the pulpit may perchance produce a good effect on the vulgar, whose ears are opener to rhetoric than logic; yet do they in no wise confirm the faith of wiser believers, who know that a good cause needs not to be pardoned by passion, but can sustain itself upon a temperate dispute.

I could never divide myself from any man upon the difference of an opinion, or be angry with his judgment for not agreeing with me in that, from which within a few days I should dissent myself. I have no genius to disputes in religion, and have often thought it wisdom to decline them, especially upon a disadvantage, or when the cause of truth might suffer in the weakness of my patronage. Where we desire to be informed, 't is good to contest with men above ourselves; but to confirm and establish our opinions, 't is best to argue with judgments below our own, that the frequent spoils and victories over their reasons, may settle in ourselves an esteem and confirmed opinion of our own. Every man is not a proper champion for truth, nor fit to take up the gauntlet in the cause of verity. Many from the ignorance of these maxims, and an inconsiderate zeal unto truth, have too rashly charged the troops of error, and remain as trophies unto the enemies of truth. A man may be in as just possession of truth as of a city, and yet be forced to surrender; 't is therefore far better to enjoy her with peace, than to hazard her on a battle. If therefore there rise any doubts in my way, I do forget them, or at least defer them, till my better settled judgment and more manly reason be able to resolve them, for I perceive every man's own reason is his best Œdipus, and will upon a reasonable truce find a way to loose those bonds wherewith the subtleties of error have enchained our more flexible and tender judgments. In philosophy, where truth seems double faced, there is no man more paradoxical than myself; but in divinity I love to keep the road; and though not in an implicit, yet an humble faith, follow the great wheel of the church, by which I move, not reserving any proper poles or motion from the epicycle of my own brain. By this means I have no gap for heresy, schisms, or errors, of which at present I hope I shall not injure truth to say I have no taint or tincture. I must confess my greener studies have been polluted with two or three, not any begotten in the latter centuries, but old and obsolete, such as could never have been revived but by such extravagant and irregular heads as mine. For indeed heresies perish not with their authors, but like the river Arethusa, though they lose their currents in one place, they rise up again in another. One general council is not able to extirpate one single heresy; it may be canceled for the present, but revolution of time, and the like aspects from heaven, will restore it, when it will flourish till it be condemned again. For as though there were metempsychosis, and the soul of one man passed into another; opinions do find after certain revolutions men and minds like those that first begat them. To see ourselves again, we need not look for Plato's year [1]: every man is not only himself; there hath been many Diogenes, and as many Timons, though but few of that name; men are lived over again, the world is now as it was in ages past; there was none then, but there hath been some one since that parallels him, and as it were his revived self.

* * *

As for those wingy mysteries in divinity, and airy subtleties in religion, which have unhinged the brains of better heads, they never stretched the *pia mater* of mine, ~~it seems to me~~ methinks there be not impossibilities enough in religion, for an active faith; the deepest mysteries ours contains, have not only been illustrated, but maintained by syllogism, and the rule of reason: I love to lose myself in a mystery, to pursue my reason to an *O altitudo!* 'T is my solitary recreation to pose my apprehension with those involved enigmas and riddles of the trinity, with incarnation and resurrection. I can answer all the objections of Satan and my rebellious reason, with that odd resolution I learned of Tertullian, *Certum est quia impossibile est* [It is certain because it is impossible]. I desire to exercise my faith in the difficultest point; for to credit ordinary and visible objects, is not faith, but persuasion. Some believe the better for seeing Christ's sepulcher; and when they have seen the Red Sea, doubt not of the miracle. Now contrarily, I bless myself, and am thankful that I lived not in the days of miracles, that I never saw Christ nor his disciples. I would not have been one of those Israelites that passed the Red Sea, nor one of Christ's patients on whom he wrought his wonders; then had my faith been thrust upon me; nor should I enjoy that greater blessing pronounced to all that believe and saw not. 'T is an easy and necessary belief, to credit what

our eye and sense hath examined: I believe he was dead and buried, and rose again; and desire to see him in his glory, rather than to contemplate him in his cenotaph or sepulcher. Nor is this much to believe; as we have reason, we owe this faith unto history: they only had the advantage of a bold and noble faith, who lived before his coming, who upon obscure prophecies and mystical types could raise a belief, and expect apparent impossibilities.

* * *

Thus there are two books from whence I collect my divinity; besides that written one of God, another of his servant nature, that universal and public manuscript, that lies expansed unto the eyes of all; those that never saw him in the one, have discovered him in the other: this was the scripture and theology of the heathens; the natural motion of the sun made them more admire him, than its supernatural station did the Children of Israel; the ordinary effects of nature wrought more admiration in them, than in the other all his miracles; surely the heathens knew better how to join and read these mystical letters, than we christians, who cast a more careless eye on these common hieroglyphics, and disdain to suck divinity from the flowers of nature. Nor do I so forget God as to adore the name of nature; which I define not with the schools, to be the principle of motion and rest, but that straight and regular line, that settled and constant course the wisdom of God hath ordained the actions of his creatures, according to their several kinds. To make a revolution every day, is the nature of the sun, because of that necessary course which God hath ordained it, from which it cannot swerve but by a faculty from that voice which first did give it motion. Now this course of nature God seldom alters or perverts, but like an excellent artist hath so contrived his work, that with the selfsame instrument, without a new creation, he may effect his obscurest designs. Thus he sweeteneth the water with a word, preserveth the creatures in the ark, which the blast of his mouth might have as easily created. For God is like a skilful geometrician, who when more easily, and with one stroke of his compass he might describe or divide a right line, had yet rather do

---

[1] A revolution of certain thousand years, when all things should return unto their former estate, and he be teaching again in his school as when he delivered this opinion.

this in a circle or longer way; according to the constituted and fore-laid principles of his art. Yet this rule of his he doth sometimes pervert, to acquaint the world with his prerogative, lest the arrogancy of our reason should question his power, and conclude he could not. And thus I call the effects of nature the works of God, whose hand and instrument she only is; and therefore to ascribe his actions unto her, is to devolve the honor of the principal agent, upon the instrument; which if with reason we may do, then let our hammers rise up and boast they have built our houses, and our pens receive the honor of our writing. I hold there is a general beauty in the works of God, and therefore no deformity in any kind of species of creature whatsoever: I cannot tell by what logic we call a toad, a bear, or an elephant ugly, they being created in those outward shapes and figures which best express those actions of their inward forms. And having passed that general visitation of God, who saw that all that he had made was good, that is, conformable to his will, which abhors deformity, and is the rule of order and beauty; there is no deformity but in monstrosity, wherein notwithstanding there is a kind of beauty. Nature so ingeniously contriving the irregular parts, as they become sometimes more remarkable than the principal fabric. To speak yet more narrowly, there was never anything ugly or mis-shapen but the chaos; wherein notwithstanding, to speak strictly, there was no deformity, because no form, nor was it yet impregnant by the voice of God. Now nature is not at variance with art, nor art with nature; they being both servants of his providence. Art is the perfection of nature: were the world now as it was the sixth day, there were yet a chaos. Nature hath made one world, and art another. In brief, all things are artificial; for nature is the art of God.

* * *

I am naturally bashful, nor hath conversation, age, or travel been able to effront, or enharden me; yet I have one part of modesty, which I have seldom discovered in another, that is (to speak truly) I am not so much afraid of death, as ashamed thereof; 't is the very disgrace and ignominy of our natures, that in a moment can so disfigure us, that our nearest friends, wife and children stand afraid and start at us. The birds and beasts of the field, that before in a natural fear obeyed us, forgetting all allegiance begin to prey upon us. This very conceit hath in a tempest disposed and left me willing to be swallowed up in the abyss of waters; wherein I had perished unseen, unpitied, without wondering eyes, tears of pity, lectures of mortality, and none had said, *Quantum mutatus ab illo* [How much changed from what he was]! Not that I am ashamed of the anatomy of my parts, or can accuse nature for playing the bungler in any part of me, or my own vicious life for contracting any shameful disease upon me, whereby I might not call myself as wholesome a morsel for the worms as any.

Some upon the courage of a fruitful issue, wherein, as in the truest chronicle, they seem to outlive themselves, can with greater patience away with death. This conceit and counterfeit subsisting in our progenies, seems to be a mere fallacy, unworthy the desires of a man, that can but conceive a thought of the next world; who, in a nobler ambition, should desire to live in his substance in heaven, rather than his name and shadow in the earth. And therefore at my death I mean to take a total adieu of the world, not caring for a monument, history, or epitaph, not so much as the memory of my name to be found anywhere, but in the universal register of God. I am not yet so cynical, as to approve the testament of Diogenes,[1] nor do I altogether allow that rodomontado of Lucan:

Caelo tegitur, qui non habet urnam.
He that unburied lies, wants not his hearse,
For unto him a tomb's the universe.

But commend in my calmer judgment, those ingenuous intentions that desire to sleep by the urns of [their] fathers, and strive to go the nearest way unto corruption. I do not envy the temper of crows and daws, nor the numerous and weary days of our fathers before the flood. If there be any truth in astrology, I may outlive a jubilee; as yet I have

---

[1] Who willed his friend not to bury him, but hang him up with a staff in his hand to fright away the crows.

not seen one revolution of Saturn, nor hath my pulse beat thirty years; and yet excepting one, have seen the ashes, and left underground, all the kings of Europe; have been contemporary to three emperors, four grand signiors, and as many popes. Methinks I have outlived myself, and begin to be weary of the sun; I have shaken hands with delight: in my warm blood and canicular days, I perceive I do anticipate the vices of age. The world to me is but a dream or mock show, and we all therein but pantalones and antics, to my severer contemplations.

It is not, I confess, an unlawful prayer to desire to surpass the days of our Savior, or wish to outlive that age wherein he thought fittest to die; yet if (as divinity affirms) there shall be no gray hairs in heaven, but all shall rise in the perfect state of men, we do but outlive those perfections in this world, to be recalled unto them by a greater miracle in the next, and run on here but to be retrograde hereafter. Were there any hopes to outlive vice, or a point to be superannuated from sin, it were worthy our knees to implore the days of Methuselah. But age doth not rectify, but incurvate our natures, turning bad dispositions into worser habits, and (like diseases) brings on incurable vices; for every day as we grow weaker in age, we grow stronger in sin; and the number of our days doth but make our sins innumerable. The same vice committed at sixteen, is not the same, though it agrees in all other circumstances, as at forty, but swells and doubles from that circumstance of our ages, wherein, besides the constant and inexcusable habit of transgressing, the maturity of our judgment cuts off pretense unto excuse or pardon. Every sin the **oftener** it is committed, the more it acquireth in the quality of evil; as it succeeds in time, so it proceeds in degrees of badness; for as they proceed they ever multiply, and like figures in arithmetic, the last stands for more than all that went before it. And though I think no man can live well once, but he that could live twice, yet for my own part I would not live over my hours past, or begin again the thread of my days: not upon Cicero's ground, because I have lived them well, but for fear I should live them worse. I find my growing judgment daily instruct me how to be better, but my untamed affections and confirmed vitiosity makes me daily do worse; I find in my confirmed age the same sins I discovered in my youth; I committed many then because I was a child, and because I commit them still, I am yet an infant. Therefore I perceive a man may be twice a child before the days of dotage, and stand in need of Æson's bath before threescore.

And truly there goes a great deal of providence to produce a man's life unto threescore. There is more required than an able temper for those years; though the radical humor contain in it sufficient oil for seventy, yet I perceive in some it gives no light past thirty: men assign not all the causes of long life, that write whole books thereof. They that found themselves on the radical balsam, or vital sulphur of the parts, determine not why Abel lived not so long as Adam. There is therefore a secret glome or bottom of our days; 't was his wisdom to determine them, but his perpetual and waking providence that fulfils and accomplisheth them; wherein the spirits, ourselves, and all the creatures of God in a secret and disputed way do execute his will. Let them not therefore complain of immaturity that die about thirty; they fall but like the whole world, whose solid and well-composed substance must not expect the duration and period of its constitution. When all things are completed in it, its age is accomplished; and the last and general fever may as naturally destroy it before six thousand, as me before forty. There is therefore some other hand that twines the thread of life than that of nature. We are not only ignorant in antipathies and occult qualities; our ends are as obscure as our beginnings. The line of our days is drawn by night, and the various effects therein by a pencil that is invisible; wherein though we confess our ignorance, I am sure we do not err if we say it is the hand of God.

* * *

begun

THE SECOND PART

Now for that other virtue of charity, without which faith is a mere notion, and of no existence, I have ever endeavored to nourish the merciful disposition and humane inclination I borrowed from my parents, and regulate it to the written and prescribed laws of charity; and if I hold the true anatomy of myself, I am delineated and naturally framed to such a piece of virtue. For I am of a constitution so general, that it comforts and sympathizeth with all things; I have no antipathy, or rather idiosyncrasy, in diet, humor, air, anything: I wonder not at the French for their dishes of frogs, snails, and toadstools; nor at the Jews for locusts and grasshoppers; but being amongst them, make them my common viands; and I find they agree with my stomach as well as theirs. I could digest a salad gathered in a churchyard, as well as in a garden. I cannot start at the presence of a serpent, scorpion, lizard, or salamander: at the sight of a toad or viper, I find in me no desire to take up a stone to destroy them. I feel not in myself those common antipathies that I can discover in others: those national repugnances do not touch me, nor do I behold with prejudice the French, Italian, Spaniard and Dutch; but where I find their actions in balance with my countrymen's, I honor, love, and embrace them in the same degree. I was born in the eighth climate, but seem for to be framed and constellated unto all: I am no plant that will not prosper out of a garden: all places, all airs make unto me one country; I am in England, everywhere, and under any meridian. I have been shipwrecked, yet am not enemy with the sea or winds; I can study, play, or sleep in a tempest. In brief, I am averse from nothing; my conscience would give me the lie if I should absolutely detest or hate any essence but the devil; or so at least abhor anything, but that we might come to composition. If there be any among those common objects of hatred I do contemn and laugh at, it is that great enemy of reason, virtue and religion, the multitude; that numerous piece of monstrosity, which taken asunder seem men, and the reasonable creatures of God; but confused together, make but one great beast, and a monstrosity more prodigious than Hydra. It is no breach of charity to call these fools; it is the style all holy writers have afforded them, set down by Solomon in canonical Scripture.

and a point of our faith to believe so. Neither in the name of multitude do I only include the base and minor sort of people; there is a rabble even amongst the gentry, a sort of plebeian heads, whose fancy moves with the same wheel as these; men in the same level with mechanics, though their fortunes do somewhat gild their infirmities, and their purses compound for their follies. But as in casting account, three or four men together come short in account of one man placed by himself below them: so neither are a troop of these ignorant Doradoes, of that true esteem and value, as many a forlorn person, whose condition doth place them below their feet. Let us speak like politicians, there is a nobility without heraldry, a natural dignity, whereby one man is ranked with another; another filed before him, according to the quality of his desert, and pre-eminence of his good parts: though the corruption of these times, and the bias of present practice wheel another way. Thus it was in the first and primitive commonwealths, and is yet in the integrity and cradle of well-ordered polities, till corruption getteth ground, ruder desires laboring after that which wiser generations contemn every one having a liberty to amass and heap up riches, and they a license or faculty to do or purchase anything.

*   *   *

To do no injury, nor take none, was a principle, which to my former years, and impatient affections, seemed to contain enough of morality; but my more settled years, and christian constitution, have fallen upon severer resolutions. I can hold there is no such thing as injury; that if there be, there is no such injury as revenge, and no such revenge as the contempt of an injury; that to hate another, is to malign himself; that the truest way to love another, is to despise ourselves. I were unjust unto mine own conscience, if I should say I am at variance with anything like myself. I find there are many pieces in this one fabric of man; this frame is raised upon a mass of antipathies. I am one methinks, but as the world; wherein notwithstanding there are a swarm of distinct essences, and in them another world of contrarieties; we carry private and domestic enemies within, public and more hostile adversaries without. The devil, that did but buffet St. Paul, plays methinks at sharp with me. Let me be nothing, if within the compass of myself I do not find the battle of Lepanto, passion against reason, reason against faith, faith against the devil, and my conscience against all. There is another man within me, that's angry with me, rebukes, commands, and dastards me. I have no conscience of marble, to resist the hammer of more heavy offenses; nor yet so soft and waxen, as to take the impression of each single peccadillo or scape of infirmity: I am of a strange belief, that it is as easy to be forgiven some sins, as to commit some others. For my original sin, I hold it to be washed away in my baptism; for my actual transgressions, I compute and reckon with God but from my last repentance, sacrament, or general absolution; and therefore am not terrified with the sins or madness of my youth. I thank the goodness of God, I have no sins that want a name. I am not singular in offenses; my transgressions are epidemical, and from the common breath of our corruption. For there are certain tempers of body, which, matched with a humorous depravity of mind, do hatch and produce vitiosities, whose newness and monstrosity of nature admits no name. * * * For the heavens are not only fruitful in new and unheard-of stars, the earth in plants and animals; but men's minds also in villainy and vices. Now the dulness of my reason, and the vulgarity of my disposition, never prompted my invention, nor solicited my affection unto any of those. Yet even those common and quotidian infirmities that so necessarily attend me, and do seem to be my very nature, have so dejected me, so broken the estimation that I should have otherwise of myself, that I repute myself the most abjectest piece of mortality. Divines prescribe a fit of sorrow to repentance; there goes indignation, anger, sorrow, hatred, into mine: passions of a contrary nature, which neither seem to be my very nature, which neither seem to suit with this action, nor my proper constitution. It is no breach of charity to ourselves, to be at variance with our vices; nor to abhor that part of us, which is an enemy to the ground of charity, our God; wherein we do but imitate our great

selves, the world, whose divided antipathies and contrary faces do yet carry a charitable regard unto the whole by their particular discords, preserving the common harmony, and keeping in fetters those powers, whose rebellions once masters might be the ruin of all.

I thank God, amongst those millions of vices I do inherit and hold from Adam, I have escaped one, and that a mortal enemy to charity, the first and [father-sin], not only of man, but of the devil, pride; a vice whose name is comprehended in a monosyllable, but in its nature not circumscribed with a world. I have escaped it in a condition that can hardly avoid it. Those petty acquisitions and reputed perfections that advance and elevate the conceits of other men add no feathers unto mine. I have seen a grammarian tower and plume himself over a single line in Horace, and show more pride in the construction of one ode, than the author in the composure of the whole book. For my own part, besides the jargon and *patois* of several provinces, I understand no less than six languages; yet I protest I have no higher conceit of myself, than had our fathers before the confusion of Babel, when there was but one language in the world, and none to boast himself either linguist or critic. I have not only seen several countries, beheld the nature of their climes, the chorography of their provinces, topography of their cities, but understood their several laws, customs and policies; yet cannot all this persuade the dulness of my spirit unto such an opinion of myself, as I behold in nimbler and conceited heads, that never looked a degree beyond their nests. I know the names, and somewhat more, of all the constellations in my horizon; yet I have seen a prating mariner, that could only name the pointers and the north star, out-talk me, and conceive himself a whole sphere above me. I know most of the plants of my country, and of those about me; yet methinks I do not know so many as when I did but know a hundred, and had scarcely ever simpled further than Cheapside. For indeed, heads of capacity, and such as are not full with a handful, or easy measure of knowledge, think they know nothing, till they know all; which being impossible, they fall upon the opinion of Socrates, and only know they know not anything. I cannot think that Homer pined away upon the riddle of the fisherman, or that Aristotle, who understood the uncertainty of knowledge, and confessed so often the reason of man too weak for the works of nature, did ever drown himself upon the flux and reflux of Euripus. We do but learn to-day, what our better advanced judgments will unteach to-morrow: and Aristotle doth not instruct us, as Plato did him; that is, to confute himself. I have run through all sorts, yet find no rest in any: though our first studies and junior endeavors may style us Peripatetics, Stoics, or Academics, yet I perceive the wisest heads prove, at last, almost all sceptics, and stand like Janus in the field of knowledge. I have therefore one common and authentic philosophy I learned in the schools, whereby I discourse and satisfy the reason of other men; another more reserved, and drawn from experience, whereby I content mine own. Solomon, that complained of ignorance in the height of knowledge, hath not only humbled my conceits, but discouraged my endeavors. There is yet another conceit that hath sometimes made me shut my books, which tells me it is a vanity to waste our days in the blind pursuit of knowledge; it is but attending a little longer, and we shall enjoy that by instinct and infusion, which we endeavor at here by labor and inquisition. It is better to sit down in a modest ignorance; and rest contented with the natural blessing of our own reasons, than buy the uncertain knowledge of this life, with sweat and vexation, which death gives every fool gratis, and is an accessory of our glorification.

I was never yet once, and commend their resolutions who never marry twice: not that I disallow of second marriage; as neither in all cases of polygamy, which considering some times, and the unequal number of both sexes, may be also necessary. The whole world was made for man, but the twelfth part of man for woman: man is the whole world, and the breath of God; woman the rib, and crooked piece of man. * * * I speak not in prejudice, nor am averse from that sweet sex, but naturally amorous of all that is beautiful; I can look a whole day with delight upon a handsome picture, though it be but of a horse. It is my temper, and I like it the better, to affect all harmony; and sure there is music even in the beauty, and the silent note which Cupid strikes, far sweeter than the sound of an instrument. For there is a music wherever there is a harmony, order or proportion; and thus far we may maintain the music of the spheres: for those well-ordered motions, and regular paces, though they give no sound unto the ear, yet to the understanding they strike a note most full of harmony. Whosoever is harmonically composed, delights in harmony; which makes me much distrust the symmetry of those heads which declaim against all church-music. For myself, not only from my obedience, but my particular genius, I do embrace it: for even that vulgar and tavern-music, which makes one man merry, another mad, strikes in me a deep fit of devotion, and a profound contemplation of the first composer. There is something in it of divinity more than the ear discovers: it is a hieroglyphical and shadowed lesson of the whole world, and creatures of God; such a melody to the ear, as the whole world well understood, would afford the understanding. In brief, it is a sensible fit of that harmony, which intellectually sounds in the ears of God. I will not say with Plato, the soul is a harmony, but harmonical, and hath its nearest sympathy unto music: thus some whose temper of body agrees, and humors the constitution of their souls, are born poets, though indeed all are naturally inclined unto rhythm. This made Tacitus in the very first line of his story, fall upon a verse,[1] and Cicero the worst of poets, but declaiming for a poet, falls in the very first sentence upon a perfect hexameter.[2] I feel not in me those sordid and unchristian desires of my profession; I do not secretly implore and wish for plagues, rejoice at famines, revolve ephemerides and almanacs, in expectation of malignant aspects, fatal conjunctions and eclipses: I rejoice not at unwholesome springs, nor unseasonable winters; my prayer goes with the husbandman's; I desire everything in its proper season, that neither men nor the times be put out of temper.

[1] Urbem Romam in principio reges habuere.
[2] *Pro Archia Poeta:* In qua me non inficior mediocriter esse.

Let me be sick myself, if sometimes the malady of my patient be not a disease unto me; I desire rather to cure his infirmities than my own necessities: where I do him no good, methinks it is scarce honest gain; though I confess 't is but the worthy salary of our well-intended endeavors. I am not only ashamed, but heartily sorry, that besides death, there are diseases incurable; yet not for my own sake, or that they be beyond my art, but for the general cause and sake of humanity, whose common cause I apprehend as mine own. And to speak more generally, those three noble professions which all civil commonwealths do honor are raised upon the fall of Adam, and are not exempt from their infirmities; there are not only diseases incurable in physic, but cases indissolvable in laws, vices incorrigible in divinity. If general councils may err, I do not see why particular courts should be infallible; their perfectest rules are raised upon the erroneous reasons of man; and the laws of one do but condemn the rules of another; as Aristotle oft-times the opinions of his predecessors, because, though agreeable to reason, yet were not consonant to his own rules, and logic of his proper principles. Again, to speak nothing of the sin against the Holy Ghost, whose cure not only, but whose nature is unknown; I can cure the gout or stone in some, sooner than divinity pride or avarice in others. I can cure vices by physic, when they remain incurable by divinity; and shall obey my pills, when they contemn their precepts. I boast nothing, but plainly say, we all labor against our own cure; for death is the cure of all diseases. There is no catholicon or universal remedy I know but this, which though nauseous to queasy stomachs, yet to prepared appetites is nectar, and a pleasant potion of immortality.

* * *

From HYDRIOTAPHIA URN-
       BURIAL

What song the Syrens sang, or what name Achilles assumed when he hid himself among women, though puzzling questions,[1] are not beyond all conjecture.

What time the persons of these ossuaries entered the famous nations of the dead,[2] and slept with princes and counsellors, might admit a wide solution. But who were the proprietaries of these bones, or what bodies these ashes made up, were a question above antiquarism, not to be resolved by man, nor easily perhaps by spirits, except we consult the provincial guardians, or tutelary observators. Had they made as good provision for their names as they have done for their relics, they had not so grossly erred in the art of perpetuation. But to subsist in bones, and be but pyramidally extant, is a fallacy in duration. Vain ashes, which, in the oblivion of names, persons, times and sexes, have found unto themselves a fruitless continuation, and only arise unto late posterity as emblems of mortal vanities, antidotes against pride, vainglory, and madding vices! Pagan vainglories, which thought the world might last forever, had encouragement for ambition, and finding no *Atropos* unto the immortality of their names, were never damped with the necessity of oblivion. Even old ambitions had the advantage of ours in the attempts of their vain-glories, who acting early, and before the probable meridian of time, have by this time found great accomplishment of their designs, whereby the ancient heroes have already out-lasted their monuments and mechanical preservations. But in this latter scene of time we cannot expect such mummies unto our memories, when ambition may fear the prophecy of Elias;[3] and Charles the Fifth can never hope to live within two Methuselahs of Hector.[4]

And therefore restless inquietude for the diuturnity of our memories unto present considerations seems a vanity almost out of date, and a superannuated piece of folly. We cannot hope to live so long in our names as some have done in their persons: one face of Janus holds no proportion to the other. 'T is too late to be ambitious. The great mutations of the world are acted, or time may be too short for our designs. To extend our memories by monuments, whose death we daily pray for, and whose duration we cannot hope without injury to our ex-

---

[1] The puzzling questions of Tiberius unto grammarians. *Marcel. Donatus in Suet.*

[2] Κλυτὰ ἔθνεα νεκρῶν. *Hom. Job.*
[3] That the world may last but six thousand years.
[4] Hector's fame lasting above two lives of Methuselah, before that famous prince was extant.

pectations in the advent of the last day, were a contradiction to our beliefs. We, whose generations are ordained in this setting part of time, are providentially taken off from such imaginations; and, being necessitated to eye the remaining particle of futurity, are naturally constituted unto thoughts of the next world, and cannot excusably decline the consideration of that duration which maketh pyramids pillars of snow, and all that's past a moment.

Circles and right lines limit and close all bodies, and the mortal right-lined circle[1] must conclude and shut up all. There is no antidote against the opium of time, which temporally considereth all things. Our fathers find their graves in our short memories, and sadly tell us how we may be buried in our survivors. Grave-stones tell truth scarce forty years.[2] Generations pass while some trees stand, and old families last not three oaks. To be read by bare inscriptions, like many in Gruter,[3] to hope for eternity by enigmatical epithets or first letters of our names, to be studied by antiquaries who we were, and have new names given us like many of the mummies, are cold consolations unto the students of perpetuity, even by everlasting languages.

To be content that times to come should only know there was such a man, not caring whether they knew more of him, was a frigid ambition in Cardan,[4] disparaging his horoscopal inclination and judgment of himself. Who cares to subsist like Hippocrates' patients, or Achilles' horses in Homer, under naked nominations, without deserts and noble acts, which are the balsam of our memories, the *entelechia* and soul of our subsistences. To be nameless in worthy deed exceeds an infamous history. The Canaanitish woman lives more happily without a name, than Herodias with one. And who had not rather have been the good thief, than Pilate?

But the iniquity of oblivion blindly scattereth her poppy, and deals with the memory of men without distinction to merit of perpetuity. Who can but pity

the founder of the pyramids? Herostratus lives that burnt the temple of Diana; he is almost lost that built it. Time hath spared the epitaph of Adrian's horse, confounded that of himself. In vain we compute our felicities by the advantage of our good names, since bad have equal durations; and Thersites is like to live as long as Agamemnon, without the favor of the everlasting register. Who knows whether the best of men be known? or whether there be not more remarkable persons forgot, than any that stand remembered in the known account of time? The first man had been as unknown as the last, and Methuselah's long life had been his only chronicle.

Oblivion is not to be hired: the greater part must be content to be as though they had not been, to be found in the register of God, not in the record of man. Twenty-seven names make up the first story, and the recorded names ever since contain not one living century. The number of the dead long exceedeth all that shall live. The night of time far surpasseth the day, and who knows when was the equinox? Every hour adds unto that current arithmetic, which scarce stands one moment. And since death must be the *Lucina* of life, and even pagans could doubt whether thus to live were to die; since our longest sun sets at right descensions, and makes but winter arches, and therefore it cannot be long before we lie down in darkness, and have our light in ashes; since the brother of death daily haunts us with dying mementoes, and time, that grows old itself, bids us hope no long duration: diuturnity is a dream and folly of expectation.

Darkness and light divide the course of time, and oblivion shares with memory a great part even of our living beings; we slightly remember our felicities, and the smartest strokes of affliction leave but short smart upon us. Sense endureth no extremities, and sorrows destroy us or themselves. To weep into stones are fables. Afflictions induce callosites, miseries are slippery, or fall like snow upon us, which notwithstanding is no stupidity. To be ignorant of evils to come, and forgetful of evils past, is merciful provision in nature, whereby we digest the mixture of our few and evil days, and our delivered senses not relapsing into

---

[1] 9 The character of death.

[2] Old ones being taken up, and other bodies laid under them.

[3] *Gruteri Inscriptiones Antiquae.*

Cuperem notum esse quòd sim, non opto ut *sciatur qualis sim. Card. in vita propria.*

cutting remembrances, our sorrows are not kept raw by the edge of repetitions. A great part of antiquity contented their hopes of subsistency with a transmigration of their souls. A good way to continue their memories, while having the advantage of plural successions, they could not but act something remarkable in such variety of beings, and enjoying the fame of their passed selves, make accumulation of glory unto their last durations. Others, rather than be lost in the uncomfortable night of nothing, were content to recede into the common being, and make one particle of the public soul of all things, which was no more than to return into their unknown and divine original again. Egyptian ingenuity was more unsatisfied, contriving their bodies in sweet consistencies to attend the return of their souls. But all was vanity,[1] feeding the wind, and folly. The Egyptian mummies, which Cambyses or time hath spared, avarice now consumeth. Mummy is become merchandise, Mizraim cures wounds, and Pharaoh is sold for balsams.

In vain do individuals hope for immortality, or any patent from oblivion, in preservations below the moon; men have been deceived even in their flatteries above the sun, and studied conceits to perpetuate their names in heaven. The various cosmography of that part hath already varied the names of contrived constellations; Nimrod is lost in Orion, and Osiris in the dog-star. While we look for incorruption in the heavens, we find they are but like the earth; durable in their main bodies, alterable in their parts: whereof, beside comets and new stars, perspectives begin to tell tales; and the spots that wander about the sun, with Phæthon's favor, would make clear conviction.

There is nothing strictly immortal but immortality; whatever hath no beginning may be confident of no end: (all others have a dependent being, and within the reach of destruction) which is the peculiar of that necessary essence that cannot destroy itself; and the highest strain of omnipotency, to be so powerfully constituted, as not to suffer even

from the power of itself. But the sufficiency of christian immortality frustrates all earthly glory, and the quality of either state after death makes a folly of posthumous memory. God, who can only destroy our souls, and hath assured our resurrection, either of our bodies or names hath directly promised no duration; wherein there is so much of chance, that the boldest expectants have found unhappy frustration; and to hold long subsistence, seems but a scape in oblivion. But man is a noble animal, splendid in ashes, and pompous in the grave, solemnizing nativities and deaths with equal luster nor omitting ceremonies of bravery in the infamy of his nature.

Life is a pure flame, and we live by an invisible sun within us. A small fire sufficeth for life, great flames seemed too little after death, while men vainly affected precious pyres, and to burn like Sardanapalus. But the wisdom of funeral laws found the folly of prodigal blazes, and reduced undoing fires, unto the rule of sober obsequies, wherein few could be so mean as not to provide wood, pitch, a mourner, and an urn.

Five languages secured not the epitaph of Gordianus. The man of God lives longer without a tomb than any by one, invisibly interred by angels, and adjudged to obscurity, though not without some marks directing human discovery. Enoch and Elias, without either tomb or burial, in an anomalous state of being, are the great examples of perpetuity in their long and living memory, in strict account being still on this side death, and having a late part yet to act upon this stage of earth. If in the decretory term of the world we shall not all die, but be changed, according to received translation, the last day will make but few graves; at least quick resurrections will anticipate lasting sepultures: some graves will be opened before they be quite closed, and Lazarus be no wonder, when many that feared to die shall groan that they can die but once. The dismal state is the second and living death, when life puts despair on the damned; when men shall wish the coverings of mountains, not of monuments, and annihilation shall be courted.

* * *

[1] *Omnia vanitas et pastio venti, νομὴ ἀνέμου, Βόσκησις ut olim Aquila et Symmachus.* v. *Drus.* Eccles.

ISAAK WALTON (1593–1683)

The *Complete Angler* (1653) is one of the best established of the English classics, holding its place through succeeding ages by its unaffected simplicity and charming naturalness. Its author, when he was not fishing and enjoying country sights and sounds, was a London linen draper with many pleasant friendships, including some of the leading men of the time; his life was happy and uneventful.

THE COMPLETE ANGLER

CHAPTER IV

OBSERVATIONS OF THE NATURE AND BREED-
ING OF THE TROUT, AND HOW TO FISH
FOR HIM; AND THE MILKMAID'S SONG

The trout is a fish highly valued both in this and foreign nations: he may be justly said, as the old poet said of wine, and we English say of venison, to be a generous fish: a fish that is so like the buck that he also has his seasons; for it is observed, that he comes in and goes out of season with the stag and buck. Gesner says his name is of a German offspring, and says he is a fish that feeds clean and purely, in the swiftest streams, and on the hardest gravel; and that he may justly contend with all fresh-water fish, as the mullet may with all sea-fish, for precedency and daintiness of taste, and that being in right season, the most dainty palates have allowed precedency to him.

And before I go further in my discourse, let me tell you, that you are to observe, that as there be some barren does that are good in summer, so there be some barren trouts that are good in winter; but there are not many that are so, for usually they be in their perfection in the month of May, and decline with the buck. Now you are to take notice that in several countries, as in Germany and in other parts, compared to ours, fish differ much in their bigness and shape, and other ways, and so do trouts: it is well known that in the Lake Leman, the Lake of Geneva, there are trouts taken of three cubits long, as is affirmed by Gesner, a writer of good credit; and Mercator says the trouts that are taken in the Lake of Geneva are a great part of the merchandise of that famous city. And you are further to know that there be certain waters that breed trouts remarkable both for their number and smallness. I know a little brook in Kent that breeds them to a number incredible, and you may take them twenty or forty in an hour, but none greater than about the size of a gudgeon: there are also in divers rivers, especially that relate to or be near to the sea, as Winchester or the Thames about Windsor, a little trout called a samlet or skegger trout (in both which places I have caught twenty or forty at a standing), that will bite as fast and as freely as minnows; these be by some taken to be young salmons; but in those waters they never grow to be bigger than a herring.

There is also in Kent, near to Canterbury, a trout called there a Fordidge trout, a trout that bears the name of the town where it is usually caught, that is accounted the rarest of fish: many of them near the bigness of salmon, but known by their different color; and in their best season they cut very white; and none of these have been known to be caught with an angle, unless it were one that was caught by Sir George Hastings, an excellent angler, and now with God: and he hath told me, he thought *that* trout bit not for hunger but wantonness; and it is rather to be believed, because both he then, and many others before him, have been curious to search into their bellies, what the food

212

was by which they lived, and have found out nothing by which they might satisfy their curiosity.

Concerning which you are to take notice that it is reported by good authors that grasshoppers and some fish have no mouths, but are nourished and take breath by the porousness of their gills, man knows not how: and this may be believed, if we consider that when the raven hath hatched her eggs, she takes no further care, but leaves her young ones to the care of the God of nature, who is said, in the Psalms, ' to feed the young ravens that call upon him.' And they be kept alive and fed by dew, or worms that breed in their nests, or some other ways that we mortals know not; and this may be believed of the Fordidge trout, which, as it is said of the stork (Jerem. viii. 7), that ' he knows his season,' so he knows his times, I think almost his day of coming into that river out of the sea, where he lives, and, it is like, feeds nine months of the year, and fasts three in the river of Fordidge. And you are to note that those townsmen are very punctual in observing the time of beginning to fish for them, and boast much that their river affords a trout that exceeds all others. And just so does Sussex boast of several fish: as namely, a Shelsey cockle, a Chichester lobster, an Arundel mullet, and an Amerly trout.

And now for some confirmation of the Fordidge trout: you are to know that this trout is thought to eat nothing in the fresh water; and it may be better believed, because it is well known that swallows and bats and wagtails, which are called half-year birds, and not seen to fly in England for six months in the year, but about Michaelmas leave us for a better climate than this; yet some of them that have been left behind their fellows, have been found many thousands at a time, in hollow trees, or clay caves; where they have been observed to live and sleep out the whole winter without meat; and so Albertus observes, that there is one kind of frog that hath her mouth naturally shut up about the end of August, and that she lives so all the winter; and though it be strange to some, yet it is known to too many among us to be doubted.

And so much for these Fordidge trouts, which never afford an angler sport, but either live their time of being in the fresh water, by their meat formerly got in the sea (not unlike the swallow or frog), or by the virtue of the fresh water only; or, as the birds of Paradise and the chameleon are said to live by the sun and the air.

There is also in Northumberland a trout called a bull trout, of a much greater length and bigness than any in the southern parts. And there are, in many rivers that relate to the sea, salmon trouts, as much different from others, both in shape and in their spots, as we see sheep in some countries differ one from another in their shape and bigness, and in the fineness of their wool. And certainly, as some pastures breed larger sheep, so do some rivers, by reason of the ground over which they run, breed larger trouts.

Now the next thing that I will commend to your consideration is that the trout is of a more sudden growth than other fish. Concerning which, you are also to take notice that he lives not so long as the perch and divers other fishes do, as Sir Francis Bacon hath observed in his History of Life and Death.

And now you are to take notice that he is not like the crocodile, which if it lives never so long, yet always thrives till his death; but 't is not so with the trout; for after he is come to his full growth, he declines in his body, and keeps his bigness or thrives only in his head till his death. And you are to know that he will about, especially before, the time of his spawning, get almost miraculously through weirs and floodgates against the streams; even through such high and swift places as is almost incredible. Next, that the trout usually spawns about October or November, but in some rivers a little sooner or later; which is the more observable, because most other fish spawn in the spring or summer, when the sun hath warmed both the earth and the water, and made it fit for generation. And you are to note, that he continues many months out of season; for it may be observed of the trout, that he is like the buck or the ox, that will not be fat in many months, though he go in the very same pasture that horses do, which will be fat in one month; and so you may observe that most other fishes recover strength, and grow sooner fat and in season, than the trout doth.

And next you are to note that till the sun gets to such a height as to warm the earth and the water, the trout is sick and lean, and lousy, and unwholesome; for you shall in winter find him to have a big head, and then to be lank, and thin, and lean; at which time many of them have sticking on them sugs, or trout-lice, which is a kind of worm, in shape like a clove or pin, with a big head, and sticks close to him and sucks his moisture: those I think the trout breeds himself, and never thrives till he free himself from them, which is when warm weather comes; and then, as he grows stronger, he gets from the dead, still water, into the sharp streams and the gravel, and there rubs off these worms or lice; and then as he grows stronger, so he gets him into swifter and swifter streams, and there lies at the watch for any fly or minnow that comes near to him; and he especially loves the May-fly, which is bred of the cod-worm or caddis; and these make the trout bold and lusty, and he is usually fatter and better meat at that end of that month [May] than at any time of the year.

Now you are to know that it is observed that usually the best trouts are either red or yellow; though some (as the Fordidge trout) be white and yet good; but that is not usual: and it is a note observable, that the female trout hath usually a less head and a deeper body than the male trout, and is usually the better meat. And note that a hog-back and a little head to either trout, salmon, or any other fish, is a sign that that fish is in season.

But yet you are to note that as you see some willows or palm-trees bud and blossom sooner than others do, so some trouts be in rivers sooner in season; and as some hollies or oaks are longer before they cast their leaves, so are some trouts in rivers longer before they go out of season.

And you are to note that there are several kinds of trouts; but these several kinds are not considered but by very few men; for they go under the general name of trouts; just as pigeons do in most places; though it is certain there are tame and wild pigeons; and of the tame, there be helmets and runts, and carriers and cropers, and indeed too many to name. Nay, the Royal Society have found and published lately that there be thirty and three kinds of spiders; and yet all, for aught I know, go under that one general name of spider. And it is so with many kinds of fish, and of trouts especially, which differ in their bigness and shape and spots and color. The great Kentish hens may be an instance, compared to other hens. And, doubtless, there is a kind of small trout, which will never thrive to be big, that breeds very many more than others do, that be of a larger size; which you may rather believe if you consider that the little wren and titmouse will have twenty young ones at a time, when usually the noble hawk or the musical thrassel or blackbird exceed not four or five.

And now you shall see me try my skill to catch a trout; and at my next walking, either this evening or to-morrow morning, I will give you direction how you yourself shall fish for him.

VENATOR [The HUNTER]. Trust me, master, I see now it is a harder matter to catch a trout than a chub; for I have put on patience and followed you these two hours, and not seen a fish stir, neither at your minnow nor your worm.

PISCATOR [The ANGLER]. Well, scholar, you must endure worse luck some time, or you will never make a good angler. But what say you now? There is a trout now, and a good one too, if I can but hold him, and two or three more turns more will tire him. Now you see he lies still, and the sleight is to land him. Reach me that landing-net; so, sir, now he is mine own. What say you now? is not this worth all my labor and your patience?

VEN. On my word, master, this is a gallant trout: what shall we do with him?

PISC. Marry, e'en eat him to supper: we'll go to my hostess, from whence we came; she told me, as I was going out of door, that my brother Peter, a good angler and a cheerful companion, had sent word that he would lodge there to-night, and bring a friend with him. My hostess has two beds, and I know you and I may have the best; we'll rejoice with my brother Peter and his friend, tell tales, or sing ballads, or make a catch, or find some harmless sport to content us and pass away a little time, without offense to God or man.

VEN. A match, good master, let's go to that house, for the linen looks white and smells of lavender, and I long to lie in a pair of sheets that smells so. Let's be going, good master, for I am hungry again with fishing.

PISC. Nay, stay a little, good scholar. I caught my last trout with a worm; now I will put on a minnow, and try a quarter of an hour about yonder trees for another; and so walk towards our lodging. Look you, scholar, thereabout we shall have a bite presently or not at all. Have with you, sir! o' my word I have hold of him. Oh! it is a great logger-headed chub; come hang him upon that willow twig, and let's be going. But turn out of the way a little, good scholar, towards yonder high honeysuckle hedge; there we'll sit and sing, whilst this shower falls so gently upon the teeming earth, and gives yet a sweeter smell to the lovely flowers that adorn these verdant meadows.

Look! under that broad beech-tree I sat down, when I was last this way a-fishing. And the birds in the adjoining grove seemed to have a friendly contention with an echo, whose dead voice seemed to live in a hollow tree, near to the brow of that primrose hill. There I sat viewing the silver streams glide silently towards their center, the tempestuous sea; yet sometimes opposed by rugged roots and pebble-stones, which broke their waves, and turned them into foam. And sometimes I beguiled time by viewing the harmless lambs; some leaping securely in the cool shade, whilst others sported themselves in the cheerful sun; and saw others craving comfort from the swollen udders of their bleating dams. As I thus sat, these and other sights had so fully possessed my soul with content, that I thought, as the poet hath happily expressed it,

I was for that time lifted above earth,
And possessed joys not promised in my birth.

As I left this place, and entered into the next field, a second pleasure entertained me; 'twas a handsome milkmaid, that had not yet attained so much age and wisdom as to load her mind with any fears of many things that will never be, as too many men too often do; but she cast away all care, and sang like a nightingale: her voice was good, and the ditty fitted for it: it was that smooth song which was made by Kit Marlow, now at least fifty years ago; and the milkmaid's mother sang an answer to it, which was made by Sir Walter Raleigh in his younger days.

They were old-fashioned poetry, but choicely good; I think much better than the strong lines that are now in fashion in this critical age. Look yonder; on my word, yonder they both be a-milking again. I will give her the chub, and persuade them to sing those two songs to us.

God speed you, good woman! I have been a-fishing and am going to Bleak Hall to my bed, and having caught more fish than will sup myself and friend, I will bestow this upon you and your daughter, for I use to sell none.

MILK-W. Marry, God requite you, sir, and we'll eat it cheerfully; and if you come this way a-fishing two months hence, a grace of God, I'll give you a syllabub of new verjuice in a new-made hay-cock for it, and my Maudlin shall sing you one of her best ballads; for she and I both love all anglers, they be such honest, civil, quiet men: in the meantime will you drink a draft of red cow's milk? you shall have it freely.

PISC. No, I thank you; but, I pray, do us a courtesy that shall stand you and your daughter in nothing, and yet we will think ourselves still something in your debt; it is but to sing us a song that was sung by your daughter when I last passed over this meadow, about eight or nine days since.

MILK-W. What song was it, I pray? Was it Come, shepherds, deck your heads? or, As at noon Dulcina rested? or, Phillida flouts me? or, Chevy Chase? or, Johnny Armstrong? or, Troy Town?

PISC. No, it is none of those; it is a song that your daughter sang the first part, and you sang the answer to it.

MILK-W. Oh, I know it now. I

learned it the first part in my golden age, when I was about the age of my poor daughter; and the latter part, which indeed fits me best now, but two or three years ago, when the cares of the world began to take hold of me: but you shall, God willing, hear them both, and sung as well as we can, for we both love anglers. Come, Maudlin, sing the first part to the gentlemen with a merry heart, and I'll sing the second, when you have done.

THE MILKMAID'S SONG

Come, live with me, and be my love,   15
And we will all the pleasures prove
That valleys, groves, or hills, or field,
Or woods and steepy mountains yield;

Where we will sit upon the rocks,   20
And see the shepherds feed our flocks
By shallow rivers, to whose falls
Melodious birds sing madrigals.

And I will make thee beds of roses,   25
And then a thousand fragrant posies.
A cap of flowers, and a kirtle
Embroidered all with leaves of myrtle;

A gown made of the finest wool   30
Which from our pretty lambs we pull;
Slippers lined choicely for the cold,
With buckles of the purest gold;

A belt of straw and ivy-buds,   35
With coral clasps and amber studs:
And if these pleasures may thee move,
Come, live with me, and be my love.

Thy silver dishes for my meat,   40
As precious as the gods do eat,
Shall on an ivory table be
Prepared each day for thee and me.

The shepherd swains shall dance and sing, 45
For thy delight, each May morning.
If these delights thy mind may move,
Then live with me, and be my love.

VEN. Trust me, master, it is a choice 50 song, and sweetly sung by honest Maudlin. I now see it was not without cause that our good Queen Elizabeth did so often wish herself a milkmaid all the month of May, because they are not 55 troubled with fears and cares, and sing sweetly all the day and sleep securely all the night; and without doubt, honest,

innocent, pretty Maudlin does so. I'll bestow Sir Thomas Overbury's milkmaid's wish upon her, 'That she may die in the spring, and being dead, may have good store of flowers stuck round about her winding-sheet.'

THE MILKMAID'S MOTHER'S ANSWER

If all the world and love were young,
And truth in every shepherd's tongue,
These pretty pleasures might me move
To live with thee, and be thy love.

But time drives flocks from field to fold,
When rivers rage and rocks grow cold;
Then Philomel becometh dumb,
And age complains of care to come.

The flowers do fade, and wanton fields
To wayward winter reckoning yields.
A honey tongue, a heart of gall,
Is fancy's spring, but sorrow's fall.

Thy gowns, thy shoes, thy beds of roses,
Thy cap, thy kirtle, and thy posies,
Soon break, soon wither, soon forgotten,
In folly ripe, in reason rotten.

Thy belt of straw and ivy-buds,
Thy coral clasps and amber studs,
All these in me no means can move
To come to thee, and be thy love.

What should we talk of dainties then,
Of better meat than's fit for men?
These are but vain; that's only good
Which God hath blest, and sent for food.

But could youth last and love still breed,
Had joys no date nor age no need;
Then those delights my mind might move
To live with thee, and be thy love.

PISC. Well sung, good woman; I thank you. I'll give you another dish of fish one of these days, and then beg another song of you. Come, scholar, let Maudlin alone; do not you offer to spoil her voice. Look, yonder comes mine hostess, to call us to supper. How now? Is my brother Peter come?

HOST. Yes, and a friend with him, they are both glad to hear that you are in these parts, and long to see you, and long to be at supper, for they be very hungry.

THOMAS FULLER (1608–1661)

Fuller retained more than his contemporaries of the Elizabethan quaintness and humor. Although a clergyman and an army chaplain during the Civil War, he was not a keen partisan, and kept his position at Waltham Abbey under the Commonwealth. At the Restoration he was made chaplain to the king, and would have become a bishop, if he had not been suddenly carried off by a fever. His chief works were *The Holy State* (1642) and *The Worthies of England*, published the year after his death.

THE LIFE OF SIR FRANCIS DRAKE

FROM THE HOLY STATE, BK. II, CH. XXII

Francis Drake was born nigh South Tavistock in Devonshire, and brought up in Kent; God dividing the honor betwixt two counties, that the one might have his birth, and the other his education. His father, being a minister, fled into Kent, for fear of the Six Articles, wherein the sting of Popery still remained in England, though the teeth thereof were knocked out, and the Pope's supremacy abolished. Coming into Kent, he bound his son Francis apprentice to the master of a small bark, which traded into France and Zealand, where he underwent a hard service; and pains, with patience in his youth, did knit the joints of his soul, and made them more solid and compacted. His master, dying unmarried, in reward of his industry, bequeathed his bark unto him for a legacy.

For some time he continued his master's profession; but the narrow seas were a prison for so large a spirit, born for greater undertakings. He soon grew weary of his bark; which would scarce go alone, but as it crept along by the shore: wherefore, selling it, he unfortunately ventured most of his estate with Captain John Hawkins into the West Indies, in 1567; whose goods were taken by the Spaniards at St. John de Ulva, and he himself scarce escaped with life: the king of Spain being so tender in those parts, that the least touch doth wound him; and so jealous of the West Indies, his wife, that willingly he would have none look upon her: he therefore used them with the greater severity.

Drake was persuaded by the minister of his ship, that he might lawfully recover in value of the king of Spain, and repair his losses upon him anywhere else. The case was clear in sea-divinity; and few are such infidels, as not to believe doctrines which make for their own profit. Whereupon Drake, though a poor private man, hereafter undertook to revenge himself on so mighty a monarch; who, as not contented that the sun riseth and setteth in his dominions, may seem to desire to make all his own where he shineth. And now let us see how a dwarf, standing on the mount of God's providence, may prove an overmatch for a giant.

After two or three several voyages to gain intelligence in the West Indies, and some prizes taken, at last he effectually set forward from Plymouth with two ships, the one of seventy, the other twenty-five tons, and seventy-three men and boys in both. He made with all speed and secrecy to Nombre de Dios, as loath to put the town to too much charge (which he knew they would willingly bestow) in providing beforehand for his entertainment; which city was then the granary of the West Indies, wherein the golden harvest brought from Panama was hoarded up till it could be conveyed into Spain. They came hard aboard the shore, and lay quiet all night, intending to attempt the town in the dawning of the day.

But he was forced to alter his resolution, and assault it sooner; for he heard his men muttering amongst themselves of the strength and greatness of the town: and when men's heads are once fly-blown with buzzes of suspicion, the vermin multiply instantly, and one

217

jealousy begets another. Wherefore, he raised them from their nest before they had hatched their fears; and, to put away those conceits, he persuaded them it was day-dawning when the moon rose, and instantly set on the town, and won it, being unwalled. In the market-place the Spaniards saluted them with a volley of shot; Drake returned their greeting with a flight of arrows, the best and ancient English compliment, which drave their enemies away. Here Drake received a dangerous wound, though he valiantly concealed it a long time; knowing if his heart stooped, his men's would fall, and loath to leave off the action, wherein if so bright an opportunity once setteth, it seldom riseth again. But at length his men forced him to return to his ship, that his wound might be dressed; and this unhappy accident defeated the whole design. Thus victory sometimes slips through their fingers who have caught it in their hands.

But his valor would not let him give over the project as long as there was either life or warmth in it; and therefore, having received intelligence from the negroes called Symerons, of many mules'-lading of gold and silver, which was to be brought from Panama, he, leaving competent numbers to man his ships, went on land with the rest, and bestowed himself in the woods by the way as they were to pass, and so intercepted and carried away an infinite mass of gold. As for the silver, which was not portable over the mountains, they digged holes in the ground and hid it therein.

There want not those who love to beat down the price of every honorable action, though they themselves never mean to be chapmen. These cry up Drake's fortune herein to cry down his valor; as if this his performance were nothing, wherein a golden opportunity ran his head, with his long forelock, into Drake's hands beyond expectation. But, certainly, his resolution and unconquerable patience deserved much praise, to adventure on such a design, which had in it just no more probability than what was enough to keep it from being impossible. Yet I admire not so much at all the treasure he took, as at the rich and deep mine of God's providence.

Having now full freighted himself with wealth, and burnt at the House of Crosses above two hundred thousand pounds' worth of Spanish merchandise, he returned with honor and safety into England, and, some years after (December 13th, 1577) undertook that his famous voyage about the world, most accurately described by our English authors: and yet a word or two thereof will not be amiss.

Setting forward from Plymouth, he bore up for Cabo-verd, where, near to the island of St. Jago, he took prisoner Nuno de Silva, an experienced Spanish pilot, whose direction he used in the coasts of Brazil and Magellan Straits, and afterwards safely landed him at Guatulco in New Spain. Hence they took their course to the Island of Brava; and hereabouts they met with those tempestuous winds whose only praise is, that they continue not an hour, in which time they change all the points of the compass. Here they had great plenty of rain, poured (not, as in other places, as it were out of sieves, but) as out of spouts, so that a butt of water falls down in a place; which, notwithstanding, is but a courteous injury in that hot climate far from land, and where otherwise fresh water cannot be provided. Then cutting the Line, they saw the face of that heaven which earth hideth from us, but therein only three stars of the first greatness, the rest few and small compared to our hemisphere; as if God, on purpose, had set up the best and biggest candles in that room wherein his civilest guests are entertained.

Sailing the south of Brazil, he afterwards passed the Magellan Straits (August 20th, 1578) and then entered *Mare Pacificum* [the Pacific Ocean], came to the southernmost land at the height of 55½ latitudes; thence directing his course northward, he pillaged many Spanish towns, and took rich prizes of high value in the kingdoms of Chili, Peru, and New Spain. Then, bending eastwards, he coasted China, and the Moluccas, where, by the king of Terrenate, a true gentleman Pagan, he was most honorably entertained. The king told them, they and he were all of one religion in this respect,— that they believed not in gods made of stocks and stones, as did the Portugals. He furnished them also with all necessaries that they wanted.

On January 9th following (1579), his ship, having a large wind and a smooth sea, ran aground on a dangerous shoal, and struck twice on it; knocking twice at the door of death, which, no doubt, had opened the third time. Here they stuck, from eight o'clock at night till four the next afternoon, having ground too much, and yet too little to land on; and water too much, and yet too little to sail in. Had God (who, as the wise man saith, 'holdeth the winds in his fist,' Prov. xxx. 4) but opened his little finger, and let out the smallest blast, they had undoubtedly been cast away; but there blew not any wind all the while. Then they, conceiving aright that the best way to lighten the ship was, first, to ease it of the burden of their sins by true repentance, humbled themselves, by fasting, under the hand of God. Afterwards they received the communion, dining on Christ in the sacrament, expecting no other than to sup with him in heaven. Then they cast out of their ship six great pieces of ordnance, threw overboard as much wealth as would break the heart of a miser to think on it, with much sugar, and packs of spices, making a caudle of the sea round about. Then they betook themselves to their prayers, the best lever at such a dead lift indeed; and it pleased God, that the wind, formerly their mortal enemy, became their friend; which, changing from the starboard to the larboard of the ship, and rising by degrees, cleared them off to the sea again,— for which they returned unfeigned thanks to Almighty God.

By the Cape of Good Hope and west of Africa, he returned safe into England, and (November 3rd, 1580) landed at Plymouth (being almost the first of those that made a thorough light through the world), having, in his whole voyage though a curious searcher after the time, lost one day through the variation of several climates. He feasted the queen in his ship at Dartford, who knighted him for his service. Yet it grieved him not a little, that some prime courtiers refused the gold he offered them, as gotten by piracy. Some of them would have been loath to have been told, that they had *aurum Tholosanum* [gold of Spain] in their own purses. Some think, that they did it to show that

their envious pride was above their covetousness, who of set purpose did blur the fair copy of his performance, because they would not take pains to write after it.

I pass by his next West-Indian voyage (1585), wherein he took the cities of St. Jago, St. Domingo, Carthagena, and St. Augustine in Florida; as also his service performed in 1588, wherein he, with many others, helped to the waning of that half-moon, which sought to govern all the motion of our sea. I haste to his last voyage.

Queen Elizabeth, in 1595, perceiving that the only way to make the Spaniard a cripple forever, was to cut his sinews of war in the West Indies, furnished Sir Francis Drake, and Sir John Hawkins, with six of her own ships, besides twenty-one ships and barks of their own providing, containing in all two thousand five hundred men and boys, for some service on America. But, alas! this voyage was marred before begun. For, so great preparations being too big for a cover, the king of Spain knew of it, and sent a caraval of adviso to the West Indies; so that they had intelligence three weeks before the fleet set forth of England, either to fortify or remove their treasure; whereas, in other of Drake's voyages, not two of his own men knew whither he went; and managing such a design is like carrying a mine in war,— if it hath any vent, all is spoiled. Besides, Drake and Hawkins, being in joint commission, hindered each other. The latter took himself to be inferior rather in success than skill; and the action was unlike to prosper when neither would follow, and both could not handsomely go abreast. It vexed old Hawkins, that his counsel was not followed, in present sailing to America, but that they spent time in vain in assaulting the Canaries; and the grief that his advice was slighted, say some, was the cause of his death, Others impute it to the sorrow he took for the taking of his bark called 'the Francis,' which five Spanish frigates had intercepted. But when the same heart hath two mortal wounds given it together, it is hard to say which of them killeth.

Drake continued his course for Porto Rico: and, riding within the road, a shot from the Castle entered the steerage of the ship, took away the stool from under him as he sat at supper, wounded Sir Nicholas Clifford, and Brute Brown to death. 'Ah, dear Brute!' said Drake, 'I could grieve for thee, but now is no time for me to let down my spirits.' And, indeed, a soldier's most proper bemoaning a friend's death in war, is in revenging it. And, sure, as if grief had made the English furious, they soon after fired five Spanish ships of two hundred tons apiece, in despite of the Castle.

America is not unfitly resembled to an hourglass, which hath a narrow neck of land (suppose it the hole where the sand passeth), betwixt the parts thereof, — Mexicana and Peruana. Now, the English had a design to march by land over this Isthmus, from Porto Rico to Panama, where the Spanish treasure was laid up. Sir Thomas Baskerville, general of the land-forces, undertook the service with seven hundred and fifty armed men. They marched through deep ways, the Spaniards much annoying them with shot out of the woods. One fort in the passage they assaulted in vain, and heard two others were built to stop them, besides Panama itself. They had so much of this breakfast they thought they should surfeit of a dinner and supper of the same. No hope of conquest, except with cloying the jaws of death, and thrusting men on the mouth of the cannon. Wherefore, fearing to find the proverb true, that 'gold may be bought too dear,' they returned to their ships. Drake afterwards fired Nombre de Dios, and many other petty towns (whose treasure the Spaniards had conveyed away), burning the empty casks, when their precious liquor was run out before, and then prepared for their returning home.

Great was the difference betwixt the Indian cities now, from what they were when Drake first haunted these coasts. At first, the Spaniards here were safe and secure, counting their treasure sufficient to defend itself, the remoteness thereof being the greatest (almost only) resistance, and the fetching of it more than the fighting for it. Whilst the king of Spain guarded the head and heart of his dominions in Europe, he left his long legs in America open to blows; till, finding them to smart, being beaten black and blue by the English, he learned to arm them at last, fortifying the most important of them to make them impregnable.

Now began Sir Francis's discontent to feed upon him. He conceived, that expectation, a merciless usurer, computing each day since his departure, exacted an interest and return of honor and profit proportionable to his great preparations, and transcending his former achievements. He saw that all the good which he had done in this voyage, consisted in the evil he had done to the Spaniards afar off, whereof he could present but small visible fruits in England. These apprehensions, accompanying, it not causing, the disease of the flux, wrought his sudden death, January 28th, 1595. And sickness did not so much untie his clothes, as sorrow did rend at once the robe of his mortality asunder. He lived by the sea, died on it, and was buried in it. Thus an extempore performance (scarce heard to be begun before we hear it is ended!) comes off with better applause, or miscarries with less disgrace, then a long-studied and openly-premeditated action. Besides, we see how great spirits, having mounted to the highest pitch of performance, afterwards strain and break their credits in striving to go beyond it. Lastly, God oftentimes leaves the brightest men in an eclipse, to show that they do but borrow their luster from his reflexion. We will not justify all the actions of any man, though of a tamer profession than a sea-captain, in whom civility is often counted preciseness. For the main, we say that this our captain was a religious man towards God and his houses (generally sparing churches where he came), chaste in his life, just in his dealings, true of his word, and merciful to those that were under him, hating nothing so much as idleness: and therefore, lest his soul should rust in peace, at spare hours he brought fresh water to Plymouth. Careful he was for posterity (though men of his profession have as well an ebb of riot, as a float of fortune) and providently raised a worshipful family of his kindred. In a word: should those that speak against him fast till they fetch their bread where he did his, they would have a good stomach to eat it.

JEREMY TAYLOR (1613-1667)

Mr. Saintsbury, whose praise of Browne's prose style is quoted on page 200, says in another place that 'on the whole no one in English prose has so much command of the enchanter's wand as Jeremy Taylor'; and critical authority is, indeed, much divided as to the stylistic excellences of the two writers. Taylor's inferiority is more in thought than in expression, and he has the disadvantage of writing from the point of view of the theologian or cleric: Browne is a layman and has a touch of modern scepticism. Taylor was the son of a barber, spent many years at Cambridge and Oxford, became a clergyman and lost his rectory under the Commonwealth. He retired to Wales, and there composed *The Liberty of Prophesying*, a plea for toleration against Presbyterian bigotry (1647), *Holy Living* (1650), *Holy Dying* (1651), *A Course of Sermons for all the Sundays of the Year* (1651), and *The Golden Grove*, a manual of private devotion for young people (1655).

THE FAITH AND PATIENCE OF THE SAINTS

(FROM A SERMON PREACHED AT GOLDEN GROVE)

The state of the Gospel is a state of sufferings, not of temporal prosperities. This was foretold by the prophets: 'A fountain shall go out of the house of the Lord *et irrigabit torrentem spinarum* (so it is in the Vulgar Latin), and it shall water the torrent of thorns,' that is, the state or time of the Gospel, which, like a torrent, shall carry all the world before it, and, like a torrent, shall be fullest in ill weather; and by its banks shall grow nothing but thorns and briers, sharp afflictions, temporal infelicities, and persecution. This sense of the words is more fully explained in the book of the prophet Isaiah. 'Upon the ground of my people shall thorns and briers come up; how much more in all the houses of the city of rejoicing?' Which prophecy is the same in the style of the prophets, that my text is in the style of the Apostles. The house of God shall be watered with the dew of heaven, and there shall spring up briers in it: 'Judgment must begin there;' but how much more 'in the houses of the city of rejoicing?' how much more amongst 'them that are at ease in Sion,' that serve their desires, that satisfy their appetites, that are given over to their own heart's lust, that so serve themselves that they never serve God, that 'dwell in the city of rejoicing?' They are like Dives, whose portion was in this life, 'who went in fine linen, and fared deliciously every day:' they, indeed, trample upon their briers and thorns, and suffer them not to grow in their houses; but the roots are in the ground, and they are reserved for fuel of wrath in the day of everlasting burning. Thus, you see, it was prophesied, now see how it was performed; Christ was the captain of our sufferings, and he began.

He entered into the world with all the circumstances of poverty. He had a star to illustrate his birth; but a stable for his bedchamber, and a manger for his cradle. The angels sang hymns when he was born; but he was cold and cried, uneasy and unprovided. He lived long in the trade of a carpenter; he, by whom God made the world, had in his first years the business of a mean and ignoble trade. He did good wherever he went; and almost wherever he went, was abused. He deserved heaven for his obedience, but found a cross in his way thither: and if ever any man had reason to expect fair usages from God, and to be dandled in the lap of ease, softness, and a prosperous fortune, he it was only that could deserve that, or anything that can be good. But after he had chosen to live a life of virtue, of poverty, and labor, he entered into a state of death; whose shame and trouble was great

221

enough to pay for the sins of the whole world. And I shall choose to express this mystery in the words of Scripture. He died not by a single or a sudden death, but he was the 'Lamb slain from 5 the beginning of the world:' for he was massacred in Abel, saith St. Paulinus; he was tossed upon the waves of the sea in the person of Noah; it was he that went out of his country, when 10 Abraham was called from Charran, and wandered from his native soil; he was offered up in Isaac, persecuted in Jacob, betrayed in Joseph, blinded in Samson, affronted in Moses, sawed in Isaiah, 15 cast into the dungeon with Jeremiah: for all these were types of Christ suffering. And then his passion continued even after his resurrection. For it is he that suffers in all his members; it is he 20 that 'endures the contradiction of all sinners'; it is he that is 'the lord of life,' and is 'crucified again, and put to open shame' in all the sufferings of his servants, and sins of rebels, and defi- 25 ances of apostates and renegadoes, and violence of tyrants, and injustice of usurpers, and the persecutions of his church. It is he that is stoned in St. Stephen, flayed in the person of St. 30 Bartholomew; he was roasted upon St. Laurence's gridiron, exposed to lions in St. Ignatius, burnt in St. Polycarp, frozen in the lake where stood forty martyrs of Cappadocia. '*Unigenitus* 35 *enim Dei ad peragendum mortis suae sacramentum consummavit omne genus humanarum passionum,*' said St. Hilary; 'the sacrament of Christ's death is not to be accomplished but by suffering all the 40 sorrows of humanity.'

All that Christ came for was, or was mingled with, sufferings; for all those little joys which God sent, either to recreate his person, or to illustrate his 45 office, were abated or attended with afflictions, God being more careful to establish in him the covenant of sufferings than to refresh his sorrows. Presently after the angels had finished their hallelu- 50 jahs, he was forced to fly to save his life; and the air became full of shrieks of the desolate mothers of Bethlehem for their dying babes. God had no sooner made him illustrious with a voice 55 from heaven and the descent of the Holy Ghost upon him in the waters of baptism, but he was delivered over to be tempted

and assaulted by the devil in the wilderness. His transfiguration was a bright ray of glory; but then also he entered into a cloud, and was told a sad story of what he was to suffer at Jerusalem. And upon Palm Sunday, when he rode triumphantly into Jerusalem, and was adorned with the acclamations of a king and a god, he wet the palms with his tears, sweeter than the drops of manna, or the little pearls of heaven that descended upon Mount Hermon; weeping, in the midst of this triumph, over obstinate, perishing, and malicious Jerusalem. For this Jesus was like the rainbow, which God set in the clouds as a sacrament to confirm a promise and establish a grace; he was half made of the glories of the light, and half of the moisture of a cloud; in his best days he was but half triumph and half sorrow: he was sent to tell of his Father's mercies, and that God intended to spare us; but appeared not but in the company or in the retinue of a shower and of foul weather. But I need not tell that Jesus, beloved of God, was a suffering person: that which concerns this question most is that he made for us a covenant of sufferings: his doctrines were such as expressly, and by consequent, enjoin and suppose sufferings and a state of affliction; his very promises were sufferings; his beatitudes were sufferings; his rewards and his arguments to invite men to follow him were only taken from sufferings in this life and the reward of sufferings hereafter.

For if we sum up the commandments of Christ, we shall find humility, mortification, self-denial, repentance, renouncing the world, mourning, taking up the cross, dying for him, patience and poverty, to stand in the chiefest rank of christian precepts, and in the direct order to heaven: 'He that will be my disciple, must deny himself, and take up his cross and follow me.' We must follow him that was crowned with thorns and sorrows, him that was drenched in Cedron, nailed upon the cross, that deserved all good, and suffered all evil: that is the sum of christian religion, as it distinguishes from all the religions in the world. To which we may add the express precept recorded by St. James: 'Be afflicted, and mourn, and weep; let your laughter be turned into mourning' and your joy into weeping.' You see the commandments: will you also see the promises? These they are. 'In the world ye shall have tribulation; in me, ye shall have peace:—Through many tribulations ye shall enter into heaven:—He that loseth father and mother, wives and children, houses and lands, for my name's sake and the Gospel, shall receive a hundred fold in this life, with persecution:' that is part of his reward: and, 'He chastiseth every son that he receiveth;—if ye be exempt from sufferings, ye are bastards, and not sons.' These are some of Christ's promises: will you see some of Christ's blessings that he gives his church? 'Blessed are the poor: blessed are the hungry and thirsty: blessed are they that mourn: blessed are the humble: blessed are the persecuted.' Of the eight beatitudes, five of them have temporal misery and meanness, or an afflicted condition for their subject. Will you at last see some of the rewards which Christ hath propounded to his servants, to invite them to follow him? 'When I am lifted up, will draw all men after me:' when Christ is 'lifted up, as Moses lift up the serpent in the wilderness,' that is, lifted upon the cross, then 'he will draw us fter him.' 'To you it is given for Christ,' saith St. Paul, when he went to sweeten and flatter the Philippians: well, what is given to them? some great favors, surely; true; 'It is not only given you that you believe in Christ,' though that be a great matter, 'but also that you suffer for him,' that is the highest of your honor. And therefore, saith St. James, 'My brethren, count it all joy when ye enter into divers temptations:' and St. Peter; 'Communicating with the sufferings of Christ, rejoice.' And St. James again: 'We count them blessed that have suffered:' and St. Paul, when he gives his blessing to the Thessalonians, useth this form of prayer; 'Our Lord direct your hearts in the charity of God, and in the patience and sufferings of Christ.' So that if we will serve the king of sufferings, whose crown was of thorns, whose scepter was a reed of scorn, whose imperial robe was a scarlet of mockery, whose throne was the cross, we must serve him in sufferings, in poverty of spirit, in humility and mortification; and for our reward we shall have persecution, and all its blessed

consequents. '*Atque hoc est esse Christianum*' [And this is to be a christian]. Since this was done in the green tree, what might we expect should be done in the dry? Let us, in the next place, consider how God hath treated his saints and servants in the descending ages of the Gospel: that if the best of God's servants were followers of Jesus in this covenant of sufferings, we may not think it strange concerning the fiery trial, as if some new thing had happened to us. For as the Gospel was founded in sufferings, we shall also see it grow in persecutions; and as Christ's blood did cement the corner-stones and the first foundation; so the blood and sweat, the groans and sighings, the afflictions and mortifications, of saints and marytrs, did make the superstructures, and must at last finish the building.

If we begin with the apostles, who were to persuade the world to become christian, and to use proper arguments of invitations, we shall find that they never offered an argument of temporal prosperity; they never promised empires and thrones on earth, nor riches, nor temporal power: and it would have been soon confuted, if they who were whipped and imprisoned, banished and scattered, persecuted and tormented, should have promised sunshine days to others which they could not to themselves. Of all the apostles there was not one that died a natural death but only St. John; and did he escape? Yes: but he was put into a cauldron of scalding lead and oil before the Porta Latina in Rome, and escaped death by miracle, though no miracle was wrought to make him escape the torture. And, besides this, he lived long in banishment, and that was worse than St. Peter's chains. '*Sanctus Petrus in vinculis, et Johannes ante Portam Latinam*' [Saint Peter in chains, and John before the Latin Gate], were both days of martyrdom, and church-festivals. And after a long and laborious life, and the affliction of being detained from his crown, and his sorrows for the death of his fellow-disciples, he died full of days and sufferings. And when St. Paul was taken into the apostolate, his commissions were signed in these words: 'I will shew unto him how great things he must suffer for my name:' And his whole life was a continual suffering. '*Quotidie morior'* was his motto, 'I die daily;' and his lesson that he daily learned was, to 'know Christ Jesus, and him crucified;' and all his joy was 'to rejoice in the cross of Christ;' and the changes of his life were nothing but the changes of his sufferings and the variety of his labors. For though Christ hath finished his own sufferings for expiation of the world; yet there are ὑστερήματα θλίψεων, 'portions that are behind of the sufferings' of Christ, which must be filled up by his body, the church; and happy are they that put in the greatest symbol: for 'in the same measure you are partakers of the sufferings of Christ, in the same shall ye be also of the consolation.' And therefore, concerning St. Paul, as it was also concerning Christ, there is nothing or but very little in Scripture relating to his person and chances of his private life, but his labors and persecutions; as if the Holy Ghost did think nothing fit to stand upon record for Christ but sufferings.

And now began to work the greatest glory of the divine providence; here was the case of christianity at stake. The world was rich and prosperous, learned and full of wise men; the Gospel was preached with poverty and persecution, in simplicity of discourse, and in demonstration of the Spirit: God was on one side, and the devil on the other; they each of them dressed up their city; Babylon upon earth, Jerusalem from above. The devil's city was full of pleasure, triumphs, victories, and cruelty; good news, and great wealth; conquest over kings, and making nations tributary: they 'bound kings in chains, and the nobles with links of iron;' and the inheritance of the earth was theirs: the Romans were lords over the greatest part of the world; and God permitted to the devil the firmament and increase, the wars and the success of that people,

giving to him an entire power of disposing the great change of the world, so as might best increase their greatness and power; and he therefore did it, because all the power of the Roman greatness was a professed enemy to christianity. And on the other side, God was to build up Jerusalem, and the kingdom of the Gospel; and he chose to build it of hewn stone, cut and broken; the apostles he chose for preachers, and they had no learning; women and mean people were the first disciples, and they had no power; the devil was to lose his kingdom, and he wanted no malice: and therefore he stirred up, and, as well as he could, he made active all the power of Rome, and all the learning of the Greeks, and all the malice of barbarous people, and all the prejudice and the obstinacy of the Jews, against this doctrine and institution, which preached, and promised, and brought, persecution along with it. On the one side, there was *'scandalum crucis'* [the offence of the cross]; on the other, *'patientia sanctorum'* [the patience of the saints], and what was the event? They that had overcome the world, could not strangle Christianity. But so have I seen the sun with a little ray of distant light challenge all the power of darkness, and without violence and noise, climbing up the hill, hath made night so to retire, that its memory was lost in the joys and spritefulness of the morning: and christianity without violence or armies, without resistance and self-preservation, without strength or human eloquence, without challenging of privileges or fighting against tyranny, without alteration of government and scandal of princes, with its humility and meekness, with toleration and patience, with obedience and charity, with praying and dying, did insensibly turn the world into christian, and persecution into victory.

JOHN BUNYAN (1628-1688)

The greatest of English allegorical writers was a Bedfordshire tinker. ' I never went to school to Aristotle or Plato, but was brought up at my father's house in a very mean condition, among a company of poor countrymen,' he tells us in his autobiography, *Grace abounding to the Chief of Sinners* (1666). As a matter of fact, he was not a conspicuously bad character, the worst faults of which he can accuse himself being fondness for dancing, bell-ringing, and other sports and pastimes, and a habit of profanity, for which he acquired a local reputation. All this was changed, however, by his marriage, about the age of twenty, to a godly wife, who brought about his conversion. He became famous as a preacher, to the great displeasure of the regular clergy, who were ' angry with the tinker because he strove to mend souls as well as kettles and pans.' After the Restoration, when the old laws against dissenters were revived, he was arrested for holding religious services, and remained in prison for the next twelve years; he made laces for the support of his family, preached to his fellow-prisoners, studied the Bible and Foxe's Book of Martyrs, and wrote a large number of religious tracts. It was apparently during a later imprisonment that he wrote *The Pilgrim's Progress*, the first part of which was published in 1678 and became immediately popular. After two other allegorical stories — from one point of view religious tracts, from another, novels — *The Life and Death of Mr. Badman* and *The Holy War* — he wrote the second part of *Pilgrim's Progress* (1684), completing the pilgrimage of Christian, his wife Christiana, and their children. In his later years he was active as a nonconformist minister (his congregation met in a barn at Bedford) and he was known in the surrounding country as ' Bishop Bunyan'; his fame as a preacher spread to London, where he drew great crowds together on his occasional visits, and attracted the attention of royalty; but it is only in recent years that Bunyan's literary merits have been fully appreciated — his power of imagination and realistic description, and the forthright directness of his style.

FROM THE PILGRIM'S PROGRESS

Now I saw in my dream, that the highway up which Christian was to go, was fenced on either side with a wall, and that that wall was called Salvation.[1] Up this way, therefore, did burdened Christian run, but not without great difficulty, because of the load on his back.

He ran thus till he came at a place somewhat ascending, and upon that place stood a cross, and a little below, in the bottom, a sepulcher. So I saw in my dream, that just as Christian came up with the cross, his burden loosed from off his shoulders, and fell from off his back, and began to tumble, and so continued to do, till it came to the mouth of the sepulcher, where it fell in, and I saw it no more.

Then was Christian glad and lightsome, and said, with a merry heart, ' He hath given me rest by his sorrow, and life by his death.' Then he stood still awhile to look and wonder; for it was very surprising to him, that the sight of the cross should thus ease him of his burden. He looked, therefore, and looked again, even till the springs that were in his head sent the waters down his cheeks.[2] Now, as he stood looking and weeping, behold three Shining Ones came to him and saluted him with ' Peace be to thee.' So the first said to him, ' Thy sins be forgiven thee!'[3] the second stripped him of his rags, and clothed him ' with change of raiment;'[4] the third also set a mark in his forehead, and gave him a roll with a seal upon it, which he bade him look on as he ran, and that he should give it in at the Celestial Gate.[5] So they went their way. Then Christian gave three leaps for joy, and went on singing —

Thus far I did come laden with my sin;
Nor could aught ease the grief that I was in

[1] Zec. xii. 10.
[2] Zec. xii. 10.
[3] Mar. ii. 5.
[4] Zec. iii. 4.
[5] Ep. i. 13.

Till I came hither: What a place is this!
Must here be the beginning of my bliss?
Must here the burden fall from off my
　　back?
Must here the strings that bound it to me 5
　　crack?
Blest cross! blest sepulcher! blest rather be
The man that there was put to shame for
　　me!

I saw then in my dream, that he went
on thus, even until he came at a bottom,
where he saw, a little out of the way,
three men fast asleep, with fetters upon
their heels. The name of the one was 15
Simple, another Sloth, and the third Presumption.

Christian then seeing them lie in this
case, went to them, if peradventure he
might awake them, and cried, You are 20
like them that sleep on the top of a mast,
for the Dead Sea is under you — a gulf
that hath no bottom.[1] Awake, therefore,
and come away; be willing also, and I
will help you off with your irons. He 25
also told them, If he that 'goeth about
like a roaring lion' comes by, you will
certainly become a prey to his teeth.[2]
With that they looked upon him, and
began to reply in this sort: Simple 30
said, 'I see no danger;' Sloth said,
'Yet a little more sleep;' and Presumption said, 'Every fat must stand upon its
own bottom.' And so they lay down to
sleep again, and Christian went on his 35
way.

Yet was he troubled to think that
men in that danger should so little
esteem the kindness of him that so freely
offered to help them, both by awakening 40
of them, counseling of them, and proffer-
ing to help them off with their irons.
And as he was troubled thereabout he
espied two men come tumbling over the
wall, on the left hand of the narrow way; 45
and they made up apace to him. The
name of the one was Formalist, and the
name of the other Hypocrisy. So, as I
said, they drew up unto him, who thus
entered with them into discourse.   50

CHR. Gentlemen, whence came you,
and whither go you?

FORM. and HYP. We were born in the
land of Vain-glory, and are going for
praise to Mount Zion.   55

CHR. Why came you not in at the gate,
which standeth at the beginning of the
way? Know you not that it is written,
that he that cometh not in by the door,
'but climbeth up some other way, the
same is a thief and a robber?'[3]

FORM. and HYP. They said, That to go
to the gate for entrance was, by all their
countrymen, counted too far about; and
that, therefore, their usual way was to
make a short cut of it, and to climb over
the wall, as they had done.

CHR. But will it not be counted a trespass against the Lord of the city whither
we are bound, thus to violate his revealed will?

FORM. and HYP. They told him, that,
as for that, he needed not to trouble his
head thereabout; for what they did, they
had custom for; and could produce, if
need were, testimony that would witness
it for more than a thousand years.

CHR. But, said Christian, will your
practice stand a trial at law?

FORM. and HYP. They told him, That
custom, it being of so long a standing
as above a thousand years, would doubtless, now be admitted as a thing legal by
any impartial judge; and besides, said
they, if we get into the way, what's
matter which way we get in? if we are
in, we are in; thou art but in the way,
who, as we perceived, came in at the
gate; and we are also in the way, that
came tumbling over the wall; wherein,
now, is thy condition better than ours?

CHR. I walk by the rule of my Master;
you walk by the rude working of your
fancies. You are counted thieves already, by the Lord of the way; therefore,
I doubt you will not be found true men at
the end of the way. You come in by
yourselves, without his direction; and
shall go out by yourselves, without his
mercy.

To this they made him but little answer; only they bid him look to himself.
Then I saw that they went on every man
in his way, without much conference one
with another; save that these two men
told Christian, that as to laws and
ordinances, they doubted not but they
should as conscientiously do them as he;
therefore, said they, we see not wherein
thou differest from us, but by the coat
that is on thy back, which was, as we

---

[1] Pr. xxiii. 34.
[2] Pe. v. 5.

[3] Jn. x. 1.

trow, given thee by some of thy neighbors, to hide the shame of thy nakedness.

CHR. By laws and ordinances you will not be saved, since you came not in by the door.[1] And as for this coat that is on my back, it was given me by the Lord of the place whither I go; and that, as you say, to cover my nakedness with. And I take it as a token of his kindness to me; for I had nothing but rags before. And, besides, thus I comfort myself as I go: Surely, think I, when I come to the gate of the city, the Lord thereof will know me for good, since I have his coat on my back — a coat that he gave me freely in the day that he stripped me of my rags. I have, moreover, a mark in my forehead, of which, perhaps, you have taken no notice, which one of my Lord's most intimate associates fixed there in the day that my burden fell off my shoulders. I will tell you, moreover, that I had then given me a roll, sealed, to comfort me by reading, as I go on the way; I was also bid to give it in at the Celestial Gate, in token of my certain going in after it; all which things, I doubt, you want, and want them because you came not in at the gate.

To these things they gave him no answer; only they looked upon each other, and laughed. Then I saw that they went on all, save that Christian kept before, who had no more talk but with himself, and that sometimes sighingly and sometimes comfortably; also he would be often reading in the roll that one of the Shining Ones gave him, by which he was refreshed.

I beheld, then, that they all went on till they came to the foot of the Hill Difficulty; at the bottom of which was a spring. There were also in the same place two other ways besides that which came straight from the gate; one turned to the left hand, and the other to the right, at the bottom of the hill; but the narrow way lay right up the hill, and the name of the going up the side of the hill is called Difficulty. Christian now went to the spring, and drank thereof, to refresh himself,[2] and then began to go up the hill, saying —

The hill, though high, I covet to ascend,
The difficulty will not me offend;
For I perceive the way to life lies here.
Come, pluck up heart, let's neither faint
 nor fear;
Better, though difficult, the right way to go,
Than wrong, though easy, where the end
 is woe.

The other two also came to the foot of the hill; but when they saw that the hill was steep and high, and that there were two other ways to go; and supposing also that these two ways might meet again, with that up which Christian went, on the other side of the hill; therefore they were resolved to go in those ways. Now the name of one of those ways was Danger, and the name of the other Destruction. So the one took the way which is called Danger, which led him into a great wood, and the other took directly up the way to Destruction, which led him into a wide field, full of dark mountains, where he stumbled and fell, and rose no more.

I looked, then, after Christian, to see him go up the hill, where I perceived he fell from running to going, and from going to clambering upon his hands and his knees, because of the steepness of the place. Now, about the midway to the top of the hill was a pleasant arbor, made by the Lord of the hill for the refreshing of weary travelers; thither, therefore, Christian got, where also he sat down to rest him. Then he pulled his roll out of his bosom, and read therein to his comfort; he also now began afresh to take a review of the coat or garment that was given him as he stood by the cross. Thus pleasing himself awhile, he at last fell into a slumber, and thence into a fast sleep, which detained him in that place until it was almost night; and in his sleep his roll fell out of his hand. Now, as he was sleeping, there came one to him, and awaked him, saying, 'Go to the ant, thou sluggard; consider her ways, and be wise.'[3] And with that Christian suddenly started up, and sped him on his way, and went apace, till he came to the top of the hill.

Now, when he was got up to the top

[1] Ga. ii. 16.
[2] Is. xlix. 10.

[3] Pr. vi. 6.

of the hill, there came two men running
to meet him amain; the name of the one
was Timorous, and of the other Mistrust;
to whom Christian said, Sirs, what's the
matter? You run the wrong way. Timorous answered, that they were going
to the City of Zion, and had got up that
difficult place; but, said he, the further
we go, the more danger we meet with;
wherefore we turned, and are going back
again.

Yes, said Mistrust, for just before us
lie a couple of lions in the way, whether
sleeping or waking we know not, and we
could not think, if we came within reach,
but they would presently pull us in pieces.

Chr. Then said Christian, You make
me afraid, but whither shall I fly to be
safe? If I go back to mine own country,
that is prepared for fire and brimstone,
and I shall certainly perish there. If I
can get to the Celestial City, I am sure
to be in safety there. I must venture.
To go back is nothing but death; to go
forward is fear of death, and life everlasting beyond it. I will yet go forward.
So Mistrust and Timorous ran down the
hill, and Christian went on his way.
But, thinking again of what he heard
from the men, he felt in his bosom for
his roll, that he might read therein, and
be comforted; but he felt, and found it
not. Then was Christian in great distress, and knew not what to do; for he
wanted that which used to relieve him,
and that which should have been his
pass into the Celestial City. Here therefore, he began to be much perplexed, and
knew not what to do. At last, he bethought himself, that he had slept in the
arbor that is on the side of the hill; and,
falling down upon his knees, he asked
God forgiveness for that his foolish fact,
and then went back to look for his roll.
But all the way he went back, who can
sufficiently set forth the sorrow of
Christian's heart! Sometimes he sighed,
sometimes he wept, and oftentimes he
chid himself for being so foolish to fall
asleep in that place, which was erected
only for a little refreshment for his
weariness. Thus, therefore, he went
back, carefully looking on this side, and
on that, all the way as he went, if happily
he might find his roll, that had been his
comfort so many times in his journey.
He went thus, till he came again within
sight of the arbor where he sat and

slept; but that sight renewed his sorrow
the more, by bringing again, even afresh,
his evil of sleeping into his mind.[1]
Thus, therefore, he now went on bewailing his sinful sleep, saying, 'O wretched
man that I am!' that I should sleep in
the day-time! that I should sleep in the
midst of difficulty! that I should so indulge the flesh, as to use that rest for
ease to my flesh, which the Lord of the
hill hath erected only for the relief of
the spirits of pilgrims!

How many steps have I took in vain!
Thus it happened to Israel, for their sin;
they were sent back again by the way of
the Red Sea; and I am made to tread
those steps with sorrow, which I might
have trod with delight, had it not been
for this sinful sleep. How far might I
have been on my way by this time! I
am made to tread those steps thrice over,
which I needed not to have trod but
once; yea, now also I am like to be benighted, for the day is almost spent. O
that I had not slept!

Now by this time he was come to the
arbor again, where for a while he sat
down and wept; but at last, as Christian
would have it, looking sorrowfully down
under the settle, there he espied his roll;
the which he, with trembling and haste,
catched up, and put it into his bosom.
But who can tell how joyful this man
was when he had gotten his roll again!
for this roll was the assurance of his
life and acceptance at the desired haven.
Therefore he laid it up in his bosom, gave
thanks to God for directing his eye to
the place where it lay, and with joy
and tears betook himself again to his
journey. But oh, how nimbly now did
he go up the rest of the hill! Yet, before he got up, the sun went down upon
Christian; and this made him again recall the vanity of his sleeping to his
remembrance; and thus he again began
to condole with himself. O thou sinful
sleep! how, for thy sake am I like to be
benighted in my journey! I must walk
without the sun; darkness must cover the
path of my feet; and I must hear the
noise of the doleful creatures, because
of my sinful sleep.[2] Now also he remembered the story that Mistrust and
Timorous told him of, how they were

[1] Re. ii. 5.   1 Th. v. 7, 8.
[2] 1 Th. v. 6.

frighted with the sight of the lions. Then said Christian to himself again, These beasts range in the night for their prey; and if they should meet with me in the dark, how should I shift them? How should I escape being by them torn in pieces? Thus he went on his way. But while he was thus bewailing his unhappy miscarriage, he lift up his eyes, and behold there was a very stately palace before him, the name of which was Beautiful; and it stood just by the highway side.

So I saw in my dream, that he made haste and went forward, that if possible he might get lodging there. Now before he had gone far, he entered into a very narrow passage, which was about a furlong off of the porter's lodge; and looking very narrowly before him as he went, he espied two lions in the way. Now, thought he, I see the dangers that Mistrust and Timorous were driven back by. (The lions were chained, but he saw not the chains.) Then he was afraid, and thought also himself to go back after them, for he thought nothing but death was before him. But the porter at the lodge, whose name is Watchful, perceiving that Christian made a halt as if he would go back, cried unto him, saying, Is thy strength so small?[1] Fear not the lions, for they are chained, and are placed there for trial of faith where it is, and for discovery of those that have none. Keep in the midst of the path, and no hurt shall come unto thee.

Then I saw that he went on, trembling for fear of the lions, but taking good heed to the directions of the porter; he heard them roar, but they did him no harm. Then he clapped his hands, and went on till he came and stood before the gate, where the porter was. Then said Christian to the porter, Sir, what house is this? and may I lodge here to-night? The porter answered, This house was built by the Lord of the hill, and he built it for the relief and security of pilgrims. The porter also asked whence he was, and whither he was going.

CHR. I am come from the City of Destruction, and am going to Mount Zion; but because the sun is now set, I desire, if I may, to lodge here to-night.

POR. What is your name?

CHR. My name is now Christian, but my name at the first was Graceless; I came of the race of Japheth, whom God will persuade to dwell in the tents of Shem.[2]

POR. But how doth it happen that you come so late? The sun is set.

CHR. I had been here sooner, but that, 'wretched man that I am!' I slept in the arbor that stands on the hill-side; nay, I had, notwithstanding that, been here much sooner, but that, in my sleep, I lost my evidence, and came without it to the brow of the hill; and then feeling for it, and finding it not, I was forced, with sorrow of heart, to go back to the place where I slept my sleep, where I found it, and now I am come.

POR. Well, I will call out one of the virgins of this place, who will, if she likes your talk, bring you in to the rest of the family, according to the rules of the house. So Watchful, the porter, rang a bell, at the sound of which came out at the door of the house, a grave and beautiful damsel, named Discretion, and asked why she was called.

The porter answered, This man is in a journey from the City of Destruction to Mount Zion, but being weary and benighted, he asked me if he might lodge here to-night; so I told him I would call for thee, who, after discourse had with him, mayest do as seemeth thee good, even according to the law of the house.

Then she asked him whence he was, and whither he was going; and he told her. She asked him also how he got into the way; and he told her. Then she asked him what he had seen and met with in the way; and he told her. And last she asked him his name; so he said, It is Christian, and I have so much the more a desire to lodge here to-night, because, by what I perceive, this place was built by the Lord of the hill, for the relief and security of pilgrims. So she smiled, but the water stood in her eyes; and after a little pause, she said, I will call forth two or three more of the family. So she ran to the door, and call out Prudence, Piety, and Charity, who, after a little more discourse with him, had him in to the family; and many of them meeting him at the threshold

---

[1] Mar. xiii. 34–37.

[2] Ge. ix. 23.

of the house, said, 'Come in, thou blessed of the Lord;' this house was built by the Lord of the hill, on purpose to entertain such pilgrims in. Then he bowed his head, and followed them into the house. So when he was come in and sat down, they gave him something to drink, and consented together, that until supper was ready, some of them should have some particular discourse with Christian, for the best improvement of time; and they appointed Piety, and Prudence, and Charity to discourse with him; and thus they began:

PIETY. Come, good Christian, since we have been so loving to you, to receive you into our house this night, let us, if perhaps we may better ourselves thereby, talk with you of all things that have •happened to you in your pilgrimage.

CHR. With a very good will, and I am glad that you are so well disposed.

PIETY. What moved you at first to betake yourself to a pilgrim's life?

CHR. I was driven out of my native country, by a dreadful sound that was in mine ears; to wit, that unavoidable destruction did attend me, if I abode in that place where I was.

PIETY. But how did it happen that you came out of your country this way?

CHR. It was as God would have it; for when I was under the fears of destruction, I did not know whither to go; but by chance there came a man, even to me, as I was trembling and weeping, whose name is Evangelist, and he directed me to the wicket-gate, which else I should never have found, and so set me into the way that hath led me directly to this house.

PIETY. But did you not come by the house of the Interpreter?

CHR. Yes, and did see such things there, the remembrance of which will stick by me as long as I live; especially three things, to wit, how Christ, in despite of Satan, maintains his work of grace in the heart; how the man had sinned himself quite out of hopes of God's mercy; and also the dream of him that thought in his sleep the day of judgment was come.

PIETY. Why, did you hear him tell his dream?

CHR. Yes, and a dreadful one it was. I thought it made my heart ache as he was telling of it; but yet I am glad I heard it.

PIETY. Was that all that you saw at the house of the Interpreter?

CHR. No; he took me and had me where he showed me a stately palace, and how the people were clad in gold that were in it; and how there came a venturous man and cut his way through the armed men that stood in the door to keep him out; and how he was bid to come in, and win eternal glory. Methought those things did ravish my heart! I would have staid at that good man's house a twelvemonth, but that I knew I had further to go.

PIETY. And what saw you else in the way?

CHR. Saw! why, I went but a little further, and I saw one, as I thought in my mind, hang bleeding upon the tree; and the very sight of him made my burden fall off my back (for I groaned under a very heavy burden), but then it fell down from off me. It was a strange thing to me, for I never saw such a thing before; yea, and while I stood looking up, for then I could not forbear looking, three Shining Ones came to me. One of them testified that my sins were forgiven me; another stripped me of my rags, and gave me this broidered coat which you see; and the third set the mark which you see in my forehead, and gave me this sealed roll. (And with that he plucked it out of his bosom.)

PIETY. But you saw more than this, did you not?

CHR. The things that I have told you were the best, yet some other matters I saw, as, namely, I saw three men, Simple, Sloth, and Presumption, lie asleep a little out of the way, as I came, with irons upon their heels; but do you think I could awake them? I also saw Formality and Hypocrisy come tumbling over the wall, to go, as they pretended, to Zion, but they were quickly lost, even as I myself did tell them; but they would not believe. But above all, I found it hard work to get up this hill, and as hard to come by the lions' mouths; and truly if it had not been for the good man, the porter that stands at the gate, I do not know but that after all I might have gone back again; but now, I thank God I am here, and I thank you for receiving of me.

Then Prudence thought good to ask him a few questions, and desired his answer to them.

PRUD. Do you not think sometimes of the country from whence you came?

CHR. Yes, but with much shame and detestation: 'truly if I had been mindful of that country from whence I came out, I might have had opportunity to have returned; but now I desire a better country, that is, an heavenly.'[1]

PRUD. Do you not yet bear away with you some of the things that then you were conversant withal?

CHR. Yes, but greatly against my will; especially my inward and carnal cogitations, with which all my countrymen, as well as myself, were delighted; but now all those things are my grief; and might I but choose mine own things, I would choose never to think of those things more; but when I would be doing of that which is best, that which is worst is with me.[2]

PRUD. Do you not find sometimes, as if those things were vanquished, which at other times are your perplexity?

CHR. Yes, but that is but seldom; but they are to me golden hours, in which such things happen to me.

PRUD. Can you remember by what means you find your annoyances at times, as if they were vanquished?

CHR. Yes; when I think what I saw at the cross, that will do it; and when I look upon my broidered coat, that will do it; also when I look into the roll that I carry in my bosom, that will do it; and when my thoughts wax warm about whither I am going, that will do it.

PRUD. And what is it that makes you so desirous to go to Mount Zion?

CHR. Why, there I hope to see him alive that did hang dead on the cross; and there I hope to be rid of all those things that to this day are in me an annoyance to me; there, they say, there is no death; and there I shall dwell with such company as I like best.[3] For, to tell you truth, I love him, because I was by him eased of my burden; and I am weary of my inward sickness. I would fain be where I shall die no more, and with the company that shall continually cry, 'Holy, holy, holy.'

Then said Charity to Christian, Have you a family? Are you a married man?

CHR. I have a wife and four small children.

CHAR. And why did you not bring them along with you?

CHR. Then Christian wept, and said, Oh how willingly would I have done it! but they were all of them utterly averse to my going on pilgrimage.

CHAR. But you should have talked to them, and have endeavored to have shown them the danger of being behind.

CHR. So I did; and told them also what God had shown to me of the destruction of our city; 'but I seemed to them as one that mocked,' and they believed me not.[4]

CHAR. And did you pray to God that he would bless your counsel to them?

CHR. Yes, and that with much affection; for you must think that my wife and poor children were very dear unto me.

CHAR. But did you tell them of your own sorrow, and fear of destruction? for I suppose that destruction was visible enough to you.

CHR. Yes, over, and over, and over. They might also see my fears in my countenance, in my tears, and also in my trembling under the apprehension of the judgment that did hang over our heads; but all was not sufficient to prevail with them to come with me.

CHAR. But what could they say for themselves, why they came not?

CHR. Why, my wife was afraid of losing this world, and my children were given to the foolish delights of youth; so what by one thing, and what by another, they left me to wander in this manner alone.

CHAR. But did you not, with your vain life, damp all that you by words used by way of persuasion to bring them away with you?

CHR. Indeed, I cannot commend my life; for I am conscious to myself of many failings therein; I know also, that a man by his conversation may soon overthrow, what by argument or persuasion he doth labor to fasten upon others for their good. Yet this I can say, I was very wary of giving them occasion, by any unseemly action, to make them

[1] He. xi. 15, 16.
[2] Ro. vii.
[3] Is. xxv. 8. Re. xxi. 4.

[4] Ge. xix. 14.

averse to going on pilgrimage. Yea, for this very thing, they would tell me I was too precise, and that I denied myself of things, for their sakes, in which they saw no evil. Nay, I think I may say, that if what they saw in me did hinder them, it was my great tenderness in sinning against God, or of doing any wrong to my neighbor.

CHAR. Indeed Cain hated his brother, 'because his own works were evil, and his brother's righteous;'[1] and if thy wife and children have been offended with thee for this, they thereby show themselves to be implacable to good, and 'thou hast delivered thy soul from their blood.'[2]

Now I saw in my dream, that thus they sat talking together until supper was ready. So when they had made ready, they sat down to meat. Now the table was furnished 'with fat things, and with wine that was well refined:' and all their talk at the table was about the Lord of the hill; as, namely, about what he had done, and wherefore he did what he did, and why he had builded that house. And by what they said, I perceived that he had been a great warrior, and had fought with and slain 'him that had the power of death,' but not without great danger to himself, which made me love him the more.[3]

For, as they said, and as I believe (said Christian), he did it with the loss of much blood; but that which put glory of grace into all he did, was, that he did it out of pure love to his country. And besides, there were some of them of the household that said they had seen and spoke with him since he did die on the cross; and they have attested that they had it from his own lips, that he is such a lover of poor pilgrims, that the like is not to be found from the east to the west.

They, moreover, gave an instance of what they affirmed, and that was, he had stripped himself of his glory, that he might do this for the poor; and that they heard him say and affirm, 'that he would not dwell in the mountain of Zion alone.' They said, moreover, that he had made many pilgrims princes, though by nature they were beggars born, and their original had been the dunghill.[4]

Thus they discoursed together till late at night; and after they had committed themselves to their Lord for protection, they betook themselves to rest: the Pilgrim they laid in a large upper chamber, whose window opened toward the sunrising; the name of the chamber was Peace; where he slept till break of day, and then he awoke and sang —

Where am I now? Is this the love and care
Of Jesus for the men that pilgrims are?
Thus to provide! that I should be forgiven!
And dwell already the next door to heaven!

So, in the morning, they all got up; and after some more discourse, they told him that he should not depart till they had shown him the rarities of that place. And first, they had him into the study, where they showed him records of the greatest antiquity; in which, as I remember my dream, they showed him first the pedigree of the Lord of the hill, that he was the son of the Ancient of Days, and came by that eternal generation. Here also was more fully recorded the acts that he had done, and the names of many hundreds that he had taken into his service; and how he had placed them in such habitations, that could neither by length of days, nor decays of nature, be dissolved.

Then they read to him some of the worthy acts that some of his servants had done: as, how they had 'subdued kingdoms, wrought righteousness, obtained promises, stopped the mouths of lions, quenched the violence of fire, escaped the edge of the sword, out of weakness were made strong, waxed valiant in fight, and turned to flight the armies of the aliens.'[5]

They then read again in another part of the records of the house, where it was showed how willing their Lord was to receive into his favor any, even any, though they in time past had offered great affronts to his person and proceedings. Here also were several other histories of many other famous things, of all which Christian had a view; as of things both ancient and modern; to

---

[1] 1 Jn. iii. 12.
[2] Eze. iii. 19.
[3] He. ii. 14, 15.
[4] 1 Sa. ii. 8. Ps. cxiii. 7.
[5] He. xi. 33. 34.

gether with prophecies and predictions of things that have their certain accomplishment, both to the dread and amazement of enemies, and the comfort and solace of pilgrims.

The next day they took him and had him into the armory, where they showed him all manner of furniture, which their Lord had provided for pilgrims, as sword, shield, helmet, breastplate, all-prayer, and shoes that would not wear out. And there was here enough of this to harness out as many men, for the service of their Lord, as there be stars in the heaven for multitude.

They also showed him some of the engines with which some of his servants had done wonderful things. They showed him Moses' rod; the hammer and nail with which Jael slew Sisera; the pitchers, trumpets, and lamps, too, with which Gideon put to flight the armies of Midian. Then they showed him the ox's goad wherewith Shamgar slew six hundred men. They showed him, also, the jaw-bone with which Samson did such mighty feats. They showed him, moreover, the sling and stone with which David slew Goliath of Gath; and the sword, also, with which their Lord will kill the Man of Sin, in the day that he shall rise up to the prey. They showed him, besides, many excellent things, with which Christian was much delighted. This done, they went to their rest again.

Then I saw in my dream, that, on the morrow, he got up to go forward; but they desired him to stay till the next day also; and then, said they, we will, if the day be clear, show you the Delectable Mountains, which, they said, would yet further add to his comfort, because they were nearer the desired haven than the place where at present he was; so he consented and stayed. When the morning was up, they had him to the top of the house, and bid him look south; so he did; and, behold, at a great distance, he saw a most pleasant mountainous country, beautified with woods, vineyards, fruits of all sorts, flowers also, with springs and fountains, very delectable to behold.[1] Then he asked the name of the country.

[1] Is. xxxiii. 16, 17.

They said it was Immanuel's Land; and it is as common, said they, as this hill is, to and for all the pilgrims. And when thou comest there, from thence, said they, thou mayest see to the gate of the Celestial City, as the shepherds that live there will make appear.

Now, he bethought himself of setting forward, and they were willing he should. But first, said they, let us go again into the armory. So they did; and when he came there, they harnessed him from head to foot with what was of proof, lest, perhaps, he should meet with assaults in the way. He being, therefore, thus accoutred, walketh out with his friends to the gate, and there he asked the porter if he saw any pilgrims pass by. Then the porter answered, Yes.

CHR. Pray, did you know him? said he.

POR. I asked his name, and he told me it was Faithful.

CHR. Oh, said Christian, I know him; he is my townsman, my near neighbor; he comes from the place where I was born. How far do you think he may be before?

POR. He is got by this time below the hill.

CHR. Well, said Christian, good Porter, the Lord be with thee, and add to all thy blessings much increase, for the kindness that thou hast showed to me.

Then he began to go forward; but Discretion, Piety, Charity and Prudence, would accompany him down to the foot of the hill. So they went on together, reiterating their former discourses, till they came to go down the hill. Then, said Christian, as it was difficult coming up, so, so far as I can see, it is dangerous going down. Yes, said Prudence, so it is, for it is a hard matter for a man to go down into the Valley of Humiliation, as thou art now, and to catch no slip by the way; therefore, said they, are we come out to accompany thee down the hill. So he began to go down, but very warily; yet he caught a slip or two.

Then I saw in my dream that these good companions, when Christian was gone to the bottom of the hill, gave him a loaf of bread, a bottle of wine, and a cluster of raisins; and then he went on his way.

But now, in this Valley of Humiliation, poor Christian was hard put to it; for he had gone but a little way, before he espied a foul fiend coming over the field to meet him; his name is Apollyon. Then did Christian begin to be afraid, and to cast in his mind whether to go back or to stand his ground. But he considered again that he had no armor for his back; and, therefore, thought that to turn the back to him might give him the greater advantage, with ease to pierce him with his darts. Therefore he resolved to venture and stand his ground; for, thought he, had I no more in mine eye than the saving of my life, it would be the best way to stand.

So he went on, and Apollyon met him. Now the monster was hideous to behold; he was clothed with scales, like a fish (and they are his pride), he had wings like a dragon, feet like a bear, and out of his belly came fire and smoke, and his mouth was as the mouth of a lion. When he was come up to Christian, he beheld him with a disdainful countenance, and thus began to question with him.

APOL. Whence come you? and whither are you bound?

CHR. I am come from the City of Destruction, which is the place of all evil, and am going to the City of Zion.

APOL. By this I perceive thou art one of my subjects, for all that country is mine, and I am the prince and god of it. How is it, then, that thou hast run away from thy king? Were it not that I hope thou mayest do me more service, I would strike thee now, at one blow, to the ground.

CHR. I was born, indeed, in your dominions, but your service was hard, and your wages such as a man could not live on, 'for the wages of sin is death;'[1] therefore, when I was come to years, I did as other considerate persons do, look out, if, perhaps, I might mend myself.

APOL. There is no prince that will thus lightly lose his subjects, neither will I as yet lose thee; but since thou complainest of thy service and wages, be content to go back; what our country

will afford, I do here promise to give thee.

CHR. But I have let myself to another, even to the King of princes; and how can I, with fairness, go back with thee?

APOL. Thou hast done in this according to the proverb, 'Changed a bad for a worse;' but it is ordinary for those that have professed themselves his servants, after a while to give him the slip, and return again to me. Do thou so too, and all shall be well.

CHR. I have given him my faith, and sworn my allegiance to him; how, then, can I go back from this, and not be hanged as a traitor?

APOL. Thou didst the same to me, and yet I am willing to pass by all, if now thou wilt yet turn again and go back.

CHR. What I promised thee was in my nonage; and, besides, I count the Prince under whose banner now I stand is able to absolve me; yea, and to pardon also what I did as to my compliance with thee; and besides, O thou destroying Apollyon! to speak truth, I like his service, his wages, his servants, his government, his company, and country, better than thine; and, therefore, leave off to persuade me further; I am his servant, and I will follow him.

APOL. Consider again, when thou art in cool blood, what thou art like to meet with in the way that thou goest. Thou knowest that, for the most part, his servants come to an ill end, because they are transgressors against me and my ways. How many of them have been put to shameful deaths! and, besides, thou countest his service better than mine, whereas he never came yet from the place where he is to deliver any that served him out of their hands; but as for me, how many times, as all the world very well knows, have I delivered, either by power or fraud, those that have faithfully served me, from him and his, though taken by them; and so I will deliver thee.

CHR. His forbearing at present to deliver them is on purpose to try their love, whether they will cleave to him to the end; and as for the ill end thou sayest they come to, that is most glorious in their account; for, for present deliverance, they do not much expect it,

[1] Ro. vi. 23.

for they stay for their glory, and then they shall have it, when their Prince comes in his and the glory of the angels.

APOL. Thou hast already been unfaithful in thy service to him; and how dost thou think to receive wages of him?

CHR. Wherein, O Apollyon! have I been unfaithful to him?

APOL. Thou didst faint at first setting out, when thou wast almost choked in the Gulf of Despond; thou didst attempt wrong ways to be rid of thy burden, whereas thou shouldst have stayed till thy Prince had taken it off; thou didst sinfully sleep, and lose thy choice thing; thou wast, also, almost persuaded to go back, at the sight of the lions; and when thou talkest of thy journey, and of what thou hast heard and seen, thou art inwardly desirous of vainglory in all that thou sayest or doest.

CHR. All this is true, and much more which thou hast left out; but the Prince, whom I serve and honor, is merciful, and ready to forgive; but, besides, these infirmities possessed me in thy country, for there I sucked them in; and I have groaned under them, been sorry for them, and have obtained pardon of my Prince.

APOL. Then Apollyon broke out into a grievous rage, saying, I am an enemy to this Prince; I hate his person, his laws, and people; I am come out on purpose to withstand thee.

CHR. Apollyon, beware what you do; for I am in the king's highway, the way of holiness; therefore take heed to yourself.

APOL. Then Apollyon straddled quite over the whole breadth of the way, and said, I am void of fear in this matter: prepare thyself to die; for I swear by my infernal den, that thou shalt go no further; here will I spill thy soul.

And with that he threw a flaming dart at his breast; but Christian had a shield in his hand, with which he caught it, and so prevented the danger of that.

Then did Christian draw; for he saw it was time to bestir him: and Apollyon as fast made at him, throwing darts as thick as hail; by the which, notwithstanding all that Christian could do to avoid it, Apollyon wounded him in his head, his hand, and foot. This made Christian give a little back; Apollyon,

therefore, followed his work amain, and Christian again took courage and resisted as manfully as he could. This sore combat lasted for above half a day, even till Christian was almost quite spent; for you must know, that Christian, by reason of his wounds, must needs grow weaker and weaker.

Then Apollyon, espying his opportunity, began to gather up close to Christian, and wrestling with him, gave him a dreadful fall; and with that, Christian's sword flew out of his hand. Then said Apollyon, I am sure of thee now. And with that he had almost pressed him to death; so that Christian began to despair of life: but as God would have it, while Apollyon was fetching of his last blow, thereby to make a full end of this good man, Christian nimbly reached out his hand for his sword, and caught it, saying, 'Rejoice not against me, O mine enemy: when I fall, I shall arise;'[1] and with that gave him a deadly thrust, which made him give back, as one that had received his mortal wound. Christian perceiving that, made at him again, saying, 'Nay, in all these things we are more than conquerors, through him that loved us.'[2] And with that Apollyon spread forth his dragon's wings, and sped him away, that Christian for a season saw him no more.[3]

In this combat no man can imagine, unless he had seen and heard as I did, what yelling and hideous roaring Apollyon made all the time of the fight — he spake like a dragon; and, on the other side, what sighs and groans burst from Christian's heart. I never saw him all the while give so much as one pleasant look, till he perceived he had wounded Apollyon with his two-edged sword; then, indeed, he did smile and look upward; but it was the dreadfulest sight that ever I saw.

So when the battle was over, Christian said, 'I will here give thanks to him that delivered me out of the mouth of the lion, to him that did help me against Apollyon.' And so he did.

* * *

1 Mi. vii. 8.
2 Ro. viii. 37.
3 Ja. iv. 7.

JOHN MILTON (1608–1674)

Milton belonged to a London Puritan family, and when he went up to Cambridge at the end of James I's reign, it was with the intention of becoming a clergyman of the Church of England, in which the Puritans were then a party, hoping to substitute in it government by presbyters, elected by church councils, for government by bishops, appointed by the king. Changes in the administration of the national church under Charles I as well as the development of Milton's own opinions led him to abandon this purpose, towards which all his early training was directed. He has described his serious and studious boyhood in lines 201–7 of *Paradise Regained*, Book I. He was deeply versed not only in Greek and Latin, but also in Hebrew, and in French and Italian, but his early poems show no sign of the mingling of Christianity and paganism which is characteristic of Renaissance thought. On the other hand, he did not share the later Puritan intolerance of innocent amusements. Two of his earlier poems, *Arcades* (c. 1630–3) and *Comus* (1634) and one of his latest, *Samson Agonistes* (pub. 1671), were in dramatic form; in 1630 he wrote a poem in praise of Shakspere for the folio edition of the plays (see below), and in *L'Allegro* he speaks appreciatively of both Shakspere's and Jonson's comedies (see p. 238). After seven years at Christ's College, where on account of his almost girlish beauty he was known as 'our fair lady of Christ's,' he retired for further study to Horton in Buckinghamshire, where his principal early poems were written (1632–7). He then traveled on the Continent to complete his education (1638–9), and was recalled by the political crisis preceding the outbreak of the Civil War. 'I thought it base,' he wrote later, 'to be traveling for amusement abroad while my fellow citizens were fighting for liberty at home.' Milton fought, not with the sword, but with the pen. He perceived that 'there were three species of liberty which are essential to the happiness of social life — religious, domestic and civil.' In 1641–2 he took an active part in the controversy that was raging as to the government of the Church by bishops, which appeared to him contrary to religious liberty. His marriage in 1643 to Mary Powell, daughter of a Cavalier and half his own age, turned out unhappily; she found life with the poet and pamphleteer 'very solitary' and too 'philosophical,' and after a month's experience of it returned to her father's house. This led Milton to publish a series of pamphlets in favor of divorce, and he was said to be contemplating a marriage with Miss Davis, the 'virtuous young lady' of Sonnet IX (see p. 242) but, when this came to his wife's ears, she sought and obtained a reconciliation. In 1644 he wrote two important tracts — one on education, and another on the freedom of the press (*Areopagitica*). In 1649 he took up the defence of the Commonwealth for the execution of Charles I, and as Latin Secretary to the Council of State continued his task with a devotion which involved the sacrifice of his eye-sight (see Sonnets, pp. 243–4). His pen was still active on behalf of religious toleration and republican government when the Restoration drove him into hiding; he was arrested, but suffered no harm beyond a short imprisonment and the burning of his books by the hangman. He lost, of course, his Latin secretaryship, and the destruction of some of his property by the fire of London brought him into straitened circumstances; but his tastes were simple, and bating 'not a jot of heart or hope' he returned to his studies. He wrote a history, a logic, a Latin grammar, a compendium of theology; but the great works of his later years were *Paradise Lost* (published 1667), and *Paradise Regained* and *Samson Agonistes* (1671). He chose the subject of *Paradise Lost* out of some hundred which he jotted down about 1640, and wrote a small part of it, but the great design was interrupted by the Civil War, resumed in 1658, and completed in 1663 or 1665.

ON SHAKSPERE

What needs my Shakspere for his honored bones
The labor of an age in pilèd stones?
Or that his hallowed relics should be hid
Under a star-ypointing pyramid?
Dear son of memory, great heir of fame, 5
What need'st thou such weak witness of thy name?
Thou in our wonder and astonishment
Hast built thyself a livelong monument.
For whilst, to the shame of slow-endeavoring art,
Thy easy numbers flow, and that each heart
Hath from the leaves of thy unvalued book

Those Delphic lines with deep impression
   took,   12
Then thou, our fancy of itself bereaving,
Dost make us marble with too much conceiv-
   ing,
And so sepúlchered in such pomp dost lie 15
That kings for such a tomb would wish to
   die.

L'ALLEGRO

Hence, loathèd Melancholy,
Of Cerberus and blackest midnight born
In Stygian cave forlorn,
'Mongst horrid shapes, and shrieks, and
   sights unholy!
Find out some uncouth cell   5
Where brooding Darkness spreads his
   jealous wings
And the night raven sings;
There, under ebon shades and low-browed
   rocks
As ragged as thy locks,
In dark Cimmerian desert ever dwell.   10
  But come, thou goddess fair and free,
In heaven yclept Euphrosyne,
And by men heart-easing Mirth,
Whom lovely Venus, at a birth
With two sister Graces more,   15
To ivy-crowned Bacchus bore:
Or whether (as some sager sing)
The frolic wind that breathes the spring,
Zephyr with Aurora playing
As he met her once a-Maying,   20
There, on beds of violets blue
And fresh-blown roses washed in dew,
Filled her with thee, a daughter fair,
So buxom, blithe, and debonair.
  Haste thee, nymph, and bring with thee
Jest, and youthful jollity,   26
Quips, and cranks, and wanton wiles,
Nods, and becks, and wreathèd smiles,
Such as hang on Hebe's cheek
And love to live in dimple sleek;   30
Sport that wrinkled Care derides,
And Laughter holding both his sides.
Come, and trip it, as you go
On the light fantastic toe;
And in thy right hand lead with thee   35
The mountain nymph, sweet Liberty;
And, if I give thee honor due,
Mirth, admit me of thy crew,
To live with her, and live with thee,
In unreprovèd pleasures free: —   40
  To hear the lark begin his flight,
And, singing, startle the dull night,
From his watch-tower in the skies,
Till the dappled dawn doth rise;

Then to come, in spite of sorrow,   45
And at my window bid good-morrow,
Through the sweet-briar, or the vine,
Or the twisted eglantine;
While the cock, with lively din,
Scatters the rear of darkness thin,   50
And to the stack, or the barn-door,
Stoutly struts his dames before;
Oft listening how the hounds and horn
Cheerly rouse the slumbering morn,
From the side of some hoar hill,   55
Through the high wood echoing shrill;
Some time walking, not unseen,
By hedgerow elms, on hillocks green,
Right against the eastern gate
Where the great sun begins his state   60
Robed in flames and amber light,
The clouds in thousand liveries dight;
While the ploughman, near at hand,
Whistles o'er the furrowed land,
And the milkmaid singeth blithe,   65
And the mower whets his scythe,
And every shepherd tells his tale
Under the hawthorn in the dale.
  Straight mine eye hath caught new
   pleasures,
Whilst the landscape round it measures: 70
Russet lawns, and fallows gray,
Where the nibbling flocks do stray;
Mountains on whose barren breast
The laboring clouds do often rest;
Meadows trim, with daisies pied,   75
Shallow brooks, and rivers wide;
Towers and battlements it sees
Bosomed high in tufted trees,
Where, perhaps, some beauty lies,
The cynosure of neighboring eyes.   80
  Hard by, a cottage chimney smokes
From betwixt two agèd oaks,
Where Corydon and Thyrsis met,
Are at their savory dinner set
Of herbs, and other country messes,   85
Which the neat-handed Phyllis dresses;
And then in haste her bower she leaves,
With Thestylis to bind the sheaves,
Or, if the earlier season lead,
To the tanned haycock in the mead.   90
  Sometimes, with secure delight,
The upland hamlets will invite,
When the merry bells ring round,
And the jocund rebecks sound
To many a youth and many a maid   95
Dancing in the checkered shade,
And young and old come forth to play
On a sunshine holyday,
Till the livelong daylight fail;
Then to the spicy nut-brown ale,   100
With stories told of many a feat;

How fairy Mab the junkets eat;
She was pinched, and pulled she said;
And he, by friar's lantern led,
Tells how the drudging goblin sweat   105
To earn his cream-bowl duly set,
When, in one night, ere glimpse of morn,
His shadowy flail hath threshed the corn
That ten day-laborers could not end;
Then lies him down the lubber fiend,   110
And, stretched out all the chimney's length,
Basks at the fire his hairy strength,
And, crop-full, out of doors he flings,
Ere the first cock his matin rings.
Thus done the tales, to bed they creep,   115
By whispering winds soon lulled asleep.
    Towered cities please us then,
And the busy hum of men,
Where throngs of knights and barons bold,
In weeds of peace high triumphs hold,   120
With store of ladies, whose bright eyes
Rain influence, and judge the prize
Of wit or arms, while both contend
To win her grace whom all commend.
There let Hymen oft appear   125
In saffron robe, with taper clear,
And pomp, and feast, and revelry,
With mask and antique pageantry;
Such sights as youthful poets dream
On summer eves by haunted stream.   130
Then to the well-trod stage anon,
If Jonson's learnèd sock be on,
Or sweetest Shakspere, Fancy's child,
Warble his native wood-notes wild.
    And ever, against eating cares,   135
Lap me in soft Lydian airs
Married to immortal verse,
Such as the meeting soul may pierce
In notes with many a winding bout
Of linkèd sweetness long drawn out,   140
With wanton heed and giddy cunning,
The melting voice through mazes running,
Untwisting all the chains that tie
The hidden soul of harmony;
That Orpheus' self may heave his head,   145
From golden slumber on a bed
.Of heaped elysian flowers, and hear
Such strains as would have won the ear
Of Pluto to have quite set free
His half-regained Eurydice.   150
These delights if thou canst give,
Mirth, with thee I mean to live.

IL PENSEROSO

    Hence, vain deluding joys,
The brood of Folly, without father bred!
How little you bested,
Or fill the fixed mind with all your toys!

Dwell in some idle brain,   5
And fancies fond with gaudy shapes pos-
    sess
As thick and numberless
As the gay motes that people the sun
    beams,
Or likest hovering dreams,
The fickle pensioners of Morpheus' train.   10
But, hail! thou goddess sage and holy,
Hail, divinest Melancholy,
Whose saintly visage is too bright
To hit the sense of human sight,
And, therefore, to our weaker view,   15
O'erlaid with black, staid Wisdom's hue;
Black, but such as in esteem
Prince Memnon's sister might beseem,
Or that starred Ethiop queen that strove
To set her beauty's praise above   20
The sea-nymphs, and their powers offended.
Yet thou art higher far descended;
Thee bright-haired Vesta, long of yore,
To solitary Saturn bore;
His daughter she; in Saturn's reign   24
Such mixture was not held a stain.
Oft in glimmering bowers and glades
He met her, and in secret shades
Of woody Ida's inmost grove,
Whilst yet there was no fear of Jove.   30
    Come, pensive nun, devout and pure,
Sober, steadfast, and demure,
All in a robe of darkest grain
Flowing with majestic train,
And sable stole of cypress lawn   35
Over thy decent shoulders drawn.
Come, but keep thy wonted state,
With even step, and musing gait,
And looks commèrcing with the skies,
Thy rapt soul sitting in thine eyes: 40
There, held in holy passion still,
Forget thyself to marble, till,
With a sad leaden downward cast,
Thou fix them on the earth as fast.
And join with thee calm Peace and Quiet,
Spare Fast, that oft with gods doth diet,   46
And hears the Muses, in a ring,
Aye round about Jove's altar sing.
And add to these retirèd Leisure,
That in trim gardens takes his pleasure.   50
But first, and chiefest, with thee bring,
Him that yon soars on golden wing,
Guiding the fiery-wheelèd throne,
The cherub Contemplation;
And the mute silence hist along,   55
'Less Philomel will deign a song,
In her sweetest saddest plight,
Smoothing the rugged brow of Night,
While Cynthia checks her dragon yoke
Gently o'er the accustomed oak.   60

Sweet bird, that shunn'st the noise of folly,
Most musical, most melancholy!
Thee, chantress, oft, the woods among,
I woo, to hear thy even-song;
And, missing thee, I walk unseen   65
On the dry smooth-shaven green,
To behold the wandering moon
Riding near her highest noon,
Like one that had been led astray
Through the heaven's wide pathless way, 70
And oft, as if her head she bowed,
Stooping through a fleecy cloud.
  Oft, on a plat of rising ground,
I hear the far-off curfew sound
Over some wide watered shore,   75
Swinging slow with sullen roar;
Or, if the air will not permit,
Some still, removèd place will fit,
Where glowing embers through the room
Teach light to counterfeit a gloom;   80
Far from all resort of mirth,
Save the cricket on the hearth,
Or the bellman's drowsy charm
To bless the doors from nightly harm.
  Or let my lamp, at midnight hour,   85
Be seen in some high lonely tower
Where I may oft outwatch the Bear
With thrice great Hermes, or unsphere
The spirit of Plato, to unfold
What worlds or what vast regions hold   90
The immortal mind that hath forsook
Her mansion in this fleshly nook,
And of those demons that are found
In fire, air, flood, or underground,
Whose power hath a true consent,   95
With planet or with element.
Sometime let gorgeous Tragedy,
In sceptered pall, come sweeping by,
Presenting Thebes, or Pelops' line,
Or the tale of Troy divine,   100
Or what (though rare) of later age
Ennobled hath the buskined stage.
  But, O, sad virgin! that thy power
Might raise Musæus from his bower;
Or bid the soul of Orpheus sing   105
Such notes as, warbled to the string,
Drew iron tears down Pluto's cheek,
And made hell grant what love did seek;
Or call up him that left half told
The story of Cambuscan bold,   110
Of Camball, and of Algarsife,
And who had Canacé to wife
That owned the virtuous ring and glass,
And of the wondrous horse of brass,
On which the Tartar king did ride;   115
And if aught else great bards beside
In sage and solemn tunes have sung,
Of tourneys, and of trophies hung,

Of forests, and enchantments drear,
Where more is meant than meets the ear.
  Thus, Night, oft see me in thy pale career,
Till civil-suited Morn appear,
Not tricked and frounced as she was wont
With the Attic boy to hunt,
But kerchieft in a comely cloud,   125
While rocking winds are piping loud;
Or ushered with a shower still,
When the gust hath blown his fill,
Ending on the rustling leaves,
With minute drops from off the eaves.   130
And, when the sun begins to fling
His flaring beams, me, goddess, bring
To archèd walks of twilight groves,
And shadows brown, that Sylvan loves,
Of pine, or monumental oak,   135
Where the rude axe with heavèd stroke
Was never heard the nymphs to daunt
Or fright them from their hallowed haunt.
There in close covert by some brook,
Where no profaner eye may look,   140
Hide me from day's garish eye,
While the bee, with honied thigh,
That at her flowery work doth sing,
And the waters murmuring,
With such concert as they keep,   145
Entice the dewy-feathered sleep;
And let some strange mysterious dream
Wave at his wings, in airy stream
Of lively portraiture displayed,
Softly on my eyelids laid.   150
And, as I wake, sweet music breathe
Above, about, or underneath,
Sent by some spirit to mortals good,
Or the unseen genius of the wood.
  But let my due feet never fail   155
To walk the studious cloister's pale,
And love the high embowèd roof,
With antique pillars massy proof,
And storied windows richly dight,
Casting a dim religious light: 160
There let the pealing organ blow
To the full-voiced choir below
In service high and anthems clear
As may with sweetness, through mine ear,
Dissolve me into ecstasies,   165
And bring all heaven before mine eyes.
  And may at last my weary age
Find out the peaceful hermitage,
The hairy gown and mossy cell,
Where I may sit and rightly spell   170
Of every star that heaven doth shew,
And every herb that sips the dew,
Till old experience do attain
To something like prophetic strain.
   These pleasures, Melancholy, give,   175
And I with thee will choose to live.

LYCIDAS

Yet once more, O ye laurels, and once
　　more,
Ye myrtles brown, with ivy never sere,
I come, to pluck your berries harsh and
　　crude,
And with forced fingers rude
Shatter your leaves before the mellowing
　　year.　　　　　　　　　　　　　　5
Bitter constraint and sad occasion dear
Compels me to disturb your season due;
For Lycidas is dead, dead ere his prime,
Young Lycidas, and hath not left his peer;
Who would not sing for Lycidas? He
　　knew　　　　　　　　　　　　　　10
Himself to sing, and build the lofty rime.
He must not float upon his watery bier
Unwept, and welter to the parching wind
Without the meed of some melodious tear.
　Begin, then, sisters of the sacred well　15
That from beneath the seat of Jove doth
　　spring:
Begin, and somewhat loudly sweep the
　　string;
Hence with denial vain, and coy excuse:
So may some gentle muse
With lucky words favor my destined urn.
And as he passes, turn,　　　　　　　21
And bid fair peace be to my sable shroud!
　For we were nursed upon the self-same
　　hill,
Fed the same flock, by fountain, shade,
　　and rill.
Together both, ere the high lawns appeared
Under the opening eyelids of the morn, 26
We drove a-field, and both together heard
What time the gray-fly winds her sultry
　　horn,
Battening our flocks with the fresh dews
　　of night,
Oft till the star that rose at evening bright
Toward heaven's descent had sloped his
　　westering wheel.　　　　　　　　31
Meanwhile the rural ditties were not mute;
Tempered to the oaten flute
Rough satyrs danced, and fauns with cloven
　　heel
From the glad sound would not be absent
　　long:　　　　　　　　　　　　　35
And old Damœtas loved to hear our song.
　But, oh! the heavy change, now thou art
　　gone,
Now thou art gone and never must return!
Thee, shepherd, thee the woods, and desert
　　caves,
With wild thyme and the gadding vine o'er-
　　grown,　　　　　　　　　　　　40

And all their echoes, mourn:
The willows, and the hazel copses green,
Shall now no more be seen
Fanning their joyous leaves to thy soft
　　lays
As killing as the canker to the rose,　45
Or taint-worm to the weanling herds that
　　graze,
Or frost to flowers that their gay ward-
　　robe wear,
When first the white-thorn blows;
Such, Lycidas, thy loss to shepherd's ear.
　Where were ye, Nymphs, when the re-
　　morseless deep　　　　　　　　　50
Closed o'er the head of your loved Lycidas?
For neither were ye playing on the steep
Where your old bards, the famous Druids
　　lie,
Nor on the shaggy top of Mona high,
Nor yet where Deva spreads her wizard
　　stream:　　　　　　　　　　　55
Ah me! I fondly dream,
'Had ye been there': . . . for what
　　could that have done?
What could the Muse herself that Orpheus
　　bore,
The Muse herself, for her enchanting son
Whom universal nature did lament,　60
When by the rout that made the hideous
　　roar
His gory visage down the stream was
　　sent,
Down the swift Hebrus to the Lesbian
　　shore?
　Alas! what boots it with incessant care
To tend the homely, slighted, shepherd's
　　trade,　　　　　　　　　　　　65
And strictly meditate the thankless Muse?
Were it not better done, as others use,
To sport with Amaryllis in the shade,
Or with the tangles of Neæra's hair?
Fame is the spur that the clear spirit doth
　　raise　　　　　　　　　　　　70
(That last infirmity of noble mind)
To scorn delights and live laborious days:
But the fair guerdon when we hope to find,
And think to burst out into sudden blaze,
Comes the blind Fury with the abhorrèd
　　shears　　　　　　　　　　　75
And slits the thin-spun life. 'But not the
　　praise,'
Phœbus replied, and touched my trembling
　　ears:
'Fame is no plant that grows on mortal
　　soil,
Nor in the glistering foil
Set off to the world, nor in broad rumor
　　lies,

But lives and spreads aloft by those pure
    eyes
And perfect witness of all-judging Jove:
As he pronounces lastly on each deed,
Of so much fame in heaven expect thy
    meed.'
    O fountain Arethuse, and thou honored
    flood,   85
Smooth-sliding Mincius, crowned with vocal
    reeds,
That strain I heard was of a higher mood.
But now my oat proceeds,
And listens to the herald of the sea
That came in Neptune's plea;   90
He asked the waves, and asked the felon
    winds,
What hard mishap hath doomed this gentle
    swain?
And questioned every gust, of rugged wings,
That blows from off each beakèd promon-
    tory:
They know not of his story: 95
And sage Hippotades their answer brings,
That not a blast was from his dungeon
    strayed,
The air was calm, and on the level brine
Sleek Panopé with all her sisters played.
It was that fatal and perfidious bark,   100
Built in the eclipse, and rigged with curses
    dark,
That sunk so low that sacred head of thine.
    Next, Camus, reverend sire, went footing
    slow,
His mantle hairy, and his bonnet sedge
Inwrought with figures dim and on the
    edge   105
Like to that sanguine flower inscribed with
    woe.
'Ah! who hath reft,' quoth he, 'my dearest
    pledge?'
Last came, and last did go,
The pilot of the Galilean lake.
Two massy keys he bore, of metals twain,
The golden opes, the iron shuts amain.   111
He shook his mitered locks, and stern be-
    spake:
'How well could I have spared for thee,
    young swain,
Enow of such as, for their bellies' sake
Creep, and intrude, and climb into the
    fold!
Of other care they little reckoning make   116
Than how to scramble at the shearers' feast
And shove away the worthy bidden guest;
Blind mouths! that scarce themselves know
    how to hold
A sheep-hook, or have learned ought else
    the least   120

That to the faithful herdsman's art be-
    longs!
What recks it them? What need they?
    They are sped,
And, when they list, their lean and flashy
    songs
Grate on their scrannel pipes of wretched
    straw;
The hungry sheep look up, and are not
    fed,   125
But, swoln with wind and the rank mist
    they draw,
Rot inwardly, and foul contagion spread;
Besides what the grim wolf, with privy
    paw,
Daily devours apace, and nothing said.
But that two-handed engine at the door
Stands ready to smite once, and smite no
    more.'   131
    Return, Alphëus, the dread voice is past,
That shrunk thy streams; return, Sicilian
    Muse,
And call the vales, and bid them hither
    cast
Their bells and flowerets of a thousand
    hues.   135
Ye valleys low, where the mild whispers
    use
Of shades and wanton winds, and gushing
    brooks,
On whose fresh lap the swart star sparely
    looks,
Throw hither all your quaint enameled
    eyes
That on the green turf suck the honeyed
    showers,   140
And purple all the ground with vernal flow-
    ers.
Bring the rathe primrose that forsaken dies,
The tufted crow-toe, and pale jessamine,
The white pink, and the pansy freaked with
    jet,
The glowing violet,   145
The musk-rose, and the well-attired wood-
    bine,
With cowslips wan that hang the pensive
    head,
And every flower that sad embroidery
    wears;
Bid amaranthus all his beauty shed,
And daffodillies fill their cups with tears,
To strew the laureate hearse where Lycid
    lies.   151
For so, to interpose a little ease,
Let our frail thoughts dally with false sur-
    mise:
Ah me! whilst thee the shores and sound-
    ing seas

Wash far away, where 'er thy bones are
   hurled;   155
Whether beyond the stormy Hebrides,
Where thou, perhaps under the whelming
   tide,
Visit'st the bottom of the monstrous world;
Or whether thou, to our moist vows de-
   nied,
Sleep'st by the fable of Bellerus old,   160
Where the great vision of the guarded
   mount
Looks toward Namancos and Bayona's
   hold:
Look homeward, angel, now, and melt with
   ruth;
And, O ye dolphins, waft the hapless youth.
   Weep no more, woeful shepherds, weep
   no more,   165
For Lycidas, your sorrow, is not dead,
Sunk though he be beneath the watery
   floor.
So sinks the day-star in the ocean-bed,
And yet anon repairs his drooping head,
And tricks his beams, and, with new span-
   gled ore,   .   170
Flames in the forehead of the morning sky:
So Lycidas sunk low, but mounted high,
Through the dear might of Him that
   walked the waves,
Where, other groves and other streams
   along,
With nectar pure his oozy locks he laves,
And hears the unexpressive nuptial song 176
In the blest kingdoms meek of joy and
   love.
There entertain him all the saints above,
In solemn troops and sweet societies
That sing, and, singing, in their glory
   move,   .   180
And wipe the tears for ever from his eyes.
Now, Lycidas, the shepherds weep no more;
Henceforth thou art the genius of the shore
In thy large recompense, and shalt be good
To all that wander in that perilous flood.

   Thus sang the uncouth swain to the oaks
   and rills,   186
While the still morn went out with sandals
   gray;
He touched the tender stops of various
   quills,
With eager thought warbling his Doric lay;
And now the sun had stretched out all the
   hills.   190
And now was dropt into the western bay;
At last he rose, and twitched his mantle
   blue;
To-morrow to fresh woods and pastures new.

SONNETS

WHEN THE ASSAULT WAS INTENDED TO THE CITY

Captain or colonel, or knight in arms,
Whose chance on these defenseless doors
   may seize,
If deed of honor did thee ever please,
Guard them, and him within protect from
   harms.
He can requite thee; for he knows the
   charms   5
That call fame on such gentle acts as these,
And he can spread thy name o'er lands and
   seas,
Whatever clime the sun's bright circle
   warms.
Lift not thy spear against the Muses'
   bower:
The great Emathian conqueror bid spare   10
The house of Pindarus, when temple and
   tower
Went to the ground; and the repeated air
Of sad Electra's poet had the power
To save the Athenian walls from ruin bare.

[TO A VIRTUOUS YOUNG LADY]

Lady, that in the prime of earliest youth
Wisely hast shunned the broad way and the
   green,
And with those few art eminently seen
That labor up the hill of heavenly truth,   4
The better part with Mary and with Ruth
Chosen thou hast; and they that overween,
And at thy growing virtues fret their spleen,
No anger find in thee, but pity and ruth.
Thy care is fixed, and zealously attends
To fill thy odorous lamp with deeds of
   light,   10
And hope that reaps not shame. Therefore
   be sure
Thou, when the Bridegroom with his feast-
   ful friends
Passes to bliss at the mid-hour of night,
Hast gained thy entrance, virgin wise and
   pure.

ON THE DETRACTION WHICH FOLLOWED UPON MY WRITING CERTAIN TREATISES

A book was writ of late called *Tetrachordon,*
And woven close, both matter, form, and
   style;
The subject new: it walked the town a
   while,
Numbering good intellects; now seldom
   pored on.

Cries the stall-reader, 'Bless us! what a
    word on 5
A title page is this!' and some in file
Stand spelling false, while one might walk
    to Mile-
End Green. Why, is it harder, sirs, than
    Gordon,
Colkitto, or *Macdonnel,* or *Galasp?*
Those rugged names to our like mouths
    grow sleek 10
That would have made Quintilian stare and
    gasp.
Thy age, like ours, O soul of Sir John
    Cheke,
Hated not learning worse than toad or asp,
When thou taught'st Cambridge and King
    Edward Greek.

ON THE SAME

I did but prompt the age to quit their clogs
By the known rules of ancient liberty,
When straight a barbarous noise environs
    me
Of owls and cuckoos, asses, apes, and dogs;
As when those hinds that were transformed
    to frogs 5
Railed at Latona's twin-born progeny,
Which after held the sun and moon in fee.
But this is got by casting pearl to hogs,
That bawl for freedom in their senseless
    mood,
And still revolt when truth would set them
    free. 10
License they mean when they cry Liberty;
For who loves that must first be wise and
    good:
But from 'that mark how far they rove we
    see,
For all this waste of wealth and loss of
    blood.

TO THE LORD GENERAL CROMWELL MAY 1652

ON THE PROPOSALS OF CERTAIN MINISTERS AT
THE COMMITTEE FOR PROPAGATION OF THE
GOSPEL

Cromwell, our chief of men, who through
    a cloud
Not of war only, but detractions rude,
Guided by faith and matchless fortitude,
To peace and truth thy glorious way hast
    ploughed,
And on the neck of crownèd Fortune proud
Hast reared God's trophies, and his work
    pursued, 6
While Darwen stream, with blood of Scots
    imbrued,

And Dunbar field, resounds thy praises
    loud,
And Worcester's laureate wreath: yet much
    remains
To conquer still; Peace hath her victories 10
No less renowned than War: new foes
    arise,
Threatening to bind our souls with secular
    chains.
Help us to save free conscience from the
    paw
Of hireling wolves, whose Gospel is their
    maw.

ON THE LATE MASSACRE IN PIEDMONT

Avenge, O Lord, thy slaughtered saints,
    whose bones
Lie scattered on the Alpine mountains cold;
Even them who kept thy truth so pure of
    old,
When all our fathers worshipped stocks
    and stones,
Forget not: in thy book record their groans
Who were thy sheep, and in their ancient
    fold 6
Slain by the bloody Piedmontese, that rolled
Mother with infant down the rocks. Their
    moans
The vales redoubled to the hills, and they
To heaven. Their martyred blood and ashes
    sow 10
O'er all the Italian fields, where still doth
    sway
The triple Tyrant that from these may grow
A hundredfold, who, having learnt thy way,
Early may fly the Babylonian woe.

[ON HIS BLINDNESS]

When I consider how my light is spent
Ere half my days in this dark world and
    wide,
And that one talent which is death to hide
Lodged with me useless, though my soul
    more bent
To serve therewith my Maker, and present
My true account, lest he returning chide, 6
'Doth God exact day-labor, light denied?'
I fondly ask. But Patience, to prevent
That murmur, soon replies, 'God doth not
    need
Either man's work or his own gifts. Who
    best 10
Bear his mild yoke, they serve him best.
    His state
Is kingly: thousands at his bidding speed,
And post o'er land and ocean without rest;
They also serve who only stand and wait.'

[TO CYRIACK SKINNER]

Cyriack, this three years' day these eyes, though clear,
To outward view, of blemish or of spot,
Bereft of light, their seeing have forgot;
Nor to their idle orbs doth sight appear
Of sun, or moon, or star, throughout the year,   5
Or man, or woman. Yet I argue not
Against Heaven's hand or will, nor bate a jot
Of heart or hope, but still bear up and steer
Right onward. What supports me, dost thou ask?
The conscience, friend, to have lost them overplied   10
In liberty's defense, my noble task,
Of which all Europe rings from side to side.
This thought might lead me through the world's vain mask
Content though blind, had I no better guide.

[ON HIS DECEASED WIFE]

Methought I saw my late espousèd saint
Brought to me like Alcestis from the grave,
Whom Jove's great son to her glad husband gave,
Rescued from Death by force, though pale and faint.
Mine, as whom washed from spot of child-bed taint   5
Purification in the old law did save,
And such as yet once more I trust to have
Full sight of her in heaven without restraint,
Came vested all in white, pure as her mind.
Her face was veiled; yet to my fancied sight   10
Love, sweetness, goodness, in her person shined
So clear as in no face with more delight.
But, oh! as to embrace me she inclined,
I waked, she fled, and day brought back my night.

PARADISE LOST

BOOK I

THE ARGUMENT

This First Book proposes, first in brief, the whole subject,— Man's disobedience, and the loss thereupon of Paradise, wherein he was placed: then touches the prime cause of his fall,— the serpent, or rather Satan in the serpent; who,

revolting from God, and drawing to his side many legions of angels, was, by the command of God, driven out of heaven, with all his crew, into the great deep. Which action passed over, the poem hastens into the midst of things, presenting Satan, with his angels, now fallen into hell, described here, not in the center (for heaven and earth may be supposed as yet not made, certainly not yet accursed), but in a place of utter darkness, fitliest called Chaos: here Satan with his angels, lying on the burning lake, thunderstruck and astonished, after a certain space recovers, as from confusion, calls up him who next in order and dignity lay by him. They confer of their miserable fall; Satan awakens all his legions, who lay till then in the same manner confounded. They rise; their numbers; array of battle; their chief leaders named, according to the idols known afterwards in Canaan and the countries adjoining. To these Satan directs his speech, comforts them with hope yet of regaining heaven, but tells them lastly of a new world and new kind of creature to be created, according to an ancient prophecy, or report, in heaven — for, that the angels were long before this visible creation, was the opinion of many ancient fathers. To find out the truth of this prophecy, and what to determine thereon, he refers to a full council. What his associates thence attempt. Pandemonium, the palace of Satan, rises, suddenly built out of the deep: the infernal peers there sit in council.

Of Man's first disobedience, and the fruit
Of that forbidden tree, whose mortal taste
Brought death into the world, and all our woe,
With loss of Eden, till one greater Man
Restore us, and regain the blissful seat,   5
Sing, heavenly Muse, that on the secret top
Of Oreb, or of Sinai, did'st inspire
That shepherd, who first taught the chosen seed,
In the beginning how the heavens and earth
Rose out of chaos: or, if Sion hill   10
Delight thee more, and Siloa's brook that flowed
Fast by the oracle of God, I thence
Invoke thy aid to my adventurous song,
That with no middle flight intends to soar
Above the Aonian mount, while it pursues
Things unattempted yet in prose or rime.
And chiefly thou, O Spirit, that dost prefer
Before all temples the upright heart and pure,
Instruct me, for thou know'st; thou from the first
Wast present, and, with mighty wings outspread,   20
Dove-like, sat'st brooding on the vast abyss
And mad'st it pregnant: what in me is dark,
Illumine; what is low, raise and support;
That to the height of this great argument
I may assert eternal Providence.   25

And justify the ways of God to men.
  Say first — for heaven hides nothing from
    thy view,
Nor the deep tract of hell — say first, what
    cause
Moved our grand Parents, in that happy
    state,
Favored of Heaven so highly, to fall off 30
From their Creator, and transgress his will
For one restraint, lords of the world
    besides.
Who first seduced them to that foul revolt?
  The infernal Serpent; he it was, whose
    guile,
Stirred up with envy and revenge, deceived
The mother of mankind; what time his
    pride   36
Had cast him out from heaven, with all his
    host
Of rebel angels; by whose aid, aspiring
To set himself in glory above his peers,
He trusted to have equaled the Most
    High,
If he opposed; and, with ambitious aim 41
Against the throne and monarchy of God,
Raised impious war in heaven, and battle
    proud,
With vain attempt. Him the Almighty
    Power
Hurled headlong flaming from the ethereal
    sky,   45
With hideous ruin and combustion, down
To bottomless perdition; there to dwell
In adamantine chains and penal fire,
Who durst defy the Omnipotent to arms.
  Nine times the space that measures day
    and night   50
To mortal men, he with his horrid crew
Lay vanquished, rolling in the fiery gulf,
Confounded, though immortal. But his
    doom
Reserved him to more wrath; for now the
    thought
Both of lost happiness and lasting pain   55
Torments him; round he throws his baleful
    eyes, *woe*
That witnessed huge affliction and dismay,
Mixed with obdurate pride, and steadfast
    hate. *all*
At once, as far as angels' ken, he views
The dismal situation waste and wild.   60
A dungeon horrible, on all sides round,
As one great furnace, flamed; yet from
    those flames
No light; but rather darkness visible
Served only to discover sights of woe,
Regions of sorrow, doleful shades, where
    peace   65

And rest can never dwell; hope never
    comes
That comes to all; but torture without end
Still urges, and a fiery deluge, fed
With ever-burning sulphur unconsumed.
Such place eternal justice had prepared 70
For those rebellious; here their prison or-
    dained
In utter darkness, and their portion set
As far removed from God and light of
    heaven,
As from the center thrice to the utmost
    pole.
O, how unlike the place from whence they
    fell!   75
There the companions of his fall, o'er-
    whelmed
With floods and whirlwinds of tempestuous
    fire,
He soon discerns; and weltering by his
    side
One next himself in power, and next in
    crime,
Long after known in Palestine, and named
Beëlzebub. To whom the arch-enemy,   81
And thence in heaven called Satan, with
    bold words
Breaking the horrid silence, thus began:—
  'If thou beest he — but O, how fall'n!
    how changed
From him who, in the happy realms of light,
Clothed with transcendent brightness, didst
    outshine   86
Myriads, though bright! If he, whom
    mutual league,
United thoughts and counsels, equal hope
And hazard in the glorious enterprise,
Joined with me once, now misery hath
    joined   90
In equal ruin; into what pit thou seest
From what height fall'n, so much the
    stronger proved
He with his thunder: and till then who
    knew
The force of those dire arms? Yet not for
    those,
Nor what the potent victor in his rage   95
Can else inflict, do I repent or change,
Though changed in outward luster, that
    fixed mind,
And high disdain from sense of injured
    merit,
That with the Mightiest raised me to
    contend,
And to the fierce contention brought along
Innumerable force of spirits armed,   10?
That durst dislike his reign, and, me pre-
    ferring

His utmost power with adverse power op-
posed
In dubious battle on the plains of heaven,
And shook his throne. What though the
field be lost?   105
All is not lost; the unconquerable will,
And study of revenge, immortal hate,
And courage never to submit or yield,
And what is else not to be overcome;
That glory never shall his wrath or might
Extort from me. To bow and sue for
grace   111
With suppliant knee, and deify his power
Who from the terror of this arm so late
Doubted his empire — that were low indeed,
That were an ignominy, and shame beneath
This downfall; since, by fate, the strength
of gods,   116
And this empyreal substance, cannot fail:
Since, through experience of this great
event,
In arms not worse, in foresight much ad-
vanced,
We may with more successful hope resolve
To wage by force or guile eternal war,   121
Irreconcilable to our grand foe,
Who now triumphs, and, in the excess of
joy
Sole reigning, holds the tyranny of heaven.'
So spake the apostate angel, though in
pain,   125
Vaunting aloud, but racked with deep de-
spair
And him thus answered soon his bold com-
peer:—
'O prince, O chief of many-throned
powers,
That led the embattled seraphim to war
Under thy conduct, and in dreadful deeds
Fearless, endangered heaven's perpetual
King,   131
And put to proof his high supremacy,
Whether upheld by strength, or chance, or
fate;
Too well I see, and rue the dire event,
That with sad overthrow, and foul defeat,
Hath lost us heaven, and all this mighty
host   136
In horrible destruction laid thus low,
As far as gods and heavenly essences
Can perish: for the mind and spirit remain
Invincible, and vigor soon returns,   140
Though all our glory extinct, and happy
state
Here swallowed up in endless misery.
But what if he our Conqueror (whom I
now
Of force believe Almighty, since no less

Than such could have o'erpowered such
force as ours)   145
Have left us this our spirit and strength
entire,
Strongly to suffer and support our pains,
That we may so suffice his vengeful ire,
Or do him mightier service as his thralls
By right of war, whate'er his business be,
Here in the heart of hell to work in fire,
Or do his errands in the gloomy deep?
What can it then avail, though yet we feel
Strength undiminished, or eternal being
To undergo eternal punishment?'   155
    Whereto with speedy words the arch-fiend
        replied:—
'Fallen cherub, to be weak is miserable,
Doing or suffering; but of this be sure,
To do aught good never will be our task,
But ever to do ill our sole delight,   160
As being the contrary to his high will
Whom we resist. If then his providence
Out of our evil seek to bring forth good,
Our labor must be to pervert that end, 164
And out of good still to find means of evil,
Which ofttimes may succeed, so as perhaps
Shall grieve him, if I fail not, and disturb
His inmost counsels from their destined
aim.
But see, the angry Victor hath recalled
His ministers of vengeance and pursuit 170
Back to the gates of heaven; the sulphur-
ous hail,
Shot after us in storm, o'erblown, hath laid
The fiery surge, that from the precipice
Of heaven received us falling; and the
thunder,
Winged with red lightning and impetuous
rage,   175
Perhaps hath spent his shafts, and ceases
now
To bellow through the vast and boundless
deep.
Let us not slip the occasion, whether scorn
Or satiate fury yield it from our foe.
Seest thou yon dreary plain, forlorn and
wild,   180
The seat of desolation, void of light,
Save what the glimmering of these livid
flames
Casts pale and dreadful? Thither let us
tend
From off the tossing of these fiery waves;
There rest, if any rest can harbor there; 185
And, re-assembling our afflicted powers,
Consult how we may henceforth most of-
fend
Our enemy; our own loss how repair;
How overcome this dire calamity;

What reinforcement we may gain from
hope;   190
If not, what resolution from despair.'
  Thus Satan, talking to his nearest mate,
With head uplift above the wave, and eyes
That sparkling blazed; his other parts be-
    sides
Prone on the flood, extended long and large,
Lay floating many a rood; in bulk as huge
As whom the fables name of monstrous
    size,   197
Titanian, or Earth-born, that warred on
    Jove;
Briareos or Typhon, whom the den
By ancient Tarsus held; or that sea-beast
Leviathan, which God of all his works   201
Created hugest that swim the ocean stream.
Him, haply, slumbering on the Norway
    foam,
The pilot of some small night-foundered
    skiff,
Deeming some island, oft, as seamen tell,
With fixèd anchor in his scaly rind   206
Moors by his side under the lee, while night
Invests the sea, and wishèd morn delays:
So stretched out huge in length the arch-
    fiend lay
Chained on the burning lake: nor ever
    thence   210
Had risen, or heaved his head; but that the
    will
And high permission of all-ruling Heaven
Left him at large to his own dark designs;
That with reiterated crimes he might
Heap on himself damnation, while he
    sought   215
Evil to others; and, enraged, might see
How all his malice served but to bring forth
Infinite goodness, grace, and mercy, shown
On man by him seduced; but on himself
Treble confusion, wrath, and vengeance
    poured.   220
  Forthwith upright he rears from off the
    pool
His mighty stature; on each hand the
    flames,
Driven backward, slope their pointing spires,
    and rolled
In billows, leave i' the midst a horrid vale.
Then with expanded wings he steers his
    flight   225
Aloft, incumbent on the dusky air,
That felt unusual weight; till on dry land
He lights, if it were land that ever burned
With solid, as the lake with liquid fire;
And such appeared in hue, as when the
    force   230
Of subterranean wind transports a hill

Torn from Pelorus, or the shattered side
Of thundering Etna, whose combustible
And fuelled entrails thence conceiving fire,
Sublimed with mineral fury, aid the winds,
And leave a singèd bottom, all involved 236
With stench and smoke: such resting found
    the sole
Of unblest feet. Him followed his next
    mate:
Both glorying to have 'scaped the stygian
    flood,
As gods, and by their own recovered
    strength,   240
Not by the sufferance of supernal power.
  'Is this the region, this the soil, the
    clime,'
Said then the lost archangel, 'this the seat
That we must change for heaven; this
    mournful gloom
For that celestial light? Be it so, since he,
Who now is Sovereign, can dispose and bid
What shall be right: farthest from him is
    best,   247
Whom reason hath equaled, force hath
    made supreme
Above his equals. Farewell, happy fields,
Where joy for ever dwells! Hail, horrors!
    hail   250
Infernal world! and thou profoundest hell,
Receive thy new possessor — one who brings
A mind not to be changed by place or time:
The mind is its own place, and in itself 254
Can make a heaven of hell, a hell of heaven.
What matter where, if I be still the same,
And what I should be; all but less than he
Whom thunder hath made greater? Here
    at least
We shall be free: the Almighty hath not
    built
Here for his envy, will not drive us hence:
Here we may reign secure, and, in my
    choice,   261
To reign is worth ambition, though in hell;
Better to reign in hell, than serve in heaven.
But wherefore let we then our faithful
    friends,
The associates and co-partners of our
    loss,
Lie thus astonished on the oblivious pool,
And call them not to share with us their
    part   267
In this unhappy mansion; or once more
With rallied arms to try what may be yet
Regained in heaven, or what more lost in
    hell?'   270
  So Satan spake, and him Beëlzebub
Thus answered: 'Leader of those armies
    bright,

Which, but the Omnipotent, none could
   have foiled,
If once they hear that voice, their liveliest
   pledge
Of hope in fears and dangers, heard so oft
In worst extremes, and on the perilous edge
Of battle when it raged, in all assaults 277
Their surest signal, they will soon resume
New courage and revive; though now they
   lie
Groveling and prostrate on yon lake of
   fire,   280
As we erewhile, astounded and amazed;
No wonder, fall'n in such a pernicious height.'
  He scarce had ceased, when the superior
   fiend
Was moving toward the shore: his ponder-
   ous shield
Ethereal temper, massy, large, and round,
Behind him cast; the broad circumference
Hung on his shoulders like the moon, whose
   orb
Through optic glass the Tuscan artist views
At evening, from the top of Fesolé,
Or in Valdarno, to descry new lands, 290
Rivers, or mountains, in her spotty globe.
His spear, to equal which the tallest pine
Hewn on Norwegian hills, to be the mast
Of some great admiral, were but a wand,
He walked with, to support uneasy steps 295
Over the burning marl, not like those steps
On heaven's azure, and the torrid clime
Smote on him sore besides, vaulted with
   fire:
Nathless he so endured, till on the beach
Of that inflamèd sea he stood, and called
His legions, angel forms, who lay entranced,
Thick as autumnal leaves, that strew the
   brooks   302
In Vallombrosa, where the Etrurian shades,
High over-arched, embower; or scattered
   sedge
Afloat, when with fierce winds Orion armed
Hath vexed the Red Sea coast, whose waves
   o'erthrew   306
Busiris and his Memphian chivalry,
While with perfidious hatred they pursued
The sojourners of Goshen, who beheld
From the safe shore their floating carcasses
And broken chariot-wheels; so thick be-
   strewn,   311
Abject and lost lay these, covering the
   flood,
Under amazement of their hideous change.
He called so loud, that all the hollow deep
Of hell resounded. 'Princes, potentates, 315
Warriors, the flower of heaven, once yours,
  now lost,

If such astonishment as this can seize
Eternal spirits; or have ye chosen this
   place
After the toil of battle to repose   319
Your wearied virtue, for the ease you find
To slumber here, as in the vales of heaven?
Or in this abject posture have ye sworn
To adore the Conqueror? who now beholds
Cherub and seraph rolling in the flood
With scattered arms and ensigns, till anon
His swift pursuers from heaven-gates dis-
   cern   326
The advantage, and descending, tread us
   down
Thus drooping, or with linkèd thunderbolts
Transfix us to the bottom of this gulf?
Awake, arise, or be for ever fall'n!' 330
  They heard, and were abashed, and up
   they sprung
Upon the wing; as when men, wont to
   watch
On duty, sleeping found by whom they
   dread,
Rouse and bestir themselves ere well awake.
Nor did they not perceive the evil plight
In which they were, or the fierce pains not
   feel;   335
Yet to their general's voice they soon
   obeyed,
Innumerable. As when the potent rod
Of Amram's son, in Egypt's evil day,
Waved round the coast, up called a pitchy
   cloud   340
Of locusts, warping on the eastern wind,
That o'er the realm of impious Pharaoh
   hung
Like night, and darkened all the land of
   Nile:
So numberless were those bad angels seen
Hovering on wing under the cope of hell,
'Twixt upper, nether, and surrounding
   fires;   346
Till, at a signal given, the uplifted spear
Of their great sultan waving to direct
Their course, in even balance down they
   light   349
On the firm brimstone, and fill all the
   plain:
A multitude like which the populous north
Poured never from her frozen loins, to pass
Rhine or the Danube, when her barbarous
   sons
Came like a deluge on the south and spread
Beneath Gibraltar to the Libyan sands. 355
Forthwith from every squadron and each
   band
The heads and leaders thither haste where
   stood

Their great commander; godlike shapes and forms
Excelling human; princely dignities;
And powers that erst in heaven sat on thrones,   360
Though of their names in heavenly records now
Be no memorial; blotted out and rased
By their rebellion from the books of life.
Nor had they yet among the sons of Eve
Got them new names; till, wandering o'er the earth,   365
Through God's high sufferance, for the trial of man,
By falsities and lies the greater part
Of mankind they corrupted to forsake
God their Creator, and the invisible
Glory of him that made them, to transform
Oft to the image of a brute, adorned   371
With gay religions, full of pomp and gold,
And devils to adore for deities:
Then were they known to men by various names,
And various idols through the heathen world.   375
  Say, Muse, their names then known, who first, who last,
Roused from the slumber on that fiery couch,
At their great emperor's call, as next in worth,
Came singly where he stood on the bare strand,
While the promiscuous crowd stood yet aloof.   380
  The chief were those who from the pit of hell,
Roaming to seek their prey on earth, durst fix
Their seats long after next the seat of God,
Their altars by his altar, gods adored   384
Among the nations round, and durst abide
Jehovah thundering out of Sion, throned
Between the cherubim; yea, often placed
Within his sanctuary itself their shrines,
Abominations; and with cursèd things   389
His holy rites and solemn feasts profaned,
And with their darkness durst affront his light.
  First, Moloch, horrid king, besmeared with blood
Of human sacrifice, and parents' tears;
Though, for the noise of drums and timbrels loud,
Their children's cries unheard, that passed through fire   395
To his grim idol. Him the Ammonite
Worshipped in Rabba and her watery plain,

In Argob and in Basan, to the stream
Of utmost Arnon. Nor content with such
Audacious neighborhood, the wisest heart
Of Solomon he led by fraud to build   401
His temple right against the temple of God,
On that opprobrious hill; and made his grove
The pleasant valley of Hinnom, Tophet thence
And black Gehenna called, the type of hell.
Next, Chemos, the obscene dread of Moab's sons,   406
From Aroer to Nebo, and the wild
Of southmost Abarim; in Hesebon
And Horonáim, Seon's realm, beyond
The flowery dale of Sibma clad with vines,
And Eleäle to the asphaltic pool;   411
Peor his other name, when he enticed
Israel in Sittim, on their march from Nile,
To do him wanton rites, which cost them woe.
Yet thence his lustful orgies he enlarged   415
Even to that hill of scandal, by the grove
Of Moloch homicide: lust hard by hate;
Till good Josiah drove them thence to hell.
With these came they who, from the bordering flood
Of old Euphrates to the brook that parts
Egypt from Syrian ground, had general names   421
Of Baälim and Ashtaroth; those male,
These feminine; for spirits, when they please,
Can either sex assume, or both; so soft
And uncompounded is their essence pure;
Not tied or manacled with joint or limb,   426
Nor founded on the brittle strength of bones,
Like cumbrous flesh; but, in what shape they choose,
Dilated or condensed, bright or obscure,
Can execute their aëry purposes,   430
And works of love or enmity fulfil.
For those the race of Israel oft forsook
Their living Strength, and unfrequented left
His righteous altar, bowing lowly down
To bestial gods; for which their heads as low   435
Bowed down in battle, sunk before the spear
Of despicable foes. With these in troop
Came Astoreth, whom the Phenicians called
Astarté, queen of heaven, with crescent horns;
To whose bright image nightly by the moon
Sidonian virgins paid their vows and songs;
In Sion also not unsung, where stood   442
Her temple on the offensive mountain, built

By that uxorious king, whose heart, though
　　large,
Beguiled by fair idolatresses, fell　　　445
To idols foul.　Thammuz came next behind,
Whose annual wound in Lebanon allured
The Syrian damsels to lament his fate
In amorous ditties all a summer's day;
While smooth Adonis from his native rock
Ran purple to the sea, supposed with blood
Of Thammuz yearly wounded; the love-tale
Infected Sion's daughters with like heat;
Whose wanton passions in the sacred porch
Ezekiel saw, when, by the vision led,　　455
His eye surveyed the dark idolatries
Of alienated Judah.　Next came one
Who mourned in earnest, when the captive
　　ark
Maimed his brute image, head and hands
　　lopped off
In his own temple, on the grunsel edge,　460
Where he fell flat, and shamed his worship-
　　pers;
Dagon his name, sea-monster, upward man
And downward fish; yet had his temple
　　high
Reared in Azotus, dreaded through the
　　coast
Of Palestine, in Gath and Ascalon,　　465
And Accaron and Gazar's frontier bounds.
Him followed Rimmon, whose delightful
　　seat　　　　.
Was fair Damascus, on the fertile banks
Of Abbana and Pharphar, lucid streams.
He also 'gainst the house of God was bold:
A leper once he lost, and gained a king; 471
Ahaz his sottish conqueror, whom he drew
God's altar to disparage and displace
For one of Syrian mode, whereon to burn
His odious offerings, and adore the gods 475
Whom he had vanquished.　After these ap-
　　peared
A crew who, under names of old renown,
Osiris, Isis, Orus, and their train,
With monstrous shapes and sorceries abused
Fanatic Egypt and her priests, to seek　480
Their wandering gods disguised in brutish
　　forms
Rather than human.　Nor did Israel 'scape
The infection, when their borrowed gold
　　composed
The calf in Oreb; and the rebel king
Doubled that sin in Bethel and in Dan,　485
Likening his Maker to the grazèd ox —
Jehovah, who in one night, when he passed
From Egypt marching, equaled with one
　　stroke
Both her first-born and all her bleating
　　gods.

Belial came last, than whom a spirit more
　　lewd　　　　　　　　　　　　　490
Fell not from heaven, or more gross to love
Vice for itself; to him no temple stood,
Or altar smoked; yet who more oft than he
In temples and at altars, when the priest
Turns atheist, as did Eli's sons, who filled
With lust and violence the house of God?
In courts and palaces he also reigns,　　497
And in luxurious cities, where the noise
Of riot ascends above their loftiest towers,
And injury and outrage: and when night
Darkens the streets, then wander forth the
　　sons　　　　　　　　　　　　501
Of Belial, flown with insolence and wine.
Witness the streets of Sodom, and that
　　night
In Gibeah, when the hospitable door
Exposed a matron, to avoid worse rape. 505
　These were the prime in order and in
　　might:
The rest were long to tell, though far re-
　　nowned,
The Ionian gods — of Javan's issue held
Gods, yet confessed later than heaven and
　　earth,
Their boasted parents: Titan, heaven's first-
　　born　　　　　　　　　　　　510
With his enormous brood, and birthright
　　seized
By younger Saturn; he from mightier Jove,
His own and Rhea's son, like measure
　　found;
So Jove usurping reigned: these first in
　　Crete　　　　　　　　　　　514
And Ida known, thence on the snowy top
Of cold Olympus ruled the middle air,
Their highest heaven; or on the Delphian
　　cliff,
Or in Dodona, and through all the bounds
Of Doric land: or who with Saturn old
Fled over Adria to the Hesperian fields, 520
And o'er the Celtic roamed the utmost isles.
　All these and more came flocking, but
　　with looks
Downcast and damp; yet such wherein ap-
　　peared
Obscure some glimpse of joy, to have found
　　their chief
Not in despair, to have found themselves
　　not lost　　　　　　　　　　525
In loss itself; which on his countenance
　　cast
Like doubtful hue; but he, his wonted pride
Soon recollecting, with high words, that
　　bore
Semblance of worth, not substance, gently
　　raised

Their fainting courage, and dispelled their
    fears.   530
Then straight commands that at the war-
    like sound
Of trumpets loud and clarions be upreared
His mighty standard; that proud honor
    claimed
Azazel as his right, a cherub tall;
Who forthwith from the glittering staff un-
    furled   535
The imperial ensign; which, full high ad-
    vanced,
Shone like a meteor, streaming to the wind,
With gems and golden luster rich emblazed,
Seraphic arms and trophies, all the while
Sonorous metal blowing martial sounds:
At which the universal host up-sent   541
A shout, that tore hell's concave, and be-
    yond
Frighted the reign of Chaos and old Night.
All in a moment through the gloom were
    seen
Ten thousand banners rise into the air. 545
With orient colors waving; with them rose
A forest huge of spears; and thronging
    helms
Appeared, and serried shields in thick array
Of depth immeasurable; anon they move
In perfect phalanx to the Dorian mood 550
Of flutes and soft recorders; such as raised
To height of noblest temper heroes old
Arming to battle, and instead of rage,
Deliberate valor breathed, firm and un-
    moved   554
With dread of death to flight or foul re-
    treat;
Nor wanting power to mitigate and 'suage
With solemn touches troubled thoughts, and
    chase
Anguish, and doubt, and fear, and sorrow,
    and pain
From mortal or immortal minds. Thus
    they,   559
Breathing united force, with fixèd thought,
Moved on in silence, to soft pipes, that
    charmed
Their painful steps o'er the burnt soil: and
    now
Advanced in view they stand; a horrid
    front
Of dreadful length and dazzling arms, in
    guise
Of warriors old with ordered spear and
    shield,   565
Awaiting what command their mighty chief
Had to impose: he through the armèd files
Darts his experienced eye, and soon traverse
The whole battalion views, their order due,

Their visages and stature as of gods; 570
Their number last he sums. And now his
    heart
Distends with pride, and hardening in his
    strength
Glories: for never since created man
Met such embodied force as, named with
    these,
Could merit more than that small infantry
Warred on by cranes: though all the giant
    brood   576
Of Phlegra with the heroic race were joined
That fought at Thebes and Ilium, on each
    side
Mixed with auxiliar gods; and what re-
    sounds
In fable or romance of Uther's son   580
Begirt with British and Armoric knights;
And all who since, baptized or infidel,
Jousted in Aspramont, or Montalban,
Damascus, or Morocco, or Trebizond,
Or whom Biserta sent from Afric shore,
When Charlemagne with all his peerage
    fell   586
By Fontarabbia. Thus far these beyond
Compare of mortal prowess, yet observed
Their dread commander; he, above the rest
In shape and gesture proudly eminent, 590
Stood like a tower; his form had yet not
    lost
All its original brightness; nor appeared
Less than archangel ruined, and the excess
Of glory obscured: as when the sun, new
    risen,
Looks through the horizontal misty air 595
Shorn of his beams, or from behind the
    moon,
In dim eclipse, disastrous twilight sheds
On half the nations, and with fear of change
Perplexes monarchs. Darkened so, yet
    shone
Above them all the archangel; but his
    face   600
Deep scars of thunder had entrenched; and
    care
Sat on his faded cheek; but under brows
Of dauntless courage, and considerate pride
Waiting revenge; cruel his eye, but cast
Signs of remorse and passion, to behold 605
The fellows of his crime, the followers
    rather
(Far other once beheld in bliss), condemnèd
For ever now to have their lot in pain;
Millions of spirits for his fault amerced
Of heaven, and from eternal splendors
    flung   610
For his revolt; yet faithful how they stood,
Their glory withered; as when heaven's fire

Hath scathed the forest oaks, or mountain
pines,
With singèd top their stately growth, though
bare,
Stands on the blasted heath. He now pre-   615
pared
To speak; whereat their doubled ranks they
bend
From wing to wing, and half enclose him
round
With all his peers: attention held them
mute.
Thrice he essayed, and thrice, in spite of
scorn,
Tears, such as angels weep, burst forth; at
last   620
Words, interwove with sighs, found out
their way.
' O myriads of immortal spirits! O powers
Matchless, but with the Almighty; and that
strife
Was not inglorious, though the event was
dire,   624
As this place testifies, and this dire change,
Hateful to utter! but what power of mind,
Foreseeing or presaging, from the depth
Of knowledge, past or present, could have
feared
How such united force of gods, how such
As stood like these, could ever know re-
pulse?   630
For who can yet believe, though after loss,
That all these puissant legions, whose exile
Hath emptied heaven, shall fail to reascend
Self-raised, and repossess their native seat?
For me, be witness all the host of heaven,
If counsels different, or dangers shunned 636
By me, have lost our hopes. But he who
reigns
Monarch in heaven, till then as one secure
Sat on this throne upheld by old repute,
Consent or custom; and his regal state   640
Put forth at full, but still his strength con-
cealed,
Which tempted our attempt, and wrought
our fall.
Henceforth his might we know, and know
our own;
So as not either to provoke, or dread
New war, provoked; our better part re-
mains,   645
To work in close design, by fraud or guile,
What force effected not; that he no less
At length from us may find, who over-
comes
By force, hath overcome but half his foe.
Space may produce new worlds; whereof
so rife   650

There went a fame in heaven that he ere
long
Intended to create, and therein plant
A generation, whom his choice regard
Should favor equal to the sons of heaven:
Thither, if but to pry, shall be perhaps   655
Our first eruption; thither, or elsewhere;
For this infernal pit shall never hold
Celestial spirits in bondage, nor the abyss
Long under darkness cover. But these
thoughts
Full counsel must mature; peace is de-
spaired;
For who can think submission? War, then,
war,   660
Open or understood, must be resolved.'
He spake; and, to confirm his words, out
flew
Millions of flaming swords, drawn from the
thighs
Of mighty cherubim; the sudden blaze   665
Far round illumined hell; highly they raged
Against the Highest, and fierce with graspèd
arms
Clashed on their sounding shields the din
of war,
Hurling defiance toward the vault of heaven.
There stood a hill not far, whose grisly
top   670
Belched fire and rolling smoke; the rest en-
tire
Shone with a glossy scurf, undoubted sign
That in his womb was hid metallic ore,
The work of sulphur. Thither, winged with
speed,
A numerous brigade hastened: as when
bands   675
Of pioneers, with spade and pickaxe armed,
Forerun the royal camp, to trench a field,
Or cast a rampart. Mammon led them on:
Mammon, the least erected spirit that fell
From heaven; for even in heaven his looks
and thoughts   680
Were always downward bent, admiring
more
The riches of heaven's pavement, trodden
gold,
Than aught, divine or holy, else enjoyed
In vision beatific; by him first
Men also, and by his suggestion taught,   685
Ransacked the center, and with impious
hands
Rifled the bowels of their mother earth
For treasures, better hid. Soon had his
crew
Opened into the hill a spacious wound,
And digged out ribs of gold. Let none ad-
mire   690

That riches grow in hell; that soil may best
Deserve the precious bane. And here let those
Who boast in mortal things, and wondering tell
Of Babel, and the works of Memphian kings,
Learn how their greatest monuments of fame, 695
And strength and art, are easily outdone
By spirits reprobate, and in an hour
What in an age they with incessant toil
And hands innumerable scarce perform.
Nigh on the plain, in many cells prepared,
That underneath had veins of liquid fire 701
Sluiced from the lake, a second multitude
With wondrous art founded the massy ore,
Severing each kind, and scummed the bullion dross;
A third as soon had formed within the ground 705
A various mold, and from the boiling cells,
By strange conveyance, filled each hollow nook,
As in an organ, from one blast of wind,
To many a row of pipes the sound-board breathes.
Anon, out of the earth a fabric huge 710
Rose like an exhalation, with the sound
Of dulcet symphonies and voices sweet,
Built like a temple, where pilasters round
Were set, and Doric pillars overlaid
With golden architrave; nor did there want
Cornice or frieze, with bossy sculptures graven: 716
The roof was fretted gold. Not Babylon,
Nor great Alcairo, such magnificence
Equaled in all their glories, to enshrine
Belus or Serapis their gods, or seat 720
Their kings, when Egypt with Assyria strove
In wealth and luxury. The ascending pile
Stood fixed her stately height: and straight the doors,
Opening their brazen folds, discover, wide
Within, her ample spaces, o'er the smooth
And level pavement; from the archèd roof, 726
Pendent by subtle magic, many a row
Of starry lamps and blazing cressets, fed
With naphtha and asphaltus, yielded light
As from a sky. The hasty multitude 730
Admiring entered; and the work some praise,
And some the architect: his hand was known
In heaven by many a towered structure high

Where sceptered angels held their residence,
And sat as princes; whom the supreme King 735
Exalted to such power, and gave to rule,
Each in his hierarchy, the orders bright.
Nor was his name unheard or unadored
In ancient Greece; and in Ausonian land
Men called him Mulciber; and how he fell
From heaven they fabled, thrown by angry Jove 741
Sheer o'er the crystal battlements: from morn
To noon he fell, from noon to dewy eve,
A summer's day; and with the setting sun
Dropped from the zenith like a falling star.
On Lemnos, th' Ægean isle: thus they relate, 746
Erring; for he with this rebellious rout
Fell long before; nor aught availed him now
To have built in heaven high towers; nor did he 'scape 749
By all his engines, but was headlong sent
With his industrious crew to build in hell.
   Meanwhile, the wingèd heralds, by command
Of sovereign power, with awful ceremony
And trumpet's sound, throughout the host proclaim
A solemn council, forthwith to be held 755
At Pandemonium, the high capital
Of Satan and his peers: their summons called
From every band and squarèd regiment
By place or choice the worthiest; they anon,
With hundreds and with thousands, trooping came, 760
Attended; all access was thronged; the gates
And porches wide, but chief the spacious hall
(Though like a covered field, where champions bold
Wont ride in armed, and at the soldan's chair
Defied the best of paynim chivalry 765
To mortal combat, or career with lance),
Thick swarmed, both on the ground and in the air,
Brushed with the hiss of rustling wings.
   As bees
In spring-time, when the sun with Taurus rides,
Pour forth their populous youth about the hive 770
In clusters; they among fresh dews and flowers
Fly to and fro, or on the smoothèd plank,

The suburb of their straw-built citadel,
New rubbed with balm, expatiate, and con-
   fer   774
Their state affairs; so thick the aëry crowd
Swarmed and were straitened; till, the sig-
   nal given,
Behold a wonder! They, but now who
   seemed
In bigness to surpass earth's giant sons,
Now less than smallest dwarfs, in narrow
   room
Throng numberless, like that Pygmëan
   race   780
Beyond the Indian mount, or faëry elves,
Whose midnight revels, by a forest side
Or fountain, some belated peasant sees,
Or dreams he sees, while over head the
   moon
Sits arbitress, and nearer to the earth   785
Wheels her pale course; they, on their mirth
   and dance
Intent, with jocund music charm his ear;
At once with joy and fear his heart re-
   bounds.
Thus incorporeal spirits to smallest forms
Reduced their shapes immense, and were
   at large,   790
Though without number still, amidst the
   hall
Of that infernal court. But far within,
And in their own dimensions, like them-
   selves,
The great seraphic lords and cherubim
In close recess and secret conclave sat; 795
A thousand demi-gods on golden seats
Frequent and full. After short silence then,
And summons read, the great consult be-
   gan.

Book II

High on a throne of royal state, which far
Outshone the wealth of Ormus and of Ind,
Or where the gorgeous East, with richest
   hand,
Showers on her kings barbaric pearl and
   gold,
Satan exalted sat, by merit raised   5
To that bad eminence; and, from despair
Thus high uplifted beyond hope, aspires
Beyond thus high, insatiate to pursue
Vain war with Heaven; and, by success un-
   taught,
His proud imaginations thus displayed:— 10
'Powers and dominions, deities of
   heaven;
For since no deep within her gulf can hold
Immortal vigor, though oppressed and
   fallen,

I give not heaven for lost. From this de-
   scent
Celestial virtues rising, will appear   15
More glorious and more dread than from
   no fall,
And trust themselves to fear no second fate.
Me, though just right, and the fixed laws of
   heaven,
Did first create your leader; next, free
   choice,
With what besides, in council or in fight, 20
Hath been achieved of merit; yet this loss,
Thus far at least recovered, hath much more
Established in a safe unenvied throne,
Yielded with full consent. The happier
   state
In heaven, which follows dignity, might
   draw   25
Envy from each inferior; but who here
Will envy whom the highest place exposes
Foremost to stand against the Thunderer's
   aim,
Your bulwark, and condemns to greatest
   share
Of endless pain? Where there is then no
   good   30
For which to strive, no strife can grow up
   there
From faction; for none sure will claim in
   hell
Precédence; none whose portion is so small
Of present pain, that with ambitious mind
Will covet more. With this advantage, then,
To union, and firm faith, and firm accord, 36
More than can be in heaven, we now re-
   turn
To claim our just inheritance of old.
Surer to prosper than prosperity
Could have assured us; and, by what best
   way,   40
Whether of open war or covert guile,
We now debate: who can advise, may
   speak.'
   He ceased; and next him Moloch, scep-
   tered king,
Stood up, the strongest and the fiercest
   spirit
That fought in heaven, now fiercer by de-
   spair.   45
His trust was with the Eternal to be
   deemed
Equal in strength; and rather than be less,
Cared not to be at all; with that care lost
Went all his fear: of God, or hell, or
   worse,
He recked not; and these words thereafter
   spake:—   50
'My sentence is for open war: of wiles,

More unexpert, I boast not; them let those
Contrive who need, or when they need, not
now.
For, while they sit contriving, shall the
rest,
Millions that stand in arms, and longing
wait   55
The signal to ascend, sit lingering here
Heaven's fugitives, and for their dwelling-
place
Accept this dark, opprobrious den of shame,
The prison of his tyranny who reigns
By our delay? No, let us rather choose,   60
Armed with hell-flames and fury, all at
once,
O'er heaven's high towers to force resist-
less way,
Turning our tortures into horrid arms
Against the torturer; when, to meet the
noise
Of his almighty engine, he shall hear   65
Infernal thunder; and, for lightning, see
Black fire and horror shot with equal rage
Among his angels; and his throne itself
Mixed with Tartarean sulphur, and strange
fire,   -   69
His own invented torments. But perhaps
The way seems difficult and steep to scale
With upright wing against a higher foe.
Let such bethink them, if the sleepy drench
Of that forgetful lake benumb not still,
That in our proper motion we ascend   75
Up to our native seat; descent and fall
To us is adverse. Who but felt of late,
When the fierce foe hung on our broken
rear
Insulting, and pursued us through the deep,
With what compulsion and laborious flight
We sunk thus low? The ascent is easy
then;   81
The event is feared; should we again pro-
voke
Our stronger, some worse way his wrath
may find
To our destruction; if there be in hell
Fear to be worse destroyed; what can be
worse   85
Than to dwell here, driven out from bliss,
condemned
In this abhorrèd deep to utter woe;
Where pain of unextinguishable fire
Must exercise us without hope of end,
The vassals of his anger, when the scourge
Inexorable, and the torturing hour,   91
Calls us to penance? More destroyed than
thus,
We should be quite abolished, and expire.

What fear we, then? what doubt we to in-
cense
His utmost ire? which, to the height en-
raged,   95
Will either quite consume us, and reduce
To nothing this essential (happier far
Than miserable to have eternal being),
Or, if our substance be indeed divine,
And cannot cease to be, we are at worst   100
On this side nothing; and by proof we feel
Our power sufficient to disturb his heaven,
And with perpetual inroads to alarm,
Though inaccessible, his fatal throne;
Which, if not victory, is yet revenge.'   105
    He ended frowning, and his look de-
nounced
Desperate revenge, and battle dangerous
To less than gods. On the other side up-
rose
Belial, in act more graceful and humane;
A fairer person lost not heaven; he seemed
For dignity composed, and high exploit: 111
But all was false and hollow, though his
tongue
Dropt manna, and could make the worse
appear
The better reason, to perplex and dash
Maturest counsels: for his thoughts were
low: 115
To vice industrious, but to nobler deeds
Timorous and slothful; yet he pleased the
ear,
And with persuasive accent thus began: —
    'I should be much for open war, O peers,
As not behind in hate; if what was urged   120
Main reason to persuade immediate war,
Did not dissuade me most, and seem to cast
Ominous conjecture on the whole success
When he who most excels in fact of arms,
In what he counsels and in what excels   125
Mistrustful, grounds his courage on despair
And utter dissolution as the scope
Of all his aim, after some dire revenge.
First, what revenge? The towers of heaven
are filled
With armèd watch, that render all access   130
Impregnable; oft on the bordering deep
Encamp their legions; or, with obscure
wing,
Scout far and wide into the realm of night,
Scorning surprise. Or could we break our
way
By force, and at our heels all hell should
rise   135
With blackest insurrection, to confound
Heaven's purest light; yet our great enemy,
All incorruptible, would on his throne

Sit unpolluted, and the ethereal mold,
Incapable of stain, would soon expel   140
Her mischief, and purge off the baser fire,
Victorious. Thus repulsed, our final hope
Is flat despair: we must exasperate
The Almighty Victor to spend all his rage,
And that must end us; that must be our
    cure,   145
To be no more. Sad cure! for who would
    lose,
Though full of pain, this intellectual being,
Those thoughts that wander through eter-
    nity,
To perish rather, swallowed up and lost
In the wide womb of uncreated night,   150
Devoid of sense and motion? And who
    knows,
Let this be good, whether our angry foe
Can give it, or will ever? how he can,
Is doubtful; that he never will, is sure.
Will he, so wise, let loose at once his ire 155
Belike through impotence, or unaware,
To give his enemies their wish, and end
Them in his anger whom his anger saves
To punish endless? "Wherefore cease we
    then?"
Say they who counsel war. "We are de-
    creed,   160
Reserved, and destined to eternal woe;
Whatever doing, what can we suffer more,
What can we suffer worse?" In this then
    worst,
Thus sitting, thus consulting, thus in arms?
What, when we fled amain, pursued, and
    struck   165
With heaven's afflicting thunder, and be-
    sought
The deep to shelter us? this hell then
    seemed
A refuge from those wounds; or when we
    lay
Chained on the burning lake? that sure was
    worse.
What if the breath that kindled those grim
    fires,   170
Awaked, should blow them into sevenfold
    rage,
And plunge us in the flames? or, from
    above,
Should intermitted vengeance arm again
His red right hand to plague us? What
    if all   174
Her stores were opened, and this firmament
Of hell should spout her cataracts of fire,
Impendent horrors, threatening hideous fall
One day upon our heads; while we, perhaps,
Designing or exhorting glorious war,
Caught in a fiery tempest, shall be hurled 180

Each on his rock transfixed, the sport and
    prey
Of racking whirlwinds; or for ever sunk
Under yon boiling ocean, wrapt in chains;
There to converse with everlasting groans,
Unrespited, unpitied, unreprieved,   185
Ages of hopeless end? This would be
    worse.
War, therefore, open or concealed, alike
My voice dissuades; for what can force or
    guile
With him, or who deceive his mind, whose
    eye
Views all things at one view? He from
    heaven's height   190
All these our motions vain sees and de-
    rides:
Not more almighty to resist our might,
Than wise to frustrate all our plots and
    wiles.
Shall we then live thus vile, the race of
    heaven
Thus trampled, thus expelled, to suffer here
Chains and these torments? Better these
    than worse,   196
By my advice; since fate inevitable
Subdues us, and omnipotent decree,
The victor's will. To suffer, as to do,
Our strength is equal, nor the law unjust 200
That so ordains; this was at first resolved,
If we were wise, against so great a foe
Contending, and so doubtful what might
    fall.
I laugh, when those who at the spear are
    bold
And venturous, if that fail them, shrink
    and fear   205
What yet they know must follow, to en-
    dure
Exile, or ignominy, or bonds, or pain,
The sentence of their conqueror; this is
    now
Our doom; which if we can sustain and
    bear,
Our supreme foe in time may much re-
    mit   210
His anger; and perhaps, thus far removed,
Not mind us not offending, satisfied
With what is punished; whence these raging
    fires
Will slacken, if his breath stir not their
    flames.
Our purer essence then will overcome   215
Their noxious vapor; or, inured, not feel;
Or, changed at length, and to the place con-
    formed
In temper and in nature, will receive
Familiar the fierce heat, and void of pain;

This horror will grow mild, this darkness
   light;   220
Besides what hope the never-ending flight
Of future days may bring, what chance,
   what change
Worth waiting; since our present lot ap-
   pears
For happy though but ill, for ill not worst,
If we procure not to ourselves more woe.'
   Thus Belial, with words clothed in rea-
   son's garb,   226
Counseled ignoble ease, and peaceful sloth,
Not peace; and after him thus Mammon
   spake: —
'Either to disenthrone the King of heaven
We war, if war be best, or to regain   230
Our own right lost: him to unthrone we
   then
May hope, when everlasting fate shall yield
To fickle chance, and Chaos judge the
   strife:
The former, vain to hope, argues as vain
The latter; for what place can be for us 235
Within heaven's bound, unless heaven's Lord
   supreme
We overpower? Suppose he should relent,
And publish grace to all, on promise made
Of new subjection; with what eyes could we
Stand in his presence humble, and receive
Strict laws imposed, to celebrate his
   throne   241
With warbled hymns, and to his Godhead
   sing
Forced hallelujahs, while he lordly sits
Our envied sovereign, and his altar breathes
Ambrosial odors and ambrosial flowers, 245
Our servile offerings? This must be our
   task
In heaven, this our delight; how wearisome
Eternity so spent, in worship paid
To whom we hate! Let us not then pursue
By force impossible, by leave obtained 250
Unacceptable, though in heaven, our state
Of splendid vassalage; but rather seek
Our own good from ourselves, and from our
   own
Live to ourselves, though in this vast re-
   cess,
Free, and to none accountable, preferring
Hard liberty before the easy yoke   256
Of servile pomp. Our greatness will appear
Then most conspicuous, when great things
   of small,
Useful of hurtful, prosperous of adverse,
We can create; and in what place soe'er 260
Thrive under evil, and work ease out of
   pain,

Through labor and endurance. This deep
   world
Of darkness do we dread? How oft
   amidst
Thick clouds and dark doth heaven's all
   ruling Sire
Choose to reside, his glory unobscured, 265
And with the majesty of darkness round
Covers his throne; from whence deep thun-
   ders roar,
Mustering their rage, and heaven resembles
   hell!
As he our darkness, cannot we his light 269
Imitate when we please? This desert soil
Wants not her hidden luster, gems and
   gold;
Nor want we skill or art, from whence to
   raise
Magnificence; and what can heaven show
   more?
Our torments also may in length of time
Become our elements; these piercing fires
As soft as now severe, our temper changed
Into their temper; which must needs re-
   move   277
The sensible of pain. All things invite
To peaceful counsels, and the settled state
Of order, how in safety best we may 280
Compose our present evils, with regard
Of what we are, and where; dismissing
   quite
All thoughts of war. Ye have what I ad-
   vise.'
   He scarce had finished, when such mur-
   mur filled
The assembly, as when hollow rocks re-
   tain   285
The sound of blustering winds which all
   night long
Had roused the sea, now with hoarse ca-
   dence lull
Seafaring men o'er-watched, whose bark by
   chance
Or pinnace anchors in a craggy bay 289
After the tempest: such applause was heard
As Mammon ended, and his sentence
   pleased,
Advising peace; for such another field
They dreaded worse than hell; so much the
   fear
Of thunder and the sword of Michael
Wrought still within them, and no less de-
   sire   295
To found this nether empire, which might
   rise
By policy, and long process of time,
In emulation opposite to heaven.

Which when Beëlzebub perceived, than
    whom,   299
Satan except, none higher sat, with grave
Aspect he rose, and in his rising seemed
A pillar of state; deep on his front en-
    graven
Deliberation sat, and public care;
And princely counsel in his face yet shone,
Majestic, though in ruin; sage he stood. 305
With Atlantean shoulders fit to bear
The weight of mightiest monarchies; his
    look
Drew audience and attention still as night
Or summer's noontide air, while thus he
    spake: —
'Thrones and imperial powers, offspring
    of heaven,   310
Ethereal virtues! or these titles now
Must we renounce, and, changing style, be
    called
Princes of hell, for so the popular vote
Inclines, here to continue and build up here
A growing empire; doubtless, while we
    dream,   315
And know not that the King of heaven hath
    doomed
This place our dungeon; not our safe re-
    treat
Beyond his potent arm; to live exempt
From heaven's high jurisdiction, in new
    league   319
Banded against his throne, but to remain
In strictest bondage, though thus far re-
    moved,
Under the inevitable curb, reserved
His captive multitude; for he, be sure,
In height or depth, still first and last will
    reign   324
Sole king, and of his kingdom lose no part
By our revolt, but over hell extend
His empire, and with iron scepter rule
Us here, as with his golden those in heaven.
What sit we then projecting peace and war?
War hath determined us, and foiled with
    loss   330
Irreparable; terms of peace yet none
Vouchsafed or sought; for what peace will
    be given
To us enslaved but custody severe,
And stripes, and arbitrary punishment
Inflicted? and what peace can we return, 335
But to our power hostility and hate,
Untamed reluctance, and revenge, though
    slow,
Yet ever plotting how the Conqueror least
May reap his conquest, and may least re-
    joice   339

In doing what we most in suffering feel?
Nor will occasion want, nor shall we need
With dangerous expedition to invade
Heaven, whose high walls fear no assault
    or siege,
Or ambush from the deep. What if we
    find
Some easier enterprise? There is a place
(If ancient and prophetic fame in heaven 346
Err not), another world, the happy seat
Of some new race, called Man, about this
    time
To be created like to us, though less
In power and excellence, but favored more
Of him who rules above; so was his will 351
Pronounced among the gods; and by an
    oath
That shook heaven's whole circumference
    confirmed.
Thither let us bend all our thoughts, to
    learn
What creatures there inhabit, of what mold
Or substance, how endued, and what their
    power,   356
And where their weakness, how attempted
    best,
By force or subtlety. Though heaven be
    shut,
And heaven's high Arbitrator sit secure
In his own strength, this place may lie ex-
    posed,   360
The utmost border of his kingdom, left
To their defense who hold it; here per-
    haps
Some advantageous act may be achieved
By sudden onset; either with hell-fire
To waste his whole creation, or possess 365
All as our own, and drive, as we were
    driven,
The puny habitants; or, if not drive,
Seduce them to our party, that their God
May prove their foe, and with repenting
    hand
Abolish his own works. This would sur-
    pass   370
Common revenge, and interrupt his joy
In our confusion, and our joy upraise
In his disturbance, when his darling sons,
Hurled headlong to partake with us, shall
    curse
Their frail original and faded bliss,   375
Faded so soon. Advise, if this be worth
Attempting, or to sit in darkness here
Hatching vain empires.' Thus Beëlzebub
Pleaded his devilish counsel, first devised
By Satan, and in part proposed; for whence
But from the author of all ill could spring

So deep a malice, to confound the race 382
Of mankind in one root, and earth with
   hell
To mingle and involve, done all to spite
The great Creator? But their spite still
   serves   385
His glory to augment. The bold design
Pleased highly those infernal states, and
   joy
Sparkled in all their eyes: with full assent
They vote: whereat his speech he thus re-
   news: —
  'Well have ye judged, well ended long
   debate,   390
Synod of gods, and, like to what ye are,
Great things resolved, which from the
   lowest deep
Will once more lift us up, in spite of fate,
Nearer our ancient seat: perhaps in view
Of those bright confines, whence, with
   neighboring arms,   395
And opportune excursion, we may chance
Re-enter heaven; or else in some mild zone
Dwell, not unvisited of heaven's fair light,
Secure; and at the brightening orient beam
Purge off this gloom; the soft delicious air,
To heal the scar of these corrosive fires, 401
Shall breathe her balm. But first, whom
   shall we send
In search of this new world? whom shall
   we find
Sufficient? who shall tempt with wandering
   feet
The dark, unbottomed, infinite abyss,   405
And through the palpable obscure find out
His uncouth way, or spread his aëry flight,
Upborne with indefatigable wings,
Over the vast abrupt, ere he arrive
The happy isle? What strength, what art,
   can then   410
Suffice, or what evasion bear him safe
Through the strict senteries and stations
   thick
Of angels watching round? Here he had
   need
All circumspection, and we now no less
Choice in our suffrage; for, on whom we
   send,   415
The weight of all, and our last hope relies.'
  This said, he sat; and expectation held
His look suspense, awaiting who appeared
To second, or oppose, or undertake
The perilous attempt: but all sat mute, 420
Pondering the danger with deep thoughts;
   and each
In other's countenance read his own dismay,
Astonished: none among the choice and
   prime

Of those heaven-warring champions could
   be found
So hardy as to proffer or accept,   425
Alone, the dreadful voyage; till at last
Satan, whom now transcendent glory raised
Above his fellows, with monarchal pride,
Conscious of highest worth, unmoved thus
   spake: —
'O progeny of heaven! empyreal thrones!
With reason hath deep silence and demur
Seized us, though undismayed. Long is the
   way   432
And hard, that out of hell leads up to
   light;
Our prison strong; this huge convex of fire,
Outrageous to devour, immures us round
Ninefold; and gates of burning adamant,
Barred over us, prohibit all egress.   437
These passed, if any pass, the void profound
Of unessential night receives him next,
Wide-gaping, and with utter loss of being
Threatens him plunged in that abortive
   gulf.   441
If thence he 'scape into whatever world
Or unknown region, what remains him less
Than unknown dangers and as hard escape?
But I should ill become this throne, O peers,
And this imperial sovereignty, adorned   446
With splendor, armed with power, if aught
   proposed
And judged of public moment, in the shape
Of difficulty or danger, could deter
Me from attempting. Wherefore do I
   assume   450
These royalties, and not refuse to reign,
Refusing to accept as great a share
Of hazard as of honor, due alike
To him who reigns, and so much to him due
Of hazard more, as he above the rest 455
High honored sits? Go, therefore, mighty
   powers,
Terror of heaven, though fallen; intend at
   home
(While here shall be our home) what best
   may ease
The present misery, and render hell
More tolerable; if there be cure or charm
To respite, or deceive, or slack the pain 461
Of this ill mansion; intermit no watch
Against a wakeful foe, while I abroad
Through all the coasts of dark destruction
   seek
Deliverance for us all: this enterprise 465
None shall partake with me.' Thus saying,
   rose
The monarch, and prevented all reply;
Prudent, lest from his resolution raised
Others among the chief might offer now

(Certain to be refused) what erst they
   feared;   470
And, so refused, might in opinion stand
His rivals; winning cheap the high repute
Which he through hazard huge must earn.
   But they
Dreaded not more the adventure than his
   voice
Forbidding; and at once with him they rose.
Their rising all at once was as the sound
Of thunder heard remote. Towards him
   they bend   477
With awful reverence prone; and as a god
Extol him equal to the Highest in heaven.
Nor failed they to express how much they
   praised   480
That for the general safety he despised
His own: for neither do the spirits damned
Lose all their virtue; lest bad men should
   boast
Their specious deeds on earth, which glory
   excites   484
Or close ambition varnished o'er with zeal.
   Thus they their doubtful consultations
   dark
Ended, rejoicing in their matchless chief.
As when from mountain-tops the dusky
   clouds
Ascending, while the north wind sleeps,
   o'erspread
Heaven's cheerful face, the louring element
Scowls o'er the darkened landscape snow or
   shower;   491
If chance the radiant sun, with farewell
   sweet,
Extend his evening beam, the fields revive,
The birds their notes renew, and bleating
   herds   494
Attest their joy, that hill and valley rings.
O shame to men! devil with devil damned
Firm concord holds, men only disagree
Of creatures rational, though under hope
Of heavenly grace; and, God proclaiming
   peace,
Yet live in hatred, enmity, and strife   500
Among themselves, and levy cruel wars,
Wasting the earth, each other to destroy:
As if (which might induce us to accord)
Man had not hellish foes enough besides,
That day and night for his destruction wait.
       * * *   (1667)

From AREOPAGITICA

A SPEECH FOR THE LIBERTY OF UNLI-
CENSED PRINTING TO THE PARLIAMENT
OF ENGLAND

   Lords and Commons of England, consider what nation it is whereof ye are,
and whereof ye are the governors: a
nation not slow and dull, but of a quick,
ingenious, and piercing spirit, acute to
invent, subtle and sinewy to discourse,
not beneath the reach of any point the
highest that human capacity can soar to.
Therefore the studies of learning in her
deepest sciences have been so ancient and
so eminent among us, that writers of good
antiquity and ablest judgment have been
persuaded that even the school of Pythagoras and the Persian wisdom took beginning from the old philosophy of this
island. And that wise and civil Roman, Julius Agricola, who governed
once here for Cæsar, preferred the natural wits of Britain, before the labored
studies of the French. Nor is it for
nothing that the grave and frugal Tran-
sylvanian sends out yearly from as far
as the mountainous borders of Russia,
and beyond the Hercynian wilderness,
not their youth, but their staid men, to
learn our language, and our theologic
arts. Yet that which is above all this,
the favor and the love of Heaven we
have great argument to think in a peculiar manner propitious and propending
towards us. Why else was this nation
chosen before any other, that out of her
as out of Sion should be proclaimed and
sounded forth the first tidings and trumpet of Reformation to all Europe? And
had it not been the obstinate perverse-
ness of our prelates against the divine
and admirable spirit of Wyclif, to suppress him as a schismatic and innovator,
perhaps neither the Bohemian Huss and
Jerome, no, nor the name of Luther, or
of Calvin had been ever known: the
glory of reforming all our neighbors
had been completely ours. But now, as
our obdurate clergy have with violence
demeaned the matter, we are become
hitherto the latest and the backwardest
scholars, of whom God offered to have
made us the teachers. Now once again
by all concurrence of signs, and by the
general instinct of holy and devout men,
as they daily and solemnly express their
thoughts, God is decreeing to begin some
new and great period in his church, even
to the reforming of Reformation itself:
what does he then but reveal himself to
his servants, and as his manner is, first
to his Englishmen; I say as his manner
is, first to us, though we mark not the
method of his counsels, and are un-

worthy. Behold now this vast city: a city of refuge, the mansion house of liberty, encompassed and surrounded with his protection. The shop of war hath not there more anvils and hammers waking, to fashion out the plates and instruments of armed justice in defense of beleaguered truth, than there be pens and heads there, sitting by their studious lamps, musing, searching, revolving new notions and ideas wherewith to present, as with their homage and their fealty, the approaching Reformation; others as fast reading, trying all things, assenting to the force of reason and convincement. What could a man require more from a nation so pliant and so prone to seek after knowledge? What wants there to such a towardly and pregnant soil, but wise and faithful laborers, to make a knowing people, a nation of prophets, of sages, and of worthies? We reckon more than five months yet to harvest; there need not be five weeks; had we but eyes to lift up, the fields are white already. Where there is much desire to learn, there of necessity will be much arguing, much writing, many opinions; for opinion in good men is but knowledge in the making. Under these fantastic terrors of sect and schism, we wrong the earnest and zealous thirst after knowledge and understanding which God hath stirred up in this city. What some lament of, we rather should rejoice at, should rather praise this pious forwardness among men, to reassume the ill-deputed care of their religion into their own hands again. A little generous prudence, a little forbearance of one another, and some grain of charity might win all these diligences to join, and unite in one general and brotherly search after truth, could we but forego this prelatical tradition of crowding free consciences and christian liberties into canons and precepts of men. I doubt not, if some great and worthy stranger should come among us, wise to discern the mold and temper of a people, and how to govern it, observing the high hopes and aims, the diligent alacrity of our extended thoughts and reasonings in the pursuance of truth and freedom, but that he would cry out as Pyrrhus did, admiring the Roman docility and courage, If such were my Epirots, I would

not despair the greatest design that could be attempted to make a church or kingdom happy. Yet these are the men cried out against for schismatics and sectaries; as if, while the temple of the Lord was building, some cutting, some squaring the marble, others hewing the cedars, there should be a sort of irrational men who would not consider there must be many schisms and many dissections made in the quarry and in the timber, ere the house of God can be built. And when every stone is laid artfully together, it cannot be united into a continuity, it can but be contiguous in this world; neither can every piece of the building be of one form; nay, rather the perfection consists in this, that out of many moderate varieties and brotherly dissimilitudes that are not vastly disproportional, arises the goodly and the graceful symmetry that commends the whole pile and structure. Let us therefore be more considerate builders, more wise in spiritual architecture, when great reformation is expected. For now the time seems come, wherein Moses the great prophet may sit in heaven rejoicing to see that memorable and glorious wish of his fulfilled, when not only our seventy elders, but all the Lord's people, are become prophets. No marvel then though some men, and some good men too, perhaps, but young in goodness, as Joshua then was, envy them. They fret, and out of their own weakness are in agony, lest those divisions and subdivisions will undo us, The adversary again applauds, and waits the hour, when they have branched themselves out (saith he) small enough into parties and partitions, then will be our time. Fool! he sees not the firm root, out of which we all grow, though into branches; nor will beware until he see our small divided maniples cutting through at every angle of his ill-united and unwieldy brigade. And that we are to hope better of all these supposed sects and schisms, and that we shall not need that solicitude (honest perhaps though over-timorous) of them that vex in this behalf, but shall laugh in the end, at those malicious applauders of our differences, I have these reasons to persuade me.

First, when a city shall be as it were besieged and blocked about, her navig·

able river infested, inroads and incursions round, defiance and battle oft rumored to be marching up even to her walls and suburb trenches, that then the people, or the greater part, more than at other times, wholly taken up with the study of highest and most important matters to be reformed, should be disputing, reasoning, reading, inventing, discoursing, even to a rarity and admiration, things not before discoursed or written of, argues first a singular goodwill, contentedness and confidence in your prudent foresight, and safe government, Lords and Commons; and from thence derives itself to a gallant bravery and well grounded contempt of their enemies, as if there were no small number of as great spirits among us, as his was, who when Rome was nigh besieged by Hannibal, being in the city, bought that piece of ground at no cheap rate, whereon Hannibal himself encamped his own regiment. Next, it is a lively and cheerful presage of our happy success and victory. For as in a body, when the blood is fresh, the spirits pure and vigorous, not only to vital, but to rational faculties, and those in the acutest and the pertest operations of wit and subtlety, it argues in what good plight and constitution the body is, so when the cheerfulness of the people is so sprightly up, as that it has, not only wherewith to guard well its own freedom and safety, but to spare, and to bestow upon the solidest and sublimest points of controversy and new invention, it betokens us not degenerated, nor drooping to a fatal decay, but casting off the old and wrinkled skin of corruption to outlive these pangs and wax young again, entering the glorious ways of truth and prosperous virtue destined to become great and honorable in these latter ages. Methinks I see in my mind a noble and puissant nation, rousing herself like a strong man after sleep, and shaking her invincible locks. Methinks I see her as an eagle mewing her mighty youth, and kindling her undazzled eyes at the full midday beam; purging and unscaling her long-abused sight at the fountain itself of heavenly radiance; while the whole noise of timorous and flocking birds, with those also that love the twilight, flutter about, amazed at what she means, and in their envious gabble would prognosticate a year of sects and schisms.

What should ye do then, should ye suppress all this flowery crop of knowledge and new light sprung up and yet springing daily in this city, should ye set an oligarchy of twenty engrossers over it, to bring a famine upon our minds again, when we shall know nothing but what is measured to us by their bushel? Believe it, Lords and Commons, they who counsel ye to such a suppressing, do as good as bid ye suppress yourselves; and I will soon show how. If it be desired to know the immediate cause of all this free writing and free speaking, there cannot be assigned a truer than your own mild, and free, and humane government; it is the liberty, Lords and Commons, which your own valorous and happy counsels have purchased us, liberty which is the nurse of all great wits. This is that which hath rarefied and enlightened our spirits like the influence of heaven; this is that which hath enfranchised, enlarged, and lifted up our apprehensions degrees above themselves. Ye cannot make us now less capable, less knowing, less eagerly pursuing of the truth, unless ye first make yourselves, that made us so, less the lovers, less the founders of our true liberty. We can grow ignorant again, brutish, formal, and slavish, as ye found us; but you then must first become that which ye cannot be, oppressive, arbitrary, and tyrannous, as they were from whom ye have freed us. That our hearts are now more capacious, our thoughts more erected to the search and expectation of greatest and exactest things, is the issue of your own virtue propagated in us; ye cannot suppress that unless ye reinforce an abrogated and merciless law, that fathers may despatch at will their own children. And who shall then stick closest to ye, and excite others? not he who takes up arms for coat and conduct, and his four nobles of danegelt. Although I dispraise not. the defense of just immunities, yet love my peace better, if that were all. Give me the liberty to know, to utter, and to argue freely according to conscience, above all liberties.

What would be best advised, then, if it be found so hurtful and so unequal to suppress opinions for the newness, or the unsuitableness to a customary acceptance, will not be my task to say. I only shall repeat what I have learned from one of your own honorable number, a right noble and pious lord, who, had he not sacrificed his life and fortunes to the church and commonwealth, we had not now missed and bewailed a worthy and undoubted patron of this argument. Ye know him I am sure; yet I for honor's sake, and may it be eternal to him, shall name him the Lord Brook. He writing of episcopacy and by the way treating of sects and schisms, left ye his vote, or rather now the last words of his dying charge, which I know will ever be of dear and honored regard with ye, so full of meekness and breathing charity, that next to his last testament, who bequeathed love and peace to his disciples, I cannot call to mind where I have read or heard words more mild and peaceful. He there exhorts us to hear with patience and humility those, however they be miscalled, that desire to live purely, in such a use of God's ordinances, as the best guidance of their conscience gives them, and to tolerate them, though in some disconformity to ourselves. The book itself will tell us more at large, being published to the world, and dedicated to the Parliament by him who both for his life and for his death deserves that what advice he left be not laid by without perusal.

And now the time in special is, by privilege to write and speak what may help to the further discussing of matters in agitation. The temple of Janus with his two controversal faces might now not unsignificantly be set open. And though all the winds of doctrine were let loose to play upon the earth, so Truth be in the field, we do injuriously by licensing and prohibiting to misdoubt her strength. Let her and Falsehood grapple; who ever knew Truth put to the worse, in a free and open encounter? Her confuting is the best and surest suppressing. He who hears what praying there is for light and clearer knowledge to be sent down among us, would think of other matters to be constituted beyond the discipline of Geneva, framed and fabricked already to our hands. Yet when the new light which we beg for shines in upon us, there be who envy and oppose, if it come not first in at their casements. What a collusion is this, whenas we are exhorted by the wise man to use diligence, to seek for wisdom as for hidden treasures early and late, that another order shall enjoin us to know nothing but by statute? When a man hath been laboring the hardest labor in the deep mines of knowledge, hath furnished out his findings in all their equipage, drawn forth his reasons as it were a battle ranged, scattered and defeated all objections in his way, calls out his adversary into the plain, offers him the advantage of wind and sun, if he please, only that he may try the matter by dint of argument — for his opponents then to skulk, to lay ambushments, to keep a narrow bridge of licensing where the challenger should pass, though it be valor enough in soldiership, is but weakness and cowardice in the wars of Truth. For who knows not that Truth is strong, next to the Almighty; she needs no policies, no stratagems, no licensings to make her victorious; those are the shifts and the defenses that error uses against her power: give her but room, and do not bind her when she sleeps, for then she speaks not true, as the old Proteus did, who spake oracles only when he was caught and bound, but then rather she turns herself into all shapes, except her own, and perhaps tunes her voice according to the time, as Micaiah did before Ahab, until she be adjured into her own likeness. Yet it is not impossible that she may have more shapes than one. What else is all that rank of things indifferent, wherein Truth may be on this side, or on the other, without being unlike herself? What but a vain shadow else is the abolition of those ordinances, that hand-writing nailed to the cross, what great purchase is this christian liberty which Paul so often boasts of? His doctrine is, that he who eats or eats not, regards a day or regards it not, may do either to the Lord. How many other things might be tolerated in peace, and left to conscience, had we but charity, and were it not the chief stronghold of our hypocrisy to be ever judging one another. I fear yet this iron yoke of outward conformity hath left a slavish print upon our necks; the ghost of a linen decency yet haunts us. We stumble and are impatient at the least dividing of one visible congregation from another, though it be not in fundamentals; and through our forwardness to suppress, and our backwardness to recover any enthralled piece of truth out of the grip of custom, we care not to keep truth separated from truth, which is the fiercest rent and disunion of all. We do not see that while we still affect by all means a rigid external formality, we may as soon fall again into a gross conforming stupidity, a stark and dead congealment of wood, and hay, and stubble forced and frozen together, which is more to the sudden degenerating of a church than many subdichotomies of petty schisms. Not that I can think well of every light separation, or that all in a church is to be expected gold and silver and precious stones. It is not possible for man to sever the wheat from the tares, the good fish from the other fry; that must be the angels' ministry at the end of mortal things. Yet if all cannot be of one mind, (as who looks they should be?) this doubtless is more wholesome, more prudent, and more christian that many be tolerated, rather than all compelled. I mean not tolerated popery, and open superstition, which, as it extirpates all religions and civil supremacies, so itself should be extirpate, provided first that all charitable and compassionate means be used to win and regain the weak and the misled: that also which is impious or evil absolutely either against faith or manners, no law can possibly permit that intends not to unlaw itself. But those neighboring differences, or rather indifferences, are what I speak of, whether in some point of doctrine or of discipline, which though they may be many, yet need not interrupt the unity of Spirit, if we could but find among us the bond of peace. In the meanwhile if any one would write, and bring his helpful hand to the slow-moving reformation which we labor under, if Truth have spoken to him before others, or but seemed at least to speak, who hath so bejesuited us that we should trouble that man with asking license to do so worthy a deed? and not consider this, that if it come to prohibiting, there is not aught more likely to be prohibited than truth itself; whose first appearance to our eyes bleared and dimmed with prejudice and custom, is more unsightly and unplausible than many errors, even as the person is of many a great man slight and contemptible to see to. And what do they tell us vainly of new opinions, when this very opinion of theirs, that none must be heard but whom they like, is the worst and newest opinion of all others; and is the chief cause why sects and schisms do so much abound, and true knowledge is kept at distance from us; besides yet a greater danger which is in it. For when God shakes a kingdom with strong and healthful commotions to a general reforming, 't is not untrue that many sectaries and false teachers are then busiest in seducing; but yet more true it is, that God then raises to his own work men of rare abilities, and more than common industry, not only to look back and revise what hath been taught heretofore, but to gain further and go on, some new enlightened steps in the discovery of truth. For such is the order of God's enlightening his church, to dispense and deal out by degrees his beam, so as our earthly eyes may best sustain it. Neither is God appointed and confined, where and out of what place these his chosen shall be first heard to speak; for he sees not as man sees, chooses not as man chooses, lest we should devote ourselves again to set places, and assemblies, and outward callings of men; planting our faith one while in the old Convocation House, and another while in the Chapel at Westminster; when all the faith and religion that shall be there canonized, is not sufficient without plain convincement, and the charity of patient instruction to supple the least bruise of conscience, to edify the meanest christian, who desires to walk in the Spirit, and not in the letter of human trust, for all the number of voices that can be there made — no, though Harry VII himself there, with all his liege tombs about him, should lend them voices from the dead, to swell their number. And if the men be erroneous who appear to be the leading schismatics, what withholds us but our sloth, our self-will, and distrust in the right cause, that we do not give them gentle meetings and gentle dismissions, that we debate not and examine the matter thoroughly with liberal and frequent audience; if not for their sakes, yet for our own? Seeing no man who hath tasted learning, but will confess the many ways of profiting by those who, not contented with stale receipts, are able to manage and set forth new positions to the world. And were they but as the dust and cinders of our feet, so long as in that notion they may yet serve to polish and brighten the armory of Truth, even for that respect they were not utterly to be cast away. But if they be of those whom God hath fitted for the special use of [5] these times with eminent and ample gifts, and those perhaps neither among the Priests, nor among the Pharisees, and we in the haste of a precipitant zeal shall make no distinction, but resolve to [10] stop their mouths, because we fear they come with new and dangerous opinions, as we commonly forejudge them ere we understand them, no less than woe to us, while thinking thus to defend the Gospel, [15] we are found the persecutors.

There have been not a few since the beginning of this Parliament, both of the Presbytery and others, who by their unlicensed books to the contempt of an Imprimatur [20] first broke that triple ice clung about our hearts, and taught the people to see day. I hope that none of those were the persuaders to renew upon us this bondage which they themselves have [25] wrought so much good by contemning. But if neither the check that Moses gave to young Joshua, nor the countermand which our Savior gave to young John, who was so ready to prohibit those whom [30] he thought unlicensed, be not enough to admonish our Elders, how unacceptable to God their testy mood of prohibiting is; if neither their own remembrance what evil hath abounded in the Church [35] by this let of licensing, and what good they themselves have begun by transgressing it, be not enough, but that they will persuade, and execute the most Dominican part of the Inquisition over [40] us, and are already with one foot in the stirrup so active at suppressing, it would be no unequal distribution in the first place to suppress the suppressors themselves: whom the change of their con- [45] dition hath puffed up, more than their late experience of harder times hath made wise.

And as for regulating the Press, let no man think to have the honor of advising [50] ye better than yourselves have done in that order published next before this, ' that no book be printed, unless the printer's and the author's name, or at least the printer's be registered.' Those [55] which otherwise come forth, if they be found mischievous and libelous, the fire and the executioner will be the timeliest and the most effectual remedy, that man's prevention can use. For this authentic Spanish policy of licensing books, if I have said aught, will prove the most unlicensed book itself within a short while; and was the immediate image of a Star Chamber decree to that purpose made in those very times when that court did the rest of those her pious works, for which she is now fallen from the stars with Lucifer. Whereby ye may guess what kind of state prudence, what love of the people, what care of religion or good manners there was at the contriving, although with singular hypocrisy it pretended to bind books to their good behavior. And how it got the upper hand of your precedent order, so well constituted before, if we may believe those men whose profession gives them cause to inquire most, it may be doubted there was in it the fraud of some old patentees and monopolizers in the trade of bookselling; who under pretense of the poor in their Company not to be defrauded, and the just retaining of each man his several copy (which God forbid should be gainsaid), brought divers glossing colors to the House; which were indeed but colors, and serving to no end except it be to exercise a superiority over their neighbors, men who do not therefore labor in an honest profession to which learning is indebted, that they should be made other men's vassals. Another end is thought was aimed at by some of them in procuring by petition this order, that having power in their hands, malignant books might the easier 'scape abroad, as the event shows. But of these sophisms and elenchs of merchandise I skill not. This I know, that errors in a good government and in a bad are equally almost incident; for what magistrate may not be misinformed, and much the sooner, if liberty of printing be reduced into the power of a few; but to redress willingly and speedily what hath been erred, and in highest authority to esteem a plain advertisement more than others have done a sumptuous bribe, is a virtue (honored Lords and Commons) answerable to your highest actions, and whereof none can participate but greatest and wisest men.

(1644)

JOHN DRYDEN (1631–1700)

Dryden came of a good Northamptonshire family, and was educated at Westminster School and Trinity College, Cambridge. He was only eighteen when his first verses were published, but his first poem of importance was in commemoration of the death of Oliver Cromwell. Dryden's dependence as a professional writer on the party in power made his financial position insecure, hampered his genius, and ruined his reputation for consistency: his eulogy of Cromwell was followed almost immediately by poems in celebration of Charles II. The reopening of the theaters after the Restoration gave him a less equivocal opportunity for the exercise of his talents, and he led the way in the development of the new comedy (largely indebted to the French) and the heroic play with its preposterous characters and incidents and extravagant rant. After defending and perfecting the rimed couplet as a medium for tragedy, he turned to blank verse in *All for Love* (1678), founded upon Shakspere's *Antony and Cleopatra*, and generally accounted Dryden's best play. Meanwhile he had won distinction in other ways; his *Essay of Dramatic Poesy* (1668) is remarkable both for its literary insight and its vigorous and lucid style, which had an important influence on the development of English prose. In 1670 he was appointed poet laureate and historiographer with a salary of £200, which relieved his immediate necessities, but was not enough to save him from financial difficulties. The political intrigues at the end of Charles II's reign gave occasion for the bitter satirical poem *Absalom and Achitophel* (1681) which in its own kind of poetry remains unsurpassed. *Religio Laici* (1682), a poem in defense of the Church of England, was discounted by the author's conversion to Roman Catholicism on the accession of James II, though most students of Dryden's life and writings hold that his change of view was sincere. *The Hind and the Panther*, a plea for the poet's newly adopted faith, appeared in 1687. The Revolution of 1688 deprived Dryden of his offices, and he was dependent for the rest of his life upon his pen. He returned to the stage with *Don Sebastian* (1690), one of his best tragedies, wrote excellent prologues and epilogues for the plays of other men, and worked hard at criticism and translations. After enjoying for many years the literary leadership of his time, he was buried in the Poets' Corner at Westminster Abbey.

HEROIC STANZAS,

CONSECRATED TO THE MEMORY OF HIS HIGHNESS OLIVER

LATE LORD PROTECTOR OF THIS COMMON-
WEALTH &C.

Written after the celebrating of his funeral

And now 't is time; for their officious haste
Who would before have borne him to the sky,
Like eager Romans ere all rites were past,
Did let too soon the sacred eagle fly.

Though our best notes are treason to his fame 5
Joined with the loud applause of public voice,
Since Heaven what praise we offer to his name
Hath rendered too authentic by its choice;

Though in his praise no arts can liberal be,
Since they, whose muses have the highest flown, 10
Add not to his immortal memory,
But do an act of friendship to their own;

Yet 't is our duty and our interest too
Such monuments as we can build to raise,
Lest all the world prevent what we should do 15
And claim a title in him by their praise.

How shall I then begin or where conclude
To draw a fame so truly circular?
For in a round what order can be shewed,
Where all the parts so equal-perfect are? 20

His grandeur he derived from Heaven alone,
For he was great, ere Fortune made him so;

And wars, like mists that rise against the
  sun,
  Made him but greater seem, not greater
  grow.

No borrowed bays his temples did adorn, 25
  But to our crown he did fresh jewels
  bring;
Nor was his virtue poisoned, soon as born,
  With the too early thoughts of being
  king.

Fortune, that easy mistress of the young,
  But to her ancient servants coy and hard,
Him at that age her favorites ranked
  among   31
  When she her best-loved Pompey did dis-
  card.

He, private, marked the faults of others'
  sway
  And set as sea-marks for himself to
  shun;
Not like rash monarchs, who their youth
  betray   35
  By acts their age too late would wish undone.

And yet dominion was not his design;
  We owe that blessing not to him but
  Heaven,
Which to fair acts unsought rewards did
  join.
  Rewards that less to him than us were
  given.   40

Our former chiefs, like sticklers of the war,
  First sought to inflame the parties, then
  to poise;
The quarrel loved, but did the cause abhor,
  And did not strike to hurt, but make a
  noise.

War, our consumption, was their gainful
  trade;   45
  We inward bled, whilst they prolonged
  our pain;
He fought to end our fighting, and assayed
  To stanch the blood by breathing of the
  vein.

* * *

Nor died he when his ebbing fame went
  less,
  But when fresh laurels courted him to
  live;   50
He seemed but to prevent some new success.

As if above what triumphs earth could
  give.

His latest victories still thickest came,
  As near the center motion does increase;
Till he, pressed down by his own weighty
  name,   55
  Did, like the vestal, under spoils decease.

But first the ocean as a tribute sent
  That giant-prince of all her watery herd;
And the isle, when her protecting genius
  went,   59
  Upon his obsequies loud sighs conferred.

No civil broils have since his death arose,
  But faction now by habit does obey;
And wars have that respect for his repose
  As winds for halcyons when they breed
  at sea.

His ashes in a peaceful urn shall rest;   65
  His name a great example stands to show
How strangely high endeavors may be
  blessed
  Where piety and valor jointly go.

(1659)

From ASTRÆA REDUX

And welcome now, great monarch, to
  your own!
Behold the approaching cliffs of Albion.
It is no longer motion cheats your view;
As you meet it, the land approacheth you,
The land returns, and in the white it wears
The marks of penitence and sorrow bears. 6
But you, whose goodness your descent doth
  show,
Your heavenly parentage and earthly too,
By that same mildness which your father's
  crown
Before did ravish shall secure your own. 10
Not tied to rules of policy, you find
Revenge less sweet than a forgiving mind.
Thus, when the Almighty would to Moses
  give
A sight of all he could behold and live,
A voice before his entry did proclaim   15
Long-suffering, goodness, mercy, in his
  name.
Your power to justice doth submit your
  cause,
Your goodness only is above the laws,
Whose rigid letter, while pronounced by
  you,

Is softer made. So winds that tempests
　　brew,　　　　　　　　　　　　20
When through Arabian groves they take
　　their flight,
Made wanton with rich odors, lose their
　　spite.
And as those lees that trouble it refine
The agitated soul of generous wine,
So tears of joy, for your returning spilt, 25
Work out and expiate our former guilt.
Methinks I see those crowds on Dover's
　　strand,
Who in their haste to welcome you to land
Choked up the beach with their still grow-
　　ing store
And made a wilder torrent on the shore: 30
While, spurred with eager thoughts of past
　　delight,
Those who had seen you, court a second
　　sight,
Preventing still your steps and making
　　haste
To meet you often wheresoe'er you past.
How shall I speak of that triumphant
　　day,　　　　　　　　　　　　　35
When you renewed the expiring pomp of
　　May!
A month that owns an interest in your
　　name;
You and the flowers are its peculiar claim.
That star, that at your birth shone out so
　　bright
It stained the duller sun's meridian light, 40
Did once again its potent fires renew,
Guiding our eyes to find and worship you.
　　And now Time's whiter series is begun,
Which in soft centuries shall smoothly run;
Those clouds that overcast your morn shall
　　fly,　　　　　　　　　　　　　45
Dispelled to farthest corners of the sky.
Our nation, with united interest blest,
Not now content to poise, shall sway the
　　rest.
Abroad your empire shall no limits know,
But, like the sea, in boundless circles flow;
Your much-loved fleet shall with a wide
　　command　　　　　　　　　　　51
Besiege the petty monarchs of the land;
And as old Time his offspring swallowed
　　down,
Our ocean in its depths all seas shall drown.
Their wealthy trade from pirates' rapine
　　free,　　　　　　　　　　　　55
Our merchants shall no more adventurers
　　be;
Nor in the farthest East those dangers fear
Which humble Holland must dissemble
　　here.

Spain to your gift alone her Indies owes,
For what the powerful takes not he be-
　　stows;　　　　　　　　　　　60
And France that did an exile's presence
　　fear
May justly apprehend you still too near.
At home the hateful names of parties cease,
And factious souls are wearied into peace.
The discontented now are only they　　65
Whose crimes before did your just cause
　　betray;
Of those your edicts some reclaim from
　　sins,
But most your life and blest example wins.
Oh, happy prince, whom Heaven hath taught
　　the way
By paying vows to have more vows to pay!
Oh, happy age! oh, times like those alone 71
By fate reserved for great Augustus'
　　throne,
When the joint growth of arms and arts
　　foreshew
The world a monarch, and that monarch
　　you!

　　　　　　　　　　　　　(1660)

From ABSALOM AND ACHITOPHEL

　　The inhabitants of old Jerusalem
Were Jebusites; the town so called from
　　them,
And theirs the native right.
But when the chosen people grew more
　　strong,
The rightful cause at length became the
　　wrong;　　　　　　　　　　　5
And every loss the men of Jebus bore,
They still were thought God's enemies the
　　more.
Thus worn and weakened, well or ill con-
　　tent,
Submit they must to David's government:
Impoverished and deprived of all com-
　　mand,　　　　　　　　　　　10
Their taxes doubled as they lost their land;
And, what was harder yet to flesh and
　　blood,
Their gods disgraced, and burnt like com-
　　mon wood.
This set the heathen priesthood in a flame,
For priests of all religions are the same. 15
Of whatsoe'er descent their godhead be,
Stock, stone, or other homely pedigree,
In his defense his servants are as bold,
As if he had been born of beaten gold.
The Jewish rabbins, though their enemies, 20
In this conclude them honest men and wise

For 't was their duty, all the learned think,
To espouse his cause by whom they eat and
drink.
From hence began that Plot, the nation's
curse,
Bad in itself, but represented worse,   25
Raised in extremes, and in extremes de-
cried,
With oaths affirmed, with dying vows de-
nied,
Not weighed or winnowed by the multitude,
But swallowed in the mass, unchewed and
crude.
Some truth there was, but dashed and
brewed with lies   30
To please the fools and puzzle all the wise:
Succeeding times did equal folly call,
Believing nothing or believing all.
The Egyptian rites the Jebusites embraced,
Where gods were recommended by their
taste;   35
Such savory deities must needs be good
As served at once for worship and for food.
By force they could not introduce these
gods,
For ten to one in former days was odds:
So fraud was used, the sacrificer's trade; 40
Fools are more hard to conquer than per-
suade.
Their busy teachers mingled with the Jews
And raked for converts even the court and
stews:
Which Hebrew priests the more unkindly
took,
Because the fleece accompanies the flock. 45
Some thought they God's anointed meant to
slay
By guns, invented since full many a day:
Our author swears it not; but who can
know
How far the devil and Jebusites may go?
This plot, which failed for want of common
sense,   50
Had yet a deep and dangerous consequence;
For as, when raging fevers boil the blood,
The standing lake soon floats into a flood,
And every hostile humor which before
Slept quiet in its channels bubbles o'er; 55
So several factions from this first ferment
Work up to foam and threat the govern-
ment.
Some by their friends, more by themselves
thought wise,
Opposed the power to which they could not
rise.
Some had in courts been great, and thrown
from thence,   60
Like fiends were hardened in impenitence.

Some by their monarch's fatal mercy grown
From pardoned rebels kinsmen to the throne
Were raised in power and public office
high;
Strong bands, if bands ungrateful men
could tie.   65
Of these the false Achitophel was first,
A name to all succeeding ages curst:
For close designs and crooked counsels fit,
Sagacious, bold, and turbulent of wit,
Restless, unfixed in principles and place, 70
In power unpleased, impatient of disgrace;
A fiery soul, which working out its way,
Fretted the pigmy body to decay
And o'er-informed the tenement of clay.
A daring pilot in extremity,   75
Pleased with the danger, when the waves
went high,
He sought the storms; but for a calm unfit,
Would steer too nigh the sands to boast his
wit.
Great wits are sure to madness near allied
And thin partitions do their bounds di-
vide;   80
Else, why should he, with wealth and honor
blest,
Refuse his age the needful hours of rest?
Punish a body which he could not please,
Bankrupt of life, yet prodigal of ease?
And all to leave what with his toil he won
To that unfeathered two-legged thing, a
son,   86
Got, while his soul did huddled notions try,
And born a shapeless lump, like anarchy.
In friendship false, implacable in hate,
Resolved to ruin or to rule the state;   90
To compass this the triple bond he broke
The pillars of the public safety shook,
And fitted Israel for a foreign yoke;
Then, seized with fear, yet still affecting
fame,
Usurped a patriot's all-atoning name.   95
So easy still it proves in factious times
With public zeal to cancel private crimes.
How safe is treason and how sacred ill,
Where none can sin against the people's
will,
Where crowds can wink and no offense be
known,   100
Since in another's guilt they find their own!
Yet fame deserved no enemy can grudge;
The statesman we abhor, but praise the
judge.
In Israel's courts ne'er sat an abbethdin
With more discerning eyes or hands more
clean,   105
Unbribed, unsought, the wretched to redress,
Swift of dispatch and easy of access.

Oh! had he been content to serve the crown
With virtues only proper to the gown,
Or had the rankness of the soil been freed
From cockle that oppressed the noble
　　seed,　　　　　　　　　　　　　111
David for him his tuneful harp had strung
And Heaven had wanted one immortal song.
But wild ambition loves to slide, not stand,
And fortune's ice prefers to virtue's land.
Achitophel, grown weary to possess　　116
A lawful fame and lazy happiness,
Disdained the golden fruit to gather free
And lent the crowd his arm to shake the
　　tree.
Now, manifest of crimes contrived long
　　since,　　　　　　　　　　　　120
He stood at bold defiance with his prince,
Held up the buckler of the people's cause
Against the crown, and skulked behind the
　　laws.
The wished occasion of the plot he takes;
Some circumstances finds, but more he
　　makes;　　　　　　　　　　　125
By buzzing emissaries fills the ears
Of listening crowds with jealousies and
　　fears,
Of arbitrary counsels brought to light,
And proves the king himself a Jebusite.
Weak arguments! which yet he knew full
　　well　　　　　　　　　　　　　130
Were strong with people easy to rebel.
For governed by the moon, the giddy Jews
Tread the same track when she the prime
　　renews:
And once in twenty years their scribes re-
　　cord,
By natural instinct they change their lord.
Achitophel still wants a chief, and none 136
Was found so fit as warlike Absalon.
Not that he wished his greatness to create,
For politicians neither love nor hate:
But, for he knew his title not allowed　140
Would keep him still depending on the
　　crowd,
That kingly power, thus ebbing out, might
　　be
Drawn to the dregs of a democracy.
　　　　　　　　　　　　　　(1681)

* * *

THE HIND AND THE PANTHER

A milk-white Hind, immortal and un-
　　changed,
Fed on the lawns and in the forest ranged;
Without unspotted, innocent within,
She feared no danger, for she knew no sin.

Yet had she oft been chased with horns and
　　hounds　　　　　　　　　　　　5
And Scythian shafts; and many wingèd
　　wounds
Aimed at her heart; was often forced to
　　fly,
And doomed to death, though fated not to
　　die.
Not so her young; for their unequal line
Was hero's make, half human, half di-
　　vine.　　　　　　　　　　　　10
Their earthly mold obnoxious was to fate,
The immortal part assumed immortal state.
Of these a slaughtered army lay in blood,
Extended o'er the Caledonian wood,
Their native walk; whose vocal blood arose
And cried for pardon on their perjured
　　foes.　　　　　　　　　　　　16
Their fate was fruitful, and the sanguine
　　seed,
Endued with souls, increased the sacred
　　breed.
So captive Israel multiplied in chains,
A numerous exile, and enjoyed her pains. 20
With grief and gladness mixed, their mother
　　viewed
Her martyred offspring and their race re-
　　newed;
Their corpse to perish, but their kind to
　　last,
So much the deathless plant the dying fruit
　　surpassed.
　　Panting and pensive now she ranged
　　alone,　　　　　　　　　　　　25
And wandered in the kingdoms once her
　　own.
The common hunt, though from their rage
　　restrained
By sovereign power, her company disdained.
Grinned as they passed, and with a glaring
　　eye
Gave gloomy signs of secret enmity.　30
'T is true she bounded by and tripped so
　　light,
They had not time to take a steady sight;
For truth has such a face and such a mien
As to be loved needs only to be seen.
　　The bloody Bear, an independent beast, 35
Unlicked to form, in groans her hate ex-
　　pressed.
Among the timorous kind the quaking Hare
Professed neutrality, but would not swear.
Next her the buffoon Ape, as atheists use,
Mimicked all sects and had his own to
　　choose;　　　　　　　　　　　40
Still when the Lion looked, his knees he
　　bent.

And paid at church a courtier's compliment.
The bristled baptist Boar, impure as he,
But whitened with the foam of sanctity,
With fat pollutions filled the sacred place 45
And mountains leveled in his furious race;
So first rebellion founded was in grace.
But, since the mighty ravage which he made
In German forests had his guilt betrayed,
With broken tusks and with a borrowed
    name, 50
He shunned the vengeance and concealed
    the shame,
So lurked in sects unseen. With greater
    guile
False Reynard fed on consecrated spoil;
The graceless beast by Athanasius first
Was chased from Nice, then by Socinus
    nursed, 55
His impious race their blasphemy renewed,
And Nature's King through Nature's optics
    viewed;
Reversed they viewed him lessened to their
    eye,
Nor in an infant could a God descry.
New swarming sects to this obliquely tend,
Hence they began, and here they all will
    end. 61
    What weight of ancient witness can pre-
    vail,
If private reason hold the public scale?
But, gracious God, how well dost thou pro-
    vide
For erring judgments an unerring guide! 65
Thy throne is darkness in the abyss of
    light,
A blaze of glory that forbids the sight.
O teach me to believe thee thus concealed,
And search no farther than thy self re-
    vealed;
But her alone for my director take, 70
Whom thou hast promised never to for-
    sake!
My thoughtless youth was winged with vain
    desires;
My manhood, long misled by wandering
    fires,
Followed false lights; and when their
    glimpse was gone,
My pride struck out new sparkles of her
    own. 75
Such was I, such by nature still I am;
Be thine the glory and be mine the shame!
Good life be now my task; my doubts are
    done:
What more could fright my faith than
    Three in One?
Can I believe eternal God could lie 80
Disguised in mortal mold and infancy,

That the great Maker of the world could
    die?
And, after that, trust my imperfect sense
Which calls in question his omnipotence?
Can I my reason to my faith compel, 85
And shall my sight and touch and taste
    rebel?
Superior faculties are set aside;
Shall their subservient organs be my guide?
Then let the moon usurp the rule of day,
And winking tapers show the sun his way;
For what my senses can themselves per-
    ceive 91
I need no revelation to believe.
Can they, who say the host should be
    descried
By sense, define a body glorified,
Impassible, and penetrating parts? 95
Let them declare by what mysterious arts
He shot that body through the opposing
    might
Of bolts and bars impervious to the light,
And stood before his train confessed in
    open sight.
For since thus wondrously he passed, 't is
    plain 100
One single place two bodies did contain,
And sure the same omnipotence as well
Can make one body in more places dwell.
Let Reason then at her own quarry fly,
But how can finite grasp infinity? 105
    'T is urged again, that faith did first com-
    mence
By miracles, which are appeals to sense,
And thence concluded, that our sense must
    be
The motive still of credibility.
For later ages must on former wait, 110
And what began belief must propagate.
    But winnow well this thought, and you
    shall find
'T is light as chaff that flies before the wind.
Were all those wonders wrought by power
    divine
As means or ends of some more deep de-
    sign? 115
Most sure as means, whose end was this
    alone,
To prove the Godhead of the eternal Son
God thus asserted: man is to believe
Beyond what sense and reason can con-
    ceive,
And for mysterious things of faith rely 120
On the proponent Heaven's authority.
If then our faith we for our guide admit,
Vain is the farther search of human wit;
As when the building gains a surer stay,
We take the unuseful scaffolding away. 125

Reason by sense no more can understand;
The game is played into another hand.
Why chose we then like bilanders to creep
Along the coast, and land in view to keep,
When safely we may launch into the deep?
In the same vessel which our Savior bore,
Himself the pilot, let us leave the shore, 132
And with a better guide a better world ex-
plore.
Could he his godhead veil with flesh and
blood
And not veil these again to be our food?
His grace in both is equal in extent;   136
The first affords us life, the second nourish-
ment.
And if he can, why all this frantic pain
To construe what his clearest words con-
tain,
And make a riddle what he made so plain?
To take up half on trust and half to try, 141
Name it not faith, but bungling bigotry.
Both knave and fool the merchant we may
call
To pay great sums and to compound the
small,
For who would break with Heaven, and
would not break for all?   145
Rest then, my soul, from endless anguish
freed:
Nor sciences thy guide, nor sense thy creed.
Faith is the best insurer of thy bliss;
The bank above must fail before the ven-
ture miss.
But Heaven and heaven-born faith are far
from thee,   150
Thou first apostate to divinity.
Unkennelled range in thy Polonian plains;
A fiercer foe, the insatiate Wolf remains.
  Too boastful Britain, please thyself no
more
That beasts of prey are banished from thy
shore;   155
The Bear, the Boar, and every savage name,
Wild in effect, though in appearance tame,
Lay waste thy woods, destroy thy blissful
bower,
And, muzzled though they seem, the mutes
devour.
More haughty than the rest, the wolfish
race   160
Appear with belly gaunt and famished face;
Never was so deformed a beast of grace.
His ragged tail betwixt his legs he wears,
Close clapped for shame; but his rough
crest he rears,
And pricks up his predestinating ears. 165
His wild disordered walk, his haggard eyes,
Did all the bestial citizens surprise:

Though feared and hated, yet he ruled a
while,
As captain or companion of the spoil.
Full many a year his hateful head had
been   170
For tribute paid, nor since in Cambria seen;
The last of all the litter 'scaped by chance,
And from Geneva first infested France.
Some authors thus his pedigree will trace,
But others write him of an upstart race; 175
Because of Wyclif's brood no mark he
brings
But his innate antipathy to kings.
These last deduce him from the Helvetian
kind,
Who near the Leman lake his consort lined;
That fiery Zuinglius first the affection bred,
And meager Calvin blessed the nuptial bed.
In Israel some believe him whelped long
since,   182
When the proud sanhedrim oppressed the
prince,
Or, since he will be Jew, derive him higher,
When Corah with his brethren did con-
spire   185
From Moses' hand the sovereign sway to
wrest,
And Aaron of his ephod to divest;
Till opening earth made way for all to
pass,
And could not bear the burden of a class.
The Fox and he came shuffled in the dark,
If ever they were stowed in Noah's ark; 191
Perhaps not made; for all their barking
train
The Dog (a common species) will contain;
And some wild curs, who from their mas-
ters ran,
Abhorring the supremacy of man,   195
In woods and caves the rebel-race began.
  O happy pair, how well have you in-
creased!
What ills in church and state have you
redressed!
With teeth untried and rudiments of claws,
Your first essay was on your native laws:
Those having torn with ease and trampled
down,   201
Your fangs you fastened on the mitered
crown,
And freed from God and monarchy your
town.
What though your native kennel still be
small,
Bounded betwixt a puddle and a wall; 205
Yet your victorious colonies are sent
Where the North Ocean girds the conti-
nent.

Quickened with fire below, your monsters
   breed
In fenny Holland and in fruitful Tweed;
And, like the first, the last affects to be   210
Drawn to the dregs of a democracy.
As, where in fields the fairy rounds are
   seen
A rank sour herbage rises on the green;
So, springing where these midnight elves
   advance,
Rebellion prints the footsteps of the dance.
Such are their doctrines, such contempt
   they show   216
To Heaven above and to their prince be-
   low,
As none but traitors and blasphemers
   know.
God like the tyrant of the skies is placed,
And kings, like slaves, beneath the crowd
   debased.   220
So fulsome is their food that flocks refuse
To bite, and only dogs for physic use.
As, where the lightning runs along the
   ground,
No husbandry can heal the blasting wound;
Nor bladed grass nor bearded corn suc-
   ceeds,   225
But scales of scurf, and putrefaction breeds:
Such wars, such waste, such fiery tracks of
   dearth
Their zeal has left, and such a teemless
   earth.
But as the poisons of the deadliest kind
Are to their own unhappy coasts confined,
As only Indian shades of sight deprive,   231
And magic plants will but in Colchos thrive,
So Presbytery and pestilential zeal
Can only flourish in a common-weal.

* * *

These are the chief; to number o'er the
   rest   235
And stand, like Adam, naming every beast,
Were weary work; nor will the Muse de-
   scribe
A slimy-born and sun-begotten tribe,
Who, far from steeples and their sacred
   sound,
In fields their sullen conventicles found. 240
These gross, half-animated lumps I leave,
Nor can I think what thoughts they can
   conceive.
But if they think at all, 't is sure no higher
Than matter put in motion may aspire;
Souls that can scarce ferment their mass of
   clay,   245
So drossy, so divisible are they
As would but serve pure bodies for allay,

Such souls as shards produce, such beetle
   things
As only buzz to heaven with evening wings,
Strike in the dark, offending but by chance,
Such are the blindfold blows of ignorance.
They know not beings, and but hate a
   name;   252
To them the Hind and Panther are the
   same.
   The Panther, sure the noblest next the
   Hind
And fairest creature of the spotted kind;
Oh, could her inborn stains be washed
   away   256
She were too good to be a beast of prey!
How can I praise or blame, and not of-
   fend,
Or how divide the frailty from the friend?
Her faults and virtues lie so mixed, that
   she   260
Nor wholly stands condemned nor wholly
   free.
Then, like her injured Lion, let me speak;
He cannot bend her and he would not
   break.
Unkind already, and estranged in part,
The Wolf begins to share her wandering
   heart.   265
Though unpolluted yet with actual ill,
She half commits who sins but in her will.
If, as our dreaming Platonists report,
There could be spirits of a middle sort,
Too black for heaven and yet too white for
   hell,   270
Who just dropped half-way down, nor lower
   fell;
So poised, so gently she descends from
   high,
It seems a soft dismission from the sky.
Her house not ancient, whatsoe'er pretense
Her clergy heralds make in her defense 275
A second century not half-way run,
Since the new honors of her blood begun.
* * *
   Thus is the Panther neither loved nor
   feared,
A mere mock queen of a divided herd;
Whom soon by lawful power she might
   control,   280
Herself a part submitted to the whole.
Then, as the moon who first receives the
   light
By which she makes our nether regions
   bright,
So might she shine, reflecting from afar
The rays she borrowed from a better star;
Big with the beams which from her mother
   flow

And reigning o'er the rising tides below:
Now mixing with a savage crowd she goes,
And meanly flatters her inveterate foes,
Ruled while she rules, and losing every
  hour   290
Her wretched remnants of precarious
  power.
  One evening, while the cooler shade she
    sought,
Revolving many a melancholy thought,
Alone she walked, and looked around in
  vain   294
With rueful visage for her vanished train:
None of her sylvan subjects made their
  court;
Levees and couchees passed without resort.
So hardly can usurpers manage well
Those whom they first instructed to rebel.
More liberty begets desire of more;   300
The hunger still increases with the store.
Without respect they brushed along the
  wood,
Each in his clan, and, filled with loathsome
  food,
Asked no permission to the neighboring
  flood.
The Panther, full of inward discontent, 305
Since they would go, before them wisely
  went;
Supplying want of power by drinking first,
As if she gave them leave to quench their
  thirst.
Among the rest, the Hind with fearful face
Beheld from far the common watering-
  place,   310
Nor durst approach; till with an awful roar
The sovereign Lion bade her fear no more.
Encouraged thus, she brought her young-
  lings nigh,
Watching the motions of her patron's eye,
And drank a sober draft; the rest
  amazed   315
Stood mutely still and on the stranger
  gazed;
Surveyed her part by part, and sought to
  find
The ten-horned monster in the harmless
  Hind,
Such as the Wolf and Panther had
  designed.
They thought at first they dreamed: for
  't was offense   320
With them to question certitude of sense,
Their guide in faith: but nearer when they
  drew,
And had the faultless object full in view,
Lord, how they all admired her heavenly
  hue!   324

Some, who before her fellowship disdained,
Scarce, and but scarce, from inborn rage
  restrained,
Now frisked about her and old kindred
  feigned.
Whether for love or interest, every sect
Of all the savage nation showed respect.
The viceroy Panther could not awe the
  herd;   330
The more the company, the less they feared
The surly Wolf with secret envy burst,
Yet could not howl, the Hind had seen him
  first;
But what he durst not speak, the Panther
  durst.

       * * *   (1687)

ALEXANDER'S FEAST
OR THE POWER OF MUSIC

  A SONG IN HONOR OF ST. CECILIA'S DAY

I

'T was at the royal feast for Persia won
  By Philip's warlike son:
  Aloft in awful state
  The godlike hero sate
    On his imperial throne;
His valiant peers were placed around;
Their brows with roses and with myrtles
  bound
(So should desert in arms be crowned).
The lovely Thais, by his side,
Sate like a blooming Eastern bride,   10
In flower of youth and beauty's pride.
  Happy, happy, happy, pair!
    None but the brave,
    None but the brave,
  None but the brave deserves the fair. 15

CHORUS: Happy, happy, happy pair, etc.

2

  Timotheus, placed on high
    Amid the tuneful quire,
With flying fingers touched the lyre:
The trembling notes ascend the sky,   20
  And heavenly joys inspire
The song began from Jove,
Who left his blissful seats above
(Such is the power of mighty love).
A dragon's fiery form belied the god: 25
Sublime on radiant spires he rode,
When he to fair Olympia pressed:
  And while he sought her snowy breast.
Then round her slender waist he curled.

And stamped an image of himself, a
    sovereign of the world. 30
The listening crowd admire the lofty
    sound,
A present deity, they shout around;
A present deity the vaulted roofs re-
    bound:
      With ravished ears
      The monarch hears, 35
      Assumes the god,
      Affects to nod,
And seems to shake the spheres.

CHORUS: With ravished ears, etc.

3

The praise of Bacchus then the sweet
    musician sung, 40
Of Bacchus ever fair, and ever young.
The jolly god in triumph comes;
Sound the trumpets, beat the drums;
    Flushed with a purple grace
    He shows his honest face: 45
Now give the hautboys breath; he comes,
    he comes.
    Bacchus, ever fair and young,
    Drinking joys did first ordain;
    Bacchus' blessings are a treasure,
    Drinking is the soldier's pleasure; 50
      Rich the treasure,
      Sweet the pleasure,
    Sweet is pleasure after pain.

CHORUS: Bacchus' blessings are a treasure,
    etc.

4

Soothed with the sound the king grew vain;
    Fought all his battles o'er again; 56
And thrice he routed all his foes, and thrice
    he slew the slain.
The master saw the madness rise,
His glowing cheeks, his ardent eyes;
And while he heaven and earth defied, 60
Changed his hand, and checked his pride.
    He chose a mournful Muse,
    Soft pity to infuse;
    He sung Darius great and good,
    By too severe a fate, 65
    Fallen, fallen, fallen, fallen,
    Fallen from his high estate,
    And weltering in his blood;
    Deserted at his utmost need
    By those his former bounty fed! 70
    On the bare earth exposed he lies,
    With not a friend to close his eyes.
With downcast looks the joyless victor
    sate.

Revolving in his altered soul
    The various turns of chance below;
And, now and then, a sigh he stole, 76
    And tears began to flow.

CHORUS: Revolving in the altered soul, etc.

5

The mighty master smiled to see
That love was in the next degree; 80
'T was but a kindred sound to move,
For pity melts the mind to love.
    Softly sweet in Lydian measures,
    Soon he soothed his soul to pleasures.
War, he sung, is toil and trouble; 85
Honor but an empty bubble;
    Never ending, still beginning,
    Fighting still, and still destroying:
    If the world be worth thy winning,
    Think, O think it worth enjoying: 90
    Lovely Thais sits beside thee,
    Take the good the gods provide thee.
The many rend the skies with loud ap-
    plause;
So love was crowned, but Music won the
    cause.
The prince, unable to conceal his pain, 95
    Gazed on the fair
    Who caused his care,
    And sighed and looked, sighed and
      looked,
    Sighed and looked, and sighed again·
At length, with love and wine at once op-
    pressed, 100
The vanquished victor sunk upon her
    breast.

CHORUS: The prince, unable to conceal his
    pain, etc.

6

Now strike the golden lyre again;
A louder yet, and yet a louder strain.
Break his bands of sleep asunder, 105
And rouse him, like a rattling peal of
    thunder.
    Hark, hark, the horrid sound
    Has raised up his head;
    As awaked from the dead,
    And amazed, he stares around. 110
Revenge, revenge, Timotheus cries,
    See the Furies arise;
    See the snakes that they rear,
    How they hiss in their hair,
    And the sparkles that flash from their
      eyes!
    Behold a ghastly band, 116
    Each a torch in his hand!

Those are Grecian ghosts, that in battle
　　　were slain,
　　And unburied remain
　　Inglorious on the plain:　　　　120
　　Give the vengeance due
　　To the valiant crew.
Behold how they toss their torches on high,
　How they point to the Persian abodes,
And glittering temples of their hostile gods.
The princes applaud with a furious joy;
And the king seized a flambeau with zeal to
　　　　destroy;　　　　　　　　127
　　　Thais led the way,
　　　To light him to his prey,
And, like another Helen, fired another
　　　Troy.　　　　　　　　　　130
Chorus: And the king seized a flambeau
　　　zeal to destroy, etc.

7

　　Thus long ago,
Ere heaving bellows learned to blow,
　While organs yet were mute,
Timotheus, to his breathing flute 135
　And sounding lyre,
Could swell the soul to rage, or kindle soft
　　　desire.
At last divine Cecilia came,
　Inventress of the vocal frame;
The sweet enthusiast, from her sacred
　　　store,　　　　　　　　　140
　Enlarged the former narrow bounds,
　And added length to solemn sounds,
With Nature's mother-wit, and arts un-
　　　known before.
　Let old Timotheus yield the prize,
　Or both divide the crown:　　　145
He raised a mortal to the skies;
　She drew an angel down.

Grand Chorus: At last divine Cecilia
　　　came, etc.

　　　　　　　　　　　(1697)

AN ESSAY OF DRAMATIC POESY

It was that memorable day, in the first
summer of the late war, when our navy
engaged the Dutch — a day wherein the
two most mighty and best appointed fleets
which any age had ever seen, disputed
the command of the greater half of the
globe, the commerce of nations, and the
riches of the universe. While these
vast floating bodies, on either side, moved
against each other in parallel lines, and

our countrymen, under the happy conduct
of his royal highness, went breaking, by
little and little, into the line of the
enemies, the noise of the cannon from
both navies reached our ears about the
city; so that all men being alarmed with
it, and in a dreadful suspense of the
event, which they knew was then deciding, every one went following the sound
as his fancy led him. And leaving the
town almost empty, some took towards
the Park, some cross the river, others
down it; all seeking the noise in the depth
of silence.

Among the rest, it was the fortune of
Eugenius, Crites, Lisideius, and Neander,
to be in company together: three of them
persons whom their wit and quality have
made known to all the town; and whom
I have chosen to hide under these borrowed names, that they may not suffer
by so ill a relation as I am going to make
of their discourse.

Taking then a barge, which a servant
of Lisideius had provided for them, they
made haste to shoot the bridge, and left
behind them that great fall of waters
which hindered them from hearing what
they desired; after which, having disen-
gaged themselves from many vessels
which rode at anchor in the Thames, and
almost blocked up the passage towards
Greenwich, they ordered the watermen to
let fall their oars more gently; and then
every one favoring his own curiosity
with a strict silence, it was not long ere
they perceived the air to break about
them like the noise of distant thunder, or
of swallows in a chimney: those little
undulations of sound, though almost
vanishing before they reached them, yet
still seeming to retain somewhat of their
first horror which they had betwixt the
fleets.

After they had attentively listened till
such time as the sound by little and little
went from them, Eugenius, lifting up his
head, and taking notice of it, was the first
who congratulated to the rest that happy
omen of our nation's victory: adding,
that we had but this to desire in confirmation of it, that we might hear no
more of that noise which was now leaving the English coast.

When the rest had concurred in the
same opinion, Crites (a person of a
sharp judgment, and somewhat a too
delicate taste in wit, which the world

have mistaken in him for ill nature), said, smiling to us, that if the concernment of this battle had not been so exceeding great, he could scarce have wished the victory at the price he knew 5 he must pay for it, in being subject to the reading and hearing of so many ill verses as he was sure would be made on that subject. Adding, that no argument could 'scape some of those eternal 10 rimers, who watch a battle with more diligence than the ravens and birds of prey; and the worst of them surest to be first in upon the quarry; while the better able, either out of modesty writ 15 not at all, or set that due value upon their poems, as to let them be often desired, and long expected.

There are some of those impertinent people of whom you speak (answered 20 Lisideius) who, to my knowledge, are already so provided, either way, that they can produce not only a panegyric upon the victory, but, if need be, a funeral elegy on the duke; wherein, after they 25 have crowned his valor with many laurels, they will at last deplore the odds under which he fell, concluding, that his courage deserved a better destiny.

* * * 30

There are so few who write well, in this age (said Crites), that methinks any praises should be welcome. They neither rise to the dignity of the last 35 age, nor to any of the ancients: and we may cry out of the writers of this time, with more reason than Petronius of his, *Pace vestra liceat dixisse, primi omnium eloquentiam perdidistis:* You have de- 40 bauched the true old poetry so far, that Nature, which is the soul of it, is not in any of your writings!

If your quarrel (said Eugenius) to those who now write, be grounded only 45 upon your reverence to antiquity, there is no man more ready to adore those great Greeks and Romans than I am; but, on the other side, I cannot think so contemptibly of the age in which I live, or 50 so dishonorably of my own country, as not to judge we equal the ancients in most kinds of poesy, and in some surpass them. Neither know I any reason why I may not be as zealous for the reputation 55 of our age, as we find the ancients themselves were in reference to those who lived before them. For you hear your Horace saying,

Indignor quidquam reprehendi, non quia crasse
Compositum, illepideve putetur, sed quia nuper.

[I am indignant when anything is blamed, not because it is thought badly or inelegantly written, but because it is new.]

And after:

Si meliora dies, ut vina, poemata reddit,
Scire velim, pretium chartis quotus arroget annus?

[If time makes poems better, as it does wines, I should like to know what length of years gives value to writings.]

But I see I am engaging in a wide dispute, where the arguments are not like to reach close on either side; for poesy is of so large an extent, and so many, both of the ancients and moderns, have done well in all kinds of it, that in citing one against the other, we shall take up more time this evening, than each man's occasions will allow him. Therefore I would ask Crites to what part of poesy he would confine his arguments, and whether he would defend the general cause of the ancients against the moderns, or oppose any age of the moderns against this of ours.

Crites, a little while considering upon this demand, told Eugenius, that if he pleased he would limit their dispute to dramatic poesy; in which he thought it not difficult to prove, either that the ancients were superior to the moderns, or the last age to this of ours.

Eugenius was somewhat surprised, when he heard Crites make choice of that subject. For aught I see (said he), I have undertaken a harder province than I imagined; for, though I never judged the plays of the Greek or Roman poets comparable to ours, yet, on the other side, those we now see acted come short of many which were written in the last age. But my comfort is, if we are overcome, it will be only by our own countrymen; and if we yield to them in this one part of poesy, we more surpass them in all the other; for in the epic or lyric way, it will be hard for them to show us one such amongst them, as we have many now living, or who lately were. They can produce nothing so courtly writ, or which expresses so much the conversation of a gentleman, as Sir John Suckling; nothing so even, sweet, and flowing, as Mr. Waller; nothing so majestic, so correct, as Sir John Denham; nothing so elevated, so copious, and full of spirit, as Mr. Cowley. As for the Italian, French, and Spanish plays, I can make it evident that those who now write surpass them; and that the drama is wholly ours.

All of them were thus far of Eugenius his opinion, that the sweetness of English verse was never understood or practised by our fathers; even Crites himself did not much oppose it. And every one was willing to acknowledge how much our poesy is improved, by the happiness of some writers yet living, who first taught us to mold our thoughts into easy and significant words, to retrench the superfluities of expression, and to make our rime so properly a part of the verse, that it should never mislead the sense, but itself be led and governed by it.

Eugenius was going to continue this discourse, when Lisideius told him that it was necessary, before they proceeded further, to take a standing measure of their controversy; for how was it possible to be decided, who wrote the best plays, before we know what a play should be? But, this once agreed on by both parties, each might have recourse to it, either to prove his own advantages, or to discover the failings of his adversary.

He had no sooner said this, but all desired the favor of him to give the definition of a play; and they were the more importunate, because neither Aristotle, nor Horace, nor any other, who had writ of that subject, had ever done it.

Lisideius, after some modest denials, at last confessed he had a rude notion of it; indeed rather a description than a definition; but which served to guide him in his private thoughts, when he was to make a judgment of what others writ; that he conceived a play ought to be, 'A just and lively image of human nature, representing its passions and humors, and the changes of fortune to which it is subject, for the delight and instruction of mankind.'

This definition (though Crites raised a logical objection against it — that it was only *a genere et fine,* and so not altogether perfect) was yet well received by the rest; and after they had given order to the waterman to turn their barge, and row softly, that they might take the cool of the evening in their return, Crites, being desired by the company to begin, spoke on behalf of the ancients, in this manner: —

If confidence presage a victory, Eugenius, in his own opinion, has already triumphed over the ancients: nothing seems more easy to him than to overcome those whom it is our greatest praise to have imitated well; for we do not only build upon their foundations, but by their models. Dramatic poesy had time enough, reckoning from Thespis (who first invented it) to Aristophanes, to be born, to grow up, and to flourish in maturity. It has been observed of arts and sciences, that in one and the same century they have arrived to great perfection; and no wonder, since every age has a kind of universal genius, which inclines those that live in it to some particular studies. The work then being pushed on by many hands, must of necessity go forward.

Is it not evident, in these last hundred years (when the study of philosophy has been the business of all the virtuosi in christendom), that almost a new nature has been revealed to us? that more errors of the school have been detected, more useful experiments in philosophy have been made, more noble secrets in optics, medicine, anatomy, astronomy, discovered, than in all those credulous and doting ages from Aristotle to us? So true it is, that nothing spreads more fast than science, when rightly and generally cultivated.

Add to this, the more than common emulation that was in those times, of writing well; which though it be found in all ages and all persons that pretend to the same reputation, yet poesy being then in more esteem than now it is, had greater honors decreed to the professors of it, and consequently the rivalship was more high between them. They had judges ordained to decide their merit, and prizes to reward it; and historians have been diligent to record of Æschylus, Euripides, Sophocles, Lycophron, and the rest of them, both who they were that vanquished in these wars of the theater, and how often they were crowned; while the Asian kings and Grecian common-

Aristotle – unity of plot

wealths scarce afforded them a nobler subject than the unmanly luxuries of a debauched court, or giddy intrigues of a factious city. *Alit aemulatio ingenia,* (says Paterculus) *et nunc invidia, nunc admiratio incitationem accendit:* Emulation is the spur of wit; and sometimes envy, sometimes admiration, quickens our endeavors.

But now since the rewards of honor are taken away, that virtuous emulation is turned into direct malice; yet so slothful, that it contents itself to condemn and cry down others, without attempting to do better. 'T is a reputation too unprofitable, to take the necessary pains for it; yet wishing they had it, that desire is incitement enough to hinder others from it. And this, in short, Eugenius, is the reason, why you have now so few good poets, and so many severe judges. Certainly, to imitate the ancients well, much labor and long study is required; which pains, I have already shown, our poets would want encouragement to take, if yet they had ability to go through the work. Those ancients have been faithful imitators, and wise observers of that nature which is so torn and ill represented in our plays; they have handed down to us a perfect resemblance of her; which we, like ill copiers, neglecting to look on, have rendered monstrous, and disfigured. But, that you may know how much you are indebted to those your masters, and be ashamed to have so ill requited them, I must remember you, that all the rules by which we practise the drama at this day (either such as relate to the justness and symmetry of the plot; or the episodical ornaments, such as descriptions, narrations, and other beauties, which are not essential to the play) were delivered to us from the observations which Aristotle made, of those poets, who either lived before him, or were his contemporaries. We have added nothing of our own, except we have the confidence to say, our wit is better; of which none boast in this our age, but such as understand not theirs. Of that book which Aristotle has left us, περὶ τῆς Ποιητικῆς, Horace his *Art of Poetry,* is an excellent comment, and, I believe, restores to us that Second Book of his concerning comedy, which is wanting in him.

Out of these two have been extracted the famous rules which the French call *les trois unités,* or the three unities, which ought to be observed in every regular play; namely, of time, place, and action.

The unity of time they comprehend in twenty-four hours, the compass of a natural day, or as near as it can be contrived; and the reason of it is obvious to every one,—that the time of the feigned action, or fable of the play, should be proportioned as near as can be to the duration of that time in which it is represented. Since therefore all plays are acted on the theater in a space of time much within the compass of twenty-four hours, that play is to be thought the nearest imitation of nature, whose plot or action is confined within that time. And by the same rule which concludes this general proportion of time, it follows that all the parts of it are (as near as may be) to be equally subdivided; namely, that one act take not up the supposed time of half a day, which is out of proportion to the rest; since the other four are then to be straitened within the compass of the remaining half: for it is unnatural, that one act, which being spoken or written, is not longer than the rest, should be supposed longer by the audience. It is therefore the poet's duty, to take care, that no act should be imagined to exceed the time in which it is represented on the stage; and that the intervals and inequalities of time be supposed to fall out between the acts.

This rule of time, how well it has been observed by the ancients, most of their plays will witness. You see them in their tragedies (wherein to follow this rule is certainly most difficult), from the very beginning of their plays, falling close into that part of the story which they intend for the action, or principal object of it, leaving the former part to be delivered by narration: so that they set the audience, as it were, at the post where the race is to be concluded; and saving them the tedious expectation of seeing the poet set out and ride the beginning of the course, they suffer you not to behold him, till he is in sight of the goal, and just upon you.

For the second unity, which is that of place, the ancients meant by it, that the scene ought to be continued through the play, in the same place where it was laid in the beginning; for the stage, on which it is represented, being but one and the same place, it is unnatural to conceive it many; and those far distant from one another. I will not deny, but by the variation of painted scenes, the fancy (which in these cases will contribute to its own deceit) may sometimes imagine it several places, with some appearance of probability; yet it still carries the greater likelihood of truth, if those places be supposed so near each other, as in the same town or city, which may all be comprehended under the larger denomination of one place; for a greater distance will bear no proportion to the shortness of time which is allotted, in the acting, to pass from one of them to another. For the observation of this, next to the ancients, the French are to be most commended. They tie themselves so strictly to the unity of place, that you never see in any of their plays, a scene changed in the middle of an act: if the act begins in a garden, a street, or chamber, 't is ended in the same place; and that you may know it to be the same, the stage is so supplied with persons, that it is never empty all the time: he who enters second, has business with him who was on before; and before the second quits the stage, a third appears who has business with him. This Corneille calls *la liaison des scènes*, the continuity or joining of the scenes; and 't is a good mark of a well-contrived play, when all the persons are known to each other, and every one of them has some affairs with all the rest.

As for the third unity, which is that of action, the ancients meant no other by it than what the logicians do by their *finis*, the end or scope of any action; that which is the first in intention, and last in execution. Now the poet is to aim at one great and complete action, to the carrying on of which all things in his play, even the very obstacles, are to be subservient; and the reason of this is as evident as any of the former.

For two actions equally labored and driven on by the writer, would destroy the unity of the poem; it would be no longer one play, but two: not but that there may be many actions in a play, as Ben Jonson has observed in his *Discoveries;* but they must be all subservient to the great one, which our language

happily expresses in the name of underplots: such as in Terence's *Eunuch* is the difference and reconcilement of Thais and Phædria, which is not the chief business of the play, but promotes the marriage of Chærea and Chremes's sister, principally intended by the poet. There ought to be but one action (says Corneille), that is, one complete action, which leaves the mind of the audience in a full repose; but this cannot be brought to pass, but by many other imperfect actions, which conduce to it, and hold the audience in a delightful suspense of what will be.

If by these rules (to omit many other drawn from the precepts and practice of the ancients) we should judge our modern plays, 't is probable that few of them would endure the trial: that which should be the business of a day, takes up in some of them an age; instead of one action, they are the epitomes of a man's life, and for one spot of ground (which the stage should represent) we are sometimes in more countries than the map can show us.

But if we allow the ancients to have contrived well, we must acknowledge them to have written better. Questionless we are deprived of a great stock of wit in the loss of Menander among the Greek poets, and Cæcilius, Afranius, and Varius, among the Romans. We may guess at Menander's excellency, by the plays of Terence, who translated some of them; and yet wanted so much of him, that he was called by C. Cæsar the half-Menander; and may judge of Varius, by the testimonies of Horace, Martial, and Velleius Paterculus. 'T is probable that these, could they be recovered, would decide the controversy; but so long as Aristophanes and Plautus are extant, while the tragedies of Euripides, Sophocles, and Seneca, are in our hands, I can never see one of those plays which are now written, but it increases my admiration of the ancients. And yet I must acknowledge further, that to admire them as we ought, we should understand them better than we do. Doubtless many things appear flat to us, the wit of which depended on some custom or story, which never came to our knowledge; or perhaps on some criticism in their language, which being so long dead, and only remaining in their books, 't is not possible they should make us understand perfectly

To read Macrobius, explaining the propriety and elegancy of many words in Virgil, which I had before passed over without consideration, as common things, is enough to assure me, that I ought to think the same of Terence; and that in the purity of his style (which Tully so much valued, that he ever carried his works about him), there is yet left in him great room for admiration, if I knew but where to place it. In the meantime, I must desire you to take notice, that the greatest man of the last age (Ben Jonson) was willing to give place to them in all things: he was not only a professed imitator of Horace, but a learned plagiary of all the others; you track him everywhere in their snow. If Horace, Lucan, Petronius Arbiter, Seneca, and Juvenal, had their own from him, there are few serious thoughts which are new in him; you will pardon me, therefore, if I presume he loved their fashion, when he wore their clothes. But since I have otherwise a great veneration for him, and you, Eugenius, prefer him above all other poets, I will use no farther argument to you than his example: I will produce before you Father Ben, dressed in all the ornaments and colors of the ancients; you will need no other guide to our party, if you follow him; and whether you consider the bad plays of our age, or regard the good plays of the last, both the best and worst of the modern poets will equally instruct you to admire the ancients.

Crites had no sooner left speaking, but Eugenius, who had waited with some impatience for it, thus began: —

I have observed in your speech, that the former part of it is convincing, as to what the moderns have profited by the rules of the ancients; but in the latter you are careful to conceal how much they have excelled them. We own all the helps we have from them, and want neither veneration nor gratitude, while we acknowledge that to overcome them we must make use of the advantages we have received from them; but to these assistances we have joined our own industry; for, had we sat down with a dull imitation of them, we might then have lost somewhat of the old perfection, but never acquired any that was new. We draw not therefore after their lines, but those of nature; and having

the life before us, besides the experience of all they knew, it is no wonder if we hit some airs and features which they have missed. I deny not what you urge of arts and sciences, that they have flourished in some ages more than others; but your instance in philosophy makes for me: for if natural causes be more known now than in the time of Aristotle, because more studied, it follows that poesy and other arts may, with the same pains, arrive still nearer to perfection; and, that granted, it will rest for you to prove that they wrought more perfect images of human life, than we; which seeing in your discourse you have avoided to make good, it shall now be my task to show you some part of their defects, and some few excellencies of the moderns. And I think there is none among us can imagine I do it enviously, or with purpose to detract from them; for what interest of fame or profit can the living lose by the reputation of the dead? On the other side, it is a great truth which Velleius Paterculus affirms: *Audita visis libentius laudamus; et praesentia invidia, praeterita admiratione prosequimur; et his nos obrui, illis instrui credimus* [We praise things reported more willingly than those seen; and things of the present we pursue with envy, those of the past with admiration, believing ourselves to be hindered by the former and helped by the latter]. That praise or censure is certainly the most sincere, which unbribed posterity shall give us.

Be pleased then, in the first place, to take notice, that the Greek poesy, which Crites has affirmed to have arrived to perfection in the reign of the old comedy, was so far from it, that the distinction of it into acts was not known to them; or if it were, it is yet so darkly delivered to us, that we cannot make it out.

All we know of it is, from the singing of their chorus; and that too is so uncertain, that in some of their plays we have reason to conjecture they sung more than five times. Aristotle indeed divides the integral parts of a play into four. First, the *Protasis*, or entrance, which gives light only to the characters of the persons, and proceeds very little into any part of the action. Secondly, the *Epitasis*, or working up of the plot; where the play grows warmer, the design or action of it is drawing on, and you see something promising that it will come to pass. Thirdly, the *Catastasis*, called by the Romans, *Status,* the height and full growth of the play: we may call it properly the counterturn, which destroys that expectation, embroils the action in new difficulties, and leaves you far distant from that hope in which it found you; as you may have observed in a violent stream, resisted by a narrow passage,— it runs round to an eddy, and carries back the waters with more swiftness than it brought them on. Lastly, the *Catastrophe,* which the Grecians called λύσις, the French *le dénouement,* and we the discovery, or unraveling of the plot: there you see all things settling again upon their first foundations, and, the obstacles which hindered the design or action of the play once removed, it ends with that resemblance of truth and nature, that the audience are satisfied with the conduct of it. Thus this great man delivered to us the image of a play; and I must confess it is so lively, that from thence much light has been derived to the forming it more perfectly into acts and scenes; but what poet first limited to five the number of the acts, I know not; only we see it so firmly established in the time of Horace, that he gives it for a rule in comedy: — *Neu brevior quinto, neu sit productior actu* [Let it be neither shorter nor longer than five acts]. So that you see the Grecians cannot be said to have consummated this art; writing rather by entrances, than by acts, and having rather a general indigested notion of a play, than knowing how, and where to bestow the particular graces of it.

But since the Spaniards at this day allow but three acts, which they call *jornadas,* to a play, and the Italians in many of theirs follow them, when I condemn the ancients, I declare it is not altogether because they have not five acts to every play, but because they have not confined themselves to one certain number; it is building a house without a model; and when they succeeded in such undertakings, they ought to have sacrificed to Fortune, not to the Muses.

Next, for the plot, which Aristotle called τὸ μυθὸς, and often τῶν πραγμάτων σύνθεσις, and from him the Romans *Fabula,* it has already been judiciously observed by a late writer, that in their tragedies it was only some tale derived from Thebes or Troy, or at least something that happened in those two ages; which was worn so thread-bare by the pens of all the epic poets, and even by tradition itself of the talkative Greeklings (as Ben Jonson calls them), that before it came upon the stage, it was already known to all the audience; and the people, so soon as ever they heard the name of Œdipus, knew as well as the poet, that he had killed his father by a mistake, and committed incest with his mother, before the play; that they were now to hear of a great plague, an oracle, and the ghost of Laius; so that they sat with a yawning kind of expectation, till he was to come with his eyes pulled out, and speak a hundred or more verses in a tragic tone, in complaint of his misfortunes. But one Œdipus, Hercules, or Medea, had been tolerable; poor people, they escaped not so good cheap; they had still the *chapon bouillé* [boiled chicken] set before them, till their appetites were cloyed with the same dish, and, the novelty being gone, the pleasure vanished; so that one main end of dramatic poesy in its definition, which was to cause delight, was of consequence destroyed.

In their comedies, the Romans generally borrowed their plots from the Greek poets; and theirs was commonly a little girl stolen or wandered from her parents, brought back unknown to the city, there got with child by some lewd young fellow, who, by the help of his servant, cheats his father; and when her time comes to cry *Juno Lucina, fer opem* [Help me, O goddess of childbearing]! one or other sees a little box or cabinet which was carried away with her, and so discovers her to her friends, if some god do not prevent it, by coming down in a machine, and taking the thanks of it to himself.

By the plot you may guess much of the characters of the persons. An old father, who would willingly, before he dies, see his son well married; his debauched son, kind in his nature to his mistress, but miserably in want of money; a servant or slave, who has so much wit to strike in with him, and help to dupe his father; a braggadocio captain, a parasite, and a lady of pleasure.

As for the poor honest maid, on whom

the story is built, and who ought to be one of the principal actors in the play, she is commonly a mute in it; she has the breeding of the old Elizabeth way, which was for maids to be seen, and not to be heard; and it is enough you know she is willing to be married, when the fifth act requires it.

These are plots built after the Italian mode of houses,— you see through them all at once; the characters are indeed the imitations of nature, but so narrow, as if they had imitated only an eye or an hand, and did not dare to venture on the lines of a face, or the proportion of a body.

But in how straight a compass soever they have bounded their plots and characters, we will pass it by, if they have regularly pursued them, and perfectly observed those three unities of time, place, and action; the knowledge of which you say is derived to us from them. But, in the first place, give me leave to tell you, that the unity of place, however it might be practised by them, was never any of their rules: we neither find it in Aristotle, Horace, or any who have written of it, till in our age the French poets first made it a precept of the stage. The unity of time, even Terence himself, who was the best and most regular of them, has neglected: his *Heautontimorumenos*, or Self-punisher, takes up visibly two days, says Scaliger; the two first acts concluding the first day, the three last the day ensuing; and Euripides, in tying himself to one day, has committed an absurdity never to be forgiven him; for in one of his tragedies he has made Theseus go from Athens to Thebes, which was about forty English miles, under the walls of it to give battle, and appear victorious in the next act; and yet, from the time of his departure to the return of the Nuntius, who gives the relation of his victory, Æthra and the Chorus have but thirty-six verses; which is not for every mile a verse.

The like error is as evident in Terence his *Eunuch*, when Laches, the old man, enters by mistake into the house of Thais; where, betwixt his exit, and the entrance of Pythias, who comes to give ample relation of the disorders he has raised within, Parmeno, who was left upon the stage, has not above five lines to speak. *C'est bien employer un temps si court* [This is making good use of so short a time], says the French poet, who furnished me with one of the observations: and almost all their tragedies will afford us examples of the like nature.

It is true, they have kept the continuity, or, as you called it, *liaison des scènes*, somewhat better: two do not perpetually come in together, talk, and go out together; and other two succeed them, and do the same throughout the act, which the English call by the name of single scenes; but the reason is, because they have seldom above two or three scenes, properly so called, in every act; for it is to be accounted a new scene, not only every time the stage is empty, but every person who enters, though to others, makes it so; because he introduces a new business. Now the plots of their plays being narrow, and the persons few, one of their acts was written in a less compass than one of our well-wrought scenes; and yet they are often deficient even in this. To go no farther than Terence, you find in the *Eunuch*, Antipho entering single in the midst of the third act, after Chremes and Pythias were gone off: in the same play you have likewise Dorias beginning the fourth act alone; and after she has made a relation of what was done at the Soldier's entertainment (which by the way was very inartificial, because she was presumed to speak directly to the audience, and to acquaint them with what was necessary to be known, but yet should have been so contrived by the poet, as to have been told by persons of the drama to one another, and so by them to have come to the knowledge of the people), she quits the stage, and Phædria enters next, alone likewise: he also gives you an account of himself, and of his returning from the country, in monologue; to which unnatural way of narration Terence is subject in all his plays. In his *Adelphi*, or Brothers, Syrus and Demea enter after the scene was broken by the departure of Sostrata, Geta, and Canthara; and indeed you can scarce look into any of his comedies, where you will not presently discover the same interruption.

But as they have failed both in laying of their plots, and in the management, swerving from the rules of their own art, by misrepresenting nature to us, in which they have ill satisfied one intention of a play, which was delight; so in the instructive part they have erred worse: instead of punishing vice, and rewarding virtue, they have often shown a prosperous wickedness, and an unhappy piety: they have set before us a bloody image of revenge in Medea, and given her dragons to convey her safe from punishment; a Priam and Astyanax murdered, and Cassandra ravished, and the lust and murder ending in the victory of him who acted them. In short, there is no indecorum in any of our modern plays, which, if I would excuse, I could not shadow with some authority from the ancients.

And one further note of them let me leave you: tragedies and comedies were not writ then, as they are now, promiscuously, by the same person; but he who found his genius bending to the one, never attempted the other way. This is so plain, that I need not instance to you that Aristophanes, Plautus, Terence, never, any of them, writ a tragedy; Æschylus, Euripides, Sophocles, and Seneca never meddled with comedy. The sock and buskin were not worn by the same poet. Having, then, so much care to excel in one kind, very little is to be pardoned them if they miscarried in it. And this would lead me to the consideration of their wit, had not Crites given me sufficient warning not to be too bold in my judgment of it; because, the languages being dead, and many of the customs and little accidents on which it depended lost to us, we are not competent judges of it. But though I grant that, here and there, we may miss the application of a proverb or a custom, yet a thing well said will be wit in all languages; and, though it may lose something in the translation, yet to him who reads it in the original, 'tis still the same: he has an idea of its excellency, though it cannot pass from his mind into any other expression or words than those in which he finds it.

* * *

As Neander was beginning to examine *The Silent Woman,* Eugenius, earnestly regarding him: I beseech you, Neander (said he), gratify the company, and me in particular, so far as, before you speak of the play, to give us a character of the author; and tell us frankly your opinion, whether you do not think all writers,

both French and English, ought to give place to him?

I fear (replied Neander) that, in obeying your commands, I shall draw some envy on myself. Besides, in performing them, it will be first necessary to speak somewhat of Shakspere and Fletcher, his rivals in poesy; and one of them, in my opinion, at least his equal, perhaps his superior.

To begin then with Shakspere. He was the man who of all modern, and perhaps ancient poets, had the largest and most comprehensive soul. All the images of nature were still present to him, and he drew them not laboriously, but luckily: when he describes anything, you more than see it, you feel it too. Those who accuse him to have wanted learning, give him the greater commendation: he was naturally learned; he needed not the spectacles of books to read nature; he looked inwards, and found her there. I cannot say he is everywhere alike; were he so, I should do him injury to compare him with the greatest of mankind. He is many times flat, insipid; his comic wit degenerating into clenches, his serious swelling into bombast. But he is always great, when some great occasion is presented to him: no man can say, he ever had a fit subject for his wit, and did not then raise himself as high above the rest of poets,

Quantum lenta solent inter viburna cupressi.
[As the cypresses tower above low-growing shrubs.]

The consideration of this made Mr. Hales of Eton say, that there was no subject of which any poet ever writ, but he would produce it much better done in Shakspere; and however others are now generally preferred before him, yet the age wherein he lived, which had contemporaries with him, Fletcher and Jonson, never equaled them to him in their esteem: and in the last king's court, when Ben's reputation was at highest, Sir John Suckling, and with him the greater part of the courtiers, set our Shakspere far above him.

Beaumont and Fletcher, of whom I am next to speak, had with the advantage of Shakspere's wit, which was their precedent, great natural gifts, improved by study; Beaumont especially being so accurate a judge of plays, that Ben Jonson, while he lived, submitted all his writings to his censure, and 't is thought, used his judgment in correcting, if not contriving all his plots. What value he had for him, appears by the verses he writ to him; and therefore I need speak no farther of it. The first play that brought Fletcher and him in esteem, was their *Philaster;* for before that, they had written two or three very unsuccessfully: as the like is reported of Ben Jonson, before he writ *Every Man in his Humor.* Their plots were generally more regular than Shakspere's, especially those which were made before Beaumont's death; and they understood and imitated the conversation of gentlemen much better; whose wild debaucheries, and quickness of wit in repartees, no poet before them could paint as they have done. Humor, which Ben Jonson derived from particular persons, they made it not their business to describe; they represented all the passions very lively, but above all, love. I am apt to believe the English language in them arrived to its highest perfection; what words have since been taken in, are rather superfluous than ornamental. Their plays are now the most pleasant and frequent entertainments of the stage; two of theirs being acted through the year for one of Shakspere's or Jonson's: the reason is, because there is a certain gaiety in their comedies, and pathos in their more serious plays, which suits generally with all men's humors. Shakspere's language is likewise a little obsolete, and Ben Jonson's wit comes short of theirs.

As for Jonson, to whose character I am now arrived, if we look upon him while he was himself (for his last plays were but his dotages), I think him the most learned and judicious writer which any theater ever had. He was a most severe judge of himself, as well as others. One cannot say he wanted wit, but rather that he was frugal of it. In his works you find little to retrench or alter. Wit and language, and humor also in some measure, we had before

him; but something of art was wanting to the drama, till he came. He managed his strength to more advantage than any who preceded him. You seldom find him making love in any of his scenes, or endeavoring to move the passions; his genius was too sullen and saturnine to do it gracefully, especially when he knew he came after those who had performed both to such a height. Humor was his proper sphere; and in that he delighted most to represent mechanic people. He was deeply conversant in the ancients, both Greek and Latin, and he borrowed boldly from them: there is scarce a poet or historian among the Roman authors of those times, whom he has not translated in *Sejanus* and *Catiline.* But he has done his robberies so openly, that one may see he fears not to be taxed by any law. He invades authors like a monarch; and what would be theft in other poets, is only victory in him. With the spoils of these writers he so represents old Rome to us, in its rites, ceremonies, and customs, that if one of their poets had written either of his tragedies, we had seen less of it than in him. If there was any fault in his language, it was, that he weaved it too closely and laboriously, in his comedies especially: perhaps, too, he did a little too much Romanize our tongue, leaving the words which he translated almost as much Latin as he found them; wherein, though he learnedly followed their language, he did not enough comply with the idiom of ours. If I would compare him with Shakspere, I must acknowledge him the more correct poet, but Shakspere the greater wit. Shakspere was the Homer, or father of our dramatic poets; Jonson was the Virgil, the pattern of elaborate writing; I admire him, but I love Shakspere. To conclude of him; as he has given us the most correct plays, so in the precepts which he has laid down in his *Discoveries,* we have as many and profitable rules for perfecting the stage, as any wherewith the French can furnish us.

* * * (1667)

DANIEL DEFOE (1661–1731)

Defoe was the son of a nonconformist butcher, and attended a dissenting school, where, according to his own account, he received a sound training in English and other modern languages as well as in the classics; his master, Morton, was a man of advanced ideas in education, and afterwards became vice-president of Harvard University. Defoe took part in the rebellion of Monmouth, engaged unsuccessfully in trade, and welcomed the Revolution. When William III was attacked as a foreigner, Defoe took up his defence in a satirical poem, *The True-born Englishman*, which ran through twenty-one editions and was sold in thousands in the streets. He published a number of political pamphlets, and one of them, *The Shortest Way with the Dissenters*, was so successful in its irony that it deceived both parties into accepting it as a serious plea for high church principles. When it became known that the author was a dissenter and that the tract was really a plea for toleration, the high church party were furious at the fraud practised upon them, and the dissenters were too sore and bewildered to defend him. Defoe was fined, imprisoned, and condemned to be exposed to public derision in the pillory (1703). But the people covered the pillory with flowers, drank his health, and bought copies of his *Hymn to the Pillory*, in which he denounced his antagonists as ' scandals to the times,' who ' are at a loss to find his guilt, and can't commit his crimes.' Defoe was not kept long in prison, and in 1704 he began the publication of the *Review*, which was continued till 1713 and marks an important advance in the development of journalism. As a journalist Defoe showed unwearied diligence, unsurpassed enterprise and resourcefulness, and a keen sense of popular interest. There are few features of the modern newspaper which are not represented in his writings. He wrote sometimes for one party, sometimes for another, and for some years he conducted Tory papers in the interests of the Whig government, by which he was employed in the secret service. His style is remarkably simple and direct, and the ' stories ' he invented can hardly be distinguished from genuine narratives. Of his numerous works, which would make a considerable library if reprinted, the one which has earned most enduring popularity is *Robinson Crusoe* (1720), a realistic autobiography of a sailor cast away upon a desolate island. It has been translated into almost every literary language and has been followed by countless imitations.

From THE TRUE BORN ENGLISHMAN

A true born Englishman's a contradiction!
In speech, an irony; in fact, a fiction!
A banter made to be a test of fools!
Which those that use it, justly ridicules;
A metaphor invented to express   5
A man akin to all the universe!

For as the Scots, as learned men have said,
Throughout the world their wandering seed
   have spread,
So open-handed England, 't is believed,
Has all the gleanings of the world received.
Some think, of England 't was, our Savior
   meant   11
The Gospel should, to all the world be sent,
Since, when the blessed sound did hither
   reach,
They to all nations might be said to preach.

'T is well that virtue gives nobility;   15
How shall we else the want of birth and
   blood supply?
Since scarce one family is left alive,
Which does not from some foreigner de-
   rive.
Of sixty thousand English gentlemen
Whose names and arms in registers remain,
We challenge all our heralds to declare   21
Ten families which English Saxons are!

France justly boasts the ancient noble line
Of Bourbon, Montmorency, and Lorraine.
The Germans, too, their House of Austria
   show,   25
And Holland their invincible Nassau —
Lines which in heraldry were ancient grown,
Before the name of Englishman was known.
Even Scotland, too, her elder glory shows!
Her Gordons, Hamiltons, and her Monroes;

Douglas, Mackays, and Grahams, names
   well known   31
Long before ancient England knew her
   own.

But England, modern to the last degree,
Borrows or makes her own nobility,
And yet she boldly boasts of pedigree!   35
Repines that foreigners are put upon her,
And talks of her antiquity and honor!
Her S[ackvil]les, S[avi]les, C[eci]ls, Dela-
   [me]res,
M[ohu]ns and M[ontag]ues, D[ura]s, and
   V[ee]res;
Not one have English names, yet all are
   English peers!   40
Your Houblons, Papillons, and Lethuliers
Pass now for true born English knights
   and squires,
And make good senate members, or lord
   mayors,
Wealth (howsoever got) in England, makes
Lords, of mechanics! gentlemen, of rakes!
Antiquity and birth are needless here.   46
'T is impudence and money make a p[ee]r!

* * *

THE CONCLUSION

Then let us boast of ancestors no more,
Or deeds of heroes done in days of yore,
In latent records of the ages past,   50
Behind the rear of time, in long oblivion
   placed.
For if our virtues must in lines descend,
The merit with the families would end,
And intermixtures would most fatal grow,
For vice would be hereditary too;   55
The tainted blood would of necessity,
In voluntary wickedness convey!

Vice, like ill-nature, for an age or two,
May seem a generation to pursue:
But virtue seldom does regard the breed, 60
Fools do the wise, and wise men fools suc-
   ceed.
What is it to us, what ancestors we had?
If good, what better? or what worse. if
   bad?
Examples are for imitation set,
Yet all men follow virtue with regret.   65

Could but our ancestors retrieve their fate,
And see their offspring thus degenerate;
How we contend for birth and names un-
   known,
And build on their past actions, not our
   own;
They'd cancel records, and their tombs de-
   face.   70

And openly disown the vile degenerate
   race!
For fame of families is all a cheat;
'T is personal virtue only makes us great!
                  (1701)

THE SHORTEST WAY WITH THE DISSENTERS

Sir Roger L'Estrange tells us a story in his collection of Fables, of the cock and the horses. The cock was gotten to roost in the stable among the horses; and there being no racks or other conveniences for him, it seems he was forced to roost upon the ground. The horses jostling about for room and putting the cock in danger of his life, he gives them this grave advice, 'Pray, gentlefolks! let us stand still! for fear we should tread upon one another!'

There are some people in the world, who, now they are unperched, and reduced to an equality with other people, and under strong and very just apprehensions of being further treated as they deserve, begin with Esop's cock, to preach up peace and union and the christian duty of moderation; forgetting that when they had the power in their hands, those graces were strangers in their gates!

It is now near fourteen years, that the glory and peace of the purest and most flourishing church in the world has been eclipsed, buffeted, and disturbed by a sort of men whom God in his providence has suffered to insult over her, and bring her down. These have been the days of her humiliation and tribulation. She has borne with an invincible patience the reproach of the wicked; and God has at last heard her prayers, and delivered her from the oppression of the stranger.

And now, they find their day is over, their power gone, and the throne of this nation possessed by a royal, English, true, and ever constant member of, and friend to, the Church of England. Now they find that they are in danger of the Church of England's just resentments. Now, they cry out, 'Peace!' 'Union!' 'Forbearance!' and 'Charity!': as if the Church had not too long harbored her enemies under her wing, and nourished the viperous brood, till they hiss and fly in the face of the mother that cherished them!

No, gentlemen, the time of mercy is past, your day of grace is over, you should have practised peace, and moderation, and charity, if you expected any yourselves.

We have heard none of this lesson for fourteen years past. We have been huffed and bullied with your Act of Toleration. You have told us you are the Church established by law, as well as others; have set up your canting synagogues at our church doors; and the Church and her members have been loaded with reproaches, with oaths, associations, abjurations, and what not! Where has been the mercy, the forbearance, the charity you have shown to tender consciences of the Church of England that could not take oaths as fast as you made them; that, having sworn allegiance to their lawful and rightful king, could not dispense with that oath, their king being still alive, and swear to your new hodge-podge of a Dutch government? These have been turned out of their livings, and they and their families left to starve; their estates double taxed to carry on a war they had no hand in, and you got nothing by!

What account can you give of the multitudes you have forced to comply, against their consciences, with your new sophistical politics, who, like new converts in France, sin because they cannot starve? And now the tables are turned upon you, you must not be persecuted! It is not a christian spirit!

You have butchered one king, deposed another king, and made a mock king of a third, and yet, you could have the face to expect to be employed and trusted by the fourth! Anybody that did not know the temper of your party, would stand amazed at the impudence as well as the folly to think of it!

Your management of your Dutch monarch, whom you reduced to a mere King of Clubs, is enough to give any future princes such an idea of your principles as to warn them sufficiently from coming into your clutches; and, God be thanked, the Queen is out of your hands, knows you, and will have a care of you!

There is no doubt but the supreme authority of a nation has in itself a power, and a right to that power, to execute the laws upon any part of that nation it governs. The ex-ecution of the known laws of the land, and that with but a gentle hand neither, was all that the fanatical party of this land have ever called persecution. This they have magnified to a height that the sufferings of the Huguenots in France were not to be compared with them. Now to execute the known laws of a nation upon those who transgress them, after having first been voluntarily consenting to the making of those laws, can never be called persecution, but justice. But justice is always violence to the party offending, for every man is innocent in his own eyes.

The first execution of the laws against Dissenters in England was in the days of King James I; and what did it amount to? Truly, the worst they suffered was, at their own request, to let them go to New England, and erect a new colony; and give them great privileges, grants, and suitable powers; keep them under protection, and defend them against all invaders; and receive no taxes or revenue from them!

This was the cruelty of the Church of England. Fatal lenity! It was the ruin of that excellent prince, King Charles I. Had King James sent all the Puritans in England away to the West Indies, we had been a national unmixed church. The Church of England had been kept undivided and entire!

To requite the lenity of the father, they take up arms against the son, conquer, pursue, take, imprison, and at last put to death the anointed of God, and destroy the very being and nature of government: setting up a sordid impostor, who had neither title to govern, nor understanding to manage, but supplied that want, with power, bloody and desperate counsels and craft, without conscience.

Had not King James I withheld the full execution of the laws: had he given them strict justice, he had cleared the nation of them! And the consequences had been plain; his son had never been murdered by them, nor the monarchy overwhelmed. It was too much mercy shown them that was the ruin of his posterity, and the ruin of the nation's peace. One would think the Dissenters should not have the face to believe that we are to be wheedled and canted into peace and toleration, when they know that they have once requited us with a civil war, and once with an intolerable and unrighteous persecution, for our former civility.

Nay, to encourage us to be easy with them, it is apparent that they never had the upper hand of the Church but they treated her with all the severity, with all the reproach and contempt as was possible! What peace and what mercy did they show the loyal gentry of the Church of England, in the time of their triumphant Commonwealth? How did they put all the gentry of England to ransom, whether they were actually in arms for the king or not, making people compound for their estates, and starve their families! How did they treat the clergy of the Church of England, sequester the ministers, devour the patrimony of the Church and divide the spoil, by sharing the Church lands among their soldiers, and turning her clergy out to starve! Just such measure as they have meted, should be measured to them again!

Charity and love is the known doctrine of the Church of England, and it is plain she has put it in practise towards the Dissenters, even beyond what they ought, till she has been wanting to herself, and in effect unkind to her own sons; particularly, in the too much lenity of King James I, mentioned before. Had he so rooted the Puritans from the face of the land, which he had an opportunity early to have done, they had not had the power to vex the Church, as since they have done.

In the days of King Charles II, how did the Church reward their bloody doings with lenity and mercy! Except the barbarous regicides of the pretended court of justice, not a soul suffered for all the blood in an unnatural war. King Charles came in all mercy and love, cherished them, preferred them, employed them, withheld the rigor of the law and oftentimes, even against the advice of his Parliament, gave them liberty of conscience; and how did they requite him? With the villainous contrivance to depose and murder him and his successor, at the Rye House Plot!

King James II, as if mercy was the inherent quality of the family, began his reign with unusual favor to them. Nor could their joining with the Duke of Monmouth against him, move him to do himself justice upon them. But that mistaken prince, thinking to win them by gentleness and love, proclaimed a universal liberty to them, and rather discountenanced the Church of England than them. How they requited him, all the world knows!

The late reign is too fresh in the memory of all the world to need a comment. How under pretense of joining with the Church in redressing some grievances, they pushed things to that extremity, in conjunction with some mistaken gentlemen, as to depose the late king; as if the grievance of the nation could not have been redressed but by the absolute ruin of the prince.

Here is an instance of their temper, their peace, and charity!

To what height they carried themselves during the reign of a king of their own, how they crept into all places of trust and profit; how they insinuated themselves into the favor of the king, and were at first preferred to the highest places in the nation, how they engrossed the ministry; and, above all, how pitifully they managed, is too plain to need any remarks.

But particularly, their mercy and charity, the spirit of union they tell us so much of, has been remarkable in Scotland. If any man would see the spirit of a Dissenter, let him look into Scotland. There, they made entire conquest of the Church, trampled down the sacred orders and suppressed the episcopal government, with an absolute, and, as they supposed, irretrievable victory; though it is possible they may find themselves mistaken!

Now it would be a very proper question to ask their impudent advocate, the *Observator,* 'Pray how much mercy and favor did the members of the Episcopal Church find in Scotland from the Scotch Presbyterian government?' And I shall undertake for the Church of England, that the Dissenters shall still receive as much here, though they deserve but little.

In a small treatise of *The Sufferings of the Episcopal Clergy in Scotland,* it will appear what usage they met with. How they not only lost their livings; but, in several places, were plundered and abused in their persons, the ministers that could not conform, were turned out, with numerous families and no maintenance, and hardly charity enough left to relieve them with a bit of bread. The cruelties of the party were innumerable, and are not to be attempted in this short piece.

And now, to prevent the distant cloud which they perceive to hang over their heads from England, with a true Presbyterian policy, they put in for a union of nations — that England might unite their Church with the Kirk of Scotland, and their assembly of Scotch canting longcloaks in our convocation. What might have been, if our fanatic Whiggish statesmen continued, God only knows; but we hope we are out of fear of that now.

It is alleged by some of the faction, and they have begun to bully us with it, that 'if we won't unite with them, they will not settle the Crown with us again; but when her Majesty dies, will choose a king for themselves!'

If they won't, we must make them; and it is not the first time we have let them know that we are able. The crowns of these kingdoms have not so far disowned the right of succession, but they may retrieve it again; and if Scotland thinks to come off from a successive to an elective state of government, England has not promised, not to assist the right heir, and put him into possession, without any regards to their ridiculous settlements.

These are the gentlemen! these, their ways of treating the Church, both at home and abroad!

Now let us examine the reasons they pretend to give, why we should be favorable to them; why we should continue and tolerate them among us.

First. They are very numerous, they say. They are a great part of the nation, and we cannot suppress them!

To this, may be answered:

First. They are not so numerous as the Protestants in France: and yet the French king effectually cleared the nation of them at once; and we don't find he misses them at home!

But I am not of the opinion they are so numerous as is pretended. Their party is more numerous than their persons; and those mistaken people of the Church who are misled and deluded by their wheedling artifices to join with them, make their party the greater: but those will open their eyes when the government shall set

heartily about the work, and come off from them, as some animals, which they say, always desert a house when it is likely to fall.

5 Secondly. The more numerous, the more dangerous; and therefore the more need to suppress them; and God has suffered us to bear them as goads in our sides, for not utterly extinguishing them 10 long ago.

Thirdly. If we are to allow them, only because we cannot suppress them; then it ought to be tried, whether we can or not? And I am of opinion it is easy to be 15 done, and could prescribe ways and means, if it were proper: but I doubt not the government will find effectual methods for the rooting of the contagion from the face of this land.

20 Another argument they use, which is this. That this is a time of war, and we have need to unite against the common enemy.

We answer, this common enemy had 25 been no enemy, if they had not made him so. He was quiet, in peace, and no way disturbed and encroached upon us; and we know no reason we had to quarrel with him.

30 But further. We make no question but we are able to deal with this common enemy without their help: but why must we unite with them, because of the enemy? Will they go over to the enemy, 35 if we do not prevent it, by a union with them? We are very well contented they should, and make no question, we shall be ready to deal with them and the common enemy too; and better without them 40 than with them. Besides, if we have a common enemy, there is the more need to be secure against our private enemies. If there is one common enemy, we have the less need to have an enemy in our 45 bowels!

It was a great argument some people used against suppressing the old money, that 'it was a time of war, and it was too great a risk for the nation to run. 50 If we should not master it, we should be undone!' And yet the sequel proved the hazard was not so great, but it might be mastered, and the success was answerable. The suppressing the Dissenters is 55 not a harder work, nor a work of less necessity to the public. We can never enjoy a settled, uninterrupted union and tranquillity in this nation, till the spirit of Whiggism, faction, and schism is melted down like the old money!

To talk of difficulty is to frighten ourselves with chimeras and notions of a powerful party, which are indeed a party without power. Difficulties often appear greater at a distance than when they are searched into with judgment, and distinguished from the vapors and shadows that attend them.

We are not to be frightened with it! This age is wiser than that, by all our own experience, and theirs too! King Charles I had early suppressed this party, if he had taken more deliberate measures. In short, it is not worth arguing, to talk of their arms. Their Monmouths and Shaftesburys and Argyles are gone! Their Dutch sanctuary is at an end! Heaven has made way for their destruction, and if we do not close with the divine occasion, we are to blame ourselves! and may hereafter remember that we had, once, an opportunity to serve the Church of England, by extirpating her implacable enemies; and having let slip the minute that Heaven presented, may experimentally complain, *post est occasio calva* [opportunity is bald behind].

Here are some popular objections in the way.

As first, the queen has promised them to continue them in their tolerated liberty; and has told us she will be a religious observer of her word.

What her Majesty will do we cannot help, but what, as the head of the Church, she ought to do, is another case. Her Majesty has promised to protect and defend the Church of England, and if she cannot effectually do that without the destruction of the Dissenters, she must, of course, dispense with one promise to comply with another.

But to answer this cavil more effectually. Her Majesty did never promise to maintain the toleration to the destruction of the Church; but it was upon supposition that it may be compatible with the well-being and safety of the Church, which she had declared she would take especial care of. Now if these two interests clash, it is plain her Majesty's intentions are to uphold, protect, defend, and establish the Church; and this, we conceive, is impossible.

Perhaps it may be said, that the Church is in no immediate danger from the Dissenters, and therefore it is time enough.

But this is a weak answer. For first: if the danger be real, the distance of it is no argument against, but rather a spur to quicken us to prevention, lest it be too late hereafter.

And secondly: here is the opportunity, and the only one, perhaps, that ever the Church had to secure herself and destroy her enemies.

The representatives of the nation have now an opportunity. The time is come which all good men have wished for, that the gentlemen of England may serve the Church of England, now they are protected and encouraged by a Church of England queen!

What will you do for your sister in the day that she shall be spoken for?

If ever you will establish the best christian church in the world; if ever you will suppress the spirit of enthusiasm; if ever you will free the nation from the viperous brood that have so long sucked the blood of their mother; if ever you will leave your posterity free from faction and rebellion, this is the time! This is the time to pull up this heretical weed of sedition, that has so long disturbed the peace of the Church, and poisoned the good corn!

But, says another hot and cold objector, this is renewing fire and faggot, reviving the Act, *de heretico comburendo* [for the burning of heretics]. This will be cruelty in its nature, and barbarous to all the world.

I answer, it is cruelty to kill a snake or a toad in cold blood, but the poison of their nature makes it a charity to our neighbors to destroy those creatures, not for any personal injury received, but for prevention; not for the evil they have done, but the evil they may do. Serpents, toads, vipers, etc., are noxious to the body, and poison the sensitive life: these poison the soul, corrupt our posterity, ensnare our children, destroy the vitals of our happiness, our future felicity, and contaminate the whole mass!

Shall any law be given to such wild creatures? Some beasts are for sport, and the huntsmen give them the advantages of ground, but some are knocked on the head by all possible ways of violence and surprise.

I do not prescribe fire and faggot; but as Scipio said of Carthage, *Delenda est Carthago* [Carthage must be destroyed]!

they are to be rooted out of this nation, if ever we will live in peace, serve God, or enjoy our own. As for the manner, I leave it to those hands who have a right to execute God's justice on the nation's and the Church's enemies.

But if we must be frighted from this justice, under these specious pretenses, and odious sense of cruelty, nothing will be effected. It will be more barbarous to our own children and dear posterity, when they shall reproach their fathers, as we ours, and tell us, 'You had an opportunity to root out this cursed race from the world under the favor and protection of a true Church of England queen, and out of your foolish pity, you spared them, because, forsooth, you would not be cruel! And now our Church is suppressed and persecuted, our religion trampled under foot, our estates plundered, our persons imprisoned, and dragged to gaols, gibbets, and scaffolds! Your sparing this Amalekite race is our destruction! Your mercy to them proves cruelty to your poor posterity!'

How just will such reflections be when our posterity shall fall under the merciless clutches of this uncharitable generation; when our Church shall be swallowed up in schism, faction, enthusiasm, and confusion; when our government shall be devolved upon foreigners, and our monarchy dwindled into a republic!

It would be more rational for us, if we must spare this generation, to summon our own to a general massacre; and as we have brought them into the world free, to send them out so; and not betray them to destruction by our supine negligence, and then cry, 'It is mercy!'

Moses was a merciful meek man; and yet with what fury did he run through the camp, and cut the throats of three and thirty thousand of his dear Israelites that were fallen into idolatry. What was the reason? It was mercy to the rest, to make these examples, to prevent the destruction of the whole army.

How many millions of future souls we save from infection and delusion, if the present race of poisoned spirits were purged from the face of the land!

It is vain to trifle in this matter. The light foolish handling of them by mulcts, fines, etc.; 't is their glory and their advantage! If the gallows instead of the counter, and the galleys instead of the

fines were the reward of going to a conventicle to preach or hear, there would not be so many sufferers. The spirit of martyrdom is over. They that will go to church to be chosen sheriffs and mayors, would go to forty churches rather than be hanged!

If one severe law were made and punctually executed that whoever was found at a conventicle should be banished the nation, and the preacher be hanged, we should soon see an end of the tale. They would all come to church again, and one age would make us all one again.

To talk of five shillings a month for not coming to the sacrament, and one shilling per week, for not coming to church: this is such a way of converting people as was never known. This is selling them a liberty to transgress, for so much money.

If it be not a crime, why don't we give them full license? And if it be, no price ought to compound for the committing of it, for that is selling a liberty to people to sin against God and the government.

If it be a crime of the highest consequence, both against the peace and welfare of the nation, the glory of God, the good of the Church, and the happiness of the soul, let us rank it among capital offenses, and let it receive a punishment in proportion to it.

We hang men for trifles, and banish them for things not worth naming; but that an offense against God and the Church, against the welfare of the world, and the dignity of religion shall be bought off for five shillings: this is such a shame to a Christian government that it is with regret I transmit it to posterity.

If men sin against God, affront his ordinances, rebel against his church, and disobey the precepts of their superiors; let them suffer, as such capital crimes deserve. So will religion flourish, and this divided nation be once again united.

And yet the title of barbarous and cruel will soon be taken off from this law too. I am not supposing that all the Dissenters in England should be hanged or banished. But as in case of rebellions and insurrections, if a few of the ringleaders suffer, the multitude are dismissed; so a few obstinate people being made examples, there is no doubt but the severity of the law would find a stop in the compliance of the multitude.

To make the reasonableness of this matter out of question, and more unanswerably plain, let us examine for what it is that this nation is divided into parties and factions; and let us see how they can justify a separation; or we of the Church of England can justify our bearing the insults and inconveniences of the party.

One of their leading pastors, and a man of as much learning as most among them, in his *Answer* to a pamphlet entitled *An Enquiry into the Occasional Conformity*, hath these words, p. 27:—'Do the religion of the Church and the meeting houses make two religions? Wherein do they differ? The substance of the same religion is common to them both, and the modes and accidents are the things in which only they differ.' P. 28: —'Thirty-nine Articles are given us for the summary of our religion; thirty-six contain the substance of it wherein we agree; three are additional appendices, about which we have some differences.'

Now, if, as by their own acknowledgment, the Church of England is a true church, and the difference is only in a few 'modes and accidents,' why should we expect that they will suffer the gallows and galleys, corporal punishment and banishment, for these trifles? There is no question, but they will be wiser. Even their own principles won't bear them out in it.

They will certainly comply with the laws, and with reason. And though, at the first, severity may seem hard, the next age will feel nothing of it; the contagion will be rooted out. The disease being cured, there will be no need of the operation. But if they should venture to transgress, and fall into the pit, all the world must condemn their obstinacy, as being without ground from their own principles.

Thus the pretense of cruelty will be taken off, and the party actually suppressed, and the disquiets they have so often brought upon the nation, prevented.

Their numbers and their wealth make them haughty; and that is so far from being an argument to persuade us to forbear them, that it is a warning to us, without any more delay, to reconcile them to the unity of the Church, or remove them from us.

At present, Heaven be praised! they are not so formidable as they have been, and it is our own fault if ever we suffer them to be so. Providence and the Church of England seem to join in this particular, that now the destroyers of the nation's peace may be overturned; and to this end, the present opportunity seems to put into our hands.

To this end, her present Majesty seems reserved to enjoy the crown, that the ecclesiastic as well as civil rights of the nation may be restored by her hand.

To this end, the face of affairs has received such a turn in the process of a few months as never has been before. The leading men of the nation, the universal cry of the people, the unanimous request of the clergy agree in this, that the deliverance of our Church is at hand!

For this end, has Providence given such a parliament, such a convocation, such a gentry, and such a queen, as we never had before.

And what may be the consequences of a neglect of such opportunities? The succession of the crown has but a dark prospect. Another Dutch turn may make the hopes of it ridiculous, and the practice impossible. Be the house of our future princes ever so well inclined, they will be foreigners. Many years will be spent in suiting the genius of strangers to this crown, and the interests of the nation; and how many ages it may be before the English throne be filled with so much zeal and candor, so much tenderness and hearty affection to the Church, as we see it now covered with, who can imagine?

It is high time, then, for the friends of the Church of England to think of building up and establishing her in such a manner that she may be no more invaded by foreigners, nor divided by factions, schisms, and error.

If this could be done by gentle and easy methods, I should be glad: but the wound is corroded, the vitals begin to mortify, and nothing but amputation of members can complete the cure. All the ways of tenderness and compassion, all persuasive arguments have been made use of in vain.

The humor of the Dissenters has so increased among the people, that they hold the Church in defiance, and the house of God is an abomination among them. Nay, they have brought up their posterity in such prepossessed aversion to our holy religion, that the ignorant mob think we are all idolators and worshippers of Baal, and account it a sin to come within the walls of our churches. The primitive christians were not more shy of a heathen temple, or of meat offered to idols, nor the Jews of swine's flesh, than some of our Dissenters are of the church and the divine service solemnized therein.

The obstinacy must be rooted out, with the profession of it. While the generation are left at liberty daily to affront God Almighty, and dishonor his holy worship, we are wanting in our duty to God, and to our mother, the Church of England.

How can we answer it to God, to the Church, and to our posterity, to leave them entangled with fanaticism, error, and obstinacy, in the bowels of the nation; to leave them an enemy in their streets, that, in time, may involve them in the same crimes, and endanger the utter extirpation of the religion of the nation.

What is the difference betwixt this, and being subject to the power of the Church of Rome, from whence we have reformed. If one be an extreme to the one hand, and one on another, it is equally destructive to the truth to have errors settled among us, let them be of what nature they will. Both are enemies of our Church, and of our peace; and why should it not be as criminal to admit an enthusiast as a Jesuit? Why should the papist with his seven sacraments be worse than the Quaker with no sacraments at all? Why should religious houses be more intolerable than meeting houses?

Alas, the Church of England! What with popery on one hand, and schismatics on the other, how has she been crucified between two thieves. Now, let us crucify the thieves!

Let her foundations be established upon the destruction of her enemies! The doors of mercy being always open to the returning part of the deluded people, let the obstinate be ruled with the rod of iron!

Let all true sons of so holy and oppressed a mother, exasperated by her afflictions, harden their hearts against those who have oppressed her.

And may God Almighty put it into the hearts of all the friends of truth, to lift up a standard against pride and Antichrist, that the posterity of the sons of error may be rooted out from the face of this land, for ever!

(1702)

PREFACE TO THE FIRST VOLUME OF THE REVIEW

When authors present their works to the world, like a thief at the gallows, they make a speech to the people.

The author, indeed, has something like this to say, too, 'Good people all, take warning by me!' I have studied to inform and to direct the world, and what have I had for my labor?

Profit, the press would not allow; and therein I am not deceived, for I expected none. But good manners and good language, I thought I might expect, because I gave no other; and it were but just to treat mankind as we would be treated by them. But neither has this been paid me, in debt to custom and civility.

How often have my ears, my hands, and my head been to be pulled off! Impotent bullies! that attacked by truth, and their vices stormed, fill the air with rhodomontades and indecencies; but never show their faces to the resentment truth had a just cause to entertain for them.

I have passed through clouds of clamor, cavil, raillery, and objection; and have this satisfaction, that truth being the design, *Finis coronat* [The end crowns the work]!

I am never forward to value my own performances. 'Let another man's mouth praise thee!' said the Wise Man; but I cannot but own myself infinitely pleased, and more than satisfied that wise men read this paper with pleasure, own the just observations in it, and have voted it useful.

The first design I allow is not yet pursued, and indeed I must own the field is so large, the design so vast, and the necessary preliminaries so many that though I cannot yet pass for an old man, I must be so, if I live to go through with it.

This volume has passed through my descriptions of the French grandeur, with its influence on the affairs of Poland, Sweden, and Hungary. What assaults have I met with from the impatience of the readers; what uneasiness of friends, lest I was turned about to the enemy; I leave to their reading the sheets to discover.

How is this age unqualified to bear feeling truth, how unwilling to hear what we do not like, though ever so necessary to know!

And yet if this French monarchy were not very powerful, vastly strong, its power terrible, its increasing encroaching measures formidable; why do we (and justly too) applaud, extol, congratulate, and dignify the victorious Duke of Marlborough at such a rate? If it had been a mean and contemptible enemy, how shall we justify the English army's march through so many hazards; the nation's vast charge; the daily just concern in every article of this war; and (as I have frequently hinted), why not beat them, all this while?

They who have made, or may make, an ill use of the true plan of French greatness, which I have laid down, must place it to the account of their own corrupted prejudiced thoughts. My design is plain — to tell you the strength of your enemy, that you may fortify yourselves in due proportion, and n'.t go out with your ten thousands against his twenty thousands.

In like manner, I think myself very oddly handled in the case of the Swedes and the Hungarians. How many complaints of ambassadors for the one, and of fellow Protestants for the other! And yet, after the whole story is finished, I have this felicity (than which no author can desire a greater) viz., not one thing I ever affirmed, but was exactly true; not one conjecture have I made, but has appeared to be rational; not one inference drawn, but the consequences have proved just; and not one thing guessed at, but what has come to pass.

I am now come home to England, and entered a little into our own affairs. Indeed, I have advanced some things as to trade, navies, seamen, etc., which some may think a little arrogant, because perfectly new. But as I have offered nothing but what I am always ready to make appear practicable, I finish my apology by saying to the world, ' Bring me to the test; and the rest, I leave to time.'

In the bringing the story of France down to the matter of trade, I confess myself surprisingly drawn into a vast wilderness of a subject so large that I know not where it will end. The misfortune of which is, that thinking to have finished it with this volume, I found myself strangely deceived, and indeed amazed, when I found the story of it intended to be the end of this volume, and hardly enough of it entered upon to say it is begun.

However, the volume being of necessity to be closed, I am obliged to content myself with taking what is here as an introduction to the next volume; and to give this notice, that the matter of our English trade appears to be a thing of such consequence to be treated of, so much pretended to, and so little understood, that nothing could be more profitable to the readers, more advantageous to the public interest of this nation, or more suitable to the greatness of this undertaking, than to make an essay at the evils, causes, and remedies of our general negoce. *commerce*

I have been confirmed in my opinion of the consequences and benefit of this undertaking by a crowd of entreaties from persons of the best judgment, and some of extraordinary genius in these affairs; whose letters are my authority for this clause, and whose arguments are too forcible for me to resist.

And this is to me a sufficient apology for a vast digression from the affairs of France, which were really in my first design, and to which my title at first too straitly bound me.

Whoever shall live to see this undertaking finished, if the author (or some better pen after him) shall bring 20 or 30 volumes of this work on the stage, it will not look so preposterous as it seems now to have one whole volume to be employed on the most delightful as well as profitable subject of the English trade.

Things at short distance look large, and public patience is generally very short; but when remote, the case alters, and people see the reason of things in themselves. It is this remote prospect of affairs which I have before me. And this makes me not so much regard the uneasiness people show at the story being frequently broken abruptly, and running great lengths before it revolves upon itself again; but as time and the course of things will bring all about again, and make the whole to be of a piece with itself, I am content to wait the approbation of the readers, till such time as the thing itself forces it from the at present impatient readers.

Readers are strange judges when they see but part of the design. It is a new thing for an author to lay down his thoughts piece-meal. Importunate cavils assault him every day. They claim to be answered to-day! before to-morrow! and are so far from staying till the story is finished, that they can hardly stay till their letters come to hand, but follow the first with a second, that with clamor, and this sometimes with threatening scoffs, banters, and raillery!

Thus I am letter-baited by querists; and I think my trouble in writing civil private answers to teasing and querulous epistles, has been equal to, if not more troublesome than, all the rest of this work. Through these difficulties I steer with as much temper and steadiness as I can. I still hope to give satisfaction in the conclusion; and it is this alone that makes the continuing of the work tolerable to me. If I cannot, I have made my essay.

If those that know these things better than I would bless the world with further instructions, I shall be glad to see them, and very far from interrupting or discouraging them, as these do me.

Let not those gentlemen who are critics in style, in method, or manner, be angry, that I have never pulled off my cap to them, in humble excuse for my loose way of treating the world as to language, expression, and politeness of phrase. Matters of this nature differ from most things a man can write. When I am busied writing essays and matters of science, I shall address them for their aid, and take as much care to avoid their displeasure as becomes me; but when I am upon the subject of trade and the variety of casual story, I think myself a little loose from the bonds of cadence and perfections of style, and satisfy myself in my study to be explicit, easy, free, and very plain. And for all the rest, *Nec careo, nec curo* [I neither need it, nor pay attention to it]!

I had a design to say something on the entertaining part of this paper; but I have so often explained myself on that head, that I shall not trouble the world much about it.

When I first found the design of this paper (which had its birth *in tenebris*) [in darkness], I considered it would be a thing very historical, very long; and though it could be much better performed than ever I was likely to do it, this age had such natural aversion to a solemn and tedious affair, that however profitable, it would never be diverting, and the world would never read it.

To get over this difficulty, the secret hand (I make no doubt) that directed this birth into the world, dictated to make some sort of entertainment or amusement at the end of every paper, upon the immediate subject, then on the tongues of the town — which innocent diversion would hand on the more weighty and serious part of the design into the heads and thoughts of those to whom it might be useful.

I take this opportunity to assure the world that receiving or answering letters of doubts, difficulties, cases, and questions, as it is a work I think myself very meanly qualified for, so it was the remotest thing from my first design of anything in the world; and I could be heartily glad, if the readers of this paper would excuse me from it yet. But I see it cannot be, and the world will have it done. I have therefore done my best to oblige them; but as I have not one word to say for my performance that way, so I leave it where I found it, a mere circumstance casually and undesignedly annexed to the work, and a curiosity, though honestly endeavored to be complied with.

If the method I have taken in answering questions has pleased some wiser men more than I expected it would, I confess it is one of the chief reasons why I was induced to continue it.

I have constantly adhered to this rule in all my answers (and I refer my reader to his observation for the proof), that from the loosest and lightest questions, I endeavor to draw some useful inferences, and, if possible, to introduce something solid, and something solemn in applying it. The custom of the ancients in writing fables is my very laudable pattern for this; and my firm resolution, in all I write, to exalt virtue, expose vice, promote truth, and help men to serious reflection, is my first moving cause, and last directed end.

If any shall make ill use of, wrest, wrongly interpret, wilfully or otherwise mistake the honest design of this work; let such wait for the end, when I doubt not, the author will be cleared by their own vote, their want of charity will appear, and they be self-condemned till they come to acknowledge their error, and openly to justify

Their humble servant, D. F.
(1705)

THE EDUCATION OF WOMEN

FROM AN ESSAY UPON PROJECTS

I have often thought of it as one of the most barbarous customs in the world, considering us as a civilized and a christian country, that we deny the advantages of learning to women. We reproach the sex every day with folly and impertinence; while I am confident, had they the advantages of education equal to us, they would be guilty of less than ourselves.

One would wonder, indeed, how it should happen that women are conversible at all, since they are only beholden to natural parts for all their knowledge. Their youth is spent to teach them to stitch and sew, or make baubles. They are taught to read, indeed, and perhaps to write their names, or so; and that is the height of a woman's education. And I would but ask any who slight the sex for their understanding, what is a man (a gentleman, I mean) good for, that is taught no more? I need not give instances, or examine the character of a gentleman, with a good estate, of a good family, and with tolerable parts; and examine what figure he makes for want of education.

The soul is placed in the body like a rough diamond, and must be polished, or the luster of it will never appear. And 't is manifest, that as the rational soul distinguishes us from brutes, so education carries on the distinction, and makes some less brutish than others. This is too evident to need any demonstration. But why then should women be denied the benefit of instruction? If knowledge and understanding had been useless additions to the sex, God Almighty would never have given them capacities; for he made nothing needless. Besides, I would ask such, what they can see in ignorance,

that they should think it a necessary ornament to a woman? or how much worse is a wise woman than a fool? or what has the woman done to forfeit the privilege of being taught? Does she plague us with her pride and impertinence? Why did we not let her learn, that she might have had more wit? Shall we upbraid women with folly, when 't is only the error of this inhuman custom that hindered them from being made wiser?

The capacities of women are supposed to be greater, and their senses quicker than those of the men; and what they might be capable of being bred to, is plain from some instances of female wit, which this age is not without, which upbraids us with injustice, and looks as if we denied women the advantages of education, for fear they should vie with the men in their improvements. . . .

They should be taught all sorts of breeding suitable both to their genius and quality. And in particular, music and dancing, which it would be cruelty to bar the sex of because they are their darlings. But besides this, they should be taught languages, as particularly French and Italian, and I would venture the injury of giving a woman more tongues than one. They should, as a particular study, be taught all the graces of speech, and all the necessary air of conversation, which our common education is so defective in that I need not expose it. They should be brought to read books, and especially history; and so to read as to make them understand the world, and be able to know and judge of things when they hear of them.

To such whose genius would lead them to it, I would deny no sort of learning; but the chief thing, in general, is to cultivate the understandings of the sex, that they may be capable of all sorts of conversation; that their parts and judgments being improved, they may be as profitable in their conversation as they are pleasant.

Women, in my observation, have little or no difference in them, but as they are or are not distinguished by education. Tempers, indeed, may in some degree influence them, but the main distinguishing part is their breeding.

The whole sex are generally quick and

sharp — I believe, I may be allowed to say, generally so: for you rarely see them lumpish and heavy when they are children, as boys will often be. If a woman be well bred, and taught the proper management of her natural wit, she proves generally very sensible and retentive.

And, without partiality, a woman of sense and manners is the finest and most delicate part of God's creation, the glory of her Maker, and the great instance of his singular regard to man, his darling creature, to whom he gave the best gift either God could bestow or man receive. And 't is the sordidest piece of folly and ingratitude in the world, to withhold from the sex the due luster which the advantages of education give to the natural beauty of their minds.

A woman well bred and well taught, furnished with the additional accomplishments of knowledge and behavior, is a creature without comparison. Her society is the emblem of sublimer enjoyments, her person is angelic, and her conversation heavenly. She is all softness and sweetness, peace, love, wit, and delight. She is every way suitable to the sublimest wish; and the man that has such a one to his portion, has nothing to do but to rejoice in her, and be thankful.

On the other hand, suppose her to be the very same woman, and rob her of the benefit of education, and it follows: —

If her temper be good, want of education makes her soft and easy.

Her wit, for want of teaching, makes her impertinent and talkative.

Her knowledge, for want of judgment and experience, makes her fanciful and whimsical.

If her temper be bad, want of breeding makes her worse; and she grows haughty, insolent, and loud.

If she be passionate, want of manners makes her a termagant and a scold, which is much at one with lunatic.

If she be proud, want of discretion (which still is breeding) makes her conceited, fantastic, and ridiculous.

And from these she degenerates to be turbulent, clamorous, noisy, nasty, the devil! . . .

The great distinguishing difference, which is seen in the world between men and women, is in their education; and this is manifested by comparing it with the difference between one man or woman, and another.

And herein it is that I take upon me to make such a bold assertion, that all the world are mistaken in their practice about women. For I cannot think that God Almighty ever made them so delicate, so glorious creatures, and furnished them with such charms, so agreeable and so delightful to mankind, with souls capable of the same accomplishments with men; and all, to be only stewards of our houses, cooks, and slaves.

Not that I am for exalting the female government in the least; but, in short, I would have men take women for companions, and educate them to be fit for it. A woman of sense and breeding will scorn as much to encroach upon the prerogative of man, as a man of sense will scorn to oppress the weakness of the woman. But if the women's souls were refined and improved by teaching, that word would be lost. To say, the weakness of the sex, as to judgment, would be nonsense; for ignorance and folly would be no more to be found among women than men.

I remember a passage, which I heard from a very fine woman. She had wit and capacity enough, an extraordinary shape and face, and a great fortune, but had been cloistered up all her time, and for fear of being stolen, had not had the liberty of being taught the common necessary knowledge of women's affairs. And when she came to converse in the world her natural wit made her so sensible of the want of education, that she gave this short reflection on herself: 'I am ashamed to talk with my very maids,' says she, ' for I don't know when they do right or wrong. I had more need go to school, than be married.'

I need not enlarge on the loss the defect of education is to the sex, nor argue the benefit of the contrary practice. 'T is a thing will be more easily granted than remedied. This chapter is but an essay at the thing; and I refer the practice to those happy days (if ever they shall be) when men shall be wise enough to mend it.   (1697)

JONATHAN SWIFT (1667–1745)

Swift was born in Dublin — a chance which all his life he chose to resent as the first of many insults of fortune. At Kilkenny Grammar School and at Trinity College, Dublin, where he was 'wild, witty, and poor,' he had to be supported by one relative, and for the next decade, he was a discontented dependent of another, Sir William Temple. During one of his disagreements with the latter, he left in a huff, crossed to Ireland, and went into holy orders. Dryden had crushed his poetic inclinations and incurred his lasting resentment by the solid remark, 'Cousin Swift, you will never be a poet.' He did not discover his genius for satire until about his thirtieth year, when he wrote *A Tale of a Tub* and *The Battle of the Books.* These were published anonymously in 1704, preceded and followed by a rapid volley of pamphlets upon subjects then in dispute. For about ten years, he spent much of his time in London, mingled with the reigning wits in their homes and clubs, amused his leisure with squibs and verses, and projected the Scriblerus Club whose chief members, besides himself, were Pope, Arbuthnot, Atterbury, Parnell and Gay. In 1710, personal interest united with conscience to engage him on the Tory side. He edited the *Examiner* (1710–11), threw himself ferociously into political intrigue, and, for a time, wielded an extraordinary personal influence. But, though he could dictate the preferment of bishops, the author of *A Tale of a Tub* was powerless to secure a high appointment for himself. He had to be content with the Deanery of St. Patrick's, at Dublin, whither after the disruption of the Tory party in 1714, he permanently retired,— an embittered and disappointed man. Ten years later, an attempt to exploit the Irish people by a scheme of debased coinage called forth the most angry, unscrupulous, and masterly of his controversial series, the *Letters of M. B. Drapier* (1724). Here, and in his *Modest Proposal for preventing the Children of Poor People from being a Burden to their Parents,* and similar ironical extravagances, he voiced his savage indignation at the unjust and heart-rending poverty of his adopted people. After the death of 'the unfortunate Stella' (Esther Johnson), Swift's powerful faculties began to show signs of derangement. 'I shall die at the top,' he had once said, pointing to a tree which had been blasted by lightning,— and the words were prophetic. Already, in the last portions of *Gulliver's Travels* (1726), we see the horrible evidences of 'a mind diseased.' In 1741, he became 'furiously insane,' then lapsed into idiocy, and at last was laid to rest in his own cathedral, in the city of his birth, 'where,' in the words of his epitaph, which he himself composed, ferocious indignation can no longer tear the heart'—

> Ubi saeva indignatio
> Cor ulterius lacerare nequit.

In dealing with Swift, it is never safe to forget the deadly purpose and 'intent to kill' which inspires his grim horseplay. He bitterly hated the world's shams and inconsistencies. His reckless and irreverent energy of thought and the acrid irony of his style made him dangerous, to all he touched. His humor was like fire; what it played over, it consumed.

From A TALE OF A TUB

SECTION II

Once upon a time there was a man who had three sons by one wife, and all 5 at a birth, neither could the midwife tell certainly which was the eldest. Their father died while they were young; and upon his death-bed, calling the lads to him, spoke thus:— 10

'Sons, because I have purchased no estate, nor was born to any, I have long considered of some good legacies to bequeath you; and at last, with much care, as well as expense, have provided each of you (here they are) a new coat. Now, you are to understand that these coats have two virtues contained in them; one is, that with good wearing they will last you fresh and sound as long as you live; the other is, that they will grow in the same proportion with your bodies, lengthening and widening of themselves, so as to be always fit. Here; let me see them on you before I die. So; very well; pray, children, wear them clean, and brush them often. You will find in my will[1] (here it is) full instructions in every particular concerning the wearing and management of your coats; wherein you must be very exact, to avoid the penalties I have appointed for every transgression or neglect, upon which your future fortunes will entirely depend. I have also commanded in my will that you should live together in one house like brethren and friends, for then you will be sure to thrive, and not otherwise.'

Here, the story says, this good father died, and the three sons went all together to seek their fortunes.

I shall not trouble you with recounting what adventures they met for the first seven years, any farther than by taking notice that they carefully observed their father's will, and kept their coats in very good order: that they traveled through several countries, encountered a reasonable quantity of giants, and slew certain dragons.

Being now arrived at the proper age for producing themselves, they came up to town, and fell in love with the ladies, but especially three, who about that time were in chief reputation; the Duchess d'Argent, Madame de Grands Titres, and the Countess d'Orgueil. On their first appearance our three adventurers met with a very bad reception; and soon with great sagacity guessing out the reason, they quickly began to improve in the good qualities of the town; they writ, and rallied, and rhymed, and sung, and said, and said nothing; they drank, and fought, and whored, and slept, and swore, and took snuff; they went to new plays on the first night, haunted the chocolate-houses, beat the watch, lay on bulks, and got claps; they bilked hackney-coachmen, ran in debt with shop-keepers, and lay with their wives; they killed bailiffs, kicked fiddlers down stairs, eat at Locket's, loitered at Will's; they talked of the drawing-room, and never came there; dined with lords they never saw; whispered a duchess, and spoke never a word; exposed the scrawls of their laundress for billets-doux of quality; came ever just from court, and were never seen in it; attended the levee *sub dio* [in the

open air]; got a list of peers by heart in one company, and with great familiarity retailed them in another. Above all, they constantly attended those committees of senators who are silent in the house and loud in the coffee-house; where they nightly adjourn to chew the cud of politics, and are encompassed with a ring of disciples, who lie in wait to catch up their droppings. The three brothers had acquired forty other qualifications of the like stamp, too tedious to recount, and by consequence were justly reckoned the most accomplished persons in the town; but all would not suffice, and the ladies aforesaid continued still inflexible. To clear up which difficulty I must, with the reader's good leave and patience, have recourse to some points of weight, which the authors of that age have not sufficiently illustrated.

For about this time it happened a sect arose[2] whose tenets obtained and spread very far, especially in the *grand monde*, and among everybody of good fashion. They worshipped a sort of idol,[3] who, as their doctrine delivered, did daily create men by a kind of manufactory operation. This idol they placed in the highest parts of the house, on an altar erected about three foot; he was shown in the posture of a Persian emperor, sitting on a superficies, with his legs interwoven under him. This god had a goose for his ensign; whence it is that some learned men pretend to deduce his original from Jupiter Capitolinus. At his left hand, beneath the altar, hell seemed to open and catch at the animals the idol was creating; to prevent which, certain of his priests hourly flung in pieces of the uninformed mass, or substance, and sometimes whole limbs already enlivened, which that horrid gulf insatiably swallowed, terrible to behold. The goose was also held a subaltern divinity or *deus minorum gentium* [god of the lesser peoples], before whose shrine was sacrificed that creature whose hourly food is human gore, and who is in so great renown abroad for being the delight and favorite of the Egyptian Cercopithecus.[4]

[1] The New Testament.

[2] This is an occasional satire upon dress and fashion, in order to introduce what follows.
[3] By this idol is meant a tailor.
[4] The Egyptians worshipped a monkey, which animal is very fond of eating lice, styled here creatures that feed on human gore.

Millions of these animals were cruelly slaughtered every day to appease the hunger of that consuming deity. The chief idol was also worshipped as the inventor of the yard and needle; whether as the god of seamen, or on account of certain other mystical attributes, has not been sufficiently cleared.

The worshippers of this deity had also a system of their belief, which seemed to turn upon the following fundamentals. They held the universe to be a large suit of clothes, which invests everything; that the earth is invested by the air; the air is invested by the stars; and the stars are invested by the *primum mobile*. Look on this globe of earth, you will find it to be a very complete and fashionable dress. What is that which some call land but a fine coat faced with green? or the sea, but a waistcoat of water-tabby? Proceed to the particular works of the creation, you will find how curious journeyman Nature has been to trim up the vegetable beaux; observe how sparkish a periwig adorns the head of a beech, and what a fine doublet of white satin is worn by the birch. To conclude from all, what is man himself but a microcoat,[1] or rather a complete suit of clothes with all its trimmings? As to his body there can be no dispute; but examine even the acquirements of his mind, you will find them all contribute in their order towards furnishing out an exact dress: to instance no more; is not religion a cloak, honesty a pair of shoes worn out in the dirt, self-love a surtout, vanity a shirt, and conscience a pair of breeches? * * *

These postulata being admitted, it will follow in due course of reasoning that those beings, which the world calls improperly suits of clothes, are in reality the most refined species of animals; or, to proceed higher, that they are rational creatures or men. For, is it not manifest that they live, and move, and talk, and perform all other offices of human life? are not beauty, and wit, and mien, and breeding, their inseparable proprieties? in short, we see nothing but them, hear nothing but them. Is it not they who walk the streets, fill up parliament-, coffee-, play-, bawdy-houses? 'T is true,

indeed, that these animals, which are vulgarly called suits of clothes, or dresses, do, according to certain compositions, receive different appellations. If one of them be trimmed up with a gold chain, and a red gown, and white rod, and a great horse, it is called a lord-mayor: if certain ermines and furs be placed in a certain position, we style them a judge; and so an apt conjunction of lawn and black satin we entitle a bishop.

Others of these professors, though agreeing in the main system, were yet more refined upon certain branches of it; and held that man was an animal compounded of two dresses, the natural and celestial suit, which were the body and the soul: that the soul was the outward, and the body the inward clothing; that the latter was *ex traduce;* but the former of daily creation and circumfusion; this last they proved by scripture, because in them we live, and move, and have our being; as likewise by philosophy, because they are all in all, and all in every part. Besides, said they, separate these two and you will find the body to be only a senseless unsavory carcase; by all which it is manifest that the outward dress must needs be the soul.

To this system of religion were tagged several subaltern doctrines, which were entertained with great vogue: as particularly the faculties of the mind were deduced by the learned among them in this manner; embroidery was sheer wit, gold fringe was agreeable conversation, gold lace was repartee, a huge long periwig was humor, and a coat full of powder was very good raillery — all which required abundance of *finesse* and *delicatesse* to manage with advantage, as well as a strict observance after times and fashions.

I have, with much pains and reading, collected out of ancient authors this short summary of a body of philosophy and divinity, which seems to have been composed by a vein and race of thinking very different from any other systems either ancient or modern. And it was not merely to entertain or satisfy the reader's curiosity, but rather to give him light into several circumstances of the following story; that, knowing the state of dispositions and opinions in an age so remote, he may better comprehend

---

[1] Alluding to the word microcosm, or a little world, as man has been called by philosophers.

those great events which were the issue of them. I advise, therefore, the courteous reader to peruse with a world of application, again and again, whatever I have written upon this matter. And leaving these broken ends, I carefully gather up the chief thread of my story and proceed.

These opinions, therefore, were so universal, as well as the practices of them, among the refined part of court and town, that our three brother adventurers, as their circumstances then stood, were strangely at a loss. For, on the one side, the three ladies they addressed themselves to, whom we have named already, were at the very top of the fashion, and abhorred all that were below it but the breadth of a hair. On the other side, their father's will was very precise; and it was the main precept in it, with the greatest penalties annexed, not to add to or diminish from their coats one thread, without a positive command in the will. Now, the coats their father had left them were, 't is true, of very good cloth, and besides so neatly sewn, you would swear they were all of a piece; but at the same time very plain, and with little or no ornament: and it happened that before they were a month in town great shoulder-knots[1] came up — straight all the world was shoulder-knots — no approaching the ladies' *ruelles* without the *quota* of shoulder-knots. That fellow, cries one, has no soul; where is his shoulder-knot? Our three brethren soon discovered their want by sad experience, meeting in their walks with forty mortifications and indignities. If they went to the playhouse the door-keeper showed them into the twelvepenny gallery; if they called a boat, says a waterman, 'I am first sculler'; if they stepped to the Rose to take a bottle, the drawer would cry, 'Friend, we sell no ale'; if they went to visit a lady, a footman met them at the door with 'Pray send up your message.' In this unhappy case they went immediately to consult their father's will, read it over and over, but not a word of the shoulder-knot. What should they do? — what

temper should they find? — obedience was absolutely necessary, and yet shoulder-knots appeared extremely requisite. After much thought one of the brothers, who happened to be more book-learned than the other two, said he had found an expedient. ''T is true,' said he, 'there is nothing here in this will, *totidem verbis* [in so many words], making mention of shoulder-knots: but I dare conjecture we may find them *inclusive*, or *totidem syllabis* [in so many syllables].' This distinction was immediately approved by all, and so they fell again to examine the will; but their evil star had so directed the matter that the first syllable was not to be found in the whole writing. Upon which disappointment, he who found the former evasion took heart, and said, 'Brothers, there are yet hopes; for though we cannot find them *totidem verbis*, nor *totidem syllabis*, I dare engage we shall make them out *tertio modo* [by a third method] or *totidem literis* [in so many letters].' This discovery was also highly commended, upon which they fell once more to the scrutiny, and picked out S, H, O, U, L, D, E, R; when the same planet, enemy to their repose, had wonderfully contrived that a K was not to be found. Here was a weighty difficulty! but the distinguishing brother, for whom we shall hereafter find a name, now his hand was in, proved by a very good argument that K was a modern, illegitimate letter, unknown to the learned ages, nor anywhere to be found in ancient manuscripts. ''T is true,' said he, 'Calendæ hath in Q. V. C.[2] been sometimes writ with a K, but erroneously; for in the best copies it ever spelt with a C. And, by consequence, it was a gross mistake in our language to spell 'knot' with a K'; but that from henceforward he would take care it should be writ with a C. Upon this all farther difficulty vanished — shoulder-knots were made clearly out to be *jure paterno* [according to the law of the father], and our three gentlemen swaggered with as large and as flaunting ones as the best.

But, as human happiness is of a very short duration, so in those days were human fashions, upon which it entirely de-

[1] By this is understood the first introducing of pageantry, and unnecessary ornaments in the Church, such as were neither for convenience nor edification, as a shoulder-knot, in which there is neither symmetry nor use.

[2] Quibusdam veteribus codicibus; i. e. some ancient manuscripts.

pends. Shoulder-knots had their time, and we must now imagine them in their decline; for a certain lord came just from Paris, with fifty yards of gold lace upon his coat, exactly trimmed after the court fashion of that month. In two days all mankind appeared closed up in bars of gold lace:[1] whoever durst peep abroad without his complement of gold lace was as scandalous as a ———, and as ill received among the women: what should our three knights do in this momentous affair? they had sufficiently strained a point already in the affair of shoulder-knots: upon recourse to the will, nothing appeared there but *altum silentium* [primeval silence]. That of the shoulder-knots was a loose, flying, circumstantial point; but this of gold lace seemed too considerable an alteration without better warrant; it did *aliquo modo essentiae adhaerere* [in some manner belong to the essence of the matter], and therefore required a positive precept. But about this time it fell out that the learned brother aforesaid had read *Aristotelis dialectica,* and especially that wonderful piece *de interpretatione,* which has the faculty of teaching its readers to find out a meaning in everything but itself; like commentators on the Revelations, who proceed prophets without understanding a syllable of the text. 'Brothers,' said he, 'you are to be informed that of wills *duo sunt genera* [there are two kinds], nuncupatory[2] and scriptory: that in the scriptory will

here before us there is no precept or mention about gold lace, *conceditur* [it is conceded] but *si idem affirmetur de nuncupatorio, negatur* [if the same is as- 5 serted of the nuncupatory, it is denied]. For, brothers, if you remember, we heard a fellow say when we were boys that he heard my father's man say, that he heard my father say, that he would ad- 10 vise his sons to get gold lace on their coats as soon as ever they could procure money to buy it.' 'By G——! that is very true,' cries the other; 'I remember it perfectly well,' said the third. And 15 so without more ado they got the largest gold lace in the parish, and walked about as fine as lords.

A while after there came up all in fashion a pretty sort of flame-colored 20 satin for linings; and the mercer brought a pattern of it immediately to our three gentlemen; 'An please your worships,' said he, 'my lord C——[3] and Sir J. W. had linings out of this very piece last 25 night: it takes wonderfully, and I shall not have a remnant left enough to make my wife a pincushion by to-morrow morning at ten o'clock.' Upon this they fell again to rummage the will, because 30 the present case also required a positive precept — the lining being held by orthodox writers to be of the essence of the coat. After long search they could fix upon nothing to the matter in hand, 35 except a short advice of their father in the will to take care of fire[4] and put out their candles before they went to sleep. This, though a good deal for the purpose, and helping very far towards self- 40 conviction, yet not seeming wholly of force to establish a command (being resolved to avoid farther scruple as well as future occasion for scandal), says he that was the scholar, 'I remem- 45 ber to have read in wills of a codicil annexed, which is indeed a part of the will, and what it contains hath equal authority with the rest. Now, I have been considering of this same will here 50 before us, and I cannot reckon it to be complete for want of such a codicil: I will therefore fasten one in its proper place very dexterously — I have had it

[1] I cannot tell whether the author means any new innovation by this word, or whether it be only to introduce the new methods of forcing and perverting Scripture.

[2] By this is meant tradition, allowed by the Papists to have equal authority with the Scripture, or rather greater.

This is a Purgatory, whereof he speaks more particularly hereafter; but here, only to shew how Scripture was perverted to prove it, which was done by giving equal authority with the canon to Apocrypha, called here a codicil annexed. It is likely the author, in every one of these changes in the brothers' dresses, refers to some particular error in the Church of Rome, though it is not easy, I think, to apply them all: but by this of flame-colored satin, is manifestly intended Purgatory; by gold lace may perhaps be understood, the lofty ornaments and plate in the churches; the shoulder-knots and silver fringe are not so obvious, at least to me; but the Indian figures of men, women, and children, plainly relate to the pictures in the Romish churches, of God like an old man, of the Virgin Mary, and our Savior as a child.

[3] This shews the time the author writ, it being about fourteen years since those two persons were reckoned the fine gentlemen of the town.

[4] That is, to take care of hell; and, in order to do that, to subdue and extinguish their lusts.

by me some time — it was written by a dog-keeper of my grandfather's,[1] and talks a great deal, as good luck would have it, of this very flame-colored satin.' The project was immediately approved by the other two; an old parchment scroll was tagged on according to art in the form of a codicil annexed, and the satin bought and worn.

Next winter a player, hired for the purpose by the corporation of fringe-makers, acted his part in a new comedy, all covered with silver-fringe,[2] and, according to the laudable custom, gave rise to that fashion. Upon which the brothers, consulting their father's will, to their great astonishment found these words: '*item,* I charge and command my said three sons to wear no sort of silver fringe upon or about their said coats,' etc., with a penalty, in case of disobedience, too long here to insert. However, after some pause, the brother so often mentioned for his erudition, who was well skilled in criticisms, had found in a certain author, which he said should be nameless, that the same word which in the will is called fringe does also signify a broomstick: and doubtless ought to have the same interpretation in this paragraph. This another of the brothers disliked, because of that epithet silver, which could not he humbly conceived in propriety of speech be reasonably applied to a broomstick: but it was replied upon him that this epithet was understood in a mythological and allegorical sense. However, he objected again why their father should forbid them to wear a broomstick on their coats — a caution that seemed unnatural and impertinent; upon which he was taken up short, as one who spoke irreverently of a mystery, which doubtless was very useful and significant, but ought not to be over-curiously pried into or nicely reasoned upon. And, in short, their father's authority being now considerably sunk, this expedient was allowed to serve as a lawful dispensation for wearing their full proportion of silver fringe.

A while after was revived an old fashion, long antiquated, of embroidery with Indian figures of men, women, and children. Here they remembered but too well how their father had always abhorred this fashion; that he made several paragraphs on purpose, importing his utter detestation of it, and bestowing his everlasting curse to his sons whenever they should wear it. For all this, in a few days they appeared higher in the fashion than anybody else in the town. But they solved the matter by saying that these figures were not at all the same with those that were formerly worn and were meant in the will. Besides, they did not wear them in the sense as forbidden by their father; but as they were a commendable custom, and of great use to the public.[3] That these rigorous clauses in the will did therefore require some allowance and a favorable interpretation, and ought to be understood *cum grano salis* [with a grain of salt].

But fashions perpetually altering in that age, the scholastic brother grew weary of searching farther evasions, and solving everlasting contradictions. Resolved, therefore, at all hazards, to comply with the modes of the world, they concerted matters together, and agreed unanimously to lock up their father's will in a strong box, brought out of Greece or Italy (I have forgot which), and trouble themselves no farther to examine it, but only refer to its authority whenever they thought fit. In consequence whereof, a while after it grew a general mode to wear an infinite number of points, most of them tagged with silver: upon which the scholar pronounced, *ex cathedrâ* [from the bench], that points were absolutely *jure paterno,* as they might very well remember. 'T is true, indeed, the fashion prescribed somewhat more than were directly named in the will; however, that they, as heirs-general of their father, had power to make and add certain clauses for public emolument, though not deducible, *totidem verbis,* from the letter of the will, or else *multa absurda sequerentur* [many absurdities would follow]. This was understood for canonical, and therefore, on the following Sunday, they came to church all covered with points.

---

[1] I believe this refers to that part of the Apocrypha where mention is made of Tobit and his dog.

[2] This is certainly the farther introducing the pomps of habit and ornament.

[3] Here they had no occasion to examine the will; they remembered.— *First Edition.*

The learned brother, so often mentioned, was reckoned the best scholar in all that or the next street to it, insomuch as, having run something behindhand in the world, he obtained the favor of a certain lord[1] to receive him into his house, and to teach his children. A while after the lord died, and he, by long practice of his father's will, found the way of contriving a deed of conveyance of that house to himself and his heirs; upon which he took possession, turned the young squires out, and received his brothers in their stead.

* * *

SECTION IV

I have now, with much pains and study, conducted the reader to a period where he must expect to hear of great revolutions. For no sooner had our learned brother, so often mentioned, got a warm house of his own over his head than he began to look big and take mightily upon him; insomuch that, unless the gentle reader, out of his great candor, will please a little to exalt his idea, I am afraid he will henceforth hardly know the hero of the play when he happens to meet him; his part, his dress, and his mien being so much altered.

He told his brothers he would have them to know that he was their elder, and consequently his father's sole heir; nay, a while after, he would not allow them to call him brother, but *Mr.* PETER, and then he must be styled *Father* PETER; and sometimes, *My Lord* PETER. To support this grandeur, which he soon began to consider could not be maintained without a better *fonde* than what he was born to, after much thought, he cast about at last to turn projector and virtuoso, wherein he so well succeeded, that many famous discoveries, projects and machines, which bear great vogue and practice at present in the world, are owing entirely to lord PETER'S invention. I will deduce the best account I have been able to collect of the chief among them, without considering much the order they came out in; because I think authors are not well agreed as to that point.

I hope, when this treatise of mine shall be translated into foreign languages (as I may without vanity affirm that the labor of collecting, the faithfulness in recounting, and the great usefulness of the matter to the public, will amply deserve that justice), that the worthy members of the several academies abroad, especially those of France and Italy, will favorably accept these humble offers for the advancement of universal knowledge. I do also advertise the most reverend fathers, the eastern missionaries, that I have, purely for their sakes, made use of such words and phrases as will best admit an easy turn into any of the oriental languages, especially the Chinese. And so I proceed with great content of mind, upon reflecting how much emolument this whole globe of the earth is likely to reap by my labors.

The first undertaking of lord Peter was, to purchase a large continent,[2] lately said to have been discovered in *terra australis incognita* [an unknown country to the south]. This tract of land he bought at a very great pennyworth from the discoverers themselves (though some pretend to doubt whether they had ever been there), and then retailed it into several cantons to certain dealers, who carried over colonies, but were all shipwrecked in the voyage. Upon which lord Peter sold the said continent to other customers again, and again, and again, and again, with the same success.

The second project I shall mention was his sovereign remedy for the worms, especially those in the spleen. The patient was to eat nothing after supper for three nights:[3] as soon as he went to bed he was carefully to lie on one side, and when he grew weary to turn upon the other; he must also duly confine his two eyes to the same object. * * * These prescriptions diligently observed, the worms would void insensibly by perspiration, ascending through the brain.

A third invention was the erecting of a whispering-office for the public good and ease of all such as are hypochondriacal or troubled with the colic; as

---

[1] This was Constantine the Great, from whom the popes pretend a donation of St. Peter's patrimony, which they have never been able to produce.

[2] That is, Purgatory.

[3] Here the author ridicules the penances of the Church of Rome, which may be made as easy to the sinner as he pleases, provided he will pay for them accordingly.

midwives,[1] small politicians, friends fallen out, repeating poets, lovers happy or in despair, bawds, privy-counsellors, pages, parasites, and buffoons; in short, of all such as are in danger of bursting with too much wind. An ass's head was placed so conveniently that the party effected might easily with his mouth accost either of the animal's ears; to which he was to apply close for a certain space, and by a fugitive faculty, peculiar to the ears of that animal, receive immediate benefit, either by eructation, or expiration, or evomitation.

Another very beneficial project of lord Peter's was an office of insurance for tobacco-pipes,[2] martyrs of the modern zeal, volumes of poetry, shadows, ——, and rivers; that these, nor any of these, shall receive damage by fire. Whence our friendly societies may plainly find themselves to be only transcribers from this original; though the one and the other have been of great benefit to the undertakers, as well as of equal to the public.

Lord PETER was also held the original author of puppets and raree-shows;[3] the great usefulness whereof being so generally known, I shall not enlarge farther upon this particular.

But another discovery for which he was much renowned, was his famous universal pickle. For, having remarked how your common pickle[4] in use among housewives was of no farther benefit than to preserve dead flesh and certain kinds of vegetables, Peter, with great cost as well as art, had contrived a pickle proper for houses, gardens, towns, men, women, children, and cattle; wherein he could preserve them as sound as insects in amber. Now, this pickle, to the taste, the smell, and the sight, appeared exactly the same with what is in common service for beef, and butter, and herrings, and has been often that way applied with great success; but, for its many sovereign virtues, was a quite different thing. For Peter would put in a certain quantity of his powder pimperlimpimp, after which it never failed of success. The operation was performed by spargefaction, in a proper time of the moon. The patient who was to be pickled, if it were a house, would infallibly be preserved from all spiders, rats, and weasels; if the party affected were a dog, he should be exempt from mange, and madness, and hunger. It also infallibly took away all scabs, and lice, and scalled heads from children, never hindering the patient from any duty, either at bed or board.

But of all Peter's rarities he most valued a certain set of bulls, whose race was by great fortune preserved in a lineal descent from those that guarded the golden fleece. Though some, who pretended to observe them curiously, doubted the breed had not been kept entirely chaste, because they had degenerated from their ancestors in some qualities, and had acquired others very extraordinary, by a foreign mixture. The bulls of Colchis are recorded to have brazen feet; but whether it happened by ill pasture and running, by an allay from intervention of other parents, from stolen intrigues; whether a weakness in their progenitors had impaired the seminal virtue, or by a decline necessary through a long course of time, the originals of nature being depraved in these latter sinful ages of the world; whatever was the cause, it is certain that lord Peter's bulls were extremely vitiated by the rust of time in the metal of their feet, which was now sunk into common lead. However, the terrible roaring peculiar to their lineage was preserved; as likewise that faculty of breathing out fire from their nostrils, which, notwithstanding, many of their detractors took to be a feat of art, to be nothing so terrible as it appeared, proceeding only from their usual course of diet, which was of squibs and crackers.[5] However, they had two peculiar marks, which extremely distinguished them from the bulls of Jason, and which I have not met together in the description of any other monster beside that in Horace:

---

[1] As likewise of all eavesdroppers, midwives, etc. — *First Edition.*

[2] This I take to be the office of indulgences, the gross abuses whereof first gave occasion for the Reformation.

[3] I believe are the monkeries and ridiculous processions, etc., among the papists.

[4] This is easily understood to be holy water, composed of the same ingredients with many other pickles.

[5] These are the fulminations of the pope, threatening hell and damnation to those princes who offend him.

Varias inducere plumas;
[putting on gay plumage.]
Atrum desinat in piscem.
[ending in a foul fish below.]

and

For these had fishes' tails, yet upon occasion could outfly any bird in the air. Peter put these bulls upon several employs. Sometimes he would set them a-roaring to fright naughty boys,[1] and make them quiet. Sometimes he would send them out upon errands of great importance; where, it is wonderful to recount (and perhaps the cautious reader may think much to believe it), an *appetitus sensibilis* [an appetite of the senses] deriving itself through the whole family from their noble ancestors, guardians of the golden fleece, they continued so extremely fond of gold, that if Peter sent them abroad, though it were only upon a compliment, they would roar, and spit, and belch, and snivel out fire, and keep a perpetual coil, till you flung them a bit of gold; but then, *pulveris exigui jactu* [by throwing on a little dust], they would grow calm and quiet as lambs. In short, whether by secret connivance or encouragement from their master, or out of their own liquorish affection to gold, or both, it is certain they were no better than a sort of sturdy, swaggering, beggars; and where they could not prevail to get an alms, would make women miscarry, and children fall into fits, who to this very day usually call sprights and hobgoblins by the name of bull-beggars. They grew at last so very troublesome to the neighborhood, that some gentlemen of the north-west got a parcel of right English bull-dogs, and baited them so terribly that they felt it ever after.

I must needs mention one more of lord Peter's projects, which was very extraordinary, and discovered him to be master of a high reach and profound invention. Whenever it happened that any rogue of Newgate was condemned to be hanged, Peter would offer him a pardon for a certain sum of money; which, when the poor caitiff had made all shifts to scrape up and send, his lordship would return a piece of paper in this form:—[2]

[1] That is, kings who incurred his displeasure.
[2] This is a copy of a general pardon, signed servus servorum (slave of slaves).

'To all mayors, sheriffs, jailors, constables, bailiffs, hangmen, etc. Whereas we are informed that A. B. remains in the hands of you, or some of you, under the sentence of death. We will and command you, upon sight hereof, to let the said prisoner depart to his own habitation, whether he stands condemned for murder, sodomy, rape, sacrilege, incest, treason, blasphemy, etc., for which this shall be your sufficient warrant; and if you fail hereof, G— d—mn you and yours to all eternity. And so we bid you heartily farewell.

Your most humble
Man's man,
Emperor PETER.'

The wretches, trusting to this, lost their lives and money too.

I desire of those whom the learned among posterity will appoint for commentators upon this elaborate treatise, that they will proceed with great caution upon certain dark points, wherein all who are not *verè adepti* [genuine adepts] may be in danger to form rash and hasty conclusions, especially in some mysterious paragraphs, where certain *arcana* are joined for brevity sake, which in the operation must be divided. And I am certain that future sons of art will return large thanks to my memory for so grateful, so useful an *innuendo*.

It will be no difficult part to persuade the reader that so many worthy discoveries met with great success in the world; though I may justly assure him that I have related much the smallest number; my design having been only to single out such as will be of most benefit for public imitation, or which best serve to give some idea of the reach and wit of the inventor. And therefore it need not be wondered at if by this time lord Peter was become exceeding rich: but, alas! he had kept his brain so long and so violently upon the rack, that at last it shook itself, and began to turn round for a little ease. In short, what with pride, projects, and knavery, poor Peter was grown distracted, and conceived the strangest imaginations in the world. In the height of his fits, as it is usual with those who run mad out of pride, he would call himself God Almighty,[3] and some-

[3] The Pope is not only allowed to be the vicar

times monarch of the universe. I have seen him (says my author) take three old high-crowned hats,[1] and clap them all on his head three story high, with a huge bunch of keys at his girdle,[2] and an angling-rod in his hand. In which guise, whoever went to take him by the hand in the way of salutation, Peter with much grace, like a well-educated spaniel, would present them with his foot, and if they refused his civility, then he would raise it as high as their chaps, and give them a damned kick on the mouth, which hath ever since been called a salute. Whoever walked by without paying him their compliments, having a wonderful strong breath, he would blow their hats off into the dirt. Meantime his affairs at home went upside down, and his two brothers had a wretched time; where his first *boutade*[3] was to kick both their wives one morning out of doors, and his own too; and in their stead gave orders to pick up the first three strollers that could be met with in the streets. A while after he nailed up the cellar-door, and would not allow his brothers a drop of drink to their victuals.[4] Dining one day at an alderman's in the city, Peter observed him expatiating, after the manner of his brethren, in the praises of his sirloin of beef. 'Beef,' said the sage magistrate, 'is the king of meat; beef comprehends in it the quintessence of partridge, and quail, and venison, and pheasant, and plum-pudding, and custard.' When Peter came home he would needs take the fancy of cooking up this doctrine into use, and apply the precept, in default of a sirloin, to his brown loaf. 'Bread,' says he, 'dear brothers, is the staff of life; in which bread is contained, inclusive, the quintessence of beef, mutton, veal, venison, partridge, plum-pudding, and custard; and, to render all complete, there is intermingled a due quantity of water, whose crudities are also corrected by yeast or barm, through which means it becomes a wholesome

of Christ, but by several divines is called God upon earth, and other blasphemous titles.
[1] The triple crown.
[2] The keys of the Church.
[3] This word properly signifies a sudden jerk, or lash of a horse, when you do not expect it.
[4] The Pope's refusing the cup to the laity, persuading them that the blood is contained in the bread, and that the bread is the real and entire body of Christ.

fermented liquor, diffused through the mass of the bread.' Upon the strength of these conclusions, next day at dinner was the brown loaf served up in all the formality of a city feast. 'Come, brothers,' said Peter, 'fall to, and spare not; here is excellent good mutton; or hold, now my hand is in, I will help you.' At which word, in much ceremony, with fork and knife, he carves out two good slices of a loaf, and presents each on a plate to his brothers. The elder of the two, not suddenly entering into lord Peter's conceit, began with very civil language to examine the mystery. 'My lord,' said he, 'I doubt, with great submission, there may be some mistake.'— 'What,' says Peter, 'you are pleasant; come then, let us hear this jest your head is so big with.'—'None in the world, my lord; but, unless I am very much deceived, your lordship was pleased a while ago to let fall a word about mutton, and I would be glad to see it with all my heart.'—'How,' said Peter, appearing in great surprise, 'I do not comprehend this at all.' Upon which the younger interposing to set the business aright, 'My lord,' said he, 'my brother, I suppose, is hungry, and longs for the mutton your lordship has promised us to dinner.'— 'Pray,' said Peter, 'take me along with you; either you are both mad, or disposed to be merrier than I approve of; if you there do not like your piece I will carve you another; though I should take that to be the choice bit of the whole shoulder.' —'What then, my lord,' replied the first, 'it seems this is a shoulder of mutton all this while?'—'Pray, sir,' says Peter, 'eat your victuals, and leave off your impertinence, if you please, for I am not disposed to relish it at present': but the other could not forbear, being over-provoked at the affected seriousness of Peter's countenance: 'By G—, my lord,' said he, 'I can only say, that to my eyes, and fingers, and teeth, and nose, it seems to be nothing but a crust of bread.' Upon which the second put in his word: 'I never saw a piece of mutton in my life so nearly resembling a slice from a twelvepenny loaf.'—'Look ye, gentlemen,' cries Peter, in a rage; 'to convince you what a couple of blind, positive, ignorant, wilful puppies you are, I will use but this plain argument: by G—, it is true, good, natural mutton as any in Leadenhallmarket; and G— confound you both eternally if you offer to believe otherwise.' Such a thundering proof as this left no farther room for objection; the two unbelievers began to gather and pocket up their mistake as hastily as they could. 'Why truly,' said the first, 'upon more mature consideration——'—'Ay,' says the other, interrupting him, 'now I have thought better on the thing, your lordship seems to have a great deal of reason.'— 'Very well,' said Peter; 'here, boy, fill me a beer-glass of claret; here's to you both with all my heart.' The two brethren, much delighted to see him so readily appeased, returned their most humble thanks, and said they would be glad to pledge his lordship. 'That you shall,' said Peter; 'I am not a person to refuse you anything that is reasonable: wine, moderately taken, is a cordial; here is a glass a-piece for you; 'tis true natural juice from the grape, none of your damned vintner's brewings.' Having spoke thus, he presented to each of them another large dry crust, bidding them drink it off, and not be bashful, for it would do them no hurt. The two brothers, after having performed the usual office in such delicate conjectures, of staring a sufficient period at lord Peter and each other, and finding how matters were likely to go, resolved not to enter on a new dispute, but let him carry the point as he pleased; for he was now got into one of his mad fits, and to argue or expostulate farther would only serve to render him a hundred times more untractable.

I have chosen to relate this worthy matter in all its circumstances, because it gave a principal occasion to that great and famous rupture [1] which happened about the same time among these brethren, and was never afterwards made up. But of that I shall treat at large in another section.

However, it is certain that lord Peter, even in his lucid intervals, was very lewdly given in his common conversation, extremely wilful and positive, and would at any time rather argue to the death than allow himself once to be in an error. Besides, he had an abominable faculty of telling huge palpable lies upon all occasions; and not only swearing to the truth, but cursing the whole company

to hell if they pretended to make the least scruple of believing him. One time he swore he had a cow at home which gave as much milk at a meal as would fill three thousand churches; and, what was yet more extraordinary, would never turn sour. Another time he was telling of an old sign-post, [2] that belonged to his father, with nails and timber enough in it to build sixteen large men of war. Talking one day of Chinese wagons, which were made so light as to sail over mountains, 'Z—ds,' said Peter, 'where's the wonder of that? By G—, I saw a large house of lime and stone travel over sea and land (granting that it stopped sometimes to bait) above two thousand German leagues.' And that which was the good of it, he would swear desperately all the while that he never told a lie in his life; and at every word, 'By G—, gentlemen, I tell you nothing but the truth; and the d—l broil them eternally that will not believe me.'

In short, Peter grew so scandalous, that all the neighborhood began in plain words to say he was no better than a knave. And his two brothers, long weary of his ill-usage, resolved at last to leave him; but first they humbly desired a copy of their father's will, which had now lain by neglected time out of mind. Instead of granting this request he called them damned . . . rogues, traitors, and the rest of the vile names he could muster up. However, while he was abroad one day upon his projects, the two youngsters watched their opportunity, made a shift to come at the will, [3] and took a *copia vera* [true copy] by which they presently saw how grossly they had been abused; their father having left them equal heirs, and strictly commanded that whatever they got should lie in common among them all. Pursuant to which their next enterprise was to break open the cellar-door, and get a little good drink, [4] to spirit and comfort their hearts. In copying the will they had met another precept against whoring, divorce, and separate maintenance; upon which their next work [5] was to discard their concubines, and send for

---

[1] By this rupture is meant the Reformation.

[2] By the sign-post is meant the cross of our Blessed Savior.

[3] Translated the Scriptures into the vulgar tongues.

[4] Administered the cup to the laity at the communion.

[5] Allowed the marriages of priests.

their wives. While all this was in agitation there enters a solicitor from Newgate, desiring lord Peter would please procure a pardon for a thief that was to be hanged to-morrow. But the two brothers told him he was a coxcomb to seek pardons from a fellow who deserved to be hanged much better than his client; and discovered all the method of that imposture in the same form I delivered it a while ago, advising the solicitor to put his friend upon obtaining a pardon from the king.[1] In the midst of all this clutter and revolution, in comes Peter with a file of dragoons at his heels,[2] and gathering from all hands what was in the wind, he and his gang, after several millions of scurrilities and curses, not very important here to repeat, by main force very fairly kicked them both out of doors,[3] and would never let them come under his roof from that day to this.

* * *

SECTION VI

We left lord Peter in open rupture with his two brethren; both for ever discarded from his house, and resigned to the wide world, with little or nothing to trust to. Which are circumstances that render them proper subjects for the charity of a writer's pen to work on; scenes of misery ever affording the fairest harvest for great adventures. And in this the world may perceive the difference between the integrity of a generous author and that of a common friend. The latter is observed to adhere close in prosperity, but on the decline of fortune to drop suddenly off. Whereas the generous author, just on the contrary, finds his hero on the dunghill, from thence by gradual steps raises him to a throne, and then immediately withdraws, expecting not so much as thanks for his pains; in imitation of which example, I have placed lord Peter in a noble house, given him a title to wear and money to spend. There I shall leave him for some time; returning where common charity directs me, to the assistance of his two brothers at their lowest ebb. However, I shall by no means forget my character of an historian to follow the truth step by step, whatever happens, or wherever it may lead me.

The two exiles, so nearly united in fortune and interest, took a lodging together; where, at their first leisure, they began to reflect on the numberless misfortunes and vexations of their life past, and could not tell on the sudden to what failure in their conduct they ought to impute them; when, after some recollection, they called to mind the copy of their father's will, which they had so happily recovered. This was immediately produced, and a firm resolution taken between them to alter whatever was already amiss, and reduce all their future measures to the strictest obedience prescribed therein. The main body of the will (as the reader cannot easily have forgot) consisted in certain admirable rules about the wearing of their coats; in the perusal whereof, the two brothers at every period duly comparing the doctrine with the practice, there was never seen a wider difference between two things; horrible downright transgressions of every point. Upon which they both resolved, without further delay, to fall immediately upon reducing the whole exactly after their father's model.

But here it is good to stop the hasty reader, ever impatient to see the end of an adventure before we writers can duly prepare him for it. I am to record that these two brothers began to be distinguished at this time by certain names. One of them desired to be called MARTIN,[4] and the other took the appellation of JACK.[5] These two had lived in much friendship and agreement under the tyranny of their brother Peter, as it is the talent of fellow-sufferers to do; men in misfortune being like men in the dark, to whom all colors are the same: but when they came forward into the world, and began to display themselves to each other and to the light, their complexions appeared extremely different; which the present posture of their affairs gave them sudden opportunity to discover.

---

[1] Directed penitents not to trust to pardons and absolutions procured for money, but sent them to implore the mercy of God, from whence alone remission is to be obtained.

[2] By Peter's dragoons is meant the civil power, which those princes who were bigoted to the Romish superstition, employed against the reformers.

[3] The Pope shuts all who dissent from him out of the Church.

[4] Martin Luther.

[5] John Calvin.

But here the severe reader may justly tax me as a writer of short memory, a deficiency to which a true modern cannot but of necessity be a little subject. Because memory, being an employment of the mind upon things past, is a faculty for which the learned in our illustrious age have no manner of occasion, who deal entirely with invention, and strike all things out of themselves, or at least by collision from each other: upon which account we think it highly reasonable to produce our great forgetfulness as an argument unanswerable for our great wit. I ought in method to have informed the reader, about fifty pages ago, of a fancy lord Peter took, and infused into his brothers, to wear on their coats whatever trimmings came up in fashion; never pulling off any as they went out of the mode, but keeping on all together, which amounted in time to a medley the most antic you can possibly conceive; and this to a degree, that upon the time of their falling out there was hardly a thread of the original coat to be seen; but an infinite quantity of lace, and ribbons, and fringe, and embroidery, and points; I mean only those tagged with silver,[1] for the rest fell off. Now this material circumstance, having been forgot in due place, as good fortune hath ordered, comes in very properly here when the two brothers are just going to reform their vestures into the primitive state prescribed by their father's will.

They both unanimously entered upon this great work, looking sometimes on their coats; and sometimes on the will. Martin laid the first hand; at one twitch brought off a large handful of points; and, with a second pull, stripped away ten dozen yards of fringe. But when he had gone thus far he demurred a while: he knew very well there yet remained a great deal more to be done; however, the first heat being over, his violence began to cool, and he resolved to proceed more moderately in the rest of the work, having already narrowly escaped a swinging rent, in pulling off the points, which, being tagged with silver (as we have observed before), the judicious workman had, with much sagacity, double sewn, to

preserve them from falling. Resolving, therefore, to rid his coat of a great quantity of gold-lace, he picked up the stitches with much caution, and diligently gleaned out all the loose threads as he went, which proved to be a work of time. Then he fell about the embroidered Indian figures of men, women, and children; against which, as you have heard in its due place, their father's testament was extremely exact and severe; these, with much dexterity and application, were, after a while, quite eradicated or utterly defaced. For the rest, where he observed the embroidery to be worked so close as not to be got away without damaging the cloth, or where it served to hide or strengthen any flaw in the body of the coat, contracted by the perpetual tampering of workmen upon it, he concluded the wisest course was to let it remain, resolving in no case whatsoever that the substance of the stuff should suffer injury; which he thought the best method for serving the true intent and meaning of his father's will. And this is the nearest account I have been able to collect of Martin's proceedings upon this great revolution.

But his brother Jack, whose adventures will be so extraordinary as to furnish a great part in the remainder of this discourse, entered upon the matter with other thoughts and a quite different spirit. For the memory of lord Peter's injuries produced a degree of hatred and spite which had a much greater share of inciting him than any regards after his father's commands; since these appeared, at best, only secondary and subservient to the other. However, for this medley of humor he made a shift to find a very plausible name, honoring it with the title of zeal; which is perhaps the most significant word that has been ever yet produced in any language: as I think I have fully proved in my excellent analytical discourse upon that subject; wherein I have deduced a histori-theo-physi-logical account of zeal, showing how it first proceeded from a notion into a word, and thence, in a hot summer, ripened into a tangible substance. This work, containing three large volumes in folio, I design very shortly to publish by the modern way of subscription, not doubting but the nobility and gentry of the land will give me all possible en-

---

[1] Points tagged with silver are those doctrines that promote the greatness and wealth of the Church, which have been therefore woven deepest into the body of popery.

couragement; having had already such a
taste of what I am able perform.

I record, therefore, that brother Jack,
brimful of this miraculous compound, reflecting with indignation upon Peter's
tyranny, and farther provoked by the
despondency of Martin, prefaced his resolutions to this purpose. 'What,' said
he, 'a rogue that locked up his drink,
turned away our wives, cheated us of our
fortunes; palmed his damned crusts upon
us for mutton; and at last kicked us out
of doors; must we be in his fashions,
with a pox? A rascal, besides, that all
the street cries out against.' Having
thus kindled and inflamed himself as
high as possible, and by consequence in a
delicate temper for beginning a reformation, he set about the work immediately;
and in three minutes made more despatch
than Martin had done in as many hours.
For, courteous reader, you are given to
understand that zeal is never so highly
obliged as when you set it a-tearing; and
Jack, who doted on that quality in himself, allowed it at this time its full swing.
Thus it happened that, stripping down a
parcel of gold lace a little too hastily,
he rent the main body of his coat from
top to bottom; and whereas his talent
was not of the happiest in taking up a
stitch, he knew no better way than to
darn it again with packthread and a
skewer. But the matter was yet infinitely worse (I record it with tears)
when he proceeded to the embroidery:
for, being clumsy by nature, and of
temper impatient; withal, beholding millions of stitches that required the nicest
hand and sedatest constitution to extri-
cate; in a great rage he tore off the whole
piece, cloth and all, and flung them into
the kennel, and furiously thus continuing his career: 'Ah, good brother Martin,' said he, 'do as I do, for the love of
God; strip, tear, pull, rend, flay off all,
that we may appear as unlike the rogue
Peter as it is possible; I would not for
a hundred pounds carry the least mark
about me that might give occasion to the
neighbors of suspecting that I was related to such a rascal.' But Martin, who
at this time happened to be extremely
phlegmatic and sedate, begged his
brother, of all love, not to damage his
coat by any means; for he never would
get such another: desired him to consider
that it was not their business to form

their actions by any reflection upon
Peter, but by observing the rules prescribed in their father's will. That he
should remember Peter was still their
brother, whatever faults or injuries he
had committed; and therefore they should
by all means avoid such a thought as
that of taking measures for good and
evil from no other rule than of opposition to him. That it was true, the testament of their good father was very exact
in what related to the wearing of their
coats: yet it was no less penal and strict
in prescribing agreement, and friendship,
and affection between them. And therefore, if straining a point were at all dis-
pensable, it would certainly be so rather
to the advance of unity than increase of
contradiction.

MARTIN had still proceeded as gravely
as he began, and doubtless would have
delivered an admirable lecture of morality, which might have exceedingly contributed to my reader's repose both of
body and mind, the true ultimate end of
ethics; but Jack was already gone a
flight-shot beyond his patience. And as
in scholastic disputes nothing serves to
rouse the spleen of him that opposes so
much as a kind of pedantic affected
calmness in the respondent; disputants
being for the most part like unequal
scales, where the gravity of one side advances the lightness of the other, and
causes it to fly up and kick the beam;
so it happened here that the weight of
Martin's argument exalted Jack's levity,
and made him fly out, and spurn against
his brother's moderation. In short, Martin's patience put Jack in a rage; but
that which most afflicted him was, to
observe his brother's coat so well reduced
into the state of innocence; while his
own was either wholly rent to his shirt,
or those places which had escaped his
cruel clutches were still in Peter's livery.
So that he looked like a drunken beau,
half rifled by bullies; or like a fresh
tenant of Newgate, when he has refused
the payment of garnish; or like a discovered shoplifter, left to the mercy of
Exchange women; or like a bawd in her
old velvet petticoat, resigned into her
secular hands of the mobile. Like any,
or like all these, a medley of rags, and
lace, and rents, and fringes, unfortunate
Jack did now appear: he would have
been extremely glad to see his coat in

the condition of Martin's, but infinitely gladder to find that of Martin in the same predicament with his. However, since neither of these was likely to come to pass, he thought fit to lend the whole business another turn, and to dress up necessity into a virtue. Therefore, after as many of the fox's arguments as he could muster up, for bringing Martin to reason, as he called it; or, as he meant it, into his own ragged, bobtailed condition; and observing he said all to little purpose; what, alas! was left for the forlorn Jack to do, but, after a million of scurrilities against his brother, to run mad with spleen, and spite, and contradiction. To be short, here began a mortal breach between these two. Jack went immediately to new lodgings, and in a few days it was for certain reported that he had run out of his wits. In a short time after he appeared abroad, and confirmed the report by falling into the oddest whimseys that ever a sick brain conceived.

And now the little boys in the streets began to salute him with several names. Sometimes they would call him Jack the bald;[1] sometimes, Jack with a lantern;[2] sometimes, Dutch Jack;[3] sometimes, French Hugh;[4] sometimes, Tom the beggar;[5] and sometimes, Knocking Jack of the North.[6] And it was under one, or some, or all of these appellations, which I leave the learned reader to determine, that he has given rise to the most illustrious and epidemic sect of Aeolists; who, with honorable commemoration, do still acknowledge the renowned JACK for their author and founder. Of whose original, as well as principles, I am now advancing to gratify the world with a very particular account.

—Melleo contingens cuncta lepore.
[Touching everything with a honeyed charm.]

[1] That is, Calvin, from *calvus,* bald.

[2] All those who pretend to inward light.

[3] Jack of Leyden, who gave rise to the Anabaptists.

[4] The Huguenots.

[5] The Gueuses, by which name some Protestants in Flanders were called.

[6] John Knox, the reformer of Scotland.

* * *

SECTION XI

After so wide a compass as I have wandered, I do now gladly overtake and close in with my subject, and shall henceforth hold on with it an even pace to the end of my journey, except some beautiful prospect appears within sight of my way; whereof though at present I have neither warning nor expectation, yet upon such an accident, come when it will, I shall beg my reader's favor and company, allowing me to conduct him through it along with myself. For in writing it is as in traveling; if a man is in haste to be at home (which I acknowledge to be none of my case, having never so little business as when I am there), and his horse be tired with long riding and ill ways, or be naturally a jade, I advise him clearly to make the straightest and the commonest road, be it ever so dirty; but then surely we must own such a man to be a scurvy companion at best; he spatters himself and his fellow-travelers at every step; all their thoughts, and wishes, and conversation turn entirely upon the subject of their journey's end; and at every splash, and plunge, and stumble, they heartily wish one another at the devil.

On the other side, when a traveler and his horse are in heart and plight, when his purse is full and the day before him, he takes the road only where it is clean and convenient; entertains his company there as agreeably as he can; but, upon the first occasion, carries them along with him to every delightful scene in view, whether of art, of nature, or of both; and if they chance to refuse, out of stupidity or weariness, let them jog on by themselves and be d——n'd; he'll overtake them at the next town; at which arriving, he rides furiously through; the men, women and children run out of gaze; a hundred[7] noisy curs run barking after him, of which, if he honors the boldest with a lash of his whip, it is rather out of sport than revenge; but should some sourer mongrel dare too near an approach, he receives a salute on the chaps by an accidental stroke from the courser's heels, nor is any ground lost by the blow, which sends him yelping and limping home.

[7] By these are meant what the author calls the true critics.

I now proceed to sum up the singular adventures of my renowned Jack; the state of whose dispositions and fortunes the careful reader does, no doubt, most exactly remember, as I last parted with them in the conclusion of a former section. Therefore, his next care must be, from two of the foregoing, to extract a scheme of notions that may best fit his understanding for a true relish of what is to ensue.

JACK had not only calculated the first revolution of his brain so prudently as to give rise to that epidemic sect of Aeolists, but succeeding also into a new and strange variety of conceptions, the fruitfulness of his imagination led him into certain notions, which, although in appearance very unaccountable, were not without their mysteries and their meanings, nor wanted followers to countenance and improve them. I shall therefore be extremely careful and exact in recounting such material passages of this nature as I have been able to collect, either from undoubted tradition or indefatigable reading; and shall describe them as graphically as it is possible, and as far as notions of that height and latitude can be brought within the compass of a pen. Nor do I at all question but they will furnish plenty of noble matter for such whose converting imaginations dispose them to reduce all things into types; who can make shadows, no thanks to the sun; and then mould them into substances, no thanks to philosophy; whose peculiar talent lies in fixing tropes and allegories to the letter, and refining what is literal into figure and mystery.

JACK had provided a fair copy of his father's will, engrossed in form upon a large skin of parchment; and resolving to act the part of a most dutiful son, he became the fondest creature of it imaginable. For although, as I have often told the reader, it consisted wholly in certain plain, easy directions, about the management and wearing their coats, with legacies, and penalties in case of obedience or neglect, yet he began to entertain a fancy that the matter was deeper and darker, and therefore must needs have a great deal more of mystery at the bottom. 'Gentlemen,' said he, 'I will prove this very skin of parchment to be meat, drink, and cloth, to be the philosopher's stone and the universal medicine.' In consequence of which raptures, he resolved to make use of it in the necessary as well as the most paltry occasions of life.[1] He had a way of working it into any shape he pleased; so that it served him for a nightcap when he went to bed, and for an umbrella in rainy weather. He would lap a piece of it about a sore toe, or, when he had fits, burn two inches under his nose; or, if anything lay heavy on his stomach, scrape off and swallow as much of the powder as would lie on a silver penny; they were all infallible remedies. With analogy to these refinements, his common talk and conversation ran wholly in the phrase of his will, and he circumscribed the utmost of his eloquence within that compass, not daring to let slip a syllable without authority from thence. . . .

He made it a part of his religion never to say grace to his meat;[2] nor could all the world persuade him, as the common phrase is, to eat his victuals like a christian.[3]

He bore a strange kind of appetite to snap-dragon,[4] and to the livid snuffs of a burning candle, which he would catch and swallow with an agility wonderful to conceive; and, by this procedure, maintained a perpetual flame in his belly, which, issuing in a glowing steam from both his eyes, as well as his nostrils and his mouth, made his head appear, in a dark night, like the skull of an ass, wherein a roguish boy had conveyed a farthing candle, to the terror of his majesty's liege subjects. Therefore, made use of no other expedient to light himself home, but was wont to say that a wise man was his own lantern.

He would shut his eyes as he walked along the streets, and if he happened to bounce his head against a post, or fall into a kennel, as he seldom missed either to do one or both, he would tell the gib-

---

[1] The author here lashes those pretenders to purity, who place so much merit in using Scripture phrases on all occasions.

[2] The slovenly way of receiving the sacrament among the fanatics.

[3] This is a common phrase to express eating cleanly, and is meant for an invective against that indecent manner among some people in receiving the sacrament; so in the lines before, which is to be understood of the Dissenters refusing to kneel at the sacrament.

[4] I cannot well find out the author's meaning here, unless it be the hot, untimely, blind zeal of enthusiasts.

ing prentices who looked on that he submitted with entire resignation as to a trip or a blow of fate, with whom he found, by long experience, how vain it was either to wrestle or to cuff; and whoever durst undertake to do either would be sure to come off with a swinging fall or a bloody nose. 'It was ordained,' said he, 'some few days before the creation, that my nose and this very post should have a rencounter; and therefore nature thought fit to send us both into the world in the same age, and to make us countrymen and fellow-citizens. Now, had my eyes been open, it is very likely the business might have been a great deal worse; for how many a confounded slip is daily got by a man with all this foresight about him? Besides, the eyes of the understanding see best when those of the senses are out of the way; and therefore blind men are observed to tread their steps with much more caution, and conduct, and judgment, than those who rely with too much confidence upon the virtue of the visual nerve, which every little accident shakes out of order, and a drop or a film can wholly disconcert; like a lantern among a pack of roaring bullies when they scour the streets, exposing its owner and itself to outward kicks and buffets, which both might have escaped if the vanity of appearing would have suffered them to walk in the dark. But farther. if we examine the conduct of these boasted lights, it will prove yet a great deal worse than their fortune. 'T is true, I have broke my nose against this post, because fortune either forgot, or did not think it convenient, to twitch me by the elbow, and give me notice to avoid it. But let not this encourage either the present age or posterity to trust their noses into the keeping of their eyes, which may prove the fairest way of losing them for good and all. For, O ye eyes, ye blind guides; miserable guardians are ye of our frail noses; ye, I say, who fasten upon the first precipice in view, and then tow our wretched willing bodies after you to the very brink of destruction. But alas! that brink is rotten, our feet slip, and we tumble down prone into a gulf, without one hospitable shrub in the way to break the fall; a fall to which not any nose of mortal make is equal, except that of the

giant Laurcalco,[1] who was lord of the silver bridge. Most properly, therefore, O eyes, and with great justice, may you be compared to those foolish lights which conduct men through dirt and darkness, till they fall into a deep pit or a noisome bog.'

This I have produced as a scantling of Jack's great eloquence, and the force of his reasoning upon such abstruse matters.

He was, besides, a person of great design and improvement in affairs of devotion, having introduced a new deity, who has since met with a vast number of worshippers; by some called Babel, by others Chaos, who had an ancient temple of Gothic structure upon Salisbury plain, famous for its shrine and celebration by pilgrims.

When he had some roguish trick to play,[2] he would down with his knees, up with his eyes, and fall to prayers, though in the midst of the kennel. Then it was that those who understood his pranks would be sure to get far enough out of his way; and whenever curiosity attracted strangers to laugh or to listen, he would, of a sudden, . . . all bespatter them with mud.

In winter he went always loose and unbuttoned,[3] and clad as thin as possible to let in the ambient heat; and in summer lapped himself close and thick to keep it out.

In all revolutions of government[4] he would make his court for the office of hangman general; and in the exercise of that dignity, where he was very dexterous, would make use of no other vizard[5] than a long prayer.

He had a tongue so musculous and subtile, that he could twist it up into his nose, and deliver a strange kind of speech from thence. He was also the first in these kingdoms who began to improve the Spanish accomplishment of braying; and having large ears, perpetually exposed and erected, he carried his art to such perfection, that it was a point

[1] Vide [See] Don Quixote.
[2] The villainies and cruelties, committed by enthusiasts and fanatics among us, were all performed under the disguise of religion and long prayers.
[3] They affect differences in habit and behavior.
[4] They are severe persecutors and all in a form of cant and devotion.
[5] Cromwell and his confederates went, as they called it, to seek the Lord. when they resolved to murder the king.

of great difficulty to distinguish, either by the view or the sound, between the original and the copy.

He was troubled with a disease reverse to that called the stinging of the tarantula; and would run dog-mad at the noise of music, especially a pair of bagpipes. But he would cure himself again by taking two or three turns in Westminster-hall, or Billingsgate, or in the boarding-school, or the Royal Exchange, or a state coffee-house.

He was a person that feared no colors, but mortally hated all, and, upon that account, bore a cruel aversion against painters,[1] insomuch that, in his paroxysms, as he walked the streets, he would have his pockets loaden with stones to pelt at the signs.

Having, from this manner of living, frequent occasion to wash himself, he would often leap over head and ears into the water, though it were in the midst of the winter, but was always observed to come out again much dirtier, if possible, than he went in.

He was the first that ever found out the secret of contriving a soporiferous medicine to be conveyed in at the ears;[2] it was a compound of sulphur and balm of Gilead, with a little pilgrim's salve.

He wore a large plaster of artificial caustics on his stomach, with the fervor of which he could set himself a-groaning, like the famous board upon application of a red-hot iron.

He would stand in the turning of a street, and, calling to those who passed by, would cry to one, 'Worthy sir, do me the honor of a good slap in the chaps.'[3] To another, 'Honest friend, pray favor me with a handsome kick on the arse: Madam, shall I entreat a small box on the ear from your ladyship's fair hands? Noble captain, lend a reasonable thwack, for the love of God, with that cane of yours over these poor shoulders.' And when he had, by such earnest solicitations, made a shift to procure a basting sufficient to swell up his fancy and his sides, he would return home extremely comforted, and full of terrible accounts of what he had undergone for the public good. 'Observe this stroke,' said he, showing his bare shoulders; 'a plaguy janizary gave it me this very morning, at seven o'clock, as, with much ado, I was driving off the great Turk. Neighbors, mind, this broken head deserves a plaster; had poor Jack been tender of his noddle, you would have seen the pope and the French king, long before this time of day, among your wives and your warehouses. Dear christians, the great Mogul was come as far as Whitechapel, and you may thank these poor sides that he hath not (God bless us!) already swallowed up man, woman, and child.'

It was highly worth observing the singular effects of that aversion[4] or antipathy which Jack and his brother Peter seemed, even to an affectation, to bear toward each other. Peter had lately done some rogueries that forced him to abscond, and he seldom ventured to stir out before night, for fear of bailiffs. Their lodgings were at the two most distant parts of the town from each other; and whenever their occasions or humors called them abroad, they would make choice of the oddest unlikely times, and most uncouth rounds they could invent, that they might be sure to avoid one another; yet, after all this, it was their perpetual fortune to meet. The reason of which is easy enough to apprehend; for, the frenzy and the spleen of both having the same foundation, we may look upon them as two pair of compasses, equally extended, and the fixed foot of each remaining in the same center, which, though moving contrary ways at first, will be sure to encounter somewhere or other in the circumference. Besides, it was among the great misfortunes of Jack to bear a huge personal resemblance with his brother Peter. Their humor and dispositions were not only the same, but there was a close analogy in their shape, and size, and their mien. Insomuch, that nothing was more frequent than for a bailiff to

---

[1] They quarrel at the most innocent decency and ornament, and defaced the statues and paintings in all the churches in England.

[2] Fanatic preaching, composed either of hell and damnation, or a fulsome description of the joys of heaven; both in such a dirty, nauseous style, as to be well resembled to pilgrim's salve.

[3] The fanatics have always had a way of affecting to run into persecution, and count vast merit upon every little hardship they suffer.

[4] The Papists and fanatics, though they appear the most averse to each other, yet bear a near resemblance in many things, as has been observed by learned men.

seize Jack by the shoulder, and cry,
'Mr. Peter, you are the king's prisoner.'
Or, at other times, for one of Peter's
nearest friends to accost Jack with open
arms, 'Dear Peter, I am glad to see
thee; pray send me one of your best
medicines for the worms.' This, we may
suppose, was a mortifying return of
those pains and proceedings Jack had
labored in so long; and finding how
directly opposite all his endeavors had
answered to the sole end and intention
which he had proposed to himself, how
could it avoid having terrible effects
upon a head and heart so furnished as
his? However, the poor remainders of
his coat bore all the punishment; the
orient sun never entered upon his
diurnal progress without missing a piece
of it. He hired a tailor to stitch up the
collar so close that it was ready to
choke him, and squeezed out his eyes
at such a rate as one could see nothing
but the white. What little was left of
the main substance of the coat he rubbed every day for two hours against a
rough-cast wall, in order to grind away
the remnants of lace and embroidery;
but at the same time went on with so
much violence that he proceeded a
heathen philosopher. Yet, after all he
could do of this kind, the success continued still to disappoint his expectation. For, as it is the nature of rags
to bear a kind of mock resemblance to
finery, there being a sort of fluttering
appearance in both which is not to be
distinguished at a distance, in the dark,
or by short-sighted eyes, so, in those
junctures, it fared with Jack and his
tatters, that they offered to the first view
a ridiculous flaunting, which, assisting
the resemblance in person and air,
thwarted all his projects of separation,
and left so near a similitude between
them as frequently deceived the very
disciples and followers of both.

. . . .

Desunt non- . . . . .
nulla [something is wanting].   .

The old Sclavonian proverb said well,
that it is with men as with asses; whoever would keep them fast must find a
very good hold at their ears. Yet I
think we may affirm that it hath been
verified by repeated experience that —

*Effugiet tamen haec sceleratus vincula Pro-
teus.*
[Still wicked Proteus eludes these chains.]

It is good, therefore, to read the maxims of our ancestors, with great allowances to times and persons; for, if we
look into primitive records, we shall find
that no revolutions have been so great
or so frequent as those of human ears.
In former days there was a curious invention to catch and keep them, which
I think we may justly reckon among the
artes perditæ [lost arts]; and how can
it be otherwise, when in the latter centuries the very species is not only diminished to a very lamentable degree, but the
poor remainder is also degenerated so
far as to mock our skilfullest tenure?
For, if the only slitting of one ear in
a stag has been found sufficient to propagate the defect through a whole forest, why should we wonder at the
greatest consequences from so many lop-
pings and mutilations to which the ears
of our fathers, and our own, have been
of late so much exposed? It is true,
indeed, that while this island of ours was
under the dominion of grace, many endeavors were made to improve the
growth of ears once more among us.
The proportion of largeness was not only
looked upon as an ornament of the outward man, but as a type of grace in the
inward. Lastly, the devouter sisters,
who looked upon all extraordinary dilata-
tions of that member as protrusions of
zeal, or spiritual excrescences, were
sure to honor every head they sat upon
as if they had been marks of grace;[1]
but especially that of the preacher,
whose ears were usually of the prime
magnitude; which, upon that account,
he was very frequent and exact in exposing with all advantages to the people; in his rhetorical paroxysms turning
sometimes to hold forth the one, and
sometimes to hold forth the other: from
which custom the whole operation of
preaching is to this very day, among
their professors, styled by the phrase
of holding forth.

Such was the progress of the saints
for advancing the size of that member;
and it is thought the success would have
been every way answerable, if, in proc-

[1] As if they had been cloven tongues.— *First
Edition.*

ess of time, a cruel king had not risen,[1] who raised a bloody persecution against all ears above a certain standard; upon which, some were glad to hide their flourishing sprouts in a black border, others crept wholly under a periwig; some were slit, others cropped, and a great number sliced off to the stumps. But of this more hereafter in my general history of ears, which I design very speedily to bestow upon the public.

From this brief survey of the falling state of ears in the last age, and the small care had to advance their ancient growth in the present, it is manifest how little reason we can have to rely upon a hold so short, so weak, and so slippery, and that whoever desires to catch mankind fast must have recourse to some other methods. Now, he that will examine human nature with circumspection enough may discover several handles, whereof the six[2] senses afford one-a-piece, beside a great number that are screwed to the passions, and some few riveted to the intellect. Among these last, curiosity is one, and of all others, affords the firmest grasp: curiosity, that spur in the side, that bridle in the mouth, that ring in the nose, of a lazy and impatient and a grunting reader. By this handle it is, that an author should seize upon his readers; which as soon as he has once compassed, all resistance and struggling are in vain; and they become his prisoners as close as he pleases, till weariness or dulness force him to let go his grip.

And therefore, I, the author of this miraculous treatise, having hitherto, beyond expectation, maintained, by the aforesaid handle, a firm hold upon my gentle readers, it is with great reluctance that I am at length compelled to remit my grasp; leaving them, in the perusal of what remains, to that natural oscitancy inherent in the tribe. I can only assure thee, courteous reader, for both our comforts, that my concern is altogether equal to thine for my unhappiness in losing, or mislaying among my papers, the remaining part of these memoirs; which consisted of accidents, turns, and adventures, both new, agreeable, and surprising; and therefore calculated, in

all due points, to the delicate taste of this our noble age. But, alas! with my utmost endeavors, I have been able only to retain a few of the heads. Under which, there was a full account how Peter got a protection out of the king's bench; and of a reconcilement[3] between Jack and him, upon a design they had, in a certain rainy night, to trepan brother Martin into a spunging-house, and there strip him to the skin. How Martin, with much ado, showed them both a fair pair of heels. How a new warrant came out against Peter; upon which, how Jack left him in the lurch, stole his protection, and made use of it himself. How Jack's tatters came into fashion in court and city; how he got upon a great horse,[4] and eat custard.[5] But the particulars of all these, with several others which have now slid out of my memory, are lost beyond all hopes of recovery. For which misfortune, leaving my readers to condole with each other, as far as they shall find it to agree with their several constitutions, but conjuring them by all the friendship that has passed between us, from the title-page to this, not to proceed so far as to injure their healths for an accident past remedy — I now go on to the ceremonial part of an accomplished writer, and therefore, by a courtly modern, least of all others to be omitted.

* * * (1704)

A MEDITATION UPON A BROOM-STICK, ACCORDING TO THE STYLE AND MANNER OF THE HON. ROBERT BOYLE'S MEDITATIONS

This single stick, which you now behold ingloriously lying in that neglected

---

[1] This was King Charles the Second, who, at his restoration, turned out all the dissenting teachers that would not conform.

[2] Including Scaliger's.

[3] In the reign of King James the Second the Presbyterians, by the king's invitation, joined with the Papists, against the Church of England, and addressed him for repeal of the penal laws and test. The king, by his dispensing power, gave liberty of conscience, which both Papists and Presbyterians made use of; but, upon the Revolution, the Papists being down of course, the Presbyterians freely continued their assemblies, by virtue of King James's indulgence, before they had a toleration by law. This I believe the author means by Jack's stealing Peter's protection, and making use of it himself.

[4] Sir Humphry Edwyn, a Presbyterian, when lord-mayor of London, in 1697, had the insolence to go in his formalities to a conventicle, with the ensigns of his office.

[5] Custard is a famous dish at a lord-mayor's feast.

torner, I once knew in a flourishing state in a forest; it was full of sap, full of leaves, and full of boughs; but now in vain does the busy art of man pretend to vie with nature, by tying that 5 withered bundle of twigs to its sapless trunk; 't is now at best but the reverse of what it was, a tree turned upside down, the branches on the earth, and the root in the air; 't is now handled 10 by every dirty wench, condemned to do her drudgery, and, by a capricious kind of fate, destined to make other things clean, and be nasty itself; at length, worn to the stumps in the service of 15 the maids, it is either thrown out of door, or condemned to the last use, of kindling a fire. When I beheld this, I sighed, and said within myself: SURELY MAN IS A BROOMSTICK! 20 nature sent him into the world strong and lusty, in a thriving condition, wearing his own hair on his head, the proper branches of this reasoning vegetable, until the axe of intemperance has lopped 25 off his green boughs, and left him a withered trunk; he then flies to art, and puts on a periwig, valuing himself upon an unnatural bundle of hairs, all covered with powder, that never grew on 30 his head; but now should this our broomstick pretend to enter the scene, proud of those birchen spoils it never bore, and all covered with dust, though the sweepings of the finest lady's chamber, 35 we should be apt to ridicule and despise its vanity. Partial judges that we are of our own excellences, and other men's defaults!

But a broomstick, perhaps you will 40 say, is an emblem of a tree standing on its head; and pray, what is man but a topsy-turvy creature, his animal faculties perpetually mounted on his rational; his head where his heels should be, grovel- 45 ing on the earth! and yet, with all his faults, he sets up to be a universal reformer and corrector of abuses, a remover of grievances; rakes into every slut's corner of nature, bringing hidden 50 corruption to the light, and raises a mighty dust where there was none before; sharing deeply all the while in the very same pollutions he pretends to sweep away: his last days are spent in 55 slavery to women, and generally the least deserving, till, worn out to the stumps, like his brother besom, he is either kicked out of doors, or made use of to kindle flames for others to warm themselves by.

(1704)

A MODEST PROPOSAL

FOR PREVENTING THE CHILDREN OF POOR PEOPLE IN IRELAND FROM BEING A BURDEN TO THEIR PARENTS OR COUNTRY, AND FOR MAKING THEM BENEFICIAL TO THE PUBLIC

It is a melancholy object to those who 15 walk through this great town or travel in the country, when they see the streets, the roads, and cabin doors, crowded with beggars of the female sex, followed by three, four, or six children, all in rags 20 and importuning every passenger for an alms. These mothers, instead of being able to work for their honest livelihood, are forced to employ all their time in strolling to beg sustenance for their help- 25 less infants: who as they grow up either turn thieves for want of work, or leave their dear native country to fight for the pretender in Spain, or sell themselves to the Barbadoes.

I think it is agreed by all parties that this prodigious number of children in the arms, or on the backs, or at the heels of their mothers, and frequently of their fathers, is in the present deplorable state 35 of the kingdom a very great additional grievance; and, therefore, whoever could find out a fair, cheap, and easy method of making these children sound, useful members of the commonwealth, would 40 deserve so well of the public as to have his statue set up for a preserver of the nation.

But my intention is very far from being confined to provide only for the chil- 45 dren of professed beggars; it is of a much greater extent, and shall take in the whole number of infants at a certain age who are born of parents in effect as little able to support them as those 50 who demand our charity in the streets.

As to my own part, having turned my thoughts for many years upon this important subject, and maturely weighed the several schemes of other projectors, 55 I have always found them grossly mistaken in the computation. It is true, a child just dropped from its dam may be supported by her milk for a solar year, with little other nourishment; at most not above the value of 2s., which the mother may certainly get, or the value in scraps, by her lawful occupation of begging; and it is exactly at one year old that I propose to provide for them in such a manner as instead of being a charge upon their parents or the parish, or wanting food and raiment for the rest of their lives, they shall on the contrary contribute to the feeding, and partly to the clothing, of many thousands.

There is likewise another great advantage in my scheme, that it will prevent those voluntary abortions, and that horrid practice of women murdering their bastard children, alas! too frequent among us! sacrificing the poor innocent babes I doubt more to avoid the expense than the shame, which would move tears and pity in the most savage and inhuman breast.

The number of souls in this kingdom being usually reckoned one million and a half, of these I calculate there may be about two hundred thousand couple whose wives are breeders; from which number I subtract thirty thousand couples who are able to maintain their own children, although I apprehend there cannot be so many, under the present distresses of the kingdom; but this being granted, there will remain an hundred and seventy thousand breeders. I again substract fifty thousand for those women who miscarry, or whose children die by accident or disease within the year. There only remains one hundred and twenty thousand children of poor parents annually born. The question therefore is, how this number shall be reared and provided for, which, as I have already said, under the present situation of affairs, is utterly impossible by all the methods hitherto proposed. For we can neither employ them in handicraft or agriculture; we neither build houses (I mean in the country) nor cultivate land: they can very seldom pick up a livelihood by stealing, till they arrive at six years old, except where they are of towardly parts, although I confess they learn the rudiments much earlier, during which time, they can however be properly looked upon only as probationers, as I have been informed by a principal gentleman in the county of Cavan, who protested to me that he never knew above one or two instances under the age of six, even in a part of the kingdom so renowned for the quickest proficiency in that art.

I am assured by our merchants, that a boy or a girl before twelve years old is no salable commodity; and even when they come to this age they will not yield above three pounds, or three pounds and half-a-crown at most on the exchange; which cannot turn to account either to the parents or kingdom, the charge of nutriment and rags having been at least four times that value.

I shall now therefore humbly propose my own thoughts, which I hope will not be liable to the least objection.

I have been assured by a very knowing American of my acquaintance in London, that a young healthy child well nursed is at a year old a most delicious, nourishing, and wholesome food, whether stewed, roasted, baked, or boiled; and I make no doubt that it will equally serve in a fricassee or a ragout.

I do therefore humbly offer it to public consideration that of the hundred and twenty thousand children already computed, twenty thousand may be reserved for breed, whereof only one-fourth part to be males; which is more than we allow to sheep, black cattle or swine; and my reason is, that these children are seldom the fruits of marriage, a circumstance not much regarded by our savages, therefore one male will be sufficient to serve four females. That the remaining hundred thousand may, at a year old, be offered in the sale to the persons of quality and fortune through the kingdom; always advising the mother to let them suck plentifully in the last month, so as to render them plump and fat for a good table. A child will make two dishes at an entertainment for friends; and when the family dines alone, the fore or hind quarter will make a reasonable dish, and seasoned with a little pepper or salt will be very good boiled on the fourth day, especially in winter.

I have reckoned upon a medium that a child just born will weigh 12 pounds, and in a solar year, if tolerably nursed, increaseth to 28 pounds.

I grant this food will be somewhat dear, and therefore very proper for landlords, who, as they have already devoured most of the parents, seem to have the best title to the children.

Infant's flesh will be in season throughout the year, but more plentiful in March, and a little before and after; for we are told by a grave author, an eminent French physician, that fish being a prolific diet, there are more children born in Roman Catholic countries about nine months after Lent than at any other season; therefore, reckoning a year after Lent, the markets will be more glutted than usual, because the number of popish infants is at least three to one in this kingdom: and therefore it will have one other collateral advantage, by lessening the number of papists among us.

I have already computed the charge of nursing a beggar's child (in which list I reckon all cottagers, laborers, and four-fifths of the farmers) to be about two shillings per annum, rags included; and I believe no gentleman would repine to give ten shillings for the carcass of a good fat child, which, as I have said, will make four dishes of excellent nutritive meat, when he hath only some particular friend or his own family to dine with him. Thus the squire will learn to be a good landlord, and grow popular among his tenants; the mother will have eight shillings net profit, and be fit for work till she produces another child.

Those who are more thrifty (as I must confess the times require) may flay the carcass; the skin of which artificially dressed will make admirable gloves for ladies, and summer boots for fine gentlemen.

As to our city of Dublin, shambles may be appointed for this purpose in the most convenient parts of it, and butchers we may be assured will not be wanting; although I rather recommend buying the children alive than dressing them hot from the knife as we do roasting pigs.

A very worthy person, a true lover of his country, and whose virtues I highly esteem, was lately pleased in discoursing on this matter to offer a refinement upon my scheme. He said that many gentlemen of this kingdom, having of late destroyed their deer, he conceived that the want of venison might be well supplied by the bodies of young lads and maidens, not exceeding fourteen years of age nor under twelve; so great a number of both sexes in every country being now ready to starve for want of work and service; and these to be disposed of by their parents, if alive, or otherwise by their nearest relations. But with due deference to so excellent a friend and so deserving a patriot, I cannot be altogether in his sentiments; for as to the males, my American acquaintance assured me, from frequent experience, that their flesh was generally tough and lean, like that of our school-boys by continual exercise, and their taste disagreeable; and to fatten them would not answer the charge. Then as to the females, it would, I think, with humble submission be a loss to the public, because they soon would become breeders themselves; and besides, it is not improbable that some scrupulous people might be apt to censure such a practice (although indeed very unjustly), as a little bordering upon cruelty; which, I confess, hath always been with me the strongest objection against any project, however so well intended.

But in order to justify my friend, he confessed that this expedient was put into his head by the famous Psalmanazar, a native of the island Formosa, who came from thence to London above twenty years ago, and in conversation told my friend, that in his country when any young person happened to be put to death, the executioner sold the carcass to persons of quality as a prime dainty; and that in his time the body of a plump girl of fifteen, who was crucified for an attempt to poison the emperor, was sold to his imperial majesty's prime minister of state, and other great mandarins of the court, in joints from the gibbet, at four hundred crowns. Neither indeed can I deny, that if the same use were made of several plump young girls in this town, who without one single groat to their fortunes cannot stir abroad without a chair, and appear at playhouse and assemblies in foreign fineries which they never will pay for, the kingdom would not be the worse.

Some persons of a desponding spirit are in great concern about that vast number of poor people, who are aged, diseased, or maimed, and I have been desired to employ my thoughts what course may be taken to ease the nation of so grievous an encumbrance. But I am not in the least pain upon that matter, because it is very well known that they are every day dying and rotting by cold and famine, and filth and vermin, as fast as can be reasonably expected. And as to the young laborers, they are now in as hopeful a condition; they cannot get work, and consequently pine away for want of nourishment, to a degree that if at any time they are accidentally hired to common labor, they have not strength to perform it; and thus the country and themselves are happily delivered from the evils to come.

I have too long digressed, and therefore shall return to my subject. I think the advantages by the proposal which I have made are obvious and many, as well as of the highest importance.

For first, as I have already observed, it would greatly lessen the number of papists, with whom we are yearly over-run, being the principal breeders of the nation as well as our most dangerous enemies; and who stay at home on pur-pose with a design to deliver the king-dom to the pretender, hoping to take their advantage by the absence of so many good protestants, who have chosen rather to leave their country than stay at home and pay tithes against their conscience to an episcopal curate.

Secondly, The poorer tenants will have something valuable of their own, which by law may be made liable to distress and help to pay their landlord's rent, their corn and cattle being already seized, and money a thing unknown.

Thirdly, Whereas the maintenance of an hundred thousand children, from two years old and upward, cannot be com-puted at less than ten shillings a-piece per annum, the nation's stock will be thereby increased fifty thousand pounds per annum, beside the profit of a new dish introduced to the tables of all gentle-men of fortune in the kingdom who have any refinement in taste. And the money will circulate among ourselves, the goods being entirely of our own growth and manufacture.

Fourthly, The constant breeders, beside the gain of eight shillings sterling per annum by the sale of their children, will be rid of the charge of maintaining them after the first year.

Fifthly, This food would likewise bring great custom to taverns; where the vint-ners will certainly be so prudent as to procure the best receipts for dressing it to perfection, and consequently have their houses frequented by all the fine

gentlemen, who justly value themselves upon their knowledge in good eating; and a skilful cook, who understands how to oblige his guests, will contrive to make it as expensive as they please.

Sixthly, This would be a great induce ment to marriage, which all wise nations have either encouraged by rewards or enforced by laws and penalties. It would increase the care and tenderness of mothers toward their children, when they were sure of a settlement for life to the poor babes, provided in some sort by the public, to their annual profit in-stead of expense. We should see an honest emulation among the married women, which of them could bring the fattest child to the market. Men would become as fond of their wives during the time of their pregnancy as they are now of their mares in foal, their cows in calf, their sows when they are ready to far-row; nor offer to beat or kick them (as is too frequent a practice) for fear of a miscarriage.

Many other advantages might be enu-merated. For instance, the addition of some thousand carcasses in our exporta-tion of barreled beef, the propagation of swine's flesh, and improvement in the art of making good bacon, so much wanted among us by the great destruction of pigs, too frequent at our tables; which are no way comparable in taste or magnificence to a well-grown, fat, yearling child, which roasted whole will make a considerable figure at a lord mayor's feast or any other public entertainment. But this and many others I omit, being studious of brevity.

Supposing that one thousand families in this city would be constant customers for infants' flesh, beside others who might have it at merry-meetings, particularly weddings and christenings, I compute that Dublin would take off annually about twenty thousand carcasses; and the rest of the kingdom (where probably they will be sold somewhat cheaper) the remaining eighty thousand.

I can think of no one objection that will possibly be raised against this pro-posal, unless it should be urged that the number of people will be thereby much lessened in the kingdom. This I freely own, and was indeed one principal de-sign in offering it to the world. I desire the reader will observe, that I calculate my remedy for this one individual kingdom of Ireland and for no other that ever was, is, or I think ever can be upon earth. Therefore let no man talk to me of other expedients: of taxing our absentees at five shillings a pound; of using neither clothes nor household furniture except what is of our own growth and manufacture; of utterly rejecting the materials and instruments that promote foreign luxury; of curing the expensiveness of pride, vanity, idleness, and gaming in our women; of introducing a vein of parsimony, prudence, and temperance; of learning to love our country, wherein we differ even from LAPLANDERS and the inhabitants of TOPINAMBOO; of quitting our animosities and factions, nor act any longer like the Jews, who were murdering one another at the very moment their city was taken; of being a little cautious not to sell our country and conscience for nothing; of teaching landlords to have at least one degree of mercy toward their tenants; lastly, of putting a spirit of honesty, industry, and skill into our shop-keepers; who, if a resolution could now be taken to buy only our native goods, would immediately unite to cheat and exact upon us in the price, the measure, and the goodness, nor could ever yet be brought to make one fair proposal of just dealing, though often and earnestly invited to it.

Therefore I repeat, let no man talk to me of these and the like expedients, till he hath at least some glimpse of hope that there will be ever some hearty and sincere attempt to put them in practice.

But as to myself, having been wearied out for many years with offering vain, idle, visionary thoughts, and at length utterly despairing of success I fortunately fell upon this proposal; which, as it is wholly new, so it hath something solid and real, of no expense and little trouble, full in our own power, and whereby we can incur no danger in disobliging ENGLAND. For this kind of commodity will not bear exportation, the flesh being of too tender a consistence to admit a long continuance in salt, although perhaps I could name a country which would be

glad to eat up our whole nation without it.

After all, I am not so violently bent upon my own opinion as to reject any offer proposed by wise men, which shall be found equally innocent, cheap, easy, and effectual. But before something of that kind shall be advanced in contradiction to my scheme, and offering a better, I desire the author or authors will be pleased maturely to consider two points. First, as things now stand, how they will be able to find food and raiment for an hundred thousand useless mouths and backs. And secondly, there being a round million of creatures in human figure throughout this kingdom, whose whole subsistence put into a common stock would leave them in debt two millions of pounds sterling, adding those who are beggars by profession to the bulk of farmers, cottagers, and laborers, with their wives and children who are beggars in effect: I desire those politicians who dislike my overture, and may perhaps be so bold as to attempt an answer, that they will first ask the parents of these mortals, whether they would not at this day think it a great happiness to have been sold for food at a year old in the manner I prescribe, and thereby have avoided such a perpetual scene of misfortunes as they have since gone through by the oppression of landlords, the impossibility of paying rent without money or trade, the want of common sustenance, with neither house nor clothes to cover them from the inclemencies of the weather, and the most inevitable prospect of entailing the like or greater miseries upon their breed for ever.

I profess, in the sincerity of my heart that I have not the least personal interest in endeavoring to promote this necessary work, having no other motive than the public good of my country, by advancing our trade, providing for infants, relieving the poor, and giving some pleasure to the rich. I have no children by which I can propose to get a single penny; the youngest being nine years old, and my wife past child-bearing.

(1729)

SIR RICHARD STEELE (1672–1729)

Steele, like Swift, was born in Dublin. He passed, with Addison, through Charterhouse School to Oxford, but soon left the university to seek his fortune in the army. By 1701, he had gained a captaincy in the Tower Guards and was a vivacious figure among the wits who haunted the coffee-houses, clubs, and theaters of London. Several comedies, in which he made a manly and effective effort to win a place for decency on the English stage, were still sprightly enough to sustain his reputation as a wit and good fellow. He was soon taken on by the government and, in 1707, was commissioned to write *The Gazette*. While officially 'keeping that paper very innocent and very insipid,' Steele discovered the possibilities of periodical writing. Two years later he began *The Tatler*, picking up as a disguise the character of a fictitious astrologer, Isaac Bickerstaff, which Swift had let drop after provoking the town to hilarious scoffing at one Partridge, an almanac-maker. Addison soon penetrated the disguise and was eagerly welcomed as a contributor. After about a year, Steele and Addison together devised the more commodious plan of *The Spectator*. The novel periodical created and supplied a new kind of literary demand. Its freedom from party bias, and the penetrating and yet urbane irony of its portrayals and criticisms of English manners gave it a wide appeal. *The Spectator* became a part of the 'tea-equipage' in London clubs and coffee-houses and wide-awake provincial homes. It turned out a valuable pecuniary asset; but the partnership did not last. Steele was a turbulent politician; Addison disapproved of his factious spirit; and, after the earlier numbers of *The Guardian* (1713), they ceased to collaborate. None of the later periodicals of either approximated the success of *The Spectator*. Steele was now approaching the liveliest part of his life. He had a stormy parliamentary experience, was made supervisor of the Drury Lane Theater, and George I knighted him for energetic championship of the Hanoverian succession.

His prosperity was brief, however. Through his opposition to the Peerage Bill (1719), he lost the support of his party and received some sore knocks from his old friend. He was frequently in money difficulties, and finally, broken in health as well as fortune, he took refuge in Wales, not as Swift venomously rimed, 'from perils of a hundred gaols,' but from the expenses of a London establishment, so that his debts might be paid before his death. Steele's Irish imprudences are sometimes exaggerated for the sake of contrasting him with Addison. He was not, in practice, above the fashionable vices of his times, and he was sinfully reckless in money matters. He was, nevertheless, a sincere champion of virtue and lover of piety; he was chivalrous toward women, generous and forgiving toward his friends, and intrepid where his political conscience was involved. The uncalculating prodigality and sweetness of his nature are reflected in his pages, and have made many besides Thackeray 'own to liking Dick Steele the man, and Dick Steele the author, much better than much better men and much better authors.'

From THE TATLER

[No. 1.]

THE ADVERTISEMENT

Though the other papers which are published for the use of the good people of England have certainly very wholesome effects and are laudable in their particular kinds, they do not seem to come up to the main design of such narrations, which, I humbly presume, should be principally intended for the use of politic persons, who are so public-spirited as to neglect their own affairs to look into transactions of state. Now these gentlemen, for the most part, being persons of strong zeal and weak 5 intellects, it is both a charitable and necessary work to offer something whereby such worthy and well-affected members of the commonwealth may be instructed, after their reading, what to 10 think; which shall be the end and purpose of this my paper, wherein I shall from time to time report and consider all matters of what kind soever that shall occur to me, and publish such my advices and reflections every Tuesday, Thursday and Saturday in the week, for the convenience of the post. I resolve also to have something which may be of entertainment to the fair sex, in honor of whom I have invented the title of this paper. I therefore earnestly desire all persons, without distinction, to take it in for the present *gratis,* and hereafter at the price of one penny, forbidding all hawkers to take more for it at their peril. And I desire all persons to consider that I am at a very great charge for proper materials for this work, as well as that, before I resolved upon it, I had settled a correspondence in all parts of the known and knowing world. And forasmuch as this globe is not trodden upon by mere drudges of business only, but that men of spirit and genius are justly to be esteemed as considerable agents in it, we shall not upon a dearth of news present you with musty foreign edicts, or dull proclamations, but shall divide our relation of the passages which occur in action or discourse throughout this town, as well as elsewhere, under such dates of places as may prepare you for the matter you are to expect, in the following manner:

All accounts of gallantry, pleasure, and entertainment shall be under the article of White's Chocolate-house; poetry, under that of Will's Coffee-house; learning, under the title of Grecian; foreign and domestic news, you will have from Saint James's Coffee-house; and what else I have to offer on any other subject shall be dated from my own apartment.

I once more desire my reader to consider that, as I cannot keep an ingenious man to go daily to Wills under twopence each day, merely for his charges; to White's under sixpence; nor to the Grecian, without allowing him some plain Spanish, to be as able as others at the learned table; and that a good observer cannot speak with even kidney at Saint James's without clean linen; I say, these considerations will, I hope, make all persons willing to comply with my humble request (when my *gratis* stock is exhausted) of a penny a piece; especially since they are sure of some proper amusement, and that it is impossible for me to want means to entertain them, having, besides the force of my own parts, the power of divination, and that I can, by

casting a figure, tell you all that will happen before it comes to pass.

But this last faculty I shall use very sparingly, and speak but of few things until they are passed, for fear of divulging matters which may offend our superiors.   Tuesday, April 12, 1709.

* * *

[No. 181.]

A RECOLLECTION

The first sense of sorrow I ever knew was upon the death of my father, at which time I was not quite five years of age; but was rather amazed at what all the house meant than possessed with a real understanding why nobody was willing to play with me. I remember I went into the room where his body lay, and my mother sat weeping alone by it. I had my battledore in my hand, and fell a-beating the coffin, and calling ' Papa '; for I know not how, I had some slight idea that he was locked up there. My mother catched me in her arms, and transported beyond all patience of the silent grief she was before in, she almost smothered me in her embrace, and told me in a flood of tears, ' Papa could not hear me, and would play with me no more, for they were going to put him under ground, whence he could never come to us again.' She was a very beautiful woman, of a noble spirit, and there was a dignity in her grief amidst all the wildness of her transport, which, methought struck me with an instinct of sorrow which, before I was sensible of what it was to grieve, seized my very soul, and has made pity the weakness of my heart ever since. The mind in infancy is, methinks, like the body in embryo, and receives impressions so forcible that they are as hard to be removed by reason, as any mark with which a child is born is to be taken away by any future application. Hence it is that good-nature in me is no merit; but, having been so frequently overwhelmed with her tears before I knew the cause of any affliction, or could draw defenses from my own judgment, I imbibed commiseration, remorse, and an unmanly gentleness of mind, which has since insnared me into ten thousand calamities, and from whence I can reap no advantage, except it be that, in such a humor as I am now in, I can the better indulge myself in the softnesses or humanity, and enjoy that sweet anxiety which arises from the memory of past afflictions.

June 5, 1710.

From THE SPECTATOR
[No. 2.]

THE CLUB

The first of our society is a gentleman of Worcestershire, of ancient descent, a baronet, his name is Sir Roger de Coverley. His great grandfather was inventor of that famous country-dance which is called after him. All who know that shire are very well acquainted with the parts and merits of Sir Roger. He is a gentleman that is very singular in his behavior, but his singularities proceed from his good sense, and are contradictions to the manners of the world, only as he thinks the world is in the wrong. However, this humor creates him no enemies, for he does nothing with sourness or obstinacy; and his being unconfined to modes and forms, makes him but the readier and more capable to please and oblige all who know him. When he is in town, he lives in Soho Square. It is said, he keeps himself a bachelor, by reason he was crossed in love by a perverse beautiful widow of the next county to him. Before this disappointment, Sir Roger was what you call a fine gentleman, had often supped with my Lord Rochester and Sir George Etherege, fought a duel upon his first coming to town, and kicked Bully Dawson in a public coffee house for calling him youngster. But, being ill used by the above mentioned widow, he was very serious for a year and a half; and though, his temper being naturally jovial, he at last got over it, he grew careless of himself, and never dressed afterwards. He continues to wear a coat and doublet of the same cut that were in fashion at the time of his repulse, which, in his merry humors, he tells us, has been in and out twelve times since he first wore it. He is now in his fifty-sixth year, cheerful, gay, and hearty; keeps a good house both in town and country; a great lover of mankind: but there is such a mirthful cast in his behavior, that he is rather

beloved than esteemed. His tenants grow rich, his servants look satisfied, all the young women profess love to him, and the young men are glad of his com-
5 pany; when he comes into a house, he calls the servants by their names, and talks all the way up stairs to a visit. I must not omit, that Sir Roger is a justice of the *quorum;* that he fills the chair
10 at a quarter-sessions with great abilities, and three months ago, gained universal applause, by explaining a passage in the game-act.

The gentleman next in esteem and
15 authority among us, is another bachelor, who is a member of the Inner Temple; a man of great probity, wit, and understanding; but he has chosen his place of residence rather to obey the direction of
20 an old humorsome father, than in pursuit of his own inclinations. He was placed there to study the laws of the land, and is the most learned of any of the house in those of the stage. Aristotle and
25 Longinus are much better understood by him than Littleton or Coke. The father sends up every post questions relating to marriage articles, leases and tenures, in the neighborhood; all which questions he
30 agrees with an attorney to answer and take care of in the lump. He is studying the passions themselves, when he should be inquiring into the debates among men which arise from them. He knows the
35 argument of each of the orations of Demosthenes and Tully; but not one case in the reports of our own courts. No one ever took him for a fool, but none, except his intimate friends, know he has
40 a great deal of wit. This turn makes him at once both disinterested and agreeable; as few of his thoughts are drawn from business, they are most of them fit for conversation. His taste of books is
45 a little too just for the age he lives in; he has read all, but approves of very few. His familiarity with the customs, manners, actions, and writings of the ancients, makes him a very delicate ob-
50 server of what occurs to him in the present world. He is an excellent critic, and the time of the play is his hour of business; exactly at five he passes through New Inn, crosses through Russell court,
55 and takes a turn at Will's, till the play begins; he has his shoes rubbed, and his periwig powdered at the barber's as you go into the Rose. It is for the good of

the audience when he is at a play; for the actors have an ambition to please him.

The person of next consideration is Sir Andrew Freeport, a merchant of great eminence in the city of London. A person of indefatigable industry, strong reason, and great experience. His notions of trade are noble and generous, and (as every rich man has usually some sly way of jesting, which would make no great figure were he not a rich man) he calls the sea the British Common. He is acquainted with commerce in all its parts, and will tell you that it is a stupid and barbarous way to extend dominion by arms, for true power is to be got by arts and industry. He will often argue, that if this part of our trade were well cultivated, we should gain from one nation,— and if another, from another. I have heard him prove, that diligence makes more lasting acquisitions than valor, and that sloth has ruined more nations than the sword. He abounds in several frugal maxims, amongst which the greatest favorite is, 'A penny saved is a penny got.' A general trader of good sense is pleasanter company than a general scholar; and Sir Andrew having a natural unaffected eloquence, the perspicuity of his discourse gives the same pleasure that wit would in another man. He has made his fortunes himself; and says that England may be richer than other kingdoms, by as plain methods as he himself is richer than other men; though at the same time I can say this of him, that there is not a point in the compass but blows home a ship in which he is an owner.

Next to Sir Andrew in the club-room sits Captain Sentry, a gentleman of great courage, good understanding, but invincible modesty. He is one of those that deserve very well, but are very awkward at putting their talents within the observation of such as should take notice of them. He was some years a captain, and behaved himself with great gallantry in several engagements and at several sieges; but having a small estate of his own, and being next heir to Sir Roger, he has quitted a way of life, in which no man can rise suitably to his merit, who is not something of a courtier as well as a soldier. I have heard him often lament, that in a profession where merit is placed in so conspicuous a view, impudence should get the better of modesty. When he has talked to this purpose, I never heard him make a sour expression, but frankly confess that he left the world, because he was not fit for it. A strict honesty and an even regular behavior are in themselves obstacles to him that must press through crowds who endeavor at the same end with himself, the favor of a commander. He will, however, in his way of talk, excuse generals for not disposing according to men's desert, or inquiring into it: for, says he, that great man who has a mind to help me, has as many to break through to come at me, as I have to come at him: therefore, he will conclude, that the man who would make a figure, especially in a military way, must get over all false modesty, and assist his patron against the importunity of other pretenders, by a proper assurance in his own vindication. He says, it is a civil cowardice to be backward in asserting what you ought to expect, as it is a military fear to be slow in attacking when it is your duty. With this candor does the gentleman speak of himself and others. The same frankness runs through all his conversation. The military part of his life has furnished him with many adventures, in the relation of which he is very agreeable to the company; for he is never over-bearing, though accustomed to command men in the utmost degree below him; nor ever too obsequious, from an habit of obeying men highly above him.

But, that our society may not appear a set of humorists, unacquainted with the gallantries and pleasures of the age, we have among us the gallant Will Honeycomb, a gentleman who, according to his years, should be in the decline of his life, but, having ever been very careful of his person, and always had a very easy fortune, time has made but a very little impression, either by wrinkles on his forehead, or traces on his brain. His person is well turned, of a good height. He is very ready at that sort of discourse with which men usually entertain women. He has all his life dressed very well, and remembers habits as others do men. He can smile when one speaks to him, and laughs easily. He knows the history of every mode, and can inform you from what Frenchwomen our wives and daughters had this manner of curling their hair, that way of placing their hoods; and whose vanity to shew her foot made that part of the dress so short in such a year. In a word, all his conversation and knowledge have been in the female world; as other men of his age will take notice to you what such a minister said upon such and such an occasion, he will tell you, when the Duke of Monmouth danced at court, such a woman was then smitten, another was taken with him at the head of his troop in the Park. For all these important relations, he has ever about the same time received a kind glance or a blow of a fan from some celebrated beauty, mother of the present lord such-a-one.

This way of talking of his very much enlivens the conversation, among us of a more sedate turn; and I find there is not one of the company, but myself, who rarely speak at all, but speaks of him as of that sort of man who is usually called a well-bred fine gentleman. To conclude his character, where women are not concerned, he is an honest worthy man.

I cannot tell whether I am to account him whom I am next to speak of, as one of our company; for he visits us but seldom, but when he does, it adds to every man else a new enjoyment of himself. He is a clergyman, a very philosophic man, of general learning, great sanctity of life, and the most exact good breeding. He has the misfortune to be of a very weak constitution; and consequently cannot accept of such cares and business as preferments in his function would oblige him to; he is therefore among divines what a chamber-councillor is among lawyers. The probity of his mind, and the integrity of his life, create him followers, as being eloquent or loud advances others. He seldom introduces the subject he speaks upon; but we are so far gone in years that he observes, when he is among us, an earnestness to have him fall on some divine topic, which he always treats with much authority, as one who has no interest in this world, as one who is hastening to the object of all his wishes, and conceives hope from his decays and infirmities. These are my ordinary companions.

Friday, March 2, 1710–11.

[No. 6.]

SIR ROGER ON MEN OF PARTS

I know no evil under the sun so great as the abuse of the understanding, and yet there is no one vice more common. It has diffused itself through both sexes, and all qualities of mankind; and there is hardly that person to be found, who is not more concerned for the reputation of wit and sense, than honesty and virtue. But this unhappy affectation of being wise rather than honest, witty than good-natured, is the source of most of the ill habits of life. Such false impressions are owing to the abandoned writings of men of wit, and the awkward imitation of the rest of mankind.

For this reason, Sir Roger was saying last night, that he was of opinion that none but men of fine parts deserve to be hanged. The reflections of such men are so delicate upon all occurrences which they are concerned in, that they should be exposed to more than ordinary infamy and punishment, for offending against such quick admonitions as their own souls give them, and blunting the fine edge of their minds in such a manner, that they are no more shocked at vice and folly, than men of slower capacities. There is no greater monster in being, than a very ill man of great parts. He lives like a man in a palsy, with one side of him dead. While perhaps he enjoys the satisfaction of luxury, of wealth, of ambition, he has lost the taste of good will, of friendship, of innocence. Scarecrow, the beggar in Lincoln's-inn-fields, who disabled himself in his right leg, and asks alms all day to get himself a warm supper at night, is not half so despicable a wretch, as such a man of sense. The beggar has no relish above sensations; he finds rest more agreeable than motion; and while he has a warm fire, never reflects that he deserves to be whipped. Every man who terminates his satisfactions and enjoyments within the supply of his own necessities and passions is, says Sir Roger, in my eye as poor a rogue as Scarecrow. 'But,' continued he, 'for the loss of public and private virtue we are beholden to your men of fine parts forsooth; it is with them no matter what is done, so it be done with an air. But to me who am so whimsical in a corrupt age as to act according to nature and reason, a selfish man in the most shining circumstance and equipage, appears in the same condition with the fellow above mentioned, but more contemptible in proportion to what more he robs the public of and enjoys above him. I lay it down therefore for a rule, that the whole man is to move together; that every action of any importance, is to have a prospect of public good: and that the general tendency of our indifferent actions ought to be agreeable to the dictates of reason, of religion, of good breeding; without this, a man, as I have before hinted, is hopping instead of walking, he is not in his entire and proper motion.'

While the honest knight was thus bewildering himself in good starts, I looked intentively upon him, which made him, I thought, collect his mind a little. 'What I aim at,' says he, 'is, to represent, that I am of opinion, to polish our understandings and neglect our manners is of all things the most inexcusable. Reason should govern passion, but instead of that, you see, it is often subservient to it; and, as unaccountable as one would think it, a wise man is not always a good man.' This degeneracy is not only the guilt of particular persons, but also at some times of a whole people; and perhaps it may appear upon examination, that the most polite ages are the least virtuous. This may be attributed to the folly of admitting wit and learning as merit in themselves, without considering the application of them. By this means it becomes a rule, not so much to regard what we do, as how we do it. But this false beauty will not pass upon men of honest minds and true taste. Sir Richard Blackmore says, with as much good sense as virtue, 'It is a mighty dishonor and shame to employ excellent faculties and abundance of wit, to humor and please men in their vices and follies. The great enemy of mankind, notwithstanding his wit and angelic faculties, is the most odious being in the whole creation.' He goes on soon after to say, very generously, that he undertook the writing of his poem 'to rescue the Muses out of the hands of ravishers, to restore them to their sweet and chaste mansions, and to engage them in an employment suitable to their dignity.' This certainly ought to be the purpose of every man who appears in public, and whoever does not proceed upon that foundation, injures his country as fast as he succeeds in his studies. When modesty ceases to be the chief ornament of one sex, and integrity of the other, society is upon a wrong basis, and we shall be ever after without rules to guide our judgment in what is really becoming and ornamental. Nature and reason direct one thing, passion and humor another. To follow the dictates of these two latter, is going into a road that is both endless and intricate; when we pursue the other, our passage is delightful, and what we aim at easily attainable.

I do not doubt but England is at present as polite a nation as any in the world; but any man who thinks can easily see, that the affectation of being gay and in fashion, has very near eaten up our good sense and our religion. Is there anything so just as that mode and gallantry should be built upon exerting ourselves in what is proper and agreeable to the institutions of justice and piety among us? And yet is there anything more common, than that we run in perfect contradiction to them? All which is supported by no other pretension, than that it is done with what we call a good grace.

Nothing ought to be held laudable or becoming, but what nature itself should prompt us to think so. Respect to all kinds of superiors is founded, methinks, upon instinct; and yet what is so ridiculous as age? I make this abrupt transition to the mention of this vice, more than any other, in order to introduce a little story, which I think a pretty instance that the most polite age is in danger of being the most vicious.

'It happened at Athens, during a public representation of some play exhibited in honor of the commonwealth, that an old gentleman came too late for a place suitable to his age and quality. Many of the young gentlemen, who observed the difficulty and confusion he was in, made signs to him that they would accommodate him if he came where they sat. The good man bustled through the crowd accordingly; but when he came to the seats to which he was invited, the jest was to sit close and expose him, as he stood out of countenance, to the whole audience. The frolic went round all the Athenian benches. But on those occasions there were also particular places assigned for foreigners. When the good man skulked towards the boxes appointed for the Lacedæmonians, that honest people, more virtuous than polite, rose up all to a man, and with the greatest respect received him among them. The Athenians being suddenly touched with a sense of the Spartan virtue and their own degeneracy, gave a thunder of applause; and the old man cried out, "The Athenians understand what is good, but the Lacedæmonians practise it."

Wednesday, March 17, 1710–11.

[No. 113.]

SIR ROGER IN LOVE

In my first description of the company in which I pass most of my time, it may be remembered, that I mentioned a great affliction which my friend Sir Roger had met with in his youth; which was no less than a disappointment in love. It happened this evening, that we fell into a very pleasing walk at a distance from his house. As soon as we came into it, 'It is,' quoth the good old man, looking round him with a smile, 'very hard, that any part of my land should be settled upon one who has used me so ill as the perverse widow did; and yet I am sure I could not see a sprig of any bough of this whole walk of trees, but I should reflect upon her and her severity. She has certainly the finest hand of any woman in the world. You are to know, this was the place wherein I used to muse upon her; and by that custom I can never come into it, but the same tender sentiments revive in my mind, as if I had actually walked with that beautiful creature under these shades. I have been fool enough to carve her name on the bark of several of these trees; so unhappy is the condition of men in love, to attempt the removing of their passion by the methods which serve only to imprint it deeper. She has certainly the finest hand of any woman in the world.'

Here followed a profound silence; and I was not displeased to observe my friend falling so naturally into a discourse which I had ever before taken notice he industriously avoided. After a very long pause, he entered upon an account of this great circumstance in his life, with an air which I thought raised my idea of him above what I had ever had before; and gave me the picture of that cheerful mind of his, before it received that stroke which has ever since affected his words and actions. But he went on as follows: —

'I came to my estate in my twenty-second year, and resolved to follow the steps of the most worthy of my ancestors who have inhabited this spot of earth before me, in all the methods of hospitality and good neighborhood, for the sake of my fame; and in country sports and recreations, for the sake of my health. In my twenty-third year I was obliged to serve as sheriff of the county; and in my servants, officers, and whole equipage, indulged the pleasure of a young man (who did not think ill of his own person) in taking that public occasion of showing my figure and behavior to advantage. You may easily imagine to yourself what appearance I made, who am pretty tall, ride well, and was very well dressed, at the head of a whole county, with music before me, a feather in my hat, and my horse well bitted. I can assure you I was not a little pleased with the kind looks and glances I had from all the balconies and windows as I rode to the hall where the assizes were held. But, when I came there, a beautiful creature in a widow's habit sat in a court to hear the event of a cause concerning her dower. This commanding creature (who was born for the destruction of all who behold her) put on such a resignation in her countenance, and bore the whispers of all around the court with such a pretty uneasiness, I warrant you, and then recovered herself from one eye to another, until she was perfectly confused by meeting something so wistful in all she encountered, that at last, with a murrain to her, she cast her bewitching eye upon me. I no sooner met it but I bowed like a great surprised booby; and knowing her cause to be the first which came on, I cried, like a captivated calf as I was, "Make way for the defendant's witnesses." This sudden partiality made all the county immediately see the sheriff also was become a slave to the fine widow. During the time her cause was upon trial, she behaved herself, I warrant you, with such a deep attention to her business, took opportunities to have little billets handed to her counsel, then would be in such a pretty confusion, occasioned, you must know, by acting before so much company, that not only I but the whole court was prejudiced in her favor; and all that the next heir to her husband had to urge was thought so groundless and frivolous, that when it came to her counsel to reply, there was not half so much said as every one besides in the court thought he could have urged to her advantage. You must understand, sir, this perverse woman is one of those unaccountable creatures that secretly rejoice in the admiration of men, but indulge themselves in no farther consequences. Hence it is that she has ever had a train of admirers, and she removes from her slaves in town to those in the country, according to the seasons of the year. She is a reading lady, and far gone in the pleasures of friendship. She is always accompanied by a confidante, who is witness to her daily protestations against our sex, and consequently a bar to her first steps towards love, upon the strength of her own maxims and declarations.

'However, I must needs say, this accomplished mistress of mine has distinguished me above the rest, and has been known to declare Sir Roger de Coverley was the tamest and most humane of all the brutes in the country. I was told she said so by one who thought he rallied me; and upon the strength of this slender encouragement of being thought least detestable, I made new liveries, new-paired my coach-horses, sent them all to town to be bitted, and taught to throw their legs well, and move all together, before I pretended to cross the country, and wait upon her. As soon as I thought my retinue suitable to the character of my fortune and youth, I set out from hence to make my addresses. The particular skill of this lady has ever been to inflame your wishes, and yet command respect. To make her mistress of this art, she has a greater share of knowledge, wit, and good sense than is usual even among men of merit. Then she is beautiful beyond the race of women. If you will not let her go on with a certain artifice with her eyes,

and the skill of beauty, she will arm herself with her real charms, and strike you with admiration instead of desire. It is certain that if you were to behold the whole woman, there is that dignity in her aspect, that composure in her motion, that complacency in her manner, that if her form makes you hope, her merit makes you fear. But then again, she is such a desperate scholar that no country gentleman can approach her without being a jest. As I was going to tell you, when I came to her house, I was admitted to her presence with great civility; at the same time she placed herself to be first seen by me in such an attitude, as I think you call the posture of a picture, that she discovered new charms, and I at last came towards her with such an awe as made me speechless. This she no sooner observed but she made her advantage of it, and began a discourse to me concerning love and honor, as they both are followed by pretenders, and the real votaries to them. When she discussed these points in a discourse which, I verily believe, was as learned as the best philosopher in Europe could possibly make, she asked me whether she was so happy as to fall in with my sentiments on these important particulars. Her confidante sat by her, and on my being in the last confusion and silence, this malicious aid of hers turning to her, says, "I am very glad to observe Sir Roger pauses upon this subject, and seems resolved to deliver all his sentiments upon the matter when he pleases to speak." They both kept their countenances, and after I had sat half an hour meditating how to behave before such profound casuists, I rose up and took my leave. Chance has since that time thrown me very often in her way, and she as often directed a discourse to me which I do not understand. This barbarity has kept me ever at a distance from the most beautiful object my eyes ever beheld. It is thus also she deals with all mankind, and you must make love to her as you would conquer the sphinx, by posing her. But were she like other women, and that there were any talking to her, how constant must the pleasure of that man be, who could converse with a creature — But, after all, you may be sure her heart is fixed on some one or other: and yet I have been credibly informed — but who can believe half that is said! — They say she sings excellently; her voice in her ordinary speech has something in it inexpressibly sweet. You must know I dined with her at a public table the day after I first saw her, and she helped me to some tansy in the eye of all the gentlemen in the country. She has certainly the finest hand of any woman in the world. I can assure you, sir, were you to behold her, you would be in the same condition; for as her speech is music, her form is angelic. But I find I grow irregular while I am talking of her; but indeed it would be stupidity to be unconcerned at such perfection. Oh, the excellent creature! she is as inimitable to all women, as she is inaccessible to all men.'

I found my friend begin to rave, and insensibly led him towards the house, that we might be joined by some other company; and am convinced that the widow is the secret cause of all that inconsistency which appears in some parts of my friend's discourse; though he has so much command of himself as not directly to mention her, yet according to that of Martial, which one knows not how to render into English, *dum tacet hanc loquitur* [even when silent he talks of her].

Tuesday, July 10, 1711.

* * *

[No. 454.]

A DAY IN LONDON

It is an expressible pleasure to know a little of the world, and to be of no character or significancy in it.

To be ever unconcerned, and ever looking on new objects with an endless curiosity, is a delight known only to those who are turned for speculation: nay, they who enjoy it must value things only as they are the objects of speculation, without drawing any worldly advantage to themselves from them, but just as they are what contribute to their amusement, or the improvement of the mind. I lay one night last week at Richmond; and being restless, not out of dissatisfaction, but a certain busy inclination one sometimes has, I rose at four in the morning, and took boat for London, with a resolution to rove by boat and coach for the

next four-and-twenty hours, till the many different objects I must needs meet with should tire my imagination, and give me an inclination to a repose more profound than I was at that time capable of. I beg people's pardon for an odd humor I am guilty of, and was often that day, which is saluting any person whom I like, whether I know him or not. This is a particularity would be tolerated in me, if they considered that the greatest pleasure I know I receive at my eyes, and that I am obliged to an agreeable person for coming abroad into my view, as another is for a visit of conversation at their own houses.

The hours of the day and night are taken up in the cities of London and Westminster by people as different from each other as those who are born in different centuries. Men of six o'clock give way to those of nine, they of nine to the generation of twelve; and they of twelve disappear, and make room for the fashionable world, who have made two o'clock the noon of the day.

When we first put off from shore, we soon fell in with a fleet of gardeners, bound for the several market ports of London; and it was the most pleasing scene imaginable to see the cheerfulness with which those industrious people plied their way to a certain sale of their goods. The banks on each side are as well peopled, and beautified with as agreeable plantations, as any spot on the earth; but the Thames itself, loaded with the product of each shore, added very much to the landscape. It was very easy to observe by their sailing and the countenances of the ruddy virgins who were supercargoes, the parts of the town to which they were bound. There was an air in the purveyors for Covent Garden, who frequently converse with morning rakes, very unlike the seeming sobriety of those bound for Stocks Market.

Nothing remarkable happened in our voyage; but I landed with ten sail of apricot-boats, at Strand Bridge, after having put in at Nine Elms, and taken in melons, consigned by Mr. Cuffe, of that place, to Sarah Sewell and Company, at their stall in Covent Garden. We arrived at Strand Bridge at six of the clock, and were unloading, when the hackney-coachmen of the foregoing night took their leave of each other at the

Darkhouse, to go to bed before the day was too far spent. Chimney-sweepers passed by us as we made up to the market, and some raillery happened between one of the fruit-wenches and those black men about the Devil and Eve, with allusion to their several professions. I could not believe any place more entertaining than Covent Garden, where I strolled from one fruit-shop to another, with crowds of agreeable young women, around me, who were purchasing fruit for their respective families. It was almost eight of the clock before I could leave that variety of objects. I took coach and followed a young lady, who tripped into another just before me, attended by her maid. I saw immediately she was of the family of the Vainloves. There are a set of these, who, of all things, affect the play of blindman's-buff, and leading men into love for they know not whom, who are fled they know not where. This sort of woman is usually a jaunty slattern; she hangs on her clothes, plays her head, varies her posture, and changes place incessantly, and all with an appearance of striving at the same time to hide herself, and yet give you to understand she is in humor to laugh at you. You must have often seen the coachmen make signs with their fingers, as they drive by each other, to intimate how much they have got that day. They can carry on that language to give intelligence where they are driving. In an instant my coachman took the wink to pursue, and the lady's driver gave the hint that he was going through Longacre toward St. James's; while he whipped up James Street, we drove for King Street, to save the pass at St. Martin's Lane. The coachmen took care to meet, jostle, and threaten each other for way, and be entangled at the end of Newport Street and Longacre. The fright, you must believe, brought down the lady's coach-door, and obliged her, with her mask off, to inquire into the bustle,—when she sees the man she would avoid. The tackle of the coach-window is so bad she cannot draw it up again, and she drives on, sometimes wholly discovered, and sometimes half escaped, according to the accident of carriages in her way. One of these ladies keeps her seat in a hackney-coach as well as the best rider does on a managed horse. The laced shoe on her left foot, with a careless gesture, just appearing on the opposite cushion, held her both firm and in a proper attitude to receive the next jolt.

As she was an excellent coach-woman, many were the glances at each other which we had for an hour and a half in all parts of the town, by the skill of our drivers, till at last my lady was conveniently lost, with notice from her coachman to ours to make off, and he should hear where she went. This chase was now at an end, and the fellow who drove her came to us, and discovered that he was ordered to come again in an hour, for that she was a silk-worm. I was surprised with this phrase, but found it was a cant among the hackney fraternity for their best customers, women who ramble twice or thrice a week from shop to shop, to turn over all the goods in town without buying anything. The silk-worms are, it seems, indulged by the tradesmen; for, though they never buy, they are ever talking of new silks, laces, and ribbons, and serve the owners in getting them customers, as their common dunners do in making them pay.

The day of people of fashion began now to break, and carts and hacks were mingled with equipages of show and vanity, when I resolved to walk it, out of cheapness; but my unhappy curiosity is such, that I find it always my interest to take a coach, for some odd adventure among beggars, ballad-singers, or the like, detains and throws me into expense. It happened so immediately, for at the corner of Warwick Street, as I was listening to a new ballad, a ragged rascal, a beggar who knew me, came up to me, and began to turn the eyes of the good company upon me, by telling me he was extreme poor, and should die in the street for want of drink, except I immediately would have the charity to give him sixpence to go into the next ale-house and save his life. He urged with a melancholy face, that all his family had died of thirst. All the mob have humor, and two or three began to take the jest; by which Mr. Sturdy carried his point, and let me sneak off to a coach. As I drove along, it was a pleasing reflection to see the world so prettily checkered since I left Richmond, and the scene still filling with children of a new hour. This satisfaction increased as I moved towards the city; and gay signs, well-disposed streets, magnificent public structures, and wealthy shops adorned with contented faces, made the joy still rising till we came into the center of the city, and center of the world of trade, the Exchange of London. As other men in the crowds about me were pleased with their hopes and bargains, I found my account in observing them, in attention to their several interests. I, indeed, looked upon myself as the richest man that walked the Exchange that day; for my benevolence made me share the gains of every bargain that was made. It was not the least of my satisfaction in my survey, to go up stairs and pass the shops of agreeable females; to observe so many pretty hands busy in the folding of ribbons, and the utmost eagerness of agreeable faces in the sale of patches, pins, and wires, on each side of the counters, was an amusement in which I could longer have indulged myself, had not the dear creatures called to me, to ask what I wanted, when I could not answer, 'Only to look at you.' I went to one of the windows which opened to the area below, where all the several voices lost their distinction, and rose up in a confused humming, which created in me a reflection that could not come into the mind of any but of one a little too studious; for I said to myself with a kind of pun in thought, 'What nonsense is all the hurry of this world to those who are above it?' In these, or not much wiser thoughts, I had like to have lost my place at the chophouse, where every man, according to the natural bashfulness or sullenness of our nation, eats in a public room a mess of broth, or chop of meat, in dumb silence, as if they had no pretense to speak to each other on the foot of being men, except they were of each other's acquaintance.

I went afterward to Robin's, and saw people who had dined with me at the five-penny ordinary just before, give bills for the value of large estates; and could not but behold with great pleasure property lodged in and transferred in a moment from, such as would never be masters of half as much as is seemingly in them, and given from them, every day they live. But before five in the afternoon I left the city, came to my common scene of Covent Garden, and passed the evening at Will's in attending the discourses of several sets of people, who relieved each other within my hearing on the subjects of cards, dice, love, learning, and politics. The last subject kept me till I heard the streets in the possession of the bellman, who had now the world to himself, and cried, 'Past two o'clock.' This roused me from my seat; and I went to my lodgings, led by a light, whom I put into the discourse of his private economy, and made him give me an account of the charge, hazard, profit, and loss of a family that depended upon a link, with a design to end my trivial day with the generosity of sixpence, instead of a third part of that sum. When I came to my chambers, I writ down these minutes, but was at a loss what instruction I should propose to my reader from the enumeration of so many insignificant matters and occurrences; and I thought it of great use, if they could learn with me to keep their minds open to gratification, and ready to receive it from anything it meets with. This one circumstance will make every face you see give you the satisfaction you now take in beholding that of a friend; will make every object a pleasing one; will make all the good which arrives to any man an increase of happiness to yourself.

Monday, August 11, 1712.

JOSEPH ADDISON (1672–1719)

From a refined clerical home, Addison was sent to Charterhouse School and thence, at fifteen to Oxford, where he distinguished himself as a scholar and rose to a fellowship at Magdalen College (1697–99). By his twenty-second year, he was known as a cultivated writer of English and Latin verses and Dryden had welcomed him to the world of letters. While he was considering the church, the Whig government, desiring to enlist the service of his pen, granted him a pension which enabled him to spend four years in study and travel on the continent. Returning, in 1704, to a mean London lodging, he was directly sought out by the Whig leaders and commissioned to celebrate the recent victory of Marlborough at Blenheim. His poem, *The Campaign*, proved satisfactory, and he was rewarded with lucrative secretary-ships, one of which took him to Ireland, where he was eminently successful and popular. Meantime, he had become a leader among the coffee-house wits and had won the friendship of Swift. He renewed his Charterhouse intimacy with Steele, was responsible for 'many applauded strokes' in the latter's comedy, *The Tender Husband* (1705), and contributed to *The Tatler* (1709), 42 of its 271 numbers. With Steele, he started *The Spectator* (1711–12) which appeared daily and ran to 555 numbers, of which Addison wrote 274. In *The Spectator*, Addison's genius found its aptest expression. No other periodical writing has every combined, in so high a degree, immediate journalistic effectiveness and permanent literary charm. This success was promptly followed by that of his tragedy, *Cato* (1713), which, though intrinsically undramatic, became immensely famous because of its supposed political sentiments. When the Whigs returned to power, he was made chief secretary for Ireland; carried on, for a time, a party periodical called *The Freeholder;* became in 1716 commissioner for trade and the colonies, and, in 1717, secretary of state. Ill-health and, possibly, ill-success as a public speaker induced him to resign his post after a few months. In the midst of new literary plans and an unkind political squabble with his old friend Steele, he was cut off by death when only forty-seven years of age. A fine elegy, by his friend Tickell, gives us a good idea of his impressive night burial in Westminster Abbey.

Addison's central qualities are discretion and self-possession. He 'always preferred cheer-fulness to mirth,' and those who look for sensational elements, whether in style or behavior, will find him tame. A profane person once pronounced him 'a parson in a tye-wig,' and another vindictively declared, 'One day or other you'll see that man a bishop.' But the chiefs of a witty and sociable age owned that, after the bottle had been round and among friends, he was the most delightful companion alive. As a writer, he profoundly influenced English manners and morals by demonstrating that urbanity and good breeding might be associated with learning, and that virtue is not necessarily incompatible with elegance and wit. Of his merit as a prose stylist, no one has spoken more roundly than Dr. Johnson in his measured statement, that 'Whoever wishes to attain an English style, familiar but not coarse, and elegant but not ostentatious, must give his days and nights to the volumes of Addison.'

From THE SPECTATOR

[No. 1.]

THE SPECTATOR INTRODUCES HIMSELF

I have observed that a reader seldom peruses a book with pleasure, till he knows whether the writer of it be a black or a fair man, of a mild or choleric dis-10 position, married or a bachelor, with other particulars of the like nature, that conduce very much to the right under-standing of an author. To gratify this curiosity, which is so natural to a reader, I design this paper, and my next, as prefatory discourses to my following 5 writings, and shall give some account in them of the several persons that are engaged in this work. As the chief trouble of compiling, digesting, and correcting, will fall to my share, I must do myself 10 the justice to open the work with my own history.

I was born to a small hereditary estate, which, according to the tradition of the village where it lies, was bounded by the same hedges and ditches in William the Conqueror's time that it is at present, and has been delivered down from father to son whole and entire, without the loss or acquisition of a single field or meadow, during the space of six hundred years. There runs a story in the family, that my mother, near the time of my birth, dreamed that her son was become a judge; whether this might proceed from a law-suit which was then depending in the family, or my father's being a justice of the peace, I cannot determine; for I am not so vain as to think it presaged any dignity that I should arrive at in my future life, though that was the interpretation which the neighborhood put upon it. The gravity of my behavior at my very first appearance in the world seemed to favor my mother's dream: for as she often told me, I threw away my rattle before I was two months old, and would not make use of my coral until they had taken away the bells from it.

As for the rest of my infancy, there being nothing in it remarkable, I shall pass it over in silence. I find, that during my nonage, I had the reputation of a very sullen youth, but was always a favorite of my schoolmaster, who used to say, that my parts were solid, and would wear well. I had not been long at the university, before I distinguished myself by a most profound silence; for, during the space of eight years, excepting in the public exercises of the college, I scarce uttered the quantity of an hundred words; and indeed do not remember that I ever spoke three sentences together in my whole life. Whilst I was in this learned body, I applied myself with so much diligence to my studies, that there are very few celebrated books, either in the learned or the modern tongues, which I am not acquainted with.

Upon the death of my father, I was resolved to travel into foreign countries, and therefore left the university, with the character of an odd unaccountable fellow, that had a great deal of learning, if I would but shew it. An insatiable thirst after knowledge carried me into all the countries of Europe, in which there was anything new or strange to be seen; nay, to such a degree was my curiosity raised, that having read the controversies of some great men concerning the antiquities of Egypt, I made a voyage to Grand Cairo, on purpose to take the measure of a pyramid; and as soon as I had set myself right in that particular, returned to my native country with great satisfaction.

I have passed my latter years in this city, where I am frequently seen in most public places, though there are not above half-a-dozen of my select friends that know me; of whom my next paper shall give a more particular account. There is no place of general resort, wherein I do not often make my appearance: sometimes I am seen thrusting my head into a round of politicians, at Will's, and listening with great attention to the narratives that are made in those little circular audiences. Sometimes I smoke a pipe at Child's, and whilst I seem attentive to nothing but the Postman, overhear the conversation of every table in the room. I appear on Sunday nights at St. James's coffee-house, and sometimes join the little committee of politics in the inner room, as one who comes there to hear and improve. My face is likewise very well known at the Grecian, the Cocoa-tree, and in the theaters both of Drury-Lane and the Hay-market. I have been taken for a merchant upon the exchange for above these ten years, and sometimes pass for a Jew in the assembly of stock-jobbers at Jonathan's: in short, wherever I see a cluster of people, I always mix with them, though I never open my lips but in my own club.

Thus I live in the world rather as a spectator of mankind, than as one of the species, by which means I have made myself a speculative statesman, soldier, merchant and artisan, without ever meddling with any practical part in life. I am very well versed in the theory of a husband or a father, and can discern the errors in the economy, business, and diversion of others, better than those who are engaged in them; as standers-by discover blots, which are apt to escape those who are in the game. I never espoused any party with violence, and am resolved to observe an exact neutrality between the whigs and tories, unless I shall be forced to declare myself by the hostilities of either side. In short, I have acted in all the parts of my life as a looker-on, which is the character I intend to preserve in this paper.

I have given the reader just so much of my history and character, as to let him see I am not altogether unqualified for the business I have undertaken. As for other particulars in my life and adventures, I shall insert them in following papers, as I shall see occasion. In the meantime, when I consider how much I have seen, read, and heard, I begin to blame my own taciturnity; and since I have neither time nor inclination, to communicate the fulness of my heart in speech, I am resolved to do it in writing, and to print myself out, if possible, before I die. I have been often told by my friends, that it is a pity so many useful discoveries which I have made should be in the possession of a silent man. For this reason, therefore, I shall publish a sheet-full of thoughts every morning, for the benefit of my contemporaries: and if I can any way contribute to the diversion or improvement of the country in which I live, I shall leave it when I am summoned out of it, with the secret satisfaction of thinking that I have not lived in vain.

There are three very material points which I have not spoken to in this paper; and which, for several important reasons, I must keep to myself, at least for some time: I mean, an account of my name, my age, and my lodgings. I must confess, I would gratify my reader in anything that is reasonable; but as for these three particulars, though I am sensible they might tend very much to the embellishment of my paper, I cannot yet come to a resolution of communicating them to the public. They would indeed draw me out of that obscurity which I have enjoyed for many years, and expose me in public places to several salutes and civilities, which have been always very disagreeable to me; for the greatest pain I can suffer, is the being talked to, and being stared at. It is for this reason likewise, that I keep my complexion and dress as very great secrets; though it is not impossible that I may make discoveries of both in the progress of the work I have undertaken.

After having been thus particular upon myself, I shall, in to-morrow's paper, give an account of those gentlemen who are concerned with me in this work; for, as I have before intimated, a plan of it is laid and concerted, as all other matters of importance are, in a club. However, as my friends have engaged me to stand in the front, those who have a mind to correspond with me may direct their letters to the Spectator, at Mr. Buckley's in Little Britain. For I must further acquaint the reader, that, though our club meet, only on Tuesdays and Thursdays, we have appointed a committee to sit every night, for the inspection of all such papers as may contribute to the advancement of the public weal.

Thursday, March 1, 1710–11.

[No. 112.]

A COUNTRY SUNDAY

I am always very well pleased with a country Sunday, and think, if keeping holy the seventh day were only a human institution, it would be the best method that could have been thought of for the polishing and civilizing of mankind. It is certain the country people would soon degenerate into a kind of savages and barbarians, were there not such frequent returns of a stated time in which the whole village meet together with their best faces, and in their cleanliest habits, to converse with one another upon indifferent subjects, hear their duties explained to them, and join together i. adoration of the Supreme Being. Sunday clears away the rust of the whole week, not only as it refreshes in their minds the notions of religion, but as it puts both the sexes upon appearing in their most agreeable forms, and exerting all such qualities as are apt to give them a figure in the eye of the village. A country fellow distinguishes himself as much in the churchyard, as a citizen does upon the Change, the whole parish-politics being generally discussed in that place either after sermon or before the bell rings.

My friend Sir Roger, being a good churchman, has beautified the inside of his church with several texts of his own choosing: he has likewise given a handsome pulpit-cloth, and railed in the communion table at his own expense. He has often told me, that at his coming to his estate he found his parishioners very irregular; and that in order to make them kneel and join in the responses, he gave every one of them a hassock and a common-prayer book: and at the same time employed an itinerant singing master, who goes about the country for that purpose, to instruct them rightly in the tunes of the psalms; upon which they now very much value themselves, and indeed outdo most of the country churches that I have ever heard.

As Sir Roger is landlord to the whole congregation, he keeps them in very good order, and will suffer nobody to sleep in it besides himself; for if, by chance, he has been surprised into a short nap at sermon, upon recovering out of it he stands up and looks about him, and if he sees anybody else nodding, either wakes them himself, or sends his servants to them. Several other of the old knight's particularities break out upon these occasions: sometimes he will be lengthening out a verse in the singing-psalms, half a minute after the rest of the congregation have done with it; sometimes, when he is pleased with the matter of his devotion, he pronounces 'Amen' three or four times to the same prayer; and sometimes stands up when everybody else is upon their knees, to count the congregation, or see if any of his tenants are missing.

I was yesterday very much surprised to hear my old friend, in the midst of the service, calling out to one John Matthews to mind what he was about, and not disturb the congregation. This John Matthews it seems is remarkable for being an idle fellow, and at that time was kicking his heels for his diversion. This authority of the knight, though exerted in that odd manner which accompanies him in all circumstances of life, has a very good effect upon the parish, who are not polite enough to see any thing ridiculous in his behavior; besides that the general good sense and worthiness of his character makes his friends observe these little singularities as foils that rather set off than blemish his good qualities.

As soon as the sermon is finished, nobody presumes to stir till Sir Roger is gone out of the church. The knight walks down from his seat in the chancel between a double row of his tenants, that stand bowing to him on each side; and every now and then inquires how such a one's wife, or mother, or son, or father do, whom he does not see at church; which is understood as a secret reprimand to the person that is absent.

The chaplain has often told me, that upon a catechising day, when Sir Roger has been pleased with a boy that answers well, he has ordered a bible to be given him next day for his encouragement; and sometimes accompanies it with a flitch of bacon to his mother. Sir Roger has likewise added five pounds a year to the clerk's place; and that he may encourage the young fellows to make themselves perfect in the church-service, has promised, upon the death of the present incumbent, who is very old, to bestow it according to merit.

The fair understanding between Sir Roger and his chaplain, and their mutual concurrence in doing good, is the more remarkable, because the very next village is famous for the differences and contentions that rise between the parson and the squire, who live in a perpetual state of war. The parson is always preaching at the squire, and the squire to be revenged on the parson never comes to church. The squire has made all his tenants atheists, and tithe-stealers; while the parson instructs them every Sunday in the dignity of his order, and insinuates to them in almost every sermon that he is a better man than his patron. In short matters have come to such an extremity, that the squire had not said his prayers either in public or private this half year; and that the parson threatens him, if he does not mend his manners, to pray for him in the face of the whole congregation.

Feuds of this nature, though too frequent in the country, are very fatal to the ordinary people; who are so used to be dazzled with riches, that they pay as much deference to the understanding of a man of an estate, as of a man of learning: and are very hardly brought to regard any truth, how important soever it may be, that is preached to them, when they know there are several men of five hundred a year who do not believe it.

Monday, July 9, 1711.

[No. 122.]

SIR ROGER AT THE ASSIZES

A man's first care should be to avoid the reproaches of his own heart; his next, to escape the censures of the world: if the last interferes with the former, it ought to be entirely neglected; but otherwise there cannot be a greater satisfaction to an honest mind, than to see those approbations which it gives itself seconded by the applauses of the public: a man is more sure of conduct, when the verdict which he passes upon his own behavior is thus warranted and confirmed by the opinion of all that know him.

My worthy friend Sir Roger is one of those who is not only at peace within himself, but beloved and esteemed by all about him. He receives a suitable tribute for his universal benevolence to mankind, in the returns of affection and goodwill, which are paid him by every one that lives within his neighborhood. I lately met with two or three odd instances of that general respect which is shewn to the good old knight. He would needs carry Will Wimble and myself with him to the county assizes: as we were upon the road Will Wimble joined a couple of plain men who rode before us, and conversed with them for some time; during which my friend Sir Roger acquainted me with their characters.

'The first of them,' says he, 'that has a spaniel by his side, is a yeoman of about an hundred pounds a year, an honest man: he is just within the game-act, and qualified to kill an hare or a pheasant: he knocks down his dinner with his gun twice or thrice a week: and by that means lives much cheaper than those who have not so good an estate as himself. He would be a good neighbor if he did not destroy so many partridges: in short he is a very sensible man; shoots flying; and has been several times foreman of the petty jury.

'That other that rides along with him is Tom Touchy, a fellow famous for "taking the law" of everybody. There is not one in the town where he lives that he has not sued at a quarter-sessions. The rogue had once the impudence to go to law with the widow. His head is full of costs, damages, and ejectments: he plagued a couple of honest gentlemen so

long for a trespass in breaking one of his hedges, till he was forced to sell the ground it enclosed to defray the charges of the prosecution: his father left him fourscore pounds a year; but he has cast and been cast so often, that he is not now worth thirty. I suppose he is going upon the old business of the willow tree.'

As Sir Roger was giving me this account of Tom Touchy, Will Wimble and his two companions stopped short till he came up to them. After having paid their respects to Sir Roger, Will told him that Mr. Touchy and he must appeal to him upon a dispute that arose between them. Will it seems had been giving his fellow-traveler an account of his angling one day in such a hole; when Tom Touchy, instead of hearing out his story, told him that Mr. such-a-one, if he pleased, might 'take the law of him' for fishing in that part of the river. My friend Sir Roger heard them both upon a round trot; and after having paused some time, told them, with the air of a man who would not give his judgment rashly, that 'much might be said on both sides.' They were neither of them dissatisfied with the knight's determination, because neither of them found himself in the wrong by it: upon which we made the best of our way to the assizes.

The court was set before Sir Roger came; but notwithstanding all the justices had taken their places upon the bench, they made room for the old knight at the head of them; who, for his reputation in the country, took occasion to whisper in the judge's ear, 'that he was glad his lordship had met with so much good weather in his circuit.' I was listening to the proceedings of the court with much attention, and infinitely pleased with that great appearance of solemnity which so properly accompanies such a public administration of our laws; when, after about an hour's sitting, I observed to my great surprise, in the midst of a trial, that my friend Sir Roger was getting up to speak. I was in some pain for him till I found he had acquitted himself of two or three sentences, with a look of much business and great intrepidity.

Upon his first rising the court was hushed, and a general whisper ran among the country people that Sir Roger 'was up.' The speech he made was so little to the purpose, that I shall not trouble my readers with an account of it; and I believe was not so much designed by the knight himself to inform the court, as to give him a figure in my eye, and keep up his credit in the country.

I was highly delighted, when the court rose, to see the gentlemen of the country gathering about my old friend, and striving who should compliment him most; at the same time that the ordinary people gazed upon him at a distance, not a little admiring his courage, that was not afraid to speak to the judge.

In our return home we met with a very odd accident; which I cannot forbear relating, because it shews how desirous all who know Sir Roger are of giving him marks of their esteem. When we were arrived upon the verge of his estate, we stopped at a little inn to rest ourselves and our horses. The man of the house had, it seems, been formerly a servant in the knight's family; and to do honor to his old master, had some time since, unknown to Sir Roger, put him up in a sign-post before the door; so that 'the Knight's Head' had hung out upon the road about a week before he himself knew anything of the matter. As soon as Sir Roger was acquainted with it, finding that his servant's indiscretion proceeded wholly from affection and good-will, he only told him that he had made him too high a compliment; and when the fellow seemed to think that could hardly be, added with a more decisive look, that it was too great an honor for any man under a duke; but told him at the same time, that it might be altered with a very few touches, and that he himself would be at the charge of it. Accordingly, they got a painter by the knight's directions to add a pair of whiskers to the face, and by a little aggravation of the features to change it into the *Saracen's Head*. I should not have known this story, had not the inn-keeper, upon Sir Roger's alighting, told him in my hearing, that his honor's head was brought back last night with the alterations that he had ordered to be made in it. Upon this my friend with his usual cheerfulness related the particulars above-mentioned, and ordered the head to be brought into the room. I could not forbear discovering greater expressions of mirth than ordinary upon the appearance of this monstrous face, under which, notwithstand-

ing it was made to frown and stare in a most extraordinary manner, I could still discover a distant resemblance of my old friend. Sir Roger, upon seeing me laugh, desired me to tell him truly if I thought it possible for people to know him in that disguise. I at first kept my usual silence: but upon the knight's conjuring me to tell him whether it was not still more like himself than a Saracen, I composed my countenance in the best manner I could, and replied 'That much might be said on both sides.'

These several adventures, with the knight's behavior in them, gave me as pleasant a day as ever I met with in any of my travels.

Friday, July 20, 1711.

[No. 131.]

TOWN AND COUNTRY

It is usual for a man who loves country sports to preserve the game on his own grounds, and divert himself upon those that belong to his neighbor. My friend Sir Roger generally goes two or three miles from his house, and gets into the frontiers of his estate, before he beats about in search of a hare or partridge, on purpose to spare his own fields, where he is always sure of finding diversion when the worst comes to the worst. By this means the breed about his house has time to increase and multiply besides that the sport is the more agreeable where the game is the harder to come at, and where it does not lie so thick as to produce any perplexity or confusion in the pursuit. For these reasons the country gentleman, like the fox, seldom preys near his own home.

In the same manner I have made a month's excursion out of town, which is the great field of game for sportsmen of my species, to try my fortune in the country, where I have started several subjects, and hunted them down, with some pleasure to myself, and I hope to others. I am here forced to use a great deal of diligence before I can spring anything to my mind, whereas in town, whilst I am following one character, it is ten to one but I am crossed in my way by another, and put up such a variety of odd creatures in both sexes, that they foil the scent of one another, and puzzle the chase. My greatest difficulty in the country is to find sport, and in town to choose it. In the mean time, as I have given a whole month's rest to the cities of London and Westminster, I promise myself abundance of new game upon my return thither.

It is indeed high time for me to leave the country, since I find the whole neighborhood begin to grow very inquisitive after my name and character; my love of solitude, taciturnity, and particular way of life, having raised a great curiosity in all these parts.

The notions which have been framed of me are various; some look upon me as very proud, some as very modest, and some as very melancholy. Will Wimble, as my friend the butler tells me, observing me very much alone, and extremely silent when I am in company, is afraid I have killed a man. The country people seem to suspect me for a conjurer; and some of them hearing of the visit which I made to Moll White, will needs have it that Sir Roger has brought down a cunning man with him, to cure the old woman, and free the country from her charms. So that the character which I go under in part of the neighborhood, is what they here call a 'white witch.'

A justice of peace, who lives about five miles off, and is not of Sir Roger's party, has, it seems, said twice or thrice at his table, that he wishes Sir Roger does not harbor a Jesuit in his house; and that he thinks the gentlemen of the country would do very well to make me give some account of myself.

On the other side, some of Sir Roger's friends are afraid the old knight is imposed upon by a designing fellow, and as they have heard that he converses very promiscuously when he is in town, do not know but he has brought down with him some discarded Whig, that is sullen, and says nothing because he is out of place.

Such is the variety of opinions which are here entertained of me, so that I pass among some for a disaffected person, and among others for a popish priest; among some for a wizard, and among others for a murderer; and all this for no other reason, that I can imagine, but because I do not hoot, and hollow, and make a noise. It is true, my friend Sir Roger tells them that it is my way, and that I am only a philosopher; but this will not satisfy them. They think there

is more in me than he discovers, and that I do not hold my tongue for nothing.

For these and other reasons I shall set out for London to-morrow, having found by experience that the country is not a place for a person of my temper, who does not love jollity, and what they call good neighborhood. A man that is out of humor when an unexpected guest breaks in upon him, and does not care for sacrificing an afternoon to every chance comer,— that will be the master of his own time, and the pursuer of his own inclinations,— makes but a very unsociable figure in this kind of life. I shall therefore retire into the town, if I may make use of that phrase, and get into the crowd again as fast as I can, in order to be alone. I can there raise what speculations I please upon others without being observed myself, and at the same time enjoy all the advantages of company with all the privileges of solitude. In the meanwhile, to finish the month, and conclude these my rural speculations, I shall here insert a letter from my friend Will Honeycomb, who has not lived a month for these forty years out of the smoke of London, and rallies me after his way upon my country life.

'Dear Spec,

'I suppose this letter will find thee picking up daisies, or smelling to a lock of hay, or passing away thy time in some innocent country diversion of the like nature. I have however orders from the club to summon thee up to town, being all of us cursedly afraid thou wilt not be able to relish our company, after thy conversations with Moll White and Will Wimble. Pr'ythee don't send up any more stories of a cock and a bull, nor frighten the town with spirits and witches. Thy speculations begin to smell confoundedly of woods and meadows. If thou dost not come up quickly, we shall conclude that thou art in love with one of Sir Roger's dairy-maids. Service to the knight. Sir Andrew is grown the cock of the club since he left us, and if he does not return quickly, will make every mother's son of us commonwealth's men.

'Dear Spec.

'Thine eternally,
'WILL HONEYCOMB.'
Tuesday, July 31, 1711.

[No. 335.]

SIR ROGER AT THE PLAY

My friend Sir Roger de Coverley, when we last met together at the club, told me that he had a great mind to see the new tragedy with me, assuring me at the same time, that he had not been at a play these twenty years. 'The last I saw,' said Sir Roger, 'was *The Committee,* which I should not have gone to neither, had not I been told before-hand that it was a good Church of England comedy.' He then proceeded to inquire of me who this 'Distressed Mother' was; and upon hearing that she was Hector's widow, he told me that her husband was a brave man, and that when he was a school-boy he had read his life at the end of the dictionary. My friend asked me, in the next place, if there would not be some danger in coming home late, in case the Mohocks should be abroad. 'I assure you,' says he, 'I thought I had fallen into their hands last night; for I observed two or three lusty black men that followed me half way up Fleet-street, and mended their pace behind me, in proportion as I put on to get away from them. You must know,' continued the knight, with a smile, 'I fancied they had a mind to *hunt* me; for I remember an honest gentleman in my neighborhood, who was served such a trick in King Charles II's time, for which reason he has not ventured himself in town ever since. I might have shewn them very good sport, had this been their design; for as I am an old fox-hunter, I should have turned and dodged, and have played them a thousand tricks they had never seen in their lives before.' Sir Roger added, that if these gentlemen had any such intention, they did not succeed very well in it; 'for I threw them out,' says he, 'at the end of Norfolk-street, where I doubled the corner, and got shelter in my lodgings before they could imagine what was become of me. However,' says the knight, 'if Captain Sentry will make one with us to-morrow night, and if you will both of you call upon me about four o'clock, that we may be at the house before it is full, I will have my own coach in readiness to attend you, for John tells me he has got the fore-wheels mended.'

The captain, who did not fail to meet me there at the appointed hour, bid Sir Roger fear nothing, for that he had put on the same sword which he made use of at the battle of Steenkirk. Sir Roger's servants, and among the rest, my old friend the butler, had, I found, provided themselves with good oaken plants, to attend their master upon this occasion. When we had placed him in his coach, with myself at his left hand, the Captain before him, and his butler at the head of his footmen in the rear, we convoyed him in safety to the playhouse, where, having marched up the entry in good order, the Captain and I went in with him, and seated him betwixt us in the pit. As soon as the house was full, and the candles lighted, my old friend stood up and looked about him with that pleasure, which a mind seasoned with humanity naturally feels in itself, at the sight of a multitude of people who seem pleased with one another, and partake of the same common entertainment. I could not but fancy myself, as the old man stood up in the middle of the pit, that he made a very proper center to a tragic audience. Upon the entering of Pyrrhus, the knight told me that he did not believe the king of France himself had a better strut. I was indeed very attentive to my old friend's remarks, because I looked upon them as a piece of natural criticism; and was well pleased to hear him, at the conclusion of almost every scene, telling me that he could not imagine how the play would end. One while he appeared much concerned for Andromache, and a little while after as much for Hermione; and was extremely puzzled to think what would become of Pyrrhus.

When Sir Roger saw Andromache's obstinate refusal to her lover's importunities, he whispered me in the ear, that he was sure she would never have him; to which he added, with a more than ordinary vehemence, 'You can't imagine, sir, what it is to have to do with a widow.' Upon Pyrrhus his threatening afterwards to leave her, the knight shook his head, and muttered to himself, 'Ay, do if you can.' This part dwelt so much upon my friend's imagination, that at the close of the third act, as I was thinking of something else, he whispered me in my ear, ' These widows, sir, are the most perverse creatures in the world. But pray,' says he, ' you that are a critic, is this play according to your dramatic rules, as you call them? Should your people in tragedy always talk to be understood? Why, there is not a single sentence in this play that I do not know the meaning of.'

The fourth act very unluckily began before I had time to give the old gentleman an answer: ' Well,' says the knight, sitting down with great satisfaction, ' I suppose we are now to see Hector's ghost.' He then renewed his attention, and from time to time fell a-praising the widow. He made, indeed, a little mistake as to one of her pages, whom at his first entering he took for Astyanax: but he quickly set himself right in that particular, though, at the same time, he owned he should have been very glad to have seen the little boy. ' Who,' says he, ' must needs be a very fine child by the account that is given of him.' Upon Hermione's going off with a menace to Pyrrhus, the audience gave a loud clap; to which Sir Roger added, ' On my word, a notable young baggage!'

As there was a very remarkable silence and stillness in the audience during the whole action, it was natural for them to take the opportunity of the intervals between the acts, to express their opinion of the players, and of their respective parts. Sir Roger hearing a cluster of them praise Orestes, struck in with them, and told them that he thought his friend Pylades was a very sensible man; as they were afterwards applauding Pyrrhus, Sir Roger put in a second time, ' And let me tell you,' says he, ' though he speak but little, I like the old fellow in whiskers as well as any of them.' Captain Sentry, seeing two or three wags who sat near us, lean with an attentive ear towards Sir Roger, and fearing lest they should smoke the knight, plucked him by the elbow, and whispered something in his ear, that lasted till the opening of the fifth act. The knight was wonderfully attentive to the account which Orestes gives of Pyrrhus his death, and at the conclusion of it told me, it was such a bloody piece of work, that he was glad it was not done upon the stage. Seeing

afterwards Orestes in his raving fit, he grew more than ordinary serious, and took occasion to moralize (in his way) upon an evil conscience, adding, that Orestes, in his madness, looked as if he saw something.

As we were the first that came into the house, so we were the last that went out of it; being resolved to have a clear passage for our old friend, whom we did not care to venture among the justling of the crowd. Sir Roger went out fully satisfied with his entertainment, and we guarded him to his lodging in the same manner that we brought him to the playhouse; being highly pleased for my own part, not only with the performance of the excellent piece which had been presented, but with the satisfaction which it had given to the old man.

Tuesday, March 25, 1712.

[No. 517.]

THE DEATH OF SIR ROGER

We last night received a piece of ill news at our club, which very sensibly afflicted every one of us. I question not but my readers themselves will be troubled at the hearing of it. To keep them no longer in suspense, Sir Roger de Coverley is *dead*. He departed this life at his house in the country, after a few weeks' sickness. Sir Andrew Freeport has a letter from one of his correspondents in those parts, that informs him the old man caught a cold at the county sessions, as he was very warmly promoting an address of his own penning, in which he succeeded according to his wishes. But this particular comes from a whig justice of peace, who was always Sir Roger's enemy and antagonist. I have letters both from the chaplain and Captain Sentry which mention nothing of it, but are filled with many particulars to the honor of the good old man. I have likewise a letter from the butler, who took so much care of me last summer when I was at the knight's house. As my friend the butler mentions, in the simplicity of his heart, several circumstances the others have passed over in silence, I shall give my reader a copy of his letter, without any alteration or diminution.

'HONORED SIR,

'Knowing that you was my old master's good friend, I could not forbear sending you the melancholy news of his death, which has afflicted the whole country as well as his poor servants, who loved him, I may say, better than we did our lives. I am afraid he caught his death the last county sessions, where he would go to see justice done to a poor widow woman, and her fatherless children, that had been wronged by a neighboring gentleman; for you know, sir, my good master was always the poor man's friend. Upon his coming home, the first complaint he made was, that he had lost his roast-beef stomach, not being able to touch a sirloin, which was served up according to custom; and you know he used to take great delight in it. From that time forward he grew worse and worse, but still kept a good heart to the last. Indeed we were once in great hope of his recovery, upon a kind message that was sent him from the widow lady whom he had made love to the forty last years of his life, but this only proved a lightning before death. He has bequeathed to this lady, as a token of his love, a great pearl necklace, and a couple of silver bracelets set with jewels, which belonged to my good old lady his mother: he has bequeathed the fine white gelding, that he used to ride a hunting upon, to his chaplain, because he thought he would be kind to him, and has left you all his books. He has, moreover, bequeathed to the chaplain a very pretty tenement with good lands about it. It being a very cold day when he made his will, he left for mourning, to every man in the parish, a great frize-coat, and to every woman a black riding-hood. It was a moving sight to see him take leave of his poor servants, commending us all for our fidelity, whilst we were not able to speak a word for weeping. As we most of us are grown gray-headed in our dear master's service, he has left us pensions and legacies, which we may live very comfortably upon the remaining part of our days. He has bequeathed a great deal more in charity, which is not yet come to my knowledge, and it is peremptorily said in the parish, that he has left money to build a steeple to the church; for he was heard to say some time ago that if he lived two years longer, Coverley church should have a steeple to it. The chaplain tells everybody that he made a very good end, and never speaks of him without tears. He was buried, according to his own directions, among the family of the Coverleys, on the left hand of his father Sir Arthur. The coffin was carried by six of his tenants, and the pall held up by six of the *quorum:* the whole parish followed the corpse with heavy hearts, and in their mourning suits, the men in frize, and the women in riding-hoods. Captain Sentry, my master's nephew, has taken possession of the hall-house, and the whole estate. When my old master saw him a little before his death, he shook him by the hand, and wished him joy of the estate which was falling to him, desiring him only to make a good use of it, and to pay the several legacies, and the gifts of charity which he told him he had left as quit-rents upon the estate. The captain truly seems a courteous man, though he says but little. He makes much of those whom my master loved, and shews great kindness to the old house-dog, that you know my poor master was so fond of. It would have gone to your heart to have heard the moans the dumb creature made on the day of my master's death. He has never joyed himself since; no more has any of us. 'T was the melancholiest day for the poor people that ever happened in Worcestershire. This is all from,

'Honored Sir, your most sorrowful servant,

'EDWARD BISCUIT.'

'P. S. My master desired, some weeks before he died, that a book which comes up to you by the carrier, should be given to Sir Andrew Freeport, in his name.'

This letter, notwithstanding the poor butler's manner of writing it, gave us such an idea of our good old friend, that upon the reading of it there was not a dry eye in the club. Sir Andrew, opening the book, found it to be a collection of acts of parliament. There was in particular the act of uniformity, with some passages in it marked by Sir Roger's own hand. Sir Andrew found that they related to two or three points, which he had disputed with Sir Roger the last time he appeared at the club. Sir Andrew, who would have been merry at such an incident on another occasion, at the sight of the old man's hand-writing burst into tears, and put the book into his pocket. Captain Sentry informs me, that the knight has left rings and mourning for every one in the club.

Thursday, October 23, 1712.

[No. 81.]

PARTY PATCHES

About the middle of last winter I went to see an opera at the theater in the Hay-market, where I could not but take notice of two parties of very fine women, that had placed themselves in the opposite side-boxes, and seemed drawn up in a kind of battle-array one against another. After a short survey of them, I found they were Patched differently; the faces, on one hand, being spotted on the right side of the forehead, and those upon the other on the left: I quickly perceived that they cast hostile glances upon one another; and that their Patches were placed in those different situations, as party-signals to distinguish friends from foes. In the middle-boxes, between these two opposite bodies, were several ladies who patched indifferently on both sides of their faces, and seemed to sit there with no other intention but to see the opera. Upon enquiry I found, that the body of Amazons on my right hand were whigs, and those on my left, tories: and that those who had placed themselves in the middle-boxes were a neutral party, whose faces had not yet declared themselves. These last, however, as I afterwards found, diminished daily, and took their party with one side or the other; insomuch that I observed in several of them, the patches, which were before dispersed equally, are now all gone over to the whig or tory side of the face. The censorious say, that the men whose hearts are aimed at, are very often the occasions that one part of the face is thus dishonored, and lies under a kind of disgrace, while the other is so much set off and adorned by the owner; and that the Patches turn to the right or to the left, according to the principles of the man who is most in favor. But whatever may be the motives of a few fantastical coquettes, who do not

Patch for the public good so much as for their own private advantage, it is certain, that there are several women of honor who Patch out of principle, and with an eye to the interest of their country. Nay, I am informed that some of them adhere so steadfastly to their party, and are so far from sacrificing their zeal for the public to their passion for any particular person, that in a late draught of marriage-articles a lady has stipulated with her husband, that whatever his opinions are, she shall be at liberty to patch on which sides she pleases.

I must here take notice that Rosalinda, a famous whig partisan, has most unfortunately a very beautiful mole on the tory part of her forehead; which being very conspicuous, has occasioned many mistakes, and given an handle to her enemies to misrepresent her face, as though it had revolted from the whig interest. But, whatever this natural patch may seem to insinuate, it is well known that her notions of government are still the same. This unlucky mole, however, has misled several coxcombs; and like the hanging out of false colors, made some of them converse with Rosalinda in what they thought the spirit of her party, when on a sudden she has given them an unexpected fire, that has sunk them all at once. If Rosalinda is unfortunate in her mole, Nigranilla is as unhappy in a pimple, which forces her, against her inclinations, to patch on the whig side.

I am told that many virtuous matrons, who formerly have been taught to believe that this artificial spotting of the face was unlawful, are now reconciled by a zeal for their cause, to what they could not be prompted by a concern for their beauty. This way of declaring war upon one another, puts me in mind of what is reported of the tigress, that several spots rise in her skin when she is angry; or as Mr. Cowley has imitated the verses that stand as the motto of this paper,

— She swells with angry pride,
And calls forth all her spots on ev'ry side.

When I was in the theater the time above-mentioned, I had the curiosity to count the Patches on both sides, and found the tory Patches to be about twenty stronger than the whig; but to make amends for this small inequality, I the next morning found the whole puppet-shew filled with faces spotted after the whiggish manner. Whether or no the ladies had retreated hither in order to rally their forces, I cannot tell; but the next night they came in so great a body to the opera, that they out-numbered the enemy.

This account of Party-patches will, I am afraid, appear improbable to those who live at a distance from the fashionable world; but as it is a distinction of a very singular nature, and what perhaps may never meet with a parallel, I think I should not have discharged the office of a faithful SPECTATOR, had I not recorded it.

I have, in former papers, endeavored to expose this party-rage in women, as it only serves to aggravate the hatred and animosities that reign among men, and in a great measure deprives the fair sex of those peculiar charms with which nature has endowed them.

When the Romans and Sabines were at war, and just upon the point of giving battle, the women who were allied to both of them, interposed with so many tears and entreaties, that they prevented the mutual slaughter which threatened both parties, and united them together in a firm and lasting peace.

I would recommend this noble example to our British ladies, at a time when their country is torn with so many unnatural divisions, that if they continue, it will be a misfortune to be born in it. The Greeks thought it so improper for women to interest themselves in competitions and contentions, that for this reason, among others, they forbad them, under pain of death, to be present at the Olympic games, notwithstanding these were the public diversions of all Greece.

As our English women excel those of all nations in beauty, they should endeavor to outshine them in all other accomplishments proper to the sex, and to distinguish themselves as tender mothers and faithful wives, rather than as furious partisans. Female virtues are of a domestic turn. The family is the proper province for private women to shine in. If they must be showing their zeal for the public, let it not be against those who are perhaps of the same family, or at least of the same religion or nation, but against those who are the open, professed, undoubted enemies of their faith, liberty and country. When the Romans were pressed with a foreign enemy, the ladies voluntarily contributed all their rings and jewels to assist the government under the public exigence, which appeared so laudable an action in the eyes of their countrymen, that from thenceforth it was permitted by a law to pronounce public orations at the funeral of a woman in praise of the deceased person, which till that time was peculiar to men. Would our English ladies, instead of sticking on a patch against those of their own country, show themselves so truly public-spirited as to sacrifice every one her necklace against the common enemy, what decrees ought not to be made in favor of them?

Since I am recollecting upon this subject such passages as occur to my memory out of ancient authors, I cannot omit a sentence in the celebrated funeral oration of Pericles, which he made in honor of those brave Athenians that were slain in a fight with the Lacedæmonians. After having addressed himself to the several ranks and orders of his countrymen, and shown them how they should behave themselves in the public cause, he turns to the female part of his audience; 'And as for you (says he) I shall advise you in very few words: Aspire only to those virtues that are peculiar to your sex; follow your natural modesty, and think it your greatest commendation not to be talked of one way or other.'

Saturday, June 2, 1711.

[No. 253.]

DETRACTION AMONG POETS

There is nothing which more denotes a great mind, than the abhorrence of envy and detraction. This passion reigns more among bad poets, than among any other set of men.

As there are none more ambitious of fame, than those who are conversant in poetry, it is very natural for such as have not succeeded in it, to depreciate the works of those who have. For since they cannot raise themselves to the reputation of their fellow-writers, they must endeavor to sink it to their own pitch, if they would still keep themselves upon a level with them.

The greatest wits that ever were produced in one age, lived together in so good an understanding, and celebrated one another with so much generosity, that each of them receives an additional luster from his contemporaries, and is more famous for having lived with men of so extraordinary a genius, than if he had himself been the sole wonder of the age. I need not tell my reader, that I here point at the reign of Augustus, and I believe he will be of my opinion, that neither Virgil nor Horace would have gained so great a reputation in the world, had they not been the friends and admirers of each other. Indeed all the great writers of that age, for whom singly we have so great an esteem, stand up together as vouchers for one another's reputation. But at the same time that Virgil was celebrated by Gallus, Propertius, Horace, Varius, Tucca and Ovid, we know that Bavius and Mævius were his declared foes and calumniators.

In our own country a man seldom sets up for a poet, without attacking the reputation of all his brothers in the art. The ignorance of the moderns, the scribblers of the age, the decay of poetry, are the topics of detraction, with which he makes his entrance into the world; but how much more noble is the fame that is built on candor and ingenuity, according to those beautiful lines of Sir John Denham, in his poem on Fletcher's works!

But whither am I strayed? I need not raise

Trophies to thee from other men's dispraise:
Nor is thy fame on lesser ruins built,
Nor needs thy juster title the foul guilt
Of eastern Kings, who to secure their reign
Must have their brothers, sons, and kindred slain.

I am sorry to find that an author, who is very justly esteemed among the best judges, has admitted some strokes of this nature into a very fine poem, I mean *The Art of Criticism*, which was published some months since, and is a master-piece in its kind. The observa-

tions follow one another like those in Horace's *Art of Poetry*, without that methodical regularity which would have been requisite in a prose author. They are some of them uncommon, but such as the reader must assent to, when he sees them explained with that elegance and perspicuity in which they are delivered. As for those which are the most known, and the most received, they are placed in so beautiful a light, and illustrated with such apt allusions, that they have in them all the graces of novelty, and make the reader, who was before acquainted with them, still more convinced of their truth and solidity. And here give me leave to mention what Monsieur Boileau has so very well enlarged upon in the preface to his works, that wit and fine writing doth not consist so much in advancing things that are new, as in giving things that are known an agreeable turn. It is impossible for us, who live in the latter ages of the world, to make observations in criticism, morality, or in any art or science, which have not been touched upon by others. We have little else left us, but to represent the common sense of mankind in more strong, more beautiful, or more uncommon lights. If a reader examines Horace's *Art of Poetry*, he will find but very few precepts in it, which he may not meet with in Aristotle, and which were not commonly known by all the poets of the Augustan age. His way of expressing and applying them, not his invention of them, is what we are chiefly to admire.

For this reason I think there is nothing in the world so tiresome as the works of those critics who write in a positive dogmatic way, without either language, genius or imagination. If the reader would see how the best of the Latin critics writ, he may find their manner very beautifully described in the characters of Horace, Petronius, Quintilian and Longinus, as they are drawn in the essay of which I am now speaking.

Since I have mentioned Longinus, who in his reflections has given us the same kind of sublime, which he observes in the several passages that occasioned them; I cannot but take notice, that our English author has after the same manner exemplified several of his precepts in the very precepts themselves. I shall produce two or three instances of this kind. Speaking of the insipid smoothness which some readers are so much in love with, he has the following verses.

These EQUAL SYLLABLES alone require,
Though oft the ear the OPEN VOWELS tire,
While EXPLETIVES their feeble aid DO join,
And ten low words oft creep in one dull line.

The gaping of the vowels in the second line, the expletive *do* in the third, and the ten monosyllables in the fourth, give such a beauty to this passage, as would have been very much admired in an ancient poet. The reader may observe the following lines in the same view.

A NEEDLESS ALEXANDRINE ends the song,
That like a wounded snake, drags its slow length along

And afterwards,

'T 'is not enough no harshness gives offense,
The SOUND must seem an ECHO to the SENSE.
SOFT is the strain when ZEPHIR gently blows,
And the SMOOTH STREAM in SMOOTHER NUMBERS flows;
But when loud surges lash the sounding shore,
The HOARSE, ROUGH VERSE should like the TORRENT roar.
When AJAX strives, some rock's vast weight to throw,
The line too LABORS, and the words move SLOW:
Not so, when swift CAMILLA scours the plain,
Flies o'er th' unbending corn, and skims along the main.

The beautiful distich upon Ajax in the foregoing lines, puts me in mind of a description in Homer's *Odyssey*. * * * It would be endless to quote verses out of Virgil which have this particular kind of beauty in the numbers; but I may take an occasion in a future paper to shew several of them which have escaped the observation of others.

I cannot conclude this paper without taking notice, that we have three poems in our tongue, which are of the same nature, and each of them a master-piece in its kind; the *Essay on Translated Verse*, the *Essay on the Art of Poetry*, and the *Essay upon Criticism*.

Thursday, December 20, 1711.

[No. 26.]

WESTMINSTER ABBEY

When I am in a serious humor, I very often walk by myself in Westminster Abbey; where the gloominess of the place and the use to which it is applied, with the solemnity of the building, and the condition of the people who lie in it, are apt to fill the mind with a kind of melancholy, or rather thoughtfulness, that is not disagreeable. I yesterday passed a whole afternoon in the churchyard, the cloisters, and the church, amusing myself with the tombstones and inscriptions that I met with in those several regions of the dead. Most of them recorded nothing else of the buried person, but that he was born upon one day, and died upon another, the whole history of his life being comprehended in those two circumstances, that are common to all mankind. I could not but look upon these registers of existence, whether of brass or marble, as a kind of satire upon the departed persons; who had left no other memorial of them, but that they were born and that they died. They put me in mind of several persons mentioned in the battles of heroic poems, who have sounding names given them, for no other reason but that they may be killed, and are celebrated for nothing but being knocked on the head.

Γλαῦκόν τε Μέδοντά τε Θερσίλοχόν τε. Hom.
Glaucumque, Medontaque, Thersilochumque. Virg.

The life of these men is finely described in holy writ by 'the path of an arrow,' which is immediately closed up and lost.

Upon my going into the church, I entertained myself with the digging of a grave; and saw in every shovel-full of it that was thrown up, the fragment of a bone or skull intermixt with a kind of fresh moldering earth, that some time or other had a place in the composition of an human body. Upon this, I began to consider with myself what innumerable multitudes of people lay confused together under the pavement of that ancient cathedral; how men and women, friends and enemies, priests and soldiers, monks and prebendaries, were crumbled amongst one another, and blended together in the same common mass; how beauty, strength, and youth, with old-age, weakness and deformity, lay undistinguished in the same promiscuous heap of matter.

After having thus surveyed this great magazine of mortality, as it were, in the lump; I examined it more particularly by the accounts which I found on several of the monuments which are raised in every quarter of that ancient fabric. Some of them were covered with such extravagant epitaphs, that, if it were possible for the dead person to be acquainted with them, he would blush at the praises which his friends have bestowed upon him. There are others so excessively modest, that they deliver the character of the person departed in Greek or Hebrew, and by that means are not understood once in a twelvemonth. In the poetical quarter, I found there were poets who had no monuments, and monuments which had no poets. I observed indeed that the present war had filled the church with many of these uninhabited monuments, which had been erected to the memory of persons whose bodies were perhaps buried in the plains of Blenheim, or in the bosom of the ocean.

I could not but be very much delighted with several modern epitaphs, which are written with great elegance of expression and justness of thought, and therefore do honor to the living as well as to the dead. As a foreigner is very apt to conceive an idea of the ignorance or politeness of a nation, from the turn of their public monuments and inscriptions, they should be submitted to the perusal of men of learning and genius, before they are put in execution. Sir Cloudesly Shovel's monument has very often given me great offense: Instead of the brave rough English admiral, which was the distinguishing character of that plain gallant man, he is represented on his tomb by the figure of a beau, dressed in a long periwig, and reposing himself upon velvet cushions under a canopy of state. The inscription is answerable to the Monument; for instead of celebrating the many remarkable actions he had performed in the service of his country, it acquaints us only with the manner of his death, in which it was impossible for him to reap any honor. The Dutch, whom we are apt to despise for want of genius, shew an infinitely greater taste of antiquity and politeness in their buildings and works of this nature, than what we meet with in those of our own country. The monuments of their admirals, which have been erected at the public expense, represent them like themselves; and are adorned with rostral crowns and naval ornaments, with beautiful festoons of sea-weed, shells, and coral.

But to return to our subject. I have left the repository of our English kings for the contemplation of another day, when I shall find my mind disposed for so serious an amusement. I know that entertainments of this nature are apt to raise dark and dismal thoughts in timorous minds, and gloomy imaginations; but for my own part, though I am always serious, I do not know what it is to be melancholy; and can therefore take a view of nature in her deep and solemn scenes, with the same pleasure as in her most gay and delightful ones. By this means I can improve myself with those objects, which others consider with terror. When I look upon the tombs of the great, every emotion of envy dies in me; when I read the epitaphs of the beautiful, every inordinate desire goes out; when I meet with the grief of parents upon a tomb-stone, my heart melts with compassion; when I see the tomb of the parents themselves, I consider the vanity of grieving for those whom we must quickly follow; when I see kings lying by those who deposed them, when I consider rival wits placed side by side, or the holy men that divided the world with their contests and disputes, I reflect with sorrow and astonishment on the little competitions, factions and debates of mankind. When I read the several dates of the tombs, of some that died yesterday, and some six hundred years ago, I consider that great day when we shall all of us be contemporaries, and make our appearance together.

Friday, March 30, 1711.

ALEXANDER POPE (1688-1744)

Pope was born in London, the year of the protestant revolution. His parents, who were catholics, shortly retired to a country home near Windsor Forest, and there the poet passed most of his boyhood. Deformed and sickly from his birth, he was reared with great tenderness and compliance and, after his twelfth year, was chiefly self-educated. He read widely and at random among English authors and was an eager, though inexact, student of the ancient classics. At a remarkably early age, he became avid of literary fame and displayed a talent for acquainting himself with the literary personalities of the day. Before he was twelve, he had visited Will's coffee-house in order to have a look at the great Dryden and, while yet a boy, had passed from the courting to the quarreling stage with Wycherley. His precocity as a verse-maker, which he never troubled himself to disparage, is celebrated in the well-known couplet:

> As yet a child, nor yet a fool to fame,
> I lisped in numbers for the numbers came.

He claimed to have written his *Pastorals* at sixteen. They were printed in 1709, and immediately attracted attention. His *Messiah* and his *Essay on Criticism* won the encomiums of *The Spectator* and admitted him to Addison's circle. *The Rape of the Lock* (1712-14) confirmed his reputation, and his translation of the *Iliad* (1715-18) and the *Odyssey* (completed 1726) procured him a competence. 'Thanks to Homer,' he 'could live and thrive, indebted to no prince or peer alive.' He purchased a villa on the Thames at Twickenham, and there spent the last twenty-five years of his life, improving his 'grotto' and gardens, entertaining wits and social celebrities, and polishing off his rivals in finished satirical verse of which the monumental example is *The Dunciad*, published in 1728, but afterward much altered and amplified. His best known attempt at philosophical poetry is the superficial, but eminently quotable, *Essay on Man* (1732-4). Pope is chiefly valued for the smoothness and sweetness of his versification, and for his gift of turning into brief and memorable phrase 'what oft was thought, but ne'er so well expressed.' Though not a great poet in the highest sense of that term, he is often glowing and sometimes powerful in declamation; while for mischievous innuendo and sustained condensation and point he has no equal in English poetry. His satire, unlike Dryden's, is usually personal and frequently poisoned by the same envy and malice which impaired his character and conduct. 'Leave Pope as soon as you can; he is sure to play you some devilish trick else,' Addison wrote to Lady Montagu,— one victim of Pope's shiftiness to another. Pope's physical inferiority made him preternaturally sensitive and distorted his social outlook. He could be pitifully base and treacherous where his vanity was engaged, and his literary career was a tissue of trivial deceits and mean animosities. Yet we cannot but admire the indomitableness of the mind which, in spite of physical suffering and humiliation, fought its way by fair means and foul, to the chief place in the literature of its time.

AN ESSAY ON CRITICISM

I

'T is hard to say, if greater want of skill
Appear in writing or in judging ill;
But, of the two, less dangerous is the offense
To tire our patience, than mislead our sense.
Some few in that, but numbers err in this, 5

Ten censure wrong for one who writes amiss;
A fool might once himself alone expose,
Now one in verse makes many more in prose.
'T is with our judgments as our watches, none
Go just alike, yet each believes his own. 10
In poets as true genius is but rare,
True taste as seldom is the critic's share,

350

Both must alike from Heaven derive their
    light,
These born to judge, as well as those to
    write.
Let such teach others who themselves ex-
    cel,   15
And censure freely who have written well.
Authors are partial to their wit, 't is true,
But are not critics to their judgment too?
    Yet if we look more closely, we shall
    find
Most have the seeds of judgment in their
    mind: 20
Nature affords at least a glimmering light;
The lines, though touched but faintly, are
    drawn right.
But as the slightest sketch, if justly traced,
Is by ill-coloring but the more disgraced,
So by false learning is good sense defaced;
Some are bewildered in the maze of schools,
And some made coxcombs nature meant
    but fools.   27
In search of wit these lose their common
    sense,
And then turn critics in their own defense;
Each burns alike, who can, or cannot write,
Or with a rival's or an eunuch's spite.   31
All fools have still an itching to deride,
And fain would be upon the laughing
    side.
If Mævius scribble in Apollo's spite,
There are who judge still worse than he can
    write.   35
    Some have at first for wits, then poets
    passed,
Turned critics next, and proved plain fools
    at last.
Some neither can for wits nor critics
    pass,
As heavy mules are neither horse nor ass.
Those half-learned witlings, numerous in
    our isle,   40
As half-formed insects on the banks of
    Nile;
Unfinished things, one knows not what to
    call,
Their generation's so equivocal:
To tell 'em, would a hundred tongues re-
    quire,
Or one vain wit's, that might a hundred
    tire.   45
    But you who seek to give and merit fame,
And justly bear a critic's noble name,
Be sure yourself and your own reach to
    know,
How far your genius, taste, and learning
    go;
Launch not beyond your depth, but be dis-
    creet,   50

And mark that point where sense and dul-
    ness meet.
    Nature to all things fixed the limits fit,
And wisely curbed proud man's pretending
    wit.
As on the land while here the ocean gains,
In other parts it leaves wide sandy plains;
Thus in the soul while memory prevails, 56
The solid power of understanding fails;
Where beams of warm imagination play,
The memory's soft figures melt away.
One science only will one genius fit;   60
So vast is art, so narrow human wit:
Not only bounded to peculiar arts,
But oft in those confined to single parts.
Like kings we lose the conquests gained
    before,
By vain ambition still to make them more;
Each might his several province well com-
    mand,   66
Would all but stoop to what they under-
    stand.
    First follow Nature, and your judgment
    frame
By her just standard, which is still the
    same:
Unerring Nature, still divinely bright,   70
One clear, unchanged, and universal light,
Life, force, and beauty, must to all impart,
At once the source, and end, and test of
    Art.
Art from that fund each just supply pro-
    vides,
Works without show, and without pomp
    presides: 75
In some fair body thus the informing soul
With spirits feeds, with vigor fills the whole,
Each motion guides, and every nerve sus-
    tains;
Itself unseen, but in the effects, remains.
Some, to whom Heaven in wit has been pro-
    fuse,   80
Want as much more, to turn it to its use;
For wit and judgment often are at strife,
Though meant each other's aid, like man
    and wife.
'T is more to guide than spur the Muse's
    steed;   84
Restrain his fury, than provoke his speed;
The wingèd courser, like a generous horse,
Shows most true mettle when you check his
    course.
    Those rules of old discovered, not devised,
Are Nature still, but Nature methodized;
Nature, like liberty, is but restrained   90
By the same laws which first herself or-
    dained.
    Hear how learned Greece her useful rules
    indites

When to repress, and when indulge our
     flights:
High on Parnassus' top her sons she
     showed,
And pointed out those arduous paths they
     trod;   95
Held from afar, aloft, the immortal prize,
And urged the rest by equal steps to rise.
Just precepts thus from great examples
     given,
She drew from them what they derived from
     Heaven.
The generous critic fanned the poet's fire,
And taught the world with reason to ad-
     mire.   101
Then criticism the Muses' handmaid proved,
To dress her charms, and make her more
     beloved:
But following wits from that intention
     strayed,
Who could not win the mistress, wooed the
     maid;   105
Against the poets their own arms they
     turned,
Sure to hate most the men from whom they
     learned.
So modern 'pothecaries, taught the art
By doctor's bills to play the doctor's part,
Bold in the practice of mistaken rules,   110
Prescribe, apply, and call their masters
     fools.
Some on the leaves of ancient authors prey,
Nor time nor moths e'er spoiled so much
     as they.
Some dryly plain, without invention's aid,
Write dull receipts, how poems may be
     made.   115
These leave the sense, their learning to dis-
     play,
And those explain the meaning quite away.
You, then, whose judgment the right
     course would steer,
Know well each ancient's proper character;
His fable, subject, scope in every page;   120
Religion, country, genius of his age:
Without all these at once before your eyes,
Cavil you may, but never criticise.
Be Homer's works your study and delight,
Read them by day, and meditate by night;
Thence form your judgment, thence your
     maxims bring,   126
And trace the Muses upward to their
     spring.
Still with itself compared, his text peruse;
And let your comment be the Mantuan
     Muse.
When first young Maro in his boundless
     mind   130

A work to outlast immortal Rome designed,
Perhaps he seemed above the critic's law,
And but from nature's fountains scorned
     to draw:
But when to examine every part he came,
Nature and Homer were, he found, the
     same.   135
Convinced, amazed, he checks the bold de-
     sign;
And rules as strict his labored work con-
     fine,
As if the Stagirite o'erlooked each line.
Learn hence for ancient rules a just es-
     teem;
To copy nature is to copy them.   140
     Some beauties yet no precepts can declare,
For there's a happiness as well as care.
Music resembles poetry, in each
Are nameless graces which no methods
     teach,
And which a master-hand alone can
     reach.   145
If, where the rules not far enough extend,
(Since rules were made but to promote
     their end)
Some lucky license answer to the full
The intent proposed, that license is a rule.
Thus Pegasus, a nearer way to take,   150
May boldly deviate from the common track;
From vulgar bounds with brave disorder
     part,
And snatch a grace beyond the reach of
     art,
Which without passing through the judg-
     ment, gains   154
The heart, and all its end at once attains.
In prospects thus, some objects please our
     eyes,
Which out of nature's common order rise,
The shapeless rock, or hanging precipice.
Great wits sometimes may gloriously of-
     fend,
And rise to faults true critics dare not
     mend.   160
But though the ancients thus their rules in-
     vade,
(As kings dispense with laws themselves
     have made)
Moderns, beware! or if you must offend
Against the precept, ne'er transgress its end;
Let it be seldom and compelled by need;   165
And have, at least, their precedent to plead.
The critic else proceeds without remorse,
Seizes your fame, and puts his laws in force.
     I know there are, to whose presumptuous
     thoughts
Those freer beauties, even in them, seem
     faults.   170

Some figures monstrous and mis-shaped appear,
Considered singly, or beheld too near,
Which, but proportioned to their light or place,
Due distance reconciles to form and grace.
A prudent chief not always must display 175
His powers in equal ranks, and fair array,
But with the occasion and the place comply,
Conceal his force, nay, seem sometimes to fly.
Those oft are stratagems which errors seem,
Nor is it Homer nods, but we that dream.
Still green with bays each ancient altar stands,   181
Above the reach of sacrilegious hands;
Secure from flames, from envy's fiercer rage,
Destructive war, and all-involving age.
See, from each clime the learned their incense bring!   185
Hear, in all tongues, consenting peans ring!
In praise so just let every voice be joined,
And fill the general chorus of mankind.
Hail, bards triumphant! born in happier days;
Immortal heirs of universal praise!   190
Whose honors with increase of ages grow,
As streams roll down, enlarging as they flow;
Nations unborn your mighty names shall sound,
And worlds applaud that must not yet be found!
Oh, may some spark of your celestial fire,
The last, the meanest of your sons inspire,   196
(That on weak wings, from far, pursues your flights;
Glows while he reads, but trembles as he writes)
To teach vain wits a science little known,
To admire superior sense, and doubt their own!   200

II

Of all the causes which conspire to blind
Man's erring judgment, and misguide the mind,
What the weak head with strongest bias rules,
Is pride, the never-failing vice of fools.
Whatever nature has in worth denied,   205
She gives in large recruits of needful pride;
For as in bodies, thus in souls, we find

What wants in blood and spirits, swelled with wind:
Pride, where wit fails, steps in to our defense,
And fills up all the mighty void of sense.
If once right reason drives that cloud away,   211
Truth breaks upon us with resistless day.
Trust not yourself; but your defects to know,
Make use of every friend — and every foe.
A little learning is a dangerous thing; 215
Drink deep, or taste not the Pierian spring:
There shallow draughts intoxicate the brain,
And drinking largely sobers us again.
Fired at first sight with what the Muse imparts,
In fearless youth we tempt the heights of arts,   220
While from the bounded level of our mind,
Short views we take, nor see the lengths behind;
But more advanced, behold with strange surprise
New distant scenes of endless science rise!
So pleased at first the towering Alps we try,   225
Mount o'er the vales, and seem to tread the sky,
The eternal snows appear already past,
And the first clouds and mountains seem the last;
But, those attained, we tremble to survey
The growing labors of the lengthened way,
The increasing prospect tires our wandering eyes,   231
Hills peep o'er hills, and Alps on Alps arise!
A perfect judge will read each work of wit
With the same spirit that its author writ:
Survey the whole, nor seek slight faults to find   235
Where nature moves, and rapture warms the mind;
Nor lose, for that malignant dull delight,
The generous pleasure to be charmed with wit.
But in such lays as neither ebb, nor flow,
Correctly cold, and regularly low,   240
That shunning faults, one quiet tenor keep;
We cannot blame indeed, but we may sleep.
In wit, as nature, what affects our hearts
Is not the exactness of peculiar parts;
'T is not a lip, or eye, we beauty call,   245
But the joint force and full result of all.
Thus when we view some well-proportioned dome.

(The world's just wonder, and e'en thine,
　O Rome!)
No single parts unequally surprise,
All comes united to the admiring eyes;　250
No monstrous height, or breadth, or length
　appear;
The whole at once is bold, and regular.
　Whoever thinks a faultless piece to see,
Thinks what ne'er was, nor is, nor e'er shall
　be.
In every work regard the writer's end,　255
Since none can compass more than they in-
　tend;
And if the means be just, the conduct true,
Applause, in spite of trivial faults, is due;
As men of breeding, sometimes men of wit,
To avoid great errors, must the less com-
　mit:　260
Neglect the rules each verbal critic lays,
For not to know some trifles, is a praise.
Most critics, fond of some subservient art,
Still make the whole depend upon a part:
They talk of principles, but notions prize,
And all to one loved folly sacrifice.　266
　Once on a time, La Mancha's knight, they
　say,
A certain bard encountering on the way,
Discoursed in terms as just, with looks as
　sage,
As e'er could Dennis of the Grecian stage;
Concluding all were desperate sots and
　fools,　271
Who durst depart from Aristotle's rules.
Our author, happy in a judge so nice,
Produced his play, and begged the knight's
　advice;
Made him observe the subject, and the
　plot,　275
The manners, passions, unities, what not?
All which, exact to rule, were brought
　about,
Were but a combat in the lists left out.
'What! leave the combat out?' exclaims
　the knight;
Yes, or we must renounce the Stagirite.　280
'Not so, by Heaven' (he answers in a
　rage),
'Knights, squires, and steeds, must enter on
　the stage.'
So vast a throng the stage can ne'er con-
　tain.
'Then build a new, or act it in a plain.'
　Thus critics, of less judgment than
　caprice,　285
Curious not knowing, not exact but nice,
Form short ideas; and offend in arts
(As most in manners) by a love to parts.
　Some to conceit alone their taste confine,

And glittering thoughts struck out at every
　line;　290
Pleased with a work where nothing's just
　or fit;
One glaring chaos and wild heap of wit.
Poets like painters, thus unskilled to trace
The naked nature and the living grace,
With gold and jewels cover every part, 295
And hide with ornaments their want of
　art.
True wit is nature to advantage dressed,
What oft was thought, but ne'er so well ex-
　pressed;
Something, whose truth convinced at sight
　we find,
That gives us back the image of our mind
As shades more sweetly recommend the
　light,　301
So modest plainness sets off sprightly wit.
For works may have more wit than does
　'em good,
As bodies perish thro' excess of blood.　304
　Others for language all their care express
And value books, as women, men for dress:
Their praise is still,—the style is excellent:
The sense, they humbly take upon content.
Words are like leaves; and where they
　most abound,　309
Much fruit of sense beneath is rarely found;
False eloquence, like the prismatic glass,
Its gaudy colors spreads on every place;
The face of nature we no more survey,
All glares alike, without distinction gay:
But true expression, like the unchanging
　sun,　315
Clears and improves whate'er it shines upon,
It gilds all objects, but it alters none.
Expression is the dress of thought, and
　still
Appears more decent, as more suitable;
A vile conceit in pompous words expressed,
Is like a clown in regal purple dressed:　321
For different styles with different subjects
　sort,
As several garbs with country, town, and
　court.
Some by old words to fame have made
　pretense,
Ancients in phrase, mere moderns in their
　sense;　325
Such labored nothings, in so strange a
　style,
Amaze the unlearned, and make the learnèd
　smile.
Unlucky, as Fungoso in the play,
These sparks with awkward vanity display
What the fine gentleman wore yesterday; 330
And but so mimic ancient wits at best.

As apes our grandsires, in their doublets
dressed.
In words, as fashions, the same rule will
hold;
Alike fantastic, if too new, or old:
Be not the first by whom the new are tried,
Nor yet the last to lay the old aside.   336
    But most by numbers judge a poet's song;
And smooth or rough, with them, is right
or wrong:
In the bright Muse though thousand charms
conspire,   339
Her voice is all these tuneful fools admire;
Who haunt Parnassus but to please their ear,
Not mend their minds; as some to church
repair,
Not for the doctrine, but the music there.
These equal syllables alone require,   344
Though oft the ear the open vowels tire;
While expletives their feeble aid do join;
And ten low words oft creep in one dull
line:
While they ring round the same unvaried
chimes,
With sure returns of still expected rhymes;
Where'er you find 'the cooling western
breeze,'   350
In the next line, it 'whispers through the
trees';
If crystal streams 'with pleasing murmurs
creep,'
The reader's threatened (not in vain) with
'sleep':
Then, at the last and only couplet fraught
With some unmeaning thing they call a
thought,   355
A needless Alexandrine ends the song,
That, like a wounded snake, drags its slow
length along.
Leave such to tune their own dull rhymes,
and know
What's roundly smooth or languishingly
slow;
And praise the easy vigor of a line,   360
Where Denham's strength, and Waller's
sweetness join.
True ease in writing comes from art, not
chance,
As those move easiest who have learned to
dance.
'T is not enough no harshness gives offense,
The sound must seem an echo to the sense:
Soft is the strain when Zephyr gently
blows,   366
And the smooth stream in smoother num-
bers flows;
But when loud surges lash the sounding
shore,

The hoarse, rough verse should like the
torrent roar:
When Ajax strives some rock's vast weight
to throw,   370
The line too labors, and the words move
slow;
Not so, when swift Camilla scours the
plain,
Flies o'er the unbending corn, and skims
along the main.
Hear how Timotheus' varied lays surprise,
And bid alternate passions fall and rise!
While, at each change, the son of Libyan
Jove *Alexander*   376
Now burns with glory, and then melts with
love;
Now his fierce eyes with sparkling fury
glow,
Now sighs steal out, and tears begin to
flow:
Persians and Greeks like turns of nature
found,   380
And the world's victor stood subdued by
sound!
The power of music all our hearts allow,
And what Timotheus was, is Dryden now.
    Avoid extremes; and shun the fault of
such,
Who still are pleased too little or too much.
At every trifle scorn to take offense,   386
That always shows great pride, or little
sense;
Those heads, as stomachs, are not sure the
best,
Which nauseate all, and nothing can di
gest.
Yet let not each gay turn thy rapture move;
For fools admire, but men of sense ap-
prove: 391
As things seem large which we through
mists descry,
Dulness is ever apt to magnify.
    Some foreign writers, some our own de-
spise;   394
The ancients only, or the moderns prize.
Thus wit, like faith, by each man is ap-
plied
To one small sect, and all are damned be-
side.
Meanly they seek the blessing to confine,
And force that sun but on a part to shine,
Which not alone the southern wit sub-
limes,   400
But ripens spirits in cold northern climes;
Which from the first has shone on ages
past,
Enlights the present, and shall warm the
last:

Though each may feel increases and decays,
And see now clearer and now darker days.
Regard not then if wit be old or new,   406
But blame the false, and value still the
    true.
  Some ne'er advance a judgment of their
    own,
But catch the spreading notion of the town;
They reason and conclude by precedent, 410
And own stale nonsense which they ne'er in-
    vent.
Some judge of authors' names, not works,
    and then
Nor praise nor blame the writings, but the
    men.
Of all this servile herd the worst is he
That in proud dullness joins with quality. 415
A constant critic at the great man's board,
To fetch and carry nonsense for my lord.
What woeful stuff this madrigal would be,
In some starved hackney sonneteer, or me?
But let a lord once own the happy lines, 420
How the wit brightens; how the style re-
    fines!
Before his sacred name flies every fault,
And each exalted stanza teems with
    thought!
  The vulgar thus through imitation err;
As oft the learned by being singular;   425
So much they scorn the crowd, that if the
    throng
By chance go right, they purposely go
    wrong;
So schismatics the plain believers quit,
And are but damned for having too much
    wit.
Some praise at morning what they blame at
    night;   430
But always think the last opinion right.
A Muse by these is like a mistress used,
This hour she's idolized, the next abused;
While their weak heads like towns unforti-
    fied,
'Twixt sense and nonsense daily change
    their side.   435
Ask them the cause; they're wiser still,
    they say;
And still to-morrow's wiser than to-day.
We think our fathers fools, so wise we
    grow
Our wiser sons, no doubt, will think us so.
Once school-divines this zealous isle o'er-
    spread;   440
Who knew most Sentences, was deepest
    read;
Faith, Gospel, all seemed made to be dis-
    puted:
And none had sense enough to be confuted:

Scotists and Thomists, now in peace re-
    main,
Amidst their kindred cobwebs in Duck
    Lane,   445
If faith itself has different dresses worn,
What wonder modes in wit should take
    their turn?
Oft, leaving what is natural and fit,
The current folly proves the ready wit;
And authors think their reputation safe,
Which lives as long as fools are pleased to
    laugh.   451
  Some valuing those of their own side of
    mind,
Still make themselves the measure of man-
    kind:
Fondly we think we honor merit then,
When we but praise ourselves in other
    men.   455
Parties in wit attend on those of state,
And public faction doubles private hate.
Pride, malice, folly, against Dryden rose,
In various shapes of parsons, critics, beaus;
But sense survived, when merry jests were
    past;   460
For rising merit will buoy up at last.
Might he return, and bless once more our
    eyes,
New Blackmores and new Milbourns must
    arise:
Nay, should great Homer lift his awful
    head,   464
Zoilus again would start up from the dead.
Envy will merit, as its shade, pursue;
But like a shadow, proves the substance
    true;
For envied wit, like Sol eclipsed, makes
    known
The opposing body's grossness, not its own.
When first that sun too powerful beams
    displays,   470
It draws up vapors which obscure its rays;
But ev'n those clouds at last adorn its way,
Reflect new glories, and augment the day.
  Be thou the first true merit to defend,
His praise is lost, who stays till all com-
    mend.   475
Short is the date, alas, of modern rhymes,
And 't is but just to let them live betimes.
No longer now that golden age appears,
When patriarch-wits survived a thousand
    years:
Now length of fame (our second life) is
    lost,   480
And bare threescore is all ev'n that can
    boast;
Our sons their fathers' failing language
    see,

And such as Chaucer is, shall Dryden be.
So when the faithful pencil has designed
Some bright idea of the master's mind, 485
Where a new word leaps out at his command,
And ready nature waits upon his hand;
When the ripe colors soften and unite,
And sweetly melt into just shade and light;
When mellow years their full perfection give, 490
And each bold figure just begins to live,
The treacherous colors the fair art betray,
And all the bright creation fades away!
Unhappy wit, like most mistaken things,
Atones not for that envy which it brings.
In youth alone its empty praise we boast,
But soon the short-lived vanity is lost: 497
Like some fair flower the early spring supplies,
That gaily blooms, but even in blooming dies.
What is this wit, which must our cares employ? 500
The owner's wife, that other men enjoy;
Then most our trouble still when most admired,
And still the more we give, the more required;
Whose fame with pains we guard, but lose with ease, 504
Sure some to vex, but never all to please;
'T is what the vicious fear, the virtuous shun,
By fools 't is hated, and by knaves undone!
If wit so much from ignorance undergo,
Ah, let not learning too commence its foe!
Of old, those met rewards who could excel,
And such were praised who but endeavored well: 511
Though triumphs were to generals only due,
Crowns were reserved to grace the soldiers too.
Now, they who reach Parnassus' lofty crown,
Employ their pains to spurn some others down; 515
And while self-love each jealous writer rules,
Contending wits become the sport of fools:
But still the worst with most regret commend,
For each ill author is as bad a friend.
To what base ends, and by what abject ways, 520
Are mortals urged through sacred lust of praise!

Ah, ne'er so dire a thirst of glory boast,
Nor in the critic let the man be lost.
Good-nature and good-sense must ever join;
To err is human, to forgive, divine. 525
But if in noble minds some dregs remain
Not yet purged off, of spleen and sour disdain;
Discharge that rage on more provoking crimes,
Nor fear a dearth in these flagitious times.
No pardon vile obscenity should find, 530
Though wit and art conspire to move your mind;
But dulness with obscenity must prove
As shameful sure as impotence in love.
In the fat age of pleasure, wealth, and ease,
Sprung the rank weed, and thrived with large increase: 535
When love was all an easy Monarch's care;
Seldom at council, never in a war:
Jilts ruled the state, and statesmen farces writ;
Nay, wits had pensions, and young lords had wit:
The fair sat panting at a courtier's play, 540
And not a mask went unimproved away:
The modest fan was lifted up no more,
And virgins smiled at what they blushed before.
The following license of a foreign reign
Did all the dregs of bold Socinus drain; 545
Then unbelieving priests reformed the nation,
And taught more pleasant methods of salvation;
Where Heaven's free subjects might their rights dispute,
Lest God himself should seem too absolute:
Pulpits their sacred satire learned to spare
And vice admired to find a flatterer there!
Encouraged thus, wit's Titans braved the skies, 552
And the press groaned with licensed blasphemies.
These monsters, critics! with your darts engage,
Here point your thunder, and exhaust your rage! 555
Yet shun their fault, who, scandalously nice,
Will needs mistake an author into vice;
All seems infected that the infected spy,
As all looks yellow to the jaundiced eye.

* * *

(1711)

THE RAPE OF THE LOCK

CANTO I

What dire offense from amorous causes
  springs,
What mighty contests rise from trivial
  things,
I sing—This verse to Caryl, Muse! is due:
This, even Belinda may vouchsafe to view:
Slight is the subject, but not so the praise,
If she inspire, and he approve my lays.   6
  Say what strange motive, goddess! could
    compel
A well-bred lord to assault a gentle belle?
Oh, say what stranger cause, yet un-
  explored,
Could make a gentle belle reject a lord? 10
In tasks so bold, can little men engage,
And in soft bosoms dwells such mighty
  rage?
  Sol through white curtains shot a timor-
    ous ray,
And oped those eyes that must eclipse the
  day:
Now lap-dogs give themselves the rousing
  shake,   15
And sleepless lovers, just at twelve, awake:
Thrice rung the bell, the slipper knocked
  the ground,
And the pressed watch returned a silver
  sound.
Belinda still her downy pillow pressed,
Her guardian sylph prolonged the balmy
  rest: 20
'Twas he had summoned to her silent bed
The morning dream that hovered o'er her
  head;
A youth more glittering than a birth-night
  beau
(That e'en in slumber caused her cheek to
  glow),
Seemed to her ear his winning lips to lay,
And thus in whispers said, or seemed to
  say.   26
  'Fairest of mortals, thou distinguished
    care
Of thousand bright inhabitants of air!
If e'er one vision touched thy infant
  thought,
Of all the nurse and all the priest have
  taught   30
Of airy elves by moonlight shadows seen,
The silver token, and the circled green,
Or virgins visited by angel powers,
With golden crowns and wreaths of
  heavenly flowers;

Hear and believe! thy own importance
  know,   35
Nor bound thy narrow views to things
  below.
Some secret truths, from learned pride
  concealed,
To maids alone and children are revealed:
What though no credit doubting wits may
  give?
The fair and innocent shall still believe. 40
Know, then, unnumbered spirits round thee
  fly,
The light militia of the lower sky:
These, though unseen, are ever on the wing,
Hang o'er the box, and hover round the
  Ring,
Think what an equipage thou hast in air, 45
And view with scorn two pages and a chair.
As now your own, our beings were of old,
And once enclosed in woman's beauteous
  mould;
Thence, by a soft transition, we repair
From earthly vehicles to these of air.   50
Think not, when woman's transient breath
  is fled,
That all her vanities at once are dead;
Succeeding vanities she still regards,
And though she plays no more, o'erlooks
  the cards.
Her joy in gilded chariots, when alive, 55
And love of ombre, after death survive.
For when the fair in all their pride expire,
To their first elements their souls retire:
The sprites of fiery termagants in flame
Mount up, and take a salamander's name.
Soft yielding minds to water glide away, 61
And sip, with nymphs, their elemental tea.
The graver prude sinks downward to a
  gnome,
In search of mischief still on earth to roam.
The light coquettes in sylphs aloft repair, 65
And sport and flutter in the fields of air.
  'Know further yet; whoever fair and
    chaste
Rejects mankind, is by some sylph em-
  braced:
For spirits, freed from mortal laws, with
  ease
Assume what sexes and what shapes they
  please.   70
What guards the purity of melting maids,
In courtly balls, and midnight masquerades,
Safe from the treacherous friend, the
  daring spark,
The glance by day, the whisper in the dark,
When kind occasion prompts their warm
  desires,   75

When music softens, and when dancing
   fires?
'T is but their sylph, the wise celestials
   know,
Though honor is the word with men below.
Some nymphs there are, too conscious of
   their face,
For life predestined to the gnomes' em-
   brace.   80
These swell their prospects and exalt their
   pride,
When offers are disdained, and love denied:
Then gay ideas crowd the vacant brain,
While peers, and dukes, and all their sweep-
   ing train,
And garters, stars, and coronets appear, 85
And in soft sounds 'Your Grace' salutes
   their ear.
'T is these that early taint the female soul,
Instruct the eyes of young coquettes to roll,
Teach infant cheeks a bidden blush to
   know,
And little hearts to flutter at a beau.   90
  'Oft, when the world imagine women
   stray,
The sylphs through mystic mazes guide
   their way,
Through all the giddy circle they pursue,
And old impertinence expel by new.
What tender maid but must a victim fall 95
To one man's treat, but for another's ball?
When Florio speaks, what virgin could
   withstand,
If gentle Damon did not squeeze her hand?
With varying vanities, from every part,
They shift the moving toyshop of their
   heart;   100
Where wigs with wigs, with sword-knots
   sword-knots strive,
Beaux banish beaux, and coaches coaches
   drive.
This erring mortals levity may call;
Oh, blind to truth! the sylphs contrive it
   all.   104
  'Of these am I, who thy protection claim,
A watchful sprite, and Ariel is my name.
Late, as I ranged the crystal wilds of air,
In the clear mirror of thy ruling star
I saw, alas! some dread event impend,
Ere to the main this morning sun descend,
But Heaven reveals not what, or how, or
   where: 111
Warned by the sylph, O pious maid,
   beware!
This to disclose is all thy guardian can:
Beware of all, but most beware of man!'
  He said; when Shock, who thought she
   slept too long,

Leaped up, and waked his mistress with his
   tongue.   116
'T was then, Belinda, if report say true,
Thy eyes first opened on a billet-doux;
Wounds, charms, and ardors were no
   sooner read,
But all the vision vanished from thy head.
  And now, unveiled, the toilet stands dis-
   played,   121
Each silver vase in mystic order laid.
First, robed in white, the nymph intent
   adores,
With head uncovered, the cosmetic powers.
A heavenly image in the glass appears. 125
To that she bends, to that her eyes she
   rears; *maid*
The inferior priestess, at her altar's side,
Trembling begins the sacred rites of pride.
Unnumbered treasures ope at once, and here
The various offerings of the world appear;
From each she nicely culls with curious
   toil,   131
And decks the goddess with the glittering
   spoil.
This casket India's glowing gems unlocks,
And all Arabia breathes from yonder box.
The tortoise here and elephant unite, 135
Transformed to combs, the speckled, and
   the white.
Here files of pins extend their shining rows,
Puffs, powders, patches, bibles, billet-doux.
Now awful beauty puts on all its arms;
The fair each moment rises in her charms,
Repairs her smiles, awakens every grace,
And calls forth all the wonders of her
   face;   142
Sees by degrees a purer blush arise,
And keener lightnings quicken in her eyes.
The busy sylphs surround their darling
   care,   145
These set the head, and those divide the
   hair,
Some fold the sleeve, whilst others plait
   the gown;
And Betty's praised for labors not her own.

CANTO II

Not with more glories, in the ethereal plain,
The sun first rises o'er the purpled main,
Than, issuing forth, the rival of his beams
Launched on the bosom of the silver
   Thames.
Fair nymphs, and well-dressed youths
   around her shone,   5
But every eye was fixed on her alone.

On her white breast a sparkling cross she
    wore,
Which Jews might kiss, and infidels adore.
Her lively looks a sprightly mind disclose,
Quick as her eyes, and as unfixed as those;
Favors to none, to all she smiles extends;
Oft she rejects, but never once offends.
Bright as the sun, her eyes the gazers strike,
And, like the sun, they shine on all alike.
Yet graceful ease, and sweetness void of
    pride,   15
Might hide her faults, if belles had faults
    to hide;
If to her share some female errors fall,
Look on her face, and you'll forget 'em all.
    This nymph, to the destruction of man-
    kind,
Nourished two locks, which graceful hung
    behind   20
In equal curls, and well conspired to deck
With shining ringlets the smooth ivory
    neck.
Love in these labyrinths his slaves detains,
And mighty hearts are held in slender
    chains.
With hairy springes, we the birds betray, 25
Slight lines of hair surprise the finny prey,
Fair tresses man's imperial race ensnare,
And beauty draws us with a single hair.
    The adventurous baron the bright locks
    admired;
He saw, he wished, and to the prize aspired.
Resolved to win, he meditates the way, 31
By force to ravish, or by fraud betray;
For when success a lover's toil attends,
Few ask, if fraud or force attained his
    ends.
    For this, ere Phœbus rose, he had im-
    plored   35
Propitious Heaven, and every power adored,
But chiefly Love — to Love an altar built,
Of twelve vast French romances, neatly
    gilt.
There lay three garters, half a pair of
    gloves;
And all the trophies of his former loves; 40
With tender billets-doux he lights the pyre,
And breathes three amorous sighs to raise
    the fire.
Then prostrate falls, and begs with ardent
    eyes
Soon to obtain, and long possess the prize:
The powers gave ear, and granted half his
    prayer,   45
The rest, the winds dispersed in empty air.
    But now secure the painted vessel glides,
The sunbeams trembling on the floating
    tides:

While melting music steals upon the sky,
And softened sounds along the waters die;
Smooth flow the waves, the zephyrs gently
    play,   51
Belinda smiled, and all the world was gay.
All but the sylph — with careful thoughts
    oppressed,
The impending woe sat heavy on his breast.
He summons straight his denizens of air; 55
The lucid squadrons round the sails repair:
Soft o'er the shrouds aërial whispers
    breathe,
That seemed but zephyrs to the train be-
    neath.
Some to the sun their insect wings unfold,
Waft on the breeze, or sink in clouds of
    gold;   60
Transparent forms, too fine for mortal
    sight,
Their fluid bodies half dissolved in light.
Loose to the wind their airy garments flew
Thin glittering textures of the filmy dew,
Dipt in the richest tincture of the skies, 65
Where light disports in ever-mingling dyes,
While every beam new transient colors
    flings,
Colors that change whene'er they wave their
    wings.
Amid the circle, on the gilded mast,
Superior by the head, was Ariel placed; 70
His purple pinions opening to the sun,
He raised his azure wand, and thus begun.
    'Ye sylphs and sylphids, to your chief
    give ear!
Fays, fairies, genii, elves, and demons, hear!
Ye know the spheres, and various tasks
    assigned   75
By laws eternal to the aërial kind.
Some in the fields of purest ether play,
And bask and whiten in the blaze of day.
Some guide the course of wandering orbs
    on high,
Or roll the planets through the boundless
    sky.   80
Some less refined, beneath the moon's pale
    light
Pursue the stars that shoot athwart the
    night,
Or suck the mists in grosser air below,
Or dip their pinions in the painted bow,
Or brew fierce tempests on the wintry main,
Or o'er the glebe distil the kindly rain. 86
Others on earth o'er human race preside,
Watch all their ways, and all their actions
    guide:
Of these the chief, the care of nations own,
And guard with arms divine the British
    throne.   90

'Our humbler province is to tend the fair,
Not a less pleasing, though less glorious
  care;
To save the powder from too rude a gale,
Nor let the imprisoned essences exhale;
To draw fresh colors from the vernal
  flowers;   95
To steal from rainbows ere they drop in
  showers,
A brighter wash; to curl their waving hairs,
Assist their blushes, and inspire their airs;
Nay, oft in dreams, invention we bestow,
To change a flounce, or add a furbelow. 100
  'This day, black omens threat the bright-
    est fair
That e'er deserved a watchful spirit's care;
Some dire disaster, or by force, or slight;
But what, or where, the fates have wrapped
  in night.
Whether the nymph shall break Diana's
  law,   105
Or some frail china jar receive a flaw;
Or stain her honor, or her new brocade;
Forget her prayers, or miss a masquerade;
Or lose her heart, or necklace, at a ball;
Or whether Heaven has doomed that Shock
  must fall.   110
Haste, then, ye spirits! to your charge
  repair;
The fluttering fan be Zephyretta's care;
The drops to thee, Brillante, we consign;
And, Momentilla, let the watch be thine;
Do thou, Crispissa, tend her favorite lock;
Ariel himself shall be the guard of Shock.
  'To fifty chosen sylphs, of special note,
We trust the important charge, the petti-
  coat:
Oft have we known that seven-fold fence
  to fail,
Though stiff with hoops, and armed with
  ribs of whale;   120
Form a strong line about the silver bound,
And guard the wide circumference around,
  'Whatever spirit, careless of his charge,
His post neglects, or leaves the fair at large,
Shall feel sharp vengeance soon o'ertake his
  sins,   125
Be stopped in vials, or transfixed with pins;
Or plunged in lakes of bitter washes lie,
Or wedged whole ages in a bodkin's eye:
Gums and pomatums shall his flight re-
  strain,
While clogged he beats his silken wings in
  vain;   130
Or alum styptics with contracting power
Shrink his thin essence like a rivelled
  flower:
Or, as Ixion fixed, the wretch shall feel

The giddy motion of the whirling mill, 134
In fumes of burning chocolate shall glow,
And tremble at the sea that froths below!'
  He spoke; the spirits from the sails de-
    scend;
Some, orb in orb, around the nymph extend;
Some thrid the mazy ringlets of her hair;
Some hang upon the pendants of her ear;
With beating hearts the dire event they
  wait,   141
Anxious, and trembling for the birth of
  fate.

CANTO III

Close by those meads, for ever crowned
  with flowers,
Where Thames with pride surveys his ris-
  ing towers,
There stands a structure of majestic frame,
Which from the neighboring Hampton
  takes its name.
Here Britain's statesmen oft the fall fore-
  doom   5
Of foreign tyrants and of nymphs at home;
Here thou, great Anna! whom three realms
  obey,
Dost sometimes counsel take — and some-
  times tea.
  Hither the heroes and the nymphs resort,
To taste awhile the pleasures of a court; 10
In various talk the instructive hours they
  passed,
Who gave the ball, or paid the visit last;
One speaks the glory of the British queen,
And one describes a charming Indian
  screen;
A third interprets motions, looks, and eyes;
At every word a reputation dies.   16
Snuff, or the fan, supply each pause of
  chat,
With singing, laughing, ogling, and all that.
  Meanwhile, declining from the noon of
    day,
The sun obliquely shoots his burning ray;
The hungry judges soon the sentence sign,
And wretches hang that jurymen may dine;
The merchant from the Exchange returns
  in peace,
And the long labors of the toilet cease. 24
Belinda now, whom thirst of fame invites,
Burns to encounter two adventurous
  knights,
At ombre singly to decide their doom;
And swells her breast with conquests yet
  to come.
Straight the three bands prepare in arms
  to join,

Each band the number of the sacred nine. 30
Soon as she spreads her hand, the aërial
　　guard
Descend, and sit on each important card:
First, Ariel perched upon a Matadore,
Then each, according to the rank they bore;
For sylphs, yet mindful of their ancient
　　race,　　　　　　　　　　　　　　　35
Are, as when women, wondrous fond of
　　place.
　Behold, four kings in majesty revered,
With hoary whiskers and a forky beard;
And four fair queens whose hands sustain
　　a flower,
The expressive emblem of their softer
　　power;　　　　　　　　　　　　　40
Four knaves in garbs succinct, a trusty
　　band,
Caps on their heads, and halberts in their
　　hand;
And parti-colored troops, a shining train,
Draw forth to combat on the velvet plain.
　The skillful nymph reviews her force with
　　care:　　　　　　　　　　　　　　45
Let spades be trumps! she said, and trumps
　　they were.
　Now moved to war her sable Matadores,
In show like leaders of the swarthy Moors.
Spadillio first, unconquerable lord!
Led off two captive trumps, and swept the
　　board.　　　　　　　　　　　　　50
As many more Manillio forced to yield,
And marched a victor from the verdant
　　field.
Him Basto followed, but his fate more hard
Gained but one trump and one plebeian
　　card.
With his broad saber next, a chief in years,
The hoary majesty of spades appears,　56
Puts forth one manly leg, to sight revealed,
The rest, his many-colored robe concealed.
The rebel knave, who dares his prince en-
　　gage,
Proves the just victim of his royal rage. 60
Even mighty Pam, that kings and queens
　　o'erthrew,
And mowed down armies in the fights of
　　Loo,
Sad chance of war! now destitute of aid,
Falls undistinguished by the victor spade!
　Thus far both armies to Belinda yield; 65
Now to the baron fate inclines the field.
His warlike Amazon her host invades,
The imperial consort of the crown of
　　spades,
The club's black tyrant first her victim died,
Spite of his haughty mien, and barbarous
　　pride:　　　　　　　　　　　　　70

What boots the regal circle on his head,
His giant limbs, in state unwieldy spread;
That long behind he trails his pompous
　　robe,
And, of all monarchs only grasps the globe?
　The baron now his diamonds pours apace;
The embroidered king who shows but half
　. his face,　　　　　　　　　　　76
And his refulgent queen, with powers com-
　　bined,
Of broken troops an easy conquest find.
Clubs, diamonds, hearts, in wild disorder
　　seen,
With throngs promiscuous strew the level
　　green.　　　　　　　　　　　　80
Thus when dispersed a routed army runs,
Of Asia's troops, and Afric's sable sons,
With like confusion different nations fly,
Of various habit, and of various dye,
The pierced battalions disunited fall,　85
In heaps on heaps; one fate o'erwhelms
　　them all.
　The knave of diamonds tries his wily arts,
And wins (oh, shameful chance!) the queen
　　of hearts.
At this the blood the virgin's cheek forsook
A livid paleness spreads o'er all her look;
She sees, and trembles at the approaching
　　ill,　　　　　　　　　　　　　　91
Just in the jaws of ruin, and codille.
And now (as oft in some distempered state)
On one nice trick depends the general fate,
An ace of hearts steps forth; the king un-
　　seen　　　　　　　　　　　　　95
Lurked in her hand, and mourned his cap-
　　tive queen:
He springs to vengeance with an eager pace,
And falls like thunder on the prostrate ace.
The nymph exulting fills with shouts the
　　sky;
The walls, the wood, and long canals reply.
　Oh, thoughtless mortals! ever blind to
　　fate,　　　　　　　　　　　　　101
Too soon dejected, and too soon elate.
Sudden, these honors shall be snatched
　　away,
And cursed for ever this victorious day.
　For lo! the board with cups and spoons
　　is crowned,　　　　　　　　　　105
The berries crackle, and the mill turns
　　round;
On shining altars of Japan they raise
The silver lamp; the fiery spirits blaze:
From silver spouts the grateful liquors
　　glide,
While China's earth receives the smoking
　　tide:　　　　　　　　　　　　　110
At once they gratify their scent and taste,

And frequent cups prolong the rich repast.
Straight hover round the fair her airy band;
Some, as she sipped, the fuming liquor
fanned,
Some o'er her lap their careful plumes dis-
played, 115
Trembling, and conscious of the rich bro-
cade.
Coffee (which makes the politician wise,
And see through all things with his half-
shut eyes)
Sent up in vapors to the baron's brain
New stratagems the radiant lock to gain. 120
Ah, cease, rash youth! desist ere 't is too
late,
Fear the just gods, and think of Scylla's
fate!
Changed to a bird, and sent to flit in air,
She dearly pays for Nisus' injured hair!
    But when to mischief mortals bend their
will, 125
How soon they find fit instruments of ill!
Just then Clarissa drew with tempting grace
A two-edged weapon from her shining case:
So ladies in romance assist their knight,
Present the spear, and arm him for the
fight. 130
He takes the gift with reverence, and ex-
tends
The little engine on his finger's ends;
This just behind Belinda's neck he spread,
As o'er the fragrant steams she bends her
head.
Swift to the lock a thousand sprites repair,
A thousand wings, by turns, blow back the
hair; 136
And thrice they twitched the diamond in
her ear;
Thrice she looked back, and thrice the foe
drew near.
Just in that instant, anxious Ariel sought
The close recesses of the virgin's thought;
As on the nosegay in her breast reclined,
He watched the ideas rising in her mind,
Sudden he viewed, in spite of all her art,
An earthly lover lurking at her heart.
Amazed, confused, he found his power ex-
pired, 145
Resigned to fate, and with a sigh retired.
    The peer now spreads the glittering for-
fex wide,
To inclose the lock; now joins it, to divide.
Even then, before the fatal engine closed,
A wretched sylph too fondly interposed;
Fate urged the shears, and cut the sylph in
twain, 151
(But airy substance soon unites again)
The meeting points the sacred hair dissever

From the fair head, for ever, and for ever!
Then flashed the living lightning from her
eyes, 155
And screams of horror rend the affrighted
skies.
Not louder shrieks to pitying Heaven are
cast,
When husbands, or when lapdogs breathe
their last;
Or when rich China vessels, fallen from
high,
In glittering dust and painted fragments
lie! 160
'Let wreaths of triumph now my temples
twine,'
(The victor cried,) 'the glorious prize is
mine!'
While fish in streams, or birds delight in
air,
Or in a coach and six the British fair,
As long as Atalantis shall be read, 165
Or the small pillow grace a lady's bed,
While visits shall be paid on solemn days,
When numerous wax-lights in bright order
blaze,
While nymphs take treats, or assignations
give,
So long my honor, name, and praise shall
live! 170
What Time would spare, from steel receives
its date,
And monuments, like men, submit to fate!
Steel could the labor of the gods destroy,
And strike to dust the imperial towers of
Troy;
Steel could the works of mortal pride con-
found, 175
And hew triumphal arches to the ground.
What wonder then, fair nymph! thy hairs
should feel
The conquering force of unresisted steel?'

CANTO IV

But anxious cares the pensive nymph op-
pressed,
And secret passions labored in her breast.
Not youthful kings in battle seized alive,
Not scornful virgins who their charms sur-
vive,
Not ardent lovers robbed of all their bliss, 5
Not ancient ladies when refused a kiss,
Not tyrants fierce that unrepenting die,
Not Cynthia when her manteau's pinned
awry,
E'er felt such rage, resentment, and despair,

As thou, sad virgin, for thy ravished hair. 10
For, that sad moment, when the sylphs
    withdrew
And Ariel weeping from Belinda flew,
Umbriel, a dusky, melancholy sprite,
As ever sullied the fair face of light,
Down to the central earth, his proper
    scene,   15
Repaired to search the gloomy cave of
    Spleen.
    Swift on his sooty pinions flits the gnome,
And in a vapor reached the dismal dome.
No cheerful breeze this sullen region knows,
The dreaded east is all the wind that blows.
Here in a grotto, sheltered close from air, 21
And screened in shades from day's detested
    glare,
She sighs for ever on her pensive bed,
Pain at her side, and Megrim at her head.
    Two handmaids wait the throne, alike in
    place,   25
But differing far in figure and in face.
Here stood Ill-nature like an ancient maid,
Her wrinkled form in black and white
    arrayed;
With store of prayers, for mornings, nights,
    and noons,
Her hand is filled; her bosom with lam-
    poons.   30
    There Affectation, with a sickly mien,
Shows in her cheek the roses of eighteen,
Practiced to lisp, and hang the head aside,
Faints into airs, and languishes with pride,
On the rich quilt sinks with becoming woe,
Wrapped in a gown, for sickness, and for
    show.   36
The fair ones feel such maladies as these,
When each new night-dress gives a new dis-
    ease.
    A constant vapor o'er the palace flies;
Strange phantoms rising as the mists arise;
Dreadful, as hermit's dreams in haunted
    shades,   41
Or bright, as visions of expiring maids.
Now glaring fiends, and snakes on rolling
    spires,
Pale specters, gaping tombs, and purple
    fires:
Now lakes of liquid gold, Elysian scenes, 45
And crystal domes, and angels in machines.
    Unnumbered throngs on every side are
    seen,
Of bodies changed to various forms by
    Spleen.
Here living tea-pots stand, one arm held out,
One bent; the handle this, and that the
    spout: 50
A pipkin there, like Homer's tripod, walks;

Here sighs a jar, and there a goose-pie
    talks;
Men prove with child, as powerful fancy
    works,
And maids, turned bottles, call aloud for
    corks.
    Safe past the gnome through this fantastic
    band,   55
A branch of healing spleenwort in his hand.
Then thus addressed the power: 'Hail, way-
    ward queen!
Who rule the sex, to fifty from fifteen:
Parent of vapors and of female wit,
Who give the hysteric, or poetic fit,   60
On various tempers act by various ways,
Make some take physic, others scribble
    plays;
Who cause the proud their visits to delay,
And send the godly in a pet to pray.
A nymph there is, that all thy power dis-
    dains,   65
And thousands more in equal mirth main-
    tains.
But oh! if e'er thy gnome could spoil a
    grace,
Or raise a pimple on a beauteous face,
Like citron-waters matrons' cheeks inflame,
Or change complexions at a losing game; 70
If e'er with airy horns I planted heads,
Or rumpled petticoats, or tumbled beds,
Or caused suspicion when no soul was
    rude,
Or discomposed the head-dress of a prude,
Or e'er to costive lap-dog gave disease,   75
Which not the tears of brightest eyes could
    ease:
Hear me, and touch Belinda with chagrin,
That single act gives half the world the
    spleen.'
    The goddess with a discontented air
Seems to reject him, though she grants his
    prayer.   80
A wondrous bag with both her hands she
    binds,
Like that where once Ulysses held the
    winds;
There she collects the force of female lungs,
Sighs, sobs, and passions, and the war of
    tongues.
A vial next she fills with fainting fears, 85
Soft sorrows, melting griefs, and flowing
    tears.
The gnome rejoicing bears her gifts away,
Spreads his black wings, and slowly mounts
    to day.
    Sunk in Thalestris' arms the nymph he
    found,
Her eyes dejected and her hair unbound. 90

Full o'er their heads the swelling bag he
    rent,
And all the furies issued at the vent.
Belinda burns with more than mortal ire,
And fierce Thalestris fans the rising fire.
'O wretched maid!' she spread her hands,
    and cried,   95
(While Hampton's echoes, 'Wretched
    maid!' replied)
'Was it for this you took such constant
    care
The bodkin, comb, and essence to prepare?
For this your locks in paper durance bound,
For this with torturing irons wreathed
    around?
For this with fillets strained your tender
    head,   101
And bravely bore the double loads of lead?
Gods! shall the ravisher display your hair,
While the fops envy, and the ladies stare!
Honor forbid! at whose unrivalled shrine 105
Ease, pleasure, virtue, all our sex resign.
Methinks already I your tears survey,
Already hear the horrid things they say,
Already see you a degraded toast,
And all your honor in a whisper lost! 110
How shall I, then, your helpless fame de-
    fend?
'T will then be infamy to seem your friend!
And shall this prize, the inestimable prize,
Exposed through crystal to the gazing eyes,
And heightened by the diamond's circling
    rays,   115
On that rapacious hand for ever blaze?
Sooner shall grass in Hyde Park Circus
    grow,
And wits take lodgings in the sound of
    Bow;
Sooner let earth, air, sea, to chaos fall,
Men, monkeys, lap-dogs, parrots, perish
    all!'   120
    She said; then raging to Sir Plume re-
    pairs,
And bids her beau demand the precious
    hairs.
(Sir Plume, of amber snuff-box justly vain,
And the nice conduct of a clouded cane)
With earnest eyes, and round unthinking
    face,   125
He first the snuff-box opened, then the case,
And thus broke out — 'My lord, why, what
    the devil?
Z——ds! damn the lock! 'fore Gad, you
    must be civil!
Plague on 't! 't is past a jest — nay prithee,
    pox!
Give her the hair,' he spoke, and rapped his
    box.   130

'It grieves me much,' replied the peer again,
'Who speaks so well should ever speak in
    vain.
But by this lock, this sacred lock, I swear,
(Which never more shall join its parted
    hair;
Which never more its honors shall renew,
Clipped from the lovely head where late it
    grew)   136
That while my nostrils draw the vital air,
This hand, which won it, shall for ever
    wear.'
He spoke, and speaking, in proud triumph
    spread
The long-contended honors of her head.
    But Umbriel, hateful gnome! forbears not
    so;   141
He breaks the vial whence the sorrows
    flow.
Then see! the nymph in beauteous grief ap-
    pears,
Her eyes half languishing, half drowned in
    tears;
On her heaved bosom hung her drooping
    head,   145
Which, with a sigh, she raised; and thus
    she said:
    'For ever cursed be this detested day,
Which snatched my best, my favorite curl
    away!
Happy! ah, ten times happy had I been,
If Hampton Court these eyes had never
    seen!   150
Yet am not I the first mistaken maid,
By love of courts to numerous ills betrayed.
Oh, had I rather unadmired remained
In some lone isle or distant northern land;
Where the gilt chariot never marks the
    way,
Where none learn ombre, none e'er taste
    bohea!   156
There kept my charms concealed from
    mortal eye,
Like roses, that in deserts bloom and die.
What moved my mind with youthful lords
    to roam?
Oh, had I stayed, and said my prayers at
    home!   160
'T was this, the morning omens seemed to
    tell,
Thrice from my trembling hand the patch-
    box fell;
The tottering china shook without a wind.
Nay, Poll sat mute, and Shock was most
    unkind!
A sylph, too, warned me of the threats of
    fate,   165
In mystic visions, now believed too late!

See the poor remnants of these slighted
  hairs!
My hands shall rend what e'en thy rapine
  spares;
These in two sable ringlets taught to break,
Once gave new beauties to the snowy neck;
The sister lock now sits uncouth, alone, 171
And in its fellow's fate foresees its own;
Uncurled it hangs, the fatal shears demands,
And tempts once more, thy sacrilegious
  hands.   174
Oh, hadst thou, cruel! been content to seize
Hairs less in sight, or any hairs but these!'

CANTO V

She said:.the pitying audience melt in tears.
But Fate and Jove had stopped the baron's
  ears.
In vain Thalestris with reproach assails,
For who can move when fair Belinda fails?
Not half so fixed the Trojan could remain,5
While Anna begged and Dido raged in vain.
Then grave Clarissa graceful waved her
  fan;
Silence ensued, and thus the nymph began:
  'Say, why are beauties praised and
    honored most,
The wise man's passion, and the vain man's
  toast?   10
Why decked with all that land and sea
  afford,
Why angels called, and angel-like adored?
Why round our coaches crowd the white-
  gloved beaux,
Why bows the side-box from its inmost
  rows?
How vain are all these glories, all our
  pains,   15
Unless good sense preserve what beauty
  gains:
That men may say, when we the front-box
  grace:
'Behold the first in virtue as in face!'
Oh! if to dance all night, and dress all day,
Charmed the smallpox, or chased old age
  away;   20
Who would not scorn what housewife's
  cares produce,
Or who would learn one earthly thing of
  use?
To patch, nay ogle, might become a saint,
Nor could it sure be such a sin to paint.
But since, alas! frail beauty must decay, 25
Curled or uncurled, since locks will turn
  to gray;

Since painted, or not painted, all shall fade,
And she who scorns a man must die a
  maid;
What then remains but well our power to
  use,
And keep good humor still whate'er we
  lose?   30
And trust me, dear! good humor can pre-
  vail,
When airs, and flights, and screams, and
  scolding fail.
Beauties in vain their pretty eyes may roll;
Charms strike the sight, but merit wins the
  soul.'
  So spoke the dame, but no applause en-
    sued;   35
Belinda frowned, Thalestris called her
  prude.
'To arms, to arms!' the fierce virago cries,
And swift as lightning to the combat flies.
All side in parties, and begin th' attack;
Fans clap, silks rustle, and tough whale-
  bones crack;   40
Heroes' and heroines' shouts confusedly
  rise,
And bass and treble voices strike the skies.
No common weapons in their hands are
  found,
Like gods they fight, nor dread a mortal
  wound.
  So when bold Homer makes the gods en-
    gage,   45
And heavenly breasts with human passions
  rage;
'Gainst Pallas, Mars; Latona, Hermes arms;
And all Olympus rings with loud alarms:
Jove's thunder roars, Heaven trembles all
  around,
Blue Neptune storms, the bellowing deeps
  resound: 50
Earth shakes her nodding towers, the
  ground gives way,
And the pale ghosts start at the flash of
  day!
  Triumphant Umbriel on a sconce's height
Clapped his glad wings, and sat to view the
  fight:
Propped on their bodkin spears, the sprites
  survey   55
The growing combat, or assist the fray.
  While through the press enraged Thales-
    tris flies,
And scatters death around from both her
  eyes,
A beau and witling perished in the throng,
One died in metaphor, and one in song. 60
'O cruel nymph! a living death I bear,'
Cried Dapperwit, and sunk beside his chair.

A mournful glance Sir Fopling upwards
   cast,
'Those eyes are made so killing'—was his
   last.
Thus on Meander's flowery margin lies 65
The expiring swan, and as he sings he dies.
  When bold Sir Plume had drawn Clarissa
   down,
Chloe stepped in and killed him with a
   frown;
She smiled to see the doughty hero slain,
But, at her smile, the beau revived again.
Now Jove suspends his golden scales in air,
Weighs the men's wits against the lady's
   hair; 72
The doubtful beam long nods from side to
   side;
At length the wits mount up, the hairs sub-
   side.
  See, fierce Belinda on the Baron flies, 75
With more than usual lightning in her eyes:
Nor feared the chief the unequal fight to
   try,
Who sought no more than on his foe to
   die.
But this bold lord with manly strength en-
   dued,
She with one finger and a thumb subdued:
Just where the breath of life his nostrils
   drew, 81
A charge of snuff the wily virgin threw;
The gnomes direct, to every atom just,
The pungent grains of titillating dust.
Sudden, with starting tears each eye o'er-
   flows, 85
And the high dome re-echoes to his nose.
  'Now meet thy fate,' incensed Belinda
   cried,
And drew a deadly bodkin from her side.
(The same, his ancient personage to deck,
Her great great grandsire wore about his
   neck, 90
In three seal-rings; which after, melted
   down,
Formed a vast buckle for his widow's
   gown:
Her infant grandame's whistle next it
   grew,
The bells she jingled, and the whistle blew;
Then in a bodkin graced her mother's hairs,
Which long she wore, and now Belinda
   wears.) 96
  'Boast not my fall,' he cried, 'insulting
   foe!
Thou by some other shalt be laid as low,
Nor think to die dejects my lofty mind:
All that I dread is leaving you behind! 100
Rather than so, ah, let me still survive,

And burn in Cupid's flames—but burn
   alive.'
  'Restore the lock!' she cries; and all
   around
'Restore the lock!' the vaulted roofs re-
   bound.
Not fierce Othello in so loud a strain 105
Roared for the handkerchief that caused
   his pain.
But see how oft ambitious aims are crossed,
And chiefs contend till all the prize is lost!
The lock, obtained with guilt, and kept with
   pain,
In every place is sought, but sought in vain:
With such a prize no mortal must be blessed,
So Heaven decrees! with Heaven who can
   contest? 112
  Some thought it mounted to the lunar
   sphere,
Since all things lost on earth are treasured
   there.
There heroes' wits are kept in ponderous
   vases, 115
And beaux' in snuff-boxes and tweezer
   cases.
There broken vows and death-bed alms are
   found,
And lovers' hearts with ends of riband
   bound,
The courtier's promises, and sick man's
   prayers, 119
The smiles of harlots, and the tears of heirs,
Cages for gnats, and chains to yoke a flea,
Dried butterflies, and tomes of casuistry.
  But trust the Muse—she saw it upward
   rise,
Though marked by none but quick, poetic
   eyes:
(So Rome's great founder to the heavens
   withdrew, 125
To Proculus alone confessed in view)
A sudden star, it shot through liquid air,
And drew behind a radiant trail of hair.
Not Berenice's locks first rose so bright,
The heavens bespangling with dishevelled
   light. 130
The sylphs behold it kindling as it flies,
And pleased pursue its progress through the
   skies.
  This the beau monde shall from the Mall
   survey,
And hail with music its propitious ray.
This the blest lover shall for Venus take, 135
And send up vows from Rosamonda's
   lake.
This Partridge soon shall view in cloudless
   skies,
When next he looks through Galileo's eyes;

And hence the egregious wizard shall fore-
doom
The fate of Louis and the fall of Rome. 140
  Then cease, bright nymph! to mourn thy
ravished hair,
Which adds new glory to the shining
sphere!
Not all the tresses that fair head can boast,
Shall draw such envy as the lock you lost.
For, after all the murders of your eye, 145
When, after millions slain, yourself shall
die:
When those fair suns shall set, as set they
must,
And all those tresses shall be laid in dust,
This lock, the Muse shall consecrate to
fame,
And 'midst the stars inscribe Belinda's
name. 150

(1712, 1714)

From EPISTLE TO DR. ARBUTHNOT

  Why did I write? what sin to me un-
known
Dipped me in ink, my parents', or my own?
As yet a child, nor yet a fool to fame,
I lisped in numbers, for the numbers came.
I left no calling for this idle trade, 5
No duty broke, no father disobeyed.
The Muse but served to ease some friend,
not wife,
To help me through this long disease, my
life,
To second, Arbuthnot! thy art and care,
And teach the being you preserved, to
bear. . . . 10
  Soft were my numbers; who could take
offense
While pure description held the place of
sense?
Like gentle Fanny's was my flowery theme,
A painted mistress, or a purling stream. 14
Yet then did Gildon draw his venal quill;—
I wished the man a dinner, and sat still.
Yet then did Dennis rave in furious fret;
I never answered—I was not in debt.
If want provoked, or madness made them
print,
I waged no war with Bedlam or the Mint. 20
  Did some more sober critic come abroad,
If wrong, I smiled; if right, I kissed the
rod.

* * *

  Were others angry: I excused them too;
Well might they rage, I gave them but their
due,

A man's true merit 't is not hard to find; 25
But each man's secret standard in his mind,
That casting-weight pride adds to emptiness,
This, who can gratify? for who can guess?
The bard whom pilfered Pastorals renown,
Who turns a Persian tale for half a crown,
Just writes to make his barrenness appear,
And strains from hard-bound brains, eight
lines a year; 32
He, who still wanting, though he lives on
theft,
Steals much, spends little, yet has nothing
left:
And he, who now to sense, now nonsense
leaning, 35
Means not, but blunders round about a
meaning:
And he, whose fustian's so sublimely bad,
It is not poetry, but prose run mad:
All these, my modest satire bade translate,
And owned that nine such poets made a
Tate. 40
How did they fume, and stamp, and roar,
and chafe!
And swear, not Addison himself was safe.
  Peace to all such! but were there one
whose fires
True genius kindles, and fair fame inspires;
Blessed with each talent and each art to
please, 45
And born to write, converse, and live with
ease:
Should such a man, too fond to rule alone,
Bear, like the Turk, no brother near the
throne,
View him with scornful, yet with jealous
eyes,
And hate for arts that caused himself to
rise; 50
Damn with faint praise, assent with civil
leer,
And without sneering, teach the rest to
sneer;
Willing to wound, and yet afraid to strike,
Just hint a fault, and hesitate dislike;
Alike reserved to blame, or to commend, 55
A timorous foe, and a suspicious friend;
Dreading e'en fools, by flatterers besieged,
And so obliging, that he ne'er obliged;
Like Cato, give his little senate laws,
And sit attentive to his own applause; 60
While wits and Templars every sentence
raise,
And wonder with a foolish face of praise—
Who but must laugh, if such a man there
be?
Who would not weep, if Atticus were he!

* * *

(1735)

JAMES THOMSON (1700–1748)

Thomson was a Scotchman who, at the height of Pope's reign, went to seek his fortune in literary London. He arrived in need of a pair of shoes and lost the packet of recommendations which he had tied up in his handkerchief; but he was kindly received by his brother poets, and enjoyed sufficient patronage from the rich to preserve him from actual want. The four parts of *The Seasons* which appeared in rapid succession (1726–30) made his reputation, and a series of stiff tragedies in blank verse had a lukewarm success on the stage. Politically, he adhered to the opposition and was one of a group, including the poet Collins, which gathered around Lord Lyttleton at Hagley, under the 'precarious patronage' of Frederick, Prince of Wales. Thomson was an indolent man 'more fat than bard beseems,' luxurious and procrastinating, and the last fifteen years of his life originated little that was important. *The Castle of Indolence*, which commemorates the Hagley company, was begun in 1733, though not completed until two years before his death. Dull in unfamiliar society, Thomson was loyally and deeply beloved by those who intimately knew him. His warm and truthful delineations of nature and his resource in the older harmonies of English verse helped to inaugurate a new era in poetry. Notwithstanding these tendencies, Pope regarded him with respect and favor. In the next generation, Dr. Johnson abated his prejudice against blank verse in favor of *The Seasons*, and forgot his hostility to Spenserism in commenting on *The Castle of Indolence*. 'He thinks always as a man of genius; he looks round on Nature and on Life with the eye which Nature bestows only on a poet,' was Johnson's summary of his abilities.

FROM SUMMER

Iambic pentameter
blank verse

Low walks the sun, and broadens by degrees,
Just o'er the verge of day. The shifting clouds
Assembled gay, a richly gorgeous train,
In all their pomp attend his setting throne.
Air, earth, and ocean smile immense. And now, 5
As if his weary chariot sought the bowers
Of Amphitrite, and her tending nymphs —
So Grecian fable sung — he dips his orb;
Now half immersed; and now a golden curve
Gives one bright glance, then total disappears. * * * 10
  Confessed from yonder slow-extinguished clouds,
All ether softening, sober evening takes
Her wonted station in the middle air;
A thousand shadows at her beck. First this
She sends on earth; then that of deeper dye 15
Steals soft behind; and then a deeper still,
In circle following circle, gathers round,
To close the face of things. A fresher gale
Begins to wave the wood, and stir the stream,
Sweeping with shadowy gust the fields of corn: 20
While the quail clamors for his running mate.
Wide o'er the thistly lawn, as swells the breeze,
A whitening shower of vegetable down
Amusive floats. The kind impartial care
Of nature nought disdains: thoughtful to feed 25
Her lowest sons, and clothe the coming year,
From field to field the feathered seeds she wings.
  His folded flock secure, the shepherd home
Hies merry-hearted; and by turns relieves
The ruddy milkmaid of her brimming pail;
The beauty whom perhaps his witless heart — 31
Unknowing what the joy-mixed anguish means —
Sincerely loves, by that best language shewn
Of cordial glances, and obliging deeds.
Onward they pass o'er many a panting height, 35

And valley sunk, and unfrequented; where
At fall of eve the fairy people throng,
In various game and revelry, to pass
The summer night, as village stories tell.
But far about they wander from the grave 40
Of him whom his ungentle fortune urged
Against his own sad breast to lift the hand
Of impious violence. The lonely tower
Is also shunned; whose mournful chambers
    hold —
So night-struck fancy dreams — the yelling
    ghost.   45
  Among the crooked lanes, on every hedge,
The glowworm lights his gem; and through
    the dark
A moving radiance twinkles. Evening yields
The world to night; not in her winter robe
Of massy Stygian woof, but loose arrayed 50
In mantle dun. A faint erroneous ray,
Glanced from the imperfect surfaces of
    things,
Flings half an image on the straining eye;
While wavering woods, and villages, and
    streams,
And rocks, and mountain-tops, that long re-
    tained   55
The ascending gleam, are all one swimming
    scene,
Uncertain if beheld. Sudden to heaven
Thence weary vision turns; where, leading
    soft
The silent hours of love, with purest ray
Sweet Venus shines; and from her genial
    rise,   60
When daylight sickens till it springs afresh,
Unrivaled reigns, the fairest lamp of night.
                    * * *
use of color adjective (1727)

From AUTUMN

But see the fading many-colored woods,
Shade deepening over shade, the country
    round
Imbrown; a crowded umbrage dusk and dun,
Of every hue, from wan declining green
To sooty dark. These now the lonesome
    muse,   5
Low whispering, lead into their leaf-strewn
    walks,
And give the season in its latest view.
  Meantime, light shadowing all, a sober
    calm
Fleeces unbounded ether: whose least wave
Stands tremulous, uncertain where to turn 10
The gentle current: while illumined wide,
The dewy-skirted clouds imbibe the sun,

And through their lucid veil his softened
    force
Shed o'er the peaceful world. Then is the
    time,
For those whom virtue and whom nature
    charm,   15
To steal themselves from the degenerate
    crowd,
And soar above this little scene of things:
To tread low-thoughted vice beneath their
    feet;
To soothe the throbbing passions into peace;
And woo lone Quiet in her silent walks. 20
  Thus solitary, and in pensive guise,
Oft let me wander o'er the russet mead,
And through the saddened grove, where
    scarce is heard
One dying strain, to cheer the woodman's
    toil.
Haply some widowed songster pours his
    plaint,   25
Far, in faint warblings, through the tawny
    copse;
While congregated thrushes, linnets, larks,
And each wild throat, whose artless strains
    so late
Swelled all the music of the swarming
    shades,
Robbed of their tuneful souls, now shiver-
    ing sit   30
On the dead tree, a dull despondent flock:
With not a brightness waving o'er their
    plumes,
And naught save chattering discord in their
    note.
O let not, aimed from some inhuman eye,
The gun the music of the coming year 35
Destroy; and harmless, unsuspecting harm,
Lay the weak tribes a miserable prey
In mingled murder, fluttering on the ground!
  The pale descending year, yet pleasing
    still,
A gentler mood inspires; for now the leaf 40
Incessant rustles from the mournful grove;
Oft startling such as studious walk below,
And slowly circles through the waving air.
But should a quicker breeze amid the boughs
Sob, o'er the sky the leafy deluge streams;
Till choked, and matted with the dreary
    shower,   46
The forest walks, at every rising gale,
Roll wide the withered waste, and whistle
    bleak.
Fled is the blasted verdure of the fields;
And, shrunk into their beds, the flowery
    race   50
Their sunny robes resign. E'en what re-
    mained

Liking for birds

Of stronger fruits falls from the naked
  tree;
And woods, fields, gardens, orchards all
  around,
The desolated prospect thrills the soul. . . .
  The western sun withdraws the shortened
  day,   55
And humid evening, gliding o'er the sky,
In her chill progress, to the ground con-
  densed
The vapor throws. Where creeping waters
  ooze,
Where marshes stagnate, and where rivers
  wind,
Cluster the rolling fogs, and swim along 60
The dusky-mantled lawn. Meanwhile the
  moon,
Full orbed, and breaking through the scat-
  tered clouds,
Shews her broad visage in the crimsoned
  east.
Turned to the sun direct her spotted disk,
Where mountains rise, umbrageous dales de-
  scend,   65
And caverns deep as optic tube descries,
A smaller earth, gives us his blaze again,
Void of its flame, and sheds a softer day.
Now through the passing clouds she seems
  to stoop,
Now up the pure cerulean rides sublime. 70
Wide the pale deluge floats, and streaming
  mild
O'er the skied mountain to the shadowy
  vale,
While rocks and floods reflect the quivering
  gleam;
The whole air whitens with a boundless tide
Of silver radiance trembling round the
  world.   75

* * *

(1730)

From WINTER

Through the hushed air the whitening
  shower descends,
At first thin-wavering, till at last the flakes
Fall broad, and wide, and fast, dimming the
  day
With a continual flow. The cherished fields
Put on their winter robe of purest white: 5
'T is brightness all, save where the new
  snow melts
Along the mazy current. Low the woods
Bow their hoar head; and ere the languid
  sun
Faint from the west, emits his evening ray;
Earth's universal face, deep hid, and chill, 10

Is one wide dazzling waste, that buries wide
The works of man. Drooping, the laborer-
  ox
Stands covered o'er with snow, and then
  demands
The fruit of all his toil. The fowls of
  heaven,
Tamed by the cruel season, crowd around 15
The winnowing store, and claim the little
  boon
Which Providence assigns them. One alone,
The redbreast, sacred to the household gods,
Wisely regardful of the embroiling sky,
In joyless fields and thorny thickets, leaves
His shivering mates, and pays to trusted
  man   21
His annual visit. Half-afraid, he first
Against the window beats; then, brisk,
  alights
On the warm hearth; then hopping o'er the
  floor,
Eyes all the smiling family askance,   25
And pecks, and starts, and wonders where
  he is:
Till more familiar grown, the table crumbs
Attract his slender feet. The foodless
  wilds
Pour forth their brown inhabitants. The
  hare,
Though timorous of heart, and hard beset
By death in various forms, dark snares and
  dogs,   31
And more unpitying men, the garden seeks,
Urged on by fearless want. The bleating
  kine
Eye the bleak heaven, and next, the glisten-
  ing earth,
With looks of dumb despair; then, sad dis-
  persed,   35
Dig for the withered herb through heaps of
  snow.   * * *
  As thus the snows arise, and foul and
  fierce
All winter drives along the darkened air,
In his own loose revolving fields the swain
Disastered stands; sees other hills ascend, 40
Of unknown joyless brow, and other scenes,
Of horrid prospect, shag the trackless plain;
Nor finds the river nor the forest, hid
Beneath the formless wild; but wanders on
From hill to dale, still more and more
  astray,   45
Impatient flouncing through the drifted
  heaps,
Stung with the thoughts of home; the
  thoughts of home
Rush on his nerves, and call their vigor
  forth

In many a vain attempt. How sinks his
    soul!
What black despair, what horror, fills his
    heart!   50
When for the dusky spot which fancy
    feigned,
His tufted cottage rising through the snow,
He meets the roughness of the middle waste,
Far from the track and blessed abode of
    man;
While round him night resistless closes
    fast,   55
And every tempest howling o'er his head,
Renders the savage wilderness more wild.
Then throng the busy shapes into his mind,
Of covered pits, unfathomably deep,
A dire descent! beyond the power of frost;
Of faithless bogs; of precipices huge   61
Smoothed up with snow; and what is land
    unknown,
What water of the still unfrozen spring,
In the loose marsh or solitary lake,
Where the fresh fountain from the bottom
    boils.   65
These check his fearful steps, and down he
    sinks
Beneath the shelter of the shapeless drift,
Thinking o'er all the bitterness of death,
Mixed with the tender anguish nature shoots
Through the wrung bosom of the dying man,
His wife, his children, and his friends, un-
    seen.   71
In vain for him the officious wife prepares
The fire fair blazing, and the vestment
    warm:
In vain his little children, peeping out
Into the mingling storm, demand their sire
With tears of artless innocence. Alas!   76
Nor wife nor children more shall he behold,
Nor friends, nor sacred home. On every
    nerve
The deadly winter seizes, shuts up sense,
And o'er his inmost vitals creeping cold,   80
Lays him along the snows a stiffened corse,
Stretched out, and bleaching in the northern
    blast.

* * *

(1726)

A HYMN

These, as they change, Almighty Father,
    these,
Are but the varied God. The rolling year
Is full of thee. Forth in the pleasing
    Spring
Thy beauty walks, thy tenderness and love.

Wide-flush the fields; the softening air is
    balm;   5
Echo the mountains round; the forest
    smiles;
And every sense, and every heart is joy.
Then comes thy glory in the summer-
    months,
With light and heart refulgent. Then thy
    sun
Shoots full perfection through the swelling
    year: 10
And oft thy voice in dreadful thunder
    speaks;
And oft at dawn, deep noon, or falling eve,
By brooks and groves, in hollow-whispering
    gales.
Thy bounty shines in autumn unconfined,
And spreads a common feast for all that
    lives.   15
In winter awful thou! with clouds and
    storms
Around thee thrown, tempest o'er tempest
    roll'd
Majestic darkness! on the whirlwind's wing,
Riding sublime, thou bidst the world adore,
And humblest Nature with thy northern
    blast.   20

Mysterious round! what skill, what force
    divine,
Deepfelt, in these appear! a simple train,
Yet so delightful mixed, with such kind art,
Such beauty and beneficence combined: 24
Shade, unperceived, so softening into shade;
And all so forming an harmonious whole;
That, as they still succeed, they ravish still.
But wandering oft, with brute unconscious
    gaze,
Man marks not thee, marks not the mighty
    hand,
That, ever-busy, wheels the silent spheres;
Works in the secret deep; shoots, steaming,
    thence   31
The fair profusion that o'erspreads the
    spring:
Flings from the sun direct the flaming day;
Feeds every creature; hurls the tempest
    forth;
And, as on earth this grateful change re-
    volves,   35
With transport touches all the springs of
    life.

Nature, attend! join every living soul,
Beneath the spacious temple of the sky,
In adoration join; and ardent raise
One general song! To him, ye vocal gales

Breathe soft, whose spirit in your freshness
    breathes. 41
Oh, talk of him in solitary glooms,
Where o'er the rock the scarcely waving
    pine
Fills the brown shade with a religious awe,
And ye, whose bolder note is heard afar, 45
Who shake the astonished world, lift high
    to heaven
The impetuous song, and say from whom
    you rage.
His praise, ye brooks, attune, ye trembling
    rills;
And let me catch it as I muse along,
Ye headlong torrents, rapid and profound;
Ye softer floods, that lead the humid maze
Along the vale; and thou, majestic main, 52
A secret world of wonders in thyself,
Sound his stupendous praise, whose greater
    voice
Or bids you roar, or bids your roaring fall.
So roll your incense, herbs, and fruits, and
    flowers, 56
In mingled clouds to him, whose sun exalts,
Whose breath perfumes you, and whose
    pencil paints.
Ye forests, bend, ye harvests, wave to him;
Breathe your still song into the reaper's
    heart, 60
As home he goes beneath the joyous moon.
Ye that keep watch in heaven, as earth
    asleep
Unconscious lies, effuse your mildest beams;
Ye constellations, while your angels strike,
Amid the spangled sky, the silver lyre. 65
Great source of day! blest image here be-
    low
Of thy Creator, ever pouring wide,
From world to world, the vital ocean round,
On nature write with every beam his praise.
The thunder rolls: be hushed the prostrate
    world, 70
While cloud to cloud returns the solemn
    hymn.
Bleat out afresh, ye hills; ye mossy rocks,
Retain the sound; the broad responsive low,
Ye valleys, raise; for the Great Shepherd
    reigns,
And his unsuffering kingdom yet will come.
Ye woodlands, all awake; a boundless song
Burst from the groves; and when the rest-
    less day, 77
Expiring, lays the warbling world asleep,
Sweetest of birds! sweet Philomela, charm
The listening shades, and teach the night
    his praise. 80
Ye chief, for whom the whole creation
    smiles;

At once the head, the heart, the tongue of
    all,
Crown the great hymn! in swarming cities
    vast,
Assembled men to the deep organ join
The long resounding voice, oft breaking
    clear, 85
At solemn pauses, through the swelling base;
And, as each mingling flame increases each,
In one united ardor rise to heaven.
Or if you rather choose the rural shade,
And find a fame in every sacred grove, 90
There let the shepherd's lute, the virgin's
    lay,
The prompting seraph, and the poet's lyre,
Still sing the God of seasons as they roll.
For me, when I forget the darling theme,
Whether the blossom blows, the Summer
    ray 95
Russets the plain, inspiring Autumn gleams,
Or Winter rises in the blackening east —
Be my tongue mute, my fancy paint no
    more,
And, dead to joy, forget my heart to beat.
Should fate command me to the furthest
    verge 100
Of the green earth, to distant barbarous
    climes,
Rivers unknown to song; where first the
    sun
Gilds Indian mountains, or his setting beam
Flames on the Atlantic isles, 't is nought to
    me;
Since God is ever present, ever felt, 105
In the void waste as in the city full;
And where he vital breathes, there must be
    joy.
When even at last the solemn hour shall
    come,
And wing my mystic flight to future worlds,
I cheerful will obey; there with new pow-
    ers, 110
Will rising wonders sing. I cannot go
Where universal love not smiles around,
Sustaining all yon orbs, and all their suns;
From seeming evil still educing good,
And better thence again, and better still, 115
In infinite progression. But I lose
Myself in him, in light ineffable!
Come, then, expressive silence, muse his
    praise. (1730)

THE CASTLE OF INDOLENCE, Book I

O mortal man, who livest here by toil,
Do not complain of this thy hard estate;
That like an emmet thou must ever moil,

Is a sad sentence of an ancient date;
And, certes, there is for it reason great; 5
For, though sometimes it makes thee
    weep and wail,
And curse thy star, and early drudge and
    late,
Withouten that would come a heavier bale,
Loose life, unruly passions, and diseases
    pale.

In lowly dale, fast by a river's side,   10
With woody hill o'er hill encompassed
    round,
A most enchanting wizard did abide,
Than whom a fiend more fell is nowhere
    found.
It was, I ween, a lovely spot of ground:
And there a season atween June and May,
Half pranked with spring, with summer
    half imbrowned,   16
A listless climate made, where, sooth to say,
No living wight could work, ne carèd ever
    for play.

Was nought around but images of rest:
Sleep-soothing groves, and quiet lawns
    between;   20
And flowery beds that slumberous influ-
    ence kest,
From poppies breathed; and beds of pleas-
    ant green,
Where never yet was creeping creature
    seen.
Meantime unnumbered glittering stream-
    lets played,
And hurlèd everywhere their waters
    sheen;   25
That, as they bickered through the sunny
    glade,
Though restless still themselves, a lulling
    murmur made.

Joined to the prattle of the purling rills,
Were heard the lowing herds along the
    vale,
And flocks loud bleating from the distant
    hills,   30
And vacant shepherds piping in the dale:
And now and then sweet Philomel would
    wail,
Or stock-doves 'plain amid the forest
    deep,
That drowsy rustled to the sighing gale;
And still a coil the grasshopper did keep;
Yet all these sounds yblent inclinèd all to
    sleep.   36

Full in the passage of the vale above,
A sable, silent, solemn forest stood,
Where nought but shadowy forms was
    seen to move,
As Idlesse fancied in her dreaming mood:
And up the hills, on either side, a wood 41
Of blackening pines, aye waving to and
    fro,
Sent forth a sleepy horror through the
    blood;
And where this valley winded out below,
The murmuring main was heard, and
    scarcely heard, to flow.   45

A pleasing land of drowsy-head it was,
Of dreams that wave before the half-shut
    eye:
And of gay castles in the clouds that
    pass,
For ever flushing round a summer sky:
There eke the soft delights, that witch-
    ingly   50
Instill a wanton sweetness through the
    breast,
And the calm pleasures, always hovered
    nigh;
But whate'er smacked of noyance or un-
    rest,
Was far, far off expelled from this delicious
    nest.

* * *

The doors, that knew no shrill alarming
    bell,   55
Ne cursed knocker plied by villain's hand,
Self-opened into halls, where, who can
    tell
What elegance and grandeur wide ex-
    pand,
The pride of Turkey and of Persia land?
Soft quilts on quilts, on carpets carpets
    spread,   60
And couches stretched around in seemly
    band;
And endless pillows rise to prop the head;
So that each spacious room was one full-
    swelling bed.

And everywhere huge covered tables stood,
With wines high flavored and rich viands
    crowned;   65
Whatever sprightly juice or tasteful food
On the green bosom of this earth are
    found,
And all old ocean genders in his round;
Some hand unseen these silently displayed,
Even undemanded by a sign or sound;   70
You need but wish, and, instantly obeyed,
Fair ranged the dishes rose, and thick the
    glasses played

The rooms with costly tapestry were hung,
Where was inwoven many a gentle tale;
Such as of old the rural poets sung, 75
Or of Arcadian or Sicilian vale:
Reclining lovers, in the lonely dale,
Poured forth at large the sweetly tortured
   heart;
Or, sighing tender passion, swelled the
   gale,
And taught charmed echo to resound their
   smart; 80
While flocks, woods, streams, around, re-
   pose and peace impart.

Those pleased the most, where, by a cunning hand,
Depainted was the patriarchal age;
What time Dan Abraham left the Chaldee
   land,
And pastured on from verdant stage to
   stage, 85
Where fields and fountains fresh could
   best engage.
Toil was not then. Of nothing took they
   heed,
But with wild beasts the sylvan war to
   wage,
And o'er vast plains their herds and flocks
   to feed;
Blest sons of nature they! true golden age
   indeed! 90

Sometimes the pencil, in cool airy halls,
Bade the gay bloom of vernal landscapes
   rise,
Or autumn's varied shades imbrown the
   walls;
Now the black tempest strikes the astonished eyes,
Now down the steep the flashing torrent
   flies; 95
The trembling sun now plays o'er ocean
   blue,
And now rude mountains frown amid the
   skies;
Whate'er Lorraine light-touched with softening hue,
Or savage Rosa dashed, or learned Poussin
   drew.

A certain music, never known before, 100
Here lulled the pensive melancholy mind,
Full easily obtained. Behoves no more,
But sidelong, to the gently waving wind,
To lay the well-tuned instrument reclined;
From which with airy flying fingers light,

Beyond each mortal touch the most refined, 106
The god of winds drew sounds of deep
   delight;
Whence, with just cause, the harp of Æolus
   it hight.

Ah me! what hand can touch the string
   so fine?
Who up the lofty diapason roll 110
Such sweet, such sad, such solemn airs
   divine,
Then let them down again into the soul?
Now rising love they fanned; now pleas-
   ing dole
They breathed, in tender musings, through
   the heart;
And now a graver sacred strain they
   stole, 115
As when seraphic hands a hymn impart:
Wild warbling nature all, above the reach
   of art!

Such the gay splendor, the luxurious state
Of Caliphs old, who on the Tigris' shore,
In mighty Bagdad, populous and great, 120
Held their bright court, where was of
   ladies store;
And verse, love, music, still the garland
   wore;
When sleep was coy, the bard in waiting
   there
Cheered the lone midnight with the muse's
   lore;
Composing music bade his dreams be
   fair, 125
And music lent new gladness to the morn-
   ing air.

Near the pavilions where we slept, still
   ran
Soft tinkling streams, and dashing waters
   fell,
And sobbing breezes sighed, and oft began —
So worked the wizard — wintry storms to
   swell, 130
As heaven and earth they would together
   mell;
At doors and windows threatening seemed
   to call
The demons of the tempest, growling fell.
Yet the least entrance found they none at
   all;
Whence sweeter grew our sleep, secure in
   massy hall. 135

* * *

(1748)

MINOR POETS — YOUNG TO CHATTERTON

Before the 'Augustan age' of wit and common-sense had completed its course a departure from its precepts and fashions had begun. The complex of tendencies which gradually transformed literature in the course of the eighteenth century is usually referred to as 'the romantic movement.' Some, however, prefer to conserve this term for a more restricted application to the revival of medievalism which was a part of the broader movement; while still others prefer to think of these changes as the result of two related tendencies, 'the return to nature' and 'the revival of the past.' The English genius could not long content itself with the equably ironic view of human fate which found expression in the essays of Addison, or with the jaunty commendations of God and the universe which capped Pope's essentially shallow and worldly philosophy. Even Pope's *Essay on Man*, it is worth while to notice, had been preceded by Thomson's *Hymn on the Seasons*. Three-quarters of a century were to elapse before any first-rate mind should survey life with that comprehensive sympathy and penetrate it with that fresh, imaginative insight which marks the truly great and original poet. In the meantime the useful work of our 'age of prose and reason,' 'our excellent and indispensable eighteenth century,' was being done. Meantime, also, chiefly among men of second-rate and third-rate quality, we may detect evidences, stray and imperfect, of that 'longing to inquire into the mystery of this heart which beats so wild, so deep in us'— which always underlies literature of the finest power. Now, great literary changes are usually 'accompanied or heralded,' as Stevenson has phrased it, 'by a cast back to earlier and fresher models.' Thus, most of these minor writers were in some degree imitative. Discontented, first of all, with the subject-matter of poetry, its restriction to what they deemed superficial and trivial in town life, they sought the fields and 'the mountain's rugged brow.' And, just as they became interested in the solitudes and the untamed aspects of Nature, so they became interested in wild and primitive, or in simple and rustic society, where the elementary impulses of men have freer play. Discontented, too, with the artificial diction and rhetoric and the restricted couplet verse of the Pope school, they 'cast back' to the blank verse of Shakspere and Milton, to Milton's octo-syllabics, to the fluid stanza of Spenser, and to the free modulations of the old ballad stave. Emulating their models in subject, diction, rhythm,— they caught at times something of their spirit. There is hardly one of these men of slighter power, thinly descriptive or heavily didactic as they frequently are, who does not at some point flash for a moment with the loveliness, or mystery, or melancholy, or boldness, or 'fine frenzy,' of the earlier masters, or the wilding songs of the folk.

Edward Young, five years Pope's senior, an Oxford scholar of saturnine temper, a disappointed seeker after 'the bubble reputation,' first in the theater and then in the church, produced at three-score the poem for which he is remembered. *The Complaint, or Night Thoughts on Life, Death, and Immortality*, a didactic poem in ten thousand lines of blank verse, is still impressive for its nervous aphoristic force and somber magnificence of imagery and music.

John Gay, the intimate friend of Swift and Pope, was a compliant creature of his age. His prime gift was for travesty and his greatest success in this kind, *The Beggar's Opera*, created a type. *The Shepherd's Week* was intended to burlesque the Pastorals then in vogue. 'But the effect of reality and truth became conspicuous,' says Johnson, 'even when the intention was to show them groveling and degraded.'

Robert Blair was a Scotch minister. *The Grave*, in some eight hundred lines of blank verse, is an early example of the so-called 'grave-yard' school of poetry. It is somewhat singular among the poems of its time and class, in that its diction and versification suggest the influence of Elizabethan dramatic poets rather than that of Milton.

John Dyer, a Welsh landscape painter, was also a landscape poet. His *Grongar Hill* was published the year of Thomson's *Winter*. Its likeness to Milton's *L'Allegro* is sufficiently obvious. *The Ruins of Rome* (1740) and *The Fleece* (1757) are didactico-descriptive poems in blank verse, suggestive of Milton and Thomson.

William Shenstone was a somewhat spiritless bachelor and recluse who amused himself with landscape-gardening on a small scale at the Leasowes, a modest estate adjoining Lord

Littleton's acres at Hagley. His poetry is tamely elegiac and pastoral. *The Schoolmistress*, his best known poem, is a Spenserian semi-burlesque.

Mark Akenside, a physician whom a youthful addiction to poetry did not prevent from rising high in his profession, published his *Pleasures of Imagination* in his twenty-third year. His *Odes* and *Hymn to the Naiades* appeared successively the two years following. Though too abstract and coldly elegant, his poems are impregnated with the manner of Milton and tinged with romantic aspiration.

Somewhat like that of Akenside, but incomparably more exquisite, is the poetry of William Collins,—slight and fragile in everything except its hold on immortality. Collins' delicately cultivated mind was early obscured and he died in his thirty-eighth year, having written nothing for a decade. Lowell has said of his *Ode on the Popular Superstitions of the Scottish Highlands*, that it contained 'the whole Romantic School in its germ'; but his grace of spirit and the importunate loveliness of his diction are seen in purest perfection in his shorter pieces.

Thomas Warton, in his youth a friend of Thomson and Collins and, in later years, an admirer of Gray and a valued member of Johnson's club, spent most of his life at Oxford. He was an accomplished antiquarian, author of the first *History of English Poetry*, and a 'pioneer of the medieval revival.' His verse shows the confluence of many romantic elements but is too little original to be of much intrinsic value.

Thomas Chatterton spent most of his few years at Bristol, where his ancestors had been, for a century and a half, sextons of St. Mary Redcliffe. In the 'muniment room' of this church he pretended to have discovered the manuscripts of the poems which he gave to the world as those of a fifteenth century priest, Thomas Rowley. His forgeries were clever enough to impose upon Horace Walpole, though Gray readily detected the deception. In London, whither he had gone with the hope of living by his pen, the morbidly precocious boy took his own life at the age of seventeen years and nine months. His strange hectic genius and the romantic tragedy of his death exercised a spell upon the poets of the next two generations.

EDWARD YOUNG (1681-1765)

From NIGHT THOUGHTS

Tired Nature's sweet restorer, balmy Sleep!
He, like the world, his ready visit pays
Where Fortune smiles; the wretched he forsakes:
Swift on his downy pinion flies from wo,
And lights on lids unsullied with a tear. 5
From short (as usual) and disturbed repose
I wake: how happy they who wake no more!
Yet that were vain, if dreams infest the grave.
I wake, emerging from a sea of dreams
Tumultuous; where my wrecked desponding thought 10
From wave to wave of fancied misery
At random drove, her helm of reason lost.
Though now restored, 't is only change of pain —
A bitter change! — severer for severe:
The day too short for my distress; and night, 15
E'en in the zenith of her dark domain,
Is sunshine to the color of my fate.
Night, sable goddess; from her ebon throne,
In rayless majesty, now stretches forth

Her leaden scepter o'er a slumbering world.
Silence how dead! and darkness how profound! 21
Nor eye nor listening ear an object finds;
Creation sleeps. 'T is as the general pulse
Of life stood still, and Nature made a pause;
An awful pause! prophetic of her end. 25
And let her prophecy be soon fulfilled:
Fate! drop the curtain; I can lose no more.
Silence and Darkness! solemn sisters! twins
From ancient Night, who nurse the tender thought
To reason, and on reason build resolve — 30
That column of true majesty in man —
Assist me: I will thank you in the grave;
The grave your kingdom: there this frame shall fall
A victim sacred to your dreary shrine.
But what are ye? 35
Thou, who didst put to flight
Primeval Silence, when the morning stars,
Exulting, shouted o'er the rising ball;
O Thou! whose word from solid darkness struck
That spark, the sun, strike wisdom from my soul; 40
My soul, which flies to thee, her trust, her treasure,

As misers to their gold, while others rest.
  Through this opaque of nature and of
    soul,
This double night, transmit one pitying ray,
To lighten and to cheer. Oh, lead my
    mind —   45
A mind that fain would wander from its
    wo —
Lead it through various scenes of life and
    death,
And from each scene the noblest truths in-
    spire.
Nor less inspire my conduct than my song;
Teach my best reason, reason; my best will
Teach rectitude; and fix my firm resolve
Wisdom to wed, and pay her long arrear:
Nor let the phial of thy vengeance, poured
On this devoted head, be poured in vain.

* * *

This is the desert, *this* the solitude: 55
How populous, how vital is the grave!
This is creation's melancholy vault,
The vale funereal, the sad cypress gloom;
The land of apparitions, empty shades!
All, all on earth, is shadow, all beyond 60
Is substance; the reverse is folly's creed;
How solid all, where change shall be no
    more!
  This is the bud of being, the dim dawn,
The twilight of our day, the vestibule;
Life's theater as yet is shut, and death, 65
Strong death alone can heave the massy bar,
This gross impediment of clay remove,
And make us embryos of existence free
From real life; but little more remote
Is he, not yet a candidate for light,   70
The future embryo, slumbering in his sire.
Embryos we must be till we burst the shell,
Yon ambient azure shell, and spring to life,
The life of gods, O transport! and of man.
  Yet man, fool man! here buries all his
    thoughts;   75
Inters celestial hopes without one sigh.
Prisoner of earth, and pent beneath the
    moon,
Here pinions all his wishes; winged by
    heaven
To fly at infinite: and reach it there
Where seraphs gather immortality,   80
On life's fair tree, fast by the throne of
    God.
What golden joys ambrosial clustering glow
In his full beam, and ripen for the just,
Where momentary ages are no more!
Where time, and pain, and chance, and
    death expire!   85
And is it in the flight of threescore years

To push eternity from human thought,
And smother souls immortal in the dust?
A soul immortal, spending all her fires,
Wasting her strength in strenuous idleness,
Thrown into tumult, raptured or alarmed, 91
At aught this scene can threaten or indulge,
Resembles ocean into tempest wrought,
To waft a feather, or to drown a fly.

(1742)

* * *

Beggar's Opera

JOHN GAY (1685–1732)

From THE SHEPHERD'S WEEK

When fast asleep they Bowzybeus spy'd,
His hat and oaken staff lay close beside.
That Bowzybeus who could sweetly sing,
Or with the rozin'd bow torment the string:
That Bowzybeus who with finger's speed 5
Could call soft warblings from the breath-
    ing reed;
That Bowzybeus who with jocound tongue,
Ballads and roundelays and catches sung.
They loudly laugh to see the damsel's fright,
And in disport surround the drunken wight.
  Ah, Bowzybee, why didst thou stay so
    long?   11
The mugs were large, the drink was won-
    d'rous strong!
Thou shouldst have left the fair before
    't was night,
But thou sat'st toping 'till the morning
    light.
  Cic'ly, brisk maid, steps forth before the
    rout,   15
And kiss'd with smacking lip the snoring
    lout.
For custom says, 'Whoe'er this venture
    proves,
For such a kiss demands a pair of gloves.'
By her example Dorcas bolder grows,
And plays a tickling straw within his nose.
He rubs his nostril, and in wonted joke 21
The sneezing swains with stamm'ring speech
    bespoke.
To you, my lads, I 'll sing my carols o'er,
As for the maids — I've something else in
    store.   24
  No sooner 'gan he raise his tuneful song,
But lads and lasses round about him throng.
Not ballad-singer plac'd above the crowd
Sings with a note so thrilling sweet and
    loud,
Nor parish-clerk who calls the psalm so
    clear,

Like Bowzybeus sooths th' attentive ear. 30
Of nature's laws his carols first begun,
Why the grave owl can never face the sun.
For owls, as swains observe, detest the
    light,
And only sing and seek their prey by night.
How turnips hide their swelling heads be-
    low,   35
And how the closing colworts upwards
    grow;
How Will-a-Wisp misleads night-faring
    clowns,
O'er hills, and sinking bogs, and pathless
    downs.
Of stars he told that shoot with shining
    trail,
And of the glow-worm's light that gilds his
    tail.   40
He sung where wood-cocks in the summer
    feed,
And in what climates they renew their
    breed;
Some think to northern coasts their flight
    they tend,
Or to the moon in midnight hours ascend.
Where swallows in the winter season keep,
And how the drowsy bat and dormouse
    sleep,   46
How nature does the puppy's eyelid close,
Till the bright sun has nine times set and
    rose.
For huntsmen by their long experience find,
That puppies still nine rolling suns are
    blind.   50
    Now he goes on and sings of fairs and
    shows,
For still new fairs before his eyes arose.
How pedlars' stalls with glitt'ring toys are
    laid,
The various fairings of the country maid.
Long silken laces hang upon the twine, 55
And rows of pins and amber bracelets
    shine;
How the tight lass, knives, combs, and scis-
    sors spies,
And locks on thimbles with desiring eyes.
Of lott'ries next with tuneful note he told,
Where silver spoons are won, and rings of
    gold.   60
The lads and lasses trudge the street along,
And all the fair is crowded in his song.
The mountebank now treads the stage, and
    sells
His pills, his balsams, and his ague-spells;
Now o'er and o'er the nimble tumbler
    springs,   65
And on the rope the vent'rous maiden
    swings;

Jack-pudding in his parti-colored jacket
Toffs the glove, and jokes at ev'ry packet.
Of raree-shows he sung and Punch's fates,
Of pockets pick'd in crowds, and various
    cheats.   70
    Then sad he sung 'the children in the
    wood.'
Ah, barb'rous uncle, stain'd with infant
    blood!
How blackberries they pluck'd in deserts
    wild,
And fearless at the glittering fauchion
    smil'd;
Their little corpses the robin-red-breasts
    found,   75
And strewed with pious bill the leaves
    around.
Ah, gentle birds! if this verse lasts so
    long,
Your names shall live for ever in my
    song.
    For buxom Joan he sung the doubtful
    strife,
How the fly sailor made the maid a wife. 80
    To louder strains he rais'd his voice, to
    tell
What woeful wars in Chevy-Chace befell,
When 'Percy drove the deer with hound and
    horn,
Wars to be wept by children yet unborn!'
Ah, Withrington, more years thy life had
    crown'd,   85
If thou hadst never heard the horn or
    hound!
Yet shall the squire, who fought on bloody
    stumps,
By future bards be wail'd in doleful dumps.
                    * * *
    Then he was seized with a religious qualm,
And on a sudden, sung the hundredth
    psalm.   90
    He sung of Taffy Welch, and Sawney
    Scot,
Lilly-bullero and the Irish Trot.
Why should I tell of Bateman or of Shore,
Or Wantley's dragon slain by valiant
    Moore,
The bower of Rosamond, or Robin Hood,
And how the grass now grows where Troy
    town stood?   96
    His carols ceas'd: the listening maids
    and swains
Seem still to hear some soft imperfect
    strains.
Sudden he rose; and as he reels along,
Swears kisses sweet should well reward his
    song.   100
The damsels laughing fly: the giddy clown

Again upon a wheat-sheaf, drops adown;
The power that guards the drunk, his sleep
    attends,
'Till ruddy, like his face, the sun descends.
                                        (1714)

ROBERT BLAIR (1699–1746)

From THE GRAVE

Oft in the lone church-yard at night I've
    seen,
By glimpse of moon-shine, cheq'ring through
    the trees,
The school-boy, with his satchel in his hand,
Whistling aloud to bear his courage up,
And lightly tripping o'er the long flat
    stones   5
(With nettles skirted, and with moss o'er-
    grown)
That tell in homely phrase who lie below;
Sudden he starts! and hears, or thinks he
    hears,
The sound of something purring at his
    heels:
Full fast he flies, and dares not look be-
    hind him,   10
Till out of breath he overtakes his fel-
    lows;
Who gather round, and wonder at the tale
Of horrid apparition, tall and ghastly,
That walks at dead of night, or takes his
    stand
O'er some new-opened grave: and, strange
    to tell!   15
Evanishes at crowing of the cock.

* * *

What is this world?
What but a spacious burial-field unwall'd,
Strew'd with death's spoils, the spoils of
    animals,
Savage and tame, and full of dead men's
    bones?   20
The very turf on which we tread once liv'd;
And we that live must lend our carcasses
To cover our own offspring: in their turns
They too must cover theirs. 'T is here all
    meet!
The shivering Icelander, and sun-burnt
    Moor;   25
Men of all climes, that never met before;
And of all creeds, the Jew, the Turk, the
    Christian.
Here the proud prince, and favorite yet
    prouder,
His sovereign's keeper, and the people's
    scourge,

Are huddled out of sight. Here lie abash'd
The great negotiators of the earth,   31
And celebrated masters of the balance,
Deep read in stratagems, and wiles of
    courts:
Now vain their treaty-skill! Death scorns
    to treat.
Here the o'erloaded slave flings down his
    burden   35
From his gall'd shoulders; and when the
    cruel tyrant
With all his guards and tools of power
    about him,
Is meditating new unheard-of hardships,
Mocks his short arm, and quick as thought
    escapes   39
Where tyrants vex not, and the weary rest.
Here the warm lover, leaving the cool
    shade,
The tell-tale echo, and the bubbling stream,
Time out of mind the fav'rite seats of love
Fast by his gentle mistress lays him down
Unblasted by foul tongue. Here friends
    and foes   45
Lie close, unmindful of their former
    feuds.

* * *

Sure the last end
Of the good man is peace. How calm his
    exit!
Night-dews fall not more gently to the
    ground,
Nor weary worn-out winds expire so soft.
Behold him! in the evening tide of life,   51
A life well spent, whose early care it was
His riper years should not upbraid his
    green
By unperceiv'd degrees he wears away;
Yet like the sun seems larger at his set-
    ting!   55
High in his faith and hopes, look! how he
    reaches
After the prize in view! and, like a bird
That 's hamper'd, struggles hard to get
    away!
Whilst the glad gates of sight are wide
    expanded   59
To let new glories in, the first fair fruits
Of the fast-coming harvest! Then! O
    then!
Each earth-born joy grows vile, or disap-
    pears,
Shrunk to a thing of nought. O how he
    longs
To have his passport sign'd, and be dis-
    miss'd!
'T is done, and now he 's happy! The glad
    soul   62

Has not a wish uncrown'd. Even the lag
    flesh
Rests too in hope of meeting once again
Its better half, never to sunder more.
Nor shall it hope in vain: the time draws on
When not a single spot of burial-earth,   70
Whether on land, or in the spacious sea,
But must give back its long-committed dust
Inviolate: and faithfully shall these
Make up the full account; not the least
    atom
Embezzled, or mislaid, of the whole tale.
Each soul shall have a body ready-fur-
    nished;   76
And each shall have his own. Hence, ye
    profane:
Ask not how this can be. Sure the same
    power
That reared the piece at first, and took it
    down,
Can reassemble the loose scatter'd parts,
And put them as they were: Almighty
    God   81
Has done much more: Nor is his arm im-
    pair'd
Through length of days; and what he can
    he will:
His faithfulness stands bound to see it
    done.
When the dread trumpet sounds, the slum-
    bering dust,
Not unattentive to the call, shall wake;   86
And every joint possess its proper place,
With a new elegance of form, unknown
To its first state. Nor shall the conscious
    soul
Mistake its partner; but amidst the crowd,
Singling its other half, into its arms   91
Shall rush, with all the impatience of a man
That's new come home, who having long
    been absent,
With haste runs over every different room,
In pain to see the whole. Thrice happy
    meeting!   95
Nor time, nor death, shall ever part them
    more.
'T is but a night, a long and moonless
    night;
We make the grave our bed, and then are
    gone.
  Thus, at the shut of even, the weary
    bird
Leaves the wide air, and in some lonely
    brake   100
Cowers down, and dozes till the dawn of
    day;
Then claps his well-fledg'd wings and bears
    away.   (1743)

JOHN DYER (1700–1758)

GRONGAR HILL

Silent nymph, with curious eye,
Who, the purple evening, lie
On the mountain's lonely van,
Beyond the noise of busy man;
Painting fair the form of things,   5
While the yellow linnet sings;
Or the tuneful nightingale
Charms the forest with her tale;
Come, with all thy various hues,
Come, and aid thy sister muse;   10
Now, while Phœbus, riding high,
Gives luster to the land and sky!
Grongar Hill invites my song,
Draw the landscape bright and strong;
Grongar, in whose mossy cells,   15
Sweetly musing, Quiet dwells;
Grongar, in whose silent shade,
For the modest Muses made;
So oft I have, the evening still,
At the fountain of a rill,   20
Sat upon a flowery bed,
With my hand beneath my head;
While strayed my eyes o'er Towy's flood,
Over mead, and over wood,
From house to house, from hill to hill,   25
Till contemplation had her fill.
  About his checkered sides I wind,
And leave his brooks and meads behind,
And groves and grottoes where I lay,
And vistas shooting beams of day: 30
Wide and wider spreads the vale,
As circles on a smooth canal:
The mountains round, unhappy fate,
Sooner or later, of all height,
Withdraw their summits from the skies,   35
And lessen as the others rise:
Still the prospect wider spreads,
Adds a thousand woods and meads;
Still it widens, widens still,
And sinks the newly risen hill.   40
  Now I gain the mountain's brow,
What a landscape lies below!
No clouds, no vapors intervene,
But the gay, the open scene,
Does the face of nature shew,   45
In all the hues of heaven's bow;
And, swelling to embrace the light,
Spreads around beneath the sight.
  Old castles on the cliffs arise,
Proudly towering in the skies!   50
Rushing from the woods, the spires
Seem from hence ascending fires!
Half his beams Apollo sheds
On the yellow mountain heads,

Gilds the fleeces of the flocks,   55
And glitters on the broken rocks!
  Below me trees unnumbered rise,
Beautiful in various dyes:
The gloomy pine, the poplar blue,
The yellow beech, the sable yew,   60
The slender fir, that taper grows,
The sturdy oak, with broad-spread boughs.
And beyond the purple grove,
Haunt of Phyllis, queen of love!
Gaudy as the opening dawn,   65
Lies a long and level lawn,
On which a dark hill, steep and high,
Holds and charms the wandering eye!
Deep are his feet in Towy's flood,
His sides are clothed with waving wood,   70
And ancient towers crown his brow,
That cast an awful look below;
Whose ragged walls the ivy creeps,
And with her arms from falling keeps:
So both a safety from the wind   75
On mutual dependence find.
'T is now the raven's bleak abode;
'T is now the apartment of the toad;
And there the fox securely feeds,
And there the poisonous adder breeds,   80
Concealed in ruins, moss, and weeds;
While, ever and anon, there falls
Huge heaps of hoary mouldered walls.
Yet time has seen, that lifts the low,
And level lays the lofty brow,   85
Has seen this broken pile complete,
Big with the vanity of state;
But transient is the smile of fate!
A little rule, a little sway,
A sunbeam in a winter's day,   90
Is all the proud and mighty have
Between the cradle and the grave.
  And see the rivers, how they run
Through woods and meads, in shade and
    sun,
Sometimes swift, sometimes slow,   95
Wave succeeding wave, they go
A various journey to the deep,
Like human life, to endless sleep!
Thus is nature's vesture wrought,
To instruct our wandering thought;   100
Thus she dresses green and gay,
To disperse our cares away.
  Ever charming, ever new,
When will the landscape tire the view!
The fountain's fall, the river's flow,   105
The woody valleys, warm and low;
The windy summit, wild and high,
Roughly rushing on the sky!
The pleasant seat, the ruined tower,
The naked rock, the shady bower;   110
The town and village, dome and farm,
Each give each a double charm,

As pearls upon an Æthiop's arm.
  See, on the mountain's southern side,
Where the prospect opens wide,   115
Where the evening gilds the tide,
How close and small the hedges lie!
What streaks of meadows cross the eye!
A step, methinks, may pass the stream,
So little distant dangers seem;   120
So we mistake the future's face,
Eyed through hope's deluding glass;
As yon summits soft and fair,
Clad in colors of the air,
Which to those who journey near,   125
Barren, brown, and rough appear;
Still we tread the same coarse way,
The present's still a cloudy day.
O may I with myself agree,
And never covet what I see!   130
Content me with an humble shade,
My passions tamed, my wishes laid;
For while our wishes wildly roll,
We banish quiet from the soul:
'T is thus the busy beat the air,   135
And misers gather wealth and care.
  Now, even now, my joys run high,
As on the mountain turf I lie;
While the wanton zephyr sings,
And in the vale perfumes his wings;   140
While the waters murmur deep,
While the shepherd charms his sheep,
While the birds unbounded fly,
And with music fill the sky,
Now, even now, my joys run high.   145
  Be full, ye courts; be great who will;
Search for peace with all your skill;
Open wide the lofty door,
Seek her on the marble floor:
In vain you search, she is not there;   150
In vain you search the domes of care!
Grass and flowers Quiet treads,
On the meads and mountain heads,
Along with Pleasure close allied,
Ever by each other's side: 155
And often, by the murmuring rill,
Hears the thrush, while all is still,
Within the groves of Grongar Hill.
                                        (1726)

WILLIAM SHENSTONE (1714–1763)

FROM THE SCHOOLMISTRESS

Near to this dome is found a patch so
    green,
On which the tribe their gambols do dis-
    play;

And at the door imprisoning board is
    seen,
Lest weakly wights of smaller size should
    stray;
Eager, perdie, to bask in sunny day!   5
The noises intermixed, which thence re-
    sound,
Do learning's little tenement betray;
Where sits the dame, disguised in look
    profound,
And eyes her fairy throng, and turns her
    wheel around.

Her cap, far whiter than the driven
    snow,   10
Emblem right meet of decency does yield:
Her apron dyed in grain, as blue, I trow,
As is the harebell that adorns the field;
And in her hand, for scepter, she does
    wield
Tway birchen sprays; with anxious fear
    entwined,   15
With dark distrust, and sad repentance
    filled;
And steadfast hate, and sharp affliction
    joined,
And fury uncontrolled, and chastisement un-
    kind.

A russet stole was o'er her shoulders
    thrown;
A russet kirtle fenced the nipping air; 20
'T was simple russet, but it was her own;
'T was her own country bred the flock so
    fair!
'T was her own labor did the fleece pre-
    pare;
And, sooth to say, her pupils ranged
    around,
Through pious awe, did term it passing
    rare;   25
For they in gaping wonderment abound,
And think, no doubt, she been the greatest
    wight on ground.

Albeit ne flattery did corrupt her truth,
Ne pompous title did debauch her ear;
Goody, good woman, gossip, n'aunt, for-
    sooth,   30
Or dame, the sole additions she did hear;
Yet these she challenged, these she held
    right dear;
Ne would esteem him act as mought be-
    hove,
Who should not honored eld with these
    revere;
For never title yet so mean could prove,
But there was eke a mind which did that
    title love.   36

One ancient hen she took delight to feed,
The plodding pattern of the busy dame;
Which, ever and anon, impelled by need,
Into her school, begirt with chickens,
    came;   40
Such favor did her past deportment claim;
And, if neglect had lavished on the
    ground
Fragment of bread, she would collect the
    same;
For well she knew, and quaintly could
    expound,
What sin it were to waste the smallest
    crumb she found.   45

Herbs, too, she knew, and well of each
    could speak,
That in her garden sipped the silvery
    dew;
Where no vain flower disclosed a gaudy
    streak,
But herbs for use and physic, not a few,
Of gray renown, within those borders
    grew: 50
The tufted basil, pun-provoking thyme,
Fresh balm, and marigold of cheerful
    hue:
The lowly gill, that never dares to climb;
And more I fain would sing, disdaining
    here to rhyme.

Here oft the dame, on Sabbath's decent
    eve,   55
Hymnèd such psalms as Sternhold forth
    did mete;
If winter 't were, she to her hearth did
    cleave,
But in her garden found a summer-seat:
Sweet melody! to hear her then repeat
How Israel's sons, beneath a foreign king,
While taunting foemen did a song en-
    treat,   61
All, for the nonce, untuning every string,
Uphung their useless lyres — small heart
    had they to sing.

For she was just, and friend to virtuous
    lore,
And passed much time in truly virtuous
    deed;   65
And in those elfins' ears would oft de-
    plore
The times, when truth by popish rage did
    bleed,
And tortuous death was true devotion's
    meed;
And simple faith in iron chains did
    mourn.

That nould on wooden image place her
  creed;   70
And lawny saints in smouldering flames
  did burn:
Ah! dearest Lord, forefend thilk days
  should e'er return!

In elbow-chair (like that of Scottish stem,
By the sharp tooth of cankering eld de-
  faced,
In which, when he receives his diadem, 75
Our sovereign prince and liefest liege is
  placed)
The matron sat; and some with rank she
  graced,
(The source of children's and of courtiers'
  pride!)
Redressed affronts—for vile affronts
  there passed;
And warned them not the fretful to de-
  ride,   80
But love each other dear, whatever them
  betide.

Right well she knew each temper to
  descry,
To thwart the proud, and the submiss to
  raise;
Some with vile copper-prize exalt on high,
And some entice with pittance small of
  praise;   85
And other some with baleful sprig she
  frays:
Even absent, she the reins of power doth
  hold,
While with quaint arts the giddy crowd
  she sways;
Forewarned, if little bird their pranks
  behold,
T will whisper in her ear, and all the scene
  unfold.   90

Lo! now with state she utters her com-
  mand;
Eftsoons the urchins to their tasks re-
  pair,
Their books of stature small they take
  in hand,
Which with pellucid horn secured are,
To save from finger wet the letters fair:
The work so gay, that on their back is
  seen,   96
St. George's high achievements does de-
  clare;
On which thilk wight that has y-gazing
  been,
Kens the forthcoming rod—unpleasing
  sight, I ween!

Ah! luckless he, and born beneath the
  beam   100
Of evil star! it irks me whilst I write;
As erst the bard by Mulla's silver stream,
Oft, as he told of deadly dolorous plight,
Sighed as he sung, and did in tears in-
  dite;
For brandishing the rod, she doth begin
To loose the brogues, the stripling's late
  delight;   106
And down they drop; appears his dainty
  skin,
Fair as the furry coat of whitest ermilin.

O ruthful scene! when, from a nook ob-
  scure,
His little sister doth his peril see,   110
All playful as she sat, she grows demure;
She finds full soon her wonted spirits
  flee;
She meditates a prayer to set him free;
Nor gentle pardon could this dame deny—
If gentle pardon could with dames agree—
To her sad grief that swells in either
  eye,   116
And wrings her so that all for pity she
  could die.

No longer can she now her shrieks com-
  mand;
And hardly she forbears, through awful
  fear,
To rushen forth, and, with presumptuous
  hand,   120
To stay harsh justice in its mid career.
On thee she calls, on thee her parent
  dear;
(Ah! too remote to ward the shameful
  blow!)
She sees no kind domestic visage near,
And soon a flood of tears begins to flow,
And gives a loose at last to unavailing
  woe.   126

But, ah! what pen his piteous plight may
  trace?
Or what device his loud laments explain—
The form uncouth of his disguised face—
The pallid hue that dyes his looks
  amain—   130
The plenteous shower that does his cheek
  disdain?
When he, in abject wise, implores the
  dame,
Ne hopeth aught of sweet reprieve to
  gain:

Or when from high she levels well her
    aim,
And, through the thatch, his cries each fall-
    ing stroke proclaim.   135

But now Dan Phœbus gains the middle
    sky,
And liberty unbars her prison door;
And like a rushing torrent out they fly;
And now the grassy cirque han covered
    o'er
With boisterous revel rout and wild up-
    roar;   140
A thousand ways in wanton rings they
    run.
Heaven shield their short-lived pastimes
    I implore;
For well may freedom erst so dearly won
Appear to British elf more gladsome than
    the sun.

Enjoy, poor imps! enjoy your sportive
    trade,   145
And chase gay flies, and cull the fairest
    flowers;
For when my bones in grass-green sods
    are laid,
O never may ye taste more careless hours
In knightly castles or in ladies' bowers.
O vain to seek delight in earthly thing! 150
But most in courts, where proud ambition
    towers;
Deluded wight! who weens fair peace can
    spring
Beneath the pompous dome of kesar or of
    king.
                    (1742)
       * * *

MARK AKENSIDE (1721–1770)

From PLEASURES OF THE IMAGINA-
TION

Who that, from Alpine heights, his labor-
    ing eye
Shoots round the wide horizon, to survey
Nilus or Ganges rolling his bright wave
Through mountains, plains, through empires
    black with shade,
And continents of sand, will turn his gaze 5
To mark the windings of a scanty rill
That murmurs at his feet? The high-born
    soul
Disdains to rest her heaven-aspiring wing
Beneath its native quarry. Tired of earth
And this diurnal scene, she springs aloft 10

Through fields of air; pursues the flying
    storm;
Rides on the vollied lightning through the
    heavens;   ·
Or, yoked with whirlwinds and the northern
    blast,
Sweeps the long tract of day. Then high
    she soars
The blue profound, and, hovering round the
    sun,   15
Beholds him pouring the redundant stream
Of light; beholds his unrelenting sway
Bend the reluctant planets to absolve
The fated rounds of Time. Thence far
    effused,
She darts her swiftness up the long career
Of devious comets: through its burning
    signs   ·   ·   21
Exulting measures the perennial wheel
Of Nature, and looks back on all the stars,
Whose blended light, as with a milky zone,
Invest the orient. Now, amazed she views
The empyreal waste, where happy spirits
    hold,   26
Beyond this concave heaven, their calm
    abode;
And fields of radiance, whose unfading light
Has traveled the profound six thousand
    years,
Nor yet arrives in sight of mortal things. 30
Even on the barriers of the world, untired
She meditates the eternal depth below;
Till half-recciling, down the headlong steep
She plunges; soon o'erwhelmed and swal-
    lowed up
In that immense of being. There her hopes
Rest at the fated goal. For from the birth
Of mortal man, the sovereign Maker said, 37
That not in humble nor in brief delight,
Not in the fading echoes of Renown,
Power's purple robes, nor Pleasure's flowery
    lap,   40
The soul should find enjoyment: but from
    these
Turning disdainful to an equal good,
Through all the ascent of things enlarge
    her view,
Till every bound at length should disap-
    pear,
And infinite perfection close the scene. 45
                    (1744)
       * * *

       O ye dales
Of Tyne, and ye most ancient woodlands;
    where
Oft as the giant flood obliquely strides,
And his banks open and his lawns extend.

Stops short the pleasèd traveler to view,   50
Presiding o'er the scene, some rustic tower
Founded by Norman or by Saxon hands:
O ye Northumbrian shades, which overlook
The rocky pavement and the mossy falls
Of solitary Wensbeck's limpid stream!   55
How gladly I recall your well-known seats
Beloved of old, and that delightful time
When all alone, for many a summer's day,
I wandered through your calm recesses, led
In silence by some powerful hand un-
    seen.   60
Nor will I e'er forget you; nor shall e'er
The graver tasks of manhood, or the ad-
    vice
Of vulgar wisdom, move me to disclaim
Those studies which possessed me in the
    dawn   •
Of life, and fixed the color of my mind   65
For every future year: whence even now
From sleep I rescue the clear hours of morn,
And, while the world around lies over-
    whelmed
In idle darkness, am alive to thoughts
Of honorable fame, of truth divine   70
Or moral, and of minds to virtue won
By the sweet magic of harmonious verse.
                (1772)

       * * *

WILLIAM COLLINS (1721–1759)

ODE

WRITTEN IN THE BEGINNING OF THE YEAR
1746

How sleep the brave who sink to rest
By all their country's wishes blest!
When Spring, with dewy fingers cold,
Returns to deck their hallow'd mold,
She there shall dress a sweeter sod   5
Than Fancy's feet have ever trod.

By fairy hands their knell is rung,
By forms unseen their dirge is sung;
There Honor comes, a pilgrim grey,
To bless the turf that wraps their clay;   10
And Freedom shall awhile repair,
To dwell a weeping hermit there!

ODE TO EVENING

If ought of oaten stop, or pastoral song,
May hope, chaste Eve, to sooth thy modest
    ear,

Like thy own solemn springs,
Thy springs and dying gales,

O nymph reserv'd, while now the bright-
    hair'd sun   5
Sits in yon western tent, whose cloudy
    skirts,
With brede ethereal wove,
O'erhang his wavy bed:

Now air is hush'd, save where the weak-
    ey'd bat,
With short shrill shriek, flits by on leathern
    wing,   10
Or where the beetle winds
His small but sullen horn,

As oft he rises 'midst the twilight path,
Against the pilgrim borne in heedless hum:
Now teach me, maid compos'd,   15
To breathe some soften'd strain,

Whose numbers, stealing thro' thy dark-
    'ning vale
May not unseemly with its stillness suit,
As, musing slow, I hail
Thy genial lov'd return!   20

For when thy folding-star arising shews
His paly circlet, at his warning lamp
The fragrant Hours, the elves
Who slept in flow'rs the day,

And many a nymph who wreaths her brows
    with sedge,   25
And sheds the fresh'ning dew, and, lovelier
    still
The pensive Pleasures sweet,
Prepare thy shadowy car.

Then lead, calm vot'ress, where some sheety
    lake
Cheers the lone heath, or some time-hal-
    low'd pile   30
Or upland fallows grey
Reflect its last cool gleam.

But when chill blust'ring winds, or driving
    rain,
Forbid my willing feet, be mine the hut
That from the mountain's side   35
Views wilds, and swelling floods,

And hamlets brown, and dim-discover'd
    spires,
And hears their simple bell, and marks o'er
    all
Thy dewy fingers draw
The gradual dusky veil.   40

While Spring shall pour his show'rs, as oft
   he wont,
And bathe thy breathing tresses, meekest
   Eve;
  While Summer loves to sport
  Beneath thy ling'ring light;

While sallow Autumn fills thy lap with
   leaves;   45
Or Winter, yelling thro' the troublous air,
  Affrights thy shrinking train,
  And rudely rends thy robes;

So long, sure-found beneath the sylvan
   shed,
Shall Fancy, Friendship, Science, rose-lipp'd
   Health,   50
  Thy gentlest influence own,
  And hymn thy fav'rite name!
               (1746)

ODE TO SIMPLICITY

O Thou, by nature taught
To breathe her genuine thought,
In numbers warmly pure, and sweetly
   strong;
  Who first, on mountains wild,
  In fancy, loveliest child,   5
Thy babe, or pleasure's, nursed the powers
   of song!

Thou, who, with hermit heart,
Disdain'st the wealth of art,
And gauds, and pageant weeds, and trailing
   pall;
  But com'st a decent maid,   10
  In Attic robe arrayed,
O chaste, unboastful nymph, to thee I call;

By all the honeyed store
On Hybla's thymy shore;
By all her blooms, and mingled murmurs
   dear;   15
  By her whose lovelorn woe,
  In evening musings slow,
Soothed sweetly sad Electra's poet's ear:

By old Cephisus deep,
Who spread his wavy sweep,   20
In warbled wanderings, round thy green re-
   treat;
  On whose enameled side,
  When holy freedom died,
No equal haunt allured thy future feet.

O sister meek of truth,   25
To my admiring youth,

Thy sober aid and native charms infuse!
The flowers that sweetest breathe,
Though beauty culled the wreath,
Still ask thy hand to range their ordered
   hues.   30

While Rome could none esteem
But virtue's patriot theme,
You loved her hills, and led their laureat
   band:
But stayed to sing alone
To one distinguished throne;   35
And turned the face, and fled her altered
   land.

No more, in hall or bower,
The passions own thy power;
Love, only love, her forceless numbers
   mean:
For thou hast left her shrine;   40
Nor olive more, nor vine,
Shall gain thy feet to bless the servile
   scene.

Though taste, though genius, bless
To some divine excess,
Faints the cold work till thou inspire the
   whole;   45
What each, what all supply,
May court, may charm, our eye;
Thou, only thou, cans't raise the meeting
   soul!

Of these let others ask,
To aid some mighty task,   50
I only seek to find thy temperate vale;
  Where oft my reed might sound
  To maids and shepherds round,
And all thy sons, O nature, learn my tale.
              (1746)

THE PASSIONS

AN ODE FOR MUSIC

When Music, heav'nly maid, was young,
While yet in early Greece she sung,
The Passions oft, to hear her shell,
Throng'd around her magic cell,
Exulting, trembling, raging, fainting,   5
Possest beyond the Muse's painting;
By turns they felt the glowing mind
Disturb'd, delighted, rais'd, refin'd:
Till once, 't is said, when all were fir'd,
Fill'd with fury, rapt, inspir'd,   10
From the supporting myrtles round
They snatch'd her instruments of sound;
And as they oft had heard apart

Sweet lessons of her forceful art,
Each, for madness rul'd the hour,   15
Would prove his own expressive pow'r.

First Fear his hand, its skill to try,
    Amid the chords bewilder'd laid,
And back recoil'd, he knew not why,
    Ev'n at the sound himself had made.   20

Next Anger rush'd; his eyes, on fire,
    In lightnings own'd his secret stings;
In one rude clash he struck the lyre,
    And swept with hurried hand the strings.

With woeful measures wan Despair   25
    Low sullen sounds his grief beguil'd;
A solemn, strange, and mingled air;
    'T was sad by fits, by starts 't was wild.

But thou, O Hope, with eyes so fair,
    What was thy delightful measure?   30
Still it whisper'd promis'd pleasure,
    And bade the lovely scenes at distance
        hail!

Still would her touch the strain prolong,
    And from the rocks, the woods, the vale,
She call'd on Echo still thro' all the song; 35
    And where her sweetest theme she chose,
A soft responsive voice was heard at ev'ry
    close,
And Hope enchanted smil'd, and wav'd her
    golden hair.

And longer had she sung,— but with a
        frown
    Revenge impatient rose;   40
He threw his blood-stain'd sword in thun-
        der down
    And with a with'ring look
    The war-denouncing trumpet took,
And blew a blast so loud and dread,
Were ne'er prophetic sounds so full of
        woe.   45
    And ever and anon he beat
    The doubling drum with furious heat;
And tho' sometimes, each dreary pause be-
        tween,
    Dejected Pity, at his side,
    Her soul-subduing voice applied,   50
Yet still he kept his wild unalter'd mien,
    While each strain'd ball of sight seem'd
        bursting from his head.

Thy numbers, Jealousy, to nought were fix'd,
    Sad proof of thy distressful state;
Of diff'ring themes the veering song was
    mix'd,   55

And now it courted Love, now raving
    call'd on Hate.
With eyes uprais'd, as one inspir'd,
Pale Melancholy sate retir'd,
And from her wild sequester'd seat,
    In notes by distance made more sweet,   60
Pour'd thro' the mellow horn her pensive
    soul:
    And, dashing soft from rocks around,
    Bubbling runnels join'd the sound;
Thro' glades and glooms the mingled
    measure stole;
Or o'er some haunted stream with fond
    delay   65
    Round an holy calm diffusing,
    Love of peace and lonely musing,
In hollow murmurs died away.

But oh, how alter'd was its sprightlier tone,
When Cheerfulness, a nymph of healthiest
    hue,   70
    Her bow across her shoulder flung,
    Her buskins gemm'd with morning dew,
Blew an inspiring air, that dale and thicket
    rung,
    The hunter's call to faun and dryad
        known!
    The oak-crown'd sisters, and their chaste-
        ey'd queen,   75
    Satyrs, and sylvan boys, were seen,
    Peeping from forth their alleys green;
Brown Exercise rejoic'd to hear,
    And Sport leapt up, and seiz'd his
        beechen spear.

Last came Joy's ecstatic trial.   80
He, with viny crown advancing,
    First to the lively pipe his hand addrest;
But soon he saw the brisk awak'ning viol,
    Whose sweet entrancing voice he lov'd the
        best.
        They would have thought, who heard
            the strain,   85
        They saw in Tempe's vale her native
            maids
    Amidst the vestal sounding shades,
To some unwearied minstrel dancing,
While, as his flying fingers kiss'd the strings,
    Love fram'd with Mirth a gay fantastic
        round;   90
    Loose were her tresses seen, her zone un-
        bound,
    And he, amidst his frolic play,
    As if he would the charming air repay,
Shook thousand odors from his dewy wings

O Music, sphere-descended maid,   95
Friend of Pleasure. Wisdom's aid.

Why, goddess, why, to us denied,
Lay'st thou thy ancient lyre aside?
As in that lov'd Athenian bow'r
You learn'd an all-commanding pow'r   100
Thy mimic soul, O nymph endear'd,
Can well recall what then it heard.
Where is thy native simple heart,
Devote to Virtue, Fancy, Art?
Arise as in that elder time,   105
Warm, energic, chaste, sublime!
Thy wonders, in that godlike age,
Fill thy recording sister's page.—
'T is said, and I believe the tale,
Thy humblest reed could more prevail,   110
Had more of strength, diviner rage,
Than all which charms this laggard age,
Ev'n all at once together found,
Cecilia's mingled world of sound.
O, bid our vain endeavors, cease,   115
Revive the just designs of Greece,
Return in all thy simple state,
Confirm the tales her sons relate!
(1746)

A SONG FROM SHAKSPERE'S CYMBELINE

Sung by Guiderus and Arviragus over Fidele, supposed to be dead

To fair Fidele's grassy tomb
  Soft maids and village hinds shall bring
Each op'ning sweet, of earliest bloom,
  And rifle all the breathing spring.

No wailing ghost shall dare appear,   5
  To vex with shrieks this quiet grove;
But shepherd lads assemble here,
  And melting virgins own their love.

No wither'd witch shall here be seen,
  No goblins lead their nightly crew;   10
The female fays shall haunt the green,
  And dress thy grave with pearly dew.

The redbreast oft at ev'ning hours
  Shall kindly lend his little aid,
With hoary moss, and gather'd flow'rs,   15
  To deck the ground where thou art laid.

When howling winds, and beating rain,
  In tempests shake the sylvan cell,
Or midst the chase on ev'ry plain,
  The tender thought on thee shall dwell,   20

Each lonely scene shall thee restore.
  For thee the tear be duly shed:
Belov'd, till life could charm no more;
  And mourn'd, till Pity's self be dead.
(1744)

THOMAS WARTON (1728–1790)

THE GRAVE OF KING ARTHUR

Stately the feast, and high the cheer:
Girt with many an armèd peer,
And canopied with golden pall,
Amid Cilgarran's castle hall,
Sublime in formidable state,   5
And warlike splendor, Henry sate;
Prepar'd to stain the briny flood
Of Shannon's lakes with rebel blood.
  Illumining the vaulted roof,
A thousand torches flam'd aloof: 10
From massy cups, with golden gleam
Sparkled the red metheglin's stream:
To grace the gorgeous festival,
Along the lofty-window'd hall,
The storied tapestry was hung;—   15
With minstrelsy the rafters rung
Of harps, that with reflected light
From the proud gallery glitter'd bright:
While gifted bards, a rival throng
(From distant Mona, nurse of song,   20
From Teivi, fring'd with umbrage brown,
From Elvy's vale, and Cader's crown,
From many a shaggy precipice
That shades Ierne's hoarse abyss,
And many a sunless solitude   25
Of Radnor's inmost mountains rude),
To crown the banquet's solemn close,
Themes of British glory chose;
And to the strings of various chime
Attemper'd thus the fabling rhyme.   30
'O'er Cornwall's cliffs the tempest roar'd,
High the screaming sea-mew soar'd;
On Tintagell's topmost tower
Darksome fell the sleety shower;
Round the rough castle shrilly sung   35
The whirling blast, and wildly flung
On each tall rampart's thundering side
The surges of the tumbling tide:
When Arthur rang'd his red-cross ranks
On conscious Camlan's crimson'd banks: 40
By Mordred's faithless guile decreed
Beneath a Saxon spear to bleed!
Yet in vain a paynim foe
Arm'd with fate the mighty blow;
For when he fell an elfin queen,   45
All in secret, and unseen,
O'er the fainting hero threw
Her mantle of ambrosial blue;
And bade her spirits bear him far,
In Merlin's agate-axled car,   50
To her green isle's enamell'd steep,
Far in the navel of the deep.
O'er his wounds she sprinkled dew
From flowers that in Arabia grew:

On a rich enchanted bed   55
She pillow'd his majestic head;
O'er his brow, with whispers bland,
Thrice she wav'd an opiate wand;
And to soft music's airy sound,
Her magic curtains clos'd around.   60
There, renew'd the vital spring,
Again he reigns.a mighty king;
And many a fair and fragrant clime,
Blooming in immortal prime,
By gales of Eden ever fann'd,   65
Owns the monarch's high command:
Thence to Britain shall return
(If right prophetic rolls I learn),
Borne on Victory's spreading plume,
His ancient scepter to resume;   70
Once more, in old heroic pride,
His barbèd courser to bestride;
His knightly table to restore,
And brave the tournaments of yore.'

* * *
(1777)

SONNETS

WRITTEN IN A BLANK LEAF OF DUGDALE'S MONASTICON

Deem not devoid of elegance the sage,
By Fancy's genuine feelings unbeguiled
Of painful pedantry, the poring child,
Who turns of these proud tomes the his-
toric page,
Now sunk by Time, and Henry's fiercer
rage.   5
Think'st thou the warbling muses never
smiled
On his lone hours? Ingenious views en-
gage
His thoughts on themes unclassic falsely
styled,
Intent. While cloistered piety displays
Her moldering roll, the piercing eye ex-
plores   10
New manners, and the pomp of elder days,
Whence culls the pensive bard his pictured
stores.
Not rough nor barren are the winding ways
Of hoar antiquity, but strewn with flowers.
(1777)

WRITTEN AT STONEHENGE

Thou noblest monument of Albion's isle!
Whether by Merlin's aid from Scythia's
shore,
To Amber's fatal plain Pendragon bore,
Huge frame of giant-hands, the mighty pile,

T' entomb his Britons slain by Hengist's
guile: 5
Or Druid priests, sprinkled with human
gore,
Taught 'mid thy massy maze their mystic
lore:
Or Danish chiefs, enrich'd with savage
spoil,
To Victory's idol vast, an unhewn shrine,
Rear'd the rude heap: or, in thy hallow'd
round,   10
Repose the kings of Brutus' genuine line;
Or here those kings in solemn state were
crown'd:
Studious to trace thy wondrous origine,
We muse on many an ancient tale renown'd
(1777)

THOMAS CHATTERTON
(1752–1770)

BRISTOWE TRAGEDIE

OR THE DETHE OF SYR CHARLES BAWDIN

The featherd songster chaunticleer
Han wounde hys bugle horne,
And tolde the earlie villager
The commynge of the morne: 4

Kynge Edwarde sawe the ruddie streakes
Of lyghte eclypse the greie;
And herde the raven's crokynge throte
Proclayme the fated daie.   8

'Thou 'rt ryghte,' quod he, 'for, by the
Godde
That syttes enthron'd on hyghe!
Charles Bawdin, and hys fellowes twaine,
To-daie shall surelie die.'   12

Thenne wythe a jugge of nappy ale
Hys knyghtes dydd onne hymm waite;
'Goe tell the traytour, thatt to-daie
Hee leaves thys mortall state.'   16

Sir Canterlone thenne bendedd lowe,
With harte brymm-fulle of woe;
Hee journey'd to the castle-gate,
And to Syr Charles dydd goe.   20

Butt whenne hee came, hys children twaine,
And eke hys lovynge wyfe,
Wythe brinie tears dydd wett the floore,
For goode Syr Charleses lyfe.   24

'O, goode Syr Charles!' sayd Canterlone,
  'Badde tydyngs I doe brynge.'
'Speke boldlie, manne,' sayd brave Syr
    Charles,
  'Whatte says thie traytor kynge?'   28

'I greeve to telle; before yonne Sonne
  Does fromme the welkinn flye,
Hee hathe uppon hys honour sworne,
  Thatt thou shalt surelie die.'   32

'Wee all must die,' quod brave Syr Charles;
  'Of thatte I'm not affearde;
Whatte bootes to lyve a little space?
  Thanke Jesu, I'm prepar'd: 36

'Butt telle thye kynge, for myne hee's not,
  I'de sooner die to-daie
Thanne lyve hys slave, as manie are,
  Though I shoulde lyve for aie.'   40

Thenne Canterlone hee dydd goe out,
  To telle the maior straite
To gett all thynges ynne redyness
  For goode Syr Charleses fate.   44

Thenne Maister Canynge saughte the kynge,
  And felle down onne hys knee;
'I'm come,' quod hee, 'unto your grace
  To move your clemencye.'   48

Thenne quod the kynge, 'Youre tale speke
    out,
  You have been much oure friende;
Whatever youre request may bee,
  Wee wylle to ytte attende.   52

'My noble liege! alle my request,
  Ys for a nobile knyghte,
Who, though may hap hee has donne
    wronge,
  Hee thoughte ytte stylle was ryghte: 56

'He has a spouse and children twaine,
  Alle rewyn'd are for aie;
Yff that you are resolved to lett
  Charles Bawdin die to-dai.'   60

'Speke not of such a traytour vile,'
  The kynge ynn furie sayde;
'Before the evening starre doth sheene,
  Bawdin shall loose hys hedde: 64

'Justice does loudlie for hym calle,
  And hee shalle have hys meede:
Speke, maister Canynge! Whatte thynge
    else
  Att present doe you neede?'   68

'My nobile liege!' goode Canynge sayde,
  'Leave justice to our Godde,
And laye the yronne rule asyde;
  Be thyme the olyve rodde.   72

'Was Godde to serche our hertes and
    reines,
  The best were synners grete;
Christ's vycarr only knowes ne synne,
  Ynne alle thys mortall state.   76

'Lett mercie rule thyne infante reigne,
  'T wylle faste thye crowne fulle sure;
From race to race thye familie
  Alle sov'reigns shall endure: 80

'But yff wythe bloode and slaughter thou
  Beginne thy infante reigne,
Thy crowne upponne thy childrennes brows
  Wylle never long remayne.'   84

'Canynge, awaie! thys traytour vile
  Has scorn'd my power and mee;
Howe canst thou then for such a manne
  Entreate my clemencye?'   88

'My nobile liege! the trulie brave
  Wylle val'rous actions prize;
Respect a brave and nobile mynde,
  Although ynne enemies.'   92

'Canynge, awaie! By Godde ynne Heav'n
  That dydd mee beinge gyve,
I wylle nott taste a bitt of breade
  Whilst thys Syr Charles dothe lyve.   96

'By Marie, and alle Seinctes ynne Heav'n,
  Thys sunne shall be hys laste,'
Thenne Canynge dropt a brinie teare,
  And from the presence paste.   100

With herte brymm-full of gnawynge grief,
  Hee to Syr Charles dydd goe,
And sat hymm downe uponne a stoole,
  And teares beganne to flowe.   104

'Wee all must die,' quod brave Syr Charles;
  'Whatte bootes ytte howe or whenne;
Dethe ys the sure, the certaine fate
  Of all wee mortall menne.   108

'Saye why, my friende, thie honest soul
  Runns overr att thyne eye;
Is ytte for my most welcome doome
  Thatt thou dost child-lyke crye?'   112

Quod godlie Canynge, 'I doe weepe,
  Thatt thou soe soone must dye,

And leave thy sonnes and helpless wyfe;
    'Tys thys thatt wettes myne eye.'   116

'Thenne drie the tears thatt out thyne eye
    From godlie fountaines sprynge;
Dethe I despise, and alle the power
    Of Edwarde, traytour kynge.   120

'Whan through the tyrant's welcom means
    I shall resigne my lyfe,
The Godde I serve wylle soone provyde
    For bothe mye soones and wyfe.   124

'Before I sawe the lyghtsome sunne,
    Thys was appointed mee;
Shall mortall manne repyne or grudge
    What Godde ordeynes to bee?   128

'Howe oft ynne battaile have I stood
    Whan thousands dy'd arounde;
Whan smokynge streemes of crimson bloode
    Imbrew'd the fatten'd grounde: 132

'Howe dydd I knowe thatt ev'ry darte,
    That cutte the airie waie,
Myghte nott fynde passage toe my harte,
    And close myne eyes for aie?   136

'And shall I nowe, forr feere of dethe,
    Looke wanne and bee dysmayde?
Ne! fromm my herte flie childyshe feere,
    Bee alle the manne display'd.   140

'Ah! goddelyke Henrie! Godde forefende,
    And guarde thee and thye sonne,
Yff 't is hys wylle; but yff 't is nott,
    Why thenne hys wylle bee donne.   144

'My honest friende, my faulte has beene
    To serve Godde and myre prynce;
And thatt I no tyme-server am,
    My dethe wylle soone convynce.   148

'Ynne Londonne citye was I borne,
    Of parents of grete note;
My fadre dydd a nobile armes
    Emblazon onne hys cote: 152

'I make ne doubte butt hee ys gone
    Where soone I hope to goe;
Where wee for ever shall bee blest,
    From oute the reech of woe.   156

Hee taughte mee justice and the laws
    Wyth pitie to unite;
And eke hee taughte mee howe to knowe
    The wronge cause fromm the ryghte: 160

'Hee taughte mee with a prudent hande
    To feede the hungrie poore,
Ne lett mye servants dryve awaie
    The hungrie fromme my doore: 164

'And none can saye butt alle mye lyfe
    I have hys wordyes kept;
And summ'd the actyonns of the daie
    Eche nyght before I slept.   168

'I have a spouse, goe aske of her
    Yff I defyl'd her bedde?
I have a kynge, and none can laie
    Black treason onne my hedde.   172

'Ynne Lent, and onne the holie eve,
    Fromm fleshe I dydd refrayne;
Whie should I thenne appeare dismay'd
    To leave thys worlde of payne?   17:

'Ne, hapless Henrie! I rejoyce,
    I shall ne see thye dethe;
Moste willynglie ynne thye just cause
    Doe I resign my brethe.   18ა

'Oh, fickle people! rewyn'd londe!
    Thou wylt kenne peace ne moe;
Whyle Richard's sonnes exalt themselves.
    Thye brookes wythe bloude wylle flowe.

'Saie, were ye tyr'd of godlie peace,   185
    And godlie Henrie's reigne,
Thatt you dydd choppe your easie daies
    For those of bloude and peyne?   188

'Whatte though I onne a sledde be drawne,
    And mangled by a hynde,
I doe defye the traytor's pow'r,
    Hee can ne harm my mynd;   192

'Whatte though, uphoisted onne a pole,
    Mye lymbes shall rotte ynne ayre,
And ne ryche monument of brasse
    Charles Bawdin's name shall bear;   196

'Yett ynne the holie booke above,
    Whyche tyme can't eate awaie,
There wythe the servants of the Lord
    Mye name shall lyve for aie.   200

'Thenne welcome dethe! for lyfe eterne
    I leave thys mortall lyfe:
Farewell vayne world, and alle that's deare,
    Mye sonnes and lovynge wyfe!   204

'Nowe dethe as welcome to mee comes,
    As e'er the moneth of Maie;

Nor woulde I even wyshe to lyve,
  Wyth my dere wyfe to staie.'   208

Quod Canynge, ''T ys a goodlie thynge
  To bee prepar'd to die;
And from thys world of peyne and grefe
  To Godde ynne heav'n to flie.'   212

And nowe the belle began to tolle,
  And claryonnes to sound;
Syr Charles hee herde the horses feete
  A prauncyng onne the grounde: 216

And just before the officers
  His lovynge wyfe came ynne,
Weepynge unfeigned teeres of woe,
  Wythe loude and dysmalle dynne.   220

'Sweet Florence! nowe I praie forbere,
  Ynn quiet lett mee die;
Praie Godde thatt ev'ry Christian souie
  Maye looke onne dethe as I.   224

'Sweet Florence! why these brinie teers?
  Theye washe my soule awaie,
And almost make mee wyshe for lyfe,
  Wyth thee, sweete dame, to staie.   228

''T ys butt a journie I shalle goe
  Untoe the lande of blysse;
Nowe, as a proofe of husbande's love,
  Receive thys holie kysse.'   232

Thenne Florence, fault'ring ynne her saie,
  Tremblynge these wordyes spoke,
'Ah, cruele Edwarde! bloudie kynge!
  Mye herte ys welle nyghe broke: 236

Ah, sweete Syr Charles! why wylt thou
    goe,
  Wythoute thye lovynge wyfe?
The cruelle axe thatt cuttes thy necke,
  Ytte eke shall ende mye lyfe.'   240

And nowe the officers came ynne
  To brynge Syr Charles awaie,
Whoe turnedd toe hys lovynge wyfe,
  And thus to her dydd saie: 244

'I goe to lyfe, and nott to dethe;
  Truste thou ynne Godde above,
And teache thy sonnes to feare the Lorde,
  And ynne theyre hertes hym love: 248

'Teache them to runne the nobile race
  Thatt I theyre fader runne;
Florence! shou'd dethe thee take — adieu!
  Yee officers leade onne.'   252

Thenne Florence rav'd as anie madde,
  And dydd her tresses tere;
'Oh, staie, mye husbande, lorde, and lyfe!'
  Syr Charles thenne dropt a teare.   256

'T yll tyredd oute wythe ravynge loude,
  Shee fellen onne the flore;
Syr Charles exerted alle hys myghte,
  And march'd fromm oute the dore.   26r,

Uponne a sledde hee mounted thenne,
  Wythe lookes full brave and swete;
Lookes thatt enshone ne more concern
  Thanne anie ynne the strete.   264

Before hym went the council-menne,
  Ynne scarlett robes and golde,
And tassils spanglynge ynne the sunne,
  Muche glorious to beholde: 268

The Freers of Seincte Augustyne next
  Appeared to the syghte,
Alle cladd ynne homelie russett weedes,
  Of godlie monkysh plyghte: 272

Ynne diffraunt partes a godlie psaume
  Moste sweetlie theye dydd chaunt;
Behynde theyre backes syx mynstrelles
    came,
  Who tun'd the strunge bataunt.   276

Thenne fyve-and-twentye archers came;
  Echone the bowe dydd bende,
From rescue of Kynge Henries friends
  Syr Charles forr to defend.   280

Bolde as a lyon came Syr Charles,
  Drawne onne a cloth-layde sledde,
Bye two blacke stedes ynne trappynges
    white,
  Wyth plumes uponne theyre hedde: 284

Behynde hym five-and-twenty moe
  Of archers stronge and stoute,
Wyth bended bowe echone ynne hande,
  Marched ynne goodlie route;   288

Seincte Jameses Freers marched next,
  Echone hys parte dydd chaunt;
Behynde theyre backes syx mynstrelles came,
  Who tun'd the strunge bataunt: 292

Thenne came the maior and eldermenne,
  Ynne clothe of scarlett deck't;
And theyre attendynge menne echone,
  Lyke easterne princes trickt: 296

And after them, a multitude
  Of citizens dydd thronge;

The wyndowes were alle fulle of heddes,
   As hee dydd passe alonge.   300

And whenne hee came to the hyghe crosse,
   Syr Charles dydd turne and saie,
'O, thou, thatt savest manne fromme synne,
   Washe mye soule clean thys daie!'   304

Att the grete mynster wyndowe sat
   The kynge ynne mycle state,
To see Charles Bawdin goe alonge
   To hys most welcom fate.   308

Soone as the sledde drewe nyghe enowe,
   Thatt Edwarde hee myghte heare,
The brave Syr Charles hee dydd stande
     uppe,
   And thus hys wordes declare: 312

Thou seest me, Edwarde! traytour vile!
   Expos'd to infamie;
Butt bee assur'd disloyall manne!
   I 'm greaterr nowe thanne thee.   316

'Bye foule proceedyngs, murdre, bloude,
   Thou wearest nowe a crowne;
And hast appoynted mee to die,
   By power nott thyne owne.   320

'Thou thynkest I shall die to-daie;
   I have beene dede 'till nowe,
And soone shall lyve to weare a crowne
   For aie uponne my browe: 324

'Whylst thou, perhapps, for som few
     yeares,
   Shalt rule thys fickle lande,
To lett them knowe howe wyde the rule
   'Twixt kynge and tyrant hande: 328

'Thye pow'r unjust, thou traytour slave!
   Shall falle onne thye owne hedde'—
Fromm out of hearyng of the kynge
   Departed thenne the sledde.   332

Kynge Edwarde's soule rush'd to hys face,
   Hee turn'd hys hedde awaie,
And to hys broder Gloucester
   Hee thus dydd speke and saie: 336

'To hym that soe much dreaded dethe
   Ne ghastlie terrors brynge,
Beholde the manne! hee spake the truthe,
   Hee 's greater thanne a kynge!'   340

'Soe let hym die!' Duke Richarde sayde;
   'And maye echone oure foes
Bende downe theyre neckes to bloudie axe
   And feede the carryon crowes.'   344

And nowe the horses gentlie drewe
   Syr Charles uppe the hyghe hylle;
The axe dydd glysterr ynne the sunne,
   His pretious bloude to spylle.   348

Syr Charles dydd uppe the scaffold goe,
   As uppe a gilded carre
Of victory, bye val'rous chiefs
   Gayn'd ynne the bloudie warre: 352

And to the people hee dyd saie,
   'Beholde you see mee dye,
For servynge loyally mye kynge,
   Mye kynge most ryghtfullie.   356

'As longe as Edwarde rules thys land,
   Ne quiet you wylle knowe:
Your sonnes and husbandes shalle bee
     slayne
   And brookes wythe bloude shall flowe. 360

'You leave youre goode and lawfulle kynge,
   Whenne ynne adversitye;
Lyke mee, untoe the true cause stycke,
   And for the true cause dye.'   364

Thenne, hee, wyth preestes, uponne hys
     knees,
   A prayer to Godde dyd make,
Beseechynge hym unto hymselfe
   Hys partynge soule to take.   368

Thenne, kneelynge downe, hee layd hys
     hedde
   Most seemlie onne the blocke;
Whyche fromme hys bodie fayre at once
   The able heddes-manne stroke: 372

And oute the bloude beganne to flowe,
   And rounde the scaffolde twyne;
And teares, enow to washe 't awaie,
   Dydd flowe fromme each mann's eyne. 376

The bloudie axe hys bodie fayre
   Ynnto foure parties cutte;
And ev'rye parte, and eke hys hedde,
   Uponne a pole was putte.   380

One parte dydd rotte onne Kynwulph-hylle
   One onne the mynster-tower,
And one from off the castle-gate
   The crowen dydd devoure;   384

The other onne Seyncte Powle's goode gate
   A dreery spectacle;
Hys hedde was plac'd onne the hyghe crosse,
   Ynne hyghe-streete most nobile.   388

Thus was the ende of Bawdin's fate:
Godde prosper longe oure kynge,
And grante hee maye, wyth Bawdin's soule,
Ynne heav'n Godd's mercie synge!   392
(1772)

FROM ÆLLA: A TRAGYCAL ENTER-LUDE

MYNSTRELLES SONGE

O! synge untoe mie roundelaie,
O! droppe the brynie teare wythe mee,
Daunce ne moe atte hallie daie,
Lycke a reynynge[1] ryver bee;
  Mie love ys dedde,   5
  Gon to hys death-bedde,
  Al under the wyllowe tree.

Blacke hys cryne[2] as the wyntere nyghte,
Whyte hys rode[3] as the sommer snowe,
Rodde hys face as the morynynge lyghte,
Cale he lyes ynne the grave belowe;   11
  Mie love ys dedde,
  Gon to hys death-bedde,
  Al under the wyllowe tree.

Swote hys tyngue as the throstles note,
Quycke ynn daunce as thoughte canne bee,
Defte hys taboure, codgelle stote,   17
O! hee lyes bie the wyllowe tree:
  Mie love ys dedde,
  Gonne to hys death-bedde,   20
  Alle under the wyllowe tree.

Harke! the ravenne flappes hys wynge,
In the briered delle belowe;
Harke! the dethe-owle loude dothe syngg,
To the nyghte-mares as heie goe;   25

1. Running.   2. Hair.   3. Complexion.

Mie love ys dedde,
Gonne to hys death-bedde,
Al under the wyllowe tree.

See! the whyte moone sheenes onne hie;
Whyterre ys mie true loves shroude;   30
Whyterre yanne the mornynge skie,
Whyterre yanne the evenynge cloude;
  Mie love ys dedde,
  Gon to hys death-bedde,
  Al under the wyllowe tree.   35

Heere, uponne mie true loves grave,
Schalle the baren fleurs be layde,
Nee one hallie Seyncte to save
Al the celness of a mayde.
  Mie love ys dedde,   40
  Gonne to hys death-bedde,
  Alie under the wyllowe tree.

Wythe mie hondes I'lle dente the brieres
Rounde his hallie corse to gre,
Ouphante fairie lyghte youre fyres,   45
Heere mie boddie stylle schalle bee.
  Mie love ys dedde,
  Gon to hys death-bedde,
  Al under the wyllowe tree.

Comme, wythe acorne-coppe & thorne,
Drayne mie hartys blodde awaie;   51
Lyfe & all yttes goode I scorne,
Daunce bie nete, or feaste by daie.
  Mie love ys dedde,
  Gon to hys death-bedde,   55
  Al under the wyllowe tree.

Waterre wytches, crownede wythe reytes,[4]
Bere mee to yer leathalle tyde.
I die; I comme; mie true love waytes.
Thos the damselle spake, and dyed.   60
(1777)

4. Water-flags.

THOMAS GRAY (1716–1771)

The life of Gray was singularly devoid of external incident. The records of a few personal ties, a little travel, and a few scattering and reluctant publications, alone give liveliness to the ' noiseless tenor ' of his sequestered studies. At Eton he was noted for ' great delicacy and sometimes a too fastidious behavior,' but found sympathetic companions in Horace Walpole and Richard West. In 1734 he entered Pembroke Hall, Cambridge, and soon became a pensioner at Peterhouse. He devoted himself to classical literature, history, and modern languages, taking no degree on account of his dislike to mathematics. In 1739, on Walpole's invitation, Gray accompanied him to the continent and with great pleasure and profit, spent two years in Italy and France. Many of his Latin poems were written abroad and soon after his return he made his first trials in English verse. The death of his friend West, in 1742, deeply affected him and called forth the first sonnet of importance since those of Milton. About the same time, he began ' the far-famed *Elegy*,' while visiting his mother at Stoke, near Windsor. None of his poems were published until several years afterward. He now settled again at Peterhouse and when fifteen years later, he removed to Pembroke Hall, he referred to the incident as ' a sort of era in a life so barren of events as mine.' He graduated as LL.B. in 1744, but never entered the law. He made voluminous notes and collections for a History of English Poetry which was never written. Toward the end of his life he was appointed Professor of Modern History at Cambridge, but gave no lectures. A dozen poems in English, none long, were all that he published during his lifetime, and the two dozen fragments and fugitive pieces since collected add little to his fame.

By 1757 his reputation was such that he was offered, on the death of Colley Cibber, the poet laureateship; but he declined to be ' rat catcher to his Majesty.' Doctor Johnson, who is grudging in his estimate of Gray's genius, quotes without disparagement a statement that ' Perhaps he was the most learned man in Europe.' Gray was a precursor of the great romanticists in his taste for picturesque landscape, and he kept pace with the antiquarian movements of his time which were preparing the romantic revival. His *Letters*, which are among the best in the language, reveal the variety and enthusiasm of his interests. They also reveal a shrinking and fastidious taste dashed with piquant, half-cynical humor and not a little scholastic intolerance, and they help us to understand how the man who could write so tender and exquisite a poem as the *Elegy in a Country Churchyard* should have written so little else.

SONNET ON THE DEATH OF MR. RICHARD WEST

In vain to me the smiling mornings shine,
  And reddening Phœbus lifts his golden fire:
The birds in vain their amorous descant join;
  Or cheerful fields resume their green attire:
These ears, alas! for other notes repine; 5
  A different object do these eyes require:
My lonely anguish melts no heart but mine;
  And in my breast the imperfect joys expire.
Yet morning smiles the busy race to cheer,
  And new-born pleasure brings to happier men: 10
The fields to all their wonted tribute bear;
  To warm their little loves the birds complain:
I fruitless mourn to him that cannot hear,
  And weep the more, because I weep in vain.

(1774)

AN ODE

ON A DISTANT PROSPECT OF ETON COLLEGE

Ye distant spires, ye antique towers,
  That crown the watery glade,
Where grateful Science still adores
  Her Henry's holy Shade;

And ye, that from the stately brow   5
Of Windsor's heights the expanse below
Of grove, of lawn, of mead survey,
Whose turf, whose shade, whose flowers
    among
Wanders the hoary Thames along
  His silver-winding way.   10

Ah, happy hills, ah, pleasing shade,
  Ah, fields beloved in vain,
Where once my careless childhood strayed,
  A stranger yet to pain!
I feel the gales, that from ye blow,   15
A momentary bliss bestow,
  As waving fresh their gladsome wing,
My weary soul they seem to sooth,
And, redolent of joy and youth,
  To breathe a second spring.   20

Say, Father Thames, for thou hast seen
  Full many a sprightly race
Disporting on thy margent green
  The paths of pleasure trace,
Who foremost now delight to cleave   25
With pliant arm thy glassy wave?
  The captive linnet which enthrall?
What idle progeny succeed
To chase the rolling circle's speed,
  Or urge the flying ball?   30

While some on earnest business bent
  Their murmuring labors ply
'Gainst graver hours, that bring constraint
  To sweeten liberty:
Some bold adventurers disdain   35
The limits of their little reign,
  And unknown regions dare descry:
Still as they run they look behind,
They hear a voice in every wind,
  And snatch a fearful joy.   40

Gay hope is theirs by fancy fed,
  Less pleasing when possest;
The tear forgot as soon as shed,
  The sunshine of the breast:
Theirs buxom health of rosy hue,   45
Wild wit, invention ever-new,
  And lively cheer of vigor born;
The thoughtless day, the easy night,
The spirits pure, the slumbers light,
  That fly the approach of morn.   50

Alas, regardless of their doom,
  The little victims play!
No sense have they of ills to come,
  Nor care beyond to-day:
Yet see how all around 'em wait   55
The Ministers of human fate,
  And black Misfortune's baleful train!

Ah, shew them where in ambush stand
To seize their prey the murth'rous band!
  Ah, tell them, they are men!   60

These shall the fury Passions tear,
  The vultures of the mind,
Disdainful Anger, pallid Fear,
  And Shame that skulks behind;
Or pining Love shall waste their youth,   65
Or Jealousy with rankling tooth,
  That inly gnaws the secret heart,
And Envy wan, and faded Care,
Grim-visaged comfortless Despair,
  And Sorrow's piercing dart.   70

Ambition this shall tempt to rise.
  Then whirl the wretch from high,
To bitter Scorn a sacrifice,
  And grinning Infamy.
The stings of Falsehood those shall try,   75
And hard Unkindness, altered eye,
  That mocks the tear it forced to flow;
And keen Remorse with blood defiled,
And moody Madness laughing wild
  Amid severest woe.   80

Lo, in the vale of years beneath
  A griesly troop are seen,
The painful family of Death,
  More hideous than their Queen:
This racks the joints, this fires the veins, 85
That every laboring sinew strains,
  Those in the deeper vitals rage:
Lo, Poverty, to fill the band,
That numbs the soul with icy hand,
  And slow-consuming Age.   90

To each his sufferings: all are men,
  Condemned alike to groan,
The tender for another's pain;
  The unfeeling for his own.
Yet ah! why should they know their fate?   95
Since sorrow never comes too late,
  And happiness too swiftly flies.
Thought would destroy their paradise.
No more; where ignorance is bliss,
  'T is folly to be wise.   100

                   (1747)

HYMN TO ADVERSITY

Daughter of Jove, relentless power,
  Thou tamer of the human breast,
Whose iron scourge and torturing hour
  The bad affright, afflict the best!
Bound in thy adamantine chain,   5
The proud are taught to taste of pain,
And purple tyrants vainly groan

[handwritten: writing classic, leaning to romantic]

With pangs unfelt before, unpitied and
   alone.

When first thy sire to send on earth
   Virtue, his darling child, designed,   10
To thee he gave the heavenly birth,
   And bade to form her infant mind.
Stern rugged nurse! thy rigid lore
With patience many a year she bore:
What sorrow was, thou bad'st her
   know,
And from her own she learned to melt at
   others' woe.   16

Scared at thy frown terrific, fly
   Self-pleasing Folly's idle brood,
Wild Laughter, Noise, and thoughtless
   Joy,
   And leave us leisure to be good.   20
Light they disperse, and with them go
The summer friend, the flattering foe;
By vain Prosperity received,
To her they vow their truth, and are again
   believed.

Wisdom in sable garb arrayed,   25
   Immersed in rapturous thought pro-
   found,
And Melancholy, silent maid,
   With leaden eye that loves the ground,
Still on thy solemn steps attend:
Warm Charity, the general friend,   30
With Justice, to herself severe,
And Pity, dropping soft the sadly-pleasing
   tear.

Oh! gently on thy suppliant's head,
   Dread goddess, lay thy chastening
   hand!
Not in thy Gorgon terrors clad,   35
   Not circled with the vengeful band
(As by the impious thou art seen)
With thundering voice, and threatening
   mien,
With screaming Horror's funeral cry,
Despair, and fell Disease, and ghastly Pov-
   erty: 40

Thy form benign, oh goddess, wear,
   Thy milder influence impart,
Thy philosophic train be there
   To soften, not to wound, my heart.
The generous spark extinct revive   45
Teach me to love, and to forgive,
Exact my own defects to scan,
What others are to feel, and know myself a
   Man.

             (1753)

ELEGY

WRITTEN IN A COUNTRY CHURCH-YARD

The Curfew tolls the knell of parting day
   The lowing herd wind slowly o'er the lea,
The plowman homeward plods his weary way,
   And leaves the world to darkness and to
   me.

Now fades the glimmering landscape on the
   sight,   5
   And all the air a solemn stillness holds,
Save where the beetle wheels his droning
   flight,
   And drowsy tinklings lull the distant
   folds;

Save that from yonder ivy-mantled tower
   The moping owl does to the moon com-
   plain   10
Of such, as wandering near her secret
   bower,
   Molest her ancient solitary reign.

Beneath those rugged elms, that yew-tree's
   shade,
   Where heaves the turf in many a moulder-
   ing heap,
Each in his narrow cell for ever laid,   15
   The rude Forefathers of the hamlet sleep.

The breezy call of incense-breathing Morn,
   The swallow twittering from the straw-
   built shed,
The cock's shrill clarion, or the echoing
   horn,
   No more shall rouse them from their
   lowly bed.   20

For them no more the blazing hearth shall
   burn,
   Or busy housewife ply her evening care:
No children run to lisp their sire's return,
   Or climb his knees the envied kiss to
   share.

Oft did the harvest to their sickle yield,   25
   Their furrow oft the stubborn glebe has
   broke;
How jocund did they drive their team afield!
   How bowed the woods beneath their
   sturdy stroke!

Let not Ambition mock their useful toil,
   Their homely joys, and destiny obscure: 30
Nor Grandeur hear with a disdainful smile
   The short and simple annals of the poor

[handwritten: utterance 18th cent]
[handwritten: Feeling ? romantic]
[handwritten: Setting]

The boast of heraldry, the pomp of power,
And all that beauty, all that wealth e'er
  gave,
Awaits alike the inevitable hour.   35
The paths of glory lead but to the grave.

Nor you, ye Proud, impute to These the
  fault,
If Memory o'er their Tomb no Trophies
  raise,
Where through the long-drawn aisle and
  fretted vault
The pealing anthem swells the note of
  praise.   40

Can storied urn or animated bust
Back to its mansion call the fleeting
  breath?
Can Honor's voice provoke the silent dust,
Or Flattery sooth the dull cold ear of
  Death?

Perhaps in this neglected spot is laid   45
Some heart once pregnant with celestial
  fire;
Hands, that the rod of empire might have
  swayed,
Or waked to ecstasy the living lyre.

But Knowledge to their eyes her ample
  page
Rich with the spoils of time did ne'er un-
  roll;   50
Chill Penury repressed their noble rage,
And froze the genial current of the soul.

Full many a gem of purest ray serene,
The dark unfathomed caves of ocean
  bear:
Full many a flower is born to blush un-
  seen,   55
And waste its sweetness on the desert air.

Some village-Hampden, that with dauntless
  breast
The little Tyrant of his fields withstood;
Some mute inglorious Milton here may rest,
Some Cromwell guiltless of his country's
  blood.   60

The applause of listening senates to com-
  mand,
The threats of pain and ruin to despise,
To scatter plenty o'er a smiling land,
And read their history in a nation's eyes,

Their lot forbade: nor circumscribed alone
Their growing virtues, but their crimes
  confin'd: 66

Forbade to wade through slaughter to a
  throne,
And shut the gates of mercy on mankind,

The struggling pangs of conscious truth to
  hide,
To quench the blushes of ingenuous
  shame,
Or heap the shrine of Luxury and Pride   71
With incense kindled at the Muse's flame.

Far from the madding crowd's ignoble
  strife,
Their sober wishes never learned to stray;
Along the cool sequestered vale of life   75
They kept the noiseless tenor of their
  way.

Yet even these bones from insult to pro-
  tect,
Some frail memorial still erected nigh,
With uncouth rhymes and shapeless sculp-
  ture decked,
Implores the passing tribute of a sigh.   80

Their name, their years, spelt by the un-
  lettered muse,
The place of fame and elegy supply:
And many a holy text around she strews,
That teach the rustic moralist to die.

For who to dumb Forgetfulness a prey,   85
This pleasing anxious being e'er resigned,
Left the warm precincts of the cheerful
  day,
Nor cast one longing lingering look be-
  hind?

On some fond breast the parting soul re-
  lies,
Some pious drops the closing eye requires;
Ev'n from the tomb the voice of Nature
  cries,   91
Ev'n in our Ashes live their wonted Fires.

For thee, who mindful of the unhonoured
  Dead
Dost in these lines their artless tale relate;
If chance, by lonely contemplation led,   95
Some kindred Spirit shall inquire thy fate,

Haply some hoary-headed Swain may say,
'Oft have we seen him at the peep of
  dawn
Brushing with hasty steps the dews away
To meet the sun upon the upland lawn.

Drop of classic
More romanticism

'There at the foot of yonder nodding beech   101
  That wreathes its old fantastic roots so high,
His listless length at noontide would he stretch,
  And pore upon the brook that babbles by.

'Hard by yon wood, now smiling as in scorn,   105
  Muttering his wayward fancies he would rove,
Now drooping, woeful wan, like one forlorn,
  Or crazed with care, or crossed in hopeless love.

'One morn I missed him on the customed hill,
  Along the heath and near his favorite tree;   110
Another came; nor yet beside the rill,
  Nor up the lawn, nor at the wood was he;

'The next with dirges due in sad array
  Slow through the church-way path we saw him borne.
Approach and read (for thou can'st read) the lay,   115
  Graved on the stone beneath yon agèd thorn.'

THE EPITAPH

Here rests his head upon the lap of Earth
  A Youth to Fortune and to Fame unknown.
Fair Science frowned not on his humble birth,
  And Melancholy marked him for her own.

Large was his bounty, and his soul sincere,   121
  Heav'n did a recompense as largely send:
He gave to Misery all he had, a tear,
  He gained from Heaven ('twas all he wished) a friend.

No farther seek his merits to disclose,   125
  Or draw his frailties from their dread abode
(There they alike in trembling hope repose),
  The bosom of his Father and his God.
                                        (1751)

THE PROGRESS OF POESY
A PINDARIC ODE

I
The Strophe

Awake, Æolian lyre, awake,
And give to rapture all thy trembling strings
From Helicon's harmonious springs
A thousand rills their mazy progress take:
The laughing flowers, that round them blow,
Drink life and fragrance as they flow.   6
Now the rich stream of music winds along
Deep, majestic, smooth, and strong,
Through verdant vales, and Ceres' golden reign:
Now rolling down the steep amain,   10
Headlong, impetuous, see it pour:
The rocks, and nodding groves rebellow to the roar.

The Antistrophe

Oh! Sovereign of the willing soul,
Parent of sweet and solemn-breathing airs,
Enchanting shell! the sullen Cares,   15
And frantic Passions hear thy soft control.
On Thracia's hills the Lord of War,
Has curbed the fury of his car,
And dropped his thirsty lance at thy command.
Perching on the sceptered hand   20
Of Jove, thy magic lulls the feathered king
With ruffled plumes, and flagging wing:
Quenched in dark clouds of slumber lie
The terror of his beak, and lightnings of his eye.

The Epode

Thee the voice, the dance, obey,   25
Tempered to thy warbled lay.
O'er Idalia's velvet-green
The rosy-crownèd Loves are seen
On Cytherea's day
With antic Sports, and blue-eyed Pleasures,
Frisking light in frolic measures;   31
Now pursuing, now retreating,
Now in circling troops they meet:
To brisk notes in cadence beating
Glance their many-twinkling feet.   35
Slow melting strains their Queen's approach declare:
Where'er she turns the Graces homage pay
With arms sublime, that float upon the air,
In gliding state she wins her easy way:
O'er her warm cheek, and rising bosom, move   40
The bloom of young Desire, and purple light of Love

II

The Strophe

Man's feeble race what Ills await,
Labor, and Penury, the racks of Pain,
Disease, and Sorrow's weeping train,
And Death, sad refuge from the storms of
    Fate!   45
The fond complaint, my Song, disprove,
And justify the laws of Jove.
Say, has he given in vain the heavenly
    Muse?
Night, and all her sickly dews,
Her Specters wan, and Birds of boding cry,
He gives to range the dreary sky;   51
Till down the eastern cliffs afar
Hyperion's march they spy, and glittering
    shafts of war.

The Antistrophe

In climes beyond the solar road,
Where shaggy forms o'er ice-built moun-
    tains roam,
The Muse has broke the twilight-gloom   56
To cheer the shivering Native's dull abode.
And oft, beneath the odorous shade
Of Chili's boundless forests laid,
She deigns to hear the savage Youth re-
    peat   60
In loose numbers wildly sweet
Their feather-cinctured Chiefs, and dusky
    Loves.
Her track, where'er the Goddess roves,
Glory pursue, and generous Shame,
The unconquerable Mind, and Freedom's
    holy flame.   65

The Epode

Woods, that wave o'er Delphi's steep,
Isles, that crown the Ægean deep,
Fields, that cool Ilissus laves,
Or where Mæander's amber waves
In lingering Labyrinths creep,   70
How do your tuneful Echo's languish,
Mute, but to the voice of Anguish?
Where each old poetic Mountain
Inspiration breathed around:
Every shade and hallowed Fountain   75
Murmured deep a solemn sound:
Till the sad Nine in Greece's evil hour
Left their Parnassus for the Latian plains.
Alike they scorn the pomp of tyrant-Power,
And coward Vice, that revels in her chains.
When Latium had her lofty spirit lost, 81
They sought, O Albion! next thy sea-en-
    circled coast.

III

The Strophe

Far from the sun and summer-gale,
In thy green lap was Nature's Darling laid,
What time, where lucid Avon strayed,   85
To Him the mighty Mother did unveil
Her awful face: The dauntless Child
Stretched forth his little arms, and smiled
This pencil take (she said) whose colors
    clear
Richly paint the vernal year: 90
Thine too these golden keys, immortal Boy!
This can unlock the gates of Joy;
Of Horror that, and thrilling Fears,
Or ope the sacred source of sympathetic
    Tears.

The Antistrophe

Nor second He, that rode sublime   95
Upon the seraph-wings of Ecstasy,
The secrets of the Abyss to spy.
He passed the flaming bounds of Place and
    Time:
The living Throne, the sapphire-blaze,
Where Angels tremble, while they gaze, 100
He saw; but blasted with excess of light,
Closed his eyes in endless night.
Behold, where Dryden's less presumptuous
    car,
Wide o'er the fields of Glory bear
Two Coursers of ethereal race,   105
With necks in thunder clothed, and long-
    resounding pace.

The Epode

Hark, his hands the lyre explore!
Bright-eyed Fancy hovering o'er
Scatters from her pictured urn
Thoughts that breathe, and words that burn.
But ah! 't is heard no more——   111
O Lyre divine, what daring Spirit
Wakes thee now? though he inherit
Nor the pride, nor ample pinion,
That the Theban Eagle bear   115
Sailing with supreme dominion
Through the azure deep of air:
Yet oft before his infant eyes would run
Such forms, as glitter in the Muse's ray
With orient hues, unborrowed of the Sun:
Yet shall he mount, and keep his distant
    way   121
Beyond the limits of a vulgar fate,
Beneath the Good how far — but far above
    the Great.

(1757)

THE BARD

A PINDARIC ODE

I

The Strophe

'Ruin seize thee, ruthless King!
Confusion on thy banners wait,
Though fanned by Conquest's crimson wing
They mock the air with idle state.
Helm, nor Hauberk's twisted mail,   5
Nor even thy virtues, Tyrant, shall avail
To save thy secret soul from nightly fears,
From Cambria's curse, from Cambria's
  tears!'
  Such were the sounds, that o'er the crested
  pride
Of the first Edward scattered wild dismay,
As down the steep of Snowdon's shaggy
  side   11
He wound with toilsome march his long
  array.
Stout Gloster stood aghast in speechless
  trance;
To arms! cried Mortimer, and couched his
  quivering lance.

The Antistrophe

On a rock, whose haughty brow   15
Frowns o'er old Conway's foaming flood,
Robed in the sable garb of woe,
With haggard eyes the Poet stood
(Loose his beard, and hoary hair
Streamed, like a meteor, to the troubled
  air),   20
And with a Master's hand, and Prophet's
  fire,
Struck the deep sorrows of his lyre:
'Hark, how each giant-oak, and desert
  cave,
Sighs to the torrent's awful voice beneath!
O'er thee, O King! their hundred arms they
  wave,   25
Revenge on thee in hoarser murmurs
  breathe;
Vocal no more, since Cambria's fatal day,
To high-born Hoel's harp, or soft Llew-
  ellyn's lay.

The Epode

'Cold is Cadwallo's tongue,
That hushed the stormy main;   30
Brave Urien sleeps upon his craggy bed:
Mountains, ye mourn in vain
Modred, whose magic song
Made huge Plinlimmon bow his cloud-
  topped head.
On dreary Arvon's shore they lie,   35

Smeared with gore, and ghastly pale:
Far, far aloof the affrighted ravens sail;
The famished Eagle screams, and passes by.
Dear lost companions of my tuneful art,
Dear, as the light that visits these sad eyes,
Dear, as the ruddy drops that warm my
  heart,   41
Ye died amidst your dying country's
  cries —
No more I weep. They do not sleep.
On yonder cliffs, a grisly band,
I see them sit, they linger yet,   45
Avengers of their native land:
With me in dreadful harmony they join,
And weave with bloody hands the tissue of
  thy line: —

II

The Strophe

'Weave the warp, and weave the woof,
The winding sheet of Edward's race.   50
Give ample room, and verge enough
The characters of hell to trace.
Mark the year, and mark the night,
When Severn shall re-echo with affright
The shrieks of death, through Berkley's
  roofs that ring,   55
Shrieks of an agonizing King!
She-Wolf of France, with unrelenting fangs,
That tear'st the bowels of thy mangled
  Mate,
From thee be born, who o'er thy country
  hangs
The scourge of Heav'n. What Terrors
  round him wait!   60
Amazement in his van, with Flight com-
  bined,
And Sorrow's faded form, and Solitude be-
  hind.

The Antistrophe

'Mighty Victor, mighty Lord,
Low on his funeral couch he lies!
No pitying heart, no eye, afford   65
A tear to grace his obsequies.
Is the sable Warrior fled?
Thy son is gone. He rests among the
  Dead.
The Swarm, that in thy noon-tide beam were
  born?
Gone to salute the rising Morn.   70
Fair laughs the Morn, and soft the Zephyr
  blows,
While proudly riding o'er the azure realm
In gallant trim the gilded Vessel goes;
Youth on the prow, and Pleasure at the
  helm;

Regardless of the sweeping Whirlwind's
    sway, 75
That, hushed in grim repose, expects his
    evening-prey.

The Epode

Fill high the sparkling bowl,
The rich repast prepare;
Reft of a crown, he yet may share the
    feast.
Close by the regal chair 80
Fell Thirst and Famine scowl
A baleful smile upon their baffled Guest.
    Heard ye the din of battle bray,
Lance to lance, and horse to horse?
Long Years of havoc urge their destined
    course, 85
And through the kindred squadrons mow
    their way.
Ye Towers of Julius, London's lasting
    shame,
With many a foul and midnight murther
    fed,
Revere his Consort's faith, his Father's
    fame,
And spare the meek Usurper's holy head. 90
Above, below, the rose of snow,
Twined with her blushing foe, we spread:
The bristled Boar in infant-gore
Wallows beneath the thorny shade.
Now, brothers, bending o'er the accursed
    loom 95
Stamp we our vengeance deep, and ratify
    his doom.

III

The Strophe

'Edward, lo! to sudden fate
(Weave we the woof. The thread is spun)
Half of thy heart we consecrate.
(The web is wove. The work is done.)'—
    Stay, oh stay! nor thus forlorn 101
Leave me unblessed, unpitied, here to mourn!
In yon bright track, that fires the western
    skies,
They melt, they vanish from my eyes.
    But oh! what solemn scenes on Snow-
      don's height 105
Descending slow their glittering skirts un-
    roll?
Visions of glory, spare my aching sight,
Ye unborn Ages, crowd not on my soul!
No more our long-lost Arthur we bewail.
All-hail, ye genuine Kings, Britannia's Issue,
    hail! 110

The Antistrophe

'Girt with many a baron bold
Sublime their starry fronts they rear;
And gorgeous Dames, and Statesmen old
In bearded majesty, appear.
In the midst a Form divine! 115
Her eye proclaims her of the Briton-Line;
Her lion-port, her awe-commanding face,
Attempered sweet to virgin-grace.
What strings symphonious tremble in the
    air,
What strains of vocal transport round her
    play! 120
Hear from the grave, great Taliessin, hear;
They breathe a soul to animate thy clay.
Bright Rapture calls, and soaring, as she
    sings,
Waves in the eye of Heaven her many-col-
    ored wings.

The Epode

'The verse adorn again 125
Fierce War, and faithful Love,
And Truth severe, by fairy Fiction drest.
In buskined measures move
Pale Grief, and pleasing Pain,
With Horror, Tyrant of the throbbing
    breast. 130
A Voice, as of the Cherub-Choir,
Gales from blooming Eden bear;
And distant warblings lessen on my ear,
That lost in long futurity expire.
    Fond impious Man, think'st thou, yon san-
      guine cloud, 135
Raised by thy breath, has quenched the Orb
    of day?
To-morrow he repairs the golden flood,
And warms the nations with redoubled ray.
    Enough for me: With joy I see
The different doom our Fates assign. 140
Be thine Despair, and sceptered Care,
To triumph, and to die, are mine.'—
    He spoke, and headlong from the moun-
      tain's height
Deep in the roaring tide he plunged to end-
    less night.

(1757)

THE FATAL SISTERS

AN ODE

FROM THE NORSE TONGUE

Now the storm begins to lower,
(Haste, the loom of hell prepare,)
Iron-sleet of arrowy shower
Hurtles in the darkened air.

Glittering lances are the loom,   5
Where the dusky warp we strain,
Weaving many a soldier's doom,
Orkney's woe, and Randver's bane.

See the grisly texture grow,
('T is of human entrails made,)   10
And the weights, that play below,
Each a gasping warrior's head.

Shafts for shuttles, dipt in gore,
Shoot the trembling cords along.
Sword, that once a monarch bore,   15
Keep the tissue close and strong.

Mista black, terrific maid,
Sangrida, and Hilda see,
Join the wayward work to aid:
'T is the woof of victory.   20

Ere the ruddy sun be set.
Pikes must shiver, javelins sing,
Blade with clattering buckler meet,
Hauberk crash, and helmet ring.

(Weave the crimson web of war)   25
Let us go, and let us fly,
Where our friends the conflict share,
Where they triumph, where they die.

As the paths of fate we tread,
Wading through the ensanguined field: 30
Gondula, and Geira, spread
O'er the youthful king your shield.

We the reins to slaughter give,
Ours to kill, and ours to spare:

Spite of danger he shall live.   35
(Weave the crimson web of war.)

They, whom once the desert-beach
Pent within its bleak domain,
Soon their ample sway shall stretch
O'er the plenty of the plain.   40

Low the dauntless earl is laid,
Gored with many a gaping wound:
Fate demands a nobler head;
Soon a king shall bite the ground.

Long his loss shall Eirin weep,   45
Ne'er again his likeness see;
Long her strains in sorrow steep,
Strains of immortality!

Horror covers all the heath,
Clouds of carnage blot the sun.   50
Sisters, weave the web of death;
Sisters, cease, the work is done.

Hail the task, and hail the hands!
Songs of joy and triumph sing!
Joy to the victorious bands;   55
Triumph to the younger king.

Mortal, thou that hear'st the tale,
Learn the tenor of our song.
Scotland, through each winding vale
Far and wide the notes prolong.   60

Sisters, hence with spurs of speed:
Each her thundering falchion wield;
Each bestride her sable steed.
Hurry, hurry to the field.

(1768)

SAMUEL JOHNSON (1709–84)

Few personalities of famous men are so well-known to us as the personality of 'that great Cham of literature, Samuel Johnson.' The son of a poor Lichfield book-seller, Johnson had the advantages of the local grammar-school and a few poverty-stricken months at Pembroke College, Oxford; served for a time as usher in a boy's school; married for true love's sake, a woman much his senior; and set up a private academy near his native city. This enterprise proving neither agreeable nor profitable, in his twenty-eighth year, with little in his uncouth person, his ponderous genius, or in' the sturdy independence of his character, to recommend him to the rich and fortunate, Johnson had the hardihood to seek a living among the penurious publishers and starving hack writers of London. For nearly a quarter of a century, he earned a precarious subsistence by huge 'odd jobs' of literature which now have little interest except as a part of his biography. The greatest of these, his *Dictionary of the English Language*, was published in 1755, after seven years of continuous labor. During a part of this time he had supported himself by writing *The Rambler* (1750–52), and, in ensuing years, *The Idler* (1759–60) and *Rasselas* (1759) helped to defray expenses while he was preparing his edition of Shakspere (1765). He was now famous. A pension of three hundred pounds, granted by government in 1762, had relieved him from the pressure of necessity. Thereafter he wrote but little, and his social talents expanded. In 1764, he joined with Sir Joshua Reynolds in founding the renowned Literary Club which had the good fortune to gather to its convivial meetings such men as Burke, Goldsmith, Gibbon, Garrick, Adam Smith, the two Wartons, Bishop Percy of ballad fame, and many others whose names are still remembered. The previous year, Boswell had made his acquaintance and had begun to gather materials for the record of those 'nights and suppers of the gods' with which we are regaled in his *Life*. If we may trust Boswell's vivid and, apparently, accurate account, Johnson inspired in his comrades not only unusual affection, but a degree of respect which approximated reverence. His conversation was witty, powerful, and varied and gives us a higher idea of his genius than anything which he wrote. His eccentricities both of behavior and of opinion were extraordinary; but the prevailing impression left by Boswell's picture of his mind is one of massive common-sense, united with great depth and benignity of soul.

Johnson's most important contribution to literature is his *Lives of the Poets*, which he undertook toward the end of his life (1779–81), when his powers were in their fullness and after years of polite conversation had favorably affected his style. They are the outpouring of a capacious mind stored by a lifetime of reading, experience, and reflection. His judgments are often marred by his peculiar crochets of opinion or temper; but his sayings are almost always invigorating, for they are the abrupt utterances of an honest and strong man who knew much of the world and of letters.

THE LIFE OF ADDISON

Joseph Addison was born on the 1st of May, 1672, at Milston, of which his father, Lancelot Addison, was then rector, near Ambrosebury, in Wiltshire, and, appearing weak and unlikely to live, he was christened the same day. After the usual domestic education, which from the character of the father may be reasonably supposed to have given him strong impressions of piety, he was committed to the care of Mr. Naish at Ambrosebury, and afterwards of Mr. Taylor at Salisbury.

Not to name the school or the masters of men illustrious for literature, is a kind of historical fraud, by which honest fame is injuriously diminished: I would 5 therefore trace him through the whole process of his education. In 1683, in the beginning of his twelfth year, his father, being made Dean of Lichfield, naturally carried his family to his new residence, 10 and, I believe, placed him for some time, probably not long, under Mr. Shaw, then master of the school at Lichfield, father of the late Dr. Peter Shaw. Of this interval his biographers have given no account, 15 and I know it only from a story of a 'barring-out,' told me, when I was a boy, by Andrew Corbet, of Shropshire, who had heard it from Mr. Pigot, his uncle.

The practice of 'barring-out' was a savage license, practiced in many schools to the end of the last century, by which the boys, when the periodical vacation drew near, growing petulant at the approach of liberty, some days before the time of regular recess, took possession of the school, of which they barred the doors, and bade their master defiance from the windows. It is not easy to suppose that on such occasions the master would do more than laugh; yet, if tradition may be credited, he often struggled hard to force or surprise the garrison. The master, when Pigot was a schoolboy, was 'barred out' at Lichfield; and the whole operation, as he said, was planned and conducted by Addison.

To judge better of the probability of this story, I have inquired when he was sent to the Chartreux; but, as he was not one of those who enjoyed the founder's benefaction, there is no account preserved of his admission. At the school of the Chartreux, to which he was removed either from that of Salisbury or Lichfield, he pursued his juvenile studies under the care of Dr. Ellis, and contracted that intimacy with Sir Richard Steele which their joint labors have so effectually recorded.

Of this memorable friendship the greater praise must be given to Steele. It is not hard to love those from whom nothing can be feared; and Addison never considered Steele as a rival; but Steele lived, as he confesses, under an habitual subjection to the predominating genius of Addison, whom he always mentioned with reverence, and treated with obsequiousness.

Addison, who knew his own dignity, could not always forbear to show it, by playing a little upon his admirer; but he was in no danger of retort; his jests were endured without resistance or resentment. But the sneer of jocularity was not the worst. Steele, whose imprudence of generosity, or vanity of profusion, kept him always incurably necessitous, upon some pressing exigence, in an evil hour, borrowed an hundred pounds of his friend probably without

much purpose of repayment; but Addison, who seems to have had other notions of a hundred pounds, grew impatient of delay, and reclaimed his loan by an execution. Steele felt with great sensibility the obduracy of his creditor, but with emotions of sorrow rather than of anger.

In 1687 he was entered into Queen's College in Oxford, where, in 1689, the accidental perusal of some Latin verses gained him the patronage of Di. Lancaster, afterwards Provost of Queen's College; by whose recommendation he was elected into Magdalen College as a demy, a term by which that society denominates those who are elsewhere called scholars: young men who partake of the founder's benefaction, and succeed in their order to vacant fellowships. Here he continued to cultivate poetry and criticism, and grew first eminent by his Latin compositions, which are indeed entitled to particular praise. He has not confined himself to the imitation of any ancient author, but has formed his style from the general language, such as a diligent perusal of the productions of different ages happened to supply. His Latin compositions seem to have had much of his fondness, for he collected a second volume of the *Musae Anglicanae*, perhaps for a convenient receptacle, in which all his Latin pieces are inserted, and where his poem on the Peace has the first place. He afterwards presented the collection to Boileau, who from that time 'conceived,' says Tickell, 'an opinion of the English genius for poetry.' Nothing is better known of Boileau than that he had an injudicious and peevish contempt of modern Latin, and therefore his profession of regard was probably the effect of his civility rather than approbation.

Three of his Latin poems are upon subjects on which perhaps he would not have ventured to have written in his own language: — *The Battle of the Pigmies and Cranes, The Barometer,* and *A Bowling-green.* When the matter is low or scanty, a dead language, in which nothing is mean because nothing is familiar, affords great conveniences; and by the sonorous magnificence of Roman syllables, the writer conceals penury of thought, and want of novelty, often from the reader and often from himself.

In his twenty-second year he first showed his power of English poetry by some verses addressed to Dryden; and soon afterwards published a translation of the greater part of the *Fourth Georgic* upon Bees; after which, says Dryden, ' my latter swarm is hardly worth the hiving.' About the same time he composed the arguments prefixed to the several books of Dryden's *Virgil;* and produced an *Essay on the Georgics,* juvenile, superficial, and uninstructive, without much either of the scholar's learning or the critic's penetration. His next paper of verses contained a character of the principal English poets, inscribed to Henry Sacheverell, who was then, if not a poet, a writer of verses; as is shown by his version of a small part of Virgil's *Georgics,* published in the *Miscellanies;* and a Latin encomium on Queen Mary, in the *Musae Anglicanae.* These verses exhibit all the fondness of friendship; but, on one side or the other, friendship was afterwards too weak for the malignity of faction. In this poem is a very confident and discriminative character of Spenser, whose work he had then never read; so little sometimes is criticism the effect of judgment. It is necessary to inform the reader that about this time he was introduced by Congreve to Montague, then chancellor of the exchequer: Addison was then learning the trade of a courtier, and subjoined Montague as a poetical name to those of Cowley and of Dryden. By the influence of Mr. Montague, concurring, according to Tickell, with his natural modesty, he was diverted from his original design of entering into holy orders. Montague alleged the corruption of men who engaged in civil employments without liberal education; and declared that, though he was represented as an enemy to the church, he would never do it any injury but by withholding Addison from it.

Soon after (1695) he wrote a poem to King William, with a riming introduction addressed to Lord Somers. King William had no regard to elegance or literature; his study was only war; yet by a choice of ministers, whose disposition was very different from his own, he procured, without intention, a very liberal patronage to poetry. Addison was caressed both by Somers and Montague.

In 1697 appeared his Latin verses on the Peace of Ryswick, which he dedicated to Montague, and which was afterwards called, by Smith, ' the best Latin poem since the *Aeneid.*' Praise must not be too rigorously examined; but the performance cannot be denied to be vigorous and elegant. Having yet no public employment, he obtained (in 1699) a pension of three hundred pounds a year, that he might be enabled to travel. He stayed a year at Blois, probably to learn the French language; and then proceeded in his journey to Italy, which he surveyed with the eyes of a poet. While he was traveling at leisure, he was far from being idle: for he not only collected his observations on the country, but found time to write his *Dialogues on Medals,* and four acts of *Cato.* Such, at least, is the relation of Tickell. Perhaps he only collected his materials and formed his plan. Whatever were his other employments in Italy, he there wrote the letter to Lord Halifax which is justly considered as the most elegant, if not the most sublime, of his poetical productions. But in about two years he found it necessary to hasten home; being, as Swift informs us, distressed by indigence, and compelled to become the tutor of a traveling squire, because his pension was not remitted.

At his return he published his Travels, with a dedication to Lord Somers. As his stay in foreign countries was short, his observations are such as might be supplied by a hasty view, and consist chiefly in comparisons of the present face of the country with the descriptions left us by the Roman poets, from whom he made preparatory collections, though he might have spared the trouble had he known that such collections had been made twice before by Italian authors.

The most amusing passage of his book is his account of the minute republic of San Marino; of many parts it is not a very severe censure to say that they might have been written at home. His elegance of language, and variegation of prose and verse, however, gain upon the reader; and the book, though awhile neglected, became in time so much the favorite of the public that before it was reprinted it rose to five times its price.

When he returned to England (in

1702), with a meanness of appearance which gave testimony of the difficulties to which he had been reduced, he found his old patrons out of power, and was therefore, for a time, at full leisure for the cultivation of his mind; and a mind so cultivated gives reason to believe that little time was lost. But he remained not long neglected or useless. The victory at Blenheim (1704) spread triumph and confidence over the nation; and Lord Godolphin, lamenting to Lord Halifax that it had not been celebrated in a manner equal to the subject, desired him to propose it to some better poet. Halifax told him that there was no encouragement for genius; that worthless men were unprofitably enriched with public money, without any care to find or employ those whose appearance might do honor to their country. To this Godolphin replied that such abuses should in time be rectified; and that, if a man could be found capable of the task then proposed, he should not want an ample recompense. Halifax then named Addison, but required that the treasurer should apply to him in his own person. Godolphin sent the message by Mr. Boyle, afterwards Lord Carlton; and Addison, having undertaken the work, communicated it to the treasury while it was yet advanced no farther than the simile of the angel, and was immediately rewarded by succeeding Mr. Locke in the place of commissioner of appeals.

In the following year he was at Hanover with Lord Halifax: and the year after he was made under secretary of state, first to Sir Charles Hedges, and in a few months more to the Earl of Sunderland. About this time the prevalent taste for Italian operas inclined him to try what would be the effect of a musical drama in our own language. He therefore wrote the opera of *Rosamond*, which, when exhibited on the stage, was either hissed or neglected; but, trusting that the readers would do him more justice, he published it with an inscription to the Duchess of Marlborough — a woman without skill, or pretensions to skill, in poetry or literature. His dedication was therefore an instance of servile absurdity, to be exceeded only by Joshua Barnes's dedication of a Greek *Anacreon* to the Duke. His reputation had been somewhat advanced by *The Tender Husband,* a comedy which Steele dedicated to him, with a confession that he owed to him several of the most successful scenes. To this play Addison supplied a prologue.

When the Marquis of Wharton was appointed lord lieutenant of Ireland, Addison attended him as his secretary; and was made keeper of the records, in Birmingham's tower, with a salary of three hundred pounds a year. The office was little more than nominal, and the salary was augmented for his accommodation. Interest and faction allow little to the operation of particular dispositions or private opinions. Two men of personal characters more opposite than those of Wharton and Addison could not easily be brought together. Wharton was impious, profligate, and shameless; without regard, or appearance of regard, to right and wrong. Whatever is contrary to this may be said of Addison; but as agents of a party they were connected, and how they adjusted their other sentiments we cannot know.

Addison, must, however, not be too hastily condemned. It is not necessary to refuse benefits from a bad man when the acceptance implies no approbation of his crimes; nor has the subordinate officer any obligation to examine the opinions or conduct of those under whom he acts, except that he may not be made the instrument of wickedness. It is reasonable to suppose that Addison counteracted, as far as he was able, the malignant and blasting influence of the lieutenant; and that at least by his intervention some good was done, and some mischief prevented. When he was in office he made a law to himself, as Swift has recorded, never to remit his regular fees in civility to his friends: 'for,' said he, 'I may have a hundred friends; and if my fee be two guineas, I shall, by relinquishing my right, lose two hundred guineas, and no friend gain more than two; there is therefore no proportion between the good imparted and the evil suffered.' He was in Ireland when Steele, without any communication of his design, began the publication of *The Tatler;* but he was not long concealed; by inserting a remark on Virgil which Addison had given him he discovered himself. It is, indeed, not easy for any man to write upon literature or common life so as not to make himself known to those with whom he familiarly converses, and who are acquainted with his track of study, his favorite topic, his peculiar notions, and his habitual phrases.

If Steele desired to write in secret, he was not lucky; a single month detected him. His first *Tatler* was published April 22 (1709); and Addison's contribution appeared May 26. Tickell observes that *The Tatler* began and was concluded without his concurrence. This is doubtless literally true; but the work did not suffer much by his unconsciousness of its commencement, or his absence at its cessation; for he continued his assistance to December 23, and the paper stopped on January 2, 1710-11. He did not distinguish his pieces by any signature; and I know not whether his name was not kept secret till the papers were collected into volumes.

To *The Tatler,* in about two months, succeeded *The Spectator:* a series of essays of the same kind, but written with less levity, upon a more regular plan, and published daily. Such an undertaking showed the writers not to distrust their own copiousness of materials or facility of composition, and their performance justified their confidence. They found, however, in their progress many auxiliaries. To attempt a single paper was no terrifying labor; many pieces were offered, and many were received.

Addison had enough of the zeal of party; but Steele had at that time almost nothing else. *The Spectator,* in one of the first papers, showed the political tenets of its authors; but a resolution was soon taken of courting general approbation by general topics, and subjects on which faction had produced no diversity of sentiments; such as literature, morality, and familiar life. To this practice they adhered with few deviations. The ardor of Steele once broke out in praise of Marlborough; and when Dr. Fleetwood prefixed to some sermons a preface overflowing with whiggish opinions, that it might be read by the Queen, it was reprinted in *The Spectator*.

To teach the minuter decencies and inferior duties, to regulate the practice of daily conversation, to correct those depravities, which are rather ridiculous

than criminal, and remove those grievances which, if they produce no lasting calamities, impress hourly vexation, was first attempted by Casa in his book of 5 *Manners,* and Castiglione in his *Courtier;* two books yet celebrated in Italy for purity and elegance, and which, if they are now less read, are neglected only because they have effected that reforma- 10 tion which their authors intended, and their precepts now are no longer wanted. Their usefulness to the age in which they were written is sufficiently attested by the translations which almost all the nations 15 of Europe were in haste to obtain.

This species of instruction was continued, and perhaps advanced, by the French; among whom La Bruyère's *Manners of the Age* (though, as Boileau re- 20 marked, it is written without connection) certainly deserves great praise for liveliness of description and justness of observation.

Before *The Tatler* and *Spectator,* if 25 the writers for the theater are excepted, England had no masters of common life. No writers had yet undertaken to reform either the savageness of neglect, or the impertinence of civility; to show when to 30 speak, or to be silent; how to refuse, or how to comply. We had many books to teach us our more important duties, and to settle opinions in philosophy or politics; but an *arbiter elegantiarum,* a judge 35 of propriety, was yet wanting, who should survey the track of daily conversation, and free it from thorns and prickles, which tease the passer, though they do not wound him. For this purpose noth- 40 ing is so proper as the frequent publication of short papers, which we read, not as study, but amusement. If the subject be slight, the treatise likewise is short. The busy may find time, and the idle may 45 find patience. This mode of conveying cheap and easy knowledge began among us in the civil war, when it was much the interest of either party to raise and fix the prejudices of the people. At that 50 time appeared *Mercurius Aulicus, Mercurius Rusticus,* and *Mercurius Civicus.* It is said that when any title grew popular, it was stolen by the antagonist, who by this stratagem conveyed his notions to 55 those who would not have received him had he not worn the appearance of a friend. The tumult of those unhappy days left scarcely any man leisure to treasure up occasional compositions; and so much were they neglected that a complete collection is nowhere to be found.

These Mercuries were succeeded by L'Estrange's *Observator;* and that by Lesley's *Rehearsal,* and perhaps by others; but hitherto nothing had been conveyed to the people, in this commodious manner, but controversy relating to the church or state; of which they taught many to talk, whom they could not teach to judge.

It has been suggested that the Royal Society was instituted soon after the Restoration to divert the attention of the people from public discontent. *The Tatler* and *Spectator* had the same tendency; they were published at a time when two parties — loud, restless, and violent, each with plausible declarations, and each perhaps without any distinct termination of its views — were agitating the nation; to minds heated with political contest they supplied cooler and more inoffensive reflections; and it is said by Addison, in a subsequent work, that they had a perceptible influence upon the conversation of that time, and taught the frolic and the gay to unite merriment with decency — an effect which they can never wholly lose while they continue to be among the first books by which both sexes are initiated in the elegances of knowledge.

The Tatler and *Spectator* adjusted, like Casa, the unsettled practice of daily intercourse by propriety and politeness; and, like La Bruyère, exhibited the characters and manners of the age. The personages introduced in these papers were not merely ideal; they were then known, and conspicuous in various stations. Of *The Tatler* that is told by Steele in his last paper; and of *The Spectator* by Budgell in the preface to *Theophrastus,* a book which Addison has recommended, and which he was suspected to have revised, if he did not write it. Of those portraits which may be supposed to be sometimes embellished, and sometimes aggravated, the originals are now partly known, and partly forgotten. But to say that they united the plans of two or three eminent writers, is to give them but a small part of their due praise; they superadded literature and criticism,

and sometimes towered far above their predecessors; and taught, with great justness of argument and dignity of language, the most important duties and sublime truths. All these topics were happily varied with elegant fictions and refined allegories, and illuminated with different changes of style and felicities of invention.

It is recorded by Budgell, that of the characters feigned or exhibited in *The Spectator,* the favorite of Addison was Sir Roger de Coverley, of whom he had formed a very delicate and discriminated idea, which he would not suffer to be violated; and therefore when Steele had shown him innocently picking up a girl in the Temple, and taking her to a tavern, he drew upon himself so much of his friend's indignation that he was forced to appease him by a promise of forbearing Sir Roger for the time to come.

The reason which induced Cervantes to bring his hero to the grave, *para mi sola nacio Don Quixote, y yo para el* [for me alone was Don Quixote born, and I for him], made Addison declare, with undue vehemence of expression, that he would kill Sir Roger; being of opinion that they were born for one another, and that any other hand would do him wrong.

It may be doubted whether Addison ever filled up his original delineation. He describes his knight as having his imagination somewhat warped; but of this perversion he has made very little use. The irregularities in Sir Roger's conduct seem not so much the effects of a mind deviating from the beaten track of life, by the perpetual pressure of some overwhelming idea, as of habitual rusticity, and that negligence which solitary grandeur naturally generates. The variable weather of the mind, the flying vapors of incipient madness, which from time to time cloud reason without eclipsing it, it requires so much nicety to exhibit that Addison seems to have been deterred from prosecuting his own design.

To Sir Roger, who, as a country gentleman, appears to be a tory, or, as it is gently expressed, an adherent to the landed interest, is opposed Sir Andrew Freeport, a new man, a wealthy merchant, zealous for the moneyed interest, and a whig. Of this contrariety of opinions, it is probable more consequences were at first intended than could be produced when the resolution was taken to exclude party from the paper. Sir Andrew does but little, and that little seems not to have pleased Addison, who, when he dismissed him from the club, changed his opinions. Steele had made him, in the true spirit of unfeeling commerce, declare that he 'would not build an hospital for idle people'; but at last he buys land, settles in the country, and builds, not a manufactory, but an hospital for twelve old husbandmen — for men with whom a merchant has little acquaintance, and whom he commonly considers with little kindness.

Of essays thus elegant, thus instructive, and thus commodiously distributed, it is natural to suppose the approbation general, and the sale numerous. I once heard it observed that the sale may be calculated by the product of the tax, related in the last number to produce more than twenty pounds a week, and therefore stated at one-and-twenty pounds, or three pounds ten shillings a day: this, at a halfpenny a paper, will give sixteen hundred and eighty for the daily number. This sale is not great; yet this, if Swift be credited, was likely to grow less; for he declares that *The Spectator,* whom he ridicules for his endless mention of the *fair sex,* had before his recess wearied his readers.

The next year (1713), in which *Cato* came upon the stage, was the grand climacteric of Addison's reputation. Upon the death of Cato he had, as is said, planned a tragedy in the time of his travels, and had for several years the four first acts finished, which were shown to such as were likely to spread their admiration. They were seen by Pope and by Cibber, who relates that Steele, when he took back the copy, told him, in the despicable cant of literary modesty, that, whatever spirit his friend had shown in the composition, he doubted whether he would have courage sufficient to expose it to the censure of a British audience. The time, however, was now come when those who affected to think liberty in danger affected likewise to think that a stage-play might preserve it; and Addison was importuned, in the name of the tutelary deities of Britain, to show his

courage and his zeal by finishing his design.

To resume his work he seemed perversely and unaccountably unwilling; and by a request, which perhaps he wished to be denied, desired Mr. Hughes to add a fifth act. Hughes supposed him serious; and, undertaking the supplement, brought in a few days some scenes for his examination; but he had in the meantime gone to work himself, and produced half an act, which he afterwards completed, but with brevity irregularly disproportionate to the foregoing parts, like a task performed with reluctance and hurried to its conclusion.

It may yet be doubted whether *Cato* was made public by any change of the author's purpose; for Dennis charged him with raising prejudices in his own favor by false positions of preparatory criticism, and with 'poisoning the town' by contradicting in *The Spectator* the established rule of poetical justice, because his own hero, with all his virtues, was to fall before a tyrant. The fact is certain; the motives we must guess.

Addison was, I believe, sufficiently disposed to bar all avenues against all danger. When Pope brought him the prologue, which is properly accommodated to the play, there were these words, 'Britains, arise! be worth like this approved'; meaning nothing more than — Britons, erect and exalt yourselves to the approbation of public virtue. Addison was frighted, lest he should be thought a promoter of insurrection, and the line was liquidated to 'Britons, attend.'

Now 'heavily in clouds came on the day, the great, the important day,' when Addison was to stand the hazard of the theater. That there might, however, be left as little hazard as was possible, on the first night Steele, as himself relates, undertook to pack an audience. 'This,' says Pope, 'had been tried for the first time in favor of *The Distressed Mother;* and was now, with more efficacy, practised for *Cato.*' The danger was soon over. The whole nation was at that time on fire with faction. The whigs applauded every line in which liberty was mentioned, as a satire on the tories; and the tories echoed every clap, to show that the satire was unfelt. The story of Bolingbroke is well known; he called Booth to his box, and gave him fifty guineas for defending the cause of liberty so well against a perpetual dictator. 'The whigs,' says Pope, 'design a second present, when they can accompany it with as good a sentence.'

The play, supported thus by the emulation of factious praise, was acted night after night for a longer time than, I believe, the public had allowed to any drama before; and the author, as Mrs. Porter long afterwards related, wandered through the whole exhibition behind the scenes with restless and unappeasable solicitude. When it was printed, notice was given that the Queen would be pleased if it were dedicated to her; 'but as he had designed that compliment elsewhere, he found himself obliged,' says Tickell, 'by his duty on the one hand, and his honor on the other, to send it into the world without any dedication.'

Human happiness has always its abatements; the brightest sunshine of success is not without a cloud. No sooner was Cato offered to the reader than it was attacked by the acute malignity of Dennis with all the violence of angry criticism. Dennis, though equally zealous, and probably by his temper more furious than Addison, for what they called liberty, and though a flatterer of the Whig Ministry, could not sit quiet at a successful play; but was eager to tell friends and enemies that they had misplaced their admirations. The world was too stubborn for instruction; with the fate of the censurer of Corneille's Cid, his animadversions showed his anger without effect, and Cato continued to be praised.

Pope had now an opportunity of courting the friendship of Addison by vilifying his old enemy, and could give resentment its full play without appearing to revenge himself. He therefore published A Narrative of the Madness of John Dennis: a performance which left the objections to the play in their full force, and therefore discovered more desire of vexing the critic than of defending the poet.

Addison, who was no stranger to the world, probably saw the selfishness of Pope's friendship; and, resolving that he should have the consequences of his officiousness to himself, informed Dennis by Steele that he was sorry for the insult; and that, whenever he should think fit to answer his remarks, he would do it in a manner to which nothing could be objected.

The greatest weakness of the play is in the scenes of love, which are said by Pope to have been added to the original plan upon a subsequent review, in compliance with the popular practice of the stage. Such an authority it is hard to reject; yet the love is so intimately mingled with the whole action that it cannot easily be thought extrinsic and adventitious; for if it were taken away, what would be left? Or how were the four acts filled in the first draft? At the publication the wits seemed proud to pay their attendance with encomiastic verses. The best are from an unknown hand, which will perhaps lose somewhat of their praise when the author is known to be Jeffreys.

Cato had yet other honors. It was censured as a party-play by a scholar of Oxford; and defended in a favorable examination by Dr. Sewel. It was translated by Salvini into Italian, and acted at Florence; and by the Jesuits of St. Omer's into Latin, and played by their pupils. Of this version a copy was sent to Mr. Addison: it is to be wished that it could be found, for the sake of comparing their version of the soliloquy with that of Bland.

A tragedy was written on the same subject by Des Champs, a French poet, which was translated with a criticism on the English play. But the translator and the critic are now forgotten.

Dennis lived on unanswered, and therefore little read. Addison knew the policy of literature too well to make his enemy important by drawing the attention of the public upon a criticism which, though sometimes intemperate, was often irrefragable.

While Cato was upon the stage, another daily paper, called The Guardian, was published by Steele. To this Addison gave great assistance, whether occasionally or by previous engagement is not known. The character of Guardian was too narrow and too serious: it might properly enough admit both the duties and the decencies of life, but seemed not to include literary speculations, and was in some degree violated by merriment and burlesque. What had the Guardian of the Lizards to do with clubs of tall or of little men, with nests of ants, or with Strada's prolusions? Of this paper nothing is necessary to be said but that it found many contributors, and that it was a continuation of *The Spectator,* with the same elegance and the same variety, till some unlucky sparkle from a tory paper set Steele's politics on fire, and wit at once blazed into faction. He was soon too hot for neutral topics, and quitted *The Guardian* to write *The Englishman.*

The papers of Addison are marked in *The Spectator* by one of the letters in the name of Clio, and in *The Guardian* by a hand; whether it was, as Tickell pretends to think, that he was unwilling to usurp the praise of others, or as Steele, with far greater likelihood, insinuates, that he could not without discontent impart to others any of his own. I have heard that his avidity did not satisfy itself with the air of renown, but that with great eagerness he laid hold on his proportion of the profits.

Many of these papers were written with powers truly comic, with nice discrimination of characters, and accurate observation of natural or accidental deviations from propriety; but it was not supposed that he had tried a comedy on the stage, till Steele after his death declared him the author of *The Drummer.* This, however, Steele did not know to be true by any direct testimony, for when Addison put the play into his hands, he only told him it was the work of a 'gentleman in the company,' and when it was received, as is confessed, with cold disapprobation, he was probably less willing to claim it. Tickell omitted it in his collection; but the testimony of Steele, and the total silence of any other claimant, has determined the public to assign it to Addison, and it is now printed with his other poetry. Steele carried *The Drummer* to the play-house, and afterwards to the press, and sold the copy for fifty guineas.

To the opinion of Steele may be added the proof supplied by the play itself, of which the characters are such as Addison would have delineated, and the tendency such as Addison would have pro-

moted. That it should have been ill received would raise wonder, did we not daily see the capricious distribution of theatrical praise.

He was not all this time an indifferent spectator of public affairs. He wrote, as different exigences required (in 1707). *The present State of the War, and the Necessity of an Augmentation;* which, however judicious, being written on temporary topics, and exhibiting no peculiar powers, laid hold on no attention, and has naturally sunk by its own weight into neglect. This cannot be said of the few papers entitled *The Whig Examiner,* in which is employed all the force of gay malevolence and humorous satire. Of this paper, which just appeared and expired, Swift remarks, with exultation, that 'it is now down among the dead men.' He might well rejoice at the death of that which he could not have killed. Every reader of every party, since personal malice is past, and the papers which once inflamed the nation are read only effusions of wit, must wish for more of the *Whig Examiner,* on no occasion was the power of Addison more vigorously exerted, and on none did the superiority of his powers more evidently appear. His *Trial of Count Tariff,* written to expose the treaty of commerce with France, lived no longer than the question that produced it.

Not long afterwards an attempt was made to revive *The Spectator,* at a time indeed by no means favorable to literature, when the succession of a new family to the throne filled the nation with anxiety, discord, and confusion; and either the turbulence of the times, or the satiety of the readers, put a stop to the publication after an experiment of eighty numbers, which were afterwards collected into an eighth volume, perhaps more valuable than any of those that went before it. Addison produced more than a fourth part; and the other contributors are by no means unworthy of appearing as his associates. The time that had passed during the suspension of *The Spectator,* though it had not lessened his power of humor, seems to have increased his disposition to seriousness: the proportion of his religious to his comic papers is greater than in the former series.

The Spectator, from its re-commencement, was published only three times a week; and no discriminative marks were added to the papers. To Addison, Tickell has ascribed twenty-three. *The Spectator* had many contributors; and Steele, whose negligence kept him always in a hurry, when it was his turn to furnish a paper, called loudly for the letters, of which Addison, whose materials were more, made little use — having recourse to sketches and hints, the product of his former studies, which he now reviewed and completed: among these are named by Tickell the Essays on Wit, those on the Pleasures of the Imagination, and the Criticism on Milton.

When the House of Hanover took possession of the throne, it was reasonable to expect that the zeal of Addison would be suitably rewarded. Before the arrival of King George, he was made secretary to the Regency, and was required by his office to send notice to Hanover that the Queen was dead, and that the ~~~~~~~ vacant. To do this would not have ~~~~~~~ ult to any man but Addison, who w~~~~~~ ~~whelmed with the greatness of the ~~~~~~~ d so distracted by choice of express~~~~~ the lords, who could not wait for the niceties of criticism, called Mr. Southwell, a clerk in the House, and ordered him to despatch the message. Southwell readily told what was necessary in the common style of business, and valued himself upon having done what was too hard for Addison. He was better qualified for *The Freeholder,* a paper which he published twice a week, from December 23, 1715, to the middle of the next year. This was undertaken in defense of the established Government, sometimes with argument, and sometimes with mirth. In argument he had many equals; but his humor was singular and matchless. Bigotry itself must be delighted with the Tory Foxhunter. There are, however, some strokes less elegant and less decent; such as the *Pretender's Journal,* in which one topic of ridicule is his poverty. This mode of abuse had been employed by Milton against King Charles II.

Jacoboei.

Centum exulantis viscera marsuppi regis.
[A hundred Jacobuses, dregs of the purse of an exiled king.]

And Oldmixon delights to tell of some alderman of London that he had more money than the exiled princes; but that which might be expected from Milton's savageness, or Oldmixon's meanness, was not suitable to the delicacy of Addison.

Steele thought the humor of *The Freeholder* too nice and gentle for such noisy times, and is reported to have said that the ministry made use of a lute, when they should have called for a trumpet.

This year (1716) he married the Countess Dowager of Warwick, whom he had solicited by a very long and anxious courtship, perhaps with behavior not very unlike that of Sir Roger to his disdainful widow; and who, I am afraid, diverted herself often by playing with his passion. He is said to have first known her by becoming tutor to her son. 'He formed,' said Tonson, 'the design of getting that lady from the time when he was first recommended into the family.' In what part of his life he obtained the recommendation, or how long, and in what manner he lived in the family, I know not. His advances at first were certainly timorous, but grew bolder as his reputation and influence increased; till at last the lady was persuaded to marry him, on terms much like those on which a Turkish princess is espoused, to whom the Sultan is reported to pronounce, 'Daughter, I give thee this man for thy slave.' The marriage, if uncontradicted report can be credited, made no addition to his happiness; it neither found them nor made them equal. She always remembered her own rank, and thought herself entitled to treat with very little ceremony the tutor of her son. Rowe's ballad of *The Despairing Shepherd* is said to have been written, either before or after marriage, upon this memorable pair; and it is certain that Addison has left behind him no encouragement for ambitious love.

The year after (1717) he rose to his highest elevation, being made secretary of state. For this employment he might be justly supposed qualified by long practice of business, and by his regular ascent through other offices; but expectation is often disappointed; it is universally confessed that he was unequal to the duties of his place. In the House of Commons he could not speak, and therefore was useless to the defense of the government. 'In the office,' says Pope, 'he could not issue an order without losing his time in quest of fine expressions.' What he gained in rank he lost in credit; and finding by experience his own inability, was forced to solicit his dismission, with a pension of fifteen hundred pounds a year. His friends palliated this relinquishment, of which both friends and enemies knew the true reason, with an account of declining health, and the necessity of recess and quiet. He now returned to his vocation, and began to plan literary occupations for his future life. He purposed a tragedy on the death of Socrates, a story of which, as Tickell remarks, the basis is narrow, and to which I know not how love could have been appended. There would, however, have been no want either of virtue in the sentiments, or elegance in the language. He engaged in a nobler work, a *Defense of the Christian Religion,* of which part was published after his death; and he designed to have made a new poetical version of the Psalms.

These pious compositions Pope imputed to a selfish motive, upon the credit, as he owns, of Tonson; who, having quarreled with Addison, and not loving him, said that when he laid down the secretary's office he intended to take orders and obtain a bishopric; 'for,' said he, 'I always thought him a priest in his heart.'

That Pope should have thought this conjecture of Tonson worth remembrance, is a proof — but indeed, so far as I have found, the only proof — that he retained some malignity from their ancient rivalry. Tonson pretended but to guess it; no other mortal ever suspected it; and Pope might have reflected that a man who had been secretary of state in the ministry of Sunderland knew a nearer way to a bishopric than by defending religion or translating the Psalms.

It is related that he had once a design to make an *English Dictionary,* and that he considered Dr. Tillotson as the writer of highest authority. There was formerly sent to me by Mr. Locker, clerk of the Leathersellers' Company, who was eminent for curiosity and literature, a collection of examples selected from Tillotson's works, as Locker said, by Addi-

son. It came too late to be of use, so I inspected it but slightly, and remember it indistinctly. I thought the passages too short. Addison, however, did not conclude his life in peaceful studies, but relapsed, when he was near his end, to a political dispute.

It so happened that (1718-19) a controversy was agitated with great vehemence between those friends of long continuance, Addison and Steele. It may be asked, in the language of Homer, what power or what cause could set them at variance. The subject of their dispute was of great importance. The Earl of Sunderland proposed an act called The Peerage Bill; by which the number of peers should be fixed, and the king restrained from any new creation of nobility, unless when an old family should be extinct. To this the lords would naturally agree; and the king, who was yet little acquainted with his own prerogative, and, as is now well known, almost indifferent to the possessions of the crown, had been persuaded to consent. The only difficulty was found among the commons, who were not likely to approve the perpetual exclusion of themselves and their posterity. The bill, therefore, was eagerly opposed, and, among others, by Sir Robert Walpole, whose speech was published.

The lords might think their dignity diminished by improper advancements, and particularly by the introduction of twelve new peers at once, to produce a majority of tories in the last reign: an act of authority violent enough, yet certainly legal, and by no means to be compared with that contempt of national right with which some time afterwards, by the instigation of whiggism, the commons, chosen by the people for three years, chose themselves for seven. But, whatever might be the disposition of the lords, the people had no wish to increase their power. The tendency of the bill, as Steele observed in a letter to the Earl of Oxford, was to introduce an aristocracy: for a majority in the House of Lords, so limited, would have been despotic and irresistible.

To prevent this subversion of the ancient establishment, Steele, whose pen readily seconded his political passions, endeavored to alarm the nation by a pamphlet called *The Plebeian.* To this an answer was published by Addison, under the title of *The Old Whig,* in which it is not discovered that Steele was then known to be the advocate for the commons. Steele replied by a second *Plebeian;* and, whether by ignorance or by courtesy, confined himself to his question, without any personal notice of his opponent. Nothing hitherto was committed against the laws of friendship or proprieties of decency; but controvertists cannot long retain their kindness for each other. *The Old Whig* answered *The Plebeian,* and could not forbear some contempt of ' little Dicky, whose trade it was to write pamphlets.' Dicky, however, did not lose his settled veneration for his friend, but contented himself with quoting some lines of *Cato,* which were at once detection and reproof. The bill was laid aside during that session, and Addison died before the next, in which its commitment was rejected by two hundred and sixty-five to one hundred and seventy-seven.

Every reader surely must regret that these two illustrious friends, after so many years passed in confidence and endearment, in unity of interest, conformity of opinion, and fellowship of study, should finally part in acrimonious opposition. Such a controversy was *bellum plusquam civile* [worse than civil war], as Lucan expresses it. Why could not faction find other advocates? But among the uncertainties of the human state, we are doomed to number the instability of friendship. Of this dispute I have little knowledge but from the *Biographia Britannica. The Old Whig* is not inserted in Addison's works; nor is it mentioned by Tickell in his *Life;* why it was omitted, the biographers doubtless give the true reason: the fact was too recent, and those who had been heated in the contention were not yet cool.

The necessity of complying with times, and of sparing persons, is the great impediment of biography. History may be formed from permanent monuments and records; but lives can only be written from personal knowledge, which is growing every day less, and in a short time is lost for ever. What is known can seldom be immediately told; and when it might be told, it is no longer known.

The delicate features of the mind, the nice discriminations of character, and the minute peculiarities of conduct, are soon obliterated; and it is surely better that caprice, obstinacy, frolic, and folly, however they might delight in the description, should be silently forgotten, than that, by wanton merriment and unseasonable detection, a pang should be given to a widow, a daughter, a brother, or a friend. As the process of these narratives is now bringing me among my contemporaries, I begin to feel myself ' walking upon ashes under which the fire is not extinguished,' and coming to the time of which it will be proper rather to say ' nothing that is false, than all that is true.'

The end of this useful life was now approaching. Addison had for some time been oppressed by shortness of breath, which was now aggravated by a dropsy; and, finding his danger pressing, he prepared to die comfortably to his own precepts and professions. During this lingering decay, he sent, as Pope relates, a message by the Earl of Warwick to Mr. Gay, desiring to see him. Gay, who had not visited him for some time before, obeyed the summons, and found himself received with great kindness. The purpose for which the interview had been solicited was then discovered. Addison told him that he had injured him; but that, if he recovered, he would recompense him. What the injury was he did not explain, nor did Gay ever know; but supposed that some preferment designed for him had, by Addison's intervention, been withheld.

Lord Warwick was a young man, of very irregular life, and perhaps of loose opinions. Addison, for whom he did not want respect, had very diligently endeavored to reclaim him, but his arguments and expostulations had no effect. One experiment, however, remained to be tried; when he found his life near its end, he directed the young lord to be called, and when he desired with great tenderness to hear his last injunctions, told him, ' I have sent for you that you may see how a Christian can die.' What effect this awful scene had on the earl, I know not; he likewise died himself in a short time.

In Tickell's excellent Elegy on his friend are these lines: —

He taught us how to live; and, oh! too high
The price of knowledge, taught us how to die —

in which he alludes, as he told Dr. Young, to this moving interview.

Having given directions to Mr. Tickell for the publication of his works, and dedicated them on his death-bed to his friend Mr. Craggs, he died June 17, 1719, at Holland House, leaving no child but a daughter.

Of his virtue it is a sufficient testimony that the resentment of party has transmitted no charge of any crime. He was not one of those who are praised only after death; for his merit was so generally acknowledged that Swift, having observed that his election passed without a contest, adds that if he had proposed himself for king he would hardly have been refused. His zeal for his party did not extinguish his kindness for the merit of his opponents; when he was secretary in Ireland, he refused to intermit his acquaintance with Swift. Of his habits or external manners, nothing is so often mentioned as that timorous or sullen taciturnity, which his friends called modesty by too mild a name. Steele mentions with great tenderness 'that remarkable bashfulness which is a cloak that hides and muffles merit'; and tells us that his abilities were covered only by modesty, which doubles the beauties which are seen, and gives credit and esteem to all that are concealed.' Chesterfield affirms that 'Addison was the most timorous and awkward man that he ever saw.' And Addison, speaking of his own deficience in conversation used to say of himself that, with respect to intellectual wealth, 'he could draw bills for a thousand pounds, though he had not a guinea in his pocket.' That he wanted current coin for ready payment, and by that want was often obstructed and distressed; that he was oppressed by an improper and ungraceful timidity, every testimony concurs to prove; but Chesterfield's representation is doubtless hyperbolical. That man cannot be supposed very unexpert in the arts of conversation and practice of life who, without fortune or alliance, by his usefulness and dexterity became secretary of state, and who

died at forty-seven, after having not only stood long in the highest rank of wit and literature, but filled one of the most important offices of state.

The time in which he lived had reason to lament his obstinacy of silence; 'for he was,' says Steele, 'above all men in that talent called humor, and enjoyed it in such perfection that I have often reflected, after a night spent with him apart from all the world, that I had had the pleasure of conversing with an intimate acquaintance of Terence and Catullus, who had all their wit and nature, heightened with humor more exquisite and delightful than any other man ever possessed.' This is the fondness of a friend; let us hear what is told us by a rival. 'Addison's conversation,' says Pope, 'had something in it more charming than I have found in any other man. But this was only when familiar: before strangers, or perhaps a single stranger, he preserved his dignity by a stiff silence.' This modesty was by no means inconsistent with a very high opinion of his own merit. He demanded to be the first name in modern wit; and, with Steele to echo him, used to depreciate Dryden, whom Pope and Congreve defended against them. There is no reason to doubt that he suffered too much pain from the prevalence of Pope's poetical reputation; nor is it without strong reason suspected that by some disingenuous acts he endeavored to obstruct it; Pope was not the only man whom he insidiously injured, though the only man of whom he could be afraid. His own powers were such as might have satisfied him with conscious excellence. Of very extensive learning he has indeed given no proofs. He seems to have had small acquaintance with the sciences, and to have read little except Latin and French; but of the Latin poets his Dialogues on Medals show that he had perused the works with great diligence and skill. The abundance of his own mind left him little need of adventitious sentiments; his wit always could suggest what the occasion demanded. He had read with critical eyes the important volume of human life, and knew the heart of man, from the depths of stratagem to the surface of affectation. What he knew he could easily communicate. 'This,' says Steele, 'was particular in this writer — that when he had taken his resolution, or made his plan for what he designed to write, he would walk about a room and dictate it into language with as much freedom and ease as any one could write it down, and attend to the coherence and grammar of what he dictated.'

Pope, who can be less suspected of favoring his memory, declares that he wrote very fluently, but was slow and scrupulous in correcting; that many of his *Spectators* were written very fast, and sent immediately to the press; and that it seemed to be for his advantage not to have time for much revisal. 'He would alter,' says Pope, 'anything to please his friends before publication, but would not re-touch his pieces afterwards; and I believe not one word in *Cato* to which I made an objection was suffered to stand.'

The last line of *Cato* is Pope's, having been originally written —

And oh! 't was this that ended Cato's life.

Pope might have made more objections to the six concluding lines. In the first couplet the words 'from hence' are improper; and the second line is taken from Dryden's Virgil. Of the next couplet, the first verse, being included in the second, is therefore useless; and in the third Discord is made to produce Strife.

Of the course of Addison's familiar day, before his marriage, Pope has given a detail. He had in the house with him Budgell, and perhaps Philips. His chief companions were Steele, Budgell, Philips, Carey, Davenant, and Colonel Brett. With one or other of these he always breakfasted. He studied all morning; then dined at a tavern; and went afterwards to Button's.

Button had been a servant in the Countess of Warwick's family, who, under the patronage of Addison, kept a coffee-house on the south side of Russell Street, about two doors from Covent Garden. Here it was that the wits of that time used to assemble. It is said when Addison had suffered any vexation from the countess, he withdrew the company from Button's house. From the coffee-house he went again to a tavern, where he often sat late, and drank too much wine. In the bottle discontent seeks for comfort, cowardice for courage,

and bashfulness for confidence. It is not unlikely that Addison was first seduced to excess by the manumission which he obtained from the servile timidity of his sober hours. He that feels oppression from the presence of those to whom he knows himself superior will desire to set loose his powers of conversation; and who that ever asked succors from Bacchus was able to preserve himself from being enslaved by his auxiliary?

Among those friends it was that Addison displayed the elegance of his colloquial accomplishments, which may easily be supposed such as Pope represents them. The remark of Mandeville, who, when he had passed an evening in his company, declared that he was a parson in a tye-wig, can detract little from his character; he was always reserved to strangers, and was not incited to uncommon freedom by a character like that of Mandeville.

From any minute knowledge of his familiar manners the intervention of sixty years has now debarred us. Steele once promised Congreve and the public a complete description of his character; but the promises of authors are like the vows of lovers. Steele thought no more on his design, or thought on it with anxiety that at last disgusted him, and left his friend in the hands of Tickell.

One slight lineament of his character Swift has preserved. It was his practice, when he found any man invincibly wrong, to flatter his opinions by acquiescence, and sink him yet deeper in absurdity. This artifice of mischief was admired by Stella; and Swift seems to approve her admiration. His works will supply some information. It appears from his various pictures of the world, that, with all his bashfulness, he had conversed with many distinct classes of men, had surveyed their ways with very diligent observation, and marked with great acuteness the effects of different modes of life. He was a man in whose presence nothing reprehensible was out of danger; quick in discerning whatever was wrong or ridiculous, and not unwilling to expose it. 'There are,' says Steele, 'in his writings many oblique strokes upon some of the wittiest men of the age.' His delight was more to excite merriment than detestation; and he detects follies rather than crimes. If any judgment be made from his books of his moral character, nothing will be found but purity and excellence. Knowledge of mankind, indeed, less extensive than that of Addison, will show that to write, and to live, are very different. Many who praise virtue, do no more than praise it. Yet it is reasonable to believe that Addison's professions and practice were at no great variance, since amidst that storm of faction in which most of his life was passed, though his station made him conspicuous, and his activity made him formidable, the character given him by his friends was never contradicted by his enemies. Of those with whom interest or opinion united him he had not only the esteem, but the kindness; and of others whom the violence of opposition drove against him, though he might lose the love, he retained the reverence.

It is justly observed by Tickell that he employed wit on the side of virtue and religion. He not only made the proper use of wit himself, but taught it to others; and from his time it has been generally subservient to the cause of reason and of truth. He has dissipated the prejudice. that had long connected gaiety with vice, and easiness of manners with laxity of principles. He has restored virtue to its dignity, and taught innocence not to be ashamed. This is an elevation of literary character 'above all Greek, above all Roman fame.' No greater felicity can genius attain than that of having purified intellectual pleasure, separated mirth from ind cency, and wit from licentiousness; of having taught a succession of writers to bring elegance and gaiety to the aid of goodness; and, if I may use expressions yet more awful, of having 'turned many to righteousness.'

* * *

As a describer of life and manners, he must be allowed to stand perhaps the first of the first rank. His humor, which, as Steele observes, is peculiar to himself, is so happily diffused as to give the grace of novelty to domestic scenes and daily occurrences. He never 'outsteps the modesty of nature,' nor raises merriment or wonder by the violation of truth. His figures never divert by distortion nor amaze by aggravation. He copies life with so much fidelity that he can be hardly said to invent; yet his exhibitions have an air so much original, that it is difficult to suppose them not merely the product of imagination.

As a teacher of wisdom, he may be confidently followed. His religion has nothing in it enthusiastic or superstitious: he appears neither weakly credulous nor wantonly sceptical; his morality is neither dangerously lax nor impracticably rigid. All the enchantment of fancy, and all the cogency of argument, are employed to recommend to the reader his real interest, the care of pleasing the author of his being. Truth is shown sometimes as the phantom of a vision; sometimes appears half-veiled in an allegory; sometimes attracts regard in the robes of fancy; and sometimes steps forth in the confidence of reason. She wears a thousand dresses, and in all is pleasing.

Mille habet ornatus, mille decenter habet.

His prose is the model of the middle style; on grave subjects not formal, on light occasions not groveling; pure without scrupulosity, and exact without apparent elaboration; always equable, and always easy, without glowing words or pointed sentences. Addison never deviates from his track to snatch a grace; he seeks no ambitious ornaments, and tries no hazardous innovations. His page is always luminous, but never blazes in unexpected splendor.

It was apparently his principal endeavor to avoid all harshness and severity of diction; he is therefore sometimes verbose in his transitions and connections, and sometimes descends too much to the language of conversation; yet if his language had been less idiomatical it might have lost somewhat of its genuine Anglicism. What he attempted, he performed; he is never feeble, and he did not wish to be energetic; he is never rapid, and he never stagnates. His sentences have neither studied amplitude nor affected brevity; his periods, though not diligently rounded, are voluble and easy. Whoever wishes to attain an English style, familiar but not coarse, and elegant but not ostentatious, must give his days and nights to the volumes of Addison.

(1781)

LETTERS

To the Right Honorable the Earl of Chesterfield

February 7, 1755.

MY LORD:

I have lately been informed by the proprietor of *The World,* that two papers, in which my *Dictionary* is recommended to the public, were written by your lordship. To be so distinguished is an honor which, being very little accustomed to favors from the great, I know not well how to receive, or in what terms to acknowledge.

When, upon some slight encouragement, I first visited your lordship, I was overpowered, like the rest of mankind, by the enchantment of your address; and I could not forbear to wish that I might boast myself ' *Le vainqueur du vainqueur de la terre* ' [conqueror of the conqueror of the earth]; that I might obtain that regard for which I saw the world contending; but I found my attendance so little encouraged, that neither pride nor modesty would suffer me to continue it. When I had once addressed your lordship in public, I had exhausted all the art of pleasing which a retired and uncourtly scholar can possess. I had done all that I could; and no man is well pleased to have his all neglected, be it ever so little.

Seven years, my lord, have now passed, since I waited in your outward rooms, or was repulsed from your door; during which time I have been pushing on my work through difficulties, of which it is useless to complain, and have brought it at last to the verge of publication, without one act of assistance, one word of encouragement, or one smile of favor. Such treatment I did not expect, for I never had a patron before.

The shepherd in Virgil grew at last acquainted with Love, and found him a native of the rocks.

Is not a patron, my lord, one who looks with unconcern on a man struggling for life in the water, and, when he has reached ground, encumbers him with help? The notice which you have been pleased to take of my labors, had it been early, had been kind; but it has been delayed till I am indifferent, and cannot enjoy it; till I am solitary, and cannot impart it; till I am known, and do not want it. I hope it is no very cynical asperity not to confess obligations where no benefit has been received, or to be unwilling that the public should consider me as owing that to a patron, which Providence has enabled me to do for myself.

Having carried on my work thus far with so little obligation to any favorer of learning, I shall not be disappointed though I should conclude it, if less be possible, with less; for I have been long wakened from that dream of hope, in which I once boasted myself with so much exultation,

My Lord,
Your Lordship's most humble,
Most obedient servant,
SAM. JOHNSON.

MR. JAMES MACPHERSON:

I received your foolish and impudent letter. Any violence offered me I shall do my best to repel; and what I cannot do for myself the law shall do for me. I hope I shall never be deterred from detecting what I think a cheat, by the menaces of a ruffian.

What would you have me retract? I thought your book an imposture; I think it an imposture still. For this opinion I have given my reasons to the public which I here dare you to refute. Your rage I defy. Your abilities, since you Homer, are not so formidable; and what hear of your morals, inclines me to pay regard not to what you shall say, but to what you shall prove. You may print this if you will.

SAM. JOHNSON.
(1775)

To the Reverend Dr. Taylor, Ashbourne, Derbyshire

DEAR SIR:

What can be the reason that I hear nothing from you? I hope nothing disables you from writing. What I have seen, and what I have felt, gives me reason to fear everything. Do not omit giving me the comfort of knowing, that after all my losses I have yet a friend left.

I want every comfort. My life is very solitary and very cheerless. Though has pleased God wonderfully to deliver

ne from the dropsy, I am yet very weak,
and have not passed the door since the
13th of December. I hope for some help
from warm weather, which will surely
come in time.

I could not have the consent of
physicians to go to church yesterday; I
therefore received the holy sacrament
at home, in the room where I communicated with dear Mrs. Williams, a little
before her death. O! my friend, the approach of death is very dreadful. I am
afraid to think on that which I know I
cannot avoid. It is vain to look round
and round for that help which cannot be
had. Yet we hope and hope, and fancy
that he who has lived to-day may live
to-morrow. But let us learn to derive
our hope only from God.

In the meantime let us be kind to one
another. I have no friend now living but
you and Mr. Hector, that was the friend
of my youth. Do not neglect, dear Sir,
   Yours affectionately,
    SAM. JOHNSON.
London, Easter Monday,
  April 12, 1784.

FROM THE VANITY OF HUMAN WISHES

Let observation, with extensive view,
Survey mankind, from China to Peru;
Remark each anxious toil, each eager strife,
And watch the busy scenes of crowded life;
Then say how hope and fear, desire and
  hate,   5
O'erspread with snares the clouded maze of
  fate,
Where wavering man, betrayed by venturous
  pride,
To tread the dreary paths without a guide;
As treacherous phantoms in the mist delude,
Shuns fancied ills, or chases airy good. 10
How rarely reason guides the stubborn
  choice,
Rules the bold hand, or prompts the sup-
  pliant voice.
How nations sink, by darling schemes op-
  pressed,
When vengeance listens to the fool's re-
  quest.
Fate wings with every wish the afflictive
  dart,   15
Each gift of nature, and each grace of art,
With fatal heat impetuous courage glows,
With fatal sweetness elocution flows,
Impeachment stops the speaker's powerful
  breath,
And restless fire precipitates on death. 20
But scarce observed, the knowing and the
  bold,
Fall in the general massacre of gold;
Wide-wasting pest! that rages unconfined,
And crowds with crimes the records of man-
  kind;
For gold his sword the hireling ruffian
  draws,   25
For gold the hireling judge distorts the
  laws;
Wealth heaped on wealth, nor truth nor
  safety buys,
The dangers gather as the treasures rise.
Let history tell where rival kings com-
  mand,
And dubious title shakes the maddened
  land;   30
When statutes glean the refuse of the
  sword,
How much more safe the vassal than the
  lord;
Low skulks the hind beneath the rage of
  power,
And leaves the wealthy traitor in the Tower,
Untouched his cottage, and his slumbers
  sound,   35
Though confiscation's vultures hover round.
    * * *
In full-blown dignity, see Wolsey stand,
Law in his voice, and fortune in his hand:
To him the church, the realm, their powers
  consign;
Through him the rays of regal bounty shine;
Turned by his nod the stream of honor
  flows,   41
His smile alone security bestows:
Still to new heights his restless wishes
  tower;
Claim leads to claim, and power advances
  power;
Till conquest unresisted ceased to please, 45
And rights submitted, left him none to
  seize.
At length his sovereign frowns — the train
  of state
Mark the keen glance, and watch the sign
  to hate:
Where'er he turns he meets a stranger's eye,
His suppliants scorn him, and his followers
  fly;   50
Now drops at once the pride of awful state,
The golden canopy, the glittering plate,
The regal palace, the luxurious board,
The liveried army, and the menial lord.

With age, with cares, with maladies op-
   pressed,   55
He seeks the refuge of monastic rest.
Grief aids disease, remembered folly stings,
And his last sighs reproach the faith of
   kings.
Speak thou, whose thoughts at humble
   peace repine,
Shall Wolsey's wealth, with Wolsey's end
   be thine?   60
Or liv'st thou now, with safer pride con-
   tent,
The wisest Justice on the banks of Trent?
For why did Wolsey, near the steeps of
   fate,
On weak foundations raise the enormous
   weight?   64
Why, but to sink beneath misfortune's blow,
With louder ruin to the gulfs below.

      * * *

On what foundations stands the warrior's
   pride,
How just his hopes, let Swedish Charles de-
   cide;
A frame of adamant, a soul of fire,
No dangers fright him, and no labors tire;
O'er love, o'er fear, extends his wide do-
   main,   71
Unconquered lord of pleasure and of pain.
No joys to him pacific scepters yield,
War sounds the trump, he rushes to the
   field;
Behold surrounding kings their power com-
   bine,   75
And one capitulate, and one resign;
Peace courts his hand, but spreads her
   charms in vain;
'Think nothing gained,' he cries, 'till nought
   remain,
On Moscow's walls till Gothic standards fly,
And all be mine beneath the polar sky.'   80
The march begins in military state,
And nations on his eye suspended wait;
Stern famine guards the solitary coast,
And winter barricades the realms of frost:
He comes, nor want, nor cold, his course
   delay;   85
Hide, blushing glory, hide Pultowa's day:
The vanquished hero leaves his broken
   bands,

And shews his miseries in distant lands;
Condemned a needy supplicant to wait,
While ladies interpose, and slaves debate. 90
But did not Chance at length the error
   mend?
Did no subverted empire mark his end?
Did rival monarchs give the fatal wound?
Or hostile millions press him to the ground?
His fall was destined to a barren strand,
A petty fortress, and a dubious hand;   96
He left the name at which the world grew
   pale,
To point a moral, or adorn a tale.

      * * *

Where then shall Hope and Fear their
   objects find?
Must dull suspense corrupt the stagnant
   mind?   100
Must helpless man, in ignorance sedate,
Roll darkling down the torrent of his fate?
Must no dislike alarm, no wishes rise,
No cries invoke the mercies of the skies?
Enquirer, cease; petitions yet remain   105
Which Heaven may hear, nor deem Religion
   vain.
Still raise for good the supplicating voice,
But leave to Heaven the measure and the
   choice.
Safe in his power whose eyes discern afar
The secret ambush of a specious prayer;
Implore his aid, in his decisions rest,   111
Secure, whate'er he gives, he gives the best.
Yet, when the sense of sacred presence fires,
And strong devotion to the skies aspires,
Pour forth thy fervors for a healthful mind,
Obedient passions, and a will resign'd;   116
For love, which scarce collective man can
   fill;
For patience, sovereign o'er transmuted ill;
For faith, that, panting for a happier seat,
Counts death kind Nature's signal of re-
   treat.   120
These goods for man the laws of Heav'n or-
   dain,
These goods he grants, who grants the
   power to gain;
With these celestial Wisdom calms the mind,
And makes the happiness she does not find.

                (1749)

JAMES BOSWELL (1740-1795)

James Boswell was the son of a Scotch laird at Auchinleck, in Ayrshire, and was prepared for the bar at Edinburgh and Glasgow. He also studied at Utrecht, later, entered the Middle Temple in London, and, in 1786, was admitted to the English bar. He traveled widely, cultivated assiduously the society of famous men, and made literary stock of their conversation and correspondence. During one of his tours he 'gratified his curiosity much in dining with Jean Jacques Rousseau,' then an exile 'in the wilds of Neufchatel.' At another time, he got as far as Corsica, published an *Account* on his return, and, when Paoli, the Corsican patriot, took refuge in London in 1776, became his constant guest. But the acquaintance which was particularly fruitful for English literature was that with Dr. Samuel Johnson, begun in 1763 and lasting until Johnson's death. Boswell was gifted with a high degree of curiosity, acute perception and a retentive memory, and he early formed the habit of keeping an exact journal. It is reported of him that he would 'lay down his knife and fork, and take out his tablets to record a good anecdote.' In spite of toadyism and vanity and his habit of taking notes, he had the faculty of making himself agreeable as a companion and, in 1773, Johnson got him elected to the Literary Club, thus vastly extending his opportunities for observation. The same year, the two toured the Hebrides together. During this journey Boswell allowed Johnson to read portions of his journal, and the great man acknowledged that it was 'a very exact picture of a portion of his life.' The year after Johnson's death Boswell published his *Journal of a Tour to the Hebrides with Dr. Johnson,* and during the next few years, he brought to completion the *Life of Samuel Johnson, LL.D.* (1791). This remarkable book is as vital and intimate as a masterpiece of fiction and has the additional interest that it is an authentic transcript from the life of a great and influential man of peculiar social qualities, 'the whole exhibiting,' as the title page has it, 'a view of literature and literary men in Great Britain for near half a century, during which he flourished.'

From THE LIFE OF JOHNSON

The accession of George the Third to the throne of these kingdoms, opened a new and brighter prospect to men of literary merit, who had been honored with no mark of royal favor in the preceding reign. His present Majesty's education in this country, as well as his taste and beneficence, prompted him to be the patron of science and the arts; and early this year, Johnson having been represented to him as a very learned and good man, without any certain provision, his Majesty was pleased to grant him a pension of three hundred pounds a year. The Earl of Bute, who was then prime minister, had the honor to announce this instance of his sovereign's bounty, concerning which, many and various stories, all equally erroneous, have been propagated; maliciously representing it as a political bribe to Johnson, to desert his avowed principles, and become the tool of a government which he held to be founded in usurpation. I have taken care to have it in my power to refute them from the most authentic information. Lord Bute told me that Mr. Wedderburne, now Lord Loughborough, was the person who first mentioned this subject to him. Lord Loughborough told me that the pension was granted to Johnson solely as the reward of his literary merit, without any stipulation whatever, or even tacit understanding that he should write for the administration. His lordship added, that he was confident the political tracts which Johnson afterwards did write, as they were entirely consonant with his own opinions, would have been written by him though no pension had been granted to him.

Mr. Thomas Sheridan and Mr. Murphy, who then lived a good deal both with him and Mr. Wedderburne, told me that they previously talked with Johnson upon this matter, and that it was perfectly understood by all parties that the pension was merely honorary. Sir Joshua Reynolds told me, that Johnson called on him after his Majesty's intention had been notified to him, and said he wished to consult his friends as to the propriety of his accepting this mark of the royal favor, after the definitions which he had given in his *Dictionary* of 'pension' and 'pensioners.' He said he should not have Sir Joshua's answer till next day, when he would call again, and desired he might think of it. Sir Joshua answered that he was clear to give his opinion then, that there could be no objection to his receiving from the king a reward for literary merit; and that certainly the definitions in his *Dictionary* were not applicable to him. Johnson, it should seem, was satisfied, for he did not call again till he had accepted the pension, and had waited on Lord Bute to thank him. He then told Sir Joshua that Lord Bute said to him expressly, 'It is not given you for anything you are to do, but what you have done.' His lordship, he said, behaved in the handsomest manner. He repeated the words twice, that he might be sure Johnson heard them, and thus set his mind perfectly at ease. * * *

But I shall not detain my readers longer by any words of my own, on a subject on which I am happily enabled, by the favor of the Earl of Bute, to present them with what Johnson himself wrote; his lordship having been pleased to communicate to me a copy of the following letter to his father, which does great honor both to the writer and to the noble person to whom it is addressed:

'To the Right Honorable the Earl of Bute

'July 20, 1762.

'MY LORD — When the bills were yesterday delivered to me by Mr. Wedderburne, I was informed by him of the future favors which his Majesty has, by your Lordship's recommendation, been induced to intend for me.

'Bounty always receives part of its value from the manner in which it is bestowed; your Lordship's kindness includes every circumstance that can gratify delicacy, or enforce obligation. You have conferred favors on a man who has neither alliance nor interest, who has not merited them by services, nor courted them by officiousness; you have spared him the shame of solicitation, and the anxiety of suspense.

'What has been thus elegantly given, will, I hope, be not reproachfully enjoyed; I shall endeavor to give your Lordship the only recompense which generosity desires,— the gratification of finding that your benefits are not improperly bestowed. I am, my Lord,

'Your Lordship's most obliged,

'Most obedient, and most humble servant,

'SAM JOHNSON.'

This year his friend, Sir Joshua Reynolds, paid a visit of some weeks to his native county, Devonshire, in which he was accompanied by Johnson, who was much pleased with this jaunt, and declared he had derived from it a great accession of new ideas. He was entertained at the seats of several noblemen and gentlemen in the west of England,[1] but the greatest part of this time was passed at Plymouth, where the magnificence of the navy, the ship-building and all its circumstances, afforded him a grand subject for contemplation. The commissioner of the dockyard paid him the compliment of ordering the yacht to convey him and his friend to the Eddystone, to which they accordingly sailed. But the weather was so tempestuous that they could not land. * * *

Sir Joshua Reynolds, to whom I was obliged for my information concerning this excursion, mentions a very characteristical anecdote of Johnson while at Plymouth. Having observed that, in consequence of the dock-yard, a new town had arisen about two miles off as a rival to the old; and knowing, from his sagacity and just observation of human nature, that it is certain, if a man hates at all, he will hate his next neighbor, he concluded that this new and rising

[1] At one of these seats Dr. Amyat, physician in London, told me he happened to meet him. In order to amuse him till dinner should be ready, he was taken out to walk in the garden. The master of the house, thinking it proper to introduce something scientific into the conversation, addressed him thus: 'Are you a botanist, Dr. Johnson?' 'No, sir,' answered Johnson, 'I am not a botanist; and (alluding no doubt to his near-sightedness), should I wish to become a botanist, I must first turn myself into a reptile.'

town could not but excite the envy and jealousy of the old, in which conjecture he was very soon confirmed; he, therefore, set himself resolutely on the side of the old town, the *established* town, in which his lot was cast, considering it as a kind of duty to *stand by* it. He accordingly entered warmly into its interests, and upon every occasion talked of the *dockers,* as the inhabitants of the new town were called, as upstarts and aliens. Plymouth is very plentifully supplied with water by a river brought into it from a great distance, which is so abundant that it runs to waste in the town. The Dock, or New-town, being totally destitute of water, petitioned Plymouth that a small portion of the conduit might be permitted to go to them, and this was now under consideration. Johnson, affecting to entertain the passions of the place, was violent in opposition; and half-laughing at himself for his pretended zeal, where he had no concern, exclaimed, ' No, no; I am against the *dockers;* I am a Plymouth man. Rogues! let them die of thirst. They shall not have a drop!'

* * *

1763: Aetat. 54. In 1763, he furnished to *The Poetical Calendar,* published by Fawkes and Woty, a character of Collins, which he afterwards ingrafted into his entire life of that admirable poet, in the collection of lives which he wrote for the body of English poetry, formed and published by the booksellers of London. His account of the melancholy depression with which Collins was severely afflicted, and which brought him to his grave, is, I think, one of the most tender and interesting passages in the whole series of his writings. * * *

This is to me a memorable year; for in it I had the happiness to obtain the acquaintance of that extraordinary man whose memoirs I am now writing: an acquaintance which I shall ever esteem as one of the most fortunate circumstances in my life. Though then but two-and-twenty, I had for several years read his works with delight and instruction, and had the highest reverence for their author, which had grown up in my fancy into a kind of mysterious veneration, by figuring to myself a state of solemn, elevated abstraction in which I supposed him to live in the immense metropolis of London. Mr. Gentleman, a native of Ireland, who passed some years in Scotland as a player, and as an instructor in the English language, a man whose talents and worth were depressed by misfortunes, had given me a representation of the figure and manner of DICTIONARY JOHNSON! as he was then generally called; and during my first visit to London, which was for three months in 1760, Mr. Derrick, the poet, who was Gentleman's friend and countryman, flattered me with hopes that he would introduce me to Johnson, an honor of which I was very ambitious. But he never found an opportunity, which made me doubt that he had promised to do what was not in his power; till Johnson, some years afterwards, told me, ' Derrick, sir, might very well have introduced you. I had a kindness for Derrick, and am sorry he is dead.'

In the summer of 1761 Mr. Thomas Sheridan was at Edinburgh, and delivered lectures upon the English language and public speaking to large and respectable audiences. I was often in his company, and heard him frequently expatiate upon Johnson's extraordinary knowledge, talents, and virtues, repeat his pointed sayings, describe his particularities, and boast of his being his guest sometimes till two or three in the morning. At his house I hoped to have many opportunities of seeing the sage, as Mr. Sheridan obligingly assured me I should not be disappointed.

When I returned to London in the end of 1762, to my surprise and regret I found an irreconcilable difference had taken place between Johnson and Sheridan. A pension of two hundred pounds a year had been given to Sheridan. Johnson, who thought slightingly of Sheridan's art, upon hearing that he was also pensioned, exclaimed, ' What! have they given *him* a pension? Then it is time for me to give up mine.' Whether this proceeded from a momentary indignation, as if it were an affront to his exalted merit that a player should be rewarded in the same manner with him, or was the sudden effect of a fit of peevishness, it was unluckily said, and indeed cannot be justified. Mr. Sheridan's pension was granted to him not as a player, but as a sufferer in the cause of government, when he was manager of the Theater Royal in Ireland, when parties ran high in 1753. And it must also be allowed that he was a man of literature, and had considerably improved the arts of reading and speaking with distinctness and propriety. * * *

Johnson complained that a man who disliked him repeated his sarcasm to Mr. Sheridan, without telling him what followed, which was, that after a pause he added, 'However, I am glad that Mr. Sheridan has a pension, for he is a very good man.' Sheridan could never forgive this hasty contemptuous expression. It rankled in his mind; and though I informed him of all that Johnson said, and that he would be very glad to meet him amicably, he positively declined repeated offers which I made, and once went off abruptly from a house where he and I were engaged to dine, because he was told that Dr. Johnson was to be there.

I have no sympathetic feeling with such persevering resentment. It is painful when there is a breach between those who have lived together socially and cordially; and I wonder that there is not, in all such cases, a mutual wish that it should be healed. I could perceive that Mr. Sheridan was by no means satisfied with Johnson's acknowledging him to be a good man. That could not soothe his injured vanity. I could not but smile, at the same time that I was offended, to observe Sheridan in *The Life of Swift,* which he afterwards published, attempting, in the writhings of his resentment, to depreciate Johnson, by characterizing him as 'A writer of gigantic fame in these days of little men'; that very Johnson whom he once so highly admired and venerated. This rupture with Sheridan deprived Johnson of one of his most agreeable resources for amusement in his lonely evenings; for Sheridan's well-informed, animated, and bustling mind never suffered conversation to stagnate; and Mrs. Sheridan was a most agreeable companion to an intellectual man. She was sensible, ingenious, unassuming, yet communicative. I recollect, with satisfaction, many pleasing hours which I passed with her under the hospitable roof of her husband, who was to me a very kind friend.

Her novel, entitled *Memoirs of Miss Sydney Biddulph,* contains an excellent moral while it inculcates a future state of retribution; and what it teaches is impressed upon the mind by a series of as deep distress as can affect humanity, in the amiable and pious heroine who goes to her grave unrelieved, but resigned, and full of hope of 'heaven's mercy.' Johnson paid her this high compliment upon it: 'I know not, Madam, that you have a right, upon moral principles, to make your readers suffer so much.'

Mr. Thomas Davies, the actor, who then kept a bookseller's shop in Russell Street, Covent Garden, told me that Johnson was very much his friend, and came frequently to his house, where he more than once invited me to meet him; but by some unlucky accident or other he was prevented from coming to us. Mr. Thomas Davies was a man of good understanding and talents, with the advantage of a liberal education. Though somewhat pompous, he was an entertaining companion; and his literary performances have no inconsiderable share of merit. He was a friendly and very hospitable man. Both he and his wife, (who has been celebrated for her beauty), though upon the stage for many years, maintained an uniform decency of character; and Johnson esteemed them, and lived in as easy an intimacy with them, as with any family which he used to visit. Mr. Davies recollected several of Johnson's remarkable sayings, and was one of the best of the many imitators of his voice and manner, while relating them. He increased my impatience more and more to see the extraordinary man whose works I highly valued, and whose conversation was reported to be so peculiarly excellent.

At last, on Monday, the 16th of May, when I was sitting in Mr. Davies's back-parlor, after having drunk tea with him and Mrs. Davies, Johnson unexpectedly came into the shop; and Mr. Davies having perceived him, through the glass-door in the room in which we were sitting, advancing towards us,—he announced his awful approach to me, somewhat in the manner of an actor in the part of ·Horatio, when he addresses Hamlet on the appearance of his father's ghost, 'Look, my lord, it comes!' I found that I had a very perfect idea of Johnson's figure, from the portrait of him painted by Sir Joshua Reynolds soon after he had published his *Dictionary*, in the attitude of sitting in his easy chair in deep meditation. Mr. Davies mentioned my name, and respectfully introduced me to him. I was much agitated; and recollecting his prejudice against the Scotch, of which I had heard much, I said to Davies, 'Don't tell where I come from.'—'From Scotland,' cried Davies, roguishly. 'Mr. Johnson,' said I, 'I do indeed come from Scotland, but I cannot help it.' I am willing to flatter myself that I meant this as light pleasantry to soothe and conciliate him, and not as an humiliating abasement at the expense of my country. But however that might be, this speech was somewhat unlucky; for with that quickness of wit for which he was so remarkable, he seized the expression, 'come from Scotland,' which I used in the sense of being of that country; and, as if I had said that I had come away from it, or left it, retorted, 'That, sir, I find, is what a very great many of your countrymen cannot help.' This stroke stunned me a good deal; and when we had sat down, I felt myself not a little embarrassed, and apprehensive of what might come next. He then addressed himself to Davies: 'What do you think of Garrick? He has refused me an order for the play for Miss Williams, because he knows the house will be full, and that an order would be worth three shillings.' Eager to take any opening to get into conversation with him, I ventured to say, 'O sir, I cannot think Mr. Garrick would grudge such a trifle to you.' 'Sir,' said he, with a stern look, 'I have known David Garrick longer than you have done; and I know no right you have to talk to me on the **subject**.' Perhaps I deserved this check; for it was rather presumptuous in me, an entire stranger, to express any doubt of the justice of his animadversion upon his old acquaintance and pupil.[1] I now felt

myself much mortified, and began to think that the hope which I had long indulged of obtaining his acquaintance was blasted. And, in truth, had not my ardor been uncommonly strong, and my resolution uncommonly persevering, so rough a reception might have deterred me from ever making any further attempts. Fortunately, however, I remained upon the field not wholly discomfited; and was soon rewarded by hearing some of his conversation, of which I preserved the following short minute, without remarking the questions and observations by which it was produced.

'People,' he remarked, 'may be taken in once, who imagine that an author is greater in private life than other men. Uncommon parts require uncommon opportunities, for their exertion.

'In barbarous society, superiority of parts is of real consequence. Great strength or great wisdom is of much value to an individual. But in more polished times there are people to do everything for money; and then there are a number of other superiorities, such as those of birth, and fortune, and rank, that dissipate men's attention, and leave no extraordinary share of respect for personal and intellectual superiority. This is wisely ordered by Providence, to preserve some equality among mankind.'

* * *

I was highly pleased with the extraordinary vigor of his conversation, and regretted that I was drawn away from it by an engagement at another place. I had, for a part of the evening, been left alone with him, and had ventured to make an observation now and then, which he received very civilly; so that I was satisfied that, though there was a roughness in his manner, there was no ill-nature in his disposition. Davies followed me to the door, and when I complained to him a little of the hard blows which the great man had given me, he kindly took upon him to console me by saying, 'Don't be uneasy. I can see he likes you very well.'

A few days afterwards I called on Davies, and asked him if he thought I

[1] That this was a momentary sally against Garrick there can be no doubt; for at Johnson's desire he had, some years before, given a benefit-night at his theater to this very person, by which she had got two hundred pounds. Johnson, indeed, upon all other occasions, when I was in his company, praised the very liberal charity of Garrick. I once mentioned to him, 'It is observed,

Sir, that you attack Garrick yourself, but will suffer nobody else to do it.' Johnson (smiling) 'Why, Sir, that is true.'

might take the liberty of waiting on Mr. Johnson at his chambers in the Temple. He said I certainly might, and that Mr. Johnson would take it as a compliment. So, on Tuesday, the 24th day of May, [5] after having been enlivened by the witty sallies of Messieurs Thornton, Wilkes, Churchill, and Lloyd, with whom I had passed the morning, I boldly repaired to Johnson. His chambers were on the first [10] floor of No. 1, Inner Temple-lane, and I entered them with an impression given me by the Reverend Dr. Blair, of Edinburgh, who had been introduced to him not long before, and described his having [15] 'found the Giant in his den'; an expression which, when I came to be pretty well acquainted with Johnson, I repeated to him, and he was diverted at this picturesque account of himself. Dr. Blair [20] had been presented to him by Dr. James Fordyce. At this time the controversy concerning the pieces published by Mr. James Macpherson, as translations of Ossian, was at its height. Johnson had [25] all along denied their authenticity; and, what was still more provoking to their admirers, maintained that they had no merit. The subject having been introduced by Dr. Fordyce, Dr. Blair, relying [30] on the internal evidence of their antiquity, asked Dr. Johnson whether he thought any man of a modern age could have written such poems? Johnson replied, ' Yes, sir, many men, many women, [35] and many children.' Johnson, at this time, did not know that Dr. Blair had just published a *Dissertation,* not only defending their authenticity, but seriously ranking them with the poems of Homer [40] and Virgil; and when he was afterwards informed of this circumstance, he expressed some displeasure at Dr. Fordyce's having suggested the topic, and said, ' I am not sorry that they got thus much for [45] their pains. Sir, it was like leading one to talk of a book, when the author is concealed behind the door.'

He received me very courteously; but it must be confessed that his apartment, [50] and furniture, and morning dress, were sufficiently uncouth. His brown suit of clothes looked very rusty; he had on a little old shriveled unpowdered wig, which was too small for his head, his [55] shirt-neck and knees of his breeches were loose; his black worsted stockings ill

drawn up; and he had a pair of unbuckled shoes by way of slippers. But all these slovenly particularities were forgotten the moment that he began to talk. Some gentlemen, whom I do not recollect, were sitting with him; and when they went away, I also rose; but he said to me, ' Nay, don't go.' ' Sir,' said I, ' I am afraid that I intrude upon you. It is benevolent to allow me to sit and hear you.' He seemed pleased with this compliment, which I sincerely paid him, and answered ' Sir, I am obliged to any man who visits me.' I have preserved the following short minute of what passed this day: —

' Madness frequently discovers itself merely by unnecessary deviation from the usual modes of the world. My poor friend Smart showed the disturbance of his mind, by falling upon his knees, and saying his prayers in the street, or in any other unusual place. Now although, rationally speaking, it is greater madness not to pray at all, than to pray as Smart did, I am afraid there are so many who do not pray, that their understanding is not called in question.'

Concerning this unfortunate poet, Christopher Smart, who was confined in a madhouse, he had, at another time, the following conversation with Dr. Burney. BURNEY: ' How does poor Smart do, sir; is he likely to recover? '— JOHNSON: ' It seems as if his mind had ceased to struggle with the disease: for he grows fat upon it.'— BURNEY: ' Perhaps, sir, that may be from want of exercise.'— JOHNSON: ' No, sir; he has partly as much exercise as he used to have, for he digs in the garden. Indeed, before his confinement, he used for exercise to walk to the ale-house; but he was *carried* back again. I did not think he ought to be shut up. His infirmities were not noxious to society. He insisted on people praying with him, and I'd as lief pray with Kit Smart as any one else. Another charge was, that he did not love clean linen; and I have no passion for it.' Johnson continued: ' Mankind have a great aversion to intellectual labor; but even supposing knowledge to be easily attainable, more people would be content to be ignorant than would take even a little trouble to acquire it.'

' The morality of an action depends on the motive from which we act. If I fling half-a-crown to a beggar, with intention to break his head, and he picks it up and buys victuals with it, the physical effect is good; but, with respect to me, the action is very wrong. So religious exercises, if not performed with an intention to please God, avail us nothing. As our Saviour says of those who perform them from other motives, " Verily they have their reward."

' The Christian religion has very strong evidences. It, indeed, appears in some degree strange to reason; but in History we have undoubted facts, against which, reasoning à priori, we have more arguments than we have for them; but then, testimony has great weight, and casts the balance. I would recommend to every man whose faith is yet unsettled, Grotius, — Dr. Pearson,— and Dr. Clarke.'

Talking of Garrick, he said, ' He is the first man in the world for sprightly conversation.'

When I rose a second time, he again pressed me to stay, which I did.

He told me, that he generally went abroad at four in the afternoon, and seldom came home till two in the morning. I took the liberty to ask if he did not think it wrong to live thus, and not make more use of his great talents. He owned it was a bad habit. On reviewing, at the distance of many years, my journal of this period, I wonder how, at my first visit, I ventured to talk to him so freely, and that he bore it with so much indulgence.

Before we parted, he was so good as to promise to favor me with his company one evening at my lodgings; and, as I took my leave, shook me cordially by the hand. It is almost needless to add, that I felt no little elation at having now so happily established an acquaintance of which I had been so long ambitious.

My readers will, I trust, excuse me for being thus minutely circumstantial, when it is considered that the acquaintance of Dr. Johnson was to me a most valuable acquisition, and laid the foundation of whatever instruction and entertainment they may receive from my collections concerning the great subject of the work which they are now perusing.

I did not visit him again till Monday, June 13, at which time I recollect no part of his conversation, except, that

when I told him I had been to see Johnson ride upon three horses, he said, ' Such a man, sir, should be encouraged; for his performances show the extent of the human powers in one instance, and thus tend to raise our opinion of the faculties of man. He shows what may be attained by persevering application; so that every man may hope, that by giving as much application, although, perhaps, he may never ride three horses at a time, or dance upon a wire, yet he may be equally expert in whatever profession he has chosen to pursue.'

He again shook me by the hand at parting, and asked me why I did not come oftener to him. Trusting that I was now in his good graces, I answered, that he had not given me much encouragement, and reminded him of the check I had received from him at our first interview. ' Poh, poh !' said he, with a complacent smile, ' never mind these things. Come to me as often as you can. I shall be glad to see you.'

I had learnt that his place of frequent resort was the Mitre tavern in Fleet-street, where he loved to sit up late, and I begged I might be allowed to pass an evening with him there soon, which he promised I should. A few days afterwards, I met him near Temple-bar about one o'clock in the morning, and asked if he would then go to the Mitre. ' Sir,' said he, ' it is too late, they won't let us in. But I 'll go with you another night, with all my heart.'

A revolution of some importance in my plan of life had just taken place: for instead of procuring a commission in the foot guards, which was my own inclination, I had, in compliance with my father's wishes, agreed to study the law, and was soon to set out for Utrecht, to hear the lectures of an excellent civilian in that University, and then to proceed on my travels. Though very desirous of obtaining Dr. Johnson's advice and instructions on the mode of pursuing my studies, I was at this time so occupied, shall I call it? or so dissipated by the amusements of London, that our next meeting was not till Saturday, June 25, when, happening to dine at Clifton's eating-house, in Butcher-row, I was surprised to perceive Johnson come in and take his seat at another table. The mode of dining, or rather being fed, at such houses in London, is well known to many to be particularly unsocial, as there is no ordinary, or united company, but each person has his own mess, and is under no obligation to hold any intercourse with any one. A liberal and full-minded man, however, who loves to talk, will break through this churlish and unsocial restraint. Johnson and an Irish gentleman got into a dispute concerning the cause of some part of mankind being black. 'Why, sir,' said Johnson, 'it has been accounted for in three ways: either by supposing that they are the posterity of Ham, who was cursed, or that God at first created two kinds of men, one black, and another white, or that, by the heat of the sun, the skin in scorched, and so acquires a sooty hue. This matter has been much canvassed among naturalists, but has never been brought to any certain issue.' What the Irishman said is totally obliterated from my mind; but I remember that he became very warm and intemperate in his expressions; upon which Johnson rose, and quietly walked away. When he had retired, his antagonist took his revenge, as he thought by saying, 'He has a most ungainly figure, and an affection of pomposity, unworthy of a man of genius.'

Johnson had not observed that I was in the room. I followed him, however, and he agreed to meet me in the evening at the Mitre. I called on him, and we went thither at nine. We had a good supper, and port wine, of which he then sometimes drank a bottle. The orthodox high-church sound of the Mitre,—the figure and manner of the celebrated Samuel Johnson, — the extraordinary power and precision of his conversation, and the pride, arising from finding myself admitted as his companion, produced a variety of sensations, and a pleasing elevation of mind beyond what I had ever before experienced. I find in my Journal the following minute of our conversation, which though it will give but a very faint notion of what passed, is, in some degree, a valuable record; and it will be curious in this view, as showing how habitual to his mind were some opinions which appear in his works.

'Colley Cibber, sir, was by no means a blockhead, but by arrogating to himself too much, he was in danger of losing that degree of estimation to which he was entitled. His friends gave out that he *intended* his Birthday Odes should be bad; but that was not the case, sir, for he kept them many months by him, and a few years before he died he showed me one of them, with great solicitude to render it as perfect as might be, and I made some corrections, to which he was not very willing to submit. I remember the following couplet in allusion to the King and himself:—

Perched on the eagle's soaring wing,
The lowly linnet loves to sing.

Sir, he had heard something of the fabulous tale of the wren sitting upon the eagle's wing, and he had applied it to a linnet. Cibber's familiar style, however, was better than that which Whitehead had assumed. *Grand* nonsense is insupportable. Whitehead is but a little man to inscribe verses to players.'

I did not presume to controvert this censure, which was tinctured with his prejudice against players; but I could not help thinking that a dramatic poet might with propriety pay a compliment to an eminent performer, as Whitehead has very happily done in his verses to Mr. Garrick.

'Sir, I do not think Gray a first-rate poet. He has not a bold imagination, nor much command of words. The obscurity in which he has involved himself will not persuade us that he is sublime. His *Elegy in a Churchyard* has a happy selection of images, but I don't like what are called his great things. His Ode which begins

" Ruin seize thee, ruthless King,
Confusion on thy banners wait!"

has been celebrated for its abruptness, and plunging into the subject all at once. But such arts as these have no merit, unless when they are original. We admire them only once; and this abruptness has nothing new in it. We have had it often before. Nay, we have it in the old song of Johnny Armstrong:

Is there ever a man in all Scotland,
From the highest estate to the lowest degree.

And then, sir,

Yes, there is a man in Westmoreland,
And Johnny Armstrong they do him call.

There, now, you plunge at once into the subject. You have no previous narration to lead you to it. The two next lines in that Ode are, I think, very good:

"Though fanned by Conquest's crimson
    wing,
They mock the air with idle state."'

* * *

Finding him in a placid humor, and wishing to avail myself of the opportunity which I fortunately had of consulting a sage, to hear whose wisdom, I conceived, in the ardor of youthful imagination, that men filled with a noble enthusiasm for intellectual improvement would gladly have resorted from distant lands,— I opened my mind to him ingenuously, and gave him a little sketch of my life, to which he was pleased to listen with great attention.

I acknowledged that though educated very strictly in the principles of religion, I had for some time been misled into a certain degree of infidelity; but that I was come now to a better way of thinking, and was fully satisfied of the truth of the christian revelation, though I was not clear as to every point considered to be orthodox. Being at all times a curious examiner of the human mind, and pleased with an undisguised display of what had passed in it, he called to me with warmth, 'Give me your hand, I have taken a liking to you.' He then began to descant upon the force of testimony, and the little we could know of final causes; so that the objections of, 'Why was it so?' or 'Why was it not so?' ought not to disturb us: adding, that he himself had at one period been guilty of a temporary neglect of religion, but that it was not the result of argument, but mere absence of thought.

After having given credit to reports of his bigotry, I was agreeably surprised when he expressed the following very liberal sentiment, which has the additional value of obviating an objection to our holy religion, founded upon the discordant tenets of christians themselves: 'For my part, sir, I think all christians, whether papists or protestants, agree in the essential articles, and that their differences are trivial, and rather political than religious.'

We talked of belief in ghosts. He said, 'Sir, I make a distinction between what a man may experience by the mere strength of his imagination, and what imagination cannot possibly produce. Thus, suppose I should think that I saw a form, and heard a voice cry, "Johnson, you are a very wicked fellow, and unless you repent you will certainly be punished"; my own unworthiness is so deeply impressed upon my mind, that I might *imagine* I thus saw and heard, and therefore I should not believe that an external communication had been made to me. But if a form should appear, and a voice should tell me that a particular man had died at a particular place, and a particular hour, a fact which I had no apprehension of, nor any means of knowing, and this fact, with all its circumstances, should afterwards be unquestionably proved, I should in that case be persuaded that I had supernatural intelligence imparted to me.'

Here it is proper, once for all, to give a true and fair statement of Johnson's way of thinking upon the question, whether departed spirits are ever permitted to appear in this world, or in any way to operate upon human life. He has been ignorantly misrepresented as weakly credulous upon that subject; and, therefore, though I feel an inclination to disdain and treat with silent contempt so foolish a notion concerning my illustrious friend, yet, as I find it has gained ground, it is necessary to refute it. The real fact then is, that Johnson had a very philosophical mind, and such a rational respect for testimony, as to make him submit his understanding to what was authentically proved, though he could not comprehend why it was so. Being thus disposed, he was willing to inquire into the truth of any relation of supernatural agency, a general belief of which has prevailed in all nations and ages. But so far was he from being the dupe of implicit faith, that he examined the matter with a jealous attention, and no man was more ready to refute its falsehood when he had discovered it. Churchill in his poem entitled *The Ghost,* availed himself of the absurd credulity imputed to Johnson, and drew a caricature of him under the name of 'Pomposo,' representing him as one of the believers of the story of a ghost in Cock-lane, which, in the year 1762, had gained very general credit in London. Many of my readers, I am convinced, are to this hour under an impression that Johnson was thus foolishly deceived. It will therefore surprise them a good deal when they are informed upon undoubted authority, that Johnson was one of those by whom the imposture was detected. The story had become so popular, that he thought it should be investigated; and in this research he was assisted by the Rev. Dr. Douglas, now bishop of Salisbury, the great detector of impostures; who informs me that after the gentlemen who went and examined into the evidence were satisfied of its falsity, Johnson wrote in their presence an account of it, which was published in the newspapers and *Gentleman's Magazine,* and undeceived the world.

Our conversation proceeded. 'Sir,' said he, 'I am a friend to subordination as most conducive to the happiness of society. There is a reciprocal pleasure in governing and being governed.'

'Dr. Goldsmith is one of the first men we now have as an author, and he is a very worthy man too. He has been loose in his principles, but he is coming right.'

I mentioned Mallet's tragedy of *Elvira,* which had been acted the preceding winter at Drury-lane, and that the Honorable Andrew Erskine, Mr. Dempster, and myself, had joined in writing a pamphlet, entitled *Critical Strictures,* against it. That the mildness of Dempster's disposition had, however, relented; and he had candidly said, 'We have hardly a right to abuse this tragedy, for, bad as it is, how vain should either of us be to write one not near so good!' JOHNSON: 'Why, no sir; this is not just reasoning. You *may* abuse a tragedy, though you cannot write one. You may scold a carpenter who has made you a bad table, though you cannot make a table. It is not your trade to make tables.'

When I talked to him of the paternal estate to which I was heir, he said, 'Sir, let me tell you, that to be a Scotch landlord, where you have a number of families dependent upon you, and attached to you, is, perhaps, as high a situation as humanity can arrive at. A merchant upon the 'Change of London, with a hundred thousand pounds, is nothing; an English Duke, with an immense fortune, is nothing; he has no tenants who consider themselves as under his patriarchal care, and who will follow him to the field upon an emergency.'

* * *

I complained to him that I had not yet acquired much knowledge, and asked his advice as to my studies. He said, 'Don't talk of study, now. I will give you a plan; but it will require some time to consider of it.' 'It is very good of you,' I replied, 'to allow me to be with you thus. Had it been foretold to me some years ago that I should pass an evening with the author of the *Rambler,* how should I have exulted!' What I then expressed was sincerely from my heart. He was satisfied that it was, and cordially answered, 'Sir, I am glad we have met. I hope we shall pass many evenings, and mornings too, together.' We finished a couple of bottles of port, and sat till between one and two in the morning.

He wrote this year, in the *Critical Review,* the account of *Telemachus, a Mask,* by the Rev. George Graham, of Eton College. The subject of this beautiful poem was particularly interesting to Johnson. who had much experience of 'the conflict of opposite principles,' which he describes as 'the contention between pleasure and virtue, a struggle which will always be continued while the present system of nature shall subsist; nor can history or poetry exhibit more than pleasure triumphing over virtue, and virtue subjugating pleasure.'

As Dr. Oliver Goldsmith will frequently appear in this narrative, I shall endeavor to make my readers in some degree acquainted with his singular character. He was a native of Ireland, and a contemporary with Mr. Burke, at Trinity College, Dublin, but did not then give much promise of future celebrity. He, however, observed to Mr. Malone, that 'though he made no great figure in mathematics, which was a study in much repute there, he could turn an Ode of

Horace into English better than any of them.' He afterwards studied physic in Edinburgh, and upon the Continent: and, I have been informed, was enabled to pursue his travels on foot, partly by demanding, at Universities, to enter the lists as a disputant, by which, according to the custom of many of them, he was entitled to the premium of a crown, when, luckily for him, his challenge was not accepted so that, as I once observed to Johnson, he *disputed* his passage through Europe. He then came to England, and was employed successively in the capacities of an usher to an academy, a corrector of the press, a reviewer, and a writer for a newspaper. He had sagacity enough to cultivate assiduously the acquaintance of Johnson, and his faculties were gradually enlarged by the contemplation of such a model. To me and many others it appeared that he studiously copied the manner of Johnson, though, indeed, upon a smaller scale.

At this time I think he had published nothing with his name, though it was pretty generally known that *one Dr. Goldsmith* was the author of *An Inquiry into the present State of Polite Learning in Europe,* and of *The Citizen of the World,* a series of letters supposed to be written from London by a Chinese. No man had the art of displaying with more advantage, as a writer, whatever literary acquisitions he made. *Nihil quod tetigit non ornavit*[1] [There was nothing he touched he did not adorn]. His mind resembled a fertile but thin soil. There was a quick, but not a strong, vegetation, of whatever chanced to be thrown upon it. No deep root could be struck. The oak of the forest did not grow there; but the elegant shrubbery and the fragrant parterre appeared in gay succession. It has been generally circulated and believed that he was a mere fool in conversation; but, in truth, this has been greatly exaggerated. He had, no doubt, a more than common share of that hurry of ideas which we often find in his countrymen, and which sometimes produces a laughable confusion in expressing them. He was very much what the French call *un étourdi,* and from vanity and an eager desire of being conspicuous

wherever he was, he frequently talked carelessly without knowledge of the subject, or even without thought. His person was short, his countenance coarse and vulgar, his deportment that of a scholar awkwardly affecting the easy gentleman. Those who were in any way distinguished, excited envy in him to so ridiculous an excess, that the instances of it are hardly credible. When accompanying two beautiful young ladies,[2] with their mother, on a tour in France, he was seriously angry that more attention was paid to them than to him; and once at the exhibition of the *Fantoccini* in London, when those who sat next to him observed with what dexterity a puppet was made to toss a pike, he could not bear that it should have such praise, and exclaimed, with some warmth, ' Pshaw! I can do it better myself.'[3]

He, I am afraid, had no settled system of any sort, so that his conduct must not be strictly scrutinized; but his affections were social and generous, and when he had money he gave it away very liberally. His desire of imaginary consequence predominated over his attention to truth. When he began to rise into notice, he said he had a brother who was dean of Durham, a fiction so easily detected, that it is wonderful how he should have been so inconsiderate as to hazard it. He boasted to me at this time of the power of his pen in commanding money, which I believe was true in a certain degree, though in the instance he gave he was by no means correct. He told me that he had sold a novel for four hundred pounds. This was his *Vicar of Wakefield.* But Johnson informed me that he had made the bargain for Goldsmith, and the price was sixty pounds. ' And, sir,' said he, ' a sufficient price too, when it was sold; for then the fame of Goldsmith had not been elevated, as it afterwards was, by his *Traveller;* and the bookseller had such faint hopes of profit by his bargain, that he kept the manuscript by him a long time, and did not publish it till after *The Traveller* had appeared. Then,

[1] See his epitaph in Westminster Abbey, written by Dr. Johnson.

[2] Miss Hornecks, one of whom is now married to Henry Bunbury, Esq., and the other to Colonel Gwyn.
[3] He went home with Mr. Burke to supper; and broke his shin by attempting to exhibit to the company how much better he could jump over a stick than the puppets.

to be sure, it was accidentally worth more money.'

Mrs. Piozzi and Sir John Hawkins have strangely misstated the history of Goldsmith's situation and Johnson's friendly interference, when this novel was sold. I shall give it authentically from Johnson's own exact narration:—'I received one morning a message from poor Goldsmith that he was in great distress, and, as it was not in his power to come to me, begging that I would come to him as soon as possible. I sent him a guinea, and promised to come to him directly. I accordingly went as soon as I was dressed, and found that his landlady had arrested him for his rent, at which he was in a violent passion. I perceived that he had already changed my guinea, and had got a bottle of Madeira and a glass before him. I put the cork into the bottle, desired he would be calm, and began to talk to him of the means by which he might be extricated. He then told me that he had a novel ready for the press, which he produced to me. I looked into it, and saw its merits; told the landlady I should return; and, having gone to a bookseller, sold it for sixty pounds. I brought Goldsmith the money, and he discharged his rent, not without rating his landlady in a high tone for having used him so ill.'

My next meeting with Johnson was on Friday, the 1st of July, when he and I and Dr. Goldsmith supped at the Mitre.

* * *

He talked very contemptuously of Churchill's poetry, observing, that 'it had a temporary currency, only from its audacity of abuse, and being filled with living names, and that it would sink into oblivion.' I ventured to hint that he was not quite a fair judge, as Churchill had attacked him violently. JOHNSON: 'Nay sir, I am a very fair judge. He did not attack me violently till he found I did not like his poetry; and his attack on me shall not prevent me from continuing to say what I think of him, from an apprehension that it may be ascribed to resentment. No, sir, I called the fellow a blockhead at first, and I will call him a blockhead still. However, I will acknowledge that I have a better opinion of him now than I once had; for he has shown more fertility than I expected. To

be sure, he is a tree that cannot produce good fruit: he only bears crabs. But, sir, a tree that produces a great many crabs, is better than a tree which produces only a few.'

* * *

Let me here apologize for the imperfect manner in which I am obliged to exhibit Johnson's conversation at this period. In the early part of my acquaintance with him, I was so wrapt in admiration of his extraordinary colloquial talents, and so little accustomed to his peculiar mode of expression, that I found it extremely difficult to recollect and record his conversation with its genuine vigor and vivacity. In progress of time, when my mind was, as it were, *strongly impregnated with the Johnsonian aether*, I could with much more facility and exactness, carry in my memory and commit to paper the exuberant variety of his wisdom and wit.

At this time *Miss* Williams, as she was then called, though she did not reside with him in the Temple under his roof, but had lodgings in Bolt-court, Fleet-street, had so much of his attention, that he every night drank tea with her before he went home, however late it might be, and she always sat up for him. This it may be conjectured, was not alone a proof of his regard for *her*, but of his own unwillingness to go into solitude, before that unseasonable hour at which he had habituated himself to expect the oblivion of repose. Dr. Goldsmith, being a privileged man, went with him this night, strutting away, and calling to me with an air of superiority, like that of an esoteric over an exoteric disciple of a sage of antiquity, 'I go to Miss Williams.' I confess, I then envied him this mighty privilege, of which he seemed so proud; but it was not long before I obtained the same mark of distinction.

* * *

On Wednesday, July 6, he was engaged to sup with me at my lodgings in Downing-street, Westminster. But on the preceding night my landlord having behaved very rudely to me and some company who were with me, I had resolved not to remain another night in his house. I was exceedingly uneasy at the awkward appearance I supposed I should make to Johnson and the other gentlemen whom

I had invited, not being able to receive them at home, and being obliged to order supper at the Mitre. I went to Johnson in the morning, and talked of it as a serious distress. He laughed and said, 'Consider, sir, how insignificant this will appear a twelvemonth hence.' Were this consideration to be applied to most of the little vexatious incidents of life, by which our quiet is too often disturbed, it would prevent many painful sensations. I have tried it frequently with good effect. 'There is nothing,' continued he, 'in this mighty misfortune; nay, we shall be better at the Mitre.' I told him that I had been at Sir John Fielding's office, complaining of my landlord, and had been informed that though I had taken my lodgings for a year, I might, upon proof of his bad behavior, quit them when I pleased, without being under an obligation to pay rent for any longer time than while I possessed them. The fertility of Johnson's mind could show itself even upon so small a matter as this. 'Why, sir,' said he, 'I suppose this must be the law, since you have been told so in Bow-street. But if your landlord could hold you to your bargain, and the lodgings should be yours for a year, you may certainly use them as you think fit. So, sir, you may quarter two life-guardsmen upon him; or you may send the greatest scoundrel you can find into your apartments; or you may say that you want to make some experiments in natural philosophy, and may burn a large quantity of assafoetida in his house.'

I had as my guests this evening at the Mitre Tavern, Dr. Johnson, Dr. Goldsmith, Mr. Thomas Davies, Mr. Eccles, an Irish gentleman for whose agreeable company I was obliged to Mr. Davies, and the Rev. Mr. John Ogilvie, who was desirous of being in company with my illustrious friend, while I, in my turn, was proud to have the honor of showing one of my countrymen upon what easy terms Johnson permitted me to live with him.

Goldsmith, as usual, endeavored with too much eagerness to *shine*, and disputed very warmly with Johnson against the well-known maxim of the British constitution, 'the king can do no wrong'; affirming that 'what was morally false could not be politically true; and as the king might, in the exercise of his regal power, command and cause the doing of what was wrong, it certainly might be said, in sense and in reason, that he could do wrong.' Johnson: 'Sir, you are to consider that in our constitution, according to its true principles, the king is the head, he is supreme; he is above everything, and there is no power by which he can be tried. Therefore, it is, sir, that we hold the king can do no wrong; that whatever may happen to be wrong in government, may not be above our reach by being ascribed to majesty. Redress is always to be had against oppression by punishing the immediate agents. The king, though he should command, cannot force a judge to condemn a man unjustly; therefore it is the judge whom we prosecute and punish. Political institutions are formed upon the consideration of what will most frequently tend to the good of the whole, although now and then exceptions may occur. Thus it is better in general that a nation should have a supreme legislative power, although it may at times be abused. And then, sir, there is this consideration, that *if the abuse be enormous, nature will rise up, and claiming her original rights, overturn a corrupt political system.*' I mark this animated sentence with peculiar pleasure, as a noble instance of that truly dignified spirit of freedom which ever glowed in his heart, though he was charged with slavish tenets by superficial observers; because he was at all times indignant against that false patriotism, that pretended love of freedom, that unruly restlessness, which is inconsistent with the stable authority of any good government. This generous sentiment, which he uttered with great fervor, struck me exceedingly, and stirred my blood to that pitch of fancied resistance, the possibility of which I am glad to keep in mind, but to which I trust I never shall be forced.

'Great abilities,' said he, 'are not requisite for an historian, for in historical composition all the greatest powers of the human mind are quiescent. He has facts ready to his hand, so there is no exercise of invention. Imagination is not required in any high degree; only about as much as is used in the lower kinds of poetry. Some penetration, accuracy, and coloring, will fit a man for the task, if he can give the application which is necessary.'

'Bayle's *Dictionary* is a very useful work for those to consult who love the biographical part of literature, which is what I love most.'

Talking of the eminent writers in Queen Anne's reign, he observed, 'I think Dr. Arbuthnot the first man among them. He was the most universal genius, being an excellent physician, a man of deep learning, and a man of much humor. Mr. Addison was, to be sure, a great man; his learning was not profound, but his morality, his humor, and his elegance of writing set him very high.'

Mr. Ogilvie was unlucky enough to choose for the topic of his conversation, the praises of his native country. He began with saying, that there was very rich land around Edinburgh. Goldsmith, who had studied physic there, contradicted this, very untruly, with a sneering laugh. Disconcerted a little by this, Mr. Ogilvie then took a new ground, where, I suppose, he thought himself perfectly safe; for he observed, that Scotland had a great many noble wild prospects. JOHNSON: 'I believe, sir, you have a great many. Norway, too, has noble wild prospects; and Lapland is remarkable for prodigious noble wild prospects. But, sir, let me tell you, the noblest prospect which a Scotchman ever sees is the high-road that leads him to England!' This unexpected and pointed sally produced a roar of applause. After all, however, those, who admire the rude grandeur of nature, cannot deny it to Caledonia.

On Saturday, July 9, I found Johnson surrounded with a numerous levee, but have not preserved any part of his conversation. On the 14th we had another evening by ourselves at the Mitre. It happening to be a very rainy night, I made some commonplace observations on the relaxation of nerves and depression of spirits which such weather occasioned; adding, however, that it was good for the vegetable creation. Johnson, who, as we have already seen, denied that the temperature of the air had any influence on the human frame, answered, with a smile of ridicule, 'Why, yes, sir, it is good for

vegetables, and for the animals who eat those vegetables, and for the animals who eat those animals.' This observation of his, aptly enough introduced a good supper; and I soon forgot, in Johnson's company, the influence of a moist atmosphere.

Feeling myself now quite at ease as his companion, though I had all possible reverence for him, I expressed a regret that I could not be so easy with my father, though he was not much older than Johnson, and certainly, however respectable, had not more learning and greater abilities to depress me. I asked him the reason of this. JOHNSON: 'Why sir, I am a man of the world. I live in the world, and I take, in some degree, the color of the world as it moves along. Your father is a judge in a remote part of the island, and all his notions are taken from the old world. Besides, sir, there must always be a struggle between a father and a son, while one aims at power and the other at independence.' I said, I was afraid my father would force me to be a lawyer. JOHNSON: 'Sir, you need not be afraid of his forcing you to be a laborious practising lawyer; that is not in his power. For, as the proverb says, "One man may lead a horse to the water, but twenty cannot make him drink." He may be displeased that you are not what he wishes you to be; but that displeasure will not go far. If he insists only on your having as much law as is necessary for a man of property, and then endeavors to get you into parliament, he is quite in the right.'

He enlarged very convincingly upon the excellence of rime over blank verse in English poetry. I mentioned to him that Dr. Adam Smith, in his lectures upon composition, when I studied under him in the College of Glasgow, had maintained the same opinion strenuously, and I repeated some of his arguments. JOHNSON: 'Sir, I was once in company with Smith, and we did not take to each other; but had I known that he loved rime as much as you tell me he does, I should have HUGGED him.'

Talking of those who denied the truth of Christianity, he said: 'It is always easy to be on the negative side. If a man were now to deny that there is salt upon the table, you could not reduce him to an absurdity. Come, let us try this little further. I deny that Canada is taken, and I can support my denial by pretty good arguments. The French are a much more numerous people than we; and it is not likely that they would allow us to take it. "But the ministry have assured us, in all the formality of *The Gazette*, that it is taken."—Very true. But the ministry have put us to an enormous expense by the war in America, and it is their interest to persuade us that we have got something for our money. "But the fact is confirmed by thousands of men who were at the taking of it." Ay, but these men have still more interest in deceiving us. They don't want that you should think the French have beat them, but that they have beat the French. Now suppose you should go over and find that it really is taken, that would only satisfy yourself; for when you come home we will not believe you. We will say, you have been bribed. Yet, sir, notwithstanding all these plausible objections, we have no doubt that Canada is really ours. Such is the weight of common testimony. How much stronger are the evidences of the Christian religion!'

'Idleness is a disease which must be combated; but I would not advise a rigid adherence to a particular plan of study. I myself have never persisted in any plan for two days together. A man ought to read just as inclination leads him; for what he reads as a task will do him little good. A young man should read five hours in a day, and so may acquire a great deal of knowledge.'

To such a degree of unrestrained frankness had he now accustomed me that in the course of this evening I talked of the numerous reflections which had been thrown out against him, on account of his having accepted a pension from his present Majesty. 'Why, sir,' said he, with a hearty laugh, 'it is a mighty foolish noise that they make.[1] I have accepted of a pension as a reward which has been thought due to my literary merit; and now that I have this pension, I am the same man in every respect that I have ever been; I retain the same principles.

[1] When I mentioned the same idle clamor to him several years afterwards, he said, with a smile, 'I wish my pension were twice as large, that they might make twice as much noise.'

It is true, that I cannot now curse (smiling) the house of Hanover; nor would it be decent for me to drink King James's health in the wine that King George gives me money to pay for. But, sir, I think that the pleasure of cursing the house of Hanover, and drinking King James's health, are amply overbalanced by three hundred pounds a year.'

* * *

He recommended to me to keep a journal of my life, full and unreserved. He said it would be a very good exercise, and would yield me great satisfaction when the particulars were faded from my remembrance. I was uncommonly fortunate in having had a previous coincidence of opinion with him upon this subject, for I had kept such a journal for some time; and it was no small pleasure to me to have this to tell him, and to receive his approbation. He counseled me to keep it private, and said I might surely have a friend who would burn it in case of my death. From this habit I have been enabled to give the world so many anecdotes, which would otherwise have been lost to posterity. I mentioned that I was afraid I put into my journal too many little incidents. JOHNSON: 'There is nothing sir, too little for so little a creature as man. It is by studying little things that we attain the great art of having as little misery, and as much happiness as possible.'

Next morning Mr. Dempster happened to call on me, and was so much struck even with the imperfect account which I gave him of Dr. Johnson's conversation, that to his honor be it recorded, when I complained that drinking port and sitting up late with him, affected my nerves for some time after, he said, 'One had better be palsied at eighteen, than not keep company with such a man.'

On Tuesday, July 18th, I found tall Sir Thomas Robinson sitting with Johnson. Sir Thomas said, that the king of Prussia valued himself upon three things; upon being a hero, a musician, and an author. JOHNSON: 'Pretty well, sir, for one man. As to his being an author, I have not looked at his poetry; but his prose is poor stuff. He writes just as you may suppose Voltaire's footboy to do, who has been his amanuensis. He has such parts as the valet might have, and about as much of the coloring of the style as might be got by transcribing his works.' When I was at Ferney, I repeated this to Voltaire in order to reconcile him somewhat to Johnson, whom he, in affecting the English mode of expression, had previously characterized as 'a superstitious dog;' but after hearing such a criticism on Frederick the Great, with whom he was then on bad terms, he exclaimed, 'An honest fellow!'

* * *

I again begged his advice as to my method of study at Utrecht. 'Come,' said he, 'let us make a day of it. Let us go down to Greenwich and dine, and talk of it there.' The following Saturday was fixed for this excursion.

As we walked along the Strand tonight, arm in arm, a woman of the town accosted us, in the usual enticing manner. 'No, no, my girl,' said Johnson, 'it won't do.' He, however, did not treat her with harshness; and we talked of the wretched life of such women, and agreed that much more misery than happiness, upon the whole, is produced by illicit commerce between the sexes.

On Saturday, July 30, Dr. Johnson and I took a sculler at the Temple-stairs, and set out for Greenwich. I asked him if he really thought a knowledge of the Greek and Latin languages an essential requisite to a good education. JOHNSON: 'Most certainly, sir; for those who know them have a very great advantage over those who do not. Nay, sir, it is wonderful what a difference learning makes upon people even in the common intercourse of life, which does not appear to be much connected with it.' 'And yet,' said I, 'people go through the world very well and carry on the business of life, to good advantage without learning.' JOHNSON: 'Why, sir, that may be true in cases where learning cannot possibly be of any use; for instance, this boy rows us as well without learning, as if he could sing the song of Orpheus to the Argonauts, who were the first sailors.' He then called to the boy, 'What would you give, my lad, to know about the Argonauts?' 'Sir,' said the boy, 'I would give what I have.' Johnson was much pleased with his answer, and we gave him a double fare. Dr. Johnson then turning to me, 'Sir,' said he, 'a desire

of knowledge is the natural feeling of mankind; and every human being whose mind is not debauched, will be willing to give all that he has to get knowledge.'

We landed at the Old Swan, and walked to Billingsgate, where we took oars and moved smoothly along the silver Thames. It was a very fine day. We were entertained with the immense number and variety of ships that were lying at anchor, and with the beautiful country. on each side of the river.

I talked of preaching, and of the great success which those called Methodists have. JOHNSON: 'Sir, it is owing to their expressing themselves in a plain and familiar manner, which is the only way to do good to the common people, and which clergymen of genious and learning ought to do from a principle of duty, when it is suited to their congregations; a practice, for which they will be praised by men of sense. To insist against drunkenness as a crime, because it debases reason: the noblest faculty of man, would be of no service to the common people, but to tell them that they may die in a fit of drunkenness and show them how dreadful that would be, cannot fail to make a deep impression. Sir, when your Scotch clergy give up their homely manner, religion will soon decay in that country.'

I was much pleased to find myself with Johnson at Greenwich, which he celebrates in his *London* as a favorite scene.

I had the poem in my pocket, and read the lines aloud with enthusiasm:

'On Thames's banks in silent thought we stood:
Where Greenwich smiles upon the silver flood:
Pleased with the seat which gave Eliza birth,
We kneel, and kiss the consecrated earth.'

He remarked that the structure of Greenwich hospital was too magnificent for a place of charity, and that its parts were too much detached, to make one great whole.

Buchanan, he said, was a very fine poet; and observe, that he was the first who complimented a lady, by ascribing to her the different perfections of the heathen goddesses; but that Johnstone improved upon this, by making his lady, at the same time, free from their defects.

He dwelt upon Buchanan's elegant verses to Mary Queen of Scots, *Nympha Caledoniae*, [Nymph of Scotland] etc., and spoke with enthusiasm of the beauty of Latin verse. 'All the modern languages,' said he, 'cannot furnish so melodious a line as

Formosam resonare doces Amarillida silvas.
[You teach the woods to re-echo beauteous Amarillis.]

Afterwards he entered upon the business of the day, which was to give me his advice as to a course of study. And here I am to mention with much regret that my record of what he said is miserably scanty. I recollect with admiration an animating blaze of eloquence, which roused every intellectual power in me to the highest pitch, but must have dazzled me so much that my memory could not preserve the substance of his discourse; for the note which I find of it is no more than this:—'He ran over the grand scale of human knowledge; advised me to select some particular branch to excel in, but to acquire a little of every kind.' The defect of my minutes will be fully supplied by a long letter upon the subject, which he favored me with after I had been some time at Utrecht, and which my readers will have the pleasure to peruse in its proper place.

We walked in the evening, in Greenwich Park. He asked me, I suppose, by way of trying my disposition, 'Is not this very fine?' Having no exquisite relish of the beauties of nature, and being more delighted with 'the busy hum of men,' I answered, 'Yes, sir, but not equal to Fleet-street.' JOHNSON: 'You are right, sir.'

I am aware that many of my readers may censure my want of taste. Let me, however, shelter myself under the authority of a very fashionable baronet in the brilliant world, who, on his attention being called to the fragrance of a May evening in the country, observed, 'This may be very well; but, for my part, I prefer the small of a flambeau at the play-house.'

We stayed so long at Greenwich, that our sail up the river, in our return to London, was by no means so pleasant as in the morning; for the night air was so cold that it made me shiver. I was the more sensible of it from having sat up all the night before recollecting and writing in my journal what I thought worthy of preservation; an exertion which during the first part of my acquaintance with Johnson, I frequently made. I remember having sat up four nights in one week, without being much incommoded in the daytime.

Johnson, whose robust frame was not in the least affected by the cold, scolded me, as if my shivering had been a paltry effeminacy, saying, 'Why do you shiver?' Sir William Scott, of the Commons, told me that when he complained of a headache in the post-chaise, as they were traveling together to Scotland, Johnson treated him in the same manner: 'At your age, sir, I had no headache.' It is not easy to make allowance for sensations in others, which we ourselves have not at the time.

We concluded the day at the Turk's Head coffee-house very socially. He was pleased to listen to a particular account which I gave him of my family, and of its hereditary estate, as to the extent and population of which he asked questions, and made calculations; recommending, at the same time, a liberal kindness to the tenantry, as people over whom the proprietor was placed by Providence. He took delight in hearing my description of the romantic seat of my ancestors. 'I must be there, sir' said he, 'and we will live in the old castle; and if there is not a room in it remaining, we will build one.' I was highly flattered, but could scarcely indulge a hope that Auchinleck would indeed be honored by his presence, and celebrated by a description, as it afterward was, in his *Journey to the Western Islands.*

After we had again talked of my setting out for Holland, he said, 'I must see thee out of England; I will accompany you to Harwich.' I could not find words to express what I felt upon this unexpected and very great mark of his affectionate regard.

Next day, Sunday, July 31, I told him I had been that morning at a meeting of the people called Quakers, where I had heard a woman preach. Johnson: 'Sir, a woman's preaching is like a dog's walking on his hind legs. It is not done well; but you are surprised to find it done at all.'

On Tuesday, August 2 (the day of my departure from London having been fixed for the 5th), Dr. Johnson did me the honor to pass a part of the morning with me at my chambers. He said, 'that he always felt an inclination to do nothing.' I observed, that it was strange to think that the most indolent man in Britain had written the most laborious work, *The English Dictionary*.

I mentioned an imprudent publication, by a certain friend of his, at an early period of life, and asked him if he thought it would hurt him. Johnson: 'No, sir; not much. It may, perhaps, be mentioned at an election.'

I had now made good my title to be a privileged man, and was carried by him in the evening to drink tea with Miss Williams, whom, though under the misfortune of having lost her sight, I found to be agreeable in conversation, for she had a variety of literature, and expressed herself well; but her peculiar value was the intimacy in which she had long lived with Johnson, by which she was well acquainted with his habits, and knew how to lead him on to talk.

After tea he carried me to what he called his walk, which was a long narrow paved court in the neighborhood, overshadowed by some trees. There we sauntered a considerable time, and I complained to him that my love of London and of his company was such, that I shrunk almost from the thought of going away even to travel, which is generally so much desired by young men. He roused me by manly and spirited conversation. He advised me, when settled in any place abroad, to study with an eagerness after knowledge, and to apply to Greek an hour every day; and when I was moving about, to read diligently the great book of mankind.

On Wednesday, August 3, we had our last social evening at the Turk's Head coffee-house, before my setting out for foreign parts. I had the misfortune, before we parted, to irritate him unintentionally. I mentioned to him how common it was in the world to tell absurd

stories of him, and to ascribe to him very strange sayings. Johnson: 'What do they make me say, sir?' Boswell: 'Why, sir, as an instance very strange indeed,' laughing heartily as I spoke, 'David Hume told me, you said that you would stand before a battery of cannon to restore the Convocation to its full powers.' Little did I apprehend that he had actually said this: but I was soon convinced of my error; for, with a determined look he thundered out, 'And would I not, sir? Shall the Presbyterian *Kirk* of Scotland have its General Assembly, and the Church of England be denied its Convocation?' He was walking up and down the room while I told him the anecdote; but, when he uttered this explosion of high-church zeal he had come close to my chair, and his eyes flashed with indignation. I bowed to the storm, and diverted the force of it, by leading him to expatiate on the influence which religion derived from maintaining the church with great external respectability.

I must not omit to mention that he this year wrote *The Life of Ascham*, and the Dedication to the Earl of Shaftesbury, prefixed to the edition of that writer's English works, published by Mr. Bennet.

On Friday, August 5, we set out early in the morning in the Harwich stage-coach. A fat elderly gentlewoman, and a young Dutchman, seemed the most inclined among us to conversation. At the inn where we dined, the gentlewoman said that she had done her best to educate her children; and particularly, that she had never suffered them to be a moment idle. Johnson: 'I wish, madam, you would educate me too; for I have been an idle fellow all my life.' 'I am sure, sir,' said she, 'you have not been idle.' Johnson: 'Nay, madam, it is very true: and that gentleman there, pointing to me, has been idle. He was idle at Edinburgh. His father sent him to Glasgow, where he continued to be idle. He then came to London, where he has been very idle; and now he is going to Utrecht, where he will be as idle as ever.' I asked him privately how he could expose me so. Johnson: 'Poh, poh!' said he, 'they knew nothing about you, and will think of it no more.' In the afternoon the gentlewoman talked violently against the Roman Catholics, and of the horrors of the inquisition. To the utter astonishment of all the passengers but myself, who knew that he could talk upon any side of a question, he defended the inquisition, and maintained that 'false doctrine should be checked on its first appearance; that the civil power should unite with the church in punishing those who dare to attack the established religion, and that such only were punished by the inquisition.' He had in his pocket, *Pomponius Mela de Situ Orbis,* in which he read occasionally, and seemed very intent upon ancient geography. Though by no means niggardly, his attention to what was generally right was so minute, that having observed at one of the stages that I ostentatiously gave a shilling to the coachman, when the custom was for each passenger to give only sixpence, he took me aside and scolded me, saying that what I had done would make the coachman dissatisfied with all the rest of the passengers, who gave him no more than his due.

* * *

Having stopped a night at Colchester, Johnson talked of that town with veneration, for having stood a siege for Charles the First. The Dutchman alone now remained with us. He spoke English tolerably well; and thinking to recommend himself to us by expatiating on the superiority of the criminal jurisprudence of this country over that of Holland, he inveighed against the barbarity of putting an accused person to the torture, in order to force a confession. But Johnson was as ready for this as for the inquisition. 'Why, sir, you do not, I find, understand the law of your own country. To torture in Holland is considered as a favor to an accused person; for no man is put to the torture there, unless there is as much evidence against him as would amount to conviction in England. An accused person, among you, therefore, has one chance more to escape punishment than those who are tried among us.'

At supper this night he talked of good' eating with uncommon satisfaction. 'Some people,' said he, 'have a foolish way of not minding, or pretending not to mind, what they eat. For my part, I mind my belly very studiously and very carefully; for I look upon it, that he who

does not mind his belly will hardly mind anything else.' He now appeared to me *Jean Bull philosophe,* and he was for the moment not only serious, but vehement, yet I have heard him, upon other occasions, talk with great contempt of people who were anxious to gratify their palates: and the 206th number of his *Rambler* is a masterly essay against gulosity. His practice, indeed, I must acknowledge, may be considered as casting the balance of his different opinions upon this subject; for I never knew any man who relished good eating more than he did. When at table he was totally absorbed in the business of the moment: his looks seemed riveted to his plate; nor would he, unless when in very high company, say one word, or even pay the least attention to what was said by others, till he had satisfied his appetite, which was so fierce, and indulged with such intenseness, that while in the act of eating, the veins of his forehead swelled, and generally a strong perspiration was visible. To those whose sensations were delicate, this could not but be disgusting; and it was doubtless not very suitable to the character of a philosopher, who should be distinguished by self-command. But it must be owned that Johnson, though he could be rigidly *abstemious,* was not a *temperate* man either in eating or drinking. He could refrain, but he could not use moderately. He told me that he had fasted two days without inconvenience, and that he had never been hungry but once. They who beheld with wonder how much he ate upon all occasions, when his dinner was to his taste, could not easily conceive what he must have meant by hunger; and not only was he remarkable for the extraordinary quantity which he ate, but he was, or affected to be, a man of very nice discernment in the science of cookery. He used to descant critically on the dishes which had been at table where he had dined or supped, and to recollect very minutely what he had liked. I remember when he was in Scotland, his praising 'Gordon's palates' (a dish of palates at the Honorable Alexander Gordon's) with a warmth of expression which might have done honor to more important subjects. 'As for Maclaurin's imitation of a *made dish,* it was a wretched attempt.' He about the same time was so much displeased with the performances of a nobleman's French cook, that he exclaimed with vehemence, 'I'd throw such a rascal into the river;' and he then proceeded to alarm a lady at whose house he was to sup, by the following manifesto of his skill:—'I, madam, who live at a variety of good tables, am a much better judge of cookery, than any person who has a very tolerable cook, but lives much at home; for his palate is gradually adapted to the taste of his cook; whereas, madam, in trying by a wider range, I can more exquisitively judge.' When invited to dine, even with an intimate friend, he was not pleased if something better than a plain dinner was not prepared for him. I have heard him say on such an occasion. 'This was a good dinner enough to be sure; but it was not a dinner to *ask* a man to.' On the other hand, he was wont to express, with great glee, his satisfaction when he had been entertained quite to his mind.

While we were left by ourselves, after the Dutchman had gone to bed, Dr. Johnson talked of that studied behavior which many have recommended and practised. He disapproved of it; and said, 'I never considered whether I should be a grave man, or a merry man, but just let inclination, for the time, have its course.'

Next day we got to Harwich, to dinner; and my passage in the packet boat to Helvoetsluys being secured, and my baggage put on board, we dined at our inn by ourselves. I happened to say it would be terrible if he should not find a speedy opportunity of returning to London, and be confined in so dull a place. JOHNSON: 'Don't, sir, accustom yourself to use big words for little matters. It would *not* be *terrible,* though I *were* to be detained some time here.' The practice of using words of disproportionate magnitude, is, no doubt, too frequent everywhere; but, I think, most remarkable among the French, of which, all who have traveled in France must have been struck with innumerable instances.

We went and looked at the church, and having gone into it, and walked up to the altar, Johnson, whose piety was constant and fervent, sent me to my knees, saying, 'Now that you are going to leave your native country, recommend yourself to the protection of your Creator and Redeemer.'

After we came out of the church, we stood talking for some time together, of Bishop Berkeley's ingenious sophistry to prove the non-existence of matter, and that everything in the universe is merely ideal. I observed that, though we are satisfied his doctrine is not true, it is impossible to refute it. I never shall forget the alacrity with which Johnson answered, striking his foot with mighty force against a large stone, till he rebounded from it,—'I refute it *thus.*'

* * *

My revered friend walked down with me to the beach, where we embraced and parted with tenderness, and engaged to correspond by letters. I said, 'I hope, sir, you will not forget me in my absence.' JOHNSON: 'Nay, sir, it is more likely you should forget me, than that I should forget you.' As the vessel put out to sea, I kept my eyes upon him for a considerable time, while he remained rolling his majestic frame in his usual manner; and at last I perceived him walk back into the town, and he disappeared.

(1791)

* * *

EDMUND BURKE (1729-1797)

The career of Burke belongs to the history of English politics, its memorials to English literature. His father was a Dublin solicitor and a Protestant; his mother was a firm Catholic, and he spent a part of his school days under the tuition of a Quaker. He was himself brought up a Protestant, but on this as other subjects preserved a large and open mind. He took his bachelor's degree at Trinity College, Dublin, in 1748, and later read law at the Middle Temple in London. For upwards of a decade after his removal to England, in 1750, his ambition pointed to literature. In 1756 he published *A Vindication of Natural Society*, an ironical imitation of Bolingbroke intended to throw ridicule upon the political theories of that writer. 'Burke foresaw from the first,' an English statesman of our own day has said, 'what, if rationalism were allowed to run its course, would be the really great business of the second half of his century.' The same year he printed his youthful essay *On the Sublime and Beautiful* and three years later became editor of Dodsley's *Annual Register*. But his literary abilities soon marked him out for the public service. In some way, not very well understood, his financial disability was overcome, and he entered upon a career in Parliament, making his first speech in January, 1766. His *Observations on the Present State of the Nation* (1769) showed his grasp of economic detail, and his pamphlet, entitled, *Thoughts on the Present Discontents*, the following year, for the first time exhibited the full breadth of his political philosophy. Four years later the struggle with the American colonies which had been going on ever since Burke entered Parliament had reached the stage of threatened war. It was in the debate upon this great occasion that Burke's mastery of economic detail, and his broad and lucid command of principle were welded together by his gift of passionate exposition into the three documents of political philosophy which will be cherished wherever the race flourishes in whose language they were delivered. *The Speech on American Taxation* was given in April, 1774, *The Speech for Conciliation*, March 22, 1775, and the *Letter to the Sheriffs of Bristol* was issued in 1777. The other subjects upon which Burke distinguished himself as an orator were the Impeachment of Warren Hastings and the incidents of the French Revolution. His views in regard to the latter were such as sometimes to perplex his party and his friends and he was often almost solitary in his position. In spite of Goldsmith's accusation that he 'to party gave up what was meant for mankind,' Burke's gifts were not those of the successful politician. He retired from Parliament in 1794, having wielded great power at times, but having won no official position of high dignity. His achievements were such as grow more lustrous with the passage of time.

From THE SPEECH FOR CONCILIATION WITH THE COLONIES

These, sir, are my reasons for not entertaining that high opinion of untried force, by which many gentlemen, for whose sentiments in other particulars I have great respect, seem to be so greatly captivated. But there is still behind a third consideration concerning this object, which serves to determine my opinion on the sort of policy which ought to be pursued in the management of America, even more than its population and its commerce, I mean its *temper and character*.

In this character of the Americans, a love of freedom is the predominating feature which marks and distinguishes the whole; and as an ardent is always a jealous affection, your colonies become sus-5 picious, restive, and untractable, whenever they see the least attempt to wrest from them by force or shuffle from them by chicane, what they think the only advantage worth living for. This fierce 10 spirit of liberty is stronger in the English colonies probably than in any other people of the earth; and this from a great variety of powerful causes; which, to understand the true temper of their minds, 15 and the direction which this spirit takes, it will not be amiss to lay open somewhat more largely.

First, the people of the colonies are descendants of Englishmen. England, sir, is a nation which still I hope respects, and formerly adored, her freedom. The colonists emigrated from you, when this part of your character was most predominant; and they took this bias and direction the moment they parted from your hands. They are therefore not only devoted to liberty, but to liberty according to English ideas, and on English principles. Abstract liberty, like other mere abstractions, is not to be found. Liberty inheres in some sensible object; and every nation has formed to itself some favorite point, which by way of eminence becomes the criterion of their happiness. It happened, you know, sir, that the great contests for freedom in this country were from the earliest times chiefly upon the question of taxing. Most of the contests in the ancient commonwealths turned primarily on the right of election of magistrates; or on the balance among the several orders of the state. The question of money was not with them so immediate. But in England it was otherwise. On this point of taxes the ablest pens and most eloquent tongues have been exercised; the greatest spirits have acted and suffered. In order to give the fullest satisfaction concerning the importance of this point, it was not only necessary for those who in argument defended the excellence of the English constitution to insist on this privilege of granting money as a dry point of fact, and to prove that the right had been acknowledged in ancient parchments and blind usage to reside in a certain body called a House of Commons. They went much farther; they attempted to prove, and they succeeded, that in theory it ought to be so, from the particular nature of a House of Commons as an immediate representative of the people, whether the old records had delivered this oracle or not. They took infinite pains to inculcate, as a fundamental principle, that in all monarchies the people must in effect themselves, mediately or immediately, possess the power of granting their own money, or no shadow of liberty could subsist. The colonies draw from you, as with their lifeblood, these ideas and principles. Their love of liberty, as with you, fixed and attached on this specific point of taxing.

Liberty might be safe, or might be endangered, in twenty other particulars, without their being much pleased or alarmed. Here they felt its pulse; and as they found that beat, they thought themselves sick or sound. I do not say whether they were right or wrong in applying your general arguments to their own cause. It is not easy indeed to make a monopoly of theorems and corollaries. The fact is, that they did thus apply those general arguments; and your mode of governing them, whether through lenity or indolence, through wisdom or mistake, confirmed them in the imagination, that they, as well as you, had an interest in these common principles.

They were further confirmed in this pleasing error by the form of their provincial legislative assemblies. The governments are popular in a high degree; some are merely popular; in all, the popular representative is the most weighty; and this share of the people in their ordinary government never fails to inspire them with lofty sentiments, and with a strong aversion from whatever tends to deprive them of their chief importance.

If anything were wanting to this necessary operation of the form of government, religion would have given it a complete effect. Religion, always a principle of energy, in this new people is no way worn out or impaired; and their mode of professing it is also one main cause of this free spirit. The people are Protestants; and of that kind which is the most adverse to all implicit submission of mind and opinion. This is a persuasion not only favorable to liberty, but built upon it. I do not think, sir, that the reason of this averseness in the dissenting churches, from all that looks like absolute government, is so much to be sought in their religious tenets as in their history. Every one knows that the Roman Catholic religion is at least coeval with most of the governments where it prevails; that it has generally gone hand in hand with them, and received great favor and every kind of support from authority. The Church of England too was formed from her cradle under the nursing care of regular government. But the dissenting interests have sprung up in direct opposition to all the ordinary powers of the world; and could justify that opposition only on a strong claim to natural liberty. Their very existence depended on the powerful and unremitted assertion of that claim. All Protestantism, even the most cold and passive, is a sort of dissent. But the religion most prevalent in our northern colonies is a refinement on the principle of resistance; it is the dissidence of dissent, and the Protestantism of the Protestant religion. This religion, under a variety of denominations agreeing in nothing but in the communion of the spirit of liberty, is predominant in most of the northern provinces, where the Church of England, notwithstanding its legal rights, is in reality no more than a sort of private sect, not composing most probably the tenth of the people. The colonists left England when this spirit was high, and in the emigrants was the highest of all, and even that stream of foreigners, which has been constantly flowing into these colonies, has, for the greatest part, been composed of dissenters from the establishments of their several countries, and have brought with them a temper and character far from alien to that of the people with whom they mixed.

Sir, I can perceive by their manner, that some gentlemen object to the latitude of this description, because in the southern colonies the Church of England forms a large body, and has a regular establishment. It is certainly true. There is, however, a circumstance attending these colonies, which, in my opinion, fully counterbalances this difference, and makes the spirit of liberty still more high and haughty than in those to the northward. It is, that in Virginia and the Carolinas they have a vast multitude of slaves. Where this is the case in any part of the world, those who are free are by far the most proud and jealous of their freedom. Freedom is to them not only an enjoyment, but a kind of rank and privilege. Not seeing there, that freedom, as in countries where it is a common blessing, and as broad and general as the air, may be united with much abject toil, with great misery, with all the exterior of servitude, liberty looks, amongst them, like something that is more noble and liberal. I do not mean, sir, to commend the superior morality of this sentiment, which has at least as much pride as virtue in it: but I cannot alter the nature of man. The fact is so; and these people of the southern colonies are much more strongly, and with a higher and more stubborn spirit, attached to liberty, than those to the northward. Such were all the ancient commonwealths; such were our Gothic ancestors; such in our days were the Poles; and such will be all masters of slaves who are not slaves themselves. In such a people, the haughtiness of domination combines with the spirit of freedom, fortifies it, and renders it invincible.

Permit me, sir, to add another circumstance in our colonies, which contributes no mean part towards the growth and effect of this untractable spirit. I mean their education. In no country perhaps in the world is the law so general a study. The profession itself is numerous and powerful; and in most provinces it takes the lead. The greater number of the deputies sent to the Congress were lawyers. But all who read (and most do read), endeavor to obtain some smattering in that science. I have been told by an eminent bookseller, that in no branch of his business, after tracts of popular devotion, were so many books as those on the law exported to the plantations. The colonists have now fallen into the way of printing them for their own use. I hear that they have sold nearly as many of Blackstone's Commentaries in America as in England. General Gage marks out this disposition very particularly in a letter on your table. He states that all the people in his government are lawyers, or smatterers in law; and that in Boston they have been enabled, by successful chicane, wholly to evade many parts of one of your capital penal constitutions. The smartness of debate will say that this knowledge ought to teach them more clearly the rights of legislature, their obligations to obedience, and the penalties of rebellion. All this is mighty well. But my honorable and learned friend on the floor, who condescends to mark what I say for animadversion, will disdain that ground. He has heard, as well as I, that when great honors and great emoluments do not win over this knowledge to the service of the state, it is a formidable adversary to government. If the spirit be not tamed and broken by these happy methods, it is stubborn and litigious.

Abeunt studia in mores [studies develop into habits]. This study renders men acute, inquisitive, dexterous, prompt in attack, ready in defense, full of resources. In other countries, the people, more simple, and of a less mercurial cast, judge of an ill principle in government only ,by an actual grievance; here they anticipate the evil, and judge of the pressure of the grievance by the badness of the principle. They augur misgovernment at a distance; and snuff the approach of tyranny in every tainted breeze.

The last cause of this disobedient spirit in the colonies is hardly less powerful than the rest, as it is not merely moral, but laid deep in the natural constitution of things. Three thousand miles of ocean lie between you and them. No contrivance can prevent the effect of this distance in weakening government. Seas roll, and months pass, between the order and the execution; and the want of a speedy explanation of a single point is enough to defeat a whole system. You have, indeed, 'winged ministers of vengeance,' who carry your bolts in their pounces to the remotest verge of the sea. But there a power steps in, that limits the arrogance of raging passions and furious elements, and says, ' So far shalt thou go, and no farther.' Who are you, that you should fret and rage, and bite the chains of Nature? — nothing worse happens to you than does to all nations who have extensive empire; and it happens in all the forms into which empire can be thrown. In large bodies, the circulation of power must be less vigorous at the extremities. Nature has said it. The Turk cannot govern Egypt, and Arabia, and Kurdistan, as he governs Thrace; nor has he the same dominion in Crimea and Algiers which he has at Brusa and Smyrna. Despotism itself is obliged to truck and huckster. The Sultan gets such obedience as he can. He governs with a loose rein, that he may govern at all; and the whole of the force and vigor of his authority in his center is derived from a prudent relaxation in all his borders. Spain, in her provinces, is perhaps not so well obeyed as you are in yours. She complies too; she submits; she watches times. This is the immutable condition, the eternal law, of extensive and detached empire.

Then, sir, from these six capital sources; of descent; of form of government; of religion in the northern provinces; of manners in the southern; of education; of the remoteness of situation from the first mover of government; from all these causes a fierce spirit of liberty has grown up. It has grown with the growth of the people in your colonies, and increased with the increase of their wealth; a spirit, that unhappily mèeting with an exercise of power in England, which, however lawful, is not reconcilable to any ideas of liberty, much less with theirs, has kindled this flame that is ready to consume us.

I do not mean to commend either the spirit in this excess, or the moral causes which produce it. Perhaps a more smooth and accommodating spirit of freedom in them would be more acceptable to us. Perhaps ideas of liberty might be desired more reconcilable with an arbitrary and boundless authority. Perhaps we might wish the colonists to be persuaded that their liberty is more secure when held in trust for them by us (as their guardians during a perpetual minority) than with any part of it in their own hands. The question is, not whether their spirit deserves praise or blame, but what, in the name of God, shall we do with it? You have before you the object, such as it is, with all its glories with all its imperfections, on its head. You see the magnitude, the importance, the temper, the habits, the disorders. By all these considerations we are strongly urged to determine something concerning it. We are called upon to fix some rule and line for our future conduct, which may give a little stability to our politics, and prevent the return of such unhappy deliberations as the present. Every such return will bring the matter before us in a still more untractable form. For, what astonishing and incredible things have we not seen already! What monsters have not been generated from this unnatural contention! Whilst every principle of authority and resistance has been pushed, upon both sides, as far as it would go, there is nothing so solid and certain, either in reasoning or in practice, that has not been shaken. Until very lately, all authority in America seemed to be nothing but an emanation from yours. Even the popular part of the colony constitution derived all its activity, and its first vital movement, from the pleasure of the crown. We thought, sir, that the utmost which the discontented colonists could do was to disturb authority; we never dreamt they could of themselves supply it; knowing in general what an operose business it is to establish a government absolutely new. But having, for our purposes in this contention, resolved that none but an obedient assembly should sit; the humors of the people there finding all passage through the legal channel stopped, with great violence broke out another way. Some provinces have tried their experiment, as we have tried ours; and theirs has succeeded. They have formed a government sufficient for its purposes, without the bustle of a revolution, or the troublesome formality of an election. Evident necessity and tacit consent have done the business in an instant. So well they have done it, that Lord Dunmore — the account is among the fragments on your table — tells you that the new institution is infinitely better obeyed than the ancient government ever was in its most fortunate periods. Obedience is what makes government, and not the names by which it is called; not the name of Governor, as formerly, or Committee, as at present. This new government has originated directly from the people; and was not transmitted through any of the ordinary artificial media of a positive constitution. It was not a manufacture ready formed, and transmitted to them in that condition from England. The evil arising from hence is this, that the colonists having once found the possibility of enjoying the advantages of order in the midst of a struggle for liberty, such struggles will not henceforward seem so terrible to the settled and sober part of mankind as they had appeared before the trial.

Pursuing the same plan of punishing by the denial of the exercise of government to still greater lengths, we wholly abrogated the ancient government of Massachusetts. We were confident that the first feeling, if not the very prospect of anarchy, would instantly enforce a complete submission. The experiment was tried A new, strange, unexpected phase of things appeared. Anarchy is found tolerable. A vast province has now subsisted, and subsisted in a considerable degree of health and vigor, for near a twelvemonth, without Governor, without public council, without judges, without executive magistrates. How long it will continue in this state, or what may rise out of this unheard-of situation, how can the wisest of us conjecture? Our late experience has taught us that many of those fundamental principles formerly believed infallible, are either not of the importance they were imagined to be; or that we have not at all adverted to some other far more important and far more powerful principles, which entirely overrule those we had considered as omnipotent. I am much against any further experiments, which tend to put to the proof any more of these allowed opinions, which contribute o much to the public tranquillity. In effect, we suffer as much at home by this loosening of all ties, and this concussion of all established opinions, as we do abroad. For, in order to prove that the Americans have no right to their liberties, we are every day endeavoring to subvert the maxims which preserve the whole spirit of our own. To prove that the Americans ought not to be free, we are obliged to depreciate the value of freedom itself; and we never seem to gain a paltry advantage over them in debate, without attacking some of those principles, or deriding some of those feelings, for which our ancestors have shed their blood.

But, sir, in wishing to put an end to pernicious experiments, I do not mean to preclude the fullest inquiry. Far from it. Far from deciding on a sudden or partial view, I would patiently go round and round the subject, and survey it minutely in every possible aspect. Sir, if I were capable of engaging you to an equal attention, I would state that, as far as I am capable of discerning, there are but three ways of proceeding relative to this stubborn spirit, which prevails in your colonies, and disturbs your government. These are: to change that spirit, as inconvenient, by removing the causes; to prosecute it as criminal; or, to comply with it as necessary. I would not be guilty of an imperfect enumeration; I can think of but these three. Another has indeed been started, that of giving up the colonies; but it met so slight a reception, that I do not think myself obliged to dwell a great while upon it. It is nothing but a little sally of anger, like the frowardness of peevish children, who, when they cannot get all they would have, are resolved to take nothing.

The first of these plans, to change the spirit as inconvenient, by removing the causes, I think is the most like a systematic proceeding. It is radical in its principle; but it is attended with great difficulties, some of them little short, as I conceive, of impossibilities. This will appear by examining into the plans which have been proposed.

As the growing population in the colonies is evidently one cause of their resistance, it was last session mentioned in both Houses, by men of weight, and received not without applause, that in order to check this evil, it would be proper for the crown to make no further grants of land. But to this scheme there are two objections. The first, that there is already so much unsettled land in private hands as to afford room for an immense future population, although the crown not only withheld its grants, but annihilated its soil. If this be the case, then the only effect of this avarice of desolation, this hoarding of a royal wilderness, would be to raise the value of the possessions in the hands of the great private monopolists, without any adequate check to the growing and alarming mischief of population.

But if you stopped your grants, what would be the consequence? The people would occupy without grants. They have already so occupied in many places. You cannot station garrisons in every part of these deserts. If you drive the people from one place, they will carry on their annual tillage, and remove with their flocks and herds to another. Many of the people in the back settlements are already little attached to particular situations. Already they have topped the Appalachian mountains. From thence they behold before them an immense plain, one vast, rich, level meadow; a square of five hundred miles. Over this they would wander without a possibility of restraint; they would change their manners with the habits of their life; would soon forget a government by which they were disowned; would become hordes of English

Tartars; and pouring down upon your unfortified frontiers a fierce and irresistible cavalry, become masters of your governors and your counsellors, your collectors and comptrollers, and of all the slaves that adhered to them. Such would, and in no long time must, be the effect of attempting to forbid as a crime, and to suppress as an evil, the command and blessing of Providence, 'Increase and multiply.' Such would be the happy result of an endeavor to keep, as a lair of wild beasts, that earth which God, by an express charter, has *given to the children of men*. Far different, and surely much wiser, has been our policy hitherto. Hitherto we have invited our people, by every kind of bounty, to fixed establishments. We have invited the husbandman to look to authority for his title. We have taught him piously to believe in the mysterious virtue of wax and parchment. We have thrown each tract of land, as it was peopled, into districts, that the ruling power should never be wholly out of sight. We have settled all we could; and we have carefully attended every settlement with government.

Adhering sir, as I do, to this policy, as well as for the reasons I have just given, I think this new project of hedging-in population to be neither prudent nor practicable.

To impoverish the colonies in general, and in particular to arrest the noble course of their marine enterprises, would be a more easy task. I freely confess it. We have shown a disposition to a system of this kind; a disposition even to continue the restraint after the offence; looking on ourselves as rivals to our colonies, and persuaded that of course we must gain all that they shall lose. Much mischief we may certainly do. The power inadequate to all other things is often more than sufficient for this. I do not look on the direct and immediate power of the colonies to resist our violence as very formidable. In this, however, I may be mistaken. But when I consider that we have colonies for no purpose but to be serviceable to us, it seems to my poor understanding a little preposterous to make them unserviceable, in order to keep them obedient. It is, in truth, nothing more than the old, and, as I thought, exploded problem of tyranny which proposes to beggar its subjects into submission. But remember, when you have completed your system of impoverishment, that Nature still proceeds in her ordinary course; that discontent will increase with misery; and that there are critical moments in the fortune of all states, when they who are too weak to contribute to your prosperity may be strong enough to complete your ruin. *Spoliatis arma supersunt* [Arms remain to the despoiled].

The temper and character which prevail in our colonies, are, I am afraid, unalterable by any human art. We cannot, I fear, falsify the pedigree of this fierce people, and persuade them that they are not sprung from a nation in whose veins the blood of freedom circulates. The language in which they would hear you tell them this tale would detect the imposition: your speech would betray you. An Englishman is the unfittest person on earth to argue another Englishman into slavery.

I think it is nearly as little in our power to change their republican religion as their free descent; or to substitute the Roman Catholic, as a penalty; or the Church of England, as an improvement. The mode of inquisition and dragooning is going out of fashion in the Old World, and I should not confide much to their efficacy in the New. The education of the Americans is also on the same unalterable bottom with their religion. You cannot persuade them to burn their books of curious science; to banish their lawyers from their courts of laws; or to quench the lights of their assemblies, by refusing to choose those persons who are best read in their privileges. It would be no less impracticable to think of wholly annihilating the popular assemblies, in which these lawyers sit. The army, by which we must govern in their place, would be far more chargeable to us; not quite so effectual; and perhaps, in the end, full as difficult to be kept in obedience.

With regard to the high aristocratic spirit of Virginia and the southern colonies, it has been proposed, I know, to reduce it, by declaring a general enfranchisement of their slaves. This project has had its advocates and panegyrists; yet I never could argue myself into any opinion of it. Slaves are often much attached to their masters. A general wild offer of liberty would not always be accepted. History furnishes few instances of it. It is sometimes as hard to persuade slaves to be free, as it is to compel freemen to be slaves; and in this auspicious scheme we should have both these pleasing tasks on our hands at once. But when we talk of enfranchisement, do we not perceive that the American master may enfranchise too, and arm servile hands in defence of freedom? A measure to which other people have had recourse more than once, and not without success, in a desperate situation of their affairs.

Slaves as these unfortunate black people are, and dull as all men are from slavery, must they not a little suspect the offer of freedom from that very nation which has sold them to their present masters? from that nation, one of whose causes of quarrel with those masters is their refusal to deal any more in that inhuman traffic? An offer of freedom from England would come rather oddly, shipped to them in an African vessel, which is refused an entry into the ports of Virginia or Carolina, with a cargo of three hundred Angola negroes. It would be curious to see the Guinea captain attempting at the same instant to publish his proclamation of liberty, and to advertise his sale of slaves.

But let us suppose all these moral difficulties got over. The ocean remains. You cannot pump this dry; and as long as it continues in its present bed, so long all the causes which weaken authority by distance will continue. 'Ye gods, annihilate but space and time, and make two lovers happy!' was a pious and passionate prayer; but just as reasonable as many of the serious wishes of very grave and solemn politicians.

If then, sir, it seems almost desperate to think of any alternative course for changing the moral causes, and not quite easy to remove the natural, which produce prejudices irreconcilable to the late exercise of our authority, but that the spirit infallibly will continue, and, continuing, will produce such effects as now embarrass us; the second mode under consideration is to prosecute that spirit in its overt acts as criminal.

At this proposition I must pause a moment. The thing seems a great deal too big for my ideas of jurisprudence. It should seem to my way of conceiving such matters, that there is a very wide difference in reason and policy between the mode of proceeding on the irregular conduct of scattered individuals, or even of bands of men, who disturb order within the state, and the civil dissensions which may, from time to time, on great questions, agitate the several communities which compose a great empire. It looks to me to be narrow and pedantic to apply the ordinary ideas of criminal justice to this great public contest. I do not know the method of drawing up an indictment against a whole people. I cannot insult and ridicule the feelings of millions of my fellow-creatures, as Sir Edward Coke insulted one excellent individual (Sir Walter Raleigh) at the bar. I hope I am not ripe to pass sentence on the gravest public bodies, entrusted with magistracies of great authority and dignity, and charged with the safety of their fellow-citizens, upon the very same title that I am. I really think that, for wise men, this is not judicious; for sober men, not decent; for minds tinctured with humanity, not mild and merciful.

Perhaps, sir, I am mistaken in my idea of an empire, as distinguished from a single state or kingdom. But my idea of it is this: that an empire is the aggregate of many states under one common head; whether this head be a monarch, or a presiding republic. It does, in such constitutions, frequently happen (and nothing but the dismal, cold, dead uniformity of servitude can prevent its happening) that the subordinate parts have many local privileges and immunities. Between these privileges and the supreme common authority the line may be extremely nice. Of course, disputes, often, too, very bitter disputes, and much ill blood, will arise. But though every privilege is an exemption (in the case) from the ordinary exercise of the supreme authority, it is no denial of it. The claim of the privilege seems rather, *ex vi termini* [by the meaning of the term], to imply a superior power. For to talk of the privileges of a state, or of a person, who has no superior, is hardly any better than speaking nonsense. Now, in such unfortunate quarrels among the component parts of a great political union of com-

munities, I can scarcely conceive anything more completely imprudent than for the head of the empire to insist that, if any privilege is pleaded against his will, or his acts, his whole authority is denied; instantly to proclaim rebellion, to beat to arms, and to put the offending provinces under the ban. Will not this, sir, very soon teach the provinces to make no distinctions on their part? Will it not teach them that the government, against which a claim of liberty is tantamount to high treason, is a government to which submission is equivalent to slavery? It may not always be quite convenient to impress dependent communities with such an idea.

We are indeed, in all disputes with the colonies, by the necessity of things, the judge. It is true, sir. But I confess that the character of judge in my own cause is a thing that frightens me. Instead of filling me with pride, I am exceedingly humbled by it. I cannot proceed with a stern, assured, judicial confidence, until I find myself in something more like a judicial character. I must have these hesitations as long as I am compelled to recollect that, in my little reading upon such contests as these, the sense of mankind has, at least, as often decided against the superior as the subordinate power. Sir, let me add too, that the opinion of my having some abstract right in my favor would not put me much at my ease in passing sentence, unless I could be sure that there were no rights which, in their exercise under certain circumstances, were not the most odious of all wrongs, and the most vexatious of all injustice. Sir, these considerations have great weight with me, when I find things so circumstanced, that I see the same party at once a civil litigant against me in point of right; and a culprit before me, while I sit as a criminal judge on acts of his, whose moral quality is to be decided upon the merits of that very litigation. Men are every now and then put, by the complexity of human affairs, into strange situations; but justice is the same, let the judge be in what situation he will.

There is, sir, also a circumstance which convinces me that this mode of criminal proceeding is not (at least in the present stage of our contest) altogether expedient; which is nothing less than the conduct of those very persons who have seemed to adopt that mode, by lately declaring a rebellion in Massachusetts Bay, as they had formerly addressed to have traitors brought hither, under an Act of Henry the Eighth, for trial. For though rebellion is declared, it is not proceeded against as such; nor have any steps been taken towards the apprehension or conviction of any individual offender, either on our late or our former Address; but modes of public coercion have been adopted, and such as have much more resemblance to a sort of qualified hostility toward an independent power than the punishment of rebellious subjects. All this seems rather inconsistent; but it shows how difficult it is to apply these juridical ideas to our present case.

In this situation, let us seriously and coolly ponder. What is it we have got by all our menaces, which have been many and ferocious? What advantage have we derived from the penal laws we have rightly passed, and which, for the time, have been severe and numerous? What advances have we made towards our object, by the sending of a force which, by land and sea, is no contemptible strength? Has the disorder abated? Nothing less. When I see things in this situation, after such confident hopes, bold promises, and active exertions, I cannot for my life avoid a suspicion that the plan itself is not correctly right.

If then the removal of the causes of this spirit of American liberty be, for the greater part, or rather entirely, impracticable; if the ideas of criminal process be inapplicable, or if applicable, are in the highest degree inexpedient; what way yet remains? No way is open but the third and last — to comply with the American spirit as necessary; or, if you please, to submit to it as a necessary evil.

If we adopt this mode; if we mean to conciliate and concede; let us see of what nature the concession ought to be: to ascertain the nature of our concession we must look at their complaint. The colonies complain that they have not the characteristic mark and seal of British freedom. They complain that they are taxed in a parliament in which they are not represented. If you mean to satisfy them at all, you must satisfy them with regard to this complaint. If you mean to

please any people, you must give them the boon which they ask; not what you may think better for them, but of a kind totally different. Such an act may be a wise regulation, but it is no concession; whereas our present theme is the mode of giving satisfaction.

Sir, I think you must perceive that I am resolved this day to have nothing at all to do with the question of the right of taxation. Some gentlemen startle — but it is true; I put it totally out of the question. It is less than nothing in my consideration. I do not indeed wonder, nor will you, sir, that gentlemen of profound learning are fond of displaying it on this profound subject. But my consideration is narrow, confined, and wholly limited to the policy of the question. I do not examine whether the giving away a man's money be a power excepted and reserved out of the general trust of government; and how far all mankind, in all forms of polity, are entitled to an exercise of that right by the charter of Nature. Or whether, on the contrary, a right of taxation is necessarily involved in the general principle of legislation, and inseparable from the ordinary supreme power. These are deep questions, where great names militate against each other; where reason is perplexed; and an appeal to authorities only thickens the confusion. For high and reverend authorities lift up their heads on both sides; and there is no sure footing in the middle. This point 'is the great Serbonian bog. Betwixt Damiata and Mount Casius old, Where armies whole have sunk.' I do not intend to be overwhelmed in that bog, though in such respectable company. The question with me is, not whether you have a right to render your people miserable, but whether it is not your interest to make them happy. It is not what a lawyer tells me I may do, but what humanity, reason, and justice tell me I ought to do. Is a politic act the worse for being a generous one? Is no concession proper, but that which is made from your want of right to keep what you grant? Or does it lessen the grace or dignity of relaxing in the exercise of an odious claim, because you have your evidence-room full of titles, and your magazines stuffed with arms to enforce them? What signify all those titles and all those arms? Of what avail are they, when the reason of the thing tells me that the assertion of my title is the loss of my suit; and that I could do nothing but wound myself by the use of my own weapons?

Such is steadfastly my opinion of the absolute necessity of keeping up the concord of this empire by a unity of spirit, though in a diversity of operations, that, if I were sure the colonists had, at their leaving this country, sealed a regular compact of servitude; that they had solemnly abjured all the rights of citizens; that they had made a vow to renounce all ideas of liberty for them and their posterity to all generations; yet I should hold myself obliged to conform to the temper I found universally prevalent in my own day, and to govern two million of men, impatient of servitude, on the principles of freedom. I am not determining a point of law; I am restoring tranquillity; and the general character and situation of a people must determine what sort of government is fitted for them. That point nothing else can or ought to determine.

My idea, therefore, without considering whether we yield as matter of right, or grant as matter of favor, is to *admit the people of our colonies into an interest in the Constitution;* and, by recording that admission in the journals of parliament, to give them as strong an assurance as the nature of the thing will admit, that we mean for ever to adhere to that solemn declaration of systematic indulgence.

Some years ago, the repeal of a Revenue Act, upon its understood principle, might have served to show that we intended an unconditional abatement of the exercise of a taxing power. Such a measure was then sufficient to remove all suspicion, and to give perfect content. But unfortunate events, since that time, may make something further necessary; and not more necessary for the satisfaction of the colonies, than for the dignity and consistency of our own future proceedings.

* * *

(1775)

EDWARD GIBBON (1737–1794)

The greatest of English historians was born not far from London, at Putney in Surrey, where his father lived the easy life of a country gentleman. Gibbon ascribed the success of his later years to the 'golden mediocrity' of his fortunes, which preserved him on the one hand from the seductions of pleasure and, on the other, from the need of earning a living. His childhood was sickly, his education was intermittent, and he was indulged in his bent for reading which soon settled to a passion for history. At an early age he had devoured everything in that department which was accessible in English and had begun to annex other languages in order that he might gratify his hunger for original documents. He was sent at fifteen to Magdalen College, Oxford, and has left a withering indictment of the neglect and incompetence which he encountered at that seat of learning. Left to himself, he fell under the influence of a Jesuit and was converted to Roman Catholicism; whereupon his father promptly deported him to Switzerland and placed him under the care of a Calvinist minister at Lausanne. Through constant practice in the defense of his faith he became familiar with its assailable points, and soon passed to the position of scepticism which he permanently occupied. He mastered the French language and the French method of study and became deeply imbued with the French rationalistic ideas of the period. By five years of great diligence under able direction he laid the foundation of his superb equipment for the task of his life. Returning to England, he published in the French language his first book, *Essai sur l'Etude de la Litterature* [Essay on the Study of Literature] (1761). To please his father he served for two years and a half as a captain of militia. The singleness of his ambition is well illustrated by his summary of these lost years: 'The discipline and evolutions of a modern battalion gave me a clearer notion of the phalanx and the legions, and the captain of the Hampshire grenadiers — the reader may smile — has not been useless to the historian of the Roman empire.' But of this and of his later career in Parliament he was impatient as of anything which did not contribute directly to his one ambition. From his early youth he had 'aspired to the character of a historian,' but he remained unsettled as to the field he should occupy until he found himself at Rome. 'In my journal, the place and the moment of the conception are recorded,' he tells us in his *Memoirs*, 'the fifteenth of October, 1764, in the close of the evening, as I sat musing in the church of the Zoccolanti or Franciscan friars, while they were singing vespers in the temple of Jupiter on the ruins of the Capitol.' Two years elapsed before he was able to set to work, twelve before the first volume was published in London, and another twelve before he laid down his pen at Lausanne. His *History of the Decline and Fall* had been his life, the one object toward which all his reading and experience were made to converge, and is the one subject of his *Memoirs*. He quietly finished his days at Lausanne, undoubtedly justified in his feeling that this achievement had been enough for one life. The substance of Gibbon's 'candid and rational inquiry into the human causes' of the religious growth which undermined the civilization of the ancient world, has not remained totally unassailed by the modern historian; nor is Gibbon's style perfect; but it is safe to say that no other Englishman has united in an equal degree abundance and accuracy of information, sense of historical perspective and proportion, vigor of narrative, and splendor of style.

From THE DECLINE AND FALL OF THE ROMAN EMPIRE

Of the triangle which composes the figure of Constantinople, the two sides along the sea were made inaccessible to an enemy: the Propontis by nature and the harbor by art. Between the two waters, the basis of the triangle, the land side was protected by a double wall and a deep ditch of the depth of one hundred feet. Against this line of fortification, which Phranza, an eye-witness, prolongs to the measure of six miles, the Ottomans 5 directed their principal attack; and the emperor, after distributing the service and command of the most perilous stations, undertook the defence of the external wall. In the first days of the siege, 10 the Greek soldiers descended into the ditch, or sallied into the field; but they soon discovered that, in the proportion of their numbers, one christian was of more value than twenty Turks; and, after these bold preludes, they were prudently content to maintain the rampart with their missile weapons. Nor should this prudence be accused of pusillanimity. The nation was indeed pusillanimous and base; but the last Constantine deserves the name of an hero: his noble band of volunteers was inspired with Roman virtue; and the foreign auxiliaries supported the honor of the Western chivalry. The incessant volleys of lances and arrows were accompanied with the smoke, the sound, and the fire of their musketry and cannon. Their small arms discharged at the same time either five or even ten balls of lead of the size of a walnut; and, according to the closeness of the ranks and the force of the powder, several breastplates and bodies were transpierced by the same shot. But the Turkish approaches were soon sunk in trenches or covered with ruins. Each day added to the science of the christians; but their inadequate stock of gunpowder was wasted in the operations of each day. Their ordnance was not powerful either in size or number; and, if they possessed some heavy cannon, they feared to plant them on the walls, lest the aged structure should be shaken and overthrown by the explosion. The same destructive secret had been revealed to the Moslems; by whom it was employed with the superior energy of zeal, riches, and despotism. The great cannon of Mahomet has been separately noticed; an important and visible object in the history of the times: but that enormous engine was flanked by two fellows almost of equal magnitude; the long order of the Turkish artillery was pointed against the walls; fourteen batteries thundered at once on the most accessible places; and of one of these it is ambiguously expressed that it was mounted with one hundred and thirty guns, or that it discharged one hundred and thirty bullets. Yet, in the power and activity of the sultan, we may discern the infancy of the new science. Under a master who counted the moments, the great cannon could be loaded and fired no more than seven times in one day. The heated metal unfortunately burst; several

workmen were destroyed; and the skill of an artist was admired, who bethought himself of preventing the danger and the accident, by pouring oil, after each explosion, into the mouth of the cannon.

The first random shots were productive of more sound than effect; and it was by the advice of a christian that the engineers were taught to level their aim against the two opposite sides of the salient angles of a bastion. However imperfect, the weight and repetition of the fire made some impression on the walls; and the Turks, pushing their approaches to the edge of the ditch, attempted to fill the enormous chasm and to build a road to the assault. Innumerable fascines and hogsheads and trunks of trees were heaped on each other; and such was the impetuosity of the throng that the foremost and the weakest were pushed headlong down the precipice and instantly buried under the accumulated mass. To fill the ditch was the toil of the besiegers; to clear away the rubbish was the safety of the besieged; and, after a long and bloody conflict, the web that had been woven in the day was still unraveled in the night. The next resource of Mahomet was the practice of mines; but the soil was rocky; in every attempt he was stopped and undermined by the christian engineers; nor had the art been yet invented of replenishing those subterraneous passages with gunpowder and blowing whole towers and cities into the air. A circumstance that distinguishes the siege of Constantinople is the reunion of the ancient and modern artillery. The cannon were intermingled with the mechanical engines for casting stones and darts; the bullet and the battering-ram were directed against the same walls; nor had the discovery of gunpowder superseded the use of the liquid and unextinguishable fire. A wooden turret of the largest size was advanced on rollers: this portable magazine of ammunition and fascines was protected by a threefold covering of bulls' hides; incessant volleys were securely discharged from the loop-holes; in the front, three doors were contrived for the alternate sally and retreat of the soldiers and workmen. They ascended by a staircase to the upper platform, and, as high as the level of that platform, a scaling-ladder could be raised by pulleys ro form a bridge and grapple with the adverse rampart. By these various arts of annoyance, some as new as they were pernicious to the Greeks, the tower of St. Romanus was at length overturned: after a severe struggle, the Turks were repulsed from the breach and interrupted by darkness; but they trusted that with the return of light they should renew the attack with fresh vigor and decisive success. Of this pause of action, this interval of hope, each moment was improved by the activity of the emperor and Justiniani, who passed the night on the spot, and urged the labors which involved the safety of the church and city. At the dawn of day, the impatient sultan perceived, with astonishment and grief, that his wooden turret had been reduced to ashes: the ditch was cleared and restored; and the tower of St. Romanus was again strong and entire. He deplored the failure of his design; and uttered a profane exclamation that the word of the thirty-seven thousand prophets should not have compelled him to believe that such a work, in so short a time, should have been accomplished by the infidels.

The generosity of the christian princes was cold and tardy; but, in the first apprehension of a siege, Constantine had negotiated, in the isles of the Archipelago, the Morea, and Sicily, the most indispensable supplies. As early as the beginning of April, five great ships, equipped for merchandise and war, would have sailed from the harbor of Chios, had not the wind blown obstinately from the north. One of these ships bore the Imperial flag; the remaining four belonged to the Genoese; and they were laden with wheat and barley, with wine, oil, and vegetables, and, above all, with soldiers and mariners, for the service of the capital. After a tedious delay, a gentle breeze, and, on the second day, a strong gale from the south, carried them through the Hellespont and the Propontis; but the city was already invested by sea and land; and the Turkish fleet, at the entrance of the Bosphorus, was stretched from shore to shore, in the form of a crescent, to intercept, or at least to repel, these bold auxiliaries. The reader who has present to his mind the geographical picture of Constantinople. will conceive and admire the greatness of the spectacle. The five christian ships continued to advance with joyful shouts, and a full press both of sails and oars, against an hostile fleet of three hundred vessels; and the rampart, the camp, the coasts of Europe and Asia, were lined with innumerable spectators, who anxiously awaited the event of this momentous succor. At the first view that event could not appear doubtful: the superiority of the Moslems was beyond all measure or account; and, in a calm, their numbers and valor must inevitably have prevailed. But their hasty and imperfect navy had been created, not by the genius of the people, but by the will of the sultan: in the height of their prosperity, the Turks have acknowledged that, if God had given them the earth, he had left the sea to the infidels; and a series of defeats, a rapid progress of decay, has established the truth of their modest confession. Except eighteen galleys of some force, the rest of their fleet consisted of open boats, rudely constructed and awkwardly managed, crowded with troops and destitute of cannon; and, since courage arises in a great measure from the consciousness of strength, the bravest of the Janizaries might tremble on a new element. In the christian squadron, five stout and lofty ships were guided by skilful pilots, and manned with the veterans of Italy and Greece, long practised in the arts and perils of the sea. Their weight was directed to sink or scatter the weak obstacles that impeded their passage: their artillery swept the waters; their liquid fire was poured on the heads of the adversaries who, with the design of boarding, presumed to approach them; and the winds and waves are always on the side of the ablest navigators. In this conflict, the Imperial vessel, which had been almost overpowered, was rescued by the Genoese; but the Turks, in a distant and closer attack, were twice repulsed with considerable loss. Mahomet himself sat on horseback on the beach, to encourage their valor by his voice and presence, by the promise of reward, and by fear more potent than the fear of the enemy. The passions of his soul, and even the gestures of his body, seemed to imitate the actions of the combatants; and, as if he had been the lord of nature, he spurred his horse with a fearless and impotent effort into the sea. His loud reproaches, and the clamors of the camp, urged the Ottomans to a third attack, more fatal and bloody than the two former; and I must repeat, though I cannot credit, the evidence of Phranza, who affirms, from their own mouth, that they lost above twelve thousand men in the slaughter of the day. They fled in disorder to the shores of Europe and Asia, while the christian squadron, triumphant and unhurt, steered along the Bosphorus and securely anchored within the chain of the harbor. In the confidence of victory, they boasted that the whole Turkish power must have yielded to their arms; but the admiral, or captain bashaw, found some consolation for a painful wound in his eye, by representing that accident as the cause of his defeat. Baltha Ogli was a renegade of the race of the Bulgarian princes; his military character was tainted with the unpopular vice of avarice; and, under the despotism of the prince or people, misfortune is a sufficient evidence of guilt. His rank and services were annihilated by the displeasure of Mahomet. In the royal presence, the captain bashaw was extended on the ground by four slaves, and received one hundred strokes with a golden rod; his death had been pronounced; and he adored the clemency of the sultan, who was satisfied with the milder punishment of confiscation and exile. The introduction of this supply revived the hopes of the Greeks, and accused the supineness of their Western allies. Amidst the deserts of Anatolia and the rocks of Palestine, the millions of the crusades had buried themselves in a voluntary and inevitable grave; but the situation of the Imperial city was strong against her enemies, and accessible to her friends; and a rational and moderate armament of the maritime states might have saved the relics of the Roman name, and maintained a christian fortress in the heart of the Ottoman empire. Yet this was the sole and feeble attempt for the deliverance of Constantinople; the more distant powers were insensible of its danger; and the ambassador of Hungary, or at least of Huniades, resided in the Turkish camp, to remove the fears, and to direct the operations, of the sultan.

It was difficult for the Greeks to penetrate the secret of the divan; yet the Greeks are persuaded that a resistance, so obstinate and surprising, had fatigued the perseverance of Mahomet. He began to meditate a retreat, and the siege would have been speedily raised, if the ambition and jealousy of the second vizir had not opposed the perfidious advice of Calil Bashaw, who still maintained a secret correspondence with the Byzantine court. The reduction of the city appeared to be hopeless, unless a double attack could be made from the harbor as well as from the land; but the harbor was inaccessible: an impenetrable chain was now defended by eight large ships, more than twenty of a smaller size, with several galleys and sloops; and instead of forcing this barrier, the Turks might apprehend a naval sally and a second encounter in the open sea. In this perplexity, the genius of Mahomet conceived and executed a plan of a bold and marvelous cast, of transporting by land his lighter vessels and military stores from the Bosphorus into the higher part of the harbor. The distance is about ten miles; the ground is uneven, and was overspread with thickets; and, as the road must be opened behind the suburb of Galata, their free passage or total destruction must depend on the option of the Genoese. But these selfish merchants were ambitious of the favor of being the last devoured; and the deficiency of art was supplied by the strength of obedient myriads. A level way was covered with a broad platform of strong and solid planks; and to render them more slippery and smooth, they were anointed with the fat of sheep and oxen. Fourscore light galleys and brigantines of fifty and thirty oars were disembarked on the Bosphorus shore, arranged successively on rollers, and drawn forwards by the power of men and pulleys. Two guides or pilots were stationed at the helm and the prow of each vessel: the sails were unfurled to the winds; and the labor was cheered by song and acclamation. In the course of a single night, this Turkish fleet painfully climbed the hill, steered over the plain, and was launched from the declivity into the shallow waters of the harbor, far above the molestation of the deeper vessels of the Greeks. The real importance of this operation was magnified by the consternation and confidence which it inspired; but the notorious, unquestionable fact was displayed before the eyes, and is recorded by the pens, of the two nations. A similar stratagem had been repeatedly practised by the ancients; the Ottoman galleys, I must again repeat, should be considered as large boats; and, if we compare the magnitude and the distance, the obstacles and the means, the boasted miracle has perhaps been equaled by the industry of our own times. As soon as Mahomet had occupied the upper harbor with a fleet and army, he constructed, in the narrowest part, a bridge, or rather mole, of fifty cubits in breadth and one hundred in length; it was formed of casks and hogsheads, joined with rafters linked with iron, and covered with a solid floor. On this floating battery he planted one of his largest cannon, while the fourscore galleys, with troops and scaling-ladders, approached the most accessible side, which had formerly been stormed by the Latin conquerors. The indolence of the christians has been accused for not destroying these unfinished works; but their fire, by a superior fire, was controlled and silenced; nor were they wanting in a nocturnal attempt to burn the vessels as well as the bridge of the sultan. His vigilance prevented their approach; their foremost galliots were sunk or taken; forty youths, the bravest of Italy and Greece were inhumanly massacred at his command; nor could the emperor's grief be assuaged by the just though cruel retaliation of exposing from the walls the heads of two hundred and sixty Mussulman captives. After a siege of forty days, the fate of Constantinople could no longer be averted. The diminutive garrison was exhausted by a double attack; the fortifications, which had stood for ages against hostile violence, were dismantled on all sides by the Ottoman cannon; many breaches were opened; and near the gate of St. Romanus four towers had been leveled with the ground. For the payment of his feeble and mutinous troops, Constantine was compelled to despoil the churches, with the promise of a fourfold restitution; and his sacrilege offered a new reproach to the enemies of the union. A spirit of discord impaired the remnant of the christian strength: the Genoese and Venetian auxiliaries asserted the pre-eminence of their respective service; and Justiniani and the Great Duke, whose ambition was not extinguished by the common danger, accused each other of treachery and cowardice.

During the siege of Constantinople, the words of peace and capitulation had been sometimes pronounced; and several embassies had passed between the camp and the city. The Greek emperor was humbled by adversity; and would have yielded to any terms compatible with religion and royalty. The Turkish sultan was desirous of sparing the blood of his soldiers; still more desirous of securing for his own use the Byzantine treasures; and he accomplished a sacred duty in presenting to the *Gabours* the choice of circumcision, of tribute, or of death. The avarice of Mahomet might have been satisfied with an annual sum of one hundred thousand ducats; but his ambition grasped the capital of the East; to the prince he offered a rich equivalent, to the people a free toleration or a safe departure: but, after some fruitless treaty, he declared his resolution of finding either a throne or a grave under the walls of Constantinople. A sense of honor and the fear of universal reproach forbade Palæologus to resign the city into the hands of the Ottomans; and he determined to abide the last extremities of war. Several days were employed by the sultan in the preparations of the assault; and a respite was granted by his favorite science of astrology, which had fixed on the twenty-ninth of May as the fortunate and fatal hour. On the evening of the twenty-seventh, he issued his final orders; assembled in his presence the military chiefs; and dispersed his heralds through the camp to proclaim the duty and the motives of the perilous enterprise. Fear is the first principle of a despotic government; and his menaces were expressed in the Oriental style, that the fugitives and deserters, had they the wings of a bird, should not escape from his inexorable justice. The greatest part of his bashaws and Janizaries were the offspring of christian parents; but the glories of the Turkish name were perpetuated by successive adoption; and, in the gradual change of individuals, the spirit of a legion, a regiment, or an *oda* is kept alive by imitation and discipline. In this holy warfare, the Moslems were exhorted to purify their minds with prayer, their bodies with seven ablutions; and to abstain from food till the close of the ensuing day. A crowd of dervishes visited the tents, to instil the desire of martyrdom, and the assurance of spending an immortal youth amidst the rivers and gardens of paradise and in the embraces of the black-eyed virgins. Yet Mahomet principally trusted to the efficacy of temporal and visible rewards. A double pay was promised to the victorious troops: 'The city and the buildings,' said Mahomet, 'are mine; but I resign to your valor the captives and the spoil, the treasures of gold and beauty; be rich and be happy. Many are the provinces of my empire: the intrepid soldier who first ascends the walls of Constantinople shall be rewarded with the government of the fairest and most wealthy; and my gratitude shall accumulate his honors and fortunes above the measure of his own hopes.' Such various and potent motives diffused among the Turks a general ardor, re-gardless of life and impatient for action: the camp re-echoed with the Moslem shouts of 'God is God, there is but one God, and Mahomet is the apostle of God'; and the sea and land, from Ga-lata to the seven towers, were illuminated by the blaze of their nocturnal fires.

Far different was the state of the christians; who with loud and impotent complaints, deplored the guilt, or the punishment, of their sins. The celestial image of the Virgin had been exposed in solemn procession; but their divine pa-troness was deaf to their entreaties: they accused the obstinacy of the emperor for refusing a timely surrender; anticipated the horrors of their fate; and sighed for the repose and security of Turkish serv-itude. The noblest of the Greeks, and the bravest of the allies, were summoned to the palace, to prepare them, on the evening of the twenty-eighth, for the duties and dangers of the general assault. The last speech of Palæologus was the funeral oration of the Roman Empire: he promised, he conjured, and he vainly attempted to infuse the hope which was extinguished in his own mind. In this world all was comfortless and gloomy; and neither the gospel nor the church have proposed any conspicuous recom-pense to the heroes who fall in the serv-ice of their country. But the example of their prince and the confinement of a siege had armed these warriors with the courage of despair; and the pathetic scene is described by the feelings of the historian Phranza, who was himself present at this mournful assembly. They wept, they embraced; regardless of their families and fortunes, they devoted their lives; and each commander, departing to his station, maintained all night a vigi-lant and anxious watch on the rampart. The emperor, and some faithful compan-ions, entered the dome of St. Sophia, which in a few hours was to be converted into a mosque; and devoutly received, with tears and prayers, the sacrament of the holy communion. He reposed some moments in the palace, which resounded with cries and lamentations; solicited the pardon of all whom he might have in-jured; and mounted on horseback to visit the guards and explore the motions of the enemy. The distress and fall of the last Constantine are more glorious than the long prosperity of the Byzantine Cæsars.

In the confusion of darkness an assail-ant may sometimes succeed; but, in this great and general attack, the military judgment and astrological knowledge of Mahomet advised him to expect the morning, the memorable twenty-ninth of May, in the fourteen hundred and fifty-third year of the christian æra. The preceding night had been strenuously em-ployed: the troops, the cannon, and the fascines were advanced to the edge of the ditch, which, in many parts, pre-sented a smooth and level passage to the breach; and his fourscore galleys al-most touched, with the prows and their scaling-ladders, the less defensible walls of the harbor. Under pain of death, si-lence was enjoined; but the physical laws of motion and sound are not obedi-ent to discipline or fear; each individual might suppress his voice and measure his footsteps; but the march and labor of thousands must inevitably produce a strange confusion of dissonant clamors, which reached the ears of the watchmen of the towers. At daybreak, without the customary signal of the morning-gun, the Turks assaulted the city by sea and land; and the similitude of a twined or twisted thread has been applied to the closeness and continuity of their line of attack. The foremost ranks consisted of the refuse of the host, a voluntary crowd, who fought without order or command; of the feebleness of age or childhood, of peasants and vagrants, and of all who had joined the camp in the blind hope of plunder and martyrdom. The common impulse drove them onwards to the wall; the most audacious to climb were instantly precipitated; and not a dart, not a bullet of the christians was idly wasted on the accumulated throng. But their strength and ammunition were exhausted in this laborious defence; the ditch was filled with the bodies of the slain; they supported the footsteps of their companions; and of this devoted vanguard the death was more serviceable than the life. Under their respective bashaws and sanjaks, the troops of Anatolia and Romania were successively led to the charge: their progress was various and doubtful; but, after a conflict of two hours, the Greeks still maintained and improved their advantage; and the voice of the emperor was heard, encouraging his soldiers to achieve, by a last effort, the deliverance of their country. In that fatal moment, the Janizaries arose, fresh, vigorous, and invincible. The sultan himself on horseback, with an iron mace in his hand, was the spectator and judge of their valor; he was surrounded by ten thousand of his domestic troops, whom he reserved for the decisive occasion; and the tide of battle was directed and impelled by his voice and eye. His numerous ministers of justice were posted behind the line, to urge, to restrain, and to punish; and, if danger was in the front, shame and inevitable death were in the rear of the fugitives. The cries of fear and of pain were drowned in the martial music of drums, trumpets, and attaballs; and experience has proved that the mechanical operation of sounds, by quickening the circulation of the blood and spirits, will act on the human machine more forcibly than the eloquence of reason and honor. From the lines, the galleys, and the bridge, the Ottoman artillery thundered on all sides; and the camp and city, the Greeks and the Turks, were involved in a cloud of smoke, which could only be dispelled by the final deliverance or destruction of the Roman empire. The single combats of the heroes of history or fable amuse our fancy and engage our affections: the skilful evolutions of war may inform the mind, and improve a necessary though pernicious science. But, in the uniform and odious pictures of a general assault, all is blood, and horror, and confusion; nor shall I strive, at the distance of three centuries and a thousand miles, to delineate a scene of which there could be no spectators, and of which the actors themselves were incapable of forming any just or adequate idea.

The immediate loss of Constantinople may be ascribed to the bullet, or arrow, which pierced the gauntlet of John Justiniani. The sight of his blood, and the exquisite pain, appalled the courage of the chief, whose arms and counsel were the firmest rampart of the city. As he withdrew from his station in quest of a surgeon, his flight was perceived and stopped by the indefatigable emperor. 'Your wound,' exclaimed Palæologus, 'is slight; the danger is pressing; your presence is necessary; and whither will you retire?' 'I will retire,' said the trembling Genoese, 'by the same road which God has opened to the Turks;' and at these words he hastily passed through one of the breaches of the inner wall. By this pusillanimous act, he stained the honors of a military life; and the few days which he survived in Galata, or the isle of Chios, were embittered by his own and the public reproach. His example was imitated by the greatest part of the Latin auxiliaries, and the defence began to slacken when the attack was pressed with redoubled vigor. The number of Ottomans was fifty, perhaps an hundred, times superior to that of the christians; the double walls were reduced by the cannon to a heap of ruins; in a circuit of several miles, some places must be found more easy of access or more feebly guarded; and, if the besiegers could penetrate in a single point, the whole city was irrecoverably lost. The first who deserved the sultan's reward was Hassan, the Janizary, of gigantic stature and strength. With his scimitar in one hand and his buckler in the other, he ascended the outward fortification: of the thirty Janizaries, who were emulous of his valor, eighteen perished in the bold adventure. Hassan and his twelve companions had reached the summit: the giant was precipitated from 5 the rampart; he rose on one knee, and was again oppressed by a shower of darts and stones. But his success had proved that the achievement was possible: the walls and towers were instantly covered 10 with a swarm of Turks; and the Greeks, now driven from the vantage-ground, were overwhelmed by increasing multitudes. Amidst these multitudes, the emperor, who accomplished all the duties 15 of a general and a soldier, was long seen, and finally lost. The nobles who fought round his person sustained, till their last breath, the honorable names of Palæologus and Cantacuzene: his mournful ex- 20 clamation was heard, 'Cannot there be found a christian to cut off my head?' and his last fear was that of falling alive into the hands of the infidels. The prudent despair of Constantine cast away 25 purple; amidst the tumult, he fell by an unknown hand, and his body was buried under a mountain of the slain. After his death, resistance and order were no more; the Greeks fled towards the city; and 30 many were pressed and stifled in the narrow pass of the gate of St. Romanus. The victorious Turks rushed through the breaches of the inner wall; and, as they advanced into the streets, they were soon 35 joined by their brethren, who had forced the gate Phenar on the side of the harbor. In the first heat of the pursuit, about two thousand christians were put to the sword; but avarice soon prevailed 40 over cruelty; and the victors acknowledged that they should immediately have given quarter, if the valor of the emperor and his chosen bands had not prepared them for a similar opposition in 45 every part of the capital. It was thus, after a siege of fifty-three days, that Constantinople, which had defied the power of Chosroes, the Chagan, and the caliphs, was irretrievably subdued by the arms 50 of Mahomet the Second. Her empire only had been subverted by the Latins: her religion was trampled in the dust by the Moslem conquerors.

The tidings of misfortune fly with a 55 rapid wing; yet such was the extent of Constantinople that the more distant quarters might prolong, some moments, the happy ignorance of their ruin. But in the general consternation, in the feelings of selfish or social anxiety, in the tumult and thunder of the assault, a *sleepless* night and morning must have elapsed; nor can I believe that many Grecian ladies were awakened by the Janizaries from a sound and tranquil slumber. On the assurance of the public calamity, the houses and convents were instantly deserted; and the trembling inhabitants flocked together in the streets, like an herd of timid animals, as if accumulated weakness could be productive of strength, or in the vain hope that amid the crowd each individual might be safe and invisible. From every part of the capital, they flowed into the church of St. Sophia: in the space of an hour, the sanctuary, the choir, the nave, the upper and lower galleries, were filled with the multitudes of fathers and husbands, of women and children, of priests, monks, and religious virgins: the doors were barred on the inside, and they sought protection from the sacred dome which they had so lately abhorred as a profane and polluted edifice. Their confidence was founded on the prophecy of an enthusiast or impostor, that one day the Turks would enter Constantinople, and pursue the Romans as far as the column of Constantine in the square before St. Sophia; but that this would be the term of their calamities; that an angel would descend from heaven, with a sword in his hand, and would deliver the empire, with that celestial weapon, to a poor man seated at the foot of the column. 'Take this sword,' would he say, 'and avenge the people of the Lord.' At these animating words, the Turks would instantly fly, and the victorious Romans would drive them from the West, and from all Anatolia, as far as the frontiers of Persia. It is on this occasion that Ducas, with some fancy and much truth, upbraids the discord and obstinacy of the Greeks. 'Had that angel appeared,' exclaims the historian, 'had he offered to exterminate your foes if you would consent to the union of the church, even then, in that fatal moment, you would have rejected your safety or have deceived your God.'

While they expected the descent of the

tardy angel, the doors were broken with axes; and, as the Turks encountered no resistance, their bloodless hands were employed in selecting and securing the multitude of their prisoners. Youth, beauty, and the appearance of wealth attracted their choice; and the right of property was decided among themselves by a prior seizure, by personal strength, and by the authority of command. In the space of an hour, the male captives were bounds with cords, the females with their veils and girdles. The senators were linked with their slaves; the prelates with the porters of the church; and young men of a plebeian class with noble maids, whose faces had been invisible to the sun and their nearest kindred. In this common captivity, the ranks of society were confounded; the ties of nature were cut asunder; and the inexorable soldier was careless of the father's groans, the tears of the mother, and the lamentations of the children. The loudest in their wailings were the nuns, who were torn from the altar with naked bosoms, outstretched hands, and disheveled hair; and we should piously believe that few could be tempted to prefer the vigils of the haram to those of the monastery. Of these unfortunate Greeks, of these domestic animals, whole strings were rudely driven through the streets; and, as the conquerors were eager to return for more prey, their trembling pace was quickened with menaces and blows. At the same hour, a similar rapine was exercised in all the churches and monasteries, in all the palaces and habitations of the capital; nor could any palace, however sacred or sequestered, protect the persons or the property of the Greeks. Above sixty thousand of this devoted people were transported from the city to the camp and fleet; exchanged or sold according to the caprice or interest of their masters, and dispersed in remote servitude through the provinces of the Ottoman empire.

* * *

The chain and entrance of the outward harbor was still occupied by the Italian ships of merchandise and war. They had signalized their valor in the siege: they embraced the moment of retreat, while the Turkish mariners were dissipated in the pillage of the city. When they hoisted sail the beach was covered with a suppliant and lamentable crowd; but the means of transportation were scanty; the Venetians and Genoese selected their countrymen; and, notwithstanding the fairest promises of the sultan, the inhabitants of Galata evacuated their houses and embarked with their most precious effects.

In the fall and the sack of great cities, an historian is condemned to repeat the tale of uniform calamity: the same effects must be produced by the same passions; and, when those passions may be indulged without control, small, alas! is the difference between civilised and savage man. Amidst the vague exclamations of bigotry and hatred, the Turks are not accused of a wanton or immoderate effusion of christian blood; but, according to their maxims (the maxims of antiquity), the lives of the vanquished were forfeited; and the legitimate reward of the conqueror was derived from the service, the sale, or the ransom, of his captives of both sexes. The wealth of Constantinople had been granted by the sultan to his victorious troops; and the rapine of an hour is more productive than the industry of years. But, as no regular division was attempted of the spoil, the respective shares were not determined by merit; and the rewards of valor were stolen away by the followers of the camp, who had declined the toil and the danger of the battle. The narrative of their depredations could not afford either amusement or instruction: the total amount, in the last poverty of the empire, has been valued at four millions of ducats; and of this sum a small part was the property of the Venetians, the Genoese, the Florentines, and the merchants of Ancona. Of these foreigners, the stock was improved in quick and perpetual circulation; but the riches of the Greeks were displayed in the idle ostentation of palaces and wardrobes, or deeply buried in treasures of ingots and old coin, lest it should be demanded at their hands for the defence of their country. The profanation and plunder of the monasteries and churches excited the most tragic complaints. The dome of St. Sophia itself, the earthly heaven, the second firmament, the vehicle of the cherubim, the throne of the glory of God, was despoiled of the oblations of ages;

and the gold and silver, the pearls and jewels, the vases and sacerdotal ornaments, were most wickedly converted to the service of mankind. After the divine images had been stripped of all that could be valuable to a profane eye, the canvas, or the wood, was torn, or broken, or burnt, or trod under foot, or applied, in the stables or the kitchen, to the vilest uses. The example of sacrilege was imitated, however, from the Latin conquerors of Constantinople; and the treatment which Christ, the Virgin, and the saints had sustained from the guilty Catholic might be inflicted by the zealous Mussulman on the monuments of idolatry. Perhaps, instead of joining the public clamor, a philosopher will observe that in the decline of the arts the workmanship could not be more valuable than the work, and that a fresh supply of visions and miracles would speedily be renewed by the craft of the priest and the credulity of the people. He will more seriously deplore the loss of the Byzantine libraries, which were destroyed or scattered in the general confusion: one hundred and twenty thousand manuscripts are said to have disappeared; ten volumes might be purchased for a single ducat; and the same ignominious price, too high perhaps for a shelf of theology, included the whole works of Aristotle and Homer, the noblest productions of the science and literature of ancient Greece. We may reflect with pleasure that an inestimable portion of our classic treasures was safely deposited in Italy; and that the mechanics of a German town had invented an art which derides the havoc of time and barbarism.

From the first hour of the memorable twenty-ninth of May, disorder and rapine prevailed in Constantinople till the eighth hour of the same day; when the sultan himself passed in triumph through the gate of St. Romanus. He was attended by his vizirs, bashaws, and guards, each of whom (says a Byzantine historian) was robust as Hercules, dexterous as Apollo, and equal in battle to any ten of the race of ordinary mortals. The conqueror gazed with satisfaction and wonder on the strange though splendid appearance of the domes and palaces, so dissimilar from the style of Oriental architecture. In the hippodrome, or *atmeidan,* his eye was attracted by the twisted column of the three serpents; and, as a trial of his strength, he shattered with his iron mace or battle-axe the under-jaw of one of these monsters, which in the eye of the Turks were the idols or talismans of the city. At the principal door of St. Sophia, he alighted from his horse and entered the dome; and such was his jealous regard for that monument of his glory that, on observing a zealous Mussulman in the act of breaking the marble pavement, he admonished him with his scimitar that, if the spoil and captives were granted to the soldiers, the public and private buildings had been reserved for the prince. By his command the metropolis of the Eastern church was transformed into a mosque: the rich and portable instruments of superstition had been removed; the crosses were thrown down; and the walls, which were covered with images and mosaics, were washed and purified and restored to a state of naked simplicity. On the same day, or on the ensuing Friday, the *muezin* or crier ascended the most lofty turret, and proclaimed the *ezan,* or public invitation, in the name of God and his prophet; the imam preached; and Mahomet the Second performed the *namaz* of prayer and thanksgiving on the great altar, where the christian mysteries had so lately been celebrated before the last of the Cæsars. From St. Sophia he proceeded to the august but desolate mansion of an hundred successors of the great Constantine; but which, in a few hours, had been stripped of the pomp of royalty. A melancholy reflection on the vicissitudes of human greatness forced itself on his mind; and he repeated an elegant distich of Persian poetry, 'The spider has wove his web in the imperial palace; and the owl hath sung her watch-song on the towers of Afrasiab.'

* * *

(1788)

55

OLIVER GOLDSMITH (1728–1774)

The author of *The Vicar of Wakefield* was the sixth of nine children of an Irish parson farmer and passed most of his boyhood in the little hamlet of Lissoy, which he afterward idealized in *The Deserted Village*. He was regarded as 'a stupid blockhead' in the village school and when, in 1749, he succeeded in taking a degree at Trinity College, Dublin, he was lowest on the list. For a number of years he showed little ability and still less inclination to fit himself to practical life. Rejected for holy orders, he taught school for a time and, soon disgusted, tried the law with the same result. He then spent several years in the nominal study of medicine, in the course of which, he made the grand tour of Europe, setting off it is said, 'with a guinea in his pocket, one shirt to his back, and a flute in his hand.' Finding his way to London, in 1756, he existed for a couple of years in a most haphazard manner, as 'chemist's' assistant, corrector of the press, struggling physician, usher in a school, and hack writer for the *Monthly Review*. The culmination of this period arrived when he borrowed a suit of clothes to present himself for examination as a hospital mate, failed in the examination. and pawned the clothes. Soon after this, his literary successes began. It was in 1764, that Johnson following close after a guinea with which he had responded to a message of distress, 'put the cork into the bottle' for which Goldsmith had promptly changed the guinea, carried off the manuscript of *The Vicar of Wakefield* to a bookseller, and relieved the author from arrest. *The Traveler* (1764) was now published and *The Deserted Village* (1770) confirmed the reputation which this had established. His two plays, *The Good Natured Man* (1768) and *She Stoops to Conquer* (1773) brought him five hundred pounds apiece; his *History of Animated Nature*, for which he had no qualification except the ability to write, secured him eight hundred pounds; and similar hack work was similarly paid; but such was his indiscretion that he was seldom long out of difficulty. He had in a high measure the prodigality, not uncommon among clever writers, of bestowing his entire stock of wisdom on the reader and reserving none for the conduct of life. Yet his follies, like those of Steele, were the indexes of a liberal and lovable nature. When he died, at the age of forty-six, leaving debts of two thousand pounds, there was as much tenderness as humor in Johnson's deep ejaculation: 'Was ever poet so trusted?'

SONG

When lovely woman stoops to folly,
  And finds too late that men betray,
What charm can soothe her melancholy?
  What art can wash her guilt away?

The only art her guilt to cover,   5
  To hide her shame from every eye,
To give repentance to her lover,
  And wring his bosom, is — to die.

          (1766)

THE DESERTED VILLAGE

Sweet Auburn! loveliest village of the plain;
Where health and plenty cheered the laboring swain,
Where smiling spring its earliest visit paid,
And parting summer's lingering blooms delayed:

Dear lovely bowers of innocence and ease, 5
Seats of my youth, when every sport could please,
How often have I loitered o'er thy green,
Where humble happiness endeared each scene!
How often have I paused on every charm,
The sheltered cot, the cultivated farm,   10
The never-failing brook, the busy mill,
The decent church that topped the neighboring hill,
The hawthorn bush, with seats beneath the shade,
For talking age and whispering lovers made!
How often have I blest the coming day,   15
When toil remitting lent its turn to play,
And all the village train, from labor free,
Led up their sports beneath the spreading tree,
While many a pastime circled in the shade,
The young contending as the old surveyed;

And many a gambol frolicked o'er the
   ground,   21
And sleights of art and feats of strength
   went round.
And still, as each repeated pleasure tired,
Succeeding sports the mirthful band in-
   spired;
The dancing pair that simply sought re-
   nown,   25
By holding out to tire each other down;
The swain mistrustless of his smutted face,
While secret laughter tittered round the
   place;
The bashful virgin's side-long looks of love,
The matron's glance that would those looks
   reprove: 30
These were thy charms, sweet village! sports
   like these,
With sweet succession, taught even toil to
   please:
These round thy bowers their cheerful in-
   fluence shed:
These were thy charms — but all these
   charms are fled.
   Sweet smiling village, loveliest of the
     lawn,   35
Thy sports are fled, and all thy charms with-
   drawn;
Amidst thy bowers the tyrant's hand is
   seen,
And desolation saddens all thy green:
One only master grasps the whole domain,
And half a tillage stints thy smiling plain.
No more thy glassy brook reflects the day,
But, choked with sedges, works its weedy
   way;   42
Along thy glades, a solitary guest,
The hollow sounding bittern guards its
   nest;   44
Amidst thy desert walks the lapwing flies,
And tires their echoes with unvaried cries;
Sunk are thy bowers in shapeless ruin all,
And the long grass o'ertops the moldering
   wall;
And trembling, shrinking from the spoiler's
   hand,
Far, far away thy children leave the land. 50
Ill fares the land, to hastening ills a prey,
Where wealth accumulates, and men decay:
Princes and lords may flourish, or may
   fade;
A breath can make them, as a breath has
   made: 54
But a bold peasantry, their country's pride,
When once destroyed, can never be supplied.
   A time there was, ere England's griefs
   began,
When every rood of ground maintained its
   man;

For him light labor spread her wholesome
   store,
Just gave what life required, but gave no
   more: 60
His best companions, innocence and health;
And his best riches, ignorance of wealth.
   But times are altered; trade's unfeeling
   train
Usurp the land and dispossess the swain;
Along the lawn, where scattered hamlets
   rose,   65
Unwieldy wealth and cumbrous pomp re-
   pose,
And every want to opulence allied,
And every pang that folly pays to pride.
These gentle hours that plenty bade to
   bloom,
Those calm desires that asked but little
   room,   70
Those healthful sports that graced the peace-
   ful scene,
Lived in each look, and brightened all the
   green;
These, far departing, seek a kinder shore,
And rural mirth and manners are no more.
   Sweet Auburn! parent of the blissful
   hour,   75
Thy glades forlorn confess the tyrant's
   power.
Here, as I take my solitary rounds
Amidst thy tangling walks and ruined
   grounds,
And, many a year elapsed, return to view
Where once the cottage stood, the hawthorn
   grew,   80
Remembrance wakes with all her busy
   train,
Swells at my breast, and turns the past to
   pain.
   In all my wanderings round this world
   of care,
In all my griefs — and God has given my
   share —   84
I still had hopes, my latest hours to crown,
Amidst these humble bowers to lay me
   down;
To husband out life's taper at the close,
And keep the flame from wasting by repose:
I still had hopes, for pride attends us still,
Amidst the swains to show my book-learned
   skill,   90
Around my fire an evening group to draw,
And tell of all I felt, and all I saw;
And, as an hare whom hounds and horns
   pursue,
Pants to the place from whence at first she
   flew,
I still had hopes, my long vexations past, 95
Here to return — and die at home at last.

O, blest retirement, friend to life's de-
cline,
Retreats from care, that never must be mine,
How happy he who crowns in shades like
these,
A youth of labor with an age of ease; 100
Who quits a world where strong tempta-
tions try,
And, since 't is hard to combat, learns to fly!
For him no wretches, born to work and
weep,
Explore the mine, or tempt the dangerous
deep;
No surly porter stands in guilty state, 105
To spurn imploring famine from the gate;
But on he moves to meet his latter end,
Angels around befriending Virtue's friend;
Bends to the grave with unperceived decay,
While resignation gently slopes the way;
And, all his prospects brightening to the
last, 111
His heaven commences ere the world be
past!
Sweet was the sound, when oft at even-
ing's close
Up yonder hill the village murmur rose.
There, as I passed with careless steps and
slow, 115
The mingling notes came softened from be-
low;
The swain responsive as the milk-maid sung,
The sober herd that lowed to meet their
young,
The noisy geese that gabbled o'er the pool,
The playful children just let loose from
school, 120
The watch-dog's voice that bayed the
whispering wind,
And the loud laugh that spoke the vacant
mind;—
These all in sweet confusion sought the
shade,
And filled each pause the nightingale had
made.
But now the sounds of population fail, 125
No cheerful murmurs fluctuate in the gale,
No busy steps the grass-grown foot-way
tread,
For all the bloomy flush of life is fled.
All but yon widowed, solitary thing,
That feebly bends beside the plashy spring:
She, wretched matron, forced in age, for
bread, 131
To strip the brook with mantling cresses
spread,
To pick her wintry faggot from the thorn,
To seek her nightly shed and weep till
morn.

She only left of all the harmless train, 135
The sad historian of the pensive plain.
Near yonder copse, where once the garden
smiled,
And still where many a garden flower grows
wild;
There, where a few torn shrubs the place
disclose,
The village preacher's modest mansion rose.
A man he was to all the country dear, 141
And passing rich with forty pounds a year;
Remote from towns he ran his godly race,
Nor e'er had changed, nor wished to change
his place;
Unpracticed he to fawn, or seek for power,
By doctrines fashioned to the varying hour;
Far other aims his heart had learned to
prize, 147
More skilled to raise the wretched than to
rise.
His house was known to all the vagrant
train;
He chid their wanderings but relieved their
pain: 150
The long-remembered beggar was his guest,
Whose beard descending swept his aged
breast;
The ruined spendthrift, now no longer
proud,
Claimed kindred there, and had his claims
allowed;
The broken soldier, kindly bade to stay, 155
Sat by the fire, and talked the night away,
Wept o'er his wounds or, tales of sorrow
done,
Shouldered his crutch and showed how fields
were won.
Pleased with his guests, the good man
learned to glow,
And quite forgot their vices in their woe;
Careless their merits or their faults to
scan
His pity gave ere charity began. 162
Thus to relieve the wretched was his
pride,
And e'en his failings leaned to Virtue's side;
But in his duty prompt at every call,
He watched and wept, he prayed and felt for
all; 166
And, as a bird each fond endearment tries
To tempt its new-fledged offspring to the
skies,
He tried each art, reproved each dull delay,
Allured to brighter worlds, and led the way.
Beside the bed where parting life was
laid, 171
And sorrow, guilt, and pain by turns dis-
mayed.

The reverend champion stood. At his con-
trol
Despair and anguish fled the struggling soul;
Comfort came down the trembling wretch
to raise,   175
And his last faltering accents whispered
praise.
At church, with meek and unaffected
grace,
His looks adorned the venerable place;
Truth from his lips prevailed with double sway,
And fools, who came to scoff, remained to
pray.   180
The service past, around the pious man,
With steady zeal, each honest rustic ran;
Even children followed with endearing wile,
And plucked his gown to share the good
man's smile.
His ready smile a parent's warmth exprest;
Their welfare pleased him, and their cares
distrest: 186
To them his heart, his love, his griefs were
given,
But all his serious thoughts had rest in
heaven.
As some tall cliff that lifts its awful form,
Swells from the vale, and midway leaves the
storm,   190
Though round its breast the rolling clouds
are spread,
Eternal sunshine settles on its head.
Beside yon straggling fence that skirts the
way,
With blossomed furze unprofitably gay,
There, in his noisy mansion, skilled to rule,
The village master taught his little school.
A man severe he was, and stern to view; 197
I knew him well, and every truant knew;
Well had the boding tremblers learned to
trace
The day's disasters in his morning face; 200
Full well they laughed with counterfeited
glee
At all his jokes, for many a joke had he;
Full well the busy whisper circling round
Conveyed the dismal tidings when he
frowned.
Yet he was kind, or, if severe in aught, 205
The love he bore to learning was in fault;
The village all declared how much he knew:
'T was certain he could write, and cipher
too;
Lands he could measure, terms and tides
presage,
And even the story ran that he could gauge;
In arguing, too, the parson owned his skill,
For, even though vanquished, he could argue
still;   212

While words of learned length and thunder-
ing sound
Amazed the gazing rustics ranged around;
And still they gazed, and still the wonder
grew,   213
That one small head could carry all he
knew.
But past is all his fame. The very spot
Where many a time he triumphed, is forgot.
Near yonder thorn, that lifts its head on
high,
Where once the sign-post caught the pass-
ing eye,   220
Low lies that house where nut-brown
draughts inspired,
Where graybeard mirth and smiling toil re-
tired,
Where village statesmen talked with looks
profound,
And news much older than their ale went
round.
Imagination fondly stoops to trace   225
The parlor splendors of that festive place:
The white-washed wall, the nicely sanded
floor,
The varnished clock that clicked behind the
door;   228
The chest contrived a double debt to pay,
A bed by night, a chest of drawers by day,
The pictures placed for ornament and use,
The twelve good rules, the royal game of
goose;
The hearth, except when winter chilled the
day,
With aspen boughs and flowers and fennel
gay;
While broken tea-cups, wisely kept for
show,   235
Ranged o'er the chimney, glistened in a
row.
Vain transitory splendors! could not all
Reprieve the tottering mansion from its
fall?
Obscure it sinks, nor shall it more impart
An hour's importance to the poor man's
heart.   240
Thither no more the peasant shall repair
To sweet oblivion of his daily care;
No more the farmer's news, the barber's tale,
No more the woodman's ballad shall pre-
vail;
No more the smith his dusky brow shall
clear,   245
Relax his ponderous strength, and lean to
hear;
The host himself no longer shall be found
Careful to see the mantling bliss go round;
Nor the coy maid, half willing to be prest

Shall kiss the cup to pass it to the rest. 250
Yes! let the rich deride, the proud disdain,
These simple blessings of the lowly train;
To me more dear, congenial to my heart,
One native charm, than all the gloss of art.
Spontaneous joys, where Nature has its play, 255
The soul adopts, and owns their first born sway;
Lightly they frolic o'er the vacant mind,
Unenvied, unmolested, unconfined.
But the long pomp, the midnight masquerade,
With all the freaks of wanton wealth arrayed — 260
In these, ere triflers half their wish obtain,
The toiling pleasure sickens into pain;
And, even while fashion's brightest arts decoy,
The heart distrusting asks if this be joy.
Ye friends to truth, ye statesmen who survey 265
The rich man's joy increase, the poor's decay,
'T is yours to judge, how wide the limits stand
Between a splendid and an happy land.
Proud swells the tide with loads of freighted ore,
And shouting Folly hails them from her shore; 270
Hoards even beyond the miser's wish abound,
And rich men flock from all the world around.
Yet count our gains! This wealth is but a name
That leaves our useful products still the same.
Not so the loss. The man of wealth and pride 275
Takes up a space that many poor supplied;
Space for his lake, his park's extended bounds,
Space for his horses, equipage, and hounds:
The robe that wraps his limbs in silken sloth
Has robbed the neighboring fields of half their growth; 280
His seat, where solitary sports are seen,
Indignant spurns the cottage from the green:
Around the world each needful product flies,
For all the luxuries the world supplies;
While thus the land adorned for pleasure all
In barren splendor feebly waits the fall. 286
As some fair female unadorned and plain,

Secure to please while youth confirms her reign,
Slights every borrowed charm that dress supplies,
Nor shares with art the triumph of her eyes; 290
But when those charms are past, for charms are frail,
When time advances, and when lovers fail,
She then shines forth, solicitous to bless,
In all the glaring impotence of dress.
Thus fares the land by luxury betrayed: 295
In nature's simplest charms at first arrayed,
But verging to decline, its splendors rise,
Its vistas strike, its palaces surprise;
While, scourged by famine from the smiling land
The mournful peasant leads his humble band, 300
And while he sinks, without one arm to save,
The country blooms — a garden and a grave.
Where then, ah! where, shall poverty reside,
To 'scape the pressure of contiguous pride?
If to some common's fenceless limits strayed, 305
He drives his flock to pick the scanty blade,
Those fenceless fields the sons of wealth divide,
And even the bare-worn common is denied.
If to the city sped — what waits him there?
To see profusion that he must not share; 310
To see ten thousand baneful arts combined
To pamper luxury, and thin mankind;
To see those joys the sons of pleasure know
Extorted from his fellow-creature's woe.
Here while the courtier glitters in brocade, 315
There the pale artist plies the sickly trade;
Here while the proud their long-drawn pomps display,
There the black gibbet glooms beside the way.
The dome where pleasure holds her midnight reign,
Here, richly decked, admits the gorgeous train: 320
Tumultuous grandeur crowds the blazing square,
The rattling chariots clash, the torches glare.
Sure scenes like these no troubles e'er annoy!
Sure these denote one universal joy!
Are these thy serious thoughts? — Ah, turn thine eyes 325
Where the poor houseless shivering female lies.

She once, perhaps, in village plenty blest,
Has wept at tales of innocence distrest;
Her modest looks the cottage might adorn,
Sweet as the primrose peeps beneath the
　　thorn;　　　　　　　　　　　330
Now lost to all; her friends, her virtue fled,
Near her betrayer's door she lays her head,
And, pinched with cold, and shrinking from
　　the shower,
With heavy heart deplores that luckless hour,
When idly first, ambitious of the town,　335
She left her wheel and robes of country
　　brown.
　　Do thine, sweet Auburn, thine, the love-
　　liest train,
Do thy fair tribes participate her pain?
Even now, perhaps, by cold and hunger led,
At proud men's doors they ask a little
　　bread!　　　　　　　　　　　340
　　Ah, no! To distant climes, a dreary
　　scene,
Where half the convex world intrudes be-
　　tween,
Through torrid tracts with fainting steps
　　they go,　　　　　・
Where wild Altama murmurs to their woe.
Far different there from all that charmed
　　before　　　　　　　　　　　345
The various terrors of that horrid shore;
Those blazing suns that dart a downward
　　ray,
And fiercely shed intolerable day;
Those matted woods, where birds forget to
　　sing,
But silent bats in drowsy clusters cling; 350
Those poisonous fields with rank luxuriance
　　crowned,
Where the dark scorpion gathers death
　　around;
Where at each step the stranger fears to
　　wake
The rattling terrors of the vengeful snake;
Where crouching tigers wait their hapless
　　prey,　　　　　　　　　　　355
And savage men more murderous still than
　　they;
While oft in whirls the mad tornado flies,
Mingling the ravaged landscape with the
　　skies.
Far different these from every former scene,
The cooling brook, the grassy vested green,
The breezy covert of the warbling grove, 361
That only sheltered thefts of harmless love.
　　Good Heaven! what sorrows gloomed that
　　parting day,
That called them from their native walks
　　away;
When the poor exiles, every pleasure past,

Hung round the bowers, and fondly looked
　　their last,　　　　　　　　　366
And took a long farewell, and wished in
　　vain
For seats like these beyond the western
　　main,
And shuddering still to face the distant
　　deep,
Returned and wept, and still returned to
　　weep.　　　　　　　　　　　370
The good old sire, the first prepared to go
To new found worlds, and wept for others'
　　woe;
But for himself, in conscious virtue brave,
He only wished for worlds beyond the
　　grave.
His lovely daughter, lovelier in her tears, 375
The fond companion of his helpless years,
Silent went next, neglectful of her charms,
And left a lover's for a father's arms.
With louder plaints the mother spoke her
　　woes,
And blest the cot where every pleasure
　　rose,　　　　　　　　　　　380
And kist her thoughtless babes with many
　　a tear
And claspt them close, in sorrow doubly
　　dear,
Whilst her fond husband strove to lend re-
　　lief,
In all the silent manliness of grief.
　　O luxury! thou curst by Heaven's de-
　　cree,　　　　　　　　　　　385
How ill exchanged are things like these for
　　thee!
How do thy potions, with insidious joy,
Diffuse their pleasure only to destroy!
Kingdoms by thee, to sickly greatness
　　grown,
Boast of a florid vigor not their own.　390
At every draught more large and large they
　　grow,
A bloated mass of rank, unwieldy woe;
Till sapped their strength, and every part
　　unsound,
Down, down, they sink, and spread a ruin
　　round.
　　Even now the devastation is begun,　395
And half the business of destruction done;
Even now, methinks, as pondering here I
　　stand,
I see the rural virtues leave the land.
Down where yon anchoring vessel spreads
　　the sail,
That idly waiting flaps with every gale, 400
Downward they move, a melancholy band,
Pass from the shore, and darken all the
　　strand.

Contented toil, and hospitable care,
And kind connubial tenderness, are there;
And piety with wishes placed above,   405
And steady loyalty, and faithful love.
And thou, sweet Poetry, thou loveliest maid,
Still first to fly where sensual joys invade;
Unfit in these degenerate times of shame
To catch the heart, or strike for honest
    fame;   410
Dear charming nymph, neglected and de-
    cried,
My shame in crowds, my solitary pride;
Thou source of all my bliss, and all my woe,
That found'st me poor at first, and keep'st
    me so;   414
Thou guide by which the nobler arts excel,
Thou nurse of every virtue, fare thee well!
Farewell, and oh! where'er thy voice be
    tried,
On Torno's cliffs, or Pambamarca's side,
Whether where equinoctial fervors glow,
Or winter wraps the polar world in snow,
Still let thy voice, prevailing over time, 421
Redress the rigors of the inclement clime;
Aid slighted truth with thy persuasive strain;
Teach erring man to spurn the rage of
    gain;
Teach him, that states of native strength
    possest,   425
Though very poor, may still be very blest;
That trade's proud empire hastes to swift
    decay,
As ocean sweeps the labored mole away;
While self-dependent power can time defy,
As rocks resist the billows and the sky. 430
                                    (1770)

From THE RETALIATION

Here lies our good Edmund, whose genius
    was such,
We scarcely can praise it, or blame it too
    much;
Who, born for the universe, narrowed his
    mind,
And to party gave up what was meant for
    mankind:
Though fraught with all learning, yet strain-
    ing his throat   5
To persuade Tommy Townshend to lend him
    a vote;
Who, too deep for his hearers, still went on
    refining,
And thought of convincing, while they
    thought of dining;

Though equal to all things, for all things
    unfit;
Too nice for a statesman, too proud for a
    wit;   10
For a patriot too cool; for a drudge dis-
    obedient;
And too fond of the right to pursue the
    expedient.
In short, 't was his fate, unemployed or in
    place, sir,
To eat mutton cold, and cut blocks with a
    razor.
                    * * *

Here lies David Garrick, describe me who
    can,   15
An abridgment of all that was pleasant in
    man;
As an actor, confest without rival to shine;
As a wit, if not first, in the very first line;
Yet with talents like these, and an excellent
    heart,
The man had his failings, a dupe to his art;
Like an ill-judging beauty his colors he
    spread,   21
And beplastered with rouge his own natural
    red.
On the stage he was natural, simple, affect-
    ing,
'T was only that when he was off he was
    acting;
With no reason on earth to go out of his
    way,   25
He turn'd and he varied full ten times a
    day:
Though secure of our hearts, yet confound-
    edly sick
If they were not his own by finessing and
    trick;
He cast off his friends as a huntsman his
    pack,
For he knew when he pleased he could
    whistle them back.   30
Of praise a mere glutton, he swallowed
    what came,
And the puff of a dunce he mistook it for
    fame;
Till his relish grown callous, almost to dis-
    ease,
Who peppered the highest was surest to
    please.
But let us be candid, and speak out our
    mind: 35
If dunces applauded, he paid them in kind.

                    * * *

                                    (1774)

WILLIAM COWPER (1731-1800)

The son of a chaplain of George II, Cowper was derived on both sides from illustrious families and it is not unnatural to ascribe to race a certain touch of gentility in all he did or wrote. After seven years at Westminster School he was 'articled,' at eighteen, to a London attorney, with whom he spent three years, afterward going into residence in the Temple, and in 1754, he was called to the bar. His experiments in versification at this time, some of them addressed to his cousin Theodora, with whom he was in love, show few symptoms of the poetic originality which he long afterward evinced. Some of his early associates, too, Warren Hastings at Westminster, Thurlow, the fellow-clerk of his apprentice days, and the raucous and none too moral wits of the Nonsense Club, seem in their several ways incongruous associates for the shrinking and self-searching pietist whom we know in his later years. Cowper was too timid for the business of a lawyer and, in 1763, when he was thirty-two years of age, the dread of qualifying for a clerkship so preyed upon his mind that he became violently insane and attempted suicide. When he recovered, he determined to retire from the excitements of the world and found a retreat at Huntington, near Cambridge, where he entered the home of the Reverend Unwin and his wife and was converted to Methodism. On the death of Unwin, in 1767, Cowper removed with Mrs. Unwin to Olney, and here came under the influence of John Newton, with whom he joined in the writing of the *Olney Hymns*. Newton's strenuous fanaticism aggravated his religious mania and, in 1773, he again became mad and so remained for two years. On his recovery, along with other worldly diversions, such as gardening, cheerful conversation and the keeping of pet hares, which were discountenanced by his spiritual comforter, Cowper began to amuse himself by writing verses and found increasing satisfaction in the exercise. His first volume, containing *Table Talk* and other poems, was published in 1782. The liveliness of this period was increased by his acquaintance with Lady Austen, a bright young widow, who suggested the subjects of *The Task* and *The Diverting Ride of John Gilpin*. These poems, published in 1785, made his reputation national. The most exacting of his tasks, the translation of Homer, was brought to completion in 1791. He now began to sink, for the last time, under the cloud of despondency, suffering almost constantly from the conviction that he was a lost soul. Some of the darker and more intense of his short poems, such as *The Castaway*, belong to these unhappy years and were printed after his death. Cowper had a rare and intense, though not a rich nature. His gift of humor appears most conspicuously in his Letters, which some critics have not hesitated to pronounce the best in the language. Fidelity to nature and religious earnestness are the prevailing characteristics of his poetry. Byron's phrase, 'the quiet of a loving eye,' precisely fits Cowper's manner of looking about him, except in his most heightened moments.

FROM OLNEY HYMNS

WALKING WITH GOD. Gen. v. 24

Oh! for a closer walk with God,
A calm and heavenly frame;
A light to shine upon the road
That leads me to the Lamb!

Where is the blessedness I knew   5
When first I saw the Lord?
Where is the soul-refreshing view
Of Jesus and his word?

What peaceful hours I once enjoyed!
How sweet their memory still!   10

But they have left an aching void
The world can never fill.

Return, O holy Dove, return
Sweet messenger of rest!
I hate the sins that made thee mourn   15
And drove thee from my breast.

The dearest idol I have known,
Whate'er that idol be,
Help me to tear it from thy throne,
And worship only thee.   20

So shall my walk be close with God,
Calm and serene my frame;
So purer light shall mark the road
That leads me to the Lamb.

(1779)

From TABLE TALK

Pity religion has so seldom found
A skilful guide into poetic ground!
The flowers would spring where'er she
    deigned to stray,
And every Muse attend her in her way.
Virtue indeed meets many a rhyming
    friend,   5
And many a compliment politely penned;
But, unattired in that becoming vest
Religion weaves for her, and half un-
    dressed,
Stands in the desert, shivering and forlorn,
A wintry figure, like a withered thorn.   10
The shelves are full, all other themes are
    sped,
Hackneyed and worn to the last flimsy
    thread:
Satire has long since done his best, and
    cursed
And loathsome ribaldry has done his worst;
Fancy has sported all her powers away   15
In tales, in trifles, and in children's play;
And 't is the sad complaint, and almost true,
Whate'er we write, we bring forth nothing
    new.
'T were new indeed, to see a bard all fire,
Touched with a coal from Heaven, assume
    the lyre   20
And tell the world, still kindling as he
    sung,
With more than mortal music on his tongue,
That he, who dies below, and reigns above,
Inspires the song, and that his name is
    Love.

(1782)

THE TASK, Book IV

Hark! 't is the twanging horn o'er yonder
    bridge,
That with its wearisome but needful length
Bestrides the wintry flood, in which the
    moon
Sees her unwrinkled face reflected bright; —
He comes, the herald of a noisy world,   5
With spattered boots, strapped waist, and
    frozen locks;
News from all nations lumbering at his
    back.
True to his charge, the close-packed load
    behind,
Yet careless what he brings, his one con-
    cern
Is to conduct it to the destined inn: 10
And. having dropt the expected bag, pass
    on,

He whistles as he goes, light-hearted wretch,
Cold and yet cheerful: messenger of grief
Perhaps to thousands, and of joy to some;
To him indifferent whether grief or joy.   15
Houses in ashes, and the fall of stocks,
Births, deaths, and marriages, epistles wet
With tears, that trickled down the writer's
    cheeks
Fast as the periods from his fluent quill,
Or charged with amorous sighs of absent
    swains,   20
Or nymphs responsive, equally affect
His horse and him, unconscious of them all.
But oh, the important budget! ushered in
With such heart-shaking music, who can
    say
What are its tidings? have our troops
    awaked?   25
Or do they still, as if with opium drugged,
Snore to the murmurs of the Atlantic wave?
Is India free? and does she wear her
    plumed
And jeweled turban with a smile of peace,
Or do we grind her still? The grand de-
    bate,   30
The popular harangue, the tart reply,
The logic, and the wisdom, and the wit,
And the loud laugh — I long to know them
    all;
I burn to set the imprisoned wranglers free,
And give them voice and utterance once
    again.   35

Now stir the fire, and close the shutters
    fast,
Let fall the curtains, wheel the sofa round,
And while the bubbling and loud-hissing
    urn
Throws up a steamy column, and the cups,
That cheer but not inebriate, wait on
    each,   40
So let us welcome peaceful evening in.

* * *

Oh, Winter, ruler of the inverted year,
Thy scattered hair with sleet-like ashes
    filled,
Thy breath congealed upon thy lips, thy
    cheeks
Fringed with a beard made white with other
    snows   45
Than those of age, thy forehead wrapped
    in clouds,
A leafless branch thy scepter and thy throne
A sliding car indebted to no wheels,
But urged by storms along its slippery way,
I love thee, all unlovely as thou seem'st,   50
And dreaded as thou art. Thou hold'st the
    sun

A prisoner in the yet undawning East,
Shortening his journey between morn and
  noon,
And hurrying him, impatient of his stay,
Down to the rosy west; but kindly still   55
Compensating his loss with added hours
Of social converse and instructive ease,
And gathering at short notice in one group
The family dispersed, and fixing thought
Not less dispersed by daylight and its cares.
I crown the king of intimate delights,   61
Fire-side enjoyments, home-born happiness,
And all the comforts that the lowly roof
Of undisturbed retirement, and the hours
Of long uninterrupted evening know.   65
No rattling wheels stop short before these
  gates;
No powdered, pert proficients in the art
Of sounding an alarm, assault these doors
Till the street rings; no stationary steeds
Cough their own knell, while heedless of
  the sound   70
The silent circle fan themselves, and quake:
But here the needle plies its busy task,
The pattern grows, the well-depicted flower,
Wrought patiently into the snowy lawn,
Unfolds its bosom; buds and leaves and
  sprigs   75
And curly tendrils, gracefully disposed,
Follow the nimble finger of the fair;
A wreath that cannot fade, of flowers that
  blow
With most success when all besides decay.
The poet's or historian's page, by one   80
Made vocal for the amusement of the rest;
The sprightly lyre, whose treasure of sweet
  sounds
The touch from many a trembling chord
  shakes out;
And the clear voice symphonious, yet dis-
  tinct,
And in the charming strife triumphant still;
Beguile the night, and set a keener edge 86
On female industry; the threaded steel
Flies swiftly, and unfelt the task proceeds.
The volume closed, the customary rites
Of the last meal commence: a Roman
  meal,   90
Such as the mistress of the world once
  found
Delicious, when her patriots of high note,
Perhaps by moonlight, at their humble
  doors,
And under an old oak's domestic shade,
Enjoyed — spare feast! — a radish and an
  egg.   95
Discourse ensues, not trivial, yet not dull,
Nor such as with a frown forbids the play

Of fancy, or prescribes the sound of mirth;
Nor do we madly, like an impious world,
Who deem religion frenzy, and the God 100
That made them an intruder on their joys,
Start at his awful name, or deem his praise
A jarring note; themes of a graver tone
Exciting oft our gratitude and love,
While we retrace with memory's pointing
  wand   105
That calls the past to our exact review,
The dangers we have scaped, the broken
  snare,
The disappointed foe, deliverance found
Unlooked for, life preserved and peace re-
  stored,
Fruits of omnipotent eternal love: — 110
Oh, evenings worthy of the gods! exclaimed
The Sabine bard. Oh, evenings, I reply,
More to be prized and coveted than yours,
As more illumined and with nobler truths,
That I, and mine, and those we love, en-
  joy.   115

Is Winter hideous in a garb like this?
Needs he the tragic fur, the smoke of lamps,
The pent-up breath of an unsavory throng
To thaw him into feeling, or the smart
And snappish dialogue that flippant wits 120
Call comedy, to prompt him with a smile?
The self-complacent actor, when he views
(Stealing a sidelong glance at a full house)
The slope of faces from the floor to the
  roof,
As if one master-spring controlled them
  all,   125
Relaxed into an universal grin,
Sees not a countenance there that speaks a
  joy
Half so refined or so sincere as ours.
Cards were superfluous here, with all the
  tricks
That idleness has ever yet contrived   130
To fill the void of an unfurnished brain,
To palliate dulness and give time a shove.
Time, as he passes us, has a dove's wing,
Unsoiled and swift and of a silken sound.
But the world's time is time in masquerade.
Theirs, should I paint him, has his pinions
  fledged   136
With motley plumes, and, where the peacock
  shows
His azure eyes, is tinctured black and red
With spots quadrangular of diamond form,
Ensanguined hearts, clubs typical of strife,
And spades, the emblem of untimely graves.
What should be, and what was an hour-glass
  once,   142
Becomes a dice-box, and a billiard mast

Well does the work of his destructive scythe.
Thus decked he charms a world whom fashion blinds 145
To his true worth, most pleased when idle most,
Whose only happy are their wasted hours.
Even misses, at whose age their mothers wore
The back-string and the bib, assume the dress
Of womanhood, sit pupils in the school 150
Of card-devoted time, and night by night,
Placed at some vacant corner of the board,
Learn every trick, and soon play all the game.
But truce with censure. Roving as I rove,
Where shall I find an end, or how proceed? 155
As he that travels far, oft turns aside
To view some rugged rock, or moldering tower,
Which seen delights him not; then coming home,
Describes and prints it, that the world may know
How far he went for what was nothing worth; 160
So I, with brush in hand and pallet spread
With colors mixed for a far different use,
Paint cards and dolls, and every idle thing
That fancy finds in her excursive flights.

Come, Evening, once again, season of peace, 165
Return, sweet Evening, and continue long!
Methinks I see thee in the streaky west,
With matron-step slow moving, while the night
Treads on thy sweeping train; one hand employed
In letting fall the curtain of repose 170
On bird and beast, the other charged for man
With sweet oblivion of the cares of day;
Not sumptuously adorned, nor needing aid,
Like homely-featured night, of clustering gems,
A star or two just twinkling on thy brow 175
Suffices thee; save that the moon is thine
No less than hers, not worn indeed on high
With ostentatious pageantry, but set
With modest grandeur in thy purple zone,
Resplendent less, but of an ampler round.
Come, then, and thou shalt find thy votary calm, 181
Or make me so. Composure is thy gift;
And whether I devote thy gentle hours

To books, to music, or to poet's toil,
To weaving nets for bird-alluring fruit, 185
Or twining silken threads round ivory reels
When they command whom man was born to please,
I slight thee not, but make thee welcome still.

* * *

How calm is my recess! and how the frost
Raging abroad, and the rough wind, endear 190
The silence and the warmth enjoyed within!
I saw the woods and fields at close of day
A variegated show; the meadows green
Though faded, and the lands, where lately waved
The golden harvest, of a mellow brown, 195
Upturned so lately by the forceful share;
I saw far off the weedy fallows smile
With verdure not unprofitable, grazed
By flocks fast feeding, and selecting each
His favorite herb; while all the leafless groves 200
That skirt the horizon wore a sable hue,
Scarce noticed in the kindred dusk of eve.
To-morrow brings a change, a total change,
Which even now, though silently performed
And slowly, and by most unfelt, the face 205
Of universal nature undergoes.
Fast falls a fleecy shower; the downy flakes,
Descending and with never-ceasing lapse
Softly alighting upon all below,
Assimilate all objects. Earth receives 210
Gladly the thickening mantle, and the green
And tender blade, that feared the chilling blast,
Escapes unhurt beneath so warm a veil.

In such a world, so thorny, and where none
Finds happiness unblighted, or if found, 215
Without some thistly sorrow at its side,
It seems the part of wisdom, and no sin
Against the law of love, to measure lots
With less distinguished than ourselves, that thus
We may with patience bear our moderate ills, 220
And sympathize with others, suffering more.
Ill fares the traveler now, and he that stalks
In ponderous boots beside his reeking team;
The wain goes heavily, impeded sore
By congregating loads adhering close 225
To the clogged wheels, and, in its sluggish pace,
Noiseless appears a moving hill of snow.
The toiling steeds expand the nostril wide,
While every breath, by respiration strong

Forced downward, is consolidated soon 230
Upon their jutting chests. He, formed to
bear
The pelting brunt of the tempestuous night,
With half-shut eyes, and puckered cheeks,
and teeth
Presented bare against the storm, plods on;
One hand secures his hat, save when with
both 235
He brandishes his pliant length of whip,
Resounding oft, and never heard in vain.
Oh, happy, and, in my account, denied
That sensibility of pain with which
Refinement is endued, thrice happy thou!
Thy frame, robust and hardy, feels in-
deed 241
The piercing cold, but feels it unimpaired;
The learned finger never need explore
Thy vigorous pulse, and the unhealthful
East,
That breathes the spleen, and searches every
bone 245
Of the infirm, is wholesome air to thee.
Thy days roll on exempt from household
care,
Thy wagon is thy wife; and the poor beasts,
That drag the dull companion to and fro,
Thine helpless charge, dependent on thy
care. 250
Ah, treat them kindly! rude as thou ap-
pearest,
Yet show that thou hast mercy, which the
great,
With needless hurry whirled from place to
place,
Humane as they would seem, not always
show. 254

Poor, yet industrious, modest, quiet, neat,
Such claim compassion in a night like this,
And have a friend in every feeling heart.
Warmed while it lasts, by labor, all day
long
They brave the season, and yet find at eve,
Ill clad and fed but sparely, time to cool. 260
The frugal housewife trembles when she
lights
Her scanty stock of brushwood, blazing
clear,
But dying soon, like all terrestrial joys;
The few small embers left she nurses well.
And while her infant race with outspread
hands 265
And crowded knees sit cowering o'er the
sparks,
Retires, content to quake, so they be
warmed.

The man feels least, as more inured than
she
To winter, and the current in his veins
More briskly moved by his severer toil; 270
Yet he, too, finds his own distress in theirs
The taper soon extinguished, which I saw
Dangled along at the cold finger's end
Just when the day declined, and the brown
loaf
Lodged on the shelf, half-eaten, without
sauce 275
Of sav'ry cheese, or butter costlier still,
Sleep seems their only refuge. For alas,
Where penury is felt the thought is chained,
And sweet colloquial pleasures are but few.
With all this thrift they thrive not. All the
care 280
Ingenious parsimony takes, but just
Saves the small inventory, bed and stool,
Skillet and old carved chest, from public
sale.
They live, and live without extorted alms
From grudging hands, but other boast have
none 285
To soothe their honest pride that scorns to
beg,
Nor comfort els., but in their mutual love.
I praise you much, ye meek and patient pair,
For ye are worthy; choosing rather far
A dry but independent crust, hard-earned 290
And eaten with a sigh, than to endure
The rugged frowns and insolent rebuffs
Of knaves in office, partial in their work
Of distribution; liberal of their aid
To clamorous importunity in rags, 295
But ofttimes deaf to suppliants who would
blush
To wear a tattered garb however coarse,
Whom famine cannot reconcile to filth;
These ask with painful shyness, and, re-
fused
Because deserving, silently retire. 300
But be ye of good courage! Time itself
Shall much befriend you. Time shall give
increase,
And all your numerous progeny, well
trained,
But helpless, in few years shall find their
hands,
And labor too. Meanwhile ye shall not
want 305
What, conscious of your virtues, we can
spare,
Nor what a wealthier than ourselves may
send.
I mean the man, who when the distant
poor

Need help, denies them nothing but his
name.

But poverty with most, who whimper
forth 310
Their long complaints, is self-inflicted woe,
The effect of laziness or sottish waste.
Now goes the nightly thief prowling abroad
For plunder; much solicitous how best
He may compensate for a day of sloth, 315
By works of darkness and nocturnal wrong,
Woe to the gardener's pale, the farmer's
hedge
Plashed neatly and secured with driven
stakes
Deep in the loamy bank. Uptorn by
strength
Resistless in so bad a cause, but lame 320
To better deeds, he bundles up the spoil —
An ass's burden — and when laden most
And heaviest, light of foot steals fast away.
Nor does the boarded hovel better guard
The well-stacked pile of riven logs and
roots 325
From his pernicious force. Nor will he
leave
Unwrenched the door, however well se-
cured,
Where chanticleer amidst his harem sleeps
In unsuspecting pomp; twitched from the
perch
He gives the princely bird with all his
wives 330
To his voracious bag, struggling in vain,
And loudly wondering at the sudden change.
Nor this to feed his own. 'T were some
excuse
Did pity of their sufferings warp aside
His principle, and tempt him into sin 335
For their support, so destitute; but they
Neglected pine at home, themselves, as more
Exposed than others, with less scruple made
His victims, robbed of their defenceless all.
Cruel is all he does. 'T is quenchless thirst
Of ruinous ebriety that prompts 341
His every action, and imbrutes the man.
Oh, for a law to noose the villain's neck
Who starves his own; who persecutes the
blood
He gave them in his children's veins, and
hates 345
And wrongs the woman he has sworn to
love.

Pass where we may, through city, or
through town,
Village or hamlet of this merry land

Though lean and beggared, every twentieth
pace
Conducts the unguarded nose to such a
whiff 350
Of stale debauch, forth-issuing from the
styes
That law has licensed, as makes temperance
reel.
There sit involved and lost in curling clouds
Of Indian fume, and guzzling deep, the
boor,
The lackey, and the groom. The craftsman
there 355
Takes a Lethean leave of all his toil.
Smith, cobbler, joiner, he that plies the
shears,
And he that kneads the dough: all loud
alike,
All learned, and all drunk. The fiddle
screams
Plaintive and piteous, as it wept and wailed
Its wasted tones and harmony unheard; 361
Fierce the dispute, whate'er the theme; while
she,
Fell Discord, arbitress of such debate,
Perched on the sign-post, holds with even
hand
Her undecisive scales. In this she lays 365
A weight of ignorance, in that, of pride,
And smiles delighted with the eternal poise.
Dire is the frequent curse and its twin sound
The cheek-distending oath, not to be praised
As ornamental, musical, polite, 370
Like those which modern senators employ,
Whose oath is rhetoric, and who swear for
fame.
Behold the schools in which plebeian minds,
Once simple, are initiated in arts
Which some may practise with politer grace,
But none with readier skill! 'T is here they
learn 376
The road that leads from competence and
peace
To indigence and rapine; till at last
Society, grown weary of the load,
Shakes her encumbered lap, and casts them
out. 380
But censure profits little. Vain the attempt
To advertise in verse a public pest,
That, like the filth with which the peasant
feeds
His hungry acres, stinks and is of use.
The excise is fattened with the rich result
Of all this riot; and ten thousand casks, 386
For ever dribbling out their base contents,
Touched by the Midas finger of the state,
Bleed gold for Ministers to sport away.

Drink and be mad then; 't is your country
    bids!   390
Gloriously drunk, obey the important call,
Her cause demands the assistance of your
    throats; —
Ye all can swallow, and she asks no more.

Would I had fallen upon those happier
    days
That poets celebrate; those golden times 395
And those Arcadian scenes that Maro sings,
And Sidney, warbler of poetic prose.
Nymphs were Dianas then, and swains had
    hearts
That felt their virtues. Innocence, it seems,
From courts dismissed, found shelter in the
    groves;   400
The footsteps of simplicity, impressed
Upon the yielding herbage (so they sing),
Then were not all effaced. Then speech
    profane
And manners profligate were rarely found
Observed as prodigies, and soon reclaimed.
Vain wish! those days were never: airy
    dreams   406
Sat for the picture; and the poet's hand,
Imparting substance to an empty shade,
Imposed a gay delirium for a truth.
Grant it: I still must envy them an age 410
That favored such a dream, in days like
    these
Impossible, when virtue is so scarce
That to suppose a scene where she presides
Is tramontane, and stumbles all belief.   414
No. We are polished now. The rural lass,
Whom once her virgin modesty and grace,
Her artless manners and her neat attire,
So dignified, that she was hardly less
Than the fair shepherdess of old romance,
Is seen no more. The character is lost. 420
Her head adorned with lappets pinned aloft
And ribbons streaming gay, superbly raised
And magnified beyond all human size,
Indebted to some smart wig-weaver's hand
For more than half the tresses it sustains;
Her elbows ruffled, and her tottering form
Ill propped upon French heels; she might be
    deemed   427
(But that the basket dangling on her arm
Interprets her more truly) of a rank
Too proud for dairy-work, or sale of
    eggs;   430
Expect her soon with foot-boy at her heels,
No longer blushing for her awkward load,
Her train and her umbrella all her care.

The town has tinged the country; and the
    stain

Appears a spot upon the vestal's robe,   435
The worse for what it soils.
           * * *
  But slighted as it is, and by the great
Abandoned, and, which still I more regret,
Infected with the manners and the modes
It knew not once, the country wins me
    still.   440
I never framed a wish or formed a plan
That flattered me with hopes of earthly
    bliss,
But there I laid the scene. There early
    strayed
My fancy, ere yet liberty of choice
Had found me, or the hope of being free.
My very dreams were rural, rural too   446
The first-born efforts of my youthful muse,
Sportive, and jingling her poetic bells
Ere yet her ear was mistress of their pow-
    ers.
No bard could please me but whose lyre was
    tuned   450
To Nature's praises. Heroes and their feats
Fatigued me, never weary of the pipe
Of Tityrus, assembling as he sang
The rustic throng beneath his favorite beech.
Then Milton had indeed a poet's charms:
New to my taste, his Paradise surpassed 456
The struggling efforts of my boyish tongue
To speak its excellence; I danced for joy.
I marveled much that, at so ripe an age
As twice seven years, his beauties had then
    first   460
Engaged my wonder, and admiring still,
And still admiring, with regret supposed
The joy half lost because not sooner found.
Thee, too, enamored of the life I loved,
Pathetic in its praise, in its pursuit   465
Determined, and possessing it at last
With transports such as favored lovers feel,
I studied, prized, and wished that I had
    known
Ingenious Cowley: and though now, re-
    claimed
By modern lights from an erroneous taste
I cannot but lament thy splendid wit   471
Entangled in the cobwebs of the schools.
I still revere thee, courtly though retired,
Though stretched at ease in Chertsey's silent
    bowers,
Not unemployed, and finding rich amends
For a lost world in solitude and verse.   476
'T is born with all. The love of Nature's
    works
Is an ingredient in the compound, man,
Infused at the creation of the kind.
And though the Almighty Maker has
    throughout   480

Discriminated each from each, by strokes
And touches of His hand, with so much art
Diversified, that two were never found
Twins at all points — yet this obtains in all,
That all discern a beauty in his works, 485
And all can taste them: minds that have
    been formed
And tutored, with a relish more exact,
But none without some relish, none un-
    moved.
It is a flame that dies not even there,
Where nothing feeds it. Neither business,
    crowds, 490
Nor habits of luxurious city life,
Whatever else they smother of true worth
In human bosoms, quench it or abate.
The villas, with which London stands be-
    girt
Like a swarth Indian with his belt of beads,
Prove it. A breath of unadulterate air, 496
The glimpse of a green pasture, how they
    cheer
The citizen and brace his languid frame!
Even in the stifling bosom of the town,
A garden in which nothing thrives, has
    charms 500
That soothe the rich possessor; much con-
    soled
That here and there some sprigs of mourn-
    ful mint,
Of nightshade, or valerian, grace the well
He cultivates. These serve him with a hint
That Nature lives; that sight-refreshing
    green 505
Is still the livery she delights to wear,
Though sickly samples of the exuberant
    whole.
What are the casements lined with creeping
    herbs
The prouder sashes fronted with a range
Of orange, myrtle, or the fragrant weed,
The Frenchman's darling? are they not all
    proofs 511
That man, immured in cities, still retains
His inborn, inextinguishable thirst
Of rural scenes, compensating his loss
By supplemental shifts, the best he may? 515
The most unfurnished with the means of
    life,
And they that never pass their brick-wall
    bounds
To range the fields, and treat their lungs
    with air,
Yet feel the burning instinct: over-head
Suspend their crazy boxes planted thick 520
And watered duly. There the pitcher stands
A fragment, and the spoutless tea-pot there:
Sad witnesses how close-pent man regrets

The country, with what ardor he contrives
A peep at nature, when he can no more. 525

Hail, therefore, patroness of health and
    ease
And contemplation, heart-consoling joys
And harmless pleasures, in the thronged
    abode
Of multitudes unknown, hail rural life!
Address himself who will to the pursuit 530
Of honors, or emolument, or fame,
I shall not add myself to such a chase,
Thwart his attempts, or envy his success.
Some must be great. Great offices will have
Great talents. And God gives to every
    man 535
The virtue, temper, understanding, taste,
That lifts him into life, and lets him fall
Just in the niche he was ordained to fill.
To the deliverer of an injured land 539
He gives a tongue to enlarge upon, a heart
To feel, and courage to redress her wrongs;
To monarchs dignity, to judges sense;
To artists ingenuity and skill;
To me an unambitious mind, content
In the low vale of life, that early felt 545
A wish for ease and leisure, and ere long
Found here that leisure and that ease I
    wished.

                 (1785)

ON THE RECEIPT OF MY MOTHER'S PICTURE

Oh, that those lips had language! Life has
    passed
With me but roughly since I heard thee
    last.
Those lips are thine — thy own sweet smile
    I see,
The same that oft in childhood solaced me;
Voice only fails, else how distinct they
    say, 5
'Grieve not, my child, chase all thy fears
    away!'
The meek intelligence of those dear eyes
(Blessed be the art that can immortalize,
The art that baffles Time's tyrannic claim
To quench it) here shines on me still the
    same.
Faithful remembrancer of one so dear,
O welcome guest, though unexpected here!
Who bidst me honor with an artless song,
Affectionate, a mother lost so long,
I will obey, not willingly alone, 15
But gladly, as the precept were her own:
And, while that face renews my filial grief,

Fancy shall weave a charm for my relief,
Shall steep me in Elysian reverie,
A momentary dream that thou art she.   20
My mother! when I learnt that thou wast
    dead
Say, wast thou conscious of the tears I
    shed?
Hovered thy spirit o'er thy sorrowing son,
Wretch even then, life's journey just be-
    gun?
Perhaps thou gavest me, though unfelt, a
    kiss: 25
Perhaps a tear, if souls can weep in bliss —
Ah, that maternal smile! It answers —
    Yes.
I heard the bell tolled on thy burial day,
I saw the hearse that bore thee slow away,
And turning from my nursery window, drew
A long, long sigh, and wept a last adieu! 31
But was it such? — It was.— Where thou
    art gone
Adieus and farewells are a sound unknown.
May I but meet thee on that peaceful shore,
The parting word shall pass my lips no
    more!   35
Thy maidens, grieved themselves at my con-
    cern,
Oft gave me promise of thy quick return.
What ardently I wished I long believed,
And, disappointed still, was still deceived.
By expectation every day beguiled,   40
Dupe of *to-morrow* even from a child.
Thus many a sad to-morrow came and went,
Till, all my stock of infant sorrow spent,
I learned at last submission to my lot;
But, though I less deplored thee, ne'er for-
    got.   45
    Where once we dwelt our name is heard
    no more,
Children not thine have trod my nursery
    floor;
And where the gardener Robin, day by day,
Drew me to school along the public way,
Delighted with my bauble coach, and
    wrapped   50
In scarlet mantle warm, and velvet capped,
'T is now become a history little known,
That once we called the pastoral house our
    own.
Short-lived possession! but the record fair
That memory keeps, of all thy kindness
    there,   55
Still outlives many a storm that has effaced
A thousand other themes less deeply traced.
Thy nightly visits to my chamber made,
That thou mightst know me safe and
    warmly laid;
Thy morning bounties ere I left my home, 60

The biscuit, or confectionary plum;
The fragrant waters on my cheek bestowed
By thy own hand, till fresh they shone and
    glowed;
All this, and more endearing still than all,
Thy constant flow of love, that knew no
    fall,   65
Ne'er roughened by those cataracts and
    brakes
That humor interposed too often makes;
All this still legible in memory's page,
And still to be so to my latest age,
Adds joy to duty, makes me glad to pay 70
Such honors to thee as my numbers may;
Perhaps a frail memorial, but sincere,
Not scorned in heaven, though little noticed
    here.
    Could Time, his flight reversed, restore
    the hours,
When, playing with thy vesture's tissued
    flowers,   75
The violet, the pink, and jassamine,
I pricked them into paper with a pin
(And thou wast happier than myself the
    while,
Wouldst softly speak, and stroke my head
    and smile),
Could those few pleasant days again ap-
    pear,   80
Might one wish bring them, would I wish
    them here?
I would not trust my heart — the dear de-
    light
Seems so to be desired, perhaps I might.—
But no — what here we call our life is such,
So little to be loved, and thou so much, 85
That I should ill requite thee to constrain
Thy unbound spirit into bonds again.
    Thou, as a gallant bark from Albion's
    coast
(The storms all weathered and the ocean
    crossed)
Shoots into port at some well-havened isle,
Where spices breathe, and brighter seasons
    smile,   91
There sits quiescent on the floods that show
Her beauteous form reflected clear below,
While airs impregnated with incense play
Around her, fanning light her streamers
    gay;   95
So thou, with sails how swift! hast reached
    the shore,
'Where tempests never beat nor billows
    roar.'
And thy loved consort on the dangerous
    tide
Of life long since has anchored by thy side,
But me, scarce hoping to attain that rest, 100

Always from port withheld, always distressed —
Me howling blasts drive devious, tempest tost,
Sails ripped, seams opening wide, and compass lost,
And day by day some current's thwarting force
Sets me more distant from a prosperous course. 105
Yet, oh, the thought that thou art safe, and he!
That thought is joy, arrive what may to me.
My boast is not, that I deduce my birth
From loins enthroned and rulers of the earth;
But higher far my proud pretensions rise —
The son of parents passed into the skies! 111
And now, farewell — Time unrevoked has run
His wonted course, yet what I wished is done.
By contemplation's help, not sought in vain,
I seem to have lived my childhood o'er again; 115
To have renewed the joys that once were mine,
Without the sin of violating thine:
And, while the wings of Fancy still are free,
And I can view this mimic show of thee,
Time has but half succeeded in his theft —
Thyself removed, thy power to soothe me left. 121

(1798)

SONNET TO MRS. UNWIN

Mary! I want a lyre with other strings;
Such aid from Heaven as some have feigned they drew!
An eloquence scarce given to mortals, new,
And undebased by praise of meaner things!
That, ere through age or woe I shed my wings, 5
I may record thy worth, with honor due,
In verse as musical as thou art true,—
Verse, that immortalizes whom it sings!
But thou hast little need: there is a book,
By seraphs writ with beams of heavenly light, 10
On which the eyes of God not rarely look;
A chronicle of actions just and bright!

There all thy deeds, my faithful Mary, shine,
And since thou own'st that praise, I spare thee mine. (1803)

ON THE LOSS OF THE ROYAL GEORGE

Toll for the brave!
The brave that are no more!
All sunk beneath the wave,
Fast by their native shore!

Eight hundred of the brave, 5
Whose courage well was tried,
Had made the vessel heel,
And laid her on her side.

A land-breeze shook the shrouds,
And she was overset; 10
Down went the Royal George,
With all her crew complete.

Toll for the brave!
Brave Kempenfelt is gone;
His last sea-fight is fought; 15
His work of glory done.

It was not in the battle;
No tempest gave the shock;
She sprang no fatal leak;
She ran upon no rock. 20

His sword was in its sheath;
His fingers held the pen,
When Kempenfelt went down
With twice four hundred men.

Weigh the vessel up, 25
Once dreaded by our foes!
And mingle with our cup
The tears that England owes.

Her timbers yet are sound,
And she may float again 30
Full charged with England's thunder,
And plough the distant main.

But Kempenfelt is gone,
His victories are o'er;
And he and his eight hundred 35
Shall plough the wave no more.

(1803)

GEORGE CRABBE (1754–1832)

When Goldsmith sat down to sketch for all time the picture of his native village, it was after an absence of eighteen years and he saw it through a tinted haze of retrospect and soft sentimental reflection. Crabbe came to his task fresh from the hardships of his youth; he wrote 'with his eye on the object'; and he painted the cot 'as Truth will paint it and as Bards will not,' in all the reality of its hard and sordid detail. The *Village* was Aldborough, a rude fishing port on the 'frowning coast' of Suffolk. Here Crabbe was born, the eldest child of a collector of salt-duties. After a scattered education which consisted partly in loading butter and cheese in the neighboring port, he was apprenticed, at fourteen, to a surgeon near Bury St. Edmunds, who employed him in 'hoeing turnips.' After some years of study he set up as a surgeon in his native village; but his rewards were meager and he desired to marry. In the meantime, he had begun to cultivate the Muses and he resolved to try his lot in London. On the verge of starvation, he was taken up by Burke, who introduced him to his distinguished friends, aided the publication of his first successful poem, *The Library* (1781), and induced him to exchange the knife for the prayer-book. Returning to Aldborough as a curate, he became, shortly after, through Burke's introduction, a protégé of the Duke of Rutland, and was never again in want. His literary fame, during most of his life, was based on *The Village*, which he published in 1783 and followed with a silence of twenty-four years, broken only by the publication of a trifling poem, *The Newspaper* (1785). During these years he wrote and destroyed large quantities of verse and a treatise on botany and busied himself with domestic life, but was especially occupied in healing both the minds and bodies of the poor of his various parishes. His second period of publication, beginning with *The Parish Register* (1807), including *The Borough* (1810) and *Tales in Verse* (1812), and concluding with *Tales of the Hall* (1819), brought him into the world of Wordsworth, Byron, and Scott. He outlived the second and died in the same year with the last.

Crabbe's powerful realism has been greatly admired by the men of his own craft. He has, as Tennyson said, 'a world of his own.' It is a far more populous world than that of Cowper or even of Wordsworth and it is not more unlovely than that of Burns; but he brought to its interpretation little of the tenderness of the first, the 'internal brightness' of the second, or the human tears and laughter of the third. We may be stunned or impressed by Crabbe's world, but we will never love it.

THE VILLAGE, Book I

The Village Life, and every care that reigns
O'er youthful peasants and declining swains;
What labor yields, and what, that labor past,
Age, in its hour of languor, finds at last;
What form the real Picture of the Poor,   5
Demand a song — the Muse can give no more.
  Fled are those times, when, in harmonious strains,
The rustic poet praised his native plains:
No shepherds now, in smooth alternate verse,
Their country's beauty or their nymphs rehearse;   10

Yet still for these we frame the tender strain,
Still in our lays fond Corydons complain,
And shepherds' boys their amorous pains reveal,
The only pains, alas! they never feel.
  On Mincio's banks, in Cæsar's bounteous reign,   15
If Tityrus found the Golden Age again,
Must sleepy bards the flattering dream prolong,
Mechanic echoes of the Mantuan song?
From Truth and Nature shall we widely stray,
Where Virgil, not where Fancy, leads the way?   20
  Yes, thus the Muses sing of happy swains,
Because the Muses never knew their pains:

They boast their peasant's pipes; but peasants now
Resign their pipes and plod behind the plough;
And few, amid the rural tribe, have time 25
To number syllables, and play with rime;
Save honest Duck, what son of verse could share
The poet's rapture and the peasant's care?
Or the great labors of the field degrade,
With the new peril of a poorer trade? 30
  From this chief cause these idle praises spring,
That themes so easy few forbear to sing;
For no deep thought the trifling subjects ask;
To sing of shepherds is an easy task;
The happy youth assumes the common strain, 35
A nymph his mistress, and himself a swain;
With no sad scenes he clouds his tuneful prayer,
But all, to look like her, is painted fair.
  I grant indeed that fields and flocks have charms 39
For him that grazes or for him that farms;
But when amid such pleasing scenes I trace
The poor laborious natives of the place,
And see the mid-day sun, with fervid ray,
On their bare heads and dewy temples play;
While some, with feebler heads, and fainter hearts 45
Deplore their fortune, yet sustain their parts —
Then shall I dare these real ills to hide,
In tinsel trappings of poetic pride?
No; cast by Fortune on a frowning coast,
Which neither groves nor happy valleys boast; 50
Where other cares than those the Muse relates,
And other shepherds dwell with other mates;
By such examples taught, I paint the Cot,
As Truth will paint it, and as Bards will not:
Nor you, ye poor, of lettered scorn complain, 55
To you the smoothest song is smooth in vain;
O'ercome by labor, and bowed down by time,
Feel you the barren flattery of a rime?
Can poets soothe you, when you pine for bread,
By winding myrtles round your ruined shed? 60

Can their light tales your weighty griefs o'erpower,
Or glad with airy mirth the toilsome hour?
Lo! where the heath, with withering brake grown o'er,
Lends the light turf that warms the neighboring poor
From thence a length of burning sand appears, 65
Where the thin harvest waves its withered ears.
Rank weeds, that every art and care defy,
Reign o'er the land, and rob the blighted rye;
There thistles stretch their prickly arms afar,
And to the ragged infant threaten war; 70
There poppies, nodding, mock the hope of toil,
There the blue bugloss paints the sterile soil;
Hardy and high, above the slender sheaf,
The slimy mallow waves her silky leaf;
O'er the young shoot the charlock throws a shade, 75
And clasping tares cling round the sickly blade;
With mingled tints the rocky coasts abound,
And a sad splendor vainly shines around.
So looks the nymph whom wretched arts adorn,
Betrayed by man, then left for man to scorn; 80
Whose cheek in vain assumes the mimic rose,
While her sad eyes the troubled breast disclose:
Whose outward splendor is but folly's dress,
Exposing most when most it gilds distress.
  Here joyless roam a wild amphibious race, 85
With sullen woe displayed in every face;
Who, far from civil arts and social fly,
And scowl at strangers with suspicious eye.
  Here too the lawless merchant of the main
Draws from his plough the intoxicated swain; 90
Want only claimed the labor of the day,
But vice now steals his nightly rest away.
  Where are the swains, who, daily labor done,
With rural games played down the setting sun;
Who struck with matchless force the bounding ball, 95
Or made the ponderous quoit obliquely fall;
While some huge Ajax, terrible and strong,

Engaged some artful stripling of the throng.
And fell beneath him, foiled, while far
   around
Hoarse triumph rose, and rocks returned
   the sound?   100
Where now are these? — Beneath yon cliff
   they stand,
To show the freighted pinnace where to
   land;
To load the ready steed with guilty haste,
To fly in terror o'er the pathless waste,
Or, when detected, in their straggling
   course,   105
To foil their foes by cunning or by force;
Or, yielding part (which equal knaves de-
   mand),
To gain a lawless passport through the land.
Here, wandering long, amid these frown-
   ing fields,
I sought the simple life that Nature yields;
Rapine and Wrong and Fear usurped her
   place,   111
And a bold, artful, surly, savage race;
Who, only skilled to take the finny tribe,
The yearly dinner, or septennial bribe,
Wait on the shore, and, as the waves run
   high,   115
On the tossed vessel bend their eager eye,
Which to their coast directs its vent'rous
   way;
Theirs or the ocean's miserable prey.
  As on their neighboring beach yon swal-
   lows stand,
And wait for favoring winds to leave the
   land;   120
While still for flight the ready wing is
   spread:
So waited I the favoring hour, and fled;
Fled from these shores where guilt and
   famine reign,
And cried, Ah! hapless they who still re-
   main:
Who still remain to hear the ocean roar, 125
Whose greedy waves devour the lessening
   shore;
Till some fierce tide, with more imperious
   sway
Sweeps the low hut and all it holds away;
When the sad tenant weeps from door to
   door,
And begs a poor protection from the poor!
  But these are scenes where Nature's nig-
   gard hand   131
Gave a spare portion to the famished land;
Hers is the fault, if here mankind com-
   plain
Of fruitless toil and labor spent in vain;
But yet in other scenes more fair in view,

When Plenty smiles — alas! she smiles for
   few —   136
And those who taste not, yet behold her
   store,
Are as the slaves that dig the golden ore —
The wealth around them makes them doubly
   poor.
Or will you deem them amply paid in
   health,   140
Labor's fair child, that languishes with
   wealth?
Go, then! and see them rising with the sun,
Through a long course of daily toil to run;
See them beneath the Dog-star's raging
   heat,
When the knees tremble and the temples
   beat;   145
Behold them, leaning on their scythes, look
   o'er
The labor past, and toils to come explore;
See them alternate suns and showers en-
   gage,
And hoard up aches and anguish for their
   age;
Through fens and marshy moors their steps
   pursue,   150
When their warm pores imbibe the evening
   dew;
Then own that labor may as fatal be
To these thy slaves, as thine excess to thee.
  Amid this tribe too oft a manly pride
Strives in strong toil the fainting heart to
   hide;   155
There may you see the youth of slender
   frame
Contend with weakness, weariness, and
   shame·
Yet, urged along, and proudly loth to yield,
He strives to join his fellows of the field;
Till long-contending nature droops at last,
Declining health rejects his poor repast, 161
His cheerless spouse the coming danger
   sees,
And mutual murmurs urge the slow di
   ease.
  Yet grant them health, 't is not for us t
   tell,
Though the head droops not, that the heart
   is well;   165
Or will you praise that homely, healthy fare,
Plenteous and plain, that happy peasants
   share!
Oh! trifle not with wants you cannot feel,
Nor mock the misery of a stinted meal;
Homely, not wholesome, plain, not plenteous,
   such   170
As you who praise, would never deign to
   touch.

Ye gentle souls, who dream of rural ease,
Whom the smooth stream and smoother
   sonnet please;
Go! if the peaceful cot your praises share,
Go look within, and ask if peace be there;
If peace be his, that drooping weary sire;
Or theirs, that offspring round their feeble
   fire;   177
Or hers, that matron pale, whose trembling
   hand
Turns on the wretched hearth the expiring
   brand.   179
   Nor yet can Time itself obtain for these
Life's latest comforts, due respect and ease;
For yonder see that hoary swain, whose age
Can with no cares except its own engage;
Who, propped on that rude staff, looks up
   to see
The bare arms broken from the withering
   tree,   185
On which, a boy, he climbed the loftiest
   bough,
Then his first joy, but his sad emblem now.
   He once was chief in all the rustic trade;
His steady hand the straightest furrow
   made;
Full many a prize he won, and still is proud
To find the triumphs of his youth allowed;
A transient pleasure sparkles in his eyes, 192
He hears and smiles, then thinks again and
   sighs;
For now he journeys to his grave in pain;
The rich disdain him; nay, the poor disdain:
Alternate masters now their slave command,
Urge the weak efforts of his feeble hand,
And, when his age attempts its task in vain,
With ruthless taunts, of lazy poor complain.
   Oft may you see him, when he tends the
   sheep,   200
His winter charge, beneath the hillock weep;
Oft hear him murmur to the winds that
   blow
O'er his white locks and bury them in snow,
When, roused by rage and muttering in the
   morn,
He mends the broken edge with icy thorn: —
   'Why do I live, when I desire to be 206
At once from life and life's long labor free?
Like leaves in spring, the young are blown
   away,
Without the sorrows of a slow decay;
I, like yon withered leaf, remain behind, 210
Nipped by the frost, and shivering in the
   wind;
There it abides till younger buds come on
As I, now all my fellow-swains are gone;
Then from the rising generation thrust,
It falls, like me, unnoticed to the dust. 215

'These fruitful fields, these numerous
   flocks I see,
Are others' gain, but killing cares to me;
To me the children of my youth are lords,
Cool in their looks, but hasty in their words:
Wants of their own demand their care; and
   who   220
Feels his own want and succors others too?
A lonely, wretched man, in pain I go,
None need my help, and none relieve my
   woe;
Then let my bones beneath the turf be laid,
And men forget the wretch they would not
   aid.'   225
   Thus groan the old, till by disease op-
   pressed,
They taste a final woe, and then they rest.
   Theirs is yon House that holds the parish
   poor,
Whose walls of mud scarce bear the broken
   door;
There, where the putrid vapors, flagging,
   play,   230
And the dull wheel hums doleful through
   the day;
There children dwell who know no parents'
   care;
Parents, who know no children's love, dwell
   there!
Heart-broken matrons on their joyless bed,
Forsaken wives, and mothers never wed;
Dejected widows with unheeded tears, 236
And crippled age with more than childhood
   fears;
The lame, the blind, and, far the happiest
   they!
The moping idiot, and the madman gay.
   Here too the sick their final doom receive,
Here brought, amid the scenes of grief, to
   grieve,   241
Where the loud groans from some sad
   chamber flow,
Mixed with the clamors of the crowd be-
   low;
Here, sorrowing, they each kindred sorrow
   scan.
And the cold charities of man to man: 245
Whose laws indeed for ruined age provide,
And strong compulsion plucks the scrap
   from pride;
But still that scrap is bought with many a
   sigh,
And pride embitters what it can't deny.
   Say, ye, oppressed by some fantastic woes,
Some jarring nerve that baffles your repose;
Who press the downy couch, while slaves
   advance   252
With timid eye to read the distant glance;

Who with sad prayers the weary doctor
    tease,
To name the nameless ever new disease; 255
Who with mock patience dire complaints
    endure,
Which real pain and that alone can cure;
How would ye bear in real pain to lie,
Despised, neglected, left alone to die?
How would ye bear to draw your latest
    breath   260
Where all that's wretched paves the way for
    death?
  Such is that room which one rude beam
    divides,
And naked rafters form the sloping sides;
Where the vile bands that bind the thatch
    are seen,
And lath and mud are all that lie between;
Save one dull pane, that, coarsely patched,
    gives way   266
To the rude tempest, yet excludes the day:
Here, on a matted flock, with dust o'er-
    spread,
The drooping wretch reclines his languid
    head;
For him no hand the cordial cup applies, 270
Or wipes the tear that stagnates in his eyes;
No friends with soft discourse his pain be-
    guile,
Or promise hope, till sickness wears a smile.
But soon a loud and hasty summons calls,
Shakes the thin roof, and echoes round the
    walls;   275
Anon, a figure enters, quaintly neat,
All pride and business, bustle and conceit;
With looks unaltered by these scenes of
    woe,
With speed that, entering, speaks his haste
    to go,
He bids the gazing throng around him fly,
And carries fate and physic in his eye: 281
A potent quack, long versed in human ills,
Who first insults the victim whom he kills;
Whose murd'rous hand a drowsy Bench
    protect,   284
And whose most tender mercy is neglect.
  Paid by the parish for attendance here,
He wears contempt upon his sapient sneer;
In haste he seeks the bed where Misery
    lies,
Impatience marked in his averted eyes;
And, some habitual queries hurried o'er, 290
Without reply, he rushes on the door:
His drooping patient, long inured to pain,
And long unheeded, knows remonstrance
    vain;
He ceases now the feeble help to crave
Of man; and silent sinks into the grave. 295

But ere his death some pious doubts arise,
Some simple fears, which 'bold bad' men
    despise;
Fain would he ask the parish priest to prove
His title certain to the joys above:
For this he sends the murmuring nurse, who
    calls   300
The holy stranger to these dismal walls:
And doth not he, the pious man, appear,
He, 'passing rich, with forty pounds a
    year?'
Ah! no; a shepherd of a different stock:
And far unlike him, feeds this little flock:
A jovial youth, who thinks his Sunday's task
As much as God or man can fairly ask; 307
The rest he gives to loves and labors light,
To fields the morning, and to feasts the
    night;
None better skilled the noisy pack to guide,
To urge their chase, to cheer them or to
    chide;   311
A sportsman keen, he shoots through half
    the day,
And, skilled at whist, devotes the night to
    play:
Then, while such honors bloom around his
    head,
Shall he sit sadly by the sick man's bed, 315
To raise the hope he feels not, or with zeal
To combat fears that e'en the pious feel?

          * * *

  Now to the church behold the mourners
    come,
Sedately torpid and devoutly dumb;
The village children now their games sus-
    pend,   320
To see the bier that bears their ancient
    friend:
For he was one in all their idle sport,
And like a monarch ruled their little court;
The pliant bow he formed, the flying ball,
The bat, the wicket, were his labors all; 325
Him now they follow to his grave, and
    stand,
Silent and sad, and gazing hand in hand;
While bending low, their eager eyes explore
The mingled relics of the parish poor.
The bell tolls late, the moping owl flies
    round,   330
Fear marks the flight and magnifies the
    sound.
The busy priest, detained by weightier care,
Defers his duty till the day of prayer;
And, waiting long, the crowd retire dis-
    tressed,
To think a poor man's bones should lie un-
    blessed.   335
                    (1783)

WILLIAM BLAKE (1757–1827)

'I walked the other evening to the end of the heath and touched the sky with my finger.' Was the man inspired or mad who made this statement in fierce literalness, when bored by some scientific cant about 'the vastness of space'? One's answer to this question will determine one's attitude toward Blake. The ordinary biographical summary hardly seems to apply to him; yet undeniably, like the hero in the old song, 'This man was born, lived, drank, and died.' He was born in London, he spent his life there, he did not drink much and frequently had none too much to eat and wear, and in London he died, 'leaving the delusive Goddess Nature to her laws, to get into freedom from all law of the numbers, into the mind, in which every one is king and priest in his own house.' Yet this man who denied the validity of positive science and repudiated the reality of physical nature was a twofold artist, draughtsman and poet. After the bare rudiments of an education, he began at ten the study of drawing and almost as early the writing of verses. At the age of fourteen he was apprenticed to the well-known engraver, Basire. About the same time he wrote some of his published poems. He first exhibited at the Royal Academy in 1780, and three years later brought out his first volume, *Poetical Sketches*, the only one of his publications which was printed in the ordinary manner. *Songs of Innocence* (1789), *Songs of Experience* (1794), and the series of enormous, crazed, difficult, or unintelligible Prophetic Books were all engraved upon plates and embellished with designs by himself. Other published designs and engravings of importance were those for Young's *Night Thoughts* (1797), Hayley's *Life of Cowper* (1803), Blair's *The Grave* (1808), the Book of Job (1825), and Dante (1824–27).

None of his accomplishments, whether in literature or design, brought him any considerable return in money or immediate fame. He lived most of his life in almost squalid poverty which he did not seem to mind and, when he had means, bestowed them with unstinted charity and without concern for the future. His conduct was fairly within the law of conventional society and government; his doctrines were revolutionary and extreme even for the age of revolution in which he lived. With all their wildness they are sometimes startlingly modern, and it is not unlikely that the world is yet to ring with some of his ideas. As a workman in lines he was strangely original and powerful, and has been compared with the greatest artists of design that ever lived; though often crudely careless or perverse he could draw with propriety and beauty when he chose, and with tremendous energy and suggestiveness. It would be hard to conceive of finer illustrations than his 'Winter' and 'Evening' for Cowper's *Task*. His poetry speaks for itself. Like his design it is often absurdly crude and at other times his speech is something more than mortal.

'When the stars threw down their spears '—

We happen upon a line like this and we seem to have heard a voice of other worlds.

TO SPRING

O thou with dewy locks, who lookest down
Through the clear windows of the morning, turn
Thine angel eyes upon our western isle,
Which in full choir hails thy approach, O Spring!

The hills tell each other, and the listening 5
Valleys hear; all our longing eyes are turned
Up to thy bright pavilions: issue forth,
And let thy holy feet visit our clime.

Come o'er the eastern hills, and let our winds
Kiss thy perfumèd garments; let us taste 10
Thy morn and evening breath; scatter thy pearls
Upon our love-sick land that mourns for thee.

O deck her forth with thy fair fingers; pour
Thy soft kisses on her bosom; and put 14
Thy golden crown upon her languished head,
Whose modest tresses were bound up for thee. (1783)

TO THE MUSES

Whether on Ida's shady brow,
　Or in the chambers of the East,
The chambers of the sun, that now
　From ancient melody have ceased;

Whether in Heaven ye wander fair,　　5
　Or the green corners of the earth,
Or the blue regions of the air
　Where the melodious winds have birth;

Whether on crystal rocks ye rove,
　Beneath the bosom of the sea　　10
Wandering in many a coral grove,
　Fair Nine, forsaking Poetry!

How have you left the ancient love
　That bards of old enjoyed in you!
The languid strings do scarcely move!　15
The sound is forced, the notes are few!
　　　　　　　　　　(1783)

MAD SONG

The wild winds weep,
And the night is a-cold;
Come hither, Sleep;
And my griefs enfold! . . .
But lo! the morning peeps　　5
Over the eastern steeps,
And the rustling [birds] of dawn
The earth do scorn.

Lo! to the vault
Of pavèd heaven,　　10
With sorrow fraught,
My notes are driven:
They strike the ear of night,
Make weep the eyes of day;
They make mad the roaring winds,　15
And with tempests play.

Like a fiend in a cloud,
With howling woe
After night I do crowd
And with night will go;　　20
I turn my back to the east
From whence comforts have increased;
For light doth seize my brain
With frantic pain.
　　　　　　　　　　(1783)

THE PIPER

Piping down the valleys wild,
　Piping songs of pleasant glee,
On a cloud I saw a child,
　And he laughing said to me:

'Pipe a song about a Lamb!'　　5
　So I piped with merry cheer.
'Piper, pipe that song again;'
　So I piped: he wept to hear.

'Drop thy pipe, thy happy pipe;
　Sing thy songs of happy cheer:'　10
So I sang the same again,
　While he wept with joy to hear.

'Piper, sit thee down and write
　In a book, that all may read.'
So he vanished from my sight,　　15
　And I plucked a hollow reed,

And I made a rural pen,
　And I stained the water clear,
And I wrote my happy songs
　Every child may joy to hear.　　20
　　　　　　　　　　(1789)

THE SHEPHERD

How sweet is the shepherd's sweet lot!
　From the morn to the evening he strays;
He shall follow his sheep all the day,
　And his tongue shall be fillèd with praise.

For he hears the lamb's innocent call,　5
　And he hears the ewe's tender reply;
He is watchful while they are in peace,
　For they know when their shepherd is nigh.
　　　　　　　　　　(1789)

THE LITTLE BLACK BOY

My mother bore me in the southern wild,
　And I am black, but O my soul is white;
White as an angel is the English child,
　But I am black, as if bereaved of light.

My mother taught me underneath a tree,　5
　And, sitting down before the heat of day,
She took me on her lap and kissèd me,
　And, pointing to the east, began to say:

'Look on the rising sun,—there God does
　　live,
　And gives his light, and gives his heat
　　away;　　10
And flowers and trees and beasts and men
　　receive
　Comfort in morning, joy in the noonday.

'And we are put on earth a little space,
　That we may learn to bear the beams of
　　love;

And these black bodies and this sunburnt
    face   15
  Is but a cloud, and like a shady grove.

'For when our souls have learned the heat
    to bear,
  The cloud will vanish, we shall hear his
    voice,
Saying: "Come out from the grove, my
    love and care,
  And round my golden tent like lambs re-
    joice."'   20

  Thus did my mother say, and kissèd me;
  And thus I say to little English boy.
When I from black, and he from white cloud
    free,
  And round the tent of God like lambs
    we joy,

I 'll shade him from the heat, till he can
    bear   25
  To lean in joy upon our father's knee;
And then I 'll stand and stroke his silver
    hair,
  And be like him, and he will then love me.
                    (1789)

CRADLE SONG

FROM SONGS OF INNOCENCE

Sweet dreams, form a shade
O'er my lovely infant's head;
Sweet dreams of pleasant streams
By happy, silent, moony beams.

Sweet sleep, with soft down   5
Weave thy brows an infant crown.
Sweet sleep, Angel mild,
Hover o'er my happy child.

Sweet smiles, in the night
Hover over my delight;   10
Sweet smiles, mother's smiles,
All the livelong night beguiles.

Sweet moans, dovelike sighs,
Chase not slumber from thy eyes.
Sweet moans, sweeter smiles,   15
All the dovelike moans beguiles.

Sleep, sleep, happy child,
All creation slept and smil'd;
Sleep, sleep, happy sleep,
While o'er thee thy mother weep.   20

Sweet babe, in thy face
Holy image I can trace

Sweet babe, once like thee,
Thy Maker lay and wept for me.

Wept for me, for thee, for all,   25
When he was an infant small.
Thou his image ever see,
Heavenly face that smiles on thee,

Smiles on thee, on me, on all;
Who became an infant small.   30
Infant smiles are His own smiles;
Heaven and earth to peace beguiles.
                  (1789)

CRADLE SONG

FROM SONGS OF EXPERIENCE

Sleep! sleep! beauty bright,
Dreaming o'er the joys of night;
Sleep! sleep! in thy sleep
Little sorrows sit and weep.

Sweet Babe, in thy face   5
Soft desires I can trace,
Secret joys and secret smiles,
Little pretty infant wiles.

As thy softest limbs I feel,
Smiles as of the morning steal   10
O'er thy cheek, and o'er thy breast
Where thy little heart does rest.

O! the cunning wiles that creep
In thy little heart asleep.
When thy little heart does wake   15
Then the dreadful lightnings break,

From thy cheek and from thy eye,
O'er the youthful harvests nigh.
Infant wiles and infant smiles
Heaven and Earth of peace beguiles.   20
                  (1794)

A DREAM

Once a dream did weave a shade
O'er my Angel-guarded bed,
That an emmet lost its way
Where on grass methought I lay.

Troubled, 'wildered, and forlorn,   5
Dark, benighted, travel-worn,
Over many a tangled spray,
All heart-broke I heard her say:

'O, my children! do they cry?
Do they hear their father sigh?   10

Now they look abroad to see:
Now return and weep for me.'

Pitying, I dropped a tear;
But I saw a glow-worm near,
Who replied: 'What wailing wight   15
Calls the watchman of the night?

'I am set to light the ground,
While the beetle goes his round:
Follow now the beetle's hum;
Little wanderer, hie thee home.'   20
                                    (1789)

THE DIVINE IMAGE

To Mercy, Pity, Peace, and Love,
All pray in their distress,
And to these virtues of delight
Return their thankfulness.

For Mercy, Pity, Peace, and Love,   5
Is God our Father dear;
And Mercy, Pity, Peace, and Love,
Is man, his child and care.

For Mercy has a human heart;
Pity, a human face;
And Love, the human form divine:
And Peace, the human dress.

Then every man, of every clime,
That prays in his distress,
Prays to the human form divine: 15
Love, Mercy, Pity, Peace.

And all must love the human form,
In heathen, Turk, or Jew.
Where Mercy, Love, and Pity dwell,
There God is dwelling too.   20
                                    (1789)

THE CHIMNEY SWEEPER

A little black thing among the snow,
Crying 'weep! weep!' in notes of woe!
'Where are thy father and mother, say?'—
'They are both gone up to the church to
    pray.

'Because I was happy upon the heath,   5
And smiled among the winter's snow,
They clothèd me in the clothes of death,
And taught me to sing the notes of woe.

'And because I am happy and dance and
    sing.

They think they have done me no injury,   10
And are gone to praise God and his priest
    and king,
Who make up a heaven of our misery.'
                                    (1794)

THE CLOD AND THE PEBBLE

'Love seeketh not itself to please,
  Nor for itself hath any care,
But for another gives its ease,
  And builds a Heaven in Hell's despair."

So sung a little clod of clay,   5
  Trodden with the cattle's feet,
But a pebble of the brook
  Warbled out these meters meet:

'Love seeketh only self to please,
  To bind another to its delight,   1,
Joys in another's loss of ease,
  And builds a Hell in Heaven's despite.'
                                    (1794)

THE TIGER

Tiger! Tiger! burning bright
In the forests of the night,
What immortal hand or eye
Could frame thy fearful symmetry?

In what distant deeps or skies   5
Burnt the fire of thine eyes?
On what wings dare he aspire?
What the hand dare seize the fire?

And what shoulder, and what art,
Could twist the sinews of thy heart?   10
And when thy heart began to beat,
What dread hand? and what dread feet?

What the hammer? what the chain?
In what furnace was thy brain?
What the anvil? what dread grasp   15
Dare its deadly terrors clasp?

When the stars threw down their spears,
And watered heaven with their tears,
Did he smile his work to see?
Did he who made the Lamb make thee?   20

Tiger! Tiger! burning bright
In the forests of the night,
What immortal hand or eye
Dare frame thy fearful symmetry?
                                    (1794)

AH SUNFLOWER

Ah Sunflower, weary of time,
Who countest the steps of the sun,
Seeking after that sweet golden clime
Where the traveler's journey is done —

Where the youth pined away with desire, 5
And the pale virgin, shrouded in snow,
Arise from their graves, and aspire
Where my sunflower wishes to go!

(1794)

NURSE'S SONG

When the voices of children are heard on
the green
And whisperings are in the dale,
The days of my youth rise fresh in my
mind,
My face turns green and pale.

Then come home, my children, the sun is
gone down, 5
And the dews of night arise;
Your spring and your day are wasted in
play,
And your winter and night in disguise.

(1794)

A LITTLE BOY LOST.

'Nought loves another as itself,
Nor venerates another so,
Nor is it possible to thought
A greater than itself to know.

'And, father, how can I love you 5
Or any of my brothers more?
I love you like the little bird
That picks up crumbs around the door.'

The priest sat by and heard the child;
In trembling zeal he seized his hair, 10
He led him by his little coat,
And all admired the priestly care.

And standing on the altar high,
'Lo, what a fiend is here!' said he:
'One who sets reason up for judge 15
Of our most holy mystery.'

The weeping child could not be heard,
The weeping parents wept in vain:
They stripped him to his little shirt,
And bound him in an iron chain, 20

And burned him in a holy place
Where many had been burned before;
The weeping parents wept in vain.
Are such things done on Albion's shore?

(1794)

FROM MILTON

And did those feet in ancient time
Walk upon England's mountains green?
And was the holy Lamb of God
On England's pleasant pastures seen?

And did the Countenance Divine 5
Shine forth upon our clouded hills?
And was Jerusalem builded here
Among these dark Satanic Mills?

Bring me my bow of burning gold!
Bring me my arrows of desire! 10
Bring me my spear! O clouds, unfold!
Bring me my chariot of fire!

I will not cease from mental fight,
Nor shall my sword sleep in my hand,
Till we have built Jerusalem 1
In England's green and pleasant land.

(1804)

ROBERT BURNS (1759–1796)

Burns was born near 'Alloway's auld haunted kirk' on the banks of the Doon, in a two-roomed cottage which his father had built with his own hands out of rough stone and clay. A storm blew down the gable a few days after his birth, and 'A blast o' Janwar' win' Blew hansel in on Robin.' 'No wonder that one ushered into the world amid such a tempest should be the victim of stormy passions,' Burns would afterward say. His father was a poor 'renter' who moved from one farm to another while Burns was growing up. Amid 'the unceasing moil of a galley slave,' he found time for the ordinary education of a Scotch peasant lad and added considerable reading in history and English poetry; but he had known many a weary day at the plow-tail and in harvest by the time he was fifteen. It was at this age, as he has told us, that he found himself partner in the harvest-field with 'a bonnie sweet sonsie lassie.' 'Among her love-inspiring qualities, she sung sweetly; and it was her favorite reel to which I attempted giving an embodied vehicle in rime. . . . Thus with me began love and poetry.'

Farming, love, and poetry were the staples of Burns's life from now on. He tried flax-dressing at Irvine, a town of some size near-by, but succeeded only in acquiring the bad habits of the place and soon returned to the farm and to poetry. After his father's death in 1784, he and his brother Gilbert moved to the farm of Mossgiel and a little later he met Jean Armour, who after a long and irregular courtship became his wife. His first collection of poems was issued at Kilmarnock in 1786, and such was their immediate success that he went to Edinburgh and brought out a new edition the following winter. He was lionized for a season, but had bitterly to learn the difference between curiosity and social acceptance. From this publication he realized enough money to pay for a tour of the Highlands, contribute two hundred pounds to the needs of his brother, and stock a farm at Ellisland. Here he settled with his wife Jean, now regularly married, in December, 1788. But he had chosen his farm with a poet's rather than a farmer's eye, and shortly undertook to add to his earnings by securing a post in the excise at Dumfries,— 'gauging auld wives' barrels,' he called it. His next course was to give up the farm and remove his family to town. It was a perilous position for one of his temperament. Too many 'trusty drouthy cronies' clustered around him; the 'social glass' became too frequent; 'thoughtless follies laid him low, and stained his name.'

Yet even during these years of decline in health and respectability his genius burned brightly. Many of the 'old Scots songs' with which his name is inseparably connected were given to the world at this time; many equally fine were not printed until after his death. Though it is totally uncritical to think of him as merely an unlettered natural singer, Burns never had the leisure or opportunity to become a highly cultivated poet in the English language or on the grand scale. He constantly falls back upon his native dialect for his most telling phrases and his most magical bursts; and he is at his best in those brief snatches, perfect in pitch and infinite in variety, for which — and for the passionate, imperfect, human bounty of his nature — the world so deeply loves him.

SONG: MARY MORISON

O Mary, at thy window be,
  It is the wish'd, the trysted hour!
Those smiles and glances let me see,
  That make the miser's treasure poor:
How blythely wad I bide the stoure,   5
  A weary slave frae sun to sun,
Could I the rich reward secure,
  The lovely Mary Morison.

Yestreen when to the trembling string
  The dance gaed thro' the lighted ha',   10
To thee my fancy took its wing,
  I sat, but neither heard nor saw:

Tho' this was fair, and that was braw,
  And yon the toast of a' the town,
I sigh'd, and said amang them a',   15
  'Ye are na Mary Morison.'

O Mary, canst thou wreck his peace,
  Wha for thy sake wad gladly die?
Or canst thou break that heart of his,
  Whase only faut is loving thee?   20
If love for love thou wilt na gie
  At least be pity to me shown:
A thought ungentle canna be
  The thought o' Mary Morison.

(1800)

SONG: MY NANIE, O

Behind yon hills where Lugar flows,
'Mang moors an' mosses many, O,
The wintry sun the day has clos'd,
An' I'll awa to Nanie, O.

The westlin wind blaws loud an' shill: 5
  The night's baith mirk an' rainy, O;
But I'll get my plaid an' out I'll steal,
  An' owre the hill to Nanie, O.

My Nanie's charming, sweet, an' young;
  Nae artfu' wiles to win ye, O: 10
May ill befa' the flattering tongue
  That wad beguile my Nanie, O.

Her face is fair, her heart is true,
  As spotless as she's bonie, O:
The op'ning gowan, wat wi' dew,   15
  Nae purer is than Nanie, O.

A country lad is my degree,
  An' few there be that ken me, O;
But what care I how few they be?
  I'm welcome aye to Nanie, O.   20

My riches a's my penny-fee,
  An' I maun guide it cannie, O;
But warl's gear ne'er troubles me,
  My thoughts are a' my Nanie, O.

Our auld guidman delights to view   25
  His sheep an' kye thrive bonie, O;
But I'm as blythe that hauds his pleugh,
  And has nae care but Nanie, O.

Come weel, come woe, I care na by,
  I'll tak what Heav'n will sen' me, O;   30
Nae ither care in life hae I,
  But live, an' love my Nanie, O.
                    (1787)

SONG: GREEN GROW THE RASHES

CHORUS.— Green grow the rashes, O!
  Green grow the rashes, O!
    The sweetest hours that e'er I spend
  Are spent amang the lasses, O.

There's nought but care on ev'ry han',   5
  In every hour that passes, O:
What signifies the life o' man,
  An 't were na for the lasses, O?

The war'ly race may riches chase,
  An' riches still may fly them, O;   10

An' tho' at last they catch them fast,
  Their hearts can ne'er enjoy them, O.

But gie me a cannie hour at e'en,
  My arms about my dearie, O;
An' war'ly cares, an' war'ly men,   15
  May a' gae tapsalteerie, O.

For you sae douce, ye sneer at this;
  Ye're nought but senseless asses, O:
The wisest man the warl' e'er saw,
  He dearly lov'd the lasses, O.   20

Auld Nature swears, the lovely dears
  Her noblest work she classes, O:
Her prentice han' she try'd on man,
  An' then she made the lasses, O.
                    (1803)

FROM LINES TO JOHN LAPRAIK

I am nae Poet, in a sense,
But just a Rhymer like by chance,
An' hae to learning nae pretence;
    Yet what the matter?
Whene'er my Muse does on me glance,   5
    I jingle at her.

Your critic-folk may cock their nose,
And say, 'How can you e'er propose,
You wha ken hardly verse frae prose,
    To mak a sang?'   10
But, by your leave, my learned foes,
    Ye're maybe wrang.

What's a' your jargon o' your schools,
Your Latin names for horns an' stools?
If honest nature made you fools,   15
    What sairs your grammars?
Ye'd better taen up spades and shools,
    Or knappin-hammers.

A set o' dull, conceited hashes
Confuse their brains in college classes!   20
They gang in stirks and come out asses,
    Plain truth to speak;
An' syne they think to climb Parnassus
    By dint o' Greek!

Gie me ae spark o' Nature's fire,   25
That's a' the learnin I desire;
Then, tho' I drudge thro' dub an' mire
    At pleugh or cart,
My Muse, though hamely in attire,
    May touch the heart.   30
                * *
                    (1786)

TO A MOUSE

ON TURNING UP HER NEST WITH THE PLOUGH,
NOVEMBER, 1785

Wee, sleekit, cowrin, tim'rous beastie,
Oh, what a panic's in thy breastie!
Thou need na start awa sae hasty
    Wi' bickerin brattle!
I wad be laith to rin an' chase thee   5
    Wi' murd'rin pattle!

I'm truly sorry man's dominion
Has broken nature's social union,
An' justifies that ill opinion
    Which makes thee startle   10
At me, thy poor earth-born companion,
    An' fellow-mortal!

I doubt na, whyles, but thou may thieve:
What then? poor beastie, thou maun live!
A daimen icker in a thrave   15
    'S a sma' request;
I'll get a blessin wi' the lave,
    An' never miss 't!

Thy wee bit housie, too, in ruin!
Its silly wa's the win's are strewin   20
An' naething, now, to big a new ane,
    O' foggage green!
An' bleak December's winds ensuin
    Baith snell an' keen!

Thou saw the fields laid bare and waste,   25
An' weary winter comin fast,
An' cozie here beneath the blast
    Thou thought to dwell,
Till crash! the cruel coulter past
    Out thro' thy cell.   30

That wee bit heap o' leaves an' stibble
Has cost thee mony a weary nibble!
Now thou's turn'd out for a' thy trouble,
    But house or hald,
To thole the winter's sleety dribble   35
    An' cranreuch cauld!

But, Mousie, thou art no thy lane
In proving foresight may be vain:
The best laid schemes o' mice an' men
    Gang aft a-gley,   40
An' lea'e us nought but grief an' pain
    For promis'd joy.

Still thou art blest, compar'd wi' me!
The present only toucheth thee:
But, och! I backward cast my ee   45
    On prospects drear!
An' forward, tho' I canna see,
    I guess an' fear!

            (1786)

THE COTTER'S SATURDAY NIGHT

INSCRIBED TO ROBERT AIKEN, ESQ.

Let not Ambition mock their useful toil,
    Their homely joys and destiny obscure;
Nor Grandeur hear with a disdainful smile,
    The short and simple annals of the poor,
            — GRAY.

My lov'd, my honored, much respected
    friend!
No mercenary bard his homage pays;
With honest pride, I scorn each selfish
    end:
    My dearest meed a friend's esteem and
        praise.
To you I sing, in simple Scottish lays,   5
The lowly train in life's sequester'd scene;
    The native feelings strong, the guileless
        ways;
What Aiken in a cottage would have been;
Ah! tho' his worth unknown, far happier
    there, I ween!

November chill blaws loud wi' angry sugh,
    The short'ning winter day is near a
        close;   11
The miry beasts retreating frae the pleugh,
    The black'ning trains o' craws to their
        repose;
    The toil-worn Cotter frae his labor
        goes,—
This night his weekly moil is at an end,—
    Collects his spades, his mattocks and his
        hoes,   16
Hoping the morn in ease and rest to
    spend,
And weary o'er the moor, his course does
    hameward bend.

At length his lonely cot appears in view,
    Beneath the shelter of an agèd tree;   20
Th' expectant wee-things, toddlin, stacher
    through
    To meet their dad, wi' flichterin noise
        an' glee.
His wee bit ingle, blinkin bonilie,
His clean hearth-stane, his thrifty wifie's
    smile,
    The lisping infant prattling on his knee,
Does a' his weary kiaugh and care be-
    guile,   26
An' makes him quite forget his labor an'
    his toil.

Belyve, the elder bairns come drappin in,
    At service out amang the farmers roun';
Some ca the pleugh, some herd, some
    tentie rin   30
    A cannie errand to a neibor toun:
Their eldest hope, their Jenny, woman-
    grown,

In youthfu' bloom, love sparkling in her ee,
  Comes hame, perhaps to shew a braw new
      gown,
Or deposite her sair-won penny-fee,   35
To help her parents dear, if they in hard-
      ship be.

With joy unfeign'd brothers and sisters
    meet,
  An' each for other's weelfare kindly
    spiers:
The social hours, swift-wing'd, unnotic'd
    fleet;
  Each tells the uncos that he sees or
    hears.   40
The parents, partial, eye their hopeful
    years;
Anticipation forward points the view;
  The mother, wi' her needle an' her
    sheers,
Gars auld claes look amaist as weel's the
    new;
The father mixes a' wi' admonition due. 45

Their master's an' their mistress's com-
    mand
The younkers a' are warnèd to obey;
An' mind their labors wi' an eydent hand,
  An' ne'er tho' out o' sight, to jauk or
    play:
  'An' O! be sure to fear the Lord
    alway,   50
An' mind your duty, duly, morn an' night!
  Lest in temptation's path ye gang
    astray,
Implore his counsel and assisting might:
They never sought in vain that sought the
    Lord aright!'

But hark! a rap comes gently to the door.
  Jenny, wha kens the meaning o' the
    same,   56
Tells how a neibor lad cam o'er the moor,
  To do some errands, and convoy her
    hame.
  The wily mother sees the conscious
    flame
Sparkle in Jenny's ee, and flush her
    cheek;   60
Wi' heart-struck, anxious care, inquires
    his name,
While Jenny hafflins is afraid to speak;
Weel pleas'd the mother hears it's nae wild
    worthless rake.

Wi' kindly welcome Jenny brings him ben,
  A strappin youth; he takes the mother's
    eye;   65

Blythe Jenny sees the visit's no ill taen;
  The father cracks of horses, pleughs,
    and kye.
The youngster's artless heart o'erflows
    wi' joy,
But, blate and laithfu', scarce can weel
    behave;
  The mother wi' a woman's wiles can
    spy   70
What maks the youth sae bashfu' an' sae
    grave,
Weel-pleas'd to think her bairn's respected
    like the lave.

O happy love! where love like this is
    found!
  O heart-felt raptures! bliss beyond com-
    pare!
I've pacèd much this weary, mortal
    round,   75
  And sage experience bids me this de-
    clare —
  'If Heaven a draught of heavenly pleas-
    ure spare,
One cordial in this melancholy vale,
  'T is when a youthful, loving, modest
    pair,
In other's arms breathe out the tender
    tale,   80
Beneath the milk-white thorn that scents
    the ev'ning gale.'

Is there, in human form, that bears a
    heart,
  A wretch! a villain! lost to love and
    truth!
That can with studied, sly, ensnaring art
  Betray sweet Jenny's unsuspecting
    youth?   85
  Curse on his perjur'd arts! dissembling
    smooth!
Are honor, virtue, conscience, all exil'd?
  Is there no pity, no relenting ruth,
Points to the parents fondling o'er their
    child,
Then paints the ruin'd maid, and their dis-
    traction wild?   90

But now the supper crowns their simple
    board,
  The halesome parritch, chief of Scotia's
    food;
The sowpe their only hawkie does afford,
  That yont the hallan' snugly chows her
    cud.
  The dame brings forth, in complimental
    mood,   95
To grace the lad, her weel-hain'd kebbuck
    fell,

And aft he's prest, an' aft he ca's it
  guid;
The frugal wifie, garrulous, will tell,
How 't was a towmond auld, sin' lint was i'
  the bell.

The cheerfu' supper done, wi' serious
  face,   100
They round the ingle form a circle wide;
The sire turns o'er with patriarchal grace
The big ha'-bible, ance his father's pride;
His bonnet rev'rently is laid aside,
His lyart haffets wearing thin and bare;
Those strains that once did sweet in
  Zion glide,   106
He wales a portion with judicious care;
And, 'Let us worship God,' he says with
  solemn air.

They chant their artless notes in simple
  guise;
They tune their hearts, by far the noblest
  aim: 110
Perhaps *Dundee's* wild-warbling measures
  rise,
Or plaintive *Martyrs,* worthy of the
  name,
Or noble *Elgin* beats the heaven-ward
  flame,
The sweetest far of Scotia's holy lays.
Compar'd with these, Italian trills are
  tame;   115
The tickl'd ear no heart-felt raptures
  raise;
Nae unison hae they with our Creator's
  praise.

The priest-like father reads the sacred
  page,—
How Abram was the friend of God on
  high;
Or Moses bade eternal warfare wage 120
With Amalek's ungracious progeny;
Or how the royal bard did groaning lie
Beneath the stroke of heaven's avenging
  ire;
Or Job's pathetic plaint, and wailing
  cry;
Or rapt Isaiah's wild, seraphic fire; 125
Or other holy seers that tune the sacred lyre.

Perhaps the Christian volume is the
  theme,—
How guiltless blood for guilty man was
  shed;
How he, who bore in heav'n the second
  name,
Had not on earth whereon to lay his
  head: 130

How his first followers and servants
  sped;
The precepts sage they wrote to many a
  land
How he, who lone in Patmos banishèd,
Saw in the sun a mighty angel stand,
And heard great Bab'lon's doom pronounced
  by Heav'n's command.   135

Then kneeling down to Heaven's Eternal
  King,
The saint, the father, and the husband
  prays:
Hope 'springs exulting on triumphant
  wing,'
That thus they all shall meet in future
  days:
There ever bask in uncreated rays, 140
No more to sigh or shed the bitter tear,
Together hymning their Creator's praise,
In such society, yet still more dear,
While circling Time moves round in an
  eternal sphere.

Compar'd with this, how poor Religion's
  pride   145
In all the pomp of method and of art,
When men display to congregations wide
Devotion's ev'ry grace except the heart!
The Pow'r, incens'd, the pageant will
  desert,
The pompous strain, the sacerdotal stole;
But haply in some cottage far apart 151
May hear, well pleased, the language of
  the soul,
And in his book of life the inmates poor
  enrol.

Then homeward all take off their sev'ral
  way;
The youngling cottagers retire to rest;
The parent-pair their secret homage pay,
And proffer up to Heav'n the warm re-
  quest,   157
That he, who stills the raven's clam'rous
  nest
And decks the lily fair in flow'ry pride,
Would, in the way his wisdom sees the
  best,   160
For them and for their little ones pro-
  vide;
But chiefly, in their hearts with grace divine
  preside.

From scenes like these old Scotia's grandeur springs,
That makes her lov'd at home, rever'd
  abroad:

Princes and lords are but the breath of
    kings,   165
  'An honest man's the noblest work of
    God':
And certes, in fair Virtue's heavenly
    road,
The cottage leaves the palace far be-
    hind:
  What is a lordling's pomp? a cumbrous
    load,
Disguising oft the wretch of human kind,
Studied in arts of hell, in wickedness re-
    fin'd!   171

O Scotia! my dear, my native soil!
  For whom my warmest wish to Heaven
    is sent!
Long may thy hardy sons of rustic toil
  Be blest with health, and peace, and
    sweet content!   175
  And, oh! may Heaven their simple lives
    prevent
From luxury's contagion, weak and vile!
  Then, howe'er crowns and coronets be
    rent,
A virtuous populace may rise the while,
And stand a wall of fire around their much-
    lov'd isle.   180

O thou! who pour'd the patriotic tide
  That stream'd thro' Wallace's undaunted
    heart,
Who dar'd to nobly stem tyrannic pride,
  Or nobly die, the second glorious
    part,—
(The patriot's God peculiarly thou art,
  His friend, inspirer, guardian, and re-
    ward!)   186
  O never, never Scotia's realm desert,
But still the patriot, and the patriot-bard,
In bright succession raise, her ornament and
    guard!

(1786)

ADDRESS TO THE DEIL

O thou! whatever title suit thee,—
Auld Hornie, Satan, Nick, or Clootie!
Wha in yon cavern, grim an' sootie,
    Clos'd under hatches,
Spairges about the brunstane cootie   5
    To scaud poor wretches!

Hear me, auld Hangie, for a wee,
An' let poor damnèd bodies be;
I'm sure sma' pleasure it can gie,
    E'en to a deil.   10

To skelp an' scaud poor dogs like me,
    An' hear us squeel!

Great is thy pow'r, an' great thy fame;
Far ken'd an' noted is thy name;
An tho' yon lowin heugh's thy hame,   15
    Thou travels far;
An' faith! thou's neither lag nor lame,
    Nor blate nor scaur.

Whyles, rangin like a roarin lion,
For prey a' holes an' corners tryin;   20
Whyles, on the strong-wing'd tempest flyin,
    Tirlin' the kirks;
Whyles, in the human bosom pryin,
    Unseen thou lurks.

I've heard my rev'rend grannie say,   25
In lanely glens ye like to stray;
Or whare auld ruin'd castles gray
    Nod to the moon,
Ye fright the nightly wand'rer's way
    Wi' eldritch croon.   30

When twilight did my grannie summon
To say her pray'rs, douce honest woman!
Aft yont the dike she's heard you bummin,
    Wi eerie drone;
Or, rustlin, thro' the boortrees comin,   35
    Wi' heavy groan.

Ae dreary, windy, winter night,
The stars shot down wi' sklentin light,
Wi' you mysel I gat a fright
    Ayont the lough;   40
Ye like a rash-buss stood in sight
    Wi' waving sough.

The cudgel in my nieve did shake,
Each bristl'd hair stood like a stake,
When wi' an eldritch, stoor 'Quaick, quaick,'
    Amang the springs,   46
Awa ye squatter'd like a drake,
    On whistlin wings.

Let warlocks grim an' wither'd hags
Tell how wi' you on ragweed nags   50
They skim the muirs an' dizzy crags
    Wi' wicked speed;
And in kirk-yards renew their leagues,
    Owre howket dead.

Thence, countra wives wi' toil an' pain   55
May plunge an' plunge the kirn in vain;
For oh! the yellow treasure's taen
    By witchin skill;
An' dawtet, twal-pint hawkie's gaen
    As yell's the bill.   60

Thence, mystic knots mak great abuse,
On young guidmen, fond, keen, an' crouse;
When the best wark-lume i' the house,
    By cantrip wit,
Is instant made no worth a louse,   65
    Just at the bit.

When thowes dissolve the snawy hoord,
An' float the jinglin icy-boord
Then water-kelpies haunt the foord
    By your direction,   70
An' nighted trav'lers are allur'd
    To their destruction.

And aft your moss-traversing spunkies
Decoy the wight that late and drunk is:
The bleezin, curst, mischievous monkeys 75
    Delude his eyes,
Till in some miry slough he sunk is,
    Ne'er mair to rise.

When masons' mystic word and grip
In storms an' tempests raise you up,   80
Some cock or cat your rage maun stop,
    Or, strange to tell,
The youngest brither ye wad whip
    Aff straught to hell!

Lang syne, in Eden's bonie yard,   85
When youthfu' lovers first were pair'd,
And all the soul of love they shar'd,
    The raptur'd hour,
Sweet on the fragrant flow'ry swaird,
    In shady bow'r;   90

Then you, ye auld sneck-drawin dog!
Ye cam to Paradise incog,
And play'd on man a cursed brogue,
    (Black be your fa'!)
And gied the infant warld a shog,   95
    Maist ruin'd a'.

D'ye mind that day, when in a bizz,
Wi' reeket duds and reestet gizz,
Ye did present your smoutie phiz
    Mang better folk,   100
An' sklented on the man of Uz
    Your spitefu' joke?

An' how ye gat him i' your thrall,
An' brak' him out o' house and hal',
While scabs and blotches did him gall, 105
    Wi' bitter claw,
An' lows'd his ill-tongued, wicked scaul,
    Was warst ava?

But a' your doings to rehearse,
Your wily snares an' fechtin fierce, 110

Sin' that day Michael did you pierce,
    Down to this time,
Wad ding a Lallan tongue, or Erse,
    In prose or rhyme.

An' now, auld Cloots, I ken ye're thinkin,
A certain Bardie's rantin, drinkin,   116
Some luckless hour will send him linkin,
    To your black pit;
But faith! he'll turn a corner jinkin,
    An' cheat you yet.   120

But fare you weel, auld Nickie-ben!
O wad ye tak a thought an' men'!
Ye aiblins might — I dinna ken —
    Still hae a stake:
I'm wae to think upo' yon den,   125
    Ev'n for your sake!
                            (1786)

A BARD'S EPITAPH

Is there a whim-inspirèd fool,
Owre fast for thought, owre hot for rule,
Owre blate to seek, owre proud to snool?
    Let him draw near;
And owre this grassy heap sing dool,   5
    And drap a tear.

Is there a bard of rustic song,
Who, noteless, steals the crowds among,
That weekly this area throng? —
    Oh, pass not by!   10
But with a frater-feeling strong
    Here heave a sigh.

Is there a man whose judgment clear
Can others teach the course to steer,
Yet runs himself life's mad career   15
    Wild as the wave? —
Here pause — and thro' the starting tear
    Survey this grave.

The poor inhabitant below
Was quick to learn and wise to know,   20
And keenly felt the friendly glow
    And softer flame;
But thoughtless follies laid him low,
    And stain'd his name!

Reader, attend! whether thy soul   25
Soars fancy's flights beyond the pole,
Or darkling grubs this earthly hole
    In low pursuit;
Know, prudent, cautious self-control
    Is wisdom's root.   30
                            (1786)

But to our tale: — Ae market night,
Tam had got planted unco right,
Fast by an ingle, bleezin finely,
Wi' reamin swats that drank divinely; 40
And at his elbow, Souter Johnie,
His ancient, trusty, drouthy crony:
Tam lo'ed him like a vera brither;
They had been fou for weeks thegither.
The night drave on wi' sangs and clatter;
And ay the ale was growing better: 46
The landlady and Tam grew gracious
Wi' secret favors, sweet, and precious:
The souter tauld his queerest stories;
The landlord's laugh was ready chorus: 50
The storm without might rair and rustle
Tam did na mind the storm a whistle.

Care, mad to see a man sae happy,
E'en drown'd himsel amang the nappy:
As bees flee hame wi' lades o' treasure, 55
The minutes wing'd their way wi' pleasure;
Kings may be blest, but Tam was glorious,
O'er a' the ills o' life victorious!

But pleasures are like poppies spread,
You seize the flow'r, its bloom is shed; 60
Or like the snow falls in the river,
A moment white — then melts forever;
Or like the borealis race.
That flit ere you can point their place;
Or like the rainbow's lovely form 65
Evanishing amid the storm.
Nae man can tether time or tide:
The hour approaches Tam maun ride,—
That hour, o' night's black arch the key-
      stane,
That dreary hour he mounts his beast in; 70
And sic a night he taks the road in,
As ne'er poor sinner was abroad in.

The wind blew as 't wad blawn its last;
The rattling show'rs rose on the blast; 74
The speedy gleams the darkness swallow'd;
Loud, deep, and lang the thunder bellow'd:
That night, a child might understand,
The Deil had business on his hand.

Weel mounted on his grey mear, Meg,—
A better never lifted leg,— 80
Tam skelpit on thro' dub and mire,
Despising wind and rain and fire;
Whiles holding fast his guid blue bonnet,
Whiles crooning o'er some auld Scots son-
      net,
Whiles glowrin round wi' prudent cares, 85
Lest bogies catch him unawares.
Kirk-Alloway was drawing nigh,
Whare ghaists and houlets nightly cry.

By this time he was cross the ford,
Whare in the snaw the chapman smoor'd;
And past the birks and meikle stane, 91
Whare drucken Charlie brak 's neck-bane;
And thro' the whins, and by the cairn,
Whare hunters fand the murder'd bairn;
And near the thorn, aboon the well, 95
Whare Mungo's mither hang'd hersel.
Before him Doon pours all his floods;
The doubling storm roars thro' the woods;
The lightnings flash from pole to pole,
Near and more near the thunders roll; 100
When, glimmering thro' the groaning trees,
Kirk-Alloway seemed in a bleeze:
Thro' ilka bore the beams were glancing,
And loud resounded mirth and dancing.

Inspiring bold John Barleycorn! 105
What dangers thou can'st make us scorn!
Wi' tippenny we fear nae evil;
Wi' usquebae we 'll face the devil!
The swats sae ream'd in Tammie's noddle,
Fair play, he car'd na deils a boddle. 110
But Maggie stood right sair astonish'd,
Till, by the heel and hand admonish'd,
She ventur'd forward on the light;
And, wow! Tam saw an unco sight!

Warlocks and witches in a dance; 115
Nae cotillon brent-new frae France,
But hornpipes, jigs, strathspeys, and reels
Put life and mettle in their heels:
A winnock bunker in the east,
There sat Auld Nick in shape o' beast; 120
A towzie tyke, black, grim, and large,
To gie them music was his charge;
He screw'd the pipes and gart them skirl,
Till roof and rafters a' did dirl.—
Coffins stood round like open presses, 125
That shaw'd the dead in their last dresses;
And by some devilish cantraip sleight
Each in its cauld hand held a light,
By which heroic Tam was able
To note upon the haly table 130
A murderer's banes in gibbet airns;
Twa span-lang, wee, unchristen'd bairns;
A thief, new-cutted frae the rape —
Wi' his last gasp his gab did gape;
Five tomahawks, wi' blude red-rusted; 135
Five scymitars, wi' murder crusted;
A garter, which a babe had strangled;
A knife, a father's throat had mangled;
Whom his ain son o' life bereft —
The grey hairs yet stack to the heft; 140
Wi' mair o' horrible and awfu',
Which ev'n to name wad be unlawfu'.

As Tammie glowr'd, amaz'd and curious,
The mirth and fun grew fast and furious;

The piper loud and louder blew,   145
The dancers quick and quicker flew;
They reel'd, they set, they cross'd, they
          cleekit,
Till ilka carlin swat and reekit
And coost her duddies to the wark
And linket at it in her sark!   150

Now Tam, O Tam! had thae been queans,
A' plump and strapping in their teens!
Their sarks, instead o' creeshie flannen,
Been snaw-white seventeen hunder linen!—
Thir breeks o' mine, my only pair,   155
That ance were plush, o' gude blue hair,
I wad hae gien them aff my hurdies,
For ae blink o' the bonie burdies!

* * *

But Tam ken'd what was what fu'
          brawlie;
There was ae winsom wench and walie, 160
That night enlisted in the core
(Lang after ken'd on Carrick shore:
For mony a beast to dead she shot,
And perish'd mony a bonie boat,
And shook baith meikle corn and bear, 165
And kept the country-side in fear);
Her cutty sark o' Paisley harn,
That while a lassie she had worn,
In longitude tho' sorely scanty,
It was her best, and she was vauntie.   170
Ah! little kent thy reverend grannie,
That sark she coft for her wee Nannie,
Wi' twa pund Scots ('t was a' her riches),
Wad ever graced a dance o' witches!

But here my Muse her wing maun cow'r,
Sic flights are far beyond her pow'r;   176
To sing how Nannie lap and flang,
(A souple jad she was and strang,)
And how Tam stood like ane bewitch'd,
And thought his very een enrich'd;   180
Even Satan glowr'd and fidg'd fu' fain,
And hotch'd and blew wi' might and main:
Till first ae caper, syne anither,
Tam tint his reason a' thegither,
And roars out, 'Weel done, Cutty-sark!' 185
And in an instant all was dark:
And scarcely had he Maggie rallied,
When out the hellish legion sallied.
  As bees bizz out wi' angry fyke,
When plundering herds assail their byke;
As open pussie's mortal foes,   191
When pop! she starts before their nose;
As eager runs the market-crowd,
When 'Catch the thief!' resounds aloud;
So Maggie runs, the witches follow,   195
Wi' mony an eldritch skriech and hollo.

Ah, Tam! ah, Tam! thou 'll get thy fairin!
In hell they 'll roast thee like a herrin!
In vain thy Kate awaits thy comin!
Kate soon will be a woefu' woman!   200
Now, do thy speedy utmost, Meg,
And win the key-stane of the brig:
There at them thou thy tail may toss,
A running stream they dare na cross.
But ere the key-stane she could make,   205
The fient a tail she had to shake!
For Nannie, far before the rest,
Hard upon noble Maggie prest,
And flew at Tam wi' furious ettle;
But little wist she Maggie's mettle—   210
Ae spring brought aff her master hale,
But left behind her ain grey tail.

* * *   (1793)

WILLIE BREWED A PECK O' MAUT

O, Willie brew'd a peck o' maut,   1
An' Rob an' Allan cam to see:
Three blyther hearts that lee-lang night
Ye wad na found in Christendie.

CHORUS.— We are na fou, we 're nae
          that fou,   5
But just a drappie in our ee;
The cock may craw, the day may daw,
And aye we 'll taste the barley bree.

Here are we met, three merry boys,
Three merry boys, I trow, are we;   10
An' mony a night we 've merry been,
And mony mae we hope to be!

It is the moon, I ken her horn,
That 's blinkin in the lift sae hie;
She shines sae bright to wile us hame,   15
But, by my sooth, she 'll wait a wee!

Wha first shall rise to gang awa',
A cuckold, coward loon is he!
Wha first beside his chair shall fa',
He is the king amang us three!   20
                          (1790)

A WINTER NIGHT

Poor naked wretches, wheresoe'er you are,
That bide the pelting of this pitiless storm!
How shall your houseless heads and unfed sides,
Your looped and windowed raggedness, defend you
From seasons such as these?
                          — SHAKSPERE.

When biting Boreas, fell and doure,
Sharp shivers thro' the leafless bow'r;

When Phoebus gies a short lived glow'r
 Far south the lift,
Dim-darkening thro' the flaky show'r 5
 Or whirling drift;

Ae night the storm the steeples rocked,
Poor Labor sweet in sleep was locked,
While burns, wi' snawy wreaths up-choked,
 Wild-eddying swirl, 10
Or, thro' the mining outlet bocked,
 Down headlong hurl:

Listening the doors and winnocks rattle,
I thought me on the ourie cattle,
Or silly sheep, wha bide this brattle 15
 O' winter war,
An' through the drift, deep-lairing, sprattle
 Beneath a scaur.

Ilk happin bird — wee, helpless thing!—
That in the merry months o' spring 20
Delighted me to hear thee sing,
 What comes o' thee?
Whare wilt thou cow'r thy chittering wing
 An' close thy ee?

Ev'n you on murd'ring errands toil'd, 25
Lone from your savage homes exil'd,—
The blood-stain'd roost an' sheep-cot spoil'd
 My heart forgets.
While pitiless the tempest wild
 Sore on you beats. 30
   * . * *

     (1787)

HIGHLAND MARY

Ye banks, and braes, and streams around
 The castle o' Montgomery,
Green be your woods and fair your flowers,
 Your waters never drumlie!
There simmer first unfauld her robes, 5
 And there the langest tarry;
For there I took the last fareweel,
 O' my sweet Highland Mary.

How sweetly bloom'd the gay green birk,
 How rich the hawthorn's blossom, 10
As underneath their fragrant shade
 I clasp'd her to my bosom!
The golden hours, on angel wings,
 Flew o'er me and my dearie;
For dear to me as light and life, 15
 Was my sweet Highland Mary.

Wi' monie a vow and lock'd embrace
 Our parting was fu' tender;
And, pledging aft to meet again,
 We tore oursels asunder; 20

But O! fell death's untimely frost,
 That nipt my flower sae early!
Now green's the sod, and cauld's the clay,
 That wraps my Highland Mary!

O, pale, pale now, those rosy lips, 23
 I aft hae kiss'd sae fondly!
And closed for aye the sparkling glance,
 That dwelt on me sae kindly!
And mould'ring now in silent dust,
 That heart that lo'ed me dearly! 30
But still within my bosom's core
 Shall live my Highland Mary.

     (1799)

BONIE DOON

Ye flowery banks o' bonie Doon,
 How can ye blume sae fair?
How can ye chant, ye little birds,
 And I sae fu' o' care?

Thou'll break my heart, thou bonie bird, 5
 That sings upon the bough;
Thou minds me o' the happy days,
 When my fause luve was true.

Thou'll break my heart, thou bonie bird,
 That sings beside thy mate; 10
For sae I sat, and sae I sang,
 And wist na o' my fate.

Aft hae I rov'd by bonie Doon
 To see the wood-bine twine,
And ilka bird sang o' its luve, 15
 And sae did I o' mine.

Wi' lightsome heart I pu'd a rose
 Frae aff its thorny tree;
And my fause luver staw my rose
 But left the thorn wi' me. 20

     (1808)

DUNCAN GRAY

Duncan Gray came here to woo,
 Ha, ha, the wooin o't!
On blythe Yule night when we were fou,
 Ha, ha, the wooin o't!
Maggie coost her head fu' hiegh, 5
Look'd asklent and unco skiegh,
Gart poor Duncan stand abiegh;
 Ha, ha, the wooin o't!

Duncan fleech'd, and Duncan pray'd;
 Ha, ha, the wooin o't! 10
Meg was deaf as Ailsa Craig,
 Ha, ha, the wooin o't!

Duncan sigh'd baith out and in,
Grat his een baith bleer't and blin'.
Spak o' lowpin owre a linn;   15
    Ha, ha, the wooin o't!

Time and chance are but a tide,
    Ha, ha, the wooin o't!
Slighted love is sair to bide,
    Ha, ha, the wooin o't!   20
'Shall I, like a fool,' quoth he,
'For a haughty hizzie die?
She may gae to — France for me!'
    Ha, ha, the wooin o't!

How it comes let doctors tell,   25
    Ha, ha, the wooin o't!
Meg grew sick as he grew hale,
    Ha, ha, the wooin o't!
Something in her bosom wrings,
For relief a sigh she brings;   30
And O! her een, they spak sic things!
    Ha, ha, the wooin o't!

Duncan was a lad o' grace,
    Ha, ha, the wooin o't!
Maggie's was a piteous case,   35
    Ha, ha, the wooin o't!
Duncan could na be her death,
Swelling pity smoor'd his wrath;
Now they're crouse and cantie baith;
    Ha, ha, the wooin o't!   40
            (1798)

SCOTS WHA HAE

Scots, wha hae wi' Wallace bled,
Scots, wham Bruce has aften led;
Welcome to your gory bed,
    Or to victory!
Now's the day, and now's the hour;   5
See the front o' battle lour;
See approach proud Edward's power —
    Chains and slavery!

Wha will be a traitor knave?
Wha can fill a coward's grave?   10
Wha sae base as be a slave?
    Let him turn and flee!
Wha for Scotland's king and law
Freedom's sword will strongly draw,
Freeman stand, or Freeman fa',   15
    Let him follow me!

By oppression's woes and pains
By your sons in servile chains!

We will drain our dearest veins,
    But they shall be free!   20
Lay the proud usurpers low!
Tyrants fall in every foe!
Liberty's in every blow! —
    Let us do or die!
            (1794)

A MAN'S A MAN FOR A' THAT

Is there, for honest poverty,
    That hings his head, an' a' that?
The coward slave, we pass him by,
    We dare be poor for a' that!
      For a' that, an' a' that,   5
      Our toils obscure, an' a' that;
      The rank is but the guinea's stamp;
      The man's the gowd for a' that.

What tho' on hamely fare we dine,
    Wear hodden-gray, an' a' that;   10
Gie fools their silks, and knaves their wine,
    A man's a man for a' that.
      For a' that, an' a' that,
      Their tinsel show, an' a' that;
      The honest man, tho' e'er sae poor, 15
      Is king o' men for a' that.

Ye see yon birkie, ca'd a lord,
    Wha struts, an' stares, an' a' that;
Tho' hundreds worship at his word,
    He's but a coof for a' that.   20
      For a' that, an' a' that,
      His riband, star, an' a' that,
      The man o' independent mind,
      He looks and laughs at a' that.

A prince can mak a belted knight,   25
    A marquis, duke, an' a' that;
But an honest man's aboon his might,
    Guid faith he mauna fa' that!
      For a' that, an' a' that,
      Their dignities, an' a' that,   30
      The pith o' sense, an' pride o' worth,
      Are higher rank than a' that.

Then let us pray that come it may,
    As come it will for a' that,
That sense and worth, o'er a' the earth,   35
    May bear the gree, an' a' that.
      For a' that, an' a' that,
      It's coming yet, for a' that,
      That man to man, the warld o'er,
      Shall brothers be for a' that.   40
            (1800)

WILLIAM WORDSWORTH (1770-1850)

Wordsworth was born at Cockermouth in Cumberland, and educated at Hawkshead Grammar School between Esthwaite Water and Windermere in the Lake District, with which his whole life was closely connected. At St. John's College, Cambridge, according to his own account, he was neither among the 'loyal students faithful to their books,' nor among the 'honest dunces,' but one of the 'half-and-half idlers' who 'read lazily in trivial books,' amused themselves with athletic sports, 'and let the stars Come forth, perhaps, without one quiet thought.' In recollection, Wordsworth probably exaggerated his youthful idleness, for he read extensively, in both classical and modern languages, but he 'was not for that hour, nor for that place,' and he undoubtedly profited more, intellectually and spiritually, by his vacations in the Lake District and in France. He became a warm sympathizer with the French revolutionary movement, which deeply stirred his imagination. The declaration of war between France and England and the Reign of Terror in France cast him into deep melancholy, but he clung to his revolutionary principles until the Napoleonic despotism finally threw him back into agreement with his conservative fellow-countrymen.

In this spiritual crisis Wordsworth owed much to the companionship of his sister Dorothy, with whom he decided to retire from the world and devote himself to 'plain living and high thinking.' A legacy of £900 from a young admirer (Raisley Calvert) enabled the Wordsworths, who were living in the Lake District on milk and potatoes, to carry out this resolution, and in 1795 they took a cottage at Racedown, in Worcestershire, where they were visited by Coleridge. In the autumn of 1797 the three friends took a long walk together in the Quantock Hills; and to pay the expenses of the excursion, the young men planned a small volume of poetry, which was published the following year by an obscure Bristol printer under the title of *Lyrical Ballads*. Containing Coleridge's *Ancient Mariner* and *Wordsworth's Lines written above Tintern Abbey*, it marked very distinctly the two new streams of influence which were to enrich English poetry throughout the nineteenth century, and it has come to be regarded as one of the most important events in the history of literature, although at the time it attracted little attention. In the same year (1798) the Wordsworths and Coleridge sailed for Germany, where the latter plunged deep into the study of German literature and philosophy, while Wordsworth began the composition of *The Prelude*, an account of his own poetical and spiritual development, which was finished in 1805, although withheld from publication until after his death.

In 1799 Wordsworth and his sister settled permanently in the Lake District, their home for the next nine years being Dove Cottage, Grasmere. In 1800 the payment of a long deferred debt to the family enabled Wordsworth to marry a lifelong friend, Mary Hutchison, sung by him in 'She was a phantom of delight' and other poems. In 1813 he was given a government sinecure as distributor of stamps, which brought him in £400 a year, and he was able to remove to a larger house at Rydal Mount, where he stayed until his death. Most of his work now recognized as of the highest excellence was published by 1807, though his longest poem, *The Excursion*, appeared in 1814; *The White Doe of Rylstone* and *Laodamia* in 1815; *The Waggoner* and *Peter Bell* in 1819; the fine series of sonnets, *The River Duddon*, in 1820; and a less successful sequence, *Ecclesiastical Sketches*, in 1822. On the death of Southey in 1843, he was appointed Poet Laureate, and was in turn succeeded by Tennyson, who received 'the laurel greener from the brow, Of him who uttered nothing base.'

Wordsworth's most obvious service to English poetry was to free it from the bondage of the artificial diction which the school of Pope received as a tradition and hardened into a convention. Subsequent ages owe him a greater debt for opening their minds to truer and deeper relations with Nature, and their hearts to sympathy with simple things and simple people. But his greatest gift was neither a theory of diction nor a system of philosophy, but the union of high imaginative powers with a rare faculty of expression, which enabled him to enrich English poetry with priceless treasures. Matthew Arnold's conviction that 'the poetical performance of Wordsworth is after that of Shakspere and Milton . . . undoubtedly the most considerable in our language from the Elizabethan age to the present time' has been confirmed by the judgment of later critics.

PREFACE TO LATER ISSUES
OF 'LYRICAL BALLADS'

The first volume of these poems has already been submitted to general perusal. It was published as an experiment, which, I hoped, might be of some use to ascertain, how far, by fitting to metrical arrangement a selection of the real language of men in a state of vivid sensation, that sort of pleasure and that quantity of pleasure may be imparted, which a poet may rationally endeavor to impart.

I had formed no very inaccurate estimate of the probable effect of those poems: I flattered myself that they who should be pleased with them would read them with more than common pleasure; and, on the other hand, I was well aware, that by those who should dislike them, they would be read with more than common dislike. The result has differed from my expectation in this only, that a greater number have been pleased than I ventured to hope I should please.

Several of my friends are anxious for the success of these poems from a belief, that, if the views with which they were composed were indeed realized, a class of poetry would be produced well adapted to interest mankind permanently, and not unimportant in the quality and in the multiplicity of its moral relations: and on this account they have advised me to add a systematic defense of the theory upon which the poems were written. But I was unwilling to undertake the task, because I knew that on this occasion the reader would look coldly upon my arguments, since I might be suspected of having been principally influenced by the selfish and foolish hope of *reasoning* him into an approbation of these particular poems: and I was still more unwilling to undertake the task, because, adequately to display my opinions, and fully to enforce my arguments, would require a space wholly disproportionate to a preface. For to treat the subject with the clearness and coherence of which it is susceptible, it would be necessary to give a full account of the present state of the public taste in this country, and to determine how far this taste is healthy or depraved; which, again, could not be determined, without pointing out, in what manner language and the human mind act and react on each other, and without retracing the revolutions, not of literature alone, but likewise of society itself. I have therefore altogether declined to enter regularly upon this defense; yet I am sensible, that there would be some impropriety in abruptly obtruding upon the public, without a few words of introduction, poems so materially different from those upon which general approbation is at present bestowed.

It is supposed, that by the act of writing in verse an author makes a formal engagement that he will gratify certain known habits of association; that he not only thus apprises the reader that certain classes of ideas and expressions will be found in his book, but that others will be carefully excluded. This exponent or symbol held forth by metrical language must in different eras of literature have excited very different expectations: for example, in the age of Catullus, Terence, and Lucretius, and that of Statius or Claudian; and in our own country, in the age of Shakspere and Beaumont and Fletcher, and that of Donne and Cowley, or Dryden, or Pope. I will not take upon me to determine the exact import of the promise which by the act of writing in verse an author, in the present day, makes to his reader; but it will undoubtedly appear to many persons that I have not fulfilled the terms of an engagement thus voluntarily contracted. They who have been accustomed to the gaudiness and inane phraseology of many modern writers, if they persist in reading this book to its conclusion, will, no doubt, frequently have to struggle with feelings of strangeness and awkwardness: they will look round for poetry, and will be induced to inquire by what species of courtesy these attempts can be permitted to assume that title. I hope therefore the reader will not censure me, for attempting to state what I have proposed to myself to perform; and also (as far as the limits of a preface will permit) to explain some of the chief reasons which have determined me in the choice of my purpose: that at least he may be spared any unpleasant feeling of disappointment, and that I myself may be protected from one of the most dishonorable accusations which can be brought against an author, namely, that of an indolence which prevents him from endeavoring to ascertain what is his duty, or, when his duty is ascertained, prevents him from performing it.

The principal object, then, proposed in these poems was to choose incidents and situations from common life, and to relate or describe them, throughout, as far as was possible, in a selection of language really used by men, and, at the same time, to throw over them a certain coloring of imagination, whereby ordinary things should be presented to the mind in an unusual aspect, and, further, and above all, to make these incidents and situations interesting by tracing in them, truly though not ostentatiously, the primary laws of our nature: chiefly, as far as regards the manner in which we associate ideas in a state of excitement. Humble and rustic life was generally chosen, because, in that condition, the essential passions of the heart find a better soil in which they can attain their maturity, are less under restraint, and speak a plainer and more emphatic language; because in that condition of life our elementary feelings co-exist in a state of greater simplicity, and, consequently, may be more accurately contemplated, and more forcibly communicated; because the manners of rural life germinate from those elementary feelings; and from the necessary character of rural occupations, are more easily comprehended, and are more durable; and, lastly, because in that condition the passions of men are incorporated with the beautiful and permanent forms of nature. The language, too, of these men is adopted (purified indeed from what appears to be its real defects, from all lasting and rational causes of dislike or disgust) because such men hourly communicate with the best objects from which the best part of language is originally derived; and because, from their rank in society and the sameness and narrow circle of their intercourse, being less under the influence of social vanity, they convey their feelings and notions in simple and unelaborated expressions. Accordingly such a language, arising out of repeated experience and regular feelings, is a more permanent, and a far more philosophical language, than that which is frequently substituted for it by poets, who think that they are conferring honor upon themselves and their art, in proportion as they separate themselves from the sympathies of men, and indulge in arbitrary and capricious habits of expression, in order to furnish food for fickle tastes, and fickle appetites, of their own creation.

I cannot, however, be insensible to the present outcry against the triviality and meanness, both of thought and language, which some of my contemporaries have occasionally introduced into their metrical compositions; and I acknowledge that this defect, where it exists, is more dishonorable to the writer's own character than false refinement or arbitrary innovation, though I should contend at the same time, that it is far less pernicious in the sum of its consequences. From such verses the poems in these volumes will be found distinguished at least by one mark of difference, that each of them has a worthy *purpose*. Not that I always began to write with a distinct purpose formally conceived; but habits of meditation have, I trust, so prompted and regulated my feelings, as that my descriptions of such objects as strongly excite those feelings, will be found to carry along with them a *purpose*. If this opinion is erroneous, I can have little right to the name of a poet. [For all good poetry is the spontaneous overflow of powerful feelings] and though this be true, poems to which any value can be attached were never produced on any variety of subjects but by a man, who, being possessed of more than usual organic sensibility, had also thought long and deeply. For our continued influxes of feeling are modified and directed by our thoughts, which are indeed the representatives of all our past feelings; and, as by contemplating the relation of these general representatives to each other, we discover what is really important to men, so, by the repetition and continuance of this act, our feelings will be connected with important subjects, till at length, if we be originally possessed of much sensibility, such habits of mind will be produced, that, by obeying blindly and mechanically the impulses of those habits, we shall describe objects, and utter senti-ments, of such a nature, and in such connection with each other, that the un-derstanding of the reader must necessarily be in some degree enlightened, and his affections strengthened and purified.

I have said that each of these poems has a purpose. But it is proper that I should mention one other circumstance which distinguishes these poems from the popular poetry of the day; it is this, that the feeling therein developed gives im-portance to the action and situation, and not the action and situation to the feel-ing. My meaning will be rendered per-fectly intelligible by referring my reader to the poems entitled *Poor Susan* and the *Childless Father,* particularly to the last stanza of the latter poem.

I will not suffer a sense of false modesty to prevent me from asserting, that I point my reader's attention to this mark of distinction, far less for the sake of these particular poems than from the general importance of the subject. The subject is indeed important! For the human mind is capable of being excited without the application of gross and vio-lent stimulants; and he must have a very faint perception of its beauty and dignity who does not know this, and who does not further know, that one being is elevated above another, in proportion as he possesses this capability. It has there-fore appeared to me, that to endeavor to produce or enlarge this capability is one of the best services in which, at any period, a writer can be engaged; but this service, excellent at all times, is espe-cially so at the present day. For a multitude of causes, unknown to former times, are now acting with a combined force to blunt the discriminating powers of the mind, and unfitting it for all voluntary exertion, to reduce it to a state of almost savage torpor. The most ef-fective of these causes are the great national events which are daily taking place, and the increasing accumulation of men in cities, where the uniformity of their occupations produces a craving for extraordinary incident, which the rapid communication of intelligence hourly gratifies. To this tendency of life and manners the literature and theatrical exhibitions of the country have conformed themselves. The invaluable works of our elder writers, I had almost said the works of Shakspere and Milton, are driven into neglect by frantic novels, sickly and stupid German tragedies, and deluges of idle and extravagant stories in verse.— When I think upon this degrading thirst after outrageous stimulation, I am almost ashamed to have spoken of the feeble endeavor made in these volumes to coun-teract it; and, reflecting upon the mag-nitude of the general evil, I should be oppressed with no dishonorable melan-choly, had I not a deep impression of certain inherent and indestructible quali-ties of the human mind, and likewise of certain powers in the great and perma-nent objects that act upon it, which are equally inherent and indestructible; and did I not further add to this impression a belief, that the time is approaching when the evil will be systematically op-posed, by men of greater powers, and with far more distinguished success.

Having dwelt thus long on the subjects and aim of these poems, I shall request the reader's permission to apprise him of a few circumstances relating to their *style,* in order, among other reasons, that I may not be censured for not having performed what I never attempted. The reader will find that personifications of abstract ideas rarely occur in these volumes; and, I hope, are utterly re-jected, as an ordinary device to elevate the style, and raise it above prose. I have proposed to myself to imitate, and, as far as is possible, to adopt the very language of men; and assuredly such personifications do not make any natural or regular part of that language. They are, indeed, a figure of speech occasion-ally prompted by passion, and I have made use of them as such; but I have endeavored utterly to reject them as a mechanical device of style, or as a fam-ily language which writers in meter seem to lay claim to by prescription. I have wished to keep my reader in the company of flesh and blood, persuaded that by so doing I shall interest him. Others who pursue a different track will interest him likewise; I do not interfere with their claim, but wish to prefer a different claim of my own. There will also be found in these pieces little of what is usually called poetic diction; as much pains has been taken to avoid it as is ordinarily taken an ability of conjuring up in himself passions, which are indeed far from being the same as those produced by real events, yet (especially in those parts of the general sympathy which are pleasing and delightful) do more nearly resemble the passions produced by real events, than anything which, from the motions of their own minds merely, other men are accustomed to feel in themselves; whence, and from practice, he has acquired a greater readiness and power in expressing what he thinks and feels, and especially those thoughts and feelings which, by his own choice, or from the structure of his own mind, arise in him without immediate external excitement.

But, whatever portion of this faculty we may suppose even the greatest poet to possess, there cannot be a doubt but that the language which it will suggest to him must often, in liveliness and truth, fall far short of that which is uttered by men in real life, under the actual pressure of those passions, certain shadows of which the poet thus produces, or feels to be produced, in himself.

However exalted a notion we would wish to cherish of the character of a poet, it is obvious, that, while he describes and imitates passions, his employment is in some degree mechanical, compared with the freedom and power of real and substantial action and suffering. So that it will be the wish of the poet to bring his feelings near to those of the persons whose feelings he describes, nay, for short spaces of time, perhaps, to let himself slip into an entire delusion, and even confound and identify his own feelings with theirs; modifying only the language which is thus suggested to him by a consideration that he describes for a particular purpose, that of giving pleasure. Here, then, he will apply the principle of selection which has been already insisted upon. He will depend upon this for removing what would otherwise be painful or disgusting in the passion; he will feel that there is no necessity to trick out or to elevate nature: and, the more industriously he applies this principle, the deeper will be his faith that no words, which *his* fancy or imagination can suggest, will be to be compared with those which are the emanations of reality and truth.

But it may be said by those who do not object to the general spirit of these remarks, that, as it is impossible for the poet to produce upon all occasions language as exquisitely fitted for the passion as that which the real passion itself suggests, it is proper that he should consider himself as in the situation of a translator, who does not scruple to substitute excellencies of another kind for those which are unattainable by him; and endeavors occasionally to surpass his original in order to make some amends for the general inferiority to which he feels that he must submit. But this would be to encourage idleness and unmanly despair. Further, it is the language of men who speak of what they do not understand; who talk of poetry as of a matter of amusement and idle pleasure; who will converse with us as gravely about a *taste* for poetry, as they express it, as if it were a thing as indifferent as a taste for rope-dancing, or frontiniac or sherry. Aristotle, I have been told, has said, that poetry is the most philosophic of all writing: it is so: its object is truth, not individual and local, but general, and operative; not standing upon external testimony, but carried alive into the heart by passion; truth which is its own testimony, which gives competence and confidence to the tribunal to which it appeals, and receives them from the same tribunal. Poetry is the image of man and nature. The obstacles which stand in the way of the fidelity of the biographer and historian and of their consequent utility, are incalculably greater than those which are to be encountered by the poet who comprehends the dignity of his art. The poet writes under one restriction only, namely, that of the necessity of giving immediate pleasure to a human being possessed of that information which may be expected from him, not as a lawyer, a physician, a mariner, an astronomer, or a natural philosopher, but as a man. Except this one restriction, there is no object standing between the poet and the image of things; between this, and the biographer and historian there are a thousand.

Nor let this necessity of producing immediate pleasure be considered as a degradation of the poet's art. It is far otherwise. It is an acknowledgment of respecting what imagery or diction he may choose to connect with the passion, whereas, in the other, the meter obeys certain laws, to which the poet and reader both willingly submit because they are certain, and because no interference is made by them with the passion but such as the concurring testimony of ages has shown to heighten and improve the pleasure which co-exists with it.

It will now be proper to answer an obvious question, namely, Why, professing these opinions, have I written in verse? To this, in addition to such answer as is included in what I have already said, I reply, in the first place, Because, however I may have restricted myself, there is still left open to me what confessedly constitutes the most valuable object of all writing, whether in prose or verse, the great and universal passions of men, the most general and interesting of their occupations, and the entire world of nature before me to supply endless combinations of forms and imagery. Now, supposing for a moment that whatever is interesting in these objects may be as vividly described in prose, why should I be condemned, for attempting to superadd to such description the charm, which, by the consent of all nations, is acknowledged to exist in metrical language? To this, by such as are yet unconvinced, it may be answered that a very small part of the pleasure given by poetry depends upon the meter, and that it is injudicious to write in meter, unless it be accompanied with the other artificial distinctions of style with which meter is usually accompanied, and that, by such deviation, more will be lost from the shock which will thereby be given to the reader's associations than will be counterbalanced by any pleasure which he can derive from the general power of numbers. In answer to those who still contend for the necessity of accompanying meter with certain appropriate colors of style in order to the accomplishment of its appropriate end, and who also, in my opinion, greatly underrate the power of meter in itself, it might, perhaps, as far as relates to these volumes, have been almost sufficient to observe, that poems are extant, written upon more humble subjects, and in a more naked and simple style than I have aimed at,

which poems have continued to give pleasure from generation to generation. Now, if nakedness and simplicity be a defect, the fact here mentioned affords a strong presumption that poems somewhat less naked and simple are capable of affording pleasure at the present day; and, what I wished *chiefly* to attempt, at present, was to justify myself for having written under the impression of this belief.

But various causes might be pointed out why, when the style is manly, and the subject of some importance, words metrically arranged will long continue to impart such a pleasure to mankind as he who is sensible of the extent of that pleasure will be desirous to impart. The end of poetry is to produce excitement in coexistence with an overbalance of pleasure. Now, by the supposition, excitement is an unusual and irregular state of the mind; ideas and feelings do not, in that state, succeed each other in accustomed order. If the words, however, by which this excitement is produced be in themselves powerful, or the images and feelings have an undue proportion of pain connected with them, there is some danger that the excitement may be carried beyond its proper bounds. Now the co-presence of something regular, something to which the mind has been accustomed in various moods, and in a less excited state, cannot but have great efficacy in tempering and restraining the passion by an intertexture of ordinary feeling, and of feeling not strictly and necessarily connected with the passion. This is unquestionably true, and hence, though the opinion will at first appear paradoxical, from the tendency of meter to divest language, in a certain degree, of its reality, and thus to throw a sort of half consciousness of unsubstantial existence over the whole composition, there can be little doubt, but that more pathetic situations and sentiments, that is, those which have a greater proportion of pain connected with them, may be endured in metrical composition, especially in rime, than in prose. The meter of the old ballads is very artless; yet they contain many passages which would illustrate this opinion, and I hope, if the following poems be attentively perused, similar instances will be found in them. This opinion may be further illustrated by appealing to the reader's own experience of the reluctance with which he comes to the re-perusal of the distressful parts of Clarissa Harlowe, or the Gamester. While Shakspere's writings, in the most pathetic scenes, never act upon us, as pathetic, beyond the bounds of pleasure — an effect which, in a much greater degree than might at first be imagined, is to be ascribed to small, but continual and regular impulses of pleasurable surprise from the metrical arrangement.— On the other hand, (what it must be allowed will much more frequently happen,) if the poet's words should be incommensurate with the passion, and inadequate to raise the reader to a height of desirable excitement, then, (unless the poet's choice of his meter has been grossly injudicious,) in the feelings of pleasure which the reader has been accustomed to connect with meter in general, and in the feeling, whether cheerful or melancholy, which he has been accustomed to connect with that particular movement of meter, there will be found something which will greatly contribute to impart passion to the words, and to effect the complex end which the poet proposes to himself.

If I had undertaken a systematic defense of the theory here maintained, it would have been my duty to develop the various causes upon which the pleasure received from metrical language depends. Among the chief of these causes is to be reckoned a principle which must be well known to those who have made any of the arts the object of accurate reflection; I mean the pleasure which the mind derives from the perception of similitude in dissimilitude. This principle is the great spring of the activity of our minds, and their chief feeder. From this principle the direction of the sexual appetite, and all the passions connected with it, take their origin: it is the life of our ordinary conversation; and upon the accuracy with which similitude in dissimilitude, and dissimilitude in similitude are perceived, depend our taste and our moral feelings. It would not be a useless employment to apply this principle to the consideration of meter, and to show that meter is hence enabled to afford much pleasure, and to point out in what manner that pleasure

is produced. But my limits will not permit me to enter upon this subject, and I must content myself with a general summary.

I have said that poetry is the spontaneous overflow of powerful feelings; it takes its origin from emotion recollected in tranquillity; the emotion is contemplated, till, by a species of reaction, the tranquillity gradually disappears, and an emotion, kindred to that which was before the subject of contemplation, is gradually produced, and does itself actually exist in the mind. In this mood successful composition generally begins, and in a mood similar to this it is carried on; but the emotion of whatever kind, and in whatever degree, from various causes, is qualified by various pleasures, so that in describing any passions whatsoever, which are voluntarily described, the mind will, upon the whole, be in a state of enjoyment. If nature be thus cautious to preserve in a state of enjoyment a being so employed, the poet ought to profit by the lesson held forth to him, and ought especially to take care, that, whatever passions he communicates to his reader, those passions, if his reader's mind be sound and vigorous, should always be accompanied with an overbalance of pleasure. Now the music of harmonious metrical language, the sense of difficulty overcome, and the blind association of pleasure which has been previously received from works of rime or meter of the same or similar construction, an indistinct perception perpetually renewed of language closely resembling that of real life, and yet, in the circumstance of meter, differing from it so widely — all these imperceptibly make up a complex feeling of delight, which is of the most important use in tempering the painful feeling which is always found intermingled with powerful descriptions of the deeper passions. This effect is always produced in pathetic and impassioned poetry; while, in lighter compositions, the ease and gracefulness with which the poet manages his numbers are themselves confessedly a principal source of the gratification of the reader. All that it is *necessary* to say upon this subject, may be effected by affirming what few persons will deny, that, of two descriptions either of passions, manners, or characters, each of them equally well executed, the one in prose and the other in verse, the verse will be read a hundred times where the prose is read once.

Having thus explained a few of the reasons for writing in verse, and why I have chosen subjects from common life, and endeavored to bring my language near to the real language of men, if I have been too minute in pleading my own cause, I have at the same time been treating a subject of general interest; and for this reason a few words shall be added with reference solely to these particular poems, and to some defects which will probably be found in them. I am sensible that my associations must have sometimes been particular instead of general, and that, consequently, giving to things a false importance, I may have sometimes written upon unworthy subjects; but I am less apprehensive on this account, than that my language may frequently have suffered from those arbitrary connections of feelings and ideas with particular words and phrases, from which no man can altogether protect himself. Hence I have no doubt, that, in some instances, feelings, even of the ludicrous, may be given to my readers by expressions which appeared to me tender and pathetic. Such faulty expressions, were I convinced they were faulty at present, and that they must necessarily continue to be so, I would willingly take all reasonable pains to correct. But it is dangerous to make these alterations on the simple authority of a few individuals, or even of certain classes of men; for where the understanding of an author is not convinced, or his feelings altered, this cannot be done without great injury to himself: for his own feelings are his stay and support; and, if he set them aside in one instance, he may be induced to repeat this act till his mind shall lose all confidence in itself, and becomes utterly debilitated. To this it may be added, that the reader ought never to forget that he is himself exposed to the same errors as the poet, and, perhaps, in a much greater degree: for there can be no presumption in saying of most readers that it is not probable they will be so well acquainted with the various stages of meaning through which words have passed, or with the fickleness or stability of the re-

lations of particular ideas to each other; and, above all, since they are so much less interested in the subject, they may decide lightly and carelessly.

Long as the reader has been detained, I hope he will permit me to caution him against a mode of false criticism which has been applied to poetry, in which the language closely resembles that of life and nature. Such verses have been triumphed over in parodies of which Dr. Johnson's stanza is a fair specimen.

> I put my hat upon my head
> And walked into the Strand,
> And there I met another man
> Whose hat was in his hand.

Immediately under these lines I will place one of the most justly-admired stanzas of the 'Babes in the Wood.'

> These pretty babes with hand in hand
> Went wandering up and down;
> But never more they saw the Man
> Approaching from the Town.

In both these stanzas the words, and the order of the words, in no respect differ from the most unimpassioned conversation. There are words in both, for example, 'The Strand,' and 'The Town,' connected with none but the most familiar ideas; yet the one stanza we admit as admirable, and the other as a fair example of the superlatively contemptible. Whence arises this difference? Not from the meter, not from the language, not from the order of the words; but the *matter* expressed in Dr. Johnson's stanza is contemptible. The proper method of treating trivial and simple verses, to which Dr. Johnson's stanza would be a fair parallelism, is not to say, This is a bad kind of poetry, or, This is not poetry; but, This wants sense; it is neither interesting in itself, nor can *lead* to anything interesting; the images neither originate in that sane state of feeling which arises out of thought, nor can excite thought or feeling in the reader. This is the only sensible manner of dealing with such verses. Why trouble yourself about the species till you have previously decided upon the genus? Why take pains to prove that an ape is not a Newton, when it is self-evident that he is not a man?

I must make one request of my reader, which is, that in judging these poems he would decide by his own feelings genuinely, and not by reflection upon what will probably be the judgment of others. How common is it to hear a person say, 'I myself do not object to this style of composition, or this or that expression, but, to such and such classes of people, it will appear mean or ludicrous!' This mode of criticism, so destructive of all sound unadulterated judgment, is almost universal: let the reader then abide independently by his own feelings, and if he finds himself affected, let him not suffer such conjectures to interfere with his pleasure.

If an author, by any single composition, has impressed us with respect for his talents, it is useful to consider this as affording a presumption, that on other occasions where we have been displeased, he, nevertheless, may not have written ill or absurdly; and, further, to give him so much credit for this one composition as may induce us to review what has displeased us, with more care than we should otherwise have bestowed upon it. This is not only an act of justice, but, in our decisions upon poetry especially, may conduce, in a high degree, to the improvement of our own taste: for an *accurate* taste in poetry, and in all the other arts, as Sir Joshua Reynolds has observed, is an *acquired* talent, which can only be produced by thought and a long-continued intercourse with the best models of composition. This is mentioned, not with so ridiculous a purpose as to prevent the most inexperienced reader from judging for himself (I have already said that I wish him to judge for himself), but merely to temper the rashness of decision, and to suggest, that, if poetry be a subject on which much time has not been bestowed, the judgment may be erroneous; and that, in many cases, it necessarily will be so.

Nothing would, I know, have so effectually contributed to further the end which I have in view, as to have shown of what kind the pleasure is, and how that pleasure is produced, which is confessedly produced by metrical composition essentially different from that which I have here endeavored to recommend: for the reader will say that he has been

pleased by such composition; and what more can be done for him? The power of any art is limited; and he will suspect, that, if it be proposed to furnish him with new friends, that can be only upon condition of his abandoning his old friends. Besides, as I have said, the reader is himself conscious of the pleasure which he has received from such composition, composition to which he has peculiarly attached the endearing name of poetry; and all men feel an habitual gratitude, and something of an honorable bigotry for the objects which have long continued to please them; we not only wish to be pleased, but to be pleased in that particular way in which we have been accustomed to be pleased. There is in these feelings enough to resist a host of arguments; and I should be the less able to combat them successfully, as I am willing to allow, that, in order entirely to enjoy the poetry which I am recommending, it would be necessary to give up much of what is ordinarily enjoyed. But, would my limits have permitted me to point out how this pleasure is produced, many obstacles might have been removed, and the reader assisted in perceiving that the powers of language are not so limited as he may suppose; and that it is possible for poetry to give other enjoyments, of a purer, more lasting, and more exquisite nature. This part of the subject has not been altogether neglected; but it has not been so much my present aim to prove, that the interest excited by some other kinds of poetry is less vivid, and less worthy of the nobler powers of the mind, as to offer reasons for presuming, that, if my purpose were fulfilled, a species of poetry would be produced, which is genuine poetry; in its nature well adapted to interest mankind permanently, and likewise important in the multiplicity and quality of its moral relations.

From what has been said, and from a perusal of the poems, the reader will be able clearly to perceive the object which I had in view; he will determine how far it has been attained; and, what is a much more important question, whether it be worth attaining; and upon the decision of these two questions will rest my claim to the approbation of the public.

(1800)

THE PRELUDE

FROM BOOK I

Fair seed-time had my soul, and I grew up
Fostered alike by beauty and by fear:
Much favored in my birth-place, and no
   less
In that beloved Vale to which erelong
We were transplanted — there were we let
   loose   5
For sports of wider range. Ere I had told
Ten birth-days, when among the mountain
   slopes
Frost, and the breath of frosty wind, had
   snapped
The last autumnal crocus, 't was my joy
With store of springes o'er my shoulder
   hung   10
To range the open heights where woodcocks
   run
Along the smooth green turf. Through half
   the night,
Scudding away from snare to snare, I plied
That anxious visitation; — moon and stars
Were shining o'er my head. I was alone, 15
And seemed to be a trouble to the peace
That dwelt among them. Sometimes it be-
   fell
In these night wanderings, that a strong de-
   sire
O'erpowered my better reason, and the bird
Which was the captive of another's toil   20
Became my prey; and when the deed was done
I heard among the solitary hills
Low breathings coming after me, and
   sounds
Of undistinguishable motion, steps
Almost as silent as the turf they trod.   25

Nor less when spring had warmed the
   cultured Vale,
Moved we as plunderers where the mother-
   bird
Had in high places built her lodge; though
   mean
Our object and inglorious, yet the end
Was not ignoble. Oh! when I have hung 30
Above the raven's nest, by knots of grass
And half-inch fissures in the slippery rock
But ill sustained, and almost (so it seemed)
Suspended by the blast that blew amain,
Shouldering the naked crag, oh, at that time
While on the perilous ridge I hung alone, 36
With what strange utterance did the loud
   dry wind
Blow through my ear! the sky seemed not
   a sky

Of earth — and with what motion moved the
   clouds!

Dust as we are, the immortal spirit grows
Like harmony in music; there is a dark 41
Inscrutable workmanship that reconciles
Discordant elements, makes them cling to-
   gether
In one society. How strange that all
The terrors, pains, and early miseries,   45
Regrets, vexations, lassitudes interfused
Within my mind, should e'er have borne a
   part,
And that a needful part, in making up
The calm existence that is mine when I
Am worthy of myself! Praise to the end! 50
Thanks to the means which Nature deigned
   to employ;
Whether her fearless visitings, or those
That came with soft alarm, like hurtless
   light
Opening the peaceful clouds; or she may use
Severer interventions, ministry   55
More palpable, as best might suit her aim.

One summer evening (led by her) I found
A little boat tied to a willow tree
Within a rocky cave, its usual home.
Straight I unloosed her chain, and stepping
   in   60
Pushed from the shore. It was an act of
   stealth
And troubled pleasure, nor without the voice
Of mountain-echoes did my boat move on;
Leaving behind her still, on either side,
Small circles glittering idly in the moon, 65
Until they melted all into one track
Of sparkling light. But now, like one who
   rows,
Proud of his skill, to reach a chosen point
With an unswerving line, I fixed my view
Upon the summit of a craggy ridge,   70
The horizon's utmost boundary; far above
Was nothing but the stars and the gray sky.
She was an elfin pinnace; lustily
I dipped my oars into the silent lake,
And, as I rose upon the stroke, my boat 75
Went heaving through the water like a
   swan;
When, from behind that craggy steep till
   then
The horizon's bound, a huge peak, black and
   huge,
As if with voluntary power instinct
Upreared its head. I struck and struck
   again,
And growing still in stature the grim shape

Towered up between me and the stars, and
  still,
For so it seemed, with purpose of its own
And measured motion like a living thing,
Strode after me. With trembling oars I
  turned,   85
And through the silent water stole my way
Back to the covert of the willow tree;
There in her mooring-place I left my
  bark,—
And through the meadows homeward went,
  in grave
And serious mood; but after I had seen   90
That spectacle, for many days, my brain
Worked with a dim and undetermined sense
Of unknown modes of being; o'er my
  thoughts
There hung a darkness, call it solitude
Or blank desertion. No familiar shapes   95
Remained, no pleasant images of trees,
Of sea or sky, no colors of green fields;
But huge and mighty forms that do not
  live
Like living men, moved slowly through the
  mind   99
By day, and were a trouble to my dreams.

Wisdom and Spirit of the universe!
Thou Soul that art the eternity of thought,
That givest to forms and images a breath
And everlasting motion, not in vain
By day or star-light thus from my first
  dawn   105
Of childhood didst thou intertwine for me
The passions that build up our human soul;
Not with the mean and vulgar works of
  man,
But with high objects, with enduring
  things—
With life and nature—purifying thus   110
The elements of feeling and of thought,
And sanctifying, by such discipline,
Both pain and fear, until we recognize
A grandeur in the beatings of the heart. 114
Nor was this fellowship vouchsafed to me
With stinted kindness. In November days,
When vapors rolling down the valley made
A lonely scene more lonesome, among
  woods,
At noon and 'mid the calm of summer
  nights,   119
When, by the margin of the trembling lake,
Beneath the gloomy hills homeward I went
In solitude, such intercourse was mine;

Mine was it in the fields both day and
  night,
And by the waters, all the summer long.

  And in the frosty season, when the sun
Was set, and visible for many a mile   126
The cottage windows blazed through twi-
  light gloom,
I heeded not their summons: happy time
It was indeed for all of us—for me   129
It was a time of rapture! Clear and loud
The village clock tolled six,—I wheeled
  about,
Proud and exulting like an untired horse
That cares not for his home. All shod
  with steel,
We hissed along the polished ice in games
Confederate, imitative of the chase   135
And woodland pleasures,—the resounding
  horn,
The pack loud chiming, and the hunted
  hare.
So through the darkness and the cold we
  flew,
And not a voice was idle; with the din
Smitten, the precipices rang aloud;   140
The leafless trees and every icy crag
Tinkled like iron; while far distant hills
Into the tumult sent an alien sound
Of melancholy not unnoticed, while the
  stars
Eastward were sparkling clear, and in the
  west   145
The orange sky of evening died away.
Not seldom from the uproar I retired
Into a silent bay, or sportively
Glanced sideway, leaving the tumultuous
  throng,
To cut across the reflex of a star   150
That fled, and, flying still before me,
  gleamed
Upon the glassy plain; and oftentimes,
When we had given our bodies to the wind,
And all the shadowy banks on either side
Came sweeping through the darkness, spin-
  ning still   155
The rapid line of motion, then at once
Have I, reclining back upon my heels,
Stopped short; yet still the solitary cliffs
Wheeled by me—even as if the earth had
  rolled
With visible motion her diurnal round!   160
Behind me did they stretch in solemn train,
Feebler and feebler, and I stood and
  watched
Till all was tranquil as a dreamless sleep.
                                          (1850)

LINES

COMPOSED A FEW MILES ABOVE TINTERN ABBEY
ON REVISITING THE BANKS OF THE WYE
DURING A TOUR.

JULY 13, 1798

Five years have past; five summers, with
the length
Of five long winters! and again I hear
These waters, rolling from their mountain-
springs
With a soft inland murmur [1] — Once again
Do I behold these steep and lofty cliffs, 5
That on a wild secluded scene impress
Thoughts of more deep seclusion; and con-
nect
The landscape with the quiet of the sky.
The day is come when I again repose
Here under this dark sycamore, and view
These plots of cottage-ground, these or-
chard-tufts, 11
Which at this season, with their unripe
fruits,
Are clad in one green hue, and lose them-
selves
'Mid groves and copses. Once again I
see
These hedgerows, hardly hedgerows, little
lines 15
Of sportive wood run wild; these pastoral
farms,
Green to the very door; and wreaths of
smoke
Sent up in silence, from among the trees!
With some uncertain notice, as might seem,
Of vagrant dwellers in the houseless woods,
Or of some hermit's cave, where by his
fire 21
The hermit sits alone.
　　　　　　　These beauteous forms,
Through a long absence, have not been to
me
As is a landscape to a blind man's eye: 24
But oft, in lonely rooms, and mid the din
Of towns and cities, I have owed to them
In hours of weariness, sensations sweet,
Felt in the blood, and felt along the heart;
And passing even into my purer mind, 29
With tranquil restoration: — feelings, too,
Of unremembered pleasure: such perhaps,
As have no slight or trivial influence
On that best portion of a good man's
life,
His little, nameless, unremembered acts
Of kindness and of love. Nor less, I trust,

[1] The river is not affected by the tides a few
miles above Tintern.

To them I may have owed another gift, 36
Of aspect more sublime; that blessed mood,
In which the burden of the mystery,
In which the heavy and the weary weight
Of all this unintelligible world, 40
Is lightened: — that serene and blessed
mood,
In which the affections gently lead us on,—
Until, the breath of this corporeal frame,
And even the motion of our human blood
Almost suspended, we are laid asleep 45
In body, and become a living soul:
While with an eye made quiet by the
power
Of harmony, and the deep power of joy,
We see into the life of things.
　　　　　　　　　　　　If this
Be but a vain belief, yet, oh! how oft — 50
In darkness, and amid the many shapes
Of joyless daylight; when the fretful stir
Unprofitable, and the fever of the world,
Have hung upon the beatings of my heart,
How oft, in spirit, have I turned to thee,
O sylvan Wye! Thou wanderer through
the woods, 56
How often has my spirit turned to thee!

And now, with gleams of half-ex-
tinguished thought,
With many recognitions dim and faint,
And somewhat of a sad perplexity, 60
The picture of the mind revives again:
While here I stand, not only with the sense
Of present pleasure, but with pleasing
thoughts
That in this moment there is life and food
For future years. And so I dare to
hope. 65
Though, changed, no doubt, from what I
was when first
I came among these hills; when like a roe
I bounded o'er the mountains, by the sides
Of the deep rivers, and the lonely streams,
Wherever nature led; more like a man 70
Flying from something that he dreads, than
one
Who sought the thing he loved. For na-
ture then
(The coarser pleasures of my boyish days,
And their glad animal movements all gone
by)
To me was all in all.— I cannot paint 75
What then I was. The sounding cataract
Haunted me like a passion: the tall rock,
The mountain, and the deep and gloomy
wood,
Their colors and their forms, were then to
me

An appetite; a feeling and a love, 80
That had no need of a remoter charm,
By thought supplied, nor any interest
Unborrowed from the eye.— That time is past,
And all its aching joys are now no more,
And all its dizzy raptures. Not for this
Faint I, nor mourn nor murmur; other gifts 86
Have followed; for such loss, I would believe,
Abundant recompense. For I have learned
To look on nature, not as in the hour
Of thoughtless youth; but hearing oftentimes 90
The still, sad music of humanity,
Nor harsh nor grating, though of ample power
To chasten and subdue. And I have felt
A presence that disturbs me with the joy
Of elevated thoughts; a sense sublime 95
Of something far more deeply interfused,
Whose dwelling is the light of setting suns,
And the round ocean and the living air,
And the blue sky, and in the mind of man:
A motion and a spirit, that impels 100
All thinking things, all objects of all thought,
And rolls through all things. Therefore am I still
A lover of the meadows and the woods,
And mountains; and of all that we behold
From this green earth; of all the mighty world 105
Of eye, and ear,—both what they half create,
And what perceive; well pleased to recognize
In nature and the language of the sense,
The anchor of my purest thoughts, the nurse,
The guide, the guardian of my heart, and soul 110
Of all my moral being.
                        Nor perchance,
If I were not thus taught, should I the more
Suffer my genial spirits to decay:
For thou art with me here upon the banks
Of this fair river; thou my dearest Friend, 115
My dear, dear Friend; and in thy voice I catch
The language of my former heart, and read
My former pleasures in the shooting lights
Of thy wild eyes. Oh! yet a little while
May I behold in thee what I was once 120

My dear, dear Sister! and this prayer I make
Knowing that Nature never did betray
The heart that loved her; 't is her privilege
Through all the years of this our life, to lead
From joy to joy: for she can so inform 125
The mind that is within us, so impress
With quietness and beauty, and so feed
With lofty thoughts, that neither evil tongues,
Rash judgments, nor the sneers of selfish men,
Nor greetings where no kindness is, nor all 130
The dreary intercourse of daily life,
Shall e'er prevail against us, or disturb
Our cheerful faith that all which we behold
Is full of blessings. Therefore let the moon
Shine on thee in thy solitary walk; 135
And let the misty mountain-winds be free
To blow against thee: and, in after years,
When these wild ecstasies shall be matured
Into a sober pleasure; when thy mind
Shall be a mansion for all lovely forms, 140
Thy memory be as a dwelling-place
For all sweet sounds and harmonies; oh! then,
If solitude, or fear, or pain, or grief,
Should be thy portion, with what healing thoughts
Of tender joy wilt thou remember me, 145
And these my exhortations! Nor, perchance —
If I should be where I no more can hear
Thy voice, nor catch from thy wild eyes these gleams
Of past existence — wilt thou then forget
That on the banks of this delightful stream 150
We stood together; and that I, so long
A worshipper of Nature, hither came
Unwearied in that service: rather say
With warmer love — oh! with far deeper zeal
Of holier love. Nor wilt thou then forget, 155
That after many wanderings, many years
Of absence, these steep woods and lofty cliffs,
And this green pastoral landscape, were to me
More dear, both for themselves and for thy sake! 160

(1798)

STRANGE FITS OF PASSION HAVE I KNOWN

Strange fits of passion have I known:
And I will dare to tell,
But in the Lover's ear alone,
What once to me befell.

When she I loved looked every day,   5
Fresh as a rose in June,
I to her cottage bent my way,
Beneath an evening moon.

Upon the moon I fixed my eye,
All over the wide lea;   10
With quickening pace my horse drew nigh
Those paths so dear to me.

And now we reached the orchard plot;
And as we climbed the hill,
The sinking moon to Lucy's cot   15
Came near and nearer still.

In one of those sweet dreams I slept,
Kind Nature's gentlest boon!
And all the while my eyes I kept
On the descending moon.   20

My horse moved on; hoof after hoof
He raised, and never stopped:
When down behind the cottage roof,
At once, the bright moon dropped.

What fond and wayward thought will slide
Into a lover's head!—   26
'Oh, mercy!' to myself I cried,
'If Lucy should be dead!'

(1800)

SHE DWELT AMONG THE UNTRODDEN WAYS

She dwelt among the untrodden ways
  Beside the springs of Dove,
A Maid whom there were none to praise,
  And very few to love.

A violet by a mossy stone   5
  Half-hidden from the eye!
Fair as a star, when only one
  Is shining in the sky.

She lived unknown, and few could know
  When Lucy ceased to be;   10
But she is in her grave, and, oh,
  The difference to me!

(1800)

I TRAVELED AMONG UNKNOWN MEN

I traveled among unknown men,
  In lands beyond the sea;
Nor, England! did I know till then
  What love I bore to thee.

'T is past, that melancholy dream!   5
  Nor will I quit thy shore
A second time; for still I seem
  To love thee more and more.

Among thy mountains did I feel
  The joy of my desire;   10
And she I cherished turned her wheel
  Beside an English fire.

Thy mornings showed, thy nights concealed
  The bowers where Lucy played;
And thine too is the last green field   15
  That Lucy's eyes surveyed.

(1807)

THREE YEARS SHE GREW IN SUN AND SHOWER

Three years she grew in sun and shower,
Then Nature said, 'A lovelier flower
On earth was never sown;
This Child I to myself will take,
She shall be mine, and I will make   5
A Lady of my own.

'Myself will to my darling be
Both law and impulse: and with me
The Girl, in rock and plain,
In earth and heaven, in glade and bower, 10
Shall feel an overseeing power
To kindle or restrain.

'She shall be sportive as the fawn
That wild with glee across the lawn
Or up the mountain springs;   15
And hers shall be the breathing balm,
And hers the silence and the calm
Of mute insensate things.

'The floating clouds their state shall lend
To her; for her the willow bend;   20
Nor shall she fail to see
Even in the motions of the Storm
Grace that shall mold the Maiden's form
By silent sympathy.

'The stars of midnight shall be dear 25
To her; and she shall lean her ear
In many a secret place
Where rivulets dance their wayward round,
And beauty born of murmuring sound
Shall pass into her face. 30

'And vital feelings of delight
Shall rear her form to stately height,
Her virgin bosom swell;
Such thoughts to Lucy I will give
While she and I together live 35
Here in this happy dell.'

Thus Nature spake — The work was
   done —
How soon my Lucy's race was run!
She died, and left to me
This heath, this calm, and quiet scene; 40
The memory of what has been,
And never more will be.

(1800)

A SLUMBER DID MY SPIRIT SEAL

A slumber did my spirit seal;
  I had no human fears:
She seemed a thing that could not feel
  The touch of earthly years.

No motion has she now, no force; 5
  She neither hears nor sees;
Rolled round in earth's diurnal course,
  With rocks, and stones, and trees.

(1800)

MICHAEL

A PASTORAL POEM

If from the public way you turn your steps;
Up the tumultuous brook of Green-head
  Ghyll,
You will suppose that with an upright path
Your feet must struggle; in such bold
  ascent
The pastoral mountains front you face to
  face. 5
But courage! for around that boisterous
  brook
The mountains have all opened out them-
  selves,
And made a hidden valley of their own.
No habitation can be seen: but they
Who journey thither find themselves alone
With a few sheep, with rocks and stones,
  and kites 11

That overhead are sailing in the sky.
It is in truth an utter solitude;
Nor should I have made mention of this
  Dell
But for one object which you might
  pass by, 15
Might see and notice not. Beside the
  brook
Appears a straggling heap of unhewn
  stones!
And to that simple object appertains,
A story unenriched with strange events,
Yet not unfit, I deem, for the fireside, 20
Or for the summer shade. It was the first
Of those domestic tales that spake to me
Of Shepherds, dwellers in the valleys, men
Whom I already loved; — not verily
For their own sakes, but for the fields and
  hills 25
Where was their occupation and abode.
And hence this Tale, while I was yet a Boy
Careless of books, yet having felt the power
Of Nature, by the gentle agency
Of natural objects led me on to feel 30
For passions that were not my own, and
  think
(At random and imperfectly indeed)
On man, the heart of man, and human
  life.
Therefore, although it be a history 34
Homely and rude, I will relate the same
For the delight of a few natural hearts;
And, with yet fonder feeling, for the sake
Of youthful Poets who among these hills
Will be my second self when I am gone.

Upon the forest-side in Grasmere Vale
There dwelt a Shepherd, Michael was his
  name; 41
An old man, stout of heart, and strong of
  limb.
His bodily frame had been from youth to
  age
Of an unusual strength: his mind was keen,
Intense, and frugal, apt for all affairs, 45
And in his shepherd's calling he was prompt
And watchful more than ordinary men.
Hence had he learned the meaning of all
  winds,
Of blasts of every tone; and, oftentimes,
When others heeded not, He heard the
  South 50
Make subterraneous music, like the noise
Of bagpipers on distant Highland hills.
The Shepherd, at such warning, of his flock
Bethought him, and he to himself would
  say, 54
'The winds are now devising work for me!'

And, truly, at all times, the storm, that
　　drives
The traveler to a shelter, summoned him
Up to the mountains; he had been alone
Amid the heart of many thousand mists,
That came to him and left him on the
　　heights.　　　　　　　　　　60
So lived he till his eightieth year was
　　past.
And grossly that man errs, who should
　　suppose
That the green valleys, and the streams and
　　rocks,
Were things indifferent to the Shepherd's
　　thoughts.
Fields, where with cheerful spirits he had
　　breathed　　　　　　　　　　65
The common air; hills, which with vigor-
　　ous step
He had so often climbed; which had im-
　　pressed
So many incidents upon his mind　　68
Of hardship, skill or courage, joy or fear;
Which like a book preserved the memory
Of the dumb animals, whom he had saved,
Had fed or sheltered, linking to such acts,
The certainty of honorable gain;
Those fields, those hills — what could they
　　less? — had laid　　　　　　　74
Strong hold on his affections, were to him
A pleasurable feeling of blind love,
The pleasure which there is in life itself.

His days had not been passed in single-
　　ness.
His Helpmate was a comely matron, old —
Though younger than himself full twenty
　　years.　　　　　　　　　　80
She was a woman of a stirring life,
Whose heart was in her house: two wheels
　　she had
Of antique form, this large for spinning
　　wool,
That small for flax; and if one wheel had
　　rest,
It was because the other was at work.　85
The Pair had but one inmate in their house,
An only Child, who had been born to them
When Michael, telling o'er his years, began
To deem that he was old,— in shepherd's
　　phrase,　　　　　　　　　　89
With one foot in the grave. This only Son,
With two brave sheep-dogs tried in many a
　　storm,
The one of an inestimable worth,
Made all their household. I may truly say,
That they were as a proverb in the vale　94
For endless industry. When day was gone,

And from their occupations out of doors
The Son and Father were come home, even
　　then,
Their labor did not cease; unless when all
Turned to the cleanly supper-board, and
　　there,
Each with a mess of pottage and skimmed
　　milk,　　　　　　　　　　100
Sat round the basket piled with oaten
　　cakes,
And their plain home-made cheese. Yet
　　when the meal
Was ended, Luke (for so the Son was
　　named)
And his old father both betook them-
　　selves　　　　　　　　　　105
To such convenient work as might employ
Their hands by the fire-side; perhaps to
　　card
Wool for the Housewife's spindle, or re-
　　pair
Some injury done to sickle, flail, or scythe,
Or other implement of house or field.　110

Down from the ceiling by the chimney's
　　edge
That in our ancient uncouth country style
With huge and black projection overbrowed
Large space beneath, as duly as the light
Of day grew dim the Housewife hung a
　　lamp;　　　　　　　　　　115
An aged utensil, which had performed
Service beyond all others of its kind,
Early at evening did it burn and late,
Surviving comrade of uncounted hours,
Which going by from year to year had
　　found　　　　　　　　　　120
And left the couple neither gay perhaps
Nor cheerful, yet with objects and with
　　hopes,
Living a life of eager industry.
And now, when Luke had reached his
　　eighteenth year
There by the light of this old lamp they
　　sat,　　　　　　　　　　125
Father and Son, while far into the night
The Housewife plied her own peculiar
　　work,
Making the cottage through the silent hours
Murmur as with the sound of summer flies.
This light was famous in its neighborhood,
And was a public symbol of the life　131
That thrifty Pair had lived. For, as it
　　chanced,
Their cottage on a plot of rising ground
Stood single, with large prospect, north
　　and south,　　　　　　　　134
High into Easedale, up to Dunmail-Raise.

And westward to the village near the lake;
And from this constant light, so regular
And so far seen, the House itself, by all
Who dwelt within the limits of the vale,
Both old and young, was named The Even-
   ing Star.   140

  Thus living on through such a length of
   years,
The shepherd, if he loved himself, must
   needs
Have loved his Helpmate; but to Michael's
   heart
This son of his old age was yet more
   dear —   144
Less from instinctive tenderness, the same
Fond spirit that blindly works in the blood
   of all —
Than that a child, more than all other
   gifts,
That earth can offer to declining man
Brings hope with it, and forward looking
   thoughts,
And stirrings of inquietude, when they 150
By tendency of nature needs must fail.
Exceeding was the love he bare to him,
His heart and his heart's joy! For often-
   times
Old Michael, while he was a babe in arms,
Had done him female service, not alone 155
For pastime and delight, as is the use
Of fathers, but with patient mind enforced
To acts of tenderness; and he had rocked
His cradle as with a woman's gentle hand.

  And, in a later time, ere yet the Boy 160
Had put on boy's attire, did Michael love,
Albeit of a stern unbending mind,
To have the Young one in his sight, when
   he
Wrought in the field, or on his shepherd's
   stool
Sat with a fettered sheep before him
   stretched,   165
Under the large old oak, that near his door,
Stood single, and, from matchless depth of
   shade,
Chosen for the Shearer's covert from the
   sun,
Thence in our rustic dialect was called
The Clipping Tree,[1] a name which yet it
   bears.   170
There, while they two were sitting in the
   shade,
With others round them, earnest all and
   blithe,

[1] Clipping is the word used in the North of England for shearing.

Would Michael exercise his heart with
   looks
Of fond correction and reproof bestowed
Upon the Child, if he disturbed the sheep
By catching at their legs, or with his shouts
Scared them, while they lay still beneath
   the shears.   177

  And when by Heaven's good grace the
   boy grew up
A healthy Lad, and carried in his cheek
Two steady roses that were five years old,
Then Michael from a winter coppice cut 181
With his own hand a sapling, which he
   hooped
With iron, making it throughout in all
Due requisites a perfect shepherd's staff,
And gave it to the Boy; wherewith equipt
He as a watchman oftentimes was placed
At gate or gap, to stem or turn the flock;
And, to his office prematurely called, 188
There stood the urchin, as you will divine,
Something between a hindrance and a help;
And for this course not always, I believe,
Receiving from his Father hire of praise;
Though nought was left undone which
   staff or voice,
Or looks, or threatening gestures could
   perform.

  But soon as Luke, full ten years old, could
   stand   195
Against the mountain blasts; and to the
   heights,
Not fearing toil, nor length of weary ways,
He with his Father daily went, and they
Were as companions, why should I relate
That objects which the Shepherd loved be-
   fore   200
Were dearer now? that from the Boy there
   came
Feelings and emanations — things which
   were
Light to the sun and music to the wind;
And that the old Man's heart seemed born
   again.
Thus in his Father's sight the Boy grew up;
And now when he had reached his eight-
   eenth year,   206
He was his comfort and his daily hope.

  While in this sort the simple household
   lived
From day to day, to Michael's ear there
   came
Distressful tidings. Long before the time
Of which I speak, the Shepherd had been
   bound   211

In surety for his brother's son, a man
Of an industrious life, and ample means —
But unforeseen misfortunes suddenly
Had pressed upon him,— and old Michael
  now
Was summoned to discharge the forfei-
  ture,   216
A grievous penalty, but little less
Than half his substance. This unlooked
  for claim
At the first hearing, for a moment took
More hope out of his life than he supposed
That any old man ever could have lost.
As soon as he had armed himself with
  strength
To look his trouble in the face, it seemed
The Shepherd's sole resource to sell at once
A portion of his patrimonial fields.   225
Such was his first resolve; he thought
  again,
And his heart failed him. 'Isabel,' said he,
Two evenings after he had heard the news,
'I have been toiling more than seventy
  years,
And in the open sunshine of God's love 230
Have we all lived; yet if these fields of ours
Should pass into a stranger's hand, I think
That I could not lie quiet in my grave.
Our lot is a hard lot; the sun himself
Has scarcely been more diligent than I; 235
And I have lived to be a fool at last
To my own family. An evil man
That was, and made an evil choice, if he
Were false to us; and if he were not false,
There are ten thousand to whom loss like
  this   240
Had been no sorrow. I forgive him — but
'T were better to be dumb, than to talk thus.
When I began, my purpose was to speak
Of remedies and of a cheerful hope.
Our Luke shall leave us, Isabel; the land
Shall not go from us, and it shall be free;
He shall possess it free as is the wind 247
That passes over it. We have, thou know-
  est,
Another kinsman — he will be our friend
In this distress. He is a prosperous man,
Thriving in trade — and Luke to him shall
  go,   251
And with his kinsman's help and his own
  thrift
He quickly will repair this loss, and then
He may return to us. If here he stay,
What can be done? Where every one is
  poor,   255
What can be gained?' At this the old Man
  paused,
And Isabel sat silent, for her mind

Was busy, looking back into past times.
There's Richard Bateman, thought she to
  herself,
He was a parish-boy — at the church-door
They made a gathering for him, shillings,
  pence,   261
And halfpennies, wherewith the neighbors
  bought
A basket, which they filled with pedlar's
  wares;
And with this basket on his arm, the lad
Went up to London, found a master there,
Who out of many chose the trusty boy 266
To go and overlook his merchandise
Beyond the seas: where he grew wondrous
  rich,
And left estates and monies to the poor,
And at his birthplace built a chapel floored
With marble, which he sent from foreign
  lands.   271
These thoughts, and many others of like
  sort,
Passed quickly through the mind of Isabel
And her face brightened. The old Man
  was glad,
And thus resumed: — 'Well, Isabel! this
  scheme   275
These two days has been meat and drink
  to me.
Far more than we have lost is left us yet.
We have enough — I wish indeed that I
Were younger,— but this hope is a good
  hope.
Make ready Luke's best garments, of the
  best   280
Buy for him more, and let us send him
  forth
To-morrow, or the next day, or to-night:
If he *could* go, the Boy should go to-night.'

  Here Michael ceased, and to the fields
  went forth
With a light heart. The Housewife for
  five days   285
Was restless morn and night, and all day
  long
Wrought on with her best fingers to pre-
  pare
Things needful for the journey of her son.
But Isabel was glad when Sunday came
To stop her in her work: for, when she
  lay   290
By Michael's side, she through the last two
  nights
Heard him, how he was troubled in his
  sleep:
And when they rose at morning she could
  see

That all his hopes were gone. That day at
noon
She said to Luke, while they two by them-
selves   295
Were sitting at the door. 'Thou must not
go:
We have no other Child but thee to lose,
None to remember — do not go away,
For if thou leave thy Father he will die.'
The Youth made answer with a jocund
voice;   300
And Isabel, when she had told her fears,
Recovered heart. That evening her best
fare
Did she bring forth, and all together sat
Like happy people round a Christmas fire.

With daylight Isabel resumed her work;
And all the ensuing week the house ap-
peared   306
As cheerful as a grove in Spring: at length
The expected letter from their kinsman
came,
With kind assurances that he would do
His utmost for the welfare of the Boy; 310
To which, requests were added, that forth-
with
He might be sent to him. Ten times or
more
The letter was read over; Isabel
Went forth to show it to the neighbors
round;
Nor was there at that time on English land
A prouder heart than Luke's. When Isabel
Had to her house returned, the old Man
said,   317
'He shall depart to-morrow.' To this word
The Housewife answered, talking much of
things
Which, if at such short notice he should go,
Would surely be forgotten. But at length
She gave consent, and Michael was at
ease.   322

Near the tumultuous brook of Green-head
Ghyll,
In that deep valley, Michael had designed
To build a Sheep-fold; and, before he heard
The tidings of his melancholy loss, 326
For this same purpose he had gathered up
A heap of stones, which by the streamlet's
edge
Lay thrown together, ready for the work.
With Luke that evening thitherward he
walked;   330
And soon as they had reached the place he
stopped,

And thus the old Man spake to him.— 'My
son,
To-morrow thou wilt leave me: with full
heart
I look upon thee, for thou art the same
That wert a promise to me ere thy birth, 335
And all thy life hast been my daily joy.
I will relate to thee some little part
Of our two histories; 't will do thee good
When thou art from me, even if I should
touch
On things thou canst not know of.— After
thou   340
First cam'st into the world — as oft befalls
To new-born infants — thou didst sleep
away
Two days, and blessings from thy Father's
tongue
Then fell upon thee. Day by day passed
on,
And still I loved thee with increasing love.
Never to living ear came sweeter sounds
Than when I heard thee by our own fire-
side   347
First uttering, without words, a natural
tune;
While thou, a feeding babe, didst in thy
joy
Sing at thy Mother's breast. Month fol-
lowed month,   350
And in the open fields my life was passed
And on the mountains, else I think that
thou
Hadst been brought up upon thy Father's
knees.
But we were playmates, Luke: among these
hills,
As well thou know'st, in us the old and
young   355
Have played together, nor with me didst
thou
Lack any pleasure which a boy can know.'
Luke had a manly heart; but at these words
He sobbed aloud. The old Man grasped
his hand
And said, 'Nay, do not take it so — I see
That these are things of which I need not
speak.   361
Even to the utmost I have been to thee
A kind and a good Father: and herein
I but repay a gift which I myself
Received at others' hands; for, though now
old   365
Beyond the common life of man, I still
Remember them who loved me in my youth.
Both of them sleep together: here they
lived

As all their forefathers had done; and
  when
At length their time was come, they were
  not loath   370
To give their bodies to the family mold.
I wished that thou shouldst live the life
  they lived.
But 't is a long time to look back, my Son,
And see so little gain from threescore years.
These fields were burdened when they
  came to me;   375
Till I was forty years of age, not more
Than half of my inheritance was mine.
I toiled and toiled; God blessed me in my
  work,
And till these three weeks past the land was
  free.
It looks as if it never could endure   380
Another Master. Heaven forgive me, Luke,
If I judge ill for thee, but it seems good
That thou shouldst go.' At this the old
  Man paused;
Then, pointing to the stones near which
  they stood,
Thus, after a short silence, he resumed:
'This was a work for us; and now, my
  son,   386
It is a work for me. But, lay one stone —
Here, lay it for me, Luke, with thine own
  hands.
Nay, Boy, be of good hope; — we both may
  live
To see a better day. At eighty-four   390
I still am strong and hale; — do thou thy
  part,
I will do mine. — I will begin again
With many tasks that were resigned to
  thee;
Up to the heights, and in among the storms,
Will I without thee go again, and do 395
All works which I was wont to do alone,
Before I knew thy face. — Heaven bless
  thee, Boy!
Thy heart these two weeks has been beating
  fast
With many hopes; it should be so — yes
  — yes —
I knew that thou couldst never have a wish
To leave me, Luke: thou hast been bound
  to me   401
Only by links of love: when thou art gone,
What will be left to us! — But, I forget
My purposes. Lay now the corner-stone,
As I requested; and hereafter, Luke, 405
When thou art gone away, should evil men
Be thy companions, think of me, my Son,
And of this moment; hither turn thy
  thoughts,

And God will strengthen thee: amid all fear
And all temptation, Luke, I pray that thou
Mayst bear in mind the life thy Fathers
  lived,   411
Who, being innocent, did for that cause
Bestir them in good deeds. Now, fare thee
  well —
When thou return'st, thou in this place wilt
  see
A work which is not here: a covenant 415
'T will be between us — But, whatever fate
Befall thee, I shall love thee to the last,
And bear thy memory with me to the
  grave.'

    The Shepherd ended here; and Luke
  stooped down,
And, as his Father had requested, laid 420
The first stone of the Sheep-fold. At the
  sight
The old Man's grief broke from him; to
  his heart
He pressed his Son, he kissèd him and
  wept;
And to the house together they returned.
Hushed was that House in peace, or seem-
  ing peace,   425
Ere the night fell; — with morrow's dawn
  the Boy
Began his journey, and when he had
  reached
The public way, he put on a bold face;
And all the neighbors as he passed their
  doors
Came forth with wishes and with farewell
  prayers,   430
That followed him till he was out of sight.

    A good report did from their Kinsman
  come,
Of Luke and his well doing: and the Boy
Wrote loving letters, full of wondrous news,
Which, as the Housewife phrased it, were
  throughout   435
'The prettiest letters that were ever seen.'
Both parents read them with rejoicing
  hearts.
So, many months passed on: and once
  again
The Shepherd went about his daily work
With confident and cheerful thoughts; and
  now   440
Sometimes when he could find a leisure
  hour
He to that valley took his way, and there
Wrought at the sheep-fold. Meantime
  Luke began
To slacken in his duty; and at length

He in the dissolute city gave himself   445
To evil courses: ignominy and shame
Fell on him, so that he was driven at last
To seek a hiding-place beyond the seas.

There is a comfort in the strength of
    love;   449
'T will make a thing endurable, which else
Would overset the brain, or break the
    heart:
I have conversed with more than one who
    well
Remember the old Man, and what he was
Years after he had heard this heavy news.
His bodily frame had been from youth to
    age   455
Of an unusual strength. Among the rocks
He went, and still looked up to sun and
    cloud
And listened to the wind; and as before
Performed all kinds of labor for his sheep,
And for the land, his small inheritance. 460
And to that hollow dell from time to time
Did he repair, to build the fold of which
His flock had need. 'T is not forgotten yet
The pity which was then in every heart
For the old Man — and 't is believed by all
That many and many a day he thither went,
And never lifted up a single stone. √ 467

There, by the Sheep-fold, sometimes was
    he seen
Sitting alone, or with his faithful Dog,
Then old, beside him, lying at his feet. 470
The length of full seven years from time
    to time
He at the building of this Sheep-fold
    wrought,
And left the work unfinished when he died.
Three years, or little more, did Isabel
Survive her Husband: at her death the
    estate   475
Was sold, and went into a stranger's hand.
The cottage which was named the Evening
    Star
Is gone — the ploughshare has been through
    the ground
On which it stood; great changes have been
    wrought
In all the neighborhood: — yet the oak is
    left   480
That grew beside their door; and the re-
    mains
Of the unfinished Sheep-fold may be seen
Beside the boisterous brook of Green-head
    Ghyll.
                    (1800)

MY HEART LEAPS UP WHEN I BEHOLD

My heart leaps up when I behold   ¹
    A rainbow in the sky:
So was it when my life began;
So is it now, I am a man:
So be it when I shall grow old,   ⁵
    Or let me die!
The Child is father of the Man;
And I could wish my days to be
Bound each to each by natural piety.
                    (1807)

THE SPARROW'S NEST

Behold, within the leafy shade,
Those bright blue eggs together laid!
On me the chance-discovered sight
Gleamed like a vision of delight.
I started — seeming to espy   ⁵
The home and sheltered bed,—
The Sparrow's dwelling, which, hard by,
My Father's house, in wet or dry,
My sister Emmeline and I
        Together visited.   ¹⁰
She looked at it, and seemed to fear it;
Dreading, tho' wishing to be near it:

Such heart was in her, being then
A little Prattler among men.
The Blessing of my later years   ¹⁵
Was with me when a boy:
She gave me eyes, she gave me ears;
And humble cares, and delicate fears;
A heart, the fountain of sweet tears;
        And love, and thought, and joy.   ²⁰
                    (1807)

TO THE CUCKOO

O blithe New-comer! I have heard,
I hear thee and rejoice.
O Cuckoo! shall I call thee Bird,
Or but a wandering Voice?

While I am lying on the grass   ⁵
Thy twofold shout I hear;
From hill to hill it seems to pass,
At once far off, and near.

Though babbling only to the Vale,
Of sunshine and of flowers,   ¹⁰
Thou bringest unto me a tale
Of visionary hours.

Thrice welcome, darling of the Spring!
Even yet thou art to me
No bird, but an invisible thing, 15
A voice, a mystery;

The same whom in my school-boy days
I listened to; that Cry
Which made me look a thousand ways
In bush, and tree, and sky. 20

To seek thee did I often rove
Through woods and on the green;
And thou wert still a hope, a love;
Still longed for, never seen.

And I can listen to thee yet; 25
Can lie upon the plain
And listen, till I do beget
That golden time again.

O blessed Bird! the earth we pace
Again appears to be 30
An unsubstantial, faery place;
That is fit home for Thee!

(1807)

RESOLUTION AND INDEPENDENCE

There was a roaring in the wind all night;
The rain came heavily and fell in floods;
But now the sun is rising calm and bright;
The birds are singing in the distant woods:
Over his own sweet voice the Stock-dove
 broods; 5
The Jay makes answer as the Magpie chat-
 ters;
And all the air is filled with pleasant noise
 of waters.

All things that love the sun are out of
 doors:
The sky rejoices in the morning's birth;
The grass is bright with rain-drops; — on
 the moors 10
The hare is running races in her mirth;
And with her feet she from the plashy
 earth
Raises a mist; that, glittering in the sun,
Runs with her all the way, wherever she
 doth run.

I was a Traveler then upon the moor; 15
I saw the hare that raced about with joy;
I heard the woods and distant waters roar,
Or heard them not, as happy as a boy:
The pleasant season did my heart employ:
My old remembrances went from me
 wholly; 20

And all the ways of men so vain and
 melancholy!

But, as it sometimes chanceth, from the
 might
Of joy in minds that can no further go,
As high as we have mounted in delight
In our dejection do we sink as low, 25
To me that morning did it happen so;
And fears, and fancies, thick upon me
 came;
Dim sadness — and blind thoughts, I knew
 not, nor could name.

I heard the sky-lark warbling in the sky;
And I bethought me of the playful hare: 30
Even such a happy child of earth am I;
Even as these blissful creatures do I fare;
Far from the world I walk, and from all
 care;
But there may come another day to me —
Solitude, pain of heart, distress, and
 poverty. 35

My whole life I have lived in pleasant
 thought,
As if life's business were a summer mood;
As if all needful things would come un-
 sought
To genial faith, still rich in genial good;
But how can He expect that others should
Build for him, sow for him, and at his call
Love him, who for himself will take no
 heed at all? 42

I thought of Chatterton, the marvelous Boy,
The sleepless Soul that perished in his
 pride;
Of Him who walked in glory and in joy 45
Following his plough, along the mountain-
 side:
By our own spirits are we deified:
We Poets in our youth begin in gladness;
But thereof come in the end despondency
 and madness.

Now, whether it were by peculiar grace, 50
A leading from above, a something given,
Yet it befell, that, in this lonely place,
When I with these untoward thoughts had
 striven,
Beside a pool bare to the eye of heaven
I saw a Man before me unawares: 55
The oldest man he seemed that ever wore
 gray hairs.
As a huge stone is sometimes seen to lie
Couched on the bald top of an eminence;
Wonder to all who do the same espy,

By what means it could thither come, and
   whence;   60
So that it seems a thing endued with sense:
Like a sea-beast crawled forth, that on a
   shelf
Of rock or sand reposeth, there to sun itself;

Such seemed this Man, not all alive nor
   dead,
Nor all asleep — in his extreme old age: 65
His body was bent double, feet and head
Coming together in life's pilgrimage;
As if some dire constraint of pain, or rage
Of sickness felt by him in times long past,
A more than human weight upon his frame
   had cast.   70

Himself he propped, limbs, body, and pale
   face,
Upon a long gray staff of shaven wood:
And, still as I drew near with gentle pace,
Upon the margin of that moorish flood
Motionless as a cloud the old Man stood; 75
That heareth not the loud winds when they
   call;
And moveth altogether, if it move at all.

At length, himself unsettling, he the pond
Stirred with his staff, and fixedly did look
Upon the muddy water, which he conned, 80
As if he had been reading in a book:
And now a stranger's privilege I took;
And, drawing to his side, to him did say,
'This morning gives us promise of a glori-
   ous day.'

A gentle answer did the old Man make, 85
In courteous speech which forth he slowly
   drew:
And him with further words I thus bespake,
'What occupation do you there pursue?
This is a lonesome place for one like you.'
Ere he replied, a flash of mild surprise
Broke from the sable orbs of his yet vivid
   eyes.   91

His words came feebly, from a feeble chest,
But each in solemn order followed each,
With something of a lofty utterance drest;
Choice word, and measured phrase, above
   the reach   95
Of ordinary men; a stately speech;
Such as grave Livers do in Scotland use,
Religious men, who give to God and man
   their dues.

He told, that to these waters he had come
To gather leeches, being old and poor: 100
Employment hazardous and wearisome!

And he had many hardships to endure:
From pond to pond he roamed, from moor
   to moor;
Housing, with God's good help, by choice
   or chance;
And in this way he gained an honest maintenance.   105

The old Man still stood talking by my side;
But now his voice to me was like a stream
Scarce heard; nor word from word could I
   divide;
And the whole body of the man did seem
Like one whom I had met with in a dream;
Or like a man from some far region sent,
To give me human strength, by apt ad-
   monishment.   112

My former thoughts returned: the fear that
   kills;
And hope that is unwilling to be fed;
Cold, pain and labor, and all fleshly ills;
And mighty Poets in their misery dead. 116
Perplexed, and longing to be comforted,
My question eagerly did I renew,
'How is it that you live, and what is it you
   do?'

He with a smile did then his words repeat;
And said, that, gathering leeches, far and
   wide   121
He traveled; stirring thus about his feet
The waters of the pools where they abide.
'Once I could meet with them on every
   side;
But they have dwindled long by slow decay;
Yet still I persevere, and find them where I
   may.'   126

While he was talking thus, the lonely place,
The old Man's shape, and speech, all
   troubled me:
In my mind's eye I seemed to see him pace
About the weary moors continually,   130
Wandering about alone and silently.
While I these thoughts within myself pur-
   sued,
He, having made a pause, the same dis-
   course renewed.

And soon with this he other matter blended,
Cheerfully uttered, with demeanor kind, 135
But stately in the main; and when he
   ended,
I could have laughed myself to scorn to find
In that decrepit Man so firm a mind.
'God,' said I, 'be my help and stay secure;
I'll think of the leech-gatherer on the
   lonely moor!'   140
                         (1807)

TO A YOUNG LADY

WHO HAD BEEN REPROACHED FOR TAKING LONG
WALKS IN THE COUNTRY

Dear child of nature, let them rail!
There is a nest in a green dale,
A harbor and a hold,
Where thou, a Wife and Friend, shalt see
Thy own heart-stirring days, and be   5
A light to young and old.

There, healthy as a shepherd-boy,
And treading among flowers of joy,
Which at no season fade,
Thou, while thy babes around thee cling,   10
Shalt show us how divine a thing
A Woman may be made.

Thy thoughts and feelings shall not die,
Nor leave thee when gray hairs are nigh,
A melancholy slave;   15
But an old age serene and bright,
And lovely as a Lapland night,
Shall lead thee to thy grave.

(1807)

THE SOLITARY REAPER

Behold her, single in the field,
Yon solitary Highland Lass!
Reaping and singing by herself;
Stop here, or gently pass!
Alone she cuts and binds the grain,   5
And sings a melancholy strain;
O listen! for the Vale profound
Is overflowing with the sound.

No Nightingale did ever chaunt
More welcome notes to weary bands   10
Of travelers in some shady haunt,
Among Arabian sands:
A voice so thrilling ne 'er was heard
In spring-time from the Cuckoo-bird,
Breaking the silence of the seas   15
Among the farthest Hebrides.

Will no one tell me what she sings? —
Perhaps the plaintive numbers flow
For old, unhappy, far-off things,
And battles long ago: 20
Or is it some more humble lay,
Familiar matter of to-day?
Some natural sorrow, loss, or pain,
That has been, and may be again?

Whate'er the theme, the Maiden sang   25
As if her song could have no ending;

I saw her singing at her work,
And o'er the sickle bending; —
I listened, motionless and still;
And, as I mounted up the hill,   30
The music in my heart I bore,
Long after it was heard no more.

(1807)

YARROW UNVISITED

See the various Poems the scene of which is laid
upon the Banks of the Yarrow: in particular, the
exquisite Ballad of Hamilton, beginning:

'Busk ye, busk ye, my bonny, bonny bride,
Busk ye, busk ye, my winsome Marrow!

From Sterling Castle we had seen
The mazy Forth unraveled.
Had trod the banks of Clyde, and Tay,
And with the Tweed had traveled:
And when we came to Clovenford,   5
Then said my *winsome Marrow*,
'Whate'er betide, we 'll turn aside,
And see the Braes of Yarrow.

'Let Yarrow folk, *frae* Selkirk town.
Who have been buying, selling,   10
Go back to Yarrow, 't is their own;
Each maiden to her dwelling!
On Yarrow's banks let herons feed,
Hares couch, and rabbits burrow!
But we will downward with the Tweed,   15
Nor turn aside to Yarrow.

'There 's Gala Water, Leader Haughs,
Both lying right before us;
And Dryburgh, where with chiming Tweed
The lintwhites sing in chorus;   20
There 's pleasant Teviotdale, a land
Made blithe with plough and harrow:
Why throw away a needful day
To go in search of Yarrow?

'What 's Yarrow but a river bare,   25
That glides the dark hills under?
There are a thousand such elsewhere
As worthy of your wonder.'
Strange words they seemed of slight and
        scorn:
My True love sighed for sorrow: 30
And looked me in the face, to think
I thus could speak of Yarrow!

'Oh! green,' said I, 'are Yarrow's holms,
And sweet is Yarrow flowing!
Fair hangs the apple frae the rock,[1]   35

[1] See Hamilton's ballad, as above.

But we will leave it growing.
O'er hilly path, and open Strath,
We'll wander Scotland thorough;
But, though so near, we will not turn
Into the dale of Yarrow.   40

'Let beeves and home-bred kine partake
The sweets of Burn-mill meadow;
The swan on still St. Mary's Lake
Float double, swan and shadow!
We will not see them; will not go,   45
To-day, nor yet to-morrow;
Enough if in our hearts we know
There's such a place as Yarrow.

'Be Yarrow stream unseen, unknown!
It must, or we shall rue it: 50
We have a vision of our own;
Ah! why should we undo it?
The treasured dreams of times long past,
We'll keep them, winsome Marrow!
For when we're there, although 't is fair, 55
'T will be another Yarrow!

'If Care, with freezing years should come,
And wandering seem but folly,—
Should we be loath to stir from home,
And yet be melancholy;   60
Should life be dull, and spirits low,
'T will soothe us in our sorrow,
That earth has something yet to show,
The bonny holms of Yarrow!'
                            (1807)

SHE WAS A PHANTOM OF DE-
LIGHT

She was a Phantom of delight
When first she gleamed upon my sight;
A lovely Apparition, sent
To be a moment's ornament;
Her eyes as stars of Twilight fair;   5
Like Twilight's too, her dusky hair;
But all things else about her drawn
From May-time and the cheerful Dawn;
A dancing Shape, an Image gay,
To haunt, to startle, and waylay.   10

I saw her upon nearer view,
A Spirit, yet a Woman too!
Her household motions light and free,
And steps of virgin liberty;
A countenance in which did meet   15
Sweet records, promises as sweet;
A Creature not too bright or good
For human nature's daily food:

For transient sorrows, simple wiles,
Praise, blame, love, kisses, tears, and
    smiles.   20

And now I see with eye serene
The very pulse of the machine;
A Being breathing thoughtful breath,
A Traveler between life and death;
The reason firm, the temperate will,   25
Endurance, foresight, strength, and skill,
A perfect Woman, nobly planned,
To warn, to comfort, and command;
And yet a Spirit still, and bright
With something of angelic light.   30
                            (1807)

I WANDERED LONELY AS A CLOUD

I wandered lonely as a cloud
That floats on high o'er vales and hills,
When all at once I saw a crowd,
A host of golden daffodils;
Beside the lake, beneath the trees,   5
Fluttering and dancing in the breeze.

Continuous as the stars that shine
And twinkle on the milky way,
They stretched in never-ending line
Along the margin of a bay: 10
Ten thousand saw I at a glance,
Tossing their heads in sprightly dance.

The waves beside them danced, but they
Outdid the sparkling waves in glee:—
A poet could not but be gay   15
In such a jocund company:
I gazed—and gazed—but little thought
What wealth the show to me had brought.

For oft when on my couch I lie
In vacant or in pensive mood,   20
They flash upon that inward eye
Which is the bliss of solitude,
And then my heart with pleasure fills,
And dances with the daffodils.
                            (1807)

TO A SKY-LARK

Up with me! up with me into the clouds!
    For thy song, Lark, is strong;
Up with me, up with me into the clouds!
    Singing, singing,
With clouds and sky about thee ringing,   5
    Lift me, guide me till I find
That spot which seems so to thy mind.

I have walked through wildernesses dreary,
And to-day my heart is weary;
Had I now the wings of a Faery   10
Up to thee would I fly.
There is madness about thee, and joy divine
In that song of thine;
Lift me, guide me, high and high
To thy banqueting-place in the sky!   15

      Joyous as morning,
Thou art laughing and scorning;
Thou hast a nest for thy love and thy rest,
And, though little troubled with sloth,
Drunken Lark! thou wouldst be loath   20
To be such a traveler as I.
Happy, happy Liver,
With a soul as strong as a mountain river
Pouring out praise to the almighty Giver,
      Joy and jollity be with us both!   25

Alas! my journey, rugged and uneven,
Through prickly moors or dusty ways must
    wind;
But hearing thee, or others of thy kind,
As full of gladness and as free of heaven,
I, with my fate contented, will plod on, 30
And hope for higher raptures, when life's
    day is done.

               (1807)

ELEGIAC STANZAS

SUGGESTED BY A PICTURE OF PEELE CASTLE IN
A STORM PAINTED BY SIR GEORGE BEAUMONT

I was thy neighbor once, thou rugged Pile!
Four summer weeks I dwelt in sight of
    thee:
I saw thee every day; and all the while
Thy Form was sleeping on a glassy sea.

So pure the sky, so quiet was the air;   5
So like, so very like, was day to day!
Whene'er I looked, thy Image still was
    there;
It trembled, but it never passed away.

How perfect was the calm! it seemed no
    sleep;
No mood which season takes away or
    brings: 10
I could have fancied that the mighty Deep
Was even the gentlest of all gentle Things.

Ah! then, if mine had been the Painter's
hand.

To express what then I saw; and add the
    gleam
The light that never was on sea or land,   15
The consecration and the Poet's dream;

I would have planted thee, thou hoary Pile!
Amid a world how different from this!
Beside a sea that could not cease to smile;
On tranquil land, beneath a sky of bliss. 20

Thou should'st have seemed a treasure-
    house divine
Of peaceful years; a chronicle of heaven;—
Of all the sunbeams that did ever shine
The very sweetest had to thee been given.

A Picture had it been of lasting ease,   25
Elysian quiet, without toil or strife;
No motion but the moving tide, a breeze,
Or merely silent Nature's breathing life.

Such, in the fond illusion of my heart,
Such Picture would I at that time have
    made: 30
And seen the soul of truth in every part;
A steadfast peace that might not be betrayed.

So once it would have been,—'t is so no
    more;
I have submitted to a new control:
A power is gone, which nothing can re-
    store;   35
A deep distress hath humanized my Soul.

Not for a moment could I now behold
A smiling sea, and be what I have been:
The feeling of my loss will ne'er be old;
This, which I know, I speak with mind
    serene.   40

Then, Beaumont, Friend! who would have
    been the Friend,
If he had lived, of Him whom I deplore,
This work of thine I blame not, but com-
    mend;
This sea in anger, and that dismal shore.

Oh, 't is a passionate Work!—yet wise and
    well;   45
Well chosen is the spirit that is here;
That Hulk which labors in the deadly swell,
This rueful sky, this pageantry of fear!

And this huge Castle, standing here sub-
    lime,
I love to see the look with which it braves,
Cased in the unfeeling armor of old time   51
The lightning, the fierce wind, and trampling
    waves.

Farewell, farewell, the heart that lives
    alone,
Housed in a dream, at distance from the
    Kind!
Such happiness, wherever it be known, 55
Is to be pitied; for 't is surely blind.

But welcome fortitude, and patient cheer,
And frequent sights of what is to be borne!
Such sights, or worse, as are before me
    here.—   59
Not without hope we suffer and we mourn.
                                    (1807)

ODE TO DUTY

Stern Daughter of the Voice of God!
O Duty! if that name thou love,
Who art a light to guide, a rod
To check the erring, and reprove;
Thou who art victory and law   5
When empty terrors overawe;
From vain temptations dost set free;
And calm'st the weary strife of frail
    humanity!

There are who ask not if thine eye   10
Be on them; who, in love and truth,
Where no misgiving is, rely
Upon the genial sense of youth;
Glad Hearts! without reproach or blot;
Who do thy work, and know it not: 15
O if through confidence misplaced they
    fail,
Thy saving arms, dread Power! around
    them cast.

Serene will be our days and bright,
And happy will our nature be,
When love is an unerring light,   20
And joy its own security.
And they a blissful course may hold
Even now, who, not unwisely bold,
Live in the spirit of this creed;
Yet seek thy firm support, according to
    their need.   25

I, loving freedom, and untried;
No sport of every random gust,
Yet being to myself a guide,
Too blindly have reposed my trust:
And oft, when in my heart was heard   30
Thy timely mandate, I deferred
The task, in smoother walks to stray;
But thee I now would serve more strictly,
    if I may.

Through no disturbance of my soul,
Or strong compunction in me wrought, 35
I supplicate for thy control;
But in the quietness of thought:
Me this unchartered freedom tires;
I feel the weight of chance-desires:
My hopes no more must change their name,
I long for a repose that ever is the same. 41

Stern Lawgiver! yet thou dost wear
The Godhead's most benignant grace;
Nor know we anything so fair
As is the smile upon thy face: 45
Flowers laugh before thee on their beds;
And fragrance in thy footing treads;
Thou dost preserve the stars from wrong;
And the most ancient heavens, through
    Thee, are fresh and strong.

To humbler functions, awful Power!   50
I call thee: I myself commend
Unto thy guidance from this hour;
Oh, let my weakness have an end!
Give unto me, made lowly wise,
The spirit of self-sacrifice;   55
The confidence of reason give;
And in the light of truth thy Bondman let
    me live!
                                    (1807)

CHARACTER OF THE HAPPY WARRIOR

Who is the happy Warrior? Who is he
That every man in arms should wish to be?
It is the generous Spirit, who, when
    brought
Among the tasks of real life, hath wrought
Upon the plan that pleased his boyish
    thought: 5
Whose high endeavors are an inward light
That makes the path before him always
    bright:
Who, with a natural instinct to discern
What knowledge can perform, is diligent
    to learn;   9
Abides by this resolve, and stops not there,
But makes his moral being his prime care;
Who doomed to go in company with Pain,
And Fear, and Bloodshed, miserable train!
Turns his necessity to glorious gain;
In face of these doth exercise a power 15
Which is our human nature's highest
    dower;
Controls them and subdues, transmutes, be-
    reaves,
Of their bad influence, and their good re-
    ceives;

By objects, which might force the soul to
abate
Her feeling, rendered more compassionate;
Is placable — because occasions rise	21
So often that demand such sacrifice;
More skilful in self-knowledge, even more
pure,
As tempted more; more able to endure,
As more exposed to suffering and distress;
Thence, also more alive to tenderness.	26
'T is he whose law is reason; who depends
Upon that law as on the best of friends;
Whence, in a state where men are tempted
still
To evil for a guard against worse ill,	30
And what in quality or act is best
Doth seldom on a right foundation rest,
He labors good on good to fix, and owes
To virtue every triumph that he knows;
Who, if he rise to station of command,	35
Rises by open means; and there will stand
On honorable terms, or else retire,
And in himself possess his own desire;
Who comprehends his trust, and to the
same
Keeps faithful with a singleness of aim;	40
And therefore does not stoop, nor lie in
wait
For wealth, or honors or for worldly state;
Whom they must follow; on whose head
must fall,
Like showers of manna, if they come at all:
Whose powers shed round him in the com-
mon strife,	45
Or mild concerns of ordinary life,
A constant influence, a peculiar grace;
But who, if he be called upon to face
Some awful moment to which Heaven has
joined	49
Great issues, good or bad for human kind,
Is happy as a Lover; and attired
With sudden brightness, like a Man in-
spired;
And, through the heat of conflict keeps the
law
In calmness made, and sees what he fore-
saw;
Or if an unexpected call succeed,	55
Come when it will, is equal to the need:
He who though thus endued as with a sense
And faculty for storm and turbulence,
Is yet a Soul whose master-bias leans
To homefelt pleasures and to gentle scenes;
Sweet images! which, wheresoe'er he be,	61
Are at his heart; and such fidelity
It is his darling passion to approve;
More brave for this that he hath much to
love: —

'T is, finally, the Man, who, lifted high	65
Conspicuous object in a Nation's eye,
Or left unthought-of in obscurity,—
Who, with a toward or untoward lot,
Prosperous or adverse, to his wish or not,
Plays, in the many games of life, that one
Where what he most doth value must be
won:	71
Whom neither shape of danger can dismay,
Nor thought of tender happiness betray;
Who, not content that former worth stand
fast,
Looks forward, persevering to the last,	75
From well to better, daily self-surpast:
Who, whether praise of him must walk the
earth
For ever, and to noble deeds give birth,
Or he must fall to sleep without his fame,
And leave a dead unprofitable name,	80
Finds comfort in himself and in his cause;
And, while the mortal mist is gathering,
draws
His breath in confidence of Heaven's ap-
plause:
This is the happy Warrior; this is He
Whom every Man in arms should wish to
be.	85

(1807)

ODE

ON INTIMATIONS OF IMMORTALITY FROM RECOL-
LECTIONS OF EARLY CHILDHOOD

There was a time when meadow, grove and
stream,
The earth, and every common sight,
To me did seem
Appareled in celestial light,
The glory and the freshness of a dream.	5
It is not now as it hath been of yore; —
Turn wheresoe'er I may,
By night or day,
The things which I have seen I now can see
no more.

The rainbow comes and goes,	10
And lovely is the Rose,
The Moon doth with delight
Look round her when the heavens are
bare,
Waters on a starry night
Are beautiful and fair;	15
The sunshine is a glorious birth;
But yet I know, where'er I go,
That there hath past away a glory from
the earth.
Now, while the birds thus sing a joyous
song,

And while the young lambs bound 20
    As to the tabor's sound,
To me alone there came a thought of grief:
A timely utterance gave that thought re-
    lief,
    And I again am strong:
The cataracts blow their trumpets from the
    steep;   25
No more shall grief of mine the season
    wrong;
I hear the Echoes through the mountains
    throng,
The Winds come to me from the fields of
    sleep,
    And all the earth is gay;
        Land and sea   30
    Give themselves up to jollity,
    And with the heart of May
    Doth every Beast keep holiday;—
        Thou Child of Joy,
Shout round me, let me hear thy shouts,
        thou happy Shepherd-boy! 35

Ye blessèd Creatures, I have heard the
    call
    Ye to each other make; I see
The heavens laugh with you in your jubilee;
    My heart is at your festival,
    My head hath its coronal,   40
The fulness of your bliss, I feel—I feel it
    all.
    Oh evil day! if I were sullen
    While Earth herself is adorning,
    This sweet May-morning,
    And the Children are culling   45
        On every side,
    In a thousand valleys far and wide,
    Fresh flowers; while the sun shines
        warm,
And the Babe leaps up on his Mother's
    arm:—
    I hear, I hear, with joy I hear!   50
    — But there's a Tree, of many, one,
A single Field which I have looked upon,
Both of them speak of something that is
        gone:
    The Pansy at my feet
    Doth the same tale repeat: 55
Whither is fled the visionary gleam?
Where is it now, the glory and the dream?

Our birth is but a sleep and a forgetting:
The Soul that rises with us, our life's Star,
    Hath had elsewhere its setting,   60
        And cometh from afar:
    Not in entire forgetfulness,
    And not in utter nakedness,
But trailing clouds of glory do we come
    From God, who is our home: 65

Heaven lies about us in our infancy!
Shades of the prison-house begin to close
        Upon the growing Boy,
But he beholds the light, and whence it
        flows
        He sees it in his joy;   70
The Youth, who daily farther from the east
    Must travel, still is Nature's Priest,
    And by the vision splendid
    Is on his way attended;
At length the Man perceives it die away, 75
And fade into the light of common day.

Earth fills her lap with pleasures of her
        own;
Yearnings she hath in her own natural
        kind,
And even with something of a Mother's
        mind,
        And no unworthy aim,   80
    The homely Nurse doth all she can
To make her Foster-child, her Inmate Man,
    Forget the glories he hath known,
And that imperial palace whence he came.

Behold the Child among his new-born
        blisses,   85
A six years' Darling of a pigmy size!
See, where 'mid work of his own hand he
        lies,
Fretted by sallies of his mother's kisses,
With light upon him from his father's eyes!
See, at his feet, some little plan or chart, 90
Some fragment from his dream of human
        life,
Shaped by himself with newly-learned art;
    A wedding or a festival,
    A mourning or a funeral,
        And this hath now his heart,   95
    And unto this he frames his song:
        Then will he fit his tongue
To dialogues of business, love, or strife;
    But it will not be long
    Ere this be thrown aside,   100
        And with new joy and pride
The little Actor cons another part;
Filling from time to time his 'humorous
        stage'
With all the Persons, down to palsied Age,
That Life brings with her in her equipage;
        As if his whole vocation   106
        Were endless imitation.

Thou, whose exterior semblance doth belie
        Thy Soul's immensity;   109
Thou best Philosopher, who yet dost keep
Thy heritage, thou Eye among the blind,
That, deaf and silent, read'st the eternal
        deep,

Haunted for ever by the eternal mind,—
  Mighty Prophet! Seer blest!
    On whom those truths do rest,   115
Which we are toiling all our lives to find,
In darkness lost, the darkness of the grave;
Thou, over whom thy Immortality
Broods like the Day, a Master o'er a Slave,
A Presence which is not to be put by;   120
Thou little Child, yet glorious in the might
Of heaven-born freedom on thy being's
    height,
Why with such earnest pains dost thou pro-
    voke
The years to bring the inevitable yoke,
Thus blindly with thy blessedness at strife?
Full soon thy Soul shall have her earthly
    freight,   126
And custom lie upon thee with a weight,
Heavy as frost, and deep almost as life!

    Oh joy! that in our embers
    Is something that doth live,   130
    That nature yet remembers
    What was so fugitive!
The thought of our past years in me doth
    breed
Perpetual benediction: not indeed
For that which is most worthy to be blest;
Delight and liberty, the simple creed   136
Of Childhood, whether busy or at rest,
With new-fledged hope still fluttering in his
    breast: —
    Not for these I raise
    The song of thanks and praise;   140
    But for those obstinate questionings
    Of sense and outward things,
    Fallings from us, vanishings;
    Blank misgivings of a Creature
Moving about in worlds not realized,   145
High instincts before which our mortal
    nature
Did tremble like a guilty thing surprised:
    But for those first affections,
    Those shadowy recollections,
    Which, be they what they may,   150
Are yet the fountain light of all our day,
Are yet a master light of all our seeing;
    Uphold us, cherish, and have power to
    make
Our noisy years seem moments in the being
Of the eternal Silence: truths that wake,   155
    To perish never;
Which neither listlessness, nor mad en-
    deavor,
    Nor Man nor Boy.
Nor all that is at enmity with joy,
Can utterly abolish or destroy!   160
    Hence in a season of calm weather

    Though inland far we be,
Our Souls have sight of that immortal sea
    Which brought us hither,
    Can in a moment travel thither,   165
And see the Children sport upon the shore,
And hear the mighty waters rolling ever-
    more.

Then sing, ye Birds, sing, sing a joyous
    song!
    And let the young Lambs bound
    As to the tabor's sound!   170
We in thought will join your throng,
    Ye that pipe and ye that play,
    Ye that through your hearts to-day
    Feel the gladness of the May!
What though the radiance which was once
    so bright   175
Be now for ever taken from my sight,
    Though nothing can bring back the hour
Of splendor in the grass, of glory in the
    flower;
    We will grieve not, rather find
    Strength in what remains behind;   180
    In the primal sympathy
    Which having been must ever be;
    In the soothing thoughts that spring
    Out of human suffering;   184
    In the faith that looks through death,
In years that bring the philosophic mind.

And O, ye Fountains, Meadows, Hills, and
    Groves,
Forebode not any severing of our loves!
Yet in my heart of hearts I feel your
    might;
I only have relinquished one delight   190
To live beneath your more habitual sway.
I love the Brooks which down their chan-
    nels fret,
Even more than when I tripped lightly as
    they;
The innocent brightness of a new-born Day
    Is lovely yet;   195
The Clouds that gather round the setting
    sun
Do take a sober coloring from an eye
That hath kept watch o'er man's mortality;
Another race hath been, and other palms
    are won.
Thanks to the human heart by which we
    live,   200
Thanks to its tenderness, its joys, and fears,
To me the meanest flower that blows can
    give
Thoughts that do often lie too deep for
    tears.
                        (1807)

NUNS FRET NOT AT THEIR CONVENT'S NARROW ROOM

Nuns fret not at their convent's narrow
room;
And hermits are contented with their cells;
And students with their pensive citadels:
Maids at the wheel, the weaver at his loom,
Sit blithe and happy; bees that soar for
bloom, 5
High as the highest Peak of Furness Fells,
Will murmur by the hour in foxglove bells:
In truth, the prison, unto which we doom
Ourselves, no prison is: and hence for me,
In sundry moods, 'twas pastime to be
bound 10
Within the sonnet's scanty plot of ground;
Pleased if some Souls (for such there
needs must be)
Who have felt the weight of too much
liberty,
Should find brief solace there, as I have
found.

(1807)

PERSONAL TALK

I.

I am not One who much or oft delight
To season my fireside with personal talk,—
Of friends, who live within an easy walk,
Or neighbors, daily, weekly, in my sight:
And, for my chance-acquaintance, ladies
bright, 5
Sons, mothers, maidens withering on the
stalk,
These all wear out of me, like Forms, with
chalk
Painted on rich men's floors for one feast
night.
Better than such discourse doth silence long,
Long, barren silence, square with my desire;
To sit without emotion, hope, or aim, 11
In the loved presence of my cottage-fire,
And listen to the flapping of the flame,
Or kettle whispering its faint undersong.

II.

'Yet life,' you say, 'is life; we have seen
and see,
And with a living pleasure we describe;
And fits of sprightly malice do but bribe
The languid mind into activity.
Sound sense, and love itself, and mirth and
glee 5
Are fostered by the comment and the gibe.'
Even be it so, yet still among your tribe,
Our daily world's true Worldlings, rank not
me!

Children are blest, and powerful; their
world lies
More justly balanced; partly at their feet,
And part far from them—sweetest melo-
dies 11
Are those that are by distance made more
sweet;
Whose mind is but the mind of his own
eyes,
He is a Slave; the meanest we can meet!

III.

Wings have we,—and as far as we can go
We may find pleasure: wilderness and
wood, 16
Blank ocean and mere sky, support that
mood
Which with the lofty sanctifies the low.
Dreams, books, are each a world; and
books, we know 5
Are a substantial world, both pure and
good:
Round these, with tendrils strong as flesh
and blood,
Our pastime and our happiness will grow.
There find I personal themes, a plenteous
store,
Matter wherein right voluble I am, 10
To which I listen with a ready ear;
Two shall be named, preëminently dear,—
The gentle Lady married to the Moor;
And heavenly Una with her milk-white
Lamb.

IV.

Nor can I not believe but that hereby
Great gains are mine; for thus I live re-
mote
From evil-speaking; rancor, never sought,
Comes to me not; malignant truth, or lie.
Hence have I genial seasons, hence have I
Smooth passions, smooth discourse, and
joyous thought: 6
And thus from day to day my little boat
Rocks in its harbor, lodging peaceably.
Blessings be with them—and eternal
praise,
Who gave us nobler loves and nobler
cares— 10
The poets, who on earth have made us
heirs
Of truth and pure delight by heavenly lays!
Oh! might my name be numbered among
theirs,
Then gladly would I end my mortal days.

(1807)

COMPOSED UPON WESTMINSTER BRIDGE SEPT. 3 1802

Earth has not anything to show more fair:
Dull would he be of soul who could pass by
A sight so touching in its majesty:
This city now doth like a garment wear
The beauty of the morning; silent, bare, 5
Ships, towers, domes, theaters, and temples lie
Open unto the fields, and to the sky;
All bright and glittering in the smokeless air.
Never did sun more beautifully steep
In his first splendor valley, rock, or hill; 10
Ne'er saw I, never felt, a calm so deep!
The river glideth at his own sweet will:
Dear God! the very houses seem asleep;
And all that mighty heart is lying still!

(1807)

COMPOSED BY THE SEA-SIDE NEAR CALAIS AUGUST 1802

Fair Star of evening, Splendor of the west,
Star of my Country! — on the horizon's brink
Thou hangest, stooping, as might seem, to sink
On England's bosom: yet well pleased to rest,
Meanwhile, and be to her a glorious crest 5
Conspicuous to the Nations. Thou, I think,
Shouldst be my Country's emblem; and should'st wink,
Bright Star! with laughter on her banners, drest
In thy fresh beauty. There! that dusky spot
Beneath thee that is England; there she lies. 10
Blessings be on you both! one hope, one lot,
One life, one glory! I with many a fear
For my dear Country, many heartfelt sighs,
Among men who do not love her, linger here.

(1807)

IT IS A BEAUTEOUS EVENING, CALM AND FREE

It is a beauteous evening, calm and free.
The holy time is quiet as a Nun,
Breathless with adoration: the broad sun
Is sinking down in its tranquillity;
The gentleness of heaven broods o'er the sea; 5
Listen! the mighty Being is awake,
And doth with his eternal motion make
A sound like thunder — everlastingly.
Dear Child! dear Girl! that walkest with me here,
If thou appear untouched by solemn thought,
Thy nature is not therefore less divine: 11
Thou liest in Abraham's bosom all the year,
And worshipp'st at the Temple's inner shrine,
God being with thee when we know it not.

(1807)

ON THE EXTINCTION OF THE VENETIAN REPUBLIC

Once did she hold the gorgeous east in fee;
And was the safeguard of the west: the worth
Of Venice did not fall below her birth,
Venice, the eldest Child of liberty.
She was a maiden City, bright and free; 5
No guile seduced, no force could violate;
And when she took unto herself a Mate,
She must espouse the everlasting Sea!
And what if she had seen those glories fade,
Those titles vanish, and that strength decay; 10
Yet shall some tribute of regret be paid
When her long life hath reached its final day:
Men are we, and must grieve when even the Shade
Of that which once was great, is passed away.

(1807)

TO TOUSSAINT L'OUVERTURE

Toussaint, the most unhappy man of men!
Whether the whistling Rustic tend his plough
Within thy hearing, or thy head be now
Pillowed in some deep dungeon's earless den;
O miserable Chieftain! where and when 5
Wilt thou find patience? Yet die not! do thou
Wear rather in thy bonds a cheerful brow:
Though fallen thyself, never to rise again,
Live, and take comfort. Thou hast left behind
Powers that will work for thee, air, earth, and skies: 10

There's not a breathing of the common
    wind
That will forget thee; thou hast great allies;
Thy friends are exultations, agonies,
And love, and man's unconquerable mind.

(1807)

SEPTEMBER 1802 NEAR DOVER

Inland, within a hollow vale, I stood;
And saw, while sea was calm and air was
    clear,
The coast of France, the coast of France
    how near!
Drawn almost into frightful neighborhood.
I shrunk, for verily the barrier flood   5
Was like a lake, or river bright and fair,
A span of waters; yet what power is there!
What mightiness for evil and for good!
Even so doth God protect us if we be
Virtuous and wise. Winds blow, and
    waters roll,   10
Strength to the brave, and Power, and
    Deity,
Yet in themselves are nothing! One decree
Spake laws to *them,* and said that by the
    soul
Only the Nations shall be great and free!

(1807)

LONDON 1802

Milton! thou shouldst be living at this
    hour:
England hath need of thee; she is a fen
Of stagnant waters; altar, sword, and pen,
Fireside, the heroic wealth of hall and
    bower,
Have forfeited their ancient English dower
Of inward happiness. We are selfish men;
Oh! raise us up, return to us again;   7
And give us manners, virtue, freedom,
    power.
Thy soul was like a Star, and dwelt apart;
Thou hadst a voice whose sound was like
    the sea;   10
Pure as the naked heavens, majestic, free,
So didst thou travel on life's common way,
In cheerful godliness; and yet thy heart
The lowliest duties on herself did lay.

(1807)

IT IS NOT TO BE THOUGHT OF
THAT THE FLOOD

It is not to be thought of that the Flood
Of British freedom, which, to the open sea

Of the world's praise, from dark antiquity
Hath flowed, 'with pomp of waters unwith-
    stood,'
Roused though it be full often to a mood
Which spurns the check of salutary bands,
That this most famous Stream in bogs and
    sands   7
Should perish; and to evil and to good
Be lost for ever. In our halls is hung
Armory of the invincible knights of old: 10
We must be free or die, who speak the
    tongue
That Shakspere spake: the faith and morals
    hold
Which Milton held. In everything we are
    sprung
Of earth's first blood, have titles manifold.

(1807)

WHEN I HAVE BORNE IN MEMORY
WHAT HAS TAMED

When I have borne in memory what has
    tamed
Great Nations, how ennobling thoughts de-
    part
When men change swords for ledgers and
    desert
The student's bower for gold, some fears
    unnamed
I had, my Country! — am I to be blamed?
Now when I think of thee, and what thou
    art,   6
Verily, in the bottom of my heart,
Of those unfilial fears I am ashamed.
For dearly must we prize thee; we who
    find
In thee a bulwark for the cause of men; 10
And I by my affection was beguiled.
What wonder if a Poet now and then,
Among the many movements of his mind,
Felt for thee as a lover or a child!

(1807)

TO THE MEN OF KENT OCTOBER
1803

Vanguard of Liberty, ye men of Kent,
Ye children of a soil that doth advance
Her haughty brow against the coast of
    France,
Now is the time to prove your hardiment!
To France be words of invitation sent!   5
They from their fields can see the counte-
    nance
Of your fierce war, may ken the glittering
    lance

And hear you shouting forth your brave
    intent.
Left single, in bold parley, ye of yore,
Did from the Norman win a gallant wreath;
Confirmed the charters that were yours be-
    fore; —   11
No parleying now! In Britain is one
    breath;
We all are with you now from shore to
    shore:
Ye men of Kent, 't is victory or death!
                   (1807)

THOUGHT OF A BRITON ON THE SUBJUGATION OF SWITZERLAND

Two Voices are there; one is of the sea,
One of the mountains; each a mighty Voice:
In both from age to age thou didst re-
    joice,
They were thy chosen music, Liberty!
There came a Tyrant, and with holy glee 5
Thou fought'st against him; but hast vainly
    striven.
Thou from thy Alpine holds at length art
    driven,
Where not a torrent murmurs heard by thee.
Of one deep bliss thine ear hath been bereft;
Then cleave, O cleave to that which still
    is left;   10
For, high-souled Maid, what sorrow would
    it be
That Mountain floods should thunder as be-
    fore,
And Ocean bellow from his rocky shore,
And neither awful Voice be heard by thee!
                   (1807)

THE WORLD IS TOO MUCH WITH US

The world is too much with us: late and
    soon,
Getting and spending, we lay waste our
    powers;
Little we see in Nature that is ours;
We have given our hearts away, a sordid
    boon!
This Sea that bares her bosom to the moon;
The winds that will be howling at all hours, 6
And are up-gathered now like sleeping
    flowers;
For this, for everything, we are out of tune;
It moves us not.— Great God! I 'd rather be
A Pagan suckled in a creed outworn;   10
So might I, standing on this pleasant lea,

Have glimpses that would make me less for-
    lorn;
Have sight of Proteus rising from the sea;
Or hear old Triton blow his wreathèd horn.
                   (1807)

AFTER-THOUGHT TO THE RIVER DUDDON

I thought of Thee, my partner and my
    guide,
As being past away. Vain sympathies!
For, backward, Duddon! as I cast my eyes,
I see what was, and is, and will abide;
Still glides the Stream, and shall for ever
    glide;   5
The Form remains, the Function never dies;
While we, the brave, the mighty, and the
    wise,
We Men, who in our morn of youth defied
The elements, must vanish; — be it so!
Enough, if something from our hands have
    power   10
To live, and act, and serve the future hour;
And if, as towards the silent tomb we go,
Through love, through hope, and faith's
    transcendent dower,
We feel that we are greater than we know.
                   (1820)

INSIDE OF KING'S COLLEGE CHAPEL CAMBRIDGE

Tax not the royal saint with vain expense,
With ill-matched aims the Architect who
    planned,
Albeit laboring for a scanty band
Of white-robed Scholars only, this immense
And glorious Work of fine intelligence! 5
Give all thou canst; high Heaven rejects
    the lore
Of nicely-calculated less or more;
So deemed the man who fashioned for the
    sense
These lofty pillars, spread that branching
    roof
Self-poised, and scooped into ten thousand
    cells,   10
Where light and shade repose, where music
    dwells
Lingering — and wandering on as loath to
    die;
Like thoughts whose very sweetness yieldeth
    proof
That they were born for immortality.
                   (1822)

CONTINUED

They dreamt not of a perishable home
Who thus could build. Be mine, in hours
    of fear
Or groveling thought, to seek a refuge here;
Or through the aisles of Westminster to
    roam;
Where bubbles burst, and folly's dancing
    foam   5
Melts, if it cross the threshold; where the
    wreath
Of awe-struck wisdom droops: or let my
    path
Lead to that younger Pile, whose sky-like
    dome
Hath typified by reach of daring art
Infinity's embrace; whose guardian crest, 10
The silent Cross, among the stars shall
    spread
As now, when She hath also seen her breast
Filled with mementos, satiate with its part
Of grateful England's overflowing Dead.
                     (1822)

ON THE DEPARTURE OF SIR WALTER SCOTT FROM ABBOTSFORD FOR NAPLES

A trouble not of clouds, or weeping rain,
Nor of the setting sun's pathetic light
Engendered, hangs o'er Eildon's triple
    height:
Spirits of Power, assembled there, complain
For kindred Power departing from their
    sight;   5
While Tweed, best pleased in chanting a
    blithe strain,
Saddens his voice again, and yet again.
Lift up your hearts, ye Mourners! for the
    might
Of the whole world's good wishes with him
    goes;
Blessings and prayers in nobler retinue 10
Than sceptered King or laureled Conqueror
    knows,
Follow this wondrous Potentate. Be true,
Ye winds of ocean, and the midland sea,
Wafting your Charge to soft Parthenope!
                     (1835)

'THERE!' SAID A STRIPLING, POINTING WITH MEET· PRIDE

'There!' said a Stripling, pointing with
    meet pride
Towards a low roof with green trees half
    concealed,
'Is Mossgiel Farm; and that's the very
    field
Where Burns ploughed up the Daisy.' Far
    and wide
A plain below stretched sea-ward, while,
    descried   5
Above sea-clouds, the Peaks of Arran rose;
And, by that simple notice, the repose
Of earth, sky, sea, and air, was vivified.
Beneath 'the random *bield* of clod or stone'
Myriads of daisies have shone forth in
    flower   10
Near the lark's nest, and in their natural
    hour
Have passed away, less happy than the One
That by the unwilling ploughshare died to
    prove
The tender charm of Poetry and Love.
                     (1835)

CONCLUSION

Most sweet it is with unuplifted eyes
To pace the ground if path be there or
    none,
While a fair region round the traveler lies,
Which he forbears again to look upon;
Pleased rather with some soft ideal scene, 5
The work of Fancy or some happy tone
Of meditation, slipping in between
The beauty coming and the beauty gone.
If Thought and Love desert us, from that
    day
Let us break off all commerce with the
    Muse;   10
With Thought and Love companions of our
    way,
Whate'er the senses take or may refuse
The Mind's internal heaven shall shed her
    dews
Of inspiration on the humblest lay.
                     (1835)

SAMUEL TAYLOR COLERIDGE (1772-1834)

Coleridge was the son of a Devonshire clergyman, about whose eccentricities some amusing stories are told. As a 'poor, friendless boy' he came to London at the age of ten, and entered Christ's Hospital, the famous charity school founded by Edward VI, at the same time as Charles Lamb, with whom he struck up a friendship which lasted as long as they lived. Coleridge was a dreamy, precocious youth, who talked neo-platonism and recited Homer and Pindar in Greek in the play ground. In 1791 he was admitted as a 'sizar' or poor student at Jesus College, Cambridge, which he left in his second year, encumbered with debt and disappointed in love, to enlist in a dragoon regiment under the name of Silas Tomkyn Cumberback. As he could not ride or clean his horse and accoutrements, he proved unsuccessful as a cavalry soldier, and after four months was sent back to the university. He left Cambridge without a degree in 1795, having already formed with Southey, who was at Oxford, the design of the Pantisocracy, an ideal community to be founded on the banks of the Susquehanna by twelve gentlemen and twelve ladies of good education and liberal principles. Southey and Coleridge did not go to America, but they married the two Miss Frickers, who were to have been their partners in the adventure. Mrs. Coleridge complained that her husband 'would walk up and down composing poetry when he ought to have been in bed,' and the union proved an ill-assorted one, but as Coleridge brought his bride to a cottage near Bristol unfurnished with groceries or kitchen ware, the fault was not entirely on her side. Coleridge was all his life terribly impractical, as his own story of the publication of *The Watchman* at this time, given below, abundantly shows. In the same year (1796) Coleridge made the acquaintance of Wordsworth, and the two poets formed a strong friendship, based upon mutual affection, admiration, and reverence. Wordsworth thought Coleridge 'the only wonderful man he had ever met;' Coleridge said of Wordsworth, 'I feel myself a little man by his side.' The two poets were very different in appearance and disposition. Wordsworth's tall, gaunt frame, his high ascetic forehead, stately expression and reserved manner contrasted sharply with Coleridge's stockish figure, awkward gait, and good-natured face with curly black hair and ardent gray eyes. For more than a year (1797-8) the two poets were constantly together, and their communion resulted, not only in the publication of *Lyrical Ballads*, as already related (p. 503), but in the permanent enrichment of each poetic nature by contact with another, richly though differently endowed. After transitory appearances as a Unitarian minister and a London journalist, Coleridge returned from his studies in Germany to publish his translation of Schiller's *Wallenstein* (1800) and to establish his family at Greta Hall, Keswick, a few miles from the Wordsworths. His lack of will power was increased by the habit of taking laudanum, which became fixed in 1803, and grew upon him to an alarming extent. Lamb described him in 1806 as 'an archangel, a little damaged'; a less humorous account says he was 'ill, penniless, and worse than homeless.' Another attempt at periodical publication, *The Friend* (1809), was no better managed, and no more successful than *The Watchman*. His lectures in London, begun about the same time, were more profitable, both to himself and to the public, in spite of his habit of lecturing on anything but the subject announced, and his occasional failure to come at all; the scattered notes he left behind contain some most valuable contributions to Shaksperean criticism. Unable to break himself of the opium habit, Coleridge in 1816 put himself under the care of Dr. Gillman, of Highgate, a London suburb, with whom he lived until his death. His poetic productivity had practically ceased years before, but he continued to write prose (*Biographia Literaria*, 1817; *Aids to Reflection*, 1825), and to pour forth the flood of impassioned and philosophical talk he had begun as a school boy at Christ's Hospital. Some of it is preserved in *Table Talk*, published after his death.

Coleridge had all the powers of a great poet except the ordinary virtues of concentration and continuity of purpose. The only great poem he succeeded in completing was the *Ancient Mariner*, on which he worked under the spur of Wordsworth's influence. He projected innumerable literary undertakings, most of which were not even begun. Yet his influence in producing what a modern critic has called 'the renascence of wonder' was as revolutionary as that of Wordsworth in another way, and if the change in poetry is rightly named 'the romantic revival,' Coleridge must be given a place by the side of his greater friend and fellow poet as one of the makers of the new era.

BIOGRAPHIA LITERARIA

FROM CHAPTER X

An imprudent man of common goodness of heart cannot but wish to turn even his imprudences to the benefit of others, as far as this is possible. If therefore any one of the readers of this semi-narrative should be preparing or intending a periodical work, I warn him, in the first place, against trusting in the number of names on his subscription list. For he cannot be certain that the names were put down by sufficient authority; or, should that be ascertained, it still remains to be known, whether they were not extorted by some over zealous friend's importunity; whether the subscriber had not yielded his name, merely from want of courage to answer, no; and with the intention of dropping the work as soon as possible. One gentleman procured me nearly a hundred names for *The Friend,* and not only took frequent opportunity to remind me of his success in his canvass, but labored to impress my mind with the sense of the obligation, I was under to the subscribers; for, (as he very pertinently admonished me,) 'fifty-two shillings a year was a large sum to be bestowed on one individual, where there were so many objects of charity with strong claims to the assistance of the benevolent.' Of these hundred patrons ninety threw up the publication before the fourth number, without any notice; though it was well known to them, that in consequence of the distance, and the slowness and irregularity of the conveyance, I was compelled to lay in a stock of stamped paper for at least eight weeks beforehand; each sheet of which stood me in five pence previously to its arrival at my printer's; though the subscription money was not to be received till the twenty-first week after the commencement of the work; and lastly, though it was in nine cases out of ten impracticable for me to receive the money for two or three numbers without paying an equal sum for the postage.

In confirmation of my first caveat, I will select one fact among many. On my list of subscribers, among a considerable number of names equally flattering, was that of an Earl of Cork, with his address. He might as well have been an Earl of Bottle, for aught I knew of him, who had been content to reverence the peerage *in abstracto,* rather than *in concretis.* Of course *The Friend* was regularly sent as far, if I remember right, as the eighteenth number; that is, till a fortnight before the subscription was to be paid. And lo! just at this time I received a letter from his lordship, reproving me in language far more lordly than courteous for my impudence in directing my pamphlets to him, who knew nothing of me or my work! Seventeen or eighteen numbers of which, however, his lordship was pleased to retain, probably for the culinary or post-culinary conveniences of his servants.

Secondly, I warn all others from the attempt to deviate from the ordinary mode of publishing a work by the trade. I thought indeed, that to the purchaser it was indifferent, whether thirty per cent. of the purchase-money went to the booksellers or to the government; and that the convenience of receiving the work by the post at his own door would give the preference to the latter. It is hard, I own, to have been laboring for years, in collecting and arranging the materials; to have spent every shilling that could be spared after the necessaries of life had been furnished, in buying books, or in journeys for the purpose of consulting them or of acquiring facts at the fountain head; then to buy the paper, pay for the printing, and the like, all at least fifteen per cent. beyond what the trade would have paid; and then after all to give thirty per cent. not of the net profits, but of the gross results of the sale, to a man who has merely to give the books shelf or warehouse room, and permit his apprentice to hand them over the counter to those who may ask for them; and this too copy by copy, although, if the work be on any philosophical or scientific subject, it may be years before the edition is sold off. All this, I confess, must seem a hardship, and one, to which the products of industry in no other mode of exertion are subject. Yet even this is better, far better, than to attempt in any way to unite the functions of author and publisher. But the most prudent mode is to sell the copyright, at least of one or more editions, for the most that the trade will offer. By few only can a large remuneration be expected; but fifty pounds and ease of mind are of more real advantage to a literary man, than the chance of five hundred with the certainty of insult and degrading anxieties. I shall have been grievously misunderstood, if this statement should be interpreted as written with the desire of detracting from the character of booksellers or publishers. The individuals did not make the laws and customs of their trade, but, as in every other trade, take them as they find them. Till the evil can be proved to be removable, and without the substitution of an equal or greater inconvenience, it were neither wise nor manly even to complain of it. But to use it as a pretext for speaking, or even for thinking, or feeling, unkindly or opprobriously of the tradesmen, as individuals, would be something worse than unwise or even than unmanly; it would be immoral and calumnious. My motives point in a far different direction and to far other objects, as will be seen in the conclusion of the chapter.

A learned and exemplary old clergyman, who many years ago went to his reward followed by the regrets and blessings of his flock, published at his own expense two volumes octavo, entitled, *A New Theory of Redemption.* The work was most severely handled in *The Monthly* or *Critical Review,* I forget which; and this unprovoked hostility became the good old man's favorite topic of conversation among his friends. Well! (he used to exclaim,) in the second edition, I shall have an opportunity of exposing both the ignorance and the malignity of the anonymous critic. Two or three years however passed by without any tidings from the bookseller, who had undertaken the printing and publication of the work, and who was perfectly at his ease, as the author was known to be a man of large property. At length the accounts were written for; and in the course of a few weeks they were presented by the rider for the house, in person. My old friend put on his spectacles, and holding the scroll with no very firm hand, began — '*Paper, so much:* O moderate enough — not at all beyond my expectation! *Printing, so much:* well! moderate enough! *Stitching, covers, advertisements, carriage, and so forth, so*

much.' — Still nothing amiss. *Selleridge* (for orthography is no necessary part of a bookseller's literary acquirements) £3. 3*s.* 'Bless me! only three guineas for the what d'ye call it — the *selleridge?*' 'No more, sir!' replied the rider. 'Nay, but that is *too* moderate!' rejoined my old friend. 'Only three guineas for *selling* a thousand copies of a work in two volumes?' 'O sir!' (cries the young traveler) 'you have mistaken the word. There have been none of them *sold;* they have been sent back from London long ago; and this £3. 3*s.* is for the *cellaridge,* or warehouse-room in our book cellar.' The work was in consequence preferred from the ominous cellar of the publisher's to the author's garret; and, on presenting a copy to an acquaintance, the old gentleman used to tell the anecdote with great humor and still greater good nature.

With equal lack of worldly knowledge, I was a far more than equal sufferer for it, at the very outset of my authorship. Toward the close of the first year from the time, that in an inauspicious hour I left the friendly cloisters, and the happy grove of quiet, ever honored Jesus College, Cambridge, I was persuaded by sundry philanthropists and Anti-polemists to set on foot a periodical work, entitled *The Watchman,* that according to the general motto of the work, *all might know the truth, and that the truth might make us free!* In order to exempt it from the stamp-tax, and likewise to contribute as little as possible to the supposed guilt of a war against freedom, it was to be published on every eighth day, thirty-two pages, large octavo, closely printed, and price only four-pence. Accordingly with a flaming prospectus,— '*Knowledge is power,*' 'To cry the state of the political atmosphere,'— and so forth, I set off on a tour to the North, from Bristol to Sheffield, for the purpose of procuring customers, preaching by the way in most of the great towns, as a hireless volunteer, in a blue coat and white waistcoat, that not a rag of the woman of Babylon might be seen on me. For I was at that time and long after, though a Trinitarian (that is ad normam *Platonis*) in philosophy, yet a zealous Unitarian in religion; more accurately, I was a Psilanthropist, one of those who believe our Lord to have been the real son of Joseph, and who lay the main stress on the resurrection rather than on the crucifixion. O! never can I remember those days with either shame or regret. For I was most sincere, most disinterested. My opinions were indeed in many and most important points erroneous; but my heart was single. Wealth, rank, life itself then seemed cheap to me, compared with the interests of what I believed to be the truth, and the will of my Maker. I cannot even accuse myself of having been actuated by vanity; for in the expansion of my enthusiasm I did not think of myself at all.

My campaign commenced at Birmingham; and my first attack was on a rigid Calvinist, a tallow-chandler by trade. He was a tall dingy man, in whom length was so predominant over breadth, that he might almost have been borrowed for a foundry poker. O that face! a face κατ' ἔμφασιν! I have it before me at this moment. The lank, black, twine-like hair, pingui-nitescent, cut in a straight line along the black stubble of his thin gunpowder eye-brows, that looked like a scorched after-math from a last week's shaving. His coat collar behind in perfect unison, both of color and luster, with the coarse yet glib cordage, which I suppose he called his hair, and which with a bend inward at the nape of the neck,— the only approach to flexure in his whole figure,— slunk in behind his waistcoat; while the countenance lank, dark, very hard, and with strong perpendicular furrows, gave me a dim notion of some one looking at me through a used gridiron, all soot, grease, and iron! But he was one of the thorough-bred, a true lover of liberty, and, as I was informed, had proved to the satisfaction of many, that Mr. Pitt was one of the horns of the second beast in *The Revelations*, that *spake as a dragon*. A person, to whom one of my letters of recommendation had been addressed, was my introducer. It was a new event in my life, my first stroke in the new business I had undertaken of an author, yea, and of an author trading on his own account. My companion after some imperfect sentences and a multitude of hums and ha's abandoned the cause of his client; and I commenced an harangue of half an hour to Phileleutheros, the tallow-chandler, varying my notes, through the whole gamut of eloquence, from the ratiocinative to the declamatory, and in the latter from the pathetic to the indignant. I argued, I described, I promised, I prophesied; and beginning with the captivity of nations I ended with the near approach of the millennium, finishing the whole with some of my own verses describing that glorious state out of the Religious Musings:

—————————— Such delights
As float to earth, permitted visitants!
When in some hour of solemn jubilee
The massive gates of Paradise are thrown
Wide open, and forth come in fragments wild
Sweet echoes of unearthly melodies,
And odors snatched from beds of amaranth,
And they, that from the crystal river of life
Spring up on freshened wing, ambrosial gales!

My taper man of lights listened with perseverant and praiseworthy patience, though, as I was afterwards told, on complaining of certain gales that were not altogether ambrosial, it was a melting day with him. 'And what, Sir,' he said, after a short pause, 'might the cost be?' 'Only four-pence,'—(O! how I felt the anti-climax, the abysmal bathos of that four-pence!)—'Only four-pence, Sir, each number, to be published on every eighth day.'—'That comes to a deal of money at the end of a year. And how much, did you say, there was to be for the money?'—'Thirty-two pages, Sir, large octavo, closely printed.'—'Thirty and two pages? Bless me! why except what I does in a family way on the Sabbath, that's more than I ever reads, Sir! all the year round. I am as great a one, as any man in Brummagem, Sir! for liberty and truth and all them sort of things, but as to this,— no offense, I hope, sir,— I must beg to be excused.'

So ended my first canvass: from causes that I shall presently mention, I made but one other application in person. This took place at Manchester to a stately and opulent wholesale dealer in cottons. He took my letter of introduction, and, having perused it, measured me from head to foot and again from foot to head, and then asked if I had any bill or invoice of the thing. I presented my prospectus to him. He rapidly skimmed and hummed over the first side, and still more rapidly the second and concluding page; crushed it within his fingers and the palm of his hand; then most deliberately and significantly rubbed and smoothed one part against the other; and lastly putting it into his pocket turned his back on me with an 'over-run with these articles!' and so without another syllable retired into his counting-house. And, I can truly say, to my unspeakable amusement.

This, I have said, was my second and last attempt. On returning baffled from the first, in which I had vainly essayed to repeat the miracle of Orpheus with the Brummagem patriot, I dined with the tradesman who had introduced me to him. After dinner he importuned me to smoke a pipe with him, and two or three other *illuminati* of the same rank. I objected, both because I was engaged to spend the evening with a minister and his friends, and because I had never smoked except once or twice in my lifetime, and then it was herb tobacco mixed with Oronooko. On the assurance, however, that the tobacco was equally mild, and seeing too that it was of a yellow color; — not forgetting the lamentable difficulty, I have always experienced, in saying, 'No,' and in abstaining from what the people about me were doing,— I took half a pipe, filling the lower half of the bowl with salt. I was soon however compelled to resign it, in consequence of a giddiness and distressful feeling in my eyes, which, as I had drunk but a single glass of ale, must, I knew, have been the effect of the tobacco. Soon after, deeming myself recovered, I sallied forth to my engagement; but the walk and the fresh air brought on all the symptoms again, and, I had scarcely entered the minister's drawing-room, and opened a small packet of letters, which he had received from Bristol for me; ere I sank back on the sofa in a sort of swoon rather than sleep. Fortunately I had found just time enough to inform him of the confused state of my feelings, and of the occasion. For here and thus I lay, my face like a wall that is white-washing, deathly pale

and with the cold drops of perspiration running down it from my forehead, while one after another there dropped in the different gentlemen, who had been invited to meet, and spend the evening with me, to the number of from fifteen to twenty. As the poison of tobacco acts but for a short time, I at length awoke from insensibility, and looked round on the party, my eyes dazzled by the candles which had been lighted in the interim. By way of relieving my embarrassment one of the gentlemen began the conversation, with 'Have you seen a paper to-day, Mr. Coleridge?' 'Sir,' I replied, rubbing my eyes, 'I am far from convinced, that a christian is permitted to read either newspapers or any other works of merely political and temporary interest.' This remark, so ludicrously inapposite to, or rather, incongruous with, the purpose, for which I was known to have visited Birmingham, and to assist me in which they were all then met, produced an involuntary and general burst of laughter; and seldom indeed have I passed so many delightful hours, as I enjoyed in that room from the moment of that laugh till an early hour the next morning. Never, perhaps, in so mixed and numerous a party have I since heard conversation sustained with such animation, enriched with such variety of information and enlivened with such a flow of anecdote. Both then and afterwards they all joined in dissuading me from proceeding with my scheme; assured me in the most friendly and yet most flattering expressions, that neither was the employment fit for me, nor I fit for the employment. Yet, if I determined on persevering in it, they promised to exert themselves to the utmost to procure subscribers, and insisted that I should make no more applications in person, but carry on the canvass by proxy. The same hospitable reception, the same dissuasion, and, that failing, the same kind exertions in my behalf, I met with at Manchester, Derby, Nottingham, Sheffield,— indeed, at every place in which I took up my sojourn. I often recall with affectionate pleasure the many respectable men who interested themselves for me, a perfect stranger to them, not a few of whom I can still name among my friends. They will bear witness for me how opposite even then my principles were to those of Jacobinism or even of democracy, and can attest the strict accuracy of the statement which I have left on record in the tenth and eleventh numbers of *The Friend.*

From this rememberable tour I returned with nearly a thousand names on the subscription list of *The Watchman;* yet more than half convinced, that prudence dictated the abandonment of the scheme. But for this very reason I persevered in it; for I was at that period of my life so completely hag-ridden by the fear of being influenced by selfish motives, that to know a mode of conduct to be the dictate of prudence was a sort of presumptive proof to my feelings, that the contrary was the dictate of duty. Accordingly, I commenced the work, which was announced in London by long bills in letters larger than had ever been seen before, and which, I have been informed, for I did not see them myself, eclipsed the glories even of the lottery puffs. But alas! the publication of the very first number was delayed beyond the day announced for its appearance. In the second number an essay against fast days, with a most censurable application of a text from Isaiah for its motto, lost me near five hundred of my subscribers at one blow. In the two following numbers I made enemies of all my Jacobin and democratic patrons; for, disgusted by their infidelity, and their adoption of French morals with French *psilosophy;* and perhaps thinking, that charity ought to begin nearest home; instead of abusing the government and the Aristocrats chiefly or entirely, as had been expected of me, I leveled my attacks at 'modern patriotism,' and even ventured to declare my belief, that whatever the motives of ministers might have been for the sedition, or as it was then the fashion to call them, the *gagging* bills, yet the bills themselves would produce an effect to be desired by all the true friends of freedom, as far as they should contribute to deter men from openly declaiming on subjects, the principles of which they had never bottomed and from 'pleading *to* the poor and ignorant, instead of pleading *for* them.' At the same time I avowed my conviction, that national education and a concurring spread of the Gospel were the indispensable condition of any true political melioration. Thus by the time the seventh number was published, I had the mortification — (but why should I say this, when in truth I cared too little for any thing that concerned my worldly interests to be at all mortified about it?) — of seeing the preceding numbers exposed in sundry old iron shops for a penny a piece. At the ninth number I dropped the work. But from the London publisher I could not obtain a shilling; he was a ———— and set me at defiance. From other places I procured but little, and after such delays as rendered that little worth nothing; and I should have been inevitably thrown into jail by my Bristol printer, who refused to wait even for a month, for a sum between eighty and ninety pounds, if the money had not been paid for me by a man by no means affluent, a dear friend, who attached himself to me from my first arrival at Bristol, who has continued my friend with a fidelity unconquered by time or even by my own apparent neglect; a friend from whom I never received an advice that was not wise, nor a remonstrance that was not gentle and affectionate.

Conscientiously an opponent of the first revolutionary war, yet with my eyes thoroughly opened to the true character and impotence of the favorers of revolutionary principles in England, principles which I held in abhorrence,— (for it was part of my political creed, that whoever ceased to act as an individual by making himself a member of any society not sanctioned by his Government, forfeited the rights of a citizen)— a vehement Anti-Ministerialist, but after the invasion of Switzerland, a more vehement Anti-Gallican, and still more intensely an Anti-Jacobin, I retired to a cottage at Stowey, and provided for my scanty maintenance by writing verses for a London morning paper. I saw plainly, that literature was not a profession, by which I could expect to live; for I could not disguise from myself, that, whatever my talents might or might not be in other respects, yet they were not of the sort that could enable me to become a popular writer, and that whatever my opinions might be in themselves, they were almost equi-distant from all the three prominent parties, the Pittites, the Foxites, and the Democrats. Of the unsalable nature of my writings I had an amusing memento one morning from our own servant girl. For happening to rise at an earlier hour than usual, I observed her putting an extravagant quantity of paper into the grate in order to light the fire, and mildly checked her for her wastefulness; 'La, Sir!' (replied poor Nanny) 'why, it is only Watchmen.'

I now devoted myself to poetry and to the study of ethics and psychology; and so profound was my admiration at this time of Hartley's *Essay on Man,* that I gave his name to my first-born. In addition to the gentleman, my neighbor, whose garden joined on to my little orchard, and the cultivation of whose friendship had been my sole motive in choosing Stowey for my residence, I was so fortunate as to acquire, shortly after my settlement there, an invaluable blessing in the society and neighborhood of one, to whom I could look up with equal reverence, whether I regarded him as a poet, a philosopher, or a man. His conversation extended to almost all subjects, except physics and politics; with the latter he never troubled himself. Yet neither my retirement nor my utter abstraction from all the disputes of the day could secure me in those jealous times from suspicion and obloquy, which did not stop at me, but extended to my excellent friend, whose perfect innocence was even adduced as a proof of his guilt. One of the many busy sycophants of that day,— (I here use the word sycophant in its original sense, as a wretch who *flatters* the prevailing party by *informing* against his neighbors, under pretence that they are exporters of prohibited *figs* or fancies, — for the moral application of the term it matters not which)— one of these sycophantic law-mongrels, discoursing on the politics of the neighborhood, uttered the following deep remark: 'As to Coleridge, there is not so much harm in *him,* for he is a whirl-brain that talks whatever come uppermost; but that——! he is the *dark* traitor. *You never hear* HIM *say a syllable on the subject.'*

* * *

The dark guesses of some zealous *Quidnunc* met with so congenial a soil in the grave alarm of a titled Dogberry of our neighborhood, that a spy was actually sent down from the government *pour surveillance* of myself and friend. There must have been not only abundance, but variety of those 'honorable men' at the disposal of Ministers; for this proved a very honest fellow. After three weeks' truly Indian perseverance in tracking us, (for we were commonly together,) during all which time seldom were we out of doors, but he contrived to be within hearing,— and all the while utterly unsuspected; how indeed *could* such a suspicion enter our fancies? — he not only rejected Sir Dogberry's request that he would try yet a little longer, but declared to him his belief, that both my friend and myself were as good subjects, for aught he could discover to the contrary, as any in His Majesty's dominions. He had repeatedly hid himself, he said, for hours together behind a bank at the sea-side, (our favorite seat,) and overheard our conversation. At first he fancied, that we were aware of our danger; for he often heard me talk of one *Spy Nozy,* which he was inclined to interpret of himself, and of a remarkable feature belonging to him; but he was speedily convinced that it was the name of a man who had made a book and lived long ago. Our talk ran most upon books, and we were perpetually desiring each other to look at *this,* and to listen to *that;* but he could not catch a word about politics. Once he had joined me on the road; (this occurred, as I was returning home alone from my friend's house, which was about three miles from my own cottage,) and, passing himself off as a traveler, he had entered into conversation with me, and talked of purpose in a democrat way in order to draw me out. The result, it appears, not only convinced him that I was no friend of Jacobinism; but, (he added,) I had 'plainly made it out to be such a silly as well as wicked thing, that he felt ashamed though he had only *put it on.'* I distinctly remembered the occurrence, and had mentioned it immediately on my return, repeating what the traveler with his Bardolph nose had said, with my own answer; and so little did I suspect the true object of my 'tempter ere accuser,' that I expressed with no small pleasure my hope and belief that the conversation had been of some service to the poor misled malcontent. This incident therefore prevented all doubt as to the truth of the report, which through a friendly medium came to me from the master of the village inn, who had been ordered to entertain the Government gentleman in his best manner, but above all to be silent concerning such a person being in his house. At length he received Sir Dogberry's commands to accompany his guest at the final interview; and, after the absolving suffrage of the *gentleman honored with the confidence of Ministers,* answered, as follows, to the following queries: D. Well, landlord! and what do you know of the person in question? L. I see him often pass by with maister ————, my landlord, (*that is, the owner of the house,*) and sometimes with the new-comers at Holford; but I never said a word to him or he to me. D. But do you not know, that he has distributed papers and hand-bills of a seditious nature among the common people? L. No, your Honor! I never heard of such a thing. D. Have you not seen this Mr. Coleridge, or heard of, his haranguing and talking to knots and clusters of the inhabitants? — What are you grinning at, sir? L. Beg your Honor's pardon! but I was only thinking, how they'd have stared at him. If what I have heard be true, your Honor! they would not have understood a word he said. When our Vicar was here, Dr. L. the master of the great school and Canon of Windsor, there was a great dinner party at maister ————'s; and one of the farmers, that was there, told us that he and the Doctor talked real Hebrew Greek at each other for an hour together after dinner. D. Answer the question, sir! does he ever harangue the people? L. I hope your Honor ain't angry with me. I can say no more than I know. I never saw him talking with any one, but my landlord, and our curate, and the strange gentleman. D. Has he not been seen wandering on the hills towards the Channel, and along the shore, with books and papers in his hand, taking charts and maps of the country? L. Why, as to that, your Honor! I own, I have heard; I am sure, I would not wish to say ill of any body; but it is certain, that I have heard — D. Speak out, man! don't be afraid, you are doing your duty to your King and Gov-

ernment. What have you heard? L. Why, folks do say, your Honor! as how that he is a *Poet,* and that he is going to put Quantock and all about here in print; and as they be so much together, I suppose that the strange gentleman has some *consarn* in the business.— So ended this formidable inquisition, the latter part of which alone requires explanation, and at the same time entitles the anecdote to a place in my literary life. I had considered it as a defect in the admirable poem of *The Task,* that the subject, which gives the title to the work, was not, and indeed could not be, carried on beyond the three or four first pages, and that, throughout the poem, the connections are frequently awkward, and the transitions abrupt and arbitrary. I sought for a subject that should give equal room and freedom for description, incident, and impassioned reflections on men, nature, and society, yet supply in itself a natural connection to the parts, and unity to the whole. Such a subject I conceived myself to have found in a stream, traced from its source in the hills among the yellow-red moss and conical glass-shaped tufts of bent, to the first break or fall, where its drops become audible, and it begins to form a channel; thence to the peat and turf barn, itself built of the same dark squares as it sheltered; to the sheepfold; to the first cultivated plot of ground; to the lonely cottage and its bleak garden won from the heath; to the hamlet, the villages, the market-town, the manufactories, and the seaport. My walks therefore were almost daily on top of Quantock, and among its sloping coombes. With my pencil and memorandum-book in my hand, I was *making studies,* as the artists call them, and often moulding my thoughts into verse, with the objects and imagery immediately before my senses. Many circumstances, evil and good, intervened to prevent the completion of the poem, which was to have been entitled *The Brook.* Had I finished the work, it was my purpose in the heat of the moment to have dedicated it to our then committee of public safety as containing the charts and maps, with which I was to have supplied the French Government in aid of their plans of invasion. And these

too for a tract of coast that, from Clevedon to Minehead, scarcely permits the
approach of a fishing-boat!

<h2>CHAPTER XIV</h2>

During the first year that Mr. Wordsworth and I were neighbors, our conversations turned frequently on the two
cardinal points of poetry, the power of
exciting the sympathy of the reader by
a faithful adherence to the truth of nature, and the power of giving the interest
of novelty by the modifying colors of
imagination. The sudden charm, which
accidents of light and shade, which moonlight or sunset, diffused over a known
and familiar landscape, appeared to represent the practicability of combining both.
These are the poetry of nature. The
thought suggested itself (to which of us
I do not recollect) that a series of poems
might be composed of two sorts. In the
one, the incidents and agents were to
be, in part at least, supernatural; and the
excellence aimed at was to consist in
the interesting of the affections by the
dramatic truth of such emotions, as
would naturally accompany such situations, supposing them real. And real in
this sense they have been to every human being who, from whatever source
of delusion, has at any time believed himself under supernatural agency. For the
second class, subjects were to be chosen
from ordinary life; the characters and
incidents were to be such as will be
found in every village and its vicinity
where there is a meditative and feeling
mind to seek after them, or to notice
them when they present themselves.
In this idea originated the plan of the
Lyrical Ballads; in which it was agreed
that my endeavors should be directed to
persons and characters supernatural, or at
least romantic; yet so as to transfer from
our inward nature a human interest and
a semblance of truth sufficient to procure
for these shadows of imagination that
willing suspension of disbelief for the
moment, which constitutes poetic faith.
Mr. Wordsworth, on the other hand, was
to propose to himself as his object, to give
the charm of novelty to things of every
day, and to excite a feeling analogous to
the supernatural, by awakening the mind's
attention from the lethargy of custom,

and directing it to the loveliness and the
wonders of the world before us; an inexhaustible treasure, but for which, in
consequence of the film of familiarity
and selfish solicitude, we have eyes, yet
see not, ears that hear not, and hearts
that neither feel nor understand.

With this view I wrote the *Ancient
Mariner,* and was preparing, among other
poems, the *Dark Ladie,* and the *Christabel,* in which I should have more nearly
realized my ideal than I had done in my
first attempt. But Mr. Wordsworth's industry had proved so much more successful, and the number of his poems so much
greater, that my compositions, instead of
forming a balance, appeared rather an
interpolation of heterogeneous matter.
Mr. Wordsworth added two or three
poems written in his own character, in
the impassioned, lofty, and sustained
diction which is characteristic of his
genius. In this form the *Lyrical Ballads*
were published; and were presented by
him, as an experiment, whether subjects,
which from their nature rejected the
usual ornaments and extra-colloquial style
of poems in general, might not be so
managed in the language of ordinary life
as to produce the pleasurable interest
which it is the peculiar business of
poetry to impart. To the second edition
he added a preface of considerable length;
in which, notwithstanding some passages
of apparently a contrary import, he was
understood to contend for the extension
of this style to poetry of all kinds, and
to reject as vicious and indefensible all
phrases and forms of style that were not
included in what he (unfortunately, I
think, adopting an equivocal expression)
called the language of real life. From
this preface prefixed to poems in which
it was impossible to deny the presence of
original genius, however mistaken its
direction might be deemed, arose the
whole long-continued controversy. For
from the conjunction of perceived power
with supposed heresy I explain the in-
veteracy, and in some instances, I grieve
to say, the acrimonious passions, with
which the controversy has been conducted
by the assailants.

Had Mr. Wordsworth's poems been the
silly, the childish things which they were
for a long time described as being; had
they been really distinguished from the

compositions of other poets merely by meanness of language, and inanity of thought; had they indeed contained nothing more than what is found in the parodies and pretended imitations of them; they must have sunk at once, a dead weight, into the slough of oblivion, and have dragged the preface along with them. But year after year increased the number of Mr. Wordsworth's admirers. They were found, too, not in the lower classes of the reading public, but chiefly among young men of strong sensibility and meditative minds; and their admiration (inflamed perhaps in some degree by opposition) was distinguished by its intensity, I might almost say, by its religious fervor. These facts, and the intellectual energy of the author, which was more or less consciously felt, where it was outwardly and even boisterously denied, meeting with sentiments of aversion to his opinions, and of alarm at their consequences, produced an eddy of criticism, which would of itself have borne up the poems by the violence with which it whirled them round and round. With many parts of this preface, in the sense attributed to them, and which the words undoubtedly seem to authorize, I never concurred; but, on the contrary, objected to them as erroneous in principle, and as contradictory (in appearance at least) both to other parts of the same preface and to the author's own practice in the greater number of the poems themselves. Mr. Wordsworth, in his recent collection, has, I find, degraded this prefatory disquisition to the end of his second volume, to be read or not at the reader's choice. But he has not, as far as I can discover, announced any change in his poetic creed. At all events, considering it as the source of a controversy, in which I have been honored more than I deserve by the frequent conjunction of my name with his, I think it expedient to declare, once for all, in what points I coincide with his opinions, and in what points I altogether differ. But in order to render myself intelligible, I must previously, in as few words as possible, explain my ideas, first, of a poem; and secondly, of poetry itself, in kind and in essence.

The office of philosophical disquisition consists in just distinction: while it is the privilege of the philosopher to preserve himself constantly aware that distinction is not division. In order to obtain adequate notions of any truth, we must intellectually separate its distinguishable parts; and this is the technical process of philosophy. But having so done, we must then restore them in our conceptions to the unity in which they actually coexist; and this is the result of philosophy. A poem contains the same elements as a prose composition; the difference, therefore, must consist in a different combination of them, in consequence of a different object proposed. According to the difference of the object will be the difference of the combination. It is possible that the object may be merely to facilitate the recollection of any given facts or observations by artificial arrangement; and the composition will be a poem, merely because it is distinguished from prose by meter, or by rime, or by both conjointly. In this, the lowest sense, a man might attribute the name of a poem to the well-known enumeration of the days in the several months:

Thirty days hath September,
April, June, and November, etc.

and others of the same class and purpose. And as a particular pleasure is found in anticipating the recurrence of sound and quantities, all compositions that have this charm superadded, whatever be their contents, *may* be entitled poems.

So much for the superficial form. A difference of object and contents supplies an additional ground of distinction. The immediate purpose may be the communication of truths: either of truth absolute and demonstrable, as in works of science; or of facts experienced and recorded, as in history. Pleasure, and that of the highest and most permanent kind, may result from the attainment of the end; but it is not itself the immediate end. In other works the communication of pleasure may be the immediate purpose; and though truth, either moral or intellectual, ought to be the ultimate end, yet this will distinguish the character of the author, not the class to which the work belongs. Blest indeed is that state of society, in which the immediate purpose would be baffled by the perversion of the proper ultimate end; in which no charm of diction or imagery could exempt the Bathyllus even of an Anacreon, or the Alexis of Virgil, from disgust and aversion!

But the communication of pleasure may be the immediate object of a work not metrically composed; and that object may have been in a high degree attained, as in novels and romances. Would then the mere superaddition of meter, with or without rime, entitle these to the name of poems? The answer is, that nothing can permanently please, which does not contain in itself the reason why it is so, and not otherwise. If meter be superadded, all other parts must be made consonant with it. They must be such as to justify the perpetual and distinct attention to each part, which an exact correspondent recurrence of accent and sound are calculated to excite. The final definition then, so deduced, may be thus worded. A poem is that species of composition, which is opposed to works of science, by proposing for its immediate object pleasure, not truth; and from all other species (having this object in common with it) it is discriminated by proposing to itself such delight from the whole, as is compatible with a distinct gratification from each component part.

Controversy is not seldom excited in consequence of the disputants attaching each a different meaning to the same word; and in few instances has this been more striking than in disputes concerning the present subject. If a man chooses to call every composition a poem, which is rime, or measure, or both, I must leave his opinion uncontroverted. The distinction is at least competent to characterize the writer's intention. If it were subjoined, that the whole is likewise entertaining or affecting as a tale, or as a series of interesting reflections, I of course admit this as another fit ingredient of a poem, and an additional merit. But if the definition sought for be that of a legitimate poem, I answer, it must be one the parts of which mutually support and explain each other; all in their proportion harmonizing with, and supporting the purpose and known influences of metrical arrangement. The philosophic critics of all ages coincide with the ultimate judgment of all countries, in equally denying the praises of a just poem, on the one hand to a series of striking lines or distichs, each of which absorbing the whole attention of the reader to itself, disjoins it from its context, and makes it a separate whole, instead of a harmonizing part; and on the other hand, to an unsustained composition, from which the reader collects rapidly the general result unattracted by the component parts. The reader should be carried forward, not merely or chiefly by the mechanical impulse of curiosity, or by a restless desire to arrive at the final solution; but by the pleasurable activity of mind excited by the attractions of the journey itself. Like the motion of a serpent, which the Egyptians made the emblem of intellectual power; or like the path of sound through the air, at every step he pauses and half recedes, and from the retrogressive movement collects the force which again carries him onward, *Praecipitandus est liber spiritus* [The free spirit must be urged onward], says Petronius Arbiter most happily. The epithet, *liber,* here balances the preceding verb: and it is not easy to conceive more meaning condensed in fewer words.

But if this should be admitted as a satisfactory character of a poem, we have still to seek for a definition of poetry. The writings of Plato, and Bishop Taylor, and the *Theoria Sacra* of Burnet, furnish undeniable proofs that poetry of the highest kind may exist without meter, and even without the contra-distinguishing objects of a poem. The first chapter of Isaiah (indeed a very large proportion of the whole book) is poetry in the most emphatic sense; yet it would be not less irrational than strange to assert, that pleasure, and not truth, was the immediate object of the prophet. In short, whatever specific import we attach to the word poetry, there will be found involved in it, as a necessary consequence, that a poem of any length neither can be, nor ought to be, all poetry. Yet if a harmonious whole is to be produced, the remaining parts must be preserved in keeping with the poetry; and this can be no otherwise effected than by such a studied selection and artificial arrangement as will partake of one, though not a peculiar property of poetry. And this again can be no other than the property of exciting a more continuous and equal attention than the language of prose aims at, whether colloquial or written.

My own conclusions on the nature of poetry, in the strictest use of the word, have been in part anticipated in the preceding disquisition on the fancy and imagination. What is poetry? is so nearly the same question with, what is a poet? that the answer to the one is involved in the solution of the other. For it is a distinction resulting from the poetic genius itself, which sustains and modifies the images, thoughts, and emotions of the poet's own mind. The poet, described in ideal perfection, brings the whole soul of man into activity, with the subordination of its faculties to each other, according to their relative worth and dignity. He diffuses a tone and spirit of unity, that blends, and (as it were) fuses, each into each, by that synthetic and magical power, to which we have exclusively appropriated the name of imagination. This power, first put in action by the will and understanding, and retained under their irremissive, though gentle and unnoticed, control (*laxis effertur habenis* [he is borne with loose reins]), reveals itself in the balance or reconciliation of opposite or discordant qualities: of sameness, with difference; of the general, with the concrete; the idea, with the image; the individual, with the representative; the sense of novelty and freshness, with old and familiar objects; a more than usual state of emotion, with more than usual order; judgment ever awake and steady self-possession, with enthusiasm and feeling profound or vehement; and while it blends and harmonizes the natural and the artificial, still subordinates art to nature; the manner to the matter; and our admiration of the poet to our sympathy with the poetry. 'Doubtless,' as Sir John Davies observes of the soul (and his words may with slight alteration be applied, and even more appropriately, to the poetic imagination),—

Doubtless this could not be, but that she turns
Bodies to spirit by sublimation strange,
As fire converts to fire, the things it burns,
As we our food into our nature change.

From their gross matter she abstracts their forms,
And draws a kind of quintessence from things;
Which to her proper nature she transforms
To bear them light on her celestial wings.

Thus does she, when from individual states
She doth abstract the universal kinds;
Which then re-clothed in divers names and fates
Steal access through our senses to our minds.

Finally, good sense is the body of poetic genius, fancy its drapery, motion its life, and imagination the soul that is everywhere, and in each; and forms all into one graceful and intelligent whole.

(1817)

THE RIME OF THE ANCIENT MARINER

IN SEVEN PARTS

PART I

It is an ancient Mariner,
And he stoppeth one of three.
'By thy long gray beard and glittering eye,
Now wherefore stopp'st thou me?

'The Bridegroom's doors are opened wide,   5
And I am next of kin;
The guests are met, the feast is set:
May'st hear the merry din.'

He holds him with his skinny hand,
'There was a ship,' quoth he.   10
'Hold off! unhand me, graybeard loon!'
Eftsoons his hand dropt he.

He holds him with his glittering eye —
The Wedding-Guest stood still,
And listens like a three years' child: 15
The Mariner hath his will.

The Wedding-Guest sat on a stone:
He cannot choose but hear;
And thus spake on that ancient man,
The bright-eyed Mariner.   20

'The ship was cheered, the harbor cleared,
Merrily did we drop
Below the kirk, below the hill,
Below the lighthouse top.

'The sun came up upon the left,   25
Out of the sea came he!

And he shone bright, and on the right
Went down into the sea.

'Higher and higher every day,
Till over the mast at noon —'   30
The Wedding-Guest here beat his breast,
For he heard the loud bassoon.

The bride hath paced into the hall,
Red as a rose is she;
Nodding their heads before her goes   35
The merry minstrelsy.

The Wedding-Guest he beat his breast,
Yet he cannot choose but hear;
And thus spake on that ancient man,
The bright-eyed Mariner: 40

'And now the Storm-blast came, and he
Was tyrannous and strong:
He struck with his o'ertaking wings,
And chased us south along.

'With sloping masts and dipping prow,   45
As who pursued with yell and blow
Still treads the shadow of his foe,
And forward bends his head,
The ship drove fast, loud roared the blast,
And southward aye we fled.   50

'And now there came both mist and snow,
And it grew wondrous cold;
And ice, mast-high, came floating by,
As green as emerald.

'And through the drifts the snowy clifts   55
Did send a dismal sheen:
Nor shapes of men nor beasts we ken —
The ice was all between.

'The ice was here, the ice was there,
The ice was all around: 60
It cracked and growled, and roared and
        howled,
Like noises in a swound!

'At length did cross an Albatross:
Thorough the fog it came:
As if it had been a Christian soul,   65
We hailed it in God's name.

'It ate the food it ne'er had eat,
And round and round it flew.
The ice did split with a thunder-fit;
The helmsman steered us through!   70

And a good south wind sprung up behind;
The Albatross did follow,

And every day, for food or play,
Came to the mariner's hollo!

'In mist or cloud, on mast or shroud,   75
It perched for vespers nine;
Whiles all the night, through fog-smoke
        white,
Glimmered the white moon-shine.'

'God save thee, ancient Mariner!
From the fiends, that plague thee thus!— 80
Why look'st thou so?'—'With my cross-
        bow
I shot the Albatross!'

PART II

'The Sun now rose upon the right:
Out of the sea came he,
Still hid in mist, and on the left   85
Went down into the sea.

'And the good south wind still blew be-
        hind,
But no sweet bird did follow,
Nor any day, for food or play,
Came to the mariner's hollo!   90

'And I had done a hellish thing,
And it would work 'em woe;
For all averred, I had killed the bird
That made the breeze to blow.
Ah, wretch! said they, the bird to slay   95
That made the breeze to blow!

'Nor dim nor red, like God's own head,
The glorious Sun uprist:
Then all averred, I had killed the bird
That brought the fog and mist.   100
'T was right, said they, such birds to slay,
That bring the fog and mist.

'The fair breeze blew, the white foam flew,
The furrow followed free:
We were the first that ever burst   105
Into that silent sea.

'Down dropt the breeze, the sails dropt
        down,
'T was sad as sad could be;
And we did speak only to break
The silence of the sea!   110

'All in a hot and copper sky,
The bloody Sun, at noon,
Right up above the mast did stand,
No bigger than the Moon.

'Day after day, day after day, 115
We stuck, nor breath nor motion;
As idle as a painted ship
Upon a painted ocean.

'Water, water, everywhere,
And all the boards did shrink; 120
Water, water, everywhere,
Nor any drop to drink.

'The very deep did rot: O Christ!
That ever this should be!
Yea, slimy things did crawl with legs 125
Upon the slimy sea.

'About, about, in reel and rout,
The death-fires danced at night;
The water, like a witch's oils,
Burnt green, and blue, and white. 130

'And some in dreams assurèd were
Of the Spirit that plagued us so:
Nine fathom deep he had followed us,
From the land of mist and snow.

'And every tongue, through utter drought,
Was withered at the root; 136
We could not speak, no more than if
We had been choked with soot.

'Ah! well-a-day! what evil looks
Had I from old and young! 140
Instead of the cross, the Albatross
About my neck was hung.

PART III

'There passed a weary time. Each throat
Was parched, and glazed each eye.
A weary time! A weary time! 145
How glazed each weary eye!
When looking westward I beheld
A something in the sky.

'At first it seemed a little speck,
And then it seemed a mist: 150
It moved and moved, and took at last
A certain shape, I wist.

'A speck, a mist, a shape, I wist!
And still it neared and neared:
As if it dodged a water-sprite, 155
It plunged and tacked and veered.

'With throats unslaked, with black lips
baked,
We could nor laugh nor wail;
Through utter drought all dumb we stood!

I bit my arm, I sucked the blood, 160
And cried, "A sail! a sail!"

'With throats unslaked, with black lips
baked,
Agape they heard me call:
Gramercy! they for joy did grin,
And all at once their breath drew in, 165
As they were drinking all.

"See! see (I cried) she tacks no more!
Hither to work us weal;
Without a breeze, without a tide,
She steadies with upright keel!" 170

'The western wave was all a-flame:
The day was well nigh done:
Almost upon the western wave
Rested the broad bright Sun;
When that strange shape drove suddenly 175
Betwixt us and the Sun.

'And straight the Sun was flecked with bars,
(Heaven's Mother send us grace!)
As if through a dungeon grate he peered,
With broad and burning face. 180

'Alas! (thought I, and my heart beat loud)
How fast she nears and nears!
Are those her sails that glance in the Sun,
Like restless gossameres?

'Are those her ribs through which the
Sun 185
Did peer, as through a grate?
And is that Woman all her crew?
Is that a Death? and are there two?
Is Death that woman's mate?

'Her lips were red, her looks were free, 190
Her locks were yellow as gold:
Her skin was as white as leprosy,
The Nightmare Life-in-Death was she,
Who thicks man's blood with cold.

'The naked hulk alongside came, 195
And the twain were casting dice;
"The game is done! I've won, I've won!"
Quoth she, and whistles thrice.

'The Sun's rim dips; the stars rush out:
At one stride comes the dark; 200
With far-heard whisper, o'er the sea,
Off shot the specter-bark.

'We listened and looked sideways up!
Fear at my heart, as at a cup,
My life-blood seemed to sip! 205

The stars were dim, and thick the night,
The steersman's face by his lamp gleamed
    white;
From the sails the dew did drip —
Till clomb above the eastern bar
The hornèd Moon with one bright star   210
Within the nether tip.

'One after one, by the star-dogged Moon,
Too quick for groan or sigh,
Each turned his face with a ghastly pang,
And cursed me with his eye.   215

'Four times fifty living men,
(And I heard nor sigh nor groan)
With heavy thump, a lifeless lump,
They dropped down one by one.

'The souls did from their bodies fly —   220
They fled to bliss or woe!
And every soul, it passed me by,
Like the whiz of my cross-bow!'

PART IV

'I fear thee, ancient Mariner!
I fear thy skinny hand!   225
And thou art long, and lank, and brown,
As is the ribbed sea-sand.

'I fear thee and thy glittering eye,
And thy skinny hand, so brown.' —
'Fear not, fear not, thou Wedding-Guest!
This body dropt not down.   231

'Alone, alone, all, all alone,
Alone on a wide wide sea!
And never a saint took pity on
My soul in agony.   235

'The many men, so beautiful!
And they all dead did lie:
And a thousand thousand slimy things
Lived on; and so did I.

'I looked upon the rotting sea,   240
And drew my eyes away;
I looked upon the rotting deck,
And there the dead men lay.

'I looked to heaven, and tried to pray;
But or ever a prayer had gusht,   245
A wicked whisper came, and made
My heart as dry as dust.

'I closed my lids, and kept them close,
And the balls like pulses beat;
For the sky and the sea, and the sea and
    the sky,

Lay like a load on my weary eye,   251
And the dead were at my feet.

'The cold sweat melted from their limbs,
Nor rot nor reek did they:
The look with which they looked on me   255
Had never passed away.

'An orphan's curse would drag to hell
A spirit from on high;
But oh! more horrible than that
Is the curse in a dead man's eye!   260
Seven days, seven nights, I saw that curse,
And yet I could not die.

'The moving Moon went up the sky,
And nowhere did abide:
Softly she was going up,   265
And a star or two beside —

'Her beams bemocked the sultry main,
Like April hoar-frost spread;
But where the ship's huge shadow lay,
The charmèd water burnt alway   270
A still and awful red.

'Beyond the shadow of the ship,
I watched the water-snakes:
They moved in tracks of shining white,
And when they reared, the elfish light   275
Fell off in hoary flakes.

'Within the shadow of the ship
I watched their rich attire:
Blue, glossy green, and velvet black,
They coiled and swam; and every track   280
Was a flash of golden fire.

'O happy living things! no tongue
Their beauty might declare:
A spring of love gushed from my heart,
And I blessed them unaware!   285
Sure my kind saint took pity on me,
And I blessed them unaware.

'The selfsame moment I could pray;
And from my neck so free
The Albatross fell off, and sank   290
Like lead into the sea.

PART V

'Oh, sleep! it is a gentle thing,
Beloved from pole to pole!
To Mary Queen the praise be given!
She sent the gentle sleep from Heaven,   295
That slid into my soul.

'The silly buckets on the deck,
That had so long remained,
I dreamt that they were filled with dew;
And when I awoke, it rained.   300

'My lips were wet, my throat was cold.
My garments all were dank;
Sure I had drunken in my dreams,
And still my body drank.

'I moved, and could not feel my limbs:
I was so light — almost   306
I thought that I had died in sleep,
And was a blessèd ghost.

'And soon I heard a roaring wind:
It did not come anear;   310
But with its sound it shook the sails,
That were so thin and sere.

'The upper air burst into life!
And a hundred fire-flags sheen,
To and fro they were hurried about;   315
And to and fro, and in and out,
The wan stars danced between.

'And the coming wind did roar more loud,
And the sails did sigh like sedge;
And the rain poured down from one black
     cloud;   320
The Moon was at its edge.

'The thick black cloud was cleft, and still
The Moon was at its side:
Like waters shot from some high crag,
The lightning fell with never a jag,   325
A river steep and wide.

'The loud wind never reached the ship,
Yet now the ship moved on!
Beneath the lightning and the Moon
The dead men gave a groan.   330

'They groaned, they stirred, they all up-
     rose,
Nor spake nor moved their eyes;
It had been strange, even in a dream,
To have seen those dead men rise.

'The helmsman steered, the ship moved on;
Yet never a breeze up-blew;   336
The mariners all 'gan work the ropes,
Where they were wont to do:
They raised their limbs like lifeless tools —
We were a ghastly crew.   340

'The body of my brother's son
Stood by me, knee to knee:

The body and I pulled at one rope,
But he said nought to me.'

'I fear thee, ancient Mariner!'   345
'Be calm, thou Wedding-Guest!
'T was not those souls that fled in pain,
Which to their corses came again,
But a troop of spirits blest:

'For when it dawned — they dropped their
     arms,
And clustered round the mast;   351
Sweet sounds rose slowly through their
     mouths,
And from their bodies passed.

'Around, around, flew each sweet sound,
Then darted to the Sun;   355
Slowly the sounds come back again,
Now mixed, now one by one.

'Sometimes a-dropping from the sky
I heard the skylark sing;
Sometimes all little birds that are,   360
How they seemed to fill the sea and air
With their sweet jargoning!

'And now 't was like all instruments,
Now like a lonely flute;
And now it is an angel's song,   365
That makes the heavens be mute.

'It ceased; yet still the sails made on
A pleasant noise till noon,
A noise like of a hidden brook
In the leafy month of June,   370
That to the sleeping woods all night
Singeth a quiet tune.

'Till noon we quietly sailed on,
Yet never a breeze did breathe:
Slowly and smoothly went the ship,   375
Moved onward from beneath.

'Under the keel nine fathom deep,
From the land of mist and snow,
The spirit slid; and it was he
That made the ship to go.   380
The sails at noon left off their tune,
And the ship stood still also.

'The Sun, right up above the mast,
Had fixed her to the ocean;
But in a minute she 'gan stir,   385
With a short uneasy motion —
Backwards and forwards half her length.
With a short uneasy motion.

'Then like a pawing horse let go,
She made a sudden bound: 390
It flung the blood into my head,
And I fell down in a swound.

'How long in that same fit I lay,
I have not to declare;
But ere my living life return'd,   395
I heard, and in my soul discern'd
Two voices in the air.

'"Is it he?" quoth one, "is this the man?
By Him who died on cross,
With his cruel bow he laid full low   400
The harmless Albatross.

'"The spirit who bideth by himself
In the land of mist and snow,
He loved the bird that loved the man
Who shot him with his bow."   405

'The other was a softer voice,
As soft as honey-dew:
Quoth he, "The man hath penance done,
And penance more will do."

PART VI

FIRST VOICE

   "But tell me, tell me! speak again   410
Thy soft response renewing —
What makes that ship drive on so fast?
What is the ocean doing?"

SECOND VOICE

'"Still as a slave before his lord,
The ocean hath no blast;   415
His great bright eye most silently
Up to the Moon is cast —

'"If he may know which way to go;
For she guides him, smooth or grim.
See, brother, see! how graciously   420
She looketh down on him."

FIRST VOICE

'"But why drives on that ship so fast,
Without or wave or wind?"

SECOND VOICE

'"The air is cut away before,
And closes from behind.   425

'"Fly brother, fly! more high, more high!
Or we shall be belated:
For slow and slow that ship will go,
When the Mariner's trance is abated."

'I woke, and we were sailing on,   420
As in a gentle weather:
'Twas night, calm night, the moon was
     high;
The dead men stood together.

'All stood together on the deck,
For a charnel-dungeon fitter: 435
All fixed on me their stony eyes,
That in the Moon did glitter.

'The pang, the curse, with which they died,
Had never passed away:
I could not draw my eyes from theirs,   440
Nor turn them up to pray.

'And now this spell was snapt: once more
I viewed the ocean green,
And looked far forth, yet little saw
Of what had else been seen —   445

'Like one, that on a lonesome road
Doth walk in fear and dread,
And having once turned round, walks on,
And turns no more his head;
Because he knows a frightful fiend   450
Doth close behind him tread.

'But soon there breathed a wind on me,
Nor sound nor motion made:
Its path was not upon the sea,
In ripple or in shade.   455

'It raised my hair, it fanned my cheek
Like a meadow-gale of spring —
It mingled strangely with my fears,
Yet it felt like a welcoming.

'Swiftly, swiftly flew the ship,   460
Yet she sailed softly too:
Sweetly, sweetly blew the breeze —
On me alone it blew.

'Oh! dream of joy! is this indeed
The lighthouse top I see?   465
Is this the hill? is this the kirk?
Is this mine own countree?

'We drifted o'er the harbor-bar,
And I with sobs did pray —
"O let me be awake, my God!   470
Or let me sleep alway."

'The harbor-bay was clear as glass,
So smoothly it was strewn!
And on the bay the moonlight lay,
And the shadow of the Moon.   475

'The rock shone bright, the kirk no less,
That stands above the rock:
The moonlight steeped in silentness
The steady weathercock.

'And the bay was white with silent light,
Till rising from the same,   481
Full many shapes, that shadows were,
In crimson colors came.

'A little distance from the prow
Those crimson shadows were: 485
I turned my eyes upon the deck—
Oh, Christ! what saw I there!

'Each corse lay flat, lifeless and flat,
And, by the holy rood!
A man all light, a seraph-man,   490
On every corse there stood.

'This seraph-band, each waved his hand:
It was a heavenly sight!
They stood as signals to the land,
Each one a lovely light: 495

'This seraph-band, each waved his hand,
No voice did they impart—
No voice; but oh! the silence sank
Like music on my heart.

'But soon I heard the dash of oars,   500
I heard the pilot's cheer;
My head was turned perforce away,
And I saw a boat appear.

'The Pilot, and the Pilot's boy,
I heard them coming fast: 505
Dear Lord in Heaven! it was a joy
The dead men could not blast.

'I saw a third—I heard his voice:
It is the Hermit good!
He singeth loud his godly hymns   510
That he makes in the wood.
He'll shrieve my soul, he'll wash away
The Albatross's blood.

PART VII

'This Hermit good lives in that wood
Which slopes down to the sea.   515
How loudly his sweet voice he rears!
He loves to talk with marineres
That come from a far countree.

'He kneels at morn, and noon, and eve—
He hath a cushion plump: 520
It is the moss that wholly hides
The rotted old oak-stump.

'The skiff-boat neared: I heard them talk,
"Why, this is strange, I trow!
Where are those lights so many and fair,
That signal made but now?"   526

'"Strange, by my faith!" the Hermit said—
"And they answered not our cheer!
The planks look warped! and see those
    sails,
How thin they are and sere!   530
I never saw aught like to them,
Unless perchance it were ·

'"Brown skeletons of leaves that lag
My forest-brook along:
When the ivy-tod is heavy with snow,   535
And the owlet whoops to the wolf below,
That eats the she-wolf's young."

'"Dear Lord! it hath a fiendish look"—
(The pilot made reply)
"I am a-feared"—"Push on, push on!"
Said the Hermit cheerily.   541

'The boat came closer to the ship,
But I nor spake nor stirred;
The boat came close beneath the ship,
And straight a sound was heard.   545

'Under the water it rumbled on,
Still louder and more dread:
It reached the ship, it split the bay;
The ship went down like lead.

'Stunned by that loud and dreadful sound,
Which sky and ocean smote,   551
Like one that hath been seven days drowned,
My body lay afloat;
But swift as dreams, myself I found
Within the Pilot's boat.   555

'Upon the whirl, where sank the ship,
The boat spun round and round;
And all was still, save that the hill
Was telling of the sound.

'I moved my lips—the Pilot shrieked,   560
And fell down in a fit;
The holy·Hermit raised his eyes,
And prayed where he did sit.

'I took the oars: the Pilot's boy,
Who now doth crazy go,   565
Laughed loud and long, and all the while
His eyes went to and fro.
"Ha! ha!" quoth he, "full plain I see,
The Devil knows how to row."

'And now, all in my own countree, 570
I stood on the firm land!
The Hermit stepped forth from the boat,
And scarcely he could stand.

'"O shrieve me, shrieve me, holy man!"
The Hermit crossed his brow. 575
"Say quick," quoth he, "I bid thee say —
What manner of man art thou?"

'Forthwith this frame of mine was
wrenched
With a woeful agony,
Which forced me to begin my tale; 580
And then it left me free.

'Since then at an uncertain hour,
That agony returns;
And till my ghastly tale is told,
This heart within me burns. 585

'I pass, like night, from land to land;
I have strange power of speech;
That moment that his face I see,
I know the man that must hear me:
To him my tale I teach. 590

'What loud uproar bursts from that door:
The wedding-guests are there;
But in the garden-bower the bride
And bride-maids singing are;
And hark the little vesper bell, 595
Which biddeth me to prayer!

'O Wedding-Guest! this soul hath been
Alone on a wide wide sea:
So lonely 't was, that God himself
Scarce seemed there to be. 600

'O sweeter than the marriage-feast,
'T is sweeter far to me,
To walk together to the kirk
With a goodly company! —

'To walk together to the kirk, 605
And all together pray,
While each to his great Father bends,
Old men, and babes, and loving friends,
And youths and maidens gay!

'Farewell, farewell! but this I tell · 610
To thee, thou Wedding-Guest!
He prayeth well, who loveth well
Both man and bird and beast.

'He prayeth best, who loveth best
All things both great and small; 615
For the dear God who loveth us,
He made and loveth all.'

The Mariner, whose eye is bright,
Whose beard with age is hoar,
Is gone; and now the Wedding-Guest 620
Turned from the bridegroom's door.

He went like one that hath been stunned,
And is of sense forlorn:
A sadder and a wiser man
He rose the morrow morn. 625

(1798)

CHRISTABEL

Part I

'T is the middle of night by the castle clock
And the owls have awaken'd the crowing
cock;
Tu-whit! — Tu-whoo!
And hark, again! the crowing cock,
How drowsily it crew. 5
Sir Leoline, the Baron rich,
Hath a toothless mastiff, which
From her kennel beneath the rock
Maketh answer to the clock,
Four for the quarters, and twelve for the
hour; 10
Ever and aye, by shine and shower,
Sixteen short howls, not over loud;
Some say, she sees my lady's shroud.

Is the night chilly and dark?
The night is chilly, but not dark. 15
The thin gray cloud is spread on high,
It covers but not hides the sky.
The moon is behind, and at the full;
And yet she looks both small and dull.
The night is chill, the cloud is gray: 20
'T is a month before the month of May,
And the Spring comes slowly up this way.
The lovely lady, Christabel,
Whom her father loves so well,
What makes her in the wood so late, 25
A furlong from the castle gate?
She had dreams all yesternight
Of her own betrothèd knight;
And she in the midnight wood will pray
For the weal of her lover that 's far away. 30

She stole along, she nothing spoke,
The sighs she heaved were soft and low,
And naught was green upon the oak,
But moss and rarest misletoe:
She kneels beneath the huge oak tree, 35
And in silence prayeth she.

The lady sprang up suddenly,
The lovely lady, Christabel!

It moaned as near, as near can be,
But what it is she cannot tell.—   40
On the other side it seems to be,
Of the huge, broad-breasted, old oak tree.

The night is chill; the forest bare;
Is it the wind that moaneth bleak?
There is not wind enough in the air   45
To move away the ringlet curl
From the lovely lady's cheek —
There is not wind enough to twirl
The one red leaf, the last of its clan,
That dances as often as dance it can,   50
Hanging so light, and hanging so high,
On the topmost twig that looks up at the
       sky.

Hush, beating heart of Christabel!
Jesu, Maria, shield her well!
She folded her arms beneath her cloak,   55
And stole to the other side of the oak.
     What sees she there?

There she sees a damsel bright,
Drest in a silken robe of white,
That shadowy in the moonlight shone: 60
The neck that made that white robe wan,
Her stately neck, and arms were bare;
Her blue-veined feet unsandaled were;
And wildly glittered here and there
The gems entangled in her hair.   65
I guess, 't was frightful there to see
A lady so richly clad as she —
Beautiful exceedingly!

'Mary mother, save me now!'
Said Christabel, 'and who art thou?'   70

The lady strange made answer meet,
And her voice was faint and sweet: —
'Have pity on my sore distress,
I scarce can speak for weariness:
Stretch forth thy hand, and have no fear!'
Said Christabel, 'How camest thou here?'76
And the lady, whose voice was faint and
       sweet,
Did thus pursue her answer meet: —
'My sire is of a noble line,
And my name is Geraldine: 80
Five warriors seized me yestermorn,
Me, even me, a maid forlorn:
They choked my cries with force and fright,
And tied me on a palfrey white.
The palfrey was as fleet as wind,   85
And they rode furiously behind.
They spurred amain, their steeds were white:
And once we crossed the shade of night.
As sure as Heaven shall rescue me,

I have no thought what men they be;   90
Nor do I know how long it is
(For I have lain entranced, I wis)
Since one, the tallest of the five,
Took me from the palfrey's back,
A weary woman, scarce alive.   95
Some muttered words his comrades spoke:
He placed me underneath this oak;
He swore they would return with haste;
Whither they went I cannot tell —
I thought I heard, some minutes past,   100
Sounds as of a castle bell.
Stretch forth thy hand,' thus ended she,
'And help a wretched maid to flee.'

Then Christabel stretched forth her hand,
And comforted fair Geraldine: 105
'O well, bright dame, may you command
The service of Sir Leoline;
And gladly our stout chivalry
Will he send forth, and friends withal,
To guide and guard you safe and free   110
Home to your noble father's hall.'

She rose: and forth with steps they passed
That strove to be, and were not, fast.
Her gracious stars the lady blest,
And thus spake on sweet Christabel: 115
'All our household are at rest,
The hall as silent as the cell;
Sir Leoline is weak in health,
And may not well awakened be,
But we will move as if in stealth;   120
And I beseech your courtesy,
This night, to share your couch with me.'

They crossed the moat, and Christabel
Took the key that fitted well;
A little door she opened straight,   125
All in the middle of the gate;
The gate that was ironed within and with-
       out,
Where an army in battle array had marched
       out.
The lady sank, belike through pain,
And Christabel with might and main   130
Lifted her up, a weary weight,
Over the threshold of the gate:
Then the lady rose again,
And moved, as she were not in pain.

So, free from danger, free from fear,   135
They crossed the court: right glad they
       were.
And Christabel devoutly cried
To the Lady by her side;
'Praise we the Virgin all divine,
Who hath rescued thee from thy distress!'

'Alas, alas!' said Geraldine,   141
'I cannot speak for weariness.'
So, free from danger, free from fear,
They crossed the court: right glad they
    were.

Outside her kennel the mastiff old   145
Lay fast asleep, in moonshine cold.
The mastiff old did not awake,
Yet she an angry moan did make.
And what can ail the mastiff bitch?
Never till now she uttered yell   150
Beneath the eye of Christabel.
Perhaps it is the owlet's scritch:
For what can ail the mastiff bitch?

They passed the hall, that echoes still,
Pass as lightly as you will.   155
The brands were flat, the brands were dying,
Amid their own white ashes lying;
But when the lady passed, there came
A tongue of light, a fit of flame;
And Christabel saw the lady's eye,   160
And nothing else saw she thereby,
Save the boss of the shield of Sir Leoline
    tall,
Which hung in a murky old niche in the
    wall.
'O softly tread,' said Christabel,
'My father seldom sleepeth well:'   165
Sweet Christabel her feet doth bare,
And, jealous of the listening air,
They steal their way from stair to stair,
Now in glimmer, and now in gloom,
And now they pass the Baron's room,   170
As still as death, with stifled breath!
And now have reached her chamber door;
And now doth Geraldine press down
The rushes of the chamber floor.

The moon shines dim in the open air, 175
And not a moonbeam enters here.
But they without its light can see
The chamber carved so curiously,
Carved with figures strange and sweet,
All made out of the carver's brain,   180
For a lady's chamber meet:
The lamp with twofold silver chain
Is fastened to an angel's feet.
The silver lamp burns dead and dim;
But Christabel the lamp will trim.   185
She trimmed the lamp, and made it bright,
And left it swinging to and fro,
While Geraldine, in wretched plight,
Sank down upon the floor below.

  O weary lady, Geraldine,   190
I pray you, drink this cordial wine!

It is a wine of virtuous powers;
My mother made it of wild flowers.'
'And will your mother pity me,
Who am a maiden most forlorn?'   195
Christabel answered—'Woe is me!
She died the hour that I was born.
I have heard the gray-haired friar tell,
How on her death-bed she did say,
That she should hear the castle-bell 200
Strike twelve upon my wedding-day.
O mother dear! that thou wert here!'
'I would,' said Geraldine, 'she were!'

But soon, with altered voice, said she—
'Off, wandering mother! Peak and pine!
I have power to bid thee flee.'   205
Alas! what ails poor Geraldine?
Why stares she with unsettled eye?
Can she the bodiless dead espy?
And why with hollow voice cries she, 210
'Off, woman, off! this hour is mine—
Though thou her guardian spirit be,
Off, woman, off! 'tis given to me.'

Then Christabel knelt by the lady's side,
And raised to heaven her eyes so blue— 215
'Alas!' said she, 'this ghastly ride—
Dear lady! it hath wildered you!'
The lady wiped her moist cold brow,
And faintly said, ''T is over now!'
Again the wild-flower wine she drank: 220
Her fair large eyes 'gan glitter bright,
And from the floor, whereon she sank,
The lofty lady stood upright:
She was most beautiful to see,
Like a lady of a far countrée.   225

And thus the lofty lady spake—
'All they, who live in the upper sky,
Do love you, holy Christabel!
And you love them, and for their sake,
And for the good which me befell,   230
Even I in my degree will try,
Fair maiden, to requite you well.
But now unrobe yourself; for I
Must pray, ere yet in bed I lie.'

Quoth Christabel, 'So let it be!'   235
And as the lady bade, did she.
Her gentle limbs did she undress
And lay down in her loveliness.

But through her brain, of weal and woe,
So many thoughts moved to and fro,   240
That vain it were her lids to close;
So half-way from the bed she rose,
And on her elbow did recline.
To look at the lady Geraldine.

Beneath the lamp the lady bowed, 245
And slowly rolled her eyes around;
Then drawing in her breath aloud,
Like one that shuddered, she unbound
The cincture from beneath her breast:
Her silken robe, and inner vest, 250
Dropt to her feet, and full in view,
Behold! her bosom and half her side —
A sight to dream of, not to tell!
O shield her! shield sweet Christabel!

Yet Geraldine nor speaks nor stirs: 255
Ah! what a stricken look was hers!
Deep from within she seems half-way
To lift some weight with sick assay,
And eyes the maid and seeks delay;
Then suddenly, as one defied, 260
Collects herself in scorn and pride,
And lay down by the maiden's side! —
And in her arms the maid she took,
      Ah, well-a-day!
And with low voice and doleful look 265
These words did say:

'In the touch of this bosom there worketh
    a spell,
Which is lord of thy utterance, Christabel!
Thou knowest to-night, and wilt know to-
    morrow,
This mark of my shame, this seal of my
    sorrow;
    But vainly thou warrest, 271
      For this is alone in
    Thy power to declare,
      That in the dim forest
    Thou heard'st a low moaning, 275
And found'st a bright lady, surpassingly
    fair:
And didst bring her home with thee, in love
    and in charity,
To shield her and shelter her from the damp
    air.'

The Conclusion to Part I

It was a lovely sight to see
The lady Christabel, when she 280
Was praying at the old oak tree.
    Amid the jagged shadows
    Of mossy leafless boughs,
    Kneeling in the moonlight,
    To make her gentle vows; 285
Her slender palms together prest,
Heaving sometimes on her breast;
Her face resigned to bliss or bale —
Her face, oh, call it fair not pale,
And both blue eyes more bright than clear,
Each about to have a tear. 291

With open eyes (ah, woe is me!)
Asleep, and dreaming fearfully,
Fearfully dreaming, yet, I wis,
Dreaming that alone, which is — 295
O sorrow and shame! Can this be she,
The lady, who knelt at the old oak tree?
And lo! the worker of these harms,
That holds the maiden in her arms,
Seems to slumber still and mild, 300
As a mother with her child.

A star hath set, a star hath risen,
O Geraldine! since arms of thine
Have been the lovely lady's prison.
O Geraldine! one hour was thine — 305
Thou'st had thy will! By tairn and rill,
The night-birds all that hour were still.
But now they are jubilant anew,
From cliff and tower, tu-whoo! tu-whoo!
Tu-whoo! tu-whoo! from wood and fell! 310

And see! the lady Christabel
Gathers herself from out her trance;
Her limbs relax, her countenance
Grows sad and soft; the smooth thin lids
Close o'er her eyes; and tears she sheds —
Large tears that leave the lashes bright!
And oft the while she seems to smile 317
As infants at a sudden light!
Yea, she doth smile, and she doth weep,
Like a youthful hermitess, 320
Beauteous in a wilderness,
Who, praying always, prays in sleep.
And, if she move unquietly,
Perchance, 't is but the blood so free
Comes back and tingles in her feet. 325
No doubt, she hath a vision sweet.
What if her guardian spirit 't were,
What if she knew her mother near?
But this she knows, in joys and woes,
That saints will aid if men will call: 330
For the blue sky bends over all.

Part II

Each matin bell, the Baron saith,
Knells us back to a world of death.
These words Sir Leoline first said,
When he rose and found his lady dead: 335
These words Sir Leoline will say
Many a morn to his dying day!

And hence the custom and law began
That still at dawn the sacristan,
Who duly pulls the heavy bell, 340
Five and forty beads must tell
Between each stroke — a warning knell,
Which not a soul can choose but hear
From Bratha Head to Wyndermere.

Saith Bracy the bard, 'So let it knell!   345
And let the drowsy sacristan
Still count as slowly as he can!'
There is no lack of such, I ween,
As well fill up the space between.
In Langdale Pike and Witch's Lair,   350
And Dungeon-ghyll so foully rent,
With ropes of rock and bells of air
Three sinful sextons' ghosts are pent,
Who all give back, one after t' other,
The death-note to their living brother;   355
And oft too, by the knell offended,
Just as their one! two! three! is ended,
The devil mocks the doleful tale
With a merry peal from Borrowdale.

The air is still! through mist and cloud   360
That merry peal comes ringing loud;
And Geraldine shakes off her dread,
And rises lightly from the bed;
Puts on her silken vestments white,
And tricks her hair in lovely plight,   365
And nothing doubting of her spell
Awakens the lady Christabel.
'Sleep you, sweet lady Christabel?
I trust that you have rested well.'

And Christabel awoke and spied   370
The same who lay down by her side —
O rather say, the same whom she
Raised up beneath the old oak tree!
Nay, fairer yet! and yet more fair!
For she belike hath drunken deep   375
Of all the blessedness of sleep!
And while she spake, her looks, her air,
Such gentle thankfulness declare,
That (so it seemed) her girded vests
Grew tight beneath her heaving breasts.   380
'Sure I have sinned!' said Christabel,
'Now heaven be praised if all be well!'
And in low faltering tones, yet sweet,
Did she the lofty lady greet
With such perplexity of mind   385
As dreams too lively leave behind.

So quickly she rose, and quickly arrayed
Her maiden limbs, and having prayed
That He, who on the cross did groan,
Might wash away her sins unknown,   390
She forthwith led fair Geraldine
To meet her sire, Sir Leoline.
The lovely maid and the lady tall
Are pacing both into the hall,
And pacing on through page and groom,   395
Enter the Baron's presence-room.

The Baron rose, and while he prest
His gentle daughter to his breast,
With cheerful wonder in his eyes
The lady Geraldine espies,   400

And gave such welcome to the same,
As might beseem so bright a dame!

But when he heard the lady's tale,
And when she told her father's name,
Why waxed Sir Leoline so pale,   405
Murmuring o'er the name again,
Lord Roland de Vaux of Tryermaine?
Alas! they had been friends in youth;
But whispering tongues can poison truth;
And constancy lives in realms above;   410
And life is thorny; and youth is vain;
And to be wroth with one we love
Doth work like madness in the brain.
And thus it chanced, as I divine,
With Roland and Sir Leoline.   415
Each spake words of high disdain
And insult to his heart's best brother:
They parted — ne'er to meet again!
But never either found another
To free the hollow heart from paining —
They stood aloof, the scars remaining,   421
Like cliffs which had been rent asunder;
A dreary sea now flows between.
But neither heat, nor frost, nor thunder,
Shall wholly do away, I ween,   425
The marks of that which once hath been.
Sir Leoline, a moment's space,
Stood gazing on the damsel's face:
And the youthful Lord of Tryermaine
Came back upon his heart again.   430

O then the Baron forgot his age,
His noble heart swelled high with rage;
He swore by the wounds in Jesu's side
He would proclaim it far and wide,
With trump and solemn heraldry,   435
That they, who thus had wronged the dame
Were base as spotted infamy!
'And if they dare deny the same,
My herald shall appoint a week,
And let the recreant traitors seek   440
My tourney court — that there and then
I may dislodge their reptile souls
From the bodies and forms of men!'
He spake: his eye in lightning rolls!
For the lady was ruthlessly seized; and he
     kenned   445
In the beautiful lady the child of his friend!

And now the tears were on his face,
And fondly in his arms he took
Fair Geraldine, who met the embrace,
Prolonging it with joyous look.   450
Which when she viewed, a vision fell
Upon the soul of Christabel,
The vision of fear, the touch and pain!
She shrunk and shuddered, and saw again —
(Ah, woe is me! Was it for thee,   455
Thou gentle maid! such sights to see?)

Again she saw that bosom old,
Again she felt that bosom cold,
And drew in her breath with a hissing
 sound:
Whereat the Knight turned wildly round, 460
And nothing saw, but his own sweet maid
With eyes upraised, as one that prayed.

The touch, the sight, had passed away,
And in its stead that vision blest,
Which comforted her after-rest, 465
While in the lady's arms she lay,
Had put a rapture in her breast,
And on her lips and o'er her eyes
Spread smiles like light!
  With new surprise,
'What ails then my belovèd child?' 470
The Baron said — His daughter mild
Made answer, 'All will yet be well!'
I ween, she had no power to tell
Aught else; so mighty was the spell.
  * * *
  (1816)

KUBLA KHAN

In Xanadu did Kubla Khan
A stately pleasure-dome decree:
Where Alph, the sacred river, ran
Through caverns measureless to man
Down to a sunless sea. 5
So twice five miles of fertile ground
With walls and towers were girdled round:
And here were gardens bright with sinuous
 rills 8
Where blossomed many an incense-bearing
 tree;
And here were forests ancient as the hills, 10
Enfolding sunny spots of greenery.

But oh! that deep romantic chasm which
 slanted
Down the green hill athwart a cedarn cover!
A savage place! as holy and enchanted
As e'er beneath a waning moon was haunted
By woman wailing for her demon-lover! 16
And from this chasm, with ceaseless turmoil
 seething,
As if this earth in fast thick pants were
 breathing,
A mighty fountain momently was forced;
Amid whose swift half-intermitted burst 20
Huge fragments vaulted like rebounding
 hail,
Or chaffy grain beneath the thresher's flail:
And 'mid these dancing rocks at once and
 ever
It flung up momently the sacred river.
Five miles meandering with a mazy motion

Through wood and dale the sacred river
 ran, 26
Then reached the caverns measureless to
 man,
And sank in tumult to a lifeless ocean:
And 'mid this tumult Kubla heard from far
Ancestral voices prophesying war! 30

  The shadow of the dome of pleas-
   ure
  Floated midway on the waves;
  Where was heard the mingled
   measure
  From the fountain and the caves.
It was a miracle of rare device, 35
A sunny pleasure-dome with caves of
 ice!

  A damsel with a dulcimer
  In a vision once I saw:
  It was an Abyssinian maid,
  And on her dulcimer she played, 40
  Singing of Mount Abora.
  Could I revive within me
  Her symphony and song,
  To such a deep delight 't would win
   me
That with music loud and long, 45
I would build that dome in air,
That sunny dome! those caves of ice!
And all who heard should see them there,
And all should cry, Beware! Beware!
His flashing eyes, his floating hair! 50
Weave a circle round him thrice,
And close your eyes with holy dread,
For he on honey-dew hath fed,
And drunk the milk of Paradise.
  (1816)

FROST AT MIDNIGHT

The frost performs its secret ministry,
Unhelped by any wind. The owlet's cry
Came loud — and hark, again! loud as be-
 fore.
The inmates of my cottage, all at rest,
Have left me to that solitude, which suits 5
Abstruser musings: save that at my side
My cradled infant slumbers peacefully.
'T is calm indeed! so calm, that it disturbs
And vexes meditation with its strange
And extreme silentness. Sea, hill, and
 wood, 10
This populous village! Sea, and hill, and
 wood,
With all the numberless goings on of life
Inaudible as dreams! the thin blue flame
Lies on my low-burnt fire, and quivers not;

Only that film, which fluttered on the grate,
Still flutters there, the sole unquiet thing. 16
Methinks, its motion in this hush of nature
Gives it dim sympathies with me who live,
Making it a companionable form,
Whose puny flaps and freaks the idling
   Spirit   20
By its own moods interprets, every where
Echo or mirror seeking of itself,
And makes a toy of Thought.

                       But O! how oft,
How oft, at school, with most believing
   mind,   25
Presageful, have I gazed upon the bars,
To watch that fluttering stranger! and as
   oft
With unclosed lids, already had I dreamt
Of my sweet birth-place, and the old church-
   tower,
Whose bells, the poor man's only music,
   rang   30
From morn to evening, all the hot Fair-day,
So sweetly, that they stirred and haunted
   me
With a wild pleasure, falling on mine ear
Most like articulate sounds of things to
   come!
So gazed I, till the soothing things I dreamt
Lulled me to sleep, and sleep prolonged my
   dreams!   36
And so I brooded all the following morn,
Awed by the stern preceptor's face, mine
   eye
Fixed with mock study on my swimming
   book:
Save if the door half opened, and I snatched
A hasty glance, and still my heart leaped
   up,   41
For still I hoped to see the stranger's face,
Townsman, or aunt, or sister more beloved,
My play-mate when we both were clothed
   alike!

   Dear babe, that sleepest cradled by my
   side,   45
Whose gentle breathings, heard in this deep
   calm,
Fill up the interspersèd vacancies
And momentary pauses of the thought!
My babe so beautiful! it thrills my heart
With tender gladness, thus to look at thee, 50
And think that thou shalt learn far other
   lore
And in far other scenes! For I was reared
In the great city, pent 'mid cloisters dim,
And saw naught lovely but the sky and
   stars.

But thou, my babe! shalt wander like a
   breeze   55
By lakes and sandy shores, beneath the
   crags
Of ancient mountain, and beneath the clouds,
Which image in their bulk both lakes and
   shores
And mountain crags: so shalt thou see and
   hear
The lovely shapes and sounds intelligible 60
Of that eternal language, which thy God
Utters, who from eternity doth teach
Himself in all, and all things in himself.
Great universal Teacher! he shall mold
Thy spirit, and by giving make it ask.   65

   Therefore all seasons shall be sweet to
   thee,
Whether the summer clothe the general
   earth
With greenness, or the redbreast sit and
   sing
Betwixt the tufts of snow on the bare
   branch
Of mossy apple-tree, while the nigh thatch
Smokes in the sun-thaw; whether the eave-
   drops fall   71
Heard only in the trances of the blast,
Or if the secret ministry of frost
Shall hang them up in silent icicles,
Quietly shining to the quiet Moon.   75
                       (1798)

HUMILITY THE MOTHER OF CHARITY

Frail creatures are we all! To be the best
   Is but the fewest faults to have: —
Look thou then to thyself, and leave the
   rest
To God, thy conscience, and the grave.
                       (1830)

EPITAPH

Stop, Christian passer-by! — Stop, child of
   God,
And read with gentle breast. Beneath this
   sod
A poet lies, or that which once seemed he.—
O, lift one thought in prayer for S. T. C.;
That he who many a year with toil of breath
Found death in life, may here find life in
   death!   6
Mercy for praise — to be forgiven for fame
He asked, and hoped, through Christ.
      Do thou the same!
                  (Nov. 9, 1833)

CHARLES LAMB (1775–1834)

There are few English authors with whose character and circumstances we may become so closely acquainted as with Charles Lamb's, on account of his habit of self-confession in his essays, his skill and charm as a letter-writer, and his many literary friendships. The first seven years of his life were spent at the Inner Temple, where his father had rooms as clerk and confidential servant to one of the barristers; for the next seven he was a 'blue coat boy' at Christ's Hospital, along with Coleridge. Lamb was passionately fond of London, where he passed nearly all his days, but in *Mackery End in Hertfordshire* and other essays he has given us delightful glimpses of holiday visits to the country home of his grandmother Field. It was on one of these visits that he fell in love with the 'fair Alice' of *Dream Children*, but this youthful romance was cruelly cut short. There was a strain of mental weakness in the family, and Lamb's mind gave way. Not long after his restoration, his sister Mary, the 'Bridget Elia' of the essays, in a sudden fit of insanity, was the cause of her mother's death; on her recovery it was necessary that some one should be responsible for her safe keeping, and to this task Charles devoted the rest of his life. At this time he was earning a small salary as a clerk in the office of the East India Company and his first efforts in literature, apart from a few sonnets and other short poems, were directed to eking out their scanty income. *A Tale of Rosamund Gray*, published in 1798, had no great success; he could not get his tragedy, *John Woodvil*, put on the stage; his comedy, *Mr. H.*, was acted at Drury Lane and failed. He contributed 'witty paragraphs' to the morning papers at the rate of 'sixpence a joke, and it was thought pretty high, too,' as he tells us in the essay on *Newspapers Thirty-five Years Ago*. Fortune first smiled upon them in the *Tales from Shakspere*, written for children by the brother and sister together, Charles taking the tragedies and Mary the comedies. His *Specimens of English Dramatists contemporary with Shakspere* was an important contribution to the criticism of the Elizabethan drama, and his position in the world of letters was now well established. Leigh Hunt, Wordsworth, Southey, Keats, Hazlitt, De Quincey, and many other famous men of the time were among his friends, and much of his leisure was spent in conversation and convivial meetings, from which he sometimes returned, as his sister says, 'very smoky and drinky.' His ready wit and unfailing kindliness of heart endeared him to his friends, as the charm of his personality and the delicacy of his humor have to an ever-increasing circle of readers. His most characteristic work is to be found in the *Essays of Elia*, which appeared in the *London Magazine* from 1820 to 1826.

THE OLD FAMILIAR FACES

I have had playmates, I have had companions,
In my days of childhood, in my joyful school-days;
All, all are gone, the old familiar faces.

I have been laughing, I have been carousing,
Drinking late, sitting late, with my bosom cronies;   5
All, all are gone, the old familiar faces.

I loved a love once, fairest among women;
Closed are her doors on me, I must not see her —
All, all are gone, the old familiar faces.   9

I have a friend, a kinder friend has no man;
Like an ingrate, I left my friend abruptly;
Left him, to muse on the old familiar faces.

Ghost-like I paced round the haunts of my childhood,
Earth seemed a desert I was bound to traverse,
Seeking to find the old familiar faces.   15

Friend of my bosom, thou more than a brother,
Why wert not thou born in my father's dwelling?
So might we talk of the old familiar faces —   18

How some they have died, and some they have left me,
And some are taken from me; all are departed;   20
All, all are gone, the old familiar faces.

(1798)

567

MACKERY END IN HERTFORD-SHIRE

Bridget Elia has been my housekeeper for many a long year. I have obligations to Bridget, extending beyond the period of memory. We house together, old bachelor and maid, in a sort of double singleness; with such tolerable comfort, upon the whole, that I, for one, find in myself no sort of disposition to go out upon the mountains, with the rash king's offspring, to bewail my celibacy. We agree pretty well in our tastes and habits — yet so, as 'with a difference.' We are generally in harmony, with occasional bickerings — as it should be among near relations. Our sympathies are rather understood, than expressed; and once, upon my dissembling a tone in my voice more kind than ordinary, my cousin burst into tears, and complained that I was altered. We are both great readers in different directions. While I am hanging over (for the thousandth time) some passage in old Burton, or one of his strange contemporaries, she is abstracted in some modern tale, or adventure, whereof our common reading-table is daily fed with assiduously fresh supplies. Narrative teases me. I have little concern in the progress of events. She must have a story — well, ill, or indifferently told — so there be life stirring in it, and plenty of good or evil accidents. The fluctuations of fortune in fiction — and almost in real life — have ceased to interest, or operate but dully upon me. Out-of-the-way humors and opinions — heads with some diverting twist in them — the oddities of authorship please me most. My cousin has a native disrelish of anything that sounds odd or bizarre. Nothing goes down with her that is quaint, irregular, or out of the road of common sympathy. She 'holds Nature more clever.' I can pardon her blindness to the beautiful obliquities of the Religio Medici; but she must apologize to me for certain disrespectful insinuations, which she has been pleased to throw out latterly, touching the intellectuals of a dear favorite of mine, of the last century but one — the thrice noble, chaste, and virtuous,— but again somewhat fantastical, and original-brained, generous Margaret Newcastle.

It has been the lot of my cousin, oftener perhaps than I could have wished, to have had for her associates and mine, freethinkers — leaders, and disciples, of novel philosophies and systems; but she neither wrangles with, nor accepts, their opinions. That which was good and venerable to her, when a, child, retains its authority over her mind still. She never juggles or plays tricks with her understanding.

We are both of us inclined to be a little too positive; and I have observed the result of our disputes to be almost uniformly this — that in matters of fact, dates, and circumstances, it turns out, that I was in the right, and my cousin in the wrong. But where we have differed upon moral points; upon something proper to be done, or let alone; whatever heat of opposition, or steadiness of conviction, I set out with, I am sure always, in the long run, to be brought over to her way of thinking.

I must touch upon the foibles of my kinswoman with a gentle hand, for Bridget does not like to be told of her faults. She hath an awkward trick (to say no worse of it) of reading in company: at which times she will answer yes or no to a question, without fully understanding its purport — which is provoking, and derogatory in the highest degree to the dignity of the putter of the said question. Her presence of mind is equal to the most pressing trials of life, but will sometimes desert her upon trifling occasions. When the purpose requires it, and is a thing of moment, she can speak to it greatly; but in matters which are not stuff of the conscience, she hath been known sometimes to let slip a word less seasonably.

Her education in youth was not much attended to; and she happily missed all that train of female garniture, which passeth by the name of accomplishments. She was tumbled early, by accident or design, into a spacious closet of good old English reading, without much selection or prohibition, and browsed at will upon that fair and wholesome pasturage. Had I twenty girls, they should be brought up exactly in this fashion. I know not whether their chance in wedlock might not be diminished by it; but I can answer for it, that it makes (if the worst come to the worst) most incomparable old maids.

In a season of distress, she is the truest comforter; but in the teasing accidents, and minor perplexities, which do not call out the *will* to meet them, she sometimes maketh matters worse by an excess of participation. If she does not always divide your trouble, upon the pleasanter occasions of life she is sure always to treble your satisfaction. She is excellent to be at play with, or upon a visit; but best, when she goes a journey with you.

We made an excursion together a few summers since, into Hertfordshire, to beat up the quarters of some of our less-known relations in that fine corn country.

The oldest thing I remember is Mackery End; or Mackarel End, as it is spelt, perhaps more properly, in some old maps of Hertfordshire: a farm-house,— delightfully situated within a gentle walk from Wheathampstead. I can just remember having been there, on a visit to a great-aunt, when I was a child, under the care of Bridget; who, as I have said, is older than myself by some ten years. I wish that I could throw into a heap the remainder of our joint existences, that we might share them in equal division. But that is impossible. The house was at that time in the occupation of a substantial yeoman, who had married my grandmother's sister. His name was Gladman. My grandmother was a Bruton, married to a Field. The Gladmans and the Brutons are still flourishing in that part of the county, but the Fields are almost extinct. More than forty years had elapsed since the visit I speak of; and, for the greater portion of that period, we had lost sight of the other two branches also. Who or what sort of persons inherited Mackery End — kindred or strange folk — we were afraid almost to conjecture, but determined some day to explore.

By somewhat a circuitous route, taking the noble park at Luton in our way from Saint Alban's, we arrived at the spot of our anxious curiosity about noon. The sight of the old farm-house, though every trace of it was effaced from my recollec-tion, affected me with a pleasure which I had not experienced for many a year. For though *I* had forgotten it, *we* had never forgotten being there together, and we had been talking about Mackery End all our lives, till memory on my part became mocked with a phantom of itself, and I thought I knew the aspect of a place, which, when present, O how unlike it was to *that*, which I had conjured up so many times instead of it!

Still the air breathed balmily about it; the season was in the 'heart of June,' and I could say with the poet,

But thou, that didst appear so fair
To fond imagination,
Dost rival in the light of day
Her delicate creation!

Bridget's was more a waking bliss than mine, for she easily remembered her old acquaintance again — some altered features, of course, a little grudged at. At first, indeed, she was ready to disbelieve for joy; but the scene soon reconfirmed itself in her affections — and she traversed every outpost of the old mansion, to the wood-house, the orchard, the place where the pigeon-house had stood (house and birds were alike flown) — with a breathless impatience of recognition, which was more pardonable perhaps than decorous at the age of fifty odd. But Bridget in some things is behind her years.

The only thing left was to get into the house — and that was a difficulty which to me singly would have been insurmountable; for I am terribly shy in making myself known to strangers and out-of-date kinsfolk. Love, stronger than scruple, winged my cousin in without me; but she soon returned with a creature that might have sat to a sculptor for the image of Welcome. It was the youngest of the Gladmans; who, by marriage with a Bruton, had become mistress of the old mansion. A comely brood are the Brutons. Six of them, females, were noted as the handsomest young women in the county. But this adopted Bruton, in my mind, was better than they all — more comely. She was born too late to have remembered me. She just recollected in early life to have had her cousin Bridget once pointed out to her, climbing a stile. But the name of kindred, and of cousinship, was enough. Those slender ties, that prove slight as gossamer in the rending atmosphere of a metropolis, bind faster, as we found it, in hearty, homely, loving Hertfordshire. In five minutes we were as thoroughly acquainted as if we had been born and bred up together; were familiar, even to the calling each other by our christian names. So christians should call one another. To have seen Bridget, and her — it was like the meeting of the two scriptural cousins! There was a grace and dignity, an amplitude of form and stature, answering to her mind, in this farmer's wife, which would have shined in a palace — or so we thought it. We were made welcome by husband and wife equally — we, and our friend that was with us.— I had almost forgotten him — but B. F. will not so soon forget that meeting, if peradventure he shall read this on the far-distant shores where the kangaroo haunts. The fatted calf was made ready, or rather was already so, as if in anticipation of our coming; and, after an appropriate glass of native wine, never let me forget with what honest pride this hospitable cousin made us proceed to Wheathampstead, to introduce us (as some new-found rarity) to her mother and sister Gladmans, who did indeed know something more of us, at a time when she almost knew nothing.— With what corresponding kindness we were received by them also — how Bridget's memory, exalted by the occasion, warmed into a thousand half-obliterated recollections of things and persons, to my utter astonishment, and her own — and to the astoundment of B. F. who sat by, almost the only thing that was not a cousin there,— old effaced images of more than half-forgotten names and circumstances still crowding back upon her, as words written in lemon come out upon exposure to a friendly warmth,— when I forget all this, then may my country cousins forget me; and Bridget no more remember, that in the days of weakling infancy I was her tender charge — as I have been her care in foolish manhood since — in those pretty pastoral walks, long ago, about Mackery End, in Hertfordshire.   (1821)

DREAM-CHILDREN: A REVERIE

Children love to listen to stories about their elders, when *they* were children; to stretch their imagination to the conception of a traditionary great-uncle, or grandame, whom they never saw. It was in this spirit that my little ones crept about me the other evening to hear about their great-grandmother Field, who lived in a great house in Norfolk (a hundred times bigger than that in which they and papa lived) which had been the scene — so at least it was generally believed in that part of the country — of the tragic incidents which they had lately become familiar with from the ballad of the Children in the Wood. Certain it is that the whole story of the children and their cruel uncle was to be seen fairly carved out in wood upon the chimney-piece of the great hall, the whole story down to the Robin Redbreasts, till a foolish rich person pulled it down to set up a marble one of modern invention in its stead, with no story upon it. Here Alice put out one of her dear mother's looks, too tender to be called upbraiding. Then I went on to say, how religious and how good their great-grandmother Field was, how beloved and respected by everybody, though she was not indeed the mistress of this great house, but had only the charge of it (and yet in some respects she might be said to be the mistress of it too) committed to her by the owner, who preferred living in a newer and more fashionable mansion which he had purchased somewhere in the adjoining county; but still she lived in it in a manner as if it had been her own, and kept up the dignity of the great house in a sort while she lived, which afterwards came to decay, and was nearly pulled down, and all its old ornaments stripped and carried away to the owner's other house, where they were set up, and looked as awkward as if some one were to carry away the old tombs they had seen lately at the Abbey, and stick them up in Lady C.'s tawdry gilt drawing-room. Here John smiled, as much as to say, 'that would be foolish, indeed.' And then I told how, when she came to die, her funeral was attended by a concourse of all the poor, and some of the gentry too, of the neighborhood for many miles round, to show their respect for her memory, because she had been such a good and religious woman; so good indeed that she knew all the Psaltery by heart, ay, and a great part of the Testament besides. Here little Alice spread her hands. Then I told what a tall, upright, graceful person their great-grandmother Field once was; and how in her youth she was esteemed the best dancer — here Alice's little right foot played an involuntary movement, till upon my looking grave, it desisted — the best dancer, I was saying, in the county, till a cruel disease, called a cancer, came, and bowed her down with pain; but it could never bend her good spirits, or make them stoop, but they were still upright, because she was so good and religious. Then I told how she was used to sleep by herself in a lone chamber of the great lone house; and how she believed that an apparition of two infants was to be seen at midnight gliding up and down the great staircase near where she slept, but she said 'those innocents would do her no harm'; and how frightened I used to be, though in those days I had my maid to sleep with me, because I was never half so good or religious as she — and yet I never saw the infants. Here John expanded all his eyebrows and tried to look courageous. Then I told how good she was to all her grandchildren, having us to the great house in the holidays, where I in particular used to spend many hours by myself, in gazing upon the old busts of the twelve Cæsars, that had been emperors of Rome, till the old marble heads would seem to live again, or I to be turned into marble with them; how I never could be tired with roaming about that huge mansion, with its vast empty rooms, with their worn-out hangings, fluttering tapestry, and carved oaken panels, with the gilding almost rubbed out — sometimes in the spacious old-fashioned gardens, which I had almost to myself, unless when now and then a solitary gardening man would cross me — and how the nectarines and peaches hung upon the walls without my ever offering to pluck them, because they were forbidden fruit, unless now and then, — and because I had more pleasure in strolling about among the old melancholy-looking yew-trees, or the firs, and picking up the red berries, and the fir apples, which were good for nothing but to look at —

or in lying about upon the fresh grass, with all the fine garden smells around me — or basking in the orangery, till I could almost fancy myself ripening too along with the oranges and the limes in that grateful warmth — or in watching the dace that darted to and fro in the fish-pond, at the bottom of the garden, with here and there a great sulky pike hanging midway down the water in silent state, as if it mocked at their impertinent friskings,— I had more pleasure in these busy-idle diversions than in all the sweet flavors of peaches, nectarines, oranges, and such like common baits of children. Here John slyly deposited back upon the plate a bunch of grapes which, not unobserved by Alice, he had meditated dividing with her, and both seemed willing to relinquish them for the present as irrelevant. Then in somewhat a more heightened tone, I told how, though their great-grandmother Field loved all her grandchildren, yet in an especial manner she might be said to love their uncle, John L——, because he was so handsome and spirited a youth, and a king to the rest of us; and, instead of moping about in solitary corners, like some of us, he would mount the most mettlesome horse he could get, when but an imp no bigger than themselves, and make it carry him half over the county in a morning, and join the hunters when there were any out — and yet he loved the old great house and gardens too, but had too much spirit to be always pent up within their boundaries — and how their uncle grew up to man's estate as brave as he was handsome, to the admiration of everybody, but of their great-grandmother Field most especially; and how he used to carry me upon his back when I was a lame-footed boy — for he was a good bit older than me — many a mile when I could not walk for pain; — and how in after-life he became lame-footed too, and I did not always (I fear) make allowances enough for him when he was impatient, and in pain, nor remember sufficiently how considerate he had been to me when I was lame-footed; and how when he died, though he had not been dead an hour, it seemed as if he had died a great while ago, such a distance there is betwixt life and death; and how I bore his death as I thought pretty well at first, but afterwards it haunted and haunted me; and though I did not cry or take it to heart as some do, and as I think he would have done if I had died, yet I missed him all day long, and knew not till then how much I had loved him. I missed his kindness, and I missed his crossness, and wished him to be alive again, to be quarreling with him (for we quarreled sometimes), rather than not have him again, and was as uneasy without him, as he, their poor uncle, must have been when the doctor took off his limb. Here the children fell a-crying, and asked if their little mourning which they had on was not for uncle John, and they looked up, and prayed me not to go on about their uncle, but to tell them some stories about their pretty dead mother. Then I told how for seven long years, in hope sometimes, sometimes in despair, yet persisting ever, I courted the fair Alice W——n; and, as much as children could understand, I explained to them what coyness, and difficulty, and denial meant in maidens — when suddenly, turning to Alice, the soul of the first Alice looked out at her eyes with such a reality of representment, that I became in doubt which of them stood there before me, or whose that bright hair was; and while I stood gazing, both the children gradually grew fainter to my view, receding, and still receding till nothing at last but two mournful features were seen in the uttermost distance, which without speech, strangely impressed upon me the effects of speech: 'We are not of Alice, nor of thee, nor are we children at all. The children of Alice call Bartrum father. We are nothing; less than nothing, and dreams. We are only what might have been, and must wait upon the tedious shores of Lethe millions of ages before we have existence and a name'—— and immediately awaking, I found myself quietly seated in my bachelor arm-chair, where I had fallen asleep, with the faithful Bridget unchanged by my side — but John L. (or James Elia) was gone for ever. (1822)

A CHAPTER ON EARS

I have no ear.—

Mistake me not, reader,— nor imagine that I am by nature destitute of those exterior twin appendages, hanging ornaments, and (architectually speaking) handsome volutes to the human capital. Better my mother had never borne me. — I am, I think, rather delicately than copiously provided with those conduits; and I feel no disposition to envy the mule for his plenty, or the mole for her exactness, in those ingenious labyrinthine inlets — those indispensable side-intelligencers.

Neither have I incurred, or done anything to incur, with Defoe, that hideous disfigurement, which constrained him to draw upon assurance — to feel 'quite unabashed,' and at ease upon that article. I was never, I thank my stars, in the pillory; nor, if I read them aright, is it within the compass of my destiny, that I ever should be.

When therefore I say that I have no ear, you will understand me to mean — for music.— To say that this heart never melted at the concourse of sweet sounds, would be a foul self-libel.—'Water parted from the sea' never fails to move it strangely. So does 'In infancy.' But they were used to be sung at her harpsichord (the old-fashioned instrument in vogue in those days) by a gentlewoman — the gentlest, sure, that ever merited the appellation — the sweetest — why should I hesitate to name Mrs. S——, once the blooming Fanny Weatheral of the Temple — who had power to thrill the soul of Elia, small imp as he was, even in his long coats; and to make him glow, tremble, and blush with a passion, that not faintly indicated the day-spring of that absorbing sentiment, which was afterwards destined to overwhelm and subdue his nature quite, for Alice W——n.

I even think that sentimentally I am disposed to harmony. But organically I am incapable of a tune. I have been practising 'God save the King' all my life; whistling and humming of it over to myself in solitary corners; and am not yet arrived, they tell me, within many quavers of it. Yet hath the loyalty of Elia never been impeached.

I am not without suspicion that I have an undeveloped faculty of music within me. For, thrumming, in my wild way, on my friend A.'s piano, the other morning, while he was engaged in an adjoining parlor,—on his return he was pleased to say, '*he thought it could not be the maid!*' On his first surprise at hearing the keys touched in somewhat an airy and masterful way, not dreaming of me, his suspicions had lighted on *Jenny.* But a grace snatched from a superior refinement, soon convinced him that some being,— technically perhaps deficient, but higher informed from a principle common to all the fine arts,— had swayed the keys to a mood which Jenny, with all her (less-cultivated) enthusiasm, could never have elicited from them. I mention this as a proof of my friend's penetration, and not with any view of disparaging Jenny.

Scientifically I could never be made to understand (yet have I taken some pains) what a note in music is; or how one note should differ from another. Much less in voices can I distinguish a soprano from a tenor. Only sometimes the thorough bass I contrive to guess at from its being supereminently harsh and disagreeable. I tremble, however, for my misapplication of the simplest terms of *that* which I disclaim. While I profess my ignorance, I scarce know what to *say* I am ignorant of. I hate, perhaps, by misnomers. *Sostenuto* and *adagio* stand in the like relation of obscurity to me; and *Sol, Fa, Mi, Re,* is as conjuring as *Baralipton.*

It is hard to stand alone — in an age like this,— (constituted to the quick and critical perception of all harmonious combinations, 1 verily believe, beyond all preceding ages, since Jubal stumbled upon the gamut)— to remain, as it were, singly unimpressible to the magic influences of an art which is said to have such an especial stroke at soothing, elevating, and refining the passions.— Yet, rather than break the candid current of my confessions, I must avow to you, that I have received a great deal more pain than pleasure from this so cried-up faculty.

I am constitutionally susceptible of noises. A carpenter's hammer in a warm summer noon, will fret me into more than midsummer madness. But those unconnected, unset sounds are nothing to the measured malice of music. The ear is passive to those single strokes; willingly enduring stripes, while it hath no task to con. To music it cannot be passive. It will strive — mine at least will — spite of

its inaptitude, to thrid the maze; like an unskilled eye painfully poring upon hieroglyphics. I have sat through an Italian Opera, till, for sheer pain, and inexplicable anguish, I have rushed out into the noisiest places of the crowded streets, to solace myself with sounds, which I was not obliged to follow, and get rid of the distracting torment of endless, fruitless, barren attention! I take refuge in the unpretending assemblage of honest common-life sounds; — and the purgatory of the Enraged Musician becomes my paradise.

I have sat at an Oratorio (that profanation of the purposes of the cheerful playhouse) watching the faces of the auditory in the pit (what a contrast to Hogarth's Laughing Audience!) immovable, or affecting some faint emotion,— till (as some have said, that our occupations in the next world will be but a shadow of what delighted us in this) I have imagined myself in some cold theater in Hades, where some of the *forms* of the earthly one should be kept up, with none of the *enjoyment;* or like that —

———— Party in a parlor,
All silent, and all DAMNED!

Above all, those insufferable concertos, and pieces of music, as they are called, do plague and embitter my apprehension. — Words are something; but to be exposed to an endless battery of mere sounds; to be long a dying, to lie stretched upon a rack of roses; to keep up languor by unintermitted effort; to pile honey upon sugar, and sugar upon honey, to an interminable tedious sweetness; to fill up sound with feeling, and strain ideas to keep pace with it; to gaze on empty frames, and be forced to make the pictures for yourself; to read a book *all stops,* and be obliged to supply the verbal matter; to invent extempore tragedies to answer to the vague gestures of an inexplicable rambling mime — these are faint shadows of what I have undergone from a series of the ablest-executed pieces of this empty *instrumental music.*

I deny not, that in the opening of a concert, I have experienced something vastly lulling and agreeable: — afterwards followeth the languor, and the oppression. Like that disappointing book in Patmos; or, like the comings on of melancholy, described by Burton, doth music make her first insinuating approaches:—'Most pleasant it is to such as are melancholy given, to walk alone in some solitary grove, betwixt wood and water, by some brook side, and to meditate upon some delightsome and pleasant subject, which shall effect him most, *amabilis insania,* and *mentis gratissimus error.* A most incomparable delight to build castles in the air, to go smiling to themselves, acting an infinite variety of parts, which they suppose, and strongly imagine, they act, or that they see done. — So delightsome these toys at first, they could spend whole days and nights without sleep, even whole years in such contemplations, and fantastical meditations, which are like so many dreams, and will hardly be drawn from them — winding and unwinding themselves as so many clocks, and still pleasing their humors, until at last the SCENE TURNS UPON A SUDDEN, and they being now habitated to such meditations and solitary places, can endure no company, can think of nothing but harsh and distasteful subjects. Fear, sorrow, suspicion, *subrusticus pudor,* discontent, cares, and weariness of life, surprise them on a sudden, and they can think of nothing else: continually suspecting, no sooner are their eyes open, but this infernal plague of melancholy seizeth on them, and terrifies their souls, representing some dismal object to their minds; which now, by no means, no labor, no persuasions, they can avoid, they cannot be rid of, they cannot resist.'

Something like this 'SCENE-TURNING' I have experienced at the evening parties, at the house of my good Catholic friend *Nov*——; who, by the aid of a capital organ, himself the most finished of players, converts his drawing-room into a chapel, his week days into Sundays, and these latter into minor heavens.[1]

When my friend commences upon one of those solemn anthems, which peradventure struck upon my heedless ear, rambling in the side aisles of the dim abbey, some five-and-thirty years since, waking a new sense, and putting a soul of old religion into my young apprehension — (whether it be *that,* in which the psalmist, weary of the persecutions of bad men, wisheth to himself dove's wings — or *that other* which, with a like measure of sobriety and pathos, inquireth by what means the young man shall best cleanse his mind) — a holy calm pervadeth me. — I am for the time

———— rapt above earth,
And possess joys not promised at my birth.

But when this master of the spell, not content to have laid a soul prostrate, goes on, in his power, to inflict more bliss than lies in her capacity to receive — impatient to overcome her 'earthly' with his 'heavenly,' — still pouring in, for protracted hours, fresh waves and fresh from the sea of sound, or from that inexhausted *German* ocean, above which, in triumphant progress, dolphin-seated, ride those Arions *Haydn* and *Mozart,* with their attendant Tritons *Bach, Beethoven,* and a countless tribe, whom to attempt to reckon up would but plunge me again in the deeps, — I stagger under the weight of harmony, reeling to and fro at my wit's end; — clouds, as of frankincense, oppress me — priests, altars, censers, dazzle before me — the genius of *his* religion hath me in her toils — a shadowy triple tiara invests the brow of my friend, late so naked, so ingenuous — he is Pope, — and by him sits, like as in the anomaly of dreams, a she-Pope too, — tri-coroneted like himself! — I am converted, and yet a Protestant; — at once *malleus hereticorum,* and myself grand heresiarch: or three heresies center in my person: I am Marcion, Ebion, and Cerinthus — Gog and Magog — what not? — till the coming in of the friendly supper-tray dissipates the figment, and a draught of true Lutheran beer (in which chiefly my friend shows himself no bigot) at once reconciles me to the rationalities of a purer faith; and restores to me the genuine unterrifying aspects of my pleasant-countenanced host and hostess.

(1821)

A DISSERTATION UPON ROAST PIG

Mankind, says a Chinese manuscript, which my friend M. was obliging enough

---

[1] I have been there, and still would go;
'T is like a little heaven below.—*Dr. Watts.*

to read and explain to me, for the first seventy thousand ages ate their meat raw, clawing or biting it from the living animal, just as they do in Abyssinia to this day. This period is not obscurely hinted at by their great Confucius in the second chapter of his Mundane Mutations, where he designates a kind of golden age by the term Cho-fang, literally the Cooks' holiday. The manuscript goes on to say, that the art of roasting, or rather broiling (which I take to be the elder brother) was accidentally discovered in the manner following. The swine-herd, Ho-ti, having gone out into the woods one morning, as his manner was, to collect mast for his hogs, left his cottage in the care of his eldest son Bo-bo, a great lubberly boy, who being fond of playing with fire, as younkers of his age commonly are, let some sparks escape into a bundle of straw, which kindling quickly, spread the conflagration over every part of their poor mansion, till it was reduced to ashes. Together with the cottage (a sorry antediluvian makeshift of a building, you may think it), what was of much more importance, a fine litter of new-farrowed pigs, no less than nine in number, perished. China pigs have been esteemed a luxury all over the East from the remotest periods that we read of. Bo-bo was in the utmost consternation, as you may think, not so much for the sake of the tenement, which his father and he could easily build up again with a few dry branches, and the labor of an hour or two, at any time, as for the loss of the pigs. While he was thinking what he should say to his father, and wringing his hands over the smoking remnants of one of those untimely sufferers, an odor assailed his nostrils, unlike any scent which he had before experienced. What could it proceed from? — not from the burnt cottage — he had smelt that smell before — indeed this was by no means the first accident of the kind which had occurred through the negligence of this unlucky young firebrand. Much less did it resemble that of any known herb, weed, or flower. A premonitory moistening at the same time overflowed his nether lip. He knew not what to think. He next stooped down to feel the pig, if there were any signs of life in it. He burnt his fingers, and to cool them he applied

them in his booby fashion to his mouth. Some of the crumbs of the scorched skin had come away with his fingers, and for the first time in his life (in the world's life indeed, for before him no man had known it) he tasted — crackling! Again he felt and fumbled at the pig. It did not burn him so much now, still he licked his fingers from a sort of habit. The truth at length broke into his slow understanding, that it was the pig that smelt so, and the pig that tasted so delicious; and, surrendering himself up to the new-born pleasure, he fell to tearing up whole handfuls of the scorched skin with the flesh next it, and was cramming it down his throat in his beastly fashion, when his sire entered amid the smoking rafters, armed with retributory cudgel, and finding how affairs stood, began to rain blows upon the young rogue's shoulders, as thick as hail-stones, which Bo-bo heeded not any more than if they had been flies. The tickling pleasure, which he experienced in his lower regions, had rendered him quite callous to any inconveniences he might feel in those remote quarters. His father might lay on, but he could not beat him from his pig, till he had fairly made an end of it, when, becoming a little more sensible of his situation, something like the following dialogue ensued.

'You graceless whelp, what have you got there devouring? Is it not enough that you have burnt me down three houses with your dog's tricks, and be hanged to you, but you must be eating fire, and I know not what — what have you got there, I say?'

'O father, the pig, the pig, do come and taste how nice the burnt pig eats.'

The ears of Ho-ti tingled with horror. He cursed his son and he cursed himself that ever he should beget a son that should eat burnt pig.

Bo-bo, whose scent was wonderfully sharpened since morning, soon raked out another pig, and fairly rending it asunder, thrust the lesser half by main force into the fists of Ho-ti, still shouting out, 'Eat, eat, eat the burnt pig, father, only taste,— O Lord,'— with such-like barbarous ejaculations, cramming all the while as if he would choke.

Ho-ti trembled in every joint while he grasped the abominable thing, wavering whether he should not put his son to death for an unnatural young monster, when the crackling scorching his fingers, as it had done his son's, and applying the same remedy to them, he in his turn tasted some of its flavor, which, make what sour mouths he would for a pretense, proved not altogether displeasing to him. In conclusion (for the manuscript here is a little tedious) both father and son fairly sat down to the mess, and never left off till they had despatched all that remained of the litter.

Bo-bo was strictly enjoined not to let the secret escape, for the neighbors would certainly have stoned them for a couple of abominable wretches, who could think of improving upon the good meat which God had sent them. Nevertheless, strange stories got about. It was observed that Ho-ti's cottage was burnt down now more frequently than ever. Nothing but fires from this time forward. Some would break out in broad day, others in the night-time. As often as the sow farrowed, so sure was the house of Ho-ti to be in a blaze; and Ho-ti himself, which was the more remarkable, instead of chastising his son, seemed to grow more indulgent to him than ever. At length they were watched, the terrible mystery discovered, and father and son summoned to take their trial at Pekin, then an inconsiderable assize town. Evidence was given, the obnoxious food itself produced in court, and verdict about to be pronounced, when the foreman of the jury begged that some of the burnt pig, of which the culprits stood accused, might be handed into the box. He handled it, and they all handled it, and burning their fingers, as Bo-bo and his father had done before them, and nature prompting to each of them the same remedy, against the face of all the facts, and the clearest charge which judge had ever given, — to the surprise of the whole court, townsfolk, strangers, reporters, and all present — without leaving the box, or any manner of consultation whatever, they brought in a simultaneous verdict of Not Guilty.

The judge, who was a shrewd fellow, winked at the manifest iniquity of the decision; and, when the court was dismissed, went privily, and bought up all the pigs that could be had for love or money. In a few days his lordship's town house was observed to be on fire. The thing took wing, and now there was nothing to be seen but fires in every direction. Fuel and pigs grew enormously dear all over the districts. The insurance offices one and all shut up shop. People built slighter and slighter every day, until it was feared that the very science of architecture would in no long time be lost to the world. Thus this custom of firing houses continued, till in process of time, says my manuscript, a sage arose, like our Locke, who made a discovery, that the flesh of swine, or indeed of any other animal, might be cooked (burnt, as they called it) without the necessity of consuming a whole house to dress it. Then first began the rude form of a gridiron. Roasting by the string, or spit, came in a century or two later, I forget in whose dynasty. By such slow degrees, concludes the manuscript, do the most useful, and seemingly the most obvious arts, make their way among mankind.

Without placing too implicit faith in the account above given, it must be agreed, that if a worthy pretext for so dangerous an experiment as setting houses on fire (especially in these days) could be assigned in favor of any culinary object, that pretext and excuse might be found in ROAST PIG.

Of all the delicacies in the whole *mundus edibilis,* I will maintain it to be the most delicate — *princeps obsoniorum.*

I speak not of your grown porkers — things between pig and pork — those hobbydehoys — but a young and tender suckling — under a moon old — guiltless as yet of the sty — with no original speck of the *amor immunditiae,* the hereditary failing of the first parent, yet manifest his voice as yet not broken, but something between a childish treble, and a grumble — the mild forerunner, or *praeludium,* of a grunt.

He must be roasted. I am not ignorant that our ancestors ate them seethed, or boiled — but what a sacrifice of the exterior tegument!

There is no flavor comparable, I will contend, to that of the crisp, tawny, well-watched, not over-roasted, *crackling,* as it is well called — the very teeth are invited to their share of the pleasure at this banquet in overcoming the coy, brittle resistance — with the adhesive oleaginous — O call it not fat — but an indefinable sweetness growing up to it — the tender blossoming of fat — fat cropped in the bud — taken in the shoot — in the first innocence — the cream and quintessence of the child-pig's yet pure food — the lean, no lean, but a kind of animal manna — or, rather, fat and lean (if it must be so) so blended and running into each other, that both together make but one ambrosian result, or common substance.

Behold him, while he is doing — it seemeth rather a refreshing warmth, than a scorching heat, that he is so passive to. How equably he twirleth round the string! Now he is just done. To see the extreme sensibility of that tender age, he hath wept out his pretty eyes — radiant jellies — shooting stars —

See him in the dish, his second cradle, how meek he lieth! — wouldst thou have had this innocent grow up to the grossness and indocility which too often accompany maturer swinehood? Ten to one he would have proved a glutton, a sloven, an obstinate, disagreeable animal — wallowing in all manner of filthy conversation — from these sins he is happily snatched away —

Ere sin could blight, or sorrow fade,
Death came with timely care —

his memory is odoriferous — no clown curseth, while his stomach half rejecteth, the rank bacon — no coalheaver bolteth him in reeking sausages — he hath a fair sepulcher in the grateful stomach of the judicious epicure — and for such a tomb might be content to die.

He is the best of sapors. Pineapple is great. She is indeed almost too transcendent — a delight, if not sinful, yet so like to sinning, that really a tender-conscienced person would do well to pause — too ravishing for mortal taste, she woundeth and excoriateth the lips that approach her — like lovers' kisses, she biteth — she is a pleasure bordering on pain from the fierceness and insanity of her relish — but she stoppeth at the palate — she meddleth not with the appetite — and the coarsest hunger might barter her consistently for a mutton chop.

Pig — let me speak his praise — is no less provocative of the appetite, than he is satisfactory to the criticalness of the censorious palate. The strong man may batten on him, and the weakling refuseth not his mild juices.

Unlike to mankind's mixed characters, a bundle of virtues and vices, inexplicably intertwisted, and not to be unraveled without hazard, he is — good throughout. No part of him is better or worse than another. He helpeth, as far as his little means extend, all around. He is the least envious of banquets. He is all neighbors' fare.

I am one of those who freely and ungrudgingly impart a share of the good things of this life which fall to their lot (few as mine are in this kind) to a friend. I protest I take as great an interest in my friend's pleasures, his relishes, and proper satisfactions, as in mine own. 'Presents,' I often say, 'endear Absents.' Hares, pheasants, partridges, snipes, barndoor chickens (those 'tame villatic fowl'), capons, plovers, brawn, barrels of oysters, I dispense as freely as I receive them. I love to taste them, as it were, upon the tongue of my friend. But a stop must be put somewhere. One would not, like Lear, 'give everything.' I make my stand upon pig. Methinks it is an ingratitude to the Giver of all good flavors, to extradomiciliate, or send out of the house, slightingly (under pretext of friendship, or I know not what), a blessing so particularly adapted, predestined, I may say, to my individual palate — It argues an insensibility.

I remember a touch of conscience in this kind at school. My good old aunt, who never parted from me at the end of a holiday without stuffing a sweetmeat, or some nice thing into my pocket, had dismissed me one evening with a smoking plum-cake, fresh from the oven. In my way to school (it was over London Bridge) a gray-headed old beggar saluted me (I have no doubt at this time of day that he was a counterfeit). I had no pence to console him with, and in the vanity of self-denial, and the very coxcombry of charity, school-boy-like, I made him a present of — the whole cake!

I walked on a little, buoyed up, as one is on such occasions, with a sweet soothing of self-satisfaction; but before I had got to the end of the bridge, my better feelings returned, and I burst into tears, thinking how ungrateful I had been to my good aunt, to go and give her good gift away to a stranger, that I had never seen before, and who might be a bad man for aught I knew; and then I thought of the pleasure my aunt would be taking in thinking that I — I myself, and not another — would eat her nice cake — and what should I say to her the next time I saw her — how naughty I was to part with her pretty present — and the odor of that spicy cake came back upon my recollection, and the pleasure and the curiosity I had taken in seeing her make it, and her joy when she sent it to the oven, and how disappointed she would feel that I had never had a bit of it in my mouth at last — and I blamed my impertinent spirit of alms-giving, and out-of-place hypocrisy of goodness, and above all I wished never to see the face again of that insidious, good-for-nothing, old gray impostor.

Our ancestors were nice in their method of sacrificing these tender victims. We read of pigs whipt to death with something of a shock, as we hear of any other obsolete custom. The age of discipline is gone by, or it would be curious to inquire (in a philosophical light merely) what effect this process might have towards intenerating and dulcifying a substance, naturally so mild and dulcet as the flesh of young pigs. It looks like refining a violet. Yet we should be cautious, while we condemn the inhumanity, how we censure the wisdom of the practice. It might impart a gusto —

I remember an hypothesis, argued upon by the young students, when I was at St. Omer's, and maintained with much learning and pleasantry on both sides, 'Whether, supposing that the flavor of a pig who obtained his death by whipping (*per flagellationem extremam*) superadded a pleasure upon the palate of a man more intense than any possible suffering we can conceive in the animal, is man justified in using that method of putting the animal to death?' I forget the decision.

His sauce should be considered. Decidedly, a few bread crumbs, done up with his liver and brains, and a dash of mild sage. But, banish, dear Mrs. Cook, I beseech you, the whole onion tribe. Barbecue your whole hogs to your palate, steep them in shalots, stuff them out with plantations of the rank and guilty garlic; you cannot poison them, or make them stronger than they are — bu consider, he is a weakling — a flower.

(1822)

SIR WALTER SCOTT (1771-1832)

Scott's birthplace was Edinburgh. His father, a solicitor of creditable standing, had been the first of his family to adopt a town life, and Scott early evinced an innate attraction toward those ancestors who for centuries had linked their history with the stirring life of the Border. 'You will find me a rattle-skulled, half-lawyer, half-sportsman, through whose head a regiment of horse has been exercising since he was five years old,' he once wrote to a stranger. Lameness derived from a fever kept him inactive as a child and he was dreamy and fond of reading. As he grew up he entered robustly into outdoor sports; but his choicest pastime was cruising about the country-side after relics of folklore. Passing through the High-School and the College in Edinburgh, he studied law and, in 1792, became an advocate. His taste for country residence led him to settle on the Esk at Lasswade after his marriage in 1798, and from here as Sheriff of Selkirkshire, he removed to Ashestiel on the Tweed, in 1804. His *Border Minstrelsy* had appeared in 1802, and now his poems, *Lay of the Last Minstrel* (1805), *Marmion* (1808), *Lady of the Lake* (1810), and others in quick sequence began to supplement his profession as a means of livelihood. In 1812 he succeeded to a salary of £1300 as clerk of session, and he proceeded to materialize his dream of a feudal estate by purchasing, as nucleus, a hundred acres of rough land five miles down the Tweed at Abbotsford. Thither he removed with 'twenty-five cartloads of the veriest trash in nature, besides dogs, pigs, ponies, poultry, cows, calves'; he gives an amusing and significant account of 'the procession of my furniture, in which old swords, bows, targets, and lances, made a very conspicuous show. A family of turkeys was accommodated within the helmet of some *preux chevalier* of ancient border fame; and the very cows, for aught I know, were bearing banners and muskets.' From Abbotsford came the series of historical novels, beginning with *Waverly* (1814) and closing with *Castle Dangerous* (1831,—twenty-nine novels in half as many years. The quantity of energy which Scott poured into these works of fiction,— to say nothing of his Edition of Swift and *Life of Napoleon*,— while discharging his official duties and engaging in all the activities of a country-gentleman, is almost inconceivable. In addition, the work of his last years was done in sharp adversity. Soon after his marriage he had entered into a secret partnership with James and John Ballantyne, publishers of Edinburgh, and this business had been complicated with that of Constable and Co. His partners were feeble managers; only the extraordinary success of the novels had tided over a crisis for several years. It is estimated that Scott's writings earned him, during his lifetime, nearly a million dollars; but his outlay at Abbotsford and in other directions had been excessively lavish, and greatly increased after he was knighted in 1820. The crash came in 1825; Constable, the Ballantynes, and Scott went down together. From the age of fifty-five to sixty, in spite of breaking health and failing imagination, he wrought doggedly with his pen to pay off £117,000 of debt. When the end came nearly half the debt remained; but this was extinguished by his copyrights after his death. In any event, Scott's character would have lived as one signally illustrious and lovable; his last years conferred upon it the quality of heroism. The real sweep and variety of his genius is denoted in his novels. His poetry is, nevertheless, animated and stirring, and well exemplifies his power of delineating, with bold, free strokes, scenic background and enterprising action.

From MARMION, CANTO VI

Not far advanced was morning day
When Marmion did his troop array
  To Surrey's camp to ride;
He had safe-conduct for his band
Beneath the royal seal and hand,
  And Douglas gave a guide.
The ancient earl with stately grace

Would Clara on her palfrey place,
And whispered in an undertone,
'Let the hawk stoop, his prey is flown.' 10
The train from out the castle drew,
But Marmion stopped to bid adieu:
  'Though something I might plain,' he said,
'Of cold respect to stranger guest,
Sent hither by your king's behest, 15

While in Tantallon's towers I stayed,
Part we in friendship from your land,
And, noble earl, receive my hand.'—
But Douglas round him drew his cloak,
Folded his arms, and thus he spoke:— 20
'My manors, halls, and bowers shall still
Be open at my sovereign's will
To each one whom he lists, howe'er
Unmeet to be the owner's peer.
My castles are my king's alone,   25
From turret to foundation-stone—
The hand of Douglas is his own,
And never shall in friendly grasp
The hand of such as Marmion clasp.'

Burned Marmion's swarthy cheek like
    fire   30
And shook his very frame for ire,
And—'This to me!' he said,
'An 't were not for thy hoary beard,
Such hand as Marmion's had not spared
    To cleave the Douglas' head!   35
And first I tell thee, haughty peer,
He who does England's message here,
Although the meanest in her state,
May well, proud Angus, be thy mate;
And, Douglas, more I tell thee here,   40
    Even in thy pitch of pride,
Here in thy hold, thy vassals near,—
Nay, never look upon your lord,
And lay your hands upon your sword,—
    I tell thee, thou 'rt defied!
And if thou saidst I am not peer
To any lord in Scotland here,
Lowland or Highland, far or near,
    Lord Angus, thou hast lied!'
On the earl's cheek the flush of rage 50
O'ercame the ashen hue of age:
Fierce he broke forth,—'And darest thou
    then
To beard the lion in his den,
    The Douglas in his hall?
And hopest thou hence unscathed to
    go?—   55
No, by Saint Bride of Bothwell, no!
Up drawbridge, grooms—what, warder,
    ho!
Let the portcullis fall,—'
Lord Marmion turned,—well was his
    need,—
And dashed the rowels in his steed,   60
Like arrow through the archway sprung
The ponderous grate behind him rung;
To pass there was such scanty room,
The bars descending razed his plume.

The steed along the drawbridge flies   65
Just as it trembled on the rise;
Not lighter does the swallow skim

Along the smooth lake's level brim:
And when Lord Marmion reached his
    band,
He halts, and turns with clenchèd hand, 70
And shout of loud defiance pours,
And shook his gauntlet at the towers.
'Horse! horse!' the Douglas cried, 'and
    chase!'
But soon he reined his fury's pace:
'A royal messenger he came,   75
Though most unworthy of the name.—
A letter forged! Saint Jude to speed!
Did ever knight so foul a deed?[1]
At first in heart it liked me ill
When the king praised his clerkly skill. 80
Thanks to Saint Bothan, son of mine,
Save Gawain, ne'er could pen a line;
So swore I, and I swear it still,
Let my boy-bishop fret his fill.—
Saint Mary mend my fiery mood!   85
Old age ne'er cools the Douglas blood,
I thought to slay him where he stood.
'T is pity of him too,' he cried:
'Bold can he speak and fairly ride,
I warrant him a warrior tried.'   90
With this his mandate he recalls,
And slowly seeks his castle halls.

The day in Marmion's journey wore;
Yet, ere his passion's gust was o'er,
They crossed the heights of Stanrig-moor. 95
His troop more closely there he scanned,
And missed the Palmer from the band.
'Palmer or not,' young Blount did say,
'He parted at the peep of day;
Good sooth, it was in strange array.' 100
'In what array?' said Marmion quick.
'My lord, I ill can spell the trick;
But all night long with clink and bang
Close to my couch did hammers clang;
At dawn the falling drawbridge rang,   105
And from a loophole while I peep,
Old Bell-the-Cat came from the keep,
Wrapped in a gown of sables fair,
As fearful of the morning air;
Beneath, when that was blown aside,   110
A rusty shirt of mail I spied,

[1] Lest the reader should partake of the Earl's astonishment and consider the crime as inconsistent with the manners of the period, I have to remind him of the numerous forgeries (partly executed by a female assistant) devised by Robert of Artois, to forward his suit against the Countess Matilda; which, being detected, occasioned his flight into England, and proved the remote cause of Edward the Third's memorable wars in France. John Harding, also, was expressly hired by Edward IV to forge such documents as might appear to establish the claim of fealty asserted over Scotland by the English monarchs.

By Archibald won in bloody work
Against the Saracen and Turk;
Last night it hung not in the hall;
I thought some marvel would befall.   115
And next I saw them saddled lead
Old Cheviot forth, the earl's best steed,
A matchless horse, though something old,
Prompt in his paces, cool and bold.
I heard the Sheriff Sholto say   120
The earl did much the Master pray
To use him on the battle-day;
But he preferred '—'Nay, Henry, cease!
Thou sworn horse-courser, hold thy peace.—
Eustace, thou bear'st a brain—I pray,   125
What did Blount see at break of day?'

'In brief, my lord, we both descried—
For then I stood by Henry's side—
The Palmer mount and outwards ride
Upon the earl's own favorite steed.   130
All sheathed he was in armor bright,
And much resembled that same knight
Subdued by you in Cotswold fight;
Lord Angus wished him speed.'—
The instant that Fitz-Eustace spoke,   135
A sudden light on Marmion broke:—
'Ah! dastard fool, to reason lost!'
He muttered; ''T was nor fay nor ghost
I met upon the moonlight wold,
But living man of earthly mold.   140
O dotage blind and gross!
Had I but fought as wont, one thrust
Had laid De Wilton in the dust,
My path no more to cross.—
How stand we now?—he told his tale   145
To Douglas, and with some avail;
'T was therefore gloomed his rugged brow.—
Will Surrey dare to entertain
'Gainst Marmion charge disproved and vain?
Small risk of that, I trow.   150
Yet Clare's sharp questions must I shun,
Must separate Constance from the nun—
Oh! what a tangled web we weave
When first we practise to deceive!
A Palmer too!—no wonder why   155
I felt rebuked beneath his eye;
I might have known there was but one
Whose look could quell Lord Marmion.'

Stung with these thoughts, he urged to speed
His troop, and reached at eve the Tweed,   160
Where Lennel's convent closed their march
There now is left but one frail arch,
Yet mourn thou not its cells;

Our time a fair exchange has made:
Hard by, in hospitable shade   165
A reverend pilgrim dwells,
Well worth the whole Bernardine brood
That e'er wore sandal, frock, or hood.
Yet did Saint Bernard's abbot there
Give Marmion entertainment fair,   170
And lodging for his train and Clare.
Next morn the baron climbed the tower,
To view afar the Scottish power,
Encamped on Flodden edge;
The white pavilions made a show   175
Like remnants of the winter snow
Along the dusky ridge.
Long Marmion looked:—at length his eye
Unusual movement might descry
Amid the shifting lines;   180
The Scottish host drawn out appears,
For, flashing on the hedge of spears,
The eastern sunbeam shines.
Their front now deepening, now extending,
Their flank inclining, wheeling, bending,   185
Now drawing back, and now descending,
The skilful Marmion well could know
They watched the motions of some foe
Who traversed on the plain below.

Even so it was. From Flodden ridge   190
The Scots beheld the English host
Leave Barmore-wood, their evening post,
And heedful watched them as they crossed
The Till by Twisel Bridge.
High sight it is and haughty, while   195
They dive into the deep defile;
Beneath the caverned cliff they fall,
Beneath the castle's airy wall.
By rock, by oak, by hawthorn-tree.
Troop after troop are disappearing;   200
Troop after troop their banners rearing
Upon the eastern bank you see;
Still pouring down the rocky den
Where flows the sullen Till,
And rising from the dim-wood glen,   205
Standards on standards, men on men,
In slow succession still,
And sweeping o'er the Gothic arch,
And pressing on, in ceaseless march,
To gain the opposing hill.   210
That morn, to many a trumpet clang,
Twisel! thy rock's deep echo rang,
And many a chief of birth and rank,
Saint Helen! at thy fountain drank.
Thy hawthorn glade, which now we see   215
In spring-tide bloom so lavishly,
Had then from many an axe its doom.

To give the marching columns room.
And why stands Scotland idly now,
Dark Flodden! on thy airy brow,   220
Since England gains the pass the while
And struggles through the deep defile?
What checks the fiery soul of James?
Why sits that champion of the dames
   Inactive on his steed,
And sees, between him and his land,   225
Between him and Tweed's southern strand,
   His host Lord Surrey lead?
What vails the vain knight-errant's
   brand? —
O Douglas, for thy leading wand!
   Fierce Randolph, for thy speed!   230
Oh! for one hour of Wallace wight,
Or well-skilled Bruce, to rule the fight
And cry, 'Saint Andrew and our right!'
Another sight had seen that morn,
From Fate's dark book a leaf been torn,   235
And Flodden had been Bannock-
   bourne! —
The precious hour has passed in vain,
And England's host has gained the plain,
Wheeling their march and circling still
Around the base of Flodden hill.   240

Ere yet the bands met Marmion's eye,
Fitz-Eustace shouted loud and high,
'Hark! hark! my lord, an English drum!
And see ascending squadrons come
   Between Tweed's river and the hill,   245
Foot, horse, and cannon! Hap what hap,
My basnet to a prentice cap,
   Lord Surrey's o'er the Till! —
Yet more! yet more! — how fair arrayed
They file from out the hawthorn shade,   250
· And sweep so gallant by!
With all their banners bravely spread,
   And all their armor flashing high,
Saint George might waken from the dead,
   To see fair England's standards fly.'—255
'Stint in thy prate,' quoth Blount, 'thou
   'dst best,
And listen to our lord's behest.'—
With kindling brow Lord Marmion said,
'This instant be our band arrayed;
The river must be quickly crossed,   260
That we may join Lord Surrey's host.
If fight King James,— as well I trust
That fight he will, and fight he must,—
The Lady Clare behind our lines
Shall tarry while the battle joins.'   265

Himself he swift on horseback threw,
Scarce to the abbot bade adieu,
Far less would listen to his prayer
To leave behind the helpless Clare.

Down to the Tweed his band he drew,   270
And muttered as the flood they view,
'The pheasant in the falcon's claw,
He scarce will yield to please a daw;
Lord Angus may the abbot awe,
   So Clare shall bide with me.'   275
Then on that dangerous ford and deep
Where to the Tweed Leat's eddies creep,
   He ventured desperately:
And not a moment will he bide
Till squire or groom before him ride;   280
Headmost of all he stems the tide,
   And stems it gallantly.
Eustace held Clare upon her horse,
   Old Hubert led her rein,
Stoutly they braved the current's course, 285
And, though far downward driven per-
   force,
   The southern bank they gain.
Behind them straggling came to shore,
   As best they might, the train:
Each o'er his head his yew-bow bore,   290
   A caution not in vain;
Deep need that day that every string,
By wet unharmed, should sharply ring.
A moment then Lord Marmion stayed,
And breathed his steed, his men arrayed, 295
   Then forward moved his band,
Until, Lord Surrey's rear-guard won,
He halted by a cross of stone,
That on a hillock standing lone
   Did all the field command.   300

Hence might they see the full array
Of either host for deadly fray;
Their marshaled lines stretched east and
   west,
   And fronted north and south,
And distant salutation passed   305
   From the loud cannon mouth;
Not in the close successive rattle
That breathes the voice of modern battle,
   But slow and far between.
The hillock gained, Lord Marmion
   stayed,   310
'Here, by this cross,' he gently said,
   'You well may view the scene.
Here shalt thou tarry, lovely Clare:
Oh! think of Marmion in thy prayer! —
Thou wilt not? — well, no less my care   315
Shall, watchful, for thy weal prepare.—
You, Blount and Eustace, are her guard,
   With ten picked archers of my train;
With England if the day go hard,
   To Berwick speed amain.—   320
But if we conquer, cruel maid,
My spoils shall at your feet be laid,
   When here we meet again.'

He waited not for answer there,
And would not mark the maid's despair, 325
 Nor heed the discontented look
From either squire, but spurred amain,
And dashing through the battle-plain,
 His way to Surrey took.

'The good Lord Marmion, by my life! 330
 Welcome to danger's hour!—
Short greeting serves in time of strife.—
 Thus have I ranged my power:
Myself will rule this central host,
 Stout Stanley fronts their right, 335
My sons command the vaward post,
 With Brian Tunstall, stainless knight;
Lord Dacre, with his horsemen light,
 Shall be in rearward of the fight,
And succor those that need it most. 340
 Now gallant Marmion, well I know,
 Would gladly to the vanguard go;
Edmund, the Admiral, Tunstall there,
With thee their charge will blithely share;
The fight thine own retainers too 345
Beneath De Burg, thy steward true.'
'Thanks, noble Surrey!' Marmion said,
Nor further greeting there he paid,
But, parting like a thunderbolt,
First in the vanguard made a halt, 350
 Where such a shout there rose
Of 'Marmion! Marmion!' that the cry,
Up Flodden mountain shrilling high,
 Startled the Scottish foes.

Blount and Fitz-Eustace rested still 355
With Lady Clare upon the hill,
On which — for far the day was spent —
The western sunbeams now were bent;
The cry they heard, its meaning knew,
Could plain their distant comrades view: 360
 Sadly to Blount did Eustace say,
'Unworthy office here to stay!
No hope of gilded spurs to-day.—
But see! look up — on Flodden bent
The Scottish foe has fired his tent.' 365
 And sudden, as he spoke,
From the sharp ridges of the hill,
All downward to the banks of Till,
 Was wreathed in sable smoke.
Volumed and vast, and rolling far, 370
The cloud enveloped Scotland's war
 As down the hill they broke;
Nor martial shout, nor minstrel tone,
Announced their march; their tread alone,
At times one warning trumpet blown, 375
 At times a stifled hum,
Told England, from his mountain-throne
 King James did rushing come.
Scarce could they hear or see their foes

Until at weapon-point they close.— 380
They close in clouds of smoke and dust,
With sword-sway and with lance's thrust;
 And such a yell was there,
Of sudden and portentous birth,
As if men fought upon the earth, 385
 And fiends in upper air:
Oh! life and death were in the shout,
Recoil and rally, charge and rout,
 And triumph and despair.
Long looked the anxious squires; their eye 390
Could in the darkness nought descry.

At length the freshening western blast
Aside the shroud of battle cast;
And first the ridge of mingled spears
Above the brightening cloud appears, 395
And in the smoke the pennons flew,
As in the storm the white seamew.
Then marked they, dashing broad and far,
The broken billows of the war,
And plumed crests of chieftains brave 400
Floating like foam upon the wave;
 But nought distinct they see:
Wide raged the battle on the plain;
Spears shook and falchions flashed amain;
Fell England's arrow-flight like rain; 405
Crests rose, and stooped, and rose again.
 Wild and disorderly.
Amid the scene of tumult, high
They saw Lord Marmion's falcon fly;
And stainless Tunstall's banner white, 410
And Edmund Howard's lion bright,
Still bear them bravely in the fight,
 Although against them come
Of gallant Gordons many a one,
And many a stubborn Badenoch-man, 415
And many a rugged Border clan,
 With Huntly and with Home.—

Far on the left, unseen the while,
Stanley broke Lennox and Argyle,
Though there the western mountaineer 420
Rushed with bare bosom on the spear,
And flung the feeble targe aside,
And with both hands the broadsword plied.
'T was vain.— But Fortune, on the right,
With fickle smile cheered Scotland's fight. 425
Then fell that spotless banner white,
 The Howard's lion fell;
Yet still Lord Marmion's falcon flew
With wavering flight, while fiercer grew
 Around the battle-yell. 430
The Border slogan rent the sky!
A Home! a Gordon! was the cry:
 Loud were the clanging blows;

Advanced,— forced back,— now low, now
  high,
  The pennon sunk and rose;   435
As bends the bark's mast in the gale,
When rent are rigging, shrouds, and sail,
  It wavered mid the foes.
No longer Blount the view could bear:
'By heaven and all its saints! I swear   440
  I will not see it lost!
Fitz-Eustace, you with Lady Clare
May bid your beads and patter prayer,—
  I gallop to the host.'
And to the fray he rode amain,   445
Followed by all the archer train.
The fiery youth, with desperate charge,
Made for a space an opening large,—
  The rescued banner rose,—
But darkly closed the war around,   450
Like pine-tree rooted from the ground
  It sank among the foes.
Then Eustace mounted too,— yet stayed,
As loath to leave the helpless maid,
  When, fast as shaft can fly,   455
Bloodshot his eyes, his nostrils spread,
The loose rein dangling from his head,
Housing and saddle bloody red,
  Lord Marmion's steed rushed by:
And Eustace, maddening at the sight,   460
  A look and sign to Clara cast
  To mark he would return in haste,
Then plunged into the fight.

Ask me not what the maiden feels,
  Left in that dreadful hour alone: 465
Perchance her reason stoops or reels;
Perchance a courage, not her own,
  Braces her mind to desperate tone.—
The scattered van of England wheels; —
  She only said, as loud in air   470
The tumult roared. 'Is Wilton there?'—
  They fly, or, maddened by despair,
  Fight but to die,—'Is Wilton there?'
With that, straight up the hill there rode
  Two horsemen drenched with gore,   475
And in their arms, a helpless load,
  A wounded knight they bore.
His hand still strained the broken brand;
His arms were smeared with blood and
  sand.
Dragged from among the horses' feet,   480
With dinted shield and helmet beat,
The falcon-crest and plumage gone,
Can that be haughty Marmion! . . .
Young Blount his armor did unlace,
And, gazing on his ghastly face,   485
  Said, 'By Saint George, he's gone!
That spear-wound has our master sped,
And see the deep cut on his head!

Good-night to Marmion.'—
'Unnurtured Blount! thy brawling cease: 490
He opes his eyes,' said Eustace; 'peace!'

When, doffed his casque, he felt free air,
Around gan Marmion wildly stare:
'Where's   Harry   Blount?   Fitz-Eustace
  where?
Linger ye here, ye hearts of hare!   495
Redeem my pennon,— charge again!
Cry, 'Marmion to the rescue!'— Vain!
Last of my race, on battle-plain
That shout shall ne'er be heard again!—
Yet my last thought is England's — fly, 500
  To Dacre bear my signet-ring:
  Tell him his squadrons up to bring.—
Fitz-Eustace, to Lord Surrey hie:
  Tunstall lies dead upon the field,
  His lifeblood stains the spotless shield; 505
  Edmund is down; my life is reft;
  The Admiral alone is left.
Let Stanley charge with spur of fire,—
With Chester charge, and Lancashire,
Full upon Scotland's central host,   510
Or victory and England's lost.—
Must I bid twice? — hence, varlets fly!—
  Leave Marmion here alone — to die.'
They parted, and alone he lay;
Clare drew her from the sight away,   515
Till pain wrung forth a lowly moan,
And half he murmured, 'Is there none
  Of all my halls have nurst,
Page, squire, or groom, one cup to bring
Of blessed water from the spring,   520
  To slake my dying thirst!'

O Woman! in our hours of ease
Uncertain, coy, and hard to please,
And variable as the shade
By the light quivering aspen made;   525
When pain and anguish wring the brow,
A ministering angel thou!—
Scarce were the piteous accents said,
When with the baron's casque the maid
  To the nigh streamlet ran: 530
Forgot were hatred, wrongs, and fears;
The plaintive voice alone she hears,
  Sees but the dying man.
She stooped her by the runnel's side,
  But in abhorrence backward drew;   535
For, oozing from the mountain's side
Where raged the war, a dark-red tide
  Was curdling in the streamlet blue.
Where shall she turn? — behold her mark
  A little fountain cell,   540
Where water, clear as diamond spark,
  In a stone basin fell.
Above, some half-worn letters say,

Drink. weary. pilgrim. drink. and. pray.
for. the. kind. soul. of. Sibyl. Grey.
Who. built. this. cross. and. well.

She filled the helm and back she hied,
And with surprise and joy espied
    A monk supporting Marmion's head;
A pious man, whom duty brought
To dubious verge of battle fought,
    To shrive the dying, bless the dead.

Deep drank Lord Marmion of the wave,
And, as she stooped his brow to lave —
'Is it the hand of Clare,' he said,   555
'Or injured Constance, bathes my head?'
    Then, as remembrance rose, —
'Speak not to me of shrift or prayer!
    I must redress her woes.
Short space, few words, are mine to
        spare;   560
Forgive and listen, gentle Clare!'
    'Alas!' she said, 'the while. —
Oh! think of your immortal weal!
In vain for Constance is your zeal!
    She — died at Holy Isle.' —   565
Lord Marmion started from the ground
As light as if he felt no wound,
Though in the action burst the tide
In torrents from his wounded side.
'Then it was truth,' he said — 'I knew   570
That the dark presage must be true. —
I would the Fiend, to whom belongs
The vengeance due to all her wrongs,
    Would spare me but a day!
For wasting fire, and dying groan,   575
And priests slain on the altar stone,
    Might bribe him for delay.
It may not be! — this dizzy trance —
Curse on yon base marauder's lance,
And doubly cursed my failing brand!   580
A sinful heart makes feeble hand.'
Then fainting down on earth he sunk,
Supported by the trembling monk.

With fruitless labor Clara bound
And strove to stanch the gushing
        wound: 585
The monk with unavailing cares
Exhausted all the Church's prayers.
Ever, he said, that close and near,
A lady's voice was in his ear,
And that the priest he could not hear;   590
    For that she ever sung,
'In the lost battle borne down by the fly-
        ing,
Where mingles war's rattle with groans of
        the dying!'
    So the notes rung. —
'Avoid thee, Fiend! — with cruel hand   595
Shake not the dying sinner's sand! —

Oh! look, my son, upon yon sign
Of the Redeemer's grace divine;
    Oh! think on faith and bliss! —
By many a death-bed I have been,   600
And many a sinner's parting seen,
    But never aught like this.'
The war, that for a space did fail,
Now trebly thundering swelled the gale,
    And 'Stanley!' was the cry; —   605
A light on Marmion's visage spread,
    And fired his glazing eye;
With dying hand above his head
He shook the fragment of his blade,
    And shouted 'Victory! —   610
Charge, Chester, charge! On, Stanley, on!'
Were the last words of Marmion.
                    * * *
                                        (1808)

SOLDIER, REST!

Soldier, rest! thy warfare o'er,
    Sleep the sleep that knows not breaking;
Dream of battled fields no more,
    Days of danger, nights of waking.
In our isle's enchanted hall,   5
    Hands unseen thy couch are strewing,
Fairy strains of music fall,
    Every sense in slumber dewing.
Soldier, rest! thy warfare o'er,
    Dream of fighting fields no more;   10
Sleep the sleep that knows not breaking
Morn of toil, nor night of waking.

No rude sound shall reach thine ear,
    Armor's clang, or war-steed champing,
Trump nor pibroch summon here   15
    Mustering clan or squadron tramping.
Yet the lark's shrill fife may come
    At the daybreak from the fallow,
And the bittern sound his drum,
    Booming from the sedgy shallow.   20
Ruder sounds shall none be near,
Guards nor warders challenge here,
Here 's no war-steed's neigh and champ-
        ing,
Shouting clans or squadrons stamping.

Huntsman, rest! thy chase is done;   25
    While our slumbrous spells assail ye,
Dream not, with the rising sun,
    Bugles here shall sound reveillé.
Sleep! the deer is in his den;
    Sleep! thy hounds are by thee lying: 30
Sleep! nor dream in yonder glen
How thy gallant steed lay dying.
Huntsman, rest! thy chase is done;
Think not of the rising sun,
For at dawning to assail ye   35
Here no bugles sound reveillé.

                                        (1810)

GEORGE NOEL GORDON, LORD BYRON (1788–1824)

Byron's father, a military rake known as 'mad Jack Byron,' had squandered his wife's estate and terminated an ill-spent life within three years after the poet's birth in a London lodging house. His mother was a 'mad Gordon.' Byron therefore was half Scotch, and part of his childhood was spent in Scotland. His early training, chiefly at the hands of nurses and tutors, was incoherent and 'shabby-genteel.' When ten years of age he succeeded to the titles and estates of his uncle, 'the wicked Lord Byron' of Newstead. At Harrow (1801-5), in spite of a deformed ankle which the torture of surgeons had failed to correct and which his pride and sensitiveness converted into a curse, he was energetic in sports and laid the basis of those athletic habits which remained with him through life. While at Trinity College, Cambridge, he brought out his first volume of poems, *Hours of Idleness* (1807). To the ridicule of the *Edinburgh Review* he retorted angrily and with some vigor in his *English Bards and Scotch Reviewers* (1809), then left England for two years of travel in Spain, Greece and the Levant, and, on his return, published the first two cantos of *Childe Harold's Pilgrimage* (1812). The effect was electrical. Young, proud, traveled, mysteriously unhappy, romantically wicked, with a countenance of wild insolent beauty, a poet and a peer, Byron became the rage. Under such circumstances poetry is not critically scanned for its deeper elements. Byron's powers were sufficient for the occasion. From the midst of the social whirl into which he was caught up he extemporized tale after tale. *The Giaour*, *The Bride of Abydos*, *The Corsair*, *Lara*, followed each other in swift succession. Scott seemed local and tame, Marmion a schoolboy. Fashion followed and the critics fawned. Then came Byron's marriage, and a year later, his separation, and in 'one of those periodical spasms of British morality' his worshippers suddenly discovered that their idol had been a monster. Byron left England never to return alive. In Switzerland he met Shelley and the two poets spent some months together among the Alps, an intimacy of great value to both, which they afterward renewed in Italy. From this time Byron's poetry, though still unequal, showed a deeper quality and his activity increased. The third canto of *Childe Harold*, *The Prisoner of Chillon*, and many short pieces of new sincerity and strength were finished, and *Manfred* begun, in Switzerland. In the autumn of 1816 he settled at Venice, and, except for short tours, remained there until in 1819 he removed to Ravenna in order to be near the Countess Guiccioli. He became domiciled with that lady in 1819, and in 1821 they moved to Pisa. Throughout his Italian residence Byron had been greatly interested in the plans for Italian independence, and had constantly given aid and comfort to the Carbonari. In 1823 he resolved to devote his fortune and services to the cause of Greek freedom, and it was while assisting in the organization of the patriot forces in Greece, that he succumbed to a fever at Missolonghi when only thirty-six years of age. During his seven years in Italy Byron had completed *Manfred* (1817) and written seven other dramas, and had added a fourth canto to *Childe Harold*. What was more important he had discovered in *Beppo* (1818) the serio-comic vein in which his real strength lay, had produced in *The Vision of Judgment* (1821) the sublimest of parodies, and in *Don Juan* (1819-23) his masterpiece. Few poets are so difficult to represent by selections as Byron. His lyrics do not exhibit him to advantage, and extracts give but a poor idea of his variety, sweep, and vitality. Great faults and great virtues 'antithetically mixed'; a spirit hampered by mal-direction, affectation, and self-sophistication, but when it gets free, giant and fine; an imagination full of clay and crudities, but volleying at times into prodigious passion, reality, and compass; this is Byron.

SONNET ON CHILLON

Eternal Spirit of the chainless Mind!
Brightest in dungeons, Liberty! thou art,
For there thy habitation is the heart —
The heart which love of thee alone can
   bind;
And when thy sons to fetters are con-
   signed —   5
To fetters, and the damp vault's dayless
   gloom,
Their country conquers with their mar-
   tyrdom,

And Freedom's fame finds wings on every
    wind.
Chillon! thy prison is a holy place,
And thy sad floor an altar — for 't was
    trod,   10
Until his very steps have left a trace
Worn, as if thy cold pavement were a sod,
By Bonnivard! May none those marks
    efface!
For they appeal from tyranny to God.
                December 5, 1816

From CHILDE HAROLD, CANTO III

Adieu to thee, fair Rhine! How long de-
    lighted
The stranger fain would linger on his way!
Thine is a scene alike where souls united
Or lonely Contemplation thus might stray;
And could the ceaseless vultures cease to
    prey   5
On self-condemning bosoms, it were here,
Where Nature, nor too somber nor too gay,
Wild but not rude, awful yet not austere,
Is to the mellow Earth as Autumn to the
    year.

Adieu to thee again! a vain adieu!   10
There can be no farewell to scene like
    thine;
The mind is colored by thy every hue;
And if reluctantly the eyes resign
Their cherished gaze upon thee, lovely
    Rhine!
'T is with the thankful heart of parting
    praise;   15
More mighty spots may rise, more glaring
    shine,
But none unite in one attaching maze
The brilliant, fair, and soft,— the glories
    of old days,

The negligently grand, the fruitful bloom
Of coming ripeness, the white city's
    sheen,   20
The rolling stream, the precipice's gloom,
The forest's growth and Gothic walls be-
    tween,
The wild rocks shaped as they had tur-
    rets been,
In mockery of man's art; and these withal
A race of faces happy as the scene,   25
Whose fertile bounties here extend to all,
Still springing o'er thy banks, though Em-
    pires near them fall.

But these recede. Above me are the Alps,
The palaces of Nature, whose vast walls 30

Have pinnacled in clouds their snowy
    scalps,
And throned Eternity in icy halls
Of cold sublimity, where forms and falls
The avalanche — the thunderbolt of snow!
All that expands the spirit, yet appalls, 35
Gather around these summits, as to show
How earth may pierce to Heaven, yet leave
    vain man below.

But ere these matchless heights I dare to
    scan,
There is a spot should not be passed in
    vain,—
Morat! the proud, the patriot field! where
    man   40
May gaze on ghastly trophies of the slain,
Nor blush for those who conquered on that
    plain;
Here Burgundy bequeathed his tombless
    host,
A bony heap, through ages to remain,
Themselves their monument; the Stygian
    coast   45
Unsepulchered they roamed, and shrieked
    each wandering ghost.

While Waterloo with Cannæ's carnage vies,
Morat and Marathon twin names shall
    stand;
They were true Glory's stainless victories,
Won by the unambitious heart and hand 50
Of a proud, brotherly, and civic band,
All unbought champions in no princely
    cause
Of vice-entailed Corruption; they no land
Doomed to bewail the blasphemy of laws
Making kings' rights divine, by some Dra-
    conic clause.   55

By a lone wall a lonelier column rears
A gray and grief-worn aspect of old days:
'T is the last remnant of the wreck of
    years,
And looks as with the wild-bewildered gaze
Of one to stone converted by. amaze,   60
Yet still with consciousness; and there it
    stands
Making a marvel that it not decays,
When the coeval pride of human hands,
Leveled Adventicum hath strewed her sub-
    ject lands.

And there — oh! sweet and sacred be the
    name! —   65
Julia — the daughter, the devoted — gave
Her youth to Heaven; her heart, beneath
    a claim

Nearest to Heaven's, broke o'er a father's
grave.
Justice is sworn 'gainst tears, and hers
would crave
The life she lived in; but the judge was
just,   70
And then she died on him she could not
save.
Their tomb was simple, and without a bust,
And held within their urn one mind, one
heart, one dust.

But these are deeds which should not pass
away,
And names that must not wither though
the earth   75
Forgets her empires with a just decay,
The enslavers and the enslaved, their death
and birth;
The high, the mountain-majesty of worth
Should be, and shall, survivor of its woe,
And from its immortality look forth   80
In the sun's face, like yonder Alpine snow,
Imperishably pure beyond all things below.

Lake Leman woos me with its crystal face,
The mirror where the stars and moun-
tains view
The stillness of their aspect in each trace 85
Its clear depth yields of their far height
and hue;
There is too much of man here, to look
through
With a fit mind the might which I behold;
But soon in me shall Loneliness renew
Thoughts hid, but not less cherished than
of old,   90
Ere mingling with the herd had penned
me in their fold.

To fly from, need not be to hate, mankind:
All are not fit with them to stir and toil,
Nor is it discontent to keep the mind
Deep in its fountain, lest it overboil   95
In the hot throng, where we become the
spoil
Of our infection, till too late and long
We may deplore and struggle with the coil,
In wretched interchange of wrong for
wrong
Midst a contentious world, striving where
none are strong.   100

There, in a moment we may plunge our
years
In fatal penitence, and in the blight
Of our own soul turn all our blood to
tears,

And color things to come with hues of
Night;
The race of life becomes a hopeless flight
To those who walk in darkness: on the
sea   106
The boldest steer but where their ports in-
vite;
But there are wanderers o'er Eternity
Whose bark drives on and on, and anchored
ne'er shall be.

Is it not better, then, to be alone,   110
And love Earth only for its earthly sake?
By the blue rushing of the arrowy Rhone,
Or the pure bosom of its nursing lake,
Which feeds it as a mother who doth make
A fair but froward infant her own care, 115
Kissing its cries away as these awake; —
Is it not better thus our lives to wear,
Than join the crushing crowd, doomed to
inflict or bear?

I live not in myself, but I become
Portion of that around me; and to me   120
High mountains are a feeling, but the hum
Of human cities torture: I can see
Nothing to loathe in nature, save to be
A link reluctant in a fleshly chain.
Classed among creatures, when the soul can
flee,   125
And with the sky, the peak, the heaving
plain
Of ocean, or the stars, mingle, and not in
vain.

And thus I am absorbed, and this is life:
I look upon the peopled desert past,
As on a place of agony and strife,   130
Where, for some sin, to sorrow I was cast,
To act and suffer, but remount at last
With a fresh pinion; which I feel to spring,
Though young, yet waxing vigorous as the
blast
Which it would cope with, on delighted
wing,   135
Spurning the clay-cold bonds which round
our being cling.

And when, at length, the mind shall be all
free
From what it hates in this degraded form,
Reft of its carnal life, save what shall be
Existent happier in the fly and worm — 140
When elements to elements conform,
And dust is as it should be, shall I not
Feel all I see, less dazzling, but more warm?
The bodiless thought? the Spirit of each
spot?

Of which, even now, I share at times the
   immortal lot? 145

Are not the mountains, waves, and skies, a
   part
Of me and of my soul, as I of them?
Is not the love of these deep in my heart
With a pure passion? should I not contemn
All objects, if compared with these? and
   stem 150
A tide of suffering, rather than forego
Such feelings for the hard and worldly
   phlegm
Of those whose eyes are only turned below,
Gazing upon the ground, with thoughts
   which dare not glow?

But this is not my theme; and I return 155
To that which is immediate, and require
Those who find contemplation in the urn,
To look on One, whose dust was once all
   fire,
A native of the land where I respire 159
The clear air for a while — a passing guest
Where he became a being,— whose desire
Was to be glorious; 't was a foolish quest,
The which to gain and keep, he sacrificed
   all rest.

Here the self-torturing sophist, wild Rous-
   seau,
The apostle of affliction, he who threw 165
Enchantment over passion, and from woe
Wrung overwhelming eloquence, first drew
The breath which made him wretched; yet
   he knew
How to make madness beautiful and cast
O'er erring deeds and thoughts a heavenly
   hue 170
Of words, like sunbeams, dazzling as they
   past
The eyes, which o'er them shed tears feel-
   ingly and fast.

His love was passion's essence: — as a tree
On fire by lightning, with ethereal flame
Kindled he was, and blasted; for to be 175
Thus, and enamored, were in him the same.
But his was not the love of living dame,
Nor of the dead who rise upon our dreams,
But of ideal beauty, which became
In him existence, and o'erflowing teems 180
Along his burning page, distempered though
   it seems.

This breathed itself to life in Julie, *this*
Invested her with all that 's wild and sweet;
This hallowed, too, the memorable kiss

Which every morn his fevered lip would
   greet, 185
From hers, who but with friendship his
   would meet;
But to that gentle touch through brain and
   breast
Flashed the thrilled spirit's love-devouring
   heat;
In that absorbing sigh perchance more
   blest
Than vulgar minds may be with all they
   seek possest. 190

His life was one long war with self-sought
   foes,
Or friends by him self-banished; for his
   mind
Had grown Suspicion's sanctuary, and chose,
For its own cruel sacrifice, the kind,
'Gainst whom he raged with fury strange
   and blind. 195
But he was phrensied,— wherefore, who may
   know?
Since cause might be which skill could never
   find;
But he was phrensied by disease or woe,
To that worst pitch of all, which wears
   a reasoning show.

For then he was inspired, and from him
   came, 200
As from the Pythian's mystic cave of yore,
Those oracles which set the world in flame,
Nor ceased to burn till kingdoms were no
   more:
Did he not this for France? which lay be-
   fore
Bowed to the inborn tyranny of years? 205
Broken and trembling to the yoke she bore,
Till by the voice of him and his compeers
Roused up to too much wrath, which fol-
   lows o'ergrown fears?

They made themselves a fearful monument!
The wreck of old opinions — things which
   grew, 210
Breathed from the birth of time: the veil
   they rent,
And what behind it lay, all earth shall
   view.
But good with ill they also overthrew,
Leaving but ruins, wherewith to rebuild
Upon the same foundation, and renew 215
Dungeons and thrones, which the same hour
   refilled,
As heretofore, because ambition was self-
   willed.

But this will not endure, nor be endured!
Mankind have felt their strength, and made
it felt.
They might have used it better, but, allured
By their new vigor, sternly have they dealt
On one another; pity ceased to melt   222
With her once natural charities. But they
Who in oppression's darkness caved had
dwelt,
They were not eagles, nourished with the
day;   225
What marvel then, at times, if they mis-
took their prey?

What deep wounds ever closed without a
scar?
The heart's bleed longest, and but heal to
wear
That which disfigures it; and they who war
With their own hopes, and have been
vanquished, bear   230
Silence, but not submission: in his lair
Fixed Passion holds his breath, until the
hour
Which shall atone for years; none need
despair:
It came, it cometh, and will come,— the
power
To punish or forgive— in *one* we shall be
slower.   235

Clear, placid Leman! thy contrasted lake,
With the wild world I dwelt in, is a thing
Which warns me, with its stillness, to for-
sake
Earth's troubled waters for a purer spring.
This quiet sail is as a noiseless wing   240
To waft me from distraction; once I loved
Torn ocean's roar, but thy soft murmur-
ing
Sounds sweet as if a Sister's voice reproved,
That I with stern delights should e'er have
been so moved.

It is the hush of night, and all between 245
Thy margin and the mountains, dusk, yet
clear,
Mellowed and mingling, yet distinctly seen,
Save darkened Jura, whose capt heights ap-
pear
Precipitously steep; and drawing near,
There breathes a living fragrance from the
shore,   250
Of flowers yet fresh with childhood; on
the ear
Drops the light drip of the suspended oar,
Or chirps the grasshopper one good-night
carol more;

He is an evening reveler, who makes
His life an infancy, and sings his fill; 255
At intervals, some bird from out the brakes
Starts into voice a moment, then is still.
There seems a floating whisper on the hill,
But that is fancy, for the starlight dews
All silently their tears of love instil, 260
Weeping themselves away, till they infuse
Deep into nature's breast the spirit of her
hues.

Ye stars! which are the poetry of heaven!
If in your bright leaves we would read the
fate
Of men and empires,— 't is to be forgiven,
That in our aspirations to be great,   266
Our destinies o'erleap their mortal state,
And claim a kindred with you; for ye are
A beauty and a mystery, and create
In us such love and reverence from afar,
That fortune, fame, power, life, have named
themselves a star.   271

All heaven and earth are still — though not
in . sleep,
But breathless, as we grow when feeling
most;
And silent, as we stand in thoughts too
deep: —
All heaven and earth are still: From the
high host   275
Of stars, to the lulled lake and mountain
coast,
All is concentered in a life intense,
Where not a beam, nor air, nor leaf is lost,
But hath a part of being, and a sense
Of that which is of all Creator and de-
fence.   280

Then stirs the feeling infinite, so felt
In solitude, where we are *least* alone;
A truth, which through our being then doth
melt,
And purifies from self: it is a tone,
The soul and source of music, which makes
known   285
Eternal harmony, and sheds a charm
Like to the fabled Cytherea's zone,
Binding all things with beauty:— 't would
disarm
The specter Death, had he substantial power
to harm.

Not vainly did the early Persian make   290
His altar the high places, and the peak
Of earth-o'ergazing mountains, and thus take
A fit and unwalled temple, there to seek
The Spirit, in whose honor shrines are
weak,

Upreared of human hands. Come, and
  compare   295
Columns and idol-dwellings, Goth or Greek,
With Nature's realms of worship, earth and
  air,
Nor fix on fond abodes to circumscribe thy
  prayer!

The sky is changed! — and such a change!
  Oh, night,
And storm, and darkness, ye are wondrous
  strong,   300
Yet, lovely in your strength, as is the light
Of a dark eye in woman! Far along,
From peak to peak, the rattling crags
  among
Leaps the live thunder! Not from one
  lone cloud,
But every mountain now hath found a
  tongue,   305
And Jura answers, through her misty
  shroud,
Back to the joyous Alps, who call to her
  aloud!

And this is in the night: — Most glorious
  night!
Thou wert not sent for slumber! let me be
A sharer in thy fierce and far delight,—310
A portion of the tempest and of thee!
How the lit lake shines, a phosphoric sea,
And the big rain comes dancing to the
  earth!
And now again 't is black — and now, the
  glee
Of the loud hills shakes with its mountain-
  · mirth,   315
As if they did rejoice o'er a young earth-
  quake's birth.

Now, where the swift Rhone cleaves his
  way between
Heights which appear as lovers who have
  parted
In hate, whose mining depths so intervene,
That they can meet no more, though broken-
  hearted;   320
Though in their souls, which thus each other
  thwarted,
Love was the very root of the fond rage
Which blighted their life's bloom, and then
  departed:
Itself expired, but leaving them an age
Of years all winters,— war within them-
  selves to wage: 325

Now, where the quick Rhone thus hath cleft
  his way,

The mightiest of the storms hath ta'en his
  stand:
For here, not one, but many, make their
  play,
And fling their thunder-bolts from hand to
  hand,
Flashing and cast around; of all the band,
The brightest through these parted hills
  hath forked   331
His lightnings,— as if he did understand,
That in such gaps as desolation worked,
There the hot shaft should blast whatever
  therein lurked.

Sky, mountains, river, winds, lake, light-
  nings! ye!   335
With night, and clouds, and thunder, and a
  soul
To make these felt and feeling, well may
  be
Things that have made me watchful; the
  far roll
Of your departing voices, is the knoll
Of what in me is sleepless,— if I rest. 340
But where of ye, O tempests! is the goal?
Are ye like those within the human breast?
Or do ye find, at length, like eagles, some
  high nest?

Could I embody and unbosom now
That which is most within me,— could I
  wreak   345
My thoughts upon expression,. and thus
  throw
Soul, heart, mind, passions, feelings, strong
  or weak,
All that I would have *sought, and all I
  seek,
Bear, know, feel, and yet breathe — into
  one word,
And that one word were Lightning, I would
  speak;   350
But as it is, I live and die unheard,
With a most voiceless thought, sheathing
  it as a sword.

The morn is up again, the dewy morn,
With breath all incense, and with cheek all
  bloom,
Laughing the clouds away with playful
  scorn,   355
And living as if earth contained no tomb,—
And glowing into day: we may resume
The march of our existence: and thus I,
Still on thy shores, fair Leman! may find
  room
And food for meditation, nor pass by 360
Much, that may give us pause, if pondered
  fittingly.

Clarens! sweet Clarens, birthplace of deep
   Love!
Thine air is the young breath of passionate
   thought;
Thy trees take root in Love; the snows
   above
The very Glaciers have his colors caught,
And sunset into rose-hues sees them
   wrought   366
By rays which sleep there lovingly; the
   rocks,
The permanent crags, tell here of Love,
   who sought
In them a refuge from the worldly shocks,
Which stir and sting the soul with hope
   that woos, then mocks.   370

Clarens! by heavenly feet thy paths are
   trod,—
Undying Love's, who here ascends a throne
To which the steps are mountains; where
   the god
Is a pervading life and light,— so shown
Not on those summits solely, nor alone 375
In the still cave and forest; o'er the flower
His eye is sparkling, and his breath hath
   blown,
His soft and summer breath, whose tender
   power
Passes the strength of storms in their most
   desolate hour.

All things are here of *him;* from the black
   pines,   380
Which are his shade on high, and the loud
   roar
Of torrents, where he listeneth, to the
   vines
Which slope his green path downward to
   the shore,
Where the bowed waters meet him, and
   adore,
Kissing his feet with murmurs; and the
   wood,   385
The covert of old trees, with trunks all
   hoar,
But light leaves, young as joy, stands where
   it stood,
Offering to him, and his, a populous
   solitude;

A populous solitude of bees and birds,
And fairy-formed and many colored things,
Who worship him with notes more sweet
   than words,   391
And innocently open their glad wings,
Fearless and full of life: the gush of
   springs,

And fall of lofty fountains, and the bend
Of stirring branches, and the bud which
   brings   395
The swiftest thought of beauty, here extend,
Mingling, and made by Love, unto one
   mighty end.

He who hath loved not, here would learn
   that lore,
And make his heart a spirit; he who knows
That tender mystery, will love the more;
For this is Love's recess, where vain men's
   woes,   401
And the world's waste, have driven him far
   from those,
For 't is his nature to advance or die;
He stands not still, but or decays, or grows
Into a boundless blessing, which may vie
With the immortal lights, in its eternity! 406

'T was not for fiction chose Rousseau this
   spot,
Peopling it with affections; but he found
It was the scene which Passion must allot
To the mind's purified beings; 't was the
   ground   410
Where early Love his Psyche's zone un-
   bound,
And hallowed it with loveliness; 't is lone,
And wonderful, and deep, and hath a
   sound,
And sense, and sight of sweetness; here the
   Rhone
Hath spread himself a couch, the Alps have
   reared a throne.   415

Lausanne! and Ferney! ye have been the
   abodes
Of names which unto you bequeathed a
   name;
Mortals, who sought and found, by danger-
   ous roads,
A path to perpetuity of fame:
They were gigantic minds, and their steep
   aim   420
Was, Titan-like, on daring doubts to pile
Thoughts which should call down thunder,
   and the flame
Of Heaven again assailed, if Heaven the
   while
On man and man's research could deign do
   more than smile.

The one was fire and fickleness, a child 425
Most mutable in wishes, but in mind
A wit as various,— gay, grave, sage, or
   wild,—
Historian, bard, philosopher, combined;

He multiplied himself among mankind,
The Proteus of their talents: But his own
Breathed most in ridicule,— which, as the
   wind,   431
Blew where it listed, laying all things
   prone,—
Now to o'erthrow a fool, and now to shake
   a throne.

The other, deep and slow, exhausting
   thought,
And hiving wisdom with each studious
   year,   435
In meditation dwelt, with learning wrought,
And shaped his weapon with an edge severe,
Sapping a solemn creed with solemn sneer;
The lord of irony,— that master-spell,
Which stung his foes to wrath, which grew
   from fear,   440
And doomed him to the zealot's ready Hell,
Which answers to all doubts so eloquently
   well.

Yet, peace be with their ashes,— for by
   them,
If merited, the penalty is paid;
It is not ours to judge,— far less condemn;
The hour must come when such things shall
   be made   446
Known unto all, or hope and dread allayed
By slumber, on one pillow in the dust,
Which, thus much we are sure, must lie
   decayed;
And when it shall revive, as is our trust,
'T will be to be forgiven, or suffer what is
   just.   451

But let me quit man's works, again to read
His Maker's, spread around me, and sus-
   pend
This page, which from my reveries I feed,
Until it seems prolonging without end. 455
The clouds above me to the white Alps
   tend,
And I must pierce them, and survey whate'er
May be permitted, as my steps I bend
To their most great and growing region,
   where
The earth to her embrace compels the
   powers of air.   460

       * * *

I have not loved the world, nor the world
   me;
I have not flattered its rank breath, nor
   bowed
To its idolatries a patient knee,
Nor coined my cheek to smiles,, nor cried
   aloud

In worship of an echo; in the crowd 465
They could not deem me one of such; I
   stood
Among them, but not of them; in a shroud
Of thoughts which were not their thoughts,
   and still could,
Had I not filled my mind, which thus itself
   subdued.

I have not loved the world, nor the world
   me,—   470
But let us part fair foes; I do believe,
Though I have found them not, that there
   may be
Words which are things, hopes which will
   not deceive,
And virtues which are merciful, nor weave
Snares for the failing; I would also
   deem   475
O'er others' griefs that some sincerely
   grieve;
That two, or one, are almost what they
   seem,
That goodness is no name, and happiness
   no dream

       * * *

       (1817)

From CHILDE HAROLD, CANTO IV

Oh Rome! my country! City of the soul!
The orphans of the heart must turn to
   thee,
Lone mother of dead empires! and control
In their shut breasts their petty misery.
What are our woes and sufferance? Come
   and see   5
The cypress, hear the owl, and plod your
   way
O'er steps of broken thrones and temples,
   Ye!
Whose agonies are evils of a day —
A world is at our feet as fragile as our
   clay.

The Niobe of nations! there she stands 10
Childless and crownless, in her voiceless
   woe;
An empty urn within her withered hands,
Whose holy dust was scattered long ago;
The Scipios' tomb contains no ashes now;
The very sepulchers lie tenantless 15
Of their heroic dwellers: dost thou flow,
Old Tiber! through a marble wilderness?
Rise, with thy yellow waves, and mantle her
   distress.

The Goth, the Christian, Time, War, Flood,
   and Fire.

On infant Washington? Has earth no
  more   170
Such seeds within her breast, or Europe no
  such shore?

But France got drunk with blood to vomit
  crime,
And fatal have her Saturnalia been
To Freedom's cause, in every age and clime;
Because the deadly days which we have
  seen,   175
And vile Ambition, that built up between
Man and his hopes an adamantine wall,
And the base pageant last upon the scene,
Are grown the pretext for the eternal thrall
Which nips life's tree, and dooms man's
  worst — his second fall.   180

Yet, Freedom! yet thy banner, torn, but
  flying,
Streams, like the thunder-storm *against* the
  wind;
Thy trumpet voice, though broken now and
  dying,
The loudest still the tempest leaves behind;
Thy tree hath lost its blossoms, and the
  rind,   185
Chopped by the axe, looks rough and little
  worth,
But the sap lasts,— and still the seed we
  find
Sown deep, even in the bosom of the North;
So shall a better spring less bitter fruit bring
  forth.

There is a stern round tower of other
  days,   190
Firm as a fortress, with its fence of stone,
Such as an army's baffled strength delays,
Standing with half its battlements alone,
And with two thousand years of ivy grown,
The garland of eternity, where wave 195
The green leaves over all by time o'er-
  thrown: —
What was this tower of strength? within its
  cave
What treasure lay so locked, so hid? — A
  woman's grave.

But who was she, the lady of the dead,
Tombed in a palace? Was she chaste and
  fair?   200
Worthy a king's or more — a Roman's bed?
What race of chiefs and heroes did she
  bear?
What daughter of her beauties was the
  heir?
How lived, how loved, how died she? Was
  she not

So honored — and conspicuously there,   205
Where meaner relics must not dare to rot,
Placed to commemorate a more than mortal
  lot?

Was she as those who love their lords, or
  they
Who love the lords of others? such have
  been
Even in the olden time, Rome's annals
  say.   210
Was she a matron of Cornelia's mien,
Or the light air of Egypt's graceful queen,
Profuse of joy — or 'gainst it did she war,
Inveterate in virtue? Did she lean
To the soft side of the heart, or wisely
  bar   215
Love from amongst her griefs? — for such
  the affections are.

Perchance she died in youth: it may be
  bowed
With woes far heavier than the ponderous
  tomb
That weighed upon her gentle dust, a cloud
Might gather o'er her beauty, and a
  gloom   220
In her dark eye, prophetic of the doom
Heaven gives its favorites — early death; yet
  shed
A sunset charm around her, and illume
With hectic light, the Hesperus of the
  dead,
Of her consuming cheek the autumnal leaf-
  like red.   225

Perchance she died in age — surviving all,
Charms, kindred, children — with the silver
  gray
On her long tresses, which might yet recall,
It may be, still a something of the day
When they were braided, and her proud
  array   230
And lovely form were envied, praised, and
  eyed
By Rome — But whither would Conjecture
  stray?
Thus much alone we know — Metella died,
The wealthiest Roman's wife: Behold his
  love or pride!

I know not why — but standing thus by
  thee   235
It seems as if I had thine inmate known,
Thou Tomb! and other days come back to
  me
With recollected music, though the tone
Is changed and solemn, like a cloudy groan
Of dying thunder on the distant wind: 240

Yet could I seat me by this ivied stone
Till I had bodied forth the heated mind
Forms from the floating wreck which Ruin
    leaves behind;

And from the planks, far shattered o'er the
    rocks,
Built me a little bark of hope, once more
To battle with the ocean and the shocks 246
Of the loud breakers, and the ceaseless
    roar
Which rushes on the solitary shore
Where all lies foundered that was ever dear:
But could I gather from the wave-worn
    store   -   250
Enough for my rude boat, where should I
    steer?
There woos no home, nor hope, nor life, save
    what is here.

Then let the winds howl on! their har-
    mony
Shall henceforth by my music, and the
    night
The sound shall temper with the owlets'
    cry,   255
As I now hear them, in the fading light
Dim o'er the bird of darkness' native site,
Answering each other on the Palatine,
With their large eyes, all glistening gray
    and bright,
And sailing pinions.— Upon such a shrine
What are our petty griefs?— let me not
    number mine.   261

Cypress and ivy, weed and wallflower grown
Matted and massed together, hillocks heaped
On what were chambers, arch crushed,
    column strown
In fragments, choked up vaults, and fres-
    coes steeped   265
In subterranean damps, where the owl
    peeped,
Deeming it midnight:— Temples, baths, or
    halls?
Pronounce who can; for all that Learning
    reaped
From her research hath been, that these are
    walls—
Behold the Imperial Mount! 't is thus the
    mighty falls.   270

There is the moral of all human tales;
'T is but the same rehearsal of the past,
First Freedom and then Glory— when that
    fails,
Wealth, vice, corruption,— barbarism at
    last,
And history, with all her volumes vast. 275

Hath but *one* page —'t is better written here,
Where gorgeous Tyranny hath thus amassed
All treasures, all delights, that eye or ear,
Heart, soul could seek, tongue ask — Away
    with words! draw near,

Admire, exult, despise, laugh, weep,— for
    here   280
There is such matter for all feeling:—
    Man!
Thou pendulum betwixt a smile and tear,
Ages and realms are crowded in this span,
This mountain, whose obliterated plan
The pyramid of empires pinnacled,   285
Of Glory's gewgaws shining in the van
Till the sun's rays with added flame were
    filled!
Where are its golden roofs? where those
    who dared to build?

Tully was not so eloquent as thou,
Thou nameless column with the buried
    base!   290
What are the laurels of the Cæsar's brow?
Crown me with ivy from his dwelling-place
Whose arch or pillar meets me in the face,
Titus or Trajan's? No —'t is that of Time;
Triumph, arch, pillar, all he doth displace 295
Scoffing; and apostolic statues climb
To crush the imperial urn, whose ashes
    slept sublime,

Buried in air, the deep blue sky of Rome,
And looking to the stars: they had con-
    tained
A spirit which with these would find a
    home,   300
The last of those who o'er the whole earth
    reigned,
The Roman globe, for after none sustained,
But yielded back his conquests:— he was
    more
Than a mere Alexander, and, unstained
With household blood and wine, serenely
    wore   305
His sovereign virtues— still we Trajan's
    name adore.   -

* * *

Arches on arches! as it were that Rome,
Collecting the chief trophies of her line,
Would build up all her triumphs in one
    dome,
Her Coliseum stands; the moonbeams shine
As 't were its natural torches, for divine 311
Should be the light which streams here, to
    illume
This long-explored but still exhaustless
    mine

Of contemplation; and the azure gloom
Of an Italian night, where the deep skies
  assume   315

Hues which have words, and speak to ye
  of heaven,
Floats o'er this vast and wondrous monu-
  ment,
And shadows forth its glory. There is
  given
Unto the things of earth, which Time hath
  bent,
A spirit's feeling, and where he hath leant
His hand, but broke his scythe, there is a
  power   321
And magic in the ruined battlement,
For which the palace of the present hour
Must yield its pomp, and wait till ages are
  its dower.

Oh, Time! the beautifier of the dead,   325
Adorner of the ruin, comforter
And only healer when the heart hath bled;
Time! the corrector where our judgments
  err,
The test of truth, love — sole philosopher, 329
For all beside are sophists — from thy thrift,
Which never loses though it doth defer —
Time, the avenger! unto thee I lift
My hands, and eyes, and heart, and crave of
  thee a gift:

Amidst this wreck, where thou hast made a
  shrine
And temple more divinely desolate,   335
Among thy mightier offerings here are
  mine,
Ruins of years, though few, yet full of fate:
If thou hast ever seen me too elate,
Hear me not; but if calmly I have borne
Good, and reserved my pride against the
  hate   340
Which shall not whelm me, let me not have
  worn
This iron in my soul in vain — shall *they*
  not mourn?

And thou, who never yet of human wrong
Left the unbalanced scale, great Nemesis!
Here, where the ancient paid thee homage
  long —   345
Thou, who didst call the Furies from the
  abyss,
And round Orestes bade them howl and
  hiss
For that unnatural retribution — just,
Had it but been from hands less near —
  in this

Thy former realm, I call thee from the dust!
Dost thou not hear my heart? — Awake!
  thou shalt, and must.   351

It is not that I may not have incurred
For my ancestral faults or mine the wound
I bleed withal, and had it been conferred
With a just weapon, it had flowed un-
  bound;   355
But now my blood shall not sink in the
  ground;
To thee I do devote it — *thou* shalt take
The vengeance, which shall yet be sought and
  found
Which if *I* have not taken for the sake —
But let that pass — I sleep, but thou shalt yet
  awake.   360

And if my voice break forth, 't is not that
  now
I shrink from what is suffered: let him
  speak
Who hath beheld decline upon my brow,
Or seen my mind's convulsion leave it
  weak;
But in this page a record will I seek.   365
Not in the air shall these my words disperse,
Though I be ashes; a far hour shall
  wreak
The deep prophetic fulness of this verse,
And pile on human heads the mountain of
  my curse!

That curse shall be Forgiveness,— Have I
  not —   370
Hear me, my mother Earth! behold it,
  Heaven! —
Have I not had to wrestle with my lot?
Have I not suffered things to be forgiven?
Have I not had my brain seared, my heart
  riven,
Hopes sapped, name blighted, Life's life lied
  away?   375
And only not to desperation driven,
Because not altogether of such clay
As rots into the souls of those whom I sur-
  vey.

From mighty wrongs to petty perfidy
Have I not seen what human things could
  do?   380
From the loud roar of foaming calumny
To the small whisper of the as paltry few,
And subtler venom of the reptile crew,
The Janus glance of whose significant eye,
Learning to lie with silence, would *seem*
  true.   385

And without utterance, save the shrug or sigh,
Deal round to happy fools its speechless obloquy.

But I have lived, and have not lived in vain:
My mind may lose its force, my blood its fire,
And my frame perish even in conquering pain;   390
But there is that within me which shall tire
Torture and Time, and breathe when I expire;
Something unearthly, which they deem not of,
Like the remembered tone of a mute lyre,
Shall on their softened spirits sink, and move   395
In hearts all rocky now the late remorse of love.

The seal is set.— Now welcome, thou dread power!
Nameless, yet thus omnipotent, which here
Walk'st in the shadow of the midnight hour
With a deep awe, yet all distinct from fear;
Thy haunts are ever where the dead walls rear   401
Their ivy mantles, and the solemn scene
Derives from thee a sense so deep and clear
That we become a part of what has been,
And grow unto the spot, all-seeing but unseen.   405

And here the buzz of eager nations ran,
In murmured pity, or loud-roared applause,
As man was slaughtered by his fellow man.
And wherefore slaughtered? wherefore, but because
Such were the bloody Circus' genial laws,
And the imperial pleasure.— Wherefore not?   411
What matters where we fall to fill the maws
Of worms.— On battle-plains or listed spot?
Both are but theaters where the chief actors rot.

I see before me the Gladiator lie: 415
He leans upon his hand — his manly brow
Consents to death, but conquers agony,
And his drooped head sinks gradually low —
And through his side the last drops, ebbing slow
From the red gash, fall heavy, one by one,
Like the first of a thunder-shower; and now   421
The arena swims around him — he is gone,

Ere ceased the inhuman shout which hailed the wretch who won.

He heard it, but he heeded not — his eyes
Were with his heart, and that was far away;
He recked not of the life he lost nor prize,   426
But where his rude hut by the Danube lay,
There were his young barbarians all at play,
There was their Dacian mother — he, their sire,
Butchered to make a Roman holiday —   430
All this rushed with his blood — Shall he expire
And unavenged? Arise! ye Goths, and glut your ire!

But here, where Murder breathed her bloody steam;
And here, where buzzing nations choked the ways,
And roared or murmured like a mountain stream   435
Dashing or winding as its torrent strays;
Here, where the Roman millions' blame or praise
Was death or life, the playthings of a crowd,
My voice sounds much — and fall the stars' faint rays
On the arena void — seats crushed — walls bowed —   440
And galleries, where my steps seem echoes strangely loud.

A ruin — yet what ruin! — from its mass
Walls, palaces, half-cities, have been reared;
Yet oft the enormous skeleton ye pass,
And marvel where the spoil could have appeared.   445
Hath it indeed been plundered, or but cleared?
Alas! developed, opens the decay,
When the colossal fabric's form is neared:
It will not bear the brightness of the day,
Which streams too much on all, years, man have reft away.   450

But when the rising moon begins to climb
Its topmost arch, and gently pauses there;
When the stars twinkle through the loops of time,
And the low night-breeze waves along the air
The garland-forest, which the gray walls wear,   455
Like laurels on the bald first Cæsar's head;
When the light shines serene but doth not glare,

Then in this magic circle raise the dead:
Heroes have trod this spot —'t is on their
  dust ye tread.

'While stands the Coliseum, Rome shall
  stand;   460
When falls the Coliseum, Rome shall fall,
And when Rome falls — the World.'
  From our own land
Thus spake the pilgrims o'er this mighty
  wall
In Saxon times, which we are wont to call
Ancient; and these three mortal things are
  still   465
On their foundations, and unaltered all;
Rome and her Ruin past Redemption's
  skill,
The world, the same wide den — of thieves,
  or what ye will.

        * * *

                (1818)

From THE VISION OF JUDGMENT

In the first year of freedom's second
  dawn
  Died George the Third; although no
    tyrant, one
Who shielded tyrants, till each sense with-
  drawn
  Left him nor mental nor external sun;
A better farmer ne'er brushed dew from
  lawn,   5
  A worse king never left a realm undone!
He died — but left his subjects still behind,
One half as mad — and t'other no less blind.

He died! his death made no great stir on
  earth:
  His burial made some pomp; there was
    profusion   10
Of velvet, gilding, brass, and no great
  dearth
  Of aught but tears — save those shed by
    collusion.
For these things may be bought at their
  true worth;
  Of elegy there was the due infusion —
Bought also; and the torches, cloaks and
  banners,   15
Heralds, and relics of old Gothic manners,

Formed a sepulchral melodrame. Of all
  The fools who flocked to swell or see the
    show,
Who cared about the corpse? The funeral
  Made the attraction, and the black the
    woe.   20

There throbbed not there a thought which
  pierced the pall;
  And when the gorgeous coffin was laid
    low,
It seemed the mockery of hell to fold
The rottenness of eighty years in gold.

So mix his body with the dust! It might 25
  Return to what it *must* far sooner, were
The natural compound left alone to fight
  Its way back into earth, and fire, and air;
But the unnatural balsams merely blight
  What nature made him at his birth, as
    bare   30
As the mere million's base unmummied
  clay —
Yet all his spices but prolong decay.

He's dead — and upper earth with him has
  done;
  He's buried; save the undertaker's bill,
Or lapidary scrawl, the world is gone 35
  For him, unless he left a German will;
But where's the proctor who will ask his
  son?
  In whom his qualities are reigning still,
Except that household virtue, most uncom-
  mon,
Of constancy to a bad, ugly woman. 40

'God save the king!' It is a large econ-
  omy
  In God to save the like; but if he will
Be saving, all the better; for not one am I
  Of those who think damnation better still:
I hardly know too if not quite alone am I 45
  In this small hope of bettering future ill
By circumscribing, with some slight restric-
  tion,
The eternity of hell's hot jurisdiction.

I know this is unpopular; I know
  'T is blasphemous; I know one may be
    damned   50
For hoping no one else may e'er be so;
  I know my catechism; I know we've
    crammed
With the best doctrines till we quite o'er-
  flow;
  I know that all save England's church
    have shammed,
And that the other twice two hundred
  churches   55
And synagogues have made a *damned* bad
  purchase.

God help us all! God help me too! I am,
  God knows, as helpless as the devil can
    wish,

And not a whit more difficult to damn,
  Than is to bring to land a late-hooked
    fish, 60
Or to the butcher to purvey the lamb;
  Not that I'm fit for such a noble dish,
As one day will be that immortal fry
Of almost everybody born to die.

Saint Peter sat by the celestial gate, 65
  And nodded o'er his keys; when, lo! there
    came
A wondrous noise he had not heard of
    late —
  A rushing sound of wind, and stream and
    flame;
In short, a roar of things extremely great,
  Which would have made aught save a
    saint exclaim; 70
But he, with first a start and then a wink,
Said, 'There's another star gone out, I
    think!'

But ere he could return to his repose,
  A cherub flapped his right wing o'er his
    eyes —
At which St. Peter yawned, and rubbed his
    nose: 75
  'Saint porter,' said the angel, 'prithee
    rise!'
Waving a goodly wing, which glowed, as
    glows
  An earthly peacock's tail, with heavenly
    dyes:
To which the saint replied, 'Well, what's
    the matter?
Is Lucifer come back with all this clat-
    ter?' 80

'No,' quoth the cherub; 'George the Third
    is dead.'
  'And who is George the Third?' replied
    the apostle:
'What George? what Third?' 'The king
    of England,' said
  The angel. 'Well! he won't find kings to
    jostle
Him on his way; but does he wear his
    head? 85
  Because the last we saw here had a
    tussle,
And ne'er would have got into heaven's good
    graces,
Had he not flung his head in all our faces.

'He was, if I remember, king of France;
  That head of his, which could not keep
    a crown 90
On earth, yet ventured in my face to ad-
    vance

A claim to those of martyrs — like my
    own;
If I had had my sword, as I had once
  When I cut ears off, I had cut him down;
But having but my keys, and not my
    brand, 95
I only knock'd his head from out his hand.

'And then he set up such a headless howl,
  That all the saints came out and took
    him in;
And there he sits by St. Paul, cheek by
    jowl;
  That fellow Paul — the parvenú! The
    skin 100
Of St. Bartholomew, which makes his cowl
  In heaven, and upon earth redeemed his
    sin,
So as to make a martyr, never sped
Better than did this weak and wooden head.

'But had it come up here upon its shoul-
    ders, 105
  There would have been a different tale to
    tell:
The fellow-feeling in the saints' beholders
  Seems to have acted on them like a spell,
And so this very foolish head heaven
    solders
  Back on its trunk: it may be very well, 110
And seems the custom here, to overthrow
Whatever has been wisely done below.'

The angel answered, 'Peter! do not pout:
  The king who comes has head and all
    entire,
And never knew much what it was
    about — 115
  He did as doth the puppet — by its wire,
And will be judged like all the rest, no
    doubt:
  My business and your own is not to in-
    quire
Into such matters, but to mind our cue —
Which is to act as we are bid to do.' 120

While thus they spake, the angelic caravan
  Arriving like a rush of mighty wind,
Cleaving the fields of space, as doth the
    swan
  Some silver stream (say Ganges, Nile or
    Inde,
Or Thames, or Tweed), and 'midst them an
    old man 125
  With an old soul, and both extremely
    blind,
Halted before the gate, and in his shroud
Seated their fellow traveler on a cloud.

And much of earth and all the watery plain
  Of ocean called him king: through many
     a storm
His isles had floated on the abyss of time;
For the rough virtues chose them for their
    clime.   280

'He came to his scepter young; he leaves it
  old:
Look to the state in which he found his
    realm,
And left it; and his annals too behold,
  How to a minion first he gave the helm;
How grew upon his heart a thirst for gold,
  The beggar's vice, which can but over-
    whelm   286
The meanest hearts; and for the rest, but
    glance
Thine eye along America and France.

''T is true, he was a tool from first to last
  (I have the workmen safe), but as a tool
So let him be consumed. From out the
    past   291
Of ages, since mankind have known the
    rule
Of monarchs — from the bloody rolls
    amassed
Of sin and slaughter — from the Cæsar's
    school,
Take the worst pupil; and produce a reign
More drenched with gore, more cumbered
    with the slain.   296

'He ever warred with freedom and the free:
  Nations as men, home subjects, foreign
    foes,
So that they uttered the word 'Liberty!'
  Found George the Third their first op-
    ponent. Whose   300
History was ever stained as his will be
  With national and individual woes?
I grant his household abstinence; I grant
  His neutral virtues, which most monarchs
    want;

'I know he was a constant consort; own 305
  He was a decent sire, and middling lord.
All this is much, and most upon a throne;
  As temperance, if at Apicius' board,
Is more than at an anchorite's supper shown.
  I grant him all the kindest can accord; 310
And this was well for him, but not for
    those
Millions who found him what oppression
    chose.

'The New World shook him off; the Old
  yet groans
Beneath what he and his prepared, if not
Completed: he leaves heirs on many thrones
  To all his vices, without what begot 316
Compassion for him — his tame virtues;
    drones
Who sleep, or despots who have now for-
    got
A lesson which shall be re-taught them,
    wake
Upon the thrones of earth; but let them
    quake!   320

'Five millions of the primitive, who hold
  The faith which makes ye great on earth
    implored
A part of that vast all they held of old,—
  Freedom to worship — not alone your
    Lord.
Michael, but you, and you, Saint Peter!
    cold   325
  Must be your souls, if you have not
    abhorred
The foe to Catholic participation
  In all the license of a Christian nation.

'True! he allowed them to pray God; but
  as
  A consequence of prayer, refused the law
Which would have placed them upon the
    same base   331
  With those who did not hold the saints
    in awe.'
But here Saint Peter started from his place,
  And cried, 'You may the prisoner with-
    draw:
Ere heaven shall ope her portals to this
    Guelph,   335
While I am guard, may I be damned my-
    self!

'Sooner will I with Cerberus exchange
  My office (and his is no sinecure)
Than see this royal Bedlam bigot range
  The azure fields of heaven, of that be
    sure!'   340
'Saint!' replied Satan, 'you do well to
    avenge
  The wrongs he made your satellites en-
    dure;
And if to this exchange you should be
    given,
I 'll try to coax our Cerberus up to heaven!'

Here Michael interposed: 'Good saint! and
    devil!   345

Pray, not so fast; you both outrun dis-
        cretion.
Saint Peter! you were wont to be more
        civil!
Satan, excuse this warmth of his expres-
        sion,
And condescension to the vulgar's level;
    Even saints sometimes forget themselves
        in session.   350
    Have you got more to say?'—'No.'—
        'If you please,
I'll trouble you to call your witnesses.'
                                    (1822)

* * *

From DON JUAN, CANTO III

THE ISLES OF GREECE

The isles of Greece, the isles of Greece!
    Where burning Sappho loved and sung,
Where grew the arts of war and peace,—
    Where Delos rose, and Phœbus sprung!
Eternal summer gilds them yet,   5
But all, except their sun, is set.

The Scian and the Teian muse,
    The hero's harp, the lover's lute,
Have found the fame your shores refuse:
    Their place of birth alone is mute   10
To sounds which echo further west
Than your sires' 'Islands of the Blest.'

The mountains look on Marathon—
    And Marathon looks on the sea;
And musing there an hour alone,   15
    I dreamed that Greece might still be free;
For standing on the Persian's grave,
I could not deem myself a slave.

A king sate on the rocky brow
    Which looks o'er sea-born Salamis;   20
And ships, by thousands, lay below,
    And men in nations;—all were his!
He counted them at break of day—
And when the sun set, where were they?

And where are they? and where art thou, 25
    My country? On thy voiceless shore
The heroic lay is tuneless now—
    The heroic bosom beats no more!
And must thy lyre, so long divine,
Degenerate into hands like mine?   30

'Tis something, in the dearth of fame,
    Though linked among a fettered race,
To feel at least a patriot's shame,
    Even as I sing, suffuse my face;

For what is left the poet here?   35
For Greeks a blush—for Greece a tear.

Must we but weep o'er days more blest?
    Must we but blush?—Our fathers bled.
Earth! render back from out thy breast
    A remnant of our Spartan dead!   40
Of the three hundred grant but three,
To make a new Thermopylæ!

What, silent still? and silent all?
    Ah! no;—the voices of the dead
Sound like a distant torrent's fall,   45
    And answer, 'Let one living head,
But one arise,—we come, we come!'
'Tis but the living who are dumb.

In vain—in vain: strike other chords:
    Fill high the cup with Samian wine!   50
Leave battles to the Turkish hordes,
    And shed the blood of Scio's vine!
Hark! rising to the ignoble call—
How answers each bold Bacchanal!

You have the Pyrrhic dance as yet: 55
    Where is the Pyrrhic phalanx gone?
Of two such lessons, why forget
    The nobler and the manlier one?
You have the letters Cadmus gave—
Think ye he meant them for a slave?   60

Fill high the bowl with Samian wine!
    We will not think of themes like these!
It made Anacreon's song divine;
    He served—but served Polycrates—
A tyrant; but our masters then   65
Were still, at least, our countrymen.

The tyrant of the Chersonese
    Was freedom's best and bravest friend;
That tyrant was Miltiades!
    Oh! that the present hour would lend 7•
Another despot of the kind!
Such chains as his were sure to bind.

Fill high the bowl with Samian wine!
    On Suli's rock, and Parga's shore,
Exists the remnant of a line   75
    Such as the Doric mothers bore;
And there, perhaps, some seed is sown,
The Heracleidan blood might own.

Trust not for freedom to the Franks,
    They have a king who buys and sells; 8•
In native swords and native ranks,
    The only hope of courage dwells:
But Turkish force, and Latin fraud,
Would break your shield, however broad.

Fill high the bowl with Samian wine!   85
  Our virgins dance beneath the shade —
I see their glorious black eyes shine;
  But gazing on each glowing maid,
My own the burning tear-drop laves,
To think such breasts must suckle slaves.

Place me on Sunium's marbled steep,   91
  Where nothing, save the waves and I,
May hear our mutual murmurs sweep;
  There, swan-like, let me sing and die:
A land of slaves shall ne'er be mine —   95
Dash down yon cup of Samian wine!

Thus sung, or would, or could, or should
  have sung,
  The modern Greek, in tolerable verse:
If not like Orpheus quite, when Greece was
  young,
  Yet in these times he might have done
    much worse: 100
His strain displayed some feeling — right or
  wrong;
  And feeling, in a poet, is the source
Of others' feeling; but they are such liars,
And take all colors — like the hands of
  dyers.

But words are things, and a small drop of
  ink,   105
  Falling like dew, upon a thought, pro-
    duces
That which makes thousands, perhaps mil-
  lions, think;
  'T is strange, the shortest letter which man
  uses
Instead of speech, may form a lasting link
  Of ages; to what straits old Time re-
    duces   110
Frail man when paper — even a rag like
  this,
Survives himself, his tomb, and all that's
  his!

And when his bones are dust, his grave a
  blank,
  His station, generation, even his nation,
Become a thing, or nothing, save to rank 115
  In chronological commemoration,
Some dull MS. oblivion long has sank.
  Or graven stone found in a barrack's
    station
In digging the foundation of a closet,
May turn his name up, as a rare deposit. 120

And glory long has made the sages smile;
'T is something, nothing, words, illusion
  wind —

Depending more upon the historian's style
  Than on the name a person leaves be-
    hind:
Troy owes to Homer what whist owes to
  Hoyle: 125
  The present century was growing blind
To the great Marlborough's skill in giving
  knocks,
Until his late Life by Archdeacon Coxe.

Milton's the prince of poets — so we say;
  A little heavy, but no less divine: 130
An independent being in his day —
  Learned, pious, temperate in love and
    wine;
But his life falling into Johnson's way,
  We 're told this great high priest of all
    the Nine
Was whipt at college — a harsh sire — odd
  spouse,   135
For the first Mrs. Milton left his house.

All these are, *certes,* entertaining facts,
  Like Shakspere's stealing deer, Lord
    Bacon's bribes;
Like Titus' youth, and Cæsar's earliest acts;
  Like Burns (whom Doctor Currie well
    describes);   140
Like Cromwell's pranks: — but although
  truth exacts
  These amiable descriptions from the
    scribes,
As most essential to their hero's story,
They do not much contribute to his glory.

All are not moralists, like Southey, when
  He prated to the world of 'Pantisocracy:'
Or Wordsworth unexcised, unhired, who
  then   147
  Seasoned his peddler poems with democ-
    racy;
Or Coleridge, long before his flighty pen
  Let to the Morning Post its aristocracy;
When he and Southey, following the same
  path,   151
Espoused two partners (milliners of Bath).

Such names at present cut a convict figure,
  The very Botany Bay in moral geogra-
    phy:
Their royal treason, renegado rigor,   155
  Are good manure for their more bare
    biography.
Wordsworth's last quarto, by the way, is
  bigger
  Than any since the birthday of typogra-
    phy:

A drowsy frowzy poem, called the 'Excursion,'
Writ in a manner which is my aversion. 160
* * *
T' our tale.— The feast was over, the slaves gone,
  The dwarfs and dancing girls had all retired —
The Arab lore and poet's song were done,
  And every sound of revelry expired;
The lady and her lover, left alone. 165
  The rosy flood of twilight's sky admired:
Ave Maria! o'er the earth and sea,
That heavenliest hour of Heaven is worthiest thee!

Ave Maria! blessed be the hour!
  The time, the clime, the spot, where I so oft 170
Have felt that moment in its fullest power
  Sink o'er the earth so beautiful and soft,
While swung the deep bell in the distant tower,
  Or the faint dying day-hymn stole aloft,
And not a breath crept through the rosy air,
And yet the forest leaves seemed stirred with prayer. 176

Ave Maria! 't is the hour of prayer!
  Ave Maria! 't is the hour of love!
Ave Maria! may our spirits dare
  Look up to thine and to thy Son's above!
Ave Maria! oh, that face so fair! 181
  Those downcast eyes beneath the Almighty dove —
What though 't is but a pictured image strike,
That painting is no idol, — 't is too like.

Some kinder casuists are pleased to say,
  In nameless print — that I have no devotion; 186
But set those persons down with me to pray,
  And you shall see who has the properest notion
Of getting into heaven the shortest way;
  My altars are the mountains and the ocean, 190
Earth, air, stars,— all that springs from the great Whole,
Who hath produced, and will receive the soul.

Sweet hour of twilight!— in the solitude
Of the pine forest and the silent shore
Which bounds Ravenna's immemorial wood,
  Rooted where once the Adrian wave flowed o'er, 196

To where the last Cæsarean fortress stood,
  Evergreen forest! which Boccaccio's lore
And Dryden's lay made haunted ground to me,
How have I loved the twilight hour and thee! 200

The shrill cicalas, people of the pine,
  Making their summer lives one ceaseless song,
Were the sole echoes, save my steed's and mine,
  And vesper bell's that rose the boughs along;
The specter huntsman of Onesti's line, 205
  His hell-dogs, and their chase, and the fair throng
Which learned from this example not to fly
From a true lover, shadowed my mind's eye.

O Hesperus! thou bringest all good things —
  Home to the weary, to the hungry cheer, 210
To the young bird the parent's brooding wings,
  The welcome stall to the o'erlabored steer;
Whate'er of peace about our hearthstone clings,
  Whate'er our household gods protect of dear, 214
Are gathered round us by thy look of rest;
Thou bring'st the child, too, to the mother's breast.

Soft hour! which wakes the wish and melts the heart
  Of those who sail the seas, on the first day
When they from their sweet friends are torn apart; 219
  Or fills with love the pilgrim on his way
As the far bell of vesper makes him start,
  Seeming to weep the dying day's decay;
Is this a fancy which our reason scorns?
Ah! surely nothing dies but something mourns!

When Nero perished by the justest doom 225
  Which ever the destroyer yet destroyed,
Amidst the roar of liberated Rome,
  Of nations freed, and the world overjoyed,
Some hands unseen strewed flowers upon his tomb: 229
  Perhaps the weakness of a heart not void

Of feeling for some kindness done, when
    power
Had left the wretch an uncorrupted hour.

But I'm digressing; what on earth has
    Nero,
Or any such like sovereign buffoons,
To do with the transactions of my hero, 235
    More than such madmen's fellow man
    — the moon's?   235
Sure my invention must be down at zero;
    And I grown one of many 'wooden
    spoons'
Of verse (the name with which we Cantabs
    please
To dub the last of honors in degrees). 240

* * *

DON JUAN, CANTO IV

Nothing so difficult as a beginning
    In poesy, unless perhaps the end;
For oftentimes, when Pegasus seems win-
    ning
    The race, he sprains a wing, and down we
    tend,
Like Lucifer, when hurled from heaven for
    sinning;   5
    Our sin the same, and hard as his to
    mend,
Being pride, which leads the mind to soar
    too far,
Till our own weakness shows us what we
    are.

But Time, which brings all beings to their
    level,
    And sharp Adversity, will teach at last 10
Man, and — as we would hope — perhaps the
    devil,
    That neither of their intellects are vast:
While youth's hot wishes in our red veins
    revel,
    We know not this — the blood flows on
    too fast;
But as the torrent widens towards the ocean,
We ponder deeply on each past emotion. 16

As boy, I thought myself a clever fellow,
    And wished that others held the same
    opinion;
They took it up when my days grew more
    mellow,
    And other minds acknowledged my do-
    minion:
Now my sere fancy 'falls into the yellow
    Leaf,' and Imagination droops her pinion,

And the sad truth which hovers o'er my
    desk
Turns what was once romantic to burlesque.

And if I laugh at any mortal thing,   25
    'T is that I may not weep; and if I weep,
'T is that our nature cannot always bring
    Itself to apathy, for we must steep
Our hearts first in the depth of Lethe's
    spring,
    Ere what we least wish to behold will
    sleep: 30
Thetis baptized her mortal son in Styx;
A mortal mother would on Lethe fix.

Some have accused me of a strange design
    Against the creed and morals of the land,
And trace it in this poem every line: 35
    I don't pretend that I quite understand
My own meaning when I would be *very* fine;
    But the fact is, that I have nothing planned
Unless it were to be a moment merry,
A novel word in my vocabulary.   40

To the kind reader of our sober clime,
    This way of writing will appear exotic:
Pulci was sire of the half-serious rhyme,
    Who sang when chivalry was more Quix-
    otic,
And reveled in the fancies of the time, 45
    True knights, chaste dames, huge giants,
    kings despotic;
But all these, save the last, being obsolete,
I chose a modern subject as more meet.

How I have treated it, I do not know;
    Perhaps no better than they have treated
    me   50
Who have imputed such designs as show
    Not what they saw, but what they wished
    to see:
But if it gives them pleasure, be it so;
    This is a liberal age, and thoughts are
    free:
Meantime Apollo plucks me by the ear, 55
And tells me to resume my story here.

* * *

Now pillowed cheek to cheek, in loving
    sleep,
    Haidée and Juan their siesta took,
A gentle slumber, but it was not deep,
    For ever and anon a something shook 60
Juan, and shuddering o'er his frame would
    creep;
    And Haidée's sweet lips murmured like a
    brook

A wordless music, and her face so fair
Stirred with her dream, as rose-leaves with
    the air;

Or as the stirring of a deep clear stream 65
Within an Alpine hollow, when the wind
Walks o'er it, was she shaken by the dream,
    The mystical usurper of the mind —
O'erpowering us to be whate'er may seem
    Good to the soul which we no more can
      bind; 70
Strange state of being! (for 't is still to be)
Senseless to feel, and with sealed eyes to
    see.

She dreamed of being alone on the sea-
    shore,
    Chained to a rock; she knew not how, but
      stir
She could not from the spot, and the loud
    roar 75
    Grew, and each wave rose roughly, threat-
      ening her;
And o'er her upper lip they seemed to pour,
    Until she sobbed for breath, and soon they
      were
Foaming o'er her lone head, so fierce and
    high —
Each broke to drown her, yet she could not
    die. 80

Anon — she was released; and then she
    strayed
    O'er the sharp shingles with her bleeding
      feet,
And stumbled almost every step she made:
    And something rolled before her in a
      sheet,
Which she must still pursue, howe'er afraid;
    'T was white and indistinct, nor stopped
      to meet 86
Her glance or grasp, for still she gazed and
    grasped,
And ran, but it escaped her as she clasped.

The dream changed: — in a cave she stood,
    its walls
    Were hung with marble icicles: the work
Of ages on its water-fretted halls, 91
    Where waves might wash, and seals might
      breed and lurk;
Her hair was dripping, and the very balls
    Of her black eyes seemed turned to tears,
      and mirk
The sharp rocks looked below each drop
    they caught, 95
Which froze to marble as it fell — she
    thought.

And wet, and cold, and lifeless, at her feet,
    Pale as the foam that frothed on his dead
      brow,
Which she essayed in vain to clear (how
    sweet
    Were once her cares, how idle seemed
      they now!) 100
Lay Juan, nor could aught renew the beat
    Of his quenched heart; and the sea-dirges
      low
Rang in her sad ears like a mermaid's song,
And that brief dream appeared a life too
    long.

And gazing on the dead, she thought his
    face 105
    Faded, or altered into something new —
Like to her father's features, till each trace
    More like and like to Lambro's aspect
      grew —
With all his keen worn look and Grecian
    grace;
    And starting, she awoke, and what to view?
O Powers of Heaven! what dark eye meets
    she there? 111
'T is — 't is her father's — fixed upon the
    pair!

Then shrieking, she arose, and shrieking
    fell,
    With joy and sorrow, hope and fear, to
      see
Him whom she deemed a habitant where
    dwell 115
    The ocean buried, risen from death, to be
Perchance the death of one she loved
    too well:
    Dear as her father had been to Haidée,
It was a moment of that awful kind —
I have seen such — but must not call to
    mind. 120

Up Juan sprang to Haidée's bitter shriek,
    And caught her falling, and from off
    the wall
Snatched down his sabre, in hot haste to
    wreak
    Vengeance on him who was the cause of
      all;
Then Lambro, who till now forbore to
    speak, 125
    Smiled scornfully, and said, 'Within my
    call,
A thousand scimitars await the word;
Put up, young man, put up your silly
    sword.'

And Haidée clung around him: 'Juan,
  't is —
'T is Lambro —'t is my father! Kneel with
  me —   130
He will forgive us — yes — it must be —
  yes,
Oh, dearest father, in this agony
Of pleasure and of pain — even while I kiss
  Thy garment's hem with transport, can it
  be
That doubt should mingle with my filial
  joy?   135
Deal with me as thou wilt, but spare this
  boy.'

High and inscrutable the old man stood,
  Calm in his voice, and calm within his
  eye —
Not always signs with him of calmest
  mood:
He looked upon her, but gave no reply;
Then turned to Juan, in whose cheek the
  blood   141
  Oft came and went, as there resolved to
  die
In arms, at least, he stood in act to spring
On the first foe whom Lambro's call might
  bring.

'Young man, your sword!' So Lambro once
  more said;   145
  Juan replied, 'Not while this arm is
  free!'
The old man's cheek grew pale, but not with
  dread,
  But drawing from his belt a pistol, he
Replied, 'Your blood be then on your own
  head.'
Then looked close at the flint, as if to
  see   150
'T was fresh — for he had lately used the
  lock —
And next proceeded quietly to cock.

It has a strange, quick jar upon the ear,
  That cocking of a pistol, when you know
A moment more will bring the sight to bear
  Upon your person, twelve yards off, or so;
A gentlemanly distance, not too near,
  If you have got a former friend for foe;
But after being fired at once or twice,   159
The ear becomes more Irish, and less nice.

Lambro presented, and one instant more
  Had stopped this canto, and Don Juan's
  breath,
When Haidée threw herself her boy before.

Stern as her sire: 'On me,' she cried,
  'let death
Descend — the fault is mine; this fatal
  shore   165
He found — but sought not. I have
  pledged my faith;
I love him — I will die with him: I knew
Your nature's firmness — know your daughter's too.'

A minute past, and she had been all tears,
  And tenderness, and infancy; but now 170
She stood as one who championed human
  fears —
Pale, statue-like, and stern, she wooed the
  blow;
And tall beyond her sex, and their com-
  peers,
  She drew up to her height, as if to show
A fairer mark; and with a fixed eye scanned
Her father's face — but never stopped his
  hand.   176

He gazed on her, and she on him; 't was
  strange
  How like they looked! the expression was
  the same;
Serenely savage, with a little change
  In the large dark eye's mutual-darted
  flame;   180
For she, too, was as one who could avenge,
  If cause should be — a lioness, though
  tame:
Her father's blood, before her father's face
Boiled up, and proved her truly of his race.

I said they were alike, their features and 185
  Their stature differing but in sex and
  years;
Even to the delicacy of their hand
  There was resemblance, such as true blood
  wears;
And now to see them, thus divided, stand
  In fixed ferocity, when joyous tears,   190
And sweet sensations, should have wel-
  comed both,
Show what the passions are in their full
  growth.

The father paused a moment, then withdrew
  His weapon, and replaced it; but stood
  still,
And looking on her, as to look her through,
  'Not I,' he said, 'have sought this stran-
  ger's ill;   196
Not I have made this desolation; few
  Would bear such outrage, and forbear to
  kill;

But I must do my duty — how thou hast
Done thine, the present vouches for the
    past.   200

'Let him disarm; or, by my father's head,
    His own shall roll before you like a
    ball!'
He raised his whistle, as the word he said,
    And blew, another answered to the call,
And, rushing in disorderly, though led,   205
    And armed from boot to turban, one and
    all,
Some twenty of his train came, rank on
    rank;
He gave the word —'Arrest or slay the
    Frank!'

Then, with a sudden movement, he with-
    drew
    His daughter; while compressed within
    his clasp,   210
'Twixt her and Juan interposed the crew;
    In vain she struggled in her father's
    grasp —
His arms were like a serpent's coil: then
    flew
Upon their prey, as darts an angry asp,
The file of pirates; save the foremost, who
Had fallen, with his right shoulder half cut
    through.   216

The second had his cheek laid open; but
    The third, a wary, cool old sworder, took
The blows upon his cutlass, and then put
    His own well in: so well, ere you could
    look,   220
His man was floored, and helpless at his
    foot,
    With the blood running like a little
    brook,
From two smart sabre gashes, deep and
    red —
One on the arm, the other on the head.

And then they bound him where he fell,
    and bore   225
    Juan from the apartment: with a sign,
Old Lambro bade them take him to the
    shore,
    Where lay some ships which were to sail
    at nine.
They laid him in a boat, and plied the oar
    Until they reached some galliots, placed
    in line;   230
On board of one of these, and under
    hatches,
They stowed him, with strict orders to the
    watches.

The world is full of strange vicissitudes,
    And here was one exceedingly unpleas-
    ant:
A gentleman so rich in the world's goods,
    Handsome and young, enjoying all the
    present,   236
Just at the very time when he least broods
    On such a thing, is suddenly to sea
    sent,
Wounded and chained, so that he cannot
    move,
And all because a lady fell in love.   240

Here I must leave him, for I grow pathetic,
    Moved by the Chinese nymph of tears,
    green tea!
Than whom Cassandra was not more pro-
    phetic;
    For if my pure libations exceed three,
I feel my heart become so sympathetic,   245
    That I must have recourse to black Bo-
    hea:
'T is pity wine should be so deleterious,
For tea and coffee leave us much more
    serious,

Unless when qualified with thee, Cognac!
    Sweet Naïad of the Phlegethontic rill!
Ah, why the liver wilt thou thus attack,
    And make, like other nymphs, thy lovers
    ill?
I would take refuge in weak punch, but
    rack
    (In each sense of the word), whene'er I
    fill   254
My mild and midnight beakers to the brim,
Wakes me next morning with its synonym.

I leave Don Juan for the present, safe —
    Not sound, poor fellow, but severely
    wounded;
Yet could his corporal pangs amount to
    half
    Of those with which his Haidée's bosom
    bounded!   260
She was not one to weep, and rave, and
    chafe,
    And then give way, subdued, because sur-
    rounded;
Her mother was a Moorish maid, from Fez,
Where all is Eden, or a wilderness.

There the large olive rains its amber store
    In marble fonts; there grain, and flower,
    and fruit,   266
Gush from the earth, until the land runs
    o'er:
    But there, too, many a poison tree has
    root,

And midnight listens to the lion's roar,
  And long, long deserts scorch the camel's
    foot,   270
Or heaving, whelm the helpless caravan:
And as the soil is, so the heart of man.

Afric is all the sun's, and as her earth
  Her human clay is kindled: full of power
For good or evil, burning from its birth.
  The Moorish blood partakes the planet's
    hour,
And like the soil beneath, it will bring
    forth:
  Beauty and love were Haidée's mother's
    dower;
But her large dark eye showed deep Pas-
    sion's force,   279
Though sleeping like a lion near a source.

Her daughter, tempered with a milder ray,
  Like summer's clouds all silvery smooth
    and fair,
Till slowly charged with thunder, they dis-
    play
.Terror to earth, and tempest to the air,
Had held till now her soft and milky way,
  But, overwrought with passion and de-
    spair,   286
The fire burst forth from her Numidian
    veins,
Even as the Simoom sweeps the blasted
    plains.

The last sight which she saw was Juan's
    gore,
  And he himself o'ermastered, and cut
    down;   290
His blood was running on the very floor,
  Where late he trod, her beautiful, her
    own;
Thus much she viewed an instant, and no
    more —
  Her struggles ceased with one convulsive
    groan;
On her sire's arm, which, until now, scarce
    held   295
Her, writhing, fell she, like a cedar felled.

A vein had burst, and her sweet lips' pure
    dyes
  Were dabbled with the deep blood which
    ran o'er;
And her head drooped, as when the lily lies
  O'ercharged with rain: her summoned
    handmaids bore   300
Their lady to her couch, with gushing eyes;
  Of herbs and cordials they produced their
    store.

But she defied all means they could employ,
Like one life could not hold, nor death de-
    stroy.

Days lay she in that state, unchanged,
    though chill —   305
  With nothing livid, still her lips were
    red:
She had no pulse, but death seemed absent
    still;
  No hideous sign proclaimed her surely
    dead;
Corruption came not, in each mind to kill
  All hope; to look upon her sweet face,
    bred   310
New thoughts of life, for it seemed full of
    soul —
She had so much, earth could not claim the
    whole.

The ruling passion, such as marble shows
  When exquisitely chiseled, still lay there,
But fixed as marble's unchanged aspect
    throws   315
  O'er the fair Venus, but forever fair;
O'er the Laocoon's all eternal throes,
  And ever-dying Gladiator's air,
Their energy, like life, forms all their fame,
Yet looks not life, for they are still the
    same.

She woke at length, but not as sleepers
    wake,   320
  Rather the dead, for life seemed some-
    thing new,
A strange sensation which she must partake
  Perforce, since whatsoever met her view
Struck not on memory, though a heavy ache
  Lay at her heart, whose earliest beat, still
    true,   325
Brought back the sense of pain without the
    cause,
For, for a while, the furies made a pause.

She looked on many a face with vacant
    eye,
  On many a token, without knowing what;
She saw them watch her, without asking
    why,   330
  And recked not who around her pillow
    sat:
Not speechless, though she spoke not; not a
    sigh
  Relieved her thoughts; dull silence and
    quick chat
Were tried in vain by those who served;
    she gave
No sign, save breath, of having left the
    grave.   335

Her handmaids tended, but she heeded not;
　Her father watched, she turned her eyes
　　away;
She recognized no being, and no spot,
　However dear, or cherished in their day;
They changed from room to room, but all
　forgot,　　　　　　　　　　　　　340
　Gentle, but without memory, she lay;
At length those eyes, which they would fain
　be weaning
Back to old thoughts, waxed full of fearful
　meaning.

And then a slave bethought her of a harp;
　The harper came and tuned his instru-
　　ment.　　　　　　　　　　　　　345
At the first notes, irregular and sharp,
　On him her flashing eyes a moment bent,
Then to the wall she turned, as if to warp
　Her thoughts from sorrow through her
　　heart re-sent;　　　　　　　　　349
And he began a long low island song
Of ancient days, ere tyranny grew strong.

Anon her thin wan fingers beat the wall,
　In time to his old tune: he changed the
　　theme,
And sung of love; the fierce name struck
　through all　　　　　　　　　　354
　Her recollection; on her flashed the dream
Of what she was, and is, if ye could call
　To be so being: in a gushing stream
The tears rushed forth from her o'erclouded
　brain,
Like mountain mists, at length dissolved in
　rain.

Short solace, vain relief! — thought came
　too quick,　　　　　　　　　　　360
　And whirled her brain to madness; she
　　arose,
As one who ne'er had dwelt among the
　sick,
　And flew at all she met, as on her foes;
But no one ever heard her speak or shriek,
　Although her paroxysm drew towards its
　　close: —　　　　　　　　　　　365
Hers was a frenzy which disdained to rave,
Even when they smote her, in the hope to
　save.

Yet she betrayed at times a gleam of sense;
　Nothing could make her meet her father's
　　face,
Though on all other things with looks in-
　tense　　　　　　　　　　　　　370

She gazed, but none she ever could re-
　trace.
Food she refused, and raiment; no pretence
　Availed for either; neither change of
　　place,
Nor time, nor skill, nor remedy, could give
　her
Senses to sleep — the power seemed gone
　forever.　　　　　　　　　　　375

Twelve days and nights she withered thus;
　at last,
　Without a groan, or sigh, or glance, to
　　show
A parting pang, the spirit from her past:
　And they who watched her nearest, could
　　not know　　　　　　　　　　379
The very instant, till the change that cast
　Her sweet face into shadow, dull and
　　slow,
Glazed o'er her eyes — the beautiful, the
　black —
Oh! to possess such luster — and then lack!

Thus lived — thus died she; never more on
　her
　Shall sorrow light, or shame. She was
　　not made　　　　　　　　　　385
Through years or moons the inner weight
　to bear,
　Which colder hearts endure till they are
　　laid
By age in earth; her days and pleasures
　were
　Brief but delightful — such as had not
　　stayed　　　　　　　　　　　389
Long with her destiny; but she sleeps well
By the sea-shore, whereon she loved to
　dwell.

The isle is now all desolate and bare,
　Its dwellings down, its tenants passed
　　away;
None but her own and father's grave is
　there,　　　　　　　　　　　　394
　And nothing outward tells of human clay:
Ye could not know where lies a thing so fair,
　No stone is there to show, no tongue to
　　say
What was: no dirge, except the hollow
　sea's,
Mourns o'er the beauty of the Cyclades.　399

　　　　　* * *　　　　　(1821)

PERCY BYSSHE SHELLEY (1792-1822)

Shelley was the son of a country squire of large means whose utter inability to comprehend the nature of his son's convictions was an important factor in the latter's history. At Eton 'mad Shelley' became unpopular with the older boys for heading an insurrection against the school system of 'fagging,' and he had not been long at University College, Oxford, when he was expelled for circulating a revolutionary tract entitled *The Necessity of Atheism*. He was only nineteen when out of fancied chivalry he married Harriet Westbrooke, a school girl of sixteen, much below him in social station. Angered by the first indiscretion, his father was permanently estranged by the second. These two children set off for Dublin, Shelley writing to a friend, 'We go to forward as much as we can the Catholic Emancipation.' Before setting out for the scene of destiny he had printed an *Address to the Irish People*, which he now published by dropping it from windows upon such passers-by as 'looked likely.' Shelley's ingenuous faith that men needed only to be shown the truth in order to follow it was doomed to cruel disillusion. For two or three years he wandered about the British Isles pushing his propaganda of freedom, and prosecuting irregular studies in philosophy and literature. His friend Hogg declared that a splendid library might have been formed out of the books which Shelley left scattered about the three kingdoms. In 1814, he separated from Harriet and, soon after, he fell passionately in love with Mary Godwin, daughter of the author of *Political Justice*. The feeling was returned and consistently with the tenets of all concerned, except Harriet and Shelley's father, Mary became his mate. Two years later, the wife whom he had abandoned ended her life by drowning. How far Shelley should be held culpable for this unhappy event is a moot point with his biographers. In 1818, he permanently left England for Italy, partially on account of his health and partially out of a fear lest the Lord Chancellor, who had already removed from his custody the children of his first marriage, might pass a similar judgment in regard to those of the second.

In Italy, for more reasons than one can pause to enumerate, Shelley's genius flowered; but only four years of it remained. Setting out in a small sailing boat he was overtaken by a squall in the bay of Lerici. A few days later his body was found imbedded in the sand of the shore. In one pocket of his jacket was a volume of Sophocles and in the other a volume of Keats, 'doubled back as if the reader, in the act of reading, had hastily thrust it away.' A narration of the bare acts of Shelley's life leaves an impression of waywardness which is not altogether misleading. Those who were competent to judge agreed that his impulses were noble and high, that a purer spirit never breathed; but he suffered and made others suffer because he would not bind himself to the code by which society lives. To the common run of his contemporaries he was a fanatical monster; to many since it has seemed that his sufferings and errors were the fault of an irrationally organized world and that he himself belonged to a 'crowning race' of which he was 'a noble type, appearing ere the time was ripe.'

All of Shelley's poetry of importance was written after he met Mary Godwin. *Queen Mab* (1813) was a frantic poetical drama interesting only for its revolutionary doctrines. His genius first declared itself in *Alastor* (1815), and passages of great promise are scattered through his enormous revolutionary document, *The Revolt of Islam* (1817). But in Italy he matured with astonishing rapidity. To the year 1819 belonged *Prometheus Unbound*, his totally different *Cenci* which some critics regard as the most distinguished poetical tragedy since the Elizabethans, and numerous fine lyrics, including the *Ode to the West Wind*. The year 1820 was notable chiefly for its lyrics, *To a Skylark* among them. In 1821, besides *Epipsychidion*, *Adonais*, and *Hellas*, came some of the most poignant of the short lyrics. *The Triumph of Life* was uncompleted when Shelley set out to sea on Monday, July 8, 1822.

No one can estimate Shelley for us but ourselves. This is true of all poetry, but preëminently so of Shelley's because it is so preëminently poetical. When it is best it has little intellectual content. We do not, narrowly speaking, learn anything from Shelley; we surrender to an element.

HYMN TO INTELLECTUAL BEAUTY

The awful shadow of some unseen Power
  Floats though unseen amongst us,— visiting
  This various world with as inconstant wing
As summer winds that creep from flower to flower ; —
  Like moonbeams that behind some piny mountain shower, 5
  It visits with inconstant glance
  Each human heart and countenance ;
Like hues and harmonies of evening,—
  Like clouds in starlight widely spread,—
  Like memory of music fled,— 10
  Like aught that for its grace may be
Dear, and yet dearer for its mystery.

Spirit of Beauty, that dost consecrate
  With thine own hues all thou dost shine upon
  Of human thought or form,— where art thou gone ? 15
Why dost thou pass away and leave our state,
This dim vast vale of tears, vacant and desolate ?
  Ask why the sunlight not forever
  Weaves rainbows o'er yon mountain river,
Why aught should fail and fade that once is shown, 20
  Why fear and dream and death and birth
  Cast on the daylight of this earth
  Such gloom,— why man has such a scope
For love and hate, despondency and hope?

No voice from some sublimer world hath ever 25
  To sage or poet these responses given —
  Therefore the names of Dæmon, Ghost, and Heaven,
Remain the records of their vain endeavor,
Frail spells — whose uttered charm might not avail to sever,
  From all we hear and all we see, 30
  Doubt, chance, and mutability.
Thy light alone — like mist o'er mountains driven,
  Or music by the night wind sent,
  Through strings of some still instrument,
  Or moonlight on a midnight stream, 35
Gives grace and truth to life's unquiet dream.

Love, Hope, and Self-esteem, like clouds depart
  And come, for some uncertain moments lent.
Man were immortal, and omnipotent,
Didst thou, unknown and awful as thou art, 40
Keep with thy glorious train firm state within his heart.
  Thou messenger of sympathies,
  That wax and wane in lovers' eyes —
Thou — that to human thought art nourishment,
  Like darkness to a dying flame ! 45
  Depart not as thy shadow came,
  Depart not — lest the grave should be,
Like life and fear, a dark reality.

While yet a boy I sought for ghosts, and sped
  Through many a listening chamber, cave and ruin, 50
  And starlight wood, with fearful steps pursuing
Hopes of high talk with the departed dead.
I called on poisonous names with which our youth is fed ;
  I was not heard — I saw them not —
  When musing deeply on the lot 55
Of life, at the sweet time when winds are wooing
  All vital things that wake to bring
  News of birds and blossoming,—
  Sudden, thy shadow fell on me ;
I shrieked, and clasped my hands in ecstasy !

I vowed that I would dedicate my powers
  To thee and thine — have I not kept the vow ? 62
  With beating heart and streaming eyes, even now
I call the phantoms of a thousand hours
Each from his voiceless grave : they have in visioned bowers 65
  Of studious zeal or love's delight
  Outwatched with me the envious night —
They know that never joy illumed my brow
  Unlinked with hope that thou wouldst free
  This world from its dark slavery, 70
  That thou — O awful Loveliness,
Wouldst give whate'er these words cannot express.

The day becomes more solemn and serene
  When noon is past — there is a harmony
  In autumn, and a luster in its sky, 75

Which through the summer is not heard or
    seen,
As if it could not be, as if it had not been!
    Thus let thy power, which like the
    truth
    Of nature on my passive youth
Descended, to my onward life supply   80
    Its calm — to one who worships thee,
    And every form containing thee,
    Whom, Spirit fair, thy spells did bind
To fear himself, and love all human kind.

                      (1819)

OZYMANDIAS

I met a traveler from an antique land
Who said: Two vast and trunkless legs
    of stone
Stand in the desert. Near them, on the
    sand,
Half sunk, a shattered visage lies, whose
    frown,
And wrinkled lip, and sneer of cold com-
    mand,   5
Tell that its sculptor well those passions
    read
Which yet survive, (stamped on these life-
    less things,)
The hand that mocked them and the heart
    that fed;
And on the pedestal these words appear:
'My name is Ozymandias, king of kings; 10
Look on my works, ye Mighty, and despair!'
Nothing beside remains. Round the decay
Of that colossal wreck, boundless and bare
The lone and level sands stretch far away.

                      (1819)

STANZAS

WRITTEN IN DEJECTION, NEAR NAPLES

The sun is warm, the sky is clear,
    The waves are dancing fast and bright,
Blue isles and snowy mountains wear
    The purple noon's transparent might,
    The breath of the moist earth is light, 5
Around its unexpanded buds:
    Like many a voice of one delight,
The winds, the birds, the ocean floods,
The City's voice itself is soft like Solitude's.

I see the Deep's untrampled floor   10
    With green and purple seaweeds strown:
I see the waves upon the shore,
Like light dissolved in star-showers,
    thrown:
    I sit upon the sands alone,

The lightning of the noontide ocean   15
    Is flashing round me, and a tone
Arises from its measured motion,
How sweet! did any heart now share in
    my emotion.

Alas! I have nor hope nor health,
    Nor peace within nor calm around,   20
Nor that content surpassing wealth
    The sage in meditation found,
    And walked with inward glory crowned —
Nor fame, nor power, nor love, nor leisure.
    Others I see whom these surround —   25
Smiling they live, and call life pleasure; —
To me that cup has been dealt in another
    measure.

Yet now despair itself is mild,
    Even as the winds and waters are;
I could lie down like a tired child,   30
    And weep away the life of care
Which I have borne and yet must bear,
    Till death like sleep might steal on me,
    And I might feel in the warm air
My cheek grow cold, and hear the sea   35
Breathe o'er my dying brain its last
    monotony.

Some might lament that I were cold,
    As I when this sweet day is gone,
Which my lost heart, too soon grown old,
    Insults with this untimely moan;   40
    They might lament — for I am one
Whom men love not, — and yet regret,
    Unlike this day, which, when the sun
Shall on its stainless glory set,
Will linger, though enjoyed, like joy in
    memory yet.   45

                    (1842)

PROMETHEUS UNBOUND,

ACT IV

SCENE, A PART OF THE FOREST NEAR THE
CAVE OF PROMETHEUS. PANTHEA *and*
IONE *are sleeping. They awaken gradually
during the first song.*

    Voice of Unseen Spirits
    The pale stars are gone!
For the sun, their swift shepherd,
    To their folds them compelling,
    In the depths of the dawn,
Hastes, in meteor-eclipsing array, and they
    flee
    Beyond his blue dwelling,
    As fawns flee the leopard.
      But where are ye?

A train of dark Forms and Shadows passes
by confusedly, singing.

Here, oh, here:
We bear the bier   10
Of the Father of many a canceled year!
Specters we
Of the dead Hours be,
We bear Time to his tomb in eternity.

Strew, oh, strew   15
Hair, not yew!
Wet the dusty pall with tears, not dew!
Be the faded flowers
Of Death's bare bowers
Spread on the corpse of the King of Hours!

Haste, oh, haste!   21
As shades are chased,
Trembling, by day, from heaven's blue
waste.
We melt away,
Like dissolving spray,   25
From the children of a diviner day,
With the lullaby
Of winds that die
On the bosom of their own harmony!

Ione

What dark forms were they?   30

Panthea

The past Hours weak and gray,
With the spoil which their toil
Raked together
From the conquest but One could foil.

Ione

Have they past?   35

Panthea

They have past;
They outspeeded the blast,
While 't is said, they are fled:

Ione

Whither, oh, whither?

Panthea

To the dark, to the past, to the dead. 40

Voice of Unseen Spirits

Bright clouds float in heaven,
Dew-stars gleam on earth,
Waves assemble on ocean,
They are gathered and driven
By the storm of delight, by the panic of
glee!   45

They shake with emotion,
They dance in their mirth.
But where are ye?

The pine boughs are singing,
Old songs with new gladness,   50
The billows and fountains
Fresh music are flinging,
Like the notes of a spirit from land and
from sea;
The storms mock the mountains
With the thunder of gladness.   55
But where are ye?

Ione. What charioteers are these?
Panthea.   Where are their
chariots?

Semichorus of Hours

The voice of the Spirits of Air and of
Earth
Have drawn back the figured curtain of
sleep   60
Which covered our being and darkened our
birth
In the deep.

A Voice

In the deep?

Semichorus II

Oh! below the deep.

Semichorus I

An hundred ages we had been kept   65
Cradled in visions of hate and care,
And each one who waked as his brother
slept,
Found the truth —

Semichorus II

Worse than his visions were!

Semichorus I

We have heard the lute of Hope in sleep;
We have known the voice of Love in
dreams,   71
We have felt the wand of Power, and
leap —

Semichorus I

As the billows leap in the morning beams!

Chorus

Weave the dance on the floor of the
breeze.

Pierce with song heaven's silent light,
Enchant the day that too swiftly flees, 76
  To check its flight ere the cave of
    night.

Once the hungry Hours were hounds
  Which chased the day like a bleeding
    deer,
And it limped and stumbled with many
    wounds   80
  Through the nightly dells of the desert
    year.

But now, oh, weave the mystic measure
  Of music and dance, and shapes of light,
Let the Hours, and the spirits of might
    and pleasure,
  Like the clouds and sunbeams, unite.   85

A Voice
                  Unite!
Panthea. See, where the spirits of the
    human mind
Wrapt in sweet sounds, as in bright veils,
    approach.

Chorus of Spirits
  We join the throng
  Of the dance and the song,   90
By the whirlwind of gladness borne along:
  As the flying-fish leap
  From the Indian deep,
And mix with the sea-birds, half asleep.

Chorus of Hours
Whence come ye, so wild and so fleet,   95
For sandals of lightning are on your feet,
And your wings are soft and swift as
    thought,
And your eyes are as love which is veilèd
    not?

Chorus of Spirits
  We come from the mind
  Of human kind   100
Which was late so dusk, and obscene, and
    blind.
  Now 't is an ocean
  Of clear emotion,
A heaven of serene and mighty motion;

  From that deep abyss   105
  Of wonder and bliss,
Whose caverns are crystal palaces;
  From these skiey towers
  Where Thought's crowned powers
Sit watching your dance, ye happy Hours!

From the dim recesses   111
  Of woven caresses,
Where lovers catch ye by your loose
    tresses;
  From the azure isles;
  Where sweet Wisdom smiles,   115
Delaying your ships with her siren wiles.

  From the temples high
  Of Man's ear and eye,
Roofed over Sculpture and Poesy;
  From the murmurings
  Of the unsealed springs   121
Where Science bedews his Dædal wings.

  Years after years,
  Through blood and tears,
And a thick hell of hatreds, and hopes,
    and fears;   125
  We waded and flew
  And the islets were few
Where the bud-blighted flowers of happiness
    grew.

  Our feet now, every palm,
  Are sandaled with calm,   130
And the dew of our wings is a rain of
    balm;
  And, beyond our eyes,
  The human love lies
Which makes all it gazes on Paradise.

Chorus of Spirits and Hours
Then weave the web of the mystic
    measure;   135
From the depths of the sky and the ends of
    the earth,
  Come, swift Spirits of might and of
    pleasure,
Fill the dance and the music of mirth,
  As the waves of a thousand streams rush
    by   139
To an ocean of splendor and harmony!

Chorus of Spirits
  Our spoil is won,
  Our task is done,
We are free to dive, or soar, or run;
  Beyond and around,
  Or within the bound   145
Which clips the world with darkness round.

  We 'll pass the eyes
  Of the starry skies
Into the hoar deep to colonize:
  Death, Chaos, and Night,   150
  From the sound of our flight,
Shall flee, like mist from a tempest's might

And Earth, Air, and Light,
And the Spirit of Might,
Which drives round the stars in their fiery
   flight;   155
And Love, Thought, and Breath,
The powers that quell Death,
Wherever we soar shall assemble beneath.

And our singing shall build
In the void's loose field   160
A world for the Spirit of Wisdom to
   wield;
We will take our plan
From the new world of man,
And our work shall be called the Pro-
   methean.

Chorus of Hours

Break the dance, and scatter the song;   165
Let some depart, and some remain.

Semichorus I

We, beyond heaven, are driven along!

Semichorus II

Us the enchantments of earth retain;

Semichorus I

Ceaseless, and rapid, and fierce and free,
With the Spirits which build a new earth
   and sea,   170
And a heaven where yet heaven could
   never be.

Semichorus II

Solemn, and slow, and serene and bright,
Leading the Day and outspeeding the Night,
With the powers of a world of perfect
   light.

Semichorus I

We whirl, singing loud, round the gathering sphere,   175
Till the trees, and the beasts, and the clouds
   appear
From its chaos made calm by love, not
   fear.

Semichorus II

We encircle the ocean and mountains of
   earth,   178
And the happy forms of its death and birth
Change to the music of our sweet mirth.

Chorus of Hours and Spirits

Break the dance, and scatter the song,

Let some depart, and some remain,
Wherever we fly we lead along,
In leashes, like starbeams, soft yet strong.
The clouds that are heavy with love's
   sweet rain.   185

Panthea. Ha! they are gone!
Ione.   Yet feel you no delight
From the past sweetness?
Panthea.   As the bare green hill
When some soft cloud vanishes into rain,
Laughs with a thousand drops of sunny
   water   191
To the unpavilioned sky!
Ione.   Even whilst we speak
New notes arise. What is that awful
   sound?
Panthea. 'T is the deep music of the roll-
   ing world
Kindling within the strings of the waved
   air,   196
Æolian modulations.
Ione.   Listen too,
How every pause is filled with under notes,
Clear, silver, icy, keen, awakening tones,
Which pierce the sense, and live within
   the soul,   201
As the sharp stars pierce winter's crystal
   air
And gaze upon themselves within the sea.
Panthea. But see where through two
   openings in the forest
Which hanging branches overcanopy,   205
And where two runnels of a rivulet,
Between the close moss violet-inwoven,
Have made their path of melody, like
   sisters
Who part with sighs that they may meet
   in smiles,
Turning their dear disunion to an isle 210
Of lovely grief, a wood of sweet sad
   thoughts;
Two visions of strange radiance float upon
The ocean-like enchantment of strong sound,
Which flows intenser, keener, deeper yet
Under the ground and through the wind-
   less air,   215
Ione. I see a chariot like that thinnest
   boat,
In which the mother of the months is borne
By ebbing night into her western cave,
When she upsprings from interlunar
   dreams,   219
O'er which is curved an orblike canopy
Of gentle darkness, and the hills and woods
Distinctly seen through that dusk airy veil,
Regard like shapes in an enchanter's glass;
Its wheels are solid clouds, azure and gold,

Such as the genii of the thunderstorm   225
Pile on the floor of the illumined sea
When the sun rushes under it; they roll
And move and grow as with an inward
    wind;
Within it sits a wingèd infant, white
Its countenance, like the whiteness of bright
    snow,   230
Its plumes are as feathers of sunny frost,
Its limbs gleam white, through the wind
    flowing folds
Of its white robe, woof of ethereal pearl.
Its hair is white, the brightness of white
    light
Scattered in strings; yet its two eyes are
    heavens   235
Of liquid darkness, which the Deity
Within seems pouring, as a storm is poured
From jaggèd clouds, out of their arrowy
    lashes,
Tempering the cold and radiant air around,
With fire that is not brightness: in its
    hand   240
It sways a quivering moonbeam, from whose
    point
A guiding power directs the chariot's prow
Over its wheelèd clouds, which as they roll
Over the grass, and flowers, and waves,
    wake sounds,
Sweet as a singing rain of silver dew.
   Panthea. And from the other opening in
    the wood   246
Rushes, with loud and whirlwind harmony,
A sphere, which is as many thousand
    spheres,
Solid as crystal, yet through all its mass
Flow, as through empty space, music and
    light: 250
Ten thousand orbs involving and involved,
Purple and azure, white, and green, and
    golden,
Sphere within sphere; and every space be-
    tween
Peopled with unimaginable shapes,
Such as ghosts dream dwell in the lamp-
    less deep,   255
Yet each inter-transpicuous, and they whirl
Over each other with a thousand motions,
Upon a thousand sightless axles spinning,
And with the force of self-destroying swift-
    ness,
Intensely, slowly, solemnly roll on,   260
Kindling with mingled sounds, and many
    tones,
Intelligible words and music wild.
With mighty whirl the multitudinous orb
Grinds the bright brook into an azure mist

Of elemental subtlety; like light: 265
And the wild odor of the forest flowers,
The music of the living grass and air,
The emerald light of leaf-entangled beams
Round its intense yet self-conflicting speed,
Seem kneaded into one aërial mass   270
Which drowns the sense. Within the orb
    itself,
Pillowed upon its alabaster arms,
Like to a child o'erwearied with sweet toil,
On its own folded wings, and wavy hair,
The Spirit of the Earth is laid asleep,   275
And you can see its little lips are moving,
Amid the changing light of their own
    smiles,
Like one who talks of what he loves in
    dream.
   Ione. 'T is only mocking the orb's har-
    mony.
   Panthea. And from a star upon its fore-
    head, shoot,   280
Like swords of azure fire, or golden spears
With tyrant-quelling myrtle overtwined,
Embleming heaven and earth united now,
Vast beams like spokes of some invisible
    wheel
Which whirl as the orb whirls, swifter than
    thought,   285
Filling the abyss with sun-like lightenings,
And perpendicular now, and now trans-
    verse,
Pierce the dark soil, and as they pierce and
    pass,
Make bare the secrets of the earth's deep
    heart;
Infinite mine of adamant and gold,   290
Valueless stones, and unimagined gems,
And caverns on crystalline columns poised
With vegetable silver overspread;
Wells of unfathomed fire, and water springs
Whence the great sea, even as a child is
    fed,   295
Whose vapors clothe earth's monarch moun-
    tain-tops
With kingly ermine snow. The beams
    flash on
And make appear the melancholy ruins
Of canceled cycles; anchors, beaks of
    ships;
Planks turned to marble; quivers, helms,
    and spears,   300
And gorgon-headed targes, and the wheels
Of scythèd chariots and the emblazonry
Of trophies, standards, and armorial beasts,
Round which death laughed, sepulchred
    emblems
Of dead destruction, ruin within ruin!   305

The wrecks beside of many a city vast,
Whose population which the earth grew
over
Was mortal, but not human; see, they lie,
Their monstrous works, and uncouth
skeletons,
Their statues, homes and fanes: prodigious
shapes   310
Huddled in gray annihilation, split,
Jammed in the hard, black deep; and over
these,
The anatomies of unknown wingèd things,
And fishes which were isles of living scale,
And serpents, bony chains, twisted around
The iron crags, or within heaps of dust 316
To which the tortuous strength of their last
pangs
Had crushed the iron crags; and over these
The jagged alligator, and the might
Of earth-convulsing behemoth, which once
Were monarch beasts, and on the slimy
shores,   321
And weed-overgrown continents of earth,
Increased and multiplied like summer
worms
On an abandoned corpse, till the blue globe
Wrapt deluge round it like a cloak, and
they   325
Yelled, gasped, and were abolished; or some
God
Whose throne was in a comet, passed, and
cried,
Be not! And like my words they were no
more.

The Earth

The joy, the triumph, the delight, the madness!
The boundless, overflowing, bursting gladness,   330
The vaporous exultation not to be confined!
Ha! ha! the animation of delight
Which wraps me, like an atmosphere
of light,
And bears me as a cloud is borne by its own
wind.

The Moon

Brother mine, calm wanderer,   335
Happy globe of land and air,
Some Spirit is darted like a beam from
thee.
Which penetrates my frozen frame,
And passes with the warmth of flame,
With love, and odor, and deep melody 340
Through me, through me!

The Earth

Ha! ha! the caverns of my hollow
mountains,
My cloven fire-crags, sound-exulting fountains,
Laugh with a vast and inextinguishable
laughter.
The oceans, and the deserts, and the
abysses,   345
And the deep air's unmeasured wildernesses,
Answer from all their clouds and billows,
echoing after.

They cry aloud as I do. Sceptered curse,
Who all our green and azure universe
Threatenedst to muffle round with black de-
struction, sending   350
A solid cloud to rain hot thunderstones,
And splinter and knead down my chil-
dren's bones,
All I bring forth, to one void mass, bat-
tering and blending,

Until each crag-like tower, and storied
column,   354
Palace, and obelisk, and temple solemn,
My imperial mountains crowned with cloud,
and snow, and fire;
My sea-like forests, every blade and blossom
Which finds a grave or cradle in my
bosom,
Were stamped by thy strong hate into a lifeless mire.

How art thou sunk, withdrawn, covered,
drunk up   360
By thirsty nothing, as the brackish cup
Drained by a desert-troop, a little drop for
all:
And from beneath, around, within, above,
Filling thy void annihilation, love
Burst in like light on caves cloven by the
thunder-ball   365

The Moon

The snow upon my lifeless mountains
Is loosened into living fountains,
My solid oceans flow, and sing, and shine:
A spirit from my heart bursts forth,
It clothes with unexpected birth   370
My cold bare bosom: Oh! it must be thine
On mine, on mine!

Gazing on thee I feel, I know
Green stalks burst forth, and bright
flowers grow,

And living shapes upon my bosom move:
Music is in the sea and air,   376
Wingèd clouds soar here and there,
Dark with the rain new buds are dreaming
of:
'T is love, all love!

The Earth

It interpenetrates my granite mass, 380
Through tangled roots and trodden clay
doth pass,
Into the utmost leaves and delicatest flowers;
Upon the winds, among the clouds 't is
spread,
It wakes a life in the forgotten dead,
They breathe a spirit up from their obscurest
bowers,   385

And like a storm bursting its cloudy
prison
With thunder, and with whirlwind, has
arisen
Out of the lampless caves of unimagined
being:
With earthquake shock and swiftness
making shiver
Thought's stagnant chaos, unremoved for
ever,   390
Till hate, and fear, and pain, light-van-
quished shadows, fleeing,

Leave Man, who was a many-sided mirror,
Which could distort to many a shape of
error,
This true fair world of things, a sea reflecting love;
Which over all his kind as the sun's
heaven   395
Gliding o'er ocean, smooth, serene and
even
Darting from starry depths radiance and life,
doth move,

Leave Man, even as a leprous child is left,
Who follows a sick beast to some warm
cleft
Of rocks, through which the might of heal-
ing springs is poured;   400
Then when it wanders home with rosy
smile,
Unconscious, and its mother fears awhile
It is a spirit, then, weeps on her child re-
stored —

Man, oh, not men! a chain of linkèd
thought,
Of love and might to be divided not. 405

Compelling the elements with adamantine
stress;
As the sun rules, even with a tyrant's
gaze,
The unquiet republic of the maze
Of planets, struggling fierce towards heaven's
free wilderness —

Man, one harmonious soul of many a
soul,   410
Whose nature is its own divine control,
Where all things flow to all, as rivers to the
sea;
Familiar acts are beautiful through love;
Labor, and pain, and grief, in life's green
grove
Sport like tame beasts, none knew how gentle
they could be!   415

His will, with all mean passions, bad de-
lights,
And selfish cares, its trembling satel-
lites,
A spirit ill to guide, but mighty to obey,
Is as a tempest-wingèd ship whose helm
Love rules, through waves which dare not
overwhelm,   420
Forcing life's wildest shores to own its
sovereign sway.

All things confess his strength. Through
the cold mass
Of marble and of color his dreams pass;
Bright threads whence mothers weave the
robes their children wear;   425
Language is a perpetual orphic song,
Which rules with Dædal harmony a throng
Of thoughts and forms, which else sense-
less and shapeless were.

The lightning is his slave; heaven's utmost deep
Gives up her stars, and like a flock of
sheep   430
They pass before his eyes, are numbered,
and roll on!
The tempest is his steed, he strides the
air;
And the abyss shouts from her depth laid
bare,
Heaven, hast thou secrets? Man unveils
me; I have none.

The Moon

The shadow of white death has past 435
From my path in heaven at last,
A clinging shroud of solid frost and sleep;
And through my newly-woven bowers,

Wander happy paramours,
Less mighty, but as mild as those who keep
   Thy vales more deep.   441

The Earth

As the dissolving warmth of dawn may
   fold
A half unfrozen dew-globe, green and
   gold,
And crystalline, till it becomes a wingèd
   mist,
And wanders up the vault of the blue day,
Outlives the noon, and on the sun's last
   ray   446
Hangs o'er the sea, a fleece of fire and
   amethyst.

The Moon

Thou art folded, thou art lying
In the light which is undying,
Of thine own joy, and heaven's smile divine;
All suns and constellations shower   451
On thee a light, a life, a power
Which doth array thy sphere; thou pourest
   thine
   On mine, on mine!

The Earth

I spin beneath my pyramid of night,
Which points into the heavens dreaming
   delight,
Murmuring victorious joy in my enchanted
   sleep;   457
As a youth lulled in love-dreams faintly
   sighing,
Under the shadows of his beauty lying,
Which round his rest a watch of light and
   warmth doth keep.   460

The Moon

As in the soft and sweet eclipse,
When soul meets soul on lovers' lips,
High hearts are calm, and brightest eyes
   are dull;
So when thy shadow falls on me,
Then am I mute and still, by thee   465
Covered: of thy love, Orb most beautiful,
   Full, oh, too full!

Thou art speeding round the sun,
Brightest world of many a one;
Green and azure sphere which shinest   470
With a light which is divinest
Among all the lamps of Heaven
To whom light and life is given;
I, thy crystal paramour,
Borne beside thee by a power   475

Like the polar Paradise,
Magnet-like of lovers' eyes;
I, a most enamored maiden
Whose weak brain is overladen
With the pleasure of her love,   480
Maniac-like around thee move
Gazing, an insatiate bride,
On thy form from every side
Like a Mænad, round the cup
Which Agave lifted up   485
In the weird Cadmeian forest.
Brother, wheresoe'er thou soarest
I must hurry, whirl and follow
Through the heavens wide and hollow,
Sheltered by the warm embrace   490
Of thy soul from hungry space,
Drinking from thy sense and sight
Beauty, majesty, and might,
As a lover or chameleon
Grows like what it looks upon,   495
As a violet's gentle eye
Gazes on the azure sky
Until its hue grows like what it beholds,
As a gray and watery mist
Glows like solid amethyst   500
Athwart the western mountain it enfolds,
When the sunset sleeps
   Upon its snow.

The Earth

And the weak day weeps
   That it should be so.   505
Oh, gentle Moon, the voice of thy delight
Falls on me like thy clear and tender light
Soothing the seaman, borne the summer
   night,
Through isles for ever calm;
Oh, gentle Moon, thy crystal accents
   pierce   510
The caverns of my pride's deep universe,
Charming the tiger joy, whose tramplings
   fierce
Made wounds which need thy balm.
Panthea. I rise as from a bath of spark-
   ling water,
A bath of azure light, among dark rocks, 515
Out of the stream of sound.
Ione.   Ah me! sweet sister,
The stream of sound has ebbed away from
   us,
And you pretend to rise out of its wave,
Because your words fall like the clear, soft
   dew   520
Shaken from a bathing wood-nymph's limbs
   and hair.
Panthea. Peace! peace! A mighty Pow-
   er, which is as darkness,
Is rising out of Earth, and from the sky

Is showered like night, and from within the
    air
Bursts, like eclipse which had been gath-
    ered up   525
Into the pores of sunlight: the bright vis-
    ions,
Wherein the singing spirits rode and shone,
Gleam like pale meteors through a watery
    night.
  Ione. There is a sense of words upon
    mine ear.
  Panthea. An universal sound like words:
    Oh, list!   530

Demogorgon

Thou, Earth, calm empire of a happy soul,
Sphere of divinest shapes and harmonies,
Beautiful orb! gathering as thou dost roll
The love which paves thy path along the
    skies: 534

The Earth

I hear: I am as a drop of dew that dies.

Demogorgon

Thou, Moon, which gazest on the nightly
    Earth
With wonder, as it gazes upon thee;
Whilst each to men, and beasts, and the swift
    birth
Of birds, is beauty, love, calm, harmony:

The Moon

I hear: I am a leaf shaken by thee!   540

Demogorgon

Ye kings of suns and stars, Demons and
    Gods,
Ethereal Dominations, who possess
Elysian, windless, fortunate abodes
Beyond Heaven's constellated wilderness:

A Voice from above

Our great Republic hears, we are blest,
  and bless.

Demogorgon

Ye happy dead, whom beams of brightest
    verse
Are clouds to hide, not colors to portray,
Whether your nature is that universe
Which once ye saw and suffered —

A Voice from beneath

            Or as they
Whom we have left, we change and pass
  away.   551

Demogorgon

Ye elemental Genii, who have homes
  From man's high mind even to the cen-
    tral stone
Of sullen lead; from Heaven's star-fretted
    domes
To the dull weed some sea-worm battens
    on: 555

A confused Voice

We hear: thy words waken Oblivion.

Demogorgon

Spirits, whose homes are flesh: ye beasts
    and birds,
  Ye worms, and fish; ye living leaves and
    buds;
Lightning and wind; and ye untamable
    herds,
  Meteors and mists, which throng air's
    solitudes: —   560

A Voice

Thy voice to us is wind among still
  woods.

Demogorgon

Man, who wert once a despot and a slave;
A dupe and a deceiver; a decay;
A traveler from the cradle to the grave
Through the dim night of this immortal
    day: 565

All

Speak; thy strong words may never pass
  away.

Demogorgon

This is the day, which down the void
    abysm
At the Earth-born's spell yawns for
    Heaven's despotism,
  And Conquest is dragged captive through
    the deep:
Love, from its awful throne of patient
    power   570
In the wise heart, from the last giddy
    hour
  Of dead endurance, from the slippery,
    steep,
And narrow verge of crag-like agony,
    springs
And folds over the world its healing wings

Gentleness, Virtue, Wisdom, and Endurance.   575

These are the seals of that most firm as-
surance
  Which bars the pit over Destruction's
strength;
And if, with infirm hand, Eternity,
Mother of many acts and hours, should
free
  The serpent that would clasp her with his
length;   580
These are the spells by which to reassume
An empire o'er the disentangled doom.

To suffer woes which Hope thinks infinite;
To forgive wrongs darker than death or
  night;
  To defy Power, which seems omnipotent;
To love, and bear; to hope till Hope cre-
ates   586
From its own wreck the thing it contem-
plates;
  Neither to change, nor falter, nor re-
pent;
This, like thy glory, Titan, is to be
Good, great and joyous, beautiful and free;
This is alone Life, Joy, Empire, and Vic-
tory.   591
                (1820)

ODE TO THE WEST WIND

I

O, wild West Wind, thou breath of Autumn's being,
Thou, from whose unseen presence the
leaves dead
Are driven, like ghosts from an enchanter
fleeing,

Yellow, and black, and pale, and hectic red,
Pestilence-stricken multitudes: O, thou,   5
Who chariotest to their dark wintry bed

The wingèd seeds, where they lie cold and
low,
Each like a corpse within its grave, until
Thine azure sister of the spring shall blow

Her clarion o'er the dreaming earth, and
fill   10
(Driving sweet buds like flocks to feed in
air)
With living hues and odors plain and hill:

Wild Spirit, which art moving everywhere;
Destroyer and preserver; hear, O, hear!

II

Thou on whose stream, 'mid the steep sky's
commotion,   15
Loose clouds like earth's decaying leaves are
shed,
Shook from the tangled boughs of Heaven
and Ocean,

Angels of rain and lightning: there are
spread
On the blue surface of thine airy surge,
Like the bright hair uplifted from the head

Of some fierce Mænad, even from the dim
verge   21
Of the horizon to the zenith's height
The locks of the approaching storm. Thou
dirge

Of the dying year, to which this closing
night
Will be the dome of a vast sepulcher,   25
Vaulted with all thy congregated might

Of vapors, from whose solid atmosphere
Black rain, and fire, and hail will burst: O,
hear!

III

Thou who didst waken from his summer
dreams
The blue Mediterranean, where he lay,   30
Lulled by the coil of his crystalline
streams,

Beside a pumice isle in Baiæ's bay,
And saw in sleep old palaces and towers
Quivering within the wave's intenser day,

All overgrown with azure moss and flow-
ers   35
So sweet, the sense faints picturing them!
Thou
For whose path the Atlantic's level powers

Cleave themselves into chasms, while far
below
The sea-blooms and the oozy woods which
wear
The sapless foliage of the ocean, know   40

Thy voice, and suddenly grow gray with
fear,
And tremble and despoil themselves: O,
hear!

IV

If I were a dead leaf thou mightest bear;
If I were a swift cloud to fly with thee;

A wave to pant beneath thy power, and
　share　　　　　　　　　　　　　45
The impulse of thy strength, only less free
Than thou, O, uncontrollable! If even
I were as in my boyhood, and could be

The comrade of thy wanderings over heaven,
As then, when to outstrip thy skiey speed 50
Scarce seemed a vision; I would ne'er have
　striven

As thus with thee in prayer in my sore
　need.
Oh! lift me as a wave, a leaf, a cloud!
I fall upon the thorns of life! I bleed!

A heavy weight of hours has chained and
　bowed　　　　　　　　　　　　55
One too like thee: tameless, and swift, and
　proud.

V

Make me thy lyre, even as the forest is:
What if my leaves are falling like its own!
The tumult of thy mighty harmonies

Will take from both a deep, autumnal tone,
Sweet though in sadness. Be thou, spirit
　fierce,　　　　　　　　　　　　61
My spirit! Be thou me, impetuous one!

Drive my dead thoughts over the universe
Like withered leaves to quicken a new
　birth!
And, by the incantation of this verse,　65

Scatter, as from an unextinguished hearth
Ashes and sparks, my words among man-
　kind!
Be through my lips to unawakened earth

The trumpet of a prophecy! O, wind,
If Winter comes, can Spring be far be-
　hind?　　　　　　　　　　　　70
　　　　　　　　　　　　　(1820)

THE INDIAN SERENADE

I arise from dreams of thee
In the first sweet sleep of night,
When the winds are breathing low,
And the stars are shining bright:
I arise from dreams of thee,　　　5
And a spirit in my feet
Hath led me — who knows how?
To thy chamber window, Sweet!

The wandering airs they faint
On the dark, the silent stream —　　10
The Champak odors fail
Like sweet thoughts in a dream;
The nightingale's complaint,
It dies upon her heart; —
As I must on thine,　　　　　　15
O! belovèd as thou art!

O lift me from the grass!
I die! I faint! I fail!
Let thy love in kisses rain
On my lips and eyelids pale.　　20
My cheek is cold and white, alas!
My heart beats loud and fast; —
Oh! press it to thine own again,
Where it will break at last.
　　　　　　　　　　　　(1822)

THE CLOUD

I bring fresh showers for the thirsting flow-
　ers,
　From the seas and the streams;
I bear light shade for the leaves when laid
　In their noon-day dreams.
From my wings are shaken the dews that
　waken　　　　　　　　　　　5
　The sweet buds every one,
When rocked to rest on their mother's
　breast,
　As she dances about the sun.
I wield the flail of the lashing hail,
　And whiten the green plains under,　10
And then again I dissolve it in rain,
　And laugh as I pass in thunder.

I sift the snow on the mountains below,
　And their great pines groan aghast;
And all the night 't is my pillow white,　15
　While I sleep in the arms of the blast.
Sublime on the towers of my skiey bow-
　ers,
　Lightning my pilot sits;
In a cavern under is fettered the thunder,—
　It struggles and howls at fits;　　20
Over earth and ocean, with gentle motion,
　This pilot is guiding me,
Lured by the love of the genii that move
　In the depths of the purple sea;
Over the rills, and the crags, and the hills,
　Over the lakes and the plains,　　26
Wherever he dream, under mountain or
　stream,
　The Spirit he loves remains;
And I all the while bask in heaven's blue
　smile,
　Whilst he is dissolving in rains.　　30

The sanguine sunrise, with his meteor
  eyes,
  And his burning plumes outspread,
Leaps on the back of my sailing rack,
  When the morning star shines dead,
As on the jag of a mountain crag,   35
  Which an earthquake rocks and swings,
An eagle alit one moment may sit
  In the light of its golden wings.
And when sunset may breathe, from the lit
  sea beneath,
  Its ardors of rest and of love,   40
And the crimson pall of eve may fall
  From the depth of heaven above,
With wings folded I rest, on mine airy nest,
  As still as a brooding dove.

That orbèd maiden with white fire laden, 45
  Whom mortals call the moon,
Glides glimmering o'er my fleece-like floor,
  By the midnight breezes strewn;
And wherever the beat of her unseen feet,
  Which only the angels hear,   50
May have broken the woof of my tent's
  thin roof,
  The stars peep behind her and peer;
And I laugh to see them whirl and flee,
  Like a swarm of golden bees,
When I widen the rent in my wind-built
  tent,   55
  Till the calm rivers, lakes, and seas,
Like strips of the sky fallen through me on
  high,
  Are each paved with the moon and these.

I bind the sun's throne with a burning zone,
  And the moon's with a girdle of pearl; 60
The volcanoes are dim, and the stars reel
  and swim,
  When the whirlwinds my banner unfurl.
From cape to cape, with a bridge-like shape,
  Over a torrent sea,
Sunbeam-proof, I hang like a roof,   65
  The mountains its columns be.
The triumphal arch through which I march
  With hurricane, fire, and snow,
When the powers of the air are chained to
  my chair,
  Is the million-colored bow;   70
The sphere-fire above its soft colors wove,
  While the moist earth was laughing be-
  low.

I am the daughter of earth and water,
  And the nursling of the sky;
I pass through the pores of the ocean and
  shores;   75
  I change, but I cannot die.

For after the rain when, with never a stain,
  The pavilion of heaven is bare,
And the winds and sunbeams with their con-
  vex gleams
  Build up the blue dome of air,   80
I silently laugh at my own cenotaph,
  And out of the caverns of rain,
Like a child from the womb, like a ghost
  from the tomb,
  I arise and unbuild it again.

               (1820)

TO A SKYLARK

Hail to thee, blithe spirit!
  Bird thou never wert,
That from heaven, or near it,
  Pourest thy full heart
In profuse strains of unpremeditated art. 5

Higher still and higher
  From the earth thou springest
Like a cloud of fire;
  The blue deep thou wingest,
And singing still dost soar, and soaring ever
  singest.   10

In the golden lightning
  Of the sunken sun,
O'er which clouds are brightning,
  Thou dost float and run;
Like an unbodied joy whose race is just be-
  gun   15

The pale purple even
  Melts around thy flight;
Like a star of heaven
  In the broad day-light
Thou art unseen, but yet I hear thy shrill
  delight,   20

Keen as are the arrows
  Of that silver sphere,
Whose intense lamp narrows
  In the white dawn clear,
Until we hardly see, we feel that it is there.

All the earth and air   26
  With thy voice is loud,
As, when night is bare,
  From one lonely cloud
The moon rains out her beams, and heaven
  is overflowed.   30

What thou art we know not;
  What is most like thee?
From rainbow clouds there flow not

Drops so bright to see
As from thy presence showers a rain of
    melody.   35

Like a poet hidden
    In the light of thought,
Singing hymns unbidden,
    Till the world is wrought
To sympathy with hopes and fears it heeded
    not: 40

Like a high-born maiden
    In a palace tower,
Soothing her love-laden
    Soul in secret hour
With music sweet as love, which overflows
    her bower: 45

Like a glow-worm golden
    In a dell of dew,
Scattering unbeholden
    Its aërial hue
Among the flowers and grass which screen
    it from the view: 50

Like a rose embowered
    In its own green leaves,
By warm winds deflowered,
    Till the scent it gives
Makes faint with too much sweet these
    heavy-wingèd thieves.   55

Sound of vernal showers
    On the twinkling grass,
Rain-awakened flowers,
    All that ever was
Joyous, and clear, and fresh, thy music doth
    surpass.   60

Teach us, sprite or bird,
    What sweet thoughts are thine;
I have never heard
    Praise of love or wine
That panted forth a flood of rapture so di-
    vine: 65

Chorus Hymenæal,
    Or triumphal chaunt,
Matched with thine, would be all
    But an empty vaunt,
A thing wherein we feel there is some hid-
    den want.   70

What objects are the fountains
    Of thy happy strain?
What fields, or waves, or mountains?
    What shapes of sky or plain?
What love of thine own kind? what igno-
    rance of pain?   75

With thy clear keen joyance
    Languor cannot be —
Shadow of annoyance
    Never came near thee:
Thou lovest — but ne'er knew love's sad
    satiety.   80

Waking or asleep,
    Thou of death must deem
Things more true and deep
    Than we mortals dream,
Or how could thy notes flow in such a crys-
    tal stream?   85

We look before and after
    And pine for what is not:
Our sincerest laughter
    With some pain is fraught;
Our sweetest songs are those that tell of
    saddest thought.   90

Yet if we could scorn
    Hate, and pride, and fear;
If we were things born
    Not to shed a tear,
I know not how thy joy we ever should
    come near.   95

Better than all measures
    Of delightful sound —
Better than all treasures
    That in books are found —
Thy skill to poet were, thou scorner of the
    ground!   100

Teach me half the gladness
    That thy brain must know,
Such harmonious madness
    From my lips would flow,
The world should listen then — as I am lis-
    tening now.   105

                                   (1820)

A LAMENT

O world! O life! O time!
On whose last steps I climb
    Trembling at that where I had stood be-
        fore;
When will return the glory of your prime?
    No more — Oh, never more!   1

Out of the day and night
A joy has taken flight;
    Fresh spring, and summer, and winter
        hoar,

Move my faint heart with grief, but with
delight
  No more — Oh, never more!   10
              (1824)

TO ———

Music, when soft voices die,
Vibrates in the memory —
Odors, when sweet violets sicken,
Live within the sense they quicken,

Rose leaves, when the rose is dead,   5
Are heaped for the belovèd's bed;
And so thy thoughts, when thou art gone,
Love itself shall slumber on.
              (1824)

ADONAIS

I weep for Adonais — he is dead!
O, weep for Adonais! though our tears
Thaw not the frost which binds so dear
  a head!
And thou, sad Hour, selected from all
  years
To mourn our loss, rouse thy obscure
  compeers,   5
And teach them thine own sorrow! Say:
  'With me
Died Adonais; till the Future dares
Forget the Past, his fate and fame shall
  be
An echo and a light unto eternity!'

Where wert thou, mighty Mother, when
  he lay,   10
When thy Son lay, pierced by the shaft
  which flies
In darkness? where was lorn Urania
When Adonais died? With veilèd eyes,
'Mid listening Echoes, in her Paradise
She sate, while one, with soft enamored
  breath,   15
Rekindled all the fading melodies,
With which, like flowers that mock the
  corse beneath,
He had adorned and hid the coming bulk of
  death.

O, weep for Adonais — he is dead!
Wake, melancholy Mother, wake and
  weep!   20
Yet wherefore? Quench within their
  burning bed
Thy fiery tears, and let thy loud heart
  keep

Like his, a mute and uncomplaining sleep;
For he is gone, where all things wise and
  fair
Descend; — oh, dream not that the amor-
  ous Deep   25
Will yet restore him to the vital air;
Death feeds on his mute voice, and laughs
  at our despair.

Most musical of mourners, weep again!
Lament anew, Urania! — He died, —
Who was the Sire of an immortal strain,
Blind, old, and lonely, when his country's
  pride,   31
The priest, the slave, and the liberticide,
Trampled and mocked with many a loathèd
  rite
Of lust and blood; he went, unterrified,
Into the gulph of death; but his clear
  Sprite   35
Yet reigns o'er earth; the third among the
  sons of light.

Most musical of mourners, weep anew!
Not all to that bright station dared to
  climb;
And happier they their happiness who
  knew,
Whose tapers yet burn through that night
  of time   40
In which suns perished; others more sub-
  lime,
Struck by the envious wrath of man or
  God,
Have sunk, extinct in their refulgent
  prime;
And some yet live, treading the thorny
  road,
Which leads, through toil and hate, to
  Fame's serene abode.   45

But now, thy youngest, dearest one has
  perished,
The nursling of thy widowhood, who
  grew,
Like a pale flower by some sad maiden
  cherished,
And fed with true love tears, instead of
  dew;
Most musical of mourners, weep anew! 50
Thy extreme hope, the loveliest and the
  last,
The bloom, whose petals, nipped before
  they blew,
Died on the promise of the fruit, is
  waste;
The broken lily lies — the storm is over-
  past.

To that high Capital, where kingly
  Death   55
Keeps his pale court in beauty and de-
cay,
He came; and bought, with price of purest
breath,
A grave among the eternal.— Come away!
Haste, while the vault of blue Italian day
Is yet his fitting charnel-roof! while still
He lies, as if in dewy sleep he lay;   61
Awake him not! surely he takes his fill
Of deep and liquid rest, forgetful of all ill.

He will awake no more, oh, never
  more! —
Within the twilight chamber spreads
  apace,   65
The shadow of white Death, and at the
  door
Invisible Corruption waits to trace
His extreme way to her dim dwelling-
  place;
The eternal Hunger sits, but pity and awe
Soothe her pale rage, nor dares she to de-
face   70
So fair a prey, till darkness, and the law
Of change, shall o'er his sleep the mortal
  curtain draw.

O, weep for Adonais! — The quick
  Dreams,
The passion-wingèd Ministers of thought,
Who were his flocks, whom near the liv-
  ing streams   75
Of his young spirit he fed, and whom he
  taught
The love which was its music, wander
  not,—
Wander no more, from kindling brain to
  brain,
But droop there, whence they sprung;
  and mourn their lot
Round the cold heart, where, after their
  sweet pain,   80
They ne'er will gather strength, or find a
  home again.

And one with trembling hands clasps his
  cold head,
And fans him with her moonlight wings,
  and cries:
'Our love, our hope, our sorrow, is not
  dead;   84
See, on the silken fringe of his faint eyes,
Like dew upon a sleeping flower, there lies
A tear some Dream has loosened from his
  brain.'
Lost Angel of a ruined Paradise!

She knew not 't was her own; as with no
  stain
She faded, like a cloud which had outwept
  its rain.   90

One from a lucid urn of starry dew
Washed his light limbs as if embalming
  them;
Another clipped her profuse locks, and
  threw
The wreath upon him, like an anadem,
Which frozen tears instead of pearls be-
  gem;   95
Another in her wilful grief would break
Her bow and wingèd reeds, as if to stem
A greater loss with one which was more
  weak;
And dull the barbèd fire against his frozen
  cheek.

Another Splendor on his mouth alit,   100
That mouth, whence it was wont to draw
  the breath
Which gave it strength to pierce the
  guarded wit,
And pass into the panting heart beneath
With lightning and with music: the damp
  death
Quenched its caress upon his icy lips;   105
And, as a dying meteor stains a wreath
Of moonlight vapor, which the cold night
  clips,
It flushed through his pale limbs, and
  passed to its eclipse.

And others came . . . Desires and
  Adorations,
Wingèd Persuasions and veiled Destinies,
Splendors, and Glooms, and glimmering
  Incarnations   111
Of hopes and fears, and twilight Phanta-
  sies;
And Sorrow, with her family of Sighs,
And Pleasure, blind with tears, led by the
  gleam
Of her own dying smile instead of eyes,
Came in slow pomp; — the moving pomp
  might seem   116
Like pageantry of mist on an autumnal
  stream.

All he had loved, and molded into
  thought,
From shape, and hue, and odor, and sweet
  sound,
Lamented Adonais. Morning sought   120
Her eastern watch-tower, and her hair
  unbound.

Wet with the tears which should adorn
the ground,
Dimmed the aërial eyes that kindle day;
Afar the melancholy thunder moaned,
Pale Ocean in unquiet slumber lay,   125
And the wild winds flew round, sobbing in
their dismay.

Lost Echo sits amid the voiceless mountains,
And feeds her grief with his remembered
lay,
And will no more reply to winds or fountains,
Or amorous birds perched on the young
green spray,   130
Or herdsman's horn, or bell at closing
day;
Since she can mimic not his lips, more
dear
Than those for whose disdain she pined
away
Into a shadow of all sounds; — a drear
Murmur, between their songs, is all the
woodmen hear.   135

Grief made the young Spring wild, and
she threw down
Her kindling buds, as if she Autumn
were,
Or they dead leaves; since her delight is
flown,
For whom should she have waked the sul-
len year?
To Phœbus was not Hyacinth so dear   140
Nor to himself Narcissus, as to both
Thou, Adonais: wan they stand and sere
Amid the faint companions of their youth,
With dew all turned to tears; odor, to sigh-
ing ruth.

Thy spirit's sister, the lorn nightingale,
Mourns not her mate with such melodious
pain;   146
Not so the eagle, who like thee could scale
Heaven, and could nourish in the sun's
domain
Her mighty youth with morning, doth
complain,
Soaring and screaming round her empty
nest,   150
As Albion wails for thee: the curse of
Cain
Light on his head who pierced thy inno-
cent breast,
And scared the angel soul that was its
earthly guest!

Ah, woe is me! Winter is come and
gone,
But grief returns with the revolving year;
The airs and streams renew their joyous
tone;   156
The ants, the bees, the swallows reap-
pear;
Fresh leaves and flowers deck the dead
Seasons' bier;
The amorous birds now pair in every
brake,
And build their mossy homes in field and
brere;   160
And the green lizard, and the golden
snake,
Like unimprisoned flames, out of their
trance awake.

Through wood and stream and field and
hill and Ocean
A quickening life from the Earth's heart
has burst,
As it has ever done, with change and motion   165
From the great morning of the world
when first
God dawned on Chaos; in its stream immersed
The lamps of Heaven flash with a softer
light;
All baser things pant with life's sacred
thirst;
Diffuse themselves; and spend in love's
delight   170
The beauty and the joy of their renewèd
might.

The leprous corpse touched by this spirit
tender
Exhales itself in flowers of gentle breath;
Like incarnations of the stars, when splen-
dor
Is changed to fragrance, they illumine
death   175
And mock the merry worm that wakes
beneath;
Naught we know, dies. Shall that alone
which knows
Be as a sword consumed before the sheath
By sightless lightning? — the intense atom
glows
A moment, then is quenched in a most cold
repose.   180

Alas! that all we loved of him should be,
But for our grief, as if it had not been
And grief itself be mortal! Woe is me!

Whence are we, and why are we? of
    what scene
The actors or spectators? Great and
    mean   185
Meet massed in death, who lends what
    life must borrow.
As long as skies are blue, and fields are
    green,
Evening must usher night, night urge the
    morrow,
Month follow month with woe, and year
    wake year to sorrow.

He will awake no more, oh, never more!
'Wake thou,' cried Misery, 'childless
    Mother, rise   191
Out of thy sleep, and slake, in thy heart's
    core,
A wound more fierce than his with tears
    and sighs.'
And all the Dreams that watched Urania's
    eyes,
And all the Echoes whom their sister's
    song   195
Had held in holy silence, cried: 'Arise!'
Swift as a Thought by the snake Memory
    stung,
From her ambrosial rest the fading Splen-
    dor sprung.

She rose like an autumnal Night, that
    springs
Out of the East, and follows wild and
    drear   200
The golden Day, which, on eternal wings,
Even as a ghost abandoning a bier,
Had left the Earth a corpse. Sorrow
    and fear
So struck, so roused, so rapt Urania;
So saddened round her like an atmos-
    phere   205
Of stormy mist; so swept her on her way
Even to the mournful place where Adonais
    lay.

Out of her secret Paradise she sped,
Through camps and cities rough with
    stone and steel,
And human hearts, which to her aëry
    tread   210
Yielding not, wounded the invisible
Palms of her tender feet where'er they
    fell:
And barbèd tongues, and thoughts more
    sharp than they,
Rent the soft Form they never could re-
    pel,
Whose sacred blood, like the young tears
    of May,   215

Paved with eternal flowers that undeserving
    way.

In the death chamber for a moment
    Death,
Shamed by the presence of that living
    Might,
Blushed to annihilation, and the breath
Revisited those lips, and life's pale light
Flashed through those limbs, so late her
    dear delight.   221
'Leave me not wild and drear and com-
    fortless,
As silent lightning leaves the starless
    night!
Leave me not!' cried Urania: her distress
Roused Death: Death rose and smiled, and
    met her vain caress.   225

'Stay yet awhile! speak to me once again;
Kiss me, so long but as a kiss may live;
And in my heartless breast and burning
    brain
That word, that kiss shall all thoughts
    else survive,   229
With food of saddest memory kept alive,
Now thou art dead, as if it were a part
Of thee, my Adonais! I would give
All that I am to be as thou now art!
But I am chained to Time, and cannot
    thence depart!

'Oh gentle child, beautiful as thou wert,
Why didst thou leave the trodden paths of
    men   236
Too soon, and with weak hands though
    mighty heart
Dare the unpastured dragon in his den?
Defenceless as thou wert, oh, where was
    then
Wisdom the mirrored shield, or scorn the
    spear?   240
Or hadst thou waited the full cycle, when
Thy spirit should have filled its crescent
    sphere,
The monsters of life's waste had fled from
    thee like deer.

'The herded wolves, bold only to pursue;
The obscene ravens, clamorous o'er the
    dead;   245
The vultures to the conqueror's banner
    true,
Who feed where Desolation first has fed,
And whose wings rain contagion; — how
    they fled,
When like Apollo, from his golden bow,
The Pythian of the age one arrow sped 250

And smiled! — The spoilers tempt no
second blow;
They fawn on the proud feet that spurn
them lying low.

'The sun comes forth, and many reptiles
spawn;
He sets, and each ephemeral insect then
Is gathered into death without a dawn, 255
And the immortal stars awake again;
So is it in the world of living men:
A godlike mind soars forth, in its delight
Making earth bare and veiling heaven,
and when
It sinks, the swarms that dimmed or
shared its light   260
Leave to its kindred lamps the spirit's
awful night.'

Thus ceased she: and the mountain shep-
herds came,
Their garlands sere, their magic mantles
rent;
The Pilgrim of Eternity, whose fame
Over his living head like Heaven is bent,
An early but enduring monument,   266
Came, veiling all the lightnings of his
song
In sorrow: from her wilds Ierne sent
The sweetest lyrist of her saddest wrong,
And love taught grief to fall like music
from his tongue.   270

Midst others of less note, came one frail
Form,
A phantom among men, companionless
As the last cloud of an expiring storm
Whose thunder is its knell; he, as I guess,
Had gazed on Nature's naked loveliness,
Actæon-like, and now he fled astray 276
With feeble steps o'er the world's wilder-
ness,
And his own thoughts, along that rugged
way,
Pursued, like raging hounds, their father
and their prey.

A pardlike Spirit beautiful and swift — 280
A Love in desolation masked; — a Power
Girt round with weakness; — it can scarce
uplift
The weight of the superincumbent hour;
It is a dying lamp, a falling shower,
A breaking billow; — even whilst we
speak   285
Is it not broken? On the withering
flower
The killing sun smiles brightly; on a
cheek

The life can burn in blood, even while the
heart may break.

His head was bound with pansies over-
blown,
And faded violets, white, and pied, and
blue;   290
And a light spear topped with a cypress
cone,
Round whose rude shaft dark ivy tresses
grew
Yet dripping with the forest's noonday
dew,
Vibrated, as the ever-beating heart
Shook the weak hand that grasped it; of
that crew   295
He came the last, neglected and apart;
A herd-abandoned deer, struck by the
hunter's dart.

All stood aloof, and at his partial moan
Smiled through their tears; well knew
that gentle band   299
Who in another's fate now wept his own;
As, in the accents of an unknown land,
He sung new sorrow; sad Urania scanned
The Stranger's mien, and murmured:
'Who art thou?'
He answered not, but with a sudden hand
Made bare his branded and ensanguined
brow,   305
Which was like Cain's or Christ's — Oh!
that it should be so!

What softer voice is hushed over the
dead?
Athwart what brow is that dark mantle
thrown?
What form leans sadly o'er the white
death-bed,
In mockery of monumental stone,   310
The heavy heart heaving without a
moan?
If it be He, who, gentlest of the wise,
Taught, soothed, loved, honored the de-
parted one,
Let me not vex with inharmonious sighs
The silence of that heart's accepted
sacrifice.   315

Our Adonais has drunk poison — oh!
What deaf and viperous murderer could
crown
Life's early cup with such a draught of
woe?
The nameless worm would now itself dis-
own:
It felt yet could escape the magic tone 320

Whose prelude held all envy, hate, and
wrong,
But what was howling in one breast alone,
Silent with expectation of the song,
Whose master's hand is cold, whose silver
lyre unstrung.

Live thou, whose infamy is not thy fame!
Live! fear no heavier chastisement from
me,   326
Thou noteless blot on a remembered
name!
But be thyself, and know thyself to be!
And ever at thy season be thou free
To spill the venom when thy fangs o'er-
flow: 330
Remorse and Self-contempt shall cling to
thee;
Hot Shame shall burn upon thy secret
brow,
And like a beaten hound tremble thou shalt
— as now.

Nor let us weep that our delight is fled
Far from these carrion kites that scream
below;   335
He wakes or sleeps with the enduring
dead;
Thou canst not soar where he is sitting
now.—
Dust to the dust! but the pure spirit shall
flow
Back to the burning fountain whence it
came,
A portion of the Eternal, which must
glow   340
Through time and change, unquenchably
the same,
Whilst thy cold embers choke the sordid
hearth of shame.

Peace, peace! he is not dead, he doth not
sleep —
He hath awakened from the dream of
life —
'T is we who, lost in stormy visions, keep
With phantoms an unprofitable strife, 346
And in mad trance strike with our spirit's
knife
Invulnerable nothings.— *We* decay
Like corpses in a charnel; fear and grief
Convulse us and consume us day by day,
And cold hopes swarm like worms within
our living clay.   351

He has outsoared the shadow of our
night;
Envy and calumny and hate and pain,

And that unrest which men miscall de-
light,
Can touch him not and torture not again;
From the contagion of the world's slow
stain   356
He is secure, and now can never mourn
A heart grown cold, a head grown gray in
vain;
Nor, when the spirit's self has ceased to
burn,
With sparkless ashes load an unlamented
urn.   360

He lives, he wakes — 't is Death is dead,
not he;
Mourn not for Adonais.— Thou young
Dawn,
Turn all thy dew to splendor, for from
thee
The spirit thou lamentest is not gone;
Ye caverns and ye forests, cease to moan!
Cease, ye faint flowers and fountains, and
thou Air,   366
Which like a mourning veil thy scarf
hadst thrown
O'er the abandoned Earth, now leave it
bare
Even to the joyous stars which smile on
its despair!

He is made one with Nature: there is
heard   370
His voice in all her music, from the moan
Of thunder, to the song of night's sweet
bird;
He is a presence to be felt and known
In darkness and in light, from herb and
stone,
Spreading itself where'er that Power may
move   375
Which has withdrawn his being to its
own;
Which wields the world with never
wearied love,
Sustains it from beneath, and kindles it
above.

He is a portion of the loveliness
Which once he made more lovely: he doth
bear   380
His part, while the one Spirit's plastic
stress
Sweeps through the dull dense world, compelling there
All new successions to the forms they
wear;
Torturing the unwilling dross that checks
its flight

To its own likeness, as each mass may
  bear;   385
And bursting in its beauty and its might
From trees and beasts and men into the
  Heaven's light.

The splendors of the firmament of time
May be eclipsed, but are extinguished not;
Like stars to their appointed height they
  climb   390
And death is a low mist which cannot
  blot
The brightness it may veil. When lofty
  thought
Lifts a young heart above its mortal lair,
And love and life contend in it, for what
Shall be its earthly doom, the dead live
  there   395
And move like winds of light on dark and
  stormy air.

The inheritors of unfulfilled renown
Rose from their thrones, built beyond
  mortal thought,
Far in the Unapparent. Chatterton
Rose pale, his solemn agony had not 400
Yet faded from him; Sidney, as he
  fought
And as he fell and as he lived and loved,
Sublimely mild, a Spirit without spot,
Arose; and Lucan, by his death approved:
Oblivion, as they rose, shrank like a thing
  reproved.   405

And many more, whose names on Earth
  are dark
But whose transmitted effluence cannot
  die
So long as fire outlives the parent spark,
Rose, robed in dazzling immortality.
'Thou art become as one of us,' they
  cry,   410
'It was for thee yon kingless sphere has
  long
Swung blind in unascended majesty,
Silent alone amid an Heaven of Song.
Assume thy wingèd throne, thou Vesper of
  our throng!'

Who mourns for Adonais? oh, come
  forth,   415
Fond wretch! and know thyself and him
  aright.
Clasp with thy panting soul the pendu-
  lous Earth;
As from a center, dart thy spirit's light
Beyond all worlds, until its spacious might
Satiate the void circumference: then
  shrink   420

Even to a point within our day and
  night;
And keep thy heart light, lest it make
  thee sink,
When hope has kindled hope, and lured thee
  to the brink.

Or go to Rome, which is the sepulcher,
O, not of him, but of our joy: 'tis
  naught   425
That ages, empires, and religions there
Lie buried in the ravage they have
  wrought;
For such as he can lend,— they borrow
  not
Glory from those who made the world
  their prey;
And he is gathered to the kings of
  thought   430
Who waged contention with their time's
  decay,
And of the past are all that cannot pass
  away.

Go thou to Rome,— at once the Paradise,
The grave, the city, and the wilderness;
And where its wrecks like shattered
  mountains rise   435
And flowering weeds and fragrant copses
  dress
The bones of Desolation's nakedness
Pass, till the Spirit of the spot shall
  lead
Thy footsteps to a slope of green access
Where, like an infant's smile, over the
  dead,   440
A light of laughing flowers along the grass
  is spread.

And gray walls moulder round, on which
  dull Time
Feeds, like slow fire upon a hoary brand;
And one keen pyramid with wedge sub-
  lime,   444·
Pavilioning the dust of him who planned
This refuge for his memory, doth stand
Like flame transformed to marble; and
  beneath,
A field is spread, on which a newer band
Have pitched in Heaven's smile their
  camp of death,
Welcoming him we lose with scarce ex-
  tinguished breath.   450

Here pause: these graves are all too
  young as yet
To have outgrown the sorrow which consigned

Its charge to each; and if the seal is set,
Here, on one fountain of a mourning
  mind,
Break it not thou! too surely shalt thou
  find   455
Thine own well full, if thou returnest
  home,
Of tears and gall. From the world's bit-
  ter wind
Seek shelter in the shadow of the tomb.
What Adonais is, why fear we to become?

The One remains, the many change and
  pass;   460
Heaven's light forever shines, Earth's
  shadows fly;
Life, like a dome of many-colored glass,
Stains the white radiance of Eternity,
Until Death tramples it to fragments.—
  Die,
If thou wouldst be with that which thou
  dost seek!   465
Follow where all is fled!—Rome's azure
  sky,
Flowers, ruins, statues, music, words, are
  weak
The glory they transfuse with fitting truth
  to speak.

Why linger? why turn back, why shrink,
  my Heart?
Thy hopes are gone before: from all
  things here   470
They have departed; thou shouldst now
  depart!
A light is past from the revolving year,
And man, and woman; and what still is
  dear
Attracts to crush, repels to make thee
  wither.
The soft sky smiles,—the low wind whis-
  pers near;   475
'T is Adonais calls! oh, hasten thither,
No more let Life divide what Death can
  join together.

That Light whose smile kindles the
  Universe,
That Beauty in which all things work and
  move,
That Benediction which the eclipsing
  Curse   480
Of birth can quench not, that sustaining
  Love
Which, through the web of being blindly
  wove
By man and beast and earth and air and
  sea,

Burns bright or dim, as each are mirrors
  of
The fire for which all thirst, now beams
  on me,   485
Consuming the last clouds of cold mortality.

The breath whose might I have invoked
  in song
Descends on me; my spirit's bark is
  driven,
Far from the shore, far from the trem-
  bling throng
Whose sails were never to the tempest
  given;   490
The massy earth and spherèd skies are
  riven!
I am borne darkly, fearfully, afar:
Whilst burning through the inmost veil of
  Heaven,
The soul of Adonais, like a star,
Beacons from the abode where the Eternal
  are.   495

(1821)

FINAL CHORUS FROM HELLAS

The world's great age begins anew,
  The golden years return,
The earth doth like a snake renew
  Her winter weeds outworn:
Heaven smiles, and faiths and empires
  gleam,   5
Like wrecks of a dissolving dream.

A brighter Hellas rears its mountains
  From waves serener far;
A new Peneus rolls his fountains
  Against the morning-star.   10
Where fairer Tempes bloom, there sleep
Young Cyclads on a sunnier deep.

A loftier Argo cleaves the main,
  Fraught with a later prize;
Another Orpheus sings again,   15
  And loves, and weeps, and dies.
A new Ulysses leaves once more
Calypso for his native shore.

O, write no more the tale of Troy,
  If earth Death's scroll must be!   20
Nor mix with Laian rage the joy
  Which dawns upon the free:
Although a subtler Sphinx renew
Riddles of death Thebes never knew.

Another Athens shall arise,   25
  And to remoter time

Bequeath, like sunset to the skies,
  The splendor of its prime;
And leave, if naught so bright may live,
All earth can take or Heaven can give. 30

Saturn and Love their long repose
  Shall burst, more bright and good
Than all who fell, than One who rose,
  Than many unsubdued:
Not gold, not blood, their altar dowers, 35
But votive tears and symbol flowers.

O cease! must hate and death return?
  Cease! must men kill and die?
Cease! drain not to its dregs the urn
  Of bitter prophecy. 40
The world is weary of the past,
O might it die or rest at last!
                (1822)

TO NIGHT

Swiftly walk over the western wave,
  Spirit of Night!
  Out of the misty eastern cave,
Where all the long and lone daylight,
Thou wovest dreams of joy and fear, 5
Which make thee terrible and dear,—
  Swift be thy flight!

Wrap thy form in a mantle gray,
  Star in-wrought!
Blind with thine hair the eyes of Day; 10
Kiss her until she be wearied out,
Then wander o'er city, and sea, and land,
Touching all with thine opiate wand—
  Come, long sought!

When I arose and saw the dawn, 15
  I sighed for thee;
When light rode high, and the dew was
  gone,
And noon lay heavy on flower and tree,
And the weary Day turned to his rest,
Lingering like an unloved guest, 20
  I sighed for thee.

Thy brother Death came, and cried,
  Wouldst thou me?
Thy sweet child Sleep, the filmy-eyed,
Murmured like a noon-tide bee, 25
Shall I nestle near thy side?
Wouldst thou me?—And I replied,
  No, not thee!

Death will come when thou art dead,
  Soon, too soon—

Sleep will come when thou art fled; 31
Of neither would I ask the boon
I ask of thee, belovèd Night—
Swift be thine approaching flight,
  Come soon, soon! 35
                (1824)

TO——

One word is too often profaned
  For me to profane it,
One feeling too falsely disdained
  For thee to disdain it.
One hope is too like despair 5
  For prudence to smother,
And pity from thee more dear
  Than that from another.

I can give not what men call love,
  But wilt thou accept not 10
The worship the heart lifts above
  And the Heavens reject not,
The desire of the moth for the star,
  Of the night for the morrow,
The devotion to something afar 15
  From the sphere of our sorrow?
                (1824)

WITH A GUITAR, TO JANE

Ariel to Miranda.—Take
This slave of Music, for the sake
Of him who is the slave of thee,
And teach it all the harmony
In which thou canst, and only thou, 5
Make the delighted spirit glow,
Till joy denies itself again,
And, too intense, is turned to pain;
For by permission and command
Of thine own Prince Ferdinand, 10
Poor Ariel sends this silent token
Of more than ever can be spoken;
Your guardian spirit, Ariel, who,
From life to life, must still pursue
Your happiness;— for thus alone 15
Can Ariel ever find his own.
From Prospero's enchanted cell,
As the mighty verses tell,
To the throne of Naples, he
Lit you o'er the trackless sea, 20
Flitting on, your prow before,
Like a living meteor.
When you die, the silent Moon,
In her interlunar swoon,
Is not sadder in her cell 25
Than deserted Ariel.

When you live again on earth,
Like an unseen star of birth,
Ariel guides you o'er the sea
Of life from your nativity.   30
Many changes have been run,
Since Ferdinand and you begun
Your course of love, and Ariel still
Has tracked your steps, and served your
    will;
Now, in humbler, happier lot,   35
This is all remembered not;
And now, alas! the poor sprite is
Imprisoned, for some fault of his,
In a body like a grave; —
From you he only dares to crave,   40
For his service and his sorrow,
A smile to-day, a song to-morrow.

The artist who this idol wrought,
To echo all harmonious thought,
Felled a tree, while on the steep   45
The woods were in their winter sleep,
Rocked in that repose divine
On the wind-swept Apennine;
And dreaming, some of Autumn past,
And some of Spring approaching fast,   50
And some of April buds and showers,
And some of songs in July bowers,
And all of love; and so this tree,—
Oh, that such our death may be!—
Died in sleep, and felt no pain,   55
To live in happier form again:
From which, beneath Heaven's fairest star,
The artist wrought this loved Guitar,
And taught it justly to reply,
To all who question skilfully,   60
In language gentle as thine own;
Whispering in enamored tone
Sweet oracles of woods and dells,
And summer winds in sylvan cells;
For it had learnt all harmonies   65
Of the plains and of the skies,
Of the forests and the mountains,
And the many-voicèd fountains;
The clearest echoes of the hills,
The softest notes of falling rills,   70
The melodies of birds and bees,
The murmuring of summer seas,
And pattering rain, and breathing dew
And airs of evening; and it knew
That seldom-heard mysterious sound,   75
Which, driven on its diurnal round,
As it floats through boundless day,
Our world enkindles on its way —
All this it knows, but will not tell
To those who cannot question well   80
The spirit that inhabits it;
It talks according to the wit
Of its companions; and no more
Is heard than has been felt before,

By those who tempt it to betray   85
These secrets of an elder day:
But sweetly as its answers will
Flatter hands of perfect skill,
It keeps its highest, holiest tone
For our belovèd Jane alone.   90

                        (1832–1833)

LINES: WHEN THE LAMP IS SHATTERED

When the lamp is shattered
The light in the dust lies dead —
    When the cloud is scattered
The rainbow's glory is shed.
    When the lute is broken,   5
Sweet tones are remembered not;
    When the lips have spoken,
Loved accents are soon forgot.

    As music and splendor
Survive not the lamp and the lute,   10
    The heart's echoes render
No song when the spirit is mute: —
    No song but sad dirges,
Like the wind through a ruined cell,
    Or the mournful surges   15
That ring the dead seaman's knell.

    When hearts have once mingled
Love first leaves the well-built nest,
    The weak one is singled
To endure what it once possessed.   20
    O Love! who bewailest
The frailty of all things here,
    Why choose you the frailest
For your cradle, your home, and your bier?

    Its passions will rock thee   25
As the storms rock the ravens on high:
    Bright reason will mock thee,
Like the sun from a wintry sky.
    From thy nest every rafter
Will rot, and thine eagle home   30
    Leave thee naked to laughter,
When leaves fall and cold winds come.

                             (1824)

A DIRGE

Rough wind, that moanest loud
    Grief too sad for song;
Wild wind, when sullen cloud
    Knells all the night long;
Sad storm, whose tears are vain,   5
Bare woods, whose branches strain,
Deep caves and dreary main,
    Wail, for the world's wrong!

                             (1824)

JOHN KEATS (1795-1821).

The parents of John Keats were living, at the time of his birth, at the Swan-and-Hoop stable in Finsbury, London. As a boy Keats was a sturdy fellow, with a hot temper, fond of fighting, fond of 'gold-finches, tomtits, minnows, mice, tickle-backs, dace, cock-salmons, and all the whole tribe of the bushes and the brooks.' It was toward the end of his school-days that he was set dreaming by Spenser's *Faery Queen.* He persevered, however, in his medical studies, passed his surgeon's examination with credit in 1815, and proved a skilful operator. But he was excessively sensitive to the nervous strain incident to surgery and, also, he was pining for a poetic career, 'Like a sick eagle looking at the sky.' Early in 1816 he met Leigh Hunt and through him numerous poets and artists, including Shelley, Wordsworth, and the painter Haydon. Shelley took a lively interest in him and attempted to show him hospitality. Wordsworth, whom he admired highly, is said to have chilled him by remarking after Keats had recited his *Hymn to Pan* for the benefit of a company: 'A pretty piece of Paganism!' To Haydon he owed something of an initiation into art and an opportunity to lend thirty pounds. In May, 1816, Hunt published in his *Examiner* the sonnet 'O Solitude! if I with thee must dwell,' and Keats had, so to speak, his first taste of blood. He now gave himself with increasing constancy to composition. His first volume came in March, 1817, and a year later *Endymion.* Chiefly because of Keats's friendship with Hunt, who was hated for his political opinions, these earlier volumes were sneeringly reviewed. Though Keats was indignant, it was by no means, '*The Quarterly,* so savage and tartarly' that killed him. Partially from nursing his brother Tom through his last illness and partially, perhaps, from inherited susceptibility he became a victim of consumption. A few months snatched from the grave, harassed by insufficient means, 'the law's delay,' and 'the pangs of disprized love,' produced the more mature and discreet work which lies between *Endymion* and his last sonnet ('Bright Star would I were steadfast as thou art'), composed on shipboard as he was leaving for Italy to die. Brief as was Shelley's career, all his poems of real importance were written between his twenty-sixth and thirtieth years; the corresponding years Keats never knew. Yet his poetry is far more than the poetry of promise. Some of it is 'as final as Shakspere.'

KEEN, FITFUL GUSTS ARE WHISPERING HERE AND THERE

Keen, fitful gusts are whispering here and
    there
Among the bushes half leafless, and dry;
The stars look very cold about the sky,
And I have many miles on foot to fare.
Yet feel I little of the cool bleak air,   5
Or of the dead leaves rustling drearily,
Or of those silver lamps that burn on high,
Or of the distance from home's pleasant
    lair:
For I am brimful of the friendliness
That in a little cottage I have found;   10
Of fair-haired Milton's eloquent distress,
And all his love for gentle Lycid drowned;
Of lovely Laura in her light green dress,
And faithful Petrarch gloriously crowned.

(1816)

ON FIRST LOOKING INTO CHAPMAN'S HOMER

Ital. Sonnet

Much have I traveled in the realms of gold,
And many goodly states and kingdoms seen;
Round many western islands have I been
Which bards in fealty to Apollo hold.
Oft of one wide expanse had I been told   5
That deep-browed Homer ruled as his de-
    mesne;
Yet did I never breathe its pure serene
Till I heard Chapman speak out loud and bold:
Then felt I like some watcher of the skies
When a new planet swims into his ken;   10
Or like stout Cortez when with eagle eyes
He stared at the Pacific — and all his men
Looked at each other with a wild sur-
    mise —
Silent, upon a peak in Darien.

(1816)

From ENDYMION, BOOK I

PROEM

A thing of beauty is a joy for ever:
Its loveliness increases; it will never
Pass into nothingness; but still will keep
A bower quiet for us, and a sleep
Full of sweet dreams, and health, and quiet
    breathing.   5
Therefore, on every morrow, are we wreath-
    ing
A flowery band to bind us to the earth,
Spite of despondence, of the inhuman
    dearth
Of noble natures, of the gloomy days,
Of all the unhealthy and o'er-darkened
    ways   10
Made for our searching: yes, in spite of
    all,
Some shape of beauty moves away the pall
From our dark spirits. Such the sun, the
    moon,
Trees old and young, sprouting a shady
    boon
For simple sheep: and such are daffodils 15
With the green world they live in; and clear
    rills
That for themselves a cooling covert make
'Gainst the hot season; the mid-forest
    brake,
Rich with a sprinkling of fair musk-rose
    blooms:
And such too is the grandeur of the dooms
We have imagined fcr the mighty dead; 21
All lovely tales that we have heard or read:
An endless fountain of immortal drink,
Pouring unto us from the heaven's brink.

Nor do we merely feel these essences 25
For one short hour; no, even as the trees
That whisper round a temple become soon
Dear as the temple's self, so does the moon,
The passion poesy, glories infinite,
Haunt us till they become a cheering light 30
Unto our souls, and bound to us so fast,
That, whether there be shine, or gloom o'er-
    cast,
They alway must be with us, or we die.

Therefore, 't is with full happiness that I
Will trace the story of Endymion. 35
The very music of the name has gone
Into my being, and each pleasant scene
Is growing fresh before me as the green
Of our own valleys: so I will begin
Now while I cannot hear the city's din; 40
Now while the early budders are just new,

And run in mazes of the youngest hue
About old forests; while the willow trails
Its delicate amber; and the dairy pails
Bring home increase of milk. And, as the
    year   45
Grows lush in juicy stalks, I 'll smoothly
    steer
My little boat, for many quiet hours,
With streams that deepen freshly into bow-
    ers.
Many and many a verse I hope to write,
Before the daisies, vermeil rimmed and
    white,   50
Hide in deep herbage; and ere yet the bees
Hum about globes of clover and sweet peas,
I must be near the middle of my story.
O may no wintry season, bare and hoary,
See it half finished; but let Autumn bold, 55
With universal tinge of sober gold,
Be all about me when I make an end.
And now at once, adventuresome, I send
My herald thought into a wilderness:
There let its trumpet blow, and quickly dress
My uncertain path with green, that I may
    speed   61
Easily onward, thorough flowers and weed.

    (1818)

THE EVE OF ST. AGNES

St. Agnes' Eve — Ah, bitter chill it was!
The owl, for all his feathers, was a-cold;
The hare limped trembling through the
    frozen grass,
And silent was the flock in woolly fold:
Numb were the Beadsman's fingers, while
    he told   5
His rosary, and while his frosted breath,
Like pious incense from a censer old,
Seemed taking flight for heaven, without a
    death,
Past the sweet Virgin's picture, while his
    prayer he saith.   10

His prayer he saith, this patient, holy man
Then takes his lamp, and riseth from his
    knees,
And back returneth, meager, barefoot, wan,
Along the chapel aisle by slow degrees:
The sculptured dead, on each side, seem to
    freeze,   15
Emprisoned in black, purgatorial rails:
Knights, ladies, praying in dumb orat'ries,
He passeth by; and his weak spirit fails
To think how they may ache in icy hoods
    and mails

Northward he turneth through a little door,
And scarce three steps, ere Music's golden
    tongue   21
Flattered to tears this aged man and poor;
But no — already had his deathbell rung;
The joys of all his life were said and sung:
His was harsh penance on St. Agnes' Eve:
Another way he went, and soon among   26
Rough ashes sat he for his soul's reprieve,
And all night kept awake, for sinners' sake
    to grieve.

That ancient Beadsman heard the prelude
    soft;
And so it chanced, for many a door was
    wide,   30
From hurry to and fro. Soon, up aloft,
The silver, snarling trumpets 'gan to chide:
The level chambers, ready with their pride,
Were glowing to receive a thousand guests:
The carvèd angels, ever eager-eyed,   35
Stared where upon their heads the cornice
    rests,
With hair blown back, and wings put cross-
    wise on their breasts.

At length burst in the argent revelry,
With plume, tiara, and all rich array,
Numerous as shadows haunting fairily   40
The brain, new stuffed, in youth, with tri-
    umphs gay

Of old romance. These let us wish away,
And turn, sole-thoughted, to one Lady there,
Whose heart had brooded, all that wintry
    day,
On love, and winged St. Agnes' saintly care,
As she had heard old dames full many times
    declare.   46

They told her how, upon St. Agnes' Eve,
Young virgins might have visions of delight,
And soft adorings from their loves receive
Upon the honeyed middle of the night   50
11 ceremonies due they did aright;
As, supperless to bed they must retire,
And couch supine their beauties, lily white;
Nor look behind, nor sideways, but require
Of Heaven with upward eyes for all that
    they desire.   55

Full of this whim was thoughtful Made-
    line;
The music, yearning like a God in pain,
She scarcely heard: her maiden eyes di-
    vine,
Fixed on the floor, saw many a sweeping
    train
Pass by — she heeded not at all: in vain   60

Came many a tiptoe, amorous cavalier,
And back retired; not cooled by high dis-
    dain,
But she saw not: her heart was other-
    where:
She sighed for Agnes' dreams, the sweetest
    of the year.

She danced along with vague, regardless
    eyes,   65
Anxious her lips, her breathing quick and
    short:
The hallowed hour was near at hand: she
    sighs
Amid the timbrels, and the thronged re-
    sort
Of whisperers in anger, or in sport;
'Mid looks of love, defiance, hate, and
    scorn,   70
Hoodwinked with faery fancy; all amort,
Save to St. Agnes and her lambs unshorn,
And all the bliss to be before to-morrow
    morn.

So, purposing each moment to retire,
She lingered still. Meantime, across the
    moors,   75
Had come young Porphyro, with heart on
    fire
For Madeline. Beside the portal doors,
Buttressed from moonlight, stands he, and
    implores
All saints to give him sight of Madeline,
But for one moment in the tedious hours,   80
That he might gaze and worship all un-
    seen;
Perchance speak, kneel, touch, kiss — in
    sooth such things have been.

He ventures in: let no buzzed whisper tell:
All eyes be muffled, or a hundred swords
Will storm his heart, Love's fev'rous cita-
    del: 85
For him, those chambers held barbarian
    hordes,
Hyena foemen, and hot-blooded lords,
Whose very dogs would execrations howl
Against his lineage: not one breast affords
Him any mercy, in that mansion foul,   90
Save one old beldame, weak in body and
    in soul.

Ah, happy chance! the aged creature came,
Shuffling along with ivory-headed wand,
To where he stood, hid from the torch's
    flame,
Behind a broad hall-pillar, far beyond   95
The sound of merriment and chorus bland:

He startled her; but soon she knew his face,
And grasped his fingers in her palsied hand,
Saying, 'Mercy, Porphyro! hie thee from
   this place;
They are all here to-night, the whole blood-
   thirsty race!   100

Get hence! get hence! there's dwarfish Hil-
   debrand;
He had a fever late, and in the fit
He cursèd thee and thine, both house and
   land:
Then there's that old Lord Maurice, not a
   whit
More tame for his gray hairs—Alas me!
   flit!   105
Flit like a ghost away.'—'Ah, Gossip dear,
We're safe enough; here in this armchair
   sit,
And tell me how'—'Good Saints! not here,
   not here;
'Follow me, child, or else these stones will
   be thy bier.'

He followed through a lowly archèd
   way,   110
Brushing the cobwebs with his lofty plume;
And as she muttered 'Well-a—well-a-
   day!'
He found him in a little moonlight room,
Pale, latticed, chill, and silent as a tomb.
'Now tell me where is Madeline,' said he,
'O tell me, Angela, by the holy loom   116
Which none but secret sisterhood may see,
When they St. Agnes' wool are weaving
   piously.'

'St. Agnes! Ah! it is St. Agnes' Eve—
Yet men will murder upon holy days: 120
Thou must hold water in a witch's sieve,
And be liege-lord of all the Elves and
   Fays,
To venture so; it fills me with amaze
To see thee, Porphyro!—St. Agnes' Eve!
God's help! my lady fair the conjurer
   plays   125
This very night; good angels her deceive!
But let me laugh awhile, I've mickle time to
   grieve.'

Feebly she laugheth in the languid moon,
While Porphyro upon her face doth look,
Like puzzled urchin on an aged crone   130
Who keepeth closed a wond'rous riddle-
   book,
As spectacled she sits in chimney nook.
But soon his eyes grew brilliant, when she
   told

His lady's purpose; and he scarce could
   brook
Tears, at the thought of those enchantments
   cold,   135
And Madeline asleep in lap of legends old.

Sudden a thought came like a full-blown
   rose,
Flushing his brow, and in his painèd heart
Made purple riot: then doth he propose
A stratagem, that makes the beldame start:
'A cruel man and impious thou art: 141
Sweet lady, let her pray, and sleep, and
   dream
Alone with her good angels, far apart
From wicked men like thee. Go, go!—
   I deem
Thou canst not surely be the same that thou
   didst seem.'   145

'I will not harm her, by all saints I swear,'
Quoth Porphyro: 'O may I ne'er find grace
When my weak voice shall whisper its last
   prayer,
If one of her soft ringlets I displace,
Or look with ruffian passion in her face: 150
Good Angela, believe me by these tears:
Or I will, even in a moment's space,
Awake, with horrid shout, my foemen's
   ears,
And beard them, though they be more fanged
   than wolves and bears.'

'Ah! why wilt thou affright a feeble soul?
A poor, weak, palsy-stricken churchyard
   thing,   156
Whose passing-bell may ere the midnight
   toll;
Whose prayers for thee, each morn and
   evening,
Were never missed.' Thus plaining, doth
   she bring   159
A gentler speech from burning Porphyro;
So woful, and of such deep sorrowing,
That Angela gives promise she will do
Whatever he shall wish, betide her weal or
   woe.

Which was, to lead him, in close secrecy,
Even to Madeline's chamber, and there hide
Him in a closet, of such privacy   160
That he might see her beauty unespied,
And win perhaps that night a peerless
   bride,
While legioned fairies paced the coverlet,
And pale enchantment held her sleepy-
   eyed.   170
Never on such a night have lovers met,

Since Merlin paid his Demon all the monstrous debt.

'It shall be as thou wishest,' said the Dame:
'All cates and dainties shall be stored there
Quickly on this feast-night: by the tambour
    frame   175
Her own lute thou wilt see: no time to
    spare,
For I am slow and feeble, and scarce dare
On such a catering trust my dizzy head.
Wait here, my child, with patience; kneel in
    prayer
The while: Ah! thou must needs the lady
    wed,   180
Or may I never leave my grave among the
    dead.'

So saying, she hobbled off with busy fear.
The lover's endless minutes slowly passed;
The dame returned, and whispered in his
    ear
To follow her; with agèd eyes aghast   185
From fright of dim espial. Safe at last,
Through many a dusky gallery, they gain
The maiden's chamber, silken, hushed, and
    chaste;
Where Porphyro took covert, pleased amain.
His poor guide hurried back with agues in
    her brain.   190

Her falt'ring hand upon the balustrade
Old Angela was feeling for the stair,
When Madeline, St. Agnes' charmèd maid,
Rose, like a missioned spirit, unaware:
With silver taper's light, and pious care, 195
She turned, and down the agèd gossip led
To a safe level matting. Now prepare,
Young Porphyro, for gazing on that bed;
She comes, she comes again, like ring-dove
    frayed and fled.

Out went the taper as she hurried in;   200
Its little smoke, in pallid moonshine, died:
She closed the door, she panted, all akin
To spirits of the air, and visions wide!
No uttered syllable, or, woe betide!
But to her heart, her heart was voluble, 205
Paining with eloquence her balmy side;
As though a tongueless nightingale should
    swell
Her throat in vain, and die, heart-stifled, in
    her dell.

A casement high and triple arched there
    was,
All garlanded with carven imag'ries   210

Of fruits, and flowers, and bunches of knot-
    grass.
And diamonded with panes of quaint device,
Innumerable of stains and splendid dyes,
As are the tiger-mouth's deep-damasked
    wings;
And in the midst, 'mong thousand herald-
    ries,   215
And twilight saints, and dim emblazonings,
A shielded scutcheon blushed with blood of
    queens and kings.

Full on this casement shone the wintry
    moon,
And threw warm gules on Madeline's fair
    breast,
As down she knelt for **heaven's grace and**
    boon;   220
Rose-bloom fell on her hands, together
    prest,
And on her silver cross soft amethyst,
And on her hair a glory, like a saint:
She seemed a splendid angel, newly drest,
Save wings, for heaven: Porphyro grew
    faint: 225
She knelt, so pure a thing, so free from
    mortal taint.

Anon his heart revives: her vespers done,
Of all its wreathèd pearls her hair she frees;
Unclasps her warmèd jewels one by one;
Loosens her fragrant bodice; by degrees 230
Her rich attire creeps rustling to her knees;
Half-hidden, like a mermaid in seaweed,
Pensive awhile she dreams awake, and sees,
In fancy, fair St. Agnes in her bed,
But dares not look behind, or all the charm
    is fled.   235

Soon, trembling in her soft and chilly nest,
In sort of wakeful swoon, perplexed she
    lay.
Until the poppied warmth of sleep op-
    pressed
Her soothèd limbs, and soul fatigued away;
Flown, like a thought, until the morrow-
    day;   240
Blissfully havened both from joy and pain;
Clasped like a missal where swart Paynims
    pray;
Blinded alike from sunshine and from rain,
As though a rose should shut, and be a bud
    again.

Stolen to this paradise, and so entranced, 245
Porphyro gazed upon her empty dress.

And listened to her breathing, if it chanced
To wake into a slumberous tenderness;
Which when he heard, that minute did he
  bless,
And breathed himself: then from the closet
  crept,　　　　　250
Noiseless as fear in a wide wilderness,
And over the hushed carpet, silent, stepped,
And 'tween the curtains peeped, where, lo!
  — how fast she slept.

Then by the bed-side, where the faded moon
Made a dim, silver twilight, soft he set　　255
A table, and, half-anguished, threw thereon
A cloth of woven crimson, gold, and jet: —
O for some drowsy Morphean amulet!
The boisterous, midnight, festive clarion,
The kettle-drum, and far-heard clarionet,　260
Affray his ears, though but in dying tone: —
The hall door shuts again, and all the noise
  is gone.

And still she slept an azure-lidded sleep,
In blanchèd linen, smooth, and lavendered,
While he from forth the closet brought a
  heap　　　　　265
Of candied apple, quince, and plum, and
  gourd;
With jellies soother than the creamy curd.
And lucent syrops, tinct with cinnamon;
Manna and dates, in argosy transferred
From Fez; and spicèd dainties, every one,　270
From silken Samarcand to cedared Lebanon.

These delicates he heaped with glowing hand
On golden dishes and in baskets bright
Of wreathèd silver: sumptuous they stand
In the retired quiet of the night,　　　275
Filling the chilly room with perfume light.—
'And now, my love, my seraph fair, awake!
Thou art my heaven, and I thine eremite:
Open thine eyes, for meek St. Agnes' sake,
Or I shall drowse beside thee, so my soul
  doth ache.'　　　　　280

Thus whispering, his warm, unnervèd arm
Sank in her pillow. Shaded was her dream
By the dusk curtains: — 'twas a midnight
  charm
Impossible to melt as icèd stream:
The lustrous salvers in the moonlight
  gleam:　　　　　285
Broad golden fringe upon the carpet lies:
It seemed he never, never could redeem
From such a stedfast spell his lady's eyes;
So mused awhile, entoiled in woofèd phan-
  tasies.

Awakening up, he took her hollow lute,—
Tumultuous,— and, in chords that tenderest
  be,　　　　　291
He played an ancient ditty, long since mute.
In Provence called, 'La belle dame sans
  mercy:'
Close to her ear touching the melody; —
Wherewith disturbed, she uttered a soft
  moan:　　　　　295
He ceased — she panted quick — and sud-
  denly
Her blue affrayèd eyes wide open shone:
Upon his knees he sank, pale as smooth-
  sculptured stone.

Her eyes were open, but she still beheld,
Now wide awake, the vision of her sleep: 300
There was a painful change, that nigh ex-
  pelled
The blisses of her dream so pure and deep
At which fair Madeline began to weep,
And moan forth witless words with many a
  sigh;
While still her gaze on Porphyro would
  keep;　　　　　305
Who knelt, with joinèd hands and piteous
  eye,
Fearing to move or speak, she looked so
  dreamingly.

'Ah, Porphyro!' said she, 'but even now
Thy voice was at sweet tremble in mine ear,
Made tuneable with every sweetest vow; 310
And those sad eyes were spiritual and clear:
How changed thou art! how pallid, chill,
  and drear!
Give me that voice again, my Porphyro,
Those looks immortal, those complainings
  dear!
Oh, leave me not in this eternal woe,　　315
For if thou diest, my Love, I know not
  where to go.'

Beyond a mortal man impassioned far
At these voluptuous accents, he arose,
Ethereal, flushed, and like a throbbing star
Seen mid the sapphire heaven's deep re-
  pose;　　　　　320
Into her dream he melted, as the rose
Blendeth its odor with the violet,—
Solution sweet: meantime the frost wind
  blows
Like Love's alarum pattering the sharp sleet
Against the window-panes; St. Agnes' moon
  hath set.　　　　　325

'T is dark; quick pattereth the flaw-blown
  sleet:

'This is no dream, my bride, my Madeline!'
'T is dark: the icèd gusts still rave and
   beat:
'No dream, alas! alas! and woe is mine!
Porphyro will leave me here to fade and
   pine.—   330
Cruel! what traitor could thee hither bring?
I curse not, for my heart is lost in thine,
Though thou forsakest a deceivèd thing;—
A dove forlorn and lost with sick unprunèd
   wing.'

'My Madeline! sweet dreamer! lovely
   bride!   335
Say, may I be for aye thy vassal blest?
Thy beauty's shield, heart-shaped and ver-
   meil dyed?
Ah, silver shrine, here will I take my rest
After so many hours of toil and quest,
A famished pilgrim,— saved by a miracle.
Though I have found, I will not rob thy
   nest   341
Saving of thy sweet self; if thou think'st
   well
To trust, fair Madeline, to no rude infidel.

'Hark! 'tis an elfin-storm from faery
   land,
Of haggard seeming, but a boon indeed: 345
Arise — arise! the morning is at hand;—
The bloated wassailers will never heed:—
Let us away, my love, with happy speed;—
There are no ears to hear, or eyes to see,—
Drowned all in Rhenish and the sleepy
   mead;   350
Awake! arise! my love, and fearless be,
For o'er the southern moors I have a home
   for thee.'

She hurried at his words, beset with fears,
For there were sleeping dragons all around,
At glaring watch, perhaps, with ready
   spears —   355
Down the wide stairs a darkling way they
   found.—
In all the house was heard no human sound.
A chain-drooped lamp was flickering by
   each door;
The arras, rich with horseman, hawk, and
   hound,
Fluttered in the besieging wind's uproar; 360
And the long carpets rose along the gusty
   floor.

They glide, like phantoms, into the wide
   hall;
Like phantoms, to the iron porch, they
   glide:

Where lay the Porter, in uneasy sprawl,
With a huge empty flagon by his side: 365
The wakeful bloodhound rose, and shook
   his hide,
But his sagacious eye an inmate owns:
By one, and one, the bolts full easy slide:—
The chains lie silent on the footworn
   stones;—
The key turns, and the door upon its hinges
   groans.   370

And they are gone: ay, ages long ago
These lovers fled away into the storm.
That night the Baron dreamt of many a
   woe,
And all his warrior-guests, with shade and
   form
Of witch, and demon, and large coffin-
   worm,   375
Were long be-nightmared. Angela the old
Died palsy-twitched, with meager face de-
   form;
The Beadsman, after thousand aves told,
For aye unsought for slept among his ashes
   cold.

                    (1820)

ODE

Bards of Passion and of Mirth,
Ye have left your souls on earth!
Have ye souls in heaven too,
Double-lived in regions new?
Yes, and those of heaven commune   5
With the spheres of sun and moon;
With the noise of fountains wond'rous,
And the parle of voices thund'rous;
With the whisper of heaven's trees
And one another, in soft ease   10
Seated on Elysian lawns
Browsed by none but Dian's fawns;
Underneath large blue-bells tented,
Where the daisies are rose-scented,
And the rose herself has got   15
Perfume which on earth is not;
Where the nightingale doth sing
Not a senseless, trancèd thing,
But divine melodious truth;
Philosophic numbers smooth;   20
Tales and golden histories
Of heaven and its mysteries.

Thus ye live on high, and then
On the earth ye live again;
And the souls ye left behind you   25
Teach us, here, the way to find you,
Where your other souls are joying,

Never slumbered, never cloying.
Here, your earth-born souls still speak
To mortals, of their little week;   30
Of their sorrows and delights;
Of their passions and their spites;
Of their glory and their shame;
What doth strengthen and what maim.
Thus ye teach us, every day,   35
Wisdom, though fled far away.

    Bards of Passion and of Mirth,
Ye have left your souls on earth!
Ye have souls in heaven too,
Double-lived in regions new!   40
              (1820)

ROBIN HOOD

No! those days are gone away,
And their hours are old and gray,
And their minutes buried all
Under the down-trodden pall
Of the leaves of many years: 5
Many times have winter's shears,
Frozen North, and chilling East,
Sounded tempests to the feast
Of the forest's whispering fleeces.
Since men knew nor rent nor leases.   10

    No, the bugle sounds no more,
And the twanging bow no more;
Silent is the ivory shrill
Past the heath and up the hill;
There is no mid-forest laugh,   15
Where lone Echo gives the half
To some wight, amazed to hear
Jesting, deep in forest drear.

    On the fairest time of June
You may go, with sun or moon,   20
Or the seven stars to light you,
Or the polar ray to right you;
But you never may behold
Little John, or Robin bold;
Never one, of all the clan,
Thrumming on an empty can
Some old hunting ditty, while
He doth his green way beguile
To fair hostess Merriment,
Down beside the pasture Trent;   30
For he left the merry tale
Messenger for spicy ale.

    Gone, the merry morris din;
Gone, the song of Gamelyn;
Gone, the tough-belted outlaw   35
Idling in the 'grene shawe;'
All are gone away and past!

And if Robin should be cast
Sudden from his turfèd grave,
And if Marian should have   40
Once again her forest days,
She would weep, and he would craze:
He would swear, for all his oaks,
Fallen beneath the dockyard strokes,
Have rotted on the briny seas;   45
She would weep that her wild bees
Sang not to her — strange! that honey
Can't be got without hard money!

    So it is: yet let us sing,
Honor to the old bow-string!   50
Honor to the bugle-horn!
Honor to the woods unshorn!
Honor to the Lincoln green!
Honor to the archer keen!
Honor to tight Little John,   55
And the horse he rode upon!
Honor to bold Robin Hood,
Sleeping in the underwood!
Honor to Maid Marian,
And to all the Sherwood-clan!   60
Though their days have hurried by,
Let us two a burden try.
              (1820)

LINES ON THE MERMAID TAVERN

    Souls of Poets dead and gone,
What Elysium have ye known,
Happy field or mossy cavern,
Choicer than the Mermaid Tavern?
Have ye tippled drink more fine   5
Than mine host's Canary wine?
Or are fruits of Paradise
Sweeter than those dainty pies
Of venison? O generous food!
Drest as though bold Robin Hood   10
Would, with his maid Marian,
Sup and bowse from horn and can.

    I have heard that on a day
Mine host's sign-board flew away,
Nobody knew whither, till   15
An astrologer's old quill
To a sheepskin gave the story,
Said he saw you in your glory,
Underneath a new old-sign
Sipping beverage divine,   20
And pledging with contented smack
The Mermaid in the Zodiac.

    Souls of Poets dead and gone,
What Elysium have ye known,
Happy field or mossy cavern,   25
Choicer than the Mermaid Tavern?
              (1820)

ODE ON A GRECIAN URN

Thou still unravished bride of quietness,
  Thou foster-child of silence and slow time,
Sylvan historian, who canst thus express
  A flowery tale more sweetly than our rhyme:
What leaf-fringed legend haunts about thy shape 5
  Of deities or mortals, or of both,
    In Tempe or the dales of Arcady?
What men or gods are these? What maidens loth?
What mad pursuit? What struggle to escape?
  What pipes and timbrels? What wild ecstasy? 10

Heard melodies are sweet, but those unheard
  Are sweeter; therefore, ye soft pipes, play on;
Not to the sensual ear, but, more endeared,
  Pipe to the spirit ditties of no tone:
Fair youth, beneath the trees, thou canst not leave 15
  Thy song, nor ever can those trees be bare;
    Bold Lover, never, never canst thou kiss
Though winning near the goal — yet, do not grieve;
  She cannot fade, though thou hast not thy bliss,
    For ever wilt thou love, and she be fair! 20

Ah, happy, happy boughs! that cannot shed
  Your leaves, nor ever bid the Spring adieu;
And, happy melodist, unwearièd,
  For ever piping songs for ever new;
More happy love! more happy, happy love!
  For ever warm and still to be enjoyed, 26
  For ever panting, and for ever young;
All breathing human passion far above,
  That leaves a heart high-sorrowful and cloyed,
    A burning forehead, and a parching tongue. 30

Who are these coming to the sacrifice?
  To what green altar, O mysterious priest,
Lead'st thou that heifer lowing at the skies,
  And all her silken flanks with garlands dressed?

What little town by river or sea shore, 35
  Or mountain-built with peaceful citadel,
    Is emptied of this folk, this pious morn?
And, little town, thy streets for evermore
  Will silent be; and not a soul to tell
    Why thou art desolate, can e'er return. 40

O Attic shape! Fair attitude! with brede
  Of marble men and maidens over wrought,
With forest branches and the trodden weed;
  Thou, silent form, dost tease us out of thought
As doth eternity: Cold Pastoral! 45
  When old age shall this generation waste,
    Thou shalt remain, in midst of other woe
Than ours, a friend to man, to whom thou say'st,
  'Beauty is truth, truth beauty,'—that is all
    Ye know on earth, and all ye need to know. 50

(1820)

ODE TO A NIGHTINGALE

My heart aches, and a drowsy numbness pains
  My sense, as though of hemlock I had drunk,
Or emptied some dull opiate to the drains
  One minute past, and Lethe-wards had sunk:
'T is not through envy of thy happy lot, 5
  But being too happy in thine happiness,—
    That thou, light wingèd Dryad of the trees,
      In some melodious plot
Of beechen green, and shadows numberless,
  Singest of summer in full-throated ease. 10

O for a draught of vintage! that hath been
Cooled a long age in the deep-delved earth,
Tasting of Flora and the country green,
  Dance, and Provençal song, and sunburnt mirth!
O for a beaker full of the warm South, 15
  Full of the true, the blushful Hippocrene,
    With beaded bubbles winking at the brim,
      And purple-stainèd mouth;

That I might drink, and leave the world
    unseen,
  And with thee fade away into the for-
    est dim: 20

Fade far away, dissolve, and quite forget
  What thou among the leaves hast never
    known,
The weariness, the fever, and the fret
  Here, where men sit and hear each other
    groan;
Where palsy shakes a few, sad, last gray
    hairs,   25
  Where youth grows pale, and specter-thin,
    and dies;
    Where but to think is to be full of sor-
      row
      And leaden-eyed despairs,
  Where Beauty cannot keep her lustrous
    eyes,
    Or new Love pine at them beyond to-
      morrow.   30

Away! away! for I will fly to thee,
  Not charioted by Bacchus and his pards,
But on the viewless wings of Poesy,
  Though the dull brain perplexes and re-
    tards:
Already with thee! tender is the night,   35
  And haply the Queen-Moon is on her
    throne,
  Clustered around by all her starry Fays;
    But here there is no light,
  Save what from heaven is with the
    breezes blown
    Through verdurous glooms and winding
    mossy ways.   40

I cannot see what flowers are at my feet,
  Nor what soft incense hangs upon the
    boughs,
But, in embalmed darkness, guess each sweet
  Wherewith the seasonable month endows
The grass, the thicket, and the fruit-tree
  wild;   45
  White hawthorn, and the pastoral eglan-
    tine;
    Fast fading violets covered up in
      leaves;
      And mid-May's eldest child,
  The coming musk-rose, full of dewy wine,
  The murmurous haunt of flies on sum-
    mer eves.   50

Darkling I listen; and, for many a time
  I have been half in love with easeful
    Death,

Called him soft names in many a musèd
    rime,
  To take into the air my quiet breath;
Now more than ever seems it rich to die, 55
  To cease upon the midnight with no pain,
    While thou art pouring forth thy soul
    abroad
        In such an ecstasy!
  Still wouldst thou sing, and I have ears in
    vain—
    To thy high requiem become a sod.

Thou wast not born for death, immortal
    Bird!   61
  No hungry generations tread thee down:
  The voice I hear this passing night was
    heard
  In ancient days by emperor and clown:
Perhaps the self-same song that found a
    path   65
  Through the sad heart of Ruth, when, sick
    for home,
    She stood in tears amid the alien corn:
      The same that oft-times hath
Charmed magic casements, opening on the
    foam
    Of perilous seas, in faery lands forlorn.

Forlorn! the very word is like a bell   71
  To toll me back from thee to my sole
    self!
Adieu! the fancy cannot cheat so well
  As she is famed to do, deceiving elf,
Adieu! adieu! thy plaintive anthem fades
  Past the near meadows, over the still
    stream,
    Up the hill-side; and now 't is buried
    deep
      In the next valley-glades:
  Was it a vision, or a waking dream?
    Fled is that music:—Do I wake or
    sleep?   80

                    (1819)

ODE ON MELANCHOLY

No, no, go not to Lethe, neither twist
  Wolf's-bane, tight-rooted, for its poison-
    ous wine;
Nor suffer thy pale forehead to be kissed
  By nightshade, ruby grape of Proserpine;
Make not your rosary of yew-berries,   5
  Nor let the beetle, nor the death-moth
    be
    Your mournful Psyche, nor the downy
      owl
A partner in your sorrow's mysteries;

For shade to shade will come too
    drowsily,
    And drown the wakeful anguish of the
        soul.   10

But when the melancholy fit shall fall
    Sudden from heaven like a weeping
        cloud,
That fosters the droop-headed flowers all,
    And hides the green hill in an April
        shroud:
Then glut thy sorrow on a morning rose,
    Or on the rainbow of a salt sandwave,
    Or on the wealth of globèd peonies;
Or if thy mistress some rich anger shows,
    Emprison her soft hand, and let her rave,
    And feed deep, deep upon her peerless
        eyes.   20

She dwells with Beauty — Beauty that
    must die;
    And Joy, whose hand is ever at his lips
Bidding adieu; and aching Pleasure nigh,
    Turning to poison while the bee-mouth
        sips:
Ay, in the very temple of Delight   25
    Veiled Melancholy has her sovran shrine,
        Though seen of none save him whose
            strenuous tongue
Can burst Joy's grape against his palate
    fine;
    His soul shall taste the sadness of her
        might,
    And be among her cloudy trophies
        hung.   30
                                    (1820)

TO AUTUMN

Season of mists and mellow fruitfulness,
    Close bosom friend of the maturing sun:
Conspiring with him how to load and bless
    With fruit the vines that round the
        thatch-eves run;
To bend with apples the mossed cottage-
    trees,   5
    And fill all fruit with ripeness to the core;
    To swell the gourd, and plump the hazel
        shells
With a sweet kernel; to set budding more,
    And still more, later flowers for the bees,
    Until they think warm days will never
        cease,   10
        For Summer has o'er-brimmed their
            clammy cells.

Who hath not seen thee oft amid thy store?
    Sometimes whoever seeks abroad may
        find

Thee sitting careless on a granary floor,
    Thy hair soft-lifted by the winnowing
        wind;   16
Or on a half-reaped furrow sound asleep,
    Drowsed with the fume of poppies, while
        thy hook
    Spares the next swath and all its
        twinèd flowers:
And sometimes like a gleaner thou dost
    keep,   20
    Steady thy laden head across a brook;
    Or by a cider-press, with patient look,
        Thou watchest the last oozings hours
            by hours.

Where are the songs of Spring? Ay, where
    are they?
    Think not of them, thou hast thy music
        too,—   25
While barrèd clouds bloom the soft-dying
    day,
    And touch the stubble-plains with rosy
        hue;
Then in a wailful choir the small gnats
    mourn
    Among the river sallows, borne aloft
        Or sinking as the light wind lives or
            dies;   30
And full-grown lambs loud bleat from hilly
    bourn;
    Hedge-crickets sing: and now with treble
        soft
    The red-breast whistles from a garden-
        croft;
        And gathering swallows twitter in the
            skies.   (1820)

HYPERION

A FRAGMENT

BOOK I

Deep in the shady sadness of a vale
Far sunken from the healthy breath of
    morn,
Far from the fiery noon, and eve's one
    star,
Sat gray-haired Saturn, quiet as a stone,
Still as the silence round about his lair;
Forest on forest hung about his head   6
Like cloud on cloud. No stir of air was
    there,
Not so much life as on a summer's day
Robs not one light seed from the feathered
    grass,
But where the dead leaf fell, there did it
    rest.   10

A stream went voiceless by, still deadened
    more
By reason of his fallen divinity
Spreading a shàde: the Naiad 'mid her
    reeds
Pressed her cold finger closer to her lips.

Along the margin-sand large footmarks
    went,   15
No further than to where his feet had
    strayed
And slept there since. Upon the sodden
    ground
His old right hand lay nerveless, listless,
    dead,
Unsceptered; and his realmless eyes were
    closed;
While his bowed head seemed list'ning to
    the Earth,   20
His ancient mother, for some comfort yet.

It seemed no force could wake him from
    his place;
But there came one, who with a kindred
    hand
Touched his wide shoulders, after bending
    low
With reverence, though to one who knew it
    not.   25
She was a Goddess of the infant world;
By her in stature the tall Amazon
Had stood a pigmy's height: she would
    have ta'en
Achilles by the hair and bent his neck;
Or with a finger stayed Ixion's wheel. 30
Her face was large as that of Memphian
    sphinx,
Pedestaled haply in a palace court,
When sages looked to Egypt for their lore.
But oh! how unlike marble was that face:
How beautiful, if sorrow had not made 35
Sorrow more beautiful than Beauty's self.
There was a listening fear in her regard,
As if calamity had but begun:
As if the vanward clouds of evil days
Had spent their malice, and the sullen
    rear   40
Was with its storèd thunder laboring up.
One hand she pressed upon that aching spot
Where beats the human heart, as if just
    there,
Though an immortal, she felt cruel pain;
The other upon Saturn's bended neck 45
She laid, and to the level of his ear
Leaning with parted lips, some words she
    spake
In solemn tenor and deep organ tone:

Some mourning words, which in our feeble
    tongue
Would come in these like accents; O how
    frail   50
To that large utterance of the early Gods!
'Saturn, look up! — though wherefore, poor
    old King?
I have no comfort for thee, no, not one:
I cannot say, "O wherefore sleepest thou?"
For heaven is parted from thee, and the
    earth   55
Knows thee not, thus afflicted, for a God;
And ocean too, with all its solemn noise,
Has from thy scepter passed; and all the
    air
Is emptied of thine hoary majesty.
Thy thunder, conscious of the new com-
    mand,   60
Rumbles reluctant o'er our fallen house;
And thy sharp lightning in unpractised
    hands
Scorches and burns our once serene do-
    main.
O aching time! O moments big as years!
All as ye pass swell out the monstrous
    truth,   65
And press it so upon our weary griefs
That unbelief has not a space to breathe.
Saturn, sleep on: — O thoughtless, why did
    I
Thus violate thy slumbrous solitude?
Why should I ope thy melancholy eyes? 70
Saturn, sleep on! while at thy feet I weep.'

As when, upon a trancèd summer night,
Those green-robed senators of mighty
    woods,
Tall oaks, branch-charmèd by the earnest
    stars,
Dream, and so dream all night without a
    stir,   75
Save from one gradual solitary gust
Which comes upon the silence, and dies
    off,
As if the ebbing air had but one wave;
So came these words and went; the while
    in tears
She touched her fair large forehead to the
    ground,   80
Just where her falling hair might be out-
    spread
A soft and silken mat for Saturn's feet.
One moon, with alteration slow, had shed
Her silver seasons four upon the night,
And still these two were postured motion-
    less,   85
Like natural sculpture in cathedral cavern;

The frozen God still couchant on · the
    earth,
And the sad Goddess weeping at his feet:
Until at length old Saturn lifted up   89
His faded eyes, and saw his kingdom gone,
And all the gloom and sorrow of the place,
And that fair kneeling Goddess; and then
    spake,
As with a palsied tongue, and while his
    beard
Shook horrid with such aspen-malady:
'O tender spouse of gold Hyperion,   95
Thea, I feel thee ere I see thy face;
Look up, and let me see our doom in it;
Look up, and tell me if this feeble shape
Is Saturn's; tell me, if thou hear'st the
    voice   99
Of Saturn; tell me, if this wrinkling brow,
Naked and bare of its great diadem,
Peers like the front of Saturn. Who had
    power
To make me desolate? whence came the
    strength?
How was it nurtured to such bursting
    forth,
While Fate seemed strangled in my
    nervous grasp?   105
But it is so; and I am smothered up,
And buried from all godlike exercise
Of influence benign on planets pale,
Of admonitions to the winds, and seas,   109
Of peaceful sway above man's harvesting,
And all those acts which Deity supreme
Doth ease its heart of love in.— I am gone
Away from my own bosom: I have left
My strong identity, my real self,   115
Somewhere between the throne, and where
    I sit   115
Here on this spot of earth. Search, Thea,
    search!
Open thine eyes eterne, and sphere them
    round
Upon all space: space starred, and lorn of
    light;   ·
Space regioned with life-air; and barren
    void;   119
Spaces of fire, and all the yawn of hell.—
Search, Thea, search! and tell me, if thou
    seest
A certain shape or shadow, making way
With wings or chariot fierce to repossess
A heaven he lost erewhile: it must — it
    must
Be of ripe progress — Saturn must be
    King,   125
Yes, there must be a golden victory;
There must be Gods thrown down, and
    trumpets blown

Of triumph calm, and hymns of festival
Upon the gold clouds metropolitan,
Voices of soft proclaim, and silver stir   130
Of strings in hollow shells; and there
    shall be
Beautiful things made new, for the surprise
Of the sky-children; I will give com-
    mand:
Thea! Thea! Thea! where is Saturn?'   134

    This passion lifted him upon his feet,
And made his hands to struggle in the air,
His Druid locks to shake and ooze with
    sweat,
His eyes to fever out, his voice to cease.
He stood, and heard not Thea's sobbing
    deep;   139
A little time, and then again he snatched
Utterance thus.— 'But cannot I create?
Cannot I form? Cannot I fashion forth
Another world, another universe,
To overbear and crumble this to nought?
Where is another chaos? Where?'— That
    word   145
Found way unto Olympus, and made quake
The rebel three.— Thea was startled up,
And in her bearing was a sort of hope,
As thus she quick-voiced spake, yet full of
    awe.

'This cheers our fallen house: come to
    our friends,   150
O Saturn! come away, and give them heart:
I know the covert, for thence came I
    hither.'
Thus brief; then with beseeching eyes she
    went
With backward footing through the shade
    a space:
He followed, and she turned to lead the
    way   155
Through agèd boughs, that yielded like the
    mist
Which eagles cleave upmounting from their
    nest.

    Meanwhile in other realms big tears were
    shed,
More sorrow like to this, and such like woe,
Too huge for mortal tongue or pen of
    scribe;   160
The Titans fierce, self-hid, or prison-bound,
Groaned for the old allegiance once more,
And listened in sharp pain for Saturn's
    voice.
But one of the whole mammoth-brood still
    kept   164
His sov'reignty, and rule, and majesty;—

Blazing Hyperion on his orbèd fire
Still sat, still snuff'd the incense, teeming up
From man to the sun's God; yet un-
　　secure:
For as among us mortals omens drear　169
Fright and perplex, so also shuddered he —
Not at dog's howl, or gloom-bird's hated
　　screech,
Or the familiar visiting of one
Upon the first toll of his passing-bell,
Or prophesyings of the midnight lamp;　174
But horrors, portioned to a giant nerve,
Oft made Hyperion ache. His palace
　　bright
Bastioned with pyramids of glowing gold,
And touched with shade of bronzèd obe-
　　lisks,
Glared a blood-red through all its thou-
　　sand courts,
Arches, and domes, and fiery galleries;　180
And all its curtains of Aurorian clouds
Flushed angerly: while sometimes eagle's
　　wings,
Unseen before by Gods or wondering men,
Darkened the place; and neighing steeds
　　were heard,
Not heard before by Gods or wondering
　　men.　185
Also, when he would taste the spicy wreaths
Of incense, breathed aloft from sacred
　　hills,
Instead of sweets, his ample palate took
Savor of poisonous brass and metal sick:
And so, when harbored in the sleepy
　　west,　190
After the full completion of fair day,—
For rest divine upon exalted couch
And slumber in the arms of melody,
He paced away the pleasant hours of ease
With stride colossal, on from hall to hall;
While far within each aisle and deep re-
　　cess,　196
His wingèd minions in close clusters stood,
Amazed and full of fear; like anxious men
Who on wide plains gather in panting troops,
When earthquakes jar their battlements and
　　towers.　200
Even now, while Saturn, roused from icy
　　trance,
Went step for step with Thea through the
　　woods,
Hyperion, leaving twilight in the rear,
Came slope upon the threshold of the west;
Then, as was wont, his palace-door flew
　　ope　205
In smoothest silence, save what solemn
　　tubes,

Blown by the serious Zephyrs, gave of
　　sweet
And wandering sounds, slow-breathèd melo-
　　dies;
And like a rose in vermeil tint and shape,
In fragrance soft, and coolness to the eye,
That inlet to severe magnificence　211
Stood full blown, for the God to enter in.

He entered, but he entered full of wrath;
His flaming robes streamed out beyond his
　　heels,
And gave a roar, as if of earthly fire,　215
That scared away the meek ethereal Hours
And made their dove-wings tremble. On
　　he flared,
From stately nave to nave, from vault to
　　vault,
Through bowers of fragrant and enwreathèd
　　light,　219
And diamond-pavèd lustrous long arcades,
Until he reached the great main cupola;
There standing fierce beneath, he stamped
　　his foot,
And from the basements deep to the high
　　towers
Jarred his own golden region; and before
The quavering thunder thereupon had
　　ceased,　225
His voice leapt out, despite of godlike curb,
To this result: 'O dreams of day and
　　night!
O monstrous forms! O effigies of pain!
O specters busy in a cold, cold gloom!
O lank-eared Phantoms of black-weeded
　　pools!　230
Why do I know ye? why have I seen ye?
　　why
Is my eternal essence thus distraught
To see and to behold these horrors new?
Saturn is fallen, am I too to fall?　234
Am I to leave this haven of my rest,
This cradle of my glory, this soft clime,
This calm · luxuriance of blissful light,
These crystalline pavilions, and pure fanes,
Of all my lucent empire? It is left
Deserted, void, nor any haunt of mine.　240
The blaze, the splendor, and the symmetry,
I cannot see — but darkness, death and dark-
　　ness.
Even here, into my center of repose,
The shady visions come to domineer,　244
Insult, and blind, and stifle up my pomp.—
Fall! — No, by Tellus and her briny robes!
Over the fiery frontier of my realms
I will advance a terrible right arm,　248
Shall scare that infant thunderer, rebel Jove.

And bid old Saturn take his throne again.'—
He spake and ceased, the while a heavier threat
Held struggle with his throat but came not forth:
For as in theaters of crowded men   253
Hubbub increases more they call out 'Hush!'
So at Hyperion's words the Phantoms pale
Bestirred themselves, thrice horrible and cold;
And from the mirrored level where he stood
A mist arose, as from a scummy marsh.
At this, through all his bulk an agony
Crept gradual, from the feet unto the crown,   260
Like a lithe serpent vast and muscular
Making slow way, with head and neck convulsed
From over-strainèd might. Released, he fled
To the eastern gates, and full six dewy hours   264
Before the dawn in season due should blush,
He breathed fierce breath against the sleepy portals,
Cleared them of heavy vapors, burst them wide
Suddenly on the ocean's chilly streams.
The planet orb of fire, whereon he rode
Each day from east to west the heavens through,   270
Spun round in sable curtaining of clouds;
Not therefore veilèd quite, blindfold, and hid,
But ever and anon the glancing spheres,
Circles, and arcs, and broad-belting colure,
Glowed through, and wrought upon the muffling dark   275
Sweet-shapèd lightnings from the nadir deep
Up to the Zenith,— hieroglyphics old,
Which sages and keen-eyed astrologers
Then living on the earth, with laboring thought
Won from the gaze of many centuries: 280
Now lost, save what we find in remnants huge
Of stone, or marble swart; their import gone,
Their wisdom long since fled. Two wings this orb
Possessed for glory, two fair argent wings,
Ever exalted at the God's approach: 285
And now, from forth the gloom their plumes immense
Rose, one by one, till all outspreaded were;
While still the dazzling globe maintained eclipse,
Awaiting for Hyperion's command.

Fain would he have commanded, fain took throne   290
And bid the day begin, if but for change.
He might not:— No, though a primeval God:
The sacred seasons might not be disturbed.
Therefore the operations of the dawn
Stayed in their birth, even as here 't is told.
Those silver wings expanded sisterly,   296
Eager to sail their orb; the porches wide
Opened upon the dusk demesnes of night;
And the bright Titan, phrenzied with new woes,
Unused to bend, by hard compulsion bent
His spirit to the sorrow of the time; 301
And all along a dismal rack of clouds,
Upon the boundaries of day and night,
He stretched himself in grief and radiance faint.
There as he lay, the Heaven with its stars
Looked down on him with pity, and the voice   306
Of Cœlus, from the universal space,
Thus whispered low and solemn in his ear.
'O brightest of my children dear, earth-born
And sky-engendered, Son of Mysteries 310
All unrevealèd even to the powers
Which met at thy creating; at whose joy
And palpitations sweet, and pleasures soft,
I, Cœlus, wonder, how they came and whence;
And at the fruits thereof what shapes they be,   315
Distinct, and visible; symbols divine,
Manifestations of that beauteous life
Diffused unseen throughout eternal space;
Of these new-formed art thou, oh brightest child!   319
Of these, thy brethren and the Goddesses!
There is sad feud among ye, and rebellion
Of son against his sire. I saw him fall,
I saw my first-born tumbled from his throne!
To me his arms were spread, to me his voice
Found way from forth the thunders round his head!   325
Pale wox I and in vapors hid my face.
Art thou, too, near such doom? vague fear there is:
For I have seen my sons most unlike Gods.
Divine ye were created, and divine
In sad demeanor, solemn, undisturbed, 330
Unruffled like high Gods, ye lived and ruled:
Now I behold in you fear, hope, and wrath;
Actions of rage and passion; even as
I see them, on the mortal world beneath,
In men who die.— This is the grief, O Son!

Sad sign of ruin, sudden dismay, and fall!
Yet do thou strive; as thou art capable,
As thou canst move about, an evident God;
And canst oppose to each malignant hour
Ethereal presence:— I am but a voice;   340
My life is but the life of winds and tides,
No more than winds and tides can I
     avail:—
But thou canst.— Be thou therefore in the
     van
Of circumstance; yea, seize the arrow's barb
Before the tense string murmur.— To the
     earth!   345
For there thou wilt find Saturn, and his
     woes.
Meantime I will keep watch on thy bright
     sun,
And of thy seasons be a careful nurse.'—
Ere half this region-whisper had come
     down,
Hyperion arose, and on the stars   350
Lifted his curvèd lids, and kept them wide
Until it ceased; and still he kept them wide:
And still they were the same bright, patient
     stars.
Then with a slow incline of his broad
     breast,
Like to a diver in the pearly seas,   355
Forward he stooped over the airy shore,
And plunged all noiseless into the deep
     night.

               (1820)

IN A DREAR-NIGHTED DECEMBER

In a drear-nighted December,
Too happy, happy tree,
Thy branches ne'er remember
Their green felicity:
The north cannot undo them,   5
With a sleety whistle through them;
Nor frozen thawings glue them
From budding at the prime.

In a drear-nighted December,
Too happy, happy brook,   10
Thy bubblings ne'er remember
Apollo's summer look;
But with a sweet forgetting,
They stay their crystal fretting,
Never, never petting   15
About the frozen time.

Ah! would 't were so with many
A gentle girl and boy!
But were there ever any
Writhed not at passèd joy   20

To know the change and feel it,
When there is none to heal it,
Nor numbèd sense to steal it,
Was never said in rime.

               (1829)

LA BELLE DAME SANS MERCI

BALLAD

O what can ail thee, knight-at-arms!
   Alone and palely loitering!
The sedge has withered from the lake,
   And no birds sing.

O what can ail thee, knight-at-arms!   5
   So haggard and so woe-begone?
The squirrel's granary is full,
   And the harvest's done.

I see a lily on thy brow
   With anguish moist and fever dew,   10
And on thy cheeks a fading rose
   Fast withereth too.

I met a lady in the meads,
   Full beautiful—a faery's child,
Her hair was long, her foot was light,   15
   And her eyes were wild.

I made a garland for her head,
   And bracelets too, and fragrant zone;
She looked at me as she did love,
   And made sweet moan.   20

I set her on my pacing steed,
   And nothing else saw all day long.
For sidelong would she bend, and sing
   A faery's song.

She found me roots of relish sweet,   25
   And honey wild, and manna dew,
And sure in language strange she said—
   'I love thee true.'

She took me to her elfin grot,
   And there she wept, and sighed full sore,
And there I shut her wild wild eyes   31
   With kisses four.

And there she lullèd me asleep,
   And there I dreamed—Ah! woe betide!
The latest dream I ever dreamed   35
   On the cold hill's side.

I saw pale kings and princes too,
   Pale warriors, death-pale were they all;
They cried—'La Belle Dame sans Merci
   Hath thee in thrall!'   40

I saw their starved lips in the gloam,
  With horrid warning gapèd wide,
And I awoke and found me here,
  On the cold hill's side.

And this is why I sojourn here,   45
  Alone and palely loitering,
Though the sedge is withered from the lake
  And no birds sing.

                              (1820)

ON SEEING THE ELGIN MARBLES

My spirit is too weak — mortality
Weighs heavily on me like unwilling sleep,
And each imagined pinnacle and steep
Of godlike hardship tells me I must die
Like a sick Eagle looking at the sky.   5
Yet 't is a gentle luxury to weep
That I have not the cloudy winds to keep,
Fresh for the opening of the morning's eye.
Such dim-conceivèd glories of the brain
Bring round the heart an undescribable
  feud;   10
So do these wonders a most dizzy pain,
That mingles Grecian grandeur with the
  rude
Wasting of old Time — with a billowy
  main —
A sun — a shadow of a magnitude.
                              (1817)

ON THE SEA

It keeps eternal whisperings around
Desolate shores, and with its mighty swell
Gluts twice ten thousand caverns, till the
  spell
Of Hecate leaves them their old shadowy
  sound.
Often 't is in such gentle temper found,   5
That scarcely will the very smallest shell
Be moved for days from whence it some-
  time fell,
When last the winds of heaven were un-
  bound.
Oh ye! who have your eye-balls vexed and
  tired,
Feast them upon the wideness of the Sea; 10
Oh ye! whose ears are dinned with uproar
  rude,

Or fed too much with cloying melody,—
Sit ye near some old cavern's mouth, and
  brood
Until ye start, as if the sea-nymphs quired!
                              (1848)

WHEN I HAVE FEARS THAT I MAY CEASE TO BE

When I have fears that I may cease to be
Before my pen has gleaned my teeming
  brain,
Before high pilèd books, in charact'ry,
Hold like rich garners the full-ripened
  grain;
When I behold, upon the night's starred
  face,   5
Huge cloudy symbols of a high romance,
And think that I may never live to trace
Their shadows, with the magic hand of
  chance;
And when I feel, fair creature of an
  hour!
That I shall never look upon thee more,   10
Never have relish in the faery power
Of unreflecting love! — then on the shore
Of the wide world I stand alone, and think
Till Love and Fame to nothingness do sink.
                              (1848)

BRIGHT STAR! WOULD I WERE STEADFAST AS THOU ART

Bright star! would I were steadfast as thou
  art —
Not in lone splendor hung aloft the night,
And watching, with eternal lids apart,
Like Nature's patient sleepless Eremite,
The moving waters at their priestlike task
Of pure ablution round earth's human
  shores,   6
Or gazing on the new soft fallen mask
Of snow upon the mountains and the
  moors —
No — yet still steadfast, still unchangeable,
Pillowed upon my fair love's ripening breast,
To feel for ever its soft fall and swell,   11
Awake for ever in a sweet unrest,
Still, still to hear her tender-taken breath,
And so live ever — or else swoon to death.
                              (1848)

NINETEENTH CENTURY LYRICS

For lyric excellence the period of nearly one hundred years between *Lyrical Ballads* (1798) and Tennyson's *Crossing the Bar* (1889) was as eminent as any in our history. Much of this excellence lies in the work of the greater poets, all of whom, from Wordsworth to Tennyson, Browning and Swinburne, will perhaps live to after times for their short flights of song, elegy, idyl, or dramatic monologue rather than by virtue of their more ambitious work. Men of less notable power than the very greatest must particularly depend, for 'a perpetuity of fame,' upon those brief pieces or passages where their imperfect or less sustained genius gets for a moment a perfect, or happy, or distinctive utterance. Literature would be the poorer without these happier snatches of its less distinguished warblers, and the nineteenth century is peculiarly rich in minor singers of this description. One grace of the minor singer is his frequent recognition of his minority and his contentedness to sing in a light or a minor key, leaving the 'C Major of this life' to his robuster brethren. If he lack this self-denial or wisdom, time will not hesitate to do for him what he fails to do for himself. Thus, while Southey's obese epics are strangling in dust we can still enjoy a ballad or two. Landor, with all his elegance and elevation may prove too great a tax on our patience unless we can select out a few choicely cut 'gems of purest ray,' sparkling with gallantry and gracious sentiment. There may be little hope of pleasure in Campbell's *Pleasures of Hope;* but his battle hymns can still bring a tingle to the blood which has any British infusion. The inimitable joviality of Peacock's songs will tempt some to read them in their setting, his novels. Tom Hood, for his humanitarian sympathy, his tragic insight, and his literary refinement when he throws off his Comic Almanac manner, will interest as long as greater and more fortunate poets. The busiest of us can afford to listen for a moment to the bubbling pastoral music of Barnes, 'the Dorsetshire Burns.' We need not entangle ourselves among the fantastic situations and impossible characters of *Death's Jest Book* in order to feel Beddoes' tuneful diabolism; we get the essence of it in his dirges and night pieces. Not the least interesting phase of nineteenth century poetry is its inclination to plane away the barrier between poetry and prose and approach the natural or easy-going manner of colloquial speech. This careless, 'over the walnuts and the wine' kind of talk had been introduced by Byron into his *Don Juan;* the tone is happily and more innocently hit by Tennyson in *Will Waterproof's Lyrical Monologue;* and is conspicuous in Peacock's songs and in the love poetry of Coventry Patmore. Praed, Thackeray, and Locker-Lampson convey in poetry that nice blending of frivolity, light cynicism, obscured sentiment, and good breeding which characterise the gentle man-of-the-city. In Austin Dobson there is super-added a fragile renaissance of eighteenth century 'teacup times of hood and hoop, Or when the patch was worn.' Most of this poetry is tinged with delicate regret for the fresher, simpler and more heroic times that are gone. The darker and more terrible pessimism which is bred by modern cities found a voice in Thomson's *City of Dreadful Night;* the querulous rebellion of a sensitive but feebler artistic temperament may be heard in the 'Songs' of O'Shaughnessey. Of somewhat more professional scope than any of these were the poems of Mrs. Browning, the most Sapphic of English poetesses; and Miss Rossetti's sad, sweet songs of devotion and renunciation are the best of their kind. The feminine interpretation of love, humanity, and religion found in these two a more adequate expression than elsewhere in English poetry. Finally, the scholarly and sincere, if sometimes harsh, spiritual remonstrances of Arthur Hugh Clough are most worthy to supplement those of Tennyson, Browning and Matthew Arnold.

ROBERT SOUTHEY (1774–1843)

THE BATTLE OF BLENHEIM

It was a summer evening,
Old Kaspar's work was done,

And he before his cottage door
Was sitting in the sun,
And by him sported on the green   5
His little grandchild Wilhelmine.

She saw her brother Peterkin
Roll something large and round,

Which he besiue the rivulet
In playing there had found;   10
He came to ask what he had found,
That was so large, and smooth, and round.

Old Kaspar took it from the boy,
Who stood expectant by;
And then the old man shook his head,   15
And with a natural sigh,
''T is some poor fellow's skull,' said he,
'Who fell in the great victory.

'I find them in the garden,
For there 's many here about;   20
And often when I go to plough,
The ploughshare turns them out!
For many thousand men,' said he,
'Were slain in that great victory.'

'Now tell me what 't was all about,'   25
Young Peterkin, he cries;
And little Wilhelmine looks up
With wonder-waiting eyes;
'Now tell us all about the war,
And what they fought each other for.'   30

'It was the English,' Kaspar cried,
'Who put the French to rout;
But what they fought each other for,
I could not well make out;
But everybody said,' quoth he,   35
'That 't was a famous victory.

'My father lived at Blenheim then,
Yon little stream hard by;
They burnt his dwelling to the ground,
And he was forced to fly;   40
So with his wife and child he fled,
Nor had he where to rest his head.

'With fire and sword the country round
Was wasted far and wide,
And many a childing mother then,   45
And new-born baby died;
But things like that, you know, must be
At every famous victory.

'They say it was a shocking sight
After the field was won;   50
For many thousand bodies here
Lay rotting in the sun;
But things like that, you know, must be
After a famous victory.

'Great praise the Duke of Marlbro' won, 55
And our good Prince Eugene.'
'Why 't was a very wicked thing!'
Said little Wilhelmine.

'Nay, nay, my little girl,' quoth he,
'It was a famous victory.   60

'And everybody praised the Duke
Who this great fight did win.'
'But what good came of it at last?'
Quoth little Peterkin.
'Why that I cannot tell,' said he,   65
'But 't was a famous victory.'

                        (1805)

WALTER SAVAGE LANDOR
(1775–1864)

ROSE AYLMER

Ah, what avails the sceptered race,
Ah, what the form divine!
What every virtue, every grace!
Rose Aylmer, all were thine.
Rose Aylmer, whom these wakeful eyes   5
May weep, but never see,
A night of memories and of sighs
I consecrate to thee.

                        (1806)

MILD IS THE PARTING YEAR

Mild is the parting year, and sweet
The odor of the falling spray;
Life passes on more rudely fleet,
And balmless is its closing day.

I wait its close, I court its gloom,   5
But mourn that never must there fall
Or on my breast or on my tomb
The tear that would have soothed it all.

                        (1831)

PAST RUINED ILION

Past ruined Ilion Helen lives,
Alcestis rises from the shades;
Verse calls them forth; 't is verse that gives
Immortal youth to mortal maids.

Soon shall Oblivion's deepening veil   5
Hide all the peopled hills you see,
The gay, the proud, while lovers hail
These many summers you and me.

                        (1831)

THE DEATH OF ARTEMIDORA

'Artemidora! Gods invisible,
While thou art lying faint along the couch

Have tied the sandal to thy slender feet
And stand beside thee, ready to convey
Thy weary steps where other rivers flow. 5
Refreshing shades will waft thy weariness
Away, and voices like thy own come near
And nearer, and solicit an embrace.'
  Artemidora sighed, and would have
    pressed
The hand now pressing hers, but was too
  weak.   10
Iris stood over her dark hair unseen
While thus Elpenor spake. He looked into
Eyes that had given light and life erewhile
To those above them, but now dim with
  tears
And wakefulness. Again he spake of joy 15
Eternal. At that word, that sad word, *joy,*
Faithful and fond her bosom heaved once
  more:
Her head fell back; and now a loud deep
  sob
Swelled through the darkened chamber;
  't was not hers.
                  (1836)

DIRCE

Stand close around, ye Stygian set,
  With Dirce in one boat conveyed,
Or Charon, seeing, may forget
  That he is old, and she a shade.
                  (1836)

ON LUCRETIA BORGIA'S HAIR

Borgia, thou once wert almost too august
And high for adoration; now thou 'rt dust;
All that remains of thee these plaits un-
  fold,
Calm hair meandering in pellucid gold.
                (1837)

MEMORY AND PRIDE

'Do you remember me? or are you proud?'
Lightly advancing through her star-trimmed
  crowd,
  Ianthe said, and looked into my eyes.
'A *yes,* a *yes,* to both: for Memory
Where you but once have been must ever
  be,   5
  And at your voice Pride from his throne
  must rise.'
                (1846)

THE LOVE OF OTHER YEARS

No, my own love of other years!
  No, it must never be.
Much rests with you that yet endears,
  Alas! but what with me?
Could those bright years o'er me revolve 5
  So gay, o'er you so fair,
The pearl of life we would dissolve
  And each the cup might share.
You show that truth can ne'er decay,
  Whatever fate befalls;   10
I, that the myrtle and the bay
  Shoot fresh on ruined walls.
                (1846)

TO ROBERT BROWNING

There is delight in singing, though none hear
Beside the singer; and there is delight
In praising, tho' the praiser sit alone
And see the praised far off him, far above.
Shakspere is not our poet, but the world's,
Therefore on him no speech! and brief for
  thee,   6
Browning! Since Chaucer was alive and
  hale,
No man hath walked along our roads with
  step
So active, so inquiring eye, or tongue
So varied in discourse. But warmer climes
Give brighter plumage, stronger wing: the
  breeze   11
Of Alpine heights thou playest with, borne
  on
Beyond Sorrento and Amalfi, where
The Siren waits thee, singing song for song
                (1846)

ON TIMELY DEATH

Is it not better at an early hour
  In its calm cell to rest the weary head,
While birds are singing and while blooms
  the bower,
  Than sit the fire out and go starved to
  bed?
                (1846)

TO AGE

Welcome, old friend! These many years
  Have we lived door by door:
The Fates have laid aside their shears
  Perhaps for some few more.

I was indocile at an age   5
  When better boys were taught,
But thou at length hast made me sage,
  If I am sage in aught.

Little I know from other men,
  Too little they from me,   10
But thou hast pointed well the pen
  That writes these lines to thee.

Thanks for expelling Fear and Hope,
  One vile, the other vain;
One's scourge, the other's telescope,   15
  I shall not see again:

Rather what lies before my feet
  My notice shall engage —
He who hath braved Youth's dizzy heat
  Dreads not the frost of Age.   20
                                        (1853)

ON HIS SEVENTY-FIFTH BIRTHDAY

I strove with none; for none was worth my
    strife,
  Nature I loved, and next to Nature, Art;
I warmed both hands before the fire of
    life,
  It sinks, and I am ready to depart.
                                        (1853)

THOMAS CAMPBELL (1777-1844)

YE MARINERS OF ENGLAND

A NAVAL ODE

Ye mariners of England
That guard our native seas,
Whose flag has braved a thousand years
The battle and the breeze!
Your glorious standard launch again   5
To match another foe,
And sweep through the deep,
While the stormy winds do blow;
While the battle rages loud and long,
And the stormy winds do blow.   10

The spirits of your fathers
Shall start from every wave! —
For the deck it was their field of fame,
And Ocean was their grave:
Where Blake and mighty Nelson fell   15
Your manly hearts shall glow,
As ye sweep through the deep,
While the stormy winds do blow;
While the battle rages loud and long,
And the stormy winds do blow.   20

Britannia needs no bulwark,
No towers along the steep;
Her march is o'er the mountain waves,
Her home is on the deep.
With thunders from her native oak   25
She quells the floods below —
As they roar on the shore,
When the stormy winds do blow;
When the battle rages loud and long,
And the stormy winds do blow.   30

The meteor flag of England
Shall yet terrific burn,
Till danger's troubled night depart
And the star of peace return.
Then, then, ye ocean-warriors!   35
Our song and feast shall flow
To the fame of your name,
When the storm has ceased to blow;
When the fiery fight is heard no more,
And the storm has ceased to blow.   40
                                        (1801)

THOMAS MOORE (1779-1852)

OFT IN THE STILLY NIGHT

Oft, in the stilly night,
  Ere Slumber's chain has bound me,
Fond Memory brings the light
  Of other days around me;
    The smiles, the tears,   5
    Of boyhood's years,
The words of love then spoken;
    The eyes that shone,
    Now dimmed and gone,
The cheerful hearts now broken!   10
Thus, in the stilly night,
  Ere Slumber's chain has bound me,
Sad Memory brings the light
  Of other days around me.

When I remember all   15
  The friends, so linked together,
I've seen around me fall,
  Like leaves in wintry weather;
    I feel like one
    Who treads alone   20
Some banquet-hall deserted,
    Whose lights are fled,
    Whose garlands dead,
And all but he departed!
Thus, in the stilly night,   25
  Ere Slumber's chain has bound me,
Sad Memory brings the light
  Of other days around me.
                                        (1818)

THE HARP THAT ONCE THROUGH TARA'S HALLS

The harp that once through Tara's halls
  The soul of music shed,
Now hangs as mute on Tara's walls
  As if that soul were fled.
So sleeps the pride of former days,   5
  So glory's thrill is o'er,
And hearts that once beat high for praise
  Now feel that pulse no more!

No more to chiefs and ladies bright
  The harp of Tara swells;   10
The chord alone that breaks at night
  Its tale of ruin tells.
Thus Freedom now so seldom wakes,
  The only throb she gives
Is when some heart indignant breaks,   15
  To show that still she lives.

               (1808)

LEIGH HUNT (1784–1859)

RONDEAU

Jenny kissed me when we met,
  Jumping from the chair she sat in;
Time, you thief, who love to get
  Sweets into your list, put that in:
Say I'm weary, say I'm sad,   5
  Say that health and wealth have missed
    me,
Say I'm growing old, but add,
  Jenny kissed me.

THOMAS LOVE PEACOCK
(1785–1866)

THE MEN OF GOTHAM

Seamen three! what men be ye?
  Gotham's three Wise Men we be.
Whither in your bowl so free?
  To rake the moon from out the sea.
The bowl goes trim; the moon doth shine;
  And our ballast is old wine: 6
  And your ballast is old wine.

Who art thou, so fast adrift?
  I am he they call Old Care.
Here on board we will thee lift.   10
  No: I may not enter there.
Wherefore so? 'T is Jove's decree —
  In a bowl Care may not be:
  In a bowl Care may not be.

Fear ye not the waves that roll?   15
  No: in charmed bowl we swim.
What the charm that floats the bowl?
  Water may not pass the brim.
The bowl goes trim; the moon doth shine;
  And our ballast is old wine: 20
  And your ballast is old wine.

               (1818)

THE WAR-SONG OF DINAS VAWR

The mountain sheep are sweeter,
But the valley sheep are fatter;
We therefore deemed it meeter
To carry off the latter.
We made an expedition;   5
We met an host and quelled it;
We forced a strong position
And killed the men who held it.

On Dyfed's richest valley,
Where herds of kine were browsing,   10
We made a mighty sally,
To furnish our carousing.
Fierce warriors rushed to meet us;
We met them, and o'erthrew them:
They struggled hard to beat us;   15
But we conquered them, and slew them.

As we drove our prize at leisure,
The king marched forth to catch us:
His rage surpassed all measure,
But his people could not match us.   20
He fled to his hall-pillars;
And, ere our force we led off,
Some sacked his house and cellars,
While others cut his head off.

We there, in strife bewildering,   25
Spilt blood enough to swim in:
We orphaned many children
And widowed many women.
The eagles and the ravens
We glutted with our foemen: 30
The heroes and the cravens,
The spearmen and the bowmen.

We brought away from battle,
And much their land bemoaned them,
Two thousand head of cattle   35
And the head of him who owned them:
Ednyfed, King of Dyfed,
His head was borne before us;
His wine and beasts supplied our feasts.
And his overthrow, our chorus.   40

               (1829)

THE FRIAR'S SONG

Though I be now a gray, gray friar,
  Yet I was once a hale young knight:
The cry of my dogs was the only choir
  In which my spirit did take delight.
Little I recked of matin bell,   5
  But drowned its toll with my clanging
      horn
And the only beads I loved to tell
  Were the beads of dew on the spangled
      thorn.

Little I reck of matin bell,
  But drown its toll with my clanging
    horn: 10
And the only beads I love to tell
  Are the beads of dew on the spangled
      thorn.

An archer keen I was withal,
  As ever did lean on greenwood tree;
And could make the fleetest roebuck fall, 15
  A good three hundred yards from me.
Though changeful time, with hand severe,
  Has made me now these joys forego,
Yet my heart bounds whene'er I hear
  Yoicks! hark away! and tally ho!   20

Though changeful time, with hand severe,
  Has made me now these joys forego,
Yet my heart bounds whene'er I hear
  Yoicks! hark away! and tally ho!
                (1822)

CHARLES WOLFE (1791–1823)

THE BURIAL OF SIR JOHN MOORE AT CORUNNA

Not a drum was heard, not a funeral note,
  As his corse to the rampart we hurried;
Not a soldier discharged his farewell shot
  O'er the grave where our hero we buried.

We buried him darkly at dead of night,   5
  The sods with our bayonets turning;
By the struggling moonbeam's misty light,
  And the lantern dimly burning.

No useless coffin enclosed his breast,
  Not in sheet nor in shroud we wound
    him,   10
But he lay like a warrior taking his rest
  With his martial cloak around him.

Few and short were the prayers we said,
  And we spoke not a word of sorrow;
But we steadfastly gazed on the face that
    was dead,   15
And we bitterly thought of the morrow.

We thought as we hollowed his narrow bed,
  And smoothed down his lonely pillow,
That the foe and the stranger would tread
    o'er his head,
And we far away on the billow!   20

Lightly they'll talk of the spirit that's gone,
  And o'er his cold ashes upbraid him,—
But little he'll reck, if they let him sleep on
  In the grave where a Briton has laid him.

But half of our weary task was done   25
  When the clock struck the hour for re-
    tiring;
And we heard the distant and random gun
  That the foe was sullenly firing.

Slowly and sadly we laid him down,
  From the field of his fame fresh and
    gory;   30
We carved not a line, and we raised not a
    stone—
But we left him alone with his glory.
                (1817)

JOHN KEBLE (1792–1866)

UNITED STATES

Tyre of the *farther* West! be thou too
    warned,
  Whose eagle wings thine own green world
    o'erspread,
Touching two Oceans: wherefore hast thou
    scorned
  Thy fathers' God, O proud and full of
    bread?
Why lies the Cross unhonored on thy
    ground   5
  While in mid air thy stars and arrows
    flaunt?
That sheaf of darts, will it not fall un-
    bound,
  Except, disrobed of thy vain earthly vaunt,
Thou bring it to be blessed where Saints
    and Angels haunt?

The holy seed, by Heaven's peculiar grace, 10
  Is rooted here and there in thy dark
    woods;

But many a rank weed round it grows
　　　apace,
　And Mammon builds beside thy mighty
　　　floods,
O'ertopping Nature, braving Nature's God;
　O while thou yet hast room, fair fruitful
　　　land,　　　　　　　　　　　　　　15
Ere war and want have stained thy virgin
　　　sod,
　Mark thee a place on high, a glorious
　　　stand,
　Whence Truth her sign may make o'er
　　　forest, lake, and strand.

Eastward, this hour, perchance thou turn'st
　　　thine ear,
　Listening if haply with the surging sea, 20
Blend sounds of Ruin from a land once
　　　dear
　To thee and Heaven. O trying hour for
　　　thee!
Tyre mocked when Salem fell; where now
　　　is Tyre?
Heaven was against her. Nations thick as
　　　waves,
Burst o'er her walls, to Ocean doomed and
　　　fire:　　　　　　　　　　　　　　25
　And now the tideless water idly laves
　Her towers, and lone sands heap her
　　　crownèd merchants' graves.
　　　　　　　　　　　　　　　　(1836)

THOMAS HOOD (1798-1845)

FAIR INES

O saw ye not fair Ines?
She's gone into the West,
To dazzle when the sun is down,
And rob the world of rest:
She took our daylight with her,　　　5
The smiles that we love best,
With morning blushes on her cheek,
And pearls upon her breast.

O turn again, fair Ines,
Before the fall of night,　　　　　10
For fear the Moon should shine alone,
And stars unrivaled bright;
And blessèd will the lover be
That walks beneath their light,
And breathes the love against thy cheek 15
I dare not even write!

Would I had been, fair Ines,
That gallant cavalier.

Who rode so gaily by thy side,
And whispered thee so near!—　　　20
Were there no bonny dames at home
Or no true lovers here,
That he should cross the seas to win
The dearest of the dear?

I saw thee, lovely Ines,　　　　　25
Descend along the shore,
With bands of noble gentlemen,
And banners waved before;
And gentle youth and maidens gay,
And snowy plumes they wore;—　　　30
It would have been a beauteous dream,
—If it had been no more!

Alas, alas! fair Ines,
She went away with song,
With Music waiting on her steps,　　　35
And shoutings of the throng;
But some were sad and felt no mirth,
But only Music's wrong,
In sounds that sang Farewell, Farewell
To her you've loved so long.　　　40

Farewell, farewell, fair Ines!
That vessel never bore
So fair a lady on its deck,
Nor danced so light before,—
Alas for pleasure on the sea,　　　45
And sorrow on the shore!
The smile that blest one lover's heart
Has broken many more!
　　　　　　　　　　　　　　　　(1827)

THE BRIDGE OF SIGHS

One more Unfortunate,
　Weary of breath,
Rashly importunate,
　Gone to her death!

Take her up tenderly,　　　　　5
　Lift her with care;
Fashioned so slenderly,
　Young, and so fair!

Look at her garments
Clinging like cerements;　　　　10
Whilst the wave constantly
　Drips from her clothing;
Take her up instantly,
　Loving, not loathing.

Touch her not scornfully;　　　　15
Think of her mournfully,
　Gently and humanly;

Not of the stains of her,
All that remains of her
  Now is pure womanly.   20

Make no deep scrutiny
Into her mutiny
  Rash and undutiful:
Past all dishonor,
Death has left on her   25
  Only the beautiful.

Still, for all slips of hers,
  One of Eve's family —
Wipe those poor lips of hers
  Oozing so clammily.   30

Loop up her tresses
  Escaped from the comb,
Her fair auburn tresses;
Whilst wonderment guesses
  Where was her home?   35

Who was her father?
  Who was her mother?
Had she a sister?
  Had she a brother?
Or was there a dearer one   40
Still, and a nearer one
  Yet, than all other?

Alas! for the rarity
Of Christian charity
  Under the sun!   45
O, it was pitiful!
Near a whole city full,
  Home she had none.

Sisterly, brotherly,
Fatherly, motherly   50
  Feelings had changed:
Love, by harsh evidence,
Thrown from its eminence;
Even God's providence
  Seeming estranged.   55

Where the lamps quiver
So far in the river,
  With many a light
From window to casement,
From garret to basement,   60
She stood with amazement,
  Houseless by night.

The bleak wind of March
  Made her tremble and shiver;
But not the dark arch,   65
  Or the black flowing river:
Mad from life's history,

Glad to death's mystery,
  Swift to be hurled —
Anywhere, anywhere   70
  Out of the world!

In she plunged boldly —
No matter how coldly
  The rough river ran —
Over the brink of it,   75
Picture it — think of it,
  Dissolute Man!
Lave in it, drink of it,
  Then, if you can!

Take her up tenderly,   80
  Lift her with care;
Fashioned so slenderly,
  Young, and so fair!

Ere her limbs frigidly
Stiffen too rigidly,   85
  Decently, kindly,
Smooth and compose them;
And her eyes, close them,
  Staring so blindly!

Dreadfully staring   90
  Through muddy impurity,
As when with the daring
Last look of despairing
  Fixed on futurity.

Perishing gloomily,   95
Spurred by contumely,
Cold inhumanity,
Burning insanity,
  Into her rest —
Cross her hands humbly,   100
As if praying dumbly,
  Over her breast!

Owning her weakness,
  Her evil behaviour,
And leaving with meekness,   105
  Her sins to her Saviour!

           (1844)

THE SONG OF THE SHIRT

With fingers weary and worn,
  With eyelids heavy and red,
A woman sat, in unwomanly rags,
  Plying her needle and thread —
Stitch! stitch! stitch!
  In poverty, hunger, and dirt,
And still with a voice of dolorous pitch
  She sang the 'Song of the Shirt.'

'Work! work! work!
　While the cock is crowing aloof!　　10
And　work — work — work,
　Till the stars shine through the roof!
It 's Oh! to be a slave
　Along with the barbarous Turk,
Where woman has never a soul to save,　15
　If this is Christian work!

'Work — work — work,
　Till the brain begins to swim;
Work — work — work,
　Till the eyes are heavy and dim!　　20
Seam, and gusset, and band,
　Band, and gusset, and seam,
Till over the buttons I fall asleep,
　And sew them on in a dream!

'Oh, Men, with Sisters dear!　　25
　Oh, Men, with Mothers and Wives!
It is not linen you 're wearing out
　But human creatures' lives!
Stitch — stitch — stitch,
　In poverty, hunger, and dirt,　　30
Sewing at once, with a double thread,
　A Shroud as well as a Shirt.

'But why do I talk of Death?
　That Phantom of grisly bone,
I hardly fear its terrible shape,　　35
　It seems so like my own —
It seems so like my own,
　Because of the fasts I keep;
Oh, God! that bread should be so dear,
　And flesh and blood so cheap!　　40

'Work — work — work!
　My labor never flags;
And what are its wages? A bed of straw,
　A crust of bread — and rags.
That shattered roof — this naked floor — 45
　A table — a broken chair —
And a wall so blank, my shadow I thank
　For sometimes falling there!

'Work — work — work!
　From weary chime to chime,　　50
Work — work — work,
　As prisoners work for crime!
Band, and gusset, and seam,
　Seam, and gusset, and band,
Till the heart is sick, and the brain be-
　　numbed,　　55
　As well as the weary hand.

'Work — work — work,
　In the dull December light,

And work — work — work,
　When the weather is warm and bright —
While underneath the eaves　　61
　The brooding swallows cling
As if to show me their sunny backs
　And twit me with the spring.

'Oh! but to breathe the breath　　65
　Of the cowslip and primrose sweet —
With the sky above my head,
　And the grass beneath my feet;
For only one short hour
　To feel as I used to feel,　　70
Before I knew the woes of want
　And the walk that costs a meal.

'Oh! but for one short hour!
　A respite however brief!
No blessèd leisure for Love or Hope,　75
　But only time for Grief!
A little weeping would ease my heart,
　But in their briny bed
My tears must stop, for every drop
　Hinders needle and thread!'　　80

With fingers weary and worn,
　With eyelids heavy and red,
A woman sat, in unwomanly rags,
　Plying her needle and thread —
Stitch! stitch! stitch!　　85
　In poverty, hunger, and dirt,
And still with a voice of dolorous pitch,—
　Would that its tone could reach the Rich! —
She sang this 'Song of the Shirt!'
　　　　　　　　(1843)

WINTHROP MACKWORTH
PRAED (1802–1839)

THE BELLE OF THE BALL-ROOM

Years — years ago, ere yet my dreams
　Had been of being wise or witty,—
Ere I had done with writing themes,
　Or yawned o'er this infernal Chitty; —
Years — years ago,— while all my joy　　5
　Was in my fowling-piece and fillv,—
In short, while I was yet a boy,
　I fell in love with Laura Lily.

I saw her at the County Ball:
　There, when the sounds of flute and fiddle
Gave signal sweet in that old hall　　11
　Of hands across and down the middle,
Hers was the subtlest spell by far

Of all that set young hearts romancing;
She was our queen, our rose, our star;   15
And then she danced — O Heaven, her
     dancing!

Dark was her hair, her hand was white;
Her voice was exquisitely tender;
Her eyes were full of liquid light;
I never saw a waist so slender!   20
Her every look, her every smile,
Shot right and left a score of arrows;
I thought 't was Venus from her isle,
And wondered where she'd left her spar-
     rows.

She talked, — of politics or prayers, —   25
Of Southey's prose or Wordsworth's son-
     nets, —
Of danglers — or of dancing bears,
Of battles — or the last new bonnets,
By candlelight, at twelve o'clock,
To me it mattered not a tittle,   30
If those bright lips had quoted Locke,
I might have thought they murmured Lit-
     tle.

Through sunny May, through sultry June,
I loved her with a love eternal;
I spoke her praises to the moon,   35
I wrote them to the Sunday Journal:
My mother laughed; I soon found out
That ancient ladies have no feeling:
My father frowned; but how should gout
See any happiness in kneeling?   40

She was the daughter of a Dean,
Rich, fat, and rather apoplectic;
She had one brother, just thirteen,
Whose color was extremely hectic;
Her grandmother for many a year   45
Had fed the parish with her bounty;
Her second cousin was a peer,
And Lord Lieutenant of the County.

But titles, and the three per cents,
And mortgages, and great relations,   50
And India bonds, and tithes, and rents,
Oh, what are they to love's sensations?
Black eyes, fair forehead, clustering locks —
Such wealth, such honors, Cupid chooses;
He cares as little for the Stocks,   55
As Baron Rothschild for the Muses.

She sketched; the vale, the wood, the beach,
Grew lovelier from her pencil's shading:
She botanized; I envied each
Young blossom in her boudoir fading;   60
She warbled Handel; it was grand;

She made the Catalani jealous:
She touched the organ; I could stand
For hours and hours to blow the bellows.

She kept an album, too, at home,   65
Well filled with all an album's glories;
Paintings of butterflies, Rome,
Patterns for trimmings, Persian stories;
Soft songs to Julia's cockatoo,
Fierce odes to Famine and to Slaughter;
And autographs of Prince Leboo,   71
And recipes for elder-water.
And she was flattered, worshipped, bored;

Her steps were watched, her dress was
     noted,
Her poodle dog was quite adored,   75
Her sayings were extremely quoted;
She laughed, and every heart was glad,
As if the taxes were abolished;
She frowned, and every look was sad,
As if the Opera were demolished.   80

She smiled on many, just for fun, —
I knew that there was nothing in it;
I was the first — the only one
Her heart had thought of for a minute. —
I knew it, for she told me so,   85
In phrase which was divinely molded;
She wrote a charming hand, — and oh!
How sweetly all her notes were folded!

Our love was like most other loves; —
A little glow, a little shiver,   90
A rose-bud, and a pair of gloves,
And 'Fly not yet' — upon the river;
Some jealousy of some one's heir,
Some hopes of dying broken-hearted;
A miniature, a lock of hair,   95
The usual vows, — and then we parted.

We parted; months and years rolled by;
We met again four summers after:
Our parting was all sob and sigh;
Our meeting was all mirth and laughter:
For in my heart's most secret cell   101
There had been many other lodgers;
And she was not the ball-room's belle,
But only — Mrs. Something Rogers!
                    (1844)

A LETTER OF ADVICE

FROM MISS MEDORA TREVILIAN, AT PADUA, TO
MISS ARAMINTA VAVASOUR, IN LONDON

You tell me you 're promised a lover,
My own Araminta, next week:

Why cannot my fancy discover
  The hue of his coat and his cheek?
Alas! if he look like another,   5
  A vicar, a banker, a beau,
Be deaf to your father and mother,
  My own Araminta, say 'No!'

Miss Lane, at her Temple of Fashion,
  Taught us both how to sing and to speak,
And we loved one another with passion, 11
  Before we had been there a week:
You gave me a ring for a token;
  I wear it wherever I go;
I gave you a chain,— is it broken?   15
  My own Araminta, say 'No!'

O think of our favorite cottage,
  And think of our dear Lalla Rookh!
How we shared with the milkmaids their
    pottage,   19
  And drank of the stream from the brook;
How fondly our loving lips faltered,
  'What further can grandeur bestow?'
My heart is the same;— is yours altered?
  My own Araminta, say 'No!'

Remember the thrilling romances   25
  We read on the bank in the glen;
Remember the suitors our fancies
  Would picture for both of us then.
They wore the red cross on their shoulder,
  They had vanquished and pardoned their
    foe —   30
Sweet friend, are you wiser or colder?
  My own Araminta, say 'No!'

You know, when Lord Rigmarole's carriage,
  Drove off with your Cousin Justine,
You wept, dearest girl, at the marriage, 35
  And whispered 'How base she has been!'
You said you were sure it would kill you,
  If ever your husband looked so;
And you will not apostatize,— will you?
  My own Araminta, say 'No!'   40

When I heard I was going abroad, love,
  I thought I was going to die;
We walked arm in arm to the road, love,
  We looked arm in arm to the sky;
And I said 'When a foreign postilion 45
  Has hurried me off to the Po,
Forget not Medora Trevilian:
  My own Araminta, say "No"!'

We parted! but sympathy's fetters
  Reach far over valley and hill; 50
I muse o'er your exquisite letters,
  And feel that your heart is mine still;
And he who would share it with me, love.—

The richest of treasures below,—
If he 's not what Orlando should be, love, 55
  My own Araminta, say 'No!'

If he wears a top-boot in his wooing,
  If he comes to you riding a cob,
If he talks of his baking or brewing,
  If he puts up his feet on the hob, 60
If he ever drinks port after dinner,
  If his brow or his breeding is low,
If he calls himself 'Thompson' or 'Skin-
    ner,'
  My own Araminta, say 'No!'

If he studies the news in the papers 65
  While you are preparing the tea,
If he talks of the damps or the vapors
  While moonlight lies soft on the sea,
If he 's sleepy while you are capricious,
  If he has not a musical 'Oh!' 70
If he does not call Werther delicious,—
  My own Araminta, say 'No!'

If he ever sets foot in the City
  Among the stockbrokers and Jews,
If he has not a heart full of pity, 75
  If he don't stand six feet in his shoes,
If his lips are not redder than roses,
  If his hands are not whiter than snow,
If he has not the model of noses,—
  My own Araminta, say 'No!' 80

If he speaks of a tax or a duty,
  If he does not look grand on his knees,
If he 's blind to a landscape of beauty,
  Hills, valleys, rocks, waters, and trees,
If he dotes not on desolate towers, 85
  If he likes not to hear the blast blow,
If he knows not the language of flowers,—
  My own Araminta, say 'No!'

He must walk — like a god of old story
  Come down from the home of his rest; 90
He must smile — like the sun in his glory
  On the buds he loves ever the best;
And oh! from its ivory portal
  Like music his soft speech must flow! —
If he speak, smile, or walk like a mortal, 95
  My own Araminta, say 'No!'

Don't listen to tales of his bounty,
  Don't hear what they say of his birth,
Don't look at his seat in the county,
  Don't calculate what he is worth; 100
But give him a theme to write verse on,
  And see if he turns out his toe;
If he 's only an excellent person,—
  My own Araminta, say 'No!'

(1844)

WILLIAM BARNES (1801–1886)

BLACKMWORE MAIDENS

The primrwose in the sheäde do blow,
The cowslip in the zun,
The thyme upon the down do grow,
The clote where streams do run;
An' where do pretty maidens grow   5
An' blow, but where the tow'r
Do rise among the bricken tuns
In Blackmwore by the Stour.

If you could zee their comely gaït,
An' pretty feäces' smiles,   10
A-trippèn on so light o' waïght,
An' steppèn off the stiles;
A-gwain to church, as bells do swing
An' ring 'ithin the tow'r,
You 'd own the pretty maïdens' pleäce   15
Is Blackmwore by the Stour.

If you vrom Wimborne took your road,
To Stower or Paladore,
An' all the farmers' housen show'd
Their daughters at the door;   20
You 'd cry to bachelors at hwome —
'Here come: 'ithin an hour
You 'll vind ten maïdens to your mind,
In Blackmwore by the Stour.'

An' if you look'd 'ithin their door,   25
To zee em in their pleäce,
A-doèn housework up avore
Their smilèn mother's feäce;
You'd cry — 'Why, if a man would wive
An' thrive, 'ithout a dow'r,   30
Then let en look en out a wife
In Blackmwore by the Stour.'

As I upon my road did pass
A school-house back in Maÿ,
There out upon the beäten grass   35
Wer maidens at their plaÿ;
An' as the pretty souls did tweil
An' smile, I cried, 'The flow'r
O' beauty, then, is still in bud
In Blackmwore by the Stour.'   40
                              (1844)

THE SURPRISE

As there I left the road in May,
And took my way along a ground,
I found a glade with girls at play,
By leafy boughs close-hemmed around,
And there, with stores of harmless joys. 5

They plied their tongues, in merry noise;
Though little did they seem to fear
So queer a stranger might be near;
Teeh-hee! Look here! Hah! ha! Look
    there!
And oh! so playsome, oh! so fair.   10

And one would dance as one would spring,
Or bob or bow with leering smiles,
And one would swing, or sit and sing,
Or sew a stitch or two at whiles,
And one skipped on with downcast face,   15
All heedless, to my very place,
And there, in fright, in one foot out,
Made one dead step and turned about.
Heeh, hee, oh! oh! ooh! oo! — Look there!
And oh! so playsome, oh, so fair.   20

Away they scampered all, full speed,
By boughs that swung along their track,
As rabbits out of wood at feed,
At sight of men all scamper back.
And one pulled on behind her heel,   25
A thread of cotton, off her reel,
And oh! to follow that white clue,
I felt I fain could scamper too.
Teeh, hee, run here. Eeh! ee! Look
    there!
And oh! so playsome, oh! so fair.   30
                              (1868)

THOMAS LOVELL BEDDOES
(1803–1849)

DREAM-PEDLARY

If there were dreams to sell,
    What would you buy?
Some cost a passing bell;
    Some a light sigh,
That shakes from Life's fresh crown   5
Only a rose-leaf down.
If there were dreams to sell,
Merry and sad to tell,
And the crier rang the bell,
    What would you buy?   10

A cottage lone and still,
    With bowers nigh,
Shadowy, my woes to still,
    Until I die.
Such pearl from Life's fresh crown   15
Fain would I shake me down.
Were dreams to have at will,
This would best heal my ill,
    This would I buy.

But there were dreams to sell   20
  Ill didst thou buy;
Life is a dream, they tell,
  Waking, to die.
Dreaming a dream to prize,
Is wishing ghosts to rise;   25
And if I had the spell
To call the buried well,
  Which one would I?

If there are ghosts to raise,
  What shall I call,   30
Out of hell's murky haze,
  Heaven's blue pall?
Raise my loved long-lost boy,
To lead me to his joy.—
There are no ghosts to raise;   35
Out of death lead no ways;
  Vain is the call.

Know'st thou not ghosts to sue,
  No love thou hast.
Else lie, as I will do.   40
  And breathe thy last.
So out of Life's fresh crown
Fall like a rose-leaf down.
Thus are the ghosts to woo;
Thus are all dreams made true,   45
  Ever to last!

(1851)

BALLAD OF HUMAN LIFE

When we were girl and boy together,
  We tossed about the flowers
  And wreathed the blushing hours
Into a posy green and sweet.
  I sought the youngest, best,   5
  And never was at rest
Till I had laid them at thy fairy feet.
But the days of childhood they were fleet,
  And the blooming sweet-briar-breathed
    weather,
  When we were boy and girl together.   10

Then we were lad and lass together,
  And sought the kiss of night
  Before we felt aright,
Sitting and singing soft and sweet.
  The dearest thought of heart   15
  With thee 't was joy to part,
And the greater half was thine, as meet.
Still my eyelid's dewy, my veins they beat
  At the starry summer-evening weather,
  When we were lad and lass together.   20

And we are man and wife together,
  Although thy breast, once bold
  With song, be closed and cold
Beneath flowers' roots and birds' light feet.
  Yet sit I by thy tomb,   25
  And dissipate the gloom
With songs of loving faith and sorrow
    sweet.
And fate and darkling grave kind dreams do
    cheat,
  That, while fair life, young hope, despair
    and death are,
  We 're boy and girl, and lass and lad, and
    man and wife together.   30

(1851)

FROM DEATH'S JEST BOOK

TO SEA, TO SEA!

To sea, to sea! The calm is o'er;
  The wanton water leaps in sport,
And rattles down the pebbly shore;
  The dolphin wheels, the sea-cows snort,
And unseen Mermaids' pearly song   5
Comes bubbling up, the weeds among.
  Fling broad the sail, dip deep the oar:
  To sea, to sea! the calm is o'er.

To sea, to sea! our wide-winged bark
  Shall billowy cleave its sunny way,   10
And with its shadow, fleet and dark,
  Break the caved Triton's azure day,
Like mighty eagle soaring light
O'er antelopes on Alpine height.
  The anchor heaves, the ship swings free,   15
  The sails swell full. To sea, to sea!

(1850)

DIRGE

If thou wilt ease thine heart
Of love and all its smart,
    Then sleep, dear, sleep;
And not a sorrow
  Hang any tear on your eye-lashes;
    Lie still and deep,
  Sad soul, until the sea-wave washes
The rim o' the sun to-morrow,
    In eastern sky.

But wilt thou cure thine heart
Of love and all its smart,
    Then die, dear, die;

'T is deeper, sweeter,
  Than on a rose bank to lie dreaming
    With folded eye;   15
  And then alone, amid the beaming
Of love's stars, thou 'lt meet her
    In eastern sky.

               (1850)

SONG

Old Adam, the carrion crow,
  The old crow of Cairo;
He sat in the shower, and let it flow
  Under his tail and over his crest;
    And through every feather   5
    Leaked the wet weather;
  And the bough swung under his nest;
  For his beak it was heavy with marrow.
    Is that the wind dying? O no;
    It 's only two devils, that blow   10
    Through a murderer's bones, to and
      fro,
    In the ghosts' moonshine.

Ho! Eve, my gray carrion wife,
  When we have supped on king's mar-
    row,
Where shall we drink and make merry our
    life?   15
  Our nest it is Queen Cleopatra's skull,
    'T is cloven and cracked,
    And battered and hacked,
  But with tears of blue eyes it is full:
  Let us drink then, my raven of Cairo.
    Is that the wind dying? O no;   21
    It 's only two devils, that blow
    Through a murderer's bones, to and
      fro,
    In the ghosts' moonshine.

               (1850)

EDWARD FITZGERALD
(1809–1883)

From THE RUBAIYAT OF OMAR KHAYYAM

Why, if the Soul, can fling the dust aside,
And naked on the air of Heaven ride,
  Wer 't not a shame — wer 't not a shame
    for him
In this clay carcase crippled to abide?

'T is but a tent where takes his one-day's
  rest   5

A Sultán to the realm of Death addrest;
  The Sultán rises, and the dark Ferrásh
Strikes, and prepares it for another guest.

And fear not lest existence closing your
Account, and mine, should know the like no
    more;   10
  The Eternal Sáki from that bowl has
    poured
Millions of bubbles like us, and will pour.

When you and I behind the veil are past,
Oh, but the long long while the world shall
    last,
  Which of our coming and departure heeds
As the Seven Seas should heed a pebble-
    cast.   16

A moment's halt — a momentary taste
Of Being from the well amid the waste —
  And lo! — the phantom caravan has
    reached
The Nothing it set out from — Oh, make
    haste!   20
         * * *

The Moving Finger writes; and, having
    writ,
Moves on: nor all your Piety nor Wit
  Shall lure it back to cancel half a Line
Nor all your Tears wash out a Word of it.
         * * *

Yet ah, that Spring should vanish with the
    rose!   25
That Youth's sweet-scented manuscript
    should close!
  The nightingale that in the branches sang,
Ah, whence, and whither flown again, who
    knows!

Would but the desert of the fountain yield
One glimpse — if dimly, yet indeed, re-
    vealed,   30
  To which the fainting traveler might
    spring,
As springs the trampled herbage of the
    field!

Would but some winged Angel ere too late
Arrest the yet unfolded roll of fate,
  And make the stern Recorder otherwise 35
Enregister, or quite obliterate!

Ah, Love! could you and I with him con-
    spire
To grasp this sorry Scheme of Things en-
    tire,
  Would not we shatter it to bits — and then
Re-mold it nearer to the heart's desire! 40
         * * *

            (1859; 1872)

ELIZABETH BARRETT BROWNING (1809–1861)

A MUSICAL INSTRUMENT

What was he doing, the great god Pan,
  Down in the reeds by the river?
Spreading ruin and scattering ban,
Splashing and paddling with hoofs of a
  goat,
And breaking the golden lilies afloat   5
  With the dragon-fly on the river?

He tore out a reed, the great god Pan,
  From the deep cool bed of the river,
The limpid water turbidly ran,
And the broken lilies a-dying lay,   10
And the dragon-fly had fled away,
  Ere he brought it out of the river.

High on the shore sat the great god Pan,
  While turbidly flowed the river,
And hacked and hewed as a great god can 15
With his hard bleak steel at the patient reed,
Till there was not a sign of the leaf indeed
  To prove it fresh from the river.

He cut it short, did the great god Pan,
  (How tall it stood in the river!),   20
Then drew the pith, like the heart of a man,
Steadily from the outside ring,
And notched the poor dry empty thing
  In holes as he sat by the river.

'This is the way,' laughed the great god
  Pan,   25
  (Laughed while he sat by the river)
'The only way since gods began
To make sweet music, they could succeed.'
Then dropping his mouth to a hole in the
  reed,
  He blew in power by the river.   30

Sweet, sweet, sweet, O Pan!
  Piercing sweet by the river!
Blinding sweet, O great god Pan!
The sun on the hill forgot to die,
And the lilies revived, and the dragon-fly 35
  Came back to dream on the river.

Yet half a beast is the great god Pan
  To laugh, as he sits by the river,
Making a poet out of a man:
The true gods sigh for the cost and pain —
For the reed which grows never more
  again   41
  As a reed with the reeds of the river.

                (1862)

SONNETS FROM THE PORTUGUESE

I

I thought once how Theocritus had sung
Of the sweet years, the dear and wished-for
  years,
Who each one in a gracious hand appears
To bear a gift for mortals, old or young:
And, as I mused it in his antique tongue,   5
I saw in gradual vision through my tears,
The sweet, sad years, the melancholy years,
Those of my own life, who by turns had
  flung
A shadow across me. Straightway I was
  'ware,
So weeping, how a mystic Shape did move
Behind me, and drew me backward by the
  hair;   11
And a voice said in mastery while I strove,
'Guess now who holds thee?'—'Death!' I
  said. But there,
The silver answer rang: 'Not Death, but
  Love.'

V

I lift my heavy heart up solemnly,
As once Electra her sepulchral urn,
And looking in thine eyes, I overturn
The ashes at thy feet. Behold and see
What a great heap of grief lay hid in me,   5
And how the red wild sparkles dimly burn
Through the ashen grayness. If thy foot in
  scorn
Could tread them out to darkness utterly,
It might be well perhaps. But if instead
Thou wait beside me for the wind to blow
The gray dust up, . . . those laurels on
  thine head,   11
O my Belovèd, will not shield thee so,
That none of all the fires shall scorch and
  shred
The hair beneath. Stand farther off then!
  go.

VI

Go from me. Yet I feel that I shall stand
Henceforward in thy shadow. Nevermore
Alone upon the threshold of my door
Of individual life, I shall command
The uses of my soul, nor lift my hand   5
Serenely in the sunshine as before,
Without the sense of that which I forbore —
Thy touch upon the palm. The widest land
Doom takes to part us, leaves thy heart in
  mine
With pulses that beat double. What I do 10
And what I dream include thee, as the wine
Must taste of its own grapes. And when
  I sue

God for myself, he hears that name of
    thine,
And sees within my eyes the tears of two.

VII

The face of all the world is changed, I
    think,
Since first I heard the footsteps of thy soul
Move still, oh, still, beside me, as they stole
Betwixt me and the dreadful outer brink
Of obvious death, where I, who thought to
    sink,   5
Was caught up into love, and taught the
    whole
Of life in a new rhythm. The cup of dole
God gave for baptism, I am fain to drink,
And praise its sweetness, Sweet, with thee
anear.
The names of country, heaven, are changed
    away   10
For where thou art or shalt be, there or
    here;
And this . . . this lute and song . . .
    loved yesterday,
(The singing angels know) are only dear
Because thy name moves right in what they
say.

XIII

And wilt thou have me fashion into speech
The love I bear thee, finding words enough,
And hold the torch out, while the winds are
    rough,
Between our faces, to cast light on each? —
I drop it at thy feet. I cannot teach   5
My hand to hold my spirit so far off
From myself — me — that I should bring
    thee proof
In words, of love hid in me out of reach.
Nay, let the silence of my womanhood
Commend my woman-love to thy belief,—   10
Seeing that I stand unwon, however wooed,
And rend the garment of my life, in brief,
By a most dauntless, voiceless fortitude,
Lest one touch of this heart convey its
    grief.

XIV

If thou must love me, let it be for nought
Except for love's sake only. Do not say
'I love her for her smile — her look — her
    way
Of speaking gently,— for a trick of thought
That falls in well with mine, and certes
    brought   5
A sense of pleasant ease on such a day'—
For these things in themselves, Belovèd,
may

Be changed, or change for thee,— and love,
    so wrought,
May be unwrought so. Neither love me for
Thine own dear pity's wiping my cheeks
    dry,—   10
A creature might forget to weep, who bore
Thy comfort long, and lose thy love there-
    by!
But love me for love's sake, that ever-
    more
Thou mayst love on, through love's eter-
nity.

XX

Belovèd, my Belovèd, when I think
That thou wast in the world a year ago,
What time I sat alone here in the snow
And saw no footprint, heard the silence
    sink   4
No moment at thy voice, but, link by link,
Went counting all my chains as if that so
They never could fall off at any blow
Struck by thy possible hand,— why, thus I
    drink
Of life's great cup of wonder! Wonder-
    ful,
Never to feel thee thrill the day or night   10
With personal act or speech,— nor ever cull
Some prescience of thee with the blossoms
    white
Thou sawest growing! Atheists are as dull,
Who cannot guess God's presence out of
    sight.

XXXV

If I leave all for thee, wilt thou exchange
And be all to me? Shall I never miss
Home-talk and blessing and the common
    kiss
That comes to each in turn, nor count it
    strange,
When I look up, to drop on a new range   5
Of walls and floors, another home than
    this?
Nay, wilt thou fill that place by me which is
Filled by dead eyes too tender to know
    change?
That 's hardest. If to conquer love, has
    tried,
To conquer grief, tries more, as all things
    prove;   10
For grief indeed is love and grief beside.
Alas, I have grieved so I am hard to love.
Yet love me — wilt thou? Open thine heart
    wide,
And fold within the wet wings of thy dove.

XLIII

How do I love thee? Let me count the
ways.
I love thee to the depth and breadth and
height
My soul can reach, when feeling out of
sight
For the ends of Being and ideal Grace.
I love thee to the level of everyday's   5
Most quiet need, by sun and candle-light.
I love thee freely, as men strive for Right;
I love thee purely, as they turn from Praise.
I love thee with the passion put to use
In my old griefs, and with my childhood's
faith.   10
I love thee with a love I seemed to lose
With my lost saints,—I love thee with the
breath,
Smiles, tears, of all my life!—and, if God
choose,
I shall but love thee better after death.

(1850)

WILLIAM MAKEPEACE THACK-ERAY (1811-1863)

AT THE CHURCH GATE

Although I enter not,
   Yet round about the spot
     Ofttimes I hover;
And near the sacred gate,
   With longing eyes I wait,   5
     Expectant of her.

The minster bell tolls out
   Above the city's rout,
     And noise and humming;
They've hush'd the minster bell: 10
   The organ 'gins to swell;
     She's coming, she's coming!

My lady comes at last,
   Timid and stepping fast
     And hastening thither,   15
With modest eyes downcast;
   She comes—she's here, she's past!
     May heaven go with her!

Kneel undisturbed, fair saint!
   Pour out your praise or plaint   20
     Meekly and duly;
I will not enter there,
   To sully your pure prayer
     With thoughts unruly.

But suffer me to pace   25
   Round the forbidden place,
     Lingering a minute,
Like outcast spirits, who wait,
   And see, through heaven's gate,
     Angels within it.   30

(1849-50)

THE END OF THE PLAY

The play is done—the curtain drops,
   Slow falling to the prompter's bell;
A moment yet the actor stops,
   And looks around, to say farewell.
It is an irksome word and task;   5
   And when he's laughed and said his say,
He shows, as he removes the mask,
   A face that's anything but gay.

One word, ere yet the evening ends:
   Let's close it with a parting rhyme,   10
And pledge a hand to all young friends,
   As fits the merry Christmas time;
On life's wide scene you, too, have parts,
   That fate ere long shall bid you play;
Good-night!—with honest gentle hearts   15
   A kindly greeting go alway!

Good-night!—I'd say the griefs, the joys,
   Just hinted in this mimic page,
The triumphs and defeats of boys,
   Are but repeated in our age;   20
I'd say your woes were not less keen,
   Your hopes more vain, than those of men,
Your pangs or pleasures of fifteen
   At forty-five played o'er again.

I'd say we suffer and we strive   25
   Not less nor more as men than boys,
With grizzle beards at forty-five,
   As erst at twelve in corduroys,
And if, in time of sacred youth,
   We learned at home to love and pray,   30
Pray heaven that early love and truth
   May never wholly pass away.

And in the world, as in the school,
   I'd say how fate may change and shift,
The prize be sometimes with the fool,   35
   The race not always to the swift;
The strong may yield, the good may fall,
   The great man be a vulgar clown,
The knave be lifted over all,
   The kind cast pitilessly down.   40

Who knows the inscrutable design?
   Blessed be he who took and gave!
Why should your mother, Charles, not mine,
   Be weeping at her darling's grave?

We bow to heaven that willed it so,   45
  That darkly rules the fate of all,
That sends the respite or the blow,
  That's free to give or to recall.

This crowns his feast with wine and wit —
  Who brought him to that mirth and state?
His betters, see, below him sit,   51
  Or hunger hopeless at the gate.
Who bade the mud from Dives' wheel
  To spurn the rags of Lazarus?
Come, brother, in that dust we'll kneel,   55
  Confessing heaven that ruled it thus.

So each shall mourn, in life's advance,
  Dear hopes, dear friends, untimely killed,
Shall grieve for many a forfeit chance,
  And longing passion unfulfilled.   60
Amen! — whatever fate be sent,
  Pray God the heart may kindly glow,
Although the head with cares be bent,
  And whitened with the winter snow.

Come wealth or want, come good or ill,   65
  Let young and old accept their part,
And bow before the awful will,
  And bear it with an honest heart.
Who misses or who wins the prize —
  Go, lose or conquer as you can;   70
But if you fail, or if you rise,
  Be each, pray God, a gentleman.

A gentleman, or old or young!
  (Bear kindly with my humble lays;)
The sacred chorus first was sung   75
  Upon the first of Christmas days;
The shepherds heard it overhead —
  The joyful angels raised it then:
Glory to heaven on high, it said,
  And peace on earth to gentle men!   80

My song, save this, is little worth;
  I lay the weary pen aside,
And wish you health, and love, and mirth,
  As fits the solemn Christmas-tide.
As fits the holy Christmas birth,   85
  Be this, good friends, our carol still:
Be peace on earth, be peace on earth,
  To men of gentle will.

                      (1848)

ARTHUR HUGH CLOUGH
(1819–1861)

QUA CURSUM VENTUS

As ships, becalmed at eve, that lay
  With canvas drooping, side by side,
Two towers of sail at dawn of day
  Are scarce long leagues apart descried:

When fell the night, upsprung the breeze,
  And all the darkling hours they plied,
Nor dreamt but each the self-same seas
  By each was cleaving, side by side;

E'en so, but why the tale reveal
  Of those, whom year by year, un-   10
    changed,
Brief absence joined anew to feel,
  Astounded, soul from soul estranged?

At dead of night their sails were filled,
  And onward each rejoicing steered —
Ah, neither blame, for neither willed,   15
  Or wist, what first with dawn appeared!

To veer, how vain! On, onward strain,
  Brave barks! In light, in darkness too,
Through winds and tides one compass
    guides —
  To that, and your own selves, be true. 20

But O blithe breeze; and O great seas,
  Though ne'er, that earliest parting past,
On your wide plain they join again,
  Together lead them home at last.

One port, methought, alike they sought,   25
  One purpose hold where'er they fare,—
O bounding breeze, O rushing seas!
  At last, at last, unite them there!
                      (1849)

WHITHER DEPART THE BRAVE

Rome is fallen, I hear, the gallant Medici
  taken,
Noble Manara slain, and Garibaldi has lost
  il Moro; —
Rome is fallen; and fallen, or falling, heroi-
  cal Venice.
I, meanwhile, for the loss of a single small
  chit of a girl, sit
Moping and mourning here,— for her, and
  myself much smaller.   5
  Whither depart the souls of the brave that
    die in the battle,
Die in the lost, lost fight, for the cause that
  perishes with them?
Are they upborne from the field on the slumberous pinions of angels
Unto a far-off home, where the weary rest
  from their labor,
And the deep wounds are healed, and the
  bitter and burning moisture   10
Wiped from the generous eyes? or do they
  linger, unhappy.

Pining, and haunting the grave of their by-
    gone hope and endeavor?
All declamation, alas! though I talk, I
    care not for Rome nor
Italy; feebly and faintly, and but with the
    lips, can lament the
Wreck of the Lombard youth, and the vic-
    tory of the oppressor.   15
Whither depart the brave!—God knows; I
    certainly do not.

                    (1858)

WHERE LIES THE LAND

Where lies the land to which the ship would
    go?
Far, far ahead, is all her seamen know.
And where the land she travels from?
    Away,
Far, far behind, is all that they can say.

On sunny noons upon the deck's smooth
    face,   5
Linked arm in arm, how pleasant here to
    pace;
Or, o'er the stern reclining, watch below
The foaming wake far widening as we go.

On stormy nights when wild northwesters
    rave,
How proud a thing to fight with wind and
    wave!   10
The dripping sailor on the reeling mast
Exults to bear, and scorns to wish it past.

Where lies the land to which the ship would
    go?
Far, far ahead, is all her seamen know.
And where the land she travels from?
    Away,   15
Far, far behind, is all that they can say.

                    (1862)

AH! YET CONSIDER IT AGAIN!

'Old things need not be therefore true,'
O brother men, nor yet the new;
Ah! still awhile the old thought retain,
And yet consider it again!

The souls of now two thousand years   5
Have laid up here their toils and fears,
And all the earnings of their pain,—
Ah, yet consider it again!

We! what do we see? each a space
Of some few yards before his face: 10

Does that the whole wide plan explain?
Ah, yet consider it again!

Alas! the great world goes its way,
And takes its truth from each new day;
They do not quit, nor can retain,   15
Far less consider it again.

                    (1862)

IN THE DEPTHS

It is not sweet content, be sure,
    That moves the nobler Muse to song,
Yet when could truth come whole and pure
    From hearts that inly writhe with wrong?

'T is not the calm and peaceful breast   5
    That sees or reads the problem true;
They only know, on whom 't has prest
    Too hard to hope to solve it too.

Our ills are worse than at their ease
    These blameless happy souls suspect,   10
They only study the disease,
    Alas, who live not to detect.

                    (1862)

THE LATEST DECALOGUE

Thou shalt have one God only; who
Would be at the expense of two?
No graven images may be
Worshipped, except the currency:
Swear not at all; for, for thy curse   5
Thine enemy is none the worse:
At church on Sunday to attend
Will serve to keep the world thy friend:
Honor thy parents: that is, all
From whom advancement may befall;   10
Thou shalt not kill; but need'st not strive
Officiously to keep alive:
Do not adultery commit;
Advantage rarely comes of it:
Thou shalt not steal; an empty feat,   15
When it 's so lucrative to cheat:
Bear not false witness; let the lie
Have time on its own wings to fly:
Thou shalt not covet, but tradition
Approves all forms of competition.   20

                    (1862)

SAY NOT THE STRUGGLE NOUGHT AVAILETH

Say not the struggle nought availeth,
    The labor and the wounds are vain,
The enemy faints not, nor faileth,
    And as things have been they remain

If hopes were dupes, fears may be liars; 5
  It may be, in yon smoke concealed,
Your comrades chase e'en now the fliers,
  And, but for you, possess the field.

For while the tired waves, vainly breaking,
  Seem here no painful inch to gain, 10
Far back, through creeks and inlets making,
  Comes silent, flooding in, the main.

And not by eastern windows only,
  When daylight comes, comes in the light,
In front, the sun climbs slow, how slowly, 15
  But westward, look, the land is bright.

(1862)

LIFE IS STRUGGLE

To wear out heart, and nerves, and brain,
And give oneself a world of pain;
Be eager, angry, fierce, and hot,
Imperious, supple — God knows what,
For what's all one to have or not; 5
O false, unwise, absurd, and vain!
For 't is not joy, it is not gain,
It is not in itself a bliss,
Only it is precisely this
  That keeps us all alive. 10

To say we truly feel the pain,
And quite are sinking with the strain; —
Entirely, simply, undeceived,
Believe, and say we ne'er believed
The object, e'en were it achieved, 15
A thing we e'er had cared to keep;
With heart and soul to hold it cheap,
And then to go and try it again;
O false, unwise, absurd, and vain!
O, 't is not joy, and 't is not bliss, 20
Only it is precisely this
  That keeps us still alive.

(1869)

FREDERICK LOCKER-LAMPSON
(1821–1895)

TO MY GRANDMOTHER

Suggested by a picture by Mr. Romney

This relative of mine,
Was she seventy-and nine
  When she died?
By the canvas may be seen
How she looked at seventeen, 5
  As a bride.

Beneath a summer tree
Her maiden reverie
  Has a charm;
Her ringlets are in taste; 10
What an arm! and what a waist
  For an arm!

With her bridal-wreath, bouquet,
Lace farthingale, and gay
  Falbala,— 15
If Romney's touch be true,
What a lucky dog were you,
  Grandpapa!

Her lips are sweet as love;
They are parting! Do they move? 20
  Are they dumb?
Her eyes are blue, and beam
Beseechingly, and seem
  To say, 'Come!'

What funny fancy slips 25
From atween these cherry lips?
  Whisper me,
Fair Sorceress in paint,
What canon says I may n't
  Marry thee? 30

That good-for-nothing Time
Has a confidence sublime!
  When I first
Saw this Lady, in my youth,
Her winters had, forsooth, 35
  Done their worst.

Her locks, as white as snow,
Once shamed the swarthy crow;
  By-and-by
That fowl's avenging sprite 40
Set his cruel foot for spite
  Near her eye.

Her rounded form was lean,
And her silk was bombazine;
  Well I wot 45
With her needles would she sit,
And for hours would she knit,—
  Would she not?

Ah, perishable clay!
Her charms had dropt away 50
  One by one;
But if she heaved a sigh
With a burthen, it was, 'Thy
  Will be done.'

In travail, as in tears, 55
With the fardel of her years
  Overprest,

In mercy she was borne
Where the weary and the worn
  Are at rest.   60

Oh, if you now are there,
And sweet as once you were,
  Grandmamma,
This nether world agrees
You 'll all the better please   65
  Grandpapa.

                (1862)

MY MISTRESS'S BOOTS

She has dancing eyes and ruby lips,
Delightful boots — and away she skips.

They nearly strike me dumb,—
I tremble when they come
  Pit-a-pat: 5
This palpitation means
These Boots are Geraldine's —
  Think of that!

O, where did hunter win
So delicate a skin   10
  For her feet?
You lucky little kid,
You perished, so you did,
  For my Sweet.

The faery stitching gleams   15
On the sides, and in the seams,
  And reveals
That the Pixies were the wags
Who tipt these funny tags,
  And these heels.   20

What soles to charm an elf! —
Had Crusoe, sick of self,
  Chanced to view
One printed near the tide,
O, how hard he would have tried   25
  For the two!

For Gerry 's debonair,
And innocent and fair
  As a rose;
She 's an Angel in a frock,—   30
She 's an Angel with a clock,
  To her hose!

The simpletons who squeeze
Their pretty toes to please
  Mandarins,   35
Would positively flinch
From venturing to pinch
  Geraldine's!

Cinderella's left and rights
To Geraldine's were frights: 40
  And I trow
The Damsel, deftly shod,
Has dutifully trod
  Until now.

Come, Gerry, since it suits   45
Such a pretty Puss (in Boots)
  These to don,
Set your dainty hand a while
On my shoulder, Dear, and I 'll
  Put them on.   50

                (1868)

COVENTRY PATMORE
(1823–1896)

THE SPIRIT'S EPOCHS

Not in the crises of events,
  Of compassed hopes, or fears fulfilled,
Or acts of gravest consequence,
  Are life's delight and depth revealed.
The day of days was not the day;   5
  That went before, or was postponed;
The night Death took our lamp away
  Was not the night on which we groaned.
I drew my bride, beneath the moon,
  Across my threshold; happy hour!   10
But, ah, the walk that afternoon
  We saw the water-flags in flower!

                (1862)

THE MARRIED LOVER

Why, having won her, do I woo?
  Because her spirit's vestal grace
Provokes me always to pursue,
  But, spirit-like, eludes embrace;
Because her womanhood is such   5
  That, as on court-days subjects kiss
The Queen's hand, yet so near a touch
  Affirms no mean familiarness;
Nay, rather marks more fair the height
  Which can with safety so neglect   10
To dread, as lower ladies might,
  That grace could meet with disrespect;
Thus she with happy favor feeds
  Allegiance from a love so high
That thence no false conceit proceeds   15
  Of difference bridged, or state put by,
Because although in act and word
  As lowly as a wife can be,

Her manners, when they call me lord,
   Remind me 't is by courtesy;   20
Not with her least consent of will, -
   Which would my proud affection hurt,
But by the noble style that still
   Imputes an unattained desert;
Because her gay and lofty brows,   25
   When all is won which hope can ask,
Reflect a light of hopeless snows
   That bright in virgin ether bask;
Because, though free of the outer court
   I am, this Temple keeps its shrine   30
Sacred to Heaven; because in short,
   She 's not and never can be mine.

                  (1862)

IF I WERE DEAD

'If I were dead, you 'd sometimes say, Poor
   Child!'
The dear lips quivered as they spake,
   And the tears brake
From eyes which, not to grieve me, brightly
   smiled.
Poor Child, poor Child!
I seem to hear your laugh, your talk, your
   song.
It is not true that Love will do no wrong.
Poor Child!
And did you think, when you so cried and
   smiled,
How I, in lonely nights, should lie awake, 10
And of those words your full avengers
   make?
Poor Child, poor Child!
And now unless it be
That sweet amends thrice told are come to
   thee,
O God, have thou *no* mercy upon me!   15
Poor Child!

                  (1877)

SIDNEY DOBELL (1824–1874)

AMERICA

Men say, Columbia, we shall hear thy guns.
But in what tongue shall be thy battle-cry?
Not that our sires did love in years gone
   by,
When all the Pilgrim Fathers were little
   sons
In merrie homes of Englaunde? Back,
   and see   5
Thy satcheled ancestor! Behold, he runs

To mine, and, clasped, they tread the equal
   lea
To the same village-school, where side by
   side
They spell 'our Father.' Hard by, the twin-
   pride
Of that gray hall whose ancient oriel
   gleams   10
Through yon baronial pines, with looks of
   light
Our sister-mothers sit beneath one tree.
Meanwhile our Shakspere wanders past and
   dreams
His Helena and Hermia. Shall we fight?

Nor force nor fraud shall sunder us! O
   ye   15
Who north or south, on east or western
   land,
Native to noble sounds, say truth for truth,
Freedom for freedom, love for love, and
   God
For God; O ye who in eternal youth
Speak with a living and creative flood   20
This universal English, and do stand
Its breathing book; live worthy of that
   grand,
Heroic utterance — parted, yet a whole,
Far, yet unsevered,— children brave and
   free
Of the great Mother-tongue, and ye shall
   be   25
Lords of an Empire wide as Shakspere's
   soul,
Sublime as Milton's immemorial theme,
And rich as Chaucer's speech, and fair as
   Spenser's dream.

                  (1855)

CHRISTINA ROSSETTI
(1830–1894)

SONG

When I am dead, my dearest,
   Sing no sad songs for me;
Plant thou no roses at my head,
   Nor shady cypress-tree:
Be the green grass above me   5
   With showers and dewdrops wet;
And if thou wilt, remember,
   And if thou wilt, forget.

I shall not see the shadows,
   I shall not feel the rain;   10
I shall not hear the nightingale
   Sing on, as if in pain:
And dreaming through the twilight

That doth not rise nor set,
Haply I may remember,   15
And haply may forget.

(1862)

REMEMBER

Remember me when I am gone away,
Gone far away into the silent land;
When you can no more hold me by the
hand,
Nor I half turn to go yet turning stay.
Remember me when no more, day by day, 5
You tell me of our future that you planned:
Only remember me; you understand
It will be late to counsel then or pray.
Yet if you should forget me for a while
And afterwards remember, do not grieve: 10
For if the darkness and corruption leave
A vestige of the thoughts that once I had,
Better by far you should forget and smile
Than that you should remember and be sad.

(1862)

ABNEGATION

If there be any one can take my place
And make you happy whom I grieve to
grieve,
Think not that I can grudge it, but be-
lieve
I do commend you to that nobler grace,
That readier wit than mine, that sweeter
face;   5
Yea, since your riches make me rich, con-
ceive
I too am crowned, while bridal crowns I
weave,
And thread the bridal dance with jocund
pace.
For if I did not love you, it might be
That I should grudge you some one dear
delight;   10
But since the heart is yours that was mine
own,
Your pleasure is my pleasure, right my
right,
Your honorable freedom makes me free,
And you companioned I am not alone.

(1881)

TRUST

If I could trust mine own self with your
fate,
Shall I not rather trust it in God's hand?

Without whose will one lily doth not stand,
Nor sparrow fall at his appointed date;
Who numbereth the innumerable sand,   5
Who weighs the wind and water with a
weight,
To whom the world is neither small nor
great,
Whose knowledge foreknew every plan we
planned.
Searching my heart for all that touches you,
I find there only love and love's good-will
Helpless to help and impotent to do,   11
Of understanding dull, of sight most dim;
And therefore I commend you back to him
Whose love your love's capacity can fill.

(1881)

UP-HILL

Does the road wind up-hill all the way?
Yes, to the very end.
Will the day's journey take the whole long
day?
From morn to night, my friend.

But is there for the night a resting-place? 5
A roof for when the slow dark hours be-
gin.
May not the darkness hide it from my face?
You cannot miss that inn.

Shall I meet other wayfarers at night?
Those who have gone before.   10
Then must I knock, or call when just in
sight?
They will not keep you standing at that
door.

Shall I find comfort, travel-sore and weak?
Of labor you shall find the sum.
Will there be beds for me and all who
seek?   15
Yea, beds for all who come.

(1862)

CHARLES STUART CALVER-
LEY (1831–1884)

COMPANIONS

A TALE OF A GRANDFATHER

I know not of what we pondered
Or made pretty pretence to talk,
As, her hand within mine, we wandered
Toward the pool by the lime-tree walk,

While the dew fell in showers from the
    passion flowers   5
And the blush-rose bent on her stalk.

I cannot recall her figure:
    Was it regal as Juno's own?
Or only a trifle bigger
Than the elves who surround the throne 10
Of the Faëry Queen, and are seen, I ween,
    By mortals in dreams alone?

What her eyes were like I know not:
    Perhaps they were blurred with tears;
And perhaps in yon skies there glow not 15
    (On the contrary) clearer spheres.
No! as to her eyes I am just as wise
    As you or the cat, my dears.

Her teeth, I presume, were 'pearly:'
    But which was she, brunette or blonde? 20
Her hair, was it quaintly curly,
    Or as straight as a beadle's wand?
That I failed to remark: it was rather dark
    And shadowy round the pond.

Then the hand that reposed so snugly   25
    In mine,— was it plump or spare?
Was the countenance fair or ugly?
    Nay, children, you have me there!
My eyes were p'haps blurred; and besides
    I 'd heard
That it 's horribly rude to stare.   30

And I,— was I brusque and surly?
    Or oppressively bland and fond?
Was I partial to rising early?
    Or why did we twain abscond,
When nobody knew, from the public view 35
    To prowl by a misty pond?

What passed, what was felt or spoken,—
    Whether anything passed at all,—
And whether the heart was broken
    That beat under that shelt'ring shawl,— 40
(If shawl she had on, which I doubt),—
    has gone,
    Yes, gone from me past recall.

Was I haply the lady's suitor?
    Or her uncle? I can't make out;
Ask your governess, dears, or tutor.   45
    For myself, I 'm in hopeless doubt
As to why we were there, who on earth we
    were,
    And what this is all about.

                  (1872)

AUSTIN DOBSON (1840–)

A DEAD LETTER

I

I drew it from its china tomb;—
    It came out feebly scented
With some thin ghost of past perfume
    That dust and days had lent it.

An old, old letter,— folded still!   5
    To read with due composure,
I sought the sun-lit window-sill,
    Above the gray enclosure,

That glimmering in the sultry haze,
    Faint flowered, dimly shaded,   10
Slumbered like Goldsmith's Madam Blaize,
    Bedizened and brocaded.

A queer old place! You 'd surely say
    Some tea-board garden-maker
Had planned it in Dutch William's day   15
    To please some florist Quaker,

So trim it was. The yew-trees still,
    With pious care perverted,
Grew in the same grim shapes; and still
    The lipless dolphin spurted;   20

Still in his wonted state abode
    The broken-nosed Apollo;
And still the cypress-arbor showed
    The same umbrageous hollow.

Only,— as fresh young Beauty gleams   25
    From coffee-colored laces,—
So peeped from its old-fashioned dreams
    The fresher modern traces;

For idle mallet, hoop, and ball
    Upon the lawn were lying;   30
A magazine, a tumbled shawl,
    Round which the swifts were flying;

And, tossed beside the Guelder rose,
    A heap of rainbow knitting,
Where, blinking in her pleased repose,   35
    A Persian cat was sitting.

'A place to love in,— live,— for aye,
    If we too, like Tithonus,
Could find some God to stretch the gray
    Scant life the Fates have thrown us;   40

'But now by steam we run our race,
    With buttoned heart and pocket;

Our Love's a gilded, surplus grace,—
  Just like an empty locket!

"The time is out of joint." Who will,   45
  May strive to make it better;
For me, this warm old window-sill,
  And this old dusty letter.'

II

'Dear *John* (the letter ran), it can't, can't
    be,
  For Father's gone to *Chorley Fair* with
    Sam,   50
And Mother's storing Apples,—*Prue* and
    Me
Up to our Elbows making Damson Jam:
But we shall meet before a Week is gone,—
  "'T is a long Lane that has no turning,"
    John!

'Only till Sunday next, and then you'll
    wait   55
  Behind the White-Thorn, by the broken
    Stile —
We can go round and catch them at the
    Gate,
  All to Ourselves, for nearly one long
    Mile;
Dear *Prue* won't look, and Father he'll go
    on,
And *Sam's* two Eyes are all for *Cissy*,
    John!   60

'*John*, she's so smart,—with every ribbon
    new,
  Flame-colored Sack, and Crimson Pade-
    soy;
As proud as proud; and has the Vapors too,
  Just like My Lady;—calls poor *Sam* a
    Boy,
And vows no Sweet-heart's worth the
    Thinking-on   65
Till he's past Thirty . . . I know better,
    John!

'My Dear, I don't think that I thought of
    much
  Before we knew each other, I and you;
And now, why, *John*, your least, least Fin-
    ger-touch,
  Gives me enough to think a Summer
    through.
See, for I send you Something! There, 't is
    gone!
Look in this corner,—mind you find it,
    John!'

III

This was the matter of the note,—
  A long-forgot deposit,
Dropped in an Indian dragon's throat,   75
  Deep in a fragrant closet,

Piled with a dapper Dresden world,—
  Beaux, beauties, prayers, and poses,—
Bonzes with squat legs undercurled,
  And great jars filled with roses.   80

Ah, heart that wrote! Ah, lips that kissed!
  You had no thought or presage
Into what keeping you dismissed
  Your simple old-world message!

A reverent one. Though we to-day   85
  Distrust beliefs and powers,
The artless, ageless things you say
  Are fresh as May's own flowers,

Starring some pure primeval spring,
  Ere Gold had grown despotic,—   90
Ere Life was yet a selfish thing,
  Or Love a mere exotic!

I need not search too much to find
  Whose lot it was to send it,
That feel upon me yet the kind,   95
  Soft hand of her who penned it;

And see, through twoscore years of smoke,
  In by-gone, quaint apparel,
Shine from yon time-black Norway oak
  The face of Patience Caryl,—   100

The pale, smooth forehead, silver-tressed;
  The gray gown, primly flowered;
The spotless, stately coif whose crest
  Like Hector's horse-plume towered;

And still the sweet half-solemn look   105
  Where some past thought was clinging,
As when one shuts a serious book
  To hear the thrushes singing.

I kneel to you! Of those you were,
  Whose kind old hearts grow mellow,—   110
Whose fair old faces grow more fair
  As Point and Flanders yellow;

Whom some old store of garnered grief,
  Their placid temples shading,
Crowns like a wreath of autumn leaf   115
  With tender tints of fading.

Peace to your soul! You died unwed —
Despite this loving letter.
And what of John? The less that's said
Of John, I think, the better.   120

(1883)

JAMES THOMSON (1834–1882)

From THE CITY OF DREADFUL NIGHT

MELENCOLIA

Anear the center of that northern crest
Stands out a level upland bleak and bare,
From which the city east and south and
west
Sinks gently in long waves; and thronèd
there
An Image sits, stupendous, superhuman,   5
The bronze colossus of a wingèd Woman,
Upon a graded granite base foursquare.

Low-seated she leans forward massively,
With cheek on clenched left hand, the
forearm's might
Erect, its elbow on her rounded knee;
Across a clasped book in her lap the
right   11
Upholds a pair of compasses; she gazes
With full set eyes, but wandering in thick
mazes
Of somber thought beholds no outward
sight.

Words cannot picture her; but all men know
That solemn sketch the pure sad artist
wrought   16
Three centuries and three score years ago,
With fantasies of his peculiar thought:
The instruments of carpentry and science
Scattered about her feet, in strange alliance
With the keen wolf-hound sleeping undis-
traught;

Scales, hour-glass, bell, and magic-square
above;
The grave and solid infant perched beside,
With open winglets that might bear a dove,
Intent upon its tablets, heavy-eyed;   25
Her folded wings as of a mighty eagle
But all too impotent to lift the regal
Robustness of her earth-born strength and
pride;

And with those wings, and that light wreath
which seems

To mock her grand head and the knotted
frown   30
Of forehead charged with baleful thoughts
and dreams,
The household bunch of keys, the house-
wife's gown
Voluminous, indented, and yet rigid
As if a shell of burnished metal frigid,
The feet thick-shod to tread all weakness
down;   35

The comet hanging o'er the waste dark seas,
The massy rainbow curved in front of it
Beyond the village with the masts and
trees;
The snaky imp, dog-headed, from the Pit,
Bearing upon its batlike leathern pinions 40
Her name unfolded in the sun's dominions,
The 'MELENCOLIA' that transcends all
wit.

Thus has the artist copied her, and thus
Surrounded to expound her form sublime,
Her fate heroic and calamitous;   45
Fronting the dreadful mysteries of Time,
Unvanquished in defeat and desolation,
Undaunted in the hopeless conflagration
Of the day setting on her baffled prime.

Baffled and beaten back she works on still,
Weary and sick of soul she works the
more,   51
Sustained by her indomitable will:
The hands shall fashion and the brain
shall pore,
And all her sorrow shall be turned to labor,
Till Death the friend-foe piercing with his
saber   55
That mighty heart of hearts ends bitter
war.

But as if blacker night could dawn on night,
With tenfold gloom on moonless night
unstarred,
A sense more tragic than defeat and blight,
More desperate than strife with hope de-
barred,   60
More fatal than the adamantine Never
Encompassing her passionate endeavor,
Dawns glooming in her tenebrous regard:

The sense that every struggle brings de-
feat
Because Fate holds no prize to crown suc-
cess;   65
That all the oracles are dumb or cheat
Because they have no secret to express;

That none can pierce the vast black veil
   uncertain
Because there is no light beyond the curtain;
   That all is vanity and nothingness.   70

Titanic from her high throne in the north,
   That City's somber Patroness and Queen,
In bronze sublimity she gazes forth
   Over her Capital of teen and threne,
Over the river with its isles and bridges, 75
The marsh and moorland, to the stern rock-
   ridges,
   Confronting them with a coeval mien.

The moving moon and stars from east to
   west
   Circle before her in the sea of air;
Shadows and gleams glide round her sol-
   emn rest.   80
Her subjects often gaze up to her there:
The strong to drink new strength of iron
   endurance,
The weak new terrors; all, renewed assur-
   ance
   And confirmation of the old despair.
                    (1874)

ARTHUR O'SHAUGHNESSY
(1844–1881)

HAS SUMMER COME WITHOUT THE ROSE?

Has summer come without the rose,
   Or left the bird behind?
Is the blue changed above thee,
   O world! or am I blind?
Will you change every flower that grows, 5
   Or only change this spot,
Where she who said, I love thee,
   Now says, I love thee not?

The skies seemed true above thee,
   The rose true on the tree;   10
The bird seemed true the summer through,
   But all proved false to me.
World, is there one good thing in you,
   Life, love, or death — or what?

Since lips that sang, I love thee,   15
   Have said, I love thee not?

I think the sun's kiss will scarce fall
   Into one flower's gold cup;
I think the bird will miss me,
   And give the summer up.   20
O sweet place, desolate in tall
   Wild grass, have you forgot
How her lips loved to kiss me,
   Now that they kiss me not,

Be false or fair above me;   25
   Come back with any face,
Summer! — do I care what you do?
   You cannot change one place,—
The grass, the leaves, the earth, the dew,
   The grave I make the spot,—   30
Here, where she used to love me,
   Here, where she loves me not.
                    (1874)

ODE

We are the music makers,
   And we are the dreamers of dreams,
Wandering by lone sea-breakers,
   And sitting by desolate streams;—
World-losers and world-forsakers,   5
   On whom the pale moon gleams:
Yet we are the movers and shakers
   Of the world for ever, it seems.

With wonderful deathless ditties
We build up the world's great cities,   10
   And out of a fabulous story
   We fashion an empire's glory:
One man with a dream, at pleasure,
   Shall go forth and conquer a crown;
And three with a new song's measure   15
   Can trample a kingdom down.

We, in the ages lying
   In the buried past of the earth,
Built Nineveh with our sighing,
   And Babel itself in our mirth;   20
And o'erthrew them with prophesying
   To the old of the new world's worth;
For each age is a dream that is dying,
   Or one that is coming to birth.
            * * *
                    (1874)

THOMAS DE QUINCEY (1785-1859)

De Quincey's life was ill-regulated, almost from his infancy, in its material conditions. His education was interrupted by changes from one school to another, and at seventeen he ran away from the grammar school of his native city, Manchester, as he himself describes in the first of our extracts from the 'Confessions.' He made his way through Wales to London, where he wandered about in the streets and mixed with the lowest classes of society. After a year of this adventurous life he became an undergraduate at Oxford, but he gave little attention to the prescribed studies, and left without taking a degree. He spent a great deal of time on German, of which he had already learnt something from a chance meeting with a tourist during his wanderings in Wales, and he obtained a good knowledge of Kant and other philosophical writers. He wrote, years afterwards: 'Without breach of truth or modesty I may affirm that my life has been, on the whole, the life of a philosopher: from my birth I was made an intellectual creature; and intellectual in the highest sense my pursuits and pleasures have been, even from my school-boy days.' In 1807 he paid a visit to Coleridge and escorted Mrs. Coleridge and her children to the Lake District, where he met Southey and Wordsworth, and settled down for some years, marrying the daughter of a Westmoreland farmer. In 1821 he removed to London and began his literary career by contributing the *Confessions of an English Opium Eater* to the *London Magazine*. His writings consist almost entirely of essays and reviews, written for various periodicals, and covering a wide range of subjects; many of them are on German literature, which at that time was interesting the British public. The latter part of his life was spent mainly in and about Edinburgh, where his daughter kept house for him. She says: 'He was not a reassuring man for nervous people to live with, as those nights were exceptions on which he did not set something on fire, the commonest incident being for someone to look up from book or work to say casually: "Papa, your hair is on fire," of which a calm, "Is it, my love?" and a hand rubbing out of the blaze was all the notice taken.' His rooms were crowded with books and papers until they became uninhabitable and he moved elsewhere, leaving the accumulated store to the mercy of the landlady. He was incapable of managing money matters, and was often in prison for debt. He would ask for the loan of a small sum, imagining himself absolutely penniless when he had a £50 note in his pocket. His dress and his personal appearance were as odd as his habits; he was of very short stature, with a large head, and bright eyes. He had an extremely delicate ear for music and the harmonies of words; this in part accounts for the beauty of his prose style, which is molded on that of the great writers of the first half of the seventeenth century. He had a keenly analytic intellect, and some of his writings are highly philosophical and imaginative; but like Lamb, as he himself said, he had 'a furious love for nonsense — headlong nonsense '— 'rigmaroling' his friends called it — and the 'Confessions' need not be taken as literal accounts of actual fact.

From CONFESSIONS OF AN ENGLISH OPIUM EATER

I have often been asked how I first came to be a regular opium eater; and have suffered, very unjustly, in the opinion of my acquaintance, from being reputed to have brought upon myself all the sufferings which I shall have to record, by a long course of indulgence in this practice purely for the sake of creating an artificial state of pleasurable excitement. This, however, is a misrepresentation of my case. True it is, that for nearly ten years I did occasionally take opium for the sake of the exquisite pleasure it gave me: but, so long as I took it with this view, I was effectually protected from all material bad consequences, by the necessity of interposing long intervals between the several acts of indulgence, in order to renew the pleasurable sensations. It was not for the purpose of creating pleasure, but of mitigating pain in the severest degree, that I first began to use opium as an article of daily diet. In the twenty-eighth year of my age, a most painful affection of the stomach, which I had first experienced about ten years before, attacked me in great strength. This affection had originally been caused by extremities of hunger, suffered in my boyish days. During the season of hope and redundant happiness which succeeded (that is, from eighteen to twenty-four) it had slumbered; for the three following years it had revived at intervals; and now, under unfavorable circumstances, from depression of spirits, it attacked me with a violence that yielded to no remedies but opium. As the youthful sufferings, which first produced this derangement of the stomach, were interesting in themselves, and in the circumstances that attended them, I shall here briefly retrace them.

My father died when I was about seven years old, and left me to the care of four guardians. I was sent to various schools, great and small; and was very early distinguished for my classical attainments, especially for my knowledge of Greek. At thirteen I wrote Greek with ease; and at fifteen my command of that language was so great, that I not only composed Greek verses in lyric meters, but could converse in Greek fluently and without embarrassment — an accomplishment which I have not since met with in any scholar of my times, and which, in my case, was owing to the practice of daily reading off the newspapers into the best Greek I could furnish *extempore;* for the necessity of ransacking my memory and invention, for all sorts and combinations of periphrastic expressions, as equivalents for modern ideas, images, relations of things, etc., gave me a compass of diction which would never have been called out by a dull translation of moral essays, etc. 'That boy,' said one of my masters, pointing the attention of a stranger to me, 'that boy could harangue an Athenian mob, better than you and I could address an English one.' He who honored me with this eulogy was a scholar, 'and a ripe and good one;' and of all my tutors, was the only one whom I loved or reverenced. Unfortunately for me (and, as I afterwards learned, to this worthy man's great indignation) I was transferred to the care, first of a blockhead, who was in a perpetual panic, lest I should expose his ignorance; and finally, to that of a respectable scholar, at the head of a great school on an ancient foundation. This man had been appointed to his situation by —— College, Oxford; and was a sound, well-built scholar, but (like most men, whom I have known from that college) coarse, clumsy, and inelegant. A miserable contrast he presented, in my eyes, to the Etonian brilliancy of my favorite master; and beside, he could not disguise from my hourly notice, the poverty and meagerness of his understanding. It is a bad thing for a boy to be, and to know himself, far beyond his tutors, whether in knowledge or in power of mind. This was the case, so far as regarded knowledge at least, not with myself only, for the two boys who jointly with myself composed the first form were better Grecians than the head-master, though not more elegant scholars, nor at all more accustomed to sacrifice to the graces. When I first entered, I remember that we read Sophocles; and it was a constant matter of triumph to us, the learned triumvirate of the first form, to see our 'Archididascalus' (as he loved to be called) conning our lessons before we went up, and laying a regular train, with lexicon and grammar, for blowing up and blasting (as it were) any difficulties he found in the choruses; whilst *we* never condescended to open our books until the moment of going up, and were generally employed in writing epigrams upon his wig, or some such important matter. My two class-fellows were poor, and dependent for their future prospects at the university on the recommendation of the head-master; but I, who had a small patrimonial property, the income of which was sufficient to support me at college, wished to be sent thither immediately. I made earnest representations on the subject to my guardians, but all to no purpose. One, who was more reasonable, and had more knowledge of the world than the rest, lived at a distance; two of the other three resigned all their authority into the hands of the fourth; and this fourth with whom I had to negotiate, was a worthy man, in his way, but haughty, obstinate, and intolerant of all opposition to his will. After a certain number of letters and personal interviews, I found that I had nothing to hope for, not even a compromise of the matter, from my guardian; unconditional submission was what he demanded; and I prepared myself, therefore, for other measures. Summer was now coming on with hasty steps, and my seventeenth birthday was fast approaching; after which day I had sworn within myself that I would no longer be numbered amongst school-boys. Money being what I chiefly wanted, I wrote to a woman of high rank, who, though young herself, had known me from a child, and had latterly treated me with great distinction, requesting that she would 'lend' me five guineas. For upwards of a week no answer came; and I was beginning to despond, when, at length, a servant put into my hands a double letter, with a coronet on the seal. The letter was kind and obliging; the fair writer was on the sea-coast, and in that way the delay had arisen; she enclosed double of what I had asked, and good-naturedly hinted that if I should *never* repay her, it would not absolutely ruin her. Now then, I was prepared for my scheme; ten guineas, added to about two which I had remaining from my pocket money, seemed to me sufficient for an indefinite length of time; and at that happy age, if no *definite* boundary can be assigned to one's power, the spirit of hope and pleasure makes it virtually infinite.

It is a just remark of Dr. Johnson's (and what cannot often be said of his remarks, it is a very feeling one), that we never do anything consciously for the last time (of things, that is, which we have long been in the habit of doing) without sadness of heart. This truth I felt deeply, when I came to leave ——, a place which I did not love, and where I had not been happy. On the evening before I left —— for ever, I grieved when the ancient and lofty school-room resounded with the evening service, performed for the last time in my hearing and at night, when the muster-roll of names was called over, and mine (as usual) was called first, I stepped forward, and, passing the head-master, who was standing by, I bowed to him, and looked earnestly in his face, thinking to myself, 'He is old and infirm, and in this world I shall not see him again.' I was right: I never *did* see him again, nor ever shall. He looked at me complacently, smiled good-naturedly, returned my salutation (or rather, my valediction), and we parted (though he knew it not) for ever. I could not reverence him intellectually; but he had been uniformly kind to me, and had allowed me many indulgences; and I grieved at the thought of the mortification I should inflict upon him.

The morning came which was to launch me into the world, and from which my whole succeeding life has, in many important points, taken its coloring. I lodged in the head-master's house, and had been allowed, from my first entrance, the indulgence of a private room, which I used both as a sleeping room and as a study. At half after three I rose, and gazed with deep emotion at the ancient towers of ——, 'drest in earliest light,' and beginning to crimson with the radiant luster of a cloudless July morning. I was firm and immovable in my purpose; but yet agitated by anticipation of uncertain danger and troubles; and, if I could have foreseen the hurricane and perfect hail-storm of affliction which soon fell upon me, well might I have been agitated. To this agitation the deep peace of the morning presented an affecting contrast, and in some degree a medicine. The silence was more profound than that of midnight; and to me the silence of a summer morning is more touching than all other silence, because, the light being broad and strong, as that of noon-day at other seasons of the year, it seems to differ from perfect day, chiefly because man is not yet abroad; and thus, the peace of nature, and of the innocent creatures of God, seems to be secure and deep, only so long as the presence of man, and his restless and unquiet spirit, are not there to trouble its sanctity. I dressed myself, took my hat and gloves, and lingered a little in the room. For the last year and a-half this room had been my 'pensive citadel;' here I had read and studied through all the hours of night; and, though true it was, that for the latter part of this time I, who was framed for love and gentle affections, had lost my gaiety and happiness, during the strife and fever of contention with my guardian; yet, on the other hand, as a boy, so passionately fond of books, and dedicated to intellectual pursuits, I could not fail to have enjoyed many happy hours in the midst of general dejection. I wept as I looked round on the chair, hearth, writing-table, and other familiar objects, knowing too certainly, that I looked upon them for the last time. Whilst I write this, it is eighteen years ago; and yet, at this moment, I see distinctly, as if it were yesterday, the lineaments and expression of the object on which I fixed my parting gaze; it was a picture of the lovely ——, which hung over the mantelpiece; the eyes and mouth of which were so beautiful, and the whole countenance so radiant with benignity and divine tranquillity, that I had a thousand times laid down my pen, or my book, to gather consolation from it, as a devotee from his patron saint. Whilst I was yet gazing upon it, the deep tones of —— clock proclaimed that it was four o'clock. I went up to the picture, kissed it, and then gently walked out, and closed the door for ever!

. . . .

So blended and intertwisted in this life are occasions of laughter and of tears, that I cannot yet recall, without smiling, an incident which occurred at that time, and which had nearly put a stop to the immediate execution of my plan. I had a trunk of immense weight; for, besides my clothes, it contained nearly all my library. The difficulty was to get this removed to a carrier's; my room was at an aërial elevation in the house, and (what was worse) the stair-case, which communicated with this angle of the building, was accessible only by a gallery which passed the head-master's chamber door. I was a favorite with all the servants; and, knowing that any of them would screen me, and act confidentially, I communicated my embarrassment to a groom of the head-master's. The groom swore he would do anything I wished; and, when the time arrived, went upstairs to bring the trunk down. This I feared was beyond the strength of any one man; however, the groom was a man

Of Atlantean shoulders, fit to bear
The weight of mightiest monarchies;

and had a back as spacious as Salisbury Plain. Accordingly he persisted in bringing down the trunk alone, whilst I stood waiting at the foot of the last flight, in anxiety for the event. For some time I heard him descending with slow and firm steps; but unfortunately, from his trepidation, as he drew near the dangerous quarter, within a few steps of the gallery, his foot slipped; and the mighty burden, falling from his shoulders, gained such increase of impetus at each step of the descent, that, on reaching the bottom, it trundled, or rather leaped, right across, with the noise of twenty devils, against the very bed-room door of the archididascalus. My first thought was that all was lost, and that my only chance for executing a retreat was to sacrifice my baggage. However, on reflection, I determined to abide the issue. The groom was in the utmost alarm, both on his own account and on mine; but, in spite of this, so irresistibly had the sense of the ludicrous in this unhappy *contretemps* taken possession of his fancy, that he sang out a long, loud and canorous peal of laughter, that might have wakened the Seven Sleepers. At the sound of this resonant merriment, within the very ears of insulted authority, I could not myself forbear joining in it; subdued to this, not so much by the unhappy *étourderie* of the trunk, as by the effect it had upon the groom. We both expected, as a matter of course, that Dr. —— would sally out of his room; for in general, if but a mouse stirred, he sprang out like a mastiff from the kennel. Strange to say, however, on this occasion, when the noise of laughter had ceased, no sound, or rustling even, was to be heard in the bed-room. Dr. —— had a painful complaint, which, sometimes keeping him awake, made his sleep, perhaps, when it *did* come, the deeper. Gathering courage from the silence, the groom hoisted his burden again, and accomplished the remainder of his descent, without accident. I waited until I saw the trunk placed on a wheel-barrow, and on its road to the carrier's; then, ' with Providence my guide,' I set off on foot — carrying a small parcel, with some articles of dress, under my arm; a favorite English poet in one pocket, and a small 12mo. volume, containing about nine plays of Euripides, in the other.

* * *

If any man, poor or rich, were to say that he would tell us what had been the happiest day in his life, and the why and the wherefore, I suppose that we should all cry out — Hear him! hear him! As to the happiest *day*, that must be very difficult for any wise man to name; because any event that could occupy so distinguished a place in a man's retrospect of his life, or be entitled to have shed a special felicity on any one day, ought to be of such an enduring character as that (accidents apart) it should have continued to shed the same felicity, or one not distinguishably less, on many years together. To the happiest *lustrum*, however, or even to the happiest *year*, it may be allowed to any man to point without discountenance from wisdom. This year, in my case, reader, was the one which we have now reached; though it stood, I confess, as a parenthesis between years of a gloomier character. It was a year of brilliant water (to speak after the manner of jewelers), set as it were, and insulated, in the gloom and cloudy melancholy of opium. Strange as it may sound, I had a little before this time descended suddenly, and without any considerable effort, from 320 grains of opium (*i. e.*, eight [1] thousand drops of laudanum) per day to forty grains, or one-eighth part. Instantaneously, and as if by magic, the cloud of profoundest melancholy which rested upon my brain, like some black vapors that I have seen roll away from the summits of mountains, drew off in one day ($νυχθήμερον$) ; passed off with its murky banners as simultaneously as a ship that has been stranded, and is floated off by a spring-tide —

That moveth altogether, if it move at all.

Now, then, I was again happy; I now took only 1,000 drops of laudanum per day; and what was that? A latter spring had come to close up the season

[1] I here reckon twenty-five drops of laudanum as equivalent to one grain of opium, which, I believe, is the common estimate. However, as both may be considered variable quantities (the crude opium varying much in strength, and the tincture still more), I suppose that no infinitesimal accuracy can be had in such a calculation. Teaspoons vary as much in size as opium in strength. Small ones hold about 100 drops; so that 8,000 drops are about eighty times a teaspoonful. The reader sees how much I kept within Dr. Buchan's indulgent allowance.

of youth; my brain performed its functions as healthily as ever before; I read Kant again, and again I understood him, or fancied that I did. Again my feelings of pleasure expanded themselves to all around me; and if any man from Oxford or Cambridge, or from neither, had been announced to me in my unpretending cottage, I should have welcomed him with as sumptuous a reception as so poor a man could offer. Whatever else was wanting to a wise man's happiness,— of laudanum I would have given him as much as he wished, and in a golden cup. And, by the way, now that I speak of giving laudanum away, I remember, about this time, a little incident, which I mention, because, trifling as it was, the reader will soon meet it again in my dreams, which it influenced more fearfully than could be imagined. One day a Malay knocked at my door. What business a Malay could have to transact amongst English mountains, I cannot conjecture; but possibly he was on his road to a seaport about forty miles distant.

The servant who opened the door to him was a young girl born and bred amongst the mountains, who had never seen an Asiatic dress of any sort; his turban, therefore, confounded her not a little; and, as it turned out, that his attainments in English were exactly of the same extent as hers in the Malay, there seemed to be an impassable gulf fixed between all communication of ideas, if either party had happened to possess any. In this dilemma, the girl, recollecting the reputed learning of her master (and, doubtless, giving me credit for a knowledge of all the languages of the earth, besides, perhaps, a few of the lunar ones), came and gave me to understand that there was a sort of demon below, whom she clearly imagined that my art could exorcise from the house. I did not immediately go down; but, when I did, the group which presented itself, arranged as it was by accident, though not very elaborate, took hold of my fancy and my eye in a way that none of the statuesque attitudes exhibited in the ballets at the Opera House, though so ostentatiously complex, had ever done. In a cottage kitchen, but paneled on the wall with dark wood that from age and rubbing resembled oak, and looking more like a rustic hall of entrance than a kitchen, stood the Malay — his turban and loose trousers of dingy white relieved upon the dark paneling; he had placed himself nearer to the girl than she seemed to relish; though her native spirit of mountain intrepidity contended with the feeling of simple awe which her countenance expressed as she gazed upon the tiger-cat before her. And a more striking picture there could not be imagined, than the beautiful English face of the girl, and its exquisite fairness, together with her erect and independent attitude, contrasted with the sallow and bilious skin of the Malay, enameled or veneered with mahogany, by marine air, his small, fierce, restless eyes, thin lips, slavish gestures and adorations. Half-hidden by the ferocious-looking Malay, was a little child from a neighboring cottage who had crept in after him, and was now in the act of reverting its head, and gazing upwards at the turban and the fiery eyes beneath it, whilst with one hand he caught at the dress of the young woman for protection. My knowledge of the Oriental tongues is not remarkably extensive, being indeed confined to two words — the Arabic word for barley, and the Turkish for opium (madjoon), which I have learned from Anastasius. And, as I had neither a Malay dictionary, nor even Adelung's *Mithridates,* which might have helped me to a few words, I addressed him in some lines from the Iliad; considering that, of such languages as I possessed, Greek, in point of longitude, came geographically nearest to an Oriental one. He worshipped me in a most devout manner, and replied in what I suppose was Malay. In this way I saved my reputation with my neighbors; for the Malay had no means of betraying the secret. He lay down upon the floor for about an hour, and then pursued his journey. On his departure I presented him with a piece of opium. To him, as an Orientalist, I concluded that opium must be familiar; and the expression of his face convinced me that it was. Nevertheless, I was struck with some little consternation when I saw him suddenly raise his hand to his mouth, and (in the school-boy phrase) bolt the whole, divided into three pieces, at one mouthful. The quantity was enough to kill three dragoons and their horses; and I felt some alarm for the poor creature; but what could be done? I had given him the opium in compassion for his solitary life, on recollecting that if he had traveled on foot from London, it must be nearly three weeks since he could have exchanged a thought with any human being. I could not think of violating the laws of hospitality, by having him seized and drenched with an emetic, and thus frightening him into a notion that we were going to sacrifice him to some English idol. No: there was clearly no help for it; — he took his leave, and for some days I felt anxious; but as I never heard of any Malay being found dead, I became convinced that he was used [1] to opium: and that I must have done him the service I designed, by giving him one night of respite from the pains of wandering.

This incident I have digressed to mention, because this Malay (partly from the picturesque exhibition he assisted to frame, partly from the anxiety I connected with his image for some days) fastened afterwards upon my dreams, and brought other Malays with him worse than himself, that ran ' a-muck ' [2] at me, and led me into a world of troubles. But to quit this episode, and to return to my intercalary year of happiness. I have said already, that on a subject so important to us all as happiness, we should listen with pleasure to any man's experience or experiments, even though he were but a plowboy, who cannot be supposed to have plowed very deep into such an intractable soil as that of human pains and pleasures, or to have conducted

[1] This, however, is not a necessary conclusion; the varieties of effect produced by opium on different constitutions are infinite. A London Magistrate (Harriott's *Struggles through Life,* vol. iii, p. 391, Third Edition), has recorded that, on the first occasion of his trying laudanum for the gout, he took *forty* drops, the next night *sixty,* and on the fifth night *eighty,* without any effect whatever; and this at an advanced age. I have an anecdote from a country surgeon, however, which sinks Mr. Harriott's case into a trifle; and in my projected medical treatise on opium, which I will publish, provided the College of Surgeons will pay me for enlightening their benighted understandings upon this subject, I will relate it; but it is far too good a story to be published gratis.

[2] See the common accounts in any Eastern traveler or voyager of the frantic excesses committed by Malays who have taken opium, or are reduced to desperation by ill luck at gambling.

his researches upon any very enlightened principles. But I, who have taken happiness, both in a solid and a liquid shape, both boiled and unboiled, both East India and Turkey — who have conducted my experiments upon this interesting subject with a sort of galvanic battery — and have, for the general benefit of the world, inoculated myself, as it were, with the poison of 8,000 drops of laudanum per day (just, for the same reason, as a French surgeon inoculated himself lately with cancer — an English one, twenty years ago, with plague — and a third, I know not of what nation, with hydrophobia),— I (it will be admitted) must surely know what happiness is, if anybody does. And, therefore, I will here lay down an analysis of happiness; and as the most interesting mode of communicating it, I will give it, not didactically, but wrapped up and involved in a picture of one evening, as I spent every evening during the intercalary year when laudanum, though taken daily, was to me no more than the elixir of pleasure. This done, I shall quit the subject of happiness altogether, and pass to a very different one — the *pains of opium.*

Let there be a cottage, standing in a valley, eighteen miles from any town — no spacious valley, but about two miles long, by three quarters of a mile in average width; the benefit of which provision is, that all the families resident within its circuit will compose, as it were, one larger household personally familiar to your eye, and more or less interesting to your affections. Let the mountains be real mountains, between three and four thousand feet high; and the cottage a real cottage, not (as a witty author has it) 'a cottage with a double coach-house'; let it be, in fact (for I must abide by the actual scene), a white cottage, embowered with flowering shrubs, so chosen as to unfold a succession of flowers upon the walls, and clustering round the windows through all the months of spring, summer, and autumn — beginning, in fact, with May roses, and ending with jasmine. Let it, however, *not* be spring, nor summer, nor autumn — but winter in his sternest shape. This is a most important point in the science of happiness. And I am surprised to see people overlook it, and think

it matter of congratulation that winter is going, or, if coming, is not likely to be a severe one. On the contrary, I put up a petition annually, for as much snow, hail, frost, or storm, of one kind or other, as the skies can possibly afford us. Surely everybody is aware of the divine pleasures which attend a winter fireside; candles at four o'clock, warm hearth-rugs, tea, a fair tea-maker, shutters closed, curtains flowing in ample draperies on the floor, whilst the wind and rain are raging audibly without,

And at the doors and windows seem to call,
As heaven and earth they would together mell;
Yet the least entrance find they none at all;
Whence sweeter grows our rest secure in massy hall.
      — *Castle of Indolence.*

All these are items in the description of a winter evening, which must surely be familiar to everybody born in a high latitude. And it is evident that most of these delicacies, like ice-cream, require a very low temperature of the atmosphere to produce them: they are fruits which cannot be ripened without weather stormy or inclement, in some way or other. I am not '*particular*,' as people say, whether it be snow, or black frost, or wind so strong, that (as Mr. —— says) 'you may lean your back against it like a post.' I can put up even with rain, provided it rains cats and dogs; but something of the sort I must have; and, if I have it not, I think myself in a manner ill-used; for why am I called on to pay so heavily for winter, in coals, and candles, and various privations that will occur even to gentlemen, if I am not to have the article good of its kind? No: a Canadian winter for my money; or a Russian one, where every man is but a co-proprietor with the north wind in the fee-simple of his own ears. Indeed, so great an epicure am I in this matter, that I cannot relish a winter night fully if it be much past St. Thomas's day, and have degenerated into disgusting tendencies to vernal appearances; no, it must be divided by a thick wall of dark nights from all return of light and sunshine. From the latter weeks of October to Christmas Eve, therefore, is the period during which happiness is in season, which, in my judgment, enters the room with the tea-tray; for tea, though ridiculed by those who are naturally of coarse nerves, or are become so from wine-drinking, and are not susceptible of influence from so refined a stimulant, will always be the favorite beverage of the intellectual; and, for my part, I would have joined Dr. Johnson in a *bellum internecinum* against Jonas Hanway, or any other impious person, who should presume to disparage it. But here, to save myself the trouble of too much verbal description, I will introduce a painter, and give him directions for the rest of the picture. Painters do not like white cottages, unless a good deal weather-stained; but as the reader now understands that it is a winter night, his services will not be required, except for the inside of the house.

Paint me, then, a room seventeen feet by twelve, and not more than seven and a half feet high. This, reader, is somewhat ambitiously styled, in my family, the drawing-room; but, being contrived 'a double debt to pay,' it is also, and more justly, termed the library; for it happens that books are the only article of property in which I am richer than my neighbors. Of these I have about five thousand, collected gradually since my eighteenth year. Therefore, painter, put as many as you can into this room. Make it populous with books; and, furthermore, paint me a good fire; and furniture plain and modest, befitting the unpretending cottage of a scholar. And, near the fire paint me a tea-table; and (as it is clear that no creature can come to see one such a stormy night), place only two cups and saucers on the tea-tray; and, if you know how to paint such a thing symbolically, or otherwise, paint me an eternal tea-pot — eternal *à parte ante,* and *à parte post;* for I usually drink tea from eight o'clock at night to four o'clock in the morning. And, as it is very unpleasant to make tea, or to pour it out for oneself, paint me a lovely young woman, sitting at the table. Paint her arms like Aurora's, and her smiles like Hebe's.— But no, dear M——, not even in jest let me insinuate that thy power to illuminate my cottage rests upon a tenure so perishable as mere personal

beauty; or that the witchcraft of angelic smiles lies within the empire of any earthly pencil. Pass, then, my good painter, to something more within its power; and the next article brought forward should naturally be myself — a picture of the Opium-eater, with his 'little golden receptacle of the pernicious drug' lying beside him on the table. As to the opium, I have no objection to see a picture of *that,* though I would rather see the original: you may paint it if you choose; but I apprise you, that no 'little' receptacle would, even in 1816, answer *my* purpose, who was at a distance from the 'stately Pantheon,' and all druggists (mortal or otherwise). No; you may as well paint the real receptacle, which was not of gold, but of glass, and as much like a wine-decanter as possible. Into this you may put a quart of ruby-colored laudanum: that, and a book of German Metaphysics placed by its side, will sufficiently attest my being in the neighborhood; but, as to myself,— there I demur. I admit that, naturally, I ought to occupy the foreground of the picture; that being the hero of the piece, or (if you choose) the criminal at the bar, my body should be had into court. This seems reasonable; but why should I confess, on this point, to a painter? or why confess at all? If the public (into whose private ear I am confidentially whispering my confessions, and not into any painter's) should chance to have framed some agreeable picture for itself, of the Opium-eater's exterior — should have ascribed to him, romantically, an elegant person, or a handsome face, why should I barbarously tear from it so pleasing a delusion — pleasing both to the public and to me? No: paint me, if at all, according to your own fancy; and, as a painter's fancy should teem with beautiful creations, I cannot fail, in that way, to be a gainer. And now, reader, we have run through all the ten categories of my condition as it stood about 1816–17; up to the middle of which latter year I judge myself to have been a happy man; and the elements of that happiness I have endeavored to place before you, in the above sketch of the interior of a scholar's library, in a cottage among the mountains, on a stormy winter evening.   * * *   (1821)

THOMAS BABINGTON MACAULAY (1800–1859).

Macaulay's life is a remarkable story of successful endeavor. The son of a well-known philanthropist and anti-slavery agitator, he was a precocious boy, with a natural aptitude for literary composition and a phenomenal memory; he began a compendium of universal history at the age of seven, and repeated after a lapse of forty years a scrap of poetry he had read as a youth in a country newspaper and had not recalled in the interval; he knew *Paradise Lost* and *Pilgrim's Progress* by heart. He went in 1818 to Trinity College, Cambridge, and left with a fellowship which secured him a sufficient income for his personal wants for the next seven years. An essay on Milton he contributed to the *Edinburgh Review* in 1825 attracted the attention of the editor, Jeffrey, who said to him, 'The more I think, the less I can conceive where you picked up that style.' In 1830 he entered the House of Commons as member for Calne, and at once made his mark by a speech on the Reform Bill. The termination of his fellowship in 1831 put him in somewhat straitened circumstances, and he was obliged to sell the gold medals he had won at the university; but a way out of all financial difficulties was found in 1833 by his appointment as a member of the Supreme Council of India for five years at a salary of £10,000 a year. He did valuable work in India, reconstructing the educational system and drawing up a criminal code, beside doing an enormous amount of private reading. On his return home, he began his *History of England*, and published a collection of his essays, which at once obtained a very large sale. He was elected member for Edinburgh, and became Secretary for War, with a seat in the cabinet. The ministry fell in 1841, and in 1847 Macaulay was rejected by his constituency. He wrote a poem to the effect that literature had been his consolation under all the trials of life, ' of which,' says one biographer, ' it was rather difficult to make a respectable list.' The Edinburgh seat again becoming vacant, he was re-elected without any exertion on his part, but he adhered to his determination to give the rest of his life to literature. The first two volumes of his History were published in 1848, the third and fourth in 1855; from the first it enjoyed very great popularity, and his publishers sent him a check for £20,000. He was raised to the peerage, and buried in Westminster Abbey. He never married, but was devoted to his sisters and their children; his nephew, Sir G. O. Trevelyan, wrote his life, and has attained a considerable reputation as a politician and man of letters.

Macaulay has not Lamb's delicate humor, or De Quincey's philosophical imagination. He disliked speculation, and his idea of history was to present accumulated facts with the attractiveness of fiction. His worst fault is a tendency to emphasize the commonplace — 'blackening the chimney,' Sir Leslie Stephen calls it — but his judgment is generally sound, as far as it goes. His style has no subtle harmonies, but is admirable for mechanical excellences — orderly arrangement of material, careful paragraphing, and absolute clearness of statement. In these points he offers a better model for young writers than De Quincey, Carlyle, Ruskin, and other masters of a more elaborate style.

THE ROMANCE OF HISTORY

The best historians of later times have been seduced from truth, not by their imagination, but by their reason. They far excel their predecessors in the art of deducing general principles from facts. But unhappily they have fallen into the error of distorting facts to suit general principles. They arrive at a theory from looking at some of the phenomena; and the remaining phenomena they strain or curtail to suit the theory. For this purpose it is not necessary that they should assert what is absolutely false; for all questions in morals and politics are questions of comparison and degree. Any proposition 5 which does not involve a contradiction in terms may by possibility be true; and if all the circumstances which raise a probability in its favor be stated and enforced, and those which lead to an op- 10 posite conclusion be omitted or lightly passed over, it may appear to be demonstrated. In every human character and transaction there is a mixture of good and evil: a little exaggeration, a little suppression, a judicious use of epithets, a watchful and searching scepticism with respect to the evidence on one side, a convenient credulity with respect to every report or tradition on the other, may easily make a saint of Laud, or a tyrant of Henry IV.

This species of misrepresentation abounds in the most valuable works of modern historians. Herodotus tells his story like a slovenly witness, who, heated by partialities and prejudices, unacquainted with the established rules of evidence, and uninstructed as to the obligations of his oath, confounds what he imagines with what he has seen and heard, and brings out facts, reports, conjectures, and fancies, in one mass. Hume is an accomplished advocate. Without positively asserting much more than he can prove, he gives prominence to all the circumstances which support his case; he glides lightly over those which are unfavorable to it; his own witnesses are applauded and encouraged; the statements which seem to throw discredit on them are controverted; the contradictions into which they fall are explained away; a clear and connected abstract of their evidence is given. Everything that is offered on the other side is scrutinized with the utmost severity; every suspicious circumstance is a ground for comment and invective; what cannot be denied is extenuated, or passed by without notice; concessions even are sometimes made: but this insidious candor only increases the effect of the vast mass of sophistry.

We have mentioned Hume as the ablest and most popular writer of his class; but the charge which we have brought against him is one to which all our most distinguished historians are in some degree obnoxious. Gibbon, in particular, deserves very severe censure. Of all the numerous culprits, however, none is more deeply guilty than Mr. Mitford. We willingly acknowledge the obligations which are due to his talents and industry. The modern historians of Greece had been in the habit of writing as if the world had learned nothing new during the last sixteen hundred years. Instead of illustrating the events which they narrated by the philosophy of a more enlightened age, they judged of antiquity by itself alone. They seemed to think that notions, long driven from every other corner of literature, had a prescriptive right to occupy this last fastness. They considered all the ancient historians as equally authentic. They scarcely made any distinction between him who related events at which he had himself been present and him who five hundred years after composed a philosophic romance for a society which had in the interval undergone a complete change. It was all Greek, and all true! The centuries which separated Plutarch from Thucydides seemed as nothing to men who lived in an age so remote. The distance of time produced an error similar to that which is sometimes produced by distance of place. There are many good ladies who think that all the people in India live together, and who charge a friend setting out for Calcutta with kind messages to Bombay. To Rollin and Barthelemi, in the same manner, all the classics were contemporaries.

Mr. Mitford certainly introduced great improvements; he showed us that men who wrote in Greek and Latin sometimes told lies; he showed us that ancient history might be related in such a manner as to furnish not only allusions to schoolboys, but important lessons to statesmen. From that love of theatrical effect and high-flown sentiment which had poisoned almost every other work on the same subject his book is perfectly free. But his passion for a theory as false, and far more ungenerous, led him substantially to violate truth in every page. Statements unfavorable to democracy are made with unhesitating confidence, and with the utmost bitterness of language. Every charge brought against a monarch or an aristocracy is sifted with the utmost care. If it cannot be denied, some palliating supposition is suggested; or we are at least reminded that some circumstances now unknown *may* have justified what at present appears unjustifiable. Two events are reported by the same author in the same sentence; their truth rests on the same testimony; but the one supports the darling hypothesis, and the other seems inconsistent with it. The one is taken and the other is left.

The practice of distorting narrative into a conformity with theory is a vice not so unfavorable as at first sight it may appear to the interests of political science. We have compared the writers who indulge in it to' advocates; and we may add that their conflicting fallacies, like those of advocates, correct each other. It has always been held, in the most enlightened nations, that a tribunal will decide a judicial question most fairly when it has heard two able men argue, as unfairly as possible, on the two opposite sides of it; and we are inclined to think that this opinion is just. Sometimes, it is true, superior eloquence and dexterity will make the worse appear the better reason; but it is at least certain that the judge will be compelled to contemplate the case under two different aspects. It is certain that no important consideration will altogether escape notice.

This is at present the state of history. The poet laureate appears for the Church of England, Lingard for the Church of Rome. Brodie has moved to set aside the verdicts obtained by Hume; and the cause in which Mitford succeeded is, we understand, about to be reheard. In the midst of these disputes, however, history proper, if we may use the term, is disappearing. The high, grave, impartial summing up of Thucydides is nowhere to be found.

While our historians are practising all the arts of controversy, they miserably neglect the art of narration, the art of interesting the affections and presenting pictures to the imagination. That a writer may produce these effects without violating truth is sufficiently proved by many excellent biographical works. The immense popularity which well-written books of this kind have acquired deserves the serious consideration of historians. Voltaire's Charles the Twelfth, Marmontel's Memoirs, Boswell's life of Johnson, Southey's account of Nelson, are perused with delight by the most frivolous and indolent. Whenever any tolerable book of the same description makes its appearance, the circulating libraries are mobbed; the book societies are in commotion; the new novel lies uncut; the magazines and newspapers fill their columns with extracts. In the meantime histories of great empires, written by men of eminent ability, lie unread on the shelves of ostentatious libraries.

The writers of history seem to entertain an aristocratical contempt for the writers of memoirs. They think it beneath the dignity of men who describe the revolutions of nations to dwell on the details which constitute the charm of biography. They have imposed on themselves a code of conventional decencies as absurd as that which has been the bane of the French drama. The most characteristic and interesting circumstances are omitted or softened down, because, as we are told, they are too trivial for the majesty of history. The majesty of history seems to resemble the majesty of the poor King of Spain, who died a martyr to ceremony because the proper dignitaries were not at hand to render him assistance.

That history would be more amusing if this etiquette were relaxed will, we suppose, be acknowledged. But would it be less dignified or less useful? What do we mean when we say that one past event is important and another insignificant? No past event has any intrinsic importance. The knowledge of it is valuable only as it leads us to form just calculations with respect to the future. A history which does not serve this purpose, though it may be filled with battles, treaties, and commotions, is as useless as the series of turnpike tickets collected by Sir Matthew Mite.

Let us suppose that Lord Clarendon, instead of filling hundreds of folio pages with copies of state papers in which the same assertions and contradictions are repeated till the reader is overpowered with weariness, had condescended to be the Boswell of the Long Parliament. Let us suppose that he had exhibited to us the wise and lofty self-government of Hampden, leading while he seemed to follow, and propounding unanswerable arguments in the strongest forms with the modest air of an inquirer anxious for information; the delusions which misled the noble spirit of Vane; the coarse fanaticism which concealed the yet loftier genius of Cromwell, destined to control a mutinous army and a factious people, to abase the flag of Holland, to arrest the victorious arms of Sweden, and to hold the balance firm between the rival monarchies of France and Spain. Let us suppose that he had made his Cavaliers and Roundheads talk in their own style; that he had reported some of the ribaldry of Rupert's pages, and some of the cant of Harrison and Fleetwood. Would not his work in that case have been more interesting? Would it not have been more accurate?

A history in which every particular incident may be true may on the whole be false. The circumstances which have most influence on the happiness of mankind, the changes of manners and morals, the transition of communities from poverty to wealth, from knowledge to ignorance, from ferocity to humanity — these are, for the most part, noiseless revolutions. Their progress is rarely indicated by what historians are pleased to call important events. They are not achieved by armies, or enacted by senates. They are sanctioned by no treaties, and recorded in no archives. They are carried on in every school, in every church, behind ten thousand counters, at ten thousand firesides. The upper current of society presents no certain criterion by which we can judge of the direction in which the under current flows. We read of defeats and victories. But we know that nations may be miserable amidst victories and prosperous amidst defeats. We read of the fall of wise ministers and of the rise of profligate favorites. But we must remember how small a proportion the good or evil effected by a single statesman can bear to the good or evil of a great social system.

Bishop Watson compares a geologist to a gnat mounted on an elephant, and laying down theories as to the whole internal structure of the vast animal, from the phenomena of the hide. The comparison is unjust to the geologists; but is very applicable to those historians who write as if the body politic were homogeneous, who look only on the surface of affairs, and never think of the mighty and various organization which lies deep below.

In the works of such writers as these, England, at the close of the Seven Years' War, is in the highest state of prosperity: at the close of the American war she is in a miserable and degraded condition; as if the people were not on the whole as rich, as well governed, and as well educated at the latter period as at the former. We have read books called Histories of England, under the reign of George the Second, in which the rise of Methodism is not even mentioned. A hundred years hence this breed of authors will, we hope, be extinct. If it should still exist, the late ministerial interregnum will be described in terms which will seem to imply that all government was at end; that the social contract was annulled; and that the hand of every man was against his neighbor until the wisdom and virtue of the new cabinet educed order out of the chaos of anarchy. We are quite certain that misconceptions as gross prevail at this moment respecting many important parts of our annals.

The effect of historical reading is analogous, in many respects, to that produced by foreign travel. The student, like the tourist, is transported into a new state of society. He sees new fashions. He hears new modes of expression. His mind is enlarged by contemplating the wide diversities of laws, of morals and of manners. But men may travel far, and return with minds as contracted as if they had never stirred from their own market-town. In the same manner, men may know the dates of many battles and the genealogies of many royal houses, and yet be no wiser. Most people look at past times as princes look at foreign countries. More than one illustrious stranger has landed on our island amidst the shouts of a mob, has dined with the King, has hunted with the master of the stag-hounds, has seen the Guards reviewed, and a knight of the garter installed, has cantered along Regent Street, has visited Saint Paul's, and noted down its dimensions; and has then departed, thinking that he has seen England. He has, in fact, seen a few public buildings, public men, and public ceremonies. But of the vast and complex system of society, of the fine shades of national character, of the practical operation of government and laws, he knows nothing. He who would understand these things rightly must not confine his observations to palaces and solemn days. He must see ordinary men as they appear in their ordinary business and in their ordinary pleasures. He must mingle in the crowds of the exchange and the coffee-house. He must obtain admittance to the convivial table and the domestic hearth. He must bear with vulgar expressions. He must not shrink from exploring even the retreats of misery. He who wishes to understand the condition of mankind in former ages must proceed on the same principle. If he attends only to public transactions, to wars, congresses, and debates, his studies will be as unprofitable as the travels of those imperial, royal and serene sovereigns who form their judgment of our island from having gone in state to a few fine sights, and from having held formal conferences with a few great officers.

The perfect historian is he in whose work the character and spirit of an age is exhibited in miniature. He relates no fact, he attributes no expression to his characters, which is not authenticated by sufficient testimony. But, by judicious selection, rejection, and arrangement, he gives to truth those attractions which have been usurped by fiction. In his narrative a due subordination is observed: some transactions are prominent; others retire. But the scale on which he represents them is increased or diminished, not according to the dignity of the persons concerned in them, but according to the degree in which they elucidate the condition of society and the nature of man. He shows us the court, the camp, and the senate. But he shows us also the nation. He considers no anecdote, no peculiarity of manner, no familiar saying, as too insignificant for his notice which is not too insignificant to illustrate the operation of laws, of religion, and of education, and to mark the progress of the human mind. Men will not merely be described, but will be made intimately known to us. The changes of manners will be indicated, not merely by a few general phrases or a few extracts from statistical documents, but by appropriate images presented in every line.

If a man, such as we are supposing, should write the history of England, he would assuredly not omit the battles, the sieges, the negotiations, the seditions, ministerial changes. But with these he would intersperse the details which are the charm of historical romances. At Lincoln Cathedral there is a beautiful painted window, which was made by an apprentice out of the pieces of glass which had been rejected by his master. It is so far superior to every other in the church, that, according to the tradition, the vanquished artist killed himself from mortification. Sir Walter Scott, in the same manner, has used those fragments of truth which historians have scornfully thrown behind them in a manner which may well excite their envy. He has constructed out of their gleanings works which, even considered as histories, are scarcely less valuable than theirs. But a truly great historian would reclaim those materials which the novelist has appropriated. The history of the government, and the history of the people, would be exhibited in that mode in which alone they can be exhibited justly, in inseparable conjunction and intermixture. We should not then have to look for the wars and votes of the Puritans in Clarendon, and for their phraseology in Old Mortality; for one half of King James in Hume, and for the other half in the Fortunes of Nigel.

The early part of our imaginary history would be rich with coloring from romance, ballad, and chronicle. We should find ourselves in the company of knights such as those of Froissart, and of pilgrims such as those who rode with Chaucer from the Tabard. Society would be shown from the highest to the lowest,— from the royal cloth of state to the den of the outlaw; from the throne of the Legate to the chimney-corner where the begging friar regaled himself. Palmers, minstrels, crusaders,— the stately monastery, with the good cheer in its refectory and the high-mass in its chapel,— the manor-house, with its hunting and hawking,— the tournament, with the heralds and ladies, the trumpets and the cloth of gold,— would give truth and life to the representation. We should perceive, in a thousand slight touches, the importance of the privileged burgher, and the fierce and haughty spirit which swelled under the collar of the degraded villain. The revival of letters would not merely be described in a few magnificent periods. We should discern, in innumerable particulars, the fermentation of mind, the eager appetite for knowledge, which distinguished the sixteenth from the fifteenth century. In the Reformation we should see, not merely a schism which changed the ecclesiastical constitution of England and the mutual relations of the European powers, but a moral war which raged in every family, which set the father against the son, and the son against the father, the mother against the daughter, and the daughter against the mother. Henry would be painted with the skill of Tacitus. We should have the change of his character from his profuse and joyous youth to his savage and imperious old age. We should perceive the gradual progress of selfish and tyrannical passions in a mind not naturally insensible or ungenerous; and to the last we should detect some remains of that open and noble temper which endeared him to a people whom he oppressed, struggling with the hardness of despotism and the irritability of disease. We should see Elizabeth in all her weakness and in all her strength, surrounded by the handsome favorites whom she never trusted, and the wise old statesman whom she never dismissed, uniting in herself the most contradictory qualities of both her parents,— the coquetry, the caprice, the petty malice of Anne,— the haughty and resolute spirit of Henry. We have no hesitation in saying that a great artist might produce a portrait of this remarkable woman at least as striking as that in the novel of Kenilworth, without employing a single trait not authenticated by ample testimony. In the meantime, we should see arts cultivated, wealth accumulated, the conveniences of life improved. We should see the keeps, where nobles, insecure themselves, spread insecurity around them, gradually giving place to the halls of peaceful opulence, to the oriels of Longleat, and the stately pinnacles of Burleigh. We should see towns extended, deserts cultivated, the hamlets of fisherman turned into wealthy havens, the meal of the peasant improved, and his hut more commodiously furnished. We should see those opinions and feelings which produced the great struggle against the House of Stuart slowly growing up in the bosom of private families, before they manifested themselves in parliamentary debates. Then would come the Civil War. Those skirmishes on which Clarendon dwells so minutely

would be told, as Thucydides would have told them, with perspicuous conciseness. They are merely connecting links. But the great characteristics of the age, the loyal enthusiasm of the brave English gentry, the fierce licentiousness of the swearing, dicing, drunken reprobates whose excesses disgraced the royal cause, — the austerity of the Presbyterian Sabbaths in the city, the extravagance of the independent preachers in the camp, the precise garb, the severe countenance, the petty scruples, the affected accent, the absurd names and phrases which marked the Puritans,— the valor, the policy, the public spirit, which lurked beneath these ungraceful disguises,— the dreams of the raving Fifth-monarchy-man, the dreams, scarcely less wild, of the philosophic republican,— all these would enter into the representation, and render it at once more exact and more striking.

The instruction derived from history thus written would be of a vivid and practical character. It would be received by the imagination as well as by the reason. It would be not merely traced on the mind, but branded into it. Many truths, too, would be learned, which can be learned in no other manner. As the history of states is generally written, the greatest and most momentous revolutions seem to come upon them like supernatural inflictions, without warning or cause. But the fact is, that such revolutions are almost always the consequences of moral changes, which have gradually passed on the mass of the community, and which ordinarily proceed far, before their progress is indicated by any public measure. An intimate knowledge of the domestic history of nations is therefore absolutely necessary to the prognosis of political events. A narrative, defective in this respect, is as useless as a medical treatise which should pass by all the symptoms attendant on the early stage of a disease and mention only what occurs when the patient is beyond the reach of remedies.

A historian such as we have been attempting to describe would indeed be an intellectual prodigy. In his mind, powers scarcely compatible with each other must be tempered into an exquisite harmony. We shall sooner see another Shakspere or another Homer. The highest excellence to which any single faculty can be brought would be less surprising than such a happy and delicate combination of qualities. Yet the contemplation of imaginary models is not an unpleasant or useless employment of the mind. It cannot indeed produce perfection; but it produces improvement, and nourishes that generous and liberal fastidiousness which is not inconsistent with the strongest sensibility to merit, and which, while it exalts our conceptions of the art, does not render us unjust to the artist.

(1828)

THE HISTORY OF ENGLAND

(FROM VOL. I, CHAP. III, ON THE STATE OF ENGLAND IN 1685)

The coffee-house must not be dismissed with a cursory mention. It might, indeed, at that time have been not improperly called a most important political institution. No Parliament had sat for years. The municipal council of the city had ceased to speak the sense of the citizens. Public meetings, harangues, resolutions, and the rest of the modern machinery of agitation had not yet come into fashion. Nothing resembling the modern newspaper existed. In such circumstances the coffee-houses were the chief organs through which the public opinion of the metropolis vented itself.

The first of these establishments had been set up, in the time of the Commonwealth, by a Turkey merchant, who had acquired among the Mahometans a taste for their favorite beverage. The convenience of being able to make appointments in any part of the town, and of being able to pass evenings socially at a very small charge, was so great that the fashion spread fast. Every man of the upper or middle class went daily to his coffee-house to learn the news and to discuss it. Every coffee-house had one or more orators to whose eloquence the crowd listened with admiration, and who soon became, what the journalists of our time have been called, a fourth Estate of the realm. The court had long seen with uneasiness the growth of this new power in the state. An attempt had been made, during Danby's administration, to close the coffee-houses. But men of all parties missed their usual places of resort so much that there was a universal outcry. The government did not venture, in opposition to a feeling so strong and general, to enforce a regulation of which the legality might well be questioned. Since that time ten years had elapsed, and during those years the number and influence of the coffee-houses had been constantly increasing. Foreigners remarked that the coffee-house was that which especially distinguished London from all other cities; that the coffee-house was the Londoner's home, and that those who wished to find a gentleman commonly asked, not whether he lived in Fleet Street or Chancery Lane, but whether he frequented the Grecian or the Rainbow. Nobody was excluded from these places who laid down his penny at the bar. Yet every rank and profession, and every shade of religious and political opinion, had its own headquarters. There were houses near Saint James's Park where fops congregated, their heads and shoulders covered with black or flaxen wigs, not less ample than those which are now worn by the Chancellor and by the Speaker of the House of Commons. The wig came from Paris; and so did the rest of the fine gentleman's ornaments, his embroidered coat, his fringed gloves, and the tassel which upheld his pantaloons. The conversation was in that dialect, which, long after it had ceased to be spoken in fashionable circles, continued, in the mouth of Lord Foppington, to excite the mirth of theaters.[1] The atmosphere was like that of a perfumer's shop. Tobacco in any other form than that of richly scented snuff was held in abomination. If any clown, ignorant of the usages of the house, called for a pipe, the sneers of the whole assembly and the short answers of the waiters soon convinced him that he had better go somewhere else. Nor, indeed, would he have had far to go. For, in general, the coffee-rooms

[1] The chief peculiarity of this dialect was that, in a large class of words, the O was pronounced like A. Thus Lord was pronounced Lard. See Vanbrugh's Relapse. Lord Sunderland was a great master of this court tune, as Roger North calls it; and Titus Oates affected it in the hope of passing for a fine gentleman. Examen, 77, 254.

reeked with tobacco like a guard-room; and strangers sometimes expressed their surprise that so many people should leave their own firesides to sit in the midst of eternal fog and stench. Nowhere was the smoking more constant than at Will's. That celebrated house, situated between Covent Garden and Bow Street, was sacred to polite letters. There the talk was about poetical justice and the unities of place and time. There was a faction for Perrault and the moderns, a faction for Boileau and the ancients. One group debated whether Paradise Lost ought not to have been in rime. To another an envious poetaster demonstrated that Venice Preserved ought to have been hooted from the stage. Under no roof was a greater variety of figures to be seen. There were earls in stars and garters, clergymen in cassocks and bands, pert Templars, sheepish lads from the universities, translators and index-makers in ragged coats of frieze. The great press was to get near the chair where John Dryden sat. In winter that chair was always in the warmest nook by the fire; in summer it stood in the balcony. To bow to the Laureate, and to hear his opinion of Racine's last tragedy or of Bossu's treatise on epic poetry, was thought a privilege. A pinch from his snuff-box was an honor sufficient to turn the head of a young enthusiast. There were coffee-houses where the first medical men might be consulted. Dr. John Radcliffe, who, in the year 1685, rose to the largest practice in London, came daily, at the hour when the Exchange was full, from his house in Bow Street, then a fashionable part of the capital, to Garraway's, and was to be found, surrounded by surgeons and apothecaries, at a particular table. There were Puritan coffee-houses where no oath was heard, and where lank-haired men discussed election and reprobation through their noses; Jew coffee-houses where dark-eyed money changers from Venice and from Amsterdam greeted each other; and popish coffee-houses where, as good Protestants believed, Jesuits planned, over their cups, another great fire, and cast silver bullets to shoot the King.[1]

These gregarious habits had no small share in forming the character of the Londoner of that age. He was, indeed, a different being from the rustic Englishman. There was not then the intercourse which now exists between the two classes. Only very great men were in the habit of dividing the year between town and country. Few esquires came to the capital thrice in their lives. Nor was it yet the practice of all citizens in easy circumstances to breathe the fresh air of the fields and woods during some weeks of every summer. A cockney in a rural village was stared at as much as if he had intruded into a kraal of Hottentots. On the other hand, when the lord of a Lincolnshire or Shropshire manor appeared in Fleet Street, he was as easily distinguished from the resident population as a Turk or a Lascar. His dress, his gait, his accent, the manner in which he gazed at the shops, stumbled into the gutters, ran against the porters, and stood under the waterspouts, marked him out as an excellent subject for the operations of swindlers and banterers. Bullies jostled him into the kennel. Hackney coachmen splashed him from head to foot. Thieves explored with perfect security the huge pockets of his horseman's coat, while he stood entranced by the splendor of the Lord Mayor's show. Moneydroppers, sore from the cart's tail, introduced themselves to him, and appeared to him the most honest friendly gentlemen that he had ever seen. Painted women, the refuse of Lewkner Lane and Whetstone Park, passed themselves on him for countesses and maids of honor. If he asked his way to Saint James's, his informants sent him to Mile End. If he went into a shop, he was instantly discerned to be a fit purchaser of everything that nobody else would buy, of second-hand embroidery, copper rings, and watches that would not go. If he rambled into any fashionable coffee-house, he became a mark for the insolent

[1] Lettres sur les Anglois; Tom Brown's Tour; Ward's London Spy; The Character of a Coffee House, 1673; Rules and Orders of the Coffee House, 1674; Coffee Houses vindicated, 1675; A Satyr against Coffee; North's Examen, 138; Life of Guildford, 152; Life of Sir Dudley North, 249; Life of Dr. Radcliffe, published by Curll in 1715. The liveliest description of Will's is in the City and Country Mouse. There is a remarkable passage about the influence of the coffee house orators in Halstead's Succinct Genealogies, printed in 1685.

derision of fops and the grave waggery of Templars. Enraged and mortified, he soon returned to his mansion, and there, in the homage of his tenants and the conversation of his boon companions, found consolation for the vexations and humiliations which he had undergone. There he was once more a great man, and saw nothing above himself except when at the assizes he took his seat on the bench near the judge, or when at the muster of the militia he saluted the Lord Lieutenant.

The chief cause which made the fusion of the different elements of society so imperfect was the extreme difficulty which our ancestors found in passing from place to place. Of all inventions, the alphabet and the printing-press alone excepted, those inventions which abridge distance have done most for the civilization of our species. Every improvement of the means of locomotion benefits mankind morally and intellectually as well as materially, and not only facilitates the interchange of the various productions of nature and art, but tends to remove national and provincial antipathies, and to bind together all the branches of the great human family. In the seventeenth century the inhabitants of London were, for almost every practical purpose, farther from Reading than they now are from Edinburgh, and farther from Edinburgh than they now are from Vienna.

The subjects of Charles the Second were not, it is true, quite unacquainted with that principle which has, in our own time, produced an unprecedented revolution in human affairs, which has enabled navies to advance in face of wind and tide, and brigades of troops, attended by all their baggage and artillery, to traverse kingdoms at a pace equal to that of the fleetest race horse. The Marquess of Worcester had recently observed the expansive power of moisture rarefied by heat. After many experiments he had succeeded in constructing a rude steam engine, which he called a fire water work, and which he pronounced to be an admirable and most forcible instrument of propulsion.[1] But the Marquess was suspected to be a madman, and known to be a Papist. His inventions, therefore, found no favorable reception. His fire

water work might, perhaps, furnish matter for conversation at a meeting of the Royal Society, but was not applied to any practical purpose. There were no railways, except a few made of timber, on which coals were carried from the mouths of the Northumbrian pits to the banks of the Tyne.[2] There was very little international communication by water. A few attempts had been made to deepen and embank the natural streams, but with slender success. Hardly a single navigable canal had been even projected. The English of that day were in the habit of talking with mingled admiration and despair of the immense trench by which Louis the Fourteenth had made a junction between the Atlantic and Mediterranean. They little thought that their country would, in the course of a few generations, be intersected, at the cost of private adventurers, by artificial rivers making up more than four times the length of the Thames, the Severn, and the Trent together.

It was by the highways that both travelers and goods generally passed from place to place; and those highways appear to have been far worse than might have been expected from the degree of wealth and civilization which the nation had even then attained. On the best lines of communication the ruts were deep, the descents precipitous, and the way often such as it was hardly possible to distinguish, in the dusk, from the uninclosed heath and fen which lay on both sides. Ralph Thoresby, the antiquary, was in danger of losing his way on the great North road, between Barnby Moor and Tuxford, and actually lost his way between Doncaster and York.[3] Pepys and his wife, traveling in their own coach, lost their way between Newbury and Reading. In the course of the same tour they lost their way near Salisbury, and were in danger of having to pass the night on the plain.[4] It was only in fine weather that the whole breadth of the road was available for wheeled vehicles. Often the mud lay deep on the right and the left; and only a narrow track of firm ground rose above the quagmire.[5] At

[1] Century of Inventions, 1663, No. 68.

[2] North's Life of Guildford, 136.
[3] Thoresby's Diary, Oct. 21, 1680, Aug. 3, 1712.
[4] Pepys's Diary, June 12 and 16, 1668.
[5] Pepys's Diary, Feb. 28, 1660.

such times obstructions and quarrels were frequent, and the path was sometimes blocked up during a long time by carriers, neither of whom would break the way. It happened, almost every day, that coaches stuck fast, until a team of cattle could be procured from some neighboring farm to tug them out of the slough. But in bad seasons the traveler had to encounter inconveniences still more serious. Thoresby, who was in the habit of traveling between Leeds and the capital, has recorded, in his Diary, such a series of perils and disasters as might suffice for a journey to the Frozen Ocean or to the Desert of Sahara. On one occasion he learned that the floods were out between Ware and London, that passengers had to swim for their lives, and that a higgler had perished in the attempt to cross. In consequence of these tidings he turned out of the high-road, and was conducted across some meadows, where it was necessary for him to ride to the saddle skirts in water.[1] In the course of another journey he narrowly escaped being swept away by an inundation of the Trent. He was afterwards detained at Stamford four days, on account of the state of the roads, and then ventured to proceed only because fourteen members of the House of Commons, who were going up in a body to Parliament with guides and numerous attendants, took him into their company.[2] On the roads of Derbyshire, travelers were in constant fear for their necks, and were frequently compelled to alight and lead their beasts.[3] The great route through Wales to Holyhead was in such a state that, in 1685, a viceroy, going to Ireland, was five hours in traveling fourteen miles, from Saint Asaph to Conway. Between Conway and Beaumaris he was forced to walk great part of the way; and his lady was carried in a litter. His coach was, with much difficulty, and by the help of many hands, brought after him entire. In general, carriages were taken to pieces at Conway, and borne on the shoulders of stout Welsh peasants, to the Menai Straits.[4] In some parts of Kent and Sussex none but the strongest horses could, in winter, get through the bog, in which, at every step, they sank deep. The markets were often inaccessible during several months. It is said that the fruits of the earth were sometimes suffered to rot in one place, while in another place, distant only a few miles, the supply fell far short of the demand. The wheeled carriages were, in this district, generally pulled by oxen.[5] When Prince George of Denmark visited the stately mansion of Petworth in wet weather, he was six hours in going nine miles; and it was necessary that a body of sturdy hinds should be on each side of his coach, in order to prop it. Of the carriages which conveyed his retinue, several were upset and injured. A letter from one of the party has been preserved, in which the unfortunate courtier complains that, during fourteen hours, he never once alighted except when his coach was overturned or stuck fast in the mud.[6]

One chief cause of the badness of the roads seems to have been the defective state of the law. Every parish was bound to repair the highways which passed through it. The peasantry were forced to give their gratuitous labor six days in the year. If this was not sufficient, hired labor was employed, and the expense was met by a parochial rate. That a route connecting two great towns, which have a large and thriving trade with each other, should be maintained at the cost of the rural population scattered between them is obviously unjust; and this injustice was peculiarly glaring in the case of the great North road, which traversed very poor and thinly inhabited districts, and joined very rich and populous districts. Indeed it was not in the power of the parishes of Huntingdonshire to mend a highway worn by the constant traffic between the West Riding of Yorkshire and London. Soon after the Restoration this grievance attracted the notice of Parliament; and an act, the first of our many turnpike acts, was passed, imposing a small toll on travelers and goods, for the purpose of keeping some parts of this important line of

[1] Thoresby's Diary, May 17, 1695.

[2] Ibid., Dec. 27, 1708.

[3] Tour in Derbyshire, by J. Browne, son of Sir Thomas Browne, 1662. Cotton's Angler, 1676.

[4] Correspondence of Henry, Earl of Clarendon, Dec. 30, 1685, Jan. 1, 1686.

[5] Postlethwaite's Dict., Roads; History of Hawkhurst, in the Bibliotheca Topographica Britannica.

[6] Annals of Queen Anne, 1703, Appendix, No. 3.

communication in good repair.[1] This innovation, however, excited many murmurs; and the other great avenues to the capital were long left under the old system. A change was at length effected, but not without much difficulty. For unjust and absurd taxation to which men are accustomed is often borne far more willingly than the most reasonable impost which is new. It was not till many toll bars had been violently pulled down, till the troops had in many districts been forced to act against the people, and till much blood had been shed, that a good system was introduced.[2] By slow degrees reason triumphed over prejudice; and our island is now crossed in every direction by near thirty thousand miles of turnpike road.

On the best highways heavy articles were, in the time of Charles the Second, generally conveyed from place to place by stage wagons. In the straw of these vehicles nestled a crowd of passengers, who could not afford to travel by coach or on horseback, and who were prevented by infirmity, or by the weight of their luggage, from going on foot. The expense of transmitting heavy goods in this way was enormous. From London to Birmingham the charge was seven pounds a ton; from London to Exeter, twelve pounds a ton.[3] This was about fifteen pence a ton for every mile, more by a third than was afterwards charged on turnpike roads, and fifteen times what is now demanded by railway companies. The cost of conveyance amounted to a prohibitory tax on many useful articles. Coal in particular was never seen except in the districts where it was produced, or in the districts to which it could be carried by sea, and was indeed always known in the south of England by the name of sea coal.

On by-roads, and generally throughout the country north of York and west of Exeter, goods were carried by long trains of pack horses. These strong and patient beasts, the breed of which is now extinct, were attended by a class of men who seem to have borne much resemblance to the Spanish muleteers. A traveler of humble condition often found it convenient to perform a journey mounted on a pack saddle between two baskets, under the care of these hardy guides. The expense of this mode of conveyance was small. But the caravan moved at a foot's pace; and in winter the cold was often insupportable.[4]

The rich commonly traveled in their own carriages, with at least four horses. Cotton, the facetious poet, attempted to go from London to the Peak with a single pair, but found at Saint Albans that the journey would be insupportably tedious, and altered his plan.[5] A coach and six is in our time never seen, except as part of some pageant. The frequent mention therefore of such equipages in old books is likely to mislead us. We attribute to magnificence what was really the effect of a very disagreeable necessity. People, in the time of Charles the Second, traveled with six horses, because with a smaller number there was great danger of sticking fast in the mire. Nor were even six horses always sufficient. Vanbrugh, in the succeeding generation, described with great humor the way in which a country gentleman, newly chosen a member of Parliament, went up to London. On that occasion all the exertions of six beasts, two of which had been taken from the plough, could not save the family coach from being embedded in a quagmire.

* * *

[1] 15 Car. II. c. 1.
[2] The evils of the old system are strikingly set forth in many petitions which appear in the Commons' Journal of 1725–26. How fierce an opposition was offered to the new system may be learned from the Gentleman's Magazine of 1749.
[3] Postlethwaite's Dict., Roads.

[4] Loidis and Elmete; Marshall's Rural Economy of England. In 1739 Roderic Random came from Scotland to Newcastle on a packhorse.
[5] Cotton's Epistle to J. Bradshaw.

JOHN HENRY, CARDINAL NEWMAN (1801-1890)

That ferment of aspiration and unrest which produced in the nineteenth century so many forms of religious inquiry, the questioning faith of Tennyson's *In Memoriam*, Carlyle's turbid discontent with modern civilization and Ruskin's frantic anti-materialism, produced in John Henry Newman its most specialized and inspired searcher after spiritual grace,— in short, a religious genius. Newman was born in the City of London not far from the Bank. His father, a banker, was a man of cultivated tastes and is thought to have been of Jewish extraction. His mother came of a Huguenot family and Newman was instructed during his childhood in 'modified Calvinism.' As a youth he displayed singular intellectual restlessness combined with literary instinct and precocity. He was said to know the Bible by heart. His early passion for Scott provided his imagination with a background of medieval sympathies, and his memory with a piquant reference at a crucial point in the most close-knit controversy of his later life. In 1817 he entered Trinity College, Oxford, and won a scholarship at the end of his first year. The stirrings of the medieval movement were already beginning at Oxford when Newman became a fellow of Oriel College, its special home. After some terms at the law in London, Newman took orders in the Anglican church and by 1829 had become a tutor in Oriel and Vicar of St. Mary's. From contact with Hurrell Froude he soon grew deeply interested in the historic phases of Christianity; the new-old ideas of the Fathers 'came like music' to his 'inward ear,' and he conveyed them with burning effect into his clarion University Sermons at St. Mary's. In 1832, with Froude he saw Rome; he came near to death from cholera, paid devout visits to many ancient churches, wrote at Palermo, 'O, that thy creed were sound, thou Church of Rome,' and on shipboard composed in the twilight of Roman Catholicism, *Lead Kindly Light*, which one of his critics has termed 'the "March" of the tractarian movement.' The Sunday after Newman reached England, John Keble preached in his pulpit at St. Mary's the sermon on *National Apostasy*, which is held to have precipitated the Tractarian movement. To meet the rationalistic liberalism and irreligion which were threatening the church from without, two movements, broadly speaking, were advocated within it; — one, in sympathy with the temper of the age, toward more latitude of doctrine and more practical activity; the other, reactionary, toward a more zealous adherence to the forms, traditions and earlier sanctities of the church. It was this latter course that Newman and his friends espoused in the *Tracts for the Times*. Of this movement Newman was the most powerful writer. In seeking to establish the historical continuity of the English church, he gradually convinced himself of the authenticity of Romanism. He was not yet aware of the approaching position of his own mind, when he examined the subject of Apostolic Succession in his famous *Tract Ninety* (1841). The dangerousness of his position did not remain undetected by others and aroused the utmost violence of passion. Newman was compelled to leave Oxford and, soon after, it became known that he had entered the Roman fold. What followed is indescribable. Families were broken up. The entire religious world was in a state of almost tragic excitement. Newman alone preserved his calm and what was considered an ominous silence. For twenty years he addressed himself chiefly to his own parish and the men of his adopted faith. Finally, in 1864, a supreme opportunity came for him to address from a point of advantage the public which had reviled him. Charles Kingsley in a review of Froude's *History of England*, went out of his way to accuse 'Father Newman' of having justified the principle of dishonesty in the Roman priesthood. In the complicated correspondence, which was afterwards published in full, Newman had all the honors. With resistless logic and dexterity and the perfect poise and sincerity of a christian gentleman he left his assailant in an obvious position of reckless bigotry, wrong-headedness and untruth. Newman could now present to the English world the logic of his religious development, and this he did in his *Apologia pro Vita Sua* [Defense of his Life]. This is a telling presentation, full of acute personal interest, of the claims which an ancient and established religion can urge upon modern culture, and a justification of faith 'against the assaults of a fictitious enlightenment.' Upon the elevation of Pope Leo XIII, Newman was made, in 1879, a Cardinal of the Roman church.

Newman's prose style was a remarkable weapon in the hands of a controversialist. Pliant and strong, colloquial but never familiar, subtle and suave without the least insinuation of vulgar slyness, in command of all the nuances of delicate culture which it sparingly uses, it bends and thrusts like a beautifully tempered steel. Even should its matter cease to be of great interest, Newman's prose will always remain poignant for its classic purity and strength.

THE IDEA OF A UNIVERSITY

DISCOURSE VI

KNOWLEDGE VIEWED IN RELATION TO LEARNING

It were well if the English, like the Greek language, possessed some definite word to express, simply and generally, intellectual proficiency or perfection, such as 'health,' as used with reference to the animal frame, and 'virtue,' with reference to our moral nature. I am not able to find such a term; — talent, ability, genius, belong distinctly to the raw material, which is the subject-matter, not to that excellence which is the result of exercise and training. When we turn, indeed, to the particular kinds of intellectual perfection, words are forthcoming for our purpose, as, for instance, judgment, taste, and skill; yet even these belong, for the most part, to powers or habits bearing upon practice or upon art, and not to any perfect condition of the intellect, considered in itself. Wisdom, again, is certainly a more comprehensive word than any other, but it has a direct relation to conduct, and to human life. Knowledge, indeed, and science express purely intellectual ideas, but still not a state or quality of the intellect; for knowledge, in its ordinary sense, is but one of its circumstances, denoting a possession or a habit; and science has been appropriated to the subject-matter of the intellect, instead of belonging in English, as it ought to do, to the intellect itself. The consequence is that, on an occasion like this, many words are necessary, in order, first, to bring out and convey what surely is no difficult idea in itself,— that of the cultivation of the intellect as an end; next, in order to recommend what surely is no unreasonable object; and lastly, to describe and make the mind realize the particular perfection in which that object consists. Every one knows practically what are the constituents of health or of virtue; and every one recognizes health and virtue as ends to be pursued; it is otherwise with intellectual excellence, and this must be my excuse, if I seem to anyone to be bestowing a good deal of labor on a preliminary matter.

In default of a recognized term, I have called the perfection or virtue of the intellect by the name of philosophy, philosophical knowledge, enlargement of mind, or illumination; terms which are not uncommonly given to it by writers of this day: but, whatever name we bestow on it, it is, I believe, as a matter of history, the business of a university to make this intellectual culture its direct scope, or to employ itself in the education of the intellect,— just as the work of a hospital lies in healing the sick or wounded, of a riding or fencing school, or of a gymnasium, in exercising the limbs, of an almshouse, in aiding and solacing the old, of an orphanage, in protecting innocence, of a penitentiary, in restoring the guilty. I say, a university, taken in its bare idea, and before we view it as an instrument of the church, has this object and this mission; it contemplates neither moral impression nor mechanical production; it professes to exercise the mind neither in art nor in duty; its function is intellectual culture; here it may leave its scholars, and it has done its work when it has done as much as this. It educates the intellect to reason well in all matters, to reach out towards truth, and to grasp it.

This, I said in my foregoing discourse, was the object of a university, viewed in itself, and apart from the Catholic Church, or from the state, or from any other power which may use it; and I illustrated this in various ways. I said that the intellect must have an excellence of its own, for there was nothing which had not its specific good; that the word 'educate' would not be used of intellectual culture, as it is used, had not the intellect had an end of its own; that, had it not such an end, there would be no meaning in calling certain intellectual exercises 'liberal,' in contrast with 'useful,' as is commonly done; that the very notion of a philosophical temper implied it, for it threw us back upon research and system as ends in themselves, distinct from effects and works of any kind; that a philosophical scheme of knowledge, or system of sciences, could not, from the nature of the case, issue in any one definite art or pursuit, as its end; and that, on the other hand, the discovery and contemplation of truth, to which research and systematizing led, were surely sufficient ends, though nothing beyond them were added, and that they had ever been accounted sufficient by mankind.

Here then I take up the subject; and, having determined that the cultivation of the intellect is an end distinct and sufficient in itself, and that, so far as words go, it is an enlargement or illumination, I proceed to inquire what this mental breadth, or power, or light, or philosophy consists in. A hospital heals a broken limb or cures a fever: what does an institution effect, which professes the health, not of the body, not of the soul, but of the intellect? What is this good, which in former times, as well as our own, has been found worth the notice, the appropriation of the Catholic Church?

I have then to investigate, in the discourses which follow, those qualities and characteristics of the intellect in which its cultivation issues or rather consists; and, with a view of assisting myself in this undertaking, I shall recur to certain questions which have already been touched upon. These questions are three: viz. the relation of intellectual culture, first, to *mere* knowledge; secondly, to *professional* knowledge; and thirdly, to *religious* knowledge. In other words, are *acquirements* and *attainments* the scope of a university education? or *expertness in particular arts* and *pursuits?* or *moral and religious proficiency?* or something besides these three? These questions I shall examine in succession, with the purpose I have mentioned; and I hope to be excused, if, in this anxious undertaking, I am led to repeat what, either in these discourses or elsewhere, I have already put upon paper. And first, of *mere knowledge,* or learning, and its connection with intellectual illumination or philosophy.

I suppose the *prima-facie* view which the public at large would take of a university, considering it as a place of education, is nothing more or less than a place for acquiring a great deal of knowledge on a great many subjects. Memory is one of the first developed of the mental faculties; a boy's business when he goes to school is to learn, that is, to store up things in his memory. For some years his intellect is little more than an instrument for taking in facts, or a re-

ceptacle for storing them; he welcomes them as fast as they come to him; he lives on what is without; he has his eyes ever about him; he has a lively susceptibility of impressions; he imbibes information of every kind; and little does he make his own in a true sense of the word, living rather upon his neighbors all around him. He has opinions, religious, political and literary, and, for a boy, is very positive in them and sure about them; but he gets them from his schoolfellows, or his masters, or his parents, as the case may be. Such as he is in his other relations, such also is he in his school exercises; his mind is observant, sharp, ready, retentive; he is almost passive in the acquisition of knowledge. I say this in no disparagement of the idea of a clever boy. Geography, chronology, history, language, natural history, he heaps up the matter of these studies as treasures for a future day. It is the seven years of plenty with him: he gathers in by handfuls, like the Egyptians, without counting; and though, as time goes on, there is exercise for his argumentative powers in the elements of mathematics, and for his taste in the poets and orators, still, while at school, or at least, till quite the last years of his time, he acquires, and little more; and when he is leaving for the university, he is mainly the creature of foreign influences and circumstances, and made up of accidents, homogeneous or not, as the case may be. Moreover, the moral habits, which are a boy's praise, encourage and assist this result; that is, diligence, assiduity, regularity, despatch, persevering application; for these are the direct conditions of acquisition, and naturally lead to it. Acquirements, again, are emphatically producible, and at a moment; they are a something to show, both for master and scholar; an audience, even though ignorant themselves of the subjects of an examination, can comprehend when questions are answered and when they are not. Here again is a reason why mental culture is in the minds of men identified with the acquisition of knowledge.

The same notion possesses the public mind, when it passes on from the thought of a school to that of a university: and with the best of reasons so far as this, that there is no true culture without acquirements, and that philosophy presupposes knowledge. It requires a great deal of reading, or a wide range of information, to warrant us in putting forth our opinions on any serious subject; and without such learning the most original mind may be able indeed to dazzle, to amuse, to refute, to perplex, but not to come to any useful result or any trustworthy conclusion. There are indeed persons who profess a different view of the matter, and even act upon it. Every now and then you will find a person of vigorous or fertile mind, who relies upon his own resources, despises all former authors, and gives the world, with the utmost fearlessness, his views upon religion, or history, or any other popular subject. And his works may sell for a while; he may get a name in his day; but this will be all. His readers are sure to find on the long run that his doctrines are mere theories, and not the expression of facts, that they are chaff instead of bread, and then his popularity drops as suddenly as it rose.

Knowledge then is the indispensable condition of expansion of mind, and the instrument of attaining to it; this cannot be denied, it is ever to be insisted on; I begin with it as a first principle; however, the very truth of it carries men too far, and confirms to them the notion that it is the whole of the matter. A narrow mind is thought to be that which contains little knowledge; and an enlarged mind, that which holds a great deal; and what seems to put the matter beyond dispute is, the fact of the great number of studies which are pursued in a university, by its very profession. Lectures are given on every kind of subject; examinations are held; prizes awarded. There are moral, metaphysical, physical professors; professors of languages, of history, of mathematics, of experimental science. Lists of questions are published, wonderful for their range and depth, variety and difficulty; treatises are written, which carry upon their very face the evidence of extensive reading or multifarious information; what then is wanting for mental culture to a person of large reading and scientific attainments? what is grasp of mind but acquirement? where shall philosophical repose be found, but in the conscious-

ness and enjoyment of large intellectual possessions?

And yet this notion is, I conceive, a mistake, and my present business is to show that it is one, and that the end of a liberal education is not mere knowledge, or knowledge considered in its *matter;* and I shall best attain my object, by actually setting down some cases, which will be generally granted to be instances of the process of enlightenment or enlargement of mind, and others which are not, and thus, by the comparison, you will be able to judge for yourselves, gentlemen, whether knowledge, that is, acquirement, is after all the real principle of the enlargement or whether that principle is not rather something beyond it.

For instance, let a person, whose experience has hitherto been confined to the more calm and unpretending scenery of these islands, whether here or in England, go for the first time into parts where physical nature puts on her wilder and more awful forms, whether at home or abroad, as into mountainous districts; or let one, who has ever lived in a quiet village, go for the first time to a great metropolis,— then I suppose he will have a sensation which perhaps he never had before. He has a feeling not in addition or increase of former feelings, but of something different in its nature. He will perhaps be borne forward, and find for a time that he has lost his bearings. He has made a certain progress, and he has a consciousness of mental enlargement; he does not stand where he did, he has a new center, and a range of thoughts to which he was before a stranger.

Again, the view of the heavens which the telescope opens upon us, if allowed to fill and possess the mind, may almost whirl it round and make it dizzy. It brings in a flood of ideas, and is rightly called an intellectual enlargement, whatever is meant by the term.

And so again, the sight of beasts of prey and other foreign animals, their strangeness, the originality (if I may use the term) of their forms and gestures and habits, and their variety and independence of each other, throw us out of ourselves into another creation, and as if under another Creator, if I may so express the temptation which may come on the mind. We seem to have new faculties, or a new exercise for our faculties, by this addition to our knowledge; like a prisoner, who, having been accustomed to wear manacles or fetters, suddenly finds his arms and legs free.

Hence physical science generally, in all its departments, as bringing before us the exuberant riches and resources, yet the orderly course, of the universe, elevates and excites the student, and at first, I may say, almost takes away his breath, while in time it exercises a tranquilizing influence upon him.

Again the study of history is said to enlarge and enlighten the mind, and why? because, as I conceive, it gives it a power of judging of passing events and of all events, and a conscious superiority over them, which before it did not possess.

And in like manner, what is called seeing the world, entering into active life, going into society, traveling, gaining acquaintance with the various classes of the community, coming into contact with the principles and modes of thought of various parties, interests, and races, their views, aims, habits and manners, their religious creeds and forms of worship,— gaining experience how various yet how alike men are, how low-minded, how bad, how opposed, yet how confident in their opinions; all this exerts a perceptible influence upon the mind, which it is impossible to mistake, be it good or be it bad, and is popularly called its enlargement.

And then again, the first time the mind comes across the arguments and speculations of unbelievers, and feels what a novel light they cast upon what he has hitherto accounted sacred; and still more, if it gives in to them and embraces them, and throws off as so much prejudice what it has hitherto held, and, as if waking from a dream, begins to realize to its imagination that there is now no such thing as law and the transgression of law, that sin is a phantom, and punishment a bugbear, that it is free to sin, free to enjoy the world and the flesh; and still further, when it does enjoy them, and reflects that it may think and hold just what it will, that 'the world is all before it where to choose,' and what system to build up as its own private persuasion; when this torrent of wilful thoughts rushes over and inundates it.

who will deny that the fruit of the tree of knowledge, or what the mind takes for knowledge, has made it one of the gods, with a sense of expansion and elevation,— an intoxication in reality, still, so far as the subjective state of the mind goes, an illumination? Hence the fanaticism of individuals or nations, who suddenly cast off their Maker. Their eyes are opened; and, like the judgment-stricken king in the tragedy, they see two suns, and a magic universe, out of which they look back upon their former state of faith and innocence with a sort of contempt and indignation, as if they were then but fools, and the dupes of imposture.

On the other hand, religion has its own enlargement, and an enlargement, not of tumult, but of peace. It is often remarked of uneducated persons, who have hitherto thought little of the unseen world, that, on their turning to God, looking into themselves, regulating their hearts, reforming their conduct, and meditating on death and judgment, heaven and hell, they seem to become, in point of intellect, different beings from what they were. Before, they took things as they came, and thought no more of one thing than another. But now every event has a meaning; they have their own estimate of whatever happens to them; they are mindful of times and seasons, and compare the present with the past; and the world, no longer dull, monotonous, unprofitable, and hopeless, is a various and complicated drama, with parts and an object, and an awful moral.

Now from these instances, to which many more might be added, it is plain, first, that the communication of knowledge certainly is either a condition or the means of that sense of enlargement, or enlightenment of which at this day we hear so much in certain quarters: this cannot be denied; but next, it is equally plain, that such communication is not the whole of the process. The enlargement consists, not merely in the passive reception into the mind of a number of ideas hitherto unknown to it, but in the mind's energetic and simultaneous action upon and towards and among those new ideas, which are rushing in upon it. It is the action of a formative power, reducing to order and meaning the matter of our acquirements; it is a making the objects of our knowledge subjectively our own, or, to use a familiar word, it is a digestion of what we receive, into the substance of our previous state of thought; and without this no enlargement is said to follow. There is no enlargement, unless there be a comparison of ideas one with another, as they come before the mind, and a systematizing of them. We feel our minds to be growing and expanding *then*, when we not only learn, but refer what we learn to what we know already. It is not the mere addition to our knowledge that is the illumination; but the locomotion, the movement onwards, of that mental center, to which both what we know, and what we are learning, the accumulating mass of our acquirements, gravitates. And therefore a truly great intellect, and recognized to be such by the common opinion of mankind, such as the intellect of Aristotle, or of St. Thomas, or of Newton, or of Goethe (I purposely take instances within and without the Catholic pale, when I would speak of the intellect as such), is one which takes a connected view of old and new, past and present, far and near, and which has an insight into the influence of all these one on another; without which there is no whole and no center. It possesses the knowledge, not only of things, but also of their mutual and true relations; knowledge, not merely considered as acquirement but as philosophy.

Accordingly, when this analytical, distributive, harmonizing process is away, the mind experiences no enlargement, and is not reckoned as enlightened or comprehensive, whatever it may add to its knowledge. For instance, a great memory, as I have already said, does not make a philosopher, any more than a dictionary can be called a grammar. There are men who embrace in their minds a vast multitude of ideas, but with little sensibility about their real relations towards each other. These may be antiquarians, annalists, naturalists; they may be learned in the law; they may be versed in statistics; they are most useful in their own place; I should shrink from speaking disrespectfully of them; still, there is nothing in such attainments to guarantee the absence of narrowness of mind. If they are nothing more than well-read men, or men of information, they have not what specially deserves the name of culture of mind, or fulfils the type of liberal education.

In like manner, we sometimes fall in with persons who have seen much of the world, and of the men who, in their day, have played a conspicuous part in it, but who generalize nothing, and have no observation, in the true sense of the word. They abound in information in detail, curious and entertaining, about men and things; and, having lived under the influence of no very clear or settled principles, religious or political, they speak of every one and every thing, only as so many phenomena, which are complete in themselves, and lead to nothing, not discussing them, or teaching any truth, or instructing the hearer, but simply talking. No one would say that these persons, well informed as they are, had attained to any great culture of intellect or to philosophy.

The case is the same still more strikingly where the persons in question are beyond dispute men of inferior powers and deficient education. Perhaps they have been much in foreign countries, and they receive, in a passive, otiose, unfruitful way, the various facts which are forced upon them there. Seafaring men, for example, range from one end of the earth to the other; but the multiplicity of external objects, which they have encountered, forms no symmetrical and consistent picture upon their imagination; they see the tapestry of human life, as it were on the wrong side, and it tells no story. They sleep, and they rise up, and they find themselves, now in Europe, now in Asia; they see visions of great cities and wild regions; they are in the marts of commerce, or amid the islands of the South; they gaze on Pompey's Pillar, or on the Andes; and nothing which meets them carries them forward or backward, to any idea beyond itself. Nothing has a drift or relation; nothing has a history or a promise. Every thing stands by itself, and comes and goes in its turn, like the shifting scenes of a show, which leave the spectator where he was. Perhaps you are near such a man on a particular occasion, and expect him to be shocked or perplexed at something which occurs; but one thing is much the same to him as another, or, if he is perplexed, it is as not knowing what to say, whether it is right to admire, or to ridicule, or to disapprove, while conscious that some expression of opinion is expected from him; for in fact he has no standard of judgment at all, and no landmarks to guide him to a conclusion. Such is mere acquisition, and, I repeat, no one would dream of calling it philosophy.

Instances, such as these, confirm, by the contrast, the conclusion I have already drawn from those which preceded them. That only is true enlargement of mind which is the power of viewing many things at once as one whole, of referring them severally to their true place in the universal system, of understanding their respective values, and determining their mutual dependence. Thus is that form of universal knowledge, of which I have on a former occasion spoken, set up in the individual intellect, and constitutes its perfection. Possessed of this real illumination, the mind never views any part of the extended subject-matter of knowledge without recollecting that it is but a part, or without the associations which spring from this recollection. It makes everything in some sort lead to everything else; it would communicate the image of the whole to every separate portion, till that whole becomes in imagination like a spirit, everywhere pervading and penetrating its component parts, and giving them one definite meaning. Just as our bodily organs, when mentioned, recall their function in the body, as the word 'creation' suggests the Creator, and 'subjects' a sovereign, so, in the mind of the philosopher, as we are abstractedly conceiving of him, the elements of the physical and moral world, sciences, arts, pursuits, ranks, offices, events, opinions, individualities, are all viewed as one, with correlative functions, and as gradually by successive combinations converging, one and all, to the true center.

To have even a portion of this illuminative reason and true philosophy is the highest state to which nature can aspire, in the way of intellect; it puts the mind above the influences of chance and necessity, above anxiety, suspense, unsettlement, and superstition, which is the lot

of the many. Men, whose minds are possessed with some one object, take exaggerated views of its importance, are feverish in the pursuit of it, make it the measure of things which are utterly foreign to it, and are startled and despond if it happens to fail them. They are ever in alarm or in transport. Those on the other hand who have no object or principle whatever to hold by, lose their way every step they take. They are thrown out, and do not know what to think or say, at every fresh juncture; they have no view of persons, or occurrences, or facts, which come suddenly upon them, and they hang upon the opinion of others for want of internal resources. But the intellect, which has been disciplined to the perfection of its powers, which knows, and thinks while it knows, which has learned to leaven the dense mass of facts and events with the elastic force of reason, such an intellect cannot be partial, cannot be exclusive, cannot be impetuous, cannot be at a loss, cannot but be patient, collected, and majestically calm, because it discerns the end in every beginning, the origin in every end, the law in every interruption, the limit in each delay; because it ever knows where it stands, and how its path lies from one point to another. It is the τετράγωνος [four-square] of the Peripatetic, and has the *nil admirari* [to be moved by nothing] of the Stoic,—

Felix qui potuit rerum cognoscere causas,
Atque metus omnes, et inexorabile fatum
Subjecit pedibus, strepitumque Acherontis
    avari.
[Happy is he who has come to know the sequences of things, and is thus above all fear and the dread march of fate and the roar of greedy Acheron.]

There are men who, when in difficulties, originate at the moment vast ideas or dazzling projects; who, under the influence of excitement, are able to cast a light, almost as if from inspiration, on a subject or course of action which comes before them; who have a sudden presence of mind equal to any emergency, rising with the occasion, and an undaunted magnanimous bearing, and an energy and keenness which is but made intense by opposition. This is genius, this is heroism; it is the exhibition of a natural gift, which no culture can teach, at which no institution can aim: here, on the contrary, we are concerned, not with mere nature, but with training and teaching. That perfection of the intellect, which is the result of education, and its *beau ideal*, to be imparted to individuals in their respective measures, is the clear, calm, accurate vision and comprehension of all things, as far as the finite mind can embrace them, each in its place, and with its own characteristics upon it. It is almost prophetic from its knowledge of history; it is almost heart-searching from its knowledge of human nature; it has almost supernatural charity from its freedom from littleness and prejudice; it has almost the repose of faith, because nothing can startle it; it has almost the beauty and harmony of heavenly contemplation, so intimate is it with the eternal order of things and the music of the spheres.

And now, if I may take for granted that the true and adequate end of intellectual training and of a university is not learning or acquirement, but rather, is thought or reason exercised upon knowledge, or what may be called philosophy, I shall be in a position to explain the various mistakes which at the present day beset the subject of university education.

I say then, if we would improve the intellect, first of all, we must ascend; we cannot gain real knowledge on a level; we must generalize, we must reduce to method, we must have a grasp of principles, and group and shape our acquisitions by means of them. It matters not whether our field of operation be wide or limited; in every case, to command it, is to mount above it. Who has not felt the irritation of mind and impatience created by a deep, rich country, visited for the first time, with winding lanes, and high hedges, and green steeps, and tangled woods, and every thing smiling indeed, but in a maze? The same feeling comes upon us in a strange city, where we have no map of its streets. Hence you hear of practised travelers, when they first come into a place, mounting some high hill or church tower, by way of reconnoitering its neighborhood. In like manner, you must be above your knowledge, not under it, or it will oppress you: and

the more you have of it, the greater will be the load. The learning of a Salmasius or a Burman, unless you are its master, will be your tyrant. *Imperat aut servit* [it rules or it serves]; if you can wield it with a strong arm, it is a great weapon; otherwise,

> Vis consili expers
> Mole ruit suâ.
> [Brute force without intelligence falls by its own weight.]

You will be overwhelmed, like Tarpeia, by the heavy wealth which you have exacted from tributary generations.

Instances abound; there are authors who are as pointless as they are inexhaustible in their literary resources. They measure knowledge by bulk, as it lies in the rude block, without symmetry, without design. How many commentators are there on the classics, how many on Holy Scripture, from whom we rise up, wondering at the learning which has passed before us, and wondering why it passed! How many writers are there of Ecclesiastical history, such as Mosheim or Du Pin, who, breaking up their subject into details, destroy its life, and defraud us of the whole by their anxiety about the parts! The sermons, again, of the English divines in the seventeenth century, how often are they mere repertories of miscellaneous and officious learning! Of course Catholics also may read without thinking; and in their case, equally as with Protestants, it holds good, that such knowledge is unworthy of the name, knowledge which they have not thought through, and thought out. Such readers are only possessed by their knowledge, not possessed of it; nay, in matter of fact they are often even carried away by it, without any volition of their own. Recollect, the memory can tyrannize, as well as the imagination. Derangement, I believe, has been considered as a loss of control over the sequence of ideas. The mind, once set in motion, is henceforth deprived of the power of initiation, and becomes the victim of a train of associations, one thought suggesting another, in the way of cause and effect, as if by a mechanical process, or some physical necessity. No one, who has had experience of men of studious habits, but must recognize the existence of a parallel phenomenon in the case of those who have over-stimulated the memory. In such persons reason acts almost as feebly and as impotently as in the madman; once fairly started on any subject whatever, they have no power of self-control; they passively endure the succession of impulses which are evolved out of the original exciting cause; they are passed on from one idea to another and go steadily forward, plodding along one line of thought in spite of the amplest concessions of the hearer, or wandering from it in endless digression in spite of his remonstrances. Now, if, as is very certain, no one would envy the madman the glow and originality of his conceptions, why must we extol the cultivation of that intellect, which is the prey, not indeed of barren fancies but of barren facts, of random intrusions from without, though not of morbid imaginations from within? And in thus speaking, I am not denying that a strong and ready memory is in itself a real treasure; I am not disparaging a well-stored mind, though it be nothing besides, provided it be sober, any more than I would despise a bookseller's shop: — it is of great value to others, even when not so to the owner. Nor am I banishing, far from it, the possessors of deep and multifarious learning from my ideal University; they adorn it in the eyes of men; I do but say that they constitute no type of the results at which it aims; that it is no great gain to the intellect to have enlarged the memory at the expense of faculties which are indisputably higher.

Nor indeed am I supposing that there is any great danger, at least in this day, of over-education; the danger is on the other side. I will tell you, gentlemen, what has been the practical error of the last twenty years,— not to load the memory of the student with a mass of undigested knowledge, but to force upon him so much that he has rejected all. It has been the error of distracting and enfeebling the mind by an unmeaning profusion of subjects; of implying that a smattering in a dozen branches of study is not shallowness, which it really is, but enlargement which it is not; of considering an acquaintance with the learned names of things and persons and the possession of clever duodecimos, and attendance on eloquent lecturers, and membership with scientific institutions, and the sight of the experiments of a platform and the specimens of a museum, that all this was not dissipation of mind, but progress. All things now are to be learned at once, not first one thing, then another, not one well, but many badly. Learning is to be without exertion, without attention, without toil; without grounding, without advance, without finishing. There is to be nothing individual in it; and this, forsooth, is the wonder of the age. What the steam engine does with matter, the printing press is to do with the mind; it is to act mechanically, and the population is to be passively, almost unconsciously enlightened, by the mere multiplication and dissemination of volumes. Whether it be the school boy, or the school girl, or the youth at college, or the mechanic in the town, or the politician in the senate, all have been the victims in one way or other of this most preposterous and pernicious of delusions. Wise men have lifted up their voices in vain; and at length, lest their own institutions should be outshone and should disappear in the folly of the hour, they have been obliged, as far as they could with a good conscience, to humor a spirit which they could not withstand, and make temporizing concessions at which they could not but inwardly smile.

It must not be supposed that, because I so speak, therefore I have some sort of fear of the education of the people: on the contrary, the more education they have, the better, so that it is really education. Nor am I an enemy to the cheap publication of scientific and literary works, which is now in vogue: on the contrary, I consider it a great advantage, convenience, and gain; that is, to those to whom education has given a capacity for using them. Further, I consider such innocent recreations as science and literature are able to furnish will be a very fit occupation of the thoughts and the leisure of young persons, and may be made the means of keeping them from bad employments and bad companions. Moreover, as to that superficial acquaintance with chemistry, and geology, and astronomy, and political economy, and modern history, and biography, and other branches of knowledge, which periodical literature and occasional lectures and scientific institutions diffuse through the community, I think it a graceful accomplishment, and a suitable, nay, in this day a necessary accomplishment, in the case of educated men. Nor, lastly, am I disparaging or discouraging the thorough acquisition of any one of these studies, or denying that, as far as it goes, such thorough acquisition is a real education of the mind. All I say is, call things by their right names, and do not confuse together ideas which are essentially different. A thorough knowledge of one science and a superficial acquaintance with many, are not the same thing; a smattering of a hundred things or a memory for detail, is not a philosophical or comprehensive view. Recreations are not education; accomplishments are not education. Do not say, the people must be educated, when, after all, you only mean, amused, refreshed, soothed, put into good spirits and good humor, or kept from vicious excesses. I do not say that such amusements, such occupations of mind, are not a great gain; but they are not education. You may as well call drawing and fencing education as a general knowledge of botany or conchology. Stuffing birds or playing stringed instruments is an elegant pastime, and a resource to the idle, but it is not education; it does not form or cultivate the intellect. Education is a high word; it is the preparation for knowledge, and it is the imparting of knowledge in proportion to that preparation. We require intellectual eyes to know withal, as bodily eyes for sight. We need both objects and organs intellectual; we cannot gain them without setting about it; we cannot gain them in our sleep, or by haphazard. The best telescope does not dispense with eyes; the printing press or the lecture room will assist us greatly, but we must be true to ourselves, we must be parties in the work. A university is, according to the usual designation, an alma mater, knowing her children one by one, not a foundry, or a mint, or a treadmill.

I protest to you, gentlemen, that if I had to choose between a so-called university, which dispensed with residence and tutorial superintendence, and gave its degrees to any person who passed an examination in a wide range of subjects, and a university which had no professors or examinations at all, but merely brought a number of young men together for three or four years, and then sent them away as the University of Oxford is said to have done some sixty years since, if I were asked which of these two methods was the better discipline of the intellect, — mind, I do not say which is morally the better, for it is plain that compulsory study must be a good and idleness an intolerable mischief,— but if I must determine which of the two courses was the more successful in training, molding, enlarging the mind, which sent out men the more fitted for their secular duties, which produced better public men, men of the world, men whose names would descend to posterity, I have no hesitation in giving the preference to that university which did nothing, over that which exacted of its members an acquaintance with every science under the sun. And, paradox as this may seem, still if results be the test of systems, the influence of the public schools and colleges of England, in the course of the last century, at least will bear out one side of the contrast as I have drawn it. What would come, on the other hand, of the ideal systems of education which have fascinated the imagination of this age, could they ever take effect, and whether they would not produce a generation frivolous, narrow-minded, and resourceless, intellectually considered, is a fair subject for debate; but so far is certain, that the universities and scholastic establishments, to which I refer, and which did little more than bring together first boys and then youths in large numbers, these institutions, with miserable deformities on the side of morals, with a hollow profession of Christianity, and a heathen code of ethics,— I say, at least they can boast of a succession of heroes and statesmen, of literary men and philosophers, of men conspicuous for great natural virtues, for habits of business, for knowledge of life, for practical judgment, for cultivated tastes, for accomplishments, who have made England what it is,— able to subdue the earth, able to domineer over Catholics.

How is this to be explained? I suppose as follows: When a multitude of young men, keen, open-hearted, sympathetic, and observant, as young men are, come together and freely mix with each other, they are sure to learn one from another, even if there be no one to teach them; the conversation of all is a series of lectures to each, and they gain for themselves new ideas and views, fresh matter of thought, and distinct principles for judging and acting, day by day. An infant has to learn the meaning of the information which its senses convey to it, and this seems to be its employment. It fancies all that the eye presents to it to be close to it, till it actually learns the contrary, and thus by practice does it ascertain the relations and uses of those first elements of knowledge which are necessary for its animal existence. A parallel teaching is necessary for our social being, and it is secured by a large school or a college; and this effect may be fairly called in its own department an enlargement of mind. It is seeing the world on a small field with little trouble; for the pupils or students come from very different places, and with widely different notions, and there is much to generalize, much to adjust, much to eliminate, there are inter-relations to be defined, and conventional rules to be established, in the process, by which the whole assemblage is molded together, and gains one tone and one character.

Let it be clearly understood, I repeat it, that I am not taking into account moral or religious considerations; I am but saying that that youthful community will constitute a whole, it will embody a specific idea, it will represent a doctrine, it will administer a code of conduct, and it will furnish principles of thought and action. It will give birth to a living teaching, which in course of time will take the shape of a self-perpetuating tradition, or a *genius loci,* as it is sometimes called; which haunts the home where it has been born, and which imbues and forms more or less, and one by one, every individual who is successively brought under its shadow. Thus it is that, independent of direct instruction on the part of superiors, there is a sort of self-education in the academic institutions of protestant England; a characteristic tone of thought, a recognized standard of judgment is found in them, which as developed in the individual who

is submitted to it, becomes a twofold source of strength to him, both from the distinct stamp it impresses on his mind, and from the bond of union which it creates between him and others,— effects which are shared by the authorities of the place, for they themselves have been educated in it, and at all times are exposed to the influence of its ethical atmosphere. Here then is a real teaching, whatever be its standards and principles, true or false; and it at least tends towards cultivation of the intellect; it at least recognizes that knowledge is something more than a sort of passive reception of scraps and details; it is a something, and it does a something, which never will issue from the most strenuous efforts of a set of teachers, with no mutual sympathies and no intercommunion, of a set of examiners with no opinions which they dare profess, and with no common principles, who are teaching or questioning a set of youths who do not know them, and do not know each other, on a large number of subjects, different in kind, and connected by no wide philosophy, three times a week, or three times a year, or once in three years, in chill lecture-rooms or on a pompous anniversary.

Nay, self-education in any shape, in the most restricted sense, is preferable to a system of teaching which, professing so much, really does so little for the mind. Shut your college gates against the votary of knowledge, throw him back upon the searchings and the efforts of his own mind; he will gain by being spared an entrance into your babel. Few indeed there are who can dispense with the stimulus and support of instructors, or will do anything at all, if left to themselves. And fewer still (though such great minds are to be found), who will not, from such unassisted attempts, contract a self-reliance and a self-esteem, which are not only moral evils, but serious hindrances to the attainment of truth. And next to none, perhaps, or none, who will not be reminded from time to time of the disadvantage under which they lie, by their imperfect grounding, by the breaks, deficiencies, and irregularities of their knowledge, by the eccentricity of opinion and the confusion of principle which they exhibit. They will be too often ignorant of what every one knows and takes for granted, of that multitude of small truths which fall upon the mind like dust, impalpable and ever accumulating; they may be unable to converse, they may argue perversely, they may pride themselves on their worst paradoxes or their grossest truisms, they may be full of their own mode of viewing things, unwilling to be put out of their way, slow to enter into the minds of others; — but, with these and whatever other liabilities upon their heads, they are likely to have more thought, more mind, more philosophy, more true enlargement, than those earnest but ill-used persons, who are forced to load their minds with a score of subjects against an examination, who have too much on their hands to indulge themselves in thinking or investigation, who devour premise and conclusion together with indiscriminate greediness, who hold whole sciences on faith, and commit demonstrations to memory, and who too often, as might be expected, when their period of education is passed, throw up all they have learned in disgust, having gained nothing really by their anxious labors, except perhaps the habit of application.

Yet such is the better specimen of the fruit of that ambitious system which has of late years been making way among us: for its result on ordinary minds, and on the common run of students, is less satisfactory still; they leave their place of education simply dissipated and relaxed by the multiplicity of subjects, which they have never really mastered, and so shallow as not even to know their shallowness. How much better, I say, is it for the active and thoughtful intellect, where such is to be found, to eschew the college and the university altogether, than to submit to a drudgery so ignoble, a mockery so contumelious!

How much more profitable for the independent mind, after the mere rudiments of education, to range through a library at random, taking down books as they meet him, and pursuing the trains of thought which his mother wit suggests! How much healthier to wander into the fields, and there with the exiled prince to find 'tongues in the trees, books in the running brooks!' How much more genuine an education is that of the poor boy in the poem [1]— a poem, whether in conception or in execution, one of the most touching in our language — who, not in the wide world, but ranging day by day around his widowed mother's home, 'a dexterous gleaner' in a narrow field and with only such slender outfit

As the village school and books a few Supplied,

contrived from the beach, and the quay, and the fisher's boat, and the inn's fireside, and the tradesman's shop, and the shepherd's walk, and the smuggler's hut, and the mossy moor, and the screaming gulls, and the restless waves, to fashion for himself a philosophy and a poetry of his own!

But in a large subject, I am exceeding my necessary limits. Gentlemen, I must conclude abruptly; and postpone any summing up of my argument, should that be necessary, to another day.

(1852)

[1] Crabbe's *Tales of the Hall*. This poem, let me say, I read on its first publication, above thirty years ago, with extreme delight, and have never lost my love of it; and on taking it up lately, found I was even more touched by it than heretofore. A work which can please in youth and age, seems to fulfil (in logical language) the *accidental definition* of a classic. (A further course of twenty years has past, and I bear the same witness in favor of this poem.)

THOMAS CARLYLE (1795–1881)

Early struggles and privations, followed by acute dyspepsia, embittered Carlyle's temper. The son of a Scottish stone-mason, he walked eighty miles from his native village of Ecclefechan to Edinburgh to study at the university and prepare himself for the ministry. This latter purpose was soon abandoned on account of unsettled religious convictions; after graduating he earned a scanty living by teaching and tried in vain to obtain various professorships. Having married Jane Baillie Welsh, a woman of brilliant wit and some property, he retired with her to the manor house of Craigenputtock, where for six years he studied German literature and philosophy and wrote essays for the reviews, among them his first great work, *Sartor Resartus*. Under the disguise of a translation from the papers of a German professor, it is an imaginative account of his own school and college experiences, his falling in love with Margaret Gordon of Prince Edward Island, who returned to that colony as wife of the governor, his spiritual and intellectual struggles, and his philosophy of life. It had just been published in *Fraser's Magazine*, when, in 1834, the Carlyles determined to risk their little all, and leave Craigenputtock for London. Carlyle chose a house in Cheyne Row, Chelsea, and kept it for the rest of his life. The peculiar style of *Sartor* did not commend it to the public. Fraser wrote that it excited 'universal disapprobation,' and several subscribers to the magazine refused to take it any longer. Carlyle was more fortunate in his next subject, 'The French Revolution,' suggested by John Stuart Mill. When the manuscript of the first volume was finished, Carlyle lent it to Mill to read; Mill lent it in turn to a friend, whose housemaid found it on the table one morning and lit the fire with it. Carlyle was in despair at the loss of so much labor; he felt incapable of doing the work over again, and spent three months in reading Marryat's novels before he could bend his energies to the unwelcome task. The book was completed in 1837, and at once won the favor of both critics and public. He was also successful about this time as a lecturer, and his wife said that the public had evidently made up its mind that 'Carlyle was worth keeping alive at a moderate rate.' One of the courses he gave, that 'On Heroes, Hero-worship, and the Heroic in History,' when published in 1841 became one of his most popular works; it contains in the shortest and simplest form Carlyle's favorite doctrine that the history of the world is at bottom the history of its great men. After setting forth his ideas on social and political questions in *Chartism* and *Past and Present*, he returned to the study of history, and his *Life and Letters of Oliver Cromwell* made a remarkable change in the current estimate of the great Protector. The labor of a dozen years is contained in his last historical work, *Frederick the Great* (published 1858–65). The year after this was completed, Mrs. Carlyle died suddenly in her carriage from the shock caused by an accident to her pet dog, which was run over when she was driving one afternoon in Hyde Park. Carlyle in heartbroken remorse determined to tell the public not only his wife's virtues but his own unkindness to her. The publication after his death of the record of their unhappy married life injured his reputation, and led to a controversy which has not yet ended, the discretion and even the good faith of J. A. Froude, who edited the papers, being attacked by Carlyle's admirers.

PAST AND PRESENT

BOOK III

CHAPTER X

PLUGSON OF UNDERSHOT

One thing I do know: Never, on this Earth, was the relation of man to man long carried on by Cash-payment alone. If, at any time, a philosophy of Laissez-faire, Competition and Supply-and-demand, start up as the exponent of human relations, expect that it will soon end.

Such philosophies will arise: for man's 5 philosophies are usually the 'supplement of his practice;' some ornamental Logic-varnish, some outer skin of Articulate intelligence, with which he strives to render his dumb Instinctive 10 Doings presentable when they are done. Such philosophies will arise; be preached as Mammon-Gospels, the ultimate Evangel of the World; be believed with what is called belief, with much superficial bluster, and a kind of shallow satisfaction real in its way; — but they are ominous gospels! They are the sure and even swift, forerunner of great changes. Expect that the old System of Society is done, is dying and fallen into dotage, when it begins to rave in that fashion. Most Systems that I have watched the death of, for the last three thousand years, have gone just so. The Ideal, the True and Noble that was in them having faded out, and nothing now remaining but naked Egoism, vulturous Greediness, they cannot live; they are bound and inexorably ordained by the oldest Destinies, Mothers of the Universe, to die. Curious enough; they thereupon, as I have pretty generally noticed, devised some light comfortable kind of 'wine-and-walnuts philosophy' for themselves, this of Supply-and-demand or another; and keep saying, during hours of mastication and rumination, which they call hours of meditation: 'Soul, take thy ease; it is all *well* that thou art a vulture-soul;' — and pangs of dissolution come upon them, oftenest before they are aware!

Cash-payment never was, or could except for a few years be, the union-bond of man to man. Cash never yet paid one man fully his deserts to another; nor could it, nor can it, now or henceforth to the end of the world. I invite his Grace of Castle-Rackrent to reflect on this; — does he think that a Land Aristocracy when it becomes a Land Auctioneership can have long to live? Or that Sliding-scales will increase the vital stamina of it? The indomitable Plugson too, of the respected Firm of Plugson, Hunks and Company, in St. Dolly Undershot, is invited to reflect on this; for to him also it will be new, perhaps even newer. Bookkeeping by double entry is admirable, and records several things in an exact manner. But the Mother-Destinies also keep their Tablets; in Heaven's Chancery also there goes on a recording; and things, as my Moslem friends say, are 'written on the iron leaf.'

Your Grace and Plugson, it is like, go to Church occasionally: did you never in vacant moments, with perhaps a dull parson droning to you, glance into your New Testament, and the cash-account stated four times over, by a kind of quadruple entry, — in the Four Gospels there? I consider that a cash-account, and balance-statement of work done and wages paid, worth attending to. Precisely *such*, though on a smaller scale, go on at all moments under this Sun; and the statement and balance of them in the Plugson Ledgers and on the Tablets of Heaven's Chancery are discrepant exceedingly; — which ought really to teach, and to have long since taught, an indomitable common-sense Plugson of Undershot, much more an unattackable *un*common-sense Grace of Rackrent, a thing or two! — In brief, we shall have to dismiss the Cash-Gospel rigorously into its own place: we shall have to know, on the threshold, that either there is some infinitely deeper Gospel, subsidiary, explanatory and daily and hourly corrective, to the Cash one; or else that the Cash one itself and all others are fast traveling!

For all human things do require to have an Ideal in them; to have some Soul in them, as we said, were it only to keep the Body unputrefied. And wonderful it is to see how the Ideal or Soul, place it in what ugliest Body you may, will irradiate said Body with its own nobleness; will gradually, incessantly, mold, modify, new-form or reform said ugliest Body, and make it at last beautiful, and to a certain degree divine! — Oh, if you could dethrone that Brute-god Mammon, and put a Spirit-god in his place! One way or other, he must and will have to be dethroned.

Fighting, for example, as I often say to myself, Fighting with steel murder-tools is surely a much uglier operation than Working, take it how you will. Yet even of Fighting, in religious Abbot Samson's days, see what a Feudalism there had grown, — a 'glorious Chivalry,' much besung down to the present day. Was not that one of the 'impossiblest' things? Under the sky is no uglier spectacle than two men with clenched teeth, and hell-fire eyes, hacking one another's flesh, converting precious living bodies, and priceless living souls, into nameless masses of putrescence, useful only for turnip-manure. How did a Chivalry ever come out of that; how anything that was not hideous, scandalous, infernal? It will be a question worth considering by and by.

I remark, for the present, only two things: first, that the Fighting itself was not, as we rashly suppose it, a Fighting without cause, but more or less with cause. Man is created to fight; he is perhaps best of all definable as a born soldier; his life 'a battle and a march,' under the right General. It is forever indispensable for a man to fight: now with Necessity, with Barrenness, Scarcity, with Puddles, Bogs, tangled Forests, unkempt Cotton; — now also with the hallucinations of his poor fellow Men. Hallucinatory visions rise in the head of my poor fellow man; make him claim over me rights which are not his. All fighting, as we noticed long ago, is the dusty conflict of strengths, each thinking itself the strongest, or, in other words, the justest; — of Mights which do in the long-run, and forever will in this just Universe in the long-run, mean Rights. In conflict the perishable part of them, beaten sufficiently, flies off into dust; this process ended, appears the imperishable, the true and exact.

And now let us remark a second thing: how, in these baleful operations, a noble devout-hearted Chevalier will comport himself, and an ignoble godless Bucanier and Chactaw Indian. Victory is the aim of each. But deep in the heart of the noble man it lies forever legible, that as an Invisible Just God made him, so will and must God's Justice and this only, were it never so invisible, ultimately prosper in all controversies and enterprises and battles whatsoever. What an Influence; ever-present,— like a Soul in the rudest Caliban of a body; like a ray of Heaven, and illuminative creative *Fiat-Lux,* in the wastest terrestrial Chaos! Blessed divine Influence, traceable even in the horror of Battlefields and garments rolled in blood: how it ennobles even the Battlefield; and, in place of a Chactaw Massacre, makes it a Field of Honor! A Battlefield too, is great. Considered well, it is a kind of Quintessence of Labor; Labor distilled into its utmost concentration; the sig-

nificance of years of it compressed into an hour. Here too thou shalt be strong, and not in muscle only, if thou wouldst prevail. Here too thou shalt be strong of heart, noble of soul; thou shalt dread no pain or death, thou shalt not love ease or life; in rage, thou shalt remember mercy, justice; — thou shalt be a Knight and not a Chactaw, if thou wouldst prevail! It is the rule of all battles, against hallucinating fellow Men, against unkempt Cotton, or whatsoever battles they may be, which a man in this world has to fight.

Howel Davies dyes the West-Indian Seas with blood, piles his decks with plunder; approves himself the expertest Seaman, the daringest Seafighter: but he gains no lasting victory, lasting victory is not possible for him. Not, had he fleets larger than the combined British Navy all united with him in bucaniering. He, once for all, cannot prosper in his duel. He strikes down his man: yes; but his man, or his man's representative, has no notion to lie struck down; neither, though slain ten times, will he keep so lying; — nor has the Universe any notion to keep him so lying! On the contrary, the Universe and he have, at all moments, all manner of motives to start up again, and desperately fight again. Your Napoleon is flung out, at last, to St. Helena; the latter end of him sternly compensating the beginning. The Bucanier strikes down a man, a hundred or a million men: but what profits it? He has one enemy never to be struck down; nay two enemies: Mankind and the Maker of Men. On the great scale or on the small, in fighting of men or fighting of difficulties, I will not embark my venture with Howel Davies: it is not the Bucanier, it is the Hero only that can gain victory, that can do more than *seem* to succeed. These things will deserve meditating; for they apply to all battle and soldiership, all struggle and effort whatsoever in this Fight of Life. It is a poor Gospel, Cash-Gospel or whatever name it have, that does not, with clear tone, uncontradictable, carrying conviction to all hearts, forever keep men in mind of these things.

Unhappily, my indomitable friend Plugson of Undershot has, in a great degree, forgotten them: — as, alas, all the world has; as, alas, our very Dukes and Soul-Overseers have, whose special trade it was to remember them! Hence these tears.— Plugson, who has indomitably spun Cotton merely to gain thousands of pounds, I have to call as yet a Bucanier and Chactaw; till there come something better, still more indomitable from him. His hundred Thousand-pound Notes, if there be nothing other, are to me but as the hundred Scalps in a Chactaw wigwam. The blind Plugson: he was a Captain of Industry, born member of the Ultimate genuine Aristocracy of this 'Universe, could he have known it! These thousand men that span and toiled round him, they were a regiment whom he had enlisted, man by man; to make war on a very genuine enemy: Bareness of back, and disobedient Cotton-fiber, which will not, unless forced to it, consent to cover bare backs. Here is a most genuine enemy; over whom all creatures will wish him victory. He enlisted his thousand men; said to them, 'Come, brothers, let us have a dash at Cotton!' They follow with cheerful shout; they gain such a victory over Cotton as the Earth has to admire and clap hands at: but, alas, it is yet only of the Bucanier or Chactaw sort,— as good as no victory! Foolish Plugson of St. Dolly Undershot: does he hope to become illustrious by hanging up the scalps in his wigwam, the hundred thousands at his banker's, and saying, Behold my scalps? Why, Plugson, even thy own host is all in mutiny: Cotton is conquered; but the 'bare backs'— are worse covered than ever! Indomitable Plugson, thou must cease to be a Chactaw; thou and others; thou thyself, if no other!

Did William the Norman Bastard, or any of his Taillefers, *Ironcutters*, manage so? Ironcutter, at the end of the campaign, did not turn-off his thousand fighters, but said to them: 'Noble fighters, this is the land we have gained; be I Lord in it,— what we will call *Law-ward*, maintainer and *keeper* of Heaven's *Laws:* be I *Law-ward*, or in brief orthoepy *Lord* in it, and be ye Loyal Men around me in it; and we will stand by one another, as soldiers round a captain, for again we shall have need of one another!' Plugson, bucanier-like, says

to them: 'Noble spinners, this is the Hundred Thousand we have gained, wherein I mean to dwell and plant vineyards; the hundred thousand is mine, the three and sixpence daily was yours: adieu, noble spinners; drink my health with this groat each, which I give you over and above!' The entirely unjust Captain of Industry, say I; not Chevalier, but Bucanier! 'Commercial Law' does indeed acquit him; asks, with wide eyes, What else? So too Howell Davies asks, Was it not according to the strictest Bucanier Custom? Did I depart in any jot or tittle from the Laws of the Bucaniers?

After all, money, as they say, is miraculous. Plugson wanted victory; as Chevaliers and Bucaniers, and all men alike do. He found money recognized, by the whole world with one assent, as the true symbol, exact equivalent and synonym of victory;— and here we have him, a grimbrowed, indomitable Bucanier, coming home to us with a 'victory,' which the whole world is *ceasing* to clap hands at! The whole world, taught somewhat impressively, is beginning to recognize that such victory is but half a victory; and that now, if it please the Powers, we must— have the other half!

Money is miraculous. What miraculous facilities has it yielded, will it yield us; but also what never-imagined confusions, obscurations has it brought in; down almost to total extinction of the moral-sense in large masses of mankind! 'Protection of property,' of what is '*mine*,' means with most men protection of money,— the thing which, had I a thousand padlocks over it, is least of all *mine;* is, in a manner, scarcely worth calling mine! The symbol shall be held sacred, defended everywhere with tipstaves, ropes, and gibbets; the thing signified shall be composedly cast to the dogs. A human being who has worked with human beings clears all scores with them, cuts himself with triumphant completeness forever loose from them, by paying down certain shillings and pounds. Was it not the wages, I promised you? There they are, to the last sixpence,— according to the Laws of the Bucaniers! — Yes, indeed;— and, at such times, it becomes imperatively necessary to ask all persons, bucaniers and others, Whether these same respectable Laws of the Bucaniers are written on God's eternal Heavens at all, on the inner Heart of Man at all; or on the respectable Bucanier Logbook merely, for the convenience of bucaniering merely? What a question;— whereat Westminster Hall shudders to its driest parchment; and on the dead wigs each particular horsehair stands on end!

The Laws of Laissez-faire, O Westminster, the laws of industrial Captain and industrial Soldier, how much more of idle Captain and industrial Soldier, will need to be remodeled, and modified, and rectified in a hundred and a hundred ways,— and *not* in the Sliding-scale direction, but in the totally opposite one! With two million industrial Soldiers already sitting in Bastilles, and five million pining on potatoes, methinks Westminster cannot begin too soon!— A man has other obligations laid on him, in God's Universe, than the payment of cash: these also Westminster, if it will continue to exist and have board-wages, must contrive to take some charge of: — by Westminster or by another, they must and will be taken charge of; be, with whatever difficulty, got articulated, got enforced, and to a certain approximate extent put in practice. And, as I say, it cannot be too soon! For Mammonism, left to itself, has become Midaseared; and with all its gold mountains, sits starving for want of bread: and Dilettantism with its partridge-nets, in this extremely earnest Universe of ours, is playing somewhat too high a game. 'A man by the very look of him promises so much': yes; and by the rent-roll of him does he promis nothing?—

Alas, what a business will this be, which our Continental friends, groping this long while somewhat absurdly about it and about it, call 'Organization of Labor';— which must be taken out of the hand of absurd windy persons, and put into the hands of wise, laborious, modest and valiant men, to begin with it straightway; to proceed with it, and succeed in it more and more, if Europe, at any rate if England, is to continue habitable much longer. Looking at the kind of most noble Corn-Law Dukes or Practical *Duces* we have, and also of

right reverend Soul-Overseers, Christian Spiritual *Duces* 'on a minimum of four thousand five hundred,' one's hopes are a little chilled. Courage, nevertheless; there are many brave men in England! My indomitable Plugson,— nay is there not even in thee some hope? Thou art hitherto a Bucanier, as it was written and prescribed for thee by an evil world: but in that grim brow, in that indomitable heart which *can* conquer Cotton, do there not perhaps lie other ten-times nobler conquests?

CHAPTER XI

LABOR

For there is a perennial nobleness, and even sacredness, in Work. Were he never so benighted, forgetful of his high calling, there is always hope in a man that actually and earnestly works: in Idleness alone is there perpetual despair. Work, never so Mammonish, mean, *is* in communication with Nature; the real desire to get Work done will itself lead one more and more to truth, to Nature's appointments and regulations, which are truth.

The latest Gospel in this world is, Know thy work and do it. 'Know thyself': long enough has that poor 'self' of thine tormented thee; thou wilt never get to 'know' it, I believe! Think it not thy business, this of knowing thyself; thou art an unknowable individual: know what thou canst work at; and work at it, like a Hercules! That will be thy better plan.

It has been written, 'an endless significance lies in Work'; a man perfects himself by working. Foul jungles are cleared away, fair seedfields rise instead, and stately cities; and withal the man himself first ceases to be a jungle and foul unwholesome desert thereby. Consider how, even in the meanest sorts of Labor, the whole soul of a man is composed into a kind of real harmony, the instant he sets himself to work! Doubt, Desire, Sorrow, Remorse, Indignation, Despair itself, all these like helldogs lie beleaguering the soul of the poor dayworker, as of every man: but he bends himself with free valor against his task, and all these are stilled, all these shrink murmuring far off into their caves. The man is now a man. The blessed glow of Labor in him, is it not as purifying fire, wherein all poison is burnt up, and of sour smoke itself there is made bright blessed flame!

Destiny, on the whole, has no other way of cultivating us. A formless Chaos, once set it *revolving,* grows round and ever rounder; ranges itself, by mere force of gravity, into strata, spherical courses; is no longer a Chaos, but a round compacted World. What would become of the Earth, did she cease to revolve? In the poor old Earth, so long as she revolves, all inequalities, irregularities disperse themselves; all irregularities are incessantly becoming regular. Hast thou looked on the Potter's wheel,— one of the venerablest objects; old as the Prophet Ezechiel and far older? Rude lumps of clay, how they spin themselves up, by mere quick whirling, into beautiful circular dishes. And fancy the most assiduous Potter, but without his wheel; reduced to make dishes or rather amorphous botches, by mere kneading and baking! Even such a Potter were Destiny, with a human soul that would rest and lie at ease, that would not work and spin! Of an idle unrevolving man the kindest Destiny, like the most assiduous Potter without wheel, can bake and knead nothing other than a botch; let her spend on him what expensive coloring, what gilding and enameling she will, he is but a botch. Not a dish; no, a bulging, kneaded, crooked, shambling, squint-cornered, amorphous botch,— a mere enameled vessel of dishonor! Let the idle think of this.

Blessed is he who has found his work; let him ask no other blessedness. He has a work, a life-purpose; he has found it, and will follow it! How, as a free-flowing channel, dug and torn by noble force through the sour mud-swamp of one's existence, like an ever-deepening river there, it runs and flows; — draining-off the sour festering water, gradually from the root of the remotest grass-blade; making, instead of pestilential swamp, a green fruitful meadow with its clear-flowing stream. How blessed for the meadow itself, let the stream and *its* value be great or small! Labor is Life: from the inmost heart of the Worker rises his god-given Force, the sacred celestial Life-essence breathed into him by Almighty God; from his inmost heart awakens him to all

nobleness,— to all knowledge, 'self-knowledge' and much else, so soon as Work fitly begins. Knowledge? The knowledge that will hold good in working, cleave thou to that; for Nature herself accredits that, says Yea to that. Properly thou hast no other knowledge but what thou hast got by working: the rest is yet all a hypothesis of knowledge; a thing to be argued of in schools, a thing floating in the clouds, in endless logic-vortices, till we try it and fix it. 'Doubt, of whatever kind, can be ended by Action alone.'

And again, hast thou valued Patience, Courage, Perseverance, Openness to light; readiness to own thyself mistaken, to do better next time? All these, all virtues, in wrestling with the dim brute Powers of Fact, in ordering of thy fellows in such wrestle, there and elsewhere not at all, thou wilt continually learn. Set down a brave Sir Christopher in the middle of black ruined Stone-heaps, of foolish unarchitectural Bishops, redtape Officials, idle Nell-Gwyn Defenders of the Faith; and see whether he will ever raise a Paul's Cathedral out of all that, yea or no! Rough, rude, contradictory are all things and persons, from the mutinous masons and Irish hodmen, up to the idle Nell-Gwyn Defenders, to blustering red-tape Officials, foolish unarchitectural Bishops. All these things and persons are there not for Christopher's sake and his Cathedral's; they are there for their own sake mainly! Christopher will have to conquer and constrain all these,— if he be able. All these are against him. Equitable Nature herself, who carries her mathematics and architectonics not on the face of her, but deep in the hidden heart of her,— Nature herself is but partially for him; will be wholly against him, if he constrain her not! His very money, where is it to come from? The pious munificence of England lies far-scattered, distant, unable to speak, and say, 'I am here'; — must be spoken to before it can speak. Pious munificence, and all help, is so silent, invisible like the gods; impediment, contradictions manifold are so loud and near! O brave Sir Christopher, trust thou in those notwithstanding, and front all these; understand all these; by valiant patience, noble effort, insight, by man's-strength, vanquish and compel all these,

— and, on the whole, strike down victoriously the last topstone of that Paul's Edifice; thy monument for certain centuries, the stamp 'Great Man' impressed very legibly on Portland-stone there! —

Yes, all manner of help, and pious response from Men or Nature, is always what we call silent; cannot speak or come to light, till it be seen, till it be spoken to. Every noble work is at first 'impossible.' In very truth, for every noble work the possibilities will lie diffused through Immensity; inarticulate, undiscoverable except to faith. Like Gideon thou shalt spread out thy fleece at the door of thy tent; see whether under the wide arch of Heaven there be any bounteous moisture, or none. Thy heart and life-purpose shall be as a miraculous Gideon's fleece, spread out in silent appeal to Heaven: and from the kind Immensities, what from the poor unkind Localities and town and country Parishes there never could, blessed dew-moisture to suffice thee shall have fallen!

Work is of a religious nature: — work is of a *brave* nature; which it is the aim of all religion to be. All work of man is as the swimmer's: a waste ocean threatens to devour him; if he front it not bravely, it will keep its word. By incessant wise defiance of it, lusty rebuke and buffet of it, behold how it loyally supports him, bears him as its conqueror along. 'It is so,' says Goethe, 'with all things that man undertakes in this world.'

Brave Sea-captain, Norse Sea-king,— Columbus, my hero, royalest Sea-king of all! it is no friendly environment this of thine, in the waste deep waters; around thee mutinous discouraged souls, behind thee disgrace and ruin, before thee the unpenetrated veil of Night. Brother, these wild water-mountains, bounding from their deep bases (ten miles deep, I am told), are not entirely there on thy behalf! Meseems *they* have other work than floating thee forward: — and the huge Winds, that sweep from Ursa Major to the Tropics and Equators, dancing their giant-waltz through the kingdoms of Chaos and Immensity, they care little about filling rightly or filling wrongly the small shoulder-of-mutton sails in this cockle-skiff of thine! Thou art not among articulate-speaking friends, my brother; thou art among immeasurable dumb monsters, tumbling, howling wide as the world here. Secret, far off, invisible to all hearts but thine, there lies a help in them: see how thou wilt get at that. Patiently thou wilt wait till the mad Southwester spend itself, saving thyself by dextrous science of defense, the while: valiantly, with swift decision, wilt thou strike in, when the favoring East, the Possible, springs up. Mutiny of men thou wilt sternly repress; weakness, despondency, thou wilt cheerily encourage: thou wilt swallow down complaint, unreason, weariness, weakness of others and thyself; — how much wilt thou swallow down! There shall be a depth of Silence in thee, deeper than this Sea, which is but ten miles deep: a Silence unsoundable; known to God only. Thou shalt be a Great Man. Yes, my World-Soldier, thou of the World Marine-service,— thou wilt have to be *greater* than this tumultuous unmeasured World here round thee is; thou, in thy strong soul, as with wrestler's arms, shalt embrace it, harness it down; and make it bear thee on,— to new Americas, or whither God wills!

CHAPTER XII

REWARD

'Religion,' I said; for, properly speaking, all true Work is Religion: and whatsoever Religion is not Work may go and dwell among the Brahmins, Antinomians, Spinning Dervishes, or where it will; with me it shall have no harbor. Admirable was that of the old Monks, '*Laborare est Orare*, Work is Worship.'

Older than all preached Gospels was this unpreached, inarticulate. but ineradicable, forever-enduring Gospel: Work, and therein have wellbeing. Man, Son of Earth and of Heaven, lies there not, in the innermost heart of thee, a Spirit of active Method, a Force for Work; — and burns like a painfully-smoldering fire, giving thee no rest till thou unfold it, till thou write it down in beneficent Facts around thee! What is immethodic, waste, thou shalt make methodic, regulated, arable; obedient and productive to thee. Wheresoever thou findest Disorder, there is thy eternal enemy; attack him swiftly, subdue him; make Order of him, the subject not of Chaos. but of Intelligence, Divinity and Thee! The thistle that grows in thy path, dig it out, that a blade of useful grass, a drop of nourishing milk, may grow there instead. The waste cotton-shrub, gather its waste white down, spin it, weave it; that, in place of idle litter, there may be folded webs, and the naked skin of man be covered.

But above all, where thou findest Ignorance, Stupidity, Brute-mindedness,— yes, there, with or without Church-tithes and Shovel-hat, with or without Talfourd-Mahon Copyrights, or were it with mere dungeons and gibbets and crosses, attack it, I say; smite it wisely, unweariedly, and rest not while thou livest and it lives; but smite, smite, in the name of God! The Highest God, as I understand it, does audibly so command thee; still audibly, if thou have ears to hear. He, even He, with his *un*spoken voice, awfuler than any Sinai thunders or syllabled speech of Whirlwinds; for the SILENCE of deep Eternities, of Worlds from beyond the morning-stars, does it not speak to thee? The unborn Ages; the old Graves, with their long-moldering dust, the very tears that wetted it now all dry,— do not these speak to thee, what ear hath not heard? The deep Death-kingdoms, the Stars in their never-resting courses, all Space and all Time, proclaim it to thee in continual silent admonition. Thou too, if ever man should, shalt work while it is called To-day. For the Night cometh, wherein no man can work.

All true Work is sacred; in all true Work, were it but true hand-labor, there is something of divineness. Labor, wide as the Earth, has its summit in Heaven. Sweat of the brow; and up from that to sweat of the brain, sweat of the heart; which includes all Kepler calculations, Newton meditations, all Sciences, all spoken Epics, all acted Heroisms, Martyrdoms,— up to that 'Agony of bloody sweat,' which all men have called divine! O brother, if this is not 'worship,' then I say, the more pity for worship; for this is the noblest thing yet discovered under God's sky. Who art thou that complainest of thy life of toil? Complain not. Look up, my wearied brother; see thy fellow Workmen there, in God's Eternity; surviving there, they alone surviving: sacred Band of the Immortals, celestial Bodyguard of the Empire of Mankind. Even in the weak Human Memory they survive so long, as saints, as heroes, as gods; they alone surviving; peopling, they alone, the unmeasured solitudes of Time! To thee Heaven, though severe, is *not* unkind; Heaven is kind,— as a noble Mother; as that Spartan Mother, saying while she gave her son his shield, 'With it, my son, or upon it!' Thou too shalt return *home* in honor; to thy far-distant home, in honor; doubt it not,— if in the battle thou keep thy shield! Thou, in the Eternities and deepest Death-kingdoms, art not an alien; thou everywhere art a denizen! Complain not; the very Spartans did not *complain*.

And who art thou that braggest of thy life of Idleness; complacently showest thy bright gilt equipages; sumptuous cushions; appliances for folding of the hands to mere sleep? Looking up, looking down, around, behind or before, discernest thou, if it be not in Mayfair alone, any *idle* hero, saint, god, or even devil? Not a vestige of one. In the Heavens, in the Earth, in the Waters under the Earth, is none like unto thee. Thou art an original figure in this Creation; a denizen in Mayfair alone, in this extraordinary Century or Half-Century alone! One monster there is in the world: the idle man. What is his 'Religion'? That Nature is a Phantasm, where cunning beggary or thievery may sometimes find good victual. That God is a lie; and that Man and his Life are a lie.— Alas, alas, who of us *is* there that can say, I have worked? The faithfulest of us are unprofitable servants; the faithfulest of us know that best. The faithfulest of us may say, with sad and true old Samuel, 'Much of my life has been trifled away!' But he that has, and except 'on public occasions' professes to have, no function but that of going idle in a graceful or graceless manner; and of begetting sons to go idle; and to address Chief Spinners and Diggers, who at least *are* spinning and digging, 'Ye scandalous persons who produce too much'— My Corn-Law friends, on what imaginary still richer Eldorados, and true iron-spikes with law of gravitation, are ye rushing!

As to the Wages of Work there might innumerable things be said; there will and must yet innumerable things be said and spoken, in St. Stephen's and out of St. Stephen's; and gradually not a few things be ascertained and written, on Law-parchment, concerning this very matter:— 'Fair day's-wages for a fair day's-work' is the most unrefusable demand! Money-wages 'to the extent of keeping your worker alive that he may work more'; these, unless you mean to dismiss him straightway out of this world, are indispensable alike to the noblest Worker and to the least noble!

One thing only I will say here, in special reference to the former class, the noble and noblest; but throwing light on all the other classes and their arrangements of this difficult matter: The 'wages' of every noble Work do yet lie in Heaven or else Nowhere. Not in Bank-of-England bills, in Owen's Labor-bank, or any the most improved establishment of banking and money-changing, needest thou, heroic soul, present thy account of earnings. Human banks and labor-banks know thee not; or know thee after generations and centuries have passed away, and thou art clean gone from 'rewarding,'— all manner of bank-drafts, shop-tills, and Downing-street Exchequers lying very invisible, so far from thee! Nay, at bottom, dost thou need any reward? Was it thy aim and life-purpose to be filled with good things for thy heroism; to have a life of pomp and ease, and be what men call 'happy,' in this world, or in any other world? I answer for thee deliberately. No. The whole spiritual secret of the new epoch lies in this, that thou canst answer for thyself, with thy whole clearness of head and heart, deliberately, No!

My brother, the brave man has to give his Life away. Give it, I advise thee; — thou dost not expect to *sell* thy Life in an adequate manner? What price, for example, would content thee? The just price of thy LIFE to thee,— why, God's entire Creation to thyself, the whole Universe of Space, the whole Eternity of Time, and what they hold: that is the price which would content thee; that, and if thou wilt be candid, nothing short of that! It is thy all; and for it thou wouldst have all. Thou art an unreasonable mortal;— or rather thou art a poor *infinite* mortal, who, in thy narrow clay-prison here, *seemest* so unreasonable!

Thou wilt never sell thy Life, or any part of thy Life, in a satisfactory manner. Give it, like a royal heart; let the price be Nothing: thou *hast* then, in a certain sense, got All for it! The heroic man,— and is not every man, God be thanked, a potential hero?— has to do so, in all times and circumstances. · In the most heroic age, as in the most unheroic, he will have to say, as Burns said proudly and humbly of his little Scottish Songs, little dewdrops of Celestial Melody in an age when so much was unmelodious: 'By Heaven, they shall either be invaluable or of no value; I do not need your guineas for them.' It is an element which should, and must, enter deeply into all settlements of wages here below. They never will be 'satisfactory' otherwise; they cannot, O Mammon Gospel, they never can! Money for my little piece of work 'to the extent that will allow me to keep working'; yes, this,— unless you mean that I shall go my ways *before* the work is all taken out of me: but as to 'wages'—!—

On the whole, we do entirely agree with those old Monks, *Laborare est Orare*. In a thousand senses, from one end of it to the other, true Work *is* Worship. He that works, whatsoever be his work, he bodies forth the form of Things Unseen; a small Poet every Worker is. The idea, were it but of his poor Delf Platter, how much more of his Epic Poem, is as yet 'seen,' half-seen, only by himself; to all others it is a thing unseen, impossible; to Nature herself it is a thing unseen, a thing which never hitherto was;— very 'impossible,' for it is as yet a No-thing! The Unseen Powers had need to watch over such a man; he works in and for the Unseen. Alas, if he look to the Seen Powers only, he may as well quit the business; his No-thing will never rightly issue as a Thing, but as a Deceptivity, a Sham-thing,— which it had better not do!

Thy No-thing of an Intended Poem, O Poet who hast looked merely to reviewers, copyrights, booksellers, popularities, behold it has not yet become a Thing; for the truth is not in it! Though printed, hotpressed, reviewed, celebrated, sold to the twentieth edition: what is all that? The Thing, in philosophical uncommercial language, is still a No-thing, mostly semblance and deception of the sight; — benign Oblivion incessantly gnawing at it, impatient till Chaos, to which it belongs, do reabsorb it! —

He who takes not counsel of the Unseen and Silent, from him will never come real visibility and speech. Thou must descend to the *Mothers,* to the *Manes,* and Hercules-like long suffer and labor there, wouldst thou emerge with victory into the sunlight. As in battle and the shock of war,— for is not this a battle? — thou too shalt fear no pain or death, shalt love no ease or life; the voice of festive Lubberlands, the noise of greedy Acheron shall alike lie silent under thy victorious feet. Thy work, like Dante's, shall 'make thee lean for many years.' The world and its wages, its criticisms, counsels, helps, impediments, shall be as a waste ocean-flood; the chaos through which thou art to swim and sail. Not the waste waves and their weedy gulfstreams, shalt thou take for guidance: thy star alone,—' *Se tu segui tua stella!* ' Thy star alone, now clear-beaming over Chaos, nay now by fits gone out, disastrously eclipsed: this only shalt thou strive to follow. O, it is a business, as I fancy, that of weltering your way through Chaos and the murk of Hell! Green-eyed dragons watching you, threeheaded Cerberuses,— not without sympathy of *their* sort! ' *Eccovi l' uom ch' è stato all' Inferno.* ' For in fine, as Poet Dryden says, you do walk hand in hand with sheer Madness, all the way,— who is by no means pleasant company! You look fixedly into Madness, and *her* undiscovered, boundless, bottomless Night-empire; that you may extort new Wisdom out of it, as an Eurydice from Tartarus. The higher the Wisdom, the closer was its neighborhood and kindred with mere Insanity; literally so; — and thou wilt, with a speechless feeling, observe how highest Wisdom, struggling up into this world, has oftentimes carried such tinctures and adhesions of Insanity still cleaving to it hither!

All Works, each in their degree, are a making of Madness sane; — truly enough a religious operation; which cannot be carried on without religion. You have not work otherwise; you have eye-service, greedy grasping of wages, swift and ever swifter manufacture of semblances to get hold of wages. Instead of better felt-hats to cover your head, you have bigger lath-and-plaster hats set traveling the streets on wheels. Instead of heavenly and earthly Guidance for the souls of men, you have ' Black or White Surplice ' Controversies, stuffed hair-and-leather Popes; — terrestrial *Law-wards,* Lords and Law-bringers, ' organizing Labor ' in these years, by passing Corn-Laws. With all which, alas, this distracted Earth is now full, nigh to bursting. Semblances most smooth to the touch and eye; most accursed, nevertheless, to body and soul. Semblances, be they of Sham-woven Cloth or of Dilettante Legislation, which are *not* real wool or substance, but Devil's-dust, accursed of God and man! No man has worked, or can work, except religiously; not even the poor day-laborer, the weaver of your coat, the sewer of your shoes. All men, if they work not as in a Great Taskmaster's eye, will work wrong, work unhappily for themselves and you.

Industrial work, still under bondage to Mammon, the rational soul of it not yet awakened, is a tragic spectacle. Men in the rapidest motion and self-motion; restless, with convulsive energy, as if driven by Galvanism, as if possessed by a Devil; tearing asunder mountains,— to no purpose, for Mammonism is always Midaseared! This is sad, on the face of it. Yet courage: the beneficent Destinies, kind in their sternness, are apprising us that this cannot continue. Labor is not a devil, even while encased in Mammonism; Labor is ever an imprisoned god, writhing unconsciously or consciously to escape out of Mammonism! Plugson of Undershot, like Taillefer of Normandy, wants victory; how much happier will even Plugson be to have a Chivalrous victory than a Chactaw one! The unredeemed ugliness is that of a slothful People. Show me a People energetically busy; heaving, struggling, all shoulders at the wheel; their heart pulsing, every muscle swelling, with man's energy and will; — I show you a People of whom great good is already predicable; to whom all manner of good is yet certain, if their energy endure. By very working, they will learn; they have, Antæus-like, their foot on Mother Fact: how can they but learn?

The vulgarest Plugson of a Master-Worker, who can command Workers, and get work out of them, is already a considerable man. Blessed and thrice-blessed symptoms I discern of Master-Workers who are not vulgar men; who are Nobles, and begin to feel that they must act as such: all speed to these, they are England's hope at present! But in this Plugson himself, conscious of almost no nobleness whatever, how much is there! Not without man's faculty, insight, courage, hard energy, is this rugged figure. His words none of the wisest; but his actings cannot be altogether foolish. Think, how were it, stoodst thou suddenly in his shoes! He has to command a thousand men. And not imaginary commanding; no, it is real, incessantly practical. The evil passions of so many men (with the Devil in them, as in all of us) he has to vanquish; by manifold force of speech and of silence, to repress or evade. What a force of silence, to say nothing of the others, is in Plugson! For these his thousand men he has to provide raw-material, machinery, arrangement, houseroom; and ever at the week's end, wages by due sale. No Civil-List, or Goulburn-Baring Budget has he to fall back upon, for paying of his regiment; he has to pick his supplies from the confused face of the whole Earth and Contemporaneous History, by his dexterity alone. There will be dry eyes if he fail to do it!—He exclaims, at present, 'black in the face,' near strangled with Dilettante Legislation: 'Let me have elbow-room, throat-room, and I will not fail! No, I will spin yet, and conquer like a giant: what "sinews of war" lie in me, untold resources towards the Conquest of this Planet, if instead of hanging me, you husband them, and help me!'—My indomitable friend, it is *true;* and thou shalt and must be helped.

This is not a man I would kill and strangle by Corn-Laws, even if I could! No, I would fling my Corn-laws and shot-belts to the Devil; and try to help this man. I would teach him, by noble precept and law-precept, by noble example most of all, that Mammonism was not the essence of his or of my station in God's Universe; but the adscititious excrescence of it; the gross, terrene, godless embodiment of it; which would have to become, more or less, a godlike one. By noble *real* legislation, by true *noble's*-work, by unwearied, valiant, and were it wageless effort, in my Parliament and in my Parish, I would aid, constrain, encourage him to effect more or less this blessed change. I should know that it would have to be effected; that unless it were in some measure effected, he and I and all of us, I first and soonest of all, were doomed to perdition!—Effected it will be; unless it were a Demon that made this Universe; which I, for my own part, do at no moment, under no form, in the least believe.

May it please your Serene Highnesses, your Majesties, Lordships and Law-wardships, the proper Epic of this world is not now 'Arms and the Man'; how much less, 'Shirt-frills and the Man': no, it is now 'Tools and the Man': that, henceforth to all time, is now our Epic; —and you, first of all others, I think were wise to take note of that!

CHAPTER XIII

DEMOCRACY

If the Serene Highnesses and Majesties do not take note of that, then, as I perceive, *that* will take note of itself! The time for levity, insincerity, and idle babble and play-acting, in all kinds, is gone by; it is a serious, grave time. Old long-vexed questions, not yet solved in logical words or parliamentary laws, are fast solving themselves in facts, somewhat unblessed to behold! This largest of questions, this question of Work and Wages, which ought, had we heeded Heaven's voice, to have begun two generations ago or more, cannot be delayed longer without hearing Earth's voice. 'Labor' will verily need to be somewhat 'organized,' as they say,— God knows with what difficulty. Man will actually need to have his debts and earnings a little better paid by man; which, let Parliaments speak of them or be silent of them, are eternally his due from man, and cannot, without penalty and at length not without death-penalty, be withheld. How much ought to cease among us straightway; how much ought to begin straightway, while the hours yet are!

Truly they are strange results to which

this of leaving all to 'Cash'; of quietly shutting-up the God's Temple, and gradually opening wide-open the Mammon's Temple, with 'Lassez-faire, and Every man for himself,'—have led us in these days! We have Upper, speaking Classes, who indeed do 'speak' as never man spake before; the withered flimsiness, the godless baseness and barrenness of whose Speech might of itself indicate what kind of Doing and practical Governing went on under it! For Speech is the gaseous element out of which most kinds of Practice and Performance, especially all kinds of moral Performance, condense themselves, and take shape; as the one is, so will the other be. Descending, accordingly, into the Dumb Class in its Stockport Cellars and Poor-Law Bastilles, have we not to announce that they also are hitherto unexampled in the History of Adam's Posterity?

Life was never a May-game for men: in all times the lot of the dumb millions born to toil was defaced with manifold sufferings, injustices, heavy burdens, avoidable and unavoidable; not play at all, but hard work that made the sinews sore and the heart sore. As bond-slaves, *villani, bordarii, sochemanni,* nay indeed as dukes, earls and kings, men were oftentimes made weary of their life; and had to say, in the sweat of their brow and of their soul, Behold, it is not sport, it is grim earnest, and our back can bear no more! Who knows not what massacrings and harryings there have been; grinding, long-continuing, unbearable injustices,—till the heart had to rise in madness, and some '*Eu Sachsen, nimith euer sachses,* You Saxons, out with your gully-knives, then!' You Saxons, some 'arrestment,' partial 'arrestment of the Knaves and Dastards' has become indispensable!—The page of Dryasdust is heavy with such details.

And yet I will venture to believe that in no time, since the beginnings of Society, was the lot of those same dumb millions of toilers so entirely unbearable as it is even in the days now passing over us. It is not to die, or even to die of hunger, that makes a man wretched; many men have died; all men must die,—the last exit of us all is in a Fire-Chariot of Pain. But it is to live miserable we know not why; to work sore and yet gain nothing; to be heart-worn, weary, yet isolated, unrelated, girt-in with a cold universal Laissez-faire: it is to die slowly all our life long, imprisoned in a deaf, dead, Infinite Injustice, as in the accursed iron belly of a Phalaris' Bull! This is and remains forever intolerable to all men whom God has made. Do we wonder at French Revolutions, Chartisms, Revolts of Three Days? The times, if we will consider them, are really unexampled.

Never before did I hear of an Irish Widow reduced to 'prove her sisterhood by dying of typhus-fever and infecting seventeen persons,'—saying in such undeniable way, 'You *see* I was your sister!' Sisterhood, brotherhood, was often forgotten; but not till the rise of these ultimate Mammon and Shotbelt Gospels did I ever see it so expressly denied. If no pious Lord or *Law-ward* would remember it, always some pious Lady ('*Hlaf-dig,*' Benefactress, '*Loaf-giveress,*' they say she is,—blessings on her beautiful heart!) was there, with mild mother-voice and hand, to remember it; some pious thoughtful *Elder,* what we now call 'Prester,' *Presbyter* or 'Priest,' was there to put all men in mind of it, in the name of the God who had made all.

Not even in Black Dahomey was it ever, I think, forgotten to the typhus-fever length. Mungo Park, resourceless, had sunk down to die under the Negro Village-Tree, a horrible White object in the eyes of all. But in the poor Black Woman, and her daughter who stood aghast at him, whose earthly wealth and funded capital consisted of one small Calabash of rice, there lived a heart richer than *Laissez-faire:* they, with a royal munificence, boiled their rice for him; they sang all night to him, spinning assiduous on their cotton distaffs, as he lay to sleep: 'Let us pity the poor white man; no mother has he to fetch him milk, no sister to grind him corn!' Thou poor black Noble One,—thou *Lady* too: did not a God make thee too; was there not in thee too something of a God!—

Gurth, born thrall of Cedric the Saxon, has been greatly pitied by Dryasdust and others. Gurth, with the brass collar round his neck, tending Cedric's pigs in the glades of the wood, is not what I call an exemplar of human felicity: but

Gurth, with the sky above him, with the free air and tinted boscage and umbrage round him, and in him at least the certainty of supper and social lodging when he came home; Gurth to me seems happy, in comparison with many a Lancashire and Buckinghamshire man of these days, not born thrall of anybody! Gurth's brass collar did not gall him: Cedric *deserved* to be his master. The pigs were Cedric's, but Gurth too would get his parings of them. Gurth had the inexpressible satisfaction of feeling himself related indissolubly, though in a rude brass-collar way, to his fellow-mortals in this Earth. He had superiors, inferiors, equals.— Gurth is now 'emancipated' long since; has what we call 'Liberty.' Liberty, I am told, is a divine thing. Liberty when it becomes the 'Liberty to die by starvation' is not so divine!

Liberty? The true liberty of a man, you would say, consisted in his finding out, or being forced to find out the right path, and to walk thereon. To learn, or to be taught, what work he actually was able for; and then by permission, persuasion, and even compulsion, to set about doing of the same! That is his true blessedness, honor, 'liberty' and maximum of wellbeing: if liberty be not that, I for one have small care about liberty. You do not allow a palpable madman to leap over precipices; you violate his liberty, you that are wise; and keep him, were it in strait-waistcoats, away from the precipices! Every stupid, every cowardly and foolish man is but a less palpable madman: his true liberty were that a wiser man, that any and every wiser man, could, by brass collars, or in whatever milder or sharper way, lay hold of him when he was going wrong, and order and compel him to go a little righter. O, if thou really art my *Senior*, Seigneur, my *Elder*, Presbyter or Priest,— if thou art in very deed my *Wiser*, may a beneficent instinct lead and impel thee to 'conquer' me, to command me! If thou do know better than I what is good and right, I conjure thee in the name of God, force me to do it; were it by never such brass collars, whips and handcuffs, leave me not to walk over precipices! That I have been called, by all the Newspapers, a 'free man' will avail me little, if my pilgrimage have ended in death and wreck. O that the Newspaper had called me slave, coward, fool, or what it pleased their sweet voices to name me, and I had attained not death, but life!—Liberty requires new definitions.

A conscious abhorrence and intolerance of Folly, of Baseness, Stupidity, Poltroonery and all that brood of things, dwells deep in some men: still deeper in others an *un*conscious abhorrence and intolerance, clothed moreover by the beneficent Supreme Powers in what stout appetites, energies, egoisms so-called, are suitable to it;—these latter are your Conquerors, Romans, Normans, Russians, Indo-English; Founders of what we call Aristocracies. Which indeed have they not the most 'divine right' to found;— being themselves very truly *"Ἄριστοι*, BRAVEST, BEST; and conquering generally a confused rabble of WORST, or at lowest, clearly enough, of WORSE? I think their divine right, tried, with affirmatory verdict, in the greatest Law-Court known to me, was good! A class of men who are dreadfully exclaimed against by Dryasdust; of whom nevertheless beneficent Nature has oftentimes had need; and may, alas, again have need.

When, across the hundredfold poor scepticisms, trivialisms and constitutional cobwebberies of Dryasdust, you catch any glimpse of a William the Conqueror, a Tancred of Hauteville or such like,— do you not discern veritably some rude outline of a true God-made King; whom not the Champion of England cased in tin, but all Nature and the Universe were calling to the throne? It is absolutely necessary that he get thither. Nature does not mean her poor Saxon children to perish, of obesity, stupor or other malady, as yet: a stern Ruler and Line of Rulers therefore is called in,— a stern but most beneficent *perpetual House-Surgeon* is by Nature herself called in, and even the appropriate *fees* are provided for him! Dryasdust talks lamentably about Hereward and the Fen Counties; fate of Earl Waltheof; Yorkshire and the North reduced to ashes: all which is undoubtedly lamentable. But even Dryasdust apprises me of one fact: 'A child, in this William's reign, might have carried a purse of gold from end to end of England.' My erudite friend, it is a fact which outweighs a thousand! Sweep away thy constitutional, sentimental and other cobwebberies; look eye to eye, if thou still have any eye, in the face of this big burly William Bastard: thou wilt see a fellow of most flashing discernment, of most strong lion-heart; in whom, as it were, within a frame of oak and iron, the gods have planted the soul of a man of genius'! Dost thou call that nothing? I call it an immense thing! — Rage enough was in this Willelmus Conquæstor, rage enough for his occasions; — and yet the essential element of him, as of all such men, is not scorching fire, but shining illuminative *light*. Fire and light are strangely interchangeable; nay, at bottom, I have found them different forms of the same most godlike ' elementary substance' in our world: a thing worth stating in these days. The essential element of this Conquæstor is, first of all, the most sun-eyed perception of what *is* really what on this God's-Earth; — which, thou wilt find, does mean at bottom 'Justice,' and 'Virtues' not a few: *Conformity* to what the Maker has seen good to make; that, I suppose, will mean Justice and a Virtue or two? —

Dost thou think Willelmus Conquæstor would have tolerated ten years' jargon, one hour's jargon, on the propriety of killing Cotton-manufactures by partridge Corn-Laws? I fancy, this was not the man to knock out of his night's rest with nothing but a noisy bedlamism in your mouth! 'Assist us still better to bush the partridges; strangle Plugson who spins the shirts?'—'*Par la Splendeur de Dieu!*'— — Dost thou think Willelmus Conquæstor, in this new time, with Steamengine Captains of Industry on one hand of him,· and Joe-Manton Captains of Idleness on the other, would have doubted which *was* really the BEST; which did deserve strangling, and which not?

I have a certain indestructible regard for Willelmus Conquæstor. A resident House-surgeon, provided by Nature for her beloved English People, and even furnished with the requisite fees, as I said; for he by no means felt himself doing Nature's work, this Willelmus, but his own work exclusively! And his own work withal it was: informed '*par la*

Splendeur de Dieu.'—I say, it is necessary to get the work out of such a man, however harsh that be! When a world, not yet doomed for death, is rushing down to ever-deeper Baseness and Confusion, it is a dire necessity of Nature's to bring in her ARISTOCRACIES, her BEST, even by forcible methods. When their descendants or representatives cease entirely to *be* the Best, Nature's poor world will very soon rush down again to Baseness; and it becomes a dire necessity of nature's to cast them out. Hence French Revolutions, Five-point Charters, Democracies, and a mournful list of *Etceteras,* in these our afflicted times.

To what extent Democracy has now reached, how it advances irresistible with ominous, ever-increasing speed, he that will open his eyes on any province of human affairs may discern. Democracy is everywhere the inexorable demand of these ages, swiftly fulfilling itself. From the thunder of Napoleon battles, to the jabbering of Open-vestry in St. Mary Axe, all things announce Democracy. A distinguished man, whom some of my readers will hear again with pleasure, thus writes to me what in these days he notes from the Wahngasse of Weissnicht-wo, where our London fashions seem to be in full vogue. Let us hear the Herr Teufelsdröckh again, were it but the smallest word!

'Democracy, which means despair of finding any Heroes to govern you, and contented putting-up with the want of them,— alas, thou too, *mein Lieber,* seest well how close it is of kin to *Atheism,* and other sad *Isms:* he who discovers no God whatever, how shall he discover Heroes, the visible Temples of God? — Strange enough meanwhile it is, to observe with what thoughtlessness, here in our rigidly Conservative Country, men rush into Democracy with full cry. Beyond doubt, his Excellenz the Titular-Herr Ritter Kauderwälsch von Pferde-fuss-Quacksalber, he our distinguished Conservative Premier himself, and all but the thicker-headed of his Party, discern Democracy to be inevitable as death, and are even desperate of delaying it much!

'You cannot walk the streets without beholding Democracy announce itself: the very Tailor has become, if not prop·, erly Sansculottic, which to him would be ruinous, yet a Tailor unconsciously symbolizing, and prophesying with his scissors, the reign of Equality. What now is our fashionable coat? A thing of superfinest texture, of deeply meditated cut; with Malines-lace cuffs; quilted with gold; so that a man can carry, without difficulty, an estate of land on his back? *Keineswegs,* By no manner of means! The Sumptuary Laws have fallen into such a state of desuetude as was never before seen. Our fashionable coat is an amphibium between barn-sack and drayman's doublet. The cloth of it is studiously coarse; the color a speckled sootblack or rust-brown gray; the nearest approach to a Peasant's. And for shape, —thou shouldst see it! The last consummation of the year now passing over us is definable as Three Bags; a big bag for the body, two small bags for the arms, and by way of collar a hem! The first Antique Cheruscan who, of feltcloth or bear's-hide, with bone or metal needle, set about making himself a coat, before Tailors had yet awakened out of Nothing,—did not he make it even so? A loose wide poke for body, with two holes to let out the arms; this was his original coat: to which holes it was soon visible that two small loose pokes, or sleeves, easily appended, would be an improvement.

'Thus has the Tailor-art, so to speak, overset itself, like most other things; changed its center-of-gravity; whirled suddenly over from zenith to nadir. Your Stulz, with huge somerset, vaults from his high shopboard down to the depths of primal savagery,— carrying much along with him! For I will invite thee to reflect that the Tailor, as topmost ultimate froth of Human Society, is indeed swift-passing, evanescent, slippery to decipher; yet significant of much, nay of all. Topmost evanescent froth, he is churned-up from the very lees, and from all intermediate regions of the liquor. The general outcome he, visible to the eye, of what men aimed to do, and were obliged and enabled to do, in this one public department of symbolizing themselves to each other by covering of their skins. A smack of all Human Life lies in the Tailor: its wild struggles towards beauty, dignity, freedom, victory;

and how, hemmed-in by Sedan and Huddersfield, by Nescience, Dulness, Prurience, and other sad necessities and laws of Nature, it has attained just to this: Gray savagery of Three Sacks with a hem!

'When the very Tailor verges towards Sansculottism, is it not ominous? The last Divinity of poor mankind dethroning himself; sinking *his* taper too, flame downmost, like the Genius of Sleep or of Death; admonitory that Tailor time shall be no more! — For, little as one could advise Sumptuary Laws at the present epoch, yet nothing is clearer than that where ranks do actually exist, strict division of costumes will also be enforced; that if we ever have a new Hierarchy and Aristocracy, acknowledged veritably as such, for which I daily pray Heaven, the Tailor will reawaken; and be, by volunteering and appointment, consciously and unconsciously, a safeguard of that same.'— Certain farther observations, from the same invaluable pen, on our never-ending changes of mode, our 'perpetual nomadic and even ape-like appetite for change and mere change' in all the equipments of our existence, and the 'fatal revolutionary character' thereby manifested, we suppress for the present. It may be admitted that Democracy, in all meanings of the word, is in full career; irresistible by any Ritter Kauderwälsch or other Son of Adam, as times go. 'Liberty' is a thing men are determined to have.

But truly, as I had to remark in the mean while, 'the liberty of not being oppressed by your fellow man' is an indispensable, yet one of the most insignificant fractional parts of Human Liberty. No man oppresses thee, can bid thee fetch or carry, come or go, without reason shown. True; from all men thou art emancipated: but from Thyself and from the Devil — ? No man, wiser, unwiser, can make thee come or go: but thy own futilities, bewilderments, thy false appetites for Money, Windsor Georges and suchlike? No man oppresses thee, O free and independent Franchiser: but does not this stupid Porter-pot oppress thee? No Son of Adam can bid thee come or go; but this absurd Pot of Heavy-wet, this can and does! Thou art the thrall not of Cedric the Saxon, but of thy own brutal appetites and this scoured dish of liquor. And thou pratest of thy 'liberty'? Thou entire blockhead!

Heavy-wet and gin: alas, these are not the only kinds of thraldom. Thou who walkest in a vain show, looking out with ornamental dilettante sniff and serene supremacy at all Life and all Death; and amblest jauntily; perking up thy poor talk into crotchets, thy poor conduct into fatuous somnambulisms; — and *art* as an 'enchanted Ape' under God's sky, where thou mightest have been a man, had proper School-masters and Conquerors, and Constables with cat-o'-nine tails, been vouchsafed thee; dost thou call that 'liberty'? Or your unreposing Mammon-worshipper again, driven, as if by Galvanisms, by Devils and Fixed-Ideas, who rises early and sits late, chasing the impossible; straining every faculty to 'fill himself with the east wind,'— how merciful were it, could you, by mild persuasion, or by the severest tyranny so-called, check him in his mad path, and turn him into a wiser one! All painful tyranny, in that case again, were but mild 'surgery;' the pain of it cheap, as health and life, instead of galvanism and fixed-idea, are cheap at any price.

Sure enough, of all paths a man could strike into, there *is,* at any given moment, a *best path* for every man; a thing which, here and now, it were of all things *wisest* for him to do; — which could he be but led or driven to do, he were then doing 'like a man,' as we phrase it; all men and gods agreeing with him, the whole Universe virtually exclaiming Well-done to him! His success, in such case, were complete; his felicity a maximum. This path, to find this path and walk in it, is the one thing needful for him. Whatsoever forwards him in that, let it come to him even in the shape of blows and spurnings, is liberty: whatsoever hinders him, were it wardmotes, open-vestries, pollbooths, tremendous cheers, rivers of heavy-wet, is slavery.

The notion that a man's liberty consists in giving his vote at election-hustings, and saying, 'Behold, now I too have my twenty-thousandth part of a Talker in our National Palaver; will not all the gods be good to me?'— is one of the pleasantest! Nature nevertheless is kind

at present; and puts it into the heads of many, almost of all. The liberty especially which has to purchase itself by social isolation, and each man standing separate from the other, having 'no business with him' but a cash-account: this is such a liberty as the Earth seldom saw; — as the Earth will not long put up with, recommend it how you may. This liberty turns out, before it have long continued in action, with all men flinging up their caps round it, to be, for the Working Millions a liberty to die by want of food; for the Idle Thousands and Units, alas, a still more fatal liberty to live in want of work; to have no earnest duty to do in this God's-World any more. What becomes of a man in such predicament? Earth's Laws are silent; and Heaven's speak in a voice which is not heard. No work, and the ineradicable need of work, give rise to new very wondrous life-philosophies, new very wondrous life-practices! Dilettantism, Pococurantism, Beau-Brummelism, with perhaps an occasional, half-mad, protesting burst of Byronism, establish themselves: at the end of a certain period,— if you go back to 'the Dead Sea,' there is, say our Moslem friends, a very strange 'Sabbath-day' transacting itself there! — Brethren, we know but imperfectly yet, after ages of Constitutional Government, what Liberty and Slavery are.

Democracy, the chase of Liberty in that direction, shall go its full course; unrestrainable by him of Pferdefuss-Quacksalber, or any of *his* household. The Toiling Millions of Mankind, in most vital need and passionate instinctive desire of Guidance, shall cast away False-Guidance; and hope, for an hour, that No-Guidance will suffice them: but it can be for an hour only. The smallest item of human Slavery is the oppression of man by his Mock-Superiors; the palpablest, but I say at bottom the smallest. Let him shake-off such oppression, trample it indignantly under his feet; I blame him not, I pity and commend him. But oppression by your Mock-Superiors well shaken off, the grand problem yet remains to solve: That of finding government by your Real-Superiors! Alas, how shall we ever learn the solution of that, benighted, bewildered, sniffing, sneering, godforgetting unfortunates as we are?

It is a work for centuries; to be taught us by tribulations, confusions, insurrections, obstructions; who knows if not by conflagration and despair! It is a lesson inclusive of all other lessons; the hardest of all lessons to learn.

One thing I do know: Those Apes, chattering on the branches by the Dead Sea, never got it learned; but chatter there to this day. To them no Moses need come a second time; a thousand Moseses would be but so many painted Phantasms, interesting Fellow-Apes of new strange aspect,— whom they would 'invite to dinner,' be glad to meet with in lion-soirées. To them the voice of Prophecy, of heavenly monition, is quite ended. They chatter there, all Heaven shut to them, to the end of the world. The unfortunates! Oh, what is dying of hunger, with honest tools in your hand, with a manful purpose in your heart, and much real labor lying round you done, in comparison? You honestly quit your tools; quit a most muddy confused coil of sore work, short rations, of sorrows, dispiritments and contradictions, having now honestly done with it all; — and await, not entirely in a distracted manner, what the Supreme Powers, and the Silences and the Eternities may have to say to you.

A second thing I know: This lesson will have to be learned,— under penalties! England will either learn it, or England also will cease to exist among Nations. England will either learn to reverence its Heroes, and discriminate them from its Sham-Heroes and Valets and gaslighted Histrios; and to prize them as the audible God's-voice, amid all inane jargons and temporary market-cries, and say to them with heart-loyalty, 'Be ye King and Priest, and Gospel and Guidance for us:' or else England will continue to worship new and ever-new forms of Quackhood,— and so, with what resiliences and reboundings matters little, go down to the Father of Quacks! Can I dread such things of England? Wretched, thick-eyed, gross-hearted mortals, why will ye worship lies, and 'Stuffed Clothes-suits created by the ninth-parts of men'! It is not your purses that suffer; your farm-rents, your commerces, your mill-revenues, loud as ye lament over these; no, it is not these

alone, but a far deeper than these: it is your souls that lie dead, crushed down under despicable Nightmares, Atheisms, Brain-fumes; and are not souls at all, but mere succedanea for *salt* to keep your bodies and their appetites from putrefying! Your cotton-spinning and thrice-miraculous mechanism, what is this too, by itself, but a larger kind of Animalism? Spiders can spin, Beavers can build and show contrivance; the Ant lays-up accumulation of capital, and has, for aught I know, a Bank of Antland. If there is no soul in man higher than all that, did it reach to sailing on the cloud-rack and spinning seasand; then I say, man is but an animal, a more cunning kind of brute: he has no soul, but only a succedaneum for salt. Whereupon, seeing himself to be truly of the beasts that perish, he ought to admit it, I think; — and also straightway universally to kill himself; and so, in a manlike manner at least *end,* and wave these brute-worlds *his* dignified farewell! —

* * *

BOOK IV

CHAPTER VIII

THE DIDACTIC

Certainly it were a fond imagination to expect that any preaching of mine could abate Mammonism; that Bobus of Houndsditch will love his guineas less, or his poor soul more, for any preaching of mine! But there is one Preacher who does preach with effect, and gradually persuade all persons: his name is Destiny, is Divine Providence, and his Sermon the inflexible Course of Things. Experience does take dreadfully high school-wages; but he teaches like no other!

I revert to Friend Prudence the good Quaker's refusal of 'seven thousand pounds to boot.' Friend Prudence's practical conclusion will, by degrees, become that of all rational practical men whatsoever. On the present scheme and principle, Work cannot continue. Trades' Strikes, Trades' Unions, Chartisms; mutiny, squalor, rage and desperate revolt, growing ever more desperate, will go on their way. As dark misery settles down on us, and our refuges of lies fall in pieces one after one, the hearts of men, now at last serious, will turn to refuges of truth. The eternal stars shine out again, so soon as it is dark *enough.*

Begirt with desperate Trades' Unionism and Anarchic Mutiny, many an Industrial *Law-ward,* by and by, who has neglected to make laws and keep them, will be heard saying to himself: 'Why have I realized five hundred thousand pounds? I rose early and sat late, I toiled and moiled, and in the sweat of my brow and of my soul I strove to gain this money, that I might become conspicuous, and have some honor among my fellow-creatures. I wanted them to honor me, to love me. The money is here, earned with my best lifeblood; but the honor? I am encircled with squalor, with hunger, rage, and sooty desperation. Not honored, hardly even envied; only fools and the flunky-species so much as envy me. I am conspicuous, — as a mark for curses and brick-bats. What good is it? My five hundred scalps hang here in my wigwam; would to Heaven I had sought something else than the scalps; would to Heaven I had been a Christian Fighter, not a Chactaw one! To have ruled and fought not in a Mammonish but in a Godlike spirit; to have had the hearts of the people bless me, as a true ruler and captain of my people; to have felt my own heart bless me, and that God above instead of Mammon below was blessing me,— this had been something. Out of my sight, ye beggarly five hundred scalps of banker's-thousands: I will try for something other, or account my life a tragical futility!'

* * *

But truly it is beautiful to see the brutish empire of Mammon cracking everywhere; giving sure promise of dying, or of being changed. A strange, chill, almost ghastly dayspring strikes up in Yankeeland itself: my Transcendental friends announce there, in a distinct, though somewhat lankhaired, ungainly manner, that the Demiurgus Dollar is dethroned; that new unheard-of Demiurgusships, Priesthoods, Aristocracies, Growths and Destructions are already visible in the gray of coming Time. Chronos is dethroned by Jove; Odin by St. Olaf: the Dollar cannot rule in Heaven forever. No; I reckon not. Socinian Preachers quit their pulpits in Yankeeland, saying, 'Friends, this is all gone to colored cobweb, we regret to say!'— and retire into the fields to cultivate onion-beds, and live frugally on vegetables. It is very notable. Old godlike Calvinism declares that its old body is now fallen to tatters, and done; and its mournful ghost, disembodied, seeking new embodiment, pipes again in the winds;— a ghost and spirit as yet, but heralding new Spirit-worlds, and better Dynasties than the Dollar one.

Yes, here as there, light is coming into the world; men love not darkness, they do love light. A deep feeling of the eternal nature of Justice looks out among us everywhere,— even through the dull eyes of Exeter Hall; an unspeakable religiousness struggles, in the most helpless manner, to speak itself, in Puseyisms and the like. Of our Cant, all condemnable, how much is not condemnable without pity; we had almost said, without respect! The *in*articulate worth and truth that is in England goes down yet to the Foundations.

Some 'Chivalry of Labor,' some noble Humanity and practical Divineness of Labor, will yet be realized on this Earth. Or why *will;* why do we pray to Heaven, without setting our own shoulder to the wheel? The Present, if it will have the Future accomplish, shall itself commence. Thou who prophesiest, who believest, begin thou to fulfil. Here or nowhere, now equally as at any time! That outcast help-needing thing or person, trampled down under vulgar feet or hoofs, no help 'possible' for it, no prize offered for the saving of it,— canst not thou save it, then, without prize? Put forth thy hand, in God's name; know that 'impossible,' where Truth and Mercy and the everlasting Voice of Natural order, has no place in the brave man's dictionary. That when all men have said 'Impossible,' and tumbled noisily elsewhither, and thou alone art left, then first thy time and possibility have come. It is for thee now; do thou that, and ask no man's counsel, but thy own only, and God's. Brother, thou hast possibility in thee for much: the possibility of writing on the eternal skies the record of a heroic like. That noble downfallen or yet unborn 'Impossibility,' thou canst lift it up, thou canst, by thy soul's travail, bring it into clear being. That loud inane Actuality, with millions in its pocket, too 'possible' that, which rolls along there, with quilted trumpeters blaring round it, and all the world escorting it as mute or vocal flunky,— escort it not thou; say to it, either nothing, or else deeply in thy heart: 'Loud-blaring Nonentity, no force of trumpets, cash, Long-acre art, or universal flunkyhood of men, makes thee an Entity; thou art a Nonentity, and deceptive Simulacrum, more accursed than thou seemest. Pass on in the Devil's name, unworshipped by at least one man, and leave the thoroughfare clear!'

Not on Ilion's or Latium's plains; on far other plains and places henceforth can noble deeds be now done. Not on Ilion's plains; how much less in Mayfair's drawingrooms! Not in victory over poor brother French or Phrygians; but in victory over Frost-jötuns, Marshgiants, over demons of Discord, Idleness, Injustice, Unreason, and Chaos come again. None of the old Epics is longer possible. The Epic of French and Phrygians was comparatively a small Epic; but that of Flirts and Fribbles, what is that? A thing that vanishes at cockcrowing,— that already begins to scent the morning air. Gamepreserving Aristocracies, let them 'bush' never so effectually, cannot escape the Subtle Fowler. Game seasons will be excellent, and again will be indifferent, and by and by they will not be at all. The Last Partridge of England, of an England where millions of men can get no corn to eat, will be shot and ended. Aristocracies with beards on their chins will find other work to do than amuse themselves with trundling-hoops.

But it is to you, ye Workers, who do already work, and are as grown men, noble and honorable in a sort, that the whole world calls for new work and nobleness. Subdue mutiny, discord, widespread despair, by manfulness, justice, mercy and wisdom. Chaos is dark, deep as Hell; let light be, and there is instead a green flowery World. Oh, it is great, and there is no other greatness. To make some nook of God's Creation a little fruitfuller, better, more worthy of God; to make some human hearts a little wiser, manfuller, happier,— more blessed, less accursed! It is work for a God. Sooty Hell of mutiny and savagery and despair can, by man's energy, be made a kind of Heaven; cleared of its soot, of its mutiny, of its need to mutiny; the everlasting arch of Heaven's azure overspanning it too, and its cunning mechanisms and tall chimney-steeples, as a birth of Heaven; God and all men looking on it well pleased.

Unstained by wasteful deformities, by wasted tears or heart's-blood of men, or any defacement of the Pit, noble fruitful Labor, growing ever nobler, will come forth,— the grand sole miracle of Man; whereby Man has risen from the low places of this Earth, very literally, into divine Heavens. Ploughers, Spinners, Builders; Prophets, Poets, Kings; Brindleys and Goethes, Odins and Arkwrights; all martyrs, and noble men, and gods are of one grand Host; immeasurable; marching ever forward since the beginnings of the World. The enormous, all-conquering, flame-crowned Host, noble every soldier in it; sacred, and alone noble. Let him who is not of it hide himself; let him tremble for himself. Stars at every button cannot make him noble; sheaves of Bath-garters, nor bushels of Georges; nor any other contrivance but manfully enlisting in it, valiantly taking place and step in it. O Heavens, will he not bethink himself; he too is so needed in the Host! It were so blessed, thrice-blessed, for himself and for us all! In hope of the Last Partridge, and some Duke of Weimar among our English Dukes, we will be patient yet a while.

The Future hides in it
Gladness and sorrow;
We press still thorow,
Naught that abides in it
Daunting us,— onward.
     * * *

(1843)

JOHN RUSKIN (1819–1900)

Ruskin's literary career divides itself into two periods: in the first, his supreme interest was art; in the second, his attention was chiefly directed to social problems and ethical teaching. When he was only seventeen his indignation was aroused by the current depreciation of the great landscape painter, Turner, to whom he wrote offering his pen in defence. The offer was declined, but this youthful project was realized in *Modern Painters*, the first volume of which Ruskin published when he was twenty-four, and the sixth when he was forty-one. His main principles are that truth is the standard of all excellence, and nature the inspiration of all great art; he applies these tests to establish the conclusion that Turner is the only perfect landscape painter the world has ever seen. In the midst of this undertaking, which was expanded far beyond its original object, Ruskin wrote *The Seven Lamps of Architecture* — (Sacrifice, Truth, Power, Beauty, Life, Memory, Obedience). He developed his ideas further in *The Stones of Venice*, in which he defended Gothic architecture on the same grounds as he had defended Turner — truthfulness and the love of nature. These works and the successive volumes of *Modern Painters* gave him an unprecedented position as an art critic, but he was already beginning to turn his attention to other subjects. He was greatly influenced by Carlyle, with whom he formed a close friendship; and he was deeply interested in the Workmen's College conducted by Maurice and Kingsley, writing for his pupils there *The Elements of Drawing* and *The Elements of Perspective*. In 1857 he said that the kind of painting they wanted in London was painting cheeks red with health, and in the same year he gave fuller utterance to his new ideas in a course of lectures at Manchester on 'The Political Economy of Art.' Four essays which appeared in *The Cornhill Magazine* in 1860 (afterwards republished under the title *Unto This Last*) were even more outspoken, and caused so much dissatisfaction that the editor refused to continue the series; *Fraser's Magazine* a little later took the same course with the papers now included in Ruskin's works as *Munera Pulveris*. He advocated the application of christian principles to the organization of labor, and condemned the accepted political economy of the day as self-seeking and unsound. His idea of political economy was that it was not an abstract science, but 'a system of conduct founded on the sciences, and impossible, except under certain conditions of moral culture.' He accordingly devoted his main energies henceforth to arousing the upper classes to a sense of their duties to the poor, and helping the lower classes to realize their opportunities. To this end he wrote, gave his money, and labored with his own hands. *Time and Tide by Weare and Tyne* and *Fors Clavigera* are letters to workingmen; *Sesame and Lilies* and *The Crown of Wild Olive* are lectures delivered in various parts of England, dealing with political, social, and economical questions. He held the Professorship of Fine Art at Oxford for many years, and his courses there were the foundation of several of his later works on art; after his retirement he wrote a series of sketches of his past life under the title *Præterita* (things gone by). His last years were spent in seclusion at Brantwood, on the shores of Coniston Water in the Lake District. On his eightieth birthday Edward, Prince of Wales, headed an address which was signed by the most distinguished men of the time to assure Ruskin of their 'deepest respect and sincerest affection.' While there have been wide differences of opinion about his theories of art and his views of political economy and social reform, his entire singleness of aim and his preëminence as a writer of English prose are beyond dispute.

TRAFFIC

(A lecture delivered in the Town Hall, Bradford, afterwards included in The Crown of Wild Olive)

My good Yorkshire friends, you asked me down here among your hills that I might talk to you about this Exchange you are going to build: but earnestly and seriously asking you to pardon me, I am going to do nothing of the kind. I cannot talk, or at least can say very little, 5 about this same Exchange. I must talk of quite other things, though not willingly; — I could not deserve your pardon, if when you invited me to speak on one

733

subject, I *wilfully* spoke on another. But I cannot speak, to purpose, of anything about which I do not care; and most simply and sorrowfully I have to tell you, in the outset, that I do *not* care about this Exchange of yours.

If, however, when you sent me your invitation, I had answered, 'I won't come, I don't care about the Exchange of Bradford,' you would have been justly offended with me, not knowing the reasons of so blunt a carelessness. So I have come down, hoping that you will patiently let me tell you why, on this, and many other such occasions, I now remain silent, when formerly I should have caught at the opportunity of speaking to a gracious audience.

In a word, then, I do not care about this Exchange,—because *you* don't; and because you know perfectly well I cannot make you. Look at the essential conditions of the case, which you, as business men, know perfectly well, though perhaps you think I forget them. You are going to spend £30,000, which to you, collectively, is nothing; the buying a new coat is, as to the cost of it, a much more important matter of consideration to me than building a new Exchange is to you. But you think you may as well have the right thing for your money. You know there are a great many odd styles of architecture about; you don't want to do anything ridiculous; you hear of me, among others, as a respectable architectural man-milliner; and you send for me, that I may tell you the leading fashion; and what is, in our shops, for the moment, the newest and sweetest thing in pinnacles.

Now, pardon me for telling you frankly, you cannot have good architecture merely by asking people's advice on occasion. All good architecture is the expression of national life and character; and it is produced by a prevalent and eager national taste, or desire for beauty. And I want you to think a little of the deep significance of this word 'taste;' for no statement of mine has been more earnestly or oftener controverted than that good taste is essentially a moral quality. 'No,' say many of my antagonists, 'taste is one thing, morality is another. Tell us what is pretty: we shall be glad to know that; but we need no

sermons even were you able to preach them, which may be doubted.'

Permit me, therefore, to fortify this old dogma of mine somewhat. Taste is not only a part and an index of morality —it is the ONLY morality. The first, and last, and closest trial question to any living creature is, 'What do you like?' Tell me what you like, and I'll tell you what you are. Go out into the street, and ask the first man or woman you meet, what their 'taste' is, and if they answer candidly, you know them, body and soul. 'You, my friend in the rags, with the unsteady gait, what do *you* like?' 'A pipe and a quartern of gin.' I know you. 'You, good woman, with the quick step and tidy bonnet, what do you like?' 'A swept hearth and a clean tea-table, and my husband opposite me, and a baby at my breast.' Good, I know you also. 'You, little girl with the golden hair and the soft eyes, what do you like?' 'My canary, and a run among the wood hyacinths.' 'You, little boy with the dirty hands and the low forehead, what do you like?' 'A shy at the sparrows, and a game at pitch farthing.' Good; we know them all now. What more need we ask?

'Nay,' perhaps you answer: 'we need rather to ask what these people and children do, than what they like. If they *do* right, it is no matter that they like what is wrong; and if they *do* wrong, it is no matter that they like what is right. Doing is the great thing; and it does not matter that the man likes drinking, so that he does not drink; nor that the little girl likes to be kind to her canary, if she will not learn her lessons; nor that the little boy likes throwing stones at the sparrows, if he goes to the Sunday School.' Indeed, for a short time, and in a provisional sense, this is true. For if, resolutely, people do what is right, in time they come to like doing it. But they only are in a right moral state when they *have* come to like doing it; and as long as they don't like it, they are still in a vicious state. The man is not in health of body who is always thinking of the bottle in the cupboard, though he bravely bears his thirst; but the man who heartily enjoys water in the morning and wine in the evening, each in its proper quantity and time. And the entire object of true education is to make people not merely *do* the right things, but *enjoy* the right things — not merely industrious, but to love industry — not merely learned, but to love knowledge — not merely pure, but to love purity — not merely just, but to hunger and thirst after justice.

But you may answer or think, 'Is the liking for outside ornaments,— for pictures, or statues, or furniture, or architecture,— a moral quality?' Yes, most surely, if a rightly set liking. Taste for *any* pictures or statues is not a moral quality, but taste for good ones is. Only here again we have to define the word 'good.' I don't mean by 'good,' clever — or learned — or difficult in the doing. Take a picture by Teniers, of sots quarreling over their dice: it is an entirely clever picture; so clever that nothing in its kind has ever been done equal to it; but it is also an entirely base and evil picture. It is an expression of delight in the prolonged contemplation of a vile thing, and delight in that is an 'unmannered,' or 'immoral' quality. It is 'bad taste' in the profoundest sense — it is the taste of the devils. On the other hand, a picture of Titian's, or a Greek statue, or a Greek coin, or a Turner landscape, expresses delight in the perpetual contemplation of a good and perfect thing. That is an entirely moral quality — it is the taste of the angels. And all delight in fine art, and all love of it, resolve themselves into simple love of that which deserves love. That deserving is the quality which we call 'loveliness'— (we ought to have an opposite word, hateliness, to be said of the things which deserve to be hated) ; and it is not an indifferent nor optional thing whether we love this or that; but it is just the vital function of all our being. What we *like* determines what we *are,* and is the sign of what we are; and to teach taste is inevitably to form character.

As I was thinking over this, in walking up Fleet Street the other day, my eye caught the title of a book standing open in a bookseller's window. It was — 'On the necessity of the diffusion of taste among all classes.' 'Ah,' I thought to myself, 'my classifying friend, when you have diffused your taste, where will your classes be? The man who likes what you like, belongs to the same class with you, I think. Inevitably so. You may put him to other work if you choose; but, by the condition you have brought him into, he will dislike the other work as much as you would yourself. You get hold of a scavenger, or a costermonger, who enjoyed the Newgate Calendar for literature, and 'Pop goes the Weasel' for music. You think you can make him like Dante and Beethoven? I wish you joy of your lessons; but if you do, you have made a gentleman of him: — he won't like to go back to his costermongering.'

And so completely and unexceptionally is this so, that, if I had time to-night, I could show you that a nation cannot be affected by any vice, or weakness, without expressing it, legibly, and forever, either in bad art, or by want of art; and that there is no national virtue, small or great, which is not manifestly expressed in all the art which circumstances enable the people possessing that virtue to produce. Take, for instance, your great English virtue of enduring and patient courage. You have at present in England only one art of any consequence — that is, iron-working. You know thoroughly well how to cast and hammer iron. Now, do you think in those masses of lava which you build volcanic cones to melt, and which you forge at the mouths of the Infernos you have created; do you think, on those iron plates, your courage and endurance are not written forever — not merely with an iron pen, but on iron parchment? And take also your great English vice — European vice — vice of all the world —vice of all other worlds that roll or shine in heaven, bearing with them yet the atmosphere of hell — the vice of jealousy, which brings competition into your commerce, treachery into your councils, and dishonor into your wars — that vice which has rendered for you, and for your next neighboring nation, the daily occupations of existence no longer possible, but with the mail upon your breasts and the sword loose in its sheath; so that at last, you have realized for all the multitudes of the two great peoples who lead the so-called civilization of the earth,— you have realized for them all. I say, in person and in policy, what was once true only of the rough Border riders of your Cheviot hills —

> They carved at the meal
> With gloves of steel,
> And they drank the red wine through the helmet barred; —

do you think that this national shame and dastardliness of heart are not written as legibly on every rivet of your iron armor as the strength of the right hands that forged it?

Friends, I know not whether this thing be the more ludicrous or the more melancholy. It is quite unspeakably both. Suppose, instead of being now sent for by you, I had been sent for by some private gentleman, living in a suburban house, with his garden separated only by a fruit-wall from his next door neighbor's; and he had called me to consult with him on the furnishing of his drawing room. I begin looking about me, and find the walls rather bare; I think such and such a paper might be desirable — perhaps a little fresco here and there on the ceiling — a damask curtain or so at the windows. 'Ah,' says my employer, 'damask curtains, indeed! That's all very fine, but you know I can't afford that kind of thing just now!' 'Yet the world credits you with a splendid income!' 'Ah, yes,' says my friend, 'but do you know, at present, I am obliged to spend it nearly all in steel-traps?' 'Steel-traps! for whom?' 'Why, for that fellow on the other side of the wall, you know: we're very good friends, but we are obliged to keep our traps set on both sides of the wall; we could not possibly keep on friendly terms without them, and our spring guns. The worst of it is, we are both clever fellows enough; and there's never a day passes that we don't find out a new trap, or a new gun-barrel, or something; we spend about fifteen millions a year each in our traps, take it all together; and I don't see how we're to do with less.' A highly comic state of life for two private gentlemen! but for two nations, it seems to me, not wholly comic? Bedlam would be comic, perhaps, if there were only one madman in it; and your Christmas pantomime is comic, when there is only one clown in it; but when the whole world turns clown, and paints itself red with its own heart's blood instead of vermilion, it is something else than comic, I think.

Mind, I know a great deal of this is play, and willingly allow for that. You don't know what to do with yourselves for a sensation: fox-hunting and cricketing will not carry you through the whole of this unendurably long mortal life: you liked pop-guns when you were schoolboys, and rifles and Armstrongs are only the same things better made: but then the worst of it is, that what was play to you when boys, was not play to the sparrows; and what is play to you now, is not play to the small birds of State neither; and for the black eagles, you are somewhat shy of taking shots at them, if I mistake not.

I must get back to the matter in hand, however. Believe me, without farther instance, I could show you, in all time, that every nation's vice, or virtue, was written in its art: the soldiership of early Greece; the sensuality of late Italy; the visionary religion of Tuscany; the splendid human energy and beauty of Venice. I have no time to do this to-night (I have done it elsewhere before now); but I proceed to apply the principle to ourselves in a more searching manner.

I notice that among all the new buildings which cover your once wild hills, churches and schools are mixed in due, that is to say, in large proportion, with your mills and mansions; and I notice also that the churches and schools are almost always Gothic, and the mansions and mills are never Gothic. Will you allow me to ask precisely the meaning of this? For, remember, it is peculiarly a modern phenomenon. When Gothic was invented, houses were Gothic as well as churches; and when the Italian style superseded the Gothic, churches were Italian as well as houses. If there is a Gothic spire to the cathedral of Antwerp, there is a Gothic belfry to the Hôtel de Ville at Brussels; if Inigo Jones builds an Italian Whitehall, Sir Christopher Wren builds an Italian St. Paul's. But now you live under one school of architecture, and worship under another. What do you mean by doing this? Am I to understand that you are thinking of changing your architecture back to Gothic; and that you treat your churches experimentally, because it does not matter what mistakes you make in a church? Or am I to understand that you consider Gothic a pre-eminently sacred and beautiful mode of building, which you think, like the fine frankincense, should be mixed for the tabernacle only, and reserved for your religious services? For if this be the feeling, though it may seem at first as if it were graceful and reverent, at the root of the matter, it signifies neither more nor less than that you have separated your religion from your life.

For consider what a wide significance this fact has; and remember that it is not you only, but all the people of England, who are behaving thus just now.

You have all got into the habit of calling the church 'the house of God.' I have seen, over the doors of many churches, the legend actually carved, ' This is the house of God, and this is the gate of heaven.' Now, note where that legend comes from, and of what place it was first spoken. A boy leaves his father's house to go on a long journey on foot, to visit his uncle; he has to cross a wild hill-desert; just as if one of your own boys had to cross the wolds to visit an uncle at Carlisle. The second or third day your boy finds himself somewhere between Hawes and Brough, in the midst of the moors, at sunset. It is stony ground, and boggy; he cannot go one foot farther that night. Down he lies, to sleep, on Wharnside, where best he may, gathering a few of the stones together to put under his head; — so wild the place is, he cannot get anything but stones. And there, lying under the broad night, he has a dream; and he sees a ladder set up on the earth, and the top of it reaches to heaven, and the angels of God are seen ascending and descending upon it. And when he wakes out of his sleep, he says, ' How dreadful is this place; surely, this is none other than the house of God, and this is the gate of heaven.' This PLACE, observe; not this church; not this city; not this stone, even, which he puts up for a memorial — the piece of flint on which his head has lain. But this *place;* this windy slope of Wharnside: this moorland hollow, tor-

rent-bitten, snow-blighted; this *any* place where God lets down the ladder. And how are you to know where that will be? or how are you to determine where it may be, but by being ready for it always? Do you know where the lightning is to fall next? You *do* know that, partly; you can guide the lightning; but you cannot guide the going forth of the Spirit, which is as that lightning when it shines from the east to the west.

But the perpetual and insolent warping of that strong verse to serve a merely ecclesiastical purpose, is only one of the thousand instances in which we sink back into gross Judaism. We call our churches ' temples.' Now, you know perfectly well they are *not* temples. They have never had, never can have, anything whatever to do with temples. They are ' synagogues '—' gathering places '— where you gather yourselves together as an assembly; and by not calling them so, you again miss the force of another mighty text — ' Thou, when thou prayest, shalt not be as the hypocrites are; for they love to pray standing in the *churches* ' (we should translate it), ' that they may be seen of men. But thou, when thou prayest, enter into thy closet, and when thou hast shut thy door, pray to thy Father,'— which is, not in chancel nor in aisle, but ' in secret.'

Now, you feel, as I say this to you — I know you feel — as if I were trying to take away the honor of your churches. Not so; I am trying to prove to you the honor of your houses and your hills; not that the Church is not sacred — but that the whole Earth is. I would have you feel, what careless, what constant, what infectious sin there is in all modes of thought, whereby, in calling your churches only ' holy,' you call your hearths and homes ' profane '; and have separated yourselves from the heathen by casting all your household gods to the ground, instead of recognizing, in the place of their many and feeble Lares, the presence of your One and Mighty Lord and Lar.

' But what has all this to do with our Exchange? ' you ask me, impatiently. My dear friends, it has just everything to do with it; on these inner and great questions depend all the outer and little ones: and if you have asked me down here to speak to you, because you had before been interested in anything I have written, you must know that all I have yet said about architecture was to show this. The book I called 'The Seven Lamps' was to show that certain right states of temper and moral feeling were the magic powers by which all good architecture, without exception, had been produced. 'The Stones of Venice' had, from beginning to end, no other aim than to show that the Gothic architecture of Venice had arisen out of, and indicated in all its features, a state of pure national faith, and of domestic virtue; and that its Renaissance architecture had arisen out of, and in all its features indicated, a state of concealed national infidelity, and of domestic corruption. And now, you ask me what style is best to build in; and how can I answer, knowing the meaning of the two styles, but by another question — do you mean to build as Christians or as Infidels? And still more — do you mean to build as honest Christians or as honest Infidels? as thoroughly and confessedly either one or the other? You don't like to be asked such rude questions. I cannot help it; they are of much more importance than this Exchange business; and if they can be at once answered, the Exchange business settles itself in a moment. But, before I press them farther, I must ask leave to explain one point clearly.

In all my past work, my endeavor has been to show that good architecture is essentially religious — the production of a faithful and virtuous, not of an infidel and corrupted people. But in the course of doing this, I have had also to show that good architecture is not ecclesiastical. People are so apt to look upon religion as the business of the clergy, not their own, that the moment they hear of anything depending on 'religion,' they think it must also have depended on the priesthood; and I have had to take what place was to be occupied between these two errors, and fight both, often with seeming contradiction. Good architecture is the work of good and believing men; therefore, you say, at least some people say, 'Good architecture must essentially have been the work of the clergy, not of the laity.' No — a thousand times no; good archi-

tecture [1] has always been the work of the commonalty, *not* of the clergy. What, you say, those glorious cathedrals — the pride of Europe — did their builders not form Gothic architecture? No; they corrupted Gothic architecture. Gothic was formed in the baron's castle, and the burgher's street. It was formed by the thoughts, and hands, and powers of free citizens and warrior kings. By the monk it was used as an instrument for the aid of his superstition; when that superstition became a beautiful madness, and the best hearts of Europe vainly dreamed and pined in the cloister, and vainly raged and perished in the crusade — through that fury of perverted faith and wasted war, the Gothic rose also to its loveliest, most fantastic, and, finally, most foolish dreams; and, in those dreams, was lost.

I hope, now, that there is no risk of your misunderstanding me when I come to the gist of what I want to say tonight; — when I repeat, that every great national architecture has been the result and exponent of a great national religion. You can't have bits of it here, bits there — you must have it everywhere, or nowhere. It is not the monopoly of a clerical company — it is not the exponent of a theological dogma — it is not the hieroglyphic writing of an initiated priesthood; it is the manly language of a people inspired by resolute and common purpose, and rendering resolute and common fidelity to the legible laws of an undoubted God.

Now, there have as yet been three distinct schools of European architecture. I say, European, because Asiatic and African architectures belong so entirely to other races and climates, that there is no question of them here; only, in passing, I will simply assure you that whatever is good or great in Egypt, and Syria, and India, is just good or great for the same reasons as the buildings on our side of the Bosphorus. We Europeans, then, have had three great religions: the Greek, which was the worship of the God of Wisdom and Power; the Medieval, which was the Worship of the God of Judgment and Consolation; the Renaissance, which was the worship of the God of Pride and Beauty;

[1] And all other arts, for the most part; even of incredulous and secularly-minded commonalties.

these three we have had — they are past, — and now, at last, we English have got a fourth religion, and a God of our own, about which I want to ask you. But I must explain these three old ones first.

I repeat, first, the Greeks essentially worshipped the God of Wisdom; so that whatever contended against their religion, — to the Jews a stumbling block,— was, to the Greeks — *Foolishness.*

The first Greek idea of Deity was that expressed in the word, of which we keep the remnant in our words '*Di*-urnal' and '*Di*-vine'— the god of *Day,* Jupiter the revealer. Athena is his daughter, but especially daughter of the Intellect, springing armed from the head. We are only with the help of recent investigation beginning to penetrate the depth of meaning couched under the Athenaic symbols: but I may note rapidly, that her ægis, the mantle with the serpent fringes, in which she often, in the best statues, is represented as folding up her left hand for better guard, and the Gorgon on her shield, are both representative mainly of the chilling horror and sadness (turning men to stone, as it were,) of the outmost and superficial spheres of knowledge — that knowledge which separates, in bitterness, hardness, and sorrow, the heart of the full-grown man from the heart of the child. For out of imperfect knowledge spring terror, dissension, danger, and disdain; but from perfect knowledge, given by the full-revealed Athena, strength and peace, in sign of which she is crowned with the olive spray, and bears the resistless spear.

This, then, was the Greek conception of purest Deity, and every habit of life, and every form of his art developed themselves from the seeking this bright, serene, resistless wisdom; and setting himself, as a man, to do things evermore rightly and strongly;[1] not with any

[1] It is an error to suppose that the Greek worship, or seeking, was chiefly of Beauty. It was essentially of Rightness and Strength, founded on Forethought: the principal character of Greek art is not Beauty, but design: and the Dorian Apollo-worship and Athenian Virgin-worship are both expressions of adoration of divine Wisdom and Purity. Next to these great deities rank, in power over the national mind, Dionysus and Ceres, the givers of human strength and life: then, for heroic example, Hercules. There is no Venus-worship among the Greeks in the great times: and the Muses are essentially teachers of Truth, and of its harmonies. Compare Aratra Pentelici, § 200.

ardent affection or ultimate hope; but with a resolute and continent energy of will, as knowing that for failure there was no consolation, and for sin there was no remission. And the Greek architecture rose unerring, bright, clearly defined, and self-contained.

Next followed in Europe the great Christian faith, which was essentially the religion of Comfort. Its great doctrine is the remission of sins; for which cause it happens, too often, in certain phases of Christianity, that sin and sickness themselves are partly glorified, as if, the more you had to be healed of, the more divine was the healing. The practical result of this doctrine, in art, is a continual contemplation of sin and disease, and of imaginary states of purification from them; thus we have an architecture conceived in a mingled sentiment of melancholy and aspiration, partly severe, partly luxuriant, which will bend itself to every one of our needs, and every one of our fancies, and be strong or weak with us, as we are strong or weak ourselves. It is, of all architecture, the basest, when base people build it — of all, the noblest, when built by the noble.

And now note that both these religions — Greek and Medieval — perished by falsehood in their own main purpose. The Greek religion of Wisdom perished in a false philosophy —'Oppositions of science, falsely so called.' The Mediæval religion of Consolation perished in false comfort; in remission of sins given lyingly. It was the selling of absolution that ended the Medieval faith; and I can tell you more, it is the selling of absolution which, to the end of time, will mark false Christianity. Pure Christianity gives her remission of sins only by *ending* them; but false Christianity gets her remission of sins by *compounding for* them. And there are many ways of compounding for them. We English have beautiful little quiet ways of buying absolution, whether in low Church, or high, far more cunning than any of Tetzel's trading.

Then, thirdly, there followed the religion of Pleasure, in which all Europe gave itself to luxury, ending in death. First, *bals masqués* in every saloon, and then guillotines in every square. And all these three worships issue in vast temple building. Your Greek worshipped Wisdom, and built you the Parthenon — the Virgin's temple. The Medieval worshipped Consolation, and built you Virgin temples also — but to our Lady of Salvation. Then the Revivalist worshipped beauty, of a sort, and built you Versailles, and the Vatican. Now, lastly, will you tell me what *we* worship, and what *we* build?

You know we are speaking always of the real, active, continual, national worship; that by which men act while they live; not that which they talk of when they die. Now, we have, indeed, a nominal religion, to which we pay tithes of property and sevenths of time; but we have also a practical and earnest religion, to which we devote nine-tenths of our property and sixth-sevenths of our time. And we dispute a great deal about the nominal religion; but we are all unanimous about this practical one, of which I think you will admit that the ruling goddess may be best generally described as the 'Goddess of Getting-on,' or 'Britannia of the Market.' The Athenians had an 'Athena Agoraia,' or Athena of the Market; but she was a subordinate type of their goddess, while our Britannia Agoraia is the principal type of ours. And all your great architectural works, are, of course, built to her. It is long since you built a great cathedral; and how you would laugh at me, if I proposed building a cathedral on the top of one of these hills of yours, to make it an Acropolis! But your railroad mounds, vaster than the walls of Babylon; your railroad stations, vaster than the temple of Ephesus, and innumerable; your chimneys how much more mighty and costly than cathedral spires! your harbor piers; your warehouses; your exchanges! — all these are built to your great Goddess of 'Getting-on'; and she has formed, and will continue to form, your architecture, as long as you worship her; and it is quite vain to ask me to tell you how to build to *her;* you know far better than I.

There might indeed, on some theories, be a conceivably good architecture for Exchanges — that is to say, if there were any heroism in the fact or deed of exchange, which might be typically carved on the outside of your building. For,

you know, all beautiful architecture must be adorned with sculpture or painting; and for sculpture or painting, you must have a subject. And hitherto it has been a received opinion among the nations of the world that the only right subjects for either, were *heroisms* of some sort. Even on his pots and his flagons, the Greek put a Hercules slaying lions, or an Apollo slaying serpents, or Bacchus slaying melancholy giants, and earthborn despondencies. On his temples, the Greek put contests of great warriors in founding states, or of gods with evil spirits. On his houses and temples alike, the Christian put carvings of angels conquering devils; or of hero-martyrs exchanging this world for another; subjects inappropriate, I think, to our direction of exchange here. And the Master of Christians not only left his followers without any orders as to the sculpture of affairs of exchange on the outside of buildings, but gave some strong evidence of his dislike of affairs of exchange within them. And yet there might surely be a heroism in such affairs; and all commerce become a kind of selling of doves, not impious. The wonder has always been great to me that heroism has never been supposed to be in anywise consistent with the practice of supplying people with food, or clothes; but rather with that of quartering one's self upon them for food, and stripping them of their clothes. Spoiling of armor is a heroic deed in all ages; but the selling of clothes, old or new, has never taken any color of magnanimity. Yet one does not see why feeding the hungry and clothing the naked should ever become base business, even when engaged in on a large scale. If one could contrive to attach the notion of conquest to them anyhow! so that, supposing there were anywhere an obstinate race, who refused to be comforted, one might take some pride in giving them compulsory comfort![1] and as it were, '*occupying* a country' with one's gifts, instead of one's armies? If one could only consider it as much a victory to get a barren field sown, as to get an eared field stripped; and contend who should build villages, instead of who should 'carry' them! Are not all forms of heroism, conceivable in doing these

[1] Quite serious, all this, though it reads like jest.

serviceable deeds? You doubt who is strongest? It might be ascertained by push of spade, as well as push of sword. Who is wisest? There are witty things to be thought of in planning other business than campaigns. Who is bravest? There are always the elements to fight with, stronger than men; and nearly as merciless.

The only absolutely and unapproachably heroic element in the soldier's work seems to be — that he is paid little for it — and regularly: while you traffickers, and exchangers, and others occupied in presumably benevolent business, like to be paid much for it — and by chance. I never can make out how it is that a *knight*-errant does not expect to be paid for his trouble, but a *peddler*-errant always does; — that people are willing to take hard knocks for nothing, but never to sell ribbons cheap; — that they are ready to go on fervent crusades to recover the tomb of a buried God, but never on any travels to fulfil the orders of a living one; — that they will go anywhere barefoot to preach their faith, but must be well bribed to practise it, and are perfectly ready to give the Gospel gratis, but never the loaves and fishes.[1]

If you choose to take the matter up on any such soldierly principle, to do your commerce, and your feeding of nations, for fixed salaries; and to be as particular about giving people the best food, and the best cloth, as soldiers are about giving them the best gunpowder, I could carve something for you on your exchange worth looking at. But I can only at present suggest decorating its frieze with pendent purses; and making its pillars broad at the base, for the sticking of bills. And in the innermost chambers of it there might be a statue of Britannia of the Market, who may have, perhaps advisably, a partridge for her crest, typical at once of her courage in fighting for noble ideas, and of her interest in game; and round its neck the inscription in golden letters, *Perdix fovit quae non peperit*.[2] Then, for her

spear, she might have a weaver's beam; and on her shield, instead of St. George's Cross, the Milanese boar, semi-fleeced, with the town of Gennesaret proper, in the field, and the legend 'In the best market,'[3] and her corselet, of leather, folded over her heart in the shape of a purse, with thirty slits in it for a piece of money to go in at, on each day of the month. And I doubt not but that people would come to see your exchange, and its goddess, with applause.

Nevertheless, I want to point out to you certain strange characters in this goddess of yours. She differs from the great Greek and Medieval deities essentially in two things — first, as to the continuance of her presumed power; secondly, as to the extent of it.

Ist, as to the Continuance.

The Greek Goddess of Wisdom gave continual increase of wisdom, as the Christian Spirit of Comfort (or Comforter) continual increase of comfort. There was no question, with these, of any limit or cessation of function. But with your Agora Goddess, that is just the most important question. Getting on — but where to? Gathering together — but how much? Do you mean to gather always — never to spend? If so, I wish you joy of your goddess, for I am just as well off as you, without the trouble of worshipping her at all. But if you do not spend, somebody else will — somebody else must. And it is because of this (among many other such errors) that I have fearlessly declared your so-called science of Political Economy to be no science; because, namely, it has omitted the study of exactly the most important branch of the business — the study of *spending*. For spend you must, and as much as you make, ultimately. You gather corn: — will you bury England under a heap of grain; or will you, when you have gathered, finally eat? You gather gold: — will you make your house-roofs of it, or pave your streets with it? That is still one way of spending it. But if you keep it, that you may get more, I'll give you more; I'll give you all the gold you want — all you can imagine — if you can tell me what you'll do with it. You shall have thousands of

---

[1] Please think over this paragraph, too briefly and antithetically put, but one of those which I am happiest in having written.

[2] Jerem. xvii. 11 (best in Septuagint and Vulgate). 'As the partridge, fostering what she brought not forth, so he that getteth riches, not by right shall leave them in the midst of his days, and at his end shall be a fool.'

[3] Meaning fully, 'We have brought our pigs to it.'

gold pieces;—thousands of thousands—millions—mountains, of gold: where will you keep them? Will you put an Olympus of silver upon a golden Pelion—make Ossa like a wart? Do you think the rain and dew would then come down to you, in the streams from such mountains, more blessedly than they will down the mountains which God has made for you, of moss and whinstone? But it is not gold that you want to gather! What is it? greenbacks? No; not those neither. What is it then—is it ciphers after a capital I? Cannot you practise writing ciphers, and write as many as you want? Write ciphers for an hour every morning, in a big book, and say every evening, I am worth all those naughts more than I was yesterday. Won't that do? Well, what in the name of Plutus is it you want? Not gold, not greenbacks, not ciphers after a capital I? You will have to answer, after all, ' No; we want, somehow or other, money's *worth.*' Well, what is that? Let your Goddess of Getting-on discover it, and let her learn to stay therein.

II. But there is yet another question to be asked respecting this Goddess of Getting-on. The first was of the continuance of her power; the second is of its extent.

Pallas and the Madonna were supposed to be all the world's Pallas, and all the world's Madonna. They could teach all men, and they could comfort all men. But, look strictly into the nature of the power of your Goddess of Getting-on; and you will find she is the Goddess—not of everybody's getting on—but only of somebody's getting on. This is a vital, or rather deathful, distinction. Examine it in your own ideal of the state of national life which this Goddess is to evoke and maintain. I asked you what it was, when I was last here;[1]—you have never told me. Now, shall I try to tell you?

Your ideal of human life then is, I think, that it should be passed in a pleasant undulating world, with iron and coal everywhere underneath it. On each pleasant bank of this world is to be a beautiful mansion, with two wings; and

stables, and coach-houses; a moderately sized park; a large garden and hot-houses; and pleasant carriage drives through the shrubberies. In this mansion are to live the favored votaries of the Goddess; the English gentleman, with his gracious wife, and his beautiful family; always able to have the boudoir and the jewels for the wife, and the beautiful ball dresses for the daughters, and hunters for the sons, and a shooting in the Highlands for himself. At the bottom of the bank, is to be the mill; not less than a quarter of a mile long, with a steam engine at each end, and two in the middle, and a chimney three hundred feet high. In this mill are to be in constant employment from eight hundred to a thousand workers, who never drink, never strike, always go to church on Sunday, and always express themselves in respectful language.

Is not that, broadly, and in the main features, the kind of thing you propose to yourselves? It is very pretty indeed, seen from above; not at all so pretty, seen from below. For, observe, while to one family this deity is indeed the Goddess of Getting-on, to a thousand families she is the Goddess of *not* Getting-on. ' Nay,' you say, ' they have all their chance.' Yes, so has every one in a lottery, but there must always be the same number of blanks. ' Ah! but in a lottery it is not skill and intelligence which take the lead, but blind chance.' What then! do you think the old practice, that ' they should take who have the power, and they should keep who can,' is less iniquitous, when the power has become power of brains instead of fist? and that, though we may not take advantage of a child's or a woman's weakness, we may of a man's foolishness? ' Nay, but finally, work must be done, and some one must be at the top, some one at the bottom.' Granted, my friends. Work must always be, and captains of work must always be; and if you in the least remember the tone of any of my writings, you must know that they are thought unfit for this age, because they are always insisting on need of government, and speaking with scorn of liberty. But I beg you to observe that there is a wide difference between being captains or governors of work, and

[1] 'The Two Paths,' p. 115 (small edition), and p. 99 of vol. x of the ' Revised Series of the Entire Works.'

taking the profits of it. It does not follow, because you are general of an army, that you are to take all the treasure, or land, it wins (if it fight for treasure or land); neither, because you are king of a nation, that you are to consume all the profits of the nation's work. Real kings, on the contrary, are known invariably by their doing quite the reverse of this,— by their taking the least possible quantity of the nation's work for themselves. There is no test of real kinghood so infallible as that. Does the crowned creature live simply, bravely, unostentatiously? probably he *is* a King. Does he cover his body with jewels, and his table with delicates? in all probability he is *not* a King. It is possible he may be, as Solomon was; but that is when the nation shares his splendor with him. Solomon made gold, not only to be in his own palace as stones, but to be in Jerusalem as stones. But even so, for the most part, these splendid kinghoods expire in ruin, and only the true kinghoods live, which are of royal laborers governing loyal laborers; who, both leading rough lives, establish the true dynasties. Conclusively you will find that because you are king of a nation, it does not follow that you are to gather for yourself all the wealth of that nation; neither, because you are king of a small part of the nation, and lord over the means of its maintenance — over field, or mill, or mine,— are you to take all the produce of that piece of the foundation of national existence for yourself.

You will tell me I need not preach against these things, for I cannot mend them. No, good friends, I cannot; but you can, and you will; or something else can and will. Even good things have no abiding power — and shall these evil things persist in victorious evil? All history shows, on the contrary, that to be the exact thing they never can do. Change *must* come; but it is ours to determine whether change of growth, or change of death. Shall the Parthenon be in ruins on its rock, and Bolton priory in its meadow, but these mills of yours be the consummation of the buildings of the earth, and their wheels be as the wheels of eternity? Think you that 'men may come, and men may go,' but — mills — go on forever? Not so; out

of these, better or worse shall come; and it is for you to choose which.

I know that none of this wrong is done with deliberate purpose. I know, on the contrary, that you wish your workmen well; that you do much for them, and that you desire to do more for them, if you saw your way to such benevolence safely. I know that even all this wrong and misery are brought about by a warped sense of duty, each of you striving to do his best; but unhappily, not knowing for whom this best should be done. And all our hearts have been betrayed by the plausible impiety of the modern economist, that 'To do the best for yourself, is finally to do the best for others.' Friends, our great Master said not so; and most absolutely we shall find this world is not made so. Indeed, to do the best for others, is finally to do the best for ourselves; but it will not do to have our eyes fixed on that issue. The Pagans had got beyond that. Hear what a Pagan says of this matter; hear what were, perhaps, the last written words of Plato,— if not the last actually written (for this we cannot know), yet assuredly in fact and power his parting words — in which, endeavoring to give full crowning and harmonious close to all his thoughts, and to speak the sum of them by the imagined sentence of the Great Spirit, his strength and his heart fail him, and the words cease, broken off forever.

They are at the close of the dialogue called 'Critias,' in which he describes, partly from real tradition, partly in ideal dream, the early state of Athens; and the genesis, and order, and religion, of the fabled isle of Atlantis; in which genesis he conceives the same first perfection and final degeneracy of man, which in our own Scriptural tradition is expressed by saying that the Sons of God intermarried with the daughters of men, for he supposes the earliest race to have been indeed the children of God; and to have corrupted themselves, until 'their spot was not the spot of his children.' And this, he says, was the end; that indeed 'through many generations, so long as the God's nature in them yet was full, they were submissive to the sacred laws, and carried themselves lovingly to all that had kindred with them in divineness; for their uttermost spirit was faithful and true, and in every wise great; so that, in *all meekness of wisdom, they dealt with each other,* and took all the chances of life; and despising all things except virtue, they cared little what happened day by day, and *bore lightly the burden* of gold and of possessions; for they saw that, if *only their common love and virtue increased, all these things would be increased together with them;* but to set their esteem and ardent pursuit upon material possession would be to lose that first, and their virtue and affection together with it. And by such reasoning, and what of the divine nature remained in them, they gained all this greatness of which we have already told; but when the God's part of them faded and became extinct, being mixed again and again, and effaced by the prevalent mortality; and the human nature at last exceeded, they then became unable to endure the courses of fortune; and fell into shapelessness of life, and baseness in the sight of him who could see, having lost everything that was fairest of their honor; while to the blind hearts which could not discern the true life, tending to happiness, it seemed that they were then chiefly noble and happy, being filled with all iniquity of inordinate possession and power. Whereupon, the God of gods, whose Kinghood is in laws, beholding a once just nation thus cast into misery, and desiring to lay such punishment upon them as might make them repent into restraining, gathered together all the gods into his dwelling-place, which from heaven's center overlooks whatever has part in creation; and having assembled them, he said '—

The rest is silence. Last words of the chief wisdom of the heathen, spoken of this idol of riches; this idol of yours; this golden image high by measureless cubits, set up where your green fields of England are furnace-burnt into the likeness of the plain of Dura: this idol, forbidden to us, first of all idols, by our own Master and faith; forbidden to us also by every human lip that has ever, in any age or people, been accounted of as able to speak according to the purposes of God. Continue to make that forbidden deity your principal one, and soon no more art, no more science, no more pleasure will be possible. Catastrophe will come; or worse than catastrophe, slow moldering and withering into Hades. But if you can fix some conception of a true human state of life to be striven for — life good for all men as for yourselves — if you can determine some honest and simple order of existence; following those trodden ways of wisdom, which are pleasantness, and seeking her quiet and withdrawn paths, which are peace; [1]— then, and so sanctifying wealth into 'commonwealth,' all your art, your literature, your daily labors, your domestic affection, and citizen's duty, will join and increase into one magnificent harmony. You will know then how to build, well enough; you will build with stone well, but with flesh better; temples not made with hands, but riveted of hearts; and that kind of marble, crimson-veined, is indeed eternal.

[1] I imagine the Hebrew chant merely intends passionate repetition, and not a distinction of this somewhat fanciful kind; yet we may profitably make it in reading the English.

ALFRED, LORD TENNYSON (1809–1892)

Tennyson was born at Somersby Rectory in Lincolnshire. The rich level landscape of the reclaimed fen district is clearly visible in his poems. He soon began to imitate the English masters of verse and the compositions 'written between 15 and 17' in *Poems by Two Brothers* (1827) show his transitory allegiance to Byron and Scott. At Trinity College, Cambridge, he took the Newdigate prize in 1829 with a blank verse poem on *Timbuctoo*, and the next year issued *Poems, Chiefly Lyrical*. Numerous collegians, of whom many were afterward eminent in scholarship and affairs, became his sworn admirers and steadily announced that a new poet had arrived. *Poems* (1833) showed a further advance in quality and scope, but this and the preceding volume were ridiculed by the reviews for certain obvious affectations and slips of taste and Tennyson waited nine years before publishing again. During this interval, he set himself with great earnestness to comprehend the thoughts and movements of his time, enriched his mind by constant study of the classics and of English literature, recreated the best of his old poems and composed with great deliberation his new ones. When his two volumes of 1842 appeared, such poems as *The Lady of Shalott* and *The Palace of Art* had been transformed and with them came *Ulysses*, *Morte d'Arthur*, *Locksley Hall* and many others of moderate length, every one exquisitely tempered and wrought. His reputation was immediately secure, and steadily increased during fifty years more of continuous authorship. In 1850 he received the 'laurel greener from the brows of him that uttered nothing base.' *The Princess* had already appeared and *In Memoriam* which had been growing since the death of his friend Arthur Hallam in 1833, now sealed his title not only to the laureateship but to the position of chief spiritual guide to his age. *Maud* (1855) represented something of a departure from his previous methods toward a less restrained style and a more vigorous grasp on the realities of life, a departure which he carried still farther in some of his 'ballads' and in realistic studies such as *The Northern Farmer*. The chief enterprise of his later years, however, was *The Idylls of the King*, at which he wrought from 1856–59, and again in 1868–72, when the poem became substantially complete. For nearly ten years his chief energies were given to the production of his seven dramas; of these *Queen Mary*, *Harold*, and *Becket* were all written by 1879, though the last was not published until several years later. From 1880 until his death in 1892 every few years added another volume of miscellaneous poems. At least in his lyrics, Tennyson's voice remained to the last, 'unchanged to hoarse or mute,' a 'clear call' with only a few dark overtones caught from the perplexities of the new era into which his life extended. In the few years since his death, we have moved fast and far from the platforms of the Victorian age; its problems are not our problems, and still less its solutions. Our interest, then, shifts more and more from Tennyson's 'message,' which was of his time, and attaches to the rich and instructed beauty of his art, which is imperishable.

MARIANA

With blackest moss, the flower-plots
  Were thickly crusted, one and all:
The rusted nails fell from the knots
  That held the pear to the gable-wall.
The broken sheds looked sad and strange: 5
  Unlifted was the clinking latch;
  Weeded and worn the ancient thatch
Upon the lonely moated grange.
    She only said, 'My life is dreary,
      He cometh not, she said;   10
    She said, 'I am aweary, aweary,
      I would that I were dead!'

Her tears fell with the dews at even;
  Her tears fell ere the dews were dried;
She could not look on the sweet heaven, 15
  Either at morn or eventide.
After the flitting of the bats,
  When thickest dark did trance the sky,
  She drew her casement-curtain by,
And glanced athwart the glooming flats, 20
    She only said, 'The night is dreary,
      He cometh not,' she said;
    She said, 'I am aweary, aweary,
      I would that I were dead!'

Upon the middle of the night,   25
  Waking she heard the night-fowl crow:

The cock sung out an hour ere light;
From the dark fen the oxen's low
Came to her: without hope of change,
In sleep she seemed to walk forlorn,   30
Till cold winds woke the gray-eyed morn
About the lonely moated grange.
    She only said, 'My life is dreary,
      He cometh not,' she said;
    She said, 'I am aweary, aweary,   35
      I would that I were dead!'

About a stone-cast from the wall
  A sluice with blackened waters slept
And o'er it many, round and small,
  The clustered marish-mosses crept.   40
Hard by a poplar shook alway,
  All silver-green with gnarlèd bark:
For leagues no other tree did mark
  The level waste, the rounding gray.
    She only said, 'The night is dreary,
      He cometh not,' she said;   46
    She said, 'I am aweary, aweary,
      I would that I were dead!'

And ever when the moon was low,
  And the shrill winds were up and away,   50
In the white curtain, to and fro,
  She saw the gusty shadow sway.
But when the moon was very low,
  And wild winds bound within their cell,
The shadow of the poplar fell   55
Upon her bed, across her brow.
    She only said, 'My life is dreary,
      He cometh not,' she said;
    She said, 'I am aweary, aweary,
      I would that I were dead!'   60

All day within the dreamy house,
  The doors upon their hinges creaked;
The blue fly sung in the pane; the mouse
  Behind the moldering wainscot shrieked,
Or from the crevice peered about.   65
  Old faces glimmered through the doors,
  Old footsteps trod the upper floors,
Old voices called her from without.
    She only said, 'My life is dreary,
      He cometh not,' she said;   70
    She said, 'I am aweary, aweary,
      I would that I were dead!'

The sparrow's chirrup on the roof,
  The slow clock ticking, and the sound
Which to the wooing wind aloof   75
  The poplar made, did all confound
Her sense; but most she loathed the hour
  When the thick-moated sunbeam lay
  Athwart the chambers, and the day
Was sloping toward his western bower.   80

Then, said she, 'I am very dreary,
  He will not come,' she said;
She wept: 'I am aweary, aweary,
  O God, that I were dead!'

                (1830)

SONG

I

A spirit haunts the year's last hours
Dwelling amid these yellowing bowers:
  To himself he talks;
For at eventide, listening earnestly,
At his work you may hear him sob
    and sigh   5
  In the walks;
    Earthward he boweth the heavy
      stalks
Of the moldering flowers:
  Heavily hangs the broad sunflower
    Over its grave i' the earth so chilly;
  Heavily hangs the hollyhock,   11
  Heavily hangs the tiger-lily.

II

The air is damp, and hushed, and close,
As a sick man's room when he taketh
    repose
  An hour before death;   15
My very heart faints and my whole soul
    grieves
At the moist rich smell of the rotting
    leaves,
  And the breath
    Of the fading edges of box beneath,
And the year's last rose.   20
  Heavily hangs the broad sunflower
    Over its grave i' the earth so chilly;
  Heavily hangs the hollyhock,
  Heavily hangs the tiger-lily.

                (1830)

THE POET

The poet in a golden clime was born,
  With golden stars above;
Dowered with the hate of hate, the scorn of
    scorn,
  The love of love.

He saw through life and death, through
    good and ill,   5
  He saw through his own soul.
The marvel of the everlasting will,
  An open scroll,

Before him lay; with echoing feet he
    threaded
The secretest walks of fame: 10
The viewless arrows of his thoughts were
    headed
And winged with flame,

Like Indian reeds blown from his silver
    tongue,
And of so fierce a flight,
From Calpe unto Caucasus they sung,   15
Filling with light

And vagrant melodies the winds which bore
Them earthward till they lit;
Then, like the arrow-seeds of the field
    flower,
The fruitful wit   20

Cleaving took root, and springing forth
    anew
Where'er they fell, behold,
Like to the mother plant in semblance grew
A flower all gold,

And bravely furnished all abroad to fling
The wingèd shafts of truth,   26
To throng with stately blooms the breath-
    ing spring,
Of Hope and Youth.

So many minds did gird their orbs with
    beams,
Though one did fling the fire;   30
Heaven flowed upon the soul in many
    dreams
Of high desire.

Thus truth was multiplied on truth, the
    world
Like one great garden showed,
And through the wreaths of floating dark up-
    curled,   35
Rare sunrise flowed.

And Freedom reared in that august sun-
    rise
Her beautiful bold brow,
When rites and forms before his burning
    eyes
Melted like snow.   40

There was no blood upon her maiden robes
Sunned by those orient skies;
But round about the circles of the globes
Of her keen eyes

And in her raiment's hem was traced in
    flame   45
Wisdom, a name to shake
All evil dreams of power — a sacred name,
And when she spake,

Her words did gather thunder as they ran,
And as the lightning to the thunder
Which follows it, riving the spirit of man,
    Making earth wonder,   52

So was their meaning to her words. No
    sword
Of wrath her right arm whirled,
But one poor poet's scroll, and with *his*
    word   55
She shook the world.

                 (1830)

THE LADY OF SHALOTT

PART I

On either side the river lie
Long fields of barley and of rye,
That clothe the wold and meet the sky;
And through the field the road runs by
    To many-towered Camelot;   5
And up and down the people go,
Gazing where the lilies blow
Round an island there below,
    The island of Shalott.

Willows whiten, aspens quiver,   10
Little breezes dusk and shiver
Through the wave that runs for ever
By the island in the river
    Flowing down to Camelot.
Four gray walls, and four gray towers,   15
Overlook a space of flowers,
And the silent isle imbowers
    The Lady of Shalott.

By the margin, willow-veiled,
Slide the heavy barges trailed   20
By slow horses; and unhailed
The shallop flitteth silken-sailed
    Skimming down to Camelot;
But who hath seen her wave her hand?
Or at the casement seen her stand?   25
Or is she known in all the land,
    The Lady of Shalott?

Only reapers, reaping early
In among the bearded barley,
Hear a song that echoes cheerly   30
From the river winding clearly,

Down to towered Camelot;
And by the moon the reaper weary,
Piling sheaves in uplands airy,
Listening, whispers ''T is the fairy   35
    Lady of Shalott.'

PART II

There she weaves by night and day
A magic web with colors gay.
She has heard a whisper say,
A curse is on her if she stay   40
    To look down to Camelot.
She knows not what the curse may be,
And so she weaveth steadily,
And little other care hath she,
    The Lady of Shalott.   45

And moving through a mirror clear
That hangs before her all the year,
Shadows of the world appear.
There she sees the highway near
    Winding down to Camelot;   50
There the river eddy whirls,
And there the surly village-churls,
And the red cloaks of market girls,
    Pass onward from Shalott.

Sometimes a troop of damsels glad,   55
An abbot on an ambling pad,
Sometimes a curly shepherd-lad,
Or long-haired page in crimson clad,
    Goes by to towered Camelot;
And sometimes through the mirror blue   60
The knights come riding two and two:
She hath no loyal knight and true,
    The Lady of Shalott.

But in her web she still delights
To weave the mirror's magic sights,   65
For often through the silent nights
A funeral, with plumes and lights
    And music, went to Camelot;
Or when the moon was overhead,
Came two young lovers lately wed;   70
'I am half sick of shadows,' said
    The Lady of Shalott.

PART III

A bow-shot from her bower-eaves,
He rode between the barley-sheaves,
The sun came dazzling through the leaves,
And flamed upon the brazen greaves   76
    Of bold Sir Lancelot.
A red-cross knight for ever kneeled,
To a lady in his shield,
That sparkled in the yellow field,   80
    Beside remote Shalott.

The gemmy bridle glittered free,
Like to some branch of stars we see
Hung in the golden Galaxy.
The bridle bells rang merrily   85
    As he rode down to Camelot;
And from his blazoned baldric slung
A mighty silver bugle hung,
And as he rode his armor rung,
    Beside remote Shalott.   90

All in the blue unclouded weather
Thick-jeweled shone the saddle-leather,
The helmet and the helmet-feather
Burned like one burning flame together,
    As he rode down to Camelot;   95
As often through the purple night,
Below the starry clusters bright,
Some bearded meteor, trailing light,
    Moves over still Shalott.

His broad clear brow in sunlight glowed;
On burnished hooves his war-horse trode;
From underneath his helmet flowed
His coal-black curls as on he rode,
    As he rode down to Camelot.
From the bank and from the river   105
He flashed into the crystal mirror,
'Tirra lirra,' by the river
    Sang Sir Lancelot.

She left the web, she left the loom,
She made three paces through the room,   110
She saw the water-lily bloom,
She saw the helmet and the plume,
    She looked down at Camelot.
Out flew the web and floated wide;
The mirror cracked from side to side;   115
'The curse is come upon me,' cried
    The Lady of Shalott.

PART IV

In the stormy east-wind straining,
The pale yellow woods were waning,
The broad stream in his banks complaining,
Heavily the low sky raining   121
    Over towered Camelot;
Down she came and found a boat
Beneath a willow left afloat,
And round about the prow she wrote   125
    The Lady of Shalott.

And down the river's dim expanse
Like some bold seër in a trance,
Seeing all his own mischance —
With a glassy countenance   130
    Did she look to Camelot.
And at the closing of the day

She loosed the chain, and down she lay;
The broad stream bore her far away,
 The Lady of Shalott.   135

Lying, robed in snowy white
That loosely flew to left and right —
The leaves upon her falling light —
Through the noises of the night
 She floated down to Camelot; 140
And as the boat-head wound along
The willowy hills and fields among,
They heard her singing her last song,
 The Lady of Shalott.

Heard a carol, mournful, holy, 145
Chanted loudly, chanted lowly,
Till her blood was frozen slowly
And her eyes were darkened wholly
 Turned to towered Camelot.
For ere she reached upon the tide 150
The first house by the water-side,
Singing in her song she died,
 The Lady of Shalott.

Under tower and balcony,
By garden-wall and gallery, 155
A gleaming shape she floated by,
Dead-pale between the houses high,
 Silent into Camelot.
Out upon the wharfs they came,
Knight, and burgher, lord and dame, 160
And round the prow they read her name,
 The Lady of Shalott.

Who is this? and what is here?
And in the lighted palace near
Died the sound of royal cheer; 165
And they crossed themselves for fear,
 All the knights at Camelot;
But Lancelot mused a little space;
He said, 'She has a lovely face;
God in his mercy lend her grace, 170
 The Lady of Shalott.'

       (1833)

THE PALACE OF ART

I built my soul a lordly pleasure-house,
 Wherein at ease for aye to dwell.
I said, 'O Soul, make merry and carouse,
 Dear soul, for all is well.'

A huge crag-platform, smooth as burnished
  brass, 5
 I chose. The rangèd ramparts bright
From level meadow-bases of deep grass
 Suddenly scaled the light.

Thereon I built it firm. Of ledge cr shelf
 The rock rose clear, or winding stair, 10
My soul would live alone unto herself
 In her high palace there.

And 'while the world runs round and
  round,' I said,
 'Reign thou apart, a quiet king,
Still as, while Saturn whirls, his steadfast
  shade 15
 Sleeps on his luminous ring.'

To which my soul made answer readily:
 'Trust me, in bliss I shall abide
In this great mansion, that is built for me.
 So royal-rich and wide.' 20

. . . .

Four courts I made, East, West, and South
  and North,
 In each a squarèd lawn, wherefrom
The golden gorge of dragons spouted forth
 A flood of fountain-foam.

And round the cool green courts there ran
  a row 25
 Of cloisters, branched like mighty woods,
Echoing all night to that sonorous flow
 Of spouted fountain-floods.

And round the roofs a gilded gallery
 That lent broad verge to distant lands, 30
Far as the wild swan wings, to where the
  sky
 Dipped down to sea and sands.

From those four jets four currents in one
  swell
 Across the mountain streamed below
In misty folds, that floating as they fell, 35
 Lit up a torrent-bow.

And high on every peak a statue seemed
 To hang on tiptoe, tossing up
A cloud of incense of all odor steamed
 From out a golden cup. 40

So that she thought, 'And who shall gaze
  upon
 My palace with unblinded eyes,
While this great bow will waver in the sun,
 And that sweet incense rise?'

For that sweet incense rose and never
  failed, 45
 And, while day sank or mounted higher,
The light aerial gallery, golden-railed,
 Burnt like a fringe of fire.

Likewise the deep-set windows, stained and
    traced,
Would seem slow-flaming crimson fires 50
From shadowed grots of arches interlaced,
    And tipped with frost-like spires.

.   .   .   .

Full of long-sounding corridors it was,
    That over-vaulted grateful gloom,
Through which the livelong day my soul did
        pass,   55
    Well-pleased, from room to room.

Full of great rooms and small the palace
      stood,
All various, each a perfect whole
From living Nature, fit for every mood
    And change of my still soul.   60

For some were hung with arras green and
    blue,
    Showing a gaudy summer-morn,
Where with puffed cheek the belted hunter
    blew
    His wreathèd bugle-horn.

One seemed all dark and red—a tract of
    sand,   65
And some one pacing there alone,
Who paced for ever in a glimmering land,
    Lit with a low large moon.

One showed an iron coast and angry waves,
    You seemed to hear them climb and fall
And roar rock-thwarted under bellowing
    caves,   71
    Beneath the windy wall.

And one, a full-fed river winding slow
    By herds upon an endless plain,
The ragged rims of thunder brooding low,
    With shadow-streaks of rain.   76

And one, the reapers at their sultry toil.
    In front they bound the sheaves. Behind
Were realms of upland, prodigal in oil,
    And hoary to the wind.   80

And one a foreground black with stones and
    slags,
    Beyond, a line of heights, and higher
All barred with long white cloud the scorn-
    ful crags,
    And highest, snow and fire.

And one, an English home—gray twilight
    poured   85

    On dewy pastures, dewy trees,
Softer than sleep—all things in order
    stored,
    A haunt of ancient Peace.

Nor these alone, but every landscape fair,
    As fit for every mood of mind,   90
Or gay, or grave, or sweet, or stern, was
    there,
    Not less than truth designed.

.   .   .   .

Or the maid-mother by a crucifix,
    In tracts of pasture sunny-warm,
Beneath branch-work of costly sardonyx, 95
    Sat smiling, babe in arm.

Or in a clear-walled city on the sea,
    Near gilded organ-pipes, her hair
Wound with white roses, slept Saint Cecily;
    An angel looked at her.   100

Or thronging all one porch of Paradise
    A group of Houris bowed to see
The dying Islamite, with hands and eyes
    That said, We wait for thee.

Or mythic Uther's deeply-wounded son 105
    In some fair space of sloping greens
Lay, dozing in the vale of Avalon,
    And watched by weeping queens.

Or hollowing one hand against his ear,
    To list a foot-fall, ere he saw   110
The wood-nymph, stayed the Ausonian king
    to hear
    Of wisdom and of law.

Or over hills with peaky tops engrailed,
    And many a tract of palm and rice,
The throne of Indian Cama slowly sailed 115
    A summer fanned with spice.

Or sweet Europa's mantle blew unclasped,
    From off her shoulder backward borne,
From one hand drooped a crocus; one hand
    grasped
    The mild bull's golden horn.   120

Or else flushed Ganymede, his rosy thigh
    Half-buried in the eagle's down,
Sole as a flying star shot through the sky
    Above the pillared town.

Nor these alone; but every legend fair   125
    Which the supreme Caucasian mind
Carved out of Nature for itself, was there,
    Not less than life, designed.

.   .   .   .

Then in the towers I placed great bells that
　　　swung,
　Moved of themselves, with silver sound;
And with choice paintings of wise men I
　　　hung   131
　　The royal dais round.

For there was Milton like a seraph strong,
　Beside him Shakespeare bland and mild;
And there the world-worn Dante grasped
　　　his song,   135
　　And somewhat grimly smiled.

And there the Ionian father of the rest;
　A million wrinkles carved his skin;
A hundred winters snowed upon his breast,
　　From cheek and throat and chin.   140

Above, the fair hall-ceiling stately-set
　Many an arch high up did lift,
And angels rising and descending met
　　With interchange of gift.

Below was all mosaic choicely planned   145
　With cycles of the human tale
Of this wide world, the times of every land
　　So wrought, they will not fail.

The people here, a beast of burden slow,
　Toiled onward, pricked with goads and
　　　stings;   150
Here played, a tiger, rolling to and fro
　　The heads and crowns of kings;

Here rose, an athlete, strong to break or
　　　bind
　All force in bonds that might endure,
And here once more like some sick man
　　　declined,   155
　　And trusted any cure.

But over these she trod; and those great
　　　bells
　Began to chime. She took her throne;
She sat betwixt the shining oriels,
　　To sing her songs alone.   160

And through the topmost oriels' colored
　　　flame
　Two godlike faces gazed below;
Plato the wise, and large-browed Verulam,
　　The first of those who know.

And all those names that in their motion
　　　were   165
　Full-welling fountain-heads of change,
Betwixt the slender shafts were blazoned
　　　fair
　　In diverse raiment strange:

Through which the lights, rose, amber, em-
　　　erald, blue,
　Flushed in her temples and her eyes,   170
And from her lips, as morn from Mem-
　　　non, drew
　　Rivers of melodies.

No nightingale delighteth to prolong
　Her low preamble all alone,
More than my soul to hear her echoed song
　　Throb through the ribbèd stone;   176

Singing and murmuring in her feastful
　　　mirth,
　Joying to feel herself alive,
Lord over Nature, lord of the visible earth,
　　Lord of the senses five;   180

Communing with herself: 'All these are
　　　mine,
　And let the world have peace or wars,
'T is one to me.' She — when young night
　　　divine
　Crowned dying day with stars,

Making sweet close of his delicious toils —
　Lit light in wreaths and anadems,   186
And pure quintessences of precious oils
　　In hollowed moons of gems,

To mimic heaven; and clapped her hands
　　　and cried,
　'I marvel if my still delight   190
In this great house so royal-rich and wide
　　Be flattered to the height.

'O all things fair to sate my various eyes!
　O shapes and hues that please me well!
O silent faces of the Great and Wise,   195
　　My Gods, with whom I dwell!

'O Godlike isolation which art mine,
　I can but count thee perfect gain,
What time I watch the darkening droves of
　　　swine
　That range on yonder plain.   200

'In filthy sloughs they roll a prurient skin,
　They graze and wallow, breed and sleep;
And oft some brainless devil enters in,
　　And drives them to the deep.'

Then of the moral instinct would she prate
　And of the rising from the dead,   206
As hers by right of full-accomplished Fate;
　　And at the last she said:

'I take possession of man's mind and deed.
  I care not what the sects may brawl,   210
I sit as God holding no form of creed,
    But contemplating all.'

.   .   .   .

Full oft the riddle of the painful earth
  Flashed through her as she sat alone,
Yet not the less held she her solemn mirth,
    And intellectual throne.   216

And so she throve and prospered; so three
     years
  She prospered; on the fourth she fell,
Like Herod, when the shout was in his ears,
    Struck through with pangs of hell.   220

Lest she should fail and perish utterly,
  God, before whom ever lie bare
The abysmal deeps of Personality,
    Plagued her with sore despair.

When she would think, where'er she turned
     her sight,   225
  The airy hand confusion wrought,
Wrote 'Mene, mene,' and divided quite
    The kingdom of her thought.

Deep dread and loathing of her solitude
  Fell on her, from which mood was born
Scorn of herself; again, from out that
     mood   231
    Laughter at her self-scorn.

'What! is not this my place of strength,'
     she said,
  'My spacious mansion built for me,
Whereof the strong foundation-stones were
     laid   235
    Since my first memory?'

But in dark corners of her palace stood
  Uncertain shapes; and unawares
On white-eyed phantasms weeping tears of
     blood,
    And horrible nightmares,   240

And hollow shades enclosing hearts of
     flame,
  And, with dim fretted foreheads all,
On corpses three-months-old at noon she
     came,
    That stood against the wall.

A spot of dull stagnation, without light   245
  Or power of movement, seemed my soul,
Mid onward-sloping motions infinite
    Making for one sure goal.

A still salt pool, locked in with bars of sand
  Left on the shore, that hears all night   250
The plunging seas draw backward from the
     land
    Their moon led waters white.

A star that with the choral starry dance
  Joined not, but stood, and standing saw
The hollow orb of moving Circumstance   255
    Rolled round by one fixed law.

Back on herself her serpent pride had curled.
  'No voice,' she shrieked in that lone hall,
'No voice breaks thro' the stillness of this
     world:
    One deep, deep silence all!'   260

She, moldering with the dull earth's mold-
     ering sod,
  Inwrapt tenfold in slothful shame,
Lay there exilèd from eternal God,
    Lost to her place and name;

And death and life she hated equally,   265
  And nothing saw, for her despair,
But dreadful time, dreadful eternity,
    No comfort anywhere;

Remaining utterly confused with fears,
  And ever worse with growing time,   270
And ever unrelieved by dismal tears,
    And all alone in crime:

Shut up as in a crumbling tomb, girt round
  With blackness as a solid wall,
Far off she seemed to hear the dully sound
    Of human footsteps fall.   276

As in strange lands a traveler walking slow,
  In doubt and great perplexity,
A little before moonrise hears the low
    Moan of an unknown sea;   280

And knows not if it be thunder, or a sound
  Of rocks thrown down, or one deep cry
Of great wild beasts; then thinketh, 'I have
     found
    A new land, but I die.'

She howled aloud, 'I am on fire within.   285
  There comes no murmur of reply.
What is it that will take away my sin,
    And save me lest I die?'

So when four years were wholly finishèd,
  She threw her royal robes away.   290
'Make me a cottage in the vale,' she said,
    'Where I may mourn and pray.

'Yet pull not down my palace towers, that
are
So lightly, beautifully built:
Perchance I may return with others there,
When I have purged my guilt.' 296

(1833-1842)

A DREAM OF FAIR WOMEN

I read, before my eyelids dropped their
shade,
The Legend of Good Women, long ago
Sung by the morning star of song, who
made
His music heard below;

Dan Chaucer, the first warbler, whose sweet
breath 5
Preluded those melodious bursts that fill
The spacious times of great Elizabeth
With sounds that echo still.

And, for a while, the knowledge of his art
Held me above the subject, as strong gales
Hold swollen clouds from raining, though
my heart, 11
Brimful of those wild tales,

Charged both mine eyes with tears. In
every land
I saw, wherever light illumineth,
Beauty and anguish walking hand in hand 15
The downward slope to death.

Those far-renownèd brides of ancient song
Peopled the hollow dark, like burning
stars,
And I heard sounds of insult, shame, and
wrong,
And trumpets blown for wars; 20

And clattering flints battered with clanging
hoofs;
And I saw crowds in columned sanctu-
aries,
And forms that passed at windows and on
roofs
Of marble palaces;

Corpses across the threshold; heroes tall 25
Dislodging pinnacle and parapet
Upon the tortoise creeping to the wall;
Lances in ambush set;

And high shrine-doors burst through with
heated blasts

That run before the fluttering tongues of
fire; 30
White surf wind-scattered over sails and
masts,
And ever climbing higher;

Squadrons and squares of men in brazen
plates,
Scaffolds, still sheets of water, divers
woes,
Ranges of glimmering vaults with iron
grates, 35
And hushed seraglios.

So shape chased shape as swift as, when to
land
Bluster the winds and tides the self-same
way,
Crisp foam-flakes scud along the level sand,
Torn from the fringe of spray. 40

I started once, or seemed to start in pain,
Resolved on noble things, and strove to
speak,
As when a great thought strikes along the
brain,
And flushes all the cheek.

And once my arm was lifted to hew down
A cavalier from off his saddle-bow, 46
That bore a lady from a leaguered town;
And then, I know not how,

All those sharp fancies, by down-lapsing
thought
Streamed onward, lost their edges, and did
creep 50
Rolled on each other, rounded, smoothed,
and brought
Into the gulfs of sleep.

At last methought that I had wandered far
In an old wood; fresh-washed in coolest
dew
The maiden splendors of the morning star
Shook in the steadfast blue. 56

Enormous elm-tree boles did stoop and lean
Upon the dusky brushwood underneath
Their broad curved branches, fledged with
clearest green,
New from its silken sheath. 60

The dim red Morn had died, her journey
done,
And with dead lips smiled at the twilight
plain,

Half-fallen across the threshold of the sun,
  Never to rise again.

There was no motion in the dumb dead
    air,   65
Not any song of bird or sound of rill;
Gross darkness of the inner sepulchre
  Is not so deadly still

As that wide forest. Growths of jasmine
    turned
  Their humid arms festooning tree to
    tree,   70
And at the root through lush green grasses
    burned
  The red anemone.

I knew the flowers, I knew the leaves, I
    knew
  The tearful glimmer of the languid dawn
On those long, rank, dark wood-walks
    drenched in dew,   75
  Leading from lawn to lawn.

The smell of violets, hidden in the green,
  Poured back into my empty soul and
    frame
The times when I remember to have been
  Joyful and free from blame.   80

And from within me a clear undertone
  Thrilled through mine ears in that unbliss-
    ful clime,
Pass freely through; the wood is all thine
    own,
  Until the end of time.'

At length I saw a lady within call,   85
  Stiller than chiseled marble, standing
    there;
A daughter of the gods, divinely tall,
  And most divinely fair.

Her loveliness with shame and with sur-
    prise
  Froze my swift speech; she turning on
    my face   90
The star-like sorrows of immortal eyes,
  Spoke slowly in her place.

'I had great beauty; ask thou not my
    name:
  No one can be more wise than destiny.
Many drew swords and died. Where'er I
    came   95
  I brought calamity.'

'No marvel, sovereign lady: in fair field
  Myself for such a face had boldly died,'
I answered free; and turning I appealed
  To one that stood beside.   100

But she, with sick and scornful looks averse,
  To her full height her stately stature
    draws;
'My youth,' she said, 'was blasted with
    a curse:
  This woman was the cause.

'I was cut off from hope in that sad place
  Which men called Aulis in those iron
    years;   106
My father held his hand upon his face;
  I, blinded with my tears,

'Still strove to speak: my voice was thick
    with sighs
  As in a dream. Dimly I could descry
The stern black-bearded kings with wolfish
    eyes,   110
  Waiting to see me die.

'The high masts flickered as they lay afloat;
  The crowds, the temples, wavered, and
    the shore;
The bright death quivered at the victim's
    throat;
  Touched; and I knew no more.'   115

Whereto the other with a downward brow:
  'I would the white cold heavy-plunging
    foam,
Whirled by the wind, had rolled me deep
    below,
  Then when I left my home.'

Her slow full words sank through the silence
    drear,   120
  As thunder-drops fall on a sleeping sea:
Sudden I heard a voice that cried 'Come
    here,
  That I may look on thee.'

I turning saw, throned on a flowery rise,
  One sitting on a crimson scarf un-
    rolled;   125
A queen, with swarthy cheeks and bold
    black eyes,
  Brow-bound with burning gold.

She, flashing forth a haughty smile, began:
  'I governed men by change, and so I
    swayed
All moods. 'T is long since I have seen a
    man.   130
  Once, like the moon, I made

'The ever-shifting currents of the blood
  According to my humor ebb and flow.
I have no men to govern in this wood:
    That makes my only woe.   135

'Nay — yet it chafes me that I could not
    bend
  One will; nor tame and tutor with mine
    eye
That dull cold-blooded Cæsar. Prythee,
    friend,
    Where is Mark Antony?

'The man, my lover, with whom I rode sub-
    lime   140
  On Fortune's neck; we sat as God by
    God;
The Nilus would have risen before his time
  And flooded at our nod.

'We drank the Libyan Sun to sleep, and
    lit
  Lamps which out-burned Canopus. O, my
    life   145
In Egypt! O, the dalliance and the wit,
  The flattery and the strife,

'And the wild kiss, when fresh from war's
    alarms,
  My Hercules, my Roman Antony,
My mailèd Bacchus leaped into my arms,
  Contented there to die!   151

'And there he died: and when I heard my
    name
  Sighed forth with life, I would not brook
    my fear
Of the other: with a worm I balked his
    fame.
  What else was left? look here!'—   155

With that she tore her robe apart, and half
  The polished argent of her breast to sight
Laid bare. Thereto she pointed with a
    laugh,
  Showing the aspic's bite.—   159

'I died a Queen. The Roman soldier found
  Me lying dead, my crown about my brows,
A name for ever!—lying robed and
    crowned
  Worthy a Roman spouse.'

Her warbling voice, a lyre of widest range
  Struck by all passion, did fall down and
    glance   165
From tone to tone, and glided through all
    change
  Of liveliest utterance.

When she made pause I knew not for de-
    light
  Because with sudden motion from the
    ground
She raised her piercing orbs, and filled with
    light   170
  The interval of sound.

Still with their fires Love tipt his keenest
    darts:
  As once they drew into two burning rings
All beams of Love, melting the mighty
    hearts
  Of captains and of kings.   175

Slowly my sense undazzled. Then I heard
  A noise of some one coming through the
    lawn,
And singing clearer than the crested bird
  That claps his wings at dawn:

'The torrent brooks of hallowed Israel   180
  From craggy hollows pouring, late and
    soon,
Sound all night long, in falling through the
    dell,
  Far-heard beneath the moon.

'The balmy moon of blessed Israel
  Floods all the deep-blue gloom with beams
    divine;   185
All night the splintered crags that wall the
    dell
  With spires of silver shine.'

As one that museth where broad sunshine
    laves
  The lawn by some cathedral, through the
    door
Hearing the holy organ rolling waves   190
  Of sound on roof and floor

Within, and anthem sung, is charmed and
    tied
  To where he stands,— so stood I, when
    that flow
Of music left the lips of her that died
  To save her father's vow,   195

The daughter of the warrior Gileadite,
  A maiden pure; as when she went along
From Mizpah's towered gate with welcome
    light,
  With timbrel and with song.

My words leaped forth: 'Heaven heads the
    count of crimes   200
  With that wild oath.' She rendered an-
    swer high;

'Not so, nor once alone; a thousand times
    I would be born and die.

'Single I grew, like some green plant, whose
    root   204
Creeps to the garden water-pipes beneath,
Feeding the flower; but ere my flower to
    fruit
    Changed, I was ripe for death.

My God, my land, my father — these did
    move
Me from my bliss of life, that Nature
    gave,
Lowered softly with a threefold cord of
    love   210
    Down to a silent grave.

'And I went mourning, "No fair Hebrew
    boy
Shall smile away my maiden blame among
The Hebrew mothers"— emptied of all joy,
    Leaving the dance and song.   215

'Leaving the olive-gardens far below,
Leaving the promise of my bridal bower,
The valleys of grape-loaded vines that glow
    Beneath the battled tower.   219

'The light white cloud swam over us. Anon
We heard the lion roaring from his den;
We saw the large white stars rise one by
    one,
    Or, from the darkened glen,

'Saw God divide the night with flying flame,
And thunder on the everlasting hills.   225
I heard him, for he spake, and grief became
    A solemn scorn of ills.

'When the next moon was rolled into the
    sky,
    Strength came to me that equaled my de-
    sire,
How beautiful a thing it was to die   230
    For God and for my sire!

'It comforts me in this one thought to
    dwell,
That I subdued me to my father's will;
Because the kiss he gave me, ere I fell,
    Sweetens the spirit still.   235

'Moreover it is written that my race
Hewed Ammon, hip and thigh, from
    Aroer
On Arnon unto Minneth.' Here her face
    Glowed, as I looked at her.

She locked her lips; she left me where I
    stood: 240
'Glory to God,' she sang, and past afar,
Thridding the somber boskage of the wood,
    Toward the morning-star.

Losing her carol I stood pensively,
    As one that from a casement leans his
    head,   245
When midnight bells cease ringing suddenly,
    And the old year is dead.

'Alas! alas!' a low voice, full of care,
    Murmured beside me: 'Turn and look on
    me;   249
I am that Rosamond, whom men call fair,
    If what I was I be.

'Would I had been some maiden coarse and
    poor!
O me, that I should ever see the light!
Those dragon eyes of angered Eleanor
    Do hunt me, day and night.'   255

She ceased in tears, fallen from hope and
    trust;
    To whom the Egyptian: 'O, you tamely
    died!
You should have clung to Fulvia's waist,
    and thrust
    The dagger through her side.'

With that sharp sound the white dawn's
    creeping beams,   260
    Stolen to my brain dissolved the mystery
Of folded sleep. The captain of my dreams
    Ruled in the eastern sky.

Morn broadened on the borders of the dark
    Ere I saw her, who clasped in her last
    trance   265
Her murdered father's head, or Joan of
    Arc,
    A light of ancient France;

Or her who knew that Love can vanquish
    Death,
    Who kneeling, with one arm about her
    king,
Drew forth the poison with her balmy
    breath,   270
    Sweet as new buds in spring.

No memory labors longer from the deep
    Gold-mines of thought to lift the hidden
    ore
That glimpses, moving up, than I from
    sleep
    To gather and tell o'er   275

Each little sound and sight. With what
    dull pain
Compassed, how eagerly I sought to strike
Into that wondrous track of dreams again!
    But no two dreams are like.

As when a soul laments, which hath been
    blest,   280
    Desiring what is mingled with past years,
In yearnings that can never be expressed
    By sighs or groans or tears;

Because all words, though culled with choic-
    est art,   284
    Failing to give the bitter of the sweet,
Wither beneath the palate, and the heart
    Faints, faded by its heat.

            (1833)

SAINT AGNES' EVE

Deep on the convent-roof the snows
    Are sparkling to the moon:
My breath to heaven like vapor goes:
    May my soul follow soon!
The shadows of the convent-towers   5
    Slant down the snowy sward,
Still creeping with the creeping hours
    That lead me to my Lord:
Make thou my spirit pure and clear
    As are the frosty skies,   10
Or this first snowdrop of the year
    That in my bosom lies.

As these white robes are soiled and dark,
    To yonder shining ground;
As this pale taper's earthly spark,   15
    To yonder argent round;
So shows my soul before the Lamb,
    My spirit before thee;
So in mine earthly house I am,
    To that I hope to be.   20
Break up the heavens, O Lord! and far,
    Through all yon starlight keen,
Draw me, thy bride, a glittering star,
    In raiment white and clean.

He lifts me to the golden doors;   25
    The flashes come and go;
All heaven bursts her starry floors,
And strows her lights below,
And deepens on and up! the gates
    Roll back, and far within   30
For me the Heavenly Bridegroom waits,
    To make me pure of sin.
The Sabbaths of Eternity,
    One Sabbath deep and wide —

A light upon the shining sea —   35
    The Bridegroom with his bride!

            (1837)

YOU ASK ME, WHY, THOUGH ILL AT EASE

You ask me why, though ill at ease,
    Within this region I subsist,
    Whose spirits falter in the mist,
And languish for the purple seas.

It is the land that freemen till,   5
    That sober-suited Freedom chose,
    The land, where girt with friends or foes
A man may speak the thing he will;

A land of settled government,
    A land of just and old renown,   10
    Where Freedom slowly broadens down
From precedent to precedent:

Where faction seldom gathers head,
    But, by degrees to fullness wrought,
    The strength of some diffusive thought 15
Hath time and space to work and spread.

Should banded unions persecute
    Opinion, and induce a time
    When single thought is civil crime,
And individual freedom mute,   20

Though power should make from land to
    land
    The name of Britain trebly great —
    Though every channel of the State
Should fill and choke with golden sand —

Yet waft me from the harbor-mouth,   25
    Wild wind! I seek a warmer sky,
    And I will see before I die
The palms and temples of the South.

            (1842)

OF OLD SAT FREEDOM ON THE HEIGHTS

Of old sat Freedom on the heights,
    The thunders breaking at her feet:
Above her shook the starry lights:
    She heard the torrents meet.

There in her place she did rejoice,   5
    Self-gathered in her prophet-mind,
But fragments of her mighty voice
    Came rolling on the wind.

Then stepped she down through town and
   field
  To mingle with the human race,   10
And part by part to men revealed
  The fulness of her face —

Grave mother of majestic works,
  From her isle-altar gazing down,
Who, Godlike, grasps the triple forks,   15
  And, king-like, wears the crown:

Her open eyes desire the truth.
  The wisdom of a thousand years
Is in them. May perpetual youth
  Keep dry their light from tears;   20

That her fair form may stand and shine,
  Make bright our days and light our
    dreams,
Turning to scorn with lips divine
  The falsehood of extremes!
                  (1842)

SIR GALAHAD

My good blade carves the casques of men,
  My tough lance thrusteth sure,
My strength is as the strength of ten,
  Because my heart is pure.
The shattering trumpet shrilleth high,   5
  The hard brands shiver on the steel,
The splintered spear-shafts crack and fly,
  The horse and rider reel:
They reel, they roll in clanging lists,
  And when the tide of combat stands,   10
Perfume and flowers fall in showers,
  That lightly rain from ladies' hands.

How sweet are looks that ladies bend
  On whom their favors fall!
For them I battle till the end,   15
  To save from shame and thrall:
But all my heart is drawn above,
  My knees are bowed in crypt and shrine:
I never felt the kiss of love,
  Nor maiden's hand in mine.   20
More bounteous aspects on me beam,
  Me mightier transports move and thrill;
So keep I fair through faith and prayer
  A virgin heart in work and will.

When down the stormy crescent goes,   25
  A light before me swims,
Between dark stems the forest glows,
  I hear a noise of hymns:
Then by some secret shrine I ride;
  I hear a voice but none are there;   30
The stalls are void, the doors are wide,
  The tapers burning fair.

Fair gleams the snowy altar-cloth,
  The silver vessels sparkle clean,
The shrill bell rings, the censer swings,   35
  And solemn chants resound between.

Sometimes on lonely mountain-meres
  I find a magic bark;
I leap on board: no helmsman steers:
  I float till all is dark: 40
A gentle sound, an awful light!
  Three angels bear the holy Grail:
With folded feet, in stoles of white,
  On sleeping wings they sail
Ah, blessed vision! blood of God!   45
  My spirit beats her mortal bars,
As down dark tides the glory slides,
  And star-like mingles with the stars.

When on my goodly charger borne
  Through dreaming towns I go,   50
The cock crows ere the Christmas morn,
  The streets are dumb with snow.
The tempest crackles on the leads,
  And, ringing, springs from brand and
    mail;
But o'er the dark a glory spreads,   55
  And gilds the driving hail.
I leave the plain, I climb the height;
  No branchy thicket shelter yields;
But blessèd forms in whistling storms
  Fly o'er waste fens and windy fields.   60

A maiden knight — to me is given
  Such hope, I know not fear;
I yearn to breathe the airs of heaven
  That often meet me here.
I muse on joy that will not cease,   65
  Pure spaces clothed in living beams,
Pure lilies of eternal peace,
  Whose odors haunt my dreams;
And, stricken by an angel's hand,
  This mortal armor that I wear,   70
This weight and size, this heart and eyes,
  Are touched, are turned to finest air.

The clouds are broken in the sky,
  And through the mountain-walls
A rolling organ-harmony   75
  Swells up, and shakes and falls.
Then move the trees, the copses nod,
  Wings flutter, voices hover clear:
'O just and faithful knight of God!
  Ride on! the prize is near.'   80
So pass I hostel, hall, and grange;
  By bridge and ford, by park and pale,
All-armed I ride, whate'er betide,
  Until I find the holy Grail.
                  (1842)

A FAREWELL

Flow down, cold rivulet, to the sea,
  Thy tribute wave deliver:
No more by thee my steps shall be,
  For ever and for ever.

Flow, softly flow, by lawn and lea,   5
  A rivulet, then a river:
Nowhere by thee my steps shall be,
  For ever and for ever.

But here will sigh thine alder-tree,
  And here thine aspen shiver;   10
And here by thee will hum the bee,
  For ever and for ever.

A thousand suns will stream on thee,
  A thousand moons will quiver;
But not by thee my steps shall be,   15
  For ever and for ever.

              (1842)

MORTE D'ARTHUR

So all day long the noise of battle rolled
Among the mountains by the winter sea;
Until King Arthur's table, man by man,
Had fallen in Lyonnesse about their lord,
King Arthur; then, because his wound was
  deep,   5
The bold Sir Bedivere uplifted him,
Sir Bedivere, the last of all his knights,
And bore him to a chapel nigh the field,
A broken chancel with a broken cross,
That stood on a dark strait of barren
  land.
On one side lay the ocean, and on one   11
Lay a great water, and the moon was full.
  Then spake King Arthur to Sir Bedi-
  vere:
'The sequel of to-day unsolders all
The goodliest fellowship of famous knights
Whereof this world holds record. Such a
  sleep   16
They sleep — the men I loved. I think that
  we
Shall never more, at any future time,
Delight our souls with talk of knightly
  deeds,
Walking about the gardens and the halls 20
Of Camelot, as in the days that were.
I perish by this people which I made,—
Though Merlin sware that I should come
  again
To rule once more — but let what will be
  be,

I am so deeply smitten through the helm 25
That without help I cannot last till morn.
Thou therefore take my brand Excalibur,
Which was my pride; for thou rememberest
  how
In those old days, one summer noon, an
  arm
Rose up from out the bosom of the lake,
Clothed in white samite, mystic, wonder-
  ful,   31
Holding the sword —— and how I rowed
  across
And took it, and have worn it, like a king;
And, wheresoever I am sung or told
In aftertime, this also shall be known; 35
But now delay not; take Excalibur,
And fling him far into the middle mere;
Watch what thou seest, and lightly bring me
  word.'
  To him replied the bold Sir Bedivere:
'It is not meet, Sir King, to leave thee
  thus,   40
Aidless, alone, and smitten through the helm.
A little thing may harm a wounded man.
Yet I thy hest will all perform at full,
Watch what I see, and lightly bring thee
  word.'
  So saying, from the ruined shrine he stept
And in the moon athwart the place of
  tombs,   46
Where lay the mighty bones of ancient men,
Old knights, and over them the sea-wind
  sang
Shrill, chill, with flakes of foam. He, step-
  ping down
By zigzag paths, and juts of pointed rock, 50
Came on the shining levels of the lake.
  There drew he forth the brand Excalibur,
And o'er him, drawing it, the winter moon,
Brightening the skirts of a long cloud, ran
  forth
And sparkled keen with frost against the
  hilt;   55
For all the haft twinkled with diamond
  sparks,
Myriads of topaz-lights, and jacinth work
Of subtlest jewelery. He gazed so long
That both his eyes were dazzled, as he stood,
This way and that dividing the swift mind,
In act to throw; but at the last it seemed 61
Better to leave Excalibur concealed
There in the many-knotted water-flags,
That whistled stiff and dry about the marge.
So strode he back slow to the wounded
  king.   65
  Then spake King Arthur to Sir Bedivere:
'Hast thou performed my mission which
  I gave?

What is it thou hast seen, or what hast
  heard?'
And answer made the bold Sir Bedivere:
'I heard the ripple washing in the reeds, 70
And the wild water lapping on the crag.'
  To whom replied King Arthur, faint and
    pale:
'Thou hast betrayed thy nature and thy
  name,
Not rendering true answer, as beseemed
Thy fealty, nor like a noble knight;   75
For surer sign had followed, either hand,
Or voice, or else a motion of the mere.
This is a shameful thing for men to lie.
Yet now, I charge thee, quickly go again
As thou art lief and dear, and do the
  thing   80
I bade thee, watch, and lightly bring me
  word.'
  Then went Sir Bedivere the second time
Across the ridge, and paced beside the mere,
Counting the dewy pebbles, fixed in thought;
But when he saw the wonder of the hilt, 85
How curiously and strangely chased, he
  smote
His palms together, and he cried aloud:
'And if indeed I cast the brand away,
Surely a precious thing, one worthy note,
Should thus be lost forever from the earth,
Which might have pleased the eyes of many
  men.   91
What good should follow this, if this were
  done?
What harm, undone? deep harm to disobey,
Seeing obedience is the bond of rule.
Were it well to obey then, if a king de-
  mand   95
An act unprofitable, against himself?
The king is sick, and knows not what he
  does.
What record, or what relic of my lord
Should be to aftertime, but empty breath
And rumors of a doubt? but were this kept,
Stored in some treasure-house of mighty
  kings,   101
Some one might show it at a joust of arms,
Saying, "King Arthur's sword, Excalibur,
Wrought by the lonely maiden of the lake;
Nine years she wrought it, sitting in the
  deeps   105
Upon the hidden bases of the hills."
So might some old man speak in the after-
  time
To all the people, winning reverence;
But now much honor and much fame were
  lost.'
  So spake he, clouded with his own con-
  ceit,   110

And hid Excalibur the second time,
And so strode back slow to the wounded
  king.
  Then spoke King Arthur, breathing
    heavily:
'What is it thou hast seen, or what hast
  heard?'
  And answer made the bold Sir Bedi-
    vere: 115
'I heard the water lapping on the crag,
And the long ripple washing in the reeds.'
  To whom replied King Arthur, much in
    wrath:
'Ah, miserable and unkind, untrue,
Unknightly, traitor-hearted! Woe is me! 120
Authority forgets a dying king,
Laid widowed of the power in his eye
That bowed the will. I see thee what thou
  art,
For thou, the latest-left of all my knights,
In whom should meet the offices of all, 125
Thou wouldst betray me for the precious
  hilt;
Either from lust of gold, or like a girl
Valuing the giddy pleasure of the eyes.
Yet, for a man may fail in duty twice,
And the third time may prosper, get thee
  hence;   130
But, if thou spare to fling Excalibur,
I will arise and slay thee with my hands.'
  Then quickly rose Sir Bedivere, and ran,
And, leaping down the ridges lightly,
  plunged
Among the bulrush-beds, and clutched the
  sword,   135
And strongly wheeled and threw it. The
  great brand
Made lightnings in the splendor of the moon,
And flashing round and round, and whirled
  in an arch,
Shot like a streamer of the northern morn,
Seen where the moving isles of winter
  shock   140
By night, with noises of the northern sea.
So flashed and fell the brand Excalibur;
But ere he dipped the surface, rose an arm
Clothed in white samite, mystic, wonderful,
And caught him by the hilt, and brandished
  him   145
Three times, and drew him under in the
  mere.
And lightly went the other to the king.
  Then spoke King Arthur, drawing thicker
    breath:
'Now see I by thine eyes that this is done.
Speak out: what is it thou hast heard, or
  seen?'   150

And answer made the bold Sir Bedivere:
'Sir King, I closed mine eyelids, lest the gems
Should blind my purpose, for I never saw,
Nor shall see, here or elsewhere, till I die,
Not though I live three lives of mortal men,   155
So great a miracle as yonder hilt.
Then with both hands I flung him, wheeling him;
But when I looked again, behold an arm,
Clothed in white samite, mystic, wonderful,
That caught him by the hilt, and brandished him   160
Three times, and drew him under in the mere.'
    And answer made King Arthur, breathing hard:
'My end draws nigh; 't is time that I were gone.
Make broad thy shoulders to receive my weight,
And bear me to the margin; yet I fear   165
My wound hath taken cold, and I shall die.'
    So saying, from the pavement he half rose,
Slowly, with pain, reclining on his arm,
And looking wistfully with wide blue eyes
As in a picture. Him Sir Bedivere   170
Remorsefully regarded through his tears,
And would have spoken, but he found not words,
Then took with care, and kneeling on one knee,
O'er both his shoulders drew the languid hands,
And rising bore him through the place of tombs.
    But, as he walked, King Arthur panted hard,   176
Like one that feels a nightmare on his bed
When all the house is mute. So sighed the king,
Muttering and murmuring at his ear,
'Quick, quick!
I fear it is too late, and I shall die.'   180
But the other swiftly strode from ridge to ridge,
Clothed with his breath, and looking, as he walked,
Larger than human on the frozen hills.
He heard the deep behind him, and a cry
Before. His own thought drove him like a goad.   185
Dry clashed his harness in the icy caves
And barren chasms, and all to left and right

The bare black cliff clanged round him, as he based
His feet on juts of slippery crag that rang
Sharp-smitten with the dint of armèd heels —   190
And on a sudden, lo! the level lake,
And the long glories of the winter moon.
    Then saw they how there hove a dusky barge,
Dark as a funeral scarf from stem to stern,
Beneath them; and descending they were ware   195
That all the decks were dense with stately forms
Black-stoled, black-hooded, like a dream —
by these
Three queens with crowns of gold — and from them rose
A cry that shivered to the tingling stars,
And, as it were one voice, an agony   200
Of lamentation, like a wind that shrills
All night in a waste land, where no one comes,
Or hath come, since the making of the world.
    Then murmured Arthur, 'Place me in the barge,'
And to the barge they came. There those three queens   205
Put forth their hands, and took the king, and wept.
But she that rose the tallest of them all
And fairest, laid his head upon her lap,
And loosed the shattered casque, and chafed his hands,
And called him by his name, complaining loud,   210
And dropping bitter tears against his brow
Striped with dark blood; for all his face was white
And colorless, and like the withered moon
Smote by the fresh beam of the springing east;
And all his greaves and cuisses dashed with drops   215
Of onset; and the light and lustrous curls —
That made his forehead like a rising sun
High from the dais-throne — were parched with dust;
Or, clotted into points and hanging loose,
Mixed with the knightly growth that fringed his lips.   220
So like a shattered column lay the king;
Not like that Arthur who, with lance in rest,
From spur to plume a star of tournament,
Shot through the lists at Camelot, and charged

Before the eyes of ladies and of kings. 225
Then loudly cried the bold Sir Bedivere:
'Ah! my Lord Arthur, whither shall I go?
Where shall I hide my forehead and my
eyes?
For now I see the true old times are dead,
When every morning brought a noble
chance,   230
And every chance brought out a noble
knight.
Such times have been not since the light
that led
The holy Elders with the gift of myrrh.
But now the whole ROUND TABLE is dis-
solved   234
Which was an image of the mighty world;
And I, the last, go forth companionless,
And the days darken round me, and the
years,
Among new men, strange faces, other
minds.'
  And slowly answered Arthur from the
barge:
'The old order changeth, yielding place to
new,   240
And God fulfils himself in many ways,
Lest one good custom should corrupt the
world.
Comfort thyself: what comfort is in me?
I have lived my life, and that which I have
done
May he within himself make pure! but
thou,   245
If thou shouldst never see my face again,
Pray for my soul. More things are wrought
by prayer
Than this world dreams of. Wherefore, let
thy voice
Rise like a fountain for me night and
day.   249
For what are men better than sheep or goats
That nourish a blind life within the brain,
If, knowing God, they lift not hands of
prayer
Both for themselves and those who call them
friend?
For so the whole round earth is every
way
Bound by gold chains about the feet of
God.   255
But now farewell. I am going a long way
With these thou seëst — if indeed I go —
(For all my mind is clouded with a doubt)
To the island-valley of Avilion;   259
Where falls not hail, or rain, or any snow,
Nor ever wind blows loudly; but it lies
Deep-meadowed, happy, fair with orchard
lawns

And bowery hollows crowned with summer
sea,
Where I will heal me of my grievous
wound.'
  So said he, and the barge with oar and
sail   265
Moved from the brink, like some full-
breasted swan
That, fluting a wild carol ere her death,
Ruffles her pure cold plume, and takes the
flood
With swarthy webs. Long stood Sir Bedi-
vere
Revolving many memories, till the hull 270
Looked one black dot against the verge of
dawn,
And on the mere the wailing died away.
(1842)

ULYSSES

It little profits that an idle king,
By this still hearth, among these barren
crags,
Matched with an agèd wife, I mete and dole
Unequal laws unto a savage race,
That hoard, and sleep, and feed, and know
not me.   5
I cannot rest from travel; I will drink
Life to the lees. All times I have enjoyed
Greatly, have suffered greatly, both with
those
That loved me, and alone; on shore, and
when   9
Through scudding drifts the rainy Hyades
Vext the dim sea. I am become a name;
For always roaming with a hungry heart
Much have I seen and known,— cities of
men
And manners, climates, councils, govern-
ments,
Myself not least, but honored of them
all;   15
And drunk delight of battle with my peers,
Far on the ringing plains of windy Troy.
I am a part of all that I have met;
Yet all experience is an arch wherethro'
Gleams that untraveled world whose margin
fades   20
For ever and for ever when I move.
How dull it is to pause, to make an end,
To rust unburnished, not to shine in use!
As though to breathe were life! Life piled
on life
Were all too little, and of one to me 25
Little remains; but every hour is saved
From that eternal silence, something more.

A bringer of new things; and vile it were
For some three suns to store and hoard my-
    self,
And this gray spirit yearning in desire   30
To follow knowledge like a sinking star,
Beyond the utmost bound of human thought.

This is my son, mine own Telemachus,
To whom I leave the scepter and the isle —
Well-loved of me, discerning to fulfil   35
This labor, by slow prudence to make mild
A rugged people, and through soft degrees
Subdue them to the useful and the good.
Most blameless is he, centered in the sphere
Of common duties, decent not to fail   40
In offices of tenderness, and pay
Meet adoration to my household gods,
When I am gone. He works his work, I
    mine.

There lies the port; the vessel puffs her
    sail:
There gloom the dark, broad seas. My
    mariners,   45
Souls that have toiled and wrought, and
    thought with me —
That ever with a frolic welcome took
The thunder and the sunshine, and opposed
Free hearts, free foreheads — you and I are
    old;
Old age hath yet his honor and his toil.   50
Death closes all; but something ere the end,
Some work of noble note, may yet be done,
Not unbecoming men that strove with Gods.
The lights begin to twinkle from the rocks;
The long day wanes; the slow moon climbs;
    the deep   55
Moans round with many voices. Come, my
    friends,
'T is not too late to seek a newer world.
Push off, and sitting well in order smite
The sounding furrows; for my purpose
    holds
To sail beyond the sunset, and the baths   60
Of all the western stars, until I die.
It may be that the gulfs will wash us down;
It may be we shall touch the Happy Isles,
And see the great Achilles, whom we knew.
Though much is taken, much abides; and
    though   65
We are not now that strength which in old
    days
Moved earth and heaven, that which we are,
    we are;
One equal temper of heroic hearts,
Made weak by time and fate, but strong in
    will   69
To strive, to seek, to find, and not to yield.
        (1842)

LOCKSLEY HALL

Comrades, leave me here a little, while as
    yet 't is early morn:
Leave me here, and when you want me,
    sound upon the bugle-horn.

'T is the place, and all around it, as of old,
    the curlews call,
Dreary gleams about the moorland flying
    over Locksley Hall;

Locksley Hall, that in the distance overlooks
    the sandy tracts,   5
And the hollow ocean-ridges roaring into
    cataracts.

Many a night from yonder ivied casement,
    ere I went to rest,
Did I look on great Orion sloping slowly
    to the West.

Many a night I saw the Pleiads, rising
    through the mellow shade,
Glitter like a swarm of fire-flies tangled in a
    silver braid.   10

Here about the beach I wandered, nourish-
    ing a youth sublime
With the fairy tales of science, and the
    long result of Time;

When the centuries behind me like a fruitful
    land reposed;
When I clung to all the present for the
    promise that it closed:

When I dipped into the future far as human
    eye could see;   15
Saw the Vision of the world, and all the
    wonder that would be.—

In the Spring a fuller crimson comes upon
    the robin's breast;
In the Spring the wanton lapwing gets him-
    self another crest;

In the Spring a livelier iris changes on the
    burnished dove;
In the Spring a young man's fancy lightly
    turns to thoughts of love.   20

Then her cheek was pale and thinner than
    should be for one so young,
And her eyes on all my motions with a mute
    observance hung.

And I said, 'My cousin Amy, speak, and
    speak the truth to me,

Trust me, cousin, all the current of my
   being sets to thee.'

On her pallid cheek and forehead came a
   color and a light,   25
As I have seen the rosy red flushing in the
   northern night.

And she turned — her bosom shaken with a
   sudden storm of sighs —
All the spirit deeply dawning in the dark
   of hazel eyes —

Saying, 'I have hid my feelings, fearing
   they should do me wrong';
Saying, 'Dost thou love me, cousin?' weeping, 'I have loved thee long.'   30

Love took up the glass of time, and turned
   it in his glowing hands;
Every moment, lightly shaken, ran itself in
   golden sands.

Love took up the harp of Life, and smote
   on all the chords with might;
Smote the chord of Self, that, trembling,
   passed in music out of sight.

Many a morning on the moorland did we
   hear the copses ring,   35
And her whisper thronged my pulses with
   the fulness of the Spring.

Many an evening by the waters did we
   watch the stately ships,
And our spirits rushed together at the
   touching of the lips.

O my cousin, shallow-hearted! O my Amy,
   mine no more!
O the dreary, dreary moorland! O the barren, barren shore!   40

Falser than all fancy fathoms, falser than
   all songs have sung,
Puppet to a father's threat, and servile to a
   shrewish tongue!

Is it well to wish thee happy? having known
   me — to decline
On a range of lower feelings and a narrower heart than mine!

Yet it shall be; thou shalt lower to his level
   day by day,   45
What is fine within thee growing coarse to
   sympathize with clay.

As the husband is, the wife is; thou art
   mated with a clown,
And the grossness of his nature will have
   weight to drag thee down.

He will hold thee, when his passion shall
   have spent its novel force,
Something better than his dog, a little dearer
   than his horse.   50

What is this? his eyes are heavy; think not
   they are glazed with wine.
Go to him, it is thy duty; kiss him, take his
   hand in thine.

It may be my lord is weary, that his brain
   is overwrought;
Soothe him with thy finer fancies, touch him
   with thy lighter thought.

He will answer to the purpose, easy things
   to understand —   55
Better thou wert dead before me, though I
   slew thee with my hand!

Better thou and I were lying, hidden from
   the hearts' disgrace,
Rolled in one another's arms, and silent in
   a last embrace.

Cursèd be the social wants that sin against
   the strength of youth!
Cursèd be the social lies that warp us from
   the living truth!   60

Cursèd be the sickly forms that err from
   honest Nature's rule!
Cursèd be the gold that gilds the straitened
   forehead of the fool!

Well — 't is well that I should bluster! —
   hadst thou less unworthy proved —
Would to God — for I had loved thee more
   than ever wife was loved.

Am I mad, that I should cherish that which
   bears but bitter fruit?   65
I will pluck it from my bosom, though my
   heart be at the root.

Never, though my mortal summers to such
   length of years should come
As the many-wintered crow that leads the
   clanging rookery home.

Where is comfort? in division of the records of the mind?
Can I part her from herself, and love her,
   as I knew her, kind?   70

I remember one that perished; sweetly did
    she speak and move;
Such a one do I remember, whom to look
    at was to love.

Can I think of her as dead, and love her for
    the love she bore?
No — she never loved me truly; love is love
    for evermore.

Comfort? comfort scorned of devils! this is
    truth the poet sings,   75
That a sorrow's crown of sorrow is remem-
    bering happier things.

Drug thy memories, lest thou learn it, lest
    thy heart be put to proof,
In the dead unhappy night, and when the
    rain is on the roof.

Like a dog, he hunts in dreams, and thou
    art staring at the wall,
Where the dying night-lamp flickers, and
    the shadows rise and fall.   80

Then a hand shall pass before thee, pointing
    to his drunken sleep,
To thy widowed marriage-pillows, to the
    tears that thou wilt weep.

Thou shalt hear the 'Never, never,' whis-
    pered by the phantom years,
And a song from out the distance in the
    ringing of thine ears;

And an eye shall vex thee, looking ancient
    kindness on thy pain.   85
Turn thee, turn thee on thy pillow; get thee
    to thy rest again.

Nay, but Nature brings thee solace; for a
    tender voice will cry,
'T is a purer life than thine, a lip to drain
    thy trouble dry.

Baby lips will laugh me down; my latest
    rival brings thee rest.
Baby fingers, waxen touches, press me from
    the mother's breast.   90

O, the child too clothes the father with a
    dearness not his due.
Half is thine and half is his; it will be
    worthy of the two.

O, I see thee old and formal, fitted to thy
    petty part,
With a little hoard of maxims preaching
    down a daughter's heart.

'They were dangerous guides, the feelings
    — she herself was not exempt —   95
Truly, she herself had suffered'— Perish in
    thy self-contempt!

Overlive it — lower yet — be happy! where-
    fore should I care?
I myself must mix with action, lest I
    wither by despair.

What is that which I should turn to, light-
    ing upon days like these?
Every door is barred with gold, and opens
    but to golden keys.   100

Every gate is thronged with suitors, all the
    markets overflow.
I have but an angry fancy; what is that
    which I should do?

I had been content to perish, falling on the
    foeman's ground,
When the ranks are rolled in vapor, and the
    winds are laid with sound.

But the jingling of the guinea helps the hurt
    that Honor feels,   105
And the nations do but murmur, snarling
    at each other's heels.

Can I but relive in sadness? I will turn
    that earlier page.
Hide me from my deep emotion, O thou
    wondrous Mother-Age!

Make me feel the wild pulsation that I felt
    before the strife,
When I heard my days before me, and the
    tumult of my life;   110

Yearning for the large excitement that the
    coming years would yield,
Eager-hearted as a boy when first he leaves
    his father's field,

And at night along the dusky highway near
    and nearer drawn,
Sees in heaven the light of London flaring
    like a dreary dawn;

And his spirit leaps within him to be gone
    before him then,   115
Underneath the light he looks at, in among
    the throngs of men;

Men, my brothers, men the workers, ever
    reaping something new;
That which they have done but earnest of
    the things that they shall do.

For I dipped into the future, far as human
    eye could see.
Saw the Vision of the world, and all the
    wonder that would be;   120

Saw the heavens fill with commerce, ar-
    gosies of magic sails,
Pilot of the purple twilight, dropping down
    with costly bales;

Heard the heavens fill with shouting, and
    there rained a ghastly dew
From the nations' airy navies grappling in
    the central blue;

Far along the world-wide whisper of the
    south-wind rushing warm,   125
With the standards of the peoples plunging
    through the thunder-storm;

Till the war-drum throbbed no longer, and
    the battle-flags were furled
In the Parliament of man, the Federation of
    the world.

There the common sense of most shall hold
    a fretful realm in awe,
And the kindly earth shall slumber, lapped
    in universal law.   130

So I triumphed ere my passion sweeping
    through me left me dry,
Left me with the palsied heart, and left me
    with the jaundiced eye;

Eye, to which all order festers, all things
    here are out of joint;
Science moves, but slowly slowly, creeping
    on from point to point;

Slowly comes a hungry people, as a lion,
    creeping nigher,   135
Glares at one that nods and winks behind a
    slowly-dying fire.

Yet I doubt not through the ages one in-
    creasing purpose runs,
And the thoughts of men are widened with
    the process of the suns.

What is that to him that reaps not harvest
    of his youthful joys,
Though the deep heart of existence beat for
    ever like a boy's?   140

Knowledge comes, but wisdom lingers, and
    I linger on the shore,
And the individual withers, and the world is
    more and more.

Knowledge comes, but wisdom lingers, and
    he bears a laden breast,
Full of sad experience, moving toward the
    stillness of his rest.

Hark, my merry comrades call me, sounding
    on the bugle-horn,   145
They to whom my foolish passion were a
    target for their scorn:

Shall it not be scorn to me to harp on such
    a moldered string?
I am shamed through all my nature to have
    loved so slight a thing.

Weakness to be wroth with weakness!
    woman's pleasure, woman's pain —
Nature made them blinder motions bounded
    in a shallower brain: 150

Woman is the lesser man, and all thy pas-
    sions, matched with mine,
Are as moonlight unto sunlight, and as
    water unto wine —

Here at least, where nature sickens, noth-
    ing. Ah, for some retreat
Deep in yonder shining Orient, where my
    life began to beat,

Where in wild Mahratta-battle fell my
    father evil-starred; —   155
I was left a trampled orphan, and a selfish
    uncle's ward.

Or to burst all links of habit — there to
    wander far away,
On from island unto island at the gate-
    ways of the day.

Larger constellations burning, mellow moons
    and happy skies,
Breadths of tropic shade and palms in clus-
    ter, knots of Paradise.   160

Never comes the trader, never floats an
    European flag,
Slides the bird o'er lustrous woodland,
    swings the trailer from the crag;

Droops the heavy-blossomed bower, hangs
    the heavy-fruited tree —
Summer isles of Eden lying in dark-purple
    spheres of sea.

There methinks would be enjoyment more
    than in this march of mind,   165
In the steamship, in the railway, in the
    thoughts that shake mankind.

There the passions cramped no longer shall
    have scope and breathing space;
I will take some savage woman, she shall
    rear my dusky race.

Iron-jointed, supple-sinewed, they shall dive,
    and they shall run,
Catch the wild goat by the hair, and hurl
    their lances in the sun;   170

Whistle back the parrot's call, and leap the
    rainbows of the brooks,
Not with blinded eyesight poring over mis-
    erable books —

Fool, again the dream, the fancy! but I
    know my words are wild,
But I count the gray barbarian lower than
    the Christian child.

I, to herd with narrow foreheads, vacant of
    our glorious gains,   175
Like a beast with lower pleasures, like a
    beast with lower pains!

Mated with a squalid savage — what to me
    were sun or clime!
I the heir of all the ages, in the foremost
    files of time —

I that rather held it better men should perish
    one by one,
Than that earth should stand at gaze like
    Joshua's moon in Ajalon!   180

Not in vain the distance beacons. Forward,
    forward let us range,
Let the great world spin for ever down the
    ringing grooves of change.

Through the shadow of the globe we sweep
    into the younger day;
Better fifty years of Europe than a cycle of
    Cathay.

Mother-Age,— for mine I knew not,— help
    me as when life begun;   185
Rift the hills, and roll the waters, flash the
    lightnings, weigh the sun.

O, I see the crescent promise of my spirit
    hath not set.
Ancient founts of inspiration well through
    all my fancy yet.

Howsoever these things be, a long farewell
    to Locksley Hall!

Now for me the woods may wither, now for
    me the roof-tree fall.   190

Comes a vapor from the margin, blackening
    over heath and holt,
Cramming all the blast before it, in its
    breast a thunderbolt.

Let it fall on Locksley Hall, with rain or
    hail, or fire or snow;
For the mighty wind arises, roaring seaward,
    and I go.

                    (1842)

BREAK, BREAK, BREAK

Break, break, break,
    On thy cold gray stones, O Sea!
And I would that my tongue could utter
    The thoughts that arise in me.

O well for the fisherman's boy,   5
    That he shouts with his sister at play!
O well for the sailor lad,
    That he sings in his boat on the bay!

And the stately ships go on
    To their haven under the hill;   10
But O for the touch of a vanished hand,
    And the sound of a voice that is still!

Break, break, break,
    At the foot of thy crags, O Sea!
But the tender grace of a day that is dead
    Will never come back to me.   16

                    (1842)

THE POET'S SONG

The rain had fallen, the Poet arose,
    He passed by the town and out of the
        street,
A light wind blew from the gates of the
        sun,
    And waves of shadow went over the
        wheat,
And he sat him down in a lonely place,   5
    And chanted a melody loud and sweet,
That made the wild-swan pause in her cloud,
    And the lark drop down at his feet.

The swallow stopped as he hunted the fly,
    The snake slipped under a spray,   10
The wild hawk stood with the down on his
        beak,
    And stared, with his foot on the prey.

And the nightingale thought, 'I have sung
　　many songs,
　But never a one so gay,
For he sings of what the world will be　15
When the years have died away.'

(1842)

SONGS

FROM THE PRINCESS

Tears, idle tears, I know not what they
　　mean,
Tears from the depth of some divine de-
　　spair
Rise in the heart, and gather to the eyes,
In looking on the happy Autumn-fields,
And thinking of the days that are no
　　more.　5

Fresh as the first beam glittering on a
　　sail,
That brings our friends up from the under-
　　world,
Sad as the last which reddens over one
That sinks with all we love below the verge;
So sad, so fresh, the days that are no
　　more.　10

Ah, sad and strange as in dark summer
　　dawns
The earliest pipe of half-awakened birds
To dying ears, when unto dying eyes
The casement slowly grows a glimmering
　　square;
So sad, so strange, the days that are no
　　more.　15

Dear as remembered kisses after death,
And sweet as those by hopeless fancy
　　feigned
On lips that are for others; deep as love,
Deep as first love, and wild with all regret;
O Death in Life, the days that are no
　　more!　20

(1847)

The splendor falls on castle walls
　And snowy summits old in story;
The long light shakes across the lakes,
　And the wild cataract leaps in glory.
Blow, bugle, blow, set the wild echoes fly-
　　ing,　5
Blow, bugle; answer, echoes, dying, dying,
　dying.

O, hark, O, hear! how thin and clear,
　And thinner, clearer, farther going!
O, sweet and far from cliff and scar
　The horns of Elfland faintly blowing!　10
Blow, let us hear the purple glens replying;
Blow, bugle; answer, echoes, dying, dying,
　dying.

O love, they die in yon rich sky,
　They faint on hill or field or river;
Our echoes roll from soul to soul,　15
　And grow for ever and for ever.
Blow, bugle, blow, set the wild echoes fly-
　ing,
And answer, echoes, answer, dying, dying,
　dying.

(1850)

————

Thy voice is heard through rolling drums
　That beat to battle where he stands;
Thy face across his fancy comes,
　And gives the battle to his hands:
A moment, while the trumpets blow,　5
　He sees his brood about thy knee;
The next, like fire he meets the foe,
　And strikes him dead for thine and thee.

(1850)

————

Home they brought her warrior dead;
　She nor swooned nor uttered cry:
All her maidens, watching, said,
　'She must weep or she will die.'

Then they praised him, soft and low,　5
　Called him worthy to be loved,
Truest friend and noblest foe;
　Yet she neither spoke nor moved.

Stole a maiden from her place,
　Lightly to the warrior stepped,　10
Took the face-cloth from the face;
　Yet she neither moved nor wept.

Rose a nurse of ninety years,
　Set his child upon her knee —
Like summer tempest came her tears —　15
　'Sweet my child, I live for thee.'

(1850)

————

Ask me no more: the moon may draw the
　　sea;
　The cloud may stoop from heaven and
　　take the shape,
　With fold to fold, of mountain or of
　　cape;

But O too fond, when have I answered
  thee?
      Ask me no more.   5

Ask me no more: what answer should I
  give?
I love not hollow cheek or faded eye:
Yet, O my friend, I will not have thee
  die!
Ask me no more, lest I should bid thee live;
      Ask me no more.   10

Ask me no more: thy fate and mine are
  sealed;
I strove against the stream and all in
  vain;
Let the great river take me to the main.
No more, dear love, for at a touch I yield;
      Ask me no more.   15
          (1850)

IN MEMORIAM A. H. H.

OBIIT MDCCCXXXIII

Strong Son of God, immortal Love,
  Whom we, that have not seen thy face,
  By faith, and faith alone, embrace,
Believing where we cannot prove;

Thine are these orbs of light and shade; 5
  Thou madest Life in man and brute;
  Thou madest Death; and lo, thy foot
Is on the skull which thou hast made.

Thou wilt not leave us in the dust;
  Thou madest man, he knows not why, 10
  He thinks he was not made to die;
And thou hast made him: thou art just.

Thou seemest human and divine,
  The highest, holiest manhood, thou:
  Our wills are ours, we know not how; 15
Our wills are ours, to make them thine.

Our little systems have their day,
  They have their day and cease to be;
  They are but broken lights of thee,
And thou, O Lord, art more than they. 20

We have but faith: we cannot know;
  For knowledge is of things we see;
  And yet we trust it comes from thee,
A beam in darkness: let it grow.

Let knowledge grow from more to more, 25
  But more of reverence in us dwell;

That mind and soul, according well,
May make one music as before,

But vaster. We are fools and slight;
  We mock thee when we do not fear: 30
  But help thy foolish ones to bear;
Help thy vain worlds to bear thy light.

Forgive what seemed my sin in me;
  What seemed my worth since I began;
  For merit lives from man to man, 35
And not from man, O Lord, to thee.

Forgive my grief for one removed,
  Thy creature, whom I found so fair.
  I trust he lives in thee, and there
I find him worthier to be loved. 40

Forgive these wild and wandering cries,
  Confusions of a wasted youth;
  Forgive them where they fail in truth,
And in thy wisdom make me wise.

III

O Sorrow, cruel fellowship,
  O Priestess in the vaults of Death,
  O sweet and bitter in a breath,
What whispers from thy lying lip?

'The stars,' she whispers, 'blindly run; 5
  A web is woven across the sky,
  From out waste places comes a cry,
And murmurs from the dying sun;

'And all the phantom, Nature, stands —
  With all the music in her tone, 10
  A hollow echo of my own, —
A hollow form with empty hands.'

And shall I take a thing so blind,
  Embrace her as my natural good;
  Or crush her, like a vice of blood, 15
Upon the threshold of the mind?

XIX

The Danube to the Severn gave
  The darkened heart that beat no more;
  They laid him by the pleasant shore,
And in the hearing of the wave.

There twice a day the Severn fills; 5
  The salt sea-water passes by,
  And hushes half the babbling Wye,
And makes a silence in the hills.

The Wye is hushed nor moved along,
  And hushed my deepest grief of all, 10

When filled with tears that cannot fall,
I brim with sorrow drowning song.

The tide flows down, the wave again
  Is vocal in its wooded walls;
  My deeper anguish also falls,   15
And I can speak a little then.

XXVII

I envy not in any moods
  The captive void of noble rage,
  The linnet born within the cage,
That never knew the summer woods;

I envy not the beast that takes   5
  His license in the field of time,
  Unfettered by the sense of crime,
To whom a conscience never wakes;

Nor, what may count itself as blest,
  The heart that never plighted troth   10
  But stagnates in the weeds of sloth;
Nor any want-begotten rest.

I hold it true, whate'er befall;
  I feel it, when I sorrow most;
  'T is better to have loved and lost   15
Than never to have loved at all.

LV

The wish, that of the living whole
  No life may fail beyond the grave,
  Derives it not from what we have
The likest God within the soul?

Are God and Nature then at strife,   5
  That Nature lends such evil dreams?
  So careful of the type she seems,
So careless of the single life;

That I, considering everywhere
  Her secret meaning in her deeds,   10
  And finding that of fifty seeds
She often brings but one to bear,

I falter where I firmly trod,
  And falling with my weight of cares
  Upon the great world's altar-stairs,   15
That slope through darkness up to God,

I stretch lame hands of faith, and grope,
  And gather dust and chaff, and call
  To what I feel is Lord of all,
And faintly trust the larger hope.   20

LXIV

Dost thou look back on what hath been,
  As some divinely gifted man,

Whose life in low estate began
And on a simple village green;

Who breaks his birth's invidious bar,   5
  And grasps the skirts of happy chance,
  And breasts the blows of circumstance,
And grapples with his evil star;

Who makes by force his merit known
  And lives to clutch the golden keys,   10
  To mold a mighty state's decrees,
And shape the whisper of the throne;

And moving up from high to higher,
  Becomes in Fortune's crowning slope
  The pillar of a people's hope,   15
The center of a world's desire;

Yet feels, as in a pensive dream,
  When all his active powers are still,
  A distant dearness in the hill,
A secret sweetness in the stream,   20

The limit of his narrower fate,
  While yet beside its vocal springs
  He played at counselors and kings
With one that was his earliest mate;

Who ploughs with pain his native lea   25
  And reaps the labor of his hands,
  Or in the furrow musing stands:
'Does my old friend remember me?'

LXVII

When on my bed the moonlight falls,
  I know that in thy place of rest
  By that broad water of the west
There comes a glory on the walls;

Thy marble bright in dark appears,   5
  As slowly steals a silver flame,
  Along the letters of thy name,
And o'er the number of thy years.

The mystic glory swims away;
  From off my bed the moonlight dies;   10
  And closing eaves of wearied eyes
I sleep till dusk is dipped in gray:

And then I know the mist is drawn
  A lucid veil from coast to coast,
  And in the dark church like a ghost   15
Thy tablet glimmers to the dawn.

LXXXVIII

Wild bird, whose warble, liquid sweet,
  Rings Eden through the budded quicks,
  O, tell me where the senses mix,
O. tell me where the passions meet.

Whence radiate: fierce extremes employ 5
  Thy spirits in the darkening leaf,
  And in the midmost heart of grief
Thy passion clasps a secret joy;

And I — my harp would prelude woe —
  I cannot all command the strings, 10
  The glory of the sum of things
Will flash along the chords and go.

CXXIII

There rolls the deep where grew the tree.
  O earth, what changes hast thou seen!
  There where the long street roars, hath
    been
The stillness of the central sea.

The hills are shadows, and they flow 5
  From form to form, and nothing stands;
  They melt like mist, the solid lands,
Like clouds they shape themselves and go.

But in my spirit will I dwell,
  And dream my dream, and hold it true; 10
  For though my lips may breathe adieu,
I cannot think the thing farewell.

CXXX

Thy voice is on the rolling air;
  I hear thee where the waters run;
  Thou standest in the rising sun,
And in the setting thou art fair.

What art thou then? I cannot guess; 5
  But though I seem in star and flower,
  To feel thee some diffusive power,
I do not therefore love thee less.

My love involves the love before;
  My love is vaster passion now; 10
  Though mixed with God and Nature thou,
I seem to love thee more and more.

Far off thou art, but ever nigh;
  I have thee still, and I rejoice;
  I prosper, circled with thy voice; 15
I shall not lose thee though I die.

CXXXI

O living will that shalt endure
  When all that seems shall suffer shock,
  Rise in the spiritual rock,
Flow through our deeds and make them
    pure,

That we may lift from out of dust 5
  A voice as unto him that hears.

A cry above the conquered years
To one that with us works, and trust,

With faith that comes of self-control,
  The truths that never can be proved 10
  Until we close with all we loved,
And all we flow from, soul in soul.
                (1850)

* * *

MAUD; A MONODRAMA

PART I

I

I hate the dreadful hollow behind the little
    wood,
Its lips in the field above are dabbled with
    blood-red heath,
The red-ribbed ledges drip with a silent hor-
    ror of blood,
And Echo there, whatever is asked her, an-
    swers 'Death.'

For there in the ghastly pit long since a
    body was found, 5
His who had given me life — O father! O
    God! was it well? —
Mangled and flattened, and crushed, and
    dinted into the ground:
There yet lies the rock that fell with him
    when he fell.

Did he fling himself down? who knows? for
    a vast speculation had failed,
And ever he muttered and maddened, and
    ever wanned with despair, 10
And out he walked, when the wind like a
    broken worldling wailed,
And the flying gold of the ruined wood-
    lands drove through the air.

I remember the time, for the roots of my
    hair were stirred
By a shuffled step, by a dead weight trailed,
    by a whispered fright,
And my pulses closed their gates with a
    shock on my heart as I heard 15
The shrill-edged shriek of a mother divide
    the shuddering night.

Villainy somewhere! whose? One says, we
    are villains all.
Not he: his honest fame should at least by
    me be maintained.
But that old man, now lord of the broad es-
    tate and the Hall,

Dropped off gorged from a scheme that had left us flaccid and drained.

Why do they prate of the blessings of Peace? we have made them a curse, 20
Pickpockets, each hand lusting for all that is not its own;
And lust of gain, in the spirit of Cain, is it better or worse
Than the heart of the citizen hissing in war on his own hearthstone?

But these are the days of advance, the works of the men of mind,
When who but a fool would have faith in a tradesman's ware or his word? 25
Is it peace or war? Civil war, as I think, and that of a kind
The viler, as underhand, not openly bearing the sword.

Sooner or later I too may passively take the print
Of the golden age — why not, I have neither hope nor trust;
May make my heart as a millstone, set my face as a flint, 30
Cheat and be cheated, and die; who knows? we are ashes and dust.

Peace sitting under her olive, and slurring the days gone by,
When the poor are hoveled, and hustled together, each sex, like swine,
When only the ledger lives, and when only not all men lie;
Peace in her vineyard — yes! — but a company forges the wine. 35

And the vitriol madness flushes up in the ruffian's head,
Till the filthy by-lane rings to the yell of the trampled wife,
And chalk and alum and plaster are sold to the poor for bread,
And the spirit of murder works in the very means of life,

And Sleep must lie down armed, for the villainous center-bits 40
Grind on the wakeful ear in the hush of the moonless nights,
While another is cheating the sick of a few last gasps, as he sits
To pestle a poisoned poison behind his crimson lights.

When a Mammonite mother kills her babe for a burial fee,
And Timour-Mammon grins on a pile of children's bones, 45
Is it peace or war? better, war! loud war by land and by sea,
War with a thousand battles, and shaking a hundred thrones.

For I trust if an enemy's fleet came yonder round by the hill,
And the rushing battle-bolt sang from the three-decker out of the foam,
That the smooth-faced snubnosed rogue would leap from his counter and till, 50
And strike, if he could, were it but with his cheating yardwand, home.—

What! am I raging alone as my father raged in his mood?
Must I too creep to the hollow and dash myself down and die
Rather than hold by the law that I made, nevermore to brood
On a horror of shattered limbs and a wretched swindler's lie? 55

Would there be sorrow for me? there was love in the passionate shriek,
Love for the silent thing that had made false haste to the grave —
Wrapt in a cloak, as I saw him, and thought he would rise and speak
And rave at the lie and the liar, ah, God, as he used to rave.

I am sick of the Hall, and the hill, I am sick of the moor and the main. 60
Why should I stay? can a sweeter chance ever come to me here?
O, having the nerves of motion as well as the nerves of pain,
Were it not wise if I fled from the place and the pit and the fear?

Workmen up at the Hall! — they are coming back from abroad;
The dark old place will be gilt by the touch of a millionaire; 65
I have heard, I know not whence, of the singular beauty of Maud;
I played with the girl when a child; she promised then to be fair.

Maud with her venturous climbings, and tumbles and childish escapes,
Maud the delight of the village, the ringing joy of the Hall,

Maud with her sweet purse-mouth when my
   father dangled the grapes,   70
Maud the beloved of my mother, the moon-
   faced darling of all,—

What is she now? My dreams are bad.
   She may bring me a curse,
No, there is fatter game on the moor; she
   will let me alone.
Thanks, for the fiend best knows whether
   woman or man be the worse.
I will bury myself in myself, and the Devil
   may pipe to his own.   75

III

Cold and clear-cut face, why come you so
   cruelly meek,
Breaking a slumber in which all spleenful
   folly was drowned,
Pale with the golden beam of an eyelash
   dead on the cheek,
Passionless, pale, cold face, star-sweet on a
   gloom profound;
Woman-like, taking revenge too deep for a
   transient wrong   80
Done but in thought to your beauty, and
   ever as pale as before
Growing and fading and growing upon me
   without a sound,
Luminous, gem-like, ghost-like, death-like,
   half the night long
Growing and fading and growing, till I
   could bear it no more,
But arose, and all by myself in my own
   dark garden ground,   85
Listening now to the tide in its broad-flung
   shipwrecking roar,
Now to the scream of a maddened beach
   dragged down by the wave,
Walked in a wintry wind by a ghastly glimmer, and found
The shining daffodil dead, and Orion low in
   his grave.

V

A voice by the cedar tree   90
In the meadow under the Hall!
She is singing an air that is known to me,
A passionate ballad gallant and gay,
A martial song like a trumpet's call!
Singing alone in the morning of life,   95
In the happy morning of life and of May,
Singing of men that in battle array,
Ready in heart and ready in hand,
March with banner and bugle and fife,
To the death, for their native land.   100

Maud with her exquisite face,
And wild voice pealing up to the sunny sky,
And feet like sunny gems on an English
   green,
Maud in the light of her youth and her
   grace,
Singing of Death, and of Honor that can-
   not die,   105
Till I well could weep for a time so sordid
   and mean,
And myself so languid and base.

Silence, beautiful voice!
Be still, for you only trouble the mind
With a joy in which I cannot rejoice,   110
A glory I shall not find.
Still! I will hear you no more.
For your sweetness hardly leaves me a
   choice
But to move to the meadow and fall before
Her feet on the meadow grass, and adore,
Not her, who is neither courtly nor kind,
Not her, not her, but a voice.   117

XI

O, let the solid ground
   Not fail beneath my feet
Before my life has found   120
   What some have found so sweet;
Then let come what come may,
What matter if I go mad,
I shall have had my day.

Let the sweet heavens endure,   125
   Not close and darken above me
Before I am quite quite sure
   That there is one to love me;
Then let come what come may
To a life that has been so sad,   130
I shall have had my day.

XII

Birds in the high Hall-garden,
   When twilight was falling,
Maud, Maud, Maud, Maud,
   They were crying and calling.   135

Where was Maud? in our wood;
   And I — who else? — was with her,
Gathering woodland lilies,
   Myriads blow together.

Birds in our wood sang   140
   Ringing through the valleys,
Maud is here, here, here
   In among the lilies.

I kissed her slender hand,
　　She took the kiss sedately;　　　145
Maud is not seventeen,
　　But she is tall and stately.

I to cry out on pride
　　Who have won her favor!
O, Maud were sure of heaven　　　150
　　If lowliness could save her!

I know the way she went
　　Home with her maiden posy,
For her feet have touched the meadows
　　And left the daisies rosy.　　　155

Birds in the high Hall-garden
　　Were crying and calling to her,
Where is Maud, Maud, Maud?
　　One is come to woo her.

Look, a horse at the door,　　　160
　　And little King Charley snarling!
Go back, my lord, across the moor,
　　You are not her darling.

XVII

Go not, happy day,
　　From the shining fields,　　　165
Go, not, happy day,
　　Till the maiden yields.
Rosy is the West,
　　Rosy is the South,
Roses are her cheeks,　　　170
　　And a rose her mouth.
When the happy Yes
　　Falters from her lips,
Pass and blush the news
　　Over glowing ships;　　　175
Over blowing seas,
　　Over seas at rest,
Pass the happy news,
　　Blush it through the West;
Till the red man dance　　　180
　　By his red cedar-tree,
And the red man's babe
　　Leap, beyond the sea.
Blush from West to East,
　　Blush from East to West,　　　185
Till the West is East,
　　Blush it through the West.
Rosy is the West,
　　Rosy is the South,
Roses are her cheeks,　　　190
　　And a rose her mouth.

XVIII

I have led her home, my love, my only
　　friend.
There is none like her, none.
And never yet so warmly ran my blood
And sweetly, on and on　　　195
Calming itself to the long-wished-for end,
Full to the banks, close on the promised
　　good.

None like her, none.
Just now the dry-tongued laurels' pattering
　　talk
Seemed her light foot along the garden
　　walk,　　　200
And shook my heart to think she comes
　　once more;
But even then I heard her close the door;
The gates of heaven are closed, and she is
　　gone.

There is none like her, none,
Nor will be when our summers have de-
　　ceased.　　　205
O, art thou sighing for Lebanon
In the long breeze that streams to thy de-
　　licious East,
Sighing for Lebanon,
Dark cedar, though thy limbs have here in-
　　creased,
Upon a pastoral slope as fair,　　　210
And looking to the South and fed
With honeyed rain and delicate air,
And haunted by the starry head
Of her whose gentle will has changed my
　　fate,
And made my life a perfumed altar-flame,
And over whom thy darkness, must have
　　spread　　　216
With such delight as theirs of old, thy great
Forefathers of the thornless garden, there
Shadowing the snow-limbed Eve from
　　whom she came?

Here will I lie, while these long branches
　　sway,　　　220
And you fair stars that crown a happy day
Go in and out as if at merry play,
Who am no more so all forlorn
As when it seemed far better to be born
To labor and the mattock-hardened hand　225
Than nursed at ease and brought to under-
　　stand
A sad astrology, the boundless plan
That makes you tyrants in your iron skies,
Innumerable, pitiless, passionless eyes,
Cold fires, yet with power to burn and
　　brand,　　　230

His nothingness into man.
But now shine on, and what care I
Who in this stormy gulf have found a
    pearl
The countercharm of space and hollow sky,
And do accept my madness, and would die
To save from some slight shame one simple
    girl? —   236

Would die, for sullen-seeming Death may
    give
More life to Love than is or ever was
In our low world, where yet 't is sweet to
    live.
Let no one ask me how it came to pass;
It seems that I am happy, that to me   241
A livelier emerald twinkles in the grass,
A purer sapphire melts into the sea.

Not die, but live a life of truest breath,
And teach true life to fight with mortal
    wrongs,   245
O, why should Love, like men in drinking
    songs,
Spice his fair banquet with the dust of
    death?
Make answer, Maud my bliss,
Maud made my Maud by that long loving
    kiss,   249
Life of my life, wilt thou not answer this?
'The dusky strand of Death inwoven here
With dear Love's tie, makes Love himself
    more dear.'

Is that enchanted moan only the swell
Of the long waves that roll in yonder bay?
And hark the clock within, the silver knell
Of twelve sweet hours that past in bridal
    white,   256
And died to live, long as my pulses play;
But now by this my love has closed her
    sight,
And given false death her hand, and stolen
    away
To dreamful wastes where footless fancies
    dwell   260
Among the fragments of the golden day.
May nothing there her maiden grace af-
    fright!
Dear heart, I feel with thee the drowsy
    spell.
My bride to be, my evermore delight,
My own heart's heart, my ownest own, fare-
    well;   265
It is but for a little space I go,
And ye meanwhile far over moor and fell
Beat to the noiseless music of the night!

Has our whole earth gone nearer to the
    glow
Of your soft splendors that you look so
    bright?   270
I have climbed nearer out of lonely Hell.
Beat, happy stars, timing with things be-
    low,
Beat with my heart more blest than heart
    can tell,
Blest, but for some dark undercurrent woe,
That seems to draw — but it shall not be so:
Let all be well, be well.   276

XXI

Rivulet crossing my ground,
And bringing me down from the Hall
This garden-rose that I found,
Forgetful of Maud and me,   280
And lost in trouble and moving round
Here at the head of a tinkling fall,
And trying to pass to the sea;
O rivulet, born at the Hall,
My Maud has sent it by thee —   285
If I read her sweet will right —
On a blushing mission to me,
Saying in odor and color, 'Ah, be
Among the roses to-night.'

XXII

Come into the garden, Maud,   290
    For the black bat, night, has flown,
Come into the garden, Maud,
    I am here at the gate alone;
And the woodbine spices are wafted
    abroad,
    And the musk of the rose is blown 295

For a breeze of morning moves,
    And the planet of love is on high,
Beginning to faint in the light that she
    loves
    On a bed of daffodil sky,
To faint in the light of the sun she loves
    To faint in his light, and to die.   301

All night have the roses heard
    The flute, violin, bassoon;
All night has the casement jessamine stirred
    To the dancers dancing in tune;   305
Till a silence fell with the waking bird,
    And a hush with the setting moon.

I said to the lily, 'There is but one,
    With whom she has heart to be gay.
When will the dancers leave her alone?   310
    She is weary of dance and play.'
Now half to the setting moon are gone,
    And half to the rising day;

Low on the sand and loud on the stone
  The last wheel echoes away.   315

I said to the rose, 'The brief night goes
  In babble and revel and wine.
O young lord-lover, what sighs are those,
  For one that will never be thine?
But mine, but mine,' so I sware to the rose,
  'Forever and ever, mine.'   321

And the soul of the rose went into my
    blood,
  As the music clashed in the Hall;
And long by the garden lake I stood,
  For I heard your rivulet fall   325
From the lake to the meadow and on to the
    wood,
  Our wood, that is dearer than all;

From the meadow your walks have left so
    sweet
  That whenever a March-wind sighs
He sets the jewel-print of your feet   330
  In violets blue as your eyes,
To the woody hollows in which we meet
  And the valleys of Paradise.

The slender acacia would not shake
  One long milk-bloom on the tree;   335
The white lake-blossom fell into the lake
  As the pimpernel dozed on the lea;
But the rose was awake all night for your
    sake,
  Knowing your promise to me;
The lilies and roses were all awake,   340
  They sighed for the dawn and thee.

Queen rose of the rosebud garden of girls,
  Come hither, the dances are done,
In gloss of satin and glimmer of pearls,
  Queen lily and rose in one;   345
Shine out, little head, sunning over with
    curls,
  To the flowers, and be their sun.

There has fallen a splendid tear
  From the passion-flower at the gate,
She is coming, my dove, my dear;   350
  She is coming, my life, my fate.
The red rose cries, 'She is near, she is
    near;'
And the white rose weeps, 'She is late;'
The larkspur listens, 'I hear, I hear;'
  And the lily whispers, 'I wait.'

She is coming, my own, my sweet;   356
  Were it ever so airy a tread,

My heart would hear her and beat,
  Were it earth in an earthy bed;
My dust would hear her and beat,   360
  Had I lain for a century dead;
Would start and tremble under her feet,
  And blossom in purple and red.

PART II

II

See what a lovely shell,
Small and pure as a pearl,   365
Lying close to my foot,
Frail, but a work divine,
Made so fairly well
With delicate spire and whorl,
How exquisitely minute,   370
A miracle of design!

What is it? a learned man
Could give it a clumsy name,
Let him name it who can,
The beauty would be the same.   375

The tiny cell is forlorn,
Void of the little living will
That made it stir on the shore.
Did he stand at the diamond door
Of his house in a rainbow frill?   380
Did he push, when he was uncurled,
A golden foot or a fairy horn
Through his dim water-world?

Slight, to be crushed with a tap
Of my finger-nail on the sand,   385
Small, but a work divine,
Frail, but of force to withstand,
Year upon year, the shock
Of cataract seas that snap
The three-decker's oaken spine   390
Athwart the ledges of rock,
Here on the Breton strand!

Breton, not Briton; here
Like a shipwrecked man on a coast
Of ancient fable and fear—   395
Plagued with a flitting to and fro,
A disease, a hard mechanic ghost
That never came from on high
Nor ever arose from below,
But only moves with the moving eye,   400
Flying along the land and the main—

Why should it look like Maud?
Am I to be overawed
By what I cannot but know
Is a juggle born of the brain?   405

Back from the Breton, coast,
Sick of a nameless fear,
Back to the dark sea-line
Looking, thinking of all I have lost;
An old song vexes my ear;   410
But that of Lamech is mine.

For years, a measureless ill,
For years, for ever, to part —
But she, she would love me still;
And as long, O God, as she   415
Have a grain of love for me,
So long, no doubt, no doubt,
Shall I nurse in my dark heart,
However weary, a spark of will
Not to be trampled out.   420

Strange, that the mind, when fraught
With a passion so intense
One would think that it well
Might drown all life in the eye,—
That it should, by being so overwrought,
Suddenly strike on a sharper sense   426
For a shell, or a flower, little things
Which else would have been past by!
And now I remember, I,
When he lay dying there,   430
I noticed one of his many rings
(For he had many, poor worm) and thought
It is his mother's· hair.

Who knows if he be dead?
Whether I need have fled   435
Am I guilty of blood?
However this may be,
Comfort her, comfort her, all things good,
While I am over the sea!
Let me and my passionate love go by,   440
But speak to her all things holy and high,
Whatever happen to me!
Me and my harmful love go by;
But come to her waking, find her asleep,
Powers of the height, Powers of the deep,
And comfort her though I die.   446

III

Courage, poor heart of stone,
I will not ask thee why
Thou canst not understand
That thou art left for ever alone: 450
Courage, poor stupid heart of stone.—
Or, if I ask thee why,
Care not thou to reply;
She is but dead, and the time is at hand
When thou shalt more than die.   455

IV

O that 't were possible
After long grief and pain

To find the arms of my true love
Round me once again!
When I was wont to meet her   460
In the silent woody places
By the home that gave me birth,
We stood tranced in long embraces
Mixed with kisses sweeter, sweeter
Than anything on earth.   465

A shadow flits before me,
Not thou, but like to thee,
Ah Christ, that it were possible
For one short hour to see
The souls we loved, that they might tell us
What and where they be!   471

It leads me forth at evening,
It lightly winds and steals
In a cold white robe before me,
When all my spirit reels   475
At the shouts, the leagues of lights,
And the roaring of the wheels.

Half the night I waste in sighs,
Half in dreams I sorrow after
The delight of early skies;   480
In a wakeful doze I sorrow
For the hand, the lips, the eyes,
For the meeting of the morrow,
The delight of happy laughter,
The delight of low replies.   485

'T is a morning pure and sweet.
And a dewy splendor falls
On the little flower that clings
To the turrets and the walls;
'T is a morning pure and sweet,   490
And the light and shadow fleet;
She is walking in the meadow,
And the woodland echo rings;
In a moment we shall meet;
She is singing in the meadow,   495
And the rivulet at her feet
Ripples on in light and shadow
To the ballad that she sings.

Do I hear her sing as of old,
My bird with the shining head,   500
My own dove with the tender eye?
But there rings on a sudden, a passionate
      cry,
There is some one dying or dead,
And a sullen thunder is rolled;
For a tumult shakes the city,   505
And I wake, my dream is fled;
In the shuddering dawn, behold,
Without knowledge, without pity,
By the curtains of my bed

That abiding phantom cold!   510
Get thee hence, nor come again,
Mix not memory with doubt,
Pass, thou death-like type of pain,
Pass and cease to move about!
'T is the blot upon the brain   515
That *will* show itself without.

Then I rise, the eave-drops fall,
And the yellow vapors choke
The great city sounding wide;
The day comes, a dull red ball   520
Wrapt in drifts of lurid smoke
On the misty river-tide.

Through the hubbub of the market
I steal, a wasted frame;
It crosses here, it crosses there,   525
Through all that crowd confused and loud,
The shadow still the same;
And on my heavy eyelids
My anguish hangs like shame.

Alas, for her that met me,   530
That heard me softly call,
Came glimmering through the laurels
At the quiet evenfall,
In the garden by the turrets
Of the old manorial hall!   535

Would the happy spirit descend
From the realms of light and song,
In the chamber or the street,
As she looks among the blest,
Should I fear to greet my friend   540
Or to say 'Forgive the wrong,'
Or to ask her, 'Take me, sweet,
To the regions of thy rest'?

But the broad light glares and beats,
And the shadow flits and fleets   545
And will not let me be;
And I loathe the squares and streets,
And the faces that one meets,
Hearts with no love for me.
Always I long to creep   550
Into some still cavern deep,
There to weep, and weep, and weep
My whole soul out to thee.

(1855)

SONG: From GUINEVERE

'Late, late, so late! and dark the night
and chill!
Late, late, so late! but we can enter still.
Too late, too late! ye cannot enter now.

'No light had we; for that we do repent;
And learning this, the bridegroom will relent.   5
Too late, too late! ye cannot enter now.

'No light! so late! and dark and chill the
night!
O, let us in, that we may find the light!
Too late, too late! ye cannot enter now.

'Have we not heard the bridegroom is so
sweet?   10
O, let us in, though late, to kiss his feet!
No, no, too late! ye cannot enter now.'

(1859)

TITHONUS

The woods decay, the woods decay and fall,
The vapors weep their burthen to the
ground,
Man comes and tills the field and lies be-
neath,
And after many a summer dies the swan.
Me only cruel immortality   5
Consumes; I wither slowly in thine arms,
Here at the quiet limit of the world,
A white-haired shadow roaming like a dream
The ever-silent spaces of the East,
Far-folded mists, and gleaming halls of
morn.   10
Alas! for this gray shadow, once a man —
So glorious in his beauty and thy choice,
Who madest him thy chosen, that he
seemed
To his great heart none other than a God!
I asked thee, 'Give me immortality.'   15
Then didst thou grant mine asking with a
smile,
Like wealthy men who care not how they
give.
But thy strong Hours indignant worked
their wills,
And beat me down and marred and wasted
me,
And though they could not end me, left me
maimed   20
To dwell in presence of immortal youth,
Immortal age beside immortal youth,
And all I was, in ashes. Can thy love,
Thy beauty, make amends, though even now,
Close over us, the silver star, thy guide, 25
Shines in those tremulous eyes that fill with
tears
To hear me? Let me go; take back thy
gift;

Why should a man desire in any way
To vary from the kindly race of men,
Or pass beyond the goal of ordinance   30
Where all should pause, as is most meet for
    all?
A soft air fans the cloud apart; there comes
A glimpse of that dark world where I was
    born.
Once more the old mysterious glimmer steals
From thy pure brows, and from thy shoul-
    ders pure,   35
And bosom beating with a heart renewed.
Thy cheek begins to redden through the
    gloom,
Thy sweet eyes brighten slowly close to
    mine,
Ere yet they blind the stars, and the wild
    team
Which love thee, yearning for thy yoke,
    arise,   40
And shake the darkness from their loosened
    manes,
And beat the twilight into flakes of fire.
Lo! ever thus thou growest beautiful
In silence, then before thine answer given
Departest, and thy tears are on my cheek. 45
    Why wilt thou ever scare me with thy
        tears,
And make me tremble lest a saying learnt,
In days far-off, on that dark earth, be true?
'The Gods themselves cannot recall their
    gifts.'
    Ay me! ay me! with what another heart 50
In days far-off, and with what other eyes
I used to watch — if I be he that watched —
The lucid outline forming round thee; saw
The dim curls kindle into sunny rings;
Changed with thy mystic change, and felt
    my blood   55
Glow with the glow that slowly crimsoned
    all
Thy presence and thy portals, while I lay,
Mouth, forehead, eyelids, growing dewy-
    warm
With kisses balmier than half-opening buds
Of April, and could hear the lips that kissed
Whispering I knew not what of wild and
    sweet,   61
Like that strange song I heard Apollo sing,
While Ilion like a mist rose into towers.
    Yet hold me not for ever in thine East;
How can my nature longer mix with thine?
Coldly thy rosy shadows bathe me, cold   66
Are all thy lights, and cold my wrinkled
    feet
Upon thy glimmering thresholds, when the
    steam
Floats up from those dim fields about the
    homes

Of happy men that have the power to die, 70
And grassy barrows of the happier dead.
Release me, and restore me to the ground;
Thou seest all things, thou wilt see my
    grave;
Thou wilt renew thy beauty morn by morn;
I earth in earth forget these empty courts, 75
And thee returning on thy silver wheels.
                                        (1860)

MILTON

(ALCAICS)

O mighty-mouthed inventor of harmonies,
O skilled to sing of Time or Eternity,
    God-gifted organ-voice of England,
        Milton, a name to resound for ages:
Whose Titan angels, Gabriel, Abdiel,   5
Starred from Jehovah's gorgeous armories,
    Tower, as the deep-domed empyrean
        Rings to the roar of an angel onset!
Me rather all that bowery loneliness,
The brooks of Eden mazily murmuring,   10
    And bloom profuse and cedar arches
        Charm, as a wanderer out in ocean,
Where some refulgent sunset of India
Streams o'er a rich ambrosial ocean isle,
    And crimson-hued the stately palm-woods
        Whisper in odorous heights of even. 16
                                        (1863)

NORTHERN FARMER

OLD STYLE

Wheer 'asta bean saw long and mea liggin'
    'ere aloan?
Noorse? thoort nowt o' a noorse; whoy,
    Doctor's abean an' agoan;
Says that I moant 'a naw moor aale, but I
    beänt a fool;
Git ma my aale, fur I beänt a-gawin' to break
    my rule.

Doctors, they knaws nowt, fur a says what's
    nawways true;   5
Naw soort o' koind o' use to saay the things
    that a do.
I've 'ed my point o' aale ivry noight sin' I
    bean 'ere.
An' I've 'ed my quart ivry market-noight
    for foorty year.

Parson's a bean loikewoise, an' a sittin' ere
    o' my bed.
'The Amoighty's a taakin o' you to 'issén,
    my friend,' a said,   10

An' a towd ma my sins, an' 's toithe were
　　due, an' I gied it in hond;
I done moy duty boy 'um, as I 'a done boy
　　the lond.

Larn'd a ma' bea. I reckons I 'annot sa
　　mooch to larn.
But a cast oop, thot a did, 'bout Bessy Mar-
　　ris's barne.
Thaw a knaws I hallus voated wi' Squoire
　　an' choorch an' staate,　　　　　　15
An' i' the woost o' toimes I wur niver agin
　　the raate.

An' I hallus coom'd to 's choorch afoor moy
　　Sally wur dead,
An' 'eard 'um a bummin' awaay loike a buz-
　　zard-clock ower my 'ead,
An' I niver knaw'd whot a mean'd but I
　　thowt a 'ad summut to saay,
An' I thowt a said whot a owt to 'a said, an'
　　I coom'd awaay.　　　　　　　　20

Bessy Marris's barne! tha knaws she laaid
　　it to mea.
Mowt a bean, mayhap, for she wur a bad
　　un, shea.
'Siver, I kep 'um, I kep 'um, my lass, tha
　　mun understond;
I done moy duty boy 'um, as I 'a done boy
　　the lond.

But Parson a cooms an' a goas, an' a says
　　it easy an' frea:　　　　　　　　25
'The Amoighty 's a taakin o' you to 'issén,
　　my friend,' says 'ea.
I weant saay men be loiars, thaw summun
　　said it in 'aaste;
But 'e reads wonn sarmin a weak, an' I 'a
　　stubb'd Thurnaby waaste.

D' ya moind the waaste, my lass? naw, naw,
　　tha was not born then;
Theer wur a boggle in it, I often 'eard 'um
　　mysén;　　　　　　　　　　　30
Moast loike a butter-bump, fur I 'eard 'um
　　about an' about,
But I stubb'd 'um oop wi' the lot, an' raäved
　　an' rembled 'um out.

Keaper's it wur; fo' they fun 'um theer
　　a-laaid of 'is faace
Down i' the woild 'enemies afoor I coom'd
　　to the plaace.
Noaks or Thimbleby—toaner 'ed shot 'um
　　as dead as a naail.
Noaks wur 'ang'd for it oop at 'soize—but
　　git ma my aale.

Dubbut looök at the waaste; theer warn't
　　not feead for a cow;
Nowt at all but bracken an' fuzz, an' loook
　　at it now—
Warn't worth nowt a haacre, an' now theer
　　's lots o' feead,
Fourscoor yows upon it, an' some on it down
　　i' seead.　　　　　　　　　　　40

Nobbut a bit on it 's left, an' I mean'd to 'a
　　stubb'd it at fall,
Done it ta-year I mean'd, an' runn'd plow
　　thruff it an' all,
If Godamoighty an' parson 'ud nobbut let
　　ma aloan,—
Mea, wi' haate hoonderd haacre o' Squoire's,
　　an lond o' my oan.

Do Godamoighty knaw what a's doing a-
　　taakin' o' mea?　　　　　　　　45
I beant wonn as saws 'ere a bean an yonder
　　a pea;
An' Squoire 'ull be sa mad an' all—a' dear,
　　a' dear!
And I 'a managed for Squoire coom
　　Michaelmas thutty year.

A mowt 'a taaen owd Joanes, as 'ant not a
　　'aapoth o' sense,
Or a mowt a' taaen young Robins—a niver
　　mended a fence;　　　　　　　50
But Godamoighty a moost taake mea an'
　　taake ma now,
Wi' aaf the cows to cauve an' Thurnaby
　　hoalms to plow!

Looök 'ow quoloty smoiles when they seeas
　　ma a passin' boy,
Says to thessén, naw doubt, 'What a man
　　a bea sewerloy!'
Fur they knaws what I bean to Squoire sin'
　　fust a coom'd to the 'All;　　　55
I done moy duty by Squoire an' I done moy
　　duty boy hall.

Squoire 's i' Lunnon, an' summun I reckons
　　'ull 'a to wroite,
For whoa 's to howd the lond ater mea thot
　　muddles ma quoit;
Sartin-sewer I bea thot a weant niver give
　　it to Joanes,
Naw, nor a moant to Robins—a niver rem-
　　bles the stoans.　　　　　　　60

But summun 'ull come ater mea mayhap wi'
　　'is kittle o' steam
Huzzin' an' maazin' the blessed fealds wi'
　　the divil's oan team.

Sin' I mun doy I mun doy, thaw loife they
   says is sweet,
But sin' I mun doy I mun doy, for I couldn
   abear to see it.

What atta stannin' theer fur, an' doesn
   bring ma the aale?   65
Doctor's a 'toattler, lass, an a's hallus i' the
   owd taale;
I weant break rules fur Doctor, a knaws
   naw moor nor a floy;
Git ma my aale, I tell tha, an' if I mun doy
   I mun doy.

                              (1864)

THE REVENGE

A BALLAD OF THE FLEET

I

At Flores in the Azores Sir Richard Gren-
   ville lay,
And a pinnace, like a fluttered bird, came
   flying from far away;
'Spanish ships of war at sea! we have
   sighted fifty-three!'
Then sware Lord Thomas Howard: ''Fore
   God I am no coward;
But I cannot meet them here, for my ships
   are out of gear,   5
And the half my men are sick. I must fly,
   but follow quick.
We are six ships of the line; can we fight
   with fifty-three?'

II

Then spake Sir Richard Grenville: 'I know
   you are no coward;
You fly them for a moment to fight with
   them again.
But I've ninety men and more that are lying
   sick ashore.   10
I should count myself the coward if I left
   them, my Lord Howard,
To these Inquisition dogs and the devildoms
   of Spain.'

III

So Lord Howard passed away with five
   ships of war that day,
Till he melted like a cloud in the silent sum-
   mer heaven;
But Sir Richard bore in hand all his sick
   men from the land   15
Very carefully and slow,
Men of Bideford in Devon,

And we laid them on the ballast down below:
For we brought them all aboard,
And they blest him in their pain, that they
   were not left to Spain,   20
To the thumb-screw and the stake, for the
   glory of the Lord.

IV

He had only a hundred seamen to work the
   ship and to fight
And he sailed away from Flores till the
   Spaniard came in sight,
With his huge sea-castles heaving upon the
   weather bow.
'Shall we fight or shall we fly?   25
Good Sir Richard, tell us now,
For to fight is but to die!
There'll be little of us left by the time this
   sun be set.'
And Sir Richard said again: 'We be all
   good English men.
Let us bang these dogs of Seville, the chil-
   dren of the devil,   30
For I never turned my back upon Don or
   devil yet.'

V

Sir Richard spoke and he laughed, and we
   roared a hurrah, and so
The little Revenge ran on sheer into the
   heart of the foe,
With her hundred fighters on deck, and her
   ninety sick below;
For half of their fleet to the right and half
   to the left were seen,   35
And the little Revenge ran on through the
   long sea-lane between.

VI

Thousands of their soldiers looked down
   from their decks and laughed,
Thousands of their seamen made mock at
   the mad little craft
Running on and on, till delayed
By their mountain-like San Philip that, of
   fifteen hundred tons,   40
And up-shadowing high above us with her
   yawning tiers of guns,
Took the breath from our sails, and we
   stayed.

VII

And while now the great San Philip hung
   above us like a cloud
Whence the thunderbolt will fall
Long and loud.

Four galleons drew away
From the Spanish fleet that day,
And two upon the larboard and two upon
the starboard lay,
And the battle-thunder broke from them all.

VIII

But anon the great San Philip, she bethought herself and went,   50
Having that within her womb that had left
her ill content;
And the rest they came aboard us, and they
fought us hand to hand,
For a dozen times they came with their
pikes and musqueteers,
And a dozen times we shook 'em off as a
dog that shakes his ears
When he leaps from the water to the land.

IX

And the sun went down, and the stars came
out far over the summer sea,   56
But never a moment ceased the fight of the
one and the fifty-three.
Ship after ship, the whole night long, their
high-built galleons came,
Ship after ship, the whole night long, with
her battle-thunder and flame;
Ship after ship, the whole night long, drew
back with her dead and her shame.   60
For some were sunk and many were shattered, and so could fight us no more —
God of battles, was ever a battle like this
in the world before?

X

For he said, ' Fight on! fight on! '
Though his vessel was all but a wreck;
And it chanced that, when half of the short
summer night was gone,   65
With a grisly wound to be drest he had left
the deck,
But a bullet struck him that was dressing it
suddenly dead,
And himself he was wounded again in the
side and the head,
And he said, ' Fight on! fight on! '

XI

And the night went down, and the sun
smiled out far over the summer sea, 70
And the Spanish fleet with broken sides lay
round us all in a ring;
But they dared not touch us again, for they
feared that we still could sting,
So they watched what the end would be.
And we had not fought them in vain,
But in perilous plight were we,   75

Seeing forty of our poor hundred were
slain,
And half of the rest of us maimed for life
In the crash of the cannonades and the des-
perate strife;
And the sick men down in the hold were
most of them stark and cold,
And the pikes were all broken or bent, and
the powder was all of it spent;   80
And the masts and the rigging were lying
over the side;
But Sir Richard cried in his English pride:
' We have fought such a fight for a day and
a night
As may never be fought again!
We have won great glory, my men!   85
And a day less or more
At sea or ashore,
We die — does it matter when?
Sink me the ship, Master Gunner — sink
her, split her in twain!
Fall into the hands of God, not into the
hands of Spain! '   90

XII

And the gunner said, ' Ay, ay,' but the sea-
men made reply:
' We have children, we have wives,
And the Lord hath spared our lives.
We will make the Spaniard promise, if we
yield, to let us go;
We shall live to fight again and to strike
another blow.'   95
And the lion there lay dying, and they
yielded to the foe.

XIII

And the stately Spanish men to their flag-
ship bore him then,
Where they laid him by the mast, old Sir
Richard caught at last,
And they praised him to his face with their
courtly foreign grace;   99
But he rose upon their decks, and he cried:
' I have fought for Queen and Faith like a
valiant man and true;
I have only done my duty as a man is bound
to do.
With a joyful spirit I Sir Richard Gren-
ville die! '
And he fell upon their decks, and he died.

XIV

And they stared at the dead that had been
so valiant and true,   105
And had holden the power and glory of
Spain so cheap

That he dared her with one little ship and
his English few;
Was he devil or man? He was devil for
aught they knew,
But they sank his body with honor down
into the deep,
And they manned the Revenge with a
swarthier alien crew,   110
And away she sailed with her loss and
longed for her own;
When a wind from the lands they had ruined
awoke from sleep,
And the water began to heave and the
weather to moan,
And or ever that evening ended a great
gale blew,
And a wave like the wave that is raised by
an earthquake grew,   115
Till it smote on their hulls and their sails
and their masts and their flags,
And the whole sea plunged and fell on the
shot-shattered navy of Spain,
And the little Revenge herself went down
by the island crags
To be lost evermore in the main.
(1878)

TO VIRGIL

Roman Virgil, thou that singest Ilion's lofty
temples robed in fire,
Ilion falling, Rome arising, wars, and filial
faith, and Dido's pyre;

Landscape-lover, lord of language more than
he that sang the 'Works and Days,'
All the chosen coin of fancy flashing out
from many a golden phrase;

Thou that singest wheat and woodland, tilth
and vineyard, hive and horse and herd; 5
All the charm of all the Muses often flowering in a lonely word;

Poet of the happy Tityrus piping underneath his beechen bowers;
Poet of the poet-satyr whom the laughing
shepherd bound with flowers;

Chanter of the Pollio, glorying in the blissful years again to be,
Summers of the snakeless meadow, unla-
borious earth and oarless sea;   10

Thou that seest Universal Nature moved by
Universal Mind;
Thou majestic in thy sadness at the doubtful
doom of human kind;

Light among the vanished ages; star that
gildest yet this phantom shore;
Golden branch amid the shadows, kings and
realms that pass to rise no more;

Now thy Forum roars no longer, fallen every
purple Cæsar's dome —   15
Though thine ocean-roll of rhythm sound
forever of Imperial Rome —

Now the Rome of slaves hath perished, and
the Rome of freemen holds her place,
I, from out the Northern Island sundered
once from all the human race,

I salute thee, Mantovano, I that loved thee
since my day began,
Wielder of the stateliest measure ever
molded by the lips of man.   20
(1882)

'FRATER AVE ATQUE VALE'

Row us out from Desenzano, to your Sir-
mione row!
So they rowed, and there we landed — 'O
venusta Sirmio!'
There to me through all the groves of olive
in the summer glow,
There beneath the Roman ruin where the
purple flowers grow,
Came that 'Ave atque Vale' of the Poet's
hopeless woe,   5
Tenderest of Roman poets nineteen hun-
dred years ago,
'Frater Ave atque Vale' — as we wandered
to and fro,
Gazing at the Lydian laughter of the Garda
Lake below,
Sweet Catullus's all-but-island, olive-silvery
Sirmio!
(1883)

VASTNESS

Many a hearth upon our dark globe sighs
after many a vanished face,
Many a planet by many a sun may roll with
the dust of a vanished race.

Raving politics, never at rest — as this poor
earth's pale history runs, —
What is it all but a trouble of ants in the
gleam of a million million of suns?

Lies upon this side, lies upon that side,
truthless violence mourned by the wise, 5

Thousands of voices drowning his own in a
    popular torrent of lies upon lies;

Stately purposes, valor in battle, glorious
    annals of army and fleet,
Death for the right cause, death for the
    wrong cause, trumpets of victory, groans
    of defeat;

Innocence seethed in her mother's milk, and
    Charity setting the martyr aflame;
Thraldom who walks with the banner of
    Freedom, and recks not to ruin a realm
    in her name.   10

Faith at her zenith, or all but lost in the
    gloom of doubts that darken the schools;
Craft with a bunch of all-heal in her hand,
    followed up by her vassal legion of
    fools;

Trade flying over a thousand seas with her
    spice and her vintage, her silk and her
    corn;
Desolate offing, sailorless harbors, famish-
    ing populace, wharves forlorn;

Star of the morning, Hope in the sunrise;
    gloom of the evening, Life at a close; 15
Pleasure who flaunts on her wide downway
    with her flying robe and her poisoned
    rose;

Pain that has crawled from the corpse of
    Pleasure, a worm which writhes all day,
    and at night
Stirs up again in the heart of the sleeper,
    and stings him back to the curse of the
    light;

Wealth with his wines and his wedded har-
    lots; honest Poverty, bare to the bone;
Opulent Avarice, lean as Poverty; Flattery
    gilding the rift in a throne;   20

Fame blowing out from her golden trumpet
    a jubilant challenge to Time and to
    Fate;
Slander, her shadow, sowing the nettle on
    all the laureled graves of the great;

Love for the maiden, crowned with mar-
    riage, no regrets for aught that has
    been,
Household happiness, gracious children,
    debtless competence, golden mean;

National hatreds of whole generations, and
    pigmy spites of the village spire;   25

Vows that will last to the last death-ruckle,
    and vows that are snapped in a mo-
    ment of fire;

He that has lived for the lust of the min-
    ute, and died in the doing it, flesh with-
    out mind;
He that has nailed all flesh to the Cross, till
    Self died out in the love of his kind;

Spring and Summer and Autumn and Win-
    ter, and all these old revolutions of
    earth;
All new-old revolutions of Empire — change
    of the tide — what is all of it worth? 30

What the philosophies, all the sciences,
    poesy, varying voices of prayer?
All that is noblest, all that is basest, all
    that is filthy with all that is fair?

What is it all, if we all of us end but in
    being our own corpse-coffins at last?
Swallowed in Vastness, lost in Silence,
    drowned in the deeps of a meaningless
    Past?

What but a murmur of gnats in the gloom,
    or a moment's anger of bees in their
    hive? —   35

.   .   .   .   .   .

Peace, let it be! for I loved him, and love
    him for ever: the dead are not dead
    but alive.   (1885)

CROSSING THE BAR

Sunset and evening star,
    And one clear call for me!
And may there be no moaning of the bar,
    When I put out to sea,

But such a tide as moving seems asleep,   5
    Too full for sound and foam,
When that which drew from out the bound-
    less deep
    Turns again home.

Twilight and evening bell,
    And after that the dark!   10
And may there be no sadness of farewell,
    When I embark;

For though from out our bourne of Time
    and Place
    The flood may bear me far,
I hope to see my Pilot face to face   15
    When I have crossed the bar.

        (1889)

ROBERT BROWNING (1812--1889).

Browning, born in Camberwell, a London suburb, was the son of a clerk in the Bank of England, who gave him a good education and encouraged his youthful inclination towards poetry. His first poem, *Pauline, the Fragment of a Confession*, was published anonymously in 1833; it is strongly marked by the influence of Shelley, and gives only a hint of its author's later style. After a visit to Russia, he produced *Paracelsus* (1835), which shows a considerable advance in artistic power, especially in the delineation of character. It brought about an invitation from Macready, the leading actor-manager of the day, to write a play, and in response *Strafford* was written and acted in 1837, with only moderate success. Browning wrote other plays, some for the stage and others for the study, *A Blot in the 'Scutcheon* being his best tragedy, and *Colombe's Birthday* his best comedy. Meanwhile he was working at a long narrative poem, *Sordello*, discussing the philosophic issues raised in connection with the life of a medieval troubadour; for the historical background he made elaborate studies in the British Museum and in Italy, to which he paid his first visit in 1838. *Sordello* was published in 1840, and had an unfavorable reception, owing to its extraordinarily concise and allusive style, which made it exceedingly difficult to understand. Browning was compelled to issue his next volumes in very cheap form at his own expense; the early numbers of the *Bells and Pomegranates* series, as he called it, could be bought for a few cents. The first issue, a dramatic poem entitled *Pippa Passes*, at once became popular, but many years elapsed before the injury done to the poet's reputation by *Sordello* was overcome.

The crucial event in Browning's life and in his poetic career was his marriage in 1846 to the most gifted of English poetesses, Elizabeth Barrett: owing partly to the state of her health and partly to her father's disapproval of the match, they lived in Italy, chiefly at Florence, till Mrs. Browning's death in 1861. During his married life Browning produced his best work — the dramatic monologues included in the volume known as *Men and Women* (1855). His wife's influence is also to be discerned in another collection of shorter poems, *Dramatis Personæ* (1864), and in his longest narrative poem, *The Ring and the Book* (1868-9), an elaborate treatment of a Roman murder trial, of which Browning found the pleadings in an old book he picked up from a second-hand book stall at Florence. He did not return to Florence after the death of his wife, but resided in London, and slowly won for himself a leading place in public esteem along with Tennyson, with whom he was on very friendly terms. His later work is marred by an excessive tendency to philosophical speculation and psychological analysis as well as grotesqueness of expression, but these defects are naturally most noticeable in his longer poems. He continued to produce beautiful lyrics and dramatic monologues of unsurpassed power and intensity until his death at Venice in 1889.

It is probably by his shorter rather than by his longer poems that Browning will hold his place among the leading English poets. He is unsurpassed as a master of the dramatic monologue — a short poem in which the speaker reveals his soul at some critical moment by telling his thoughts or his story to someone else. Although Browning had unusual metrical facility, he indulged at times in abrupt transitions and grotesque rimes which give to his work an appearance of oddity and sometimes of obscurity. The charge of intentional obscurity sometimes leveled against him is, of course, absurd. He wrote to an admirer who drew attention to this accusation: 'I can have little doubt that my writing has been in the main too hard for many I should have been pleased to communicate with; but I never designedly tried to puzzle people, as some of my critics have supposed. On the other hand, I never pretended to offer such literature as should be a substitute for a cigar or a game at dominoes to an idle man. So, perhaps, on the whole I get my deserts, and something over — not a crowd, but a few I value more.' Swinburne's comment was that Browning is 'something too much the reverse of obscure; he is too brilliant and subtle for the ready reader of a ready writer to follow with any certainty the track of an intelligence which moves with such incessant rapidity. . . . He never thinks but at full speed; and the rate of his thought is to that of another man's as the speed of a railway to that of a waggon, or the speed of a telegraph to that of a railway.' Fortunately for the ordinary reader, his best poems are not his most difficult ones, and the patient student will find that even his worst are marked by extraordinary intellectual vigor and insight into character. While his reputation has hardly kept the supreme place given to it by his admirers at the close of the Victorian era, he remains one of the greatest figures in English poetry, remarkable alike for his message to his time and for the skill and power with which he delivered it.

SONGS FROM 'PIPPA PASSES'

I

ALL SERVICE RANKS THE SAME WITH GOD

All service ranks the same with God:
If now, as formerly he trod
Paradise, his presence fills
Our earth, each only as God wills
Can work — God's puppets, best and worst, 5
Are we; there is no last nor first.

II

THE YEAR'S AT THE SPRING

The year's at the spring
And day's at the morn;
Morning's at seven;
The hill-side's dew-pearled;
The lark's on the wing; 5
The snail's on the thorn:
God's in his heaven —
All's right with the world!

III

GIVE HER BUT A LEAST EXCUSE TO LOVE ME

Give her but a least excuse to love me!
When — where —
How — can this arm establish her above me,
If fortune fixed her as my lady there,
There already, to eternally reprove me? 5
('Hist!'— said Kate the Queen;
But 'Oh!'— cried the maiden, binding her
    tresses,
''T is only a page that carols unseen,
Crumbling your hounds their messes!')

Is she wronged?— To the rescue of her
    honor, 10
My heart!
Is she poor? — What costs it to be styled a
    donor?
Merely an earth to cleave, a sea to part.
But that fortune should have thrust all this
    upon her!
('Nay, list!'— bade Kate the Queen; 15
And still cried the maiden, binding her
    tresses,
''Tis only a page that carols unseen,
Fitting your hawks their jesses!')

                                (1841)

MY LAST DUCHESS

FERRARA

That's my last Duchess painted on the wall,
Looking as if she were alive. I call
That piece a wonder, now: Frà Pandolf's
    hands
Worked busily a day, and there she stands.

Will 't please you sit and look at her? 1
    said 5
'Frà Pandolf' by design, for never read
Strangers like you that pictured countenance,
The depth and passion of its earnest glance,
But to myself they turned (since none puts
    by
The curtain I have drawn for you, but I) 10
And seemed as they would ask me, if they
    durst,
How such a glance came there; so, not the
    first
Are you to turn and ask thus. Sir, 't was
    not
Her husband's presence only, called that
    spot
Of joy into the Duchess' cheek: perhaps 15
Frà Pandolf chanced to say, 'Her mantle
    laps
Over my lady's wrist too much,' or 'Paint
Must never hope to reproduce the faint
Half-flush that dies along her throat:' such
    stuff
Was courtesy, she thought, and cause
    enough 20
For calling up that spot of joy. She had
A heart — how shall I say?— too soon made
    glad,
Too easily impressed; she liked whate'er
She looked on, and her looks went every-
    where.
Sir, 't was all one! My favor at her breast,
The dropping of the daylight in the West, 26
The bough of cherries some officious fool
Broke in the orchard for her, the white
    mule
She rode with round the terrace — all and
    each
Would draw from her alike the approving
    speech, 30
Or blush, at least. She thanked men,—
    good! but thanked
Somehow — I know not how — as if she
    ranked
My gift of a nine-hundred-years-old name
With anybody's gift. Who'd stoop to blame
This sort of trifling? Even had you skill 35
In speech — (which I have not)— to make
    your will
Quite clear to such an one, and say, 'Just
    this
Or that in you disgusts me; here you miss,
Or there exceed the mark'— and if she let
Herself be lessoned so, nor plainly set 40
Her wits to yours, forsooth, and made ex-
    cuse,
— E'en then would be some stooping; and I
    choose

Never to stoop. Oh, sir, she smiled, no
doubt,
Whene'er I passed her; but who passed with-
out
Much the same smile? This grew; I gave
commands; 45
Then all smiles stopped together. There she
stands
As if alive. Will 't please you rise? We 'll
meet
The company below then. I repeat,
The Count your master's known munificence
Is ample warrant that no just pretense 50
Of mine for dowry will be disallowed;
Though his fair daughter's self, as I
avowed
At starting, is my object. Nay, we 'll go
Together down, sir. Notice Neptune,
though,
Taming a sea-horse, thought a rarity, 55
Which Claus of Innsbruck cast in bronze
for me!

(1842)

COUNT GISMOND

AIX IN PROVENCE

I

Christ God who savest man, save most
Of men Count Gismond who saved me!
Count Gauthier, when he chose his post,
Chose time and place and company
To suit it; when he struck at length 5
My honor, 't was with all his strength.

II

And doubtlessly ere he could draw
All points to one, he must have schemed!
That miserable morning saw
Few half so happy as I seemed, 10
While being dressed in queen's array
To give our tourney prize away.

III

I thought they loved me, did me grace
To please themselves; 't was all their
deed;
God makes, or fair or foul, our face; 15
If showing mine so caused to bleed
My cousins' hearts, they should have
dropped
A word, and straight the play had stopped.

IV

They, too, so beauteous! Each a queen
By virtue of her brow and breast; 20

Not needing to be crowned, I mean,
As I do. E'en when I was dressed,
Had either of them spoke, instead
Of glancing sideways with still head!

V

But no: they let me laugh, and sing 25
My birthday song quite through, adjust
The last rose in my garland, fling
A last look on the mirror, trust
My arms to each an arm of theirs,
And so descend the castle-stairs — 30

VI

And come out on the morning-troop
Of merry friends who kissed my cheek,
And called me queen, and made me stoop
Under the canopy — (a streak
That pierced it, of the outside sun, 35
Powdered with gold its gloom's soft dun) —

VII

And they could let me take my state
And foolish throne amid applause
Of all come there to celebrate
My queen's-day — Oh, I think the cause 40
Of much was, they forgot no crowd
Makes up for parents in their shroud!

VIII

Howe'er that be, all eyes were bent
Upon me, when my cousins cast
Theirs down; 't was time I should present
The victor's crown, but . . . there, 't
will last 46
No long time . . . the old mist again
Blinds me as then it did. How vain!

IX

See! Gismond's at the gate, in talk
With his two boys: I can proceed. 50
Well, at that moment, who should stalk
Forth boldly — to my face, indeed —
But Gauthier, and he thundered, 'Stay!'
And all stayed. 'Bring no crowns, I say!

X

'Bring torches! Wind the penance-sheet 55
About her! Let her shun the chaste,
Or lay herself before their feet!
Shall she whose body I embraced
A night long, queen it in the day?
For honor's sake no crowns, I say!' 60

XI

I? What I answered? As I live,
I never fancied such a thing

As answer possible to give.
What says the body when they spring
Some monstrous torture-engine's whole   65
Strength on it? No more says the soul.

XII

Till out strode Gismond; then I knew
That I was saved. I never met
His face before, but, at first view,
I felt quite sure that God had set   70
Himself to Satan; who would spend
A minute's mistrust on the end?

XIII

He strode to Gauthier, in his throat
Gave him the lie, then struck his mouth
With one back-handed blow that wrote   75
In blood men's verdict there. North,
South,
East, West, I looked. The lie was dead,
And damned, and truth stood up instead.

XIV

This glads me most, that I enjoyed
The heart of the joy, with my content   80
In watching Gismond unalloyed
By any doubt of the event:
God took that on him — I was bid
Watch Gismond for my part: I did.

XV

Did I not watch him while he let   85
His armorer just brace his greaves,
Rivet his hauberk, on the fret
The while! His foot . . . my memory
leaves
No least stamp out, nor how anon
He pulled his ringing gauntlets on.   90

XVI

And e'en before the trumpet's sound
Was finished, prone lay the false knight,
Prone as his lie, upon the ground:
Gismond flew at him, used no sleight
O' the sword, but open-breasted rove,   95
Cleaving till out the truth he clove.

XVII

Which done, he dragged him to my feet
And said, 'Here die, but end thy breath
In full confession, lest thou fleet
From my first, to God's second death!   100
Say, hast thou lied?' And, 'I have lied
To God and her,' he said, and died.

XVIII

Then Gismond, kneeling to me, asked
— What safe my heart holds, though no
word

Could I repeat now, if I tasked   105
My powers for ever, to a third
Dear even as you are. Pass the rest
Until I sank upon his breast.

XIX

Over my head his arm he flung
Against the world; and scarce I felt   110
His sword (that dripped by me and swung)
A little shifted in its belt;
For he began to say the while
How South our home lay many a mile.

XX

So 'mid the shouting multitude   115
We two walked forth to never more
Return. My cousins have pursued
Their life, untroubled as before
I vexed them. Gauthier's dwelling-place
God lighten! May his soul find grace!   120

XXI

Our elder boy has got the clear
Great brow; though when his brother's
black
Full eye shows scorn, it . . . Gismond
here?
And have you brought my tercel back?
I just was telling Adela   125
How many birds it struck since May.

                       (1842)

INCIDENT OF THE FRENCH CAMP

I

You know, we French stormed Ratisbon;
A mile or so away,
On a little mound, Napoleon
Stood on our storming-day;
With neck out-thrust, you fancy how,   5
Legs wide, arms locked behind,
As if to balance the prone brow
Oppressive with its mind.

II

Just as perhaps he mused, 'My plans
That soar, to earth may fall,   10
Let once my army-leader Lannes
Waver at yonder wall,'—
Out 'twixt the battery-smokes there flew
A rider, bound on bound
Full-galloping; nor bridle drew   15
Until he reached the mound.

III

Then off there flung in smiling joy,
And held himself erect
By just his horse's mane, a boy:
You hardly could suspect —   20

(So tight he kept his lips compressed,
  Scarce any blood came through)
You looked twice ere you saw his breast
  Was all but shot in two.

IV

'Well,' cried he, 'Emperor, by God's grace
  We've got you Ratisbon!   26
The Marshal's in the market-place,
  And you'll be there anon
To see your flag-bird flap his vans
  Where I, to heart's desire,   30
Perched him!' The chief's eye flashed; his
    plans
  Soared up again like fire.

V

The chief's eye flashed; but presently
  Softened itself, as sheathes
A film the mother-eagle's eye   35
  When her bruised eaglet breathes;
'You're wounded!' 'Nay,' the soldier's
    pride
  Touched to the quick, he said:
'I'm killed, Sire!' And his chief beside,
  Smiling the boy fell dead.   40

          (1842)

THE ITALIAN IN ENGLAND

That second time they hunted me
From hill to plain, from shore to sea,
And Austria, hounding far and wide
Her blood-hounds through the country-side,
Breathed hot and instant on my trace,—   5
I made six days a hiding-place
Of that dry green old aqueduct
Where I and Charles, when boys, have
    plucked
The fire-flies from the roof above,
Bright creeping through the moss they love:
—How long it seems since Charles was
    lost!   11
Six days the soldiers crossed and crossed
The country in my very sight;
And when that peril ceased at night,
The sky broke out in red dismay   15
With signal fires; well, there I lay
Close covered o'er in my recess,
Up to the neck in ferns and cress,
Thinking on Metternich our friend,
And Charles's miserable end,   20
And much beside, two days; the third,
Hunger o'ercame me when I heard
The peasants from the village go
To work among the maize; you know,
With us in Lombardy, they bring   25

Provisions packed on mules, a string
With little bells that cheer their task,
And casks, and boughs on every cask
To keep the sun's heat from the wine;
These I let pass in jingling line.   30
And, close on them, dear noisy crew,
The peasants from the village, too;
For at the very rear would troop
Their wives and sisters in a group
To help, I knew. When these had passed, 35
I threw my glove to strike the last,
Taking the chance: she did not start,
Much less cry out, but stooped apart,
One instant rapidly glanced round,
And saw me beckon from the ground.   40
A wild bush grows and hides my crypt;
She picked my glove up while she stripped
A branch off, then rejoined the rest
With that; my glove lay in her breast.
Then I drew breath; they disappeared: 45
It was for Italy I feared.

    An hour, and she returned alone
Exactly where my glove was thrown.
Meanwhile came many thoughts; on me
Rested the hopes of Italy.   50
I had devised a certain tale
Which, when 't was told her, could not fail
Persuade a peasant of its truth;
I meant to call a freak of youth
This hiding, and give hopes of pay,   55
And no temptation to betray.
But when I saw that woman's face,
Its calm simplicity of grace,
Our Italy's own attitude
In which she walked thus far, and stood,   60
Planting each naked foot so firm,
To crush the snake and spare the worm—
At first sight of her eyes, I said,
'I am that man upon whose head
They fix the price, because I hate   65
The Austrians over us; the State
Will give you gold—oh, gold so much—
If you betray me to their clutch,
And be your death, for aught I know,
If once they find you saved their foe.   70
Now, you must bring me food and drink,
And also paper, pen and ink,
And carry safe what I shall write
To Padua, which you'll reach at night
Before the duomo shuts; go in,   75
And wait till Tenebræ begin;
Walk to the third confessional,
Between the pillar and the wall,
And kneeling whisper, *Whence comes peace?*
Say it a second time, then cease;   80
And if the voice inside returns,
From Christ and Freedom; what concerns

The cause of Peace?— for answer, slip
My letter where you placed your lip;
Then come back happy we have done　85
Our mother service — I, the son,
As you the daughter of our land!'

Three mornings more, she took her stand
In the same place, with the same eyes:
I was no surer of sunrise　　　　90
Than of her coming. We conferred
Of her own prospects, and I heard
She had a lover — stout and tall,
She said — then let her eyelids fall,
'He could do much'— as if some doubt　95
Entered her heart,— then, passing out,
'She could not speak for others, who
Had other thoughts; herself she knew;'
And so she brought me drink and food.
After four days, the scouts pursued　100
Another path; at last arrived
The help my Paduan friends contrived
To furnish me: she brought the news.
For the first time I could not choose
But kiss her hand, and lay my own　105
Upon her head —'This faith was shown
To Italy, our mother; she
Uses my hand and blesses thee.'
She followed down to the sea-shore;
I left and never saw her more.　　110

How very long since I have thought
Concerning — much less wished for — aught
Beside the good of Italy,
For which I live and mean to die!
I never was in love; and since　115
Charles proved false, what shall now con-
　vince
My inmost heart I have a friend?
However, if I pleased to spend
Real wishes on myself — say, three —
I know at least what one should be.　120
I would grasp Metternich until
I felt his red wet throat distil
In blood through these two hands. And
　next
— Nor much for that am I perplexed —
Charles, perjured traitor, for his part,　125
Should die slow of a broken heart
Under his new employers. Last
— Ah, there, what should I wish? For fast
Do I grow old and out of strength.
If I resolved to seek at length　130
My father's house again, how scared
They all would look, and unprepared!
My brothers live in Austria's pay
— Disowned me long ago, men say;
And all my early mates who used　135
To praise me so — perhaps induced

More than one early step of mine —
Are turning wise: while some opine
'Freedom grows license,' some suspect
'Haste breeds delay,' and recollect　140
They always said, such premature
Beginnings never could endure!
So, with a sullen 'All's for best,'
The land seems settling to its rest.
I think then, I should wish to stand　145
This evening in that dear, lost land,
Over the sea the thousand miles,
And know if yet that woman smiles
With the calm smile; some little farm
She lives in there, no doubt; what harm　150
If I sat on the door-side bench,
And, while her spindle made a trench
Fantastically in the dust,
Inquired of all her fortunes — just
Her children's ages and their names,　155
And what may be the husband's aims
For each of them. I'd talk this out,
And sit there, for an hour about,
Then kiss her hand once more, and lay
Mine on her head, and go my way.　160

So much for idle wishing — how
It steals the time! To business now.
　　　　　　　　　　　　(1845)

THE LOST LEADER

I

Just for a handful of silver he left us,
　Just for a riband to stick in his coat —
Found the one gift of which fortune bereft
　us,
　Lost all the others she lets us devote;
They, with the gold to give, doled him out
　silver,　　　　　　　　　　　　5
So much was theirs who so little allowed:
How all our copper had gone for his serv-
　ice!
Rags — were they purple, his heart had
　been proud!
We that had loved him so, followed him,
　honored him,
Lived in his mild and magnificent eye,　10
Learned his great language, caught his
　clear accents,
Made him our pattern to live and to die!
Shakspere was of us, Milton was for us,
　Burns, Shelley, were with us,— they watch
　from their graves!
He alone breaks from the van and the free-
　men,　　　　　　　　　　　　15
　— He alone sinks to the rear and the
　slaves!

II

We shall march prospering,— not through
  his presence;
Songs may inspirit us,— not from his lyre;
Deeds will be done,— while he boasts his
  quiescence,
Still bidding crouch whom the rest bade
  aspire;   20
Blot out his name, then, record one lost
  soul more,
One task more declined, one more foot-
  path untrod,
One more devil's-triumph and sorrow for
  angels,
One wrong more to man, one more insult
  to God!
Life's night begins: let him never come back
  to us!   25
There would be doubt, hesitation and
  pain,
Forced praise on our part — the glimmer
  of twilight,
Never glad confident morning again!
Best fight on well, for we taught him —
  strike gallantly,
Menace our heart ere we master his own;
Then let him receive the new knowledge
  and wait us,   31
Pardoned in heaven, the first by the
  throne!

                             (1845)

HOME-THOUGHTS FROM ABROAD

I

Oh, to be in England,
Now that April's there,
And whoever wakes in England
Sees, some morning, unaware,
That the lowest boughs and the brush-wood
  sheaf   5
Round the elm-tree bole are in tiny leaf,
While the chaffinch sings on the orchard
  bough
In England — now!

II

And after April, when May follows,
And the white-throat builds, and all the
  swallows!   10
Hark, where my blossomed pear-tree in
  the hedge
Leans to the field and scatters on the clover
Blossoms and dewdrops — at the bent spray's
  edge —
That's the wise thrush; he sings each song
twice over,

Lest you should think he never could re-
  capture   15
The first fine careless rapture!
And though the fields look rough with
  hoary dew,
All will be gay when noontide wakes anew
The buttercups, the little children's dower
— Far brighter than this gaudy melon-
  flower!   20

                             (1845)

HOME-THOUGHTS FROM THE SEA

Nobly, nobly, Cape Saint Vincent to the
  Northwest died away;
Sunset ran, one glorious blood-red, reeking
  into Cadiz Bay;
Bluish 'mid the burning water, full in face
  Trafalgar lay;
In the dimmest Northeast distance dawned
  Gibraltar, grand and gray;
'Here and here did England help me: how
  can I help England?'— say,   5
Whoso turns as I, this evening, turn to God
  to praise and pray,
While Jove's planet rises yonder, silent over
  Africa.

                             (1845)

SAUL

I

Said Abner, 'At last thou art come! Ere
  I tell, ere thou speak,
Kiss my cheek, wish me well!' Then I
  wished it, and did kiss his cheek.
And he: 'Since the King, O my friend, for
  thy countenance sent,
Neither drunken nor eaten have we; nor
  until from his tent
Thou return with the joyful assurance the
  King liveth yet,   5
Shall our lip with the honey be bright, with
  the water be wet.
For out of the black mid-tent's silence, a
  space of three days,
Not a sound hath escaped to thy servants,
  of prayer nor of praise,
To betoken that Saul and the Spirit have
  ended their strife,
And that, faint in his triumph, the monarch
  sinks back upon life.

II

'Yet now my heart leaps, O beloved! God's
  child with his dew
On thy gracious gold hair, and those lilies
  still living and blue

Just broken to twine round thy harp-strings,
    as if no wild heat
Were now raging to torture the desert.'

III

Then I, as was meet,
Knelt down to the God of my fathers, and
    rose on my feet,   15
And ran o'er the sand burnt to powder.
    The tent was unlooped;
I pulled up the spear that obstructed, and
    under I stooped;
Hands and knees on the slippery grass-
    patch, all withered and gone,
That extends to the second enclosure, I
    groped my way on
Till I felt where the foldskirts fly open.
    Then once more I prayed,   20
And opened the foldskirts and entered, and
    was not afraid
But spoke, 'Here is David, thy servant!'
    And no voice replied.
At the first I saw naught but the black-
    ness; but soon I descried
A something more black than the blackness
    — the vast, the upright
Main prop which sustains the pavilion; and
    slow into sight   25
Grew a figure against it, gigantic and black-
    est of all.
Then a sunbeam, that burst through the
    tent roof, showed Saul.

IV

He stood as erect as that tent-prop, both
    arms stretched out wide
On the great cross-support in the center,
    that goes to each side;
He relaxed not a muscle, but hung there
    as, caught in his pangs   30
And waiting his change, the king serpent all
    heavily hangs,
Far away from his kind, in the pine, till de-
    liverance come
With the spring-time,— so agonized Saul,
    drear and stark, blind and dumb.

V

Then I tuned my harp,— took off the lilies
    we twine round its chords
Lest they snap 'neath the stress of the noon-
    tide — those sunbeams like swords!   35
And I first played the tune all our sheep
    know, as, one after one,
So docile they come to the pen-door till
    folding be done.
They are white and untorn by the bushes,
    for lo, they have fed

Where the long grasses stifle the water with-
    in the stream's bed;
And now one after one seeks its lodging, as
    star follows star   40
Into eve and the blue far above us,— so
    blue and so far!

VI

— Then the tune, for which quails on the
    cornland will each leave his mate
To fly after the player; then, what makes
    the crickets elate
Till for boldness they fight one another;
    and then, what has weight
To set the quick jerboa a-musing outside
    his sand-house —   45
There are none such as he for a wonder,
    half bird and half mouse!
God made all the creatures and gave them
    our love and our fear,
To give sign, we and they are his children,
    one family here.

VII

Then I played the help-tune of our reapers,
    their wine-song, when hand
Grasps at hand, eye lights eye in good
    friendship, and great hearts expand   50
And grow one in the sense of this world's
    life.— And then, the last song
When the dead man is praised on his jour-
    ney —'Bear, bear him along
With his few faults shut up like dead
    flowerets! Are balm-seeds not here
To console us? The land has none left
    such as he on the bier.
Oh, would we might keep thee, my brother!'
    — And then, the glad chaunt   55
Of the marriage,— first go the young
    maidens, next, she whom we vaunt
As the beauty, the pride of our dwelling.
    — And then, the great march
Wherein man runs to man to assist him and
    buttress an arch
Naught can break; who shall harm them,
    our friends? — Then, the chorus in-
    toned
As the Levites go up to the altar in glory
    enthroned.   60
But I stopped here: for here in the dark-
    ness Saul groaned.

VIII

And I paused, held my breath in such
    silence, and listened apart;
And the tent shook, for mighty Saul shud-
    dered: and sparkles 'gan dart

From the jewels that woke in his turban, at
  once with a start,
All its lordly male-sapphires, and rubies
  courageous at heart.   65
So the head; but the body still moved not,
  still hung there erect.
And I bent once again to my playing, pursued it unchecked,
As I sang: —

IX

'Oh, our manhood's prime vigor! No
  spirit feels waste,
Not a muscle is stopped in its playing nor
  sinew unbraced.
Oh, the wild joys of living! the leaping
  from rock up to rock,   70
The strong rending of boughs from the fir-
  tree, the cool silver shock
Of the plunge in a pool's living water, the
  hunt of the bear,
And the sultriness showing the lion is
  couched in his lair.
And the meal, the rich dates yellowed over
  with gold dust divine,
And the locust-flesh steeped in the pitcher,
  the full draft of wine,   75
And the sleep in the dried river-channel
  where bulrushes tell
That the water was wont to go warbling
  so softly and well.
How good is man's life, the mere living?
  how fit to employ
All the heart and the soul and the senses
  forever in joy!
Hast thou loved the white locks of thy
  father, whose sword thou didst guard 80
When he trusted thee forth with the armies,
  for glorious reward?
Didst thou see the thin hands of thy
  mother, held up as men sung
The low song of the nearly-departed, and
  hear her faint tongue
Joining in while it could to the witness,
  " Let one more attest
I have lived, seen God's hand through a
  lifetime, and all was for best?"   85
Then they sung through their tears in
  strong triumph, not much, but the rest.
And thy brothers, the help and the contest,
  the working whence grew
Such result as, from seething grape-bundles,
  the spirit strained true:
And the friends of thy boyhood — that boy-
  hood of wonder and hope,
Present promise and wealth of the future
  beyond the eye's scope,—   90

Till lo, thou art grown to a monarch; a
  people is thine:
And all gifts, which the world offers singly,
  on one head combine!
On one head, all the beauty and strength,
  love and rage (like the throe
That, a-work in the rock, helps its labor and
  lets the gold go),
High ambition and deeds which surpass it,
  fame crowning them,— all   95
Brought to blaze on the head of one creature — King Saul.'

X

And lo, with that leap of my spirit,— heart,
  hand, harp and voice,
Each lifting Saul's name out of sorrow,
  each bidding rejoice
Saul's fame in the light it was made for —
  as when, dare I say,
The Lord's army, in rapture of service,
  strains through its array,   100
And upsoareth the cherubim-chariot —
  'Saul!' cried I, and stopped,
And waited the thing that should follow.
  Then Saul, who hung propped
By the tent's cross-support in the center,
  was struck by his name.
Have ye seen when Spring's arrowy sum-
  mons goes right to the aim,
And some mountain, the last to withstand
  her, that held (he alone,   105
While the vale laughed in freedom and
  flowers) on a broad bust of stone
A year's snow bound about for a breast-
  plate,— leaves grasp of the sheet?
Fold on fold all at once it crowds thunder-
  ously down to his feet,
And there fronts you, stark, black, but
  alive yet, your mountain of old,
With his rents, the successive bequeathings
  of ages untold —   110
Yea, each harm got in fighting your battles,
  each furrow and scar
Of his head thrust 'twixt you and the
  tempest — all hail, there they are!
— Now again to be softened with verdure,
  again hold the nest
Of the dove, tempt the goat and its young
  to the green on his crest
For their food in the ardors of summer.
  One long shudder thrilled   115
All the tent till the very air tingled, then
  sank and was stilled
At the King's self left standing before me,
  released and aware.
What was gone, what remained? All to
  traverse 'twixt hope and despair;

Death was past, life not come: so he
waited. Awhile his right hand
Held the brow, helped the eyes left too
vacant, forthwith to remand 120
To their place what new objects should
enter: 't was Saul as before.
I looked up, and dared gaze at those eyes,
nor was hurt any more
Than by slow pallid sunsets in autumn, ye
watch from the shore,
At their sad level gaze o'er the ocean — a
sun's slow decline
Over hills which, resolved in stern silence,
o'erlap and entwine 125
Base with base to knit strength more intensely; so, arm folded arm
O'er the chest whose slow heavings subsided.

XI

What spell or what charm
(For, awhile there was trouble within me),
what next should I urge
To sustain him where song had restored
him? — Song filled to the verge
His cup with the wine of this life, pressing all that it yields 130
Of mere fruitage, the strength and the
beauty: beyond, on what fields,
Glean a vintage more potent and perfect to
brighten the eye,
And bring blood to the lip, and commend
them the cup they put by?
He saith, ' It is good;' still he drinks not:
he lets me praise life,
Gives assent, yet would die for his own
part. 135

XII

Then fancies grew rife
Which had come long ago on the pasture,
when round me the sheep
Fed in silence — above, the one eagle
wheeled slow as in sleep;
And I lay in my hollow and mused on the
world that might lie
'Neath his ken, though I saw but the strip
'twixt the hill and the sky:
And I laughed — ' Since my days are or-
dained to be passed with my flocks, 140
Let me people at least, with my fancies, the
plains and the rocks,
Dream the life I am never to mix with, and
image the show
Of mankind as they live in those fashions
I hardly shall know!
Schemes of life, its best rules and right
uses, the courage that gains,

And the prudence that keeps what men
strive for!' And now these old trains
Of vague thought came again; I grew
surer; so, once more the string 146
Of my harp made response to my spirit, as
thus —

XIII

'Yea, my King,'
I began — ' thou dost well in rejecting mere
comforts that spring
From the mere mortal life held in common
by man and by brute:
In our flesh grows the branch of this life,
In our soul it bears fruit. 150
Thou hast marked the slow rise of the tree,
— how its stem trembled first
Till it passed the kid's lip, the stag's antler;
then safely outburst
The fan-branches all round; and thou mind-
est when these too, in turn
Broke a-bloom and the palm-tree seemed
perfect: yet more was to learn,
E'en the good that comes in with the palm-
fruit. Our dates shall we slight, 155
When their juice brings a cure for all sor-
row? or care for the plight
Of the palm's self whose slow growth produced them? Not so! stem and branch
Shall decay, nor be known in their place,
while the palm-wine shall stanch
Every wound of man's spirit in winter. I
pour thee such wine.
Leave the flesh to the fate it was fit for!
the spirit be thine! 160
By the spirit, when age shall o'ercome thee,
thou still shalt enjoy
More indeed, than at first when inconscious,
the life of a boy.
Crush that life, and behold its wine running! Each deed thou hast done
Dies, revives, goes to work in the world;
until e'en as the sun
Looking down on the earth, though clouds
spoil him, though tempests efface, 165
Can find nothing his own deed produced
not, must everywhere trace
The results of his past summer-prime, —
so, each ray of thy will,
Every flash of thy passion and prowess,
long over, shall thrill
Thy whole people, the countless, with ardor,
till they too give forth
A like cheer to their sons; who in turn, fill
the South and the North 170
With the radiance thy deed was the germ of.
Carouse in the past!
But the license of age has its limit; thou
diest at last:

As the lion when age dims his eyeball,
  the rose at her height,
So with man — so his power and his beauty
  for ever take flight.
No! Again a long draft of my soul-wine!
  Look forth o'er the years!   175
Thou hast done now with eyes for the ac-
  tual; begin with the seer's!
Is Saul dead? In the depth of the vale
  make his tomb — bid arise
A gray mountain of marble heaped four-
  square, till, built to the skies,
Let it mark where the great First King
  slumbers: whose fame would ye know?
Up above see the rock's naked face, where
  the record shall go   180
In great characters cut by the scribe, — Such
  was Saul, so he did;
With the sages directing the work, by the
  populace chid,—
For not half, they'll affirm, is comprised
  there! Which fault to amend,
In the grove with his kind grows the cedar,
  whereon they shall spend
(See, in tablets 't is level before them) their
  praise, and record   185
With the gold of the graver, Saul's story,—
  the statesman's great word
Side by side with the poet's sweet comment.
  The river's a-wave
With smooth paper-reeds grazing each other
  when prophet-winds rave:
So the pen gives unborn generations their
  due and their part
In thy being! Then, first of the mighty,
  thank God that thou art!'   190

XIV

And behold while I sang . . . but O
  thou who didst grant me that day,
And before it not seldom hast granted thy
  help to essay,
Carry on and complete an adventure,— my
  shield and my sword
In that act where my soul was thy servant,
  thy word was my word,—
Still be with me, who then at the summit
  of human endeavor   195
And scaling the highest, man's thought could,
  gazed hopeless as ever
On the new stretch of heaven above me —
  till, mighty to save,
Just one lift of thy hand cleared that distance — God's throne from man's grave!
Let me tell out my tale to its ending — my
  voice to my heart
Which can scarce dare believe in what marvels last night I took part,   200

As this morning I gather the fragments,
  alone with my sheep,
And still fear lest the terrible glory evanish
  like sleep!
For I wake in the gray dewy covert, while
  Hebron upheaves
The dawn struggling with night on his shoul-
  der, and Kidron retrieves
Slow the damage of yesterday's sunshine.   205

XV

        I say then,— my song
While I sang thus, assuring the monarch,
  and, ever more strong,
Made a proffer of good to console him —
  he slowly resumed
His old motions and habitudes kingly. The
  right hand replumed
His black locks to their wonted composure,
  adjusted the swathes
Of his turban, and see — the huge sweat
  that his countenance bathes,   210
He wipes off with the robe; and he girds
  now his loins as of yore,
And feels slow for the armlets of price,
  with the clasp set before.
He is Saul, ye remember in glory,— ere
  error had bent
The broad brow from the daily communion;
  and still, though much spent
Be the life and the bearing that front you,
  the same, God did choose,   215
To receive what a man may waste, desecrate,
  never quite lose.
So sank he along by the tent-prop, till,
  stayed by the pile
Of his armor and war-cloak and garments,
  he leaned there awhile,
And sat out my singing,— one arm round
  the tent-prop, to raise
His bent head, and the other hung slack —
  till I touched on the praise   220
I foresaw from all men in all time, to the
  man patient there;
And thus ended, the harp falling forward.
  Then first I was 'ware
That he sat, as I say, with my head just
  above his vast knees
Which were thrust out on each side around
  me, like oak roots which please
To encircle a lamb when it slumbers. I
  looked up to know   225
If the best I could do had brought solace:
  he spoke not, but slow
Lifted up the hand slack at his side, till he
  laid it with care
Soft and grave, but in mild settled will, on
  my brow: through my hair

The large fingers were pushed, and he bent
    back my head, with kind power —
All my face back, intent to peruse it, as men
    do a flower.   230
Thus held he me there with his great eyes
    that scrutinized mine —
And oh, all my heart how it loved him! but
    where was the sign?
I yearned — 'Could I help thee, my father,
    inventing a bliss,
I would add, to that life of the past, both
    the future and this;
I would give thee new life altogether, as
    good, ages hence,   235
As this moment,— had love but the warrant,
    love's heart to dispense!'

XVI

Then the truth came upon me. No harp
    more — no song more! outbroke —

XVII

'I have gone the whole round of creation:
    I saw and I spoke:
I, a work of God's hand for that purpose,
    received in my brain
And pronounced on the rest of his handwork
    — returned him again   240
His creation's approval or censure: I spoke
    as I saw,
I report, as a man may of God's work —
    all's love, yet all's law.
Now I lay down the judgeship he lent me.
    Each faculty tasked
To perceive him has gained an abyss, where
    a dewdrop was asked.
Have I knowledge? confounded it shrivels
    at Wisdom laid bare.   245
Have I forethought? how purblind, how
    blank, to the Infinite Care!
Do I task any faculty highest, to image suc-
    cess?
I but open my eyes,— and perfection, no
    more and no less,
In the kind I imagined, full-fronts me, and
    God is seen God
In the star, in the stone, in the flesh, in the
    soul and the clod.   250
And thus looking within and around me,
    I ever renew
(With that stoop of the soul which in bend-
    ing upraises it too)
The submission of man's nothing-perfect to
    God's all-complete,
As by each new obeisance in spirit, I climb
    to his feet.
Yet with all this abounding experience, this
    deity known,   255

I shall dare to discover some province, some
    gift of my own.
There's a faculty pleasant to exercise, hard
    to hoodwink,
I am fain to keep still in abeyance (I laugh
    as I think)
Lest, insisting to claim and parade in it, wot
    ye, I worst
E'en the Giver in one gift.— Behold, I could
    love if I durst!   260
But I sink the pretension as fearing a man
    may o'ertake
God's own speed in the one way of love:
    I abstain for love's sake.
— What, my soul? see thus far and no
    farther? when doors great and small,
Nine-and-ninety flew ope at our touch,
    should the hundredth appal?
In the least things have faith, yet distrust
    in the greatest of all?   265
Do I find love so full in my nature, God's
    ultimate gift,
That I doubt his own love can compete with
    it? Here, the parts shift?
Here, the creature surpass the Creator,— the
    end, what Began?
Would I fain in my impotent yearning do
    all for this man,
And dare doubt he alone shall not help him,
    who yet alone can?   270
Would it ever have entered my mind, the
    bare will, much less power,
To bestow on this Saul what I sang of, the
    marvelous dower
Of the life he was gifted and filled with? to
    make such a soul,
Such a body, and then such an earth for in-
    sphering the whole?
And doth it not enter my mind (as my warm
    tears attest),   275
These good things being given, to go on, and
    give one more, the best?
Ay, to save and redeem and restore him,
    maintain at the height
This perfection,— succeed with life's day-
    spring, death's minute of night?
Interpose at the difficult minute, snatch Saul
    the mistake,
Saul the failure, the ruin he seems now,—
    and bid him awake   280
From the dream, the probation, the prelude,
    to find himself set
Clear and safe in new light and new life,—
    a new harmony yet
To be run and continued, and ended — who
    knows?— or endure!
The man taught enough by life's dream, of
    the rest to make sure;

By the pain-throb, triumphantly winning in-
tensified bliss, 285
And the next world's reward and repose, by
the struggles in this.

XVIII

'I believe it! 'T is thou, God, that givest,
't is I who receive:
In the first is the last, in thy will is my
power to believe.
All 's one gift: thou canst grant it moreover,
as prompt to my prayer
As I breathe out this breath, as I open these
arms to the air. 290
From thy will, stream the worlds, life and
nature, thy dread Sabaoth:
I will?—the mere atoms despise me! Why
am I not loth
To look that, even that in the face too?
Why is it I dare
Think but lightly of such impuissance?
What stops my despair?
This;—'t is not what man Does which ex-
alts him, but what man Would do! 295
See the King—I would help him but can-
not, the wishes fall through.
Could I wrestle to raise him from sorrow,
grow poor to enrich,
To fill up his life, starve my own out, I
would—knowing which,
I know that my service is perfect. Oh,
speak through me now!
Would I suffer for him that I love? So
wouldst thou—so wilt thou! 300
So shall crown thee the topmost, ineffablest,
uttermost crown—
And thy love fill infinitude wholly, nor leave
up nor down
One spot for the creature to stand in! It
is by no breath,
Turn of eye, wave of hand, that salvation
joins issue with death!
As thy Love is discovered almighty, al-
mighty be proved 305
Thy power, that exists with and for it, of
being Beloved!
He who did most, shall bear most; the
strongest shall stand the most weak.
'T is the weakness in strength, that I cry
for! my flesh, that I seek
In the Godhead! I seek and I find it. O
Saul, it shall be
A Face like my face that receives thee; a
Man like to me, 310
Thou shalt love and be loved by, for ever:
a Hand like this hand
Shall throw open the gates of new life to
thee! See the Christ stand!'

XIX

I know not too well how I found my way
home in the night.
There were witnesses, cohorts about me, to
left and to right,
Angels, powers, the unuttered, unseen, the
alive, the aware: 315
I repressed, I got through them as hardly,
as strugglingly there,
As a runner beset by the populace famished
for news—
Life or death. The whole earth was awakened, hell loosed with her crews;
And the stars of night beat with emotion,
and tingled and shot
Out in fire the strong pain of pent knowledge: but I fainted not, 320
For the hand still impelled me at once and
supported, suppressed
All the tumult, and quenched it with quiet,
and holy behest,
Till the rapture was shut in itself, and the
earth sank to rest.
Anon at the dawn, all that trouble had
withered from earth—
Not so much, but I saw it die out in the
day's tender birth; 325
In the gathered intensity brought to the
gray of the hills;
In the shuddering forests' held breath; in
the sudden wind-thrills;
In the startled wild beasts that bore off,
each with eye sidling still,
Though averted with wonder and dread; in
the birds stiff and chill
That rose heavily as I approached them,
made stupid with awe: 330
E'en the serpent that slid away silent,—he
felt the new law.
The same stared in the white humid faces
upturned by the flowers;
The same worked in the heart of the cedar
and moved the vine-bowers:
And the little brooks witnessing murmured,
persistent and low,
With their obstinate, all but hushed voices
—'E'en so, it is so!' 335

(1845–1855)

LOVE AMONG THE RUINS

I

Where the quiet-colored end of evening
smiles
Miles and miles
On the solitary pastures where our sheep
Half-asleep

Tinkle homeward through the twilight, stray
   or stop   5
  As they crop—
Was the site once of a city great and gay
  (So they say),
Of our country's very capital, its prince
  Ages since   10
Held his court in, gathered councils, wield-
   ing far
  Peace or war.

II

Now,—the country does not even boast a
   tree,
  As you see,
To distinguish slopes of verdure, certain
   rills   15
  From the hills
Intersect and give a name to (else they run
  Into one),
Where the domed and daring palace shot
   its spires
  Up like fires   20
O'er the hundred-gated circuit of a wall
  Bounding all,
Made of marble, men might march on nor
   be pressed,
  Twelve abreast.

III

And such plenty and perfection, see, of
   grass   25
  Never was!
Such a carpet as, this summer-time, o'er-
   spreads
  And embeds
Every vestige of the city, guessed alone,
  Stock or stone—   30
Where a multitude of men breathed joy
   and woe
  Long ago;
Lust of glory pricked their hearts up, dread
   of shame
  Struck them tame;
And that glory and that shame alike, the
   gold   35
  Bought and sold.

IV

Now,—the single little turret that remains
  On the plains,
By the caper overrooted, by the gourd
  Overscored,   40
While the patching houseleek's head of blos-
   som winks
  Through the chinks—
Marks the basement whence a tower in an-
   cient time
  Sprang sublime,

And a burning ring, all round, the chariots
   traced   45
  As they raced,
And the monarch and his minions and his
   dames
  Viewed the games.

V

And I know—while thus the quiet-colored
   eve
  Smiles to leave   50
To their folding, all our many tinkling fleece
  In such peace,
And the slopes and rills in undistinguished
   gray
  Melt away—
That a girl with eager eyes and yellow hair
  Waits me there   56
In the turret whence the charioteers caught
   soul
  For the goal,
When the king looked, where she looks now,
   breathless, dumb
  Till I come.   60

VI

But he looked upon the city, every side,
  Far and wide,
All the mountains topped with temples, all
   the glades'
  Colonnades,
All the causeys, bridges, aqueducts,—and
   then,   65
  All the men!
When I do come, she will speak not, she will
   stand,
  Either hand
On my shoulder, give her eyes the first em-
   brace
  Of my face,   70
Ere we rush, ere we extinguish sight and
   speech
  Each on each.

VII

In one year they sent a million fighters forth
  South and North,
And they built their gods a brazen pillar
   high   75
  As the sky,
Yet reserved a thousand chariots in full
   force—
  Gold, of course.
Oh heart! oh blood that freezes, blood that
   burns!
  Earth's returns   80

For whole centuries of folly, noise and sin!
  Shut them in,
With their triumphs and their glories and
    the rest!
Love is best.

(1855)

A WOMAN'S LAST WORD

I

Let's contend no more, Love,
  Strive nor weep:
All be as before, Love,
  — Only sleep!

II

What so wild as words are?   5
  I and thou
In debate, as birds are,
  Hawk on bough!

III

See the creature stalking
  While we speak!   10
Hush and hide the talking,
  Cheek on cheek.

IV

What so false as truth is,
  False to thee?
Where the serpent's tooth is   15
  Shun the tree —

V

Where the apple reddens
  Never pry —
Lest we lose our Edens,
  Eve and I.   20

VI

Be a god and hold me
  With a charm!
Be a man and fold me
  With thine arm!

VII

Teach me, only teach, Love!   25
  As I ought
I will speak thy speech, Love,
  Think thy thought —

VIII

Meet, if thou require it,
  Both demands,   30
Laying flesh and spirit
  In thy hands.

IX

That shall be to-morrow,
  Not to-night:
I must bury sorrow   35
  Out of sight:

X

— Must a little weep, Love,
  (Foolish me!),
And so fall asleep, Love
  Loved by thee.   40

(1855)

A TOCCATA OF GALUPPI'S

I

Oh, Galuppi, Baldassare, this is very sad to
  find!
I can hardly misconceive you; it would
  prove me deaf and blind;
But although I take your meaning, 't is with
  such a heavy mind!

II

Here you come with your old music, and
  here's all the good it brings.
What, they lived once thus at Venice where
  the merchants were. the kings,   5
Where St. Mark's is, where the Doges used
  to wed the sea with rings?

III

Ay, because the sea's the street there; and
  't is arched by . . . what you call
. . . Shylock's bridge with houses on it,
  where they kept the carnival:
I was never out of England — it's as if I
  saw it all.

IV

Did young people take their pleasure when
  the sea was warm in May?   10
Balls and masks begun at midnight, burning
  ever to mid-day,
When they made up fresh adventures for
  the morrow, do you say?

V

Was a lady such a lady, cheeks so round
  and lips so red,—
On her neck the small face buoyant, like a
  bell-flower on its bed,
O'er the breast's superb abundance where
  a man might base his head?   15

VI

Well, and it was graceful of them — they 'd
　　break talk off and afford
— She, to bite her mask's black velvet — he,
　　to finger on his sword,
While you sat and played Toccatas, stately
　　at the clavichord?

VII

What? Those lesser thirds so plaintive,
　　sixths diminished, sigh on sigh,
Told them something? Those suspensions,
　　those solutions —'Must we die?'　　20
Those commiserating sevenths —'Life might
　　last! we can but try!'

VIII

'Were you happy?'—'Yes.'—'And are you
　　still as happy?'—'Yes. And you?'
—'Then, more kisses!'—'Did _I_ stop them,
　　when a million seemed so few?'
Hark, the dominant's persistence till it must
　　be answered to!

IX

So, an octave struck the answer. Oh, they
　　praised you, I dare say!　　25
'Brave Galuppi! that was music! good alike
　　at grave and gay!
I can always leave off talking when I hear
　　a master play!'·

X

Then they left you for their pleasure: till
　　in due time, one by one,
Some with lives that came to nothing, some
　　with deeds as well undone,
Death stepped tacitly and took them where
　　they never see the sun.　　30

XI

But when I sit down to reason, think to take
　　my stand nor swerve,
While I triumph o'er a secret wrung from
　　nature's close reserve,
In you come with your cold music till I
　　creep through every nerve.

XII

Yes, you, like a ghostly cricket, creaking
　　where a house was burned:
'Dust and ashes, dead and done with,
　　Venice spent what Venice earned.　　35
The soul, doubtless, is immortal — where a
　　soul can be discerned

XIII

'Yours for instance: you know physics,
　　something of geology,
Mathematics are your pastime; souls shall
　　rise in their degree;
Butterflies may dread extinction,— you 'll not
　　die, it cannot be!

XIV

'As for Venice and her people, merely born
　　to bloom and drop,　　40
Here on earth they bore their fruitage, mirth
　　and folly were the crop:
What of soul was left, I wonder, when
　　the kissing had to stop?

XV

'Dust and ashes!' So you creak it, and I
　　want the heart to scold.
Dear dead women, with such hair, too —
　　what's become of all the gold
Used to hang and brush their bosoms? I
　　feel chilly and grown old.　　45

(1855)

MY STAR

All that I know
　　Of a certain star
Is, it can throw
　　(Like the angled spar)
Now a dart of red,　　5
　　Now a dart of blue;
Till my friends have said
　　They would fain see, too,
My star that dartles the red and the blue!
Then it stops like a bird; like a flower,
　　hangs furled:　　10
　　They must solace themselves with the
　　　　Saturn above it.
What matter to me if their star is a world?
　　Mine has opened its soul to me; therefore
　　　　I love it.

(1855)

THE LAST RIDE TOGETHER

I

I said — Then, dearest, since 't is so,
Since now at length my fate I know,
Since nothing all my love avails,
Since all, my life seemed meant for, fails,
Since this was written and needs must
　　be —　　5

My whole heart rises up to bless
Your name in pride and thankfulness!
Take back the hope you gave,— I claim
Only a memory of the same,
—And this beside, if you will not blame, 10
  Your leave for one more last ride with
  me.

II

My mistress bent that brow of hers;
Those deep dark eyes where pride demurs
When pity would be softening through,
Fixed me a breathing-while or two 15
  With life or death in the balance: right!
The blood replenished me again;
My last thought was at least not vain:
I and my mistress, side by side
Shall be together, breathe and ride, 20
So, one day more am I deified.
  Who knows but the world may end to-
  night?

III

Hush! if you saw some western cloud
All billowy-bosomed, over-bowed
By many benedictions — sun's 25
And moon's and evening-star's at once —
  And so, you, looking and loving best,
Conscious grew, your passion drew
Cloud, sunset, moonrise, star-shine too,
Down on you, near and yet more near, 30
Till flesh must fade for heaven was here! —
Thus leant she and lingered — joy and fear!
  Thus lay she a moment on my breast.

IV

Then we began to ride. My soul
Smoothed itself out, a long-cramped scroll 35
Freshening and fluttering in the wind.
Past hopes already lay behind.
  What need to strive with a life awry?
Had I said that, had I done this,
So might I gain, so might I miss. 40
Might she have loved me? just as well
She might have hated, who can tell!
Where had I been now if the worst befell?
  And here we are riding, she and I.

V

Fail I alone, in words and deeds? 45
Why, all men strive, and who succeeds?
We rode; it seemed my spirit flew,
Saw other regions, cities new,
  As the world rushed by on either side.
I thought,— All labor, yet no less 50
Bear up beneath their unsuccess.
Look at the end of work, contrast
The petty done, the undone vast,
This present of theirs with the hopeful past!
  I hoped she would love me; here we ride.

VI

What hand and brain went ever paired? 56
What heart alike conceived and dared?
What act proved all its thought had been?
What will but felt the fleshly screen?
  We ride and I see her bosom heave. 60
There's many a crown for who can reach.
Ten lines, a statesman's life in each!
The flag stuck on a heap of bones,
A soldier's doing! what atones?
They scratch his name on the Abbey-
  stones. 65
  My riding is better, by their leave.

VII

What does it all mean, poet? Well,
Your brains beat into rhythm, you tell
What we felt only; you expressed
You hold things beautiful the best, 70
  And pace them in rhyme so, side by side.
'T is something, nay 't is much: but then,
Have you yourself what's best for men?
Are you — poor, sick, old ere your time —
Nearer one whit your own sublime 75
Than we who never have turned a rhyme?
  Sing, riding's a joy! For me, I ride.

VIII

And you, great sculptor — so, you gave
A score of years to Art, her slave,
And that's your Venus, whence we turn 80
To yonder girl that fords the burn!
  You acquiesce, and shall I repine?
What, man of music, you grown gray
With notes and nothing else to say,
Is this your sole praise from a friend, 85
'Greatly his opera's strains intend,
But in music we know how fashions end!
  I gave my youth; but we ride, in fine.

IX

Who knows what's fit for us? Had fate
Proposed bliss here should sublimate 90
My being — had I signed the bond —
Still one must lead some life beyond,
  Have a bliss to die with, dim-descried.
This foot once planted on the goal,
This glory-garland round my soul, 95
Could I descry such? Try and test!
I sink back shuddering from the quest.
Earth being so good, would heaven seem
  best?
  Now, heaven and she are beyond this
  ride.

X

And yet — she has not spoke so long! 100
What if heaven be that, fair and strong

At life's best, with our eyes upturned
Whither life's flower is first discerned,
  We, fixed so, ever should so abide?
What if we still ride on, we two,   105
With life for ever old yet new,
Changed not in kind but in degree,
The instant made eternity,—
And heaven just prove that I and she
  Ride, ride together, for ever ride?   110
                                   (1855)

MEMORABILIA

I

Ah, did you once see Shelley plain,
  And did he stop and speak to you,
And did you speak to him again?
  How strange it seems and new!

II

But you were living before that,   5
  And also you are living after;
And the memory I started at —
  My starting moves your laughter!

III

I crossed a moor, with a name of its own
  And a certain use in the world no doubt,
Yet a hand's-breadth of it shines alone   11
  'Mid the blank miles round about:

IV

For there I picked up on the heather
  And there I put inside my breast
A moulted feather, an eagle-feather!   15
  Well, I forget the rest.
                                   (1855)

'DE GUSTIBUS—'

Your ghost will walk, you lover of trees,
  (If our loves remain)
  In an English lane,
By a cornfield-side a-flutter with poppies.
Hark, those two in the hazel coppice —   5
A boy and a girl, if the good fates please,
  Making love, say,—
  The happier they!
Draw yourself up from the light of the
    moon,
And let them pass, as they will too soon, 10
  With the beanflowers' boon,
  And the blackbird's tune,
And May, and June!

What I love best in all the world
Is a castle, precipice-encurled,   15
In a gash of the wind-grieved Apennine.
Or look for me, old fellow of mine,
(If I get my head from out the mouth
O' the grave, and loose my spirit's bands,
And come again to the land of lands)—   20
In a sea-side house to the farther South,
Where the baked cicala dies of drouth,
And one sharp tree—'t is a cypress—
    stands,
By the many hundred years red-rusted,
Rough iron-spiked, ripe fruit-o'ercrusted,
My sentinel to guard the sands   26
To the water's edge. For, what expands
Before the house, but the great opaque
Blue breadth of sea without a break?
While, in the house, forever crumbles   30
Some fragment of the frescoed walls,
From blisters where a scorpion sprawls.
A girl bare-footed brings, and tumbles
Down on the pavement, green-flesh melons,
And says there 's news to-day — the king   35
Was shot at, touched in the liver-wing,
Goes with his Bourbon arm in a sling:
— She hopes they have not caught the felons.
Italy, my Italy!
Queen Mary's saying serves for me —   40
  (When fortune's malice
  Lost her Calais)—
Open my heart and you will see
Graved inside of it, 'Italy.'
Such lovers old are I and she: 45
So it always was, so shall ever be!
                                   (1855)

ANDREA DEL SARTO

CALLED 'THE FAULTLESS PAINTER'

But do not let us quarrel any more,
No, my Lucrezia; bear with me for once:
Sit down and all shall happen as you wish.
You turn your face, but does it bring your
    heart?
I 'll work then for your friend's friend,
    never fear,   5
Treat his own subject after his own way,
Fix his own time, accept too, his own price,
And shut the money into this small hand
When next it takes mine. Will it? ten-
    derly?
Oh, I 'll content him,— but to-morrow, Love!
I often am much wearier than you think,   11
This evening more than usual, and it seems
As if — forgive now — should you let me
    sit

Here by the window with your hand in
mine
And look a half-hour forth on Fiesolé, 15
Both of one mind, as married people use,
Quietly, quietly the evening through,
I might get up to-morrow to my work
Cheerful and fresh as ever. Let us try.
To-morrow, how you shall be glad for this!
Your soft hand is a woman of itself, 21
And mine the man's bared breast she curls
inside.
Don't count the time lost, neither; you must
serve
For each of the five pictures we require:
It saves a model. So! keep looking so — 25
My serpentining beauty, rounds on rounds!
- -How could you ever prick those perfect
ears,
Even to put the pearl there! oh, so sweet —
My face, my moon, my everybody's moon,
Which everybody looks on and calls his, 30
And, I suppose, is looked on by in turn,
While she looks — no one's: very dear, no
less.
You smile? why, there's my picture ready
made,
There's what we painters call our harmony!
A common grayness silvers everything,— 35
All in a twilight, you and I alike
— You, at the point of your first pride in
me
(That's gone you know),—but I, at every
point;
My youth, my hope, my art, being all toned
down
To yonder sober pleasant Fiesolé. 40
There's the bell clinking from the chapel-
top;
That length of convent-wall across the way
Holds the trees safer, huddled more inside;
The last monk leaves the garden; days de-
crease,
And autumn grows, autumn in everything. 45
Eh? the whole seems to fall into a shape
As if I saw alike my work and self
And all that I was born to be and do,
A twilight-piece. Love, we are in God's
hand.
How strange now looks the life he makes
us lead; 50
So free we seem, so fettered fast we are!
I feel he laid the fetter: let it lie!
This chamber for example — turn your
head —
All that's behind us! You don't under-
stand
Nor care to understand about my art, 55
But you can hear at least when people
speak:

And that cartoon, the second from the door
— It is the thing, Love! so such thing should
be —
Behold Madonna! — I am bold to say.
I can do with my pencil what I know, 60
What I see, what at bottom of my heart
I wish for, if I ever wish so deep —
Do easily, too — when I say, perfectly,
I do not boast, perhaps: yourself are judge,
Who listened to the Legate's talk last week,
And just as much they used to say in
France. 66
At any rate, 'tis easy, all of it!
No sketches first, no studies, that's long
past:
I do what many dream of all their lives,
—Dream? strive to do, and agonize to do, 70
And fail in doing. I could count twenty
such
On twice your fingers, and not leave this
town,
Who strive — you don't know how the others
strive
To paint a little thing like that you smeared
Carelessly passing with your robes afloat,—
Yet do much less, so much less, Someone
says, 76
(I know his name, no matter)— so much
less!
Well, less is more, Lucrezia: I am judged.
There burns a truer light of God in them,
In their vexed beating stuffed and stopped-
up brain,
Heart, or whate'er else, than goes on to 80
prompt
This low-pulsed forthright craftsman's hand
of mine.
Their works drop groundward, but them-
selves, I know,
Reach many a time a heaven that's shut to
me,
Enter and take their place there sure
enough, 85
Though they come back and cannot tell the
world.
My works are nearer heaven, but I sit here.
The sudden blood of these men! at a word —
Praise them, it boils, or blame them, it boils
too.
I, painting from myself, and to myself, 90
Know what I do, am unmoved by men's
blame
Or their praise either. Somebody remarks
Morello's outline there is wrongly traced,
His hue mistaken; what of that? or else,
Rightly traced and well ordered; what of
that? 95
Speak as they please, what does the mountain
care?

Ah, but a man's reach should exceed his
    grasp,
Or what's a heaven for? All is silver-
    gray
Placid and perfect with my art: the worse!
I know both what I want and what might
    gain,   100
And yet how profitless to know, to sigh
'Had I been two, another and myself,
Our head would have o'erlooked the world!'
    No doubt.
Yonder's a work now, of that famous youth
The Urbinate who died five years ago.   105
('T is copied, George Vasari sent it me.)
Well, I can fancy how he did it all,
Pouring his soul, with kings and popes to
    see,
Reaching, that heaven might so replenish
    him,
Above and through his art — for it gives
    way;   110
That arm is wrongly put — and there
    again —
A fault to pardon in the drawing's lines,
Its body, so to speak: its soul is right,
He means right — that, a child may under-
    stand.
Still, what an arm! and I could alter it: 115
But all the play, the insight and the
    stretch —
Out of me, out of me! And wherefore out?
Had you enjoined them on me, given me
    soul,
We might have risen to Rafael, I and you!
Nay, Love, you did give all I asked, I
    think —   120
More than I merit, yes, by many times.
But had you — oh, with the same perfect
    brow,
And perfect eyes, and more than perfect
    mouth,
And the low voice my soul hears, as a
    bird
The fowler's pipe, and follows to the snare —
Had you, with these the same, but brought a
    mind!   126
Some women do so. Had the mouth there
    urged
'God and the glory! never care for gain.
The present by the future, what is that?
Live for fame, side by side with Agnolo! 130
Rafael is waiting: up to God, all three!'
I might have done it for you. So it seems:
Perhaps not. All is as God overrules.
Beside, incentives come from the soul's
    self;
The rest avail not. Why do I need you?
What wife had Rafael, or has Agnolo? 136
In this world, who can do a thing, will not;

And who would do it, cannot, I perceive:
Yet the will's somewhat — somewhat, too,
    the power —
And thus we half-men struggle. At the
    end,   140
God, I conclude, compensates, punishes.
'T is safer for me, if the award be strict,
That I am something underrated here,
Poor this long while, despised, to speak the
    truth.
I dared not, do you know, leave home all
    day,   145
For fear of chancing on the Paris lords.
The best is when they pass and look aside;
But they speak sometimes; I must bear it
    all.
Well may they speak! That Francis, that
    first time,
And that long festal year at Fontainebleau!
I surely then could sometimes leave the
    ground,   151
Put on the glory, Rafael's daily wear,
In that humane great monarch's golden
    look,—
One finger in his beard or twisted curl
Over his mouth's good mark that made the
    smile,   155
One arm about my shoulder, round my neck,
The jingle of his gold chain in my ear,
I painting proudly with his breath on me,
All his court round him, seeing with his
    eyes,
Such frank French eyes, and such a fire of
    souls   160
Profuse, my hand kept plying by those
    hearts,—
And, best of all, this, this, this face be-
    yond,
This in the background, waiting on my work,
To crown the issue with a last reward! 164
A good time, was it not, my kingly days?
And had you not grown restless . . . but
    I know —
'T is done and past; 't was right, my in-
    stinct said;
Too live the life grew, golden and not gray,
And I'm the weak-eyed bat no sun should
    tempt
Out of his grange whose four walls make
    his world.   170
How could it end in any other way?
You called me, and I came home to your
    heart.
The triumph was — to reach and stay there;
    since
I reached it ere the triumph, what is lost?
Let my hands frame your face in your
    hair's gold,   175
You beautiful Lucrezia that are mine!

'Rafael did this, Andrea painted that;
The Roman's is the better when you pray,
But still the other's Virgin was his wife'—
Men will excuse me. I am glad to judge
Both pictures in your presence; clearer
grows   181
My better fortune, I resolve to think.
For, do you know, Lucrezia, as God lives,
Said one day Agnolo, his very self,
To Rafael . . . I have known it all
these years . . .   185
(When the young man was flaming out his
thoughts
Upon a palace-wall for Rome to see,
Too lifted up in heart because of it)
'Friend, there's a certain sorry little scrub
Goes up and down our Florence, none cares
how,   190
Who, were he set to plan and execute
As you are, pricked on by your popes and
kings,
Would bring the sweat into that brow of
yours!'
To Rafael's!—And indeed the arm is
wrong.
I hardly dare . . . yet, only you to see,
Give the chalk here—quick, thus the line
should go!   196
Ay, but the soul! he's Rafael! rub it out!
Still, all I care for, if he spoke the truth
(What he? why, who but Michel Agnolo?
Do you forget already words like those?),
If really there was such a chance, so lost,—
Is, whether you're—not grateful—but
more pleased.   202
Well, let me think so. And you smile in-
deed!
This hour has been an hour! Another
smile?
If you would sit thus by me every night 205
I should work better, do you comprehend?
I mean that I should earn more, give you
more.
See, it is settled dusk now; there's a star;
Morello's gone, the watch-lights show the
wall,
The cue-owls speak the name we call them
by.   210
Come from the window, Love,—come in,
at last,
Inside the melancholy little house
We built to be so gay with. God is just.
King Francis may forgive me; oft at nights,
When I look up from painting, eyes tired
out,   215
The walls become illumined, brick from
brick
Distinct, instead of mortar, fierce bright
gold,

That gold of his I did cement them with!
Let us but love each other. Must you go?
That Cousin here again? he waits outside?
Must see you—you, and not with me?
Those loans?   221
More gaming debts to pay? you smiled for
that?
Well, let smiles buy me! have you more to
spend?
While hand and eye and something of a
heart
Are left me, work's my ware, and what's
it worth?   225
I'll pay my fancy. Only let me sit
The gray remainder of the evening out,
Idle, you call it, and muse perfectly
How I could paint, were I but back in
France,
One picture, just one more—the Virgin's
face,   230
Not yours this time! I want you at my
side
To hear them—that is, Michel Agnolo—
Judge all I do and tell you of its worth.
Will you? To-morrow, satisfy your friend.
I take the subjects for his corridor,   235
Finish the portrait out of hand—there,
there,
And throw him in another thing or two
If he demurs; the whole should prove
enough
To pay for this same Cousin's freak. Be-
side,
What's better and what's all I care about,
Get you the thirteen scudi for the ruff!   241
Love, does that please you? Ah, but what
does he,
The Cousin! what does he to please you
more?

I am grown peaceful as old age to-night.
I regret little, I would change still less.   245
Since there my past life lies, why alter it?
The very wrong to Francis!—it is true
I took his coin, was tempted and complied,
And built this house and sinned, and all is
said.
My father and my mother died of want. 250
Well, had I riches of my own? you see
How one gets rich! Let each one bear his
lot.
They were born poor, lived poor, and poor
they died:
And I have labored somewhat in my time
And not been paid profusely. Some good
son   255
Paint my two hundred pictures—let him
try!

No doubt, there's something strikes a
    balance. Yes,
You loved me quite enough, it seems to-
    night.
This must suffice me here. What would
    one have?
In heaven, perhaps, new chances, one more
    chance —   260
Four great walls in the new Jerusalem,
Meted on each side by the angel's reed,
For Leonard, Rafael, Agnolo and me
To cover — the three first without a wife,
While I have mine! So — still they over-
    come   265
Because there's still Lucrezia,— as I choose.

Again the Cousin's whistle! Go, my Love.
                                   (1855)

THE GUARDIAN-ANGEL

A PICTURE AT FANO

I

Dear and great Angel, wouldst thou only
    leave
    That child, when thou hast done with him,
        for me!
Let me sit all the day here, that when eve
Shall find performed thy special ministry,
And time come for departure, thou, suspend-
    ing,   5
Thy flight, may'st see another child for
    tending,
    Another still, to quiet and retrieve.

II

Then I shall feel thee step one step, no
    more,
    From where thou standest now, to where
        I gaze,
— And suddenly my head is covered o'er   10
    With those wings, white above the child
        who prays
Now on that tomb — and I shall feel thee
    guarding
Me, out of all the world; for me, discard-
    ing
    Yon heaven thy home, that waits and opes
        its door.

III

I would not look up thither past thy head   15
    Because the door opes, like that child, I
        know,
For I should have thy gracious face instead,
    Thou bird of God! And wilt thou bend
        me low

Like him, and lay, like his, my hands to-
    gether,
And lift them up to pray, and gently tether
Me, as thy lamb there, with thy garment's
    spread?   21

IV

If this was ever granted, I would rest
    My head beneath thine, while thy healing
        hands
Close-covered both my eyes beside thy
    breast,
    Pressing the brain, which too much
        thought expands,   25
Back to its proper size again, and smooth-
    ing
Distortion down till every nerve had sooth-
    ing,
    And all lay quiet, happy and suppressed.

V

How soon all worldly wrong would be re-
    paired!
    I think how I should view the earth and
        skies   30
And sea, when once again my brow was
    bared
    After thy healing, with such different eyes.
O world, as God has made it! All is
    beauty:
And knowing this, is love, and love is duty.
    What further may be sought for or de-
        clared?   35

VI

Guercino drew this angel I saw teach
    (Alfred, dear friend!) — that little child
        to pray,
Holding the little hands up, each to each
    Pressed gently,— with his own head
        turned away
Over the earth where so much lay before
    him   40
Of work to do, though heaven was open-
    ing o'er him,
    And he was left at Fano by the beach.

VII

We were at Fano, and three times we went
    To sit and see him in his chapel there,
And drink his beauty to our soul's content 45
    — My angel with me too: and since I
        care
For dear Guercino's fame (to which in
    power
And glory comes this picture for a dower,
    Fraught with a pathos so magnificent) —

VIII

And since he did not work thus earnestly 50
  At all times, and has else endured some
    wrong —
I took one thought his picture struck from
  me,
  And spread it out, translating it to song.
My love is here. Where are you, dear old
  friend?
How rolls the Wairoa at your world's far
  end? 55
  This is Ancona, yonder is the sea.

                    (1855)

A GRAMMARIAN'S FUNERAL

SHORTLY AFTER THE REVIVAL OF LEARNING IN
EUROPE

Let us begin and carry up this corpse,
  Singing together.
Leave we the common crofts, the vulgar
    thorpes
  Each in its tether
Sleeping safe on the bosom of the plain, 5
  Cared-for till cock-crow:
Look out if yonder be not day again
  Rimming the rock-row!
That's the appropriate country; there, man's
    thought,
  Rarer, intenser, 10
Self-gathered for an outbreak, as it ought,
  Chafes in the censer.
Leave we the unlettered plain its herd and
    crop;
  Seek we sepulture
On a tall mountain, citied to the top, 15
  Crowded with culture!
All the peaks soar, but one the rest excels;
  Clouds overcome it;
No! yonder sparkle is the citadel's
  Circling its summit. 20
Thither our path lies; wind we up the
    heights:
  Wait ye the warning?
Our low life was the level's and the night's;
  He's for the morning.
Step to a tune, square chests, erect each
    head, 25
  'Ware the beholders!
This is our master, famous calm and dead,
  Borne on our shoulders.

Sleep, crop and herd! sleep, darkling thorpe
    and croft,
  Safe from the weather! 30
He, whom we convoy to his grave aloft,
  Singing together,

He was a man born with thy face and
    throat.
  Lyric Apollo!
Long he lived nameless: how should spring
    take note 35
  Winter would follow?
Till lo, the little touch, and youth was gone!
  Cramped and diminished,
Moaned he, 'New measures, other feet
    anon!
  My dance is finished?' 40
No, that's the world's way: (keep the
    mountain-side,
  Make for the city!)
He knew the signal, and stepped on with
    pride
  Over men's pity;
Left play for work, and grappled with the
    world - 45
  Bent on escaping:
'What's in the scroll,' quoth he, 'thou keep-
    est furled?
  Show me their shaping,
Theirs who most studied man, the bard and
    sage,—
  Give!'— So, he gowned him, 50
Straight got by heart that book to its last
    page:
  Learnèd, we found him.
Yea, but we found him bald too, eyes like
    lead,
  Accents uncertain:
'Time to taste life,' another would have
    said, 55
  'Up with the curtain!'
This man said rather, 'Actual life comes
    next?
  Patience a moment!
Grant I have mastered learning's crabbed
    text,
  Still there's the comment. 60
Let me know all! Prate not of most or
    least,
  Painful or easy!
Even to the crumbs I'd fain eat up the
    feast,
  Ay, nor feel queasy.'
Oh, such a life as he resolved to live, 65
  When he had learned it,
When he had gathered all books had to
    give!
  Sooner, he spurned it.
Image the whole, then execute the parts —
  Fancy the fabric 70
Quite, ere you build, ere steel strike fire
    from quartz,
  Ere mortar dab brick.

(Here's the town-gate reached; there's the
    market-place
    Gaping before us.)
Yea, this in him was the peculiar grace 75
    (Hearten our chorus!)
That before living he'd learn how to live —
    No end to learning.
Earn the means first — God surely will con-
    trive
    Use for our earning.   80
Others mistrust and say, 'But time escapes:
    Live now or never!'
He said, 'What's time? Leave Now for
    dogs and apes!
    Man has Forever!'
Back to his book then: deeper drooped his
    head;   85
    Calculus racked him:
Leaden before, his eyes grew dross of lead:
    Tussis attacked him.
'Now, master, take a little rest!'—not he!
    (Caution redoubled,   90
Step two abreast, the way winds narrowly!)
    Not a whit troubled,
Back to his studies, fresher than at first,
    Fierce as a dragon
He (soul-hydroptic with a sacred thirst) 95
    Sucked at the flagon.
Oh, if we draw a circle premature,
    Heedless of far gain,
Greedy for quick returns of profit, sure
    Bad is our bargain!   100
Was it not great? did not he throw on
    God
    (He loves the burthen) —
God's task to make the heavenly period
    Perfect the earthen,
Did not he magnify the mind, show clear
    Just what it all meant?   106
He would not discount life, as fools do
    here,
    Paid by instalment.
He ventured neck or nothing — heaven's
    success
    Found, or earth's failure: 110
'Wilt thou trust death or not?' He an-
    swered 'Yes:
    Hence with life's pale lure!'
That low man seeks a little thing to do,
    Sees it and does it;
This high man, with a great thing to pur-
    sue,   115
    Dies ere he knows it.
That low man goes on adding one to one,
    His hundred's soon hit;
This high man, aiming at a million,
    Misses an unit.   120

That, has the world here — should he need
    the next,
    Let the world mind him!
This, throws himself on God, and unper-
    plexed
    Seeking shall find Him.
So, with the throttling hands of death at
    strife,   125
    Ground he at grammar;
Still, through the rattle, parts of speech
    were rife:
    While he could stammer
He settled *Hoti's* business — let it be! —
    Properly based *Oun* —   130
Gave us the doctrine of the enclitic *De*,
    Dead from the waist down.
Well, here's the platform, here's the proper
    place:
    Hail to your purlieus,
All ye highfliers of the feathered race, 135
    Swallows and curlews!
Here's the top-peak, the multitude below
    Live, for they can, there:
This man decided not to Live but Know —
    Bury this man there?   140
Here — here's his place, where meteors
    shoot, clouds form,
    Lightnings are loosened,
Stars come and go! Let joy break with
    the storm,
    Peace let the dew send!
Lofty designs must close in like effects: 145
    Loftily lying,
Leave him — still loftier than the world sus-
    pects,
    Living and dying.

                    (1855)

ONE WORD MORE

TO E. B. B.

I

There they are, my fifty men and women
Naming me the fifty poems finished!
Take them, Love, the book and me together:
Where the heart lies, let the brain lie also.

II

Rafael made a century of sonnets,   5
Made and wrote them in a certain volume
Dinted with the silver-pointed pencil
Else he only used to draw Madonnas:
These, the world might view — but one, the
    volume.
Who that one, you ask? Your heart in-
    structs you.

Did she live and love it all her lifetime?
Did she drop, his lady of the sonnets,
Die, and let it drop beside her pillow
Where it lay in place of Rafael's glory,
Rafael's cheek so duteous and so loving — 15
Cheek, the world was wont to hail a
    painter's,
Rafael's cheek, her love had turned a poet's?

III

You and I would rather read that volume
(Taken to his beating bosom by it)
Lean and list the bosom-beats of Rafael, 20
Would we not? than wonder at Madonnas —
Her, San Sisto names, and Her, Foligno,
Her, that visits Florence in a vision,
Her, that's left with lilies in the Louvre —
Seen by us and all the world in circle. 25

IV

You and I will never read that volume.
Guido Reni, like his own eye's apple,
Guarded long the treasure-book and loved
    it.
Guido Reni dying, all Bologna
Cried, and the world cried too, 'Ours, the
    treasure!' 30
Suddenly, as rare things will, it vanished.

V

Dante once prepared to paint an angel:
Whom to please? You whisper 'Beatrice.'
While he mused and traced it and retraced
    it
(Peradventure with a pen corroded 35
Still by drops of that hot ink he dipped
    for,
When, his left-hand i' the hair o' the
    wicked,
Back he held the brow and pricked its
    stigma,
Bit into the live man's flesh for parchment,
Loosed him, laughed to see the writing
    rankle, 40
Let the wretch go festering through Flor-
    ence) —
Dante, who loved well because he hated,
Hated wickedness that hinders loving,
Dante, standing, studying his angel —
In there broke the folk of his Inferno. 45
Says he —'Certain people of importance'
(Such he gave his daily dreadful line to)
'Entered and would seize, forsooth, the
    poet.'
Says the poet —'Then I stopped my paint-
    ing.'

VI

You and I would rather see that angel, 50
Painted by the tenderness of Dante,
Would we not? — than read a fresh Inferno

VII

You and I will never see that picture.
While he mused on love and Beatrice,
While he softened o'er his outlined angel, 55
In they broke, those 'people of importance':
We and Bice bear the loss forever.

VIII

What of Rafael's sonnets, Dante's picture?
This: no artist lives and loves, that longs
    not
Once, and only once, and for one only 60
(Ah, the prize!), to find his love a
    language
Fit and fair and simple and sufficient —
Using nature that's an art to others,
Not, this one time, art that's turned his
    nature.
Ay, of all the artists living, loving, 65
None but would forego his proper dowry,
Does he paint? he fain would write a poem,
Does he write? he fain would paint a
    picture,—
Put to proof art alien to the artist's.
Once, and only once, and for one only, 70
So to be the man and leave the artist,
Gain the man's joy, miss the artist's sorrow.

IX

Wherefore? Heaven's gift takes earth's
    abatement!
He who smites the rock and spreads the
    water,
Bidding drink and live a crowd beneath him,
Even he, the minute makes immortal, 76
Proves, perchance, but mortal in the
    minute,
Desecrates, belike, the deed in doing.
While he smites, how can he but remem-
    ber,
So he smote before, in such a peril, 80
When they stood and mocked —'Shall smit-
    ing help us?'
When they drank and sneered —'A stroke
    is easy!'
When they wiped their mouths and went
    their journey,
Throwing him for thanks —'But drought
    was pleasant.'
Thus old memories mar the actual
    triumph; 85
Thus the doing savors of disrelish;

Thus achievement lacks a gracious some-
   what;
O'er-importuned brows becloud the mandate,
Carelessness or consciousness — the gesture,
For he bears an ancient wrong about him, 90
Sees and knows again those phalanxed faces,
Hears, yet one time more, the 'customed pre-
   lude —
'How shouldst thou, of all men, smite, and
   save us?'
Guesses what is like to prove the sequel —
'Egypt's flesh-pots — nay, the drought was
   better.'   95

X

Oh, the crowd must have emphatic warrant!
Theirs, the Sinai-forehead's cloven bril-
   liance,
Right-arm's rod-sweep, tongue's imperial
   fiat.
Never dares the man put off the prophet.

XI

Did he love one face from out the thou-
   sands   100
(Were she Jethro's daughter, white and
   wifely,
Were she but the Æthiopian bondslave)
He would envy yon dumb, patient camel,
Keeping a reserve of scanty water
Meant to save his own life in the desert, 105
Ready in the desert to deliver
(Kneeling down to let his breast be opened)
Hoard and life together for his mistress.

XII

I shall never, in the years remaining,
Paint you pictures, no, nor carve you
   statues,   110
Make you music that should all-express me;
So it seems: I stand on my attainment,
This of verse alone, one life allows me;
Verse and nothing else have I to give you,
Other heights in other lives, God willing: 115
All the gifts from all the heights, your own,
   Love!

XIII

Yet a semblance of resource avails us —
Shade so finely touched, love's sense must
   seize it.
Take these lines, look lovingly and nearly,
Lines I write the first time and the last
   time.   120
He who works in fresco, steals a hair-brush,
Curbs the liberal hand, subservient proudly,
Cramps his spirit, crowds its all in little,
Makes a strange art of an art familiar,
Fills his lady's missal-marge with flowerets.

He who blows through bronze may breathe
   through silver,   126
Fitly serenade a slumbrous princess.
He who writes, may write for once as I do.

XIV

Love, you saw me gather men and women,
Live or dead or fashioned by my fancy, 130
Enter each and all, and use their service,
Speak from every mouth,— the speech, a
   poem.
Hardly shall I tell my joys and sorrows,
Hopes and fears, belief and disbelieving:
I am mine and yours — the rest be all
   men's,   135
Karshish, Cleon, Norbert, and the fifty.
Let me speak this once in my true person,
Not as Lippo, Roland, or Andrea,
Though the fruit of speech be just this sen-
   tence:
Pray you, look on these my men and
   women,   140
Take and keep my fifty poems finished;
Where my heart lies, let my brain lie also!
Poor the speech; be how I speak, for all
   things.

XV

Not but that you know me! Lo, the moon's
   self!
Here in London, yonder late in Florence, 145
Still we find her face, the thrice-transfigured.
Curving on a sky imbrued with color,
Drifted over Fiesolé by twilight,
Came she, our new crescent of a hair's-
   breadth.
Full she flared it, lamping Samminiato, 150
Rounder 'twixt the cypresses and rounder,
Perfect till the nightingales applauded.
Now, a piece of her old self, impoverished,
Hard to greet, she traverses the house-roofs,
Hurries with unhandsome thrift of silver,
Goes dispiritedly, glad to finish.   156

XVI

What, there's nothing in the moon note-
   worthy?
Nay: for if that moon could love a mortal,
Use, to charm him (so to fit a fancy),
All her magic ('t is the old sweet mythos),
She would turn a new side to her mortal, 161
Side unseen of herdsman, huntsman, steers-
   man —
Blank to Zoroaster on his terrace,
Blind to Galileo on his turret,
Dumb to Homer, dumb to Keats — him,
   even!   165

Think, the wonder of the moonstruck mortal —
When she turns round, comes again in heaven,
Opens out anew for worse or better!
Proves she like some portent of an iceberg
Swimming full upon the ship it founders, 170
Hungry with huge teeth of splintered crystals?
Proves she as the paved work of a sapphire,
Seen by Moses when he climbed the mountain?
Moses, Aaron, Nadab, and Abihu
Climbed and saw the very God, the Highest, 175
Stand upon the paved work of a sapphire.
Like the bodied heaven in his clearness
Shone the stone, the sapphire of that paved work,
When they ate and drank and saw God also!

XVII

What were seen? None knows, none ever shall know. 180
Only this is sure — the sight were other,
Not the moon's same side, born late in Florence,
Dying now impoverished here in London.
God be thanked, the meanest of his creatures
Boasts two soul-sides, one to face the world with, 185
One to show a woman when he loves her!

XVIII

This I say of me, but think of you, Love!
This to you — yourself my moon of poets!
Ah, but that's the world's side, there's the wonder,
Thus they see you, praise you, think they know you! 190
There, in turn I stand with them and praise you —
Out of my own self, I dare to phrase it.
But the best is when I glide from out them,
Cross a step or two of dubious twilight,
Come out on the other side, the novel 195
Silent silver lights and darks undreamed of,
Where I hush and bless myself with silence.

XIX

Oh, their Rafael of the dear Madonnas,
Oh, their Dante of the dread Inferno,
Wrote one song — and in my brain I sing it,
Drew one angel — borne, see, on my bosom! 201

R. B. (1855)

ABT VOGLER

AFTER HE HAS BEEN EXTEMPORIZING UPON THE MUSICAL INSTRUMENT OF HIS INVENTION

I

Would that the structure brave, the manifold music I build,
  Bidding my organ obey, calling its keys to their work,
Claiming each slave of the sound, at a touch, as when Solomon willed
  Armies of angels that soar, legions of demons that lurk,
Man, brute, reptile, fly,— alien of end and of aim, 5
  Adverse, each from the other heaven-high, hell-deep removed,—
Should rush into sight at once as he named the ineffable Name,
  And pile him a palace straight, to pleasure the princess he loved!

II

Would it might tarry like his, the beautiful building of mine,
  This which my keys in a crowd pressed and importuned to raise! 10
Ah, one and all, how they helped, would dispart now and now combine,
  Zealous to hasten the work, heighten their master his praise!
And one would bury his brow with a blind plunge down to hell,
  Burrow awhile and build, broad on the roots of things,
Then up again swim into sight, having based me my palace well, 15
  Founded it, fearless of flame, flat on the nether springs.

III

And another would mount and march, like the excellent minion he was,
  Ay, another and yet another, one crowd but with many a crest,
Raising my rampired walls of gold as transparent as glass,
  Eager to do and die, yield each his place to the rest: 20
For higher still and higher (as a runner tips with fire,
  When a great illumination surprises a festal night —
Outlining round and round Rome's dome from space to spire)

Up, the pinnacled glory reached, and the
pride of my soul was in sight.

IV

In sight? Not half! for it seemed, it was
certain, to match man's birth,   25
Nature in turn conceived, obeying an impulse as I;
And the emulous heaven yearned down,
made effort to reach the earth,
As the earth had done her best, in my passion, to scale the sky:
Novel splendors burst forth, grew familiar
and dwelt with mine,
Not a point nor peak but found and fixed
its wandering star;   30
Meteor-moons, balls of blaze: and they did
not pale nor pine,
For earth had attained to heaven, there
was no more near nor far.

V

Nay more; for there wanted not who walked
in the glare and glow,
Presences plain in the place; or, fresh
from the Protoplast,
Furnished for ages to come, when a kindlier
wind should blow,   35
Lured now to begin and live, in a house to
their liking at last;
Or else the wonderful Dead who have
passed through the body and gone,
But were back once more to breathe in an
old world worth their new:
What never had been, was now; what was,
as it shall be anon;
And what is,— shall I say, matched both?
for I was made perfect too.   40

VI

All through my keys that gave their sounds
to a wish of my soul,
All through my soul that praised as its
wish flowed visibly forth,
All through music and me! For think, had
I painted the whole,
Why, there it had stood, to see, nor the
process so wonder-worth:
Had I written the same, made verse — still,
effect proceeds from cause,   45
Ye know why the forms are fair, ye hear
how the tale is told;
It is all triumphant art, but art in obedience
to laws,
Painter and poet are proud in the artist-
list enrolled: —

VII

But here is the finger of God, a flash of the
will that can,
Existent behind all laws, that made them
and, lo, they are!   50
And I know not if, save in this, such gift
be allowed to man
That out of three sounds he frame, not a
fourth sound, but a star.
Consider it well: each tone of our scale in
itself is naught:
It is everywhere in the world — loud, soft,
and all is said:
Give it to me to use! I mix it with two in
my thought: 55
And there! Ye have heard and seen: consider and bow the head!

VIII

Well, it is gone at last, the palace of music
I reared;
Gone! and the good tears start, the praises
that come too slow;
For one is assured at first, one scarce can
say that he feared,
That he even gave it a thought, the gone
thing was to go.   60
Never to be again! But many more of the
kind
As good, nay, better perchance: is this
your comfort to me?
To me, who must be saved because I cling
with my mind
To the same, same self, same love, same
God: ay, what was, shall be.

IX

Therefore to whom turn I but to thee, the ineffable Name?   65
Builder and maker, thou, of houses not
made with hands!
What, have fear of change from thee who
art ever the same?
Doubt that thy power can fill the heart that
thy power expands?
There shall never be one lost good! What
was, shall live as before;
The evil is null, is naught, is silence implying sound;   70
What was good shall be good, with, for evil,
so much good more;
On the earth the broken arcs; in the
heaven a perfect round.

X

All we have willed or hoped or dreamed of
good shall exist;

Not its semblance, but itself; no beauty,
    nor good, nor power
Whose voice has gone forth, but each sur-
    vives for the melodist   75
    When eternity affirms the conception of
    an hour.
The high that proved too high, the heroic
    for earth too hard,
    The passion that left the ground to lose
    itself in the sky,
Are music sent up to God by the lover and
    the bard;
    Enough that he heard it once: we shall
    hear it by and by.   80

XI

And what is our failure here but a triumph's
    evidence
    For the fullness of the days? Have we
    withered or agonized?
Why else was the pause prolonged but that
    singing might issue thence?
    Why rushed the discords in, but that har-
    mony should be prized?
Sorrow is hard to bear, and doubt is slow to
    clear,   85
    Each sufferer says his say, his scheme of
    the weal and woe:
But God has a few of us whom he whispers
    in the ear;
    The rest may reason and welcome: 't is we
    musicians know.

XII

Well, it is earth with me; silence resumes
    her reign:
    I will be patient and proud, and soberly
    acquiesce.   90
Give me the keys. I feel for the common
    chord again,
    Sliding by semitones till I sink to the
    minor,— yes,
And I blunt it into a ninth, and I stand on
    alien ground,
    Surveying awhile the heights I rolled from
    into the deep;
Which, hark, I have dared and done, for my
    resting-place is found,   95
    The C Major of this life: so, now I will
    try to sleep.

                  (1864)

RABBI BEN EZRA

I

Grow old along with me!
The best is yet to be,

The last of life, for which the first was
    made:
Our times are in His hand
Who saith, 'A whole I planned,
Youth shows but half; trust God: see all,
    nor be afraid!'

II

Not that, amassing flowers,
Youth sighed, 'Which rose make ours,
Which lily leave and then as best recall?'
Not that, admiring stars,   10
It yearned, 'Nor Jove, nor Mars;
Mine be some figured flame which blends,
    transcends them all!'

III

Not for such hopes and fears
Annulling youth's brief years,
Do I remonstrate: folly wide the mark!   15
Rather I prize the doubt
Low kinds exist without,
Finished and finite clods, untroubled by a
    spark.

IV

Poor vaunt of life indeed,
Were man but formed to feed   20
On joy, to solely seek and find and feast;
Such feasting ended, then
As sure an end to men;
Irks care the crop-full bird? Frets doubt
    the maw-crammed beast?

V

Rejoice we are allied   25
To That which doth provide
And not partake, effect and not receive!
A spark disturbs our clod;
Nearer we hold of God
Who gives, than of his tribes that take, I
    must believe.   30

VI

Then, welcome each rebuff
That turns earth's smoothness rough,
Each sting that bids nor sit nor stand but
    go!
Be our joys three-parts pain!
Strive, and hold cheap the strain;   35
Learn, nor account the pang; dare, never
    grudge the throe!

VII

For thence,— a paradox
Which comforts while it mocks,—

Shall life succeed in that it seems to fail:
What I aspired to be, 40
And was not, comforts me:
A brute I might have been, but would not
sink i' the scale.

VIII

What is he but a brute
Whose flesh has soul to suit,
Whose spirit works lest arms and legs want
play? 45
To man, propose this test —
Thy body at its best,
How far can that project thy soul on its
lone way?

IX

Yet gifts should prove their use:
I own the Past profuse 50
Of power each side, perfection every turn:
Eyes, ears took in their dole,
Brain treasured up the whole;
Should not the heart beat once 'How good
to live and learn'?

X

Not once beat 'Praise be thine! 55
I see the whole design,
I, who saw power, see now love perfect too:
Perfect I call thy plan:
Thanks that I was a man!
Maker, remake, complete,— I trust what thou
shalt do!' 60

XI

For pleasant is this flesh;
Our soul, in its rose-mesh
Pulled ever to the earth, still yearns for rest:
Would we some prize might hold
To match those manifold 65
Possessions of the brute,— gain most, as we
did best!

XII

Let us not always say,
'Spite of this flesh to-day
I strove, made head, gained ground upon
the whole!'
As the bird wings and sings, 70
Let us cry, 'All good things
Are ours, nor soul helps flesh more, now,
than flesh helps soul!'

XIII

Therefore I summon age
To grant youth's heritage,

Life's struggle having so far reached its
term: 75
Thence shall I pass, approved
A man, for aye removed
From the developed brute; a God though in
the germ.

XIV

And I shall thereupon
Take rest, ere I be gone 80
Once more on my adventure brave and new:
Fearless and unperplexed,
When I wage battle next,
What weapons to select, what armor to in-
due.

XV

Youth ended, I shall try 85
My gain or loss thereby;
Leave the fire ashes, what survives is gold:
And I shall weigh the same,
Give life its praise or blame:
Young, all lay in dispute; I shall know,
being old. 90

XVI

For, note when evening shuts,
A certain moment cuts
The deed off, calls the glory from the gray:
A whisper from the west
Shoots —'Add this to the rest, 95
Take it and try its worth: here dies another
day.'

XVII

So, still within this life,
Though lifted o'er its strife,
Let me discern, compare, pronounce at last,
'This rage was right i' the main, 100
That acquiescence vain:
The Future I may face now I have proved
the Past.'

XVIII

For more is not reserved
To man, with soul just nerved
To act to-morrow what he learns to-day: 105
Here, work enough to watch
The Master work, and catch
Hints of the proper craft, tricks of the
tool's true play.

XIX

As it was better, youth
Should strive, through acts uncouth, 110

Toward making, than repose on aught found
    made:
So, better, age, exempt
From strife, should know, than tempt
Further. Thou waitedst age: wait death nor
    be afraid!

XX

Enough now, if the Right   115
And Good and Infinite
Be named here, as thou callest thy hand
    thine own,
With knowledge absolute,
Subject to no dispute
From fools that crowded youth, nor let thee
    feel alone.   120

XXI

Be there, for once and all,
Severed great minds from small,
Announced to each his station in the Past!
Was I, the world arraigned,
Were they, my soul disdained,   125
Right? Let age speak the truth and give us
    peace at last!

XXII

Now, who shall arbitrate?
Ten men love what I hate,
Shun what I follow, slight what I receive;
Ten, who in ears and eyes   130
Match me: we all surmise,
They, this thing, and I, that: whom shall
    my soul believe?

XXIII

Not on the vulgar mass
Called 'work,' must sentence pass,
Things done, that took the eye and had the
    price;   135
O'er which, from level stand,
The low world laid its hand,
Found straightway to its mind, could value
    in a trice:

XXIV

But all, the world's coarse thumb,
And finger failed to plumb,   140
So passed in making up the main account;
All instincts immature,
All purposes unsure,
That weighed not as his work, yet swelled
    the man's amount:

XXV

Thoughts hardly to be packed   145
Into a narrow act,
Fancies that broke through language and
    escaped;
All I could never be,
All, men ignored in me,
This, I was worth to God, whose wheel the
    pitcher shaped.   150

XXVI

Ay, note that Potter's wheel,
That metaphor! and feel
Why time spins fast, why passive lies our
    clay,—
Thou, to whom fools propound,
When the wine makes its round,   155
'Since life fleets, all is change; the Past
    gone, seize to-day!'

XXVII

Fool! All that is, at all,
Lasts ever, past recall;
Earth changes, but thy soul and God stand
    sure:
What entered into thee,   160
That was, is, and shall be:
Time's wheel runs back or stops: Potter
    and clay endure.

XXVIII

He fixed thee mid this dance
Of plastic circumstance,
This Present, thou, forsooth, wouldst fain
    arrest: 165
Machinery just meant
To give thy soul its bent,
Try thee and turn thee forth, sufficiently
    impressed.

XXIX

What though the earlier grooves
Which ran the laughing loves   170
Around thy base, no longer pause and press?
What though about thy rim,
Skull-things in order grim
Grow out, in graver mood, obey the sterner
    stress?

XXX

Look not thou down but up!   175
To uses of a cup!
The festal board, lamp's flash and trumpet's
    peal,

The new wine's foaming flow,
The Master's lips a-glow!
Thou, heaven's consummate cup, what
    need'st thou with earth's wheel?   180

XXXI

But I need, now as then,
Thee, God, who moldest men;
And since, not even while the whirl was
    worst,
Did I — to the wheel of life
With shapes and colors rife,   185
Bound dizzily,— mistake my end, to slake
    thy thirst:

XXXII

So, take and use thy work,
Amend what flaws may lurk,
What strain o' the stuff, what warpings past
    the aim!
My times be in thy hand!   190
Perfect the cup as planned!
Let age approve of youth, and death com-
    plete the same!

           (1864)

PROSPICE

Fear death? to feel the fog in my throat,
    The mist in my face,
When the snows begin, and the blasts de-
    note
    I am nearing the place,
The power of the night, the press of the
    storm,   5
    The post of the foe;
Where he stands, the Arch Fear in a visible
    form,
    Yet the strong man must go:
For the journey is done and the summit at-
    tained,
    And the barriers fall,   10
Though a battle's to fight ere the guerdon
    be gained,
    The reward of it all.
I was ever a fighter, so — one fight more,
    The best and the last!
I would hate that death bandaged my eyes,
    and forbore,   15
    And bade me creep past.
No! let me taste the whole of it, fare like my
    peers
    The heroes of old,
Bear the brunt, in a minute pay glad life's
    arrears
    Of pain, darkness and cold.   20

For sudden the worst turns the best to the
    brave,
    The black minute's at end,
And the elements' rage, the fiend-voices that
    rave,
    Shall dwindle, shall blend,
Shall change, shall become first a peace out
    of pain,   25
    Then a light, then thy breast,
O thou soul of my soul! I shall clasp thee
    again,
    And with God be the rest!

           (1864)

HERVÉ RIEL

On the sea and at the Hogue, sixteen hun-
    dred ninety-two,
    Did the English fight the French,— woe to
    France!
And, the thirty-first of May, helter-skelter
    through the blue,
Like a crowd of frightened porpoises a shoal
    of sharks pursue,
    Came crowding ship on ship to Saint Malo
    on the Rance,   5
With the English fleet in view.

II

'T was the squadron that escaped, with the
    victor in full chase;
First and foremost of the drove, in his great
    ship, Damfreville;
    Close on him fled, great and small,
    Twenty-two good ships in all;   10
And they signaled to the place
'Help the winners of a race!
    Get us guidance, give us harbor, take us
    quick — or, quicker still,
    Here's the English can and will!'

III

Then the pilots of the place put out brisk
    and leapt on board;   15
    'Why, what hope or chance have ships
    like these to pass?' laughed they:
'Rocks to starboard, rocks to port, all the
    passage scarred and scored,
Shall the "Formidable" here with her
    twelve and eighty guns
    Think to make the river-mouth by the
    single narrow way,
Trust to enter where 't is ticklish for a craft
    of twenty tons,   20

And with flow at full beside?
Now, 't is slackest ebb of tide.
Reach the mooring? Rather say,
While rock stands or water runs,
Not a ship will leave the bay!'   25

IV

Then was called a council straight.
Brief and bitter the debate:
'Here 's the English at our heels; would you
    have them take in tow
All that 's left us of the fleet, linked together
    stern and bow,
For a prize to Plymouth Sound?   30
Better run the ships aground!'
    (Ended Damfreville his speech).
'Not a minute more to wait!
    Let the Captains all and each
    Shove ashore, then blow up, burn the ves-
      sels on the beach!   35
France must undergo her fate.

V

'Give the word!' But no such word
Was ever spoke or heard;
    For up stood, for out stepped, for in struck
      amid all these
—A Captain? A Lieutenant? A Mate—
    first, second, third?   40
No such man of mark, and meet
With his betters to compete!
But a simple Breton sailor pressed by
    Tourville for the fleet,
A poor coasting-pilot he, Hervé Riel the
    Croisickese.

VI

And 'What mockery or malice have we
    here?' cried Hervé Riel: 45
'Are you mad, you Malouins? Are you
    cowards, fools, or rogues?
Talk to me of rocks and shoals, me who
    took the soundings, tell
On my fingers every bank, every shallow,
    every swell
'Twixt the offing here and Grève where the
    river disembogues?
Are you bought by English gold? Is it love
    the lying 's for?   50
    Morn and eve, night and day,
    Have I piloted your bay,
Entered free and anchored fast at the foot
    of Solidor.
Burn the fleet and ruin France? That
    were worse than fifty Hogues!
    Sirs, they know I speak the truth! Sirs,
    believe me there 's a way!   55

Only let me lead the line,
    Have the biggest ship to steer,
    Get this "Formidable" clear,
Make the others follow mine,
And I lead them, most and least, by a
    passage I know well,   60
Right to Solidor past Grève,
    And there lay them safe and sound;
    And if one ship misbehave,
    —Keel so much as grate the ground,
Why, I 've nothing but my life,—here 's my
    head!' cries Hervé Riel.   65

VII

Not a minute more to wait.
'Steer us in, then, small and great!
    Take the helm, lead the line, save the
      squadron!' cried its chief.
Captains, give the sailor place!
    He is Admiral, in brief.   70
Still the north-wind, by God's grace!
See the noble fellow's face
As the big ship, with a bound,
Clears the entry like a hound,
Keeps the passage as its inch of way were
    the wide sea's profound!   75
    See, safe through shoal and rock,
    How they follow in a flock,
Not a ship that misbehaves, not a keel that
    grates the ground,
    Not a spar that comes to grief!
The peril, see, is past,   80
All are harbored to the last,
And just as Hervé Riel hollas 'Anchor!'—
    sure as fate,
Up the English come—too late!

VIII

So, the storm subsides to calm:
    They see the green trees wave   85
    On the heights o'erlooking Grève.
Hearts that bled are stanched with balm.
'Just our rapture to enhance,
    Let the English rake the bay,
Gnash their teeth and glare askance   90
    As they cannonade away!
'Neath rampired Solidor pleasant riding on
    the Rance!'
How hope succeeds despair on each Captain's
    countenance!
Out burst all with one accord,
    'This is Paradise for Hell!   95
    Let France, let France's King
    Thank the man that did the thing!'
What a shout, and all one word,
    'Hervé Riel!'

As he stepped in front once more,   100
 Not a symptom of surprise
In the frank blue Breton eyes.
Just the same man as before.

IX

Then said Damfreville, ' My friend,
I must speak out at the end,   105
 Though I find the speaking hard.
Praise is deeper than the lips:
You have saved the King his ships,
 You must name your own reward.
'Faith, our sun was near eclipse!   110
Demand whate'er you will,
France remains your debtor still.
Ask to heart's content and have! or my
 name 's not Damfreville.'

X

Then a beam of fun outbroke
On the bearded mouth that spoke,   115
As the honest heart laughed through
Those frank eyes of Breton blue:
' Since I needs must say my say,
 Since on board the duty 's done,
 And from Malo Roads to Croisic Point,
 what is it but a run? —   120
Since 't is ask and have, I may —
 Since the others go ashore —
Come! A good whole holiday!
 Leave to go and see my wife, whom I call
 the Belle Aurore!'
That he asked and that he got,— nothing
 more.   125

XI

Name and deed alike are lost:
Not a pillar nor a post
 In his Croisic keeps alive the feat as it
 befell:
Not a head in white and black
On a single fishing-smack,   130
In memory of the man but for whom had
 gone to wrack
 All that France saved from the fight
 whence England bore the bell.
Go to Paris: rank on rank
 Search the heroes flung pell-mell
On the Louvre, face and flank!   135
 You shall look long enough ere you come
 to Hervé Riel.
So, for better and for worse,
Hervé Riel, accept my verse!
In my verse, Hervé Riel, do thou once more
Save the squadron, honor France, love thy
 wife the Belle Aurore!   140
 (1871)

THE TWO POETS OF CROISIC

PROLOGUE

Such a starved bank of moss
 Till, that May-morn,
Blue ran the flash across:
 Violets were born!

Sky — what a scowl of cloud
 Till, near and far,
Ray on ray split the shroud:
 Splendid, a star!

World — how it walled about
 Life with disgrace   10
Till God's own smile came out:
 That was thy face!

EPILOGUE

I

What a pretty tale you told me
 Once upon a time
— Said you found it somewhere (scold me!)
 Was it prose or was it rhyme,   16
Greek or Latin? Greek, you said,
While your shoulder propped my head.

II

Anyhow there 's no forgetting
 This much if no more,   20
That a poet (pray, no petting!)
 Yes, a bard, sir, famed of yore,
Went where suchlike used to go,
Singing for a prize, you know.

III

Well, he had to sing, not merely   25
 Sing but play the lyre;
Playing was important clearly
 Quite as singing: I desire,
Sir, you keep the fact in mind
For a purpose that 's behind.   30

IV

There stood he, while deep attention
 Held the judges round,
— Judges able, I should mention,
 To detect the slightest sound
Sung or played amiss: such ears   35
Had old judges, it appears!

V

None the less he sang out boldly,
 Played in time and tune.

Till the judges, weighing coldly
  Each note's worth, seemed, late or soon, 40
Sure to smile 'In vain one tries
Picking faults out: take the prize!'

VI

When, a mischief! Were they seven
  Strings the lyre possessed?
Oh, and afterwards eleven,   45
  Thank you! Well, sir,— who had guessed
Such ill luck in store?— it happed
One of those same seven strings snapped.

VII

All was lost, then! No! a cricket
  (What 'cicada?' Pooh!)   50
— Some mad thing that left its thicket
  For mere love of music — flew
With its little heart on fire,
Lighted on the crippled lyre.

VIII

So that when (Ah, joy!) our singer   55
  For his truant string
Feels with disconcerted finger,
  What does cricket else but fling
Fiery heart forth, sound the note
Wanted by the throbbing throat?   60

IX

Ay, and ever to the ending,
  Cricket chirps at need,
Executes the hand's intending,
  Promptly, perfectly,— indeed
Saves the singer from defeat   65
With her chirrup low and sweet.

X

Till, at ending, all the judges
  Cry with one assent,
'Take the prize — a prize who grudges
  Such a voice and instrument?   70
Why, we took your lyre for harp,
So it thrilled us forth F sharp!'

XI

Did the conqueror spurn the creature,
  Once its service done?
That's no such uncommon feature   75
  In the case when Music's son
Finds his Lotte's power too spent
For aiding soul-development.

XII

No! This other on returning
  Homeward, prize in hand,   80

Satisfied his bosom's yearning:
  (Sir, I hope you understand!)
— Said 'Some record there must be
Of this cricket's help to me!'

XIII

So, he made himself a statue: 85
  Marble stood, life-size;
On the lyre, he pointed at you,
  Perched his partner in the prize;
Never more apart you found
Her, he throned, from him, she crowned. 90

XIV

That's the tale: its application?
  Somebody I know
Hopes one day for reputation
  Through his poetry that's — Oh,
All so learned and so wise   95
And deserving of a prize!

XV

If he gains one, will some ticket,
  When his statue's built,
Tell the gazer ''T was a cricket
  Helped my crippled lyre, whose lilt   100
Sweet and low, when strength usurped
Softness' place i' the scale, she chirped?

XVI

'For as victory was nighest,
  While I sang and played,—
With my lyre at lowest, highest   105
  Right alike,— one string that made
"Love" sound soft was snapt in twain,
Never to be heard again,—

XVII

'Had not a kind cricket fluttered,
  Perched upon the place   110
Vacant left, and duly uttered
  "Love, Love, Love," whene'er the bass
Asked the treble to atone
For its somewhat somber drone.'

XVIII

But you don't know music! Wherefore 115
  Keep on casting pearls
To a — poet? All I care for
  Is — to tell him that a girl's
'Love' comes aptly in when gruff
Grows his singing. (There, enough!)   120

(1878)

PHEIDIPPIDES

χαίρετε, νικῶμεν.

First I salute this soil of the blessed, river
and rock!
Gods of my birthplace, dæmons and heroes,
honor to all!
Then I name thee, claim thee for our patron,
co-equal in praise
— Ay, with Zeus the Defender, with Her
of the ægis and spear!
Also, ye of the bow and the buskin, praised
be your peer,   5
Now, henceforth and for ever,— O latest
to whom I upraise
Hand and heart and voice! For Athens,
leave pasture and flock!
Present to help, potent to save, Pan — patron
I call!

Archons of Athens, topped by the tettix,
see, I return!
See, 't is myself here standing alive, no spec-
ter that speaks!   10
Crowned with the myrtle, did you command
me, Athens and you,
'Run, Pheidippides, run and race, reach
Sparta for aid!
Persia has come, we are here, where is She?'
Your command I obeyed,
Ran and raced: like stubble, some field
which a fire runs through,
Was the space between city and city: two
days, two nights did I burn   15
Over the hills, under the dales, down pits
and up peaks.

Into their midst I broke: breath served but
for 'Persia has come.
Persia bids Athens proffer slaves'-tribute,
water and earth;
Razed to the ground is Eretria — but Athens,
shall Athens sink,
Drop into dust and die — the flower of
Hellas utterly die,   20
Die with the wide world spitting at Sparta,
the stupid, the stander-by?
Answer me quick, what help, what hand do
you stretch o'er destruction's brink?
How,— when? No care for my limbs!—
there's lightning in all and some —
Fresh and fit your message to bear, once lips
give it birth!'

O my Athens — Sparta love thee? Did
Sparta respond?   25

Every face of her leered in a furrow of
envy, mistrust,
Malice,— each eye of her gave me its glitter
of gratified hate!
Gravely they turned to take counsel, to cast
for excuses. I stood
Quivering,— the limbs of me fretting as fire
frets, an inch from dry wood:
'Persia has come, Athens asks aid, and still
they debate?   30
Thunder, thou Zeus! Athene, are Spartans
a quarry beyond
Swing of thy spear? Phoibos and Artemis,
clang them "Ye must"!'

No bolt launched from Olumpos! Lo, their
answer at last!
'Has Persia come,— does Athens ask aid,—
may Sparta befriend?
Nowise precipitate judgment — too weighty
the issue at stake!   35
Count we no time lost time which lags
through respect to the gods!
Ponder that precept of old, 'No warfare,
whatever the odds
In your favor, so long as the moon, half-
orbed, is unable to take
Full-circle her state in the sky!' Already
she rounds to it fast:
Athens must wait, patient as we — who
judgment suspend.'   40

Athens,— except for that sparkle,— thy
name, I had moldered to ash!
That sent a blaze through my blood; off, off
and away was I back,
— Not one word to waste, one look to lose
on the false and the vile!
Yet 'O gods of my land!' I cried, as each
hillock and plain,
Wood and stream, I knew, I named, rush-
ing past them again,   45
'Have ye kept faith, proved mindful of
honors we paid you erewhile?
Vain was the filleted victim, the fulsome
libation! Too rash
Love in its choice, paid you so largely service so slack!

'Oak and olive and bay,— I bid you cease
to enwreathe
Brows made bold by your leaf! Fade at
the Persian's foot,   50
You that, our patrons were pledged, should
never adorn a slave!

Rather I hail thee, Parnes,— trust to thy
    wild waste tract!
Treeless, herbless, lifeless mountain! What
    matter if slacked
My speed may hardly be, for homage to
    crag and to cave
No deity deigns to drape with verdure? —
    at least I can breathe,   55
Fear in thee no fraud from the blind, no
    lie from the mute!'

Such my cry as, rapid, I ran over Parnes'
    ridge;
Gully and gap I clambered and cleared till,
    sudden, a bar
Jutted, a stoppage of stone against me,
    blocking the way.
Right! for I minded the hollow to traverse,
    the fissure across: 60
'Where I could enter, there I depart by!
    Night in the fosse?
Athens to aid? Though the dive were
    through Erebos, thus I obey —
Out of the day dive, into the day as bravely
    arise! No bridge
Better!'— when — ha! what was it I came
    on, of wonders that are?

There, in the cool of a cleft, sat he —
    majestical Pan!   65
Ivy drooped wanton, kissed his head, moss
    cushioned his hoof:
All the great god was good in the eyes
    grave-kindly — the curl
Carved on the bearded cheek, amused at a
    mortal's awe
As, under the human trunk, the goat-thighs
    grand I saw.
'Halt, Pheidippides!'— halt I did, my brain
    of a whirl: 70
'Hither to me! Why pale in my presence?'
    he gracious began:
'How is it,— Athens, only in Hellas, holds
    me aloof?

'Athens, she only, rears me no fane, makes
    me no feast!
Wherefore? Than I what godship to
    Athens more helpful of old?
Ay, and still, and forever her friend!
    Test Pan, trust me!   75
Go, bid Athens take heart, laugh Persia to
    scorn, have faith
In the temples and tombs! Go, say to
    Athens, "The Goat-God saith:

When Persia — so much as strews not the
    soil — is cast in the sea,
Then praise Pan who fought in the ranks
    with your most and least,
Goat-thigh to greaved-thigh, made one cause
    with the free and the bold!"   80

'Say Pan saith: "Let this, foreshowing the
    place, be the pledge!"'
(Gay, the liberal hand held out this her-
    bage I bear
— Fennel,— I grasped it a-tremble with
    dew — whatever it bode)
'While, as for thee . . ,' But enough!
    He was gone. If I ran hitherto —
Be sure that the rest of my journey, I ran
    no longer, but flew.   85
Parnes to Athens — earth no more, the air
    was my road:
Here am I back. Praise Pan, we stand no
    more on the razor's edge!
Pan for Athens, Pan for me! I too have
    a guerdon rare!

Then spoke Miltiades. 'And thee, best
    runner of Greece,
Whose limbs did duty indeed,— what gift
    is promised thyself?   90
Tell it us straightway,— Athens the mother
    demands of her son!'
Rosily blushed the youth: he paused; but,
    lifting at length
His eyes from the ground, it seemed as he
    gathered the rest of his strength
Into the utterance— 'Pan spoke thus: "For
    what thou hast done
Count on a worthy reward! Henceforth be
    allowed thee release   95
From the racer's toil, no vulgar reward in
    praise or in pelf!"

'I am bold to believe, Pan means reward
    the most to my mind!
Fight I shall, with our foremost, where-
    ever this fennel may grow,—
Pound — Pan helping us — Persia to dust,
    and, under the deep,
Whelm her away forever; and then,— no
    Athens to save,—   100
Marry a certain maid, I know keeps faith
    to the brave,—
Hie to my house and home: and, when my
    children shall creep
Close to my knees,— recount how the God
    was awful yet kind,

Promised their sire reward to the full —
  rewarding him — so!'

———

Unforeseeing one! Yes, he fought on the
  Marathon day: 105
So, when Persia was dust, all cried 'To
  Akropolis!
Run, Pheidippides, one race more! the meed
  is thy due!
"Athens is saved, thank Pan," go shout!'
  He flung down his shield,
Ran like fire once more: and the space
  'twixt the Fennelfield
And Athens was stubble again, a field which
  a fire runs through,   110
Till in he broke: 'Rejoice, we conquer!'
  Like wine through clay,
Joy in his blood bursting his heart, he died
  — the bliss!
So, to this day, when friend meets friend,
  the word of salute
Is still 'Rejoice'— his word which brought
  rejoicing indeed.
So is Pheidippides happy forever,— the
  noble strong man   115
Who could race like a god, bear the face of
  a god, whom a god loved so well;
He saw the land saved he had helped to
  save, and was suffered to tell
Such tidings, yet never decline, but,
  gloriously as he began,
So to end gloriously — once to shout, thereafter be mute: '
Athens is saved!'— Pheidippides dies in the
  shout for his meed.   120

(1879)

ASOLANDO

EPILOGUE

At the midnight in the silence of the sleep
  time,
  When you set your fancies free,
Will they pass to where — by death, fools
  think, imprisoned —
Low he lies who once so loved you, whom
  you loved so.—
              — Pity me?   5
Oh, to love so, be so loved, yet so mis-
  taken!
What had I on earth to do
With the slothful, with the mawkish, the
  unmanly?
Like the aimless, helpless, hopeless, did I
  drivel
              — Being — who?   10

One who never turned his back but marched
  breast forward,
  Never doubted clouds would break,
Never dreamed, though right were worsted,
  wrong would triumph,
Held we fall to rise, are baffled to fight
  better,
              Sleep to wake.   15

No, at noonday in the bustle of man's work-
  time
  Greet the unseen with a cheer!
Bid him forward, breast and back as either
  should be,
'Strive and thrive!' cry 'Speed,— fight on.
  fare ever
              There as here!'   20

(1890)

MATTHEW ARNOLD (1822-1888)

From his father, Dr. Thomas Arnold, afterward headmaster of Rugby, Matthew Arnold may well have inherited the academic tastes that dominated his life. After a schooling at Winchester and Rugby, Arnold won a classical scholarship, in 1841, at Balliol College, Oxford. During his second year at the university, he gained the Newdigate prize by a poem on Cromwell, and in 1845 he was elected to a fellowship at Oriel College. Arnold abandoned Oxford presently, however, in order to become private secretary to the Marquis of Lansdowne, who procured for him, in 1851, an appointment as inspector of schools, from which he was released only a short time before his death. In 1848 he became known to a small circle of readers by his first volume of poems, *The Strayed Reveller and other Poems*, and during the next few years his poetical influence greatly increased, especially through the poems contained in *Poems by Matthew Arnold* (1853), a volume to which he prefaced a notable critical essay on poetry. In 1857 Arnold was elected to the professorship of poetry at Oxford, which he held for ten years, and which provided him the stimulus for writing certain of his best critical essays. The substantial classic *On Translating Homer: Three Lectures given at Oxford* (1861) was followed by *Essays in Criticism* (1865), which promptly fascinated and influenced English readers, as did also the published lectures, *On the Study of Celtic Literature* (1867). From pure literary criticism Arnold passed, for a time, to studies in religion, ethics, and politics, such as *Culture and Anarchy* (1869), *Friendship's Garland* (1871), *Literature and Dogma* (1873), and *Last Essays on Church and Religion* (1877). He returned subsequently, however, to literary criticism, occupying himself largely in editing, in making selections from poets, and in writing prefaces. In 1883 Arnold received a civil service pension of £250, which enabled him to retire from his duties as inspector of schools. In the winter of 1883-84, he lectured in America, as he did also in 1886. The lectures delivered during his first American tour were published in 1885 as *Discourses in America*.

Arnold's poetry, small in volume, is of almost invariable excellence. Although it makes no strong popular appeal, it has always held a large audience through its grace, gravity, and melody. As a critic, Arnold is preëminent. For a generation or two his canons of poetry, securely expressed in a poised, gentle, and precise style, have dominated English literary criticism.

THE STUDY OF POETRY

'The future of poetry is immense, because in poetry, where it is worthy of its high destinies, our race, as time goes on, will find an ever surer and surer stay. There is not a creed which is not shaken, not an accredited dogma which is not shown to be questionable, not a received tradition which does not threaten to dissolve. Our religion has materialized itself in the fact, in the supposed fact; it has attached its emotion to the fact, and now the fact is failing it. But for poetry the idea is everything; the rest is a world of illusion, of divine illusion. Poetry attaches its emotion to the idea; the idea *is* the fact. The strongest part of our religion to-day is its unconscious poetry.'

Let me be permitted to quote these words of my own, as uttering the thought which should, in my opinion, go with us and govern us in all our study of poetry. 5 In the present work it is the course of one great contributory stream to the world-river of poetry that we are invited to follow. We are here invited to trace the stream of English poetry. But 10 whether we set ourselves, as here, to follow only one of the several streams that make the mighty river of poetry, or whether we seek to know them all, our governing thought should be the 15 same. We should conceive of poetry worthily, and more highly than it has been the custom to conceive of it. We should conceive of it as capable of higher uses and called to higher destinies, than those which in general men have assigned to it hitherto. More and more mankind will discover that we have to turn to poetry to interpret life for us, to console us, to sustain us. Without poetry, our science will appear incomplete; and most of what now passes with us for religion and philosophy will be replaced by poetry. Science, I say, will appear incomplete without it. For finely and truly does Wordsworth call poetry 'the impassioned expression which is in the countenance of all science;' and what is a countenance without its expression? Again, Wordsworth finely and truly calls poetry 'the breath and finer spirit of all knowledge:' our religion, parading evidences such as those on which the popular mind relies now; our philosophy, pluming itself on its reasonings about causation and finite and infinite being; what are they but the shadows and dreams and false shows of knowledge? The day will come when we shall wonder at ourselves for having trusted to them, for having taken them seriously; and the more we perceive their hollowness, the more we shall prize 'the breath and finer spirit of knowledge' offered to us by poetry.

But if we conceive thus highly of the destinies of poetry, we must also set our standard for poetry high, since poetry, to be capable of fulfilling such high destinies, must be poetry of a high order of excellence. We must accustom ourselves to a high standard and to a strict judgment. Sainte-Beuve relates that Napoleon one day said, when somebody was spoken of in his presence as a charlatan: 'Charlatan as much as you please; but where is there not charlatanism?' 'Yes,' answers Sainte-Beuve, 'in politics, in the art of governing mankind, that is perhaps true. But in the order of thought, in art, the glory, the eternal honor is that charlatanism shall find no entrance; herein lies the inviolableness of that noble portion of man's being.' It is admirably said, and let us hold fast to it. In poetry, which is thought and art in one, it is the glory, the eternal honor, that charlatanism shall find no entrance; that this noble sphere be kept inviolate and inviolable. Charlatanism is for confusing or obliterating the distinctions between excellent and inferior,

sound and unsound or only half-sound, true and untrue or only half-true. It is charlatanism, conscious or unconscious, whenever we confuse or obliterate these. And in poetry, more than anywhere else, it is unpermissible to confuse or obliterate them. For in poetry the distinction between excellent and inferior, sound and unsound or only half-sound, true and untrue or only half-true, is of paramount importance. It is of paramount importance because of the high destinies of poetry. In poetry, as a criticism of life under the conditions fixed for such a criticism by the laws of poetic truth and poetic beauty, the spirit of our race will find, we have said, as time goes on and as other helps fail, its consolation and stay. But the consolation and stay will be of power in proportion to the power of the criticism of life. And the criticism of life will be of power in proportion as the poetry conveying it is excellent rather than inferior, sound rather than unsound or half-sound, true rather than untrue or half-true.

The best poetry is what we want; the best poetry will be found to have a power of forming, sustaining, and delighting us, as nothing else can. A clearer, deeper sense of the best in poetry, and of the strength and joy to be drawn from it, is the most precious benefit which we can gather from a poetical collection such as the present. And yet in the very nature and conduct of such a collection there is inevitably something which tends to obscure in us the consciousness of what our benefit should be, and to distract us from the pursuit of it. We should therefore steadily set it before our minds at the outset, and should compel ourselves to revert constantly to the thought of it as we proceed.

Yes; constantly, in reading poetry, a sense for the best, the really excellent, and of the strength and joy to be drawn from it, should be present in our minds and should govern our estimate of what we read. But this real estimate, the only true one, is liable to be superseded, if we are not watchful, by two other kinds of estimate, the historic estimate and the personal estimate, both of which are fallacious. A poet or a poem may count to us historically, they may count to us on grounds personal to ourselves, and they may count to us really. They may count to us historically. The course of development of a nation's language, thought, and poetry, is profoundly interesting; and by regarding a poet's work as a stage in this course of development we may easily bring ourselves to make it of more importance as poetry than in itself it really is, we may come to use a language of quite exaggerated praise in criticizing it; in short, to overrate it. So arises in our poetic judgments the fallacy caused by the estimate which we may call historic. Then, again, a poet or a poem may count to us on grounds personal to ourselves. Our personal affinities, likings, and circumstances, have great power to sway our estimate of this or that poet's work, and to make us attach more importance to it as poetry than in itself it really possesses, because to us it is, or has been, of high importance. Here also we overrate the object of our interest, and apply to it a language of praise which is quite exaggerated. And thus we get the source of a second fallacy in our poetic judgments,— the fallacy caused by an estimate which we may call personal.

Both fallacies are natural. It is evident how naturally the study of the history and development of a poetry may incline a man to pause over reputations and works once conspicuous but now obscure, and to quarrel with a careless public for skipping, in obedience to mere tradition and habit, from one famous name or work in its national poetry to another, ignorant of what it misses, and of the reason for keeping what it keeps, and of the whole process of growth in its poetry. The French have become diligent students of their own early poetry, which they long neglected; the study makes many of them dissatisfied with this so-called classical poetry, the court-tragedy of the seventeenth century, a poetry which Pellisson long ago reproached with its want of the true poetic stamp, with its *politesse stérile et rampante* [sterile and servile politeness], but which nevertheless has reigned in France as absolutely as if it had been the perfection of classical poetry indeed. The dissatisfaction is natural; yet a lively and accomplished critic, M. Charles d'Héricault, the editor of Clément Marot,

goes too far when he says that 'the cloud of glory playing round a classic is a mist as dangerous to the future of a literature as it is intolerable for the purposes of history.' 'It hinders,' he goes on, 'it hinders us from seeing more than one single point, the culminating and exceptional point; the summary, fictitious and arbitrary, of a thought and of a work. It substitutes a halo for a physiognomy, it puts a statue where there was once a man, and hiding from us all trace of the labor, the attempts, the weaknesses, the failures, it claims not study but veneration; it does not show us how the thing is done, it imposes upon us a model. Above all, for the historian this creation of classic personages is inadmissible; for it withdraws the poet from his time, from his proper life, it breaks historical relationships, it blinds criticism by conventional admiration, and renders the investigation of literary origins unacceptable. It gives us a human personage no longer, but a God seated immovable amidst his perfect work, like Jupiter on Olympus; and hardly will it be possible for the young student, to whom such work is exhibited at such a distance from him, to believe that it did not issue ready made from that divine head.'

All this is brilliantly and tellingly said, but we must plead for a distinction. Everything depends on the reality of a poet's classic character. If he is a dubious classic, let us sift him; if he is a false classic, let us explode him. But if he is a real classic, if his work belongs to the class of the very best (for this is the true and right meaning of the word *classic, classical*), then the great thing for us is to feel and enjoy his work as deeply as ever we can, and to appreciate the wide difference between it and all work which has not the same high character. This is what is salutary, this is what is formative; this is the great benefit to be got from the study of poetry. Everything which interferes with it, which hinders it, is injurious. True, we must read our classic with open eyes, and not with eyes blinded with superstition; we must perceive when his work comes short, when it drops out of the class of the very best, and we must rate it, in such cases, at its proper value. But the use of this negative criticism is not in itself, it is entirely in its enabling us to have a clearer sense and a deeper enjoyment of what is truly excellent. To trace the labor, the attempts, the weaknesses, the failures of a genuine classic, to acquaint oneself with his time and his life and his historical relationships, is mere literary dilettantism unless it has that clear sense and deeper enjoyment for its end. It may be said that the more we know about a classic the better we shall enjoy him; and, if we lived as long as Methuselah and had all of us heads of perfect clearness and wills of perfect steadfastness, this might be true in fact as it is plausible in theory. But the case here is much the same as the case with the Greek and Latin studies of our schoolboys. The elaborate philological groundwork which we require them to lay is in theory an admirable preparation for appreciating the Greek and Latin authors worthily. The more thoroughly we lay the groundwork, the better we shall be able, it may be said, to enjoy the authors. True, if time were not so short, and schoolboys' wits not so soon tired and their power of attention exhausted; only, as it is, the elaborate philological preparation goes on, but the authors are little known and less enjoyed. So with the investigator of 'historic origins' in poetry. He ought to enjoy the true classic all the better for his investigations; he often is distracted from the enjoyment of the best, and with the less good he overbusies himself, and is prone to overrate it in proportion to the trouble which it has cost him.

The idea of tracing historic origins and historical relationships cannot be absent from a compilation like the present. And naturally the poets to be exhibited in it will be assigned to those persons for exhibition who are known to prize them highly, rather than to those who have no special inclination towards them. Moreover the very occupation with an author, and the business of exhibiting him, disposes us to affirm and amplify his importance. In the present work, therefore, we are sure of frequent temptation to adopt the historic estimate, or the personal estimate, and to forget the real estimate; which latter, nevertheless, we must employ if we are to make poetry yield us its full benefit. So high is that

benefit, the benefit of clearly feeling and of deeply enjoying the really excellent, the truly classic in poetry, that we do well, I say, to set it fixedly before our minds as our object in studying poets and poetry, and to make the desire of attaining it the one principle to which, as the *Imitation* says, whatever we may read or come to know, we always return. *Cum multa legeris et cognoveris, ad unum semper oportet redire principium* [When you have read and known many things, you ought always to revert to the one beginning].

The historic estimate is likely in especial to affect our judgment and our language when we are dealing with ancient poets; the personal estimate when we are dealing with poets our contemporaries, or at any rate modern. The exaggerations due to the historic estimate are not in themselves, perhaps, of very much gravity. Their report hardly enters the general ear; probably they do not always impose even on the literary men who adopt them. But they lead to a dangerous abuse of language. So we hear Cædmon, amongst our own poets, compared to Milton. I have already noticed the enthusiasm of one accomplished French critic for 'historic origins.' Another eminent French critic, M. Vitet, comments upon that famous document of the early poetry of his nation, the *Chanson de Roland*. It is indeed a most interesting document. The *joculator* or *jongleur* Taillefer, who was with William the Conqueror's army at Hastings, marched before the Norman troops, so said the tradition, singing 'of Charlemagne and of Roland and of Oliver, and of the vassals who died at Roncevaux'; and it is suggested that in the *Chanson de Roland* by one Turoldus or Théroulde, a poem preserved in a manuscript of the twelfth century in the Bodleian Library at Oxford, we have certainly the matter, perhaps even some of the words of the chaunt which Taillefer sang. The poem has vigor and freshness; it is not without pathos. But M. Vitet is not satisfied with seeing in it a document of some poetic value, and of very high historic and linguistic value; he sees in it a grand and beautiful work, a monument of epic genius. In its general design he finds the grandiose concep tion, in its details he finds the constant union of simplicity with greatness, which are the marks, he truly says, of the genuine epic, and distinguish it from the artificial epic of literary ages. One thinks of Homer; this is the sort of praise which is given to Homer, and justly given. Higher praise there cannot well be, and it is the praise due to epic poetry of the highest order only, and to no other. Let us try, then, the *Chanson de Roland* at its best. Roland, mortally wounded, lays himself down under a pine tree, with his face turned toward Spain and the enemy:

De plusurs choses à remembrer li prist
De tantes teres cume li bers cunquist,
De dulce France, des humes de sun lign,
De Carlemagne sun seignor ki l'nurrit.[1]

That is primitive work, I repeat, with an undeniable poetic quality of its own. It deserves such praise and such praise is sufficient for it. But now turn to Homer:

῝Ως φάτο, τοὺς δ' ἤδη κατέχεν φυσίζοος αἶα
ἐν Λακεδαίμονι αὖθι, φίλῃ ἐν πατρίδι γαίῃ.[2]

We are here in another world, another order of poetry altogether; here is rightly due such supreme praise as that which M. Vitet gives to the *Chanson de Roland*. If our words are to have any meaning, if our judgments are to have any solidity, we must not heap that supreme praise upon poetry of an order immeasurably inferior.

Indeed there can be no more useful help for discovering what poetry belongs to the class of the truly excellent, and can therefore do us most good, than to have always in one's mind lines and expressions of the great masters, and to apply them as a touchstone to other poetry. Of course we are not to require this other poetry to resemble them: it may be very dissimilar. But if we have any tact we shall find them, when we have lodged them well in our minds, an infallible touchstone for detecting the presence or absence of high poetic quality, and also the degree of this quality, in all other poetry which we may place beside them. Short passages, even single lines, will serve our turn quite sufficiently. Take the two lines which I have just quoted from Homer, the poet's comment on Helen's mention of her brothers; or take his

᾿Α δειλώ τί σφῶϊ δόμεν Πηλῆϊ ἄνακτι
θνητῷ; ὑμεῖς δ' ἐστὸν ἀγήρω τ' ἀθανάτω τε.
ἦ ἵνα δυστήνοισι μετ' ἀνδράσιν ἄλγε' ἔχητον;[3]

the address of Zeus to the horses of Peleus; or, take finally, his

Καὶ σέ, γέρον, τὸ πρὶν μὲν ἀκούομεν ὄλβιον εἶναι[4]

the words of Achilles to Priam, a suppliant before him. Take that incomparable line and a half of Dante, Ugolino's tremendous words:

Io no piangeva; sì dentro impietrai.
Piangevan elli . .

take the lovely words of Beatrice to Virgil:

Io son fatta da Dio, sua mercè, tale,
Che la vostra miseria non mi tange,
Nè fiamma d'esto incendio non
        m'assale . . . [6]

take the simple, but perfect, single line:

In la sua volontade è nostra pace.[7]

Take of Shakespeare a line or two of Henry the Fourth's expostulation with sleep:

Wilt thou upon the high and giddy mast

---

[1] 'Then began he to call many things to remembrance,— all the lands which his valor conquered, and pleasant France, and the men of his lineage, and Charlemagne his liege lord who nourished him.'— *Chanson de Roland*, iii. 939-942.

[2] 'So said she; they long since in Earth's soft arms were reposing,
There, in their own dear land, their fatherland, Lacedæmon.'
Iliad, iii. 243-4 (translated by Dr. Hawtrey).

[3] 'Ah, unhappy pair, why gave we you to King Peleus, to a mortal? but ye are without old age, and immortal. Was it that with men born to misery ye might have sorrow?'— *Iliad*, xvii. 443-445.

[4] 'Nay, and thou too, old man, in former days wast, as we hear, happy.'— *Iliad*, xxiv. 543.

[5] 'I wailed not. so of stone grew I within;— they wailed.'— *Inferno*, xxxiii. 39, 40.

[6] 'Of such sort hath God, thanked be his mercy, made me, that your misery toucheth me not, neither doth the flame of this fire strike me.'— *Inferno*, ii. 91-93.

[7] 'In His will is our peace.'— *Paradiso*, iii. 85.

Seal up the ship-boy's eyes, and rock his
   brains
In cradle of the rude imperious
   surge . . .

   . . .

and take, as well, Hamlet's dying request
to Horatio:

If thou didst ever hold me in thy heart,
Absent thee from felicity awhile,
And in this harsh world draw thy breath
   in pain
To tell my story . . .
Take of Milton that Miltonic passage:

       Darkened so, yet shone
Above them all the archangel; but his face
Deep scars of thunder had intrenched, and
   care
Sat on his faded cheek . . .

add two such lines as:

And courage never to submit or yield
And what is else not to be overcome . . .

and finish with the exquisite close to the
loss of Proserpine, the loss

   . . . which cost Ceres all that pain
To seek her through the world.

These few lines, if we have tact and can
use them, are enough even of themselves
to keep clear and sound our judgments
about poetry, to save us from fallacious
estimates of it, to conduct us to a real
estimate.

The specimens I have quoted differ
widely from one another, but they have
in common this: the possession of the
very highest poetical quality. If we are
thoroughly penetrated by their power, we
shall find that we have acquired a sense
enabling us, whatever poetry may be laid
before us, to feel the degree in which a
high poetical quality is present or wanting there. Critics give themselves great
labor to draw out what in the abstract
constitutes the characters of a high
quality of poetry. It is much better
simply to have recourse to concrete examples: — to take specimens of poetry
of the high, the very highest quality, and
to say: The characters of a high quality
of poetry are what is expressed *there*.
They are far better recognized by being
felt in the verse of the master, than by

being perused in the prose of the critic.
Nevertheless if we are urgently pressed
to give some critical account of them,
we may safely, perhaps, venture on laying down, not indeed how and why the
characters arise, but where and in what
they arise. They are in the matter and
substance of the poetry, and they are in
its manner and style. Both of these, the
substance and matter on the one hand,
the style and manner on the other, have
a mark, an accent, of high beauty, worth,
and power. But if we are asked to define this mark and accent in the abstract,
our answer must be: No, for we should
thereby be darkening the question, not
clearing it. The mark and accent are as
given by the substance and matter of that
poetry, by the style and manner of that
poetry, and of all other poetry which is
akin to it in quality.

Only one thing we may add as to the
substance and matter of poetry, guiding
ourselves by Aristotle's profound observation that the superiority of poetry over
history consists in its possessing a higher
truth and a higher seriousness (φιλοσοφώ-
τερον καὶ σπουδαιότερον) [more philosophic
and more serious]. Let us add, therefore, to what we have said, this: that the
substance and matter of the best poetry
acquire their special character from
possessing, in an eminent degree, truth
and seriousness. We may add yet further, what is in itself evident, that to the
style and manner of the best poetry their
special character, their accent, is given
by their diction, and, even yet more, by
their movement. And though we distinguish between the two characters, the two
accents, of superiority, yet they are
nevertheless vitally connected one with
the other. The superior character of
truth and seriousness, in the matter and
substance of the best poetry, is inseparable from the superiority of diction and
movement marking its style and manner.
The two superiorities are closely related,
and are in steadfast proportion one to the
other. So far as high poetic truth and
seriousness are wanting to a poet's matter
and substance, so far also we may be
sure, will a high poetic stamp of diction
and movement be wanting to his style
and manner. In proportion as this high
stamp of diction and movement, again,
is absent from a poet's style and manner,

we shall find, also, that high poetic truth and seriousness are absent from his substance and matter.

So stated, these are but dry generalities; their whole force lies in their application. And I could wish every student of poetry to make the application of them for himself. Made by himself, the application would impress itself upon his mind far more deeply than made by me. Neither will my limits allow me to make any full application of the generalities above propounded; but in the hope of bringing out, at any rate, some significance in them, and of establishing an important principle more firmly by their means, I will, in the space which remains to me, follow rapidly from the commencement the course of our English poetry with them in my view.

Once more I return to the early poetry of France, with which our own poetry, in its origins, is indissolubly connected. In the twelfth and thirteenth centuries, that seed-time of all modern language and literature, the poetry of France had a clear predominance in Europe. Of the two divisions of that poetry, its productions in the *langue d' oil* and its productions in the *langue d' oc,* the poetry of the *langue d' oc,* of southern France, of the troubadours, is of importance because of its effect on Italian literature; — the first literature of modern Europe to strike the true and grand note, and to bring forth, as in Dante and Petrarch it brought forth, classics. But the predominance of French poetry in Europe, during the twelfth and thirteenth centuries, is due to its poetry of the *langue d' oil,* the poetry of northern France and of the tongue which is now the French language. In the twelfth century the bloom of this romance-poetry was earlier and stronger in England, at the court of our Anglo-Norman kings, than in France itself. But it was a bloom of French poetry; and as our native poetry formed itself, it formed itself out of this. The romance-poems which took possession of the heart and imagination of Europe in the twelfth and thirteenth centuries are French; 'they are,' as Southey justly says, 'the pride of French literature, nor have we anything which can be placed in competition with them.' Themes were supplied from all quarters; but the ro-

mance-setting which was common to them all, and which gained the ear of Europe, was French. This constituted for the French poetry, literature, and language, at the height of the Middle Age, an unchallenged predominance. The Italian Brunetto Latini, the master of Dante, wrote his *Treasure* in French because, he says, ' *la parleure en est plus délitable et plus commune à toutes gens.*' In the same century, the thirteenth, the French romance-writer, Christian of Troyes, formulates the claims, in chivalry and letters, of France, his native country, as follows:

Or vous ert par ce livre apris,
Que Gresse ot de chevalerie
Le premier los et de clergie;
Puis vint chevalerie à Rome,
Et de la clergie la some,
Qui ore est en France venue.
Diex doinst qu'ele i soit retenue,
Et que li lius li abelisse
Tant que de France n'isse
L'onor qui s'i est arestée!

' Now by this book you will learn that first Greece had the renown for chivalry and letters; then chivalry and the primacy in letters passed to Rome, and now it is come to France. God grant it may be kept there; and that the place may please it so well, that the honor which has come to make stay in France may never depart thence!'

Yet it is now all gone, this French romance-poetry, of which the weight of substance and the power of style are not unfairly represented by this extract from Christian of Troyes. Only by means of the historic estimate can we persuade ourselves now to think that any of it is of poetical importance.

But in the fourteenth century there comes an Englishman nourished on this poetry, taught his trade by this poetry, getting words, rime, meter from this poetry; for even of that stanza which the Italians used, and which Chaucer derived immediately from the Italians, the basis and suggestion was probably given in France. Chaucer (I have already named him) fascinated his contemporaries, but so too did Christian of Troyes and Wolfram of Eschenbach. Chaucer's power of fascination, however, is enduring; his poetical importance does not need the assistance of the historic estimate, it is real. He is a genuine source of joy and strength which is flowing still for us and will flow always. He will be read, as time goes on, far more generally than he is read now. His language is a cause of difficulty for us; but so also, and I think in quite as great a degree, is the language of Burns. In Chaucer's case, as in that of Burns, it is a difficulty to be unhesitatingly accepted and overcome.

If we ask ourselves wherein consists the immense superiority of Chaucer's poetry over the romance-poetry, why it is that in passing from this to Chaucer we suddenly feel ourselves to be in another world, we shall find that his superiority is both in the substance of his poetry and in the style of his poetry. His superiority in substance is given by his large, free, simple, clear yet kindly view of human life,— so unlike the total want, in the romance-poets, of all intelligent command of it. Chaucer has not their helplessness; he has gained the power to survey the world from a central, a truly human point of view. We have only to call to mind the Prologue to *The Canterbury Tales*. The right comment upon it is Dryden's: ' It is sufficient to say, according to the proverb, that *here is God's plenty*.' And again: ' He is a perpetual fountain of good sense.' It is by a large, free, sound representation of things, that poetry, this high criticism of life, has truth of substance; and Chaucer's poetry has truth of substance.

Of his style and manner, if we think first of the romance-poetry and then of Chaucer's divine liquidness of diction, his divine fluidity of movement, it is difficult to speak temperately. They are irresistible, and justify all the rapture with which his successors speak of his ' gold dew-drops of speech.' Johnson misses the point entirely when he finds fault with Dryden for ascribing to Chaucer the first refinement of our numbers, and says that Gower also can show smooth numbers and easy rimes. The refinement of our numbers means something far more than this. A nation may have versifiers with smooth numbers and easy rimes, and yet may have no real poetry at all. Chaucer is the father of our splendid English poetry, he is our ' well of English undefiled,' because by the lovely charm of his diction, the lovely charm of his movement, he makes an epoch and founds a tradition. In Spenser, Shakspere, Milton, Keats, we can follow the tradition of the liquid diction, the fluid movement, of Chaucer; at one time it is his liquid diction of which in these poets we feel the virtue, and at another time it is his fluid movement. And the virtue is irresistible.

Bounded as is my space, I must yet find room for an example of Chaucer's virtue, as I have given examples to show the virtue of the great classics. I feel disposed to say that a single line is enough to show the charm of Chaucer's verse; that merely one line like this:

O martyr souded [1] in virginitee!

has a virtue of manner and movement such as we shall not find in all the verse of romance-poetry; — but this is saying nothing. The virtue is such as we shall not find, perhaps, in all English poetry, outside the poets whom I have named as the special inheritors of Chaucer's tradition. A single line, however, is too little if we have not the strain of Chaucer's verse well in our memory; let us take a stanza. It is from *The Prioress's Tale*, the story of the Christian child murdered in a Jewry: —

My throte is cut unto my nekke-bone,
Saidè this child, and as by way of kinde
I should have deyd, yea, longè time agone;
But Jesu Christ, as ye in bookès finde,
Will that his glory last and be in minde
And for the worship of his mother dere
Yet may I sing O *Alma* loud and clere.

Wordsworth has modernized this Tale, and to feel how delicate and evanescent is the charm of verse, we have only to read Wordsworth's first three lines of this stanza after Chaucer's: —

My throat is cut unto the bone, I trow,
Said this young child, and by the law of kind
I should have died, yea, many hours ago.

The charm is departed. It is often said that the power of liquidness and fluidity in Chaucer's verse was dependent

[1] The French *soudé;* soldered, fixed fast.

upon a free, a licentious dealing with language, such as is now impossible; upon a liberty, such as Burns too enjoyed, of making words like *neck, bird,* into a dissyllable by adding to them, and words like *cause, rime,* into a dissyllable by sounding the *e* mute. It is true that Chaucer's fluidity is conjoined with this liberty, and is admirably served by it; but we ought not to say that it was dependent upon it. It was dependent upon his talent. Other poets with a like liberty do not attain to the fluidity of Chaucer; Burns himself does not attain to it. Poets again, who have a talent akin to Chaucer's, such as Shakspere or Keats, have known how to attain to his fluidity without the like liberty.

And yet Chaucer is not one of the great classics. His poetry transcends and effaces, easily and without effort, all the romance-poetry of Catholic Christendom; it transcends and effaces all the English poetry contemporary with it, it transcends and effaces all the English poetry subsequent to it down to the age of Elizabeth. Of such avail is poetic truth of substance, in its natural and necessary union with poetic truth of style. And yet, I say, Chaucer is not one of the great classics. He has not their accent. What is wanting to him is suggested by the mere mention of the name of the first great classic of Christendom, the immortal poet who died eighty years before Chaucer,— Dante. The accent of such verse as

In la sua volontade è nostra pace . . .

is altogether beyond Chaucer's reach; we praise him, but we feel that this accent is out of the question for him. It may be said that it was necessarily out of the reach of any poet in the England of that stage of growth. Possibly; but we are to adopt a real, not a historic, estimate of poetry. However we may account for its absence, something is wanting, then, to the poetry of Chaucer, which poetry must have before it can be placed in the glorious class of the best. And there is no doubt what that something is. It is the σπουδαιότης, the high and excellent seriousness, which Aristotle assigns as one of the grand virtues of poetry. The substance of Chaucer's poetry, his view of things and his criticism of life, has

largeness, freedom, shrewdness, benignity; but it has not this high seriousness. Homer's criticism of life has it, Dante's has it, Shakspere's has it. It is this chiefly which gives to our spirits what they can rest upon; and with the increasing demands of our modern ages upon poetry, this virtue of giving us what we can rest upon will be more and more highly esteemed. A voice from the slums of Paris, fifty or sixty years after Chaucer, the voice of poor Villon out of his life of riot and crime, has at its happy moments (as, for instance, in the last stanza of *La Belle Heaulmière*[1]) more of this important poetic virtue of seriousness than all the productions of Chaucer. But its apparition in Villon, and in men like Villon, is fitful; the greatness of the great poets, the power of their criticism of life, is that their virtue is sustained.

To our praise, therefore, of Chaucer as a poet there must be this limitation; he lacks the high seriousness of the great classics, and therewith an important part of their virtue. Still, the main fact for us to bear in mind about Chaucer is his sterling value according to that real estimate which we firmly adopt for all poets. He has poetic truth of substance, though he has not high poetic seriousness, and corresponding to his truth of substance he has an exquisite virtue of style and manner. With him is born our real poetry.

But for my present purpose I need not dwell on our Elizabethan poetry, or on the continuation and close of this poetry in Milton. We all of us profess to be

[1] The name *Heaulmière* is said to be derived from a head-dress (helm) worn as a mark by courtesans. In Villon's ballad, a poor old creature of this class laments her days of youth and beauty. The last stanza of the ballad runs thus: —

> Ainsi le bon temps regretons
> Entre nous, pauvres vieilles sottes,
> Assises bas, à croppetons,
> Tout en ung tas comme pelottes;
> A petit feu de chenevottes
> Tost allumées, tost estainctes.
> Et jadis fusmes si mignottes!
> Ainsi en prend à maintz et maintes.

Thus amongst ourselves we regret the good time, poor silly old things, low-seated on our heels, all in a heap like so many balls; by a little fire of hempstalks, soon lighted, soon spent. And once we were such darlings! So fares it with many and many a one.'

agreed in the estimate of this poetry; we all of us recognize it as great poetry, our greatest, and Shakspere and Milton as our poetical classics. The real estimate, here, has universal currency. With the next age of our poetry divergency and difficulty begin. An historic estimate of that poetry has established itself; and the question is, whether it will be found to coincide with the real estimate.

The age of Dryden, together with our whole eighteenth century which followed it, sincerely believed itself to have produced poetical classics of its own, and even to have made advance, in poetry, beyond all its predecessors. Dryden regards as not seriously disputable the opinion 'that the sweetness of English verse was never understood or practised by our fathers.' Cowley could see nothing at all in Chaucer's poetry. Dryden heartily admired it, and, as we have seen, praised its matter admirably; but of its exquisite manner and movement all he can find to say is that 'there is the rude sweetness of a Scotch tune in it, which is natural and pleasing, though not perfect.' Addison, wishing to praise Chaucer's numbers, compares them with Dryden's own. And all through the eighteenth century, and down even into our own times, the stereotyped phrase of approbation for good verse found in our early poetry has been, that it even approached the verse of Dryden, Addison, Pope, and Johnson.

Are Dryden and Pope poetical classics? Is the historic estimate, which represents them as such, and which has been so long established that it cannot easily give way, the real estimate? Wordsworth and Coleridge, as is well known, denied it; but the authority of Wordsworth and Coleridge does not weigh much with the young generation, and there are many signs to show that the eighteenth century and its judgments are coming into favor again. Are the favorite poets of the eighteenth century classics?

It is impossible within my present limits to discuss the question fully. And what man of letters would not shrink from seeming to dispose dictatorially of the claims of two men who are, at any rate, such masters in letters as Dryden and Pope; two men of such admirable talent, both of them. and one of them. Dryden,

a man, on all sides, of such energetic and genial power? And yet, if we are to gain the full benefit from poetry, we must have the real estimate of it. I cast about for some mode of arriving, in the present case, at such an estimate without offence. And perhaps the best way is to begin, as it is easy to begin, with cordial praise.

When we find Chapman, the Elizabethan translator of Homer, expressing himself in his preface thus: 'Though truth in her very nakedness sit in so deep a pit, that from Gades to Aurora and Ganges few eyes can sound her, I hope yet those few here will so discover and confirm, that, the date being out of her darkness in this morning of our poet, he shall now gird his temples with the sun,' — we pronounce that such a prose is intolerable. When we find Milton writing: 'And long it was not after, when I was confirmed in this opinion, that he, who would not be frustrate of his hope to write well hereafter in laudable things, ought himself to be a true poem,'— we pronounce that such a prose has its own grandeur, but that it is obsolete and inconvenient. But when we find Dryden telling us: 'What Virgil wrote in the vigor of his age, in plenty and at ease, I have undertaken to translate in my declining years, struggling with wants, oppressed with sickness, curbed in my genius, liable to be misconstrued in all I write,'— then we exclaim that here at last we have the true English prose, a prose such as we would all gladly use if we only knew how. Yet Dryden was Milton's contemporary.

But after the Restoration the time had come when our nation felt the imperious need of a fit prose. So, too, the time had likewise come when our nation felt the imperious need of freeing itself from the absorbing preoccupation which religion in the Puritan age had exercised. It was impossible that this freedom should be brought about without some negative excess, without some neglect and impairment of the religious life of the soul; and the spiritual history of the eighteenth century shows us that the freedom was not achieved without them. Still, the freedom was achieved; the preoccupation, an undoubtedly baneful and retarding one if it had continued, was got rid of. And as with religion amongst us at that period, so it was also with letters. A fit prose was a necessity; but it was impossible that a fit prose should establish itself amongst us without some touch of frost to the imaginative life of the soul. The needful qualities for a fit prose are regularity, uniformity, precision, balance. The men of letters, whose destiny it may be to bring their nation to the attainment of a fit prose, must of necessity, whether they work in prose or in verse, give a predominating, an almost exclusive attention to the qualities of regularity, uniformity, precision, balance. But an almost exclusive attention to these qualities involves some repression and silencing of poetry.

We are to regard Dryden as the puissant and glorious founder, Pope as the splendid high-priest, of our age of prose and reason, of our excellent and indispensable eighteenth century. For the purposes of their mission and destiny their poetry, like their prose, is admirable. Do you ask me whether Dryden's verse, take it almost where you will, is not good?

A milk-white Hind, immortal and unchanged,
Fed on the lawns and in the forest ranged.

I answer: Admirable for the purposes of the inaugurator of an age of prose and reason. Do you ask me whether Pope's verse, take it almost where you will, is not good?

To Hounslow Heath I point, and Banstead Down;
Thence comes your mutton, and these chicks my own.

I answer: Admirable for the purposes of the high-priest of an age of prose and reason. But do you ask me whether such verse proceeds from men with an adequate poetic criticism of life, from men whose criticism of life has a high seriousness, or even, without that high seriousness, has poetic largeness, freedom, insight, benignity? Do you ask me whether the application of ideas to life in the verse of these men, often a powerful application, no doubt, is a powerful *poetic* application? Do you ask me whether the poetry of these men has

either the matter or the inseparable manner of such an adequate poetic criticism; whether it has the accent of

Absent thee from felicity awhile . . .

or of

And what is else not to be overcome . . .

or of

O martyr souded in virginitee!

I answer: It has not and cannot have them; it is the poetry of the builders of an age of prose and reason. Though they may write in verse, though they may in a certain sense be masters of the art of versification, Dryden and Pope are not classics of our poetry, they are classics of our prose.

Gray is our poetical classic of that literature and age; the position of Gray is singular, and demands a word of notice here. He has not the volume or the power of poets who, coming in times more favorable, have attained to an independent criticism of life. But he lived with the great poets, he lived, above all, with the Greeks, through perpetually studying and enjoying them; and he caught their poetic point of view for regarding life, caught their poetic manner. The point of view and the manner are not self-sprung in him, he caught them of others; and he had not the free and abundant use of them. But whereas Addison and Pope never had the use of them, Gray had the use of them at times. He is the scantiest and frailest of classics in our poetry, but he is a classic.

And now, after Gray, we are met, as we draw towards the end of the eighteenth century, we are met by the great name of Burns. We enter now on times where the personal estimate of poets begins to be rife, and where the real estimate of them is not reached without difficulty. But in spite of the disturbing pressures of personal partiality, of national partiality, let us try to reach a real estimate of the poetry of Burns.

By his English poetry Burns in general belongs to the eighteenth century, and has little importance for us.

Mark ruffian Violence, distained with
    crimes,
Rousing elate in these degenerate times;
View unsuspecting Innocence a prey,
As guileful Fraud points out the erring way; 5
While subtle Litigation's pliant tongue
The life-blood equal sucks of Right and
    Wrong!

Evidently this is not the real Burns, or 10
his name and fame would have disappeared long ago. Nor is Clarinda's love-
poet, Sylvander, the real Burns either.
But he tells us himself: 'These English
songs gravel me to death. I have not the 15
command of the language that I have of
my native tongue. In fact, I think that
my ideas are more barren in English than
in Scotch. I have been at *Duncan Gray*
to dress it in English, but all I can do is 20
desperately stupid.' We English turn
naturally, in Burns, to the poems in our
own language, because we can read them
easily; but in those poems we have not
the real Burns.   25

The real Burns is of course in his
Scotch poems. Let us boldly say that of
much of this poetry, a poetry dealing
perpetually with Scotch drink, Scotch
religion, and Scotch manners, a Scotch- 30
man's estimate is apt to be personal. A
Scotchman is used to this world of Scotch
drink, Scotch religion, and Scotch manners; he has a tenderness for it; he meets
its poet half way. In this tender mood 35
he reads pieces like the *Holy Fair* or
Halloween. But this world of Scotch
drink, Scotch religion, and Scotch manners is against a poet, not for him, when
it is not a partial countryman who reads 40
him; for in itself it is not a beautiful
world, and no one can deny that it is of
advantage to a poet to deal with a beautiful world. Burn's world of Scotch drink,
Scotch religion, and Scotch manners, is 45
often a harsh, a sordid, a repulsive world;
even the world of his *Cotter's Saturday
Night* is not a beautiful world. No doubt
a poet's criticism of life may have such
truth and power that it triumphs over its 50
world and delights us. Burns may triumph over his world, often he does triumph over his world, but let us observe
how and where. Burns is the first case
we have had where the bias of the per- 55
sonal estimate tends to mislead; let us
look at him closely, he can bear it.

Many of his admirers will tell us that
we have Burns, convivial, genuine, delightful, here:

Leeze me on drink! it gies us mair
    Than either school or college;
It kindles wit, it waukens lair,
    It pangs us fou o' knowledge,
Be 't whiskey gill or penny wheep
    Or ony stronger potion,
It never fails, on drinking deep,
    To kittle up our notion
          By night or day.

There is a great deal of that sort of thing
in Burns, and it is unsatisfactory, not
because it is bacchanalian poetry, but because it has not that accent of sincerity
which bacchanalian poetry, to do it justice, very often has. There is something
in it of bravado, something which
makes us feel that we have not the man
speaking to us with his real voice; something, therefore, poetically unsound.

With still more confidence will his admirers tell us that we have the genuine
Burns, the great poet, when his strain
asserts the independence, equality, dignity, of men, as in the famous song *For
a' that and a' that:*

A prince can mak' a belted knight,
    A marquis, duke, and a' that;
But an honest man 's aboon his might,
    Guid faith he mauna fa' that!
        For a' that and a' that,
            Their dignities, and a' that,
            The pith o' sense, and pride o' worth,
            Are higher rank than a' that.

Here they find his grand, genuine
touches; and still more, when this puissant genius, who so often set morality at
defiance, falls moralizing:

The sacred lowe o' weel-placed love
    Luxuriantly indulge it;
But never tempt th' illicit rove,
    Tho' naething should divulge it.

I waive the quantum o' the sin,
    The hazard o' concealing,
But och! it hardens a' within,
    And petrifies the feeling.

Or in a higher strain:

Who made the heart, 't is he alone
    Decidedly can try us;

He knows each chord, its various tone;
　Each spring, its various bias.
Then at the balance let's be mute,
　We never can adjust it;
What's *done* we partly may compute,
　But know not what's resisted.

Or in a better strain yet, a strain, his
admirers will say, unsurpassable:

To make a happy fire-side clime
　　To weans and wife,
That's the true pathos and sublime
　　Of human life.

There is criticism of life for you, the
admirers of Burns will say to us; there
is the application of ideas to life! There
is, undoubtedly. The doctrine of the
last-quoted lines coincides almost exactly
with what was the aim and end, Xenophon tells us, of all the teaching of
Socrates. And the application is a
powerful one; made by a man of vigorous understanding, and (need I say?) a
master of language.

But for supreme poetical success more
is required than the powerful application
of ideas to life; it must be an application
under the conditions fixed by the laws
of poetic truth and poetic beauty. Those
laws fix as an essential condition, in the
poet's treatment of such matters as are
here in question, high seriousness; — the
high seriousness which comes from absolute sincerity. The accent of high
seriousness, born of absolute sincerity, is
what gives to such verse as

In la sua volontade è nostra pace . . .

to such criticism of life as Dante's, its
power. Is this accent felt in the passages which I have been quoting from
Burns? Surely not; surely, if our sense
is quick, we must perceive that we have
not in those passages a voice from the
very inmost soul of the genuine Burns;
he is not speaking to us from these
depths, he is more or less preaching.
And the compensation for admiring such
passages less, from missing the perfect
poetic accent in them, will be that we
shall admire more the poetry where that
accent is found.

No; Burns, like Chaucer, comes short
of the high seriousness of the great
classics, and the virtue of matter and

manner which goes with that high seriousness is wanting to his work. At
moments he touches it in a profound and
passionate melancholy, as in those four
immortal lines taken by Byron as a
motto for *The Giaour,* but which have in
them a depth of poetic quality such as
resides in no verse of Byron's own:

Had we never loved sae kindly,
Had we never loved sae blindly,
Never met, or never parted,
We had ne'er been broken-hearted.

But a whole poem of that quality Burns
cannot make; the rest, in the *Farewell to
Nancy,* is verbiage.

We arrive best at the real estimate of
Burns, I think, by conceiving his work
as having truth of matter and truth of
manner, but not the accent or the poetic
virtue of the highest masters. His genuine criticism of life, when the sheer
poet in him speaks, is ironic; it is not:

Thou Power Supreme, whose mighty scheme
　These woes of mine fulfil,
Here firm I rest, they must be best
　Because they are Thy will!

It is far rather: *Whistle owre the lave
o' t!* Yet we may say of him as of
Chaucer, that of life and the world, as
they come before him, his view is large,
free, shrewd, benignant,— truly poetic,
therefore; and his manner of rendering
what he sees is to match. But we must
note, at the same time, his great difference from Chaucer. The freedom of
Chaucer is heightened, in Burns, by a
fiery, reckless energy; the benignity of
Chaucer deepens, in Burns, into an overwhelming sense of the pathos of things;
— of the pathos of human nature, the
pathos, also, of non-human nature. Instead of the fluidity of Chaucer's manner,
the manner of Burns has spring, bounding swiftness. Burns is by far the
greater force, though he has perhaps less
charm. The world of Chaucer is fairer,
richer, more significant than that of
Burns; but when the largeness and freedom of Burns get full sweep, as in *Tam
o' Shanter,* or still more in that puissant
and splendid production, *The Jolly Beggars,* his world may be what it will, his
poetic genius triumphs over it. In the

world of the *Jolly Beggars* there is more than hideousness and squalor, there is bestiality; yet the piece is a superb poetic success. It has a breadth, truth, and power which make the famous scene in Auerbach's Cellar, of Goethe's *Faust,* seem artificial and tame beside it, and which are only matched by Shakspere and Aristophanes.

Here, where his largeness and freedom serve him so admirably, and also in those poems and songs, where to shrewdness he adds infinite archness and wit, and to benignity infinite pathos, where his manner is flawless, and a perfect poetic whole is the result,— in things like the address to the Mouse whose home he had ruined, in things like *Duncan Gray, Tam Glen, Whistle and I'll come to you, my lad, Auld lang syne* (the list might be made much longer),— here we have the genuine Burns, of whom the real estimate must be high indeed. Not a classic, nor with the excellent σπουδαιότης [seriousness] of the great classics, nor with a verse rising to a criticism of life and a virtue like theirs; but a poet with thorough truth of substance and an answering truth of style, giving us a poetry sound to the core. We all of us have a leaning towards the pathetic, and may be inclined perhaps to prize Burns most for his touches of piercing, sometimes almost intolerable, pathos; for verse like:

We twa hae paidl't i' the burn
  From mornin' sun till dine;
But seas between us braid hae roar'd,
  Sin auld lang syne . . .

where he is as lovely as he is sound. But perhaps it is by the perfection of soundness of his lighter and archer masterpieces that he is poetically most wholesome for us. For the votary misled by a personal estimate of Shelley, as so many of us have been, are, and will be,— of that beautiful spirit building his many-colored haze of words and images

Pinnacled dim in the intense inane —

no contact can be wholesomer than the contact with Burns at his archest and soundest. Side by side with the

On the brink of the night and the morning
  My coursers are wont to respire,
But the Earth has just whispered a warning,
  That their flight must be swifter than
    fire . . .

of *Prometheus Unbound,* how salutary, how very salutary, to place this from *Tam Glen:*

My minnie does constantly deave me
  And bids me beware o' young men;
They flatter, she says, to deceive me;
  But wha can think sae o' Tam Glen?

But we enter on burning ground as we approach the poetry of times so near to us, poetry like that of Byron, Shelley, and Wordsworth, of which the estimates are so often not only personal, but personal with passion. For my purpose, it is enough to have taken the single case of Burns, the first poet we come to of whose work the estimate formed is evidently apt to be personal, and to have suggested how we may proceed, using the poetry of the great classics as a sort of touchstone, to correct this estimate, as we had previously corrected by the same means the historic estimate where we met with it. A collection like the present, with its succession of celebrated names and celebrated poems, offers a good opportunity to us for resolutely endeavoring to make our estimates of poetry real. I have sought to point out a method which will help us in making them so, and to exhibit it in use so far as to put any one who likes in a way of applying it for himself.

At any rate the end to which the method and the estimate are designed to lead, and from leading to which, if they do lead to it, they get their whole value, — the benefit of being able clearly to feel and deeply to enjoy the best, the truly classic, in poetry,— is an end, let me say it once more at parting, of supreme importance. We are often told that an era is opening in which we are to see multitudes of a common sort of readers, and masses of a common sort of literature; that such readers do not want and could not relish anything better than such literature, and that to provide it is becoming a vast and profitable industry. Even if good literature entirely lost currency with the world, it would still be abundantly worth while to continue to enjoy it by oneself. But it never will lose currency with the world, in spite of momentary appearances; it never will lose supremacy. Currency and supremacy are insured to it, not indeed by the world's deliberate and conscious choice, but by something far deeper,— by the instinct of self-preservation in humanity.

(1880)

SHAKSPERE

Others abide our question. Thou art free.
We ask and ask: Thou smilest and art still,
Out-topping knowledge. For the loftiest hill
That to the stars uncrowns his majesty,
Planting his steadfast footsteps in the sea, 5
Making the heaven of heavens his dwelling-place,
Spares but the cloudy border of his base
To the foiled searching of mortality:
And thou, who didst the stars and sunbeams know,
Self-schooled, self-scanned, self-honored, self-secure, 10
Didst tread on earth unguessed at. Better so!
All pains the immortal spirit must endure,
All weakness that impairs, all griefs that bow,
Find their sole voice in that victorious brow.

(1849)

THE FORSAKEN MERMAN

Come, dear children, let us away,
Down and away below!
Now my brothers call from the bay,
Now the great winds shoreward blow,
Now the salt tides seaward flow, 5
Now the wild white horses play,
Champ, and chafe, and toss in the spray,
Children dear, let us away!
This way, this way!

Call her once before you go, 10
Call once yet!
In a voice that she will know:
'Margaret! Margaret!'
Children's voices should be dear
(Call once more!) to a mother's ear; 15
Children's voices, wild with pain:
Surely she will come again!
Call her once and come away;

This way, this way!
'Mother dear, we cannot stay; 20
The wild white horses foam and fret.'
Margaret! Margaret!

Come, dear children, come away down;
Call no more!
One last look at the white-walled town, 25
And the little gray church on the windy shore;
Then come down!
She will not come though you call all day:
Come away, come away!

Children dear, was it yesterday 30
We heard the sweet bells over the bay?
In the caverns where we lay,
Through the surf and through the swell,
The far-off sound of a silver bell?
Sand-strewn caverns, cool and deep, 35
Where the winds are all asleep;
Where the spent lights quiver and gleam,
Where the salt weed sways in the stream,
Where the sea-beasts, ranged all round,
Feed in the ooze of their pasture-ground; 40
Where the sea-snakes coil and twine,
Dry their mail and bask in the brine;
Where great whales come sailing by,
Sail and sail, with unshut eye,
Round the world for ever and aye; 45
When did music come this way?
Children dear, was it yesterday?

Children dear, was it yesterday
(Call yet once!) that she went away?
Once she sate with you and me, 50
On a red gold throne in the heart of the sea,
And the youngest sate on her knee.
She combed its bright hair, and she tended it well,
When down swung the sound of a far-off bell.
She sighed, she looked up through the clear green sea; 55
She said: 'I must go, for my kinsfolk pray
In the little gray church on the shore to-day.
'T will be Easter-time in the world, ah me!
And I lose my poor soul, merman! here with thee.'
I said: 'Go up, dear heart, through the waves:— 60
Say thy prayer, and come back to the kind sea-caves!'
She smiled, she went up through the surf in the bay.
Children dear, was it yesterday?

Children dear, were we long alone?
'The sea grows stormy: the little ones
    moan:—   65
Long prayers,' I said, 'in the world they
    say;
Come!' I said; and we rose through the
    surf in the bay.
We went up the beach, by the sandy down
Where the sea-stocks bloom, to the white-
    walled town;
Through the narrow paved streets, where
    all was still,   70
To the little gray church on the windy
    hill.
From the church came a murmur of folk at
    their prayers,
But we stood without in the cold blowing
    airs.
We climbed on the graves, on the stones
    worn with rains,
And we gazed up the aisle through the small
    leaded panes.   75
She sate by the pillar; we saw her clear:
'Margaret, hist! come quick, we are here!
Dear heart,' I said, 'we are long alone:
The sea grows stormy; the little ones
    moan.'
But, ah, she gave me never a look,   80
For her eyes were sealed to the holy book.
Loud prays the priest; shut stands the door.
Come away, children, call no more!
Come away, come down, call no more!

Down, down, down!   85
Down to the depths of the sea—
She sits at her wheel in the humming town,
Singing most joyfully.
Hark what she sings: 'O joy, O joy,
For the humming street, and the child with
    its toy!   90
For the priest, and the bell, and the holy
    well;
For the wheel where I spun,
And the blessèd light of the sun!'
And so she sings her fill,
Singing most joyfully,   95
Till the spindle drops from her hand,
And the whizzing wheel stands still.
She steals to the window, and looks at the
    sand,
And over the sand at the sea;
And her eyes are set in a stare: 100
And anon there breaks a sigh,
And anon there drops a tear,
From a sorrow-clouded eye,
And a heart sorrow-laden;
A long, long sigh   105

For the cold strange eyes of a little mer
    maiden
And the gleam of her golden hair.

Come away, away, children;
Come children, come down!—
The hoarse wind blows coldly;   110
Lights shine in the town.
She will start from her slumber
When gusts shake the door;
She will hear the winds howling,
Will hear the waves roar.   115
We shall see, while above us
The waves roar and whirl,
A ceiling of amber,
A pavement of pearl.
Singing: 'Here came a mortal,   120
But faithless was she!
And alone dwell for ever
The kings of the sea.'
But, children, at midnight,
When soft the winds blow,   125
When clear falls the moonlight,
When spring-tides are low;
When sweet airs come seaward
From heaths starred with broom,
And high rocks throw mildly   130
On the blanched sands a gloom;
Up the still, glistening beaches,
Up the creeks, we will hie,
Over banks of bright seaweed
The ebb-tide leaves dry.   135
We will gaze, from the sand-hills,
At the white, sleeping town;
At the church on the hill-side:
And then come back down,
Singing: 'There dwells a loved one,   140
But cruel is she!
She left lonely for ever
The kings of the sea.'

(1849)

THE BURIED LIFE

Light flows our war of mocking words,
    and yet,
Behold, with tears mine eyes are wet!
I feel a nameless sadness o'er me roll.
Yes, yes, we know that we can jest,
We know, we know that we can smile!   5
But there's a something in this breast,
To which thy light words bring no rest,
And thy gay smiles no anodyne.
Give me thy hand, and hush awhile,
And turn those limpid eyes on mine,   10
And let me read there love! thy inmost
    soul.

Alas! is even love too weak
To unlock the heart, and let it speak?
Are even lovers powerless to reveal
To one another what indeed they feel?   15
I knew the mass of men concealed
Their thoughts, for fear that if revealed
They would by other men be met
With blank indifference, or with blame re-
    proved;
I knew they lived and moved   20
Tricked in disguises, alien to the rest
Of men, and alien to themselves — and yet
The same heart beats in every human
    breast!

But we, my love! — doth a like spell be-
    numb
Our hearts, our voices? — must we too be
    dumb?   25

Ah! well for us, if even we,
Even for a moment, can get free
Our heart, and have our lips unchained;
For that which seals them hath been deep-
    ordained!

Fate, which foresaw   30
How frivolous a baby man would be —
By what distractions he would be possessed,
How he would pour himself in every strife,
And well-nigh change his own identity —
That it might keep from his capricious play
His genuine self, and force him to obey   36
Even in his own despite his being's law,
Bade through the deep recesses of our
    breast
The unregarded river of our life
Pursue with indiscernible flow its way;   40
And that we should not see
The buried stream, and seem to be
Eddying at large in blind uncertainty,
Though driving on with it eternally.

But often, in the world's most crowded
    streets,   45
But often, in the din of strife,
There rises an unspeakable desire
After the knowledge of our buried life;
A thirst to spend our fire and restless force
In tracking out our true, original course;   50
A longing to inquire
Into the mystery of this heart which beats
So wild, so deep in us — to know
Whence our lives come and where they go.
And many a man in his own breast then
    delves,   55

But deep enough, alas! none ever mines.
And we have been on many thousand lines,
And we have shown, on each, spirit and
    power;
But hardly have we, for one little hour,
Been on our own line, have we been our-
    selves —   60
Hardly had skill to utter one of all
The nameless feelings that course through
    our breast,
But they course on for ever unexpressed,
And long we try in vain to speak and act
Our hidden self, and what we say and do   65
Is eloquent, is well — but 't is not true!
And then we will no more be racked
With inward striving, and demand,
Of all the thousand nothings of the hour
Their stupefying power;   70
Ah, yes, and they benumb us at our call!
Yet still, from time to time, vague and for-
    lorn,
From the soul's subterranean depth up-
    borne
As from an infinitely distant land,
Come airs, and floating echoes, and convey   75
A melancholy into all our day.

Only — but this is rare —
When a belovèd hand is laid in ours,
When, jaded with the rush and glare
Of the interminable hours,   80
Our eyes can in another's eyes read clear,
When our world-deafened ear
Is by the tones of a loved voice caressed —
A bolt is shot back somewhere in our
    breast,
And a lost pulse of feeling stirs again.   85
The eye sinks inward, and the heart lies
    plain,
And what we mean, we say, and what we
    would, we know.
A man becomes aware of his life's flow,
And hears its winding murmur; and he sees
The meadows where it glides, the sun, the
    breeze.   90

And there arrives a lull in the hot race
Wherein he doth for ever chase
That flying and elusive shadow, rest.
An air of coolness plays upon his face,
And an unwonted calm pervades his breast.
And then he thinks he knows   95
The hills where his life rose,
And the sea where it goes.

                    (1852)

SELF-DEPENDENCE

Weary of myself, and sick of asking
What I am, and what I ought to be,
At this vessel's prow I stand, which bears
　　me
Forwards, forwards, o'er the starlit sea.

And a look of passionate desire　　　5
O'er the sea and to the stars I send:
' Ye who from my childhood up have calmed
　　me,
Calm me, ah, compose me to the end!

' Ah, once more,' I cried, ' ye stars, ye
　　waters,
On my heart your mighty charm renew; 10
Still, still let me, as I gaze upon you,
Feel my soul becoming vast like you!'

From the intense, clear, star-sown vault of
　　heaven,
Over the lit sea's unquiet way,
In the rustling night-air came the answer:
' Wouldst thou be as these are? Live as
　　they.　　　　　　　　　　　16

' Unaffrighted by the silence round them,
Undistracted by the sights they see,
These demand not that the things without
　　them
Yield them love, amusement, sympathy.　20

' And with joy the stars perform their shin-
　　ing,
And the sea its long moon-silvered roll;
For self-poised they live, nor pine with
　　noting
All the fever of some differing soul.

' Bounded by themselves, and unregardful 25
In what state God's other works may be,
In their own tasks all their powers pouring,
These attain the mighty life you see.'

O air-born voice! long since, severely clear,
A cry like thine in mine own heart I hear:
' Resolve to be thyself; and know that he, 31
Who finds himself, loses his misery!'
　　　　　　　　　　　　　(1852)

MORALITY

We cannot kindle when we will
The fire which in the heart resides;
The spirit bloweth and is still,

In mystery our soul abides.
　　But tasks in hours of insight willed,　5
　　Can be through hours of gloom fulfilled.

With aching hands and bleeding feet
We dig and heap, lay stone on stone;
We bear the burden and the heat
Of the long day, and wish 't were done. 10
　　Not till the hours of light return,
　　All we have built do we discern.

Then, when the clouds are off the soul,
When thou dost bask in Nature's eye,
Ask, how she viewed thy self-control,　15
Thy struggling, tasked morality —
　　Nature, whose free, light, cheerful air,
　　Oft made thee, in thy gloom, despair.

And she, whose censure thou dost dread,
Whose eye thou wast afraid to seek,　20
See, on her face a glow is spread,
A strong emotion on her cheek!
　　' Ah, child!' she cries, ' that strife divine,
　　Whence was it, for it is not mine?

' There is no effort on my brow —　　25
I do not strive, I do not weep;
I rush with the swift spheres and glow
In joy, and when I will, I sleep.
　　Yet that severe, that earnest air,
　　I saw, I felt it once — but where?　30

' I knew not yet the gauge of time,
Nor wore the manacles of space;
I felt it in some other clime,
I saw it in some other place.
　　'T was when the heavenly house I trod,
　　And lay upon the breast of God.'　36
　　　　　　　　　　　　　(1852)

SOHRAB AND RUSTUM

AN EPISODE

And the first gray of morning filled the east,
And the fog rose out of the Oxus stream.
But all the Tartar camp along the stream
Was hushed, and still the men were plunged
　　in sleep;
Sohrab alone, he slept not: all night long 5
He had lain wakeful, tossing on his bed;
But when the gray dawn stole into his tent,
He rose, and clad himself, and girt his
　　sword,
And took his horseman's cloak, and left his
　　tent,
And went abroad into the cold wet fog,　10

Through the dim camp to Peran-Wisa's tent.
  Through the black Tartar tents he passed,
    which stood
Clustering like bee-hives on the low flat
    strand
Of Oxus, where the summer floods o'er-
    flow
When the sun melts the snows in high Pa-
    mere: 15
Through the black tents he passed, o'er that
    low strand,
And to a hillock came, a little back
From the stream's brink, the spot where first
    a boat,
Crossing the stream in summer, scrapes the
    land.
The men of former times had crowned the
    top   20
With a clay fort: but that was fall'n; and
    now
The Tartars built there Peran-Wisa's tent,
A dome of laths, and o'er it felts were
    spread.
And Sohrab came there, and went in, and
    stood
Upon the thick-piled carpets in the tent, 25
And found the old man sleeping on his bed
Of rugs and felts, and near him lay his
    arms.
And Peran-Wisa heard him, though the step
Was dulled; for he slept light, an old man's
    sleep;
And he rose quickly on one arm, and said: 30
  'Who art thou? for it is not yet clear
    dawn.
Speak! is there news, or any night alarm?'
  But Sohrab came to the bedside, and said:
'Thou knowest me, Peran-Wisa: it is I.
The sun is not yet risen, and the foe   35
Sleep; but I sleep not; all night long I lie
Tossing and wakeful, and I come to thee.
For so did King Afrasiab bid me seek
Thy counsel, and to heed thee as thy son,
In Samarcand, before the army marched; 40
And I will tell thee what my heart desires.
Thou know'st if, since from Ader-baijan,
    first
I came among the Tartars, and bore arms,
I have still served Afrasiab well, and shown,
At my boy's years, the courage of a man. 45
This too thou know'st, that, while I still bear
    on
The conquering Tartar ensigns through the
    world,
And beat the Persians back on every field,
I see one man, one man, and one alone — 49

Rustum, my father; who, I hoped, should
    greet,
Should one day greet, upon some well-
    fought field,
His not unworthy, not inglorious son.
So I long hoped, but him I never find.
Come then, hear now, and grant me what I
    ask.
Let the two armies rest to-day: but I   55
Will challenge forth the bravest Persian
    lords
To meet me, man to man; if I prevail,
Rustum will surely hear it; if I fall —
Old man, the dead need no one, claim no
    kin.
Dim is the rumor of a common fight,   60
Where host meets host, and many names
    are sunk:
But of a single combat Fame speaks
    clear.'
  He spoke: and Peran-Wisa took the hand
Of the young man in his, and sighed, and
    said:
  'O Sohrab, an unquiet heart is thine!   65
Canst thou not rest among the Tartar
    chiefs,
And share the battle's common chance with
    us
Who love thee, but must press forever first,
In single fight incurring single risk,
To find a father thou hast never seen? 70
That were far best, my son, to stay with us
Unmurmuring; in our tents, while it is war,
And when 't is truce, then in Afrasiab's
    towns.
But, if this one desire indeed rules all,
To seek out Rustum — seek him not through
    fight: 75
Seek him in peace, and carry to his arms,
O Sohrab, carry an unwounded son!
But far hence seek him, for he is not here,
For now it is not as when I was young,   79
When Rustum was in front of every fray:
But now he keeps apart, and sits at home,
In Seïstan, with Zal, his father old.
Whether that his own mighty strength at
    last
Feels the abhorred approaches of old age;
Or in some quarrel with the Persian King.
  There go: — Thou wilt not? Yet my
    heart forebodes   86
Danger of death awaits thee on this field.
Fain would I know thee safe and well,
    though lost
To us: fain therefore send thee hence, in
    peace

To seek thy father, not seek single fights 90
In vain: — but who can keep the lion's cub
From ravening? and who govern Rustum's
    son?
Go: I will grant thee what thy heart de-
    sires.'
    So said he, and dropped Sohrab's hand,
    and left   94
His bed, and the warm rugs whereon he lay,
And o'er his chilly limbs his woolen coat
He passed, and tied his sandals on his feet,
And threw a white cloak round him, and he
    took
In his right hand a ruler's staff, no sword;
And on his head he set his sheep-skin
    cap,   100
Black, glossy, curled, the fleece of Kara-
    Kul;
And raised the curtain of his tent, and called
His herald to his side, and went abroad.
    The sun, by this, had risen, and cleared
    the fog
From the broad Oxus and the glittering
    sands: 105
And from their tents the Tartar horsemen
    filed
Into the open plain; so Haman bade;
Haman, who next to Peran-Wisa ruled
The host, and still was in his lusty prime.
From their black tents, long files of horse,
    they streamed: 110
As when, some gray November morn, the
    files,
In marching order spread, of long-necked
    cranes,
Stream over Casbin, and the southern
    slopes
Of Elburz, from the Aralian estuaries,
Or some frore Caspian reed-bed, southward
    bound   115
For the warm Persian sea-board: so they
    streamed.
The Tartars of the Oxus, the King's guard,
First, with black sheep-skin caps and with
    long spears;
Large men, large steeds; who from Bokhara
    come   119
And Khiva, and ferment the milk of mares.
Next, the more temperate Toorkmuns of the
    south,
The Tukas, and the lances of Salore,
And those from Attruck and the Caspian
    sands;
Light men, and on light steeds, who only
    drink   124
The acrid milk of camels, and their wells.
And then a swarm of wandering horse, who
    came

From far, and a more doubtful service
    owned;
The Tartars of Ferghana, from the banks
Of the Jaxartes, men with scanty beards
And close-set skull-caps; and those wilder
    hordes   130
Who roam o'er Kipchak and the northern
    waste,
Kalmuks and unkempt Kuzzaks, tribes who
    stray
Nearest the Pole, and wandering Kirghizzes,
Who come on shaggy ponies from Pamere.
These all filed out from camp into the plain.
    And on the other side the Persians
    formed: 136
First a light cloud of horse, Tartars they
    seemed,
The Ilyats of Khorassan: and behind,
The royal troops of Persia, horse and foot,
Marshaled battalions bright in burnished
    steel.   140
But Peran-Wisa with his herald came
Threading the Tartar squadrons to the front,
And with his staff kept back the foremost
    ranks.
And when Ferood, who led the Persians,
    saw
That Peran-Wisa kept the Tartars back, 145
He took his spear, and to the front he came,
And checked his ranks, and fixed them
    where they stood.
And the old Tartar came upon the sand
Betwixt the silent hosts, and spake, and
    said:
    'Ferood, and ye, Persians and Tartars,
    hear!   150
Let there be truce between the hosts to-
    day.
But choose a champion from the Persian
    lords
To fight our champion Sohrab, man to man.'
As, in the country, on a morn in June, 154
When the dew glistens on the pearlèd ears,
A shiver runs through the deep corn for
    joy —
So, when they heard what Peran-Wisa said,
A thrill through all the Tartar squadrons
    ran
Of pride and hope for Sohrab, whom they
    loved.
    But as a troop of peddlers, from Cabool,
Cross underneath the Indian Caucasus, 161
That vast sky-neighboring mountain of milk
    snow;
Crossing so high, that, as they mount, they
    pass
Long flocks of traveling birds dead on the
    snow.

Choked by the air, and scarce can they them-
selves 165
Slake their parched throats with sugared
mulberries —
In single file they move, and stop their
breath,
For fear they should dislodge the o'erhang-
ing snows —
So the pale Persians held their breath with
fear.
    And to Ferood his brother chiefs came
up 170
To counsel. Gudurz and Zoarrah came,
And Feraburz, who ruled the Persian host
Second, and was the uncle of the King:
These came and counseled; and then Gudurz
said:
    'Ferood, shame bids us take their chal-
lenge up, 175
Yet champion have we none to match this
youth.
He has the wild stag's foot, the lion's heart.
But Rustum came last night; aloof he sits
And sullen, and has pitched his tents
apart:
Him will I seek, and carry to his ear 180
The Tartar challenge, and this young man's
name.
Haply he will forget his wrath, and fight,
Stand forth the while, and take their chal-
lenge up.'
    So spake he; and Ferood stood forth and
cried: 184
'Old man, be it agreed as thou hast said.
Let Sohrab arm, and we will find a man.'
    He spake; and Peran-Wisa turned, and
strode
Back through the opening squadrons to his
tent.
But through the anxious Persians Gudurz
ran,
And crossed the camp which lay behind,
and reached, 190
Out on the sands beyond it, Rustum's tents.
Of scarlet cloth they were, and glittering
gay,
Just pitched: the high pavilion in the midst
Was Rustum's, and his men lay camped
around.
And Gudurz entered Rustum's tent, and
found 195
Rustum: his morning meal was done, but
still
The table stood before him, charged with
food —
A side of roasted sheep, and cakes of
bread,

And dark green melons; and there Rustum
sate
Listless, and held a falcon on his wrist, 200
And played with it; but Gudurz came and
stood
Before him; and he looked, and saw him
stand;
And with a cry sprang up, and dropped the
bird,
And greeted Gudurz with both hands, and
said:
    'Welcome! these eyes could see no better
sight. 205
What news? but sit down first, and eat and
drink.'
    But Gudurz stood in the tent-door, and
said:
'Not now: a time will come to eat and
drink,
But not to-day: to-day has other needs.
The armies are drawn out, and stand at
gaze: 210
For from the Tartars is a challenge brough:
To pick a champion from the Persian lords
To fight their champion — and thou know'st
his name —
Sohrab men call him, but his birth is hid.
O Rustum, like thy might is this young
man's! 215
He has the wild stag's foot, the lion's heart.
And he is young, and Iran's chiefs are old,
Or else too weak; and all eyes turn to
thee.
Come down and help us, Rustum, or we
lose.'
    He spoke: but Rustum answered with a
smile: — 220
'Go to! if Iran's chiefs are old, then I
Am older: if the young are weak, the king
Errs strangely: for the king, for Kai-
Khosroo,
Himself is young, and honors younger men,
And lets the agèd molder to their graves.
Rustum he loves no more, but loves the
young — 226
The young may rise at Sohrab's vaunts,
not I.
For what care I, though all speak Sohrab's
fame?
For would that I myself had such a son,
And not that one slight helpless girl I
have, 230
A son so famed, so brave, to send to war,
And I to tarry with the snow-haired Zal,
My father, whom the robber Afghans vex,
And clip his borders short, and drive his
herds, 234

And he has none to guard his weak old age.
There would I go, and hang my armor up,
And with my great name fence that weak
old man,
And spend the goodly treasures I have got,
And rest my age, and hear of Sohrab's
fame,
And leave to death the hosts of thankless
kings,   240
And with these slaughterous hands draw
sword no more.'
  He spoke, and smiled; and Gudurz made
reply:
'What then, O Rustum, will men say to
this,
When Sohrab dares our bravest forth, and
seeks,
Thee most of all, and thou, whom most he
seeks,   245
Hidest thy face? Take heed, lest men
should say,
"Like some old miser, Rustum hoards his
fame,
And shuns to peril it with younger men."'
And, greatly moved, then Rustum made re-
ply:
'O Gudurz, wherefore dost thou say such
words?   250
Thou knowest better words than this to
say.
What is one more, one less, obscure or
famed,
Valiant or craven, young or old, to me?
Are not they mortal, am not I myself?
But who for men of naught would do great
deeds?   255
Come, thou shall see how Rustum hoards
his fame.
But I will fight unknown, and in plain arms;
Let not men say of Rustum, he was
matched
In single fight with any mortal man.'
  He spoke, and frowned; and Gudurz
turned, and ran   260
Back quickly through the camp in fear and
joy,
Fear at his wrath, but joy that Rustum
came.
But Rustum strode to his tent-door, and
called
His followers in, and bade them bring his
arms,
And clad himself in steel: the arms he
chose   265
Were plain, and on his shield was no de-
vice,
Only his helm was rich, inlaid with gold,

And from the fluted spine atop, a plume
Of horsehair waved, a scarlet horsehair
plume.
So armed, he issued forth; and Ruksh, his
horse,   270
Followed him, like a faithful hound, at heel,
Ruksh, whose renown was noised through
all the earth,
The horse, whom Rustum on a foray once
Did in Bokhara by the river find
A colt beneath its dam, and drove him home,
And reared him; a bright bay, with lofty
crest,   276
Dight with a saddle-cloth of broidered green
Crusted with gold, and on the ground were
worked
All beasts of chase, all beasts which hunters
know:
So followed, Rustum left his tents, and
crossed   280
The camp, and to the Persian host ap-
peared.
And all the Persians knew him, and with
shouts
Hailed; but the Tartars knew not who he
was.
And dear as the wet diver to the eyes
Of his pale wife who waits and weeps on
shore,   285
By sandy Bahrein, in the Persian Gulf,
Plunging all day in the blue waves, at night,
Having made up his tale of precious pearls,
Rejoins her in their hut upon the sands — 289
So dear to the pale Persians Rustum came.
  And Rustum to the Persian front ad-
vanced,
And Sohrab armed in Haman's tent, and
came.
And as afield the reapers cut a swath
Down through the middle of a rich man's
corn,   295
And on each side are squares of standing
corn,
And in the midst a stubble, short and bare;
So on each side were squares of men, with
spears
Bristling, and in the midst, the open sand.
And Rustum came upon the sand, and cast
His eyes toward the Tartar tents, and saw
Sohrab come forth, and eyed him as he
came.   301
  As some rich woman, on a winter's morn,
Eyes through her silken curtains the poor
drudge
Who with numb blackened fingers makes
her fire —
At cock-crow on a starlit winter's morn, 303

When the frost flowers the whitened win-
dow-panes —
And wonders how she lives, and what the
thoughts
Of that poor drudge may be; so Rustum
eyed
The unknown adventurous youth, who from
afar 309
Came seeking Rustum, and defying forth
All the most valiant chiefs: long he perused
His spirited air, and wondered who he was.
For very young he seemed, tenderly reared;
Like some young cypress, tall, and dark, and
straight, 314
Which in a queen's secluded garden throws
Its slight dark shadow on the moonlit turf,
By midnight, to a bubbling fountain's
sound —
So slender Sohrab seemed, so softly reared.
And a deep pity entered Rustum's soul
As he beheld him coming; and he stood, 320
And beckoned to him with his hand, and
said:
'O thou young man, the air of heaven is
soft,
And warm, and pleasant; but the grave is
cold.
Heaven's air is better than the cold dead
grave.
Behold he: I am vast, and clad in iron, 325
And tried; and I have stood on many a
field
Of blood, and I have fought with many a
foe:
Never was that field lost, or that foe saved.
O Sohrab, wherefore wilt thou rush on
death?
Be governed: quit the Tartar host, and come
To Iran, and be as my son to me, 331
And fight beneath my banner till I die.
There are no youths in Iran brave as thou.'
So he spake, mildly: Sohrab heard his
voice, 334
The mighty voice of Rustum; and he saw
His giant figure planted on the sand,
Sole, like some single tower, which a chief
Hath builded on the waste in former years
Against the robbers; and he saw that head,
Streaked with its first gray hairs: hope filled
his soul; 340
And he ran forwards and embraced his
knees,
And clasped his hand within his own and
said:
'Oh, by thy father's head! by thine own
soul!
Art thou not Rustum? Speak! art thou not
he?'

But Rustum eyed askance the kneeling
youth, 345
And turned away, and spake to his own
soul:
'Ah me, I muse what this young fox
may mean.
False, wily, boastful, are these Tartar boys.
For if I now confess this thing he asks, 349
And hide it not, but say, "Rustum is here,"
He will not yield indeed, nor quit our foes,
But he will find some pretext not to fight,
And praise my fame, and proffer courteous
gifts,
A belt or sword perhaps, and go his way.
And on a feast-day, in Afrasiab's hall, 355
In Samarcand, he will arise and cry —
"I challenged once, when the two armies
camped
Beside the Oxus, all the Persian lords
To cope with me in single fight; but they
Shrank; only Rustum dared: then he and I
Changed gifts, and went on equal terms
away." 361
So will he speak, perhaps, while men ap-
plaud.
Then were the chiefs of Iran shamed
through me.'
And then he turned, and sternly spake
aloud:
'Rise! wherefore dost thou vainly question
thus 365
Of Rustum? I am here, whom thou hast
called
By challenge forth: make good thy vaunt, or
yield.
Is it with Rustum only thou wouldst fight?
Rash boy, men look on Rustum's face and
flee.
For well I know, that did great Rustum
stand 370
Before thy face this day, and were re-
vealed,
There would be then no talk of fighting
more.
But being what I am, I tell thee this:
Do thou record it in thine inmost soul:
Either thou shalt renounce thy vaunt, and
yield; 375
Or else thy bones shall strew this sand, till
winds
Bleach them, or Oxus with his summer
floods,
Oxus in summer wash them all away.'
He spoke: and Sohrab answered, on his
feet: —
'Art thou so fierce? Thou wilt not fright
me so. 380
I am no girl, to be made pale by words.

Yet this thou hast said well, did Rustum
stand
Here on this field, there were no fighting
then.
But Rustum is far hence, and we stand
here.
Begin: thou art more vast, more dread
than I,   385
And thou art proved, I know, and I am
young —
But yet success sways with the breath of
heaven.
And though thou thinkest that thou know-
est sure   388
Thy victory, yet thou canst not surely know.
For we are all, like swimmers in the sea,
Poised on the top of a huge wave of Fate,
Which hangs uncertain to which side to
fall.
And whether it will heave us up to land,
Or whether it will roll us out to sea,
Back out to sea, to the deep waves of
death,   395
We know not, and no search will make us
know:
Only the event will teach us in its hour.'
  He spoke; and Rustum answered not, but
hurled
His spear: down from the shoulder, down
it came   399
As on some partridge in the corn a hawk
That long has towered in the airy clouds
Drops like a plummet: Sohrab saw it come,
And sprang aside, quick as a flash: the
spear
Hissed, and went quivering down into the
sand,
Which it sent flying wide: — then Sohrab
threw   405
In turn, and full struck Rustum's shield:
sharp rang
The iron plates rang sharp, but turned the
spear.
And Rustum seized his club, which none
but he
Could wield: an unlopped trunk it was, and
huge,
Still rough; like those which men in treeless
plains   410
To build them boats fish from the flooded
rivers,
Hyphasis or Hydaspes, when, high up
By their dark springs, the wind in winter-
time
Has made in Himalayan forests wrack,
And strewn the channels with torn boughs;
so huge   415

The club which Rustum lifted now, and
struck
One stroke; but again Sohrab sprang aside
Lithe as the glancing snake, and the club
came
Thundering to earth, and leapt from Rus-
tum's hand.
And Rustum followed his own blow, and
fell   420
To his knees, and with his fingers clutched
the sand:
And now might Sohrab have unsheathed his
sword,
And pierced the mighty Rustum while he
lay
Dizzy, and on his knees, and choked with
sand:
But he looked on, and smiled, nor bared his
sword,   425
But courteously drew back, and spoke, and
said:
  'Thou strik'st too hard: that club of thine
will float
Upon the summer-floods, and not my bones.
But rise, and be not wroth; not wroth
am I:
No, when I see thee, wrath forsakes my
soul.   430
Thou say'st thou art not Rustum: be it so.
Who art thou then, that canst so touch my
soul?
Boy as I am, I have seen battles too;
Have waded foremost in their bloody waves,
And heard their hollow roar of dying men;
But never was my heart thus touched be-
fore.   436
Are they from heaven, these softenings of
the heart?
O thou old warrior, let us yield to heaven!
Come, plant we here in earth our angry
spears,   439
And make a truce, and sit upon this sand,
And pledge each other in red wine, like
friends,
And thou shalt talk to me of Rustum's
deeds.
There are enough foes in the Persian host
Whom I may meet, and strike, and feel no
pang;   444
Champions enough Afrasiab has, whom thou
Mayst fight; fight them, when they confront
thy spear.
But oh, let there be peace 'twixt thee and
me!'
  He ceased: but while he spake, Rustum
had risen,
And stood erect, trembling with rage: his
club   449

He left to lie, but had regained his spear,
Whose fiery point now in his mailed right-
hand
Blazed bright and baleful, like that autumn
star,
The baleful sign of fevers: dust had soiled
His stately crest, and dimmed his glittering
arms.
His breast heaved; his lips foamed; and
twice his voice   455
Was choked with rage: at last these words
broke way:
  'Girl! nimble with thy feet, not with thy
hands!
Curled minion, dancer, coiner of sweet
words!
Fight; let me hear thy hateful voice no
more!
Thou art not in Afrasiab's gardens now   460
With Tartar girls, with whom thou art wont
to dance;
But on the Oxus sands, and in the dance
Of battle, and with me, who make no play
Of war: I fight it out, and hand to hand.
Speak not to me of truce, and pledge, and
wine!   465
Remember all thy valor; try thy feints
And cunning: all the pity I had is gone:
Because thou hast shamed me before both
the hosts
With thy light skipping tricks, and thy
girl's wiles.'
  He spoke: and Sohrab kindled at his
taunts,   470
And he too drew his sword: at once they
rushed
Together, as two eagles on one prey
Come rushing down together from the
clouds,
One from the east, one from the west:
their shields   474
Dashed with a clang together, and a din
Rose, such as that the sinewy woodcut-
ters
Make often in the forest's heart at morn,
Of hewing axes, crashing trees: such blows
Rustum and Sohrab on each other hailed.
And you would say that sun and stars took
part   480
In that unnatural conflict; for a cloud
Grew suddenly in heaven, and darked the
sun
Over the fighters' heads; and a wind rose
Under their feet, and moaning swept the
plain,
And in a sandy whirlwind wrapped the
pair.   485

In gloom they twain were wrapped, and
they alone;
For both the on-looking hosts on either
hand
Stood in broad daylight, and the sky was
pure,
And the sun sparkled on the Oxus stream.
But in the gloom they fought, with blood-
shot eyes   490
And laboring breath; first Rustum struck
the shield
Which Sohrab held stiff out: the steel-spiked
spear
Rent the tough plates, but failed to reach
the skin,
And Rustum plucked it back with angry
groan.
Then Sohrab with his sword smote Rustum's
helm,   495
Nor clove its steel quite through; but all
the crest
He shore away, and that proud horsehair
plume,
Never till now defiled, sank to the dust;
And Rustum bowed his head; but then the
gloom   499
Grew blacker: thunder rumbled in the air,
And lightnings rent the cloud; and Ruksh,
the horse,
Who stood at hand, uttered a dreadful cry:
No horse's cry was that, most like the roar
Of some pained desert lion, who all day   504
Hath trailed the hunter's javelin in his side,
And comes at night to die upon the sand:
The two hosts heard that cry, and quaked
for fear,
And Oxus curdled as it crossed his stream.
But Sohrab heard, and quailed not, but
rushed on,   509
And struck again; and again Rustum bowed
His head; but this time all the blade, like
glass,
Sprang in a thousand shivers on the helm,
And in his hand the hilt remained alone.
Then Rustum raised his head; his dreadful
eyes
Glared, and he shook on high his menacing
spear,   515
And shouted, 'Rustum!' Sohrab heard that
shout,
And shrank amazed: back he recoiled one
step,
And scanned with blinking eyes the advanc-
ing form:
And then he stood bewildered; and he
dropped   520
His covering shield, and the spear pierced
his side.

He reeled, and staggering back, sank to the
ground.
And then the gloom dispersed, and the wind
fell,
And the bright sun broke forth, and melted
all
The cloud; and the two armies saw the
pair;   524
Saw Rustum standing, safe upon his feet,
And Sohrab, wounded, on the bloody sand.
  Then with a bitter smile, Rustum began:
'Sohrab, thou thoughtest in thy mind to
kill
A Persian lord this day, and strip his corpse,
And bear thy trophies to Afrasiab's tent. 530
Or else that the great Rustum would come
down
Himself to fight, and that thy wiles would
move
His heart to take a gift, and let thee go.
And then that all the Tartar host would
praise
Thy courage or thy craft, and spread thy
fame,   535
To glad thy father in his weak old age.
Fool! thou art slain, and by an unknown
man!
Dearer to the red jackals shalt thou be,
Than to thy friends, and to thy father old.'
  And, with a fearless mien, Sohrab re-
plied: 540
'Unknown thou art; yet thy fierce vaunt is
vain.
Thou dost not slay me, proud and boastful
man!
No! Rustum slays me, and this filial heart.
For were I matched with ten such men as
thee,
And I were he who till to-day I was, 545
They should be lying here, I standing there.
But that belovèd name unnerved my arm —
That name, and something, I confess, in
thee,
Which troubles all my heart, and made my
shield
Fall; and thy spear transfixed an unarmed
foe,   550
And now thou boastest, and insult'st my
fate.
But hear thou this, fierce man, tremble to
hear!
The mighty Rustum shall avenge my death!
My father, whom I seek through all the
world,
He shall avenge my death, and punish
thee!'   555
  As when some hunter in the spring hath
found

A breeding eagle sitting on her nest,
Upon the craggy isle of a hill-lake,
And pierced her with an arrow as she
rose,
And followed her to find her where she fell
Far off; — anon her mate comes winging
back   561
From hunting, and a great way off descries
His huddling young left sole; at that, he
checks
His pinion, and with short uneasy sweeps
Circles above his eyry, with loud screams
Chiding his mate back to her nest; but
she   566
Lies dying, with the arrow in her side,
In some far stony gorge out of his ken,
A heap of fluttering feathers: never more
Shall the lake glass her, flying over it; 570
Never the black and dripping precipices
Echo her stormy scream as she sails by: —
As that poor bird flies home, nor knows his
loss —
So Rustum knew not his own loss, but
stood
Over his dying son, and knew him not. 575
  But with a cold, incredulous voice, he
said:
'What prate is this of fathers and revenge?
The mighty Rustum never had a son.'
  And, with a failing voice, Sohrab replied:
'Ah, yes, he had! and that lost son am I. 580
Surely the news will one day reach his ear,
Reach Rustum, where he sits, and tarries
long,
Somewhere, I know not where, but far from
here;
And pierce him like a stab, and make him
leap   584
To arms, and cry for vengeance upon thee.
Fierce man, bethink thee, for an only son!
What will that grief, what will that ven-
geance be!
Oh, could I live, till I that grief had seen!
Yet him I pity not so much, but her,
My mother, who in Ader-baijan dwells 590
With that old king, her father, who grows
gray
With age, and rules over the valiant Koords.
Her most I pity, who no more will see
Sohrab returning from the Tartar camp,
With spoils and honor, when the war is
done.   595
But a dark rumor will be bruited up,
From tribe to tribe, until it reach her ear;
And then will that defenceless woman learn
That Sohrab will rejoice her sight no more;
But that in battle with a nameless foe, 600
By the far distant Oxus, he is slain.'

He spoke; and as he ceased he wept
  aloud,
Thinking of her he left, and his own
  death.
He spoke; but Rustum listened, plunged in
  thought.
Nor did he yet believe it was his son 605
Who spoke, although he called back names
  he knew;
For he had had sure tidings that the babe,
Which was in Ader-baijan born to him,
Had been a puny girl, no boy at all: 609
So that sad mother sent him word, for fear
Rustum should seek the boy, to train in
  arms;
And so he deemed that either Sohrab took,
By a false boast, the style of Rustum's
  son;
Or that men gave it him, to swell his fame.
So deemed he; yet he listened, plunged in
  thought; 615
And his soul set to grief, as the vast tide
Of the bright rocking ocean sets to shore
At the full moon: tears gathered in his
  eyes;
For he remembered his own early youth,
And all its bounding rapture; as, at dawn,
The shepherd from his mountain-lodge
  descries 621
A far, bright city, smitten by the sun,
Through many rolling clouds; — so Rustum
  saw
His youth; saw Sohrab's mother, in her
  bloom;
And that old king, her father, who loved
  well · 625
His wandering guest, and gave him his fair
  child
With joy; and all the pleasant life they led,
They three, in that long-distant summer-
  time —
The castle, and the dewy woods, and hunt
And hound, and morn on those delightful
  hills 630
In Ader-baijan. And he saw that youth,
Of age and looks to be his own dear son,
Piteous and lovely, lying on the sand,
Like some rich hyacinth, which by the scythe
Of an unskilful gardener has been cut, 635
Mowing the garden grass-plots near its bed,
And lies, a fragrant tower of purple bloom,
On the mown, dying grass; — so Sohrab
  lay,
Lovely in death, upon the common sand.
Aud Rustum gazed on him with grief, and
  said: — 640
  'O Sohrab, thou indeed art such a son

Whom Rustum, wert thou his, might well
  have loved!
Yet here thou errest, Sohrab, or else men
Have told thee false; — thou art not Rus-
  tum's son.
For Rustum had no son: one child he had —
But one — a girl: who with her mother
  now 646
Plies some light female task, nor dreams of
  us —
Of us she dreams not, nor of wounds, nor
  war.'
  But Sohrab answered him in wrath; for
  now
The anguish of the deep-fixed spear grew
  fierce, 650
And he desirèd to draw forth the steel,
And let the blood flow free, and so to die;
But first he would convince his stubborn
  foe —
And, rising sternly on one arm, he said:
  'Man, who art thou who dost deny my
  words? 655
Truth sits upon the lips of dying men,
And falsehood, while I lived, was far from
  mine.
I tell thee, pricked upon this arm I bear
That seal which Rustum to my mother
  gave,
That she might prick it on the babe she
  bore.' 660
  He spoke: and all the blood left Rustum's
  cheeks;
And his knees tottered, and he smote his
  hand,
Against his breast, his heavy mailèd hand,
That the hard iron corslet clanked aloud:
And on his heart he pressed the other hand,
And in a hollow voice he spake, and said:
  'Sohrab, that were a proof which could
  not lie. 667
If thou show this, then art thou Rustum's
  son.'
  Then, with weak hasty fingers, Sohrab
  loosed
His belt, and near the shoulder bared his
  arm, 670
And showed a sign in faint vermilion points
Pricked: as a cunning workman, in Pekin,
Pricks with vermilion some clear porcelain
  vase,
An emperor's gift — at early morn he paints,
And all day long, and, when night comes,
  the lamp 675
Lights up his studious forehead and thin
  hands: —
So delicately pricked the sign appeared

On Sohrab's arm, the sign of Rustum's
   seal.
It was that Griffin, which of old reared Zal,
Rustum's great father, whom they left to
   die,   680
A helpless babe, among the mountain rocks.
Him that kind creature found, and reared,
   and loved —
Then Rustum took it for his glorious sign.
And Sohrab bared that image on his arm,
And himself scanned it long with mournful
   eyes,   685
And then he touched it with his hand and
   said:
  'How say'st thou? Is that sign the proper
   sign
Of Rustum's son, or of some other man's?'
  He spoke: but Rustum gazed, and gazed,
   and stood
Speechless; and then he uttered one sharp
   cry —   690
'O boy — thy father!'— and his voice
   choked there.
And then a dark cloud passed before his
   eyes,
And his head swam, and he sank down to
   earth.
But Sohrab crawled to where he lay, and
   cast
His arms about his neck, and kissed his
   lips,   695
And with fond faltering fingers stroked his
   cheeks,
Trying to call him back to life: and life
Came back to Rustum, and he oped his
   eyes,
And they stood wide with horror; and he
   seized
In both his hands the dust which lay around,
And threw it on his head, and smirched his
   hair,   701
His hair, and face, and beard, and glittering
   arms:
And strong convulsive groanings shook his
   breast,
And his sobs choked him; and he clutched
   his sword,
To draw it, and forever let life out.   705
But Sohrab saw his thought, and held his
   hands,
And with a soothing voice he spake, and
   said:
  'Father, forbear: for I but meet to-day
The doom that at my birth was written
   down
In heaven, and thou art heaven's uncon-
   scious hand.   710

Surely my heart cried out that it was thou,
When first I saw thee; and thy heart spoke
   too,
I know it: but Fate trod those promptings
   down
Under its iron heel; Fate, Fate engaged
The strife, and hurled me on my father's
   spear.   715
But let us speak no more of this: I find
My father; let me feel that I have found.
Come, sit beside me on this sand, and take
My head betwixt thy hands, and kiss my
   cheeks,
And wash them with thy tears, and say:
   "My son!"   720
Quick! quick! for numbered are my sands
   of life,
And swift; for like the lightning to this
   field
I came, and like the wind I go away —
Sudden, and swift, and like a passing wind.
But it was writ in heaven that this should
   be.'   725
  So said he: and his voice released the
   heart
Of Rustum, and his tears broke forth; he
   cast
His arms round his son's neck, and wept
   aloud,
And kissed him. And awe fell on both the
   hosts
When they saw Rustum's grief: and Ruksh,
   the horse,   730
With his head bowing to the ground, and
   mane
Sweeping the dust, came near, and in mute
   woe
First to the one, then to the other moved
His head, as if inquiring what their grief
Might mean; and from his dark, compas-
   sionate eyes,   735
The big warm tears rolled down, and caked
   the sand.
But Rustum chid him with stern voice, and
   said:
  'Ruksh, now thou grievest; but O Ruksh,
   thy feet
Should first have rotted on their nimble
   joints,
When first they bore thy master to this
   field.'   740
  But Sohrab looked upon the horse and
   said:
'Is this then Ruksh? How often, in past
   days,
My mother told me of thee, thou brave
   steed!

My terrible father's terrible horse; and said,
That I should one day find thy lord and
 thee. 745
Come, let me lay my hand upon thy mane.
O Ruksh, thou art more fortunate than I;
For thou hast gone where I shall never go,
And snuffed the breezes of my father's
 home.
And thou hast trod the sands of Seïstan,
And seen the river of Helmund, and the
 Lake 751
Of Zirrah; and the agèd Zal himself
Has often stroked thy neck, and given thee
 food,
Corn in a golden platter soaked with wine,
And said —"O Ruksh! bear Rustum
 well!"—but I 755
Have never known my grandsire's furrowed
 face,
Nor seen his lofty house in Seïstan,
Nor slaked my thirst at the clear Helmund
 stream:
But lodged among my father's foes, and
 seen
Afrasiab's cities only, Samarcand, 760
Bokhara, and lone Khiva in the waste,
And the black Toorkmun tents; and only
 drunk
The desert rivers, Moorghab and Tejend,
Kohik, and where the Kalmuks feed their
 sheep,
The northern Sir; and this great Oxus
 stream — 765
The yellow Oxus, by whose brink I die.'
 And, with a heavy groan, Rustum be-
 wailed:
'Oh, that its waves were flowing over me!
Oh, that I saw its grains of yellow silt
Roll tumbling in the current o'er my head!'
 And, with a grave mild voice, Sohrab re-
 plied: 771
'Desire not that, my father: thou must live.
For some are born to do great deeds, and
 live,
As some are born to be obscured, and die.
Do thou the deeds I die too young to do,
And reap a second glory in thine age. 776
Thou art my father, and thy gain is mine.
But come: thou seest this great host of
 men
Which follow me; I pray thee, slay not
 these:
Let me entreat for them: what have they
 done? 780
They followed me, my hope, my fame, my
 star.
Let them all cross the Oxus back in peace.

But me thou must bear hence, not send with
 them,
But carry me with thee to Seïstan,
And place me on a bed, and mourn for me,
Thou, and the snow-haired Zal, and all thy
 friends. 786
And thou must lay me in that lovely earth,
And heap a stately mound above my bones,
And plant a far-seen pillar over all;
That so the passing horseman on the waste
May see my tomb a great way off, and
 cry: 791
"Sohrab, the mighty Rustum's son, lies
 there,
Whom his great father did in ignorance
 kill"—
And I be not forgotten in my grave.'
 And, with a mournful voice, Rustum re-
 plied:— 795
'Fear not; as thou hast said, Sohrab, my
 son,
So shall it be; for I will burn my tents
And quit the host, and bear thee hence with
 me,
And carry thee away to Seïstan.
And place thee on a bed, and mourn for
 thee, 800
With the snow-headed Zal, and all my
 friends,
And I will lay thee in that lovely earth,
And heap a stately mound above thy bones,
And plant a far-seen pillar over all: 804
And men shall not forget thee in thy grave.
And I will spare thy host: yea, let them go:
Let them all cross the Oxus back in peace.
What should I do with slaying any more?
For would that all whom I have ever slain
Might be once more alive; my bitterest
 foes, 810
And they who were called champions in
 their time,
And through whose death I won that fame I
 have;
And I were nothing but a common man,
A poor, mean soldier, and without renown;
So thou mightest live too, my son, my son!
Or rather would that I, even I myself, 816
Might now be lying on this bloody sand,
Near death, and by an ignorant stroke of
 thine,
Not thou of mine; and I might die, not
 thou;
And I, not thou, be borne to Seïstan; 820
And Zal might weep above my grave, not
 thine;
And say —"O son, I weep thee not too
 sore.

For willingly, I know, thou met'st thine
    end."
But now in blood and battles was my youth,
And full of blood and battles is my age;
And I shall never end this life of blood.'
    Then, at the point of death, Sohrab re-
        plied: 827
'A life of blood indeed, thou dreadful man!
But thou shalt yet have peace; only not
    now.   829
Not yet: but thou shalt have it on that day,
When thou shalt sail in a high-masted ship,
Thou and the other peers of Kai Khosroo,
Returning home over the salt blue sea,
From laying thy dear master in his grave.'
    And Rustum gazed in Sohrab's face, and
        said: 835
'Soon be that day, my son, and deep that
    sea!
Till then, if fate so wills, let me endure.'
    He spoke; and Sohrab smiled on him, and
        took
The spear, and drew it from his side, and
    eased
His wound's imperious anguish; but the
    blood   840
Came welling from the open gash, and life
Flowed with the stream; all down his cold
    white side
The crimson torrent ran, dim now and
    soiled,
Like the soiled tissue of white violets
Left, freshly gathered, on their native bank,
By children whom their nurses call with
    haste   846
Indoors from the sun's eye; his head
    drooped low,
His limbs grew slack: motionless, white,
    he lay,
White, with eyes closed, only when heavy
    gasps,
Deep heavy gasps, quivering through all
    his frame,   850
Convulsed him back to life, he opened them.
And fixed them feebly on his father's face;
Till now all strength was ebbed; and from
    his limbs
Unwillingly the spirit fled away,
Regretting the warm mansion which it left,
And youth, and bloom, and this delightful
    world,   856
    So, on the bloody sand, Sohrab lay dead:
And the great Rustum drew his horse-
    man's cloak
Down o'er his face, and sate by his dead
    son.
As those black granite pillars, once high-
    reared,   860

By Jemshid in Persepolis, to bear
His house, now 'mid their broken flights
    of steps,
Lie prone, enormous, down the mountain
    side:
So, in the sand, lay Rustum by his son.
    And night came down over the solemn
        waste,   865
And the two gazing hosts, and that sole
    pair,
And darkened all; and a cold fog, with
    night,
Crept from the Oxus. Soon a hum arose,
As of a great assembly loosed, and fires
Began to twinkle through the fog; for now
Both armies moved to camp, and took their
    meal: 871
The Persians took it on the open sands
Southward, the Tartars, by the river marge:
And Rustum and his son were left alone.
    But the majestic river floated on,   875
Out of the mist and hum of that low land,
Into the frosty starlight, and there moved,
Rejoicing, through the hushed Chorasmian
    waste,
Under the solitary moon: he flowed
Right for the polar star, past Orgunjè, 880
Brimming, and bright, and large; then sands
    began
To hem his watery march, and dam his
    streams,
And split his currents, that for many a
    league
The shorn and parceled Oxus strains along
Through beds of sand and matted rushy
    isles;   885
Oxus, forgetting the bright speed he had,
In his high mountain-cradle in Pamere,
A foiled circuitous wanderer: till at last
The longed-for dash of waves is heard, and
    wide   889
His luminous home of waters opens, bright
And tranquil, from whose floor the new-
    bathed stars
Emerge, and shine upon the Aral Sea.
                                        (1853)

THE SCHOLAR GIPSY

Go, for they call you, shepherd, from the
    hill;
Go, shepherd, and untie the wattled cotes:
    No longer leave thy wistful flock unfed,
    Nor let thy bawling fellows rack their
        throats,
    Nor the cropped grasses, shoot another
        head.   5
        But when the fields are still,

And the tired men and dogs all gone to
    rest,
  And only the white sheep are some-
    times seen
Cross and recross the strips of moon-
    blanched green;
    Come, shepherd, and again renew the
    quest.   10

Here, where the reaper was at work of late,
In this high field's dark corner, where he
    leaves
  His coat, his basket, and his earthen
    cruise,
And in the sun all morning binds the
    sheaves,
  Then here, at noon, comes back his
    stores to use;   15
    Here will I sit and wait,
While to my ear from uplands far away,
  The bleating of the folded flocks is
    borne;
  With distant cries of reapers in the
    corn —
    All the live murmur of a summer's
    day.   20

Screened is this nook o'er the high, half-
    reaped field,
And here till sun-down, shepherd, will I
    be.
Through the thick corn the scarlet
    poppies peep
And round green roots and yellowing
    stalks I see
  Pale blue convolvulus in tendrils creep;
    And air-swept lindens yield   26
Their scent, and rustle down their per-
    fumed showers
Of bloom on the bent grass where I
    am laid,
  And bower me from the August sun
    with shade;
  And the eye travels down to Oxford's
    towers.   30

And near me on the grass lies Glanvil's
    book —
Come, let me read the oft-read tale again,
  The story of that Oxford scholar poor,
Of shining parts and quick inventive
    brain,
  Who, tired of knocking at preferment's
    door,   35
    One summer-morn forsook
His friends, and went to learn the gipsy
    lore,

  And roamed the world with that wild
    brotherhood,
  And came, as most men deemed, to
    little good,
    But came to Oxford and his friends
    no more.   40

But once, years after, in the country lanes,
  Two scholars whom at college erst he
    knew,
  Met him, and of his way of life en-
    quired.
Whereat he answered, that the gipsy
    crew,
  His mates, had arts to rule as they de-
    sired,   45
    The workings of men's brains;
And they can bind them to what thoughts
    they will:
  'And I,' he said, 'the secret of their art,
  When fully learned, will to the world
    impart;
    But it needs happy moments for this
    skill.'   50

This said, he left them, and returned no
    more,
  But rumors hung about the country side
  That the lost scholar long was seen to
    stray,
Seen by rare glimpses pensive and tongue-
    tied,
  In hat of antique shape, and cloak of
    gray,   55
    The same the gipsies wore.
Shepherds had met him on the Hurst in
    spring:
  At some lone alehouse in the Berkshire
    moors,
  On the warm ingle-bench, the smock-
    frocked boors
    Had found him seated at their enter-
    ing.   60

But, 'mid their drink and clatter, he would
    fly,
  And I myself seem half to know thy
    looks,
  And put the shepherds, wanderer, on
    thy trace;
And boys who in lone wheat fields
    scare the rooks
  I ask if thou hast passed their quiet
    place;   65
    Or in my boat I lie
Moored to the cool bank in the summer
    heats,

'Mid wide grass meadows which the
    sunshine fills,
And watch the warm green-muffled
    Cumner hills,
    And wonder if thou haunt'st their
      shy retreats.   70

For most, I know, thou lov'st retirèd
    ground.
Thee, at the ferry, Oxford riders blithe,
Returning home on summer nights, have
    met
Crossing the stripling Thames at Bab-
    lock-hithe,
    Trailing in the cool stream thy fingers
      wet,   75
      As the punt's rope chops round:
And leaning backwards in a pensive
    dream,
    And fostering in thy lap a heap of
      flowers
    Plucked in shy fields and distant Wych-
      wood bowers,
      And thine eyes resting on the moon-
        lit stream.   80

And then they land, and thou art seen no
    more.
Maidens who from the distant hamlets
    come
    To dance around the Fyfield elm in
      May,
Oft through the darkening fields have
    seen thee roam,
    Or cross a stile into the public way. 85
    Oft thou hast given them store
Of flowers — the frail-leafed, white anem-
    one —
    Dark bluebells drenched with dews of
      summer eves —
And purple orchises with spotted
    leaves —
    But none hath words she can report
      of thee.

And, above Godstow Bridge, when hay-
    time's here   91
In June, and many a scythe in sunshine
    flames,
    Men who through those wide fields of
      breezy grass
Where black-winged swallows haunt the
    glittering Thames,
    To bathe in the abandoned lasher pass,
    Have often passed thee near   96
Sitting upon the river bank o'ergrown;
Marked thine outlandish garb, thy
    figure spare,

    Thy dark vague eyes, and soft ab-
      stracted air;
    But, when they came from bathing,
      thou wast gone.   100

At some lone homestead in the Cumner
    hills,
Where at her open door the housewife
    darns,
    Thou hast been seen, or hanging on a
      gate
To watch the threshers in the mossy
    barns.
    Children, who early range these slopes
      and late   105
      For cresses from the rills,
Have known thee eying, all an April day,
    The springing pastures and the feed-
      ing kine;
    And marked thee, when the stars come
      out and shine,
      Through the long dewy grass move
        slow away.   110

In Autumn, on the skirts of Bagley Wood —
    Where most the gipsies by the turf-edged
      way
    Pitch their smoked tents, and every
      bush you see
With scarlet patches tagged and shreds
    of gray,
    Above the forest-ground called Thes-
      saly —   115
      The blackbird picking food.
Sees thee, nor stops his meal, nor fears
    at all;
    So often has he known thee past him
      stray,
Rapt, twirling in thy hand a withered
    spray,
    And waiting for the spark from
      heaven to fall.   120

And once, in winter, on the causeway chill
Where home through flooded fields foot-
    travelers go,
Have I not passed thee on the wooden
    bridge
Wrapt in thy cloak and battling with the
    snow,
    Thy face toward Hinskey and its win-
      try ridge?   125
      And thou hast climbed the hill,
And gained the white brow of the Cum-
    ner range,
    Turned once to watch, while thick the
      snowflakes fall,

The line of festal light in Christ Church
   hall —
  Then sought thy straw in some se-
    questered grange.   130

But what — I dream! Two hundred years
   are flown
Since first thy story ran through Oxford
   halls,
  And the grave Glanvil did the tale in-
    scribe
That thou wert wandered from the studi-
   ous walls
To learn strange arts, and join a gipsy
   tribe: 135
  And thou from earth art gone
Long since, and in some quiet churchyard
   laid;
  Some country nook, where o'er thy un-
    known grave
  Tall grasses and white flowering nettles
    wave —
   Under a dark red-fruited, yew-tree's
    shade.   140

— No, no, thou hast not felt the lapse of
   hours,
  For what wears out the life of mortal
    men?
  'T is that from change to change their
    being rolls:
  'T is that repeated shocks, again, again,
   Exhaust the energy of strongest souls,
   And numb the elastic powers.   146
Till having used our nerves with bliss
   and teen,
  And tired upon a thousand schemes
    our wit,
  To the just-pausing Genius we remit
   Our worn-out life, and are — what we
    have been.   150

Thou hast not lived, why should'st thou
   perish, so?
  Thou had'st *one* aim, *one* business, *one*
    desire;
  Else wert thou long since numbered
    with the dead —
  Else hadst thou spent, like other men, thy
    fire.
  The generations of thy peers are fled,
   And we ourselves shall go;   156
But thou possessest an immortal lot,
  And we imagine thee exempt from age,
  And living as thou liv'st on Glanvil's
    page,
  Because thou hadst — what we, alas,
    have not!   160

For early didst thou leave the world, with
   powers
Fresh, undiverted to the world without,
  Firm to their mark, not spent on other
    things;
Free from the sick fatigue, the languid
   doubt,
  Which much to have tried, in much
    been baffled, brings.   165
  O life unlike to ours!
Who fluctuate idly without term or
   scope,
  Of whom each strives, nor knows for
    what he strives,
  And each half lives a hundred different
    lives;
  Who wait like thee, but not, like thee,
    in hope.   170

Thou waitest for the spark from heaven:
   and we,
  Light half-believers of our casual creeds,
  Who never deeply felt, nor clearly
    willed,
Whose insight never has borne fruit in
   deeds,
  Whose vague resolves never have been
    fulfilled;   175
  For whom each year we see
Breeds new beginnings, disappointments
   new;
  Who hesitate and falter life away,
  And lose to-morrow the ground won to-
    day —
   Ah, do not we, wanderer, await it
    too?   180

Yes, we await it, but it still delays,
  And then we suffer; and amongst us one,
  Who most has suffered, takes deject-
    edly
His seat upon the intellectual throne;
  And all his store of sad experience he
   Lays bare of wretched days;   186
Tells us his misery's birth and growth and
   signs,
  And how the dying spark of hope was
    fed,
  And how the breast was soothed, and
    how the head,
  And all his hourly varied anodynes.

This for our wisest: and we others pine,
  And wish the long unhappy dream would
    end,   192
   And waive all claim to bliss, and try to
    bear
With close-lipped patience for our only
   friend.

Sad patience, too near neighbor to de-
    spair,   195
But none has hope like thine.
Thou through the fields and through the
    woods dost stray,
Roaming the country side, a truant boy,
Nursing thy project in unclouded joy,
    And every doubt long blown by time
        away.   200

O born in days when wits were fresh and
    clear,
And life ran gaily as the sparkling
    Thames;
Before this strange disease of modern
    life,
With its sick hurry, its divided aims,
    Its heads o'ertaxed, its palsied hearts,
        was rife —   205
    Fly hence, our contact fear!
Still fly, plunge deeper in the bowering
    wood!
Averse, as Dido did with gesture stern
From her false friend's approach in
    Hades turn,   209
    Wave us away, and keep thy solitude.

Still nursing the unconquerable hope,
Still clutching the inviolable shade,
    With a free onward impulse brushing
        through,
By night, the silvered branches of the
    glade —
Far on the forest skirts, where none
    pursue,   215
On some mild pastoral slope
Emerge, and resting on the moonlit pales,
Freshen thy flowers, as in former years,
With dew, or listen with enchanted ears,
    From the dark dingles, to the night-
        ingales.   220

But fly our paths, our feverish contact fly,
    For strong the infection of our mental
        strife,
    Which, though it gives no bliss, yet
        spoils for rest;
And we should win thee from thy own
    fair life,
Like us distracted, and like us unblest.
    Soon, soon thy cheer would die,   226
Thy hopes grow timorous, and unfixed
    thy powers,
And thy clear aims be cross and shift-
    ing made:
And then thy glad perennial youth
    would fade,
    Fade, and grow old at last, and die
    like ours.   230

Then fly our greetings, fly our speech and
    smiles!
— As some grave Tyrian trader, from the
    sea,
Descried at sunrise an emerging prow
Lifting the cool-haired creepers stealthily,
    The fringes of a southward-facing brow
        Among the Ægean isles;   236
And saw the merry Grecian coaster come,
    Freighted with amber grapes, and Chian
    wine,
    Green bursting figs, and tunnies steeped
    in brine;
    And knew the intruders on his an-
        cient home,   240

The young light-hearted masters of the
    waves;
And snatched his rudder, and shook out
    more sail,
And day and night held on indignantly
O'er the blue Midland waters with the
    gale,
    Betwixt the Syrtes and soft Sicily,
    To where the Atlantic raves   246
Outside the Western Straits; and unbent
    sails
There, where down cloudy cliffs
    through sheets of foam,
    Shy traffickers, the dark Iberians come;
    And on the beach undid his corded
    bales.   250
                        (1853)

REQUIESCAT

Strew on her roses, roses,
    And never a spray of yew!
In quiet she reposes;
    Ah, would that I did too!

Her mirth the world required;   5
    She bathed it in smiles of glee.
But her heart was tired, tired,
    And now they let her be.

Her life was turning, turning,
    In mazes of heat and sound.   10
But for peace her soul was yearning,
    And now peace laps her round.

Her cabined, ample spirit,
    It fluttered and failed for breath.
To-night it doth inherit   15
    The vasty hall of death.
                        (1853)

RUGBY CHAPEL

NOVEMBER 1857

Coldly, sadly descends
The autumn evening. The field
Strewn with its dank yellow drifts,
Of withered leaves, and the elms,
Fade into dimness apace,   5
Silent; — hardly a shout
From a few boys late at their play!
The lights come out in the street,
In the school-room windows; — but cold,
Solemn, unlighted, austere,   10
Through the gathering darkness, arise
The chapel-walls, in whose bound
Thou, my father! art laid.

There thou dost lie, in the gloom
Of the autumn evening. But ah,   15
That word, *gloom,* to my mind
Brings thee back, in the light
Of thy radiant vigor, again;
In the gloom of November we passed
Days not dark at thy side;   20
Seasons impaired not the ray
Of thy buoyant cheerfulness clear.
Such thou wast! and I stand
In the autumn evening, and think
Of bygone autumns with thee.   25

Fifteen years have gone round
Since thou arosest to tread,
In the summer-morning, the road
Of death, at a call unforeseen,
Sudden. For fifteen years,   30
We who till then in thy shade
Rested as under the boughs
Of a mighty oak, have endured
Sunshine and rain as we might,
Bare, unshaded, alone,   35
Lacking the shelter of thee.

O strong soul, by what shore
Tarriest thou now? For that force,
Surely, has not been left vain!
Somewhere, surely, afar,   40
In the sounding labor-house vast
Of being, is practised that strength,
Zealous, beneficent, firm!

Yes, in some far-shining sphere,
Conscious or not of the past,   45
Still thou performest the word
Of the Spirit in whom thou dost live —
Prompt, unwearied, as here!
Still thou upraisest with zeal
The humble good from the ground,   50
Sternly repressest the bad!

Still, like a trumpet, dost rouse
Those who with half-open eyes
Tread the border-land dim
'Twixt vice and virtue; reviv'st   55
Succorest! This was thy work,
This was thy life upon earth.

What is the course of the life
Of mortal men on the earth?
Most men eddy about   60
Here and there — eat and drink,
Chatter and love and hate,
Gather and squander, are raised
Aloft, are hurled in the dust.
Striving blindly, achieving   65
Nothing; and then they die —
Perish; — and no one asks
Who or what they have been,
More than he asks what waves,
In the moonlit solitudes mild   70
Of the midmost Ocean, have swelled,
Foamed for a moment, and gone.

And there are some, whom a thirst
Ardent, unquenchable, fires,
Not with the crowd to be spent,   75
Not without aim to go round
In an eddy of purposeless dust,
Effort unmeaning and vain.
Ah, yes! some of us strive
Not without action to die   80
Fruitless, but something to snatch
From dull oblivion, nor all
Glut the devouring grave!
We, we have chosen our path —
Path to a clear-purposed goal,   85
Path of advance! — but it leads
A long, steep journey, through sunk
Gorges, o'er mountains in snow.
Cheerful, with friends, we set forth —
Then, on the height, comes the storm.   90
Thunder crashes from rock
To rock, the cataracts reply,
Lightnings dazzle our eyes.
Roaring torrents have breached
The track, the stream-bed descends   95
In the place where the wayfarer once
Planted his footstep — the spray
Boils o'er its borders! aloft
The unseen snow-beds dislodge
Their hanging ruin! alas,   100
Havoc is made in our train!
Friends, who set forth at our side,
Falter, are lost in the storm.
We, we only are left!
With frowning foreheads, with lips   105
Sternly compressed, we strain on,
On — and at nightfall at last

Come to the end of our way,
To the lonely inn 'mid the rocks;
Where the gaunt and taciturn host   110
Stands on the threshold, the wind
Shaking his thin white hairs —
Holds his lantern to scan
Our storm-beat figures, and asks:
Whom in our party we bring,   115
Whom we have left in the snow?

Sadly we answer: We bring
Only ourselves! we lost
Sight of the rest in the storm.
Hardly ourselves we fought through,   120
Stripped, without friends, as we are.
Friends, companions, and train,
The avalanche swept from our side.

But thou would'st not *alone*
Be saved, my father! *alone*   125
Conquer and come to thy goal,
Leaving the rest in the wild.
We were weary, and we
Fearful, and we in our march
Fain to drop down and to die.   130
Still thou turnedst, and still
Beckonedst the trembler, and still
Gavest the weary, thy hand.

If, in the paths of the world,
Stones might have wounded thy feet,   135
Toil or dejection have tried
Thy spirit, of that we saw
Nothing — to us thou wast still
Cheerful, and helpful, and firm!
Therefore to thee it was given   140
Many to save with thyself;
And, at the end of thy day,
O, faithful shepherd! to come,
Bringing thy sheep in thy hand.

And through thee I believe   145
In the noble and great who are gone;
Pure souls honored and blest
By former ages, who else —
Such, so soulless, so poor,
Is the race of men whom I see —   150
Seemed but a dream of the heart,
Seemed but a cry of desire.
Yes! I believe that there lived
Others like thee in the past,
Not like the men of the crowd   155
Who all round me to-day
Bluster or cringe, and make life
Hideous, and arid, and vile;

But souls tempered with fire,   160
Fervent, heroic, and good,
Helpers and friends of mankind.

Servants of God! — or sons
Shall I not call you? because
Not as servants ye knew
Your Father's innermost mind,   165
His, who unwillingly sees
One of his little ones lost —
Yours is the praise, if mankind
Hath not as yet in its march
Fainted, and fallen, and died!   170

See! In the rocks of the world
Marches the host of mankind,
A feeble, wavering line.
Where are they tending? — A God
Marshaled them, gave them their goal.   175
Ah, but the way is so long!
Years they have been in the wild!
Sore thirst plagues them, the rocks,
Rising all round, overawe;
Factions divide them, their host   180
Threatens to break, to dissolve.
— Ah, keep, keep them combined!
Else, of the myriads who fill
That army, not one shall arrive;
Sole they shall stray; on the rocks   185
Batter for ever in vain,
Die one by one in the waste.

Then, in such hour of need
Of your fainting, dispirited race,
Ye, like angels, appear,   190
Radiant with ardor divine!
Beacons of hope, ye appear!
Languor is not in your heart,
Weakness is not in your word,
Weariness not on your brow.   195
Ye alight in our van! at your voice,
Panic, despair, flee away.
Ye move through the ranks, recall
The stragglers, refresh the outworn,
Praise, re-inspire the brave!   200
Order, courage, return.
Eyes rekindling, and prayers,
Follow your steps as ye go.
Ye fill up the gaps in our files,
Strengthen the wavering line,   205
Stablish, continue our march,
On, to the bound of the waste,
On, to the City of God.

                              (1867)

DANTE GABRIEL ROSSETTI (1828–1882)

Although as a very young boy Rossetti showed a talent for versifying, he attained distinction first as a painter. After spending five years at King's College School and in art academies in London, he became a pupil of Ford Madox Brown, and later joined Holman Hunt, Millais, and others, in that revival of mystical interpretation and detailed elaboration in painting commonly called the Pre-Raphaelite movement. No considerable part of Rossetti's poems appeared in print before the publication of *Poems*, in 1870. The following year Robert Buchanan, in an article entitled *The Fleshly School in Poetry*, savagely attacked the alleged immorality of Rossetti's poems. Although Rossetti stoutly resisted the assault, it aggravated the mental depression which had begun with the death of his wife, and which persisted until his death. The last ten years of his life were tragically clouded by mental weakness and by the habit of taking chloral. Even during this period, however, creative flashes of his mind resulted in both poems and paintings of great beauty.

Poems (1870), *Dante and His Circle* (1874), and *Ballads and Sonnets* (1881) contain substantially all of Rossetti's poetry. The volume of 1881 brought out *The King's Tragedy*, and added sonnets to complete the *House of Life*, the first sonnets of which had appeared in 1870. Rossetti's only imaginative work in prose is *Hand and Soul* (1850). His poetry, often subtly mystical in thought, has been called, significantly, 'painter's poetry,' from its delicate picturesqueness and visual beauty.

MY SISTER'S SLEEP

She fell asleep on Christmas Eve:
    At length the long-ungranted shade
    Of weary eyelids overweighed
The pain naught else might yet relieve.

Our mother, who had leaned all day   5
    Over the bed from chime to chime,
    Then raised herself for the first time,
And as she sat her down, did pray.

Her little work-table was spread
    With work to finish. For the glare   10
    Made by her candle, she had care
To work some distance from the bed.

Without, there was a cold moon up,
    Of winter radiance sheer and thin;
    The hollow halo it was in   15
Was like an icy crystal cup.

Through the small room, with subtle sound
    Of flame, by vents the fireshine drove
    And reddened. In its dim alcove
The mirror shed a clearness round.   20

I had been sitting up some nights,
    And my tired mind felt weak and blank;
    Like a sharp strengthening wine it drank
The stillness and the broken lights.

Twelve struck. That sound, by dwindling years   25
    Heard in each hour, crept off; and then
    The ruffled silence spread again,
Like water that a pebble stirs.

Our mother rose from where she sat:
    Her needles, as she laid them down,   30
    Met lightly, and her silken gown
Settled: no other noise than that.

'Glory unto the Newly Born!'
    So, as said angels, she did say;
    Because we were in Christmas Day   35
Though it would still be long till morn.

Just then in the room over us
    There was a pushing back of chairs,
    As some who had sat unawares
So late, now heard the hour, and rose.   40

With anxious softly-stepping haste
    Our mother went where Margaret lay,
    Fearing the sounds o'er head — should they
Have broken her long watched-for rest!

She stooped an instant, calm, and turned,   45
    But suddenly turned back again;
    And all her features seemed in pain
With woe, and her eyes gazed and yearned.

For my part, I but hid my face,
  And held my breath, and spoke no word:
  There was none spoken: but I heard 51
The silence for a little space.

Our mother bowed herself and wept:
  And both my arms fell, and I said,
  'God knows I knew that she was dead.' 55
And there, all white, my sister slept.

Then kneeling, upon Christmas morn
  A little after twelve o'clock,
  We said, ere the first quarter struck,
'Christ's blessing on the newly born!' 60
                    (1850)

THE BLESSED DAMOZEL

The blessed damozel leaned out
  From the golden bar of heaven;
Her eyes were deeper than the depth
  Of waters stilled at even;
She had three lilies in her hand, 5
  And the stars in her hair were seven.

Her robe, ungirt from clasp to hem,
  No wrought flowers did adorn,
But a white rose of Mary's gift,
  For service meetly worn; 10
Her hair that lay along her back
  Was yellow like ripe corn.

Her seemed she scarce had been a day
  One of God's choristers;
The wonder was not yet quite gone 15
  From that still look of hers;
Albeit, to them she left, her day
  Had counted as ten years.

(To one, it is ten years of years.
  . . . Yet now, and in this place, 20
Surely she leaned o'er me — her hair
  Fell all about my face. . . .
Nothing: the autumn-fall of leaves.
  The whole year sets apace.)

It was the rampart of God's house 25
  That she was standing on;
By God built over the sheer depth
  The which is Space begun;
So high, that looking downward thence
  She scarce could see the sun. 30

It lies in heaven, across the flood
  Of ether, as a bridge.
Beneath, the tides of day and night
  With flame and darkness ridge

The void, as low as where this earth 35
  Spins like a fretful midge.

Around her, lovers, newly met
  'Mid deathless love's acclaims,
Spoke evermore among themselves
  Their heart-remembered names; 40
And the souls mounting up to God
  Went by her like thin flames.

And still she bowed herself and stooped
  Out of the circling charm;
Until her bosom must have made 45
  The bar she leaned on warm,
And the lilies lay as if asleep
  Along her bended arm.

From the fixed place of Heaven she saw
  Time like a pulse shake fierce 50
Through all the worlds. Her gaze still
    strove,
  Within the gulf to pierce
Its path: and now she spoke as when
  The stars sang in their spheres.

The sun was gone now; the curled moon 55
  Was like a little feather
Fluttering far down the gulf; and now
  She spoke through the still weather.
Her voice was like the voice the stars
  Had when they sang together. 60

(Ah, sweet! Even now, in that bird's song,
  Strove not her accents there,
Fain to be hearkened? When those bells
  Possessed the mid-day air,
Strove not her steps to reach my side 65
  Down all the echoing stair?)

'I wish that he were come to me,
  For he will come,' she said.
'Have I not prayed in Heaven? — on earth,
  Lord, Lord, has he not prayed? 70
Are not two prayers a perfect strength?
  And shall I feel afraid?

'When round his head the aureole clings,
  And he is clothed in white,
I'll take his hand and go with him 75
  To the deep wells of light;
As unto a stream we will step down,
  And bathe there in God's sight.

'We two will stand beside that shrine,
  Occult, withheld, untrod, 80
Whose lamps are stirred continually
  With prayer sent up to God;
And see our old prayers, granted, melt
  Each like a little cloud.

'We two will lie i' the shadow of 85
That living mystic tree
Within whose secret growth the Dove
Is sometimes felt to be,
While every leaf that his plumes touch
Saith his name audibly. 90

'And I myself will teach to him,
I myself, lying so,
The songs I sing here; which his voice
Shall pause in, hushed and slow,
And find some knowledge at each pause, 95
Or some new thing to know.'

(Alas! We two, we two, thou say'st!
Yea, one wast thou with me
That once of old. But shall God lift
To endless unity 100
The soul whose likeness with thy soul
Was but its love for thee?)

'We two,' she said, 'will seek the groves
Where the lady Mary is,
With her five handmaidens, whose names
Are five sweet symphonies, 106
Cecily, Gertrude, Magdalen,
Margaret and Rosalys.

'Circlewise sit they, with bound locks
And foreheads garlanded; 110
Into the fine cloth white like flame
Weaving the golden thread,
To fashion the birth-robes for them
Who are just born, being dead.

'He shall fear, haply, and be dumb: 115
Then will I lay my cheek
To his, and tell about our love,
Not once abashed or weak;
And the dear Mother will approve
My pride, and let me speak. 120

'Herself shall bring us, hand in hand,
To him round whom all souls
Kneel, the clear-ranged unnumbered heads
Bowed with their aureoles:
And angels meeting us shall sing 125
To their cithers and citoles.

'There will I ask of Christ the Lord
Thus much for him and me: —
Only to live as once on earth
With Love, only to be, 130
As then awhile, forever now
Together, I and he.'

She gazed and listened and then said,
Less sad of speech than mild,—

'All this is when he comes.' She ceased.
The light thrilled towards her, filled 136
With angels in strong level flight.
Her eyes prayed, and she smiled.

(I saw her smile.) But soon their path
Was vague in distant spheres: 140
And then she cast her arms along
The golden barriers,
And laid her face between her hands,
And wept. (I heard her tears.)

(1850)

FRANCESCA DA RIMINI

(From DANTE)

. . .

When I made answer, I began: 'Alas!
How many sweet thoughts and how much
desire
Led these two onward to the dolorous
pass!'
Then turned to them, as who would fain
inquire,
And said: 'Francesca, these thine agonies *
Wring tears for pity and grief that they
inspire: —
But tell me,— in the season of sweet
sighs,
When and what way did Love instruct
you so
That he in your vague longings made you
wise?'
Then she to me: 'There is no greater
woe 10
Than the remembrance brings of happy
days
In Misery; and this thy guide doth know.
But if the first beginnings to retrace
Of our sad love can yield thee solace here,
So will I be as one that weeps and says. 15
One day we read, for pastime and sweet
cheer,
Of Lancelot, how he found Love tyrannous;
We were alone and without any fear.
Our eyes were drawn together, reading thus,
Full oft, and still our cheeks would pale
and glow; 20
But one sole point it was that conquered us.
For when we read of that great lover,
how
He kissed the smile which he had longed to
win,—
Then he whom naught can sever from me
now
Forever, kissed my mouth, all quivering. 25

A Galahalt was the book, and he that
    writ:
Upon that day we read no more therein.'
  At the tale told, while one soul uttered it,
The other wept: a pang so pitiable
    That I was seized, like death, in swoon-
      ing-fit,   30
And even as a dead body falls, I fell.
                                    (1861)

LOVE'S NOCTURN

Master of the murmuring courts
  Where the shapes of sleep convene!—
Lo! my spirit here exhorts
    All the powers of thy demesne
    For their aid to woo my queen.   5
        What reports
    Yield thy jealous courts unseen?

Vaporous, unaccountable,
  Dreamworld lies forlorn of light,
Hollow like a breathing shell.   10
    Ah! that from all dreams I might
    Choose one dream and guide its flight!
        I know well
    What her sleep should tell to-night.

There the dreams are multitudes: 15
  Some that will not wait for sleep,
Deep within the August woods;
    Some that hum while rest may steep
    Weary labor laid a-heap;
        Interludes,   20
    Some, of grievous moods that weep.

Poet's fancies all are there;
  There the elf-girls flood with wings
Valleys full of plaintive air;
    There breathe perfumes; there in rings
    Whirl the foam-bewildered springs;   26
        Siren there
    Winds her dizzy hair and sings.

Thence the one dream mutually
  Dreamed in bridal unison,
Less than walking ecstasy;   30
    Half-formed visions that make moan
    In the house of birth alone;
        And what we
    At death's wicket see, unknown.   35

But for mine own sleep, it lies
  In one gracious form's control,
Fair with honorable eyes,
    Lamps of a translucent soul:

O their glance is loftiest dole,   40
        Sweet and wise,
  Wherein Love descries his goal.

Reft of her, my dreams are all
  Clammy trance that fears the sky;
Changing footpaths shift and fall;   45
    From polluted coverts nigh,
    Miserable phantoms sigh;
        Quakes the pall,
    And the funeral goes by.

Master, is it soothly said   50
  That, as echoes of man's speech
Far in secret clefts are made,
    So do all men's bodies reach
    Shadows o'er thy sunken beach,—
        Shape or shade   55
    In those halls portrayed of each?

Ah! might I, by thy good grace
  Groping in the windy stair
(Darkness and the breath of space
    Like loud waters everywhere),   60
    Meeting mine own image there
        Face to face,
    Send it from that place to her!

Nay, not I; but oh! do thou,
  Master, from thy shadowkind   65
Call my body's phantom now:
    Bid it bear its face declined
    Till its flight her slumbers find,
        And her brow
    Feel its presence bow like wind.   70

Where in groves the gracile Spring
  Trembles, with mute orison
Confidently strengthening,
    Water's voice and wind's as one
    Shed an echo in the sun.   75
        Soft as Spring,
    Master, bid it sing and moan

Song shall tell how glad and strong
  Is the night she soothes alway;
Moan shall grieve with that parched tongue
    Of the brazen hours of day: 81
    Sounds as of the springtide they,
        Moan and song,
    While the chill months long for May.

Not the prayers which with all leave   85
  The world's fluent woes prefer,—
Not the praise the world doth give,
    Dulcet fulsome whisperer;—
    Let it yield my love to her,
        And achieve   90
    Strength that shall not grieve or err.

Wheresoe'er my dreams befall,
  Both at night-watch (let it say),
And where round the sun-dial
  The reluctant hours of day,   95
Heartless, hopeless of their way,
      Rest and call; —
  There her glance doth fall and stay.

Suddenly her face is there:
  So do mounting vapors wreathe   100
Subtle-scented transports where
  The black fir-wood sets its teeth
Part the boughs, and looks beneath —
      Lilies share
  Secret waters there, and breathe.   105

Master, bid my shadow bend
  Whispering thus till birth of light,
Lest new shapes that sleep may send
  Scatter all its work to flight; —
Master, master of the night,   110
      Bid it spend
  Speech, song, prayer, and end aright.

Yet, ah, me! if at her head
  There another phantom lean
Murmuring o'er the fragrant bed,   115
  Ah! and if my spirit's queen
Smile those alien prayers between,—
      Ah! poor shade!
  Shall it strive, or fade unseen?

How should love's own messenger   120
  Strive with love and be love's foe?
Master, nay! If thus, in her,
  Sleep a wedded heart should show,—
Silent let mine image go,
      Its old share   125
  Of thy spell-bound air to know.

Like a vapor wan and mute,
  Like a flame, so let it pass;
One low sigh across her lute,
  One dull breath against her glass; 130
And to my sad soul, alas!
      One salute
  Cold as when death's foot shall pass.

Then, too, let all hopes of mine,
  All vain hopes by night and day,   135
Slowly at thy summoning sign
  Rise up pallid and obey.
Dreams, if this is thus, were they: —
      Be they thine,
  And to dreamworld pine away.   140

Yet from old time, life, not death,
  Master, in thy rule is rife:

Lo! through thee, with mingling breath,
  Adam woke beside his wife.
O Love, bring me so, for strife,   145
      Force and faith,
  Bring me so not death but life!

Yea, to Love himself is poured
  This frail song of hope and fear,
Thou art Love, of one accord   150
  With kind Sleep to bring her near,
Still-eyed, deep-eyed, ah, how dear!
      Master, Lord,
  In her name implored, O hear!

                              (1870)

THE CLOUD CONFINES

The day is dark and the night
  To him that would search their heart;
No lips of cloud that will part
Nor morning song in the light:
  Only, gazing alone,   5
  To him wild shadows are shown,
  Deep under deep unknown,
And height above unknown height.
    Still we say as we go,—
    'Strange to think by the way,   10
    Whatever there is to know,
    That shall we know one day.'

The Past is over and fled;
  Named new, we name it the old;
Thereof some tale hath been told,   15
But no word comes from the dead ·
  Whether at all they be,
  Or whether as bond or free,
  Or whether they too were we,
Or by what spell they have sped.   20
    Still we say as we go,—
    'Strange to think by the way,
    Whatever there is to know,
    That shall we know one day.'

What of the heart of hate   25
  That beats in thy breast, O Time? —
Red strife from the furthest prime,
  And anguish of fierce debate;
  War that shatters her slain,
  And peace that grinds them as grain, 30
  And eyes fixed ever in vain
On the pitiless eyes of Fate.
    Still we say as we go,—
    'Strange to think by the way,
    Whatever there is to know,   35
    That shall we know one day.'

What of the heart of love
  That bleeds in thy breast, O Man ?

Thy kisses snatched 'neath the ban
Of fangs that mock them above;   40
Thy bells prolonged unto knells,
Thy hope that a breath dispels,
Thy bitter forlorn farewells
And the empty echoes thereof?
    Still we say as we go,—   45
     'Strange to think by the way,
    Whatever there is to know,
     That shall we know one day.'

The sky leans dumb on the sea,
  Aweary with all its wings;   50
And oh! the song the sea sings
Is dark everlastingly.
    Our past is clean forgot,
    Our present is and is not,
    Our future's a sealed seedplot,   55
And what betwixt them are we?—
    We who say as we go,—
     'Strange to think by the way,
    Whatever there is to know,
     That shall we know one day.'   60
                   (1872)

THREE SHADOWS

I looked and saw your eyes
  In the shadow of your hair,
As a traveler sees the stream
  In the shadow of the wood;
And I said, 'My faint heart sighs,   5
  Ah me! to linger there,
To drink deep and to dream
  In that sweet solitude.'

I looked and saw your heart
  In the shadow of your eyes,   10
As a seeker sees the gold
  In the shadow of the stream;
And I said, 'Ah me! what art
  Should win the immortal prize,
Whose want must make life cold   15
  And heaven a hollow dream?'

I looked and saw your love
  In the shadow of your heart,
As a diver sees the pearl
  In the shadow of the sea;   20
And I murmured, not above
  My breath, but all apart,—
Ah! you can love, true girl,
  And is your love for me?'
                  (1881)

THE KING'S TRAGEDY

JAMES I OF SCOTS — 20TH FEBRUARY 1473

I Catherine am a Douglas born,
  A name to all Scots dear;
And Kate Barlass they've called me now
  Through many a waning year.

This old arm's withered now. 'T was once
  Most deft 'mong maidens all   6
To rein the steed, to wing the shaft,
  To smite the palm-play ball.

In hall adown the close-linked dance
  It has shone most white and fair;   10
It has been the rest for a true lord's head,
And many a sweet babe's nursing-bed,
  And the bar to a King's chambère.

Aye, lasses, draw round Kate Barlass,
  And hark with bated breath   15
How good King James, King Robert's son,
  Was foully done to death.

Through all the days of his gallant youth
  The princely James was pent,
By his friends at first and then by his foes,
  In long imprisonment.   21

For the elder prince, the kingdom's heir,
  By treason's murderous brood
Was slain; and the father quaked for the child
  With the royal mortal blood   25

I' the Bass Rock fort, by his father's care,
  Was his childhood's life assured;
And Henry the subtle Bolingbroke,
Proud England's king, 'neath the southron yoke
  His youth for long years immured.   30

Yet in all things meet for a kingly man
  Himself did he approve;
And the nightingale through his prison-wall
  Taught him both lore and love.

For once, when the bird's song drew him close 35
  To the opened window-pane,
In her bower beneath a lady stood,
A light of life to his sorrowful mood,
  Like a lily amid the rain.

And for her sake, to the sweet bird's note,
  He framed a sweeter song,
More sweet than ever a poet's heart
  Gave yet to the English tongue.

She was a lady of royal blood;
  And when, past sorrow and teen   45
He stood where still through his crownless years
  His Scottish realm had been,
At Scone were the happy lovers crowned,
  A heart-wed king and queen.

But the bird may fall from the bough of youth,   50
  And song be turned to moan,
And love's storm-cloud be the shadow of hate,
When the tempest-waves of a troubled state
  Are beating against a throne.

Yet well they loved; and the god of love,   55
  Whom well the king had sung,
Might find on the earth no truer hearts
  His lowliest swains among.

From the days when first she rode abroad
  With Scottish maids in her train,   60
I Catherine Douglas won the trust
  Of my mistress sweet Queen Jane.

And oft she sighed, 'To be born a King!'
  And oft along the way
When she saw the homely lovers pass   65
  She has said, 'Alack the day!'

Years waned,— the loving and toiling years:
  Till England's wrong renewed
Drove James, by outrage cast on his crown,
  To the open field of feud.   70

'T was when the king and his host were met
  At the leaguer of Roxbro' hold,
The queen o' the sudden sought his camp
  With a tale of dread to be told.

And she showed him a secret letter writ   75
  That spoke of treasonous strife,
And how a band of his noblest lords
  Were sworn to take his life.

'And it may be here or it may be there,
  In the camp or the court,' she said: 80
'But for my sake come to your people's arms
  And guard your royal head.'

Quoth he, ''T is the fifteenth day of the siege,
  And the castle's nigh to yield.'
'O face your foes on your throne,' she cried,
  'And show the power you wield;   86

And under your Scottish people's love
  You shall sit as under your shield.'

At the fair queen's side I stood that day
  When he bade them raise the siege,   90
And back to his court he sped to know
  How the lords would meet their liege.

But when he summoned his parliament,
  The louring brows hung round,
Like clouds that circle the mountain-head   95
  Ere the first low thunders sound.

For he had tamed the nobles' lust
  And curbed their power and pride,
And reached out an arm to right the poor
  Through Scotland far and wide;   100
And many a lordly wrong-doer
  By the headsman's axe had died.

'T was then upspoke Sir Robert Græme,
  The bold o'ermastering man: —
'O King, in the name of your Three Estates   105
  I set you under their ban!

'For, as your lords made oath to you
  Of service and fealty,
Even in like wise you pledged your oath
  Their faithful sire to be: —   110

'Yet all we here that are nobly sprung
  Have mourned dear kith and kin
Since first for the Scottish Barons' curse
  Did your bloody rule begin.'

With that he laid his hands on his king: —
  'Is this not so, my lords?'   116
But of all who had sworn to league with him
  Not one spake back to his words.

Quoth the King: —'Thou speak'st but for one Estate,
  Nor doth it avow thy gage.   120
Let my liege lords hale this traitor hence!'
  The Græme fired dark with rage: —
'Who works for lesser men than himself,
  He earns but a witness wage!'

But soon from the dungeon where he lay   125
  He won by privy plots,
And forth he fled with a price on his head
  To the country of the Wild Scots.

And word there came from Sir Robert Græme
  To the King of Edinbro': —   130

'No liege of mine thou art; but I see
From this day forth alone in thee
God's creature, my mortal foe.

'Through thee are my wife and children
    lost,
    My heritage and lands;   135
And when my God shall show me a way,
Thyself my mortal foe will I slay
    With these my proper hands.'

Against the coming of Christmastide
    That year the king bade call   140
I' the Black Friars' Charterhouse of Perth
    A solemn festival.

And we of his household rode with him
    In a close-ranked company;
But not till the sun had sunk from his
    throne   145
    Did we reach the Scottish Sea.

That eve was clenched for a boding storm,
    'Neath a toilsome moon, half seen;
The cloud stooped low and the surf rose
    high;
And where there was a line of the sky,   150
    Wild wings loomed dark between.

And on a rock of the black beach-side
    By the veiled moon dimly lit,
There was something seemed to heave with
    life
    As the king drew nigh to it.   155

And was it only the tossing furze
    Or brake of the waste sea-wold?
Or was it an eagle bent to the blast?
When near we came, we knew it at last
    For a woman tattered and old.   160

But it seemed as though by a fire within
    Her writhen limbs were wrung;
And as soon as the king was close to her,
    She stood up gaunt and strong.

'Twas then the moon sailed clear of the
    rack   165
    On high in her hollow dome;
And still as aloft with hoary crest
    Each clamorous wave rang home,
Like fire in snow the moonlight blazed
    Amid the champing foam.   170

And the woman held his eyes with her
    eyes: —
    'O King, thou art come at last;

But thy wraith has haunted the Scottish Sea
    To my sight for four years past.

'Four years it is since first I met,   175
    'Twixt the Duchray and the Dhu,
A shape whose feet clung close in a shroud,
    And that shape for thine I knew.

'A year again, and on Inchkeith Isle
    I saw thee pass in the breeze,   180
With the cerecloth risen above thy feet
    And wound about thy knees.

'And yet a year, in the Links of Forth,
    As a wanderer without rest,
Thou cam'st with both thine arms i' the
    shroud   185
    That clung high up thy breast.

'And in this hour I find thee here,
    And well mine eyes may note
That the winding-sheet hath passed thy
    breast
    And risen around thy throat.   190

'And when I meet thee again, O King,
    That of death hast such sore drouth,—
Except thou turn again on this shore,—
The winding-sheet shall have moved once
    more
    And covered thine eyes and mouth.   195

'O King, whom poor men bless for their
    king,
    Of thy fate be not so fain;
But these my words for God's message
    take.
And turn thy steed, O King, for her sake
    Who rides beside thy rein!'   200

While the woman spoke, the king's horse
    reared
    As if it would breast the sea,
And the queen turned pale as she heard on
    the gale
    The voice die dolorously.

When the woman ceased, the steed was still,
    But the king gazed on her yet,   206
And in silence save for the wail of the sea
    His eyes and her eyes met.

At last he said: —'God's ways are his own;
    Man is but shadow and dust.   210
Last night I prayed by his altar-stone;
To-night I wend to the Feast of His Son;
    And in him I set my trust.

'I have held my people in sacred charge,
  And have not feared the sting   215
Of proud men's hate,—to his will resigned
Who has but one same death for a hind
  And one same death for a king.

'And if God in his wisdom have brought
    close
The day when I must die,   220
That day by water or fire or air
My feet shall fall in the destined snare
  Wherever my road may lie.

'What man can say but the Fiend hath set
  Thy sorcery on my path,   225
My heart with the fear of death to fill,
And turn me against God's very will
  To sink in his burning wrath?'

The woman stood as the train rode past,
  And moved nor limb nor eye;   230
And when we were shipped, we saw her
    there
  Still standing against the sky.

As the ship made way, the moon once more
  Sank slow in her rising pall;
And I thought of the shrouded wraith of the
    king,   235
  And I said, 'The heavens know all.'

And now, ye lasses, must ye hear
  How my name is Kate Barlass:—
But a little thing, when all the tale
  Is told of the weary mass   240
Of crime and woe which in Scotland's realm
  God's will let come to pass.

'T was in the Charterhouse of Perth
  That the king and all his court
Were met, the Christmas Feast being done,
  For solace and disport.   246

'T was a wind-wild eve in February,
  And against the casement-pane
The branches smote like summoning hands
  And muttered the driving rain.   250

And when the wind swooped over the lift
  And made the whole heaven frown,
It seemed a grip was laid on the walls
  To tug the housetop down.

And the queen was there, more stately fair
  Than a lily in garden set;   256
And the king was loth to stir from her side;
For as on the day when she was his bride,
  Even so he loved her yet.

And the Earl of Athole, the king's false
  friend,   260
  Sat with him at the board;
And Robert Stuart the chamberlain
  Who had sold his sovereign lord.

Yet the traitor Christopher Chaumber there
  Would fain have told him all,   265
And vainly four times that night he strove
  To reach the king through the hall.

But the wine is bright at the goblet's brim
  Though the poison lurk beneath;
And the apples still are red on the tree   270
Within whose shade may the adder be
  That shall turn thy life to death.

There was a knight of the king's fast friends
  Whom he called the King of Love;
And to such bright cheer and courtesy   275
  That name might best behoove.

And the king and queen both loved him well
  For his gentle knightliness;
And with him the king, as that eve wore on,
  Was playing at the chess.   280

And the king said, (for he thought to jest
  And soothe the queen thereby)—
'In a book 't is writ that this same year
  A king shall in Scotland die.

'And I have pondered the matter o'er,   285
  And this have I found, Sir Hugh,—
There are but two kings on Scottish ground,
  And those kings are I and you.

'And I have a wife and a newborn heir,
  And you are yourself alone;   290
So stand you stark at my side with me
  To guard our double throne.

'For here sit I and my wife and child,
  As well your heart shall approve,
In full surrender and soothfastness,   295
  Beneath your Kingdom of Love.'

And the knight laughed, and the queen too
  smiled;
  But I knew her heavy thought,
And I strove to find in the good king's
  jest
  What cheer might thence be wrought.   300

And I said, 'My Liege, for the queen's dear
  love
  Now sing the song that of old
You made, when a captive prince you lay,

And the nightingale sang sweet on the spray,
  In Windsor's castle-hold.'   305

Then he smiled the smile I knew so well
  When he thought to please the queen;
The smile which under all bitter frowns
  Of hate that rose between,
For ever dwelt at the poet's heart   310
  Like the bird of love unseen.

And he kissed her hand and took his harp,
  And the music sweetly rang;
And when the song burst forth, it seemed
  'T was the nightingale that sang.   315

'*Worship, ye lovers, on this May:*
  Of bliss your kalends are begun:
Sing with us, Away, Winter, away!
  Come, Summer, the sweet season and sun!
Awake for shame,—your heaven is won,—
And amorously your heads lift all: 321
Thank Love, that you to his grace doth call!'

But when he bent to the queen and sang
  The speech whose praise was hers,
It seemed his voice was the voice of the
      spring   325
  And the voice of the bygone years.

'*The fairest and the freshest flower*
That ever I saw before that hour,
The which o' the sudden made to start
The blood of my body to my heart.   330
        . . .
Ah sweet, are ye a worldly creature
Or heavenly thing in form of nature?'

And the song was long, and richly stored
  With wonder and beauteous things;
And the harp was tuned to every change
  Of minstrel ministerings;   336
But when he spoke of the queen at the last,
  Its strings were his own heart-strings.

'*Unworthy but only of her grace,*
  Upon Love's rock that's easy and sure, 340
In guerdon of all my love's space
  She took me her humble creäture.
  Thus fell my blissful aventure
In youth of love that from day to day
Flowereth aye new, and further I say. 345

'*To reckon all the circumstance*
  As it happed when lessen gan my sore,
Of my rancor and woful chance,
  It were too long,—I have done therefor.
  And of this flower I say no more 350

But unto my help her heart hath tended
  And even from death her man defended.'

'Aye, even from death,' to myself I said;
  For I thought of the day when she
Had borne him the news, at Roxbro' siege,
  Of the fell confederacy.   354

But Death even then took aim as he sang
  With an arrow deadly bright;
And the grinning skull lurked grimly aloof,
  And the wings were spread far over the
      roof   360
  More dark than the winter night.

Yet truly along the amorous song
  Of Love's high pomp and state,
There were words of Fortune's trackless
      doom
  And the dreadful face of Fate.   365

And oft have I heard again in dreams
  The voice of dire appeal
In which the king then sang of the pit
  That is under Fortune's wheel.

'*And under the wheel beheld I there*   370
  An ugly pit as deep as hell,
That to behold I quaked for fear:
  And this I heard, that who therein fell
Came no more up, tidings to tell:
Whereat, astound of the fearful sight,   375
I wist not what to do for fright.'

And oft has my thought called up again
  These words of the changeful song: —
'*Wist thou thy pain and thy travâil*
To come, well might'st thou weep and wail!'
  And our wail, O God! is long.   381

But the song's end was all of his love;
  And well his heart was graced
With her smiling lips and her tear-bright
      eyes
  As his arm went round her waist.   385

And on the swell of her long fair throat
  Close clung the necklet-chain
As he bent her pearl-tired head aside,
And in the warmth of his love and pride
  He kissed her lips full fain.   390

And her true face was a rosy red,
  The very red of the rose
That, couched on the happy garden-bed,
  In the summer sunlight glows.

And all the wondrous things of love   395
  That sang so sweet through the song
Were in the look that met in their eyes,
  And the look was deep and long.

'T was then a knock came at the outer gate,
  And the usher sought the king.   400
'The woman you met by the Scottish Sea,
  My Liege, would tell you a thing;
And she says that her present need for
    speech
  Will bear no gainsaying.'

And the king said: 'The hour is late;   405
  To-morrow will serve, I ween.'
Then he charged the usher strictly, and
    said:
  'No word of this to the queen.'

But the usher came again to the king.
  'Shall I call her back?' quoth he: 410
'For as she went on her way, she cried,
  "Woe! woe! then the thing must be!"'

And the king paused, but he did not speak.
  Then he called for the voidee-cup:
And as we heard the twelfth hour strike,   415
There by true lips and false lips alike
  Was the draught of trust drained up.

So with reverence meet to king and queen,
  To bed went all from the board;
And the last to leave of the courtly train
Was Robert Stuart the chamberlain   421
  Who had sold his sovereign lord.

And all the locks of the chamber-door
  Had the traitor riven and brast;
And that Fate might win sure way from
    afar,   425
He had drawn out every bolt and bar
  That made the entrance fast.

And now at midnight he stole his way
  To the moat of the outer wall,
And laid strong hurdles closely across   430
  Where the traitors' tread should fall.

But we that were the queen's bower-maids
  Alone were left behind;
And with heed we drew the curtains close
  Against the winter wind.   435

And now that all was still through the hall,
  More clearly we heard the rain
That clamored ever against the glass
  And the boughs that beat on the pane.

But the fire was bright in the ingle-nook, 440
  And through empty space around
The shadows cast on the arrased wall
'Mid the pictured kings stood sudden and
    tall
  Like specters sprung from the ground.

And the bed was dight in a deep alcove; 445
  And as he stood by the fire
The king was still in talk with the queen
  While he doffed his goodly attire.

And the song had brought the image back
  Of many a bygone year;   450
And many a loving word they said
With hand in hand and head laid to head;
  And none of us went anear.

But Love was weeping outside the house,
  A child in the piteous rain;   455
And as he watched the arrow of Death,
He wailed for his own shafts close in the
    sheath
  That never should fly again.

And now beneath the window arose
  A wild voice suddenly: 460
And the king reared straight, but the queen
    fell back
  As for bitter dule to dree;
And all of us knew the woman's voice
  Who spoke by the Scottish Sea.

'O King,' she cried, 'in an evil hour   465
  They drove me from thy gate;
And yet my voice must rise to thine ears;
  But alas! it comes too late!

'Last night at mid-watch, by Aberdour,
  When the moon was dead in the skies, 470
O King, in a death-light of thine own
  I saw thy shape arise.

'And in full season, as erst I said,
  The doom had gained its growth;
And the shroud had risen above thy neck 475
  And covered thine eyes and mouth.

'And no moon woke, but the pale dawn
    broke,
  And still thy soul stood there;
And I thought its silence cried to my soul
  As the first rays crowned its hair.   480

'Since then have I journeyed fast and fain
  In very despite of Fate,
Lest hope might still be found in God's
    will:
  But they drove me from thy gate.

'For every man on God's ground, O King,
　　His death grows up from his birth　486
In a shadow-plant perpetually;
　　And thine towers high, a black yew-tree,
　O'er the Charterhouse of Perth!'

That room was built far out from the house;
　　And none but we in the room　491
Might hear the voice that rose beneath,
　Nor the tread of the coming doom.

For now there came a torchlight-glare,
　　And a clang of arms there came;　495
And not a soul in that space but thought
　Of the foe Sir Robert Græme.

Yea, from the country of the Wild Scots,
　O'er mountain, valley, and glen,
He had brought with him in murderous
　　league　500
　Three hundred armèd men.

The king knew all in an instant's flash,
　　And like a king did he stand;
But there was no armor in all the room,
　Nor weapon lay to his hand.　505

And all we women flew to the door
　And thought to have made it fast;
But the bolts were gone and the bars were
　　gone
And the locks were riven and brast.

And he caught the pale, pale queen in his
　　arms　510
　As the iron footsteps fell,—
Then loosed her, standing alone, and said,
　'Our bliss was our farewell!'

And 'twixt his lips he murmured a prayer,
　　And he crossed his brow and breast;　515
And proudly in royal hardihood
　Even so with folded arms he stood,—
　The prize of the bloody quest.

Then on me leaped the queen like a deer:—
　'O Catherine, help!' she cried.　520
And low at his feet we clasped his knees
　Together side by side.
'Oh! even a king, for his people's sake,
　From treasonous death must hide!'

'For *her* sake most!' I cried, and I marked
　The pang that my words could wring.　526
And the iron tongs from the chimney-nook
　I snatched and held to the king:—
'Wrench up the plank! and the vault be-
　　neath
　Shall yield safe harboring.'

With brows low-bent, from my eager hand
　The heavy heft did he take;
And the plank at his feet he wrenched and
　　tore;
And as he frowned through the open floor,
　Again I said, 'For her sake!'　535

Then he cried to the queen, 'God's will be
　　done!'
　For her hands were clasped in prayer.
And down he sprang to the inner crypt;
And straight we closed the plank he had
　　ripped,
　And toiled to smooth it fair.　540

(Alas! in that vault a gap once was
　Wherethro' the king might have fled:
But three days since close-walled had it
　　been
By his will; for the ball would roll therein
　When without at the palm he played.)　545

Then the queen cried, 'Catherine, keep the
　　door,
　And I to this will suffice!'
At her word I rose all dazed to my feet,
　And my heart was fire and ice.

And louder ever the voices grew,　550
　And the tramp of men in mail;
Until to my brain it seemed to be
As though I tossed on a ship at sea
　In the teeth of a crashing gale.

Then back I flew to the rest; and hard　555
　We strove with sinews knit
To force the table against the door
　But we might not compass it.

Then my wild gaze sped far down the hall
　To the place of the hearthstone-sill;　560
And the queen bent ever above the floor,
　For the plank was rising still.

And now the rush was heard on the stair,
　And 'God, what help?' was our cry.
And was I frenzied or was I bold?　565
I looked at each empty stanchion-hold,
　And no bar but my arm had I!

Like iron felt my arm, as through
　The staple I made it pass:—
'Alack! it was flesh and bone—no more!　570
'T was Catherine Douglas sprang to the door,
　But I fell back Kate Barlass.

With that they all thronged into the hall,
　Half dim to my failing ken;

And the space that was but a void before 575
Was a crowd of wrathful men.

Behind the door I had fall'n and lay,
Yet my sense was widely aware,
And for all the pain of my shattered arm
I never fainted there. 580

Even as I fell, my eyes were cast
Where the king leaped down to the pit;
And lo! the plank was smooth in its place,
And the queen stood far from it.

And under the litters and through the bed
And within the presses all 586
The traitors sought for the king, and pierced
The arras around the wall.

And through the chamber they ramped and stormed
Like lions loose in the lair, 590
And scarce could trust to their very eyes,—
For behold! no king was there.

Then one of them seized the queen, and cried,—
'Now tell us, where is thy lord?'
And he held the sharp point over her heart: 595
She drooped not her eyes nor did she start,
But she answered never a word.

Then the sword half pierced the true true breast:
But it was the Græme's own son
Cried, 'This is a woman,—we seek a man!'
And away from her girdle-zone 601
He struck the point of the murderous steel;
And that foul deed was not done.

And forth flowed all the throng like a sea,
And 't was empty space once more; 605
And my eyes sought out the wounded queen
As I lay behind the door.

And I said: 'Dear Lady, leave me here,
For I cannot help you now;
But fly while you may, and none shall reck
Of my place here lying low.' 611

And she said, 'My Catherine, God help thee!'
Then she looked to the distant floor,
And clasping her hands, 'O God help *him*,'
She sobbed, 'for we can no more!' 615

But God he knows what help may mean,
If it mean to live or to die;
And what sore sorrow and mighty moan
On earth it may cost ere yet a throne
Be filled in his house on high. 620

And now the ladies fled with the queen;
And through the open door
The night-wind wailed round the empty room
And the rushes shook on the floor.

And the bed drooped low in the dark recess
Whence the arras was rent away; 626
And the firelight still shone over the space
Where our hidden secret lay.

And the rain had ceased, and the moonbeams lit
The window high in the wall,— 630
Bright beams that on the plank that I knew
Through the painted pane did fall
And gleamed with the splendor of Scotland's crown
And shield armorial.

But then a great wind swept up the skies, 635
And the climbing moon fell back;
And the royal blazon fled from the floor,
And naught remained on its track;
And high in the darkened window-pane
The shield and the crown were black. 640

And what I say next I partly saw
And partly I heard in sooth,
And partly since from the murderers' lips
The torture wrung the truth.

For now again came the armèd tread, 645
And fast through the hall it fell;
But the throng was less: and ere I saw,
By the voice without I could tell
That Robert Stuart had come with them
Who knew that chamber well. 650

And over the space the Græme strode dark
With his mantle round him flung;
And in his eye was a flaming light
But not a word on his tongue.

And Stuart held a torch to the floor, 655
And he found the thing he sought;
And they slashed the plank away with their swords;
And O God! I fainted not!

And the traitor held his torch in the gap,
All smoking and smoldering; 660

And through the vapor and fire, beneath
  In the dark crypt's narrow ring,
With a shout that pealed to the room's high
    roof
  They saw their naked king.

Half nakèd he stood, but stood as one   665
  Who yet could do and dare:
With the crown, the king was stript away,—
The knight was reft of his battle-array,—
  But still the man was there.

From the rout then stepped a villain forth,
  Sir John Hall was his name;   671
With a knife unsheathed he leapt to the
    vault
  Beneath the torchlight-flame.

Of his person and stature was the king
  A man right manly strong,   675
And mightily by the shoulder-blades
  His foe to his feet he flung.

Then the traitor's brother, Sir Thomas Hall,
  Sprang down to work his worst;
And the king caught the second man by the
    neck   680
  And flung him above the first.

And he smote and trampled them under
    him;
  And a long month thence they bare
All black their throats with the grip of his
    hands
  When the hangman's hand came there. 685

And sore he strove to have had their knives,
  But the sharp blades gashed his hands.
Oh! James so armed, thou hadst battled
    there
  Till help had come of thy bands;
And oh! once more thou hadst held our
    throne   690
  And ruled thy Scottish lands!

But while the king o'er his foes still raged
  With a heart that naught could tame,
Another man sprang down to the crypt;
And with his sword in his hand hard-
    gripped,   695
  There stood Sir Robert Græme.

(Now shame on the recreant traitor's heart
  Who durst not face his king,
Till the body unarmed was wearied out
  With two-fold combating!   700

Ah! well might the people sing and say,
  As oft ye have heard aright:—

O Robert Græme, O Robert Græme,
Who slew our king, God give thee shame!'
  For he slew him not as a knight.)   705

And the naked king turned round at bay,
  But his strength had passed the goal,
And he could but gasp:—'Mine hour is
    come;
But oh! to succor thine own soul's doom,
  Let a priest now shrive my soul!'   710

And the traitor looked on the king's spent
    strength
  And said:—'Have I kept my word?—
Yea, King, the mortal pledge that I gave?
No black friar's shrift thy soul shall have,
  But the shrift of this red sword!'   715

With that he smote his king through the
    breast;
  And all they three in the pen
Fell on him and stabbed and stabbed him
    there
  Like merciless murderous men.

Yet seemed it now that Sir Robert Græme,
  Ere the king's last breath was o'er,   721
Turned sick at heart with the deadly sight
  And would have done no more.

But a cry came from the troop above:—
  'If him thou do not slay,   725
The price of his life that thou dost spare
  Thy forfeit life shall pay!'

O God! what more did I hear or see,
  Or how should I tell the rest,
But there at length our king lay slain   730
  With sixteen wounds in his breast.

O God! and now did a bell boom forth,
  And the murderers turned and fled;—
Too late, too late, O God, did it sound?—
And I heard the true men mustering round,
  And the cries and the coming tread. 736

But ere they came, to the black death-gap
  Somewise did I creep and steal;
And lo! or ever I swooned away,
Through the dusk I saw where the white
    face lay   740
  In the pit of Fortune's wheel.

And now, ye Scottish maids who have heard
  Dread things of the days grown old,—
Even at the last, of true Queen Jane
  May somewhat yet be told.   745

And how she dealt for her dear lord's sake
  Dire vengeance manifold.

'T was in the Charterhouse of Perth,
  In the fair-lit Death-chapelle,
That the slain King's corpse on bier was
    laid   750
  With chaunt and requiem-knell.

And all with royal wealth of balm
  Was the body purified;
And none could trace on the brow and lips
  The death that he had died.   755

In his robes of state he lay asleep
  With orb and scepter in hand;
And by the crown he wore on his throne
  Was his kingly forehead spanned.

And, girls, 't was a sweet sad thing to see
  How the curling golden hair,   761
As in the day of the poet's youth,
  From the king's crown clustered there.

And if all had come to pass in the brain
  That throbbed beneath those curls,   765
Then Scots had said in the days to come
That this their soul was a different home
  And a different Scotland, girls!

And the queen sat by him night and day,
  And oft she knelt in prayer,   770
All wan and pale in the widow's veil
  That shrouded her shining hair.

And I had got good help of my hurt:
  And only to me some sign
She made; and save the priests that were
    there   775
  No face would she see but mine.

And the month of March wore on apace;
  And now fresh couriers fared
Still from the country of the Wild Scots
  With news of the traitors snared.   780

And still as I told her day by day,
  Her pallor changed to sight,
And the frost grew to a furnace-flame,
  That burnt her visage white.

And evermore as I brought her word,   785
  She bent to her dead King James,
And in the cold ear with fire-drawn breath,
  She spoke the traitors' names.

But when the name of Sir Robert Græme
  Was the one she had to give,   790

I ran to hold her up from the floor;
  For the froth was on her lips, and sore
  I feared that she could not live.

And the month of March wore nigh to its
    end,
  And still was the death-pall spread;   795
For she would not bury her slaughtered
    lord
  Till his slayers all were dead.

And now of their dooms dread tidings came,
  And of torments fierce and dire;
And naught she spake,— she had ceased to
    speak,   800
  But her eyes were a soul on fire.

But when I told her the bitter end
  Of the stern and just award,
She leaned o'er the bier, and thrice three
    times
  She kissed the lips of her lord.   805

And then she said,— 'My King, they are
    dead!'
  And she knelt on the chapel-floor,
And whispered low with a strange proud
    smile,
  'James, James, they suffered more!'

Last she stood up to her queenly height,
  But she shook like an autumn leaf,   811
As though the fire wherein she burned
Then left the body, and all were turned
  To winter of life-long grief.

And 'O James!' she said,—'My James!'
    she said,—   815
  'Alas for the woeful thing,
That a poet true and a friend of man,
In desperate days of bale and ban,
  Should needs be born a King!'

                                (1881)

SONNETS from THE HOUSE OF LIFE

A Sonnet is a moment's monument,—
Memorial from the Soul's eternity,
To one dead deathless hour. Look that it
    be,
Whether for lustral rite or dire portent,
Of its own arduous fulness reverent: 5
Carve it in ivory or in ebony,
As Day or Night may rule; and let Time
    see
Its flowering crest impearled and orient.
A Sonnet is a coin: its face reveals

The soul,— its converse, to what Power 't is
due: — 10
Whether for tribute to the august appeals
Of Life, or dower in Love's high retinue,
It serve; or, 'mid the dark wharf's cavernous
breath,
In Charon's palm it pay the toll to Death.

IV. LOVE-SIGHT

When do I see thee most, belovèd one?
When in the light the spirits of mine eyes
Before thy face, their altar, solemnize
The worship of that Love through thee
made known?
Or when in the dusk hours, (we two alone,)
Close-kissed and eloquent of still replies, 6
Thy twilight-hidden glimmering visage lies,
And my soul only sees thy soul its own?
O love, my love! if I no more should see
Thyself, nor on the earth the shadow of
thee, 10
Nor image of thine eyes in any spring,—
How then should sound upon Life's darken-
ing slope,
The ground-whirl of the perished leaves of
Hope,
The wind of Death's imperishable wing?

XIX. SILENT NOON

Your hands lie open in the long fresh
grass,—
The finger-points look through like rosy
blooms:
Your eyes smile peace. The pasture gleams
and glooms
'Neath billowing skies that scatter and
amass. 4
All round our nest, far as the eye can pass,
Are golden kingcup-fields with silver edge
Where the cow-parsley skirts the hawthorn-
hedge.
'T is visible silence, still as the hour-glass.
Deep in the sun-searched growths the
dragon-fly,
Hangs like a blue thread loosened from the
sky: — 10
So this winged hour is dropt to us from
above.
Oh! clasp we to our hearts, for deathless
dower,
This close-companioned inarticulate hour
When two-fold silence was the song of love.

XXI. LOVE-SWEETNESS

Sweet dimness of her loosened hair's downfall
About thy face; her sweet hands round thy
head

In gracious fostering union garlanded;
Her tremulous smiles; her glances' sweet
recall
Of love; her murmuring sighs memorial; 5
Her mouth's culled sweetness by thy kisses
shed
On cheeks and neck and eyelids, and so led
Back to her mouth which answers there for
all: —
What sweeter than these things, except the
thing
In lacking which all these would lose their
sweet: — 10
The confident heart's still fervor; the swift
beat •
And soft subsidence of the spirit's wing,
Then when it feels in cloud-girt wayfaring
The breath of kindred plumes against its
feet?

XXVI. MID-RAPTURE

Thou lovely and belovèd, thou my love;
Whose kiss seems still the first; whose sum-
moning eyes,
Even now, as for our love-world's new sun-
rise,
Shed very dawn; whose voice, attuned
above
All modulation of the deep-bowered dove,
Is like a hand laid softly on the soul; 6
Whose hand is like a sweet voice to control
Those worn tired brows it hath the keeping
of: —
What word can answer to thy word,— what
gaze
To thine, which now absorbs within its
sphere 10
My worshipping face, till I am mirrored
there
Light-circled in a heaven of deep-drawn
rays?
What clasp, what kiss mine inmost heart can
prove,
O lovely and belovèd, O my love?

LV. STILLBORN LOVE

The hour which might have been yet might
not be,
Which man's and woman's heart conceived
and bore
Yet whereof life was barren,— on what
shore
Bides it the breaking of Time's weary sea?
Bondchild of all consummate joys set free, 5
It somewhere sighs and serves, and mute be-
fore
The house of Love, hears through the
echoing door

His hours elect in choral consonancy.
But lo! what wedded souls now hand in
  hand
Together tread at last the immortal strand 10
With eyes where burning memory lights
  love home?
Lo! how the little outcast hour has turned
And leaped to them and in their faces
  yearned: —
'I am your child: O parents, ye have come!'

LXIII. INCLUSIVENESS

The changing guests, each in a different
  mood,
Sit at the roadside table and arise:
And every life among them in likewise
Is a soul's board set daily with new food.
What man has bent o'er his son's sleep, to
  brood   5
How that face shall watch his when cold it
  lies? —
Or thought, as his own mother kissed his
  eyes,
Of what her kiss was when his father
  wooed?
May not this ancient room thou sitt'st in
  dwell
In separate living souls for joy or pain? 10
Nay, all its corners may be painted plain?
Where heaven shows pictures of some life
  spent well;
And may be stamped, a memory all in vain,
Upon the sight of lidless eyes in hell.

LXV. KNOWN IN VAIN

As two whose love, first foolish, widening
  scope,
Knows suddenly, to music high and soft,
The holy of holies; who because they scoffed
Are now amazed with shame, nor dare to
  cope
With the whole truth aloud, lest heaven
  should ope;   5
Yet, at their meetings, laugh not as they
  laughed
In speech; nor speak, at length; but sitting
  oft
Together, within hopeless sight of hope
For hours are silent: — So it happeneth
When Work and Will awake too late, to
  gaze   10
After their life sailed by, and hold their
  breath.
Ah! who shall dare to search through what
  sad maze
Thenceforth their incommunicable ways
Follow the desultory feet of Death?

LXXI. THE CHOICE. I

Eat thou and drink; to-morrow thou shalt
  die.
Surely the earth, that's wise being very old,
Needs not our help. Then loose me, love,
  and hold
Thy sultry hair up from my face; that I
May pour for thee this golden wine, brim-
  high,   5
Till round the glass thy fingers glow like
  gold.
We'll drown all hours; thy song, while
  hours are tolled,
Shall leap, as fountains veil the changing
  sky.
Now kiss, and think that there are really
  those,
My own high-bosomed beauty, who increase
Vain gold, vain lore, and yet might choose
  our way!   11
Through many years they toil; then on a
  day
They die not,— for their life was death,—
  but cease;
And round their narrow lips the mold
  falls close.

LXXII. THE CHOICE. II

Watch thou and fear; to-morrow thou
  shalt die.
Or art thou sure thou shalt have time for
  death?
Is not the day which God's word promiseth
To come man knows not when? In yon-
  der sky,
Now while we speak, the sun speeds forth:
  can I   5
Or thou assure him of his goal? God's
  breath
Even at this moment haply quickeneth
The air to a flame; till spirits, always nigh
Though screened and hid, shall walk the
  daylight here.
And dost thou prate of all that man shall
  do?   10
Canst thou, who hast but plagues, presume
  to be
Glad in his gladness that comes after thee?
Will *his* strength slay *thy* worm in hell?
  Go to:
Cover thy countenance, and watch, and
  fear.

LXXIII. THE CHOICE. III

Think thou and act; to-morrow thou shalt
  die.

Outstretched in the sun's warmth upon the
  shore,
Thou say'st: 'Man's measured path is all
  gone o'er;
Up all his years, steeply, with strain and
  sigh,
Man clomb until he touched the truth; and
  I,
Even I, am he whom it was destined for.'
How should this be? Art thou then so
  much more
Than they who sowed, that thou shouldst
  reap thereby?
Nay, come up hither. From this wave-
  washed mound
Unto the furthest flood-brim look with
  me;   10
Then reach on with thy thought till it be
  drowned.
Miles and miles distant though the last line
  be,
And though thy soul sail leagues and
  leagues beyond,—
Still, leagues beyond those leagues, there is
  more sea.

LXXXVI. LOST DAYS

The lost days of my life until to-day,
What were they, could I see them on the
  street
Lie as they fell? Would they be ears of
  wheat
Sown once for food but trodden into clay?
Or golden coins squandered and still to
  pay?   5
Or drops of blood dabbling the guilty feet?
Or such spilt water as in dreams must cheat
The undying throats of hell, athirst alway?
I do not see them here; but after death
God knows I know the faces I shall see,   10
Each one a murdered self, with low last
  breath.
'I am thyself,— what hast thou done to
  me?'
'And I— and I— thyself,' (lo! each one
  saith)
'And thou thyself to all eternity!'

XCVII. A SUPERSCRIPTION

Look in my face; my name is Might-have-
  been;
I am also called No-more, Too-late, Fare-
  well;
Unto thine ear I hold the dead-sea shell
Cast up thy Life's foam-fretted feet between;
Unto thine eyes the glass where that is
  seen   5
Which had Life's form and Love's, but by
  my spell
Is now a shaken shadow intolerable,
Of ultimate things unuttered the frail
  screen.
Mark me, how still I am! But should
  there dart
One moment through thy soul the soft sur-
  prise   10
Of that winged Peace which lulls the breath
  of sighs,—
Then shalt thou see me smile, and turn
  apart
Thy visage to mine ambush at thy heart,
Sleepless with cold commemorative eyes.

CI. THE ONE HOPE

When vain desire at last and vain regret
Go hand in hand to death, and all is vain,
What shall assuage the unforgotten pain
And teach the unforgetful to forget?
Shall Peace be still a sunk stream long un-
  met,—   5
Or may the soul at once in a green plain
Stoop through the spray of some sweet life-
  fountain
And cull the dew-drenched flowering amu-
  let?
Ah! when the wan soul in that golden air
Between the scriptured petals softly blown 10
Peers breathless for the gift of grace un-
  known,—
Ah! let none other alien spell soe'er
But only the one Hope's one name be
  there,—
Not less nor more, but even that word alone.

(1869, 1870, 1881)

WILLIAM MORRIS (1834-1896)

After a youth of wide reading and varied schooling, Morris reached Exeter College, Oxford, in 1853, with broad information and strongly developed intellectual tendencies. Aside from a notable achievement in general reading, the most important result of his Oxford residence was a close friendship with Edward Burne-Jones, with whom he continued to live in the closest intimacy. A propensity toward Romanism, and then toward Anglicanism, resolved itself ultimately into an enthusiam for art, for social reform, and for the utterances of Carlyle, Ruskin, and Kingsley. Travels in northern France, in 1854 and 1855, together with his permanent love for French Gothic art, led to his decision to become an architect. After he had studied architecture sincerely for a year or so, Rossetti persuaded him to take a studio and devote himself to painting. Morris found his true vocation, however, when, in 1861, with Rossetti, Burne-Jones, and others, he established a firm in London for designing and manufacturing artistic furniture and household decorations. The scope of the enterprise was eventually enlarged to include the manufacture of textiles, dyeing, book-illumination, and printing. In 1890, Morris founded the famous Kelmscott Press, at Hammersmith. In advancing the minor arts and in sustaining the principle that every object and utensil should be beautiful, Morris did more than any other man of his time. In 1885, he became an active socialist, lecturing freely to workingmen, and contributing to *The Commonweal*, the organ of the Socialistic League.

Except during certain periods of interruption, Morris wrote voluminously throughout his life. *The Defence of Guinevere* (1858), his earliest considerable publication, is among his best. From the Arthurian themes of this work, he turned with facility to the Greek, Old French, and Norse stories seen in *Life and Death of Jason* (1867), *The Earthly Paradise* (1868-70), and *Sigurd the Volsung and the Fall of the Niblungs* (1876). Aside from these original poetical writings, Morris's chief works are his romances,— in prose, or in prose and verse,— of which the most important are *A Tale of the House of the Wolfings* (1889), *The Roots of the Mountains* (1890), *The Story of the Glittering Plain* (1891) and *The Well at the World's End* (1896). Of his translations the most notable are the *Grettis Saga* (1869) and the *Völsunga Saga* (1870). Morris stands preëminent in the literature of the nineteenth century as a charming story-teller. In his stories we find neither humor nor a dramatic grasp of situations, but rather, dreamy narrative idealizations of an alluring past.

THE EARTHLY PARADISE

Of Heaven or Hell I have no power to
   sing,
I cannot ease the burden of your fears,
Or make quick-coming death a little thing,
Or bring again the pleasure of past years,
Nor for my words shall ye forget your
   tears,   5
Or hope again for aught that I can say,
The idle singer of an empty day.

But rather, when aweary of your mirth,
From full hearts still unsatisfied ye sigh,
And, feeling kindly unto all the earth,   10
Grudge every minute as it passes by,
Made the more mindful that the sweet days
   die,—
Remember me a little then, I pray,
The idle singer of an empty day.

The heavy trouble, the bewildering care 15
That weighs us down who live and earn
   our bread,
These idle verses have no power to bear,
So let me sing of names rememberèd,
Because they, living not, can ne'er be dead,
Or long time take their memory quite
   away   20
From us poor singers of an empty day.

Dreamer of dreams, born out of my due
   time,
Why should I strive to set the crooked
   straight?
Let it suffice me that my murmuring rime
Beats with light wing against the ivory
   gate,   25
Telling a tale not too importunate
To those who in the sleepy region stay,
Lulled by the singer of an empty day.

Folk say, a wizard to a northern king
At Christmas-tide such wondrous things
   did show,   30
That through one window men beheld the
   spring,
And through another saw the summer
   glow,
And through a third the fruited vines
   arow,
While still, unheard, but in its wonted way,
Piped the drear wind of that December
   day.   35

So with this Earthly Paradise it is,
If ye will read aright and pardon me,
Who strive to build a shadowy isle of bliss
Midmost the beating of the steely sea,
Where tossed about all hearts of men must
   be;   40
Whose ravening monsters mighty men shall
   slay,
Not the poor singer of an empty day.

ATALANTA'S RACE

Atalanta, daughter of King Schœneus, not willing to lose her virgin's estate, made it a law
   to all suitors that they should run a race with
   her in the public place, and if they failed to
   overcome her should die unrevenged; and thus
   many brave men perished. At last came Milanion, the son of Amphidamas, who, outrunning
   her with the help of Venus, gained the virgin
   and wedded her.

I

Through thick Arcadian woods a hunter
   went,
Following the beasts up, on a fresh spring
   day;
But since his horn-tipped bow, but seldom
   bent,
Now at the noontide naught had happed to
   slay,
Within a vale he called his hounds away, 5
Hearkening the echoes of his lone voice
   cling
About the cliffs and through the beech-
   trees ring.

But when they ended, still awhile he stood,
And but the sweet familiar thrush could
   hear,
And all the day-long noises of the wood, 10
And o'er the dry leaves of the vanished
   year
His hounds' feet pattering as they drew
   anear,

And heavy breathing from their heads low
   hung,
To see the mighty cornel bow unstrung.

Then smiling did he turn to leave the
   place,   15
But with his first step some new fleeting
   thought
A shadow cast across his sunburnt face:
I think the golden net that April brought
From some warm world his wavering soul
   had caught;
For, sunk in vague sweet longing, did he
   go   20
Betwixt the trees with doubtful steps and
   slow.

Yet howsoever slow he went, at last
The trees grew sparser, and the wood was
   done;
Whereon one farewell, backward look he
   cast,
Then, turning round to see what place was
   won,   25
With shaded eyes looked underneath the
   sun,
And o'er green meads and new-turned furrows brown
Beheld the gleaming of King Schœneus'
   town.

So thitherward he turned, and on each
   side
The folk were busy on the teeming land, 30
And man and maid from the brown fur-
   rows cried,
Or midst the newly blossomed vines did
   stand,
And as the rustic weapon pressed the hand
Thought of the nodding of the well-filled
   ear,
Or how the knife the heavy bunch should
   shear.   35

Merry it was: about him sung the birds,
The spring flowers bloomed along the firm
   dry road,
The sleek-skinned mothers of the sharp-
   horned herds
Now for the barefoot milking-maidens
   lowed;
While from the freshness of his blue
   abode,   40
Glad his death-bearing arrows to forget,
The broad sun blazed, nor scattered
   plagues as yet.

Through such fair things unto the gates
  he came,
And found them open, as though peace
  were there;
Wherethrough, unquestioned of his race or
  name,   45
He entered, and along the streets 'gan fare,
Which at the first of folk were wellnigh
  bare;
But pressing on, and going more hastily,
Men hurrying too he 'gan at last to see.

Following the last of these, he still pressed
  on,   50
Until an open space he came unto,
Where wreaths of fame had oft been lost
  and won,
For feats of strength folk there were wont
  to do.
And now our hunter looked for something
  new,
Because the whole wide space was bare,
  and stilled   55
The high seats were, with eager people
  filled.

There with the others to a seat he gat,
Whence he beheld a broidered canopy,
'Neath which in fair array King Schœneus
  sat
Upon his throne with councilors thereby; 60
And underneath his well-wrought seat and
  high,
He saw a golden image of the sun,
A silver image of the fleet-foot one.

A brazen altar stood beneath their feet
Whereon a thin flame- flickered in the wind;
Nigh this a herald clad in raiment meet   66
Made ready even now his horn to wind,
By whom a huge man held a sword, in-
  twined
With yellow flowers; these stood a little
  space
From off the altar, nigh the starting-place.

And there two runners did the sign abide, 71
Foot set to foot,— a young man slim and
  fair,
Crisp-haired, well-knit, with firm limbs often
  tried
In places where no man his strength may
  spare;
Dainty his thin coat was, and on his hair 75
A golden circlet of renown he wore,
And in his hand an olive garland bore.

But on this day with whom shall he con-
  tend?
A maid stood by him like Diana clad
When in the woods she lists her bow to
  bend,   80
Too fair for one to look on and be glad,
Who scarcely yet has thirty summers had,
If he must still behold her from afar;
Too fair to let the world live free from
  war.

She seemed all earthly matters to forget; 85
Of all tormenting lines her face was clear,
Her wide gray eyes upon the goal were set
Calm and unmoved as though no soul were
  near.
But her foe trembled as a man in fear,
Nor from her loveliness one moment turned
His anxious face with fierce desire that
  burned.   91

Now through the hush there broke the trum-
  pet's clang
Just as the setting sun made eventide.
Then from light feet a spurt of dust there
  sprang,
And swiftly were they running side by side;
But silent did the thronging folk abide   96
Until the turning-post was reached at last,
And round about it still abreast they passed.

But when the people saw how close they
  ran,
When half-way to the starting-point they
  were,   100
A cry of joy broke forth, whereat the man
Headed the white-foot runner, and drew
  near
Unto the very end of all his fear;
And scarce his straining feet the ground
  could feel,
And bliss unhoped-for o'er his heart 'gan
  steal.   105

But midst the loud victorious shouts he
  heard
Her footsteps drawing nearer, and the
  sound
Of fluttering raiment, and thereat afeard
His flushed and eager face he turned
  around,
And even then he felt her past him bound
Fleet as the wind, but scarcely saw her
  there   111
Till on the goal she laid her fingers fair.

There stood she breathing like a little child
Amid some warlike clamor laid asleep,

For no victorious joy her red lips smiled, 115
Her cheek its wonted freshness did but
   keep;
No glance lit up her clear gray eyes and
   deep,
Though some divine thought softened all
   her face
As once more rang the trumpet through the
   place.

But her late foe stopped short amidst his
   course,   120
One moment gazed upon her piteously,
Then with a groan his lingering feet did
   force
To leave the spot whence he her eyes could
   see;
And, changed like one who knows his time
   must be
But short and bitter, without any word
He knelt before the bearer of the sword; 126

Then high rose up the gleaming deadly
   blade,
Bared of its flowers, and through the
   crowded place
Was silence now, and midst of it the maid
Went by the poor wretch at a gentle pace,
And he to hers upturned his sad white
   face;   131
Nor did his eyes behold another sight
Ere on his soul there fell eternal night.

II
So was the pageant ended, and all folk
Talking of this and that familiar thing
In little groups from that sad concourse
   broke;
For now the shrill bats were upon the wing,
And soon dark night would slay the even-
   ing,   5
And in dark gardens sang the nightingale
Her little-heeded, oft-repeated tale.

And with the last of all the hunter went,
Who, wondering at the strange sight he had
   seen,
Prayed an old man to tell him what it
   meant,   10
Both why the vanquished man so slain had
   been,
And if the maiden were an earthly queen,
Or rather what much more she seemed to
   be,
No sharer in the world's mortality.

'Stranger,' said he, 'I pray she soon may
   die   15

Whose lovely youth has slain so many an
   one!
King Schœneus' daughter is she verily,
Who when her eyes first looked upon the
   sun
Was fain to end her life but new begun,
For he had vowed to leave but men alone
Sprung from his loins when he from earth
   was gone.   21

'Therefore he bade one leave her in the
   wood,
And let wild things deal with her as they
   might;
But this being done, some cruel god thought
   good
To save her beauty in the world's despite: 25
Folk say that her, so delicate and white
As now she is, a rough root-grubbing bear
Amidst her shapeless cubs at first did rear.

'In course of time the woodfolk slew her
   nurse,
And to their rude abode the youngling
   brought,   30
And reared her up to be a kingdom's curse,
Who, grown a woman, of no kingdom
   thought,
But armed and swift, mid beasts destruction
   wrought,
Nor spared two shaggy centaur kings to
   slay,
To whom her body seemed an easy prey. 35

'So to this city, led by fate, she came,
Whom, known by signs, whereof I cannot
   tell,
King Schœneus for his child at last did
   claim;
Nor otherwhere since that day doth she
   dwell,
Sending too many a noble soul to hell.— 40
What! thine eyes glisten? what then! think-
   est thou
Her shining head unto the yoke to bow?

'Listen, my son, and love some other maid,
For she the saffron gown will never wear,
And on no flower-strewn couch shall she
   be laid,   45
Nor shall her voice make glad a lover's
   ear;
Yet if of Death thou hast not any fear,
Yea, rather, if thou lovest him utterly,
Thou still may'st woo her ere thou comest
   to die,

Fulfilled delight, or death to end my pain?
Right glad were I if it could be to-day, 195
And all my doubts at rest forever lay.'

'Nay,' said King Schœneus, 'thus it shall
not be,
But rather shalt thou let a month go by,
And weary with thy prayers for victory
What god thou know'st the kindest and
most nigh. 200
So doing, still perchance thou shalt not die;
And with my good-will wouldst thou have
the maid,
For of the equal gods I grow afraid.

'And until then, O Prince, be thou my guest,
And all these troublous things awhile for-
get. 205
'Nay,' said he, 'couldst thou give my soul
good rest,
And on mine head a sleepy garland set,
Then had I 'scaped the meshes of the net,
Nor shouldst thou hear from me another
word;
But now, make sharp thy fearful heading
sword. 210

'Yet will I do what son of man may do,
And promise all the gods may most de-
sire,
That to myself I may at least be true;
And on that day my heart and limbs so
tire,
With utmost strain and measureless desire,
That, at the worst, I may but fall asleep 216
When in the sunlight round that sword shall
sweep.'

He went with that, nor anywhere would
bide,
But unto Argos restlessly did wend;
And there, as one who lays all hope aside,
Because the leech has said his life must
end, 221
Silent farewell he bade to foe and friend,
And took his way unto the restless sea,
For there he deemed his rest and help might
be.

III

Upon the shore of Argolis there stands
A temple to the goddess that he sought,
That, turned unto the lion-bearing lands,
Fenced from the east, of cold winds hath no
thought,
Though to no homestead there the sheaves
are brought, 5

No groaning press torments the close-clipped
murk,
Lonely the fane stands, far from all men's
work.

Pass through a close, set thick with myrtle-
trees,
Through the brass doors that guard the holy
place,
And, entering, hear the washing of the
seas 10
That twice a day rise high above the base,
And, with the southwest urging them, em-
brace
The marble feet of her that standeth there,
That shrink not, naked though they be and
fair.

Small is the fane through which the sea-wind
sings 15
About Queen Venus' well-wrought image
white;
But hung around are many precious things,
The gifts of those who, longing for delight,
Have hung them there within the goddess'
sight,
And in return have taken at her hands 20
The living treasures of the Grecian lands.

And thither now has come Milanion,
And showed unto the priests' wide-open
eyes
Gifts fairer than all those that there have
shown,—
Silk cloths, inwrought with Indian fantasies,
And bowls inscribed with sayings of the
wise 26
Above the deeds of foolish living things,
And mirrors fit to be the gifts of kings.

And now before the sea-born one he stands,
By the sweet veiling smoke made dim and
soft; 30
And while the incense trickles from his
hands,
And while the odorous smoke-wreaths hang
aloft,
Thus doth he pray to her: 'O thou who
oft
Hast holpen man and maid in their dis-
tress,
Despise me not for this my wretchedness!

'O goddess, among us who dwell below, 36
Kings and great men, great for a little
while,
Have pity on the lowly heads that bow,

Nor hate the hearts that love them without
  guile;
Wilt thou be worse than these, and is thy
  smile   40
A vain device of him who set thee here,
An empty dream of some artificer?

'O great one, some men love, and are
  ashamed;
Some men are weary of the bonds of love;
Yea, and by some men lightly art thou
  blamed,   45
That from thy toils their lives they cannot
  move,
And mind the ranks of men their manhood
  prove.
Alas! O goddess, if thou slayest me
What new immortal can I serve but thee?

'Think then, will it bring honor to thy head
If folk say, "Everything aside he cast,   51
And to all fame and honor was he dead,
And to his one hope now is dead at last,
Since all unholpen he is gone and past:
Ah! the gods·love not man, for certainly 55
He to his helper did not cease to cry."

'Nay, but thou wilt help: they who died be-
  fore
Not single-hearted, as I deem, came here;
Therefore unthanked they laid their gifts
  before
Thy stainless feet, still shivering with their
  fear,   60
Lest in their eyes their true thought might
  appear,
Who sought to be the lords of that fair
  town,
Dreaded of men and winners of renown.

'O Queen, thou knowest I pray not for
  this:
O, set us down together in some place   65
Where not a voice can break our heaven of
  bliss,
Where naught but rocks and I can see her
  face,
Softening beneath the marvel of thy grace,
Where not a foot our vanished steps can
  track,—
The golden age, the golden age come back!

'O fairest, hear me now, who do thy will, 71
Plead for thy rebel that she be not slain,
But live and love and be thy servant still:
Ah! give her joy and take away my pain,
And thus two long-enduring servants gain.
An easy thing this is to do for me,   76

What need of my vain words to weary
  thee?

'But none the less this place will I not
  leave
Until I needs must go my death to meet,
Or at thy hands some happy sign receive 80
That in great joy we twain may one day
  greet
Thy presence here and kiss thy silver feet,
Such as we deem thee, fair beyond all
  words,
Victorious o'er our servants and our lords.'

Then from the altar back a space he drew,
But from the queen turned not his face
  away,   86
But 'gainst a pillar leaned, until the blue
That arched the sky, at ending of the day,
Was turned to ruddy gold and changing
  gray,
And clear, but low, the nigh-ebbed windless
  sea   90
In the still evening murmured ceaselessly.

And there he stood when all the sun was
  down;
Nor had he moved when the dim golden
  light,
Like the far luster of a godlike town,
Had left the world to seeming hopeless
  night;   95
Nor would he move the more when wan
  moonlight
Streamed through the pillars for a little
  while,
And lighted up the white queen's changeless
  smile.

Naught noted he the shallow flowing sea,
As step by step it set the wrack a-swim; 100
The yellow torchlight nothing noted he
Wherein with fluttering gown and half-bared
  limb
The temple damsels sung their midnight
  hymn;
And naught the doubled stillness of the
  fane
When they were gone and all was hushed
  again.   105

But when the waves had touched the marble
  base,
And steps the fish swim over twice a day,
The dawn beheld him sunken in his place
Upon the floor; and sleeping there he lay,
Not heeding aught the little jets of spray 110

The roughened sea brought nigh, across
  him cast,
For as one dead all thought from him had
  passed.

Yet long before the sun had showed his
  head,
Long ere the varied hangings on the wall
Had gained once more their blue and green
  and red,   115
He rose as one some well-known sign doth
  call
When war upon the city's gates doth fall,
And scarce like one fresh risen out of sleep,
He 'gan again his broken watch to keep.

Then he turned round; not for the sea-
  gull's cry   120
That wheeled above the temple in his flight,
Not for the fresh south-wind that lovingly
Breathed on the new-born day and dying
  night,
But some strange hope 'twixt fear and great
  delight
Drew round his face, now flushed, now pale
  and wan,   125
And still constrained his eyes the sea to
  scan.

Now a faint light lit up the southern sky,—
Not sun or moon, for all the world was
  gray,
But this a bright cloud seemed, that drew
  anigh,
Lighting the dull waves that beneath it
  lay   130
As toward the temple still it took its way,
And still grew greater, till Milanion
Saw naught for dazzling light that round
  him shone.

But as he staggered with his arms out-
  spread,   134
Delicious unnamed odors breathed around;
For languid happiness he bowed his head,
And with wet eyes sank down upon the
  ground,
Nor wished for aught, nor any dream he
  found
To give him reason for that happiness,
Or make him ask more knowledge of his
  bliss.   140

At last his eyes were cleared, and he could
  see
Through happy tears the goddess face to
  face

With that faint image of divinity,
Whose well-wrought smile and dainty
  changeless grace   144
Until that morn so gladdened all the place;
Then he unwitting cried aloud her name,
And covered up his eyes for fear and shame.

But through the stillness he her voice could
  hear
Piercing his heart with joy scarce bearable,
That said, 'Milanion, wherefore dost thou
  fear?   150
I am not hard to those who love me well;
List to what I a second time will tell,
And thou mayest hear perchance, and live
  to save
The cruel maiden from a loveless grave.

'See, by my feet three golden apples lie,—
Such fruit among the heavy roses falls, 156
Such fruit my watchful damsels carefully
Store up within the best loved of my walls,
Ancient Damascus, where the lover calls
Above my unseen head, and faint and light
The rose-leaves flutter round me in the
  night.   161

'And note that these are not alone most
  fair
With heavenly gold, but longing strange they
  bring
Unto the hearts of men, who will not care,
Beholding these, for any once-loved thing
Till round the shining sides their fingers
  cling.   166
And thou shalt see thy well-girt swiftfoot
  maid
By sight of these amid her glory stayed.

'For bearing these within a scrip with thee,
When first she heads thee from the starting-
  place   170
Cast down the first one for her eyes to see,
And when she turns aside make on apace,
And if again she heads thee in the race
Spare not the other two to cast aside
If she not long enough behind will bide. 175

'Farewell, and when has come the happy
  time
That she Diana's raiment must unbind,
And all the world seems blessed with Sa-
  turn's clime,
And thou with eager arms about her twined
Beholdest first her gray eyes growing kind,
Surely, O trembler, thou shalt scarcely then
Forget the helper of unhappy men.'   182

Milanion raised his head at this last word,
For now so soft and kind she seemed to be
No longer of her godhead was he feared; 185
Too late he looked, for nothing could he
　　see
But the white image glimmering doubtfully
In the departing twilight cold and gray,
And those three apples on the steps that
　　lay.

These then he caught up, quivering with
　　delight,　　　　　　　　　　　190
Yet fearful lest it all might be a dream,
And though aweary with the watchful night,
And sleepless nights of longing, still did
　　deem
He could not sleep; but yet the first sun-
　　beam
That smote the fane across the heaving
　　deep　　　　　　　　　　　195
Shone on him laid in calm untroubled sleep.

But little ere the noontide did he rise,
And why he felt so happy scarce could tell
Until the gleaming apples met his eyes.
Then, leaving the fair place where this be-
　　fell,　　　　　　　　　　　200
Oft he looked back as one who loved it
　　well,
Then homeward to the haunts of men 'gan
　　wend
To bring all things unto a happy end.

IV

Now has the lingering month at last gone
　　by,
Again are all folk around the running-place.
Nor other seems the dismal pageantry
Than heretofore, but that another face
Looks o'er the smooth course ready for the
　　race,　　　　　　　　　　　5
For now, beheld of all, Milanion
Stands on the spot he twice has looked
　　upon.

But yet — what change is this that holds the
　　maid?
Does she indeed see in his glittering eye
More than disdain of the sharp shearing
　　blade,　　　　　　　　　　　10
Some happy hope of help and victory?
The others seemed to say, 'We come to
　　die;
Look down upon us for a little while,
That, dead, we may bethink us of thy smile.'

But he — what look of mastery was this 15
He cast on her? Why were his lips so
　　red?
Why was his face so flushed with happi-
　　ness?
So looks not one who deems himself but
　　dead,
E'en if to death he bows a willing head;
So rather looks a god well pleased to find
Some earthly damsel fashioned to his mind.

Why must she drop her lids before his
　　gaze,　　　　　　　　　　　22
And even as she casts adown her eyes
Redden to note his eager glance of praise,
And wish that she were clad in other guise?
Why must the memory to her heart arise 26
Of things unnoticed when they first were
　　heard,
Some lover's song, some answering maid-
　　en's word?

What makes these longings, vague, without
　　a name,
And this vain pity never felt before, 30
This sudden languor, this contempt of fame,
This tender sorrow for the time past
　　o'er,
These doubts that grow each minute more
　　and more?
Why does she tremble as the time grows
　　near,
And weak defeat and woful victory fear? 35

But while she seemed to hear her beating
　　heart,
Above their heads the trumpet blast rang
　　out,
And forth they sprang; and she must play
　　her part.
Then flew her white feet, knowing not a
　　doubt,
Though, slackening once, she turned her
　　head about,　　　　　　　　　40
But then she cried aloud and faster fled
Than e'er before, and all men deemed him
　　dead.

But with no sound he raised aloft his hand,
And thence what seemed a ray of light there
　　flew　　　　　　　　　　　44
And past the maid rolled on along the sand;
Then trembling she her feet together drew,
And in her heart a strong desire there grew
To have the toy: some god she thought had
　　given
That gift to her, to make of earth a heaven.

Then from the course with eager steps she
  ran, 50
And in her odorous bosom laid the gold.
But when she turned again, the great-limbed
  man
Now well ahead she failed not to behold,
And, mindful of her glory waxing cold,
Sprang up and followed him in hot pursuit,
Though with one hand she touched the
  golden fruit. 56

Note, too, the bow that she was wont to
  bear
She laid aside to grasp the glittering prize,
And o'er her shoulder from the quiver fair
Three arrows fell and lay before her eyes 60
Unnoticed, as amidst the people's cries
She sprang to head the strong Milanion,
Who now the turning-post had wellnigh
  won.

But as he set his mighty hand on it,
White fingers underneath his own were laid,
And white limbs from his dazzled eyes did
  flit; 66
Then he the second fruit cast by the maid,
But she ran on awhile, then as afraid
Wavered and stopped, and turned and made
  no stay 69
Until the globe with its bright fellow lay.

Then, as a troubled glance she cast around,
Now far ahead the Argive could she see,
And in her garment's hem one hand she
  wound
To keep the double prize, and strenuously
Sped o'er the course, and little doubt had
  she 75
To win the day, though now but scanty
  space
Was left betwixt him and the winning-
  place.

Short was the way unto such wingèd feet;
Quickly she gained upon him, till at last
He turned about his eager eyes to meet, 80
And from his hand the third fair apple
  cast.
She wavered not, but turned and ran so
  fast
After the prize that should her bliss fulfil,
That in her hand it lay ere it was still.

Nor did she rest, but turned about to win 85
Once more an unblest woful victory —
And yet — and yet — why does her breath
  begin
To fail her, and her feet drag heavily?

Why fails she now to see if far or nigh
The goal is? Why do her gray eyes grow
  dim? • 90
Why do these tremors run through every
  limb?

She spreads her arms abroad some stay to
  find,
Else must she fall, indeed, and findeth this,
A strong man's arms about her body twined.
Nor may she shudder now to feel his kiss, 95
So wrapped she is in new unbroken bliss;
Made happy that the foe the prize hath
  won,
She weeps glad tears for all her glory done.

V

Shatter the trumpet, hew adown the posts!
Upon the brazen altar break the sword,
And scatter incense to appease the ghosts
Of those who died here by their own award.
Bring forth the image of the mighty lord, 5
And her who unseen o'er the runners hung,
And did a deed forever to be sung.

Here are the gathered folk; make no de-
  lay,
Open King Schœneus' well-filled treasury,
Bring out the gifts long hid from light of
  day,— 10
The golden bowls o'erwrought with imagery,
Gold chains, and unguents brought from over
  sea,
The saffron gown the old Phœnician
  brought,
Within the temple of the goddess wrought.

O ye, O damsels, who shall never see 15
Her, that Love's servant bringeth now to
  you,
Returning from another victory,
In some cool bower do all that now is due!
Since she in token of her service new 19
Shall give to Venus offerings rich enow,—
Her maiden zone, her arrows, and her bow.

THE LADY OF THE LAND

A certain man having landed on an island in the
Greek Sea, found there a beautiful damsel,
whom he would fain have delivered from a
strange and dreadful doom, but failing herein,
he died soon afterwards.

It happened once, some men of Italy
Midst the Greek Islands went a sea-roving,
And much good fortune had they on the
  sea:

Of many a man they had the ransoming,
And many a chain they gat, and goodly
    thing;   5
And midst their voyage to an isle they
    came,
Whereof my story keepeth not the name.

Now though but little was there left to
    gain,
Because the richer folk had gone away,
Yet since by this of water they were fain 10
They came to anchor in a land-locked bay,
Whence in a while some went ashore to
    play,
Going but lightly armed in twos or threes,
For midst that folk they feared no enemies.

And of these fellows that thus went ashore,
One was there who left all his friends be-
    hind;   16
Who going inland ever more and more,
And being left quite alone, at last did find
A lonely valley sheltered from the wind,
Wherein, amidst an ancient cypress wood, 20
A long-deserted ruined castle stood.

The wood, once ordered in fair grove and
    glade,
With gardens overlooked by terraces,
And marble-pavèd pools for pleasure made,
Was tangled now, and choked with fallen
    trees;   25
And he who went there, with but little ease
Must stumble by the stream's side, once
    made meet
For tender women's dainty wandering feet.

The raven's croak, the low wind choked and
    drear,
The baffled stream, the gray wolf's doleful
    cry,   30
Were all the sounds that mariner could
    hear,
As through the wood he wandered painfully;
But as unto the house he drew anigh,
The pillars of a ruined shrine he saw,
The once fair temple of a fallen law.   35

No image was there left behind to tell
Before whose face the knees of men had
    bowed;
An altar of black stone, of old wrought well,
Alone beneath a ruined roof now showed
The goal whereto the folk were wont to
    crowd,   40
Seeking for things forgotten long ago,
Praying for heads long ages laid a-low.

Close to the temple was the castle-gate,
Doorless and crumbling; there our fellow
    turned,
Trembling indeed at what might chance to
    wait   45
The prey entrapped, yet with a heart that
    burned
To know the most of what might there be
    learned,
And hoping somewhat too, amid his fear,
To light on such things as all men hold
    dear.

Noble the house was, nor seemed built for
    war,   50
But rather like the work of other days,
When men, in better peace than now they
    are,
Had leisure on the world around to gaze,
And noted well the past times' changing
    ways;
And fair with sculptured stories it was
    wrought,   55
By lapse of time unto dim ruin brought.

Now as he looked about on all these things,
And strove to read the moldering histories,
Above the door an image with wide wings,
Whose unclad limbs a serpent seemed to
    seize,   60
He dimly saw, although the western breeze,
And years of biting frost and washing rain,
Had made the carver's labor well-nigh vain.

But this, though perished sore, and worn
    away,
He noted well, because it seemed to be, 65
After the fashion of another day,
Some great man's badge of war, or armory;
And round it a carved wreath he seemed
    to see:
But taking note of these things, at the last
The mariner beneath the gateway passed. 70

And there a lovely cloistered court he found,
A fountain in the midst o'erthrown and dry,
And in the cloister briers twining round
The slender shafts; the wondrous imagery
Outworn by more than many years gone by;
Because the country people, in their fear 76
Of wizardry, had wrought destruction here;

And piteously these fair things had been
    maimed;
There stood great Jove, lacking his head of
    might;
Here was the archer, swift Apollo, lamed; 80

The shapely limbs of Venus hid from sight
By weeds and shards; Diana's ankles light
Bound with the cable of some coasting
    ship;
And rusty nails through Helen's maddening
    lip.

Therefrom unto the chambers did he pass, 85
And found them fair still, midst of their de-
    cay,
Though in them now no sign of man there
    was,
And everything but stone had passed away
That made them lovely in that vanished
    day;
Nay, the mere walls themselves would soon
    be gone   90
And naught be left but heaps of moldering
    stone.

But he, when all the place he had gone
    o'er,
And with much trouble clomb the broken
    stair,
And from the topmost turret seen the shore
And his good ship drawn up at anchor
    there,   95
Came down again, and found a crypt most
    fair
Built wonderfully beneath the greatest hall,
And there he saw a door within the wall,

Well-hinged, close shut; nor was there in
    that place
Another on its hinges, therefore he   100
Stood there and pondered for a little space,
And thought, ' Perchance some marvel I
    shall see,
For surely here some dweller there must be,
Because this door seems whole, and new,
    and sound,
While naught but ruin I can see around.' 105

So with that word, moved by a strong de-
    sire,
He tried the hasp, that yielded to his hand,
And in a strange place, lit as by a fire
Unseen but near, he presently did stand;
And by an odorous breeze his face was
    fanned,   110
As though in some Arabian plain he stood,
Anigh the border of a spice-tree wood.

He moved not for awhile, but looking
    round,
He wondered much to see the place so fair,
Because, unlike the castle above ground, 115
No pillager or wrecker had been there:

It seemed that time had passed on other-
    where,
Nor laid a finger on this hidden place,
Rich with the wealth of some forgotten
    race.

With hangings, fresh as when they left the
    loom,   120
The walls were hung a space above the
    head,
Slim ivory chairs were set about the room,
And in one corner was a dainty bed,
That seemed for some fair queen apparelèd;
And marble was the worst stone of the
    floor,   125
That with rich Indian webs was covered
    o'er.

The wanderer trembled when he saw all
    this,
Because he deemed by magic it was
    wrought;
Yet in his heart a longing for some bliss,
Whereof the hard and changing world knows
    naught,   130
Arose and urged him on, and dimmed the
    thought
That there perchance some devil lurked to
    slay
The heedless wanderer from the light of
    day.

Over against him was another door
Set in the wall; so, casting fear aside, 135
With hurried steps he crossed the varied
    floor,
And there again the silver latch he tried
And with no pain the door he opened wide,
And entering the new chamber cautiously
The glory of great heaps of gold could see.

Upon the floor uncounted medals lay,   141
Like things of little value; here and there
Stood golden caldrons, that might well out-
    weigh
The biggest midst an emperor's copper-ware,
And golden cups were set on tables fair, 145
Themselves of gold; and in all hollow things
Were stored great gems, worthy the crowns
    of kings.

The walls and roof with gold were overlaid,
And precious raiment from the wall hung
    down;
The fall of kings that treasure might have
    stayed,   150
Or gained some longing conqueror great re-
    nown.

Or built again some god-destroyed old
    town;
What wonder, if this plunderer of the sea
Stood gazing at it long and dizzily?

But at the last his troubled eyes and dazed
He lifted from the glory of that gold,   156
And then the image, that well-nigh erased
Over the castle-gate he did behold,
Above a door well wrought in colored gold
Again he saw; a naked girl with wings   160
Enfolded in a serpent's scaly rings.

And even as his eyes were fixed on it
A woman's voice came from the other side,
And through his heart strange hopes began
    to flit
That in some wondrous land he might abide
Not dying, master of a deathless bride,   166
So o'er the gold he scarcely now could see
He went, and passed this last door eagerly.

Then in a room he stood wherein there
    was
A marble bath, whose brimming water yet
Was scarcely still; a vessel of green glass
Half full of odorous ointment was there
    set   172
Upon the topmost step that still was wet,
And jeweled shoes and women's dainty gear,
Lay cast upon the varied pavement near. 175

In one quick glance these things his eyes
    did see,
But speedily they turned round to behold
Another sight, for throned on ivory
There sat a girl, whose dripping tresses
    rolled
On to the floor in waves of gleaming gold,
Cast back from such a form as, erewhile
    shown   181
To one poor shepherd, lighted up Troy
    town.

Naked she was, the kisses of her feet
Upon the floor a dying path had made
From the full bath unto her ivory seat; 185
In her right hand, upon her bosom laid,
She held a golden comb, a mirror weighed
Her left hand down, aback her fair head lay
Dreaming awake of some long vanished
    day.

Her eyes were shut, but she seemed not to
    sleep,   190
Her lips were murmuring things unheard
    and low,

Or sometimes twitched as though she needs
    must weep
Though from her eyes the tears refused to
    flow,
And oft with heavenly red her cheek did
    glow,
As if remembrance of some half-sweet
    shame   195
Across the web of many memories came.

There stood the man, scarce daring to draw
    breath
For fear the lovely sight should fade away;
Forgetting heaven, forgetting life and death,
Trembling for fear lest something he should
    say   200
Unwitting, lest some sob should yet betray
His presence there, for to his eager eyes
Already did the tears begin to rise.

But as he gazed, she moved, and with a
    sigh
Bent forward, dropping down her golden
    head;   205
'Alas, alas! another day gone by,
Another day and no soul come,' she said;
'Another year, and still I am not dead!'
And with that word once more her head she
    raised,
And on the trembling man with great eyes
    gazed.   210

Then he imploring hands to her did reach,
And toward her very slowly 'gan to move
And with wet eyes her pity did beseech,
And seeing her about to speak, he strove
From trembling lips to utter words of love;
But with a look she stayed his doubtful
    feet,   216
And made sweet music as their eyes did
    meet.

For now she spoke in gentle voice and
    clear,
Using the Greek tongue that he knew full
    well;
'What man art thou, that thus hast wan-
    dered here,   220
And found this lonely chamber where I
    dwell?
Beware, beware! for I have many a spell;
If greed of power and gold have led thee
    on,
Not lightly shall this untold wealth be won.

'But if thou com'st here, knowing of my
    tale,   225

In hope to bear away my body fair,
Stout must thine heart be, nor shall that
  avail
If thou a wicked soul in thee dost bear;
So once again I bid thee to beware,
Because no base man things like this may
  see,   230
And live thereafter long and happily.'

'Lady,' he said, 'in Florence is my home,
And in my city noble is my name;
Neither on peddling voyage am I come,
But, like my fathers, bent to gather fame;
And though thy face has set my heart
  a-flame   236
Yet of thy story nothing do I know,
But here have wandered heedlessly enow.

'But since the sight of thee mine eyes did
  bless,
What can I be but thine? what wouldst thou
  have?   240
From those thy words, I deem from some
  distress
By deeds of mine thy dear life I might save;
O then, delay not! if one ever gave
His life to any, mine I give to thee;
Come, tell me what the price of love must
  be?   245

'Swift death, to be with thee a day and
  night
And with the earliest dawning to be slain?
Or better, a long year of great delight,
And many years of misery and pain?
Or worse, and this poor hour for all my
  gain?   250
A sorry merchant am I on this day,
E'en as thou willest so must I obey.'

She said, 'What brave words! naught di-
  vine am I,
But an unhappy and unheard-of maid
Compelled by evil fate and destiny   255
To live, who long ago should have been
  laid
Under the earth within the cypress shade.
Hearken awhile, and quickly shalt thou
  know
What deed I pray thee to accomplish now.

'God grant indeed thy words are not for
  naught!   260
Then shalt thou save me, since for many
  a day
To such a dreadful life I have been brought:
Nor will I spare with all my heart to pay

What man soever takes my grief away;
Ah! I will love thee, if thou lovest me   265
But well enough my savior now to be.

'My father lived a many years agone
Lord of this land, master of all cunning,
Who ruddy gold could draw from out gray
  stone,
And gather wealth from many an uncouth
  thing;   270
He made the wilderness rejoice and sing,
And such a leech he was that none could
  say
Without his word what soul should pass
  away.

'Unto Diana such a gift he gave,
Goddess above, below, and on the earth, 275
That I should be her virgin and her slave
From the first hour of my most wretched
  birth;
Therefore my life had known but little
  mirth
When I had come unto my twentieth year
And the last time of hallowing drew anear.

'So in her temple had I lived and died   281
And all would long ago have passed away,
But ere that time came, did strange things
  betide,
Whereby I am alive unto this day;
Alas, the bitter words that I must say!   285
Ah! can I bring my wretched tongue to
  tell
How I was brought unto this fearful hell?

'A queen I was, what gods I knew I loved,
And nothing evil was there in my thought,
And yet by love my wretched heart was
  moved   290
Until to utter ruin I was brought!
Alas! thou sayest our gods were vain and
  naught;
Wait, wait, till thou hast heard this tale of
  mine,
Then shalt thou think them devilish or di-
  vine.

'Hearken! in spite of father and of vow 295
I loved a man; but for that sin I think
Men had forgiven me — yea, yea, even thou;
But from the gods the full cup must I drink,
And into misery unheard of sink,
Tormented, when their own names are for-
  got,   300
And men must doubt if they e'er lived or
  not.

'Glorious my lover was unto my sight,
Most beautiful,— of love we grew so fain
That we at last agreed, that on a night
We should be happy, but that he were slain
Or shut in hold; and neither joy nor
  pain   306
Should else forbid that hoped-for time to
  be;
So came the night that made a wretch of
  me.

'Ah! well do I remember all that night,
When through the window shone the orb of
  June,   310
And by the bed flickered the taper's light,
Whereby I trembled, gazing at the moon:
Ah me! the meeting that we had, when
  soon
Into his strong, well-trusted arms I fell,
And many a sorrow we began to tell. 315

'Ah me! what parting on that night we
  had!
I think the story of my great despair
A little while might merry folk make sad;
For, as he swept away my yellow hair
To make my shoulder and my bosom bare,
I raised mine eyes, and shuddering could
  behold   321
A shadow cast upon the bed of gold:

'Then suddenly was quenched my hot de-
  sire
And he untwined his arms; the moon so pale
A while ago, seemed changed to blood and
  fire,   325
And yet my limbs beneath me did not fail,
And neither had I strength to cry or wail,
But stood there helpless, bare, and shiver-
  ing,
With staring eyes still fixed upon the thing.

'Because the shade that on the bed of
  gold   330
The changed and dreadful moon was throw-
  ing down
Was of Diana, whom I did behold,
With knotted hair, and shining girt-up
  gown,
And on the high white brow, a deadly
  frown
Bent upon us, who stood scarce drawing
  breath,   335
Striving to meet the horrible sure death.

'No word at all the dreadful goddess said,
But soon across my feet my lover lay,
And well indeed I knew that he was dead;

And would that I had died on that same
  day!   340
For in a while the image turned away,
And without words my doom I understood,
And felt a horror change my human blood.

'And there I fell, and on the floor I lay
By the dead man, till daylight came on
  me,   345
And not a word thenceforward could I
  say
For three years; till of grief and misery,
The lingering pest, the cruel enemy,
My father and his folk were dead and
  gone,
And in this castle I was left alone: 350

'And then the doom foreseen upon me fell,
For Queen Diana did my body change
Into a fork-tongued dragon, flesh and fell,
And through the island nightly do I range,
Or in the green sea mate with monsters
  strange,   355
When in the middle of the moonlit night
The sleepy mariner I do affright.

'But all day long upon this gold I lie
Within this place, where never mason's
  hand
Smote trowel on the marble noisily;   360
Drowsy I lie, no folk at my command,
Who once was called the Lady of the
  Land;
Who might have bought a kingdom with a
  kiss,
Yea, half the world with such a sight as
  this.'

And therewithal, with rosy fingers light, 365
Backward her heavy-hanging hair she threw,
To give her naked beauty more to sight;
But when, forgetting all the things he knew,
Maddened with love unto the prize he drew,
She cried, 'Nay, wait! for wherefore wilt
  thou die,   370
Why should we not be happy, thou and I?

'Wilt thou not save me? once in every year
This rightful form of mine that thou dost
  see
By favor of the goddess have I here
From sunrise unto sunset given me,   375
That some brave man may end my misery.
And thou — art thou not brave? can thy
  heart fail,
Whose eyes e'en now are weeping at my
  tale?

'Then listen! when this day is overpast,
A fearful monster shall I be again,   380
And thou may'st be my savior at the last;
Unless, once more, thy words are naught
   and vain.
If thou of love and sovereignty art fain,
Come thou next morn, and when thou seest
   here
A hideous dragon, have thereof no fear, 385

'But take the loathsome head up in thine
   hands,
And kiss it, and be master presently
Of twice the wealth that is in all the lands
From Cathay to the head of Italy;
And master also, if it pleaseth thee,   390
Of all thou praisest as so fresh and bright,
Of what thou callest crown of all delight.

'Ah! with what joy then shall I see again
The sunlight on the green grass and the
   trees,
And hear the clatter of the summer rain, 395
And see the joyous folk beyond the seas.
Ah, me! to hold my child upon my knees,
After the weeping of unkindly tears,
And all the wrongs of these four hundred
   years.

'Go now, go quick: leave this gray heap of
   stone;   400
And from thy glad heart think upon thy
   way,
How I shall love thee — yea, love thee
   alone,
That bringest me from dark death unto
   day;
For this shall be thy wages and thy pay;
Unheard-of wealth, unheard-of love is near,
If thou hast heart a little dread to bear.' 406

Therewith she turned to go; but he cried
   out,
'Ah! wilt thou leave me then without one
   kiss,
To slay the very seeds of fear and doubt,
That glad to-morrow may bring certain
   bliss?   410
Hast thou forgotten how love lives by this,
The memory of some hopeful close embrace,
Low whispered words within some lonely
   place?'

But she, when his bright glittering eyes she
   saw,
And burning cheeks, cried out, 'Alas, alas!
Must I be quite undone, and wilt thou
   draw   416

A worse fate on me than the first one was?
O haste thee from this fatal place to pass!
Yet, ere thou goest, take this, lest thou
   shouldst deem
Thou hast been fooled by some strange mid-
   day dream.'   420

So saying, blushing like a new-kissed maid,
From off her neck a little gem she drew,
That, 'twixt those snowy rose-tinged hillocks
   laid,
The secrets of her glorious beauty knew;
And ere he well perceived what she would
   do,   425
She touched his hand, the gem within it lay,
And, turning, from his sight she fled away.

Then at the doorway where her rosy heel
Had glanced and vanished, he awhile did
   stare,
And still upon his hand he seemed to feel
The varying kisses of her fingers fair;   431
Then turned he toward the dreary crypt
   and bare,
And dizzily throughout the castle passed,
Till by the ruined fane he stood at last.

Then weighing still the gem within his
   hand,   435
He stumbled backward through the cypress
   wood,
Thinking the while of some strange lovely
   land,
Where all his life should be most fair and
   good
Till on the valley's wall of hills he stood,
And slowly thence passed down unto the
   bay   440
Red with the death of that bewildering
   day.

The next day came, and he, who all the
   night
Had ceaselessly been turning in his bed,
Arose and clad himself in armor bright,
And many a danger he rememberèd;   445
Storming of towns, lone sieges full of dread,
That with renown his heart had borne him
   through
And this thing seemed a little thing to do.

So on he went, and on the way he thought
Of all the glorious things of yesterday, 450
Naught of the price whereat they must be
   bought,
But ever to himself did softly say,
'No roaming now, my wars are passed
   away;

No long dull days devoid of happiness,
When such a love my yearning heart shall
    bless.'   455

Thus to the castle did he come at last,
But when unto the gateway he drew near,
And underneath its ruined archway passed
Into a court, a strange noise did he hear,
And through his heart there shot a pang
    of fear;   460
Trembling, he gat his sword into his hand,
And midmost of the cloisters took his stand.

But for a while that unknown noise in-
    creased,
A rattling, that with strident roars did
    blend,
And whining moans; but suddenly it
    ceased,   465
A fearful thing stood at the cloister's end,
And eyed him for a while, then 'gan to
    wend
Adown the cloisters, and began again
That rattling, and the moan like fiends in
    pain.

And as it came on towards him, with its
    teeth   470
The body of a slain goat did it tear,
The blood whereof in its hot jaws did
    seethe,
And on its tongue he saw the smoking hair;
Then his heart sank, and standing trembling
    there,
Throughout his mind wild thoughts and
    fearful ran,   475
'Some fiend she was,' he said, 'the bane of
    man.'

Yet he abode her still, although his blood
Curdled within him: the thing dropped the
    goat,
And creeping on, came close to where he
    stood,
And raised its head to him, and wrinkled
    throat,   480
Then he cried out and wildly at her smote,
Shutting his eyes, and turned and from the
    place
Ran swiftly, with a white and ghastly face.

But little things rough stones and tree-
    trunks seemed,

And if he fell, he rose and ran on still; 485
No more he felt his hurts than if he
    dreamed,
He made no stay for valley or steep hill,
Heedless he dashed through many a foam-
    ing rill,
Until he came unto the ship at last
And with no word into the deep hold
    passed.   490

Meanwhile the dragon, seeing him clean
    gone,
Followed him not, but crying horribly,
Caught up within her jaws a block of stone
And ground it into powder, then turned
    she,
With cries that folk could hear far out at
    sea,   495
And reached the treasure set apart of old,
To brood above the hidden heaps of gold.

Yet was she seen again on many a day
By some half-waking mariner, or herd,
Playing amid the ripples of the bay,   500
Or on the hills making all things afeard,
Or in the wood, that did that castle gird,
But never any man again durst go
To seek her woman's form, and end her
    woe.

As for the man, who knows what things he
    bore?   505
What mournful faces peopled the sad night,
What wailings vexed him with reproaches
    sore,
What images of that nigh-gained delight!
What dreamed caresses from soft hands
    and white,
Turning to horrors ere they reached the
    best;   510
What struggles vain, what shame, what
    huge unrest?

No man he knew, three days he lay and
    raved,
And cried for death, until a lethargy
Fell on him, and his fellows thought him
    saved;
But on the third night he awoke to die; 515
And at Byzantium doth his body lie
Between two blossoming pomegranate trees,
Within the churchyard of the Genoese.

                          (1868)

ALGERNON CHARLES SWINBURNE (1837-1909)

The poet's parents were Admiral Charles Henry Swinburne and Lady Henrietta Jane, daughter of the third Earl of Ashburnham. After a schooling of five years at Eton, Swinburne went to Balliol College, Oxford, where he contributed prose and verse to *Undergraduate Papers*, distinguished himself in Latin, Greek, French, and Italian, and began friendships with William Morris, Dante Gabriel Rossetti, and Edward Burne-Jones. After leaving Oxford, in 1860, he traveled on the continent, visiting Landor in Florence. The greater part of his life Swinburne spent quietly in England. After living for a time in London, with the Rossetti brothers, he retired to spend most of his later years at Putney Hill.

Swinburne first distinguished himself in literature as a dramatist, by the publication of *Rosamond* (1860), *The Queen Mother* (1860), *Atalanta in Calydon* (1865), and *Chastelard* (1865). By the publication of *Poems and Ballads* (1866), he aroused a moral commotion that has never been equaled in the history of English literature. To his assailants,— some of whom admired his rhythmical mastery as genuinely as they deprecated his unbridled utterances of passion,— Swinburne replied scornfully in *Notes on Poems and Reviews* (1866). The huge volume of Swinburne's poetical production, in which the lapses from lyrical and dramatic power are only occasional, is best represented by such publications as *Songs before Sunrise* (1871), *Bothwell: a Tragedy* (1874), *Erechtheus* (1876), *Studies in Song* (1880), *Mary Stuart: a Tragedy* (1881), *Tristram of Lyonesse, and Other Poems* (1882), *The Tale of Balen* (1896), and *A Channel Passage, and Other Poems* (1904). Swinburne's achievement in poetry, moreover, did not prevent his attaining a firm place in prose, chiefly through his critical studies of Elizabethan dramatists, such as *George Chapman* (1875), *A Study of Shakspere* (1880), *A Study of Ben Jonson* (1889), and *The Age of Shakspere* (1908).

Swineburne's earlier poems expressed, no doubt, a definite defiance of established social, political, and religious conventions that probably prevented, ultimately, his succession to the laureateship upon the death of Tennyson. His later poems are less defiant, and contain a more incisive appreciation of nature and more narrative charm. The severest of Swinburne's critics have never questioned his absolute mastery of the rhythmical possibilities of the English language, a mastery that resulted in his most serious poetical defect,— the substitution, in some cases, of a superb sonorousness for genuine ideas.

CHORUSES FROM ATALANTA IN CALYDON

CHORUS

When the hounds of spring are on winter's
    traces,
  The mother of months in meadow or
    plain
Fills the shadows and windy places
  With lisp of leaves and ripple of rain;
And the brown bright nightingale amorous 5
Is half assuaged for Itylus,
For the Thracian ships and the foreign
    faces,
  The tongueless vigil, and all the pain.

Come with bows bent and with emptying
    of quivers,
  Maiden most perfect, lady of light,   10

With a noise of winds and many rivers,
  With a clamor of waters, and with might;
Bind on thy sandals, O thou most fleet,
  Over the splendor and speed of thy feet;
For the faint east quickens, the wan west
    shivers,   15
  Round the feet of the day and the feet of
    the night.

Where shall we find her, how shall we sing
    to her,
  Fold our hands round her knees, and
    cling?
O that man's heart were as fire and could
    spring to her,
  Fire, or the strength of the streams that
    spring!   20
For the stars and the winds are unto her
  As raiment, as songs of the harp-player;

For the risen stars and the fallen cling
    to her,
  And the southwest-wind, and the west-
    wind sing.

For winter's rains and ruins are over, 25
  And all the season of snows and sins;
The days dividing lover and lover,
  The light that loses, the night that wins;
And time remembered is grief forgotten,
And frosts are slain and flowers begotten,
And in green underwood and cover   31
  Blossom by blossom the spring begins.

The full streams feed on flower of rushes,
  Ripe grasses trammel a traveling foot,
The faint fresh flame of the young year
    flushes   35
  From leaf to flower and flower to fruit;
And fruit and leaf are as gold and fire,
And the oat is heard above the lyre,
And the hoofèd heel of a satyr crushes
  The chestnut-husk at the chestnut-root. 40

And Pan by noon and Bacchus by night,
  Fleeter of foot than the fleet-foot kid,
Follows with dancing and fills with delight
  The Mænad and the Bassarid;
And soft as lips that laugh and hide   45
The laughing leaves of the trees divide,
And screen from seeing and leave in sight
  The god pursuing, the maiden hid.

The ivy falls with the Bacchanal's hair
  Over her eyebrows hiding her eyes;   50
The wild vine slipping down leaves bare
  Her bright breast shortening into sighs;
The wild vine slips with the weight of its
    leaves,
But the berried ivy catches and cleaves
To the limbs that glitter, the feet that scare
  The wolf that follows, the fawn that
    flies.   56

CHORUS

Before the beginning of years
  There came to the making of man
Time, with a gift of tears;
  Grief, with a glass that ran;
Pleasure,—with pain for leaven;   5
  Summer, with flowers that fell;
Remembrance fallen from heaven,
  And madness risen from hell;
Strength without hands to smite;
  Love that endures for a breath;   10
Night, the shadow of light,
  And life, the shadow of death.

And the high gods took in hand
  Fire, and the falling of tears,
And a measure of sliding sand   15
  From under the feet of the years
And froth and drift of the sea;
  And dust of the laboring earth;
And bodies of things to be
  In the houses of death and of birth; 20
And wrought with weeping and laughter,
  And fashioned with loathing and love,
With life before and after
  And death beneath and above,
For a day and a night and a morrow,   25
  That his strength might endure for a span
With travail and heavy sorrow,
  The holy spirit of man.

From the winds of the north and the south
  They gathered as unto strife;   30
They breathed upon his mouth,
  They filled his body with life;
Eyesight and speech they wrought
  For the veils of the soul therein,
A time for labor and thought,   35
  A time to serve and to sin;
They gave him light in his ways,
  And love, and a space for delight,
And beauty and length of days,
  And night, and sleep in the night.   40
His speech is a burning fire;
  With his lips he travaileth;
In his heart is a blind desire,
  In his eyes foreknowledge of death;
He weaves, and is clothed with derision; 45
  Sows, and he shall not reap;
His life is a watch or a vision
  Between a sleep and a sleep.

CHORUS

We have seen thee, O Love, thou art fair;
  thou art goodly, O Love;
Thy wings make light in the air as the
  wings of a dove.
Thy feet are as winds that divide the stream
  of the sea;
Earth is thy covering to hide thee, the garment of thee.
Thou art swift and subtle and blind as a
  flame of fire;   5
Before thee the laughter, behind thee the
  tears of desire;
And twain go forth beside thee, a man with
  a maid;
Her eyes are the eyes of a bride whom delight makes afraid;
As the breath in the buds that stir is her
  bridal breath;

But Fate is the name of her; and his name
    is Death.   10

For an evil blossom was born
  Of sea-foam and the frothing of blood,
    Blood-red and bitter of fruit,
      And the seed of it laughter and tears,
And the leaves of it madness and scorn; 15
  A bitter flower from the bud,
    Sprung of the sea without root,
      Sprung without graft from the years.

The weft of the world was untorn   19
  That is woven of the day on the night,
  The hair of the hours was not white
Nor the raiment of time overworn,
  When a wonder, a world's delight,
  A perilous goddess was born;
    And the waves of the sea as she came 25
Clove, and the foam at her feet,
    Fawning, rejoiced to bring forth
  A fleshly blossom, a flame
Filling the heavens with heat
    To the cold white ends of the north.

And in air the clamorous birds,   31
  And men upon earth that hear
Sweet articulate words
    Sweetly divided apart,
  And in shallow and channel and mere 35
The rapid and footless herds,
    Rejoiced, being foolish of heart.

For all they said upon earth,
  She is fair, she is white like a dove, 39
    And the life of the world in her breath
Breathes, and is born at her birth;
  For they knew thee for mother of love,
  And knew thee not mother of death.

What hadst thou to do being born,
  Mother, when winds were at ease,   45
As a flower of the springtime of corn,
  A flower of the foam of the seas?
For bitter thou wast from thy birth,
  Aphrodite, a mother of strife;
For before thee some rest was on earth, 50
  A little respite from tears,
  A little pleasure of life;
For life was not then as thou art,
  But as one that waxeth in years
Sweet-spoken, a fruitful wife;   55
  Earth had no thorn, and desire
No sting, neither death any dart;
  What hadst thou to do amongst these,
  Thou, clothed with a burning fire,
Thou, girt with sorrow of heart,   60
  Thou, sprung of the seed of the seas

As an ear from a seed of corn,
  As a brand plucked forth of a pyre,
As a ray shed forth of the morn,
  For division of soul and disease,   65
For a dart and a sting and a thorn?
What ailed thee then to be born?

Was there not evil enough,
  Mother, and anguish on earth
  Born with a man at his birth,   70
Wastes underfoot, and above
  Storm out of heaven, and dearth
Shaken down from the shining thereof,
  . Wrecks from afar overseas
  And peril of shallow and firth,   75
    And tears that spring and increase
In the barren places of mirth,
That thou, having wings as a dove,
  Being girt with desire for a girth,
    That thou must come after these,   80
That thou must lay on him love?

Thou shouldst not so have been born:
  But death should have risen with thee,
  Mother, and visible fear,
    Grief, and the wringing of hands,   85
And noise of many that mourn;
  The smitten bosom, the knee
  Bowed, and in each man's ear
    A cry as of perishing lands,
A moan as of people in prison,   90
  A tumult of infinite griefs;
  And thunder of storm on the sands,
    And wailing of wives on the shore;
And under thee newly arisen
  Loud shoals, and shipwrecking reefs,   95
    Fierce air and violent light;
  Sail rent and sundering oar,
    Darkness, and noises of night;
Clashing of streams in the sea,
Wave against wave as a sword,   100
  Clamor of currents, and foam;
    Rains making ruin on earth,
  Winds that wax ravenous and roam
As wolves in a wolfish horde;
Fruits growing faint in the tree,   105
    And blind things dead in their birth;
  Famine, and blighting of corn,
When thy time was come to be born.

All these we know of; but thee
  Who shall discern or declare?   110
In the uttermost ends of the sea
  The light of thine eyelids and hair,
  The light of thy bosom as fire
    Between the wheel of the sun
And the flying flames of the air?   115
  Wilt thou turn thee not yet nor have
    pity,

But abide with despair and desire
  And the crying of armies undone,
    Lamentation of one with another
    And breaking of city by city;   120
The dividing of friend against friend,
    The severing of brother and brother;
  Wilt thou utterly bring to an end?
    Have mercy, mother!

For against all men from of old   125
  Thou hast set thine hand as a curse,
    And cast out gods from their places
    These things are spoken of thee.
Strong kings and goodly with gold   129
  Thou hast found out arrows to pierce,
    And made their kingdoms and races
    As dust and surf of the sea.
All these, overburdened with woes
  And with length of their days waxen
    weak,
    Thou slewest; and sentest moreover 135
    Upon Tyro an evil thing,
Rent hair and a fetter and blows
  Making bloody the flower of the cheek,
    Though she lay by a god as a lover,
    Though fair, and the seed of a king.
For of old, being full of thy fire,   141
  She endured not longer to wear
    On her bosom a saffron vest,
    On her shoulder an ashwood quiver;
Being mixed and made one through desire,
  With Enipeus, and all her hair   146
    Made moist with his mouth, and her
      breast
    Filled full of the foam of the river.
                                                    (1865)

THE GARDEN OF PROSERPINE

Here, where the world is quiet;
  Here, where all trouble seems
Dead winds' and spent waves' riot
  In doubtful dreams of dreams;
I watch the green field growing   5
For reaping folk and sowing,
For harvest-time and mowing,
  A sleepy world of streams.

I am tired of tears and laughter,
  And men that laugh and weep;   10
Of what may come hereafter
  For men that sow to reap:
I am weary of days and hours,
Blown buds of barren flowers,
Desires and dreams and powers   15
  And everything but sleep.

Here life has death for neighbor,
  And far from eye or ear
Wan waves and wet winds labor,
  Weak ships and spirits steer;   20
They drive adrift, and whither
They wot not who make thither;
But no such winds blow hither,
  And no such things grow here.

No growth of moor or coppice,   25
  No heather-flower or vine,
But bloomless buds of poppies,
  Green grapes of Proserpine,
Pale beds of blowing rushes,
Where no leaf blooms or blushes   30
Save this whereout she crushes
  For dead men deadly wine.

Pale, without name or number,
  In fruitless fields of corn,
They bow themselves and slumber   35
  All night till light is born;
And like a soul belated,
In hell and heaven unmated,
By cloud and mist abated
  Comes out of darkness morn.   40

Though one were strong as seven,
  He too with death shall dwell,
Nor wake with wings in heaven,
  Nor weep for pains in hell;
Though one were fair as roses,   45
His beauty clouds and closes;
And well though love reposes,
  In the end it is not well.

Pale, beyond porch and portal,
  Crowned with calm leaves, she stands 50
Who gathers all things mortal
  With cold immortal hands;
Her languid lips are sweeter
Than love's who fears to greet her,
To men that mix and meet her   55
  From many times and lands.

She waits for each and other,
  She waits for all men born;
Forgets the earth her mother,
  The life of fruits and corn;   60
And spring and seed and swallow
Take wing for her and follow
Where summer song rings hollow
  And flowers are put to scorn.

There go the loves that wither,   65
  The old loves with wearier wings;
And all dead years draw thither,

And all disastrous things;
Dead dreams of days forsaken,
Blind buds that snows have shaken,   70
Wild leaves that winds have taken,
    Red strays of ruined springs.

We are not sure of sorrow;
    And joy was never sure;
To-day will die to-morrow;   75
    Time stoops to no man's lure;
And love, grown faint and fretful,
With lips but half regretful
Sighs, and with eyes forgetful
    Weeps that no loves endure.   80

From too much love of living,
    From hope and fear set free,
We thank with brief thanksgiving
    Whatever gods may be
That no life lives for ever;   85
That dead men rise up never;
That even the weariest river
    Winds somewhere safe to sea.

Then star nor sun shall waken,
    Nor any change of light: 90
Nor sound of waters shaken,
    Nor any sound or sight:
Nor wintry leaves nor vernal,
Nor days nor things diurnal;
Only the sleep eternal   95
    In an eternal night.

                              (1866)

HERTHA

I am that which began;
    Out of me the years roll;
Out of me God and man;
    I am equal and whole;
God changes, and man, and the form of
    them bodily; I am the soul.   5

Before ever land was,
    Before ever the sea,
Or soft hair of the grass,
    Or fair limbs of the tree,
Or the flesh-colored fruit of my branches, I
    was, and thy soul was in me.   10

First life on my sources
    First drifted and swam;
Out of me are the forces
    That save it or damn;
Out of me, man and woman, and wild-
    beast and bird; before God was, I
    am.   15

Beside or above me
    Naught is there to go;
Love or unlove me,
    Unknow me or know,
I am that which unloves me and loves; I
    am stricken, and I am the blow.   20

I the mark that is missed
    And the arrows that miss,
I the mouth that is kissed
    And the breath in the kiss.
The search, and the sought, and the seeker,
    the soul and the body that is.   25

I am that thing which blesses
    My spirit elate;
That which caresses
    With hands uncreate
My limbs unbegotten that measure the
    length of the measure of fate.   30

But what thing dost thou now,
    Looking Godward, to cry
'I am I, thou art thou,
    I am low, thou art high?'
I am thou, whom thou seekest to find him;
    find thou but thyself, thou art I.   35

I the grain and the furrow,
    The plough-cloven clod
And the plough-share drawn thorough,
    The germ and the sod,
The deed and the doer, the seed and the
    sower, the dust which is God.   40

Hast thou known how I fashioned thee,
    Child, underground?
Fire that impassioned thee,
    Iron that bound,
Dim changes of water, what thing of all
    these hast thou known of or
    found?   45

Canst thou say in thine heart
    Thou hast seen with thine eyes
With what cunning of art
    Thou wast wrought in what wise,
By what force of what stuff thou wast
    shapen, and shown on my breast to
    the skies?   50

Who hath given, who hath sold it thee,
    Knowledge of me?
Hath the wilderness told it thee?
    Hast thou learnt of the sea?
Hast thou communed in spirit with night?
    have the winds taken counsel with
    thee?   55

Have I set such a star
  To show light on thy brow
That thou sawest from afar
  What I show to thee now?
Have ye spoken as brethren together, the
    sun and the mountains and thou?

What is here, dost thou know it?   61
  What was, hast thou known?
Prophet nor poet
  Nor tripod nor throne
Nor spirit nor flesh can make answer, but
    only thy mother alone.   65

Mother, not maker,
  Born, and not made;
Though her children forsake her,
  Allured or afraid,
Praying prayers to the God of their fashion,
    she stirs not for all that have
    prayed.   70

A creed is a rod,
  And a crown is of night;
But this thing is God,
  To be man with thy might,
To grow straight in the strength of thy
    spirit, and live out thy life as the
    light.   75

I am in thee to save thee,
  As my soul in thee saith;
Give thou as I gave thee,
  Thy life-blood and breath,
Green leaves of thy labor, white flowers of
    thy thought, and red fruit of thy
    death.   80

Be the ways of thy giving
  As mine were to thee;
The free life of thy living,
  Be the gift of it free;
Not as servant to lord, nor as master to
    slave, shalt thou give thee to me.

O children of banishment,   86
  Souls overcast,
Were the lights ye see vanish meant
  Always to last,
Ye would know not the sun overshining the
    shadows and stars overpast.   90

I that saw where ye trod
  The dim paths of the night
Set the shadow called God
  In your skies to give light;
But the morning of manhood is risen, and
    the shadowless soul is in sight. 95

The tree many-rooted
  That swells to the sky
With frondage red-fruited
  The life-tree am I;
In the buds of your lives is the sap of
    my leaves: ye shall live and not
    die.   100

But the gods of your fashion
  That take and that give,
In their pity and passion
  That scourge and forgive,
They are worms that are bred in the bark
    that falls off, they shall die and not
    live.   105

My own blood is what stanches
  The wounds in my bark;
Stars caught in my branches
  Make day of the dark,
And are worshipped as suns till the sunrise
    shall tread out their fires as a
    spark.   110

Where dead ages hide under
  The live roots of the tree,
In my darkness the thunder
  Makes utterance of me;
In the clash of my boughs with each other
    ye hear the waves sound of the
    sea.   115

That noise is of Time,
  As his feathers are spread
And his feet set to climb
  Through the boughs overhead,
And my foliage rings round him and
    rustles, and branches are bent with
    his tread.   120

The storm-winds of ages
  Blow through me and cease,
The war-wind that rages,
  The spring-wind of peace,   124
Ere the breath of them roughen my tresses,
    ere one of my blossoms increase.

All sounds of all changes,
  All shadows and lights
On the world's mountain-ranges,
  And stream-riven heights,
Whose tongue is the wind's tongue and
    language of storm-clouds on earth-
    shaking nights;   130

All forms of all faces,
  All works of all hands
In unsearchable places

Of time-stricken lands,
All death and all life, and all reigns and
 all ruins, drop through me as
 sands. 135

Though sore be my burden
 And more than ye know,
And my growth have no guerdon
 But only to grow, 139
Yet I fail not of growing for lightnings
 above me or death-worms below.

These too have their part in me,
 As I too in these;
Such fire is at heart in me,
 Such sap is this tree's,
Which hath in it all sounds and all secrets
 of infinite lands and of seas. 145

In the spring-colored hours
 When my mind was as May's,
There brake forth of me flowers
 By centuries of days,
Strong blossoms with perfume of manhood,
 shot out from my spirit as rays. 150

And the sound of them springing
 And smell of their shoots
Were as warmth and sweet singing,
 And strength to my roots;
And the lives of my children made perfect
 with freedom of soul were my
 fruits. 155

I bid you but be;
 I have need not of prayer;
I have need of you free
 As your mouths of mine air;
That my heart may be greater within me,
 beholding the fruits of me fair. 160

More fair than strange fruit is
 Of faiths ye espouse;
In me only the root is
 That blooms in your boughs; 164
Behold now your god that ye made you,
 to feed him with faith of your vows.

In the darkening and whitening
 Abysses, adored,
With dayspring and lightning
 For lamp and for sword, 169
God thunders in heaven, and his angels are
 red with the wrath of the Lord.

O my sons, O too dutiful
 Towards gods not of me,
Was not I enough beautiful?

Was it hard to be free? 174
For behold, I am with you, am in you and
 of you; look forth now and see.

Lo, winged with world's wonders,
 With miracles shod,
With the fires of his thunders
 For raiment and rod,
God trembles in heaven, and his angels are
 white with the terror of God. 180

For his twilight is come on him,
 His anguish is here;
And his spirits gaze dumb on him,
 Grown gray from his fear;
And his hour taketh hold on him stricken,
 the last of his infinite year. 185

Thought made him and breaks him,
 Truth slays and forgives;
But to you, as time takes him,
 This new thing it gives,
Even love, the belovèd Republic, that feeds
 upon freedom and lives. 190

For truth only is living,
 Truth only is whole,
And the love of his giving
 Man's polestar and pole;
Man, pulse of my center, and fruit of my
 body, and seed of my soul. 195

One birth of my bosom;
 One beam of mine eye;
One topmost blossom
 That scales the sky;
Man, equal and one with me, man that is
 made of me, man that is I. 200
      (1871)

A FORSAKEN GARDEN

In a coign of the cliff between lowland and
 highland,
 At the sea-down's edge between windward
 and lee,
Walled round with rocks as an inland
 island,
 The ghost of a garden fronts the sea.
A girdle of brushwood and thorn encloses 5
 The steep square slope of the blossomless
 bed
Where the weeds that grew green from the
 graves of its roses
 Now lie dead.

The fields fall southward, abrupt and
 broken.

To the low last edge of the long lone
    land.   10
If a step should sound or a word be spoken,
    Would a ghost not rise at the strange
    guest's hand?
So long have the gray bare walks lain guest-
    less,
    Through branches and briers if a man
    make way,
He shall find no life but the sea-wind's
    restless   15
    Night and day.

The dense hard passage is blind and
    stifled
That crawls by a track none turn to climb
To the strait waste place that the years
    have rifled
    Of all but the thorns that are touched
    not of time.   20
The thorns he spares when the rose is
    taken;
    The rocks are left when he wastes the
    plain;
The wind that wanders, the weeds wind-
    shaken,
    These remain.

Not a flower to be pressed of the foot that
    falls not;   25
    As the heart of a dead man the seed-plots
    are dry;
From the thicket of thorns whence the
    nightingale calls not,
    Could she call, there were never a rose
    to reply.
Over the meadows that blossom and wither,
    Rings but the note of a sea-bird's song.
Only the sun and the rain come hither 31
    All year long.

The sun burns sear, and the rain dishevels
    One gaunt bleak blossom of scentless
    breath.
Only the wind here hovers and revels,   35
    In a round where life seems barren as
    death.
Here there was laughing of old, there was
    weeping,
    Haply, of lovers none ever will know,
Whose eyes went seaward a hundred sleep-
    ing
    Years ago.   40

Heart handfast in heart as they stood,
    'Look thither,'
    Did he whisper? 'Look forth from the
    flowers to the sea;

For the foam-flowers endure when the rose-
    blossoms wither,
    And men that love lightly may die — but
    we?'
And the same wind sang, and the same
    waves whitened,   45
    And or ever the garden's last petals were
    shed,
In the lips that had whispered, the eyes that
    had lightened,
    Love was dead.

Or they loved their life through, and then
    went whither?
    And were one to the end — but what end
    who knows?   50
Love deep as the sea as a rose must wither,
    As the rose-red seaweed that mocks the
    rose.
Shall the dead take thought for the dead
    to love them?
    What love was ever as deep as a grave?
They are loveless now as the grass above
    them   55
    Or the wave.

All are at one now, roses and lovers,
    Not known of the cliffs and the fields and
    the sea.
Not a breath of the time that has been
    hovers
    In the air now soft with a summer to
    be.   60
Not a breath shall there sweeten the
    seasons hereafter
    Of the flowers or the lovers that laugh
    now or weep,
When as they that are free now of weep-
    ing and laughter
    We shall sleep.

Here death may deal not again for ever; 65
    Here change may come not till all change
    end.
From the graves they have made they shall
    rise up never.
    Who have left naught living to ravage
    and rend.
Earth, stones, and thorns of the wild ground
    growing,
    While the sun and the rain live, these
    shall be;   70
Till a last wind's breath, upon all these
    blowing,
    Roll the sea.

Till the slow sea rise, and the sheer cliff
    crumble.

Till terrace and meadow the deep gulfs
   drink,
Till the strength of the waves of the high
   tides humble   75
The fields that lessen, the rocks that
   shrink,
Here now in his triumph where all things
   falter,
Stretched out on the spoils that his own
   hand spread,
As a god self-slain on his own strange altar,
   Death lies dead.

(1876)

THALASSIUS

Upon the flowery forefront of the year,
One wandering by the gray-green April sea
Found on a reach of shingle and shallower
   sand,
Inlaid with starrier glimmering jewelry
Left for the sun's love and the light wind's
   cheer   5
Along the foam-flowered strand,
Breeze-brightened, something nearer sea
   than land,
Though the last shoreward blossom-fringe
   was near,
A babe asleep, with flower-soft face that
   gleamed
To sun and seaward as it laughed and
   dreamed,   10
Too sure of either love for either's fear,
Albeit so birdlike slight and light, it seemed,
Nor man, nor mortal child of man, but fair
As even its twin-born tenderer spray-
   flowers were,   14
That the wind scatters like an Oread's hair.

For when July strewed fire on earth and
   sea
The last time ere that year,
Out of the flame of morn Cymothoë,
Beheld one brighter than the sun-bright
   sphere
Move toward her from its fieriest heart,
   whence trod   20
The live sun's very god,
Across the foam-bright water-ways that are
As heavenlier heavens, with star for answer-
   ing star;
And on her eyes and hair and maiden
   mouth
Felt a kiss falling fierier than the South, 25
And heard above afar
A noise of songs and wind-enamored wings,
And lutes and lyres of milder and mightier
   strings,

And round the resonant radiance of his
   car
Where depth is one with height,   30
Light heard as music, music seen as light,
And with that second moondawn of the
   spring's
That fosters the first rose,
A sun-child whiter than the sunlit snows
Was born out of the world of sunless
   things   35
That round the round earth flows and ebbs
   and flows.

But he that found the sea-flower by the
   sea,
And took to foster like a graft of earth,
Was born of man's most highest and
   heavenliest birth,
Free-born as winds and stars and waves
   are free;   40
A warrior gray with glories more than
   years,
Though more of years than change the
   quick to dead
Had rained their light and darkness on his
   head;
A singer that in time's and memory's ears
Should leave such words to sing as all his
   peers   45
Might praise with hallowing heat of rap-
   turous tears,
Till all the days of human flight were fled.
And at his knees his fosterling was fed,
Not with man's wine and bread,   49
Nor mortal mother-milk of hopes and fears,
But food of deep memorial days long sped;
For bread with wisdom, and with song for
   wine,
Clear as the full calm's emerald hyaline.
And from his grave glad lips the boy would
   gather
Fine honey of song-notes, goldener than
   gold,   55
More sweet than bees make of the breath-
   ing heather,
That he, as glad and bold,
Might drink as they, and keep his spirit
   from cold.
And the boy loved his laurel-laden hair
As his own father's risen on the eastern
   air,   60
And that less white brow-binding bayleaf
   bloom,
More than all flowers his father's eyes re-
   lume,
And those high songs he heard,
More than all notes of any landward bird,
More than all sounds less free   65
Than the wind's quiring to the choral sea.

High things the high song taught him:
  how the breath,
Too frail for life, may be more strong than
  death;
And this poor flash of sense in life, that
  gleams
As a ghost's glory in dreams,   70
More stable than the world's own heart's
  root seems,
By that strong faith of lordliest love, which
  gives
To death's own sightless-seeming eyes a
  light
Clearer, to death's bare bones a verier
  might,
Than shines or strikes from any man that
  lives;   75
How he that loves life overmuch shall die
The dog's death, utterly;
And he that much less loves it than he
  hates
All wrong-doing that is done,
Anywhere always underneath the sun,   80
Shall live a mightier life than time's or
  fate's.
One fairer thing he showed him, and in
  might
More strong than day and night,
Whose strengths build up time's towering
  period;
Yea, one thing stronger and more high than
  God,   85
Which, if man had not, then should God
  not be:
And that was Liberty.
And gladly should man die to gain, he
  said,
Freedom; and gladlier, having lost, lie dead.
For man's earth was not, nor the sweet sea-
  waves   90
His, nor his own land, nor its very graves,
Except they bred not, bore not, hid not
  slaves;
But all of all that is,
Were one man free in body and soul, were
  his.

And the song softened, even as heaven by
  night   95
Softens, from sunnier down to starrier
  light,
And with its moon-bright breath
Blessed life for death's sake, and for life's
  sake death;
Till as the moon's own beam and breath
  confuse,
In one clear hueless haze of glimmering
  hues   100

The sea's line, and the land's line, and the
  sky's,
And light for love of darkness almost dies,
As darkness only lives for light's dear love,
Whose hands the web of night is woven of:
So in that heaven of wondrous words were
  life   .   105
And death brought out of strife;
Yea, by that strong spell of serene in-
  crease,
Brought out of strife to peace.

And the song lightened, as the wind at
  morn
Flashes, and even with lightning of the
  wind   110
Night's thick-spun web is thinned,
And all its weft unwoven and overworn
Shrinks, as might love from scorn,
And as when wind and light, on water and
  land,
Leap as twin gods from heavenward, hand
  in hand,   115
And with the sound and splendor of their
  leap
Strike darkness dead, and daunt the spirit
  of sleep,
And burn it up with fire;
So with the light that lightened from the
  lyre,
Was all the bright heat in the child's heart
  stirred,   120
And blown with blasts of music into flame,
Till even his sense became
Fire, as the sense that fires the singing bird,
Whose song calls night by name.   124
And in the soul within the sense began
The manlike passion of a godlike man,
And in the sense within the soul again
Thoughts that make men of gods, and gods
  of men.

For love the high song taught him,— love
  that turns
God's heart toward man as man's to God-
  ward; love   130
That life and death and life are fashioned
  of,
From the first breath that burns
Half-kindled on the flower-like yeanling's
  lip
So light and faint that life seems like to
  slip,
To that yet weaklier drawn   135
When sunset dies of night's devouring
  dawn;
But the man dying not wholly as all men
  dies

If aught be left of his in live men's eyes
Out of the dawnless dark of death to rise;
If aught of deed or word   140
Be seen for all time, or of all time heard.
Love, that though body and soul were over-
    thrown,
Should live for love's sake of itself alone,
Though spirit and flesh were one thing
    doomed and dead.
Not wholly annihilated.   145
Seeing even the hoariest ash-flake that the
    pyre
Drops, and forgets the thing was once afire,
And gave its heart to feed the pile's full
    flame
Till its own heart its own heat overcame,
Outlives its own life, though by scarce a
    span,   150
As such men dying outlive themselves in
    man,
Outlive themselves for ever; if the heat
Outburn the heart that kindled it, the sweet
Outlast the flower whose soul it was, and
    flit,
Forth of a body of it   155
Into some new shape of a strange perfume
More potent than its light live spirit of
    bloom,—
How shall not something of that soul re-
    live,
That only soul that had such gifts to give
As lighten something even of all men's
    doom,   160
Even from the laboring womb,
Even to the seal set on the unopening
    tomb?
And these the loving light of song and love
Shall wrap and lap round, and impend
    above,   164
Imperishable; and all springs born illume
Their sleep with brighter thoughts than
    wake the dove
To music, when the hillside winds resume
The marriage-song of heather-flower and
    broom
And all the joy thereof.

    And hate the song, too, taught him,— hate
    of all   170
That brings or holds in thrall
Of spirit or flesh, free born ere God be-
    gan,
The holy body and sacred soul of man.
And wheresoever a curse was, or a chain,
A throne for torment or a crown for bane
Rose, molded out of poor men's molten
    pain,   176
There, said he, should man's heaviest hate
    be set

Inexorably, to faint not or forget
Till the last warmth bled forth of the last
    vein
In flesh that none should call a king's again,
Seeing wolves and dogs and birds that
    plague-strike air   181
Leave the last bone of all the carrion bare.

    And hope the high song taught him,—
    hope whose eyes
Can sound the seas unsoundable, the skies
Inaccessible of eyesight; that can see   185
What earth beholds not, hear what wind
    and sea
Hear not, and speak what all these crying
    in one
Can speak not to the sun.
For in her sovereign eyelight all things are
Clear as the closest seen and kindlier star
That marries morn and even and winter and
    spring   191
With one love's golden ring.
For she can see the days of man, the birth
Of good, and death of evil things on earth
Inevitable and infinite, and sure   195
As present pain is, or herself is pure.
Yea, she can hear and see, beyond all things
That lighten from before Time's thunderous
    wings
Through the awful circle of wheel-winged
    periods,
The tempest of the twilight of all gods; 200
And, higher than all the circling course they
    ran,
The sundawn of the spirit that was man.

    And fear the song, too, taught him,— fear
    to be
Worthless the dear love of the wind and
    sea
That bred him fearless, like a sea-mew
    reared   205
In rocks of man's foot feared,
Where naught of wingless life may sing or
    shine.
Fear to wax worthless of that heaven he
    had,
When all the life in all his limbs was glad,
And all the drops in all his veins were
    wine,   210
And all the pulses music; when his heart,
Singing, bade heaven and wind and sea
    bear part
In one live song's reiterance, and they bore;
Fear to go crownless of the flower he wore
When the winds loved him, and the waters
    knew   215
The blithest life that clove their blithe life
    through

With living limbs exultant, or held strife
More amorous than all dalliance aye anew
With the bright breath and strength of
  their large life,
With all strong wrath of all sheer winds
  that blew, 220
All glories of all storms of the air that fell
Prone, ineluctable,
With roar from heaven of revel, and with
  hue
As of a heaven turned hell.
For when the red blast of their breath had
  made, 225
All heaven aflush with light more dire than
  shade,
He felt it in his blood and eyes and hair
Burn as if all the fires of the earth and air
Had laid strong hold upon his flesh, and
  stung
The soul behind it as with serpent's tongue,
Forked like the loveliest lightnings; nor
  could bear 231
But hardly, half distraught with strong de-
  light,
The joy that like a garment wrapped him
  round,
And lapped him over and under
With raiment of great light, 235
And rapture of great sound
At every loud leap earthward of the
  thunder
From heaven's most furthest bound:
So seemed all heaven in hearing and in
  sight,
Alive and mad with glory and angry joy,
That something of its marvelous mirth and
  might 241
Moved even to madness, fledged as even for
  flight,
The blood and spirit of one but mortal
  boy.

* * *

(1880)

ÉTUDE REALISTE

I

A baby's feet, like sea-shells pink,
  Might tempt, should heaven see meet,
An angel's lips to kiss, we think,
  A baby's feet.

Like rose-hued sea-flowers toward the heat
  They stretch and spread and wink 6
Their ten soft buds that part and meet.

No flower-bells that expand and shrink
  Gleam half so heavenly sweet

As shine on life's untrodden brink 10
  A baby's feet.

II

A baby's hands, like rosebuds furled
  Whence yet no leaf expands,
Ope if you touch, though close upcurled,
  A baby's hands. 15

Then, fast as warriors grip their brands
  When battle's bolt is hurled,
They close, clenched hard like tightening
  bands.

No rosebuds yet by dawn impearled
  Match, even in loveliest lands, 20
The sweetest flowers in all the world —
  A baby's hands.

III

A baby's eyes, ere speech begin,
  Ere lips learn words or sighs,
Bless all things bright enough to win 25
  A baby's eyes.

Love, while the sweet thing laughs and lies,
  And sleep flows out and in,
Sees perfect in them Paradise.

Their glance might cast out pain and sin, 30
  Their speech make dumb the wise,
By mute glad godhead felt within
  A baby's eyes.

(1883)

THE ROUNDEL

A roundel is wrought as a ring or a star-
  bright sphere,
With craft of delight and with cunning of
  sound unsought,
That the heart of the hearer may smile if to
  pleasure his ear
    A roundel is wrought.

Its jewel of music is carven of all or of
  aught — 5
Love, laughter, or mourning — remembrance
  of rapture or fear —
That fancy may fashion to hang in the ear
  of thought.

As a bird's quick song runs round, and the
  hearts in us hear
Pause answer to pause, and again the same
  strain caught,

So moves the device whence, round as a
  pearl or tear,   10
      A roundel is wrought.

                  (1883)

ON A COUNTRY ROAD

Along these low pleached lanes, on such a
  day,
So soft a day as this, through shade and
  sun,
With glad grave eyes that scanned the glad
  wild way,
And heart still hovering o'er a song begun,
And smile that warmed the world with benison,   5
Our father, lord long since of lordly rime,
Long since hath haply ridden, when the
  lime
Bloomed broad above him, flowering where
  he came.
Because thy passage once made warm this
  clime,
Our father Chaucer, here we praise thy
  name.   10

Each year that England clothes herself with
  May,
She takes thy likeness on her. Time hath
  spun
Fresh raiment all in vain and strange ar-
  ray
For earth and man's new spirit, fain to
  shun
Things past for dreams of better to be
  won,   15
Through many a century since thy funeral
  chime
Rang, and men deemed it death's most dire-
  ful crime
To have spared not thee for very love or
  shame;
And yet, while mists round last year's mem-
  ories climb,
Our father Chaucer, here we praise thy
  name.   20

Each turn of the old wild road whereon we
  stray,
Meseems, might bring us face to face with
  one
Whom seeing we could not but give thanks,
  and pray
For England's love our father and her son
To speak with us as once in days long
  done   25

With all men, sage and churl and monk and
  mime,
Who knew not as we know the soul sublime
That sang for song's love more than lust of
  fame.
Yet, though this be not, yet, in happy time,
Our father Chaucer, here we praise thy
  name.   30

Friend, even as bees about the flowering
  thyme,
Years crowd on years, till hoar decay be-
  grime
Names once beloved; but, seeing the sun the
  same,
As birds of autumn fain to praise the prime,
Our father Chaucer, here we praise thy
  name.   35

                  (1884)

THE ARMADA
1588 : 1888

I

I

England, mother born of seamen, daughter
  fostered of the sea,
Mother more beloved than all who bear not
  all their children free,
  Reared and nursed and crowned and cher-
    ished by the sea-wind and the sun,
  Sweetest land and strongest, face most
    fair and mightiest heart in one,
Stands not higher than when the centuries
  known of earth were less by three, 5
When the strength that struck the whole
  world pale fell back from hers undone.

II

At her feet were the heads of her foes
  bowed down, and the strengths of the
  storm of them stayed,
And the hearts that were touched not with
  mercy with terror were touched and
  amazed and affrayed:
  Yea, hearts that had never been molten
    with pity were molten with fear as
    with flame,
And the priests of the Godhead whose temple is hell, and his heart is of iron
  and fire,   10
And the swordsmen that served and the
  seamen that sped them, whom peril
  could tame not or tire.

Were as foam on the winds of the waters
of England which tempest can tire
not or tame.

III

They were girded about with thunder, and
lightning came forth of the rage of
their strength,
And the measure that measures the wings
of the storm was the breadth of their
force and the length:
And the name of their might was Invincible, covered and clothed with the terror of God;   15
With his wrath were they winged, with his
love were they fired, with the speed
of his winds were they shod;
With his soul were they filled, in his trust
were they comforted; grace was upon
them as night,
And faith as the blackness of darkness: the
fume of their balefires was fair in his
sight,
The reek of them sweet as a savor of myrrh
in his nostrils: the world that he
made,
Theirs was it by gift of his servants: the
wind, if they spake in his name, was
afraid,   20
And the sun was a shadow before it, the
stars were astonished with fear of it:
fire
Went up to them, fed with men living, and
lit of men's hands for a shrine or a
pyre;
And the east and the west wind scattered
their ashes abroad, that his name
should be blest
Of the tribes of the chosen whose blessings
are curses from uttermost east unto
west.

II

I

Hell for Spain, and heaven for England,—
God to God, and man to man,—   25
Met confronted, light with darkness, life
with death: since time began,
Never earth nor sea beheld so great a
stake before them set,
Save when Athens hurled back Asia from
the lists wherein they met;
Never since the sands of ages through the
glass of history ran
Saw the sun in heaven a lordlier day than
this that lights us yet.   30

II

For the light that abides upon England, the
glory that rests on her godlike name,
The pride that is love and the love that is
faith, a perfume dissolved in flame,
Took fire from the dawn of the fierce July
when fleets were scattered as foam
And squadrons as flakes of spray; when
galleon and galliass that shadowed the
sea
Were swept from her waves like shadows
that pass with the clouds they fell
from, and she   35
Laughed loud to the wind as it gave to her
keeping the glories of Spain and
Rome.

III

Three hundred summers have fallen as
leaves by the storms in their season
thinned,
Since northward the war-ships of Spain
came sheer up the way of the south-
west wind:
Where the citadel cliffs of England are
flanked with bastions of serpentine,
Far off to the windward loomed their hulls,
an hundred and twenty-nine,   40
All filled full of the war, full-fraught with
battle and charged with bale;
Then store-ships weighted with cannon; and
all were an hundred and fifty sail.
The measureless menace of darkness an-
hungered with hope to prevail upon
light,
The shadow of death made substance, the
present and visible spirit of night,
Came, shaped as a waxing or waning moon
that rose with the fall of day,   45
To the channel where couches the Lion in
guard of the gate of the lustrous
bay.
Fair England, sweet as the sea that shields
her, and pure as the sea from stain,
Smiled, hearing hardly for scorn that stirred
her the menace of saintly Spain.

III

I

'They that ride over ocean wide with
hempen bridle and horse of tree,'
How shall they in the darkening day of
wrath and anguish and fear go free? 50
How shall these that have curbed the seas
not feel his bridle who made the sea?

God shall bow them and break them now:
    for what is man in the Lord God's
    sight?
Fear shall shake them, and shame shall
    break, and all the noon of their pride
    be night:
These that sinned shall the ravening wind
    of doom bring under, and judgment
    smite.

England broke from her neck the yoke, and
    rent the fetter, and mocked the rod: 55
Shrines of old that she decked with gold
    she turned to dust, to the dust she trod:
What is she, that the wind and sea should
    fight beside her, and war with God?

Lo, the cloud of his ships that crowd her
    channel's inlet with storm sublime,
Darker far than the tempests are that sweep
    the skies of her northmost clime;
Huge and dense as the walls that fence the
    secret darkness of unknown time. 60

Mast on mast as a tower goes past, and sail
    by sail as a cloud's wing spread;
Fleet by fleet, as the throngs whose feet
    keep time with death in his dance of
    dread;
Galleons dark as the helmsman's bark of
    old that ferried to hell the dead.

Squadrons proud as their lords, and loud
    with tramp of soldiers and chant of
    priests;
Slaves there told by the thousandfold, made
    fast in bondage as herded beasts; 65
Lords and slaves that the sweet free waves
    shall feed on, satiate with funeral feasts.

Nay, not so shall it be, they know; their
    priests have said it; can priesthood lie?
God shall keep them, their God shall sleep
    not: peril and evil shall pass them by:
Nay, for these are his children; seas and
    winds shall bid not his children die.

II

So they boast them, the monstrous host
    whose menace mocks at the dawn: and
    here 70
They that wait at the wild sea's gate, and
    watch the darkness of doom draw near,
How shall they in their evil day sustain the
    strength of their hearts for fear?

Full July in the fervent sky sets forth her
    twentieth of changing morns:

Winds fall mild that of late waxed wild:
    no presage whispers or wails or warns:
Far to west on the bland sea's breast a sail-
    ing crescent uprears her horns. 75

Seven wide miles the serene sea smiles be-
    tween them stretching from rim to rim:
Soft they shine, but a darker sign should
    bid not hope or belief wax dim:
God's are these men, and not the sea's: their
    trust is set not on her but him.

God's? but who is the God whereto the
    prayers and incense of these men rise?
What is he, that the wind and sea should
    fear him, quelled by his sunbright eyes?
What, that men should return again, and
    hail him Lord of the servile skies? 81

Hell's own flame at his heavenly name leaps
    higher and laughs, and its gulfs re-
    joice:
Plague and death from his baneful breath
    take life and lighten, and praise his
    choice:
Chosen are they to devour for prey the
    tribes that hear not and fear his voice.

Ay, but we that the wind and sea gird
    round with shelter of storms and
    waves 85
Know not him that ye worship, grim as
    dreams that quicken from dead men's
    graves:
God is one with the sea, the sun, the land
    that nursed us, the love that saves.

Love whose heart is in ours, and part of all
    things noble and all things fair;
Sweet and free as the circling sea, sublime
    and kind as the fostering air;
Pure of shame as is England's name, whose
    crowns to come are as crowns that
    were. 90

IV

I

But the Lord of darkness, the God whose
    love is a flaming fire,
The master whose mercy fulfils wide hell
    till its torturers tire,
He shall surely have heed of his servants
    who serve him for love, not hire.

They shall fetter the wing of the wind
    whose pinions are plumed with foam:

For now shall thy horn be exalted, and now
    shall thy bolt strike home;   95
Yea, now shall thy kingdom come, Lord God
    of the priests of Rome.

They shall cast thy curb on the waters, and
    bridle the waves of the sea:
They shall say to her, Peace, be still: and
    stillness and peace shall be:
And the winds and the storms shall hear
    them, and tremble, and worship thee.

Thy breath shall darken the morning, and
    wither the mounting sun;   100
And the daysprings, frozen and fettered,
    shall know thee, and cease to run;
The heart of the world shall feel thee, and
    die, and thy will be done.

The spirit of man that would sound thee,
    and search out causes of things,
Shall shrink and subside and praise thee:
    and wisdom, with plume-plucked wings,
Shall cower at thy feet and confess thee,
    that none may fathom thy springs.   105

The fountains of song that await but the
    wind of an April to be
To burst the bonds of the winter, and speak
    with the sound of a sea,
The blast of thy mouth shall quench them:
    and song shall be only of thee.

The days that are dead shall quicken, the
    seasons that were shall return;
And the streets and the pastures of England,
    the woods that burgeon and yearn,   110
Shall be whitened with ashes of women and
    children and men that burn.

For the mother shall burn with the babe
    sprung forth of her womb in fire,
And the bride with bridegroom, and brother
    with sister, and son with sire;
And the noise of the flames shall be sweet
    in thine ears as the sound of a lyre.

Yea, so shall thy kingdom be stablished,
    and so shall the signs of it be: 115
And the world shall know, and the wind
    shall speak, and the sun shall see,
That these are the works of thy servants,
    whose works bear witness to thee.

II

But the dusk of the day falls fruitless,
    whose light should have lit them on:
Sails flash through the gloom to shoreward,
    eclipsed as the sun that shone:

And the west wind wakes with dawn, and
    the hope that was here is gone.   120

Around they wheel and around, two knots
    to the Spaniard's one,
The wind-swift warriors of England, who
    shoot as with shafts of the sun,
With fourfold shots for the Spaniard's, that
    spare not till day be done.

And the wind with the sundown sharpens,
    and hurtles the ships to the lee,
And Spaniard on Spaniard smites, and shat-
    ters, and yields; and we,   125
Ere battle begin, stand lords of the battle,
    acclaimed of the sea.

And the day sweeps round to the night-
    ward; and heavy and hard the waves
Roll in on the herd of the hurtling galleons:
    and masters and slaves
Reel blind in the grasp of the dark strong
    wind that shall dig their graves.

For the sepulchers hollowed and shaped of
    the wind in the swerve of the seas,   130
The graves that gape for their pasture, and
    laugh, thrilled through by the breeze,
The sweet soft merciless waters, await and
    are fain of these.

As the hiss of a Python heaving in menace
    of doom to be
They hear through the clear night round
    them, whose hours are as clouds that
    flee,
The whisper of tempest sleeping, the heave
    and the hiss of the sea.   135

But faith is theirs, and with faith are they
    girded and helmed and shod:
Invincible are they, almighty, elect for a
    sword and a rod;
Invincible even as their God is omnipotent,
    infinite, God.

In him is their strength, who have sworn
    that his glory shall wax not dim:
In his name are their war-ships hallowed
    as mightiest of all that swim: 140
The men that shall cope with these, and
    conquer, shall cast out him.

In him is the trust of their hearts; the de-
    sire of their eyes is he;
The light of their ways, made lightning for
    men that would fain be free:
Earth's hosts are with them, and with them
    is heaven: but with us is the sea

V

I

And a day and a night pass over;   145
  And the heart of their chief swells high;
For England, the warrior, the rover,
  Whose banners on all winds fly,
Soul-stricken, he saith, by the shadow of
      death, holds off him, and draws not
      nigh.

And the wind and the dawn together   150
  Make in from the gleaming east:
And fain of the wild glad weather
  As famine is fain of feast,
And fain of the fight, forth sweeps in its
      might the host of the Lord's high
      priest.

And lightly before the breeze   155
  The ships of his foes take wing:
Are they scattered, the lords of the seas?
  Are they broken, the foes of the king?
And ever now higher as a mounting fire
      the hopes of the Spaniard spring.

And a windless night comes down: 160
  And a breezeless morning, bright
With promise of praise to crown
  The close of the crowning fight,
Leaps up as the foe's heart leaps, and glows
      with lustrous rapture of light.

And stinted of gear for battle   165
  The ships of the sea's folk lie,
Unwarlike, herded as cattle,
  Six miles from the foeman's eye
That fastens as flame on the sight of them
      tame and offenceless, and ranged as
      to die.

Surely the souls in them quail,   170
  They are stricken and withered at heart,
When in on them, sail by sail,
  Fierce marvels of monstrous art,
Tower darkening on tower till the sea-winds
      cower crowds down as to hurl them
      apart.

And the windless weather is kindly,   175
  And comforts the host in these;
And their hearts are uplift in them blindly,
  And blindly they boast at ease
That the next day's fight shall exalt them,
      and smite with destruction the lords
      of the seas.

II

And lightly the proud hearts prattle,   18c
  And lightly the dawn draws nigh,
The dawn of the doom of the battle
  When these shall falter and fly;
No day more great in the roll of fate filled
      ever with fire the sky.

To fightward they go as to feastward,   185
  And the tempest of ships that drive
Sets eastward ever and eastward,
  Till closer they strain and strive;
And the shots that rain on the hulls of
      Spain are as thunders afire and
      alive.

And about them the blithe sea smiles   190
  And flashes to windward and lee
Round capes and headlands and isles
  That heed not if war there be;
Round Sark, round Wight, green jewels of
      light in the ring of the golden sea.

But the men that within them abide   195
  Are stout of spirit and stark
As rocks that repel the tide,
  As day that repels the dark;
And the light bequeathed from their swords
      unsheathed shines lineal on Wight
      and on Sark.

And eastward the storm sets ever,   200
  The storm of the sails that strain
And follow and close and sever
  And lose and return and gain;
And English thunder divides in sunder the
      holds of the ships of Spain.

Southward to Calais, appalled   205
  And astonished, the vast fleet veers;
And the skies are shrouded and palled,
  But the moonless midnight hears
And sees how swift on them drive and drift
      strange flames that the darkness
      fears.

They fly through the night from shore-
      ward,   210
  Heart-stricken till morning break,
And ever to scourge them forward
  Drives down on them England's Drake,
And hurls them in as they hurtle and spin
      and stagger, with storm to wake.

VI

I

And now is their time come on them.
  For eastward they drift and reel.   215

With the shallows of Flanders ahead, with
   destruction and havoc at heel,
With God for their comfort only, the God
   whom they serve; and here
Their Lord, of his great loving-kindness,
   may revel and make good cheer;
Though ever his lips wax thirstier with
   drinking, and hotter the lusts in him
   swell;
For he feeds the thirst that consumes him
   with blood, and his winepress fumes
   with the reek of hell.   220

II

Fierce noon beats hard on the battle; the
   galleons that loom to the lee
Bow down, heel over, uplifting their shel-
   terless hulls from the sea:
From scuppers aspirt with blood, from
   guns dismounted and dumb,
The signs of the doom they looked for,
   the loud mute witnesses come.
They press with sunset to seaward for
   comfort: and shall not they find it
   there?   225
O servants of God most high, shall his
   winds not pass you by, and his waves
   not spare?

III

The wings of the south-west wind are
   widened; the breath of his fervent lips,
More keen than a sword's edge, fiercer than
   fire, falls full on the plunging ships.
The pilot is he of their northward flight,
   their stay and their steersman he;
A helmsman clothed with the tempest, and
   girdled with strength to constrain the
   sea.   230
And the host of them trembles and quails,
   caught fast in his hand as a bird in the
   toils;
For the wrath and the joy that fulfil him
   are mightier than man's, whom he slays
   and spoils.
And vainly, with heart divided in sunder,
   and labor of wavering will,
The lord of their host takes counsel with
   hope if haply their star shine still,
If haply some light be left them of chance
   to renew and redeem the fray;   235
But the will of the black south-wester is
   lord of the councils of war to-day.
One only spirit it quells not, a splendor un-
   darkened of chance or time;
Be the praise of his foes with Oquendo for
   ever, a name as a star sublime.

But here what aid in a hero's heart, what
   help in his hand may be?
For ever the dark wind whitens and black-
   ens the hollows and heights of the sea
And galley by galley, divided and desolate,
   founders; and none takes heed,   240
Nor foe nor friend, if they perish; forlorn,
   cast off in their uttermost need,
They sink in the whelm of the waters, as
   pebbles by children from shoreward
   hurled,
In the North Sea's waters that end not, nor
   know they a bourn but the bourn of the
   world.
Past many a secure unavailable harbor, and
   many a loud stream's mouth,   245
Past Humber and Tees and Tyne and
   Tweed, they fly, scourged on from the
   south,
And torn by the scourge of the storm-wind
   that smites as a harper smites on a
   lyre,
And consumed of the storm as the sacrifice
   loved of their God is consumed with
   fire,
And devoured of the darkness as men that
   are slain in the fires of his love are devoured,
And deflowered of their lives by the storms
   as by priests is the spirit of life deflowered.   250
For the wind, of its godlike mercy, relents
   not, and hounds them ahead to the
   north,
With English hunters at heel, till now is
   the herd of them past the Forth,
All huddled and hurtled seaward; and now
   need none wage war upon these,
Nor huntsmen follow the quarry whose fall
   is the pastime sought of the seas.
Day upon day upon day confounds them,
   with measureless mists that swell,   255
With drift of rains everlasting and dense
   as the fumes of ascending hell.
The visions of priest and of prophet beholding his enemies bruised of his rod
Beheld but the likeness of this that is fallen
   on the faithful, the friends of God.
Northward, and northward, and northward
   they stagger and shudder and swerve
   and flit,
Dismantled of masts and of yards, with
   sails by the fangs of the storm-wind
   split.   260
But north of the headland whose name is
   Wrath, by the wrath or the ruth of the
   sea,

They are swept or sustained to the westward, and drive through the rollers
aloof to the lee.
Some strive yet northward for Iceland, and
perish: but some through the storm-
hewn straits
That sunder the Shetlands and Orkneys are
borne of the breath which is God's or
fate's:
And some, by the dawn of September, at
last give thanks as for stars that smile,
For the winds have swept them to shelter
and sight of the cliffs of a Catholic
isle.   266
Though many the fierce rocks feed on, and
many the merciless heretic slays,
Yet some that have labored to land with
their treasure are trustful, and give God
praise.
And the kernes of murderous Ireland,
athirst with a greed everlasting of
blood,
Unslakable ever with slaughter and spoil,
rage down as a ravening flood,   270
To slay and to flay of their shining apparel
their brethren whom shipwreck spares;
Such faith and such mercy, such love and
such manhood, such hands and such
hearts are theirs.
Short shrift to her foes gives England, but
shorter doth Ireland to friends; and
worse
Fare they that come with a blessing· on
treason than they that come with a
curse.
Hacked, harried, and mangled of axes and
skenes, three thousand naked and dead
Bear witness of Catholic Ireland, what sons
of what sires at her breasts are bred. 276
Winds are pitiful, waves are merciful, tempest and storm are kind:
The waters that smite may spare, and the
thunder is deaf, and the lightning is
blind:
Of these perchance at his need may a man,
though they know it not, yet find grace;
But grace, if another be hardened against
him, he gets not at this man's face.   280
For his ear that hears and his eye that
sees the wreck and the wail of men,
And his heart that relents not within him,
but hungers, are like as the wolf's in
his den.
Worthy are these to worship their master,
the murderous Lord of lies,
Who hath given to the pontiff his servant
the keys of the pit and the keys of the
skies

Wild famine and red-shod rapine are cruel,
and bitter with blood are their feasts;
But fiercer than famine and redder than
rapine the hands and the hearts of
priests.   286
God, God bade these to the battle; and here,
on a land by his servants trod,
They perish, a lordly blood-offering, subdued by the hands of the servants of
God.
These also were fed of his priests with
faith, with the milk of his word and
the wine;
These too are fulfilled with the spirit of
darkness that guided their quest divine.   290
And here, cast up from the ravening sea on
the mild land's merciful breast,
This comfort they find of their fellows in
worship; this guerdon is theirs of their
quest.
Death was captain, and doom was pilot, and
darkness the chart of their way;
Night and hell had in charge and in keep-·
ing the host of the foes of day.
Invincible, vanquished, impregnable, shattered, a sign to her foes of fear,   295
A sign to the world and the stars of laughter, the fleet of the Lord lies here.
Nay, for none may declare the place of the
ruin wherein she lies;
Nay, for none hath beholden the grave
whence never a ghost shall rise.
The fleet of the foemen of England hath
found not one but a thousand graves;
And he that shall number and name them
shall number by name and by tale the
waves.   300

VII

I

Sixtus, Pope of the Church whose hope
takes flight for heaven to dethrone the
sun,
Philip, king that wouldst turn our spring to
winter, blasted, appalled, undone,
Prince and priest, let a mourner's feast give
thanks to God for your conquest won.

England's heel is upon you: kneel, O priest,
O prince, in the dust, and cry,
'Lord, why thus? art thou wroth with us
whose faith was great in thee, God
most high?   305
Whence is this, that the serpent's hiss derides us? Lord, can thy pledged word
lie?

'God of hell, are its flames that swell
  quenched now for ever, extinct and
  dead?
Who shall fear thee? or who shall hear
  the word thy servants who feared thee
  said?
Lord, art thou as the dead gods now, whose
  arm is shortened, whose rede is read?

'Yet we thought it was not for naught thy
  word was given us, to guard and guide:
Yet we deemed that they had not dreamed
  who put their trust in thee. Hast thou
  lied?   311
God our Lord, was the sacred sword we
  drew not drawn on thy Church's side?

'England hates thee as hell's own gates;
  and England triumphs, and Rome bows
  down:
England mocks at thee; England's rocks
  cast off thy servants to drive and
  drown:
England loathes thee; and fame betroths
  and plights with England her faith for
  crown.   315

'Spain clings fast to thee; Spain, aghast
  with anguish, cries to thee; where art
  thou?
Spain puts trust in thee; lo, the dust that
  soils and darkens her prostrate brow!
Spain is true to thy service; who shall raise
  up Spain for thy service now?

'Who shall praise thee, if none may raise
  thy servants up, nor affright thy foes?
Winter wanes, and the woods and plains
  forget the likeness of storms and
  snows: 320
So shall fear of thee fade even here: and
  what shall follow thee no man knows.'

Lords of night, who would breathe your
  blight on April's morning and August's
  noon,
God your Lord, the condemned, the abhorred, sinks hellward, smitten with
  deathlike swoon:
Death's own dart in his hateful heart now
  thrills, and night shall receive him
  soon.

God the Devil, thy reign of revel is here
  for ever eclipsed and fled: 325
God the Liar, everlasting fire lays hold at
  last on thee, hand and head:
God the Accurst, the consuming thirst that
  burns thee never shall here be fed.

II

England, queen of the waves whose green
  inviolate girdle enrings thee round,
Mother fair as the morning, where is now
  the place of thy foemen found?
Still the sea that salutes us free proclaims
  them stricken, acclaims thee crowned.

Times may change, and the skies grow
  strange with signs of treason and fraud
  and fear: 331
Foes in union of strange communion may
  rise against thee from far and near:
Sloth and greed on thy strength may feed as
  cankers waxing from year to year.

Yet, though treason and fierce unreason
  should league and lie and defame and
  smite,
We that know thee, how far below thee the
  hatred burns of the sons of night,   335
We that love thee, behold above thee the
  witness written of life in light.

Life that shines from thee shows forth
  signs that none may read not but eyeless
  foes:
Hate, born blind, in his abject mind grows
  hopeful now but as madness grows:
Love, born wise, with exultant eyes adores
  thy glory, beholds and glows.

Truth is in thee, and none may win thee
  to lie, forsaking the face of truth: 340
Freedom lives by the grace she gives thee,
  born again from thy deathless youth:
Faith should fail, and the world turn pale,
  wert thou the prey of the serpent's
  tooth.

Greed and fraud, unabashed, unawed, may
  strive to sting thee at heel in vain:
Craft and fear and mistrust may leer and
  mourn and murmur and plead and
  plain: 344
Thou art thou: and thy sunbright brow is
  hers that blasted the strength of Spain.

Mother, mother belovèd, none other could
  claim in place of thee England's place:
Earth bears none that beholds the sun so
  pure of record, so clothed with grace:
Dear our mother, nor son nor brother is
  thine, as strong or as fair of face.

How shalt thou be abased? or how shall
  fear take hold of thy heart? of thine.

England, maiden immortal, laden with charge
    of life and with hopes divine?   350
Earth shall wither, when eyes turned hither
    behold not light in· her darkness shine.

England, none that is born thy son, and
    lives, by grace of thy glory, free,
Lives and yearns not at heart and burns
    with hope to serve as he worships thee;
None may sing thee: the sea-wind's wing
    beats down our songs as it hails the
    sea.

                 (1889)

COR CORDIUM

O Heart of hearts, the chalice of love's fire,
Hid round with flowers and all the bounty
    of bloom;
O wonderful and perfect heart, for whom
The lyrist liberty made life a lyre;
O heavenly heart, at whose most dear de-
    sire   5
Dead love, living and singing, cleft his
    tomb,
And with him risen and regent in death's
    room
All day thy choral pulses rang full choir;
O heart whose beating blood was running
    song,
O sole thing sweeter than thine own songs
    were,   10
Help us for thy free love's sake to be free,
True for thy truth's sake, for thy strength's
    sake strong,
Till very liberty make clean and fair
The nursing earth as the sepulchral sea.

                 (1871)

'NON DOLET'

It does not hurt. She looked along the
    knife
Smiling, and watched the thick drops mix
    and run
Down the sheer blade: not that which had
    been done
Could hurt the sweet sense of the Roman
    wife,
But that which was to do yet ere the
    strife   5
Could end for each for ever, and the sun:
Nor was the palm yet nor was peace yet
    won
While pain had power upon her husband's
    life.
It does not hurt, Italia. Thou art more
Than bride to bridegroom: how shalt thou
    not take   10

The gift love's blood has reddened for thy
    sake?
Was not thy life-blood given for us be-
    fore?
And if love's heart-blood can avail thy need,
And thou not die, how should it hurt in-
    deed?   (1871)

ON THE DEATHS OF THOMAS CAR-LYLE AND GEORGE ELIOT

Two souls diverse out of our human sight
Pass, followed one with love and each with
    wonder:
The stormy sophist with his mouth of thun-
    der,
Clothed with loud words and mantled in the
    might
Of darkness and magnificence of night;   5
And one whose eye could smite the night
    in sunder,
Searching if light or no light were there-
    under,
And found in love of loving-kindness light.
Duty divine and Thought with eyes of fire
Still following Righteousness with deep de-
    sire   10
Shone sole and stern before her and· above
Sure stars and sole to steer by; but more
    sweet
Shone lower the loveliest lamp for earthly
    feet,—
The light of little children, and their love.

                 (1881)

CHRISTOPHER MARLOWE

Crowned, girdled, garbed, and shod with
    light and fire,
Son first-born of the morning, sovereign
    star!
Soul nearest ours of all, that wert most far,
Most far off in the abysm of time, thy lyre
Hung highest above the dawn-enkindled
    quire   5
Where all ye sang together, all that are,
And all the starry songs behind thy car
Rang sequence, all our souls acclaim thee
    sire.

'If all the pens that ever poets held
Had fed the feeling of their masters'
    thoughts,'   10
And as with rush of hurtling chariots
The flight of all their spirits were impelled
Toward one great end, thy glory — nay, not
    then,
Not yet mightst thou be praised enough of
    men.

                 (1882)

WALTER HORATIO PATER (1839-1894)

Pater began his life-long academic career at King's School, Canterbury, from which he proceeded to Queen's College, Oxford, where he took his bachelor's degree in 1862. As an undergraduate Pater knew few men, devoting himself closely to books, especially to Greek literature, in which Benjamin Jowett gave him much encouragement. After graduation he was elected to the Old Mortality, an essay society, through which he came into contact with the stimulating personalities of T. H. Green, A. C. Swinburne, and others. In 1864, he was elected fellow of Brasenose College, and except for visits to the Continent and a short residence in London, he remained in Oxford for the rest of his life. In 1865, a sojourn in Italy gave Pater those impressions of Renaissance art that appear conspicuously in his later writing. The quiet poise of his life as Oxford tutor and author was disturbed by nothing more eventful than an occasional vacation tour in France or Germany.

Pater's most significant mission was in interpreting to his age the spirit of the Renaissance in art and literature. His first essays, which had begun to appear in periodicals in 1867, were collected and published in a considerable volume, *Studies in the History of the Renaissance*, in 1873. In 1885 appeared Pater's finest single work. *Marius the Epicurean*, a historical romance expounding the best phases of Epicureanism. His *Imaginary Portraits* (1887) contains fine studies in philosophic fiction, and his *Appreciations, with an Essay on Style* (1889) reveals bits of his most subtle literary criticism. *Plato and Platonism* (1893) is a notable result of his early classical studies. Pater's somewhat painful seeking for precision of expression resulted in a style more delicate and rhythmical than direct and simple. His philosophy of temperance, discipline, and asceticism in art has had a permanent and refining influence upon English criticism.

STYLE

Since all progress of mind consists for the most part in differentiation, in the resolution of an obscure and complex object into its component aspects, it is surely the stupidest of losses to confuse things which right reason has put asunder, to lose the sense of achieved distinctions, the distinction between poetry and prose, for instance, or, to speak more exactly, between the laws and characteristic excellences of verse and prose composition. On the other hand, those who have dwelt most emphatically on the distinction between prose and verse, prose and poetry, may sometimes have been tempted to limit the proper functions of prose too narrowly; and this again is at least false economy, as being, in effect, the renunciation of a certain means or faculty, in a world where after all we must needs make the most of things. Critical efforts to limit art *a priori*, by anticipations regarding the natural incapacity of the material with which this or that artist works, as the sculptor with solid form, or the prose-writer with the ordinary language of men, are always liable to be discredited by the facts of artistic production; and while prose is actually found to be a colored thing with Bacon, picturesque with Livy and Carlyle, musical with Cicero and Newman, mystical and intimate with Plato and Michelet and Sir Thomas Browne, exalted or florid, it may be, with Milton and Taylor, it will be useless to protest that it can be nothing at all, except something very tamely and narrowly confined to mainly practical ends — a kind of 'good round-hand'; as useless as the protest that poetry might not touch prosaic subjects as with Wordsworth, or an abstruse matter as with Browning, or treat contemporary life nobly as with Tennyson. In subordination to one essential beauty in all good literary style, in all literature as a fine art, as there are many beauties of poetry, so the beauties of prose are many, and it is the business of criticism to estimate them as such; as it is good in the criticism of verse to look for those hard, logical and quasi-prosaic excellences which that too has, or needs. To find in the poem, amid the flowers, the allusions, the mixed perspectives, of *Lycidas* for instance, the thought, the logical structure: — how wholesome! how delightful! as to identify in prose what we call the poetry, the imaginative power, not treating it as out of place and a kind of vagrant intruder, but by way of an estimate of its rights, that is, of its achieved powers, there.

Dryden, with the characteristic instinct of his age, loved to emphasize the distinction between poetry and prose, the protest against their confusion with each other, coming with somewhat diminished effect from one whose poetry was so prosaic. In truth, his sense of prosaic excellence affected his verse rather than his prose, which is not only fervid, richly figured, poetic, as we say, but vitiated, all unconsciously, by many a scanning line. Setting up correctness, that humble merit of prose, as the central literary excellence, he is really a less correct writer than he may seem, still with an imperfect mastery of the relative pronoun. It might have been foreseen that, in the rotations of mind, the province of poetry in prose would find its assertor; and, a century after Dryden, amid very different intellectual needs, and with the need therefore of great modifications in literary form, the range of the poetic force in literature was effectively enlarged by Wordsworth. The true distinction between prose and poetry he regarded as the almost technical or accidental one of the absence or presence of metrical beauty, or, say! metrical restraint; and for him the opposition came to be between verse and prose of course; but, as the essential dichotomy in this matter, between imaginative and unimaginative writing, parallel to De Quincey's distinction between 'the literature of power and the literature of knowledge,' in the former of which the composer gives us not fact, but his peculiar sense of fact, whether past or present.

Dismissing then, under sanction of Wordsworth, that harsher opposition of poetry to prose, as savoring in fact of the arbitrary psychology of the last century, and with it the prejudice that there can be but one only beauty of prose style, I propose here to point out certain qualities of all literature as a fine art, which, if they apply to the literature of fact, apply still more to the literature of the imaginative sense of fact, while they apply indifferently to verse and prose, so far as either is really imaginative — certain conditions of true art in both alike, which conditions may also contain in them the secret of the proper discrimination and guardianship of the peculiar excellences of either.

The line between fact and something quite different from external fact is, indeed, hard to draw. In Pascal, for instance, in the persuasive writers generally, how difficult to define the point where, from time to time, argument which, if it is to be worth anything at all, must consist of facts or groups of facts, becomes a pleading — a theorem no longer, but essentially an appeal to the reader to catch the writer's spirit, to think with him, if one can or will — an expression no longer of fact but of his sense of it, his peculiar intuition of a world prospective, or discerned below the faulty conditions of the present, in either case changed somewhat from the actual world. In science, on the other hand, in history so far as it conforms to scientific rule, we have a literary domain where the imagination may be thought to be always an intruder. And as, in all science, the functions of literature reduce themselves eventually to the transcribing of fact, so all the excellences of literary form in regard to science are reducible to various kinds of painstaking; this good quality being involved in all 'skilled work' whatever, in the drafting of an act of parliament, as in sewing. Yet here again, the writer's sense of fact, in history especially, and in all those complex subjects which do but lie on the borders of science, will still take the place of fact, in various degrees. Your historian, for instance, with absolutely truthful intention, amid the multitude of facts presented to him must needs select, and in selecting assert something of his own humor, something that comes not of the world without but of a vision within. So Gibbon molds his unwieldy material to a preconceived view. Livy, Tacitus, Michelet, moving full of poignant sensibility amid the records of the past, each, after his own sense, modifies — who can tell where and to what degree? — and becomes something else than a transcriber; each, as he thus modifies, passing into the domain of art proper. For just in proportion as the writer's aim, consciously or unconsciously, comes to be the transcribing, not of the world, not of mere fact, but of his sense of it, he becomes an artist, his work *fine* art; and good art (as I hope ultimately to show) in proportion to the truth of his presentment of that sense; as in those humbler or plainer functions of literature also, truth — truth to bare fact, there — is the essence of such artistic quality as they may have. Truth! there can be no merit, no craft at all, without that. And further, all beauty is in the long run only *fineness* of truth, or what we call expression, the finer accommodation of speech to that vision within.

— The transcript of his sense of fact rather than the fact, as being preferable, pleasanter, more beautiful to the writer himself. In literature, as in every other product of human skill, in the molding of a bell or a platter for instance, wherever this sense asserts itself, wherever the producer so modifies his work as, over and above its primary use or intention, to make it pleasing (to himself, of course, in the first instance) there, 'fine' as opposed to merely serviceable art, exists. Literary art, that is, like all art which is in any way imitative or reproductive of fact — form, or color, or incident — is the representation of such fact as connected with soul, of a specific personality, in its preferences, its volition and power.

Such is the matter of imaginative or artistic literature — this transcript, not of mere fact, but of fact in its infinite variety, as modified by human preference in all its infinitely varied forms. It will be good literary art not because it is brilliant or sober, or rich, or impulsive, or severe, but just in proportion as its representation of that sense, that soul-fact, is true, verse being only one department of such literature, and imaginative prose, it may be thought, being the special art of the modern world.

That imaginative prose should be the special and opportune art of the modern world results from two important facts about the latter: first, the chaotic variety and complexity of its interests, making the intellectual issue, the really master currents of the present time incalculable — a condition of mind little susceptible of the restraint proper to verse form, so that the most characteristic verse of the nineteenth century has been lawless verse; and secondly, an all-pervading naturalism, a curiosity about everything whatever as it really is, involving a certain humility of attitude, cognate to what must, after all, be the less ambitious form of literature. And prose thus asserting itself as the special and privileged artistic faculty of the present day, will be, however critics may try to narrow its scope, as varied in its excellence as humanity itself reflecting on the facts of its latest experience — an instrument of many stops, meditative, observant, descriptive, eloquent, analytic, plaintive, fervid. Its beauties will be not exclusively 'pedestrian': it will exert, in due measure, all the varied charms of poetry, down to the rhythm which, as in Cicero, or Michelet, or Newman, at their best, gives its musical value to every syllable.

The literary artist is of necessity a scholar, and in what he proposes to do will have in mind, first of all, the scholar and the scholarly conscience — the male conscience in this matter, as we must think it, under a system of education which still to so large an extent limits real scholarship to men. In his self-criticism, he supposes always that sort of reader who will go (full of eyes) warily, considerately, though without consideration for him, over the ground which the female conscience traverses so lightly, so amiably. For the material in which he works is no more a creation of his own than the sculptor's marble. Product of a myriad various minds and contending tongues, compact of obscure and minute association, a language has its own abundant and often recondite laws, in the habitual and summary recognition of which scholarship consists. A writer, full of a matter he is before all things anxious to express, may think of those laws, the limitations of vocabulary, structure, and the like, as a restriction, but if a real artist, will find in them an opportunity. His punctilious observance of the proprieties of his medium will diffuse through all he writes a general air of sensibility, of refined usage. *Exclusiones debitae naturae* — the exclusions, or rejections, which nature demands — we know how large a part these play, according to Bacon, in the science of nature. In a somewhat changed sense, we might say that the art of the scholar is summed up in the observance of those rejections demanded by the nature of his medium, the material he must use. Alive to the value of an atmosphere in which every term finds its utmost degree of expression, and with all the jealousy of a lover of words, he will resist a constant tendency on the part of the majority of those who use them to efface the distinctions of language, the facility of writers often reinforcing in this respect the work of the vulgar. He will feel the obligation not of the laws only, but of those affinities, avoidances, those mere preferences, of his language, which through the associations of literary history have become a part of its nature, prescribing the rejection of many a neology, many a license, many a gipsy phrase which might present itself as actually expressive. His appeal, again, is to the scholar, who has great experience in literature, and will show no favor to short-cuts, or hackneyed illustration, or an affectation of learning designed for the unlearned. Hence a contention, a sense of self-restraint and renunciation, having for the susceptible reader the effect of a challenge for minute consideration; the attention of the writer, in every minutest detail, being a pledge that it is worth the reader's while to be attentive too, that the writer is dealing scrupulously with his instrument, and therefore, indirectly, with the reader himself also, that he has the science of the instrument he plays on, perhaps, after all, with a freedom which in such case will be the freedom of a master.

For meanwhile, braced only by those restraints, he is really vindicating his liberty in the making of a vocabulary, an entire system of composition, for himself, his own true manner; and when we speak of the manner of a true master we mean what is essential in his art. Pedantry being only the scholarship of *le cuistre* (we have no English equivalent), he is no pedant, and does but show his intelligence of the rules of language in his freedoms with it, addition or expansion, which like the spontaneities of manner in a well-bred person will still further illustrate good taste. — The right vocabulary! Translators have not invariably seen how all-important that is in the work of translation, driving for the most part at idiom or construction; whereas, if the original be first-rate, one's first care should be with its elementary particles, Plato, for instance, being often reproducible by an exact following, with no variation in structure, of word after word, as the pencil follows a drawing under tracing-paper, so only each word or syllable be not of false color, to change my illustration a little.

Well! that is because any writer worth translating at all has winnowed and searched through his vocabulary, is conscious of the words he would select in systematic reading of a dictionary, and still more of the words he would reject were the dictionary other than Johnson's; and doing this with his peculiar sense of the world ever in view, in search of an instrument for the adequate expression of that, he begets a vocabulary faithful to the coloring of his own spirit, and in the strictest sense original. That living authority which language needs lies, in truth, in its scholars, who recognizing always that every language possesses a genius, a very fastidious genius, of its own, expand at once and purify its very elements, which must needs change along with the changing thoughts of living people. Ninety years ago, for instance, great mental force, certainly, was needed by Wordsworth, to break through the consecrated poetic associations of a century, and speak the language that was his, that was to become in a measure the language of the next generation. But he did it with the tact of a scholar also. English, for a quarter of a century past, has been assimilating the phraseology of pictorial art; for half a century, the phraseology of the great German metaphysical movement of eighty years ago; in part also the language of mystical theology: and none but pedants will regret a great consequent increase of its resources. For many years to come its enterprise may well lie in the naturalization of the vocabulary of science, so only it be under the eye of sensitive scholarship — in a liberal naturalization of the ideas of science too, for after all, the chief stimulus of good style is to possess a full, rich, complex matter to grapple with. The literary artist, therefore, will be well aware of physical science; science also attaining, in its turn, its true literary ideal. And then, as the scholar is nothing without the historic sense, he will be apt to restore not really obsolete or really worn-out words, but the finer edge of words still in use: *ascertain, communicate, discover* — words like these it has been part of our 'business' to misuse. And still, as language was made for man, he will be no authority for correctnesses which, limiting freedom of utterance, were yet but accidents in their origin; as if one vowed not to say '*its*,' which ought to have been in Shakspere; '*his*' and '*hers*,' for inanimate objects, being but a barbarous and really inexpressive survival. Yet we have known many things like this. Racy Saxon monosyllables, close to us as touch and sight, he will intermix readily with those long, savorsome, Latin words, rich in 'second intention.' In this late day certainly, no critical process can be conducted reasonably without eclecticism. Of such eclecticism we have a justifying example in one of the first poets of our time. How illustrative of monosyllabic effect, of sonorous Latin, of the phraseology of science, of metaphysic, of colloquialism even, are the writings of Tennyson; yet with what a fine, fastidious scholarship throughout!

A scholar writing for the scholarly, he will of course leave something to the willing intelligence of his reader. 'To go preach to the first passer-by,' says Montaigne, 'to become tutor to the ignorance of the first I meet, is a thing I abhor;' a thing, in fact, naturally distressing to the scholar, who will therefore ever be shy of offering uncomplimentary assistance to the reader's wit. To really strenuous minds there is a pleasurable stimulus in the challenge for a continuous effort on their part, to be rewarded by securer and more intimate grasp of the author's sense. Self-restraint, a skilful economy of means, *ascêsis,* that too has a beauty of its own; and for the reader supposed, there will be an esthetic satisfaction in that frugal closeness of style which makes the most of a word, in the exaction from every sentence of a precise relief, in the just spacing out of word to thought, in the logically filled space connected always with the delightful sense of difficulty overcome.

Different classes of persons, at different times, make, of course, very various demands upon literature. Still, scholars, I suppose, and not only scholars, but all disinterested lovers of books, will always look to it, as to all other fine art, for a refuge, a sort of cloistral refuge, from a certain vulgarity in the actual world. A perfect poem like *Lycidas,* a perfect fiction like *Esmond,* the perfect handling of a theory like Newman's *Idea of a University,* has for them something of the uses of a religious 'retreat.' Here, then, with a view to the central need of a select few, those 'men of a finer thread' who have formed and maintain the literary ideal, everything, every component element will have undergone exact trial, and, above all, there will be no uncharacteristic or tarnished or vulgar decoration, permissible ornament being for the most part structural, or necessary. As the painter in his picture, so the artist in his book, aims at the production by honorable artifice of a peculiar atmosphere. 'The artist,' says Schiller, 'may be known rather by what he *omits;*' and in literature, too, the true artist may be best recognized by his tact of omission. For to the grave reader words too are grave; and the ornamental word, the figure, the accessory form or color or reference, is rarely content to die to thought precisely at the right moment, but will inevitably linger awhile, stirring a long 'brain-wave' behind it of perhaps quite alien associations.

Just there, it may be, is the detrimental tendency of the sort of scholarly attentiveness of mind I am recommending. But the true artist allows for it. He will remember that, as the very word ornament indicates what is in itself non-essential, so the 'one beauty' of all literary style is of its very essence, and independent, in prose and verse alike, of all removable decoration; that it may exist in its fullest luster, as in Flaubert's *Madame Bovary,* for instance, or in Stendhal's *Le Rouge et Le Noir,* in a composition utterly unadorned, with hardly a single suggestion of visibly beautiful things. Parallel, allusion, the allusive way generally, the flowers in the garden: — he knows the narcotic force of these upon the negligent intelligence to which any *diversion,* literally, is welcome, any vagrant intruder, because one can go wandering away with it from the immediate subject. Jealous, if he have a really quickening motive within, of all that does not hold directly to that, of the facile, the otiose, he will never depart from the strictly pedestrian process, unless he gains a ponderable something thereby. Even assured of its congruity, he will still question its serviceableness. Is it worth while, can we afford, to attend to just that, to just that figure or literary reference, just then? — Surplusage! he will dread that, as the runner on his muscles. For in truth all art does but consist in the removal of surplusage, from the last finish of the gem-engraver blowing away the last particle of invisible dust, back to the earliest divination of the finished work to be, lying somewhere, according to Michelangelo's fancy, in the rough-hewn block of stone.

And what applies to figure or flower must be understood of all other accidental or removable ornaments of writing whatever; and not of specific ornament only, but of all that latent color and imagery which language as such carries in it. A lover of words for their own sake, to whom nothing about them is unimportant, a minute and constant observer of their physiognomy, he will be on the alert not only for obviously mixed metaphors of course, but for the metaphor that is mixed in all our speech, though a rapid use may involve no cognition of it. Currently recognizing the incident, the color, the physical elements or particles in words like *absorb, consider, extract,* to take the first that occur, he will avail himself of them. As further

adding to the resources of expression. The elementary particles of language will be realized as color and light and shade through his scholarly living in the full sense of them. Still opposing the constant degradation of language by those who use it carelessly, he will not treat colored glass as if it were clear; and while half the world is using figure unconsciously, will be fully aware not only of all that latent figurative texture in speech, but of the vague, lazy, half-formed personification — a rhetoric, depressing, and worse than nothing, because it has no really rhetorical motive — which plays so large a part there, and, as in the case of more ostentatious ornament, scrupulously exact of it, from syllable to syllable, its precise value.

So far I have been speaking of certain conditions of the literary art arising out of the medium or material in or upon which it works, the essential qualities of language and its aptitudes for contingent ornamentation, matters which define scholarship as science and good taste respectively. They are both subservient to a more intimate quality of good style: more intimate, as coming nearer to the artist himself. The otiose, the facile, surplusage: why are these abhorrent to the true literary artist, except because, in literary as in all other art, structure is all-important, felt, or painfully missed, everywhere? — that architectural conception of work, which foresees the end in the beginning and never loses sight of it, and in every part is conscious of all the rest, till the last sentence does but, with undiminished vigor, unfold and justify the first — a condition of literary art, which, in contra-distinction to another quality of the artist himself, to be spoken of later, I shall call the necessity of *mind* in style.

An acute philosophical writer, the late Dean Mansel (a writer whose works illustrate the literary beauty there may be in closeness, and with obvious repression or economy of a fine rhetorical gift) wrote a book, of fascinating precision in a very obscure subject, to show that all the technical laws of logic are but means of securing, in each and all of its apprehensions, the unity, the strict identity with itself, of the apprehending mind. All the laws of good writing aim at a similar unity or identity of the mind in all the processes by which the word is associated to its import. The term is right, and has its essential beauty, when it becomes, in a manner, what it signifies, as with the names of simple sensations. To give the phrase, the sentence, the structural member, the entire composition, song, or essay, a similar unity with its subject and with itself: —style is in the right way when it tends towards that. All depends upon the original unity, the vital wholeness and identity, of the initiatory apprehension or view. So much is true of all art, which therefore requires always its logic, its comprehensive reason — insight, foresight, retrospect, in simultaneous action — true, most of all, of the literary art, as being of all the arts most closely cognate to the abstract intelligence. Such logical coherency may be evidenced not merely in the lines of composition as a whole, but in the choice of a single word, while it by no means interferes with, but may even prescribe, much variety, in the building of the sentence for instance, or in the manner, argumentative, descriptive, discursive, of this or that part or member of the entire design. The blithe, crisp sentence, decisive as a child's expression of its needs, may alternate with the long-contending, victoriously intricate sentence; the sentence, born with the integrity of a single word, relieving the sort of sentence in which, if you look closely, you can see much contrivance, much adjustment, to bring a highly qualified matter into compass at one view. For the literary architecture, if it is to be rich and expressive, involves not only foresight of the end in the beginning, but also development or growth of design, in the process of execution, with many irregularities, surprises, and after-thoughts; the contingent as well as the necessary being subsumed under the unity of the whole. As truly, to the lack of such architectural design, of a single, almost visual, image, vigorously informing an entire, perhaps very intricate, composition, which shall be austere, ornate, argumentative, fanciful, yet true from first to last to that vision within, may be attributed those weaknesses of conscious or unconscious repetition of word, phrase,

motive, or member of the whole matter, indicating, as Flaubert was aware, an original structure in thought not organically complete. With such foresight, the actual conclusion will most often get itself written out of hand, before, in the more obvious sense, the work is finished. With some strong and leading sense of the world, the tight hold of which secures true *composition* and not mere loose accretion, the literary artist, I suppose, goes on considerably, setting joint to joint, sustained by yet restraining the productive ardor, retracing the negligences of his first sketch, repeating his steps only that he may give the reader a sense of secure and restful progress, readjusting mere assonances even, that they may soothe the reader, or at least not interrupt him on his way; and then, somewhere before the end comes, is burdened, inspired, with his conclusion, and betimes delivered of it, leaving off, not in weariness and because he finds *himself* at an end, but in all the freshness of volition. His work now structurally complete, with all the accumulating effect of secondary shades of meaning, he finishes the whole up to the just proportion of that ante-penultimate conclusion, and all becomes expressive. The house he has built is rather a body he has informed. And so it happens, to its greater credit, that the better interest even of a narrative to be recounted, a story to be told, will often be in its second reading. And though there are instances of great writers who have been no artists, an unconscious tact sometimes directing work in which we may detect, very pleasurably, many of the effects of conscious art, yet one of the greatest pleasures of really good prose literature is in the critical tracing out of that conscious artistic structure, and the pervading sense of it as we read. Yet of poetic literature too; for, in truth, the kind of constructive intelligence here supposed is one of the forms of the imagination. That is the special function of mind, in style. Mind and soul,— hard to ascertain philosophically, the distinction is real enough practically, for they often interfere, are sometimes in conflict, with each other. Blake, in the last century, is an instance of preponderating soul, embarrassed, at a loss, in an era of preponderating mind. As a quality of style, at all events, soul is a fact, in certain writers — the way they have of absorbing language, of attracting it into the peculiar spirit they are of, with a subtlety which makes the actual result seem like some inexplicable inspiration. By mind, the literary artist reaches us, through static and objective indications of design in his work, legible to all. By soul, he reaches us, somewhat capriciously perhaps, one and not another, through vagrant sympathy and a kind of immediate contact. Mind we cannot choose but approve where we recognize it; soul may repel us, not because we misunderstand it. The way in which theological interests sometimes avail themselves of language is perhaps the best illustration of the force I mean to indicate generally in literature, by the word *soul*. Ardent religious persuasion may exist, may make its way, without finding any equivalent heat in language: or, again, it may enkindle words to various degrees, and when it really takes hold of them doubles its force. Religious history presents many remarkable instances in which, through no mere phrase-worship, an unconscious literary tact has, for the sensitive, laid open a privileged pathway from one to another. 'The altar-fire,' people say, 'has touched those lips!' The Vulgate, the English Bible, the English Prayer-Book, the writings of Swedenborg, the Tracts for the Times: — there, we have instances of widely different and largely diffused phases of religious feeling in operation as soul in style. But something of the same kind acts with similar power in certain writers of quite other than theological literature, on behalf of some wholly personal and peculiar sense of theirs. Most easily illustrated by theological literature, this quality lends to profane writers a kind of religious influence. At their best, these writers become, as we say sometimes, 'prophets'; such character depending on the effect not merely of their matter, but of their matter as allied to, in 'electric affinity' with, peculiar form, and working in all cases by an immediate sympathetic contact, on which account it is that it may be called soul, as opposed to mind, in style. And this too is a faculty

of choosing and rejecting what is congruous or otherwise, with a drift towards unity — unity of atmosphere here, as there of design — soul securing color (or perfume, might we say?) as mind secures form, the latter being essentially finite, the former vague or infinite, as the influence of a living person is practically infinite. There are some to whom nothing has any real interest, or real meaning, except as operative in a given person; and it is they who best appreciate the quality of soul in literary art. They seem to know a *person,* in a book, and make way by intuition: yet, although they thus enjoy the completeness of a personal information, it is still a characteristic of soul, in this sense of the word, that it does but suggest what can never be uttered, not as being different from, or more obscure than, what actually gets said, but as containing that plenary substance of which there is only one phase or facet in what is there expressed.

If all high things have their martyrs, Gustave Flaubert might perhaps rank as the martyr of literary style. In his printed correspondence, a curious series of letters, written in his twenty-fifth year, records what seems to have been his one other passion — a series of letters which, with its fine casuistries, its firmly repressed anguish, its tone of harmonious gray, and the sense of disillusion in which the whole matter ends, might have been, a few slight changes supposed, one of his own fictions. Writing to Madame X. certainly he does display, by 'taking thought' mainly, by constant and delicate pondering, as in his love for literature, a heart really moved, but still more, and as the pledge of that emotion, a loyalty to his work. Madame X., too, is a literary artist, and the best gifts he can send her are precepts of perfection in art, counsels for the effectual pursuit of that better love. In his love-letters it is the pains and pleasures of art he insists on, its solaces: he communicates secrets, reproves, encourages, with a view to that. Whether the lady was dissatisfied with such divided or indirect service, the reader is not enabled to see; but sees that, on Flaubert's part at least, a living person could be no rival of what was, from first to last, hi₌

leading passion, a somewhat solitary and exclusive one.

'I must scold you,' he writes, 'for one thing, which shocks, scandalizes me, the small concern, namely, you show for art just now. As regards glory be it so: there, I approve. But for art!— the one thing in life that is good and real — can you compare with it an earthly love? — prefer the adoration of a relative beauty to the *cultus* of the true beauty? Well! I tell you the truth. That is the one thing good in me: the one thing I have, to me estimable. For yourself, you blend with the beautiful a heap of alien things, the useful, the agreeable, what not? —

'The only way not to be unhappy is to shut yourself up in art, and count everything else as nothing. Pride takes the place of all beside when it is established on a large basis. Work! God wills it. That, it seems to me, is clear.—

'I am reading over again the *Æneid,* certain verses of which I repeat to myself to satiety. There are phrases there which stay in one's head, by which I find myself beset, as with those musical airs which are forever returning, and cause you pain, you love them so much. I observe that I no longer laugh much, and am no longer depressed. I am ripe. You talk of my serenity, and envy me. It may well surprise you. Sick, irritated, the prey a thousand times a day of cruel pain, I continue my labor like a true working-man, who, with sleeves turned up, in the sweat of his brow, beats away at his anvil, never troubling himself whether it rains or blows, for hail or thunder. I was not like that formerly. The change has taken place naturally, though my will has counted for something in the matter.—

'Those who write in good style are sometimes accused of a neglect of ideas, and of the moral end, as if the end of the physician were something else than healing, of the painter than painting — as if the end of art were not, before all else, the beautiful.'

What, then, did Flaubert understand by beauty, in the art he pursued with so much fervor, with so much self-command? Let us hear a sympathetic commentator: —

'Possessed of an absolute belief that there exists but one way of expressing one thing, one word to call it by, one adjective to qualify, one verb to animate it, he gave himself to superhuman labor for the discovery, in every phrase, of that word, that verb, that epithet. In this way, he believed in some mysterious harmony of expression, and when a true word seemed to him to lack euphony still went on seeking another, with invincible patience, certain that he had not yet got hold of the *unique* word. . . . A thousand preoccupations would beset him at the same moment, always with this desperate certitude fixed in his spirit: Among all the expressions in the world, all forms and turns of expression, there is but *one* — one form, one mode — to express what I want to say.'

The one word for the one thing, the one thought, amid the multitude of words, terms, that might just do: the problem of style was there! — the unique word, phrase, sentence, paragraph, essay, or song, absolutely proper to the single mental presentation or vision within. In that perfect justice, over and above the many contingent and removable beauties with which beautiful style may charm us, but which it can exist without, independent of them yet dexterously availing itself of them, omnipresent in good work, in function at every point, from single epithets to the rhythm of a whole book, lay the specific, indispensable, very intellectual, beauty of literature, the possibility of which constitutes it a fine **art.**

One seems to detect the influence of a philosophic idea there, the idea of a natural economy, of some preëxistent adaptation, between a relative, somewhere in the world of thought, and its correlative, somewhere in the world of language — both alike, rather, somewhere in the mind of the artist, desiderative, expectant, inventive — meeting each other with the readiness of 'soul and body reunited,' in Blake's rapturous design; and, in fact, Flaubert was fond of giving his theory philosophical expression.—

'There are no beautiful thoughts,' he would say, 'without beautiful forms, and conversely. As it is impossible to extract from a physical body the qualities which really constitute it — color, extension, and the like — without reducing it to a hollow abstraction, in a word, without destroying it; just so it is impossible to detach the form from the idea, for the idea only exists by virtue of the form.'

All the recognized flowers, the removable ornaments of literature (including harmony and ease in reading aloud, very carefully considered by him) counted certainly; for these too are part of the actual value of what one says. But still, after all, with Flaubert, the search, the unwearied research, was not for the smooth, or winsome, or forcible word, as such, as with false Ciceronians, but quite simply and honestly for the word's adjustment to its meaning. The first condition of this must be, of course, to know yourself, to have ascertained your own sense exactly. Then, if we suppose an artist, he says to the reader,— I want you to see precisely what I see. Into the mind sensitive to 'form,' a flood of random sounds, colors, incidents, is ever penetrating from the world without, to become, by sympathetic selection, a part of its very structure, and, in turn, the visible vesture and expression of that other world it sees so steadily within, nay, already with a partial conformity thereto, to be refined, enlarged, corrected, at a hundred points; and it is just there, just at those doubtful points that the function of style, as tact or taste, intervenes. The unique term will come more quickly to one than another, at one time than another, according also to the kind of matter in question. Quickness and slowness, ease and closeness alike, have nothing to do with the artistic character of the true word found at last. As there is a charm of ease, so there is also a special charm in the signs of discovery, of effort and contention towards a due end, as so often with Flaubert himself — in the style which has been pliant, as only obstinate, durable metal can be, to the inherent perplexities and recusancy of a certain difficult thought.

If Flaubert had not told us, perhaps we should never have guessed how tardy and painful his own procedure really was, and after reading his confession may think that his almost endless hesitation had much to do with diseased nerves. Often, perhaps, the felicity supposed will be the product of a happier, a more exuberant nature than Flaubert's. Aggravated, certainly, by a morbid physical condition, that anxiety in 'seeking the phrase,' which gathered all the other small *ennuis* of a really quiet existence into a kind of battle, was connected with his lifelong contention against facile poetry, facile art — art, facile and flimsy; and what constitutes the true artist is not the slowness or quickness of the process, but the absolute success of the result. As with those laborers in the parable, the prize is independent of the mere length of the actual day's work. 'You talk,' he writes, odd, trying lover, to Madame X.—

'You talk of the exclusiveness of my literary tastes. That might have enabled you to divine what kind of a person I am in the matter of love. I grow so hard to please as a literary artist, that I am driven to despair. I shall end by not writing another line.'

'Happy,' he cries, in a moment of discouragement at that patient labor, which for him, certainly, was the condition of a great success.—

'Happy those who have no doubts of themselves! who lengthen out, as the pen runs on, all that flows forth from their brains. As for me, I hesitate, I disappoint myself, turn round upon myself in despite: my taste is augmented in proportion as my natural vigor decreases, and I afflict my soul over some dubious word out of all proportion to the pleasure I get from a whole page of good writing. One would have to live two centuries to attain a true idea of any matter whatever. What Buffon said is a big blasphemy: genius is not long-continued patience. Still, there is some truth in the statement, and more than people think, especially as regards our own day. Art! art! art! bitter deception! phantom that glows with light, only to lead one on to destruction.'

Again —

'I am growing so peevish about my writing. I am like a man whose ear is true but who plays falsely on the violin: his fingers refuse to reproduce precisely those sounds of which he has the inward sense. Then the tears come rolling down from the poor scraper's eyes and the bow falls from his hand.'

Coming slowly or quickly, when it comes, as it came with so much labor of mind, but also with so much luster, to Gustave Flaubert, this discovery of the word will be, like all artistic success and felicity, incapable of strict analysis: effect of an intuitive condition of mind, it must be recognized by like intuition on the part of the reader, and a sort of immediate sense. In every one of those masterly sentences of Flaubert there was, below all mere contrivance, shaping and afterthought, by some happy instantaneous concourse of the various faculties of the mind with each other, the exact apprehension of what was *needed* to carry the meaning. And that it fits with absolute justice will be a judgment of immediate sense in the appreciative reader. We all feel this in what may be called inspired translation. Well! all language involves translation from inward to outward. In literature, as in all forms of art, there are the absolute and the merely relative or accessory beauties; and precisely in that exact proportion of the term to its purpose is the absolute beauty of style, prose or verse. All the good qualities, the beauties, of verse also, are such, only as precise expression.

In the highest as in the lowliest literature, then, the one indispensable beauty is, after all, truth: — truth to bare fact in the latter, as to some personal sense of fact, diverted somewhat from men's ordinary sense of it, in the former; truth there as accuracy, truth here as expression, that finest and most intimate form of truth, the *vraie vérité*. And what an eclectic principle this really is! employing for its one sole purpose — that absolute accordance of expression to idea — all other literary beauties and excellences whatever: how many kinds of style it covers, explains, justifies, and at the same time safeguards! Scott's facility, Flaubert's deeply pondered evocation of 'the phrase,' are equally good art. Say what you have to say, what you have a will to say, in the simplest, the most direct and exact manner possible, with no surplusage: — there, is the justification of the sentence so fortunately born, 'entire, smooth, and round,' that it needs no punctuation, and also (that is the point!) of the most elaborate period, if it be right in its elaboration. Here is the office of ornament: here also the purpose of restraint in ornament. As the exponent of truth, that austerity (the beauty, the function, of which in literature Flaubert understood so well) becomes not the correctness or purism of the mere scholar, but a security against the otiose, a jealous exclusion of what does not really tell towards the pursuit of relief, of life and vigor in the portraiture of one's sense. License again, the making free with rule, if it be indeed, as people fancy, a habit of genius, flinging aside or transforming all that opposes the liberty of beautiful production, will be but faith to one's own meaning. The seeming baldness of *Le Rouge et Le Noir* is nothing in itself; the wild ornament of *Les Misérables* is nothing in itself; and the restraint of Flaubert, amid a real natural opulence, only redoubled beauty — the phrase so large and so precise at the same time, hard as bronze, in service to the more perfect adaptation of words to their matter. Afterthoughts, retouchings, finish, will be of profit only so far as they too really serve to bring out the original, initiative, generative, sense in them.

In this way, according to the well-known saying, 'The style is the man,' complex for simple, in his individuality, his plenary sense of what he really has to say, his sense of the world; all cautions regarding style arising out of so many natural scruples as to the medium through which alone he can expose that inward sense of things, the purity of this medium, its laws or tricks of refraction: nothing is to be left there which might give conveyance to any matter save that. Style in all its varieties, reserved or opulent, terse, abundant, musical, stimulant, academic, so long as each is really characteristic or expressive, finds thus its justification, the sumptuous good taste of Cicero being as truly the man himself, and not another, justified, yet insured inalienably to him, thereby, as would have been his portrait by Raphael, in full consular splendor, on his ivory chair.

A relegation, you may say perhaps — a relegation of style to the subjectivity, the mere caprice, of the individual, which must soon transform it into mannerism. Not so! since there is, under the conditions supposed, for those elements of the man, for every lineament of the vision within, the one word, the one acceptable word, recognizable by the sensitive, by others 'who have intelligence' in the matter, as absolutely as ever anything can be in the evanescent and delicate region

.of human language. The style, the manner, would be the man, not in his unreasoned and really uncharacteristic caprices, involuntary or affected, but in absolutely sincere apprehension of what is most real to him. But let us hear our French guide again.—

'Styles,' says Flaubert's commentator, 'Styles, as so many peculiar molds, each of which bears the mark of a particular writer, who is to pour into it the whole content of his ideas, were no part of his theory. What he believed in was *Style*: that is to say, a certain absolute and unique manner of expressing a thing, in all its intensity and color. For him the *form* was the work itself. As in living creatures, the blood, nourishing the body, determines its very contour and external aspect, just so, to his mind, the *matter*, the basis, in a work of art, imposed necessarily, the unique, the just expression, the measure, the rhythm — the *form* in all its characteristics.'

If the style be the man, in all the color and intensity of a veritable apprehension, it will be in a real sense 'impersonal.'

I said, thinking of books like Victor Hugo's *Les Misérables*, that prose literature was the characteristic art of the nineteenth century, as others, thinking of its triumphs since the youth of Bach, have assigned that place to music. Music and prose literature are, in one sense, the opposite terms of art; the art of literature presenting to the imagination, through the intelligence, a range of interests, as free and various as those which music presents to it through sense. And certainly the tendency of what has been here said is to bring literature too under those conditions, by conformity to which music takes rank as the typically perfect art. If music be the ideal of all art whatever, precisely because in music it is impossible to distinguish the form from the substance or matter, the subject from the expression, then, literature, by finding its specific excellence in the absolute correspondence of the term to its import, will be but fulfilling the condition of all artistic quality in things everywhere, of all good art.

Good art, but not necessarily great art; the distinction between great art and good art depending immediately, as regards literature at all events, not on its form, but on the matter. Thackeray's *Esmond*, surely, is greater art than *Vanity Fair*, by the greater dignity of its interests. It is on the quality of the matter it informs or controls, its compass, its variety, its alliance to great ends, or the depth of the note of revolt, or the largeness of hope in it, that the greatness of literary art depends, as *The Divine Comedy, Paradise Lost, Les Misérables, The English Bible,* are great art. Given the conditions I have tried to explain as constituting good art; — then, if it be devoted further to the increase of men's happiness, to the redemption of the oppressed, or the enlargement of our sympathies with each other, or to such presentment of new or old truth about ourselves and our relation to the world as may ennoble and fortify us in our sojourn here, or immediately, as with Dante, to the glory of God, it will be also great art; if, over and above those qualities I summed up as mind and soul — that color and mystic perfume, and that reasonable structure, it has something of the soul of humanity in it, and finds its logical, its architectural place, in the great structure of human life. (1888)

ROBERT LOUIS STEVENSON (1850–1894).

Stevenson's great-grandfather, grandfather, and father were engineers to the Board of Northern Lighthouses, and he was educated for the family profession. At twenty-one he asked to be allowed to give up engineering for literature, and his father consented on condition that he qualified for the Scottish Bar. Stevenson fulfilled the condition, but took as little interest in his legal as in his engineering studies, setting far more store 'by certain other odds and ends that he came by in the open street while he was playing truant.' At his chosen pursuit of literature, however, he toiled incessantly. He says: 'I imagine nobody had ever such pains to learn a trade as I had; but I slogged at it day in and day out; and I frankly believe (thanks to my dire industry) I have done more with smaller gifts than almost any man of letters in the world.' As a schoolboy he edited magazines and wrote essays, stories and plays; his first novel was turned into a historical essay and privately printed when he was sixteen. As an undergraduate at Edinburgh he established the University Magazine which 'ran four months in undisturbed obscurity and died without a gasp.' In 1873-4 he had half-a-dozen articles in various magazines, and his first book, *An Inland Voyage,* was published in 1878. It is an account of a canoe trip in Belgium and France made two years earlier. About this time Stevenson met and fell in love with Mrs. Fanny Osbourne, an American lady who came to study art in France. In 1878 she returned to California, and thither in 1879 Stevenson followed her. Some of his experiences in crossing the Atlantic and the American continent (though by no means all the sufferings he endured) are told in *The Amateur Emigrant* and *Across the Plains.* He arrived at San Francisco in desperate straits of health and pocket, and only Mrs. Osbourne's devoted nursing saved his life. After his recovery, they were married, and spent their honeymoon in the neighboring mountains, described in *The Silverado Squatters.* His first volume of essays, *Virginibus Puerisque,* was highly appreciated, but only by a few: it was a book for boys, *Treasure Island,* which made him suddenly famous. *Dr. Jekyll and Mr. Hyde* and *Kidnapped* were equally successful. During these years he was living in various health resorts in Europe and America; in 1888 he went for a long voyage in the Pacific, at the end of which he bought an estate and settled in Samoa. He endeared himself to the natives, and in spite of continued illness, did some of his best literary work. The year before his death he wrote: 'For fourteen years I have not had a day's real health; I have wakened sick and gone to bed weary; and I have done my work unflinchingly. I have written in bed, and written out of it, written in hemorrhages, written in sickness, written torn by coughing, written when my hand swam for weakness; and for so long, it seems to me I have won my wager and recovered my glove. I am better now, have been, rightly speaking, since first I came to the Pacific; and still, few are the days when I am not in some physical distress. And the battle goes on — ill or well, is a trifle: so as it goes. I was made for a contest, and the Powers have so willed that my battlefield should be this dingy, inglorious one of the bed and the physic bottle.' He was buried at the top of the mountain overlooking his Samoan home in a tomb inscribed with his own *Requiem:*

> Under the wide and starry sky,
> Dig the grave and let me lie.
> Glad did I live and gladly die,
> And I laid me down with a will.
> This be the verse you grave for me:
> *Here he lies where he longed to be;*
> *Home is the sailor, home from sea,*
> *And the hunter home from the hill.*

THE FOREIGNER AT HOME

'This is no my ain house;
   I ken by the biggin' o't.'

Two recent books,[1] one by Mr. Grant
White on England, one on France by the
diabolically clever Mr. Hillebrand, may
well have set people thinking on the divisions of races and nations. Such
thoughts should arise with particular congruity and force to inhabitants of that
United Kingdom, people from so many
different stocks, babbling so many different dialects, and offering in its extent
such singular contrasts, from the busiest
over-population to the unkindliest desert,
from the Black Country to the Moor of
Rannoch. It is not only when we cross
the seas that we go abroad; there are
foreign parts of England; and the race
that has conquered so wide an empire
has not yet managed to assimilate the
islands whence she sprang. Ireland,
Wales, and the Scottish mountains still
cling, in part, to their old Gaelic speech.
It was but the other day that English
triumphed in Cornwall, and they still
show in Mousehole, on St. Michael's Bay,
the house of the last Cornish-speaking
woman. English itself, which will now
frank the traveler through the most of
North America, through the greater South
Sea Islands, in India, along much of the
coast of Africa, and in the ports of China
and Japan, is still to be heard, in its home
country, in half a hundred varying stages
of transition. You may go all over the
States, and — setting aside the actual in-
trusion and influence of foreigners, negro,
French, or Chinese — you shall scarce
meet with so marked a difference of accent as in the forty miles between Edinburgh and Glasgow, or of dialect as in
the hundred miles between Edinburgh and
Aberdeen. Book English has gone round
the world, but at home we still preserve
the racy idioms of our fathers, and every
county, in some parts every dale, has its
own quality of speech, vocal or verbal.
In like manner, local custom and
prejudice, even local religion and local
law, linger on into the latter end of the
nineteenth century — *imperia in imperio*
[kingdoms within the kingdom], foreign
things at home.

In spite of these promptings to reflection, ignorance of his neighbors is the
character of the typical John Bull. His
is a domineering nature, steady in fight,
imperious to command, but neither curious nor quick about the life of others.
In French colonies, and still more in the
Dutch, I have read that there is an immediate and lively contact between the
dominant and the dominated race, that a
certain sympathy is begotten, or at the
least a transfusion of prejudices, making
life easier for both. But the Englishman sits apart, bursting with pride and
ignorance. He figures among his vassals
in the hour of peace with the same disdainful air that led him on to victory.
A passing enthusiasm for some foreign
art or fashion may deceive the world, it
cannot impose upon his intimates. He
may be amused by a foreigner as by a
monkey, but he will never condescend to
study him with any patience. Miss Bird,
an authoress with whom I profess myself
in love, declares all the viands of Japan
to be uneatable — a staggering pretension.
So, when the Prince of Wales's marriage
was celebrated at Mentone by a dinner
to the Mentonese, it was proposed to give
them solid English fare — roast beef and
plum pudding, and no tomfoolery. Here
we have either pole of the Britannic folly.
We will not eat the food of any foreigner;
nor, when we have the chance, will we
suffer him to eat of it himself. The same
spirit inspired Miss Bird's American
missionaries, who had come thousands of
miles to change the faith of Japan, and
openly professed their ignorance of the
religions they were trying to supplant.

I quote an American in this connection
without scruple. Uncle Sam is better
than John Bull, but he is tarred with the
English stick. For Mr. Grant White the
States are the New England States and
nothing more. He wonders at the amount
of drinking in London; let him try San
Francisco. He wittily reproves English
ignorance as to the status of women in
America; but has he not himself forgotten
Wyoming? The name Yankee, of which
he is so tenacious, is used over the most
of the great Union as a term of reproach.
The Yankee States, of which he is so
staunch a subject, are but a drop in the
bucket. And we find in his book a vast
virgin ignorance of the life and prospects
of America; every view partial, parochial,

[1] 1881.

not raised to the horizon; the moral feeling proper, at the largest, to a clique of States; and the whole scope and atmosphere not American, but merely Yankee. I will go far beyond him in reprobating the assumption and the incivility of my countryfolk to their cousins from beyond the sea; I grill in my blood over the silly rudeness of our newspaper articles; and I do not know where to look when I find myself in company with an American and see my countrymen unbending to him as to a performing dog. But in the case of Mr. Grant White example were better than precept. Wyoming, is, after all, more readily accessible to Mr. White than Boston to the English, and the New England self-sufficiency no better justified than the Britannic.

It is so, perhaps, in all countries; perhaps in all, men are most ignorant of the foreigners at home. John Bull is ignorant of the States; he is probably ignorant of India; but considering his opportunities, he is far more ignorant of countries nearer his own door. There is one country, for instance — its frontier not so far from London, its people closely akin, its language the same in all essentials with the English — of which I will go bail he knows nothing. His ignorance of the sister kingdom cannot be described; it can only be illustrated by anecdote. I once traveled with a man of plausible manners and good intelligence,— a university man, as the phrase goes,— a man, besides, who had taken his degree in life and knew a thing or two about the age we live in. We were deep in talk, whirling between Peterborough and London; among other things, he began to describe some piece of legal injustice he had recently encountered, and I observed in my innocence that things were not so in Scotland. 'I beg your pardon,' said he, 'this is a matter of law.' He had never heard of the Scots law; nor did he choose to be informed. The law was the same for the whole country, he told me roundly; every child knew that. At last, to settle matters, I explained to him that I was a member of a Scottish legal body, and had stood the brunt of an examination in the very law in question. Thereupon he looked me for a moment full in the face and dropped the conversation. This is a monstrous instance, if you like,

but it does not stand alone in the experience of Scots.

England and Scotland differ, indeed, in law, in history, in religion, in education, and in the very look of nature and men's faces, not always widely, but always trenchantly. Many particulars that struck Mr. Grant White, a Yankee, struck me, a Scot, no less forcibly; he and I felt ourselves foreigners on many common provocations. A Scotchman may tramp the better part of Europe and the United States, and never again receive so vivid an impression of foreign travel and strange lands and manners as on his first excursion into England. The change from a hilly to a level country strikes him with delighted wonder. Along the flat horizon there arise the frequent venerable towers of churches. He sees at the end of airy vistas the revolution of the windmill sails. He may go where he pleases in the future; he may see Alps, and Pyramids, and lions; but it will be hard to beat the pleasure of that moment. There are, indeed, few merrier spectacles than that of many windmills bickering together in a fresh breeze over a woody country; their halting alacrity of movement, their pleasant business, making bread all day with uncouth gesticulations, their air, gigantically human, as of a creature half alive, put a spirit of romance into the tamest landscape. When the Scotch child sees them first he falls immediately in love; and from that time forward windmills keep turning in his dreams. And so, in their degree, with every feature of the life and landscape. The warm, habitable age of towns and hamlets, the green, settled, ancient look of the country; the lush hedgerows, stiles and privy pathways in the fields; the sluggish, brimming rivers; chalk and smock-frocks; chimes of bells and the rapid, pertly sounding English speech — they are all new to the curiosity; they are all set to English airs in the child's story that he tells himself at night. The sharp edge of novelty wears off; the feeling is scotched, but I doubt whether it is ever killed. Rather it keeps returning, ever the more rarely and strangely, and even in scenes to which you have been long accustomed suddenly awakes and gives a relish to enjoyment or heightens the sense of isolation.

One thing especially continues unfamiliar to the Scotchman's eye — the domestic architecture, the look of streets and buildings; the quaint, venerable age of many, and the thin walls and warm coloring of all. We have, in Scotland, far fewer ancient buildings, above all in country places; and those that we have are all of hewn or harled masonry. Wood has been sparingly used in their construction; the window-frames are sunken in the wall, not flat to the front, as in England; the roofs are steeper-pitched; even a hill farm will have a massy, square, cold, and permanent appearance. English houses, in comparison, have the look of cardboard toys, such as a puff might shatter. And to this the Scotchman never becomes used. His eye can never rest consciously on one of these brick houses — rickles of brick, as he might call them — or on one of these flat-chested streets, but he is instantly reminded where he is, and instantly travels back in fancy to his home. 'This is no my ain house; I ken by the biggin' o't.' And yet perhaps it is his own, bought with his own money, the key of it long polished in his pocket; but it has not yet, and never will be, thoroughly adopted by his imagination; nor does he cease to remember that, in the whole length and breadth of his native country, there was no building even distantly resembling it.

But it is not alone in scenery and architecture that we count England foreign. The constitution of society, the very pillars of the empire, surprise and even pain us. The dull, neglected peasant, sunk in matter, insolent, gross, and servile, makes a startling contrast with our own long-legged, long-headed, thoughtful, Bible-quoting plowman. A week or two in such a place as Suffolk leaves the Scotchman gasping. It seems incredible that within the boundaries of his own island a class should have been thus forgotten. Even the educated and intelligent, who hold our own opinions and speak in our own words, yet seem to hold them with a difference or from another reason, and to speak on all things with less interest and conviction. The first shock of English society is like a cold plunge. It is possible that the Scot comes looking for too much, and to be sure his first experiment will be in the wrong direction. Yet surely his complaint is grounded; surely the speech of Englishmen is too often lacking in generous ardor, the better part of the man too often withheld from the social commerce, and the contact of mind with mind evaded as with terror. A Scotch peasant will talk more liberally out of his own experience. He will not put you by with conversational counters and small jests; he will give you the best of himself, like one interested in life and man's chief end. A Scotchman is vain, interested in himself and others, eager for sympathy, setting forth his thoughts and experience in the best light. The egoism of the Englishman is self-contained. He does not seek to proselytize. He takes no interest in Scotland or the Scotch, and, what is the unkindest cut of all, he does not care to justify his indifference. Give him the wages of going on and being an Englishman, that is all he asks; and in the meantime, while you continue to associate, he would rather not be reminded of your baser origin. Compared with the grand, tree-like self-sufficiency of his demeanor, the vanity and curiosity of the Scot seem uneasy, vulgar, and immodest. That you should continually try to establish human and serious relations, that you should actually feel an interest in John Bull, and desire and invite a return of interest from him, may argue something more awake and lively in your mind, but it still puts you in the attitude of a suitor and a poor relation. Thus even the lowest class of the educated English towers over a Scotchman by the head and shoulders.

Different indeed is the atmosphere in which Scotch and English youth begin to look about them, come to themselves in life, and gather up those first apprehensions which are the material of future thought and, to a great extent, the rule of future conduct. I have been to school in both countries, and I found, in the boys of the North, something at once rougher and more tender, at once more reserve and more expansion, a greater habitual distance checkered by glimpses of a nearer intimacy, and on the whole wider extremes of temperament and sensibility. The boy of the South seems more wholesome, but less thoughtful; he gives himself to games as to a business, striving to excel, but is not readily transported by imagination; the type remains with me as cleaner in mind and body, more active, fonder of eating, endowed with a lesser and a less romantic sense of life and of the future, and more immersed in present circumstances. And certainly, for one thing, English boys are younger for their age. Sabbath observance make a series of grim, and perhaps serviceable, pauses in the tenor of Scotch boyhood — days of great stillness and solitude for the rebellious mind, when in the dearth of books and play, and in the intervals of studying the Shorter Catechism, the intellect and senses prey upon and test each other. The typical English Sunday, with the huge midday dinner and the plethoric afternoon, leads perhaps to different results. About the very cradle of the Scot there goes a hum of metaphysical divinity; and the whole of two divergent systems is summed up, not merely speciously, in the two first questions of the rival catechisms, the English tritely inquiring, 'What is your name?' the Scottish striking at the very roots of life with, 'What is the chief end of man?' and answering nobly, if obscurely, 'To glorify God and to enjoy Him forever.' I do not wish to make an idol of the Shorter Catechism; but the fact of such a question being asked opens to us Scotch a great field of speculation; and the fact that it is asked of all of us, from the peer to the plowboy, binds us more nearly together. No Englishman of Byron's age, character, and history, would have had patience for long theological discussions on the way to fight for Greece; but the daft Gordon blood and the Aberdonian schooldays kept their influence to the end. We have spoken of the material conditions; nor need much more be said of these: of the land lying everywhere more exposed, of the wind always louder and bleaker, of the black, roaring winters, of the gloom of high-lying, old stone cities, imminent on the windy seaboard; compared with the level streets, the warm coloring of the brick, the domestic quaintness of the architecture, among which English children begin to grow up and come to themselves in life. As the stage of the university approaches, the contrast becomes more express. The English lad goes to Oxford or Cambridge; there,

in an ideal world of gardens, to lead a semi-scenic life, costumed, disciplined, and drilled by proctors. Nor is this to be regarded merely as a stage of education: it is a piece of privilege besides, and a step that separates him further from the bulk of his compatriots. At an earlier age the Scottish lad begins his greatly different experience of crowded classrooms, of a gaunt quadrangle, of a bell hourly booming over the traffic of the city to recall him from the public-house where he has been lunching, or the streets where he has been wandering fancy-free. His college life has little of restraint, and nothing of necessary gentility. He will find no quiet clique of the exclusive, studious, and cultured; no rotten borough of the arts. All classes rub shoulders on the greasy benches. The raffish young gentleman in gloves must measure his scholarship with the plain, clownish laddie from the parish school. They separate, at the session's end, one to smoke cigars about a watering-place, the other to resume the labors of the field beside his peasant family. The first muster of a college class in Scotland is a scene of curious and painful interest; so many lads, fresh from the heather, hang round the stove in cloddish embarrassment, ruffled by the presence of their smarter comrades, and afraid of the sound of their own rustic voices. It was in these early days, I think, that Professor Blackie won the affection of his pupils, putting these uncouth, umbrageous students at their ease with ready human geniality. Thus, at least, we have a healthy democratic atmosphere to breathe in while at work; even when there is no cordiality there is always a juxtaposition of the different classes, and in the competition of study the intellectual power of each is plainly demonstrated to the other. Our tasks ended, we of the North go forth as freemen into the humming, lamplit city. At five o'clock you may see the last of us hiving from the college gates, in the glare of the shop windows, under the green glimmer of the winter sunset. The frost tingles in our blood; no proctor lies in wait to intercept us; till the bell sounds again, we are the masters of the world; and some portion of our lives is always Saturday, *la trêve de Dieu* [the truce of God].

Nor must we omit the sense of the nature of his country and his country's history gradually growing in the child's mind from story and from observation. A Scottish child hears much of shipwreck, outlying iron skerries, pitiless breakers, and great sea-lights; much of heathery mountains, wild clans, and hunted Covenanters. Breaths come to him in song of the distant Cheviots and the ring of foraying hoofs. He glories in his hard-fisted forefathers, of the iron girdle and the handful of oatmeal, who rode so swiftly and lived so sparely on their raids. Poverty, ill-luck, enterprise, and constant resolution are the fibers of the legend of his country's history. The heroes and kings of Scotland have been tragically fated; the most marking incidents in Scottish history — Flodden, Darien, or the Forty-five — were still either failures or defeats; and the fall of Wallace and the repeated reverses of the Bruce combine with the very smallness of the country to teach rather a moral than a material criterion for life. Britain is altogether small, the mere taproot of her extended empire; Scotland, again, which alone the Scottish boy adopts in his imagination, is but a little part of that, and avowedly cold, sterile, and unpopulous. It is not so for nothing. I once seemed to have perceived in an American boy a greater readiness of sympathy for lands that are great, and rich, and growing, like his own. It proved to be quite otherwise: a mere dumb piece of boyish romance, that I had lacked penetration to divine. But the error serves the purpose of my argument; for I am sure, at least, that the heart of young Scotland will be always touched more nearly by paucity of number and Spartan poverty of life.

So we may argue, and yet the difference is not explained. That Shorter Catechism which I took as being so typical of Scotland, was yet composed in the city of Westminster. The division of races is more sharply marked within the borders of Scotland itself than between the countries. Galloway and Buchan, Lothian and Lochaber, are like foreign parts; yet you may choose a man from any of them, and, ten to one, he shall prove to have the headmark of a Scot. A century and a half ago the Highlander wore a different costume, spoke a different language, worshipped in another church, held different morals, and obeyed a different social constitution from his fellow-countrymen either of the South or North. Even the English, it is recorded, did not loathe the Highlander and the Highland costume as they were loathed by the remainder of the Scotch. Yet the Highlander felt himself a Scot. He would willingly raid into the Scotch lowlands; but his courage failed him at the border, and he regarded England as a perilous, unhomely land. When the Black Watch, after years of foreign service, returned to Scotland, veterans leaped out and kissed the earth at Port Patrick. They had been in Ireland, stationed among men of their own race and language, where they were well liked and treated with affection; but it was the soil of Galloway that they kissed at the extreme end of the hostile lowlands, among a people who did not understand their speech, and who had hated, harried, and hanged them since the dawn of history. Last, and perhaps most curious, the sons of chieftains were often educated on the continent of Europe. They went abroad speaking Gaelic; they returned speaking, not English, but the broad dialect of Scotland. Now, what idea had they in their minds when they thus, in thought, identified themselves with their ancestral enemies? What was the sense in which they were Scotch and not English, or Scotch and not Irish? Can a bare name be thus influential on the minds and affections of men, and a political aggregation blind them to the nature of facts? The story of the Austrian Empire would seem to answer, No; the far more galling business of Ireland clenches the negative from nearer home. Is it common education, common morals, a common language, or a common faith, that joins men into nations? There were practically none of these in the case we are considering.

The fact remains: in spite of the difference of blood and language, the Lowlander feels himself the sentimental countryman of the Highlander. When they meet abroad, they fall upon each other's necks in spirit; even at home there is a kind of clannish intimacy in their talk. But from his compatriot in the South the Lowlander stands consciously apart. He has had a different training; he obeys different laws; he makes his will in other terms, is otherwise divorced and married; his eyes are not at home in an English landscape or with English houses; his ear continues to remark the English speech; and even though his tongue acquire the Southern knack, he will still have a strong Scotch accent of the mind.

(1882)

FRANÇOIS VILLON, STUDENT, POET, AND HOUSEBREAKER

Perhaps one of the most curious revolutions in literary history is the sudden bull's-eye light cast by M. Longnon on the obscure existence of François Villon.[1] His book is not remarkable merely as a chapter of biography exhumed after four centuries. To readers of the poet it will recall, with a flavor of satire, that characteristic passage in which he bequeaths his spectacles — with a humorous reservation of the case — to the hospital for blind paupers known as the Fifteen-Score. Thus equipped, let the blind paupers go and separate the good from the bad in the cemetery of the Innocents! For his own part the poet can see no distinction. Much have the dead people made of their advantages. What does it matter now that they have lain in state beds and nourished portly bodies upon cakes and cream! Here they all lie, to be trodden in the mud; the large estate and the small, sounding virtue and adroit or powerful vice, in very much the same condition; and a bishop not to be distinguished from a lamplighter with even the strongest spectacles.

Such was Villon's cynical philosophy. Four hundred years after his death, when surely all danger might be considered at an end, a pair of critical spectacles have been applied to his own remains; and though he left behind him a sufficiently ragged reputation from the first, it is only after these four hundred years that his delinquencies have been finally tracked home, and we can assign him to his proper place among the good or wicked.

[1] *Etude Biographique sur François Villon.* Paris: H. Menu.

It is a staggering thought, and one that affords a fine figure of the imperishability of men's acts, that the stealth of the private inquiry office can be carried so far back into the dead and dusty past. We are not so soon quit of our concerns as Villon fancied. In the extreme of dissolution, when not so much as a man's name is remembered, when his dust is scattered to the four winds, and perhaps the very grave and the very graveyard where he was laid to rest have been forgotten, desecrated, and buried under populous towns,— even in this extreme let an antiquary fall across a sheet of manuscript, and the name will be recalled, the old infamy will pop out into daylight like a toad out of a fissure in the rock, and the shadow of the shade of what was once a man will be heartily pilloried by his descendants. A little while ago and Villon was almost totally forgotten; then he was revived for the sake of his verses; and now he is being revived with a vengeance in the detection of his misdemeanors. How unsubstantial is this projection of a man's existence, which can lie in abeyance for centuries and then be brushed up again and set forth for the consideration of posterity by a few dips in an antiquary's inkpot! This precarious tenure of fame goes a long way to justify those (and they are not few) who prefer cakes and cream in the immediate present.

A WILD YOUTH.

François de Montcorbier, *alias* François des Loges, *alias* François Villon, *alias* Michel Mouton, Master of Arts in the University of Paris, was born in that city in the summer of 1431. It was a memorable year for France on other and higher considerations. A great-hearted girl and a poor-hearted boy made, the one her last, the other his first appearance on the public stage of that unhappy country. On the 30th of May the ashes of Joan of Arc were thrown into the Seine, and on the 2d of December, our Henry Sixth made his joyous entry dismally enough into disaffected and depopulating Paris. Sword and fire still ravaged the open country. On a single April Saturday twelve hundred persons, besides children, made their escape out of the starving capital. The hangman, as is no°

uninteresting to note in connection with Master Francis, was kept hard at work in 1431; on the last of April and on the 4th of May alone, sixty-two bandits swung from Paris gibbets.[1] A more confused or troublous time it would have been difficult to select for a start in life. Not even a man's nationality was certain; for the people of Paris there was no such thing as a Frenchman. The English were the English, indeed, but the French were only the Armagnacs, whom, with Joan of Arc at their head, they had beaten back from under their ramparts not two years before. Such public sentiment as they had centered about their dear Duke of Burgundy, and the dear Duke had no more urgent business than to keep out of their neighborhood. . . . At least, and whether he liked it or not, our disreputable troubadour was tubbed and swaddled as a subject of the English crown.

We hear nothing of Villon's father except that he was poor and of mean extraction. His mother was given piously, which does not imply very much in an old Frenchwoman, and quite uneducated. He had an uncle, a monk in an abbey at Angers, who must have prospered beyond the family average, and was reported to be worth five or six hundred crowns. Of this uncle and his moneybox the reader will hear once more. In 1448 Francis became a student of the University of Paris; in 1450 he took the degree of Bachelor, and in 1452 that of Master of Arts. His *bourse,* or the sum paid weekly for his board, was of the amount of two sous. Now two sous was about the price of a pound of salt butter in the bad times of 1417; it was the price of half-a-pound in the worse times of 1419; and in 1444, just four years before Villon joined the University, it seems to have been taken as the average wage for a day's manual labor.[2] In short, it cannot have been a very profuse allowance to keep a sharp-set lad in breakfast and supper for seven mortal days; and Villon's share of the cakes and pastry and general good cheer, to which he is never weary of referring, must have been slender from the first.

The educational arrangements of the University of Paris were, to our way of thinking, somewhat incomplete. Worldly and monkish elements were presented in a curious confusion, which the youth might disentangle for himself. If he had an opportunity, on the one hand, of acquiring much hair-drawn divinity and a taste for formal disputation, he was put in the way of much gross and flaunting vice upon the other. The lecture room of a scholastic doctor was sometimes under the same roof with establishments of a very different and peculiarly unedifying order. The students had extraordinary privileges, which by all accounts they abused extraordinarily. And while some condemned themselves to an almost sepulchral regularity and seclusion, others fled the schools, swaggered in the street ' with their thumbs in their girdle,' passed the night in riot, and behaved themselves as the worthy forerunners of Jehan Frollo in the romance of *Notre Dame de Paris.* Villon tells us himself that he was among the truants, but we hardly needed his avowal. The burlesque erudition in which he sometimes indulged implies no more than the merest smattering of knowledge; whereas his acquaintance with blackguard haunts and industries could only have been acquired by early and consistent impiety and idleness. He passed his degrees, it is true; but some of us who have been to modern universities will make their own reflections on the value of the test. As for his three pupils, Colin Laurent, Girard Gossouyn, and Jehan Marceau — if they were really his pupils in any serious sense — what can we say but God help them! And sure enough, by his own description, they turned out as ragged, rowdy, and ignorant as was to be looked for from the views and manners of their rare preceptor.

At some time or other, before or during his university career, the poet was adopted by Master Guillaume de Villon, chaplain of Saint Benoit-le-Bétourné near the Sorbonne. From him he borrowed the surname by which he is known to posterity. It was most likely from his house, called the *Porte Rouge,* and situated in a garden in the cloister of Saint Benoit, that Master Francis heard the bell of the Sorbonne ring out the Angelus while he was finishing his *Small Testa-*

---

[1] *Bourgeois de Paris,* ed Panthéon, pp. 688, 689.
[2] *Bourgeois,* pp. 627, 626, and 725.

ment at Christmastide in 1456. Toward this benefactor he usually gets credit for a respectable display of gratitude. But with his trap and pitfall style of writing, it is easy to make too sure. His sentiments are about as much to be relied on as those of a professional beggar; and in this, as in so many other matters, he comes toward us whining and piping the eye, and goes off again with a whoop and his finger to his nose. Thus, he calls Guillaume de Villon his 'more than father,' thanks him with a great show of sincerity for having helped him out of many scrapes, and bequeaths him his portion of renown. But the portion of renown which belonged to a young thief, distinguished (if, at the period when he wrote this legacy, he was distinguished at all) for having written some more or less obscene and scurrilous ballads, must have been little fitted to gratify the self-respect or increase the reputation of a benevolent ecclesiastic. The same remark applies to a subsequent legacy of the poet's library, with specification of one work which was plainly neither decent nor devout. We are thus left on the horns of a dilemma. If the chaplain was a godly, philanthropic personage, who had tried to graft good principles and good behavior on this wild slip of an adopted son, these jesting legacies would obviously cut him to the heart. The position of an adopted son toward his adoptive father is one full of delicacy; where a man lends his name he looks for great consideration. And this legacy of Villon's portion of renown may be taken as the mere fling of an unregenerate scapegrace who has wit enough to recognize in his own shame the readiest weapon of offense against a prosy benefactor's feelings. The gratitude of Master Francis figures, on this reading, as a frightful *minus* quality. If, on the other hand, those jests were given and taken in good humor, the whole relation between the pair degenerates into the unedifying complicity of a debauched old chaplain and a witty and dissolute young scholar. At this rate the house with the red door may have rung with the most mundane minstrelsy; and it may have been below its roof that Villon, through a hole in the plaster, studied, as

he tells us, the leisures of a rich ecclesiastic.

It was, perhaps, of some moment in the poet's life that he should have inhabited the cloister of Saint Benoît. Three of the most remarkable among his early acquaintances are Catherine de Vauselles, for whom he entertained a short-lived affection and an enduring and most unmanly resentment; Regnier de Montigny, a young blackguard of good birth; and Colin de Cayeux, a fellow with a marked aptitude for picking locks. Now we are on a foundation of mere conjecture, but it is at least curious to find that two of the canons of Saint Benoît answered respectively to the names of Pierre de Vaucel and Etienne de Montigny, and that there was a householder called Nicolas de Cayeux in a street — the Rue des Poirées — in the immediate neighborhood of the cloister. M. Longnon is almost ready to identify Catherine as the niece of Pierre; Regnier as the nephew of Etienne, and Colin as the son of Nicolas. Without going so far, it must be owned that the approximation of names is significant. As we go on to see the part played by each of these persons in the sordid melodrama of the poet's life, we shall come to regard it as even more notable. Is it not Clough who has remarked that, after all, everything lies in juxtaposition? Many a man's destiny has been settled by nothing apparently more grave than a pretty face on the opposite side of the street and a couple of bad companions round the corner.

Catherine de Vauselles (or de Vaucel — the change is within the limits of Villon's license) had plainly delighted in the poet's conversation; near neighbors or not, they were much together; and Villon made no secret of his court, and suffered himself to believe that his feeling was repaid in kind. This may have been an error from the first, or he may have estranged her by subsequent misconduct or temerity. One can easily imagine Villon an impatient wooer. One thing, at least, is sure: that the affair terminated in a manner bitterly humiliating to Master Francis. In presence of his lady-love, perhaps under her window and certainly with her connivance, he was unmercifully thrashed by one Noë le Joly — beaten, as he says himself, like dirty linen on the washing-board. It is characteristic that his malice had notably increased between the time when he wrote the *Small Testament* immediately on the back of the occurrence, and the time when he wrote the *Large Testament* five years after. On the latter occasion nothing is too bad for his 'damsel with the twisted nose,' as he calls her. She is spared neither hint nor accusation, and he tells his messenger to accost her with the vilest insults. Villon, it is thought, was out of Paris when these amenities escaped his pen; or perhaps the strong arm of Noë le Joly would have been again in requisition. So ends the love story, if love story it may properly be called. Poets are not necessarily fortunate in love; but they usually fall among more romantic circumstances and bear their disappointment with a better grace.

The neighborhood of Regnier de Montigny and Colin de Cayeux was probably more influential on his after life than the contempt of Catherine. For a man who is greedy of all pleasures, and provided with little money and less dignity of character, we may prophesy a safe and speedy voyage downward. Humble or even truckling virtue may walk unspotted in this life. But only those who despise the pleasures can afford to despise the opinion of the world. A man of a strong, heady temperament, like Villon, is very differently tempted. His eyes lay hold on all provocations greedily, and his heart flames up at a look into imperious desire; he is snared and broached to by anything and everything, from a pretty face to a piece of pastry in a cook-shop window; he will drink the rinsing of the wine cup, stay the latest at the tavern party; tap at the lit windows, follow the sound of singing, and beat the whole neighborhood for another reveler, as he goes reluctantly homeward; and grudge himself every hour of sleep as a black empty period in which he cannot follow after pleasure. Such a person is lost if he have not dignity, or, failing that, at least pride, which is its shadow and in many ways its substitute. Master Francis, I fancy, would follow his own eager instincts without much spiritual struggle. And we soon find him fallen among thieves in sober, literal earnest,

and counting as acquaintances the most disreputable people he could lay his hands on: fellows who stole ducks in Paris Moat; sergeants of the criminal court, and archers of the watch; blackguards who slept at night under the butchers' stalls, and for whom the aforesaid archers peered about carefully with lanterns; Regnier de Montigny, Colin de Cayeux, and their crew, all bound on a favoring breeze toward the gallows; the disorderly abbess of Port Royal, who went about at fair time with soldiers and thieves, and conducted her abbey on the queerest principles; and most likely Perette Mauger, the great Paris receiver of stolen goods, not yet dreaming, poor woman! of the last scene of her career when Henry Cousin, executor of the high justice, shall bury her, alive and most reluctant, in front of the new Montigny gibbet.[1] Nay, our friend soon began to take a foremost rank in this society. He could string off verses, which is always an agreeable talent; and he could make himself useful in many other ways. The whole ragged army of Bohemia, and whosoever loved good cheer without at all loving to work and pay for it, are addressed in contemporary verses as the 'Subjects of François Villon.' He was a good genius to all hungry and unscrupulous persons; and became the hero of a whole legendary cycle of tavern tricks and cheateries. At best. these were doubtful levities, rather too thievish for a schoolboy, rather too gamesome for a thief. But he would not linger long in this equivocal border land. He must soon have complied with his surroundings. He was one who would go where the cannikin clinked, not caring who should pay; and from supping in the wolves' den, there is but a step to hunting with the pack. And here, as I am on the chapter of his degradation, I shall say all I mean to say about its darkest expression, and be done with it for good. Some charitable critics see no more than a *jeu d'esprit*, a graceful and trifling exercise of the imagination, in the grimy ballad of Fat Peg (*Grosse Margot*). I am not able to follow these gentlemen to this polite extreme. Out of all Villon's works that ballad stands forth in flaring reality, gross and ghastly, as a thing written in a contraction of

[1] *Chronique Scandaleuse*, ed. Panthéon, p. 237.

disgust. M. Longnon shows us more and more clearly at every page that we are to read our poet literally, that his names are the names of real persons, and the events he chronicles were actual events. But even if the tendency of criticism had run the other way, this ballad would have gone far to prove itself. I can well understand the reluctance of worthy persons in this matter; for of course it is unpleasant to think of a man of genius as one who held, in the words of Marina to Boult —

A place, for which the pained'st fiend
Of hell would not in reputation change.

But beyond this natural unwillingness, the whole difficulty of the case springs from a highly virtuous ignorance of life. Paris now is not so different from the Paris of then; and the whole of the doings of Bohemia are not written in the sugar-candy pastorals of Murger. It is really not at all surprising that a young man of the fifteenth century, with a knack of making verses, should accept his bread upon disgraceful terms. The race of those who do is not extinct; and some of them to this day write the prettiest verses imaginable. . . . After this, it were impossible for Master Francis to fall lower: to go and steal for himself would be an admirable advance from every point of view, divine or human.

And yet it is not as a thief, but as a homicide, that he makes his first appearance before angry justice. On June 5, 1455, when he was about twenty-four, and had been Master of Arts for a matter of three years, we behold him for the first time quite definitely. Angry justice had as it were, photographed him in the act of his homicide; and M. Longnon, rummaging among old deeds, has turned up the negative and printed it off for our instruction. Villon had been supping — copiously we may believe — and sat on a stone bench in front of the Church of St. Benoît, in company with a priest called Gilles and a woman of the name of Isabeau. It was nine o'clock, a mighty late hour for the period, and evidently a fine summer's night. Master Francis carried a mantle, like a prudent man, to keep him from the dews (serain), and had a sword below it dangling from his girdle.

So these three dallied in front of St. Benoît, taking their pleasure (pour soy esbatre). Suddenly there arrived upon the scene a priest, Philippe Chermoye or Sermaise, also with sword and cloak, and accompanied by one Master Jehan le Mardi. Sermaise, according to Villon's account, which is all we have to go upon, came up blustering and denying God; as Villon rose to make room for him upon the bench, thrust him rudely back into his place; and finally drew his sword and cut open his lower lip, by what I should imagine was a very clumsy stroke. Up to this point, Villon professes to have been a model of courtesy, even of feebleness; and the brawl in his version, reads like the fable of the wolf and the lamb. But now the lamb was roused; he drew his sword, stabbed Sermaise in the groin, knocked him on the head with a big stone, and then, leaving him to his fate, went away to have his own lip doctored by a barber of the name of Fouquet. In one version, he says that Gilles, Isabeau, and Le Mardi ran away at the first high words, and that he and Sermaise had it out alone; in another, Le Mardi is represented as returning and wresting Villon's sword from him: the reader may please himself. Sermaise was picked up, lay all that night in the prison of Saint Benoît, where he was examined by an official of the Châtelet and expressly pardoned Villon, and died on the following Saturday in the Hôtel Dieu.

This, as I have said, was in June. Not before January of the next year could Villon extract a pardon from the king; but while his hand was in, he got two. One is for 'François des Loges, alias (autrement dit) de Villon'; and the other runs in the name of François de Montcorbier. Nay, it appears there was a further complication; for in the narrative of the first of these documents, it is mentioned that he passed himself off upon Fouquet, the barber-surgeon, as one Michel Mouton. M. Longnon has a theory that this unhappy accident with Sermaise was the cause of Villon's subsequent irregularities; and that up to that moment he had been the pink of good behavior. But the matter has to my eyes a more dubious air. A pardon necessary for Des Loges and another for Montcorbier? and these two the same person? and one or both of them known by the *alias* of Villon, however honestly come by? and lastly, in the heat of the moment, a fourth name thrown out with an assured countenance? A ship is not to be trusted that sails under so many colors. This is not the simple bearing of innocence. No — the young master was already treading crooked paths; already, he would start and blench at a hand upon his shoulder, with the look we know so well in the face of Hogarth's Idle Apprentice; already, in the blue devils, he would see Henry Cousin, the executor of high justice, going in dolorous procession toward Montfaucon, and hear the wind and the birds crying around Paris gibbet.

A GANG OF THIEVES

In spite of the prodigious number of people who managed to get hanged, the fifteenth century was by no means a bad time for criminals. A great confusion of parties and great dust of fighting favored the escape of private housebreakers and quiet fellows who stole ducks in Paris Moat. Prisons were leaky; and as we shall see, a man with a few crowns in his pocket and perhaps some acquaintance among the officials, could easily slip out and become once more a free marauder. There was no want of a sanctuary where he might harbor until troubles blew by; and accomplices helped each other with more or less good faith. Clerks, above all, had remarkable facilities for a criminal way of life; for they were privileged, except in cases of notorious incorrigibility, to be plucked from the hands of rude secular justice and tried by a tribunal of their own. In 1402, a couple of thieves, both clerks of the University, were condemned to death by the Provost of Paris. As they were taken to Montfaucon, they kept crying 'high and clearly' for their benefit of clergy, but were none the less pitilessly hanged and gibbeted. Indignant Alma Mater interfered before the king; and the Provost was deprived of all royal offices, and condemned to return the bodies and erect a great stone cross, on the road from Paris to the gibbet, graven with the effigies of these two holy martyrs.[1] We shall hear more of the benefit of clergy; for after this the reader will not be sur-

prised to meet with thieves in the shape of tonsured clerks, or even priests and monks.

To a knot of such learned pilferers our poet certainly belonged; and by turning over a few more of M. Longnon's negatives, we shall get a clear idea of their character and doings. Montigny and De Cayeux are names already known; Guy Tabary, Petit-Jehan, Dom Nicolas, little Thibault, who was both clerk and goldsmith, and who made picklocks and melted plate for himself and his companions — with these the reader has still to become acquainted. Petit-Jehan and De Cayeux were handy fellows and enjoyed a useful preëminence in honor of their doings with the picklock. '*Dictus des Cahyeus est fortis operator crochetorum* [the said De Cayeux is an able manipulator of picklocks],' says Tabary's interrogation, '*sed dictus Petit-Jehan, ejus socius, est forcius operator* [but the said Petit-Jehan, his companion, is a more able manipulator].' But the flower of the flock was little Thibault; it was reported that no lock could stand before him; he had a persuasive hand; let us salute capacity wherever we may find it. Perhaps the term *gang* is not quite properly applied to the persons whose fortunes we are now about to follow; rather they were independent malefactors, socially intimate, and occasionally joining together for some serious operation, just as modern stock-jobbers form a syndicate for an important loan. Nor were they at all particular to any branch of misdoing. They did not scrupulously confine themselves to a single sort of theft, as I hear is common among modern thieves. They were ready for anything, from pitch-and-toss to manslaughter. Montigny, for instance, had neglected neither of these extremes, and we find him accused of cheating at games of hazard on the one hand, and on the other of the murder of one Thevenin Pensete in a house by the Cemetery of St. John. If time had only spared us some particulars, might not this last have furnished us with the matter of a grisly winter's tale?

At Christmas-time in 1456, readers of Villon will remember that he was engaged on the *Small Testament*. About the same period, *circa festum nativitatis Domini* [about the feast of the birth

[1] Monstrelet: *Panthéon Littéraire*, p. 26.

of Our Lord], he took part in a memorable supper at the Mule Tavern, in front of the church of St. Mathurin. Tabary, who seems to have been very much Villon's creature, had ordered the supper in the course of the afternoon. He was a man who had had troubles in his time and languished in the Bishop of Paris's prisons on a suspicion of picking locks; confiding, convivial, not very astute — who had copied out a whole improper romance with his own right hand. This supper-party was to be his first introduction to De Cayeux and Petit-Jehan, which was probably a matter of some concern to the poor man's muddy wits; in the sequel, at least, he speaks of both with an undisguised respect, based on professional inferiority in the matter of picklocks. Dom Nicolas, a Picardy monk, was the fifth and last at table. When supper had been despatched and fairly washed down, we may suppose, with white Baigneux or red Beaune, which were favorite wines among the fellowship, Tabary was solemnly sworn over to secrecy on the night's performances; and the party left the Mule and proceeded to an unoccupied house belonging to Robert de Saint-Simon. This, over a low wall, they entered without difficulty. All but Tabary took off their upper garments; a ladder was found and applied to the high wall which separated Saint-Simon's house from the court of the College of Navarre; the four fellows in their shirtsleeves (as we might say) clambered over in a twinkling; and Master Guy Tabary remained alone beside the overcoats. From the court the burglars made their way into the vestry of the chapel, where they found a large chest, strengthened with iron bands and closed with four locks. One of these locks they picked, and then, by levering up the corner, forced the other three. Inside was a small coffer, of walnut wood, also barred with iron, but fastened with only three locks, which were all comfortably picked by way of the keyhole. In the walnut coffer — a joyous sight by our thieves' lantern — were five hundred crowns of gold. There was some talk of opening the aumries, where, if they had only known, a booty eight or nine times greater lay ready to their hand; but one of the party (I have a humorous suspicion it was Dom Nicolas, the Picardy monk) hurried them away. It was ten o'clock when they mounted the ladder; it was about midnight before Tabary beheld them coming back. To him they gave ten crowns, and promised a share of a two-crown dinner on the morrow; whereat we may suppose his mouth watered. In course of time, he got wind of the real amount of their booty and understood how scurvily he had been used; but he seems to have borne no malice. How could he, against such superb operators as Petit-Jehan and De Cayeux; or a person like Villon, who could have made a new improper romance out of his own head, instead of merely copying an old one with mechanical right hand?

The rest of the winter was not uneventful for the gang. First they made a demonstration against the Church of St. Mathurin after chalices, and were ignominiously chased away by barking dogs. Then Tabary fell out with Casin Chollet, one of the fellows who stole ducks in Paris Moat, who subsequently became a sergeant of the Châtelet and distinguished himself by misconduct, followed by imprisonment and public castigation, during the wars of Louis Eleventh. The quarrel was not conducted with a proper regard to the king's peace, and the pair publicly belabored each other until the police stepped in, and Master Tabary was cast once more into the prisons of the Bishop. While he still lay in durance, another job was cleverly executed by the band in broad daylight, at the Augustine Monastery. Brother Guillaume Coiffier was beguiled by an accomplice to St. Mathurin to say mass; and during his absence, his chamber was entered and five or six hundred crowns in money and some silver-plate successfully abstracted. A melancholy man was Coiffier on his return! Eight crowns from this adventure were forwarded by little Thibault to the incarcerated Tabary; and with these he bribed the jailer and reappeared in Paris taverns. Some time before or shortly after this, Villon set out for Angers, as he had promised in the *Small Testament*. The object of this excursion was not merely to avoid the presence of his cruel mistress or the strong arm of Noë le Joly, but to plan a deliberate robbery on his uncle the monk. As soon as he had properly studied the ground, the others were to go over in force from Paris — picklocks and all — and away with my uncle's strongbox! This throws a comical sidelight on his own accusation against his relatives, that they had 'forgotten natural duty' and disowned him because he was poor. A poor relation is a distasteful circumstance at the best, but a poor relation who plans deliberate robberies against those of his blood, and trudges hundreds of weary leagues to put them into execution, is surely a little on the wrong side of toleration. The uncle at Angers may have been monstrously undutiful; but the nephew from Paris was upsides with him.

On the 23d April, that venerable and discreet person, Master Pierre Marchand, Curate and Prior of Paray-le-Monial, in the diocese of Chartres, arrived in Paris and put up at the sign of the Three Chandeliers, in the Rue de la Huchette. Next day, or the day after, as he was breakfasting at the sign of the Armchair, he fell into talk with two customers, one of whom was a priest and the other our friend Tabary. The idiotic Tabary became mighty confidential as to his past life. Pierre Marchand, who was an acquaintance of Guillaume Coiffier's and had sympathized with him over his loss, pricked up his ears at the mention of picklocks, and led on the transcriber of improper romances from one thing to another, until they were fast friends. For picklocks the Prior of Paray professed a keen curiosity; but Tabary, upon some late alarm, had thrown all his into the Seine. Let that be no difficulty, however, for was there not little Thibault, who could make them of all shapes and sizes, and to whom Tabary, smelling an accomplice, would be only too glad to introduce his new acquaintance? On the morrow, accordingly, they met; and Tabary, after having first wet his whistle at the Prior's expense, led him to Notre Dame and presented him to four or five 'young companions,' who were keeping sanctuary in the church. They were all clerks, recently escaped, like Tabary himself, from the episcopal prisons. Among these we may notice Thibault, the operator, a little fellow of twenty-six, wearing long hair behind. The prior expressed, through Tabary, his anxiety to become their accomplice and altogether such as they were (*de leur sorte et le leurs complices*). Mighty polite they showed themselves, and made him many fine speeches in return. But for all that, perhaps because they had longer heads than Tabary, perhaps because it is less easy to wheedle men in a body, they kept obstinately to generalities and gave him no information as to their exploits, past, present, or to come. I suppose Tabary groaned under this reserve; for no sooner were he and the Prior out of the church than he fairly emptied his heart to him, gave him full details of many hanging matters in the past, and explained the future intentions of the band. The scheme of the hour was to rob another Augustine monk, Robert de la Porte, and in this the Prior agreed to take a hand with simulated greed. Thus, in the course of two days, he had turned this wineskin of a Tabary inside out. For a while longer the farce was carried on; the Prior was introduced to Petit-Jehan, whom he describes as a little, very smart man of thirty, with a black beard and a short jacket; an appointment was made and broken in the de la Porte affair; Tabary had some breakfast at the Prior's charge and leaked out more secrets under the influence of wine and friendship; and then all of a sudden, on the 17th of May, an alarm sprang up, the Prior picked up his skirts and walked quietly over to the Châtelet to make a deposition, and the whole band took to their heels and vanished out of Paris and the sight of the police.

Vanish as they like, they all go with a clog about their feet. Sooner or later, here or there, they will be caught in the fact, and ignominiously sent home. From our vantage of four centuries afterward, it is odd and pitiful to watch the order in which the fugitives are captured and dragged in.

Montigny was the first. In August of that same year, he was laid by the heels on many grievous counts; sacrilegious robberies, frauds, incorrigibility, and that bad business about Thevenin Pensete in the house by the Cemetery of St. John. He was reclaimed by the ecclesiastical authorities as a clerk; but the claim was rebutted on the score of incorrigibility, and ultimately fell to the ground; and he was condemned to death by the Provost of Paris. It was a very rude hour for Montigny, but hope was not yet over. He was a fellow of some birth; his father had been king's pantler; his sister, probably married to some one about the Court, was in the family way, and her health would be endangered if the execution was proceeded with. So down comes Charles the Seventh with letters of mercy, commuting the penalty to a year in a dungeon on bread and water, and a pilgrimage to the shrine of St. James in Galicia. Alas! the document was incomplete; it did not contain the full tale of Montigny's enormities; it did not recite that he had been denied benefit of clergy, and it said nothing about Thevenin Pensete. Montigny's hour was at hand. Benefit of clergy, honorable descent from king's pantler, sister in the family way, royal letters of commutation — all were of no avail. He had been in prison in Rouen, in Tours, in Bordeaux, and four times already in Paris; and out of all these he had come scathless; but now he must make a little excursion as far as Montfaucon with Henry Cousin, executor of high justice. There let him swing among the carrion crows.

About a year later, in July, 1458, the police laid hands on Tabary. Before the ecclesiastical commissary he was twice examined, and, on the latter occasion, put to the question ordinary and extraordinary. What a dismal change from pleasant suppers at the Mule, where he sat in triumph with expert operators and great wits! He is at the lees of life, poor rogue; and those fingers which once transcribed improper romances are now agonizingly stretched upon the rack. We have no sure knowledge, but we may have a shrewd guess of the conclusion. Tabary, the admirer, would go the same way as those whom he admired.

The last we hear of is Colin de Cayeux. He was caught in autumn 1460, in the great Church of St. Leu d'Esserens, which makes so fine a figure in the pleasant Oise valley between Creil and Beaumont. He was reclaimed by no less than two bishops; but the Procureur for the Provost held fast by incorrigible Colin.

1460 was an ill-starred year: for justice was making a clean sweep of 'poor and indigent persons, thieves, cheats, and lockpickers,' in the neighborhood of Paris;[1] and Colin de Cayeux, with many others, was condemned to death and hanged.[2]

VILLON AND THE GALLOWS

Villon was still absent on the Angers expedition when the Prior of Paray sent such a bombshell among his accomplices; and the dates of his return and arrest remain undiscoverable. M. Campaux plausibly enough opined for the autumn of 1457, which would make him closely follow on Montigny, and the first of those denounced by the Prior to fall into the toils. We may suppose, at least, that it was not long thereafter; we may suppose him competed for between lay and clerical Courts; and we may suppose him alternately pert and impudent, humble and fawning, in his defense. But at the end of all supposing, we come upon some nuggets of fact. For first, he was put to the question by water. He who had tossed off so many cups of white Baigneux or red Beaune, now drank water through linen folds, until his bowels were flooded and his heart stood still. After so much raising of the elbow, so much outcry of fictitious thirst, here at last was enough drinking for a lifetime. Truly, of our pleasant vices, the gods make whips to scourge us. And secondly he was condemned to be hanged. A man may have been expecting a catastrophe for years, and yet find himself unprepared when it arrives. Certainly, Villon found, in this legitimate issue of his career, a very staggering and grave consideration. Every beast, as he says, clings bitterly to a whole skin. If everything is lost, and even honor, life still remains; nay, and it becomes, like the ewe lamb in Nathan's parable, as dear as all the rest. 'Do you fancy,' he asks, in a lively ballad, 'that I had not enough

[1] *Chron. Scand.* ut supra.

[2] Here and there, principally in the order of events, this article differs from M. Longnon's own reading of his material. The ground on which he defers the execution of Montigny and De Cayeux beyond the date of their trials seems insufficient. There is a law of parsimony for the construction of historical documents; simplicity is the first duty of narration; and hanged they were.

philosophy under my hood to cry out: I appeal? If I had made any bones about the matter, I should have been planted upright in the fields, by the St. Denis Road '— Montfaucon being on the way to St. Denis. An appeal to Parliament, as we saw in the case of Colin de Cayeux, did not necessarily lead to an acquittal or a commutation; and while the matter was pending, our poet had ample opportunity to reflect on his position. Hanging is a sharp argument, and to swing with many others on the gibbet adds a horrible corollary for the imagination. With the aspect of Montfaucon he was well acquainted; indeed, as the neighborhood appears to have been sacred to junketing and nocturnal picnics of wild young men and women, he had probably studied it under all varieties of hour and weather. And now, as he lay in prison waiting the mortal push, these different aspects crowded back on his imagination with a new and startling significance; and he wrote a ballad, by way of epitaph for himself and his companions, which remains unique in the annals of mankind. It is, in the highest sense, a piece of his biography: —

La pluye nous a debuez et lavez,
Et le soleil dessechez et noirciz;
Pies, corbeaulx, nous ont les yeux cavez,
Et arrachez la barbe et les sourcilz.
Jamais, nul temps, nous ne sommes rassis;
Puis çà, puis là, comme le vent varie,
A son plaisir sans cesser nous charie,
Plus becquetez d' oiseaulx que dez à couldre.
Ne soyez donc de nostre confrairie,
Mais priez Dieu que tous nous vueille absouldre.

[The rain has soaked us and washed us, and the sun has dried us and tanned us; magpies and crows have pecked out our eyes, and snatched away our beards and eye-brows. Never, never are we at rest! Now here, now there, as the wind shifts, it carries us along at its pleasure, ceaselessly, more pecked by birds than thimbles for sewing. Do not join, then, our band, but pray God that he may be willing to absolve us.]

Here is some genuine thieves' literature after so much that was spurious; sharp as an etching, written with a shuddering soul. There is an intensity of consideration in the piece that shows it to be the transcript of familiar thoughts. It is the quintessence of many a doleful nightmare on the straw, when he felt himself swing helpless in the wind, and saw the birds turn about him, screaming and menacing his eyes.

And, after all, the Parliament changed his sentence into one of banishment; and to Roussillon, in Dauphiny, our poet must carry his woes without delay. Travelers between Lyons and Marseilles may remember a station on the line, some way below Vienne, where the Rhone fleets seaward between vine-clad hills. This was Villon's Siberia. It would be a little warm in summer, perhaps, and a little cold in winter in that draughty valley between two great mountain fields; but what with the hills, and the racing river, and the fiery Rhone wines, he was little to be pitied on the conditions of his exile. Villon, in a remarkably bad ballad, written in a breath, heartily thanked and fulsomely belauded the Parliament; the *envoi*, like the proverbial postscript of a lady's letter, containing the pith of his performance in a request for three days' delay to settle his affairs and bid his friends farewell. He was probably not followed out of Paris, like Antoine Fradin, the popular preacher, another exile of a few years later, by weeping multitudes;[1] but I dare say one or two rogues of his acquaintance would keep him company for a mile or so on the south road, and drink a bottle with him before they turned. For banished people, in those days, seem to have set out on their own responsibility, in their own guard, and at their own expense. It was no joke to make one's way from Paris to Roussillon alone and penniless in the fifteenth century. Villon says he left a rag of his tails on every bush. Indeed, he must have had many a weary tramp, many a slender meal, and many a to-do with blustering captains of the Ordonnance. But with one of his light fingers, we may fancy that he took as good as he gave; for every rag of his tail, he would manage to indemnify himself upon the population in the shape of food, or wine, or ringing money; and his route would be traceable across France and

[1] *Chron. Scand.*, p. 338.

Burgundy by housewives and inn-keepers lamenting over petty thefts, like the track of a single human locust. A strange figure he must have cut in the eyes of the good country people: this ragged, black-guard city poet, with a smack of the Paris student, and a smack of the Paris street arab, posting along the highways, in rain or sun, among the green fields and vine-yards. For himself, he had no taste for rural loveliness; green fields and vine-yards would be mighty indifferent to Master Francis; but he would often have his tongue in his cheek at the simplicity of rustic dupes, and often, at city gates, he might stop to contemplate the gibbet with its swinging bodies, and hug himself on his escape.

How long he stayed at Roussillon, how far he became the protégé of the Bour-bons, to whom that town belonged, or when it was that he took part, under the auspices of Charles of Orleans, in a riming tournament to be referred to once again in the pages of the present volume, are matters that still remain in dark-ness, in spite of M. Longnon's diligent rummaging among archives. When we next find him, in summer 1461, alas! he is once more in durance: this time at Méun-sur-Loire, in the prisons of Thi-bault d'Aussigny, Bishop of Orleans. He had been lowered in a basket into a noisome pit, where he lay, all summer, gnawing hard crusts and railing upon fate. His teeth, he says, were like the teeth of a rake: a touch of haggard portraiture all the more real for being excessive and burlesque, and all the more proper to the man for being a caricature of his own misery. His eyes were 'bandaged with thick walls.' It might blow hurricanes overhead; the lightning might leap in high heaven; but no word of all this reached him in his noisome pit. '*Il n'entre, ou gist, n'escler ni tourbillon* [Where he lies neither light-ning nor whirlwind enters].' Above all, he was fevered with envy and anger at the freedom of others; and his heart flowed over into curses as he thought of Thibault d'Aussigny, walking the streets in God's sunlight, and blessing people with extended fingers. So much we find sharply lined in his own poems. Why he was cast again into prison — how he had again managed to shave the gallows

— this we know not, nor, from the de-struction of authorities, are we ever likely to learn. But on October 2d, 1461, or some day immediately preceding, the new King, Louis Eleventh, made his joyous entry into Méun. Now it was a part of the formality on such occasions for the new King to liberate certain prisoners; and so the basket was let down into Villon's pit,' and hastily did Master Francis scramble in, and was most joy-fully hauled up, and shot out, blinking and tottering, but once more a free man, into the blessed sun and wind. Now or never is the time for verses! Such a happy revolution would turn the head of a stocking-weaver, and set him jingling rimes. And so — after a voyage to Paris, where he finds Montigny and De Cayeux clattering their bones upon the gibbet, and his three pupils roystering in Paris streets, 'with their thumbs under their girdles,'— down sits Master Fran-cis to write his *Large Testament,* and perpetuate his name in a sort of glorious ignominy.

THE 'LARGE TESTAMENT'

Of this capital achievement and, with it, of Villon's style in general, it is here the place to speak. The *Large Testament* is a hurly-burly of cynical and senti-mental reflections about life, jesting leg-acies to friends and enemies, and, in-terspersed among these many admirable ballades, both serious and absurd. With so free a design, no thought that occurred to him would need to be dismissed with-out expression; and he could draw at full length the portrait of his own bedeviled soul, and of the bleak and blackguardly world which was the theater of his ex-ploits and sufferings. If the reader can conceive something between the slap-dash inconsequence of Byron's *Don Juan* and the racy humorous gravity and brief noble touches that distinguish the ver-nacular poems of Burns, he will have formed some idea of Villon's style. To the latter writer — except in the ballades, which are quite his own, and can be paralleled from no other language known to me — he bears a particular resem-blance. In common with Burns he has a certain rugged compression, a brutal vivacity of epithet, a homely vigor, a delight in local personalities, and an interest in many sides of life, that are often despised and passed over by more effete and cultured poets. Both also, in their strong, easy, colloquial way, tend to become difficult and obscure; the obscurity in the case of Villon passing at times into the absolute darkness of cant language. They are perhaps the only two great masters of expression who keep sending their readers to a glossary.

'Shall we not dare to say of a thief,' asks Montaigne, 'that he has a handsome leg'? It is a far more serious claim that we have to put forward in behalf of Villon. Beside that of his contemporaries, his writing, so full of color, so eloquent, so picturesque, stands out in an almost miraculous isolation. If only one or two of the chroniclers could have taken a leaf out of his book, history would have been a pastime, and the fifteenth century as present to our minds as the age of Charles Second. This gallows-bird was the one great writer of his age and country, and initiated modern literature for France. Boileau, long ago, in the period of perukes and snuff-boxes, recognized him as the first articulate poet in the language; and if we measure him, not by priority of merit, but living duration of influence; not on a comparison with obscure forerunners, but with great and famous successors, we shall install this ragged and disreputable figure in a far higher niche in glory's temple than was ever dreamed of by the critic. It is, in itself, a memorable fact that, before 1542, in the very dawn of printing, and while modern France was in the making, the works of Villon ran through seven different editions. Out of him flows much of Rabelais; and through Rabelais, directly and indirectly, a deep, permanent, and growing inspiration. Not only his style, but his callous pertinent way of looking upon the sordid and ugly sides of life, becomes every day a more specific feature in the literature of France. And only the other year, a work of some power appeared in Paris, and appeared with infinite scandal, which owed its whole inner significance and much of its outward form to the study of our riming thief.

The world to which he introduces us is, as before said, blackguardly and bleak. Paris swarms before us, full of famine, shame, and death; monks and the servants of great lords hold high wassail upon cakes and pastry; the poor man licks his lips before the baker's window; people with patched eyes sprawl all night under the stall; chuckling Tabary transcribes an improper romance; barebosomed lasses and ruffling students swagger into the streets; the drunkard goes stumbling homeward; the graveyard is full of bones; and away on Montfaucon, Colin de Cayeux and Montigny hang draggled in the rain. Is there nothing better to be seen than sordid misery and worthless joys? Only where the poor old mother of the poet kneels in church below painted windows, and makes tremulous supplication to the Mother of God.

In our mixed world, full of green fields and happy lovers, where not long before, Joan of Arc had led one of the highest and noblest lives in the whole story of mankind, this was all worth chronicling that our poet could perceive. His eyes were indeed sealed with his own filth. He dwelt all his life in a pit more noisome than the dungeon at Méun. In the moral world, also, there are large phenomena not cognizable out of holes and corners. Loud winds blow, speeding home deep-laden ships and sweeping rubbish from the earth; the lightning leaps and cleans the face of heaven; high purposes and brave passions shake and sublimate men's spirits; and meanwhile, in the narrow dungeon of his soul, Villon is mumbling crusts and picking vermin.

Along with this deadly gloom of outlook, we must take another characteristic of his work: its unrivaled insincerity. I can give no better similitude of this quality than I have given already: that he comes up with a whine, and runs away with a whoop and his finger to his nose. His pathos is that of a professional mendicant who should happen to be a man of genius; his levity that of a bitter street arab, full of bread. On a first reading, the pathetic passages preoccupy the reader, and he is cheated out of an alms in the shape of sympathy. But when the thing is studied the illusion fades away: in the transitions, above all, we can detect the evil, ironical temper of the man; and instead of a flighty work, where many crude but genuine feelings tumble together for the mastery as in the lists of tournament, we are tempted to think of the *Large Testament* as of one long-drawn epical grimace, pulled by a merry-andrew, who has found a certain despicable eminence over human respect and human affections by perching himself astride upon the gallows. Between these two views, at best, all temperate judgments will be found to fall; and rather, as I imagine, toward the last.

There were two things on which he felt with perfect and, in one case, even threatening sincerity.

The first of these was an undisguised envy of those richer than himself. He was forever drawing a parallel, already exemplified from his own words, between the happy life of the well-to-do and the miseries of the poor. Burns, too proud and honest not to work, continued through all reverses to sing of poverty with a light, defiant note. Béranger waited till he was himself beyond the reach of want, before writing the *Old Vagabond* or *Jacques*. Samuel Johnson, although he was very sorry to be poor, 'was a great arguer for the advantages of poverty' in his ill days. Thus it is that brave men carry their crosses, and smile with the fox burrowing in their vitals. But Villon, who had not the courage to be poor with honesty, now whiningly implores our sympathy, now shows his teeth upon the dung-heap with an ugly snarl. He envies bitterly, envies passionately. Poverty, he protests, drives men to steal, as hunger makes the wolf sally from the forest. The poor, he goes on, will always have a carping word to say, or, if that outlet be denied, nourish rebellious thoughts. It is a calumny on the noble army of the poor. Thousands in a small way of life, ay, and even in the smallest, go through life with tenfold as much honor and dignity and peace of mind, as the rich gluttons whose dainties and state-beds awakened Villon's covetous temper. And every morning's sun sees thousands who pass whistling to their toil. But Villon was the '*mauvais pauvre*': defined by Victor Hugo, and, in its English expression, so admirably stereotyped by Dickens. He was the first wicked *sans-culotte* [tatterdemalion]. He is the man of genius with the moleskin cap. He is mighty pathetic and

beseeching here in the street, but I would not go down a dark road with him for a large consideration.

The second of the points on which he was genuine and emphatic was common to the middle ages; a deep and somewhat sniveling conviction of the transitory nature of this life and the pity and horror of death. Old age and the grave, with some dark and yet half-sceptical terror of an after-world — these were ideas that clung about his bones like a disease. An old ape, as he says, may play all the tricks in its repertory, and none of them will tickle an audience into good humor. *Tousjours vieil synge est desplaisant.* It is not the old jester who receives most recognition at a tavern party, but the young fellow, fresh and handsome, who knows the new slang, and carries off his vice with a certain air. Of this, as a tavern jester himself, he would be pointedly conscious. As for the women with whom he was best acquainted, his reflections on their old age, in all their harrowing pathos, shall remain in the original for me. Horace has disgraced himself to something the same tune; but what Horace throws out with an ill-favored laugh, Villon dwells on with an almost maudlin whimper.

It is in death that he finds his truest inspiration; in the swift and sorrowful change that overtakes beauty; in the strange revolution by which great fortunes and renowns are diminished to a handful of churchyard dust; and in the utter passing away of what was once lovable and mighty. It is in this that the mixed texture of his thought enables him to reach such poignant and terrible effects, and to enhance pity with ridicule, like a man cutting capers to a funeral march. It is in this, also, that he rises out of himself into the higher spheres of art. So, in the ballade by which he is best known, he rings the changes on names that once stood for beautiful and queenly women, and are now no more than letters and a legend. 'Where are the snows of yester year?' runs the burden. And so, in another not so famous, he passes in review the different degrees of bygone men, from the holy Apostles and the golden Emperor of the East, down to the heralds, pursuivants, and trumpeters, who also bore their part in the world's pageantries and ate greedily at great folks' tables: all this to the refrain of 'So much carry the winds away!' Probably, there was some melancholy in his mind for a yet lower grade, and Montigny and Colin de Cayeux clattering their bones on Paris gibbet. Alas, and with so pitiful an experience of life, Villon can offer us nothing but terror and lamentation about death! No one has ever more skilfully communicated his own disenchantment; no one ever blown a more ear-piercing note of sadness. This unrepentant thief can attain neither to Christian confidence, nor to the spirit of the bright Greek saying, that whom the gods love die early. It is a poor heart, and a poorer age, that cannot accept the conditions of life with some heroic readiness.

. . . . . .

The date of the *Large Testament* is the last date in the poet's biography. After having achieved that admirable and despicable performance, he disappears into the night from whence he came. How or when he died, whether decently in bed or trussed up to a gallows, remains a riddle for foolhardy commentators. It appears his health had suffered in the pit at Méun; he was thirty years of age and quite bald; with the notch in his under lip where Sermaise had struck him with the sword, and what wrinkles the reader may imagine. In default of portraits, this is all I have been able to piece together, and perhaps even the baldness should be taken as a figure of his destitution. A sinister dog, in all likelihood, but with a look in his eye, and the loose flexile mouth that goes with wit and an overweening sensual temperament. Certainly the sorriest figure on the rolls of fame.

(1877)

From A CHILD'S GARDEN OF VERSES

WHOLE DUTY OF CHILDREN

A child should always say what's true,
And speak when he is spoken to,
And behave mannerly at table:
At least as far as he is able.

BED IN SUMMER

In winter I get up at night
And dress by yellow candle-light.
In summer, quite the other way,—
I have to go to bed by day.

I have to go to bed and see
The birds still hopping on the tree,
Or hear the grown-up people's feet
Still going past me in the street.

And does it not seem hard to you,
When all the sky is clear and blue,
And I should like so much to play,
To have to go to bed by day?

SYSTEM

Every night my prayers I say,
And get my dinner every day;
And every day that I've been good,
I get an orange after food.

The child that is not clean and neat,
With lots of toys and things to eat,
He is a naughty child, I'm sure —
Or else his dear papa is poor.

HAPPY THOUGHT

The world is so full of a number of things,
I'm sure we should all be as happy as kings.

TO AUNTIE

Chief of our aunts — not only I,
But all your dozen of nurslings cry —
What did the other children do?
And what were childhood, wanting you?

(1885)

IN THE STATES

With half a heart I wander here
  As from an age gone by,
A brother — yet though young in years,
  An elder brother, I.

You speak another tongue than mine,
  Though both were English born.
I towards the night of time decline,
  You mount into the morn.

Youth shall grow great and strong and free,
  But age must still decay:
To-morrow for the States,— for me,
  England and Yesterday.

(1887)

San Francisco.

HEATHER ALE:

A GALLOWAY LEGEND

From the bonny bells of heather
  They brewed a drink long-syne,
Was sweeter far than honey,
  Was stronger far than wine.
They brewed it and they drank it,   5
  And lay in a blessed swound
For days and day together
  In their dwellings underground.

There rose a king in Scotland,
  A fell man to his foes,   10
He smote the Picts in battle,
  He hunted them like roes.
Over miles of the red mountain
  He hunted as they fled,
And strewed the dwarfish bodies   15
  Of the dying and the dead.

Summer came in the country,
  Red was the heather bell;
But the manner of the brewing
  Was none alive to tell.   20
In graves that were like children's
  On many a mountain head,
The Brewsters of the Heather
  Lay numbered with the dead.

The king in the red moorland   25
  Rode on a summer's day;
And the bees hummed, and the curlews
  Cried beside the way.
The king rode, and was angry,
  Black was his brow and pale,   30
To rule in a land of heather
  And lack the Heather Ale.

It fortuned that his vassals,
  Riding free on the heath,
Came on a stone that was fallen   35
  And vermin hid beneath.
Rudely plucked from their hiding,
  Never a word they spoke:
A son and his aged father —
  Last of the dwarfish folk.   40

And the king sat high on his charger,
  He looked on the little men;
And the dwarfish and swarthy couple
  Looked at the king again.

Down by the shore he had them;   45
  And there on the giddy brink —
'I will give you life, ye vermin,
  For the secret of the drink.'

There stood the son and father;
  And they looked high and low;   50
The heather was red around them,
  The sea rumbled below.
And up and spoke the father,
  Shrill was his voice to hear:
'I have a word in private,   55
  A word for the royal ear.

'Life is dear to the aged,
  And honor a little thing;
I would gladly sell the secret,'
  Quoth the Pict to the King.   60
His voice was small as a sparrow's,
  And shrill and wonderful clear:
'I would gladly sell my secret,
  Only my son I fear.

'For life is a little matter,   65
  And death is naught to the young;
And I dare not sell my honor
  Under the eye of my son.
Take _him_, O king, and bind him,
  And cast him far in the deep;   70
And it's I will tell the secret
  That I have sworn to keep.'

They took the son and bound him,
  Neck and heels in a thong,
And a lad took him and swung him,   75
  And flung him far and strong,
And the sea swallowed his body,
  Like that of a child of ten; —
And there on the cliff stood the father,
  Last of the dwarfish men.   80

'True was the word I told you:
  Only my son I feared;
For I doubt the sapling courage
  That goes without the beard.
But now in vain is the torture,   85
  Fire shall never avail:
Here dies in my bosom
  The secret of Heather Ale.'

(1891)

GEORGE MEREDITH (1828-1909)

Meredith is perhaps most widely known by his novels, but during recent years his poetry has come in for an increasing share of attention. His radical ideas, especially with respect to the emancipation of women, which are suggested rather than openly advocated in the novels, are explicitly avowed in the poems; and the form of his poetry, while no less characteristic than the style of his prose, is equally distinguished, and at times exquisitely musical. Meredith had to wait a long time to come by his own; his first volume of poems was published as long ago as 1851, and his first work of fiction, *The Shaving of Shagpat*, appeared in 1856. *The Ordeal of Richard Feverel* (1859) established his position in the world of fiction, as *Modern Love* (1862) won him recognition as one of the leading poets of the day; an unappreciative review provoked Swinburne to a letter of vigorous protest, in the course of which he said: 'Mr. Meredith is one of the three or four poets now alive whose work, perfect or imperfect, is always as noble in design as it is often faultless in result.' But after winning the suffrages of contemporary men of letters, Meredith had still to conquer the public. *The Egoist* (1879) is usually regarded as turning the tide in his favor, but in reviewing the *Poems and Lyrics of the Joy of Earth* in 1883 Mark Pattison could still write: 'Mr. Meredith is well known, by name, to the widest circle of readers — the novel readers. By name, because his name is a label warning them not to touch.' *Diana of the Crossways* (1885) opened the way for a larger circle of readers not only of this, but of the earlier and later novels, especially in the United States; the poems have made their way much more slowly to any considerable popularity, if indeed they can be said, as a whole, to have won it yet. Except in a few love lyrics and wayside studies, Meredith makes large demands upon his readers' powers of comprehension. He has his own system of philosophy, which needs some familiarity with his modes of expressing it before it can be understood. 'Where other writers appeal to the christian divinities or to humanity,' says a recent critic, 'he speaks, somewhat insistently, of the Earth, a term to which he attaches his own mystic meaning. The Earth is Nature, considered not as the malign stepmother which she is in pessimistic theory, but as a stern yet genial mother and instructress. The Earth gives us our bodies, our fund of power, and our basis of instinct. Life is an adjustment and realization of the inward forces that the Earth generates, and love it is that both tasks and rewards most completely our power of controlling these forces.' These are high themes for young readers, and they may well leave them till they are older and wiser. If they can appreciate Meredith's simpler poems, the understanding of the more difficult ones will come later.

Of the external events of Meredith's life there is little to be said. Of Welsh descent, he was born in Hampshire, and educated in Germany. During his early manhood he worked as a journalist, and in 1866 he was a war correspondent in Italy and Austria, his sympathy with the cause of Italian unity and independence being shown in his novel *Vittoria*, published the following year. The last thirty years of his life were spent in quiet retirement at Boxhill, near London, and the enjoyment of the admiration of an ever-widening circle of readers. In 1905 he received the Order of Merit, perhaps the most distinguished of British decorations, and in 1908, on his eightieth birthday, an address of congratulation was presented to him from the leading writers of the English-speaking world.

LOVE IN THE VALLEY

Under yonder beech-tree single on the
    greensward,
  Couched with her arms behind her golden
    head,
Knees and tresses folded to slip and ripple
    idly,
  Lies my young love sleeping in the shade.
Had I the heart to slide an arm beneath
    her,   5

Press her parting lips as her waist I
    gather slow,
Waking in amazement she could not but em-
    brace me:
Then would she hold me and never let me
    go?

Shy as the squirrel and wayward as the
    swallow,
Swift as the swallow along the river's
    light   10

Circleting the surface to meet his mirrored
    winglets,
  Fleeter she seems in her stay than in her
    flight.
Shy as the squirrel that leaps among the
    pine-tops,
  Wayward as the swallow overhead at set
    of sun,
She whom I love is hard to catch and
    conquer   15
  Hard, but oh, the glory of the winning
    were she won!

When her mother tends her before the
    laughing mirror,
  Tying up her laces, looping up her hair,
Often she thinks, were this wild thing
    wedded,
  More love should I have, and much less
    care.   20
When her mother tends her before the
    lighted mirror,
  Loosening her laces, combing down her
    curls,
Often she thinks, were this wild thing
    wedded,
  I should miss but one for many boys and
    girls.

Heartless she is as the shadow in the
    meadows   25
  Flying to the hills on a blue and breezy
    noon.
No, she is athirst and drinking up her
    wonder;
  Earth to her is young as the slip of the
    new moon.
Deals she an unkindness, 't is but her rapid
    measure,
  Even as in a dance; and her smile can
    heal no less: 30
Like the swinging May-cloud that pelts the
    flowers with hailstones
  Off a sunny border, she was made to
    bruise and bless.

Lovely are the curves of the white owl
    sweeping
  Wavy in the dusk lit by one large star.
Lone on the fir-branch, his rattle-note un-
    varied,   35
  Brooding o'er the gloom, spins the brown
    eve-jar.
Darker grows the valley, more and more
    forgetting:
  So were it with me if forgetting could be
    willed.
Tell the grassy hollow that holds the bub-
    bling well-spring,

Tell it to forget the source that keeps it
    filled.   40

Stepping down the hill with her fair com-
    panions,
  Arm in arm, all against the raying West,
Boldly she sings, to the merry tune she
    marches,
  Brave in her shape, and sweeter un-
    possessed.
Sweeter, for she is what my heart first
    awaking   45
  Whispered the world was; morning light
    is she.
Love that so desires would fain keep her
    changeless;
  Fain would fling the net, and fain have
    her free.

Happy happy time, when the white star
    hovers
  Low over dim fields fresh with bloomy
    dew,   50
Near the face of dawn, that draws athwart
    the darkness,
  Threading it with color, as yewberries
    the yew.
Thicker crowd the shades while the grave
    East deepens
  Glowing, and with crimson a long cloud
    swells.
Maiden still the morn is; and strange she
    is, and secret;   55
  Strange her eyes; her cheeks are cold as
    cold sea-shells.

Sunrays, leaning on our southern hills and
    lighting
  Wild cloud-mountains that drag the hills
    along,
Oft ends the day of your shifting brilliant
    laughter
  Chill as a dull face frowning on a song. 60
Ay, but shows the South-west a ripple-
    feathered bosom
  Blown to silver while the clouds are
    shaken and ascend
Scaling the mid-heavens as they stream,
    there comes a sunset
  Rich, deep like love in beauty without
    end.

When at dawn she sighs, and like an in-
    fant to the window   65
  Turns grave eyes craving light, released
    from dreams,
Beautiful she looks, like a white water-lily,
  Bursting out of bud in havens of the
    streams.

When from bed she rises clothed from
    neck to ankle
  In her long nightgown sweet as boughs
    of May,   70
Beautiful she looks, like a tall garden-lily,
  Pure from the night, and splendid for the
    day.

Mother of the dews, dark eye-lashed twi-
    light;
  Low-lidded twilight, o'er the valley's
    brim,
Rounding on thy breast sings the dew-
    delighted skylark,   75
  Clear as though the dew-drops had their
    voice in him.
Hidden where the rose-flush drinks the ray-
    less planet,
  Fountain-full he pours the spraying
    fountain-showers.
Let me hear her laughter, I would have her
    ·ever
  Cool as dew in twilight, the lark above
    the flowers.   80

All the girls are out with their baskets for
    the primrose;
  Up lanes, woods through, they troop in
    joyful bands.
My sweet leads: she knows not why, but
    now she loiters,
  Eyes the bent anemones, and hangs her
    hands.
Such a look will tell that the violets are
    peeping,   85
  Coming the rose; and unaware a cry
Springs in her bosom for odors and for
    color,
  Covert and the nightingale; she knows
    not why.

Kerchiefed head and chin she darts between
    her tulips,
  Streaming like a willow gray in arrowy
    rain: 90
Some bend beaten cheek to gravel, and
    their angel
  She will be; she lifts them, and on she
    speeds again.
Black the driving raincloud breasts the iron
    gate-way;
  She is forth to cheer a neighbor lacking
    mirth.
So when sky and grass met rolling dumb
    for thunder   95
  Saw I once a white dove, sole light of
    earth.

Prim little scholars are the flowers of her
    garden,
  Trained to stand in rows, and asking
    if they· please.
I might love them well but for loving more
    the wild ones;
  O my wild ones! they tell me more than
    these,   100
You, my wild one, you tell of honied field-
    rose,
  Violet, blushing eglantine in life; and
    even as they,
They, by the wayside are earnest of your
    goodness,
  You are of life's on the banks that line
    the way.

Peering at her chamber the white crowns
    the red rose,   105
  Jasmine winds the porch with stars two
    and three.
Parted is the window; she sleeps; the
    starry jasmine
  Breathes a falling breath that carries
    thoughts of me.
Sweeter unpossessed, have I said of her my
    sweetest?
  Not while she sleeps: while she sleeps the
    jasmine breathes,   110
Luring her to love; she sleeps; the starry
    jasmine
  Bears me to her pillow under white rose-
    wreaths.

Yellow with birdfoot-trefoil are the grass-
    glades;
  Yellow with cinquefoil of the dew-gray
    leaf;
Yellow with stonecrop; the moss-mounds
    are yellow;   115
  Blue-necked the wheat sways, yellowing
    to the sheaf.
Green-yellow, bursts from the copse the
    laughing yaffle,
  Sharp as a sickle is the edge of shade
    and shine:
Earth in her heart laughs looking at the
    heavens,
  Thinking of the harvest: I look and think
    of mine.   120

This I may know: her dressing and un-
    dressing
  Such a change of light shows as when
    the skies in sport
Shift from cloud to moonlight; or edging
    over thunder

Slips a ray of sun; or sweeping into
 port
White sails furl; or on the ocean borders 125
 White sails lean along the waves leaping
 green.
Visions of her shower before me, but
 from eyesight
 Guarded she would be like the sun were
 she seen.

Front door and back of the mossed old
 farmhouse
Open with the morn, and in a breezy
 link 130
Freshly sparkles garden to stripe-shadowed
 orchard,
 Green across a rill where on sand the
 minnows wink.
Busy in the grass the early sun of summer
 Swarms, and the blackbird's mellow
 fluting notes
Call my darling up with round and roguish
 challenge: 135
 Quaintest, richest carol of all the singing throats!

Cool was the woodside; cool as her white
 dairy
 Keeping sweet the cream-pan; and there
 the boys from school,
Cricketing below, rushed brown and red
 with sunshine;
 O the dark translucence of the deep-eyed
 cool! 140
Spying from the farm, herself she fetched
 a pitcher
 Full of milk, and tilted for each in turn
 the beak.
Then a little fellow, mouth up and on tip-
 toe,
 Said, 'I will kiss you': she laughed and
 leaned her cheek.

Doves of the fir-wood walling high our red
 roof 145
 Through the long noon coo, crooning
 through the coo.
Loose droop the leaves, and down the
 sleepy roadway
 Sometimes pipes a chaffinch; loose droops
 the blue.
Cows flap a slow tail knee-deep in the
 river,
 Breathless, given up to sun and gnat and
 fly, 150
Nowhere is she seen; and if I see her nowhere,

Lightning may come, straight rains and
 tiger sky.

O the golden sheaf, the rustling treasure-
 armful!
 O the nutbrown tresses nodding interlaced!
O the treasure-tresses one another over 155
 Nodding! O the girdle slack about the
 waist!
Slain are the poppies that shot their random
 scarlet
 Quick amid the wheat-ears: wound about
 the waist,
Gathered, see these brides of Earth one
 blush of ripeness!
 O the nutbrown tresses nodding interlaced! 160

Large and smoky red the sun's cold disk
 drops,
 Clipped by naked hills, on violet shaded
 snow:
Eastward large and still lights up a bower
 of moonrise,
 Whence at her leisure steps the moon
 aglow.
Nightlong on black print-branches our
 beech-tree 165
 Gazes in this whiteness: nightlong could
 I.
Here may life on death or death on life be
 painted.
 Let me clasp her soul to know she can-
 not die!

Gossips count her faults! they scour a narrow chamber
 Where there is no window, read not
 heaven or her. 170
'When she was a tiny,' one agèd woman
 quavers,
 Plucks at my heart and leads me by the
 ear.
Faults she had once as she learned to run
 and tumbled:
 Faults of feature some see, beauty not
 complete.
Yet, good gossips, beauty that makes holy
 Earth and air, may have faults from
 head to feet. 176

Hither she comes; she comes to me; she
 lingers,
 Deepens her brown eyebrows, while in
 new surprise
High rise the lashes in wonder of a
 stranger,

Yet am I the light and living of her eyes.
Something friends have told her fills her
 heart to brimming,   181
 Nets her in her blushes, and wounds her,
  and tames.—
Sure of her haven, O like a dove alighting,
 Arms up, she dropped; our souls were in
  our names.

Soon will she lie like a white frost sun-
 rise.   185
 Yellow oats and brown wheat, barley pale
  as rye,
Long since your sheaves have yielded to
 the thresher,
 Felt the girdle loosened, seen the tresses
  fly.
Soon will she lie like a blood-red sunset.
 Swift with the to-morrow, green-winged
  Spring!   190
Sing from the South-west, bring her back
 the truants,
 Nightingale and swallow, song and dip-
  ping wing.

Soft new beech-leaves, up to beamy April
 Spreading bough on bough a primrose
  mountain, you
Lucid in the moon, raise lilies to the sky-
 fields,   195
 Youngest green transfused in silver shin-
  ing through:
Fairer than the lily, than the wild white
 cherry:
 Fair as in image my seraph love appears
Born to me by dreams when dawn is at my
 eyelids;
 Fair as in the flesh she swims to me on
  tears.   200

Could I find a place to be alone with
 heaven,
 I would speak my heart out: heaven is my
  need.
Every woodland tree is flushing like the
 dogwood,
 Flashing like the whitebeam, swaying
  like the reed.
Flushing like the dogwood crimson in
 October;   205
 Streaming like the flag-reed south-west
  blown,
Flashing as in gusts the sudden-lighted
 whitebeam:
 All seem to know what is for heaven
  alone.

          (1851–78)

THE LAST WORDS OF JUGGLING JERRY

Pitch here the tent, while the old horse
 grazes:
 By the old hedge-side we'll halt a stage.
It's nigh my last above the daisies:
 My next leaf'll be man's blank page,
Yes, my old girl! and it's no use crying: 5
 Juggler, constable, king, must bow.
One that outjuggles all's been spying
 Long to have me, and has me now.

We've traveled times to this old common: 9
 Often we've hung our pots in the gorse.
We've had a stirring life, old woman!
 You, and I, and the old gray horse.
Races, and fairs, and royal occasions,
 Found us coming to their call:
Now they'll miss us at our stations: 15
 There's a Juggler outjuggles all!

Up goes the lark, as if all were jolly!
 Over the duck-pond the willow shakes,
It's easy to think that grieving's folly,
 When the hand's firm as driven stakes! 20
Ay, when we're strong, and braced, and
 manful,
 Life's a sweet fiddle: but we're a batch
Born to become the Great Juggler's han'ful:
 Balls he shies up, and is safe to catch.

Here's where the lads of the village
 cricket: 25
 I was a lad not wide from here:
Couldn't I juggle the bale off the wicket?
 Like an old world those days appear!
Donkey, sheep, geese and thatched ale-
 house — I know 'em!
 They are old friends of my halts, and
  seem,   30
Somehow, as if kind thanks I owe 'em:
 Juggling don't hinder the heart's esteem.

Juggling's no sin, for we must have victual:
 Nature allows us to bait for the fool.
Holding one's own makes us juggle no
 little;   35
 But, to increase it, hard juggling's the
  rule.
You that are sneering at my profession,
 Haven't you juggled a vast amount?
There's the Prime Minister, in one Session,
 Juggles more games than my sins'll
  count.   40

I've murdered insects with mock thunder:
 Conscience, for that, in men don't quail.

I've made bread from the bump of wonder:
  That's my business, and there's my tale.
Fashion and rank all praised the professor;
  Ay! and I've had my smile from the
    Queen: 46
Bravo, Jerry! she meant: God bless her!
Ain't this a sermon on that scene?

I've studied men from my topsy-turvy
  Close, and, I reckon, rather true. 50
Some are fine fellows: some, right scurvy;
  Most, a dash between the two.
But it's a woman, old girl, that makes me
  Think more kindly of the race:
And it's a woman, old girl, that shakes
    me 55
  When the Great Juggler I must face.

We two were married, due and legal:
  Honest we've lived since we've been one.
Lord! I could then jump like an eagle:
  You danced bright as a bit o' the sun. 60
Birds in a May-bush we were! right merry!
  All night we kissed, we juggled all day.
Joy was the heart of Juggling Jerry!
  Now from his old girl he's juggled away.

It's past parsons to console us; 65
  No, nor no doctor fetch for me:
I can die without my bolus;
  Two of a trade, lass, never agree!
Parson and Doctor! — don't they love
    rarely,
  Fighting the devil in other men's fields! 70
Stand up yourself and match him fairly:
  Then see how the rascal yields!

I, lass, have lived no gipsy, flaunting
  Finery while his poor helpmate grubs:
Coin I've stored, and you won't be wanting:
  You sha'n't beg from the troughs and
    tubs. 76
Nobly you've stuck to me, though in his
    kitchen
  Duke might kneel to call you Cook!
Palaces you could have ruled and grown
    rich in,
  But your old Jerry you never forsook. 80

Hand up the chirper! ripe ale winks in it;
  Let's have comfort and be at peace.
Once a stout draft made me light as a
    linnet.
  Cheer up! the Lord must have his lease.
May be — for none see in that black hol-
    low — 85
  It's just a place where we're held in
    pawn,

And, when the Great Juggler makes as to
    swallow,
  It's just the sword-trick — I ain't quite
    gone.

Yonder came smells of the gorse, so nutty,
  Gold-like and warm: it's the prime of
    May. 90
Better than mortar, brick, and putty,
  Is God's house on a blowing day.
Lean me more up the mound; now I feel it;
  All the old heath-smells! Ain't it
    strange?
There's the world laughing, as if to conceal
    it! 95
  But He's by us, juggling the change.

I mind it well, by the sea-beach lying,
  Once — it's long gone — when two gulls
    we beheld,
Which, as the moon got up, were flying
  Down a big wave that sparked and
    swelled.
Crack went a gun; one fell: the second 100
  Wheeled round him twice, and was off for
    new luck:
There in the dark her white wing
    beckoned; —
  Give me a kiss — I'm the bird dead-
    struck!

(1859)

THE OLD CHARTIST

Whate'er I be, old England is my dam!
  So there's my answer to the judges,
    clear.
I'm nothing of a fox, nor of a lamb;
  I don't know how to cheat, nor how to
    leer:
    I'm for the nation! 5
That's why you see me by the wayside
    here,
  Returning home from transportation.

It's Summer in her bath this morn, I think,
  I'm fresh as dew, and chirpy as the birds:
And just for joy to see old England wink 10
  Thro' leaves again, I could harangue the
    herds:
    Is n't it something
To speak out like a man when you've got
    words,
  And prove you're not a stupid dumb
    thing?

They shipped me off for it: I'm here
    again.
  Old England is my dam, whate'er I be. 16

Says I, I'll tramp it home, and see the
grain:
  If you see well, you're king of what you
  see:
    Eyesight is having,
If you 're not given, I said, to gluttony. 20
Such talk to ignorance sounds as raving.

You dear old brook, that from his Grace's
park
  Come bounding! on you run near my old
  town:
My lord can't lock the water; nor the lark,
  Unless he kills him, can my lord keep
  down.   25
    Up, is the song-note!
I've tried it, too:— for comfort and re-
nown,
  I rather pitched upon the wrong note.

I'm not ashamed: Not beaten's still my
boast:
  Again I'll rouse the people up to strike. 30
But home's where different politics jar
most.
  Respectability the women like.
    This form, or that form—
The Government may be hungry pike,
  But don't you mount a Chartist plat-
form!   35

Well, well! Not beaten—spite of them, I
shout;
  And my estate is suffering for the
Cause.—
Now, what is yon brown water-rat about,
  Who washes his old poll with busy paws?
    What does he mean by 't?   40
It's like defying all our natural laws,
  For him to hope that he'll get clean by 't.

His seat is on a mud-bank, and his trade
  Is dirt:— he's quite contemptible; and
  yet
The fellow's all as anxious as a maid   45
  To show a decent dress, and dry the wet.
    Now it's his whisker,
And now his nose, and ear; he seems to get
  Each moment at the motion brisker!

To see him squat like little chaps at school,
  I can't help laughing out with all my
  might.   51
He peers, hangs both his fore-paws: bless
that fool,
  He's bobbing at his frill now! what a
  sight!
    Licking the dish up,

As if he thought to pass from black to
  white,   55
  Like parson into lawny bishop.

The elms and yellow reed-flags in the sun,
  Look on quite grave:— the sunlight
  flecks his side;
And links of bindweed-flowers round him
  run,
  And shine up doubled with him in the
  tide.   60
    I'm nearly splitting,
But nature seems like seconding his pride,
  And thinks that his behavior's fitting.

That isle o' mud looks baking dry with gold.
  His needle-muzzle still works out and in.
It really is a wonder to behold,   66
  And makes me feel the bristles of my
  chin.
    Judged by appearance,
I fancy of the two I'm nearer Sin,
  And might as well commence a clearance.

And that's what my fine daughter said:—
  she meant: 71
  Pray hold your tongue, and wear a Sun-
  day face.
Her husband, the young linendraper, spent
  Much argument thereon:— I'm their
  disgrace.
    Bother the couple!   75
I feel superior to a chap whose place
  Commands him to be neat and supple.

But if I go and say to my old hen:
  I'll mend the gentry's boots, and keep
  discreet,
Until they grow too violent,— why, then, 80
  A warmer welcome I might chance to
  meet:
    Warmer and better.
And if she fancies her old cock is beat,
  And drops upon her knees — so let her!

She suffered for me:— women, you'll
  observe,   85
  Don't suffer for a Cause, but for a man,
When I was in the dock she showed her
  nerve:
  I saw beneath her shawl my old tea-can
    Trembling . . . she brought it
To screw me for my work: she loathed my
  plan,   90
  And therefore doubly kind I thought it.

I've never lost the taste of that same tea:
  That liquor on my logic floats like oil,
When I state facts, and fellows disagree.

For human creatures all are in a coil; 95
  All may want pardon.
I see a day when every pot will boil
Harmonious in one great Tea-garden!

We wait the setting of the Dandy's day,
  Before that time!—He's furbishing his
    dress—   100
He will be ready for it!—and I say
  That yon old dandy rat amid the cress,—
    Thanks to hard labor!—
If cleanliness is next to godliness,
  The old fat fellow's Heaven's neighbor!

You teach me a fine lesson, my old boy! 106
I've looked on my superiors far too long,
And small has been my profit as my joy.
  You've done the right while I've de-
    nounced the wrong.
  Prosper me later!   110
Like you I will despise the sniggering
    throng,
  And please myself and my Creator.

I'll bring the linendraper and his wife
  Some day to see you; taking off my hat.
Should they ask why, I'll answer: in my
    life   115
  I never found so true a democrat.
  Base occupation
Can't rob you of your own esteem, old rat!
  I'll preach you to the British nation.
             (1862)

FRANCE 1870

We look for her that sunlike stood
  Upon the forehead of our day,
An orb of nations, radiating food
  For body and for mind alway.
  Where is the Shape of glad array; 5
  The nervous hands, the front of steel,
The clarion tongue? Where is the bold
    proud face?
    We see a vacant place;
    We hear an iron heel.

O she that made the brave appeal 10
  For manhood when our time was dark,
And from our fetters struck the spark
  Which was as lightning to reveal
New seasons, with the swifter play
  Of pulses, and benigner day; 15
She that divinely shook the dead
From living man; that stretched ahead
  Her resolute forefinger straight,
And marched towards the gloomy gate

Of earths Untried, gave note, and in 20
The good name of Humanity
  Called forth the daring vision! she,
  She likewise half corrupt of sin,
  Angel and Wanton! Can it be?
  Her star has foundered in eclipse, 25
  The shriek of madness on her lips;
  Shreds of her, and no more, we see.
There is a horrible convulsion, smothered
    din,
  As of one that in a grave-cloth struggles
    to be free.

  Look not on spreading boughs 30
  For the riven forest tree.
Look down where deep in blood and mire
Black thunder plants his feet and plows
  The soil for ruin; that is France:
    Still thrilling like a lyre, 35
Amazed to shivering discord from a fall
Sudden as that the lurid hosts recall
Who met in Heaven the irreparable mis-
    chance.
  O that is France!
The brilliant eyes to kindle bliss, 40
The shrewd quick lips to laugh and kiss,
Breasts that a sighing world inspire,
And laughter-dimpled countenance
Whence soul and senses caught desire!

Ever invoking fire from Heaven, the fire 45
Has seized her, unconsumable, but framed
For all the ecstasies of suffering dire.
Mother of Pride, her sanctuary shamed:
Mother of Delicacy, and made a mark
For outrage: Mother of Luxury, stripped
    stark:
Mother of Heroes, bondsmen; through the
    rains,
Across her boundaries, lo the league-long
    chains!
Fond mother of her martial youth; they
    pass,
They are specters in her sight, are mown as
    grass!
Mother of Honor, and dishonored: Mother
Of Glory, she condemned to crown with
    bays 56
Her victor, and be fountain of his praise.
Is there another curse? There is another:
Compassionate her madness: is she not
Mother of Reason? she that sees them
    mown, 60
Like grass, her young ones! Yea, in the
    low groan,
And under the fixed thunder of this hour
Which holds the animate world in one foul
    blot

Tranced circumambient while relentless
   Power
Beaks at her heart and claws her limbs
   down-thrown,   65
She, with the plunging lightnings overshot,
With madness for an armor against pain,
With milkless breasts for little ones athirst,
And round her all her noblest dying in
   vain,
Mother of Reason is she, trebly cursed,   70
To feel, to see, to justify the blow;
Chamber to chamber of her sequent brain
Gives answer of the cause of her great woe,
Inexorably echoing through the vaults,
''T is thus they reap in blood, in blood
   who sow: 75
This is the sum of self-absolvèd faults.'
Doubt not that through her grief, with sight
   supreme,
Through her delirium and despair's last
   dream,
Through pride, through bright illusion and
   the brood
Bewildering of her various Motherhood,   80
The high strong light within her, though
   she bleeds,
Traces the letters of returned misdeeds.
She sees what seed long sown, ripened of
   late,
Bears this fierce crop; and she discerns
   her fate
From origin to agony, and on   85
As far as the wave washes long and wan
Off one disastrous impulse: for of waves
Our life is, and our deeds are pregnant
   graves
Blown rolling to the sunset from the
   dawn.

Ah, what a dawn of splendor, when her
   sowers   90
Went forth and bent the necks of popula-
   tions,
And of their terrors and humiliations
Wove her the starry wreath that earthward
   lowers
Now in the figure of a burning yoke!
Her legions traversed North and South
   and East,   95
Of triumph they enjoyed the glutton's
   feast:
They grafted the green sprig, they lopped
   the oak.
They caught by the beard the tempests, by
   the scalp
The icy precipices, and clove sheer through
The heart of horror of the pinnacled Alp,
Emerging not as men whom mortals knew.

They were the earthquake and the hurri-
   cane,   102
The lightnings and the locusts, plagues of
   blight,
Plagues of the revel: they were Deluge
   rain,
And dreaded Conflagration; lawless Might.
Death writes a reeling line along the
   snows,   106
Where under frozen mists they may be
   tracked,
Who men and elements provoked to foes,
And Gods: they were of God and Beast
   compact:
Abhorred of all. Yet, how they sucked
   the teats   110
Of Carnage, thirsty issue of their dam,
Whose eagles, angrier than their ori-
   flamme,
Flushed the vext earth with blood, green
   earth forgets.
The gay young generations mask her
   grief;
Where bled her children hangs the loaded
   sheaf.   115
Forgetful is green earth; the Gods alone
Remember everlastingly: they strike
Remorselessly, and ever like for like.
By their great memories the Gods are
   known.

They are with her now, and in her ears,
   and known.   120
'T is they that cast her to the dust for
   Strength,
Their slave, to feed on her fair body's
   length,
That once the sweetest and the proudest
   shone;
Scoring for hideous dismemberment
Her limbs, as were the anguish-taking
   breath   125
Gone out of her in the insufferable de-
   scent
From her high chieftainship; as were she
   death,
Who hears a voice of justice, feels the
   knife
Of torture, drinks all ignominy of life.
They are with her, and the painful Gods
   might weep,   130
If ever rain of tears came out of Heaven
To flatter Weakness and bid Conscience
   sleep,
Viewing the woe of this Immortal, driven
For the soul's life to drain the maddening
   cup
Of her own children's blood implacably:

Unsparing even as they to furrow up 136
The yellow land to likeness of a sea:
The bountiful fair land of vine and grain,
Of wit and grace and ardor, and strong
    roots,
Fruits perishable, imperishable fruits; 140
Furrowed to likeness of the dim gray main
Behind the black obliterating cyclone.

Behold, the Gods are with her, and are
    known.
Whom they abandon misery persecutes
No more: them half-eyed apathy may loan
The happiness of the pitiable brutes. 146
Whom the just Gods abandon have no
    light,
No ruthless light of introspective eyes
That in the midst of misery scrutinize
The heart and its iniquities outright. 150
They rest, they smile and rest; they have
    earned perchance
Of ancient service quiet for a term;
Quiet of old men dropping to the worm;
And so goes out the soul. But not of
    France.
She cries for grief, and to the gods she
    cries, 155
For fearfully their loosened hands chas-
    tise,
And mercilessly they watch the rod's ca-
    ress
Ravage her flesh from scourges merciless,
But she, inveterate of brain, discerns
That Pity has as little place as Joy 160
Among their roll of gifts; for Strength
    she yearns,
For Strength, her idol once, too long her
    toy.
Lo, Strength is of the plain root-Virtues
    born:
Strength shall ye gain by service, prove
    in scorn,
Train by endurance, by devotion shape. 165
Strength is not won by miracle or rape.
It is the offspring of the modest years,
The gift of sire to son, through those sound
    laws
Which we name Gods, which are the
    righteous cause,
The cause of man, and Manhood's minis-
    ters. 170
Could France accept the fables of her
    priests,
Who blest her banners in this game of
    beasts,
And now bid hope that Heaven will in-
    tercede

To violate its laws in her sore need,
She would find comfort in their opiates. 175
Mother of Reason! can she cheat the
    Fates?
Would she, the champion of the open
    mind,
The Omnipotent's first gift — the gift of
    growth —
Consent even for a night-time to be blind,
And sink her soul on the delusive sloth 180
For fruits ethereal and material, both,
In peril of her place among mankind?
The Mother of the many Laughters might
Call one poor shade of laughter in the
    light
Of her unwavering lamp to mark what
    things 185
The world puts faith in, careless of the
    truth:
What silly puppet-bodies danced on strings,
Attached by credence, we appear in sooth,
Demanding intercession, direct aid,
When the whole tragic tale hangs on a for-
    feit blade! 190

She swung the sword for centuries; in a
    day
It slipped her, like a stream cut from its
    source.
She struck a feeble hand, and tried to
    pray,
Clamored of treachery, and had recourse
To drunken outcries in her dream that
    Force 195
Needed but to hear her shouting to obey.
Was she not formed to conquer? The
    bright plumes
Of crested vanity shed graceful nods:
Transcendent in her foundries, Arts and
    looms,
Had France to fear the vengeance of the
    Gods? 200
Her Gods were then the battle-roll of
    names
Sheathed in the records of old war; with
    dance
And song she thrilled her warriors and
    her dames,
Embracing her Dishonorer: gave him .
    France
From head to foot, France present and to
    come, 205
So she might hear the trumpet and the
    drum —
Bellona and Bacchante! rushing forth
On those stout marching Schoolmen of the
    North.

Inveterate of brain, well knows she why
Strength failed her, faithful to himself the
        first;   210
Her dream is done, and she can read the
        sky,
And she can take into her heart the worst
Calamity to drug the shameful thought
Of days that made her as the man she
        served,
A name of terror, but a thing unnerved;
Buying the trickster, by the trickster
        bought,   216
She for dominion, he to patch a throne.

Behold the Gods are with her now, and
        known:
And to know them, not suffering for their
        sake,
Is madness to the souls that may not take
The easy way of death, being divine.   221
Her frenzy is not Reason's light extinct
In fumes of foul revenge and desperate
        sense,
But Reason rising on the storm intense,
Three-faced, with present, past, and future
        linked;   225
Informed three-fold with duty to her line.
By sacrifice of blood must she atone,
(Since thus the foe decrees it) to her
        own:
That she who cannot supplicate, nor cease,
Who will not utter the false word for
        Peace,   230
May burn to ashes, with a heart of stone,
Whatso has made her of all lands the
        flower,
To spring in flame for one redeeming hour,
For one propitious hour arise from prone,
Athwart Ambition's path, and have and
        wrench   235
His towering stature from the bitter trench,
Retributive, by her taskmasters shown,—
The spectral trench where bloody seed was
        sown.

Henceforth of her the Gods are known,
Open to them her breast is laid.   240
Inveterate of brain, heart-valiant,
Never did fairer creature pant
Before the altar and the blade!

Swift fall the blows, and men upbraid,
And friends give echo blunt and cold,   245
The echo of the forest to the axe.
Within her are the fires that wax
For resurrection from the mold.

She snatched at Heaven's flame of old,
And kindled nations: she was weak: 250

Frail sister of her heroic prototype,
The Man; for sacrifice unripe,
She too must fill a Vulture's beak.

Once more, O earthly fortune, speak!
Has she a gleam of victory? one   255
Outshining of her old historic sun?
For a while! for an hour!
And sunlight on her banner seems
A miracle conceived in dreams,
The faint reflux of orient beams   260
Through a lifting shower.

Now is she in the vulture-grasp of Power,
And all her sins are manifest to men.
Now may they reckon with punctilious pen
Her list of misdemeanors, and her dower
Of precious gifts that gilded the rank fen
Where lay a wanton greedy to devour.   267

Now is she in the vulture-grasp of Power.
The harlot sister of the man sublime,
Prometheus, she, though vanquished will
        not cower.   270
Offending Heaven, she groveled in the
        slime;
Offending Man, she aimed beyond her time;
Offending Earth, her Pride was like a
        tower.

O like the banner on the tower,
Her spirit was, and toyed and curled   275
Among its folds to lure the world —
It called to follow. But when strong men
        thrust
The banner on the winds, 't was flame,
And pilgrim-generations tread its dust,
And kiss its track. Disastrously unripe,
Imperfect, changeful, full of blame,   281
Still the Gods love her, for that of high
        aim
Is this good France, the bleeding thing they
        stripe.

She shall rise worthier of her prototype
Through her abasement deep; the pain that
        runs   285
From nerve to nerve some victory achieves.
They lie like circle-strewn soaked Autumn-
        leaves
Which stain the forest scarlet, her fair
        sons!
And of their death her life is: of their
        blood
From many streams now urging to a flood,
No more divided, France shall rise
        afresh.   291
Of them she learns the lesson of the
        flesh: —

The lesson writ in red since first Time ran
A hunter hunting down the beast in man:
That till the chasing out of its last vice, 295
The flesh was fashioned but for sacrifice.
Cast hence the slave's delights, the wan-
    ton's lures,
O France! and of thy folly pay full price;
The limitary nature that immures
A spirit dulled in clay shall break, as
    thrice   300
It has broken on a night of blood and
    tears,
To give thy ghost free breath, and joy thy
    peers.

Immortal mother of a mortal host!
Thou suffering of the wounds that will not
    slay,
Wounds that bring death but take not life
    away!—   305
Stand fast and hearken while thy victors
    boast:
Hearken, and loathe that music evermore.
Slip loose thy garments woven of pride
    and shame:
The torture lurks in them, with them the
    blame
Shall pass to leave thee purer than be-
    fore.   310
Undo thy jewels, thinking whence they
    came,
For what, and of the abominable name
Of her who in imperial beauty wore.

O Mother of a fated fleeting host
Conceived in the past days of sin, and
    born   315
Heirs of disease and arrogance and scorn,
Surrender, yield the weight of thy great
    ghost,
Like wings on air, to what the Heavens
    proclaim
With trumpets from the multitudinous
    mounds
Where peace has filled the hearing of thy
    sons: 320
Albeit a pang of dissolution rounds
Each new discernment of the undying
    Ones,
Stoop to these graves here scattered thick
    and wide
Along thy fields, as sunless billows roll;
These ashes have the lesson for the soul. 325
'Die to thy Vanity, and to thy Pride,
And to thy Luxury: that thou may'st live,
Die to thyself,' they say, 'as we have died
From dear existence, and the foe forgive,
Nor pray for aught save in our little space

To warm good seed to greet the fair
    earth's face.'   331
O mother! take their counsel, and so shall
The broader world breathe in on this thy
    home,
Light clear for thee the counter-changing
    dome,
Fire lift thee to the heights meridional, 335
Strength give thee, like an ocean's vast ex-
    panse
Off mountain cliffs, the generations all,
Not whirling in their narrow rings of
    foam,
But like a river forward. Soaring France!
Now is Humanity on trial in thee: 340
Now may'st thou gather humankind in fee:
Now prove that Reason is a quenchless
    scroll;
Make of calamity thine aureole,
And bleeding lead us through the troubles
    of the sea.

                                    (1871)

THE LARK ASCENDING

He rises and begins to round,
He drops the silver chain of sound,
Of many links without a break,
In chirrup, whistle, slur and shake,
All intervolved and spreading wide,   5
Like water-dimples down a tide
Where ripple ripple overcurls
And eddy into eddy whirls;
A press of hurried notes that run
So fleet they scarce are more than one,   10
Yet changingly the trills repeat
And linger ringing while they fleet,
Sweet to the quick o' the ear, and dear
To her beyond the handmaid ear,
Who sits beside our inner springs,   15
Too often dry for this he brings,
Which seems the very jet of earth
At sight of sun, her music's mirth,
As up he wings the spiral stair,
A song of light, and pierces air   20
With fountain ardor, fountain play,
To reach the shining tops of day,
And drink in everything discerned
An ecstasy to music turned,
Impelled by what his happy bill   25
Disperses; drinking, showering still,
Unthinking save that he may give
His voice the outlet, there to live
Renewed in endless notes of glee,
So thirsty of his voice is he,   30
For all to hear and all to know
That he is joy, awake, aglow,

The tumult of the heart to hear
Through pureness filtered crystal-clear,
And know the pleasure sprinkled bright   35
By simple singing of delight,
Shrill, irreflective, unrestrained,
Rapt, ringing, on the jet sustained
Without a break, without a fall,
Sweet-silvery, sheer lyrical,   40
Perennial, quavering up the chord
Like myriad dews of sunny sward
That trembling into fullness shine,
And sparkle dropping argentine;
Such wooing as the ear receives,   45
From zephyr caught in choric leaves
Of aspens when their chattering net
Is flushed to white with shivers wet;
And such the water-spirit's chime
On mountain heights in morning's prime,   50
Too freshly sweet to seem excess,
Too animate to need a stress;
But wider over many heads
The starry voice ascending spreads,
Awakening, as it waxes thin,   55
The best in us to him akin;
And every face to watch him raised,
Puts on the light of children praised,
So rich our human pleasure ripes
When sweetness on sincereness pipes,   60
Though naught be promised from the seas,
But only a soft-ruffling breeze
Sweep glittering on a still content,
Serenity in ravishment.

For singing till his heaven fills,   65
'T is love of earth that he instils,
And ever winging up and up,
Our valley is his golden cup;
And he the wine which overflows
To lift us with him as he goes,   70
But not from earth is he divorced,
He joyfully to fly enforced;
The woods and brooks, the sheep and kine,
He is, the hills, the human line,
The meadows green, the fallows brown, 75
The dreams of labor in the town;
He sings the sap, the quickened veins,
The wedding song of sun and rains
He is, the dance of children, thanks
Of sowers, shout of primrose-banks,   80
And eye of violets while they breathe;
All these the circling song will wreathe,
And you shall hear the herb and tree,
The better heart of men shall see,
Shall feel celestially, as long   85
As you crave nothing save the song.

Was never voice of ours could say
Our inmost in the sweetest way,
Like yonder voice aloft, and link
All hearers in the song they drink: 90
Our wisdom speaks from failing blood,
Our passion is too full in flood,
We want the key of his wild note
Of truthful in a tuneful throat,
The song seraphically free   95
Of taint of personality,
So pure that it salutes the suns
The voice of one for millions,
In whom the millions rejoice
For giving their one spirit voice.   100

Yet men have we, whom we revere,
Now names, and men still housing here,
Whose lives, by many a battle-dint
Defaced, and grinding wheels on flint,
Yield substance, though they sing not,
       sweet   105
For song our highest heaven to greet,
Whom heavenly singing gives us new,
Enspheres them brilliant in our blue,
From firmest base to farthest leap,
Because their love of Earth is deep,   110
And they are warriors in accord
With life to serve and pass reward,
So touching purest, and so heard
In the brain's reflex of yon bird;
Wherefore their soul in me, or mine,   115
Through self-forgetfulness divine,
In them, that song aloft maintains,
To fill the sky and thrill the plains
With showerings drawn from human store
As he to silence nearer soars,   120
Extends the world at wings and dome,
More spacious making more our home,
Till lost on his aërial rings
In light, and then the fancy sings.

(1881)

THE WOODS OF WESTERMAIN

I

Enter these enchanted woods,
       You who dare.
Nothing harms beneath the leaves
More than waves a swimmer cleaves.
Toss your heart up with the lark,   5
Foot at peace with mouse and worm,
       Fair you fare.
Only at a dread of dark
Quaver, and they quit their form:
Thousand eyeballs under hoods   10
       Have you by the hair.
Enter these enchanted woods,
       You who dare.

II

Here the snake across your path
Stretches in his golden bath: 15
Mossy footed squirrels leap
Soft as winnowing plumes of Sleep:
Yaffles on a chuckle skim
Low to laugh from branches dim:
Up the pine, where sits the star,   20
Rattles deep the moth-winged jar,
Each has business of his own;
But should you distrust a tone,
        Then beware.
Shudder all the haunted roods,   25
All the eyeballs under hoods
        Shroud you in their glare.
Enter these enchanted woods,
        You who dare.

III

Open hither, open hence,   30
Scarce a bramble weaves a fence,
Where the strawberry runs red,
With white star-flower overhead;
Cumbered by dry twig and cone,
Shredded husks of seedlings flown,   35
Mine of mole and spotted flint:
Of dire wizardry no hint,
Save mayhap the print that shows
Hasty outward-tripping toes,
Heels to terror, on tne mold.   40
These, the woods of Westermain,
Are as others to behold,
Rich of wreathing sun and rain;
Foliage lusterful around
Shadowed leagues of slumbering sound.   45
Wavy tree-tops, yellow whins,
Shelter eager minikins,
Myriads, free to peck and pipe:
Would you better? Would you worse?
You with them may gather ripe   50
Pleasures flowing not from purse.
Quick and far as Color flies
Taking the delighted eyes,
You of any well that springs,
May unfold the heaven of things;   55
Have it homely and within,
And thereof its likeness win,
Will you so in soul's desire:
This do sages grant t' the lyre.
This is being bird and more,   60
More than glad musician this;
Granaries you will have a store
Past the world of woe and bliss;
Sharing still its bliss and woe;
Harnessed to its hungers, no.   65
On the throne Success usurps,
You shall seat the joy you feel

Where a race of water chirps,
Twisting hues of flourished steel:
Or where light is caught in hoop   70
Up a clearing's leafy rise,
Where the crossing deerherds troop
Classic splendors, knightly dyes.
Or, where old-eyed oxen chew
Speculation with the cud,   75
Read their pool of vision through
Back to hours when mind was mud;
Nigh the knot, which did untwine
Timelessly to drowsy suns;
Seeing Earth a slimy spine,   80
Heaven a space for winging tons,
Farther, deeper, may you read,
Have you sight for things afield.
Where peeps she, the Nurse of seed,
Cloaked, but in the peep revealed;   85
Showing a kind face and sweet:
Look you with the soul you see 't.
Glory narrowing to grace,
Grace to glory magnified,
Following that will you embrace   90
Close in arms or aëry wide.
Banished is the white Foam-born
Not from here, nor under ban
Phœbus lyrist, Phœbe's horn,
Pipings of the reedy Pan.   95
Loved of Earth of old they were,
Loving did interpret her,
And the sterner worship bars
None whom Song has made her stars.
You have seen the huntress moon   100
Radiantly facing dawn,
Dusky meads between them strewn
Glimmering like downy awn;
Argent Westward glows the hunt,
East the blush about to climb;   105
One another fair they front,
Transient, yet outshine the time;
Even as dewlight off the rose
In the mind a jewel sows.
Thus opposing grandeurs live   110
Here if Beauty be their dower:
Doth she of her spirit give,
Fleetingness will spare her flower.
This is in the tune we play,
Which no spring of strength would quell,
In subduing does not slay;   115
Guides the channel, guards the well:
Tempered holds the young blood-heat,
Yet through measured grave accord,
Hears the heart of wildness beat   120
Like a centaur's hoof on sward.
Drink the sense the notes infuse,
You a larger self will find:
Sweetest fellowship ensues
With the creatures of your kind.   125

Ay, and Love, if Love it be
Flaming over *I* and *ME*,
Love meet they who do not shove
Cravings in the van of Love.
Courtly dames are here to woo,   130
Knowing love if it be true.
Reverence the blossom-shoot
Fervently, they are the fruit.
Mark them stepping, hear them talk,
Goddess, is no myth inane,   135
You will say of those who walk
In the woods of Westermain.
Waters that from throat and thigh
Dart the sun his arrows back;
Leaves that on a woodland sigh   140
Chat of secret things no lack;
Shadowy branch-leaves, waters clear,
Bare or veiled they move sincere;
Not by slavish terrors tripped;
Being anew in nature dipped,   145
Growths of what they step on, these;
With the roots the grace of trees.
Casket-breasts they give, nor hide,
For a tyrant's flattered pride,
Mind, which nourished not by light,   150
Lurks the shuffling trickster sprite:
Whereof are strange tales to tell;
Some in blood writ, tombed in hell.
Here the ancient battle ends,
Joining two astonished friends,   155
Who the kiss can give and take
With more warmth than in that world
Where the tiger claws the snake,
Snake her tiger clasps infurled,
And the issue of their fight   160
Peoples lands in snarling plight.
Here her splendid beast she leads
Silken-leashed and decked with weeds
Wild as he, but breathing faint
Sweetness of unfelt constraint.   165
Love, the great volcano, flings
Fires of lower Earth to sky;
Love, the sole permitted, sings
Sovereignly of *ME* and *I*.
Bowers he has of sacred shade,   170
Spaces of superb parade,
Voiceful. . . . But bring you a note
Wrangling, howsoe'er remote,
Discords out of discord spin
Round and round derisive din: 175
Sudden will a pallor pant
Chill at screeches miscreant;
Owls or specters, thick they flee;
Nightmare upon horror broods;
Hooded laughter, monkish glee,   180
        Gaps the vital air.
Enter these enchanted woods
        You who dare.

IV

You must love the light so well
That no darkness will seem fell.   185
Love it so you could accost
Fellowly a livid ghost,
Whish! The phantom wisps away,
Owns him smoke to cocks of day.
In your breast the light must burn   190
Fed of you, like corn in quern
Ever plumping while the wheel
Speeds the mill and drains the meal.
Light to light sees little strange,
Only features heavenly new;   195
Then you touch the nerve of Change,
Then of Earth you have the clue;
Then her two-sexed meanings melt
Through you, wed the thought and felt.
Sameness locks no scurfy pond   200
Here for Custom, crazy-fond:
Change is on the wing to bud
Rose in brain from rose in blood.
Wisdom throbbing shall you see
Central in complexity;   205
From her pasture 'mid the beasts
Rise to her ethereal feasts,
Not, though lightnings track your wit
Starward, scorning them you quit:
For be sure the bravest wing   210
Preens it in our common spring,
Thence along the vault to soar,
You with others, gathering more,
Glad of more, till you reject
Your proud title of elect,   215
Perilous even here while few
Roam the arched greenwood with you.
        Heed that snare.
Muffled by his cavern-cowl
Squats the scaly Dragon-fowl,   220
Who was lord ere light you drank,
And lest blood of knightly rank
Stream, let not your fair princess
Stray: he holds the leagues in stress,
        Watches keenly there.   225
Oft has he been riven; slain
Is no force in Westermain.
Wait, and we shall forge him curbs,
Put his fangs to uses, tame,
Teach him, quick as cunning herbs,   230
How to cure him sick and lame.
Much restricted, much enringed,
Much he frets, the hooked and winged,
        Never known to spare.
'T is enough: the name of Sage   235
Hits no thing in nature, naught,
Man the least, save when grave Age
From yon Dragon guards his thought.
Eye him when you hearken dumb
To what words from Wisdom come.   240

When she says how few are by
Listening to her, eye his eye.
　　Self, his name declare.
Him shall Change, transforming late,
Wonderously renovate,　　　　　　245
Hug himself the creature may:
What he ,hugs is loathed decay.
Crying, slip thy scales, and slough!
Change will strip his armor off;
Make of him who was all maw,　　250
Inly only thrilling-shrewd,
Such a servant as none saw
Through his days of dragonhood.
Days when growling o'er his bone,
Sharpened he for mine and thine;　255
Sensitive within alone;
Scaly as in clefts of pine.
Change, the strongest son of Life,
Has the Spirit here to wife.
Lo, their young of vivid breed,　　260
Bear the lights that onward speed,
Threading thickets, mounting glades,
Up the verdurous colonnades,
Round the fluttered curves, and down,
Out of sight of Earth's blue crown,　265
Whither, in her central space,
Spouts the Fount and Lure o' the chase.
Fount unresting, Lure divine!
There meet all: too late look most.
Fire in water hued as wine,　　　270
Springs amid a shadowy host;
Circled: one close-headed mob,
Breathless, scanning divers heaps
Where a Heart begins to throb,
Where it ceases, slow, with leaps.　275
And 't is very strange, 't is said,
How you spy in each of them
Semblance of that Dragon red,
As the oak in bracken-stem.
And, 't is said, how each and each:　280
Which commences, which subsides:
First my Dragon! doth beseech
Her who food for all provides.
And she answers with no sign;
Utters neither yea nor nay;　　　285
Fires the water hued as wine;
Kneads another spark in clay.
Terror is about her hid;
Silence of the thunders locked;
Lightnings lining the shut lid;　　290
Fixity on quaking rocked.
Lo, you look at Flow and Drought
Interflashed and interwrought:
Ended is begun, begun
Ended, quick as torrents run.　　295
Young Impulsion spouts to sink;
Luridness and luster link;
'T is your come and go of breath;

Mirrored pants the Life, the Death;
Each of either reaped and sown;　　300
Rosiest rosy wanes to crone.
See you so? your senses drift;
'T is a shuttle weaving swift.
Look with spirit past the sense,
Spirit shines in permanence.　　　305
That is She, the view of whom
Is the dust within the tomb,
Is the inner blush above,
Look to loathe, or look to love;
Think her Lump, or know her Flame;　310
Dread her scourge, or read her aim;
Shoot your hungers from their nerve:
Or, in her example, serve.
Some have found her sitting grave;
Laughing, some; or, browed with sweat,　315
Hurling dust of fool and knave
In a hissing smithy's jet.
More it were not well to speak;
Burn to see, you need but seek.
Once beheld she gives the key　　320
Airing every doorway, she.
Little can you stop or steer
Ere of her you are the seër.
On the surface she will witch,
Rendering Beauty yours, but gaze　325
Under, and the soul is rich
Past computing, past amaze.
Then is courage that endures
Even her awful tremble yours.
Then, the reflex of that Fount　　330
Spied below, will Reason mount
Lordly and a quenchless force,
Lighting Pain to its mad source,
Scaring Fear till Fear escapes,
Shot through all its phantom shapes.　335
Then your spirit will perceive
Fleshly seed of fleshly sins;
Where the passions interweave,
How the serpent tangle spins
Of the sense of Earth misprised,　340
Brainlessly unrecognized;
She being Spirit in her clods,
Footway to the God of Gods.
Then for you are pleasures pure,
Sureties as the stars are sure:　　345
Not the wanton beckoning flags
Which, of flattery and delight,
Wax to the grim Habit-Hags
Riding souls of men to night:
Pleasures that through blood run sane,　350
Quickening spirit from the brain.
Each of each in sequent birth,
Blood and brain and spirit, three
(Say the deepest gnomes of Earth),
Join for true felicity.　　　　　355
Are they parted, then expect

Some one sailing will be wrecked:
Separate hunting are they sped,
Scan the morsel coveted.
Earth that Triad is: she hides   360
Joy from him who that divides;
Showers it when the three are one
Glassing her in union.
Earth your haven, Earth your helm,
You command a double realm;   365
Laboring here to pay your debt,
Till your little sun shall set;
Leaving her the future task:
Loving her too well to ask.
Eglantine that climbs the yew,   370
She her darkest wreathes for those
Knowing her the Ever-new,
And themselves the kin o' the rose.
Life, the chisel, axe and sword,
Wield who have her depths explored: 375
Life, the dream, shall be their robe,
Large as air about the globe;
Life, the question, hear its cry
Echoed with concordant Why;
Life, the small self-dragon ramped,   380
Thrill for service to be stamped,
Ay, and over every height
Life for them shall wave a wand;
That, the last, where sits affright,
Homely shows the stream beyond.   385
Love the light and be its lynx
You will track her and attain;
Read her as no cruel Sphinx
In the woods of Westermain.
Daily fresh the woods are ranged;   390
Glooms which otherwhere appal,
Sounded: here, their worths exchanged,
Urban joins with pastoral:
Little lost, save what may drop
Husk-like, and the mind preserves.   395
Natural overgrowths they lop,
Yet from nature neither swerves,
Trained or savage: for this cause:
Of our Earth they ply the laws,
Have in Earth their feeding root,   400
Mind of man and bent of brute.
Hear that song; both wild and ruled.
Hear it: is it wail or mirth?
Ordered, bubbled, quite unschooled?
None, and all: it springs of Earth.   405
O but hear it! 't is the mind;
Mind that with deep Earth unites,
Round the solid trunk to wind
Rings of clasping parasites.
Music have you there to feed   410
Simplest and most soaring need.
Free to wind, and in desire
Winding, they to her attached
Feel the trunk a spring of fire,

And ascend to heights unmatched,   415
Whence the tidal world is viewed
As a sea of windy wheat,
Momently black, barren, rude;
Golden-brown, for harvest meet;
Dragon-reaped from folly-sown;   420
Bride-like to the sickle-blade:
Quick it varies, while the moan,
Moan of a sad creature strayed,
Chiefly is its voice. So flesh
Conjures tempest-flails to thresh   425
Good from worthless. Some clear lamps
Light it; more of dead marsh-damps.
Monster is it still, and blind,
Fit but to be led by Pain.
Glance we at the paths behind,   430
Fruitful sight has Westermain.
There we labored, and in turn
Forward our blown lamps discern,
As you see on the dark deep
Far the loftier billows leap,   435
    Foam for beacon bear.
Hither, hither, if you will,
Drink instruction, or instil,
Run the woods like vernal sap,
Crying, hail to luminousness!   440
    But have care.
In yourself may lurk the trap:
On conditions they caress.
Here you meet the light invoked:
Here is never secret cloaked.   445
Doubt you with the monster's fry
All his orbit may exclude;
Are you of the stiff, the dry,
Cursing the not understood;
Grasp you with the monster's claws;   450
Govern with his truncheon-saws;
Hate, the shadow of a grain;
You are lost in Westermain;
Earthward swoops a vulture sun,
Nighted upon carrion: 455
Straightway venom wine cups shout
Toasts to One whose eyes are out:
Flowers along the reeling floor
Drip henbane and hellebore:
Beauty, of her tresses shorn,   460
Shrieks as nature's maniac:
Hideousness on hoof and horn
Tumbles, yapping in her track:
Haggard Wisdom, stately once,
Leers fantastical and trips: 465
Allegory drums the sconce,
Impiousness nibblenips.
Imp that dances, imp that flits,
Imp o' the demon-growing girl,
Maddest! whirl with imp o' the pits   470
Round you, and with them you whirl
Fast where pours the fountain-rout

Out of Him whose eyes are out;
Multitudes on multitudes,
Drenched in wallowing devilry: 475
And you ask where you may be,
  In what reek of a lair
Given to bones and ogre-broods:
  And they yell you Where.
Enter these enchanted woods,   480
  You who dare.

                                    (1883)

FROM MODERN LOVE

XVI

In our old shipwrecked days there was an
    hour
When, in the firelight steadily aglow,
Joined slackly, we beheld the red chasm
    grow
Among the clicking coals. Our library-
    bower
That eve was left to us; and hushed we sat
As lovers to whom Time is whispering.   6
From sudden-opened doors we heard them
    sing:
The nodding elders mixed good wine with
    chat.
Well knew we that Life's greatest treasure
    lay
With us, and of it was our talk. 'Ah,
    yes!   10
Love dies!' I said: I never thought it less.
She yearned to me that sentence to unsay.
Then when the fire domed blackening, I
    found
Her cheek was salt against my kiss, and
    swift
Up the sharp scale of sobs her breast did
    lift: —   15
Now am I haunted by that taste! that
    sound.

XLIII

Mark where the pressing wind shoots
    javelin-like,
Its skeleton shadow on the broad-backed
    wave!
Here is a fitting spot to dig Love's grave;
Here where the ponderous breakers plunge
    and strike,
And dart their hissing tongues high up
    the sand: 5
In hearing of the ocean, and in sight
Of those ribbed wind-streaks running into
    white.
If I the death of Love had deeply planned,

I never could have made it half so sure,
As by the unblest kisses which upbraid   10
The full-waked senses; or failing that, de-
    grade!
'Tis morning: but no morning can restore
What we have forfeited. I see no sin:
The wrong is mixed. In tragic life, God
    wot,
No villain need be! Passions spin the plot:
We are betrayed by what is false within. 16

XLVII

We saw the swallows gathering in the sky
And in the osier-isle we heard them noise.
We had not to look back on summer joys,
Or forward to a summer of bright dye:
But in the largeness of the evening earth 5
Our spirits grew as we went side by side.
The hour became her husband and my bride.
Love that had robbed us so, thus blessed
    our dearth!
The pilgrims of the year waxed very loud
In multitudinous chatterings, as the flood 10
Full brown came from the West, and like
    pale blood
Expanded to the upper crimson cloud.
Love that had robbed us of immortal
    things,
This little moment mercifully gave,
Where I have seen across the twilight
    wave   15
The swan sail with her young beneath her
    wings.

L

Thus piteously Love closed what he begat:
The union of this ever-diverse pair!
These two were rapid falcons in a snare,
Condemned to do the flitting of the bat.
Lovers beneath the singing sky of May,   5
They wandered once; clear as the dew on
    flowers.
But they fed not on the advancing hours:
Their hearts held cravings for the buried
    day.
Then each applied to each that fatal knife,
Deep questioning, which probes to endless
    dole.   10
Ah! what a dusty answer gets the soul
When hot for certainties in this our life! —
In tragic hints here see what evermore
Moves dark as yonder midnight ocean's
    force,
Thundering like ramping hosts of warrior
    horse,   15
To throw that faint thin line upon the
    shore.

                                    (1851–62)

VICTORIAN AND LATER ESSAYISTS

Victorian prose offers such a bewildering variety of matter and manner that it seems hopeless to think of bringing even its leading examples under any simple classification. Carlyle's potent rhetoric and Ruskin's gorgeous periods give place to the more restrained mannerisms of Pater and Stevenson, and by the side of these conscious artists there are a number of writers who are much more concerned with what they have to say than with how they say it. The scientific movement, which during the second half of the nineteenth century was the predominant influence in almost every field of intellectual activity, also encouraged the stylistic virtues of clearness, simplicity, and directness. Not all the scientists were themselves examples of these virtues, and Huxley's preëminence among them is due more to his literary sympathies and power of presentation than to his original contributions to knowledge, although these were considerable.

Later writers like Butler, Shaw, and Wells, though no longer champions of evolution — for that was a won battle — carry on the freedom and independence of discussion which marked the earlier Victorian evolutionists, and leave few traditional theories and institutions uncriticized. All three write in a lively unaffected style which is, in the best sense, popular. So do Mr. Galsworthy and Mr. Chesterton, though their point of view and method of approach are entirely different from those of the writers mentioned. It was an age of intellectual unrest, of strongly marked personalities, and of widely divergent views. Although it is now separated from us by the chasm created by the Great War, it is still too near for us to formulate any sure judgment upon its general character and tendency, but that it was a time of a great deal of vigorous thinking and much excellent writing there can be no doubt.

THOMAS HENRY HUXLEY
(1825–1895)

From LAY SERMONS

EMANCIPATION — BLACK AND WHITE

Quashie's plaintive inquiry, ' Am I not a man and a brother?' seems at last to have received its final reply — the recent decision of the fierce trial by battle on the other side of the Atlantic fully concurring with that long since delivered here in a more peaceful way.

The question is settled; but even those who are most thoroughly convinced that the doom is just, must see good grounds for repudiating half the arguments which have been employed by the winning side; and for doubting whether its ultimate results will embody the hopes of the victors, though they may more than realize the fears of the vanquished. It may be quite true that some negroes are better than some white men; but no rational man, cognizant of the facts, believes that the average negro is the equal, still less the superior, of the average white man. And, if this be true, it is simply incredible that, when all his disabilities are removed, and our prognathous relative has a fair field and no favor, as well as no oppressor, he will be able to compete successfully with his bigger-brained and smaller-jawed rival, in a contest which is to be carried on by thoughts and not by bites. The highest places in the hierarchy of civilization will assuredly not be within the reach of our dusky cousins, though it is by no means necessary that they should be restricted to the lowest. But whatever the position of stable equilibrium into which the laws of social gravitation may bring the negro, all responsibility for the result will henceforward lie between Nature and him. The white man may wash his hands of it, and the Caucasian conscience be void of reproach for evermore. And this, if we look to the bottom of the matter, is the real justification of the abolition policy.

The doctrine of equal natural rights may be an illogical delusion; emancipation may convert the slave into a pauperized man; mankind may even have to do without cotton shirts; but all these evils must be faced if the moral law, that no human being can arbitrarily dominate over another without grievous damage to his own nature, be, as many think, as readily demonstrable by experiment as any physical truth. If this be true, no slavery can be abolished without a double emancipation, and the master will benefit by freedom more than the freed-man.

The like considerations apply to all the other questions of emancipation which are at present stirring the world — the multifarious demands that classes of mankind shall be relieved from restrictions imposed by the artifice of man, and not by the necessities of Nature. One of the most important, if not the most important, of all these, is that which daily threatens to become the 'irrepressible' woman question. What social and political rights have women? What ought they to be allowed, or not allowed to do, be, and suffer? And, as involved in, and underlying all these questions, how ought they to be educated?

There are philogynists as fanatical as any 'misogynists' who, reversing our antiquated notions, bid the man look upon the woman as the higher type of humanity; who ask us to regard the female intellect as the clearer and the quicker, if not the stronger; who desire us to look up to the feminine moral sense as the purer and nobler; and bid man abdicate his usurped sovereignty over Nature in favor of the female line. On the other hand, there are persons not to be outdone in all loyalty and just respect for womankind, but by nature hard of head and haters of delusion, however charming, who not only repudiate the new womanworship which so many sentimentalists and some philosophers are desirous of setting up, but, carrying their audacity further, deny even the natural equality of the sexes. They assert, on the contrary, that in every excellent character, whether mental or physical, the average woman is inferior to the average man, in the sense of having that character less in quantity, and lower in quality. Tell these persons of the rapid perceptions and the instinctive intellectual insight of women, and they reply that the feminine mental peculiarities, which pass under these names,

are merely the outcome of a greater impressibility to the superficial aspects of things, and of the absence of that restraint upon expression, which, in men, is imposed by reflection and a sense of responsibility. Talk of the passive endurance of the weaker sex, and opponents of this kind remind you that Job was a man, and that, until quite recent times, patience and long-suffering were not counted among the specially feminine virtues. Claim passionate tenderness as especially feminine, and the inquiry is made whether all the best love-poetry in existence (except, perhaps, the 'Sonnets from the Portuguese') has not been written by men; whether the song which embodies the ideal of pure and tender passion — Adelaida — was written by *Frau* Beethoven; whether it was the Fornarina, or Raphael, who painted the Sistine Madonna. Nay, we have known one such heretic go so far as to lay his hands upon the ark itself, so to speak, and to defend the startling paradox that, even in physical beauty, man is the superior. He admitted, indeed, that there was a brief period of early youth when it might be hard to say whether the prize should be awarded to the graceful undulations of the female figure, or the perfect balance and supple vigor of the male frame. But while our new Paris might hesitate between the youthful Bacchus and the Venus emerging from the foam, he averred that, when Venus and Bacchus had reached thirty, the point no longer admitted of a doubt; the male form having then attained its greatest nobility, while the female is far gone in decadence; and that, at this epoch, womanly beauty, so far as it is independent of grace or expression, is a question of drapery and accessories.

Supposing, however, that all these arguments have a certain foundation; admitting for a moment, that they are comparable to those by which the inferiority of the negro to the white man may be demonstrated, are they of any value as against woman-emancipation? Do they afford us the smallest ground for refusing to educate women as well as men? No mistake is so commonly made by clever people as that of assuming a cause to be bad because the arguments of its supporters are, to a great extent, nonsensical. And we conceive that those who may laugh at the arguments of the extreme philogynists, may yet feel bound to work heart and soul towards the attainment of their practical ends.

As regards education, for example. Granting the alleged defects of women, is it not somewhat absurd to sanction and maintain a system of education which would seem to have been specially contrived to exaggerate all these defects?

Naturally not so firmly strung, nor so well balanced, as boys, girls are in a great measure debarred from the sports and physical exercises which are justly thought absolutely necessary for the full development of the vigor of the more favored sex. Women are, by nature, more excitable than men — prone to be swept by tides of emotion, proceeding from hidden and inward, as well as from obvious and external causes; and female education does its best to weaken every physical counterpoise to this nervous mobility — tends in all ways to stimulate the emotional part of the mind and to stunt the rest. We find girls naturally timid, inclined to dependence, born conservatives; and we teach them that independence is unladylike; that blind faith is the right frame of mind; and that whatever we may be permitted, and indeed encouraged, to do to our brother, our sister is to be left to the tyranny of authority and tradition. With few insignificant exceptions, girls have been educated either to be drudges, or toys, beneath a man; or a sort of angels above him; the highest ideal aimed at oscillating between Clärchen and Beatrice. The possibility that the ideal of womanhood lies neither in the fair saint, nor in the fair sinner; that the female type of character is neither better nor worse than the male, but only weaker; that women are meant neither to be men's guides nor their playthings, but their comrades, their fellows and their equals, so far as Nature puts no bar to that equality, does not seem to have entered into the minds of those who have had the conduct of the education of girls.

If the present system of female education stands self-condemned, as inherently absurd; and if that which we have just indicated is the true position of woman, what is the first step towards a better state of things? We reply, emancipate girls. Recognize the fact that they share the senses, perceptions, feelings, reasoning powers, emotions, of boys, and that

the mind of the average girl is less different from that of the average boy, than the mind of one boy is from that of another; so that whatever argument justifies a given education for all boys, justifies its application to girls as well. So far from imposing artificial restrictions upon the acquirement of knowledge by women, throw every facility in their way. Let our Faustinas, if they will, toil through the whole round of

'Juristerei und Medizin,
Und leider! auch Philosophie.'

Let us have 'sweet girl graduates' by all means. They will be none the less sweet for a little wisdom; and the 'golden hair' will not curl the less gracefully outside the head by reason of there being brains within. Nay, if obvious practical difficulties can be overcome, let those women who feel inclined to do so descend into the gladiatorial arena of life, not merely in the guise of *retiariae*, as heretofore, but as bold *sicariae*, breasting the open fray. Let them, if they so please, become merchants, barristers, politicians. Let them have a fair field, but let them understand, as the necessary correlative, that they are to have no favor. Let Nature alone sit high above the lists, 'rain influence and judge the prize.'

And the result? For our parts, though loth to prophesy, we believe it will be that of other emancipations. Women will find their place, and it will neither be that in which they have been held, nor that to which some of them aspire. Nature's old salique law will not be repealed, and no change of dynasty will be effected. The big chests, the massive brains, the vigorous muscles and stout frames, of the best men will carry the day, whenever it is worth their while to contest the prizes of life with the best women. And the hardship of it is, that the very improvement of the women will lessen their chances. Better mothers will bring forth better sons, and the impetus gained by the one sex will be transmitted, in the next generation, to the other. The most Darwinian of theorists will not venture to propound the doctrine, that the physical disabilities under which women have hitherto labored, in the struggle for existence with men, are likely to be removed by even the most skilfully conducted process of educational selection.

We are, indeed, fully prepared to believe that the bearing of children may, and ought, to become as free from danger and disability, to the civilized woman, as it is to the savage; nor is it improbable that, as society advances towards its right organization, motherhood will occupy a less space of woman's life than it has hitherto done. But still, unless the human species is to come to an end altogether — a consummation which can hardly be desired by even the most ardent advocate of 'women's rights'— somebody must be good enough to take the trouble of annually adding to the world exactly as many people as die out of it. In consequence of some domestic difficulties, Sydney Smith is said to have suggested that it would have been good for the human race had the model offered by the hive been followed, and had all the working part of the female community been neuters. Failing any thorough-going reform of this kind, we see nothing for it but the old division of humanity into men potentially, or actually, fathers, and women potentially, if not actually, mothers. And we fear that so long as this potential motherhood is her lot, woman will be found to be fearfully weighted in the race of life.

The duty of man is to see that not a grain is piled upon that load beyond what Nature imposes; that injustice is not added to inequality.

(1865)

should be no mystery or reserve. None but the corrupt will wish to corrupt facts; honest people will accept them eagerly, whatever they may prove to be, and will convey them to others as accurately as they can. On what pretext therefore can it be well that knowledge should be withheld from the universal gaze upon a matter of such universal interest? It cannot be pretended that there is nothing to be known on these matters beyond what unaided boys and girls can be left without risk to find out for themselves. Not one in a hundred who remembers his own boyhood will say this. How, then, are they excusable who have the care of young people and yet leave a matter of such vital importance so almost absolutely to take care of itself, although they well know how common error is, how easy to fall into and how disastrous in its effects both upon the individual and the race?

Next to sexual matters there are none upon which there is such complete reserve between parents and children as on those connected with money. The father keeps his affairs as closely as he can to himself and is most jealous of letting his children into a knowledge of how he manages his money. His children are like monks in a monastery as regards money and he calls this training them up with the strictest regard to principle. Nevertheless he thinks himself ill-used if his son, on entering life, falls a victim to designing persons whose knowledge of how money is made and lost is greater than his own.

SAMUEL BUTLER (1835–1902)

From THE NOTE-BOOKS

YOUNG PEOPLE

With regard to sexual matters, the best opinion of our best medical men, the practice of those nations which have proved most vigorous and comely, the evils that have followed this or that, the good that has attended upon the other should be ascertained by men who, being neither moral nor immoral and not caring two straws what the conclusion arrived at might be, should desire only to get hold of the best available information. The result should be written down with some fullness and put before the young of both sexes as soon as they are old enough to understand such matters at all. There

THE FAMILY

I

I believe that more unhappiness comes from this source than from any other — I mean from the attempt to prolong family connection unduly and to make people hang together who would never naturally do so. The mischief among the lower classes is not so great, but among the middle and upper classes it is killing a large number daily. And the old people do not really like it much better than the young.

II

On my way down to Shrewsbury some time since I read the Bishop of Carlisle's

Walks in the Regions of Science, then just published, and found the following on p. 129 in the essay which is entitled 'Man's Place in Nature.' After saying that young sparrows or robins soon lose sight of their fellow-nestlings and leave off caring for them, the bishop continues:

'Whereas "children of one family" are constantly found joined together by a love which only grows with years, and they part for their posts of duty in the world with the hope of having joyful meetings from time to time, and of meeting in a higher world when their life on earth is finished.'

I am sure my great-grandfather did not look forward to meeting his father in heaven — his father had cut him out of his will; nor can I credit my grandfather with any great longing to rejoin my great-grandfather — a worthy man enough, but one with whom nothing ever prospered. I am certain my father, after he was 40, did not wish to see my grandfather any more — indeed, long before reaching that age he had decided that Dr. Butler's life should not be written, though R. W. Evans would have been only too glad to write it. Speaking for myself, I have no wish to see my father again, and I think it likely that the Bishop of Carlisle would not be more eager to see his than I mine.

UNCONSCIOUS HUMOR

'Writing to the Hon. Mrs. Watson in 1856, Charles Dickens says: "I have always observed within my experience that *the men who have left home very young* have, *many long years afterwards,* had the tenderest regard for it. That's a pleasant thing to think of as one of the wise adjustments of this life of ours."'

HOMER'S *ODYSSEY*

From the description of the meeting between Ulysses and Telemachus it is plain that Homer considered it quite as dreadful for relations who had long been separated to come together again as for them to separate in the first instance. And this is about true.

MELCHISEDEC

He was a really happy man. He was without father, without mother and without descent. He was an incarnate bachelor. He was a born orphan.

BACON FOR BREAKFAST

Now (1893), when I am abroad, being older and taking less exercise, I do not want any breakfast beyond coffee and bread and butter, but when this note was written (1880) I liked a modest rasher of bacon in addition, and used to notice the jealous indignation with which heads of families who enjoyed the privilege of Cephas and the brethren of our Lord regarded it. There were they with three or four elderly unmarried daughters as well as old mama — how could they afford bacon? And there was I, a selfish bachelor — The appetizing, savory smell of my rasher seemed to drive them mad. I used to feel very uncomfortable, very small and quite aware how low it was of me to have bacon for breakfast and no daughters instead of daughters and no bacon. But when I consulted the oracles of heaven about it, I was always told to stick to my bacon and not to make a fool of myself. I despised myself but have not withered under my own contempt so completely as I ought to have done.

GOD AND MAN

To love God is to have good health, good looks, good sense, experience, a kindly nature and a fair balance of cash in hand. 'We know that all things work together for good to them that love God.' To be loved by God is the same as to love Him. We love Him because He first loved us.

THE HOMERIC DEITY AND THE *PALL MALL GAZETTE*

A writer in the *Pall Mall Gazette* (I think in 1874 or 1875, and in the autumn months, but I cannot now remember) summed up Homer's conception of a god as that of a 'superlatively strong, amorous, beautiful, brave and cunning man.' This is pretty much what a good working god ought to be, but he should also be kind and have a strong sense of humor, together with a contempt for the vices of meanness and for the meannesses of virtue. After saying what I have quoted above the writer in the *Pall Mall Gazette* goes on, 'An impartial critic can judge for himself how far, if at all, this is elevated above the level of mere fetish worship.' Perhaps it is that I am not an impartial critic, but, if I am allowed to be so, I should say that the elevation above mere fetish worship was very considerable.

GOOD BREEDING THE SUMMUM BONUM

When people ask what faith we would substitute for that which we would destroy, we answer that we destroy no faith and need substitute none. We hold the glory of God to be the summum bonum, and so do Christians generally. It is on the question of what is the glory of God that we join issue. We say it varies with the varying phases of God as made manifest in his works, but that, so far as we are ourselves concerned, the glory of God is best advanced by advancing that of man. If asked what is the glory of man we answer 'Good breeding'—using the words in their double sense and meaning both the continuance of the race and that grace of manner which the words are more commonly taken to signify. The double sense of the words is all the more significant for the unconsciousness with which it is passed over.

ADVICE TO THE YOUNG

You will sometimes find your elders laying their heads together and saying what a bad thing it is for young men to come into a little money — that those always do best who have no expectancy, and the like. They will then quote some drivel from one of the Kingsleys about the deadening effect an income of £300 a year will have upon a man. Avoid any one whom you may hear talk in this way. The fault lies not with the legacy (which would certainly be better if there were more of it) but with those who have so mismanaged our education that we go in even greater danger of losing the money than other people are.

RELIGION

Is there any religion whose followers can be pointed to as distinctly more amiable and trustworthy than those of any other? If so, this should be enough. I find the nicest and best people generally profess no religion at all, but are ready to like the best men of all religions.

HEAVEN AND HELL

Heaven is the work of the best and kindest men and women. Hell is the work of prigs, pedants and professional truthtellers. The world is an attempt to make the best of both.

PRIGGISHNESS

The essence of priggishness is setting up to be better than one's neighbor. Better may mean more virtuous, more clever, more agreeable or what not. The worst of it is that one cannot do anything outside eating one's dinner or taking a walk without setting up to know more than one's neighbors. It was this that made me say in *Life and Habit* that I was among the damned in that I wrote at all. So I am; and I am often very sorry that I was never able to reach those more saintly classes who do not set up as instructors of other people. But one must take one's lot.

LOHENGRIN

He was a prig. In the bedroom scene with Elsa he should have said that her question put him rather up a tree but that, as she wanted to know who he was, he would tell her and would let the Holy Grail slide.

SWELLS

People ask complainingly what swells have done, or do, for society that they should be able to live without working. The good swell is the creature towards which all nature has been groaning and travailing together until now. He is an ideal. He shows what may be done in the way of good breeding, health, looks, temper and fortune. He realizes men's dreams of themselves, at any rate vicariously. He preaches the gospel of grace. The world is like a spoilt child, it has this good thing given it at great expense and then says it is useless!

SCIENCE AND RELIGION

These are reconciled in amiable and sensible people but nowhere else.

GENTLEMAN

If we are asked what is the most essential characterization that underlies this word, the word itself will guide us to gentleness, to absence of such things as brow-beating, overbearing manners and fuss, and generally to the consideration for other people.

THE FINEST MEN

I suppose an Italian peasant or a Breton, Norman or English fisherman, is about the best thing nature does in the way of men — the richer and the poorer being alike mistakes.

ON BEING A SWELL ALL ROUND

I have never in my life succeeded in being this. Sometimes I get a new suit and am tidy for a while in part, meanwhile the hat, tie, boots, gloves and underclothing all clamor for attention and, before I have got them well in hand, the new suit has lost its freshness. Still, if ever I do get any money, I will try and make myself really spruce all round till I find out, as I probably shall in about a week, that if I give my clothes an inch they will take an ell.

(1880)

MONEY

is the last enemy that shall never be subdued. While there is flesh there is money — or the want of money; but money is always on the brain so long as there is a brain in reasonable order.

A LUXURIOUS DEATH

Death in anything like luxury is one of the most expensive things a man can indulge himself in. It costs a lot of money to die comfortably, unless one goes off pretty quickly.

MONEY, HEALTH AND REPUTATION

Money, if it live at all, that is to say if it be reproductive and put out at any interest, however low, is mortal and doomed to be lost one day, though it may go on living through many generations of one single family if it be taken care of. No man is absolutely safe. It may be said to any man, 'Thou fool, this night thy money shall be required of thee.' And reputation is like money: it may be required of us without warning. The little unsuspected evil on which we trip may swell up in a moment and prove to be the huge, Janus-like mountain of unpardonable sin. And his health may be required of any fool, any night or any day.

A man will feel the loss of money more keenly than loss of his bodily health, so long as he can keep his money. Take his money away and deprive him of the means of earning any more, and his health will soon break up; but leave him his money and, even though his health breaks up and he dies, he does not mind it so much as we think. Money losses are the worst, loss of health is next worse and loss of reputation comes in a bad third. All other things are amusements provided money, health and good name are untouched.

SOLICITORS

A man must not think he can save himself the trouble of being a sensible man and a gentleman by going to his solicitor, any more than he can get himself a sound constitution by going to his doctor; but a solicitor can do more to keep a tolerably well-meaning fool straight than a doctor can do for an invalid. Money is to the solicitor what souls are to the parson or life to the physician. He is our money-doctor.

DOCTORS

Going to your doctor is having such a row with your cells that you refer them to your solicitor. Sometimes you, as it were, strike against them and stop their food, when they go on strike against yourself. Sometimes you file a bill in Chancery against them and go to bed.

PRIESTS

We may find an argument in favor of priests if we consider whether man is capable of doing for himself in respect of his moral and spiritual welfare (than which nothing can be more difficult and intricate) what it is so clearly better for him to leave to professional advisers in the case of his money and his body which are comparatively simple and unimportant.

GEORGE MOORE (1853–)

FROM MODERN PAINTING

THE ORGANIZATION OF ART

No fact is more painful to the modern mind than that men are not born with equal brains; and every day we grow more and more determined to thwart Nature's desire of inequality by public education. Whether everybody should be taught to read and write I leave to politicians — the matter is not important; but that the nation should not be instructed in drawing, music, painting, and English literature I will never cease to maintain. Everything that has happened in England for the last thirty years goes to prove that systematized education in art means artistic decadence.

To the ordinary mind there is something very reassuring in the words institutions, professors, examinations, medals, and titles of all kinds. All these things have been given of late years to art, and parents and guardians need no longer have any fear for those confided to their charge: the art of painting has been recognized as a profession! The principal institution where this profession is practised is called the Royal Academy. It owes its existence to the taste of a gentleman known as George the Third, and it has been dowered by the State to the extent of at least three hundred thousand pounds. Professors from Oxford, even bishops, dine there. The members of this institution put R.A. after their names; the president has been made a baronet; there was even a rumor that he was to be made a lord, and that he was not we must consider as another blow dealt against the dignity of art.

Literature does not offer so much scope for organization as painting; but strenuous efforts are being made to organize it, and, by the aid of academies, examinations, and crowns, hopes are entertained that, before long, it will be brought into line with the other professions. And the journalists too are anxious to 'erect their craft to the dignity of a profession which shall confer upon its members *certain social status* like that of the barrister and the lawyer.' Entrance is to be strictly conditional; no one is to have the right to practise without a diploma, and members are to be entitled to certain letters after their names. A movement is on foot to Churton-Collinise English literature at the universities, and every month Mr. Walter Besant raises a wail in the *Author* that the peerage is not as open to three-volume novelists as it is to brewers. He bewails the fact that no eminent man of letters, with the exception of Lord Tennyson, has been made the enforced associate of brewers and politicians. Mr. Besant does not think that titles in these democratic days are foolish and absurd, pitiful in the personality of those who own them by inheritance, grotesque in the personality of those on whom they have been conferred. Mr. Besant does not see that the desire of the baker, the brewer, the butcher, and I may add the three-volume novelist, to be addressed by small tradesmen and lackeys as 'yer lordship,' raises a smile on the lips of even the most *blasé*.

I am advocating an unpopular *régime* I know, for the majority believe that art is in Queer Street if new buildings are not being raised, if official recognition of merits is not proclaimed, and if the newspapers do not teem with paragraphs concerning the homes of the Academicians. The wailing and gnashing of teeth that were heard when an intelligent portion of the Press induced Mr. Tate to withdraw his offer to build a gallery and furnish it with pictures by Messrs. Herkomer, Fildes, Leader, Long, are not forgotten. It was not urged that the pictures were valuable pictures; the merit or demerit of the pictures was not what interested, but the fact that a great deal of money was going to be spent, and that titles, badges, medals, crowns, would be given to those whose pictures were enshrined in the new temple of art. The Tate Gallery touched these folk as would an imposing review of troops, a procession of judges, or a coronation in Westminster Abbey. Their senses were tickled by the prospect of a show, their minds were stirred by some idea of organization — something was about to be organized, and nothing appeals so much to the vulgar mind as organization.

An epoch is represented by a word, and to organize represents the dominant idea of our civilization. To organize is to be respectable, and as every one wants to be respectable, every one dreams of new schemes of organization. Soldiers, sailors, policemen, members of parliament, independent voters, clerks in the post office, bus drivers, dockers, every imaginable variety of worker, domestic servants — it is difficult to think of any class that has not been organized of late years. There is a gentleman in parliament who is anxious to do something in the way of social organization for the gipsies. The gipsies have not appealed to him; they have professed no desire to have their social status raised; they have, I believe, disclaimed through their king, whoever he may be, all participation in the scheme of this benevolent gentleman. Nor does any sense of the absurdity of his endeavor blight the worthy gentleman's ardor. How should it? He, like the other organizers, is an unreasoning instrument in a great tendency of things. To organize something — or, put it differently, to educate some one — is to-day every man's ambition. So long as it is not himself, it matters no jot to him whom he educates. The gipsy under the hedge, the artist painting under a hill, it matters not. A technical school of instruction would enable the gipsy to harness his horse better than he does at present; and the artist would paint much better if he were taught to stipple, and examined by salaried professors in stipple, and given prizes for stippling. The general mind of our century is with education and organization of every kind, and from this terrible general mind art seems unable to escape. Art, that poor little gipsy whose very condition of existence is freedom, who owns no code of laws, who evades all regulations, who groups himself under no standards, who can live only in disastrous times, when the world's attention is drawn to other things, and allows him life in shelter of the hedges, and dreams in sight of the stars, finds himself forced into a uniform — poor little fellow, how melancholy he looks on his high stool in the South Kensington Museum, and notwithstanding the professors his hand drops from the drawing-board, unable to accomplish the admired stipple.

But solemn members of parliament are certain that official recognition must be extended to art. Art is an educational influence, and the Kensington galleries are something more than agreeable places, where sweethearts can murmur soft nothings under divine masterpieces. The utilitarian M.P. must find some justification for art; he is not sensible enough to understand that art justifies its own existence, that it is its own honor and glory; and he nourishes a flimsy lie, and votes that large sums of money shall be spent in endowing schools of art and founding picture galleries. Then there is another class — those who have fish to fry, and to whom art seems a convenient frying-pan. Mr. Tate craves for a museum to be called Tate's; or, if his princely gift gained him a title, which it may, the museum would be called — What would be an appropriate name? There are men too who have trifles to sell, and they talk loudly of the glories of modern art, and the necessity of a British Luxembourg.

That France should have a Luxembourg is natural enough; that we should have one would be anomalous. We are a free-trading country. I pass over the failure of the Luxembourg to recognize genius, to save the artist of genius a struggle with insolent ignorance. What did the Luxembourg do for Corot, Millet, Manet, Degas, Monet, Renoir, Sisley, Pissaro? The Luxembourg chose rather to honor such pretentious mediocrities as Bouguereau, Jules Lefebvre, Jules Breton, and their like. What has our Academy done to rescue struggling genius from poverty and obscurity? Did it save Alfred Stevens, the great sculptor of his generation, from the task of designing fire-irons? How often did the Academy refuse Cecil Lawson's pictures? When did they accept him, was it not because he had become popular in spite of the Academy? Did not the Academy refuse Mr. Whistler's portrait of his mother, and was it not hung at the last moment owing to a threat of one of the Academicians to resign if a place was not found for it? Place was found for it seven feet above the line. Has not the Academy for the last five-and-twenty years lent the whole stress and authority of its name to crush Mr. Whistler? Happily his genius was sufficient for the fight, and it was not until he had conquered past all question that he left this country. The record of the Academy is a significant one. But if it has exercised a vicious influence in art, its history is no worse than that of other academies. Here, as elsewhere, the Academy has tolerated genius when it was popular, and when it was not popular it has trampled upon it.

We have Free Trade in literature, why should we not have Free Trade in art? Why should not every artist go into the market without title or masquerade that blinds the public to the value of what he has to sell? I would turn art adrift, titleless, R.A.-less, out into the street and field, where, under the light of his original stars, the impassioned vagrant might dream once more, and for the mere sake of his dreams.

GEORGE BERNARD SHAW
(1856–)

From DRAMATIC OPINIONS AND ESSAYS

THE CASE FOR THE CRITIC-DRAMATIST

A discussion has arisen recently as to whether a dramatic critic can also be a dramatic author without injury to his integrity and impartiality. The feebleness with which the point has been debated may be guessed from the fact that the favorite opinion seems to be that a critic is either an honest man or he is not. If honest, then dramatic authorship can make no difference to him. If not, he will be dishonest whether he writes plays or not. This childish evasion cannot, for the honor of the craft, be allowed to stand. If I wanted to ascertain the melting-point of a certain metal, and how far it would be altered by an alloy of some other metal, and an expert were to tell me that a metal is either fusible or it is not — that if not, no temperature will melt it; and if so, it will melt anyhow — I am afraid I should ask that expert whether he was a fool himself or took me for one. Absolute honesty is as absurd an abstraction as absolute temperature or absolute value. A dramatic critic who would die rather than read an American pirated edition of a copyright English book might be considered an absolutely honest man for all practical purposes on that one particular subject — I say on that one, because very few men have more than one point of honor; but as far as I am aware, no such dramatic critic exists. If he did, I should regard him as a highly dangerous monomaniac. That honesty varies inversely with temptation is proved by the fact that every additional penny on the income-tax yields a less return than the penny before it, showing that men state their incomes less honestly for the purpose of taxation at sevenpence in the pound than sixpence. The matter may be tested by a simple experiment. Go to one of the gentlemen whose theory is that a man is either honest or he is not, and obtain from him the loan of half-a-crown on some plausible pretext of a lost purse or some such petty emergency. He will not ask you for a written acknowledgment of the debt. Return next day and ask for a loan of £500 without a promissory note, on the ground that you are either honest or not honest, and that a man who will pay back half a crown without compulsion will also pay back £500. You will find that the theory of absolute honesty will collapse at once.

Are we then to believe that the critic-dramatist who stands to make anything from five hundred to ten thousand pounds by persuading a manager to produce his plays, will be prevented by his honesty from writing about that manager otherwise than he would if he had never written a play and were quite certain that he never should write one? I can only say that people who believe such a thing would believe anything. I am myself a particularly flagrant example of the critic-dramatist. It is not with me a mere case of an adaptation or two raked up against me as incidents in my past. I have written half-a-dozen 'original' plays, four of which have never been performed; and I shall presently write half-a-dozen more. The production of one of them, even if it attained the merest success of esteem, would be more remunerative to me than a couple of years of criticism. Clearly, since I am no honester than other people, I should be the most corrupt flatterer in London if there were nothing but honesty to restrain me. How is it, then, that the most severe criticisms of managers come from me and from my fellow critic-dramatists, and that the most servile puffery comes from writers whose every sentence proved that they have nothing to hope or fear from any manager? There are a good many answers to this question, one of the most obvious being that as the respect inspired by a good criticism is permanent, whilst the irritation it causes is temporary, and as, on the other hand, the pleasure given by a venal criticism is temporary, and the contempt it inspires permanent, no man really secures his advancement as a dramatist by making himself despised as a critic. The thing has been tried extensively during the last twenty years; and it has failed. For example, the late Frank Marshall, a dramatist and an extravagantly enthusiastic admirer of Sir Henry Irving's genius, followed a fashion which at one time made the Lyceum Theatre a sort of court formed by a retinue of literary gentlemen. I need not question either their sincerity or the superiority of Canute to their idolatry; for Canute never produced their plays: 'Robert Emmet' and the rest of their masterpieces remain unacted to this day. It may be said that this brings us back to honesty as the best policy; but honesty has nothing to do with it: plenty of the men who know that they can get along faster fighting than crawling, are no more honest than the first Napoleon was. No virtue, least of all courage, implies any other virtue. The cardinal guarantee for a critic's integrity is simply the force of the critical instinct itself. To try to prevent me from criticizing by pointing out to me the superior pecuniary advantages of puffing is like trying to keep a young Irving from going on the stage by pointing out the superior pecuniary advantages of stockbroking. If my own father were an actor-manager, and his life depended on his getting favorable notices of his performance, I should orphan myself without an instant's hesitation if he acted badly. I am by no means the willing victim of this instinct. I am keenly susceptible to contrary influences — to flattery, which I swallow greedily if the quality is sufficiently good; to the need of money, to private friendship or even acquaintanceship, to the pleasure of giving pleasure and the pain of giving pain, to consideration of other people's circumstances and prospects, to personal likes and dislikes, to sentimentality, pity, chivalry, pugnacity and mischief, laziness and cowardice, and a dozen other human conditions which make the critic vulnerable; but the critical instinct gets the better of them all. I spare no effort to mitigate its inhumanity, trying to detect and strike out of my articles anything that would give pain without doing any good. Those who think the things I say severe, or even malicious, should just see the things I do *not* say. I do my best to be partial, to hit out at remediable abuses rather than at accidental shortcomings, and at strong and responsible people rather than weak and helpless ones. And yet all my efforts do not alter the result very much. So stubborn is the critic within me, that with every disposition to be as good-natured and as popular an authority as the worst enemy of art could desire, I am to all intents and purposes incorruptible. And that is how the dramatist-critic, if only he is critic enough, 'slates' the actor-manager in defiance of the interest he has in conciliating him. He cannot help himself, any more than the ancient mariner could help telling his story. And the actor-manager can no more help listening than the wedding guest could. In short, the better formula would have been, that a man is either a critic or not a critic; that to the extent to which he is one he will criticize the managers in spite of heaven and earth; and that to the extent to which he is not, he will flatter them anyhow, to save himself trouble.

The advantage of having a play criticized by a critic who is also a playwright is as obvious as the advantage of having a ship criticized by a critic who is also a master shipwright. Pray observe that I do not speak of the criticism of dramas and ships by dramatists and shipwrights who are not also critics; for that would be no more convincing than the criticism of acting by actors. Dramatic authorship no more constitutes a man a critic than actorship constitutes him a dramatic author; but a dramatic critic learns as much from having been a dramatic author as Shakespeare or Mr. Pinero from having been actors. The average London critic, for want of practical experience, has no real confidence in himself: he is always searching for an imaginary 'right' opinion, with which he never dares to identify his own. Consequently every public man finds that as far as the press is concerned his career divides itself into two parts: the first, during which the critics are afraid to praise him; and the second, during which they are afraid to do anything else. In the first, the critic is uncomfortably trying to find faults enough to make out a case for his timid coldness: in the second, he is eagerly picking out excellencies to justify his eulogies. And of course he blunders equally in both phases. The faults he finds are either inessential or are positive reforms, or he blames the wrong people for them: the triumphs of acting which he announces are stage tricks that any old hand could play. In criticizing actresses he is an open and shameless voluptuary. If a woman is pretty, well dressed, and self-satisfied enough to be at her ease on the stage, he is delighted; and if she is a walking monument of handsome incompetence, so much the better, as your voluptuary rarely likes a woman to be cleverer than himself, or to force him to feel deeply or think energetically when he only wants to wallow in her good looks. Confront him with an actress who will not condescend to attack him on this side — who takes her work with thorough seriousness and self-respect — and his resentment, his humiliation, his sense of being snubbed, break out ludicrously in his writing, even when he dare not write otherwise than favorably. No dramatist begins by writing plays merely as excuses for the exhibition of pretty women on the stage. He comes to that ultimately perhaps; but at first he does his best to create real characters and make them pass through three acts of real experiences. Bring a critic who has done this face to face with the practical question of selecting an actress for his heroine, and he suddenly realizes for the first time that there is not such a galaxy of talent on the London stage as he thought, and that the handsome walking ladies whom he always thought good enough for other people's plays are not good enough for his own. That is already an immense step in his education. There are other steps, too, which he will have taken before the curtain falls on the first public representation of his play; but they may be summed up in the fact that the author of a play is the only person who really wants to have it well done in every respect, and who therefore has every drawback brought fully home to him. The man who has had that awakening about one play will thenceforth have his eyes open at all other plays; and there you have at once the first moral with the first technical qualification of the critic — the determination to have every play as well done as possible, and the knowledge of what is standing in the way of that consummation. Those of our critics who, either as original dramatists or adapters and translators, have superintended the production of plays with paternal anxiety, are never guilty of the wittily disguised indifference of clever critics who have never seen a drama through from its first beginnings behind the scenes. Compare the genuine excitement of Mr. Clement Scott, or the almost Calvinistic seriousness of Mr. Wm. Archer with the gaily easy what-does-it-matterness of Mr. Walkley, and you see at once how the two critic-dramatists influence the drama, whilst the critic-playgoer only makes it a pretext for entertaining his readers. On the whole there is only as much validity in the theory that a critic should not be a dramatist, as in the theory that a judge should not be a lawyer nor a general a soldier. You cannot have qualifications without experience; and you cannot have experience without personal interest and bias. That may not be an ideal arrangement; but it is the way the world is built; and we must make the best of it.

JOSEPH CONRAD (1857–1924).

From A PERSONAL RECORD

WITH THE MARSEILLES PILOTS

Shortly before midnight I walked down the quay of the *Vieux Port* to join the pilot-boat of my friends. I knew where she would be waiting for her crew, in the little bit of a canal behind the fort at the entrance of the harbor. The deserted quays looked very white and dry in the moonlight, and as if frost-bound in the sharp air of that December night. A prowler or two slunk by noiselessly; a custom-house guard, soldier-like, a sword by his side, paced close under the bowsprits of the long row of ships moored bows on opposite the long, slightly curved, continuous flat wall of the tall houses that seemed to be one immense abandoned building with innumerable windows shuttered closely. Only here and there a small, dingy café for sailors cast a yellow gleam on the bluish sheen of the flag-stones. Passing by, one heard a deep murmur of voices inside — nothing more. How quiet everything was at the end of the quays on the last night on which I went out for a service cruise as a guest of the Marseilles pilots! Not a footstep, except my own, not a sigh, not a whisper-ing echo of the usual revelry going on in the narrow, unspeakable lanes of the Old Town reached my ear — and suddenly, with a terrific jingling rattle of iron and glass, the omnibus of the Jolliette on its last journey swung round the corner of the dead wall which faced across the paved road the characteristic angular mass of the Fort St. Jean. Three horses trotted abreast, with the clatter of hoofs on the granite setts, and the yellow, uproarious machine jolted violently behind them, fan-tastic, lighted up, perfectly empty, and with the driver apparently asleep on his swaying perch above that amazing racket. I flattened myself against the wall and gasped. It was a stunning experience. Then after staggering on a few paces in the shadow of the fort, casting a dark-ness more intense than that of a clouded night upon the canal, I saw the tiny light of a lantern standing on the quay, and became aware of muffled figures making toward it from various directions. Pilots of the Third Company hastening to em-bark. Too sleepy to be talkative, they step on board in silence. But a few low grunts and an enormous yawn are heard. Somebody even ejaculates: 'Ah! Coquin de sort!' and sighs wearily at his hard fate.

The *patron* of the Third Company (there were five companies of pilots at that time, I believe) is the brother-in-law of my friend Solary (Baptistin), a broad-shouldered, deep-chested man of forty, with a keen, frank glance which always seeks your eyes. He greets me by a low, hearty '*Hé, l'ami. Comment va?*' With his clipped mustache and massive open face, energetic and at the same time placid in expression, he is a fine specimen of the southerner of the calm type. For there is such a type in which the volatile southern passion is transmuted into solid force. He is fair, but no one could mis-take him for a man of the north even by the dim gleam of the lantern standing on the quay. He is worth a dozen of your ordinary Normans or Bretons, but then, in the whole immense sweep of the Med-iterranean shores, you could not find half a dozen men of his stamp.

Standing by the tiller, he pulls out his watch from under a thick jacket and bends his head over it in the light cast into the boat. Time's up. His pleasant voice commands, in a quiet undertone, '*Lar-guez.*' A suddenly projected arm snatches the lantern off the quay — and, warped along by a line at first, then with the reg-ular tug of four heavy sweeps in the bow, the big half-decked boat full of men glides out of the black, breathless shadow of the fort. The open water of the *avant-port* glitters under the moon as if sown over with millions of sequins, and the long white breakwater shines like a thick bar of solid silver. With a quick rattle of blocks and one single silky swish, the sail is filled by a little breeze keen enough to have come straight down from the frozen moon, and the boat, after the clat-ter of the hauled-in sweeps, seems to stand at rest, surrounded by a mysterious whispering so faint and unearthly that it may be the rustling of the brilliant, over-powering moonrays breaking like a rain-shower upon the hard, smooth, shadowless sea.

I may well remember that last night spent with the pilots of the Third Com-pany. I have known the spell of moon-light since, on various seas and coasts — coasts of forests, of rocks, of sand dunes — but no magic so perfect in its revela-tion of unsuspected character, as though one were allowed to look upon the mystic nature of material things. For hours I suppose no word was spoken in that boat. The pilots, seated in two rows facing each other, dozed, with their arms folded and their chins resting upon their breasts. They displayed a great variety of caps: cloth, wool, leather, peaks, ear-flaps, tas-sels, with a picturesque round *béret* or two pulled down over the brows; and one grandfather, with a shaved, bony face and a great beak of a nose, had a cloak with a hood which made him look in our midst like a cowled monk being carried off goodness knows where by that silent com-pany of seamen — quiet enough to be dead.

My fingers itched for the tiller, and in due course my friend, the *patron*, surren-dered it in the same spirit in which the family coachman lets a boy hold the reins on an easy bit of road. There was a great solitude around us; the islets ahead, Monte Cristo and the Chateau d'If in full light, seemed to float toward us — so steady, so imperceptible was the progress of our boat. 'Keep her in the furrow of the moon,' the *patron* directed me, in a quiet murmur, sitting down ponderously in the stern-sheets and reaching for his pipe.

The pilot station in weather like this was only a mile or two to the westward of the islets; and presently, as we approached the spot, the boat we were going to relieve swam into our view suddenly, on her way home, cutting black and sinister into the wake of the moon under a sable wing, while to them our sail must have been a vision of white and dazzling radiance. Without altering the course a hair's breadth we slipped by each other within an oar's length. A drawling, sardonic hail came out of her. Instantly, as if by magic, our dozing pilots got on their feet in a body. An incredible babel of bantering shouts burst out, a jocular, passionate, voluble chatter, which lasted till the boats were stern to stern, theirs all bright now, and, with a shining sail to our eyes, we turned all black to their vision, and drew away from them under a sable wing. That extraordinary uproar died away almost as suddenly as it had begun; first one had enough of it and sat down, then another, then three or four together; and when all had left off with mutters and growling half-laughs the sound of hearty chuckling became audible, persistent, unnoticed. The cowled grandfather was very much entertained somewhere within his hood.

He had not joined in the shouting of jokes, neither had he moved the least bit. He had remained quietly in his place against the foot of the mast. I had been given to understand long before that he had the rating of a second-class able seaman (*matelot léger*) in the fleet which sailed from Toulon for the conquest of Algeria in the year of grace 1830. And, indeed, I had seen and examined one of the buttons of his old brown, patched coat, the only brass button of the miscellaneous lot, flat and thin, with the words *Equipages de ligne* engraved on it. That sort of button, I believe, went out with the last of the French Bourbons. 'I preserved it from the time of my navy service,' he explained, nodding rapidly his frail, vulture-like head. It was not very likely that he had picked up that relic in the street. He looked certainly old enough to have fought at Trafalgar — or, at any rate, to have played his little part there as a powder-monkey. Shortly after we had been introduced he had informed me in a Franco-Provençal jargon, mumbling tremulously with his toothless jaws, that when he was a 'shaver no higher than that' he had seen the Emperor Napoleon returning from Elba. It was at night, he narrated vaguely, without animation, at a spot between Fréjus and Antibes, in the open country. A big fire had been lit at the side of the cross-roads. The population from several villages had collected there, old and young — down to the very children in arms, because the women had refused to stay at home. Tall soldiers wearing high, hairy caps stood in a circle, facing the people silently, and their stern eyes and big mustaches were enough to make everybody keep at a distance. He, 'being an impudent little shaver,' wriggled out of the crowd, creeping on his hands and knees as near as he dared to the grenadiers' legs, and peeping through discovered, standing perfectly still in the light of the fire, 'a little fat fellow in a three-cornered hat, buttoned up in a long straight coat, with a big, pale face inclined on one shoulder, looking something like a priest. His hands were clasped behind his back. . . . It appears that this was the Emperor,' the ancient commented, with a faint sigh. He was staring from the ground with all his might, when 'my poor father,' who had been searching for his boy frantically everywhere, pounced upon him and hauled him away by the ear.

The tale seems an authentic recollection. He related it to me many times, using the very same words. The grandfather honored me by a special and somewhat embarrassing predilection. Extremes touch. He was the oldest member by a long way in that company, and I was, if I may say so, its temporarily adopted baby. He had been a pilot longer than any man in the boat could remember; thirty — forty years. He did not seem certain himself, but it could be found out, he suggested, in the archives of the Pilot-office. He had been pensioned off years before, but he went out from force of habit; and, as my friend the *patron* of the company once confided to me in a whisper, 'the old chap did no harm. He was not in the way.' They treated him with rough deference. One and another would address some insignificant remark to him now and again, but nobody really took any notice of what he had to say. He had survived his strength, his usefulness, his very wisdom. He wore long, green, worsted stockings pulled up above the knee over his trousers, a sort of woolen nightcap on his hairless cranium, and wooden clogs on his feet. Without his hooded cloak he looked like a peasant. Half a dozen hands would be extended to help him on board, but afterward he was left pretty much to his own thoughts. Of course he never did any work, except, perhaps, to cast off some rope when hailed, '*Hé, l'Ancien!* let go the halyards there, at your hand'— or some such request of an easy kind.

No one took notice in any way of the chuckling within the shadow of the hood. He kept it up for a long time with intense enjoyment. Obviously he had preserved intact the innocence of mind which is easily amused. But when his hilarity had exhausted itself, he made a professional remark in a self-assertive but quavering voice:

'Can't expect much work on a night like this.'

No one took it up. It was a mere truism. Nothing under canvas could be expected to make a port on such an idle night of dreamy splendor and spiritual stillness. We would have to glide idly to and fro, keeping our station within the appointed bearings, and, unless a fresh breeze sprang up with the dawn, we would land before sunrise on a small islet that, within two miles of us, shone like a lump of frozen moonlight, to 'break a crust and take a pull at the wine bottle.' I was familiar with the procedure. The stout boat emptied of her crowd would nestle her buoyant, capable side against the very rock — such is the perfectly smooth amenity of the classic sea when in a gentle mood. The crust broken and the mouthful of wine swallowed — it was literally no more then that with this abstemious race — the pilots would pass the time stamping their feet on the slabs of sea-salted stone and blowing into their nipped fingers. One or two misanthropists would sit apart, perched on boulders like man-like sea-fowl of solitary habits; the so-ciably disposed would gossip scandalously in little gesticulating knots; and there would be perpetually one or another of my hosts taking aim at the empty horizon with the long, brass tube of the telescope, a heavy, murderous-looking piece of collective property, everlastingly changing hands with brandishing and leveling movements. Then about noon (it was a short turn of duty — the long turn lasted twenty-four hours) another boatful of pilots would relieve us — and we should steer for the old Phœnician port, dominated, watched over from the ridge of a dust-gray, arid hill by the red-and-white striped pile of the Notre Dame de la Garde.

All this came to pass as I had foreseen in the fullness of my very recent experience. But also something not foreseen by me did happen, something which causes me to remember my last outing with the pilots. It was on this occasion that my hand touched, for the first time, the side of an English ship.

No fresh breeze had come with the dawn, only the steady little draught got a more keen edge on it as the eastern sky became bright and glassy with a clean, colorless light. It was while we were all ashore on the islet that a steamer was picked up by the telescope, a black speck like an insect posed on the hard edge of the offing. She emerged rapidly to her water-line and came on steadily, a slim hull with a long streak of smoke slanting away from the rising sun. We embarked in a hurry, and headed the boat out for our prey, but we hardly moved three miles an hour.

She was a big, high-class cargo-steamer of a type that is to be met on the sea no more — black hull, with low, white super-structures, powerfully rigged with three masts and a lot of yards on the fore; two hands at her enormous wheel — steam steering-gear was not a matter of course in these days — and with them on the bridge three others, bulky in thick blue jackets, ruddy-faced, muffled up, with peak caps — I suppose all her officers. There are ships I have met more than once and known well by sight whose names I have forgotten; but the name of that ship once seen so many years ago in the clear flush of a cold, pale sunrise I have not forgotten. How could I — the first English ship on whose side I ever laid my hand! The name — I read it letter by letter on the bow — was *James Westoll.* Not very romantic, you will say. The name of a very considerable, well-known, and universally respected ship-owner, I believe. James Westoll! What better name could an honorable hard-working ship have? To me the very grouping of the letters is alive with the romantic feeling of her reality as I saw her floating motionless and borrowing an ideal grace from the austere purity of the light.

We were then very near her and, on a sudden impulse, I volunteered to pull bow in the dinghy which shoved off at once to put the pilot on board while our boat, fanned by the faint air which had attended us all through the night, went on gliding gently past the black, glistening length of the ship. A few strokes brought us alongside, and it was then that, for the very first time in my life, I heard myself addressed in English — the speech of my secret choice, of my future, of long friendships, of the deepest affections, of hours of toil and hours of ease, and of solitary hours, too, of books read, of thoughts pursued, of remembered emotions — of my very dreams! And if (after being thus fashioned by it in that part of me which cannot decay) I dare not claim it aloud as my own, then, at any rate, the speech of my children. Thus small events grow memorable by the passage of time. As to the quality of the address itself I cannot say it was very striking. Too short for eloquence and devoid of all charm of tone, it consisted precisely of the three words 'Look out there!' growled out huskily above my head.

It proceeded from a big fat fellow (he had an obtrusive, hairy double chin) in a blue woolen shirt and roomy breeches pulled up very high, even to the level of his breast-bone, by a pair of braces quite exposed to public view. As where he stood there was no bulwark, but only a rail and stanchions, I was able to take in at a glance the whole of his voluminous person from his feet to the high crown of his soft black hat, which sat like an absurd flanged cone on his big head. The grotesque and massive aspect of that deckhand (I suppose he was that — very likely the lamp-trimmer) surprised me very much. My course of reading, of dreaming, and longing for the sea had not prepared me for a sea brother of that sort. I never met again a figure in the least like

his except in the illustrations to Mr. W. W. Jacobs's most entertaining tales of barges and coasters; but the inspired talent of Mr. Jacobs for poking endless fun at poor, innocent sailors in a prose which, however extravagant in its felicitous invention, is always artistically adjusted to observed truth, was not yet. Perhaps Mr. Jacobs himself was not yet. I fancy that, at most, if he had made his nurse laugh it was about all he had achieved at that early date.

Therefore, I repeat, other disabilities apart, I could not have been prepared for the sight of that husky old porpoise. The object of his concise address was to call my attention to a rope which he incontinently flung down for me to catch. I caught it, though it was not really necessary, the ship having no way on her by that time. Then everything went on very swiftly. The dinghy came with a slight bump against the steamer's side; the pilot, grabbing the rope ladder had scrambled half-way up before I knew that our task of boarding was done; the harsh, muffled clanging of the engine-room telegraph struck my ear through the iron plate; my companion in the dinghy was urging me to 'shove off — push hard'; and when I bore against the smooth flank of the first English ship I ever touched in my life, I felt it already throbbing under my open palm.

Her head swung a little to the west, pointing toward the miniature lighthouse of the Jolliette breakwater, far away there, hardly distinguishable against the land. The dinghy danced a squashy, splashy jig in the wash of the wake; and, turning in my seat, I followed the *James Westoll* with my eyes. Before she had gone in a quarter of a mile she hoisted her flag, as the harbor regulations prescribe for arriving and departing ships. I saw it suddenly flicker and stream out on the flagstaff. The Red Ensign! In the pellucid, colorless atmosphere of that southern land, the livid islets, the sea of pale, glassy blue under the pale, glassy sky of that cold sunrise, it was, as far as the eye could reach, the only spot of ardent color — flame-like, intense, and presently as minute as the tiny red spark the concentrated reflection of a great fire kindles in the clear heart of a globe of crystal. The Red Ensign — the symbolic, protecting, warm bit of bunting flung wide upon the seas, and destined for so many years to be the only roof over my head.

H. G. WELLS (1866–)

From SOCIAL FORCES IN ENGLAND AND AMERICA

THE CONTEMPORARY NOVEL

It is no new discovery that the novel, like the drama, is a powerful instrument of moral suggestion. This has been understood in England ever since there has been such a thing as a novel in England. This has been recognized equally by novelists, novel-readers, and the people who wouldn't read novels under any condition whatever. Richardson wrote deliberately for edification, and *Tom Jones* is a powerful and effective appeal for a charitable, and even indulgent, attitude towards loose-living men. But excepting Fielding and one or two other of those partial exceptions that always occur in the case of critical generalizations, there is a definable difference between the novel of the past and what I may call the modern novel. It is a difference that is reflected upon the novel from a difference in the general way of thinking. It lies in the fact that formerly there was a feeling of certitude about moral values and standards of conduct that is altogether absent to-day. It wasn't so much that men were agreed upon these things — about these things there have always been enormous divergences of opinion — as that men were emphatic, cock-sure, and unteachable about whatever they did happen to believe to a degree that no longer obtains. This is the Balfourian age, and even religion seeks to establish itself on doubt. There were, perhaps, just as many differences in the past as there are now, but the outlines were harder — they were, indeed, so hard as to be almost, to our sense, savage. You might be a Roman Catholic, and in that case you did not want to hear about Protestants, Turks, Infidels, except in tones of horror and hatred. You knew exactly what was good and what was evil. Your priest informed you upon these points, and all you needed in any novel you read was a confirmation, implicit or explicit, of these vivid, rather than charming, prejudices. If you were a Protestant you were equally clear and unshakable. Your sect, whichever sect you belonged to, knew the whole of truth and included all the nice people. It had nothing to learn in the world, and it wanted to learn nothing outside its sectarian convictions. The unbelievers, you know, were just as bad, and said their creeds with an equal fury — merely interpolating *nots*. People of every sort — Catholic, Protestant, Infidel, or what not — were equally clear that good was good and bad was bad, that the world was made up of good characters whom you had to love, help and admire, and of bad characters to whom one might, in the interests of goodness, even lie, and whom one had to foil, defeat and triumph over shamelessly at every opportunity. That was the quality of the times. The novel reflected this quality of assurance, and its utmost charity was to unmask an apparent villain and show that he or she was really profoundly and correctly good, or to unmask an apparent saint and show the hypocrite. There was no such penetrating and pervading element of doubt and curiosity — and charity, about the rightfulness and beauty of conduct, such as one meets on every hand to-day.

The novel-reader of the past, therefore, like the novel-reader of the more provincial parts of England to-day, judged a novel by the convictions that had been built up in him by his training and his priest or his pastor. If it agreed with these convictions he approved; if it did not agree he disapproved — often with great energy. The novel, where it was not unconditionally banned altogether as a thing disturbing and unnecessary, was regarded as a thing subordinated to the teaching of the priest or pastor, or whatever director and dogma was followed. Its modest moral confirmations began when authority had completed its direction. The novel was good — if it seemed to harmonize with the graver exercises conducted by Mr. Chadband — and it was bad and outcast if Mr. Chadband said so. And it is over the bodies of discredited and disgruntled Chadbands that the novel escapes from its servitude and inferiority.

Now the conflict of authority against criticism is one of the eternal conflicts of humanity. It is the conflict of organization against initiative, of discipline against freedom. It was the conflict of the priest against the prophet in ancient Judæa, of the Pharisee against the Nazarene, of the Realist against the Nominalist, of the Church against the Franciscan and the Lollard, of the Respectable Person against the Artist, of the hedgeclippers of mankind against the shooting buds. And to-day, while we live in a period of tightening and extending social organizations, we live also in a period of adventurous and insurgent thought, in an intellectual spring unprecedented in the world's history. There is an enormous criticism going on of the faiths upon which men's lives and associations are based, and of every standard and rule of conduct. And it is inevitable that the novel, just in the measure of its sincerity and ability, should reflect and coöperate in the atmosphere and uncertainties and changing variety of this seething and creative time.

And I do not mean merely that the novel is unavoidably charged with the representation of this wide and wonderful conflict. It is a necessary part of the conflict. The essential characteristic of this great intellectual revolution amidst which we are living to-day, that revolution of which the revival and restatement of nominalism under the name of pragmatism is the philosophical aspect, consists in the reassertion of the importance of the individual instance as against the generalization. All our social, political, moral problems are being approached in a new spirit, in an inquiring and experimental spirit, which has small respect for abstract principles and deductive rules. We perceive more and more clearly, for example, that the study of social organization is an empty and unprofitable study until we approach it as a study of the association and inter-reaction of individualized human beings inspired by diversified motives, ruled by traditions, and swayed by the suggestions of a complex intellectual atmosphere. And all our conceptions of the relationships between man and man, and of justice and rightfulness and social desirableness, remain something misfitting and inappropriate, something uncomfortable and potentially injurious, as if we were trying to wear sharp-edged clothes made for a giant out of tin, until we bring them to the test and measure of realized individualities.

And this is where the value and opportunity of the modern novel comes in. So far as I can see, it is the only medium through which we can discuss the great majority of the problems which are being raised in such bristling multitude by our contemporary social development. Nearly every one of those problems has at its core a psychological problem, and not merely a psychological problem, but one in which the idea of individuality is an essential factor. Dealing with most of these questions by a rule or generalization is like putting a cordon round a jungle full of the most diversified sort of game. The hunting only begins when you leave the cordon behind you and push into the thickets.

Take, for example, the immense cluster of difficulties that arises out of the increasing complexity of our state. On every hand we are creating officials, and compared with only a few years ago the private in a dozen fresh directions comes into contact with officialdom. But we still do practically nothing to work out the interesting changes that occur in this sort of man and that, when you withdraw him as it were from the common crowd of humanity, put his mind if not his body into uniform and endow him with powers and functions and rules. It is manifestly a study of the profoundest public and personal importance. The process of social and political organization that has been going on for the last quarter of a century is pretty clearly going on now if anything with increasing vigor — and for the most part the entire dependence of the consequences of the whole problem upon the reaction between the office on the one hand and the weak, uncertain, various human beings who take office on the other does n't seem even to be suspected by the energetic, virtuous and more or less amiable people whose activities in politics and upon the back stairs of politics bring about these developments. They assume that the sort of official they need, a combination of godlike virtue and intelligence with unfailing mechanical obedience, can be made out of just any young nephew. And I know of no means of persuading people that this is a rather unjustifiable assumption, and of creating an intelligent controlling criticism of officials and of assisting conscientious officials to an effective self-examination, and generally of keeping the atmosphere of official life sweet and healthy, except the novel. Yet so far the novel has scarcely begun its attack upon this particular field of human life, and all the attractive varied play of motive it contains.

Of course we have one supreme and devastating study of the illiterate minor official in Bumble. That one figure lit up and still lights the whole problem of Poor Law administration for the English reading community. It was a translation of well-meant regulations and pseudo-scientific conceptions of social order into blundering, arrogant, ill-bred flesh and blood. It was worth a hundred Royal Commissions. You may make your regulations as you please, said Dickens in effect; this is one sample of the stuff that will carry them out. But Bumble stands almost alone. Instead of realizing that he is only one aspect of officialdom, we are all too apt to make him the type of all officials, and not an urban district council can get into a dispute about its electric light without being denounced as a Bumbledom by some whirling enemy or other. The burden upon Bumble's shoulders is too heavy to be borne, and we want the contemporary novel to give us a score of other figures to put beside him, other aspects and reflections upon this great problem of officialism made flesh. Bumble is a magnificent figure of the follies and cruelties of ignorance in office — I would have every candidate for the post of workhouse master pass a severe examination upon Oliver Twist — but it is not only caricature and satire I demand. We must have not only the fullest treatment of the temptations, vanities, abuses, and absurdities of office, but all its dreams, its sense of constructive order, its consolations, its sense of service, and its nobler satisfactions. You may say that is demanding more insight and power in our novels and novelists than we can possibly hope to find in them. So much the worse for us. I stick to my thesis that the complicated social organization of to-day cannot get along without the amount of mutual understanding and mutual explanation such a range of characteristics in our novels implies. The success of civilization amounts ultimately to a success of sympathy and understanding. If people cannot be brought to an interest in one another greater than they feel to-day, to curiosities and criticisms far keener, and

coöperations far subtler, than we have now; if class cannot be brought to measure itself against, and interchange experience and sympathy with class, and temperament with temperament, then we shall never struggle very far beyond the confused discomforts and uneasiness of today, and the changes and complications of human life will remain as they are now, very like the crumplings and separations and complications of an immense avalanche that is sliding down a hill. And in this tremendous work of human reconciliation and elucidation, it seems to me it is the novel that must attempt most and achieve most.

You may feel disposed to say to all this: We grant the major premises, but why look to the work of prose fiction as the main instrument in this necessary process of, so to speak, sympathizing humanity together? Cannot this be done far more effectively through biography and autobiography, for example? Isn't there the lyric; and, above all, is n't there the play? Well, so far as the stage goes, I think it is a very charming and exciting form of human activity, a display of actions and surprises of the most moving and impressive sort; but beyond the opportunity it affords for saying startling and thought-provoking things — opportunities like Mr. Shaw, for example, has worked to the utmost limit — I do not see that the drama does much to enlarge our sympathies and add to our stock of motive ideas. And regarded as a medium for startling and thought-producing things, the stage seems to me an extremely clumsy and costly affair. One might just as well go about with a pencil writing up the thought-provoking phrase, whatever it is, on walls. The drama excites our sympathies intensely, but it seems to me it is far too objective a medium to widen them appreciably, and it is that widening, that increase in the range of understanding, at which I think civilization is aiming. The case for biography, and more particularly autobiography, as against the novel, is, I admit, at the first blush stronger. You may say: Why give us these creatures of a novelist's imagination, these phantom and fantastic thinkings and doings, when we may have the histories of real lives, really lived — the intimate record of actual men and women? To which one answers: 'Ah, if one could!' But it is just because biography does deal with actual lives, actual facts, because it radiates out to touch continuing interests and sensitive survivors, that it is so unsatisfactory, so untruthful. Its inseparable falsehood is the worst of all kinds of falsehood — the falsehood of omission. Think what an abounding, astonishing, perplexing person Gladstone must have been in life, and consider Lord Morley's *Life of Gladstone*, cold, dignified — not a life at all, indeed, so much as embalmed remains; the fire gone, the passions gone, the bowels carefully removed. All biography has something of that post-mortem coldness and respect, and as for autobiography — a man may show his soul in a thousand half-unconscious ways, but to turn upon oneself and explain oneself is given to no one. It is the natural liars and braggarts, your Cellinis and Casanovas, men with a habit of regarding themselves with a kind of objective admiration, who do best in autobiography. And, on the other hand, the novel has neither the intense self-consciousness of autobiography nor the paralyzing responsibilities of the biographer. It is by comparison irresponsible and free. Because its characters are figments and phantoms, they can be made entirely transparent. Because they are fictions, and you know they are fictions, so that they cannot hold you for an instant as soon as they cease to be true, they have a power of veracity beyond that of actual records. Every novel carries its own justification and its own condemnation in its success or failure to convince you that *the thing was so*. Now history, biography, blue-book, and so forth, can hardly ever get beyond the statement that the superficial fact was so.

You see now the scope of the claim I am making for the novel; it is to be the social mediator, the vehicle of understanding, the instrument of self-examination, the parade of morals and the exchange of manners, the factory of customs, the criticism of laws and institutions and of social dogmas and ideas. It is to be the home confessional, the initiator of knowledge, the seed of fruitful self-questioning. Let me be very clear here. I do not mean for a moment that the novelist is to set up as a teacher, as a sort of priest with a pen, who will make men and women believe and do this and that. The novel is not a new sort of pulpit; humanity is passing out of the phase when men *sit under* preachers and dogmatic influences. But the novelist is going to be the most potent of artists, because he is going to present conduct, devise beautiful conduct, discuss conduct, analyze conduct, suggest conduct, illuminate it through and through. He will not teach, but discuss, point out, plead, and display. And this being my view you will be prepared for the demand I am now about to make for an absolutely free hand for the novelist in his choice of topic and incident and in his method of treatment; or, rather, if I may presume to speak for other novelists, I would say it is not so much a demand we make as an intention we proclaim. We are going to write, subject only to our limitations, about the whole of human life. We are going to deal with political questions and religious questions and social questions. We cannot present people unless we have this free hand, this unrestricted field. What is the good of telling stories about people's lives if one may not deal freely with the religious beliefs and organizations that have controlled or failed to control them? What is the good of pretending to write about love, and the loyalties and treacheries and quarrels of men and women, if one must not glance at those varieties of physical temperament and organic quality, those deeply passionate needs and distresses from which half the storms of human life are brewed? We mean to deal with all these things and it will need very much more than the disapproval of provincial librarians, the hostility of a few influential people in London, the scurrility of one paper, and the deep and obstinate silences of another, to stop the incoming tide of aggressive novel-writing. We are going to write about it all. We are going to write about business and finance and politics and precedence and pretentiousness and decorum and indecorum, until a thousand pretenses and ten thousand impostures shrivel in the cold, clear air of our elucidations. We are going to write of wasted opportunities and latent beauties until a thousand new ways of living open to men and women. We are going to appeal to the young and the hopeful and the curious, against the established, the dignified, and defensive. Before we have done, we will have all life within the scope of the novel.

JOHN GALSWORTHY (1867–)

From A COMMENTARY

THE LOST DOG

It was the first October frost. Outside a half-built house, before a board on which was written, 'Jolly Bros., Builders,' I saw a man, whose eyes seemed saying: 'In the winter building will stop; if I am homeless and workless now, what shall I be in two months' time?' Turning to me he said: 'Can you give me a job, Sir? I don't mind what I do.'

His face was in mourning for a shave, his clothes were very ragged, and he was so thin that there seemed hardly any man behind those ragged clothes. He smelt, not indeed of whisky, but as though bereaved of it; and his blue and watery eyes were like those of a lost dog.

We looked at each other, and this conversation passed between our eyes:

'What are you? Where did you work last? How did you get into this condition? Are you married? How many children? Why don't you apply to the proper authorities? I have money, and you have none; it is my right to ask these questions.'

'I am a lost dog.'

'But I have no work for you; if you are really hungry I can give you sixpence; I can also refer you to a Society who will examine your affairs, but if they find you a man for whom life has been too much, they will tell me so, and warn me not to help you. Is that what you want?'

'I am a lost dog.'

'I dare say; but what can I do? I can't make work! I know nothing about you, I dare n't recommend you to my friends. No man gets into the condition you are in without the aid of his own folly. You say you fell ill; yes, but you all say that. Why could n't you look ahead and save some money? You see now that you ought to have? And yet you come to me! I have a great many calls — societies, old people, and the sick; the rates are very high — you know that — partly on your account!'

'I am a lost dog.'

'Ah! but I am told daily by the just, the orderly, the practical, who have never been lost or hungry, that I must not give to casuals. You know yourself it would be pure sentiment; you know yourself it would be mere luxury. I wonder you can ask me!'

'I am a lost dog.'

'You have said that before. It's not as if I did n't know you! I have seen and talked with you — with dozens of you. I have found you asleep on the Thames Embankment. I have given you sixpence when you were shambling empty away after running a mile behind a cab. One night, don't you remember, in the Cromwell Road — well, not you, but your twin brother — we talked together in the rain, and the wind blew your story against the shuttered windows of the tall, closed houses. Once you were with me quite six weeks, cutting up a dead tree in my garden. Day after day you sat there, working very slowly to keep the tree from coming to an end, and showing me in gratitude each morning your waistbelt filling out. With the saw in your hand and your weak smile you would look at me, and your eyes would say: "You don't know what a rest it is for me to come here and cut up wood all day." At all events, you *must* remember how you kept yourself from whisky until I went away, and how you excused yourself when I returned and found you speaking thickly in the morning: "I can't *help* rememberin' things!" It was not you, you say? No; it was your double.'

'I am a lost dog.'

'Yes, yes, yes! You are one of those men that our customs breed. You had no business to be born — or at any rate you should have seen to it that you were born in the upper classes. What right had you to imagine you could ever tackle the working-man's existence — up to the mark all day and every day? You, a man with a soft spot? You knew, or your parents ought to have known, that you could n't stand more than a certain pressure from life. You are diseased, if not physically, then in your disposition. Am I to excuse you because of that? Most probably I should be the same if life pressed hard enough. Am I to excuse myself because of that? Never — until it happens! Being what you are you chose deliberately — or was it chosen for you? — to run the risks of being born; and now you complain of the consequences, and come to me for help? To me — who may myself at some time be in need, if not of physical, of moral bread? Is it right, or reasonable?'

'I am a lost dog.'

'You are getting on my nerves! Your chin is weak — I can see that through your beard; your eyes are wistful, not like the professional beggar's pebbly eyes; you have a shuffling walk, due perhaps a little to the nature of your boots; yes, there are all the marks of amiability about you. Can you look me in the face and say it would be the slightest use to put you on your legs and thrust you again, equipped, into the ranks of battle? Can you, now? Ah! if you could only get some clothes on you, and some work to do! But don't you know that, three weeks hence, that work would be lost, those clothes in pawn, and you be on the drink? Why should I waste my charity on *you* — "the deserving" are so many! There's "something against you" too? Oh! nothing much — you're not the sort that makes a criminal; if you were you would not be in such a state. You would be glad enough to do your fellows a good turn yourself; and you are not ungrateful, you would attach yourself to any one who showed you kindness. But you are hopeless, hopeless, hopeless — are n't you now?'

'I am a lost dog.'

'You know our methods with lost dogs? Have you never heard of the lethal chamber? A real tramp, living from hand to mouth in sun and rain and dirt and rags, enjoys his life. But *you* don't enjoy the state you're in. You're afraid of the days when you've nothing to eat, afraid of the nights when you've nowhere to sleep, afraid of crime, afraid even of this begging; twice since we've been standing here I've seen you looking round. If you knew you'd be afraid like this, what made you first desert the narrow path? Something came over you? How could you let it come like that? It still comes over you? You were tired, you wanted something new — something a little new. We all want that something, friend, and get it if we can; but we can't recognize that *your* sort of human creature is entitled, for you see what's come of it?'

'I am a lost dog.'

'You say that as if you thought there were one law for the rich and another for the poor. You are making a mistake. If I am had up for begging as well as you, we shall both of us go to prison. The fact that I have no need to steal or beg, can pay for getting drunk and taking holidays, is hardly to the point — you must see that! Do not be led away by sentimental talk; if we appear before a judge, we both must suffer punishment. I am not so likely to appear as you perhaps, but that's an accident. No, please don't say that dreadful thing again! I wish to help you. There is Canada, but they don't want you. I would send you anywhere to stop your eyes from haunting me, but they don't want you. Where do they want you? Tell me, and you shall go.'

'I am a lost dog.'

'You remind me of that white shadow with little liver spots that my spaniel dog and I picked up one night when we were going home.

'"Master," he said, "there's such an amusing cur out there in the middle of the road."

'"Behave yourself! Don't pick up with anything you come across like this!"

'"Master, I know it is a thin and dirty cur, but the creature follows me."

'"Keep to heel! The poor dog will get lost if you entice him far from home."

'"Oh, master! that's just what's so amusing. He has n't any."

'And like a little ghost the white dog crept along behind. We took him home — and how he ate, and how he drank! But my spaniel said to me:

'"Master, what is the use of bringing in a dog like this? Can't you see what he is like? He has eaten all my meat, drunk my bowl dry, and now he is sleeping in my bed."

'I said to him: "My dear, you ought to like to give this up to this poor dog."

'And he said to me: "Master, I *don't!* He is no good, this dog; I am cleaner and fatter than he. And don't you know there's a place the other side of the water for all this class of dog? When are we going to take him there?"

'And I said to him: "My dear, don't ask me; *I don't know.*" . . .

'And you are like that dog, standing there with those eyes of yours and that weak chin and those weak knees, before this half-built house with the winter coming on. And I am like my spaniel, who knows there is a proper place for all your kind of creature. Man! what shall I do with you?'

'I am a lost dog.'

GILBERT K. CHESTERTON
(1873–)

From A SHORT HISTORY OF ENGLAND

THE RETURN OF THE BARBARIAN

The only way to write a popular history, as we have already remarked, would be to write it backwards. It would be to take common objects of our own street and tell of how each of them came to be in the street at all. And for my immediate purpose it is really convenient to take two objects we have known all our lives, as features of fashion or respectability. One, which has grown rarer recently, is what we call a top-hat; the other, which is still a customary formality, is a pair of trousers. The history of these humorous objects really does give a clue to what has happened in England for the last hundred years. It is not necessary to be an æsthete in order to regard both objects as the reverse of beautiful, as tested by what may be called the rational side of beauty. The lines of human limbs can be beautiful, and so can the lines of loose drapery, but not cylinders too loose to be the first and too tight to be the second. Nor is a subtle sense of harmony needed to see that while there are hundreds of differently proportioned hats, a hat that actually grows larger towards the top is somewhat top-heavy. But what is largely forgotten is this, that these two fantastic objects, which now strike the eye as unconscious freaks, were originally conscious freaks. Our ancestors, to do them justice, did not think them casual or commonplace; they thought them, if not ridiculous, at least rococo. The top-hat was the topmost point of a riot of Regency dandyism, and bucks wore trousers while business men were still wearing knee-breeches. It will not be fanciful to see a certain oriental touch in trousers, which the later Romans also regarded as effeminately oriental; it was an oriental touch found in many florid things of the time—in Byron's poems or Brighton Pavilion. Now, the interesting point is that for a whole serious century these instantaneous phantasies have remained like fossils. In the carnival of the Regency a few fools got into fancy dress, and we have all remained in fancy dress. At least, we have remained in the dress, though we have lost the fancy.

I say this is typical of the most important thing that happened in the Victorian time. For the most important thing was that nothing happened. The very fuss that was made about minor modifications brings into relief the rigidity with which the main lines of social life were left as they were at the French Revolution. We talk of the French Revolution as something that changed the world; but its most important relation to England is that it did not change England. A student of our history is concerned rather with the effect it did not have than the effect it did. If it be a splendid fate to have survived the Flood, the English oligarchy had that added splendour. But even for the countries in which the Revolution was a convulsion, it was the last convulsion—until that which shakes the world to-day. It gave their character to all the commonwealths, which all talked about progress, and were occupied in marking time. Frenchmen, under all superficial reactions, remained republican in spirit, as they had been when they first wore top-hats. Englishmen, under all superficial reforms, remained oligarchical in spirit, as they had been when they first wore trousers. Only one power might be said to be growing, and that in a plodding and prosaic fashion—the power in the North-East whose name was Prussia. And the English were more and more learning that this growth need cause them no alarm, since the North Germans were their cousins in blood and their brothers in spirit.

The first thing to note, then, about the nineteenth century is that Europe remained herself as compared with the Europe of the great war, and that England especially remained herself as compared even with the rest of Europe. Granted this, we may give their proper importance to the cautious internal changes in this country, the small conscious and the large unconscious changes. Most of the conscious ones were much upon the model of an early one, the great Reform Bill of 1832, and can be considered in the light of it. First, from the standpoint of most real reformers, the chief thing about the Reform Bill was that it did not reform. It had a huge tide of popular enthusiasm behind it, which wholly disappeared when the people found themselves in front of it. It enfranchised large masses of the middle classes; it disfranchised very definite bodies of the working classes; and it so struck the balance between the conservative and the dangerous elements in the commonwealth that the governing class was much stronger than before. The date, however, is important, not at all because it was the beginning of democracy, but because it was the beginning of the best way ever discovered of evading and postponing democracy. Here enters the homœopathic treatment of revolution, since so often successful. Well into the next generation Disraeli, the brilliant Jewish adventurer who was the symbol of the English aristocracy being no longer genuine, extended the franchise to the artisans, partly, indeed, as a party move against his great rival, Gladstone, but more as the method by which the old popular pressure was first tired out and then toned down. The politicians said the working-class was now strong enough to be allowed votes. It would be truer to say it was now weak enough to be allowed votes. So in more recent times Payment of Members, which would once have been regarded (and resisted) as an inrush of popular forces, was passed quietly and without resistance, and regarded merely as an extension of parliamentary privileges. The truth is that the old parliamentary oligarchy abandoned their first line of trenches because they had by that time constructed a second line of defense. It consisted in the concentration of colossal political funds in the private and irresponsible power of the politicians, collected by the sale of peerages and more important things, and expended on the gerrymandering of the enormously expensive elections. In the presence of this inner obstacle a vote became about as valuable as a railway ticket when there is a permanent block on the line. The façade and outward form of this new secret government is the merely mechanical application of what is called the Party System. The Party System does not consist, as some suppose, of two parties, but of one. If there were two real parties, there could be no system.

But if this was the evolution of parliamentary reform, as represented by the first Reform Bill, we can see the other side of it in the social reform attacked immediately after the first Reform Bill. It is a truth that should be a tower and a landmark, that one of the first things done by the Reform Parliament was to establish those harsh and dehumanized workhouses which both honest Radicals and honest Tories branded with the black title of the New Bastille. This bitter name lingers in our literature, and can be found by the curious in the works of Carlyle and Hood, but it is doubtless interesting rather as a note of contemporary indignation than as a correct comparison. It is easy to imagine the logicians and the legal orators of the parliamentary school of progress finding many points of differentiation and even of contrast. The Bastille was one central institution; the workhouses have been many, and have everywhere transformed local life with whatever they have to give of social sympathy and inspiration. Men of high rank and great wealth were frequently sent to the Bastille, but no such mistake has ever been made by the more business administration of the workhouse. Over the most capricious operations of the *Lettres de Cachets* there still hovered some hazy traditional idea that a man is put in prison to punish him for something. It was a discovery of a later social science that men who cannot be punished can still be imprisoned. But the deepest and most decisive difference lies in the better fortune of the New Bastille, for no mob has ever dared to storm it, and it never fell.

The new Poor Law was indeed not wholly new in the sense that it was the culmination and clear enunciation of a principle foreshadowed in the earlier Poor Law of Elizabeth, which was one of the many anti-popular effects of the Great Pillage. When the monasteries were swept away and the medieval system of hospitality destroyed, tramps and beggars became a problem, the solution of which has always tended towards slavery, even when the question of slavery has been cleared of the irrelevant question of cruelty. It is obvious that a desperate man might find Mr. Bumble and the Board of Guardians less cruel than cold weather and the bare ground — even if he were allowed to sleep on the ground, which (by a veritable nightmare of nonsense and injustice) he is not. He is actually punished for sleeping under a bush on the specific and stated ground that he cannot afford a bed. It is obvious, however, that he may find his best physical good by going into the workhouse, as he often found it in pagan times by selling himself into slavery. The point is that the solution remains servile, even when Mr. Bumble and the Board of Guardians ceased to be in common sense cruel. The pagan might have the luck to sell himself to a kind master. The principle of the new Poor Law, which has so far proved permanent in our society, is that the man lost all his civic rights and lost them solely through poverty. There is a touch of irony, though hardly of mere hypocrisy, in the fact that the Parliament which effected this reform had just been abolishing black slavery by buying out the slave-owners in the British colonies. The slave-owners were bought out at a price big enough to be called blackmail, but it would be misunderstanding the national mentality to deny the sincerity of the sentiment. Wilberforce represented in this the real wave of Wesleyan religion which had made a humane reaction against Calvinism, and was in no mean sense philanthropic. But there is something romantic in the English mind which can always see what is remote. It is the strongest example of what men lose by being long-sighted. It is fair to say that they gain many things also, the poems that are like adventures and the adventures that are like poems. It is a national savor, and therefore in itself neither good nor evil, and it depends on the application whether we find a scriptural text for it in the wish to take the wings of the morning and abide in the uttermost parts of the sea, or merely in the saying that the eyes of a fool are in the ends of the earth.

Anyhow, the unconscious nineteenth-century movement, so slow that it seems stationary, was altogether in this direction, of which workhouse philanthropy is the type. Nevertheless, it had one national institution to combat and overcome; one institution all the more intensely national because it was not official, and in a sense not even political. The modern Trade Union was the inspiration and creation of the English; it is still largely known throughout Europe by its English name. It was the English expression of the European effort to resist the tendency of Capitalism to reach its natural culmination in slavery. In this it has an almost weird psychological interest, for it is a return to the past by men ignorant of the past, like the subconscious action of some man who has lost his memory. We say that history repeats itself, and it is even more interesting when it unconsciously repeats itself. No man on earth is kept so ignorant of the Middle Ages as the British workman, except perhaps the British business man who employs him, yet all who know even a little of the Middle Ages can see that the modern Trade Union is a groping for the ancient Guild. It is true that those who look to the Trade Union, and even those clear-sighted enough to call it the Guild, are often without the faintest tinge of medieval mysticism, or even of medieval morality. But this fact is itself the most striking and even staggering tribute to medieval morality. It has all the clinching logic of coincidence. If large numbers of the most hardheaded atheists had evolved, out of their own inner consciousness, the notion that a number of bachelors or spinsters ought to live together in celibate groups for the good of the poor, or the observation of certain hours and offices, it would be a very strong point in favor of the monasteries. It would be all the stronger if the atheists had never heard of monasteries; it would be strongest of all if they hated the very name of monasteries. And it is all the stronger because the man who puts his trust in Trades Unions does not call himself a Catholic or even a Christian, if he does call himself a Guild Socialist.

The Trade Union movement passed through many perils, including a ludicrous attempt of certain lawyers to condemn as a criminal conspiracy that Trade Union solidarity of which their own profession is the strongest and most startling example in the world. The struggle culminated in gigantic strikes which split the country in every direction in the earlier part of the twentieth century. But another process, with much more power at its back, was also in operation. The principle represented by the new Poor Law proceeded in its course, and in one important respect altered its course, though it can hardly be said to have altered its object. It can most correctly be stated by saying that the employers themselves, who already organized business, began to organize social reform. It was more picturesquely expressed by a cynical aristocrat in Parliament who said, " We are all Socialists now." The Socialists, a body of completely sincere men led by several conspicuously brilliant men, had long hammered into their heads the hopeless sterility of mere non-interference in exchange. The Socialists proposed that the State should not merely interfere in business but should take over the business, and pay all men as equal wage-earners, or at any rate as wage-earners. The employers were not willing to surrender their own position to the State, and this project has largely faded from politics; but the wiser of them were willing to pay better wages, and they were specially willing to bestow various other benefits so long as they were bestowed after the manner of wages. Thus we had a series of social reforms which, for good or evil, all tended in the same direction; the permission to employees to claim certain advantages *as* employees, and as something permanently different from employers. Of these the obvious examples were Employers' Liability, Old Age Pensions, and, as marking another and more decisive stride in the process, the Insurance Act.

The latter in particular, and the whole plan of the social reform in general, were modeled upon Germany. Indeed the whole English life of this period was overshadowed by Germany. We had now reached, for good or evil, the final fulfilment of that gathering influence which began to grow on us in the seventeenth century, which was solidified by the military alliances of the eighteenth century, and which in the nineteenth century had been turned into a philosophy — not to say a mythology. German metaphysics had thinned our theology, so that many a man's most solemn conviction about Good Friday was that Friday was named after

Freya. German history had simply annexed English history, so that it was almost counted the duty of any patriotic Englishman to be proud of being a German. The genius of Carlyle, the culture preached by Matthew Arnold, would not, persuasive as they were, have alone produced this effect but for an external phenomenon of great force. Our internal policy was transformed by our foreign policy; and foreign policy was dominated by the more and more drastic steps which the Prussian, now clearly the prince of all the German tribes, was taking to extend the German influence in the world. Denmark was robbed of two provinces; France was robbed of two provinces; and though the fall of Paris was felt almost everywhere as the fall of the capital of civilization, a thing like the sacking of Rome by the Goths, many of the most influential people in England still saw nothing in it but the solid success of our kinsmen and old allies of Waterloo. The moral methods which achieved it, the juggling with the Augustenberg claim, the forgery of the Ems telegram, were either successfully concealed or were but cloudily appreciated. The Higher Criticism had entered into our ethics as well as our theology. Our view of Europe was also distorted and made disproportionate by the accident of a natural concern for Constantinople and our route to India, which led Palmerston and later premiers to support the Turk and see Russia as the only enemy. This somewhat cynical reaction was summed up in the strange figure of Disraeli, who made a pro-Turkish settlement full of his native indifference to the Christian subjects of Turkey, and sealed it at Berlin in the presence of Bismarck. Disraeli was not without insight into the inconsistencies and illusions of the English; he said many sagacious things about them, and one especially when he told the Manchester School that their motto was " Peace and Plenty amid a starving people, and with the world in arms." But what he said about peace and plenty might well be parodied as a comment on what he himself said about Peace with Honor. Returning from that Berlin Conference he should have said, " I bring you Peace with Honor; peace with the seeds of the most horrible war of history; and honor as the dupes and victims of the old bully in Berlin."

But it was, as we have seen, especially in social reform that Germany was believed to be leading the way, and to have found the secret of dealing with the economic evil. In the case of Insurance, which was the test case, she was applauded for obliging all her workmen to set apart a portion of their wages for any time of sickness; and numerous other provisions, both in Germany and England, pursued the same ideal, which was that of protecting the poor against themselves. It everywhere involved an external power having a finger in the family pie; but little attention was paid to any friction thus caused, for all prejudices against the process were supposed to be the growth of ignorance. And that ignorance was already being attacked by what was called education — an enterprise also inspired largely by the example, and partly by the commercial competition of Germany. It was pointed out that in Germany governments and great employers thought it well worth their while to apply the grandest scale of organization and the minutest inquisition of detail to the instruction of the whole German race. The government was the stronger for training its scholars as it trained its soldiers; the big businesses were the stronger for manufacturing mind as they manufactured material. English education was made compulsory; it was made free; many good, earnest, and enthusiastic men labored to create a ladder of standards and examinations, which would connect the cleverest of the poor with the culture of the English universities and the current teaching in history or philosophy. But it cannot be said that the connection was very complete, or the achievement so thorough as the German achievement. For whatever reason, the poor Englishman remained in many things much as his fathers had been, and seemed to think the Higher Criticism too high for him even to criticize.

And then a day came, and if we were wise, we thanked God that we had failed. Education, if it had ever really been in question, would doubtless have been a noble gift: education in the sense of the central tradition of history, with its freedom, its family honor, its chivalry which is the flower of Christendom. But what would our populace, in our epoch, have actually learned if they had learned all that our schools and universities had to teach? That England was but a little branch on a large Teutonic tree; that an unfathomable spiritual sympathy, all-encircling like the sea, had always made us the natural allies of the great folk by the flowing Rhine; that all light came from Luther and Lutheran Germany, whose science was still purging Christianity of its Greek and Roman accretions; that Germany was a forest fated to grow; that France was a dung-heap fated to decay — a dung-heap with a crowing cock on it. What would the ladder of education have led to, except a platform on which a posturing professor proved that a cousin german was the same as a German cousin! What would the guttersnipe have learnt as a graduate, except to embrace a Saxon because he was the other half of an Anglo-Saxon? The day came, and the ignorant fellow found he had other things to learn. And he was quicker than his educated countrymen, for he had nothing to unlearn.

He in whose honor all had been said and sung stirred, and stepped across the border of Belgium. Then were spread out before men's eyes all the beauties of his culture and all the benefits of his organization; then we beheld under a lifting daybreak what light we had followed and after what image we had labored to refashion ourselves. Nor in any story of mankind has the irony of God chosen the foolish things so catastrophically to confound the wise. For the common crowd of poor and ignorant Englishmen, because they only knew that they were Englishmen, burst through the filthy cobwebs of four hundred years and stood where their fathers stood when they knew that they were Christian men. The English poor, broken in every revolt, bullied by every fashion, long despoiled of property, and now being despoiled of liberty, entered history with a noise of trumpets, and turned themselves in two years into one of the iron armies of the world. And when the critic of politics and literature, feeling that this war is after all heroic, looks around him to find the hero, he can point to nothing but the mob.

The later nineteenth century produced no poets of sufficient distinction to fill the places left vacant by Tennyson and Browning or even to reach to the eminences still occupied by Swinburne and Meredith; but, nevertheless, just before and after the beginning of the present era a considerable body of poetry was written which will hold a permanent and honorable place in the great record of English literature. The individuality of the poets is as strongly marked as that of the prose writers, and it would be hard to trace any characteristics as common to all. Among much excellent workmanship and remarkable felicity of phrasing, variety of expression is as noteworthy as a wide range of divergence in subjects treated and ideas presented. While some aim at a perfection of form almost classic in its self-restraint, others gain their effects by abruptness, irregularity and intentional disregard of poetic convention and tradition. The examples given below, necessarily restricted by lack of space and other considerations, still afford some suggestion of the characteristic themes chosen by each poet, his individual point of view and mode of expression. Along with these should be read the ' Poems of the Great War ' which are, for convenience of classification, placed under a separate heading.

ROBERT BRIDGES (1844–)

THE GROWTH OF LOVE

(SONNET NO. 50)

The world comes not to an end: her city-
hives
Swarm with the tokens of a changeless trade,
With rolling wheel, driver and flagging jade,
Rich men and beggars, children, priests and
wives.
New homes on old are set, as lives on lives; 5
Invention with invention overlaid:
But still or tool or toy or book or blade
Shaped for the hand, that holds and toils and
strives.

The men to-day toil as their fathers taught,
With little better'd means; for works depend   10
On works and overlap, and thought on
thought:
And thro' all change the smiles of hope
amend
The weariest face, the same love changed in
nought:
In this thing too the world comes not to an
end.

MOONLIGHT

May Marigold is frolic,
She laughs till summer is done;

She hears the Grillie chirping
All day i' the blazing sun.
But when the pale moon rises,   5
She fain her face would hide;
For the high Queen of sorrows
Disdains her empty pride.

Fair Primrose haunts the shadow
With children of the Spring,   10
Till in the bloomy woodland
The nightingale will sing.
And when he lauds the May-night
And spirits throng the grove,
The moon shines thro' the branches   15
And floods her heart with love.

ALICE MEYNELL (1848–1922)

PARTED

Farewell to one now silenced quite,
Sent out of hearing, out of sight, –
My friend of friends, whom I shall miss,—
He is not banished, though, for this,—
Nor he, nor sadness, nor delight.   5

Though I shall talk with him no more,
A low voice sounds upon the shore.
He must not watch my resting-place,
But who shall drive a mournful face
From the sad winds about my door?   10

I shall not hear his voice complain,
But who shall stop the patient rain?

His tears must not disturb my heart,
But who shall change the years, and part
The world from every thought of pain?   15

Although my life is left so dim,
The morning crowns the mountain-rim;
Joy is not gone from summer skies,
Nor innocence from children's eyes,
And all these things are part of him.   20

He is not banished, for the showers
Yet wake this green warm earth of ours.
How can the summer but be sweet?
I shall not have him at my feet
And yet my feet are on the flowers.   25

THE LADY POVERTY

The Lady Poverty was fair:
But she has lost her looks of late,
With change of times and change of air.
Ah, slattern! she neglects her hair,
Her gown, her shoes; she keeps no state   5
As once when her pure feet were bare.

Or—almost worse, if worse can be—
She scolds in parlors, dusts and trims,
Watches and counts. Oh, is this she
Whom Francis met, whose step was free   10
Who with obedience carolled hymns,
In Umbria walked with Chastity?

Where is her ladyhood? Not here,
Not among modern kinds of men;
But in the stony fields, where clear   15
Through the thin trees the skies appear,
In delicate spare soil and fen,
And slender landscape and austere.

THE SHEPHERDESS

She walks—the lady of my delight—
A shepherdess of sheep.
Her flocks are thoughts. She keeps them
white;
She guards them from the steep;
She feeds them on the fragrant height, . 5
And folds them in for sleep.

She roams maternal hills and bright,
Dark valleys safe and deep.
Into that tender breast at night
The chastest stars may peep.   10
She walks—the lady of my delight—
A shepherdess of sheep.

She holds her little thoughts in sight,
Though gay they run and leap.
She is so circumspect and right;   15
She has her soul to keep.
She walks—the lady of my delight—
A shepherdess of sheep.

WILLIAM ERNEST HENLEY
(1849–1903)

OUT OF THE NIGHT THAT COVERS
ME

Out of the night that covers me,
    Black as the pit from Pole to Pole,
I thank whatever gods may be
    For my unconquerable soul.

In the fell clutch of circumstance   5
    I have not winced nor cried aloud;
Under the bludgeonings of chance
    My head is bloody, but unbowed.

Beyond this place of wrath and tears
    Looms but the Horror of the shade,   10
And yet the menace of the years
    Finds and shall find me unafraid.

It matters not how strait the gate,
    How charged with punishments the scroll:
I am the master of my fate;   15
    I am the captain of my soul.

PRO REGE NOSTRO

What have I done for you,
    England, my England?
What is there I would not do,
    England, my own?
With your glorious eyes austere,   5
As the Lord were walking near,
Whispering terrible things and dear
    As the song on your bugles blown,
        England—
Round the world on your bugles blown!   10

Where shall the watchful Sun,
    England, my England,
Match the master-work you've done,
    England, my own?
When shall he rejoice agen   15
Such a breed of mighty men

As come forward, one to ten,
  As the song on your bugles blown,
    England —
Round the world on your bugles blown!   10

Ever the faith endures,
  England, my England: —
'Take and break us: we are yours,
  England, my own!
Life is good, and joy runs high   25
Between English earth and sky:
Death is death; but we shall die
  To the Song on your bugles blown,
    England —
  To the stars on your bugles blown!'   30

They call you proud and hard,
  England, my England:
You with worlds to watch and ward,
  England, my own!
You whose mailed hand keeps the keys   35
Of such teeming destinies,
You could know nor dread nor ease,
  Were the Song on your bugles blown,
    England —
  Round the Pit on your bugles blown!   40

Mother of Ships whose might,
  England, my England,
Is the fierce old Sea's delight,
  England, my own,
Chosen daughter of the Lord,   45
Spouse-in-Chief of the ancient Sword,
There 's the menace of the Word
  In the Song on your bugles blown,
    England —
  Out of heaven on your bugles blown!   50

SIR WILLIAM WATSON
(1856-)

WORDSWORTH'S GRAVE

II

Poet who sleepest by this wandering wave!
  When thou wast born, what birth-gift
    hadst thou then?
To thee what wealth was that the Immortals
    gave,
  The wealth thou gavest in thy turn to men?

Not Milton's keen, translunar music thine; 5
  Not Shakespeare's cloudless, boundless hu-
    man view;

Not Shelley's flush of rose on peaks divine;
  Nor yet the wizard twilight Coleridge
    knew.

What hadst thou that could make so large
    amends
  For all thou hadst not and thy peers pos-
    sessed,   10
Motion and fire, swift means to radiant
    ends? —
  Thou hadst, for weary feet, the gift of
    rest.

From Shelley's dazzling glow or thunderous
    haze,
  From Byron's tempest-anger, tempest-
    mirth,
Men turned to thee and found — not blast
    and blaze,   15
  Tumult of tottering heavens, but peace on
    earth.

Nor peace that grows by Lethe, scentless
    flower,
  There in white languors to decline and
    cease;
But peace whose names are also rapture,
    power,
  Clear sight, and love: for these are parts
    of peace.   20

JOHN DAVIDSON (1857-1909)

THIRTY BOB A WEEK

I couldn't touch a stop and turn a screw,
  And set the blooming world a-work for me,
Like such as cut their teeth — I hope, like
    you —
  On the handle of a skeleton gold key;
I cut mine on a leek, which I eat it every
    week;   5
  I 'm a clerk at thirty bob as you can see.

But I don't allow it 's luck and all a toss;
  There 's no such thing as being starred and
    crossed;
It 's just the power of some to be a boss,
  And the bally power of others to be
    bossed: 10
I face the music, sir; you bet I ain't a cur;
  Strike me lucky if I don't believe I 'm lost!

For like a mole I journey in the dark,
  A-traveling along the underground

From my Pillar'd Halls and broad Suburban
Park,   15
  To come the daily dull official round;
And home again at night with my pipe all
    alight,
  A-scheming how to count ten bob a pound.

And it's often very cold and wet,
  And my missis stitches towels for a hunks;
And the Pillar'd Halls is half of it to let — 21
  Three rooms about the size of traveling
    trunks.
And we cough, my wife and I, to dislocate
    a sigh,
  When the noisy little kids are in their
    bunks.

But you never hear her do a growl or whine,
  For she's made of flint and roses, very
    odd;   26
And I've got to cut my meaning rather fine,
  Or I'd blubber, for I'm made of greens
    and sod:
So p'r'aps we are in Hell for all that I can
    tell,
  And lost and damn'd and served up hot
    to God.   30

I ain't blaspheming, Mr. Silver-tongue;
  I'm saying things a bit beyond your art:
Of all the rummy starts you ever sprung,
  Thirty bob a week's the rummiest start!
With your science and your books and your
    the'ries about spooks,   35
  Did you ever hear of looking in your
    heart?

I didn't mean your pocket, Mr., no:
  I mean that having children and a wife,
With thirty bob on which to come and go,
  Isn't dancing to the tabor and the fife: 40
When it doesn't make you drink, by Heaven!
    it makes you think,
  And notice curious items about life.

I step into my heart and there I meet
  A god-almighty devil singing small,
Who would like to shout and whistle in the
    street,   45
  And squelch the passers flat against the
    wall;
If the whole world was a cake he had the
    power to take,
  He would take it, ask for more, and eat
    them all.

And I meet a sort of simpleton beside,
  The kind that life is always giving beans;

With thirty bob a week to keep a bride   51
  He fell in love and married in his teens:
At thirty bob he stuck; but he knows it is n't
    luck:
  He knows the seas are deeper than tureens.

And the god-almighty devil and the fool   55
  That meet me in the High Street on the
    strike,
When I walk about my heart a-gathering
    wool,
  Are my good and evil angels if you like.
And both of them together in every kind of
    weather
  Ride me like a double-seated bike.   60

That's rough a bit and needs its meaning
    curled.
  But I have a high old hot un in my mind —
A most engrugious notion of the world,
  That leaves your lightning 'rithmetic be-
    hind:
I give it at a glance when I say 'There ain't
    no chance,   65
  Nor nothing of the lucky-lottery kind.'

And it's this way that I make it out to be
  No fathers, mothers, countries, climates —
    none;
Not Adam was responsible for me,
  Nor society, nor systems, nary one: 70
A little sleeping seed, I woke — I did, in-
    deed —
  A million years before the blooming sun.

I woke because I thought the time had come;
  Beyond my will there was no other cause;
And everywhere I found myself at home,   75
  Because I chose to be the thing I was;
And in whatever shape of mollusc or of ape
  I always went according to the laws.

I was the love that chose my mother out;
  I joined two lives and from the union
    burst;   80
My weakness and my strength without a
    doubt
  Are mine alone forever from the first:
It's just the very same with a difference in
    the name
  As 'Thy will be done.' You say it if you
    durst!

They say it daily up and down the land   85
  As easy as you take a drink, it's true;
But the difficultest go to understand,
  And the difficultest job a man can do,

Is to come it brave and meek with thirty bob
    a week,
And feel that that's the proper thing for
    you.   90

It's a naked child against a hungry wolf;
It's playing bowls upon a splitting wreck;
It's walking on a string across a gulf
    With millstones fore-and-aft about your
    neck;
But the thing is daily done by many and
    many a one;   95
And we fall, face downward, fighting, on
    the deck.

FRANCIS THOMPSON
(1859–1907)

THE HOUND OF HEAVEN

I fled Him, down the nights and down the
    days;
I fled Him, down the arches of the years;
I fled Him, down the labyrinthine ways
Of my own mind; and in the mist of tears
I hid from Him, and under running laugh-
    ter.   5
    Up vistaed hopes, I sped;
    And shot, precipitated,
Adown Titanic glooms of chasmèd fears,
From those strong Feet that followed, fol-
    lowed after.

    But with unhurrying chase,   10
    And unperturbèd pace,
Deliberate speed, majestic instancy,
    They beat — and a Voice beat
    More instant than the Feet —
'All things betray thee, who betrayest Me.'

    I pleaded, outlaw-wise,   16
By many a hearted casement, curtained red,
Trellised with intertwining charities;
(For, though I knew His love Who fol-
    lowèd,
    Yet was I sore adread   20
Lest, having Him, I must have naught be-
    side.)
But, if one little casement parted wide,
    The gust of His approach would clash it to.
    Fear wist not to evade as Love wist to
    pursue.
Across the margent of the world I fled,   25
And troubled the gold gateways of the
    stars,

Smiting for shelter on their clangèd bars;
    Fretted to dulcet jars
And silvern chatter the pale ports o' the
    moon.
I said to dawn: Be sudden; to eve: Be
    soon —   30
With thy young skyey blossoms heap me
    over
    From this tremendous Lover!
Float thy vague veil about me, lest He see!
I tempted all His servitors, but to find
My own betrayal in their constancy,   35
In faith to Him their fickleness to me,
    Their traitorous trueness, and their loyal
    deceit.
To all swift things for swiftness did I sue;
    Clung to the whistling mane of every wind.
      But whether they swept, smoothly
      fleet,   40
      The long savannahs of the blue;   41
      Or whether, Thunder-driven,
      They clanged His chariot 'thwart a
      heaven,
Plashy with flying lightnings round the
    spurn o' their feet: —
    Fear wist not to evade as Love wist to pur-
    sue.   45

    Still with unhurrying chase,
    And unperturbèd pace,
Deliberate speed, majestic instancy,
    Came on the following Feet,
    And a Voice above their beat —   50
'Naught shelters thee, who wilt not shel-
    ter Me.'

I sought no more that after which I strayed
    In face of man or maid;
But still within the little children's eyes
    Seems something, something that re-
    plies,   55
They at least are for me, surely for me!
I turned me to them very wistfully;
But just as their young eyes grew sudden
    fair
    With dawning answers there,
Their angel plucked them from me by the
    hair.   60
'Come then, ye other children, Nature's —
    share
With me' (said I) 'your delicate fellowship;
    Let me greet you lip to lip,
    Let me twine with you caresses,
      Wantoning   65
    With our Lady-Mother's vagrant tresses,
      Banqueting
With her in her wind-walled palace,
    Underneath her azured daïs,

Quaffing, as your taintless way is,   70
  From a chalice
Lucent-weeping out of the dayspring.'
  So it was done:
I in their delicate fellowship was one —
Drew the bolt of Nature's secrecies.   75
  I knew all the swift importings
  On the wilful face of skies;
  I knew how the clouds arise,
  Spumèd of the wild sea-snortings;
All that's born or dies   80
Rose and drooped with; made them shapers
Of mine own moods, or wailful or divine —
  With them joyed and was bereaven.
  I was heavy with the even,
When she lit her glimmering tapers   85
  Round the day's dead sanctities.
  I laughed in the morning's eyes.
I triumphed and I saddened with all weather,
  Heaven and I wept together,
And its sweet tears were salt with mortal
    mine;   90
Against the red throb of its sunset-heart
  I laid my own to beat,
  And share commingling heat;
But not by that, by that, was eased my human smart.
In vain my tears were wet on Heaven's gray
    cheek.   95
For ah! we know not what each other says,
  These things and I; in sound *I* speak —
Their sound is but their stir, they speak by
    silences.
Nature, poor stepdame, cannot slake my
    drouth;
  Let her, if she would owe me,   100
Drop yon blue bosom-veil of sky, and show
    me
  The breasts o' her tenderness:
Never did any milk of hers once bless
  My thirsting mouth.
  Nigh and nigh draws the chase,   105
  With unperturbèd pace,
  Deliberate speed, majestic instancy,
  And past those noisèd Feet
  A Voice comes yet more fleet —
  'Lo! naught contents thee, who contentst not Me.'   110

Naked I wait Thy love's uplifted stroke!
My harness piece by piece Thou hast hewn
    from me,
  And smitten me to my knee;
  I am defenseless utterly.
  I slept, methinks, and woke.   115
And, slowly gazing, find me stripped in sleep.

In the rash lustihead of my young powers,
  I shook the pillaring hours
And pulled my life upon me; grimed with
    smears,
I stand amid the dust o' the mounded years —
My mangled youth lies dead beneath the
    heap.   121
My days have crackled and gone up in smoke,
Have puffed and burst as sun-starts on a
    stream.
  Yea, faileth now even dream
The dreamer, and the lute the lutanist;   125
Even the linked fantasies, in whose blossomy twist
I swung the earth a trinket at my wrist,
Are yielding; cords of all too weak account
For earth, with heavy griefs so overplussed.
  Ah! is Thy love indeed   130
A weed, albeit an amaranthine weed,
Suffering no flowers except its own to
    mount?
  Ah! must —
  Designer infinite! —
Ah! must Thou char the wood ere Thou
  canst limn with it?   135
My freshness spent its wavering shower i'
    the dust;
And now my heart is as a broken fount,
Wherein tear-drippings stagnate, spilt down
    ever
  From the dank thoughts that shiver
Upon the sighful branches of my mind.   140
  Such is; what is to be?
The pulp so bitter, how shall taste the rind?
I dimly guess what Time in mists confounds;
Yet ever and anon a trumpet sounds
From the hid battlements of Eternity: 145
Those shaken mists a space unsettle, then
Round the half-glimpsèd turrets slowly wash
    again;
  But not ere him who summoneth
  I first have seen, enwound
With glooming robes purpureal, cypress-
    crowned;   150
His name I know, and what his trumpet saith.
Whether man's heart or life it be which
    yields
  Thee harvest, must Thy harvest fields
  Be dunged with rotten death?

  Now of that long pursuit   155
  Comes on at hand the bruit;
That Voice is round me like a bursting sea:
  'And is thy earth so marred,
  Shattered in shard on shard?
Lo, all things fly thee, for thou fliest Me!
  Strange, piteous, futile thing!   161
Wherefore should any set thee love apart?

Seeing none but I makes much of naught'
   (He said),
'And human love needs human meriting:
   How hast thou merited —   165
Of all man's clotted clay the dingiest clot?
   Alack, thou knowest not
How little worthy of any love thou art!
Whom wilt thou find to love ignoble thee,
   Save Me, save only Me?   170
All which I took from thee I did but take,
   Not for thy harms,

But just that thou might'st seek it in My
   arms.
   All which thy child's mistake
Fancies as lost, I have stored for thee at
   home: 175
   Rise, clasp My hand, and come!'

   Halts by me that footfall:
   Is my gloom, after all,
Shade of His hand, outstretched caress-
   ingly?
   'Ah, fondest, blindest, weakest,   180
   I am He Whom thou seekest!
Thou dravest love from thee, who dravest
   Me.'

ALFRED EDWARD HOUSMAN
(1859–)

A SHROPSHIRE LAD

IV.— REVEILLE

Wake: the silver dusk returning
   Up the beach of darkness brims,
And the ship of sunrise burning
   Strands upon the eastern rims.

Wake: the vaulted shadow shatters,   5
   Trampled to the door it spanned,
And the tent of night in tatters
   Straws the sky-pavilioned land.

Up, lad, up, 't is late for lying:
   Hear the drums of morning play;   10
Hark, the empty highways crying
   'Who 'll beyond the hills away?'

Towns and countries woo together,
   Forelands beacon, belfries call;
Never lad that trod on leather   15
   Lived to feast his heart on all.

Up, lad: thews that lie and cumber
   Sunlit pallets never thrive;
Morns abed and daylight slumber
   Were not meant for man alive.   20

Clay lies still, but blood 's a rover;
   Breath 's a ware that will not keep.
Up, lad: when the journey 's over
   There 'll be time enough to sleep.

V

Oh, see how thick the goldcup flowers
   Are lying in field and lane,
With dandelions to tell the hours
   That never are told again.
Oh, may I squire you round the meads   5
   And pick you posies gay?
—'T will do no harm to take my arm.
   'You may, young man, you may.'

Ah, spring was sent for lass and lad,
   'T is now the blood runs gold,   10
And man and maid had best be glad
   Before the world is old.
What flowers to-day may flower to-mor-
   row,
   But never as good as new.
— Suppose I wound my right arm
   round —   15
   ''T is true, young man, 't is true.'

Some lads there are, 't is shame to say,
   That only court to thieve,
And once they bear the bloom away
   'T is little enough they leave.   20
Then keep your heart for men like me
   And safe from trustless chaps.
My love is true for all and you.
   'Perhaps, young man, perhaps.'

Oh, look in my eyes then, can you doubt?
   — Why, 't is a mile from town.   26
How green the grass is all about!
   We might as well sit down.
—Ah, life, what is it but a flower?
   Why must true lovers sigh?   30
Be kind, have pity, my own, my pretty,—
   'Good-by, young man, good-by.'

XXXIV.— THE NEW MISTRESS

'Oh, sick I am to see you, will you never let
   me be?
You may be good for something but you are
   not good for me.

Oh, go where you are wanted, for you are
    not wanted here.'
And that was all the farewell when I parted
    from my dear.

'I will go where I am wanted, to a lady born
    and bred,   5
Who will dress me free for nothing in a uni-
    form of red;
She will not be sick to see me if I only keep
    it clean;
I will go where I am wanted for a soldier of
    the Queen.

'I will go where I am wanted, for the ser-
    geant does not mind;
He may be sick to see me but he treats me
    very kind: 10
He gives me beer and breakfast and a rib-
    bon for my cap,
And I never knew a sweetheart spend her
    money on a chap.

'I will go where I am wanted, where there's
    room for one or two,
And the men are none too many for the
    work there is to do;
Where the standing line wears thinner and
    the dropping dead lie thick;   15
And the enemies of England they shall see
    me and be sick.'

XLI

In my own shire, if I was sad,
Homely comforters I had:
The earth, because my heart was sore,
Sorrowed for the son she bore;
And standing hills, long to remain,   5
Shared their short-lived comrade's pain.
And bound for the same bourn as I,
On every road I wandered by,
Trod beside me, close and dear,
The beautiful and death-struck year: 10
Whether in the woodland brown
I heard the beechnut rustle down,
And saw the purple crocus pale
Flower about the autumn dale;
Or littering far the fields of May   15
Lady-smocks a-bleaching lay,
And like a skylit water stood
The bluebells in the azured wood.
Yonder, lightening other loads,
The seasons range the country roads,   20
But here in London streets I ken
No such helpmates, only men;
And these are not in plight to bear,
If they would, another's care.
They have enough as 't is: I see   25

In many an eye that measures me
The mortal sickness of a mind
Too unhappy to be kind.
Undone with misery, all they can
Is to hate their fellow man;   30
And till they drop they needs must still
Look at you and wish you ill.

XLIX

Think no more, lad; laugh, be jolly:
    Why should men make haste to die?
Empty heads and tongues a-talking
Make the rough road easy walking,
And the feather pate of folly   5
    Bears the falling sky.
Oh, 't is jesting, dancing, drinking
    Spins the heavy world around.
If young hearts were not so clever,
Oh, they would be young forever: 10
Think no more; 't is only thinking
    Lays lads underground.

SIR HENRY NEWBOLT
(1862–)

DRAKE'S DRUM

Drake he's in his hammock an' a thousand
    mile away,
    (Capten, art tha sleepin' there below?),
Slung atween the round shot in Nombre Dios
    Bay,
    An' dreamin' arl the time o' Plymouth Hoe.
Yarnder lumes the Island, yarnder lie the
    ships,   5
    Wi' sailor lads a dancin' heel-an'-toe,
An' the shore-lights flashin', an' the night-
    tide dashin',
    He sees et arl so plainly as he saw et long
    ago.

Drake he was a Devon man, an' ruled the
    Devon seas,
    (Capten, art tha sleepin' there below?),   10
Rovin' tho' his death fell, he went wi' heart
    at ease,
    An' dreamin' arl the time o' Plymouth Hoe.
'Take my drum to England, hang et by the
    shore,
    Strike et when your powder 's runnin' low;
If the Dons sight Devon, I 'll quit the port
    o' Heaven,   15
    An' drum them up the Channel as we
    drummed them long ago.'

Drake he 's in his hammock till the great
 Armadas come,
(Capten, art tha sleepin' there below?),
Slung atween the round shot, listenin' for
 the drum,
An' dreamin' arl the time o' Plymouth
 Hoe.   20
Call him on the deep sea, call him up the
 Sound,
Call him where ye sail to meet the foe;
Where the old trade 's plyin' an' the old flag
 flyin'
They shall find him ware an' wakin', as
 they found him long ago!

VITAI LAMPADA

There 's a breathless hush in the Close to-
 night —
Ten to make and the match to win —
A bumping pitch and a blinding light,
An hour to play and the last man in.
And it 's not for the sake of a ribboned
 coat,   5
Or the selfish hope of a season's fame,
But his Captain's hand on his shoulder
 smote —
'Play up! play up! and play the game!'

The sand of the desert is sodden red,—
 Red with the wreck of a square that
 broke; —   10
The Gatling 's jammed and the Colonel dead,
 And the regiment blind with dust and
 smoke.
The river of death has brimmed his banks,
 And England 's far, and Honor a name,
But the voice of a schoolboy rallies the
 ranks: 15
'Play up! play up! and play the game!'

This is the word that year by year,
 While in her place the School is set,
Every one of her sons must hear,
 And none that hears it dare forget. 20
This they all with a joyful mind
 Bear through life like a torch in flame,
And falling fling to the host behind —
 'Play up! play up! and play the game!'

CLIFTON CHAPEL

This is the Chapel: here. my son,
 Your father thought the thoughts of youth,
And heard the words that one by one
 The touch of Life has turned to truth.

Here in a day that is not far,   5
 You too may speak with noble ghosts
Of manhood and the vows of war
 You made before the Lord of Hosts.

To set the cause above renown,
 To love the game beyond the prize, 10
To honor, while you strike him down,
 The foe that comes with fearless eyes;
To count the life of battle good,
 And dear the land that gave you birth,
And dearer yet the brotherhood   15
 That binds the brave of all the earth —

My son, the oath is yours: the end
 Is His, Who built the world of strife,
Who gave His children Pain for friend,
 And Death for surest hope of life. 20
To-day and here the fight 's begun,
 Of the great fellowship you 're free;
Henceforth the School and you are one,
 And what You are the race shall be.

God send you fortune: yet be sure, 25
 Among the lights that gleam and pass,
You 'll live to follow none more pure
 Than that which glows on yonder brass.
'Qui procul hinc,' the legend 's writ,—
 The frontier-grave is far away — 30
'Qui ante diem periit:
 Sed miles, sed pro patriâ.'

RUDYARD KIPLING (1865-)

THE BALLAD OF EAST AND WEST

Oh, East is East, and West is West, and
 never the twain shall meet,
Till Earth and Sky stand presently at God's
 great Judgment Seat;
But there is neither East nor West, Border,
 nor Breed. nor Birth,
When two strong men stand face to face,
 tho' they come from the ends of the
 earth!

Kamal is out with twenty men to raise the
 Border side,   5
And he has lifted the Colonel's mare that is
 the Colonel's pride:
He has lifted her out of the stable-door be-
 tween the dawn and the day,
And turned the calkins upon her feet, and
 ridden her far away.
Then up and spoke the Colonel's son that led
 a troop of the Guides:

'Is there never a man of all my men can say
where Kamal hides?'   10
Then up and spoke Mahommed Khan, the
son of the Ressaldar,
'If ye know the track of the morning-mist,
ye know where his pickets are.
'At dusk he harries the Abazai — at dawn
he is into Bonair,
'But he must go by Fort Bukloh to his own
place to fare,
'So if ye gallop to Fort Bukloh as fast as a
bird can fly,
'By the favor of God ye may cut him off ere
he win to the tongue of Jagai,
'But if he be passed the Tongue of Jagai,
right swiftly turn ye then,
'For the length and the breadth of that grisly
plain is sown with Kamal's men.   15
'There is rock to the left, and rock to the
right, and low lean thorn between,
'And ye may hear a breech-bolt snick where
never a man is seen.'
The Colonel's son has taken a horse, and a
raw rough dun was he,
With the mouth of a bell and the heart of
Hell, and the head of the gallows-tree.
The Colonel's son to the Fort has won, they
bid him stay to eat —   20
Who rides at the tail of a Border thief, he
sits not long at his meat.
He 's up and away from Fort Bukloh as fast
as he can fly,
Till he was aware of his father's mare in the
gut of the Tongue of Jagai,
Till he was aware of his father's mare with
Kamal upon her back,
And when he could spy the white of her eye,
he made the pistol crack.   25
He has fired once, he has fired twice, but the
whistling ball went wide.
'Ye shoot like a soldier,' Kamal said. 'Show
now if ye can ride.'
It 's up and over the Tongue of Jagai, as
blown dust-devils go,
The dun he fled like a stag of ten, but the
mare like a barren doe.
The dun he leaned against the bit and slugged
his head above,   30
But the red mare played with the snaffle-
bars, as a maiden plays with a glove.
There was rock to the left and rock to the
right, and low lean thorn between,
And thrice he heard a breech-bolt snick tho'
never a man was seen.
They have ridden the low moon out of the
sky, their hoofs drum up the dawn,
The dun he went like a wounded bull, but
the mare like a new-roused fawn.   35

The dun he fell at a water-course — in a woeful heap fell he,
And Kamal has turned the red mare back,
and pulled the rider free.
He has knocked the pistol out of his hand —
small room was there to strive,
''T was only by favor of mine,' quoth he, 'ye
rode so long alive:
'There was not a rock for twenty mile, there
was not a clump of tree,   40
'But covered a man of my own men with his
rifle cocked on his knee.
'If I had raised my bridle-hand, as I have
held it low,
'The little jackals that flee so fast, were
feasting all in a row:
'If I had bowed my head on my breast, as
I have held it high,
'The kite that whistles above us now were
gorged till she could not fly.'   45
Lightly answered the Colonel's son: —'Do
good to bird and beast,
'But count who come for the broken meats
before thou makest a feast.
'If there should follow a thousand swords
to carry my bones away,
'Belike the price of a jackal's meal were
more than a thief could pay.
'They will feed their horse on the standing
crop, their men on the garnered grain, 50
'The thatch of the byres will serve their
fires when all the cattle are slain.
'But if thou thinkest the price be fair, — thy
brethren wait to sup,
'The hound is kin to the jackal-spawn, —
howl, dog, and call them up!
'And if thou thinkest the price be high, in
steer and gear and stack,
'Give me my father's mare again, and I 'll
fight my own way back!'   55
Kamal has gripped him by the hand and set
him upon his feet.
'No talk shall be of dogs,' said he, 'when
wolf and gray wolf meet.
'May I eat dirt if thou hast hurt of me in
deed or breath;
'What dam of lances brought thee forth to
jest at the dawn with Death?'
Lightly answered the Colonel's son, 'I hold
by the blood of my clan:
'Take up the mare for my father's gift —
by God, she has carried a man!'
The red mare ran to the Colonel's son, and
nuzzled against his breast,   60
'We be two strong men,' said Kamal then,
'but she loveth the younger best.
'So she shall go with a lifter's dower, my
turquoise-studded rein,

'My broidered saddle and saddle-cloth, and
    silver stirrups twain.'
The Colonel's son a pistol drew and held it
    muzzle-end,
'Ye have taken the one from a foe,' said he;
    'will ye take the mate from a friend?' 65
'A gift for a gift,' said Kamal straight; 'a
    limb for the risk of a limb.
'Thy father has sent his son to me, I'll
    send my son to him!'
With that he whistled his only son, that
    dropped from a mountain-crest —
He trod the ling like a buck in spring, and
    he looked like a lance in rest.
'Now here is thy master,' Kamal said, 'who
    leads a troop of the Guides,   70
'And thou must ride at his left side as shield
    on shoulder rides.
'Till Death or I cut loose the tie, at camp
    and board and bed,
'Thy life is his — thy fate it is to guard him
    with thy head.
'So thou must eat the White Queen's meat,
    and all her foes are thine,
'And thou must harry thy father's hold for
    the peace of the Border-line,   75
'And thou must make a trooper tough and
    hack thy way to power —
'Belike they will raise thee to Ressaldar when
    I am hanged in Peshawur.'

They have looked each other between the
    eyes, and there they have found no fault,
They have taken the Oath of the Brother-in-
    Blood on leavened bread and salt:
They have taken the Oath of the Brother-in-
    Blood on fire and fresh-cut sod,   80
On the hilt and the haft of the Khyber knife,
    and the Wondrous Names of God.
The Colonel's son he rides the mare and
    Kamal's boy the dun,
And two have come back to Fort Bukloh
    where there went forth but one.
And when they drew to the Quarter-Guard,
    full twenty swords flew clear —
There was not a man but carried his feud
    with the blood of the mountaineer.   85
'Ha' done! ha' done!' said the Colonel's son.
    'Put up the steel at your sides!
'Last night ye had struck at a Border thief
    — to-night 't is a man of the Guides!'

Oh, East is East, and West is West, and
    never the two shall meet,
Till Earth and Sky stand presently at God's
    great Judgment Seat;
But there is neither East nor West, Border,
    nor Breed, nor Birth,   90

When two strong men stand face to face, tho'
    they come from the ends of the earth.

DANNY DEEVER

What are the bugles blowin' for?' said Files-
    on-Parade.
'To turn you out, to turn you out,' the Color-
    Sergeant said.
'What makes you look so white, so white?'
    said Files-on-Parade.
'I'm dreadin' what I've got to watch,' the
    Color-Sergeant said.

For they're hangin' Danny Deever, you
    can 'ear the Dead March play,   5
The regiment's in 'ollow square — they're
    hangin' him to-day;
They've taken of his buttons off an' cut
    his stripes away,
An' they're hangin' Danny Deever in the
    mornin'.

'What makes the rear-rank breathe so 'ard?'
    said Files-on-Parade.
'It's bitter cold, it's bitter cold,' the Color-
    Sergeant said.   10
'What makes that front-rank man fall
    down?' says Files-on-Parade.
'A touch o' sun, a touch o' sun,' the Color-
    Sergeant said.

They are hangin' Danny Deever, they are
    marchin' of 'im round,
They 'ave 'alted Danny Deever by 'is coffin
    on the ground;
An' 'e'll swing in 'arf a minute for a
    sneakin' shootin' hound —   15
O they're hangin' Danny Deever in the
    mornin'!

''Is cot was right-'and cot to mine,' said
    Files-on-Parade.
''E's sleepin' out an' far to-night,' the Color-
    Sergeant said.
'I've drunk 'is beer a score o' times,' said
    Files-on-Parade.
''E's drinkin' bitter beer alone,' the Color-
    Sergeant said.   20

They are hangin' Danny Deever, you must
    mark 'im to 'is place,
For 'e shot a comrade sleepin' — you must
    look 'im in the face;

Nine 'undred of 'is country an' the regiment's disgrace,
While they 're hangin' Danny Deever in the mornin'.

'What's that so black agin the sun?' said Files-on-Parade.   25
'It's Danny fightin' 'ard for life,' the Color-Sergeant said.
'What's that that whimpers over'ead?' said Files-on-Parade.
'It's Danny's soul that's passin' now,' the Color-Sergeant said.

For they 're done with Danny Deever, you can 'ear the quickstep play,
The regiment's in column, an' they 're marchin' us away;   30
Ho! the young recruits are shakin', an' they 'll want their beer to-day,
After hangin' Danny Deever in the mornin'.

RECESSIONAL

God of our fathers, known of old
    Lord of our far-flung battle-line —
Beneath whose awful hand we hold
    Dominion over palm and pine —
Lord God of Hosts, be with us yet,   5
Lest we forget — lest we forget!

The tumult and the shouting dies —
    The captains and the kings depart —
Still stands Thine ancient sacrifice,
    An humble and a contrite heart.   10
Lord God of Hosts, be with us yet,
Lest we forget — lest we forget!

Far-called our navies melt away —
    On dune and headland sinks the fire —
Lo, all our pomp of yesterday   15
    Is one with Nineveh and Tyre!
Judge of the Nations, spare us yet,
Lest we forget — lest we forget!

If, drunk with sight of power, we loose
    Wild tongues that have not Thee in awe —
Such boasting as the Gentiles use   21
    Or lesser breeds without the Law —
Lord God of Hosts, be with us yet,
Lest we forget — lest we forget!

For heathen heart that puts her trust   25
    In reeking tube and iron shard —
All valiant dust that builds on dust,
    And guarding calls not Thee to guard —
For frantic boast and foolish word,
Thy Mercy on Thy People, Lord!   30
                    Amen.

WILLIAM BUTLER YEATS
(1865–)

THE LAKE ISLE OF INNISFREE

I will arise and go now, and go to Innisfree,
And a small cabin build there, of clay and
    wattles made;
Nine bean rows will I have there, a hive for
    the honey bee,
And live alone in the bee-loud glade.

And I shall have some peace there, for peace
    comes dropping slow,   5
Dropping from the veils of the morning to
    where the cricket sings;
There midnight's all a glimmer, and noon a
    purple glow,
And evening's full of the linnet's wings.

I will arise and go now, for always night
    and day
I hear lake water lapping with low sounds
    by the shore;   10
While I stand on the roadway, or on the
    pavements gray,
I hear it in the deep heart's core.

INTO THE TWILIGHT

Out-worn heart, in an out-worn time,
Come clear of the nets of wrong and right;
Laugh heart again in the gray twilight,
Sigh heart again in the dew of the morn,

Your mother Eire is always young,   5
Dew ever shining and twilight gray;
Though hope fall from you and love decay
Burning in fires of a slanderous tongue.

Come heart, where hill is heaped on hill;
For there the mystical brotherhood   10
Of sun and moon and hollow wood
And river and stream work out their will.

And God stands winding his lonely horn,
And time and the world are ever in flight,

And love is less kind than the gray twilight,
And hope is less dear than the dew of the
morn.   16

RED HANRAHAN'S SONG ABOUT IRELAND

The old brown thorn trees break in two high
    over Cummen Strand,
Under a bitter black wind that blows from
    the left hand;
Our courage breaks like an old tree in a black
    wind and dies,
But we have hidden in our hearts the flame
    out of the eyes
Of Cathleen, the daughter of Houlihan.   5

The wind has bundled up the clouds high
    over Knocknarea,
And thrown the thunder on the stones for
    all that Maeve can say.
Angers that are like noisy clouds have set
    our hearts abeat;
But we have all bent low and low and kissed
    the quiet feet
Of Cathleen, the daughter of Houlihan.   10

The yellow pool has overflowed high up on
    Clooth-na-Bare,
For the wet winds are blowing out of the
    clinging air;
Like heavy flooded waters our bodies and
    our blood;
But purer than a tall candle before the Holy
    Rood
Is Cathleen, the daughter of Houlihan.   15

SONG from THE LAND OF HEART'S DESIRE

The wind blows out of the gates of the day,
The wind blows over the lonely of heart,
And the lonely of heart is withered away
While the faeries dance in a place apart,
Shaking their milk-white feet in a ring,   5
Tossing their milk-white arms in the air;
For they hear the wind laugh and murmur
    and sing
Of a land where even the old are fair,
And even the wise are merry of tongue;
But I heard a reed of Coolaney say,   10
' When the wind has laughed and murmured
    and sung,
The lonely of heart is withered away.'

" A. E." [GEORGE RUSSELL] (1862–)

THE EARTH BREATH

From the cool and dark-lipped furrows
    Breathes a dim delight
Through the woodland's purple plumage
    To the diamond night.
Aureoles of joy encircle   5
    Every blade of grass
Where the dew-fed creatures silent
    And enraptured pass.
And the restless plowman pauses,
    Turns and, wondering,   10
Deep beneath his rustic habit
    Finds himself a king;
For a fiery moment looking
    With the eyes of God
Over fields a slave at morning   15
    Bowed him to the sod.
Blind and dense with revelation
    Every moment flies,
And unto the Mighty Mother,
    Gay, eternal, rise   20
All the hopes we hold, the gladness,
    Dreams of things to be.
One of all thy generations,
    Mother, hails to thee.
Hail, and hail, and hail forever,   25
    Though I turn again
From thy joy unto the human
    Ves019ture of pain.
I, thy child who went forth radiant
    In the golden prime,   30
Find thee still the mother-hearted
    Through my night in time;
Find in thee the old enchantment
    There behind the veil
Where the gods, my brothers, linger.   35
    Hail, forever, hail!

HILAIRE BELLOC (1870–)

THE SOUTH COUNTRY

When I am living in the midlands,
    That are sodden and unkind,
I light my lamp in the evening:
    My work is left behind;
And the great hills of the South Country   5
    Come back into my mind.

The great hills of the South Country
    They stand along the sea,

And it's there, walking in the high woods,
  That I could wish to be,   10
And the men that were boys when I was a
  boy
  Walking along with me.

The men that live in North England
  I saw them for a day:
Their hearts are set upon the waste fells, 15
  Their skies are fast and gray;
From their castle-walls a man may see
  The mountains far away.

The men that live in West England
  They see the Severn strong,   20
A-rolling on rough water brown
  Light aspen leaves along.
They have the secret of the rocks,
  And the oldest kind of song.

But the men that live in the South Country
  Are the kindest and most wise.   26
They get their laughter from the loud surf,
  And the faith in their happy eyes
Comes surely from our Sister the Spring
  When over the sea she flies;   30
The violets suddenly bloom at her feet,
  She blesses us with surprise.

I never get between the pines
  But I smell the Sussex air;
Nor I never come on a belt of sand   35
  But my home is there.
And along the sky the line of the Downs
  So noble and so bare.

A lost thing could I never find,
  Nor a broken thing mend: 40
And I fear I shall be all alone
  When I get towards the end.
Who will be there to comfort me
  Or who will be my friend?

I will gather and carefully make my friends
  Of the men of the Sussex Weald   46
They watch the stars from silent folds,
  They stiffly plow the field.
By them and the God of the South Country
  My poor soul shall be healed.   50

If I ever become a rich man,
  Or if ever I grow to be old,
I will build a house with deep thatch
  To shelter me from the cold,
And there shall the Sussex songs be sung 55
  And the story of Sussex told.

I will hold my house in the high wood,
  Within a walk of the sea,

And the men that were boys when I was a
  boy
  Shall sit and drink with me.   60

WALTER DE LA MARE (1873–)

ALL THAT'S PAST

Very old are the woods;
  And the buds that break
Out of the briar's boughs,
  When March winds wake,
So old with their beauty are —   5
  Oh, no man knows
Through what wild centuries
  Roves back the rose.

Very old are the brooks;
  And the rills that rise   10
Where snow sleeps cold beneath
  The azure skies
Sing such a history
  Of come and gone,
Their every drop is as wise   15
  As Solomon.

Very old are we men;
  Our dreams are tales
Told in dim Eden
  By Eve's nightingales;   20
We wake and whisper awhile,
  But, the day gone by,
Silence and sleep like fields
  Of amaranth lie.

MISS LOO

When thin-strewn memory I look through,
I see most clearly poor Miss Loo,
Her tabby cat, her cage of birds,
Her nose, her hair — her muffled words,
And how she'd open her green eyes,   5
As if in some immense surprise,
Whenever as we sat at tea,
She made some small remark to me.

It's always drowsy summer when
From out the past she comes again;   10
The westering sunshine in a pool
Floats in her parlor still and cool;
While the slim bird its lean wires shakes,
As into piercing song it breaks;
Till Peter's pale-green eyes ajar   15
Dream, wake; wake, dream, in one brief bar;

And I am sitting, dull and shy,
And she with gaze of vacancy,
And large hands folded on the tray,
Musing the afternoon away;   20
Her satin bosom heaving slow
With sighs that softly ebb and flow,
And her plain face in such dismay,
It seems unkind to look her way:
Until all cheerful back will come   25
Her cheerful gleaming spirit home:
And one would think that poor Miss Loo
Asked nothing else, if she had you.

JOHN MASEFIELD (1874–)

SEA-FEVER

I must down to the seas again, to the lonely
    sea and the sky,
And all I ask is a tall ship and a star to steer
    her by,
And the wheel's kick and the wind's song
    and the white sail's shaking,
And a gray mist on the sea's face and a gray
    dawn breaking.

I must down to the seas again, for the call
    of the running tide   5
Is a wild call and a clear call that may not
    be denied;
And all I ask is a windy day with the white
    clouds flying,
And the flung spray and the blown spume,
    and the sea-gulls crying.

I must down to the seas again to the vagrant
    gipsy life,
To the gull's way and the whale's way where
    the wind's like a whetted knife;   10
And all I ask is a merry yarn from a laugh-
    ing fellow-rover,
And quiet sleep and a sweet dream when the
    long trick's over.

FRANK TAYLOR (1873–1913)

ENGLAND'S DEAD

('Make them to be numbered with thy Saints: in
glory everlasting.')

Homeward the long ships leap; swift-shod
    with joy,
  Striding the deep sea-dykes fast home they
    fare,—

Where is my wedded love? Where is my
    boy?
  Where go the dead that died for England
    where?

Homeward the long ships leap; but not with
    these   5
  Thy boy, thy wedded love, O gentle-eyed
Woman of England, nor far over seas
  Mixing with dull earth sleep the dead that
    died

For England. They, in God's completed
    aims,
  Bear each his part; unseen of bounded
    sight,   10
Down the vast firmament there floats and
    flames,
  Crested with stars and panoplied in light,

Of strenuous clean souls a long array,
  With lambent lance and white, bright,
    blinding sword,
All riding upon horses,— what are they? 15
  They are the dead which died in Christ
    their Lord

For England, from old time; with God made
    one,
  As on the mount the triple vision shone,
So shine they now, and like the noontide sun
  Before them all the fair Saint George rides
    on.   20

There goes the boy of Crécy whispering low
  To him of Agincourt, a kingly pair,
With many mighty men which bent the
    bow,—
  There go the dead that died for England,
    there;

There go those quenchless Talbots, there the
    flower   25
  Of Devon, Grenville, Gilbert, mariners
    rare,
She too who thought foul scorn of Philip's
    power,—
  There go the dead that died for England,
    there;

And Sidney who the rippling cup resigned,
  And happy Wolfe; wan Pitt released from
    care,   30
Nelson the well-beloved and all his kind,—
  There go the dead that died for England,
    there;

And he who brake the Corsican's strong spell,
  And Nicholson, impatient of despair,

And Gordon, faithful, desolate sentinel,— 35
  There go the dead that died for England,
  there;

And there unhelmeted, ungirt of brand,
  Victoria moves with mild, maternal air,
Still vigilant, still prayerful for the land,—
  There go the dead that died for England,
  there.   40

Nor ride they idly nor with indolent rein,
  Irresolute, as men that seek no foe,
But by the pathless sea, by peak and plain,
  Bright-eyed, stern-lipped, all day, all night,
  they go

Forth as a fire that snatches and devours 45
  Wind-withered woods, so go they swift
  and fell,
Warring with principalities and powers,
  Hunting through space the swart, old bands
  of Hell;

And all the sounding causeways of the
  spheres
  Ring like white iron with the rhythmic
  tread   50
Of these and their innumerable peers;
  But most round England muster England's
  dead,

Round England cradled in her roaring seas,
  With Arctic snows white-girdled, bathed in
  suns
Asian and Australasian, there go these;   55
  And where one solitary trader runs

His English keel, and where one lonely
  sword
  Glimmers for England, one unsleeping
  brain
Watches and works for England, thitherward
  Gather the bright souls of her servants
  slain   60

For her, and lock their shimmering ranks,
  and sweep
  Round England's child as sweeps the
  northern gale
Round some stark pine-tree on the moorland
  steep,
  And from the flash and rattle of their mail

Hell's pale marauders shudderingly recoil
  Frustrate. O glad condition and sublime

Of our undying dead, to fight and foil
  The ancient foe, continually to climb

Through God's high order of His Saints,
  to meet
  Some soul whose star-like name lit all
  their course,   70
And commune with him, to discern and greet
  Old kindred, love, and friendship, hound
  and horse;

To see God face to face, and still to see
  And labor for the loves that grope on
  earth,
To wait serenely till all souls shall be   75
  One in God's aristocracy of worth,—

O glad condition and sublime! whereto
  That southern tomb thy hands may never
  tend
Was but the gateway thy loved boy passed
  through,
  Thy wedded love passed through, that he
  might wend   80

Homeward to thee; thou can'st not see the
  blaze
  Of his great blade nor hear his trumpets
  blare,
Yet thick as brown leaves round about thy
  ways,
  There go the dead that died for England,
  there.

RUPERT BROOKE (1887–1915)

THE OLD VICARAGE, GRANT-CHESTER

(Café des Westens, Berlin, May, 1912)

Just now the lilac is in bloom,
All before my little room;
And in my flower-beds, I think,
Smile the carnation and the pink;
And down the borders, well I know,   5
The poppy and the pansy blow . . .
Oh! there the chestnuts, summer through,
Beside the river make for you
A tunnel of green gloom, and sleep
Deeply above; and green and deep   10
The stream mysterious glides beneath,
Green as a dream and deep as death.
— Oh, damn! I know it! and I know
How the May fields all golden show,
And when the day is young and sweet, 15

Gild gloriously the bare feet
That run to bathe. . . .
Du lieber Gott!

Here am I, sweating, sick, and hot,
And there the shadowed waters fresh   20
Lean up to embrace the naked flesh.
Temperamentvoll German Jews
Drink beer around; — and *there* the dews
Are soft beneath a morn of gold.
Here tulips bloom as they are told;   25
Unkempt about those hedges blows
An English unofficial rose;
And there the unregulated sun
Slopes down to rest when day is done,
And wakes a vague unpunctual star,   30
A slippered Hesper; and there are
Meads towards Haslingfield and Coton
Where *das Betreten* 's not *verboten*.

εἴθε, γενοίμην . . . would I were
In Grantchester, in Grantchester! —   35
Some, it may be, can get in touch
With Nature there, or Earth, or such.
And clever modern men have seen
A Faun a-peeping through the green,
And felt the Classics were not dead,   40
To glimpse a Naiad's reedy head,
Or hear the Goat-foot piping low: . . .
But these are things I do not know.
I only know that you may lie
Day long and watch the Cambridge sky,   45
And, flower-lulled in sleepy grass,
Hear the cool lapse of hours pass,
Until the centuries blend and blur
In Grantchester, in Grantchester. . . .
Still in the dawnlit waters cool   50
His ghostly Lordship swims his pool,
And tries the strokes, essays the tricks,
Long learnt on Hellespont, or Styx.
Dan Chaucer hears his river still
Chatter beneath a phantom mill.   55

Tennyson notes, with studious eye,
How Cambridge waters hurry by . . .
And in that garden, black and white,
Creep whispers through the grass all night;
And spectral dance, before the dawn,   60
A hundred vicars down the lawn;
Curates, long dust, will come and go
On lissom, clerical, printless toe;
And oft between the boughs is seen
The sly shade of a Rural Dean . . .   65
Till, at a shiver in the skies,
Vanishing with Satanic cries,
The prim ecclesiastic rout
Leaves but a startled sleeper-out,

Gray heavens, the first bird's drowsy calls, 70
The falling house that never falls.

God! I will pack, and take a train,
And get me to England once again!
For England's the one land, I know,
Where men with Splendid Hearts may go; 75
And Cambridgeshire, of all England,
The shire for Men who Understand;
And of *that* district I prefer
The lovely hamlet Grantchester.
For Cambridge people rarely smile,   80
Being urban, squat, and packed with guile;
And Royston men in the far South
Are black and fierce and strange of mouth;
At Over they fling oaths at one,
And worse than oaths at Trumpington,   85
And Ditton girls are mean and dirty,
And there's none in Harston under thirty,
And folks in Shelford and those parts
Have twisted lips and twisted hearts,
And Barton men make Cockney rhymes,   90
And Coton's full of nameless crimes,
And things are done you'd not believe
At Madingley on Christmas Eve.
Strong men have run for miles and miles
When one from Cherry Hinton smiles;   95
Strong men have blanched, and shot their
    wives,
Rather than send them to St. Ives;
Strong men have cried like babes, bydam,
To hear what happened at Babraham.
But Grantchester! ah, Grantchester!   100
There's peace and holy quiet there,
Great clouds along pacific skies,
And men and women with straight eyes,
Lithe children lovelier than a dream,
A bosky wood, a slumbrous stream,   105
And little kindly winds that creep
Round twilight corners, half asleep.
In Grantchester their skins are white;
They bathe by day, they bathe by night;
The women there do all they ought;   110
The men observe the rules of Thought.
They love the Good; they worship Truth;
They laugh uproariously in youth;
(And when they get to feeling old,
They up and shoot themselves, I'm told) . . .

    Ah God! to see the branches stir   116
Across the moon at Grantchester!
To smell the thrilling-sweet and rotten
Unforgettable, unforgotten
River-smell, and hear the breeze   120
Sobbing in the little trees.
Say, do the elm-clumps greatly stand
Still guardians of the holy land?

The chestnuts shade, in reverend dream,
The yet unacademic stream? 125
Is dawn a secret shy and cold
Anadyomene, silver-gold?
And sunset still a golden sea
From Haslingfield to Madingley?
And after, ere the night is born, 130
Do hares come out about the corn?
Oh, is the water sweet and cool,
Gentle and brown, above the pool?
And laughs the immortal river still
Under the mill, under the mill? 135
Say, is there Beauty yet to find?
And Certainty? and Quiet kind?
Deep meadows yet, for to forget
The lies, and truths, and pain? . . . oh! yet
Stands the Church clock at ten to three? 140
And is there honey still for tea?

FRANCIS LEDWIDGE (1891–1917)

THE DEATH OF AILILL

When there was heard no more the war's
loud sound,
And only the rough corn-crake filled the
hours,
And hill winds in the furze and drowsy flowers,

Maeve in her chamber with her white head
bowed
On Ailill's heart was sobbing: 'I have
found 5
The way to love you now,' she said, and he
Winked an old tear away and said: 'The
proud
Unyielding heart loves never.' And then
she:
'I love you now, tho' once when we were
young
We walked apart like two who were es-
tranged 10
Because I loved you not, now all is changed.'
And he who loved her always called her name
And said: 'You do not love me; 't is your
tongue
Talks in the dusk; you love the blazing gold
Won in the battles, and the soldier's fame. 15
You love the stories that are often told
By poets in the hall.' Then Maeve arose
And sought her daughter Findebar: 'Oh,
child,
Go tell your father that my love went wild
With all my wars in youth, and say that
now 20
I love him stronger than I hate my foes. . . .'
And Findebar unto her father sped
And touched him gently on the rugged brow,
And knew by the cold touch that he was
dead.

POEMS OF THE GREAT WAR

Much of the poetry of the later nineteenth and early twentieth century is inspired by a strong spirit of national self-consciousness, and the division between this section and the preceding one is made for convenience only. English poetry before and after the beginning of the Great War has the same general characteristics, though the immensity of the struggle and the tremendous issues involved gave to the work of some of the younger poets a depth of significance which they had not shown up to that time. This is especially true of the men who themselves fought, such as Rupert Brooke, who died on his way to the Dardanelles on April 23, 1915; Julian Grenfell, who died from wounds received at Ypres in May of the same year; Charles Hamilton Sorley, killed in action in France in October, 1915; and Viscount Stuart, killed in action in France in September, 1915. It is heartrending to think of what these young poets might have achieved if they had lived, but one has at least the small consolation that the War in which they laid down their lives stirred them to heights and depths of emotion which are not ordinarily reached in the 'piping times of peace.' They lived greatly in the all too short span of life allotted to them, and wrote nobly at a time when every element of beauty in modern civilization seemed destined to destruction.

FOR THE FALLEN

With proud thanksgiving, a mother for her
   children,
England mourns for her dead across the sea.
Flesh of her flesh they were, spirit of her
   spirit,
Fallen in the cause of the free.

Solemn the drums thrill: Death august and
   royal   5
Sings sorrow up into immortal spheres.
There is music in the midst of desolation
And a glory that shines upon our tears.

They went with songs to the battle, they were
   young,
Straight of limb, true of eye, steady and
   aglow.   10
They were stanch to the end against odds
   uncounted,
They fell with their faces to the foe.

They shall grow not old, as we that are left
   grow old:
Age shall not weary them, nor the years condemn.
At the going down of the sun and in the
   morning   15
We will remember them.

They mingle not with their laughing comrades again;
They sit no more at familiar tables of home;

They have no lot in our labor of the day-
   time;
They sleep beyond England's foam.   20

But where our desires are and our hopes
   profound,
Felt as a well-spring that is hidden from
   sight,
To the innermost heart of their own land
   they are known
As the stars are known to the Night;

As the stars that shall be bright when we
   are dust,   25
Moving in marches upon the heavenly plain;
As the stars that are starry in the time of
   our darkness,
To the end, to the end, they remain.
            —Laurence Binyon.

THE SOLDIER

If I should die, think only this of me:
   That there's some corner of a foreign
   field
That is forever England. There shall be
   In that rich earth a richer dust concealed;
A dust whom England bore, shaped, made
   aware,   5
   Gave, once, her flowers to love, her ways
   to roam,
A body of England's, breathing English air,
   Washed by the rivers, blest by suns of
   home.

And think, this heart, all evil shed away,
  A pulse in the eternal mind, no less   10
  Gives somewhere back the thoughts by
    England given;
Her sights and sounds; dreams happy as her
    day;
  And laughter, learnt of friends; and gen-
    tleness,
    In hearts at peace, under an English
    heaven.
                     — *Rupert Brooke.*

AFTERMATH

Yes, he is gone, there is the message, see!
Slain by a Prussian bullet as he led
The men that loved him — dying, cheered
  them on —
My son, my eldest son. So be it, God!

This is no time for tears, no time to mourn, 5
No time for somber draperies of woe.
Let the aggressors weep! for they have
  sinned
The sin of Satan. Lust of power and pride,
Mean envy of their neighbors' weal, a plot
Hatched amidst glozing smiles and prate of
  peace   10
Through the false years; until the Day, the
  Day
When all this worship at the Devil's feet
Should win the world. Aye, let them weep!
                       But we
With eyes undimmed march on; our mourn-
  ing robes   15
Be-jeweled by the deeds of those that die,
Luster on luster, till no sable patch
Peeps through their brilliance.
              In the years to come,
When we have done our work, and God's
  own peace,   20
The Peace of Justice, Mercy, Righteousness,
Like the still radiance of a summer's dawn,
With tranquil glory floods a troubled world;
Why then, perhaps, in the old hall at home,
Where once I dreamed my eldest-born should
  stand   25
The master, as I stand the master now,
Our eyes, my wife, shall meet and gleam, and
  mark
Niched on the walls in sanctity of pride,
Hal's sword, Dick's medal, and the cross he
  won
Yet never wore. That is the time for tears,
Drawn from a well of love deep down; deep
  down,   31

Deep as the mystery of immortal souls,
That is the time for tears; not now, not now!
                  — *Burghclere.*

THE WIFE OF FLANDERS

Low and brown barns thatched and re-
  patched and tattered
Where I had seven sons until to-day,
A little hill of hay your spur has scattered . . .
This is not Paris. You have lost the way.

You, staring at your sword to find it brittle,   5
Surprised at the surprise that was your
  plan,
Who, shaking and breaking barriers not a
  little,
Find never more the death-door of Sedan.

Must I for more than carnage call you claimant,
Paying you a penny for each son you slay?
Man, the whole globe in gold were no repayment   11
For what *you* have lost. And how shall I
  repay?

What is the price of that red spark that
  caught me
From a kind farm that never had a name?
What is the price of that dead man they
  brought me?   15
For other dead men do not look the same.

How should I pay for one poor graven steeple
Whereon you shattered what you shall not
  know,
How should I pay you, miserable people?
How should I pay you everything you
  owe?   20

Unhappy, can I give you back your honor?
Though I forgave would any man forget?
While all the great green land has trampled
  on her
The treason and terror of the night we
  met.

Not any more in vengeance or in pardon   25
An old wife bargains for a bean that's
  hers.
You have no word to break; no heart to
  harden.
Ride on and prosper. You have lost your
  spurs.
              — *Gilbert K. Chesterton.*

A HARROW GRAVE IN FLANDERS

Here in the marshland, past the battered
    bridge,
  One of a hundred grains untimely sown,
Here, with his comrades of the hard-won
    ridge
  He rests, unknown.

His horoscope had seemed so plainly drawn,
  School triumphs, earned apace in work and
    play;   6
Friendships at will; then love's delightful
    dawn
  And mellowing day.

Home fostering hope; some service to the
    State;
  Benignant age; then the lost tryst to keep
Where in the yew-tree shadow congregate 11
  His fathers sleep.

Was here the one thing needful to distil
  From life's alembic, through this holier
    fate,
The man's essential soul, the hero-will? 15
  We ask; and wait.
              — *Crewe.*

'HOW SLEEP THE BRAVE'

Nay, nay, sweet England, do not grieve!
  Not one of these poor men who died
But did within his soul believe
  That death for thee was glorified.

Ever they watched it hovering near   5
  That mystery 'yond thought to plumb,
Perchance sometimes in loathèd fear
  They heard cold Danger whisper, Come! —

Heard and obeyed. Oh, if thou weep
  Such courage and honor, beauty, care, 10
Be it for joy that those who sleep
  Only thy joy could share.
          — *Walter de la Mare.*

THE DEFENDERS

His wage of rest at nightfall still
  He takes, who sixty years has known
Of plowing over Cotsall hill
  And keeping trim the Cotsall stone.

He meditates the dusk, and sees   5
  Folds of his wonted shepherdings

And lands of stubble and tall trees
  Becoming insubstantial things.

And does he see on Costall hill —
  Thrown even to the central shire — 10
The funnelled shapes forbidding still
  The stranger from his cottage fire?
          — *John Drinkwater.*

RAINING

The night I left my father said:
  'You'll go and do some stupid thing.
You've no more sense in that fat head
  Than Silly Billy Witterling.

'Not sense to come in when it rains — 5
  Not sense enough for that, you've got.
You'll get a bullet through your brains,
  Before you know, as like as not.'

And now I'm lying in the trench
  And shells and bullets through the night 10
Are raining in a steady drench,
  I'm thinking the old man was right.
          — *W. W. Gibson.*

THE QUESTION

I wonder if the old cow died or not.
Gey bad she was the night I left, and sick.
Dick reckoned she would mend. He knows
  a lot —
At least he fancies so himself, does Dick.

Dick knows a lot. But maybe I did wrong 5
To leave the cow to him, and come away.
Over and over like a silly song
These words keep bumming in my head all
  day.

And all I think of, as I face the foe
And take my lucky chance of being shot, 10
Is this — that if I'm hit I'll never know
Till Doomsday if the old cow died or not.
          — *W. W. Gibson.*

HIS FATHER

I quite forgot to put the spigot in.
It's just come over me. . . . And it is queer
To think he'll not care if we lose or win
And yet be jumping-mad about that beer.

I left it running full. He must have said 5
A thing or two. I'd give my stripes to hear

What he will say if I'm reported dead
Before he gets me told about that beer!
— *W. W. Gibson.*

THE DEAD

TO ONE KILLED IN ACTION

Dear love, they say thou art at rest.
  I heed them not, though thou art long,
  Dreaming that thou, with heart still strong
For fighting, followest some far quest.

They say, dear heart, I must forget.   5
  Nay, though the agony be deep,
  That memory can never sleep.
Thy passioned kisses linger yet.

They say, dear love, the daisies blithe
  Shall o'er thy head in summer spring.   10
  Daisies! . . . I see thy body swing
Lithe and strong-limbed, above the scythe.

Dear love, they say that in the light
  Of Heaven's joy our souls shall meet.
  Dear God! I want thee now, the sweet   15
Sight of thee — not in Heaven — to-night!
              — *Violet Gillespie.*

THE AIRMAN

Wild wind, and drear, beneath the pale stars
    blowing,
  Whom do you hunt to-night?
Out of the west into the storm-cloud glow-
    ing
  A biplane wings her flight.

In the gray day-dawn was there no return-
    ing,   5
  No homewards for the dead: —
Only a broken wing, a biplane burning,
  A shattered airship shed!

O Nation proud, on whose red altar gladly
  One more young Life is laid,   10
Scatter the news — flutter the posters
    madly —
  'Triumph of British raid!'

What of the Cross they brought to her — his
    Mother?
  Wanly her dumb lips smiled,
Then whispered: 'Give back *him* — I had
    no other —   15
  My Son — my only child.'
              — *Gregg Goddard.*

INTO BATTLE

The naked earth is warm with Spring,
  And with green grass and bursting trees
Leans to the sun's gaze glorying,
  And quivers in the sunny breeze;

And Life is Color and Warmth and Light, 5
  And a striving evermore for these;
And he is dead who will not fight;
  And who dies fighting has increase.

The fighting man shall from the sun
  Take warmth, and life from the glowing
    earth;   10
Speed with the light-foot winds to run,
  And with the trees to newer birth;
And find, when fighting shall be done,
  Great rest, and fullness after dearth.

All the bright company of Heaven   15
  Hold him in their high comradeship,
The Dog-Star and the Sisters Seven,
  Orion's Belt and sworded hip.

The woodland trees that stand together,
  They stand to him each one a friend;   20
They gently speak in the windy weather;
  They guide to valley and ridges' end.

The kestrel hovering by day,
  And the little owls that call by night,
Bid him be swift and keen as they,   25
  As keen of ear, as swift of sight.

The blackbird sings to him, 'Brother, brother,
  If this be the last song you shall sing
Sing well, for you may not sing another;
  Brother, sing.'

In dreary doubtful waiting hours,   30
  Before the brazen frenzy starts,
The horses show him nobler powers;
  O patient eyes, courageous hearts!

And when the burning moment breaks,
  And all things else are out of mind,   35
And only Joy-of-Battle takes
  Him by the throat, and makes him blind,

Through joy and blindness he shall know,
  Not caring much to know, that still
Nor lead nor steel shall reach him, so   40
  That it be not the Destined Will.

The thundering line of battle stands,
  And in the air Death moans and sings;

But Day shall clasp him with strong hands,
　And Night shall fold him in soft wings.　45
　　　　　　　　　—*Julian Grenfell.*
　　Flanders, April, 1915.

THE WYKHAMIST

In the wake of the yellow sunset one pale
　star
Hangs over the darkening city's purple haze.
An errand-boy in the street beneath me plays
On a penny whistle.　Very faint and far
Comes the scroop of tortured gear on a bat-
　tered car.　5
A hyacinth nods pallid blooms on the window
　sill,
Swayed by the tiny wind.　St. Catherine's
　Hill
Is a place of mystery, a land of dreams.
The tramp of soldiers, barrack-marching,
　seems
A thing remote, untouched by fate or time. 10
... A year ago you heard Cathedral's chime,
You hurried up to books — a year ago;
— Shouted for 'Houses' in New Field be-
　low.
... You ... 'died of wounds' ... they
　told me
　　　　　　　... yet your feet　15
Pass with the others down the twilit street.
　　　　　　　　　—*Nora Griffiths.*

NON-COMBATANT

Before one drop of angry blood was shed
　I was sore hurt and beaten to my knee;
Before one fighting man reeled back and died
　The War-Lords struck at me.

They struck me down — an idle, useless
　mouth,　5
　As cumbrous — nay, more cumbrous — than
　　the dead,
With life and heart afire to give and give
　I take a dole instead.

With life and heart afire to give and give
　I take and eat the bread of charity.　10
In all the length of all this eager land,
　No man has need of me.

That is my hurt — my burning, beating
　wound;
　That is the spear-thrust driven through my
　　pride!

With aimless hands, and mouth that must be
　fed,　15
　I wait and stand aside.

Let me endure it, then, with stiffened lip:
　I, even I, have suffered in the strife!
Let me endure it then — I give my pride
　Where others give a life.
　　　　　　　　　—*Cicely Hamilton.*

SOLDIER, SOLDIER

Soldier, soldier, off to war,
Take me a letter to my sweetheart O.
He's gone away to France
With his carbine and his lance,
And a lock of brown hair of his sweetheart
　O.　5

Fair maid of London, happy may you be
To know so much of your sweetheart O.
There's not a handsome lad,
To get the chance he's had,
But would skip, with a kiss for his sweet-
　heart O.　10

Soldier, soldier, whatever shall I do
If the cruel Germans take my sweetheart O?
They'll pen him in the jail
And starve him thin and pale,
With never a kind word from his sweet-
　heart O.　15

Fair maid of London, is that all you see
Of the lad you've taken for your sweet-
　heart O?
He'll make his prison ring
With his God Save the King
And his God bless the blue eyes of my sweet-
　heart O!　20

Soldier, soldier, if by shot or shell
They wound him, my dear lad, my sweet-
　heart O,
He'll lie bleeding in the rain
And call me, all in vain.
Crying for the fingers of his sweetheart O. 25

Pretty one, pretty one, now take a word
　from me:
Don't you grudge the life-blood of your
　sweetheart O.
For you must understand
He gives it to our land,
And proud should fly the colors of his sweet-
　heart O.　30

Soldier, soldier, my heart is growing cold —
If a German shot kill my sweetheart O!
I could not lift my head
If my dear love lay dead
With his wide eyes waiting for his sweetheart O.   35

Poor child, poor child, go to church and pray,
Pray God to spare you your sweetheart O.
But if he live or die
The English flag must fly,
And England take care of his sweetheart
O!   40
                        — *Maurice Hewlett.*

THE OLD WAY

[' I deeply regret to report the loss of H. M.
ships . . .'— Sir John Jellicoe's dispatch. (The
Times, July 7th, 1916.)]

There 's a sea that lies uncharted far beyond
the setting sun,
And a gallant Fleet was sailing there whose
fighting days are done,
Sloop and Galleon, Brig and Pinnace, all the
rigs you never met,
Fighting Frigate, grave Three-decker, with
their snowy canvas set;
Dozed and dreamed, when, on a sudden,
ev'ry sail began to swell,   5
For the breeze has spoken strangers, with a
stirring tale to tell,
And a thousand eager voices flung the challenge out to sea:
Come they hither in the old way, in the
only way that 's free?

And the flying Breeze called softly: ' In
the old way,
' Through the winters and the waters of
the North,   10
' They have waited, ah the waiting, in the
old way,
' Strong and patient, from the Pentlands
to the Forth.
' There was fog to blind and baffle off the
headlands,
' There were gales to beat the worst that
ever blew,
' But they took it, as they found it, in the
old way,   15
' And I know it often helped to think of
you.'

'T was a Frigate, under stun-sails, as she
gently gathered way

Spoke in jerks, like all the Frigates, who
have little time to stay:
' We 'd to hurry, under Nelson, thank my
timbers I was tough,
' For he worked us as he loved us, and he
never had enough —   20
' Are the English mad as ever? were the
Frigates just as few?
(' Will their sheets be always stranding, ere
the rigging 's rove anew?)
' Just as Saxon slow at starting, just as
weirdly wont to win?
' Had they Frigates out and watching? Did
they pass the signals in?'

And the laughing Breeze made answer:
' In the old way;   25
' You should see the little cruisers spread
and fly,
' Peering over the horizon, in the old way,
' And a seaplane up and wheeling in the
sky.
' When the wireless snapped "The enemy
is sighted,"
' If his accents were comparatively new, 30
' Why, the sailor men were cheering, in
the old way,
' So I naturally smiled, and thought of
you.'

Then a courtly voice and stately from a tall
Three-decker came —
She 'd the manners of a monarch and a story
in her name:
' We 'd a winter gale at even, and my shrouds
are aching yet,   35
' It was more than time for reefing when the
upper sails were set.
' So we chased in woeful weather, till we
closed in failing light,
' Then we fought them, as we caught them,
just as Hawke had bid us fight;
' And we swept the sea by sunrise, clear and
free beyond a doubt.
' Was it thus the matter ended when the
enemy was out?'   40

Cried the Breeze: ' They fought and followed in the old way,
' For they raced to make a record all the
while,
' With a knot to veer and haul on, in the
old way,
' That had never even met the measured
mile —
' And the guns were making merry in the
twilight.   45
' That the enemy was victor may be true,

'Still — he hurried into harbor — in the
  old way —
'And I wondered if he'd ever heard of
  you.'

Came a gruff and choking chuckle, and a
  craft as black as doom
Lumbered laughing down to leeward, as the
  bravest gave her room.   50
'Set 'un blazin', good your Lordships, for
  the tide be makin' strong,
'Proper breeze to fan a fireship, set 'un
  drivin' out along!
''T is the "Torch," wi' humble duty, from
  Lord Howard 'board the Ark.
'We'm a laughin'-stock to Brixham, but a
  terror after dark,
'Hold an' bilge anigh to burstin', pitch and
  sulphur, tar an' all,   55
'Was it so, my dear, they'm fashioned for
  my Lord High Admiral?'

  Cried the Breeze: 'You'd hardly know it
    from the old way
  ('Gloriana, did you waken at the fight?),
  'Stricken shadows, scared and flying, in
    the old way
  'From the swift destroying specters of the
    night,   60
  'There were some that steamed and scat-
    tered south for safety,
  'From the mocking western echo "Where
    be tu?"
  'There were some that — got the message
    — in the old way,
  'And the flashes in the darkness spoke of
    you.'

There's a wondrous Golden Harbor, far beyond the setting sun,   65
Where a gallant ship may anchor when her
  fighting days are done,
Free from tempest, rock and battle, toil and
  tumult safely o'er,
Where the breezes murmur softly and there's
  peace for evermore.
They have climbed the last horizon, they are
  standing in from sea,
And the Pilot makes the Haven where a ship
  is glad to be: 70
Comes at last the glorious greeting, strangely
  new and ages old,
See the sober gray is shining like the Tudor
  green and gold!

  And the waiting jibs are hoisted, in the
    old way,
  As the guns begin to thunder down the
    line;

Hear the silver trumpets calling, in the old
  way!   75
Over all the silken pennons float and shine,
  'Did you voyage all unspoken, small and
    lonely?
  'Or with fame, the happy fortune of the
    few?
  'So you win the Golden Harbor, in the
    old way,
  'There's the old sea welcome waiting
    there for you.'   80
            — *Ronald A. Hopwood.*

A LEGEND OF YPRES

Before the throne the spirits of the slain
  With a loud voice importunately cried,
  'O Lord of Hosts, whose name be glori-
    fied,
Scarce may the line one onslaught more sus-
  tain
Wanting our help. Let it not be in vain,   5
  Not all in vain, O God, that we have died.'
  And smiling on them our good Lord re-
    plied,
'Begone then, foolish ones, and fight again.'
Our eyes were holden, that we saw them not;
  Disheartened foes beheld — our prisoners
    said —
Behind us massed, a mighty host indeed,
Where no host was. On comrades unforgot
  We thought, and knew that all those val-
    iant dead
Forwent their rest to save us at our need.
            — *Elinor Jenkins.*

(See note on "The First Battle of Ypres," by
Mrs. Margaret L. Woods, p. 1024.)

THE SPIRES OF OXFORD

I saw the spires of Oxford
  As I was passing by,
The gray spires of Oxford
  Against a pearl-gray sky.
My heart was with the Oxford men   5
  Who went abroad to die.

The years go fast in Oxford,
  The golden years and gay,
The hoary Colleges look down
  On careless boys at play.   10
But when the bugles sounded war
  They put their games away.

They left the peaceful river,
  The cricket-field, the quad,
The shaven lawns of Oxford   15

To seek a bloody sod —
They gave their merry youth away
For country and for God.

God rest you, happy gentlemen,
  Who laid your good lives down,   20
Who took the khaki and the gun
  Instead of cap and gown.
God bring you to a fairer place
  Than even Oxford town.
               — *Winifred M. Letts.*

MANY SISTERS TO MANY BROTHERS

When we fought the campaigns (in the long
    Christmas rains)
  With soldiers spread in troops on the floor,
I shot as straight as you, my losses were as
    few,
  My victories as many, or more.
And when in naval battle, amid cannon's
    rattle,   5
Fleet met fleet in the bath,
My cruisers were as trim, my battleships as
    grim,
  My submarines cut as swift a path.
Or, when it rained too long, and the strength
    of the strong
  Surged up and broke a way with blows,   10
I was as fit and keen, my fists hit as clean,
  Your black eye matched my bleeding nose.
Was there a scrap of play in which you, the
    boy,
  Could better me? You could not climb
    higher,
Ride straighter, run as quick (and to smoke
    made you sick)   15
  . . . But I sit here, and you 're under fire.

Oh, it 's you that have the luck, out there in
    blood and muck:
  You were born beneath a kindly star;
All we dreamt, I and you, you can really go
    and do,
  And I can't, the way things are.   20
In a trench you are sitting, while I am knit-
    ting
  A hopeless sock that never gets done.
Well, here 's luck, my dear; — and you 've got
    it, no fear;
  But for me . . . a war is poor fun.
               — *Rose Macaulay.*

THE ISLAND OF SKYROS

Here, where we stood together, we three
    men,
Before the war had swept us to the East
Three thousand miles away, I stand again
And hear the bells, and breathe, and go to
    feast.
We trod the same path, to the self-same
    place,   5
Skyros whose shadows the great seas erase,
Yet here I stand, having beheld their graves,
And Seddul Bahr that ever more blood
    craves.
So, since we communed here, our bones have
    been
Nearer, perhaps, than they again will be,   10
Earth and the world-wide battle lie between,
Death lies between, and friend-destroying
    sea.
Yet here, a year ago, we talked and stood
As I stand now, with pulses beating blood.

I saw her like a shadow on the sky   15
In the last light, a blur upon the sea,
Then the gale's darkness put the shadow by,
But from one grave that island talked to me;
And, in the midnight, in the breaking storm,
I saw its blackness and a blinking light,   20
And thought, 'So death obscures your gen-
    tle form,
So memory strives to make the darkness
    bright;
And, in that heap of rocks, your body lies,
Part of the island till the planet ends,
My gentle comrade, beautiful and wise,   25
Part of this crag this bitter surge offends,
While I, who pass, a little obscure thing,
War with this force, and breathe, and am its
    king.'
               — *John Masefield.*

THE SEARCHLIGHTS

Political morality differs from individual morality because there is no power above the state.—
GENERAL VON BERNHARDI.

Shadow by shadow, stripped for fight
  The lean black cruisers search the sea.
Night-long their level shafts of light
  Revolve, and find no enemy.
Only they know each leaping wave   5
May hide the lightning, and their grave.

And in the land they guard so well
  Is there no silent watch to keep?

An age is dying, and the bell
  Rings midnight on a vaster deep.   10
But over all its waves, once more
The searchlights move, from shore to shore.

And captains that we thought were dead,
  And dreamers that we thought were dumb,
And voices that we thought were fled,   15
  Arise, and call us, and we come;
And 'search in thine own soul,' they cry;
'For there, too, lurks thine enemy.'

Search for the foe in thine own soul,
  The sloth, the intellectual pride;   20
The trivial jest that veils the goal
  For which our fathers lived and died;
The lawless dreams, the cynic Art,
That rend thy nobler self apart.

Not far, not far into the night,   25
  These level swords of light can pierce;
Yet for her faith does England fight,
  Her faith in this our universe,
Believing Truth and Justice draw
From founts of everlasting law;   30

The law that rules the stars, our stay,
  Our compass through the world's wide sea,
The one sure light, the one sure way,
  The one firm base of Liberty;
The one firm road that men have trod   35
Through Chaos to the throne of God.

Therefore a Power above the State,
  The unconquerable Power returns.
The fire, the fire that made her great
  Once more upon her altar burns,   40
Once more, redeemed and healed and whole,
She moves to the Eternal Goal.
              — *Alfred Noyes.*

WIRELESS

Now to those who search the deep —
  Gleam of Hope and *Kindly Light,*
Once, before you turn to sleep,
  Breathe a message through the night
Never doubt that they'll receive it.   5
  Send it, once, and you'll believe it.

Think you these aerial wires
  Whisper more than spirits may?
Think you that our strong desires
  Touch no distance when we pray?   10
Think you that no wings are flying
'Twixt the living and the dying?

Inland, here, upon your knees,
  You shall breathe from urgent lips
Round the ships that guard your seas   15
  Fleet on fleet of angel ships;
Yea, the guarded may so bless them
That no terrors can distress them.

You shall guide the darkling prow,
  Kneeling — thus — and far inland;   20
You shall touch the storm-beat brow,
  Gently as a spirit-hand.
Even a blindfold prayer may speed them,
And a little child may lead them.
              — *Alfred Noyes.*

KILMENY

Dark, dark lay the drifters against the red
    West,
  As they shot their long meshes of steel
    overside,
And the oily green waters were rocking to
    rest,
  When Kilmeny went out, at the turn of the
    tide;
And nobody knew where that lassie would
    roam,   5
  For the magic that called her was tapping
    unseen,
It was well nigh a week ere Kilmeny came
    home;
  And nobody knew where Kilmeny had
    been.

She'd a gun at her bow that was Newcastle's
    best,
  And a gun at her stern that was fresh from
    the Clyde;   10
And a secret her skipper had never con-
    fessed,
  Not even at dawn, to his newly-wed bride;
And a wireless that whispered above, like a
    gnome,
  The laughter of London, the boasts of Ber-
    lin;
Oh, it may have been mermaids that lured
    her from home;   15
  But nobody knew where Kilmeny had been.

It was dark when Kilmeny came home from
    her quest,
  With a bridge dabbed red where her skip-
    per had died,
But she moved like a bride with a rose at
    her breast,
  And 'Well done, Kilmeny,' the Admiral
    cried.   20

Now, at sixty-four fathom, a conger may
    come,
  And nose at the bones of a drowned sub-
    marine;   .
But — late in the evening Kilmeny came
    home;
  And nobody knew where Kilmeny had
    been.

There's a wandering shadow that stares at
    the foam —   25
  Though they sing all the night to old Eng-
    land, their queen —
Late, late in the evening, Kilmeny came
    home;
  And nobody knew where Kilmeny had
    been.
                — *Alfred Noyes.*

CANADIANS

With arrows on their quarters and with
    numbers on their hoofs,
With the trampling sound of twenty that re-
    echoes in the roofs,
Low of crest and dull of coat, wan and wild
    of eye,
Through our English village the Canadians
    go by.

Shying at a passing cart, swerving from a
    car,   5
Tossing up an anxious head to flaunt a
    snowy star,
Racking at a Yankee gait, reaching at the
    rein,
Twenty raw Canadians are tasting life again!

Hollow-necked and hollow-flanked, lean of
    rib and hip,
Strained and sick and weary with the wallow
    of the ship,   10
Glad to smell the turf again, hear the robin's
    call,
Tread again the country road they lost at
    Montreal!

Fate may bring them dule and woe; better
    steeds than they
Sleep beside the English guns a hundred
    leagues away;
But till war hath need of them lightly lie
    their reins,   15
Softly fall the feet of them along the Eng-
    lish lanes.
               — *Will H. Ogilvie.*

MASTER AND PUPIL

(To J. F. R.)

Two years ago I taught him Greek,
  And used to give him hints on bowling:
His classics were a trifle weak;
  His 'action' needed some controlling.
Convinced of my superior *nous*   5
  I thought him crude, and I was rather
Inclined, as master of his House,
  To treat him like a heavy father.

I wrote the usual reports
  Upon his 'lack of concentration';   10
Though certainly at winter Sports
  He did not earn this condemnation.
I took him out San Moritz way
  One Christmas, and our *rôles* inverted,
For in the land of ski and sleigh   15
  His mastery was soon asserted.

I thought him just a normal lad,
  Well-mannered, wholesome, unaffected;
The makings of a Galahad
  In him I had not yet detected;   20
And when I strove to mend his style,
  Blue-penciling his exercises,
I little guessed that all the while
  His soul was ripe for high emprises.

Two years ago! and here I am,   25
  Rejected as unfit; still trying
(As Verrall taught me on the Cam)
  To make Greek Plays electrifying.
And he who, till he was eighteen,
  Found life one long excuse for laughing, 30
For eighteen solid months has been
  Continuously 'strafed' or 'strafing.'

He writes me letters from the front
  Which prove, although he does n't know it,
That though his words are plain and blunt, 35
  He has the vision of a poet;
And lately, on his eight days' rest,
  After long months of hard campaigning,
He came, and lo! an angel guest
  I was aware of entertaining.   40

About himself he seldom spoke,
  But often of his widowed mother,
And how she nobly bore the stroke
  That robbed them of his sailor brother.
And still, from loyalty or whim,   45
  He would defer to my opinion,
Unconscious how I envied him
  His hard-earned gift of self-dominion.

For he had faced the awful King
  Of Shadows in the darksome Valley,   50
And scorned the terrors of his sting
  In many a perilous storm and sally.
Firm in the faith that never tires
  Or thinks that man is God-forsaken,
From war's fierce seven-times-heated fires 55
  He had emerged unseared, unshaken.

There are, alas! no sons of mine
  To serve their country in her trial,
Embattled in the cause divine
  Of sacrifice and self-denial;   60
But if there were, I could not pray
  That God might shield them from dis-
    aster
More strongly than I plead to-day
  For this my pupil and my master.
                —*O. M.*

REVENGE FOR RHEIMS

Thou Permanence amid all things that pass!
Unchanging Thought amid the drift of
    change;
Thou Rally of the Soul in days of dross;
  How art Thou fallen!

Thou Prayer, that ever-rising, yet remained,
That for seven hundred years didst sing and
    soar,   5
Spirit with wings outspread tip-toe on Earth,
  How art Thou fallen!

Thou Vision frozen, and Thou Sigh trans-
    fixed;
Thou Camp of dreams, Thou Fort of faith
    unstormed,   10
Time-worn, yet wearying t'ward Eternity,
  How art Thou fallen!

Thou wast to France her Inspiration old,
Thou hadst for ivy earliest memories;
From Thee her Knights, her Angels long
    looked down;   15
  How art Thou fallen!

What vengeance for Thy ruin shall She hurl?
Oh, be that vengeance, that the ruin stand,
Only those Choirs forever unrestored!
  Ever unfallen!   20
           —*Stephen Phillips.*

SOCKS

Shining pins that dart and click
  In the fireside's sheltered peace

Check the thoughts that cluster thick—
  20 plain and then decrease.

He was brave—well, so was I—
  Keen and merry, but his lip
Quivered when he said good-by—
  Purl the seam-stitch, purl and slip.

Never used to living rough,
  Lots of things he'd got to learn;   10
Wonder if he's warm enough—
  Knit 2, catch 2, knit 1, turn.

Hark! The paper-boys again!
  Wish that shout could be suppressed;
Keeps one always on the strain—   15
  Knit off 9, and slip the rest.

Wonder if he's fighting now,
  What he's done an where he's been;
He'll come out on top, somehow—
  Slip 1, knit 2, purl 14.
           —*Jessie Pope.*

'FORM FOURS'

A VOLUNTEER'S NIGHTMARE

If you're Volunteer Artist or Athlete, or if
  you defend the Home,
You sacrifice 'Ease' for 'Attention,' and
  march like a metronome;
But of all elementary movements you learn
  in your Volunteer Corps
The one that is really perplexing is known
  as the Forming of Fours.

Imagine us numbered off from the right:
  the Sergeant faces the squad,   5
And says that the odd files do not move—I
  never seem to be odd!
And then his instructions run like this (very
  simple in black and white) —
'A pace to the rear with the left foot, and
  one to the right with the right.'

Of course if you don't think deeply, you do
  it without a hitch;
You have only to know your right and left,
  and remember which is which;   10
But as soon as you try to be careful, you get
  in the deuce of a plight,
With 'a pace to the right with the left foot,
  and one to the rear with the right!'

Besides, when you're thoroughly muddled
  the Sergeant doubles your doubt

By saying that rules reverse themselves, as
  soon as you 're 'turned about ';
So round you go on your right heel, and
  practise until you are deft   15
At 'pace to the front with the right foot,
  and one to the left with the left.'

In my dreams the Sergeant, the Kaiser, and
  Kipling mix my feet,
Saying 'East is left, and Right is Might, and
  never the twain shall meet!'
In my nightmare squad *all* files are odd, and
  their Fours are horribly queer,
With 'a pace to the left with the front foot,
  and one to the right with the rear!'   20
           — *Frank Sidgwick.*

'ALL THE HILLS AND VALES ALONG'

All the hills and vales along
Earth is bursting into song,
And the singers are the chaps
Who are going to die perhaps.
  O sing, marching men,   5
  Till the valleys ring again.
  Give your gladness to earth's keeping,
  So be glad, when you are sleeping.

Cast away regret and rue,
Think what you are marching to.   10
Little live, great pass.
Jesus Christ and Barabbas
Were found the same day.
This died, that went his way.
  So sing with joyful breath.   15
  For why, you are going to death.
  Teeming earth will surely store
  All the gladness that you pour.

Earth that never doubts nor fears,
Earth that knows of death, not tears,   20
Earth that bore with joyful ease
Hemlock for Socrates,
Earth that blossomed and was glad
'Neath the cross that Christ had,
Shall rejoice and blossom too   25
When the bullet reaches you.
  Wherefore, men marching
  On the road to death, sing!
  Pour your gladness on earth's head,
  So be merry, so be dead.   30

From the hills and valleys earth
Shouts back the sound of mirth,
Tramp of feet and lilt of song
Ringing all the road along.

All the music of their going,   35
Ringing, swinging, glad song-throwing,
Earth will echo still, when foot
Lies numb and voice mute.
  On, marching men, on
  To the gates of death with song.   40
  Sow your gladness for earth's reaping,
  So you may be glad, though sleeping.
  Strew your gladness on earth's bed,
  So be merry, so be dead.
         — *Charles Hamilton Sorley.*

SAILOR, WHAT OF THE DEBT WE OWE YOU?

Sailor, what of the debt we owe you?
  Day or night is the peril more?
Who so dull that he fails to know you,
  Sleepless guard of our island shore?

Safe the corn to the farmyard taken;   5
  Grain ships safe upon all the seas;
Homes in peace and a faith unshaken —
  Sailor, what do we owe for these?

Safe the clerk at his desk; the trader
  Counts unruined his honest gain;   10
Safe though yonder the curs't invader
  Pours red death over hill and plain.

Sailor, what of the debt we owe you?
  Now is the hour at last to pay,
Now in the stricken field to show you   15
  What is the spirit you guard to-day.
         — *Andrew John Stuart.*

A GIRL'S SONG

The Meuse and Marne have little waves;
  The slender poplars o'er them lean.
One day they will forget the graves
  That give the grass its living green.

Some brown French girl the rose will wear 5
  That springs above his comely head;
Will twine it in her russet hair,
  Nor wonder why it is so red.

His blood is in the rose's veins,
  His hair is in the yellow corn.   10
My grief is in the weeping rains
  And in the keening wind forlorn.

Flow softly, softly, Marne and Meuse;
  Tread lightly all ye browsing sheep;

Fall tenderly, O silver dews,   15
  For here my dear Love lies asleep.

The earth is on his sealèd eyes,
  The beauty marred that was my pride;
Would I were lying where he lies,
  And sleeping sweetly by his side!   20

The Spring will come by Meuse and Marne,
  The birds be blithesome in the tree.
I heap the stones to make his cairn
  Where many sleep as sound as he.
                                        — *Katharine Tynan.*

FROM A FLEMISH GRAVEYARD

(January, 1915)

A year hence may the grass that waves
O'er English men in Flemish graves,
Coating this clay with green of peace
And softness of a year's increase,
Be kind and lithe as English grass   5
To bend and nod as the winds pass;
It was for grass on English hills
These bore too soon the last of ills.

And may the wind be brisk and clean,
And singing cheerfully between   10
The bents a pleasant-burdened song
To cheer these English dead along;
For English songs and English winds
Are they that bred these English minds.

And may the circumstantial trees   15
Dip, for these dead ones, in the breeze,
And make for them their silver play
Of spangled boughs each shiny day.
Thus may these look above, and see
And hear the wind in grass and tree,   20
And watch a lark in heaven stand,
And think themselves in their own land.
                                     — *Iolo Aneurin Williams.*

THE FIRST BATTLE OF YPRES [1]

Gray field of Flanders, grim old battle-plain,
What armies held the iron line round Ypres
      in the rain,

1 AUTHOR'S NOTE.— In the first battle of Ypres,
which was fought in October–November, 1914, a
thin line of British, supported on each wing by small
bodies of French, stopped the push of an immense
German army on Calais. The allusion in the latter
part of the poem is not to "the angels of Mons,"
but to a story received from a very competent witness. On three occasions the Germans broke

From Bixschoote to Baecelaere and down to
      the Lys river?

      Merry men of England,
      Men of the green shires,   5
      From the winding waters,
      The elm-trees and the spires,
And the lone village dreaming in the down-
      land yonder.
Half a million Huns broke over them in
      thunder,
Roaring seas of Huns swept on and sunk
      again,   10
Where fought the men of England round
      Ypres in the rain,
On the grim plain of Flanders, whose earth
      is fed with slaughter.

North-country fighting men from the mine
      and the loom,
Highlander and lowlander stood up to death
      and doom;
From Bixschoote to Baecelaere and down to
      the Lys river.   15

      London men and Irish,
      Indian men and French,
      Charging with the bayonet,
      Firing in the trench,
Fought in that furious fight, shoulder to
      shoulder,   20
Leapt from their saddles to charge in fierce
      disorder,
The Life Guards, mud and blood for the
      scarlet and the plume,
And they hurled back the foemen as the wind
      the sea spume,
From Bixschoote to Baecelaere and down to
      the Lys river.

But the huge Hun masses yet mounted more
      and more,   25
Like a giant wave gathering to whelm the
      sweet shore,
While swift the exultant foam runs on be-
      fore and over.

      Where that foam was leading,
      With bayonets, or witn none,
      The cooks and the service men   30
      Ran upon the Hun.

through our line, then paused and retired, for no
apparent reason. On each of these occasions prisoners, when asked the cause of their retirement,
replied: "We saw your enormous Reserves." We
had no Reserves. This story was incidentally confirmed by the remark of another officer on the curious conduct of the Germans in violently shelling
certain empty fields behind our lines.

The cooks and the service men charged and
    charged together
Moussy's cuirassiers, on foot, with spur and
    saber;
Helmed and shining fought they as warriors
    fought of yore —
Till calm fell sinister as the hush at the
    whirlwind's core,   35
From Bixschoote to Baecelaere and down to
    the Lys river.

Lo! the Emperor launched on us his guard
    of old renown,
Stepping in parade-march, as they step
    through Berlin town,
On the chill road to Gheluveldt, in the dark
    before the dawning.

    Heavily tolled on them   40
    Mortal mouths of guns,
    Gallantly, gallantly
    Came the flower of the Huns.
Proud men they marched, like an avalanche
    on us falling,
Prouder men they met, in the dark before
    the dawning.   45
Seven to one they came against us to shatter
    us and drown,
One to seven in the woodland we fought
    them up and down.
In the sad November woodland, when all the
    skies were mourning.

The long battle thundered till a waxing moon
    might wane,
Thrice they broke the exhausted line that
    held them on the plain,   50
And thrice like billows they went back, from
    viewless bounds retiring.

    Why paused they and went back-
      ward,
    With never a foe before
    Like a long wave dragging
    Down a level shore   55
Its fierce reluctant surges, that came tri-
    umphant storming
The land, and powers invisible drive to its
    deep returning?
On the gray field of Flanders again and yet
    again
The Huns beheld the Great Reserves on the
    old battle-plain,

The blood-red field of Flanders where all the
    skies were mourning.   60

The fury of their marshalled guns might
    plow no dreadful lane
Through those Reserves that waited in the
    ambush of the rain
On the riven plain of Flanders where hills of
    men lay moaning.

    They hurled upon an army
    The bellowing heart of Hell,   65
    We saw but the meadows
    Torn with their shot and shell.
We heard not the march of the succors that
    were coming,
Their old forgotten bugle-calls the fifes and
    the drumming,
But they gathered and they gathered from
    the graves where they had lain
A hundred years, hundreds of years, on the
    old battle-plain,   71
And the young graves of Flanders, all fresh
    with dews of mourning.

Marlborough's men and Wellington's, the
    burghers of Courtrai,
The warriors of Plantagenet, King Louis'
    Gants glacés —
And the young, young dead from Mons and
    the Marne River.   75

    Old heroic fighting men,
    Who fought for chivalry,
    Men who died for England,
    Mother of Liberty.
In the world's dim heart, where the waiting
    spirits slumber,   80
Sounded a roar when the walls were rent
    asunder
That parted Earth from Hell, and summon-
    ing them away,
Tremendous trumpets blew, as at the Judg-
    ment Day —
And the dead came forth, each to his former
    banner.

On the grim field of Flanders, the old battle
    plain,   85
Their armies held the iron line round Ypres
    in the rain,
From Bixschoote to Baecelaere and down to
    the Lys river.
        —*Margaret L. Woods.*

CONTEMPORARY PROSE

MAX BEERBOHM (1872–)

WILLIAM AND MARY

Memories, like olives, are an acquired taste. William and Mary (I give them the Christian names that were indeed theirs —the joint title by which their friends always referred to them) were for some years an interest in my life, and had a hold on my affection. But a time came when, though I had known and liked them too well ever to forget them, I gave them but a few thoughts now and then. How, being dead, could they keep their place in the mind of a young man surrounded with large and constantly renewed consignments of the living? As one grows older, the charm of novelty wears off. One finds that there is no such thing as novelty—or, at any rate, that one has lost the faculty for perceiving it. One sees every newcomer not as something strange and special, but as a ticketed specimen of this or that very familiar genus. The world has ceased to be remarkable; and one tends to think more and more often of the days when it was so very remarkable indeed.

I suppose that had I been thirty years older when first I knew him William would have seemed to me little worthier of attention than a penny-halfpenny postage-stamp seems to-day. Yet, no: William really had some oddities that would have caught even an oldster's eye. In himself he was commonplace enough (as I, coeval though I was with him, soon saw). But in details of surface he was unusual. In them he happened to be rather ahead of his time. He was a Socialist, for example. In 1890 there was only one other Socialist in Oxford, and he not at all an undergraduate, but a retired chimneysweep, named Hines, who made speeches, to which nobody, except perhaps William, listened, near the Martyrs' Memorial. And William wore a flannel shirt, and rode a bicycle—very strange habits in those days, and very horrible. He was said to be (though he was short-sighted and wore glasses) a first-rate 'back' at football; but, as football was a thing frowned on by the rowing men, and coldly ignored by the bloods, his talent for it did not help him: he was one of the principal pariahs of our College; and it was rather in a spirit of bravado, and to show how sure of myself I was, that I began, in my second year, to cultivate his acquaintance.

We had little in common. I could not think Political Economy 'the most exciting thing in the world,' as he used to call it. Nor could I without yawning listen to more than a few lines of Mr. William Morris's interminable smoth Icelandic Sagas, which my friend, pious young Socialist that he was, thought 'glorious.' He had begun to write an Icelandic Saga himself, and had already achieved some hundreds of verses. None of these pleased him, though to me they seemed very like his master's. I can see him now, standing on his hearth-rug, holding his MS. close to his short-sighted eyes, declaiming the verses and trying, with many angular gestures of his left hand, to animate them —a tall, broad, raw-boned fellow, with long brown hair flung back from his forehead, and a very shabby suit of clothes. Because of his clothes and his socialism, and his habit of offering beer to a guest, I had at first supposed him quite poor; and I was surprised when he told me that he had from his guardian (his parents being dead) an allowance of £350, and that when he came of age he would have an income of £400. 'All out of dividends,' he would groan. I would hint that Mr. Hines and similar zealots might disembarrass him of this load, if he asked them nicely. 'No,'

1026

he would say quite seriously, 'I can't do that,,' and would read out passages from 'Fabian Essays' to show that in the present anarchical conditions only mischief could result from sporadic dispersal of rent. 'Ten, twelve years hence—' he would muse more hopefully. 'But by that time,' I would say, 'You'll probably be married, and your wife mightn't quite—', whereat he would hotly repeat what he had said many times: that he would never marry. Marriage was an anti-social anachronism. I think its survival was in some part due to the machinations of Capital. Anyway, it was doomed. Temporary civil contracts between men and women would be the rule "ten, twelve years hence"; pending which time the lot of any man who had civil sense must be celibacy, tempered perhaps with free love.

Long before that time was up, nevertheless, William married. One afternoon in the spring of '95 I happened to meet him at a corner of Trafalgar Square. I wondered at the immense cordiality of his greeting; for our friendship, such as it was, had waned in our two final years at Oxford. 'You look very flourishing, and,' I said, 'you're wearing a new suit!' 'I'm married,' he replied, obviously without a twinge of conscience. He told me he had been married just a month. He declared that to be married was the most splendid thing in all the world; but he weakened the force of this generalization by adding that there never was any one like his wife. 'You must see her,' he said; and his impatience to show her proudly off to some one was so evident, and so touching, that I could but accept his invitation to go and stay with them for two or three days— 'why not next week?' They had taken and furnished 'a sort of cottage' in —— shire, and this was their home. He had 'run up for the day, on business—journalism' and was now on his way to Charing Cross. 'I know you'll like my wife,' he said at parting. 'She's—well, she's glorious.'

As this was the epithet he had erst applied to 'Beowulf' and to 'Sigurd the Volsung' it raised no high hopes. And indeed, as I was soon to find, he had again misused it. There was nothing glorious about his bride. Some people might even have not thought her pretty. I myself did not, in the flash of first sight. Neat, insignificant, pleasing, was what she ap-

peared to me, rather than pretty, and far rather than glorious. In an age of fringes, her brow was severely bare. She looked 'practical.' But an instant later, when she smiled, I saw that she was pretty, too. And presently I thought her delightful. William had met me in a 'governess cart,' and we went to see him unharness the pony. He did this in a fumbling, experimental way, confusing the reins with the traces, and profiting so little by his wife's directions that she began to laugh. And her laugh was a lovely thing; quite a small sound, but exquisitely clear and gay, coming in a sequence of notes that neither rose nor fell, that were quite even; a trill of notes, and then another, and another, as though she were pulling repeatedly a little silver bell. . . As I describe it, perhaps the sound may be imagined irritating. I can only say it was enchanting.

I wished she would go on laughing; but she ceased, she darted forward and (William standing obediently aside, and I helping unhelpfully) unharnessed the pony herself, and led it into its small stable. Decidedly, she was 'practical,' but—I was prepared now to be lenient to any quality she might have.

Had she been feckless, no doubt I should have forgiven her that, too; but I might have enjoyed my visit less than I did, and might have been less pleased to go often again. I had expected to 'rough it' under William's roof. But everything thereunder, within the limits of a strict Arcadian simplicity, was well-ordered. I was touched, when I went to my bedroom, by the precision with which the very small maid had unpacked and disposed my things. And I wondered where my hostess had got the lore she had so evidently imparted. Certainly not from William. Perhaps (it only now strikes me) from a handbook. For Mary was great at handbooks. She had handbooks about gardening, and others about poultry, and one about 'the stable,' and others on cognate themes. From these she had filled up the gaps left in her education by her father, who was a widower and either a doctor or a solicitor—I forget which—in one of the smallest towns of an adjoining county. And I daresay she may have had, somewhere hidden away, a manual for young hostesses. If so, it must have been a good one. But to say this is to belittle Mary's powers of intuition. It was they, sharpened by her adoration of William, and by her intensity for everything around him, that made her so efficient a housewife.

If she possessed a manual for young house-hunters, it was assuredly not by the light of this that she had chosen the home they were installed in. The 'sort of cottage' had been vacant for many years—an unpromising and ineligible object, a mile away from a village, and three miles away from a railway station. The main part of it was an actual cottage, of seventeenth-century workmanship; but a little stuccoed wing had been added to each side of it, in 1850 or thereabouts, by an eccentric old gentleman who at that time chose to make it his home. He had added also the small stable, a dairy, and other appanages. For these, and for garden, there was plenty of room, as he had purchased and enclosed half an acre of the surrounding land. Those two stuccoed, very Victorian wings of his, each with a sash-window above and a French window below, consorted queerly with the old red brick and the latticed panes. And the long wooden veranda that he had invoked did not unify the trinity. But one didn't want it to. The wrongness had a character all its own. The wrongness was right—at any rate after Mary had hit on it for William. As a spinster, she would, I think, have been happiest in a trim modern villa. But it was a belief of hers that she had married a man of strange genius. She had married him for himself, not for his genius; but this added grace in him was a thing to be reckoned with, ever so much; a thing she must coddle to the utmost in a proper setting. She was a year older than he (though, being so small and slight, she looked several years younger), and in her devotion the maternal instinct played a great part. William, as I have already conveyed to you, was not greatly gifted. Mary's instinct, in this matter, was at fault. But endearingly, rightly at fault. And, as William *was* outwardly odd, wasn't it well that his home should be so, too? On the inside, comfort was what Mary always aimed at for him, and achieved.

The ground floor had all been made one room, into which you stepped straight from the open air. Quite a long big room (or so it seemed, from the lowness of the ceiling); well-freshened in its antiquity, with rush-mats here and there on the irregular red-tiles, and very white white-wash on the plaster between the rafters. This was the dining-room, drawing-room, and general focus throughout the day, and was called simply the Room. William had a 'den' on the ground floor of the left wing; and there, in the mornings, he used to write a great deal. Mary had no special place of her own: her place was wherever her duties needed her. William wrote reviews of books for the *Daily* ——. He did also creative work. The vein of poetry in him had worked itself out—or rather, it expressed itself for him in Mary. For technical purposes the influence of Ibsen had superseded that of Morris. At the time of my first visit, he was writing an extraordinarily gloomy play about an extraordinarily unhappy marriage. In subsequent seasons (Ibsen's disc having been somehow eclipsed for him by George Gissing's) he was usually writing novels in which everyone—or do I exaggerate? —had made a disastrous match. I think Mary's belief in his genius had made him less diffident than he was at Oxford. He was always emerging from his den, with fresh pages of MS., into the Room. 'You don't mind?' he would say, waving his pages, and then would shout 'Mary!' She was always promptly forthcoming— sometimes from the direction of the kitchen, in a white apron, sometimes from the garden, in a blue one. She never looked at him while he read. To do so would have been lacking in respect for his work. It was on this that she must concentrate her whole mind, privileged auditor that she was. She sat looking straight before her, with her lips slightly compressed, and one hand beneath her chin. I used to wonder that there had been that first moment when I did not think her pretty. Her eyes were of a very light hazel, seeming all the lighter because her hair was of so dark a brown; and they were beautifully set in a face of that 'pinched oval' kind which is rather rare in England. Mary as listener would have atoned to me for any defects there may have been in dear old William's work. Nevertheless, I sometimes wished this work had some comic relief in it. Publishers, I believe, shared this wish; hence the eternal absence of William's name from among their announcements. For Mary's sake, and his, I should have liked him to be 'successful.' But at any rate he didn't need money. He didn't need, in addition to what he had, what he made by his journalism. And as for success—well didn't Mary think him a genius? And wasn't he Mary's husband? The main reason why I wished for light passages in what he read to us was that they would have been cues for Mary's laugh. This was a thing always new to me. I never tired of that little bell-like euphony; those funny little lucid and level trills.

There was no stint of that charm when William was not reading to us. Mary was in no awe of him, apart from his work, and in no awe at all of me: she used to laugh at us both, for one thing and another—just the same laugh as I had first heard when William tried to unharness the pony. I cultivated in myself whatever amused her in me; I drew out whatever amused her in William; I never let slip any of the things that amused her in herself. 'Chaff' is a great bond; and I should have enjoyed our bouts of it even without Mary's own special *obbligato*. She used to call me (for I was very urban in those days) the Gentleman from London. I used to call her the Brave Little Woman. Whatever either of us said or did could be twisted easily into relation to those two titles; and our bouts, to which William listened with a puzzled, benevolent smile, used to cease only because Mary regarded me as a possible purveyor of what William, she was sure, wanted and needed, down there in the country, alone with her: intellectual conversation, after his work. She often, I think, invented duties in garden or kitchen so that he should have this stimulus, or luxury, without hindrance. But when William was alone with me it was about her that he liked to talk, and that I myself liked to talk too. He was very sound on the subject of Mary; and so was I. And if, when I was alone with Mary, I seemed to be sounder than I was on the subject of William's wonderfulness, who shall blame me?

Had Mary been a mother, William's wonderfulness would have been less greatly important. But he was her child as well as her lover. And I think, though I do not know, she believed herself content that this should always be, if so it were destined. It was not destined so. On the first night of a visit I paid them in April, 1899, William, when we were alone, told me news. I had been vaguely conscious, throughout the evening, of some change; conscious that Mary had grown gayer, and less gay—somehow different, somehow remote. William said that her child would be born in September, if all went well. 'She's immensely happy,' he told me. I realized that she was indeed happier than ever. . . . 'And of course it would be a wonderful thing, for both of us,' he said presently, 'to have a son—or a daughter.' I asked him which he would rather it were, a son or a daughter. 'Oh, either,' he answered wearily. It was evident that he had misgivings and fears. I tried to reason him out of them. He did not, I am thankful to say, ever let Mary suspect them. She had no misgivings. But it was destined that her child should live only for an hour, and that she should die in bearing it.

I had stayed again at the cottage in July, for some days. At the end of that month I had gone to France, as was my custom, and a week later had written to Mary. It was William that answered this letter, telling me of Mary's death and burial. I returned to England next day. William and I wrote to each other several times. He had not left his home. He stayed there, 'trying,' as he said in a grotesque and heartrending phrase, 'to finish a novel.' I saw him in the following January. He wrote to me from the Charing Cross Hotel, asking me to lunch with him there. After our first greetings, there was a silence. He wanted to talk of—what he could not talk of. We stared helplessly at each other, and then, in the English way, talked of things at large. England was engaged in the Boer War. William was the sort of man whom one would have expected to be violently Pro-boer. I was surprised at his fervor for the stronger side. He told me he had tried to enlist, but had been rejected on account of his eyesight. But there was, he said, a good chance of his being sent out, almost immediately, as one of the *Daily* ——'s special correspondents. 'And then,' he exclaimed, 'I shall see something of it.' I had a presentiment that he would not return, and a belief that he did not want to return. He did not return. Special correspondents were not so carefully shepherded in that war as they have since been. They were more at liberty to take risks, on behalf of the journals to which they were accredited. William was killed a few weeks after he had landed at Cape Town.

And there came, as I have said, a time when I did not think of William and Mary often; and then a time when I did more often think of them. And especially much did my mind hark back to them in the late autumn of last year; for on the way to the place I was staying at I had passed the little railway station, whose name had always linked itself for me with the names of those two friends. There were but four intervening stations. It was not a difficult pilgrimage that I made some days later— back towards the past, for that past's sake and honor. I had thought I should not remember the way, the three miles of way, from the station to the cottage; but I found myself remembering it perfectly, without a glance at the fingerposts. Rain had been falling heavily, driving the late leaves off the trees; and everything looked rather sodden and misty, though the sun was now shining. I had known this landscape only in spring, summer, early autumn. Mary had held to a theory that at other seasons I could not be acclimatized. But there were groups of trees that I knew, even without their leaves; and farmhouses and small stone bridges that had not at all changed. Only what mattered was changed. Only what mattered was gone. Would what I had come to see be there still? In comparison with what it had held, it was not much. But I wished to see it, melancholy spectacle though it must be for me if it were extant, and worse than melancholy if it held something new. I began to be sure it had been demolished, built over. At the corner of the lane that had led to it, I was almost minded to explore no further, to turn back. But I went on, and suddenly I was at the four-barred iron gate, that I remembered, between the laurels. It was rusty, and fastened with a rusty padlock, and beyond it there was grass where a winding 'drive' had been. From the lane the cottage never had been visible, even when these laurels were lower and sparser than they were now. Was the cottage still standing? Presently, I climbed over the gate, and walked through the long grass, and—yes, there was Mary's cottage; still there; William's and Mary's cottage.

Trite enough, I have no doubt, were the thoughts that possessed me as I stood gazing. There is nothing new to be thought about the evanescence of human things; but there is always much to be felt about it by one who encounters in his maturity some such intimate instance and reminder as confronted me, in that cold sunshine, across that small wilderness of long rank wet grass and weeds.

Incredibly woebegone and lonesome the house would have looked even to one for whom it contained no memories; all the more because in its utter dereliction it looked so durable. Some of the stucco had fallen off the walls of the two wings; thick flakes of it lay on the discolored roof of the veranda, and thick flakes of it could be seen lying in the grass below. Otherwise, there were few signs of actual decay. The sash-window and the French window of each wing were shuttered, and, from where I was standing, the cream-colored paint of those shutters behind the glass looked almost fresh. The latticed windows between had all been boarded up from within. The house was not to be let perish soon.

I did not want to go nearer to it; yet I did go nearer, step by step, across the wilderness, right up to the edge of the veranda itself, and within a yard of the frontdoor.

I stood looking at that door. I had never noticed it in the old days, for then it had always stood open. But it asserted itself now, master of the threshold.

It was a narrow door—narrow even for its height, which did not exceed mine by more than two inches or so; a door that even when it was freshly painted must have looked mean. How much meaner now, with its paint all faded and mottled, cracked and blistered! It had no knocker, not even a slit for letters. All that it had was a large-ish key-hole. On this my eyes rested; and presently I moved to it, stooped down to it, peered through it. I had a glimpse of—darkness impenetrable. Strange it seemed to me, as I stood back, that there the Room was, the remembered Room itself, separated from me by nothing but this unremembered door . . . and a quarter of a century, yes. I saw it all, in my mind's eye, just as it had been: the way the sunlight came into it through this same doorway and through the lattices of these same four windows;

the way the little bit of a staircase came down into it, so crookedly yet so confidently; and how uneven the tiled floor was, and how low the rafters were, and how littered the whole place was with books brought in from his den by William, and how bright with flowers brought in by Mary from her garden. The rafters, the stairs, the tiles, were still existing changeless in despite of cobwebs and dust and darkness, all quite changeless on the other side of the door, so near to me. I wondered how I should feel if by some enchantment the door slowly turned on its hinges, letting in light. I should not enter, I felt, not even look, so much must I hate to see those inner things lasting when all that had given to them a meaning was gone from them, taken away from them, finally. And yet, why blame them for their survival? And how know that *nothing* of the past ever came to them, revisiting, hovering? Something—sometimes— perhaps? One knew so little. How not be tender to what, as it seemed to me, perhaps the dead loved?

So strong in me now was the wish to see again all those things, to touch them and, as it were, commune with them, and so queerly may the mind be wrought upon in a solitude among memories, that there were moments when I almost expected that the door would obey my will. I was recalled to a clearer sense of reality by something which I had not before noticed. In the door-post to the right was a small knob of rusty iron—mocking reminder that to gain admission to a house one does not 'will' the door: one rings the bell— unless it is rusty and has quite obviously no one to answer it; in which case one goes away. Yet I did not go away. The movement that I made, in despite of myself, was towards the knob itself. But, I hesitated, suppose I did what I half meant to do, and there were no sound. That would be ghastly. And surely there *would* be no sound. And if sound there were, wouldn't that be worse still? My hand drew back, wavered, suddenly closed on the knob. I heard the scrape of the wire— and then, from somewhere within the heart of the shut house, a tinkle.

It had been the weakest, the puniest of noises. It had been no more than is a fledgling's first attempt at a twitter. But I was not judging it by its volume. Deafening peals from steeples had meant less to me than that one single note breaking the silence—in there. In there, in the dark, the bell that had answered me was still quivering, I supposed, on its wire. But there was no one to answer *it*, no footstep to come hither from those recesses, making prints in the dust. Well, *I* could answer it; and again my hand closed on the knob, unhesitatingly this time, pulling further. That was my answer; and the rejoinder to it was more than I had thought to hear—a whole quick sequence of notes, faint but clear, playful, yet poignantly sad, like a trill of laughter echoing out of the past, or even merely out of this neighboring darkness. It was so like something I had known, so recognizable and oh, recognizing, that I was lost in wonder.

And long must I have remained standing at that door, for I heard the sound often, often. I must have rung again and again, tenaciously, vehemently, in my folly.

ARNOLD BENNETT (1867–   )

From OUR WOMEN

SALARY EARNING GIRLS

(Copyright, 1920, by George H. Doran Co., Publishers)

Young girls have always been held to be very mysterious. To-day they are held to be more mysterious than ever. Such at any rate is the view taken by people of middle-age, both men and women, and their attitude to the 'typical' young girl has in it a certain amount of reproach. But whether young men regard their feminine contemporaries as specially mysterious I doubt. And the young are the best judges of the young. (Though old, I assert it.)

Before going further, let me interject that when I say 'young girl' I mean what the French mean when they say 'jeune fille,' that is, an unmarried adult virgin who is not old enough to be called a spinster. I will not attempt to determine at what age an unmarried virgin begins to incur the terrible imputation of spinsterhood; it varies, being dependent on a lot of things, such as color of hair, litheness of frame, complexion, ankles, chin (the under part), style of talk and of glance. I have known spinsters of twenty-five, and young girls of at least forty   Henceforward in this chapter I intend to discuss that very large middle class of girls whose members wholly or partly earn their own living. Unfortunately this class does not yet by a long way comprise all girls; nevertheless, its demeanor towards life influences and explains the demeanor towards life of the 'leisured class' of girls above it, and therefore in some degree it is representative of that class also.

The root of modern feminism is, of course, the desire for money—money that can be transformed into personal satisfactions. True, the pioneers of feminism did not think primarily of money when they set out on those adventurous careers which too often involved obloquy and even martyrdom. They thought primarily of freedom—freedom to fulfill themselves according to their individual instincts. But freedom includes, and must include, economic freedom; and economic freedom signifies the control of the means of living.

How many pioneers would, for example, have given up the fight against the medical societies for the right to practise as doctors if the medical societies had said to them: 'You may practise as doctors, but you must not charge fees?' None. The right to earn, to be economically free, was the essence of the struggle.

After the pioneers had turned the tide of the battle, and cleared many paths for the multitude, the multitude began to follow from no other motive than an economic motive. The mass of girls saw a chance of obtaining for themselves a share of that strange and delectable commodity, money, and they took it. If they did not take it of their own accord their parents little by little insisted on their taking it, and finally, in the middle-class under review, the general rule was established that girls must earn. A few of them go out into the world against their will. On the other hand, a few would have gone out even if no money had resulted from the process, simply to escape an oppressive atmosphere at home, and to breathe the fresh winds of the world. But the great mass, the all-but totality, go out solely in search of money and the economic freedom which money confers on its possessors.

The consequences were not entirely advantageous. The girls lost the old girlish air of ignorance, of being simpletons in the world. But that was an advantage.

They lost the attractiveness of perfect inexperience. That, too, was an advantage, for such attractiveness appealed chiefly to the perverse and the Oriental in the male sex. They lost much futile leisure; that too was an advantage. They lost some of their ideals, and that, though not an unrelieved disadvantage, was a disadvantage. They lost, thousands of them, a measure of health; for, being raw and eager, they were, and still are, often exploited in the conditions of employment, overworked, and sweated. That was an unrelieved disadvantage, and all the more so because it filled them with a sense of resentment against the men who exploited them and against the innocent men who received (and still receive) more pay than they for precisely the same work.

But the gain on the whole was enormous. There was, at first, the novel and dignifying sensation of the performance of a useful function in society. Certainly the mere novelty of the sensation soon departed, and girls of the present and the future do not, and probably will not, recapture it. But the sensation itself remains, though it is chiefly subconscious, and though it may be mingled with the quite different sensation of the oppressiveness of work. People, even enthusiastic girls, as a rule start the week's work with the complaint uttered or unexpressed; 'Monday morning again! What a grind!' They do not rise on Monday morning with hearts full of heavenly gratitude for the privilege of being allowed to perform a useful function in society. Still, the gratitude vaguely persists and it gives birth to pleasurable pride.

Then, there is the advantage of meeting men other than near relatives. Under the old régime, middle-class and also lower-middle-class girls met men in a sort of ceremonial—except sometimes when they met them by ingenious and conspiratorial design. They elaborately prepared themselves for meeting men. Before meeting men they pondered long over the encounter, and after meeting men they pondered long over the encounter. Under the new régime girls who work meet as many men in a day as their predecessors of similar standing met in a month. Indeed, many of their predecessors met men (other than relatives) about as often as they met giraffes. It is, I admit, a fact that girls who work, particularly those whose work is clerical, are now during working hours confined more and more to the companionship of girls. Frequently in large establishments they find girls on either side of them, in front of them and behind them; they are supervised by girls and they have girls under them. And they might be excused for thinking that they had fallen into a nunnery instead of into a factory or an office. But those vast interiors are not after all nunneries. The male is there and the influence of the male is there: and, further, the morning and evening promiscuity of the public vehicle has to be brought into account.

Save in highly exceptional instances, the girl who earns her living abroad acquires in doing so one of the most important and healthy experiences of feminine life—familiarity with the masculine. She is bound to be constantly correcting her dreams of men by the reality of men. And the correction, stretching over a considerable period, is less violent and distressing than it would be if concentrated into, say a month of marriage.

Lastly, the salary-earning girl gains knowledge of the world. This knowledge may be superficial, imperfect, one-sided, mischievous in certain respects, but it is far better than ignorance. She does get some sort of a notion of the structure and working of society; she does get some sort of a notion of real values; which notions, even if they be pitifully vague, do enable her on frequent occasions to reject the dangerous poison of sentimentality which would otherwise be poured into her by the older persons whose object in life seems to be to confuse that which ought to be with that which is. To anybody who demands sceptically: 'But after all can the girl teach her grandmother to suck eggs?' I would reply: 'As a rule, she can.' How does she gain this knowledge of the world? It would be more reasonable to ask how she could avoid gaining it. All day the world is rubbing off information on to her. Even if she sits with a thousand girl-colleagues in some clacking interior of a Chicago mail-order house and does nothing for eight hours but tap out bills on a typewriter, she is learning about the kind of things that people really do want and how much they want them and what wild sums they are ready to pay for them. She cannot travel with regu-

larity through a city on the top of a 'bus, or under a city in a tube, without effectively learning more about the world than she would learn from a hundred books and a hundred parents in a hundred years.

She reads the newspaper. It teaches her. She may read it simply for distraction on the daily journey. It teaches her. It may teach her badly. It teaches her. She may not read a newspaper, but only look at the pictures in a newspaper. The pictures teach her. I would sooner that she read the newspaper than any of the vast majority of novels. If she reads the latest old-fashioned sweet novels she is severely handicapped, for the latest old-fashioned novelists are still catering for the girl's grandmother, and the perusal of one of them may almost undo in half an hour's train journey at night all the solid educational work that contact with the world has accomplished in ten hours.

Then she visits restaurants, either public or private—not places where there is a conspiracy of waiters to convince her that she is a most high queen surrounded by slaves; but hurrying, realistic places where the principles which rule the world stand forth naked, and everybody not merely knows, but openly admits, what is what; and she will not obtain value for her money in such places until she has genuinely obtained a grasp of the aforesaid principles.

And when she reaches home and sits down to the family meal she finds that the conversation is much more instructive, candid, catholic, and interesting than it used to be before she went into the world. The most arrogantly male father, the most head-burying ostrich of a mother, cannot decently pretend that exactly the same girl has come home who went forth. And the conversation improves accordingly.

GILBERT CANNAN (1884–)

From SAMUEL BUTLER, A CRITICAL STUDY

THE ENGLISH NOVEL

It is to be feared that many readers have laid down 'The Way of All Flesh,' for it has none of those quips and graces which modern novelists have invented to save their readers the trouble of reading for themselves, telling them what to think, what to feel, what to imagine, without disturbing what they think, feel, and imagine in everyday life; so that it is possible to pass from the columns of a newspaper to the pages of a novel without jolt or jar. A writer who honors Swift, Fielding and Defoe, enough to have read their books constantly, cannot do less than endeavor to uphold the standard they set up in style, construction, and manners—as between author and reader. If their standard is not upheld there is small hope of it ever being surpassed, for their tradition will be lost, and it must take generations to build up a new tradition fit to rank with it in the history of literature. Probably Butler did not care a fig for the history of literature or its traditions or the development of the English novel. If he had cared he would very likely have turned his own novel into a guide-book and ruined it. As it was, approaching novel-writing as an amateur, he was concerned only to make it as near as possible to the best he knew. He could not write a novel in the temper of the novelists of his time, for it was alien to his temper. They were too conscious of their public, too eager to please and too reckless in their means of doing so. Disraeli had said good things, but was hardly a novelist, a *flaneur* and, in his way, as unscrupulous as the sentimentalists who had made a property of the public ear. Dickens had enormous creative force, but his manners with his reader were atrocious, Pecksniff and old Martin Chuzzlewit. George Eliot was simply an inexplicable phenomenon, thriving, apparently, on the immense capacity of the public for being bored. A public encouraged in that capacity for generations was not at all suited to a temper like Butler's, nor could he, as a scientific writer, arrange not to jog the public out of its boredom by the mention of subjects which literary fashion had decreed to be unmentionable. Even less could he adopt the mode of hitching his work on to the popular movements of thought of the period. A practical impossibility that, for he was going to take his time over it, and a popular movement would not last long enough. Moreover, an author's first and last duty is to his subject. The public is an accessory after the fact. An author hits the taste of his time, because it happens to be his taste also, and a really popular author is so by his vices as well as by his virtues. An author whose taste is below that of his time is inconceivable: he could never emerge; but an author whose taste is above that of his contemporaries can only be popular by force of genius; skill, cunning and craftsmanship avail him nothing against indifference. Thackeray, being as much above Dickens in taste as he was below him in genius, could never overtake him in the matter of popularity. Sterne by force of genius routed the learned Smelfungus. And as taste is lowered by the weakness of writers and the advent of uneducated readers the task of genius grows more difficult. Butler's genius could no more have succeeded with his novel than it did with his guide-books. The difficulty was solved by not facing it. It was impossible to face it, because the novel contained portraits of persons who had already been pained by the author's conduct—though such reasons do not act as a deterrent on the flood of novels brought in with the spring and autumn. In this case, however, fastidious scruples postponed the publication of the book for twenty years, until after the author's death, when public taste had so far deteriorated, as, even after that long interval since composition, to find it unpalatable. So little known is 'The Way of All Flesh' that Mr. Bernard Shaw has had to complain, years after its publication, of his Butlerisms being ascribed to Ibsen and Nietzsche. The fact is, that taste needs to be cultivated before irony can be appreciated or even perceived. Now irony is one of the essential ingredients of your true novel, which is a species distinct from the romance, and begins with the application in Don Quixote of irony to romance. A novel is an epic with its wings clipped, that is, with its action and characters viewed ironically. The modern story in which action and characters are viewed sentimentally is not, properly speaking, a novel at all. Only success justifies its existence, that is, if success is a justification. (Perhaps it is for ephemeræ.) As for the story in which action and characters are regarded only in relation to political and sociological considerations, that is a fearful wildfowl, wingless, featherless, strange and indecent. Your true novel is such that if the controlling irony were removed it would soar into the region of the epic, there, as a new arrival, young, fresh and a little absurd, to receive a nod from Homer. Such a novel is 'Tom Jones,' such are 'Pickwick,' 'Jude the Obscure,' 'War and Peace,' 'The Idiot,' and such, in a smaller way, is 'The Way of All Flesh.' If it were released from all its irony it would be too humble for the Homeric company. That is not altogether the fault of the author. It is in part an inherent weakness in his subject, a weakness which is also the reason of the book's unpopularity, for, to explain it, there must be added to the general dislike of irony the very proper objection to the application of irony in art to persons who are already sufficiently reduced in stature by the irony of life and circumstance. Jests at the expense of the clergy are popular enough, but they must be broad and humorous, not witty and acid: they may be as equivocal as you will, but they must be respectful. A clergyman, after all, cannot help the uniform he wears, either in cloth or in ideas, and he stands for something to which the general hope of virtue is attached. His position with regard to his fellow-men is weakened by his strong position with regard to God, and he cannot bear the brunt of an onslaught of human ridicule. Voltaire's reputation in England has had to suffer most unjustly for his attacks on priests and Butler's has been cramped in the same way. The misunderstanding is serious, much more so indeed than that which has advertised the immorality of 'Tom Jones' and thereby prevented the development of the English novel. It is more serious because, while the objection to (alleged) immorality can be surmounted, the objection to the use of irony exacerbates irony in authors and brings it dangerously near to spleen, which will vent itself only on those characters which are circumscribed enough not to retaliate. The characters in a book can retaliate on the author of it, and, if they are unfairly treated, they never hesitate about wrecking his work. An author knows this and, if he is splenetic, will choose his characters accordingly.

SIR PHILIP GIBBS (1877–)

From PEOPLE OF DESTINY
WHAT ENGLAND THINKS OF AMERICA

Apart from individual theorists, of the 'cranky' kind, the main body of intellectual opinion in England, as far as I know it, looks to the United States as the arbitrator of the world's destiny, and the leader of the world's democracies, on peaceful and idealistic lines. There is a conviction among many of us—not killed by the controversy over the Peace Treaty—that the spirit of the American people as a whole is guided by an innate common sense free from antiquated spellwords, facing the facts of life shrewdly and honestly, leaning always to the side of popular liberty against all tyrannies of castes, dynasties, and intolerance. Aloof from the historical enmities that still divide the nations of Europe, yet not aloof in sympathy with the sufferings, the strivings, and the sentiment of these peoples, the United States is able to play the part of a reconciling power, in any league of nations, with a detached and disinterested judgment. It is above all because it is disinterested that Europe has faith and trust in its sense of justice. It is not out for empire, for revenge, or for diplomatic vanity. Its people are supporters of President Wilson's ideal of 'open covenants openly arrived at,' and of the 'self-determination of nations,' however violently they challenge the authority by which their President pledged them to definite clauses in an unpopular contract. They are a friendly and not unfriendly folk in their instincts and in their methods. They respond quickly and generously to any appeal to honest sentiment, though they have no patience with hypocrisy. They are realists, and hate sham, pose, and falsehood. Give them a 'square deal' and they will be scrupulous to a high standard of business morality. Because of the infusion of foreign blood in their democracy which has been slowly produced from the great melting-pot of nations, they are subject to all the sensibilities of the human race and not narrowly fixed to one racial idea or type of mind. The Celt, the Slav, the Saxon, the Teuton, the Hebrew, and the Latin strains are present in the sub-consciousness of the American people, so that they are capable of an enormous range of sympathy with human nature in its struggle upward to the light. They are the new People of Destiny in the world of progress, because after their early adventures of youth, their time of preparation, their immense turbulent growth, their forging of tools, and training of soul, they stand now in their full strength and maturity, powerful with the power of a great, free, confident people.

To some extent, and I think in an increasing way, the old supremacy which Europe had is passing westward. Europe is stricken, tired, and poor. America is hearty, healthy, and rich. Intellectually it is still boyish and young and raw. There is the wisdom as well as the sadness of old age in Europe. We have more subtlety of brain, more delicate sense of art, a literature more expressive of the complicated emotions which belong to an old heritage of civilization, luxury, and philosophy. But I look for a Golden Age of literature and art in America which shall be like our Elizabethan period, fresh and springlike, and rich in vitality and promise. I am bound to believe that out of the fusion of races in America, and out of their present period of wealth and power, and out of this new awakening to the problems of life outside their own country, there will come great minds, and artists, and leaders of thought, surpassing any that have yet revealed themselves. All our reading of history points to that evolution. The flowering-time of America seems due to arrive, after its growing pains.

Be that as it may, it is clear, at least, that the destiny of the American people is now marked out for the great mission of leading the world to a new phase of civilization. By the wealth they have, and by their power for good or evil, they have a controlling influence in the reshaping of the world after its convulsions. They cannot escape from that power, even though they shrink from its responsibility. Their weight thrown one way or the other will turn the scale of all the balance of the world's desires. People of destiny, they have the choice of arranging the fate of many peoples. By their action they may plunge the world into strife again or settle its peace. They may kill or cure. They may be reconcilers or destroyers. They may be kind or cruel. It is a terrific power for any people to hold. If I were a citizen of the United States I should be afraid—afraid lest my country should by passion, or by ignorance, or by sheer carelessness take the wrong way.

I think some Americans have that fear. I have met some who are anxious and distressed. But I think that the majority of Americans do not realize the power that has come to them nor their new place in the world. They have a boisterous sense of importance and prestige, but rather as a young college man is aware of his lustiness and vitality without considering the duties and the dangers that have come to him with manhood. They are inclined to a false humility, saying: 'We aren't our brothers' keepers, anyway. We needn't go fussing around. Let's keep to our own job and let the other people settle their own affairs.' But meanwhile the other people know that American policy, American decisions, the American attitude in world problems, will either make or mar them. It is essential for the safety of the world, and of civilization itself, that the United States should realize its responsibilities and fulfill the destiny that has come to it by the evolution of history. To those whom I call the People of Destiny I humbly write the words: Let the world have peace.

W. H. HUDSON (1862–1922)

From FAR AWAY AND LONG AGO

MY FIRST VISIT TO BUENOS AYRES

The happiest time of my boyhood was at that early period, a little past the age of six, when I had my own pony to ride on, and was allowed to stay on his back just as long and go as far from home as I liked. I was like the young bird when on first quitting the nest it suddenly becomes conscious of its power to fly. My early flying days were, however, soon interrupted, when my mother took me on my first visit to Buenos Ayres; that is to say, the first I remember, as I must have been taken there once before as an infant in arms, since we lived too far from town for any missionary-clergyman to travel all that distance just to baptize a little baby. Buenos Ayres is now the wealthiest, most populous Europeanized city in South America; what it was like at that time these glimpses into a far past will serve to show. Coming as a small boy of an exceptionally impressionable mind, from that green plain where people lived the simple pastoral life, everything I saw in the city impressed me deeply, and the sights which impressed me the most are as vivid in my mind to-day as they ever were. I was a solitary little boy in my rambles about the streets, for though I had a younger brother who was my only playmate, he was not yet five, and too small to keep me company in my walks. Nor did I mind having no one with me. Very, very early in my boyhood I had acquired the habit of going about alone to amuse myself in my own way, and it was only after years, when my age was about twelve, that my mother told me how anxious this singularity in me used to make her. She would miss me when looking out to see what the children were doing, and I would be called and searched for, to be found hidden away somewhere in the plantation. Then she began to keep an eye on me, and when I was observed stealing off she would secretly follow and watch me, standing motionless among the tall weeds or under the trees by the half-hour, staring at vacancy. This distressed her very much; then to her great relief and joy she discovered that I was there with a motive which she could understand and appreciate: that I was watching some living thing, an insect perhaps, but oftener a bird—a pair of little scarlet flycatchers building a nest of lichen on a peach tree, or some such beautiful thing. And as she loved all living things herself she was quite satisfied that I was not going queer in my head, for that was what she had been fearing.

The strangeness of the streets was a little too much for me at the start, and I remember that on first venturing out by myself a little distance from home I got lost. In despair of ever finding my way back I began to cry, hiding my face against a post at a street corner, and was there soon surrounded by quite a number of passers-by; then a policeman came up, with brass buttons on his blue coat and a sword at his side, and taking me by the arm he asked me in a commanding voice where I lived—the name of the street and the number of the house. I couldn't tell him; then I began to get frightened on account of his sword and big black moustache and loud rasping voice, and suddenly ran away, and after running for about six or eight minutes found myself back at home, to my surprise and joy.

The house where we stayed with English friends was near the front, or what was then the front, that part of the city which faced the Plata river, a river which was like the sea, with no visible shore beyond; and like the sea it was tidal, and differed only in its color, which was a muddy red instead of blue or green. The house was roomy, and like most of the houses at that date had a large courtyard paved with red tiles and planted with small lemon trees and flowering shrubs of various kinds. The streets were straight and narrow, paved with round boulder stones the size of a football, the pavements with brick or flagstones, and so narrow they would hardly admit of more than two persons walking abreast. Along the pavements on each side of the street were rows of posts placed at a distance of ten yards apart. These strange looking rows of posts, which foreigners laughed to see, were no doubt the remains of yet ruder times, when ropes of hide were stretched along the side of the pavements to protect the foot-passengers from runaway horses, wild cattle driven by wild men from the plains, and other dangers of the narrow streets. As they were then paved the streets must have been the noisiest in the world, on account of the immense numbers of big springless carts in them. Imagine the thunderous racket made by a long procession of these carts, when they were returning empty, and the drivers, as was often the case, urged their horses to a gallop, and they bumped and thundered over the big round stones!

Just opposite the house we stayed at there was a large church, one of the largest of the numerous churches of the city, and one of my most vivid memories relates to a great annual festival at the church—that of the patron saint's day. It had been open to worshippers all day, but the chief service was held about three o'clock in the afternoon; at all events it was at that hour when a great attendance of fashionable people took place. I watched them as they came in couples, families and small groups, in every case the ladies, beautifully dressed, attended by their cavaliers. At the door of the church the gentleman would make his bow and withdraw to the street before the building, where a sort of outdoor gathering was formed of all those who had come as escorts to the ladies, and where they would remain until the service was over. The crowd in the street grew and grew until there were about four or five hundred gentlemen, mostly young, in the gathering, all standing in small groups, conversing in an animated way, so that the street was filled with the loud humming sound of their blended voices. These men were all natives, all of the good or upper class of the native society, and all dressed exactly alike in the fashion of that time. It was their dress and the uniform appearance of so large a number of persons, most of them with young, handsome, animated faces, that fascinated me and kept me on the spot gazing at them until the big bells began to thunder at the conclusion of the service and the immense concourse of gaily-dressed ladies swarmed out, and immediately the meeting broke up, the gentlemen hurrying back to meet them.

They all wore silk hats and the glossiest black broadcloth, not even a pair of trousers of any other shade was seen; and all wore the scarlet silk or fine cloth waistcoat which, at that period, was considered the right thing for every citizen of the republic to wear; also, in lieu of buttonhole, a scarlet ribbon pinned to the lapel of the coat. It was a pretty sight, and the concourse reminded me of a flock of military starlings, a black or dark-plumaged bird with a scarlet breast, one of my feathered favorites.

My rambles were almost always on the front, since I could walk there a mile or two from home, north or south, without getting lost, always with the vast expanse of water on one hand, with many big ships looking dim in the distance, and numerous lighters or belanders coming from them with cargoes of merchandise which they unloaded into carts, these going out a quarter of a mile in the shallow water to meet them. Then there were the water-carts going and coming in scores and hundreds, for at that period there was no water supply to the houses, and every house-holder had to buy muddy water by the bucket at his own door from the watermen.

One of the most attractive spots to me was the congregating place of the lavenderas, south of my street. Here on the broad beach under the cliff one saw a whiteness like a white cloud, covering the ground for a space of about a third of a mile; and the cloud, as one drew near, resolved itself into innumerable garments, sheets and quilts, and other linen pieces, fluttering from long lines, and covering the low rocks washed clean by the tide and the stretches of green turf between. It was the spot where the washer-women were allowed to wash all the dirty linen of Buenos Ayres in public. All over the ground the women, mostly negresses, were seen on their knees, beside the pools among the rocks, furiously scrubbing and pounding away at their work, and like all negresses they were exceedingly vociferous, and their loud gabble, mingled with yells and shrieks of laughter, reminded me of the hubbub made by a great concourse of gulls, ibises, godwits, geese, and other noisy water-fowl on some marshy lake. It was a wonderfully animated scene, and drew me to it again and again: I found, however, that it was necessary to go warily among these women, as they looked with suspicion at idling boys, and sometimes, when I picked my way among the spread garments, I was sharply ordered off. Then, too, they often quarrelled over their right to certain places and spaces among themselves; then very suddenly their hilarious gabble would change to wild cries of anger and torrents of abuse. By and by I discovered that their greatest rages and worst language were when certain young gentlemen of the upper classes visited the spot to amuse themselves by baiting the lavenderas. The young gentleman would saunter about in an absent-minded manner and presently walk right on to a beautifully embroidered and be-laced nightdress or other dainty garment spread out to dry on the sward or rock, and, standing on it, calmly proceed to take out and light a cigarette. Instantly the black virago would be on her feet confronting him and pouring out a torrent of her foulest expressions and deadliest curses. He, in a pretended rage, would reply in even worse language. That would put her on her mettle; for now all her friends and foes scattered about the ground would suspend their work to listen with all their ears; and the contest of words growing louder and fiercer would last until the combatants were both exhausted and unable to invent any more new and horrible expressions of opprobrium to hurl at each other. Then the insulted young gentleman would kick the garment away in a fury and hurling the unfinished cigarette in his adversary's face would walk off with his nose in the air.

I laugh to recall these unseemly word-battles on the beach, but they were shocking to me when I first heard them as a small, innocent-minded boy, and it only made the case worse when I was assured that the young gentleman was only acting a part, that the extreme anger he exhibited, which might have served as an excuse for using such language, was all pretence.

Another favorite pastime of these same idle, rich young gentlemen offended me as much as the one I have related. The night-watchmen, called *serenos,* of that time interested me in an extraordinary way. When night came it appeared that the fierce policemen, with their swords and brass buttons, were no longer needed to safeguard the people, and their place in the streets was taken by a quaint, frowsy-looking body of men, mostly old, some almost decrepit, wearing big cloaks and carrying staffs and heavy iron lanterns with a tallow candle alight inside. But what a pleasure it was to lie awake at night and listen to their voices calling the hours! The calls began at the stroke of eleven, and then from beneath the window would come the wonderful long drawling call of *Las ón——ce han dá—— do y se——ré——no,* which means eleven of the clock and all serene, but if clouded the concluding word would be *nu——blá——do,* and so on, according to the weather. From all the streets, from all over the town, the long-drawn calls would float to my listening ears, with infinite variety in the voices —the high and shrill, the falsetto, the harsh, raucous note like the caw of the carrion-crow, the solemn booming bass, and then some fine, rich, pure voice that soared heavenwards above all the others and was like the pealing notes of an organ.

I loved the poor night-watchmen and their cries, and it grieved by little soft heart to hear that it was considered fine sport by the rich young gentlemen to sally forth at night and do battle with them, and to deprive them of their staffs and lanterns, which they took home and kept as trophies.

Another human phenomenon which annoyed and shocked my tender mind, like that of the contests on the beach between young gentlemen and washerwomen, was the multitude of beggars which infested the town. These were not like our dignified beggar on horseback, with his red poncho, spurs and tall straw hat, who rode to your gate, and having received his tribute, blessed you and rode away to the next estancia. These city beggars on the pavement were the most brutal, even fiendish, looking men I had ever seen. Most of them were old soldiers, who, having served their ten, fifteen, or twenty years, according to the nature of the crime for which they had been condemned to the army, had been discharged or thrown out to live like carrion-hawks on what they could pick up. Twenty times a day at least you would hear the iron gate opening from the courtyard into the street swung open, followed by the call or shout of the beggar demanding charity in the name of God. Outside you could not walk far without being confronted by one of these men, who would boldly square himself in front of you on the narrow pavement and beg for alms. If you had no change and said, '*Perdon, por Dios,*' he would scowl and let you pass; but if you looked annoyed or disgusted, or ordered him out of the way, or pushed by without a word, he would glare at you with a concentrated rage which seemed to say, 'Oh, to have you down at my mercy, bound hand and foot, a sharp knife in my hand!' And this would be followed by a blast of the most horrible language.

One day I witnessed a very strange thing, the action of a dog, by the waterside. It was evening and the beach was forsaken; cartmen, fishermen, boatmen all gone, and I was the only idler left on the rocks; but the tide was coming in, rolling quite big waves on to the rocks, and the novel sight of the waves, the freshness, the joy of it, kept me at that spot, standing on one of the outermost rocks not yet washed over by the water. By and by a gentleman, followed by a big dog, came down on to the beach and stood at a distance of forty or fifty yards from me, while the dog bounded forward over the flat, slippery rocks and through pools of water until he came to my side, and sitting on the edge of the rock began gazing intently down at the water. He was a big, shaggy, round-headed animal, with a greyish coat with some patches of light reddish color on it; what his breed was I cannot say, but he looked somewhat like a sheep-dog or an otter-hound. Suddenly he plunged in, quite disappearing from sight, but quickly reappeared with a big shad of about three and a half or four pounds weight in his jaws. Climbing on to the rock he dropped the fish, which he did not appear to have injured much, as it began floundering about in an exceedingly lively manner. I was astonished and looked back at the dog's master; but there he stood in the same place, smoking and paying no attention to what his animal was doing. Again the dog plunged in and brought out a second big fish and dropped it on the flat rock, and again and again he dived, until there were five big shads all floundering about on the wet rock and likely soon to be washed back into the water.

The shad is a common fish in the Plata and the best to eat of all its fishes, resembling the salmon in its rich flavor, and is eagerly watched for when it comes up from the sea by the Buenos Ayres fishermen, just as our fishermen watch for mackerel on our coasts. But on this evening the beach was deserted by every one, watchers included, and the fish came and swarmed along the rocks, and there was no one to catch them—not even some poor hungry idler to pounce upon and carry off the five fishes the dog had captured. One by one I saw them washed back into the water, and presently the dog, hearing his master whistling to him, bounded away.

For many years after this incident I failed to find any one who had even seen or heard of a dog catching fish. Eventually, in reading I met with an account of fishing-dogs in Newfoundland and other countries.

One other strange adventure met with on the front remains to be told. It was about eleven o'clock in the morning and I was on the Parade, walking north, pausing from time to time to look over the sea-wall to watch the flocks of small birds that came to feed on the beach below. Presently my attention was drawn to a young man walking on before me, pausing and peering too from time to time over the wall, and when he did so throwing something at the small birds. I ran on and overtook him, and was rather taken aback at his wonderfully fine appearance. He was like one of the gentlemen of the gathering before the church, described on a few pages back, and wore a silk hat and fashionable black coat and trousers and scarlet silk waistcoat; he was also a remarkable handsome young gentleman, with a golden-brown curly beard and moustache and dark liquid eyes that studied my face with a half-amused curiosity when I looked up at him. In one hand he carried a washleather bag by its handle, and holding a pebble in his right hand he watched the birds, the small parties of crested song sparrows, yellow house sparrows, siskins, field finches, and other kinds, and from time to time he would hurl a pebble at the bird he had singled out forty yards down below us on the rocks. I did not see him actually hit a bird, but his precision was amazing, for almost invariably the missile, thrown from such a distance at so minute an object, appeared to graze the feathers and to miss killing by but a fraction of an inch.

I followed him for some distance, my wonder and curiosity growing every minute to see such a superior-looking person engaged in such a pastime. For it is a fact that the natives do not persecute small birds. On the contrary, they despise the aliens in the land who shoot and trap them. Besides, if he wanted small birds for any purpose, why did he try to get them by throwing pebbles at them? As he did not order me off, but looked in a kindly way at me every little while, with a slight smile on his face, I at length ventured to tell him that he would never get a bird that way—that it would be impossible at that distance to hit one with a small pebble. 'Oh, no, not impossible,' he returned, smiling and walking on, still with an eye on the rocks. 'Well, you haven't hit one yet,' I was bold enough to say, and at that he stopped, and putting his finger and thumb in his waistcoat pocket he pulled out a dead male siskin and put it in my hands.

This was the bird called 'goldfinch' by the English resident in La Plata, and to the Spanish it is also goldfinch; it is, however, a siskin, *Chrysomitris magellanica*, and has a velvet-black head, the rest of its plumage being black, green, and shining yellow. It was one of my best-loved birds, but I had never had one in my hand, dead or alive, before, and now its wonderful unimagined loveliness, its graceful form, and the exquisitely pure flower-like yellow hue affected me with a delight so keen that I could hardly keep from tears.

After gloating a few moments over it, touching it with my finger-tips and opening the little black and gold wings, I looked up pleadingly and begged him to let me keep it. He smiled and shook his head: he would not waste his breath talking; all his energy was to be spent in hurling pebbles at other lovely little birds.

'Oh, señor, will you not give it to me?' I pleaded still; and then, with sudden hope, 'Are you going to sell it?'

He laughed, and taking it from my hand put it back in his waistcoat pocket; then, with a pleasant smile and a nod to say that the interview was now over, he went on his way.

Standing on the spot where he left me, and still bitterly regretting that I had failed to get the bird, I watched him until he disappeared from sight in the distance, walking towards the suburb of Palermo; and a mystery he remains to this day, the one and only Argentine gentleman, a citizen of the Athens of South America, amusing himself by killing little birds with pebbles. But I do not know that it was an amusement. He had perhaps in some wild moment made a vow to kill so many siskins in that way, or a bet to prove his skill in throwing a pebble; or he might have been practising a cure for some mysterious deadly malady, prescribed by some wandering physician from Bagdad or Ispahan; or, more probable still, some heartless, soulless woman he was in love with had imposed this fantastical task on him.

Perhaps the most wonderful thing I saw during that first eventful visit to the capital was the famed Don Eusebio, the court jester or fool of the President or Dictator Rosas, the 'Nero of South America,' who lived in his palace at Palermo, just outside the city. I had been sent with my sisters and little brother to spend the day at the house of an Anglo-Argentine family in another part of the town, and we were in the large courtyard playing with the children of the house when some one opened a window above us and called out, 'Don Eusebio!' That conveyed nothing to me, but the little boys of the house knew what it meant; it meant that if we went quickly out to the street we might catch a glimpse of the great man in all his glory. At all event, they jumped up, flinging their toys away, and rushed to the street door, and we after them. Coming out we found quite a crowd of lookers-on, and then down the street, in his general's dress—for it was one of the Dictator's little jokes to make his fool a general —all scarlet, with a big scarlet three-cor-

nered hat surmounted by an immense aigrette of scarlet plumes, came Don Eusebio. He marched along with tremendous dignity, his sword at his side, and twelve soldiers, also in scarlet, his bodyguard, walking six on each side of him with drawn swords in their hands.

We gazed with joyful excitement at this splendid spectacle, and it made it all the more thrilling when one of the boys whispered in my ear that if any person in the crowd laughed or made any insulting or rude remark, he would be instantly cut to pieces by the guard. And they looked truculent enough for anything.

The great Rosas himself I did not see, but it was something to have had this momentary sight of General Eusebio, his fool, on the eve of his fall after a reign of over twenty years, during which he proved himself one of the bloodiest as well as the most original-minded of the Caudillos and Dictators, and altogether, perhaps, the greatest of those who have climbed into power in this continent of republics and revolutions.

JOHN MAYNARD KEYNES
(1883-)

FROM THE ECONOMIC CONSEQUENCES OF THE PEACE
EUROPE BEFORE THE WAR

What an extraordinary episode in the economic progress of man that age was which came to an end in August, 1914! The greater part of the population, it is true, worked hard and lived at a low standard of comfort, yet were, to all appearances, reasonably contented with this lot. But escape was possible, for any man of capacity or character at all exceeding the average, into the middle and upper classes, for whom life offered, at a low cost and with the least trouble, conveniences, comforts, and amenities beyond the compass of the richest and most powerful monarchs of other ages. The inhabitant of London could order by telephone, sipping his morning tea in bed, the various products of the whole earth, in such quantity as he might see fit, and reasonably expect their early delivery upon his doorstep; he could at the same moment and by the same means adventure his wealth in the natural resources and new enterprises of any quarter of the world, and share, without exertion or even trouble, in their prospective fruits and advantages; or he could decide to couple the security of his fortunes with the good faith of the towns-people of any substantial municipality in any continent that fancy or information might recommend. He could secure forthwith, if he wished it, cheap and comfortable means of transit to any country or climate without passport or other formality, could despatch his servant to the neighboring office of a bank for such supply of the precious metals as might seem convenient, and could then proceed abroad to foreign quarters, without knowledge of their religion, language, or customs, bearing coined wealth upon his person, and would consider himself greatly aggrieved and much surprised at the least interference. But, most important of all, he regarded this state of affairs as normal, certain, and permanent, except in the direction of further improvement, and any deviation from it as aberrant, scandalous, and avoidable. The projects and politics of militarism and imperialism, of racial and cultural rivalries, of monopolies, restrictions, and exclusion, which were to play the serpent to this paradise, were little more than the amusements of his daily newspaper, and appeared to exercise almost no influence at all on the ordinary course of social and economic life, the internationalization of which was nearly complete in practice.

* * *

Europe was so organized socially and economically as to secure the maximum accumulation of capital. While there was some continuous improvement in the daily conditions of life of the mass of the population, Society was so framed as to throw a great part of the increased income into the control of the class least likely to consume it. The new rich of the nineteenth century were not brought up to large expenditures, and preferred the power which investment gave them to the pleasures of immediate consumption. In fact, it was precisely the 'inequality' of the distribution of wealth which made possible those vast accumulations of fixed wealth and of capital improvements which distinguished that age from all others. Herein lay, in fact, the main justification of the Capitalist System. If the rich had spent their new wealth on their own enjoyments, the world would long ago have found such a régime intolerable. But like bees they saved and accumulated, not less to the advantage of the whole community because they themselves held narrower ends in prospects.

The immense accumulations of fixed capital which, to the great benefit of mankind, were built up during the half century before the war, could never have come about in a Society where wealth was divided equitably. The railways of the world, which that age built as a monument to posterity, were, not less than the Pyramids of Egypt, the work of labor which was not free to consume in immediate enjoyment the full equivalent of its efforts.

Thus this remarkable system depended for its growth on a double bluff or deception. On the one hand the laboring classes accepted from ignorance or powerlessness, or were compelled, persuaded, or cajoled by custom, convention, authority, and the well-established order of Society into accepting, a situation in which they could call their own very little of the cake that they and Nature and the capitalists were co-operating to produce. And on the other hand the capitalist classes were allowed to call the best part of the cake theirs and were theoretically free to consume it, on the tacit underlying condition that they consumed very little of it in practice. The duty of 'saving' became nine-tenths of virtue and the growth of the cake the object of true religion. There grew round the non-consumption of the cake all those instincts of puritanism which in other ages has withdrawn itself from the world and has neglected the arts of production as well as those of enjoyment. And so the cake increased; but to what end was not clearly contemplated. Individuals would be exhorted not so much to abstain as to defer, and to cultivate the pleasures of security and anticipation. Saving was for old age or for your children; but this was only in theory—the virtue of the cake was that it was never to be consumed, neither by you nor by your children after you.

In writing thus I do not necessarily disparage the practices of that generation. In the unconscious recesses of its being Society knew what it was about. The cake was really very small in proportion to the appetites of consumption, and no one, if it were shared all round, would be much the better off by the cutting of it. Society was working not for the small pleasures of to-day but for the future security and improvement of the race—in fact for 'progress.' If only the cake were not cut but was allowed to grow in the geometrical proportion predicted by Malthus of population, but not less true of compound interest, perhaps a day might come when there would at last be enough to go round, and when posterity could enter into the enjoyment of *our* labors. In that day overwork, overcrowding, and underfeeding would have come to an end, and men, secure of the comforts and necessities of the body, could proceed to the nobler exercises of their faculties. One geometrical ratio might cancel another, and the nineteenth century was able to forget the fertility of the species in a contemplation of the dizzy virtues of compound interest.

There were two pitfalls in this prospect: lest, population still outstripping accumulation, our self-denials promote not happiness but numbers; and lest the cake be after all consumed, prematurely, in war, the consumer of all such hopes.

But these thoughts lead too far from my present purpose. I seek only to point out that the principle of accumulation based on inequality was a vital part of the pre-war order of Society and of progress as we then understood it, and to emphasize that this principle depended on unstable psychological conditions, which it may be impossible to recreate. It was not natural for a population, of whom so few enjoyed the comforts of life, to accumulate so hugely. The war has disclosed the possibility of consumption to all and the vanity of abstinence to many. Thus the bluff is discovered; the laboring classes may be no longer willing to forego so largely, and the capitalist classes, no longer confident of the future, may seek to enjoy more fully their liberties of consumption so long as they last, and thus precipitate the hour of their confiscation.

The accumulative habits of Europe before the war were the necessary condition of the greatest of the external factors which maintained the European equipoise.

Of the surplus capital goods accumulated by Europe a substantial part was exported abroad, where its investment made possible the development of the new resources of food, materials, and transport, and at the same time enabled the Old World to stake out a claim in the natural wealth and virgin potentialities of the New. This last factor came to be of the vastest importance. The Old World employed with an immense prudence the annual tribute it was thus entitled to draw. The benefit of cheap and abundant supplies, resulting from the new developments which its surplus capital had made possible, was, it is true, enjoyed and not postponed. But the greater part of the money interest accruing on these foreign investments was re-invested and allowed to accumulate, as a reserve (it was then hoped) against the less happy day when the industrial labor of Europe could no longer purchase on such easy terms the produce of other continents, and when the due balance would be threatened between its historical civilizations and the multiplying races of other climates and environments. Thus the whole of the European races tended to benefit alike from the development of new resources whether they pursued their culture at home or adventured it abroad.

Even before the war, however, the equilibrium thus established between old civilizations and new resources was being threatened. The prosperity of Europe was based on the facts that, owing to the large exportable surplus of foodstuffs in America, she was able to purchase food at a cheap rate measured in terms of the labor required to produce her own exports, and that, as a result of her previous investments of capital, she was entitled to a substantial amount annually without any payment in return at all. The second of these factors then seemed out of danger, but, as a result of the growth of population overseas, chiefly in the United States, the first was not so secure. When first the virgin soils of America came into bearing, the proportions of the population of those continents themselves, and consequently of their own local requirements, to those of Europe were very small. As lately as 1890 Europe had a population three times that of North and South America added together. But by 1914 the domestic requirements of the United States for wheat were approaching their production, and the date was evidently near when there would be an exportable surplus only in years of exceptionally favorable harvest. Indeed, the present domestic requirements of the United States are estimated at more than ninety per cent of the average yield of the five years 1909-1913.[1] At that time, however, the tendency towards stringency was showing itself, not so much in a lack of abundance as in a steady increase of real cost. That is to say, taking the world as a whole, there was no deficiency of wheat, but in order to call forth an adequate supply it was necessary to offer a higher real price. The most favorable factor in the situation was to be found in the extent to which Central and Western Europe was being fed from the exportable surplus of Russia and Roumania.

In short, Europe's claim on the resources of the New World was becoming precarious; the law of diminishing returns was at last reasserting itself, and was making it necessary year by year for Europe to offer a greater quantity of other commodities to obtain the same amount of bread; and Europe, therefore, could by no means afford the disorganization of any of her principal sources of supply.

Much else might be said in an attempt to portray the economic peculiarities of the Europe of 1914. I have selected for emphasis the three or four greatest factors of instability—the instability of an excessive population dependent for its livelihood on a complicated and artificial organization, the psychological instability of the laboring and capitalist classes, and the instability of Europe's claim, coupled with the completeness of her dependence, on the food supplies of the New World.

The war had so shaken this system as to endanger the life of Europe altogether. A great part of the Continent was sick and dying; its population was greatly in excess of the numbers for which a livelihood was available; its organization was destroyed, its transport system ruptured, and its food supplies terribly impaired.

It was the task of the Peace Conference to honor engagements and to satisfy justice; but not less to re-establish life and to heal wounds. These tasks were dictated as much by prudence as by the magnanimity which the wisdom of antiquity approved in victors. We will examine in the following chapters the actual character of the Peace.

HUGH WALPOLE (1884–)
From JOSEPH CONRAD
ROMANCE AND REALISM

I

The terms, Romance and Realism, have been used of late years very largely as a means of escape from this business of the creation of character. The purely romantic novel may now be said to be, in England at any rate, absolutely dead. Mr. Frank Swinnerton, in his study of 'Robert Louis Stevenson,' said: 'Stevenson, reviving the never-very-prosperous romance of England, created a school which has brought romance to be the sweepings of an old costume-chest; . . . if romance is to be conventional in a double sense, if it springs not from a personal vision of life, but is only a tedious virtuosity, a pretence, a conscious toy, romance as an art is dead. The art was jaded when Reade finished his vociferous carpet-beating; but it was not dead. And if it is dead, Stevenson killed it!'

We may differ very considerably from Mr. Swinnerton with regard to his estimate of Stevenson's present and future literary value without denying that the date of the publication of St. Ives was also the date of the death of the purely romantic novel.

But, surely, here, as Mr. Swinnerton himself infers, the term 'Romantic' is used in the limited and truncated idea that has formed, lately the popular idea of Romance. In exactly the same way the term 'Realism' has, recently, been most foolishly and uncritically handicapped. Romance, in its modern use, covers everything that is removed from reality: 'I like romances,' we hear the modern reader say, 'because they take me away from real life, which I desire to forget.' In the same way Realism is defined by its enemies as a photographic enumeration of unimportant facts by an observant pessimist. 'I like realism,' admirers of a cer-

[1] Even since 1914 the population of the United States has increased by seven or eight millions. As their annual consumption of wheat per head is not less than 6 bushels, the pre-war scale of production in the United States would only show a substantial surplus over present domestic requirements in about one year out of five. We have been saved for the moment by the great harvests of 1918 and 1919, which have been called forth by Mr. Hoover's guaranteed price. But the United States can hardly be expected to continue indefinitely to raise by a substantial figure the cost of living in its own country, in order to provide wheat for a Europe which cannot pay for it.

tain order of novel exclaim, 'because it is so like life. It tells me just what I myself see every day—I know where I am.'

Nevertheless, impatient though we may be of these utterly false ideas of Romance and Realism, a definition of those terms that will satisfy everyone is almost impossible. I cannot hope to achieve so exclusive an ambition—I can only say that to myself Realism is the study of life with all the rational faculties of observation, reason and reminiscence—Romance is the study of life with the faculties of imagination. I do not mean that Realism may not be emotional, poetic, even lyrical, but it is based always upon truth perceived and recorded—it is the essence of observation. In the same way Romance may be, indeed must be, accurate and defined in its own world, but its spirit is the spirit of imagination, working often upon observation and sometimes simply upon inspiration. It is, at any rate, understood here that the word Romance does not, for a moment, imply a necessary divorce from reality, nor does Realism imply a detailed and dusty preference for morbid and unagreeable subjects. It is possible for Romance to be as honestly and clearly perceptive as Realism, but it is not so easy for it to be so because imagination is more difficult of discipline than observation. It is possible for Realism to be as eloquent and potential as Romance, although it cannot so easily achieve eloquence because of its fear of deserting truth. Moreover, with regard to the influence of foreign literature upon the English novel, it may be suggested that the influence of the French novel, which was at its strongest between the years 1885 and 1895, was towards Realism, and that the influence of the Russian novel, which has certainly been very strongly marked in England during the last years, is all towards Romantic-Realism. If we wished to know exactly what is meant by Romantic-Realism, such a novel as 'The Brothers Karamazov,' such a play as 'The Cherry Orchard' are there before us, as the best possible examples. We might say, in a word, that 'Karamazov' has, in the England of 1915, taken the place that was occupied, in 1890, by Madame Bovary. . . .

II

It is Joseph Conrad whose influence is chiefly responsible for this development in the English novel. Just as, in the early nineties, Mr. Henry James and Mr. Rudyard Kipling, the one potential, the other kinetic, influenced, beyond all contemporary novelists, the minds of their younger generation, so to-day, twenty-five years later, do Mr. Joseph Conrad and Mr. H. G. Wells, the one potential, the other kinetic, hold that same position.

Joseph Conrad, from the very first, influenced though he was by the French novel, showed that Realism alone was not enough for him. That is to say that, in presenting the case of Almayer, it was not enough for him merely to state as truthfully as possible the facts. Those facts, sordid as they are, make the story of Almayer's degradation sufficiently realistic, when it is merely recorded and perceived by any observer. But upon these recorded facts Conrad's imagination, without for a moment deserting the truth, worked, beautifying, ennobling it, giving it pity and terror, above all putting it into relation with the whole universe, the whole history of the cycle of life and death.

As I have said, the Romantic novel, in its simplest form, was used, very often, by writers who wished to escape from the business of the creation of character. It had not been used for that purpose by Sir Walter Scott, who was, indeed, the first English Romantic-Realist, but it was so used by his successors, who found a little optimism, a little adventure, a little color and a little tradition go a long way towards covering the required ground.

Conrad had, from the first, a poet's— that is to say, a romantic—mind, and his determination to use that romance realistically was simply his determination to justify the full play of his romantic mind in the eyes of all honest men.

In that intention he has absolutely succeeded; he has not abated one jot of his romance—'Nostromo,' 'Lord Jim,' 'Heart of Darkness' are amongst the most romantic things in all our literature —but the last charge that any critic can make against him is falsification, whether of facts, of inference or of consequences. The whole history of his development has for its key-stone this determination to save his romance by his reality, to extend his reality by his romance. He found in English fiction little that could assist him in this development; the Russian novelists were to supply him with his clue,

This whole question of Russian influence is difficult to define, but that Conrad has been influenced by Turgéniev a little and by Dostoievsky very considerably, cannot be denied. 'Crime and Punishment,' 'The Idiot,' 'The Possessed,' 'The Brothers Karamazov' are romantic realism at the most astonishing heights that this development of the novel is ever likely to attain. We will never see again the heroes of the Prince Myshkin, Dmitri Karamazov, Nicolas Stavrogin build, men so real to us that no change of time or place, age or sickness can take them from us, men so beautifully lit with the romantic passion of Dostoievsky's love of humanity that they seem to warm the whole world, as we know it, with the fire of their charity. That power of creating figures typical as well as individual has been denied to Conrad. Captain Anthony, Nostromo, Jim do not belong to the whole world, nor do they escape the limitations and confinements that their presentation as 'cases' involves on them. Moreover, Conrad does not love humanity. He feels pity, tenderness, admiration, but love, except for certain of his sea heroes, never, and even with his sea heroes it is love built on his scorn of the land. Dostoievsky scorned no one and nothing; as relentless in his pursuit of the truth as Stendhal or Flaubert, he found humanity, as he investigated it, beautiful because of its humanity —Conrad finds humanity pitiable because of its humanity.

Nevertheless he has been influenced by the Russian writer continuously and sometimes obviously. In at least one novel, 'Under Western Eyes,' the influence has led to imitation. For that reason, perhaps, that novel is the least vital of all his books, and we feel as though Dostoievsky had given him Razumov to see what he could make of him, and had remained too overwhelmingly curious an onlooker to allow independent creation. What, however, Conrad has in common with the creator of Raskolnikov is his thrilling pursuit of the lives. the hearts,

the minutest details of his characters. Conrad alone of all English novelists shares this zest with the great Russian. Dostoievsky found his romance in his love of his fellow-beings, Conrad finds his in his love of beauty, his poet's cry for color, but their realism they find together in the hearts of men—and they find it not as Flaubert, that they may make of it a perfect work of art, not as Turgéniev, that they may extract from it a flower of poignant beauty, not as Tolstoi, that they may, from it, found a gospel—simply they pursue their quest because the breathless interest of the pursuit is stronger than they. They have, both of them, created characters simply because characters demanded to be created. We feel that Emma Bovary was dragged, painfully, arduously, against all the strength of her determination, out of the shades where she was lurking. Myshkin, the Karamazovs, and, in their own degree, Nostromo, Almayer, M'Whirr, demanded that they should be flung upon the page.

Instead of seizing upon Romance as a means of avoiding character, he has triumphantly forced it to aid him in the creation of the lives that, through him, demand existence. This may be said to be the great thing that Conrad has done for the English novel—he has brought the zest of creation back into it; the French novelists used life to perfect their art—the Russian novelists used art to liberate their passion for life. That at this moment in Russia the novel has lost that zest, that the work of Kouprin, Artzybashev, Sologub, Merejkovsky, Andreiev, shows exhaustion and sterility means nothing; the stream will soon run full again. Meanwhile we, in England, know once more what it is to feel, in the novel, the power behind the novelist, to be ourselves in the grip of a force that is not afraid of romance nor ashamed of realism, that cares for life as life and not as a means of proving the necessity for form, the danger of too many adjectives, the virtues of the divorce laws or the paradise of free love.

JOSEPH CAMPBELL (1881–)

I AM THE MOUNTAINY SINGER

I am the mountainy singer—
  The voice of the peasant's dream,
The cry of the wind on the wooded hill,
  The leap of the fish in the stream.

Quiet and love I sing—   5
  The carn on the mountain crest,
The cailin in her lover's arms,
  The child at its mother's breast.

Beauty and peace I sing—
  The fire on the open hearth,   10
The cailleach spinning at her wheel,
  The plough in the broken earth.

Travail and pain I sing—
  The bride on the childing bed,
The dark man laboring at his rhymes,   15
  The ewe in the lambing shed.

Sorrow and death I sing—
  The canker come on the corn,
The fisher lost in the mountain loch,
  The cry at the mouth of morn.   20

No other life I sing,
  For I am spring of the stock
That broke the hilly land for bread,
  And built the nest in the rock.

PADRAIC COLUM (1881--)

THE PLOUGHER

Sunset and silence! A man: around him
  earth savage, earth broken;
Beside him two horses—a plough!

Earth savage, earth broken, the brutes, the
  dawn-man there in the sunset,
And the Plough that is twin to the Sword,
  that is founder of cities!   4

'Brute-tamer, plough-maker, earth-breaker!
  Can'st hear? There are ages between us.
Is it praying you are as you stand there alone
  in the sunset?

'Surely our sky-born gods can be naught to
  you, earth child and earth master?
Surely your thoughts are of Pan, or of
  Wotan, or Dana?

'Yet, why give thought to the gods? Has
  Pan led your brutes where they stumble?
Has Dana numbed pain of the child-bed, or
  Wotan put hands to your plough?   10

'What matter your foolish reply! O man
  standing lone and bowed earthward,
Your task is a day near its close. Give
  thanks to the night-giving God.'

.   .   .   .   .   .

Slowly the darkness falls, the broken lands
  blend with the savage;
The brute-tamer stands by the brutes, a
  head's breadth only above them.

A head's breadth? Ay, but therein is hell's
  depth, and the height up to heaven, 15
And the thrones of the gods and their halls,
  their chariots, purples, and splendors.

WHAT THE SHUILER SAID AS SHE LAY BY THE FIRE IN THE FARMER'S HOUSE

I'm glad to lie on a sack of leaves
By a wasted fire and take my ease.
For the wind would strip me bare as a tree—
The wind would blow old age upon me.
And I'm dazed with the wind, the rain, and
  the cold.   5
If I had only the good red gold
To buy me the comfort of a roof,
And under the thatch the brown of the
  smoke!

I'd lie up in my painted room
Until my hired girl would come;   10
And when the sun had warmed my walls
I'd rise up in my silks and shawls,
And break my fast before the fire.
And I'd watch them that had to sweat
And shiver for shelter and what they ate.   15
The farmer digging in the fields;
The beggars going from gate to gate;
The horses striving with their loads,
And all the sights upon the roads.

I'd live my lone without clan or care,   20
And none about me to crave a share.
The young have mocking, impudent ways,
And I'd never let them a-nigh my place.
And a child has often a pitiful face.

I'd give the rambling fiddler rest,   25
And for me he would play his best.
And he'd have something to tell of me
From the Moat of Granard down to the sea!
And, though I'd keep distant, I'd let in
Old women who would card and spin   30
And clash with me, and I'd hear it said,
'Mór who used to carry her head
As if she was a lady bred—
Has little enough in her house, they say—
And such-a-one's child I saw on the way   35
Scaring crows from a crop, and glad to get,
In a warmer house, the bit to eat.
O! none are safe, and none secure,
And it's well for some whose bit is sure!'

I'd never grudge them the weight of their
    lands   40
If I had only the good red gold
To huggle between my breast and hands!

WILLIAM H. DAVIES (1870–)

LEISURE

What is this life if, full of care,
We have no time to stand and stare.

No time to stand beneath the boughs
And stare as long as sheep or cows.

No time to see, when woods we pass,   5
Where squirrels hide their nuts in grass.

No time to see, in broad daylight,
Streams full of stars, like stars at night.

No time to turn at Beauty's glance,
And watch her feet, how they can dance.   10

No time to wait till her mouth can
Enrich that smile her eyes began.

A poor life this if, full of care,
We have no time to stand and stare.

MONEY

When I had money, money, O!
  I knew no joy till I went poor;
For many a false man as a friend
  Came knocking all day at my door.

Then felt I like a child that holds   5
  A trumpet that he must not blow
Because a man is dead; I dared
  Not speak to let this false world know.

Much have I thought of life, and seen
  How poor men's hearts are ever light; 10
And how their wives do hum like bees
  About their work from morn till night.

So, when I hear these poor ones laugh
  And see the rich ones coldly frown—
Poor men, think I, need not go up   15
  So much as rich men should come down.

When I had money, money, O!
  My many friends proved all untrue;
But now I have no money, O!
  My friends are real, though very few.   20

SHEEP

When I was once in Baltimore,
  A man came up to me and cried,
'Come, I have eighteen hundred sheep,
  And we will sail on Tuesday's tide.

'If you will sail with me, young man,   5
  I'll pay you fifty shillings down;
These eighteen hundred sheep I take
  From Baltimore to Glasgow town.'

He paid me fifty shillings down,
  I sailed with eighteen hundred sheep; 10
We soon had cleared the harbor's mouth,
  We soon were in the salt sea deep.

The first night we were out at sea
  Those sheep were quiet in their mind;
The second night they cried with fear— 15
  They smelt no pastures in the wind.

They sniffed, poor things, for their green
    fields,
  They cried so loud I could not sleep:
For fifty thousand shillings down
  I would not sail again with sheep.   20

THE MUSE

I have no ale,
  No wine I want;
No ornaments,
  My meat is scant.

No maid is near,   5
  I have no wife;
But here's my pipe
  And, on my life:

With it to smoke,
  And woo the Muse,   10
To be a king
  I would not choose.

But I crave all,
  When she does fail—
Wife, ornaments,   15
  Meat, wine and ale.

HELEN PARRY EDEN

AN IDOL OF THE MARKET PLACE

Decorum and the butcher's cat
  Are seldom far apart—
From dawn when clouds surmount the air,
Piled like a beauty's powdered hair,
Till dusk, when down the misty square   5
  Rumbles the latest cart

He sits in coat of white and grey
  Where the rude cleaver's shock
Horrid from time to time descends,
And his imposing presence lends   10
Grace to a platform that extends
  Beneath the chopping-block.

How tranquil are his close-piled cheeks,
  His paws, sequestered warm!
An oak-grained panel backs his head   15
And all the stock-in-trade is spread,
A symphony in white and red,
  Round his harmonious form.

The butcher's brave cerulean garb
  Flutters before his face,   20
The cleaver dints his little roof

Of furrowed wood; remote, aloof,
He sits superb and panic proof
  In his accustomed place.

Threading the columned County Hall,   25
  Midmost before his eyes,
Alerter dog and loitering maid
Cross from the sunlight to the shade,
And small amenities of trade
  Under the gables rise;   30

Cats of the town, a shameless crew,
  Over the way he sees
Propitiate with lavish purr
An unresponsive customer,
Or, meek with sycophantic fur,   35
  Caress the children's knees.

But he, betrothed to etiquette,
  Betrays nor head nor heart;
Lone as the Ark on Ararat,
A monument of fur and fat,   40
Decorum and the butcher's cat
  Are seldom far apart.

ARS IMMORTALIS

Betsey, when all the stalwarts left
  Us women to our tasks befitting,
Your little fingers, far from deft,
  Coped for an arduous week with knitting;
And, though the meekness of your hair   5
  Drooped o'er the task disarmed my stric-
    tures,
The Army gained when in despair
  You dropped its socks to paint it pictures.

I, knowing well your guileless brush,
  Urged that there wanted something subtler
To put Meissonier to the blush   11
  And snatch the bays from Lady Butler;
And so your skies retained their blue,
  Nor reddened with the wrath of nations,
To prove at least one artist knew   15
  Her public and her limitations.

A dozen warriors far away
  Craved of your skill to keep them posted,
With colored pictures day by day,
  In aught of note their birthplace boasted;
Hence these 'Arriving Refugees'   21
  (Cheerful in burnt sienna) hurry
To soothe your uncle's hours of ease
  In some congested hut in Surrey.

I hear that Nurse's David gets   25
  (His valor is already French's)

Your 'Market' with the cigarettes
  His sister forwards to the trenches;
This 'Cat' (for Rupert in the East),
  Limned in its moments of inertia,   30
You send that he may show the beast
  To its progenitors in Persia.

Daily your brush depicts a home
  Such as our duller pens are mute on;
Squanders Vermilion, Lake and Chrome   35
  And Prussian Blue—that furious Teuton.
Paper beneath your fingers calls
  For forms and figures to divide it,
Colors and cock-eyed capitals
  And kisses cruciform to hide it.   40

Till brushes sucked and laid apart,
  And candles lit and daylight dying
And you asleep, your works of art
  Ranged on the mantelpiece and drying—
We elders (older when you're gone)   45
  Muse on our country's gains and losses . . .
Ah, Betsey, is it you alone
  Who send your kisses shaped like crosses?

JAMES ELROY FLECKER
(1884-1915)

THE BALLAD OF ISKANDER

Aflatun and Aristu and King Iskander
Are Plato, Aristotle, Alexander

Sultan Iskander sat him down
On his golden throne, in his golden crown,
And shouted 'Wine and flute-girls three,   5
And the Captain, ho! of my ships at sea.'

He drank his bowl of wine; he kept
The flute-girls dancing till they wept,
Praised and kissed their painted lips,
And turned to the Captain of All his Ships.
                                                10
And cried, 'O Lord of my Ships that go
From the Persian Gulf to the Pits of Snow,
Inquire for men unknown to man!'
Said Sultan Iskander of Yoonistan.

'Daroosh is dead, and I am King   15
Of Everywhere and Everything:
Yet leagues and leagues away for sure
The lion-hearted dream of war.

'Admiral, I command you sail!
Take you a ship of silver mail,   20
And fifty sailors, young and bold,
And stack provision deep in the hold.

'And seek out twenty men that know
All babel tongues which flaunt and flow;
And stay! Impress those learned two,   25
Old Aflatun, and Aristu.

'And set your prow South-western ways
A thousand bright and dimpling days,
And find me lion-hearted Lords   •
With breasts to feed Our rusting swords.'
                                                30
The Captain of the Ships bowed low.
'Sir,' he replied, 'I will do so.'
And down he rode to the harbor mouth,
To choose a boat to carry him South.

And he launched a ship of silver mail,   35
With fifty lads to hoist the sail,
And twenty wise—all tongues they knew,
And Aflatun, and Aristu.

There had not dawned the second day
But the glittering galleon sailed away,   40
And through the night like one great bell
The marshalled armies sang farewell.

In twenty days the silver ship
Had passed the Isle of Serendip,
And made the flat Araunian coasts   45
Inhabited, at noon, by Ghosts.

In thirty days the ship was far
Beyond the land of Calcobar,
Where men drink Dead Men's Blood for
        wine,
And dye their beards alizarine.   50

But on the hundredth day there came
Storm with his windy wings aflame,
And drave them out to that Lone Sea   \
Whose shores are near Eternity.

        .   .   .   .

For seven years and seven years   55
Sailed those forgotten mariners,
Nor could they spy on either hand
The faintest level of good red land.

Bird or fish they saw not one;
There swam no ship beside their own,   60
And day-night long the lilied Deep
Lay round them, with its flowers asleep.

The beams began to warp and crack,
The silver plates turned filthy black
And drooping down on the carven rails   65
Hung those once lovely silken sails.

And all the great ship's crew who were
Such noble lads to do and dare
Grew old and tired of the changeless sky
And laid them down on the deck to die. 70

And they who spake all tongues there be
Made antics with solemnity,
Or closely huddled each to each
Talked ribald in a foreign speech.

And Aflatun and Aristu 75
Let their Beards grow, and their Beards grew
Round and about the mainmast tree
Where they stood still, and watched the sea.

And day by day their Captain grey
Knelt on the rotting poop to pray: 80
And yet despite ten thousand prayers
They saw no ship that was not theirs.

.   .   .   .

When thrice the seven years had passed
They saw a ship, a ship at last!
Untarnished glowed its silver mail, 85
Windless bellied its silken sail.

With a shout the grizzled sailors rose
Cursing the years of sick repose,
And they who spake in tongues unknown
Gladly reverted to their own. 90

The Captain leapt and left his prayers
And hastened down the dust-dark stairs,
And taking to hand a brazen Whip
He woke to life the long dead ship.

But Aflatun and Aristu, 95
Who had no work that they could do,
Gazed at the stranger Ship and Sea
With their beards around the mainmast tree.

Nearer and nearer the new boat came,
Till the hands cried out on the old ship's
shame— 100
'Silken sail to a silver boat,
We too shone when we first set float!'

Swifter and swifter the bright boat sped,
But the hands spake thin like men long
dead—
'How striking like that boat were we 105
In the days, sweet days, when we put to sea.'

The ship all black and the ship all white
Met like the meeting of day and night,
Met, and there lay serene dark green
A twilight yard of the sea between. 110

And the twenty masters of foreign speech
Of every tongue they knew tried each;
Smiling, the silver Captain heard,
But shook his head and said no word.

Then Aflatun and Aristu 115
Addressed the silver Lord anew,
Speaking their language of Yoonistan
Like countrymen to a countryman.

And 'Whence,' they cried, 'O Sons of Pride,
Sail you the dark eternal tide? 120
Lie your halls to the South or North,
And who is the King that sent you forth?'

'We live,' replied that Lord with a smile,
'A mile beyond the millionth mile.
We know not South and we know not North,
And SULTAN ISKANDER sent us forth.'

Said Aristu to Aflatun—
'Surely our King, despondent soon,
Has sent this second ship to find
Unconquered tracts of humankind.' 130

But Aflatun turned round on him
Laughing a bitter laugh and grim.
'Alas,' he said, 'O Aristu,
A white weak thin old fool are you.

'And does yon silver Ship appear 135
As she had journeyed twenty year?
And has that silver Captain's face
A mortal or Immortal grace?

'Theirs is the land (as well I know)
Where live the Shapes of Things Below: 140
Theirs is the country where they keep
The Images men see in Sleep.

'Theirs is the Land beyond the Door,
And theirs the old ideal shore.
They steer our ship: behold our crew 145
Ideal, and our Captain too.

'And lo! beside that mainmast tree
Two tall and shining forms I see,
And they are what we ought to be,
Yet we are they, and they are we.' 150

He spake, and some young Zephyr stirred,
The two ships touched: no sound was heard;
The Black Ship crumbled into air;
Only the Phantom Ship was there.

And a great cry rang round the sky 155
Of glorious singers sweeping by,
And calm and fair on waves that shone
The Silver Ship sailed on and on.

JOHN FREEMAN (1885–)

ENGLISH HILLS

Oh that I were
Where breaks the pure cold light
On English hills,
And peewits rising cry,
And gray is all the sky.   5

Or at evening there
When the faint slow light stays,
And far below
Sleeps the last lingering sound,
And night leans all around.   10

O then, O there
'Tis English haunted ground.
The diligent stars
Creep out, watch, and smile;
The wise moon lingers a while.   15

For surely there
Heroic shapes are moving,
Visible thoughts,
Passions, things divine,
Clear beneath clear star-shine.   20

O that I were
Again on English hills,
Seeing between
Laborious villages
Her cool dark loveliness.   25

HAPPY IS ENGLAND NOW

There is not anything more wonderful
Than a great people moving towards the deep
Of an unguessed and unfeared future; nor
Is aught so dear of all held dear before
As the new passion stirring in their veins 5
When the destroying Dragon wakes from
    sleep.

Happy is England now, as never yet!
And though the sorrows of the slow days fret
Her faithfullest children, grief itself is proud.
Ev'n the warm beauty of this spring and
    summer   10
That turns to bitterness turns them to glad-
    ness
Since for this England the beloved ones died.

Happy is England in the brave that die
For wrongs not hers and wrongs so sternly
    hers;
Happy in those that give, give, and endure   15

The pain that never the new years may cure;
Happy in all her dark woods, green fields,
    towns,
Her hills and rivers and her chafing sea.

What'er was dear before is dearer now.
There's not a bird singing upon his bough 20
But sings the sweeter in our English ears:
There's not a nobleness of heart, hand, brain
But shines the purer; happiest is England now
In those that fight, and watch with pride
    and tears.

THE RETURN

I heard the rumbling guns. I saw the smoke,
The unintelligible shock of hosts that still,
Far off, unseeing, strove and strove again:
And Beauty flying naked down the hill.
From morn to eve: and then stern night
    cried Peace!   5
And shut the strife in darkness: all was still.
Then slowly crept a triumph on the dark—
And I heard Beauty singing up the hill.

ROBERT GRAVES (1895–)

GOLIATH AND DAVID

*(For D. C. T., killed at Fricourt, March,
1916.)*

Once an earlier David took
Smooth pebbles from the brook
Out between the lines he went
To that one-sided tournament,
A shepherd boy who stood out fine   5
And young to fight a Philistine
Clad all in brazen mail. He swears
That he's killed lions, he's killed bears,
And those that scorn the God of Zion
Shall perish so like bear or lion.   10
But . . . the historian of that fight
Had not the heart to tell it right.

Striding within javelin range,
Goliath marvels at this strange
Goodly-faced boy so proud of strength.   15
David's clear eye measures the length;
With hand thrust back, he cramps one knee,
Poises a moment thoughtfully,
And hurls with a long vengeful swing.
The pebble, humming from the sling   20
Like a wild bee, flies a sure line
For the forehead of the Philistine;
Then . . . but there comes a brazen clink,

And quicker than a man can think
Goliath's shield parries each cast.   25
Clang! clang! and clang! was David's last.
Scorn blazes in the Giant's eye,
Towering unhurt six cubits high.
Says foolish David, 'Damn your shield!
And damn my sling! but I'll not yield.'   30
He takes his staff of Mamre oak,
A knotted shepherd-staff that's broke
The skull of many a wolf and fox
Come filching lambs from Jesse's flocks.

Loud laughs Goliath, and that laugh   35
Can scatter chariots like blown chaff
To rout; but David, calm and brave,
Holds his ground, for God will save.
Steel crosses wood, a flash, and oh!
Shame for beauty's overthrow!   40
(God's eyes are dim, His ears are shut.)
One cruel backhand sabre-cut—
'I'm hit! I'm killed!' young David cries,
Throws blindly forward, chokes . . . and
    dies.
And look, spike-helmeted, grey, grim,   45
Goliath straddles over him.

NOT DEAD

Walking through trees to cool my heat and
    pain,
I know that David's with me here again.
All that is simple, happy, strong, he is.
Caressingly I stroke
Rough bark of the friendly oak.   5
A brook goes bubbling by: the voice is his.
Turf burns with pleasant smoke;
I laugh at chaffinch and at primroses.
All that is simple, happy, strong, he is.
Over the whole wood in a little while   10
Breaks his slow smile.

OVER THE BRAZIER

What life to lead and where to go
  After the War, after the War?
  We'd often talked this way before
But I still see the brazier glow
That April night, still feel the smoke   5
And stifling pungency of burning coke.

I'd thought: 'A cottage in the hills,
  North Wales, a cottage full of books,
  Pictures and brass and cozy nooks
And comfortable broad window-sills,   10
Flowers in the garden, walls all white,
I'd live there peacefully, and dream and write.'

But Willy said: 'No, Home's played out:
  Old England's quite a hopeless place:
  I've lost all feeling for my race: 15
The English stay-at-home's a tout,
A cad; I've done with him for life.
I'm off to Canada with my wee wife.

'Come with us, Mac, old thing,' but Mac
  Drawled: 'No, A Coral Isle for me,   20
  A warm green jewel in the South Sea.
Of course you'll sneer, and call me slack,
And Colonies are quite jolly . . . but—
Give me my hot beach and my cocoanut.'

So then we built and stocked for Willy   25
  A log-hut, and for Mac a calm
  Rockabye cradle on a palm—
Idyllic dwellings—but this silly
Mad War has now wrecked both, and what
Better hopes has my little cottage got?   30

THOMAS HARDY (1840–)

FOR LIFE I HAD NEVER CARED
GREATLY

For Life I had never cared greatly,
  As worth a man's while;
  Peradventures unsought,
Peradventures that finished in nought,
Had kept me from youth and through man-
      hood till lately   5
  Unwon by its style.

In earliest years—why I know not—
  I viewed it askance;
  Conditions of doubt,
Conditions that leaked slowly out,   10
May haply have bent me to stand and to
      show not
  Much zest for its dance.

With symphonies soft and sweet color
  It courted me then,
  Till evasions seemed wrong,   15
Till evasions gave in to its song,
And I warmed, until living aloofly loomed
      duller
  Than life among men.

Anew I found nought to set eyes on,
  When, lifting its hand,   20
  It uncloaked a star,
Uncloaked it from fog-damps afar,
And showed its beams burning from pole to
      horizon
  As bright as a brand.

And so, the rough highway forgetting,   25
 I pace hill and dale
 Regarding the sky,
 Regarding the vision on high,
And thus re-illumed have no humor for
    letting
 My pilgrimage fail.   30

AFTERWARDS

When the Present has latched its postern
    behind my tremulous stay,
 And the May month flaps its glad green
    leaves like wings,
Delicate-filmed as new-spun silk, will the
    neighbors say,
 'He was a man who used to notice such
    things.'

If it be in the dusk when, like an eyelid's
    soundless blink,   5
 The dewfall-hawk comes crossing the
    shades to alight
Upon the wind-warped upland thorn, will a
    gazer think,
 'To him this must have been a familiar
    sight'?

If I pass during some nocturnal blackness,
    mothy and warm,
 When the hedgehog travels furtively over
    the lawn,   10
Will they say, 'He strove that such innocent
    creatures should come to no harm,
 But he could do little for them; and now
    he is gone'?

If, when hearing that I have been stilled at
    last, they stand at the door,
 Watching the full-starred heavens that
    winter sees,
Will this thought rise on those who will meet
    my face no more,   15
 'He was one who had an eye for such
    mysteries'?

And will any say when my bell of quittance
    is heard in the gloom,
 And a crossing breeze cuts a pause in its
    outrollings,
Till they rise again, as they were a new bell's
    boom,
 'He hears it not now, but used to notice
    such things'?   20

THE COMING OF THE END

How it came to an end!
The meeting afar from the crowd,
And the love-looks and laughters unpenned,
The parting when much was avowed,
How it came to an end!   5

It came to an end;
Yes, the outgazing over the stream,
With the sun on each serpentine bend,
Or, later, the luring moon-gleam;
It came to an end.   10

It came to an end,
The housebuilding, furnishing, planting,
As if there were ages to spend
In welcoming, feasting, and jaunting;
It came to an end.   15

It came to an end,
That journey of one day a week:
('It always goes on,' said a friend,
'Just the same in bright weathers or bleak');
But it came to an end.   20

'How will come to an end
This orbit so smoothly begun,
Unless some convulsion attend?'
I often said. 'What will be done
When it comes to an end?'   25

Well, it came to an end
Quite silently—stopped without jerk;
Better close no prevision could lend;
Working out as One planned it should work
Ere it came to an end.   30

RALPH HODGSON (1879-   )

EVE

Eve, with her basket, was
Deep in the bells and grass
Wading in bells and grass
Up to her knees,
Picking a dish of sweet   5
Berries and plums to eat,
Down in the bells and grass
Under the trees.

Mute as a mouse in a
Corner the cobra lay,   10
Curled round a bough of the
Cinnamon tall . . .
Now to get even and
Humble proud heaven and

Now was the moment or 15
Never at all.

'Eva!' Each syllable
Light as a flower fell,
'Eva!' he whispered the
Wondering maid, 20
Soft as a bubble sung
Out of a linnet's lung,
Soft and most silverly
'Eva!' he said.

Picture that orchard sprite, 25
Eve, with her body white,
Supple and smooth to her
Slim finger tips,
Wondering, listening,
Listening, wondering, 30
Eve with a berry
Half-way to her lips.

Oh had our simple Eve
Seen through the make-believe!
Had she but known the 35
Pretender he was!
Out of the boughs he came,
Whispering still her name,
Tumbling in twenty rings
Into the grass. 40

Here was the strangest pair
In the world anywhere,
Eve in the bells and grass
Kneeling, and he
Telling his story low . . . 45
Singing birds saw them go
Down the dark path to
The Blasphemous Tree.

Oh what a clatter when
Titmouse and Jenny Wren 50
Saw him successful and
Taking his leave!
How the birds rated him,
How they all hated him!
How they all pitied 55
Poor motherless Eve!

Picture her crying
Outside in the lane,
Eve, with no dish of sweet
Berries and plums to eat, 60
Haunting the gate of the
Orchard in vain . . . .
Picture the lewd delight
Under the hill to-night—
'Eva!' the toast goes round, 65
'Eva!' again.

THE BULL

See an old unhappy bull,
Sick in soul and body both,
Slouching in the undergrowth
Of the forest beautiful,
Banished from the herd he led, 5
Bulls and cows a thousand head.

Cranes and gaudy parrots go
Up and down the burning sky;
Tree-top cats purr drowsily
In the dim-day green below; 10
And troops of monkeys, nutting, some,
All disputing, go and come;

And things abominable sit
Picking offal buck or swine,
On the mess and over it 15
Burnished flies and beetles shine,
And spiders big as bladders lie
Under hemlocks ten foot high;

And a dotted serpent curled
Round and round and round a tree, 20
Yellowing its greenery,
Keeps a watch on all the world,
All the world and this old bull
In the forest beautiful.

Bravely by his fall he came; 25
One he led, a bull of blood
Newly come to lustihood,
Fought and put his prince to shame,
Snuffed and pawed the prostrate head
Tameless even while it bled. 30

There they left him, every one,
Left him there without a lick,
Left him for the birds to pick,
Left him there for carrion,
Vilely from their bosom cast 35
Wisdom, worth and love at last.

When the lion left his lair
And roared his beauty through the hills,
And the vultures pecked their quills
And flew into the middle air, 40
Then this prince no more to reign
Came to life and lived again.

He snuffed the herd in far retreat,
He saw the blood upon the ground,
And snuffed the burning airs around 45
Still with beevish odors sweet,
While the blood ran down his head
And his mouth ran slaver red.

Pity him, this fallen chief,
All his splendor, all his strength 50

All his body's breadth and length
Dwindled down with shame and grief,
Half the bull he was before,
Bones and leather, nothing more.

See him standing dewlap-deep   55
In the rushes at the lake,
Surly, stupid, half asleep,
Waiting for his heart to break
And the birds to join the flies
Feasting at his bloodshot eyes,—   60

Standing with his head hung down
In a stupor, dreaming things:
Green savannas, jungles brown,
Battlefields and bellowings,
Bulls undone and lions dead   65
And vultures flapping overhead.

Dreaming things: of days he spent
With his mother gaunt and lean
In the valley warm and green,
Full of baby wonderment,   70
Blinking out of silly eyes
At a hundred mysteries;

Dreaming over once again
How he wandered with a throng
Of bulls and cows a thousand strong,   75
Wandered on from plain to plain,
Up the hill and down the dale,
Always at his mother's tail;

How he lagged behind the herd,
Lagged and tottered, weak of limb,   80
And she turned and ran to him
Blaring at the loathly bird
Stationed always in the skies,
Waiting for the flesh that dies,

Dreaming maybe of a day   85
When her drained and drying paps
Turned him to the sweets and saps,
Richer fountains by the way,
And she left the bull she bore
And he looked to her no more;   90

And his little frame grew stout,
And his little legs grew strong,
And the way was not so long;
And his little horns came out,
And he played at butting trees   95
And boulder-stones and tortoises,

Joined a game of knobby skulls
With the youngsters of his year,
All the other little bulls,
Learning both to bruise and bear.   100

Learning how to stand a shock
Like a little bull of rock.

Dreaming of a day less dim,
Dreaming of a time less far,
When the faint but certain star   105
Of destiny burned clear for him,
And a fierce and wild unrest
Broke the quiet of his breast,

And the gristles of his youth
Hardened in his comely pow,   110
And he came to fighting growth,
Beat his bull and won his cow,
And flew his tail and trampled off
Past the tallest, vain enough,

And curved about in splendor full   115
And curved again and snuffed the airs
As who should say, Come out who dares!
And all beheld a bull, a Bull,
And knew that here was surely one
That backed for no bull, fearing none.   120

And the leader of the herd
Looked and saw, and beat the ground,
And shook the forest with his sound,
Bellowed at the loathly bird
Stationed always in the skies,   125
Waiting for the flesh that dies.

Dreaming, this old bull forlorn
Surely dreaming of the hour
When he came to sultan power,
And they owned him master-horn,   130
Chiefest bull of all among
Bulls and cows a thousand strong.

And in all the tramping herd
Not a bull that barred his way,
Not a cow that said him nay,   135
Not a bull or cow that erred
In the furnace of his look
Dared a second, worse rebuke;

Not in all the forest wide,
Jungle, thicket, pasture, fen,   140
Not another dared him then,
Dared him and again defied;
Not a sovereign buck or boar
Came a second time for more.

Not a serpent that survived   145
Once the terrors of his hoof
Risked a second time reproof,
Came a second time and lived,
Not a serpent in its skin
Came again for discipline;   150

Not a leopard bright as flame,
Flashing fingerhooks of steel,
That a wooden tree might feel,
Met his fury once and came
For a second reprimand,   155
Not a leopard in the land.

Not a lion of them all,
Not a lion of the hills,
Hero of a thousand kills,
Dared a second fight and fail,   160
Dared that ram terrific twice,
Paid a second time the price.

Pity him this dupe of dream,
Leader of the herd again
Only in his daft old brain,   165
Once again the bull supreme
And bull enough to bear the part
Only in his tameless heart.

Pity him that he must wake;
Even now the swarm of flies   170
Blackening his bloodshot eyes
Bursts and blusters round the lake,
Scattered from the feast half-fed,
By great shadows overhead.

And the dreamer turns away   175
From his visionary herds
And his splendid yesterday,
Turns to meet the loathly birds
Flocking round him from the skies,
Waiting for the flesh that dies.   180

D. H. LAWRENCE (1885–)

THE BRIDE

(Copyright 1916 by B. W. Huebsch, New York)

My love looks like a girl to-night,
  But she is old.
The plaits that lie along her pillow
  Are not gold,
But threaded with filigree,   5
  And uncanny cold.

She looks like a young maiden, since her brow
  Is smooth and fair,
Her cheeks are very smooth, her eyes are
  closed,
She sleeps a rare   10
Still winsome sleep, so still, and so composed.

Nay, but she sleeps like a bride, and dreams
  her dreams

Of perfect things.
She lies at last, the darling, in the shape of
  her dream,
And her dead mouth sings   15
By its shape, like the thrushes in clear eve-
  nings.

STUDY

(Copyright 1916 by B. W. Huebsch, New York)

Somewhere the long mellow note of the
  blackbird
Quickens the unclasping hands of hazel,
Somewhere the wind-flowers fling their
  heads back,
Stirred by an impetuous wind. Some ways'll
All be sweet with white and blue violet.   5
  (*Hush now, hush, Where am I?—Biuret—*)

On the green wood's edge a shy girl hovers
From out of the hazel-screen on to the grass,
Where wheeling and screaming the petulant
  plovers
Wave frighted. Who comes? A laborer,
  alas!   10
Oh the sunset swims in her eyes' swift pool.
  (*Work, work, you fool——!*)

Somewhere the lamp hanging low from the
  ceiling
Lights the soft hair of a girl as she reads,
And the red firelight steadily wheeling   15
Weaves the hard hands of my friend in
  sleep.
And the white dog snuffs the warmth, ap-
  pealing
For the man to heed lest the girl shall weep.
(*Tears and dreams for them; for me
Bitter science—the exams. are near.*   20
I wish I bore it more patiently.
I wish you did not wait, my dear,
For me to come: since work I must:
Though it's all the same when we are dead.—
I wish I was only a bust,   25
  All head.)

SUSAN L. MITCHELL

(From 'Secret Springs of Dublin Song,' published
  by The Talbot Press, Ltd., Dublin)

AMBITION IN CUFFE STREET

When I grow big I'll smoke and swear
And drink like my old fellow there,
I'll smoke till all the air is thick,

I'll drink five pints and not feel sick,
And use bad language to my fill,   5
    I will!

On a high stool for hours I'll sit,
Or lean against the door and spit;
I'll drink each pint to the last sup,
And tell the man to hurry up,   10
Till I have had five tankards, yes,
    No less!

I'll talk with Jemmy Cassidy,
He'll have grown old and fat like me,
We'll talk of women and everything,   15
And then perhaps we'll start to sing,
We'll start to sing and fight and shout,
'Twill take three men to chuck us out,
By God, the things that I could do—
    Whew!   20

HOW WOULD IT BE?

How would it be if we should fare,
    By whispering to the pillar-box
A spell of which I am aware,
To some grey mountain whence the bear
May turn him to the West and stare   5
Nor yet see known land anywhere,
    And find there carven of the rocks
An idol that can answer prayer?

Or winding up a palace stair,
    Beyond the hills of Let's Pretend,   10
Come suddenly and unaware
Upon a monarch seated there,
Whose eyes were angry and whose hair
    Was frizzled there at World's End
By the sun's triumphant glare.   15

And now, indeed, how would it be
    If songs and little tales were true?
And we should find the jujube tree,
And galleons still should cross the sea,
And elves should lurk by every tree,   20
    And dragons amble two by two,
While nobody should cry 'Dear me!'

HAROLD MONRO (1879–   )

THE REBELLIOUS VINE

One day, the vine
    That clomb on God's own house
Cried, 'I will not *grow*,'
And, 'I will *not* grow,'

And, 'I *will* not grow.'   5
And, 'I will not grow.'
So God leaned out his head,
And said:
'You need not.' Then the Vine
Fluttered its leaves, and cried to all the
    winds: 10
'Oh, have I not permission from the Lord
And may I not begin to cease to grow?'
But that wise God had pondered on the vine
Before he made it.
And, all the while it labored *not* to grow   15
It grew; it grew;
And all the time God knew.

CHANGE OF MIND

How the rain tumbles. Lord!—
Only last week I would have gone all night
Dripping and scurrying, of my own accord,
For just one sight
Of you. How can I be so bored   5
Now at your short imploring note?
I curse the ugly rain and you.
I know exactly how you wrote,
Smiling—and sobbing too. . . .
I will stay here. I will not go to you.   10

I know precisely how you'll look;
I can imagine every word you'll say;
I want to close you like a finished book:
Please let me have my way.

Why must I tell you that our love is done?
It lasted well, but now you have begun   16
To sorrow me. Be wise and understand.
Whatever purpose can be served indeed
By going two enormous rainy miles
To hold your hand?   20
Or is there any need
To trudge the lane, and climb the slippery
    stiles,
When, by this fire, and snugly in my brain,
I, without effort, may
Press your dry lips and hold your hands
    again,   25
And answer every word you'll have to say?

But I'm forgetting something . . . Who
    was that
Loafing about your cottage all last week?
How cool he was, and always sat
Watching you, and would not speak.   30
Why was he there; and is he still?
It's raining less, I think. Who can he be?
Shall I put on my coat? I think I will.
He may—may not, be gone. I'll go and see.
I'll go and find out why you sent for me.

SUBURB

Dull and hard the low wind creaks
  Among the rustling pampas plumes.
Drearily the year consumes
Its fifty-two insipid weeks.

Most of the grey-green meadow land   5
Was sold in parsimonious lots;
The dingy houses stand
Pressed by some stout contractor's hand
Tightly together in their plots.

Through builded banks the sullen river   10
Gropes, where its houses crouch and shiver.
Over the bridge the tyrant train
Shrieks, and emerges on the plain.

In all the better gardens you may pass,
(Product of many careful Saturdays),   15
Large red geraniums and tall pampas grass
Adorn the plots and mark the graveled ways.

Sometimes in the background may be seen
A private summer-house in white or green.
Here on warm nights the daughter brings
Her vacillating clerk
To talk of small exciting things

And touch his fingers through the dark.
He, in the uncomfortable breach
Between her trilling laughters,   25
Promises, in halting speech,
Hopeless immense Hereafters.

She trembles like the pampas plumes,
Her strained lips haggle. He assumes
The serious quest. . . .   30

Now as the train is whistling past
He takes her in his arms at last.
It's done. She blushes at his side
Across the lawn—a bride, a bride.

              .   .   .   .

The stout contractor will design,   35
The lazy laborers will prepare,
Another villa on the line;
In the little garden-square
Pampas grass will rustle there.

MILK FOR THE CAT

When the tea is brought at five o'clock,
And all the neat curtains are drawn with
      care,
The little black cat with bright green eyes
Is suddenly purring there.

At first she pretends, having nothing to do,
She has come in merely to blink by the grate,
But, though tea may be late or the milk may
      be sour,
She is never late.

And presently her agate eyes
Take a soft large milky haze,   10
And her independent casual glance
Becomes a stiff hard gaze.

Then she stamps her claws or lifts her ears
Or twists her tail and begins to stir,
Till suddenly all her lithe body becomes   15
One breathing trembling purr.

The children eat and wriggle and laugh;
The two old ladies stroke their silk:
But the cat is grown small and thin with de-
      sire,
Transformed to a creeping lust for milk. 20

The white saucer like some full moon de-
      scends
At last from the clouds of the table above;
She sighs and dreams and thrills and glows,
Transfigured with love.

She nestles over the shining rim,   25
Buries her chin in the creamy sea;
Her tail hangs loose; each drowsy paw
Is doubled under each bending knee.

A long dim ecstasy holds her life;
Her world is an infinite shapeless white, 30
Till her tongue has curled the last holy drop,
Then she sinks back into the night.

Draws and dips her body to heap
Her sleepy nerves in the great arm-chair,
Lies defeated and buried deep   35
Three or four hours unconscious there.

SIEGFRIED SASSOON (1886-   )

THE OLD HUNTSMAN

(By permission. Copyright 1918 by E. P. Dutton
      & Co.)

I've never ceased to curse the day I signed
A seven years' bargain for the Golden Fleece.
'Twas a bad deal all round; and dear enough
It cost me, what with my daft management,
And the mean folk as owed and never paid
      me,   5
And backing losers; and the local bucks
Egging me on with whiskies while I bragged
The man I was when huntsman to the Squire.

I'd have been prosperous if I'd took a farm
Of seventy acres, drove by gig and haggled
At Monday markets; now I've squandered all
My savings; nigh three hundred pound I got
As testimonial when I'd grown too stiff
And slow to press a beaten fox.

The Fleece!   15
'Twas the damned Fleece that wore my Emily out,
The wife of thirty years who served me well;
(Not like this beldam clattering in the kitchen,
That never trims a lamp nor sweeps the floor,
And brings me greasy soup in a foul crock.)
       20
Blast the old harridan! What's fetched her now,
Leaving me in the dark, and short of fire?
And where's my pipe? 'Tis lucky I've a turn
For thinking, and remembering all that's past.
And now's my hour, before I hobble to bed,
To set the works a-wheezing, wind the clock
That keeps the time of life with feeble tick
Behind my bleared old face that stares and wonders.

．　．　．　．　．　．

It's queer how, in the dark, comes back to mind
Some morning of September. We've been digging   30
In a steep, sandy warren, riddled with holes,
And I've just pulled the terrier out and left
A sharp-nosed cub-face blinking there and snapping,
Then in a moment seen him mobbed and torn
To strips in the baying hurly of the pack. 35
I picture it so clear: the dusty sunshine
On bracken, and the men with spades, that wipe
Red faces: one tilts up a mug of ale.
And, having stooped to clean my gory hands,
I whistle the jostling beauties out o' the wood.   40

I'm but a daft old fool! I often wish
The Squire were back again—ah, he was a man!
They don't breed men like him these days; he'd come
For sure, and sit and talk and suck his briar
Till the old wife brings up a dish of tea. 45

Ay, those were days, when I was serving Squire!

I never knowed such sport as '85,
The winter afore the one that snowed us silly.

．　．　．　．　．　．

Once in a way the parson will drop in
And read a bit o' the Bible, if I'm bad,— 50
Pray the Good Lord to make my spirit whole
In faith: he leaves some 'baccy on the shelf,
And wonders I don't keep a dog to cheer me,
Because he knows I'm mortal fond of dogs!

I ask you, what's a gent like that to me, 55
As wouldn't know Elijah if I saw him,
Nor have the wit to keep him on the talk?
'Tis kind of parson to be troubling still
With such as me; but he's a town-bred chap,
Full of his college notions and Christmas hymns.   60

Religion beats me. I'm amazed at folk
Drinking the gospels in and never scratching
Their heads for questions. When I was a lad
I learned a bit from mother, and never thought
To educate myself for prayers and psalms.
      65
But now I'm old and bald and serious-minded,
With days to sit and ponder. I'd no chance
When young and gay to get the hang of all
This Hell and Heaven; and when the clergy hoick
And holloa from their pulpits, I'm asleep,
However hard I listen; and when they pray
It seems we're all like children sucking sweets
In school, and wondering whether master sees.

I used to dream of Hell when I was first
Promoted to a huntsman's job, and scent 75
Was rotten, and all the foxes disappeared,
And hounds were short of blood: and officers
From barracks over-rode 'em all day long
On weedy, whistling nags that knocked a hole
In every fence; good sportsmen to a man 80
And brigadiers by now, but dreadful hard
On a young huntsman keen to show some sport.

Ay, Hell was thick with captains, and I rode
The lumbering brute that's beat in half a mile,
And blunders into every blind old ditch. 85
Hell was the coldest scenting land I've known.

And both my whips were always lost, and
   hounds
Would never get their heads down; and a
   man
On a great yawing chestnut trying to cast 'em
While I was in a corner pounded by   90
The ugliest hog-backed stile you've clapped
   your eyes on.
There was an iron-spiked fence round all the
   coverts,
And civil-spoken keepers I couldn't trust,
And the main earth unstopp'd. The fox I
   found
Was always a three-legged 'un from a bag 95
Who reeked of aniseed and wouldn't run.
The farmers were all ploughing their old
   pasture
And bellowing at me when I rode their beans
To cast for beaten fox, or galloped on
With hounds to a lucky view. I'd lost my
   voice   100
Although I shouted fit to burst my guts,
And couldn't blow my horn.

        And when I woke,
Emily snored, and barn-cocks started crow-
   ing,
And morn was at the window; and I was
   glad   105
To be alive because I heard the cry
Of hounds like church-bells chiming on a
   Sunday,—
Ay, that's the song I'd wish to hear in
   Heaven!
The cry of hounds was Heaven for me: I
   know
Parson would call me crazed and wrong to
   say it,   110
But where's the use of life and being glad
If God's not in your gladness?

        I've no brains
For book-learned studies; but I've heard men
   say
There's much in print that clergy have to
   wink at;   115
Though many I've met were jolly chaps, and
   rode
To hounds, and walked me puppies; and
   could pick
Good legs and loins and necks and shoulders,
   ay,
And feet,—'twas necks and feet I looked at
   first.

Some hounds I've known were wise as half
   your saints,   120

And better hunters. That old dog of the
   Duke's,
Harlequin; what a dog he was to draw!
And what a note he had, and what a nose
When foxes ran down wind and scent was
   catchy!
And that light lemon bitch of the Squire's,
   old Dorcas,—   125
She were a marvelous hunter, were old
   Dorcas!

Ay, oft I've thought: 'If there were hounds
   in Heaven,
With God as Master, taking no subscription;
And all His blessed country farmed by
   tenants;
And a straight-necked old fox in every
   gorse!'   130
But when I came to work it out, I found
There'd be too many huntsmen wanting
   places,—
Though some I've known might get a job
   with Nick!

I've come to think of God as something like
The figure of a man the old Duke was   135
When I was turning hounds to Nimrod King,
Before his Grace was took so bad with gout,
And had to quit the saddle. Tall and spare,
Clean-shaved and grey, with shrewd, kind,
   eyes, that twinkled,
And easy walk; who, when he gave good
   words,   140
Gave them whole-hearted; and would never
   blame
Without just cause. Lord God might be
   like that,
Sitting alone in a great room of books
Some evening after hunting.

        Now I'm tired   145
With hearkening to the tick-tack on the shelf;
And pondering makes me doubtful.

        Riding home
On a moonless night of cloud that feels like
   frost
Though stars are hidden, (hold your feet up,
   horse!)   150
And thinking what a task I had to draw
A pack with all those lame 'uns, and the lot
Wanting a rest from all this open weather,—
That's what I'm doing now.

        And likely, too,   155
The frost'll be a long 'un, and the night

One sleep. The parsons say we'll wake to
  find
A country blinding-white with dazzle of
  snow.

The naked stars make men feel lonely,—
  wheeling
And glinting on the puddles in the road.   160
And then you listen to the wind, and wonder
If folk are quite such bucks as they appear
When dressed by London tailors, looking
  down
Their boots at covert side, and thinking big.

     .   .   .   .   .

This world's a funny place to live in. Soon
I'll need to change my country; but I know
'Tis little enough I've understood my life,
And a power of sights I've missed, and for-
  eign marvels.

I used to feel it, riding on spring days
In meadows pied with sun and chasing
  clouds,   170
And half forget how I was there to catch
The foxes; lose the angry, eager feeling
A huntsman ought to have, that's out for
  blood,
And means his hounds to get it!

        Now I know   175
It's God that speaks to us when we're be-
  witched,
Smelling the hay in June and smiling quiet;
Or when there's been a spell of summer
  drought,
Lying awake and listening to the rain.

     .   .   .   .   .

I'd like to be the simpleton I was   180
In the old days when I was whipping-in
To a little harrier-pack in Worcestershire,
And loved a dairymaid, but never knew it
Until she'd wed another. So I've loved
My life; and when the good years are gone
  down,   185
Discover what I've lost.

        I never broke
Out of my blundering self into the world,
But let it all go past me, like a man
Half-asleep in a land that's full of wars.   190

What a grand thing 'twould be if I could go
Back to the kennels now and take my hounds
For summer exercise: be riding out
With forty couple when the quiet skies
Are streaked with sunrise, and the silly birds
Grown hoarse with singing; cobwebs on the
  furze
Up on the hill, and all the country strange,
With no one stirring; and the horses fresh,
Sniffing the air I'll never breathe again.

     .   .   .   .   .

You've brought the lamp then, Martha? I've
  no mind   200
For newspaper to-night, nor bread and cheese.
Give me the candle, and I'll get to bed.

JAMES STEPHENS (1882–)
WHAT TOMAS AN BUILE SAID IN A
PUB

I saw God. Do you doubt it?
  Do you dare to doubt it?
I saw the Almighty Man. His hand
Was resting on a mountain, and
He looked upon the World and all about it:
I saw him plainer than you see me now,   6
  You mustn't doubt it.

He was not satisfied;
  His look was all dissatisfied.
His beard swung on a wind far out of sight
Behind the world's curve, and there was light
Most fearful from His forehead, and He
  sighed,   12
'That star went always wrong, and from the
  start
  I was dissatisfied.'

He lifted up His hand—   15
  I say He heaved a dreadful hand
Over the spinning Earth; then I said, 'Stay,
You must not strike it, God; I'm in the way;
And I will never move from where I stand.'
He said, 'Dear child, I feared that you were
  dead,'   20
  And stayed His hand.

EDWARD THOMAS (1878–1917)
SOWING

It was a perfect day
For sowing; just
As sweet and dry was the ground
As tobacco-dust.

I tasted deep the hour   5
Between the far

Owl's chuckling first soft cry
And the first star.

A long stretched hour it was;   10
Nothing undone
Remained; the early seeds
All safely sown.

And now, hark at the rain,
Windless and light,
Half a kiss, half a tear,   15
Saying good-night.

BRIGHT CLOUDS

Bright clouds of May
Shade half the pond.
Beyond,
All but one bay
Of emerald   5
Tall reeds
Like criss-cross bayonets
Where a bird once called,
Lies bright as the sun.
No one heeds.   10
The light wind frets
And drifts the scum
Of May-blossom.
Till the moorhen calls   15
Again
Naught's to be done
By birds or men.
Still the May falls.

THE GALLOWS

There was a weasel lived in the sun
With all his family,
Till a keeper shot him with his gun
And hung him up on a tree,
Where he swings in the wind and rain,   5
In the sun and in the snow,
Without pleasure, without pain,
On the dead oak tree bough.

There was a crow who was no sleeper,
But a thief and a murderer   10
Till a very late hour; and this keeper
Made him one of the things that were,
To hang and flap in rain and wind,
In the sun and in the snow.
There are no more sins to be sinned   15
On the dead oak tree bough.

There was a magpie, too,
Had a long tongue and a long tail;
He could both talk and do—
But what did that avail?   20
He, too, flaps in the wind and rain
Alongside weasel and crow
Without pleasure, without pain,
On the dead oak tree bough.

And many other beasts   25
And birds, skin, bone and feather,
Have been taken from their feasts
And hung up there together,
To swing and have endless leisure
In the sun and in the snow,   30
Without pain, without pleasure,
On the dead oak tree bough.

EARLY ENGLISH POEMS: NOTES

BEOWULF

The translation is that of John Earle.

i. *a.* 12. *ethelings,* warriors of noble descent.

13. *Scyld of the Sheaf.* The story goes that the founder of the Danish royal house was Scyld, who as a lone child drifted ashore in a boat, in which he had used as a pillow a sheaf of grain. See genealogical table below.

23. *trewage,* tribute.

b. 10. *Beowulf.* This Beowulf, son of Scyld, is not the hero of the poem, who was not a Dane, but a Great (Goth). The name Beowulf in the passage before us is probably formed from that of the god Beaw, by contamination. See genealogical tables below.

11. *Scedelands,* Denmark.

13. *largesses,* liberal gifts.

ii. *a.* 3. *Scyldings,* followers of Scyld, *i.e.,* Danes.

5. *hithe,* port, haven.

15. *bills,* swords.

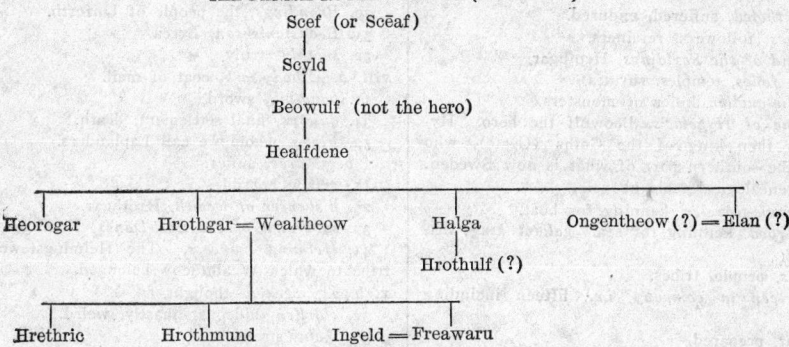

THE DANISH ROYAL FAMILY (SCYLDINGS)

Scef (or Scēaf)
Scyld
Beowulf (not the hero)
Healfdene

Heorogar — Hrothgar = Wealtheow — Halga — Ongentheow (?) = Elan (?)

Hrothulf (?)

Hrethric — Hrothmund — Ingeld = Freawaru

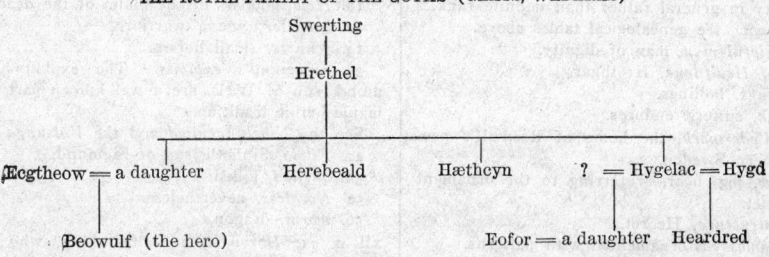

THE ROYAL FAMILY OF THE GOTHS (GEATS, WEDERAS)

Swerting
Hrethel

Ecgtheow = a daughter — Herebeald — Hæthcyn — ? = Hygelac = Hygd

Beowulf (the hero) — Eofor = a daughter — Heardred

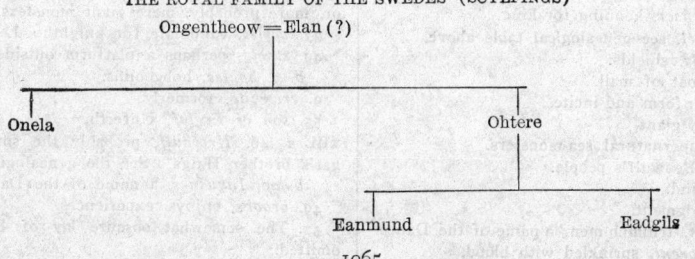

THE ROYAL FAMILY OF THE SWEDES (SCYLFINGS)

Ongentheow = Elan (?)

Onela — Ohtere

Eanmund — Eadgils

25. *holm*, sea.

43. *Healfdene*, son of Beowulf the Dane. For genealogy, see the table above.

46-8. *Heorogar . . . Hrothgar . . . Halga . . . Elan.* See genealogical table above.

49. *the warlike Scylfing*, Ongentheow. See table above.

57. *mead-house*, hall for gatherings and for drinking mead.

b. 12. *Heorot*, a name meaning 'hart,' or 'stag.' The hall was situated on the coast of Denmark.

43. *Grendel.* The name may mean 'grinder.' *mark-ranger*, one who dwells on the borders.

47. *Cain's posterity.* According to tradition, Cain was the ancestor of hateful monsters. See Section xix of the text.

54. *eotens*, giants.

iii. *a.* 23. *tholed*, suffered, endured.

24. *thanes*, followers, retainers.

45. *friend of the Scyldings*, Hrothgar.

b. 23. *fanes*, temples, shrines.

24. *goblin-queller*, killer of monsters.

53. *thane of Hygelac's*, Beowulf the hero. Hygelac was then king of the Goths (Geats), who occupied the southern part of what is now Sweden. See the genealogical table above.

iv. *a.* 1. *wave-traveler*, kenning for boat.

3. *swan-road*, kenning for sea. *gallant king*, i.e., Hrothgar.

10. *leeds*, people, tribes.

11. *fourteen in company*, i.e., fifteen including Beowulf.

17. *dight*, prepared.

32. *Weder leeds*, Goth people.

34. *sarks*, shirts of mail.

b. 3. *eorls*, noble freemen. The word indicates nobility in general rather than definite rank.

28. *Ecgtheow*, see genealogical tables above.

31. *worshipful man*, man of dignity.

33. *son of Healfdene*, Hrothgar.

50. *seethings*, boilings.

51. *tholeth*, suffers, endures.

v. *a.* 12. *Wedermark*, the home of Beowulf's people in southern Sweden.

21. *farrow*, pig, boar,—referring to the ornament on the helmet.

24. *hall structure*, Heorot.

b. 2. *damasked*, ornamented with patterns.

11. *leed of the Wederas*, Beowulf.

20. *Wendlas*, perhaps Vandals.

22. *Thereanent*, in regard to that.

24. *ring-dispenser*, kenning for king.

vi. *a.* 2. *Hrethel*, see genealogical table above.

29. *war-boards*, shields.

41. *byrnie*, coat of mail.

55. *insense*, inform and incite.

b. 2. *eoten*, giant.

3. *nickers*, supernatural sea-monsters.

5. *Wederas*, Beowulf's people.

23. *mood*, mind.

29. *doom*, judgment.

33. *Hrethmen*, 'triumph-men,' a name of the Danes.

36. *blood-besprent*, sprinkled with blood.

42. *Hild*, personification of battle.

45. *Hrethla*, Hrethel. See genealogical table. *Weland*, the Vulcan of Germanic mythology.

46. *Wyrd*, Destiny, Fate.

vii. *a.* 2. *banesman of Heatholaf . . . Wylfings.* Beowulf's father, Ecgtheow, had killed Healtholaf of the tribe of Wylfings.

11. *Heorogar.* See genealogical table above.

13. *I composed the feud.* The Danish king came to the aid of Beowulf's father, by settling the feud with the Wylfings.

b. 3. *Unferth*, spokesman of Hrothgar.

13. *Breca.* Concerning this person we know only what is here recounted.

20. *meted*, measured.

23. *sennight*, a week.

26. *Heathoram people*, perhaps in southern Norway.

29. *Brondings*, the people of Unferth.

31. *Beanstan's son*, Breca.

32. *soothly*, truly.

viii. *a.* 4. *body-sark*, coat of mail.

11. *hand-bill*, sword.

34. *quietus*, final settlement, death.

52. *Finns*, whom we call Laplanders.

b. 3. *dree*, suffer.

11. *grisly*, horrible.

25. *dispenser of wealth*, Hrothgar.

37. *sovereign of the East-Danes*, Hrothgar.

41. *Helming princess.* The Helmings were the tribe to which Wealhtheow belonged.

x. *b.* 24. *weened*, thought.

32. *eldritch*, hideous, ghastly, weird.

37. *main*, strength.

51. *heirloom*, i.e. sword.

xi. *a.* 15. *warlock*, monster.

b. 3. *mere*, water, lake.

10. *Hela*, goddess of the realm of the dead.

12. *bachelor*, young warrior.

14. *jennets*, small horses.

38. *Sigemund's exploits.* The exploits of Sigmund, son of Wæls, are a well-known part of Germanic heroic tradition.

See the *Nibelungenlied* and the *Volsunga Saga*.

42. *Fitela*, Sinfiotli, son of Sigmund.

50. *quelled*, killed.

54. *Nathless*, nevertheless.

56. *worm*, dragon.

xii. *a.* 11. *Heremod*, a Danish king, who is here cited as a stock example of a bad king, a burden to his people.

13. *Eotens*, may be the name of a human enemy, or, more probably, mere giant monsters.

33. *varlet*, candidate for knighthood.

49. *staple*, perhaps a platform outside the hall.

b. 7. *bogles*, hobgoblins.

9. *erewhile*, formerly.

55. *son of Ecglaf*, Unferth.

xiii. *a.* 46. *Hrothulf*, probably the son of Hrothgar's brother Halga. See the genealogical table.

b. 20. *Ingwines*, a name of the Danes.

49. *brooks*, enjoys, experiences.

57. The somewhat obscure lay of Finn is here omitted.

xiv. *a.* 19. *lady of the Scyldings,* Wealtheow.

41. *Hrethric and Hrothmund,* see genealogical table.

56. *carcanets,* circlets of gold and jewels.

b. 3. *necklace of the Brisings,* originally the famous necklace of the goddess Freyja.

7. *grandson of Swerting,* see genealogical table.

11. *feud with the Frisians.* A reference to the raid of Hygelac into the territory of the Frisians about 512 A.D. Hygelac was killed in this expedition. See p. i.

24. *Brook,* use, enjoy, wear.

28. *these boys,* Wealhtheow's sons, Hrethric and Hrothmund.

xv. *a.* 28. *beldam,* hag.

29. *troll-wife,* giantess.

b. 24. *blood-sprent,* blood-sprinkled.

32. *his chiefest thane,* Æschere; see text, Section xx.

xvi. *a.* 13. *quell,* kill.

28. *mark-stalkers,* boundary-stalkers.

45. *rimy,* covered with hoar-frost.

b. 41. *crull-maned,* curly-maned.

45. *weald,* any open country.

47. *warlock,* monster.

52. *scion of Ethelings,* Beowulf.

xvii. *a.* 57. *Hrothgar's orator,* Unferth.

b. 11. *Ecglaf's son,* Unferth.

37. *Hild,* personification of battle.

41. *master of the Goths . . . Hrethel's son,* Hygelac.

48. *damasked,* ornamented with patterns.

xviii. *a.* 30. *carline,* old woman.

46. *damascened,* ornamented with patterns.

b. 34. *eotenish,* fit for an eoten. or giant.

41. *Fetelhilt,* 'chain-hilt,' *i.e.* the sword.

46. *bill,* sword.

xix. *a.* 34. *gold-friend,* Hrothgar.

xx. *a.* 42. *Scania,* used as the name of the Danish kingdom.

b. 17. *Heremod,* a Danish king, stock example of a bad ruler.

18. *descendants of Ecgwela,* the Danes. Nothing is known of Ecgwela.

54. *carking,* vexatious.

xxi. *a.* 43. *eftsoons,* very soon.

47. *eld,* old-age.

b. 12. *settle,* seat.

xxii. *a.* 23. *whilom,* formerly.

32. *Hrethric,* elder son of Hrothgar.

45. *Hrethel,* see genealogical table.

b. 5. *gannet,* a water bird.

31. *gold-bedight,* adorned with gold.

49. *bachelors,* young knights.

xxiii. *a.* 25. *hithe-warden,* guard of the harbor.

40. *Consequently, etc.* The passage omitted from the present text contains as its chief item Beowulf's account to Hygelac of his encounter with Grendel and with Grendel's mother. At the end of the omitted passage we are informed of the death of Hygelac.

46. *ethel-warden,* prince.

b. 54. *intayled,* engraved, cut in.

xxiv. *b.* 19. *fire-gleeds,* fire-flames.

xxv. *a.* 27. *Beowulf uttered, etc.* The omitted passage contains an account of certain of Beowulf's former achievements.

b. 14. *burn,* streamlet.

18. *prince of the Storm-Goths,* Beowulf.

39. *hoised,* raised.

xxvi. *a.* 33. *Scylfings,* the reigning Swedish dynasty.

39. *Wægmundings,* the family to which Beowulf and Wiglaf belonged.

b. 15. *mead,* a strong fermented drink, containing honey.

30. *our liege lord behooves,* is needful to our liege lord.

37. *Me thinketh it,* it seems to me.

xxvii. *a.* 11. *gleeds,* flames.

xxviii. *b.* 25. *brook,* use, wear.

xxix. *b.* 12. *escheat,* revert to former owners.

51. *Hugas,* a name for the Franks.

53. *Hetware,* the tribe against whom Hygelac made the raid in which he was killed. See p. i, Introduction.

xxx. *a.* 3. *the Merwing, i.e.,* the Frankish king.

8. *Ongentheow slew Hæthcyn, etc.* 'Onela and Ohthere are sons of Ongentheow, and often raid Geatland [*i.e.* the land of Hygelac and Beowulf]; . . . Hæthcyn replies with a raid on Swedish soil. He seizes Ongentheow's queen. But the old king follows the foe, defeats him, and kills Hæthcyn, whose men are in desperate case, surrounded by enemies in Ravenswood. But now comes Hygelac with another Geatish army . . ., defeats the Swedes, whose queen again is captured, and besieges Ongentheow in his citadel. Ongentheow is finally killed by Eofor, whose brother Wulf has been disabled in fierce fight with the desperate old hero. Eofor is then married to Hygelac's daughter.' (Gummere.) See genealogical tables above.

10. *Scylfings,* Swedes.

b. 25. *Hygelac's valiant thane,* Eofor.

53. *bestowed upon Eofor his only daughter.* See genealogical table above.

xxxii. *a.* 29. *ruck,* mess, clutter.

SIR GAWAIN AND THE GREEN KNIGHT

The translation is that of Miss Jessie L. Weston.

xxxiv. *a.* 11. *Romulus.* According to Roman tradition, Romulus founded Rome in 753 B. C.

14. *Ticius.* The person intended cannot be identified with certainty.

15. *Langobard.* The Germans who, in 568, founded the kingdom of Lombardy in Northern Italy were called in Latin, Langobardi.

16. *Felix Brutus,* Brutus, the great-grandson of Æneas, the fabled founder of the kingdom of Britain. The name Felix may be the invention of the writer.

31. *Camelot,* a legendary spot in England where Arthur is said to have held his court.

b. 3. *carols,* dances accompanied by song.

33. *Tars,* a name of uncertain identification. This place is often mentioned in medival literature as famous for silks and tapestries.

xxxv. *a.* 28. *Agravain à la dure main,* Agravain of the hard hand.

b. 19. *gauds,* ornaments.

51. *hauberk,* a part of the armor intended originally for the protection of the neck and shoulders.

52. *gorget,* a piece of armor protecting the throat.

NOTES

xxxvi. *a.* 20, *mustered,* surveyed.

38. *doubt,* fear.

xxxvii. *b.* 3. *redest,* understandest or, perhaps, advisest.

xxxviii. *b.* 6. *dossal,* a hanging of rich, heavy cloth, against the wall.

xxxix. *a.* 8. *Michaelmas,* Sept. 29.

11. *All Hallows Day,* Nov. 1.

57. *cuisses,* armor for the thighs.

b. 1. *byrnie,* coat of mail.

7. *surcoat,* an outer garment.

9. *bawdrick,* a kind of belt.

32. *ventail,* a movable piece of armor extending downward from the front of the helmet.

5. *turtle,* turtle-dove.

43. *pentangle,* a heraldic device with five corners.

xl. *a.* 54. *Logres,* here used as a name for England in general.

b. 3. *Anglesey,* an island of the northwest coast of Wales.

4. *foreland,* headland.

5. *Holyhead,* a small island west of Anglesey.

6. *wilderness of Wirral,* in Cheshire.

xli. *a.* 12. matins, the first of the series of eight daily devotional offices called collectively the Canonical Office.

31. *Saint Julian.* This saint was noted for hospitality.

34. *hostel,* lodging.

46. *corbels,* ornamental brackets for supporting moldings.

49. *barbican,* an outwork of a castle or fortified place.

xlii. *a.* 24. *samite,* a heavy silk material.

39. *sodden,* boiled.

57. *keep,* a stronghold.

b. 22. *evensong,* vespers.

xliii. *a.* 45. *in his degree,* according to his rank.

b. 3. *Saint John's Day,* Dec. 27.

23. *behest,* command, request.

38. *wend,* go.

xliv. *a.* 17. *solace,* pleasure.

27. *waked,* kept awake, sat up.

xlv. *a.* 46. *rede,* advise.

xlvi. *a.* 49. *tale,* number, sum.

xlviii. *b.* 52. *prime,* probably about 9 o'clock.

xlix. *a.* 29. *spinney,* a clump of trees or shrubs.

l. *a.* 24. *marks.* A mark was reckoned at approximately 13 shillings.

b. 37. *assoiled,* absolved, shrived.

li. *b.* 11. *deal the doom of my weird,* to suffer the judgment of my fate.

lii. *a.* 13. *did on,* put on.

15. *cognizance,* the crest by which a man in complete armor could be recognized.

liii. *a.* 26. *let,* detain, hinder.

41. *greet,* weep.

b. 25. *kirk,* church.

liv. *a.* 3. *bent,* field.

lv. *b.* 25-6. *Samson . . . Delilah.* See Judges xvi.

27-8. *David . . . Bathsheba.* See ii Samuel xi.

lvi. *b.* 32. *book of Brutus.* Works treating the early legendary history of Britain were sometimes called *Brut.* See, for example, in English, Layamon's *Brut,* written about the year 1200.

PEARL

The translation is by Dr. S. Weir Mitchell, **The** Century Company, 1906.

lvii. 1. *pleasance,* delight. *enow,* enough.

43. *gromwell,* a plant.

lviii. 63. *ghost,* spirit.

75. *boles,* trunks of trees.

76. *blue of Inde,* indigo.

110. *beryl,* a precious mineral.

118. *gent,* elegant.

123. *hale,* safe, free from infirmity.

127. *mere,* water.

131. *wight,* person.

lix. 158. *lissome,* supple, lithe.

184. *empery,* the status of an emperor.

185. *amice,* a white linen cloth commonly worn about the head or neck by priests when celebrating the Roman Mass.

189. *ween,* think.

192. *bedight,* adorned.

194. *margerys,* pearls.

lx. 237. *weird,* fate.

246. *perdue,* lost.

275. *trow,* believe.

286. *yore-father,* ancestor, referring to Adam.

289. *dole,* grief.

301. *demoiselle,* maiden.

306. *misericorde,* pity, mercy.

lxi. 358. *phenix of Araby,* a mythical bird, fabled to be the only one of its kind.

389. *pater,* the Lord's Prayer, or *Pater noster.*

393. *par ma fay,* by my faith.

401. *Matthew.* See Matthew xx. 1-16.

lxii. 433. *evensong,* Vespers.

442. *waxed,* grew.

lxiii. 550. *The priest doth show,* a reference to the consecration of the Bread and Wine in the Roman Mass.

THE CHESTER PLAYS

NOAH'S FLOOD

The text of the play is modernized from that of Deimling in the Early English Text Society, Extra Series, Vol. LXII. The stage-directions are translated from the Latin. Stage-directions not in the original text are enclosed in square brackets. *Noah's Flood* is the third play in the cycle, as may be seen in the following complete list of the Chester plays:

1. The Fall of Lucifer
2. The Creation of the World; Cain and Abel
3. Noah's Flood
4. Abraham and Isaac
5. King Balack and Balaam
6. Octavian and the Sibyl; the Nativity
7. The Adoration of the Shepherds
8. Herod and the Magi
9. The Adoration of the Magi
10. The Slaughter of the Innocents
11. Christ in the Temple
12. The Temptation of Christ; the Woman taken in Adultery

13. The Raising of Lazarus
14. Christ's Entry into Jerusalem
15. The Last Supper
16. The Trial and Scourging of Christ
17. The Crucifixion
18. The Harrowing of Hell
19. The Resurrection
20. The Journey to Emmaus
21. The Ascension
22. Pentecost
23. The Prophets
24. Antichrist
25. The Last Judgment

Noah's Flood should be compared with its Biblical source in Genesis vi–ix.

lxiv. 1. *Stage-direction.* In this stage-direction, and in others in the play, it will be observed that, although the stage was merely a large wagon, the stage-setting was in some respects ambitious. It is not safe, however, to speculate too closely upon the nature of the 'clouds' demanded in the present instance.

5. *ghost,* spirit.
6. *fone,* foe.
7. *six score years.* It will be noticed that the period of 120 years during which God promises to delay punishing mankind conforms to the period of 'a hundred winters and twenty' (line 149) occupied by Noah in building the Ark.
8. *blyn,* cease.
23. *slake,* slack.

lxv. 27. *fonge,* take.
35. *flow,* flood.
43. *spill,* destroy.
44. *soothly,* truly.
46. *grill,* annoy.
53. *bowne,* prepared.
73. *slich,* pitch, or oily substance.
75. *stitch,* fragment.
78. *in fere,* all together.
79. *dight,* prepare.
95. *weete,* wet weather.
100. *frankish fare,* nonsense.
101. *rede,* advice.

lxvi. 103. *By Christ.* This asseveration, like that in line 112, is an obvious anachronism. See also lines 203 and 205.
109. *bere,* noise.
111. *ween,* think.
114. *hie,* make haste.
119. *make,* mate.
122. *mo,* more.

132. *bydene,* in haste.
145. *bayne,* ready.
149. *A hundred winters and twenty.* See note to line 7.
154. *Hie you,* make haste.
170. *fulmart,* polecat.
172. *cowle,* tub or similar large vessel.

lxvii. 178. *crowse,* lively, jolly.
182. *bittour,* bittern.
195. *on God's half,* for God's sake.
202. *gone,* go.
209. *wraw,* angry.
211. *trow,* trust.
224. *doubt,* fear.
225. *gossips,* companions.
234. *childer,* children.
236. *bought,* redeemed. The reference to events of the New Testament is an obvious anachronism.
240. *Stage-direction.* This stage-direction is somewhat inadequate, for Noah's sons obviously apply force to their recalcitrant mother. The situation provides a notable opportunity for a scuffle on the stage.
242. *mote,* talking, chatter.

lxviii. 250. *wood,* mad.
256. *Stage-direction.* The Psalm sung is the fifty-fourth.
261. *again,* back.
262. *sayne,* say.
269. From this stanza one line has been lost.
271. *hend,* gentle. The second dove mentioned in the stage-direction after this line seems to be a mechanical contrivance.
286. *fay,* faith.
297. *hight,* haste.
298. *dight,* prepare.
307. *bowne,* ready.
312. *able,* pleasing.
315. *myn,* think.

lxix. 324. *flytte,* swim.
325. *behite,* promise.
326. *let,* hesitate.
329. *bore,* born.
332. *in fere,* together.
335. *let,* leave alone.
344. *foreword,* covenant.
348. *hest,* promise.
351. *spill,* destroy.
352. *My bow.* On the origin of the rainbow see Genesis ix, 12–15.
360. *been,* be.
362. *teen,* anger.

READINGS: NOTES

CHAUCER: THE CANTERBURY TALES

THE PROLOGUE

The following are a few practical suggestions as to pronunciation, comparison being made to sounds in modern words:

VOWELS

a — as in father.
e long (often written *ee*) — as the *a* in hate.
e short — as in get.
i (often *y*) long — as the vowel in feet.
i (often *y*) short — as in fin.
o (often *oo*) long — as in hope.
o short — as in not.
u (sometimes *ew*) long — as in French *nature*, German *grün*.
u short — as in full. Note the absence of our modern so-called 'short u,' as in modern English but.

DIPHTHONGS

ai, ay, ei, ey — as in straight.
au, aw — as *ow* in now.
ou, ow — as in through.

CONSONANTS

ch — as *tch* in itch.
h (not initial), *gh* — guttural as *ch* in German *Nacht*.

---

2. 1. *shoures soote,* sweet showers.
2. *droghte,* dryness.
3. *swich licour,* such liquor (sap).
4. *vertu,* power.
5. *Zephirus,* the west wind. *eek,* also.
6. *holt,* wood, grove. *heeth,* heath, open country.
7. *croppes,* shoots. *yonge sonne,* young sun,— young because it had recently entered upon its annual course through the signs of the zodiac.
8. *Hath . . . y-ronne. Ram,* one of the signs of the zodiac, Aries. 'Hath run his half-course in the Ram' means that it was past the eleventh of April.
9. *fowles,* birds in general.
10. *yë,* eye.
11. *So . . . corages,* so nature excites them in their hearts (feelings).
13. *palmers,* pilgrims to foreign parts. Originally, a palmer was one who made a pilgrimage to the Holy Land and brought home a palm-branch as a token. *strondes,* shores.
14. *ferne halwes couthe,* distant shrines known.
16. *wende,* go.
17. *blisful,* blessed. *martir,* Thomas à Becket. *seke,* seek.
18. *That . . . seke,* 'who hath helped them when they were sick.' Notice the riming,— *seke . . . seke,*— of identical forms that have different meanings.
19. *bifel,* it befell.
20. *Southwerk,* Southwark, on the south bank of the Thames, across from London. *Tabard,* an inn of which the sign was a tabard, or sleeveless jacket.
22. *corage,* heart.
24. *wel,* full, quite.
25–26. *by aventure . . . felawshipe,* by chance fallen into association.
27. *wolden ryde,* wished to ride.
28. *wyde,* spacious.
29. *esed atte beste,* accommodated in the best manner.
30. *to reste,* gone to rest, set.
31. *everichon,* every one.
32. *of hir felawshipe anon,* of their company immediately.
33. *forward,* agreement.
34. *ther . . . devyse,* to that place that I tell you of.
35. *natheles,* nevertheless.
37. *Me . . . resoun,* it seems to me reasonable.
38. *condicioun,* standing.
39–40. *Of . . . aegree,* Of each of them, as it appeared to me, and of what sort they were, and of what social class.
41. *eek,* also. *array,* dress.
43. *worthy,* honorable.
45. *chivalrye,* knighthood.
46. *fredom,* liberality.
47. *werre,* war.
48. *therto,* besides that. *ferre,* farther.
49. *hethenesse,* heathen lands.
51. *Alisaundre,* Alexandria.
52–53. *Ful . . . Pruce,* Very many times, in Prussia, he had been placed at the head of the table, above the knights of all other nations.
54. *Lettow,* Lithuania. *reysed,* made a military expedition. *Ruce,* Russia.
55. *degree,* rank.
56. *Gernade,* Granada.
57. *Algezir,* modern Algeciras. *Belmarye,* a Moorish kingdom in Africa.

58. *Lyeys*, in Armenia. *Satalye*, on the south coast of Asia Minor.

59. *Grete See*, the Mediterranean.

60. *aryve*, landing of troops.

62. *Tramissene*, a Moorish kingdom in Africa.

63. *In . . . foo*, In the lists (field of combat at a tournament) thrice, and always slain his antagonist.

64. *ilke*, same.

65. *Somtyme*, at one time. *Palatye*, in Asiatic Turkey.

66. *Ageyn*, against.

67. *sovereyn prys*, great renown.

68. *wys*, wise.

69. *port*, bearing.

70. *vileinye*, low speech.

71. *un-to no maner wight*, to no kind of man.

72. *verray parfit gentil knight*, very perfect gentle knight.

73. *array*, dress, costume.

74. *hors*, horses. *gay*, gaudily dressed.

75. *fustian*, stout, coarse cloth. *wered*, wore. *gipoun*, a short coat worn under the armor.

76. *bismotered*, spotted. *habergeoun*, coat of mail.

77. *late y-come from his viage*, lately come from his journey.

79. *Squyer*, esquire, one who attended a knight.

80. *lovyer*, lover. *lusty*, joyful, gay. *bacheler*, a young candidate for knighthood.

81. *lokkes crulle*, locks curled.

83. *evene lengthe*, good stature.

84. *delivere*, active.

85. *chivachye*, military expedition.

89. *Flaundres*, Flanders, an ancient country of Europe, extending along the North Sea from the Strait of Dover to the mouth of the Schelde. *Artoys*, *Picardye*, Artois, Picardy, ancient provinces of northern France.

87. *space*, length of time.

88. *lady*, genitive singular, without 's.

89. *embrouded*, embroidered. *mede*, mead.

91. *floytinge*, playing the flute.

95. *coude*, knew how. *endyte*, relate, compose.

96. *juste*, joust. *purtreye*, draw, paint.

97. *nightertale*, night-time.

98. *sleep*, slept.

99. *lowly*, modest. *servisable*, helpful.

100. *carf*, carved.

101. *yeman*, yeoman: a servant of the next degree above a groom. *namo*, no more.

102. *him liste ryde*, it pleased him to ride.

104. *A sheef of pecok arwes*, a sheaf of arrows fitted with peacocks' feathers.

106. *takel*, implements; here arrows.

109. *not-heed*, hair closely cut.

111. *bracer*, a guard for the coat-sleeve, used by archers to avoid the friction of the string against the cloth.

112. *bokeler*, buckler; a small shield.

114. *harneised*, equipped.

115. *Cristofre*, 'a figure of St. Christopher, used as a brooch (Wright).'

116. *bawdrik*, baldric, belt.

117. *forster*, forester.

119. *coy*, quiet, modest.

120. *sëynt Loy*, Saint Eligius.

121. *cleped*, called.

124. *fetisly*, neatly, excellently.

125. *After . . . Bowe*, after the manner of Stratford-le-Bow. This was a monastery near London. The French of the prioress was dialectical, not Parisian.

132. *lest*, pleasure.

134. *ferthing*, a fourth part; hence a small bit.

136. *raughte*, reached.

137. *sikerly*, certainly. *of great disport*, readily amused.

138. *port*, carriage.

139–141. *And peyned . . . reverence*, and took pains to imitate courtly behavior, and to be stately in her deportment, and to be esteemed worthy of reverence.

142. *conscience*, feeling, tenderness.

143. *pitous*, compassionate.

147. *wastel breed*, bread made of fine flour.

148. *weep*, wept.

149. *yerde*, rod.

150. *conscience*, tenderness.

151. *wimpel*, a covering for the neck. *pinched* closely pleated.

152. *tretys*, long and well-proportioned.

153. *ther-to*, besides.

156. *hardily*, certainly. *undergrowe*, undergrown, stunted.

157. *fetis*, neat, well-made.

159. *peire*, set. *gauded al with grene*, provided with green *gawdies*. *Gawdies* were the larger beads in the set.

160. *heng*, hung. *shene*, bright.

162. *Amor vincit omnia*, love conquers all things (Virgil, *Eclog.*, X, 69).

164. *chapeleyne*. The prioress has a female chaplain.

165. *a fair for the maistrye*, a fair one for superiority.

166. *out-rydere*, outrider, the monastic officer who visited the outlying manors belonging to the house. *venerye*, hunting.

172. *Ther as*, where. *keper*, head. *celle*, cell; a small monastery or nunnery dependent on a larger one.

173. *seint Maure*, St. Maur (d. 584). *seint Beneit*, St. Benedict (d. 543). St. Benedict founded the Benedictine order, and St. Maur was his disciple.

174. *som-del streit*, somewhat narrow, strict.

175. *ilke*, same.

176. *space*, course.

177. *yaf*, gave. *pullèd*, plucked.

182. *thilke*, that.

184. *What*, why. *wood*, mad.

185. *poure*, pore.

186. *swinken*, work.

187. *Austin*, St. Augustine (d. 604), after whom the Augustinian Canons were named.

187. *bit*, contracted from 3d. person singular present, *biddeth*.

188. *swink*, toil.

189. *pricasour*, a hard rider.

191. *priking*, riding.

193. *seigh*, saw. *purfiled*, fringed.

194. *grys*, costly grey fur.

199. *anoint*, anointed.

200. *in good point*, in good condition. Cf. French *en bon point*.

201. *stepe*, prominent.

202. *stemed*, shone. *Leed*, caldron.

203. *botes souple*, boots soft.

205. *for-pyned goost*, tormented ghost.

207. *palfrey*, riding-horse.

208. *frere*, friar. *wantown*, brisk, lively.

209. *limitour*, a begging friar to whom was assigned a certain district, within which he might solicit alms. *ful solempne*, very important.

210 *ordres foure*. The four orders of mendicant friars were: (1) the Dominicans, or Black Friars; (2) the Franciscans, or Grey Friars; (3) the Carmelites, or White Friars; (4) the Augustin, or Austin Friars. These orders arose in the early part of the thirteenth century. *can*, knows.

211. *daliaunce and fair language*, gossip and flattery.

216. *frankeleyns*, wealthy farmers. *over-al*, everywhere.

219. *curat*, parish priest.

220. *licentiat*, provided with a licence from the Pope to hear confession in all places.

223. *yeve*, give.

224. *Ther . . . pitaunce*, where he knew he was sure to have good things to eat.

225. *povre*, poor. *yive*, give.

226. *y-shrive*, confessed, shriven.

227. *yaf*, gave. *dorste make avaunt*, dared make boast, dared assert confidently.

228. *wiste*, knew.

230. *He . . . smerte*, He cannot weep, although it may pain him sorely.

232. *Men moot yeve*, one ought to give.

233. *tipet*, hood. *farsed*, stuffed.

236. *rote*, a kind of violin.

237. *yeddinges*, songs. *prys*, prize.

238. *flour-de-lys*, lily.

239. *champioun*, athlete.

241. *hostiler*, inn-keeper. *tappestere*, female tapster.

242. *Bet . . . beggestere*, better than a leper or a female beggar.

244. *as by his facultee*, considering his ability.

246. *honest*, becoming. *avaunce*, profit.

247. *poraille*, poor people, rabble.

248. *riche*, rich people. *vitaille*, victuals.

249–250. *And over-al . . . servyse*, And everywhere where profit was likely to arise, he was polite, and humble in offering his services.

251. *vertuous*, efficient.

253. *sho*, shoe.

254. *In principio*, In the beginning,— the opening words of the Gospel according to St. John.

256. *purchas*, proceeds from begging. *rente*, regular income.

257. *rage*, romp. *as . . whelpe*, exactly as if he were a puppy.

258. *love-dayes*, days fixed for settling differences by umpire, without having recourse to law or violence. *mochel*, greatly.

260. *cope*, an outer vestment for a cleric.

262. *semi-cope*, short cope.

263. *presse*, mold.

264. *lipsed*, lisped.

271. *mottelee*, motley costume. *hye*, high.

273. *fetisly*, see 1. 124.

274. *resons*, opinions.

275. *Sowninge . . . winning*, tending always to the increase of his profit.

276. *kept*, guarded.

277. *Middelburgh*, a port on an island off the coast of the Netherlands. *Orewelle*, an English port, across the North Sea from Middelburgh, at the mouth of the Orwell River.

278. *Wel . . . selle*, well knew how to sell crowns in exchange. *Sheeldes*, or crowns, were valued at 3 shillings 4 pence.

279. *bisette*, used.

280. *wiste*, knew.

281–282. *So estatly . . . chevisaunce*, So ceremoniously did he order his bargains and agreements for borrowing money.

283. *sothe*, truly.

284. *noot*, know not.

285. *Clerk*, scholar.

286. *y-go*, gone.

288. *nas*, was not.

289. *holwe*, hollow. *soberly*, adj. sad, solemn.

290. *overest courtepy*, uppermost short cloak.

291. *benefice*, a church office endowed with a revenue.

292. *office*, secular office.

293. *him . . . have*, it was dearer to him to have.

295. *Aristotle*, Greek philosopher, 384–322 B. C.

296. *fithele*, fiddle. *sautrye*, psaltery; an instrument like a zither, having a sounding-box under the strings.

297–8. *philosophre*, used in the double sense of philosopher and alchemist. It was commonly believed that alchemists could produce gold.

299. *hente*, seize, get.

302. *Of hem . . . scoleye*, of those who gave him (money) with which to go to school.

303. *cure*, care.

304. *O*, one.

305. *in . . . reverence*, in due form and dignity.

306. *hy sentence*, lofty meaning.

307. *sowninge in*, conducive to.

309. *Sergeant of the Lawe*, a law officer of the crown. *war*, cautious.

310. *parvys*, church-porch. It was customary for lawyers to meet for consultation at the portico of St. Paul's, London.

312. *reverence*, dignity.

313. *swich*, such.

314. *assyse*, session of a court.

315. *By patente . . . commissioun*, by letter patent (definite legal authorization) or by full (unlimited) authorization.

318. *purchasour*, conveyancer.

319. *fee simple*, held in absolute possession.

320. *purchasing*, conveyancing. *infect*, invalid.

323. *In termes . . . alle*, he had (in mind) exactly all the cases and decisions.

325. *Therto*, moreover. *endyte*, write. *make* draw up.

326. *pinche at,* find fault with.

327. *coude . . . rote,* knew he fully by rote.

328. *medlee cote,* a coat of mixed stuff or color.

329. *ceint,* girdle. *barres,* ornaments, or studs, of a girdle.

330. *array,* costume.

331. *Frankeleyn,* a wealthy farmer.

332. *berd,* beard. *dayesye,* daisy.

333. 'The old school of medicine, following Galen, supposed that there were four "humours," *viz.* hot, cold, moist, and dry, and four complexions or temperaments of men, *viz.* the sanguine, the choleric, the phlegmatic, and the melancholy. The man of sanguine complexion abounded in hot and moist humours (Skeat).' See note to line 421.

334. *by the morwe,* in the morning. *a sop in wyn,* wine with pieces of cake in it.

335. *delyt,* pleasure. *wone,* custom.

336. *Epicurus* (d. 270 B. C.), a Greek philosopher who assumed pleasure to be the highest good.

337. *pleyn,* full.

340. *Seynt Iulian;* 'St. Julian was eminent for providing his votaries with good lodgings and accommodations of all sorts (Chambers).'

341. *alwey after oon,* always up to the standard.

342. *envyned,* stored with wine.

343. *bake mete,* meat pie.

344. *plentevous,* plenteous.

345. *snewed,* snowed.

347. *after,* according to.

348. *soper,* supper.

349. *mewe,* coop.

350. *breem,* bream, a fresh water fish. *luce,* pike. *stewe,* fishpond.

351. *but-if,* unless.

352. *gere,* utensils.

353. *table dormant,* a table fixed to the floor, irremovable. The Franklin kept open house.

355. *sessiouns,* meetings of the justices of the peace.

357. *anlas,* a knife or dagger. *gipser,* pouch.

358. *heng,* hung. *morne,* morning.

359. *shirreve,* 'governor of a county (Skeat)'; our modern word *sheriff. countour,* accountant.

360. *vavasour,* a sub-vassal of a king's vassal.

362. *Webbe,* weaver. *Tapicer,* upholsterer.

363. *in o liveree,* in one livery.

364. *solempne,* dignified. *fraternitee,* gild.

365. *hir gere apyked,* their apparel trimmed.

366. *y-chaped,* provided with *chapes,* caps of metal at the end of the sheath.

368. *everydeel,* every part.

369. *burgeys,* burgess, citizen.

370. *To . . . deys,* to sit on a dais in a gild-hall.

371. *Everich,* each. *can,* knows.

372. *shaply,* adapted, fit.

373. *catel,* property. *ynogh,* enough. *rente,* income.

376. *y-clept,* called.

377. *vigilyës.* 'It was the manner in times past, upon festival evens, called *vigiliae,* for parishioners to meet in their church-houses or church-yards, and there to have a drinking-fit for the time (Speght).' *al bifore,* before all the others.

378. *roialliche y-bore,* royally borne.

379. *for the nones,* for the occasion.

380. *mary-bones,* marrow-bones.

381. *poudre-marchant,* a sharp flavoring powder. *galingale,* root of sweet cyperus.

384. *mortreux,* a kind of soup.

385. *thoughte me,* seemed to me.

386. *mormal,* cancer, open sore.

387. *blankmanger,* 'a compound made of capon minced, with rice, milk, sugar, and almonds (Skeat).'

388. *woning . . . weste,* dwelling far westward.

389. *woot,* know. *Dertemouthe,* Dartmouth, an important sea-port on the southwest coast of England.

390. *rouncy,* nag. *couthe,* knew how.

391. *falding,* coarse cloth.

392. *laas,* cord, lace.

396–7. *Ful . . . sleep,* Very many a draught of wine had he drawn (stolen!) from Bordeaux-way, while the merchant slept.

398. *Of nyce . . . keep,* He had no regard for a fussy conscience.

400. *By water . . . lond, i.e.,* he made them 'walk the plank.'

402. *stremes,* currents. *him bisydes,* near him.

403. *herberwe,* harbor. *mone,* moon. *lodemenage,* pilotage.

404. *Hulle,* Hull. *Cartage,* Carthage.

405. *undertake,* assume responsibility.

408. *Gootlond,* Gottland, an island in the Baltic sea. *Finistere,* Cape Finisterre, on the northern coast of Spain.

409. *cryke,* creek, inlet.

414. *astronomye,* astrology.

415. *kepte,* watched.

416. *houres,* astrological hours. 'A great portion of the medical science of the middle ages depended upon astrological and other superstitious observances (Wright).'

417. *fortunen,* predict. *ascendent,* the point of the zodiacal circle which happens to be ascending above the horizon at a given moment.

418. *images.* 'It was believed that images of men and animals could be made of certain substances and *at certain times,* and could be so treated as to cause good or evil to a patient, by means of magical and planetary influences (Skeat).'

421. *humour.* The four elementary qualities, or *humours,* were hot, cold, dry, and moist. The excess of some one humor was thought to cause disease. The mixture of humors in a man determined his *complexion,* or temperament. The *sanguine complexion* was thought to be hot and moist; the *phlegmatic,* cold and moist; the *choleric,* hot and dry; the *melancholy,* cold and dry.

422. *parfit practisour,* perfect practitioner.

424. *bote,* remedy.

426. *drogges,* drugs. *letuaries,* electuaries, syrups.

428. *Hir,* their.

429. *Esculapius,* Æsculapius, god of medicine.

430. *Deiscorides,* Dioscorides, a Greek physician of the 2d century. *Rufus,* a Greek physician of the 1st century.

772. *shapen yow*, intend. *talen*, tell tales.

775. *disport*, sport.

776. *erst*, first.

777. *And . . . alle*, And if it is pleasing to you all.

781. *fader*, genitive singular. *deed*, dead.

782. *But*, unless. *heed*, head.

784. *seche*, seek.

785. *Us . . . wys*, It seemed to us not worth while to make it a matter of deliberation.

786. *avys*, consideration.

787. *as him leste*, as it pleased him.

788. *herkneth*, listen, 2d pers. plur. imperative.

791. *shorte*, make short.

792. *viage*, journey. *tweye*, two.

795. *aventures*, occurrences. *whylom*, formerly. *han*, have.

798. *sentence*, meaning, content. *solas*, amusement.

799. *our aller cost*, the cost of us all.

805. *withseye*, oppose.

807. *vouche-sauf*, grant.

809. *shape me therfore*, prepare myself for it.

810. *othes swore*, oaths sworn.

816. *devys*, direction.

819. *fet*, fetched.

820. *echoon*, each one.

823. *our aller cok*, cock of us all.

824. *gadrede*, gathered.

825. *riden*, rode. *pas*, foot-pace.

826. St. Thomas a Watering was two miles from Southwark.

828. *herkneth*; see note to l. 788. *if you leste*, if it pleases you.

829. *woot*, know. *forward*, agreement. *yow recorde*, call to your mind.

830. *If . . . acorde*, If even-song (vespers) and matins agree; *i.e.*, if you are minded this morning as you were last night.

832. *As . . . ale*, As surely as I ever hope to be able to drink wine or ale.

835. *draweth*, draw, 2d pers. plur. imperative. *ferrer twinne*, farther depart.

838. *acord*, agreement.

839. *neer*, nearer.

842. *wight*, person.

844. *sort*, lot, destiny.

845. *fil*, fell.

847. *resoun*, reasonable.

848. *forward*, agreement. *composicioun*, compact.

850. *saugh*, saw.

854. *a*, in.

855. *riden*, rode.

THE NUN'S PRIEST'S TALE

1. *widwe*, widow. *stope*, advanced.

2. *whylom*, formerly. *narwe*, narrow, small.

5. *thilke*, that.

6. *ladde*, led.

7. *catel*, property. *rente*, income.

8. *housbondrye*, economy.

9. *fond*, found, supported. *doghtren*, daughters.

11. *highte*, was called.

12. *bour*, bower, inner room.

13. *sclendre meel*, slender meal.

14. *Of . . . deel*, Of poignant sauce she had not the slightest need.

15. *thurgh*, through.

17. *Repleccioun*, overeating.

19. *hertes suffisaunce*, heart's satisfaction.

20. *lette hir no-thing*, prevented her not at all.

21. *poplexye shente*, apoplexy hurt.

25. *Seynd*, singed. *ey or tweye*, egg or two.

26. *deye*, dairy-woman.

28. *dich*, ditch.

30. *nas*, was not.

31. *merier*, pleasanter, sweeter.

32. *messe-dayes*, mass-days.

33. *sikerer*, more certain. *logge*, lodging-place.

34. *orlogge*, clock.

35-8. The cock crew every hour, for fifteen degrees of the equinoctial make an hour. *Thanne*, then.

39. *fyn*, fine.

40. *batailed*, indented like a battlement.

41. *bile*, bill. *Ieet*, jet.

42. *toon*, toes.

47. *paramours*, lovers.

48. *as of*, as to.

50. *cleped*, called.

51. *debonaire*, gracious.

52. *compaignable*, companionable.

53. *thilke*, that same.

54. *in hold*, in possession.

55. *loken in every lith*, locked in every limb.

59. *'my lief . . . londe,'* 'my beloved has gone away.' Probably the refrain of a popular song.

61. *briddes*, birds.

62. *bifel*, happened.

67. *drecched*, troubled.

70. *eyleth*, ails.

71. *verray*, true.

73. *agrief*, amiss.

74. *me mette*, I dreamed. *meschief*, mishap.

76. *my . . . aright*, interpret my dream favorably.

78. *me mette*, I dreamed.

79. *saugh*, saw.

81. *deed*, dead.

85. *tweye*, two.

86. *deye*, die.

88. *Avoy*, fie. *herteles*, coward.

94. *free*, generous.

95. *secree*, secret, discreet.

96. *tool*, weapon.

97. *avauntour*, boaster.

99. *aferd*, afraid.

101. *swevenis*, dreams.

103. *replecciouns*, gluttony.

104. *fume*, vapor arising from gluttony. *complecciouns*; see note to *Prologue*, l. 421.

106. *met*, dreamed.

108. *rede colera*, 'red cholera caused by too much bile and blood (Skeat).'

110. *lemes*, gleams.

112. *contek*, strife.

113. *humour of malencolye*, *i.e.*, black choler.

115. *boles blake*, bulls black.

120. *Catoun*, Cato's *Distichs*. This collection of

sayings, of uncertain authorship, was well known as early as the 4th century.

121. *do no fors,* pay no heed to.

122. *flee,* fly. *bemes,* beams, perches.

124. *Up,* upon.

130. *prow,* profit.

131. *tho,* the.

132. *kynde,* nature.

133. *binethe,* beneath.

135. *colerik of compleccioun;* see note to l. 104.

136. *Ware,* beware.

137. *humours hote;* see note to *Prologue,* l. 421.

138. *grote,* groat.

139. *fevere terciane,* tertian fever, a fever occurring every second day.

143. *lauriol,* laurel. *centaure,* the herb centaury. *fumetere,* the herb fumitory.

144. *ellebor,* hellebore.

145. *catapuce,* the herb spurge. *gaytres beryis,* dogwood berries.

146. *yve,* ivy. *mery,* pleasant. The herbs mentioned are disagreeable to the taste!

148. *fader kyn,* father's kinsmen.

149. *Dredeth,* 2d pers. plur. imperative.

150. *graunt mercy,* great thanks.

151. *daun,* dan, Lord, a title given to monks, and to many other sorts of persons.

156. *so moot I thee,* as I may prosper. An expletive phrase.

157. *sentence,* sense.

163. *verray preve,* true proof.

164. *Oon . . . auctours,* refers to Cicero's *De Divinatione.*

165. *whylom,* formerly.

169. *streit of herbergage,* cramped of lodging, lacking in quarters.

170. *o,* one.

173. *departen,* separate.

175. *as . . . falle,* as it chanced.

177. *Fer,* far.

179. *aventure,* chance.

180. *That . . . commune,* That governs us all alike.

182. *mette,* dreamed.

185. *ther,* where.

188. *abrayde,* started suddenly.

190. *took . . . keep,* paid no heed to this.

191. *Him thoughte,* it seemed to him. *nas,* was not.

194. *slawe,* slain.

196. *morwe-tyde,* morning-time.

198. *donge,* dung.

200. *Do . . . arresten,* have that cart stopped.

201. *sooth to sayn,* to say the truth.

206. *in,* inn.

210. *agon,* gone.

213. *mette,* dreamed.

214. *lette,* delay.

216. *to donge,* to put dung upon.

222. *upright,* lying flat on his back.

223. *ministres,* officers of justice.

224. *kepe and reulen,* guard and rule.

225. *Harrow,* a cry of distress. *lyth,* lies.

226. *What,* why.

227. *out-sterte,* started out.

231. *biwreyest,* makest known.

233. *wlatsom,* loathsome.

235. *it heled be,* it to be concealed.

238. *ministres,* officers of justice.

239. *han hent,* have seized. *pyned,* punished.

240. *engyned,* tortured.

241. *biknewe,* confessed.

246. *gabbe,* lie, jest.

247. *han,* have.

248. *fer,* far.

251. *mery,* pleasant.

252. *agayn,* toward.

253. *as hem leste,* as they desired.

254. *Iolif,* cheerful. *hir,* their.

255. *casten hem,* plan.

256. *oo,* one.

258. *mette,* dreamed. *agayn,* toward.

259. *Him thoughte,* it seemed to him.

260. *abyde,* wait.

261. *wende,* go away.

262. *dreynt,* drowned.

263. *wook,* woke. *mette,* dreamed.

264. *And . . . lette,* And urged him to abandon his journey.

265. *abyde,* stay.

268. *agaste,* terrify.

269. *lette . . . thinges,* give up doing my business.

271. *swevenes,* dreams. *Iapes,* deceptions.

273. *mase,* maze.

274. *shal,* shall be.

276. *for-sleuthen,* lose through sloth. *tyde,* time.

277. *God . . . me,* God knows it causes me sorrow.

279. *y-seyled,* sailed.

280. *eyled,* ailed.

281. *botme rente,* bottom burst.

286. *ensamples,* examples. *maistow lere,* mayest thou learn.

287. *recchelees,* careless.

290. *seint Kenelm.* 'Kenelm succeeded his father Kenulph on the throne of the Mercians in 821 at the age of seven years, and was murdered by order of his aunt, Quenedreda. He was subsequently made a saint (Wright).'

292. *Mercenrike,* Mercia. *mette,* dreamed.

293. *A lyte er,* a little while before.

294. *avisioun,* vision. *say,* saw.

295. *norice,* nurse. *del,* part, bit.

296. *kepe,* guard.

297. *For traisoun,* for fear of treason. *nas,* was not.

298. *litel . . . told,* little heed hath he paid.

300. *levere,* rather.

301. *legende,* life of a saint.

302. *yow,* to you.

303-4. *Macrobeus.* Macrobius (early 5th century) wrote a commentary on Cicero's *Somnium Scipionis.*

305. *Affermeth,* confirms.

307. *loketh, look,* 2d pers. plur. imperative.

308. *Daniel.* See Daniel, ii.

310-315. *Joseph.* See Genesis, xxxix-xli.

311. *Wher,* whether, or where.

312. *falle,* occur.

316. *actes,* history. *remes,* realms, kingdoms.

318. *Cresus,* Crœsus. *Lyde,* Lydia.

12. *Sangreal*, Holy Grail.

16. *to-fore*, before.

20. *paynims*, pagans.

24. *Hector*, son of Priam, and champion of the Trojans.

26. *Alexander the Great* (356–323 B. C.), the famous king of Macedon.

b (col. 2). 1. *Julius Cæsar* (100–44 B. C.), the famous Roman general, statesman, and writer.

6. *Joshua*, the successor of Moses as leader of the Israelites. See the Book of Joshua.

7. *behest*, promise.

8. *David*, the second king of Israel, 1055–1015 B. C.

9. *Judas Maccabæus* (d. 160 B. C.), a famous Jewish patriot and warrior.

13. *stalled*, installed, placed.

18. *Charlemagne*, king of the Franks and emperor of the Romans. Crowned emperor, 800 A. D.

21. *Godfrey of Boloine*, Godefroy de Bouillon (1061–1100), a leader of the first Crusade.

24. *King Edward the Fourth*, king of England 1461–83.

25. *instantly*, insistently, earnestly.

20. *a*. 21. *aretted*, reckoned.

25. *Glastonbury*, a town in Somerset, England, seat of an abbey.

26. *Polichronicon.* Ranulf Higden (died c. 1363), a monk of Chester, wrote *Polychronicon*, a general history, in Latin.

29. *translated*, removed.

31. *Bochas*, Boccacio (1313–1375), a celebrated Italian novelist and poet. *De Casu Principum* [On the Fall of Princes] recounts the misfortunes of famous men.

33. *Galfridus*, Geoffrey of Monmouth (c. 1100–1152?), whose fabulous Latin *History of the Kings of Britain* purported to be based largely upon a 'British book.'

40–1. *Patricius . . . Imperator*, 'Noble Arthur, Emperor of Britain, Gaul, Germany and Dacia.'

b. 1. *Camelot*, a legendary spot in England where Arthur was said to have had his court.

23. *conning*, knowledge, skill.

25. *emprised*, undertaken.

21. *a*. 28. *gat*, begot.

36. *assotted*, infatuated, besotted.

b. 43. *did do make*, had made.

47. *made a parliament*, called a council.

57. *prefixed*, set, decided upon.

22. *a*. 6. *longed*, belonged.

12. *garnished*, furnished, supplied.

14. *wist*, heard, learned.

21. *prevail*, avail.

29. *sithen*, afterward.

37. *book and bell and candle*, a reference to formal ecclesiastical curses.

49. *orgulist*, most arrogant, insolent.

b. 1. *sonds*, messages.

12. *made write*, had written.

18. *depraved*, calumniated, vilified.

34. *term*, length of time.

46. *new-fangle*, fickle.

58. *carracks*, large, round-built vessels.

23. *a*. 1. *let*, prevent.

12. *maugre*, in spite of. *power*, army.

31. *affiance*, trust, confidence.

44. *cankered*, inveterate.

45. *danger*, subjection, control.

51. *cedle*, schedule, note.

56. *French book.* As Caxton explains in his preface, Malory's sources are chiefly French.

b. 27. *straitly bestead*, hard pressed.

29. *let . . . king*, had him crowned king.

24. *a*. 2. *pight a new field*, prepared for another battle. *Barham Down*, a short distance south of Canterbury.

31. *Trinity Sunday*, the eighth Sunday after Easter.

45. *chaflet*, platform.

b. 9. *weened*, thought.

23. *an*, if.

27. *parties*, sides.

33. *as to-morn*, to-morrow.

34–5. *proffer you largely*, make liberal offers.

38. *worshipfully*, honorably, respectfully.

44. *wightly*, swiftly, strongly.

46. *avision*, vision.

25. *a*. 16. *everych*, each, every one.

43. *beams*, horns.

51. *leaning*, thrusting.

b. 1. *devoir*, duty, service.

3. *stinted*, ceased.

7. *wood*, mad.

41. *Tide*, befall.

54. *foin*, thrust.

58. *bur*, an iron ring, to prevent the hand from slipping.

26. *a*. 17. *wit*, know.

20. *yede*, went.

22. *pillers*, pillagers.

31. *rede*, advice.

53. *brast*, burst.

b. 19. *lightly*, quickly.

46. *wap*, ripple. *wan*, grow wan.

27. *a*. 39. *Avilion*, or Avalon, the Land of the Blessed in Celtic mythology.

48. *holt*, a hill with a grove on it.

b. 3. *graven*, dug.

6. *flemed*, put to flight.

10. *deeming*, judging.

15. *besant*, a gold coin, first coined at Byzantium.

20. *still*, always.

39. *read*, tell.

28. *a*. 55. *let*, prevent.

b. 10. *hard bestead*, hard pressed.

21. *unhap*, misfortune.

35. *will my worship*, wish my honor.

43. *spered*, asked, inquired.

29. *a*. 4. *dole*, alms.

14. *Requiem*, the mass for the dead, the first words of the Introit being *Requiem aeternam dona eis.*

19. *dured*, lasted.

29. *sithen*, since.

32. *disease*, trouble.

50. *still*, always, constantly.

53. *boot*, use, advantage.

b. 30. *wrack*, ruin.

30. *a*. 4. *perfection*, the religious or monastic life.

21-2. *gray or white*, referring to the habit, or costume.

52. *assoil*, absolve.

b. 10-11. *overthwart and endlong*, across and up and down.

28. *still*, continually.

30. *lust*, desire.

43. *took no force*, paid no heed.

50. *by then*, when.

53. *purvey*, provide.

53. *horse bier*, bier drawn by horses.

31. *a.* 12. *yede*, went.

35. *Dirige*. An antiphon in the office for the dead begins with the word *Dirige* ('direct').

37. *brenning*, burning.

53. *cered cloth of Raines*, waxed cloth of Raines (in Brittany).

b. 13. *careful*, troubled.

15. *orgulity*, arrogance, pride.

32. *dwined*, dwindled.

48. *steven*, voice.

49. *longeth*, belong.

50. *need you*, be necessary to you.

55-6. *will into*, wills to go into.

58. *houseled*, given the Eucharist.

32. *a.* 1. *anealed*, anointed.

30. *dretching of swevens*, tormenting of dreams.

53. *quire*, choir.

58. *worship*, honor, dignity.

b. 45. *rest*, a loop or hook attached to the armor, to steady the spear in a charge.

33. *a.* 18. *favor of makers*, fabrication of poets.

22. *quick*, alive.

b. 32. *Caxton . . . fecit*, 'Caxton caused me to be made.'

THE NUT-BROWN MAID

It is to be observed that this poem is a dialogue in stanzas, between a lover and his lass. The man speaks the first stanza.

34. 3. *dele*, bit. *agayne*, in return.

11. *mone*, moan.

20. *use*, practice.

27. *ton*, one.

29. *red*, advice, course. *can*, know.

33. *departe*, separate.

37. *distrayne*, distress.

35. 45. *leve*, stay, remain.

47. *anoon*, at once.

49. *rede*, advise.

58. *parte*, share.

59. *thoo*, those.

64. *lyeve*, live.

65. *than*, then.

71. *ony*, any.

75. *rescous*, rescue.

82. *greeve*, grieve, hurt, wound.

88. *rove*, roof.

89. *than*, then.

91. *Syth*, since.

93. *oo*, one.

98. 94. *perdé*, French *par dieu*, less strong than 'by God.'

97. *lust*, desire, wish.

103. *dere*, animals.

104. *vitayle*, victuals, food.

106. *hele*, health.

110. *here*, hair. *ere*, ear.

127. *bee*, by, concerning.

131. *dey*, die.

135. *power*, poor. *yede*, should go.

136. *be*, by.

137. *red*, advice. *can*, know.

146. *purveid me*, provided myself.

37. 153. *curteis*, courteous. *our*, hour.

165. *on the splene*. The meaning of this expression is uncertain.

172. *be*, by.

179. *echeon*, each one.

ENGLISH AND SCOTTISH POPULAR BALLADS

ROBIN HOOD AND GUY OF GISBORNE

Although tradition has persistently maintained that Robin Hood was actually a historical character of the early 14th century, the early historians seem to have had no information concerning him except what they found in the ballads themselves. In any case, whatever his origin, Robin Hood was the hero of ballads of outlawry as early as 1377. His generosity, fair-dealing, tenderness, and wit subsequently established him as a true English hero.

38. 1. *shawes*, groves. *sheene*, beautiful. *shradds* coppices.

5. *woodweele*, woodlark.

6. *a lyne*, of linden.

7. *wight*, stout.

10. *froe*, from.

12. *wrocken*, avenged. *towe*, two.

13. *Sweavens*, dreams.

17. *Buske*, dress, prepare. *bowne*, prepare.

39. 29. *capull-hyde*, horse-hide.

36. *ffarley*, strange.

39. *ken*, know.

40. *And*, if.

43. *bale*, evil.

50. *slade*, valley.

52. *stockes*, wooden blocks, stumps.

56. *Crist his*, Christ's. *mayne*, strength.

58. *ffaine*, glad.

59. *veiwe*, yew.

60. *ffetteled*, prepared.

63. *Woe worth thee*, woe be to thee.

66. *boote*, help.

77. *tane*, taken.

88. *lyne*, linden.

95. *wilfull*, astray.

96. *tyde*, time.

103. *tow*, two. *whether*, which of the two.

40. 107. *masteryes*, trials of skill.

110. *steven*, hour.

111. *shroggs*, wands.

113. *in twinn*, apart.

114. *prickes*, targets, bull's eyes.

122. *cold*, could.

124. *garlande*, 'the ring within which the prick (or bull's eye) was set.'

126. *pricke-wande*, pole, stick.

150. *ffettled*, made ready.

151. *reacheles*, careless.

156. *moy*, maiden.

161. *awkwarde*, back-handed.
177. *capull-hyde*, horse-hide.
41. 186. *lowe*, hill.
192. *tyde*, time.
208. *steven*, voice.
209. *loset*, loosed.
212. *belive*, quickly.
222. *boote*, help.
224. *rawstye*, rusty.
234. *in twinn*, in twain.

ROBIN HOOD'S DEATH AND BURIAL

3. *broom*, a kind of shrub.
12. *win*, go.
42. 48. *dree*, endure, hold out.
53. *boon*, favor.

THE BATTLE OF OTTERBURN

During the reign of **Richard II** (1377–1399), the Scots frequently harried in the northern part of England. In 1388 an army of Scots, under James, Earl of Douglas, besieged Newcastle for three days. At this time Douglas met Harry Percy, 'Hotspur,' in single combat, captured his lance and banner, and boasted that he would raise the banner on the Scottish castle at Dalkeith. Percy collected a force, pursued the Scots, and attacked them at night in a hand to hand fight, at Otterburn, near the frontier. Although Douglas was killed, the English were defeated and Percy was taken prisoner.

1. *Lamasse*, Lammas, August 1st.
2. *wynnes*, dry.
3. *bowynd*, prepared.
4. *praye*, prey.
5. *yerlle of Fyffe*. The Earl of Fife, son of the Scottish king, was ravaging in the northwest of England, about Carlisle. He passed over the Solway Firth.
7. *wolde*, would.
8. *raysse*, raid.
9–11. The places mentioned are in old Northumberland.
12. *Styrande*, stirring.
13. *brente*, burned.
16. *bowyn*, prepared.
17. *berne*, man. *bent*, field.
43. 31. *march-man*, warrior of the border.
32. *kepte Barwyke* guarded Berwick upon Tweed.
34. *on hyght*, aloud.
35. *and thow byste*, if thou art.
39. *syne*, since. *logeyng*, lodging.
46. *envye*, injury.
48. *tone*, one.
52. *logeed*, lodged.
53. *roo*, roe. *rinnes*, runs.
59. *the tyll*, to thee.
65. *pype*, pipe, a measure for wine,— 126 wine-gallons.
73. *pyght*, fixed.
74. *gettyng*, booty.
75. *syne*, afterwards.
76. *gresse*, grass.
77. *hoved*, tarried. *bent*, field.
78. *wache*, watch, sentinel.
79. *ware on*, aware of.
81. *prycked*, rode.

86. *wynne*, joy.
91. *brede*, broad.
92. *haylle*, hale, strong.
96. *garre*, make, cause.
98. *and . . . lesse*, if it were a lie.
100. *peysse*, peace.
101. *yerle of Mentaye*, Earl of Menteith. *eme*, uncle.
102. *forwarde*, van.
103. *cawte and kene*, wary and bold.
105. *Bowghan*, Buchan.
110. *bowen*, ready.
44. 115. *can*, gan, did.
116. *hyght*, promised.
121. *agayne*, back.
122. *upon hye*, in a loud voice.
128. *schoote*, sent.
130. *ryall*, royal. *rowght*, rout, company.
132. *rowynde*, round.
138. *layne*, lie.
140. *agayne*, against.
155. *Wende*, go.
156. *yee*, eye.
161. *weynde . . . growende*, go from this ground.
162. *onfowghten*, not fought, without fight.
165. *rynde*, flayed.
166. *mykkel maye*, powerful maid.
168. *Wyth*, by.
171. *waryson*, reward.
174. 'And cross himself in the name of the Trinity.'
181. *perte*, part, side.
183. *lucettes*, pikes (fish).
199. *swapped*, smote. *whyll that the*, until they.
200. *collayne*, Cologne steel.
45. 201. *bassonnettes*, steel caps, helmets.
202. *roke*, reek, steam.
210. *rede*, guessed.
215. *thee*, they. *beette*, beat.
218. *stounde*, hour, time.
225. *eke a*, every.
229. *freke*, man.
230. *stowre*, battle.
231. *drye*, endure.
238. *Grysely*, fearfully.
263. *Seyng*, seeing.
268. *makes*, mates, husband. *fette*, fetched.
276. *borowed*, ransomed.

CAPTAIN CAR OR EDOM O GORDON

Adam Gordon was deputy, in 1571, for Queen Mary in the north of Scotland, where he encountered the hostility of the Forbeses, who supported the king's party. On one occasion he sent his soldiers to take the castle of Towie in the queen's name. After the lady of the house had refused, the eager soldiers were commanded by their leader, Captain Ker, to set fire to the castle. Tradition has it that the lady and twenty-seven others were burned to death.

1. *Martynmas*, Nov. 11th.
4. *holde*, castle.
46. 5. *Syck*, sike, sick. *to-lowe*, too-too.
9. *wether*, whither.
17. *lend*, leaned.

34. *bande*, bond, agreement.
36. *ere*, possess.
38. *whitt and redda*, white and red.
45. *pestilett*, pistol.
50. *pellettes*, bullets.
54. *lowne*, servant, worthless person.
60. *eare*, heir.
64. *waran*, protection, surety.
70. *knet*, knotted.
80. *smoldereth*, smothers.
82. *ffee*, property.
86. *the*, thee.
47. 101. *busk*, prepare. *bowne*, make ready.
104. *or*, before.
108. *dele*, deal, bit.
121. *ought*, had.

THE WIFE OF USHER'S WELL

7. *carline wife*, old woman, or perhaps, wealthy woman, low-born woman.
8. *gane*, gone.
14. *fashes*, troubles.
17. *Martinmass*, Nov. 11th.
20. *birk*, birch.
21. *syke*, ditch, trench.
22. *sheugh*, ditch, furrow.
27. *a'*, all.
41. *daw*, dawn.
42. *channerin*, fretting.
43. *Gin*, if.
44. *sair*, sore. *maun*, must.
46. *byre*, cow-house.

KEMP OWYNE

Kemp Owyne is Owain, one of King Arthur's knights. The adventure here ascribed to him is that of disenchantment through kisses.
6. *dee*, do.
28. 12. *borrow*, set free, ransom.
34. *wi*, with.

THE DÆMON LOVER

20. *kend*, knew.
30. *baith*, both.
31. *ain*, own.
29. 35. *taffetie*, fine silk.
41. *drumlie*, gloomy, frightened. *ee*, eye.
53. *win*, arrive.
58. *strack*, struck.

LORD RANDALL

4. *wald*, would.
11. *broo*, water in which something has been boiled.

SIR PATRICK SPENS

3. *guid*, good.
9. *braid*, broad.
14. *lauch*, laugh.
50. 29. *laith*, loth.
31. *owre a'*, ere all.
32. *aboone*, above.
38. *kems*, combs.
39. *ain*, own.
41. *owre*, over.

THOMAS RYMER

There is considerable evidence that Thomas the Rimer was one Thomas of Erceldoune, who lived in southern Scotland in the 13th century. Tradition has it that he was a prophet, as well as a poet and that he was frequently visited by fairies.
4. *fernie brae*, ferny hill.
7. *ilka tett*, every lock.
10. *till*, to.
17. *maun*, must.
20. *wae*, woe.
44. *fairlies*, wonders.
49. *braid*, broad.
50. *lillie leven*, pleasant lawn.
56. *gae*, go.
59. *gin ae*, if one.
61. *even*, smooth.

BONNY BARBARA ALLAN

51. 1. *Martinmass*, Nov. 11th.
8. *Gin*, if.
9. *hooly*, slowly.
17. *dinna*, do not.
19. *gae*, go.
28. *reft*, deprived.
31. *jow*, stroke. *geid*, gave.

THE TWA SISTERS

1. *bowr*, bower.
10. *brotch*, brooch.
12. *sair*, sore.
15. *brast*, burst.
22. *stane*, stone.
25. *jaw*, wave, current.
27. *Ise*, I shall. *mack*, make. *a' my lan*, all my land.
29. *goud*, gold.
32. *fa*, fall. *han*, hand.
33. 'It separated me and my world's mate.'
35. *Gars*, makes. *gae*, go.
52. 46. *sma*, small.
47. *braw*, fine, handsome.
49. *sae gryte*, so great.
58. *nextin*, next. *syne*, afterwards.

THE CRUEL BROTHER

1. *ba*, ball.
5. *baith*, both.
18. *maun*, must. *frae a'*, from all.
31. *closs*, court-yard.
46. *pall*, cloak.
48. *gowden*, golden.
53. 57. *sair*, sore.
58. *rive*, tear.

EDWARD

1. *dois*, does. *brand*, sword, knife.
4. *gang*, go.
7. *guid*, good.
8. *mair*, more.
13. *reid-roan steid*, red-roan steed.
16. *frie*, good.
20. *dule ye drie*, sorrow ye suffer.
25. *drie*, suffer.
35. *ha*, hall.

37. *tul*, till.　*fa*, fall.
45. *thrae*, through.
53. *sall*, shall.　*beir*, bear.

WYATT: A RENOUNCING OF LOVE

55. 3. *Senec*, Lucius Annæus Seneca (4 B. C.–65 A. D.), a famous Roman Stoic philosopher and writer of tragedies. *Plato* (429 or 427–347 B. C.), a famous Greek philosopher.
8. *lever*, dearer.

AN EARNEST SUIT

4. *grame*, sorrow.

THE LOVER COMPLAINETH

7. *grave*, make an impression upon, engrave.
56. 24. *playn*, to complain.

OF THE MEAN AND SURE ESTATE

John Poins (died 1558), an intimate friend of Wyatt, lived chiefly at the English court.
6. *souse*, drench.
10. *dight*, put in order.
14. *store*, supply, abundance. *stroyèd*, destroyed.
26. *cater*, caterer.
28. *charge*, care, burden.
31. *jape*, jest.
53. *steaming*, gleaming.
61. *tho*, then.
57. 88. *hay*, snare.　*conies*, rabbits.
105. *dome*, judgment.

HENRY HOWARD: DESCRIPTION OF SPRING

58. 1. *soote*, sweet.
2. *eke*, also.
4. *turtle*, turtle-dove.　*make*, mate.
5. *spray*, branch, stem.　*springs*, sprouts.
8. *flete*, float.
11. *mings*, mixes.

DESCRIPTION AND PRAISE OF HIS LOVE GERALDINE

1. *Tuscan*, Tuscany.
2. *her*, their.
3. *Western isle*. See line 5.
4. *Camber's cliffs*, the cliffs of Wales.
59. 9. *Hunsdon*, in Hertfordshire, some 30 miles north of London.
11. *Hampton*, Hampton Court, a royal palace near London.
12. *Windsor*, Windsor Castle.
13. *kind*, nature.

COMPLAINT OF THE LOVER DISDAINED

1. *Cyprus*. The island of Cyprus was the especial home of Venus.

COMPLAINT OF THE ABSENCE OF HER LOVER

4. *eke*, also.
5. *wonted*, was accustomed.
14. *avail*, profit, advantage.
60. 33. *drencheth*, drowns.
38. *doubtful*, full of fear.

A PRAISE OF HIS LOVE

4. *sayn*, say.
7. *troth*, fidelity.
8. *Penelope*, the proverbially faithful wife of Odysseus.
11. *mo*, more.
21. *kind*, nature.
25. *sith*, since.

DESCRIPTION OF THE RESTLESS STATE OF A LOVER

19. *list*, please.
24. *use*, practice.
31. *plain*, complain.
61. 44. *agazed*, wrapt, amazed.
51. *teen*, sorrow.

THE MEANS TO ATTAIN HAPPY LIFE

1. *Martial* (43–104 A. D.), a Latin poet. Wrote chiefly epigrams.
5. *egall*, equal.
9. *mean*, moderate.
13. *debate*, dispute, quarrel.

OF THE DEATH OF SIR THOMAS WYATT

7. *stithe*, anvil.
14. *reft*, bereft.
17. *served in foreign realms*. See p. 54 above.
21. *none affect*, no affection.

VIRGIL'S ÆNEID

1. *whisted*, became silent.
6. *Phrygian*, of Phrygia, that country or division of Asia Minor in which Troy was situated. *wailful*, lamentable.
10. *Myrmidon*. The Myrmidons were led to the Trojan War by Achilles. *Dolopës*. The Dolopës came from Thessaly to fight on the Greek side before Troy.
62. 17. *plaint eschews*, avoids complaint.
35. *fet*, fetched, reached.
40. *Pyrrhus*, a famous Greek hero of the Trojan War. *pight*, camped.
42. *scathful*, harmful.
43. *Behight*, promised.

SACKVILLE: THE INDUCTION

63. 2. *treen*, trees.
3. *Saturnus*, Saturn, one of the planets, of unpropitious influence.
7. *tapets*, tapestries, figuratively used for foliage. *bloom*, flower.
10. *soote*, sweet.
11. *Boreas*, the north wind.
21. *whereas*, where.
24. *Venus*, goddess of love. *Hermes*, Mercury, messenger of Jupiter.
25. *Mars*, god of war. *will*, desire, urge.
27. *Virgo*, the Virgin, one of the constellations, and a sign of the zodiac.
28. *Thetis*, goddess of the sea.
29. *Scorpio*, *Sagittarius*, Scorpion and Archer, signs of the zodiac.
30. *prest*, ready.
32. *Bear*, a constellation.

26. *Phaeton,* son of the sun-god.

38. *prest,* ready.

40. *stent,* end.

42. *Titan,* the sun personified.

43. *Cynthea,* the moon.

64. 48. *chare,* car, chariot.

51. *lusty,* pleasant.

53. *fade,* faded.

57. *leams,* flames, rays.

60. *Phœbus,* the sun-god.

68. *peers,* noblemen of especial dignity.

69. *descrive,* describe.

74. *wight,* creature, person. *forewaste,* completely wasted.

75. *brast,* burst.

76. *fold,* folded.

77. *ruth,* pity.

80. *welkèd,* withered, pale. *besprent,* sprinkled.

90. *doom,* judgment.

93. *distrained,* pained, torn.

96. *apart,* set aside.

97. *dewie,* lamentation, sorrow.

100. *stint,* cease. *spill,* destroy, kill.

102. *dure,* last, endure. *attaint,* tainted, afflicted.

103. *forefaint,* very faint.

106. *distrained,* distressed.

109. *Furies,* the Eumenides: Alecto, Megæra, and Tisiphone.

111. *Lethe,* the river of oblivion, in Hades.

112. *reave,* take away.

65. 119. *dure,* last, endure.

120. *brayed,* started.

122. *shright,* shrieked.

123. *to-dashed,* dashed to pieces.

125. *eft,* again.

131. *avale,* abate.

134. *sith,* since.

141. *stike,* stich, verse, stanza.

143. *Æölus,* god of the winds.

145. *bedrent,* drenched.

161. *won,* dwelling.

166. *silly,* simple, innocent.

175. *shright,* shrieked.

176. *grisly,* dreadful.

179. *whilom,* formerly, once. *bare swing,* bore sway.

191. *unmeet,* unseemly, unusual.

66. 202. *Astoined,* astounded.

208. *yeding,* going.

210. *clepèd,* called. *Avern,* a small lake near modern Naples, anciently believed to be the entrance to the infernal regions.

212. *swelth,* overflow.

219. *besprent,* sprinkled.

221. *stent,* cease.

223. *thoughtful,* sorrowful.

233. *proffered,* put forth.

236. *staring of his hair,* hair standing on end.

237. *'Stoined,* astounded.

243. *far forth,* extremely, excessively.

250. *fet,* fetched.

253. *somedeal,* somewhat.

257. *clouts,* tatters, rags.

258. *scrip,* wallet.

260. *for most,* chiefly.

262. *wot,* knows.

67. 268. *ruth,* pity.

271. *breres,* briars.

284. *keep,* heed.

291. *Reaver,* robber, one who deprives.

292. *tide,* happen.

294. *Crœsus,* the fabulously wealthy king of Lydia, who came to the throne in 560 B. C. Thus, in Homeric legend, a beggar of gigantic stature.

297. *cheer,* countenance. *still,* ever, always.

299. *the sisters,* the fates: Clotho, Lachesis, and Atropos.

306. *forewaste,* wasted away.

308. *beseeck,* beseech.

309. *But and,* although.

313. *eld,* old age.

328. *fain,* eagerly.

333. *pilled,* bare. *with eld forlore,* wasted with age.

68. 336. *For brief,* in brief.

340. *brook,* use, endure, enjoy.

342. *recure,* recovery.

346. *grisly,* terrible.

361. *maw,* stomach.

371. *Enthrilling,* forcing in. *reave,* deprive.

374. *daunts,* subdues (by fear).

376. *peers,* noblemen.

381. *eftsoons,* forthwith, immediately.

382. *affrayèd,* frightened.

383. *dight,* provided. *pardé,* French *par Dieu.*

389. *imbrued,* covered.

393. *whilom,* formerly, once.

398. *forehewed,* hewed to pieces.

399. *targe,* shield.

401. *Debate,* dispute, contest, war.

402. *fillet,* a band for tying about the hair.

405. *Darius,* king of Persia 521–486 B. C. *power,* army.

407. *Macedo,* Alexander the great (356–323 B. C.), king of Macedonia.

69. 409. *daunted,* subdued.

410–418. *Hannibal* (247–183 B. C.), a famous Carthaginian general, among whose victories against the Romans are those of the Trebia, of Lake Trasimene, and of Cannæ. At Cannæ the Roman consul Paulus was killed. Hannibal was finally defeated by Scipio Africanus Major, at Zama, in 202 B. C.

419. *Cæsar . . . Pompey.* The civil war between Julius Cæsar and Pompey was ended by the total defeat of Pompey at Pharsalia in 48 B. C.

423. *Sulla and Marius.* The civil war between the Romans Marius and Sulla began in 88 B. C.

425. *Cyrus,* the Great (d. 529 B. C.), founded the Persian empire.

428. *Xerxes* (c. 519–464 B. C.), king of Persia.

432. *Thebes,* a city in Bœotia, Greece, destroyed by Alexander the Great.

433. *Tyrus,* Tyre, despoiled by Alexander the Great.

440. *Priam,* king of Troy.

441. *lin,* restrain myself.

442. *sith,* since.

445. *quail,* fall.

449. *Hector,* son of Priam.

451. *boot*, reward, outcome.

452. *hugy horse*, the wooden horse by means of which the Greeks gained entrance into Troy.

463. *Cassandra*, a prophetess, daughter of Priam. By command of Apollo, her prophecies, though true, were always discredited.

464. *Pallas' house*, temple of Pallas. *spercled*, disheveled.

465. *rout*, mob. *empaled*, pierced.

469. *Pyrrhus*, the Greek who slew Priam.

468. *baign*, bath.

475. *Ilium*, the citadel of Troy. *gledes*, flames.

476. *Neptunus*, god of the sea.

480. *Acheron*, a river in Hades.

70. 482. *grisly*, terrible. *Charon*, the ferryman who transported the souls of the dead over the rivers of the underworld.

486. *rout*, crowd.

491. *fraughted*, freighted, laden.

494. *hoise*, hoist.

499. *Cerberus*, the three-headed watch-dog at the entrance to the infernal regions.

501. *Foredinning*, filling with a din.

504. *peased*, held his peace, became silent.

512. *puled*, whined.

517. *yfear*, together.

527. *whilom*, formerly, once.

530. *erewhile*, a while ago.

532. *kesar*, emperor. *peer*, nobleman.

ROGER ASCHAM: THE SCHOOLMASTER

71. *a*. 6. *Circe's Court*. In Greek mythology Circe was an enchantress who, attended by four nymphs, feasted all persons who approached her dwelling. Anyone, however, who tasted the contents of her magic cup was turned into a beast.

32. *Inglese . . . incarnato*, 'An Englishman Italianate is a devil incarnate.'

b. 19. *policy*, cunning.

24. *discoursing*, reasoning, argumentative.

32. *fond*, foolish.

35. *honest*, virtuous.

72. *a*. 2. *charge*, duty, office.

5. *Paul's Cross*, a cross situated near the northeast angle of old St. Paul's, in the churchyard. From it great public assemblies were addressed and sermons preached. The 'Paul's Cross Sermons' are still preached on Sunday morning.

13. *Louvain*, a city in the province of Brabant, Belgium. Religious books were often printed here.

14. *wink*, close the eyes.

25. *St. Paul saith*, Galatians, v, 19ff.

57. *canons*, ecclesiastics retained for the performance of divine service in a cathedral or collegiate church. *Morte Arthur*, a compilation of prose romances on the life and death of King Arthur and the knights of the Round Table, translated largely from French romances by Sir Thomas Malory and printed by Caxton in 1485. See p. 19.

b. 6. *shifts*, tricks. *Sir Launcelot*, 'Launcelot of the Lake,' one of the most famous of the knights of the Round Table, who guiltily loved Arthur's queen, Guinevere.

6-7. *Wife of King Arthur*, Guinevere.

7. *Sir Tristram*, of Lyonesse, another famous Knight of the Round Table. His love for Isolde, wife of King Mark of Cornwall, forms the subject of many romances.

9. *Sir Lamerock*, a knight of the Round Table. *wife of King Lot*. King Lot in Malory's *Morte d'Arthur* was a King of Orkney who married Margawse, sister of Arthur.

23. *fond*, foolish.

73. *a*. 6. *lewd*, unlearned, vulgar.

16. *Plato* (429 or 427-547 B. C.), a famous Greek philosopher, disciple of Socrates and teacher of Aristotle.

18. *abominabiles . . . suis*, 'made destestable in their studies.'

20. *Dixit insipiens in corde suo no est Deus*, 'The fool hath said in his heart there is no God,' Psalm. xiv, 1.

29. *Triumphs of Petrarch*, an allegorical work by the celebrated Italian poet Petrarch (1304-1374).

31. *Tully's Offices*. Marcus Tullius Cicero (106-43 B. C.) was a famous Roman orator, statesman, and philosopher. The work here referred to is his *De Officiis* (On Duties).

32. *Boccaccio* (1313-1375), eminent Italian writer, author of *The Decameron*, a collection of 100 tales.

45. *Whether*, which.

50. *general councils*, composed of bishops and theologians from different nations, convened to consider questions of church doctrine, discipline, and the like.

53. *Luther*, Martin Luther (1483-1546), leader of the Protestant Reformation in Germany.

b. 2. *epicures*, those who held the opinions of the Greek philosopher Epicurus (342-270 B. C.), who taught that pleasure is the only possible end of rational action and that ultimate pleasure is freedom.

22. *list*, like, choose.

23. *Mysteries of Moses*, the rites of the Jewish religion instituted by Moses. See the Book of Leviticus. *Law and ceremonies*. See Deuteronomy.

29. *Horace*, Roman poet (65-8 B. C.). Quotation from *Satires*, i, 5, 100.

51. *Pygius*, Pighius (1490-1542), a theologian whose writings were opposed by Calvin. *Machiavelli* (1469-1527), celebrated Italian statesman and author. He was imprisoned and put to the torture on suspicion of conspiring against Giovanni de Medici, but was released and after retiring to his country estate wrote *The Prince*. His name is synonymous with all that is cunning and unscrupulous in diplomacy.

74. *a*. 3-6. *where Christ's doctrine . . . special regard*, Germany.

16. *lust*, desire.

17. *pantocle*, a slipper.

34. *bent enemy*, cf. 'bent on mischief.'

50. *Bridewell*, a celebrated London prison or house of detention. The name has become a generic term for a house of correction or lock-up.

55. *present Pope*, Pius V (1566-1572).

57. *meed*, a reward, gift.

b. 57. *lust*, desire.

75. *a. 2. Guelph,* the papal and popular party in Italy during the struggle between the papacy and the Empire in the Middle Ages. *Ghibelin,* the imperial and aristocratic party in the same struggle.

10. *let,* hindrance; archaic except in the common phrase 'without let or hindrance.'

JOHN LYLY: EUPHUES AND HIS ENGLAND

76. *a. 4. This queen.* Mary was queen from 1553 to 1558.

5. *age of twenty-two years.* At her accession to the throne, in 1558, Elizabeth (born 1533) was actually twenty-five years of age.

8. *a prisoner.* Queen Mary had imprisoned Elizabeth in the Tower of London. *Prince,* used properly, by extension of meaning, to designate a royal personage of either sex.

28. *Zeno,* a philosopher of Elea (born c. 488 B. C.), was mentioned in classical times as an example of patience.

29. *Eretricus,* apparently Lyly's own invention.

30. *Lycurgus,* either the Spartan legislator (9th century B. C.), or the Athenian orator (c. 396–c. 323 B. C.).

b. 9. spill, destroy.

10. *proffer,* offer.

14. *Aristides* (d. 468 B. C.?), an Athenian general and politician, was exiled through the influence of his great rival, Themistocles.

16. *Alexander.* Lyly's reference is uncertain.

21. *bills,* requests.

23. *resembling Julius Cæsar.* There is no authority for this comparison.

33. *government,* reign.

35. *racking,* stretching.

77. *a. 2. Antoninus* (emperor of Rome 138–161 A. D.), surnamed 'Pius.'

12–13. *gun that was shot off.* This was, for Lyly, a recent occurrence, of the summer of 1579.

24. *close,* secret.

29. *in the whale's belly.* An allusion to the story of Jonah. See Jonah i–ii.

31. *in the hot oven.* An allusion to the story of Shadrach, Meshach, and Abednego. See Daniel iii.

40. *list,* please.

43. *Theodosius,* an allusion, perhaps, to the repentance of Theodosius I (c. 346–395), Emperor of the East, after his massacre of the rebels of Thessalonica in 390.

45–8. *Augustus . . . write.* This anecdote is recounted not of Augustus, but of Nero, emperor of Rome 54–68.

47. *we,* royal use of plural for singular.

b. 18. Praxitiles, born at Athens near the end of the 5th century B. C. A famous sculptor. His statues of Venus and Cupid are known, but not his paintings.

19. *her son,* Cupid.

28. *Zeuxis,* a famous Greek painter who flourished at the end of the 5th century B. C.

36. *table,* probably a slab, or tablet.

39. *Apelles,* a famous Greek painter who flourished in the early part of the 4th century B. C.

54. *narrowly,* closely.

78. *a. 6. mold,* pattern, model.

16. *forty years,* actually forty-seven years!

26. *tickle,* uncertain.

27. *twist,* thread.

36. *the bird Ibis.* There is a slender tradition that this bird was distinguished for sweetness of odor.

52–3. *Nicaulia the queen of Saba.* A Nicaulis is mentioned in Josephus' *Antiquities of the Jews,* Bk. viii, Ch. 6.

54. *Nicostrata,* a legendary or mythological Greek prophetess.

58. *Amalasunta,* ruled at Ravenna as queen of the Ostrogoths 522–530 A. D. Tradition ascribes to her numerous literary accomplishments.

58. *b. 1. Aspasia . . . Pericles.* Aspasia was an accomplished woman to whom the famous Athenian statesman, Pericles (c. 495–429 B. C.), was notoriously attached.

2. *Themistoclea . . . Pythagoras.* Pythagoras (c. 582–c. 500 B. C.), a famous Greek philosopher and mathematician, is said to have received instruction from one Aristocleia, a priestess.

7. *escapes,* mistakes.

23. *twice . . . universities.* Queen Elizabeth visited Cambridge for a few days in 1564, and Oxford for a few days in 1566. In both places she attended disputations, and made speeches in Greek and Latin.

39. *Sybarites,* inhabitants of Sybaris in southern Italy, who were noted for luxurious living.

49. *withal,* with.

58. *whenas,* since.

79. *a. 4. gallery of Olympia.* Reference to a famous echoing gallery at Olympia, in Greece.

34. *curses of the Pope.* Pope Pius V directed a bull of excommunication and deposition against Elizabeth in 1570.

b. 17. Alexander, 'the Great' (356–323 B. C.), king of Macedon. *Galba* (3 B. C.–69 A. D.), a Roman emperor.

20. *queen of Navarre,* Margaret d' Angouleme (1492–1549), queen of Henry II of Navarre. Elizabeth, while princess, translated a small book of religious meditations from the French of Margaret.

25–6. *bound . . . palm tree, i.e.,* was victorious in Egypt.

42. *silly,* innocent.

46. *whist,* silent.

47. *bird Attagen.* The habits of this bird here recounted are vouched for by Pliny (23–79 A. D.), the celebrated Roman naturalist.

50. *wade,* go.

80. *a. 21. weams,* blemishes, scars.

SONG (FROM GALLATHEA)

1. *O yes, O yes!* A development from French *oiez,* 'hear ye,' a summons to court.

SIDNEY: AN APOLOGY FOR POETRY

81. *a. 3. so long a career.* Up to this point, Sidney has considered at length the nature and value of poetry, its superiority to history, and the kinds of poetry.

15. *Musa . . . laeso.* Virgil, *Aen.* i. 8.

22. *David.* See, for example, 2 Samuel xxii.

23. *Adrian,* the emperor Hadrian (117–138 A. D.), who wrote both prose and verse. *Sophocles,* the Greek tragic poet (495?–406 B. C.). *Germanicus* (15 B. C.–19 A. D.), nephew of the Emperor Tiberius, took his name from Germany (*Germania*), where he distinguished himself in military service. He wrote prose and poetry.

26. *Robert, King of Sicily,* king of Naples, 1309–1343. He wrote prose and poetry.

27. *King Francis,* Francis I (1515–1547), a generous patron of letters.

b. 1. *King James of Scotland,* James I of Scotland (1405–1436). His *King's Quair* is a pleasant poem in the Chaucerian style.

2. *Bembus,* Pietro Bembo (1470–1547), a cardinal and papal secretary, wrote poetry and prose in both Latin and Italian. *Bibiena,* Bernardo da Bibbiena (1470–1520), one of the tutors of Pope Leo X.

3. *Beza,* Theodore Beza (1519–1605), a French Calvinistic controversialist, composed numerous Latin poems.

4. *Melanchthon,* Philip Melanchthon (1497–1560), a German supporter of Luther, and a Latin poet.

5. *Fracastorius,* Hieronymus Fracastorius (1483–1553), an Italian poet, philosopher, and scientist. *Scaliger,* Julius Cæsar Scaliger (1484–1558) was an Italian literary critic. Sidney appears to have studied diligently his treatise on poetry.

6. *Pontanus,* Johannes Jovius Pontanus (1420–1503), an Italian, wrote both prose and distinguished poetry in Latin. *Muretus,* Marc Antoine Muret (1526–1585), a French orator, jurist, and poet.

7. *George Buchanan* (1506–1582), a distinguished Scotch Latinist.

9. *Hospital of France,* Michael de l'Hospital (1505–1573), a distinguished French lawyer and statesman, wrote numerous Latin poems.

22. *when . . . loudest.* Chaucer, for example, served in the English army under Edward III (1327–1377).

24. *over-faint quietness.* Under Queen Elizabeth England had been at peace for some 25 years.

25. *strew the house,* a figure derived from the practice of strewing rushes on the floor.

27. *mountebanks at Venice,* peddlers of quack medicines, notorious at Venice.

82. *a.* 3. *troubled . . . Mars.* Vulcan, jealous over his wife, forged a net for her.

6. *a piece of a reason,* a considerable reason.

12. *Epaminondas* (418–362 B. C.), a Theban general and statesman, who began his career modestly but effectively as a sort of commissioner of sewers.

22. *Helicon,* a mountain in Bœotia haunted by the Muses.

27. *Queis . . . Titan,* Juvenal, *Sat.* xiv. 36.

40. *Pallas,* Minerva, goddess of wisdom and war.

b. 9. *Dædalus,* invented wings for himself and for his son Icarus.

15. *withal,* with.

27. *Ovid's verse.* Cf. Ovid, *Tristia,* iv. 10. 26.

36. *Troilus and Criseyde.* See p. 4.

43. *Mirror for Magistrates.* See p. 63.

44. *Earl of Surrey's lyrics.* See p. 58.

47. *Shepherd's Calendar.* See p. 104.

48. *eclogues,* pastoral poems.

52. *Theocritus,* a Greek idyllic poet of the 3d century B. C.

53. *Sannazaro* (1458–1530), a famous Italian poet.

83. *a.* 11. *Gorboduc,* or *Ferrex and Porrex,* a tragedy by Thomas Sackville (see p. 63) and Thomas Norton, was first acted in 1561.

15. *Seneca's style.* Lucius Annæus Seneca (c. 4 B. C.–65 A. D.), a Roman philosopher and writer of tragedies.

22. *faulty both in place and time, i.e.,* a violation of the 'unity of place,' which required that all the action of a play occur in one place, and of the 'unity of time,' which required that the time represented by the action should not exceed one revolution of the sun.

27. *Aristotle's precept.* Aristotle (384–322 B. C.) was the most influential of Greek philosophers. The principles of dramatic writing are discussed in his *Poetics.*

53. *traverses,* difficulties.

b. 5. *Eunuch in Terence.* Terence (c. 185–c. 159 B. C.), a Roman comic poet. The *Eunuchus* is not the only play of Terence that violates the 'unity of time.'

10. *Plautus . . . amiss.* Plautus (died 184 B. C.), a Roman writer of comedies. We cannot be certain as to the particular play here referred to.

26. *Calicut,* the capital of Malabar, India.

27. *Pacolet's horse,* the magic horse of Pacolet, a dwarf in the French romance, *Valentine et Orson.* By turning a pin in the horse's head, the rider could convey himself instantly to any part of the world.

29. *Nuntius.* In Greek and Roman tragedy the catastrophe was not usually presented on the stage, but was reported by a messenger.

33. *Horace,* a Roman poet (65–8 B. C.), wrote a work called, *The Art of Poetry.*

34. *Ab ovo* means, 'from the remotest origin.'

38–53. *Polydorus . . . Euripides.* Polydorus was the youngest son of Priam, king of Troy. The story is told in the *Hecuba* of Euripides, a Greek tragic poet (480–406 B. C.).

45. *Hecuba,* second wife of Priam, and mother of Polydorus.

46. *sleight,* trick.

84. *a.* 10. *Apuleius* (born c. 125 A. D.), a Roman philosopher and rhetorician, best known for his romance *The Golden Ass.* The exact significance of Sidney's reference is not clear.

15. *Amphitruo.* This is pure comedy, except for the introduction of gods and heroes.

17. *daintily,* with discrimination.

25. *tract,* course.

38. *conveniency,* suitability.

55. *go . . . bias,* take an unexpected turn. The figure is taken from the game of bowls. *Bias* means 'slope.'

b. 8–9. *Spinning . . . commandment.* Hercules, in his infatuation for Omphale, queen of Lydia, allowed himself to be dressed as a female slave, and spun wool.

20. *forbidden plainly by Aristotle,* in his *Poetics.*

31. *Nil . . . facit,* Juvenal, *Sat.* iii. 152–3. The translation is that of Samuel Johnson.

37. *Thraso,* a bragging, swaggering captain. See the *Eunuchus* of Terence, referred to above.

38–39. *a wry-transformed traveler,* a traveler who unwisely affects foreign manners.

43. *Buchanan.* See 81. *b.* 7, note.

54–5. *lyrical . . . sonnets,* a reference to such miscellanies as *Tottel's Miscellany.* See p. 54.

85. *a.* 33. *coursing of a letter,* such devices as the acrostic, in which the first letters of the several lines spell a word.

35–6. *with figures and flowers,* the printing of the lines in such a way as to form geometrical figures, flowers, and the like.

45. *Tully,* Marcus Tullius Cicero (106–43 B. C.), the Roman orator, philosopher, and statesman. *Demosthenes* (384?–322 B. C.), the greatest of the Greek orators.

47. *Nizolian paper-books,* note-books containing collections of phrases, such as the *Ciceronian Thesaurus* of Marius Nizolius, an Italian professor (born 1498).

58. *Catiline,* the Roman conspirator against whom Cicero directed certain of his most famous orations.

b. 3. *Vivit . . . venit,* from Cicero's first oration against Catiline.

9. *choler,* anger.

14. *'similiter cadences,'* 'endings of similar sound or arrangement,' such as rime in poetry, or repetition.

17. *daintiness,* discrimination.

19. *sophister,* a university term for students qualified for disputations.

29. *stories . . . fishes.* Notice the use of curious illustrations from natural history in Lyly's *Euphues* on p. 79, col. 2.

43. *Antonius and Crassus.* Marcus Antonius (145–87 B. C.), grandfather of the famous Antony of the Triumvirate, was a distinguished Roman orator, and was so honored by Cicero. Publius Licinius Crassus (175–131 B. C.) was a celebrated orator and lawyer.

45. *As Cicero testifieth,* in his dialogue *On Oratory.*

47. *not to set by it,* not to value it.

53. *knacks,* tricks, ornaments.

86. *a.* 13. *pounded,* put in a 'pound,' or enclosure.

23. *awry,* out of a straight line, wrong.

38. *Tower of Babylon.* See Genesis, Chap. xi.

45. *compositions . . . together,* compound words.

56. *Whether,* which.

b. 25. *Now for rime.* Rime is here used in the sense of rhythm.

38. *sdrucciola,* means 'slippery,' 'sliding.' This is the regular Italian term for trisyllabic rime.

87. *a.* 2. *toy,* trifle.

10. *Bembus.* See 81. *b.* 2, note.

12. *Scaliger.* See 81. *b.* 5, note.

15–16. *Clauserus . . . Cornutus.* Lucius Annæus Cornutus (fl. 1st century A. D.) wrote a treatise in Greek *On the Nature of the Gods,* which was translated into Latin by one Clauserus and published about the middle of the 16th century. Sidney is drawing from the preface of this work.

17. *Hesiod,* a Greek poet assigned to the 8th century B. C.

25. *Landin,* Cristofero Landino (1424–1504), an Italian poet and critic, is here referred to for the critical precepts of his *Disputations.*

36. *Libertino patre natus,* Horace, *Satires,* i. 6. 45.

37–8. *Herculea proles,* descendant of Hercules, i.e., royal, noble.

40. *Si . . . possunt,* Virgil, *Aeneid,* ix. 446.

44. *with Dante's Beatrice, or Virgil's Anchises,* that is, in heaven, or in the Elysian fields.

46. *dull-making,* deafening. *Nilus,* the River Nile.

47. *planet-like music,* the music of the spheres produced by the rotation of the planets.

52. *Mome,* stupid person. *Momus,* the son of Night, used as a personification of the critical spirit.

54. *Midas,* king of Phrygia. Having been chosen to judge between the musical abilities of Apollo and Marsyas, he awarded the prize to Marsyas. Apollo changed his ears into those of an ass.

55. *Bubonax.* The story goes that Hipponax, an Ephesian poet (c. 500 B. C.) so savagely satirized the sculptor Bupalus that he hanged himself. The spelling Bubonax is the error either of Sidney or of his printer.

57. *done in Ireland.* It is said that the Irish peasants had a superstitious fear of the bards.

ASTROPHEL AND STELLA

88. *a.* xv, 2. *Parnassus,* a mountain-ridge in Greece, near ancient Delphi, frequented by Apollo, the muses, and the nymphs, and hence the seat of music and poetry.

7. *Petrarch's long-deceasèd woes.* The celebrated Italian poet Petrarch (1304–1374) wrote sonnets to his Laura which later set the fashion for Elizabethan sonneteers.

8. *denizened,* made a citizen, naturalized, adopted.

9. *far-fet,* far-fetched.

10. *bewray,* reveal.

14. *endite,* compose.

xxi, 1. *caustics,* medical substances which burn animal tissue.

2. *windlass,* bewilder.

5. *Plato,* Athenian philosopher (429?–347 B. C.). *but-if,* unless.

89. *a.* lxiv, 9. *Aristotle's wit.* Aristotle (384–322 B. C.), the most famous of Greek philosophers.

10. *Cæsar's bleeding fame.* Julius Cæsar 102–44 B. C.), assassinated by Brutus, Cassius, and others in the senate-house at Rome.

ELEVENTH SONG

90. *a.* 42. *Argus' eyes.* In Greek legend, Argus is famed to have had 100 eyes.

SONG: THE NIGHTINGALE

8. *Tereus.* Tereus abandoned his wife Procné in order to dishonor her sister Philomela.

9. *Philomela.* After having been dishonored by Tereus, Philomela was metamorphosed into a nightingale.

LOVE IS DEAD

8. *franzie.* frenzy.

DORUS TO PAMELA

3. *sterve,* die.
6. *weeds,* clothes.

HAKLUYT'S VOYAGES

DEDICATORY EPISTLE

Francis Walsingham (1536–1590) was a noted English statesman and patron of learning. He served his government as member of parliament, as ambassador to France, as secretary of state, and as special ambassador to several Continental courts.

91. *a.* 8. *Westminster,* Westminster School, established in Westminster Abbey by Henry VIII, and reëstablished by Elizabeth.

11. *Middle Temple,* one of the legal societies in London which provide instruction and examinations for admitting candidates to the bar.

25. *commodities,* articles of merchandise.

b. 15. *Christ Church,* one of the largest and most fashionable of the Oxford colleges.

92. *a.* 3–4. *Sir Edward Stafford* (1552?–1605), a distinguished English diplomatist, much in favor with Queen Elizabeth.

5. *Ligier* (spelled also *lieger, leger, ledger*), an ordinary or resident ambassador.

7. *chargeable,* weighty, onerous.

b. 22. *Aleppo,* in Asiatic Turkey.

23. *Balsara,* Balsar, or Bulsar, a town of British India, on the Gulf of Cambray.

24. *Goa,* on the western coast of India.

26. *river of Plate,* the Rio de la Plata, between Uruguay and the Argentine Republic.

30. *Nova Hispania,* Mexico.

32. *South Sea,* the Pacific Ocean.

33. *Luzones,* islands in the Malay Archipelago in the South Pacific.

THE LAST FIGHT OF THE REVENGE

51. *armada,* a fleet of war-vessels.

53. *Sir Walter Raleigh* (1552–1618), an English courtier, soldier, colonizer, and writer. After a short residence at Oxford, he took up military service. He became a favorite of Elizabeth. In 1584 he began his efforts towards colonizing Virginia. In 1588 he took an active part against the Armada. In 1595 he explored the Orinoco. In 1596 and 1597 he took part in the naval expeditions against the Spanish. Charged with plotting to put Arabella Stuart on the throne, Raleigh was imprisoned in 1603. In 1616 he was released to command an expedition to Guiana and the Orinoco. The expedition failed, and on his return he was condemned and executed.

54. *Lord Thomas Howard* (1561–1626), a distinguished naval officer and statesman.

57. *pinnaces,* large ship's boats.

93. *a.* 17. *pestered,* crowded. *rummaging,* making a disturbance.

29. *recovered,* regained, returned to.

43. *shrouded,* covered, concealed.

48. *Sir Richard Grenville* (c. 1541–1591), a British naval hero, cousin of Sir Walter Raleigh. In 1585 he commanded a fleet of seven vessels which shared in the colonization of Virginia. In 1591 he

served as vice-admiral in the fleet of 16 vessels under Lord Thomas Howard which sailed to Azores to intercept the Spanish treasure-ships. He died a few days after the battle recounted in the present text.

36. *Bona Speranza,* Cape of Good Hope.

37. *St. Helena,* an island off the west coast of Africa.

b. 9–10. *sprang their luff,* sailed nearer to the wind.

22. *charged.* The sense of this word is unknown. It may mean 'timbered.'

28. *admiral,* the ship that carries the commander-in-chief. *Biscayans,* inhabitants of Biscay, a province of northern Spain.

33. *right out of her chase,* directly ahead from her bow.

94. *a.* 16. *galleons,* large unwieldy ships, usually having three or four decks.

24. *Lima,* a city of Peru, in South America.

47. *armadas,* single war-vessels.

95. *a.* 36. *galley, i.e.,* service as prisoner on a galley.

LINSCHOTEN'S TESTIMONY

Jean-Hugues van Linschoten (1563–1611), was a Dutch voyager who cruised widely in the Pacific, in the Indian Ocean, and in the northern seas.

50. *Corvo,* the most northerly of the Azores.

57. *Lord Thomas Howard,* see 92. *b.* 2, note.

b. 4. *Sir Richard Grenville,* see 93. *a.* 48, note.

THE LOSS OF SIR HUMPHREY GILBERT

Sir Humphrey Gilbert (c. 1539–1583) was an English navigator and soldier, a stepbrother of Sir Walter Raleigh. After military services in Ireland and the Netherlands, he began (1578) his voyages of exploration and discovery. On June 11, 1583, he set out for North America, and on Aug. 5 landed at St. John's, where he established the first English colony in North America. On the return voyage his vessel, the *Squirrel,* foundered in a storm.

96. *a.* 52. *large,* fair, favorable.

57. *Cape Race,* the southeastern extremity of Newfoundland.

97. *a.* 7. *St. John's,* a town on the island of Newfoundland.

b. 2. *fights,* screens designed for the protection of men during a battle.

48. *Castor and Pollux,* a name given to the electric phenomenon known as St. Elmo's Fire. The phenomenon consists of the appearance, especially in southern climates, during thunder storms, of a brush or star of light.

98. *a.* 26. *flaw,* a sudden gust of wind.

A REPORT OF VIRGINIA

38. *Sir Walter Raleigh,* see 92. *b.* 53, note.

54. *humors,* bodily fluids.

RALEIGH'S DISCOVERY OF GUIANA

Guiana signified a region extending inland from the northeast coast of South America.

b. 39. *this river,* the Caroni River.

43. *Caroli,* the Caroni River, flowing northward and emptying into the Orinoco.

51. *shot,* persons who bear firearms.

57. *casique,* or *cacique,* a native chief of the aborigines in the West Indies and adjacent parts of America.

99. *a.* 32. *footman,* pedestrian.

b. 16. *marquesite,* marcasite, crystallized forms of iron pyrites.

22. *Caracas.* A tribe of Indians, called Caracas, formerly occupied the valleys about the present city, Caracas, the capital of modern Venezuela.

29. *Inca,* the Inca Empire, ruled by the Incas, the reigning order in ancient Peru.

100. *a.* 19. *provant,* provender.

25. *Cortez,* Fernando Cortez (1485–1547), the famous Spanish soldier who conquered Mexico, the City of Mexico falling in 1521. *Pizarro,* Francisco Pizarro (c. 1471–1541), the Spanish soldier who conquered Peru. Pizarro extorted from the Inca Atahualpa a sum estimated at $15,000,000 of modern money.

39. *cama,* or *anta,* names of the common tapir.

55. *tortugas,* tortoises. *lagartos,* alligators, or crocodiles.

b. 2. *calentura,* fever.

SIR FRANCIS DRAKE AT SAN DOMINGO

100. *b.* 12. *Sir Francis Drake,* see p. 217.

101. *b.* 11. *provost martial,* an army officer who acts as head of police of a district, town, or camp.

DRAKE IN CALIFORNIA

40. *Sir Francis Drake,* see p. 217.

54. *the Line,* the equator.

102. *a.* 15. *cauls,* nets for confining the hair.

b. 33. *coney,* rabbit.

103. *b.* 25. *want,* a mole.

SPENSER: THE SHEPHEARDES CALENDAR

FEBRUARIE

104. 2. *tasswage,* to subside.

4. *gryde,* pierce.

5. *rontes,* young bullocks.

6. *doen,* do.

7. *wont,* are accustomed. *wrigle,* wriggling.

8. *Perke,* pert, brisk. *avales,* subsides, droops.

9. *Lewdly,* foolishly.

10. *wracke,* violence.

105. 16. *lusty prime,* pleasant spring-time.

22. *that,* that which.

24. *mought,* might.

26. *cheare,* countenance.

27. *nie,* nigh.

28. *wrye,* awry, crooked.

30. *Good Fryday,* Friday before Easter.

32. *unwont,* unaccustomed.

35. *heardgroomes,* herdsmen.

36. *broomes,* a kind of shrub.

38. *deemen,* deem, judge.

39. *fond,* foolish.

42. *eft,* afterwards.

43. *breme,* rough. *chamfred,* wrinkled, furrowed.

46. *cruddles,* curdles.

47. *corage accoied,* heart daunted.

49. *surquedrie,* arrogance, pride.

52. *spil,* mar, ruin.

54. *elde,* old age.

55. *sicker,* certainly. *tottie,* tottering.

56. *corbe,* crooked.

57. *lopp,* branch.

58. *Als,* also. *cropp,* cut off.

62. *hery,* praise.

65. *gelt,* gold.

66. *buegle,* bead-work.

67. *faine,* glad.

69. *fon,* a foolish fellow.

71. *brag,* ostentatious.

72. *smirke,* smart.

74. *dewelap,* throat-wattle. *lythe,* pliant.

75. *venteth,* snuffs.

77. *can,* knows.

78. *lustlesse,* listless, feeble.

80. *flocks father,* ram.

82. *crags,* necks.

83. *rather lambes,* lambs born early in the year.

86. *headlessehood,* heedlessness.

89. *ynne,* inn, abode.

90. *stoopegallaunt age,* age which subdues gallantry.

92. *cond,* learned. *Tityrus,* Chaucer. The 'tale' that follows is, of course, not from Chaucer.

95. *novells,* news, or tales. *devise,* telling.

96. *thewed,* founded in morality.

97. *bespqke,* spoke of.

98. *meete,* fitting.

104. *largely,* widely.

106. *pight,* fixed, planted.

107. *throughly,* thoroughly.

106. 108. *Whilome,* formerly.

109. *mochell mast,* many acorns. *husband,* master of the house.

110. *larded,* fattened.

111. *rine,* rind, bark.

114. *honor,* i.e., foliage.

115. *Brere,* briar.

117. *threat,* threaten.

119. *wonned,* were wont.

121. *peinct,* paint, decorate.

122. *shrowde,* take shelter.

124. *wexe,* wax, grow.

125. *cast him,* planned.

126. *snebbe,* snub, reprove. *for,* because.

131. *engrained,* dyed. *lusty,* pleasant.

133. *wast,* waste.

134. *dirks,* darkens.

135. *accloieth,* encumbers.

140. *againe,* back.

141. *adawed,* subdued.

145. *survewe,* oversee, survey.

146. *trees of state,* stately trees.

151. *Pleaseth,* 2d pers. plur. imperative. *ponder,* weigh, consider.

154. *recure,* cure, heal.

155. *doole,* grief.

157. *aghast,* amazed.

160. *painted,* false.

162. *colowred,* colored, disguised.

167. *prime,* spring-time.

169. *falls*, happens.
178. *coronall*, garland.
182. *defast*, defaced, destroyed.
184. *goodlihead*, goodness.
185. *ranckorous*, sharp.
187. *sufferance*, patience.
189. *cast him*, prepared.
190. *couth*, knew.
192. *noulde*, would not.
195. *hent*, seized.
200. *enaunter*, lest. *mought*, might, should.
202. *wast*, waste.
203. *againe*, back.
206. *eld*, old age.
209. *crewe*, cruet, cruise, vessel.
107. 211. *sike*, such.
213. *quitten*, free.
223. *pleasaunce*, pleasure.
225. *eftsones*, forthwith.
226. *Boreas*, north-wind.
242. *graffed*, grafted.
243. *frorne*, frozen.
244. *galage*, wooden shoe.
245. *ease*, pleasure. *lewd*, foolish, rude.
248-9. 'God, since he is old, makes his own in his own likeness.'
251-2. 'No old man fears God.'

OCTOBER

3. *lingring Phœbus race*, lingering daylight.
4. *Whilome thou wont*, formerly thou used.
5. *bydding base*, the game of prisoners'-base.
11. *pleasaunce*, pleasure.
12. *ligge so layd*, lie so subdued.
13. *wont*, used to.
14. *fry*, children, youth.
15. *what . . . forthy*, how am I the better for that?
23. *pleasaunce of thy vaine*, pleasure of thy vein.
24. 'To whatever it pleases thee to entice their allured wills.'
26. *routes*, crowds.
28. *shepheard, i.e.*, Orpheus. *dame, i.e.*, Eurydice.
29. *Plutoes balefull bowre i.e.*, Hades.
32. *Argus blazing eye.* The spots in the peacock's tail are said to be Argus' hundred eyes.
33. *forthy*, for that.
35. *sike*, such. *sheddeth*, disperses.
108. 37. *clowne*, lout, low fellow.
39. *giusts*, jousts.
41. *doubted*, dreaded.
42. *wexen*, wax, grow.
45. *Whither thou list*, whether thou choose. *Elisa*, Queen Elizabeth.
47. *the worthy*, the hero, *i.e.*, the Earl of Leicester.
48. *white beare*, Leicester's cognizance was a bear and a ragged staff.
49. *stounds*, efforts.
50. *slackt the tenor of*, lowered the pitch of.
51. *lustihead*, pleasure. *tho*, then.
52. *the myllers*, a kind of dance.
53. *All*, although. *thilke*, that.
54. *mought*, might.

55. *Romish Tityrus*, Virgil.
56. *Mccænas*, Mæcenas, patron of Virgil.
59. *eft*, afterwards.
62. *Augustus*, the Roman emperor.
63. *liggen*, lie.
65. *derring doe*, daring deeds.
66. *hem*, them.
68. *brought . . . ease*, brought to a bed of ease.
69. *found . . . preace*, found nothing worth putting forth for competition.
72. *pend*, penned.
75. *mote*, must. *fayne*, feign.
76. *rybaudrye*. ribaldry.
78. *Tom Piper*, the piper who accompanied Morris-dancers.
87. *peeced*, patched, imperfect.
88. *Colin, i.e.*, Spenser. *scanne*, mount.
89. *bedight*, dressed.
90. *soothe*, sweetly.
91. *fon*, foolish fellow.
95. *caytive corage*, base mind.
98. *tyranne fell*, baneful tyrant.
101. *wont*, are accustomed.
103. 'Whoever thinks to accomplish great things.'
105. 'Let him pour down plentiful draughts and nourishing food.'
106. *Bacchus fruite*, wine. *Phœbus*, god of poetry.
109. 113. *buskin*, the high-heeled boot worn by actors in tragedy.
114. *queint*, elegant. *Bellona*, goddess of war.
115. *corage*, mind, heart.
116. *Forthy*, therefore.
117. *han us assayde*, have attacked us.
118. *charme*, temper.
119. *gates*, goats.
122. 'With his urging we become inflamed, etc.'

THE FAERIE QUEENE. BOOK I

1. *whylome*, formerly. *maske*, go disguised.
2. *shephards weeds*, a graceful reference to Spenser's own earlier *Shepherd's Calendar*.
7. *areeds*, counsels.
10. *holy virgin*, refers to Clio, the muse of history.
12. *scryne*, chest for papers.
14. *Tanaquill*, a British princess, daughter of Oberon, king of fairyland. In the allegory Tanaquill is probably Queen Elizabeth.
15. *Briton Prince*, Prince Arthur, representing in the allegory, probably, the Earl of Leicester.
17. *rue*, pity.
19. *dreaded impe*, Cupid, god of love.
21. *rove*, shoot an arrow with an elevation, not point blank.
23. *heben*, ebony.
25. *Mart*, Mars.
28. *Goddesse*, Queen Elizabeth.
31. *Phœbus*, Apollo, the sun-god.
32. *eyne*, eyes.
32. *type of thine*, Una, who represents truth in the allegory.
35. *afflicted*, cast down.
36. *dearest dread*, dearest object of reverence.

CANTO I

1. *knight*, the Redcross Knight, representing the English church militant. *pricking*, riding.

6. *chide*, chafe, grind.

110. 9. *giusts*, jousts.

14. *scor'd*, traced.

15. *For soveraine hope*, as a sign of supreme hope.

17. *cheere*, countenance.

18. *ydrad*, dreaded, feared.

20. *Gloriana*, Queen Elizabeth.

22. *worshippe*, honor.

24. *earne*, yearn.

25. *puissance*, power, prowess.

27. *dragon*, 'the great dragon . . . called the devil.' Revelation, xii, 9.

28. *ladie*, Una.

31. *wimpled*, pleated.

36. *in a line*, by a cord. *lambe*, symbolizing innocence.

44. *Forwasted*, utterly wasted.

45. *compeld*, summoned.

46. *dwarfe*, symbolizing prudence, or common sense.

52. *lemans*, sweet-heart's.

53. *wight*, person, creature. *shrowd*, take shelter.

54. *fain*, glad.

55. *covert*, hiding-place.

56. *shadie grove*, the wood of Error.

60. *Not perceable with*, impervious to.

63. 'A fair shelter it seems to them when they have entered.'

69. *sayling pine*, pine used for building ships.

70. *poplar never dry*, never dry because it grows especially well in moist soil.

71. *builder oake*, oak used for building.

72. *cypresse funerall*, the cypress, emblematic of death.

73. *meed*, reward.

74. *weepeth still*, weeps always. The fir exudes a resinous substance.

75. *paramours*, lovers.

76. *eugh*, yew.

111. 77. *sallow*, a kind of willow.

78. *The mirrhe*. The Arabian myrtle exudes a bitter but fragrant gum. The allusion is to the wounding of Myrrha by her father and her metamorphosis into a tree.

79. *warlike beech*. Lances and other arms were made of beech. *ash for nothing ill*. The ash served many purposes.

80. *platane*, plane-tree.

81. *carver holme*. The evergreen oak was good for carving.

84. *weening*, thinking.

88. *doubt*, fear.

94. *about*, out of.

95. *by tract*, by trace.

98. *Eftsoones*, forthwith.

103. *doubts*, fears.

106–7. *shame . . . shade*, 'it were shameful to check forward steps for fear of an unseen danger.'

108. *wade*, walk, go, pass.

110. *wot*, know.

114. *wandring wood*, wood that causes men to go astray.

118. *greedy hardiment*, eager boldness.

122. *glooming*, gloaming, twilight.

126. *full . . . disdain*, full of vileness that breeds disgust in the beholder.

129. *boughtes*, folds, coils.

130. *bred*, were born.

133. *ill favored*, of ugly appearance.

134. *uncouth*, unknown, strange.

136. *upstart*, started up. *effraide*, frightened.

139. *entraile*, fold, coil.

112. 141. *Armed to point*, completely armed.

143. *Ay wont*, ever accustomed.

145. *Elfe*, so called because he was reputed to be the son of an elf or fairy.

147. *trenchand*, sharp, cutting.

152. *enhaunst*, raised.

154. *dint*, stroke.

158. *Tho*, then. *wrethed*, twisted.

161. *That*, so that.

163. *constraint*, distress.

168. 'His anger was aroused because of pain and great disgust.' *grate*, chafe.

170. *gorge*, throat.

172. *maw*, stomach.

174. *gobbets*, lumps, pieces.

175. *vildly*, vilely.

177. *bookes and papers*, allegorically the scurrilous Catholic pamphlets that had been launched against Elizabeth and the reformed Church of England.

180. *parbreake*, vomit.

183. *outwell*, pour out.

185. *avale*, subside.

189. *reed*, perceive.

194. *sinke*, hoard, deposit.

200. *welke*, fade, grow dim.

113. 206. *clownish*, rough, rude.

208. *bestedd*, situated.

212. *lin*, cease.

213. *manly*, human.

215. *raft*, struck away.

216. *corse*, body.

225. *eke*, also.

227. *unkindly*, unnatural.

233. *needeth him*, needs he.

234. *should contend*, should have had to contend.

239. *armory*, armor.

243. *like succeed it may*, similar successful adventures may follow.

248. *still*, ever, always.

250. *to frend*, as friend.

254. *aged sire*, Archimago, the false enchanter. In general he represents hypocrisy and the Church of Rome.

259. *shew*, appearance.

262. *louting*, bowing.

263. *him quited*, paid him back, responded.

267. *silly*, simple, innocent.

268. *Bidding his beades*, praying his prayers.

270. *sits not*, is not fitting. *Mell*, mingle, meddle.

114. 277. *weare*, spend.

279. *space*, time.

280. *wastefull*, barren.

282. *thorough*, through.

285. *forwearied*, greatly wearied.

288. *baite*, feed, refresh.

295. *take up your in*, take lodging.

301. *a little wyde*, a little way off.

302. *edifyde*, built.

303. *wont*, was wont.

315. *Ave-Mary*, Hail Mary, a prayer to the Virgin.

317. *Sad humor*, heavy moisture.

318. *Morpheus*, god of sleep.

319. *deaw*, dew.

320. *riddes*, removes.

322. *amiddes*, amid.

328. *Plutoes griesly dame*, Proserpine.

332. *Great Gorgon*, Demogorgon, whose name was not to be uttered, and who had magical power over the spirits of the lower world.

333. *Cocytus*, the river of wailing. *Styx*, the river of hate. Both rivers were in Hades.

115. 338. *fray*, frighten.

343. *spersed*, dispersed.

348. *Tethys*, the ocean.

348. *Cynthia*, the moon.

360. *takes keepe*, pays heed.

367. *still*, always.

372. *mought*, might.

373. *paine*, effort.

376. *dryer braine*, too dry brain. It was supposed that a dry brain was slow in physiological processes.

378. *all*, entirely.

381. *Hecate*, queen of demons in Hades, and ruler of witches on earth.

382. *lompish*, dull.

387. *sent*, sense.

389. *diverse*, perverse.

391. *carke*, care, anxiety.

392. *starke*, stiff.

396. *afore*, before.

116. 405. *like*, likely. *seeme for*, represent.

409. *fantasy*, fancy.

410. 'In the way in which he schooled him secretly.'

411. *without her dew*, in an unnatural manner.

429. *leman*, lover.

431. *Hymen iö Hymen*, refrain of a Roman nuptial song. Hymen was god of marriage.

432. *Flora*, goddess of flowers.

443. *guise*, appearance.

444. *despight*, indignation.

445. *sufferance*, patience.

447. 'To test his perception and prove her feigned truth.'

449. *Tho can*, then did. *ruth*, pity.

454. *blind god*, Cupid. *amate*, dismay, dishearten.

462. *bereave*, take away.

468. *frayes*, frightens.

469. *deare constraint*, grievous distress.

117. 473. *redoubted*, terrible.

476. *shend*, revile, reproach. *rew*, pity, regret.

483. *appease*, cease from.

484. *beguiled of*, disappointed in.

491. *irksome*, troubled. *spright*, spirit.

CANTO II

1. *northerne wagoner*, constellation of Boötes, situated behind the Great Bear.

2. *sevenfold teme*, seven stars of Ursa Major, the Great Bear. *stedfast starre*, the pole-star.

6. *Chaunticlere*, the cock.

7. *Phoebus fiery carre*, the sun.

13. *bootelesse*, useless.

16. *Prosperine*, queen of the infernal regions.

19. *Eftsoones*, presently.

22. *squire*, an attendant on a knight. *lustyhed*, pleasure.

26. *misdeeming*, misleading.

30. *repast*, rest, refreshment.

34. *wex*, wax, grow.

118. 37. *start*, started.

40. *ment*, mingled.

43. *yblent*, blinded.

49. *wast*, waste. *despight*, anger.

50. *Yrkesome*, weary.

51. *Hesperus*, the evening star.

56. *aged Tithones*. Tithonus is 'aged' because Aurora gave him immortality, but not eternal youth.

58. *Titan*, the sun-god.

59. *drousyhed*, drowsiness.

62. *wont to wait*, was accustomed to watch.

63. *stowre*, distress.

84. *in seeming wise*, in the way of appearance.

85. *Proteus*, a sea-god.

87. *fell*, destructive.

97. *jolly*, handsome.

99. *Saint George*, patron saint of England.

100. *semblaunt*, semblance.

119. 104. *him chaunst*, he happened.

105. *Sarazin*, used for pagans in general. *armde to point*, completely armed.

107. *Sans foy*, faithless.

108. *a point*, a speck, a bit.

109. *faire companion*, Duessa, or Falsehood, who calls herself Fidessa. She probably represents Mary Queen of Scots and the Church of Rome.

111. *Purfled*, embroidered on the edge. *assay*, quality, value.

113. *owches*, jewels.

115. *palfrey*, lady's riding-horse.

117. *bosses*, ornamental studs or knobs.

118. *disport*, play.

128. *dispiteous*, cruel.

129. *couch*, level, adjust.

130. *fell*, destructive.

135. *rebutte*, recoil.

144. *broken reliques*, shivered lances.

145. *buffe*, blow.

147. *quyteth*, pays.

148. 'Each vies with the equal power of the other.'

150. *repining*, indignant. *courage*, heart.

155. *bitter fitt*, death agony.

156. *wote*, know.

157. *forwarned*, warded off.

158. *assured sitt*, sit firm.

159. *hide thy head*, i.e., behind thy shield for protection.

160. *rigor so outrageous*, force so violent.

162. *from . . . blest*, fairly preserved him from harm.

164. *eftsoones*, forthwith.

166. *rive*, split.

120. 171. *Whether*, whither.

174. *funerall*, death.

176. *scowre*, run fast.

181. *ruefull*, sad.

183. *silly*, innocent.

188. *rueth*, touches with pity.

196. *emperour*, the Pope.

198. *Tiberis*, River Tiber.

200. *onely haire*, only heir, the dauphin of France, the first husband of Mary Queen of Scots.

203. *debonaire*, gracious, courteous.

206. *fone*, foes.

212. *assaid*, tried.

213. *corse*, body.

224. *Sansjoy*, without happiness.

225. *Sansloy*, without law.

233. *rew*, pity.

121. 239. *chear*, countenance.

241. *gainsaid*, denied, opposed.

243. *dainty . . . derth*, coyness, they say, creates desire.

250. *fearefull*, timid.

251. *ne wont*, nor was accustomed to.

258. *abide*, endure, tolerate.

261. *tide*, time.

262. *seemely pleasaunce*, pleasant courtesies.

269. *rifte*, fissure.

270. *gory bloud*, clotted blood.

273. *rynd*, bark. *embard*, imprisoned.

278. *Astond*, astonished. *hove*, rise.

280. *dreadfull passion*, passion of fear.

284. *Limbo lake*, abode of the damned.

287. *rare*, thin, faint.

288. *ruefull*, piteous.

291. *Fradubio*, 'Brother Doubtful.'

295. *Boreas*, the north-wind.

122. 316. *take in hand*, maintain.

328. *Whether*, which of the two.

329. *meede*, reward.

332. *mote*, might.

336. *cast*, planned.

342. *in place*, in that place.

348. *Eftsoones*, forthwith.

351. *treen mould*, form of a tree.

353. *unweeting*, not knowing.

355. *prime*, springtime.

358. *origane*, wild marjoram.

360. *rew*, regret.

370. *cheare*, countenance.

123. 374. *bereaved*, taken away. *quight*, quite.

376. *pight*, placed, fixed.

378. *wights*, men.

382. *living well*, a flowing well.

385. *wonted well*, accustomed well-being.

386. *suffised*, satisfied. *kynd*, nature.

391. *dreriment*, sorrow.

398. *unweeting*, unaware.

404. *all passed feare*, all fear having passed.

AMORETTI

1, 6. *lamping*, shining.

7. *spright*, spirit.

10. *Helicon*, a mountain in Bœotia, Greece, famous in mythology as the haunt of the muses.

124. XXIV, 8. *Pandora*, according to Greek mythology, the first woman, created by command of Zeus in revenge for the theft of fire from heaven by Prometheus. The gods endowed her with such attributes as should bring misfortune to man.

XXXIV, 10. *Helice*, the Great Bear.

LXX, 2. *cote-armour*, a herald's tabard.

12. *amearst*, punished.

EPITHALAMION

125. 1. *learned sisters*, the muses.

8. *wreck*, violence.

11. *dreriment*, sorrow.

22. *lustyhed*, vigor.

25. *Hymen*, god of marriage.

27. *tead*, torch. *flake*, flash.

28. *bachelor*, one in the first stage of knighthood.

30. *dight*, dress.

35. *solace*, pleasure.

40. *wel beseene*, very comely.

44. *riband*, ribbon.

45. *poses*, flowers.

51. *diapred*, variegated. *discolored*, many-colored.

56. *Mulla*, island off the coast of Scotland.

126. 75. *Tithones*, Tithonus, consort of Aurora.

77. *Phœbus*, the sun-god.

80. *mattins*, morning service.

81. *mavis*, song-thrush. *descant*, an accompanying melody.

82. *ouzell*, blackbird. *ruddock*, redbreast.

83. *consent*, harmony.

86. *meeter*, more fitting.

87. *make*, mate.

95. *Hesperus*, the evening star, and also the morning star.

98–99. *Houres*, Horæ, goddesses who presided over the changes of the seasons, and of day and night.

102. *still*, always, ever.

103. *three handmayds of the Cyprian Queene*, the Graces, who were especially associated with Venus.

104, 106. *still*, ever, always.

108. 'And as you are accustomed to sing to Venus, sing to her (my bride).'

113. *strayt*, presently, soon.

121. *Phœbus*, Apollo.

123. *mote*, may.

124. *boone*, boon, prayer, favor.

131. *tabor*, drum. *croud*, fiddle.

140. *Hymen, Iö Hymen*, the refrain of a Roman nuptial song. Hymen is god of marriage.

148. *portly*, dignified.

127. 151. *seemes*, befits.

152. *weene*, think.

165. *nathlesse*, nevertheless. *still*, ever, always.

175. *incrudded*, uncurdled.

186. *spright*, spirit.

189. *red*, saw.

190. *Medusaes mazeful hed*. Medusa was a beautiful maiden whose hair was transformed into serpents. *mazeful*, confounding.

228. *dyde in grayne*, dyed in dye.

234. *sad*, grave. *still*, ever.

128. 239. *band,* tie.

257. *Graces,* the three daughters of Zeus,— Euphrosyne, Aglaia, and Thalia,— who personified grace and beauty.

265. ff. *This day.* June 11th, St. Barnabas' day, was, according to Spenser's calendar, the day of the summer solstice.

269. *Crab,* one of the signs of the zodiac.

272. *weare,* were.

282. *fayrest planet,* the sun.

285. *gloome,* become twilight.

299. *boures,* bowers.

304. *Arras,* a town in northern France formerly noted for its manufacture of tapestries.

307. *Maia,* mother of Hermes by Zeus.

308. *Tempe,* a beautiful valley in the north of Thessaly.

310. *Acidalian brooke,* the fountain Acidalius, in Bœotia, Greece.

129. 316. *defray,* pay for.

328. *Alcmena,* mother of Hercules by Zeus.

329. *Tirynthian groome.* Hercules is said to have lived for many years at the city of Tiryns, in Greece.

331. *Majesty.* By ancient poets, Night was called the mother of all things, and she was worshipped with great solemnity.

337. *dout,* fear.

340. *helplesse,* irremediable.

341. *Pouke,* Puck, or Robin Goodfellow.

346. *still,* ever, continually.

348. *griesly,* horrible.

374. *Cynthia,* the moon.

376. *envy,* begrudge.

380. *Latmian shepard,* Endymion, loved by Cinthia.

388. *hap,* fortune, lot.

390. *Juno,* sister and wife of Jove, and protectress of marriage.

130. 398. *Genius,* a higher power that maintains life and assists at the begetting and birth of each individual.

405. *Hebe,* cup-bearer to the gods.

414. *fayne,* imagine.

421. *guerdon,* reward.

429. *Hasty accidents,* accidents due to haste.

430. *expect,* await.

433. *for,* instead of.

PROTHALAMION

Written on the occasion of the marriage, on the same day, of the two daughters of the Earl of Worcester to Henry Guilford and William Peter.

2. *Zephyrus,* the west wind.

4. *Titans beames,* the sun. *glyster,* glitter, shine.

8. *still,* always.

11. *Themmes,* Thames.

12. *rutty,* rooty.

16. *paramours,* lovers.

25. *entrayled,* intertwined.

26. *flasket,* a long, shallow basket.

27. *cropt,* cut, clipped. *feateously,* neatly.

33. *vermeil,* vermilion.

38. *lee,* stream.

40. *Pindus,* a range of mountains in northern Greece.

43. *Leda.* Leda was amorously approached by Zeus in the form of a swan.

131. 55. *Eftsoones,* forthwith.

63. *Venus silver teeme,* team of swans, according to Ovid, *Metamorphoses,* x. 708.

67. *Somers-heat,* Somerset.

78. *Peneus,* a river in Thessaly that traverses the Vale of Tempe.

79. *Tempes shore.* Tempe is a valley in Thessaly celebrated for its beauty.

100. *assoile,* absolve.

110. *undersong,* burden, refrain, chorus.

119. *foule,* fowl.

132. 121. *Cynthia,* the moon. *shend,* shame.

128. *kyndly nurse.* Spenser was born in London.

132. *whereas,* where.

132–5. *bricky towres . . . Templer Knights.* A reference to the Temple. After the order of the Knights Templar had been suppressed in the reign of Edward II (1307–1327), their property on the bank of the Thames passed eventually into the hands of the students of the common law.

137–140. *a stately place . . . that great lord.* The reference is to Leicester House, where Spenser's patron, the Earl of Leicester, dwelt for some years. See the life of Spenser, above, p. 104.

145. *a noble peer,* the Earl of Essex. After the death of Leicester, in 1588, the Earl of Essex occupied his house and gave it the name, Essex House.

147. *through all Spaine did thunder.* A reference to the capture of Cadiz in 1596. Essex commanded the land forces.

148. *Hercules two pillors,* the rocks on either side of the strait of Gibraltar.

153–4. Probably a pun on Essex's family name, *Devereux,* as if it were connected with the French *heureux,* 'happy.'

157. *Elisaes glorious name,* Queen Elizabeth.

164. *Hesper,* the evening, and also the morning star.

173. *twins of Jove,* Castor and Pollux, who became the constellation Gemini.

ELIZABETHAN LYRICS

GASCOIGNE: A STRANGE PASSION

133. 1. *bale,* suffering.

15. *eschew,* avoid.

16. *grutch,* ill-will.

134. 25. *Philomene,* the nightingale.

28. *wray,* reveal.

29. *bewray,* reveal.

DYER: MY MIND TO ME A KINGDOM IS

4. *kind,* nature.

35. *fawn,* cringe to.

RALEIGH. HIS PILGRIMAGE

1. *scallop-shell,* shell of a kind of mollusk. The scallop-shell was the badge of a pilgrim.

3. *scrip,* wallet.

135. 25. *suckets,* a dried sweetmeat, or a delicacy of any kind.

57. *palmer,* a pilgrim. Specifically, a pilgrim to Jerusalem who brought back a palm-branch as a token.

A VISION UPON THIS CONCEIT OF THE FAERY QUEEN

1. *Laura,* celebrated in Petrarch's sonnets.

2. *vestal flame.* Vesta was goddess of the hearth. The sacred fire, which was her symbol, was kept burning in her temple at home by six stainless virgins, called *vestals.*

7. *Petrarch* (1304–1374), a celebrated Italian poet.

13. *sprite,* spirit.

GREENE: THE SHEPHERD'S WIFE'S SONG

137. 18. *curds,* the thickened part of milk, eaten as food.

36. *spill,* destroy.

37. *snort,* snore.

138. 42. *tide or sithe,* time or occasion.

44. *broils,* disturbances.

DANIEL: SONNETS FROM DELIA

XIX, 2. *Cytherea's son,* Cupid.

8. *Thetis,* chief of the sea-nymphs.

10. *Hermonius' spheres,* an allusion to the music supposed to be made by the planets in their revolutions. Perhaps this line should read: And thy sweet voice give back unto the spheres.

12. *Hyrcan,* pertaining to Hyrcania, a region in Asia bordering on the Caspian Sea.

139. XXXVIII, 3. *Laura . . . Petrarch.* Petrarch's sonnets were inspired by his Laura.

13. *limnèd,* described.

L, 1. *Paladins,* the knights of Charlemagne, and hence, heroic champions in general.

2. *untimely,* archaic, obsolete.

9. *arcs,* arches.

DRAYTON: SONNETS FROM IDEA

140. IX, 9. *Bedlam,* the hospital of St. Mary of Bethlehem in London, originally a priory, but afterward used as an asylum for lunatics.

XLIV, 6. *Medea-like.* Medea was granted the power of conferring immortality upon her children.

ODE XI. TO THE VIRGINIA VOYAGE

141. 16. *Eolus,* god of the winds.

37. *Golden Age,* a fabled period of simplicity, plenty, and eternal spring.

49. *kenning,* recognition.

52. *frolic,* merry.

68. *Industrious Hakluyt.* See above, p. 91.

ODE XII. TO THE CAMBRO-BRITONS

The Cambro-Britons were the Welsh.

The battle of Agincourt was fought near the northern coast of France on Oct. 25, 1415. Henry V, with about 15,000 men, defeated 50,000 or more French soldiers under the Constable d'Albret.

5. *main,* sea.

8. *King Harry,* Henry V.

16. *power,* army.

142. 41. *Poitiers and Cressy,* famous victories of the English in France, during the Hundred Years' War. The battle of Crécy was fought on Aug. 26, 1346; the battle of Poitiers, on Sept. 19, 1356.

45. *our Grandsire.* The grandfather of Henry V was John of Gaunt, son of Edward III.

49. *Duke of York,* Edward, Duke of York, who fell at Agincourt.

50. *vanward,* advance-guard.

53. *Exeter,* the Duke of Exeter, uncle of Henry V.

66. *Erpingham,* Sir Thomas Erpingham, steward of the king's household.

82. *bilboes,* swords.

91. *ding,* strike.

94. *besprent,* sprinkled.

97–112. *Gloucester . . . Clarence . . . Warwick . . . Oxford . . . Suffolk . . . Beaumont . . . Willoughby . . . Ferrers . . . Fanhope,* English noblemen and gentlemen who fought in the battle of Agincourt.

111. *doughtily,* mightily, forcibly.

113. *Saint Crispin's Day,* Oct. 25.

MARLOWE: HERO AND LEANDER
THE FIRST SESTIAD

Leander, a youth of Abydos, in love with Hero, a priestess of Aphrodite at Sestos, swam the Hellespont every night to visit her, until he perished one night in a storm. When his body was cast up on the shore of Sestos next morning, Hero threw herself into the sea.

Sestiad is really a Latin adjective meaning 'belonging to Sestos.'

1. *Hellespont,* the Strait of Dardanelles.

143. 14. *Adonis,* a youth of model beauty loved by Venus.

15. *kirtle,* close-fitting gown.

31. *buskins,* shoes laced to a point above the ankle.

49. *wrack,* destruction.

52. *Musæus,* a Greek author of the 5th century B. C., author of a celebrated poem on Hero and Leander, upon which Marlowe's poem is based.

56. *Colchos,* Colchis was the region in Asia to which the Argonautic expedition was directed in quest of the golden fleece.

59. *Cynthia,* the moon.

61. *Circe's wand.* Circe was an enchantress who, with her wand, could transform men into beasts.

65. *Pelops.* According to a tradition, one of Pelops' shoulders was made of ivory.

77. *Hippolytus,* son of Theseus and Hippolyta.

144. 98. *glistered,* glistened.

101. *Phaëton,* son of the sun-god, obtained permission of his father to drive his chariot across the heavens; but, being unable to check the horses, he nearly set the earth on fire.

107. *that . . . star,* the moon.

108. *thirling,* quivering.

109. *Latmus' mount,* a mountain in Asia Minor, the scene of the story of Cynthia's love for Endymion.

114. *Ixion's shaggy-footed race,* the Centaurs.

137. *Proteus,* a sea-god.

146. *Vulcan and his Cyclops.* Vulcan, the god of fire and of the working of metals, had the giant Cyclops for his workmen.

148. *Silvanus,* god of the fields and forests.

152. *turtles,* turtle-doves.

153. *Vailed,* bowed.

SHAKSPERE: VENUS AND ADONIS

Adonis was a beautiful youth beloved by Venus. In spite of her favor, he died from a wound received from a boar in the chase. The flower anemone sprang from his blood. Moved by the grief of Venus, the gods of the lower world allowed Adonis to spend six months of the year with her on earth, and the remaining six among the shades.

145. 18. *coasteth,* proceeds, goes.

43. *ecstasy,* excitement.

54. *rate,* scold, upbraid.

55. *spleens,* passionate impulses.

57. *mated,* bewildered.

59. *respects,* considerations, thoughts

60. *In hand with,* undertaking.

62. *caitiff,* wretch.

146. 78. *exclaims on,* cries out against.

81. *worm,* serpent.

94. *crop,* pick.

104. *vailed,* lowered.

112. *still,* ever, always.

147. 141. *all to naught,* good for nothing.

143. *clepes,* calls.

144. *Imperious,* imperial.

148. *still,* ever.

152. *wreaked,* revenged.

158. *suspect,* suspicion.

160. *With . . . insinuate,* try to ingratiate oneself with.

169. *fond,* foolish.

175. *lure,* a call or decoy, used to attract a falcon.

200. *trenched,* gashed.

148. 207. *passions,* grieves.

231, 234. *fair,* beauty.

242. *fear,* frighten.

246. *silly,* innocent, helpless.

253. *urchin-snoutèd,* with snout like that of a hedgehog.

263. *nuzzling,* thrusting his nose in.

149. 305. *toward,* fitting.

311. *Sith,* since.

316. *A purple flower,* the anemone.

323. *crops,* plucks, breaks off.

150. 341. *Paphos,* a town in Cyprus, the chief seat of the worship of Venus.

SONNETS

XII, 2. *brave,* beautiful.

9. *question make,* consider.

XV, 9. *conceit,* conception.

11. *debateth,* combats.

XVIII, 7. *fair,* beauty.

151. XXX, 6. *dateless,* endless.

8. *moan the expense,* lament the loss.

10. *tell,* count.

XXXIII, 6. *rack,* mass of floating clouds.

LIV, 5. *canker-blooms,* dog-roses.

8. *discloses,* uncloses.

9. *for,* because.

10. *unrespected,* unregarded.

LV, 3. *in these contents,* in the contents of these verses.

LX, 7. *Crooked,* malignant.

8. *confound,* destroy.

9. *flourish,* decoration.

10. *delves the parallels,* digs the furrows.

13. *times in hope,* future times.

152. LXV, 4. *action,* perhaps in the sense of 'legal action.'

LXVI, 11. *simplicity,* folly.

153. LXXVI, 5. *still,* always.

XCVII, 7. *prime,* spring.

10. *hope of orphans,* such hope as orphans bring.

XCVIII, 2. *proud-pied,* gaily variegated.

4. *That,* so that. *Saturn,* a planet of melancholy influence.

6. *different flowers in,* flowers different in.

XCIX, 6. *for thy hand,* for stealing the whiteness of thy hand.

13. *canker,* canker-worm.

CIV, 10. *Steal from his figure,* creep away from the figure on the dial.

CVI, 8. *master,* control, possess.

154. CVII, 10. *subscribes,* yields, submits.

12. *insults o'er,* exults over.

CIX, 2. *qualify,* temper, moderate.

7. *Just . . . time,* punctual. *exchanged,* altered.

CX 2. *motley,* fool.

6. *strangely,* distantly, distrustfully.

7. *blenches,* startings-aside.

10. *grind,* whet.

CXI, 10. *eisel,* vinegar.

CXIX, 2. *limbecks,* alembics.

155. CXXVIII, 5. *jacks,* here used in the sense of 'keys' of the virginal or the harpsichord.

CXXX, 5. *damasked,* variegated.

CXLVI, 10. *aggravate,* increase.

SONG FROM LOVE'S LABOR'S LOST

8. *keel,* skim.

ENGLAND'S HELICON: PHYLLIDA AND CORYDON

157. 21. *silly,* innocent, simple.

AS IT FELL UPON A DAY

23. *King Pandion,* father of Philomela (the nightingale).

HAPPY SHEPHERDS

158. 3. *wight,* creature.

31. *Circe's wand.* Circe was an enchantress, able to transform men into beasts.

THE SHEPHERD'S COMMENDATION

19. *Cynthia's silver light,* moonlight.

26. *damask-rose,* a species of pink rose.

31. *Phœbus,* god of the sun.

32. *Thetis,* goddess of the sea.

159. 40. *Dea,* an early Roman goddess.

SEVENTEENTH CENTURY LYRICS

CAMPION: CHANCE AND CHANGE

160. 9. *toys,* trifles.

13. *point to the world,* dot in comparison with the universe.

A RENUNCIATION

3. *mere,* absolute, pure.

JONSON: AN EPITAPH ON SALATHIEL PAVY

162. 11. *three filled zodiacs,* three full years.

12. *The stage's jewel.* Salathiel Pavy was a child of Queen Elizabeth's Chapel, and, apparently, a boy actor of great talent.

15. *Parcæ,* the Fates.

TO THE MEMORY OF MY BELOVED MASTER WILLIAM SHAKSPERE

20. *Beaumont.* Francis Beaumont (1584–1616), an English dramatist and lyrist.

163. 29. *Lyly.* John Lyly (1554?–1606), an English dramatist and lyrist.

30. *Kyd.* Thomas Kyd (1557?–1595?), an English dramatist who wrote 'tragedies of blood.' *Marlowe's mighty line.* Christopher Marlowe (1564?–1593), an English poet and dramatist. Marlowe's plays are written in sonorous blank verse.

33. *Æschylus, Euripides, and Sophocles,* the great Greek writers of tragedy, of the 5th century B. C.

35. *Pacuvius,* a Roman tragic poet (c. 220–c. 129 B. C.). *Accius,* a Roman tragic poet (born c. 170 B. C.). *him of Cordova,* Seneca (c. 4 B. C.–65 A. D.), a Roman Stoic philosopher and writer of tragedy.

36. *buskin,* the cothurnus, or high boot, anciently worn by actors in tragedy.

37. *socks.* The sock (Latin *soccus*) was a light shoe worn by the ancient actors of comedy.

45. *Apollo.* Apollo, the god of light, was also patron of music and poetry.

46. *Mercury,* the messenger of the gods, noted for his versatility and power of fascination.

51. *Aristophanes,* greatest of the Greek comic poets (c. 448–c. 380 B. C.).

52. *Terence,* a celebrated Roman writer of comedy (c. 185–c. 159 B. C.). *Plautus,* a Roman writer of comedy (died 184 B. C.).

71. *Swan of Avon,* a reference to Shakspere's birthplace, Stratford-upon-Avon.

74. *Eliza,* Queen Elizabeth. *James,* James I.

A PINDARIC ODE

Pindar (c. 522–433 B. C.), the greatest of the Greek lyric poets, was especially famous for his odes. Sir Lucius Cary (c. 1610–1643) was a politician and a man of letters. He married the sister of Sir Henry Morison.

1. *infant of Saguntum.* Saguntum was a town in Spain besieged and taken by the great Carthaginian general, Hannibal, in 219 B. C. The story here recounted by Jonson was actually recorded by Pliny, the Roman historian.

9. *summed.* complete.

164. 43. *Morison fell young.* Morison died before the marriage of Cary in 1630.

89. *asterism,* cluster of stars.

93. *Dioscuri,* the sons of Zeus, Castor and Pollux. Even after their burial they were kept alive, living and dying on alternate days.

DONNE: SONG

165. 2. *mandrake root.* The root of the mandrake somewhat resembles the human body in shape. It was used in amorous incantations, and was the focus of numerous superstitions.

THE CANONIZATION

166. 23. *The phoenix riddle.* It was said that the phoenix, after living 500 (or 1,000) years, made a nest of spices, burned itself to ashes, and came forth with renewed life for another similar period.

FORGET

167. 11. *Lethean flood.* Lethe was one of the streams of Hades, the waters of which caused those who drank of them to forget their previous existence.

FLETCHER: SONG TO BACCHUS

168. 1. *Lyæus,* a surname of Bacchus.

3. *lusty,* pleasant, healthy.

5. *mazer's brim.* A mazer is a bowl or large drinking cup.

BROWNE: BRITANNIA'S PASTORALS, BOOK II, SONG I

170. 8. *Willy.* In this song Browne is paying a tribute to William Ferrar, son of an eminent London merchant. The boy died young at sea.

171. 9. *Thetis' train.* Thetis was the mythical queen of the nereids, or sea-nymphs.

25. *Arion-like.* Arion, a Greek poet of Lesbos, flourished probably about 700 B. C. The story runs that while he was returning from a musical contest in Sicily, he was thrown into the sea by the sailors, but was saved and carried to shore by dolphins that had gathered about the ship to listen to his lyre.

BOOK II, SONG V

12. *Mona's . . . isle,* the island of Anglesea off the northwest coast of Wales.

26. *Teneriffe,* a peak upon the largest of the Canary Islands.

27. *hernshaw,* heron.

32. *Nestor's years.* Nestor was famous as the oldest councilor of the Greeks while they were besieging Troy.

44. *brave,* handsome. *Latmus,* a mountain in Caria, in Asia Minor, the scene of the story of Selené (the moon) and Endymion.

52. *Tellus' hair.* Tellus was a goddess personifying the earth.

ON THE COUNTESS DOWAGER OF PEMBROKE

Mary Sidney, Countess of Pembroke (1557–1621), was a sister of Sir Philip Sidney. To her he dedicated his *Arcadia.*

172. 10. *Niobe.* Too proud of her numerous

progeny, Niobe provoked the anger of Apollo and Artemis, who slew her children with arrows. Zeus metamorphosed Niobe into stone.

HERRICK: CORINNA'S GOING A-MAYING

10. *matins,* the first of the ecclesiastical services for the day.

17. *Flora,* goddess of the spring and of flowers.
25. *Titan,* the sun personified.
28. *beads,* prayers.
173. 66. *shade,* ghost.

AN ODE FOR BEN JONSON

174. 5-6. *Sun, Dog, Triple Tun,* names of taverns.
7. *clusters,* gatherings of persons.

A THANKSGIVING TO GOD

12. *state,* show, formality.
22. *unflead,* not stripped.
28. *pulse,* seeds of leguminous plants.
31. *worts,* plants, greens. *purslain,* purslane, a plant often used in salads.
39. *wassail bowls,* bowls for drinking healths.

GRACE FOR A CHILD

3. *paddocks,* toads.
5. *benison,* blessing.

HERBERT: THE COLLAR

175. 5. *store,* abundance.
14. *bays,* garlands or crowns bestowed as prizes.

CAREW: SONG

276. 3. *orient,* bright and clear.
18. *Phœnix.* See note to Donne: *The Canonization,* p. 166, l. 23.

SONG

177. 6. *orbs,* spheres. An allusion to the music made by the revolving of the spheres.

THE PROTESTATION

11. *Lethe,* one of the streams of Hades, the waters of which caused those who drank to forget their previous existence.

WALLER: THE STORY OF PHŒBUS AND DAPHNE

178. 3. *Phœbus,* Apollo, god of light, poetry, and music.
4. *Daphne,* a nymph.
29. *bays,* garlands.

SUCKLING: A DOUBT OF MARTYRDOM

179. 5. *Whether,* which. *chaplets,* wreaths.
19. *Elysium,* the abode of the souls of the good.
23. *Sophonisba,* a Carthaginian woman (died c. 204 B.C.) who was betrothed to a Numidian prince Masinissa, afterwards married Syphax, and later married Masinissa, after he had conquered her husband.
26-8. *Philoclea . . . Pirocles . . . Amphialus,* characters in Sir Philip Sidney's pastoral romance *Arcadia.* See p. 81.

CRASHAW: IN THE HOLY NATIVITY OF OUR LORD GOD

180. 15-16. *Tityrus . . . Thyrsis,* conventional names for shepherds.
46. *phœnix.* See 166. 23, note.
181. 98. *Maia,* an old Italian goddess of spring.

DENHAM: ON MR. ABRAHAM COWLEY'S DEATH

For selections from Cowley, see p. 183.
182. 7. *Aurora,* the dawn. *Spenser.* See above, pp. 104 ff.
10. *Phœbus,* Apollo, god of poetry and music.
11. *Jonson.* See p. 161. *Fletcher.* See p. 168.
16. *bays,* wreaths.
35. *Horace,* Quintus Horatius Flaccus (65-8 B.C.), a famous Roman lyric and satirical poet. *state,* stateliness.
40. *Jason.* Jason with other Argonauts made an expedition to Colchis, in Asia, to obtain the Golden Fleece.
43. *Flaccus,* the Roman poet Horace.
44. *The Theban Swan,* Pindar (c. 522-443 B.C.), the greatest of the Greek lyric poets.

LOVELACE: THE ROSE

183. 5. *Flora,* goddess of spring and flowers.
6. *Aurora,* the dawn.
11. *coverled,* coverlet.
14. *Silenus,* the foster-father of Bacchus, and leader of the satyrs.

COWLEY: THE SWALLOW

4-5. *Tereus . . . Philomel.* Tereus, after dishonoring his sister-in-law Philomela, deprived her of her tongue. Philomela was afterward metamorphosed into a nightingale.

MARVEL: THE GARDEN

184. 2. *bays,* wreaths, often of laurel.
5. *narrow-verged,* of narrow margin.
29. *Apollo . . . Daphne.* Daphne, daughter of the river-god Peneus, was pursued by Apollo, who had been charmed by her beauty. She prayed for aid, and was metamorphosed into a laurel-tree.
31. *Pan . . . Syrinx.* Syrinx, an Arcadian maid, when pursued by Pan was, as the result of her own prayer, metamorphosed into a reed.

TO HIS COY MISTRESS

185. 5. *Ganges,* the sacred river of India.
7. *Humber,* an estuary on the eastern coast of England.
40. *slow-chapt,* slowly cracked, or, perhaps, slowly devouring.

BACON: ESSAYS

I.— OF TRUTH

187. *a.* 5. *jesting Pilate.* See John xviii, 38.
7. *in giddiness,* in quick change of opinion.
b. 2. *at a stand,* at a loss.
8. *masques, mummeries, triumphs.* Evening shows or entertainments.

188. *a.* 3. *One of the fathers.* Both Jerome and Augustine have a similar saying; neither uses exactly these words.

29. *The poet,* Lucretius (1st century B. C.) in the Latin poem *On the Nature of Things.*

30. *the sect,* of the Epicureans.

52. *round,* straightforward, or as we should say, square.

b. 4. *Montaigne.* Essays ii, 18.

17. *it being foretold.* Luke xviii, 8.

V.— OF ADVERSITY

24. *Seneca.* The Roman philosopher and tutor of Nero (4 B. C.–65 A. D.). Both the passages quoted are from his Epistles.

39. *transcendencies,* hyperboles, exaggerations.

53. *in a mean,* in a moderate or prosaic style.

54. *temperance,* moderation.

VII.— OF PARENTS AND CHILDREN

189. *a.* 53. *Solomon saith.* Proverbs x, 1.

b. 7. *shifts,* subterfuges.

37. *the precept.* Ascribed by Plutarch to the Pythagoreans. Plutarch (1st century A. D.) wrote in Greek, but Bacon doubtless read him in a Latin translation.

VIII.— OF MARRIAGE AND SINGLE LIFE

51. *impediments,* hindrances, in the sense that they may deter a man from taking big risks.

190. *a.* 20. *humorous,* subject to humors, or moods.

29. *churchmen,* clergymen.

36. *hortatives,* exhortations.

44. *exhaust,* exhausted. The form Bacon uses is taken directly from the Latin past participle.

50. *Ulysses* refused to share immortality with the goddess Calypso, and returned home to his wife Penelope.

b. 4. *a quarrel,* a pretext or excuse.

5. *one of the wise men.* The saying quoted is ascribed by Plutarch and Montaigne to the Greek philosopher, Thales.

X.— OF LOVE

35. *Marcus Antonius* (83–30 B. C.), the lover of Cleopatra.

37. *Appius Claudius,* the Roman decemvir who became enamored of Virginia 449 B. C. See Macaulay's *Lays of Ancient Rome.*

45. *saying of Epicurus.* Quoted by Seneca, Epistle vii.

56. *braves,* exaggerates.

191. *a.* 2. *it hath been well said.* By Plutarch.

9. *it was well said.* The reference may be to Publius Syrus, or to Plutarch.

16. *the reciproque,* mutual affection.

22. *he that preferred Helena.* Paris, who awarded the apple to Venus in return for the gift of Helen, rejecting the offers of Juno (the sovereignty of Asia) and Pallas (renown in war).

34. *keep quarter,* keep within bounds.

36. *check,* interfere.

XII.— OF BOLDNESS

191. *b.* 1. *Demosthenes.* The story of the great Greek orator (385–322 B. C.) is told by Cicero and by Plutarch.

29. *popular,* democratic.

34. *mountebanks,* quacks who sell their medicines from public stages.

39. *grounds,* principles.

54. *slight it over,* make nothing of it.

192. *a.* 11. *stale at chess,* a drawn game which neither party wins.

XVII.— OF SUPERSTITION

54. *Augustus Cæsar,* Emperor of Rome 31 B. C.–14 A. D. *civil,* peaceful.

56. *primum mobile,* the origin or cause of motion, according to the old astronomy.

b. 5. *Council of Trent,* a great ecclesiastical council of the Roman Catholic Church held 1545–1563.

6. *schoolmen.* Mediæval philosophers.

XXIII.— OF WISDOM FOR A MAN'S SELF

50. *shrewd,* harmful. Bacon is wrong as to the fact.

52. *waste,* injure.

58. *right earth,* exactly like the earth.

193. *a.* 12. *crooked,* distorts, perverts.

13. *essentric to,* having a different center or motive from.

18. *accessory,* secondary.

29. *bias,* a weight inserted in a bowl to make it run in a curve.

38. *and,* if.

43. *respect,* consideration.

XXV.— OF DISPATCH

b. 10. *Affected,* excessively desired.

24. *false periods,* apparent conclusions, which do not really end the matter.

31. *a wise man.* Sir Amyas Paulet.

32. *byword,* proverb.

55. *moderator,* presiding officer.

56. *actor,* speaker.

194. *a.* 4. *curious,* elaborate, highly wrought.

6. *passages,* transitions.

10. *bravery,* extravagance of dress, meant for show, not use.

11. *being too material,* keeping too close to the point.

XXVI.— OF SEEMING WISE

46. *the Apostle.* Paul, 2 Timothy iii, 5.

51. *magno conatu nugas.* Quoted from Terence, the Roman writer of comedies.

55. *prospectives,* stereoscopes.

b. 14. *bear it,* carry their point.

16. *by admittance,* for granted.

17. *make good,* prove.

20. *curious,* trifling.

22. *difference,* distinction.

24. *blanch the matter,* gloss over or shirk the issue.

46. *opinion,* credit.

48. *you were better,* it would be better for you.

XXVIII.— OF EXPENSE

58. *worth,* importance.

195. *a.* 2. *kingdom of heaven.* See Matthew xix, 24.

10. *of even hand.* His outgo equal to his income.
18. *broken,* bankrupt.
20. *searching,* probing.
23. *new.* Servants.
26. *certainties,* fixed amounts.
38. *disadvantageable,* disadvantageous.

XXXII.— OF DISCOURSE

b. 5. *want,* lack.
18. *jade,* spur, overdrive.
28. *would be bridled,* ought to be restrained.
30. *Parce — loris.* Ovid, *Metamorphoses* ii, 127.
35. *saltness,* wit.
47. *poser,* an examiner putting questions.
53. *galliard,* a lively dance.
196. *a.* 8. *himself pretendeth,* he himself lays claim.
9. *of touch,* reflecting upon or wounding.
10. *as a field,* open, general.
17. *flout or dry blow,* an insulting jest or hard knock.

XXXIV.— OF RICHES

50. *conceit,* fancy, imagination. *saith Solomon.* Ecclesiastes v, 11.
56. *dole and donative,* gifts small and large.
b. 1. *feigned,* fictitious.
7. *Solomon saith.* Proverbs xviii, 11.
12. *sold,* betrayed.
25. *Solomon.* Proverbs xxviii, 20.
29. *poets.* The saying quoted is found in the Greek prose writer Lucian (2nd century A. D.).
43. *enrich,* become rich.
52. *husbandry,* industry.
54. *audits,* accounts.
57. *collier,* owner of coal mines.
197. *a.* 4. *observed by one.* In Plutarch.
8. *expect the prime,* wait for the most favorable condition.
9. *overcome,* take advantage of.
12. *mainly,* greatly.
19. *broke,* do business, negotiate.
22. *chapmen,* buyers.
24. *chopping of bargains,* speculation by middle-men.
52. *co-emption,* the modern trust.
58. *service,* to a monarch or nobleman.
b. 25. *glorious,* ostentatious.
29. *advancements,* gifts.

XLII.— OF YOUTH AND AGE

53. *Septimius Severus,* Roman Emperor 193–211 A. D.
54. *it is said.* By Spartianus.
198. *a.* 3. *Cosmos,* usually called Cosimo de' Medici, made Grand Duke of Tuscany, 1570.
Gaston De Foix, a celebrated French general, made Duke of Nemours in 1505.
6. *composition,* disposition, temperament. *Young men,* &c. Suggested by an observation of Plutarch.
12. *them,* old men (implied in *age*).
13. *abuseth,* deceives.
17. *manage,* management.
23. *absurdly* qualifies *pursue. care,* hesitate.
32. *period,* conclusion.
40. *extern,* external.

45. *A certain rabbin.* Isaac Abrabanel (1437–1508).
b. 2. *Hermogenes,* a famous rhetorician of the second century B. C.
9. *Tully.* Cicero. Hortensius was his great rival at the Roman bar.
16. *Scipio Africanus.* Roman general (234–183 B. C.).
16. *Livy.* Roman historian (59–17 B. C.).
17. *Ultima primis.* Quoted from Ovid. What Livy says is that Scipio in his later life had no opportunity for the military exploits for which he was naturally fitted.

XLVII.— OF NEGOTIATING

33. *tender,* delicate or difficult.
43. *success,* result.
48. *affect,* are inclined to.
50. *quickeneth,* spurs on, encourages.
199. *a.* 2. *prescription,* prestige, reputation previously won.
7. *in appetite,* eager for advancement.
10. *upon conditions.* A. agrees to do something if B. will do something. Who is to do his part first? A. must unless (1) B.'s part necessarily comes first; or (2) A. will still need B. for some other part of the scheme; *or* (3) A. is known to be more trustworthy and B. can therefore depend on him.
18. *practice,* negotiation. *discover,* to ascertain a man's plans or character. *work,* to induce a man to do something.
24. *know.* This verb governs *nature, fashions, ends, weakness, disadvantages, those.*

L.— OF STUDIES

46. *expert,* practised, experienced.
54. *humor,* fanciful peculiarity, foible.
b. 17. *curiously,* with elaborate care.
21. *would,* should.
25. *flashy,* tasteless.
29. *confer,* converse.
35. *moral grave,* studies in moral philosophy make men serious and dignified.
38. *stond,* drawback, hindrance.
42. *stone and reins,* bladder and kidneys.
52. *beat over matters,* take a broad general view of many things.
56. *receipt,* prescribed remedy.

BROWNE: RELIGIO MEDICI

200. *a.* 6. *general scandal of my profession.* According to the old saying, 'Where there are three physicians, there are two atheists.'
b. 12. *nothing but the name.* 'Protestant, as carrying with it an insinuation of enmity and discord, inconsistent with the peace and harmony prescribed by the gospel.'
25. *the person.* Luther.
201. *a.* 3. *shaken hands with,* parted from.
4. *desperate resolutions.* These words, with the dependent relative clauses up to *what they have been,* refer to the Roman Catholics.
6. *bottom,* ship.

8. *all* (doctrines).

11. *in diameter*, in diametrical opposition.

13. *improperations*, taunts, reproaches.

15. *difference*, show the difference of.

20. *am not scrupulous*, do not hesitate.

22. *in defect of ours*, where ours do not exist.

44. *morosity*, moroseness.

49. *violate*, injure.

b. 12. *consorts*, companions.

15. *questionless*, unquestionably.

34. *mediocrity*, moderation.

46. *difference myself*, distinguish my opinions.

202. *a.* 7. *humor*, mood.

10. *disproving*, disapproving.

11. *disavouched*, disavowed.

12. *Council of Trent.* See 192. *b.* 5, note.

13. *Dort.* In the Netherlands, where a great Protestant Synod was held in 1618–19.

18. *Geneva.* The center of Protestantism on the European Continent.

20. *scandal*, objection.

28. *the state of Venice* had a dispute with Pope Paul V in 1606.

41. *reaction*, recrimination.

b. 28. *Œdipus* solved the riddle of the Sphinx.

203. *a.* 10. *Diogenes*, the Cynic, a Greek philosopher (412–323 B.C.). *Timon*, of Athens, a famous misanthrope, contemporary with Socrates.

22. *pia mater*, a membrane enveloping the brain.

23. *impossibilities*, apparent impossibilities, difficulties calling for the exercise of faith.

29. *O altitudo.* A height beyond human comprehension.

35. *Tertullian of Carthage*, one of the fathers of the Church (2nd and 3rd centuries).

b. 18. *expansed*, spread out.

23. *admire*, wonder at.

27. *the other* (people), *i.e.*, the Israelites.

204. *a.* 37. *the chaos*, i.e., before the Creation.

b. 24. *away with*, put up with.

51. *temper*, constitution.

52. *crows and daws*, proverbially long-lived birds.

205. *a.* 1. *revolution of Saturn.* The year of Saturn is 10,759 days.

10. *canicular days*, dog days. Latin. *dies caniculares*, the hottest days of summer, ascribed in ancient astrology to the malignant influence of the dog star.

13. *pantalones and antics*, pantaloons and clowns.

28. *Methuselah* lived 969 years. See Genesis v, 27.

29. *rectify*, straighten, improve.

30. *incurvate*, deteriorate.

55. *Cicero* says in his treatise *On Old Age:* I am not sorry to have lived: since I have so lived that I do not think I was born in vain.

b. 10. *Æson*, an old man in classical mythology whom Medea restored to youth by a magical bath.

13. *providence*, foresight.

15. *able temper*, sound constitution.

16. *radical humor*, vital juice.

24. *glome or bottom*, a ball of thread.

206. *a.* 32. *climate*, a space measured on the earth's surface; England was in the eighth.

55. *Hydra*, a many-headed monster slain by Hercules.

58. *Solomon.* See Proverbs i, 7, 22, &c.

b. 15. *Doradoes*, rich men; literally *gold-fishes*

18. *politicians*, statesmen.

54. *as the world* (is one).

207. *a.* 2. *buffet*, box.

3. *at sharp*, with pointed weapons.

5. *Lepanto*, a battle between the Italians and Turks, 1571.

10. *dastards*, intimidates.

28. *epidemical*, common to all people.

b. 1. *the world*, the macrocosm which man, the microcosm, resembles.

21. *grammarian*, student of Latin grammar.

23. *construction*, construing.

30. *Babel.* See Genesis xi, 1–9.

35. *chorography*, description of countries.

46. *pointers*, the Dipper.

53. *simpled*, collected simples, or herbs. *Cheapside*, a famous London herb market.

208. *a.* 9. *Euripus*, a strait dividing Attica from Eubœa, where the tide, according to classical tradition, ebbed and flowed seven times a day. The story that Aristotle drowned himself there because he could not discover the cause of the phenomenon is discussed by Browne, along with the fable as to the death of Homer because he could not guess the fisherman's riddle, in *Pseudodoxia epidemica*, Bk. VII, ch. 13.

16. *Peripatetics, Stoics, Academics.* Classical schools of philosophy.

19. *Janus*, facing both ways.

33. *attending*, waiting.

35. *which* (knowledge).

43. *glorification* (in heaven).

46. *disallow*, disapprove.

b. 9. *music of the spheres.* The ancients had a fancy that the rotation of the planets produced music; this kept its place in poetry after it had been denied by the astronomers. See *Merchant of Venice*, V. i, 60–62.

24. *first composer.* God.

48. *ephemerides*, astrological tables.

HYDRIOTAPHIA, URNBURIAL

209. *b.* 1. *ossuaries*, receptacles for bones. In this essay Browne discourses about some urns containing bones, dug up in Norfolk and supposed to be of Roman origin.

10. *tutelary observators*, guardian spirits of the place.

15. *pyramidally*, by means of a tombstone.

25. *Atropos*, the Greek Fate who cut the thread of human life.

31. *meridian*, the noon of the world's lifetime.

39. *Charles V* (1500–1558), Emperor of Germany.

47. *Janus*, facing past and future.

210. *a.* 25. *Gruter*, Dutch philologist (1560–1627)

35. *Cardan*, a celebrated Italian (1501–1576).

38. *Hippocrates*, famous Greek physician (460–357, B.C.).

42. *entelechia*, actual being, a term in the philosophy of Aristotle.

45. *Canaanitish woman.* See Matthew x, 4.
Mark iii, 18.

46. *Herodias.* See Matthew xiv, 1–12.

48. *good thief.* See Luke xxiii, 39–43.

b. 1. Herostratus — Diana. At Ephesus 356
B. C.

4. *Adrian* (76–138 A. D.), Emperor of Rome.

8. *Thersites,* the foul-mouthed rogue of Homer's
Iliad, in which *Agamemnon* is one of the heroes.

23. *the first story.* See Genesis, v.

24. *one living century,* a hundred people still remembered.

31. *Lucina,* the goddess of childbirth.

211. *a. 23. Cambyses,* king of Persia and conqueror
of Egypt, d. 521 B. C.

25. *Mizraim,* the brother of Cush, is the Hebrew
name of Egypt.

26. *Pharaoh,* the name of many kings of ancient
Egypt. In Browne's time Egyptian mummies were
used for medical prescriptions.

36. *Nimrod,* the founder of the Babylonian Empire. See Genesis x, 8–12. In Hebrew astronomy
he corresponds to the Greek constellation Orion.

37. *Osiris,* an Egyptian deity.

42. *perspectives,* telescopes.

b. 12. scape, a momentary chance.

23. *Sardanapalus,* the last Assyrian king of
Nineveh, unable to withstand a siege there, burnt
himself and his household on a huge funeral pile
876 B. C.

30. *Gordianus.* Emperor of Rome, third century.
The Man of God. Moses. See Deuteronomy
xxxiv, 1–6.

34. *Enoch.* See Genesis v, 24.

35. *Elias, Elijah.* See 2 Kings ii, 1–11.

48. *Lozarus.* See John xi.

50. *die but once.* See Revelations xxi, 8.

53. *coverings of mountains.* See Revelations vi,
15–17.

WALTON: THE COMPLETE ANGLER

This chapter is in the form of an open-air dialogue between the Angler (Piscator), who represents
the author, and the Hunter, who is his pupil. The
Angler continues the discourse he had begun in
Chapter III, on the chub.

212. *a. 12. generous,* originally high born, and
hence full of spirit, rich and full of strength, invigorating.

16. *Gesner,* a Swiss physician and naturalist who
wrote a book *On Animals* (1551–8).

17. *offspring,* origin; there is little doubt, however, that the word *trout* comes through the Latin
trutta from the Greek τρώκτης. The trout of the Great
American Lakes is sometimes even larger.

b. 2. Mercator, a Flemish scientist who died
in 1594.

25. *Fordidge trout* are salmon trout and live in
the ordinary way: so do grasshoppers. Walton's
aspersions on the mother raven are groundless.

213. *a. 44. Michaelmas,* September 29.

51. *Albertus,* Magnus (1193–1280), a German

Dominican monk, who wrote more than twenty volumes on natural philosophy.

215. *a. 2. the best.* Men were readier at sharing a
bed in those days.

4. *catch,* a short part-song for three or more
voices.

b. 34. verjuice, acid of the crab-apple, or other
fruits.

53. *Troy Town,* a ballad about Dido and Æneas.

216. *b. 2. Overbury's — wish.* In the 'characters'
subjoined to *The Wife* (1604).

17. *Philomel,* the nightingale.

Walton found both these songs in *England's Helicon* (1600). The first is ascribed with some certainty to Christopher Marlowe, the second, more
doubtfully, to Sir Walter Raleigh.

FULLER: LIFE OF SIR FRANCIS DRAKE

217. *a. 10. Six Articles* of Faith, which Henry
VIII required the clergy to sign.

218. *a. 44. chapmen,* merchants, *i.e.,* adventurers.

55. *admire,* wonder.

b. 12. Cabo-verd, Cape Verde.

57. *Portugals,* Portuguese.

219. *a. 30. caudle,* a warm drink, consisting of
weak gruel, mixed with ale or wine, sweetened and
spiced.

47. *curious,* careful.

b. 12. half moon, the power of Spain, which
was broken by the destruction of the Armada in
1588.

28. *caraval of adviso,* a messenger-ship.

37. *vent,* outlet, *i.e.,* publicity.

220. *b. 49. fresh water .. Plymouth.* It is indeed
one of the striking instances of Drake's public-spirited enterprise that in the intervals of adventure he
devised a municipal water supply.

TAYLOR: THE PATIENCE OF THE SAINTS

221. *a. 26. my text.* 'For the time is come that
judgment must begin at the house of God: and if
it first begin at us, what shall the end be of them
that obey not the Gospel of God? And if the
righteous scarcely be saved, where shall the ungodly and the sinner appear?' — 1 Peter iv, 17, 18.

b. 2. Dives, the rich man of Luke xvi, 19–
31.

222. *a. 26. renegadoes,* renegades, those who have
denied the true fraith.

b. 15. rainbow . . . grace. See Genesis
ix, 13–17.

31. *consequent,* consequence.

223. *b. 3. green tree . . . dry.* See Luke,
xxiii 31. This is a good example of the way in
which Taylor's whole phraseology is colored by
reminiscences of Scripture.

BUNYAN: PILGRIM'S PROGRESS

227. *b. 29. going,* walking.

228. *a. 43. fact,* deed.

231. *b. 51. conversation,* manner of life.

232. *a. 7. tenderness in,* sensitiveness about, scrupulous care against.

MILTON: ON SHAKSPERE

Printed among the commendatory verses prefixed to the Shakspere folio of 1632.

236. 4. *star-ypointing*, pointing to the stars; not a correctly formed word, *y* being properly a prefix for the past participle only.

11. *unvalued*, invaluable.

237. 12. *Delphic*, oracular. The oracle of Apollo was at Delphi.

L'ALLEGRO

Published 1645; written probably at Horton about 1634.

2. *Cerberus,* the three-headed monstrous dog which guarded the classic hell.

3. *Stygian*, belonging to the Styx, *i.e.*, infernal.

5. *uncouth*, unknown, hence strange, monstrous.

8. *ebon*, black.

10. *Cimmerian desert*, according to Homer, a land of perpetual darkness 'beyond the ocean-stream.'

12. *yclept*, called. *Euphrosyne*, Mirth, one of the thre Graces of classical mythology.

19. *Zephyr*, the West Wind. *Aurora*, the Dawn.

29. *Hebe*, goddess of Youth, Jove's cupbearer.

62. *dight*, decked.

67. *tells his tale*, counts his sheep.

80. *cynosure*, center of attraction; in Greek the name of the constellation containing the pole-star.

Corydon, Thyrsis, Thestylis, Phillis, conventional names in pastoral poetry.

54. *rebecks*, fiddles.

238. 102. *fairy Mab.* See *Romeo and Juliet*, I, iv, 25.

103. *she — he*, members of the group of storytellers.

104. *friar's lantern*, will o' the wisp.

105. *drudging goblin*, Robin Goodfellow, the Puck of *Midsummer Night's Dream*, a mischievous but helpful fairy.

110. *lubber*, clumsy, awkward.

120. *weeds*, garments.

122. *rain influence*, like the stars.

125. *Hymen*, the god of marriage.

132. *sock*, Latin *soccus*, the low-heeled shoe worn in classical comedy. For tragedy the buskin was used.

136. *Lydian*, the softest and sweetest kind of Greek music.

139. *bout*, turn.

145. *Orpheus* with his music won Pluto to release his wife Eurydice from hell on condition that he did not look back to see if she were following him to the upper world: he could not withstand the temptation, and she was lost.

147. *elysian*, heavenly.

IL PENSEROSO

A companion poem to the foregoing, written and printed with it.

3. *bested*, avail, profit.

10. *Morpheus*, god of dreams.

18. *Memnon*, a handsome Ethiopian prince who fought in the Trojan war.

19. *starred Ethiop Queen*, Cassiope, changed into the constellation Cassiopœia.

23. *Vesta*, goddess of the fireside.

24. *Saturn*, father of Jupiter.

29. *Ida*, a mountain near Troy.

39. *commércing*, having commerce or intercourse with.

56. *Philomel*, the nightingale.

59. *Cynthia*, the moon.

239. 74. *curfew*, the evening bell.

87. *Bear*, the Great Bear which never sets in the latitude of Great Britain. To *outwatch the Bear* is therefore to stay awake till all the stars have faded in the light of day.

88. *Hermes*, an ancient Egyptian philosopher.

95. *consent*, sympathy.

99. *Thebes — Troy*, subjects of classical tragedy.

102. *buskined*, tragic. See **238.** 132, note.

109. *him that left half told*, Chaucer in the Squire's Tale.

113. *virtuous*, magical.

124. *Attic boy.* Cephalus, beloved of Aurora.

134. *Sylvan*, the god of woods.

148. *his*, of sleep.

154. *genius*, guardian spirit.

156. *pale*, enclosure.

159. *storied*, adorned with stories from Scripture

170. *spell*, read slowly.

LYCIDAS

The purpose of the poem is best explained in Milton's own words: —'In this monody the author bewails a learned friend, unfortunately drowned in his passage from Chester on the Irish seas, 1637, and by occasion foretells the ruin of our corrupted clergy, then in their height.' Milton's friend was Edward King, of Christ's College, Cambridge. *Lycidas* was written in 1637 and published along with other elegies in a memorial volume for King in 1638.

240. 8. *Lycidas*, a name used in the Seventh Idyll of Theocritus, the founder of pastoral poetry. *ere his prime.* King was 25.

15. *sacred well*, the fountain of the Muses on Mount Helicon.

27. *drove* (our flocks).

29. *battening*, fattening.

36. *Damœtas*, a conventional name in pastoral poetry. Possibly Milton's college tutor is meant. Both Milton and King wrote Latin verse of merit.

46. *weanling*, weaned.

52–55. The Welsh hills, Mona (Anglesea), and the River Dee bound the Irish sea on the east.

59. *the Muse*, Calliope, mother of Orpheus; he was torn to pieces by Thracian women, and his head floated down the river Hebrus to Lesbos.

64. *boots*, profits.

68. *Amaryllis, Neæra*, maidens of classical pastoral.

75. *blind Fury.* More properly the Fate Atropos, who cuts the thread of human life.

77. *Phœbus.* Apollo, the god of poetry.

79. *glistering foil*, glittering tinsel.

241. 82. *Jove,* God.

85. *Arethuse, Mincius,* rivers of Greek and Latin pastoral poetry.

88. *oat,* oaten pipe.

91. *felon,* criminal, cruel.

95. *his,* of Lycidas. *Hippotades,* Æolus, who controlled the winds.

99. *Panope,* a nymph, one of the fifty daughters of Nereus.

100. *fatal,* fated to destruction. *perfidious,* treacherous, unworthy of trust.

101. *the eclipse,* a time of evil omen.

103. *Camus,* the river at Cambridge personified as a g l. *footing slow.* The Cam flows gently.

106. *sanguine flower,* the hyacinth which the ancients held to be marked ' Ai, Ai,' in lamentation for Hyacinthus.

107. *reft,* bereaved me of.

109. *pilot of the Galilean lake,* St. Peter.

110. *keys.* See Matthew xvi, 19.

112. *mitered.* St. Peter was the first bishop of Rome. The miter is the official headdress of a Roman bishop.

114. *Enow,* enough.

120. *sheep-hook.* Milton has now turned from the shepherd as poet to the shepherd as pastor.

122. *recks,* concerns. *sped,* provided for.

123. *flashy.* See 199. *b.* 25, note.

124. *scrannel,* screeching.

130. *two-handed engine,* the axe.

132. *Alphëus,* a classical river, lover of Arethusa.

133. *Sicilian Muse,* Theocritus. Milton is returning to the more conventional tone of pastoral poetry.

138. *swart star,* the dog-star, which was supposed to blast vegetation.

142. *rathe,* early. *forsaken,* unsought for, or perhaps there is an allusion to an old myth of the wooing of certain flowers by the sun. See Shakspere's *Winter's Tale,* IV, iv, 122–5.

144. *freaked,* freckled, sprinkled.

149. *amaranthus,* emblem of immortality.

151. *laureate,* adorned with the poet's laurel. *hearse,* a platform adorned with black hangings and containing an effigy of the deceased.

152. *so,* by imagining that the body of Lycidas has been recovered.

242. 156. *Hebrides,* islands to the far north of Scotland.

160. *Bellerus.* Land's End, the most western point of England, was anciently called Bellerium. Near it is St. Michael's Mount, a rocky island with a fortress on top and a craggy seat from which visions of St. Michael were seen.

162. *Namancos,* in Spain, near Cape Finisterre and the Castle of Bayona.

163. *ruth,* pity.

169. *anon,* immediately. *repairs,* refreshes.

170. *tricks,* sets in order, adorns. *ore,* brightness.

173. *Through — waves.* See Matthew xiv, 22–3.

176. *unexpressive,* inexpressible.

183. *genius,* protecting deity, guardian angel.

186. *uncouth,* unknown, uncultivated.

188. *quills,* reeds.

189. *Doric,* pastoral, rude, as or a shepherd.

193. A forecast of the very different occupations of the poet during the next few years.

SONNETS

WHEN THE ASSAULT WAS INTENDED TO THE CITY

Written Nov., 1642; pub. 1645.

10. *Emathian conqueror.* Alexander of Macedon, when he sacked Thebes in 333 B. C., spared the house of the poet Pindar, who died almost a century before.

13. *Electra,* one of the tragedies of Euripides, the recital of whose verses are said to have saved the walls of Athens from destruction after the capture of the city by Lysander the Spartan in 404 B. C.

TO A VIRTUOUS YOUNG LADY

2. *the broad way.* See Matthew vii, 13.

5. *Mary . . . Ruth.* See Luke x, 42; Ruth i, 14–17.

12. *the Bridegroom.* See Matthew xxv, 1–13.

ON THE DETRACTION WHICH FOLLOWED UPON MY WRITING CERTAIN TREATISES

1. *Tetrachordon,* one of Milton's pamphlets in favor of divorce, the full title being *Tetrachordon: Expositions upon the four chief places of Scripture which treat of marriage.*

243. 7–8. *Mile-End Green,* in Milton's time, one of the London suburbs.

8–9. *Gordon . . . Galasp,* names of Scottish generals during the war of 1644–5, soon after which apparently this sonnet was written. This and the following sonnet were not included in the edition of 1645; they first appeared in 1673.

10. *our like,* like ours.

11. *Quintilian,* the great Latin writer on literary style.

12. *Sir John Cheke* (1514–1557), first professor of Greek at Cambridge and tutor of Edward VI.

ON THE SAME

6. *Latona's twin-born progeny,* Apollo and Diana.

TO THE LORD GENERAL CROMWELL, MAY 1652

The Puritan Parliament had a committee for *propagation of the gospel,* to which proposals were submitted by certain ministers that the Puritan preachers should be maintained at the public expense. Milton was a strong believer in the voluntary system, and objected to any interference of the government with religious matters.

7. *Darwen stream,* in Lancashire, the scene of Cromwell's victory over the Scots, Aug. 17–19, 1648.

8. *Dunbar field,* another victory, Sept. 30, 1650.

9. *Worcester's laureate wreath.* Cromwell was accustomed to speak of his success at Worcester (Sept. 3, 1651) as the ' crowning mercy ' of God.

11. *new foes,* a section of the Independents who proposed to accept state aid, as Milton's old foes, the Anglicans and Presbyterians, wished to do.

12. *secular chains,* government control.

14. *maw,* stomach. Compare *Lycidas,* ll. 114–125, p. 241.

ON THE LATE MASSACRE IN PIEDMONT

The Protestants of Piedmont were in 1655 subjected to a cruel persecution by the Court of Turin.

whose soldiery evicted them from their homes with extraordinary ferocity. The English government, through Milton, who was then Latin secretary, sent a solemn protest against the massacre to the Duke of Savoy. The sonnet expresses Milton's personal feeling.

7–8. The English agent in Piedmont narrated the following incident: 'A mother was hurled down a mighty rock with a little infant in her arms; and three days after was found dead with the child alive, but fast clasped between the arms of the mother, which were cold and stiff, insomuch that those that found them had much ado to get the child out.'

12. *The triple Tyrant,* the Pope, from his wearing a triple tiara.

14. *Babylonian woe.* The Puritans identified Rome with the Babylon of *Revelation* and of 1 Peter v, 13.

ON HIS BLINDNESS

Milton became completely blind about 1653: this sonnet was probably written not long after.

ON HIS DECEASED WIFE

244. 1. *late espousèd saint.* Catherine Woodcock, Milton's second wife, died in childbirth, in February, 1658, fifteen months after their marriage.

2. *like Alcestis.* According to the classical myth, Alcestis, who gave her life to save her husband, was rescued from death by Hercules.

6. *the old law.* Leviticus xii.

10. *her face was veiled.* Although Milton was devotedly attached to his wife, probably he had never seen her. See above as to his blindness.

PARADISE LOST, BOOK I

2. *forbidden tree.* See Genesis iii.

4. *one greater Man.* The Messiah. See Romans, v, 19.

7. *Sinai,* the lower part of the mountain range of Horeb, where God appeared to Moses. See Exodus iii and xix.

8. *first taught.* In Genesis i.

12. *fast,* close. *oracle,* the temple at Jerusalem.

15. *Aonian mount,* Helicon in Bœotia, the seat of the Greek muses. *pursues,* treats of — a classical usage.

19–22. See Genesis i, 2.

21. *Dove-like.* See Luke iii, 22.

25. *assert,* vindicate.

245. 29. *grand,* first.

32. *For,* because of; or (perhaps) but for.

36. *what time,* when; a Latin construction.

39. *peers,* equals. Latin *pares.*

45–6. See Luke x, 18.

48. See 2 Peter ii, 4.

58. *obdurate.* Accent on second syllable.

66–7. Reminiscent of Euripides and Dante.

73–4. Milton's ideas of cosmography were founded on the Ptolemaic system, and are illustrated in the accompanying figures. Fig. 1 represents the Universe before the fall, and Fig. 2 after the fall of the Angels. Fig. 3 shows the stellar world, hanging by a golden chain from the floor of heaven.

At the center of this is the earth, and around it the planets revolve in their several spheres, enclosed by the *primum mobile.* The distance from heaven to hell is three times the radius of the stellar universe.

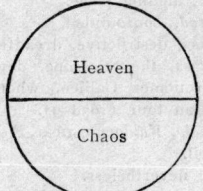

Fig. 1 — Before the fall of the Angels

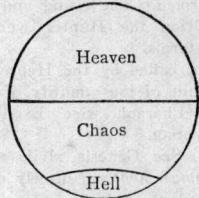

Fig. 2 — After the fall of the Angels

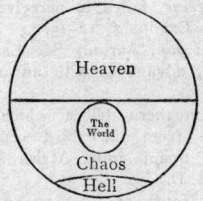

Fig. 3 — After the creation of the World

81. *Beelzebub,* the sun-god of the Philistines.

82. *Satan* 'the adversary.'

84. See Isaiah xiv, 12.

246. 114. *Doubted,* feared for.

120. *successful hope,* hope of success.

130. *conduct,* command.

148. *suffice,* satisfy.

167. *if I fail not,* if I am not mistaken. Latin construction.

172. *laid* (to rest).

178. *slip,* let slip.

187. *offend,* harm. Latin *offendere.*

247. 193. *uplift,* uplifted.

197. *whom,* those whom.

197–200. *fables,* of classical mythology, according to which the Titans rebelled against their father Uranus, as the Giants did later against Zeus or Jove. *Briareos* was a Titan, *Typhon* a Giant. The latter is described by the Greek poets living in a 'Cilician den.' *Tarsus* is the capital of Cilicia.

201. *Leviathan,* a Hebrew word meaning any huge monster. The translators of the Bible identified it with the whale, as Milton does here.

204. *night-foundered,* overtaken and enveloped by night.

226. *incumbent on,* lying on, supported by.

232–3. *Pelorus,* N. E. promontory of Sicily near Mt. *Etna.*

244. *change for,* take in exchange for.

257. *all but,* only.

266. *astonished,* astounded, thunderstruck. *Oblivious,* making forgetful.

268. *mansion,* abiding place.

248. 281. *amazed,* confounded.

282. *pernicious,* destructive, dreadful.

288. *optic glass,* the telescope, developed by the Florentine astronomer Galileo, whom Milton saw during his Italian tour (1638–9).

289–290. *Fesolé, Valdarno,* near Florence.

296. *marl,* soil.

299. *Nathles,* nevertheless.

303. *Vallombrosa,* eighteen miles from Florence in Tuscany, anciently named Etruria.

305. *Orion armed.* The rising and setting of the constellation Orion the Hunter were traditionally attended with storms.

306. *Red Sea,* called by the Hebrews the Sea of Sedge, on account of the quantity of seaweed in it.

307. *Busiris,* Pharaoh. See Exodus xiv, 5–29. *Memphian,* Egyptian.

309. *Goshen.* See Genesis xlvii, 27.

313. *Under amazement of,* utterly confounded by.

317. *If,* dependent on *lost.*

320. *virtue,* valor. Latin *virtus.*

335. *not perceive,* failed to perceive.

338–343. See Exodus x, 12–15.

339. *Amram's son,* Aaron. See Exodus vi, 20.

341. *warping,* advancing with an undulating motion.

351–5. The northern tribes which invaded the Roman empire from the third century onwards crossed from Spain into Africa and captured Carthage 439 A. D.

355. *beneath,* south of.

249. 360. *erst,* formerly.

363. *books.* Milton probably dictated '*Book*' and was misunderstood by his amanuensis. See Revelations iii, 5.

372. *religions,* religious ceremonies.

392. *Moloch.* See 1 Kings xi, 7; 2 Kings xxiii, 10; Psalm cvi, 37, 38. Sandys, whose book of travels in Palestine was known to Milton, describes the idol as 'hollow within, filled with fire,' the children offered for sacrifice being placed in his arms. 'And lest their lamentable shrieks should sadden the hearts of their parents, the priests of Moloch did deafen their ears with the continual clang of trumpets and timbrels.'

397. *Rabba,* capital of Ammon, 'the city of waters.'

398–9. *Argob, Basan, Arnon,* east of the river Jordan.

401. *Solomon.* See 1 Kings xi, 5–7; 2 Kings xxiii, 13.

403. *opprobrious hill.* The Mount of Olives, where Solomon established the worship of Moloch, was later called the 'Mount of Corruption' and 'Mount of Offence.'

404. *Hinnom,* south of Olivet.

405. *Gehenna,* the Greek form of the Hebrew *Ge Hinnom,* valley of Hinnom.

406. *Chemos,* the god of Moab, the neighbors of Ammon.

409. *Seon,* king of the Amorites. See Numbers xxi, 26.

410. *Sibma.* See Isaiah xvi, 8.

411. *the asphaltic pool,* the Dead Sea.

413. *Sittim.* See Numbers xxv.

416. *scandal,* offence.

418. *good Josiah.* See Kings xxiii, 10.

420. *the brook,* Besor, 'the river of Egypt.'

422. *Baälim and Ashtaroth,* the collective names of the various manifestations of the deities of the sun and moon respectively.

438. *Astoreth,* the same as the Assyrian Istar, the Greek Aphrodite, and the Latin Venus.

441. Sidon was the oldest city of Phenicia.

250. 444. *uxorious king,* Solomon.

446. *Thammuz,* 'Sun of Life,' the Greek Adonis, god of the solar year.

450. *Adonis,* the name of a river flowing from the heights of Lebanon, and colored in spring by the red mud gathered there.

455. *Ezekiel.* See Ezekiel viii, 14.

457. *came one.* Dagon, god of the Philistines. See 1 Samuel v, 4.

460. *grunsel,* threshold.

464–6. *Azotus . . . Gazar,* the five chief cities of the Philistines.

467. *Rimmon,* god of Damascus.

471. *leper,* Naaman. See 2 Kings v.

472. *Ahaz.* See 2 Kings xvi. *sottish,* foolish.

478. *Osiris, Isis, Orus,* Egyptian deities, worshipped under the shape of the bull, cow, and sun.

479. *abused,* deceived.

483. *borrowed,* from the Egyptians. See Exodus xii, 35–6.

484. *calf in Oreb.* See Exodus xxxii. *rebel king,* Jeroboam. 1 Kings xii, 20, 28, 29.

487. *he,* Israel. See Exodus xii.

495. *Eli's sons.* See 1 Samuel ii, 12–17.

498. *luxurious,* lustful.

502. *flown,* flushed.

503–4. *Sodom, Gibeah.* Genesis xix, Judges xix.

506. *prime,* leaders.

508. *Ionian,* Greek. *Javan,* son of Japhet. Genesis x, 2.

509. *Heaven and Earth,* Uranus and Ge, whose 12 giant children were Titans. One of them, Cronos (Saturn in Roman mythology), deposed Uranus, and was in turn deposed by his own son Zeus (Jove), whose mother was Rhea.

515–6. *Ida* in Crete was the birthplace of Zeus, *Olympus,* north of Thessaly, his abode, according to Greek mythology.

517. *Delphian cliff,* Apollo's oracle on Mt. Parnassus.

518. *Dodona,* an oracle of Zeus, in Epirus.

519. *Doric,* Greek.

520. *Adria,* the Adriatic. *Hesperian,* western, *i.e.,* Italy.

521. *Celtic,* France and Spain. *utmost isles,* of Britain.

523. *damp,* depressed.

528. *recollecting,* recovering.

251. 534. *Azazel.* Leviticus xvi, 8.

536. *advanced,* raised.

538. *emblazed,* emblazoned.

546. *orient,* bright.

547. *helms,* helmets.

548. *serried,* locked together.

550. *Dorian mood,* the kind of Greek music adapted to military exercises.

551. *recorder,* a kind of flute.

556. *'suage,* assuage.

563. *horrid,* bristling with spears. Latin *horridus.*

568. *traverse,* across.

573. *since created man,* after the creation of man.

574. *embodied,* assembled in a body. *named,* compared.

575. *small infantry,* the Pygmies. Homer's *Iliad* iii, 5.

577. *Phlegra,* in Macedonia where the Gods defeated the Giants. See l. 509.

578. *Thebes and Ilium,* the chief battle grounds of Greek tradition.

580. *fable,* Geoffrey of Monmouth's History of the Britons. *romance,* Malory's *Morte D'Arthur.*

581. *Armoric,* Breton.

583–6. The references are to scenes famous in medieval romances.

586. *peerage,* the twelve peers of the *Chanson de Roland.*

588. *observed,* obeyed.

596–9. Curiously enough, this was the only passage in the poem objected to by the official Licenser for the Press (chaplain to the Archbishop of Canterbury), when the book was first printed. Either he did not like the suggestion of a 'change' of government, or he would not admit that Charles II could be 'perplexed' even by an eclipse.

597. *disastrous,* threatening disaster.

603. *considerate,* thoughtful, reflective.

605. *remorse and passion,* pity and suffering.

609. *amerced,* condemned to loss.

613. *scathed,* injured.

252. 615. *blasted,* withered.

624. *event,* outcome.

632. *exile.* Accent on second syllable.

646. *work,* accomplish.

656. *eruption,* expedition, sortie.

662. *understood,* agreed on secretly.

670. *grisly,* horrible.

675. *brigade.* Pronounce brigad.

678. *Mammon,* riches (Syriac). See Matthew vi, 24.

686. *ransacked the center,* dug into the earth.

690. *ribs,* bars. *admire,* wonder.

253. 694. *Babel.* See Genesis xi, 1–9. *Memphian,* Egyptian, *i.e.,* the Pyramids.

703. *founded,* melted.

704. *severing,* separating.

713. *pilasters,* pillars set in a wall and lightly projecting from it. *overlaid,* surmounted.

715. *architrave,* the main beam.

716. *cornice, frieze,* adornments of the architrave. *bossy,* in relief, projecting.

717. *fretted,* worked in designs.

720. *Belus,* the Assyrian god Bel or Baal. *Serapis,* an Egyptian deity.

728. *cresset,* an iron lantern.

738. *his name,* Hephaistos or Vulcan.

739. *Ausonian land,* Italy.

740. *Mulciber,* the welder of metals.

746. *Lemnos,* sacred to Hephaistos. The story of his fall is told in Homer's *Iliad* i, 591.

750. *engines,* machines, contrivances.

756. *Pandemonium,* the place of all the demons.

764. *wont,* were wont to. *soldan,* sultan.

765. *paynim,* pagan.

769. The sun is in *Taurus* (one of the signs of the zodiac) April 19–May 20.

254. 774. *expatiate,* walk abroad. Latin use. *confer,* discuss.

780–1. Pliny placed the Pygmies beyond the source of the Ganges.

781–5. Reminiscent of *A Midsummer Night's Dream* and the *Æneid.*

785. *arbitress,* witness. The moon was supposed to be influenced by fairy incantations.

795. *recess,* retirement. *conclave,* the name given to a meeting of Cardinals in the Roman Church.

797. *frequent,* crowded. Latin use.

798. *consult,* consultation.

BOOK II

2. *Ormus,* Persia.

9. *success,* result, experience.

16. *from no fall,* if they had not fallen.

27. *whom,* him whom.

29. *Your bulwark,* as your defense.

50. *recked,* cared.

255. 52. *unexpert,* inexperienced.

59. *of,* imposed by.

60. *By,* in consequence of.

63. *our tortures,* what tortures us.

69. *Tartarean,* infernal.

73. *such,* those who think so.

74. *forgetful,* making forgetful.

75. *proper,* natural.

77. *who but felt,* who did not feel?

82. *event,* outcome.

83. *stronger,* superior in strength.

89. *exercise,* harass, torment. Latin usage.

97. *essential,* substance.

100. *at worst,* as badly off as we can be short of annihilation.

101. *proof,* experience.

104. *fatal,* established by fate.

106. *denounced,* betokened, threatened.

113. *manna.* See Exodus xvi, 31.

124. *fact,* deed.

127. *scope,* mark, aim, its original meaning in the Greek.

130. *watch,* watchmen; hence the plural verb.

132. *obscure.* Accent on first syllable.

133. *Scout,* act as scouts, reconnoiter.

256. 139. *mold,* substance. Milton imagines the angels as made of fire (see Psalm civ, 4) and the argument is that the fiery substance of the angels would expel the *baser fire* of hell.

143. *flat*, absolute.

156. *Belike*, probably. Used ironically. *impotence*, lack of self-restraint. Latin use.

165. *amain*, with all speed.

175. *Her*, of hell.

176. *cataracts*, torrents, floods.

203. *fall*, befall, happen.

210. *supreme*. Accent on first syllable.

216. *inured*, accustomed to it.

257. 224. *For happy*, in point of happiness.

231–2. *then — when*, i.e., never.

234. *former*, 'to disenthrone.' *argues*, proves.

235. *latter*, ' to regain.'

245. *Ambrosial*, divinely excellent.

249. *pursue*, seek to regain.

251. *unacceptable*. Accent on second syllable.

263–5. See Psalms xvii, 11, 13; xcvii, 2.

277. *needs*, of necessity.

278. *sensible*, sense; adj. for noun.

281. *Compose*, arrange, adjust.

288. *o'er watched*, worn out with watching.

294. *Michael*, the leading archangel, whose discomfiture of Satan and his followers is described later: vi, 320–327.

258. 301. *aspect*. Accent on second syllable.

303. *public care*, care for the common weal.

305. *Majestic* qualifies face.

306. *Atlantean*, worthy of Atlas, a Titan condemned by Zeus to bear the skies on his shoulders.

324. *first and last*. See Revelation i, 11.

330. *determined*, made an end of.

336. *to*, to the extent of.

337. *Untamed reluctance*, invincible resistance.

341. *want*, be wanting.

346. *fame*, report. Latin *fama*.

367. *puny*, literally, later born; hence, weaker.

375. *original*, origin, or perhaps originator.

376. *Advise*, consider.

380. *By Satan*. See I, 650–654.

259. 382. *confound*, utterly destroy.

387. *states*, authorities, or bodies of representatives, as in the phrase, 'the three estates of the realm,' meaning the King, Lords, and Commons in Great Britain.

391. *Synod*, assembly, meeting.

404. *tempt*, try.

406. *obscure*, obscurity. Adj. for noun.

407. *uncouth*, unknown.

409. *abrupt*, abyss, *i.e.*, between hell and the world. *arrive*, reach.

410. *isle*, the World, hung like a globe in Chaos from the floor of Heaven.

413. *had need*, would have need of.

415. *Choice*, careful selection.

418. *suspense*, in suspense. Latin form.

423. *Astonished*, astounded.

425. *hardy*, bold, courageous.

429. *unmoved*. Contrasted with *Astonished*, l. 424.

431. *demur*, hesitation.

434. *convex*, circle.

441. *abortive*, monstrous.

443. *remains*, awaits.

452. *Refusing*, if I refuse.

457. *intend*, consider, devise.

461. *deceive*, beguile. Latin use. *slack*, mitigate.

462. *mansion*, abode.

467. *prevented*, forestalled.

468. *raised*, encouraged. Refers to *Others*.

260. 470. *erst*, before.

471. *opinion*, reputation.

478. *awful*, full of awe.

485. *close*, concealed. *varnished o'er*, speciously covered with.

490. *louring element*, dark and threatening sky.

491. *Scowls*, covers the face of nature with a dark cloud of rain or snow.

492. *If chance*, if it chances that.

503. *accord*, agreement.

AREOPAGITICA

In November, 1644, when this pamphlet was published, the parliamentary cause was triumphant in the field, and high hopes were entertained for its future success in the promotion of 'real and substantial liberty — whose existence depends not so much on the terror of the sword as on sobriety of conduct and integrity of life.' But Parliament was already showing an inclination to adopt the intolerant and tyrannical measures which it had condemned in its adversaries, and it was against one of these — an order that books should not be printed without license — that Milton was here directing his efforts. His object was to secure the free publication of thought,—' that the power of determining what was true and what was false; what ought to be published and what to be suppressed, might no longer be entrusted to a few illiterate and illiberal individuals, who refused their sanction to any work which contained views or sentiments at all above the level of the vulgar superstition.' Beside Milton's general devotion to the cause of liberty, he had a special incentive in the attempt which was being made by the Stationers Company to suppress his divorce pamphlets, which had aroused a good deal of hostile feeling.

260. *b.* 15. *Julius Agricola*, governor of Britain 78–85 A. D.

16. *Cæsar*, a general name for the Roman Emperor. *preferred* — French. This statement is made on the authority of Tacitus.

22. *Hercynian*, a name given by the Romans to the mountainous and wooded region in the south and center of Germany; the country beyond it, *Transylvania*, which became part of the Austrian Empire in 1689, had during the Commonwealth friendly relations with England.

28. *propending*, inclining.

31. *as out of Sion*. See Joel ii, 1.

36. *Wyclif*, the English ecclesiastical reformer of the fourteenth century.

38. *Huss, Jerome* (of Prague), *Luther, Calvin*, leaders of the great Protestant Reformation on the Continent.

44. *demeaned*, conducted, managed.

46. *of whom*, of those of whom.

261. *a.* 2. *mansion house*, abiding place, manorial seat.

5. *plates*, armor. *instruments*, weapons.

14. *trying*, testing.

26. *white already*. See John iv, 35.

31. *fantastic*, fancied, imaginary.

38. *ill-deputed*, i.e., to the clergy.

56. *Pyrrhus*, after fighting against the Romans at Heraclea (280 B. C.) is said to have exclaimed: ' How easy it would be for me to conquer the world if I had Roman soldiers.'

b. 10. *schisms, dissections*, literally, cuttings.

28. *Moses.* See Numbers xii, 29.

35. *Joshua.* See Numbers xii, 28.

46. *maniple*, a company in the Roman army, consisting of about 60 men serving under the same ensign.

52. *vex*, worry.

58. *besieged.* Two years before the publication of Milton's pamphlet the Royalists had advanced almost to the gates of London. See Milton's first sonnet printed on p. 242.

262. *a.* 4. *suburb trenches.* The suburbs were defended by trenches made by the loyal citizens, even women and children helping.

10. *to a rarity*, to an extraordinary extent or degree.

12. *argues*, proves.

16. *derives itself to*, develops into.

20. *nigh*, closely. The incident here referred to is recounted by Livy xxvi, 11.

28. *to*, as to.

30. *pertest*, sprightliest.

34. *sprightly up*, lively and excited.

41. *old and wrinkled skin.* Like a snake.

48. *strong man.* Samson. See Judges xvi, 13, 14.

50. *mewing*, renewing; originally used of a hawk molting.

54. *noise*, noisy crew.

55. *flocking*, not daring to act independently.

b. 1. *prognosticate*, foretell, like the astrologers and almanac makers.

7. *engrossers*, merchants who dealt in large quantities, and often made a corner to raise prices. Milton compares to these the Licensers of Printing, who will set up a monopoly in knowledge.

21. *purchased*, obtained.

24. *influence*, mystic power; the original reference is to astrology.

43. *law.* The Roman law gave fathers power of life and death over children.

44. *despatch*, slay.

45. *stick closest*, be most faithful. See Proverbs xviii, 24.

47. *for coat — dangelt*, merely to resist illegal taxation, the former part of the phrase referring to the clothing and conveyance of troops, the latter to ship-money. Milton is arguing for a nobler freedom than that of not paying unjust taxes.

51. *utter*, publish.

55. *unequal*, unjust.

263. *a.* 13. *vote*, solemn wish.

18. *last testament.* See John xiv, 27.

27. *dis-conformity*, dissent.

38. *controversal*, opposite. The temple was open in war, closed in peace.

46. *Her confuting*, confutation by her.

51. *the discipline of Geneva*, the form of faith and of church government accepted as perfect by the Presbyterians.

52. *fabricked*, fabricated, manufactured.

56. *casements*, windows. *collusion*, deception.

58. *wise man*, Solomon. See also Matthew xiii, 44.

b. 6. *equipage*, equipment.

8. *battle*, army.

22. *shifts*, sleights, contrivance

31. *Micaiah.* See 1 Kings xxii, 1–2

40. *nailed to the cross.* See Colossians ii, 14. *purchase*, boon, achievement.

42. *His doctrine.* Romans xiv, 5–9.

50. *outward conformity*, under royal and episcopal government.

52. *linen decency*, the outward conformity of a white surplice is abolished, but the spirit remains.

264. *a.* 1. *care not*, do not take care, *truth separated from truth*, i.e., essentials from non-essentials.

8. *wood, and hay, and stubble.* See 1 Corinthians iii, 12.

11. *subdichotomies*, sub-divisions.

16. *wheat from the tares.* See Matthew xiii, 24-43.

17. *fry*, small fish; properly, spawn.

27. *extirpate*, extirpated.

38. *unity of Spirit.* Ephesians iv, 3.

45. *bejesuited*, made into Jesuits.

53. *unplausible*, unappreciated.

56. *see to*, look upon.

b. 30. *Convocation House*, where the governing body of the Church of England met.

31. *Chapel.* The Puritan Assembly of Divines met in Henry VII's Chapel at Westminster in 1643, and drew up a Confession of Faith and two Catechisms.

53. *canonized*, embodied in canons or rules.

34. *convincement*, argument and conviction.

35. *supple*, cure.

36. *edify*, build up, establish.

41. *liege tombs.* Henry VII's Chapel contains several royal tombs beside his own.

47. *that we do not give*, from giving. Latin construction.

56. *manage*, handle.

265. *a.* 8. *Priests, Pharisees.* See Matthew v, 20.

9. *precipitant*, precipitate.

18. *the beginning of this Parliament.* Nov. 3, 1640.

20. *Imprimatur.* The Licenser's stamp or inscription, ' Let it be printed.'

27. *Moses.* See Numbers xi, 28–29.

29. *young John.* See Luke ix, 50.

32. *elders*, the leaders of the Presbyterians.

36. *let*, hindrance.

40. *Inquisition.* One of the duties of the Inquisition was the prohibition of heretical books. The Dominican Order was especially active in the campaign against heresy. Both the Inquisition and the Dominicans were especially unpopular as Roman Catholic institutions to the Puritan readers to whom Milton was appealing.

52. *next before this.* The earlier order was passed on Jan. 29, 1642.

57. *fire — executioner.* Seditious books were burnt in public by the hangman.

b. 3. *authentic,* genuine, so-called and really so.

7. *Star Chamber,* abolished by the Puritans in 1641 owing to its unjust exactions. It had charge, among other things, of licensing.

12. *Lucifer.* See Isaiah xiv, 12.

17. *bind,* by recognizances, as people enter into bonds for their good behavior in the English courts.

19. *precedent,* of Jan. 29, 1642.

22. *doubted,* suspected.

24. *monopolizers.* The order of 1643 recognized the monopoly of the Stationers' Company, who applied the fees for licensing in part to the 'relief and maintenance of their poor.'

29. *divers glossing colors,* various specious misrepresentations.

32. *exercise a superiority,* exert authority, have an advantage.

33. *neighbors,* fellow booksellers.

34–5. *therefore — that,* to the end that.

36. *vassals,* subjects.

40. *malignant,* seditious, royalist.

42. *sophisms and elenchs of merchandise,* trade sophistries and fallacies.

43. *skill not,* am not versed in or concerned about.

45. *incident,* inevitable.

49. *what hath been erred,* the mistakes that have been made. Latin construction.

50. *in,* for those in.

51. *advertisement,* warning.

DRYDEN: HEROIC STANZAS

Cromwell died on September 3, 1658, and was buried on November 23. When this poem was published in 1659, there was every appearance that Richard Cromwell was firmly established as his father's successor. Dryden's family was Puritan, and his admiration of the great Protector was no doubt sincere, though his expression of it was conventional and exaggerated.

266. 1–4. *And now 't is time.* At the end of a Roman emperor's funeral ceremonials, they let fly *the sacred eagle* which was supposed to carry his soul to heaven.

8. *authentic,* authoritative, beyond dispute.

15. *prevent,* anticipate.

18. *circular,* perfectly rounded.

267. 25. *bays,* garlands.

32. *Pompey,* who acquired the title of 'Great' before he was thirty, and brought his career to a culminating point on his forty-fifth birthday B. C. 61 in a great trimphal procession, after that declined before the growing influence of Julius Cæsar. Cromwell came into public notice at 45, became Protector at 54, and died at the height of his fame at 59 — about the same age as Pompey when he was assassinated.

41. *Our former chiefs,* the parliamentary generals at the beginning of the war did not press the campaign against the king with vigor. *sticklers,* umpires, not combatants.

42. *poise,* balance.

45. *consumption,* destruction.

48. *breathing,* letting. When Dryden became a

royalist poet, his enemies interpreted this line as a condonation of the execution of Charles I.

49. *went,* became.

51. *prevent,* anticipate.

56. *the vestal.* Tarpeia was crushed to death by the shields of the Sabines to whom she betrayed the citadel of Rome on the promise of the shields as reward.

58. *That giant-prince.* Blake, the great Puritan admiral, died and was buried in Westminster Abbey about a year before Cromwell.

64. *halcyons,* kingfishers. It was an ancient myth that the sea was calm during their breeding season. *sea,* correctly rimed with *obey,* according to the pronunciation of the time.

ASTRÆA REDUX

Immediately after the Restoration Dryden welcomed that event as a return of the golden age of Justice, this being the significance of the title of his poem. The contrast with the political sentiments of the previous poem is as marked as it was sudden.

5. *the white* (cliffs of Dover).

10. *ravish,* take away.

13–16. *Moses — name.* See Exodus xxxiii, 20; xxxiv, 6.

268. 33. *Preventing,* running before.

36. *May.* Charles II entered London in 1660 on May 29, his birthday.

39. *That star,* Venus, which on the day of Charles II's birth shone brightly at noon.

43. *whiter,* more fortunate. A Latinism.

45. *morn,* youth.

53. *Cronos* (later identified with Chronos, Time) in Greek mythology, was said to devour his own offspring.

58. *Holland,* at this time England's great rival in the eastern trade. Each nation accused the other of misdoings in its foreign possessions, and denied the accusation when leveled against itself.

61. *France* had reluctantly been Charles II's host during part of his exile.

72. *Augustus,* the first Roman emperor, whose reign was marked by peace, prosperity, and progress in the arts.

ABSALOM AND ACHITOPHEL

This satirical poem, written, it is said, at the suggestion of Charles II, was directed against Shaftesbury, the minister whom Charles had dismissed, and who had retaliated by arousing public alarm in connection with the Popish Plot and by furthering the claims of the Duke of Monmouth, the king's illegitimate son, to the throne, in opposition to the lawful heir, Charles's brother, the Duke of York, who later succeeded as James II. In November, 1681, when the poem was published, Shaftesbury was a prisoner in the Tower on a charge of high treason, and Dryden's attack was no doubt meant to influence public feeling (and the jury) against him. In this respect it failed, for Shaftesbury was acquitted; but it made a great sensation and remains the most remarkable example of political satire in the English language. The scriptural allegory is not closely adhered to and serves as a transparent veil for personal vituperation.

1. *Jerusalem,* London.

9. *David,* Charles II.

14. *heathen,* Roman Catholic.

20. *Jewish rabbins,* leading clergy of the Church of England.

269. 24. *Plot,* the Popish Plot, a Jesuit conspiracy, which if it ever existed, was greatly exaggerated for political purposes.

34. *Egyptian,* French.

35–37. This blasphemous sneer at the Roman Catholic doctrine of transubstantiation must have been regretted by Dryden after his conversion.

43. *court and stews.* The king was (justly) suspected of being a Roman Catholic; his mistresses were known to be; so was the Duke of York, his brother.

44. *Hebrew priests,* Church of England clergymen.

46. *God's anointed,* the king. One of the reports circulated about the Popish Plot was that the conspirators had planned the assassination of Charles II and the placing of his brother, who was a Roman Catholic, on the throne.

57. *threat,* threaten.

66. *Achitophel,* Anthony Ashley Cooper, Earl of Shaftesbury, formerly Lord Chancellor, at this time the leader of the party in favor of making the Duke of Monmouth the next heir to the throne and excluding the Duke of York as a Roman Catholic.

68. *close,* secret.

73. *pigmy body.* Shaftesbury was of small stature and his frame was enfeebled by disease.

78. *boast his wit,* show off his skill.

86. *unfeathered two-legged thing.* A humorous description of man ascribed to Plato. Shaftesbury's heir was a man of 'no ability and insignificant character.'

87. *huddled,* confused.

91. *the triple bond,* the Triple Alliance of England, Holland, and Sweden against France, made in 1668 and exceedingly popular in England. It was broken in 1670 without Shaftesbury's knowledge by Charles II, who made a secret treaty with the French king.

96–107. Added in the second edition, after Shaftesbury's acquittal.

104. *abbethdin,* president of the Jewish judicature. Shaftesbury was Lord Chancellor 1672–3.

270. 111. *cockle,* weed.

113. *wanted,* lacked. Dryden's compliment to himself as David, the sweet singer of Israel, is shameless, but true. His poem has proved 'immortal.'

120. *manifest,* convicted. A Latinism.

125. *more he makes.* The charge that Shaftesbury invented the Plot is absurd; but he undoubtedly used it for political purposes by fomenting public agitation.

129. *Jebusite.* One of the stories current at the time was that the king himself had become a Roman Catholic. It is now known that it was true.

135. *instinct.* Accent on second syllable.

137. *warlike Absalom,* the favorite son of the Biblical David, here signifying the Duke of Monmouth, Charles II's favorite son, though illegitimate. He had commanded an expedition sent to suppress a Scottish rising.

140. *title not allowed.* Monmouth's claim to the succession was barred by his illegitimacy.

143. *democracy,* then a form of government in disfavor. Dryden was so fond of this line that he repeated it in *The Hind and the Panther* (p. 273, l. 211).

THE HIND AND THE PANTHER

In this religious and satirical allegory, which appeared two years after James II's accession and about a year after Dryden's conversion to Roman Catholicism, the 'milk-white Hind' stands for the Church of Rome; the Panther, fair but spotted, for the Church of England; and the less attractive beasts for the Puritan sects which were most bitterly opposed to Romanism.

6. *Scythians,* famous archers of antiquity.

8. *doomed,* sentenced, condemned.

11. *obnoxious,* liable to injury from.

13–16. The Roman martyrs in Great Britain since the Reformation.

35. *Bear,* the Independent, or modern Congregationalist.

37. *Hare,* Quaker.

39. *Ape,* Freethinker.

41. *Lion,* King of England.

271. 43. *Boar,* Anabaptist. The following lines refer to the excesses committed in connection with the Anabaptist rising in Germany in the sixteenth century.

53. *Reynard,* the Arian. Arius, one of the early heretics of the Christian Church, held that God the Son was not co-existent or co-equal with God the Father; this doctrine was combated by Athanasius and condemned at the Council of Nice.

55. *Socinus,* an Italian nobleman who revived Arian beliefs in the sixteenth century.

70. *her,* the Roman Church.

79. *Three in One,* the doctrine of the Trinity.

93. *host,* the consecrated wafer of the Eucharist.

95. *Impassible,* incapable of suffering.

96–9. See John xx, 19–26.

104. *quarry,* game, object of pursuit.

121. *proponent,* proposing, putting forth.

272. 128. *bilanders,* a Dutch word for small coasting vessels.

135. A reference to the Roman doctrine of transubstantiation.

139. *His clearest words.* 'This is my body.' See Luke xxii, 19.

144. *compound,* compromise.

152. *Polonian,* Polish. The Polish Protestants adopted Socinianism. See ll. 54–55.

153. *Wolf,* Presbyterian.

165. An allusion at once to the Presbyterian doctrine of predestination and the Puritan habit of cropping the hair close, which made the ears project.

168. *ruled a while.* During the Commonwealth.

171. *Cambria,* Wales. The wolf was exterminated in Wales by the exaction of wolves' heads as tribute.

173. *Geneva — France.* Calvin, originally a Frenchman, was appointed in 1536 Professor of Divinity at Geneva, where he drew up the system of faith and church government afterwards adopted by the French and other Protestants.

176. *Wyclif,* the English reformer of the fourteenth century.

178. *Helvetian,* Swiss.

179. *Leman,* Geneva.

180. *Zwinglius,* a Swiss Reformer a little earlier than Calvin.

183. *sanhedrim,* Parliament.

185. *Corah.* See Numbers xvi.

187. *ephod,* priestly garment.

189. *class,* a term in the Presbyterian system of church government.

190. *Fox,* Reynard, the Arian.

205. *a puddle and a wall,* the Lake of Geneva and the Alps.

273. 211. See *Absalom and Achitophel,* p. 270, l. 143.

228. *teemless,* unproductive.

232. *Colchos,* the home of the sorceress Medea.

234. *common-weal,* republic.

236. *Adam* was supposed to have given the beasts their names in the Garden of Eden.

247. *allay,* alloy.

248. *shards,* dung, which, it was thought, produced beetles.

262. *Lion,* the King.

267. *commits* (sin).

274. 297. *Levees and couchees,* early and late entertainments at court.

312. James II's Declaration of Indulgence to all dissenters from the Church of England was issued just before the poem was published. The royal favor and protection for Romanism had, of course, been shown before.

333. It was a classical tradition — reversed here by Dryden on his own authority — that the wolf had power to take away the voice of a man it saw first.

ALEXANDER'S FEAST

This ode was written for a London musical society, which held an annual festival on Nov. 22, the day of St. Cecilia, reputed the inventor of the organ and the patron saint of music.

1. *for Persia won,* for the winning of Persia.

2. *By Philip's* warlike son, Alexander, son of Philip of Macedon, and the conqueror of Persia.

9. *Thais,* a famous Athenian courtesan who accompanied Alexander into Asia, and, according to the tradition which Dryden makes use of in this poem, induced him to fire the palace of Persepolis.

17. *Timotheus,* Alexander's favorite musician.

22. *from,* with.

275. 64. *Darius,* the Persian king whom Alexander had conquered.

83. *Lydian,* soft, sensuous.

113–4. *rear — hair.* Correctly rimed according to the pronunciation of the time.

276. 139. *vocal frame,* organ.

147. The tradition was that Cecilia, owing to her virtue and piety, was visited by an angel.

ESSAY OF DRAMATIC POESY

a. 1. *that memorable day,* June 3, 1665.

b. 1. *conduct,* leadership.

2. *his royal highness,* the Duke of York, afterwards James II.

16. *Eugenius,* Sackville, Lord Buckhurst, who later became Earl of Dorset. *Crites,* Sir Robert Howard, Dryden's brother-in-law. *Lisideius,* Sir Charles Sedley. *Neander,* Dryden himself.

26. *the bridge,* London bridge.

278. 2. *Sir John Suckling.* See p. 179.

4. *Mr. Waller.* See p. 178.

5. *Sir John Denham.* See p. 181.

7. *Mr. Cowley.* See p. 183.

57. *a genere et fine,* a definition of class and object.

b. 16. *Thespis* (c. 540 B.C.), the somewhat fabulous inventor of Greek drama.

17. *Aristophanes* (448–c. 388 B.C.), the great Greek comic writer.

30. *virtuosi,* those skilled in the fine arts.

45. *pretend,* lay claim.

279. *a.* 25. *want,* lack.

37. *remember,* remind.

b. 11. *fable,* plot.

280. *a.* 33. *Corneille* (1606–84), the great French dramatist, contemporary with Dryden.

b. 7. *intended,* aimed at.

36. *wanted,* fell short.

281. *a.* 1. *Macrobius,* c. beginning of fifth century A.D.

7. *Tully,* Marcus Tullius Cicero (106–43 B.C.).

282. *a.* 25. *lively,* lifelike.

283. *a.* 35. *Scaliger* (Julius Cæsar), 1484–1558.

b. 33. *inartificial,* inartistic.

284. *a.* 15. *shadow,* palliate.

28. *sock and buskin,* the stage shoe of comedy and tragedy respectively.

57. *the author,* Ben Jonson.

b. 28. *clenches,* playing upon words.

41. *Mr. Hales* (1584–1656), Greek Professor at Oxford and Fellow of Eton College.

58. *precedent,* predecessor, model.

285. *a.* 4. *censure,* opinion.

27. *apt,* inclined.

b. 20. *taxed,* accused.

37. *comply with,* observe.

DEFOE: THE TRUE BORN ENGLISHMAN

This poem was a reply to an attack on William III and the Dutch nation, entitled *The Foreigners.* It was so successful in turning popular opinion in the king's favor that he had Defoe sent for to express his obligations to the writer.

286. 11–14. See Matthew xxviii, 19.

THE SHORTEST WAY WITH THE DISSENTERS

The succession of Queen Anne in 1702 disappointed Defoe and his nonconformist friends, while it correspondingly encouraged the tory and high church party. The latter pressed for severe measures against the dissenters, who had been tolerated under William III, and allowed to compromise by 'occasional conformity,' *i.e.*, by going to church on official occasions and attending their own place of worship at other times. Defoe in his pamphlet endeavored to show the absurdity of the high church position by making extravagant claims on their behalf, although he took occasion to aim a blow now and then at the inconsistency of his own side. The result was that he offended both parties, although for a while the high church clergy were so deceived that, according to Defoe, one of them wrote to him that next to the Holy Bible and Sacred Comments he held *The Shortest Way with the Dissenters* 'as the most valuable thing I can have. I look upon it as the Only Method! and I pray God to put it into the heart of our most gracious Queen, to put what is there proposed in execution.'

257. *b.* 10. *Sir Roger L'Estrange,* a prolific pamphleteer, the founder in 1665 of the *Gazette,* the first English newspaper which has continued to appear regularly ever since. It is the official organ of the British Government.

22. *some people,* the Nonconformists.

33. *fourteen years,* from the Revolution of 1688 to 1702.

35. *church,* the Church of England.

37. *sort,* set, lot.

41. *reproach of the wicked.* Writing in the character of a high church clergyman, Defoe imitates Scripture phraseology.

288. *a.* 8. *Act of Toleration* (1689), relieving the nonconformists from penalties for not attending the services of the Church of England.

15. *abjurations.* The clergy were required to take an oath of fidelity to William III and abjure their allegiance to James. Many refused and were deprived of their livings.

28. *a war.* William engaged, with varying success, in a prolonged struggle against Louis XIV of France.

34. *in France.* After the Revocation of the Edict of Nantes in 1685, the Huguenots were forced to conform or leave the country.

38–40. *one king — another . . . a third.* Charles I, James II, William III.

42. *the fourth,* Anne.

b. 40. *a sordid impostor,* Oliver Cromwell.

289. *a.* 23–4. *Just such measure — again.* See Matthew vii, 2.

41. *regicides,* the judges who condemned Charles I.

52. *Rye House Plot* (1682–3), a conspiracy to assassinate Charles II and his brother James.

55. *unusual favor.* James was in favor of toleration to both Puritan and Roman Catholic dissenters; but the Puritans, suspecting that his designs were really directed to Roman Catholic supremacy, joined in the movement against him.

b. 20. *a king of their own,* William III.

31. *Scotland.* The Church of Scotland, with the consent of William III, abolished episcopacy, and has ever since been presbyterian in its form of government.

290. *a.* 32. *the right heir.* The high church Tories who had remained loyal to James II looked forward to putting his son on the throne at the death of

Anne. The Elector of Hanover, who became George I, was not in the direct line of succession.

34. *ridiculous settlements.* The act of Settlement, passed by Parliament in 1701, vested the succession in the House of Hanover.

48. *French king.* Louis XIV expelled 400,000 Huguenots.

b. 2. *some animals,* rats.

22. *the common enemy,* France.

291. *a.* 17. *Monmouth,* beheaded after the rebellion of 1685.

18. *Shaftesbury,* died in exile 1683. *Argyle,* head of a Scottish rising against James; executed 1685.

28. *experimentally,* as a result of experience.

56. *impossible* (if the dissenters are tolerated).

b. 18–19. *What will — spoken for?* See Song of Solomon viii, 8.

22. *enthusiasm* was associated with dissenters, and generally regarded with disfavor in the eighteenth century.

45. *sensitive,* of the senses, physical. *these,* the dissenters.

292. *a.* 24. *Amalekite race.* The enemies of Israel in Canaan. See 1 Samuel xv.

42. *Moses — Israelites.* See Exodus xxxii, 28 The number given there is, however, three thousand.

57. *gallows instead of the counter,* hanging instead of imprisonment.

58. *counter,* a city prison. *galleys,* enslavement to the oar in a galley.

b. 1. *conventicle,* a gathering of dissenters for worship.

5 *sheriffs and mayors.* It was the custom of dissenters to go to Church on their appointment to official positions, in accordance with the law.

34. *hang men for trifles.* Hanging was the punishment for stealing in England up to 1823.

293. *b.* 53. *humor,* spirit, influence.

294. *a.* 39. *religious houses,* convents, which were at this time illegal.

40. *meeting houses,* for nonconformist worship.

PREFACE TO THE REVIEW

The *Review,* begun on Feb. 19, 1704, and published first once, then twice a week, for nine years gave Defoe scope for his talents as a journalist. The original title was *A Review of the Affairs of France and of all Europe, as influenced by that Nation,* France being at that time the center of European politics. Defoe discussed not only politics but trade and current gossip; he invented not only editorial comment, which was before unknown, but personal interviews, scandalous personalities, answers to correspondents, and many other features of the modern newspaper. The numbers of the *Review* were issued afterwards in annual volumes, and in this preface to Vol. I Defoe sets forth his motives and aims in the undertaking.

294. *b.* 42. *the Wise Man,* Solomon.

47. *first design.* See the original title, as given above.

295. *a.* 15. *Marlborough,* the great English general who defeated the French at Blenheim, Aug. 13, 1704. The war continued for several years.

b. 24. *negoce,* commerce.

296. *b. 2. its birth.* The design of the *Review* was conceived by Defoe in prison.

297. *a. 10. D. F.* Daniel Foe. The name Defoe was adopted by the author a year later.

THE EDUCATION OF WOMEN

The *Essay upon Projects,* from which this paper is taken, was written in 1692, but first printed in 1697.

297. *a. 27. conversible,* fit for human intercourse.

b. 13. wit, intellectual ability.

32. *more tongues than one.* Milton is reported to have said that one tongue was enough for any woman.

43. *genius,* natural ability.

298. *a. 17. female government,* government by women.

SWIFT: A TALE OF A TUB

299. *A Tale of a Tub.*

' Seamen have a custom, when they meet a whale, to fling him out an empty tub by way of amusement, to divert him from laying violent hands upon the ship . . . the whale was interpreted to be Hobbes's *Leviathan* . . . whence the wits of our age are said to borrow their weapons . . . and it was decreed, that, in order to prevent these Leviathans from tossing and sporting with the Commonwealth . . . they should be diverted from that game by a Tale of a Tub.' (Swift's Preface.)

300. *a. 32. d'Argent,* of wealth. *de Grands Titres,* of distinguished titles.

33. *d'Orgueil,* of pride.

49. *Locket's,* a famous ordinary, or tavern, at Charing Cross. *Will's* coffee-house. See below, 325. *a.* 34, note.

b. 24. grande monde, world of fashion.

37. *Jupiter Capitolinus.* From his temple on the Capitoline Hill, Rome.

301. *a. 12. They held the universe to be a large suit of clothes, etc.* Compare Carlyle's *Sartor Resartus.*

16. *primum mobile.* In the Ptolemaic cosmogony, the outer or tenth revolving sphere.

b. 21. ex traduce. From the root: from the original stock.

302. *a. 32. shoulder-knots.* This fashion had been introduced from France in the reign of Charles II. See *Tatler,* No. 82.

35. *ruelles,* private gatherings.

303. *a. 38. nuncupatory and scriptory,* verbal and written.

b. 23. my lord C— and Sir J. W. have not been identified.

305. *a. 41. fonde,* fund, stock, capital.

307. *a. 1–3. Varias inducere . . . piscem.* Horace, *Ars Poetica,* ll. 2 and 4.

312. *b. 49. Newgate.* The London prison for debtors and malefactors.

52. *Exchange women.* Women who kept shops in the piazzas of the Royal Exchange. For Steele's description, see p. 333.

54. *the mobile,* the mob. Latin, *mobile vulgus.*

314. *a. 58. The philosopher's stone and the universal medicine.* Sought by medieval alchemists and mystics.

315. *b. 1. the giant Laurcalco.* Inaccurate allusion to the passage (*Don Quixote,* Bk. I, Chap. XVIII) in which Don Quixote mistakes a flock of sheep for an army. ' That knight — is the valorous Laurcalco, Lord of the Silver Bridge.'

b. 16–17. an ancient temple . . . upon Salisbury plain. Probably Stonehenge.

316. *a. 4. a disease . . . the stinging of the tarantula.* Tarantism, or dancing mania, was supposed to be so caused, and curable only by music or dancing.

a. 9. Westminster-hall, etc. Places noteworthy for their noises; Westminster Hall frequented by lawyers; Billingsgate famous for the bad language of its fish-wives; the Royal Exchange a center for brokers and merchants of all nations.

b. 7. janizary, a mercenary soldier in the bodyguard of the Sultan, in the middle ages.

318. *b. 10. a spunging house.* A tavern for the temporary detention of persons arrested for debt.

A MEDITATION UPON A BROOMSTICK

Hon. Robert Boyle (1627–1691). A celebrated scientist, ' The father of chemistry and brother to the Earl of Cork.' One of the original members of the Royal Society. Swift's essay travesties the platitudinous moralizing of his religious meditations.

A MODEST PROPOSAL

321. *b. 25. the famous Psalmanazar.* George Psalmanazar, a notorious impostor, pretended to be a native of Formosa, of which he published a *Description* in 1705.

323. *a. 16. Topinamboo.* A district of Brazil.

STEELE: THE TATLER

325. *a. 33. White's Chocolate-house.* In St. James's Street. Famous for gambling.

34. *Will's Coffee-house.* No. 1, Bow Street, Covent Garden. Originally kept by William Urwin. Pepy's *Diary* mentions it, Feb. 3, 1663, as a resort of Dryden and notable for ' very witty and pleasant discourse.'

35. *Grecian.* Coffee-house in the Strand, originally kept by a Greek named Constantine, had been a resort of Newton, other members of the Royal Society, and Templars.

36. *Saint James's Coffee-house.* Near St. James's Palace. A resort of Whig statesmen, military men, and men of fashion.

45. *plain Spanish.* A simple wine.

48. *kidney,* temper, humor. A pun on the name of one of the waiters.

b. 1. casting a figure. Determining the horoscope.

THE SPECTATOR

326. *a. 39. Lord Rochester.* John Wilmot, Earl of Rochester (1647–80), a fashionable rake and poet of the Restoration period. *Sir George Etherege* (1639–94). The Restoration dramatist. Like Rochester, a courtly rake.

41. *Bully Dawson.* d. 1699. A notorious swaggerer and gamester.

b. 15. *Inner Temple.* One of the Inns of Court.

24. *Aristotle,* etc. The reference is to his *Poetics.*

25. *Longinus.* Greek Philosopher, third century A. D., to whom the essay, *On Sublimity,* is doubtfully ascribed.

26. *Littleton or Coke.* Sir Thomas Littleton (1402–1481) and Sir Edward Coke (1552–1634) were members of the Inner Temple (above, *b.* 15). A work of the first with commentary by the second used to be the English authority on the law of real property.

36. *Demosthenes.* The greatest Greek Orator (384–322 B. C.). *Tully.* Marcus Tullius Cicero (106–43 B. C.), Roman orator and philosopher.

5–8. *The Rose.* A tavern adjoining Drury Lane Theater.

327. *a.* 6. *the city of London.* The central or business district is so called. Again below, 334. *b.* 11.

328. *a.* 10. *Duke of Monmouth.* The Absolom of Dryden's *Absolom and Achitophel.* See above, 268

329. *a.* 43. *Sir Richard Blackmore* (c. 1650–1729). Physician to William III, and a poet of repute in his day.

332. *a.* 29. *Martial* (Bk. I, 69), Latin poet, first century A. D.

b. 55. *Strand Bridge.* A landing pier at the foot of Strand Lane, giving access to the Strand.

333. *a.* 19. *The Vainloves.* Vainlove is 'a capricious lover' in Congreve's comedy, *The Old Bachelor.*

334. *b.* 1. *Robin's.* A coffee-house in Exchange Alley, frequented by brokers.

11. *the city.* See 327. *a.* 6, note.

ADDISON: THE SPECTATOR

336 *b.* 22 *Child's.* Coffee-house in St. Paul's Churchyard.

30. *the Cocoa-tree.* A chocolate-house frequented by tories as St. James's by whigs. The Spectator pretends to patronize both.

31–2. *Drury Lane and the Haymarket.* The two principal theaters of London. The Theater Royal in Drury Lane, designed by Sir Christopher Wren, had been opened in 1674. The Haymarket Opera House, designed and built by Sir John Van Brugh, had been opened in 1705.

36. *Jonathan's.* Coffee-house in Cornhill. 'The general mart for stock-jobbers.' (*Tatler,* No. 38.)

337. *b.* 8. *Mr. Buckley's.* Buckley was the publisher.

9. *Little Britain.* A street in London.

341. *a.* 25. *Moll White* The witch described in *Spectator,* No. 117

342. *a.* 11. *The Committee* (1665). Comedy by Sir Robert Howard.

15. *Distressed Mother.* Adaptation, by Ambrose Philips, of Racine's *Andromaque.* Produced 1712.

24. *The Mohocks.* Some ruffianly carousers of the upper classes assumed this name. They committed a series of outrages in 1712.

345. *b.* 49. *Mr. Cowley,* etc. See Cowley's *Davideis* iii, 403–4.

26. *Gallus,* Caius Cornelius (c. 69–26). Roman poet and general.

Propertius, Sextus (c. 50–16 B. C.), poet.

27. *Horace.* Quintus Horatius Flaccus (65–8 B. C.)., the Roman poet.

Varius. Lucius Varius Rufus, 1st century B. C. *Tucca,* Plotius Tucca and Lucius *Varius* were Virgil's literary executors.

Ovid. Publius Ovidius Naso (43 B. C.–c. 17 A. D.).

28. *Bavius and Maevius.* Inferior Roman poets mentioned by Virgil (*Ecl.* iii) and Horace (*Epode* x).

347. *a.* 40. *Sir John Denham.* See p. 181.

56. *The Art of Criticism.* Pope's *Essay on Criticism.* See p. 350.

b. 18. *Boileau* (1636–1711). French critic and poet.

48. *Petronius Arbiter.* Roman satirical author. Died c 66 A. D.

Quintilian. Marcus Fabius Quintilianus (c. 35–c. 95 A. D.), Roman rhetorician.

49. *Longinus.* See 326. *b.* 25, note.

348. *b.* 1–2. *Essay on Translated Verse.* By Wentworth Dillon, Earl of Roscommon (1634–85).

2–3. *Essay on the Art of Poetry.* By John Sheffield, Duke of Buckinghamshire (1649–1721).

47. *The path of an arrow.' Wisdom of Solomon,* v, 12–13. The quotation is inaccurate.

349. *a.* 47. *Sir Cloudesley Shovel.* Commander of the British fleets from 1705. Drowned 1707.

POPE: AN ESSAY ON CRITICISM

351. 34. *Maevius.* See Addison's comment, p. 347.

352. 129–30. *the Mantuan Muse . . . young Maro.* Virgil. See 783. 19, note.

138. *the Stajirite.* Aristotle.

353. 180. *Homer nods.* Allusion to Horace, *Ars Poetica,* 359.

216. *the Pierian Spring.* Pieria in Thessaly was the reputed birthplace of the Muses.

354 248. *E'en thine, O Rome.* St. Peter's.

267. *La Mancha's Knight.* Don Quixote.

270. *Dennis — stage.* John Dennis, the critic and playwright, made sententious references to the dramatic precepts of Aristotle. This allusion and another, lines 585–591, initiated Pope's quarrel with him.

328. *Fungoso.* A character in Ben Jonson's *Every Man Out of His Humour,* who tries, without success, to keep up with court fashions.

355. 356. *Alexandrine.* The succeeding line is an example.

361. *Denham.* See p. 181 *Waller.* See p. 178.

372. *Camilla.* In Virgil's *Aeneid* vii, 808–11.

374–383. Compare Dryden's *Alexander's Feast,* p. 274.

376. *Son of Libyan Jove.* Alexander the Great.

391. *Approve,* test, put to the proof.

356. 441. *Sentences.* The *Sententiae* of Peter Lombard, 12th century.

444. *Scotists and Thomists.* Followers of the thirteenth century schoolmen, Duns Scotus and Thomas Aquinas.

463. *Blackmores.* See 329. *a.* 43, note. B. attacked Dryden in 'A Satire on Wit.'

Milbourns. Luke Milbourn, a clergyman, attacked Dryden's translation of Virgil.

465. *Zoilus.* Greek critic of the 4th century B. C., said to have been put to death for criticizing Homer.

357. 483. *Such as Chaucer is.* Pope and his generation regarded Chaucer as obsolete.

527. *Spleen,* anger, ill-temper.

536. *love was all an easy Monarch's care.* The reign of Charles II is referred to.

544. *a foreign reign.* That of William III.

545. *Socinus.* Italian unitarian of the sixteenth century.

THE RAPE OF THE LOCK

CANTO I

358. 3. *Caryl.* John Caryl, a friend and correspondent of Pope.

4. *Belinda.* Miss Arabella Fermor, a belle of the period from whom the lock celebrated in the poem was stolen.

8. *a well-bred lord.* Lord Petre, who had stolen the curl.

17. *the slipper knocked the ground.* Rapping for the servant.

56. *ombre.* See 362. 27, note.

73. *Spark.* A beau, a lady-killer.

CANTO II

360. 25. *springes.* Snares. cf. *Hamlet,* I. iii, 115.

361. 113. *drops,* earrings.

133. *Ixion.* For an offense to Zeus, fastened to an eternally revolving wheel in Hades.

CANTO III

3. *a structure of majestic frame.* Hamptca Court, one of the royal residences.

27. *ombre.* A game of cards, of Spanish origin, usually played by three persons.

362. 47. *Matadores.* The three highest cards at ombre.

49. *Spadillio.* Ace of Spades.

51. *Manillio.* The two of a black, 'he seven of a red, trump.

53. *Basto.* Ace of clubs.

61. *Pam.* Knave of clubs, the highest card in the game of loo.

92. *codille.* Failure to get the requisite tricks.

363. 122–24. *Scylla's fate . . . Nisus' injured hair.* Pope's note refers to Ovid, *Metam.* viii.

151. *cut the sylph in twain.* Compare Par. Lost vi, 330.

165. *Atalantis.* A book of contemporary scandal by Mrs. Manley, *The New Atalantis* (1709).

CANTO IV

364. 16. *Spleen.* See 357. 527, note.

24. *Megrim* Tired feeling, the blues.

89. *Thalestris.* One Mrs. Morley.

365. 118. *the sound of Bow.* St. Mary Le Bow, in Cheapside, the heart of the city, was famous for its peal of bells.

121. *Sir Plume.* Sir George Brown. He threatened Pope with violence for this delightfully malicious caricature.

156. *bohea.* A kind of tea, from the Chinese province whence it was first imported in 1666.

CANTO V

366. 5. *The Trojan.* Æneas. See *Æneid* iv, 296 ff.

62. *Dapperwit.* 'A brisk, conceited, half-witted fellow of the town' bears this name in Wycherley's *Love in a Wood.*

367. 63. *Sir Fopling.* Suggested, perhaps, by Sir Fopling Flutter in Etherege's *The Man of Mode.*

65. *Meander.* A river of Asia Minor frequently mentioned in classical poetry. Celebrated for its windings.

125. *Rome's great founder.* Romulus.

126. *Proculus.* The legend is given in Livy I, 6.

136. *Rosamonda's lake.* A pond in St. James's Park.

137. *Partridge.* An astrologer and almanac maker ridiculed by Swift in his Bickerstaff papers.

138. *Galileo's eyes.* The telescope.

368. 140. *Louis.* Louis XIV, King of France. *Rome.* The Papacy.

EPISTLE TO DR. ARBUTHNOT

Dr. John Arbuthnot was Pope's friend and physician, a wit and a man of letters.

13. *gentle Fanny's.* John, Lord Hervey, a friend of Lady Mary Wortley Montagu, was frequently lampooned by Pope, under this name.

15. *Gildon,* Charles (1665–1724). A hack writer. Pope pretended to believe that Addison had paid Gildon to defame him; hence, 'venal.'

20. *Bedlam.* Bethlehem hospital for the insane. *the Mint.* A part of Southwark London, in which criminals and debtors could take refuge from arrest.

29. *The bard . . . renown.* Ambrose Philips, whose pastorals had excited Pope's jealousy.

40. *Tate,* Nahum, a poetaster of the Restoration period, celebrated for his atrocious adaptations of Shakspere's plays.

59. *Cato.* An allusion to Addison's drama.

THOMSON: SUMMER

370. 50. *Stygian,* dark. From Styx, one of the rivers of Hades.

THE CASTLE OF INDOLENCE

374. 32. *Philomel,* the nightingale.

375. 75. *the rural poets.* Those who treated pastoral subjects.

76. *Arcadian.* See Life of Sidney, p. 81. *Sicilian.* Sicily was the home of a group of pastoral poets of whom the chief was Theocritus.

98. *Lorraine.* Claude Lorrain (1600–82), French landscape painter.

99. *Rosa,* Salvator (c. 1615–1673). Neapolitan painter noted for his battle pieces.

Poussin. Doubtless Nicholas Poussin (1594–1665). French landscape and historical painter.

131. *mell,* mingle, mix.

MINOR POETS — YOUNG TO CHATTERTON

JOHN GAY: THE SHEPHERD'S WEEK

379. 67. *Jack Pudding.* A popular nickname for a clown or mountebank's assistant.

68. *Toffs,* doffs, draws off. There is an old popular amusement called ' draw the glove.' See Brand's *Popular Antiquities.*

69. *raree-shows,* peep-shows.

71. ' *the children in the wood.*' This famous old ballad is in Percy's *Reliques.*

74. *fauchion,* falchion. See 404. 62, note.

79–80. *For buxom Joan . . . the maid a wife.* The words and music of this song are in D'Urfey's *Pills to Purge Melancholy,* Vol. III, pp. 220–221.

82. *Chevy-Chace.* For this ballad, see p. 42.

91. *He sung of Taffy Welch, and Sawney Scot.* *Taffy* (Davy) is the regular nickname for a Welshman, *Sawney* (Sandy) for a Scotchman. The reference may be to *The National Quarrel,* D'Urfey's *Pills to Purge Melancholy,* Vol. II, p. 76.

92. *Lilly-bullero.* A political ballad which was popular during the Protestant Revolution of 1688. The refrain is drawn from an old Irish song.

The Irish Trot. Possibly the ribald old song, called *The Irish Jigg,* which is given in D'Urfey's collection, v, 108.

93. *Bateman.* The reference is to *Bateman's Tragedy,* preserved in Ritson's *Ancient Songs,* etc. (ed. Hazlitt), p. 231.

Shore. Jane Shore, the mistress of King Edward IV, was a celebrated character in ballad and drama. See Percy, *Reliques,* and D'Urfey's *Pills to Purge Melancholy,* iv, 273.

94. *Wantley's Dragon . . . Moore.* The air and words are in D'Urfey's collection, Vol. III, p. 10.

95. *the bower of Rosamond.* Rosamond Clifford, the mistress of King Henry II, was the subject of many popular legends, among which was that of the subterranean labyrinth known as Rosamond's bower. *Fair Rosamond* is the title of a ballad in Percy's *Reliques.*

Robin Hood. For examples (the Robin Hood ballads, see pp. 38–42.

96. *And how the grass,* etc. The ballad of Troy town is in Percy's *Reliques.* In D'Urfey's *Pills to Purge Melancholy,* iv, 266, we meet with a ballad called *The Wandering Prince of Troy,* which contains the line, ' And corn now grows where Troy town stood.'

JOHN DYER: GRONGAR HILL

331. 23. *Towy's flood.* The river Towy, in Wales, flows south into Caermarthen Bay.

WILLIAM SHENSTONE: THE SCHOOLMISTRESS

383. 15. *Tway,* two.

56. *Sternhold,* Thomas (c. 1500–1549), with John Hopkins wrote a metrical version of the Psalms.

60–64. *How Israel's sons . . . sing.* Psalm 137.

' By the rivers of Babylon we sat down and wept,' etc.

384. 73. *like that of Scottish stem.* A stone of

supposed miraculous properties formed a part of the Scottish coronation chair at Scone. Edward I carried it off to Westminster in token of the subjugation of Scotland in 1297. It has since been a part of the chair in which all English sovereigns are crowned.

102. *Mulla's silver stream.* The river Mulla flowed near Kilcolman Castle, Spenser's home in Ireland. See Life of Spenser, p. 104.

108. *ermilin,* ermine.

WILLIAM COLLINS: ODE TO SIMPLICITY

387. 14. *Hybla's thymy shore.* Mount Hybla in Sicily is celebrated in classical poetry for the sweetness of its honey.

16–18. *By her . . . Electra's poet's ear.* ' The nightingale for which Sophocles seems to have entertained a peculiar fondness.' (Collins.)

19. *Cephisus.* A river of Attica.

35. *One distinguished throne.* Augustus Cæsar.

52. *reed.* The symbol of pastoral poetry.

388. 75. *their chaste-ey'd queen.* Diana.

86. *Tempe.* A valley adjacent to Olympus in Thessaly. See, also, 636. 11, note.

389. 104. *Devote,* devoted.

114. *Cecilia's mingled world of sound.* Compare Dryden, *Alexander's Feast,* 276. 138.

THOMAS WARTON: THE GRAVE OF KING ARTHUR

4. *Cilgarran's castle hall.* There are ruins of a thirteenth century castle at Kilgerran, in Southern Wales.

6. *Henry.* King Henry II, on his expedition for the conquest of Wales and Ireland.

8. *Shannon's lakes.* Shannon, the principal river of Ireland, flows through a chain of lakes.

12. *metheglin,* mead, liquor. A Celtic beverage.

20. *Mona,* Anglesea, an island and county of North Wales.

21. *Teivi,* the river Teifi, which flows westward into Cardigan Bay.

22. *Elvy's vale.* Valley of the river Elwy, in Northwestern Wales.

Cader's crown. Cader Idris, a mountain in Northwestern Wales.

24. *Ierne's hoarse abyss.* The Irish Sea.

26. *Radnor's . . . mountains.* Radnor is a county in the interior of Wales.

33. *Tintagell.* A village on the coast of Cornwall, the reputed birthplace of King Arthur.

40. *Camlan's crimson'd banks.* According to legend Arthur perished in the battle of Camlan (c. 542).

41. *Mordred.* See Malory's *Morte d'Arthur,* p. 19 ff.

50. *Merlin's agate-axled car.* An invention of the magician Merlin.

SONNETS: DUGDALE'S MONASTICON

A huge compilation of English monastic history by Sir William Dugdale (1605–1686) is ordinarily known as Dugdale's *Monasticon.*

390. 5. *Henry's fiercer rage.* Henry VIII's disruption of the monasteries.

WRITTEN AT STONEHENGE

Warton here summarizes the various legends known to him concerning the origin and meaning of the celebrated pre-historic ruin in Salisbury Plain, Wiltshire.

2. *Scythia's shore.* An indefinite term for northeast Europe and adjacent parts of Asia, employed with varying meaning by the ancients.

3. *Amber.* The Islands in the North Sea were vaguely known to the Greeks as the Amber Islands. *Pendragon,* Uther. The father of King Arthur.

THOMAS CHATTERTON: BRISTOWE TRAGEDIE

This poem is probably based on the story of Sir Baldwin Fulford, who was executed at Bristol in 1461. With many others who fought on the Lancastrian side he was a victim of an act of attainder which followed the accession of Edward IV. William Canynge, who figures in this and other poems of Chatterton, is a historical personage, and was mayor of Bristol at the time of Fulford's execution.

13. *nappy,* sparkling.

391. 58. *rewyn'd,* ruined.

73. *reines,* reins, kidneys.

392. 141. *goddelyke Henry.* King Henvy VI, lived in captivity for ten years after the accession of Edward.

183. *Richard's sonnes.* Richard, Duke of York, was father of Edward IV and Richard III.

393. 263. *enshone,* showed.

271. *russet weedes,* Homespun clothes.

272. *plyghte,* weave, texture.

276. *bataunt,* Chatterton's invention; no such instrument is known.

288. *route,* troop, company.

394. 306. *mycle,* much.

335. *Gloucester.* Afterward King Richard III.

347. *glysterr,* glisten.

MYNSTRELLES SONGE

395. 3. *hallie,* holy.

10. *Rodde,* red.

11. *cale,* cold.

13. *Swote,* sweet.

25. *heie,* they.

38. *Seyncte,* Saint.

39. *celness,* coldness.

43. *dente,* fasten.

44. *gre,* grow.

45. *Ouphante,* elfin.

46. *bee,* bow.

58. *leathalle,* lethal, deadly.

THOMAS GRAY: SONNET ON THE DEATH OF MR. RICHARD WEST

Richard West, son of the Lord Chancellor of Ireland, had been Gray's most intimate friend at Eton and his constant correspondent while they were at Oxford and Cambridge respectively. See also the sketch of Gray, p. 396.

AN ODE ON A DISTANT PROSPECT OF ETON COLLEGE

396. 4. *Her Henry's holy Shade.* Eton College was founded by King Henry VI in 1440. See, also, 392. a. 141, note.

397. 6. *Windsor's heights,* etc. Windsor Castle, overlooking Eton, is one of the royal residences.

HYMN TO ADVERSITY

398. 35. *Gorgon,* the terror-inspiring image on the shield of Pallas Athene, goddess of wisdom.

ELEGY WRITTEN IN A COUNTRY CHURCH YARD

399. 57. *Hampden* (John 1594–1643). One of the chief heroes of the Puritan revolt. Resisted the collection of ship-money, 1637–38.

THE PROGRESS OF POESY

400. 1. *Æolian lyre.* The lyre of Pindar who belonged to the Æolian division of the Greek race. See, also, p. 163, *A Pindaric Ode,* note.

3. *Helicon.* See 244. 15, note.

9. *Ceres' golden reign.* Fields ruled by Ceres, goddess of grain and harvest.

17. *On Thracia's hills,* etc. Thrace was thought to be a favorite haunt of Mars.

21. *the feathered king.* Jove's eagle, symbolical of the thunderbolt.

27. *Idalia.* An ancient town in Cyprus consecrated to Venus.

29. *Cytherea's Day.* The day for the worship of Venus.

401. 53. *Hyperion's march.* The sunrise.

66. *Delphi's steep.* The seat of the Greek oracle. See 450. 517, note.

68. *Ilissus.* A small stream flowing through Athens.

69. *Mæander.* The river Mæander in Asia Minor.

83–94. Shakspere.

95–102. Milton.

112. *what daring spirit,* etc. Gray himself.

115. *the Theban Eagle.* 'Pindar compares himself to that bird, and his enemies to ravens that croak and clamor in vain below, while it pursues its flight, regardless of their noise.' (Gray.)

THE BARD

'The following ode is founded on a tradition current in Wales, that Edward the First, when he completed the conquest of that country, ordered all the bards that fell into his hands to be put to death.' (Gray.) 'The massacre of the bards is a mere fable.' (J. R. Green.)

402. a. 5. *Hauberk's twisted mail.* A close-fitting shirt of steel ringlets.

8. *Cambria.* Wales.

11. *Snowdon.* The highest mountain in England or Wales. The name applies also to the mountainous tract of which this peak is a part.

13. *Gloster.* 'Gilbert de Clare, surnamed the Red, Earl of Gloucester and Hertford, son-in-law to King Edward.' (Gray.)

14. *Mortimer.* 'Edmond de Mortimer, Lord of Wigmore. A Lord Marcher.' (Gray.)

28. *high-born Hoel.* Son of Prince Owain Gwynedd of north Wales. A warrior and poet. *Llewellyn,* possibly Llewellyn ap Jorwerth, the Welsh leader, is meant.

29. *Cadwallo.* A common Welsh bardic name.

31. *Urien.* A Welsh warrior and bard of the sixth century.

33. *Modred.* No bard of this name is known.

34. *Plinlimmon.* A mountain on the border of Cardigan and Montgomery, in Wales.

35. *Arvon's shore.* The shores of Caernarvonshire opposite Anglesey. (Gray.)

54–56. *When Severn . . . an agonizing King.* Edward II was murdered in Berkeley castle in September, 1327.

57. *She-Wolf of France,* etc. Isabel of France, Edward the Second's adulterous queen.

59–66. King Edward III.

67. *the sable Warrior.* The Black Prince.

71–82. Reign of Richard II.

403. 85. *Long years of havoc.* Wars of the Roses.

87. *Towers of Julius.* The Tower of London, according to tradition, built by Julius Cæsar. See Shakspere's *Richard III,* iii, i. There is no authority to confirm the tradition. (Wheatley and Cunningham: *London Past and Present.*)

89. *his Consort's faith.* Margaret of Anjou.

his father's fame. The military glory of Henry V.

90. *the meek Usurper's holy head.* Henry VI was noted for his piety.

93. *The bristled Boar.* The insignia of Richard III.

infant gore. Of the murdered princes.

110. *ye genuine Kings.* The Tudor line, beginning with Henry VII.

111–124. *The reign of Queen Elizabeth.*

121. *Taliessin.* Cymric bard of the sixth century.

125–27. Spenser.

128–30. Shakspere.

131–34. Milton and succeeding poets.

THE FATAL SISTERS

Written in 1761. The text of the poem from which Gray derived these stanzas may be found, with a prose translation, in *Corpus Poeticum Boreale,* Vol. I, pp. 281–83. It is an Icelandic poem of the eleventh century celebrating an invasion of Ireland by a Norse hero, Sictrygg, who was assisted by Sigurd, Earl of the Orkneys. Sigurd and Brian, the Irish king, fall in the battle. The Valkries are imagined weaving the web of battle. The title of the original is *Darradar-Liod* [*Lay of the Darts*].

404. 8. *Orkney's woe.* The woe of Sigurd, Earl of Orkney.

Randver's bane. Direct from the original. Randver's destruction.

17–31. *Mista . . . Sangrida . . . Hilda . . . Gondula . . . Geira.* The names of the Valkyries in the original are Hilda, Hiorthrimol, Sangrida, and Swipol.

44. *Soon a King,* etc. Brian, King of Dublin.

45. *Eirin.* Ireland.

62. *falchion.* A short sword, bellied near the tic.

JOHNSON: THE LIFE OF ADDISON

406. *a.* 25. *the Chartreux.* Originally a Carthusian monastery in London. Endowed in 1611 as a hospital and boys' school. Usually known as the Charterhouse.

b. 36. *Boileau.* See 347. *b.* 18, note.

37. *says Tickell.* Thomas Tickell (1686–1740), Addison's friend and elegist, contributed a biographical preface to the collective edition of Addison's works published by Jacob Tonson in 1721.

411. *a.* 44. *Cibber.* In his *Apology for the Life of Mr. Colley Cibber* (1740).

b. 40. '*heavily in clouds . . . day.*' Quoted from the opening lines of *Cato.*

48. *The Distressed Mother.* See 342. *a,* 16, note.

412. *a.* 1. *Bolingbroke.* Henry St. John, Viscount Bolingbroke, the Tory leader.

2. *Booth.* Barton Booth (1681–1733), who played Cato.

13. *Mrs. Porter.* An excellent actress who played the part of Lucia.

414. *a.* 54. *Milton against King Charles II.* Defense of England against Salmasius, Chap. viii.

b. 1. *Oldmixon,* John (1653–1742), has a prominent place in Pope's *Dunciad.*

417. *a.* 38. *Chesterfield.* Philip Stanhope, Earl of Chesterfield (1694–1773). For Johnson's relations with him, see p. 420 and note.

b. 13. *Terence.* Publius Terentius Afer, Roman comic poet of the second century B. C.

Catullus, Caius Valerius. Brilliant Roman poet, contemporary with Julius Cæsar.

418. *b.* 23. *Mandeville,* Bernard (1670–1733), author of *Fable of the Bees.*

419. *a.* 35. '*above all Greek . . . fame.*' Pope, *To Augustus,* 26.

44–5. '*turned many to righteousness.*' Dan. 12, 3.

b. 24. *Mille . . . habet. Tibullus* 4, 2, 14.

LETTERS

To the . . . Earl of Chesterfield. Of the occasion of this famous letter Johnson said to Boswell: ' Sir, after making great professions, he had, for many years, taken no notice of me; but when my *Dictionary* was coming out, he fell a scribbling in *The World* about it. Upon which, I wrote him a letter expressed in civil terms, but such as might shew him that I did not mind what he said or wrote, and that I had done with him.' (Hill's Boswell, I, 301.)

420. *a.* 8. *the proprietor of The World.* Edward Moore, an old acquaintance of Johnson's.

46. *The shepherd in Virgil. Eclogue* viii, 43, ff.

58. *till I am solitary.* Johnson's wife had died three years before.

b. 22. *Mr. James Macpherson.* Johnson had publicly declared that the poems of Ossian which Macpherson claimed to have translated from the Gaelic were forgeries. Macpherson threatened physical vengeance and this celebrated letter, Johnson said, ' put an end to our correspondence.'

THE VANITY OF HUMAN WISHES

421. *37. Wolsey.* This passage is largely based on the picture of Cardinal Wolsey in Shakspere and Fletcher's *Henry VIII.*

422. *68. Swedish Charles.* Charles XII (1682–1718), defeated by Peter the Great, at Pultowa, July 8, 1709. Killed at Frederikshald, Norway.

JAMES BOSWELL: THE LIFE OF JOHNSON

423. *a. 3. The accession of George the Third.* October 25, 1760.

b. 56. Mr. Thomas Sheridan. The father of the dramatist, Richard Brinsley Sheridan.

425. *a. 39. Collins.* See p. 386.

428. *a. 7–8. Messieurs Thornton, Wilkes, Churchill, and Lloyd.* Wits of the time all of whom except Wilkes had been members, with William Cowper, of the Nonsense Club.

430. *a. 57. Colley Cibber.* Poet laureate, 1730–57.

b. 24. Whitehead, William (1715–85). He succeeded Cibber as poet laureate.

41–2. His Ode which begins, etc. *The Bard.* See p. 402.

432. *a. 33. Dr. Goldsmith.* See below, p. 463.

b. 51. Mr. Burke. See below, p. 443.

54. Mr. Malone. Edmond Malone (1741–1812), the great Shakspere scholar, assisted Boswell in preparing the *Life of Johnson* for the press.

433. *a. 35. Nihil quod tetigit,* etc. Inaccurate and often quoted in this form. Johnson wrote *Qui nullum ferè scribendi genus non tetigit, nullum quod tetigit non ornavit.* [Who left hardly any species of writing untouched and touched none that he did not adorn it.]

54. un étourdi, a rattle-head.

b. 15. Fantoccini, puppets.

434. *a. 3. Mrs. Piozzi.* Formerly the wife of Henry Thrale (d. 1781), one of Johnson's most intimate friends. She published *Anecdotes of Dr. Johnson* (1786), *Letters to and from Dr. Johnson* (1788).

Sir John Hawkins. A member of Johnson's Club, published a *Life* in 1787.

b. 24. Miss Williams. One of the many recipients of Johnson's eccentric charity.

436. *b. 42. Dr. Adam Smith* (1723–1790). Author of *The Wealth of Nations.*

438. *b. 5. The Old Swan,* Swan Stairs. The landing here and the walk to Billingsgate beyond London Bridge were made in order to avoid the risk of 'shooting the bridge.'

439. *b. 27. Turk's Head coffee-house.* In the Strand. Johnson said, on an earlier occasion, 'I encourage this house, for the mistress of it is a good civil woman and has not much business.' See below, p. 440.

442. *b. 18. Bishop Berkeley's ingenious sophistry.* In his *Principles of Human Knowledge* (1710).

BURKE: SPEECH FOR CONCILIATION

444. *a. 14. Sensible,* concrete, such as the senses can perceive.

445. *b. 7. Gothic.* We should say Teutonic.

34. *Blackstone's Commentaries.* The great law treatise published (1765–1769) by Sir William Blackstone.

35. *General Gage.* Governor of Massachusetts, 1774.

446. *a. 1. Abeunt studia,* etc. Compare Bacon, **199.** *b.* 36, and note.

with all its imperfections on its head. Hamlet I, v. 79.

447. *a. 25. Lord Dunmore.* Governor of New York, and later of Virginia.

448. *b. 10–11. 'Increase and multiply.'* Inaccurate. See Gen. I, 22 and 28.

449. *a. 11. Spoliatis arma supersunt.* Juvenal, *Sat.* viii, 124.

55. advocates and panegyrists. For example, Dr. Johnson in *Taxation no Tyranny.*

b. 39–41. ye gods annihilate, etc. This piece of bombast has never been traced beyond *The Art of Sinking Poetry,* by Arbuthnot, Swift, and Pope, where it is ostensibly quoted.

450. *a. 18. Sir Edward Coke.* Public prosecutor in 1603, when Raleigh was tried. See, also, 326, b. 26, note. *the very same title.* Popular election.

451. *a. 19. juridical,* abstractly legal.

b. 37–39. Serbonian bog, etc. Milton, *Paradise Lost* II, 592–4.

41. such respectable company. Ironical equivoke, in allusion to Milton's Satan.

452. *b. 12. the repeal of a Revenue Act.* The Stamp Act, repealed 1766.

GIBBON: THE DECLINE AND FALL OF THE ROMAN EMPIRE

The extract is from Chapter lxviii of the *Decline and Fall.* It presents the first grand culmination of Gibbon's massive study, the fall of the eastern empire. The remaining three chapters of the last volume deal with the disintegration of the empire in Italy from the eleventh to the fifteenth century. Other striking passages are the accounts of Petrarch and of Rienzi, Chapter lxx, and the 'Prospect of the Ruins of Rome in the Fifteenth Century,' Chapter lxxi.

453. *b. 3. Phranza.* The minister and friend of the Emperor Constantine.

454. *a. 57. seven times in one day.* Near an hundred years after the siege of Constantinople, the French and English fleets in the Channel were proud of firing 300 shot in an engagement of two hours. (Gibbon.)

b. 18. fascines, bundles of sticks.

455. *a. 14. Justiniani.* John Justiniani, 'a noble Genoese,' was in command of 2,000 'strangers.'

30. generosity, spirit.

455. *b. 54. The passions of his soul,* etc. I must confess that I have before my eyes the living picture which Thucydides (I. vii. c. 71) has drawn of the passions and gestures of the Athenians in a naval engagement in the great harbor of Syracuse. (Gibbon.)

456. *b. 1. the divan.* The Turkish council of state.

457. *a. 10–12. the boasted miracle . . . our own times.* I particularly allude to our own embarkations on the lakes of Canada, in the years 1776 and 1777, so great in the labor, so fruitless in the event. (Gibbon.)

457. *b.* 18. *Gabours.* Unbelievers.

51. *bashaws,* dignitaries, here probably generals.

52. *Janizaries.* Members of the central standing army of the Sultan.

57. *oda,* the unit of janizary organization.

459. *a.* 22. *sanjaks* were, formerly, bashaws of the rank entitled to wear one horse-tail.

47. *attaballs,* oriental tambours.

460. *a.* 20. *Cantacuzene.* Byzantine emperors of the fourteenth century.

50. *Chosroes.* Khusrau I, a powerful Persian king of the sixth century.

the Chagan, the Khan. The Tartar regal title. The reference here is to Jenghiz Khan, who conquered central Asia and threatened Europe early in the thirteenth century.

the caliphs. Successors of Mohammed.

b. 48. *Ducas.* A Byzantine historian who was an eye witness of the first siege of Constantinople. His history was first printed at Paris in 1649.

461. *b.* 40. *ducats.* The ducat, as a money of account, was about two dollars and thirty cents.

462. *b.* 35. *imam.* The officiating priest in Mohammedan worship.

36. *namaz.* The canonical prayer of the Moslems.

42. *the great Constantine.* Constantine I (272-337) transferred the seat of the Roman Empire in the year 330 to Byzantium, which was thereafter known as Constantinople.

GOLDSMITH: THE DESERTED VILLAGE

464. 39. *One only master,* etc. The system of enclosures is referred to.

468. 344. *wild Altama.* The river Altamaha in Georgia, U. S. A.

469. 418. *Torno's cliffs.* Lake Tornea in northern Sweden.

Pambamarca's side. A mountain in Ecuador.

THE RETALIATION

1. *Edmund.* Edmund Burke. See p. 443.

6. *Tommy Townshend.* Thomas Townshend, Viscount Sidney (1733-1780), a prominent whig statesman.

15. *David Garrick,* the actor. See Boswell's Johnson, p. 427.

COWPER: THE TASK

472. 112. *The Sabine bard.* Horace, *Sat.* ii, 6, 65. O noctes coenaeque Deum [O nights and suppers of the gods].

475. 354. *Indian fume.* Tobacco smoke.

356. *Lethean,* oblivious. From Lethe, the river of oblivion.

388. *Midas,* etc. According to the Greek myth, by a grant of Dionysus, whatever he touched turned to gold.

476. 396. *Arcadian* . . . *Maro sings.* Virgil in his *Eclogues.*

397. *Sidney.* See p. 81.

453. *Tityrus.* A shepherd in the first *Eclogue* of Virgil.

469. *Cowley.* See p. 183.

474. *Chertsey's silent bowers.* A village in Surrey not far from London. Here Cowley spent his last years.

477. 511. *The Frenchman's darling.* Mignonette.

ON THE RECEIPT OF MY MOTHER'S PICTURE

Written in 1788. Cowper's mother died in 1737, when he was little more than six years of age; yet fifty years afterward he wrote, 'Not a week passes (perhaps I might with equal veracity say a day) in which I do not think of her. The picture which suggested this poem was sent to him 'out of Norfolk,' by his cousin Anne Bodham.

ON THE LOSS OF THE ROYAL GEORGE

The *Royal George* was the flagship of Rear-Admiral Kempenfelt. While being refitted, off Spithead, she heeled and went down with crew and admiral aboard, Aug. 29, 1782. The poem was probably written the same year, though not published until after Cowper's death. The meter was determined by a tune which Cowper had in mind and the poem, therefore, must be regarded as a ballad.

GEORGE CRABBE: THE VILLAGE

480. 12. *Corydons.* Conventional shepherds of pastoral poetry, from a character of this name in Virgil's *Eclogues.*

15. *Mincio's banks.* See below, 18. *Cæsar's bounteous reign.* The reign of Augustus.

16. *If Tityrus found the Golden Age again.* Virgil, in his *Eclogues,* particularly *Eclogue IV.*

18. *Mantuan song.* Mantua, situated on an island in the river Mincio, was the home of Virgil.

481. 27. *honest Duck.* Possibly Stephen Duck, a poor thresher who was patronized by Queen Caroline, wife of George II. He is mentioned by Johnson in his *Life of Savage* (*Lives,* London, 1821, Vol. II, p. 149).

97. *Ajax.* Homer's 'strong man.'

484. 303. '*passing rich with forty pounds a year.*' Goldsmith's *Deserted Village,* 142. See p. 463.

330. *the moping owl.* Compare Gray's *Elegy,* 10, p. 398.

ROBERT BURNS: MARY MORISON

The subject of this song (written in 1781) was Ellison Begbie. Burns proposed marriage to her and was refused.

490. 5. *bide,* await, endure. *stoure,* dust, struggle.

13. *braw,* fine, handsome.

SONG: MY NANIE, O

Written in 1782.

491. 1. *Lugar,* fanciful for Stinchar.

5. *shill,* shrill, keen.

7. *plaid,* highland shawl or wrap.

15. *gowan,* daisy.

21. *penny-fee,* wages paid in money.

23. *gear,* stuff, wealth.

25. *guidman,* master.

SONG: GREEN GROW THE RASHES

Written in 1783.
1. *rashes*, rushes.
13. *cannie*, well considered, clever.
17. *douce*, solemn.
19. *The wisest man*, etc. Solomon.

LINES TO JOHN LAPRAIK

Written in 1785. The recipient of the verses was a rustic wit and poet of local reputation. When they were written Burns was still unknown to the world and quite unaware of the greatness of his own gift.
14. *horns*, probably ink-horns.
16. *sairs*, serves.
17. *shools*, shovels.
18. *knappin-hammers*. Hammers for breaking stone.
19. *hashes*, fools, weak-minded persons.
21. *stirks*, yearling steers.
23. *syne*, afterwards.

TO A MOUSE

Written in 1785.
492. 4. *brattle*, sudden sound or scamper.
6. *pattle*, paddle for scouring the plow.
13. *whyles*, at times.
15. *daimen icker*, occasional ear. *thrave*, 'shock.'
17. *lave*, remainder.
21. *big*, build.
22. *foggage*, aftermath.
34. *but*, without.
40. *a-gley*, awry.

THE COTTER'S SATURDAY NIGHT

Written in 1785.
23. *ingle*, chimney-corner.
26. *kiaugh*, worry.
28. *Belyve*, soon, directly.
30. *ca*, drive. Literally, call.
31. *toun*, a farm with its collection of buildings.
493. 34. *braw*. See 490. 13.
35. *sair-won*, hard-earned.
38. *spiers*, inquires.
40. *uncos*, news.
44. *Gars*, causes, makes.
48. *eydent*, attentive.
49. *jauk*, trifle, 'soldier.'
62. *hafflins*, halfway, partly.
67. *cracks*, chats, holds forth.
69. *blate*, bashful, embarrassed.
92. *halesome parritch*, healthful porridge (oatmeal).
93. *sowpe*, liquid.
94. *hallan'*, partition.
96. *well-hain'd kebbuck fell*. well-saved cheese, and ripe.
494. 99. *towmond*, twelve month. *lint*, flax. *bell*, blossom.
105. *lyart haffets*, grayish temples.
107. *wales*, chooses.
111-113. *Dundee's*, . . . *Martyrs*, . . . *Elgin*. Sacred melodies.

133-135. *How he, who lone in Patmos*, etc. John. See Revelation.
138. Pope's *Windsor Forest*, 112, is quoted.
495. 166. Pope's *Essay on Man*, iv, 248.
182. *Wallace's undaunted heart*. Sir William Wallace, one of the chief national heroes of Scotland, maintained a sturdy resistance to England for several years at the close of the 13th century, but was finally captured and executed at London in 1305.

ADDRESS TO THE DEIL

Written the winter of 1784-5.
495. 1-2. Imitated from the opening of Pope's *Dunciad*.
2. *Clootie*. Cloot is hoof.
5. *Spairges*, splashes. *cootie*, foot-tub.
11. *skelp*, slap.
15. *lowin heugh*, flaming cavern (gully).
17. *lag*, slow. Compare verb, to lag behind.
18. *blate*. See 493. 69, note. *scaur*, scary, timorous.
22. *Tirlin*, stripping. *kirks*, churches.
30. *eldritch*, uncanny, elvish.
32. *douce*, sober.
35. *boortrees*, elder bushes.
38. *sklentin*, slanting.
40. *lough*, lake, pond.
41. *rush-buss*, bush of rushes.
43. *neive*, fist.
45. *stoor*, harsh.
49. *warlocks*, wizards.
50. *ragweed nags*. Horses fed on ragweed, hence neglected, wild.
54. *howket*, dug up.
56. *kirn*, churn.
59. *dawtet*, petted. *Twal-pint hawkie*, twelve-pint white face. The Ayrshire breed of cattle has white markings.
60. *yell's the bill*, dry as the bull.
496. 62. *crouse*, bold.
64. *cantrip*, maliciously magical.
69. *water-kelpies*. Malevolent water-spirits in the form of black horses. Compare the 'White Horses' of Ibsen's *Rosmersholm*.
73. *spunkies*, will-o'-the-wisps.
91. *sneck-drawin*, latch-lifting, intruding.
93. *brogue*, trick.
97. *bizz*, bustling hurry.
98. *reeket*, smoky. *reestet gizz*, singed face.
101. *the man of Uz*. Job. See i, 1.
107. *lows'd*, let loose. *scaul*, scold.
108. *ava*, of all.
113. *ding*, knock, be too much for. *Lallan*, Lowland. *Erse* (strictly, Irish not Gaelic).
117. *linkin*, skipping.
119. *jinkin*, dodging.
123. *aiblins*, possibly.
124. *hae a stake*, have something to gain.

A BARD'S EPITAPH

Written in 1786.
3. *blate*, see 493. b. 69, note. *snool*, snivel, cringe.
5. *dool*, sorrow

OF A' THE AIRTS THE WIND CAN BLAW

Written in 1788.

497. 1. *airts,* quarters, directions.

3. *bonie,* winsome. This favorite Scotch word combines the ideas of good, good-looking, and good-tempered.

5. *row,* roll.

8. *my Jean.* Jean Armour, Burns's wife.

14. *shaw,* grove, woodland dell.

GO FETCH TO ME A PINT O' WINE

Written in 1788.

2. *tassie,* goblet.

4. *bonie,* see above, 3, note.

5. *Leith,* the port of Edinburgh.

7. *Berwick-law.* Berwick hill, a landmark to seamen cruising in that region.

AULD LANG SYNE

Written in 1788. The phrase auld lang syne' was an ancient one and there were other songs embodying it, the first line of the poem, and the tune, when Burns took them up. His version of the song is immeasurably superior to any which preceded it.

9. *pint-stowp,* flagon, drinking vessel.

13. *braes,* hill-sides.

14. *gowans,* see 491. 15, note.

15. *fit,* foot.

17. *paidl't i' the burn,* dabbled in the brook.

21. *fier,* comrade.

23. *waught,* draught.

JOHN ANDERSON, MY JO

Written in 1789.

1. *jo,* sweetheart.

4. *brent,* straight, steep, firm.

7. *pow,* poll, head.

11. *canty,* cheerful.

TAM GLEN

Written in 1789.

1. *tittie,* sister.

5. *braw,* handsome, fine.

6. *poortith,* poverty. *fen',* shift.

9. *laird,* landlord.

10. *ben,* the interior of the house.

11. *siller,* money.

498. 13. *minnie,* mother. *deave,* deafen, bother with noise.

17. *gin,* if (given).

18. *marks,* silver coins, each worth 26 2-3 cents.

19. *ordain'd,* a humorous allusion to the prevalent Scotch belief in foreordination.

22. *sten,* bounce.

25. *waukin,* watching, keeping awake over.

26. *my droukit sark-sleeve.* Drenched sleeve of my chemise.

28. *breeks,* breeches.

TO MARY IN HEAVEN

The subject of this poem was Mary Campbell and the parting described took place in the spring of 1788. Mary died the following autumn and the poem was written on the first anniversary of her death, after a night of agitated recollection.

TAM O' SHANTER

Written in 1790.

498. 1. *chapman billies,* peddler fellows.

4. *tak the gate,* leave town, take the road, go home.

5. *nappy,* ale.

6. *unco,* very.

7. *lang Scots miles.* The ancient Scottish mile was 1,976 yards.

8. *slaps,* openings.

16. *bonie,* see 497. a. 3, note.

19. *skellum,* scamp.

20. *blellum,* 'loud-mouth,' 'blow-hard.'

23. *ilka melder,* every grist.

24. *sill* , 497. *b.* 11, note.

25. *ev'ry naig,* etc. Every horse that was shod *ca'd,* driven.

28. *Kirkton,* the village near any church.

30. *Doon,* a charming little river near Burns's birthplace. Compare *Bonie Doon,* p. 501.

31. *warlocks,* see 495. *b.* 49, note.

33. *gars me greet,* makes me grieve.

39. *ingle,* see 492. 23, note.

499. 40. *reamin swats,* foaming ale.

41. *Souter,* cobbler.

65. *like,* as.

81. *skelpit,* clattered. *dub,* puddle.

86. *bogles,* goblins.

93. *whins,* boulders, basaltic rocks. *cairn,* stone heap.

103. *bore,* crevice.

107. *tippenny,* twopenny ale.

108. *usquebae,* whiskey.

110. *a boddle,* a copper.

116. *brent-new,* brand new.

117. *strathspeys,* Scotch dances with a peculiar catch in the time.

119. *winnock bunker.* Window box, bench.

121. *towzie tyke,* touseled cur.

123. *gart them skirl.* Made them shriek.

124. *dirl,* tingle.

127. *cantraip sleight.* Magic trick. Compare 496. 64 and note.

131. *airns,* irons.

134. *gab,* mouth.

500. 147. *cleekit,* linked.

148. *carlin,* fellow. *reekit,* smoked.

149. *duddies,* duds, clothes.

150. *linket at it.* Went at it energetically. *sark,* chemise.

151. *queans,* wenches.

153. *creeshie,* greasy.

154. *seventeen-hunder linen.* Very fine linen.

155. *Thir breeks.* These breeches.

157. *hurdies,* hips.

158. *burdies,* brides, girls.

160. *walie,* vigorous.

162. *Carrick shore.*

165. *corn,* wheat. *bear,* barley.

167. *cutty sark,* short, under-dress. *Paisley harn,* coarse linen.

170. *vauntie,* vain.

172. *coft,* bought.

173. *twa pund Scots.* The pound Scots was one twelfth of the English pound sterling.

182. *hotch'd*, hitched.
184. *tint*, lost.
189. *fyke*, fuss.
190. *byke*, nest.
191. *pussie*, the hare.
196. *eldritch*. See 495. 30, note.
197. *fairin*, reward, a present from the fair.
209. *ettle*, intention.
210. *wist*, knew.

WILLIE BREWED A PECK O' MAUT

Written in 1789.
1. *Willie*, William Nichol, a schoolmaster.
2. *Rob and Allan came to see.* Burns and Allan Masterton celebrated the occasion by composing this song, Masterton contributing the music.
8. *bree*, brew.
14. *lift*, sky.

A WINTER NIGHT

Written in 1786.
1. *Boreas*, the north wind. *doure*, grim.
501. 4. *lift*, see above, 14.
9. *burns*, brooks.
11. *bocked*, poured with a rush.
13. *winnocks*, windows.
14. *ourie*, drooping.
15. *brattle*, clamor. Compare 492. 4, note.
17. *deep-lairing*, foundering. *Sprattle*, sprawl.
18. *scaur*, scar, jutting rock.
23. *chittering*, shivering.

HIGHLAND MARY

Written in 1792. See *To Mary in Heaven*, 498. note.
1. *braes.* See note to *Auld Lang Syne*, 497. 13.
9. *birk*, birch.

BONIE DOON

Written in 1791. There are three versions of this poem, of which this is the second and best. The third version, which is the most popular, was written in 1791, and was published in Johnson's *Musical Museum*. It is given below:—

THE BANKS O' DOON

Ye banks and braes o' bonie Doon,
  How can ye bloom sae fresh and fair?
How can ye chant, ye little birds,
  And I sae weary fu' o' care!
Thou'll break my heart, thou warbling bird,
  That wantons thro' the flowering thorn!
Thou minds me o' departed joys,
  Departed never to return.

Aft hae I rov'd by bonie Doon
  To see the rose and woodbine twine,
And ilka bird sang o' its luve,
  And fondly sae did I o' mine.

Wi' lightsome heart I pu'd a rose,
  Fu' sweet upon its thorny tree!
And my fause luver staw my rose—
  But ah! he left the thorn wi' me.

1. *bonie*, see 497. 3, note. *Doon*, see 498. 30, note.
6. *bough*, pronounced in Scotch fashion this rimes perfectly with 'true,' below.
12. *wist*, knew.
19. *staw*, stole.

DUNCAN GRAY

Written in 1792. Like many of Burns's songs of this period it is an old Scotch ditty completely transformed by his rehandling. Of its tune, he wrote, 'Duncan Gray is a light-horse gallop of an air which precludes sentiment.'
2. *o't*, of it.
5. *hiegh*, high.
6. *asklent*, askance. *skeigh*, skittish.
7. *Gart*, made. *abiegh*, aside, aloof.
9. *fleech'd*, flattered.
11. *Ailsa Craig*, a small rocky island in the Firth of Clyde.
502. 14. *Grat his e'en*, etc. Wept his eyes both bleared and blind.
15. *lowpin*, leaping. *Linn*, waterfall.
17. *but a tide*, That is, they ebb and flow.
19. *sair*, sore, hard. *bide*, bear, endure.
31. *sic*, such.
38. *smoor'd*, smothered.
39. *crouse*, brisk. *cantie*, cheerful.

SCOTS WHA HAE

Written in 1793. In 1314, 100,000 Englishmen under Edward II were met on the field of Bannockburn by Robert Bruce with 30,000 Scots. Bruce's force was overwhelmingly victorious. Burns threw into a kind of Scotch ode' what Bruce might be supposed to have said 'on that eventful morning.'
1. *Wallace.* See 495. 182, note.
23. *Liberty's in every blow.* By this victory the Scotch achieved their independence.

A MAN'S A MAN FOR A' THAT

Written in 1795. Burns was strongly republican in his sentiments. His burning sense of personal worth as opposed to the privileges of station are best expressed in this piece which he called 'no song, but . . two or three pretty good prose thoughts put into rime.'
7. *guinea's stamp.* That is, merely the statement of its value which is intrinsic.
8. *gowd*, gold.
10. *hodden-gray*, coarse woollen cloth, undyed.
17. *birkie*, fine fellow.
20. *coof*, stupid lout.
28. *mauna fa' that.* Cannot accomplish that.
36. *gree*, prize.

WORDSWORTH: PREFACE TO LYRICAL BALLADS

This preface, in which Wordsworth sets forth his theory of poetry, was prefixed to the second edition of *Lyrical Ballads* in 1800, and enlarged and modified in subsequent issues to the shape in which it is here given.

A full commentary upon Wordsworth's poetic dogma will be found, considerably scattered, in Coleridge's *Biographial Literaria*. For Chapter XIV, see *Century Readings*, pp. 550-553.

Coleridge believed that Wordsworth's theories, rather than his practice, were responsible for much of the early hostility to Wordsworth's poems. "A careful and repeated examination of these confirms me in the belief, that the omission of less than a hundred lines would have precluded nine-tenths of the criticism on this work. . . . The men of business who had passed their lives chiefly in cities, and who might therefore be expected to derive the highest pleasure from acute notices of men and manners conveyed in easy, yet correct and pointed language; and all those who, reading but little poetry, are most stimulated with that species of it, which seems most distant from prose, would probably have passed by the volumes altogether. Others more catholic in their taste, and yet habituated to be most pleased when most excited, would have contented themselves with deciding, that the author had been successful in proportion to the elevation of his style and subject. . . .

"In the critical remarks, therefore, prefixed and annexed to the Lyrical Ballads, I believe, we may safely rest, as the true origin of the unexampled opposition which Mr. Wordsworth's writings have been since doomed to encounter." (*Biographia Literaria,* Chap. IV.)

504. *b.* 27-9. *Catullus* (87-47 B. C.), Terence (c. 195-158 B. C.) and Lucretius (95-55 B. C.) belong to the earlier or classical period of Roman poetry; Statius (61-96 A. D.) and Claudian (fl. c. 400 A. D.) to the later or 'Silver Age.'

505. *a.* 13-43. *a selection of language,* etc. "To this I reply; that a rustic's language, purified from all provincialism and grossness, and so far re-constructed as to be made consistent with the rules of grammar—(which are in essence no other than the laws of universal logic, applied to psychological materials)—will not differ from the language of any other man of common sense, however learned or refined he may be, except as far as the notions, which the rustic has to convey, are fewer and more indiscriminate. This will become still clearer, if we add the consideration—(equally important though less obvious)—that the rustic, from the more imperfect development of his faculties, and from the lower state of their cultivation, aims almost solely to convey insulated facts, either those of his scanty experience or his traditional belief; while the educated man chiefly seeks to discover and express those connections of things, or those relative bearings of fact to fact, from which some more or less general law is deducible. For facts are valuable to a wise man,

chiefly as they lead to the discovery of the indwelling law, which is the true being of things, the sole solution of their modes of existence, and in the knowledge of which consists our dignity and our power.

As little can I agree with the assertion, that from the objects with which the rustic hourly communicates the best part of language is formed. For first, if to communicate with an object implies such an acquaintance with it, as renders it capable of being discriminately reflected on, the distinct knowledge of an uneducated rustic would furnish a very scanty vocabulary. The few things and modes of action requisite for his bodily conveniences would alone be individualized; while all the rest of nature would be expressed by a small number of confused general terms. Secondly, I deny that the words and combinations of words derived from the objects, with which the rustic is familiar, whether with distinct or confused knowledge, can be justly said to form the best part of language. . . . The best part of human language, properly so called, is derived from reflection on the acts of the mind itself. It is formed by a voluntary appropriation of fixed symbols to internal acts, to processes and results of imagination, the greater part of which have no place in the consciousness of uneducated men; though in civilized society, by imitation and passive remembrance of what they hear from their religious instructors and other superiors, the most uneducated share in the harvest which they neither sowed, nor reaped. If the history of the phrases in hourly currency among our peasants were traced, a person not previously aware of the fact would be surprised at finding so large a number, which three or four centuries ago were the exclusive property of the universities and schools; and, at the commencement of the Reformation, had been transferred from the school to the pulpit, and thus gradually passed into common life." (*Biographia Literaria,* Chap. XVII.)

507. *b.* 50. *the language of prose and metrical composition.* See *Biographia Literaria,* Chap. XVIII, for Coleridge's correction of this doctrine.

510. *b.* 26. *Shakespere hath said. Hamlet* IV, iv, 37.

513. *a.* 5. *Clarissa Harlowe* (1748), Richardson's novel.

6. *The Gamester* (1753). A tragedy by Edward Moore portraying the horrors of gambling.

THE PRELUDE

This poem is so called because it was intended to be introductory to a great philosophical poem Wordsworth planned on retiring to the Lake District in 1799, 'with the hope of being enabled to construct a literary work that might live.' As a preliminary it seemed to him a reasonable thing 'that he should take a review of his own mind, and examine how far Nature and education had qualified him for such an employment. The philosophical poem was to be divided into three parts, and only one of these, *The Excursion,* was ever finished. But the introductory work, in which Wordsworth 'undertook to record, in verse, the origin and progress of his own powers, as far as he was acquainted with them,' was completed in 1805, although it was not published till 1850, after the poet's death, when it was given the title, *The Prelude, or Growth of a Poet's Mind; an Autobiographical Poem.* Our extract is taken from Book I, which was begun at Goslar, in Germany, and finished in the first year or two of Wordsworth's settlement at Grasmere. Lines 101–163 were published in 1809 in Coleridge's periodical *The Friend.* The whole poem was addressed to Coleridge as 'a dear friend, most distinguished for his knowledge and genius, and to whom the author's intellect is deeply indebted.'

516 2–4. Wordsworth was born at Cockermouth, in Cumberland, and in his ninth year was sent to Hawkshead Grammar School in the Vale of Esthwaite.

10. *springes,* snares. *Hamlet* I, iii, 115: 'Ay, springes to catch woodcocks.'

26. *the cultured Vale,* identified by Professor Knight with the neighbouring valley of Yewdale.

1. *object,* what we aimed at. *end,* what actually resulted.

40. *Dust as we are,* in spite of our mortal bodies.

57. *her,* Nature.

73. *elfin pinnace,* fairy bark. The 'craggy ridge' was probably Ironkeld, the 'huge peak' behind it Wetherlam; but there are other ridges and peaks about Esthwaite answering to Wordsworth's description. A similar impression may be obtained by rowing out into any lake surrounded by ridges with higher mountains behind them. It is the moral and spiritual interpretation of the impression that is Wordsworth's own.

80. *struck* with the oars.

517. 101–163. When Wordsworth published these lines in 1809 he gave them the title *Growth of Genius from the Influence of Natural Objects on the Imagination in Boyhood and Early Youth.*

101–114. The nominative of this whole sentence is 'thou,' referring to the 'Wisdom and Spirit of the universe,' addressed in the opening lines; the verb is 'didst intertwine'; and lines 108–114 are an extension of this predicate. By intertwining the passions with Nature, the Divine Spirit purifies and ennobles them; the very emotions of pain and fear, awakened by contact with Nature, gain a touch of Nature's grandeur.

133–7. What is meant exactly by 'shod with steel' and 'games confederate'?

143. *an alien sound.* The weird echo from the distant hills seemed to come from another world.

150. *reflex,* the reflection of a star in the ice.

155. *spinning still.* To the swift skater, aided by the wind, the banks seem to be moving in the contrary direction, and their motion seems to continue for a moment or two even after he has stopped, the mental impression being retained.

LINES COMPOSED ABOVE TINTERN ABBEY

Wordsworth wrote of this poem, originally published in *Lyrical Ballads:*—'No poem of mine was composed under circumstances more pleasant for me to remember than this. I began it upon leaving Tintern, after crossing the Wye, and concluded it just as I was entering Bristol in the evening, after a ramble of four or five days with my sister. Not

a line of it was altered, and not any part of it written down till I reached Bristol.'

The importance of this poem as an illustration of Wordsworth's view of Nature has been already touched on in the Introduction; but it cannot be urged too strongly. Myers says:—'To compare small things with great—or, rather, to compare great things with things vastly greater—the essential spirit of the *Lines near Tintern Abbey* was for practical purposes as new to mankind as the essential spirit of the Sermon on the Mount. Not the isolated expression of moral ideas, but their fusion into a whole in one memorable personality, is that which connects them for ever with a single name. Therefore it is that Wordsworth is venerated; because to so many men—indifferent, it may be, to literary or poetical effects, as such—he has shown by the subtle intensity of his own emotion how the contemplation of Nature can be made a revealing agency, like Love or Prayer—an opening, if indeed there be any opening, into the transcendent world.'

518. 1–2. Wordsworth's earlier visit was made, alone and on foot, in 1793.

3–5. The Wye Valley, above Tintern Abbey, is, perhaps, the most beautiful river scenery in England. Although only a few miles from the sea, the stream is free from the influence of the tide; and rocks, meadows, and wooded cliffs combine to make the scene one of romantic loveliness.

23–50. The memory has been a consolation to the poet amid the noise and loneliness of city life (23–31); it has given him, too, feelings of pleasure, which he no longer remembers, but which, he is sure, have had their influence on his moral character (31–36); and, finally, when perplexed by the mysteries of human life, he has been uplifted by the recollection of Nature's loveliness to a mood, in which the soul, endowed with spiritual insight, penetrates beyond material things to the secret of life, and sees with joy the divine harmony underlying the apparent contradictions of the world (36–50).

56. Have oppressed my spirits.

66–111. Wordsworth in this passage distinguishes three periods in his relation to Nature. In the first, Nature merely offered opportunity for boyish pleasures, such as bird-nesting, rowing, and skating, described in the extract from *The Prelude;* in the second he took delight in the forms and colors of the woods and mountains and the sound of the waterfalls—a delight of eye and ear only, for he was as yet insensible

> to the moods
> Of time and season, to the moral power,
> The affections and the spirit of the place.

In the third period, Nature had a moral and spiritual significance and helped him to understand the mystery of human life. The best commentary is a passage in *The Prelude* (Book VIII, 340–356), in which he sets forth the same succession of his delight in Nature—first, animal; second, sensuous; third, moral and contemplative.

519. 90–104. In this, which we have called the moral or contemplative period, Wordsworth sees every object in Nature as pervaded by the Spirit of God. *The Prelude*, Book II, 396–409.

108. Wordsworth noted the resemblance of this line to Young's *Night-Thoughts*, in which it is said that 'Our *senses*, as our *reason*, are divine,' 'And half-create the wondrous world they see.'

110. In nature as revealed and interpreted by the senses.

114–122. Dorothy Wordsworth was a little younger than her brother, and even in her childhood was a refining influence in his life. See what he writes of her in *The Sparrow's Nest*, p. 527. From childhood they were separated until they were both over twenty, when Dorothy became, not only her brother's constant companion and helper, but a hallowing influence in the crisis of his life.

128. *inform*, mold, inspire.

152. *Of past existence*, of my own past life. Cf. 119–123.

STRANGE FITS OF PASSION

This and the four following poems belong to what is known as the 'Lucy' group of lyrics, written in Germany in 1799. Nothing is known of the English maiden so beautifully and devoutly enshrined; she may have existed only in the poet's imagination.

520. 2. *Dove*, a river in the English Midlands.

6. *diurnal course*, daily revolution.

MICHAEL

This poem was written in Oct.–Dec., 1800, largely at the sheep-fold in Green-head Ghyll, round which the subject is centered. Wordsworth said to Mr. Justice Coleridge that there was some foundation in fact, however slight, for every poem he had ever written of a narrative kind. 'Michael was founded on the son of an old couple having become dissolute, and run away from his parents; and on an old shepherd having been seven years in building up a sheep-fold in a solitary valley.' He wrote on another occasion:—'In the two poems, *The Brothers* and *Michael*, I have attempted to draw a picture of the domestic affections, as I know they exist amongst a class of men who are now almost confined to the north of England. They are small independent *proprietors* of land, here called 'statesmen,' men of respectable education, who daily labor on their own little properties. The domestic affections will always be strong amongst men who live in a country not crowded with population, if these men are placed above poverty. But if they are proprietors of small estates which have descended to them from their ancestors, the power which these affections acquire amongst such men is inconceivable by those who have only had an opportunity of observing hired laborers, farmers, and the manufacturing poor. Their little tract of land serves as a kind of permanent rallying point for their domestic feelings, as a tablet on which they are written, which makes them objects of memory in a thousand instances, when they would otherwise be forgotten. It is a fountain fitted to the nature of social man, from which supplies of affection, as pure as his heart was intended for, are daily drawn. This class of men is rapidly disappearing.'

MY HEART LEAPS UP WHEN I BEHOLD

Wordsworth adopted the last three lines of this little poem (written in 1802) as the motto of the great Ode on Immortality, which was begun about a year later. 'Piety' is used in its original sense of 'reverence, affection.' The meaning is that the man should cherish the love of Nature he feels as a child, so that it may be a continuous inspiration, running through all his life. The sense in which 'the child is father of the man' is explained more fully in the Ode. (See p. 535.)

THE SPARROW'S NEST

Written at Grasmere in 1801. The nest was in the hedge of the garden at Cockermouth in which William and Dorothy Wordsworth played as children. In the poem as originally composed, l. 9 read: 'My sister Dorothy and I.' As to Dorothy Wordsworth see note on *Tintern Abbey*, 114–122, above.

RESOLUTION AND INDEPENDENCE

Written at Grasmere, 1802. 'This old man I met a few hundred yards from my cottage; and the account of him is taken from his own mouth. I was in the state of feeling described in the beginning of the poem, while crossing over Barton fell from Mr. Clarkson's, at the foot of Ullswater, towards Askham. The image of the hare I then observed on the ridge of the fell.' (Wordsworth's note.)

528. 12. *plashy*, marshy, swampy, boggy.

43. *Chatterton*. See pp. 377 and 390.

45. *Him*. Burns. See p. 490.

TO A YOUNG LADY

Written 1802. The poem refers either to Dorothy Wordsworth or to Mary Hutchinson — probably to the former.

530. 17. *a Lapland night*. In the far north at a certain season of the year the sun does not sink below the horizon. The winter nights are often calm and still.

THE SOLITARY REAPER

Suggested to Wordsworth by the following sentence in the MS. of his friend Wilkinson's *Tours to the British Mountains*: 'Passed a female who was reaping along; she sang in Erse, as she bended over her sickle; the sweetest human voice I ever heard; her strains were tenderly melancholy, and felt delicious long after they were heard no more.'

YARROW UNVISITED

'At Clovenford, being so near to the Yarrow, we could not but think of the possibility of going thither, but came to the conclusion of reserving the pleasure for some future time, in consequence of which, after our return, William wrote the poem which I shall here transcribe.'— From Dorothy Wordsworth's *Recollections of a Tour made in Scotland*, 1803.

When Scott sent *The Lay of the Last Minstrel* to Wordsworth, the latter returned a copy of these verses by way of acknowledgment. Scott in reply said: 'I by no means admit your apology, however ingeniously and artfully stated, for not visiting the bonny holms of Yarrow, and certainly will not rest until I have prevailed upon you to compare the ideal with the real stream. . . . I like your swan upon St. Mary's Lake. How came you to know that it is actually frequented by that superb bird?'

Wordsworth subsequently complained that Scott in one of his novels mis-quoted lines 43–44 of this poem, printing 'swans' instead of 'swan.' He added 'Never could I have written "swans" in the plural. The scene, when I saw it with its still and dim lake, under the dusky hills, was one of utter loneliness: there was *one swan*, and one only, stemming the water, and the pathetic loneliness of the region gave importance to the one companion of that swan, its own white image in the water. It was for that reason that I recorded the Swan and its Shadow. Had there been many swans and many shadows, they would have implied nothing as regards the character of that place: and I should have said nothing about them.'

530. 6. *Marrow,* companion. Dorothy Wordsworth.

20. *lintwhites,* linnets, small singing birds.

33. *holms,* flat and low-lying pieces of ground by a river, surrounded or submerged in time of flood.

531. 37. *Strath,* valley.

SHE WAS A PHANTOM OF DELIGHT

The subject of this poem, written in 1804, is Mary Hutchinson, whom Wordsworth had married two years before.

22. *machine.* This word has been objected to as unpoetical. But cf. *Hamlet* II, ii, 124: 'whilst this machine is to him?'

I WANDERED LONELY AS A CLOUD

Wordsworth says: 'The daffodils grew and still grow on the margin of Ullswater, and probably may be seen to this day as beautiful in the month of March, nodding their golden heads beside the dancing and foaming waves.'

Dorothy Wordsworth's *Journal* has the following entry under April 15, 1802: 'When we were in the woods beyond Gowbarrow Park we saw a few daffodils close to the water-side. . . . As we went along there were more, and yet more; and, at last, under the boughs of the trees, we saw there was a long belt of them along the shore. . . . I never saw daffodils so beautiful. They grew among the mossy stones, about and above them; some rested their heads on these stones as on a pillow for weariness; and the rest tossed, and reeled, and danced, and seemed as if they verily laughed with the wind that blew upon them over the lake. They looked so gay, ever glancing, ever changing.'

21–2. These lines, said by Wordsworth to be the best in the poem, were contributed by his wife. For the thought of this stanza cf. *Tintern Abbey,* lines 23–36.

TO A SKY-LARK

Cf. Shelley's poem with the same title (p. 627) and Meredith's *The Lark Ascending* (p. 960).

ELEGIAC STANZAS

There are two Peele Castles, one in the Isle of Man, the other on the coast of Lancashire. The latter is the one referred to in the poem, Wordsworth being known to have spent a four-weeks' vacation in its neighborhood.

ODE ON IMMORTALITY

Of this poem the very highest opinions have been expressed by competent judges. Principal Shairp says it 'marks the highest limit which the tide of poetic inspiration has reached in England . . . since the days of Milton.' It is, therefore, worthy of the most careful study. The best help to understanding it is given in Wordsworth's own note: — 'This was composed during my residence at Town-end, Grasmere. Two years at least passed between the writing of the four first stanzas and the remaining part. To the attentive and competent reader the whole sufficiently explains itself; but there may be no harm in adverting here to particular feelings or *experiences* of my own mind on which the structure of the poem partly rests. Nothing was more difficult for me in childhood than to admit the notion of death as a state applicable to my own being. I have said elsewhere: —

A simple child,
That lightly draws its breath,
And feels its life in every limb,
What should it know of death?

But it was not so much from feelings of animal vivacity that *my* difficulty came as from a sense of the indomitableness of the spirit within me. I used to brood over the stories of Enoch and Elijah, and almost to persuade myself that, whatever might become of others, I should be translated, in something of the same way, to heaven. With a feeling congenial to this, I was often unable to think of external things as having external existence, and I communed with all that I saw as something not apart from, but inherent in my own immaterial nature. Many times while going to school have I grasped at a wall or tree to recall myself from this abyss of idealism to the reality. At that time I was afraid of such processes. In later periods of life I have deplored, as we have all reason to do, a subjugation of an opposite character, and have rejoiced over the remembrances, as is expressed in the lines: —

Obstinate questionings
Of sense and outward things
Fallings from us, vanishings, etc.

To that dream-like vividness and splendor which invest objects of sight in childhood, every one, I believe, if he would look back, could bear testimony, and I need not dwell upon it here; but having in the poem regarded it as presumptive evidence of a prior state of existence, I think it right to protest against a conclusion, which has given pain to some good and pious persons, that I meant to inculcate such a belief. It is far too shadowy a notion to be recommended to faith as more than an element in our instincts of immortality. But let us bear in mind that, though the idea is not advanced in revelation, there is nothing there to contradict it, and the fall of man presents an analogy in its favour. Accordingly, a pre-existent state has entered into the popular creeds of many nations, and, among all persons acquainted with classic literature, is known as an ingredient in Platonic philosophy. Archimedes said that he could move the world if he had a point whereon to rest his machine. Who has not felt the same aspirations as regards the world of his own mind? Having to wield some of its elements when I was impelled to write this poem on the "Immortality of the Soul," I took hold of the notion of pre-existence as having sufficient foundation in humanity for authorizing me to make for my purpose the best use of it I could as a poet.'

Wordsworth's view of childish reminiscences of a previous existence was, however, probably not suggested by Plato, but by the seventeenth century poet Vaughan, in *Childhood* and *The Retreat.* See p. 185.

534. 4. Cf. lines 4–5 of the *Sonnet Composed upon Westminster Bridge* (p. 538), and *Elegiac Stanzas* 14–16 (p. 532).

13. *bare,* of clouds.

535. 21. *tabor,* a small drum.

22. *a thought of grief,* the thought expressed in the last two lines of the preceding stanza.

26. *wrong,* offend by lack of sympathy.

28. *the fields of sleep,* 'from the dark beyond the dawn,' or possibly 'from the sleeping [*i.e.,* quiet] fields.'

40. *coronal,* garland.

56–7. Cf. lines 4–5 and note above.

72. *Nature's Priest,* the Minister and Interpreter of the Divinity.

81. *homely,* humble — in contrast with the glories of man's divine origin.

85–9. Probably suggested by the sight of Hartley Coleridge, to whom Wordsworth addressed a poem *To H. C., Six Years Old,* beginning: 'O thou! whose fancies from afar are brought.'

102–7. Referring to Shakspere's well-known lines in *As You Like It,* II, vii, 139–166, 'All the world 's a stage,' etc.

536. 112. *the eternal deep,* the deep mysteries of eternity.

126. *earthly freight,* 'burden of earthly cares.' (Webb.)

132. *fugitive,* evanescent, quickly disappearing.

141–5. Professor Bonamy Price, walking one day with Wordsworth by the side of Rydal Water, asked him the meaning of these lines: —'The venerable old man raised his aged form erect; he was walking in the middle, and passed across me to a five-barred gate in the wall which bounded the road on the side of the lake. He clenched the top bar firmly with his right hand, pushed strongly against it, and then uttered these ever-memorable words, "There was a time in my life when I had to push against something that resisted, to be sure that there was anything outside of me. I was sure of my own mind; everything else fell away and vanished into thought." Thought he was sure of; matter for him, at the moment, was an unreality.'

181. *primal sympathy,* the child's intuitive sympathy with Nature.

183–4. Cf. *Tintern Abbey,* lines 92–5 (p. 518).

185. *through,* beyond.

189. *yet,* still, even now.

196–9. The sunset has no longer 'a celestial light, the glory and the freshness of a dream,' but suggests serious reflections to the Man who has pondered on the issues of Life and Death. The poet's final thought is that acquaintance with the world, while robbing Nature of its first glory, increases its significance by awakening sympathy with the joys and sorrows of humanity. Professor Dowden has well observed that the last two lines of the *Ode* are 'often quoted as an illustration of Wordsworth's sensibility to external nature; in reality, they testify to his enriching the sentiment of nature with feeling derived from the heart of man and from the experience of human life.'

NUNS FRET NOT

537. 3. *pensive citadels,* refuges in which they can think, secure from interruption.

6. *Furness-fells,* the hills of the district of Furness, in or near which Wordsworth spent the greater part of his life.

8–9. Cf. Lovelace, *To Althea from Prison,* p. 182.

PERSONAL TALK, III

13. Desdemona in *Othello.*

14. See Spenser *Faery Queen,* ll. 27 ff. (p. 110).

COMPOSED UPON WESTMINSTER BRIDGE

Wordsworth appears to have been mistaken as to the date he assigned to this sonnet, which was written when he left London for Dover on his way to Calais early in the morning of July 30th, 1802. The following is the entry in his sister's diary under that date: 'Left London between five and six o'clock of the morning outside the Dover coach. A beautiful morning. The city, St. Paul's, with the river — a multitude of little boats, made a beautiful sight as we crossed Westminster Bridge; the houses not overhung by their clouds of smoke, and were spread out endlessly; yet the sun shone so brightly, with such a pure light, that there was something like the purity of one of Nature's own grand spectacles.'

IT IS A BEAUTEOUS EVENING

538. 9. *Dear Child!* Dorothy Wordsworth.

12. *Abraham's bosom.* In the presence of God. See Luke xvi, 22.

ON THE EXTINCTION OF THE VENETIAN REPUBLIC

1–2. At the beginning of the thirteenth century the Venetians, with the help of France, captured Constantinople, and added to their dominions a large part of the Eastern Empire. They protected Western Europe from the incursions of the Turks for centuries.

4. Venice was founded in the fifth century in the marshes of the Adriatic by inhabitants of the mainland who fled before the conquering Huns under Attila.

7–8. The Venetians having protected Pope Alexander III against the German Emperor, whom they defeated in a sea fight in 1177, the Pope gave the Doge a ring and bade him wed with it the Adriatic that posterity might know that the sea was subject to Venice, 'as a bride is to her husband.' The ceremony was observed annually by a solemn naval procession, after which the Doge threw a ring into the sea.

9–14. Venice was robbed of much of her power in 1508 by the League of Cambrai, but the real cause of her decay was the discovery of the New World, which made the Atlantic the highway of trade instead of the Mediterranean, and shifted the commercial center from Italy to England and Holland. The Republic, however, remained free and independent, though greatly enfeebled, until 1797, when Austria and France divided its territory between them. Venice remained under Austrian dominion (except for brief intervals) until it became a part of the kingdom of Italy in 1866.

TO TOUSSAINT L'OUVERTURE

This sonnet was written in August, 1802, when Toussaint L'Ouverture, the liberator of St. Domingo, was lying in prison at Paris, where he died a few months later. He was born in 1743, the child of African slaves, and showed great political and military ability; but he was unable to resist the French fleet sent against him by Napoleon, who reestablished slavery in the island in 1801.

TO THE MEN OF KENT

Written when Britain was in fear of a Napoleonic invasion.

539. 4. *hardiment*, hardihood, courage.

540. 10. *from the Norman*, at the battle of Hastings, 1066.

ON THE SUBJUGATION OF SWITZERLAND

Switzerland was conquered by the French in 1798, and three of its cantons were annexed to the Republic. The sonnet appears to have been suggested by the Act of Mediation, by which Napoleon arranged for the government of Switzerland in 1803; he became Emperor a few months afterwards, and at the time the sonnet was written had made himself master of Europe, England alone having resisted him successfully. It was the attack upon the liberties of Switzerland which gave the final blow to the French sympathies of both Coleridge and Wordsworth, and united them with their fellow-countrymen in antagonism to Napoleon.

THE WORLD IS TOO MUCH WITH US

13–14. Proteus and Triton were sea-deities in the old Greek mythology. Wordsworth means that he would rather be a heathen with some sense of the Divinity in Nature than a professed Christian whose heart is so given to the pursuit of wealth and worldly ambition that he is out of harmony with the beautiful sights and sounds of land and sea.

THE RIVER DUDDON

This is the concluding sonnet of a beautiful series which Wordsworth wrote under the above title. The Duddon is a small stream which rises on the borders of Westmoreland, Cumberland, and Lancashire, and flows into the Irish Sea.

KING'S COLLEGE CHAPEL

This beautiful chapel was built by Henry VI for the scholars of the College, which up to a few years ago was reserved to students from Eton.

CONTINUED

541. 4. *Westminster* Abbey.

8. *younger Pile.* St. Paul's Cathedral, built by Sir Christopher Wren in the seventeenth century. It is a more modern structure than the Abbey, and contains the ashes of many great men for whom room could not be found in the older national burial place. It is surmounted by a great dome and cross.

ON THE DEPARTURE OF SIR WALTER SCOTT

This was the journey which Scott took in the hope of recovery from what proved to be his last illness. Abbotsford, on the Tweed, was his home.

3. *Eildon,* three hills near Abbotsford, famous in Scottish legend.

14. *Parthenope,* one of the Sirens, said to be burned at Naples.

'THERE!' SAID A STRIPLING

'Mossgiel was thus pointed out to me by a young man on the top of the coach on my way from Glasgow to Kilmarnock.' (Wordsworth's note.)

9. *bield,* lodging, dwelling, place of shelter.

CONCLUSION

This and the former sonnet were among the 'Poems composed or suggested during a tour in the summer of 1833,' published two years later.

COLERIDGE: BIOGRAPHIA LITERARIA

543. *a.* 24. *The Friend.* A periodical published by Coleridge in 1809–10.

544. *b.* 37. *stamp tax,* levied at this time upon all newspapers and weekly periodicals.

39. *a war against freedom,* against France.

54. *ad normam Platonis,* after the rule of Plato, the Greek philosopher.

κατ᾽ἔμφασιν, in appearance rather than reality.

545. *a.* 26. *pingui-nitescent,* shining with fat.

b. 1. *Phileleutheros,* lover of freedom.

31. *ambrosial,* heavenly.

546. *a.* 19. *Orpheus,* the musician of classical mythology whose strains persuaded even stones and trees to follow him.

24. *illuminati,* illuminated or inspired ones.

547. *a.* 1. *Jacobinism,* revolutionary principle. Jacobin means, originally, a friar of the order of St. Dominic. Hence one of a faction in the French revolution, so called from the *Jacobin* club, which first met in the hall of the Jacobin friars in Paris, Oct. 1789.

8. *The Watchman* ran from March 1 to May 13 1796.

30. *text from Isaiah.* 'My bowels shall sound like an harp.' xvi, 11.

36. *psilosophy.* See 544. *h.* 37.

46. *gagging bills.* The bills introduced into Parliament to restrict public meetings and the freedom of the press.

b. 1. *melioration,* improvement.

21. *a dear friend.* Thomas Poole.

29. *first revolutionary war,* against the French revolutionists.

44. *Stowey.* In Somersetshire.

46. *morning paper. The Post.*

548. *a.* 25. *a poet.* Wordsworth came to Stowey in July, 1797.

53. *Quidnunc,* an idle gossip, continually asking 'what now?'

55. *Dogberry,* the pompous, ignorant constable of *Much Ado about Nothing.*

57. *pour surveillance of,* to exercise supervision over.

b. 25. *Spy Nozy,* the great Jewish philosopher Spinoza (1632-1677), in whose teaching Wordsworth and Coleridge were greatly interested.

26. *a remarkable feature,* a red nose.

552. *a.* 3. *Anacreon,* Greek lyric poet of the sixth century B. C.

b. 34. *Bishop Taylor.* See p. 221.

35. *Burnet* (1635–1715), a distinguished philosopher and divine. His *Sacred Theory of the Earth* is a fanciful and ingenious speculation.

553. *a.* 47. *Sir John Davies* (1570–1626).

THE ANCIENT MARINER

The circumstances under which this poem was written and published have been already related (see p. 503). Some further particulars of the suggestions made by Wordsworth may here be given, from his own account:

'In the autumn of 1797 Mr. Coleridge, my sister and myself started from Alfoxden pretty late in the afternoon with a view to visit Linton and the Valley of Stones near to it; and as our united funds were very small, we agreed to defray the expense of the tour by writing a poem, to be sent to the *New Monthly Magazine.* Accordingly we set off and proceeded along the Quantock Hills towards Watchet; and in the course of this walk was planned the poem of the "Ancient Mariner," founded on a dream, as Mr. Coleridge said, of his friend Mr. Cruikshank. Much the greatest part of the story was Mr. Coleridge's invention, but certain parts I suggested.

'For example, some crime was to be committed which should bring upon the Old Navigator, as Coleridge afterwards delighted to call him, the spectral persecution, as a consequence of that crime, and his own wanderings. I had been reading in Shelvocke's *Voyages* a day or two before that, while doubling Cape Horn, they frequently saw albatrosses in that latitude, the largest sort of sea-fowl, some extending their wings twelve or thirteen feet. "Suppose," said I, "you represent him as having killed one of these birds on entering the South Sea, and that the tutelary spirits of these regions take upon them to avenge the crime." The incident was thought fit for the purpose, and adopted accordingly. I also suggested the navigation of the ship by the dead men, but do not recollect that I had anything more to do with the scheme of the poem. The gloss with which

it was subsequently accompanied was not thought of by either of us at the time; at least not a hint of it was given to me, and I have no doubt it was a gratuitous afterthought. We began the composition together on that, to me, memorable evening. I furnished two or three lines at the beginning of the poem, in particular: —

> And listened like a three years' child:
> The Mariner had his will.'

Coleridge seems later to have had doubts whether Wordsworth's suggestion of moral responsibility was consistent with the imaginative character of the poem as a whole. He is reported as saying in his *Table Talk* on May 31, 1830: —'Mrs. Barbauld once told me that she admired *The Ancient Mariner* very much, but that there were two faults in it,— it was improbable, and had no moral. As for the probability, I owned that that might admit some question; but as to the want of a moral, I told her that in my own judgment the poem had too much; and that the only. or chief fault, if I might say so, was the obtrusion of the moral sentiment so openly on the reader as a principle or cause of action in a work of pure imagination. It ought to have had no more moral than the *Arabian Nights'* tale of the merchant's sitting down to eat dates by the side of a well and throwing the shells aside, and lo! a genie starts up and says he *must* kill the aforesaid merchant *because* one of the date shells had, it seems, put out the eye of the genie's son.'

A marginal gloss was added by Coleridge in the edition of 1817, together with a Latin motto from Burnet, of which the following is a translation: —'I readily believe that there are more invisible beings in the universe than visible. But who shall explain to us the nature, the rank and kinship, the distinguishing marks and graces of each? What do they do? Where do they dwell? The human mind has circled round this knowledge, but never attained to it. Yet there is profit, I do not doubt, in sometimes contemplating in the mind, as in a picture, the image of a greater and better world: lest the intellect, habituated to the petty details of daily life, should be contracted within too narrow limits and settle down wholly on trifles. But, meanwhile, a watchful eye must be kept on truth, and proportion observed, that we may distinguish the certain from the uncertain, day from night.'

It has been thought that Coleridge took some hints from the *Strange and Dangerous Voyage* of Captain Thomas James (London, 1633), and from an earlier story of Saint Paulinus, but his borrowings from these sources were certainly slight. The invention of the subject, as well as its imaginative treatment, is substantially his own.

553. 11. *loon,* an idle, stupid, worthless fellow.

12. *eftsoons,* forthwith, immediately. These obsolete words are used to recall the style of the old ballads, which Coleridge was trying to revive, and to suggest that the time of the story was somewhat remote. What other words in Part I produce the same impression?

Notice what a vivid picture of the Mariner is brought before the mind by the mention of successive details of his personal appearance.

23–4. As the ship sailed further away from the harbor, first the church, then the hill, and last the top of the lighthouse upon the hill disappeared from view.

25. If the sun rose on the left, in what direction was the ship sailing?

554. 29–30. At the equator the noon sun is never far out of the perpendicular, and during the equinoxes it is directly overhead. See lines 111–114.

32. bassoon. This particular detail was probably suggested to Coleridge by the fact that during his residence at Stowey, his friend, Poole, added a bassoon to the instruments used in the village church.

36. minstrelsy, band of minstrels.

41. drawn (in the marginal note) seems to be a printer's mistake for 'driven,' but it is the reading given in all the editions during Coleridge's lifetime.

46–48. Write out this metaphor in your own words so as to make sure that you understand it.

55–57. clifts, cliffs. **sheen,** brightness, splendour. **ken,** see, discern. Compare notes above on lines 10–11.

58. between the ship and the land.

62. in a swound, heard in a swoon.

75. shroud, a rope running from the mast-head to the ship's side.

76. vesper, (Latin) evening; in its plural form the term is usually applied to the evening service of the Roman Catholic church.

81. crossbow. This suggests that the time of the story was at the end of the sixteenth or beginning of the seventeenth century, when the crossbow was still in common use.

83. Why 'upon the right?' The reader should trace the voyage of the ship on a map; it must have been now about nine days' sail from a point between Cape Horn and the South Pole.

98. uprist, used instead of 'uprose' (as 'eat' instead of 'eaten' in line 67) to give the suggestion of language of the olden time.

104. In the edition of 1817 Coleridge altered this line to read

The furrow streamed off free,

and added in a footnote: 'In the former edition the line was —

The furrow followed free;

but I had not been long on board a ship before I perceived that this was the image as seen by a spectator from the shore, or from another vessel. From the ship itself the wake appears like a brook flowing off from the stern.' But in 1828 and after, the original reading was restored.

107. Notice the sudden check in the verse at the end of this line, and the contrast with the swift movement of the preceding stanza.

555. 128. death-fires, phosphorescent lights, to which the sailors attached a superstitious significance.

139. well-a-day, an antique exclamation of lament, as 'gramercy' in line 164 is of joy and thankfulness.

152. wist, knew. See notes above on use of old words.

164. 'I took the thought of "grinning for joy"

from poor Burnett's remark to me, when we had climbed to the top of Plinlimmon, and were nearly dead with thirst. We could not speak for the constriction, till we found a little puddle under a stone. He said to me, "You grinned like an idiot!" He had done the same.' (Table Talk.)

184. gossameres, fine spider-threads.

185–9. Coleridge made considerable alterations, omissions and additions in this part of the poem after it was first published. Another version of this stanza reads:

'Are those her ribs which flecked the sun
    Like bars of a dungeon grate?
Are these two all, all of the crew,
    That woman and her mate?'

And he left the following additional stanza in manuscript:

'This ship it was a plankless thing
A bare Anatomy!
A plankless Spectre — and it moved
Like a being of the Sea!
The woman and a fleshless man
Therein sate merrily.'

197. What is it that the Woman Life-in-Death has won, and what difference does this make to the story?

199–200. A fine description of the sudden darkness of the tropics.

556. 209–11. A star within the lower tip of the crescent moon is never seen. This is Coleridge's imaginative way of using what he describes in a manuscript note as the 'common superstition among sailors that something evil is about to happen whenever a star dogs the moon.'

223. Notice at the end of each part the repeated reference to the crime the Ancient Mariner has committed.

226–7. 'For the last two lines of this stanza I am indebted to Mr. Wordsworth. It was on a delightful walk from Nether Stowey to Dulverton, with him and his sister, in the autumn of 1797, that this poem was planned and in part composed.'— Coleridge's note in the edition of 1817.

254. reek, give off vapor.

267–8. The white moonlight, as if in mockery, covered the hot sea with a sheen like that of April hoar frost.

294. Note this and other indications that the religious setting of the poem is Roman Catholic — another way of suggesting the atmosphere of antiquity.

557. 297. The buckets looked silly because they had stayed so long dry and useless.

302. dank, wet.

314. sheen, bright. The reference seems to be to the Polar Lights, known in the Northern Hemisphere as the Aurora Borealis.

319. sedge, coarse grass growing in a swamp.

333. had been (subjunctive mood), would have been.

558. 394. I have not the power; I cannot.

435. charnel-dungeon, a vault for the bones of the dead.

559. 489. *rood,* cross.

512. *shrieve* (usually pronounced and written 'shrive') to absolve after confession.

524. *trow,* trust, believe, think.

535. *ivy-tod,* ivy-bush.

560. 575. *crossed his brow,* made the sign of the cross on his forehead to warn off evil spirits.

623. *of sense forlorn,* one who has lost his senses.

CHRISTABEL

Christabel was begun in 1797–8, and continued in 1800. Scot heard it recited while it was still in manuscript, and the melody of the verse made such an impression on his mind that he adopted it for *The Lay of the Last Minstrel. Christabel* in its fragmentary state was printed in 1816; Coleridge said in 1821, 'Of my poetic works I would fain finish *Christabel*,' but he never succeeded in doing so. It remains, however, one of the most wonderful and beautiful poems of the Romantic Revival.
564. 408–426. Said by Coleridge to be 'the best and sweetest lines I ever wrote.'

KUBLA KHAN

In a note to this poem on its publication in 1816, Coleridge relates the circumstances of its composition. Being in ill-health, he had retired to a lonely farmhouse on Exmoor, and an anodyne had been prescribed, from the effects of which he fell asleep in his chair at the moment that he was reading the following sentence from the old book of travels known as *Purchas his Pilgrimage:*—'In Xamdu did Cublai Can build a stately palace, encompassing sixteen miles of plain ground with a wall, wherein are fertile meadows, pleasant springs, delightful streams, and all sorts of beasts of chase and game, and in the midst thereof a sumptuous house of pleasure.' Coleridge adds:—'The Author continued for about three hours in a profound sleep, at least of the external senses, during which time he has the most vivid confidence that he could not have composed less than from two to three hundred lines; if that indeed can be called composition in which all the images rose up before him as *things,* with a parallel production of the correspondent expressions, without any sensation or consciousness of effort. On awaking he appeared to himself to have a distinct recollection of the whole, and taking his pen, ink, and paper, instantly and eagerly wrote down the lines that are here preserved. At this moment he was unfortunately called out by a person on business from Porlock, and detained by him above an hour, and on his return to his room, found, to his no small surprise and mortification, that though he still retained some vague and dim recollection of the general purport of the vision, yet, with the exception of some eight or ten scattered lines and images, all the rest had passed away like the images on the surface of a stream into which a stone had been cast, but, alas! without the after restoration of the latter!'

Kubla Khan in the thirteenth century founded the Mogul dynasty in China, and made Pekin the capital of his empire, which was the largest that has ever existed in Asia. He was an enlightened but ambitious ruler, very fond of pomp and splendor.

565. 13. *athwart a cedarn cover,* across a cedar wood.

41. *Abora,* apparently a mountain of Coleridge's imagination.

FROST AT MIDNIGHT

Mrs. Coleridge was wont to complain to her friends that her husband '*would* walk up and down composing poetry instead of coming to bed at proper hours.' This poem was the outcome of a midnight meditation in his cottage at Stowey in February, 1798, and was published in the same year.
566. 27. *stranger,* a film of soot sticking to the bars of the grate, which, according to a common English superstition, betokens the coming of a visitor.

29–30. As to Coleridge's birth and school days, see Life, p. 542.

38. *stern preceptor.* Coleridge, in his *Biographia Literaria,* says: 'At school I enjoyed the inestimable advantage of a very sensible, though at the same time, a very severe master.' He goes on to speak at length of Boyer's merits as a teacher, 'whose severities, even now, not seldom furnish the dreams, by which the blind fancy would fain interpret to the mind the painful sensations of distempered sleep; but neither lessen nor dim the deep sense of my moral and intellectual obligations.' Coleridge writes also in his *Table Talk:* 'The discipline at Christ's Hospital in my time was ultra Spartan; all domestic ties were to be put aside. "Boy!" I remember Boyer saying to me once when I was crying the first day of my return after the holidays, "Boy! the school is your father! Boy! the school is your mother! Boy! the school is your brother! Boy! the school is your sister! the school is your first cousin, and your second cousin, and all the rest of your relations! Let's have no more crying!"' Coming under the influence of Voltaire, Coleridge professed himself an infidel. 'So, sirrah, you are an infidel, are you?' said Boyer; 'then I'll flog your infidelity out of you!' Coleridge said it was the 'only just flogging he ever received.'

43–44. Coleridge was very fond of his sister Ann, who was five years older than himself and had been his playmate when he was still in petticoats. She died in 1791, to his great grief.

52–54. At Christ's Hospital Coleridge used to lie on the roof and gaze upon the clouds and stars.

55–65. There was no likelihood at this time that Coleridge would live in the Lake District, but he fulfilled his own prophecy in 1800 by removing to Greta Hall, Keswick, from which he writes, soon after his settlement there, of his little son's enjoyment of nature: 'I look at my doted-on Hartley—he moves, he lives, he finds impulses from within and from without, he is the darling of the sun and the breeze. Nature seems to bless him as a thing of her own. He looks at the clouds, the mountains, the living beings of the earth, and vaults and jubilates.'

HUMILITY THE MOTHER OF CHARITY

The date appended to this poem is that of composition.

EPITAPH

This poem like the preceding bears the date of its composition.

LAMB: THE OLD FAMILIAR FACES

This was written in Jan., 1798, at the time of the central tragedy of Lamb's life, the poem in its original form beginning: —

> 'Where are they gone, the old familiar faces?
> I had a mother, but she died and left me,
> Died prematurely in a day of horrors —
> All, all are gone, the old familiar faces.'

The last stanza began with the word 'For,' and the words 'And some are taken from me' in l. 20 were italicized, referring no doubt to Mary Lamb, whose illness was probably the occasion of the poem. The 'friend' of l. 10 was Charles Lloyd, with whom Lamb had a temporary difference about this time; the 'more than brother' of l. 16, Coleridge.

MACKERY END, IN HERTFORDSHIRE

All these essays appeared in the *London Magazine*, 1821–22, and were afterwards included in the *Essays of Elia*.

Mackrye End may now be easily reached from Wheathampstead Station on the Great Northern Railway. The old farmhouse, with some additions since Lamb's day, is still standing.

568. *a.* 4. *Bridget Elia*, Mary Lamb. See biographical sketch, **p.** 567.

12. *the rash king's offspring*, Jephthah's daughter. Judges xi, 30–40.

15. *'with a difference.'* Ophelia in *Hamlet* IV, v. 183, 'O, you must wear your rue with a difference.'

17. *bickerings*, little quarrels.

20. *dissembling*, simulating. This is contrary to the established usage, according to which dissemble is to pretend not to be something that you are.

26. *Burton*, the author of *The Anatomy of Melancholy* (1621).

33. *a story.* Mary Lamb's passion for novel-reading is spoken of by others.

39. *humors*, eccentricities.

43. *bizarre*, whimsical, fantastic.

46. *'holds Nature more clever'*—a quotation from Gay, *Epitaph of Byewords.*

48. *obliquities*, irregularities.

49. *Religio Medici*, the chief work of Sir Thomas Browne, whose curious notions and elaborate style made him a favorite with Lamb. See p. 200.

52. *intellectuals*, reasoning powers, intelligence.

b. 1. *Margaret Newcastle*, an eccentric Restoration noblewoman, of high character and remarkable talents, for whom Lamb often expressed his admiration.

34. *derogatory*, disparaging.

42. *stuff of the conscience*, quoted from *Othello* I, ii, 2.

50. *good old English reading*, in the library of Samuel Salt of the Inner Temple.

569. *a.* 18. *beat up the quarters of*, arouse, disturb, visit unceremoniously. The expression is used in exactly the same way by Richardson in *Pamela*.

20. *corn country.* Hertfordshire is mainly agricultural and grows a large quantity of wheat.

35. *substantial yeoman*, well-to-do farmer.

b. 13. *'heart of June,'* quoted from Ben Jonson.

14. *the poet*, Wordsworth. See *Yarrow Visited*, stanza 6, 'than which' (Lamb wrote to Wordsworth) 'I think no lovelier stanza can be found in the wide world of poetry.'

21. *waking bliss*, conscious enjoyment, less like a dream; quoted from Milton's *Comus.*

570. *a.* 5. *gossamer*, spider thread. *rending*, separating.

14. *the two scriptural cousins*, Mary and Elizabeth. Luke i, 39–40.

23. *B. F.*, Baron Field, an English barrister, who in 1816 became Judge of the Supreme Court of New South Wales. To him Lamb addressed the Elia essay entitled *Distant Correspondents.*

24. *peradventure*, by chance.

26. *The fatted calf.* See the Parable of the Prodigal Son, Luke xv, 23.

43. *astoundment*, intense surprise.

50. *I forget all this.* A reminiscence of Psalm cxxxvii, 5: 'If I forget thee, O Jerusalem, let my right hand forget her cunning.'

DREAM-CHILDREN: A REVERIE

The death of Lamb's brother John on Oct. 26, 1821, appears to have suggested the tender vein of reminiscence and musing on 'what might have been' in this essay, which is justly regarded as one of the most delicate in pathos and perfect in workmanship Lamb ever wrote. But this kind of reverie was not unusual with him. He writes in an earlier essay (*New Year's Eve*): 'Being without wife or family . . . and having no offspring of my own to dally with, I turn back upon memory, and adopt my own early idea, as my heir and favorite.'

b. 11. *Norfolk.* Lamb's grandmother, Mary Field, was housekeeper for more than fifty years at Blakesware in Hertfordshire, the seat of the Plumers, described in the Elia essay, *Blakesmoor in H——shire.* William Plumer, who lived in another family seat (also in Hertfordshire), and dismantled Blakesware, was still living when *Dream-Children* was published, and this may have been the reason why Lamb altered the name of the county to Norfolk, the scene of the legend of the children in the wood.

23. *Robin Redbreasts*, which at the end of the ballad cover the bodies of the murdered children with leaves.

50. *tawdry*, showy, pretentious and yet worthless. **571.** *a.* 3. *Psaltery*, the Psalms. Psalter is the more usual and correct form.

5. *spread her hands*, in amazement at such learning.

14. *cancer*, the actual cause of Mrs. Field's death.

21. *apparition of two infants.* There was a legend in the Plumer family about the mysterious disappearance of two children in the seventeenth century.

36. *the old busts.* These were among the things removed by Mr. Plumer from Blakesware.

49. *nectarines,* a variety of peach thought particularly delicious.

52. *forbidden fruit.* See Genesis ii, 16–17, and the opening lines of *Paradise Lost.*

b. 3. *basking,* lying in the sun; originally a Norse word, meaning 'to bathe one's self.'

11. *impertinent,* because the pike eats dace. It is a sluggish fish, while dace are very lively.

20. *irrelevant,* not to the purpose, not worth attention.

30. *mettlesome,* high-spirited.

43. *a lame-footed boy.* It is not known whether Lamb was ever temporarily lame in boyhood. John Lamb's lameness was caused by the fall of a stone in 1796, just before the tragedy which made such a difference in Charles Lamb's life. Writing to Coleridge just afterwards he says: 'I had the whole weight of the family thrown on me; for my brother, little disposed (I speak not without tenderness for him) at any time to take care of old age and infirmities, had now, with his bad leg, an exemption from such duties, and I was now left alone.' John Lamb was self-indulgent, and in manhood they saw little of each other, but Charles felt his loss severely, as is shown by the letters he wrote at the time. A fuller account of John Lamb, written before his death, will be found in the Elia essay, *My Relations.*

572. *a.* 13. *took off his limb.* This is a detail supplied from Lamb's imagination.

22. *Alice W——n,* Winterton in Lamb's Key, but he adds that it is a feigned name. The real name of the village girl 'with the bright yellow Hertfordshire hair, and eye of watchet hue' was probably Ann Simmons. She seems to have lived in one of the cottages near Blakesware and married Mr. Bartram, or Bartrum, a London pawnbroker. Lamb probably idealized this youthful passion, which, if his 'seven long years' are to be taken literally, must have begun when he was a boy of fourteen. He writes in *New Year's Eve:* 'I would scarce now have any of my life reversed. I would no more alter them than the incidents of some well-contrived novel. Methinks it is better that I should have pined away seven of my goldenest years, when I was thrall to the fair hair, and fairer eyes, of Alice W——n, than that so passionate a love-adventure should be lost.'

25. *difficulty,* shyness, reserve, reluctance to be won.

28. *representment,* re-incarnation.

31. *whose, i.e.,* the first or the second Alice's.

42. *might have been,* if he had married Alice.

44. *Lethe,* the river of Hades, which made those who drank of it completely forget their past life. Virgil in the *Æneid* (VI, 703–751) says that after thousands of years the soul, having drunk of Lethe, returns to earth in another body. Some such far-off incarnation is all that is possible for the creations of the dreamer's imagination.

49. *Bridget . . . James Elia,* the names given by Lamb to his sister and brother in *My Relations.*

50. *gone for ever.* This was the only part of the dream that remained true.

A CHAPTER ON EARS

Lamb exaggerates his lack of appreciation for music in this essay, as in his verses, *Free Thoughts on Several Eminent Composers,* beginning:

> ' Some cry up Haydn, some Mozart,
> Just as the whim bites; for my part
> I do not care a farthing candle
> For either of them, or for Handel.'

As a matter of fact he was a fervent admirer of Braham, whose singing of Handel's oratorio, *Israel in Egypt,* is commended in the essay on *Imperfect Sympathies.* Lamb wrote of this great singer: ' He was a rare composition of the Jew, the gentleman, and the angel; yet all these elements mixed up so kindly in him that you could not tell which preponderated.'

b. 3. *volutes,* spiral ornaments at the sides of the capital or top of Ionic and Corinthian pillars.

6. *conduits,* channels, usually for water, here for sound.

8. *the mole* has small ears but keen hearing.

9. *labyrinthine,* winding, intricate.

10. *side-intelligencers,* side passages, conveying information to the brain.

13. *to draw upon assurance,* to rely upon impudence.

14. '*quite unabashed.*' Lamb gave the reference in a foot-note in the *London Magazine* to Pope's *Dunciad* (II, 147):

> ' Earless on high stood unabashed Defoe.'

15. *upon that article,* in that particular.

17. *pillory,* a frame in which the offender's head and hands were fixed in an uncomfortable and helpless position while he was exposed to the jeers and insults of the mob. This mode of punishment was practised in Great Britain up to the beginning of Queen Victoria's reign. Defoe was subjected to it for his satirical tract, *The Shortest Way with the Dissenters* (see p. 287), but the barbarous practice of cutting off the ears, which often accompanied exposure in the pillory, was in his case not carried out.

23. *concourse of sweet sounds. The Merchant of Venice* V, i, 83–5.

24. '*Water parted from the sea.*' This and '*In infancy*' are both songs from Arne's opera *Artaxerxes,* Lamb's *First Play.*

27. *harpsichord,* the forerunner of the modern pianoforte.

32. *Mrs. S——,* not identified beyond the name ' Spinkes' given in Lamb's Key.

42. *Alice W——n.* See notes to *Dream Children* above.

56. *A.,* William Ayrton, a well-known musical critic of the time.

573. *a.* 29. *Sostenuto and adagio,* Italian musical terms indicating that a passage is to be played in a ' sustained' or ' leisurely' manner.

31. *Sol, Fa, Mi, Re,* names of notes used in singing.

32. *conjuring,* mysterious, magical. *Baralipton,* a meaningless word invented by the scholastic philosophers for the purpose of exercises in logic.

37. *Jubal* ' was the father of all such as handle the harp and organ '— Genesis iv, 21.

38. *gamut*, the scale, from Gamma-ut, the ancient name of the first note.

39. *singly unimpressible to*, alone incapable of receiving impressions from.

41. *stroke*, effect.

46. *cried-up*, extravagantly praised.

51. *midsummer madness*. Olivia, in *Twelfth Night* III, iv, 61: ' Why, this is very midsummer madness.' The midsummer moon was believed a cause of insanity.

56. *con*, learn by heart.

　　b. 1. *thrid*, thread, follow all the windings of.

2. *hieroglyphics*, the sacred picture-writings of the ancient Egyptians.

8. *follow*, with . e mind, in the attempt to connect what went before with what comes after.

13. *the Enraged Musician*, a picture by Hogarth of a musician almost driven mad by street noises.

15. *Oratorio*, a sacred musical performance without scenery or special dress.

18. *pit*, the part of the theatre on the ground floor, a little removed from the stage, chiefly frequented by devoted theatre-goers who cannot afford to pay for dearer seats.

19. *Laughing Audience*, a wonderful picture by Hogarth representing varieties of mirth as seen on different human faces at a play. There is a good description of it in Dowden, *Shakspere's Mind and Art*, pp. 338–9.

30. *Party in a parlor*, etc. Quoted from the first edition of Wordsworth's *Peter Bell*. The stanza was omitted from subsequent editions, but in the meantime Shelley had taken it for the motto of his burlesque *Peter Bell the Third*.

33. *concertos*, elaborate pieces of music for one or more instruments, accompanied by an orchestra.

46. *all stops*, all punctuation marks, no words.

50. *mime*, a mimic actor of farces. Latin *mimus*.

574. *a.* 1. *book in Patmos*. See Revelation x, 10.

3. *Burton*. *Anatomy of Melancholy* I, ii, 2, 6.

6. *melancholy given*, given or inclined to melancholy.

10. *amabilis insania*, delightful ecstasy. Horace, *Odes* III, iv, 5.

11. *mentis gratissimus error*, a most welcome deception of the mind, a pleasing hallucination. Horace, *Epistles* II, ii, 140.

17. *toys*, trifles, innocent amusements.

26. *habitated*, habituated, accustomed.

30. *subrusticus pudor*, awkward bashfulness. Cicero, *Epistolae ad Familiares* V, xii, first sentence.

44. *Nov——*, Vincent Novello, a well-known organist and composer.

53. *abbey*, Westminster.

　　b. 3. *dove's wings*. Psalm lv, 6: ' Oh that I had wings like a dove! ' Barron Field says that Lamb was especially fond of the setting of these words by Kent, the English composer of the previous century. Mendelssohn's anthem, ' O for the wings of a dove,' was not yet composed.

6. *cleanse his mind*. Psalm cxix, 9: ' Wherewithal shall a young man cleanse his way?' An-

thems to these words were written by the English composers Cook and Boyce.

10. *rapt above earth*, etc. Walton's *Complete Angler* I, iv. See p. 212.

17. ' *earthly* ' . . . ' *heavenly.*' See 1 Corinthians xv, 48–9.

21. *German ocean*, of music by German composers.

23. *Arion* (long i), a musician of Lesbos, who, according to the Greek legend, when threatened with death by pirates, obtained permission to play one last tune. This attracted a shoal of dolphins, and upon the back of one of these he escaped to land.

24. *Tritons*, sea gods, half men, half fishes. Modern opinion would not agree with Lamb in making Bach and Beethoven subordinate to Haydn and Mozart.

28. *at my wit's end*. See Psalm cvii, 26–7.

31. *dazzle*, gleam confusedly. This is a curious use of the word, which is a diminutive of ' daze,' and means to make or become confused. *his*, Novello's.

33. *tiara*, an elaborate head-dress; originally Persian, now used with special reference to the triple crown worn by the Pope on ceremonial occasions.

34. *naked*, unadorned, frank.

38. *malleus hereticorum*, the heretics' hammer, the title of an attack upon Luther and other early Protestants.

39. *heresiarch*, chief of heretics.

41. *Marcion, Ebion, Cerinthus*, heretics of the first century, each of whom had a view inconsistent with the opinions of the other two.

42. *Gog and Magog*. See Revelation xx, 8, where they stand for all unbelievers. *what not*, anything and everything.

44. *dissipates the figment*, dispels the vision.

45. *Lutheran*, Protestant. Ben Jonson has a jesting reference to ' Luther's beer ' (*Epigram* 101). Ollier in his reminiscences of Lamb says: ' Once at a musical party at Leigh Hunt's, being oppressed with what to him was nothing better than a prolonged noise . . . he said —" If one only had a pot of porter, one might get through this." It was procured for him, and he weathered the Mozartian storm.'

47. *rationalities of a purer faith*, reasonable views of Protestantism.

A DISSERTATION UPON ROAST PIG

' The idea of the discovery of roasting pigs I borrowed from my friend Manning,' Lamb says in a letter written six months later. Manning had been in China for some years, and this fact may have suggested to Lamb his fantastic setting of the story, which in its bald outlines is a commonplace of literature going back to the third century. With the exception of the name of the Chinese philosopher Confucius (sixth century B. C.), the details are, of course, Lamb's own invention.

575. *a.* 11. *broiling*, exposing to a fierce heat; roasting, to a moderate one.

12. *the elder brother*, of earlier date.

16. *mast, beech nuts*, used to feed pigs.

18. *lubberly*, awkward.

20. *younker*, a Shaksperean word conveying the idea of youth associated with either gaiety or greenness.

25. *antediluvian*, before the flood.

28. *new-farrowed*, new-born.

35. *tenement*, habitation.

50. *firebrand*, used in the double sense of ' incendiary ' and ' mischievous rogue.'

52. *premonitory moistening*. He was forewarned of the delicacies in store for him by his mouth watering.

54. *nether*, lower.

b. 1. *booby*, stupid.

6. *crackling*, the crisp skin of roast pork.

19. *retributory*, avenging, punishing.

25. *lower regions*, stomach.

27. *remote quarters*, his shoulders, on which the blows were raining.

31. *sensible*, conscious, aware.

36. *me*, the indirect object of advantage or disadvantage, often used in Shakspere. See *Taming of the Shrew*, beginning of I, ii: ' Knock me at this gate.'

42. *eats*, quasi-passive. Goldsmith, *Vicar of Wakefield:* ' If the cakes at tea eat short and crisp.' Used in the same sense by Shakspere.

50. *the lesser half*, keeping the larger share for himself.

54. *cramming*, stuffing the pig into his mouth.

55. *would choke*, wished to choke himself.

576. a. 13. *litter*, of nine pigs.

26. *farrowed*, brought forth young.

34. *assize town*, in England a county town to which the judges come to hold the assizes. Used here to give a burlesque effect of historic detail. So with the whole circumstances of the trial, which are distinctively modern and English.

46. *charge*, direction as to the law of the case given by an English judge.

49. *box*, the shut-in benches where the jury sit during an English trial. After hearing the evidence, they are conducted to a private room for consultation, unless they are ready to give a unanimous verdict offhand, as Lamb imagines to have been the case in this instance. The taste of the burnt pig had such an effect upon their minds that they at once agreed upon a verdict in direct contradiction to the judge's charge and the evidence.

54. *winked at*, shut his eyes to. This meaning is common in the Bible and Shakspere.

b. 3. *took wing*, was noised abroad.

15. *Locke*, the great English philosopher (1632–1704).

23. *dynasty*, succession of sovereigns of the same family. Lamb is still writing in the mock-historic style.

32. *culinary*, connected with cooking. Latin, *culina*, a kitchen.

36. *mundus edibilis*, world of eatables.

37. *princeps obsoniorum*, chief of dainties.

39. *between pig and pork*, too old to roast and too young to salt.

40. *hobbydehoy* (or hobbledehoy), a clumsy youth, ' neither a man nor a boy.'

41. *suckling*, babe at the breast. *moon*, month.

Month means the period of time measured by the moon. *guiltless* . . . *of*, unpolluted by.

43. *amor immunditiae*, love of filth. The allusion is to the doctrine of original sin, the fall of Adam which involved all his offspring.

45. *broken*, commonly used only of the passage of a boy's voice to the deeper tones of manhood.

48. *praeludium*, prelude, music played by way of introduction.

51. *exterior tegument*, outer skin. The longer words are used in mock seriousness for comic effect.

54. *tawny*, yellowish-brown.

577. a. 2. *olcaginous*, oily.

7. *quintessence*, essence five times distilled.

10. *manna*, the food sent from heaven to the Israelites in the wilderness. See Exodus xvi, 14, 15.

10. *if it must be so*, if we must use terms so gross.

13. *ambrosian*, heavenly, like ambrosia, the food of the Greek gods.

15. *doing*, being cooked.

17. *passive*, submissive.

18. *equably*, smoothly, evenly, with mind undisturbed.

20. *sensibility*, sensitiveness.

22. *radiant jellies — shooting stars*. There is an ancient superstition that shooting stars leave jellies where they fall. The prosaic fact is, of course, that the young pig's eyes drop out because of the heat to which they are exposed.

30. *conversation*, manner of life, as in 2 Peter ii, 7, ' the filthy conversation of the wicked.'

34. *Ere sin could blight*, etc. This couplet is quoted, with exquisite humor, from Coleridge's *Epitaph on a Young Infant*, published in 1796 in a little volume of poems to which Lamb himself contributed.

42. *epicure*, one devoted to the pleasures of the table. The modern use of the word is a slander on the philosopher Epicurus, who was devoted to the pleasures of the intellect. *for such a tomb might be content to die*, probably a reminiscence of the last line of Milton's verses on Shakspere, ' that kings for such a tomb would wish to die.' See p. 236.

44. *sapors*, tastes, flavors.

50. *excoriateth*, takes the skin off — an exaggeration of the keenness of the flavour.

54. *stoppeth at the palate*, satisfies the taste, not the stomach.

b. 6. *censorious*, inclined to find fault without sufficient cause.

7. *batten*, fatten.

14–15. *helpeth . . . all around*, may be served and do good to everybody.

15. *is the least envious*, excites the least envy, because all parts are equally good.

17. *neighbors' fare*, food promoting neighborly or friendly feeling.

18. *I am one of those*, etc. This paragraph and the next are merely the elaboration of a letter Lamb wrote to Coleridge on March 9, 1822 — six months before the essay was published. The story of the old gray impostor and some other hints are to be found in the letter, which was evidently the foundation of the essay, the main addition being the fable of the

origin of the art of roasting, suggested by Manning.

24. *proper*, peculiar to himself. Latin, *proprius*, one's own.

26. *Absents*, those absent. The odd form adds force to the pun.

27. '*tame villatic fowl*,' quoted from Milton, *Samson Agonistes*. *villatic*, of the village.

28. *brawn*, boar's flesh pickled or potted.

33. '*give everything*.' *Lear* II, iv, 253: 'I gave you all.'

36. *extra-domiciliate*, a word of Lamb's own invention, from the Latin, *extra*, outside, and *domicilium*, a dwelling-house.

37. *slightingly*, without due appreciation.

39. *predestined*, decreed beforehand by fate.

41. *insensibility*, lack of feeling.

43. *aunt*, Sarah Lamb, Charles's Aunt Hetty, described by him more fully in the Elia essay, *My Relations*. In a letter to Coleridge in 1797 Lamb describes her as 'the kindest, goodest creature to me when I was at school; who used to toddle there to bring me good things, when I, school-boy like, only despised her for it, and used to be ashamed to see her come and sit herself down on the old coal-hole steps as you went into the old grammar-school, and open her apron, and bring out her bason, with some nice thing she had caused to be saved for me.'

52. *a counterfeit*, an impostor.

55. *the very coxcombry of charity*, the height of conceit disguising itself as charity.

578. *a.* 23. *impertinent*, irrelevant, inappropriate.

29. *nice*, discriminating.

33. *obsolete*, gone out of use. *The age of discipline*, of the use of the rod. The clause echoes a famous phrase of Burke's, 'the age of chivalry is gone.'

b. 2. *intenerating and dulcifying*, making tender and sweet.

5. *refining a violet*. See *King John* IV, ii, 11.

9. *gusto*, relish, flavor.

12. *St. Omer's*, a Jesuit college in France. Lamb was never there. Canon Ainger remarks upon this as an instance of Lamb's 'audacious indifference to fact.' The phrase on the preceding page 'over London Bridge' has also been regarded as a wilful mystification; but this is at least doubtful. Lamb had certainly no hesitation in adding fictitious details according to his fancy.

16. *per flagellationem extremam*, by whipping to death.

21. *I forget the decision*. This is the final touch of affected seriousness, the whole incident being, of course, a playful invention.

28. *barbecue*, to roast whole after splitting and stuffing. The derivation '*barbe à queue*' sometimes given is fanciful and erroneous. It comes from an Indian word, meaning a wooden frame for smoking or roasting meat. *to your palate*, with stuffing to your taste.

29. *shalots*, strong onions.

30. *rank*, strong-smelling.

31. *guilty*, harmful, poisonous, a translation of Horace's phrase (*Epodes* III, 3) *cicutis allium nocentius*.

32. *stronger*, in scent and flavor.

SCOTT: MARMION

580. 16. *Tantallon's towers*. Tantallon Castle on the coast of Haddingtonshire, Scotland.

82. *Save Gawain*. Gawain Douglas (c. 1474–1522), poet, scholar, and translator of Virgil's *Æneid*.

107. *Old Bell-the-Cat*. A phrase applied to persons of acknowledged intrepidity. From the fable of the mice and the cat.

581. 194. *The Till by Twisel Bridge*. On the evening previous to the memorable battle of Flodden, Surrey's headquarters were at Barmorewood, and King James held an inaccessible position on the ridge of Flodden-hill, one of the last and lowest eminences detached from the ridge of Cheviot. The Till, a deep and slow river, winded between the armies. On the morning of the 9th September, 1513, Surrey marched in a northwesterly direction, and crossed the Till, with his van and artillery, at Twisel-bridge, nigh where that river joins the Tweed, his rearguard column passing about a mile higher, by a ford. This movement had the double effect of placing his army between King James and his supplies from Scotland and of striking the Scottish monarch with surprise, as he seems to have relied on the depth of the river in his front. But as the passage, both over the bridge and through the ford, was difficult and slow, it seems possible that the English might have been attacked to great advantage, while struggling with these natural obstacles. (Scott.)

583. 363. Gilded spurs. The rewards of victory.

BYRON: SONNET ON CHILLON

587. 13. *Bonnivard*. Francois de Bonnivard (1496–1570) was held for six years as a political prisoner in the dungeon of the Castle of Chillon, near Geneva. Byron's well-known tale, *The Prisoner of Chillon*, presents an imaginary history of his confinement.

CHILDE HAROLD, CANTO III

40. *Morat*. The Swiss gained a decisive victory at the village of Morat in 1476.

43. *Burgundy*. Charles the Bold, Duke of Burgundy.

45. *the Stygian coast*, etc. An allusion to the Greek superstition that the shades of unburied men could not pass the river Styx which bounded Hades.

47. *Waterloo*. The Battle of Waterloo which ended the military career of Napoleon was fought June 18, 1815. It is described in an earlier section of this canto.

Cannæ. A battle in which Hannibal defeated the Roman army, 216 B. C.

48. *Marathon*. The Greeks defeated the Persians on the plains of Marathon, 490 B. C.

55. *Draconic*. Because of its free use of the death penalty, the code of Draco, an Athenian lawgiver of the seventh century, is proverbially said to have been written in blood.

64. *Adventicum*. The Roman name for Avenche the ancient capital of Helvetia, or Switzerland.

66. *Julia.* This passage is based upon the epitaph of Julia Alpinula, ' Deae Aventiae Sacerdos [Priestess of the goddess Aventia],' now known to be a modern forgery.

588. 81. *like yonder Alpine snow.* Byron records that Mont Blanc was visible in the distance.

83. *Lake Leman.* Lake Geneva, the largest lake in Switzerland.

589. 164. *Rousseau.* Jean Jacques Rousseau (1712–1778), a Swiss-French philosopher of brilliant though morbid originality whose writings are held to have been a strong influence in precipitating the French Revolution.

182. *Julie.* The heroine of Rousseau's *New Héloïse* (1761).

194. *the kind.* Civilized man.

201. *Pythian's mystic cave.* The prophetess of the Delphic oracle was called ' The Pythia '; while the god she served was known as the Pythian Apollo.

590. 248. *Jura.* A mountain chain in France and Switzerland, visible from Geneva.

287. *Cytherea's zone.* The zone or girdle of the Cytherean Aphrodite, or Venus.

592. 362. *Clarens.* A village on Lake Leman celebrated in Rousseau's *New Héloïse* and in his *Confessions.*

410. *Love his Psyche's zone,* etc. An allusion to the legend of Cupid and Psyche.

421. *Titan-like.* The Titans piled the hills on each other, attempting to ascend the sky, in their war with Zeus.

425. *The one.* Voltaire.

593. 430. *Proteus.* The son of Oceanus who could assume any shape at will.

434. *The other.* Gibbon. See p. 453.

CHILDE HAROLD, CANTO IV

10. *Niobe.* According to the Greek myth Niobe brought upon her children the wrath of Artemis and Apollo, by boasting over their mother Leto who had only those two. The modern currency of the legend is largely due to a remarkable group of antique statues preserved in the Uffizi Gallery at Florence.

14. *The Scipio's tomb.* A group of tombs on the Appian Way is called ' The tombs of the Scipios.' The most famous Roman generals of this name flourished at the beginning of the second century B. C.

594. 39. *when Brutus,* etc. An allusion to the assassination of Julius Cæsar.

41. *Tully's voice.* The oratory of Cicero.

42. *Livy's pictured page.* Titus Livius (B. C. 59–17 A. D.). The greatest Roman historian.

47. *Sylla.* Lucius Cornelius Sulla (c. 138–78 B. C.). Famous for his wholesale proscription of Roman citizens.

88. *Nemesis.* The Greek personification of fortune and hence retribution.

89. *Pompey.* Cneus Pompeius Magnus (106–48 B. C.). The passage is evidently influenced by Shakspere's description in *Julius Cæsar.* See also, 267. 32, note.

92. *She-wolf.* Allusion to a bronze group which is supposed to represent Romulus and Remus, the founders of Rome, suckled by a wolf.

595. 107. *Save one vain man.* Napoleon, at the time this was written, a prisoner on the island of St. Helena.

116. *Alcides with the distaff.* Hercules, in expiation of the murder of Iphitus, sold himself for three years to Omphale, queen of Lydia. During this time according to some poets he sat among women and spun wool.

135. *Renew thy rainbow, God!* Compare Gen. ix, 13–17.

166. *Sprung forth a Pallas.* According to the Greek myth, the goddess of wisdom sprang, full-armed, from the brain of Jove.

596. 173. *Saturnalia.* A Roman feast in honor of Saturn in which great license was customary.

211. *Cornelia's,* etc. Celebrated Roman matron, daughter of Scipio Africanus the Elder.

212. *Egypt's graceful queen.* Cleopatra.

597. 252. *There woos no home.* Allusion to his separation from his wife and exile from England.

258. *the Palatine.* One of the ' seven hills ' of Rome. It is adjacent to the site of the Forum, and was a favorite place of residence with the Roman emperors.

268. *All that learning,* etc. There have been great additions to the knowledge of Roman antiquities since Byron's day.

294. *Titus or Trajan's.* It is now believed to have been erected by Trajan, 113 A. D.

304. *A mere Alexander.* A mere military conqueror.

598. 337. *Ruins of years, though few.* Byron was thirty.

347. *Orestes,* the son of Agamemnon and Clytemnestra and brother of Electra. After the return of Agamemnon from the Trojan Wars he was murdered by Clytemnestra and her paramour, Aegisthus. They were in turn slain by Orestes and he tormented by the Furies for the killing of his mother. The *Agamemnon* and *The Furies* of Aeschylus, the *Electra* and the *Orestes* of Euripides, and the *Electra* of Sophocles, are based upon this legend.

353. *For my ancestral faults.* The parallel with Orestes is here continued.

384. *Janus.* The Roman guardian of doors and gateways was represented with two faces. Compare our epithet, ' two-faced.'

599. 415. *the Gladiator.* The statue in the Museum of the Capitol upon which this passage is based is now usually called ' The Dying Gaul,' not as formerly, ' The Dying Gladiator,' and is believed to represent a warrior wounded in battle.

429. *their Dacian mother.* The region north of the Lower Danube was conquered by Trajan and made into the Roman province of Dacia, 101 B. C. Ten thousand captives were carried to Rome and exhibited in combats for the amusement of the Roman populace.

432. *Arise! ye Goths,* etc. Alludes to the taking of Rome by the Barbarians, in 410 A. D.

456. *the bald first Cæsar's head.* ' Suetonius informs us that Julius Cæsar was particularly gratified by that decree of the senate which enabled him to wear a wreath of laurel on all occasions. He was anxious, not to show that he was the conqueror of

the world, but to hide that he was bald.' (Byron.) This stroke of bold bathos is very characteristic of Byron and anticipates his manner in *Don Juan*.

600. 463. *Thus spake the pilgrims*. Byron refers in his note on this passage to Gibbon's *Decline and Fall*. His familiarity with Gibbon is conspicuous throughout this canto.

THE VISION OF JUDGMENT

This poem is an indignant parody upon a poem of the same title in which Robert Southey, poet laureate, had celebrated the passing of George III. Byron's anger was augmented by the fact that Southey had arraigned him in his preface as the chief of a 'Satanic School' of English poetry. Southey had been a strong radical in his earlier years, but had now become a complacent servant of the government. The situation is tersely stated in a sentence of Byron's *Preface:* 'These apostate Jacobins furnish rich rejoinders.'

36. *A German will*. Probably this means only obscure, difficult. Byron's jibes at Germans were frequent.

37. *his son*, George IV.

602. 160. *Captain Parry's crew*. A narrative of Parry's arctic expedition had appeared in 1821.

168. *Johanna Southcote*. A fanatical Englishwoman of low birth who created a popular religious sensation at the beginning of the century. Died 1814.

200. *champ clos*, closed field, lists.

604. 281. *He came to his scepter young; he leaves it old*. George III reigned from 1760 to 1820.

308. *Apicius' board*. Marcus Gabius Apicius, the most celebrated Roman epicure, flourished in the time of Augustus and Tiberius.

327. *The foe to Catholic participation*. The political disability of Catholics was not removed until 1829.

355. *Guelph*. The House of Hanover was descended from Guelph stock. The allusion seems inappropriate here, inasmuch as the Guelphs were friends of the Papacy.

357. *Cerberus*. The watchdog at the entrance of the infernal regions. See 237. 2, note.

359. *Bedlam*. Bethlehem hospital for the insane, in London; hence, proverbially, the madhouse.

DON JUAN, CANTO III

605. 2. *Sappho*. Greek poetess (c. 600 B.C.).

4. *Delos*. An island of the Cyclades, Apollo's birthplace, hence Apollo.

4. *Phoebus*. One of the epithets of Apollo, god of poetry.

7. *Scian*. The island of Scio was a home of epic poetry and laid claim to Homer.

the Teian muse. Anacreon. See below, 63-64.

13. *Marathon*. See 587. 48, note.

20. *Salamis*. An island off Attica, near which the Greeks won their decisive naval victory over the fleet of Xerxes, 480 B.C.

55. *Pyrrhic dance*. An ancient martial dance in quick time.

63-64. *Anacreon's song* . . . *Polycrates*. From his birthplace, Teos in Asia Minor, Anacreon went to the court of the tyrant, Polycrates (d. 522 B.C.),

in the island of Samos. His poetry celebrates the pleasures of love and wine.

67-69. *Chersonese* . . . *Miltiades*. Miltiades whom Peisistratus had appointed master of the Chersonesus in Crete was the leader to whom the Greeks owed much of their success in Marathon.

74. *Suli's rock*. Suli, a mountain district in Albania, European Turkey, was the home of a warlike race, Suliotes. They played an important part in the Greek rebellion with which Byron was later associated.

Parga's shore. Parga was an Albanian sea-port.

76. *Doric*. One of the divisions of the Greek race. Here, Spartan.

78. *Heracleidan blood*. Race of Hercules, Spartans.

79. *Franks*. Western Europeans generally.

606. 91. *Sunium's marbled steep*. Cape Colonna with its ruins of a temple of Athene.

99. *Orpheus*. The earliest poet in Greek legend. See 238. 145, note.

127. *the great Marlborough's skill*. He won the battle of Blenheim, 1704.

128. *Life by Archdeacon Coxe*. Like many of Byron's allusions, this one is strictly 'up-to-date.' The Memoirs of Marlborough appeared in 1718-19.

133. *his life* . . . *Johnson's way*, etc. Dr. Johnson's life of Milton in his *Lives of the English Poets* (1779-80).

138. *Bacon's bribes*. See p. 187.

139. *Titus' Youth*. The reign of Titus Vespasianus (A.D. 79-81) was popular; but his youth, though brilliant, had been marked by luxury and indiscretion.

Cæsar's earliest acts. The youth of Julius Cæsar is said to have been voluptuous.

140. *Doctor Currie*. James Currie (1756-1805), a Scottish physician, edited the first collective edition of Burns's works (1800).

146. *Pantisocracy*. See the sketch of Coleridge, p. 542.

148. *peddler poems*. A hit at the humbleness of Wordsworth's characters.

152. *Milliners of Bath*. The implication is false. The Misses Fricker were respectable young women of Bristol, although they had lived for a time at Bath.

154. *Botany Bay*. An inlet near Sydney, Australia, the seat of a colony of transported criminals.

607. 198. *Boccaccio's lore*. The reference is to the eighth tale of the fifth day of the *Decameron*.

199. *Dryden's lay*. Dryden's *Theodore and Honoria*, is an adaptation of the above-mentioned tale by Boccaccio.

205. *Onesti's line*. Boccaccio's Nastagio degli Onesti is Dryden's Theodore.

608. 238. *Cantabs*. Those associated with the University of Cambridge.

DON JUAN, CANTO IV

21. '*falls into the yellow leaf*.' From *Macbeth* V, 3, 23.

55. *Apollo plucks me by the ear*. Compare *Lycidas*, 'and touched my trembling ears,' 240. 77.

611. 417. *Cognac*. A French brandy.

418. *Naïad*. A water nymph.

418. *Phlegethontic rill.* Playful allusion to Phlegethon, the river of fire in Hades.

431. *Fez.* A province of Morocco.

612. 456. *the Simoom.* A hot wind of the desert much dreaded in the Mediterranean countries.

484. *the fair Venus.* The statue described by Byron in *Childe Harold,* Canto IV, St. xlix, is the Venus de Medici.

485. *Laocoon's . . . throes.* An antique group in the Vatican, Rome. It is described by Byron, *Childe Harold,* Canto IV, St. clx.

486. *ever-dying Gladiator's air.* See 599. 415, and note.

SHELLEY: PROMETHEUS UNBOUND, ACT IV

The conception of *Prometheus Unbound* was suggested to Shelley by the *Prometheus Bound* of Æschylus. The Titan, Prometheus, having offended Zeus by his gift to man of fire and the arts, is bound to a rocky mountain-side and subjected to appalling tortures. Nothing can subdue his will and he disappears at the end in a tremendous storm. Shelley represents Prometheus, after the lapse of ages, adding love to power and endurance; whereupon he is released by Hercules and united with Asia, who typifies the generative principle in nature. Act IV is purely lyrical and portrays the elements rejoicing in the overthrow of Jupiter, the evil potency which has hitherto ruled the universe and the bulk of humanity.

619. 197. *Æolian,* wind-born. From Æolus, god of winds.

620. 291. *valueless,* priceless, beyond valuation.

621. 348. *Sceptered curse.* Jupiter.

622. 427. *Dædal,* cunningly contriving or creative.

623. 484. *Mænad,* Bacchante.

485. *Agave,* the daughter of Cadmus.

486. *Cadmeian,* Theban; from Cadmus, the mythical founder of Thebes. A world of oriental mystery envelops the Cadmeian legend.

522. *A mighty Power.* Demogorgon, who seems to represent, in Shelley's mythology, the ultimate force which presides over the destinies of the universe.

ODE TO THE WEST WIND

625. 21. *Mænad.* See 623. 484, note.

32. *pumice,* a light, porous, volcanic substance.

32. *Baiæ's bay.* Modern Baja, in Campania, Italy. Baiæ was a favorite resort of the luxurious in the days of the Early Empire.

THE INDIAN SERENADE

626. 11. *Champak.* An Indian tree, planted about temples. The perfume of its flowers is often celebrated in Hindu poetry.

THE CLOUD

627. 81. *cenotaph.* An honorary tomb to a person whose remains are lost, or who is buried elsewhere.

ADONAIS

628. This elegy was written in memory of John Keats, for whom, see p. 639.

12. *Urania.* The celestial Muse. She is the Heavenly Muse of Milton's *Paradise Lost.* Shelley's conception has been influenced by that of Milton.

630. 55. *that high Capital.* Rome.

631. 127-35. *Lost Echo,* etc. Narcissus. insensible to love, was caused to fall in love with his own image and pined away until he was turned into a flower. The nymph Echo, disappointed of his love, died from grief.

140. *to Phœbus was not Hyacinth.* Apollo fell in love with a beautiful youth, Hyacinthus, who died and was turned into a flower. See 241. 106, note.

141. *Narcissus.* See above, 127-35, note.

160. *brere,* brier.

632. 238. *the unpastured dragon.* The selfish and greedy world.

244. *The herded wolves.* The banded critics who execute the will of successful politicians.

250. *The Pythian of the age.* Lord Byron in his *English Bards and Scotch Reviewers,* by allusion to the Pythian Apollo, slayer of the Python.

633. 264. *The Pilgrim of Eternity.* The author of *Childe Harold's Pilgrimage,* Byron.

268. *Ierne,* Ireland. Thomas Moore is meant.

271. *Midst others of less note,* etc. Shelley himself.

276. *Actæon-like.* According to a Greek myth the hunter Actæon, having seen Diana bathing, was changed into a stag and destroyed by his own hounds.

280. *pardlike,* leopardlike.

307-15. *What softer voice,* etc. Keats's nearest friend among literary men, Leigh Hunt.

634. 325. *Live thou, whose infamy,* etc. The unknown critic who had assailed Keats in the *Quarterly Review.*

635. 399. *Chatterton.* See p. 377.

401. *Sidney.* Sir Philip Sidney (1554-86). See p. 81.

404. *Lucan.* Marcus Annæus Lucanus (39-65 A. D.), Roman poet. He committed suicide to prevent his execution for joining a conspiracy against Nero.

439. *A slope of green access.* The protestant burial ground at Rome, where Keats was buried, and where Shelley's ashes were placed a few months after these lines were written.

FINAL CHORUS FROM HELLAS

636. The conception of this poem and many of the details are adapted from Virgil's fourth *Eclogue.*

9. *Peneus.* The principal river in Thessaly.

11. *Tempes.* The vale of Tempe, in Thessaly, between Olympus and Ossa and traversed by the river Peneus, is celebrated for its beauty.

12. *Cyclads.* The islands known as the Cyclades are in the Ægean Sea, about Delos. Among those frequently mentioned in Greek history are Ceos, Naxos, and Paros.

13. *Argo.* The ship in which Jason and the Argonauts sought the golden fleece.

15. *Orpheus.* See 238. 145, note.

18. *Calypso.* At the opening of the *Odyssey,* Ulysses is being detained by the nymph Calypso

upon her island, where he has been for seven years.

21. *Laian.* As of Laius, king of Thebes and father to Œdipus, whose family was pursued by strange misfortunes.

23. *A subtler Sphinx,* etc. Œdipus solved the riddle of the Sphinx; whereupon she slew herself.

637. 31. *Saturn and Love.* The age of gold, supposed to have existed before Saturn was overthrown by Jupiter, was thought of as one of perfect happiness and love.

WITH A GUITAR, TO JANE

1. *Ariel to Miranda.* The reference is, of course, to the characters in Shakspere's *Tempest.* Ariel is Shelley, and Miranda is Mrs. Williams.

10. *Prince Ferdinand.* Edward Williams, a young English officer with whom Shelley was intimate towards the end of his life. He and Shelley were drowned together. See Life, p. 614.

KEATS: KEEN, FITFUL GUSTS ARE WHISPERING HERE AND THERE

639. 10. *a little cottage.* Leigh Hunt's home at Hampstead Heath. Hunt was deeply interested in Italian poetry.

12. *gentle Lycid drowned.* For Milton's Lycidas, see p. 240.

13. *Laura.* The lady to whom Petrarch addressed his sonnets. According to one theory she was the wife of Hugues de Sade and mother of eleven children.

14. *Petrarch gloriously crowned.* Francesco Petrarca (1304–1374). He was crowned poet laureate, at Rome, in 1341.

ON FIRST LOOKING INTO CHAPMAN'S HOMER

4. *Apollo.* As patron of poetry.

8. *Chapman.* George Chapman published his translation of Homer in instalments between 1598 and 1616. It is still prized as one of the greatest of English poetical translations.

11. *stout Cortez.* Not Cortez, but Balboa actually discovered the Pacific Ocean.

14. *Darien.* The mountain from which Balboa first sighted the Pacific was nearly a month's journey from his base at Darien.

ENDYMION, BOOK I

640. 35. *the story of Endymion.* The most famous English treatment of the legend before Keats was that of John Lyly in his drama, *Endymion* (1579).

THE EVE OF ST. AGNES

1. *St. Agnes' Eve,* January 20, in popular opinion, apt to be the coldest night of the year. St. Agnes suffered martyrdom under Diocletian. The chief superstitions connected with the Eve of St. Agnes are given in the course of the poem, especially ll. 47–55.

643. 172. *Since Merlin paid his Demon.* According to the legend with which Keats was familiar, Merlin had been begotten by demons. He was beguiled by an enchantress who employed one of his own spells to imprison him forever in a tree in the forest of Broceliande. Immediately afterward, a terrific tempest swept the forest. The legend forms the basis of Tennyson's *Merlin and Vivien* in *The Idylls of the King.*

643. 242. *missal where swart Paynims pray.* A prayer-book bearing upon its margin pictures of converted heathen in the act of prayer.

644. 270. *Fez.* See **611.** 431, note.

271. *Samarcand.* A city in Turkestan, more important in the middle ages than now. It was the capital of the conqueror Tamerlane.

271. *cedared Lebanon.* A mountain range in Syria, famed from remote antiquity for its cedars.

293. *In Provence called, 'La belle dame sans mercy.'* This is the title of a poem by Alain Chartier, a translation of which Keats had seen in a volume of Chaucer. The ascription of it to Provence is fanciful. The same words suggested to Keats the poem of this title, p. 654.

645. 350. *Rhenish,* wine from the vineyards of the Rhine.

350. *mead,* a liquor made by fermenting honey, much prized by the ancient Teutons.

ROBIN HOOD

For the ballads of Robin Hood, see above. pp. 38–42.

LINES ON THE MERMAID TAVERN

646. 4. *the Mermaid Tavern.* A favorite resort of Elizabethan dramatists, Shakspere, Ben Jonson, Beaumont, etc.

6. *Canary wine.* Wine made in the Canary islands. It was the 'sack' of Shakspere and his contemporaries.

ODE ON A GRECIAN URN

647. 7. *Tempe.* See **636.** 11, note.

7. *Arcady.* Arcadia, celebrated in pastoral poetry as the house of a carefree shepherd life.

41. *brede,* embroidery. Strictly, braid.

ODE TO A NIGHTINGALE

4. *Lethe-wards.* Towards the river of oblivion.

7. *Dryad,* a tree nymph.

13. *Flora,* goddess of the flowers and the spring.

14. *Provencal song.* Medieval lyric began in Provence. See **644.** 293, and note.

16. *Hippocrene,* the Muses' fountain on Mount Helicon.

648. 32. *Bacchus and his pards.* The leopard or, more strictly, the panther, was associated with the god of wine. He was sometimes represented in a chariot drawn by leopards.

37. *Fays,* fairies.

66. *Ruth.* See Ruth ii.

ODE ON MELANCHOLY

1. *Lethe.* The river of oblivion, in Hades.

4. *Proserpine.* Queen of the infernal regions.

7. *Psyche,* the soul. Her symbol was the butterfly.

HYPERION

Of the design of this poem Keats's friend, Woodhouse, wrote in his annotated copy: ' The poem, if completed, would have treated of the dethronement of Hyperion, the former god of the sun, by Apollo — and incidentally of those of Oceanus by Neptune, of Saturn by Jupiter, etc., and of the war of the Giants for Saturn's reëstablishment — with other events, of which we have but very dark hints in the mythological poets of Greece and Rome.'

650. 4. *Saturn*, an Italic deity, supposed to have ruled in the golden age; he was identified with the Greek Cronus, father and predecessor of Zeus. See, also, 250. 509, note.

23. *there came one*. Thea, sister of Hyperion, one of the female Titans.

30. *Ixion's wheel*. See 361. 133, note.

31. *Memphian sphinx*. A purely hypothetical sphinx. Memphis was an early capital of Egypt.

651. 147. *The rebel three*. Jupiter, Neptune, and Apollo.

652. 166. *Blazing Hyperion*. Hyperion was the pre-Olympian god of the sun. He was supplanted by Apollo.

181. *Aurorian*. Of Aurora, goddess of the dawn.

653. 246. *Tellus*, the earth goddess.

274. *broad-belting colure*. The colures are the two great circles which belt the celestial sphere, intersecting each other at right angles at the poles of the equator.

307. *Cœlus*, god of the firmament.

LA BELLE DAME SANS MERCI

See 644. 293, note.

ON SEEING THE ELGIN MARBLES

Between 1801 and 1803 the Earl of Elgin brought from Athens and deposited in the British Museum a superb collection of Greek sculptures. Keats derived not a little of his sympathy with Greek conceptions of beauty from the study of these antiquities.

BRIGHT STAR! WOULD I WERE STEAD-FAST AS THOU ART

This is believed to have been the last poem written by Keats. It was composed on shipboard just before his departure for Italy and written across a blank page of Shakspere's poems.

4. *eremite*, hermit.

NINETEENTH CENTURY LYRICS

ROBERT SOUTHEY: THE BATTLE OF BLENHEIM

657. 56. *Prince Eugene*. François Eugene de Savoie-Carignan (1663–1736), a distinguished Austrian general, in alliance with Marlborough defeated the French and Bavarians at Blenheim, Aug. 13, 1704.

WALTER SAVAGE LANDOR: ROSE AYLMER

657. The subject of this poem was a beautiful Welsh girl who had died in Italy. She was of an ancient and titled family; hence, 'the sceptred race.'

PAST RUINED ILION

1. *Ilion*, Troy.

2. *Alcestis*, the heroine of Euripides' drama of that name.

ARTEMIDORA

658. 11. *Iris stood over her dark hair*. Iris the messenger of the gods was supposed to loosen the hair of dying persons and, until she did so, their spirits were unable to depart.

DIRCE

1. *Stygian*, of the river Styx; here, destined for Hades.

3. *Charon*. The ferryman of the river Styx.

ON LUCRETIA BORGIA'S HAIR

Lucretia Borgia (1480–1519), Duchess of Ferrara, was famed for beauty, wit, and wickedness.

MEMORY AND PRIDE

3. *Ianthè*, Sophia Jane Swift, afterwards Countess de Molandé, Landor's early 'flame' and life-long friend. Many of his lyrics of gallantry were addressed to her.

TO ROBERT BROWNING

10–14. *But warmer climes,* etc. Browning had just married Elizabeth Barrett and left England for Italy.

TO AGE

3. *The Fates . . . shears*. Compare 240. 75, and note.

THOMAS CAMPBELL: YE MARINERS OF ENGLAND

659. 15. *Blake*. Robert Blake, the famous admiral of the Commonwealth, died at sea, 1757.

Nelson fell. Horatio, first Viscount Nelson, the chief naval hero of England, died at Trafalgar, October 21, 1805. He 'fell' severely wounded, at the Battle of Copenhagen, April 2, 1801.

THOMAS MOORE: THE HARP THAT ONCE THROUGH TARA'S HALLS

Tara, the ancient capital of one branch of the Irish race, is frequently named in early Irish poetry.

JOHN KEBLE: UNITED STATES

661. 1. This poem had been preceded in the *Lyra Apostolica* by John Henry Newman's similar apostrophe to England, beginning 'Tyre of the West.'

23. *Tyre*, the great trading center of ancient Phenicia, was constantly execrated by the Hebrew prophets for its worldliness and commercial prosperity. *Salem*, Jerusalem.

WINTHROP MACKWORTH PRAED: THE BELLE OF THE BALL-ROOM

665. 31. *Locke*. John Locke (1632–1704), author of *Essay Concerning Human Understanding*, etc.

32. *Little*. A pseudonym of Thomas Moore.

61. *Handel*. Georg Friederich Händel lived for a long time in London and died there in 1759. His compositions were popular in England.

6a. *the Catalani*. Angelica Catalani, an Italian singer.

70. *Fierce odes*, etc. Probably an allusion to Coleridge's *Fire, Famine, and Slaughter*.

71. *Prince Leboo*. Jean Louis Joseph Lebeau (b. 1794) was a distinguished Belgian diplomat who carried on important negotiations in England, 1830–31.

666. 67. *the vapors*, a 'Queen Anne' term for the blues.

71. *Werther*. Goethe's sentimental novel, *The Sorrows of Werther*.

73. *The City*. The business district of London.

WILLIAM BARNES: BLACKMORE MAIDENS

The peculiarities of the spelling are intended to suggest the Dorsetshire pronunciation.

667. 4. *Clote*, waterlily.

7. *bricken tuns*. Brick-built vats.

37. *tweil*, toil.

EDWARD FITZGERALD: THE RUBAIYAT

669. 7. *the dark Ferrash*, servant, camp-follower.

11. *Sáki*, wine-bearer.

ELIZABETH BARRETT BROWNING: A MUSICAL INSTRUMENT

670. 1. *Pan*. God of forests and flocks, the special deity of Arcadia. To him was imputed the invention of the shepherd's flute.

SONNETS FROM THE PORTUGUESE

This sonnet series is based upon the courtship of Robert Browning and Elizabeth Barrett (see p. 785). When the poems were published the description 'from the Portuguese' was adopted for the sake of disguising their personal import.

I

1–2. *Theocritus had sung . . . years. Idyl* xv, 104–5.

13. '*Death'! I said*. Miss Barrett had been for years an invalid.

V

2. *As once Electra*, etc. An allusion to a passage in the *Electra* of Sophocles in which the heroine, holding as she supposes the urn containing the ashes of her brother Orestes, experiences a sudden revulsion of feeling when she finds him alive before her.

11. *those laurels*, etc. Browning's poetical fame.

XXXV

671. 1. *If I leave all*, etc. The marriage with Browning, because of the character and attitude of Miss Barrett's father, involved the severing of all home ties.

SIDNEY DOBELL: AMERICA

These sonnets are from a series published during the Crimean War, when America was supposed to be hostile to Great Britain.

677. 6. *satcheled*. Compare *As You Like It*, II, 7, 145, 'the schoolboy with his satchel,' etc.

AUSTIN DOBSON: A DEAD LETTER

679. 11. *Goldsmith's Madam Blaize*. An allusion to Goldsmith's ridiculous poem *An elegy on the Glory of her Sex, Mrs. Mary Blaize*.

14. *tea-board garden-maker*. Apparently, one designing a garden on the scale of a tea-tray.

15. *Dutch William's day*. William of Orange's time, 1688 and after.

38. *Tithonus*. See p. 778 and note.

680. 52. *Damson Jam*. Jam made of the damson, or damask plum.

62. *Padesoy*, paduasoy, a rich heavy silk from Padua.

63. *the Vapors*. See 666. 67, note.

79. *Bonzes*, images of Buddhist priests.

112. *Point and Flanders*. Lace.

JAMES THOMSON: MELENCOLIA

16. *the pure sad artist*. Albrecht Dürer (1471–1528), Nuremberg, painter and engraver. The sketch here described is one of his works on copper.

74. *teen and threne* Sorrow and lamentation.

DE QUINCEY: CONFESSIONS OF AN ENGLISH OPIUM EATER

The version of the 'Confessions' adopted in the text is that of the original issue in the *London Magazine* (1821), which has been generally preferred, both by the critics and the public, to the enlarged edition published by De Quincey in his collected works thirty-five years later. On account of his tendency to digression, De Quincey's second thoughts are sometimes less effective than his first. The additional details given in the later version have been used in the notes and are distinguished by quotation marks.

684. *a. 1. an affection of the stomach*. Opium is said to be a remedy for gastrodynia, or neuralgia of the stomach.

20. *My father*. Thomas Quincey, merchant, of Manchester, d. July 18, 1793.

50. '*and a ripe and good one*.' See *Henry VIII*, IV, ii, 51–2. The master in question was a Mr. Morgan, of Bath Grammar School.

55. *a blockhead*. The master of Winkfield, a small private school.

b. 1. a respectable scholar. Mr. Lawson, head of Manchester Grammar School.

4. —— *College*, Brasenose.

9. *Etonian* Up to 1851 the curriculum at Eton was entirely classical.

27. *Archididascalus*. Greek for head master.

685. *a. 11. a woman of high rank*, Lady Carbery. 'A young woman some ten years older than myself, and who was remarkable for her intellectual pretensions as she was for her beauty and her benevolence.'

15. *five guineas*, $25.

35. *of Dr. Johnson's*, at the end of the last article in his periodical, *The Idler*.

44. *I had not been happy*. The chief reasons of De Quincey's unhappiness at Manchester Grammar School were (1) the state of his health, the school hours not permitting him to take sufficient exercise;

(2) his dislike of the head master; (3) the refusal of his guardian to allow him to go to Oxford, as explained above.

  b. 3. *valediction,* farewell.

  21. *towers of* ——, the 'old church,' now the cathedral of the modern diocese of Manchester.

  49. '*pensive citadel.*' See Wordsworth's sonnet *Nuns fret not,* 537. 3, and note.

686. *a.* 9. *eighteen years ago,* when De Quincey wrote the 'Confessions' about Christmas, 1820; really nineteen when they were published, the following September and October.

  13. *lovely* ——. A portrait of an unknown lady, reputed in the school to be a copy from Vandyke (1598–1641).

  22. —— *clock,* 'the old church clock.'

  54–55. See *Paradise Lost* II, 306–7, p. 258.

  56. *Salisbury Plain,* in Wiltshire.

  b. 3. *contretemps,* mishap, unlucky accident.

  25. *canorous,* resonant, ringing.

686. *b.* 27. *the Seven Sleepers,* seven Christian youths of Ephesus, who took refuge in a cave from persecution, and, according to the legend, slept there for 230 years.

  32. *étourderie,* heedless, giddy behaviour.

  35. *Dr.* ——. 'The head-master at that time was Mr. Charles Lawson. In former editions of this work I created him a doctor; my object being to evade too close an approach to the realities of the case, and consequently to personalities, which (though indifferent to myself) would have been in some cases displeasing to others.'

  50. '*with Providence my guide.*' *Paradise Lost,* closing lines:

'The world was all before them, where to choose
Their place of rest, and Providence their guide.
They, hand in hand, with wandering steps and slow,
Through Eden took their solitary way.'

687. *a.* 16. *lustrum,* period of five years.

  38. νυχθήμερον, a night and a day.

  42. *That moveth.* See Wordsworth's *Resolution and Independence,* 529. 77.

  44. *Now, then, I was again happy.* This was in 1816, the year of De Quincey's marriage, which induced him to suddenly cut down from 8,000 to 1,000 drops his daily allowance of opium. 'Instantaneously, and as if by magic, the cloud of profoundest melancholy which rested upon my brain, like some black vapors that I have seen roll away from the summit of a mountain, drew off in one week.' De Quincey began to take opium in 1804 as a remedy for 'excruciating rheumatic pains of the head and face'; but he did not become a regular and confirmed opium eater till 1813, when he was attacked by 'a most appalling irritation of the stomach.' De Quincey made repeated efforts to free himself from thraldom to the drug, which brought on severe depression and made him at times incapable of mental exertion, but he never entirely succeeded.

  b. 3. *Kant,* Immanuel Kant (1724–1804), the founder of 'Transcendental' Philosophy.

  22. *Malay.* There has been an inclination to regard this as a fictitious personage invented by De Quincey to give variety and color to his narra-

tive; he himself protested that he had recorded the incident 'most faithfully.' He adds a note to the later edition: 'Between the sea-faring populations on the coast of Lancashire and the corresponding populations on the coast of Cumberland (such as Ravenglass, Whitehaven, Workington, Maryport, etc.) there was a slender current of interchange constantly going on, and especially in the days of press-gangs — in part by sea, but in part also by land.'

  28. *a young girl.* 'This girl, Barbara Lewthwaite, was already at that time a person of some poetic distinction, being (unconsciously to herself) the chief speaker in a little pastoral poem of Wordsworth's. That she was really beautiful, and not merely so described by me for the sake of improving the picturesque effect, the reader will judge from this line in the poem, written perhaps ten years earlier, when Barbara might be six years old: —

'Twas little Barbara Lewthwaite, a child of beauty rare!'

De Quincey adds in an appendix that subsequently, when a young woman, she entered unconsciously into the composition of Wordsworth's Ode, *Intimations of Immortality from Recollections of Early Childhood.* Wordsworth, however, writing in 1843, when Barbara Lewthwaite was still living at Ambleside, says that she was not in fact the child whom he had seen and overheard as described in *The Pet Lamb.* Within a few months after the publication of the poem, it came to Barbara's knowledge, 'and alas! I had the mortification of hearing that she was very vain of being thus distinguished: and, in after-life, she used to say that she remembered the incident and what I said to her upon the occasion.'

688. *a.* 32. *Anastasius,* a novel published in 1819, and in 1821 'both of high reputation and of great influence amongst the leading circles of society.' Its hero was a Greek who ate opium, and it included a glossary of the Oriental terms used in the story.

  34. *Mithridates,* King of Pontus, was said to be able to speak the twenty two dialects of his kingdom. For this reason the German philologer Adelung gave this title to a universal dictionary of languages he published in 1806.

  b. 29. '*a-muck,*' Malay *amoq,* 'rushing in a state of frenzy to the commission of indiscriminate murder.'

  32. *intercalary,* interpolated, intervening. An intercalary day is one inserted to make the calendar agree with the solar year, as the 29th of February in leap year.

  32. *happiness, i.e.,* opium.

689. *a.* 21. *didactically,* in the way of teaching, by direct instruction.

  26. *elixir,* the philosopher's stone, which the alchemists imagined would confer perpetual youth.

  30. *a cottage standing in a valley.* 'The cottage and valley concerned in this description were not imaginary: the valley was the lovely one, *in those days,* of Grasmere: and the cottage was occupied for more than twenty years by myself, as immediate

successor, in the year 1809, to Wordsworth. Looking to the limitation here laid down — viz. *in those days* — the reader will inquire in what way *Time* can have affected the beauty of Grasmere. Do the Westmoreland valleys turn grey-headed? O reader! this is a painful memento for some of us! Thirty years ago, a gang of vandals (nameless, I thank heaven, to me), for the sake of building a mail-coach road that never would be wanted, carried, at a cost of £3,000 to the defrauded parish, a horrid causeway of sheer granite masonry, for three-quarters of a mile, right through the loveliest succession of secret forest dells and shy recesses of the lake, margined by unrivalled ferns, amongst which was the *Osmunda regalis*. This sequestered angle of Grasmere is described by Wordsworth, as it unveiled itself on a September morning, in the exquisite poems on the "Naming of Places." From this also — viz. this spot of ground, and this magnificent crest (the *Osmunda*)— was suggested that unique line, the finest independent line through all the records of verse:

> Or lady of the lake,
> Sole-sitting by the shores of old romance.

Rightly, therefore, did I introduce this limitation. The Grasmere before and after this outrage were two different vales.'

689. *a.* 42. *a witty author,* Coleridge in *The Devil's Thoughts:*

> He saw a cottage with a double coach-house,
> A cottage of gentility!
> And the Devil did grin, for his darling sin
> Is pride that apes humility.

b. 21. *The Castle of Indolence,* by Thomson, Canto I, Stanza 43. See p. 373.

25. *a high latitude,* far north. Lord Dufferin's travels in Iceland are described in *Letters from High Latitudes.*

32. *'particular,'* precise, exactly. De Quincey puts the word in quotation marks because this use of it is a Northern provincialism.

34. *Mr. ——,* 'Anti-slavery Clarkson,' the author of a *History of the Abolition of the Slave Trade.*

45. *a Canadian winter.* De Quincey seems to have been in earnest in this preference. At one time he thought of retiring to the woods of Lower Canada to devote himself to philosophic studies, and he had even fixed upon the situation for a cottage and a considerable library seventeen miles below Quebec. He gives the following reasons for this choice: 'My object was simply profound solitude, such as cannot now be had in any part of Great Britain — with two accessory advantages, also peculiar to countries situated in the circumstances and under the climate of Canada: viz. the exalting presence in an under-consciousness of forests endless and silent, the everlasting sense of living mongst forms so ennobling and impressive, together with the pleasure attached to natural agencies, such as frosts, more powerfully manifested than in English latitudes, and for a much longer period. I

hope there is nothing fanciful in all this. It is certain that in England and in all moderate climates, we are too slightly reminded of nature or the forces of nature. Great heats or great colds (and in Canada there are both) or great hurricanes, as in the West Indian latitudes, recall us continually to the sense of a powerful presence, investing our path on every side: whereas in England it is possible to forget that we live amongst greater agencies than those of men and human institutions.'

48. *fee-simple,* a legal phrase for absolute ownership.

51. *St. Thomas's day,* December 21.

53. *vernal,* spring.

690. *a.* 10. *bellum internecinum,* war to the death. Hanway wrote an *Essay on Tea* (1756), which Dr. Johnson reviewed and condemned, declaring himself 'a hardened and shameless tea-drinker, . . . whose kettle has scarcely time to cool.' A lively controversy resulted. See Boswell's *Life of Johnson* (Macmillan's edition — Library of English Classics), I, pp. 224–5.

27. *' a double debt to pay.'* Goldsmith's *Deserted Village,* 466. 229–30.

46. eternal *à parte ante* and *à parte post,* from everlasting to everlasting, having no beginning and no end.

53. *Aurora . . . Hebe,* beautiful Greek goddesses, the former the personification of Dawn, the latter of Youth.

54. *dear M——,* Margaret, De Quincey's wife.

b. 8. *' little golden receptacle, etc.,'* quoted from the *Anastasius* mentioned above.

16. *' stately Pantheon,'* a London theatre, so described by Wordsworth, near which was the druggist's shop from which De Quincey first obtained opium, as described in an earlier passage in the 'Confessions' not included in our extracts.

29. *my body should be had into court,* adapted from the wording of the writ of habeas corpus.

37. *the Opium-eater's exterior.* As was pointed out in the introductory biography, De Quincey's personal appearance was peculiar. Carlyle describes him as 'one of the smallest men you ever in your life beheld; but with a most gentle and sensible face, only the teeth are destroyed by opium, and the little bit of an under lip projects like a shelf.' 'Blue-eyed, blonde-haired, sparkling face,— had there not been a something, too, which said, "Ecovi, this child has been in hell!"' Professor Masson writes: 'In addition to the general impression of his diminutiveness and fragility, one was struck with the peculiar beauty of his head and forehead, rising disproportionately high over his small, wrinkly visage and gentle, deep-set eyes.' The effect of his childish figure and odd gait was increased by his eccentricities of dress. 'His clothes had generally a look of extreme age, and also of having been made for a person somewhat larger than himself.' He was fond of list slippers for outdoor wear and sometimes forgot to put on one or both stockings.

48. *categories,* of Aristotle: 1 Substance or Being, 2 Quantity, 3 Quality, 4 Relation, 5 Place, 6 Time, etc.

THOMAS BABINGTON MACAULAY: THE ROMANCE OF HISTORY

The article of which the latter part is here printed was professedly a review in the *Edinburgh,* May, 1828, of a new book by a popular writer of that day, Henry Neele, entitled, ' The Romance of History. England '; but this served Macaulay merely as an opportunity to set forth his own ideas as to how history should be written. He had stated the same opinions before in a review of Mitford's *History of Greece,* and he re-stated them in reviews of the historical works of Hallam and Mackintosh before he was able to put them into practice in his own *History of England from the Accession of James II.* In spite of his extraordinary aptitude for the undertaking, he carried out his scheme for only fifteen years of the century and a half for which the work was planned; no one man, even in a long life, could have executed the design with such a broad canvas and in such minute detail as Macaulay attempted. Much of the higher side of life was omitted, and many of his judgments have not stood the test of subsequent investigation. The modern historian aims at far greater accuracy as well as a more profound inquiry into causes; but no one has been more successful than Macaulay in writing a historical narrative of unfailing interest to the general reader.

692. *a. 7. Laud,* Archbishop of Canterbury, 1633–45, and the director of Charles I's ecclesiastical policy. Curiously enough, the very faults of which Macaulay here accuses other historians have since been urged against himself, and Laud is one of the instances cited. Professor Montague says: ' Macaulay, who regarded this period of English history in a peculiarly partisan spirit, uniformly wrote of Laud's personal character with a loathing, and of his abilities with a contempt, unbecoming the gravity of a historian.'

11. *Herodotus,* ' the father of history ' and the first important writer of Greek prose. Macaulay says of him earlier in this same article: ' Of the romantic historians Herodotus is the earliest and the best. His animation, his simple-hearted tenderness, his wonderful talent for description and dialogue, and the pure, sweet flow of his language, place him at the head of narrators. . . . He has written something better perhaps than the best history; but he has not written a good history; he is, from the first to the last chapter, an inventor.' Fuller knowledge has proved that Herodotus is much more accurate and trustworthy than Macaulay here makes out.

41. *Hume's History of England* was published in 1754–61 and still retained its popularity in 1825, as Macaulay admits in his essay on Milton, in which he says that Hume ' hated religion so much that he hated liberty for having been allied with religion, and has pleaded the cause of tyranny with the dexterity of an advocate, while affecting the impartiality of a judge.' This comment Professor Montague describes as ' mere childish petulance,' adding that ' Hume sympathized with the Stuarts because he was a Scotchman and distrusted popular government because he was a sceptic.' The fact is, as Professor

Huxley points out in his essay on Hume, that Hume wrote history from the Tory point of view, Macaulay from that of the Whigs.

46. *obnoxious,* open, liable. *Gibbon* published his *Decline and Fall of the Roman Empire* in 1776–88. It has stood the test of time much better than Macaulay's own work and has still a very high reputation for impartiality and accuracy.

49. *Mitford,* who died the year before this criticism appeared, published his *History of Greece* in 1784–1818. Macaulay had reviewed it with some severity in 1824, with the object, to use his own words, of ' reducing an over-praised writer to his proper level.'

b. 15. *Plutarch* (first century A. D.) wrote the Lives of 46 eminent Greeks and Romans, arranged in pairs so as to bring out contrasts of character and point moral and political lessons. Sir Thomas North's English version, made from Amyot's French translation of the Greek original, was the foundation of Shakspere's Roman tragedies.

15. *Thucydides,* the second great Greek historian (fifth century B. C.), wrote the history of the long struggle between Athens and Sparta which ended in the ruin of the former. Macaulay says earlier in this essay that ' Thucydides has surpassed all his rivals in the art of historical narration, in the art of producing an effect on the imagination, by skilful selection and disposition, without indulging in the license of invention.'

23. *Calcutta . . . Bombay* both in India, but at opposite ends of it. So, it is said, English people coming to Montreal are charged with messages for friends in Vancouver.

24. *Rollin and Barthelemi,* French historians of the seventeenth and eighteenth centuries, who in Macaulay's time had not ceased to be read.

693. *a. 17. make the worse appear the better reason.* Milton of Belial in *Paradise Lost,* II, 112–4. See p. 255.

24. *the poet Laureate,* Southey, who wrote excellent biographies of Nelson and Wesley, but no historical works of any value. His *Book of the Church,* Macaulay wrote a year or two later, ' contains some stories very prettily told; the rest is mere rubbish.' Southey was a copious writer of reviews and miscellaneous articles, in which he frequently attacks Lingard, who was a Roman Catholic. The latter's *History of England* (first edition 1819–25) at once became a standard work on account of its learning and insight; it is still held in high esteem.

26. *Brodie,* author of *A History of the British Empire from the Accession of Charles I to the Restoration* (1822). In 1836 he was appointed Historiographer Royal for Scotland.

29. *about to be reheard.* Macaulay no doubt refers to the *History of Greece* by George Grote, written with much more sympathy for democracy than Mitford's. It was not published till 1846–56, but the author began to collect materials as early as 1823.

37. *neglect the art of narration.* This was Macaulay's repeated complaint about the historians of his day; it was an art in which he himself excelled.

49. *the most frivolous and indolent.* This passage is an instance, not only of Macaulay's exaggeration of statement, but of his misconception of popular tastes. He writes in his review of Sir James Mackintosh:—'A history of England, written throughout in this manner, would be the most fascinating book in the language. It would be more in request at the circulating libraries than the last novel.' In his own History Macaulay went further than any one else towards justifying the claim he here puts forward; but he could not altogether succeed. The comparison with the historical novel, on which Macaulay so often insisted, is misleading, as Professor Montague points out. 'A novel and a history can never really be occupied with the same matter. Imaginative writing, whether in prose or verse, is always and above all concerned with the individual, and everything else is only accessory. History concerns itself with the great organized masses of men known as people or states and treats of individuals only in relation to such masses and the effect produced upon them by uncommon personal qualities.' Moreover, history deals with what actually happened, the historical novel with what might have happened.

b. 10. *conventional decencies . . . of the French drama,* the rules of classical tragedy which forbid the introduction of comic or commonplace elements and the representation of acts of violence on the stage, all the murders, etc., being reported by messengers. The bane of the French drama, from the English point of view, has been rather the observance of the Unities of Time and Place, the restriction of the plot to one critical event, and the consequent exclusion of incident.

15. *too trivial for the majesty of history.* This is a favorite idea with Macaulay. In 1824 he wrote that the true historian 'will not think anything too trivial for the gravity of history which is not too trivial to promote or diminish the happiness of man.' In the opening of his History (1848) he says: 'I shall cheerfully bear the reproach of having descended below the dignity of history, if I can succeed in placing before the English of the nineteenth century a true picture of the life of their ancestors.'

18. *King of Spain,* Philip III, who was said to have died from a fever brought on by the excessive heat of a fire, which the courtiers refused to damp because it was contrary to etiquette, the nobleman whose office it was being absent. But Lafuente in his *History of Spain* says the story was a pure invention of the French Ambassador, Bassompierre.

29. *The knowledge of it is valuable,* etc. It is characteristic of Macaulay that he has no appreciation of knowledge for its own sake.

35. *turnpike,* tollgate.

36. *Sir Matthew Mite,* the principal character in Foote's farce *The Nabob* (1772), described by Macaulay in his essay on Clive as 'an Anglo-Indian chief, dissolute, ungenerous, and tyrannical, ashamed of the humble friends of his youth, hating the aristocracy, yet childishly eager to be numbered among them, squandering his wealth on panders and flatterers, tricking out his chairmen with the most costly hot-house flowers, and astounding the igno-

rant with jargon about rupees, lacs, and jaghires.' He uses the fortune he has made in India to bribe his way into Parliament, becomes a member of the Antiquarian Society, and commits scores of extravagant follies similar to that referred to in the text.

37. *Lord Clarendon,* Charles II's chief minister and author of the *History of the Great Rebellion.*

46. *Hampden,* Oliver Cromwell's cousin and the man on the Parliamentary side whom Macaulay most admired. In his essay, *John Hampden,* he describes him as 'the first of those great English commoners whose plain addition of Mister has, to our ears, a more majestic sound than the proudest of the feudal titles.'

51. *Vane* was 'a singular combination of the statesman and the mystic.' According to Clarendon 'he did at some time believe that he was the person deputed to reign over the saints upon earth for a thousand years.' He was at one time Governor of Massachusetts, and his statue adorns the entrance hall of the Boston Public Library. He was a leading member of the Long Parliament and after the Restoration was put to death as a traitor.

694. *a.* 5. *Rupert* (Prince), nephew of Charles I and commander of the Royalist cavalry in the Civil War.

6. *Harrison and Fleetwood,* leaders on the Parliamentary side, who were famous for their religious zeal.

40. *Bishop Watson* (1737–1816), a distinguished defender of revealed religion against Tom Paine and other sceptical writers.

53. *at the close of the Seven Years' War* (1763), when France gave up Canada to Great Britain and acknowledged British supremacy in India.

55. *American war* of Independence.

b. 9. *late ministerial interregnum,* in 1827, on the death of Canning, when Goderich kept the ministry together for a few months, giving place in January, 1828, to a new government under Wellington and Peel.

695. *b.* 7. *Sir Walter Scott,* whose novels Macaulay praises in this and the following pages, is not now so highly esteemed as a historical authority for the customs and phraseology of the sixteenth and seventeenth centuries.

32. *Froissart* was the chronicler, as Chaucer was the poet, of fourteenth century chivalry. The Tabard Inn, in Southwark, is the scene of the opening of the *Canterbury Tales.*

38. *Legate,* the ambassador of the Pope.

40. *palmers,* strictly, pilgrims who had been to the Holy Land and were therefore entitled to carry a branch or leaf of palm, but often used of pilgrims generally, and especially of those who gave all their lives to pilgrimage.

42. *refectory,* dining-hall.

52. *villain* (Low Latin *villanus*), a medieval villager or serf, who was bound to the soil and subject to the lord of the manor.

696. *a.* 11. *Tacitus* is described by Macaulay earlier in this essay as unrivaled for the delineation of character and certainly the greatest of the Latin historians.

40. *keep,* the central tower or stronghold of a medieval castle.

44. *oriel,* a window built out so as to form a recess. It is one of the features of Elizabethan domestic architecture, of which Longleat and Burleigh were conspicuous examples. The houses of the nobility built at this time surpassed all that had been built before in comfort and magnificence and all that have been built since in beauty.

b. 18. *Fifth-monarchy-man,* one of those who in the seventeenth century believed that the second coming of Christ was immediately at hand, and that it was the duty of Christians to be prepared to assist in establishing his reign by force, and in the meantime to repudiate all allegiance to any other government. The allusion is to the fifth kingdom foretold in Daniel ii, 44.

THE HISTORY OF ENGLAND

This short extract cannot give any adequate impression of the scope and methods of the great history, but it may be enough to suggest some idea of the way in which Macaulay carried out his conception of how history should be written.

697. *b.* 1. *Danby's administration.* 1674–9.

45. *clown,* country bumpkin.

698. *a.* 12. *Perrault* (1628–1703), a member of the French academy, the advocate of the superiority of modern literature against *Boileau,* who upheld the classics.

17. *Venice Preserved* (1682), a tragedy by Thomas Otway.

22. *Templars,* barristers or law students, of the Inner or Middle Temple.

30. *Racine* (1660–1699).

31. *Bossu* (1631–1680).

b. 33. *Lord Mayor's show,* a magnificent allegorical procession through the streets of London made every year when the Lord Mayor assumes office.

34. *Moneydroppers,* coiners or distributors of false money. *cart's tail,* at which they were whipped through the city.

699. *b.* 38. *Thoresby* (1658–1725).

42. *Pepys* (1632–1703), the great diarist.

700. *a.* 20. *higgler,* a wandering dealer in poultry and dairy produce.

b. 34. *parochial,* levied on the parish, the smallest territorial division in England.

51. *turnpike acts,* acts of parliament establishing trusts for the maintenance of roads on which tolls were collected. The toll-gates or toll-bars were abolished about the middle of the nineteenth century.

701. *a.* 31. *seven pounds,* nearly $35.

33. *fifteen pence,* 30c.

b. 37. *Vanbrugh* (1666–1726), writer of witty and licentious comedy.

NEWMAN: THE IDEA OF A UNIVERSITY

This discourse is one of a series given before the University of Dublin and addressed primarily to Catholic educators.

706. *a.* 54–55. *' the world is all before it where to choose.' Paradise Lost,* XII, 646.

707. *a.* 24. *St. Thomas.* Thomas Aquinas, the famous schoolman of the thirteenth century.

b. 46. *Pompey's Pillar,* a shaft of the Corinthian order near Alexandria. Its traditional association with Pompey is no longer believed to have any foundation in fact.

708. *b.* 33. *the Peripatetic,* an epithet applied to the school of Aristotle, traditionally because his discussions were carried on while walking about in the Lyceum.

35. *the Stoic,* the school of Greek philosophy founded by Zeno, about 340–265 B. C.

37–39. *Felix qui potuit,* etc. Virgil's *Georgics* II, 490–92.

709. *a.* 23. *the music of the spheres.* A proberbial phrase founded on the old belief that the celestial spheres were of crystal and made a harmonious sound as they revolved.

b. 2. *Salmasius.* A Dutch scholar, chiefly remembered by Englishmen for his controversy with Milton.

3. *Burman.* Francois Burmann, Dutch theologian of the seventeenth century.

4. *Imperat aut servit* collecta pecunia cuique [a man's money is either his master or his servant]. Horace, *Ep.* 1, x, 48.

8–10. *Vis consili,* etc. Horace, *Odes* 3, iv, 65.

15. *Tarpeia.* According to legend, she betrayed the Roman citadel to the Sabines for promised treasure, but was crushed to death by the shields they threw upon her.

29. *Mosheim.* Johann Lorenz von Mosheim (1694–1755).

30. *Du Pin,* Louis Ellies (1657–1719), French ecclesiastical historian.

711. *a.* 54. *a so-called university,* etc. The University of London, a corporation for the giving of examinations and conferring of degrees had been founded in 1836.

b. 5–6. *the University of Oxford . . . some sixty years since.* One may read in this connection Gibbon's account of Oxford, in his *Memoirs.*

712. *a.* 46. *genius loci.* Spirit of the place.

713. *b.* 9–10. *' tongues in the trees . . . brooks.'* Slightly inaccurate quotation of *As You Like It,* II, i, 16.

CARLYLE: PAST AND PRESENT

This pamphlet, written during the first seven weeks of 1843, and published in April, has two sides: its historical side is founded on the twelfth century Chronicle of Jocelin de Brakelonde, describing the government of the Abbey of St. Edmund's, which had been printed in 1840 by the Camden Society; its social and political side is concerned with the England of 1842, alarmed by Chartist riots and at a loss which way to turn for relief of popular discontent. Carlyle was not in sympathy with any of the existing political parties; his pamphlet aimed at arousing the laboring classes, their employers, and the landed aristocracy to nobler ideals and a sense of their obligations to each other.

714. *a.* 11. *Laissez-faire,* freedom of manufacture, originally a protest against artificial restrictions of industry, but later the motto of the English free-traders. Carlyle denounced their policy because they were opposed to all state-interference with industry.

715. *a.* 1. *Mammon-Gospels.* Matthew vi, 24: 'Ye cannot serve God and Mammon.' *Evangel.* Gospel.

22. '*wine-and-walnuts philosophy.*' Philosophy suited to be taken with wine and walnuts after a good dinner.

27. '*Soul, take thy ease.*' See Luke xii, 19–20.

36. *his Grace of Castle-Rackrent.* Duke with an estate on which exorbitant rents are charged to the tenants.

39. *Land Auctioneership,* selling land to the highest bidder.

41. *Sliding-scales,* adjusting the duty on corn to the price of wheat.

42. *Plugson,* the typical manufacturer.

51. *Chancery,* the principal English court for dealing with business matters.

b. 12. *are discrepant,* disagree, show discrepancies.

48. *Abbot Samson,* the hero of the Chronicle of Jocelin de Brakelonde. See introductory note above.
716. *a.* 36. *Bucanier and Chactaw.* Carlyle's own spellings, which it has seemed best to leave, along with his profuse capitals.

46. *Caliban.* The monster in *The Tempest.*

48. *Fiat-Lux.* 'Let there be light.' See Genesis i, 3.

51. *garments rolled* in blood. See Isaiah ix, 5.

b. 11. *unkempt,* uncombed, raw.

15. *Howel Davies.* Not found in the Dictionary of National Biography. There was a famous West Indian pirate, Edward Davis, who flourished 1683–1702, and had at one time command of about 3,000 men.
717. *a.* 2. *Soul-Overseers.* Bishops, the Greek ἐπίσκοπος, from which the word is derived, meaning literally an overseer.

3. *Hence these tears. Hinc illae lacrumae,* a saying in Terence's *Andria,* quoted by Cicero and Horace, and since established as a commonplace of literature.

44. *William the Norman Bastard.* William I, Duke of Normandy and King of England, was of illegitimate birth.

45. *Taillefer* (literally 'cut-iron'), a minstrel of William's who at the battle of Hastings obtained from him the privilege of striking the first blow.

52. *orthoepy,* right speech.

b. 44. *tipstaves,* bailiffs, constables.
718. *a.* 7. *Westminster* Hall, one of the oldest English places of legislation and the administration of justice. Charles I was tried here in 1649.

20. *Bastille,* a great prison in Paris, destroyed at the French Revolution. Carlyle applies the term to the workhouses, in which the poor take refuge in England when they have no employment.

21. *Westminster.* Parliament.

30. *articulated,* systematized, organized.

34. *Midas-eared.* Midas, a mythological king of Phrygia, who had asses' ears, and who obtained from the gods the embarrassing gift that everything he touched turned to gold.

57. *Duces,* leaders (Latin).

'*on a minimum of four thousand five hundred.*' Some one had said that £4,500 (about $20,000) was a minimum salary for an English bishop.

b. 24. *Mammonish,* done merely to get money.
719. *a.* 18. *Ezechiel.* There is no reference to the potter's wheel in Ezechiel. Carlyle probably trusted to his remembrance of Jeremiah xviii, 1–6, and ascribed the passage to the wrong prophet.

23. *amorphous,* shapeless.

35. *shambling,* unable to stand straight.

35. *squint-cornered,* irregular.

37. *vessel of dishonor.* Romans ix, 21: 'Hath not the potter power over the clay, of the same lump to make one vessel unto honor, and another unto dishonor?'

47. *festering,* stagnant, decaying.

51. *How blessed,* etc., blessed for the man's life, no matter what kind of work it is.

57. *awakens,* nominative 'force' two lines above.

b. 10. *schools,* of philosophy.

11. *vortices,* whirlpools.

23. *Sir Christopher* Wren, after St. Paul's was destroyed by the great fire of London (1666) was appointed architect of the new Cathedral, and carried his design to accomplishment in 1710, in spite of the many difficulties Carlyle here refers to. Nell Gwyn was a popular actress of the time, a great favorite with Charles II, who spoke of her on his death-bed. 'Defender of the Faith' is a title conferred by the Pope upon Henry VIII for his answer to Luther, and retained by all the English sovereigns since.

41. *architectonics,* the principles of building.
720. *a.* 3. *monument.* Sir Christopher Wren's tomb in St. Paul's bears the inscription: '*Si monumentum quaeris circumspice.*' 'If you seek his monument, look around you.'

50. *Ursa Major,* the Great Bear, a group of stars near the North Pole, popularly known as Charles's Wain or the Dipper.

b. 33. '*Religion.*' Carlyle now returns to the thought of the last paragraph but one.

36. *Brahmins,* the highest caste in the Hindoo religion.

Antinomians, a sect who maintained that the moral law was not binding upon Christians.

37. *Spinning Dervishes,* Mohammedan friars who whirl round and round in a state of religious excitement 'till collapse ensue and sometimes death.'

51. *immethodic,* without method, irregular.
721. *a.* 12. *Shovel-hat,* a broad-brimmed hat, turned up at the sides and projecting in front, worn by some clergymen.

Talfourd-Mahon Copyright Act (1842) gave the author copyright for forty-two years. The meaning is that people should attack Ignorance, without waiting to be invested with authority, or promised reward and legal protection.

22. *Sinai thunders.* See Exodus xix, 16–19.

23. *speech of Whirlwinds.* See 1 Kings xix, 11–12.

34. *work,* etc. John ix, 4: 'I must work the works of him that sent me, while it is day: the night cometh, when no man can work.'

43. *Kepler* (1571–1630), *Newton* (1642–1727), two of the world's greatest mathematicians and astronomers.

46. '*Agony of bloody sweat.*' See Luke xxii, 44

b. 15. *denizen,* one born in the country, having rights of citizenship; opposed to 'foreigner.'

24. *Mayfair,* the fashionable quarter of London.

34. *Phantasm,* an appearance, not a reality.

40. *unprofitable servants.* See Luke xvii, 10.

53. *Eldorado,* the 'golden' land dreamed of by the Spanish explorers of America.

722. *a.* 1. *St. Stephen's.* The Houses of Parliament.

20. *Owen,* Robert (1771–1858), a socialist reformer, who, amid many other projects intended to benefit working people, established in 1832 an 'Equitable Labor Exchange.' It proved a failure.

29. *Downing-*street, where many of the government offices are in London.

723. *a.* 8. *Manes,* the deified souls of the departed, the gods of the Lower World.

15. *Acheron,* a river in the Lower World; often used as synonym for the Lower World itself.

17. *Dante* (1265–1321), the great Italian poet from whose *Divine Comedy* (*Inferno* xv, 55) Carlyle quotes below.

25. *Se tu segui la tua stella.* 'If thou followest thy star.'

33. *Cerberus,* the dog who guarded Hades.

30. *Eccovi . . . all' Inferno.* 'Behold the man who has been in hell.'

36. *Dryden.* See 269. 79.

42. *Eurydice,* beloved of Orpheus, who went down to Tartarus to rescue her.

b. 3. *lath-and-plaster hats.* Used for advertisements.

7. *Controversies* were raging at this time in the Church of England as to whether the preacher should wear a black gown or a white surplice.

10. *Corn-Laws,* imposing duties on wheat, which made bread dear, and pampered industry by increasing wages. Abolished 1846.

23. *Great Taskmaster's eye.* Milton's Sonnet *On his having arrived at the age of 23* ends

All is, if I have grace to use it so,
As ever in my great Task-Master's eye.

31. *Galvanism,* electricity.

55. *Antæus,* a giant in classical mythology, who renewed his strength by contact with the earth, his mother.

724. *a.* 56. *adscititious,* accidental.

b. 19. *the proper Epic,* not of military heroes, or of tailors, but of captains of industry.

725. *a.* 18. *Stockport,* a manufacturing town in the North of England, where, at this time, many working people lived in cellars.

19. *Poor-Law Bastilles,* workhouses.

30. *villani, bordarii, sochemanni,* mediæval Latin terms for serfs.

43. *arrestment,* arrest.

46. *Dryasdust,* the scholarly historian or mediæval chronicler.

b. 6. *Phalaris,* a tyrant of ancient Sicily, who was said to burn men alive in a bronze bull.

31. *Dahomey,* a kingdom in West Africa.

33. *Mungo Park* (1771–1806), an African explorer who tells in his *Travels* the incident referred to by Carlyle.

40. *Calabash,* a tree common in tropical America,

but said to have been introduced from Guinea. The hard shell of the fruit is used for bottles, cups, and other vessels.

52. *Gurth . . . Cedric the Saxon.* Characters in Scott's *Ivanhoe.*

726. *a.* 2. *boscage and umbrage,* wood and shade.

b. 35. *Tancred of Hauteville* (1078–1112), one of the leaders of the first crusade.

38. *cased in tin.* The Champion of England, who appears at the Coronation ceremony, wears armor — a survival of ancient custom which Carlyle wishes to ridicule.

49. *Hereward,* a Saxon hero who withstood William I in the Fen Counties, on the east coast of England.

51. *Waltheof,* Earl of Northumberland, beheaded in 1076 for conspiring against William I.

727. *a.* 35. *Corn-Laws,* maintained for the advantage of the country landowners, whose main activity, according to Carlyle, was the preservation and slaughter of partridges.

37. *bedlamism,* lunacy.

38. *bush,* to plant bushes on game preserves so as to prevent the use of nets by poachers.

40. *Par la Splendeur de Dieu,* a Norman oath. 'By God's Splendor.'

44. *Joe Manton* (d. 1835), a famous London gun maker.

b. 14. *Charter.* The agitation for the People's Charter was coming to a height when *Past and Present* was written. The six 'points' in it were (1) manhood suffrage; (2) equal electoral districts; (3) vote by ballot; (4) annual parliaments; (5) abolition of the property qualification for members of the House of Commons; (6) payment of members of parliament.

25. *St. Mary Axe,* a London parish.

30. *Wahngasse of Weissnichtwo,* the imaginary street of 'Nowhere,' in which lived Terr Teufelsdröckh (Devil's dung), the hero of Carlyle's *Sartor Resartus.* Carlyle here returns to the style and thought of his earlier work, and quotes from his own hero — really from himself, for Teufelsdröckh is merely Carlyle under a thin disguise.

41. *mein Lieber,* my dear fellow. The imaginary German philosopher intersperses his speech with scraps of his native language.

728. *a.* 1. *Sansculottic,* revolutionary.

2. *ruinous,* because *sansculottic* literally means 'without breeches.'

10. *Keineswegs,* by no means.

11. *Sumptuary Laws,* regulating the dress and way of living of various classes.

14. *amphibium,* a compromise, neither one thing nor another.

24. *Cheruscan,* a German tribe mentioned by Julius Cæsar.

b. 1. *Sedan,* a town on the French frontier with many cloth factories; now more famous for its surrender by Napoleon III to the Germans in 1870. *Huddersfield,* one of the centers of the Yorkshire cloth trade. *Nescience,* ignorance.

50. *Windsor Georges,* decorations or titles.

53. *Franchiser,* voter, elector.

56. *Heavy-wet,* ale.

729. a. 48. *wardmotes*, meetings of the voters of a small district.

55. *Palaver*, Parliament, which literally means 'talking-place.'

b. 24. *Pococurantism*, carelessness, inattention.

25. *Beau-Brummelism*, dandyism.

27. *Byronism*, sentimental egotism. *Dead Sea*, in Palestine, on the site of the once flourishing 'cities of the plain.'

30. *Sabbath-day*, of witches and apes.

730. a. 16. *lion-soirées*, evening entertainments given for the exhibition of social 'lions' or notabilities.

27. *dispiritments*, discouragements.

40. *Histrios*, actors.

47. *Quackhood*, quackery.

54. *ninth-parts of men*, tailors.

b. 5. *succedanea*, substitutes.

36. *Bobus* Higgins, 'Sausage-maker on the great scale . . . with his cash-accounts and larders dropping fatness, with his respectabilities, warm garnitures, and pony-chaise,' is Carlyle's incarnation of commercial success.

47. *Friend Prudence.* 'Prudence keeps a thousand workmen; has striven in all ways to attach them to him; has provided conversational soirées; play-grounds, bands of music for the young ones; went even "the length of buying them a drum"; all which has turned out to be an excellent investment. For a certain person, marked here by a black stroke, whom we shall name Blank, living over the way — he also keeps somewhere about a thousand men; but has done none of these things for them, nor any other thing, except due payment of the wages by supply-and-demand. Blank's workers are perpetually getting into mutiny, into broils and coils: every six months, we suppose, Blank has a strike; every one month, every day and every hour, they are fretting and obstructing the short-sighted Blank, pilfering from him, wasting and idling for him, omitting and committing for him. "I would not," says Friend Prudence, "exchange my workers for his *with seven thousand pounds to boot.*" '

8. *Law-ward*, 'maintainer and keeper of Heaven's laws' — Carlyle's interpretation of the word 'lord.' Its true origin is, however, *hlaf-weard*, loaf-ward or keeper of bread, as that of 'lady' is *hlaf-dige*, kneader of bread. Cf. 725. b. 21.

731. a. 23. *flunky-species*, people with the ideas of footmen.

Chactaw, Indian, heathen.

48. *my Transcendental friends.* Carlyle was in correspondence with two of the New England Transcendentalists — Ralph Waldo Emerson and George Ripley. The latter defined Transcendentalists as people who 'believe in an order of truth that transcends the sphere of the external senses. Their leading idea is the supremacy of mind over matter. Hence they maintain that the truth of religion does not depend on tradition or historical facts, but has an unswerving witness in the soul.' As may be gathered from the text, Carlyle was not altogether in sympathy with his Transcendental admirers. He wrote to Emerson in 1842: 'You seem to me in danger of dividing yourselves from the

Fact of this present Universe, in which alone, ugly as it is, can I find any anchorage, and soaring away after Ideas, Beliefs, Revelations, and such like — into perilous altitudes, as I think.'

52. *Demiurgusships*, Lordships. The Demiurgus is in the Platonic philosophy the Maker of the world. It means literally 'one who works for the people,' and in some Greek states was the title of a magistrate.

56. *Chronos*, in Greek mythology Kronos, the ruler of heaven and earth until his son Zeus (Latin Jupiter or Jove) drove him from the throne. *Odin*, the All-father of Norse mythology, the same as the Old English Woden, whose name is preserved in 'Wednesday.'

57. *St. Olaf*, who early in the eleventh century converted Norway to Christianity. *the Dollar*, etc. The promised change in American ideals was probably suggested to Carlyle by Emerson, who wrote to him from Concord on Oct. 30, 1840: 'We are all a little wild here with numberless projects of social reform. Not a reading man but has a draft of a new Community in his waistcoat pocket. I am gently mad myself, and am resolved to live cleanly. George Ripley is talking up a colony of agriculturists and scholars, with whom he threatens to take the field and the book. One man renounces the use of animal food; and another of coin; and another of domestic hired service; and another of the state; and on the whole we have a commendable share of reason and hope.'

b. 2. *Socinian* from two Italian theologians of the sixteenth century named Socinus, who did not believe that Christ was God. Emerson and Ripley had both resigned their charges as Unitarian ministers.

5. *retire into the fields*, etc. Carlyle here refers to the Brook Farm Institute of Agriculture and Education, which Emerson mentions in the passage quoted above. Emerson, though in sympathy with the enterprise, took no active part in it. The leader was George Ripley, and another active member, John S. Dwight, had also been a Unitarian minister. The Farm was managed on a system of 'brotherly co-operation,' and no one was paid more than a dollar a day; provision was made for educational courses of an advanced character, but after a year or two it was found that the income did not meet the expenditure. Nathaniel Hawthorne was one of the original members of the community, and has left an account of his experiences in *The Blithedale Romance.*

20. *Exeter Hall*, the meeting place of various Evangelical societies every May. It is in the Strand and has since been bought by the Y. M. C. A.

22. *Puseyism*, from Pusey, an Oxford professor and one of the leaders of the High Church movement which was attracting public attention about this time.

32. *why will*, why not *shall*, expressing determination on the part of the speaker.

732. a. 11. *Long-acre*, a London street where carriages were sold. A witness in a famous trial in 1823 had described a certain person as 'respectable,' and when asked why, answered, 'he always

kept a gig.' This furnished Carlyle with a text on which he was never tired of preaching against the superficiality of current standards of worth.

14. *Simulacrum* (Latin), image.

18. *Ilion,* Troy; *Latium,* the country about Rome, scenes of the *Iliad* and the *Æneid. Mayfair,* a fashionable part of London, east of Hyde Park; so called from a Fair formerly held there in the month of May.

23. *Phrygians,* inhabitants of Asia Minor, Trojans.

24. *jötuns,* a supernatural race of giants in Scandinavian mythology. The heroism of the future will consist in overcoming the forces of nature and the evil passions of the heart of man.

30. *Fribbles,* triflers.

' *bush,*' preserve game. See 727. *a.* 38, note.

35. *the Subtle Fowler,* Destiny.

42. *with beards on their chins,* grown men, no longer children.

b. 24. *Brindley* (1716–72), engineer of the Bridgewater and Grand Trunk Canals.

25. *Goethe,* ' for the last hundred years, by far the notablest of all Literary Men.'— Heroes and Hero Worship. *Odin,* celebrated by Carlyle in his lecture on ' The Hero as Divinity.' *Arkwright* (1732–92), inventor of cotton spinning machinery.

35. *Bath-garter.* The orders of the Garter and the Bath are among the highest honors conferred by the English sovereign. Carlyle confuses the two, for the purpose of expressing contempt for such decorations regarded as claims to respect.

36. *George,* the jewel which forms part of the insignia of the Order of the Garter.

43. *Duke of Weimar.* Carlyle had written in the previous chapter: ' A modern Duke of Weimar, not a god he either, but a human duke, levied, as I reckon, in rents and taxes and all incomings whatsoever, less than several of our English Dukes do in rent alone. The Duke of Weimar, with these incomings, had to govern, judge, defend, everyway administer *his* Dukedom. He does all this as few others did: and he improves lands besides all this, makes river-embankments, maintains not soldiers only but Universities and Institutions;— and in his Court were these four men: Wieland, Herder, Schiller, Goethe. . . . I reckon that this one Duke of Weimar did more for the Culture of his Nation than all the English Dukes and *Duces* now extant, or that were extant since Henry the Eighth gave them the Church Lands to eat, have done for theirs! '

47. *The Future hides in it,* etc. This is a stanza from Goethe's poem ' Symbolum,' introductory to the series entitled ' Loge.' Carlyle had given a translation of the whole poem earlier in *Past and Present* (end of Bk. III). He now recalls it as the final thought he wishes to impress upon the minds of his readers.

49. *thorow,* through.

RUSKIN: TRAFFIC

734. *a.* 12. *carelessness,* lack of interest.

b. 28. *pitch farthing,* pitch and toss, ' matching ' coppers

735. *a.* 18. Teniers (1582–1649), the great Dutch realist painter.

29. *Titian* (1477–1576), the leading artist of the Venetian school.

30. *Turner* (1775–1851), the greatest of English landscape painters and Ruskin's particular favorite. See introductory biography, 733. 4.

49. *Fleet Street,* a great London thoroughfare, where many London publishers have offices.

54. *classifying,* dividing into classes.

b. 7. *costermonger,* peddler of apples (' costards ') and other small fruits.

8. *Newgate Calendar,* a publication giving accounts of sensational crimes. Newgate is a London prison.

736. *a.* 4–6. Quoted from Scott's *Lay of the Last Minstrel,* Canto I.

38. *steel-traps . . . spring guns.* Appliances used against poachers, but here allegorically signifying the armaments of modern nations.

54. *Bedlam,* the monastery of St. Mary of Bethlehem in London, later used as an asylum for the insane.

b. 13. *Armstrongs,* big guns manufactured by the great English firm of Armstrong.

19. *black eagles* of Austria. Ruskin means that the English let the great military nations alone.

52. *Inigo Jones . . . Sir Christopher Wren,* the great English architects of the seventeenth century. The former planned the royal palace of Whitehall in London, the latter St. Paul's Cathedral, both in the Italian style.

737. *a.* 50. *This is none other than the house of God.* See Genesis xxviii, 10–17.

b. 25. *Thou, when thou prayest.* See Matthew vi, 5–6.

49. *Lares,* Latin gods of the hearth, household gods.

738. *a.* 5. *The Seven Lamps.* See introductory biography, p. 733.

b. 48. *Bosphorus,* the strait dividing Europe from Asia.

739. *a.* 9. *to the Jews.* See I Corinthians i, 23.

b. 51. *Tetzel,* a seller of papal indulgences who provoked the indignation of Luther.

b. 55. *bals masqués,* masked balls. They were a feature of the French frivolity which preceded the Revolution and the guillotine.

740. *a.* 6. *Revivalist,* of classical architecture, as seen in the royal palace of Versailles, near Paris, and the papal palace of the Vatican at Rome.

17. *sevenths of time,* Sunday, one-seventh of the week.

38. *Acropolis,* the hill overlooking Athens; the site of the Parthenon and other Greek temples.

39. *walls of Babylon . . . temple of Ephesus,* monuments of antiquity.

b. 23. *affairs of exchange.* See Matthew xxi, 12–13.

34. *quartering.* As armies do when they occupy a country. *color,* pretence.

55. ' *carry.*' At the point of the bayonet.

741. *b.* 2. *St. George,* the English national saint.

3. *semi-fleeced . . . proper . . . fields,* terms of heraldry.

23. *Comforter,* the Holy Ghost. See John xiv, 16–17.

27. *Agora,* market.

742. *a.* 4. *Olympus . . . Pelion . . . Ossa.* Mountains of classical antiquity. See *Hamlet* V, i, 304–7.

743. *a.* 21. *Solomon made gold.* See 1 Kings x, 14–17.

51. *Bolton priory,* a beautiful abbey in Wharfedale, Yorkshire.

56. *' men may come.'* Quoted from Tennyson's *The Brook.*

744. *b.* 7. *plain of Dura,* where Nebuchadnezzar set up a golden image. See Daniel iii, 1.

25. *pleasantness . . . peace.* See Proverbs iii, 17.

35. not made with hands. See 2 Corinthians v, i.

TENNYSON: MARIANA

745. 8. *moated grange.* Tennyson printed, as the motto of this poem, the phrase, ' Mariana in the moated grange,' adapted from a passage in Shakspere's *Measure for Measure,* III, i. The situation of Shakspere's Mariana, then, probably furnished the germ of Tennyson's conception.

THE POET

747. 15. *Calpe,* Gibraltar. *Caucasus,* the Caucasian Mountains.

THE LADY OF SHALOTT

This was probably Tennyson's earliest study from the Arthurian legend. It may be compared with his later embodiment of the story in *Lancelot and Elaine.*

5. *Camelot.* In Cornwall. The legendary seat of King Arthur's court.

9. *Shalott.* Malory's Astolat. According to Palgrave, this poem was suggested to Tennyson by an Italian romance upon the *Donna di Scalotta.* This would account for the form, Shalott.

748. 84. *the golden Galaxy.* The Milky Way.

107. *' Tirra Lirra.'* Tirelirer, in French, signifies to sing like a lark.

THE PALACE OF ART

The ethical burden of this poem has been well stated by Tennyson's friend, James Spedding. The poem ' represents allegorically the condition of a mind which, in the love of beauty and the triumphant consciousness of knowledge and intellectual supremacy, in the intense enjoyment of its own power and glory, has lost sight of its relation to man and God.'

750. 99. *Saint Cecily.* Compare 276. 138–47, and note.

105. *Uther's deeply-wounded son,* King Arthur. See below, p. 758.

111. *The wood-nymph,* Egeria. *The Ausonian king,* Numa Pompilius.

115. *Indian Cama.* The Hindu god of love.

117. *Europa.* According to the Greek myth, Europa, sister of Cadmus, was carried to Crete by Zeus who assumed the form of a white bull.

' Europa and the Bull' is the subject of a famous painting by Titian.

121. *Ganymede,* the cup-bearer of Zeus, who was conveyed to Olympus by an eagle.

137. *the Ionian father,* etc. Homer.

163. *Verulam.* Francis Bacon was created Baron Verulam in 1618. See pp. 187–199.

171–2. *as morn from Memnon,* etc. A colossus near Thebes, Egypt, was believed by the Greeks to represent this solar deity and to give forth a musical sound when reached by the rays of the rising sun.

752. 219. *Like Herod,* etc. See Acts xii, 21–23.

226. *The airy hand,* etc. See Daniel v, 24–27.

A DREAM OF FAIR WOMEN

753. 2. *The Legend of Good Women.* For its place among Chaucer's works, see p. 4.

27. *tortoise,* the roof formed by the shields of soldiers held over their heads.

754. 87. *a daughter of the gods,* etc. Helen.

100. *One that stood beside.* Iphigenia, the daughter of Agamemnon. Part of the details are drawn from Aeschylus' *Agamemnon,* 225–49, and from Lucretius' *De Rerum Natura,* I, 85–100.

122. *Sudden I heard,* etc. The description of Cleopatra is based chiefly on Shakspere's *Antony and Cleopatra,* though there are touches from Horace, *Ode* i.

755. 145. *Canopus.* One of the brightest of the first magnitude stars. It is not visible in our middle northern latitudes.

154. *the other.* Octavius Cæsar.

176. *Then I heard,* etc. Jephthah's daughter. See Judges xi.

756. 250. *Rosamond.* See 375. 95, note.

254. *Eleanor,* Henry II's queen. She is said to have slain Rosamond with her own hand or to have forced her to drink poison.

260. *Fulvia.* Antony's first wife. Cleopatra means, ' You should have slain your rival.'

264. *The captain of my dreams.* The morning star, an allusion to l. 3.

265–6. *her, who clasped . . . father's head.* Margaret Roper, the daughter of Sir Thomas More, is said to have rescued his head from London Bridge where it had been placed after his execution for high treason, and to have kept it until she died.

267–71. *Or her who knew,* etc. Eleanor, wife of Edward I, who saved his life by applying her lips to his wound after he had been stabbed with a poisoned dagger.

ST. AGNES EVE

See 640. 1, note.

OF OLD SAT FREEDOM ON THE HEIGHTS

758. 15. *the triple forks.* The trident of Neptune symbolic of maritime supremacy.

SIR GALAHAD

25. *When down the stormy crescent goes.* After a victory over the Saracen.

53. *the leads.* The roofs of lead.

84. *Until I find the holy Grail.* The sacred vessel in which the blood of the Lord was caught as

he hung upon the Cross, was said to have been carried to Britain by Joseph of Arimathea. It was an object of quest among the knights of the Round Table, but only Galahad was pure enough to achieve it. See Tennyson's *Holy Grail* in *The Idylls of the King* and Malory's *Morte d' Arthur.*

A FAREWELL

759. The Tennysons left their old home at Somersby in 1837. There are references to the incident and to the same brook in *In Memoriam.*

MORTE D'ARTHUR

For Malory's *Morte d' Arthur*, Bk. XXI, upon which this poem is based, see p. 21. The poem was afterward incorporated, with additions, into *The Idylls of the King.*

4. *Lyonnesse.* A mythical region, off the shores of Cornwall, now supposedly submerged by the sea.
15. *The goodliest fellowship*, etc. The Round Table.
21. *Camelot.* See 747. 5, note.
23. *Merlin.* The wise magician of Arthur's court.
31. *samite*, a kind of silk.
43. *hest*, behest, command.
760. 139. *the northern morn.* Aurora borealis.
140. *isles of winter*, icebergs.
761. 186. *harness*, armor.
215. *greaves*, shin pieces. *cuisses*, thigh pieces.
762. 259. *the island valley of Avilion.* Tennyson's description is influenced by classical conceptions of the Fortunate Islands. See 763. 63, note.

ULYSSES

The germ of this poem is to be found in Dante's *Inferno* xxvi, 85-142.
2. *these barren crags*, the bleak island of Ithaca.
3. *mete*, measure.
10. *the rainy Hyades.* A part of the constellation Taurus, supposed to bring rain. Virgil's *pluvias Hyadas.*
763. 63. *the Happy Isles.* Vaguely thought of by the ancients as somewhere in the Atlantic off the west coast of Africa, perhaps the Cape Verde or the Canary Islands. Tennyson's description of Avilion borrows from classical sources. See 762. 259, ff.

LOCKSLEY HALL

Suggestions for this poem were derived from the *Amriolkais*, an Arabian poem translated by Sir William Jones. *Works*, Vol. IV, pp. 247-57.
8. *Orion.* A conspicuous constellation often mentioned by Tennyson.
9. *the Pleiads.* A group of stars in the constellation Taurus. A similar reference occurs in the *Amriolkais.*
765. 75. *Comfort scorned of devils.* The reference is to *Paradise Lost*, Books I and II, *passim.*
75-76. *this is truth the poet sings*, etc. *Nessun maggior dolore, Che ricordarsi del tempo felice Nella miseria.*— Dante, *Inferno* v, 121-3.
766. 155. *Mahratta-battle.* With the Mahrattas, a warlike and powerful Hindu people of mid-India, the British had a number of serious wars between 1750 and 1818.

767. 180. *Joshua's moon in Ajalon.* See Joshua x, 12-13.
182. *the ringing grooves of change.* Tennyson has explained that when he traveled by the first train from Liverpool to Manchester in 1830 it was night and he thought that the wheels ran in a groove. 'Then I wrote this line.'
184. *Cathay*, China.

BREAK, BREAK, BREAK

Composed 'in a Lincolnshire lane at five o'clock in the morning between blossoming hedges.' (Tennyson.)

IN MEMORIAM A. H. H.

Arthur Henry Hallam died at Vienna, in September, 1833. He had been Tennyson's most intimate friend at Cambridge and was betrothed to Tennyson's sister. He was a youth of great intellectual promise and exceptional purity of spirit. The 'elegies' as they were called which make up *In Memoriam*, were composed at various times during the seventeen years which intervened between Hallam's death and their publication in 1850.
769. 5. *orbs of light and shade.* The eyes.
8. *the skull.* As symbolizing death.
35. *merit lives from man to man.* That is, man in comparison with man.
42. *Confusions of a wasted youth.* This section of the poem was written in 1849, while much of the poem had been composed years before.

XIX

1-4. *The Danube to the Severn*, etc. Vienna, where Hallam died, is on the Danube; while Clevedon Church, where he is buried, is on the river Severn near its confluence with Bristol Channel.
5-8. *There twice a day the Severn fills*, etc. The tide pushes back into the Severn and up the tributary Wye.

LV

770. 7-8. *So careful of the type*, etc. Type, species. In lvi, Tennyson points out that types, as well as individuals, become extinct.

LXIV

1. *thou*, the spirit of Hallam.

LXVII

3. *that broad water of the west.* The mouth of the Severn. See xix, 1-4, note.

LXXXVIII

2. *quicks*, hedges. Literally, living things.

MAUD; A MONODRAMA

772. 36. *vitriol madness.* The frenzy produced by chemicalized liquor.
40. *center-bits.* The drills of the safe-blower.
43. *poisoned poison.* Adulterated drugs.
45. *Timour-Mammon.* Timour (Tamerlane), 'the Scourge of the World,' is united with the god of riches to name an evil potency of the modern world.
773. 89. *Orion.* Compare *Locksley Hall*, 763. 8, and note.

132. *Birds in the high Hall-garden,* etc. Tennyson called attention to the imitation of the cries of the rooks, ll. 134 and 158, and of the smaller birds, l. 142.

774. 206. *Lebanon.* The cedars of Lebanon are said to have been brought into England by the crusaders, on their return from the Holy Land.

227. *A sad astrology.* The old astrology was based upon a belief that the movements of stars controlled the destiny of men; but modern science teaches us that they have no such significance.

775. 297. *the planet of love.* Venus, as morning star.

392. *the Breton Strand.* The coast of Brittainy, in France.

777. 411. *that of Lamech.* 'I have slain a man to my wounding, and a young man to my hurt.' Genesis iv, 23.

456. *O that 't were possible,* etc. This section of the poem, in slightly different form, had been published in *The Tribute,* 1837. Tennyson's friend, Sir John Simeon, who greatly admired the verses, suggested that they needed some introduction to make them fully intelligible. Tennyson undertook to carry out the suggestion, and *Maud* was the result.

TITHONUS

Although not published until 1860, this poem was written at about the same time as *Ulysses.* It is based upon the Greek myth according to which Tithonus, a mortal, being beloved by Eos, goddess of the dawn, the gods conferred upon him the gift of immortality. As they had neglected the gift of immortal youth, he gradually dwindled away and was metamorphosed into a grasshopper. The poem should be read as a myth of the dawn.

MILTON

This is one of a group of poems which Tennyson styled 'experiments in quantity.' It imitates the Alcaic stanza of Horace and other classical poets. To those who are unacquainted with classical prosody perhaps the best advice is that which Tennyson gave in regard to a similar experiment: 'Read it as prose and the meter will come right.'

The following time scheme may, however, be found useful in interpreting the meter:

— | ‿́ ◡ | ‿́ — ‖ ‿́ ◡ ◡ | ‿́ ◡ | ‿́
— | ‿́ ◡ | ‿́ — ‖ ‿́ ◡ ◡ | ‿́ ◡ | ‿́
— | ‿́ ◡ | ‿́ — | ‿́ ◡ | ‿́ ◡ |
‿́ ◡ ◡ | ‿́ ◡ ◡ | ‿́ ◡ | ‿́ ◡ |

NORTHERN FARMER

This poem is written in the Lincolnshire dialect with which Tennyson was familiar from childhood. It will be more easily understood if read aloud.

779. 1. *'asta,* hast thou. *liggin',* lying.

2. *nowt,* nothing.

10. *issen,* himself.

780. 11. *towd,* told. *toithe,* tithe.

14. *barne,* bairn, child.

16. *roate,* tax.

18. *buzzard-clock,* cockchafer.

23. *'Siver,* howsoever.

27. *thaw summun said it.* Though some may have said it.

28. *stubb'd,* grubbed, cleared.

30. *boggle,* goblin, bogle.

31. *butter-bump,* bittern.

32. *raäved,* rived, tore. *rembled,* removed.

34. *'enemies,* anemones.

35. *toaner,* the one or the other.

36. *'soize,* the assizes.

37. *Dubbut,* do but.

38. *bracken,* brake, fern. *fuzz,* furze, gorse.

41. *nobbut,* only.

49. *'aapoth,* half-penny's worth.

52. *hoalms,* flats, lowlands.

54. *sewerloy,* surely.

61. *kittle o' steam,* steam-engine.

62. *Huzzin' an' maazin'.* Buzzing and amazing.

781. 65. *atta,* art thou.

66. *'toattler,* teetotaler. *a's haollus i' the oud taale,* he 's always at the old story.

THE REVENGE

Compare the account from Hakluyt, above, p. 92 ff.

TO VIRGIL

783. 1. *Ilion's . . . fire.* The reference is to Æneas's description of the burning of Troy. *Æneid* II.

3. *he that sang the 'Works and Days.'* Hesiod.

5. *Thou that singest . . . herd.* Reference to the *Georgics.*

7. *Tityrus.* See *Eclogue* I.

8. *the poet-satyr.* See *Eclogue* VI.

9. *the Pollio.* See *Eclogue* IV.

11. *Thou that seest Universal Nature,* etc. See *Æneid* VI, 727.

14. *Golden branch,* etc. See *Æneid* VI, 208.

16. *the Northern Island,* etc. See *Eclogue,* I, 67.

19. *Mantovano,* Mantuan. From Mantua, Virgil's birthplace.

FRATER AVE ATQUE VALE

The refrain, 'Brother, hail and farewell,' is from Catullus's invocation at his brother's tomb. See Catullus, ci.

1. *Desenzano . . . Sirmione.* Villages on the Lago di Garda, largest of the northern Italian lakes.

2. *O venusta Sirmio* [O Ancient Sirmio]. See Catullus xxxi.

8. *Lydian laughter of the Garda Lake.* See Catullus xxxi.

CROSSING THE BAR

Tennyson requested of his son that these verses should be placed at the close of all collections of his poems. They were written in his eighty-first year and 'came in a moment.'

784. 3. *moaning of the bar.* The poem was suggested by the popular superstition that the tide moans in going out, whenever a death has occurred.

15. *my Pilot* 'that Divine and Unseen who is always guiding us.' (Tennyson.)

BROWNING: SONGS FROM 'PIPPA PASSES'

Browning was walking alone in a wood on the outskirts of London when the image flashed upon him of 'someone walking thus alone through life; one apparently too obscure to leave a trace of his or her passage, yet exercising a lasting, though unconscious, influence at every step of it.' This original conception is charmingly worked out in the character of Felippa or Pippa, the little silk winder of Asolo, a hill town in North Italy which had taken Browning's fancy during his first visit. Pippa is introduced in her humble room springing out of bed on her one holiday — New Year's Day, and singing the first of her songs, as here given. During the day she passes in and out of the village, singing her artless songs, and unconsciously influencing the lives of those about her. The second song, 'The year 's at the Spring,' awakens two wicked people to a sense of their guilt and the divine government of the world. The third, 'Give her but a least excuse to love me,' rouses a young painter to a higher conception of love and art. The explanation of this song is given in the lines which follow in the original: —

What name was that the little girl sang forth?
Kate? The Cornaro, doubtless, who renounced
The crown of Cyprus to be lady here
At Asolo, where still her memory stays,
And peasants sing how once a certain page
Pined for the grace of her so far above
His power of doing good to 'Kate the Queen —
She never could be wronged, be poor,' he sighed,
'Need him to help her!'

Browning gives us in the first five lines of each stanza the page's song; in the last four the comments of the Queen and her maid, who overhear him. Caterina (or Kate) Cornaro was a Venetian citizen who married the King of Cyprus, and after his death, resigning her authority to the Republic, retired to keep a small court at the Venetian village of Asolo, where she 'wielded her little sceptre for her people's good, and won their love by gentleness and grace.'

786. 18. *jesses.* Straps for hawks' legs.

MY LAST DUCHESS

Ferrara, which Browning gives as the scene of this poem, is a town in North Italy, not far from Venice. It was the capital of the House of Este, who were among the most accomplished and the most cruel of the tyrants of the Italian Renascence. Symonds says in his *Age of the Despots:* 'Under the House of Este, Ferrara was famous throughout Italy for its gaiety and splendor. No city enjoyed more brilliant or more frequent public shows. Nowhere did the aristocracy retain so much feudal magnificence and chivalrous enjoyment. The square castle of red brick, which still stands in the middle of the town, was thronged with poets, players, fools who enjoyed an almost European reputation, court flatterers, knights, pages, scholars, and fair ladies. But beneath its cube of solid masonry, on a level with the moat, shut out from daylight by the sevenfold series of iron bars, lay dungeons in which the objects of the Duke's displeasure clanked chains and sighed their lives away.'

3. *Frà.* The painter, who is an imaginary character, was a monk like Fra Angelico and other Italian artists of the Renascence.

787. 45–6. There has been much discussion as to whether these two lines imply that the Duke gave orders for his wife's execution. Professor Corson put the question to Browning himself, and quotes his answer thus: '"Yes, I meant that the commands were the should be put to death." And th after a pause he added with a characteristic dash of expression, as if the thought had just started in his mind, "Or he might have had her shut up in a convent."'

56. *Claus of Innsbruck.* An imaginary artist. Innsbruck is in the Tyrol. It is famous for the bronze work on the tomb of the emperor Maximilian.

The teacher should take care that the student masters all the points in this exquisite example of the dramatic monologue, Browning's favorite art form.

COUNT GISMOND

This stirring narrative, in which Browning concentrates the heroic spirit of mediæval chivalry, tells in the very words of the heroine of the incident a straight-forward story which needs no comment; but the reader should not miss the charming equivocation with which the heroine avoids telling her husband that she has been boasting to her friend of his prowess.

INCIDENT OF THE FRENCH CAMP

Ratisbon is in Bavaria, on the right bank of the Danube. It was stormed by Napoleon in 1809, after an obstinate defence by the Austrians. Mrs. Orr says: 'The story is true; but its actual hero was a man.'

788. 1. *we French.* The story is told by a spectator.

7. *prone.* Bending or leaning forward.

11. *Lannes.* One of Napoleon's generals.

789. 29. *flag-bird.* The Napoleonic standard was a tricolor powdered with golden bees, with an eagle on the central stripe.

vans. Wings. Latin *vannus,* a fan for winnowing grain.

34–5. *film* is nominative to *sheathes.*

THE ITALIAN IN ENGLAND

Browning was proud to remember that the Italian patriot Mazzini used to read this poem to his fellow exiles in England to show how an Englishman could sympathize with them. (Mrs. Orr.)

8. *Charles.* Charles Albert, Prince of Carignano belonged to the royal house of Savoy, but was brought up among the people, and as a young man expressed sympathy with revolutionary principles. He was afterward accused of betraying Italy, and was bitterly denounced by his former friends.

19. *Metternich our friend.* Said ironically. Metternich, the Austrian statesman and diplomatist, was the most determined enemy of Italian independence.

20. See note above on Charles Albert.

41. *crypt.* Place of concealment; commonly used of a place for burial.

46. My fears were not for myself, but for my country; 'on me Rested the hopes of Italy.'

35, 75. *duomo.* (Italian) Cathedral.

75. *Tenebræ.* A service of the Roman Catholic Church, which involves the gradual extinction of the lights on the altar. The Latin word literally means 'darkness.'

81. It was not unusual for a priest to render service to the cause of Italian liberty.

790. 125-7. Charles Albert became King of Sardinia in 1831 and resigned the crown to his son, Victor Emmanuel, in 1849. He retired to Portugal, where he died in the same year, 'broken-hearted and misunderstood.' The patriot's wish as expressed by Browning was, therefore, fulfilled four years after the poem was published. Charles Albert's position was a very difficult one, and historians generally take a more favorable view of his conduct than is here given. Browning has merely given characteristic expression to the sentiment of the ardent Italian patriots of the time.

138-44. These lines forcefully represent the division of opinion in Italy during the apparently fruitless struggles for independence.

THE LOST LEADER

The suggestion for this early poem as undoubtedly Wordsworth's abandonment of the Liberal principles of his youth for the reactionary Conservatism of his old age; but it was only a suggestion. 'Once call my fancy portrait Wordsworth,' Browning wrote, 'and how much more ought one to say.' In another letter he speaks of Wordsworth's 'moral and intellectual superiority,' and protests against taking this poem as an attempt to draw his real likeness. It is really a character study from Browning's own imagination, and should be so regarded, in justice to both poets.

791. 29-30. It is best for him to fight for the side he has chosen as well as he can, to fight so well indeed as to threaten us with defeat before the hour of our final triumph. 'Then let him receive,' etc.

HOME THOUGHTS FROM ABROAD

It is interesting to contrast Browning's preference for English birds and flowers, expressed in this poem after his earlier visits to the Continent, with the love of Italy breathed in '*De Gustibus —*' p. 802, which was written after his settlement with his wife in Florence.

HOME THOUGHTS FROM THE SEA

Written off Gibraltar during Browning's first voyage to Italy in 1838.

1-7. *Cape St. Vincent, Cadiz Bay, Trafalgar* are all associated with English victories. *Gibraltar,* the famous rock-fortress which guards the entrance to the Mediterranean, has been held by Great Britain since its capture in 1704. These glorious memories inspire the poet with a sense of his duty to his country, and he mingles prayer for the future with praise for the past. *Say* is imperative 'Whoso turns, etc. . . . let him say "How can I help England?"'

SAUL

Browning found the suggestion for this, one of his finest religious poems, in the Old Testament narrative of Saul's depression and its relief by the harping of David, the shepherd boy — 1 Samuel xvi, 14-23, which the teacher would do well to read to the class in order to show how the poet has filled with life and color the mere hints of the original. Browning has read into the ancient story not only doctrines and ideas taken from the New Testament, but modern religious views and sentiments.

Abner. The son of Ner, captain of Saul's host. See 1 Samuel xxvi, 5.

792. 36-41. Professor Albert S. Cook suggests that Browning obtained his hints for these tunes from Longus's romance of *Daphnis and Chloe.* The first is found on pp. 303-4 (Smith's Translation, Bohn ed.), 'He ran through all variations of pastoral melody, he played the tune which the oxen obey, and which attracts the goats — that which the sheep delight,' etc.; pp. 332-4, '. . . . standing under the shade of a beech-tree, he took his pipe from his scrip and breathed into it very gently. The goats stood still, merely raising up their heads Next he played the pasture tune, upon which they all put down their heads and began to graze. Now he produced some notes soft and sweet in tone; at once his herd lay down. After this he piped in a sharp key, and they ran off to the wood, as if a wolf were in sight.' In answer to the question as to whether there is any historical foundation for David's songs, Rabbi Charles Fleischer of Boston replied in a letter to the editors: 'I believe that David's songs in Browning's poem *Saul* are the inspired melodies of our nineteenth century David rather than the songs of Israel's poetic shepherd-king. . . . While, then, I believe that these melodies in *Saul* were not current among the Jews of old, I know that they would serve well to express beliefs and ideals characteristic of the best minds among the Jews of to-day.'— Porter and Clarke.

45. *Jerboa.* The jumping hare.

795. 203. *Hebron* was one of the cities of refuge, but Browning evidently takes it as the name of a mountain.

204. *Kidron.* A brook near Jerusalem.

The first nine stanzas of this poem (to line 96) were published in *Dramatic Romances and Lyrics* in 1845; the later stanzas were written after his marriage, and published in *Men and Women* (1855). The latter part shows a marked advance in intensity of religious conviction, probably due to Mrs. Browning's influence. The student should note that David first played on his harp (36-60); then sang (68-190); and finally spoke (237-312). The inner structure of the poem should be carefully studied so as to bring out the gradual rise of theme from external nature to human activities and sympathies, from the glory of kingship to the glory of fame, and so to the culmination of Divine Love as manifested in the Incarnation.

LOVE AMONG THE RUINS

This poem was written when Browning was in Rome in the winter of 1853–4, and is said to have been suggested by the contrast between the present desolation of the Campagna and its former magnificence; but the scene is imaginatively treated, and cannot be identified with any place in particular. The living love, even of an obscure boy and girl, counted for more with Browning than all the dead glories of the earth.

A WOMAN'S LAST WORD

The title refers to the old proverb, ' a woman will always have the last word in a quarrel.' This ' woman's last word,' however, is not one of recrimination, but of reconciliation and submission. She will even sacrifice what she believes to be true (st. iv), lest she should lose her domestic peace as Eve lost Paradise.

A TOCCATA OF GALUPPI'S

Baldassare Galuppi (1706–85), a musical composer of some note in his day, who was for the last years of his life organist at St. Mark's Cathedral, Venice, is here taken by Browning as an exponent and critic of the frivolous, empty life with which the name of this Italian city has long been associated. But the toccata speaks to the man who plays it — a student of science — not only of the emptiness of life at Venice in the eighteenth century, but of the emptiness of life in general, for st. xiii is, of course, to be taken ironically; as he thinks of the beauty and gaiety of Venice all turned to ' dust and ashes,' he feels ' chilly and grown old,' for even so all human activities seem to pass away into nothingness.

The *toccata* is marked by the repetition of phrases calculated to display a peculiar facility of touch (It. *toccare*, to touch) on the musician's part.

799. 6. ' The ceremony of wedding the Adriatic was instituted in 1174 by Pope Alexander III, who gave the Doge a gold ring from his own finger in token of the victory achieved by the Venetian fleet at Istria over Frederick Barbarossa, in defense of the Pope's quarrel. When his Holiness gave the ring, he desired the Doge to throw a similar ring into the sea annually, in commemoration of the event.' (Brewer.)

8. *Shylock's bridge.* The Rialto.

18. *clavichord.* An old-fashioned instrument, with keys and strings, the predecessor of the modern pianoforte.

The musical technicalities made use of are thus elucidated by Porter and Clarke, *Poems of Robert Browning:* —' The technical musical allusions in the poem are all to be found in the 7th, 8th, and 9th stanzas. The *lesser thirds* (line 19) are minor thirds (intervals containing three semitones), and are of common occurrence, but the diminished sixth is an interval rarely used. Ordinarily a *diminished sixth* (seven semitones), exactly the same interval as a perfect fifth, instead of giving a plaintive, mournful, or minor impression, would suggest a feeling of rest and satisfaction. There is one way, however, in which it can be used — as a suspension, in which the root of the chord on the *lowered* supertonic of the scale is suspended from above into the chord with added seventh on the super-tonic, making a diminished sixth between the root of the first and third of the second chord. The effect of this progression is most dismal, and possibly Browning had it in mind. *Suspensions* (line 20) are notes which are held over from one chord into another, and must be made according to certain strict musical rules. This holding over of a note always produces a dissonance, and must be followed by a concord — in other words, a *solution*. Sevenths are very important dissonances in music, and a *commiserating seventh* (line 21) is most likely the variety called a minor seventh. Being a somewhat less mournful interval than the lesser thirds and the diminished sixths, whether real or imaginary, yet not so final as " those solutions " which seem to put an end to all uncertainty, and therefore to life, they arouse in the listeners to Galuppi's playing a hope that life may last, although in a sort of dissonantal, Wagnerian fashion. The " commiserating sevenths " are closely connected with the " dominant's persistence " (line 24). The dominant chord in music is the chord written on the fifth degree of the scale, and it almost always has a seventh added to it, and in a large percentage of cases is followed by the tonic, the chord on the first degree of the scale. Now, in fugue form a theme is first presented in the tonic key, then the same theme s repeated in the dominant key, the latter being called the answer; after some development of the theme the fugue comes to what is called an episode, after which the theme is presented first, in the dominant. " Hark! the dominant's persistence " alludes to this musical fact; but according to rule this dominant must be answered in the tonic an octave above the first presentation of the theme, and " So an octave struck the answer." Thus the inexorable solution comes in after the dominant's persistence. Although life seemed possible with commiserating sevenths, the tonic, a resistless fate, strikes the answer that all must end.'

MY STAR

This poem has been interpreted as having personal reference to Mrs. Browning; but there is no reason to set it apart from the other poems described by Browning as ' always dramatic in principle, and so many utterances of so many imaginary persons.'

800. 4. *angled spar.* ' A prism of Iceland spar has the property of polarizing or dividing a ray of light into two parts. Suppose this polarized ray be passed through a plate of Iceland spar, at a certain angle, and a second prism of Iceland spar be rotated in front of it, different colors will be given out, complementary tints being ninety degrees apart, and four times during the rotation the light will vanish completely. Some such experiment as this was probably in the poet's mind when he made the comparison with the angled spar.' (Porter and Clarke.)

THE LAST RIDE TOGETHER

The utter devotion of this poem is, in Browning's view, characteristic of true love.

801. 62. *Ten lines.* Of history or biography.

65. *the Abbey.* Westminster Abbey, where England's heroes are commemorated.

67-88. Cf. *In a Balcony,* 664-7: —

'We live, and they experiment on life —
Those poets, painters, all who stand aloof
To overlook the farther. Let us be
The thing they look at!'

MEMORABILIA

'Things worth remembering.' This poem is said to have been suggested to Browning by overhearing a man say in a shop that he had met and spoken to Shelley. By the metaphor of the eagle's feather, Browning conveys to the reader that if such a piece of good fortune had happened to him, it would have been enough to blot out all other incidents.

'DE GUSTIBUS'

The Latin proverb 'De gustibus non est disputandum,' corresponds to the English one 'There's no accounting for tastes.' Browning says that if our preferences persist after death, his will be, not for England, but for Italy.

802. 22. *cicala,* the tree-cricket, often heard in Italy in the heat of summer.

36. *liver-wing,* right arm. The Bourbon rule in Southern Italy was exceedingly unpopular, and numerous attempts were made to cast it off; the king here referred to was Ferdinand II, whose cruelties were denounced by Gladstone in 1851. He was succeeded by his son, who was expelled in 1860, and Naples was incorporated with the new kingdom of Italy. Browning sympathized with all the Italians' attempts to regain their liberty and independence, even when they went the length of assassination.

ANDREA DEL SARTO

This is one of the most remarkable of Browning's shorter poems, whether regarded as a study of character or of art. It was written when he was living in Florence, in answer to a request from a friend in England for a copy of the portrait of Andrea del Sarto and his wife in the Pitti Palace. Browning could not get one, and sent the poem instead. Mr. Ernest Radford thus describes the picture:—'The artist and his wife are presented at half length. Andrea turns towards her with a pleading expression on his face. . . . His right arm is round her; he leans forward as if searching her face for the strength that has gone from himself. . . . She holds the letter in her hand, and looks neither at that nor at him, but straight out of the canvas. And the beautiful face with the red-brown hair is passive and unruffled, and awfully expressionless. There is silent thunder in this face if there ever was, but there is no anger. It suggests only a very mild, and at the same time immutable determination to have her own way.'

Browning develops, in his favorite form of the dramatic monologue, the suggestion given by Andrea's portrait of himself; for the details he is chiefly indebted to Vasari's *Life of Andrea del Sarto,* as will be seen from the following extracts (translation by Blashfield and Hopkins, with Mrs. Foster's notes): —'Had this master possessed a somewhat bolder and more elevated mind, had he been as much distinguished for higher qualifications as he was for genius and depth of judgment in the art he practised, he would, beyond all doubt, have been without an equal. But there was a certain timidity of mind, a sort of diffidence and want of force in his nature, which rendered it impossible that those evidences of ardor and animation, which are proper to the more exalted character, should ever appear in him; nor did he at any time display one particle of that elevation which, could it but have been added to the advantages wherewith he was endowed, would have rendered him a truly divine painter. . . . At that time there was a most beautiful girl in the Via di San Gallo, who was married to a cap-maker, and who, though born of a poor and vicious father, carried about her as much pride and haughtiness as beauty and fascination. She delighted in trapping the hearts of men, and among others ensnared the unlucky Andrea, whose immoderate love for her soon caused him to neglect the studies demanded by his art, and in great measure to discontinue the assistance which he had given his parents. Now it chanced that a sudden and grievous illness seized the husband of this woman, who rose no more from his bed, but died thereof. Without taking counsel of his friends therefore; without regard to the dignity of his art or the consideration due to his genius, and to the eminence he had attained with so much labor; without a word, in short, to any of his kindred, Andrea took this Lucrezia di Baccio del Fede, such was the name of the woman, to be his wife; her beauty appearing to him to merit thus much at his hands, and his love for her having more influence over him than the glory and honor towards which he had begun to make such hopeful advances. But when this news became known in Florence the respect and affection which his friends had previously borne to Andrea changed to contempt and disgust, since it appeared to them that the darkness of this disgrace had obscured for a time all the glory and renown obtained by his talents. But he destroyed his own peace as well as estranged his friends by this act, seeing that he soon became jealous, and found that he had besides fallen into the hands of an artful woman, who made him do as she pleased in all things. He abandoned his own poor father and mother, for example, and adopted the father and sisters of his wife in their stead; insomuch that all who knew the facts mourned over him, and he soon began to be as much avoided as he had previously been sought after.' Andrea found this mode of life so oppressive that, on the advice of his friends, he put his wife in safe keeping and went to Paris, where he was richly rewarded by the King of France for his work. But a pitiful letter from his wife induced him to return. 'Taking the money which the king confided to him for the purchase of pictures, statues and other fine things, he set off, therefore, having first sworn on the gospels to return in a few months. Arrived happily in Florence, he lived joyously with his wife for some time, making large presents to her father and sisters, but doing nothing for his own parents, whom he would not even see, and who, at the end of a certain period, ended their lives in great poverty and misery.' Having spent the money entrusted to him in building a house and indulging himself in various other pleasures, Andrea was afraid to return to France, and remained in Florence in the very lowest position, ' procuring a livelihood and passing his time as he best might.'

So says Vasari, who at one time was Andrea's pupil, and published his *Lives of the Painters* while Andrea's widow was still in Florence; but recent investigation has failed to reveal the slightest evidence in support of the charge of embezzlement made by Vasari against Andrea, and it has been generaly discredited.

803. 15. *Fiesolé.* The village on the top of the ridge overlooking the quarter of Florence in which Andrea lived.

25. *It saves a model.* ' Andrea rarely painted the countenance of a woman in any place that he did not avail himself of the features of his wife; and if at any time he took his model from any other face there was always a resemblance to hers in the painting, not only because he had this woman constantly before him and depicted her so frequently but also and what is still more, because he had her lineaments engraven on his heart; it thus happens that almost all his female heads have a certain something which recalls that of his wife.' (Vasari.)

32. *no one's.* Not even his.

36–45. Lucrezia has lost only her first pride in her husband; he has lost all his youthful ambitions and aspirations, as the day loses its noontide splendor, and the glory of summer changes to the decay of autumn.

43. *huddled more inside.* The trees are huddled together within the convent wall, and have no room to grow; but they are, perhaps, safer — so, perhaps, too, is the painter in his own home, though he misses the inspiration and development that come from contact with the world. Andrea acquiesces in his seclusion, but he cannot help regretting his lost opportunities.

93. *Morello.* A mountain near Florence.

804. 105. *the Urbinate.* Raphael of Urbino, the most famous of Italian painters; he died in ten years before Andrea. Vasari says that copied a portrait by Raphael with such exactness that Raphael's own pupils, who had helped in the painting, could not tell the copy from the original.

130. *Agnolo.* The great Italian painter usually called Michael Angelo in English; he was doubtless the ' Someone ' of line 76; Andrea refers to him again in line 184.

150. *Fontainebleau.* A royal palace not far from Paris.

166. See quotation from Vasari above for Andrea's recall from France by his wife's importunities.

173. *there.* In your heart.

174. *ere the triumph.* Of my genius in art.

805. 189–193. Pecchi, in his *Beauties of Florence,* states that Michael Angelo said to Raphael, referring to Andrea: — ' There is a little man in Florence, who, if he were employed upon such great works as have been given to you, would bring the sweat to your brow.'

199. Lucrezia has interrupted to ask Andrea about whom and what he is talking. She is evidently paying no attention.

209–10. Mount Morello can no longer be seen, the lights on the city wall are lit, and the little owls, named in Italy from their call, *Chiu,* are crying; darkness is falling on the house, as on Andrea's life.

212–18. See above for the charge against Andrea of building a house for himself with the money entrusted to him by King Francis to buy pictures with.

220. The cousin (or lover) who waits outside is the third character in the little drama — silent and unseen, but profoundly affecting the situation.

806. 263. *Leonard.* Leonardo da Vinci, the third great Italian painter of the time; he died the year before Raphael.

266. Andrea at last acknowledges to himself that his wife has been a hindrance instead of a help a drag preventing his ascent from the second rank to the first: but he prefers this to the sacrifice of giving her up.

THE GUARDIAN ANGEL

In the Church of St. Augustine at Fano, on the Adriatic, there is a picture called ' The Guardian Angel,' by Guercino, an Italian painter of the seventeenth century. It presents an angel with outspread wings embracing a kneeling child, whose hands he folds in prayer.

6. *another child.* The poet himself.

7. *retrieve.* Bring back to the right way.

14–16. In the picture cherubs point to the opened heaven, and the child looks upward past the angel's head.

18. *bird of God.* This beautiful expression is translated from Dante's *Purgatorio.*

20–21. The angel seems to be enfolding the child with the skirt of his robe, held in his left hand.

39–40. The angel's head is turned away, but the reason given is Browning's own.

46. *My angel with me, too.* His wife. See line 54.

807. 54. *dear old friend.* Alfred Domett, a much-prized friend of Browning's youth, who in 1842 settled in New Zealand.

55. *Ancona.* On the Italian coast, near Fano. Browning and his wife visited both places soon after their first settlement in Italy in 1846, and the poem was doubtless written at the time. Mrs. Browning writes of the visit to her friend, Miss Mitford: — "So we went to Ancona — a striking sea city, holding up against the brown rocks, and elbowing out the purple tides — beautiful to look upon. An exfoliation of the rock itself you would call the houses that seem to grow there — so identical is the color and character."

A GRAMMARIAN'S FUNERAL

This poem 'exhibits something of the life of the Scaligers and the Casaubons, of many an early scholar, like Roger Bacon's friend Pierre Maricourt, working at some region of knowledge, and content to labor without fame so long as he mastered thoroughly whatever he undertook.' (*Contemporary Review*, IV, 135.)

The scholars are bearing their master to his tomb in one of the Italian hill-cities, perched on the top of the rocks, like Orvieto or Perugia.

3. *croft*. Enclosed tilled or pasture land. *thorpe*. Little village.

34. *Apollo*. The classical ideal of manly beauty. His statues usually represent him holding the lyre.

39. *Moaned he*. Did he moan?

45. *the world*. Of classical lore, which was bent on escaping.

56. *the curtain*. Of the play of life.

68. *Sooner*. Before he had gathered all books had to give.

808. 86. *Calculus*. The stone.

88. *Tussis*. Cough.

95. *soul-hydroptic*. 'Every lust is a kind of hydropic distemper, and the more we drink the more we shall thirst.' (Tillotson, quoted by Webster.) *hydroptic,* dropsical.

96–100. Cf. *Abt Vogler*, l. 72, p. 812.

113–124. Cf. *Rabbi ben Ezra*, stanzas xxiii-xxv, p. 815.

129–131. *Hoti*, . . . *Oun*, . . . *De*. Greek particles, meaning respectively 'that,' 'therefore,' 'towards.' As to the last, Browning wrote to the editor of the *London Daily News* on Nov. 20, 1874, as follows:—'In a clever article you speak of "the doctrine of the enclitic *De*"—"which with all deference to Mr. Browning, in point of fact, does not exist." No, not to Mr. Browning: but pray defer to Herr Buttmann, whose fifth list of "enclitics" ends "with the inseparable *De*"—or to Curtius, whose fifth list ends also with "*De* (meaning 'towards,* and as a demonstrative appendage)." That this is not to be confounded with the accentuated "*De*, meaning but," was the "Doctrine" which the Grammarian bequeathed to those capable of receiving it.'

ONE WORD MORE

A special interest attaches to this poem because it is the only one addressed by Browning, directly and avowedly, to his wife, Elizabeth Barrett Browning. It was originally appended to the collection of poems, called *Men and Women* (1855). Browning uses the sonnets written by Raphael and a portrait painted by Dante to illustrate the desire of the artist to show his personal affection in some other way than that of his familiar craft, which has become professional and belongs to the world, so that everybody feels entitled to criticize. But as the poet cannot paint pictures, or carve statues, or make music to show his love, a semblance of resource remains in the use of a slightly different form of art from that which he commonly practises. Instead of writing dramatically, he may write, for once in his own person; for just as, according to the ancient myth,

the moon would turn to her lover a side unseen by other mortals, so the poet has two soul-sides, 'one to face the world with, One to show a woman when he loves her.' While he says this of himself, he likes to think it of her, his 'moon of poets.' Her poetry is the world's side, and he too admires her from that point of view; but the best is when he leaves the standpoint of literary appreciation for the more intimate relation of personal knowledge and affection. Then it is that he realizes the love that Raphael sought to express by his sonnets and Dante by his picture.

5. *a century of sonnets*. Guido Reni had a book of 100 drawings of Raphael's, but Raphael is only known to have made four sonnets. Raphael never married, but he was very much in love with a certain lady, who has been identified, not very convincingly, with the original of one or other of the portraits attributed to his hand.

809. 22–24. The Sistine Madonna is now in the Dresden Art Gallery, the Madonna di Foligno is in the Vatican at Rome. 'The Madonna at Florence is that called del Granduca, which represents her as "appearing to a votary in a vision"—so say the describers; it is in the earlier manner, and very beautiful. I think I meant La Belle Jardinière—but am not sure—for the picture in the Louvre. (Browning to W. J. Rolfe.) The Louvre Madonna is seated in the midst of a garden, in which there are lilies. All these are among the most famous works of Raphael.

27. *Guido Reni*. A celebrated Italian painter about a century later than Raphael. See note on line 5.

32. *Dante*. The first great Italian poet (1265–1321), who in *The Divine Comedy* attached eternal opprobrium to his enemies by assigning to them conspicuous places in Hell. Stanzas v, vi, and vii refer to a passage in his *Vita Nuova*, in which he has idealized his love for Beatrice, whom he had known as a young girl:—'On that day which fulfilled the year since my lady had been made of the citizens of eternal life; remembering me of her as I sat alone, I betook myself to draw the resemblance of an angel upon certain tablets. And while I did thus, chancing to turn my head, I perceived that some were standing beside me to whom I should have given courteous welcome, and that they were observing what I did: also I learned afterwards that they had been there a while before I perceived them. Perceiving whom, I rose for salutation and said: "Another was with me." Afterwards, when they had left me, I set myself again to the same occupation, to wit, the drawing figures of angels.' (Section 35, Rossetti's translation.) It will be noticed that Browning's interpretation of the incident goes somewhat beyond the original, which gives no indication that those who interrupted Dante were people he scarified in the *Inferno*.

33. *Beatrice*. Four syllables — *ba ah tre' tshe*.

57. *Bice*. Two syllables — *be' tshe*. A contraction of endearment of Beatrice.

74–93. There are two accounts in the Pentateuch of the smiting of the rock by Moses.— Exodus xvii, 1–7, and Numbers xx, 2–64. The latter reads:

'And Moses and Aaron gathered the congregation together before the rock, and he said unto them, Hear now, ye rebels; must we fetch you water out of this rock? . . . And the Lord spake unto Moses and Aaron, Because ye believed me not, to sanctify me in the eyes of the children of Israel, therefore ye shall not bring this congregation into the land which I have given them.' Here, again, Browning has allowed his imagination to play round the original record.

810. 94–5. When the children of Israel were rebellious against Moses, they cried, 'Would to God we had died by the hand of the Lord in the land of Egypt, when we sat by the flesh pots' (Exodus xvi, 3).

97. Exodus xxxiv, 29–35. *cloven*, because, following the Latin translation of this passage, the early painters represented Moses with two horns on his forehead. The original means to shine out or dart forth like rays of light.

101–2. Moses married Zipporah, Jethro's daughter (Exodus ii, 16–21), and an Ethiopian woman (Numbers xii, 1).

121. *fresco*. Painting in fresh plaster, usually done on the inside wall of a church.

125. *missal-marge*. The margin of a prayer book.

136–8. *Karshish, Cleon, Norbert, Lippo, Roland* and *Andrea* were among the characters in *Men and Women*, originally fifty in number.

143. *how I speak*. The personal instead of the dramatic mode of expression.

145. *Here in London*. The poem was written in London in September, 1855.

150. *Samminiato*. The common pronunciation of San Miniato, an old church, surrounded by cypress trees, overlooking Florence.

160. *mythos*. The old myth or story of the love of Diana, the moon-goddess, for the mortal Endymion.

163. *Zoroaster* (589–513 B.C.), founder of the Persian religion and a famous astronomer.

164. *Galileo* (1564–1642). Professor at Padua, and one of the founders of modern science. After being condemned by the church, he continued his studies in his house at Florence, which overlooks the city from the same side as San Miniato.

165. *Homer*. In allusion to the *Hymn to the Moon*.

Keats. The author of *Endymion*. Browning expressed special admiration for him in the poem entitled *Popularity*.

811. 172–9. Exodus xxiv, 9–11: 'Then went up Moses and Aaron, Nadab and Abihu, and seventy of the elders of Israel: And they saw the God of Israel: and there was under his feet as it were a paved work of a sapphire stone, and as it were the body of heaven in his clearness . . . also they saw God, and did eat and drink.'

ABT VOGLER

George Joseph Vogler (1749–1814), the priest-musician, composer, and teacher of Weber and Meyerbeer, was especially celebrated as an improviser, and traveled all over Europe giving performances on his orchestrion.

7. *Name*, Jehovah, used by Solomon as a talisman, according to oriental tradition.

22. *festal night*. Easter at St. Peter's, Rome.

812. 32. *no more near nor far*. 'Music frees us from the phenomena of time and space.'

34. *Protoplast*. 'The thing first formed as a model to be imitated.' The *presences* are either of the future or of the past.

70. *The evil is null*. The teaching of Spinoza, Hegel, and Emerson, as well as of the Kabbalists, founded on that of the Gnostics and Neo-Platonists.

813. 91. *the common chord* 'consists of the fundamental, with a major (four semitones), or minor (three semitones) third, and a perfect fifth (seven semitones) over it.'

93. *a ninth* 'if major, contains an octave and two semitones; if minor, an octave and one semitone. These last lines of the poem, stripped of their symbolic meaning, may be taken as an exact explanation of a simple harmonic modulation.' (Porter and Clarke.)

RABBI BEN EZRA

Ibn Ezra, or Abenezra (1092–1167), was a great Jewish scholar, poet, philosopher, and physician, who wandered over Europe, Asia, and Africa in pursuit of knowledge. As will be seen from the notes, his writings contain some of the views expressed by Browning's sage.

1. The Rabbi seems to be at the end of middle age, just where old age begins. He looks back to youth, forward to old age.

4. A poem of Abenezra's, quoted by Dr. Michael Sachs, has the same thought: 'In deiner Hand liegt mein Geschick.'

Stanzas ii and iii should be taken together. The sense is: 'I do not remonstrate because youth, amassing flowers, sighed . . .' He does not find fault with the foolish ambitions of his youth, for these aspirations, though they are vain, are what distinguish man from the beasts. This thought is expressed by Abenezra in his Commentary on Job xxxv, 11: 'Man has the sole privilege of becoming superior to the beast and the fowl.'

25–30. Stanza v expresses a favorite thought of Browning's. Cf. *A Death in the Desert*, 576–8: —

Progress, man's distinctive mark alone,
Not God's and not the beasts': God is, they are,
Man partly is and wholly hopes to be.

40–42. Cf. *Saul*, lines 160 and 295.

814. 48. *soul on its lone way*. 'The soul of man is called lonely because it is separated during its union with the body from the universal soul.' (Abenezra's Commentary on Psalm xxii, 22.)

57. Cf. *Saul*, line 242.

815. 151. *Potter's wheel*. Cf. Isaiah lxiv, 8: 'We are the clay and thou our Potter.' This is a favorite scriptural and oriental metaphor, used also by Quarles and in Fitzgerald's translation of the *Rubaiyat* of Omar Khayyam, but by no previous poet with such deep significance as here.

PROSPICE

'Look forward.' This noble defiance of death was written in the autumn after Browning lost his wife, and appeared first in the *Atlantic Monthly* for June, 1864.

816. 19. *life's arrears.* All the pain that a man might fairly have expected to suffer in life, but missed.

23. *fiend-voices.* The ancient belief was that the soul at the moment of separation from the body is the object of a struggle between the angels, whose office is to bear away the freed spirit (Luke xvi, 22) and the powers of darkness who strive to snatch it from salvation. For this reason fervent prayers are offered for a soul on the point of departure.

27–28. Browning had a strong faith in immortality, and repeatedly expressed it in both prose and verse. He said: 'I know I shall meet my dearest friends again.'

HERVÉ RIEL

Browning was in France when it was invaded by Prussia in 1870, and escaped from the country with some difficulty before the outbreak of the disorders which followed the collapse of the French resistance. Desiring to express his sympathy for the sufferers by the siege of Paris, he sold this poem to *Cornhill Magazine* for £100, which he gave as a subscription to the Relief Fund. It was written in 1867 and first published in 1871. The incident it relates was first denied in France, but the records of the admiralty of the time proved that Browning was correct, except in one small detail: the reward Hervé Riel asked and received was '*un congé absolu*'— a holiday for the rest of his life.

1. *the Hogue.* Cap La Hogue, where the French fleet was attacked in 1692 by the English and Dutch, and forced to retire. The expedition aimed at the restoration of James II, who watched the defeat from the Norman coast.

5. *St. Malo,* at the mouth of the Rance River, in Brittany, has a harbor which is described as 'safe, but difficult of approach.' In the sixteenth and seventeenth centuries it was a flourishing port, and from it Jacques Cartier sailed in 1535 to explore the River St. Lawrence. *the Rance.* A small stream with picturesque steep banks. The town is situated on a rock between the harbor and the mouth of the river.

18. *twelve and eighty.* French, quatre-vingt-douze.

817. 30. *Plymouth Sound.* In the West of England, an important harbor and naval station.

43. *pressed.* Forced to serve.

Tourville. The French admiral.

44. *Croisickese.* Of Croisic, a little fishing village of Brittany, where Browning liked to stay. See the title of the next poem in this selection. It was no doubt at Croisic that Browning picked up the story.

46. *Malouins.* Men of St. Malo.

49. *Grève.* La Grande Grève, the sandy shallows of the coast about St. Malo, especially to the east.

53. *Solidor.* A small harbor near the mouth of the Rance, beside the town of St. Servan. A fort of the same name defends it.

75. *profound* (here used as a noun). Depths.

92. *rampired.* Protected by ramparts or fortifications.

95. *for.* Instead of.

818. 135. *the Louvre.* A famous palace at Paris, now used as an art museum. On its external walls there are eighty-six statues of notable Frenchmen, but not, of course, one of the forgotten hero, Hervé Riel.

THE TWO POETS OF CROISIC

The Prologue and the Epilogue are connected with the main poem (which is here omitted) only by the thought, common to all three, that love is a necessary part of the poet's life and art. The Prologue may cause a little difficulty to begin with by its extraordinary conciseness, but this only adds to its charm when the meaning has been grasped. The grammatical construction and the relation of the stanzas to each other are indicated in the following prose rendering: 'As a bank of moss stands bare till some May morning it is made beautiful by the sudden growth of the violets; as the night sky is dark and louring till a bright star pierces the concealing clouds; so the world seemed to him in my life with disgrace till your face appeared to brighten it with the smile of God — the divine gift of love.'

In the Epilogue it is a young girl who repeats to the poet the 'pretty tale' he has once told her, and makes her own application of its significance. The story is found in Greek literature both in prose and in verse.

819. 50. Here, as in lines 15 and 21, the poet has attempted to interrupt.

77. *Lotte.* The pet name of Charlotte Buff, upon whom Goethe modelled the heroine of *The Sorrows of Young Werther.* The reference here, however, is rather to Goethe's way of treating women in general than to the particular case of Lotte, for she was already engaged to be married when he met her.

100–2. The sweet lilt of the treble was supplied by the chirping of the cricket, when its absence would have allowed the predominance of the sombre bass. Cf. lines 112–4.

120. (*There, enough!*) To what interruption of the poet's does this reply?

PHEIDIPPIDES

This is Browning's romantic setting of an incident of the Persian war which is thus recounted by the Greek historian Herodotus (VI, 105. Rawlinson's translation): —

'And first, before they left Athens, the generals sent off to Sparta a herald, one Pheidip'pides, who was by birth an Athenian, and by birth and practice a trained runner. This man, according to the account which he gave to the Athenians on his return, when he was near Mount Parthenium, above Tegea, fell in with the god Pan, who called him by his name, and bade him ask the Athenians 'wherefore they neglected him so entirely, when he was kindly disposed towards them, and had often helped them in times past, and would do so again in time to come?' The Athenians, entirely believing in the truth of this report, as soon as their affairs were once more in good order, set up a temple to Pan under the Acropolis, and, in return for the message which I have recorded, established in his honor yearly sacrifices and a torch-race.

'On the occasion of which we speak, when Pheidippides was sent by the Athenian generals, and, according to his own account saw Pan on his journey, he reached Sparta on the very next day after quitting the city of Athens. Upon his arrival he went before the rulers, and said to them:—

'"Men of Lacedæmon, the Athenians beseech you to hasten to their aid, and not allow that state, which is the most ancient in all Greece, to be enslaved by the barbarians. Eretria, look you, is already carried away captive, and Greece weakened by the loss of no mean city."

'Thus did Pheidippides deliver the message committed to him. And the Spartans wished to help the Athenians, but were unable to give them any present succor, as they did not like to break their established law. It was the ninth day of the first decade, and they could not march out of Sparta on the ninth, when the moon had not reached the full. So they waited for the full of the moon.'

It will be seen that the original story makes no mention of a reward promised by Pan to Pheidippides. This was Browning's own invention, following a later tradition. In connection with the Marathon race at the Olympic games this was the subject of a considerable discussion, to which Professor Ernest A. Gardner contributed the following note as to Pheidippides: 'His great exploit, as recorded by Herodotus, was to run from Athens to Sparta within two days, for the practical purpose of summoning the Spartans to help against the Persian invader. The whole Athenian army made a forced march back to Athens immediately after the battle, also for a practical purpose; but there is no reason to suppose that Pheidippides or any one else ran the distance. The tale of his bearing the message of victory and falling dead when he arrived is probably an invention of some later rhetorician; it is referred to by Lucian, as well as by Robert Browning, but the two authorities are about of equal value for an occurrence of the fifth century B. C. It is most unlikely that Herodotus would have omitted such a story if it had been current in his time.'

χαίρετε, νικῶμεν, the Greek words prefixed by Browning to the poem, form the message which Plutarch and Lucian attribute to the dying runner after Marathon. Browning translates them 'Rejice; we conquer!' and in lines 113–114 makes effective use of the fact that χαίρετε ('Hail!' or be of good cheer!') was also the customary form of salutation with the Greeks. Here again he was indebted to a suggestion derived from Lucian.

820. 4. *Her of the ægis and spear.* Athene. *ægis,* shield.

5. *ye of the bow and the buskin.* Apollo and Artemis. *buskin,* laced boot.

9. *Archons.* Rulers or magistrates. *tettix.* The golden grasshopper worn by Athenians to show that they were autochthons (natives of the country).

11. *Crowned with the myrtle.* This still refers to *Archons.* Browning is strictly accurate in these points of detail.

18. *water and earth.* The emblems of subjection. This demand was made in 493 B. C. The invading Persians were defeated at Marathon three years later.

19. *Eretria.* The chief city of the island of Eubœa, a little north of Athens.

20. *Hellas.* Greek civilization regarded as a whole.

25–40. Herodotus, as quoted above, says: 'So they waited for the full of the moon.' Grote ascribes the delay of the Spartans to conservatism, Rawlinson to envy; there was long-standing jealousy between Athens and Sparta, who were rivals for the leadership of Hellas. Sparta later sent 2,000 men, who arrived after the battle.

32–33. *Phoibos. Olumpos.* Browning preferred to retain the Greek spelling instead of the Latinized forms 'Phœbus' and 'Olympus.'

47. *filleted.* Adorned for sacrifice with wreaths and ribbons.

821. 52. *Parnes.* In North Attica. But according to Herodotus as quoted above, Pan appeared to Pheidippides near Mount Parthenium in Argolis. This would be on his way from Athens to Sparta: Parnes would not. Professor John Macnaughton suggests that Browning made the change deliberately. 'He must have an Attic hill at all costs, when what he wants to say is that it is the spirit of her own mountains, her own autochthonous vigor, which is going to save Athens. He consciously sacrifices, in a small and obvious point, literal accuracy to the larger truth.' (*Queen's Quarterly,* April, 1903.)

62. *Erebos.* The darkness under the earth — Erebus.

72–80. After Marathon, the Athenians built a temple to Pan and established yearly sacrifices and a torch-race in acknowledgment of the help the god had given them in the battle by affecting the Persians with 'panic'— the headlong fear Pan was supposed to inspire.

83. *Fennel.* Marathon, the name of the place where the battle was fought, is also Greek for fennel. This touch is Browning's own.

87. *on the razor's edge.* In a critical position — a proverbial phrase in Greek.

89. *Miltiades.* The leading Athenian citizen of the time and commander of the forces at Marathon.

822. 106. *Akropolis.* The citadel of Athens.

109. *the Fennel-field.* Marathon. See note on line 83.

Pheidippides is in a measure of Browning's own, composed of dactyls and spondees, each line ending in a half foot or pause. It gives the impression of firm, continuous, and rhythmic emotion, and is generally fitted to convey the exalted sentiment and heroic character of the poem. (Mrs. Orr.)

The metrical scheme should be carefully analysed. Dr. D. G. Brunton uses this poem as an illustration of Browning's employment of rime 'merely as a means of heightening his secondary rhythm. The riming words are so far apart that we are aware

only of a faint melodious echo. The always artificial and somewhat mechanical effect of rime is
thus avoided, while its rhythmic essence is retained.'

EPILOGUE TO ASOLANDO

We have given at the foot of each poem the date
of its publication, and the volume to which this
little poem is the Epilogue bears the date 1890;
it was actually issued in London on Dec. 12, 1889,
the day of Browning's death at Venice. 'The report of his illness had quickened public interest in
the forthcoming work, and his son had the satisfaction of telling him of its already realized success,
while he could still receive a warm, if momentary
pleasure from the intelligence.' (Mrs. Orr.)
Browning prepared the volume for publication while
staying in the Asolo villa of his friend Mrs. Arthur
Bronson, to whom it is dedicated. The fanciful
title is derived from the Italian verb *asolare* — ' to
disport in the open air, amuse one's self at random '
— popularly ascribed, Browning tells us, to Cardinal
Bembo, who was Queen Cornaro's secretary, and
in his dialogue, *Gli Asolani*, described the discussions on platonic love and kindred subjects the little court at Asolo used to indulge in. To Mrs.
Bronson Browning justified the title in the following sentence: ' I use it for love of the place and
in requital of your pleasant assurance that an early
poem of mine first attracted you thither.' This was,
no doubt, *Pippa Passes*.

The Epilogue is a final expression of Browning's
profound belief in a future life of hopeful activity.
When reading the poem in proof, he said of the
third stanza: —' It almost looks like bragging to say
this, and as if I ought to cancel it, but it's the
simple truth; and as it's true, it shall stand.'

As in life he had faith in right, so in death —
which only fools think of as a prison of the soul —
he would be, not pitied, but encouraged by the good
wishes of those who are working in the world.

17. *the unseen.* The poet himself after death.

ARNOLD: THE STUDY OF POETRY

This essay was published as the *Introduction* to
The English Poets, edited by T. H. Ward, London,
1880.

823. *b.* 1. *these words of my own,* quoted — not
quite exactly — from Arnold's introduction to *The
Hundred Greatest Men*, Vol. I, London, 1879.

5. *In the present work,* in *The English Poets*,
edited by Ward.

824. *a.* 11, 15. *Wordsworth . . . Again Wordsworth.* These two quotations are taken from the
Preface to the Second edition of *Lyrical Ballads*,
1800.

38. *Sainte-Beuve,* Charles Augustin Sainte-Beuve
(1804–1869), an eminent French critic.

825. *a.* 48. *Pellisson,* Paul Pellisson (1624–1693), a
French man of letters and politician.

56. *Charles d' Héricault* (born 1823), French historian, novelist, and editor.

57. *Clément Marot,* a noted French poet (1497–
1544).

826. *a.* 13. *Methuselah,* see Genesis v, 25–27.

b. 8. *the Imitation, The Imitation of Christ,*
a religious treatise commonly ascribed to Thomas à
Kempis (1380–1471). The passage quoted is found
in Bk. iii, Ch. 43, § 2.

28. *Cædmon,* an Anglo-Saxon poet who is said to
have flourished about the year 670. The Biblical
paraphrases long ascribed to Cædmon are now regarded as of uncertain authorship.

33. *M. Vitet,* a French critic and politician (1802–
1873).

35. *Chanson de Roland,* the oldest French national epic, written, probably, during the closing
years of the 11th century.

37. *joculator or jongleur,* well enough understood
by our English word *minstrel*.

39. *Hastings,* battle of Hastings, in 1066

43. *Roncevaux,* a pass in the Pyrenees, in Spain,
notable as the scene of the events recounted in the
Chanson de Roland.

44. *Turoldus or Théroulde.* The last line of the
Chanson in the Oxford manuscript may be translated, ' Here ends the geste that *Turoldus* tells.'
Turoldus may be the name of the minstrel who
sang or recited the poem rather than that of the
poet who composed it.

827. *b.* 27. *Dante,* Dante Alighieri (1265–1321),
the greatest of Italian poets. His great work, *The
Divine Comedy*, consisted of three parts: *Hell,
Purgatory,* and *Paradise*. Ugolino, Ugolino della
Gherardesca (d. 1289), a partisan leader in Pisa.
With his two sons and two nephews he was starved
to death in prison.

32. *Beatrice to Virgil.* According to *The Divine Comedy*, Virgil guided Dante through Hell
and Purgatory. In Paradise, Beatrice became
Dante's guide.

44. *Henry the Fourth's expostulation,* 2 *Henry
IV*, Act iii, Scene 1.

828. *a.* 6. *Hamlet's dying request.* In the closing
scene of the play.

14. *that Miltonic passage, Paradise Lost,* I, 599–
602.

17. *intrenched,* cut, furrowed.

21. *two such lines, Paradise Lost,* I, 108–9.

27. *exquisite close, Paradise Lost,* IV. 271–2.

829. *a.* 53. *Southey,* Robert Southey (1774–1843),
an English poet and prose-writer.

b. 7. *Brunetto Latini* (1230–1294), an Italian
poet, scholar, and orator. His chief work is an en-
cyclopedia, *Trésor* (Treasure), in French.

13. *Christian of Troyes.* The passage here quoted
is from *Cligès*, lines 30–39.

48. *that stanza.* To which of the Chaucerian
stanzas Arnold refers we cannot be certain. In
the matter of stanza forms Chaucer borrowed much
from France, and practically nothing at all from
Italy.

54. *Wolfram of Eschenbach,* a German poet (ff.
c. 1200).

830. *a.* 30. *Dryden's.* Quoted from the *Preface
to the Fables*. See edition of Scott and Saintsbury,
Vol. XI, p. 230.

49. *Gower,* John Gower (1325?–1408), an English poet.

b. 40. *worship,* honor.

41. *O Alma,* the beginning of a hymn to the Virgin.

831. *b.* 12. *Villon,* François Villon (1431–1484?), a French poet of irregular life.

832. *a.* 20. *Cowley,* Abraham Cowley (1618–1667), an English poet. See p. 183.

21–8. *Dryden . . . there . . . perfect.* See *Preface to the Fables,* edition of Scott and Saintsbury, Vol. XI, p. 224.

b. 10. *Chapman,* George Chapman 1559?–1634), an English poet and dramatist, best known for his translation of Homer.

14. *Gades,* a Phenician colony on the spot where Cadiz now stands, on the western coast of Spain. *Aurora,* the dawn, the East.

15. *Ganges,* the sacred river of India.

21. *Milton writing.* See Milton's *An Apology for Smectymnuus,* Prose Works (ed. Bohn), Vol. III, pp. 117–118.

29. *Dryden telling us.* See the *Postscript to the Reader* appended to Dryden's translation of the Æneid.

41. *Restoration,* the reëstablishment of the English monarchy with the return of Charles II in 1660.

833. *a.* 30–31. *A milk-white Hind . . . ranged,* the opening lines of *The Hind and the Panther.*

40–44. *To Hounslow Heath . . . my own, Second Satire,* lines 143–4.

b. 23. *Gray.* See p. 396.

834. *a.* 1. *Mark ruffian Violence,* etc., from *On the Death of Robert Dundas, Esq.*

12. *Clarinda's love-poet Sylvander.* Over the name Sylvander, Burns carried on a correspondence with Mrs. Maclehose, whom he called Clarinda.

15. *gravel,* pave.

b. 5. *Leeze me on,* dear to me is. The quotation is from *The Holy Fair. gies,* gives. *mair,* more.

7. *waukens lair,* wakes learning.

8. *pangs,* crams, stuffs. *fou,* full.

9. *gill,* a pint of ale. *penny wheep,* small ale.

12. *kittle,* tickle, enliven.

33. *aboon,* above.

34. *mauna fa',* may not get.

43. *falls moralizing.* See *Epistle to a Young Friend.*

45. *lowe,* flame.

47. *rove,* roving.

50. *quantum,* quantity.

56. *Who made,* etc., from *Address to the Unco Guid.*

835. *a.* 11. *To make,* etc., from *To Dr. Blacklock.*

12. *weans,* children.

20–22. *Xenophon . . . Socrates.* In his *Memorabilia,* the Greek historian and essayist, Xenophon (born about 430, died after 357 B.C.), defends the memory of his master Socrates.

b. 27. *Thou Power Supreme,* etc., from *Winter.*

32. *lave,* remainder.

836. *a.* 6. *Auerbach's Cellar of Goethe's Faust.* Johann Wolfgang von Goethe (1749–1832) is the greatest name in German literature. The scene in

Auerbach's Cellar is to be found near the beginning of the First Part of *Faust.*

9. *Aristophanes* (c. 450–c. 380 B.C.), the greatest of the Greek writers of comedy.

36. *We twa,* etc., from *Auld Lang Syne. paidl'i,* paddled. *burn,* stream, brook.

37. *dine,* dinner-time.

38. *braid,* broad.

39. *Sin auld lang syne,* since old times.

52. *Pinnacled . . . inane,* Shelley's *Prometheus Unbound,* Act III, Sc. iv, l. 204.

b. 1. *On the brink,* etc., from Shelley's *Prometheus Unbound,* Act II, Sc. v.

10. *minnie,* mother. *deave,* pester.

SOHRAB AND RUSTRUM

840. 2. *Oxus,* the chief river of central Asia, flowing northwest into the Aral Sea.

3. *Tartar camp.* The Tartars were nomadic tribes of central Asia and southern Russia.

841. 11. *Peran-Wisa,* a chief of central Asia, in command of Afrasiab's army of various Tartar tribes.

15. *Pamere,* a plateau region of central Asia.

38. *Afrasiab,* king of the Tartars.

40. *Samarcand,* a city in Turkestan.

42. *Ader-baijan,* the northwest province of Persia.

60. *common fight,* general engagement.

82. *Seistan,* a province of southwest Afghanistan bordering on Persian territory.

85. *Persian King,* Kai Khosroo. See line 223.

842. 101. *Kara-Kul,* a district in the southern part of central Asia.

107. *Haman,* a leader of the Tartars, next to Peran-Wisa in command.

113. *Casbin,* a fortified city in the northern part of Persia.

114. *Elburz,* mountains on the northern border of Persia. *Aralian,* on the Aral Sea, in central Asia.

115. *frore,* frozen.

119. *Bokhara,* a large district in central Asia, of which Bokhara, is the capital.

120. *Khiva,* a district in the valley of the lower Oxus.

121. *Toorkmuns,* a branch of the Turkish race, living in central Asia, east of the Caspian Set.

122. *Tukas,* from northwest Persia. *Salore,* a tribe living east of the Caspian Sea.

123. *Attruck,* a river in northern Persia.

128. *Ferghana,* a district in Turkestan.

129. *Jaxartes,* an ancient name of the Sir-Daria River, which flows northwest through Turkestan into the Aral Sea.

131. *Kipchak,* a district in central Asia.

132. *Kalmucks,* Mongolian nomads dwelling in western Siberia.

Kuzzaks, Cossacks, a warlike people in southern Russia and in various parts of Asia.

133. *Kirghizzes,* a nomadic people in northern Turkestan.

138. *Ilyats of Khorassan.* Khorassan is a province in northeastern Persia.

156. *corn,* grain.

160. *Cabool,* an important commercial city of northern Afghanistan.

161. *Indian Caucasus,* a range of mountains on the boundary between Turkestan and Afghanistan.

843. 217. *Iran's,* Persia's.

844. 257. *plain arms,* arms not emblazoned with devices. See line 266.

277. *Dight,* adorned, harnessed.

286. *Bahrein,* or Aval Islands, in the Persian Gulf, celebrated for their pearl-fisheries.

288. *tale,* reckoning, count.

846. 412. *Hyphasis, Hydaspes,* two rivers in northern India.

414. *wrack,* ruin.

847. 452. *autumn-star,* Sirius, the Dog Star.

497. *shore,* cut.

508. *curdled,* thickened.

848. 590. *Ader-baijan.* See l. 42.

592. *Koords,* a semi-independent people of western Persia.

596. *bruited up,* noised abroad.

849. 613. *style,* name.

851. 750. *Seistan.* See l. 82.

751. *Helmund,* a river in Seistan, in Afghanistan.

752. *Zirrah,* a lake in Seistan.

763-4. *Moorghab, Tejend, Hohik,* rivers in Turkestan.

765. *The northern Sir,* the Maxartes. See l. 129.

852. 861. *Jemshid,* a mythical king. *Persepolis,* an ancient capital of Persia.

878. *Chorasmian waste,* a region of Turkestan.

880. *Right . . . star,* i.e., due north. *Orgunje,* a village near the delta of the Oxus.

887. *Pamere.* See l. 15.

890. *luminous home,* the Aral Sea.

THE SCHOLAR GIPSY

'There was very lately a lad in the University of Oxford who was by his poverty forced to leave his studies there and at last to join himself to a company of vagabond gipsies. Among these extravagant people, by the insinuating subtilty of his carriage, he quickly got so much of their love and esteem that they discovered to him their mystery. After he had been a pretty while exercized in the trade, there chanced to ride by a couple of scholars who had formerly been of his acquaintance. They quickly spied out their old friend among the gipsies, and he gave them an account of the necessity which drove him to that kind of life, and told them that the people he went with were not such impostors as they were taken for, but that they had a traditional kind of learning among them, and could do wonders by the power of imagination, their fancy binding that of others; that himself had learned much of their art, and when he had compassed the whole secret, he intended, he said, to leave their company, and give the world an account of what he had learned.' (Glanvil's *Vanity of Dogmatizing,* 1661.)

2. *wattled cotes,* sheep-folds.

853. 19. *corn,* grain.

31. *Glanvil's book.* See note above.

42. *erst,* formerly.

57. *Hurst,* Cumner Hurst, a hill a few miles southwest of Oxford.

58. *Berkshire,* a county south of Oxford.

59. *ingle-bench,* bench in the chimney-corner.

854. 74. *Bab-lock-hithe,* a village about four miles southwest of Oxford.

79. *Wychwood bowers,* Wychwood Forest, ten miles or so northwest from Oxford.

83. *Fyfield elm in May,* the May-pole dance at Fyfield, some six miles southwest of Oxford.

91. *Godstow Bridge,* about two miles up the Thames from Oxford.

95. *lasher pass,* mill race.

111. *Bagley Wood,* southwest of Oxford.

114. *tagged,* marked.

115. *Thessaly,* the name of the northeastern district of ancient Greece, here given to a ground near Bagley Wood.

125. *Hinksey,* a village a short distance south of Oxford.

855. 129. *Christ-Church,* a large and fashionable college in Oxford.

133. *Glanvil,* Joseph Glanvil (1636–1680), an English clergyman and writer.

147. *teen,* sorrow.

856. 208-9. *Averse . . . turn.* Dido, queen of Carthage, deserted by her lover Æneas, slew herself. When Æneas encountered her on his journey through Hades, she turned scornfully away from him.

220. *dingles,* wooded dells.

232. *Tyrian,* a city of Phenicia, anciently an important commercial center.

236. *Ægean isles,* islands of the Ægean Sea, east of Greece.

238. *Chian wine.* Chios, an island in the Ægean, was noted for its wine.

239. *tunnies,* a kind of fish.

244. *Midland waters,* Mediterranean Sea.

245. *Syrtes,* Gulf of Sidra, on northern coast of Africa.

247. *western straits,* Strait of Gibraltar.

250. *Iberians,* inhabitants of Spain and Portugal.

RUGBY CHAPEL

Written in memory of the poet's father, Dr. Thomas Arnold (1795–1842), head-master of Rugby, whose remains are interred in Rugby Chapel.

ROSSETTI: FRANCESCA DA RIMINI

Francesca da Rimini, an Italian lady of the thirteenth century, became the wife of Giovanni Malatesta. Having discovered the love between Francesca and his young brother Paolo, Giovanni killed them both. An incident in the love-story of Paolo and Francesca is put into the mouth of Francesca in Dante's *Divine Comedy, Hell,* Canto v, whence it is here rendered by Rossetti.

861. 17. *Lancelot,* the lover of Queen Guenevere, in several medieval romances.

862. 26. *A Galahalt.* Galahalt was the go-between for Lancelot and Guenevere. Hence the book that brought Paolo and Francesca together is here called 'a Galahalt,'

THE KING'S TRAGEDY

'Tradition says that Catherine Douglas, in honor of her heroic act when she barred the door with her arm against the murderers of James the First of Scots, received popularly the name of "Barlass." This name remains to her descendants, the Barlas family, in Scotland, who bear for their crest a broken arm. She married Alexander Lovell of Bolunnie.

A few stanzas from King James's lovely poem, known as *The King's Quair*, are quoted in the course of this ballad. The writer must express regret for the necessity which has compelled him to shorten the ten-syllabled lines to eight syllables, in order that they might harmonize with the ballad meter.' (Rossetti.)

The passages from *The King's Quair* quoted in the present poem are printed in italics.

James I was murdered at Perth, Feb. 20, 1437, by the Earl of Atholl and Robert Graham (Græme). **864.** 8. *palm-play ball*, an old kind of tennis in which the ball was struck with the hand rather than with a racket.

25. *Bass Rock*, an islet at the entrance of the Firth of Forth.

29. *England's king*, Henry IV.

30. *long years immured*. In 1405, on his way from Scotland to France, James was captured by the English, and detained in one English prison or another until 1424.

37. *a lady*, Joan Beaufort, daughter of the Earl of Somerset. She became the wife of James in 1424.

41. *a sweeter song*, a reference to King James' poem, *The King's Quair*.

865. 45. *teen*, sorrow, grief.

48. *At Scone . . . crowned*. Scone, in Perthshire, Scotland, was the traditional scene of Scottish coronations. The coronations of James I and Joan occurred on May 21, 1424.

72. *leaguer*, siege. *Roxbro' hold*, Roxburgh Castle, on the Tweed, near the English border, besieged by James I in 1436.

106. *Three Estates*, that is, the nobility, the clergy, and the common people.

122. *Græme*. See introductory note above.

866. 157. *sea-wold*, open land on the sea.

162. *writhen*, twisted.

165. *rack*, floating mass of clouds.

176. *Duchray . . . Dhu*. The Duchray is probably the smallest stream west of Loch Lomond. A Loch Dhu is found in southwest Aberdeenshire.

179. *Inchkeith Isle*, a small island in the Firth of Forth.

181. *cerecloth*, waxed cloth, used in burial.

183. *Links of Forth*, slightly undulating land on the Firth of Forth.

192. *drouth*, thirst, lack.

867. 217. *hind*, peasant.

246. *solace and disport*, pleasure and entertainment.

251. *lift*, sky, air.

868. 305. *Windsor's castle-hold*. During the period of his detention in England, James was for a time imprisoned in Windsor Castle.

316. *Worship, ye lovers*. The lines printed in italics are adapted from King James' *The King's Quair*.

343. *blissful aventure*, happy chance.

388. *pearl-tired*, attired in pearls.

869. 414. *voidee-cup*, a drink of spiced wine served well after dinner-time and before bed-time.

424. *riven and brast*, torn and broken.

430. *hurdles*, narrow boards.

440. *ingle-nook*, a corner by the fire.

442. *arrased wall*, hung with tapestries from Arras.

445. *dight*, prepared, placed.

448. *doffed*, took off.

462. *dule to dree*, sorrow to suffer.

469. *Aberdour*, north of Edinburgh, on the north shore of the Firth of Forth.

870. 532. *heft*, handle.

871. 585. *litters*, movable bed-frames.

873. 751. *requiem-knell*, the bell at requiem-mass for the dead.

MORRIS: THE EARTHLY PARADISE

The Earthly Paradise is a collection of stories related, supposedly, at fortnightly feasts alternately by the Wanderers, who are Norwegian mariners, and by certain men of a 'Western land' whose guests they have become. Twenty-four tales are eventually told in the course of the year. *Atalanta's Race* and *The Lady of the Land* are the first and eighth stories, respectively.

ATALANTA'S RACE

I

878. 1. *Arcadian woods*. Arcadia was an inland country of Peloponnesian Greece.

14. *cornel*, the tough wood of the cornel-tree.

28. *King Schœneus' town*, probably Tegea or Mantinea, these being two of the larger towns of Arcadia.

879. 63. *the fleet-foot one*, Hermes, Mercury.

79. *Diana*, patroness of hunting and woodland sports.

II

881. 51. *the sea-born one*, Venus.

65. *presently*, at once.

73. *Dryads*, wood-nymphs.

75. *Adonis' bane*. Adonis was killed by a wild boar that he had wounded.

78. *Argive cities*, cities of the Grecian state of Argolis.

91. *must*, new wine not yet fermented.

882. 142. *three-formed goddess*, Diana.

149. *framer of delights*, Venus.

168. *Artemis*, Diana.

883. 207. *sleepy garland*, poppy wreath.

210. *heading*, beheading.

III

1. *Argolis*, one of the states of Greece.

2. *the goddess*, Venus.

6. *murk*, what is left of fruit after the juice has been extracted.

8. *close*, enclosure.

884. 54. *unholpen*, unhelped.

70. *the golden age*, a fabled age of innocence and plenty.

100. *wrack*, seaweeds cast up on the shore.

885. 169. *scrip*, wallet.

IV

887. 72. *the Argive*, Milanion, whose father was king of Argolis.

V

1. *the posts*, the starting and turning posts.

5. *mighty lord*, Zeus.

6. *her*, Venus.

16. *Love's servant*, Milanion.

21. *maiden zone*, a girdle worn by maidens before marriage.

THE LADY OF THE LAND

888. 35. *law*, belief, religion.

890. 182. *poor shepherd*, Paris.

892. 310. *orb of June*, the moon.

893. 389. *Cathay*, a mediæval name for a vague region in eastern Asia.

894. 467. *wend*, go.

SWINBURNE: ATALANTA IN CALYDON

FIRST CHORUS

895. 5–8. *nightingale . . . Itylus . . . Thracian ships . . . tongueless vigil.* Philomela and Procné were daughters of Pandion, king of Attica, who gave Procné in marriage to his ally, the Thracian king Tereus. After Procné had borne a son, Itys (Itylus), Tereus concealed her in the country, that he might dishonor her sister Philomela. Having accomplished his purpose, he deprived Philomela of her tongue. By embroidering her story on a robe, however, Philomela communicated the truth to Procné, whereupon Procné killed her son and served his flesh on a dish before Tereus. When Tereus pursued the fleeing sisters, the gods granted them an escape by transforming Procné into a swallow and Philomela into a nightingale.

10. *Maiden most perfect*, Artemis.

896. 41. *Pan*, god of flocks and shepherds.

44. *Mænad*, a female worshipper of Bacchus. *Bassarid*, a Lydian or Thracian bacchanal.

THIRD CHORUS

897. 49. *Aphrodite*, Venus, goddess of love.

136, 146. *Tyro, Enipeus.* Tyro was the wife of Cretheus, beloved by the river-god Enipeus in Thessaly.

THE GARDEN OF PROSERPINE

898. 28. *Prosperpine*, queen of the infernal regions. During the six months of the year that she passed in Olympus she was considered an amiable and propitious divinity; but during the six months in Hades she was stern and terrible. She personified the changing seasons.

HERTHA

Hertha, or Nerthus was the Germanic goddess of the earth, of fertility, and of growth.

A FORSAKEN GARDEN

The scene of this poem is East Dene, Bonchurch, Isle of Wight.

THALASSIUS

903. 15. *Oread*, a nymph of the hills.

18. *Cymothoë*, a nereid, or nymph of the sea.

37. *he*, Walter Savage Landor. See p. 657.

904. 88–9. *And gladly . . . dead.* A rendering of the epitaph written by Landor for the Spanish troops who died resisting the invasion of Napoleon:

Emeriti lubenter quiescerimus
Libertate parta;
Quiescimus amissa perlubenter.

THE ROUNDEL

The roundel in Swinburne's sense is illustrated by this poem. It consists of nine complete lines arranged as follows: *a b a, b a b, a b a*, part of the first line being repeated as a refrain after the third and ninth lines. The refrain is usually so selected as to rime with the *b* lines.

THE ARMADA

Written for the three hundredth anniversary of the defeat of the Spanish Armada by the English.

907. 8. *affrayed*, frightened.

908. 28. *when Athens hurled back Asia*. A reference to the wars between the Persians and the Greeks, which began in 500 B. C. and ended about 449 B. C.

33. *the fierce July.* The Armada descended upon England in July, 1588.

34. *galleon*, a large, unwieldy vessel, usually having 3 or 4 decks. *galliass*, a large galley carrying, usually, 3 masts and some 20 guns.

39. *bastions of serpentine.* A bastion is a part of a fortification projecting from the main rampart. A serpentine is a kind of cannon.

41. *charged with bale*, laden with destruction.

46. *the Lion*, the symbol of England.

909. 63. *the helmsman's bark*, boat of Charon, in which souls were ferried across the Styx.

65. *told*, counted.

910. 110. *burgeon*, bud, sprout. *yearn*, feel desire.

124. *hurtles*, knocks violently, dashes.

133. *Python*, a huge serpent which lived on Mount Parnassus.

911. 194. *Sark*, one of the Channel Islands, off the northern coast of France. *Wight*, the Isle of Wight.

213. *England's Drake*, Sir Francis Drake, vice-admiral to Lord Howard.

912. 238. *Oquendo*, Miguel de Oquendo, the most valiant of the captains under the Spanish admiral, the Duke of Medina.

246. *Humber, Tees, Tyne, Tweed*, English rivers emptying into the North Sea.

252. *Forth*, the Firth of Forth, in Scotland.

254. *quarry*, game.

262. *ruth*, pity.

913. 264. *Shetlands and Orkneys*, groups of islands off the northern coast of Scotland.

284. *the pontiff*, the pope.

290. *fulfilled*, filled full.

292. *guerdon*, reward.

301. *Sixtus*, Sixtus V, Pope 1585–90.

302. *Philip*, Philip II, King of Spain 1556–98.

914. 309. *rede is read*, doom is assigned.

COR CORDIUM

Cor cordium, 'Heart of Hearts,'— the words on Shelley's tomb in Rome.

NON DOLET

4 *the Roman wife.* 'Pætus Cæcina was ordered by the Emperor Claudius to take his own life; and when he hesitated, his wife Arria stabbed herself, crying, "Pæte, non dolet" (Pætus, it does not hurt).' (Beatty.)

ON THE DEATHS OF THOMAS CARLYLE AND GEORGE ELIOT

Carlyle and George Eliot died in the same year, 1881.

CHRISTOPHER MARLOWE

9–10. These two lines are quoted from Marlowe's *Tamburlaine*, Part I, Act v, Scene 1.

PATER: STYLE

916. *b. 7. Bacon.* See above, p. 187.

8. *Livy*, Titus Livius (59 B. C.–17 A. D.), greatest of the Roman historians. *Carlyle.* See p. 714.

9. *Cicero*, Marcus Tullius Cicero (106 B. C.–43 B. C.), the celebrated orator, philosopher, and statesman. *Newman.* See p. 702.

10. *Plato* (429 or 427–347 B. C.), a famous Greek philosopher. *Michelet*, Jules Michelet (1798–1874), French historian and man of letters. *Sir Thomas Browne.* See p. 200.

12. *Milton.* See p. 236. *Taylor.* See p. 221.

917. *a. 7. Lycidas.* See p. 240.

15. *Dryden.* See p. 266.

46. *dichotomy*, a division into two parts.

48. *De Quincey.* See p. 683.

b. 17. Pascal, Blaise Pascal (1623–1662), French mathematician, philosopher, and man of letters.

56. *Gibbon.* See p. 453.

918. *a. 1. Tacitus*, Cornelius Tacitus (c. 55–after 117), an eminent Roman historian and orator.

919. *a. 31. neology*, innovation in language.

b. 4. le cuistre, the pedantic fellow.

31. *Johnson.* See p. 405.

920. *a. 51. Montaigne*, Michel Eyquem de Montaigne (1533–1592), a famous French essayist.

b. 6. ascêsis, a transliteration of a Greek word meaning 'exercise, training, art.'

25. *Esmond*, a historical novel, *Henry Esmond*, by William Makepeace Thackeray (1811–1863).

26. *Newman's Idea of a University.* See p. 703.

41. *Schiller*, Johann Christoph Friedrich von Schiller (1759–1805), a celebrated German poet, dramatist, and historian.

921. *a. 6. Flaubert's Madame Bovary.* a novel by

the French man of letters, Gustave Flaubert (1821–1880).

8. *Stendhal's Le Rouge et Le Noir*, a novel by Marie Henri Beyle (1783–1842), best known by his pseudonym ' De Stendhal.'

36. *Michelangelo*, Michelagnolo Buonarroti (1475–1564), a famous Italian sculptor, painter, architect, and poet.

b. 47. Dean Mansel, Henry Longueville Mansel (1820–1871), dean of St. Paul's, an English metaphysician.

922. *b. 30. ante-penultimate*, immediately preceding that one of a series which is next to the last one.

55. *Blake.* See p. 485.

923. *a. 36. Swedenborg*, Emanuel Swedenborg (1688–1772), a Swedish philosopher and theosophist. *Tracts of the Times*, a series of 90 pamphlets published at Oxford from 1833–1841, to which Newman, Pusey, and others contributed. See p. 702.

b. 29–39. series of letters. . . . Madame X. Flaubert's letters to Madame X., in which he so often disparages human love and exalts the love of art, were written during the latter half of the year 1846. *Madame X.* was Madame Colet.

924. *a. 55. a sympathetic commentator*, Guy de Maupassant, who wrote an introduction to *Lettres de Gustave Flaubert à George Sand*. The passage here quoted will be found in the edition of Paris, 1884, pp. lxii–lxv.

b. 48. Blake's rapturous design. See p. 485.

925. *b. 2. ennuis*, wearinesses, vexations.

37. *Buffon*, the Comte de Buffon (1707–1788), a celebrated French naturalist. Especially known to literary criticism for his *Discours sur le style* (1853).

926. *a. 41. Scott's facility.* See p. 579.

b. 13. Les Misérables, a famous novel by Victor Marie Hugo (1802–1885).

44. *Raphael*, Raphael Santi (1483–1520), a famous Italian painter.

927. *a. 8. Flaubert's commentator*, Guy de Maupassant. See *Lettres de Gustave Flaubert à George Sand*, Paris, 1884, pp. lxi–lxii.

32. *Bach*, Johann Sebastian Bach (1685–1750), one of the greatest of German musicians.

b. 22. The Divine Comedy, the greatest work of the greatest of Italian poets, Dante Alighieri (1265–1321).

STEVENSON: THE FOREIGNER AT HOME

929. *a. 4. biggin'*, building.

17. *Black Country.* In the English Midlands. *Moor of Rannoch.* In Perthshire.

b. 22. Miss Bird. Isabella L. Bird, authoress of a popular book of travel, *Unbeaten Tracks in Japan.*

930. *a. 35. plausible*, pleasing, acceptable.

52. *roundly*, plainly, flatly.

53. *a Scottish legal body.* The Society of Scottish Advocates, whose examinations Stevenson passed at his father's request, though he never practiced law. See his *Apology for Idlers.*

b. 27. bickering, flushing, quivering.

931. *a.* 9. *harled,* rough-cast with lime mingled with small gravel.

 b. 5. *commerce,* conversation, intercourse.

 10. *counters,* remarks that mean nothing, not true coin.

 25. *Give him the wages of going on.* A reminiscence of Tennyson's poem entitled *Wages,* in which the poet says of Virtue, ' Give her the wages of going on, and not to die.'

932. *a.* 37. *Byron* did actually discuss theology on his way to take part in the Greek war of independence. As to his descent and schooldays, see the biographical sketch on p. 586.

 b. 3. *proctors,* officers who supervise the behavior of students at Oxford and Cambridge.

 18. *rotten borough.* The constituencies which before the Reform Act were in the gift of great patrons were so-called; they were regarded as safe refuges for unknown or unpopular politicians, and some of the greatest of English statesmen made their entrance into Parliament — Gladstone for instance — in this way.

 21. *raffish,* fashionable.

 35. *Professor Blackie* (1809–95), a popular professor of Greek at the University of Edinburgh.

 37. *umbrageous,* suspicious, shy.

933. *a.* 6. *iron skerries,* rocks projecting from the sea, hard as iron.

 13. *girdle,* griddle, gridiron.

 20. *Flodden* Field, where James IV of Scotland was defeated in 1513.

 21. *Darien,* an attempt in 1698 to plant Scottish settlers on the Isthmus of Panama, which caused considerable loss of life and widespread disappointment.

 Forty-five, the rebellion of 1745, which was crushed by the defeat of the Scotch at Culloden the following year.

 24. *Wallace,* the Scottish hero who was defeated by the English at Falkirk in 1298.

 25. *Bruce* defeated the English at Bannockburn in 1314; he was King of Scotland, 1306–29, and suffered many reverses.

 47. *Shorter Catechism,* adopted at an Assembly of Puritan divines held at Westminster during the Commonwealth.

 b. 3. *another church.* The Highlanders were, for the most part, Roman Catholics.

 8. *Highland costume,* the kilt, a short plaited skirt, coming to the knees.

 15. *Black Watch,* a famous Highland regiment.

 43. *Ireland,* though in the ' political aggregation ' of the British Empire, retains its own religion and customs.

FRANÇOIS VILLON

934. *a.* 24. *exhumed,* dug out of the grave.

 b. 20. *pilloried,* exposed to public disgrace.

935. *a.* 21. *tubbed and swaddled,* washed and wrapped in baby clothes.

 26. *given piously,* addicted to pious practices.

 b. 24. *Notre Dame de Paris,* a novel by Victor Hugo (1831).

936. *a.* 9. *piping the eye,* pretending to cry.

54. *the red door,* the *Porte Rouge* of the previous column, 1.

 b. 32. *Clough.* See p. 673.

937. *b.* 41. *cannikin clinked.* A reminiscence of Iago's drinking song, *Othello* II, iii, 71.

938. *a.* 12. *words of Mariana. Pericles* IV, vi, 173–4.

 25. *Murger* (1822–61), author of *Scènes de la Vie de Bohème.*

939. *a.* 11. *Hogarth* (1697–1764), the great English caricaturist. One of his most famous series portrayed the careers of *The Industrious and the Idle Apprentice.*

 b. 42. *pitch-and-toss.* ' Matching ' coppers.

940. *a.* 55. *aumries,* boxes in which the offerings for the poor were kept.

 b. 21. *made a demonstration against,* attempted to break into.

941. *a.* 19. *was upsides with him,* had the advantage of him.

942. *a.* 7. *pantler,* butler.

 39. *extraordinary,* by torture.

 b. 26. *put to the question,* tortured.

 35. *of our pleasant vices. Lear* V, iii, 170–171: —

  The gods are just, and of our pleasant vices
  Make instruments to plague us.

 48. *Nathan's parable.* See ii Samuel xii, 3.

943. *a.* 4. *planted upright,* buried alive. See 937. *b.* 20.

 22. *mortal push,* hand of death.

 51. *more pecked,* pecked more full of holes.

944. *a.* 26. *present volume. Familiar Studies of Men and Books* (1882).

 b. 21. *roystering,* swaggering.

945. *a.* 43. *Rabelais* (1483–1553), the great humorous writer of the French Renaissance.

 51. *a work of some power.* Perhaps Albert Glatigny's *L'Illustre Brezacier,* which made some sensation in 1873. Stevenson's essay appeared first in *Cornhill,* August, 1877.

946. *a.* 23. *Béranger* (1780–1857), the most popular of French lyrical poets.

 26. *Johnson.* See p. 405.

 31. *fox burrowing.* Like the Spartan boy of ancient fable, who concealed under his cloak a fox he had stolen.

 52. *mauvais pauvre,* wicked poor man.

 53. *Victor Hugo* (1802–85), the great French poet of the century.

 57. *mole-skin cap,* sometimes worn by the lower classes in England.

 b. 27. *for me,* so far as I am concerned. I will not translate it.

 52. *yester,* last.

A CHILD'S GARDEN OF VERSES

Stevenson began this collection of ' Rimes for Children ' (as he once intended to call them — another rejected title was ' Penny Whistles ') in 1881. They were dedicated when published in 1885 to his old nurse Alison Cunningham, the ' Cummy ' of his own childhood.

HEATHER ALE

Among the curiosities of human nature, this legend claims a high place. It is needless to remind the reader that the Picts were never exterminated, and form to this day a large proportion of the folk of Scotland: occupying the eastern and the central parts, from the Firth of Forth, or perhaps the Lammermoors, upon the south, to the Ord of Caithness on the north. That the blundering guess of a dull chronicler should have inspired men with imaginary loathing for their own ancestors is already strange: that it should have begotten this wild legend seems incredible. Is it possible the chronicler's error was merely nominal? that what he told, and what the people proved themselves so ready to receive, about the Picts, was true or partly true of some anterior and perhaps Lappish savages, small of stature, black of hue, dwelling underground — possibly also the distillers of some forgotten spirit? See Mr. Campbell's *Tales of the West Highlands.* (Stevenson's own Note.)

948. 2. *long-syne,* long ago.

6. *Swound,* swoon.

8. *underground.* The ballad tells of the early race of men who dwelt in caves.

10. *feld,* fierce, dreadful.

12. *roes,* deer.

15. *dwarfish.* This ancient race was of small stature.

21. *like children's.* They were so small.

23. *Brewsters.* Brewers.

27. *curlews.* Characteristic birds of the Scottish moorlands, with a peculiarly piercing, haunting cry.

33. *fortuned,* happened.

34. *free.* Not on the road.

36. *vermin.* The despised cave-dwellers.

43. *swarthy.* It was a small dark race.

MEREDITH: LOVE IN THE VALLEY

First published in 1851; here printed in the fuller and more perfect version of 1878.

950. 24. *for,* in return for, instead of.

32. *Off a sunny border,* the sunlit edge of the cloud.

50. *bloomy,* like blossom.

951. 77. *the rose-flush drinks the rayless planet.* The rising sun absorbs the morning star in its brighter rays.

88. *Covert,* thick wood.

117. *yaffle,* the European green woodpecker, noted for its loud laugh-like note.

952. 128. *like the sun.* By her blinding beauty.

132. *wink,* flash with quick darting motion.

134. *Swarms,* quivers like a swarm of bees.

148. *blue* (sky).

152. *tiger,* striped like a tiger, or, perhaps, fierce.

154. *nutbrown tresses,* of the wheat.

156. *girdle,* of straw about the sheaf.

162. *Clipped,* cut off, or, perhaps, embraced. *violet shaded,* by the purple shadows of the setting sun. *snow,* the season has changed from autumn to winter.

165. *black print-branches,* the shadows of the branches printed black on the snow in the moonlight.

JUGGLING JERRY

178. *Deepens,* lowers.

179. *of,* at.

953. 183. *in our names,* as we greeted each other.

188. *girdle . . . tresses.* See ll. 154 and 156.

193. *beamy,* with sunbeams between the showers.

200. *tears,* evoked by the vision seen before waking.

203. *dogwood,* which has red branches.

204. *whitebeam,* a tree with leaves white underneath, which are suddenly lighted up by a gust of wind.

208. *what is for heaven alone,* the secret which I wish to breathe to heaven. See ll. 201-2.

7. *One that outjuggles all.* Death.

25. *cricket,* play at cricket.

27. *bale,* a small piece of wood placed on top of the wickets, and whipped off by the wicket keeper to put the batsman ' out.'

33. *victual,* pronounced ' vittle.'

39. *session* (of Parliament).

41. *mock thunder* of the juggler's pistol.

954. 45. *professor* of juggling.

67. *bolus,* a large pill.

70. *fields,* souls or bodies.

81. *chirper,* glass.

88. *sword-trick,* by which a sword appears to be swallowed.

THE OLD CHARTIST

The Chartists were political revolutionaries, whose agitation came to a head in 1848. See first note on Carlyle's *Past and Present.* Some of them were transported on charges of sedition. The hero of the poem has returned to England after serving his sentence.

7. *transportation,* imprisonment beyond the seas.

955. 22. *his Grace's,* the Duke's.

28. *wrong note,* too high, in advance of the time.

39. *poll,* head.

56. *parson . . . bishop,* from the black-gowned parson into the bishop with his sleeves of white lawn.

65. *needle-muzzle,* sharp nose.

76. *place,* situation as a linen draper or dry goods salesman.

87. *dock.* At the police court.

FRANCE 1870

This ode was written in the hour of France's bitter humiliation by Germany, when Paris was in the hands of the enemy. Meredith regards France as the nation which brought political enlightenment and freedom to the world at the Revolution, but surrendered her ideals at the instigation of Napoleon III, whom he despises as a trickster. The Franco-Prussian war, he thinks, did France a service by showing her the hollowness of the pretensions of her sham-hero, and by recalling her to the path of light and freedom from which she had been beguiled by the Emperor's dreams of military glory. France is treated throughout under the similitude of the mythological Prometheus, who brought fire from heaven for the service of man, and was punished by Zeus by being chained on a rock with a vulture perpetually tearing his vitals: being immortal, he suffered unending agony, although the bringer of light and fire — the foundation of all the arts — to men. He is first mentioned by name in l. 270.

11. *when our time was dark.* Before the Revolution of 1788.

12. *fetters,* of feudal serfdom. *spark,* of freedom.

24. *Angel and Wanton.* Half an angel of light, and half sunk in vice. The state of private and public morality under Napoleon III was low.

31. *riven,* split by lightning.

37-8. *the lurid hosts who . . . irreparable mischance.* The Fallen-Angels in Milton's *Paradise Lost.*

45. *fire from heaven.* Here the Prometheus metaphor begins.

48. *Mother of Pride.* The past is contrasted with the present, which is pictured in the words that follow.

51. *Heroes, bondsmen.* The contrast continued.

56. *crown with bays.* The King of Prussia was made Emperor of Germany in the Palace of Versailles, on the outskirts of Paris.

957. 64. *Tranced circumambient.* The world is imaged as a circle of spectators, struck dumb with astonishment.

65. *Beaks.* As the vulture tore the entrails of Prometheus with its beak.

72. *Chamber* (gives answer) to chamber. *sequent,* logical, reasoning.

74. *vaults* (of the brain).

84. *long,* long ago.

100. *pinnacled Alp.* A reference to the crossing of the Alps by Napoleon I, a feat up to that time thought impossible.

106. *along the snows.* Napoleon I's retreat from Moscow.

112. *oriflamme,* the banner of ancient France, which gave place to the imperial eagle under Napoleon I.

113. *forgets,* how they sucked, etc. (l. 110), during the wars of Napoleon I. Earth covers the slain with the green grass, but the gods do not forget; they punish after the lapse of many years.

120. *They,* the gods.

133. *Immortal.* Again the Prometheus metaphor. 958. 136. *Unsparing.* The gods are merciless as were the children of France in their hour of triumph over Europe under Napoleon I.

140. *perishable,* material, the vine and grain of l. 138. *imperishable,* spiritual.

153. *worm,* grave.

161. *their,* the gods'.

171. *fables of her priests.* Napoleon III had the support of the Roman Catholic clergy, who, when the tide of battle went against France, prayed for a special intervention of Providence.

182. *In peril of,* at the risk of losing.

190. *a forfeit blade.* Meredith changed this afterwards to ' a broken blade.' His point is that France

was defeated because of the insufficiency of her military organization, which, under the laxity and corruption of the administration of Napoleon III, had been allowed to fall into decay.

194. *Clamored of treachery.* At the surrender of Sedan, which was the turning point of the war, there were outcries that France had been betrayed to the Germans by her leaders.

204. *her Dishonorer,* Napoleon III.

206. *Bellona and Bacchante,* the goddesses of War and Bacchic Frenzy.

207. *Schoolmen of the North,* the Germans, who planned the campaign scientifically long before it began.

959. 210. *faithful to himself,* to the law of strength. See ll. 161-170.

215. *A name of terror.* Napoleon III was much dreaded in Europe, but was suffering from severe illness, and showed a lack of self-control at critical moments.

216. *trickster.* Napoleon III.

217. *for dominion.* Napoleon had gained military successes and territory in previous wars. *to patch a throne.* The war against Germany was said to be undertaken to divert the public attention from internal misgovernment and secure the succession of Napoleon III's son, the Prince Imperial.

220. *for their sake, i.e.,* in a righteous cause.

221. *divine,* and therefore immortal.

228. *her own* (line). *That,* so that.

229. *cease,* die.

231. *burn . . . Whatso.* Destroy her charms with a resolute heart, which is left unconsumed.

234. *from prone,* from the position of humiliation, to which she has been stricken down.

236. *His,* Ambition's.

237. Shown by her taskmasters (the Germans) to be the retribution for her misdeeds in the past.

252. *The Man.* Prometheus.

284. *prototype.* Prometheus, the light-bringer. See l. 251.

960. 302. *ghost,* spirit.

322. *the undying Ones.* The gods, or eternal principles of right.

334. *counter-changing,* interchanging, checkered.

335. *meridional,* of the sun at noon.

341. *in fee,* in lordship, placing them under an everlasting obligation.

343. *aureole,* crown of glory.

THE LARK ASCENDING

Cf. Wordsworth (p. 531) and Shelley *To a Sky Lark* (p. 627). The different ways in which the subject is treated by the three poets should not be overlooked.

13. *quick o' the ear,* inmost nerve of the ear.

14. *her,* the brain.

16. *dry* (referring to springs) unresponsive. *he* the lark.

961. 44. *argentine,* silvery.

46. *choric,* dancing in the wind.

48. *shivers wet.* In a storm of wind and rain.

49. *chime* (of a waterfall).

56. *him,* the lark.

64. The sentence here ended runs on continuously

from the beginning of the poem, like the lark's song.

75. *fallows,* fields lying fallow.

101–124. In associating the lark's song with human intellectual activities, Meredith strikes a characteristic note, different from that of the older poets of the nineteenth century.

110. *Earth.* See biographical sketch, p. 949.

THE WOODS OF WESTERMAIN

This is more difficult than the preceding poems, and had perhaps better not be attempted by students who have not attained some mastery of Meredith's habits of thought and modes of expression.

The first three stanzas are similar in structure, the first part in each indicating the consequences of an attitude of trustfulness towards Nature, the second part the consequences of an attitude of distrust. At the beginning of each stanza, the poet says: 'You may enter the enchanted woods safely, if you do so trustingly;' at the end, 'If you enter distrustfully, you do so at your own risk.' The fourth stanza passes into a general discussion of the conduct of life, considered allegorically under the similitude of a wood.

5–7. If you toss your heart up — you fare successfully.

8–9. But if you show a sign of fear, they change their form.

962. 15. *golden bath,* of sunlight.

17. *winnowing plumes,* fanlike wings.

18. *on a chuckle,* chuckling.

21. *jar,* a bird with wings mottled like those of a moth.

23. Note the change of thought.

25. *rood,* a small plot of ground, a fraction of an acre.

30–40. The wood opens in various directions with bramble bushes, and wild strawberries, topped by the star-flower; the ground is encumbered by fallen twigs, fir cones, seed pods, mole hills, and particolored flint stones; here and there in the earth are to be seen the foot prints of small animals that have fled in fear.

46. *whins,* low shrubs.

47. *minikins,* small birds.

51. *flowing not from purse,* not dependent upon the power of money.

58. If you desire it with all your soul.

59. *t' the lyre,* to the poet.

62. *Granaries,* treasures.

65. Not enslaved to worldly appetites.

66–73. In the place too often usurped by mere worldly success, you will enthrone the joy evoked by such natural beauties as a brook or a waterfall, or a clearing in the wood, where the light shines through, and the deer pass, stately and magnificent as the knights of old.

74–81. Or the dull eyes of cattle chewing the cud may take your mind back to the primeval ages, before mind was developed, when Earth was mere rocks and slime, and the sky was a place for ungainly winged creatures — the pterodactyls.

84. *The Nurse of seed.* The principle of reproduction.

88–91. If you follow Nature, you will embrace closely her glory narrowed down to beauty, or take in arms spread wide as air her beauty enlarged to magnificence.

92. *white Foam-born,* Venus, the goddess of Love.

94. *Phœbus,* Apollo, the god of song. *Phœbus,* Diana the huntress, goddess of chastity.

95 *Pan,* the god of untamed Nature.

97. *her,* Nature.

98. *sterner worship,* of modern science, which regards them not as deities but as natural forces.

99. *her,* Nature.

103. *awn,* the delicate silky growth that terminates the grain-sheath of barley, oats, etc.

104. *Argent,* silvery. The moon is imaged as Diana the huntress.

105. *the blush,* of sunrise.

107. Passing, and eternally recurring.

110. *opposing grandeurs,* as of moonlight and sunrise. The spirit of beauty saves their glory from death ('fleetings').

114–121. The divine harmony of Nature destroys no spring (fountain) of strength; it subdues, but does not slay, guiding the course of the stream, but preserving its source; it tempers the heat of young blood, but hears the heart of its wildness beat through self-restraint, like the solemn yet ardent dance of centaurs on the greensward.

122–9. If you catch the sense of Nature's harmony, it will open the way to a larger fellowship with humanity, and to a Love, instinct with passion, soaring beyond egotism, if you do not put the sensual appetites in the foreground.

963. 132–3. Womanhood, the supreme triumph of Nature, demands reverence for Nature's earlier developments.

138. *throat and thigh.* The waterfall, reflecting the rays of the sun, is pictured as a human being.

143. *Bare or veiled.* The 'courtly dames' are compared to the open waters and whispering leaves, with which they share the sincerity of Nature.

146. Part of the Nature, by which they are surrounded, and of which they are the outcome.

147. They have the surety of the tree's roots and the grace of its branches.

148–151. They reveal the treasures of their hearts, and do not conceal those of their minds, in order to flatter the pride of the tyrant, Man; for when the mind is not open to the light of day, darkness breeds trickery. Of woman's wiles when oppressed and their consequences, strange and terrible stories are told.

154. *the ancient battle,* between the sexes.

155. *astonished friends,* man and woman, astonished at the charm of the new relation of friendship.

158. *the tiger,* man. *the snake,* woman.

162–165. Now the woman leads the man in a silken leash, decked with wild flowers, and unconscious of the constraint, though feeling its sweetness.

166–169. Love ennobles the senses, and develops individuality.

172. The dots indicate the change of thought.

181. *Gaps,* rends.

185. *fell,* savage, dreadful.

187. *Fellowly,* in the spirit of comradeship.

189. *cocks of day,* harbingers of dawn.

191. *quern,* mill.

199. *thought and felt,* what is thought and what is felt.

200–1. Nature flows on, ever-changing, like the brook, not foolishly standing still in established customs, like a stagnant pool.

209. *them you quit,* the fellow mortals you leave behind.

210–211. The most soaring spirit gains by contact with common humanity.

215–16. The sense of superiority to one's fellows is always dangerous.

218. Again the thought changes.

220. *Dragon-fowl,* of selfishness. See 1. 243.

226–7. No force, not even that of egotism, is destroyed, but is controlled and turned to noble uses.

235–8. Nothing in nature is philosophically wise, least of all man, except when long experience has freed his mind from egotism.

239. *him.* The dragon of selfishness.

dumb, with astonishment. Beware of self-esteem, even when you seem to be drinking in wisdom.

964. 241. *she,* wisdom. When you feel that you only are wise, then above all beware.

244. *late* in the history of the race.

250. *Maw,* stomach, material desires.

251. Shrewd only for his own material interests.

256. *within.* See 1. 251.

257. Like the pine, soft within, but obdurate to all outside himself.

265–7. Out of sight of heaven, to the very heart of Earth, the source of her activity and the spring of progress.

270–287. Humanity is imagined as a crowd gazing on the source of Nature, and discovering in the history of the race the slow beginnings of human sensibility. In all these beginnings are described the efforts of man to demand of Nature the satisfaction of material and selfish desires. But Nature cares nothing for the individual, and gives no sign in answer to the cravings of egotism. She proceeds with her task of developing the human spirit out of sensual desires.

293–305. Regarded merely from the physical side, the history of the race appears only a constant interchange of beginnings and endings, darkness and light, life and death, youth and age; but regarded spiritually, beyond the mere senses, Nature is seen to be permanent.

306–9. We may regard Nature with loathing, gazing on the dust in the tomb, or with love, keeping in mind the spiritual sense of living men.

312–3. Yield to the sensual appetites, or, like Nature, give yourself to service.

321. *Airing,* opening.

323. *seer,* the prophet or beholder of Nature.

324. *witch,* bewitch, play the witch, charming you with external beauty.

329. *her awful tremble.* What is dreadful in Nature, as well as what appears beneficent.

330. *Fount.* The source of Nature. See 11. 266–7.

346–9. Not the pleasures of sense, which, wantonly followed, grow into habits, and like hags ride the souls of men to destruction.

350–1. Pleasures that keep the senses under the control of the intellect.

352. *sequent birth.* Body, mind, and spirit developed in orderly succession.

356–363. 'It is fatal to neglect either blood, or brain, or soul. If we part company with any one of these three we shall be wrecked. The attempt to develop soul without blood, or worse still, without brain, is to court certain disaster, of which the chronicles of religion are full. The athletic craze for training the blood alone, is no better; and if the brain of the mere intellectual be a higher development, it is not in itself perfect, or satisfying, or secure.' (G. M. Trevelyan.)

965. 363. *Glassing her,* mirroring Earth or Nature.

370. *Eglantine,* the wild-rose.

371. *darkness.* Dark eglantine in thought most beautiful.

372. *Knowing,* who know.

373. *kin o' the rose.* Short-lived, but beautiful while it lasts.

374. Those who have explored the depths of Nature use life as a tool or weapon.

379. If they ask the secret of life, the answer is the same as the question 'Why?' With this answer they are content. See 1. 369.

380. *ramped,* held in check. Selfishness being subdued, they will thrill to be marked for service.

384–5. So that in the hour of death, where fear sits, they will still see the stream of life flowing on.

386. *lynx.* Eyeing it without fear. *her,* Nature.

388. *Sphinx.* Riddle.

396. *lop,* trim, keep within bounds.

418. *Momently,* for a moment.

430. *at the paths behind,* at the past history of the race.

441. Again the note of warning.

446–452. If with the sons of selfishness you fear all that is outside of your personal interests. All these are conditional clauses, dependent on 1. 453.

455. *Nighted,* descending by night, like a vulture.

457. *One whose eyes are out.* Ignorance.

463. *yapping,* barking.

466. *drums the sconce,* confuses the intelligence.

467. *nibblenips,* pinches, torments.

469. *demon-growing girl,* the girl being transformed into a demon.

479. *yell you Where,* yell to you where you are.

MODERN LOVE

This beautiful series of sixteen line stanzas in its entirety tells the tragedy of an ill-assorted pair. In the first here given, the husband looks back to an evening before the shipwreck of their love. The second describes a meeting by the sea after a hollow though well-meant reconciliation. The third commemorates a moment of peaceful companionship. The last analyses the causes of their failure, and contrasts the immense forces of passion with their pitiful outcome when not wisely guided and controlled.

HUXLEY: EMANCIPATION—BLACK AND WHITE

967. *a.* 9. *Quashie,* a nickname at one time applied to the negro.

a. 13. *fierce trial by battle,* the American Civil War, which was just finished when the essay was written.

b. 21. *Caucasian,* the white division of mankind.

968. *b.* 19. *Adelaida,* a Beethoven song for soprano.

b. 20. *Fornarina,* literally, baker's daughter. Marguerita, a baker's daughter with whom Raphael was in love, is said to have been the model for some of his pictures. The Sistine Madonna is now in the Dresden gallery.

969. *a.* 37. *Clärchen,* a simple cottage girl in Goethe's tragedy, *Egmont.* She is in love with the hero and takes poison when he dies.

Beatrice, the idealized object of Dante's Platonic devotion.

b. 10. *Faustinas,* mother and daughter, wives of Roman emperors, who founded schools for orphan girls in their honour.

b. 12. *Juristerei etc.*

'Jurisprudence and Medicine,
And even, alas! Philosophy'

These lines are taken from the first scene in Goethe's *Faust.*

b. 24. *retiariae.* A *retiarius* was a gladiator who endeavored to hold his adversary by throwing a net over his head—hence a fighter with feeble weapons.

b. 25. *sicariae.* A *sicarius* was an assassin armed with a curved dagger. Huxley is exhorting women to fight with effective weapons.

b. 39. *salique law.* The Salic Law provided for inheritance in the male line only.

970. *a.* 17. *Sydney Smith,* a well-known wit of the early nineteenth century.

BUTLER: THE NOTE BOOKS

Butler began, while still young, to make jottings of his experiences and impressions, as well as his thoughts. As time passed, the number of notes grew tremendous. They were intended for his own use, but after his death they were arranged and edited by his literary executor, Henry Festing Jones.

THE FAMILY

971. *a.* 28. *R. W. Evans,* archdeacon of Westmoreland and author of the time, who was educated under Dr. Butler at Shrewsbury, where Samuel Butler was also a pupil.

UNCONSCIOUS HUMOR

a. 37. *the Hon. Mrs. Watson* and her husband were intimate friends of Dickens, and *David Copperfield* was dedicated to them.

HOMER'S ODYSSEY

a. 48. *meeting between Ulysses and Telemachus. Odyssey* xvi, 180–320 describes the meeting of Ulysses after his long absence with his son, Telemachus. Both father and son wept.

MELCHISEDEC

a. 56. *Melchisedec* is described in Hebrews vii, 3, as being 'without father, without mother, without descent.'

BACON FOR BREAKFAST

b. 13. *privilege of Cephas and the brethren of our Lord.* Cephas, the Greek for Peter, was the surname given by Christ to Simon. I Corinthians ix, 5: 'Have we not power to lead about a sister, a wife, as well as the Brethren of the Lord, and Cephas.'

GOOD BREEDING THE SUMMUM BONUM

972. *a.* 10. *Summum Bonum,* highest good.

ADVICE TO THE YOUNG

a. 42. *the Kingsleys,* popular writers of the time.

LOHENGRIN

b. 31. Wagner's opera, *Lohengrin,* is founded on the medieval legend of the search for the Holy Grail, the vessel from which Christ ate the Last Supper, and in which Joseph of Arimathea caught the blood of Our Lord. In the opera, Elsa, whom Lohengrin has married, asks his name in spite of the fact that he has forbidden it. Owing to a spell, it would be impossible for him to find the Grail if he answered her. He refuses to do so and leaves her.

MONEY, HEALTH AND REPUTATION

973. *b.* 9. *Janus-like mountain of unpardonable sin.* In Roman mythology, Janus was a god with two faces, one looking east, the other west. The unpardonable sin, mentioned in Matthew xii, 31–32, may be variously interpreted; hence, it also seems to look both ways.

DOCTORS

b. 49. *file a bill in Chancery.* The Chancery
Court in England was at one time notorious for delays.

GEORGE MOORE: THE ORGANIZATION
OF ART

974. *a.* 38. *Royal Academy,* founded by George III
in 1768.

b. 9. *Churton-Collinise.* John Churton Collins,
journalist and scholar, lectured in 1880 for the
London Extension Society and later for the American University Extension Society, both organizations for the popularization of learning.

b. 11. *Mr. Walter Besant,* novelist and first
chairman of the Society of Authors.

b. 31. *in Queer Street,* colloquial expression
meaning 'in a hole.'

b. 38. *Mr. Tate,* a wealthy merchant, had a
large art collection which he wished to give to the
National Gallery. As some of his pictures were
thought mediocre, his offer could not be accepted,
and he then built the Tate Gallery, with part of
his collection as a nucleus.

b. 40. *Herkomer, Fildes, Leader, Long,* popular painters of their day.

975. *a.* 53. *South Kensington Museum,* includes the
National Art Training Schools.

b. 23. *Luxembourg,* an art gallery in Paris,
second only to the Louvre.

b. 31. *Corot, Millet, Manet, etc.,* modern
painters, mainly of the impressionistic school.

SHAW: THE CASE FOR THE CRITIC-
DRAMATIST

977. *a.* 14. *Frank Marshall,* a playwright and
dramatic critic, who, with others, edited 'The Henry
Irving Edition' of Shakespeare.

a. 16. *Sir Henry Irving,* a distinguished
actor and manager. The Lyceum Theatre was at
one time under his entire control.

a. 21. *Canute,* the king of England whose
flattering courtiers declared that even the tide
would obey him.

a. 23. *Robert Emmet.* Marshall's play which
deals with the Irish patriot, Emmet, has never been
produced.

b. 48. *Mr. Pinero,* Sir Arthur Pinero, a successful English playwright, whose first connection
with the stage was as an actor.

978. *b.* 14. *Mr. Clement Scott, Mr. Wm. Archer
and Mr. Walkley,* all London dramatic critics, the
two first also playwrights.

CONRAD: WITH THE MARSEILLES PILOTS

b. 42. *Vieux Port,* Marseilles.

979. *a.* 41. *patron,* coxswain.

a. 48. *'Hé, l'ami, Comment va?'* Hey, friend,
how goes it?

b. 9. *'Larguez,'* cast off.

b. 16. *avant-port,* outer harbor.

b. 47. *béret,* a sort of Tam o' Shanter.

980. *a.* 53. *Equipages de ligne,* Crews of the Line.

b. 8. *Franco-Provençal jargon,* a mixture of
French and the Romance tongue of Provence, the
Langue d'oc of southern France.

b. 14. *Fréjus and Antibes.* Antibes is a sea-
port of southern France and Fréjus is a town not
far away.

981. *a.* 19. *l'ancien,* Old Nick.

b. 13. *old Phœnician port.* Marseilles was
founded by Greek colonists from Phocæa about
600 B.C. and was used by Phœnician traders.

982. *b.* 1. *Mr. W. W. Jacobs,* an author of humorous short stories which deal largely with 'old
salts.'

b. 47. *The Red Ensign,* the merchant ensign
of Great Britain.

WELLS: THE CONTEMPORARY NOVEL

983. *a.* 21. *Samuel Richardson,* 1689–1761, called
'the founder of the English domestic novel.' His
heroes and heroines were Sunday-School perfections, and he took care always to reward virtue.

a. 22. *Tom Jones,* the title of a novel by
Fielding, one of the first realists, who began the
writing of novels to satirize Richardson's sentimentality and moralizing.

a. 44. *Balfourian Age.* A. J., now Lord Bal-
four, published in 1879 a *Defence of Philosophic
Doubt.*

b. 50. *Mr. Chadband,* a hypocritical minister
much given to platitudes, in Dickens's *Bleak House.*

984. *a.* 4. *the Realist against the Nominalist.* In
philosophy realism denotes the medieval metaphysical theory that universals have an existence
independent of individual objects. Directly opposed
to this is nominalism, the philosophical theory that
only individual objects have real existence, and
that the universals are nothing but names given in
common to actually different objects having nothing
else in common.

a. 5. *the Church against the Franciscan and
the Lollard.* The founding of these orders by
St. Francis and Wyclif was a protest against the
greed and unworthiness of the regular clergy.

985. *a.* 8. *Bumble,* a self-important and officious
beadle in *Oliver Twist.*

986. *a.* 21. *Cellinis.* Benvenuto Cellini, an Italian
sculptor and worker in gold of the sixteenth century,
has left in his *Autobiography* accounts of his own
courage and success in amorous adventure.

a. 21. *Casanovas.* Casanova was an Italian
poet and adventurer of the eighteenth century, the
author of scandalous memoirs in which he gleefully
exposes his immorality.

GALSWORTHY: THE LOST DOG

987. *b.* 9. *Thames Embankment,* a street with side-
walks on either side running along the north bank
of the Thames in London—like Riverside Drive in
New York City.

CHESTERTON: THE RETURN OF THE BARBARIAN

989. *a.* 52. *Regency,* the period in English history during which George IV, then Prince of Wales, was Regent. Socially, it was a time which followed its leader, Beau Brummel, in fashion and elegance.

b. 2. *Brighton Pavilion.* The Royal Pavilion at Brighton, a fashionable watering place, was founded by the Regent.

990. *b.* 21. *Hood,* Thomas Hood, nineteenth century poet, author of the *Song of the Shirt.* See p. 663 of this volume.

b. 38. *Lettres de Cachet,* written orders for imprisonment without trial, which in France before the Revolution could be secured against innocent men, for personal revenge.

b. 54. *the Great Pillage.* In 1536 Henry VIII dissolved the monasteries in England and confiscated their property.

991. *a.* 35. *Wilberforce,* the English humanitarian whose fight against slavery resulted in the final passage of the bill for abolition, 1807.

992. *b.* 1. *Freya,* in Norse mythology the wife of Odin.

b. 16. *Denmark was robbed of two provinces,* Schleswig and Holstein.

b. 17. *France was robbed of two provinces,* Alsace and Lorraine.

b. 25. *Augustenburg claim.* The duchies of Schleswig and Holstein had been fiefs of the King of Denmark. When the royal house became extinct at the death of Frederick VII, Prince Frederick of Augustenburg put forward claims of his house to the succession to the duchies. The German Diet supported this claim, and from that time on the two provinces became pawns in the game of German Unification, being finally ceded to Austria and Prussia.

b. 27. *Ems telegram.* In 1870 Bismarck was anxious to bring about a war with France over the succession to the Spanish throne. France demanded that the King of Prussia withdraw the name of his cousin, Prince Leopold, as candidate, and this was done. Then the French ambassador visited the King of Prussia at the watering-place of Ems and asked for a promise that Leopold's name should never be brought up in the future. The King refused courteously and telegraphed what he had done to Bismarck, who deliberately condensed the despatch so that the King's words seemed insulting to the French and made the Prussians feel that their sovereign had been insulted. When the despatch was published the French fell into the trap and declared war.

b. 35. *Palmerston,* Foreign Secretary and Prime Minister during the Eastern crisis and Crimean War, in which England supported Turkey against Russia.

b. 47. *Manchester School,* a group of English economic and political writers and speakers, who, under the leadership of Cobden and Bright, advocated a policy of Free Trade and Laissez-faire.

993. *a.* 46. *Higher Criticism,* inquiry into the origin, authorship and meaning of the various books of the Bible.

BRIDGES: MOONLIGHT

994. *b.* 1. *Grillie,* from the French *grillon,* a cricket.

b. 7. *Queen of Sorrows,* the moon.

HENLEY: OUT OF THE NIGHT THAT COVERS ME

995. 13. *strait,* narrow.

Pro Rege Nostro, for our King.

WATSON: WORDSWORTH'S GRAVE

996. Wordsworth was buried at Grasmere in the Lake District which he loved. He was born near and lived in the District for the greater part of his life.

5. *translunar,* literally, beyond the moon; figuratively, ethereal, visionary.

17. *Lethe,* a river of Hades whose waters brought oblivion and forgetfulness of former existence to the dead.

DAVIDSON: THIRTY BOB A WEEK

Bob, a shilling, rather less than 25c.

THOMPSON: THE HOUND OF HEAVEN

998. 8. *Titanic,* the Titans, a race in Greek Mythology, were taken as types of enormousness.

12. *instancy,* insistency.

17. *hearted casement,* heart-shaped window.

24. *wist,* knew.

25. *margent,* margin.

41. *savannahs,* in reality, flat treeless plains.

44. *Plashy,* speckled as if splashed with colour.

66. *Lady-Mother,* Nature.

999. 100. *owe,* own.

112. *harness,* armor.

117. *Shook the pillaring hours,* as Samson made an end.

123. *sun-starts,* reflections of the sun.

129. *overplussed,* overweighted.

131. *amaranthine.* The amaranth was a fabulous flower supposed never to fade.

159. *shard,* fragment.

HOUSMAN: A SHROPSHIRE LAD

1000. 17. *thews,* sinews.

THE NEW MISTRESS

1001. 8. *soldier of the Queen,* Queen Victoria.

XLI

7. *bourn,* destination.

16. *ladysmocks,*

'Daisies pied and violets blue
And lady-smocks all silver-white.'
Shakespeare, *Love's Labour Lost.*

13. *San Moritz way.* Saint Moritz is a resort in Switzerland which attracts holiday-makers for its winter sports.

24. *emprises,* adventurous enterprises.

27. *Verral,* Professor at Cambridge and a famous interpreter and translator of Greek plays.

the Cam, the river on which the town of Cambridge is situated. 'Next Camus, reverend sire, went footing slow.'—*Lycidas.* See p. 241.

PHILLIPS: REVENGE FOR RHEIMS

1022. The Cathedral of Rheims, built in the thirteenth century and one of the most beautiful buildings in the world, was irreparably damaged by the German bombardment of the city in 1914.

SORLEY: ALL THE HILLS AND VALES ALONG

1023. 12. *Barabbas,* the robber, who, by the choice of the people, was released instead of Christ.

22. *Hemlock for Socrates.* The great Greek philosopher was accused of impiety, condemned and forced to drink hemlock.

TYNAN: A GIRL'S SONG

1. *Meuse and Marne* are rivers flowing through that part of France which saw the death and devastation of the Western Front.

WILLIAMS: FROM A FLEMISH GRAVEYARD

1024. 15. *circumstantial.* The word is used in its literal sense, surrounding.

WOODS: THE FIRST BATTLE OF YPRES

Joffre is reported to have called this 'the greatest battle of the world.' The Channel ports, whose possession might have meant German victory, would have been reached if the Germans had broken through the Allied line.

3. *From Bixschoote to Baecelaere and down to the Lys river.* Bixschoote is north of Ypres, and Baecelaere is on the east. The river Lys is on the south.

17. *Indian men,* native troops from India, Gurkhas.

1025. 33. *Moussy's cuirassiers.* When the Germans were pouring in more troops in preparation for the crisis of the battle, the British asked the French for reinforcements for their part of the line, and were joined by Moussy with five battalions and three batteries.

39. *Gheluveldt.* The area around this was the scene of the critical point of the battle. The Germans took the village and drove a gap in the British line. The situation was one of extreme peril to the Allies.

73. *burghers of Courtrai,* a city in Belgium where, in 1302 the Flemings defeated the French at the Battle of the Spurs.

74. *Gants glacés,* literally, kid gloves—the name of a crack regiment of ancient France.

BEERBOHM: WILLIAM AND MARY

1027. *a.* 3. *Fabian Essays.* The Fabian Society was a moderate Socialistic group formed in London in 1884, by young literary men, including H. G. Wells, Bernard Shaw, and Sidney Webb. The Fabian Essays, its most important publication, began to appear in 1889.

a. 24. *Trafalgar Square,* one of the principal squares in London, which contains the Nelson Monument.

a. 51. *Beowulf,* the Anglo-Saxon epic.

Sigurd the Volsung, hero of the Norse sagas, corresponding to the later German Siegfried.

b. 30. *feckless,* shiftless.

1028. *b.* 16. *Ibsen,* the great Norwegian dramatist whose plays are serious and often gloomy.

Morris, William Morris, the poet, who, in his later years, was interested in spreading Socialism.

b. 22. *George Gissing,* the novelist, whose effort to depict 'the ignobly decent' often results in dreariness.

1029. *a.* 25. *obbligato,* an accompaniment.

CANNAN: THE ENGLISH NOVEL

1033. *b.* 54. *'The Way of All Flesh,'* Samuel Butler's novel which contains many of his sceptical criticisms and original opinions on the institution of the family, etc.

1034. *a.* 6. *Swift, Fielding and Defoe,* eighteenth century writers.

a. 31. *flaneur,* a gossip.

b. 11. *Sterne,* a novelist and humorist of the eighteenth century.

b. 12. *Smelfungus,* a name given by Sterne to Smollett, on account of the pessimism of Smollett's 'Travels.'

HUDSON: MY FIRST VISIT TO BUENOS AYRES

1038. *b.* 33. *lavenderas,* wash-women.

1039. *b.* 2. *estancia,* farm.

b. 21. *Perdon, por Dios,* Pardon, in God's name.

1041. *a.* 37. *Rosas, the Nero of South America* governed Buenos Ayres about the middle of the 19th century as an absolute dictator and with tyrannical cruelty.

b. 22. *Caudillo,* commander or leader.

KEYNES: EUROPE BEFORE THE WAR

1043. *a.* 9. *Malthus,* an English economist who argued that since population tends to increase in geometrical ratio and the means of subsistence only in arithmetical ratio, restriction of population was the only means of removing poverty and its evils.

WALPOLE: ROMANCE AND REALISM

1044. *b.* 32. *Reade,* Charles Reade, novelist and dramatist, author of *The Cloister and the Hearth.*

b. 40. *St. Ives,* a story by Stevenson, finished

by Sir Arthur Quiller-Couch and published after Stevenson's death.

1045. *a.* 48. *'The Brothers Karamazov,'* a novel by Dostoievsky.

    a. 49. *'The Cherry Orchard,'* a play by Chekhov.

    a. 54. *Madame Bovary,* Flaubert's great realistic novel.

    b. 14. *Almayer,* the chief character in Conrad's first novel, *Almayer's Folly.*

1046. *a.* 5. *'Crime and Punishment,' 'The Idiot,' 'The Possessed,' 'The Brothers Karamazov,'* works of Dostoievsky.

    11. *Prince Myshkin,* a character in *The Idiot.*

    Dmitri Karamazov, one of the Brothers Karamazov.

    Nicolas Stavrogin, a character in Dostoievsky's *The Possessed.*

    a. 21. *Captain Anthony,* a character in Conrad's *Chance.*

    a. 32. *Stendhal,* the pseudonym of Henri Beyle, distinguished French critic and novelist.

    a. 44. *Razumov,* a character in Conrad's novel *Under Western Eyes,* which deals with Russian revolutionaries.

    a. 49. *Raskolnikov,* a character in *Crime and Punishment.*

    b. 23. *M'Whirr,* the sea captain in Conrad's *Typhoon.*

    b. 38. *Kouprin, Artzybashev, Sologub, Merejkovsky, Andreiev,* modern and contemporary Russian writers.

CAMPBELL: I AM THE MOUNTAINY SINGER

1047. 6. *carn,* a rock or heap of rocks.

    7. *cailin,* maiden.

    11. *cailleach,* crone.

    18. *canker,* rust.

COLUM: THE PLOUGHER

8. *Pan,* see note for p. 1010, line 42.

Wotan, Woden or Odin, the chief god of northern mythology who created the world.

Dana, a great nature goddess identified with the Greek Artemis.

WHAT THE SHUILER SAID AS SHE LAY BY THE FIRE IN THE FARMER'S HOUSE

Shuiler, a beggar.

1048. 20. *clan,* crowd.

    42. *huggle,* cuddle.

EDEN: ARS IMMORTALIS

1049. 11. *Meissonier,* a nineteenth-century French artist whose work, chiefly on military subjects, was done on an exceedingly small scale.

12. *Lady Butler,* an English artist of the nineteenth century, whose large military pictures, 'Balaklava' etc., met with a furor of popularity.

FLECKER: THE BALLAD OF ISKANDER

1050. *Aflatun, Aristu,* and *Iskander* are the Turkish forms for Plato, Aristotle and Alexander.

    44. *Isle of Serendip,* an ancient name for Ceylon.

    50. *alizarine,* a dye which produces Turkey reds, shades of orange, violet, etc.

1051. 151. *Zephyr,* a personification of the west wind.

GRAVES: GOLIATH AND DAVID

1053. 31. *Mamre,* a place in Palestine, near Hebron.

    34. *Jesse,* the father of David.

HARDY: AFTERWARDS

1054. 6. *dewfall-hawk,* night hawk.

HODGSON: EVE

1055. 48. *The Blasphemous Tree,* the tree of knowledge of good and evil.

    64. *under the hill.* Elves and other spirits have their abode under mounds.

THE BULL

1056. 55. *dewlap-deep,* up to the dewlap, a fold of skin which hangs from the neck of cattle.

    110. *pow,* head.

LAWRENCE: STUDY

1057. 6. *Biuret,* a chemical term. The young man drags himself from dreams to study his chemistry.

MITCHELL: AMBITION IN CUFFE STREET

Cuffe Street, a street in Dublin.

HOW WOULD IT BE?

1058. 18. *jujube tree,* a small tree which grows in Syria, India and China.

    19. *galleons,* ships used by the Spaniards especially for treasure.

SASSOON: THE OLD HUNTSMAN

1059. 2. *Golden Fleece,* his public house.

1060. 69. *hoick,* a call used in hunting to incite the hounds.

STEPHENS: WHAT TOMAS AN BUILE SAID IN A PUB.

1062. *Pub,* a public-house or saloon.

Professor Gilbert Murray in a preface to a collection of Oxford poetry published just before the Great War pointed to the earlier collection entitled *Georgian Poetry 1911–12* as the beginning of a period 'which may take rank in due time with the several great poetic ages of the past.' This new 'Georgian Period' has not perhaps altogether fulfilled the high expectations which Professor Murray formed of it at that time, but what he said of its poets is still true:—'Each writer has his own special quality and character, and hardly any two of them are much alike. There is no remotest sign of a school, a clique, or a coterie. These writers are not Futurists, nor Unanimists, nor Paroxysts, nor Asphyxiasts, nor members of any other rising doctrinal body. They have written as suited them best, and their work has been judged for its poetry, not its tendency.' A few biographical details may, however, be helpful.

Joseph Campbell and Padraic Colum are Irishmen who have also published a good deal in the United States. Padraic Colum at the time of writing still lives in this country.

William H. Davies was born in Newport (Monmouthshire), and had a wayward youth in England before he became a professional tramp in the United States. In attempting to steal a ride in Canada he lost a foot on the railroad, and returned to England to undergo considerable privations before he was able to establish his reputation as a lyric poet. His early poems about English lodging houses won him a small government pension which has sufficed for his simple wants and has enabled him to publish a number of volumes of poetry and some prose works, including *The Autobiography of a Super-tramp*, or *A Poet's Pilgrimage*, and *Later Days* (1925).

Helen Parry Eden was born in 1885, the daughter of a well-known London and Manchester Judge who was also noteworthy as a man of letters. She was educated at Roedean School and the University of Manchester, where she won a History Scholarship and the Vice-Chancellor's prize in English Verse. She then took up the study of painting and in 1907 married the artist, Denis Eden. She has since contributed to *Punch* and published several articles and poems, which are better known in England than in America.

James Elroy Flecker was, to quote J. C. Squire, 'an artist of extreme precocity.' He went to one of the most famous English Public schools, Uppingham, and won there an open classical scholarship to Trinity College, Oxford, where he was told by the Professor of English Literature, Sir Walter Raleigh, that he was the coming poet of his time. From Oxford he went to Cambridge University to prepare for the Consular service and there too met friends who encouraged him in creative work. In June, 1910, he went to the East and fell under its glamour, which is reproduced in the poems he published before his lamented death at the age of thirty early in 1915. He said of his Oriental drama, *Hassan*: 'It is a masterpiece, but I shall never live to see it come into its own.' *Hassan* came into its own when it received a magnificent production at His Majesty's Theatre, London, in the spring of 1924,—about ten years too late to give the young poet the substantial encouragement for which he was longing. 'When he died,' says Mr. Squire, 'he had written enough to prove that, had he survived, he would have been amongst the greatest of English poets.'

Robert Graves is one of the Oxford poets and his address is still 'The World's End, Islip, Oxon.,' though the London publishers have issued several volumes of his verse, and he is a frequent contributor to the *London Mercury, Nation* and *Athenæum, New Statesman* and other English periodicals.

Thomas Hardy, at the time of writing the Dean of English Letters at the age of 85, received the cherished distinction of the Order of Merit in succession to George Meredith. He is better known to the English and American public as a writer of fiction than as a poet, although since 1897 he has published no novels and several volumes of poetry, of which the last was *Human Show* (Macmillan, 1925). His most considerable achievement is an 'epic drama' entitled *The Dynasts*, published in three parts 1903–1908.

Ralph Hodgson is an English journalist of an unusually retiring disposition; he refuses to be interviewed or to have anything said about himself in the books of reference. He writes chiefly for the sporting papers and is the leading English authority on bull terriers. The volume of his published poetry is small but it is of unusually high quality; it has melody and charm.

D. H. Lawrence was born in a coal miner's cottage on the borders of Nottinghamshire and Derbyshire, and the scene of many of the novels upon which his reputation mainly rests is laid in that district. Since the destruction of *The Rainbow*, by order of an English police court in 1915, he has lived a great deal abroad, principally in Italy and on a western ranch in the United States. Susan L. Mitchell is a disciple of the Irish mystic 'A. E.,' (George William Russell) but she can also write realistically about life in the Dublin slums and satirise the mythology of W. B. Yeats and other poets of the early Irish School.

Harold Monro is a London poet, closely associated with the Poetry Book Shop. He has written several volumes of poetry, some of them published at the Book Shop, and has also criticised his contemporaries in *Some Contemporary Poets* (1920).

Siegfried Sassoon was educated at Marlborough and Clare College, Cambridge, and served in France and Palestine, 1915–1918. His collected *War Poems* published in 1919 attracted general attention by the grim strength of his descriptions of the realities of the great struggle. About the same time he visited the United States and spoke or read his poems in various leading cities.

James Stephens was born in Ireland and discovered by 'A. E.' while working as a typist for a Dublin lawyer. His *Irish Fairy Tales, A Crock of Gold, The Demi-Gods, The Adventures of Seumas Beg,* and *In the Land of Youth* (1924) are delightful for their whimsical imaginativeness. Among his books of verse are *The Hill of Vision,* (1912), *Songs from the Plain* (1914), and *Reincarnations* (1917).

Edward Thomas was educated at St. Paul's School, London, and at Oxford; he served in the War and was killed in action on April 9, 1916. He is best known in England for his imaginative and reflective books of travel recounting his experiences and his inner life during many solitary journeys on foot. Although English by education, he had Welsh blood in his veins and his 'temperamental melancholy' is revealed both in his prose works and in his poems. He was an eager and profound student of literature and his death was lamented as among the most serious losses sustained by English literature during the War. He was a friend of Robert Frost, the American poet, to whom he dedicated the first volume of his poems published in 1917 in the United States. He did a large amount of literary work, and though his poetry is small in extent it is highly esteemed for the perfection of its workmanship and its successful expression of an atmosphere in a few carefully chosen words.

INDEX OF AUTHORS, NOTES AND TEXT

1187

INDEX OF FIRST LINES

Abbotsford D 2
Aberdour C 1
Aldborough (Aldeburgh) H 5
Alfoxden C 6
Alnwick E 2
Anglesey (Mona) B 4
Annan C 3
Arundel F 7
Ashestiel D 2
Auchinleck B 2
Avon (River) E 5
Ayr B 2
Ayr (River) B 2

Baldeswelle (Bawdeswell) H 5
Bamborough D 2
Bannockburn C 1
Barham H 6
Bath D 6
Bedford F 5
Berwick D 2
Birmingham E 5
Blean Forest H 6
Blee (See Blean)
Bow H 2
Box Hill G 3
Bradford E 4
Brantwood C 3
Bristol D 6
Brummagen (See Birmingham)
Bury St Edmunds G 5

Cader Idris (Mt.) C 5
Cambridge G 5
Canterbury H 6
Chester D 4
Chichester F 7
Clevedon D 6
Clyde, Firth of B 2
Cockermouth C 3
Colchester G 6
Conway (River) C 4
Craigenputtock C 2

Dalkeith C 2
Dartmouth C 7
Deptford H 1–F 6
Derby E 5
Dertemouthe (See Dartmouth)
Doon (River) B 2
Dover H 6
Duddon (River) C 3
Dumfermline (Dumferling) C 1
Dumfries C 2
Dunbar D 1

Earlston D 2
Ecclefechan C 2
Edinburgh C 2
Ellisland C 2
Elwy (River) C 4
Erceldoune (See Earlston)
Eton F 2
Exeter C 7

Farringford E 7
Flodden Field D 2
Fordidge H 6
Fordwich (See Fordidge)
Forth, Firth of C 1

Glasgow B 2
Glastonbury D 6
Grantchester G 5
Grasmere C 3
Greenwich H 1–6
Grongar Hill B 6

Hagley D 5
Hampstead G 2
Hampton G 2
Hampton Court G 2
Harrow G 2
Harwich H 6
Hatfield E 4
Highgate H 2
Horton F 2–6
Hull (Hulle) F 4
Humber (River) F 4
Hunsdon G 6
Huntingdon F 5
Huntington C 5

Irvine B 2

Katrine (Lake) B 1
Keswick C 3
Kilgerran B 5
Kilmarnock B 2

Lasswade C 2
Leasowes D 5
Leeds E 4
Lichfield E 5
Lindisfarne E 2
Liverpool D 4
London F 6
Lynmouth C 6

Manchester D 4
Mona (See Anglesey) B 4
Nether Stowey C 6
Newbold E 5
Newcastle E 3
Newstead Abbey E 4
Norwich H 5
Nottingham E 5

Olney F 5
Orwell (Orewelle) H 6
Otterburn D 2
Oxford (Oxenford) E 6
Plinlimmon (Mt.) C 5
Plymouth B 7
Putney G 2

Quantock Hills (Mt.) C 6

Racedown D 7
Richmond G 2
Rochester G 6
Rugby E 5

Salisbury E 6
Scarborough F 3
Severn (River) D 5
Sheffield E 4
Shrewsbury D 5
Snowdon (Mt.) B 4
Solway Firth C 3
Somersby G 4
Southampton E 7
Southwark F 6–H 2
Sterling C 1
Stoke F 2
Stonehenge E 6
Stour (River) D 7
Stowey (See Nether Stowey)
Stratford-at-Bow (See Bow)
Stratford-on-Avon E 5
Sussex Weald G 6

Tavistock B 7
Teifi (River) B 5
Thames (River) E 6
Tintagel B 7
Tintern Abbey D 6
Towy (River) B 6
Trossachs B 1
Tweed (River) D 2
Twickenham G 2
Tyne (River) D 3

Wakefield E 4
Ware F 6
Whitby F 3
Wilton E 6
Wimborne E 7
Winchester E 6
Windermere D 3
Windermere (Lake) D 3
Windsor F 2
Worcester D 5
Wye (River) D 5

Yarrow (River) C 2
York E 4

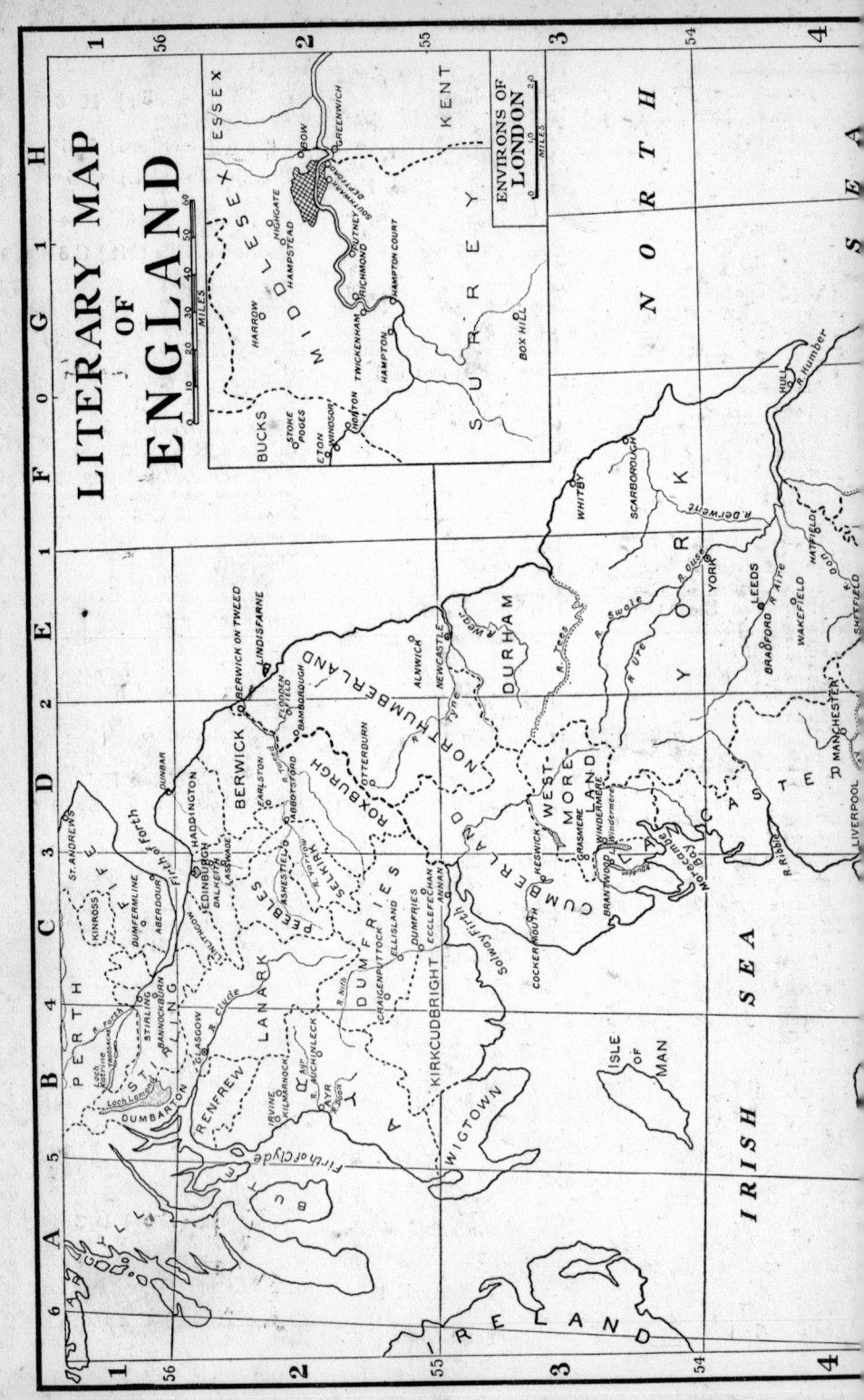